CONTENTS

Preface   7

Authors to Appear in Future Volumes   9

Appendix   633

Cumulative Index to Authors   649

Cumulative Index to Critics   651

Nineteenth-Century Literature Criticism

Nineteenth-Century Literature Criticism

Excerpts from Criticism of the
Works of Novelists, Poets, Playwrights,
Short Story Writers, and Other Creative Writers
Who Lived between 1800 and 1900,
from the First Published Critical
Appraisals to Current Evaluations

Laurie Lanzen Harris

Editor

Gale Research Company
Book Tower
Detroit, Michigan 48226

STAFF

Laurie Lanzen Harris, *Editor*

Sheila Fitzgerald and Anna C. Wallbillich, *Senior Assistant Editors*

Emily Wade Barrett, Ann K. Crowley, Denise Michlewicz,
Robert Bruce Young, Jr., *Assistant Editors*

Phyllis Carmel Mendelson, *Contributing Editor*

Carolyn Bancroft, *Production Supervisor*
Lizbeth A. Purdy, *Production Coordinator*

Robert J. Elster, *Research Coordinator*
Robert Hill and Carol Angela Thomas, *Research Assistants*

Linda Marcella Pugliese, *Manuscript Coordinator*
Donna DiNello, *Manuscript Assistant*

Cherie D. Abbey, Elizabeth Babini, Laura L. Britton, Frank James Borovsky, Lee Ferency,
Jeanne A. Gough, Denise B. Grove, Serita Lanette Lockard, Brenda Marshall, Marie M. Mazur,
Francine M. Melotti-Bacon, Gloria Anne Williams, *Editorial Assistants*

L. Elizabeth Hardin, *Permissions Supervisor*
Filomena Sgambati, *Permissions Coordinator*
Anna Maria DiNello, Judy Kowalsky, Janice M. Mach, Mary P. McGrane,
Susan D. Nobles, Patricia A. Seefelt, *Permissions Assistants*

Copyright © 1982 by Gale Research Company

Library of Congress Catalog Card Number 81-6943
ISBN 0-8103-5802-6
ISSN 0732-1864

(Reprinted from Volume One)

Library of Congress Cataloging in Publication Data

Main entry under title:

Ninteenth-century literature criticism.

"Excerpts from criticism of the works of
novelists, poets, playwrights, short story writers
and other creative writers who lived between 1800
and 1900, from the first published critical
appraisals to current evaluations."
Bibliography: p.
Includes index.
1. Literature, Modern--19th century--History
and criticism--Addresses, essays, lectures.
2. Literature, Modern--19th century--Bio-bibliog-
raphy. I. Harris, Laurie Lanzen. II. Gale
Research Company.
PN761.N5   809'.04   81-6943
ISBN 0-8103-5801-8 (v. 1)   AACR2

PREFACE

The nineteenth century was a time of tremendous growth in human endeavor: in science, in social history, and particularly in literature. The era saw the development of the novel, witnessed radical changes from classicism to romanticism to realism, and contained intellectual and artistic ideas that continue to inspire authors of our own century. The importance of the writers of the nineteenth century is twofold, for they provide insight into their own time as well as into the universal nature of human experience.

The literary criticism of an era can also give us insight into the moral and intellectual atmosphere of the past, for the criteria by which a work of art is judged reflect current philosophical and social attitudes. Literary criticism takes many forms: the traditional essay, the book or play review, even the parodic poem. Criticism can also be of several kinds: normative, descriptive, interpretive, textual, appreciative, generic. Collectively, the range of critical response helps us to understand a work of art, an author, an era.

The Scope of the Work

The success of Gale's two current literary series, *Contemporary Literary Criticism (CLC)* and *Twentieth Century Literary Criticism (TCLC),* which excerpt criticism of creative writing from the twentieth century, suggested an equivalent need among students and teachers of literature of the nineteenth century. Moreover, since the critical analysis of this literature spans almost two hundred years, a vast amount of critical material confronts the student.

Nineteenth-Century Literature Criticism (NCLC) presents significant passages from published criticism on authors who died between 1800 and 1900. Those customers who ordered the series from the sample or from early promotional material will note a small but significant change in the title of *NCLC*. In order to accurately reflect the content of *NCLC* the title was changed from *Nineteenth-Century Literary Criticism* to *Nineteenth-Century Literature Criticism,* thus indicating that it is the *literature* and the *authors* of the nineteenth century and not the *literary criticism* of that century alone with which we are concerned. Indeed, to indicate the full range of critical response to the authors covered in the series, we must draw upon the criticism of the eighteenth, nineteenth, and twentieth centuries.

The author list for each volume of *NCLC* is carefully compiled to represent a variety of genres and nationalities and to cover authors who are currently regarded as the most important writers of an era as well as those whose contribution to literature and literary history is significant. The truly great writers are rare, and in the intervals between them lesser but genuine artists, as well as writers who enjoyed immense popularity in their own time and in their own countries, are important to the study of nineteenth-century literature. The length of each author's entry is intended to represent the author's critical reception in English. Articles and books that have not been translated into English are excluded. Each author entry represents a historical overview of the critical response to the author's work: early criticism is presented to indicate initial responses, later selections represent any rise or decline in the author's literary reputation. We have also attempted to identify and include excerpts from the seminal essays on each author, and to include recent critical comment providing modern perspectives on the writer. Thus, *NCLC* is designed to serve as an introduction for the student of nineteenth-century literature to the authors of that period and to the most significant commentators on these authors.

NCLC entries are intended to be definitive overviews and approximately 30 authors are included in each 600-page volume, compared to about 100 authors in a *CLC* volume of similar size. Because of the great quantity of critical material available on many authors, and because of the resurgence of criticism generated by events such as an author's centennial or anniversary celebration, the republication of an author's works, or publication of a newly translated work or volume of letters, an author may appear more than once.

The Organization of the Book

An author section consists of the following elements: author heading; bio-critical introduction; principal works; excerpts of criticism (each followed by a citation); and an annotated bibliography of additional reading.

- The *author heading* consists of the author's full name, followed by birth and death dates. The unbracketed portion of the name denotes the form under which the author most commonly wrote. If

7

an author wrote consistently under a pseudonym, the pseudonym will be listed in the author heading and the real name given in parentheses on the first line of the bio-critical introduction. Also located at the beginning of the bio-critical introduction are any name variations under which an author wrote, including transliterated forms for authors whose languages use nonroman alphabets. Uncertainty as to a birth or death date is indicated by a question mark.

- The *bio-critical introduction* contains biographical and other background information that elucidates his or her creative output.

- The list of *principal works* is chronological by date of first publication and indentifies genres. In those instances where the first publication was in other than the English language, the title and date of the first English-language edition is given in brackets. Unless otherwise indicated, dramas are dated by the first performance, rather than first publication.

- *Criticism* is arranged chronologically in each author section to provide a perspective on any changes in critical evaluation over the years. In the text of each author entry, titles by the author are printed in boldface type. This allows the reader to ascertain without difficulty the works discussed. For purposes of easier identification, the critic's name and the publication date of the essay are given at the beginning of each piece of criticism. Unsigned criticism is preceded by the title of the journal in which it appeared. For an anonymous essay later attributed to a critic, the critic's name appears in brackets in the heading and in the citation.

- A complete *bibliographical citation* designed to facilitate the location of the original essay or book follows each piece of criticism. An asterisk (*) at the end of the citation indicates that the essay is on more than one author.

- The *annotated bibliography* appearing at the end of each author section suggests further reading on the author. In some cases it includes essays for which the editors could not obtain reprint rights. An asterisk (*) at the end of a citation indicates that the essay is on more than one author.

Each volume of *NCLC* includes a cumulative index to critics. Under each critic's name is listed the authors on whom the critic has written and the volume and page where the criticism appears. *NCLC* also includes a cumulative index to authors with the volume number in which the author appears.

An appendix is included which lists the sources from which material in the volume is reprinted. It does not, however, list every book or periodical consulted for the volume.

Acknowledgments

No work of this scope can be accomplished without the cooperation of many people. The editors especially wish to thank the copyright holders of the excerpts included in this volume, the permissions managers of the book and magazine publishing companies for assisting us in securing reprint rights, and the staffs of the Detroit Public Library, University of Michigan Library, and Wayne State University Library for making their resources available to us. We are also grateful to Fred S. Stein for his assistance with copyright research and Norma J. Merry for her editorial assistance.

Suggestions Are Welcome

The editors welcome the comments and suggestions of readers to expand the coverage and enhance the usefulness of the series.

AUTHORS TO APPEAR
IN FUTURE VOLUMES

ABOUT, Edmond François 1828-1885
AGUILÓ I FUSTER, Marià 1825-1897
AINSWORTH, William Harrison 1805-1882
AKSAKOV, Konstantin 1817-1860
ALCOTT, Louisa May 1832-1888
ALEARDI, Aleadro 1812-1878
ALECSANDRI, Vasile 1821-1890
ALENCAR, José 1829-1877
ALFIERI, Vittorio 1749-1803
ALGER, Horatio 1834-1899
ALLINGHAM, William 1824-1889
ALMQUIST, Carl Jonas Love 1793-1866
ALORNA, Leonor de Almeida 1750-1839
ALSOP, Richard 1761-1815
ALTIMIRANO, Ignacio Manuel 1834-1893
ALVARENGA, Manuel Inâcio da Silva 1749-1814
ALVARES DE AZEVEDO, Manuel Antônio 1831-1852
AMIEL, Henri-Frédéric 1821-1881
ANDERSEN, Hans Christian 1805-1875
ANZENGRUBER, Ludvig 1839-1889
ARANY, János 1817-1882
ARÈNE, Paul 1843-1893
ARJONA DE CUBAS, Manuel Mariá de 1771-1820
ARNIM, Achim von 1781-1831
ARNIM, Bettina von 1785-1859
ARNOLD, Matthew 1822-1888
ASACHI, Gheorghe 1788-1869
ASBJÖRNSEN, Peter Christen 1812-1885
ASCASUBI, Hilario 1807-1875
ASNYK, Adam 1838-1897
ATTERBOM, Per Daniel Amadeus 1790-1855
AUERBACH, Berthold 1812-1882
AUGIER, Guillaume V.F. 1820-1889
AZEGLIO, Massimo D' 1798-1866
AZEVEDO, Guilherme de 1839-1882
BAKIN (pseud. of Takizawa Okikani) 1767-1848
BALZAC, Honoré de 1799-1850
BANVILLE, Théodore de 1823-1891
BARNES, William 1801-1886
BARONIAN, Hagop 1842-1891
BAUDELAIRE, Charles Pierre 1821-1867
BEATTIE, James 1735-1803
BECKFORD, William 1760-1844
BECQUE, Henry François 1837-1899
BÉCQUER, Gustavo Adolfo 1836-1870
BEDDOES, Thomas Lovell 1803-1849
BELINSKY, Vissarion Grigor'yevich 1811-1848
BELLAMY, Edward 1850-1898
BELLO, Andrés 1781-1865
BENTHAM, Jeremy 1748-1832
BÉRANGER, Jean-Pierre de 1780-1857
BERCHET, Giovanni 1783-1851
BERZSENYI, Dániel 1776-1836
BILDERDYK, Willem 1756-1831
BLACK, William 1841-1898
BLAIR, Hugh 1718-1800
BLAKE, William 1757-1827
BLICHER, Steen Steensen 1782-1848
BOCAGE, Manuel Maria Barbosa du 1765-1805
BODTCHER, Ludvig 1793-1874
BORATYNSKY, Yevgeny 1800-1844
BOREL, Pétrus 1809-1859

BOREMAN, Yokutiel 1825-1890
BORROW, George 1803-1881
BOSBOOM-TOUSSAINT, Anna L.G. 1812-1886
BOTEV, Hristo 1778-1842
BRACKENRIDGE, Hugh Henry 1748-1816
BREMER, Fredrika 1801-1865
BRINCKMAN, John 1814-1870
BRONTË, Anne 1820-1849
BRONTË, Charlotte 1816-1855
BRONTË, Emily 1812-1848
BROWN, Charles Brockden 1777-1810
BROWNING, Robert 1812-1889
BRYANT, William Cullen 1794-1878
BÜCHNER, Georg 1813-1837
BURNEY, Fanney 1752-1840
CABALLERO, Fernan 1796-1877
CALVERLEY, Charles Stuart 1831-1884
CAMPBELL, James Edwin 1867-1895
CAMPBELL, Thomas 1777-1844
CARELTON, William 1794-1869
CARLYLE, Thomas 1795-1881
CASTELO BRANCO, Camilo 1825-1890
CASTRO, Rosalia de 1837-1885
CASTRO ALVES, Antônio de 1847-1871
CHAMISSO, Adalbert von 1781-1838
CHANNING, William Ellery 1780-1842
CHATEAUBRIAND, Vic. François-René de 1768-1848
CHATTERJE, Bankin Chanda 1838-1894
CHODERLOS DE LACLOSE, Pierre 1741-1803
CLARE, John 1793-1864
CLAUDIUS, Matthais 1740-1815
CLOUCH, Arthur Hugh 1819-1861
COBBETT, William 1762-1835
COLENSO, John William 1814-1883
COLERIDGE, Hartley 1796-1849
COLERIDGE, Samuel T. 1772-1834
COLLETT, Camilla 1813-1895
CONRAD, Robert T. 1810-1858
CONSCIENCE, Hendrik 1812-1883
CONSTANT, Benjamin 1767-1830
COOKE, John Esten 1830-1886
CORBIÈRE, Edouard 1845-1875
COWPER, William 1731-1800
CRABBE, George 1754-1832
CRAWFORD, Isabella Valancy 1850-1886
CRUZ E SOUSA, João da 1861-1898
DE QUINCEY, Thomas 1785-1859
DESBORDES-VALMORE, Marceline 1786-1859
DESCHAMPS, Antony 1800-1869
DESCHAMPS, Émile 1791-1871
DEUS, João de 1830-1896
DICKENS, Charles 1812-1870
DICKINSON, Emily 1830-1886
DINIS, Júlio 1839-1871
DINSMOOR, Robert 1757-1836
DOBROLYUBOV, Nikolay Aleksanrovich 1836-1861
DRENNAN, John Swanick 1809-1893
DROSTE-HÜLSHOFF, Annette von 1797-1848
DUMAS, Alexandre (père) 1802-1870
DUMAS, Alexandre (fils) 1824-1895
DU MAURIER, George 1834-1896
DWIGHT, Timothy 1752-1817
ECHEVERRIA, Esteban 1805-1851
EICHENDORFF, Joseph von 1788-1857

ELIOT, George 1819-1880
EMINESCY, Mihai 1850-1889
ERBEN, Karel Jaromír 1811-1870
ERTER, Isaac 1792-1851
ESPRONCEDA, José 1808-1842
ETTINGER, Solomon 1799-1855
EUCHEL, Isaac 1756-1804
FERGUSON, Samuel 1810-1886
FERNANDEZ DE LIZARDI, José Joaquín 1776-1827
FERNANDEZ DE MORAITN, Leandro 1760-1828
FET, Afanasy 1820-1892
FEUILLET, Octave 1821-1890
FIELD, Eugene 1850-1895
FITZGERALD, Edward 1809-1883
FONTANE, Theodor 1819-1898
FORSTER, John 1812-1876
FOSCOLO, Ugo 1778-1827
FREDERIC, Harold 1856-1898
FREDRO, Aleksander 1793-1876
FREYTAG, Gustav 1816-1895
FULLER, Sarah Margaret 1810-1850
GABORIAU, Emile 1835-1873
GANIVET, Angel 1865-1898
GARRETT, Almeida 1799-1854
GARSHIN, Vscvolod Mikhaylovich 1855-1888
GASKELL, E.C. 1810-1865
GEZELLE, Guido 1830-1899
GHÁLIB, Asadullah Khán 1797-1869
GODWIN, William 1756-1836
GOETHE, Johann Wolfgang von 1749-1832
GOGOL, Nikolay Vasilievich 1809-1852
GOLDSCHMIDT, Meir Aron 1819-1887
GOMEZ DE AVELLANEDA, Gertrudis 1814-1873
GONÇALVES DIAS, Antonio 1823-1864
GONCOURT, Edmond 1822-1896
GONCOURT, Jules 1830-1870
GORDON, Yehuda Leib 1812-1891
GOZZI, Carlo 1720-1806
GRIBOYEDOV, Aleksander Sergeyevich 1795-1829
GRIGOR'YEV, Appolon Aleksandrovich 1822-1864
GRIMM, Jacob Ludwig Karl 1785-1863
GRIMM, Wilhelm Karl 1786-1859
GROTH, Klaus 1819-1899
GROSSI, Tommaso 1790-1853
GRÜN, Anastasius (pseud. of Anton Alexander Graf von Auersperg) 1806-1876
GUERRAZZI, Francesco Domenico 1804-1873
GUTIÉRREZ NÁJERA, Manuel 1859-1895
HA-KOHEN, Shalom 1772-1845
HALLECK, Fitz-Greene 1790-1867
HAMMON, Jupiter 1711-1800
HARRIS, George Washington 1814-1869
HAYNE, Paul Hamilton 1830-1886
HAZLITT, William 1778-1830
HEBBEL, Christian Friedrich 1813-1863
HEBEL, Johann Peter 1760-1826
HEGEL, Georg Wilhelm Friedrich 1770-1831
HEIBERG, Johan Ludvig 1813-1863
HEINE, Heinrich 1797-1856
HERCULANO, Alexandre 1810-1866
HERDER, Johann Gottfried 1744-1803

HERNANDEZ, José 1834-1886
HERTZ, Henrik 1798-1870
HERWEGH, Georg 1817-1875
HERZEN, Alexander I. 1812-1870
HOFFMAN, Charles Fenno 1806-1884
HOFFMANOWA, Klementyna 1798-1845
HOGG, James 1770-1835
HOLDERLIN, Friedrich 1770-1843
HOLMES, Oliver Wendell 1809-1894
HOOD, Thomas 1799-1845
HOPKINS, Gerard Manley 1844-1889
HUGHES, Thomas 1822-1896
HUGO, Victor 1802-1885
IMLAY, Gilbert 1754?-1828?
IMMERMANN, Karl Lebrecht 1796-1840
IRWIN, Thomas Caulfield 1823-1892
ISSACS, Jorge 1837-1895
JACOBSEN, Jens Peter 1847-1885
JEAN PAUL (pseud. of Johann Paul Friedrich Richter) 1763-1825
JIPPENSHA, Ikku 1765-1831
KARADZIĆ, Vuk Stefanovic 1787-1864
KARAMZIN, Nikolai 1766-1826
KEATS, John 1759-1821
KEBLE, John 1792-1866
KHOMYAKOV, Alexey S. 1804-1860
KIERKEGAARD, Søren 1813-1855
KINGLAKE, Alexander W. 1809-1891
KINGSLEY, Charles 1819-1875
KIVI, Alexis 1834-1872
KLOPSTOCK, Friedrich Gottlieb 1724-1803
KOLLÁR, Jan 1793-1852
KOLTSOV, Alexey Vasilyevich 1809-1842
KOTZEBUE, August von 1761-1819
KRASICKI, Ignacy 1735-1801
KRASIŃKI, Zygmunt 1812-1859
KRASZEWSKI, Josef Ignacy 1812-1887
KREUTZWALD, Friedrich Reinhold 1803-1882
KROCHMAL, Nahman 1785-1840
LACLOS, Pierre Choderlos de 1741-1803
LAFORGUE, Jules 1860-1887
LAMARTINE, Alphonse 1790-1869
LAMB, Charles 1775-1834
LAMPMAN, Archibald 1861-1899
LANDON, Letitia Elizabeth 1802-1838
LANDOR, Walter Savage 1775-1864
LANIER, Sidney 1842-1881
LARMINIE, William 1850-1899
LARRA Y SÁNCHEZ DE CASTRO, Mariano 1809-1837
LAUTRÉAMONT (pseud. of Isodore Ducasse) 1846-1870
LEAR, Edward 1812-1888
LEBENSOHN, Micah Joseph 1828-1852
LECONTE DE LISLE, Charles-Marie-René 1818-1894
LE FANU, Joseph Sheridan 1814-1873
LENAU, Nikolaus 1802-1850
LEONTYEV, Konstantin 1831-1891
LEOPARDI, Giacoma 1798-1837
LERMONTOV, Mikhail 1814-1841
LESKOV, Nikolai 1831-1895
LEVER, Charles James 1806-1872
LEVISOHN, Solomon 1789-1822
LEWIS, Matthew Gregory 1775-1810
LEYDEN, John 1775-1811
LONGSTREET, Augustus Baldwin 1790-1870

LÓPEZ DE AYOLA Y HERRERA, Adelardo 1819-1871
LOVER, Samuel 1797-1868
LUZZATTO, Samuel David 1800-1865
MACEDO, Joaquim Manuel de 1820-1882
MÁCHA, Karel Hynek 1810-1836
MACKENZIE, Henry 1745-1831
MAGALHÃES, Domingos José 1811-1882
MAIMON, Solomon 1754-1800
MALLARMÉ, Stéphane 1842-1898
MANGAN, James Clarence 1803-1849
MANZONI, Alessandro 1785-1873
MAPU, Abraham 1808-1868
MARKOVIC, Sv. 1846-1875
MARRYAT, Frederick 1792-1848
MARII, José 1853-1895
MARTINEZ DE LA ROSA, Francisco 1787-1862
MATHEWS, Cornelius 1817-1889
MATURIN, Charles Robert 1780-1824
McCULLOCH, Thomas 1776-1843
MELVILLE, Herman 1819-1891
MÉRIMÉE, Prosper 1803-1870
MERRIMAN, Brian 1747-1805
MEYER, Conrad Ferdinand 1825-1898
MICKIEWICZ, Adam 1798-1855
MILES, George H. 1824-1871
MITFORD, Mary Russell 1787-1855
MOE, Jörgen Ingebretsen 1813-1882
MONTAGU, Elizabeth 1720-1800
MONTGOMERY, James 1771-1854
MOODIE, Susanna 1803-1885
MOORE, Thomas 1779-1852
MORIKE, Eduard 1804-1875
MORRIS, William 1834-1898
MORTON, Sarah Wentworth 1759-1846
MOTOORI Noringa 1730-1801
MÜLLER, Friedrich 1749-1825
MULTATULE (pseud. of E.D. Dekker) 1820-1887
MURGER, Henri 1822-1861
MUSSET, Alfred de 1810-1857
NEKRASOV, Nikolai 1821-1877
NEMCOVÁ, Bozena 1820-1862
NERUDA, Jan 1834-1891
NESTROY, Johann 1801-1862
NEWMAN, John Henry 1801-1890
NICCOLINI, Giambattista 1782-1861
NIEVO, Ippolito 1831-1861
NJEGOS, Petar 1813-1851
NODIER, Charles 1780-1844
NORTH, Christopher (pseud. of John Wilson) 1785-1854

NORWID, Cyprian 1821-1883
NOVALIS (pseud. of Friedrich von Hardenberg) 1772-1801
OBRADOVIC, Dositej 1742-1811
OEHLENSCHLÄGER, Adam 1779-1850
OLIPHANT, Margaret 1828-1897
O'NEDDY, Philothée (pseud. of Théophile Dondey) 1811-1875
O'SHAUGHNESSY, Arthur William Edgar 1844-1881
OSTROVSKY, Alexander 1823-1886
PAINE, Thomas 1737-1809
PALSSON, Gestur 1852-1891
PALUDAN-MILLER, Frederick 1809-1876
PARKMAN, Francis 1823-1893
PATER, Walter 1839-1894
PATMORE, Coventry Kersey Dighton 1823-1896
PEACOCK, Thomas Love 1785-1866
PERK, Jacques 1859-1881
PISEMSKY, Alexey F. 1820-1881
PLATEN-HALLERMÜNDE, August 1796-1835
POMPÉIA, Raul D'Avila 1863-1895
POPOVIC, Jovan Sterija 1806-1856
POTGEITER, Everardus Johannes 1808-1875
PRAED, Winthrop Mackworth 1802-1839
PRATI, Giovanni 1814-1884
PRERADOVIC, Petar 1818-1872
PRESEREN, France 1800-1849
PRINGLE, Thomas 1789-1834
PUSHKIN, Aleksander 1799-1837
PYE, Henry James 1745-1813
QUENTAL, Antero Tarquínio de 1842-1891
QUINTANA, Manuel José 1772-1857
RADCLIFFE, Ann 1764-1823
RADISHCHEV, Aleksander 1749-1802
RAFTERY, Anthony 1784-1835
RAIMUND, Ferdinand 1790-1836
REID, Mayne 1818-1883
RENAN, Ernest 1823-1892
REUTER, Fritz 1810-1874
RIMBAUD, Arthur 1854-1891
ROGERS, Samuel 1763-1855
ROSSETTI, Dante 1828-1882
RÜCKERT, Friedrich 1788-1866
RUNEBERG, Johan 1804-1877
RYDBERG, Viktor 1828-1895
RYUTEI TANEHIKO 1783-1842
SAAVEDRA Y RAMÍREZ DE BOQUEDANO, Angel de 1791-1865

SADE, Marquis de 1740-1814
SAINT-BEUVE, Charles 1804-1869
SALTYKOV-SHCHEDRIN, Mikhail 1826-1892
SANTO KYODEN 1761-1816
SATANOV, Isaac 1732-1805
SCHILLER, Friedrich 1759-1805
SCHLEGEL, August 1767-1845
SCHLEGEL, Karl 1772-1829
SCOTT, Sir Walter 1771-1832
SCRIBE, Augustin Eugene 1791-1861
SENOA, August 1838-1881
SHELLEY, Mary W. 1797-1851
SHELLEY, Percy Bysshe 1792-1822
SHERIDAN, Richard 1751-1816
SHEVCHENKO, Taras 1814-1861
SHULMAN, Kalman 1819-1899
SILVA, José Asunción 1865-1896
SIMMS, William Gilmore 1806-1870
SLAVEYKOV, Petko 1828-1895
SLOWACKI, Juliusz 1809-1848
SMITH, Richard Penn 1799-1854
SMOLENSKIN, Peretz 1842-1885
SOARES DE PASSOS, António Augusto de 1826-1860
SOGA, Tiyo 1829-1871
SOLOMOS, Dionysios 1798-1857
SOUTHEY, Robert 1774-1843
STAËL, Mme. de 1766-1817
STAGNELIUS, Erik Johan 1793-1823
STARING, Antonie Christiaan Wynand 1767-1840
STENDHAL (pseud. of Henri Beyle) 1783-1842
STEVENSON, Robert Louis 1850-1894
STIFTER, Adalbert 1805-1868
STONE, John Augustus 1801-1834
STOWE, Harriet Beecher 1811-1896
STUR, L'udovit 1815-1856
SURTEES, Robert Smith 1803-1894
SYROKOMLA, Wladyslaw (pseud. of Ludwik Kondratowicz) 1823-1862
TAUNAY, Alfredo d' Ecragnole 1843-1899
TAYLOR, Bayard 1825-1878
TENNYSON, Alfred, Lord 1809-1892
TERRY, Lucy (Lucy Terry Prince) 1730-1821
THACKERAY, William 1811-1863
THOMPSON, Daniel Pierce 1795-1868
THOMPSON, Samuel 1766-1816
THOMSON, James 1834-1882
THOREAU, Henry David 1817-1862
TIECK, Ludvig 1773-1853
TIEDGE, Christoph August 1752-1841
TIMROD, Henry 1828-1867

TOLENTINO DE ALMEIDA, Nicolau 1740-1811
TOMMASEO, Nicolo 1802-1874
TOMPA, Mihály 1817-1888
TOPELIUS, Zachris 1818-1898
TOPSØE, Vilhelm 1840-1881
TROLLOPE, Anthony 1815-1882
TURGENEV, Ivan 1818-1883
TYUTCHEV, Fedor I. 1803-1873
UHLAND, Ludvig 1787-1862
VAJDA, János 1827-1899
VALAORITIS, Aristotelis 1824-1879
VALLÈS, Jules 1832-1885
VERDE, Cesário 1855-1886
VERY, Jones 1813-1880
VIGNY, Alfred Victor de 1797-1863
VILLAVERDE, Cirilio 1812-1894
VILLIERS DE L'ISLE-ADAM, P.A. 1840-1889
VINJE, Aasmund Olavsson 1818-1870
VON FALLERSLEBEN, August Heinrich (pseud. of August Heinrich Hoffmann) 1798-1874
VÖRÖSMARTY, Mihaly 1800-1855
WAGNER, Richard 1813-1883
WARREN, Mercy Otis 1728-1814
WEIGELAND, Henrik Arnold 1808-1845
WEISSE, Christian Felix 1726-1804
WELHAVEN, Johan S. 1807-1873
WERGELAND, Henrik Arnold 1808-1845
WERNER, Zacharius 1768-1823
WESCOTT, Edward Noyes 1846-1898
WESSELY, Nattali Herz 1725-1805
WHEATLEY, Phyllis 1753-1784
WHITMAN, Sarah Helen 1803-1878
WHITMAN, Walt 1819-1892
WHITTIER, John Greenleaf 1807-1892
WIELAND, Christoph Martin 1733-1813
WOOLSON, Constance Fenimore 1840-1894
WORDSWORTH, William 1770-1850
ZHUKOVSKY, Vasily 1783-1852
ZORRILLA Y MORAL, José 1817-1893

Sergei Timofeyvich Aksakov

1791-1859

(Also transliterated as Serge, Serghei, Sergey; also Timofee-vich, Timoféyvich; also Aksakoff, Aksákoff, Aksákov) Russian autobiographer, essayist, short story writer, translator, and critic.

Considered one of the founders of Russian realism, Aksakov is best known for his evocative autobiographical works depicting the patriarchal life of old Russia. He was born in Ufa, in the eastern steppes of Russia. Educated at home, he later attended the University of Kazan, and, upon graduation, secured a government post in Moscow. He began to contribute essays and criticism to periodicals, and also produced a few rather ineffectual translations of French dramatic classics.

It was not until the 1830s that Aksakov began to write important original work. In 1832, he met Nikolai Gogol, who influenced his creative life. It was Gogol who encouraged Aksakov to write of his early life in the country, and to express his memoirs in a realistic prose style. A first attempt at this new method, his short story *Buran* (The Snowstorm), is considered an immature yet important work, for it contains the seeds of Aksakov's objective realism that were to germinate in his later prose masterpieces, *Semeinaia khronika (The Family Chronicle)* and *Detskie gody Bagrova-vnuka (Years of Childhood)*. These fictionalized reminiscences of Aksakov's family contain a historically accurate yet warmly objective re-creation of rural life. Like the works of Marcel Proust in their evocation of an elusory past, they have earned Aksakov a place among the masters of Russian prose.

His love for the old way of life in Russia was passed on to at least two of his fourteen children, his sons Ivan and Konstantin, who became central figures of the Russian Slavophile movement of the mid-nineteenth century. Aksakov characterized the nature and appeal of his work in this way: "To the end of a long life I have preserved warmth and liveliness of imagination; and that is why talents that are not extraordinary have produced extraordinary effect."

PRINCIPAL WORKS

Buran (short story) 1834
Zapiski ob uzhenyi ryby (essays) 1847
Zapiski ruzheynogo okhotnika (essays) 1852
Semeinaia khronika (autobiography) 1856
    [*Memoirs of the Aksakov Family*, 1871; also published as
      A Russian Gentleman, 1917; also published as *The*
      Family Chronicle, 1961]
*Vospominania (autobiography) 1856
    [*A Russian Schoolboy*, 1917]
Detskie gody Bagrova-vnuka (autobiography) 1858
    [*Years of Childhood*, 1916; also published as *The Years of*
      Childhood of Bagrov, the Grandson, 1924]
Literaturnye i teatralnye vospominaniya (memoirs) 1858
Istoriya moega znakomstva s Gogolem (unfinished
    memoirs) 1890

*This work was originally published with the author's *Semeinaia khronika*.

MAURICE BARING (essay date 1915)

Just as the camp of Reform produced in Herzen a supreme writer of memoirs, that of the Slavophiles also produced a unique memoir writer in [Serge Aksakov] . . . , who describes the life of the end of the eighteenth century, and the age of Alexander [in the *Family Chronicle*]. This book, one of the most valuable historical documents in Russian, and a priceless collection of biographical portraits, is also a gem of Russian prose, exact in its observation, picturesque and perfectly balanced in its diction. (pp. 154-55)

The story is as vivid and as interesting as that of any novel, as that of the novels of Russian writers of genius, and it has the additional value of being true. And yet we never feel that Aksakov has a thought of compiling a historical document for the sake of its historical interest. He is making history unawares . . . ; and, whether he was aware of it or not, he wrote perfect prose. No more perfect piece of prose writing exists. The style flows on like a limpid river; there is nothing superfluous, and not a hesitating touch. It is impossible to put down the narrative after once beginning it, and I have heard of children who read it like a fairy-tale. One has the sensation, in reading it, of being told a story by some enchanting nurse, who, when the usual question, "Is it true?" is put to her, could truthfully answer, "Yes, it is true." The pictures of nature, the portraits of the people, all the good and all the bad of the good and the bad old times pass before one with epic simplicity and the magic of a fairy-tale. One is spellbound by the charm, the dignity, the good-nature, the gentle, easy accent of the speaker. . . . (pp. 156-57)

> *Maurice Baring, "The Age of Prose," in his* An Outline of Russian Literature *(reprinted by permission of the Estate of the late Maurice Baring), Williams & Norgate, 1915, pp. 126-58.**

J. D. DUFF   (essay date 1915)

Aksakoff was always keenly interested in literature and wrote a number of books; but his reputation, which stands very high in Russia, depends mainly upon two volumes of Memoirs which he wrote at the end of his life. The first of these he called *A Family History,* and the second . . . *Years of Childhood.* The first volume begins with the history of his grandfather, and goes on with his own school and college days, so that the right place of [the] second volume is in the middle of the first. (pp. vii-viii)

[*Years of Childhood*] was Aksakoff's last book: he wrote it when he was almost blind, a prisoner to his room, and suffering constant pain for which death was the only cure; yet he never once alludes to the conditions under which it was written. If his powers of observation and memory are extraordinary, his power of self-control is hardly less wonderful. (p. viii)

> *J. D. Duff, "Translator's Preface" (1915), in* Years of Childhood *by Serge Aksakoff, translated by J. D. Duff, Edward Arnold Inc., 1916 (and reprinted by Hyperion Press, Inc., 1977), pp. vii-ix.*

L. PEARSALL SMITH   (essay date 1918)

[In Aksakoff's work there] is in the first place the charm of geography and local colour; for if Aksakoff's experiences themselves are not unusual, their setting is quite strange and unfamiliar to us; we are transported to one of the remotest corners of Europe, to the slopes of the Ural Mountains in South-East Russia, near the Kirghiz Steppes and the borders of Asia—into a half-barbaric country full of Tartars and nomad tribes; and the life of this region is presented to us with extraordinary richness. Books of this kind, steeped in the atmosphere of some special place; picturing for us not only the landscape but the life and thoughts of the people who inhabit it—books which fill out for us some featureless expanse on the world's map with infinite circumstance and detail, are always delightful, but always rare, for very special gifts are needed to write them. But these gifts Aksakoff possessed as few writers have ever possessed them; he conveys to us his impressions of sound and sight with such vividness that all the local life of this region, the climate, atmosphere and landscape, the immense bird-haunted steppes, the loud songs of the nightingales in the woods and valleys, the rush of the swift clear rivers, the very splash of the fish in them, seem to become a part of the reader's own experience—he has almost the hallucination of bodily presence, as if he too had spent his youth in that country, and knew it better than almost any other corner of the world.

But it is not only Russian geography but Russian character that is presented to us in these books. Aksakoff shares to the full that capacity for passionate and uncontrolled feeling which we

have come to regard as peculiarly Russian; and if his boyish experiences seem at first sight, for all the difference of geographical setting, not unlike the experiences of English boys, yet the depths of joy and terror, the storms of frantic emotion that accompany them, make them very unlike anything we read of in our literature. . . .

Combined with this capacity for deep and passionate feeling we find in Aksakoff another Russian characteristic—that of cool, acute, disinterested observation. Not only does he watch himself and keep an accurate record of his most extravagant transports, but he watches with equal coolness and detachment the people whom he most dearly loves, and dispassionately describes their eccentricities and faults and failings. . . .

[By] presenting them as they were, with that mixture of good and bad, of folly and wisdom, which is the very texture of human nature, he has done them a greater service than if he had tried to make them into ideal figures, for he has bestowed a kind of immortality upon them; they live in our imaginations like people whom we have known and loved. (p. 355)

> *L. Pearsall Smith, "Aksakoff," in* New Statesman *(© 1918 The Statesman Publishing Co. Ltd.), Vol. X, No. 249, January 12, 1918, pp. 354-55.*

J. D. DUFF   (essay date 1922)

Aksákoff lived for twenty years after his retirement [in 1839], and all his best work as a writer was done during those twenty years. All his life his interest in literature was keen, but he was surprisingly long in finding out where his real strength lay. . . . Gógol's influence and example were decisive. Aksákoff cast off the French shackles which bound him, and made himself immortal by descriptions of what he knew and loved, Russian landscape and Russian character. (pp. vi-vii)

Aksákoff is a classic in his own country. Every educated Russian knows these books. 'At the present time,' wrote a Russian man of letters in 1912, 'the normal education of a child in Russia is inconceivable unless Aksákoff's *Family History* and Tolstóy's *Childhood* form part of it.' His vocabulary is purely Russian, without any admixture of foreign words; his style is charming in its purity and simplicity. He had astonishing powers of observation and memory: he seems to have noticed everything and forgotten nothing. His vivid and minute account of Russian family life in the reign of the Empress Catherine is an important contribution to history. And even these are not his highest merits. His books are fragrant with the flavour of a marked and most attractive personality. . . . And lastly, Aksákoff, for all his air of simplicity, is a great literary artist. If any reader is inclined to doubt this, let him consider the way in which each chapter of this narrative is brought to a conclusion; and he will not remain in doubt for long.

A Russian Gentleman is a suitable title . . . , because the whole stage, on which a large number of actors play their parts, is dominated by the tremendous personality of Aksákoff's grandfather, Stepán Miháilovitch. Plain and rough in his appearance and habits, but proud of his long descent; capable of furious anger and extreme violence in his anger, but also capable of steadfast and even chivalrous affection; a born leader of men and the very incarnation of truth and honesty—Stepán Miháilovitch is more like a Homeric hero than a man of modern times. This portrait of his grandfather is the masterpiece in Aksákoff's gallery; and his descriptions of his parents' courtship and marriage are just as vivid and minute as his pictures of his own early childhood.

The reader, when he reflects that this narrative ends with the day of the narrator's own birth, will be inclined to think that Aksákoff must have had a lively imagination. But Skabitchévsky, a critic of reputation, begins his review of Aksákoff's work by saying:

> Aksákoff's books are remarkable, first of all on this account, that one finds in them no trace of creative or inventive power.

I venture, however, to differ from the Russian critic on this point. Aksákoff's mother may have told him much, and he may have remembered all she told him, but I am convinced that most of the detail in which these books abound can have been derived from no other source than his own imagination. (pp. viii-x)

> *J. D. Duff, "Introduction" (1922), in* A Russian Gentleman *by Serghei Aksakoff, translated by J. D. Duff (reprinted by permission of Oxford University Press), Oxford University Press, London, 1923, pp. v-x.*

D. S. MIRSKY (essay date 1927)

Dostoyévsky's method of evolving a new style by the *fusion* of extremes was not followed by any of his contemporaries, who preferred to arrive at a golden mean by the avoidance of extremes. This triumph of a *middle* style is the characteristic feature of Russian realism from the forties to Chékhov. It was first achieved in the work of three writers, all of them belonging to the settled and propertied class of gentlemen and not to the rootless plebeian intelligentsia: Aksákov, Goncharóv and Turgénev.

The oldest of them was Sergéy Timoféyevich Aksákov. . . . He was a man of a much older generation, older even than either Púshkin or Griboyédov, and has consequently many features to distinguish him from the strictly realistic generation. But he was born to literature through the influence (exercised to a rather unexpected result) of Gógol, and all his work belongs to the period of the realistic triumph. (p. 185)

[It] was Gógol who revealed to Aksákov the possibility of a new attitude towards reality, an attitude that had not been foreseen by the classicists—the possibility of taking life as it comes, of making use of the whole material of life, without necessarily forcing it into the molds of classical form. Of course this truth might have been revealed to Aksákov in some other way besides the evidently more-than-that route of Gógol, but it so happened that it was Gógol's art that removed the film of obligatory stylization from Aksákov's eyes. His first attempt in a new, realistic manner was a short descriptive story, *The Blizzard [Buran]*. . . . It is distinctly experimental and immature. . . . In the following years Aksákov published a series of books on sport in his native Orenbúrg country. They were enthusiastically reviewed by Turgénev, and Gógol wrote to the author: "Your birds and fishes are more alive than my men and women." (pp. 185-86)

The principal characteristic of Aksákov's work is its objectivity. His art is purely receptive. Even when he is introspective, as he is in the greater part of *Years of Childhood,* he is objectively introspective. He remains unmoved by any active desire except to find once again the time that has been lost—"*retrouver le temps perdu.*" The Proustian phrase is not out of

place, for Aksákov's sensibility is curiously and strikingly akin to that of the French novelist; only he was as sane and normal as Proust was perverse and morbid, and instead of the close and stuffy atmosphere of the never aired flat of the boulevard Haussmann, there breathes in Aksákov's books the air of the open steppe. Like Proust, Aksákov is all senses. His style is transparent. One does not notice it, for it is entirely adequate to *what* it expresses. It possesses, moreover, a beautiful Russian purity and an air of distinction and unaffected grace that gives it a fair chance of being recognized as the best, the standard, Russian prose. If it has a defect, it is the defect of its merit—a certain placidity, a certain excessive "creaminess," a lack of the thin, "daimonic," mountain air of poetry. It is of the earth earthy: the air one breathes in it is a fresh and open air, but it is the air of the lowermost atmospheric layers of a country without mountains. This is why, all said and done, it must be regarded as second in quality when compared with Lérmontov's.

The most characteristic and Aksakovian of Aksákov's books is unquestionably *Years of Childhood of Bagróv-Grandson.* . . . The most memorable passages in it are perhaps those which refer to nature. . . . Many readers who prefer incident to the everyday, and the exceptional to the humdrum, find *Years of Childhood* tedious. But if ordinary life, unruffled by unusual incident, is a legitimate subject of literature, Aksákov, in *Years of Childhood,* wrote a masterpiece of realistic narrative. In it he came nearer than any other Russian writer, even than Tolstóy in *War and Peace,* to a modern, evolutionary, continuous presentation of human life, as distinct from the dramatic and incidental presentation customary to the older novelists.

A Family Chronicle is less exclusively personal and more entertaining. It is fuller of incident, and, being the story of the author's grandparents and parents before his own birth, it is necessarily free from introspection. It is also strikingly and unusually objective. . . . [*A Family Chronicle*] is so dispassionate that it could be used by socialists as a weapon to strike at the Russian gentry, and by the conservatives to defend it. . . . [The story] is perfect from beginning to end and is quite unique in modern literature for its tone at once so primaevally magnifying and so scrupulously objective.

The other works of Aksákov are of less universal appeal. *Recollections,* the story of his life from eight to sixteen, is interesting rather as a picture of Russian provincial culture about 1805 than as a revelation of a great literary temperament. The same may be said of his *Literary and Theatrical Reminiscences [Literaturnye i teatralnye vospominaniya],* in which he tells of his relations with the actors and playwrights of 1810-30. They are delightful and at times amusing, but the portraits he paints are visual impressions left on a sensitive retina, not profound intuitions into other people's souls. The same applies to his delightful sketch of Admiral Shishkóv (who had been an early patron of Aksákov's) but not to the remarkable *Recollections of Gógol [Istoriya moega znakomstva s Gogolem].* These have a place apart. . . . [The elusive and evasive personality of Gógol caused Aksákov] such bitter disappointment and disillusionment that he was forced to make an exceptional effort to understand the workings of the strange man's mind, where genius and baseness were so strangely mingled. The effort was painful but extraordinarily successful, and Aksákov's memoir is to this day our principal approach to the problem of Gógol.

Aksákov's objectivity and impartiality are enough to mark him off from the rest of the Russian novelists of the mid-nineteenth century. (pp. 186-88)

D. S. Mirsky, "The Age of Realism: The Novelists (I)" (originally published in his A History of Russian Literature from the Earliest Times to the Death of Dostoyevsky (1881), *Alfred A. Knopf, Inc., 1927), in his* A History of Russian Literature from Its Beginnings to 1900, *edited by Francis J. Whitfield (copyright © 1926, 1927, 1949, 1958 by Alfred A. Knopf, Inc.; reprinted by permission of Alfred A. Knopf, Inc.),* Vintage Books, 1958, pp. 177-214.*

JANKO LAVRIN   (essay date 1942)

[We] look in vain in Aksakov for any traces of Gogol's tedium or morbid subjectivity. Even in literature he remains a landowner of the old patriarchal type—with the manor as the centre of his world. And he describes his family estate near Ufa with such love and affection that he is often referred to as the Homer of the Russian manor. . . . Devoid of any plot, [*A Family Chronicle*] is a leisurely panorama of manor life under his grandfather's firm but just rule. Wavering between memoirs and fiction proper, the author not only turns the reconstructed facts into art, but presents all the characters and happenings with such refreshing homeliness as to make them memorable for ever. (p. 56)

Aksakov's *Recollections* and *The Childhood of Bagrov's Grandson* are autobiographic. Devoid of affectation, they are written, like the rest of his work, in that colloquial Russian which tallies so well with the author's broad and genial personality. Shunning any questions of the day, Aksakov transcends, as it were, the 'natural school' by his very naturalness. Even such a burning topic as serfdom is ignored by him as a problem. There certainly was not much of a 'repentant nobleman' in him. Essentially honest and decent in his patriarchal views, he did not worry about things which he took for granted. (pp. 56-7)

Janko Lavrin, "From Gogol to Turgenev," in his An Introduction to the Russian Novel *(Canadian rights by permission of Janko Lavrin), Methuen & Co. Ltd., 1942, pp. 53-66.*

V. S. PRITCHETT   (essay date 1943)

To Aksakov, childhood was the Golden Age. Not a bird song, not the flight of a butterfly or flash of a fish was forgotten. They were embalmed in the stillness of an unhesitating recollection. Like Goncharov's recollections of his childhood in *Oblomov*, Aksakov's [recollections in *A Russian Schoolboy*] have the warmth of some tale of the folk, where the sun always shines and where even the wickedness of man or the savagery of nature charms us as legends do, illuminating our lives without overpowering them. Aksakov's recollections are a retrospect without remorse. We are endeared by the permanence of human types and the profit and loss of living. The turbulent emotion of Aksakov's adoration of his mother has calmed into one of those deep and now untroubled feelings so beneficent to works of art. No other Russian writer, not even Tolstoy, has achieved the extraordinary stillness and ecstasy of Aksakov's picture of family life. No other Russian writer has held the mirror up to life so steadily, so that we see how the hours pass at Ufa in all their enchanting detail, without a tremor of the glass. In Proust, the act of remembering, the search for the past, the sensibility of the seeker, are important, perhaps the most important elements, in the task of memory; in Aksakov's mirror the agitation and flaws of such a brilliant egoism are not there to distract. Aksakov is not speculative. He is simple,

tender, comic, delicate and factual. . . . How is it that so still, so conservative a memory nevertheless conveys to us an impression of animation, excitement and suspense? . . . The answer must be that Aksakov's memory conceals the act of remembering, that his imagination works in hiding; he holds the mirror so still that we see not the writer but the movement of life itself, as the hunter or watcher of birds does when he sits in the fields unmoving for hours until life has the courage to resume its business. We watch with Aksakov and observe the huge suspense that hangs upon every detail of life from minute to minute. (pp. 416-18)

One reads Aksakov now with a natural nostalgia—not indeed for the past, not for the delectable life of landed prosperity; not even for the abundance of food and drink—for what is the story of family life but the story of the hours spent between one meal and the next?—but for the fixed state of living, some settled condition of judgment. Aksakov's grandfather sat watching the happy young couple, Sofya Nicolayevna and her husband:

> His happiness had a shade of fear and of disbelief in the solidity and permanence of a state of things in itself so charming. He would have liked to speak his mind on the subject, to give them some hints or some useful advice; but whenever he began, he could not find the right words for thoughts and feelings which he could not make clear even to himself; and he went no farther than those trivial commonplaces, which, for all their triviality, have been bequeathed to us by the practical wisdom of past generations and are verified by our own experience.

What is it we admire about these words? We admire their closeness to a simple mind. But above all we admire the spaciousness of the experience from which they come. (p. 419)

V. S. Pritchett, "A Russian Cinderella" (originally published in The New Statesman, Vol. XXVI, No. 670, December 25, 1943), in his* The Living Novel and Later Appreciations *(copyright 1947 © 1964; renewed 1975 by V. S. Pritchett; reprinted by permission of Random House, Inc.; in Canada by Literistic, Ltd.), revised edition, Random House, 1964, pp. 413-19.*

MARC SLONIM   (essay date 1950)

The Realistic tradition took many paths, and not infrequently the same writer would follow several of them. Most novelists attempted to sum up the past, feeling it their duty to capture the failing light of a disappearing society. (pp. 220-21)

[Serghei Aksakov] author of *Family Chronicles* and *The Childhood Years of Bagrov's Grandson* [is a leading representative of this tendency], although his case presents certain peculiarities. . . . It is hardly enough to say that his descriptions of family life on an estate near Ufa, in Eastern Russia, were realistic. Aksakov, who had not been too keen on Pushkin but was enthusiastic about his friend Gogol, was a realist *sui generis*. Almost photographic in his portrayal of Bagrov, an irascible old gentleman of the eighteenth century, in his vignettes of country meals, excursions, and family intrigues, or in the recollections of his school days in Kazan, Aksakov focused his attention on fidelity to fact, on scrupulously exact images. There is nothing critical about his limpid prose, which lacks the ethical note that seemed obligatory in his times. He follows no particular style and has no social implication or any other purpose in his writings. He wrote for the pure joy of recollection, because he loved the life and the people he described—and he tried merely to be faithful to the memory of his senses. Mirsky has called him an 'ocular realist.'

Aksakov was attached to everything purely Russian; he was close to Mother Earth, and his readers could smell the fields and forests and see the rivers and steppes of their land from his descriptions—in a beautiful racy idiom. And these descriptions, on the whole poetic without being sentimental, had a distinctly idyllic quality. In this Aksakov was close to the mood of most of the Patrician Writers who, regardless of their political opinions, felt nostalgic about the doomed nests of the gentlefolk. (p. 221)

> *Marc Slonim, "Literary Trends of the 'Sixties," in his* The Epic of Russian Literature: From Its Origins Through Tolstoy *(copyright 1950 by Oxford University Press, Inc.; renewed 1977 by Tatiana Slonim; reprinted by permission of the publisher), Oxford University Press, New York, 1964, pp. 219-30.**

THE TIMES LITERARY SUPPLEMENT (essay date 1959)

If not everyone has descried in Aksakov one of the major delights of a literary lifetime, it is partly because his books are not easily come by. (Only his last, **Years of Childhood,** is at present in print . . .). His subject matter [is difficult]: Aksakov is taken by those who have not read him to be a kind of rustic memorialist—the father-founder, what is more, of those "sensitive evocations of childhood" which bulk so deplorably large in recent English literature. The notion has got about, in short, that Aksakov's *oeuvre* consists of an endless Mahlerian *adagio,* a parade of country sights and sounds such as has been mounted as well and more briefly by many an English writer.

These are illusions. Adult passions run as high, in *A Russian Gentleman,* as in any of the great Russian novels of the 1860s and 1870s. The attempted abduction of Natasha in *War and Peace* has few equals in fiction for narrative power and intensity of feeling; but one of them is Aksakov's account of the marriage of Mihail Maximovitch Kurolyessov. Turgenev is our touchstone, where delicacy of feeling is concerned; but nothing in Turgenev is superior, in this respect, to the wooing of Sofya Nikolaevna in *A Russian Gentleman.* And if it is the privilege of literature to set before us recurrent human types to whom we should not otherwise be able to set a name—why, then, Stepan Mihailovitch Bagrov must rank with Penelope, and Electra, and Falstaff, and Alceste in *Le Misanthrope,* and Natasha herself as one of the definitive creations of European literature.

Creative, in the strict sense, he was not, of course: Aksakov is an autobiographer, not a novelist, and "old Bagrov" was the name that he gave to his own grandfather. . . .

Much in Aksakov is on an epic scale in respect alike of the events described—the migrations, the patriarchal social structures, the creation from its first beginnings of a complete new society—and of their Eden-like environment. . . . The particularity of his style lies . . . in the perfect regularity of its tread. Yet it is not a regularity which courts monotony; on the contrary: such is the crystalline character of the narrative that we are borne forward without effort, as if in a dream. Almost never does Aksakov employ a metaphor or an unexpected turn of speech: all is transparency. The simplest of words, and the most exact: such are his instruments, and he works in intimacy

with his subject, never obtruding himself, rarely proffering a comment.

To Maurice Baring, writing in 1914, it seemed that "the story of Aksakov's grandfather might be the story of any country gentleman, in any country, at any epoch." But we ourselves prize it for quite a different reason. We find in it a kind of Russian life which, if not quite extinct, is inaccessible to western visitors; and, almost more precious, a kind of Russian character which, in international negotiations at any rate, is not now much to the fore. Human characteristics so deeply rooted, so elemental in their range and force, cannot be driven underground for ever: that is one of the things in Aksakov from which we may draw comfort. . . .

Aksakov excelled in the poetic recreation of country sports—fishing for perch with crayfish-tails, setting a hawk to catch a quail, or watching Philip, the old falconer, bring down a mallard. And he brings to all this a golden equanimity (Mirsky called it "a beautiful Russian purity and an air of distinction and unaffected grace" [see excerpt above]) which makes us loath to take leave of the Bashkiria of a hundred and fifty years ago. . . .

[Aksakov possessed] that form of hyper-excitability which is, if anything, a hindrance to creative work, so completely does it absorb its possessor's energies. . . . [And] even in middle age he had a way of expressing admiration so immoderate that the objects of it shrank back in embarrassment.

The more remarkable, therefore, is the perfected equilibrium which is one of Aksakov's master-qualities as a writer. Rarely do we see so well demonstrated the capacity of the creative impulse to re-direct those aspects of a given personality which cannot be turned to immediate creative advantage.

> *"Abramtsevo Revisted," in* The Times Literary Supplement *(© Times Newspapers Ltd. (London) 1959; reproduced from* The Times Literary Supplement *by permission), No. 3003, September 18, 1959, p. 530.*

RALPH E. MATLAW (essay date 1961)

[Aksakov's] reminiscences of theatrical life between 1812 and 1830 [in *Literaturnye i teatralnye vospominaniya*] contain material that is primarily of anecdotal and antiquarian interest, being concerned with writers, actors and stage conditions. . . . His views on naturalness in acting, on repertoire, on the modern and the classical theatre occasionally show a genuine attempt to modernize the stage and eliminate its artificiality. According to all reports, Aksakov was an extraordinary reader and actor in his own right, but as a member of the gentry, he could only appear in amateur theatricals and recitations, distinguishing himself by the depth of his interpretations and the range of his roles. His original work and criticism during this period are at best second rate, however, and by 1830 he had almost completely stopped writing. (pp. ix-x)

[In 1832, Gogol'] convinced Aksakov of the possibility of presenting material without forcing it into arbitrary and artificial literary forms, and by his own example showed the extent to which the commonplace and even the sordid might serve literary ends. Apparently under this influence Aksakov wrote *The Snowstorm* [*Buran*] . . . , a short description of the onset of a snowstorm in the steppe that communicates the elemental beauty and force of the storm far more than it does its danger, a description that adumbrates the visual clarity and the verbal simplicity of Aksakov's later works. (p. x)

[His *Notes on Fishing (Zapiski ob uzhenyi ryby)*] received great acclaim. Like Izaak Walton's *Compleat Angler,* it is both a practical and a literary guide to fishing, but Aksakov does not expatiate upon the pleasures of the sport, nor does he present fishing as a pastoral idyll. It contains no digressions or ruminative dialogue. Aksakov addresses himself to the reader, tackle and fish. The pleasures of the sport are communicated through the loving detail and expert analyses of angling and of fishes. The reader is constantly amazed by the remarkable observations Aksakov has made on the habits and peculiarities of various species, by the extent of Aksakov's knowledge of nature, and by the bounty of the streams he must have frequented. (p. xi)

In keenness of observation [*Notes of an Orenburg Province Rifle Hunter (Zapiski ruzheynogo okhotnika)*] matches Jean Henri Fabre's *Souvenirs Entomologiques,* but the dispassionate quality of its summaries precludes the fascination that Fabre's marvelous narratives of the insect world possess for the reader.

Like its predecessor on fishing, this is a book whose descriptions of equipment and of hunting are very matter of fact, but are greatly impressive in the steady manner in which they convey the richness and variety of nature. (p. xii)

[In *Notes of an Orenburg Province Rifle Hunter*] Aksakov's unique style is in full evidence, a style entirely devoid of "literariness," a style which sounds almost conversational, not as Herzen's brilliant conversational style deals with ideas, but in the sense of a rich and supple discourse that is capable of dealing with its subject without losing its air of spontaneity and reality. It is in part, no doubt, the result of oral composition, or at least of dictation, but it is also a consciously wrought style. In any case, it is the expression of something completely grounded in the native tradition, of a purity of vocabulary unequaled in Russian. Foreign words are introduced rarely, and for the most part are only such words as have already been assimilated into the language. On rare occasions they appear when Aksakov wants to create a special effect. A key instance is the title of his masterpiece (*The Family Chronicle* [*Semeinaia Khronika*]), where he utilizes the Greek derivative *khronika* rather than the Russian *letopis',* precisely to avoid the connotations of antiquity and historical authority connected with the *letopisi,* the Russian chronicles. On the other hand, Aksakov's style is equally free of archaisms and dialectical expressions.

The books on hunting and fishing are further characteristic of Aksakov's mature work in the way that nature dominates them and in the kind of detail Aksakov adduces. It has already been mentioned that Aksakov's description of a snowstorm vividly presents the physical phenomenon without attempting to communicate its effect on the peasants caught in it, without evaluating its horror or psychological effect. Similarly, in his other works nature is always depicted with an astonishing clarity and exactness, independent of man, sufficient unto itself, with life and movement and grandeur that endow it with a kind of active existence. To be sure, man moves and acts within it through ordinary necessity, for his pleasure or his livelihood, and man is dependent on nature's state. But few writers (Thoreau is a notable exception) communicate so well the total acceptance of nature, the joy in its beauties, without forgetting that man participates in it only as one of its lesser dependents. It is part of Aksakov's conception of nature as a viable entity that accounts for his ability constantly to present natural phenomena in sharp outline and clear detail. (pp. xii-xiv)

In the *Childhood of Grandson Bagrov* [there is a scene that illustrates Aksakov's conception of nature]:

> The sky sparkled with stars, the air was full of the sweet scents of the ripening steppe grasses, the stream gurgled in its course, the fire glowed and threw a bright light over our men, who sat around the fire eating hot buckwheat porridge and cheerfully chatting together; the horses, which had been loosed to get at their oats, were also lit up on one side by a streak of light. "Isn't it your bedtime, Seryosha?" my father asked.

There is no attempt here to evoke a mood, but rather to present a picture where things, even at night, have a clear and palpable shape. There are therefore few adjectives and no attempt to refine them. . . . There is no attempt to philosophize about nature, to develop the implications of the scene except to note that it is past the young boy's bedtime. What makes Aksakov's descriptions so much more impressive in their context, particularly in the narrative framework of *The Family Chronicle* and *The Childhood of Grandson Bagrov,* is the sense of this nature existing in a pristine and inviolate state, of a freshness and immediacy of vision by and large lost to the refined sophisticate who may, like Turgenev, love nature deeply and describe it movingly, but in his own rather than in its terms.

In a primary sense, nature thus plays the leading role in Aksakov's work. Nature acts as the instructor of mankind—from it one learns about the richness and complexity of life, the limits of man's activity. The reader also gauges the characters that Aksakov introduces from their attitudes toward nature, from the degree to which they are attuned to it or are indifferent to it. As with nature, Aksakov follows a similar procedure in describing his characters: his observation is delicate, his comprehension and analysis of human beings profound, but he is content to present it to the reader without offering extensive qualification and explanation. (pp. xv-xvi)

The Childhood of Grandson Bagrov best illustrates [many of Aksakov's literary virtues]: grandeur of nature, for the most part benign, the unhurried passage of time, and the even-paced calmness, all of which emphasize the permanence and immutability of life. There is nothing in Russian literature to compare with its celebration of the manorial life. In Goncharov's masterpiece [*Oblomov*], Oblomov's dream demonstrates the total concentration on physical well-being in the bountiful lap of nature which dehumanizes the participants. But in Aksakov the awareness of nature's gifts and active participation in it bespeak a far higher level of awareness and consciousness, in fact, a morality of its own. The long book is plotless, but it is organized according to an internal principle of structure rather than according to mere temporal sequence. The added distance between Aksakov the writer and Sergey Bagrov the subject serves to increase the illusion of objectivity and to impose a larger meaning on the recital of youthful events. The book is not without development. . . . The book, indeed, goes far beyond childhood in its range of experience and knowledge. Although *The Childhood of Grandson Bagrov* is a unique book, it still occupies a secondary place to Aksakov's masterpiece, *The Family Chronicle.*

Of all books in Russian literature, *The Family Chronicle* is the one that at first glance should appeal most to Americans. But for the fact that Stepan Bagrov faces east and our pioneers faced west, the situation is exactly comparable: the limitless expanse of the new frontier, the sense of space and freedom, the abundance of the land, the simplicity and occasional starkness of life, the necessity for self-reliance, and the moral fiber that manifests itself in the process. It is also a strange fact that these qualities are otherwise rather ignored in Russian literature. We read in the main of control and confinement in the artificial cities, rather than of the immensity of Russia and the implications of its sense of space. Similarly, there is no great American work dealing with the subject. The outstanding novel of that time, *Moby-Dick,* presents its microcosm of America contained and "federated along one keel" of the *Pequod,* relentlessly pursuing leviathans of the sea and monsters of the mind.

Aksakov conveys the special qualities of frontier life primarily through the colossal figure of his grandfather, Stepan Bagrov, who is presented in the first of the work's five sections, and dominates the rest of the work. . . . (pp. xviii-xix)

Stepan Bagrov is presented as an elemental creature in spontaneous communion with life and nature. Aksakov's portrait is the more successful because this elemental quality is never reduced. Bagrov is inarticulate and uncultured, though fully formed morally. . . . There is a fine, moving passage near the end when Bagrov meets his son's wife and forms a strong attachment to her. Aksakov very delicately shows the expressions of this attachment in the understanding between the two. . . . (p. xx)

The section that follows is the antithesis of the first. Its events are extraordinary; its central character a villain bereft not only of morality but even of any decency; its implications a reversal of the first. An officer named Kurolesov, a social charmer who courts Stepan Bagrov's cousin and incurs Bagrov's dislike, manages, after much manipulation and maneuvering on the part of the family, to marry the heiress. After some years odd rumors are heard of his behavior on one of his wife's distant estates, where he spends much time. He has established a harem there, and heads a gang which appropriates whatever it wishes, insults, maims, and occasionally kills those who oppose it, and is so powerful that even the provincial forces dare not institute proceedings. When the wife learns of this, she goes to verify matters for herself, is incarcerated by her husband, beaten and threatened in order to extort from her a power of attorney for all her property. Stepan Bagrov is alerted by a runaway peasant, arrives on the scene when the band is asleep and incapacitated after a lengthy carouse, and rescues his cousin. Shortly after his fall from power Kurolesov is murdered by two of his cronies.

It seems odd that Aksakov should have portrayed such criminal oppression and mistreatment and that he should have shown authority so helpless against such flagrant abuses. Unlike many of those writing at that time, however, Aksakov had no intention of serving a political or civic cause, and was not interested in writing of these events merely to air injustice in the Russian land (he even toned down the events which were more horrifying than he presented them). The episode has a distinct function in developing a major theme of *The Family Chronicle:* the relationship between power and character. Bagrov's violence is an expression of his elemental personality; Kurolesov's actions are petty and directed only to personal enjoyment, and turn out to be vicious. Mere confrontation of frontiers and wilderness does not suffice to elicit man's nobility; it may as easily enable him to fulfill his meanest drives. Aksakov makes a particular point of setting the episode back in time, to give

it the specious appearance of an age less civilized than the present. (pp. xxi-xxii)

Kurolesov anticipates the cruel and quasi-demented characters in Dostoevsky and elsewhere in later Russian literature, people who find their only outlet in dissipation of an extraordinary kind. But the reason for such behavior, the motivating force behind Kurolesov, is never examined by Aksakov. The character merely exists. Nor does Aksakov elaborate on the wife's reaction. She refuses to take steps against her husband, maintaining that she still loves him. There is material here for a great novel, but Aksakov again contents himself merely with indicating the possibility without developing it.

Against the background of these two episodes the concluding sections deal with the courtship and marriage of Aksakov's father. Here Aksakov finally gives full range to his narrative talent in depicting the endless maneuvering, struggles and bitter recriminations involved in the playing out of what would be an excellent comedy had it not been shown from the first that the characters were too seriously taken with their jealousies and with the kind of strife a powerful figure like Bagrov is bound to breed in those around him. (p. xxii)

The courtship of Sofya Nicolaevna might well have served for a novel; the career of Kurolesov for a story; the figure of Stepan Bagrov for a sketch. Aksakov was able to mold the material he derived from family tradition in such a way that each episode far extends the range and depth of the other. His narrative constantly maintains the illusion of simplicity, of forthright statement, even of a kind of ingenuousness. In the struggle for usable forms, solved so conspicuously by Russian novelists such as Gogol', Turgenev and Dostoevsky, Aksakov may well have achieved far more than his modest role as chronicler indicates. (pp. xxiii-xxiv)

Aksakov's work appears simple, but it is a simplicity achieved through clarity of artistic vision and mastery of style. He was able to imbue his recital of a time long past with a sense of the fullness and acceptance of life that speaks eloquently and unequivocally to the reader today. The form of the work, like other idiosyncratic masterpieces, is sufficiently unusual to obscure its originality, but not its quality. (p. xxiv)

> *Ralph E. Matlaw, "Sergey Aksakov: The Genius of Ingenuousness" (copyright, ©, 1961, by E. P. Dutton & Co., Inc.; reprinted by permission of the publisher, E. P. Dutton), in* The Family Chronicle *by Sergey Aksakov, translated by M. C. Beverly, Dutton, 1961, pp. vii-xxiv.*

ALEX de JONGE   (essay date 1978)

[Aksakov] loved the Russian countryside and wrote about it magnificently, especially about hawking, shooting, and above all fishing. He is brilliant on water, with the ability to make a mill pond, stream or eddy come alive in a way that makes any fisherman green with envy as he longs to fish there too. He puts across the fever of hooking a monster, as his servant tells him to 'pull away, little master, pull away', and renders the desperate need to get to the water despite an anxious mother's attempts to stop him. He also gives a marvellous account of what it was like to travel in those days, crossing rivers in particular, on rafts, or, more dangerously, on ice that was about to break up. As he puts himself back into his childhood, going out with rod, hawk or gun and staying out while daylight lasted, we might almost think of him as a Russian Richard Jefferies. . . .

Although this is what Aksakov seems to represent for most Russians he does actually spend much of his time writing about a very different kind of Russian favourite sport—family rows and emotional upheavals. This is the stuff *The Family Chronicle* is made of, with the family in question displaying what might to Anglo-Saxon eyes appear quite unbelievable bitchiness to one another, while to a Russian it appears to convey the benign warmth of true feeling; a million miles away from the deadly state of emotional 'cold'.

> *Alex de Jonge, "Growing Up," in* The Spectator *(©1978 by* The Spectator; *reprinted by permission of* The Spectator*), Vol. 241, No. 7846, November 18, 1978, p. 20.*

THE NEW YORKER   (essay date 1979)

[Aksákov,] though little known in the West, was, with Pushkin and Gogol, one of the founders of modern Russian literature, and if Mr. Duff's translation [of *A Russian Schoolboy*] is an accurate rendering, he was a writer of unusual clarity, simplicity, and charm. . . . [*A Russian Schoolboy*] is a window, open and sunlit, on a long-vanished place and time and culture.

> *"Briefly Noted: 'A Russian Schoolboy'," in* The New Yorker *(© 1979 by The New Yorker Magazine, Inc.), Vol. LV, No. 20, July 2, 1979, p. 96.*

Washington Allston

1779-1843

American poet, novelist, and essayist.

Best known as a Romantic painter, Allston was also a moderately influential literary figure in his own time. He was an important contributor to the theory of Romantic aesthetics, an associate of distinguished artists and writers in Europe and America, and was an important link between European and American artists and philosophers. Allston's writings serve as a verbal counterpart to his paintings, reflecting the shift from neoclassicism to Romanticism that he helped advance in the United States.

Allston was born in South Carolina, schooled from age seven in Rhode Island, and graduated from Harvard. Determined to become a painter, Allston sold his patrimonial estate and sailed for Europe, where he spent seven years studying painting in London, Paris, and Rome. He was influenced artistically by the work of the Italian Renaissance masters, especially in his use of color. In England, where he lived from 1811 to 1818, Allston completed his finest paintings: *Dead Man Revived by Touching the Bones of the Prophet Elisha, Uriel in the Sun,* and the portrait *Samuel Taylor Coleridge.* Coleridge was a close friend who during this time introduced Allston to Romanticism. His interest in its supernatural aspects influenced his painting and won him approval of art critics. During this period Allston also composed *The Sylphs of the Seasons, with Other Poems,* verses exalting nature and artistic imagination, which Robert Southey, William Wordsworth, and Coleridge praised.

Allston's acceptance in England greatly enhanced the reputation of American art. When he returned to Boston permanently in 1818, artists and literati recognized Allston as a master and regarded him as a symbol of the value of American art. While Allston continued to paint, perhaps his greatest contribution was spreading European philosophies to his contemporaries. Critics credit Allston for disseminating the Romantic concepts that form the heart of transcendental thought: the belief in the importance of the relationship between humankind and nature, and the primacy of the individual consciousness and imagination.

In beginning his essay on self-reliance, Ralph Waldo Emerson wrote of Allston: "I read the other day some verses written by an eminent painter which were original and not conventional. Always the soul hears admonition in such lines . . .". Although his literary output was of neither the volume nor the quality to make him a major American writer, Allston was important for the Romantic "admonition" expressed in his books and paintings. (See also *Dictionary of Literary Biography, Vol. 1: The American Renaissance in New England.*)

PRINCIPAL WORKS

The Sylphs of the Seasons, with Other Poems (poetry) 1813
Monaldi (novel) 1841
Lectures on Art, and Poems (essays and poetry) 1850

RICHARD HENRY DANA (essay date 1817)

[*The Sylphs of the Seasons*] was written, we believe, in what were Mr. Allston's moments of rest from his professional pursuits, at odd times, and with great rapidity. We would not set up for the author the old and impudent apology of "leisure hours", nor urge the quickness with which it was written, as an excuse for negligence in the finish. Indeed, we do not think that it discovers such negligence, but hold it as one among many instances of powerful and tasteful minds working surest and to most effect the more rapidly they move. The imagination and feelings are then excited, and there is at the same time a truth of touch which makes them turn off from what is out of form or place. (p. 107)

The first poem ["**The Sylphs of the Seasons**"], and that on "**Eccentricity,**" are sketchy, and would have been improved by filling up. The others are, perhaps, as complete as the nature of their several subjects, and the sprightly narrative manner in which they are treated, would admit of. Without intending to take from their merit, we should rank them with the lighter kind of poetry. They have not the continual shifting and bustling scenes and breathless speed of Scott; nor does Mr. Allston, like Byron, stir the fiery passions within you, or carry you down into the dark and mysterious depths of the soul, moving you to and fro in their wild and fearful workings. He is not majestic and epic; nor does he make you serious, like Wordsworth, or show you a stained world, and dejected virtue, throwing a hue of thoughtfulness over brightest joys. His mind seems to have in it the glad, but gentle brightness of a star, as you look up to it, sending pure influences into your heart, and making it kind and cheerful. He paints with a particularity and truth, which show that he has looked upon nature with his own eyes, and not through those of other men. He has not only an eye for nature, but a heart too, and his imagination gives them a common language, and they talk together. As we said of the poetry of the present day, so with him, every thing has soul and sense. Never has he turned toward a morning or evening sky, but

> The clouds were touched,
> And in their silent faces did he read
> Unutterable love. . . .

[Allston] views his scenes with a curious and exquisite eye, instilling some delicate beauty into the most common thing that springs up in them, imparting to it a gay and fairy spirit, and throwing over the whole a pure, floating glow. He searches into what is excellent and fair in creation, and, even in his satires, plays with the follies of mankind with an undisturbed gentleness of heart, and turns away from their vices, and shuts out their loathsomeness from his mind. He seems to look upon the world in the spirit in which it was made,—the spirit of love; and, though marred, to see the beauty in which it was ordained, and feel its purity through all its defilements. (pp. 108-09)

[The] poems before us sometimes run up into the wild, visionary, and magnificent; and the eye brightens and enlarges, and the spirits are lifted, as we look. All, however, partakes of the same joyous temperament; for if the scene, viewed alone, would be dark and awing, you find it in the midst of satire and humour, and the lights of these are observed playing and sparkling over it,—as in **"The Paint King,"** and **"The Two Painters."** And this brings us on our way to other qualities in these poems,—the character of their satire and wit. . . . [All] good satire in verse is not necessarily high poetry too. Not that satire may not be poetry, truly and distinctively poetry, permeated by, and indeed often springing from, deep sentiment, vivid, varied, and ascending fancy, and expansive imagination. With this fancy, and with even something of this faculty of imagination, we think the satirical portion of [*The Sylphs of the Seasons*] more or less imbued. We find it relieved by natural scenery both beautiful and grand, and the regions of the imagination travelled over to find objects for it. Rather, we should say, perhaps, the spirit of satire travels over these,—and, were it taken away, would leave behind a wild yet lovely prospect, such as the eyes of few satirists have looked upon. Yet, with all this, the satire is not made subordinate to the scenery through which it passes. There is nothing bitter or hard in it. But it appears so bright and playful, that the fairest prospects look gladder in it. . . . (pp. 110-11)

We trust that we shall not be charged with bestowing over-praise, when we say, that, in easy and familiar narrative style, [**"The Two Painters"**] reminds us of the tales of Swift, Prior, and Gay. Here we find satire sparkling over poetic imagery, and blending with scenes wild and picturesque. (pp. 117-18)

We must express the hope that Mr. Allston will write no more "didactic poems," as they are styled. To be sure, no man

would part with those of Cowper, for instance; yet, for the most part, they are apt to act in way of restraint upon the invention, and to shut it up from plot, and varied incidents, and freshly created worlds. Certainly, an intellect like Mr. Allston's, delighting in the fanciful, sacrifices its best powers in this lecture-room of the Muses. They should be left for men of the character of Queen Anne's time, who were formed to shine in such works, and were little at home with thoughts and images belonging to minds of our author's cast. We do not object to the satire and character-drawing; but we should always be glad to see them enlivened by incidents, with something of dramatic activity, and placed in scenes as new and poetical as those in which we find **"The Two Painters."** (pp. 125-26)

[*The Sylphs of the Seasons*] is clearly original in its character. We do not find in it imitations of the style, or borrowing of the circumstances, situations, or images of other authors. Many of its subjects are new, and all are marked by the peculiar cast of our author's mind. To this very novelty may be, in a measure, attributed its want of popularity. (p. 129)

Mr. Allston's verse is easy, and reads as if it were produced with unusual facility; and his language, too, is good. Yet we think that both would have been richer, had he made the old master-poets more his study in early life. But while the poets of the present times have done well in freeing themselves of much that was introduced at the Restoration, we hardly look for the return of that affluent, poetic diction, that rich and varied tone and deep harmony, which, with its individual varieties, marked the works of Spenser, Shakespeare, and Milton. (p. 130)

> *Richard Henry Dana, "Allston's 'Sylphs of the Seasons'" (originally published in* The North American Review, *Vol. 5, No. 3, 1817), in his* Poems and Prose Writings, Vol. II, *Baker and Scribner, 1849, pp. 101-31.*

C. C. FELTON   (essay date 1842)

[Were it not for Allston's] overshadowing fame as the foremost painter of his age, he would unquestionably have been renowned as one of our most graceful and imaginative poets. [*The Sylphs of the Seasons*] shows the invention, and fancy, and curious felicity of expression, that mark the true son of song; and, had Mr. Allston followed out the poetical career, he would most certainly have reached, ere this, the same eminence as a writer, to which his genius has borne him in art. (p. 397)

The story of [Allston's novel] *Monaldi* turns upon jealousy. This passion is the least respectable of all the methods taken by foolish men to make themselves miserable. We have never had a strong liking for tales of distress, founded upon jealousy. (p. 399)

Mr. Allston has wrought into this tale materials enough for two or three common novels; and we are not sure that he would not have done better to draw out the varied passions of the story at greater length; to paint with greater minuteness, and in a fuller style, the scenes and events through which his characters are made to pass; to soften somewhat the suddenness of the transitions, and thus to explain and justify, more completely than he has done, the overwhelming catastrophe, in which virtue, genius, beauty, and fame are swallowed up. Many hints and intimations, which the observing reader notices in a second perusal, do this for the few; but the great mass of readers, who never take up a book but once, will remain discontented with the manner in which the destinies of Monaldi and Rosalia Landi are wrought out. The great artist, studying as he does the effects of particular moments,—working up striking historical or tragic crises, and trusting to the imagination of the spectator to supply what goes before or follows; presenting, as the very conditions and materials of his art force him to do, the passions, attitudes, groups, of a single second only to the senses,—is apt to apply the same methods, and use the same principles, when he passes from art to literature, from the canvass or the marble to the printed page. (pp. 400-01)

In the conduct of [*Monaldi*], we think we see that Mr. Allston has been true to the artist's character. And though, as we have said before, hints and intimations are sufficiently thrown in to guide the careful reader to the right conclusion, yet the intervals between the great moments are not sufficiently filled out for a novel. We have no doubt this passionate story exists in his mind in the form of a series of pictures; at least it would afford half a dozen glorious subjects for his pencil. (p. 401)

We perceive the artist, not only in the respects we have above alluded to, but in the able delineation and skilful contrast of characters. The two leading personages, Maldura and Monaldi, are of equal excellence, and are brought out with the greater effect by being set off against each other with such admirable judgment. They are traced from the first traits and impulses of schoolboy days, to the finished characters of the matured men; and we cannot help admiring the delicate and subtile manner in which the diverging motives and influences, under which the two are gradually formed to such perfect opposites, are from time to time brought to light. (pp. 401-02)

The sensual villain, Count Fialto, is a remarkable and well-drawn figure, necessary to the purposes of the plot, and strongly contrasting with the intellectual profligacy of his employer. But the character which sheds a divine charm over the dark picture, and harmonizes all its terrible elements into a serene and heavenly beauty, is that of Rosalia Landi. The delineation of a perfect woman with natural traits, without exaggeration; the blending of all these ingredients of character in just proportion; the gentleness without weakness, and the firmness free from masculine hardness; the soft compliance joined to unbending love of truth and honor; which make up the admirable woman in real life; this portraiture is, we are inclined to think the rarest and most difficult achievement of the writer's art. But rare and difficult as it is, Mr. Allston has achieved the task in his Rosalia Landi. (pp. 402-03)

[*Monaldi* is] remarkable for its rich and harmonious prose. The nice selection of epithets, the faultless arrangement of the members of the sentences, and the rhythmical cadence to which thought and expression seem to move united, combine to make it one of the most finished works in American literature. We fall here and there upon a most delicately wrought picture of some natural scene, which betrays the artist's eye and hand; then a deep moral reflection, speaking a varied experience and observation of life, arrests our attention and awakens a train of solemn thought; then a maxim of art, worthy to be laid up among the treasures of memory, is modestly put forth, but bears under its simple expression the wisdom of studious and thoughtful years. Such, in our judgment, is the character of this little volume by our great artist; it is a work of high genius, of rare beauty, and of a moral purity and religious elevation, which distinguish it from most literary works of the age. (p. 403)

C. C. Felton, "'Monaldi'," in The North American Review, *Vol. LIV, No. 115, April, 1842, pp. 397-419.*

W. G. SIMMS (essay date 1843)

Allston was not a poet in the high, perhaps the only proper sense of the term. He was not an original thinker in verse,—not a seer,—not inspired. His writings are rather those of the accomplished and educated gentleman,—the man of taste and purity, of grace and sentiment, than the poet. They are not the overflow of a swelling imagination,—a brain bursting with big conceptions. They rather declare the gently contemplative mood, stirred into utterance by emotions which are equally passing and agreeable. . . . The "Sylphs of the Seasons," is the first, but not the longest poem in [the collection of the same name]. We should judge it, however, to be the best. "The Two Painters;—a tale," by which it is followed, is scarcely so pleasing a production, though it contains certain excellent morals, as well as artistical hints, to painters, which it might be well for them to study. (pp. 381-82)

["**Two Painters**"] is satirical in its character, but not personal, although the satire is based in part upon the faults, moral and professional, of well known artists. It does not strike us as a very felicitous performance. (p. 384)

["**Eccentricity**", another poem in a satirical vein,] is a forcible sketch, but not a poetical and scarcely a pleasant one. The verse, though not harsh, is not musical, and betrays the uphill toil of the unpractised workman. "**The Paint King**" is a lively ballad, in imitation of the style of Monk Lewis, and a very happy imitation it is. . . . The rest of [*The Sylphs of the Seasons*] is yielded to smaller pieces. Several of these are sonnets, educed by the contemplation of the works of ancient artists. These are energetic and thoughtful, rather than poetical. Two or three little ballads close the volume, which, as the reader may infer, is no unworthy evidence of the taste and talent of our great painter, in the exercise of a kindred art. But we turn to some better proofs of the poetic faculty of Mr. Allston. The few fugitive poems which, of late years, have escaped from his pen, take far higher rank, in the poetic scales, than any of his more youthful performances. Of these we have but few, but they are such as to awaken a desire for more. . . . [They] seem to have embodied the mental or spiritual ideals for some of his smaller pictures. This of "**Rosalie**" is said to have been the conception of beauty from which he painted one of his loveliest, and, we believe, latest pictures. The tone of sweet, sad, spiritual meaning, by which it seems burdened, is very touching and should commend it to every reader of sensibility. . . . (p. 385)

The apostrophe of "**America to Great Britain**," quoted by Coleridge in his Sybilline leaves, is a fine and spirited imitation of one of the popular odes of Campbell, and speaks equally well for the poet's love of country and powers of versification. (p. 386)

The sweet and pensive poem, "**The Tuscan Maid**," cannot be passed without recognition. It deserves a place with the two preceding. How sweetly does it describe that nice mingling, or rather melting, of one into the other, of the several transition periods in the life of maidenhood;—and how true and philosophical, as well as poetical and natural, are the descriptive passages which betray the development of that moral nature, which, we believe, the artist has striven successfully to delineate, along with the physical, in all of those works of art in which he has labored to pourtray, the contemplative. The picture which follows, tinged, as it is, in a manner equally true and delicate with the finest spiritual hues, seems to us among the most exquisite things of its kind,—keeping, as it does, within the boundaries of common sense, and plain reason, while rising in its tone and signification into the highest regions of spiritual song. . . . (pp. 387-88)

We have no means of ascertaining what degree of success attended the publication of Allston's poems in London. The probability is that it was very slight. The volume was not of a kind to awaken any sensation. It possessed no startling characteristics, had nothing of novelty, and, perhaps, but for the great success of the author in another department of art, would not now be remembered either in England or America. Though exhibiting the possession of powers, not merely fanciful, but creative, it still did not evince a mind of that degree of original resource, which is calculated to take hold of the public ear, and fasten it either in sudden or lasting allegiance. The song was one of grace and sweetness,—nothing more. . . . We repeat that we do not regard **"The Sylphs of the Seasons"** as a performance calculated to obtain for its author any higher credit than is due to a good taste, and a buoyant and artist-fancy. (p. 389)

[Allston's tale, **"Monaldi,"**] wild, tender, passionate,—full of thought, and instinct with all the graces and delicacies of the mind of the author, is one equally significant of the poet and the painter. It is not less a poem because written in prose. It is a fine specimen of artistical performance, in which the nice method and elaborate skill, are perhaps more obvious, than the originality or the propriety of the tale. This, indeed, is only another form of the old story of Italian subtlety, susceptibility to jealousy, blind passion and unhesitating vengeance. We see in it sufficient proofs of that early passion for like materials which Allston, as a painter, exhibited in his first achievements in art. But, in his hands, this material differs very greatly from the same sort of stuff in the hands of Mrs. Radcliffe. Mr. Allston was too much a man of taste, too much of the artist, too happy in his conceptions, too correct in his judgment, to attempt any of the vulgar tricks of the ordinary novelist. . . . Though **"Monaldi"** turns upon events which have been used time out of mind, by the novelist and dramatist, yet his proceedings are all effected by means which are equally probable and interesting. It is as free from the common-places of the romancer as any publication that we have ever read. The story, though comparatively simple, is yet productive of fine issues for the artist;—by which he is able to bring about frequent trials of strength between his parties,—by which the conflict between vice and virtue,—truth and falsehood,—pride and shame,—is continually going on;—with the best results to morals, though, perhaps, with such as are humbling to those whom we love, and distressing to our finest sympathies. (pp. 394-95)

"Monaldi" is a painful but a pleasing story,—painfully pleasing. . . . [At] the very opening of [Allston's] book, written in a style the most clear and forcible, is the contrasted analysis of the two persons [Monaldi and Maldura], whose antagonist moral natures are to operate as foils throughout the volume. (pp. 395-96)

The story is, indeed, a woeful one—perhaps one of a too much exaggerated woe. . . . But its chief merit is not in the story. That, as we have already said, is composed of materials which have been long since in common use. It is in the manner in which these materials have been used; in the felicitous discrimination of character; in the happy language, the appropriate illustrations, and the occasional fancies and reflections, naturally suggested, by which the details are elevated into classical forms, and made instinct with the mind of the author. The true description—the delicate fancy—the pure taste, and the correct

judgment, which this story betrays, throughout, are the distinct possessions of the genuine artist. **"Monaldi"** is a work of art. (p. 412)

W.G. Simms, "The Writings of Washington Allston," in Southern Quarterly Review, Vol. IV, No. 8, October, 1843, pp. 363-414.

THE AMERICAN REVIEW   (essay date 1848)

Monaldi is to be loved . . . because it is a delightful old-fashioned tale, full of reflection, observation, philosophy, character, pictures, true affection—all excellent qualities; because it charms the reader and draws him onward, so that when it is begun it presses to be gone through with; because it takes him into a new and beautiful region, a modification of one that was already familiar, a peculiar Italy, wherein the real and the romantic are brought into actual harmonious contact; because it is told in a pure simple style, that often rises to the most passionate eloquence; because Rosalia is so lovely and so truly intellectual a lady; or to sum up all in one, as Beatrice does her love to Benedict, "for all these bad parts together," or simply because not to like it is impossible. . . .

[We] commend *Monaldi* as an *unique* in our literature—a short story of love, ambition, revenge, and jealousy, highly dramatic and picturesque, yet embodying thought enough to give it rank with Rasselas or any similar production in the language. Though written in the form of a tale, it has all the condensation of a tragedy; every page hurries along the action, and every page teems also with suggestive reflection. Its style is pure, and finished with the most extreme care; yet it is also perfectly natural and easy. (p. 351)

But the style of *Monaldi,* though pure, is not rigid; it bends to the story, and this shows how naturally it must have been written. In the opening chapters, it is quiet and reflective, suited to the tone of the thoughtful character-drawing with which the piece commences; as it goes on, we have a vivid epigrammatic dialogue; then the most passionate scenes, all built upon the original reflective back-ground, which is ever coming in, like a prevailing harmony, to sustain the unity of the tone. Finally, nothing can be finer for harmony of style with the thought and with its previous level, than the conclusion. There, where there was so much temptation to be falsely eloquent, the author has so resolutely preserved the dominant tone, that the very melody of the sentences almost gives an effect that we are approaching a concluding harmony; the end begins to be felt a long way off, and at last it dies away with the lofty grandeur of an old Handelian cadence. (p. 352)

[Some parts of *Monaldi* contain art criticism,] of that sort which sinks into the mind and is never forgotten. There is hardly a technical word in it, but yet it goes at once to the very root of the matter. It deserves to be treasured along with Mozart's humorous oracular decisions in music. . . . For they are great simple truths, as obvious as the presence of matter, and at the same time as little considered. (pp. 354-55)

Had only the principles which might be deduced from the few passages respecting painting, in the opening chapters of this story, . . . been brought out, illustrated, *invested,* with the care a person would have used toward them to whom they were his whole stock in trade, we should have had volumes instead of paragraphs. But the author of *Monaldi* was too rich in ideas of his art, and its works, to care to husband his thoughts; neither could he be profuse or ostentatious in the display of them. He simply introduces them because they are essential to the development of his ideal character, whom he, naturally enough, made a painter. And the result is, that they are in reality far more effective than they could have been in the garb of formal criticism.

For they come to us under the modifying influences of the author's imaginative power. That is to say, the tone and keeping of the tale, the expression which seems to clothe the face of him who is all through talking with us, his character as here written down, gives a force and meaning to his words which otherwise they could not have. (p. 355)

> G.W.P., "'Monaldi'," in The American Review, Vol. 1, No. IV, April, 1848, pp. 341-57.

THE NORTH AMERICAN REVIEW   (essay date 1850)

[Allston's collection, **Lectures on Art, and Poems,** is] a welcome gift, not only to all the lovers of art, but to all who take an interest in elegant literature. The spirit of beauty which breathes through his poetical writings—the offspring of hours of rest from the labors of the pencil—will fill with delight the breasts of those who fly to the Muse for solace amidst the multiplying cares of life, or seek in poetry for the graceful embellishments that idealize the business of the crowded day. (p. 150)

Mr. Allston's poetical style is remarkable for the careful finishing hand with which he elaborated every part of every poem. He never fell into the negligent, slip-shod, vague, and half expressed mannerism, so common in these days. His practice as an artist was carried into his writings, and applied scrupulously to every production of his pen. The exquisite purity of his language, reminding us constantly of the fine coloring of his pencil, shows how thoroughly his taste was guarded, in the atmosphere of beauty that accompanied his mind, from all touch of contemporary faults. Loving heartily every genial variety of literature, whether belonging to the past or present, and showing, both in conversation and writing, with what a ready and versatile power he could work in different forms, he yet subjected his own style to a rigid self-criticism that harmonizes with the principles of an earlier and more classical age, rather than with the romantic outflow of the present. His poetical writings, therefore, will not undergo the changes of opinion incident to the fleeting popularity of temporary mannerism. They will stand the test of time. The criticism of posterity will find in them the same qualities to praise that have commended them to the approbation of the wisest contemporary judges. (pp. 151-52)

The portion of the volume which will excite the most interest and attention at the present moment, consists of the **Lectures on Art.** . . . We regard them as the most important addition to the literature of art which has been made within our memory. . . . (p. 156)

We are constantly impressed, in Mr. Allston's writings on art, with the completeness of his intellectual view, and the freedom with which he moves through the whole compass of thought in the domain of art and through all the provinces connected with it. The earlier influences of the profound and affluent genius of Coleridge left unmistakable traces upon his mind, and decided the peculiar coloring of his speculative views; but he has nowhere wandered into the obscurities which too often darkened the struggling conceptions of that great writer. Whatever of Coleridge's philosophy retained its hold upon Mr. Allston was so blended with his independent meditations, that it served only to heighten them by the hues of a spiritual manner of thinking, harmonizing admirably with the poetical light thrown by his own genius over all the objects of thought. (p. 158)

[Allston's **Lectures on Art**] are, like his poems, totally free from the mannerisms of the times, and are, in the highest and best sense of the word, original. They have their root in his inmost nature, and they have ripened into the bright consummate flower by a gradual, slow, and organic progress. They have the completeness of his works of art, while the fresh vitality of the most intense intellectual life flows through every part of them. As we read them, we are in the presence of the very soul of Allston; and whether we agree or not with all of his philosophical statements, we are drawn into perfect sympathy with the lofty spirit of their author. . . . (pp. 158-59)

The charm of Mr. Allston's exquisite style is here displayed in its highest perfection. Polished to that point where the fullest vigor and the nicest finish meet, it is moulded into forms of expression fitly adapted to the depth, completeness, and elegance of the thought. It is richly wrought, where the subject naturally lifts itself into the stately sweep of harmonious expression, and again falls into an unadorned simplicity, and sometimes even a rigid precision of phrase, where clearness of statement or subtlety of reasoning breaks and varies the vivid flow of the composition; and it passes through all these changes with such an equable and gentle movement, that we seem listening, as it were, to the rising and falling of an Æolian harp. (p. 159)

[**Lectures on Art, and Poems**] will sink deeply into the mind of the age, and its influence will slowly but surely extend itself through the whole domain of American culture. (p. 168)

> "Allston's Poems and Lectures on Art," in The North American Review, Vol. LXXI, No. CXLVIII, July, 1850, pp. 149-68.

THE NEW ENGLANDER   (essay date 1850)

We are not satisfied that the **Lectures on Art** give us a well developed and self-consistent "Theory of art," for we are not quite certain that we fully understand what the author would lay down as the fundamental principle, or what the Germans might call the constitutive idea of art. But of this we are well assured, that they contain most important contributions to the criticism of works of art. They are such contributions as no one but an artist himself could furnish. If we remember that these remarks are the principles which Allston himself applied, that he developed them one by one through a life of constant and thoughtful labor, and that they are for the most part amply illustrated by images of exquisite beauty and often by criticisms and descriptions of the great masters, we should be prepared to expect the highest satisfaction from the perusal of them. We are quite sure that no one who is in the least conversant with the study of pictures or engravings, can read these lectures without substantial profit and exquisite delight.

One or two features of these criticisms have forcibly impressed our mind, on the somewhat hasty reading which is all that we have had time to give them. The first is the good sense that pervades them. When we use the term good sense, we intend by it . . . the absence of that vague and indefinite strain which is common with the would-be critics on art. . . . [Readers of **Lectures on Art**] will find no splendid generalizations, but on the contrary a rigid and almost metaphysical analysis. Of technical terms there are not as many in the 160 pages as are often ostentatiously obtruded in a single paragraph of newspaper criticism upon the annual exhibitions. No terms are too strong to express the gratification which we feel at finding this character of good sense so strikingly pervading these criticisms. It will serve both as an example and a reproof, both to artists and critics. (pp. 447-48)

We would not leave the impression that these lectures are dull and prosaic. On the contrary, they are in the highest degree exciting. Their interest is most various. We have clear analyses pithily and pointedly expressed, felicitous illustrations beautifully imaged forth, just and discriminating thought surprising us at each turn by throwing floods of light upon subjects beyond the reach of most men, and now and then rare and wonderful descriptions which none but a man like the author, at once a painter, a poet and a critic, could have written. (pp. 448-49)

It is interesting to see how, in the lectures on art, the strong religious feeling of Allston, unconsciously reveals itself; and how naturally a line of thought is made to terminate in the beauty of holiness, and to lead up even to the wonderful presence of Jehovah. There is no effort, no affectation. The effort would be to avoid this direction, the affectation would be to repress and turn back the thought from God. The reader feels that not merely the man, but the artist lived upon such thoughts and was animated by such feelings, and the character so beautified with the halo of genius, seems also to shine with a saintly splendor and to be adorned with somewhat of a celestial majesty. (p. 451)

> *"Allston's Lectures," in* The New Englander, *Vol. VIII, No. XXXI, August, 1850, pp. 445-52.*

RUFUS WILMOT GRISWOLD   (essay date 1870)

All the specimens that I have seen of [Allston's] prose indicate a remarkable command of language, great descriptive powers, and rare philosophical as well as imaginative talent. *Monaldi* is his principal and indeed only acknowledged performance of any length. It is a tale of Italian life written with the vigour and method of a practised romancist. The mind of the true artist appears in several discussions, which are very naturally introduced, on the merits of the old masters; and it is no less evident in the character of the hero, who is a painter, as well as in many very graphic descriptions of scenery. Some of the lights and shades of the landscape are given as they could have been only by one familiar with the practice of art. The style of *Monaldi* is remarkably concise and unaffected, frequently rising into eloquence and never becoming tame. Its particular merits as a story consist in the masterly analysis of human passion, the lovely unfolding of female character, and the dramatic management of events. There is great metaphysical truth in the development of love and jealousy, which is its chief purpose. Indeed if Allston had never painted Prophets, these written pictures would have established his fame as an author. The work shows how capable he was of achieving a wide and permanent literary reputation, and forms a most interesting and valuable addition to our romantic fiction. (p. 132)

> *Rufus Wilmot Griswold, "Washington Allston," in his* The Prose Writers of America: With a Survey of the Intellectual History, Condition, and Prospects of the Country, *revised edition, Porter & Coates, 1870, pp. 131-32.*

E. P. RICHARDSON   (essay date 1948)

[Allston's *The Sylphs of the Seasons, with Other Poems*] belongs to the period of transition between the eighteenth century and the new romantic style which followed Coleridge's *Christabel*. It is the book of an amateur rather than a professional poet. . . . Its value for our time is that it throws an additional light on a more subtle and complex artistic personality than had ever before developed in this country, as its value for its own time was its quickening effect upon the nascent literary consciousness of the New England group. The most interesting work in the volume is the title poem, **"The Sylphs of the Seasons."** (p. 94)

The significance of **"The Sylphs of the Seasons"** is that it describes the four seasons of the year and the influences of each upon the mind in terms of the imagination. It is, in other words, the romantic challenge to fresh sources of feeling opened to us by a new awareness of nature, which was to be stated again in bolder terms and to a wider audience by Emerson and Thoreau. The poet's work in the world, which is as important as utilitarian effort, says the Prologue, is to create a dream. . . . The poem shows an acute and sensitive observation of nature and a variety of mood. (p. 95)

The meter and the jingle of double and triple rhymes are unfortunate. The poem interests us not for its technique, which is amateur and often poor and thin, but for its revelation of a fresh and inventive sensibility, awake to nature in all its variety of moods, and for its deliberate statement of "a world within his mind" as the artist's goal. (p. 96)

[The] most important and the most neglected of [Allston's] writings are the *Lectures on Art*. . . . (p. 158)

Allston is the only American theorist on art who combined the experience of a creative artist with a philosophical culture. He had been in touch with philosophical idealism through Coleridge, and he had, as the *Lectures* show, a methodical mind. His book is thus different from the collections of illuminating intuitions about art mingled with practical precepts which were written by Greenough, La Farge, and Henri, as it was different from the histories of Dunlap, Tuckerman, and Isham. (p. 159)

In essence [his] is a theory of art as (1) creation and (2) communication. On the one hand, the old theories of art as imitation and that of Beauty as a quality in the object contemplated are plainly set aside. "The several characteristics, Originality, Poetic Truth, Invention, each imply a something not inherent in the objects imitated (i.e.: represented) but which must emanate alone from the mind of the Artist." On the other hand, the response to a work of art is described as arising from a universal principle essential to the human mind, called "Human" or "Poetic Truth," which is independent both of the will and of the reflective faculties and whose operation is imperative (though widely different in its degree of activity in different individuals), because it is "the life, or truth within, answering to the life, or rather its sign, before us." The aim of the artist is, then, not to please but to be true to that life within us.

It is not necessary to explain to those familiar with the course of aesthetic theory in modern times how interesting it is to find such a theory put forward in 1840. (p. 163)

[Allston's] poems and tales are, as Southey said, the work of a poetic mind but are imperfect in form. [They] are the writing of a gifted amateur. (p. 172)

It is as a philosopher and sage that Allston has left writings still of value. (p. 173)

E. P. Richardson, in his Washington Allston: A Study of the Romantic Artist in America *(reprinted by permission of the author), University of Chicago Press, 1948 (and reprinted by Thomas Y. Crowell Company, 1967), 233 p.*

ROBERT L. WHITE (essay date 1961)

[Allston's] *Monaldi* is in no way a good book, but any one who bothers to read it must immediately be struck by the fact that the image of Italy to be discerned in this wildly Gothic romance is not at all in tune with the image of Italy apparent in his paintings. The Italy of his paintings is an Arcadia, a land of beauty and grace; the Italy of his romance is a land corrupt and festering beneath a mask of beauty.

The opposed images of Italy to be discerned in Allston's painting and fiction are not unique, for the preponderant majority of Americans who visited Italy had mixed reactions to the charm of the peninsula; it is unusual, however, to find this ambivalence so neatly exemplified in the creative work of one artist—one who was both painter and writer. And it is significant that the double attitudes are clearly marked in the work of one of the first Americans to visit Italy. Allston's paintings of the Italian landscape did much to shape one aspect of the American image of Italy. His romance was not so influential, but it foreshadowed the image of Italy to be seen in the fiction of such authors as Hawthorne and the early Howells. (pp. 387-88)

[It] may be said that the American painters who visited Italy during the first two-thirds of the century repeated over and over, with varying degrees of skill, Allston's vision of Italy as a calm and picturesque land of ideal beauty and grace; American writers, however, constructed an image of Italy as a land beset with violence, insanity and unspeakable moral corruption. Not many American writers denied the beauty of the Italian landscape, but the beauty of Italy was dramatized as a treacherous mask for the unwholesome spell lurking beneath the surface. (p. 396)

Monaldi is modeled directly upon Mrs. Radcliffe's and W. G. Lewis' tales of violence and horror.

The popularity of Italy as a locale for the Gothic novels and of Italians as Gothic villains undoubtedly had as much to do with Allston's selection of Italy as a setting for his tale as did the fact that he had resided in Italy; at any rate, it is certain that the Italy of *Monaldi* bears a closer resemblance to the cloudland of [Radcliffe's] *The Mysteries of Udolpho* and *The Italian* than it does to the actual Italy of the end of the eighteenth century. And it is as readily apparent that the Italy of *Monaldi* is neither the Italy of Allston's and Irving's and Coleridge's strolls through the Roman gardens nor the placid and serene country of Allston's landscapes. Actually, in spite of Allston's proficiency as a painter, there is but little pictorial description of Italy in the novel; what little there is, however, runs directly counter to the image of Italy which is formulated in his landscapes. The most lengthy descriptive passage in the tale provides a panoramic view of Rome, but the passage evokes an image of oppressive heat and nerve-jangling tension that has nothing in common with the idealized vision of Allston's Italian landscapes; instead, it surprisingly calls to mind Corot's early sketches of the Italian countryside. . . . (p. 397)

[In one] passage, Maldura is standing above the bay of Naples. Gnawed by remorse for his crimes, he turns away from the beauty of the scene (which Allston does not detail, remarking that it is "not to be painted by words") and looks toward Vesuvius: "But even from that he shrank; for the terrible Vesuvius was now smiling in purple, and reposing beneath his pillar of smoke as under a gorgeous canopy: the very type of himself—gay and peaceful without, yet restless and racked with fire within." This notion of the violence lurking beneath the smiling exterior of the Italian landscape (and of Italians) was not unique with Allston, of course; its significance lies in its total departure from the peaceful and calm image of Italy to be found in his romantic landscapes. (p. 398)

[*Monaldi*] emphasizes and wallows in libertinism, treachery, bloodshed and madness. It portrays the Italian character as sensual, unstable, misanthropic and irreligious. Allston has more than scant admiration for Monaldi's artistic gifts and sympathetic personality but he remarks that the root of his tragedy was his lack of "RELIGION: the only unchanging source of moral harmony. . . . Not that he was wholly without religion: . . . but he wanted that vital faith which mingles with every thought and foreruns every action, ever looking through time to their fruits in eternity." Allston does not openly set himself up as a critic of Catholicism, and Monaldi's wife, Rosalia, does seem to possess this viable sort of religion, but the tale does suggest a strong disapproval of Catholicism. (p. 400)

[The seduced nun described in *Monaldi,* with her "strange mixture" of loveliness and decay, is] an excellent symbol of the charming and corrupted Italy that lured and repelled several generations of American travelers who followed on the path of Allston's pilgrimage. (p. 401)

Robert L. White, "Washington Allston: Banditti in Arcadia," in American Quarterly *(copyright, Fall, 1961 Trustees of the University of Pennsylvania), Vol. XIII, No. 3, Fall, 1961, pp. 387-401.*

GEORGE P. WINSTON (essay date 1962)

[In his *Lectures on Art,* Washington Allston] used the term "Objective Correlative" in presenting one of the vital concepts of his aesthetic theory. As far as one can determine, Allston himself had coined the phrase. Nearly one hundred years later, T. S. Eliot in *The Sacred Wood* again brought this term into use. (p. 95)

In context, [Allston's] use of the term is not, at first anyway, particularly striking or unusual. It comes up quite naturally in the course of Allston's attempts to answer the standard questions in respect to the nature and source of the art experience. Nor does Allston himself appear to be aware of having coined a remarkable phrase.

His approach to the idea of the direct relationship between the artist and the natural world follows the characteristic spiral pattern of most of his arguments. Rather than begin by naming the arts or the effects of art, he comes forth with the term "mental pleasures" and the insistence that one may not use the term "sensations." Much of his discussion is designed to mark out his path among the well-known philosophical terms of his day, a necessary clarification of exactly what he wanted those terms to connote. His first goal is to locate the source of these pleasures as being within the mind, and to insist on the passive nature both of the senses and of the external objects. . . . [Allston reasons that if the cause of any emotion] lay in the object, all men who are not deaf would hear and respond quickly to a piece of music by Mozart or, he might have added, all who are not blind would respond to a rose or a sunset. Since this is obviously not what happens, the inference is that the object is passive and its emotional appeal lies outside itself. (p. 97)

[If] the source of the emotional pleasure is in the mind, what is the function, in his pattern, of the external world? In his customary way, [Allston] defines his terms by means of a parallel:

> No possible modification in degree or proportion of elements can change the specific form as that of a cabbage to that of a cauliflower—it must ever remain a cabbage, small or large, good or bad. So, too, is the external world to the mind; which needs also as the condition of its manifestation its *objective correlative* [italics mine]. Hence the presence of some outward object predetermined to correspond to the preëxisting idea in its living power, is essential to its proper end,—the pleasurable emotion.

Nature is thus the first objective correlative—the concrete symbol of the moral universe, operating within a rigid framework of moral laws. It is the language through which man converses with God, the words in themselves nothing, the value in the truth which they convey. The flower, the bird, the work of art (when faithful to nature) are objective correlatives; they are the means by which the spark of the divine, lying within the human mind, communicates with the Idea. In his novel, *Monaldi*, Allston says that there is a voice in nature that is ever audible to the heart. When he describes the artist, Monaldi, as hearing this voice of nature, he is but using a shorter way of saying that the voice within Monaldi responds to the truth objectified through nature. (p. 99)

If there is any distinction to be made between Allston's meaning of *objective correlative* and Eliot's, it is largely a matter of focus of attention. When Allston brings up the idea in his discussion of theory, he is primarily concerned with finding a means by which a perceptive human being can communicate or translate to the real his awareness of the Ideal. He does not, in fact, go beyond the first step of recognizing or defining the real world as the receptacle for the many aspects of the Ideal: Whatever Platonic leanings Eliot may or may not have in general, he is . . . attempting to emphasize the process by which art can successfully communicate the abstract emotion of experience—the process of concretizing or objectifying the emotion. Once Allston descends to the level of the real to consider the actual problem of the arts the distinction becomes hardly discernible. (p. 101)

The truth is that when Allston moves specifically to the level of the real, of man and art, he becomes much more aware of the specific and the particular. It may very well be that he deliberately avoids naming a work of art as an objective correlative in order to maintain the separation between creation by God and a creation by man: art is still an imitation of nature. (p. 102)

If in rescuing the phrase *objective correlative*, T. S. Eliot seems to have passed by the higher level and settled for a more psychological than religious angle, he has inescapably retained the duality of abstract and concrete, of emotion and external object. As he himself was well aware, the overtones are still present. The striking similarity between the two men as they deal with the correlative is a reminder once again of the vital role which Allston played in the history of American aesthetics. (p. 108)

George P. Winston, "Washington Allston and the Objective Correlative," in Bucknell Review, *Vol. XI, No. 1, December, 1962, pp. 95-108.*

NATHALIA WRIGHT   (essay date 1966)

The chief characteristic of Allston's painting . . . is its subjectivity. He was the first American painter to transcend external forms and project the visions within his own mind. His landscapes, on the whole his most successful works, are in effect reveries on nature, the figures in them appearing as dreamers. . . . Even his portraits have this dream-like character, without accessory objects as they are and seeming to probe the inner life of the subject. Those of Coleridge, W. E. Channing, and himself are particularly notable. (pp. v-vi)

Varied as all [Allston's] writings are, they have a distinctly homogeneous character, and they form a kind of literary counterpart of his painting.

Most of Allston's poems and pieces of fiction are minor in aim and achievement and obviously indebted to the Romantic tradition. When all of them are considered as one body of writing, however, it is seen, significantly, to be pervaded by a single theme and dominated by one character type: the theme of an interior life, independent of nature and of society, and the character of a dreamer or an artist whose works embody what are essentially his own visions or memories. The mind or soul of man is the main concern of several poems: the rather conventional **"Man"** and **"Fragment"** ("Who knows himself must needs in prophecy"); the orthodox **"The Atonement"** and **"Immortality"**; **"Gloria Mundi,"** with its typically mystical picture of the negative nature of the soul's experience; and the sonnet **"Thought,"** which is more Allstonian in its repeated question. . . . (p. vi)

A few other poems are typically transcental in their picture of nature taking its life from the human spirit. Even spring cannot bring hope and joy to the miserable man, the poet declares in **"Written in Spring."** . . .

The interior life is seen chiefly in Allston's poems, however, as the experience of certain characters or speakers, who have withdrawn from the physical scene around them either in surrender to a new emotion or in the exercise of memory or who as artists have produced works inspired by that life.

Two young girls—Ursulina in **"The Tuscan Girl"** and Rosalie in the poem of that name—experience the birth of a new consciousness in which earthly scenes take on a supernal appearance, the first in the process of passing from childhood into womanhood, the second as she falls in love. Both poems, incidentally, are matched by Allston paintings of the same names. . . . (p. vii)

Allston himself is a dreamer in several poems. In the complimentary **"The Magic Slippers"** . . . he fancies that he received the slippers from fairy boats in a spring beside which he lay musing. (p. viii)

The supremely creative dreamers in Allston's poems are, indeed, poets and artists. In **"The Sylphs of the Seasons, A Poet's Dream,"** the Poet is wooed in a dream by the spirits of the four seasons. Though he wakes before making his choice, winter clearly has the most pressing claims. The other sylphs are able only "Through mortal *sense* to reach the mind," she tells him, but it was her "purer" power that ministered to him. . . . (p. ix)

In his poems dealing with historical artists and works of art Allston applies a single standard of judgment: the great works are representations of the artists' own inner experiences rather than of natural forms. Michelangelo gave birth

> To forms unseen to man, unknown to Earth.
> Now living habitants;

he responded to the touch of art "that brought to view / The invisible Idea." . . . (p. x)

The title character in Allston's Gothic romance *Monaldi* . . . is also an artist who draws his inspiration from his own inner life. Apparently passive and even vacant, he shuts out the external world in order "to combine and give another life to the images it had left in his memory; as if he would sleep to the real and be awake only to a world of shadows." . . .

In contrast to Monaldi is the poet Maldura, who lives "only in externals," cannot see "beyond the regions of discovered knowledge," and lacks the "realizing quality" that "gives the living principle to thought." He is only temporarily successful. Nevertheless Monaldi is destroyed by the machinations of Maldura and his accomplice Count Fialtro. . . . In terms of Allston's allegory, Maldura and Fialtro represent the influences of the world and of evil or sin, which are equally hostile to the pure interior life of the true artist. (p. xii)

Allston's most important prose literary compositions are his **"Lectures on Art."** . . . [In themselves] they constitute a coherent treatise and one which has several distinctions. It is not only the first American art treatise, but the only one which combines actual creative experience and a clearly defined philosophical position. It is also the only treatise on art in English during the Romantic period which is based on the German idealist philosophy pervading the Romantic movement. In its conception of art as expression and communication, moreover, it anticipates developments in aesthetic theory in the present century. (p. xiii)

[Because] Allston's **"Lectures on Art"** emphasize the subjective element in the creation and the appreciation of a work of art they presuppose the existence of an interior life capable of projecting itself in its own terms. His theory is thus peculiarly consonant with his own painting and generally parallel with the theme of many of his poems and of his fiction. (p. xiv)

Allston belongs in the forefront, indeed at the very head of the whole company of American creative dreamers—writers as well as artists. Later artists like Page, Ryder, Vedder, Burchfield, and Andrew Wyeth have depicted the intangible reaches of landscapes, the thoughts and feelings of those whose portraits they painted, and unique figures of their own imaginations. Writers like Poe, Emerson, Hawthorne, Melville, James, and Faulkner have explored the dream world and the remembered past through their characters or speakers and have recorded their own transcendental visions. Only Allston, however, has left a comprehensive record of this type of art and artist, in his brooding canvases, in his poems of memories and dreams, and in his fictional and expository accounts of the creative mind. (p. xx)

> *Nathalia Wright, "Introduction" (1966), in* Lectures on Art and Poems (1850) and Monaldi (1841) *by Washington Allston, Scholars' Facsimiles & Reprints, 1967, pp. v-xx.*

JOHN R. WELSH (essay date 1971)

[The most important of Allston's writings] was the carefully worked out creed in the **'Lectures on Art'**. . . . The art lectures show Allston's romantic idealism as the principal and unifying theme of his theories, whether he be dealing with form, composition, or the idea of art in general. Basically, he attributes man's sense of beauty and inspiration to an ideal power beyond this world, the source of 'the visionary virtues' or 'intuitive Powers which are above, and beyond, both the senses and the understanding'. The individual intuition is assigned the utmost importance, and in the imagination lie thousands of unknown forms to be awakened, perhaps by the great minds and truths of the past, which are not to be imitated but are to inspire the artist 'to look into those mysterious chambers of our being'. Allston acknowledged the value of intellectual training, but such wisdom, to be effective, had to be in harmony with the higher spiritual truth. All of this is good Platonic mysticism, of course, but it also seems almost a blueprint for Emerson's familiar transcendentalist individualism. In addition, Allston presaged the didactic nature-admiration of other New England romantics: he asked, for instance, 'whether a simple flower may not sometimes be of higher use than a labor saving machine'. And, finally, he summed up the typical romantic attitude when he wrote, 'If it be true, then, that even the commonplaces of life must all in some degree partake of the mental, there can be but one rule by which to determine the proper rank of any object or pursuit, and that is by its nearer or more remote relation to our inward nature'.

Tracing influences, though, usually evolves into a tenuous matter, at best, and romanticism would have flowered in New England regardless of whether Allston had come back there to live. But the presence of this admired intimate of the English worthies served to expedite the acceptance and development of romantic tenets. Allston, because of his friendship with Coleridge, provided a definite connexion between the already established English romanticism and the burgeoning American movement. (pp. 90-1)

> *John R. Welsh, "An Anglo-American Friendship: Allston and Coleridge," in* Journal of American Studies *(© Cambridge University Press 1971), Vol. 5, No. 1, April, 1971, pp. 81-92.**

DONALD A. RINGE (essay date 1973)

[For many American writers of the early nineteenth century,] the Gothic mode derives from important theories of human psychology, and [Charles Brockden Brown, Richard Henry Dana, Sr., and Washington Allston,] in particular, make it a significant vehicle for the presentation of serious themes. In their hands, it became a means for presenting some major insights into the workings of the human mind. (p. 3)

Allston and Dana, . . . both somewhat younger than Brown, were among the first Americans to read and understand the works of Samuel Taylor Coleridge and were strongly influenced by his theory of the Romantic Imagination, a power that could transform the world of sensation into a new and different thing. For this reason, both lay particular stress on the mental make-up of their characters. . . . Because they adopt a Romantic theory of knowledge, Dana and Allston handle the Gothic mode in a way somewhat different from Brown. Their devices are often the same as his, but their theory of the Imagination enabled them to draw a closer relation between the Gothic world they project and the minds of their protagonists. In all three writers, of course, the mental state of the characters transforms external reality in such a way that they perceive only what their minds have predisposed them to see. . . . Between these extremes, however, are other, and perhaps more interesting, characters who exist precariously on the line between madness and sanity, and whose aberrations are projected for the reader into the setting of the story. Here the difference between Brown and his successors becomes most apparent. Their Gothic effects derive explicitly from the Imaginations of the protagonists, but his do not. (p. 4)

[Both Dana and Allston are quite explicit in using symbolic geography to reflect the minds of their protagonists.] When Maldura [in *Monaldi*] encounters Fialtro on the highway at night and decides to use him as the instrument of his revenge, the men proceed to a place where they may settle their bargain. They enter first a thick wood, but soon strike out of it "to ascend a wild and barren country." . . . They ascend "a narrow, broken path" and stop "at the foot of a steep rock, forming the base of a cliff." They enter "a cleft, overhung with bushes about midway up the rock," where finding a door, they enter a cavern . . . . In this enclosure, they plot Maldura's revenge on Monaldi.

Like Dana, Allston makes much of the role of the Imagination in coloring the world that his characters perceive. As Maldura accompanies Fialtro to the cavern, he looks out upon the darkness and feels "as if it had compressed his soul to a point, as if his whole being, once spread abroad, modifying, and modified by, the surrounding elements, were now suddenly gathered back, like the rays of an extinguished lamp, and absorbed in one black feeling of revenge." . . . Two ideas are important here. Maldura, like [Dana's] Paul Felton, has turned inward to give free play to the evil that lies within him. But the internal state of the man also stands in a reciprocal relation to external reality. It transforms the outside world into a mirror of what lies within, but is itself altered in turn by what it perceives there. In this way, Maldura, like Paul Felton, is entrapped in a mesh of his own evil doing. But he is not the only character involved in this complex pattern. Monaldi, too, is deeply affected by it.

In Monaldi's case, however, the imaginative vision is projected not so much into the external world as into the universe of his art. . . . It is in his paintings, however, that Monaldi's inner self is most clearly revealed. We see in his picture of "the first sacrifice of Noah after the subsiding of the waters" both the "rare union of intense feeling and lofty imagination which characterized" him, and the affirmative vision that he projects. (pp. 6-7)

Another picture, in sharp contrast to this one, is painted after he has been duped by Maldura and has stabbed his wife because of her supposed infidelity. Like Paul Felton, Monaldi has in him something of the devil that drives him to murder . . . and although he does not actually kill Rosalia, he loses his mind and runs off raving. Maldura, on the other hand, begins to repent what he has done, and when a chance event leads him to the hut of the mad Monaldi, he tries to help him. Monaldi recovers his sanity, recognizes Maldura, and speaks of him as his best and earliest friend, who has traced him to his hut out of the kindness of his heart. Such unmerited praise is too much for Maldura, who eventually reveals the truth, not only that Rosalia lives, but that he, out of hatred for Monaldi's success, had hired Fialtro to deceive him. At this point, Monaldi relapses into madness. That he was duped by the plot of Maldura and Fialtro is bad enough, but this revelation strikes at the very nature of his being. Throughout his entire life he has mistaken the character of his supposed friend, reading into him from his

own innocence a goodness that was never there. Small wonder, then, that Maldura appears to him now as a winged devil. . . .

That this Gothic image is a projection of Monaldi's inner vision after he learns the truth about Maldura is clearly underscored in the novel. He begins to paint it after that revelation, and he tells his father-in-law, Signor Landi, that although it is only a picture, he has perceived the original: "What is there, I have *seen.*" . . . The image of Maldura as winged and Satanic has, of course, no objective reality. It is simply a projection of Monaldi's imagination induced by the knowledge that his trusted friend has deliberately sought revenge on him. This, in turn, has altered Monaldi's perception of reality. Instead of projecting an image of goodness, as he has heretofore done, he now depicts on canvas a vision of enticing evil. (p. 7)

Unlike Brown and Dana, therefore, Washington Allston turned to his major interest, painting, to project the most important part of his theme in *Monaldi*. This difference, however, is not a crucial one and should not be allowed to obscure the really important relation among the works of these three men. All differences aside, Brown, Dana, and Allston are much alike in their concern with the complexities of human psychology and in their use of the Gothic mode to present their themes. One sees in their work, as well, a forecast of what was soon to come in the tales of Poe and Hawthorne. . . . [The] images of enclosure to be found in the works of Brown, Dana, and Allston appear in the tales of their successors as similar images of mind. The stories of Poe and Hawthorne are filled with them.

Yet one must not claim too much for Brown, Dana, and Allston. They cannot be seen as the "source" for Poe or Hawthorne in any specific sense. Allston's *Monaldi*, after all, appeared too late to serve this purpose, and whatever influence Brown or Dana may have had should perhaps be seen as general. The works of all three men were conceived and written in a time of great intellectual ferment when the problems engendered by the concept of a perceived reality were much in the minds of men and when the Gothic mode was available as a convenient means for revealing the aberrations of a disturbed mind or the influence of the inner man in transforming his vision of reality. [These writers] developed out of this ferment and found the Gothic mode a suitable vehicle for expressing their themes. Seen in these terms, the Gothic works of Brown, Dana, and Allston may be considered early stages in a developing intellectual position and symbolic mode of expression that were to achieve their most complex form in the works of their great successors. (pp. 7-8)

Donald A. Ringe, "Early American Gothic: Brown, Dana and Allston," in American Transcendental Quarterly *(copyright 1973 by Kenneth Walter Cameron), No. 19, Parts 1 & 2, Summer, 1973, pp. 3-8.**

ADDITIONAL BIBLIOGRAPHY

Brooks, Van Wyck. "Longfellow in Cambridge." In his *The Flowering of New England: 1815-1865*, pp. 147-71. New York: The Modern Library, 1936.*
    Description of Allston's later, artistically thwarted years in Cambridge.

Flagg, Jared B. *The Life and Letters of Washington Allston.* New York: Charles Scribner's Sons, 1892, 435 p.

Detailed biography incorporating letters and journal entries of Allston and his contemporaries.

Irving, Washington. "Washington Allston." In his *Biographies and Miscellanies,* edited by Pierre M. Irving, pp. 174-82. New York, London: G. P. Putnam's Sons, 1866.
Memoir and character sketch of Allston by his close friend.

Soria, Regina. "Washington Allston's Lectures on Art: The First American Art Treatise." *The Journal of Aesthetics and Art Criticism* XVIII, No. 3 (March 1960): 329-44.
An appraisal of the importance of Allston's critical theories in relation to European and American traditions. The critic emphasizes Allston's position as a link between Coleridge's ideas and American aesthetic trends.

Welsh, John R. "Washington Allston, Cosmopolite and Early Romantic." *The Georgia Review* XXI, No. 4 (Winter 1967): 491-502.
Asserts that Allston's influence over the American artists of his day makes him a more important figure in the American romantic movement than is generally recognized.

Wolf, Bryan J. "Washington Allston and the Aesthetics of Parody." *The Georgia Review* XXXIV, No. 2 (Summer 1980): 333-56.
Detailed discussion based on the premise that the "Romantic text often harbors within itself meanings subversive of its surface intent . . . which not only explicates its own metaphoric structure, but *criticizes* it as well." Wolf examines this "rhetoric of self-criticism" as it appears in Allston's paintings and in *Monaldi.*

Joanna Baillie

1762-1851

Scottish poet and dramatist.

Baillie was born in Bothwell, Lanarkshire, Scotland, but lived most of her life in Hampstead, England. The daughter of a rigid, ascetic clergyman, she projected the strong moral background of her childhood throughout her works. Her goal in writing for the stage was not so much to "take the house by storm," but rather to take the heart by truth. She was like a religious teacher, whose duty is to show that a free individual can secure happiness in the practice of virtue, or reap misery as the fruit of vice. *A Series of Plays: In Which It Is Attempted to Delineate the Stronger Passions of the Mind, Each Passion Being the Subject of a Tragedy and a Comedy*, commonly referred to as "The Plays on the Passions," with themes of love, hatred, fear, religion, jealousy, revenge, and remorse demonstrate Baillie's belief that "the way of the transgressor is hard." They impress on the mind that wisdom's ways are "ways of pleasantness, and all her paths are peace."

Fugitive Verses was Baillie's first publication. It received little attention until after she had established a literary career. *A Series of Plays: Volume I* was her first critically acclaimed work. Published anonymously, as was *Fugitive Verses*, it was much celebrated at the time. However, once the reading public discovered that the plays were written by an unknown woman, sales declined. Sir Walter Scott, a close friend, encouraged her to produce more dramas. The popular reception of her dramas and poems was rekindled and Baillie became one of the most significant female writers of her time.

Of her twenty-six plays, only five were ever staged; her dramas were considered untheatrical, better read than performed. Before her time, success on the stage had been a prerequisite for the publication of a drama. In Baillie's case, the order was reversed. Scott's praise was sometimes extravagant: "If you want to speak of a real poet, Joanna Baillie is now the highest genius in the country." He also contributed an introduction to her *Metrical Legends of Exalted Characters* and *The Family Legend*. Lord Byron said of her, "Women, except Joanna Baillie, cannot write tragedy."

Baillie lived with her older sister, Agnes, during her adult life. In one of her last works, *Lines to Agnes Baillie on Her Birthday*, the reader comes to know something of the childhood years of the two sisters, and the personality of the author. Another inspiration for Baillie's work came from her experience of London while living in the borough of Hampstead, which was at that time a literary and artistic center. Fame made little difference to Baillie's mode of life, and she was not given to an artistic temperament. Today, the plays are of interest to historians, as they illustrate the difference between literature and theatrical literature in the early nineteenth century. Some critics remark on the lack of art and taste in Baillie's management of her themes and in the structure of her verse, but she is generally considered an author of historical, if not artistic, importance.

PRINCIPAL WORKS

Fugitive Verses (poetry) 1790
*A Series of Plays: In Which It Is Attempted to Delineate the Stronger Passions of the Mind, Each Passion Being

Culver Pictures

the Subject of a Tragedy and a Comedy. 3 Vols.* (drama) 1798-1812
**Miscellaneous Plays* (drama) 1804
***The Family Legend* (drama) 1810
***Metrical Legends of Exalted Characters* (drama) 1821
A Collection of Poems [editor] (poetry) 1823
A View of the General Tenor of the New Testament regarding the Nature and Dignity of Jesus Christ (poetry) 1831
***Dramas* (drama) 1836
Fugitive Verses [enlarged edition] (poetry) 1840
Ahalya Baee (poetry) 1849
Lines to Agnes Baillie on Her Birthday (poetry) 1849

*This is the date of first publication rather than first performance. This series is often referred to as "Plays on the Passions."

**This is the date of first publication rather than first performance.

BRITISH CRITIC AND QUARTERLY THEOLOGICAL REVIEW
(essay date 1799)

The purpose of [*A Series of Plays, Vol. I*], is to exhibit the passions in such points of view, as may alarm the unthinking, and convince them how dreadful are the effects of ungoverned propensities. In order to do this, the author has drawn his principal characters as possessed of every virtue, and alone rendered miserable or unamiable, by the frailties arising from one fatal passion. (pp. 284-85)

To separate and individualize the passions . . . is to leave the path of Nature; and to make the possessor of one bad propensity in all other respects virtuous, is to apologize for vice, and to make us pity rather than abhor it. Here then appears an error in the construction of the plan; and the author will do well, in his subsequent plays, to make his heroes more of the colour of their fellow creatures, by displaying the less dangerous passions as the frailties of human nature only, and the blacker . . . more intimately connected with each other.

The endeavour to exhibit the passions in such lights as may influence the actions of others, and improve their hearts by convincing their understandings, is always laudable, although it has proved so often unsuccessful; and he who thinks he has discovered a better method to do it than those who have gone before him, deserves the thanks of his fellow creatures for a well-meant, even though it should still prove an unsuccessful attempt. The present volume [*A Series of Plays, Vol. I*] . . . contains three plays: *Count Basil,* a Tragedy; *The Tryal,* a Comedy; and *De Monfort,* A Tragedy. In the Introductory Discourse, which abounds in imagery, the author has exhibited much knowledge of the human mind, and has displayed his information and discernment in such a style, as convinces the reader, at the outset, that he is not incompetent to the arduous task he has undertaken. He treats at great length, and with much ingenuity, on the construction of the drama; in which, . . . he has not adhered to his own rules. He expresses his approbation of those styles of writing which apply more forcibly to the heart than to the fancy, and thinks the drama the most approved vehicle. (p. 285)

There are many sentences which struck us as strongly resembling passages in other authors; but of those the author very candidly expresses himself sensible, and therefore will expect indulgence; and, indeed, there is original merit enough throughout to demand it. The remainder of our talk will chiefly be to praise. *Count Basil* is a tragedy replete with beauties; it abounds in happy thoughts, and bold and beautiful images. The language is generally good, and frequently excellent. (p. 287)

The Comedy of the *Tryal* is not worthy of much attention; it wants plot, wit, interest, and incident; but has, nevertheless, an easy flowing style, and evinces a capability for better things.

The Tragedy of *De Monfort* is still superior to *Basil.* The hero is a more original character, and more forcibly drawn; but it is too diffuse. The last act might be omitted altogether with advantage, adding a little only at the end of the fourth. With these improvements it would make an excellent play, and one which, we have no doubt, would be received with the greatest pleasure by an English audience. (p. 289)

It is with great pleasure that we notice a publication, in which so much original genius for dramatic poetry is evidently displayed. May we not hope that, in the unknown author of these Dramas, exists the long wished-for talent, which is to remove the present opprobrium of our theatres, and supply them with productions of native growth, calculated not for the destruction of idle time, but, for the amusement of ages? We are willing, in some degree, to cherish the expectation. (p. 290)

"'A Series of Plays, Vol. I'," in British Critic and Quarterly Theological Review, *Vol. XIII, March, 1799, pp. 284-90.*

BRITISH CRITIC AND QUARTERLY THEOLOGICAL REVIEW (essay date 1802)

[On] the careful perusal of [*A Series of Plays, Vol. II*], we have felt, undoubtedly, that more time and more consideration might have increased its value. Let us not be understood to mean, that the present publication has diminished our admiration of Miss J. Baillie's powers and genius; it has, in some respects, increased it. But though, judging from her own fertility of invention, she deems the interval considerable, between her former publication [*A Series of Plays, Vol. I*] and the present, and for composition it has been undoubtedly sufficient, yet for correction it was not so ample. (p. 185)

Of Miss J. B.'s Comedies, the prevailing opinion seems to be, that they are much inferior to her Tragedies; and it is true, that comic writing does not appear to be the line to which her genius is particularly directed. They do not abound with the *vis comica,* or with situations of comic effect; nor are the plots remarkable for much contrivance in their conduct, and still less in their development. Yet, after all, it is to *herself* that she is chiefly inferior, for, in many respects, even her Comedies appear to us to have merits which few of her contemporaries can rival. In the invention of characters, so formed and circumstanced as to exemplify the passions she designs to illustrate, she is no less happy in the comic than in the tragic drama; and many of these characters are not only new to the theatre, but of a very theatrical kind. The two Comedies in this volume belong to the subjects of *Hatred* and *Ambition.* . . . [The two main characters in *The Election,* on the subject of Hatred,] are well drawn, and skilfully contrasted. Nor are the secondary characters ill conceived, or ill supported. (pp. 185-86)

The other Comedy [*The Second Marriage*] . . . , to sketch it in the same brief manner, is dedicated to the passion of Ambition. . . . [The] plot of this Comedy, after opening extremely well, is hurried towards the end, so as to form a tissue of improbabilities; and a continuance is given to it, in the supported time of action, which not only offends against critical rules, but is not rendered probable to the reader or spectator, by the mode of conducting it. . . . [There are many changes within the five acts], as they are here managed, [and] no mind can follow with sufficient acquiescence. Faults of this kind, in the two Comedies here published, but particularly the latter, are not to be counterbalanced, except by that fertility of dramatic genius which cannot fail to command admiration; or those bright and powerful touches of character, which prove a strong poetic intuition respecting human life. A longer delay of publication might have enabled the very ingenious and amiable author to discover and remove many of these defects, which, as we take a lively interest in every step of genius, would have given us a much higher satisfaction. As it is, we can by no means join with the multitude in an indiscriminate condemnation; nor shut our eyes to the beauties and merits of the Comedies, because they are not in all respects such as we could have wished to find them.

The tragic view of *Ambition* is given in . . . [*Ethwald*], or rather a history, upon the old English model, divided into two parts. The history is fictitious, but is well invented. . . . (pp. 186-87)

[The character of the hero, Ethwald,] is maintained throughout with the utmost consistency and beauty. As we proceed in the history, we meet with many inequalities; and the whole character of Woggarwolfe [a marauding and barbarous Thane] might well be spared. It is disgusting from its coarseness; and does not so materially assist the progress of the events, but that other means might be contrived. If we thus acknowledge, as we must, that we find in these two Tragedies, particularly the first, parts that are unequal to their general merit, still it is the inequality of genius; and we are led through various ways to new beauties, and new felicities of invention. (pp. 191-92)

We must now, though reluctantly, take our leave of these efforts of singular and native genius: not doubting that, after all the objections which many readers will delight to circulate, this second volume will add greatly to the permanent fame of the fair Poetess. That a few passages are unworthy of the rest, and a very few inaccuracies of language here and there occur, will not materially diminish the praise thus deservedly achieved; and Miss J. Baillie, even if her pen were not to be inactive, which is not likely, would be always celebrated among the brightest luminaries of the present period. (p. 194)

> '''A Series of Plays, Vol. II','' in British Critic and Quarterly Theological Review, Vol. XX, August, 1802, pp. 184-94.

[FRANCIS JEFFREY]   (essay date 1803)

[*A Series of Plays, Vol. II* requires] a double criticism; first, as to the merit of the peculiar plan upon which [the plays] are composed; and, secondly, as to their own intrinsic excellence.

To such peculiar plans, in general, we confess that we are far from being partial; they necessarily exclude many beauties, and ensure nothing but constraint: the only plan of a dramatic writer should be, to please and to interest as much as possible; but when, in addition to this, he resolves to write upon nothing but scriptural subjects, or to imitate the style of Shakespeare, or to have a siege, or the history of a passion in every one of his pieces, he evidently cuts himself off from some of the means of success, puts fetters upon the freedom of his own genius, and multiplies the difficulties of a very arduous undertaking.

The writer of the pieces before us, has espoused the patronage of what she has been pleased to call *characteristic truth,* as the great charm of dramatic composition; and, in order to magnify its importance, has degraded all the other requisites of a perfect drama to the rank of very weak and unprofitable auxiliaries. With a partiality not at all unusual in the advocates of a peculiar system, she admits, indeed, that a play may have qualities that give nearly as much pleasure; but maintains, that this is altogether owing to the *folly* of mankind, and that if we were constituted as we ought to be, we should care very little for any thing but the just representation of character in our dramatic performances. (p. 269)

[If] we could agree with Miss Baillie, that the striking delineation of character was the cardinal excellence of the drama, we should find great difficulty in admitting that her plan was the most likely to ensure its attainment. The peculiarity of that plan consists in limiting the interest of the piece, in a great degree, to the developement of some one great passion in the principal character, and in exhibiting this passion in all the successive stages of its progress, from its origin to its final

catastrophe. It does not appear to us that either of these observances is well calculated to increase the effect of any dramatic production. (pp. 270-71)

[To] confine the whole interest of the story to the developement of a single passion, seems to us to be altogether impracticable, and could not even be attempted, in a very imperfect degree, without violating that unity of action by which the general effect of the piece would be very materially impaired. To confine the attention, and tie down the sympathies to the observance of one master passion through a whole play, is plainly impossible; first, because that passion, in order to prove its strength, must have some other passion to encounter and overcome in the bosom where it is at last to reign; and, secondly, because a certain portion of our sympathy must necessarily be reserved for the fate and the feelings of those who are the objects and the victims of this ruling passion in the hero. The first partition of our sympathy is altogether unavoidable; and Miss Baillie herself has accordingly been forced to submit to it. *Count Basil* is distracted between love and a passion for military glory; and the interest and sympathy excited by the whole story, may be referred to the one passion, just as properly as to the other. *De Monfort* is represented as struggling between a high sense of honour, and a frantic and disgraceful antipathy; nor could the latter have been made interesting in any degree, unless our sympathy had first been very powerfully engaged for the former. *Ethwald,* in like manner, is agitated by ambition, and gratitude, and personal attachment; and pleases us as much by his generosity and kind affections, as he terrifies us by the consequences of his thirst for power. The second division of interest that is claimed by those who inspire or oppose the domineering passion of the chief personage, is scarcely less necessary. . . . The only way in which the interest we take in the story can be in any degree engrossed by the hero, is to provide him with a succession of inferior patients and observers, through whom he moves in the grand career of his passion, and who are successively forgotten for the sake of those who replace them. By this contrivance, which is but seldom practicable, it is very obvious, however, that the interest of the piece is impaired and dissipated, and the unity of the action entirely broken. Miss Baillie has had recourse to it in the tragedy that occupies so large a portion of [*A Series of Plays, Vol.II*]; and every reader of 'Ethwald' must acknowledge, that the interest of the play is exceedingly diminished by the constant introduction and renewal of the inferior characters; and that the catastrophe, which is accomplished by persons with whom we have scarcely any previous acquaintance, is but ill calculated to produce any strong or satisfactory impression.

The peculiarity of Miss Baillie's plan, however, does not consist so much in reducing any play to the exhibition of a single passion, as in attempting to comprehend within it a complete view of the origin, growth, and consummation of this passion, under all its aspects of progress and maturity. This plan seems to us almost as unpoetical as that of the bard who began the tale of the Trojan war from the egg of Leda; and really does not appear very well calculated for a species of composition, in which the time of the action represented has usually been more circumscribed than in any other. Miss Baillie, however, is of opinion, that it will turn out to be a very valuable discovery; and insists much upon the advantage that will be gained by adhering to it, both in the developement of character, the increase of interest, and the promotion of moral improvement. We are afraid that these expectations are more sanguine than reasonable. (pp. 271-72)

A play, which discriminates its characters only by the great and leading passions that are essential to the parts they have to sustain, must be as deficient in interest and effect, therefore, as a picture which shows no more of the figures than is necessary to explain its subject; that displays the hand of the murderer, and the bleeding bosom of his victim, but omits all representation of the countenance and gestures of either, or of those circumstances in the surrounding scenery which may suggest aggravations or apologies for the crime. By the plan of Miss Baillie, however, these subordinate and arbitrary traits of character appear to be in a great measure excluded. Her heroes are to be mere personifications of single passions; and the growth and varied condition of one grand feature is to be incessantly held out to our observation, while an impenetrable shade is to be spread upon all the rest of the physiognomy. Among the debasements of modern tragedy, against which Miss Baillie declaims with so much animation, there is none, perhaps, so material as this, which her doctrine has so evident a tendency to sanction. . . . (p. 274)

As to the *moral* effect of the drama . . . , we confess that we are disposed to be very sceptical. . . . Plays have, for the most part, no moral effect at all: they are seen or read for amusement and curiosity only; and the study of them forms so small a part of the occupation of any individual, that it is really altogether fantastical to ascribe to them any sensible effect in the formation of his character. (p. 275)

If there be any passions to which Miss Baillie's dramatic warnings can be applicable, they can only be those . . . that are intrinsically and fundamentally vicious, and against the remotest approaches of which we ought to be continually on our guard. Hatred, jealousy, envy, and some others, are in this class; and it may be conceived, that, to trace these to their origin, may contribute to the preservation of our morality, by enabling us to detect them in their rudiments, and to resist them in their infancy. It has happened, however, that Miss B., by a very singular infelicity in the execution of her plan, has been at the trouble to trace the origin and progress of love and ambition with great care and exactness, while she has only given us a view of hatred in its matured and confirmed state. . . . If Miss B. really believed that her readers would be better able to resist the influence of bad passions, by studying their natural history and early symptoms, in her plays, she ought certainly to have traced this of hatred to its origin, more carefully than any other, since there is none of which it would be so desirable to cut off the shoots, or extirpate the seeds, at the beginning. (p. 276)

[We] cannot leave the subject without making one remark upon the spontaneous addition that is made to its difficulties, by the extraordinary resolution of making every separate passion the subject of a tragedy and a comedy. Passion, perhaps, is not essential to comedy at all; but the distribution of passions into tragical and comical, is so old, so obvious, and so natural, that we really are at a loss to conceive what strange caprice could have tempted this ingenious writer into so wanton a violation of it. A comedy upon Hatred, sounds as paradoxical to our ears, as an elegy on a wedding, and implies as great a violation of all our customary associations. The constraint that must be submitted to, in order to make out this fantastic piece of uniformity, would deserve our most cordial compassion. . . .

Upon the whole, then, we are pretty decidedly of opinion, that Miss Baillie's plan of composing separate plays upon the passions, is, in so far as it is at all new or original, in all respects extremely injudicious; and we have been induced to express

this opinion more fully and strongly, from the anxiety that we feel to deliver her pleasing and powerful genius from the trammels that have been imposed upon it by this unfortunate system. It is paying no great compliment, perhaps, to her talents, to say, that they are superior to those of any of her contemporaries among the English writers of tragedy; and that, with proper management, they bid fair to produce something that posterity will not allow to be forgotten. Without perplexing herself with the observances of an arbitrary system, she will find that all tragical subjects imply the agency of the greater passions: and that she will have occasion for all her skill, in the delineation of character, and all her knowledge of the human heart, although she should only aim (as Shakespeare and Otway have done before her) at the excitation of virtuous sympathy, and the production of a high pathetic effect. Her readers, and her critics, will then discover those moral lessons, which she is now a little too eager to obtrude upon their notice; and will admire, more freely, the productions of a genius, that seems less incumbered with its task, and less conscious of its exertions. (p. 277)

If Miss Baillie had delighted us less with some passages of her tragedies, we should, perhaps, have had more reluctance in saying that we think she ought to write no more comedies. There is no flagrant violation of nature in these productions; and the language is for the most part unusually pure and easy. But there is no comic effect in them; a certain placid cheerfulness and gay good sense runs through the whole of them; but though these qualities form the greatest charm of real life, they are somewhat deficient in lustre and brilliancy for the stage. Though Miss Baillie's taste seems, upon the whole, to be tolerably correct as to the proper tone of pleasing conversation; yet she has no great powers, either of wit or humour, and appears to have made her observations on manners, with great judgment and sagacity, without having acquired the faculty of giving much life or animation to her characters. The story moves on too slowly, and the characters unfold themselves so very gently and leisurely, that even when the delineation is completed, the impression is but indistinct and feeble. Her comedies, therefore, have more the effect of moral tales, than of proper dramatic pieces. . . . (p. 278)

After these general remarks upon Miss Baillie's comedies, we need not detain our readers with any particular account of **"The Election, a comedy on Hatred."** . . . The humours of an election are not represented by Miss Baillie with any great spirit or effect; and, setting these aside, the piece is rather deficient in incident or variety. The characters are as fully developed in the second act, as in the fifth; and as we care very little for the issue of an election in an imaginary borough, we cannot help wishing for the close of the poll a good while before it is announced to us. The incidents that do occur, in the mean time, are certainly of a kind that do not naturally arise out of the character or situation of the parties. . . . This comedy, we are afraid, will not live to mend the morals of posterity.

It is rather unfortunate for Miss Baillie's tragedies on Ambition [the two parts of '**Ethwald**'] that they can scarcely be read by any body who is not familiar with Shakespeare's Macbeth. We do not remember any instance in which so notorious a model has been so exactly imitated. . . . Besides [the] transcript of Macbeth in the main fable, there are many subordinate scenes that are not less evidently borrowed from the same great author. (pp. 278-79)

There is a good deal too much fighting and slaughtering in these tragedies. There are at least three pitched battles fought upon the stage, each of them lasting through two or three busy scenes. . . . There are also five or six assassinations perpetrated in the sight of the audience; and a head is fairly struck off, and held up to them, towards the conclusion of the piece. None of the dramas that are usually quoted as proofs of the bloodiness of the English theatre, and the barbarity of our national taste, come up to the horrors delineated in these tragedies by the delicate hand of a female.

In the conduct of the fable, there are two great defects. The story goes on a great deal too slowly, and it goes on a great deal too long. Every thing, especially towards the beginning of the piece, is described and transacted at full length before us. The conceptions of the author are commonly good, and they are generally brought out very completely; but it is done with so much labour, so slowly, and at so great length, that it frequently gives a great heaviness to the composition. Miss Baillie cannot insinuate any thing, without expressing it; and is afraid to trust her meaning to a short and incidental intimation. She spreads a broad canvas before her, and puts in every thing that presents itself with the full colouring, and the full proportions of reality. (p. 280)

The diction and poetry of [*Ethwald*] is certainly entitled to very considerable praise. There is no part of Miss Baillie's introductory remarks better founded, than that in which she condemns the artificial stateliness and wearisome pomp of our modern tragedy. . . . [Taking] for her model the middle style of Shakespeare's versification, [Miss Baillie] has ventured to bespeak the public attention to a species of composition in which so many of her contemporaries have miscarried. There is something certainly very meritorious in this attempt, and its success has been such as should encourage the author to proceed in it. The principal peculiarity, in the style of these tragedies, is the free use of antiquated terms and phraseology. Miss Baillie has not only imitated the manner of Shakespeare, but has revived his language; and, not contented with making her characters speak more like real men and women than modern dramatists have usually done, she has thought it necessary to make them speak like men and women of the sixteenth century. Now, though something is undoubtedly gained in this way by the poetical and pleasing associations which the genius of Shakespeare has connected with this obsolete diction, it rather appears to us, that Miss Baillie has carried the practice a little into excess, and taken something both from the originality and the ease of her composition, by this decided predilection for a language that is no longer natural. (p. 282)

The last play in this volume, is entitled, **"The Second Marriage, a comedy on Ambition;"** and we are sensible that we do not speak at all equivocally of its merits, when we say, that it is by far the worst of Miss Baillie's dramatic performances. A more puerile or insipid performance, indeed, is not to be found. . . .

Upon the whole, we think there is no want of genius in this book, although there are many errors of judgment; and are persuaded, that if Miss Baillie will relinquish her plan of producing twin dramas on each of the passions, and consent to write tragedies without any deeper design than that of interesting her readers, we shall soon have the satisfaction of addressing her with more unqualified praise, than we have yet bestowed upon any poetical adventurer. (p. 286)

[Francis Jeffrey,] "'A Series of Plays, Vol. II'," in The Edinburgh Review, Vol. XI, No. IV, July, 1803, pp. 269-86.

[FRANCIS JEFFREY]   (essay date 1805)

[*Miscellaneous Plays* consists] of two tragedies and a comedy; and the fair writer, in the preface, is particularly earnest in requesting that her reader would lay down the book at the end of each play, and only take it up again after the lapse of several days. . . . The reader is first directed to pause so long after every play, as may enable him to proceed to the next with the same feelings as if it had stood first in the collection: and then he is informed, that the comedy is placed between the two tragedies, that he may enjoy 'a little flickering of the sunbeams as he passes from one sombre gloom to another.' Indeed, the only motive which Miss Baillie's modesty allows her to state for having published the said comedy, is this humane anxiety to support the spirits of her reader under these tragical impressions. . . . (pp. 405-06)

The first play is entitled 'Rayner,' and was written, we are happy to find, many years ago. Miss Baillie cannot possibly write a tragedy, not an act indeed of tragedy, without showing genius, and exemplifying a more dramatic conception and expression than any of her modern competitors; but she is always deficient in the conduct of her fable, and frequently injudicious in the selection of the incidents upon which it is made to depend. . . . If Miss Baillie had not previously achieved a very high reputation as a dramatic writer, we should have been inclined, after perusing this production, to say that nothing at all approaching to excellence could ever be expected from a writer who could build up a tragedy on a series of such miserable common-places. (p. 406)

Miss Baillie's style and diction, with some quaintness and much inequality, has in it, upon the whole, more vigour, nature and animation, than that of any of our modern dramatists. It has all the substantial characters of poetry, too, with scarcely any thing of the vulgar poetical diction; and is always a great deal richer in conception and imagery, than in melody and phrases. . . .

We come now to the comedy which is called '**The Country Inn.**' Miss Baillie positively must not write comedies. She wants that talent; and she has higher talents. There are strong indications of good sense indeed, and good humour, in the speeches of her favorite characters; and the diction throughout has the merit of being very natural, and of approaching more nearly to the tone of real conversation, than is usual in the modern drama. But the dialogue, along with the case of common conversation, has a good deal of its *fadeur* and insipidity; and there is a lamentable deficiency both of incident and character, for which no atonement could be made by the utmost accomplishment of expression. (p. 411)

The last play is a tragedy called '**Constantine Paleologus.**' . . . It is by far the best in the collection; and, though 'horribly stuffed with circumstance of war,' and composed throughout in a style rather more turgid and ambitious than any of Miss Baillie's other compositions, approaches much nearer to the standard of '**Count Basil**' and '**De Monfort**' than the preceding contents of the volume had permitted us to expect. (p. 412)

Miss Baillie says, somewhere in her preface, that this play was written with a view to being represented on the stage, and apologizes for the quantity of pomp and scenery which it exhibits, from the desire she felt of indulging the taste of the spectators in these particulars. Now, if we had not read this explanation, we will confess that we should have been disposed to seek an apology for the peculiarity to which she alludes, in the very opposite supposition, and should have excused several of the marginal expositions of the scene, by suggesting that the play was not intended for actual representation. (p. 417)

With a number of very gross defects in the management and execution, ['**Constantine Paleologus**'] has, in most of the important scenes, a degree of truth, simplicity and vigour, which are of the best example in the present state of British drama: and the diction, though in some measure distorted by too sedulous an imitation of Massinger and Shakespeare, is always sustained by a spirit of poetry which would redeem greater deficiencies.

Upon the whole, however, we are afraid that this volume will by no means add to Miss Baillie's reputation. A pretty large proportion of it is unequivocally bad, and those parts which might have appeared excellent in an unknown writer, make but an indifferent figure when contrasted with her own previous productions. . . . That she has very extraordinary talents for dramatic poetry, is unquestionable; but the more rare and precious those talents are, the more it must excite our regret to see them wasted in injudicious exertions, or disappointed of their high reward by precipitate, profuse, or unadvised publication. We have great respect for Miss Baillie's qualifications; but we wish her to respect herself, and to respect the public, a little more than she seems to do. Hers are not the talents that are calculated to enchant an idle and undistinguishing multitude; her voice is pitched for a narrower and more select audience; and she ought to recollect that, in such circles, the praise that is gained by genius may easily be forfeited by security. We carefully exhort Miss Baillie to write no more comedies; to keep her assay tragedies in her portfolio; and not to give any new ones to the world, till she has submitted them to the revision of some experienced and impartial friend: her originality cannot now be subjected to any imputation, and though she will not easily meet with a superior in genius, it will not be difficult for her to find an instructor in taste. (pp. 420-21)

> [*Francis Jeffrey,*] *"'Miscellaneous Plays',"* in The Edinburgh Review, *Vol. V, No. X, January, 1805, pp. 405-21.*

BRITISH CRITIC AND QUARTERLY THEOLOGICAL REVIEW (essay date 1806)

The first tragedy in [*Miscellaneous Plays, Rayner,* is] drama as full of poetical merit, nearly, as it is of verses; abounding with original conceptions, and fine situations; and displaying much knowledge of the human heart. . . . As far as we perceive, there is but one material error . . . in the play; and this, though a gross one, is so easily removed, that the consideration of it could not occupy ten minutes. We allude only to the incident, certainly altogether comic, by which the execution of the hero is at present delayed. Remove that, which almost a stroke of the pen would do, and all would be consistent and good. Exclusive of this, there cannot be a doubt that the play contains many fine and truly original situations; much, as we conceive, that must infallibly excite interest. . . . (p. 22)

[*Miscellaneous Plays*] contains three dramas: not written on the subject of particular passions, like those which Miss B. has published before, but with the less limited design of common dramas. The first of the three is *Rayner*, a tragedy. . . . The second is a comedy, entitled, *The Country Inn*. The third, a tragedy on a great historical subject, entitled, *Constantine Paleologus, or the last of the Caesars.*

Of the comedy, the less is said the better. With the majority of readers, we have always thought the talents of the writer much less formed for the comic than the serious drama. But, if in her former comedies she stood greatly below her tragic station, in the present she is far inferior to what she has before attempted. *The Country Inn* is, indeed, so feeble in character, incident, and dialogue, that, with all our knowledge of authorial partiality, we can hardly account for its introduction into this volume.

In the tragedy of Constantine are well delineated the leading circumstances of that great event, the taking of Constantinople by the Turks, which put an end to the imperial line of Caesars. (pp. 25-6)

Difficult as it must be to give on the stage the ideas of a general assault to a great city, we think that the author has well selected the circumstances for that purpose. The character of Constantine is also rendered interesting, and is, throughout, well drawn. (p. 27)

It will detract very little from the merit of these two tragedies to mention, that here and there, though in very few instances, we have observed inaccuracy of language. . . . It is a very high praise of Miss J. Baillie's poetry, that it is perfectly free from modern affectations. She employs our language as she finds it prepared for her in pure and classical writers, and a noble instrument it is in her employment of it. . . . The words of this poetess have all the weight she wishes to give them, and cause no surprise, but such as is consistent with admiration, and with pathos. (p. 28)

> *"Miss J. Baillie's 'Miscellaneous Plays',"* in British Critic and Quarterly Theological Review, *Vol. XXVII, January, 1806, pp. 22-8.*

WALTER SCOTT (essay date 1808)

We have Miss Baillie here at present, who is certainly the best dramatic writer whom Britain has produced since the days of Shakespeare and Massinger. I hope you have had time to look into her tragedies (the comedies you may [pass] over without any loss), for I am sure you will find much to delight you, and I venture to prophesy you will one day have an excellent opportunity to distinguish yourself in some of her characters.

> *Walter Scott, in an extract from his letter to Miss Smith on March 4, 1808, in his* Familiar Letters of Sir Walter Scott, *Vol. 1, Houghton Mifflin & Company, 1894, p. 99.*

WALTER SCOTT (essay date 1810)

I write these few lines to inform you that your laurels flourish in all their original verdure. Through this whole week the theatre has been fully attended, and by all the fashionable people in town; . . . and the most enthusiastic approbation was express'd in every quarter. All this while the [*Family Legend*] has been the only subject of town talk, where praise and censure were of course mingled. The weight of criticism falls on the head of Duart, and I observe that the fair critics in general think that he gives up the lady too easily. I begin heartily to wish that the play was printed. . . . [My] reasons are that the characters of Benlora, and especially Lochtarish, are so defaced by action that it is impossible to suppose their having the necessary influence upon Maclean's mind. Suppose we had never read Othello in our closet and saw Iago represented by a very bad actor, I suspect the same criticism would precisely apply. (pp. 167-68)

Walter Scott, in his letter to Joanna Baillie on February 6, 1810, in his Familiar Letters of Sir Walter Scott, Vol. 1, *Houghton Mifflin & Company, 1894, pp. 167-68.*

[FRANCIS JEFFREY] (essay date 1812)

It is now, we think, something more than nine years since we first ventured to express our opinion of Miss Baillie's earlier productions [see excerpt above]; and to raise our warning voice against those narrow and peculiar views of dramatic excellence, by which, it appeared to us, that she had imprudently increased the difficulties of a very difficult undertaking. Not withstanding this admonition, Miss Baillie has gone on . . . in her own way; and has become . . . both less popular and less deserving of popularity, in every successive publication. [*A Series of Plays, Vol. III*], we are afraid, is decidedly inferior to any of her former volumes; . . . at the same time that it contains indications of talent that ought not to be overlooked, and specimens of excellence, which make it a duty to examine into the causes of its general failure. (p. 261)

Miss Baillie, it appears to us, has attempted to unite the excellences of [Grecian and Continental tragic] styles;—and has produced a combination of their defects. (p. 263)

To endeavour to effect a combination of two styles so radically different, must be allowed to have been rather a bold undertaking. But it appears to us to be no less certain that Miss Baillie has made the attempt, than that she has failed in it. . . . She has united the familiar and irregular tone of our old drama, with the simple plot, and the scanty allowance of incident, that are characteristic of the Continental stage; and has given us the homely style and trifling adventures of the one school, without its copiousness and variety—and the langour and uniformity of the other, without its elevation, dignity, or polish. The events with which she is occupied, in short, are neither great nor many; and the style in which they are represented neither natural nor majestic. (p. 265)

She attempts to copy Shakespeare . . . in making her characters disclose themselves by slight incidental occurrences, and casual bursts of temper, in matters unconnected with the main story; but there is no spirit of originality either in the outline or in the touches by which it is thus sought to be animated; and the traits that are lent to it in this style of high pretension, are borrowed, for the most part, from the most obvious and commonplace accompaniments of their leading qualities. . . . (p. 266)

[Miss Baillie] is in no danger of being thus overmastered by the phantoms of her own creation; who are so far from appearing to have a being independent of her control, or an activity which she cannot repress, that it is with difficulty that they get through the work which is set before them, or that the reader can conceive of them as anything else than the limited and necessary causes of the phenomena which they produce.

This, however, is a fault by no means peculiar to Miss Baillie; and one which we should scarcely have thought ourselves bound to take any notice, if she had not insisted so largely upon the necessity of attending to the delineation of each character, and brought forward the traits of her own in a way so obtrusive, as to show very plainly that she thought her pretensions in this department proof against any sort of scrutiny. For the same

reason, we think it our duty to say, farther, that besides this want of the talent of giving individuality to her scenic personages, it appears to us that she is really disqualified from representing the higher characters of the tragic drama, by an obvious want of sympathy or admiration for such characters. . . . It is impossible, we think, to read any one of her plays, without feeling that the character which Miss Baillie thinks (and with great reason) the most amiable and engaging of all others, is that of cheerful good sense, united to calm, equable, and indulgent affections,—the character, in short, of rationality and habitual benevolence;—of which we think it must be admitted that, whatever precedence it may claim over more brilliant qualifications in real life, it is just as ill fitted to give spirit and effect to the fictions of the drama, as the qualities that shine most there, are to soothe the moments of domestic privacy. (pp. 267-68)

We come now to the last chapter of this fair writer's offences, or those which relate to the matter of style and diction; which, we are concerned to say, appears to us the heaviest of the whole; not however so much because her taste is bad, as because her stock is deplorably scanty. . . . [The] leading character of her style . . . is a poorness and narrowness of diction altogether . . .—and only rendered more conspicuous by the constrained and unnatural air produced by her affectation of antiquated phraseology, and the contrast which this affords to the carelessness, copiousness, and freedom of the true old style. . . . She seems to have no ear for the melody of blank verse,—and especially of that easy and colloquial verse which is alone suited to the purpose of the drama . . . [and her verses have a] heavy, lifeless, and unwieldy structure . . . when compared with the light and capricious undulations of [Shakespeare, or Beaumont and Fletcher.] (p. 270)

[The] tone of good sense and amiable feeling . . . pervades every part of her performances; . . . [and] wherever they are found to be habitual and unaffected, impart a charm, even to poetical compositions, which compensates for the want of many more splendid attributes. Miss Baillie is not only very moral, and intelligently moral; but there is, in all her writings, a character of indulgent and vigilant affection for her species, and of a goodness that is both magnanimous and practical, which we do not know that we have traced, in the same degree, in the compositions of any other writer. . . . She has a very considerable knowledge of human nature, and an uncommon talent of representing (though not in the best dramatical form) the peculiar symptoms and natural development of various passions; so that her plays may always be read with a certain degree of instruction and cannot be read without feelings of great respect for the penetration and sagacity of their author. . . . [We] think Miss Baillie [is] entitled to very high and unmingled praise, for the beauty of many detached passages in every one of her metrical compositions;—passages that possess many of the higher qualities of fine and original poetry. . . . (p. 273)

The merit of [*The Dream*] is, that it is short and intelligible, and tells its story without vexatious entanglement, and with a good deal of solemn effect. Its fault is, that there is not enough of story, and scarcely any variety of interest or passion. (p. 282)

The third piece in the volume is *The Siege;* a comedy . . . on the subject of Fear,—to which we really cannot afford even the very moderate praise of being better than Miss Baillie's other comedies. The story is neither striking nor probable; and the principal characters are the old hackneyed ones. . . . Poor as this play is . . . in contrivance and character, and destitute of comic effect, it could not have been written by an ordinary person. There is a chastity in the style, and a tone of strong good sense in much of the dialogue, that place it far beyond the things that have lately been produced as comedies in our theatres.

The last piece in the volume is the shortest, and the best. It is entitled, *The Beacon;* a serious drama . . . in blank verse, and interspersed with songs. The subject is Hope, and the story is very simple, and without any pretensions to probability. (pp. 283-84)

The merit of this piece certainly does not consist in the fable— nor in the delineation of character . . . , but in the fanciful and poetical cast of the whole composition—the multitude of pleasing images with which it abounds, and the beauty of several of the songs with which it is intermingled. The poetry is of a less laboured kind than that which Miss Baillie usually attempts, and has less pretension and less heaviness. The songs have all a great deal of beauty—and are thick set with images and ideas. Indeed, the whole style is more richly adorned with figures of thought and of speech than in any of her other performances. . . . (p. 286)

We do not know that [these songs] are very lyrical; but they have undoubtedly very great merit, and are more uniformly good, than any passages of equal length in the blank verse of the same writer. . . . [Whatever] be the causes of their excellence, it affords us great pleasure to bear testimony to the fact; and it would go far to console us for the determination which Miss Baillie announces, to publish no more plays on the passions during her life, if we could be permitted to hope that she will favour us now and then with a little volume of such verses. . . . (p. 290)

> [Francis Jeffrey,] "'A Series of Plays: In Which It Is Attempted to Delineate the Stronger Passions of the Mind, Vol. III'," in The Edinburgh Review, *Vol. XIX, No. XXXVIII, February, 1812, pp. 261-90.*

THE ECLECTIC REVIEW   (essay date 1813)

Miss Baillie is decidedly of the good old school of the English drama. . . . [Therefore, the personages she creates] are not always ranting or whining, in the extasies of love, or the agonies of despair, or the madness of rage: they really do talk . . . like men and women of this world. . . . (pp. 167-68)

From the old school, however, in which she has studied, Miss B. has not adopted the abundance and variety of incident, which characterize their drama. (p. 168)

[In regards to her stage-directions,] Miss B. relies too much upon her marginal notices; her pages are sometimes a tissue of mingled narrative and dialogue. To say nothing of the awkwardness of this, its effect in drawing the mind from the work to the author is truly lamentable. . . .

Miss Baillie's incidents are not only few but trivial. After all that may be said of the familiarity to which tragedy may very properly descend, she is never to become childish, and lisp and totter. (p. 169)

[We wish] that Miss Baillie would oftener take her subjects from history. She has succeeded sufficiently well in '**Constantine Paleologus**' to go forward vigorously in that path. . . .

[As for the creation of characters,] the author has great merit. . . . Miss B. has managed [to depict tragic heroic characters]

with great skill. [They] are strongly marked, and yet highly poetical, frail and infirm, and yet very interesting . . . [Her characters are] conceived in the true spirit of poetry, and touched and finished with the hand of a master. (p. 170)

It is not in the deep pathetic that she excels; [Miss Baillie] never rends the heart, or drowns the reader in tears. . . . She produces, therefore, fine and solemn poetry, and not undramatic, inasmuch as it strongly interests the feelings, but she does not melt and overwhelm. (p. 171)

It is, however, in the delineation of quiet and domestic scenes that we think Miss B. principally excels; in painting the humble cares, and unambitious pursuits, and kindly affections, and homefelt enjoyments of private life. (p. 180)

We cannot take our leave of Miss B. . . . , without expressing our regret at the resolution she has taken of keeping whatever plays she may henceforward write, 'intra penetralia vestae.' Why should the public be deprived of so great, and . . . so highly prized an entertainment, because forsooth, the *managers of playhouses* have not thought fit to bring her tragedies forward on the stage? . . . In criticising Miss Baillie's plays we have regarded them solely as dramatic *writings*. We have considered them as furnishing a high intellectual entertainment, totally unconnected with the grossness of the theatre, and its long inseparable train of evils. The fair author's partiality for *the boards* appears to us a weakness much to be regretted: for we are well convinced it has had, in many instances, an unhappy effect on her genius, in making her address the senses rather than the imagination, and in placing before her the mimic representations of things rather than the realities themselves. (pp. 185-86)

> "'A Series of Plays', 'Miscellaneous Plays', and 'The Family Legend'," in The Eclectic Review, *Vol. X, August, 1813, pp. 167-86.*

THE MONTHLY REVIEW   (essay date 1821)

[It is a high and noble] instrument of poetical music which Joanna Baillie is qualified to strike [as witnessed in her *Metrical Legends of Exalted Characters*]. She seems to us condescending from the due station of her genius, when in company with Sir Walter Scott she walks down into the regions of octosyllabic verse, and quits her early manner of treating heroic subjects in heroic strains. (p. 76)

[Miss Baillie] attempts impossibilities: for [she] endeavours to reconcile the *literal* record of any portion *even of heroic* story with *poetical* effect; to rob from *prose,* in a word, its own character of impressive simplicity, its own implicit *truth;* and to gain the effect, without paying the tax, of the essential decorations of verse. . . . We can experience no continuity of ideal charm, no sustained delight of the imagination, when we are so frequently recalled to news-paper-details in a verse. . . . (p. 78)

The most pleasing tale in [*Metrical Legends of Exalted Characters*] is the legend of '*Lady Griseld Baillie*.' . . . [The] manner in which Miss Baillie has related the extraordinary and most touching instances of filial affection, in this her family-heroine, does infinite credit to her heart as well as to her poetical genius.—Although a domestic subject, in the general character of the story, it is rendered susceptible of the most elegant poetry in many parts of it by the exquisite tact of the writer; and, where she fails in *verse*, she remains an interesting *prose*-narrator of singular events. . . . (pp. 78-9)

There is no *poetical* verisimilitude in ['*Lady Griseld Baillie*']. It might have been related *in prose* that a child *said so and so:* but when she is represented *in verse*, . . . [it is *all* so indissolubly connected.] This is the curse of Ballad Poetry. (p. 79)

We conclude with . . . [a] most courteous bow to the distinguished authoress whose work we have been examining; assuring her that, whatever unwelcome remarks our duty may have inflicted on her *Metrical Legends,* she has few more firm and decided admirers than ourselves. (p. 81)

> "*Miss Baillie's 'Metrical Legends',*" *in* The Monthly Review, *Vol. XCVI, September, 1821, pp. 72-81.*

THE NORTH AMERICAN REVIEW   (essay date 1823)

The highest rank attained of late years in [the composition of dramas must be assigned to Miss Baillie, who has done much towards effacing the old reproach; but her tragedies, though full of spirit and possessing a strong scenical interest, would not be found very manageable at the theatre, and certainly an aptness to public exhibition is an important consideration in the plan of every dramatic work. (p. 284)

> "'*The Golden Fleece*'," *in* The North American Review, *Vol. 16, April, 1823, pp. 283-99.**

BLACKWOOD'S EDINBURGH MAGAZINE   (essay date 1824)

[We are] delighted with the opportunity afforded us of offering our tribute of admiration to one, who, in point of genius, is inferior to no individual on the rolls of modern celebrity—whose labours have given a tone and character to the poetic literature of our nation—whose works were the manuals of our earliest years; . . .—whose touching portraitures of the workings of the human soul awakened in us an enthusiasm; . . .—whose deep and affecting morals, illustrated by the moving examples of her scenes, touched the heart and nerved the mind, and improved the understanding by the delightful means of an excited imagination—and whose pages we have never returned to, in our days of more matured judgment, without reviving the fading tints of admiration, and justifying our early estimate of her high intellectual superiority. . . .

When the first volume of *Plays on the Passions* was presented to the public, nothing could be much more degraded than the state of our poetic literature. (p. 162)

The public taste had been awakened a moment to the tones of nature; but it was too weak and enervated to sustain the excitement, and fell back exhausted into its habitual slumbers in the arms of art.

In this calm and listless moment—in this be-darkened hour of our poetic literature, the deep tones of Joanna Baillie's genius struck upon the ear with a thrilling sublimity, like the voice of her own *De Monfort*. . . . She penetrated the real cause of the evil, and she meditated its cure. She saw that poetry . . . had appeared to languish in exhaustion, because it had been charged with burthens that were not its own, and urged to repugnant efforts, among scenes that were foreign to its character, and in an atmosphere that oppressed its aspirations. She endeavoured to correct this melancholy perversion; she sought to direct the taste of the nation, and the exertions of its authors, to the legitimate objects of poetry; she brought to the task her counsel and her example. . . . [In the Introductory Essay to *Plays on the Passions, Vol. I*,] our authoress appeared as the

advocate of nature, against the false refinements and exaggerations of art; and exhibiting her own peculiar and highly philosophical views of the scope of Tragedy, and the means by which its purposes might be best accomplished, she asserted the reformation, which her works were calculated to achieve, with a masterly force and distinctness of conception, with a nervous eloquence of style, with a brilliant copiousness of expression, and an aptness and beauty of illustration, which must for ever rank her name among the classics of English prose composition. (pp. 163-64).

That Joanna Baillie produced the change which has been wrought in the public taste by the instrumentality of the drama, may account for the peculiarly dramatic character which is perceptible in nearly all the most favourite productions of our time. And this . . . establishes that the reformation, and the merit of the reformation, is hers. . . .

That an individual to whom literature is so deeply indebted, should have her reputation so little bruited by the public voice, may appear somewhat extraordinary. Her works have never yet obtained a success proportioned to their merits. The celebrity of Joanna Baillie has been of a most peculiar nature—her fame has had about it a kind of virgin purity. It has been the unparticipated treasure of the world of taste and intellect. The admiration of her lofty talents never made itself heard in the loud huzzas of the Theatre, or in those unmeaning expressions of approval. . . . She was never *written up* . . . in the Reviews and Magazines. She was placed . . . above any communication with those mere drudges and mercenaries of literature, into whose hands the fame of our living authors is entrusted, and by whose daring pens and uncultivated opinions the public taste is so very generally directed. (p. 165)

Joanna Baillie has discovered the true origin of our interest in the Drama. . . . [In] making each passion the subject of a separate play, she has directed her talents to an object legitimately dramatic. . . . [The] author has placed [the passions] in situations skilfully designed to call forth its attributes, to shew its extent and bearing, and to evince the malignity of its consequences. . . . (p. 167)

We shall say a very few words upon our authoress's scheme of composing a tragedy and comedy on each passion of the mind. It must be immediately perceived, that any objections against such a design, can have no real bearing on the plays themselves. . . . On Joy, there was no necessity to attempt a tragedy. It was only with the permanent dispositions of the mind that Joanna Baillie had proposed to occupy her talents, and she had expressly stated that Joy and Anger were excluded from her plan, as being the results of the gratification or the irritation of those deeper affections which her scheme was designed to embrace. . . . With respect to a tragedy on Hope . . . we can scarcely conceive a more exquisite subject for that sweet, and touching, and domestic interest. . . . (pp. 167-68)

It is said that comedies cannot be written on Hatred and Revenge—Nonsense! The bad and violent passions are only grand as long as they are terrific. . . .

The end which Joanna Baillie proposed to herself in undertaking this laborious work, was to warn the mind against the access of passion—to disclose to our observation the progress of the enemy, and to point out those stages in his approach, where he might most successfully be combated, and where the suffering him to pass may be considered as occasioning all the misery that ensues:—This is an object worthy of the exalted talents which were dedicated to its accomplishment. . . . (p. 168)

[*The Plays on Passions*] *instruct by pleasing*. The mind is, as it were, self-taught by the reflections awakened as the scene proceeds, without being wearied by the dry discussion of abstract questions of ethics; and the affections, deeply touched, retain an apprehension of horrors and consequences of guilt, which could never have been inspired by the cold and systematic precepts of the moral philosopher. (p. 169)

The characters of [*Count Basil*] are most skilfully delineated. . . . [They are] a group so forcibly depicted, and so skilfully assorted and diversified, that it is only in the volumes of Shakespeare that we could have any chance of discovering its equal. (p. 170)

Of *De Monfort* we shall not speak. It is too well known to require our recommendation. . . . It was, at its first representation, worthily supported by the finest performance that can be conceived. . . .

The two parts of *Ethwald*, are Tragedies on Ambition . . . [which Miss Baillie has delineated] with such a persuasive truth of sentiment, of manners, and of character, as almost to induce the reader to seek in the pages of authentic history for the records of her hero's actions. (p. 171)

The tragedy of *Rayner* is, though containing many beautiful passages, almost a failure. It was an early effort. The plot—to use a word of Garrick's—is ill *concocted;* the subject is unpleasing; and it is altogether a scrambling and uninteresting play.

Constantine Paleologus is perhaps the very finest of our author's works. (pp. 176-77)

The Dream, a prose tragedy, in three acts, we should class, with *Rayner,* in the inferior class of Joanna Baillie's writings; except that the opening and the concluding scenes are very far superior to anything contained in the earlier published play.

The beautiful little sketch, the *Beacon,* concludes her volumes. . . . The third scene of the second act is faultless. It is the perfection of natural tenderness, of delicacy of thought and feeling, and of grace of expression. (p. 177)

We have not mentioned the Comedies of our authoress, because, though they are evidently the productions of a very clever woman, they are by no means entitled to the high distinction of being placed in contact with the more splendid efforts of Joanna Baillie's genius.—We wish they had not been published; for, to have disappointed, in one branch of literature, the expectations which have been excited by an author's success in another, will always, to a certain degree, impair the lustre of any, even the brightest, reputation. . . .

[If] the authoress of *Plays on the Passions* would consent to publish an edition of her collected works, omitting all the comedies and the few tragedies that are unworthy of her, and adding only such among her manuscripts as are equal to the best efforts of her pen . . . ; [we] should say that there were no productions of any living writer so certain of encountering few impediments to their progress, and securing the admiration of posterity, as those of Joanna Baillie. Her powers are not inferior to those of the most illustrious of her contemporaries. . . . She is not a writer for any particular age or fashion, but trusts . . . for the success of her works to the general sympathies of our race, and appeals to those permanent affections which are common to us all. There is a peculiarity in her style and language, which casts over the moving picture of her scenes a sweet, autumnal hue . . . ; but she is far superior to all that mannerism of thought and feeling which is engendered of narrow views of life, and of a poor and bounded imagination. . . . [We] call on her to cast aside much that we should regret to lose, but this advice is given in a spirit of zealous admiration that cannot be distrusted. We wish her to cut away the weaker branches to secure the preservation of the thriving trunk; the works already published cannot, perhaps, be totally recalled, but the world will think kindlier of their errors when they are no longer sanctioned by the protection of so powerful a parent. . . . (p. 178)

"Celebrated Female Writers: Joanna Baillie," in Blackwood's Edinburgh Magazine, *Vol. XVI, No. XCI, August, 1824, pp. 162-78.*

THE ATHENAEUM   (essay date 1836)

[The coming of *Dramas* by the authoress of **'Plays on the Passions'**] has pleased and surprised us. We had long since ceased to look to "Sister Joanna," as Scott loved to call her, for either dramas or lyrics, in both of which she has excelled. . . .

In our estimation, these new dramas exhibit all the genius of her earlier works: they have the same moral grandeur of conception, the same massive vigour of thought, and the same felicity of language—but they are not so sustained nor so well united; neither have they the consummate propriety of action and character. They are full of matter and full of incident; but the matter is scarcely diffused enough through the veins of the story, and some of the incidents seem to come more by force than by free will. These remarks concern the Comedies rather than the Tragedies, and were it not for the pleasure derived from a scene or two, we could almost wish that she had abstained from mirth. Her chief strength lies in seriousness . . . ; her language is nervous and compact. . . .

Our poetess, we see, imputes to the vast size of our principal theatres the falling off in dramatic composition. . . . The actors require to stare and writhe beyond the limits of all natural emotion to be seen in the more distant boxes, and rant as if they desired to drown thunder, if they wish to make their words heard in the upper galleries. In the stormier parts of the dialogue, no doubt, the remotest auditor cannot fail to take an interest; but when it subsides into more subdued pathos or tranquil humour, the whole genius of the scene is lost to the ear and mind, and is visible only to the eye. Though Miss Baillie has not written her plays expressly for the stage, we cannot help feeling that most of them would seize on the hearts of an audience, through their heroic feeling and deep pathos, both of sentiment and situation; we should like much to see some of them tried. . . .

The tragedy of **'Romiero'** stands first in these volumes. . . . There is much dignity in the dialogue. **'Henriquez'** is a tragedy. . . . The remorse of Henriquez, and his calm heroic determination to die for his fault, are given in our author's best manner. (p. 4)

The drama of **'The Martyr'** has some fine pictures of calm Christian heroism: though divided into three acts, and also into scenes, it was not, the writer says, intended for representation, yet we think it would succeed with any audience delighting in noble sentiments and fine situations: some of the songs, or rather hymns, are beautiful.

Of **'The Separation'** we shall say little. **'The Stripling'** has affected us much more. . . . This drama is written wholly in prose: the strength of the authoress lies, we think, in blank verse; she has erred in not throwing her poetic mantle over the story.

'The Phantom' is a Scottish musical drama, in two acts. (pp. 4-5)

'Witchcraft' is another drama. . . . It has been the pleasure of Miss Baillie to write this tragedy wholly in prose: the beauty and the innocence, and the distress . . . , would, we apprehend, have been more effective in verse. . . .

We have not space to speak of **'The Homicide,'** nor inclination to discuss the merits of **'The Bride,'** they are neither the best nor the worst in these volumes. We must now bid farewell— and, we fear, for ever—to one who, with many faults, is, without question, the greatest of all living poetesses. (p. 5)

> *"'Dramas','" in* The Athenaeum, *No. 427, January, 1836, pp. 4-5.*

BLACKWOOD'S EDINBURGH MAGAZINE   (essay date 1836)

[Joanna Baillie's *Plays on the Passions* exhibit] mastery over the emotions and passions of the human heart, embodied in action. . . . Imagination builds her own airy stage, and sees her own phantoms passing along its enchanted floor. In reading a Tragedy of Joanna Baillie's . . . we behold it acted in a theatre where no noisy acclamations disturb the on-goings of events, and we enjoy in silence the uninterrupted flow of passion bearing on the agents to the catastrophe of their fate. . . .

[Joanna Baillie's plays are] found far better acting plays than the best of her contemporaries. . . . (p. 267)

Jealousy is the subject of **"Romiero,"** who is represented as naturally jealous . . . ; and fine as it is, this tragedy is far from being equal to [Miss Baillie's] **"Henriquez."** (p. 268)

[Some scenes from **"Romiero"** belong], we fear, to comedy rather than to tragedy; but Miss Baillie was resolved to prove that inveterate jealousy is an incurable disease. (p. 276)

> *"'Dramas'—by Joanna Baillie," in* Blackwood's Edinburgh Magazine, *Vol. XXXIX, No. CCXLIV, February, 1836, pp. 265-80.*

[FRANCIS JEFFREY]   (essay date 1836)

[The contents of *Dramas*] will not, on the whole, disappoint expectation. [They] are, however, of very unequal merit; for whilst some are of the highest excellence, and every way worthy of the authoress of **'Count Basil,' 'De Monfort,'** and **'Constantine Palaeologus,'** there are others which we confess we think might have been omitted with advantage to her reputation. Miss Baillie, it is true, never writes any thing on which the stamp of her strong mind is not here and there impressed; and there are none of the dramas contained in these volumes which do not, to some extent, awaken curiosity and interest. But placed beside the more sustained excellence of others, they appear as failures. The reader whose mind has been elevated to the high pitch and tragic grandeur of **'Henriquez'** and **'Romiero,'** cannot willingly descend to the almost melo-dramatic level of **'The Stripling,'** and **'Witchcraft;'** and even the **'Homicide'** and the **'Phantom,'** though of a higher cast than those we have named—and adorned, particularly the latter, by scenes and passages of great poetical beauty,—scarcely possess that finish, that dramatic compactness which entitle them to a place beside the **'Plays of the Passions.'** (pp. 73-4)

[Miss Baillie's] great work then is completed—and in a manner worthy of its commencement: a noble monument of the powerful mind and the pure and elevated imagination of its author. Looking on it, as it now stands before us,—a finished whole, we owe it to Miss Baillie and to ourselves to say, that we regard it with pride and admiration. (p. 74)

When we compare the dramas of Miss Baillie with most of the other dramatic productions of our own times, we are struck with their superiority, in one point, namely, their unity of design,—their careful subordination of the parts to the whole— and the steady and visible movement of every thing towards the proposed end. She forms her plan of a character carefully, and having done so, no temptation induces her to deviate from it for the sake of transitory effect. . . . Her mind, with all its imagination, is a strong and logical one,—delighting in sequence and consistency, and accustomed in all things to wide and comprehensive views. 'She sees as from a tower the end of all;' and keeping in view all the parts of her subject, she places them in their due relation and proportion to her intended whole. (p. 75)

[The plays of Miss Baillie] afford a very remarkable contrast to those of most of her contemporaries. However different and inferior in degree, her mind resembles Shakespeare's in kind. She plans her characters deliberately; she executes them with undeviating consistency; her pictures of passion are all leavened and penetrated by general and elevated reflection,—making her scenes something more than mere pictures of an individual situation; she is powerful, where the scene requires it, in the expression of its strongest feeling, but more so in the delineation of the previous stages which have led to it, or the exhaustion and despondency which follow; she is natural, even homely at times . . . ;—impressing us in all she writes with the idea of a well-ordered and self-concentered mind, in which each quality has its appropriate but limited sphere of action, and all dwell and work together in unity. Comprehension and grasp of mind are qualities which we involuntarily associate with all her works; and it is indeed singular that this quality, so seldom found in connexion with even the best works of the best female writers, should be thus conspicuous in the works of a woman, when its presence is so rare in those of her male competitors. (p. 79)

We formerly objected, and we think with justice, to certain minor defects of style, which were rather annoyingly conspicuous in Miss Baillie's dramas;—her fondness for the use of antiquated words, many of them of the least euphonious and agreeable character;—and the occasional awkwardness and carelessness of her versification. In the former of these particulars, we are inclined to think a very obvious improvement is visible in the [*Dramas*]. These intrusive archaisms occur but rarely; and some of the most objectionable of them have, to our great relief, disappeared entirely. The style has assumed, we think, a more modern, natural, and easy air, without any injury to its dignity, or poetical beauty; just, as we are inclined also to think, that in the better plays in these volumes, the dramatic interest and movement of the piece proceed with more rapidity and liveliness. (p. 84)

[We will not pursue the plot of **'Romiero'**]; for whatever may be the skill with which it develops all the mean and revolting features of the passion of jealousy, . . . the result of the picture, as a whole, is rather a painful and unsatisfactory one. Not so that of the drama which follows—'**Henriquez**,'—in which Jealousy also plays a principal part, but Jealousy of a different kind;—the feeling as it appears in a nature to which it is foreign—which struggles against its entrance and its growth, and only yields when a fatal combination of circumstances appear to furnish irresistible proof of guilt. (p. 86)

['**Henriquez**'] is unquestionably the finest in these volumes. The '**Separation**,' which approaches nearest to it in dramatic effect, is still far inferior as a whole. . . . [We cannot but feel that Miss Baillie's] success is . . . imperfect, and the general effect of the drama unsatisfactory. (p. 99)

We feel little inclination to dwell on what may be considered the minor performances in these volumes. There are some stirring and forcible scenes in the prose tragedy of '**Witchcraft;**' and much delightful poetry is wasted upon a most intractable groundwork in the '**Phantom.**' (p. 100)

The '**Homicide**,' though containing some striking scenes, is more interesting from situation than from the development of character; and the '**Stripling**,' we fairly confess, seems to us unworthy of Miss Baillie. The '**Martyr**,' however, is in a higher style;—and though not perhaps very dramatic, has a tone of nobleness and devotion about it which are highly attractive. Of the comedies we say nothing, because we can say little that would be agreeable to Miss Baillie or to ourselves.

Since this article was written, we perceive that Miss Baillie has obtained one object of her wishes, and that the '**Separation**' and '**Henriquez**' have been represented on the stage; but neither with any brilliant success. That the '**Separation**' should not have succeeded we feel little surprise; for its faults are great as well as its beauties. . . . But nothing has led us so completely to despair of the revival of true dramatic taste among us, as the announcement we have just noticed in a newspaper that '**Henriquez**,' when represented before a London audience, had been treated, like its predecessors, with comparative coldness; and that its announcement for repetition had been received with some token of disapprobation. (pp. 100-01)

[*Francis Jeffrey,*] "'*Dramas*'," *in* The Edinburgh Review, *Vol. LXIII, No. CXXVII, April, 1836, pp. 73-101.*

QUARTERLY REVIEW OF LITERATURE   (essay date 1841)

Unversed in the ancient languages and literatures, by no means accomplished in those of her own age, or even her own country, this remarkable woman [Joanna Baillie, owed her success] partly to the simplicity of a Scotch education, partly to the influence of the better portions of Burns's poetry, but chiefly to the spontaneous action of her own forceful genius, that she was able at once, and apparently without effort, to come forth the mistress of a masculine style of thought and diction, which constituted then, as it still constitutes, the characteristic merit of her writings, and which at the time contributed most beneficially to the already commenced reformation of the literary principles of the country. (p. 437)

[Weak and pointless as the] *Plays on the Passions* have appeared when tried on the stage, they are pre-eminently entertaining . . . to the leisurely student: the want of that unicity, growth, and consummation of interest, which is essential to the acted drama, is to the reader partly compensated by the diffusion of a gentle and more equal interest throughout all the parts and partly by the easy vigour and flowing originality of the dialogue. In this lies the peculiar strength of Joanna Baillie; in

this she is as unquestionably superior to the present fashionable playwrights as they are to her in producing an effect by striking positions and startling development. The colloquial inaccuracies omitted, . . . the style of these tragedies is almost faultless. It is never affected, never forced, never stuffed with purple patches of rhetoric; it has no ranting harangues or claptrap epigrams; it is always clear, direct, sensible; it is tender and passionate, grave and dignified, and, rising upon occasion, rises with a natural spring, and soars, like all true passion, but for a moment.

It was no doubt a mistake to set about composing separate plays on separate passions. It is not according to the course of human action: no man in his senses is ever so under the dominion of any one passion or impression as that he can be truly taken to be a permanently embodied representation of it. . . . Another ill effect of Mrs. Joanna Baillie's plan is that her principal characters have too much the air of puppets, predestined to a certain precise path of action, and yet undignified by any such dark incumbency of Fate as seems to brood over the noble struggles of the old Greek drama. . . . It is indeed the crucial test of first-rate dramatic genius so to reciprocate the action of circumstance and mind, of force and will, as to present a conspicuous and an interesting picture of that which we every one of us exhibit day by day. . . . We are far from meaning that Mrs. Joanna Baillie has always failed before this test; but we think she has often so failed, and that the plan upon which she wrote had a natural tendency to make her so fail. (pp. 439-40)

[Let] us again express our admiration of the wonderful elasticity and masculine force of mind exhibited in [*The Plays on the Passions*]. Unequal as some of them are in merit, there is not one that will not well repay perusal. The writing is sometimes plain. . . . Where the line is not poetic it is at least good sense; and the spirit breathing everywhere is a spirit of manly purity and moral uprightness. Few books of entertainment can be placed in the hands of the young so safely and profitably as Mrs. Joanna Baillie's plays, taken generally. . . . [Mere] curiosity is the craving least gratified by the *Plays on the Passions*: they appeal to higher aspirations; and we can truly say that, great as our youthful admiration was, a critical re-perusal in middle life has deepened the impression we had always retained of their excellence. (p. 441)

The characteristic qualities of Mrs. Joanna Baillie's poetry in her Dramas are, to a considerable extent, to be found in the very charming collection of poems, which, under the title of *Fugitive Verses,* she has with equal good sense and modesty just given to the world. . . . It contains the productions of the poetess in her earliest and latest years, and in all of them we have the same healthful tone, the same abundance of thought, the same clear and forcible style, frecked with the same amount of petty inaccuracies of language. . . . It is a pity that there should be any drawback whatever to the praise with which this volume, and indeed the other poetical works of this excellent writer, might be accompanied. (p. 446)

The poems in [*Fugitive Verses*] are in various styles, and in them all the authoress seems to us successful, except in her '**Scotch Songs**,' and '**Hymns for the Kirk**.' Of the former, we should say that they have a forced air, as if the writer had set about inditing them with no genius but that of patriotism to aid her. . . . Neither do we think the Hymns designed for the use of the Kirk at all calculated for such a purpose. . . . [We] think the Kirk had good grounds for not recommending them for general adoption. In fact, they are not composed with an insight into the peculiar nature and spirit of congregational singing, or, as we should venture to conjecture, with any knowledge of music on the part of the author. (pp. 447-48)

Mrs. Joanna Baillie has, we think, succeeded very well in her ballads in a romantic and supernatural vein. They are all, more or less, good; especially the **'Elden-Tree'** and **'Lord John of the East.'** **'Sir Maurice'** is not so clearly narrated as it should be—but it is still a very striking poem; and there is great power of the same kind shown in **'Malcolm's Heir.'** . . .

Highly, however, as we estimate her **'Ballads of Wonder,'** we by no means think them the best parts of this volume. She is more impressive and original in passages of ordinary life, and in the expression of domestic affection. There are many small poems in this collection of that gentler character which appear to us beautiful; and amongst these we particularly notice the **'Lovers' Farewels,'** the **'Banished Man,'** the **'Two Brothers,'** and the **'Parrot.'** (p. 449)

[We] think it well to conclude these few remarks, trusting that nothing in them will be found inconsistent with the profound respect we feel for Mrs. Joanna Baillie's name, and that the freedom in which we have indulged will be accepted as a guarantee for the sincerity of our praise. (p. 452)

> *"'Fugitive Verses',"* in Quarterly Review of Literature, *Vol. LXVII, No. CXXXIV, 1841, pp. 437-52.*

HARPER'S NEW MONTHLY MAGAZINE (essay date 1851)

Joanna Baillie, the most illustrious of the female poets of England, unless that place be assigned to Elizabeth Barrett Browning, . . . died at Hampstead, on the 23d of February at the age of 90 years. . . . To Miss Baillie and Wordsworth, more than to any others is to be attributed the redemption of our poetry from that florid or insipid sentimentalism which was its prevailing characteristic at the beginning of the present century. . . . Her dramas are wrought wholly out from her own conceptions, and exhibit great originality and invention. Her power of portraying the darker and sterner passions of the human heart has rarely been surpassed. . . . [Her dramas are] so full of life, action, and vivacity. Their spirit is . . . akin to the stern and solemn repose of the Greek dramas. They have little of the form and pressure of real life. The catastrophe springs rather from the characters themselves than from the action of the drama. The end is seen from the beginning. . . . Her female characters are delineated with great elevation and purity. . . . Miss Baillie was a conspicuous instance of high poetic powers existing in a mind capable of fulfilling the ordinary duties of life. . . . In her has set one of the last and brightest stars of that splendid constellation of genius, which arose during the early part of the present century. (p. 709)

> *"Monthly Record of Current Events: Obituaries,"* in Harper's New Monthly Magazine, *Vol. II, No. XI, April, 1851, pp. 708-09.**

MARY RUSSELL MITFORD (essay date 1852)

[Of] Mrs. Joanna Baillie, the praised of Scott, and of all whose praise is best worth having for half a century, what can I say, but that many an age to come will echo back their applause!

Her tragedies have a boldness and grasp of mind, a firmness of hand, and a resonance of cadence, that scarcely seem within the reach of a female writer; while the tenderness and sweetness of her heroines—the grace of the love-scenes—and the trem-

bling outgushings of sensibility, as in *Orra,* for instance, in the fine tragedy on Fear—would seem exclusively feminine, if we did not know that a true dramatist . . . has the wonderful power of throwing himself, mind and body, into the character that he portrays. That Mrs. Joanna *is* a true dramatist, as well as a great poet, I, for one, can never doubt, although it has been the fashion to say that her plays do not act. (pp. 152-53)

> *Mary Russell Mitford, "Female Poets: Joanna Baillie—Catherine Fanshawe,"* in her Recollections of a Literary Life; or, Books, Places, and People, *Harper & Brothers, Publishers, 1852, pp. 152-68.**

CATHERINE J. HAMILTON (essay date 1892)

[When Joanna Baillie] was twenty-nine she published anonymously a volume of miscellaneous poems [*Fugitive Verses*]. It was a failure; only one critic ventured to give a faint word of praise to the descriptions of Nature; the rest were silent, and the book died stillborn. Failure depresses the weak; it rouses the strong; . . . it now prompted Joanna Baillie to turn her talents into the right direction. . . . She had a regular plan, from which she never swerved by a hair's-breadth. One particular Passion was to be illustrated by a tragedy and a comedy; it was to be developed from its source upwards; first the germ, then the bud, and so on to the end. . . . Joanna intended to work a reform in play-writing; the interest was to depend, not on the circumstances, but on the characters of the people that moved and spoke. She studied Shakespeare, no doubt, but she studied her own ideas far more; they were her principal guide. . . . [In] a play much must be conveyed rather than expressed plainly; a word, a sentence, a passing exclamation, may reveal a whole history of emotion; the author must never indulge in his own reflections; he must be solely occupied in making his people speak for themselves as such people ought to speak. In this power Joanna Baillie stood pre-eminent; she wrote comedies, but she did not excel in the lighter scenes of life; it was when she came to represent a human soul torn with violent passion that her real power came out. (pp. 117-19)

Her life was as placid and uneventful as a life could be, and yet what stirring scenes passed before her mind's eye! Ambition, hatred, remorse, jealousy, rose like armed spectres and demanded that she should set down their fatal progress, and trace them through every varying phase. She did so, and though her life-purpose was to a certain extent defeated, she at any rate delivered her own soul and spoke her message to those who would hear it. (p. 131)

> *Catherine J. Hamilton, "Joanna Baillie (1762-1851),"* in her Women Writers: Their Words and Ways, first series, *Ward, Lock, Bowden and Co., 1892, pp. 110-31.*

ALICE MEYNELL (essay date 1921)

Would Joanna Baillie's *Plays on the Passions* have been so shunned by later generations and then so forgotten, if the writers of Literary Histories had remembered to mention the 'Comedies on the Passions' as well as the 'Tragedies'? For every tragedy Joanna Baillie . . . wrote also a comedy; and one at least of these sprightlier plays is so buoyant, so busy, so apt in speech, and so pleasant, within the limits of eighteenth-century wit, that a modern manager might surely do worse than try his luck with it. (p. 56)

Joanna Baillie would by no means permit you to slight her art. She has a passage [in her introduction to the *Plays on the Passions*] in which she disclaims the crude intention of setting up the image of a single passion as the whole nature of a man. If there were no conflict, she says, there would be no force, for the passion would have nothing to compel, to break or bend, within the passionate heart. But neither will she allow the units of humankind to puzzle us on the tragic stage with their asymmetry of nature. . . . She will not endure, as she tells us, eccentricity. (p. 57)

[Joanna Baillie's] plays seem to be built up and locked together soundly; they close with a conventional but not obtrusive dignity. . . . Vivacity among the smaller characters, and some of the strength of the ages . . . in the greater, leave her tragedies in no mean place. . . . (pp. 57-8)

It is the comedy following the tragedy of **'Basil'** that takes my fancy. Love seems to be the passion in hand, and Joanna Baillie makes such pretty eighteenth-century sport of her theme . . . that it is not easy to realize that she passed the middle of the nineteenth century, albeit in extreme old age. Of the preceding tragedy I will say merely that one may detect in it a fancy of Antiquity, as the eighteenth century dressed it, which is wonderfully pleasing. . . . (pp. 58-9)

[The comedy called **'The Trial'**], turns upon the device, since repeated, perhaps, more than once, of shuffling a couple of heroines, so that she who is the heiress may disguise herself in the dresses of her penniless cousin, and receive impertinences, suffer neglect, and also test the true heart proffered in intention to her as a girl without wealth. It is the exceeding sweetness of the two good girls bent upon their frolic . . . that makes the charm of this happy play. (p. 59)

Hardly less pleasant is the comedy on 'Hatred,' [**'De Monfort'**]. . . .

She, who had this humour, to be called 'the highest genius in our country', and to be so taken up with 'the passions of human kind'! One of the eulogists of her tragic power calls her 'undeviating'; yet she deviated delightfully. (p. 61)

Alice Meynell, "Joanna Baillie," in her The Second Person Singular and Other Essays, *Oxford University Press, New York, 1921, pp. 56-61.*

G. WILSON KNIGHT   (essay date 1962)

The dramas of Joanna Baillie were deliberately devised to illustrate the workings of various passions. . . . [Her] *De Monfort* is a study of envious hate working up to a typical accumulation of gloomy forest, night time, owls, Gothic convent, tolling bell, monks and corpse. De Monfort, despite his proud heart, has 'bursts of natural goodness'. . . . It is a strong and psychologically coherent study of the human paradox. Joanna Baillie has always a stern control: sensationalism never clogs psychology or drama. *De Monfort* was acted, and her other plays are stage-worthy.

The two parts of *Ethwald* . . . form an elaborate study of ambition. . . . Though the theme is not new, there are new subtleties in the psychology of self-deception and the exact gradations of the hero's rise and fall: much of it reads like a commentary on Napoleon. (pp. 209-10)

Joanna Baillie's strength is in her firm sense of psychological and psychic truth. Her avoidance of actual ghosts—except in *Ethwald,* where they are invisible to the hero—marks no disbelief in the other world but rather a reluctance to commit herself to any superstitious forms. Without ceasing to be dramatic her work is diagnostic and scientific; she aims at no such theatric grandeurs, such tragic positives, as we find in Shakespeare, and which both Sotheby, and Maturin attempt, and this is certainly a limitation. However, her intellectual quality serves peculiarly well to link the Gothic mode with the dramas of our greater romantic poets. (p. 212)

G. Wilson Knight, "Gothic," in his The Golden Labyrinth: A Study of British Drama *(copyright © 1962 by G. Wilson Knight; reprinted by permission of the author), Phoenix House, 1962, pp. 203-28.**

DONALD H. REIMAN   (essay date 1976)

[Joanna Baillie] wrote plays that were only moderately successful on the stage in her own time and that have never been revived or read by a large public. Yet her verse tragedies have been called "the best ever written by a woman." . . . (p. v)

[The] blank verse in Baillie's early plays is, perhaps, the best dramatic blank verse of the age—simple and natural, supple and original. It lacks the Renaissance echoes and overtones of Coleridge's *Remorse* and Shelley's *Cenci* and the intellectual vitality of Byron's dramas, but it seems closer to the natural speech—not of real people—but of real actors, given their roles and situations. (p. vii)

[An] egalitarian view of human psychology shines forth from Baillie's early plays and from the long "Introductory Discourse" to her *Series of Plays*. . . . Baillie's interest in ballads derives, perhaps, from her faith in the universality of human emotions, rather than (as in Scott) from a yearning for chivalric snows of yesteryear. In this respect Baillie, a Unitarian, shows her roots in the Enlightenment.

Baillie's moralistic bias . . . is—like Wordsworth's "simplicity"—more evident in her theory than in her dramas, where the characters are more nearly rounded and vital than her theory would lead one to expect and do not differ greatly in motivation from the characters of other English dramas written on different principles. . . . (pp. vii-viii)

[When Baillie] abandoned her theme of universal passions to write historical poems and plays dealing with Scottish heroes or Columbus, her work lost its vitality and originality. She became a bad antiquary and scholar instead of a stong psychological moralist. Neither is her rhymed poetry as good as her blank verse, for her genius was essentially bent toward naturalness rather than higher artifice.

Basil and *De Monfort* . . . mark Baillie's highest achievement. As she came under criticism and made friends among other poets, her talent . . . was hobbled by rules which she never believed in but deigned to obey. Had she . . . followed her own genius, she might have achieved more than she did. As it is, she remains one of the more significant poets of her age and one of the most noteworthy female writers in English before the twentieth century. (p. viii)

Donald H. Reiman, in his introduction to The Family Legend and Metrical Legends of Exalted Characters *by Joanna Baillie, Garland Publishers, 1976 (and reprinted in* Miscellaneous Plays *by Joanna Baillie, Garland, 1977), pp. v-viii.*

ADDITIONAL BIBLIOGRAPHY

Carhart, Margaret S. *The Life and Work of Joanna Baillie*. Yale Studies in English, edited by Albert S. Cook, Vol. LXIV. New Haven: Yale University Press, 1923, 215 p.
    A collection of criticism covering the entire life and works of Joanna Baillie.

Carswell, Donald. "Joanna Baillie." In his *Sir Walter: A Four-Part Study in Biography*, pp. 262-86. London: John Murray, 1932.
    Biography of Joanna Baillie and her family.

Insch, A. G. "Joanna Baillie's *De Monfort* in Relation to Her Theory of Tragedy." *The Durham University Journal* n.s. XXIII, No. 3 (June 1962): 114-20.
    Discusses whether or not Joanna Baillie achieved the goals she outlined for herself before writing *De Monfort*, considered her best tragedy.

Norton, M. "The Plays of Joanna Baillie." *The Review of English Studies* 23, No. 90 (April 1947): 131-43.
    The success of Baillie's dramas, discussion of her methods in writing them, and Baillie's comments on their performance.

Scott, Walter. "Prologue." In *"The Family Legend" and "Metrical Legends of Exalted Characters,"* by Joanna Baillie, pp. iii-iv. Romantic Context Poetry: Significant Minor Poetry, 1789-1830, edited by Donald H. Reiman. 1810, 1821. Reprint. New York: Garland, 1976.
    Scott's introduction to Baillie's plays, dedicated to her.

Scott, Walter. *Familiar Letters of Sir Walter Scott, Vol. 1*. Boston: Houghton, Mifflin & Co., 1894, 445 p.*
    Several letters to, from, and about Joanna Baillie.

Scott, Walter. "Walter Scott and Joanna Baillie." *The Edinburgh Review* 216 and 217 (October 1912; January 1913): 365-71, 170-81.
    Unpublished letters of Sir Walter Scott to Joanna Baillie. The essay contains Scott's remarks on several of Baillie's plays.

William Wells Brown

1816(?)-1884

American novelist, dramatist, and historian.

Brown's importance to American literary history is great: he was the first black novelist and playwright, as well as one of the most significant of the early black American historians. Born the son of a white slave owner and a black slave, Brown spent the first twenty years of his life as a slave on a plantation in Lexington, Kentucky. He escaped to freedom in Cincinnati in 1834, and became passionately devoted to the cause of abolition. He was befriended by a Quaker, Wells Brown, whose name the former slave took as his own. Brown first settled in Cleveland, where he worked as a handyman and continued to aid in the escape of other slaves. He eventually moved to Buffalo, where he came to the attention of William Lloyd Garrison, who enlisted him as a lecturer in the abolitionist cause.

Brown's first publication, *Narrative of William W. Brown, a Fugitive Slave, Written by Himself,* was a great success, and established him as an important social reformer. The success of the *Narrative* encouraged Brown, and in 1848 he collected a group of antislavery songs and published them under the title *The Anti-Slavery Harp: A Collection of Songs for Anti-Slavery Meetings.*

Because of his ability as a speaker, Brown was chosen by the American Peace Society as its representative to the Paris Peace Congress of 1849. These activities, as well as his extensive travels in England as an antislavery lecturer, are chronicled in his next publication, *Three Years in Europe; or, Places I Have Seen and People I Have Met.* Brown, at this time, was still a fugitive slave, and it was not until several English friends raised the money to pay his indenture that he became a free man.

While in England, he published the first novel by a black American, *Clotel; or, The President's Daughter: A Narrative of Slave Life in the United States,* which proved to be a popular success and something of a scandal. Drawing on the legend that Thomas Jefferson had fathered many children by his slave mistresses, Brown cast his heroine, Clotel, as the slave daughter of the former president. Brown shows, simply and effectively, both the horror and the irony of the institution of slavery in a system which would allow the daughter of a president to be sold into bondage. For the American version of the novel, Brown chose not to suggest presidential parentage for his heroine, concentrating instead on the heroism of his black characters in their fight for freedom.

Brown also published the first play by a black American, *The Escape; or, A Leap for Freedom.* Though the work was not performed, Brown gave many readings of the play, largely to antislavery gatherings in the North. It was not a dramatic success, marred, as was so much of Brown's work, by his didacticism. Brown was passionate and polemical in all that he wrote, and strove to impress his audience with the content, rather than the form, of his work.

It is perhaps as a historian of the black American experience that Brown best deserves to be remembered. In such works as *The Black Man: His Antecedents, His Genius, and His*

Achievements, Brown illustrates the importance of blacks to the American culture as they emerged after the Civil War. In his last work, *My Southern Home; or, The South and Its People,* Brown presents essays of a nostalgic nature, combining his political and social concerns in a reminiscence of the South.

Brown committed his life and his work to the freedom and dignity of his people and to the abolitionist cause. Self-educated and strong-willed, he defied the barriers of racial prejudice to contribute the first novel, the first play, and some of the first notable works of history by a black American, enriching the lives of all Americans through an explication of the black experience. (See also *Dictionary of Literary Biography, Vol. 3: Antebellum Writers in New York and the South*)

PRINCIPAL WORKS

A Lecture Delivered before the Female Anti-Slavery Society of Salem (essay) 1847
Narrative of William W. Brown, a Fugitive Slave, Written by Himself (autobiography) 1847
The Anti-Slavery Harp: A Collection of Songs for Anti-Slavery Meetings [editor] (songs) 1848

Three Years in Europe; or, Places I Have Seen and People I Have Met   (travel essays)   1852; published in the United States as *The American Fugitive in Europe: Sketches of Places and People Abroad,* 1855
*Clotel; or, The President's Daughter: A Narrative of Slave Life in the United States   (novel)   1853
St. Domingo: Its Revolutions and Its Patriots   (essay) 1855
**The Escape; or, A Leap for Freedom   (drama)   1858
The Black Man: His Antecedents, His Genius, and His Achievements   (history)   1863
The Negro in the American Rebellion, His Heroism and His Fidelity   (history)   1867
The Rising Son; or, Antecedents and Advancement of the Colored Race   (history)   1874
My Southern Home; or, The South and Its People (narrative essays)   1880

*This novel was revised as *Miralda; or, The Beautiful Quadroon,* 1861-62; also revised as *Clotelle: A Tale of the Southern States,* 1864; also revised as *Clotelle; or, The Colored Heroine,* 1867

**This is the date of first publication rather than first performance.

EDMUND QUINCY   (essay date 1847)

I heartily thank you for the privilege of reading the manuscript of your [*Narrative of William W. Brown, a Fugitive Slave*]. I have read it with deep interest and strong emotion. I am much mistaken if it be not greatly successful and eminently useful. It presents a different phase of the infernal slave-system from that portrayed in the admirable story of Mr. Douglass, and gives us a glimpse of its hideous cruelties in other portions of its domain. (p. v)

What I have admired, and marvelled at, in your *Narrative* is the simplicity and calmness with which you describe scenes and actions which might well "move the very stones to rise and mutiny" against the National Institution which makes them possible. (pp. v-vi)

I trust and believe that your *Narrative* will have a wide circulation. I am sure it deserves it. At least, a man must be differently constituted from me, who can rise from the perusal of your *Narrative* without feeling that he understands slavery better, and hates it worse, than he ever did before. (p. vi)

> *Edmund Quincy, in his letter to William Wells Brown on July 1, 1847, in* Narrative of William W. Brown: A Fugitive Slave *by William Wells Brown, The Anti-Slavery Office, 1847 (and reprinted as a chapter in* Five Slave Narratives: A Compendium, *edited by William Loren Katz, Arno Press, 1968, pp. v-vi).*

THE LIBERATOR   (essay date 1847)

'**Narrative of W. W. Brown, a Fugitive Slave, Written by Himself,**' is the title of a thin duodecimo put into our hands by a colored friend at the request of the author, and which we have perused with deep interest. It is written in a clear, simple and touching style, and is we presume, a fair history of the better class of slaves. We would recommend it to the perusal of all such as feel any interest in the slaves—it will quicken their devotion to the cause. We would advise the indifferent

to read it—it will touch the chords of their being and make them vibrate in sympathy for the oppressed bondman.

> *"New Bedford Bulletin: 'Narrative of W. W. Brown, a Fugitive Slave, Written by Himself',"* in The Liberator, *Vol. XVII, No. 36, September 3, 1847, p. 141.*

THE ATHENAEUM   (essay date 1852)

[*Three Years in Europe; or, Places I Have Seen and People I Have Met*] is a bit of genuine writing. The "fugitive slave," Mr. W. W. Brown, was a coloured person much seen about London in the year of the Great Exhibition—and heard of in Paris at the Peace Congress,—and we have in these pages the record of his sayings and doings in France and in England. A narrative of his life and sufferings as a slave has been already published; . . . [we] recommend this volume of letters to such friends of the African in this country as may like their flavour. There are a simplicity and an ingenuousness in these confessions which make us merry and sad by turns. . . . (p. 1056)

> *"Reviews: 'Three Years in Europe; or, Places I Have Seen and People I Have Met',"* in The Athenaeum, *No. 1301, October 2, 1852, pp. 1056-57.*

ECLECTIC REVIEW   (essay date 1852)

The extraordinary excitement produced by 'Uncle Tom' will, we hope, prepare the public of Great Britain and America for this lively book of travels, ['**Three Years in Europe; or, Places I Have Seen, and People I Have Met**'] by a *real* Fugitive Slave. (p. 616)

Though he never had a day's schooling in his life, he has produced a literary work not unworthy of a highly-educated gentleman. Our readers will find in these 'Letters' much instruction, not a little entertainment, and the beatings of a manly heart on behalf of a down-trodden race, with which they will not fail to sympathize. (p. 617)

> *"Brief Notices: 'Three Years in Europe; or, Places I Have Seen, and People I Have Met',"* in Eclectic Review, *n.s. Vol. IV, November, 1852, pp. 616-17.*

THE LIBERATOR   (essay date 1854)

'That a man,' says the London *Weekly News and Chronicle,* referring to Mr. Brown's '**Three Years in Europe,**' 'who was a slave for the first twenty years of his life, and who has never had a day's schooling, should produce such a book as this, cannot but astonish those who speak disparagingly of the African race.' Of the present work, '**Clotel,**' the English journals speak in terms of the warmest commendation. For a copy of it, we are greatly obliged to the author; and, having read it, we wish it might be reprinted in this country, believing it would find many readers. While the Declaration of Independence is preserved, the memory of Thomas Jefferson, its author, will be cherished, for the clear recognition it makes of the natural equality of mankind, and the inalienable right of every human being to freedom and the pursuit of happiness. But it will also be to his eternal disgrace that he lived and died a slave-holder, emancipating none of his slaves at his death, and, it is well understood, leaving some of his own children to be sold to the slave speculators, and thus to drag out a miserable life of servitude. . . .

Mr. Brown has skillfully embodied in his affecting tale numerous well-authenticated occurrences, which have transpired at the South within a comparatively short period—all calculated to intensify the moral indignation of the world against American slavery.

> *"New Work by William W. Brown,"* in The Liberator, *Vol. XXIV, No. 5, February 3, 1854, p. 19.*

NEW YORK DAILY TRIBUNE (essay date 1854)

Apart from the merits of [*Sketches of Places and People Abroad*], as a lively and entertaining record of foreign travel, its peculiar origin makes it a novelty in literature worthy the attention of our modern D'Israelis. It was written by a fugitive slave, who till the age of twenty was "held to labor" in one of the Southern States, and who never enjoyed the advantage of a day's schooling in his life. . . .

The volume before us is filled with notices of his public tours, sketches of celebrated people, and remarks on English society in general. . . . [It] will be seen that he holds a ready pen, keeps his eyes open on his travels, and knows as well how to bear himself on all occasions as if only the purest Caucasian blood ran in his veins. Without respect to its authorship, the volume is far superior to the ordinary run of books of foreign travel.

> *"New Publications: 'Sketches of Places and People Abroad',"* in New York Daily Tribune, *December 12, 1854, p. 6.*

VERNON LOGGINS (essay date 1931)

[*A Lecture Delivered before the Female Anti-Slavery Society of Salem*, written by William Wells Brown,] contains too many press clippings to be effective as popular oratory; but it has for a conclusion one of those sounding outbursts by which, unfortunately, the worth of an antislavery orator was to a great extent measured. . . . (p. 159)

[*St. Domingo: Its Revolutions and its Patriots*,] produced when Brown was at his maturity, shows a marked improvement. It is in the main a vivid and interesting narrative of the rise and fall of Toussaint L'Ouverture, with few words wasted in the attempt to be florid. Moreover, it is important in Brown's career as an author in that it is one of his earliest efforts in the field in which he was to be most industrious, that of Negro history. (p. 160)

[*Narrative of William W. Brown*] is one of the most readable of the slave autobiographies, mainly because it is developed with incident rather than with comment. . . . However much the sensationalism in the book might tax the credulity of the reader, there is interest in it. The character most completely presented, Walker, the slave trader, far more diabolic than the terrible Covey of Douglass' autobiographies, is perhaps as near an approach to the melodramatic villain as antislavery literature had to offer before Simon Legree appeared in *Uncle Tom's Cabin*. The style of the *Narrative* is all the more telling because of its simplicity. The idiom throughout is almost monosyllabic, such as one might expect from a runaway slave who had never been to school. Brown drew freely from the *Narrative*, copying passages word for word, for the autobiographical sketches with which he prefaced a number of his later books. . . . (p. 161)

[While] he was enlarging and bringing out new editions of his *Narrative*, Brown published *The Anti-Slavery Harp*. . . . The pieces included are by many hands, and considered as verse are perhaps as mean as any that ever got into print. Yet one reviewer referred to the collection as containing "the best songs of previous publications, with many that have not before been published", and there was a demand for a second edition. . . . (p. 162)

During the spring and summer of 1852, Brown got ready for the press a travel book, which was published in the autumn as *Three Years in Europe; or, Places I Have Seen and People I Have Met*. A volume written by an American Negro could not hve been issued in England at a more propitious time. The excitement over *Uncle Tom's Cabin* was at its highest. However, readers who bought *Three Years in Europe* because the author was styled on the title-page "A Fugitive Slave" must have been disappointed in the book. There is constant allusion to slavery in it, but little realistic picturing of slavery in the United States. Presented as a series of letters, it is Brown's own story of his experiences and impressions from the day he sailed from Boston, July 18, 1849, until the late spring of 1852. . . . Whoever and whatever he sees are vitally real to Brown. Being in Europe is to him a rebirth. Whether he approves or disapproves of what he runs upon, he is in high spirits. Because of the enthusiasm which he poured into it, and because of the rough naturalness of the style, *Three Years in Europe* is what a critic in the *Literary Gazette* of London called it at the time it was published—"a pleasing and amusing volume." (pp. 162-64)

The great weakness of *Clotel* is that enough material for a dozen novels is crowded into its two hundred and forty-five pages. Excellent stories have been written after much worse plans. But Brown did not realize the drama of his plot. He was too eager, it seems, to get to the end of the tale. The movement is so fast that we never see any one person in the story at any time long enough to get a clear impression of his character. A scene which might stir the emotions is sketched in a few sentences and passed by as completed. The humor is often close to the heart of the Negro. For example, there is a minor character, Sam, who, although he is a submissive slave, is in the habit of saying things with a double meaning and of making up half defiant rimes, such as:

> The big bee flies high,
> The little bee makes the honey;
> The black folks makes the cotton,
> And the white folks gets the money.

However, what humor there is is introduced in digressive episodes, the main characters being at all times deadly serious. *Clotel* was by no means what Brown probably intended to make it, a successor to *Uncle Tom's Cabin*. But it was a promising beginning for American Negro fiction. (pp. 166-67)

[The] American edition of *Three Years in Europe* appeared as *Sketches of Places and People Abroad*. It is a considerable and judicious enlargement of the original, and was commented on most favorably by the antislavery reviewers, a number of whom hailed Brown as "the Fugitive Slave turned Author." Although an immediate American edition of *Clotel* was urged, it did not come until 1864. The novel, possibly because it was based on a scandalous rumor which the author had evidently made no attempt to prove as true, had not won the approval in England which had been accorded *Three Years in Europe*. Brown must have recognized his mistake in making Jefferson the focus of the story; for when the American edition did finally appear, Jefferson was replaced by an "unnamed Senator," and the new title adopted was *Clotelle: a Tale of the Southern States*. Numerous changes were made, all, with the exception of dropping Jefferson, for the worse. Certain passages were so mutilated that they are not intelligible. Since the copyright was secured by the publisher, one might reasonably accept the edition as brought out without Brown's knowledge if he himself had not in 1867 copyrighted an almost perfect facsimile of it, which was published as *Clotelle; or, The Colored Heroine*. (pp. 167-68)

[We] must take Brown's *The Escape; or, A Leap for Freedom*, . . . as the American Negro's first definitely known attempt to write a play.

Brown claimed that he wrote *The Escape* for his "own amusement." He said:

> I read it privately, however, to a circle of friends,
> and through them was invited to read it before
> a Literary Society. Since then the Drama has
> been given in various parts of the country.

He meant, of course, that he had given it as a reading; and it seems that the public for a time preferred it to his lectures. The play is made up of five acts, each divided into many scenes. Some of the farcical episodes are diverting, but the attempts at seriousness are unpardonably forced. . . . *The Escape* as a play is far more feeble than *Clotel* is as a novel. However, since *The Escape* is a pioneer venture of the American Negro into the field of the drama, it is a landmark in his literature. (pp. 168-69)

[Brown's] first extensive attempt at history [was] *The Black Man: His Antecedents, His Genius, and His Achievements*. Following the plan for historical accounts of the Negro made popular by Henri Grégoire in his *De la littérature des nègres* (1808), Brown opened the work with a discussion of ancient civilization in Egypt and Ethiopia, and then followed it with biographical essays of more than fifty Negroes who had gained distinction of some sort in Western civilization. The publication came at a most convenient time for attracting sales, just after Lincoln issued the Emancipation Proclamation. Many of the essays, such as the one on Nat Turner, were provided with the sensationalism which Brown always depended upon for gaining a hearing. . . . It continued to be reprinted after the publication of Brown's second historical work, *The Negro in the American Rebellion: His Heroism and His Fidelity*. . . . He had no true historical perspective on his material; but he treated it in an informal and gossipy style, and thus made of *The Negro in the American Rebellion* a readable book.

In his most pretentious and most important historical work, *The Rising Son*, . . . Brown reprinted much of the serious matter which he had included in *The Black Man* and in *The Negro in the American Rebellion*. . . . . [The] book is an effort to treat in a methodic and orderly manner the history of the Negro in ancient Africa, modern Europe, South America, the West Indies, and the United States. At the time it was published it was the most complete and thorough general history of the Negro which had been produced in America. . . . While the style of *The Rising Son* is far less exciting than that of the earlier histories, the work is in the main propaganda brought out through entertaining episodes. The public accepted the book as readable—to the extent of buying ten thousand copies within less than a year from the time of its publication.

In his last book, *My Southern Home: or, The South and Its People*, . . . Brown reverted to fiction. But fortunately, this work, his nearest approach to real literature, is neither a novel nor a play. It is a series of narrative essays, made up, as Brown tells us in the preface, dated May, 1880, of memories of his childhood and impressions gathered on trips to the South after the Civil War. The stories told in many of the essays, a number of which are presented in dramatized form, had been used in his earlier books. But given as the reminiscences of an old man, they gain in effect. Humor and picturesqueness are the characteristics which dominate. . . . Unfortunate for the general artistic effect of *My Southern Home* is the fact that in each story, in each anecdote, and in each song Brown is present as the propagandist. But the message which the book brings to his people is perhaps the most important he ever preached. He summarized it in the concluding sentence, "Black men, don't be ashamed to show your colors, and to own them!" (pp. 169-72)

Vernon Loggins, "Writings of the Leading Negro Antislavery Agents, 1840-1865," in his The Negro Author: His Development in America to 1900 (copyright 1931, 1959; Columbia University Press; copyright renewed © 1959 by Vernon Loggins; reprinted by permission of the publisher), Columbia University Press, 1931 (and reprinted by Kennikat Press, Inc., 1964, pp. 127-75.).*

J. SAUNDERS REDDING　(essay date 1939)

The most unusual figure in the literary history of the American Negro is William Wells Brown. A great deal of the interest which attaches to him is, perhaps, artificial, growing out of the confusion and variety of the stories he told about himself. (p. 23)

William Wells Brown was the first serious creative prose writer of the Negro race in America. Three editions of the *Narrative of William Wells Brown*, his first considerable work, appeared under the sponsorship of the Massachusetts Anti-Slavery Society. . . . *The Black Man, St. Domingo*, and *Three Years in Europe* were published before the close of the Civil War, and though the first two of these were attempts at objective historical writing and the third was a travel account, Brown was so dominated by "the cause of my countrymen" that his facts are garbled to serve the ends of propaganda.

When the slavery controversy had settled into well-defined patterns and the cause for which he had begun his career was no longer so pressing, Brown lauched his purely imaginative efforts. (pp. 24-5)

In facility of expression, in artistic discrimination, and in narrative skill Brown advanced steadily from the *Narrative* to the essays which comprise his last work. Historically more important in the development of Negro literature than any of his contemporaries, he was also the most representative Negro of the age, for he was simply a man of slightly more than ordinary talents doing his best in a cause that was his religion. . . . Almost without forethought, like an inspired prophet, Brown gave expression to the hope and despair, the thoughts and yearnings, of thousands of what he was pleased to call his "countrymen."

Brown had the vital energy that is part of the equipment of all artists. He wrote with force, with clarity, and at times with beauty. There is in his work, however, a repetitious amplification that is not altogether accountable to a desire for perfection. (pp. 25-6)

Brown was driven by the necessity for turning out propaganda in a cause that was too close to him for emotional objectivity and reasonable perspective. He had power without the artist's control, but in spite of this his successes are considerable and of great importance to the history of Negro creative literature. First novelist, first playwright, first historian: the list argues his place. (p. 26)

At its best Brown's language is cursive and strong, adapted to the treatment he gives his material. When he held his bitterness in check, he was inclined to lay on a heavy coating of sentimental morality. Often his lack of control did hurt to an otherwise good passage. . . .

Though it is possible that Brown was true to fact . . . , there is nevertheless a loss of force. This loss is due to his failure to see *truth* beyond mere fact. It may be that his mother did talk and act as he has her talk and act in [a] passage of *Narrative,* but she is not real to us either as an individual or a type. (p. 27)

The play *The Escape* in five acts and seventeen scenes, shows clearly that Brown knew nothing of the stage. Loosely constructed according to the formula of the day and marred by didacticism and heroic sentimentality, its chief characters are but pawns in the hands of Purpose. . . . The unconscious irony in creating such characters is very sharp, whispering his unmentionable doubt of the racial equality he preached. His characters are no more representative of the Negroes he was supposed to depict than are Eliza and Uncle Tom. (p. 28)

Brown's work as historian and commentator is far more substantial than his work in the purely creative field. . . . Using key episodes and men as the basis for historical narratives of more than ordinary interest, *The Rising Son* is an outline of history rather than a detailed relation of it. In this work Brown's blunt prejudices are shown softened into calmer rationalism: the swords he usually ground are here beaten into crude ploughshares. It should not be expected that after fifty years he could change precipitantly and wholly, but there is no doubt that in the end the artistic core of him rose up to assert itself.

Even more evident of the victory of his artistic consciousness over his social consciousness is his last work, *My Southern Home.* He came at last to the recognition of permanent literary values over the ephemeral sensational. He is a composed Brown in *My Southern Home,* writing charmingly and interestingly of experiences close to him and of people who are *people.* Humor and pathos, sense and nonsense are skillfully blended in pieces that show his narrative skill at its best. He does not avoid propaganda altogether, but he administers it sparingly and in sugar-coated doses. The warmth and sunshine of the South glows over his pages. It is completely right that *My Southern Home,* his last book, should be also his best. (pp. 29-30)

J. Saunders Redding, "Let Freedom Ring," in his To Make a Poet Black, *University of North Carolina Press, 1939 (and reprinted by McGrath Publishing Company, 1968), pp. 19-48.**

EDWARD M. COLEMAN (essay date 1945)

Every fair-minded and objective appraisal of an author's work must take into account due appreciation of the writer's background and preparation. On this point William Wells Brown is very clear and direct. On page iv of his preface to *The American Fugitive in Europe* he asks his readers ". . . to remember that the author was a slave in one of the Southern States of America until he had attained the age of twenty years;

and that the education he has acquired was by his own exertions, he never having had a day day's schooling in his life." In the light of this statement one recognizes at once that perhaps the most remarkable fact about this ex-slave is that he ever wrote anything at all. (p. 50)

[*Narrative of William W. Brown, A Fugitive Slave*] is really the autobiography of a slave, in which the author gives a vivid account of his own early life; his varied experiences as a bondsman; and his escape at the age of twenty. In several respects this is one of his best efforts. His style is clear, simple, and interesting as well as convincing. The descriptions of persons, places, and emotions are realistic and often charming. . . . It is, however, in this early work that Brown also displays quite often a weakness which detracts somewhat from the historical merit of this autobiography and which was to grow even more serious with the passing years. This was his tendency to indulge in moralizing, sentimental, or philosophical digressions. Nevertheless, the book does achieve very effectively the double purpose for which it was written, namely: the faithful narration of the essential facts regarding the early life of the author; and supplying true-to-life materials for those individuals and agencies engaged in doing their utmost to expose the shame, injustice, and brutality of slavery in an effort to destroy that institution. (pp. 51-2)

[While the two editions of Brown's travel essays, *The American Fugitive in Europe* and *Three Years in Europe,*] contain many fine descriptions of persons, cities, daily life, and places of interest the reader who is familiar with the author's style and diction soon gets the impression that Brown is making a deliberate effort to imitate some of the more famous writers whose works he admits having read on the voyage or after his arrival in Europe. The effect of this apparent effort at imitation is to give these works a certain artificial and decorative quality which, in spite of the clarity of the language used, would hardly be approved by modern historians. Moreover, these two works are at times so repetitious as to be almost boring to the reader who, having read his earlier works and either one of the two under discussion, then attempts to read the other. Another fact of significance in appraising the author's work and historical instinct is seen very clearly when one remembers that Brown was sent on this trip to Europe as a delegate to the Peace Conference. Yet in writing about his travels and activities abroad he almost completely ignores the program, problems, and work of the Conference and confines himself to descriptions of persons met, places visited, and the racial attitudes of the French people. At times his descriptions come very close to being gossipy. He sums up his impression of the Conference in these words: "They put padlocks on their mouths and handed the keys to the government." (pp. 53-4)

From the point of view of the present-day historian one of the best passages, if not the *very* best in either of these books is [found in]. . .*The American Fugitive in Europe* in which Brown describes a visit to a night session of the House of Commons. Here the reader will find a collection of brief, clear, quite accurate, comprehensive, and thoroughly interesting thumbnail sketches of some of England's leading statesman. Among those described are Joseph Hume, Richard Cobden, John Bright, William E. Gladstone, Benjamin Disraeli, Lord Palmerston, and Lord John Russell. Included with each sketch is a statement of the person's political views, party position, and a word on how he was regarded by his countrymen. These are all done with such charm, originality, and precision as would do credit to even the most modern of today's writers. But even when fullest credit had been given for some exceptionally good passages these works can hardly be considered as measuring up to the demands of modern scholarship.

The Black Man: His Antecedents, His Genius, and His Achievements . . . is one of the works upon which Brown's best claim as an historian rests. . . . The treatment [of the black man in this book] almost completely ignores the true historical background of the Negro and launches, instead, into an elaborate and very able *defense* of the Negro; a refutation of the charges of indolence and inferiority; and a strong and worthy plea for liberty, justice, opportunity, and the Negro's right to win equality and a dignified place in American life and society. (pp. 54-5)

My Southern Home, or The South and Its People, . . . written thirty years after his ***Three Years in Europe*** and seventeen years after the end of the Civil War, is a collection of undocumented accounts and memories clearly and interestingly written. Often the accounts and descriptions are dramatic, colorful, and graphic and fit well into the general pattern of the slave-society of the old South, but are written without evidence or documentation other than Brown's own memory. He writes of the cholera of 1832, fifty years before his publication, and of many other events, people, and conditions during the early 1830's, 1840's, and 1850's. Obviously, therefore, one cannot avoid the necessity of seriously questioning the authenticity of much that is presented in this book. There are 29 chapters, 15 of which deal with the South before 1860. On the whole, despite its admitted charm, the work is sentimental, argumentative, and of questionable accuracy. (p. 55)

[***The Rising Son; or the Antecedents and Advancement of the Colored Race***] is the second of Brown's two best historical works. . . . Reading this work is almost like reading two separate books—one a very incomplete and sketchy general account of the Negro in both the Old World and the New; the other, a collection of *very* brief and inadequate biographical notices on 67 Negro men and women, many of whom had been previously dealt with in ***The Black Man.*** These 67 notices . . . are handled in such a fashion as to leave the reader wishing he knew *a great deal* more about the persons mentioned. The treatment is highly laudatory and often very flattering. (p. 56)

As in ***The Black Man,*** so in ***The Rising Son,*** Brown shows very little regard for documentation. Aside from a few references to such sources as the writings of Herodotus, Homer, the Bible, and a few more recent secular writers footnotes are most conspicuous by their absence. Neither will the reader find a bibliography in either ***The Black Man, The Rising Son,*** or any of the other works written by Brown. Quotations are freely used but only on rare occasions does the author, in *any* of his works, take the trouble to acknowledge in footnotes the sources from which the quotations are drawn. More often than not, even on the rare occasions when the sources are cited in footnotes, the citations are incomplete since the titles of the works and the page-references are omitted. Anecdotes and tales of various kinds—many, at best, hardly more than hearsay—are scattered throughout his ***Rising Son.***

Gaps in chronology and in the sequence of events, which are found all too frequently, are simply passed over in silence and left to the reader's imagination. Inaccurate or misleading statements, exaggerated statements, and statements of questionable authenticity are not infrequent and are left to rest solely upon the author's unsupported assertion. One cannot escape the conclusion that the book was put together without proper regard

for the relationship of chapters to each other, or to the logical development of a closely woven and accurate account with a definite historical objective. Its scope is too broad and the work suffers greatly from the very obvious lack of adequate research by its author. The lack of objectivity and the strong racial bias are apparent throughout both [***The Rising Son***] and ***The Black Man.*** The critical reader is also forced to conclude that, on the whole, and in spite of the fact that each of these works does contain some very finely handled passages and much sound information about the Negro, both ***The Black Man*** and ***The Rising Son*** are quite superficial, inadequate, and unscientific when judged by the standards and requirements of present-day methodology. His was the vigorous pen of an able and relentless crusader, rather than that of an objective and scientific historian. (pp. 57-8)

> Edward M. Coleman, "William Wells Brown as an Historian" (originally an address delivered at the Annual Meeting of the Association for the Study of Negro Life and History, October 26-28, 1945), in The Journal of Negro History, *Vol. XXXI, No. 1, January, 1946, pp. 47-59.*

W. EDWARD FARRISON (essay date 1948)

In the autumn of 1852 Brown published the very kind of book by which many journalists since his time have been heralded as promising authors. The book is entitled ***Three Years in Europe; Or, Places I Have Seen and People I Have Met.*** In form the book consists principally of letters Brown had written to friends and newspapers in America between the summer of 1849 and the spring of 1852. In substance it is a summary of the more or less recent observations and experiences of one who, in spite of the deprivations of his early life, had read profitably as well as extensively in literature and history, had developed a wholesome and refreshing sense of humor, and had gained remarkable insight into men and affairs. (pp. 17-18)

Among the people Brown saw and sketched in ***Three Years in Europe*** was Thomas Carlyle, whom he saw in an omnibus in London one day in June, 1851. His remarks concerning that "prophet" are . . . much more independent and original than are the comments not infrequently repeated in academic discussions of Victorian literature. . . . (p. 19)

Even though some might have been displeased with Brown's bold and truthful remarks concerning Carlyle, on the whole, ***Three Years in Europe*** was well received by the British reading public. . . . It did not by any means ignore the cause of human freedom, which was so dear to its author's heart, but it did more to satisfy desires for wholesome entertaining reading than to move readers to the right sides of great issues. It is still a good, though not a great, example of travel literature.

Coming within eighteen months after the first British edition of Mrs. Harriet Beecher Stowe's *Uncle Tom's Cabin,* with which it could be compared to no advantage, [***Clotel; or, The President's Daughter***] attracted no especially remarkable attention in England, and this version of the story was never published in America. (pp. 19-20)

Like ***Clotel,*** [***The Escape; or, A Leap for Freedom***] is based on actual experiences and is primarily an anti-slavery argument. The subject matter of both the novel and the play belonged to the same department of the "peculiar institution"—the department of romances between masters and beautiful slave women, usually mixed-breeds. (p. 22)

Although *The Escape* is no *Hamlet,* some parts of which Brown seems to have imitated unsuccessfully, and although it is only melodrama, in plot and setting it is a better melodrama than *Clotel* is a novel. I do not yet know whether it has ever been performed; but despite the large number of artificial speeches it contains, it might well have been tried on the stage. (pp. 22-3)

> *W. Edward Farrison, "Phylon Profile, XVI: William Wells Brown," in* PHYLON: The Atlanta University Review of Race and Culture, 9 *(copyright, 1948, copyright renewed © 1975, by Atlanta University; reprinted by permission of* PHYLON*), Vol. IX, No. 1, First Quarter (March, 1948), pp. 13-23.*

ARNA BONTEMPS (essay date 1966)

The period in which the slave narrative flourished was, of course, the period in which the Negro spiritual reached its flowering. One was poetry, the other prose. Indeed, words from the spirituals are often quoted in the narratives. But the connection between the narratives and the subsequent literary expression they stimulated is more direct and immediate than that between the spirituals and the music they came eventually to influence.

William Wells Brown is the link. One of the three men [Brown, Charles Remond and Frederick Douglas] who, in Saunders Redding's judgment, best reflected "the temper and opinion of the Negro in those years," Brown is elected as "the most representative Negro of the age." . . . All three devoted their lives to the cause of abolition, and only Remond did not leave an autobiography. All three could write effectively when the need arose, but only Brown's writing evolved into what might be called a literary career. Here his place among American Negroes is secure. (p. 867)

[The heroine of *Clotelle; or, The President's Daughter*] was a beautiful near-white girl, and there was an implication that it was based on truth, making a tie-in with gossip that was then current. This became a bit more restrained in the Boston edition published almost a decade later with a new subtitle: *A Tale of the Southern States.* According to Saunders Redding, "Brown was driven by the necessity for turning out propaganda in a cause that was too close to him for emotional objectivity and reasonable perspective. He had power without the artist's control, but in spite of this his successes are considerable and of great importance to the history of Negro creative literature. First novelist, first playwright, first historian: the list argues his place."

A quotation from *Clotelle* suggests the mixture. Following a description of a Richmond slave market where a beautiful quadroon girl is offered to bidders, Brown summarizes:

> This was a Virginia slave-auction, at which the bones, sinews, blood and nerves of a young girl of eighteen were sold for $500: her moral character for $200; her superior intellect for $100; the benefits supposed to accrue from her having been sprinkled and immersed, together with a warranty of her devoted Christianity, for $300; her ability to make a good prayer, for $200; and her chastity for $700 more. This, too, in a city thronged with churches, whose tall spires look like so many signals pointing to heaven, but whose ministers preach that slavery is a God-ordained institution.

Brown's writings after the Civil War have been described as "more reasonable." With the campaign over and tensions relaxed, he settled down and began to produce histories and narrative essays that still do him credit, nearly a hundred years later. *The Negro in the American Rebellion,* . . . *The Rising Son,* . . . and *My Southern Home,* . . . are representative. (p. 869)

> *Arna Bontemps, "The Negro Contribution to American Letters," in* The American Negro Reference Book, *edited by John P. Davis (© 1966 by Prentice-Hall, Inc.; reprinted by permission of Prentice-Hall, Inc., Englewood Cliffs, New Jersey 07632), Prentice-Hall, 1966, pp. 850-78.**

DORIS M. ABRAMSON (essay date 1968)

[*The Escape; Or, A Leap for Freedom: A Drama, In Five Acts*] turned out to be a fascinating literary and social document. (p. 371)

The Escape; Or, A Leap for Freedom has been characterized as "a hodge-podge with some humor and satire and much melodrama." It would be difficult to defend the play against these charges, but it is fair to say that such charges could be brought against most plays by white playwrights of the period. And *The Escape* did carry a message of importance to abolitionist audiences. In his preface the author stated that many incidents in the play came from his experience of eighteen years "at the South"; the characters were based on real persons then residing in Canada. There is something admirable in the concluding sentence of the preface: "The play, no doubt, abounds in defects, but as I was born in slavery, and never had a day's schooling in my life, I owe the public no apologies for errors."

The Escape, a drama in five acts, is set in the Mississippi valley, a clearing in the forest, a Quaker home in a free state, and finally at the Canadian border. Clearly it is autobiographical. Just as clearly it is nineteenth-century melodrama. Boucicault, with all his education in the theatre of England and France, would have been pleased with the plot and might have written some of the dialogue.

The chief antagonists are a white couple, Dr. and Mrs. Gaines, who mouth Christian sentiments while threatening to whip their slaves. When a clergyman, Reverend John Pinchen, visits Mrs. Gaines, he recounts a dream he has had of Paradise and of old friends he visited there. The slave Hannah asks him, "Massa Pinchen, did you see my ole man Ben up dar in hebben?" The ensuing dialogue may be rather blatant in its humor; it is, nevertheless, telling:

> MR. P.: No, Hannah; I didn't go amongst the niggers.
>
> MRS. G.: No, of course Brother Pinchen didn't go among the Blacks, what are you asking questions for? Never mind, my lady, I'll whip you well when I am done here. I'll skin you from head to foot. (*Aside*) Do go on with your heavenly discourse, Brother Pinchen; it does my very soul good, this is indeed a precious moment for me. I do love to hear of Christ and Him crucified.
>
> (p. 372)

Although reviews of Mr. Brown's play readings praised his message and fervor rather than his skill as a playwright, it is true that *The Escape* is a well-made play by standards of the period. Written in five acts, the play has variety of characterization, careful exposition, a well-designed if obvious plot, and spine-chilling scenes of seduction and revenge. The last-minute escape in the boat is not the only stage effect familiar to readers and viewers of English and American plays of the period. . . .

William Wells Brown turned the drama of his own experience into the melodrama acceptable in the theatre of his day. That his plays were not produced may have been due to his being a Negro. On the other hand, as a militant reformer he may have chosen the platform over the stage. The combination of his overwhelming anti-slavery bias and what he learned of dramaturgy from playwrights of his time make *The Escape; Or, A Leap For Freedom* an interesting document both from a social and a theatrical point of view. (p. 375)

> *Doris M. Abramson, "William Wells Brown: America's First Negro Playwright," in* Educational Theatre Journal *(© 1968 University College Theatre Association of the American Theatre Association), Vol. XX, No. 3, October, 1968, pp. 370-75.*

MAXWELL WHITEMAN (essay date 1969)

Brown, a prolific nineteenth century author, has not yet found his rightful place in black letters. . . . [The importance of his novel *Clotel*] goes beyond the claim of a pioneer novel; it established a theme of sex and race which weaves through the fiction of generations of black novelists. Whatever structural weaknesses are present in *Clotel*, its interest does not diminish. The same fate was not in store for the prioneer black drama by the same author, *The Escape; or, A Leap For Freedom.*

In his voluminous biographical work on black Americans, William J. Simmons writes of a play by Brown by the title of *Doughface* (*Dough Face*) which it is believed to precede *The Escape.* No record of a stage production or publication of *Doughface* has been located. *The Escape* which Brown describes in his preface to the play, was designed to be read, and again no evidence has been found thus far to show that it was performed. But its private reception was such that Brown had it published.

The five acts and many scenes that make up *The Escape* lack the excitement of *Clotel*. They are too contrived; and the theme of the slave-holder abusing the virtues of Melinda the slave heroine, while accurately presented, does not reveal Brown as an adept in drama techniques.

> *Maxwell Whiteman, in his bibliographical note to* The Escape; or, A Leap for Freedom: A Drama in Five Acts *by William Wells Brown, Rhistoric Publications, 1969, p. iii.*

WILLIAM EDWARD FARRISON (essay date 1969)

Letter 22 [in *Three Years in Europe*], entitled **"A Narrative of American Slavery,"** represents Brown's first attempt to write an antislavery romance. According to the story, one of the participants in Nat Turner's insurrection of August, 1831, was a white slave named George, the nineteen-year-old son of a mulatto slave woman and "a member of the American Congress." (p. 204)

In writing [**"A Narrative of American Slavery"**] Brown was, of course, less interested in achieving a literary success than in developing a persuasive antislavery argument. As he was

doubtless aware, however, although the story portrayed various evils which were inherent in slavery, it was also a love story abounding in surprising incidents motivated only by chance. He could hardly have missed foreseeing, therefore, that as a whole it might be considered not much more than a romance in the popular sense of the word. If it was taken for that, his explanation implied, it should at least be considered a romance with a factual basis. (pp. 206-07)

Although Brown did not write [*Three Years in Europe*] primarily to win distinction as an author, and although he seems not to have claimed authorship as his profession until 1860, this book may be said to have launched him on his career as a professional writer. It was indeed a good beginning—one which, alas, gave promise of more than Brown ever achieved as an author. Because of its simplicity and fluency of style and its quality of perennial human interest, it is still a good example of travel literature. (p. 209)

As busy as he was traveling and lecturing during the first six weeks after his return to America, Brown found time to revise and enlarge his *Three Years in Europe* for publication under a new title—*The American Fugitive in Europe. Sketches of Places and People Abroad*. This work has been generally referred to only by the second half of its title. (p. 252)

Sketches of Places and People Abroad is not a remarkably good revision of *Three Years in Europe*. In it Brown corrected some of the imperfections of the first version, left some as they were, and added some new ones. He did not arrange the new chapters in chronological order. In fact he seems to have left them without order, unless it was the order in which he happened to write them. They are arranged as if he might have written some of them hurriedly in response to his printers' requests for more copy while other things were demanding his attention. Had time together with inclination permitted him to reorganize the subject matter as he might well have reorganized it, and to improve the style of the work as he presumably could have improved it, he might have made this not only his best book but also an American classic. As it is, it is not a much better book than *Three Years in Europe*. (p. 254)

In [*St. Domingo: Its Revolutions and Its Patriots*] Brown intended to make the history of the Haitian revolution serve the United States as a warning and a reminder—a warning that Negroes, like other human beings, not only desired freedom but would fight unto death to win and maintain it, and a reminder that a slave revolt had actually succeeded. . . .

Although *St. Domingo* was Brown's first attempt to write history, it is as good writing of the kind as he ever did; and it is far from being an example of the worst kind of popular historical writing. Especially remarkable is the human interest with which its subject matter is endued, as well as its simplicity of diction and sentence structure and its freedom from rhetorical flourishes, even though it was originally prepared for the platform in the age of Delsartian oratory. Because of these qualities it was probably easy to listen to, and it still makes easy as well as interesting reading. (p. 258)

In [*The Negro in the American Rebellion: His Heroism and His Fidelity*] as in three earlier works, Brown proved himself a pioneer—in this instance a pioneer in the writing of the military history of the American Negro. There had been previous sketches of the part Negroes had played in the American Revolution and the War of 1812, notably those of William C. Nell and George Livermore, but Brown's was at once the first attempt to write a history of the Negro's part in the Civil War and the first attempt to bring together in one work the history of the Negro's part in all three of these wars.

More than half of *The Negro in the American Rebellion* . . . deals with events of the last two years of the war. Even more than the preceding parts, this part of the work is discursive and without chronological order—as if Brown recorded the information as it became available to him and without much concern for coherence. There are accounts of the recruiting of Negro regiments in the North, of about a dozen battles in various parts of the South in which Negro soldiers had prominent parts, of Northern opposition to the war, as was evinced by the draft riot in New York City in July, 1863, and of the refusal of the federal government for more than a year to grant Negro soldiers pay equal to that granted to white soldiers. There are also examples of verse, folk songs, and wit and humor as well as of other things incidental to the war. (p. 413)

While Brown was busiest with the cause of temperance, he was also busy writing his fourth and last historical work, which proved to be his longest book. This is *The Rising Son; or, The Antecedents and Advancement of the Colored Race.* (p. 437)

It may be readily observed that Brown's historical works are fraught with defects. In all of them there are inaccuracies in details and considerable repetition. None of them evince any study of manuscripts or many official documents on the part of the author. None of them except *The Negro in the American Rebellion* and *The Rising Son* contain footnotes or other specific references of any kind, and many of the references in these works are either vague or inaccurate. Doubtless Brown could and would have removed these defects had he known much about historiography and the methodology of research, but he knew little or nothing about the technicalities of these things, because he had had no opportunity to study them. (p. 444)

Brown's last but hardly his best book is *My Southern Home: Or, The South and Its People.* (p. 446)

In this history of slave life, Brown's technique, although not much of his subject matter, was different from that which he had used when he was an antislavery crusader. As a rule he did not argue now as he had done then; he simply related incidents as interestingly and convincingly as he could—some of them being intentionally humorous—and left his readers to draw their own conclusions. He admitted in one passage that some slaves were happy, but he remembered that "It was indeed, a low kind of happiness, existing only where masters were disposed to treat their servants kindly, and where the proverbial lightheartedness of the latter prevailed." Nowhere did he idealize the "peculiar institution," as writers of the school of Joel Chandler Harris and Thomas Nelson Page were already beginning to do apologetically if not defensively. (pp. 447-48)

William Edward Farrison, in his William Wells Brown: Author & Reformer *(reprinted by permission of The University of Chicago Press; © 1969 by The University of Chicago), University of Chicago Press, 1969, 482 p.*

J. NOEL HEERMANCE (essay date 1969)

Brown's first published speech was made under the auspices of the Massachusetts Anti-Slavery Society. . . . It was *A Lecture Delivered before the Female Anti-Slavery Society of Salem* and was given November 14, 1847 at that town's Lyceum Hall. Significantly, the lecture begins—and also ends—with the stan-

dard, purposeful "apology" of every fugitive slave who spoke before educated abolitionist audiences. (p. 46)

The "apology" is deftly made and it has its desired effects. On the one hand, it does relieve the ex-slave orator of any grammatical or formal clumsiness which his language may be heir to and does, as well, emphasize the authenticity of his speech as "a fugitive slave." On the most important other hand, it is a damning indictment of the South and its treatment of Negroes, and is, simultaneously, a testament to the Negro's inherent abilities as a man—specifically his ability to learn and cultivate himself to the level of public speaking despite the many obstacles which slavery had put in his way. (p. 47)

[A] "lecture" such as this is more a dramatic compendium than a neatly laid-out, logical argument. Nor is this bad. In fact, this is what the fugitive slave address was meant to be— a large, realistic, rambling-yet-concrete indictment of all of slavery's many cruelties and ironies in as many approaches to the audience as practicable.

In stressing the large, loping formlessness here, however, we shouldn't let ourselves believe that there was no planning to such a speech or that there was no structured approach at all. Just the fact that so many of the standard anti-slavery techniques and ironies make their presence known here shows how much this address had been "planned" for variety. The only point is that with this emphasis on variety and the substances which make up that variety, the individual beads of the didactic necklace become far more important than the string which holds them together or the necklace's overall form and beauty. Variety, juxtaposition, and concrete action—these were the important aspects of the fugitive slave oration. (p. 55)

There is a good deal of repetition of ideas and feelings which [Brown] had introduced earlier, just as there is repetition within the passage itself and within so many passages throughout the address; and this is what was intended. For the blatant evils of slavery could not be over-emphasized in the eyes of the Abolitionists, and thus this constant citation and re-citation of those evils was deemed a necessary part of the orator's delivery. (pp. 56-7)

J. Noel Heermance, in his William Wells Brown and "Clotelle": A Portrait of the Artist in the First Negro Novel *(copyright © 1969 by The Shoe String Press, Inc.), Archon Books (Shoe String Press, Inc.), Hamden, Connecticut, 1969, 309 p.*

JEAN FAGAN YELLIN (essay date 1972)

[*Three Years in Europe; or, Places I Have Seen and People I Have Met*] is an important contribution to nineteenth-century American travel literature not because of its easy style or the freshness of some of its matter, but because of its special point of view toward the United States, perhaps most clearly expressed in an open letter written by Brown to his last owner, Enoch Price:

> I will not yield to you in affection for America, but I hate her institution of Slavery. I love her, because I am identified with her enslaved millions by every tie that should bind man to his fellow man. The United States has disfranchized me, and declared that I am not a citizen, but a chattel: her Constitution dooms me to be your slave. But while I feel grieved that I am alienated and driven from my own country, I

rejoice that, in this Land, I am regarded as a man. I am in England what I can never be in America while Slavery exists there.

At a time when our classic white writers examined the Old World and returned home with visions of a native literature, our first black author, more akin to their expatriate descendants, saw Europe as a refuge from American tyranny. (p. 170)

The main narrative [of *Clotel; or, The President's Daughter*], much of which clearly derives from Lydia Maria Child's sentimental antislavery tale "The Quadroons," concerns the fate of . . . Clotel. In Brown's novel, as in Mrs. Child's tale, the beautiful girl is a white slave victimized by the institution of slavery and its ideology of racism, which make her the property of her white aristocratic sweetheart but do not permit her to marry him, though she bears his child. But Brown changes Mrs. Child's pathetic story. When Clotel is cast off by her weak lover and sold by his jealous wife, instead of dying of a broken heart like Mrs. Child's rejected heroine, she disguises herself as Ellen Craft had, and escapes North with another slave masquerading as her black servant. . . .

Brown's final white-slave plot, like Mrs. Child's, concerns his heroine's daughter. But intead of the pathetic chronicle of betrayal, rape, and suicide described in "The Quadroons," Brown retells the romance of Mary and George, complete with happy ending, which he had included in his travel book. (p. 172)

What makes *Clotel* unique among the many antislavery novels published after *Uncle Tom's Cabin* is that in addition to interspersing the standard snatches of poetry and polemic among his melodramatic plots, its fugitive slave author inserts powerful realistic scenes of slave life. (p. 173)

> *Jean Fagan Yellin, "William Wells Brown," in her* The Intricate Knot: Black Figures in American Literature, 1776-1863 *(reprinted by permission of New York University Press; copyright © 1972 by New York University), New York University Press, 1972, pp. 154-82.*

ADDISON GAYLE, JR. (essay date 1975)

Brown may be immediately dismissed as a novelist of style, one who observed people well enough to portray them without reliance upon old stereotypes. In neither version of the novel, *Clotel*, does he improve in technical efficiency, is he capable of singularity of plot, organizational unity, or apt characterization. Like his successor, Sutton Griggs, his novels are marked by nothing so much as structural chaos. This chaos bears resemblance to the chaotic life of an ex-slave, one of little organization, where people and incidents too often assume the guise of the grotesque. Brown, the ex-slave, was forced to learn of man on the run, to live a disorganized existence; it is not surprising that being forced to come by ideas secondhand, secondhand ideas proliferate in his works.

To speak of him as the great borrower is not to defame him, nor to denigrate his accomplishment, though one of the most important factors in his work is his ability to borrow from whatever source he deemed necessary. From the eighteenth-century neoclassicists, he borrowed diction; from the nineteenth-century English and American Romantics, he borrowed sentimentality and a sense of the Gothic. The nuances of plot he borrowed from American history. What he did not borrow, what he came upon firsthand, was his belief in the perfectability

of man, a belief that led him to conclude, with Copernicus, that man was the center of the universe. (pp. 5-6)

At a crucial time for black people, when the novelist should have been engaged in redefining definitions, in moving to rebut both Mrs. Stowe and her detractors, Brown is found lacking. His solution to the problem of images is to offer counterimages, more appealing to whites and the black middle class than to those on the slave plantation who bore the brunt of the Southerners' attacks. *Clotel*, the octoroon heroine of his novel, is no less a romantic image than that concocted by the imagination of Mrs. Stowe and Grayson. The only difference is that the former was acceptable to many Blacks while the latter was acceptable only to whites. Thus after Brown's pen falls silent in 1874, the black novelist must reap the fruit of the bitter harvest which he helped to plant, must turn to confront a world constructed along lines which he did not oppose, must do battle with a society in which Blacks join whites as the major upholders of Anglo-Saxon values. He is not to be censured because he was a poor novelist, because he did not match his white contemporaries in mastery of the fictional form. Censure must be leveled against him for his failure, as a black novelist, to undertake the war against the American imagists. The struggle for man's freedom begins with the mind and Brown's inability to recognize this fact was his major drawback as a novelist. (pp. 6-7)

Brown recognized no dichotomy between propaganda and art. Living in an age of tumult and chaos, he would have championed the argument that art must be intrumental in liberating the people. This objective, prevalent in each version of [*Clotel*], depicts him as the moral propagandist. Any device that damages the institution of slavery—sentimentality, melodrama, contrived plots, or stolen phrases—is to be used by the writer. In this regard, sexual license granted the owner and his family over black women are singled out for special concern. For Brown, illegitimacy, the result of the ravaging of black women, which leads to the breakup of the familial structure, is the foundation of corruption inherent in the institution of slavery. Arguing Sewall's point in *The Selling of Joseph*, with more factual evidence than the former author possessed, Brown notes that the Pharaohs are in reality selling their own children. To give this thesis validity, therefore, he peoples his novel with those like Clotel, who "was not darker than other white children."

She inhabits what might be called the world in between, one populated by octoroons, quadroons, and mulattoes, and, at least in the final version of the novel, is allowed to escape the fate of the outcast—the total isolation assigned the mulatto in fiction by whites—and evidences her ability to move freely between the white and black worlds by marriage to first a white man, then a Black. Her life ends in philanthropy, her "trials and tribulations" rewarded by service to others. For those freed Blacks, now beginning to constitute the hierarchy based upon color, she is a heroine, who for all practical purposes has the skin color, morals, and ethical values of white people. To call Brown the first novelist of the black bourgeoisie is not too far wrong; despite the apologia of his biographer, each version of *Clotel* singles him out as the conscious or unconscious propagator of assimilationism. Given her choice of several worlds in the novel, Clotel retained a more than casual affinity for the white. (pp. 8-9)

> *Addison Gayle, Jr., "Paradigms of the Early Past," in his* The Way of the New World: The Black Novel in America *(copyright © 1975 by Addison Gayle,*

Jr.; reprinted by permission of Doubleday & Company, Inc.), Anchor Press, 1975, pp. 1-24.*

ROBERT B. STEPTO　(essay date 1979)

In an authenticating narrative, represented . . . by William Wells Brown's *Narrative of the Life and Escape of William Wells Brown* (not to be confused with Brown's 1847 volume, *Narrative of William Wells Brown, a Fugitive Slave, Written by Himself*), the narrator exhibits considerable control of his narrative by becoming an editor of disparate texts for authentication purposes, far more than for the goal of recounting personal history. The texts Brown displays include passages from his speeches and other writings, but for the most part they are testimonials from antislavery groups in both America and England, excerpts from reviews of his travel book, *Three Years in Europe* . . . , selections from antislavery verse, and, quite significantly, letters to Brown's benefactors from his last master in slavery, Mr. Enoch Price of St. Louis. Brown's control of his narrative is comparable to Douglass's, but while Douglass gains control by improving upon the narrative failures of authors like Henry Bibb, Brown's control represents a refinement of the authenticating strategies used by publishers like Bibb's Lucius Matlack, who edited and deployed authenticating documents very much like those gathered by Brown. In this way, Brown's narrative is not so much a tale of personal history as it is a conceit upon the authorial mode of the white guarantor. Control and authentication are achieved, but at the enormous price of abandoning the quest to present personal history in and as literary form.

Brown's "Preface," written notably by himself and not by a white guarantor, is peculiar in that it introduces both his narrative and the text authenticated by the narrative, *Clotel; or, The President's Daughter*. By and large, the tone of the "Preface" is sophisticated and generally that of a self-assured writer. . . . Brown does not skirmish with other authenticators for authorial control of the text, nor is he anxious about competition from other literary quarters of the antislavery ranks. . . . That Brown introduces a personal narrative and a somewhat fictive narrative (*Clotel*) with language and intentions commonly reserved for works of history and journalism constitutes his first admission of being motivated by extraliterary concerns. His second admission emerges from his persistent use of the term "memoir." In contrast to a confession or autobiography, a memoir refers specifically to an author's recollections of his public life, far more than to his rendering of personal history as literary form or metaphor. This former kind of portrait is, of course, exactly what Brown gives us in his narrative.

The narrative is, as I have indicated, bereft of authorship. Brown rarely renders in fresh language those incidents of which he has written elsewhere; he simply quotes himself. His posture as the editor and not the author of his tale disallows any true expression of intimacy with his personal past. This feature is reinforced by certain objectifying and distancing qualities created by third-person narration. Brown's 1847 narrative begins, "I was born in Lexington, Ky. The man who stole me as soon as I was born, recorded the births of all the infants which he claimed to be born his property, in a book which he kept for that purpose. . . ." Thus, it inaugurates the kind of personal voice and hardboiled prose which is Brown's contribution to early Afro-American letters. In contrast, the opening of the 1852 narrative is flat, without pith or strength: "William Wells Brown, the subject of this narrative, was born a slave in Lexington, Kentucky, not far from the residence of the late Hon.

Henry Clay." These words do not constitute effective writing, but that is not Brown's goal. The goal is, rather, authentication, and the seemingly superfluous aside about Henry Clay—which in another narrative might very well generate the first ironic thrust against America's moral blindness—appears for the exclusive purpose of validation. In this way Brown commences an authentication strategy which he will pursue throughout the tale. (pp. 26-8)

The Enoch Price letters are undoubtedly the most interesting documents in Brown's compendium, and he makes good narrative use of them. While the other assembled documents merely serve the authenticating strategy, Price's letters, in their portrait of a slaveholder ironically invoking the dictates of fair play while vainly attempting to exact a bargain price for Brown from his benefactors, actually tell us something about Brown's circumstances. . . . As the editor of his résumé—his present circumstance—Brown must acknowledge slavery's looming presence in his life, but he can also attempt to bury it beneath a mountain of antislavery rhetoric and self-authenticating documentation. Through the act of self-authentication Brown may contextualize slavery and thereby control it. In these terms, then, the heroic proportions to Brown's editorial act of including and manipulating Enoch Price's letters become manifest.

Brown's personal narrative most certainly authenticates himself, but how does it also authenticate *Clotel*? The answer takes us back to Brown's "Preface," where he outlines the extraliterary goals of both narratives, and forward to the concluding chapter of *Clotel,* where he writes:

> My narrative has now come to a close. I may
> be asked, and no doubt shall, Are the various
> incidents and scenes related founded in truth?
> I answer, Yes. I have personally participated
> in many of those scenes. Some of the narratives
> I have derived from other sources; many from
> the lips of those who, like myself, have run
> away from the land of bondage. . . . To Mrs.
> Child, of New York, I am indebted for part of
> a short story. American Abolitionist journals
> are another source from whence some of the
> characters appearing in my narrative are taken.
> All these combined have made up my story.

Brown's personal narrative functions, then, as a successful rhetorical device, authenticating his *access* to the incidents, characters, scenes, and tales, which collectively make up *Clotel*. In the end, we witness a dynamic interplay between the two narratives, established by the need of each for resolution and authentication within the other. Since *Clotel* is not fully formed as either a fiction or a slave narrative, it requires completion of some sort, and finds this when it is transofrmed into a fairly effective antislavery device through linkage with its prefatory authenticating text. Since Brown's personal narrative is not fully formed as either an autobiography or a slave narrative, it requires fulfillment as a literary form through intimacy with a larger, more developed but related text. *Clotel* is no more a novel than Brown's preceding personal narrative is autobiography, but together they represent a roughly hewn literary tool which is, despite its defects, a sophisticated departure from the primary phases of slave narration and authentication. (pp. 29-30)

Robert B. Stepto, "I Rose and Found My Voice: Narration, Authentication, and Authorial Control in Four Slave Narratives," in his From Behind the Veil:

A Study of Afro-American Narrative *(© 1979 by the Board of Trustees of the University of Illinois; reprinted by permission of the author and the University of Illinois Press), University of Illinois Press, 1979, pp. 3-31.**

ADDITIONAL BIBLIOGRAPHY

Bardolph, Richard. "Out of the House of Bondage." In his *The Negro Vanguard*, pp. 19-130. New York: Vintage Books, 1959.*
   A brief biographical account of Brown.

Bone, Robert. "Novels of the Talented Tenth: Abolitionist Novels." In his *The Negro Novel in America*. Rev. ed., pp. 30-2. New Haven: Yale University Press, 1968.*
   Brief plot summary of *Clotel; or, The President's Daughter*.

Brawley, Benjamin. "William Wells Brown." In his *Early Negro American Writers: Selections with Biographical and Critical Introductions*, pp. 168-70. New York: Dover Publications, 1935.
   Outlines Brown's publishing history.

Brown, Josephine. *Biography of an American Bondman, by His Daughter*. Boston: Robert F. Wallcut, 1856, 104 p.
   A biography of Brown written by his daughter.

Cottrol, Robert J. "Heroism and the Origins of Afro-American History." *The New England Quarterly* LI, No. 2 (June 1978): 256-63.*
   Discusses Brown as a historian.

Ellison, Curtis W., and Metcalf, E. W. Jr. *William Wells Brown and Martin R. Delany: A Reference Guide*. Boston: G. K. Hall & Co., 1978, 276 p.*
   An extensive annotated bibliography.

Yellin, Jean Fagan. Introduction to *Clotel*, by William Wells Brown, pp. i-viii. New York: Arno Press and the New York Times, 1969.
   Discusses the accuracy with which Brown depicted the nineteenth-century black experience, and assesses *Clotel*'s significance as the first American Negro novel.

George Gordon (Noel) Byron, Lord Byron

1788-1824

English poet, dramatist, and satirist.

Although many of his original critics considered his work immoral and inferior, Byron is now considered one of the most important poets of the nineteenth century. His literary reputation has varied more from one era to another than that of any other major English poet. Enormously popular during his lifetime, Byron was almost forgotten in the latter half of his century. Since then, however, his critical acclaim has been restored.

Born to "Mad Jack" Byron, a dissipated nobleman from an old and revered English family, and to Catherine Gordon, a hot-tempered descendant of a Scottish noble family, Byron soon displayed the unconventional traits of his personality. He was notoriously proud of his noble heritage, and was often accused of pretension. A club foot was a major source of embarrassment throughout his life. Unable to tolerate criticism, he was quick to anger, and often used his rage as a source of inspiration.

Byron's first publication was a collection of juvenilia, *Hours of Idleness*, which drew a scathing attack in the *Edinburgh Review*. He replied with a vicious satire in the work *English Bards and Scotch Reviewers*. It lashes out at authors and critics alike, saving an especially vitriolic section for Francis Jeffrey, to whom Byron had mistakenly attributed the review of *Hours of Idleness*. Although the satire in *English Bards* is often unfair, it earned Byron the respect, or at least the fear, of his critics. However, he felt a career in writing to be below his rank, and decided to try politics. After taking his seat in the House of Lords and making several stirring speeches in the cause of reform, he journeyed to Europe and the Near East. When he returned, he casually handed the first two cantos of *Childe Harold's Pilgrimage* to a friend, thinking it not worthy of publication. Consequently, when it appeared in print, Byron was probably as surprised as anyone when it became, almost instantly, an enormous success. He was the toast of London society and England's most popular author.

For the next few years, Byron wrote verse tales, all of which sold well, though critics disagree about their quality. But the great turning point in his life was upon him. After a prolonged affair with the vivacious "little volcano," Lady Caroline Lamb (so distressed upon their separation that she burned him in effigy), Byron married Annabella Milbanke. Though their marriage seems to have gone well for a time, Annabella left Byron in 1816. The reason for the separation is still not certain. Rumor and allegation of incest between Byron and his half-sister, Augusta, may have caused the rift, but clear evidence of the matter has never been substantiated. Many critics cite Byron's relationship with Augusta as the inspiration for his later drama, *Manfred*.

When the scandal surrounding his marital separation spread through England, Byron was vilified by press and public alike, and he left the country. After travels throughout Europe, he met Percy Bysshe Shelley, with whom he stayed in Italy. Shelley, Byron, and Leigh Hunt launched an ill-fated magazine, *The Liberal*, which published Byron's *The Vision of Judgment*,

a satire on Robert Southey's poem of the same name. It was also in Europe that Byron began what is generally regarded as his masterpiece, *Don Juan. Don Juan* is a mock epic which reveals the many sides of Byron's character as aristocratic, rebellious, satiric, tender, and vengeful. "I have no character at all. . . . I am so changeable, being everything by turns and nothing long," Byron said of himself, and the complexity of *Don Juan* bears this out. It has been criticized as meandering and careless, but most modern critics perceive *Don Juan* to be meticulously constructed, providing his most competent use of varied narrative perspectives.

Because of the satiric nature of much of his work, Byron is difficult to place within the Romantic movement. He had a decided distaste for poetic theory, and ridiculed the critical work of William Wordsworth and Samuel Taylor Coleridge. And though he was a friend to Shelley, Byron was not a part of the mystic tradition of Romanticism. His most notable contribution to Romanticism is the Byronic hero: a melancholy man, often with a dark past, who, eschewing societal and religious strictures, seeks for truth and happiness in an apparently meaningless universe.

Still drawn to politics, Byron left Italy for Greece in 1823 to join a group of insurgents fighting for independence from the

Turks. He died of a fever at Missolonghi. The England that had scorned him only eight years before now mourned him as a national hero. Despite his enormous influence in Europe— both Johann Wolfgang von Goethe and Aleksander Pushkin saw him as a master poet—his own country did not give its complete critical approval until almost a century after his death. Today Byron, a sometimes careless but always fluid and interesting writer, is now regarded as a major poet.

PRINCIPAL WORKS

Hours of Idleness (poetry) 1807
English Bards and Scotch Reviewers (satire) 1809
Childe Harold's Pilgrimage: A Romaunt (poetry) 1812
The Bride of Abydos: A Turkish Tale (poetry) 1813
The Giaour: A Fragment of a Turkish Tale (poetry) 1813
Waltz: An Apostrophic Hymn (poetry) 1813
The Corsair (poetry) 1814
Lara (poetry) 1814
Ode to Napoleon Buonaparte (poetry) 1814
Hebrew Melodies (poetry) 1815
Childe Harold's Pilgrimage: Canto the Third (poetry) 1816
Parisina (poetry) 1816
The Prisoner of Chillon, and Other Poems (poetry) 1816
The Siege of Corinth (poetry) 1816
The Lament of Tasso (poetry) 1817
Manfred (dramatic poetry) 1817
Beppo: A Venetian Story (poetry) 1818
Childe Harold's Pilgrimage: Canto the Fourth (poetry) 1818
Mazeppa (poetry) 1819
Don Juan, Cantos I-XVI. 6 vols. (poetry) 1819-1824
Cain (drama) 1821
Marino Faliero, Doge of Venice (drama) 1821
Sardanapalus (drama) 1821
The Two Foscari (drama) 1821
The Vision of Judgment (poetry) 1822
Heaven and Earth (poetry) 1823
The Island; or, Christian and His Comrades (poetry) 1823
Werner (drama) 1823
The Deformed Transformed (drama) 1824
Letters and Journals. 11 vols. (letters and journals) 1975-1981

---

fectly clear. It is a plea available only to the defendant; no plaintiff can offer it as a supplementary ground of action. Thus, if any suit could be brought against Lord Byron, for the purpose of compelling him to put into court a certain quantity of poetry; and if judgement were given against him; it is highly probable that an exception would be taken, were he to deliver *for poetry*, the contents of this volume. To this he might plead *minority;* but as he now makes voluntary tender of the article, he hath no right to sue, on that ground, for the price in good current praise, should the goods be unmarketable. . . . [We] all remember the poetry of Cowley at ten, and Pope at twelve; and so far from hearing, with any degree of surprise, that very poor verses were written by a youth from his leaving school to his leaving college, inclusive, we really believe this to be the most common of all occurrences; that it happens in the life of nine men in ten who are educated in England; and that the tenth man writes better verse than Lord Byron. (p. 833)

[The] mere rhyming of the final syllable, even when accompanied by the presence of a certain number of feet; nay, although (which does not always happen) those feet should scan regularly, and have been all counted accurately upon the fingers,—is not the whole art of poetry. We would entreat him to believe, that a certain portion of liveliness, somewhat of fancy, is necessary to constitute a poem; and that a poem in the present day, to be read, must contain at least one thought, either in a little degree different from the ideas of former writers, or differently expressed. (p. 834)

But whatever judgment may be passed on the poems of this noble minor, it seems we must take them as we find them, and be content; for they are the last we shall ever have from him. He is at best, he says, but an intruder into the groves of Parnassus; he never lived in a garret, like thorough-bred poets; and 'though he once roved a careless mountaineer in the Highlands of Scotland,' he has not of late enjoyed this advantage. Moreover, he expects no profit from his publication; and whether it succeeds or not, 'it is highly improbable, from his situation and pursuits hereafter,' that he should again condescend to become an author. Therefore, let us take what we get and be thankful. (p. 835)

[*Henry Brougham*,] "'*Hours of Idleness*'," *in* Edinburgh Review, *Vol. XI, January, 1808 (and reprinted in* The Romantics Reviewed, Contemporary Reviews of British Romantic Writers: Byron and Regency Society Poets, *Vol. II, edited by Donald H. Reiman, Garland Publishing, Inc., 1972, pp. 833-35).*

[HENRY BROUGHAM] (essay date 1808)

[*Hours of Idleness*] belongs to the class which neither gods nor men are said to permit. Indeed, we do not recollect to have seen a quantity of verse with so few deviations in either direction from that exact standard. His effusions are spread over a dead flat, and can no more get above or below the level, than if they were so much stagnant water. As an extenuation of this offence, the noble author is peculiarly forward in pleading minority. We have it in the title-page, and on the very back of the volume; it follows his name like a favourite part of his *style*. Much stress is laid upon it in the preface, and the poems are connected with this general statement of his case, by particular dates, substantiating the age at which each was written. Now, the law upon the point of minority, we hold to be per-

LORD BYRON (essay date 1809)

Still must I hear?—shall hoarse Fitzgerald bawl
His creaking couplets in a tavern hall,
And I not sing, lest, haply, Scotch reviews
Should dub me scribbler, and denounce my muse?
Prepare for rhyme—I'll publish, right or wrong:
Fools are my theme, let satire be my song.

Oh! nature's noblest gift—my grey goosequill!
Slave of my thoughts, obedient to my will,
Torn from thy parent bird to form a pen,
That mighty instrument of little men!
The pen! foredoom'd to aid the mental throes
Of brains that labour, big with verse or prose,
Though nymphs forsake, and critics may deride,
The lover's solace, and the author's pride.

What wits, what poets dost thou daily raise!
How frequent is thy use, how small thy praise!
Condemn'd at length to be forgotten quite,
With all the pages which 't was thine to write.
But thou, at least, mine own especial pen!
Once laid aside, but now assumed again,
Our task complete, like Hamet's shall be free;
Though spurn'd by others, yet beloved by me:
Then let us soar to-day; no common theme,
No eastern vision, no distemper'd dream
Inspires—our path, though full of thorns, is plain;
Smooth be the verse, and easy be the strain.

When Vice triumphant holds her sov'reign sway,
Obey'd by all who nought beside obey;
When Folly, frequent harbinger of crime,
Bedecks her cap with bells of every clime;
When knaves and fools combined o'er all prevail,
And weigh their justice in a golden scale;
E'en then the boldest start from public sneers,
Afraid of shame, unknown to other fears,
More darkly sin, by satire kept in awe,
And shrink from ridicule, though not from law.

(p. 112)

I too can scrawl, and once upon a time
I pour'd along the town a flood of rhyme,
A schoolboy freak, unworthy praise or blame;
I printed—older children do the same.
"T is pleasant, sure, to see one's name in print;
A book's a book, although there's nothing in't.
Not that a title's sounding charm can save
Or scrawl or scribbler from an equal grave:
This Lambe must own, since his patrician name
Fail'd to preserve the spurious farce from shame.
No matter, George continues still to write,
Though now the name is veil'd from public sight.
Moved by the great example, I pursue
The self-same road, but make my own review;
Not seek great Jeffrey's, yet, like him, will be
Self-constituted judge of poesy.

A man must serve his time to every trade
Save censure—critics all are ready made.
Take hackney'd jokes from Miller, got by rote,
With just enough of learning to misquote;
A mind well skill'd to find or forge a fault;
A turn for punning, call it Attic salt;
To Jeffrey go, be silent and discreet,
His pay is just ten sterling pounds per sheet:
Fear not to lie, 't will seem a sharper hit;
Shrink not from blasphemy, 't will pass for wit;
Care not for feeling—pass your proper jest,
And stand a critic, hated yet caress'd.

And shall we own such judgment? no—as soon
Seek roses in December—ice in June;
Hope constancy in wind, or corn in chaff;
Believe a woman or an epitaph,
Or any other thing that's false, before
You trust in critics, who themselves are sore;
Or yield one single thought to be misled
By Jeffrey's heart, or Lambe's Boeotian head.
To these young tyrants, by themselves misplaced,
Combined usurpers on the throne of taste;
To these, when authors bend in humble awe,
And hail their voice as truth, their word as law—

While these are censors, 't would be sin to spare;
While such are critics, why should I forbear?
But yet, so near all modern worthies run,
'T is doubtful whom to seek, or whom to shun;
Nor know we when to spare, or where to strike,
Our bards and censors are so much alike.

Then should you ask me, why I venture o'er
The path which Pope and Gifford trod before;
If not yet sicken'd, you can still proceed:
Go on; my rhyme will tell you as you read.
"But hold!" exclaims a friend, "here's some neglect:
This—that—and t' other line seem incorrect."
What then? the self-same blunder Pope has got,
And careless Dryden—"Ay, but Pye has not:"—
Indeed!—'t is granted, faith!—but what care I?
Better to err with Pope, than shine with Pye.

(pp. 112-13)

Lord Byron, "English Bards and Scotch Reviewers"
(originally published as an unsigned poem in 1809),
in his The Poetical Works of Lord Byron, *John Mur-*
ray, 1837 (and reprinted by Henry Frowde, 1904,
pp. 111-24).*

SYLVANUS URBAN [pseudonym of John Nichols]
(essay date 1809)

At length comes forth a poetical work that possesses not only the three avowedly grand recommendations of *time, place,* and *circumstance*—of such moment in *all* worldly matters; but, so far as regards Literature, the three no less important, though, alas! far less frequent, recommendations, of defying *enemies*—rendering the favourable sentiments of *friends* superfluous—and the quackery of *the trade* wholly unnecessary. (p. 1074)

[*English Bards and Scotch Reviewers*] is unquestionably the result of an impassioned yet diligent study of the best masters, grounded on a fine taste and very happy natural endowments. It unites much of the judgment of the "Essay on Criticism," the playful yet poignant smile and frown of indignation and ridicule of the Dunciad, with the versification of the Epistle to Arbuthnot, and the acuteness of the "Imitations of Horace" of the same Author; at the same time that we think we have discovered a resemblance of the best epigrammatic points and brilliant turns of the "Love of Fame." And with all this it is unquestionably an original work. In a word, many years have passed since the English press has given us a performance so replete with mingled genius, good sense, and spirited animadversion. (p. 1076)

Sylvanus Urban [pseudonym of John Nichols], "'En-
glish Bards and Scotch Reviewers'," in Gentleman's
Magazine, *Vol. LXXIX, March, 1809 (and reprinted*
in The Romantics Reviewed, Contemporary British
Romantic Writers: Byron and Regency Society Poets,
Vol. III, edited by Donald H. Reiman, Garland Pub-
lishing, Inc., 1972, pp. 1074-77).

[GEORGE ELLIS] (essay date 1812)

We have been in general much gratified, and often highly delighted, during our perusal of [**'Childe Harold's Pilgrimage'**], which contains, besides the two first cantos of the **'Pilgrimage,'** and the notes by which they are accompanied, a few smaller poems of considerable merit; together with an Appendix, communicating a good deal of curious information concerning the present state of literature and language in modern Greece. The principal poem is styled 'A Romaunt;' an appellation, perhaps, rather too quaint, but which, inasmuch as it has been always used with a considerable latitude of meaning, and may be considered as applicable to all the anomalous and non-descript classes of poetical composition, is not less suited than any other title to designate the *metrical itinerary* which we are about to examine. (p. 1985)

We do not know whether Lord Byron ever had it in contemplation to write an epic poem, but we conceive that the subject, which he selected, is perfectly suited to such a purpose; that the foundation which he has laid is sufficiently solid, and his materials sufficiently ample for the most magnificent superstructure; but we doubt whether his plan be well conceived, and we are by no means disposed to applaud, in every instance, the selection of his ornaments.

Of the plan indeed we are unable to speak with perfect confidence, because it has not been at all developed in the two cantos which are now given to the public; but it appears to us that the **'Childe Harold,'** whom we suppose, in consequence of the author's positive assurance, to be a mere creature of the imagination, is so far from effecting the object for which he is introduced, and 'giving some connection to the piece,' that he only tends to embarrass and obscure it. (pp. 1990-91)

The metre adopted throughout this 'Romaunt' is the stanza of Spenser; and we admit that, for every ancient word employed by the modern poet, the authority of Spenser may be pleaded. But we think that to intersperse such words as ee, moe, feere, ne, losel, eld, &c. amidst the richest decorations of modern language, is to patch embroidery with rags. Even if these words had not been replaced by any substitutes, and if they were always correctly inserted, their uncouth appearance would be displeasing; but Lord Byron is not always correct in his use of them. (p. 1991)

Lord Byron has shewn himself, in some passages, a tolerably successful copyist; but we like him much better in those where he forgets or disdains to copy; and where, without sacrificing the sweetness and variety of pause by which Spenser's stanza is advantageously distinguished from the heroic couplet, he employs a pomp of diction suited to the splendour of the objects which he describes. We rejoice when, dismissing from his memory the wretched scraps of a musty glossary, he exhibits to us, in natural and appropriate language, the rich scenery and golden sunshine of countries which are the

> Boast of the aged, lesson of the young;
> Which sages venerate, and bards adore,
> As Pallas and the Muse unveil their awful lore.

But we have not yet exhausted our complaints against the wayward hero of the poem, whose character, we think, is most capriciously and uselessly degraded. The moral code of chivalry was not, we admit, quite pure and spotless; but its laxity in some points was redeemed by the noble spirit of gallantry which it inspired; a gallantry which courted personal danger in the defence of the sovereign, because he is the fountain of honour; of women, because they are often lovely and always helpless; and of the priesthood, because they are at once disarmed and sanctified by their profession. Now Childe Harold, if not absolutely craven and recreant, is at least a mortal enemy to all exertions, a scoffer at the fair sex, and apparently disposed to consider all religions as different modes of superstition. (p. 1992)

The second feature in Childe Harold's character, which was introduced, we presume, for the purpose of giving to it an air of originality, renders it, if not quite unnatural, at least very unpoetical. Of this indeed the author seems to have been aware; but instead of correcting what was harsh and exaggerated in his sketch of the woman hater, he has only had recourse to the expedient of introducing, under various pretexts, those delineations of female beauty which a young poet may be naturally supposed to pen with much complacency. This we think ill judged. The victim of violent and unrequited passion, whether crushed into the sullenness of apathy, or irritated into habitual moroseness, may become, in the hands of an able poet, very generally and deeply interesting; the human heart is certainly disposed to beat in unison with the struggles of strong and concentrated feeling; but the boyish libertine whose imagination is chilled by his sated appetites, whose frightful gloom is only the result of disappointed selfishness; and 'whose kiss had been pollution,' cannot surely be expected to excite any tender sympathy, and can only be viewed with unmixed disgust. Some softening of such a character would become necessary even if it were distinguished by peculiar acuteness of remark, or by dazzling flashes of wit. But there is not much wit in designating women as 'wanton *things*,' or as 'lovely harmless *things*'; or in describing English women as '*Remoter* females *famed for sickening prate*.' . . . (pp. 1992-93)

It is now time to take leave—we hope not a long leave—of Childe Harold's migrations; but we are unwilling to conclude our article without repeating our thanks to the author for the amusement which he has afforded us. The applause which he has received has been very general, and, in our opinion, well deserved. We think that the poem exhibits some marks of carelessness, many of caprice, but many also of sterling genius. On the latter we have forborne to expatiate, because we apprehend that our readers are quite as well qualified as ourselves to estimate the merits of pleasing versification, of lively conception, and of accurate expression. Of those errors of carelessness from which few poems are, in the first instance, wholly exempt, we have not attempted to form a catalogue, because they can scarcely fail to be discovered by the author, and may be silently corrected in a future edition. But it was our duty attentively to search for, and honestly to point out the faults arising from caprice, or from a disregard of general opinion; because it is a too common, though a very mischievous prejudice, to suppose that genius and eccentricity are usual and natural companions; and that, to discourage extravagance is to check the growth of excellence. Lord Byron has shewn that his confidence in his own powers is not to be subdued by illiberal and unmerited censure; and we are sure that it will not be diminished by our animadversions: we are not sure that we should have better consulted his future fame, or our own character for candour, if we had expressed our sense of his talents in terms of more unqualified panegyric. (p. 1995)

[*George Ellis*,] "'*Childe Harold*', *I-II*," *in* Quarterly Review, *Vol. VII, March, 1812 (and reprinted in* The Romantics Reviewed, Contemporary Reviews of British Romantic Writers: Byron and Regency Society Poets, *Vol. V, edited by Donald H. Reiman, Garland Publishing, Inc., 1972, pp. 1984-95).*

[FRANCIS JEFFREY]   (essay date 1813)

[*The Giaour, a Fragment of a Turkish Tale*], we think, is very beautiful—or, at all events, full of spirit, character, and originality;—nor can we think that we have any reason to envy the

Turkish auditors of the entire tale, while we have its fragments thus served up by a *restaurateur* of such taste as Lord Byron. (p. 842)

Giaour is the Turkish word for Infidel; and signifies, upon this occasion, a daring and amorous youth, who, in one of his rambles into Turkey, had been smitten with the charms of the favourite of a rich Emir; and had succeeded not only in winning her affections, but in finding opportunities for the indulgence of their mutual passion. . . .

What the noble author has most strongly conceived and most happily expressed, is the character of the Giaour;—of which, though some of the elements are sufficiently familiar in poetry, the sketch which is here given appears to us in the highest degree striking and original. . . . The whole poem, indeed, may be considered as an exposition of the doctrine, that the enjoyment of high minds is only to be found in the unbounded vehemence and strong tumult of the feelings; and that all gentler emotions are tame and feeble, and unworthy to move the soul that can bear the agency of the greater passions. It is the force and feeling with which this sentiment is expressed and illustrated, which gives the piece before us its chief excellence and effect; and has enabled Lord Byron to turn the elements of an ordinary tale of murder into a strain of noble and impassioned poetry.

The images are sometimes strained and unnatural—and the language sometimes harsh and neglected, or abrupt and disorderly; but the effect of the whole is powerful and pathetic; and, when we compare the general character of the poem to that of the more energetic parts of Campbell's O'Connor's Child, though without the softness, the wildness, or the occasional weakness, of that enchanting composition, and to the better parts of Crabbe's lyrical tales, without their coarseness or details,—we have said more to recommend this little volume to all true lovers of poetry, than if we had employed a much larger space than it occupies with a critique and analysis of its contents. (p. 843)

The Oriental *costume* is preserved, as might be expected, with admirable fidelity through the whole of this poem; and the Turkish original of the tale is attested, to all but the bolder sceptics of literature, by the great variety of untranslated words which perplex the unlearned reader in the course of these fragments. *Kiosks, Caiques* and *Muezzins*, indeed, are articles with which all readers of modern travels are forced to be pretty familiar; but *Chiaus, palampore,* and *ataghan,* are rather more puzzling: They are well sounding words, however; and as they probably express things for which we have no appropriate words of our own, we shall not now object to their introduction. But we cannot extend the same indulgence to *Phingari,* which signifies merely the moon; which, though an humble monosyllable, we maintain to be a very good word either for verse or prose, and can, on no account, allow to be supplanted, at this time of day, by any such new and unchristian appellation. . . .

We hope, however, that he will go on, and give us more fragments from his Oriental collections; and, powerful as he is in the expression of the darker passions and more gloomy emotions from which the energy and the terrors of poetry are chiefly derived, we own we should like now and then to meet in his pages with something more cheerful, more amiable, and more tender. . . . Energy of character and intensity of emotion are sublime in themselves, and attractive in the highest degree as objects of admiration; but the admiration which they excite, when presented in combination with worthlessness and guilt, is one of the most powerful corrupters and perverters of our moral nature; and is the more to be lamented, as it is most apt to exert its influence on the noblest characters. The poetry of Lord Byron is full of this perversion; and it is because we conceive it capable of producing other and still more delightful sensations than those of admiration, that we wish to see it employed upon subjects less gloomy and revolting than these to which it has hitherto been almost exclusively devoted. (p. 847)

> [*Francis Jeffrey,*] " '*The Giaour*'," *in* Edinburgh Review, *Vol. XXI, July, 1813 (and reprinted in* The Romantics Reviewed, Contemporary Reviews of British Romantic Writers: Byron and Regency Society Poets, *Vol. II, edited by Donald H. Reiman, Garland Publishing, Inc., 1972, pp. 842-47).*

[WILLIAM ROBERTS]   (essay date 1814)

[We] cannot think [*The Bride of Abydos*] at all worthy of the reputation or ability of the poet. The verses are in general very puerile and flat, and too much like the exercise of a schoolboy. One cannot but be greatly surprised, that a writer who has shewn himself so capable of sustaining the melody of the Spenser stanza should have wandered into so many forms of metre in this little poem, all of them, as it appears to us, ill chosen, and certainly very improperly blended together. The poem commences with a specimen of the amphibrachys or cretic, a metre of rare use in our language; and principally occuring on sportive, familiar, rustic, or satirical occasions. It is said to have been the metre of the fescennine verses at Rome, sung at marriage feasts and harvest home, among the Romans, and full, as is well known, of coarse and obscene allusions, and abusive satire. It is obviously ill-suited to the subject of this poem. . . . Will his lordship allow plain men to tell him that the real and radical reason of his late failures is his prurience for the press? He appears to possess a truly poetical genius, perhaps the truest that belongs to any living poet; but he seems not to be fully aware that a poet, like other people, must economise and replenish his fund in proportion to his expenditure. The field of what is called fashionable life produces nothing that can nourish the imagination, or on which the heart and affections can feed. It is from nature that the poet must be always drawing fresh accessions of ideas, and renewing the decays of his mind. (pp. 419-20)

> [*William Roberts,*] " '*The Bride of Abydos*'," *in* British Review, *Vol. V, February, 1814 (and reprinted in* The Romantics Reviewed, Contemporary Reviews of British Romantic Writers: Byron and Regency Society Poets, *Vol. I, edited by Donald H. Reiman, Garland Publishing, Inc., 1972, pp. 416-20).*

SCOTS MAGAZINE   (essay date 1814)

[*The Corsair*], we think, is decidedly the best poem of Lord Byron, and a very fine one indeed. The beauties are equal or superior, and the faults less conspicuous than those of its predecessors. The narrative, though not very artificially constructed, is free from that obscurity which enveloped some of his former stories. . . . Neither does there appear any necessity to attempt an estimate of the general merits of Lord Byron's composition, since this has been already repeatedly, and very recently done. (p. 2155)

> "'*The Corsair*'," *in* Scots Magazine, *Vol. LXXVI, February, 1814 (and reprinted in* The Romantics

Reviewed, Contemporary Reviews of British Romantic Writers: Byron and Regency Society Poets, *Vol. V, edited by Donald H. Reiman, Garland Publishing, Inc., 1972, pp. 2155-58).*

ANTIJACOBIN REVIEW (essay date 1814)

[*Ode to Napoleon Buonaparte*] has been universally imputed to the noble author of the *Corsair,* and the imputation has never been repelled. If it really be the production of his lordship's muse, his forbearance to acknowledge it must be ascribed to the recent declaration of his intention to write no more, for some years. The present unexpected occasion, however, might fully justify a departure from such intention, without subjecting him to the charge of inconstancy. However men may differ on great political questions, or upon matters of internal economy, no difference of opinion it is conceived, can subsist, among those who are friendly to civil liberty, and to the best interests of society, on the downfall of one of the most odious tyrants that ever disgraced human nature. (p. 50)

[Byron's] keenness of sarcasm, and this vein of irony, are admirable! And yet there are miscreants still in France to exclaim *Vive L'Empereur!* Aye, and there are still greater miscreants in this country to deplore his downfall, and to sigh for his restoration! . . .

The two last stanzas (particularly the last) want simplicity and perspicuity. The mixed allusion to sacred and profane History, to Prometheus and to Satan, is not consistent with that classical taste which marks the rest of the ode, which is creditable to the author's talents and principles. (p. 51)

> *"'Ode to Napoleon Buonaparte',"* in Antijacobin Review, *Vol. XLVI, May, 1814 (and reprinted in* The Romantics Reviewed, Contemporary Reviews of British Romantic Writers: Byron and Regency Society Poets, Vol. I, *edited by Donald H. Reiman, Garland Publishing, Inc., 1972, pp. 50-3).**

[WASHINGTON IRVING] (essay date 1814)

Among the cluster of poets that have lately sprung up in Great Britain, the most fashionable, at the present day, is Lord Byron. Independent of his literary merits, his popularity may be attributed, in some degree, to his rank, youth, and the eccentric and romantic cast of his private character. (p. 68)

Shortly after leaving school, and before he was of age, he published a volume of miscellaneous poems, entitled "**Hours of Idleness,** by Lord Byron, *a minor.*" This volume fell under the lash of the Edinburgh reviewers, who animadverted upon it in a strain of coarse but highly ludicrous satire. Their strictures, though severe, were in general just, and though their ridicule may have been galling to the individual, yet if it could operate in any degree to restrain that fatal eagerness to rush into notoriety, which is the misfortune of so many young writers, we cannot but think it highly beneficial. Still we consider their censure of the poems as too unqualified—many passages in the volume are stamped with considerable poetical merit; several of the poems, which, from their date, must have been written when his lordship was but fifteen years of age, are surprising productions for such early youth, and, indeed, the whole collection, as the writings of "a minor," certainly bore the air of very great promise.

One of the best of the poems is an elegy on Newstead Abbey, the family seat of the Byrons. Here his lordship dwells on the former power and feudal grandeur of his ancestors, recounts their gallant exploits, and pours forth, in elevated language, the feelings of a high-born soul, meditating on the ruins of past magnificence. (pp. 69-70)

The success of ["**English Bards and Scotch Reviewers**"] at once stamped his reputation; it met with vast circulation, and universal applause. The million were delighted with it, from the relish that almost every one has for any thing pungent and satirical; some authors extolled it, because they had formerly suffered under the lash of the critics themselves, and rejoiced in any thing that could reach their feelings, or prove their fallibility: while many others joined in the plaudits, by way of making favour with the poet, least they should at some future time suffer under the satire of his excursive muse.

The poem, indeed, was intrinsically excellent, possessing much of the terseness and vigour of Roman satire; and though he lay about him with an unsparing hand, and often cut down where he should merely have lopped off, still, we think, the garden of poetry would be wonderfully benefited by frequent visitations of the kind. The most indifferent part of the poem is that where the author meant to be most severe; his animadversions on the critics have too much of pique and anger; the heat of his feelings has taken out the temper of his weapon; and when he mentions Jeffrey he becomes grossly personal, and sinks beneath the dignity of his muse. (p. 71)

The limits of this brief article will not allow us to enter into any examination of the merits of ["**Childe Harold's Pilgrimage**"] which, indeed, has been thoroughly scrutinized by every periodical publication of the times. . . .

The subsequent writings of Lord Byron are too well known to need recapitulation. He has published a succession of brilliant little eastern tales, decorated with appropriate and splendid imagery. These are in every one's hands, and are the hackneyed subjects of every review. . . . In the introduction to his last poem he expresses a determination not to publish again for several years; and we understand he is about once more to depart on his poetic rambles in the east. We hope he may keep to his determination, and give time for that poetical genius, which has hitherto manifested itself in brilliant sparks and flashes, to kindle up into a fervent and a lasting flame. (p. 72)

> [*Washington Irving,*] *"Lord Byron,"* in The Analectic Magazine, *Vol. IV, July, 1814, pp. 68-72.*

[JOSIAH CONDER] (essay date 1814)

We have, in ['**Lara**'], a sequel to '**The Corsair.**' Whether Lord Byron thought that the narrative demanded a sequel, or that the character, a favourite production, probably, of its Author's, seemed to require further development,—whether he thought that it would subserve a moral purpose, to exhibit, in their progressive tendency and ultimate result, the gloomy passions of such a being as Conrad, or whether his Lordship wrote '**Lara**' simply to form a companion poem to his friend [Samuel] Rogers's 'Jacqueline,' we are not curious to inquire. Whatever was the cause of its being written, the reader will not regret that any circumstance should have operated as an inducement sufficiently strong, to change his Lordship's determination not to appear again before the public in the poetical character. . . . (p. 727)

[We] must express our regret that Lord Byron should not see the false taste, to say nothing of the inexcusable impiety, of the almost atheistical insinuations by which some of the finest passages in his poetry are disfigured. There is something exceedingly revolting in such a phrase, for instance, as, 'the wound that sent his soul to rest,' applied to a character like Lara's. The naked infidelity of the sentiment, is not rescued by any dignity of expression, from the charge of being vulgarly profane. . . . Of all descriptions of cant, the cant of scepticism is the most offensive, and the most nearly allied to absurdity. We do not mean to arraign, either the principles or the motives of the Noble Author; but we could have wished, for his own sake, no less than for that of his readers, that he had not forced from us these probably unwelcome remarks. (p. 729)

> [*Josiah Conder,*] *" 'Lara',—'Jacqueline'," in* Eclectic Review, *n.s. Vol. II, October, 1814 (and reprinted in* The Romantics Reviewed, Contemporary Reviews of British Romantic Writers: Byron and Regency Society Poets, *Vol. II, edited by Donald H. Reiman, Garland Publishing, Inc., 1972, pp. 727-30).*

AUGUSTAN REVIEW   (essay date 1815)

We have seldom hailed the appearance of any work with pleasure more genuine than that which [*Hebrew Melodies*] has excited. This does not arise from the superior excellence of the poetry—from the felicity of the diction, or the harmony of the numbers; but from the consideration of the noble author's muse being at length directed to the pure fountain of sacred song. We have long regretted that the richness of Lord Byron's fancy should have been reflected only on objects dreary and revolting; and that the force of his mind should have been spent in assailing the bulwarks of human consolation. . . . But now we see him in the fields of pure inspiration. He has abandoned the streams of Acheron, for "Siloa's brook that flows fast by the oracle of God"; he has escaped from the horrors of a cold, *unpoetical* scepticism, into the regions to which Milton delighted to soar. (p. 59)

[Although] we rejoice to see Lord Byron touching tenderly the harp of David, we estimate him more by his promise, than by his immediate performance.

There are traits of exquisite feeling and beauty in these little specimens. And we are the most delighted with them, as we lately feared that their author was capable of employing only the dark and the terrific machinery he has so successfully wielded. . . .

[If] Lord Byron will but keep a steady eye on the sublime objects he has been contemplating, he may elicit tones sweet and affecting as "the echo of the song of angels." (p. 60)

> *" 'Hebrew Melodies'," in* Augustan Review, *Vol. I, July, 1815 (and reprinted in* The Romantics Reviewed, Contemporary Reviews of British Romantic Writers: Byron and Regency Society Poets, *Vol. I, edited by Donald H. Reiman, Garland Publishing, Inc., 1972, pp. 57-60).*

[JOSIAH CONDER]   (essay date 1816)

If Lord Byron can produce nothing better than [**"The Siege of Corinth"** and **"Parsina"**], we care not how many of these we get from him. But with regard to the public, who are apt to mistake the recurrence of obvious traits of style, and similarity of sentiment, for the sameness of impoverished genius, and to grow, in consequence, fastidious, and at length unjust, towards the productions of their favourite, we fear that his Lordship

will gain little reputation by such publications. It is requisite that an Author should, on every fresh appearance, exceed himself, in order to keep pace with the expectations of the public. Still each successive poem will be inquired for with eagerness, and it may be a matter of indifference to his Lordship, what the many may think of their purchase.

We profess ourselves pleased to obtain productions like these from Lord Byron, provided he can do nothing better: and the repetition of similar publications, at uncertain intervals, would seem to betray in the Author a consciousness of not being able to achieve greater things. When, by a series of such performances as these, a writer has shewed us all he can do, we begin to be let into the secret of what he *cannot* accomplish, and this discovery must tend to lower the estimate of his genius, drawn from the promise of his first production. We do not scruple however to pronounce **"the Siege of Corinth,"** one of the most successful of his Lordship's efforts. The first ten stanzas are, indeed, tame, common-place, and wordy; the structure of many of the sentences is involved, and the rhymes are not infrequently absolutely Hudibrastic. The character of the whole is feebleness, and we are led to conclude, either that these stanzas were supplied at the Printing office, or that Lord Byron purposely framed them of this unpretending description, in order to give more striking effect to the exquisite passage which they serve to produce. (p. 733)

We shall say little of **"Parisina."** It is not deficient in merit. The first stanza, which has appeared before in a different form, is very beautiful; and we might select several other fine passages. His Lordship will set us down among the fastidious objectors to such stories, which he deems sufficiently authorized by 'the Greek Dramatists and some of the best of our old English writers'. Our objections, however, originate rather in taste than respect for morality. The subject of the tale is purely unpleasing, and the manner in which it is treated, does not tend to reconcile us to it. The use which was made of facts or fables of this sort, by our old dramatic writers, was, to afford occasion for the development of character, or to impart a mysterious interest to the plot. In Lord Byron's poem of Parisina, there is neither plot nor character. The story is given in the nakedness of history. A hundred similar stories, as gross and as revolting, might doubtless be extracted from the domestic histories of feudal times: but what moral emotion—not to speak of any moral end—are they calculated to excite, when imbodied in confessedly beautiful poetry? (p. 735)

We are far from depreciating Lord Byron's genius. In energy of expression, and in the power of giving to words the life and breath of poetry, we think he is almost unequalled by any contemporary. We conclude that his powers are circumscribed, from the way in which he has employed them, rather than from any other circumstance. To go down to posterity, however, as a great poet, something more than genius is requisite. There must be a high and holy ambition of legitimate fame; there must be a moral discipline of the intellect and feelings: the good, the true, and the beautiful, must, as ideal archetypes, occupy the visions of the poet; and he must be the partaker of an elevating and purifying faith, by which his mind may be brought into contact with "things unseen" and infinite. All these requisites must meet in a great poet; and there must be an appearance at least of approximation to them, in the character of any one that aspires to maintain, by means of his writings, a permanent influence over the minds and sympathies of his fellow men. There must be at least the semblance of virtue, or of the love of virtue. (pp. 735-36)

[Josiah Conder,] "'The Siege of Corinth' and 'Parisina'," in Eclectic Review, n.s. Vol. V, March, 1816 (and reprinted in The Romantics Reviewed, Contemporary Reviews of British Romantic Writers: Byron and Regency Society Poets, Vol. II, edited by Donald H. Reiman, Garland Publishing, Inc., 1972, pp. 732-36).

[FRANCIS JEFFREY] (essay date 1817)

[*Manfred*] is a very strange—not a very pleasing—but unquestionably a very powerful and most poetical production. The noble author, we find, still deals with that dark and overawing Spirit, by whose aid he has so often subdued the minds of his readers, and in whose might he has wrought so many wonders. In Manfred, we recognise at once the gloom and potency of that soul which burned and blasted and fed upon itself in Harold, and Conrad, and Lara—and which comes again in this piece, more in sorrow than in anger—more proud, perhaps, and more awful than ever—but with the fiercer traits of its misanthropy subdued, as it were, and quenched in the gloom of a deeper despondency. (p. 881)

This piece is properly entitled a dramatic Poem—for it is merely poetical, and is not at all a drama or play in the modern acceptation of the term. It has no action; no plot—and no characters; Manfred merely muses and suffers from the beginning to the end. His distresses are the same at the opening of the scene and at its closing—and the temper in which they are borne is the same. A hunter and a priest, and some domestics, are indeed introduced; but they have no connexion with the passions or sufferings on which the interest depends; and Manfred is substantially alone throughout the whole piece. . . . To delineate his character indeed—to render conceivable his feelings—is plainly the whole scope and design of the poem; and the conception and execution are, in this respect, equally admirable. It is a grand and terrific vision of a being invested with superhuman attributes, in order that he may be capable of more than human sufferings, and be sustained under them by more than human force and pride. To object to the improbability of the fiction is, we think, to mistake the end and aim of the author. Probabilities, we apprehend, did not enter at all into his consideration—his object was, to produce effect—to exalt and dilate the character through whom he was to interest or appal us—and to raise our conception of it, by all the helps that could be derived from the majesty of nature, or the dread of superstition. It is enough, therefore, if the situation in which he has placed him is *conceivable*—and if the supposition of its reality enhances our emotions and kindles our imagination;—for it is Manfred only that we are required to fear, to pity, or admire. If we can once conceive of him as a real existence, and enter into the depth and the height of his pride and his sorrows, we may deal as we please with the means that have been used to furnish us with this impression, or to enable us to attain to this conception. We may regard them but as types, or metaphors, or allegories: But *he* is the thing to be expressed, and the feeling and the intellect of which all these are but shadows. (p. 882)

There are great faults, it must be admitted, in this poem;—but it is undoubtedly a work of genius and originality. Its worst fault, perhaps, is, that it fatigues and overawes us by the uniformity of its terror and solemnity. Another is the painful and offensive nature of the circumstance on which its distress is ultimately founded. It all springs from the disappointment or fatal issue of an incestuous passion; and incest, according to

our modern ideas—for it was otherwise in antiquity—is not a thing to be at all brought before the imagination. The lyrical songs of the Spirits are too long, and not all excellent. There is something of pedantry in them now and then; and even Manfred deals in classical allusions a little too much. If we were to consider it as a proper drama, or even as a finished poem, we should be obliged to add, that it is far too indistinct and unsatisfactory. But this we take to be according to the design and conception of the author. He contemplated but a dim and magnificent sketch of a subject which did not admit of more accurate drawing, or more brilliant colouring. Its obscurity is a part of its grandeur;—and the darkness that rests upon it, and the smoky distance in which it is lost, are all devices to increase its majesty, to stimulate our curiosity, and to impress us with deeper awe. (p. 887)

[Francis Jeffrey,] "'Manfred'," in Edinburgh Review, Vol. XXVIII, August, 1817 (and reprinted in The Romantics Reviewed, Contemporary Reviews of British Romantic Writers: Byron and Regency Society Poets, Vol. II, edited by Donald H. Reiman, Garland Publishing, Inc., 1972, pp. 881-87).

[JOHN WILSON] (essay date 1817)

["The Lament of Tasso"] possesses much of the tenderness and pathos of the **"Prisoners of Chillon"**. . . . Lord Byron has not delivered himself unto any one wild and fearful vision of the imprisoned Tasso,—he has not dared to allow himself to rush forward with headlong passion into the horrors of his dungeon, and to describe, as he could fearfully have done, the conflict and agony of his uttermost despair,—but he shews us the Poet sitting in his Cell, and singing there—a low, melancholy, wailing lament, sometimes, indeed, bordering on utter wretchedness, but oftener partaking of a settled grief, occasionally subdued into mournful resignation, cheered by delightful remembrances, and elevated by the confident hope of an immortal Fame. (p. 126)

The Lament closes, as it ought to do, with a strain of exultation, and we bid farewell to Tasso with elevating music in our hearts. (p. 127)

[John Wilson,] "'Lament of Tasso'," in Blackwood's Edinburgh Magazine, Vol. II, November, 1817 (and reprinted in The Romantics Reviewed, Contemporary Reviews of British Romantic Writers: Byron and Regency Society Poets, Vol. I, edited by Donald H. Reiman, Garland Publishing, Inc., 1972, pp. 125-27).

[FRANCIS JEFFREY] (essay date 1818)

Though there is as little serious meaning or interest in this extraordinary performance [*Beppo, a Venetian Story*], as can easily be imagined, we think it well entitled to a place in our fastidious Journal—and that, not merely because it is extremely clever and amusing, but because it affords a very curious and complete specimen of a kind of diction and composition of which our English literature has hitherto afforded very few examples. It is, in itself, absolutely a thing of nothing—without story, characters, sentiments, or intelligible object;—a mere piece of lively and loquacious prattling, in short, upon all kinds of frivolous subjects,—a sort of gay and desultory babbling about Italy and England, Turks, balls, literature and fish sauces. But still there is something very engaging in the uniform gayety, politeness, and good humour of the author—and something still more striking and admirable in the matchless facility with which he has cast into regular, and even difficult versification, the unmingled, unconstrained, and unselected language of the most light, familiar, and ordinary conversation. . . . The great charm is in the simplicity and naturalness of the language—the free but guarded use of all polite idioms, and even of all phrases of temporary currency that have the stamp of good company upon them,—with the exclusion of all scholastic or ambitious eloquence, all profound views, and all deep emotions.

The unknown writer before us has accomplished all these objects with skill and felicity; and, in particular, has furnished us with an example, unique we rather think in our language, of about one hundred stanzas of good verse, entirely composed of common words, in their common places; never presenting us with one sprig of what is called poetical diction, or even making use of a single inversion, either to raise the style or assist the rhyme—but running on in an inexhaustible series of good easy colloquial phrases, and finding them fall into verse by some unaccountable and happy fatality. In this great and characteristic quality it is almost invariably excellent. In some other respects it is more unequal. About one half is as good as possible, in the style to which it belongs; the other half bears perhaps too many marks of that haste with which we take it for granted that such a work must necessarily be written. Some passages are rather too foolish, some too snappish, and some run too much on the cheap and rather plebeian humour of out-of-the-way rhymes and strange sounding words and epithets. But the greater part is very pleasant, amiable, and gentlemanlike. (p. 889)

We are not in the secret of this learned author's incognito; and, at our distance from the metropolis, shall not expose ourselves by guessing. We cannot help thinking, however, that we have seen him before, and that 'we do know that fine Roman hand.' At all events, we hope we shall see him again; and if he is not one of our old favourites, we are afraid we may be tempted to commit an infidelity on his account,—and let him supplant some of the less assiduous of the number. (p. 893)

> [*Francis Jeffrey,*] " '*Beppo*'," *in* Edinburgh Review, *Vol. XXIX, February, 1818 (and reprinted in* The Romantics Reviewed, Contemporary Reviews of British Romantic Writers: Byron and Regency Society Poets, *Vol. II, edited by Donald H. Reiman, Garland Publishing, Inc., 1972, pp. 888-93).*

MONTHLY REVIEW   (essay date 1819)

Although our opinion of the varied powers of the noble author, who has now given us an additional proof of them in *Don Juan,* though perhaps not in *Mazeppa,* has altered with his productions since his first appearance, which we hailed with gladness, to the epoch during which he has risen to his present eminence; yet we always regarded him as superior in versatility of thought and numbers to any single poet of our times. (pp. 1796-97)

While his sentiments are peculiar, and often false, his philosophical observations become obscure; and his restlessness of feeling often breaks through the connection of his thoughts, to surprize us with comparisons neither agreeable nor true. He is the real poet of passion: but he describes passion of an untamed nature, which recoils with increasing force from every weight that is laid on it. He is likewise too fond of anatomizing, and unfolding to our view, the inclinations rather than the duties or the finer action of our nature. This perversion of mind is

busy with incongruous images, with which it may illustrate its subject; we must not therefore expect those pleasing pictures of melancholy truth which Shakspeare gives, and which are the offspring of pity, not of misanthropy.

The story of *Mazeppa* possesses the novelty of a lively vein introduced into the octo-syllabic measure, which was before sacred to the author's *dreadful* heroes: but it is certainly not one of his happiest efforts, although it contains some good description of Siberian scenery. . . .

As the basis of this narrative, viz. a love-intrigue, is in conformity with Lord Byron's favourite contemplations, so the horrors of the result are congenial to the general nature of his pictures. Something new, however, is certainly presented in this incident, together with the descriptions and feelings to which it gives rise; and in these particulars the poem has its chief and perhaps its only merit. (p. 1797)

[*Don Juan* is a singular and very superior poem] which has also such demerits, that neither his Lordship nor his usual publisher has chosen to acknowledge it: but which, if originality and variety be the surest test of genius, has certainly the highest title to it; and which, we think, would have puzzled Aristotle with all his strength of Poetics to explain, have animated Longinus with some of its passages, have delighted Aristophanes, and have choked Anacreon with joy instead of with a grape. . . . He has here exhibited that wonderful versatility of style and thought which appear almost incompatible within the scope of a single subject; and the familiar and the sentimental, the witty and the sublime, the sarcastic and the pathetic, the gloomy and the droll, are all touched with so happy an art, and mingled together with such a power of union, yet such a discrimination of style, that a perusal of the poem appears more like a pleasing and ludicrous dream, than the sober feeling of reality. It is certainly one of the strangest though not the best of dreams; and it is much to be wished that the author, before he lay down to sleep, had invoked, like Shakspeare's Lysander, some good angel to protect him against the *wicked* spirit of slumbers. We hope, however, that his readers have learnt to admire his genius without being in danger from its influence; and we must not be surprized if a poet *will* not always write to instruct as well as to please us. Still we must explicitly condemn and reprobate various passages and expressions in the poem, which we shall not insult the understanding, the taste, or the feeling of our readers by pointing out. . . . (pp. 1798-99)

Voluptuous, then, as is his delineation of the delight which [ladies] confer on us in this world, and powerful as are the varied attractions of his pen, it requires some exertion to withdraw ourselves from his spell, and to bestow merited censure on all the abuses which he commits both as a painter and as a writer. (p. 1802)

> "*Lord Byron's 'Mazeppa' and 'Don Juan', I-II,*" *in* Monthly Review, *n.s., Vol. LXXXIX, July, 1819 (and reprinted in* The Romantics Reviewed, Contemporary Reviews of British Romantic Writers: Byron and Regency Society Poets, *Vol. IV, edited by Donald H. Reiman, Garland Publishing, Inc., 1972, pp. 1796-802).*

[WILLIAM HAZLITT]   (essay date 1821)

We cannot speak in terms of very enthusiastic praise of [*Marino Faliero, Doge of Venice*]. Indeed, it hardly corresponds to its title. It has little of a local or circumstantial air about it. We are not violently transported to the time or scene of action. We know not much about the plot, about the characters, about the motives of the persons introduced, but we know a good deal about their sentiments and opinions on matters in general, and hear some very fine descriptions from their mouths; which would, however, have become the mouth of any other individual in the play equally well, and the mouth of the noble poet better than that of any of his characters. We have, indeed, a previous theory, that Lord Byron's genius is not dramatic, and the present performance is not one, that makes it absolutely necessary for us to give up that theory. It is very inferior to *Manfred,* both in beauty and interest. . . . [Here] he descends to the ground of fact and history; and we cannot say, that in that circle, he treads with the same firmness of step, that he has displayed boldness and smoothness of wing, in soaring above it. He paints the cloud, or the rainbow in the cloud; or dives into the secret and subterraneous workings of his own breast; but he does not, with equal facility or earnestness, wind into the march of human affairs upon the earth, or mingle in the throng and daily conflict of human passions. There is neither action nor reaction in his poetry; both which are of the very essence of the Drama. He does not commit himself in the common arena of man; but looks down, from the high tower of his rank, nay, of his genius, on the ignobler interests of humanity, and describes them either as a dim and distant phantasmagoria or a paltry fantoccini exhibition, scarce worth his scorn. (pp. 1591-92)

Marino Faliero is without a plot, without characters, without fluctuating interest, and without the spirit of dialogue. The events hang together very slenderly and unaccountably (p. 1592)

> [*William Hazlitt,*] " '*Marino Faliero*'," *in* Baldwin's London Magazine, *Vol. III, May, 1821 (and reprinted in* The Romantics Reviewed, Contemporary Reviews of British Romantic Writers: Byron and Regency Society Poets, *Vol. I, edited by Donald H. Reiman, Garland Publishing, Inc., 1972, pp. 1591-95).*

[WILLIAM ROBERTS]   (essay date 1822)

Sardanapalus and the *Two Foscari,* distant as they are from each other in their subjects, have one bond of affinity,—they meet at the same point of deteriority,—they are equally feeble and puerile. To say this gives us no pleasure, but, on the contrary, disappointment. No works by the same hand contain so many decorous sentiments, and so little shock the wise and virtuous. They exhibit, to be sure, some clumsy efforts to be good, and some blundering about holiness and duty; but first attempts are entitled to great allowance, and considering the importance of any indications of improvement in the character of Lord Byron's poetry, we are willing sometimes to accept what he tenders for virtue, though short of the standard of legal currency.

Whimsical as it may be to receive lectures on social morality from the mouth of the effeminate King of Assyria, we are content to take upon any terms what is good in this way from Lord Byron, protesting only against the probable union of such manners as history attributes to Sardanapalus, with such dispositions as are in this tragedy assigned to him by the poet. (p. 495)

With respect to the construction of the play of Sardanapalus, the author is not to be held responsible for the want of incident. He could only draw his materials from history; but he is still

responsible for the choice of his subject. He does not assert the merit of having adhered strictly to the unities of the drama, if there be merit in such conformity; but he talks in his preface with some complacency, of his having *approached* the "unities,"—a compromise not very intelligible. As there is neither mystery nor unravelment in the plot, it was not easy to violate the unity of action. . . . Without plot, no fault can be found with the management of the fable; without rudder or rigging, no error can be committed in the navigation. With respect to the *unity of time,* the author seems to us to have sinned against it in the only way in which it could be sinned against. He has not erred by supposing a succession of events impossible to have happened within the compass of time which may be imagined to have been taken up in the representation; but he has erred in allotting a period of time for the successive transactions, involving the catastrophe of the play, within which it was impossible for them to be completed. . . . The piece before us has aimed at satisfying what is called the unity of time, by a violent compression of the incidents of the story into the compass of a day, in contempt of history and probability.

The great fault that we find with this poem is simply this,— that it is not poetry. It is only in name any thing but the dullest prose. . . . It is not a little singular that Lord Byron, who has, if we mistake not, expressed all due contempt for that absurd ambition of simplicity which has sunk poetry below the standard of conversation, should, on this occasion, have retrograded into the flattest province of prose, and outstripped all competition in the race of deteriority. We have always, indeed, been presumptuous enough to doubt the correctness of his lordship's poetical ear. He is deficient in delicacy of perception, and fineness of tact. (p. 498)

The *Two Foscari,* besides its defect of unity of action, is very deficient in dramatic requisites. To scenic effect it makes no pretensions. Respecting his competency to compose a tragedy that is to be acted, Lord Byron has practically decided the public judgment; which, but for his unsuccessful attempts, might have regretted his neglect of the tragic muse. The transactions on which the play is founded have very little capability. Of suffering there is enough; but those transitions of fortune, those trials of the heart, those conflicts of passion, which transmit their impressions to the bosoms of the spectator or the reader, and keep the sympathies in constant vibration, are not produced by the incidents of this calamitous tale. . . .

In the exhibition even of those transient passions or affections, such as terror, anger, joy, or grief, Lord Byron has not, in our judgment, the talent of a master-genius; but in respect to the more prominent passions, such as love, hatred, jealousy, and revenge, which occupy and engross the soul,—which condemn it to lasting inquietude, and determine it to fatal purposes, and which require to be kept singly in view, from their elementary beginnings through all the stages of their increase, from the first spark that sets the bosom on fire, to the conflagration that desolates the scene of its fury, he is singularly defective. His great excellence lies in the picturesque part of poetry;—in a luxuriant display of sensible forms, and a tonic description of natural scenery. To the sentiments that float on the surface of sensibility, Lord Byron has occasional pretensions; but, with the deep and central pathos of the passions, his bosom holds no communion. (p. 502)

[Of *Cain*] we shall say but little. We have heard it remarked, that a great deal of premeditated mischief is couched under the plausible reasonings put into the mouths of Cain and Lucifer. This may or may not be a just conclusion. We have no right to say that Lord Byron adopts the apologies of Cain or the dialectics of the Devil. All that can be fairly said on this subject is this—that it has been a part of the poet's plan to throw as much ingenuity into the arguments both of Cain and his mentor as it was competent to his lordship to furnish, and that he has left those arguments without refutation or answer to produce their unrestricted influence on the reader. (p. 506)

With respect to the execution of [*Cain*], we will not deny that there are passages in it of considerable merit; and in the drawing of Cain himself there is much vigorous expression. It seems, however, as if, in the effort to give Lucifer that "spiritual politeness" which the poet professes to have in view, he has reduced him rather below the standard of diabolic dignity which was necessary to his dramatic interest. He has scarcely "given the devil his due." We thought Lord Byron knew him better. (p. 507)

> [*William Roberts,*] " '*Sardanapalus*'," *in* British Review, *Vol. XIX, March, 1822 (and reprinted in* The Romantics Reviewed, Contemporary Reviews of British Romantic Writers: Byron and Regency Society Poets, *Vol. I, edited by Donald H. Reiman, Garland Publishing, Inc., 1972, pp. 495-510).*

SYLVANUS URBAN [pseudonym of John Nichols]
(essay date 1822)

[Byron's *The Vision of Judgement*] professes to be a parody upon Mr. Southey's poem, but upon what pretence we are unable to say; for it has not even Tom Errand's resemblance to Beau Clincher; it does not wear the same clothes, the style and metre being as dissimilar as possible. The subject of the (so called) parody is the same as that of Mr. Southey's poem— the great account of George the Third. After a great deal of the most shocking profaneness, we at length arrive at something, which, relating to human subjects, is less unfit for the public eye—the trial of the late King. After a long string of virulent drivelling against that sainted Monarch, put with great propriety into the Devil's mouth, the witnesses are called. . . . (pp. 1134-35)

Then follows the author's vengeance upon the Laureat. With great felicity the author has selected Asmodeus, the fiend of lust and malignity, who may in some sort be called his Lordship's patron daemon, as the instrument of his vindictive feeling against Mr. Southey. (p. 1135)

From the Noble Lord, [the public] will learn that Mr. Southey once entertained principles far more popular than those which he now professes: like every young man of generous feeling, he thought once too well of the mass of mankind, and therefore imagined the restraints of law and government needless; but those thoughts which are rarely developed in others, were in him rendered conspicuous by his talents and his zeal.

This is the amount of the charge against Mr. Southey; and against this he sets off that his accuser is no less a changeling than himself; that he abandoned the Christian Religion for the religion of Childe Harold; that he changed his disgust, at Mr. Moore's too warm painting, for a taste indicated by the incestuous ravings of Manfred; that he resigned his respect for the free government of Britain, for a love of democracy which he has inculcated in theory, and a preference for Turkish or Austrian despotism, which he has manifested in practice; that, once the admirer of Milton, Dryden, Pope, he has become the associate of the Cockney Bluestockings, and the panegyrist of Lady Morgan; or to give one which comprehends all other

degrees of metamorphosis and degradation, he has sunk from the station of an English nobleman, and the highest place in English literature, to be the colleague of Mr. Leigh Hunt, the author of *Don Juan,* and a contributor to "The Liberal." (p. 1137)

> *Sylvanus Urban [pseudonym of John Nichols], " 'Vision of Judgement'," in* Gentleman's Magazine, *Vol. XCI, No. ii, October, 1822 (and reprinted in* The Romantics Reviewed, Contemporary Reviews of British Romantic Writers: Byron and Regency Society Poets, *Vol. III, edited by Donald H. Reiman, Garland Publishing, Inc., 1972, pp. 1134-37).*

[JOHN WILSON]   (essay date 1823)

It is impossible to suppose two poems more nearly diametrically opposite to each other in object and execution than the "Loves of the Angels," by Mr. Moore, and **"Heaven and Earth, a Mystery,"** by Lord Byron. The first is all glitter and point, like a piece of Derbyshire spar—and the other is dark and massy, like a block of marble. In the one, angels harangue each other, like authors wishing to make a great public impression; in the other, they appear silent and majestic, even when their souls have been visited with human passions. . . . Moore writes with a crow-quill, on hot-press wire-wove card-paper, adorned with Cupids sporting round Venus on a couch. Byron writes with an eagle's plume, as if upon a broad leaf taken from some great tree that afterwards perished in the flood.

The great power of [**"Heaven and Earth"**] is in its fearless and daring simplicity. Byron faces at once all the grandeur of his sublime subject. He seeks for nothing, but it rises before him in its death-doomed magnificence. Man, or angel, or demon, the being who mourns, or laments, or exults, is driven to speak by his own soul. The angels of the "Mystery" deign not to use many words, even to their beautiful paramours, and they scorn Noah and his sententious sons. (p. 196)

We confess that we see little or nothing objectionable in [**"Heaven and Earth"**], either as to theological orthodoxy, or general human feeling. It is solemn, lofty, fearful, wild, wicked, and tumultuous, and shadowed all over with the darkness of a dreadful disaster. Of the angels who love the daughters of men we see little, and know less—and not too much of the love and passion of the fair lost mortals. The inconsolable despair preceding and accompanying an incomprehensible catastrophe, pervades the whole composition, and its expression is made sublime by the noble strain of poetry in which it is said or sung. Sometimes there is heaviness—dulness—as if it were pressed in on purpose, intended, perhaps, to denote the occasional stupefaction, drowsiness, and torpidity of soul produced by the impending destruction upon the latest of the Antediluvians. But, on the whole, it is not unworthy of Byron. . . . (p. 201)

> [*John Wilson,*] " '*Heaven and Earth*'," *in* Blackwood's Edinburgh Magazine, *Vol. XII, January, 1823 (and reprinted in* The Romantics Reviewed, Contemporary Reviews of British Romantic Writers: Byron and Regency Society Poets, *Vol. I, edited by Donald H. Reiman, Garland Publishing, Inc., 1972, pp. 196-201).*

***ECLECTIC REVIEW*   (essay date 1823)**

Werner is by far the least dull of all Lord Byron's tragedies: the story is extremely interesting, and the characters highly dramatic. But neither the story nor the characters are his own. His Lordship frankly avows, that the drama is taken entirely from a tale by Miss Harriet Lee, which appeared many years ago in a work entitled "Canterbury Tales." And not only the plan, but the language of many parts of the story has been adopted in the poem. All the merit, therefore, to which Lord Byron can lay claim, is that of having dramatised the story, and turned it into a tolerable play. As his Lordship is an idle man, he might have been worse employed. . . . (p. 780)

On the whole, this is a better play and a worse poem than any which has hitherto appeared under his Lordship's name. But as all that is dramatic in the piece, except the arrangement, is borrowed, it has not shaken the opinion we have constantly expressed, that the drama is not his Lordship's forte,—that he has not the power of conception requisite to produce an historical character,—that with all his great talents, he wants the transcendent faculty of dramatic or epic invention. As much as this is almost tacitly admitted by the Author of **Werner,** when, having failed in his original dramas, he becomes, in this, a copyist, aspiring to no higher merit than that of an ingenious play-wright. (p. 784)

> "'Don Carlos'—'Werner'," in Eclectic Review, n.s. Vol. XIX, February, 1823 (and reprinted in The Romantics Reviewed, Contemporary Reviews of British Romantic Writers: Byron and Regency Society Poets, Vol. II, edited by Donald H. Reiman, Garland Publishing, Inc., 1972, pp. 774-84).*

[WILLIAM MAGINN]   (essay date 1823)

I was just going to seal up, when your new packet came to hand.—Well, I have read the three new Cantos [of *Don Juan*].

ALAS! POOR BYRON!

Not ten times a-day, dear Christopher, but ten times a-page, as I wandered over the intense and incredible stupidities of this duodecimo, was the departed spirit of the genius of Childe Harold saluted with this exclamation. Alas! that one so gifted—one whose soul gave such appearance of being deeply imbued with the genuine spirit of poetry—one, to whom we all looked as an ornament of our literature, and who indeed has contributed in no small degree towards spreading a strain of higher mood over our poetry—should descend to the composition of heartless, heavy, dull, anti-British garbage, to be printed by the Cockneys, and puffed in the Examiner. . . .

But so it is. Here we have three cantos of some hundred verses, from which it would be impossible to extract twenty, distinguished by any readable quality. Cant I never speak, and, with the blessing of God, never will speak—especially to *you;* and accordingly, though I was thoroughly disgusted with the scope and tendency of the former cantos of the Don—though there were passages in them which, in common with all other men of upright minds and true feelings, I looked on with indignation—yet I, for one, never permitted my moral or political antipathies so to master my critical judgment, as to make me whiningly decry the talent which they often wickedly, sometimes properly, exhibited. But here we are in a lower deep—we are wallowing in a sty of mere filth. Page after page presents us with a monotonous unmusical drawl, decrying chastity, sneering at matrimony, cursing wives, abusing monarchy, deprecating lawful government, lisping dull double-entendres, hymning Jacobinism, in a style and manner so little relieved by any indication of poetic power, that I feel a moral conviction that his lordship must have taken the Examiner, the Liberal,

the Rimini, the Round Table, as his model, and endeavoured to write himself down to the level of the capacities and the swinish tastes of those with whom he has the misfortune, originally, I believe, from charitable motives, to associate. This is the most charitable hypothesis which I can frame. (p. 205)

Talking of language, it is indeed *luce clarius* that Lord B.'s residence in Italy has been much too long protracted. He has positively lost his ear, not only for the harmony of English verse, but for the very jingle of English rhymes. He makes *will* rhyme to *will* in stanza 33 of Canto VI. "Patience" is the rhyme to "fresh ones" in another place. "*John Murray*" rhymes to "*necessary*" in a third; and "*had in her*" to "*Wladimir*" in a fourth. (p. 207)

I don't remember anything so complete as the recent fall of Lord Byron's literary name. I don't mean to insinuate that people of taste think less highly now, than they did five, six, seven, or eight years ago, of the genius of Byron, in his true works of genius. But what I mean to say is this, that his name can no more sell a book now, than Jeremy Bentham's. . . .

I do *not* believe Lord Byron to be a bad man—I mean a deliberately, resolvedly wicked man. I know him to be a man of great original power and genius, and, from report, I know him to be a kind friend where his friendship is wanted. . . . He must adopt an entire change of system, or give the thing up altogether. (p. 209)

> [William Maginn,] "'Don Juan', VI-VIII," in Blackwood's Edinburgh Magazine, Vol. XIV, July, 1823 (and reprinted in The Romantics Reviewed, Contemporary Reviews of British Romantic Writers: Byron and Regency Society Poets, Vol. I, edited by Donald H. Reiman, Garland Publishing, Inc., 1972, pp. 205-09).

BALDWIN'S LONDON MAGAZINE   (essay date 1824)

[The] **Deformed Transformed** is, for what we have seen, a work, in our opinion, totally unworthy of the illustrious author; monstrous in design, flimsy in composition, meagre in imagery, wretched in versification,—a hasty, crude, and extravagant thing. But no one can read it, without acknowledging that it is the effusion of a great and extraordinary mind, an audacious fancy, and a splendid genius. Lord Byron may write below himself, but he never can write below *us.* Alas! that he does not write a page, where he writes a poem! (p. 1627)

> "'The Deformed Transformed'," in Baldwin's London Magazine, Vol. IX, March, 1824 (and reprinted in The Romantics Reviewed, Contemporary Reviews of British Romantic Writers: Byron and Regency Society Poets, Vol. I, edited by Donald H. Reiman, Garland Publishing, Inc., 1972, pp. 1621-27).

WALTER SCOTT   (essay date 1824)

Amidst the general calmness of the political atmosphere, we have been stunned, from another quarter, by one of those deathnotes, which are pealed at intervals, as from an archangel's trumpet, to awaken the soul of a whole people at once. Lord Byron, who has so long and so amply filled the highest place in the public eye, has shared the lot of humanity. . . . That mighty Genius, which walked amongst men as something superior to ordinary mortality, and whose powers were beheld with wonder, and something approaching to terror, as if we knew not whether they were of good or of evil, is laid as soundly to rest as the poor peasant whose ideas never went beyond his daily task. The voice of just blame, and that of malignant censure, are at one silenced; and we feel almost as if the great luminary of Heaven had suddenly disappeared from the sky, at the moment when every telescope was levelled for the examination of the spots which dimmed its brightness. It is not now the question, what were Byron's faults, what his mistakes; but how is the blank which he has left in British literature to be filled up? Not, we fear, in one generation, which, among many highly gifted persons, has produced none who approached Byron in ORIGINALITY, the first attribute of genius. Only thirty-seven years old—so much already done for immortality—so much time remaining, as it seemed to us shortsighted mortals, to maintain and to extend his fame, and to atone for errors in conduct and levities in composition,—who will not grieve that such a race has been shortened, though not always keeping the straight path, such a light extinguished, though sometimes flaming to dazzle and to bewilder? (pp. 343-44)

We are not, however, Byron's apologists, for *now,* alas! he needs none. His excellences will *now* be universally acknowledged, and his faults (let us hope and believe) not remembered in his epitaph. It will be recollected what a part he has sustained in British literature since the first appearance of *Childe Harold,* a space of nearly sixteen years. There has been no reposing under the shade of his laurels, no living upon the resource of past reputation; none of that *coddling* and petty precaution, which little authors call "taking care of their fame." Byron let his fame take care of itself. His foot was always in the arena, his shield hung always in the lists; and although his own gigantic renown increased the difficulty of the struggle, since he could produce nothing, however great, which exceeded the public estimate of his genius, yet he advanced to the honourable contest again and again and again, and came always off with distinction, almost always with complete triumph. As various in composition as Shakspeare himself, (this will be admitted by all who are acquainted with his *Don Juan,*) he has embraced every topic of human life, and sounded every string on the divine harp, from its slightest to its most powerful and heart-astounding tones. There is scarce a passion, or a situation, which has escaped his pen; and he might be drawn, like Garrick, between the Weeping and the Laughing Muse, although his most powerful efforts have certainly been dedicated to Melpomene. His genius seemed as prolific as various. The most prodigal use did not exhaust his powers, nay, seemed rather to increase their vigour. Neither *Childe Harold,* nor any of the most beautiful of Byron's earlier tales, contain more exquisite morsels of poetry than are to be found scattered through the cantos of *Don Juan,* amidst verses which the author appears to have thrown off with an effort as spontaneous as that of a tree resigning its leaves to the wind.—But that noble tree will never more bear fruit or blossom! It has been cut down in its strength, and the past is all that remains to us of Byron. We can scarce reconcile ourselves to the idea—scarce think that the voice is silent for ever, which, bursting so often on our ear, was often heard with rapturous admiration, sometimes with regret, but always with the deepest interest. (pp. 347-48)

Walter Scott, "Death of Lord Byron" (originally published in Edinburgh Weekly Journal, *May 19, 1824), in his* The Miscellaneous Prose Works of Sir Walter Scott: Biographical Memoirs of Eminent Novelists, and Other Distinguished Persons, *Vol. IV, Robert Cadell, 1834, pp. 343-99.*

VICTOR HUGO   (essay date 1824?)

After our prodigious revolutions, two political orders were struggling on the same soil. An old society had crumbled; a new society was beginning to rise. On one side ruins; on the other, rude outlines. Lord Byron, in his gloomy lamentations, has given expression to the last convulsions of society expiring. . . . By the sadness of his genius, by the pride of his character, by the tempests of his life, Lord Byron is the type of the class of poetry of which he is the poet. All his works are profoundly marked by the stamp of his individuality. It is always his haughty and sombre figure that the reader sees pass before his eyes in each poem as if across a pall of mourning. Sometimes, though like all profound thinkers, subject to vagueness and obscurity, he has words which sound the depths of the entire soul, sighs that relate the experiences of an entire existence. It seems as if his heart half opens to every thought that springs from it like a volcano that vomits forth the lightning. Sorrow, joy, passion, have for him no mystery; and if he presents real objects to view only through a veil, he shows the regions of the ideal without any disguise. We may reproach him with absolute neglect of the orderly arrangement of his poems,—a grave defect, for a poem that lacks order is a building without carpentry or a picture without perspective. He goes too far also in his lyrical disdain of transitions; and we would sometimes desire that one who is so faithful a painter of the interior emotions should throw on his physical descriptions less fantastic lights and less vaporous tints. His genius too often resembles an aimless traveller musing as he walks, and so absorbed in his own profound intuitions that he brings back with him but a confused image of the places he has traversed. However this may be, his capricious imagination rises, even in his less beautiful works, to heights none can reach without wings. (pp. 325-26)

[Let us] pardon his faults, his errors, nay, even those works in which he has appeared to stoop from the twofold height of his character and his talent; let us pardon him, he has died so nobly! he has fallen so well! He seemed yonder some warlike representative of the modern muse in the native land of the ancient muses. The generous auxiliary of glory, of religion, and of liberty, he carried his sword and his lyre to the descendants of the first warriors and the first poets; and the weight of his laurels was already inclining the balance in favour of the unfortunate Hellenes. We owe him, we particularly, deep gratitude. He has proved to Europe that the poets of the new school, although they no longer adore the gods of pagan Greece, always admire its heroes; and that, if they have deserted Olympus, they have at least never said adieu to Thermopylae. (p. 328)

Victor Hugo, "Lord Byron," in his Things Seen (Choses vues): Essays, Estes and Lauriat, *1824(?), pp. 320-29.*

WILLIAM HAZLITT   (essay date 1825)

[Lord Byron] is like a solitary peak, all access to which is cut off not more by elevation than distance. He is seated on a lofty eminence, 'cloud-capt,' or reflecting the last rays of setting suns, and in his poetical moods reminds us of the fabled Titans, retired to a ridgy steep, playing on their Pan's-pipes, and taking up ordinary men and things in their hands with haughty indifference. He raises his subject to himself, or tramples on it; he neither stoops to, nor loses himself in it. He exists not by sympathy, but by antipathy. He scorns all things, even himself. Nature must come to him to sit for her picture: he does not go to her. . . . All is strained, or petulant in the extreme. His thoughts are sphered and crystalline; his style 'prouder than when blue Iris blends'; his spirit fiery, impatient, wayward, indefatigable. Instead of taking his impressions from without, in entire and almost unimpaired masses, he moulds them according to his own temperament, and heats the materials of his imagination in the furnace of his passions. Lord Byron's verse glows like a flame. . . . (pp. 92-3)

Even in those collateral ornaments of modern style, slovenliness, abruptness and eccentricity (as well as in terseness and significance) Lord Byron, when he pleases, defies competition and surpasses all his contemporaries. Whatever he does, he must do in a more decided and daring manner than any one else; he lounges with extravagance, and yawns so as to alarm the reader! Self-will, passion, the love of singularity, a disdain of himself and of others (with a conscious sense that this is among the ways and means of procuring admiration) are the proper categories of his mind: he is a lordly writer, is above his own reputation, and condescends to the Muses with a scornful grace! (p. 94)

[Sir Walter Scott] gives us man as he is, or as he was, in almost every variety of situation, action and feeling. Lord Byron makes man after his own image, woman after his own heart; the one is a capricious tyrant, the other a yielding slave; he gives us the misanthrope and the voluptuary by turns; and with these two characters, burning or melting in their own fires, he makes out everlasting centos of himself. . . . [Scott] draws aside the curtain, and the veil of egotism is rent; and he shows us the crowd of living men and women, the endless groups, the landscape background, the cloud and the rainbow, and enriches our imaginations and relieves one passion by another, and expands and lightens reflection, and takes away that tightness at the breast which arises from thinking or wishing to think that there is nothing in the world out of a man's self!

In this point of view, the Author of *Waverley* is one of the greatest teachers of morality that ever lived, by emancipating the mind from petty, narrow, and bigoted prejudices: Lord Byron is the greatest pamperer of those prejudices, by seeming to think there is nothing else worth encouraging but the seeds or the full luxuriant growth of dogmatism and self-conceit. (pp. 95-6)

Intensity is the great and prominent distinction of Lord Byron's writings. He seldom gets beyond force of style, nor has he produced any regular work or masterly whole. He does not prepare any plan beforehand, nor revise and retouch what he has written with polished accuracy. His only object seems to be to stimulate himself and his readers for the moment—to keep both alive, to drive away *ennui*, to substitute a feverish and irritable state of excitement for listless indolence or even calm enjoyment. For this purpose he pitches on any subject at random without much thought or delicacy. . . . He grapples with his subject, and moves, penetrates and animates it by the electric force of his own feelings. He is often monotonous, extravagant, offensive; but he is never dull or tedious, but when he writes prose.

Lord Byron does not exhibit a new view of nature, or raise insignificant objects into importance by the romantic associations with which he surrounds them, but generally (at least) takes common-place thoughts and events, and endeavours to express them in stronger and statelier language than others. His poetry stands like a Martello tower by the side of his subject. (p. 97)

Lord Byron's earlier productions, *Lara,* the *Corsair,* etc., were wild and gloomy romances, put into rapid and shining verse. They discover the madness of poetry, together with the inspiration: sullen, moody, capricious, fierce, inexorable: gloating on beauty, thirsting for revenge: hurrying from the extremes of pleasure to pain, but with nothing permanent, nothing healthy or natural. The gaudy decorations and the morbid sentiments remind one of flowers strewed over the face of death! In his *Childe Harold* . . . he assumes a lofty and philosophic tone, and 'reasons high of providence, fore-knowledge, will, and fate.' He takes the highest points in the history of the world, and comments on them from a more commanding eminence. He shows us the crumbling monuments of time; he invokes the great names, the mighty spirit of antiquity. The universe is changed into a stately mausoleum: in solemn measures he chaunts a hymn to fame. (p. 98)

Lord Byron's tragedies, *Faliero, Sardanapalus,* etc., are not equal to his other works. They want the essence of the drama. They abound in speeches and descriptions, such as he himself might make either to himself or others, lolling on his couch of a morning, but do not carry the reader out of the poet's mind to the scenes and events recorded. They have neither action, character, nor interest, but are a sort of *gossamer* tragedies, spun out and glittering, and spreading a flimsy veil over the face of nature. . . . *Manfred* is merely himself with a fancy-drapery on. . . .

We must say we think little of our author's turn for satire. His *English Bards and Scotch Reviewers* is dogmatical and insolent, but without refinement or point. He calls people names, and tries to transfix a character with an epithet, which does not stick, because it has no other foundation than his own petulance and spite. . . . (p. 99)

The *Don Juan* indeed has great power; but its power is owing to the force of the serious writing, and to the contrast between that and the flashy passages with which it is interlarded. From the sublime to the ridiculous there is but one step. You laugh and are surprised that any one should turn round and *travestie* himself: the drollery is in the utter discontinuity of ideas and feelings. He makes virtue serve as a foil to vice; *dandyism* is (for want of any other) a variety of genius. A classical intoxication is followed by the splashing of sodawater, by frothy effusions of ordinary bile. After the lightning and the hurricane, we are introduced to the interior of the cabin and the contents of the wash-hand basins. (pp. 100-01)

The noble Lord is almost the only writer who has prostituted his talents in this way. He hallows in order to desecrate, takes a pleasure in defacing the images of beauty his hands have wrought, and raises our hopes and our belief in goodness to Heaven only to dash them to the earth again, and break them in pieces the more effectually from the very height they have fallen. Our enthusiasm for genius or virtue is thus turned into a jest by the very person who has kindled it, and who thus fatally quenches the spark of both. (p. 101)

William Hazlitt, "Lord Byron," in his The Spirit of the Age; or, Contemporary Portraits, *Oxford University Press, London, 1825 (and reprinted by Oxford University Press, 1947), pp. 92-105.*

FRASER'S MAGAZINE FOR TOWN AND COUNTRY
(essay date 1832)

[Lord Byron] was the creature of circumstances—but no free man. And even as a poet, from the spirit of the age came his inspiration; he was not the spirit of the age. A mere wind instrument, he gave forth the sounds which had breathed into him from the living minds of his own and former times; but he understood not the meaning of the words. He was rather actor than author, though he performed not on a stage, but in a book. . . . And so he fretted and strutted his hour on this world's stage; and will soon, however famous now, be heard no more. For his life was

> a tale
> Told by an idiot, full of sound and fury,
> Signifying nothing.

(p. 204)

> *"Lord Byron's Juvenile Poems," in* Fraser's Magazine for Town and Country, *Vol. VI, No. XXXII, September, 1832, pp. 183-204.*

JOHN RUSKIN (essay date 1836)

We have known minds, and great ones too, which were filled with such a horror of Byron's occasional immorality, as to be unable to separate his wheat from his chaff—unable to bask themselves in the light of his glory, without fearing to be scorched by his sin. These we have pitied, and they deserve pity, for they are debarred from one of the noblest feasts that ever fed the human intellect. We do not hesitate to affirm that, with the sole exception of Shakespeare, Byron was the greatest poet that ever lived, because he was perhaps the most miserable man. His mind was from its very mightiness capable of experiencing greater agony than lower intellects, and his poetry was wrung out of his spirit by that agony. We have said that he was the greatest poet that ever lived, because his talent was the most universal. Excelled by Milton and Homer only in the vastness of their epic imaginations, he was excelled in nothing else by any man. He was overwhelming in his satire, irresistible in the brilliancy of the coruscations of his wit, unequalled in depth of pathos, or in the melancholy of moralising contemplation. We may challenge every satirist and every comic poet that ever lived to produce specimens of wit or of comic power at all equal to some that might be selected from **"Don Juan."** We might challenge every lyric poet that ever existed to produce such a piece of lyric poetry as the

> long, low island song
> Of ancient days, ere tyranny grew strong,

which soothes the dying hour of Haidée [in **"Don Juan"**]. Take (and we name them at random) the death of Haidée, the dirge at the end of **"The Bride of Abydos,"** and **"The Dream,"** and match their deep, their agonising pathos, if it be possible, from the works of any other poet. Take his female characters from his tragedies—and Shakespeare will not more than match them—take his moralising stanzas from **"Childe Harold."** What other moralist ever felt so deeply? In every branch of poetry he is supereminent; there is no heart whose peculiar tone of feeling he does not touch. We have not words mighty enough to express our astonishment—our admiration. Tell us not that such writing is immoral; we know, for we have felt, what a light of illimitable loveliness, what a sickness of hushed awe, what a fire of resistless inspiration, what a glory of expansive mind fills the heart and soul, as we listen to the swell of such numbers; there is a river of rushing music that sweeps through our thoughts, resistless as a whirlwind, yet whose waves sing, as they pass onward, so softly, so lowly, so holily, half-maddening with their beauty of sweet sound, until we are clasped in the arms of the poetry as if borne away on the wings of an archangel, and our rapture is illimitable, and we are elevated and purified and ennobled by the mightiness of the influence that overshadows us. There is not, there cannot be, a human being "of soul so dead" as not to feel that he is a better man, that his ideas are higher, his heart purer, his feelings nobler, his spirit less bound by his body, after feeding on such poetry. But our enthusiasm has drawn us into a false inference. There *are* animals who neither have felt this inspiration themselves nor believe that others can feel it. They talk about Byron's immorality as if he were altogether immoral, and they actually appear to imagine that *they! they!!* yes, *they!!!* will be able to wipe away his memory from the earth. Our risibility has been excited by the Laird of Balmawhapple's humorous assertion [in Scott's *Waverly*] of his dignity by discharging his horse-pistol against the crags of Stirling Castle; but this is but typical of the audacity of these pismires, these dogs that bay the moon, these foul snails that crawl on in their despicable malice, leaving their spume and filth on the fairest flowers of literature, but are inferior to the slug in this respect, that their slime can neither shine nor injure. (pp. 373-75)

> *John Ruskin, "Essay on Literature" (1836), in* The Works of John Ruskin: Early Prose Writings, 1834 to 1843, *Vol. I, edited by E. T. Cook and Alexander Wedderburn, Longmans, Green, and Co., 1903, pp. 357-75.*

ALGERNON CHARLES SWINBURNE (essay date 1866)

Even at its best, the serious poetry of Byron is often so rough and loose, so weak in the screws and joints which hold together the framework of verse, that it is not easy to praise it enough without seeming to condone or to extenuate such faults as should not be overlooked or forgiven. No poet is so badly represented by a book of selections. It must show something of his weakness; it cannot show all of his strength. Often, after a noble overture, the last note struck is either dissonant or ineffectual. His magnificent masterpiece, which must endure for ever among the precious relics of the world, will not bear dissection or extraction. The merit of **"Don Juan"** does not lie in any part, but in the whole. There is in that great poem an especial and exquisite balance and sustenance of alternate tones which cannot be expressed or explained by the utmost ingenuity of selection. . . . Much of the poet's earlier work is or seems unconsciously dishonest; this, if not always or wholly unaffected, is as honest as the sunlight, as frank as the sea-wind. Here, and here alone, the student of his work may recognise and enjoy the ebb and flow of actual life. Here the pulse of vital blood may be felt in tangible flesh. Here for the first time the style of Byron is beyond all praise or blame: a style at once swift and supple, light and strong, various and radiant. Between **"Childe Harold"** and **"Don Juan"** the same difference exists which a swimmer feels between lake-water and sea-water: the one is fluent, yielding, invariable; the other has in it a life and pulse, a sting and a swell, which touch and excite the nerves like fire or like music. Across the stanzas of **"Don Juan"** we swim forward as over "the broad backs of the sea"; they break and glitter, hiss and laugh, murmur and move, like waves that sound or that subside. There is in them a delicious resistance, an elastic motion, which salt water has and fresh water has not. . . . Here, as at sea, there is enough and too much of fluctuation and intermission; the ripple flags and falls in loose and lazy lines: the foam flies wide of any mark, and the breakers collapse here and there in sudden ruin and violent failure. But the violence and weakness of the sea are preferable to the smooth sound and equable security of a lake: its buoyant and progressive impulse sustains and propels those who would sink through weariness in the flat and placid shallows. (pp. 242-43)

No poet of equal or inferior rank ever had so bad an ear. His smoother cadences are often vulgar and facile; his fresher notes are often incomplete and inharmonious. His verse stumbles and jingles, stammers and halts, where there is most need for a swift and even pace of musical sound. The rough sonorous changes of the songs in the **"Deformed Transformed"** rise far higher in harmony and strike far deeper into the memory than the lax easy lines in which he at first indulged; but they slip too readily into notes as rude and weak as the rhymeless tuneless verse in which they are so loosely set, as in a cheap and casual frame. (p. 246)

Except in the lighter and briefer scenes of **"Don Juan,"** [Byron] was never able to bring two speakers face to face and supply them with the right words. In structure as in metre his elaborate tragedies are wholly condemnable; filled as they are in spirit with the overflow of his fiery energy. **"Cain"** and **"Manfred"** are properly monologues decorated and set off by some slight appendage of ornament or explanation. In the later and loftier poem there is no difference perceptible, except in strength and knowledge, between Lucifer and Cain. Thus incompetent to handle the mysteries and varieties of character, Byron turns always with a fresh delight and a fresh confidence thither where he feels himself safe and strong. No part of his nature was more profound and sincere than the vigorous love of such inanimate things as were in tune with his own spirit and senses. . . . [When] once clear of men and confronted with elements, he casts the shell of pretence and drops the veil of habit; then, as in the last and highest passage of a poem which has suffered more from praise than any other from dispraise, his scorn of men caught in the nets of nature and necessity has no alloy of untruth; his spirit is mingled with the sea's, and overlooks with a superb delight the ruins and the prayers of men.

This loftiest passage in **"Childe Harold"** has been so often mouthed and mauled by vulgar admiration that it now can scarcely be relished. Like a royal robe worn out, or a royal wine grown sour, it seems the worse for having been so good. But in fact, allowing for one or two slips and blots, we must after all replace it among the choice and high possessions of poetry. After the first there is hardly a weak line; many have a wonderful vigour and melody; and the deep and glad disdain of the sea for men and the works of men passes into the verse in music and fills it with a weighty and sonorous harmony grave and sweet as the measured voice of heavy remote waves. No other passage in the fourth canto will bear to be torn out from the text; and this one suffers by extraction. The other three cantos are more loosely built and less compact of fabric; but in the first two there is little to remember or to praise. Much of the poem is written throughout in falsetto; there is a savour in many places as of something false and histrionic. (pp. 247-49)

His few sonnets, unlike Shelley's, are all good; the best is that on Bonnivard, one of his noblest and completest poems. The versified narratives which in their day were so admirable and famous have yielded hardly a stray sheaf to the gleaner. They have enough of vigour and elasticity to keep life in them yet; but once chipped or broken their fabric would crumble and collapse. The finest among them is certainly either the **"Giaour"** or the **"Siege of Corinth"**; the weakest is probably either **"Parisina"** or the **"Bride of Abydos."** But in none of these is there even a glimpse of Byron's higher and rare faculty. All that can be said for them is that they gave tokens of a talent singularly fertile, rapid and vivid; a certain power of action and motion which redeems them from the complete stagnation of dead verses; a command over words and rhymes never of the best and never of the worst. In the **"Giaour,"** indeed, there is something of a fiery sincerity which in its successors appears diluted and debased.

The change began in Byron when he first found out his comic power, and rose at once beyond sight or shot of any rival. His early satires are wholly devoid of humour, wit, or grace; the verse of **"Beppo,"** bright and soft and fluent, is full at once of all. The sweet light music of its few and low notes was perfect as a prelude to the higher harmonies of laughter and tears, of scorn and passion, which as yet lay silent in the future. It is mere folly to seek in English or Italian verse a precedent or a parallel. The scheme of metre is Byron's alone; no weaker hand than his could ever bend that bow, or ever will. . . . Before the appearance of **"Beppo"** no one could foresee what a master's hand might make of the instrument; and no one could predict its further use and its dormant powers before the advent of **"Don Juan."** In the **"Vision of Judgment"** it appears finally perfected; the metre fits the sense as with close and pliant armour, the perfect panoply of Achilles. A poem so short and hasty, based on a matter so worthy of brief contempt and long oblivion as the funeral and the fate of George III., bears about it at first sight no great sign or likelihood of life. But this poem which we have by us stands alone, not in Byron's work only, but in the work of the world. Satire in earlier times had changed her rags for robes; Juvenal had clothed with fire, and Dryden with majesty, that wandering and bastard Muse. Byron gave her wings to fly with, above the reach even of these. (pp. 250-52)

Side by side with the growth of his comic and satiric power, the graver genius of Byron increased and flourished. As the tree grew higher it grew shapelier; the branches it put forth on all sides were fairer of leaf and fuller of fruit than its earlier offshoots had promised. But from these hardly a stray bud or twig can be plucked off by way of sample. No detached morsel of **"Don Juan,"** no dismembered fragment of **"Cain,"** will serve to show or to suggest the excellence of either. These poems are coherent and complete as trees or flowers; they cannot be split up and parcelled out like a mosaic of artificial jewellery, which might be taken to pieces by the same artisan who put it together. (p. 254)

It would be waste of words and time here to enlarge at all upon the excellence of the pure comedy of **"Don Juan."** From the first canto to the sixteenth; from the defence of Julia, which is worthy of Congreve or Molière, to the study of Adeline, which is worthy of Laclos or Balzac; the elastic energy of humour never falters or flags. (pp. 255-56)

As a poet, Byron was surpassed, beyond all question and all comparison, by three men at least of his own time; and matched, if not now and then overmatched, by one or two others. The verse of Wordsworth, at its highest, went higher than his; the verse of Landor flowed clearer. But his own ground, where none but he could set foot, was lofty enough, fertile and various. Nothing in Byron is so worthy of wonder and admiration as the scope and range of his power. New fields and ways of work, had he lived, might have given room for exercise and matter for triumph to [the man Shelley called] "that most fiery spirit." (pp. 257-58)

Algernon Charles Swinburne, "Byron" (1866), in his Essays and Studies, *second edition, Chatto and Windus, 1876, pp. 238-58.*

MATTHEW ARNOLD (essay date 1881)

[Although] there may be little in Byron's poetry which can be pronounced either worthless or faultless, there are portions of it which are far higher in worth and far more free from fault than others. And although, again, the abundance and variety of his production is undoubtedly a proof of his power, yet I question whether by reading everything which he gives us we are so likely to acquire an admiring sense even of his variety and abundance, as by reading what he gives us at his happier moments. Varied and abundant he amply proves himself even by this taken alone. Receive him absolutely without omission or compression, follow his whole outpouring stanza by stanza and line by line from the very commencement to the very end, and he is capable of being tiresome.

Byron has told us himself that the **Giaour** 'is but a string of passages'. He has made full confession of his own negligence. 'No one', says he, 'has done more through negligence to corrupt the language.' This accusation brought by himself against his poems is not just. . . . '**Lara**', he declares, 'I wrote while undressing after coming home from balls and masquerades, in the year of revelry, 1814. The **Bride** was written in four, the **Corsair** in ten days.' He calls this 'a humiliating confession, as it proves my own want of judgment in publishing, and the public's in reading, things which cannot have stamina for permanence'. Again he does his poems injustice; the producer of such poems could not but publish them, the public could not but read them. Nor could Byron have produced his work in any other fashion; his poetic work could not have first grown and matured in his own mind, and then come forth as an organic whole; Byron had not enough of the artist in him for this, nor enough of self-command. . . . [It] was inevitable that works so produced should be, in general, 'a string of passages', poured out, as he describes them, with rapidity and excitement, and with new passages constantly suggesting themselves, and added while his work was going through the press. It is evident that we have here neither deliberate scientific construction, nor yet the instinctive artistic creation of poetic wholes; and that to take passages from work produced as Byron's was is a very different thing from taking passages out of the *Oedipus* or the *Tempest*, and deprives the poetry far less of its advantage.

Nay, it gives advantage to the poetry, instead of depriving it of any. Byron, I said, has not a great artist's profound and patient skill in combining an action or in developing a character,—a skill which we must watch and follow if we are to do justice to it. But he has a wonderful power of vividly conceiving a single incident, a single situation; of throwing himself upon it, grasping it as if it were real and he saw and felt it, and of making us see and feel it too. The **Giaour** is, as he truly called it, 'a string of passages', not a work moving by a deep internal law of development to a necessary end; and our total impression from it cannot but receive from this, its inherent defect, a certain dimness and indistinctness. But the incidents of the journey and death of Hassan, in that poem, are conceived and presented with a vividness not to be surpassed; and our impression from them is correspondingly clear and powerful. In **Lara,** again, there is no adequate development either of the character of the chief personage or of the action of the poem; our total impression from the work is a confused one. Yet such an incident as the disposal of the slain Ezzelin's body passes

before our eyes as if we actually saw it. And in the same way as these bursts of incident, bursts of sentiment also, living and vigorous, often occur in the midst of poems which must be admitted to be but weakly-conceived and loosely-combined wholes. Byron cannot but be a gainer by having attention concentrated upon what is vivid, powerful, effective in his work, and withdrawn from what is not so. (pp. 314-15)

To the poetry of Byron the world has ardently paid homage; full justice from his contemporaries, perhaps even more than justice, his torrent of poetry received. His poetry was admired, adored, 'with all its imperfections on its head',—in spite of negligence, in spite of diffuseness, in spite of repetitions, in spite of whatever faults it possessed. His name is still great and brilliant. Nevertheless the hour of irresistible vogue has passed away for him; even for Byron it could not but pass away. The time has come for him, as it comes for all poets, when he must take his real and permanent place, no longer depending upon the vogue of his own day and upon the enthusiasm of his contemporaries. Whatever we may think of him, we shall not be subjugated by him as they were; for, as he cannot be for us what he was for them, we cannot admire him so hotly and indiscriminately as they. His faults of negligence, of diffuseness, of repetition, his faults of whatever kind, we shall abundantly feel and unsparingly criticize; the mere interval of time between us and him makes disillusion of this kind inevitable. But how then will Byron stand, if we relieve him too, so far as we can, of the encumbrance of his inferior and weakest work, and if we bring before us his best and strongest work in one body together? (pp. 315-16)

We will take three poets, among the most considerable of our century: Leopardi, Byron, Wordsworth. Giacomo Leopardi was ten years younger than Byron, and he died thirteen years after him; both of them, therefore, died young—Byron at the age of thirty-six, Leopardi at the age of thirty-nine. Both of them were of noble birth, both of them suffered from physical defect, both of them were in revolt against the established facts and beliefs of their age; but here the likeness between them ends. . . . Leopardi has the very qualities which we have found wanting to Byron; he has the sense for form and style, the passion for just expression, the sure and firm touch of the true artist. Nay, more, he has a grave fulness of knowledge, an insight into the real bearings of the questions which as a sceptical poet he raises, a power of seizing the real point, a lucidity, with which the author of **Cain** has nothing to compare. (p. 323)

[Wordsworth's superiority] is in the power with which [he] feels the resources of joy offered to us in nature, offered to us in the primary human affections and duties, and in the power with which, in his moments of inspiration, he renders this joy, and makes us, too, feel it; a force greater than himself seeming to lift him and to prompt his tongue, so that he speaks in a style far above any style of which he has the constant command, and with a truth far beyond any philosophic truth of which he has the conscious and assured possession. (p. 324)

[Like Wordsworth's,] Byron's poetic value is also greater, on the whole, than Leopardi's; and his superiority turns in the same way upon the surpassing worth of something which he had and was, after all deduction has been made for his shortcomings. We talk of Byron's *personality*, 'a personality in eminence such as has never been yet, and is not likely to come again'; and we say that by this personality Byron is 'different from all the rest of English poets, and in the main greater'. (p. 325)

There is the Byron who posed, there is the Byron with his affectations and silliness, the Byron whose weakness Lady Blessington, with a woman's acuteness, so admirably seized: 'His great defect is flippancy and a total want of self-possession.' But when this theatrical and easily criticized personage betook himself to poetry, and when he had fairly warmed to his work, then he became another man; then the theatrical personage passed away; then a higher power took possession of him and filled him; then at last came forth into light that true and puissant personality, with its direct strokes, its ever-welling force, its satire, its energy, and its agony. This is the real Byron; whoever stops at the theatrical preludings does not know him. (pp. 326-27)

[As] a poet, he has no fine and exact sense for word and structure and rhythm; he has not the artist's nature and gifts. Yet a personality of Byron's force counts for so much in life, and a rhetorician of Byron's force counts for so much in literature! . . . Along with his astounding power and passion he had a strong and deep sense for what is beautiful in nature, and for what is beautiful in human action and suffering. When he warms to his work, when he is inspired, Nature herself seems to take the pen from him as she took it from Wordsworth, and to write for him as she wrote for Wordsworth, though in a different fashion, with her own penetrating simplicity. . . . [His] verse then exhibits quite another and a higher quality from the rhetorical quality,—admirable as this also in its own kind of merit is,—of such verse as

     Minions of splendour shrinking from distress,

and of so much more verse of Byron's of that stamp. Nature, I say, takes the pen for him; and then, assured master of a true poetic style though he is not, any more than Wordsworth, yet as from Wordsworth at his best there will come such verse as

     Will no one tell me what she sings?

so from Byron, too, at his best, there will come such verse as

     He heard it, but he heeded not; his eyes
     Were with his heart, and that was far away.

Of verse of this high quality, Byron has much; of verse of a quality lower than this, of a quality rather rhetorical than truly poetic, yet still of extraordinary power and merit, he has still more. To separate, from the mass of poetry which Byron poured forth, all this higher portion, so superior to the mass, and still so considerable in quantity, and to present it in one body by itself, is to do a service, I believe, to Byron's reputation, and to the poetic glory of our country. (pp. 327-28)

Wordsworth's value is of another kind. Wordsworth has an insight into permanent sources of joy and consolation for mankind which Byron has not; his poetry gives us more which we may rest upon than Byron's,—more which we can rest upon now, and which men may rest upon always. I place Wordsworth's poetry, therefore, above Byron's on the whole, although in some points he was greatly Byron's inferior, and although Byron's poetry will always, probably, find more readers than Wordsworth's, and will give pleasure more easily. But these two, Wordsworth and Byron, stand, it seems to me, first and pre-eminent in actual performance, a glorious pair, among the English poets of this century. Keats had probably, indeed, a more consummate poetic gift than either of them; but he died having produced too little and being as yet too immature to rival them. I for my part can never even think of equalling with them any other of their contemporaries;—either Coleridge, poet and philosopher wrecked in a mist of opium;

or Shelley, beautiful and ineffectual angel, beating in the void his luminous wings in vain. Wordsworth and Byron stand out by themselves. When the year 1900 is turned, and our nation comes to recount her poetic glories in the century which has then just ended, the first names with her will be these. (pp. 329-30)

> *Matthew Arnold, in his preface to* Poetry of Byron *by Lord Byron, Macmillan, 1881 (and reprinted as "Byron," in his* Essays in Criticism, *first and second series, Dutton, 1964, pp. 312-30).*

WILLIAM MINTO (essay date 1894)

When we turn to 'Childe Harold' now, our interest is all in the poet, and we skip with comparative indifference the stanza after stanza of description and reflection to fasten on the autobiographical portions. But in the stanzas that we now skip, the readers of the writer of 1812 found powerful expression given to thoughts that were agitating their own minds, concerning scenes and events that had for them an intensity of interest such as men rarely feel except about their own personal concerns. . . . [Napoleon's] arms had hardly received a check, except from English troops in the Peninsula. Great Britain seemed the only Power capable of checking his course, and there was an intensity of excitement throughout our country such as had never been experienced before and has never been since. (p. 216)

The strain in which [Byron] addressed the public was not the most obviously opportune one of drum and trumpet exhortation. It was full of irregular, almost capricious changes, varying through many moods, from fierce delight in battle and fiery enthusiasm for freedom to cynical mockery of ambition and despondent meditation on the fleeting character of human happiness and national greatness. It was the work of a distempered mind, and it spoke out with passionate sincerity what was in that mind; and so doing, as the age itself was moody and distempered with prolonged and feverish excitement, it was a revelation to thousands of readers of their own inmost thoughts. Macaulay in a well-known passage describes Byron as having interpreted Wordsworth to the multitude. Looking at this—his first production—purely from the literary point of view, there is much truth in this, for the pilgrimage of Childe Harold was undoubtedly the spontaneous overflow of powerful feeling; the poem was evolved by the poet's imagination out of genuine personal emotion; the satisfaction of this emotion was the motive that set the imagination at work. Byron's poetry came from the heart. In this respect, and also in the matter of poetic diction, he may truly be said to have interpreted Wordsworth's theories to the multitude. But he did more than this: he interpreted the multitude to themselves; he showed them as in a glass what they had been on the point of thinking. (p. 218)

This close harmony with the moods of the time is greatly left out of sight in attempts to explain the rapidity with which Byron gained the ear of his audience. Too much stress is laid in these explanations on the romantic character of the hero, driven into his pilgrimage by a strange unrest, satiated with pleasure, rendered joyless by the excess of it, prematurely penetrated by the conviction that all is vanity; a wanderer, not because he hopes for relief from change, but because change is an imperative necessity to him. It was not the character of Childe Harold that first drew attention to the poem; it was the interest in the poem that drew attention to the character of the poet, with whom the public, in spite of his protests, persisted in identifying him. We must not credit the readers of the first two cantos of **'Childe Harold'** with knowing all that we can now learn about Byron, from works of which this first effort, with all its revelation power, was comparatively but a feeble and one-sided instalment. Their interest was principally in the poem itself, which enthralled them before they knew much or anything about the author; and if we try to look at it with their eyes, following its movement with the interest they naturally had in its incidents, we find abundant reason for their admiration in the impetuous vehemence with which the poet hurries from theme to theme, fixing one impression after another with a few powerful strokes, moving with the ease of a giant in the fetters of a difficult stanza, controlling the rhymes with a master's hand into the service of his fervent feeling, instead of allowing them to direct and check and hamper its flow as is the way with rhymesters of less resource. The interest of the public, once kindled in the poem, turned naturally to the poet, and they would have it that in his strange hero, a new character in poetry, he had drawn the picture of himself. (pp. 220-21)

> William Minto, "Byron," in his The Literature of the Georgian Era, edited by William Knight, William Blackwood and Sons, 1894, pp. 215-33.

STEPHEN PHILLIPS   (essay date 1898)

[If] one is to say of Byron that his poetry is mere rhetoric, that he is slipshod, theatrical, and insincere, it would be mere futility to attempt to point out any redeeming feature whatsoever. In the present article, however, I entirely dissent from this judgment as a whole, though admitting that superficially much can be said for it. Let it be conceded at once that Byron is in no scientific sense a master of verse. He had evidently never studied, as many lesser modern men have done, the system of pauses, the value of an 'i' or an 'a.' Yet, this notwithstanding, is it possible to produce, in English literature, verse of so natural and yet excellent a quality as is to be found in **'Don Juan'** and **'The Vision of Judgment'**? Indeed so complete, in a sense, is Byron's mastery over verse that he appears now to sing, now to rave, now to talk with perfect metrical ease. . . . I am aware that in quoting from Byron's poetry I am taking a somewhat unfair advantage, as very many literary men and women who perpetually sneer at him have never read any of his best verse. To take for a moment the contention that Byron's verse is slipshod, and, in fact, not verse at all—is there any other poet in the whole range of English literature who could have written verse so perfect, so natural, so irresistible, as appears in the description of Satan's appearance at the bar of heaven to claim the soul of George III [in **'The Vision of Judgement'**]? Let any unprejudiced reader read aloud the following verses, and then say whether any verse so light, so exact, and yet so strong, has been produced since the days of Elizabeth:—

> While thus they spake, the angelic caravan,
>   Arriving like a rush of mighty wind,
> Cleaving the fields of space, as doth some swan
>   Some silver stream (say Ganges, Nile, or Inde,
> Or Thames or Tweed), and midst them an old man
>   With an old soul, and both extremely blind,
> Halted before the gate, and in his shroud
> Seated their fellow traveller on a cloud.

The whole of this verse, and especially the last two lines, shows consummate metrical ability. It is done, however, with the lightest possible touch. But with equal ease the poet makes in the next verse an ineffaceable and tragic impression.

> But bringing up the rear of that bright host,
>   A spirit of a different aspect waved
> His wings, like thunder-clouds above some coast
>   Whose barren beach with frequent wrecks is paved;
> His brow was like the deep when tempest tossed;
>   Fierce and unfathomable thoughts engraved
> Eternal wrath on his immortal face,
> And *where* he gazed, a gloom pervaded space.

This description, if not on so mighty a scale as that of Milton, is more direct and no less haunting.

In the next verse the poet, maintaining the grand note in the first two lines, descends without difficulty to the satiric in his description of the fright of St. Peter.

> As he drew near, he gazed upon the gate
>   Ne'er to be entered more by him or sin,
> With such a glance of supernatural hate
>   As made Saint Peter wish himself within;
> He pattered with his keys at a great rate,
>   And sweated through his apostolic skin;
> Of course his perspiration was but ichor,
> Or some such other spiritual liquor.

All this verse is, in fact, written as easily as though the man were talking after supper; and yet, of its kind, of what supreme quality it is! . . . Is it possible to deny to verse of this kind, even from the most technical point of view, an incomparable case and lightness together with a certain majesty and pathetic evidence? **'The Vision of Judgment'** is undoubtedly Byron's greatest poem, and he by no means always writes at this height. But when it is said that he was not a master of verse, and that his rhythm is false and irregular, it is as well to disprove such assertions at once and finally. It may, however, be said, though it is nothing to the point, that Byron's sole gift was satire, and that in a satiric poem he wrote verse of which at other times he was incapable. (pp. 17-18)

The other great charge hurled against Byron, besides the weak quality of his verse, is 'insincerity.' In the days when Mr. Swinburne was a poet and a critic, it is somewhat curious to recall that it was this very quality of sincerity for which he gave Byron credit. But the fact is that it is impossible to convince the average reader that a man may be superficially insincere, and at heart most sincere. That Byron loved to assume a melodramatic pose is undoubted; that he frequently wrote verse which is on the face of it hollow and unconvincing, is unquestionable. . . . Yet it is none the less true that in all that really matters—in the great and deep questions of life—he was eminently courageous and sincere. In his faith in freedom he never for an instant wavered; in his hate of the England of his time, which was for the most part petty and hypocritical, he was steadfast enough: and in his portraits of himself, exaggerated and theatrical as they are, it is easy enough to see the genuine fire and the flame that leaps up from time to time in some splendid verse. . . . [Was] anything more 'sincere,' more truly and deeply felt, than the whole of that chief of English satires, **'The Vision of Judgment'**? Is there a more sincere poem—in the artistic sense—than **'Don Juan'**? Its frequent lapses, its immorality may be quarrelled with; but, both in truth of conception and in faithfulness of depiction, few poems can stand beside it. It is really time that this cant of 'insincerity,' as applied to Byron, was dismissed. In spite of self-deceptions, of tawdriness, and of a perfectly childish pretence, Byron remains perhaps the most sincere of all our poets. Having said something with regard to the chief charges made against this poetry, let us look for a moment at its excellences. Byron never went so deep as Wordsworth, never sang so purely as Shelley, had not that overpowering sense of the soul of beauty that we find in Keats; nor had he the fine-wrought melody and dainty touch of Tennyson. But, if we are to regard range of power as a factor in reputation, where will Byron eventually stand? As a satirist alone, it would be absurd for one moment to compare any of the poets just named with him. And his satire is of the best kind—a mingling of the grotesque with the really tragic, a deep hatred and a deep love—disguised by a light and easy manner. Above all, his satire is poetry, and, at its best, poetry of a very high order. As a satirist, then, he stands quite unchallenged among modern poets. In a power of pictorial description, more especially in his sea-pieces, I know no modern poet who can pretend for a moment to stand by him. He does not probe the soul of Nature so deeply as others have done, but he can paint her with a freedom and a zest which few have approached. **'Don Juan'** especially is full of such passages, which seem to actually bring the sea wind across the page and the lap of water into the ears. As a dramatic poet Byron has been much assailed, and from one point of view rightly enough. It is complained that he never drew any one but himself. This is true enough; but what is one to say of the personality which could so multiply and transform itself, which could always interest, and at other times fascinate and appal? Then though this inability to draw a variety of characters precludes him from taking rank as a great dramatist, still he grips 'a situation,' as they say on the stage, with singular power. An opportunity offers to compare him for once with Shakspeare. The scene where Macbeth compels the witches to unveil the future for him has a very near parallel in the scene where Manfred compels the demons to raise the phantom of Astarte.

Looking at these scenes side by side, it is possible to admit the superiority of Shakspeare, and yet impossible to deny to Byron the real dramatic gift. (pp. 20-2)

In the quality of pure imagination Byron cannot for one moment be ranked with the greatest of poets. At the same time he had a great gift of imagination, and of a high quality. But it is said that he is without imagination. In the drama of **'Cain'** it is possible to compare Byron with Milton, as we have already compared him with Shakspeare. He will not of course stand such a test; but again he contrives, in his description of the flight through space, to leave on the mind a deep sense of the illimitable. (pp. 23-4)

But though I have protested against the notion that Byron had no dramatic power and no imagination, it is rather as the teller of a story that he is likely to be most remembered. The greatest story-teller in verse that the English race has ever produced is no doubt Chaucer; and an opportunity offers of comparing Byron with the author of the 'Canterbury Tales.' (p. 24)

Byron cannot tell a story with the same directness and unsought pathos that Chaucer had at command. Still, in **'The Prisoner of Chillon,'** in **'The Giaour,'** and many another tale, he has proved his right to be considered the best narrator in verse since Chaucer.

Byron, then, is to be estimated chiefly by his range of power. In satire he is supreme, in description excellent, in power of narration the second of English poets. As a dramatist he is infinitely below the Elizabethans, yet he has dramatic grip; in imagination he is infinitely below Milton and one or two others,

but imagination he has, and of a real quality. I have no intention of 'placing' or attempting to 'place' Byron in English literature. Undoubtedly there are three English poets who are head and shoulders above the rest: Chaucer, Shakspeare, and Milton. . . . After these three is a gulf fixed. Then there is a huge throng of poets, whom it is difficult to class in any accurate order. Among the second throng, however, time will give Byron a high, probably the highest place, by virtue of his elemental force, his satire, and his width of range. He is to be set 'a little lower than the angels,' but to be 'crowned with glory and worship.' (p. 26)

Stephen Phillips, "The Poetry of Byron: An Anniversary Study," in The Cornhill Magazine *(© John Murray 1898; reprinted by permission of John Murray (Publishers) Ltd.), Vol. IV, No. 19, January, 1898, pp. 16-26.*

G. K. CHESTERTON   (essay date 1902)

Everything is against our appreciating the spirit and the age of Byron. The age that has just passed from us is always like a dream when we wake in the morning, a thing incredible and centuries away. And the world of Byron seems a sad and faded world, a weird and inhuman world, where men were romantic in whiskers, ladies lived, apparently, in bowers, and the very word has the sound of a piece of stage scenery. Roses and nightingales recur in their poetry with the monotonous elegance of a wall-paper pattern. The whole is like a revel of dead men, a revel with splendid vesture and half-witted faces.

But the more shrewdly and earnestly we study the histories of men, the less ready shall we be to make use of the word "artificial." Nothing in the world has ever been artificial. (pp. 31-2)

The remarkable fact is, however, and it bears strongly on the present position of Byron, that when a thing is unfamiliar to us, when it is remote and the product of some other age or spirit, we think it not savage or terrible, but merely artificial. (pp. 32-3)

But Byron and Byronism were something immeasurably greater than anything that is represented by such a view as this: their real value and meaning are indeed little understood. The first of the mistakes about Byron lies in the fact that he is treated as a pessimist. True, he treated himself as such, but a critic can hardly have even a slight knowledge of Byron without knowing that he had the smallest amount of knowledge of himself that ever fell to the lot of an intelligent man. The real character of what is known as Byron's pessimism is better worth study than any real pessimism could ever be. (pp. 34-5)

Byron had a sensational popularity, and that popularity was, as far as words and explanations go, founded upon his pessimism. He was adored by an overwhelming majority, almost every individual of which despised the majority of mankind. But when we come to regard the matter a little more deeply we tend in some degree to cease to believe in this popularity of the pessimist. The popularity of pure and unadulterated pessimism is an oddity; it is almost a contraction in terms. Men would no more receive the news of the failure of existence or of the harmonious hostility of the stars with ardour or popular rejoicing than they would light bonfires for the arrival of cholera or dance a breakdown when they were condemned to be hanged. When the pessimist is popular it must always be not because he shows all things to be bad, but because he shows some things to be good. . . . And this was emphatically the case with Byron and the Byronists. Their real popularity was founded not upon the fact that they blamed everything, but upon the fact that they praised something. They heaped curses upon man, but they used man merely as a foil. The things they wished to praise by comparison were the energies of Nature. Man was to them what talk and fashion were to Carlyle, what philosophical and religious quarrels were to Omar, what the whole race after practical happiness was to Schopenhauer, the thing which must be censured in order that somebody else may be exalted. It was merely a recognition of the fact that one cannot write in white chalk except on a blackboard. (pp. 37-9)

Matters are very different with the more modern school of doubt and lamentation. The last movement of pessimism is perhaps expressed in Mr. Aubrey Beardsley's allegorical designs. Here we have to deal with a pessimism which tends naturally not towards the oldest elements of the cosmos, but towards the last and most fantastic fripperies of artificial life. Byronism tended towards the desert; the new pessimism towards the restaurant. . . . The Byronic young man had an affectation of sincerity; the decadent, going a step deeper into the avenues of the unreal, has positively an affectation of affectation. And it is by their fopperies and their frivolities that we know that their sinister philosophy is sincere; in their lights and garlands and ribbons we read their indwelling despair. It was so, indeed, with Byron himself; his really bitter moments were his frivolous moments. He went on year after year calling down fire upon mankind, summoning the deluge and the destructive sea and all the ultimate energies of nature to sweep away the cities of the spawn of man. But through all this his sub-conscious mind was not that of a despairer; on the contrary, there is something of a kind of lawless faith in thus parleying with such immense and immemorial brutalities. It was not until the time in which he wrote **'Don Juan'** that he really lost this inward warmth and geniality, and a sudden shout of hilarious laughter announced to the world that Lord Byron had really become a pessimist.

One of the best tests in the world of what a poet really means is his metre. He may be a hypocrite in his metaphysics, but he cannot be a hypocrite in his prosody. And all the time that Byron's language is of horror and emptiness, his metre is a bounding 'pas de quatre.' (pp. 40-3)

The truth is that Byron was one of a class who may be called the unconscious optimists, who are very often, indeed, the most uncompromising conscious pessimists, because the exuberance of their nature demands for an adversary a dragon as big as the world. But the whole of his essential and unconscious being was spirited and confident, and that unconscious being, long disguised and buried under emotional artifices, suddenly sprang into prominence in the face of a cold, hard, political necessity. In Greece he heard the cry of reality, and at the time that he was dying, he began to live. He heard suddenly the call of that buried and sub-conscious happiness which is in all of us, and which may emerge suddenly at the sight of the grass of a meadow or the spears of the enemy. (p. 44)

> G. K. Chesterton, "The Optimism of Byron," in his Twelve Types, Arthur L. Humphreys, 1902, pp. 31-44.

ARTHUR SYMONS (essay date 1909)

Byron's fame, which was never, like that of every other English poet, in his lifetime, a merely English reputation, has been kept alive in other countries, more persistently than in our own, and comes back to us now from abroad with at times almost the shock of a new discovery. It is never possible to convince a foreigner that Byron is often not even correct as a writer of verse. His lines, so full of a kind of echoing substance, ring true to the ear which has not naturalised itself in English poetry; and, hearing them march so directly and with such obvious clangour, the foreigner is at a loss to understand why one should bring what seems to him a petty charge against them. The magic of words, in which Byron is lacking, the poverty of rhythm, for which he is so conspicuous, do not tell with any certainty through the veil of another idiom. How many Englishmen know quite how bad, as verse, is the verse of the French Byron, as he has been called, Alfred de Musset, and quite why it is bad? And as Byron's best verse, even more than Musset's, is worldly verse, it is still more difficult to detect a failure in accent, in that finer part of what Byron calls 'the poetry of speech'; so delicate a difference separating what may be almost the greatest thing in poetry, a line of Dante, from something, like too much of Byron, which is commoner than the commonest prose. (pp. 242-43)

In narrative verse Byron finally made for himself a form of his own which exactly suited him, but in lyrical verse he never learnt to do much that he could not already do in the **'Hours of Idleness.'** His 'last lines' are firmer in measure, graver in substance, but they are written on exactly the same principle as the **'Well! thou art happy'** of 1808. There is the same strained simplicity of feeling, in which a really moved directness comes through the traditional rhetoric of the form. Every stanza says something, and it says exactly what he means it to say, without any of the exquisite evasions of a more purely poetic style; without, too, any of the qualifying interruptions of a more subtle temperament. Byron's mind was without subtlety; whatever he felt he felt without reservations, or the least thinking about feeling: hence his immediate hold upon the average man or woman, who does not need to come to his verse, as the verse of most other poets must be approached, with a mind already prepared for that communion. There is force, clearness, but no atmosphere; everything is seen detached, a little bare, very distinct, in a strong light without shadows. (p. 244)

Wordsworth wearies us by commonplace of thought and feeling, by nervelessness of rhythm, by a deliberate triviality; Coleridge offers us metaphysics for poetry; Browning offers us busy thinking about life for meditation; there is not a scene in Shakespeare which is perfect as a scene of Sophocles is perfect; but with Byron the failure is not exceptional, it is constant; it is like the speech of a man whose tongue is too large for his mouth. There are indeed individual good lines in Byron, a great number of quite splendid lines, though none indeed of the very finest order of poetry; but there is not a single poem, not a single passage of the length of 'Kubla Khan,' perhaps not a single stanza, which can be compared as poetry with a poem or passage or stanza of Keats or Shelley, such as any one will find by merely turning over the pages of those poets for five minutes at random. What is not there is precisely the magic which seems to make poetry its finer self, the perfume of the flower, that by which the flower is remembered, after its petals have dropped or withered. . . . Byron, when he meditates, meditates with fixed attention; if he dreams, he dreams with open eyes, to which the darkness is aglow with tumultuous action; he is at the mercy of none of those wandering sounds, delicate spirits of the air, which come entreating their liberty from the indefinite, in the releasing bondage of song. He has certain things to say, he has certain impulses to embody; he has, first, a certain type of character, then a view of the world which is more obviously the prose than the poetic view of the world, but certainly a wide view, to express; and it remains for him, in this rejection or lack of all the lesser graces, to be either Michael Angelo or Benjamin Haydon.

Or at least, so it would seem; and yet, so it does not seem to be. Byron is not Michael Angelo, not merely because his conceptions were not as great as Michael Angelo's, but because he had not the same power of achieving his conceptions, because he had not the same technical skill. . . . To leave an appealing or terrifying or lamentable incompleteness, where before there had been the clear joy of what is finished and finite: there, precisely, was the triumph of [Haydon's] technique. But Byron is not Haydon, because he is not a small man struggling to be a great man, painting large merely because he cannot paint small, and creating chaos on the canvas out of ambition rather than irresistible impulse. He is fundamentally sincere, which is the root of greatness; he has a firm hold on himself and on the world; he speaks to humanity in its own voice, heightened to a pitch which carries across Europe. No poet had ever seemed to speak to men so directly, and it was through this directness of his vision of the world, and of his speech about it, that he became a poet, that he made a new thing of poetry. (pp. 245-46)

Byron loved the world for its own sake and for good and evil. His quality of humanity was genius to him, and stood to him in the place of imagination. Whatever is best in his work is full . . . of raw or naked humanity. It is the solid part of his rhetoric, and is what holds us still in the apparently somewhat theatrical addresses to the Dying Gladiator and the like. Speaking straight, in **'Don Juan'** and **'The Vision of Judgment,'** it creates almost a new kind of poetry, the poetry of the world, written rebelliously, but on its own level, by a man to whom the world was the one reality. Only Byron, and not Shelley, could lead the revolt against custom and convention, against the insular spirit of England, because to Byron custom and convention and the insular spirit were so much more actual things. . . . His very idealism was a challenge and a recoil. He went about Europe like a man with a hazel wand in his hand, and wherever the forked branch dipped, living water rose to him out of the earth. Every line he wrote is a reminiscence, the reminiscence of a place or a passion. His mind was a cracked mirror, in which everything reflected itself directly, but as if scarred. His mind was never to him a kingdom, but always part of the tossing democracy of humankind. And so, having no inner peace, no interior vision, he was never for long together the master or the obedient vassal of his imagination; and he has left us tumultuous fragments, in which beauty comes and goes fitfully, under pained disguises, or like a bird with impatient wings, tethered at short range to the ground. (pp. 247-48)

To Byron life itself was imaginative, not the mere raw stuff out of which imagination could shape something quite different, something far more beautiful, but itself, its common hours, the places he passed on the way, a kind of poem in action. All his verse is an attempt to make his own poetry out of fragments of this great poem of life, as it came to him on his heedful way through the midst of it. All Byron's poetry is emphasis, and he obtains his tremendous emphasis by a really impersonal interest in the circumstances of the drama which he knew himself to be acting. Building entirely on his personal, his directly personal emotion, he never allows that emotion to overpower

him. He makes the most of it, even with what may easily pass for a lack of sincerity, but is only an astonishing way of recovering himself after an abandonment to feeling. Imagination comes to him as self-control. . . . It may seem to be the quality of a man rather than of a poet, and is indeed one of the reasons why without Byron the man no one would have cared for Byron the poet. But it is more than this; it becomes in him a poetic quality, the actual imaginative force by which he dramatises himself, not as if it were his own little naked human soul, shiveringly alone with God, but as a great personage, filling the world, like Napoleon, and seen always against a background of all the actual pomps of the world. (pp. 248-49)

Byron has power without wisdom, power which is sanity, and human at heart, but without that vision which is wisdom. His passion is without joy, the resurrection, or that sorrow deeper than any known unhappiness, which is the death by which we attain life. He has never known what it is to be at peace, with himself or with outward things. There is a certain haste in his temper, which does not allow him to wait patiently upon any of the spiritual guests who only come unbidden, and to those who await them. His mind is always full of busy little activities, with which a more disinterested thinker would not be concerned. Himself the centre, he sees the world revolving about him, seemingly as conscious of him as he of it. It is not only that he never forgets himself, but he never forgets that he is a lord, and that one of his feet is not perfect. (p. 253)

Neither Keats nor Shelley, not even Wordsworth, much less Coleridge, was content with our language as we have it; all, on theory or against theory, used inversions, and wrote otherwise than they would speak; it was Byron, with his boisterous contempt for rules, his headlong way of getting to the journey's end, who discovered that poetry, which is speech as well as song, and speech not least when it is most song, can be written not only with the words we use in talking, but in exactly the same order and construction. . . . Who in English poetry before Byron has ever talked in verse? (pp. 254-55)

Never, in English verse, has a man been seen who was so much a man and so much an Englishman. It is not man in the elemental sense, so much as the man of the world, whom we find reflected, in a magnificent way, in this poet for whom (like the novelists, and unlike all other poets) society exists as well as human nature. No man of the world would feel ashamed of himself for writing poetry like **'Don Juan,'** if he could write it; and not only because the poet himself seems conscious of all there is ridiculous in the mere fact of writing in rhyme, when everything can be so well said in prose. It is the poetry of middle age (premature with Byron, *'ennuyé* at nineteen,' as he assures us), and it condenses all the temporary wisdom, old enough to be a little sour and not old enough to have recovered sweetness, of perhaps the least profitable period of life. It is sad and cynical with experience, and is at the stage between storm and peace; it doubts everything, as everything must be doubted before it can be understood rightly and rightly apprehended; it regrets youth, which lies behind it, and hates the thought of age, which lies before it, with a kind of passionate self-pity; it has knowledge rather than wisdom, and is a little mirror of the world, turned away from the sky, so that only the earth is visible in it. (pp. 255-56)

Byron gives us, in an overwhelming way, the desire of life, the enjoyment of life, and the sense of life's deceit, as it vanishes from between our hands, and slips from under our feet, and is a voice and no more. In his own way he preaches 'vanity of vanities,' and not less cogently because he has been drunk with life, like Solomon himself, and has not yet lost the sense of what is intoxicating in it. He has given up the declamation of despair, as after all an effect, however sincere, of rhetoric; his jesting is more sorrowful than his outcries, for it shows him to have surrendered.

> We live and die,
> But which is best, you know no more than I.

All his wisdom (experience, love of nature, passion, tenderness, pride, the thirst for knowledge) comes to that in the end, not even a negation. (pp. 262-63)

> *Arthur Symons, "George Gordon, Lord Byron (1788-1824)," in his* The Romantic Movement in English Poetry, *Archibald Constable & Co. Ltd., 1909, pp. 239-63.*

SAMUEL C. CHEW, JR. (essay date 1915)

Byron's plays are weakest on the technical side. Of this he was probably himself aware. The fact that they violate various principles of technique is a partial explanation of their small vogue at the time of their publication and of the generally low estimate in which they are held. . . .

The beginning of the struggle in which the will of the protagonist is engaged with an opposing force, must take place either within the confines of the drama itself, or at some time previous to the opening scene. Divergence in this matter sharply differentiates the classical from the romantic drama. In Shakespeare the actual beginning of the conflict is presented in the play. (p. 41)

In the "regular" drama, concomitant with the limitation of time, is the almost invariable exclusion from the drama of the beginning of the external conflict. This is one of the great restrictions of the classical model, which cannot portray the causes, in their inception and development, as well as the consequences, of the struggle. (pp. 41-2)

This is the method which Byron employs in his historical plays. All three open with the opposing forces already arrayed. In *Marino Faliero,* had the plot been of Shakespeare's handling, one can imagine an opening scene in which Steno would have been shown scratching his wanton insult upon the wall and revealing incidentally adequate reasons for so doing. This would have been followed by the discovery of the inscription by Faliero. . . . Had Byron constructed *Sardanapalus* along the lines of English tragedy there might have been an opening scene in which would have been depicted the court of Nineveh darkened only by a distant cloud of discontent; this followed by the representation of Arbaces and Beleses in conference, planning their conspiracy and revealing their motives in undertaking it. But in the play as designed by Byron these events had to be presupposed, and knowledge of them conveyed to the audience in the exposition. So also in *The Two Foscari* the action begins in the last stages of the conflict. Even in *Werner* the hero has lost his birth-right and been driven from home years before the opening of the play. There is thus at the commencement of Byron's plays a strong obstacle to their success. Readers are asked to interest themselves in the final stages of the fortunes of people with whom they have had no previous acquaintance. . . . This was a reasonable demand upon the Greek audience, for classical tragedy had for subjects myths known to all. The story being familiar, the audience willingly dispensed with the earlier portions and watched the climax and catastrophe. Not so with Byron; his three tragedies upon historical subjects dealt with the fortunes of persons of whom many Englishmen had never heard. It was therefore his duty to cultivate an interest in the character of the protagonist by the gradual development of the tragic situation and the gradual unfolding of the elements of his characters. Instead of so doing, Byron hurls his reader not merely *in medias res* but into the very conclusion of the whole matter. He thus gains that compactness which he sought so anxiously, but he loses more than he gains. He risks the interest of all readers. (pp. 42-3)

The first part of a drama—the "introduction" or "exposition"—must convey information of events preceding the opening of the play, knowledge of which is needed for an understanding of the situation. It may also be a sort of prelude, serving to indicate the tone of the piece, somewhat as does the "Vorspiel" to an opera. . . . This may be imparted in various ways: by a prologue more or less disconnected from the actual drama, by a soliloquy delivered by one of the *dramatis personae,* or by dialogue. Of these the second and third methods, and perhaps the first, are employed by Byron. (pp. 43-4)

Byron uses the [soliloquy] device twice. In *Manfred,* largely monologue and only pseudodramatic, it is the natural way of bringing the reader into touch with the situation. Here he had, moreover, the authority of Goethe. The opening scene of *Sardanapalus* cannot be so justified. The long soliloquy of Salamenes contains no information that could not be, and hardly any that is not, given in the following dialogue-scene. (pp. 44-5)

Artistic exposition is generally best attained by means of dialogue. In Shakespearean drama it is almost always employed, and is often combined with action. . . . Byron never reaches such heights of dramatic art. His method is rather akin to that used in *A Comedy of Errors,* before Shakespeare was a master of technique, and in *The Tempest,* when he could afford to be careless of such externals. (p. 45)

The exposition of a drama is followed by the "rise" towards the climax. This "rise" is sometimes introduced by a brief transition, called the "exciting force" or stimulus. The initial complication commences when first, however obscurely, the protagonist feels that the expression of his individuality clashes with the general good, or rather,—since often he has, or thinks he has, the general good at heart,—with the pervading spirit of his surroundings. This animating force varies greatly in length, in prominence, and in position. . . . It is sometimes present from the very beginning of the exposition. This is the case in *Richard III,* in which it is the villainy of the protagonist, well defined from the first, that precipitates the tragic conflict. So also in *Sardanapalus,* the self-indulgent ease of the king is the stimulus. In these examples the force is subjective, propelling from within the soul of the protagonist. In others it is objective; as when the thought of killing Caesar is introduced into Brutus' mind, or when Iago tempts and deceives Othello. It is often a matter of gradual growth. Thus the wrongs done the state by the aristocracy have for long weighed upon the mind of Faliero. Yet often some one thing, slight in itself, *added to what has gone before,* becomes the actual exciting power that brings disaster. This is admirably illustrated by the insult offered by Steno to the Doge Faliero. Some critics have complained that the motivation of the play is too petty for tragedy. This is to miss the point. Faliero says:

> "A spark creates the flame—'tis the last drop
> Which makes the cup run o'er, and mine was full
> Already" . . .

Steno's gibe is thus a perfect example of the ''exciting force,'' in itself of little moment, yet fraught with consequence. Shakespeare would have put it at the conclusion of the exposition; Byron has imagined it occurring before the commencement of the play. Its full significance is thus lost, and we are left to gather from dialogue the relation that it bears to the real causes of the Doge's treason. (pp. 49-50)

The climax is the culmination of the rising action. Here occurs that event of utmost significance, through which the forces of opposition win the ascendancy, and gaining on the protagonist, gradually drive him down from the position of vantage which, isolated from the norm, he has been able to assume. . . . The climax must justify its technical name. What of Byron's?

In *Manfred* it is well marked. After lesser exhibitions of power over the world of spirits, by conjuring up the spirits of the universe, and the Witch of the Alps, Manfred penetrates to the abode of the Evil Principle and gains converse with the dead. This is the utmost of his power. Thence by swift decline he goes down to death. He has sought for death; therefore the very moment of the climax may be fixed at Astarte's words ''To-morrow ends thine earthly ills'' . . . , while the first indications of the ''return action'' lie in the words

> ''This is to be a mortal,
> And seek the things beyond mortality.'' . . .

The entrance of the Doge into the house in which the conspirators are met together marks the climax of *Marino Faliero* . . . , for with his appearance among them the fortunes of the plot reach the highest point. . . . [Byron has] well indicated the highest point of the rising action. He has erred, however, as he often does, in not making it sharp and incisive enough; the Doge ''protests too much.''

Sardanapalus is better. The climax is a scene of fine theatrical possibilities and appeals to the imagination of the reader. (pp. 53-4)

Here, as in almost every technical point, *The Two Foscari* is a failure. There has been no rising action; hence there can be no real climax. The piece has moved downwards towards the destruction of the protagonist. (p. 54)

The action of *Cain* is so simple and it is so far from regular dramatic form that a definite climax is hardly possible. There is a climax in the thought of the poem at the conclusion of the second act, for it is to this position that the arguments of Lucifer have been tending, and it is from his defiant assertion of the powers and privileges of the human mind that the final expression of Cain's revolt comes. *Heaven and Earth* stops at the climax, breaking off at the point of sharpest clash between the will of God and the defiance of the rebels. The catastrophe would have had its beginning at the point where the piece now concludes. *Werner* is as unsatisfactory here as in all other respects. It is difficult to pick out the scene intended for the climax, as all are on the same dead level of attainment. . . . It is impossible to find any regular climax in so formless a fragment as *The Deformed Transformed*.

From the climax to the catastrophe the descent is generally more swift than the rising action has been, though this varies in individual plays. (p. 55)

Manfred shows conflict to the last gasp of the protagonist. Sardanapalus fights and foils his enemies even in death. The elder Foscari protests to the last against his fate, but the effect of the end is marred by the certainty of its nature from the

commencement of the play. The catastrophe of *Cain* is finely conceived, and veiled in mystery. In all the plays the force of individual will is shown finally succumbing to the power of the norm.

This review of Byron's general constructive abilities in the drama has shown how faulty his technique was. In part this was due to wilful disregard of the rules of the drama, in part to ignorance and inexperience. (p. 56)

In a moment of discouragement Byron wrote . . . , ''Many people think my talent *'essentially undramatic,'* and I am not at all clear that they are not right.'' To a great extent they *were* right; the merits of his dramas are not those which belong exclusively or even chiefly to dramatic literature. Had the same amount of care and energy been expended in work native to his genius—imagine ten more cantos of *Don Juan*!—the world had been the gainer. But Byron chose otherwise; and there is much of worth and wisdom in the result of his choice, worth and wisdom preserved to us though they are through a medium foreign to his genius and faulty in technique. (pp. 58-9)

> *Samuel C. Chew, Jr., in his* The Dramas of Lord Byron: A Critical Study, *The Johns Hopkins University Press, 1915 (and reprinted by Russell & Russell, Inc., 1964), 181 p.*

CLEMENT TYSON GOODE   (essay date 1920)

Byron's equipment for criticism, from his nature, education, and travel, was far above the average. He esteemed the rôle of critic an honorable one. His first sustained effort of any kind was a critical triumph against the degrading practices of the time. He interested himself, for a while thereafter, actively in periodical criticism. And but for the sudden and unparalleled success of his occasional poetry, he probably would have adopted a critical career.

He is not, in total outline, in his criticism the confirmed reactionary that he is usually represented. He held principles of hia art, in his more constant character, conformably with his practice, and expressed them deliberately and definitely. There was, as well, a substantial strain of conservatism in his nature, such as is often the basis of technique. (p. 302)

The reformation of two great literary types is contemporaneous with Byron's critical activities—drama and criticism itself. He wrought consciously and valiantly for the betterment of both these forms, by the construction of severe models for the guidance of the one, and by combatting, often by its own methods, the evil practices of the other. The emergence, almost immediately after, of higher types in both forms is conclusive evidence of his influence and service in each.

Byron's professional critical ''scribblement'' is less creditable to his powers than any other part of his criticism. And yet only the controversial portion of it is the source of his unenviable reputation as a critic. (pp. 302-03)

His best criticism is in isolated passages—pretty frequent at that—in his letters and journals and in his poetry. It is a part of the elemental impressionism of his nature, is interpretative in character, and wherever it is inspired by his creative talent, it is at one with his great poetry. (p. 303)

Of the sum total of Byron's criticism, it may be said first that it is unusually strong and vigorous. It more often goes beyond the mark than wide of it. Its very strength and vehemence have brought against him the charge of exaggeration, of wildness, hence of unreliability. Such an attitude is illiberal in an age which applauds Swinburne's apotheosis of Victor Hugo, Carlyle's dictum that Macaulay had less intelligence than a hare, Voltaire's declaration that *Athalie* is the masterpiece of the human mind, and Schlegel's pronouncement that Calderon is the last summit of romantic poetry.

Byron's criticism, as a part of his far-reaching censoriousness, is largely destructive. He had the power of a Titan, and he used it wilfully and fearlessly, but with discretion nevertheless, that is, seldom where there was not cause for destruction.

His early death prevented his attainment of true and constant greatness as a critic. His nature was endowed with judicial elements, critical and censorious, he believed in the early subsidence of the poetical faculty, and before his death a real philosophical calm was beginning to appear. Criticism was now rid of its old shackles, largely from his own exertions, and was in the full progress of its new freedom. His "corruption" from a poet, in the event of any change in his vocation, could hardly have been into anything less than a powerful critic. Poetry may not have lost more in his untimely death than has criticism. (pp. 303-04)

> *Clement Tyson Goode, in his* Byron as Critic *(originally a thesis presented at Cornell University in 1920; reprinted by permission of the Estate of Clement Tyson Goode), R. Wagner, 1923 (and reprinted by Haskell House, 1964), 312 p.*

EDMUND WILSON   (essay date 1922)

Byron's gift was for living rather than for literature. He had neither the intensity nor the fineness to fue, for perdurable brilliants, the shifting moods of the soul. Don Juan, after all, was always more real than Childe Harold. The windy storms of passion that were blown off in *Childe Harold* and the tragedies were never the most solid realities of that deeply sensuous life. If he had only not tried to live in England, if the women only hadn't set their hearts on him, what an amiable figure he might have been! There is nothing more exhilarating in literature than Byron's first trip to Greece—his duels and skirmishings with bandits, his heroic swimming of the Hellespont. . . . To read Byron is to watch a panorama of the Europe of the early nineteenth century—the morrow of the French Revolution and of the victory of Napoleon seen through the eyes of a sophisticated man who is as much alive to how people are feeling and to what sort of struggles they are waging as to how they are drinking and making love. How amusing he makes Milan and Geneva and Venice! (pp. 59-60)

Yet this record, as we follow it further, produces an effect of depression that at last becomes almost unbearable. For one thing, life had played poor Byron not the least annoying of its tricks: by the time he had acquired enough judgment not to make any further disastrous mistakes and to be sure in what manner of life his hope for happiness lay, he had already hurt others and himself so grievously in the process of learning that both his peaceful pursuits and his pleasures were forever impaired by the wounds. Among the motley baggage of his soul, there was a sort of Calvinistic conscience (supposed to have been implanted by his early education in Edinburgh) which gnawed its nails and gnashed its teeth amid the very laughter of Venice. (pp. 60-1)

Well, art has its origin in the need to pretend that human life is something other than it is, and, in a sense, by pretending this, it succeeds to some extent in transforming it. What we see when we turn back our eyes to the age of Shelley and Byron is not the ignominy of mute broken hearts. of hurriedly muffled-up births, but a blaze of divine white light and the smoky torches of rebellion. And yet, poor Jane Claremont, to have set her heart on a love affair with a poet! Poor Annabella Milbanke, to have been so naïve and misguided as to marry an inspired rake! Poor Shelley and poor Byron, to have carried in their hearts the consciousness of such guilt as no wine could for long disguise, no songs could forever relieve. Poor male and female human beings, who, understanding life in different fashions and unfitted to live together, yet cannot leave each other alone! For a moment, as we read these letters, the very splendors of *Childe Harold* and *Prometheus* seem dwindled and insubstantial like witch-fires above a bog. (p. 62)

> *Edmund Wilson, "Byron in the Twenties: The New Byron Letters" (1922), in his* The Shores of Light: A Literary Chronicle of the Twenties and Thirties *(reprinted by permission of Farrar, Straus & Giroux, Inc.; copyright 1952 by Edmund Wilson; copyright renewed © 1980 by Helen Miranda Wilson), Farrar, Straus & Giroux, 1952, pp. 57-62.*

HOWARD MUMFORD JONES   (essay date 1924)

That Byron is an uneven versifier; that he dealt too frequently in rhetoric and too little in poetry; that his themes are monotonous and his heroes always the same; that he attempted to write plays without knowing the theatre and to enter the critical arena without understanding what was going on there; that he admired and imitated Pope when he should have scorned Pope and written like Byron—these are the indictments that are brought against him. The standard criticism, moreover, with more truth herein than elsewhere, has set aside his formal satires, his verse tales, and most of his dramas in favor of **"Childe Harold," "Manfred," "Cain," "The Vision of Judgment,"** and **"Don Juan."** (pp. 732-33)

In Byron only is it made a fault that much which he wrote is not read.

The rest of the accusations are, it must be admitted, mainly true. As a versifier Byron achieved some of the worst work in the language. Any schoolboy (O useful myth!) can put an unerring finger on the brazen rhetoric and theatrical falseness of **"Lara"** and **"The Bride of Abydos"**; any tyro in college English can see that **"Manfred"** is as much like **"Lara"** as **"Lara"** is like **"The Giaour."** Nobody reads Byron's stage-plays nowadays unless he has to, and, except for **"Sardanapalus,"** there is no reason why anybody should. (p. 733)

Byron used to be an awful instance of marital infidelity; he has latterly become the stock example of all the poetic sins. As a place to pin tags he is easy, accessible, and obvious. The critics have sat on him, the verdict is in, and the trial is over. The only difficulty with the decision is that it finds most of his contemporaries, the great luminaries of the romantic age, also guilty on most of the counts.

For it is a fact that Byron, who was in his own day the scapegoat of a brilliant and careless society has become since his death the whipping post at which a brilliant and careless poetry has been vicariously scourged by literary critics too indifferent or too ignorant to see that the literary sins of Byron are in a startling degree the literary sins of Shelley and Coleridge, of Wordsworth and Scott, and even of Keats. (pp. 733-34)

The original verdict is not unjust, but the continued iteration of that verdict, coupled with the silence of criticism concerning the numerous infelicities of Byron's contemporaries—therein it is that the critics and the professors have betrayed their notable capacity for calf paths.

If this be special pleading I am tempted to say, make the most of it, but I do not believe it is so. For the faults commonly alleged against Byron are basically the faults of the epoch, which, as they are most vehemently set forth concerning him, are made to appear his alone. Byron did not possess the artistic conscience of Shelley or Keats, though he certainly had more of it than did Wordsworth, and quite as much as Coleridge or Scott; and yet, when all is said, the only impeccable workman of the group was Landor, who perhaps does not belong in this galley at all. The plain truth is that the Romanticists care very much less for workmanship (in our sense of the word), and very much more for ideas (in their sense of the word) than either the critics or the anthologies will allow. (pp. 734-35)

Byron was, it is true, an imperfect artist. Most of his contemporaries were, in the same sense, imperfect artists. It was inevitable that they should be so. Literary art, for perhaps the first time in English history, had come to grips with society and was struggling with it. . . . Every poem was a piece of propaganda, every utterance was a pamphlet, every lyric a political platform. The consequences for poetry were enormous. On the one hand, poetry possessed an electric vitality which it has not since possessed. On the other hand, it digested only imperfectly this strange and heavy food; it had to abandon the courtly aloofness which had distinguished it since the days of Spenser, and which it did not recover until the days of Rossetti and Pater. (pp. 735-36)

Byron, who was as much opposed to the current order as was Shelley, who wrote narrative poems like Scott, who argued ardently in verse like Keats and rhetorically like Wordsworth, shares therefore in the great faults of a great age. He has the impatience of an orator, and the orator's contempt for finicky concerns of style. He was angry with mankind as Shelley was, with the difference that Byron saw mankind as it really is, and Shelley saw it as it ought to be. Now, art to an angry man is a weapon, not a ritual; and when, in that gigantic warfare, the sword got hacked and the shining armor badly dinted, it seems a bit ungracious to complain that the muses do not have their daily toilettes.

There is, then, much in Byron of his own time, but there is also much in him that comes from an earlier epoch than the age of Waterloo. It is true that he was the child of the Revolution, but the phrase means also that he was the child of the eighteenth century. Byron is at once the foremost of the Romanticists and the last of the sentimentalists. . . . (pp. 736-37)

These eighteenth-century qualities in Byron go deeper than his love for rhymed couplets and his fondness for formal satire. They are essentially part of him as they were part of the age in which he lived. (p. 737)

The best in Byron is his naked cry for sincerity in an insincere and brutal time.

The supreme picture of this period will always be **"Don Juan."** **"Don Juan"** is, so to speak, curiously eighteenth-century. . . .

Typical of eighteenth-century manners is the social pirate who is sometimes a gentleman. He is in the novels, the plays, and the history of that time. It was apparently a great age for unscrupulous social climbing, and the typical adventurer, hardly a scoundrel, not yet a gentleman, is best described as being, in an age suddenly conscious of society, one who was as yet imperfectly socialized. (p. 738)

Byron is like these men and understands them. Despite the antiquity of his family there is a dubious quality in his social status which accounts in part for his determination to play the great lord. . . .

Because his poems came to him so immediately, this half-aristocratic individualism passed at once into his stories until much that we call Romantic is found on examination to be only the belated eighteenth-century pretending that the world will never change. Thus the arrogance of Manfred is the arrogance of a French nobleman. (p. 739)

That other side of the eighteenth century about which there is just now much to-do—the sticky side—that is in Byron also. He is a great sentimentalist in both the technical and the general senses, whereat insular criticism is astounded and seeks a cause. Surely the cause is not far to seek. Byron is not solitary. If it is natural that his interpretation of nature comes from the deists, it is also reasonable that the sham misanthropy of his gloomy gentlemen springs from Rousseau, who thought so highly of human life that he despised mankind. People—in fiction, at least—were acutely conscious of their passions before **"Childe Harold,"** because sentimental doctrine had taught them so to be. . . . The Byronic hero was not new, he was simply done over from the toy misanthropy of the late eighteenth century. (p. 740)

[Byron's] stark individualism is not merely aristocratic and antisocial, it is Northern and stubborn and proud. The core of it is Scottish. The poet who had something of the careless fascination of the Stuarts, had also the obstinacy of King James. Indeed, that Byron is a Stuart, a Gordon, and half a Scotsman is a fact often forgotten in discussions of him. . . . It is clear that his pride, his brooding over theology, his parsimony and extravagance, his love for rhetoric, and (as he himself tells us) his enthusiasm for wild nature are among the traits which may have their sources in his Caledonian blood.

It is possibly absurd to assume that there are national traits in literary expression, but if we choose at random four or five literary Scotsmen and observe their common characteristics, it is illuminating to see how much Byron has in common with them, and how many things fall into focus that were scattered and meaningless before. It is at least a curious coincidence that Robert Burns, Sir Walter Scott, Thomas Carlyle, and John Davidson, and Byron, should all be artists of imperfect utterance, never quite certain whether the thing under their hands was poetry or rhetoric; that in each of them there is the same proud individualism . . . ; and finally that, saving for Scott, and perhaps not even with that exception, the thought of these five men should come again and again to the solution of a theological riddle. God is with each of them a thing to worry about, whether in Scott that anxiety softens into a proud ethical idealism, or in Burns turns into angry denunciation of religious hypocrisy, or in Carlyle and Davidson results in queer readings of life, or in Byron, with childishly imperfect weapons, seeks to storm the last citadel of heaven in the name of man. (pp. 741-42)

They have therefore something of the instinct of great preachers; their phrases are bronze and resonant, and they will employ, if necessary, the clangors of oratory provided that they can thereby rid themselves of what they are destined to say.

They are as far from Pater and Swinburne, it is clear, as they are removed from Tennyson and Coleridge. And if now we remove from Byron much that is superficial and accidental, it is surprising to see how much more he is like the Scotsmen than the Englishmen. (pp. 742-43)

Byron is the first modern man in British poetry—that is to say, the first man to whom, as to us, society was at once a responsibility and an irritation. He has our interest in the large political situation and our scorn of petty politics, our hatred of sham and phariseeism and plausible platitude and hollow respectability. I think that he had more courage than we possess, especially when it came to denunciation. (p. 744)

Mainly he has to-day to give us something that was in him a defect, and that is his own tonic lack of respect for art. We think that Art died with Oscar Wilde, and looking back upon the purple curtains of the eighteen-nineties, thank God we are not aesthetes, ignoring meanwhile the fact that we have merely fallen into the Intellectual Decadence. We are to-day connoisseurs of poetic clevernesses, hushed and holy devotees in the temple of Freud. Poetry, which was once a giant shillalah, has become once more a curious tool for the carving of mental cherry-stones. Nobody has believed in it as a weapon since everybody ceased to believe in it as a god. Yet, in the march of ideas, great poetry has always been a way of getting things done—like pamphleteering. So it was with Dante and Milton, with Wordsworth and Goethe, with Shelley and Byron. Their verses bit and swirled and scratched. Verse-making was not to them a craft, it was an armory. Byron, with all his faults upon his head, never committed our own peculiar sin: he never put the muses to lapidary work on the emotions. He is therefore a greater man than we are. . . . (p. 745)

Howard Mumford Jones, "The Byron Centenary," in The Yale Review, *Vol. XIII, No. 4, July, 1924, pp. 730-45.*

LAFCADIO HEARN (essay date 1927)

[Byron's] poetry was everything which the poetry of the Lake School had not been, and it was also something more. It openly mocked all conventions that society loved and that Byron hated; it even mocked at common notions of morality, it preached revolt against rigid beliefs and fixed rules of every kind—and yet it delighted people. There was something more in it than the spirit of revolt—a new spirit of tolerance, a large sense of indulgence for human weakness. . . . [Byron] attacked hypocrisy and cant of every sort; and he did it so well that sensible people could forgive him for occasional mockery of a less pardonable kind. And he created sympathy in all his poems for some imaginary hero or demi-god or adventurer or renegade, represented in rebellion against law and order—yet for all that in nowise really bad at heart. People said that these characters were just so many pictures of Byron himself—which is probably true. They can be criticized from many points of view. But they gave to English literature a new element of color, and a new quality of feeling. Apart from the mere question of poetic value Byron's verses deserve the gratitude of literature, simply because they helped to give literature a kind of freedom never enjoyed before—at least not in England. (pp. 519-20)

A word about the peculiar class of poets which he represents. In Italy, from old times, there has been always a class of poets who compose poetry whenever asked to do so, immediately—not writing it, but speaking it, composing as fast as they can speak, making perfectly correct verse, rhymes and all, and pronouncing it just as if they were reading from a book. . . . Scott was essentially an improvisator, in the fact that he wrote his political romances off-hand. . . . Byron was a still greater improvisator—the greatest in all English literature—though his work is more defective than that of Scott. No other poet ever wrote so much, in so many different forms of verse, in so many different kinds of compositions without study—without preparation—without correction—without even caring to read over again and to revise a great deal of the work done. . . . He was not only a lyric poet, but also a narrative poet, a poet of description, a dramatist of considerable range, a satirist, and a translator from various languages. But most of this work can be classed only as poetry of improvisation; and that is why it has so many faults—faults even against grammar;—that is why Byron cannot rank with such poets as Wordsworth or Coleridge. Defective in form, nevertheless, his immediate influence was prodigious. . . . Byron affected every existing European literature. He influenced German literature in the case of even such men as Heine and Goethe; he influenced French literature, to the extent that the French romantic movement will always be connected with his name;—he influenced the younger literature of northern Europe as well as those of Latin countries; and even modern Russian literature owes to him not a little of the stimulus that made its awakening.

Now you must remember that Byron's poetry was known in other countries than England only through translation; and that most of the translations were in prose. . . . You will see at once that his power as a poet could not have depended upon form. In one sense, the translations improved upon him;—the faults of his verse disappeared in the French and German and other prose translations. But the fact speaks for itself. If Byron could influence all European literature through prose translations, the mere faults of his verse, no more than the merits of his verse, can determine his great place in the history of literature. He was, in one way—in form—rather a great improvisator than a great poet; but his power proves to be a real power of sentiment and feeling. (pp. 522-24)

I have told you before that he brought into literature an entirely new element of feeling. He brought into it a new spirit of revolt against conventions and against shams of every kind. . . . Poets before him had tried to make their readers sympathize chiefly with good men or good women unjustly persecuted or wronged. But Byron struck a different note: he taught the world to sympathize with what society would call bad men or bad women in revolt against established authority. He forced people to think: "Are we really right in judging such splendid persons as bad?" Then this first doubt naturally suggested another— "Are the standards of right and wrong—the standards of the 18th century—by which we have been judging everybody's conduct, just and correct? And when you set people thinking about whether established customs and conventions are good or bad, you are really shaking the whole foundations of the existing fabric of received opinion. Byron could do that, not only for England, but for almost every country of the time. He obliged nations to think and to feel in a new way. (p. 524)

Lafcadio Hearn, "Pre-Victorian Poets: Byron," in A History of English Literature in a Series of Lectures, *Vol. II,* The Hokuseido Press, *1927, pp. 518-26.*

MARIO PRAZ (essay date 1930)

With Milton, the Evil One definitely assumes an aspect of fallen beauty, of splendour shadowed by sadness and death;

he is 'majestic though in ruin'. The Adversary becomes strangely beautiful. . . . Accursed beauty is a permanent attribute of Satan; the thunder and stink of Mongibello, the last traces of the gloomy figure of the medieval Fiend, have now disappeared.

Is the reversal of values which some critics have tried to discover really to be found in Milton? Is the justification of the ways of God to men only the seeming aim of the poem, the poet himself in reality being 'of the Devil's party without knowing it', as Blake declared? (p. 56)

[It] was Byron who brought to perfection the rebel type, remote descendant of Milton's Satan.

Milton's type of Satan is immediately recognizable in the shrewd portrait of Byron outlined by the Earl of Lovelace in *Astarte*, the first book to throw light on the mystery of the life of his grandfather the poet.

> He had a fancy for some Oriental legends of pre-existence, and in his conversation and poetry took up the part of a fallen or exiled being, expelled from heaven, or sentenced to a new avatar on earth for some crime, existing under a curse, predoomed to a fate really fixed by himself in his own mind, but which he seemed determined to fulfil. At times this dramatic imagination resembled a delusion; he would play at being mad, and gradually get more and more serious, as if he believed himself to be destined to wreck his own life and that of everyone near him.

This is a sketch which reproduces in dim outline the sombre portrait of his idealized self drawn by Byron in [*Lara*]. . . . (pp. 61-2)

The Corsair and the Giaour have the same characteristics [as those outlined in *Lara*]. The Corsair has a pale, high forehead, and hides dark passions beneath an appearance of calm. The furrows of his face and his frequent change of colour attract the eye and at the same time leave it bewildered,

> As if within that murkiness of mind
> Work'd feelings fearful, and yet undefined.

But no one knows exactly what his secret may be. . . . Finally the Giaour, the first in order of time of these Byronic heroes, shows plainly his relationship with Mrs. Radcliffe's Schedoni. The Giaour, who by his passion has indirectly caused the death of Leila, hides his sinister past beneath a monk's gown. . . . The pale face furrowed by an ancient grief, the rare Satanic smile, the traces of obscured nobility ('a noble soul and lineage high') worthy of a better fate—Byron might be said to have derived all these characteristics, by an almost slavish imitation, from Mrs. Radcliffe. (pp. 64-6)

It is quite possible that Mrs. Radcliffe drew the figure of the sinister monk Schedoni mainly from her own study of the books which, as a literary blue-stocking, she used to read: but Byron's case is more complex. Did he not, in any case, declare that 'the *Corsair* was written *con amore*, and much from *existence*'? Given the vanity of his own nature, what is more probable than that he should have deliberately modelled himself upon the figure of the accursed angel? Who can be sure that he may not have studied every detail in front of a mirror, even to the terrible oblique look with which he frightened people, particularly his mistresses? But however artificial the methods by which Byron

cultivated his character of Fatal Man, he possessed by nature not only 'le physique du rôle', but also the psychological tendency handed down to him from a long chain of ancestors who conformed more or less to the type of the 'noble ruffian'.

Cave a signatis: in his very physical deformity Byron saw the sign of his destiny. To what point, as an actor, he was convinced by his own role it is impossible to say, but he was always sincere in feeling himself 'a marked man', stamped with a sign among ordinary mortals, 'an outlaw'. Does the whole Byronic legend then stand on no firmer a pedestal than a club foot? A club foot, hence the *besoin de la fatalité*. . . .

The question is more complicated than that. Yet, though not denying the importance of small matters, one would not wish to reduce Byron to the level of the man who, having received a present of a gold-topped stick, felt it his duty to put the rest of his costume in harmony with it, and so ran up debts, was ruined, and finished up with his corpse at the Morgue. (pp. 69-70)

It was in transgression that Byron found his own life-rhythm. . . . Byron sought in incest a spice for love ('great is their love who love in sin and fear': *Heaven and Earth* . . .), and . . . he required the feeling of guilt to arouse in him the phenomena of the moral sense, and the feeling of fatality in order to appreciate the flow of life. (pp. 70-1)

It seems a paradox, and yet the most genuine thing that this monster of energy—if ever there was one—possessed, was the force of inertia. The function which violent exercise and a drastic régime fulfilled for him physically, checking his tendency to grow fat, was fulfilled for his moral nature, which was naturally idle, by tumultuous emotions. 'Passion is the element in which we live: without it we but vegetate', said Byron in his mature years to Lady Blessington. . . . He had to key up his life to such a high state of tension in order to make it yield him anything, that when it came to the post-mortem it was found that both brain and heart showed signs of very advanced age: the sutures of the brain were entirely obliterated and the heart bore signs of incipient ossification. Yet Byron was only thirty-six. His blood had to boil like lava for him to feel it beating in his pulses: did not the Giaour say of his own blood

> But mine was like the lava flood
> That boils in Ætna's breast of flame?

Paroxysm became his natural atmosphere; hence the jarring and clamorous discords which strike one in so many of his productions. This necessity of forcing the tones may account for Byron's behaviour during what he called his 'treacle-moon'. His conduct towards his wife seems to have been of a moral cruelty so exceptional as to make one for a moment doubt the reliability of the historical evidence. But one quickly comes to see that no episode in Byron's life is more true to type than this. (pp. 71-2)

What Manfred said of Astarte ('I loved her, and destroy'd her'), what Byron wished to be able to say of Augusta and of Annabella (see the Incantation in *Manfred*), was to become the motto of the 'fatal' heroes of Romantic literature. They diffuse all round them the curse which weighs upon their destiny, they blast, like the simoon, those who have the misfortune to meet with them (the image is from *Manfred* . . .); they destroy themselves, and destroy the unlucky women who come within their orbit. Their relations with their mistresses are those of an incubus-devil with his victim. (pp. 74-5)

Mario Praz, "The Metamorphoses of Satan," in his
The Romantic Agony, translated by Angus Davidson
(© Oxford University Press 1970; reprinted by permission of Oxford University Press; originally published as La Carne, la morte e il diavolo nella let-
teratura romantica, Soc. editrice "La Cultura," 1930),
second edition, Oxford University Press, 1951 (and
reprinted by Meridian Books, 1956), pp. 53-91.*

WILLIAM J. CALVERT   (essay date 1935)

[In] *English Bards and Scotch Reviewers* and in *Hints from
Horace* [Byron] had said all that he had to say in conventional
satire. Any repetition of his success would have been repetition
merely; he had no spur to prick his intent. His new experiences,
even his reading, were not the most appropriate matter for the
older satire; he needed a newer, more elastic form, which would
admit the enthusiasms and the raptures he was experiencing.
This form he happened upon in *Childe Harold.* (p. 108)

The poem is noticeably a medley, from many sources, without
conscious aim or conscious selection, having more unity in its
derivation than in its destination. It derives artistically from
the traditional Spenserian stanza, through Thomson, Shen-
stone, and above all Beattie, with that stanza's characteristic
rhythms and its pseudo-archaic diction. Into its composition
enter the many strains of influence from Byron's reading, more
notably from those modern productions against which he had
fulminated in the *English Bards.* The songs of Moore, the
immorality of Strangford, the narrative style of Scott, verbal
tricks and turns of the ballad, and the weaker more fantastic
neoclassic diction sometimes reminiscent of Pope's *Iliad,* but
more often of lesser poetasters, intrude upon the original tone
of the Spenserian stanza. . . . The strength is in the conception
of the hero and the spirit and fire of the poetry. The unity is
entirely one of tone, not of artistic structure.

The poem, briefly, is not a conscious work of art at all, in its
broader outlines. It is essentially a travelogue, a poetical diary
of Byron's journey, a series of poetical impressions of scenery
and people with notes attached for accuracy and for additional
information. Evidently, though it absorbed Byron's attention
for the while, he did not look upon it as a great effort of the
imagination. . . . The poem is written with a minimum of
artistic will. It is a travelogue not because Byron admired
travelogues and was particularly anxious to compose one, but
because while he was traveling it was the easiest and most
natural thing to write. He was giving way to the poetic impulse
to express his emotions, without any very assured intention of
ever publishing the result. (pp. 108-09)

The genesis of the poem, finally, may be traced back to Byron's
old motive and excuse for writing—escape from the moment
and relief of his feelings. . . . Byron broke out into poetry as
into a rash, from fever, and wrote, not because he had any
ultimate end in view, but merely because poetry, the more
personal and emotional the better, was for the moment necessary. He had no reason either from his motives or, in his
judgment, from his accomplishment, to be proud of the composition. (p. 110)

He had attempted, with the publication of the poem, to forestall
any identification of himself with his hero. For this reason he
objected to the appearance of his name on the title-page, and
added a warning in the preface, that the Childe was a fictious
character introduced to give some connection to the piece. But
in spite of his protests, the public accepted him as that dark

and sinister person whom he had described. He could never
quite escape from this creature of his imagination. (p. 111)

The impression effected by the poem was far-reaching in its
influence upon the character and career of the man. He was
received everywhere less as a poet than as a striking, romantic,
and mysterious figure. Such a reception could not but react,
finally, on his idea of himself. . . . His imagination itself was
made captive. His heroes in successive romances are but slight
modifications of the Childe, undergoing adventures Byron
liked to imagine for himself, and eternally the victims of brooding misanthropy and lawless desire.

That Childe Harold is not a very original figure, in his combination of characteristics, is generally recognized. He is another phase of an already fashionable type, of which Moore's
Zeluco, Mrs. Radcliffe's Schedoni, Lewis's Ambrosio, and
Scott's Marmion were outstanding examples. He is the ideal
hero of the Gothic novels with which the young imagination
of Byron had been fed. But to name the sources or the predecessors of the character is merely to explain why the material
was ready to his hand. The Byronic hero is not a mere compendium of inherited vices and virtues, nor is he a pale reflection of someone else's idea, but a striking personality, very
much alive. (pp. 112-13)

William J. Calvert, in his Byron: Romantic Paradox,
*University of North Carolina Press, 1935 (and re-
printed by Russell & Russell, Inc., 1962), 235 p.*

T.S. ELIOT   (essay date 1937)

One reason for the neglect of Byron is, I think, that he has
been admired for what are his most ambitious attempts to be
poetic; and these attempts turn out, on examination, to be fake:
nothing but sonorous affirmations of the commonplace with
no depth of significance. (p. 226)

The qualities of narrative verse which are found in *Don Juan*
are no less remarkable in the earlier tales. Before undertaking
this essay I had not read these tales since the days of my
schoolboy infatuation, and I approached them with apprehension. They are readable. However absurd we find their view
of life, they are, as tales, very well told. As a *tale-teller* we
must rate Byron very high indeed: I can think of none other
since Chaucer who has a greater readability, with the exception
of Coleridge whom Byron abused and from whom Byron learned
a great deal. And Coleridge never achieved a narrative of such
length. Byron's plots, if they deserve that nature, are extremely
simple. What makes the tales interesting is first a torrential
fluency of verse and a skill in varying it from time to time to
avoid monotony; and second a genius for divagation. Digression, indeed, is one of the valuable arts of the storyteller. The
effect of Byron's digressions is to keep us interested in the
story-teller himself, and through this interest to interest us more
in the story. (p. 227)

It is, I think, worth nothing, that Byron developed the verse
conte considerably beyond Moore and Scott, if we are to see
his popularity as anything more than public caprice or the
attraction of a cleverly exploited personality. These elements
enter into it, certainly. But first of all, Byron's verse tales
represent a more mature stage of this transient form than Scott's,
as Scott's represent a more mature stage than Moore's. Moore's
Lalla Rookh is a mere sequence of tales joined together by a
ponderous prose account of the circumstances of their narration
[modelled upon the *Arabian Nights*]. Scott perfected a straight-

forward story with the type of plot which he was to employ in his novels. Byron combined exoticism with actuality, and developed most effectively the use of *suspense*. (p. 230)

Childe Harold seems to me inferior to this group of poems [*The Giaour, The Bride of Abydos, The Corsair, Lara,* etc.]. Time and time again, to be sure, Byron awakens fading interest by a purple passage, but Byron's purple passages are never good enough to do the work that is expected of them in *Childe Harold:*

> Stop! for thy tread is on an Empire's dust!

is just what is wanted to revive interest, at that point; but the stanza that follows, on the Battle of Waterloo, seems to me quite false; and quite representative of the falsity in which Byron takes refuge whenever he *tries* to write poetry:

> Stop! for thy tread is on an Empire's dust!
> An Earthquake's spoil is sepulchred below!
> Is the spot mark'd with no colossal bust?
> Nor column trophied for triumphal show?
> None; but the moral's truth tells simpler so,
> As the ground was before, so let it be;—
> How that red rain hath made the harvest grow!
> And is this all the world has gained by thee,
> Thou first and last of fields! king-making victory?

It is all the more difficult, in a period which has rather lost the appreciation of the kind of virtues to be found in Byron's poetry, to analyse accurately his faults and vices. Hence we fail to give credit to Byron for the instinctive art by which, in a poem like *Childe Harold,* and still more efficiently in *Beppo* or *Don Juan,* he avoids monotony by a dexterous turn from one subject to another. He has the cardinal virtue of being never dull. But, when we have admitted the existence of forgotten virtues, we still recognize a falsity in most of those passages which were formerly most admired. To what is this falsity due?

Whatever it is, in Byron's poetry, that is 'wrong', we should be mistaken in calling it rhetoric. Too many things have been collected under that name; and if we are going to think that we have accounted for Byron's verse by calling it 'rhetorical', then we are bound to avoid using that adjective about Milton and Dryden, about both of whom [in their very different kinds] we seem to be saying something that has meaning, when we speak of their 'rhetoric'. (pp. 231-32)

Of Byron one can say, as of no other English poet of his eminence, that he added nothing to the language, that he discovered nothing in the sounds, and developed nothing in the meaning, of individual words. I cannot think of any other poet of his distinction who might so easily have been an accomplished foreigner writing English. The ordinary person talks English, but only a few people in every generation can write it; and upon this undeliberate collaboration between a great many people talking a living language and a very few people writing it, the continuance and maintenance of a language depends. Just as an artisan who can talk English beautifully while about his work or in a public bar, may compose a letter painfully written in a dead language bearing some resemblance to a newspaper leader, and decorated with words like 'maelstrom' and 'pandemonium': so does Byron write a dead or dying language.

This imperceptiveness of Byron to the English word—so that he has to use a great many words before we become aware of him—indicates for practical purposes a defective sensibility. I say 'for practical purposes' because I am concerned with the sensibility in his poetry, not with his private life; for if a writer has not the language in which to express feelings they might as well not exist. . . . Byron did for the language very much what the leader writers of our journals are doing day by day. I think that this failure is much more important than the platitude of his intermittent philosophizing. Every poet has uttered platitudes, every poet has said things that have been said before. It is not the weakness of the ideas, but the schoolboy command of the language, that makes his lines seem trite and his thought shallow. . . . (pp. 232-33)

All things worked together to make *Don Juan* the greatest of Byron's poems. The stanza that he borrowed from the Italian was admirably suited to enhance his merits and conceal his defects, just as on a horse or in the water he was more at ease than on foot. His ear was imperfect, and capable only of crude effects. . . . [He] seems always to be reminding us that he is not really trying very hard and yet producing something as good or better than that of the solemn poets who take their verse-making more seriously. And Byron really is at his best when he is not trying too hard to be poetic. . . . (p. 234)

[At] a lower intensity he gets a surprising range of effect. His genius for digression, for wandering away from his subject [usually to talk about himself] and suddenly returning to it, is, in *Don Juan,* at the height of its power. The continual banter and mockery, which his stanza and his Italian model serve to keep constantly in his mind, serve as an admirable antacid to the high-falutin which in the earlier romances tends to upset the reader's stomach; and his social satire helps to keep him to the objective and has a sincerity that is at least plausible if not profound. The portrait of himself comes much nearer to honesty than any that appears in his earlier work. This is worth examining in some detail.

Charles Du Bos, in his admirable *Byron et le besoin de la fatalité* [*Byron and the Need of Fatality*], quotes a long passage of self-portraiture from *Lara.* Du Bos deserves full credit for recognizing its importance; and Byron deserves all the credit that Du Bos gives him for having written it. This passage strikes me also as a masterpiece of self-analysis, but of a self that is largely a deliberate fabrication—a fabrication that is only completed in the actual writing of the lines. . . . Byron made a vocation out of what for most of us is an irregular weakness, and deserves a certain sad admiration for his degree of success. But in *Don Juan,* we get something much nearer to genuine self-revelation. For Juan, in spite of the brilliant qualities with which Byron invests him—so that he may hold his own among the English aristocracy——is not an heroic figure. There is nothing absurd about his presence of mind and courage during the shipwreck, or about his prowess in the Turkish wars: he exhibits a kind of physical courage and capacity for heroism which we are quite willing to attribute to Byron himself. But in the accounts of his relations with women, he is not made to appear heroic or even dignified; and these impress us as having an ingredient of the genuine as well as of the make-believe (pp. 234-35)

The last four cantos are, unless I am greatly mistaken, the most substantial of the poem. To satirize humanity in general requires either a more genial talent than Byron's, such as that of Rabelais, or else a more profoundly tortured one, such as Swift's. But in the latter part of *Don Juan* Byron is concerned with an English scene, in which there was for him nothing romantic left; he is concerned with a restricted field that he had known well, and for the satirizing of which an acute animosity sharpened his powers of observation. His understanding may remain superficial, but it is precise. . . . Lord Henry and Lady Adeline Amundeville are persons exactly on the level of Byron's capacity for understanding and they have a reality for which their author has perhaps not received due credit.

What puts the last cantos of *Don Juan* at the head of Byron's works is, I think, that the subject matter gave him at last an adequate object for a genuine emotion. The emotion is hatred of hypocrisy; and if it was reinforced by more personal and petty feelings, the feelings of the man who as a boy had known the humiliation of shabby lodgings with an eccentric mother, who at fifteen had been clumsy and unattractive and unable to dance with Mary Chaworth, who remained oddly alien among the society that he knew so well—this mixture of the origin of his attitude towards English society only gives it greater intensity. . . . Byron's satire upon English society, in the latter part of *Don Juan,* is something for which I can find no parallel in English literature. He was right in making the hero of his house-party a Spaniard, for what Byron understands and dislikes about English society is very much what an intelligent foreigner in the same position would understand and dislike.

One cannot leave *Don Juan* without calling attention to another part of it which emphasizes the difference between this poem and any other satire in English: the Dedicatory Verses. The dedication to Southey seems to me one of the most exhilarating pieces of abuse in the language:

> Bob Southey! You're a poet—Poet Laureate,
> And representative of all the race;
> Although 'tis true that you turn'd out a Tory at
> Last, yours has lately been a common case:
> And now, my Epic Renegade! what are ye at? . . .

kept up without remission to the end of seventeen stanzas. This is not the satire of Dryden, still less of Pope; it is perhaps more like Hall or Marston, but they are bunglers in comparison. This is not indeed English satire at all; it is really a *flyting.* . . . (pp. 237-39)

I do not pretend that Byron is Villon. . . , but I have come to find in him certain qualities, besides his abundance, that are too uncommon in English poetry, as well as the absence of some vices that are too common. And his own vices seem to have twin virtues that closely resemble them. With his charlatanism, he has also an unusual frankness; with his pose, he is also a *poète contumace* is a solemn country; with his humbug and self-deception he has also a reckless raffish honesty; he is at once a vulgar patrician and a dignified toss-pot; with all his bogus diabolism and his vanity of pretending to disreputability, he is genuinely superstitious and disreputable. I am speaking of the qualities and defects visible in his work, and important in estimating his work: not of the private life, with which I am not concerned. (p. 239)

> *T. S. Eliot, "Byron" (originally published in* From Ann to Victoria, *edited by Bonamy Dobree, Cassell & Co., 1937), in his* On Poetry and Poets *(reprinted by permission of Farrar, Straus and Giroux, Inc.; in Canada by Faber and Faber Limited; copyright © 1957 by T. S. Eliot), Farrar, Straus and Cudahy, 1957, pp. 223-39.*

C. KEITH   (essay date 1946-47)

Byron? And you think of Don Juan, a tangle of women, perhaps Missolonghi—that is, if you are English. For on the Continent it would take much more than a line to tell all they think of Byron. And the accent would be different—Don Juan! In tones of rapture. Did it not envisage a whole new political set-up? An Englishman with ideas, this milord! . . . To this day, up and down the blue Aegean, the fisherman's cockle-shell, the village inn, the smoky cargo steamer still bear his Lordship's name.

And when you read his *Letters,* you don't wonder. Their vital quality, their directness, their humanity, sweeping across the century like the gust of a keen Nor'-Easter, bring his personality before you as if he were writing to you last night. Not all his letters, of course. It took a long time and much misfortune before Byron could write a letter that posterity would always want to read. Though no longer, perhaps, than is usual with the great letter-writers. For nobody young can write a good letter. Sound and fury are but poor substitutes for the maturity, urbanity and rich experience that characterise letters like Scott's or Samuel Rutherford's or the masterpieces of Cowper. . . . By November [1816], when Byron reached Venice, where he was to stay for the next two-and-a-half years, mind and body were alike braced for the high, poetic achievement that lay ahead. Incidentally, he could also now write a good letter. (pp. 468-70)

Sometimes in the *Letters* you get a glimpse, unique in English literature, of how great poetry is made. The time is not in the poet's power, either when to do it or when not. "It comes over me in a kind of rage every now and then, and then if I don't write to empty my mind, I go mad." But you would be wrong if you thought with the Romantics that the process is all inspiration and the poet a mere medium. . . . And after all, what is poetry, anyway? "If one's years can't be better employed than in sweating poesy, a man had better be a ditcher." There speaks the son of the Gordons of Gight. For wasn't there Venice all around you? "I write in a passion and a sirocco and I was up till six this morning at the Carnival"; or Venice at sunrise: "It is four and the dawn gleams over the Grand Canal and unshadows the Rialto. I must to bed; up all night but, as George Philpot says, 'it's life, though, damme, it's life'." . . . [Politics] as well as city life and the beauty of the lagoons, drew you in Venice. Back at Harrow Byron had watched Europe being re-made, and watched it, not with English eyes either. Here was new life stirring, a new order rising, the rotten old monarchies toppling to their ruin. "I don't want him here", wrote Byron in 1813, appraising Napoleon, "but I shouldn't wonder if he banged them yet." And politics held him to the end. Almost the last letters that led him to Missolonghi scintillate with it. And in a diction that other great letter-writers avoid. But Byron adored it. You could say things so quickly in slang. And so tersely too. People got your meaning at once. So that when you read the letters now, with phrases like "Love and all that", "Wine and women dished me", it is hard to realise that the writer is not of to-day, but contemporary with the dignified Scott (still eighteenth century in his epistolary language) and the pompous Wordsworth, already Victorian in his full dress. But Byron's Italian letters fizzle and crackle down the century and far beyond it, seeking in vain a mate till they come to as modern a writer as Rupert Brooke. "The two first acts are the best. The third so-so—but I was blown with the first and second heats." That might have come from Brooke's unceremonious *Letters from America,* but in effect it is Byron on his own tragedy of *Manfred* almost a century earlier. . . . Not that this informality augurs an unawareness of the quality of his work. Byron was fully conscious of the divine fire within him and of the immortality it was to bring. (pp. 474-75)

By 1821 Byron had even learned how to write to his wife. Six years ago, when they parted, how the words would have stung her with their resentment and fury! But six years is a large part of a poet's life and Byron had spent most of these in learning. England and her way of living were ages apart from him now, and the tone of this farewell letter is tranquil and mellow. "We both made a bitter mistake, but now it is over and irrevocably so." Not only is the thought direct, but the expression has a rhythm rare in a Byron letter. . . . It is the last, perhaps, of the notable letters and shows the long road he has travelled from the stiff 'Dear Madam' of the early letters to his mother. A long road and an unequal one. But the very inequalities bring him nearer to his everyday reader. People that shy at the glittering perfection of a Horace Walpole letter are not intimidated by a letter on soda-water and biscuits (Byron's favourite meal). The hot Left Winger that finds Scott's measured Whig and Tory talk but yesterday's baked-meats, leaps to the live wire of Byron's politics with its slogans of liberation and tyranny. He is high enough for any highbrow with his theories of Art— good company and on a night out, over Marianna's black eyes. Up and down the ladder of humanity, more familiarly than any of the other great letter-writers, Byron moves. And with an unexpectedness that kindles your imagination. For the legendary Byron of the melodramatic poses and the theatrical melancholy—however that may fill his poetry—finds no place in his letters. Their abundant health, their sanity of outlook, their originality of thought—these are the memories that remain with you from even the most cursory perusal. And—acid test of a good letter—a cursory perusal will do. For Byron's mind makes its impact instantaneously. Some flash of his thought will stay with you—an unconventional flash, most likely, for no writer ever was more unconventional—as in the question of Heaven's attractiveness. "No existence with eternity in it", declares Byron flatly, "is even tolerable", and sets you wondering. The later Italian letters are perpetually flinging such stones into the millpond of orthodox thought—casually, in the midst of everyday talk. It is this unexpectedness that holds you. Potent, as on the day he wrote them, Byron's magnetism lives on. (pp. 476-77)

> *C. Keith, "Byron's 'Letters'," in* Queen's Quarterly, *Vol. LIII, No. 4, Winter, 1946-47, pp. 468-77.*

L. C. MARTIN   (essay date 1948)

If we say that Byron often seems to have lacked the degree of artistic detachment observed or recommended by [certain of his] critics we may, indeed we must in fairness, add that by his forthright habit his work gains something in immediacy, in urgency and directness of effect. . . . (p. 8)

Byron's personality in his lyric verse is apt to impress itself because of the strength and sincerity of his conception, because the conception is so little modified by any considerable process of artistic incubation and shaping, because of the very fact that his words and rhythms were neither far-sought nor greatly pondered and tested. Of course he runs the risk of the banal and the platitudinous.

> There's not a joy the world can give like that it
> takes away,

or

> The days of our youth are the days of our glory,

this last from a poem characteristically composed during a journey on horseback; but there are moments when the unstu-

died forthright procedure has its rewards and there is something elemental and universal in what he writes while he also reveals himself. . . . Perhaps half the lyrics that Byron wrote would be double as good if they were half as long. *Nesciit quod bene cessit relinquere*. But that is not true of his best lyrics, which can be called classical, not just because they show a knowledge of what to say and when to leave off, but because in them mere personality is transcended, and the style is simple without *simplesse*. Byron can write with that avoidance of cliché and that reliance upon bare emotive phrasing which critics so different as Boileau and Wordsworth have agreed to respect and which can be exemplified in almost any period of English poetry. (pp. 8-10)

But Byron's lyrics of amorous attachment and separation and lost opportunities are rather numerous and it is possible to have too much of them at a sitting. . . . And I think it is arguable that as a lyrical poet Byron was more often to be admired when his theme takes him further away from himself, or when the form he chooses to write in involves some technical difficulty to check his otherwise headlong profusion. On such occasions, when self is forgotten or facility hindered, or both, Byron can achieve a strength of sentiment and a dignity of utterance which place him among the masters of the English impersonal lyric— his becomes a medium of 'soul-animating strains', and never more so than when the strain is of liberty or endurance or the power of man to rise above his mortal nature.

I think something of this can be clearly seen even on the level of youthful experimentation represented by *Hours of Idleness*, a collection illustrating only too well what mischief can be found for idle hands to do. But there is more to it than that, for besides all the welter of amorous outpourings, the annals of likings and partings, reproaches and protestations, often conveyed in scampering anapaestic verse which really does not serve the purpose at all well,—in addition to all this there is evidence that some of the hours were spent not in idleness but in something more like fundamental and rewarding brain-work. (pp. 10-11)

[*The Destruction of Sennacherib*] stands out as the apex, the crown of Byron's lyrical writings. We may prefer to regard it as a narrative rather than a lyrical poem, but these at best are but uncertain categories. Call it if you wish a lyrical ballad or a dramatic lyric. At any rate the narrative element is not paramount and it is no more just to take this as a compressed story than as an expanded interjection, called forth by thoughts on the transience of all life and the vanity of human wishes.

> Like the leaves of the forest when Summer
> is green,
> That host with their banners at sunset were
> seen:
> Like the leaves of the forest when Autumn
> hath blown,
> That host on the morrow lay withered and
> strown.

Here, though not here alone, the anapaestic measure which Byron so often employed with effects of triviality and bathos is marvellously effective. The success seems to depend on keeping elastic but strong and relentless the movement of words which are all on the same plane of poetic quality, so that diction and rhythm co-operate to drive home the concept of swift visitation and inevitable doom. . . . (p. 15)

We ought indeed to take Byron with some seriousness as a technician in verse, not merely because so much has been made of his lapses, but because by art as well as by nature, he could manage so well to give those appearances of spontaneity and untrammelled movement which lyric verse, of all verse, may be expected to present; for when all is said and done, when the poet has produced words without song and the musician songs without words, the old relationship and sympathy between poetry and music has not been destroyed. (p. 17)

We also, if we would properly appreciate Byron's artistry, do well to take account of the finer shades which may appear if we think not merely of the abstract metre but of the words which give it substance. The name of a metre is less important than its local habitation. Then we can see, for instance, that when Byron writes a song for music he can so choose his words as to make it tolerably easy to take in at once the words and the music. His simplicity of thought serves him well in this and also his liking for words not too alien from the spoken idiom or the current poetic conventions; but there is more than that for we can also see art (or is it just rightness of instinct?) in the generous allowance of long vowels, the variety of vowels and consonants, and the likeness within the differences effected by internal rhymes or other devices, as in

> She walks in Beauty, like the night
> Of cloudless climes and starry skies. . . .
>
> (p. 19)

I am willing to grant that Byron is not one of the subtlest of lyrical poets. But there is one glory of the lyric wherein more is meant than meets the ear, and another glory, not necessarily to be less admired, of the lyric which states its meaning with simplicity but also with force, and comes home unerringly to men's business and bosoms because its concerns are important to all. A great thought in simple language—that in the century preceding Byron's was a recognized definition of the sublime. (p. 24)

> L. C. Martin, in his Byron's Lyrics, *The University of Nottingham, 1948, 25 p.*

CARL LEFEVRE   (essay date 1952)

Lord Byron has been interpreted overmuch in terms of a personal life notoriously dramatic and romantic. Yet paradoxically, close attention to biography, coupled with widespread belief from his day to ours that his verse is autobiographical in a sense that is peculiar—that is, Byronic—has not so far produced an accurate account of a major type of Byronic hero, the fiery convert of revenge. (p. 468)

In describing Alp, the central figure of *The Siege of Corinth* . . . , Byron formulated the political essence of the convert of revenge hero with exquisite precision of phrase. He is *the renegade, the fiery convert of revenge,* suffering the proverbial intensity and auto-intoxication of all converts.

The fiery-tempered Alp is the very type of aristocratic Byronic hero. Provoked beyond endurance by the accumulated social rejections and personal insults of his peers, he seeks retribution by turning fiercely against his class allies, whom he has come to hate, and leagues himself cynically with the vulgar, his class enemies, whom he has always scorned. In the ensuing resort to arms, the apostate noble dies a hero's death in battle, and the seditious followers he has demagogically led for his own purposes are annihilated, to a man. . . .

> They did not know how pride can stoop,
> When baffled feelings withering droop;

> They did not know how hate can burn
> In hearts once changed from soft to stern;
> Nor *all the false and fatal zeal*
> *The convert of revenge can feel.*

The theme thus brilliantly expressed in the final couplet (italics added) is of intense concern to Byron throughout his works, a surprising number of which portray the convert of revenge. (pp. 468-69)

As a character, this Byronic hero openly displays his superiority and fiery temperament to both peers and underlings. Except for his instinctive executive function, he is aloof and distant from all mankind, preoccupied with his own lofty thoughts and a profound sense of guilt and crime. In religion he is often a ruggedly individualistic pagan—an infidel from all points of view. He has a dark glance, a haughty mien, and a curling lip, but at the same time is strong, brave, handsome, skilled in manly sports and feats of arms. Above all, he is a born military genius. The noble traitor's pure love for his lady is the one bright, unblemished jewel on his blotched and ancient 'scutcheon; at his death, she often dies of heartbreak, perhaps going out of her mind first.

The complete plot, in all its wild improbability, is the counterfeit tragedy of a treacherous noble, spurned by his peers, who betrays his class and dies attempting to establish himself as a benevolent despot by demagogically rallying the mob to support him in a suicidal uprising.

Typically, the fiery convert traces his noble blood a long, long way back, but he has fallen on evil days, in a period of aristocratic decline. His social position is precarious, if not actually forfeit, and his degenerate peers misrule the populace, some even stooping to base trade. There is much seditious grumbling among the lower orders, who are ripe for revolt, awaiting only a leader to organize them and give political effectiveness to their numbers. Into this breach strides the fiery convert of revenge, fatally provoked by some crowning insult, cynically manipulating the popular forces to his own treasonable ends. In his demagogy he is a prototype of the man on horseback, but in his action he is a death-seeking hero who dies trying to turn the clock back. Like Milton's Samson in one respect, he brings destruction upon himself; significantly unlike Samson, however, he does not involve the tyrannical rulers in his own destruction, but instead destroys their rebellious class enemies, whom he has falsely led. For the fiery convert of revenge, a noble death "for the cause"—a suicidal, lost cause—is the crowning achievement of life.

A most absorbing aspect of Byron's handling of this theme is the seeming contradiction between the hero's aspirations and his achievements. The poet indulges these noble criminals in the fullest expression of their treasonable ambitions, in words, and allows them to contrive sudden and ingenious subversive plots, but he invariably causes them to fail in action. . . . The final merging of the twin themes of self-expression and self destruction resolves the apparent contradiction between the hero's rhetoric and his action. Revolutionary language, mouthed by the convert of revenge, is silenced by the counter-revolutionary action which he has provoked from his peers: extinction for the renegade aristocrat, and, of course, annihilation for his upstart followers.

In additional to *The Siege of Corinth,* three works will serve to evoke the fiery convert and exhibit the development of this theme in Byron's poetry. Of the half-dozen early tales, *The Corsair* and its sequel *Lara* . . . are among the best written of these contemporarily popular, histrionic poems of exotic adventure, and portray two distinct stages of the early convert of revenge. Lord Conrad, pirate chieftain of *The Corsair,* is the very type of aristocratic renegade adventurist, and Lara is the same noble expatriate returned to his native land and baronial castle, aching and burning with all the mortal ills of the typical Byronic hero. On the other hand, *Marino Faliero, Doge of Venice* . . . presents the same hero at a much later stage, more richly, with greater maturity, and as it were, with finality. The fiery convert in the early tales is considerably more of a juvenile delinquent than the criminal elder statesman of the Venetian political play, but they are the same blue-blooded male animal at different ages. Neither is altogether grown up, nor a whole man. (pp. 469-71)

As a dramatic figure, [the convert of revenge] is stunted by his own internal ambivalences and ambiguities, so that he is better than immature, ineffective, and finally suicidal; and suicide, no matter how complex and fascinating it may be made to appear, is not of itself an action for a great protagonist. As an aristocratic traitor who betrays his class allies in words and his class enemies in deeds, the political convert has greater interest, but his elaborate duplicity has a wishful, nightmarish quality and is never satisfactorily resolved. Perhaps here is the reason why Byron returned to this theme time after time. The inadequacy of the convert of revenge as hero, and the poet's recurrent failure to bring the theme to a satisfactory conclusion, suggest that Lord Byron himself, in politics as in love, was not so much a man of rational ideas as one of violent passion. (p. 487)

> Carl Lefevre, "Lord Byron's Fiery Convert of Revenge," in Studies in Philology, *Vol. XLIX, No. 3, July, 1952, pp. 468-87.*

NORTHROP FRYE   (essay date 1959)

The main appeal of Byron's poetry is in the fact that it is Byron's. To read Byron's poetry is to hear all about Byron's marital difficulties, flirtations, love for Augusta, friendships, travels, and political and social views. And Byron is a consistently interesting person to hear about, this being why Byron, even at his worst of self-pity and egotism and blither and doggerel, is still so incredibly readable. He proves what many critics declare to be impossible, that a poem can make its primary impact as a historical and biographical document. The critical problem involved here is crucial to our understanding of not only Byron but literature as a whole. Even when Byron's poetry is not objectively very good, it is still important, because it is Byron's. But who was Byron to be so important? certainly not an exceptionally good or wise man. Byron is, strictly, neither a great poet nor a great man who wrote poetry, but something in between: a tremendous cultural force that was life and literature at once. (p. 174)

Byron's lyrical poetry affords a good exercise in critical catholicity, because it contains nothing that "modern" critics look for: no texture, no ambiguities, no intellectualized ironies, no intensity, no vividness of phrasing, the words and images being vague to the point of abstraction. The poetry seems to be a plain man's poetry, making poetic emotion out of the worn and blunted words of ordinary speech. Yet it is not written by a plain man: it is written, as Arnold said, with the careless ease of a man of quality [see excerpt above], and its most striking and obvious feature is its gentlemanly amateurism. It is, to be sure, in an amateur tradition, being a romantic, sub-

jective, personal development of the kind of Courtly Love poetry that was written by Tudor and Cavalier noblemen in earlier ages. . . . Byron held the view that lyrical poetry was an expression of passion, and that passion was essentially fitful, and he distrusted professional poets, who pretended to be able to summon passion at will and sustain it indefinitely. . . . *Childe Harold* has the stretches of perfunctory, even slapdash writing that one would expect with such a theory.

In Byron's later lyrics, especially the *Hebrew Melodies*. . . , where he was able to add some of his Oriental technicolor to the Old Testament, more positive qualities emerge, particularly in the rhythm. (pp. 174-75)

Byron did not find the Byronic hero as enthralling as his public did, and he made several efforts to detach his own character from Childe Harold and his other heroes, with limited success. He says of Childe Harold that he wanted to make him an objective study of gloomy misanthropy, hence he deliberately cut humor out of the poem in order to preserve a unity of tone. But Byron's most distinctive talents did not have full scope in this part of his work. . . . His sardonic and ribald wit, his sense of the concrete, his almost infallible feeling for the common-sense perspective on every situation, crackles all through his letters and journals, even through his footnotes. But it seems to be locked out of his serious poetry, and only in the very last canto of *Don Juan* did he succeed in uniting fantasy and humor.

Byron's tales are, on the whole, well-told and well-shaped stories. Perhaps he learned something from his own ridicule of Southey, who was also a popular writer of verse tales, sometimes of mammoth proportions. In any case he is well able to exploit the capacity of verse for dramatizing one or two central situations, leaving all the cumbersome apparatus of plot to be ignored or taken for granted. But he seemed unable to bring his various projections of his inner ghost to life: his heroes, like the characters of a detective story, are thin, bloodless, abstract, and popular. (pp. 178-79)

The same inability to combine seriousness and humor is also to be found in the plays, where one would expect more variety of tone. The central character is usually the Byronic hero again, and again he seems to cast a spell over the whole action. Byron recognized this deficiency in his dramas, and to say that his plays were not intended for the stage would be an understatement. Byron had a positive phobia of stage production, and once tried to get an injunction issued to prevent a performance of *Marino Faliero.* . . . [With] the exception of *Werner,* a lively and well-written melodrama based on a plot by somebody else, Byron's plays are so strictly closet dramas that they differ little in structure from the tales.

The establishing of the Byronic hero was a major feat of characterization, but Byron had little power of characterization apart from this figure. Like many brilliant talkers, he had not much ear for the rhythms and nuances of other people's speech. (pp. 179-80)

But if Byron's plays are not practicable stage plays, they are remarkable works. *Manfred,* based on what Byron had heard about Goethe's *Faust,* depicts the Byronic hero as a student of magic whose knowledge has carried him beyond the limits of human society and given him superhuman powers, but who is still held to human desire by his love for his sister (apparently) Astarte. At the moment of his death the demons he has controlled, with a sense of what is customary in stories about magicians, come to demand his soul, but Manfred, in a crisp incisive speech which retains its power to surprise through any number of rereadings, announces that he has made no bargain with them, that whatever he has done, they can go to hell, and he will not go with them. The key to this final scene is the presence of the Abbot. Manfred and the Abbot differ on all points of theory, but the Abbot is no coward and Manfred is no villain: they face the crisis together, linked in a common bond of humanity which enables Manfred to die and to triumph at the same time.

Two of Byron's plays *Cain* and *Heaven and Earth*, are described by Byron as "mysteries," by which he meant Biblical plays like those of the Middle Ages. Wherever we turn in Byron's poetry, we meet the figure of Cain, the first man who never knew Paradise, and whose sexual love was necessarily incestuous. In Byron's "mystery" Cain is Adam's eldest son and heir, but what he really inherits is the memory of a greater dispossession. "Dost thou not live?" asks Adam helplessly. "Must I not die?" retorts Cain. Adam cannot comprehend the mentality of one who has been born with the consciousness of death. . . . And just as Milton tries to show us that we in Adam's place would have committed Adam's sin, so Byron makes us feel that we all have something of Cain in us: everybody has killed something that he wishes he had kept alive, and the fullest of lives is wrapped around the taint of an inner death. As the princess says in [Horace Walpole's] *The Castle of Otranto:* "This can be no evil spirit: it is undoubtedly one of the family."

The other "mystery," *Heaven and Earth*, deals with the theme of the love of angels for human women recorded in some mysterious verses of Genesis, and ends with the coming of Noah's flood. Angels who fall through sexual love are obvious enough subjects for Byron, but *Heaven and Earth* lacks the clear dramatic outline of *Cain*. (pp. 180-81)

Don Juan is traditionally the incautious amorist, the counterpart in love to Faust in knowledge, whose pursuit of women is so ruthless that he is eventually damned, as in the last scene of Mozart's opera *Don Giovanni*. Consequently he is a logical choice as a mask for Byron, but he is a mask that reveals the whole Byronic personality, instead of concealing the essence of it as Childe Harold does. The extroversion of Byron's temperament has full scope in *Don Juan*. There is hardly any characterization in the poem: even Don Juan never emerges clearly as a character. We see only what happens to him, and the other characters, even Haidée, float past as phantasmagoria of romance and adventure. What one misses in the poem is the sense of engagement or participation. Everything happens to Don Juan, but he is never an active agent, and seems to take no responsibility for his life. He drifts from one thing to the next, appears to find one kind of experience as good as another, makes no judgements and no commitments. As a result the gloom and misanthropy, the secret past sins, the gnawing remorse of the earlier heroes is finally identified as a shoddier but more terrifying evil—boredom, the sense of the inner emptiness of life that is one of Byron's most powerfully compelling moods, and has haunted literature ever since, from the *ennui* of Baudelaire to the *Angst and nausée* of our own day. (p. 184)

The Vision of Judgment is Byron's most original poem, and therefore his most conventional one; it is his wittiest poem, and therefore his most serious one. Southey, Byron's favorite target among the Lake poets, had become poet laureate, and his political views, like those of Coleridge and Wordsworth, had shifted from an early liberalism to a remarkably complacent Toryism. On the death of George III in 1820 he was ill-advised

enough to compose, in his laureate capacity, a "Vision of Judgment" describing the apotheosis and entry into heaven of the stammering, stupid, obstinate, and finally lunatic and blind monarch whose sixty-year reign had lost America, alienated Ireland, plunged the country into the longest and bloodiest war in its history, and ended in a desolate scene of domestic misery and repression. . . . The apotheosis of a dead monarch, as a literary form, is of classical origin, and so is its parody, Byron's poem being in the tradition of Seneca's brilliant mockery of the entry into heaven of the Emperor Claudius. (p. 185)

We have not yet shaken off our nineteenth-century inhibitions about Byron. A frequent twentieth-century jargon term for him is "immature," which endorses the Carlyle view that Byron is a poet to be outgrown. . . . There is certainly something youthful about the Byronic hero, and for some reason we feel more defensive about youth than about childhood, and more shamefaced about liking a poet who has captured a youthful imagination. If we replace "youthful" with the loaded term "adolescent" we can see how deeply ingrained this feeling is.

Among intellectuals the Southey type, who makes a few liberal gestures in youth to quiet his conscience and then plunges into a rapturous authoritarianism for the rest of his life, is much more common than the Byron type, who continues to be baffled by unanswered questions and simple anomalies, to make irresponsible jokes, to set his face against society, to respect the authority of his own mood—in short, to retain the rebellious or irreverent qualities of youth. Perhaps it is as dangerous to eliminate the adolescent in us as it is to eliminate the child. In any case the kind of poetic experience that Byronism represents should be obtained young, and in Byron. It may later by absorbed into more complex experiences, but to miss or renounce it is to impoverish whatever else we may attain. (pp. 188-89)

Northrop Frye, "Lord Byron," in Major British Writers, Vol. II, *edited by G. B. Harrison (© 1959 by Harcourt Brace Jovanovich, Inc.; reprinted by permission of the publisher), Harcourt, 1959 (and reprinted in his* Fables of Identity: Studies in Poetic Mythology, *Harcourt, 1963, pp. 168-89).*

PAUL WEST (essay date 1960)

Byron had no philosophy, was no great social wit, and was not even essentially a writer. This is not to debunk Byron but to penetrate the mist of Byronism. He thought best when malicious; his most impressive displays are those in which he grafts a grotesquely inappropriate item on to a revered growth: the crippled outsider devising malign prosthetics to shock the literary bourgeois and their betters. . . . Reduce everything he ever wrote, and you will find an essential act of repulsion: either self-emptying into a *persona,* or a repudiation. He pushes away what he is; he repudiates even the *persona* of *Don Juan*. He has the insecure person's fierce need of elimination; he needs to feel unobliged to his subject-matter, his friends, his publisher, his mistresses, his house, his rôle, his reputation. And yet, by a method approaching 'double-think', he seeks to eliminate this lust for elimination; and so he lands up with inappropriate impedimenta—the wrong woman, the wrong type of poem, the wrong reputation, the wrong stanza-form, and so on. His was a multiple nature, chameleonic and irresponsible. (pp. 12-13)

Only when he wrote farcically or confessionally was he a writer without reserve. And when he wrote confessionally he was eventually obliged to evoke *Childe Harold*. Even in *Don Juan* he can be sincerely himself only when writing from the viewpoint of farce. For in farce there is no considerateness, no sensitivity and no response. The personages are inhuman; they lack 'presence'—in its religious sense, and are not *obliged* in any way. And, in Byron's writing, just as there is a farce of personages, there is—consummate in *Don Juan*—a farce of language. The serious poet at his dignified best or portentous worst is obliged to maintain a high seriousness, to ensure congruity and decorum. From all this, the *farceur* is exempt. So it is that Byron develops into the master of hyperbole and bathos, the verbal ostler yoking heterogeneous images by violence together, the arch reducer and inflater, the mutilator crassly misrelating by rhyme, the raper of decorum.

Such a performer could assail with impunity; reputation he had lost but could disregard; ideas he handled laxly—his work testifies that epigrammatists have no monopoly of shallow thinking. . . . He aims at the maximum of maxim with the minimum of sincerity—a fraudulent, self-mocking sage. The pleasure we get from this is that of the combinations: they are unexpected and sudden. The astonishing thing is that the rhyme leads the sententiousness by the nose and yanks it into being. The rest is easy, for euphony and neatness ensur for the content an attention it hardly merits as thought. But this is not deception: to read *Don Juan* is to engage in a conspiracy against some putative bourgeoisie of the mind—those who think poetry should be sincere, edifying and craftly. Instead, we are to let the gustily confidential manner ('a little quietly facetious upon everything') bounce us into a disorganized hoax. *Don Juan* is the creation of the bored and sloppy puppeteer, but only in so far as people are concerned. After all, if you think life ridiculous, it matters little what aspect of it you select to prove your point. . . . But the word-play of the poem is brilliant and ingenious—the poet works by denotation alone, thus ensuring a clash now and then of connotations:

> But first of little Leila we'll dispose;
> For like a day-dawn she was young and pure,
> Or like the old comparison of snows,
> Which are more pure than pleasant to be sure.

His policy is clear: any 'old comparison' is to be upset, made to look silly. The aim is not the serious one of minting phrases for posterity to treasure. Rather, it is something more casual and ephemeral; disrespect for the solemnized verbal union and travesty of rhyming decorum:

> Her thoughts were theorems, her words a problem,
> As if she deem'd that mystery would ennoble 'em.

It is the inaccuracy which is funny, with its echo of the slangy impropriety—'nobble 'em'. In order to secure that effect of stumbling invention and lapsing taste, the poet has to be a satirist, certainly; but more too. He owes no allegiances; and it has always seemed to me that the need to eliminate was fulfilled much more nearly to Byron's satisfaction in his farce with literary language than in his 1816 hegira to the Continent. (pp. 13-15)

He is one of the most isolated figures in literature; he was lonely early on; and, late, he feared even to cherish the principle of elimination itself—for fear of being typed once again. The ironic disclaimers are ready built-in, in the same way as his need was. His style does not develop, does not improve between *English Bards* . . . and *Don Juan*. He rejects unsuitable verse-forms as he goes, and singles out the *ottava rima*. But his only advance, other than that from impudent to prudent choice, is from the compact to the sprawling, from the por-

tentous to the knack of making it look preposterous as he winks at the reader and disclaims deep interest in the whole thing anyway.

We do him no injustice, I suggest, if we formulate his compulsions in the following terms. Sensitive, he dissembled as he matured. Wishing to identify loneliness with independence, he turned into farce his legend and his sensitivity. He blunted all his responses, to people, style and ideas. He thus found himself perfectly equipped for literary farce—and yet able to preserve his paradoxical nature by the greatest commitment and response of all, in Greece. In a few words, he is elimination, farce and paradox. (p. 16)

There are few of Byron's works which present a subtle and balanced attitude to life; *The Two Foscari* is one of the few. Usually he is out of touch with reality: in *Childe Harold* he either catalogues without responding or sets down feelings which flood the object contemplated. The romances are stereotyped and artificial, rather like first drafts for an Errol Flynn filmscript—satisfactory in their kind but lacking convincingness. *The Vision of Judgment* is superb fun. *Beppo* is the idyll travestied by the new standard of irony. And *Don Juan,* urbane and disconcerting to anyone but its author, is a patchwork of distorted sequences and repudiated values, a sustained hoot at social pieties. The other poems are melodramatic and oversimplified. . . . (p. 17)

> *Paul West, "Poet in Person," in his* Byron and the Spoiler's Art *(© Paul West 1960), Chatto & Windus, 1960, pp. 11-28.*

ANDREW RUTHERFORD   (essay date 1961)

[While] *Don Juan* is always witty, always penetrating, always entertaining, it sometimes seems to lack coherence—formal, emotional, and intellectual. It is thus a very great poem, but a flawed one.

The Vision of Judgment, on the other hand, has all *Don Juan*'s strengths and none of its weaknesses. (p. 216)

Byron had come to feel a serious concern for the present state of English poetry, and to despise the Lake Poets as producers of bad poetry, disseminators of bad theories of poetry, and corrupters of the public taste, especially with regard to poetry of the eighteenth century. Southey (with less genius than any of the group) had now published in his official capacity as Poet Laureate [*The Vision of Judgement*], a work feeble in itself, a work which in listing great poets among England's Elder Worthies made no mention of Dryden or Pope, a work, finally, in which he had followed the Lake Poets' unfortunate practice of constructing some half-baked theory, and then writing in accordance with it. (pp. 218-19)

[Byron's] political objections to the poem, however, were even more important than this critical distaste. [He] despised the Lake Poets as a set of renegades, and Southey, with the Laureateship as a reward for his apostasy, seemed the very type of a successful turncoat. . . . *Vision* demonstrated how conservative and loyalist he had now become. The dedication is addressed in terms of fulsome flattery to George IV, congratulating him on the glories, military, political, and cultural, of his reign and regency. . . . Byron found this peculiarly offensive, coming from a man who had once been both a revolutionary and a pacifist, and the poem itself was just as bad, with its vilification of men who had worked or fought for Liberty. It gave, moreover, a completely false impression of George

III's reign, and of George III himself: it was an outrageous attempt to whitewash him. . . . (pp. 219-20)

Byron chose now to return to his *ottava rima* style, and *The Vision of Judgment* shows his complete mastery of this medium. In the first fifteen stanzas he uses it with great economy and flexibility to get the story under way and to suggest the values on which his satire will be based; and though his style is just as lively and varied as it was throughout *Don Juan,* it is now consistently subordinated to the poem's satiric purpose. . . . Byron's poetic manner thus establishes at the very outset a mood of patronising, amused indulgence towards the machinery of Southey's Heaven.

Almost immediately, however, he proceeds to modulate the tone to express his horror at events on earth, and we pass from the ludicrous predicament of the overworked Recording Angel to a completely serious indictment of war—an expression of violent disgust at the crime and suffering which culminated in the battle Southey saw as the highest point of Britain's military glory. . . . (pp. 222-24)

Southey's poem, then, was at once the occasion of Byron's answer and a cause of its success, for it provided him with what he lacked in some parts of *Don Juan*—a single major target and a clearly defined satiric purpose: his *Vision,* he told Hobhouse, was "by way of reversing rogue Southey's," and this object was always before his eyes. In this poem, therefore, as in *Beppo,* all his detailed effects contribute to the total meaning of the work, for while the local excellence of Byron's style is as high as ever, it is now the instrument, precise and perfectly controlled, of his artistic-moral purpose. Although he runs through the whole gamut of his moods, from flippant irreverence to solemn denunciation, they do not result in any inconsistency or confusion, for he now shows the great satirist's complete control of tone, manipulating it according to the poem's needs. (His cynical humour and urge to deflate, which sometimes run riot in *Don Juan,* are never allowed to weaken his own beliefs or feelings in the *Vision*—they are used instead to discredit Southey's work in all its aspects.) And he speaks himself of the poem's being written in his "finest . . . Caravaggio style," meaning presumably that the light and the dark—or in this case the humorous and the serious—are united in a pattern of deliberate contrasts, all of which contribute to the composition as a whole. The structure of the *Vision* is as admirable as the style: Southey's plot provided a framework for the poem, but Byron shows brilliant originality and artistic skill in his adaptation of the Laureate's work—in his selection of some parts of it for detailed treatment, in his reversal of its values, and in his abandoning its sequence of events at exactly the right moment, so as to achieve his own superb conclusion. The result is a narrative-meditative poem in which the narrative is extremely entertaining but also completely functional, being designed to ridicule one set of values and to assert another, while the comments and digressions are designed to reinforce the narrative and bring out its full implications. Hence the poem is as coherent and compact, as economical, as aesthetically satisfying, as *Beppo*—and it is fully as amusing. Yet its implications are as profound as those of the best cantos of *Don Juan:* Southey's poem embodied so many corrupt values in small compass that an attack on it involved the assertion of Byron's political, moral, and critical beliefs, and the whole poem is directed to this end. Sometimes the *ottava rima* style seems to act as a mirror, reflecting all the casual and contradictory elements in Byron's mind, but *The Vision of Judgment* (like the best parts of *Don Juan*) is more like a burning-glass, which focusses all his relevant ideas and feelings on the subject, and presents them with maximum effectiveness. It has, in fact, the characteristic excellences of *Don Juan,* with none of the longer poem's faults, just as it has the artistic perfection of *Beppo* without any of its triviality. *The Vision of Judgment* is Byron's masterpiece, aesthetically perfect, intellectually consistent, highly entertaining, and morally profound—the supreme example of satire as it could be written by an English poet-aristocrat. (pp. 236-37)

> *Andrew Rutherford, in his* Byron: A Critical Study *(with the permission of the publisher, Stanford University Press; copyright 1961), Stanford University Press, 1961, 253 p.*

W. H. AUDEN   (essay date 1962)

Most of the literary works with which we are acquainted fall into one of two classes, those we have no desire to read a second time—sometimes, we were never able to finish them—and those we are always happy to reread. There are a few, however, which belong to a third class; we do not feel like reading one of them very often but, when we are in the appropriate mood, it is the only work we feel like reading. Nothing else, however good or great, will do instead.

For me, Byron's *Don Juan* is such a work. In trying to analyze why this should be so, I find helpful a distinction which, so far as I have been able to discover, can only be made in the English language, the distinction between saying, "So-and-so or such-and-such is *boring,*" and saying, "So-and-so or such-and-such is a *bore.*" (pp. 386-87)

Perhaps the principle of the distinction can be made clearer by the following definitions:

> A. The absolutely boring but absolutely not a bore: the time of day.
> B. The absolutely not boring but absolute bore: God.

Don Juan is sometimes boring but pre-eminently an example of a long poem which is not a bore. To enjoy it fully, the reader must be in a mood of distaste for everything which is to any degree a bore, that is, for all forms of passionate attachment, whether to persons, things, actions or beliefs.

This is not a mood in which one can enjoy satire, for satire, however entertaining, has its origin in passion, in anger at what is the case, desire to change what is the case into what ought to be the case, and belief that the change is humanly possible. (p. 387)

In defending his poem against the charge of immorality, Byron said on one occasion: "*Don Juan* will be known bye-a-bye for what it is intended—a Satire on abuses of the present state of Society": but he was not telling the truth. The poem, of course, contains satirical passages. . . .

But, as a whole, *Don Juan* is not a satire but a comedy, and Byron knew it, for in a franker mood he wrote to Murray:

> I have no plan—I had no plan; but I had or
> have materials; though if, like Tony Lumpkin,
> I am to be "snubbed so when I am in spirits,"
> the poem will be naught and the poet turn serious again . . . You are too earnest and eager about a work which was never intended to be

serious. Do you suppose that I could have any intention but to giggle and make giggle.

Satire and comedy both make use of the comic contradiction, but their aims are different. Satire would arouse in readers the desire to act so that the contradictions disappear; comedy would persuade them to accept the contradictions with good humor as facts of life against which it is useless to rebel. (p. 388)

Byron's choice of the word *giggle* rather than *laugh* to describe his comic intention deserves consideration.

All comic situations show a contradiction between some general or universal principle and an individual or particular person or event. In the case of the situation at which we giggle, the general principles are two:

1) The sphere of the sacred and the sphere of the profane are mutually exclusive.
2) The sacred is that at which we do not laugh.

Now a situation arises in which the profane intrudes upon the sacred but without annulling it. If the sacred were annulled, we should laugh outright, but the sacred is still felt to be present, so that a conflict ensues between the desire to laugh and the feeling that laughter is inappropriate. (pp. 389-90)

The terms "sacred" and "profane" can be used relatively as well as absolutely. Thus, in a culture that puts a spiritual value upon love between the sexes, such a love, however physical, will seem sacred in comparison with physical hunger. When the shipwrecked Juan wakes and sees Haidée bending over him, he sees she is beautiful and is thrilled by her voice, but the first thing he longs for is not her love but a beefsteak. (p. 391)

Cannibalism, on the other hand, is a crime which is regarded with sacred horror. The survivors from the shipwreck in Canto II are not only starving but also have a craving for meat to which their upbringing has conditioned them. Unfortunately, the only kind of meat available is human. . . . The men in Byron's poem pay with their lives for their act, not because it is a sacred crime but for the profane reason that their new diet proves indigestible.

> By night chilled, by day scorched, there one by one
> They perished until withered to a few,
> But chiefly by a species of self-slaughter
> In washing down Pedrillo with salt water.

It is the silly mistake of drinking salt water, not the sacred crime of consuming a clergyman, that brings retribution. Most readers will probably agree that the least interesting figure in *Don Juan* is its official hero, and his passivity is all the more surprising when one recalls the legendary monster of depravity after whom he is named. The Don Juan of the myth is not promiscuous by nature but by will; seduction is his vocation. Since the slightest trace of affection will turn a number on his list of victims into a name, his choice of vocation requires the absolute renunciation of love. (pp. 391-92)

When he chose the name Don Juan for his hero, Byron was well aware of the associations it would carry for the public, and he was also aware that he himself was believed by many to be the heartless seducer and atheist of the legend. His poem is, among other things, a self-defense. He is saying to his accusers, as it were: "The Don Juan of the legend does not exist. I will show you what the sort of man who gets the reputation for being a Don Juan is really like." (p. 392)

Far from being a defiant rebel against the laws of God and man, his most conspicuous trait is his gift for social conformity. I cannot understand those critics who have seen in him a kind of Rousseau child of Nature. Whenever chance takes him, to a pirate's lair, a harem in Mohammedan Constantinople, a court in Greek Orthodox Russia, a country house in Protestant England, he immediately adapts himself and is accepted as an agreeable fellow. Had Byron continued the poem as he planned and taken Juan to Italy to be a *cavaliere servente* and to Germany to be a solemn Werther-faced man, one has no doubt that he would have continued to play the roles assigned to him with tact and aplomb. In some respects Juan resembles the Baudelairian dandy but he lacks the air of *insolent* superiority which Baudelaire considered essential to the true dandy; he would never, one feels, say anything outrageous or insulting. (pp. 392-93)

When one compares Don Juan with what we know of his creator, he seems to be a daydream of what Byron would have liked to be himself. Physically he is unblemished and one cannot imagine him having to diet to keep his figure; socially, he is always at his ease and his behavior in perfect taste. (p. 393)

Byron's poetry is the most striking example I know in literary history of the creative role which poetic form can play. . . . He knew Italian well, he had read Casti's *Novelle Galanti* and loved them, but he did not realize the poetic possibilities of the mock-heroic ottava-rima until he read Frere's *The Monks and the Giants*.

Take away the poems he wrote in this style and meter, *Beppo, The Vision of Judgment, Don Juan,* and what is left of lasting value? A few lyrics, though none of them is as good as the best of Moore's, two adequate satires though inferior to Dryden or Pope, **"Darkness,"** a fine piece of blank verse marred by some false sentiment, a few charming occasional pieces, half a dozen stanzas from *Childe Harold,* half a dozen lines from *Cain,* and that is all. (p. 394)

So long as Byron tried to write Poetry with a capital P, to express deep emotions and profound thoughts, his work deserved that epithet he most dreaded, *una seccatura.* As a thinker he was, as Goethe perceived, childish, and he possessed neither the imaginative vision—he could never invent anything, only remember—nor the verbal sensibility such poetry demands. (p. 395)

What had been Byron's defect as a serious poet, his lack of reverence for words, was a virtue for the comic poet. Serious poetry requires that the poet treat words as if they were persons, but comic poetry demands that he treat them as things and few, if any, English poets have rivaled Byron's ability to put words through the hoops. (p. 399)

There have been poets—Keats is the most striking example—whose letters and poems are so different from each other that they might have been written by two different people, and yet both seem equally authentic. But, with Byron, this is not the case. From the beginning, his letters seem authentic but, before *Beppo,* very little of his poetry; and the more closely his poetic *persona* comes to resemble the epistolary *persona* of his letters to his male friends—his love letters are another matter—the more authentic his poetry seems. (p. 401)

[Byron's] visual descriptions of scenery or architecture are not particularly vivid, nor are his portrayal of states of mind particularly profound, but at the description of things in motion or the way in which the mind wanders from one thought to another he is a great master.

Unlike most poets, he must be read very rapidly as if the words were single frames in a movie film; stop on a word or a line and the poetry vanishes—the feeling seems superficial, the rhyme forced, the grammar all over the place—but read at the proper pace, it gives a conviction of watching the real thing which many profounder writers fail to inspire for, though motion is not the only characteristic of life, it is an essential one.

If Byron was sometimes slipshod in his handling of the language, he was a stickler for factual accuracy. . . . (p. 405)

The material of his poems is always drawn from events that actually happened, either to himself or to people he knew, and he took great trouble to get his technical facts, such as sea terms, correct. (p. 406)

> *W. H. Auden, "'Don Juan'" (© 1962 by W. H. Auden; reprinted by permission of Random House, Inc.), in his* Dyer's Hand and Other Essays, *Random House, 1962, pp. 386-406.*

WILLIAM H. MARSHALL (essay date 1962)

Both *English Bards and Scotch Reviewers* and *Childe Harold's Pilgrimage,* Cantos I and II, appear to be constructed after established models, the Popean and the Spenserian, and for this reason these poems have been taken by many to represent, respectively, Byron's "early classicism" and his departure into "romanticism." The generalization usually passes unchallenged, but analysis of the poems themselves offers somewhat less than full support of it. . . . Despite the outer support given each poem by the facts of its origins and genre, neither *English Bards and Scotch Reviewers* nor the first *Childe Harold* reveals a sustained structure, either intellectual or dramatic.

English Bards and Scotch Reviewers appears to be essentially a series of sketches which have little inner relation other than the fact that each concerns a literary or historical figure. Such is not entirely the case, for the speaker (in this instance one not distinct from the poet) attempts, for conventional purposes, to imply the nature of the ideal and the one by describing explicitly the real and the many. That he fails to do so may be ultimately, and perhaps rather obviously, attributed to that Byronic incapacity, already described, to conceive of other than a fragmentary universe, so that the antithesis which should sustain the structure of the poem collapses. A symptom of collapse and thereby a more immediate cause for failure is the overemphasis of the multiplicity of bad bards and reviewers. Despite the quality that is apparent in some short passages, the poem is not sustained in its length, which becomes thereby excessive. The structural failure can best be understood perhaps in terms of Byron's use but final abandonment of a metaphor that should become the cohesive force in the poem, the traditional equation between priest and poet. Described simply, the speaker's employment of this metaphor is incomplete, never passing beyond the proposition that the bards and reviewers "in these degenerate days" are not priestlike, as others once were. He points to Pope and Dryden as historical ideals; but in describing the lesser bards of the contemporary scene, the speaker does not reveal, by ironic implication or otherwise, the nature of the quality of the older poets. (pp. 27-8)

The fact is often overlooked that the title [*Childe Harold's Pilgrimage*] specifies that the poem is about a "Pilgrimage," and that the poem is subtitled *A Romaunt.* Within the tradition,

the protagonist of the verse romance is sent upon a mission, the fulfillment of which will prove his courage and other qualities needed for moral survival; the end of the pilgrimage must be the test itself. In the Preface to *Childe Harold, I* and *II,* however, the poet qualifies the direction that the title seems to give to the poem. The work is primarily descriptive, he proposes, "written, for the most part, amidst the scenes which it attempts to describe"; but in order to give "some connection to the piece," structural cohesiveness, he has introduced a protagonist, who, he implies, must not be taken too seriously for what the title suggests he is. . . . (pp. 36-7)

The assertion expressed through the title remains before us, however, though its aesthetic force has been significantly weakened; the object of the pilgrimage is still justifiably a consideration. . . . In early lines of the first canto of *Childe Harold* . . . it is made explicit that the basis for affirmation which Harold has lost and would regain is either psychological or metaphysical rather than merely social. (p. 37)

The frame of the poem—the quest of the Hero, his Night Journey—suggests the possibility of irony developing within the poem itself: the Hero would appear to seek that which for him can have no being, so that the poem becomes a kind of inverted romance. But in the first two cantos of *Childe Harold* such promise fails in fulfillment, primarily because the protagonist himself does not emerge. He is introspective to the degree that, from an external viewpoint, he appears unmotivated. Whatever has dissillusioned him has no apparent relation to anything beyond the Self to which he would direct action or thought: it is given no significant dramatic projection. Harold is essentially fleeing rather than searching; he seeks only to escape. . . . A split becomes obvious between the force of the descriptions of scenes through which Harold passes and the limited degree to which these affect him. This, which might seem to be an inevitable and consistent result of his own fragmented world view is in fact an immediate result of the fragmentary nature of the narrative structure of the poem. . . . Within the frame of Harold's travels, narrated as they are by a third person, there is no dramatic tension. This might have been at least established by the elementary device of protagonist-antagonist conflict; or by the more complex instrument of dramatic irony, achieved by the juxtaposition in the speaker of the conscious and unconscious levels of expression, by which the potential offered by the split described above could be realized.

But there is none of this. The first two cantos of *Childe Harold's Pilgrimage* do not essentially pass far beyond that point at which they begin, that of "descriptive poetry"; and the phrase itself, if it is taken to mean poetry that describes without the use of symbolic or dramatic structures, is self-contradictory. At best the method of the poem is only narrative when the supposed subject, Harold as a complex personality, demands that it become dramatic. (pp. 37-9)

The early tales are constructed primarily through the interaction of the elementary themes of Love and Death. In the simpler of the Tales, the principal characters tend, in varying degrees, to assume allegorical dimensions, largely representing either Love, Death or a fusion of both; in the more complex Tales, the characters no longer serve primarily the single, self-evident demands made by the narrative but move toward the achievement of dramatic intensity through the obvious juxtaposition of their conscious and unconscious beings. Of the first type *The Bride of Abydos* and *The Corsair* are examples. *Lara* and *The Siege of Corinth,* read in context as personal recollections by their respective speakers, illustrate the transition to the second type, of which *Parisina* (completed shortly after, but published with, *The Siege of Corinth*) represents the full development. (p. 40)

The relatively slight critical consideration given *Parisina* has been primarily concerned with the question of the poet's failure to bring moral judgment to the work. If this is the criterion, then he failed indeed, for . . . the poet offers neither comment nor implication regarding the good or evil of the actions of the characters. Instead, he presents an essentially dramatic situation, of which the psychological aspects are inescapable. (p. 62)

The third canto of *Childe Harold's Pilgrimage* has been adversely judged on occasion because Byron does not sustain Harold as the central character but, instead, allows the "I" of the poem to usurp Harold's position. Despite the rather apparent fact that the poem lacks the degree of cohesiveness found in the monologues and certain other poems of the later periods, there is reason to attribute greater organization to the poem than this estimate suggests.

The poem may be regarded as a dramatic utterance. The speaker, having failed to achieve interior resolution of his problem, attempts to project it; he strives to create a dream world, in which Harold, the image of the Self or the alter ego, is to assume and dramatize (thereby possibly resolving into harmony) the emotional elements disturbing the speaker. That the speaker is unable to do this simply gives dramatic emphasis to the essential fact that he himself has not found emotional resolution and that, in his conscious attempts to reconstruct a meaningful system of belief out of his experiences, he has not escaped the limits of the Self. Ironically, the failure of the speaker to sustain the image of Harold strengthens rather than weakens the poem.

Isolation, the principal theme of *Childe Harold, III,* is dramatized by the speaker's apostrophe to his daughter, with which the poem opens and to which he returns as he approaches conclusion. . . . Few have failed to notice the general unity that this device imposes upon the poem, but most have found little evidence beyond this of structural cohesion. The highly personal quality of the utterances obviously renders the speaker's isolation emotionally more credible; moreover, it emphasizes that despite his attempts to project, even to universalize, his isolation (thereby, ironically, destroying it by sharing it), he retains it necessarily as an element of the Self as it was in the beginning. Within this framework the elements of the speaker's attempted projection, though they clearly do not form a mechanical unit, follow an organic pattern. . . . (pp. 72-4)

Manfred is not, as it has often been considered, a play that is essentially concerned with the relation between good and evil. The frame of the morality play is in itself misleading if we fail to realize that the play deals not with external verities that seem to strive for Manfred's spirit but with the reaction of his spirit itself to those apparent verities: they do not alter him, but rather in his own consciousness he creates and destroys them, or simply fails to do so. Many have recognized the fact that *Manfred* is a one-character drama, but few seem to have become fully aware of the implications therein. In the several scenes in which Manfred is not actually present, the image of his being dominates all other characters; only as psychological subordinates do these characters themselves achieve structural significance. The question of their origin, in other words, is not crucial and perhaps hardly meaningful—whether they are, within the play as an extended monologue, entirely figmental,

or (the earthly beings at least) in part objectively real. Only in the impact upon the mind of Manfred of the forces or values which these characters represent are they significant. The play is certainly not about things; but only slightly more is it about ideas. Essentially concerned with the consciousness or the Self, it is, broadly, a psychological rather than a philosophic drama. (p. 97)

The pivotal concern of *The Lament of Tasso* is madness, arising quite expectedly from the fact of the speaker's confinement. That Tasso denies outright madness in the opening of the poem but comes to admit a degree of disturbance somewhat later is quite apparent. Of greater significance is the manner in which he demonstrates the nature of his mental state. In the opening lines of the poem he is obviously reversing what to his captors is the normal course of affairs, for he sees himself as one who is not confined because he is mad but, instead, is afflicted with a canker of the mind because he has been confined. . . . The heart itself, affected as much as the brain, images for him both poetic inspiration and the impulse which is at once the cause for his confinement and the means by which he will justify his being and actions in a hostile world. The justification itself, however, is somewhat less than rationally ordered. After briefly describing the conditions "in the cave/ Which is my lair, and— it may be—my grave," Tasso remarks, with perhaps surprising moderation: "All this hath somewhat worn me, and may wear, / But must be borne. I stoop not to despair." (pp. 111-12)

Quite simply, there are in Tasso's consciousness two images of the Self, one of a being indomitable and the other of "a broken reed" with its "last bruise," and much of the tension in the poem arises from the conflict between them. As this becomes crucial and appears to be unresolvable, the speaker seems to break away from what has led to an awareness of the conflict and, as it were, begins again. . . . The thematic distinction between mind and heart is essential to his recurring protest of innocence and sanity, for he has willed no evil: "That thou wert beautiful, and I not blind, / Hath been the sin which shuts me from mankind." He has reached the point of making a substitution for the emotional sustenance given him by the composition of the *Gerusalemme;* it is worth observing that in his rationale the love for Leonora, which we might expect to be his primary mover, now at least appears to become the substitute for literary composition as the source of psychological endurance. . . . His assertion is fully messianic. With all the satisfaction that self-sacrifice brings comes a fusion, for the moment at least, of the two images of the Self, one of the "wretchéd" and the other of the "faithful." . . . (pp. 113-14)

Mazeppa is at once both more serious and more humorous than has been suggested. From the time of its publication many of those commenting upon it have taken the view that it demonstrates either a lack of creative seriousness on the part of the poet or a failure to understand his subject, for the final scene in the poem, in which Charles XII is discovered to have been sleeping for an hour when Mazeppa ends his story, has seemed discordant, in fact destructive of the emotional intensity which the story has developed. But this view does not represent a full understanding of the relation between the situation in which Mazeppa finds himself and the tale which that situation frames, to which the emotional reaction on the part of Mazeppa himself becomes the object of a satire that implies the essential question of the poem—whether experience can yield an organized moral view of the universe such as Mazeppa has appeared to develop. The central character in the poem is a garrulous old man who recounts his youthful adventure in such a way that it becomes the basis for belief in a providential system that will render the present experience endurable. Within the context of the situation, Mazeppa's attempt at rationalization appears absurd, and the abrupt close of the poem, following the end of the story, is justified. (pp. 120-21)

Cain, unlike *Manfred,* is principally concerned with the conflict between good and evil. It offers no resolution, for by the very nature of the total point of view of the play, there is none to offer. The figure upon whom the intellectual question of the play is centered is, to a far more limited degree than Manfred, a total personality: he is largely a consciousness reacting to certain propositions but not so centrally involved as Manfred in the inner conflict between awareness and affirmation. Dominated by his sense of logic, he is moved, as only an absolutist can be moved, toward resolution of the conflict between apparent cosmic injustice and his own sense of right, between the image of his father's God and his own ideal of Good. There is of course to be no resolution. . . . Though he shifts his intellectual position, from his own early absolutism toward Lucifer's cosmic relativism, he cannot make the emotional transition that this demands and in the end responds to the need for absolute action. (p. 136)

Though *Heaven and Earth* is frequently compared with *Cain,* there is but limited intellectual similarity. *Cain* questions the validity and thereby the truth of the essential Hebraic-Christian theodicy. *Heaven and Earth,* far more restricted in both its subject and implications, is certainly simpler in both its structure and its arguments. The principal intellectual concern of the drama, the justice of Divine Election, never is made the object of an exhaustive inquiry. The total viewpoint is clearly anti-Calvinistic, but despite assertion and dramatization, it is not insistently so; near the conclusion, Japhet, without excessive difficulty though little conviction, can accede to his father's wishes and accept the reality, if not the justice, of his father's cosmogony. (p. 155)

Though for both historical and critical reasons *Beppo* and *Don Juan* traditionally fall together in a consideration of Byron's poetry, there are significant differences between the two poems. Of these, length and narrative completeness are most obvious. Equally important is the relative structural complexity, particularly as this is determined in each poem by the nature of the speaker. In *Beppo* he appears to be one, but in *Don Juan* an indefinite many, whose elements kaleidoscopically fall together in an unending sequence so that identical forms never seem quite to reoccur.

The speaker in *Beppo,* though a single figure, is nevertheless an ironic one, whose naïveté and simplicity clash sharply with the nature of the story he is going to tell. At best his protagonist ("His name Giuseppe, called more briefly 'Beppo'") is the least significant of the three principals; the story is really about only Beppo's wife and her lover, the Count. Of this fact the speaker appears to be unaware; similarly, he seems not to know that for the most part his narrative is lost among his digressions. . . . Sexuality is clearly a major theme in *Beppo,* but it is treated with no more direct seriousness than that with which Beppo himself is regarded as the protagonist or Italian society (rather than its antithesis, English society) is seen as the actual object of the speaker's examination. The fact that the speaker seems largely oblivious to what he is doing is perhaps the central reason that the nickname "Beppo" becomes an instrument for the pervading irony in the poem rather than merely a term of familiarity. . . . The speaker's setting and subject are emphatically particular, but, unknown to him, they become, through irony, general and human.

The speaker assumes the center of attention, which might expectedly be held by the protagonist. Through the first twenty stanzas he digresses, but even the digressions do not form a composite image of a personality or Self, any more than the cosmogony of the protagonist in one of the early Tales becomes a compelling whole. (pp. 167-68)

The suggestion that *Don Juan* is constructed largely upon the use of dramatic irony, which the poet began to use early in his career and developed more or less consistently thereafter, runs counter to the dominant tendency in Byron criticism. Many of those who have written about the poem have regarded nearly all utterances in the first person as primarily, and often exclusively, Byron's own. Such a viewpoint arises from excessive literalness in particular instances and from a basic failure to understand the structure of the poem; on occasion it has led critics toward the quest for such values as "sincerity" and perhaps even "consistency."

In most instances the speaker refers to situations or events which Byron actually experienced or observed, and it is perfectly reasonable in a study of the whole being of the poem to point to these and in fact to explore all possibilities of autobiographical reference; this approach is obviously necessary if we are to appreciate the poem as Byron's contemporaries did. But in various cases we know that the speaker cannot have been Byron in his own person. And obvious example is found in that section of the first canto (ccix-ccxi) in which the speaker reports that for a favorable review of the poem he has "bribed my grandmother's review—the British"; William Roberts, editor of *The British Review,* confusing the poet and a persona, emphatically denied that he had received a bribe. . . . To insist in all instances upon the autobiographical aspect of the speaker's utterance leads along *some* false paths; to insist in any instance upon an exclusively autobiographical approach to the poem deprives us of the opportunity to understand what is happening at that point and throughout the poem as a whole. (pp. 174-75)

Some may seek a basis for the assurance of unity in the poem by looking at the tale itself rather than by making extensive biographical correlation. Set amid digression, the narrative in *Don Juan* reminds us, for rather different reasons, of Dr. Johnson's remark about Richardson's novels: "Why, sir, if you were to read Richardson for the story, your impatience would be so much fretted that you would hang yourself." Unlike *Pamela* and *Clarissa,* Byron's poem cannot of course be read for its moral. We approach the hero, seeking that force whose dominance will give unity to the work. What we find is totally ironic. Taken from a tradition of strong heroes, he, like the Anglicized form that is pointedly given his name, is sufficiently altered to be merely a mockery of the prototype. From the speaker's original announcement, "I want a hero," and his decision to take a traditional hero because the present age offers neither heroes nor heroism, it is ironically apparent that this protagonist is especially unheroic. (pp. 175-76)

What then is left? Only the seeming myriad of speakers in the poem. For long sections, occurring more frequently as the poem progresses, the narrative and its protagonist are unceremoniously abandoned. One after another, in sequence or in conflict, the various speakers emerge. Some readers have complained that the principal fault of *Don Juan* is its lack of consistency. This is, instead, its dominant virtue in terms of what it is supposed to do and what it does. At one moment the speaker emerging is naïve, prudish, perhaps stupid; he may be prudent to the point of absurdity, sometimes concerned with exasperating details, elsewhere frightened at the implications of what he recounts. At other times, however, the speaker is worldly, indiscreet, perhaps cynical. . . . The use of various speakers, ironic and among each other inconsistent, to comment upon the method and structure of the poem is perhaps too abundant and in many instances too obvious to require illustration.

In their dramatic function, in *how* they say rather than in *what* they say, the speakers in *Don Juan* achieve the irony that dominates the poem, thereby intensifying what is revealed in its panoramic view: the imperfection in Man's powers, the acute limitations upon what he can achieve for himself, and in fact the impossibility of his achieving an integrated and continuous view of the Self and therefore of the world upon which that Self must impose meaning. *Don Juan* should be regarded as a vast literary joke (some have called it a farce), which is humorous in its means but, beneath the clownish leer, serious in its implications. It is not satire, for it ultimately offers, in its description of the absurdities of the real, no suggestion of the ideal. Its irony is terminal rather than instrumental; this is achieved and sustained principally through a complex of individual monologues, in which the speakers, often unaware of the full situational context for their speeches, frequently reveal to us far more than they intend. (pp. 176-77)

> *William H. Marshall, in his* The Structure of Byron's Major Poems *(© 1962 by the Trustees of the University of Pennsylvania), University of Pennsylvania Press, 1962, 191 p.*

LESLIE A. MARCHAND   (essay date 1965)

Byron was of the world worldly—he had nothing of the transcendental Romanticist's sense of being a seer poet, the voice of some divine afflatus. More than Wordsworth he was "a man speaking to men," not in the language of inspired poetry, but in that of reason and honest feeling.

Byron's slight regard for poetry as an end in itself resulted in verbal carelessness (as well as a reluctance to revise or polish), a cavalier attitude toward formal beauty or symmetry, and a willingness to digress and ramble even in his Popean satires. But his very contempt for poetry contributed to a uniqueness in his literary product which must be considered a compensation for the resultant imperfections of style and structure. Literature as an aesthetic entity, a thing in itself to be admired like a painting or a statue for its artistic qualities, never won his sympathies. (p. 243)

Yet it would be a mistake to accept unqualifiedly the assumption that Byron's poetry is all bad technically. Negligent and offhand as he seemed to be in matters of form and structure, his manuscripts show that he often sought with meticulous care for the words that would match accurately the nuances of his thought or mood. And frequently when he did not revise it was because he had miraculously lighted on the most felicitous phrase in the first spring of his imagination. (pp. 243-44)

He can be subtle when one least expects it. When he says in *Don Juan* that he hates inconstancy he both means it and doesn't mean it. One has to be most on guard when he is mocking. Does he really mean to renounce all amorous writing as he announces at the beginning of the fifth canto, or is the irony forthright and meant to emphasize the opposite point of view?

He means to eschew the kind of amorous writing that Petrarch indulged in—he is going to deal with love realistically and not sentimentally—and he is making sport of the pious critics who have thought his realism conducive to immorality. But even more in his metaphysical speculations, he balances the tensions of unresolved attitudes. His ironic comments on Bishop Berkeley's "sublime discovery" that makes the "Universe universal egotism . . . *all ourselves!*" gives him an inward glimpse of the true nature of his own romantic longings, never abandoned wholly even in his most mocking moments in *Don Juan*. And he can say with both irony and conviction:

> I would shatter
> Gladly all matters down to stone or lead,
> Or adamant, to find the World a spirit.

It may be that Byron's final appeal to a disillusioned world, whether in the nineteenth century or the twentieth, is that he is as honest as we wish we could be. It may be the honesty of an anarchic mind, but it has its wholesome qualities, the strength of its weaknesses in formal poetic expression and in consistency. (pp. 244-45)

[While] present-day readers lean strongly toward the realistic and satiric in Byron, and while it is the fashion to point out that he had one foot (presumably the sound one) firmly planted in the eighteenth century—in its rationalism, its common sense, and its distrust of what Byron called "entusymusy"—it is still important to remember that the other foot, even though halt, stood as firmly in the romantic nineteenth century. The core of his thinking and the basis of his poetry is romantic aspiration. The final picture is one of a man who, reluctantly, because he is still the romantic, has come to terms with an imperfect world—at least to the point of finding it an amusing place. His romantic zest for life and experience lends vigor to both the comic and the tragic aspects of the discrepancy between reality and appearance, between imperfections and pretensions. (p. 245)

> *Leslie A. Marchand, in his* Byron's Poetry: A Critical Introduction *(copyright © 1965 by Leslie A. Marchand; reprinted by permission of Houghton Mifflin Company), Houghton Mifflin, 1965, 261 p.*

W. PAUL ELLEDGE   (essay date 1968)

To begin an essay on Byron by pointing to the poet's dualistic nature is perhaps a critical commonplace, but it is nevertheless the proper point of departure for any study of his poetry, not necessarily because the personality of the poet lurks threateningly beneath the verse, but because the distinguishing feature of his thought and art is a vacillation between the poles of orthodox dualism and romantic monism. All of the other paradoxes in his works are ultimately traceable to this fundamental and conscious dichotomy: the fluctuation between emphasis on intellect and emotion, classicism and relativistic subjectivism, pantheism and realism, flesh and spirit, stasis and change, spontaneity and ratiocination, impressionism and formalism, vastness and finitude, energy and ennui—this oscillation is rooted in an exceedingly flexible temperament which refused to settle on one metaphysical doctrine as the governing principle of the universe. (p. 4)

What must be stressed, however, is Byron's absolute fidelity to accurate factual and emotional representation in his poetry, his unqualified sincerity in presenting what at any given moment his mood might have convinced him was truth. (p. 5)

Byron's flexibility of thought was the most characteristic feature of his mind. In all likelihood, Byron had no more abandoned a mechanistic view than he had finally accepted a dynamic view, no matter how attractive either one might have appeared. Consequently, the dialectical tension generated by his emotional desire for absolutism and his intellectual recognition of the relativistic or pluralistic had two effects: it produced in the life a psychological restiveness which eliminated any prospect of emotional stability; but it issued in poetry vital with the persistence of a questing intelligence, dubious but not despairing of terminal reconciliation.

Given the elastic and exploratory qualities of Byron's thought, then, one might expect the most frequent and representative images in his poetry to bear upon the dichotomies in man's character. . . . [Similarities,] analogies, correspondences among two or more ostensibly disparate objects, concepts, or experiences are distinguished by the poet for the purpose of illuminating afresh some facet of human existence. Since poetry—even Byron's poetry, I would insist—is a severely concentrative form, the writer will necessarily not only depend to a large degree upon the evocative value—the connotative richness—of his images for the communication of his themes, but he will also require of those images clear elucidation of the complex relationships which they attempt to establish. If such relationships are made explicit, relevant, and intelligible—if, that is, some sort of order and control is imposed upon metaphorical complexity and diversity—and if the connotative value of the image assists in clarifying the idea being communicated, the image may be judged successful. Byron's images, I think, function actively as complements and reinforcements to his themes; thus they represent, in small, the ultimate union of his intellectual and imaginative faculties.

"Fire" and "clay" are Byron's favorite metaphorical vehicles for illustrating the paradoxical composition of human nature: the first representing variously passion, aspiration, freedom, motion, emotion, energy, infinity, and divinity; and the second typifying intellect, frustration, bondate, ennui, sterility, finitude, and mortality. . . . This fire-clay antinomy, however, is but one member (although the most significant one) of Byron's quartet of preferred imagistic motifs. Subordinate to it but frequently used in conjunction with it are, on the one hand, antipodal images of light and darkness, and on the other, images of organic growth and mechanical stasis—the figures of light and growth generally corresponding in symbolic and connotative value to the qualities of fire imagery noted above, and the figures of darkness and stasis having a similar relationship to clay imagery. Finally, the image of the counterpart (or the *Doppelgänger* motif) appears with sufficient frequency to merit inclusion here: the counterpart configuration may be defined as an actual or imaginary persona or phenomenon which reflects all or part of a protagonist's character, or, more precisely, what the protagonist should have been or desires to become. In each of these image patterns, polarities are juxtaposed; and . . . the thematic purpose of the juxtaposition is twofold. Byron means first of all to figure forth the essential dichotomy of human nature, and second, to dramatize the pathos and tragedy of mortality, precipitated by man's efforts to reconcile the antithetical impulses of his being. That such a reconciliation is finally impossible is suggested again and again by Byron's antipodal imagistic construct.

The poet's assumptions about the character of human existence are not confined, or course, to metaphorical representation in these four motifs. Concomitant with them are minor figurative

patterns which extend and reinforce the philosophical statements advanced through the principal imagistic substructure. The theme of man's "fatality," for instance, is frequently encapsulated in figures of decomposition and waste; or, conversely, Byron finds in the more spectacular natural phenomena—sun, moon, star, thundercloud, lightning, mountain-peak—figures to complement his representation of man's divine qualities. (pp. 7-9)

In three of the early . . . oriental romances, *The Corsair, Lara,* and *Parisina,* Byron dramatizes the efforts of three protagonists to harmonize their visions of an ideal realm with their rational perceptions of the real world; and he reinforces these conflicts with imagistic patterns opposing sunlight and darkness, heat and cold, solidity and fragility, dreams and realities. Whatever psychological equilibrium Conrad the Corsair and Lara achieve, furthermore, is in part due to the influence of their respective counterparts, Medora and Kaled; and the depicture of Azo's *(Parisina)* attempt to integrate his intellectual faculties (presented in statuesque and metallic figures) with his emotional tendencies (presented in images of fire, sunlight, and fertile vegetation) is a clear presentiment of similar metaphorical use in Byron's later dramas.

The poems of Byron's second period . . . —*The Prisoner of Chillon, Childe Harold's Pilgrimage,* Canto III, and *Manfred*—are basically organized by the theme of the disparity between the sensuous and imaginative worlds. The inability of the Prisoner, for example, to reconcile his sensory and intellectual faculties is imaged throughout the poem in the juxtaposition of light, plant, and bird configurations with figures of darkness, stones, and chains. Harold and Manfred, both unable to bridge the gulf between the claims of the flesh and the aspirations of the spirit, attempt empathic identification with arresting natural and preternatural phenomena. Accompanying and complementing their egoistic projections are figures of meteoric flight and spectacular collapse, flaming desire and icy frustration, cosmic freedom and enslaved mortality—all of them designed to picture a mortal wracked by the incompatibility of body and soul. (p. 10)

Three dramas, *Marino Faliero, Sardanapalus,* and *Cain,* constitute my examination of Byron's third period. . . . In the first, the ethical ambivalence of the hero's thought and action—his reluctance to commit himself either to the dictates of his mind or the desires of his heart—is effectively figured in patterns of half-light; and this basic pattern is supported by minor motifs emphasizing blood, bestial, statuesque, and organic figures. In *Sardanapalus,* the twin tendencies of the hero's character toward rational and authoritative rulership and toward passivity and self-indulgence are depicted in his bisexuality; again, duality of character is marked by the opposition of metallic (or stone) figures with floral images. The evolution of Sardanapalus' "divinity," moreover, initiated and sustained by his counterpart Myrrah, is figured in images of light and darkness. Physical, intellectual, and theological darkness and light, vastness and finitude, freedom and slavery, clear-sightedness and myopia are the chief resources for Byron's imagistic explorations in *Cain:* the hero soars only to plunge, sees only to be blinded, is emancipated only to be rebound. Here, too, the figure of the counterpart finds its most singular representation in Adah, the wife and sister of the hero. Cain is indeed the most genuinely pitiable victim in Byron's works, for to him alone is verified what all the other protagonists only sense—the deplorable minuteness of man amidst the universal immensity. (p. 11)

My purpose is not to demonstrate any marked progression of thought in Byron's verse or to show that the dichotomies of the poetry are finally reconciled. Byron's development must be measured in terms of multi-leveled accumulation rather than linear progression; and, judged by this standard, the rich and complex poetry of the later dramas shows a decisive advance over the crude use of imagery in the early tales. . . . Beginning with an assumption about the duality of human character, he designed a dialectical figurative pattern to encompass the implications of his assumption, and elaborated, with impressive diversity, upon that fundamental pattern. The complexity and variety of his imagery emphatically show that

> From the star
> To the winding worm all life is motion; and
> In life *commotion* is the extremest point
> Of life.

Despite the mixture of metaphors here, the passage illustrates the poet's refusal to be restrained by any single world, philosophy, attitude, or mode of conduct. Forever spinning between the poles of dualism and monism, intellect and emotion, flesh and spirit, clay and fire, he represents with extraordinary passion and insight, through his imagery, the irreconcilable opposites which are responsible for the "commotion" of moral existence. (pp. 11-12)

> *W. Paul Elledge, in his* Byron and the Dynamics of
> Metaphor *(copyright © 1968 by Vanderbilt Univer-*
> *sity Press), Vanderbilt University Press, 1968, 155 p.*

JAMES TWITCHELL   (essay date 1975)

Manfred is Byron's most "Romantic" work, both in character and in theme. Here is an almost Faustian man, who has spent his life pushing towards a union of himself and invisible forces beyond. . . . Like his peers Prometheus or Endymion, Manfred finally does what no eighteenth-century character could ever do: he transcends body and mind of this world to enter a "world beyond." But unlike them he is not seeking the future; like the Ancient Mariner, he is fleeing the past.

Despite the Romantic character of its hero, other attributes of *Manfred* make it an uneasy ally of "The Rime of the Ancient Mariner," *Prometheus Unbound* or *Endymion.* The most common problem that critics have faced is that the "world beyond" that Byron created has little in common with the imaginary worlds of Coleridge, Shelley, and Keats. For the super-naturalism Byron created above Manfred is rigorously and logically organized; it is not as much a creation of the imagination as it is the result of imaginative borrowing. With the other Romantic poets, it is not always necessary to understand precisely how their supernatural worlds operate, for their poems can be read and appreciated in spite of the supernatural machinery. But in *Manfred* this is not the case. Here there are no loose ends, no supernumeraries in the heavens.

Like a Neoclassicist, Byron has built a very sturdy Chain of Being; but like a Romantic, he has used it not to keep man in his place, but to show that there are certain links man can snap and certain ones he cannot. (p. 601)

There has been almost no attempt to dismantle the world above and around Manfred, partly because critics have assumed that *Manfred,* like other supernatural Romantic poems, really does not depend on the spirit level for "meaning." It has been assumed that the spirits in *Manfred,* like the Polar Spirit in "The Rime of the Ancient Mariner" or the spirits in *Endymion*

or at the end of *Prometheus Unbound,* are included more for adornment than for actual thematic consequences. They are important, but they are not crucial to an understanding. But to understand Manfred, it is necessary to understand what is above him. For what Byron has done, especially in the second act, is to create a world above his protagonist that mirrors the psychological world within.

There is ample evidence that the farther Manfred moves away from natural states, the closer he moves to psychological phenomena. This is most obvious with Arimanes, where Manfred is dealing not so much with the power behind external evil as with the personification of deeply-buried impulses for evil within himself. This gradual change as the play progresses from natural to psychological, from surface to myth, is part of what makes *Manfred* such a Romantic poem. And this change is achieved, as it is in many other Romantic poems, through the use of a supernatural spirit world. (p. 602)

To understand what kind of magician Byron intended Manfred to be, it is helpful to remember that 1) at the turn of the century there was a revival in interest in Near Eastern mythologies; and that 2) in 1816 Byron, mainly as the result of his association with Shelley, became fascinated with the works of the ancient Neoplatonic mystics of Alexandria: Iamblichus, Plotinus, Porphyry, and a number of others. A brief explanation of their cosmic system will show why it was so adaptable to Byron's artistic needs.

The Alexandrian Neoplatonists believed in a graduated cosmos which emanated in steps from the One downward to the phenomenal world. The most obvious attraction for such a cosmic picture is easily seen, for wherever there are plateaus in this cosmic staircase, there is the potentiality for psychological correspondences. This is the basic principle behind all myth, namely that the outer world will mirror inner space, and the Neoplatonic mythologies are no exception. They simply are more organized and logical than most. (p. 603)

Iamblichus believed that at the very top of this cosmic pyramid is the One—the force of unity for all life. Below this point— the point of God—emanate the rational and universal souls downward through the angelic, archonic, heroic, and daemonic orders to man.

The chief concern of Iamblichus' *On the Mysteries* is not, however, the topography of the cosmos or psyche, but rather the problem of how the magician can communicate with the daemons which exist in the lowest of the material spheres or plateaus. This is of considerable importance, for the theurgist (a "white magician" as opposed to the goetist, or "black magician") is responsible for preserving material harmony on the earth. He is responsible for making things go. And to do this he energies different types of daemons. These daemons who mediate between the gods and the material world are organized into distinct hierarchies. (p. 605)

According to Iamblichus, these spirits have no bodies of their own but can assume bodies on command. . . . They are also without passions. . . . In *Manfred* the daemons never appear physically and are distinguished only by their voices. In unison the Seventh Spirit and the six daemons claim that

> We have no forms, beyond the elements
> Of which we are the mind and principle:
> But choose a form—in that we will appear, . . .

and when Manfred is unable to choose a form it is the Seventh Spirit, not the six daemons, who has the power or will to assume physical shape.

Since the daemons are the productive and operative executors of nature. . . , they have power only over the four elements, not over the mind or psyche of man. (p. 606)

Next higher in Byron's Chain of Being is the enigmatic Seventh Spirit of the "star with rules thy destiny.". . .

But it is obvious from the play that the star does not control Manfred, nor does Manfred control the star. . . . Once the metaphysical pattern has been understood, the role of the Seventh Spirit is understandable. The Neoplatonists believed that everyone received a personal daemon at the hour of birth, which then controlled both body and environment. These "celestial animals of the gods" exist in higher heavenly spheres and therefore are more powerful than the other daemons since they are closer to the "One."

Manfred's star, however, has become

> A wandering mass of shapeless flame,
> A pathless comet, and a curse,
> The menace of the universe, . . .

which serves to heighten the awfulness of Manfred's fate in much the same way that Childe Harold's birth "beneath some remote inglorious star" substantiates his melancholy. Byron's use of star lore is probably not drawn directly from the Neoplatonists; more likely it is a syncretism of ancient and then-current astrological beliefs. What is interesting, however, is that the Seventh Spirit's place in the Chain of Being of *Manfred* is consistent with his place in the hierarchies of the Alexandrian mystics. (pp. 607-08)

As we move higher up through the "daemonic realm" we start to move deeper into Manfred. The characters become more organic and personalized. Above the daemons and Manfred's star, both chronologically and spatially, is the Witch of the Alps. She resembles Shelley's Witch of Atlas only in the sense that they both resemble the "Venus Genetrix" of Lucretius' *On the Nature of Things*. Once again Manfred conjures her presence by use of a theurgitic sign, but unlike the invisible wisps of daemons previously conjured, she has a form in which

> The charms of Earth's least mortal daughters grow
> To an unearthly stature, in an essence
> Of purer elements. . . .

As the ruling principle of material beauty, or as the "Mighty Mother" of all earthly life, it is implied . . . , she controls the purpose of the six daemons. In other words, she would probably be at the level of "god" in the Neoplatonic hierarchy. But the Witch of the Alps' role is more important structurally than thematically. She binds the Neoplatonic and the Zoroastrian, allowing Manfred opportunity to explain "my sciences, / My long pursued and superhuman art," and to refer obliquely to Astarte, his "heart-crushed love" Both of these points in tandem are important, for it is guilt-possessed Manfred who actively seeks out the higher celestial powers with his magic, not vice versa. He is "possessed" only in the sense that he must remember and be slave to those memories. But he still has the power to will. (p. 609)

[When] the Witch asks why she has been called, Manfred answers,

> To look upon thy beauty—nothing further.
> The face of the earth hath maddened me, and I
> Take refuge in her mysteries, and pierce
> To the abodes of those who govern her—

But they can nothing aid me. I have sought
From them what they could not bestow, and now
I search no further. . . .

But when he realizes that such a life demands that he "swear obedience to [her] will, and do / [Her] bidding" . . . , he refuses and discharges her. Manfred is now more alone than ever. On the supernatural level he has transcended the world of the Intermediary Spirits and on the psychological level he has refused a Lotus-Eater's life in Nature. He is now to pit himself against his own mind and the "unnatural" universe.

This unnatural universe takes on a singularly malicious quality when Byron next draws from the mythologies of Zoroastrianism to complete the metaphysical pattern. Whereas Manfred's powers over the daemons of Nature, his star, and the Witch of the Alps were not complete, at least he had the power to evoke and discharge. With the phantoms of the second act, Manfred's powers are less distinct and this is psychologically sensible, for man has more control of the world outside than the one within.

The cosmos of the Zoroastrian religion that Byron knew was one split and united by the constant tensions between Good and Evil. Ormazd, the Lord of Goodness and Light, wages constant war against Ahriman, the Lord of Evil and Darkness. Beneath these great patriarchs extend vast sublunar worlds of daemons, who are good or evil depending on which hierarchy they are in, that of Ormazd or that of Ahriman. This dualism is marked and distinct—man is given the choice of worshiping either the Good or the Evil. . . . Not only is the Chain of Being maintained as it is in Neoplatonism, but even the same numerology is employed, except that now the six spirits are actively and consciously malefic, whereas in Neoplatonism they are noisy but innocuous.

After Manfred has refused the solace of submission to the Witch of the Alps . . . , he appears in the court of Arimanes . . . , presumably by his own volition as there is no mention of his being conjured "up" or of his conjuring Arimanes "down." Byron himself glosses "Arimanes" as being Ahriman, the evil principle of Zoroastrianism. (pp. 609-10)

Surrounding Arimanes are six Spirits whose proximity to the godhead indicates that these are the six Spirits who minister the will of the veil principle to the lower spirits, in this case to the three Destinies. In Zoroastrian mythology each of these is charged with the working of a specific evil. But in *Manfred* these six Spirits seem to have no function other than to pester Manfred with commands to kneel and praise Arimanes.

One thing they do, however, is to provide Manfred with an opportunity to allude to a still higher (in fact, the highest) power in the hierarchy. Manfred demands that Arimanes

> bow down to that which is above him
> That overruling Infinte—The Maker
> Who made him not for worship—let him kneel,
> And we kneel together. . . .

Whether or not this "overruling Infinite" is Ormazd . . . the Neoplatonic One, or what Iamblichus calls "First God and King," it makes little difference. What is important is that it established the topmost or innermost limit as being Good and ultimately victorious. There is the implication that even in this imperfect universe redemption and salvation are possible to those who resist the compromise with evil. (pp. 611-12)

What is intrinsic to both [the Neoplatonic and the Zoroastrian systems] is their fundamental dualism. In Zoroastrianism, it is a dualism of Good and Evil in the cosmos. In Neoplatonism, it is a dualism of the higher and lower souls of men. As we have seen in the first act, Manfred's magic, made possible by the control of his higher soul, allows him some power over the material daemons. But his power is useless, for the six daemons can direct only the forces of nature, not the will of man. In the second act we learn that it is his once-detested will that prevents Manfred from succumbing to the evil forces of Arimanes. Ironically, what saves Manfred from capitulation to evil is the same thing that he had once wanted to destroy. And in the third act we get a kind of synthetic restatement of the theme, this time in a Christian context, with the Abbot begging Manfred to "reconcile thyself with thy own soul, / And thy own soul in Heaven." . . . This is the final redoubling of the psychological and metaphysical, inside-and-outside patterns dovetailed. The tension between Manfred and his soul is mirrored in the tensions between his soul and a spirit world beyond. (p. 613)

Manfred was fated to be born free, and in the cosmic system which Byron created, freedom is only slavery. Byron develops his own special brand of irony by creating a tragedy that traces neither the fall of a "high" man nor the demise of a "common" man, but rather one which shows a superhuman character fated by the very nature of his mind and the universe to be destroyed not but defeated. He is a very sophisticated Byronic hero; we are never sure that he "comes out on top." . . .

Manfred's cosmos allows spiritual victory to come from physical destruction. Manfred realizes that he is chained to the natural and purposeless world by his mortality, and accepts death as meaningless because it is inevitable.

This reading is reinforced by what we see happening within Manfred. As with any psychodrama, the battle is with evil, not with death; within the mind, not within the cosmos. In this context it is the refusal to submit to Arimanes, a refusal in his own self to give in to the tyranny of evil, that destroys and saves Manfred.

Only in the terms of the microcosm-macrocosm, the world inside and the world outside, do we find Byron in the tradition of Spenser, Shakespeare, Milton, and Pope. Philosophically he is far removed from them and is closer to the Romantics. The symbolism inherent in the supernatural hierarchy magnifies Manfred's capacity to think and feel, since he can move between the two by virtue of his magic. As one might expect, his emotions become extreme. His thoughts and actions gain an almost cosmic significance through the supernatural quality of his powers. Whereas for the earlier poets the macrocosm was an imperturbable system "out there" of which this world is a dull reflection, a characteristically iconoclastic Byron conjoins the two. And in doing so, he becomes uncharacteristically Romantic. (p. 614)

> *James Twitchell, "The Supernatural Structure of Byron's 'Manfred'," in* Studies in English Literature, 1500-1900 *(© 1975 William Marsh University), Vol. XV, No. 4, Autumn, 1975, pp. 601-14.*

JOHN D. JUMP (essay date 1975)

[Most] of those who are interested in Byron seem . . . to regard his letters and journals as a mass of autobiographical documents which happen to make entertaining reading rather than as a body of writings with some claim to the kind of attention we normally reserve for more deliberate literary works. (p. 16)

Their most conspicuous quality is their spontaneity. Never, we feel, can written utterance have been less premeditated, less rehearsed, less inhibited, less controlled. Even his complaints of boredom and depression become exuberant. (p. 17)

Byron's letters are remarked for their freshness, their unhesitating, uncensored response to the immediate situation. Many of them are gay, mocking, irreverent. Even when his recurrent melancholy weighs heavily upon him, he remains capable of asserting himself humorously against it. Sometimes he writes earnestly and purposefully. On such occasions, his humour may manifest itself as grim or savage satire. Whatever his mood, his correspondence exhibits an unfailing exuberance and vigour. Inconsistencies among his attitudes and opinions do not trouble him. If each of two incompatible positions seems to him to be tenable, he occupies both and cheerfully laughs off the contradiction.

He seems always to write with his correspondent vividly in mind. To Hobhouse his manner is frank, hearty, forthright, and trenchant. While he never quite forgets that he is an aristocrat and John Murray a tradesman, he soon comes to address his publisher as a respected friend. His warm fondness for Moore finds frequent and very cordial expression. A slightly patronising playfulness enlivens his affectionate letters to his half-sister, Augusta. A similar tone makes itself felt in his early letters to young Harness; for example, he parodies the kind of advice that most men think age authorises them to dispense to their juniors:

> Now, Child, what art thou doing? *reading I
> trust*. I want to see you take a degree, remember
> this is the most important period of your life,
> & don't disappoint your Papa & your Aunts &
> all your kin, besides myself, don't you know
> that all male children were begotten for the
> express purpose of being Graduates?
> (8 December 1811)
> (pp. 25-6)

Every characteristic letter of Byron's is accurately adapted for its particular recipient. Equally, it springs directly from the unique situation in which he wrote it. (p. 26)

In his journals, Byron has naturally no opportunity of exhibiting that astute awareness of each individual correspondent that delights us in the letters. At the same time, he does not seem in his journals to be writing merely for himself. . . . [Even] in the journals of 1813-14 and 1821 he appears to have an audience in view. A writer who wished merely to put something on record for his own interest would surely make less use of the oaths and exclamations, repetitions, parentheses, and abrupt halts which have the effect of projecting Byron dramatically upon his readers' imaginations. Since he certainly did not write his journals for immediate publication, any audience that he had in mind must have belonged to posterity. Judging by the tone and feeling of his journals, he must have imagined it as composed preponderantly of men like his friends Hobhouse, Murray, Moore, and Kinnaird. (p. 29)

In journals and letters alike, Byron allows his natural mobility of temperament to reveal itself in rapid and sometimes subversive fluctuations of mood; vigorously and racily, he sets down what he has observed; and he comments wittily, sympathetically, humorously, or mockingly upon whatever has excited his interest. He is one of the most versatile and provocative of our letter-writers and diarists; and more than any other he has left us a collection of writings that constitute a brilliant and incisive self-portrait, above all a dramatic self-portrait, of one whom we can never know too well. (p. 34)

John D. Jump, ''Byron's Prose,'' in Byron: A Symposium, *edited by John D. Jump (copyright 1975 by John D. Jump; reprinted by permission of Barnes & Noble Books, a Division of Littlefield, Adams & Co.), Barnes & Noble, 1975, pp. 16-34.*

FREDERICK W. SHILSTONE   (essay date 1979)

Byron is an anomaly among the major poets of his age in appearing to violate the principle that Romantics write best when they write briefly; while many of his longer works certainly have strongly lyrical elements, the fame that drew [composer Isaac Nathan, Byron's collaborator for the *Hebrew Melodies,*] to him was based on the satire of *English Bards and Scotch Reviewers* and the narrative exoticism of *Childe Harold's Pilgrimage* and the *Turkish Tales.* . . . Byron had several reasons for avoiding lyric poetry; his only previous attempt to publish a collection of short songs, *Hours of Idleness,* had met with strong critical hostility, and he had since found easy fame in the broader plane of *Childe Harold* and the narratives based on his adventures in the Orient. . . .

Once convinced to lend his name to the *Hebrew Melodies,* Byron found in that project the quality he needed to stir his lyric impulses: the large expanse of the *collection* of short poems in which he could play songs off one against another and thus achieve the broader effects of a work like *Childe Harold.* (p. 45)

Beyond merely providing Byron with the larger canvas he required, the *Melodies* scheme had several other fortuitous qualities. Fundamentally, these poems were to be given harmonic accompaniment and were to cover the history of a society in which music, in the form of David's harp, was assigned almost mystical power. In this knowledge, Byron, writing new lyrics and revising some he already had in manuscript, made the *Hebrew Melodies* into a discourse on the power of song, in which each poem, in addition to standing alone, informs the overall development of the collection. Byron began with an awareness of the relationship between the power of music and the expressive force of his own verse and wrote lyrics exploring the connection between his poetry and the world in which he found materials for it. To this end, the *Hebrew Melodies* tend to cluster in identifiable groups based on common themes, images, and rhythms. . . . The unity of the collection depends upon the reader's total absorption of all the melodies; the effect of the poems is cumulative rather than developmental. More like a tapestry than a written narrative, the *Melodies* unfold their meaning differently depending upon the sequence in which they are read, but they unfold it completely nonetheless.

The *Melodies* fall into four groups, identifiable by the technical and thematic connections among their individual members. Though these groups are neither rigid nor mutually exclusive, they broadly represent the various parts in the aesthetic dialogue the *Hebrew Melodies* comprise. Some of the lyrics clearly serve as an introduction to the overriding concerns of the collection: the power of music and how it relates to artistic expression in general. Others find their subject in the tragic history of the Jews and in general human themes illustrated by that history. The remaining biblical poems in the collection are visionary;

their subject is not the course of history, but, rather, the timeless realm of miracles and a possible afterlife. Finally, there are those lyrics, some of them written before the *Hebrew Melodies* plan developed, that are not directly concerned with sacred themes or the history of the Jews. Their very inclusion shows Byron's aim of making the collection more than a simple transcription of biblical passages; the relationship between these secular verses and their sacred counterparts is the vital link among all the *Melodies.* (p. 46)

The ''monarch minstrel'' of Byron's poem is of course David, under whose reign music gained a prominent role in the celebration of sacred rites. As a result, David becomes a major symbol . . . in the *Hebrew Melodies* collection; his harp is the most powerful force in the verses, since it holds the ability to transform men more radically than any other human invention, including the political structures often emphasized in discussions of the *Hebrew Melodies,* can do:

> No ear so dull, no soul so cold
> That felt not, fired not to the tone,
> 'Till David's Lyre grew mightier than his throne! . . .

The harp and its music transcend the simple realities of this world and possess a force beyond any we can know here. Further, the harp represents a universal; while its specific chords are ''heard on earth no more'' . . . , as the modern Jew Byron has created to speak these lines indicates, its power lives on in the abstractions ''Devotion and her daughter Love'' . . . , legacies that are the visionary embodiments of an ideal left vague in this particular work. Generally, though David's songs become associated in this poem with ideal creatures of the imagination; both equally raise man above the corrupting processes of earth. (p. 47)

The *Hebrew Melodies* are . . . Byron's discourse on art, an examination of how poetry takes the materials of a transient world of process and lends them the grace of immortality. As such, these poems comprise an important experiment in genre, a true lyric *collection,* and thus prepare for more elaborate volumes like Robert Lowell's *Notebook* and John Berryman's *Dream Songs.* This experiment is one of Byron's gifts to the history of literary form. On a more immediate and personal level, the *Melodies* represent an atypical moment in Byron's collected works, an almost Keatsian interlude between the unbridled melancholy and defiance of the *Turkish Tales* and the suicidal vision of *Manfred,* the first major result of the poet's exile from England. That Byron realized he was engaged in the most unstinting celebration of art in his career is made obvious in the Hebrew melody **''My Soul is Dark.''** While this poem is a dramatic versification of I Samuel 16: 14-23, it is clear that Byron chose this text because he could use it to reveal his own thoughts. The speaker here finds himself in a melancholy fit, one only the famous ''harp'' can cure; through song, he states, relief is possible. His heart is ''. . . doomed to know the worst, / And break at once—or yield to song.'' . . . In *Hebrew Melodies,* Byron found himself able, at least temporarily, to ''yield to song'' and thus to celebrate the palliative nature of the art that was, if primarily in its satiric and narrative forms, making him more and more famous. (p. 51)

Frederick W. Shilstone, ''The Lyric Collection As Genre: Byron's 'Hebrew Melodies','' in Concerning Poetry *(copyright © 1979, Western Washington University), Vol. 12, No. 1, Spring, 1979, pp. 45-52.*

ADDITIONAL BIBLIOGRAPHY

Ashton, Thomas L. "Byronic Lyrics for David's Harp: *The Hebrew Melodies.*" *Studies in English Literature 1500-1900* XII, No. 4 (Autumn 1972): 665-81.

    Claims that Byron wrote the lyrics with music in mind, and that they fit into the tragic concepts of his work as a whole.

Brandes, Georg. "Byron: The Passionate Personality," "Byron: His Self-Absorption," "Byron: The Revolutionary Spirit," "Comic and Tragic Realism," "Culmination of Naturalism," and "Byron's Death." In his *Naturalism in Nineteenth Century Literature,* pp. 251-364. New York: Russell & Russell, 1957.

    Examines the whole of Byron's career—literary and political—in the context of the influence it had on other European thinkers. These essays claim that Byron was the major influence on both French and German thought of the early nineteenth century.

Du Bos, Charles. *Byron and the Need of Fatality.* Translated by Ethel Colburn Mayne. London and New York: Putnam, 1932, 287 p.

    A speculative biography dealing with the years 1812-1816. This book concentrates almost completely on Byron's character, and examines possible causes of his (presumed) incest.

Elton, Oliver. "The Present Value of Byron." In his *Essays and Addresses,* pp. 44-69. New York: Longmans, Green & Co., 1939.

    Critical investigation of Byron's ability as a narrative writer and lyricist.

Farrell, John P. "Byron: Rebellion and Revolution." In his *Revolution as Tragedy: The Dilemma of the Moderate from Scott to Arnold,* pp. 131-86. Ithaca and London: Cornell University Press, 1980.

    Places Byron in the tradition of the aristocratic moderate, claiming that personal rebellion, rather than popular revolution, was his main goal.

Gleckner, Robert F. *Byron and the Ruins of Paradise.* Baltimore: The Johns Hopkins Press, 1967, 365 p.

    Sees Byron's recurrent metaphor as the eternal loss of paradise and a continuing hell on earth.

Hunt, Leigh. *Lord Byron and Some of His Contemporaries; with Recollections of the Author's Life, and of His Visit to Italy.* 2 vols. London: Henry Colburn, 1828.*

    A cranky account of many of Byron's frailties, which many see as an unjustified and sometimes false personal attack.

Joseph, M. K. *Byron the Poet.* London: Victor Gollancz Ltd., 1964, 352 p.

    A comprehensive view of Byron's poetry, which synthesizes previous work and adds new insights. This book has a particularly enlightening section on *Don Juan.*

Knight, G. Wilson. "The Two Eternities: An Essay on Byron." In his *The Burning Oracle: Studies in the Poetry of Action.* Folcroft, PA: The Folcroft Press, Inc., 1939, 292 p.

    An insightful essay concerning Byron's merging of inner and outer states.

Leavis, F. R. "The Augustan Tradition: Byron's Satire." In his *Revaluation: Tradition & Development in English Poetry,* pp. 148-53. New York: George W. Stewart, Publisher, Inc., 1947.

    Claims that Byron failed in his attempts to write satire in the Augustan mode, and that *The Vision of Judgment* has power precisely because he found a way to write satire ignoring the Augustan virtues.

Lovell, Ernest J., Jr. *Byron: The Record of a Quest; Studies in a Poet's Concept and Treatment of Nature.* Austin: The University of Texas Press, 1949, 270 p.

    Sees Byron's quest in terms of religion, psychology, and intellectualism, and relates his various attitudes to his treatment of nature in his work.

Marchand, Leslie A. *Byron: A Biography.* 3 vols. New York: Alfred A. Knopf, 1957.

    A comprehensive critical biography by a major Byron scholar. This book is the definitive modern source for Byron's life.

Moore, Thomas. *The Life of Lord Byron; with His Letters and Journals.* 2 vols. Philadelphia: Lippincott, Grambo, & Co., 1853.

    A rather impartial biography, considering its having been written by a friend, with some interesting anecdotes and valuable primary material.

Quennell, Peter. *Byron: The Years of Fame.* New York: The Viking Press, 1935, 320 p.

    A vivid account of Byron's last years in England. This book sketches Byron and the people around him in great detail.

Robertson, J. Michael. "Aristocratic Individualism in Byron." *Studies in English Literature 1500-1900* XVII, No. 4 (Autumn 1977): 639-55.

    Discusses Byron's views on the aristocracy—how he both identifies with and sets himself apart from it.

Russell, Bertrand. "Byron." In his *A History of Western Philosophy,* pp. 746-52. New York: Simon and Schuster, 1945.

    Discusses the "aristocratic rebel" in the context of the development of western culture.

Trueblood, Paul G. "Byron's Political Realism." *The Byron Journal,* No. 1 (1973): 50-8.

    Describes Byron's preference of political action to idealism and exaltation of the imagination.

Wesche, Ulrich. "Goethe's Faust and Byron's Manfred: The Curious Transformation of a Motif." *Revue de litterature comparée* 50, No. 3 (July-Sept. 1976): 286-90.*

    Explains how Byron took a minor theme in *Faust*—"the curse of self-consciousness"—and turned it into one of the most important themes in *Manfred.*

Lewis Carroll

1832-1898

(Pseudonym of Charles Lutwidge Dodgson) English novelist, poet, satirist, and essayist.

Carroll led a dual career. Most of the time he was C. L. Dodgson, the shy, stammering mathematics professor, but on occasion he became Lewis Carroll, the dynamic fantasist and parodist. Dodgson may be viewed as having had an interesting blend of two personalities. One embodied the conventional, Victorian reserve and repression while the other one rejected such restraints with his creative impulse. The great artistry of his fantasy assures him a dignified place in the history of letters. Today, the question of his alleged prurient interest in young girls (he has been criticized for photographing nude children) draws little more than a giggle from critics. And whether critics psychoanalyze Carroll's works, or look at them as brilliant nonsense, they are almost unanimous in proclaiming his great talent.

The son of a country pastor, Dodgson led a quiet childhood, showing a precocity in mathematics and parody. He went to Oxford at age 18, and was made a fellow of Christ Church two and a half years later. He was to remain there for the rest of his life, lecturing in mathematics and writing an occasional parody on a local political matter.

He began publishing in 1860, with *A Syllabus of Plane Algebraical Geometry*, an uninspired mathematical treatise. But the greatest influence on the works for which he is remembered was an inquisitive young girl named Alice Liddell, the daughter of the dean of Christ Church. It is reported that *Alice's Adventures in Wonderland* is a transcription of a story Carroll told Alice and her two sisters on a boating trip in 1862. Though critics now believe that the book shows much more careful workmanship than a spontaneous recitation would provide, there is little doubt that the basic outline of the story was framed on that day.

Encouraged to publish his tale, Carroll hired *Punch's* cartoonist, John Tenniel, to do the illustrations. This collaboration was an enormous success, and the popularity of the book exceeded all expectations. *Alice* and its sequel, *Through the Looking Glass, and What Alice Found There*, describe the world as seen through a bewildered, but intelligent, child's eyes. Carroll savagely parodies the Victorian attitude toward children, and also the ways in which adults treat children intellectually. These books can indeed be enjoyed by children, but the ideas Carroll presents, disguised as "nonsense," are provocative enough to enthrall critic and philosopher alike.

Through the Looking Glass also contains *Jabberwocky*, a nonsense poem and skillful parody of poetic language. *Jabberwocky* has been seen by critics as a forerunner to James Joyce's *Finnegans Wake*, and the analysis of the poem by Humpty Dumpty seems a witty anticipation of modern critical technique. Carroll's work moves forward with an inexorable, if covert, logic, in an exploration of the possibilities of the use of language.

Most critics feel that Carroll's later works, with the possible exception of *The Hunting of the Snark: An Agony, in Eight*

Fits, lack the consummate artistry of the *Alice* books. The mathematical treatises written under his real name are interesting, but added little to scholarship. Aside from *Alice*, Carroll's most important achievement is his photography. Whatever his motivations were, his photographic studies of children rank with the best of his time. While remaining a strict and proper Victorian, he managed to capture the essence of childhood, both in his books and in his photographs. The *Alice* books seem destined to be enduring classics.

PRINCIPAL WORKS

A Syllabus of Plane Algebraical Geometry (essay) 1860
Alice's Adventures in Wonderland [as Lewis Carroll]
  (novel) 1865
The Dynamics of a Particle (satire) 1865
Phantasmagoria and Other Poems [as Lewis Carroll]
  (poetry) 1869
The New Belfry [as D.C.L.] (satire) 1872
Through the Looking Glass, and What Alice Found There
  [as Lewis Carroll] (novel) 1872
The Hunting of the Snark: An Agony, in Eight Fits [as Lewis
  Carroll] (poetry) 1876

THE ATHENAEUM   (essay date 1865)

[*Alice's Adventures in Wonderland*] is a dream-story; but who can, in cold blood, manufacture a dream, with all its loops and ties, and loose threads, and entanglements, and inconsistencies, and passages which lead to nothing, at the end of which Sleep's most diligent pilgrim never arrives? Mr. Carroll has laboured hard to heap together strange adventures, and heterogeneous combinations; and we acknowledge the hard labour. . . . We fancy that any real child might be more puzzled than enchanted by this stiff, over-wrought story.

> *"Children's Books: 'Alice's Adventures in Wonder-land'," in* The Athenaeum, *No. 1990, December 16, 1865, p. 844.*

A. LANG   (essay date 1876)

[Though] it is hard to write boisterously about the pantomime, and in a Rabelaisian tone about Rabelais, it is only too easy to write snarkishly about *The Hunting of the Snark*. One of the features of this mysterious creature was, to put it mildly, its uffishness—

> Its slowness in taking a jest—
>   Should you happen to venture on one,
> It will sigh like a thing that is deeply distressed;
>   And it always looks grave at a pun.

To tell the truth, a painful truth it is, this quality of the snark has communicated itself to the reviewer.

In the first place, he is disappointed to discover that the *Hunting* is written in verse. Why did not Mr. Carroll stick to what Walt Whitman calls the free heaven of prose? The details of the chase would have made an episode in some nonsense epic very admirably, but as a mere fragment of poetry the *Hunting* is not so satisfactory. . . . [In **'Alice in Wonderland'**] much of the effect of Alice was got by the contrast of her childish niceness and naturalness with the absurd and evanescent character of the creatures in Wonderland. Now there is no sense in the territory of the Snark at all, except that mature and solemn experience of life which the reader brings with him. He is introduced to a bellman, a butcher who can only kill beavers, a beaver which makes lace, a banker, a barrister, a baker who can only make bridecake, a bonnet-maker, and so on, all just landed in the isle where the Jubjub bird sings to the Jabberwock. He sees them in themselves, he does not see them with the eyes of the child who, as in *Alice,* takes them as natural persons in a world not understood.

This is the sad position of the elderly reader, and, looking at the nonsense as nonsense for children, one does not think they will see much fun in the Barrister's dream about "Ancient Manorial Rights," "Alibis," "Insolvency," "Treason," and "Desertion," or in the Banker's presenting the "frumious Bandersnatch" with a crossed cheque for seven pounds ten. . . .

If the book is rather disappointing, it is partly the fault of the too attractive title. "We had a vision of our own," and it has proved somewhat of a Boojum. (p. 327)

> *A. Lang, "Literature : 'The Hunting of the Snark'," in* The Academy, *Vol. IX, No. 205, April 8, 1876, pp. 326-27.*

THE ATHENAEUM   (essay date 1876)

It may be that the author of **'Alice's Adventures in Wonderland'** is still suffering from the attack of Claimant on the brain, which some time ago numbed or distracted so many intellects. Or it may be that he has merely been inspired by a wild desire to reduce to idiotcy as many readers, and more especially reviewers, as possible. At all events, he has published what we may consider the most bewildering of modern poems [**'The Hunting of the Snark: An Agony in Eight Fits'**], not even excepting that which is said to have induced a convalescent to despair of his wits, and a coroner's jury to modify a verdict. . . .

What a Snark is seems to be one of those problems which no fellow—not even a mathematical Student of Christ Church—can solve. On its nature the author throws little light. . . .

That the author, when not driven wild by the modern improvements on ancient Oxonian architecture, or by the eloquence of irrepressibly bellowing barristers, can write seriously, intelligibly, and sympathetically, is proved by the dedicatory verses. . . .

> *"Novels of the Week: 'The Hunting of the Snark: An Agony in Eight Fits'," in* The Athenaeum, *No. 2528, April 8, 1876, p. 495.*

THE ATHENAEUM   (essay date 1890)

Being written by Mr. Lewis Carroll, it is needless to say that [**'Sylvie and Bruno'**] is full of amusing things, and not without some of "the graver thoughts of human life"; nevertheless it falls far below **'Alice in Wonderland'**. . . . The narrator is an impersonal being who comes and goes like Miss Meadows and the girls in "Uncle Remus," and never takes much more shape. He lapses into fairyland every time he falls asleep, and returns without any sense of strangeness; and so well is this managed that we accompany him thither with perfect ease, and are quite as able to make the best of both worlds as he is. The characters are numerous. There is a warden who is deposed from his wardenship, and finds refuge in fairyland as king—a sub-warden with a wicked and very stout wife, who "looks like a haystack out of temper"—a distinguished doctor who has "actually *invented* three new diseases, besides a new way of breaking your collar-bone!" He wears boots specially made for horizontal weather, and is so clever that "sometimes he says things that *nobody* can understand." There is another professor who lectures with his back turned to the audience, and a gardener who breaks out into snatches of song which have the old ring:—

He thought he saw an Elephant,
    That practised on the fife;
He looked again, and found it was
    A letter from his wife.
"At length I realize," he said,
    "The bitterness of Life!"

All these characters, and others too, are amusing, but Sylvie and Bruno are, as they ought to be, more interesting and amusing still. From first to last they are delightful. (pp. 11-12)

Padding, according to Mr. Lewis Carroll, may be fitly defined as "that which all can write and none can read." He does not absolutely affirm that there is none in the 395 pages in which the story of Sylvie and Bruno is told, but does affirm that it is confined to a few lines here and there, which have been inserted to eke out a page in order to bring a picture into its proper place. . . . A free use of padding is, however, a charge that could never be brought against so gay and witty a writer as Lewis Carroll, and if his definition be true, proof will be given that padding is absent, for **'Sylvie and Bruno'** is sure to be much read. (p. 12)

> *"Literature: 'Sylvie and Bruno',"* in The Athenaeum, *No. 3245, January 4, 1890, pp. 11-12.*

THE SPECTATOR   (essay date 1894)

What a loss the world had when Lewis Carroll took to writing sense! That is a reflection which must have been made a hundred times by all persons capable of forming an opinion on the subject. The author of **Alice in Wonderland** writes nonsense supremely well. His sense is but indifferent. Who then will fail to regret that [*Sylvie and Bruno Concluded*] is more than half sense? . . . He has still the power of making good nonsense, but he has not chosen to use it to the full, or rather, he has chosen so to mingle and dilute his nonsense with sense that the mixture is, for the most part, stale, flat, and we should also fear, unprofitable; though this would, we are well aware, be the last thing which Lewis Carroll would consider. . . .

In noticing *Sylvie and Bruno Concluded*, we propose to ignore altogether that portion of the book which is not nonsense. Let it be as if it were not. Let a cloud rest upon it, and blot it out for ever. In the new volume, Sylvie and Bruno, the fairy children, act much the same parts that they acted in the first volume, and the Professor, the other Professor, and the Gardener also appear. There is besides a new wonderland character—"Mein Herr"—a University Professor, who comes from a land where they have the habit of pressing things to their logical conclusion. In this land they have done away with the evils of drowning by "constantly selecting the lightest people, so that now everybody is lighter than water." (p. 408)

There is a great deal of verse scattered up and down the pages of *Sylvie and Bruno;* but though all is pleasant to read, and some quite good, none of it is up to the **Alice** level. Perhaps the best is a poem called **"To the Rescue,"** which is a variant of the nursery rhyme, "There was a little man and he had a little gun.". . .

Another excellent piece of fooling is the Professor's lecture, illustrated by experiments, in making "black light," and in getting a weight so used to being held up that it cannot fall any more. . . .

Let us hope that Mr. Lewis Carroll's next book will be all fancy and nonsense, and that he will not by writing sense lure

[his illustrator, Mr. Harry Furniss], into such vulgarities as his Lady Muriel and "the old man." That is a sin which ought to lie heavy on his conscience, and make him repent that he was ever unwise enough to stoop to real people. (p. 409)

> *"Books: 'Sylvie and Bruno',"* in The Spectator, *Vol. 72, No. 3,430, March 24, 1894, pp. 408-09.*

MAX BEERBOHM   (essay date 1900)

Between us and children—even the least "reserved" children—there is always a certain veil of mystery. . . . The punning of which Lewis Carroll was too prodigal, and which delighted us as children, may, for aught I know, bore children nowadays as greatly as it bores us. Their ringing peals may be a mere affectation. Again, do they, I wonder, really share our delight in Carroll's philosophic *aperçus*? We laugh long when some one, to whom Alice has declared that she likes the Carpenter better than the Walrus "because *he* was just a little bit sorry for the poor oysters," replies. "Yes, but he ate more of them"; we find in that reply a more deliciously just indictment of sentimentalism than ever was made, even by Mr. Meredith. The children laugh, too; but their laughter may be hollow mimicry of ours. Through the veil of mystery, we can but make wild shots at their true tastes. My own personal shot is that they do really like **"Alice,"** as a story, by reason of its perfect blend of fantasy with moral edification. I believe the love of these two separate things to be implanted in the child for all time, and I believe that Carroll's inimitable conjunction of them keeps, and will keep, **"Alice"** really popular in nurseries. Behind Lewis Carroll, the weaver of fantastic dreams, the delighter in little children, there was always Mr. Dodgson, the ascetic clergyman, the devoted scholar in mathematics. And the former had to pay constant toll to the latter—to report himself, as it were, at very brief intervals. It was as though the writer never could quite approve of his deviations into the sunny path that he loved best. When he was not infusing mathematics into his humour, he was stiffening out his fantasy with edification. In his later books, mathematics and morals triumphed. Humour lay crushed in **"The Tangled Skein,"** fantasy in **"Sylvie and Bruno."** . . . In [Carroll] the fair luxuriance of a Pagan fancy was gradually overcome by the sense of duty to his cloth, and by the tyranny of an exact science. In the two books about Alice [**"Alice's Adventures in Wonderland"** and **"Through the Looking Glass"**], however, you have a perfect fusion of the two opposing elements in his nature. In them the morality is no more than implicit, and the mathematics are not thrust on you. Though modern adults are apt to resent even implicit morality in a book for children, children delight in it. They delight in feeling that, in some way or other, Alice is being "improved" by her adventures. Orally, she seems to be an awful prig, but various internal evidence makes them suspect her of having "a past"—of having been naughty; and they feel that, somehow or other, the Caterpillar and the Red Queen and all the rest of them are working out her redemption. (pp. 139-41)

> *Max Beerbohm, "'Alice' Again Awakened" (originally published in* The Saturday Review, *London, December 22, 1900), in his* Around Theatres, *Vol. I, Alfred A. Knopf, 1939, pp. 137-41.*

GEORGE B. MASSLICH   (essay date 1921)

[*Alice in Wonderland*] is on the one hand so nonsensical that children sometimes feel ashamed to have been interested in anything "so silly." On the other hand it is so deep as to yield results in exegesis almost beyond belief. Interwoven in a dream fabric of rare verisimilitude is a psychological study of the reaction of the immature mind to academic training, particularly to instruction in logic and mathematics. . . . In the Introduction to his most valuable contribution to mathematical literature entitled *Euclid and His Modern Rivals,* which is cast in the form of a drama and abounds in humor, he says: "Subjects there are no doubt which are in their essence too serious to admit of any lightness of treatment—but I cannot recognize geometry as one of them." *Sylvia and Bruno* . . . is full of childish prattle and nonsense verses, but embodies the author's concepts of Christianity and philanthropy. One may conjecture that this teacher of mathematics and lover of children unconsciously drew upon the comedies (and tragedies) of the schoolroom for his fun. (pp. 122-23)

The author of *Alice* taught geometry for many years and was said to have been well liked as an instructor. Might it not have been because he went far afield for illustration of knotty points. For example, in his book *The Game of Logic,* which proved most useful in teaching logic to children, he uses such a quaint syllogism as this:

> Caterpillars are not eloquent;
> Jones is eloquent;
> Therefore: Jones is not a caterpillar.
>
> (p. 126)

Perhaps Lewis Carroll never meant that we should get anything more out of *Alice* than most of us do get. The world owes him a debt for what he calls this "childish story." May it not owe him a debt for its hidden meanings—for a philosophy which would protect little children from school work that is too hard for them and from books they are too young to understand? One wonders what sort of dream story he could have written had he been, say, a chemist or a physicist or a linguist instead of a mathematician. Or does the charm of *Alice in Wonderland* come from the insight of the true teacher? (p. 129)

> *George B. Masslich, "A Book within a Book," in*
> The English Journal, *Vol. X, No. 3, March 1921,*
> *pp. 119-29.*

J. B. PRIESTLEY (essay date 1923)

It is not difficult to imagine what will happen when the *Alice* books are well known [in Germany], for we know what happened to Shakespeare. A cloud of commentators will gather, and a thousand solemn Teutons will sit down to write huge volumes of comment and criticism; they will contrast and compare the characters . . . , and will offer numerous conflicting interpretations of the jokes. After that, Freud and Jung and their followers will inevitably arrive upon the scene, and they will give us appalling volumes on the "Sexualtheorie" of *Alice in Wonderland,* on the "Assoziationsfähigkeit und Assoziationsstudien" of Jabberwocky, on the inner meaning of the conflict between Tweedledum and Tweedledee from the "psychoanalytische und psychopathologische" point of view. . . . I, for one, am not going to be the first to disillusion the wistful shade of Lewis Carroll; may he remain in ignorance a little longer as to what there really was in Alice's mind, the Wonderland (save the mark!) in Alice.

How will Humpty Dumpty fare among the German critics and commentators? I shall be interested to learn, for there has always seemed to me about Humpty Dumpty the air of a solemn

literary man, and I was driven to thinking about him only a few days ago, when I had been reading the work of a rather pontifical and humourless young critic. . . . There is quite a little school of youngish critics in this country and America whose work, at once pretentious and barren, has always seemed to me to have a certain "note" in it that was vaguely familiar; but it was not until the other day that I realized where it was I had caught that manner, heard those accents, before. It was in *Through the Looking-Glass.* Humpty Dumpty has not had justice done to him; he is a prophetic figure, and Lewis Carroll, in drawing him, was satirizing a race of critics that did not then exist. Now that they do exist and put their insufferable writings before us at every turn, it is high time we learned to appreciate Carroll's character-sketch for what it is—a masterstroke of satire in anticipation. (pp. 191-93)

Alice, you will remember, discovers Humpty Dumpty (who has just been an egg in a shop) sitting on the top of a high and extremely narrow wall, and she takes him for a stuffed figure. This is, you will observe, our introduction to him: notice the *high* wall, so narrow that Alice "wondered how he could keep his *balance*" (the italics are mine) and the *stuffed figure.* . . . [He] asks Alice what her name *means* and is annoyed because she does not know, a significant procedure, that needs no comment from me. (pp. 193-94)

Notice that Humpty Dumpty thinks that every simple question is a riddle, something for him to solve triumphantly, and he cannot understand that Alice, standing firmly on the ground, may be wiser than he and may be really giving advice and not seeking the answers to trifling conundrums. He, of course, prefers to be in the air, and the very *narrowness* of his wall appeals to him. . . . Very typical too is the pedantry he displays, shortly afterwards, in the discussion about Alice's age—

> "I thought you meant 'How old *are* you?'" Alice exclaimed.
>
> "If I'd meant that, I'd have said it," said Humpty Dumpty.

And the next moment, he shows his hand again by remarking: "Now, if you'd asked *my* advice, I'd have said, 'Leave off at seven'—but it's too late now." Here is that characteristic reluctance to come to terms with reality, that love of fixed standards, rigidity, arrested development, that hatred of change and evolution, which always mark this type of mind. (pp. 194-96)

After the talk about unbirthday presents, Humpty Dumpty, it will be remembered, exclaims: "There's glory for you!" Alice, of course, does not understand what he means by "glory," and says so, upon which he smiles contemptuously and cries: "Of course you don't—till I tell you." At every step now the satire becomes more and more direct, until we reach the very climax in Humpty Dumpty's cry of "Impenetrability! That's what I say!" Who does not know those superior beings who, when they write what they allege to be literary criticism, talk of "planes" and "dimensions," of "static" and "dynamic," of "objective correlative," and Jargon only knows what else! And here is Humpty Dumpty, swaying on his high and narrow wall and crying, in a kind of ecstasy, "Impenetrability"— Humpty Dumpty—the very type and symbol of all such jargoneers. Alice, as usual, speaks for the sane mass of mankind when she remarks so thoughtfully, "That's a great deal to make one word mean." Of course it is a great deal, but then Humpty Dumpty and his kind pester us with their uncouth and inappropriate terms so that they may be spared the labour of thought and yet may convey the impression of great profundity. . . . Alice is made to speak for all of us when she exclaims, as she walks away from the absurd figure perched on the high and narrow wall, "Of all the unsatisfactory people I *ever* met . . .". There is clearly no more to be said; the episode is at an end; Humpty Dumpty and all his later followers are annihilated. (pp. 196-99)

J. B. Priestley, "A Note on Humpty Dumpty," in his I for One *(reprinted by permission of the author), John Lane, 1923 (and reprinted by Books for Libraries Press, 1967; distributed by Arno Press, Inc.), pp. 191-201.*

GEORGE SHELTON HUBBELL   (essay date 1927)

In Lewis Carroll's nonsense world [of *Alice in Wonderland*], we are privileged to see our familiar adult society (somewhat exaggerated, so that we are sure to get the joke) through the thought of the wise child Alice. We are even imbued with a natural childish misgiving that possibly she may be wrong, and all the other people so big and imposing, right. For grown-up stupidity *is* impressive. The more idiotic we are, the more impressive we adults have to seem in order to carry our point. That is why statesmen, clergy, professors, and soldiers like to wear special clothes. And in Alice's nonsense world, accordingly, an enormous amount of dignity, arbitrariness, and paraded prestige are necessary to bolster up the absurd pretentions of the incompetent. Nevertheless there is in her world the underlying joyful certainty that they are incompetent, absurd, only a pack of cards after all. (pp. 392-93)

The bustling, spruce, worried Rabbit is at heart a poor, foolish, timid creature. The arbitrary, bloody Queen of Hearts is an ineffective, abysmally stupid person. The wordy semblance of profundity which is the essence of Humpty Dumpty turns out to be more amusing than authentic. The strenuously rapid Red Queen boasts that in her country "it takes all the running *you* can do to stay in the same place". One hardly needs to point out that this is a heightening of the effect which our stupid adult life must make upon a child like Alice. And nonsense is more welcome than sense to Alice because sense would present these same matters solemnly, as if they were real and to be taken at their face value; but nonsense holds up to all things the mirror which does not lie. And this dream world, then, is the actual world, the only satisfactory, honest, enjoyable world.

It is lucky that the author knew the conventional world which he ridiculed. He had to know it in order to be fair, and therefore effectively devastating. Alice herself could not have turned the trick. Nobody but an unusually learned man could have done it. (pp. 393-94)

I have no desire to turn over all the sly wisdom of the Alice books. . . . [Madness,] as usually defined, is a comparative term. Adults are compared only with other adults, and so the standard of sanity is low. Lewis Carroll suggests a new criterion. A learned man, rather extraordinarily well acquainted with the lore of modern culture, he throws his erudition and philosophy at the feet of an understanding child. Straightway the accumulated wisdom of the ages appears as nothing but ridiculous bombast. All the chattering creatures of adultdom, coming in contact with the touchstone mind of Alice, fall to the level of the March Hare and the Mad Hatter. Thus for once we get a sane view of society. (p. 398)

George Shelton Hubbell, "The Sanity of Wonderland," in The Sewanee Review, *Vol. XXXV, No. 4, October, 1927, pp. 387-98.*

G. K. CHESTERTON   (essay date 1932)

Nobody indeed would have been more shocked than Mr. Dodgson at being classed with the anarchical artists who talked about *l'art pour l'art*. But, in spite of himself, he was a much more original artist than they. He had realised that certain images and arguments could sustain themselves in the void by a sort of defiant folly; an incongruous congruity; the very aptitude of ineptitude. It was not only very new but very national. We may even say that for some time it was a secret of the English. (p. 112)

Any educated Englishman, and especially any educational Englishman (which is worse), will tell you with a certain gravity that *Alice in Wonderland* is a classic. Such is indeed the horrid truth. The original hilarity that was born on that summer afternoon among the children, in the mind of a mathematician on a holiday, has itself hardened into something almost as cold and conscientious as a holiday task. That logician's light inversion of all the standards of logic has itself, I shudder to say, stiffened into a standard work. It is a classic; that is, people praise it who have never read it. It has a secure position side by side with the works of Milton and Dryden. . . . I am sorry to say it, but the soap-bubble which poor old Dodgson blew from the pipe of poetry, in a lucid interval of lunacy, and sent floating into the sky, has been robbed by educationists of much of the lightness of the bubble, and retained only the horrible healthiness of the soap.

This is not the fault of Lewis Carroll, but it is in one sense the fault of Charles Dodgson; at least the fault of the world which he inhabited and incorporated and to some extent encouraged and carried forward. His nonsense is a part of the peculiar genius of the English; but a part also of the elusive paradox of the English. None but they could have produced such nonsense; but none but they, having produced such nonsense, would ever have attempted to take it seriously. . . . It is a moral duty to listen to reason, but it is not a moral duty to listen to unreason. It is only a lark, and no admirer of Lewis Carroll can outstrip me in liking it as a lark. . . . Men may be told to listen, and in a sense even made to listen, when a man of adequate authority is talking sense. But we cannot be made to listen to a man who is talking nonsense; it sins against the whole spirit and atmosphere of the occasion, which is a holiday. Yet I have a dreadful fear that the works of Lewis Carroll are now a part of education, which in these liberal modern days means compulsory education. I once lectured before a congress of elementary schoolmasters, trying to persuade them to tolerate anything so human as Penny Dreadfuls or Dime Novels about Dick Turpin and Buffalo Bill. And I remember that the Chairman, with a refined and pained expression said, "I do not think Mr. Chesterton's brilliant paradoxes have persuaded us to put away our *Alice in Wonderland* and our"—something else, possibly *The Vicar of Wakefield* or *Pilgrim's Progress*. It never struck him that the nonsense tale is as much an escape from educational earnestness as the gallop after Buffalo Bill. . . . I thought to myself, with a sinking heart, "Poor, poor little Alice! She has not only been caught and made to do lessons; she has been forced to inflict lessons on others. Alice is now not only a schoolgirl but a schoolmistress. The holiday is over and Dodgson is again a don." (pp. 113-14)

I will give only one deadly and devastating fact, to show how Nonsense, in the case of Alice's story, has been allowed to become cold and monumental like a classic tomb. It has been parodied. People sit down solemnly to burlesque this burlesque. They imagine they can make it funny, or at least make it funnier, by twisting its features into paltry political caricatures. . . . Now that is a thing that nobody would dream of doing with anything he really thought *funny*. It is only serious, and even solemn things, that can be made funny. It may be said that Sheridan burlesqued Shakespeare; at least he burlesqued the sham Shakespearean historical drama in *The Critic*. But nobody could burlesque *The Critic*. . . . We have had Comic Histories of England and Comic Latin Grammars, because there remains a tradition that there is something serious, and even sacred, about the story of the English nation and the strong tongue of Rome. But even those who can enjoy, more than I can, what is now called a Comic Strip, would not think it a promising venture to bring out a Comic Comic Strip.

But, in the case of **Alice in Wonderland,** so strangely solid was this impression that the thing was a national institution, an educational classic, a well of English undefiled, a historic heritage like *Othello* or the *Samson Agonistes*, that satirists set seriously to work on it to make it amusing. Political parodists actually thought it a sort of improvement to give all that pure and happy pointlessness a point. They even felt, I think, a tingle of timid daring, in taking liberties with this monumental Victorian volume. . . . [Each] of them felt almost like a Red Republican when he took liberties with the Red Queen.

It is a delightful but difficult enterprise to liberate Lewis Carroll from the custody of Charles Dodgson. It is a hard though happy task to try to recapture the first fresh careless rapture of the days when Nonsense was new. We have to put ourselves in an utterly different attitude from that of the admirers who have come after the achievement, and feel something of the first stir and movement that went before it. . . . To appreciate it we must appreciate more deeply the paradox of the whole people and its literature, and the really comic contrast between its responsible and its irresponsible moods. There were a great many things that Charles Dodgson took only too seriously; but the things which his devotees have taken seriously were the things which he took lightly. (pp. 115-16)

Superficially speaking, the most curious thing about him was that it was only through these iron gates of reason that he entered his own private paradise of unreason. All that part of the man that might have been, and in a literary man often has been, loose or light or irresponsible, was in his case particularly prim and respectable and responsible. It was only his intellect that took a holiday; his emotions never took a holiday; and certainly his conscience never took a holiday. . . . He had no outlet, even of imagination, on the moral or social or philosophical side: he had it only on the mathematical side. Though a conscientious mathematical teacher, he could imagine something that made plus equal to minus. But though a conscientious Christian, he could not really imagine anything that made the first last and the last first; that put down the mighty from their seat or exalted the humble and the poor. His remarks about social justice and reform, in **Sylvie and Bruno,** are more worthy of a feeble curate in a farce than of a Christian priest teaching in a historic seat of learning. He was, in the ordinary sense, limited everywhere by convention; and yet it was he who with one wild leap burst the very limits of reason. It was this stodgy and stuffy Victorian parson, who followed the wild vision of utter unreason further than it was ever pursued by any wild

poet working without a conscience or an aim; by any wild painter when he dips his brush in hues of earthquake and eclipse. (pp. 116-17)

The natural extension of [Carroll's] imagination was all in the direction of the inverted ideas of the intellect. He could see the logical world upside down; he could not see any other kind of world even right side up. He took his triangles and turned them into toys for a favourite little girl; he took his logarithms and syllogisms and twisted them into nonsense. But, in a rather special sense, there is nothing but nonsense in his nonsense. There is no sense in his nonsense; as there is in the more human nonsense of Rabelais or the more bitter nonsense of Swift. If he had been suggesting any moral or metaphysical ideas, they would never have been so deep or grand as those of Rabelais or Swift. But he was only playing The Game of Logic; and it is his glory that it was a new game, and a nonsensical game, and one of the best games in the world. (pp. 117-18)

> *G. K. Chesterton, "Lewis Carroll" (originally published in* The New York Times, *January 24, 1932), in his* A Handful of Authors: Essays on Books & Writers, *edited by Dorothy Collins (reprinted by permission of the Estate of G. K. Chesterton), Sheed and Ward 1953, pp. 112-19.*

EDMUND WILSON (essay date 1932)

[If] Dodgson and his work were shown as an organic whole, his "nonsense" would not seem the anomaly which it is usually represented as being. It is true that on one of his sides he was a pompous and priggish don. . . . Under the crust of the pious professor was a mind both rebellious and skeptical. The mathematician who invented Alice was one of those semimonastic types—like Walter Pater and A. E. Housman—that the English universities breed: vowed to an academic discipline but cherishing an intense originality, painfully repressed and incomplete but in the narrow field of their art somehow both sound and bold. A good deal of the piquancy of the *Alice* books is due to their merciless irreverence: in Alice's dreaming mind, the bottoms dismayingly drop out of the didactic little poems by Dr. Watts and Jane Taylor, which Victorian children were made to learn, and their simple and trite images are replaced by grotesque and silly ones, which have rushed in like goblins to take possession. And in the White Knight's song about the aged man a-sitting on a gate, a parody of Wordsworth's "Leech-Gatherer," Lewis Carroll, in his subterranean fashion, ridiculed the stuffed-shirt side of Wordsworth as savagely as Byron had ever done. Wordsworth was a great admiration of Dodgson's; yet as soon as he enters his world of dreams, Lewis Carroll is moved to stick pins in him. (pp. 199-200)

It is curious what ordination as a clergyman of the Church of England can do to an original mind. The case of Dodgson is somewhat similar to those of Donne and Swift—though Dodgson was shy and stammered and never took priest's orders; and he was closer, perhaps, to Swift and Donne than to the merely whimsical writer like Barrie or A. A. Milne, for Dodgson had a first-rate mind of a very unusual sort: he was a logician who was also a poet.

The poetry and the logic in Dodgson were closely bound up together. It has often been pointed out that only a mind primarily logical could have invented the jokes of the *Alice* books, of which the author is always conscious that they are examples of faulty syllogisms. But it also worked the other way: his eccentric imagination invaded his scholarly work. His **Symbolic**

Logic (which had nothing to do with the subject called by the same name of which A. N. Whitehead and Bertrand Russell laid the foundation in their *Principia Mathematica*) contains syllogisms with terms as absurd as any in the *Alice* books:

> A prudent man shuns hyenas;
> No banker is imprudent.
> No banker fails to shun hyenas.

Dodgson's *Euclid and His Modern Rivals* had nothing to do with non-Euclidean geometry, but in the section called "A New Theory of Parallels" of his *Curiosa Mathematica* he grazed one of the conceptions of relativist theory; and is there not a touch of Einstein in the scenes in which the Red Queen has to keep running in order to remain in the same place and in which the White Queen gives a scream of pain before she has pricked her finger?

In literature, Lewis Carroll went deeper than his contemporaries realized and than he usually gets credit for even today. As studies in dream psychology, the *Alice* books are most remarkable: they do not suffer by comparison with the best serious performances in this field—with Strindberg or Joyce or Flaubert's *Tentation de Saint Antoine*. One of Alice's recent editors says that the heroine's personality is kept simple in order to throw into relief the eccentrics and monsters she meets. But the creatures that she meets, the whole dream, *are* Alice's personality and her waking life. They are the world of teachers, family, and pets, as it appears to a little girl and also the little girl who is looking at this world. . . . Lewis Carroll is never sentimental about Alice, though he is later on to become so, in the messiest Victorian way, in the *Sylvie and Bruno* books. Yet *Sylvie and Bruno*, too, has considerable psychological interest, with its alternations of dream and reality and the elusive relationships between them. The opening railway journey, in which the narrator is dozing and mixes with the images of his dream his awareness of the lady sitting opposite him, is of an almost Joycean complexity and quite inappropriate for reading to children. (pp. 200-02)

[I do not think] that the *Alice* that grownups read is really a different work from the *Alice* that is read by children. The grownups understand it better, but the prime source of the interest is the same. Why is it that very young children listen so attentively to *Alice*, remember it all so well and ask to hear it again, when many other stories seem to leave little impression? It is surely the psychological truth of these books that lays its hold on us all. . . . The shiftings and the transformations, the mishaps and the triumphs of Alice's dream, the mysteries and the riddles, the gibberish that conveys unmistakable meanings, are all based upon relationships that contradict the assumptions of our conscious lives but that are lurking not far behind them. In the "straight" parts of *Sylvie and Bruno*, Lewis Carroll was mawkishly Victorian to the point of unintentional parody (having produced in **"The Three Voices"** a masterpiece of intentional parody!), but in the *Alice* books he quite got away from the upholstery and the gloomy institutions of the nineteenth-century world. I believe that they are likely to survive when a good deal of the more monumental work of that world—the productions of the Carlyles and the Ruskins, the Spencers and the George Eliots—shall have sunk with the middle-class ideals of which they were the champions as well as the critics. Charles Dodgson who, in morals and religion, in his attitude toward social institutions, was professedly, as he himself believed, more conventional than any of these, had over them the curious advantage of working at once with the abstract materials of mathematical and logical conceptions and with the irrationalities of dreams. His art has a purity that is almost unique in a period so cluttered and cumbered, in which even the preachers of doom to the reign of materialism bore the stamp and the stain of the industrial system in the hard insistence of their sentences and in the turbidity of their belchings of rhetoric. They have shrunk now, but *Alice* still stands. (p. 202)

> Edmund Wilson, "C. L. Dodgson: The Poet Logician" (1932), in his The Shores of Light: A Literary Chronicle of the Twenties and Thirties *(reprinted by permission of Farrar, Straus, & Giroux, Inc.; copyright 1952 by Edmund Wilson; copyright renewed © 1980 by Helen Miranda Wilson), Farrar, Straus & Giroux, Inc, 1952 (and reprinted in* Aspects of Alice: Lewis Carroll's Dreamchild as Seen through the Critics' Looking-Glasses, 1865-1971, *edited by Robert Phillips, The Vanguard Press Inc., 1971, pp. 198-206).*

WALTER de la MARE (essay date 1932)

[Both *Alice's Adventures in Wonderland* and *Through the Looking Glass*] have a structural framework—in the one playing-cards, in the other a game of chess, the moves in which Dodgson only to some extent attempted to justify. These no doubt suggested a few of his chief characters, or rather their social status; but what other tale-teller could have made Carroll's use of them? . . . Both stories, too—and this is a more questionable contrivance, particularly as it introduces a rather sententious elder sister—turn out to be dreams. . . .

All this however affects the imaginative reality—the supreme illusion—of the *Alices* [very little] . . . . In reading the Carroll stories, that is, we scarcely notice, however consistent and admirable it may be, their ingenious design. . . . Indeed the genius in Carroll seems to have worked more subtly than the mind which it was possessed by realized. It is a habit genius has. (pp. 51-2)

The reason is in service to the imagination, not *vice versa*. (pp. 52-3)

The intellectual thread, none the less, which runs through the *Alices* is the reverse of being negligible. It is on this that their translucent beads of phantasy are strung, and it is the more effective for being so consistent and artfully concealed. As in the actual writing of poetry the critical faculties of the poet are in a supreme and constant activity, so with the *Alices*. Their 'characters', for example, in all their rich diversity are in exquisite keeping with one another. (p. 53)

It is [a] rational poise in a topsy-turvy world . . . that gives the two tales their exquisite balance. For though laws there certainly are in the realm of Nonsense, they are all of them unwritten laws. Its subjects obey them unaware of any restrictions. Anything may happen there except only what can't happen *there*. Its kings and queens are kings and queens for precisely the same reason that the Mock Turtle is a Mock Turtle, even though once he was a real Turtle—by a divine right, that is, on which there is no need to insist. (pp. 55-6)

Carroll's Wonderland indeed is a (queer little) universe of the mind resembling Einstein's in that it is a finite infinity endlessly explorable though never to be explored. How blue are its heavens, how grass-green its grass—its fauna and flora being more curiously reviving company not only than any but the pick of *this* world's but than those of almost any other book I know. And even for variety and precision, from the Mad Hatter down to Bill the Lizard, that company is rivalled only by the novelists who are as generous as they are skilled—an astonishing feat, since Carroll's creations are not only of his own species but of his own genus. (p. 57)

And what of the visionary light, the colour, the scenery; that wonderful seascape, for example, in *The Walrus and the Carpenter,* as wide as Milton's in *Il Penseroso*—the quality of its sea, its sands, its space and distances? . . . All this is of the world of dreams and of that world alone. The *Alices* indeed have the timelessness, the placelessness, and an atmosphere resembling in their own odd fashion not only those of the *Songs of Innocence* and [Thomas] Traherne's [*Centuri Meditations*], but of the medieval descriptions of paradise and many of the gem-like Italian pictures of the fifteenth century. This atmosphere is conveyed, as it could alone be conveyed, in a prose of limpid simplicity, as frictionless as the unfolding of the petals of an evening primrose in the cool of twilight. . . . (pp. 62-3)

> *Walter de la Mare, in his* Lewis Carroll *(reprinted by permission of the Literary Trustees of Walter de la Mare and The Society of Authors as their representatives), Faber and Faber Ltd., 1932, 67 p.*

A.M.E. GOLDSCHMIDT (essay date 1933)

Long before reaching the end [of *Alice in Wonderland,* Carroll] tells us, he had "drained the wells of fancy dry," and the rest "had to be hammered out." In this latter part, even the nonsense is systematic—as, owing to the prearranged scheme of the chess problem, it remains in *Through the Looking-Glass.* But in the first part there is no system, the incidents and images are suggested by the subconscious, and their nature is erotic.

The symbolism begins almost at once. Alice runs down the rabbit-hole after the White Rabbit and suddenly finds herself falling down "what seemed to be a very deep well." Here we have what is perhaps the best-known symbol of coitus. Next, the dreamer (who identifies himself with Alice throughout) is seen pursuing the White Rabbit down a series of passages. . . . Now the dreamer enters a "long, low hall," round which are a number of doors, all locked. Alice despairs of getting out; but "suddenly she came upon a little three-legged table"; she finds upon it [a small key]. . . . (p. 280)

Here we find the common symbolism of lock and key representing coitus; the doors of normal size represent adult women. These are disregarded by the dreamer and the interest is centered on the little door, which symbolizes a female child; the curtain before it represents the child's clothes.

The colorful language suggests the presence, in the subconscious, of an abnormal emotion of considerable strength. (p. 281)

The symbol of the door is replaced later in the story by that of a little house about four feet high, but meanwhile have occurred a series of incidents whose meaning we may briefly indicate here, although in the book they are as elaborate as they are striking. Alice alternately grows and shrinks—first on drinking the bottle marked "Drink Me," then on eating a cake, then on nibbling the mushroom. The phallic significance of these incidents is clear, and is borne out by the illustrations, particularly that of Alice's "immense length of neck, which seemed to rise like a stalk out of a sea of green leaves which lay far below her." . . .

The whole course of the story is perhaps to be explained by the desire for complete virility, conflicting with the desire for abnormal satisfaction. If sexual emotions may be divided into the lumbar and the thoracic, we can form a clearer idea of what is involved. The whole aim of the dreamer is to fulfill the thoracic emotion; the one, however, always involves the other; and on this occasion conflicts with it. The importance of the latter, however, in the dreamer's subconscious, when disconnected from the extraverted emotion, is seen by two further incidents, of an autoerotic significance, those of the sneezing baby and of the flamingo. Later, as we have said, the story comes under the control of the conscious mind, and there are no irrelevant incidents. But the reader, if he accepts our thesis in its main lines, may proceed to find for himself, in the earlier part, symbols of minor importance. (p. 282)

> *A.M.E. Goldschmidt, "'Alice in Wonderland' Psychoanalyzed," in* The New Oxford Outlook, *edited by Richard Crossman, Gilbert Highet, and Derek Kahn (copyright 1933 by Basil Blackwell; reprinted by permission of Clarissa Kaldor), Basil Blackwell, 1933 (and reprinted in* Aspects of Alice: Lewis Carroll's Dreamchild as Seen through the Critics' Looking-Glasses, 1865-1971, *edited by Robert Phillips, The Vanguard Press Inc., 1971, pp. 279-82).*

WILLIAM EMPSON (essay date 1935)

It must seem a curious thing that there has been so little serious criticism of the *Alices,* and that so many critics, with so militant and eager an air of good taste, have explained that they would not think of attempting it. . . . There seems to be a feeling that real criticism would involve psychoanalysis, and that the results would be so improper as to destroy the atmosphere of the books altogether. Dodgson was too conscious a writer to be caught out so easily. For instance it is an obvious bit of interpretation to say that the Queen of Hearts is a symbol of 'uncontrolled animal passion' seen through the clear but blank eyes of sexlessness; obvious, and the sort of thing critics are now so sure would be in bad taste; Dodgson said it himself, to the actress who took the part when the thing was acted. The books are so frankly about growing up that there is no great discovery in translating them into Freudian terms; it seems only the proper exegesis of a classic even where it would be a shock to the author. On the whole the results of the analysis, when put into drawing-room language, are his conscious opinions; and if there was no other satisfactory outlet for his feelings but the special one fixed in his books the same is true in a degree of any original artist. I shall use psycho-analysis where it seems relevant, and feel I had better begin by saying what use it is supposed to be. Its business here is not to discover a neurosis peculiar to Dodgson. The essential idea behind the books is a shift onto the child, which Dodgson did not invent, of the obscure tradition of pastoral. The formula is now '*child-become-judge,*' and if Dodgson identifies himself with the child so does the writer of the primary sort of pastoral with his magnified version of the swain. (pp. 253-54)

Dodgson will only go half-way with the sentiment of the child's unity with nature, and has another purpose for his heroine; she is the free and independent mind. Not that this is contradictory; because she is right about life she is independent from all the other characters who are wrong. But it is important to him because it enables him to clash the Wordsworth sentiments with the other main tradition about children derived from rogue-sentiment. (p. 262)

One might say that the *Alices* differ from other versions of pastoral in lacking the sense of glory. Normally the idea of including all sorts of men in yourself brings in an idea of reconciling yourself with nature and therefore gaining power over it. The *Alices* are more self-protective; the dream cuts out the real world and the delicacy of the mood is felt to cut out the lower classes. This is true enough, but when Humpty Dumpty says that glory means a nice knock-down argument he is not far from the central feeling of the book. There is a real feeling of isolation and yet just that is taken as the source of power.

The obvious parody of Wordsworth is the poem of the White Knight, an important figure for whom Dodgson is willing to break the language of humour into the language of sentiment. It takes off *Resolution and Independence,* a genuine pastoral poem if ever there was one; the endurance of the leechgatherer gives Wordsworth strength to face the pain of the world. . . . The parody here will have no truck with the dignity of the leechgatherer, but the point of that is to make the unworldly dreaminess of the Knight more absurd; there may even be a reproach for Wordsworth in the lack of consideration that makes him go on asking the same question. One feels that the Knight has probably imagined most of the old man's answers, or anyway that the old man was playing up to the fool who questioned him. At any rate there is a complete shift of interest from the virtues of the leechgatherer onto the childish but profound virtues of his questioner. (pp. 262-63)

One reason for the moral grandeur of the Knight, then, is that he stands for the Victorian scientist, who was felt to have invented a new kind of Roman virtue; earnestly, patiently, carefully (it annoyed Samuel Butler to have these words used so continually about scientists) without sensuality, without self-seeking, without claiming any but a fragment of knowledge, he goes on labouring at his absurd but fruitful conceptions. But the parody makes him stand also for the poet. . . . (pp. 264-65)

The talking animal convention and the changes of relative size appear in so different a children's book as *Gulliver;* they evidently make some direct appeal to the child whatever more sophisticated ideas are piled onto them. Children feel at home with animals conceived as human; the animal can be made affectionate without its making serious emotional demands on them, does not want to educate them, is at least unconventional in the sense that it does not impose its conventions, and does not make a secret of the processes of nature. So the talking animals here are a child-world. . . . But talking animals in children's books had been turned to didactic purposes ever since Aesop; the schoolmastering tone in which the animals talk nonsense to Alice is partly a parody of this—they are really childish but try not to look it. On the other hand, this tone is so supported by the way they can order her about, the firm and surprising way their minds work, the abstract topics they work on, the useless rules they accept with so much conviction, that we take them as real grown-ups contrasted with unsophisticated childhood. (pp. 265-66)

The changes of size are more complex. In *Gulliver* they are the impersonal eye; to change size and nothing else makes you feel 'this makes one see things as they are in themselves.' It excites Wonder but of a scientific sort. . . . Children like to think of being so small that they could hide from grown-ups and so big that they could control them, and to do this dramatises the great topic of growing up, which both *Alices* keep to consistently. In the same way the charm of Jabberwocky is

that it is a code language, the language with which grown-ups hide things from children or children from grown-ups. (p. 267)

Both books also keep to the topic of death—the first two jokes about death in *Wonderland* come on pages 3 and 4—and for the child this may be a natural connection; I remember believing I should have to die in order to grow up, and thinking the prospect very disagreeable. There seems to be a connection in Dodgson's mind between the death of childhood and the development of sex, which might be pursued into many of the details of the books. Alice will die if the Red King wakes up, partly because she is a dream-product of the author and partly because the pawn is put back in its box at the end of the game. . . . The trial is meant to be a mystery; Alice is told to leave the court, as if a child ought not to hear the evidence, and yet they expect her to give evidence herself. . . . And it is the refusal to let her stay that makes her revolt and break the dream. It is tempting to read an example of this idea into the poem that introduces the *Looking-Glass.*

> Come, hearken then, ere voice of dread,
>   With bitter summons laden,
> Shall summon to unwelcome bed
>   A melancholy maiden.

After all the marriage-bed was more likely to be the end of the maiden than the grave, and the metaphor firmly implied treats them as identical.

The last example is obviously more a joke against Dodgson than anything else, and though the connection between death and the development of sex is I think at work it is not the main point of the conflict about growing up. Alice is given a magical control over her growth by the traditionally symbolic caterpillar, a creature which has to go through a sort of death to become grown-up, and then seems a more spiritual creature. It refuses to agree with Alice that this process is at all peculiar, and clearly her own life will be somehow like it, but the main idea is not its development of sex. . . . Alice knows several reasons why she should object to growing up, and does not at all like being an obvious angel, a head out of contact with its body that has to come down from the sky, and gets mistaken for the Paradisal serpent of the knowledge of good and evil, and by the pigeon of the Annunciation, too. But she only makes herself smaller for reasons of tact or proportion; the triumphant close of *Wonderland* is that she has outgrown her fancies and can afford to wake and despise them. The *Looking-Glass* is less of a dream-product, less concentrated on the child's situation, and (once started) less full of changes of size; but it has the same end; the governess shrinks to a kitten when Alice has grown from a pawn to a queen, and can shake her. Both these clearly stand for becoming grown-up and yet in part are a revolt against grown-up behaviour; there is the same ambivalence as about the talking animals. (pp. 268-70)

The symbolic completeness of Alice's experience is I think important. She runs the whole gamut; she is a father in getting down the hole, a foetus at the bottom, and can only be born by becoming a mother and producing her own amniotic fluid. Whether [Dodgson's] mind played the trick of putting this into the story or not he has the feelings that would correspond to it. A desire to include all sexuality in the girl child, the least obviously sexed of human creatures, the one that keeps its sex in the safest place, was an important part of their fascination for him. He is partly imagining himself as the girl-child (with these comforting characteristics) partly as its father (these together make *it* a father) partly as its lover—so it might be a mother—but then of course it is clever and detached enough to do everything for itself. . . . So far from its dependence, the child's independence is the important thing, and the theme behind that is the self-centred emotional life imposed by the detached intelligence.

The famous cat is a very direct symbol of this ideal of intellectual detachment; all cats are detached, and since this one grins it is the amused observer. It can disappear because it can abstract itself from its surroundings into a more interesting inner world; it appears only as a head because it is almost a disembodied intelligence, and only as a grin because it can impose an atmosphere without being present. (pp. 272-73)

The Gnat gives a more touching picture of Dodgson; he treats nowhere more directly of his actual relations with the child. He feels he is liable to nag at it, as a gnat would, and the gnat turns out, as he is, to be alarmingly big as a friend for the child, but at first it sounds tiny because he means so little to her. It tries to amuse her by rather frightening accounts of other dangerous insects, other grown-ups. It is reduced to tears by the melancholy of its own jokes, which it usually can't bear to finish; only if Alice had made them, as it keeps egging her on to do, would they be at all interesting. That at least would show the child had paid some sort of attention, and he could go away and repeat them to other people. The desire to have jokes made all the time, he feels, is a painful and obvious confession of spiritual discomfort, and the freedom of Alice from such a feeling makes her unapproachable. (p. 274)

This sort of 'analysis' is a peep at machinery; the question for criticism is what is done with the machine. . . . The praise of the child in the *Alices* mainly depends on a distaste not only for sexuality but for all the distortions of vision that go with a rich emotional life; the opposite idea needs to be set against this, that you can only understand people or even things by having such a life in yourself to be their mirror. . . . (pp. 277-78)

> *William Empson, "'Alice in Wonderland'," in his* Some Versions of Pastoral *(copyright © 1974 by William Empson; all rights reserved; reprinted by permission of New Directions Publishing Corporation; in Canada by Chatto and Windus Ltd), Chatto & Windus, 1935 (and reprinted by New Directions, 1950), pp. 253-94.*

GUY BOAS (essay date 1937)

Of the literary adventures of the Victorian age surely the most singular of all is the adventure of the Christ Church mathematical don in **'Wonderland'** and **'Through the Looking-Glass.'** It might indeed be claimed with truth of 'Alice' that her dream-history constitutes one of the most remarkable books in our language, a phenomenon as well as a book, comparable with Boswell's 'Life of Johnson,' 'The Compleat Angler,' or 'Robinson Crusoe.' (p. 740)

It is the first paradox about **'Alice'** that, designed as a tale for children, it is, in fact, an encyclopaedic study of adult psychology. The number of our authors who have created type characters, as Fielding's Mr Allworthy, Sheridan's Joseph Surface, Thackeray's Colonel Newcome, are legion. But the number who have fashioned characters wrought of the full subtlety, surprise, and flavour of which Nature is capable, are few. . . . But Lewis Carroll in **'Alice'** did it, and did it again and again with something like Shakespearean wealth. Humpty-Dumpty, the White Knight, the Mad Hatter, the Queens White and Red, Tweedledum and Tweedledee, the White Rabbit, the Cook, the Duchess, even the Caterpillar, the Dodo, and the Mock Turtle—these have only to look round a corner of the story and they become stamped on our experience and memories for ever, distinct and complete personalities, so realistic that we know them better than our friends, so vital that they are immortal, so distinguished that no one like them has existed, before or after, and so rounded that not only do we know what on every occasion they said and did, but we should like to know also in any given circumstances outside the story what would be their opinions and reactions. They are, in a word, Dynamic: creatures not merely of the author's imagination, but a permanent stimulus to imagination in others. They are not only witty in their place, but continually pop out of the tale at odd moments in our lives and are witty about whatever is going forward. . . . [The] shells and the gas and the trenches, the name of Flanders and even of Armageddon, will pass away, but the reality of Dodgson's dream-kingdom will remain, impervious and invulnerable, for the most that a shell can do is to wake a dreamer: it cannot touch his dream.

Over both the worlds of **'Alice'** lies that mysterious quality, atmosphere. . . . (pp. 740-41)

The secret of this atmosphere of **'Alice,'** if the secret of so delicate a mystery can be guessed, is contained, I fancy, in the word "Oxford." It is the magic of Oxford, I suggest, the dreaming spires, the lazy Cherwell, the strange pathetic union of youth and age in "the home of lost causes and impossible loyalties" that we feel, when ostensibly we are mesmerised by the Lands of Looking-Glass and the Chessboard. (p. 741)

[If] ever the mental attitude and personal characteristics of a body of human beings have been caught and set down for the joy and instruction of posterity, the genus don lives for ever enshrined among the characters of Wonderland. (pp. 742-43)

The Caterpillar is the don dyspeptic, but there are others in profusion. There is the don peevish, who is Tweedledum; the don inventive, who is the White Knight; the don nervous, who is the White Rabbit; the don crazy, the Mad Hatter; the don lugubrious, the Mock Turtle; the don majestic, the Dodo; the don ferocious, the Queen of Hearts; the don pacific, the King of Hearts; the don precise, the Red Queen; the don vague, the White Queen; the don elusive, the Cheshire Cat; the don pugnacious, the Unicorn; and the don magnificent, who is Humpty-Dumpty. (p. 744)

The puns of the Mock Turtle, the riddles of the Hatter, the inventions of the White Knight, the poetic propensities of so many of the creatures, their uniform command of Socratic question, their unanswerable logic and crushing repartee, together with the disconcerting and totally unself-conscious eccentricity of their conduct, all serve to create the perfect picture of the don as Oxford has made him or as he has made Oxford, and as Dodgson has painted him, mind, imagination, and soul. (p. 745)

Out of his jumble of ridiculous creatures talking preposterous sophistry, and peopling a world as kaleidoscopically impossible as dreams, as exasperatingly contradictious as human nature, and yet as pure as Arithmetic and childhood, this reserved, testy, sentimental Christ Church don fashioned a mental universe which seems to have as solid a place in the time-scheme as the universe of 'The Pilgrim's Progress.' (p. 746)

> *Guy Boas, "Alice" (© William Blackwood & Sons Ltd 1937; reprinted by permission of the Estate of*

the author), in Blackwood's Magazine, *Vol. 243, No. 1466, December, 1937, pp. 740-46.*

EVELYN WAUGH　(essay date 1939)

It is easy to see why [*Sylvie and Bruno* and *Sylvie and Bruno Concluded*] failed to achieve the fame of *Alice*. They are wholly different in temper and only the explicit statements of the author's preface and of certain apostrophes in the text can convince the reader that they were ever intended for children. The main story, in which the fanciful passages are embedded, is a typical Victorian novel. . . .

The peculiarity of [*Sylvie and Bruno*] lies in the fact that the narrator of this simple tale is intermittently haunted by two dream-children named Sylvie and Bruno. Sylvie has some undefined affinity to [the heroine] Lady Muriel, but Bruno, her junior, is a creation of unique horror, who babbles throughout in baby-talk, like the "control" of a "medium." These children first appear as characters in a dream and are part of a Ruritanian State named Outland. Soon, however, Outland and its intrigues disappear, and the children pop up during the narrator's waking hours. . . . Bruno becomes so concrete that only the rival lover's gallantry saves him from being run down by a railway train. Except for this single occasion, however, they play no part in the main story; they are not supernatural visitants of the type of *A Midsummer Night's Dream*, who appear in order to solve or complicate the affairs of the world, but aberrations of the narrator's mind which, one cannot help guessing, correspond to some psychological peculiarity of Dodgson's. . . .

It seems to me likely that Dodgson was tortured by religious scepticism; his abnormal tenderness of conscience with regard to blasphemy is explicable if we think of him as treasuring a religious faith so fragile that a child's prattle endangered it. He believed that the only way he could protect his faith was by escaping more and more from contemporary life—in his scholarship into remote and fanciful abstractions, in literature into nonsense. In order to keep his mind from rational speculation he cultivated a habit of day-dreaming and peopled his consciousness with fantastic characters. Children became for him the symbols of innocent faith and accordingly the only tolerable companions; converse with them gave his fantasies literary form.

Evelyn Waugh, "Carroll and Dodgson," in The Spectator *(© 1939 by* The Spectator; *reprinted by permission of A D Peters & Co Ltd), Vol. 163, No. 5807, October 13, 1939, p. 511.*

VIRGINIA WOOLF　(essay date 1939)

The complete works of Lewis Carroll have been issued . . . in a stout volume of 1293 pages. So there is no excuse—Lewis Carroll ought once and for all to be complete. We ought to be able to grasp him whole and entire. But we fail—once more we fail. We think we have caught Lewis Carroll; we look again and see an Oxford clergyman. We think we have caught the Rev. C. L. Dodgson—we look again and see a fairy elf. The book breaks in two in our hands. (p. 81)

In order to make us into children, [Lewis Carroll] first makes us asleep. "Down, down, down, would the fall *never* come to an end?" Down, down, down we fall into that terrifying, wildly inconsequent, yet perfectly logical world where time races, then stands still; where space stretches, then contracts.

It is the world of sleep; it is also the world of dreams. Without any conscious effort dreams come; the white rabbit, the walrus, and the carpenter, one after another, turning and changing one into the other, they come skipping and leaping across the mind. It is for this reason that the two Alices are not books for children; they are the only books in which we become children. President Wilson, Queen Victoria, *The Times* leader writer, the late Lord Salisbury—it does not matter how old, how important, or how insignificant you are, you become a child again. To become a child is to be very literal; to find everything so strange that nothing is surprising; to be heartless, to be ruthless, yet to be so passionate that a snub or a shadow drapes the world in gloom. It is to be Alice in Wonderland.

It is also to be Alice Through the Looking Glass. It is to see the world upside down. Many great satirists and moralists have shown us the world upside down, and have made us see it, as grown-up people see it, savagely. Only Lewis Carroll has shown us the world upside down as a child sees it, and has made us laugh as children laugh, irresponsibly. (pp. 82-3)

And then we wake. None of the transitions in Alice in Wonderland is quite so queer. For we wake to find—is it the Rev. C. L. Dodgson? Is it Lewis Carroll? Or is it both combined? This conglomerate object intends to produce an extra-Bowdlerised edition of Shakespeare for the use of British maidens; implores them to think of death when they go to the play; and always, always to realise that "the true object of life is the development of *character*. . . ." Is there, then, even in 1293 pages, any such thing as "completeness"? (p. 83)

Virginia Woolf, "Lewis Carroll" (1939), in her The Moment and Other Essays *(copyright 1948 by Harcourt Brace Jovanovich, Inc.; copyright 1976 by Harcourt Brace Jovanovich, Inc. and Marjorie T. Parsons; reprinted by permission of the publisher; in Canada by the author's literary Estate and The Hogarth Press Ltd.), Harcourt, 1948, pp. 81-3.*

ROGER W. HOLMES　(essay date 1959)

Have you ever seen Nobody? What would your world be like if objects had no names? Can you remember what will happen week after next? How many impossible things can you believe before breakfast—*if* you hold your breath and shut your eyes? These questions transport us to the world of Lewis Carroll: to Wonderland, with the White Rabbit and the Mock Turtle. . . . They also transport us to the realm of Philosophy.

Alice's Adventures in Wonderland and *Through the Looking-Glass* belong most obviously and particularly to children whether in nurseries or bomb shelters. . . . [Both] Wonderland and the Looking-Glass country belong to the logician and the philosopher as much as to parents and children. These regions are crowded with the problems and paraphernalia of logic and metaphysics and theory of knowledge and ethics. Here are superbly imaginative treatments of logical principles, the uses and meanings of words, the functions of names, the perplexities connected with time and space, the problem of personal identity, the status of substance in relation to its qualities, the mind-body problem. (pp. 159-60)

Sometimes Carroll finds an unforgettable illustration of a major principle. We know that if all apples are red, it does not follow that all red things are apples: the logician's technical description of this is the nonconvertibility *simpliciter* of universal proportions. (p. 161)

Most often Carroll uses the absurd hilarity of Wonderland to bring difficult technical concepts into sharp focus; and for this gift teachers of logic and philosophy have unmeasured admiration and gratitude. . . . Lewis Carroll reminds us that we often refer to this curious but important logical entity. The White King is waiting for his messengers and asks Alice to look along the road to see if they are coming:

> "I see nobody on the road," said Alice.
>
> "I only wish *I* had such eyes," the King remarked in a fretful tone. "To be able to see Nobody! And at that distance too! Why, it's as much as I can do to see real people, by this light."

This is amusing and, without benefit of logic, it is also confusing. When the messenger finally arrives, several pages later, confusion is doubly confounded:

> "Who did you pass on the road?" the King went on. . . .
>
> "Nobody," said the Messenger.
>
> "Quite right," said the King; "this young lady saw him too. So of course Nobody walks slower than you."
>
> "I do my best," the Messenger said in a sullen tone. "I'm sure nobody walks much faster than I do!"
>
> "He can't do that," said the King, "or else he'd have been here first."

"Nobody" may stand for no person, but you had better be careful how you talk about him! (pp. 161-62)

[Alice boasts] to the Gnat that she can name the insects:

> "Of course they answer to their names?" the Gnat remarked carelessly.
>
> "I never knew them to do that."
>
> "What's the use of their having names," the Gnat said, "if they won't answer to them?"
>
> "No use to *them*," said Alice, "but it's useful to the people that name them, I suppose. If not, why do things have names at all?"

Why, indeed? Medieval philosophers fought bitterly about this. Alice seems to be a Nominalist, suggesting that names are tags by which we can conveniently denote objects without having to point. But a few pages later she comes to the Wood-where-things-have-no-names and quickly discovers what the Medieval Realists knew: that names have a connotation as well as a denotation. . . . [Names] are more than tags: they convey information. Such a wood evokes fascinating philosophic speculation. Suppose we could remember no names. Not only would it be impossible to communicate with anyone about objects except by pointing, but also we should be unable to generalize and should have to rely entirely on conditioned responses. (p. 162)

The most complex discussion of the function of words takes place between Alice and the White Knight when the latter offers to sing Alice a song. This passage is a classic. The Knight announces that the name of the song "is called 'Haddock's Eyes'" and the following famous conversation ensues:

> "Oh, that's the name of the song, is it?" Alice said, trying to feel interested.
>
> "No, you don't understand," the Knight said, looking a little vexed. "That's what the name is *called*. The name really is *'The Aged Aged Man.'*"
>
> "Then I ought to have said 'That's what the song is called'?" Alice corrected herself.
>
> "No, you oughtn't: that's quite another thing! The *song* is called *'Ways and Means'*: but that's only what it's *called,* you know!"
>
> "Well, what *is* the song, then?" said Alice, who was by this time completely bewildered.
>
> "I was coming to that," the Knight said. "The song really is *'A-sitting On A Gate. . . .'*"

The issues it raises are technical and abstract, but not without excitement. Pause and analyze the situation which the White Knight describes. There are two things involved, the name of the song and the song itself. Of the name it can be said a) what the name *is,* b) what the name *is called.* And of the song itself it can be said a) what *the song* is, and b) what *the song* is called. (p. 164)

The word "call" is ambiguous. We call a person by name or nickname: if I had known Keats intimately I might *call* him "Jack." In another sense I describe him to someone else; then I *call* him "England's greatest romantic poet" or "one whose name is writ in water." The first illustrates what a name is called, and is the arbitrary assigning of a tag to an individual. The second is an example of what a thing is called, and how information is conveyed. You might say that Keats was so many inches tall; he could then be called a man of such-and-such a stature. You might call a day a period of so many minutes, or a pebble on the beach of Time. Here is essentially the difference between a dictionary and an encyclopedia: the one gives information about names, the other provides data about things. Except, as the White Knight made clear, the items in a dictionary are not properly names at all!

We come, finally, to the thing itself. And here Lewis Carroll was definitely pulling our leg. The White Knight said that the song he was singing *was* "A-sitting On A Gate"—but remember that that was not its name! It was not even what the thing was called—a sad song or a lengthy one. What could it be, if it is neither the name of the song nor a description of the song? It could only be *the thing itself.* . . . To be consistent, the White Knight, when he had said that the song *is* . . . , could only have burst into the song itself. Whether consistent or not, the White Knight is Lewis Carroll's cherished gift to logicians. (p. 165)

The wealth of material which Lewis Carroll presents for the illuminating of philosophy is almost without end. . . . Alice wondered what happens to the flame of a candle when the candle is put out, while she was shutting up like a telescope during her first adventure in Wonderland, wondered whether she would go out altogether—"like a candle." The Pre-Socratics enjoyed that problem. What *does* happen to the flame?

Some of the philosophic problems are perennial. In her bewilderment at the sudden changes in her size and the conversations with a unique rabbit who wore a vest and gloves and carried a watch, Alice asks herself, "Who in the world am I? Ah, *that's* the great puzzle." And it is one of the greatest of philosophic puzzles, the problem of personal identity. (pp. 166-67)

Another passage of major philosophic interest from the **Looking-Glass** book has to do with dreams. Tweedledum and Tweedledee and Alice are watching the Red King, who is sleeping fit to snore his head off, as Tweedledum remarked:

> "He's dreaming now," said Tweedledee, "and what do you think he's dreaming about?"
>
> Alice said, "Nobody can guess that."
>
> "Why, about *you!*" Tweedledee explained, clapping his hands triumphantly. "And if he left off dreaming about you, where do you suppose you'd be?"
>
> "Where I am now, of course," said Alice.
>
> "Not you!" Tweedledee retorted contemptuously. "You'd be nowhere. Why, you're only a sort of thing in his dream!"
>
> "If that there King was to wake," added Tweedledum, "you'd go out—bang!—just like a candle."
>
> "I shouldn't!" Alice exclaimed indignantly. "Besides if I'm only a sort of thing in his dream, what are *you*, I should like to know?"
>
> "Ditto," said Tweedledum.
>
> "Ditto, ditto!" cried Tweedledee.

The Red King performs the function of God in the philosophy of Bishop Berkeley, for whom the tree in the forest exists when there are no humans to perceive it. To be is to be perceived, ultimately in the mind of God—or the Red King. (p. 169)

Lewis Carroll is at his best when he considers time. The Looking-Glass country was a place in which time moved backwards. Through a playful reference to memory, he approaches the curious character of Looking-Glass punishment:

> "What sort of things do *you* remember best?" Alice ventured to ask.
>
> "Oh, things that happened the week after next," the Queen replied in a careless tone. "For instance, now," she went on, sticking a large piece of plaster on her finger as she spoke, "there's the King's Messenger. He's in prison now, being punished; and the trial doesn't even begin till next Wednesday; and of course the crime comes last of all."
>
> "Suppose he never commits the crime?" said Alice.
>
> "That would be all the better, wouldn't it?" the Queen said, as she bound the plaster around her finger with a bit of ribbon. . . .

Alice was sure there was a mistake somewhere. It reminds one of the story about the irate father who spanked his son for fighting. When the boy insisted he had not been in a fight the father replied, as he continued to apply the hairbrush, that even if he had not been in one that day he was sure to be in one soon. (pp. 170-71)

It just does not make sense. Punishment exists in a Bergsonian time-with-direction. As everyone knows who has seen movies run backwards, most human actions so lose their significance when reversed as to appear hilarious. (p. 171)

One final temporal reference has also to do with the poor disheveled White Queen, who couldn't keep her shawl straight and who had got her brush so tangled in her hair that Alice had to retrieve it for her. Alice said she thought the Queen should have a lady's maid to take care of her:

> "I'm sure I'll take *you* with pleasure!" the Queen said. "Twopence a week, and jam every other day."
>
> Alice couldn't help but laughing, as she said, "I don't want you to hire *me*—and I don't care for jam."
>
> "It's very good jam," said the Queen.
>
> "Well, I don't want any *today,* at any rate."
>
> "You couldn't have it if you *did* want it," the Queen said. "The rule is jam tomorrow and jam yesterday—but never jam *today*."
>
> "It *must* come sometime to 'jam today,'" Alice objected.
>
> "No, it can't," said the Queen. "It's jam every *other* day; today isn't any other day, you know."
>
> "I don't understand you," said Alice. "It's dreadfully confusing!"

And so it is. The difficulty is partly the result of one of Lewis Carroll's favorite devices in entertaining children, the play on words. It is also in part the philosophic problem of knowing when the present becomes the past and the future the present. It is the problem with which James was concerned when he described time as shaped like a saddle. It is the problem that bothers the Idealist when he realizes that he can never know the present: to know it is to make it an object of our thinking and hence to put it into the past. Can the present ever be known? Can we ever have jam in the todayness of tomorrow? By its nature tomorrow must come; also, by its very definition, it can never come. (p. 173)

The world of Lewis Carroll is more extensive than most travelers in it realize. Less familiar, though unforgettable once visited, is the wild region of the Snark and the Boojum and the Bellman's problem with the bowsprit that got mixed with the rudder sometimes, in **The Hunting of the Snark.** The more conventional land of the story of **Sylvie and Bruno** and the amusing architecture of Lewis Carroll's logic exercises are now seldom included in an itinerary. There is even a vacation spot for students of government, the little-known **"The Dynamics of a Particle,"** involving plain superficiality, obtuse anger, and acute anger (the inclination of two voters to one another whose views are not in the same direction); a world in which a speaker may digress from one point to another, a controversy be raised about any question and at any distance from that question. . . .

If this essay has any "porpoise" it is to send you, the reader, to the pleasures of philosophy and logic by way of the unique fascination of Lewis Carroll. And do not get caught in the elusiveness of Alice's jam. Do not promise yourself the delights of philosophy tomorrow. Enjoy them now: take Lewis Carroll down from the shelf tonight. (p. 174)

Roger W. Holmes, "The Philosopher's 'Alice in Wonderland'," in The Antioch Review *(copyright © 1959 by The Antioch Review Inc.; reprinted by permission of the Editors), Vol. XIX, No. 2, Summer, 1959 (and reprinted in* Aspects of Alice: Lewis Carroll's Dreamchild as Seen through the Critics' Looking-Glasses, 1865-1971, *edited by Robert Phillips, The Vanguard Press Inc., 1971, pp. 159-74).*

PATRICIA MEYER SPACKS   (essay date 1961)

Only in the shallowest sense . . . does the trip through the Looking-Glass reveal disorder and nonsense. Carroll's world of fantasy is most profoundly, in its semantic aspects at least, the sort of world for which such a logician as Charles Dodgson might yearn: a world of truth and order. That it *seems* disorderly is a condemnation of the ordinary sloppy thinking of the reader and the sloppy traditions of his language; the apparent disorder concealing deep logic is an effective satiric weapon. (p. 269)

In the actual world, no real relation exists between the bark of a dog and the bark of a tree, and flowers in hard ground are as speechless as flowers in soft. In the topsy-turvy world behind the Looking-Glass, on the other hand, there is far more regard for the import of words: their meaning cannot be evaded simply by making distinctions between "bow-wow" and "bough-wough." And the unavoidable suggestion is that our everyday use of language is largely arbitrary and unaccountable.

The same sort of pun continues throughout the book, with ever deepening effect. The Rocking-horse-fly is made of wood and gets about by swinging itself from branch to branch; the Bread-and-butter-fly consists of thin slices of bread and butter, a crust, and a lump of sugar, and lives on weak tea with cream in it. . . . The Frog can't understand why anyone should answer the door unless it has been asking something; he admonishes Alice for knocking at it: "Wexes it, you know." Alice, become a queen, is rebuked for attempting to slice a leg of mutton after she has been presented to it: "It isn't etiquette to cut anyone you've been introduced to."

All of this is extremely confusing for Alice, as confusing as dreams usually are. Yet the confusion is really a product of her own initial commitment to the ordinary world: she, not her Looking-Glass interlocutors, is actually illogical. And to the extent that readers participate in the sense of dream-chaos, the joke is on them—for the apparent illogic of the dream-world comes actually from a profound absence of chaos. (pp. 269-70)

In a modern classic of semantics, *The Meaning of Meaning,* C. K. Ogden and I. A. Richards examine the usage of several noted modern philosophers with regard to the word "meaning." This is their conclusion: "In spite of a tacit assumption that the term is sufficiently understood, no principle governs its usage, nor does any technique exist whereby confusion may be avoided." Yet the most elementary principle of semantics is that agreement about the use of signs rather than the signs themselves enables us to communicate. With Humpty Dumpty's method of dealing with words, chaos is come again. For the severe social discipline of language suggested by the puns previously noted, he substitutes an altogether solipsistic discipline—but Ogden and Richards stand as eloquent witnesses to the prevalence of Solipsism in the usage of the real world. Again, the Looking-Glass world has the logical advantage: if Humpty Dumpty's technique would end by making communication impossible, at least he is clear-sighted enough to know what he is doing. In our world, failures of communication from similar causes are frequently complicated by our unwillingness to recognize high-handed dealings with language. (pp. 270-71)

[The] ultimate point of Humpty Dumpty's method with language is the same as the point of the Gnat's exposition of Looking-Glass insect life. In both cases, the central revelation is the same: that language, the symbolic representation of experience, has power of its own. Thus anthropologists find that primitive magic depends upon an equation between the *names* of things and their souls, and semanticists learn that a shift of words in a crucial context equals a shift of emotion. . . . [Alice] is accustomed to a world in which language is used more loosely: it is never used loosely in Looking-Glass Land. (pp. 271-72)

Even the use of nursery rhymes here, so different from anything in *Alice in Wonderland,* is a demonstration of the force of language. The existence of the rhymes itself seems to determine the course of the action related to them: again, a dictum of Ogden and Richards is supported—that "the power of words is the most conservative force in our life." It is the power of words that eliminates the possibility of change from the Looking-Glass world: actions are by words eternally fixed, and no deviation from them is conceivable. Tweedledum and Tweedledee fight over their rattle not because they want to—quite the contrary—but because, in effect, the rhyme says they do, and therefore they must. They are forced on by a special sort of fate, the sort most appropriate to a work so largely dominated by preoccupation with language. (pp. 272-73)

So it seems apparent that language is a theme underlying virtually all the episodes of *Through the Looking-Glass.* Through four main devices Lewis Carroll makes his points about language: through the punning which demonstrates the looseness with which words are ordinarily used; through the personal discipline imposed on language by Humpty Dumpty and, less extensively, by the White Knight; through the emphasis on the importance of names; and through the convention that existent sets of words can determine patterns of events. The attitudes thus communicated add a special emphasis to the more obvious motif of the difficulty of distinguishing between appearance and reality.

This problem of appearance and reality is, of course, implicit or explicit in all dream narratives: if the action of the dream seems true, it implies the question of whether it is not essentially as true as the more solid waking world. In *Through the Looking-Glass,* the problem is certainly explicit. Tweedledum and Tweedledee show Alice the Red King asleep under a tree, and tell her that he is dreaming of her. . . . The final question of the book is "who it was that dreamed it all," Alice or the Red King. (pp. 273-74)

The question of who is real, Alice or the Red King; which is real, the everyday world or the dream-world, is given added intensity by the special attitude toward language so closely involved in the narrative. For the dream-world is, as I have tried to show, a world which has as a dominant characteristic a high regard for the demands of language, a world in which language is taken seriously. It seems, to this extent, closer the realm of absolute truth than the existence from which Alice escapes. If, in other words, it is not actually truer than the other world, it, in a sense, should be; by being more logical, it *seems* more true. (p. 274)

[Carroll's] play with words, playful though it is, depends for its satiric effect on the assumed existence of some realm of absolutes, in which there is a real equation between a truth and its symbolic expression. The Looking-Glass world is far from this realm of absolutes, but not so far as the "real" world, where play with language is not so free, and where we too often fail to recognize the possibility that there may indeed be a significant difference between what a song is called and what it really is. As Swift, in his discussion of Houyhnhnms and Yahoos [in *Gulliver's Travels*], sheds doubts on man's claim to be a rational animal, so Carroll, with none of Swift's venom but with equally high standards, suggests in *Through the Looking-Glass* the dubiety of the assumption that human communication is logical and accurate. Both men are concerned with modes of human action; Carroll's special genius, perhaps, lies in his ability to disguise charmingly the seriousness of his concern, to make the most playful quality of his work at the same time its didactic crux. (pp. 274-75)

> *Patricia Meyer Spacks, "Logic and Language in 'Through the Looking-Glass'," in* ETC. *(copyright 1961 by the International Society for General Semantics; reprinted by permission of the International Society for General Semantics), Vol. XVIII, No. 1, April, 1961 (and reprinted in* Aspects of Alice: Lewis Carroll's Dreamchild as Seen through the Critics' Looking-Glasses, 1865-1971, *edited by Robert Phillips, The Vanguard Press Inc., 1971, pp. 267-78).*

ELSIE LEACH   (essay date 1964)

What Dodgson was doing in *Alice in Wonderland* can be seen if the reader compares the book to standard fare written earlier for children. . . . [Few] authors chose to model their stories upon the fairy tale or to incorporate fairy-tale elements into new narratives for children. . . . English books written for children were supposed to be realistic in order to provide essential instruction in religion and/or morality, that the child might become a virtuous, reasonable adult. But unlike earlier English writers, Dodgson used a number of characteristics found in fairy tales. . . . Perhaps it is not irrelevant that his heroine is the small child turned out into a magical world as in so many folk tales. Of course, *Alice* differs from the folk tale in that the heroine's antagonists are not clearly defined as "black" villains or villainesses, and no magical formula guides her to triumphant vindication. But the similarities to the fairy tale help mark the book as a departure from the norm of contemporary stories written for children.

The choice of fairy-tale elements is just one indication that in writing *Alice* Dodgson rejected the rational approach of earlier writers for children, that is, their insistent appeal to the reason of their readers. Nothing could be more antirational than Dodgson's narrative, for he chose a *dream* situation as central (and this dream is no orderly allegory). Conscious exercise of reason is not apparent in the situations which occur or in Alice's particular attempts to cope with them. (pp. 89-90)

The character of Alice herself is a bit puzzling, even to the modern child, because it does not fit a stereotype. How much more unusual she must have seemed to Victorian children, used to girl angels fated for an early death (in Dickens, Stowe, and others), or to impossibly virtuous little ladies, or to naughty girls who eventually reform in response to heavy adult pressure. . . . But Alice is neither naughty nor overly nice. Her curiosity leads her into the initial adventure and most of the later ones of the book, yet she is not punished for it, nor does she regret what she has done. On the other hand, we are not left with the feeling that Alice's experiences have been especially rewarding either. (p. 90)

Indeed, one of the most striking features of the book, especially if one reviews what was standard fare for children of the time, is the strong reaction *against* didacticism which so many of the episodes illustrate. Dodgson's parodies of the instructive verse which children were made to memorize and recite ridicule its solemnity and the practice of inflicting it upon the young. (p. 91)

[In the episode of the croquet game], the Duchess's motto is "Everything's got a moral, if only you can find it," and she becomes more and more extravagant and nonsensical in her application of axioms to everything Alice says and does. When Dodgson makes a ridiculous character like the Duchess praise and practice moralizing in this manner, he clearly indicates his attitude toward didactism directed against children. (pp. 91-2)

Not only is the Duchess inconsistent, unpleasant, and pointlessly didactic, but she is of no help to Alice in her predicament. Nor are the other characters Alice meets, with the exception of the amiable Cheshire Cat, the only one to admit he is mad; they snap at her, preach to her, confuse her, or ignore her. . . . Throughout the book Dodgson describes sympathetically the child's feelings of frustration at the illogical ways of adults—their ponderous didacticism, and contradictory behavior. They aren't consistent and they aren't fair. And their puzzling use of language is one very important manifestation of their bullying and condescension; it is primarily a mode of self-exposure rather than an exercise in logic and semantics. The underlying message of *Alice,* then, is a rejection of adult authority, a vindication of the rights of the child, even the right of the child to self-assertion. . . . The child-adult conflict of *Alice* gives direction to the heroine's adventures and controls all the notable features of the work—the kind of character Alice is, her relationships with the other characters, the texture of the dialogue, and the placement of the incidents. Thus the work can be read as a meaningful whole, and its meaning is not very esoteric after all. (p. 92)

> *Elsie Leach, "'Alice in Wonderland' in Perspective," in* The Victorian Newsletter *(copyright 1964 by* The Victorian Newsletter; *reprinted by permission of* The Victorian Newsletter*), No. 25, Spring, 1964 (and reprinted in* Aspects of Alice: Lewis Carroll's Dreamchild as Seen through the Critics' Looking-Glasses, 1865-1971, *edited by Robert Phillips, The Vanguard Press Inc., pp. 88-92).*

JUDITH BLOOMINGDALE   (essay date 1971)

Alice's Adventures in Wonderland and *Through the Looking-Glass* can best be described as the harrowing of the Victorian Hell. Alice herself is Carroll's Beatrice—the Muse of his Comedy. Her fall down the rabbit-hole is that of Eve—Adam's soul mate, or *anima*—and her ultimate coronation as Queen of the Looking-Glass World is an unconscious anticipation of the Assumption of Mary as Queen of Heaven, which became Catholic dogma in 1950. As Mary completes with Her maternal nature the incompleteness of the Trinity and fulfills in this divine destiny the task given Her on earth, Alice in her own time is Victoria Regina, heiress of all the ages. (pp. 378-79)

Circumstances led Carroll to personify his inner image of woman in Alice, the heroine of his most famous books. She figures in the drama of Wonderland-Looking-Glass as a positive *anima* who moves from innocence to experience, unconsciousness to consciousness. . . .

To complicate matters, Alice is in turn possessed by the *animus,* the image of man that compensates the feminine consciousness. The *animus* corresponds to the *Logos,* or Word, and influences a woman's thinking. Both powers are notably disturbed in their functioning in the worlds of Wonderland and the Looking-Glass. Alice, who is significantly at the age of reason, suffers memory losses and tries vainly to make "sense" of nonsense—*logic* is the key theme of the book. (p. 379)

The endless moralizing endemic to [the patriarchal Victorian system of education] typifies Alice's every encounter with the figures in Wonderland and the Looking-Glass World. This is surely the way Victorian society must have appeared to a little (Liddell) girl intent on making sense of a preeminently "sensible" world whose denial of social equality to women typically sentimentalized its feminine unconscious either as angel or whore. It is precisely this sentimentality that Carroll attacks by way of his art. The little sisters who live at the bottom of the treacle well are obviously in danger of drowning in sugar, spice, and everything nice before Carroll comes to their rescue.

It is the heroine Alice who enables Carroll to perform his own heroic artistic task. By serving as the Beatrice of his journey, she becomes the *mediatrix* to his psychic universe. (p. 380)

The figure of the mother with nursing baby, the Madonna, can be seen in grotesque form in the "Pig and Pepper" chapter of *Wonderland,* when the hideous Duchess shouts a violent lullaby—"Speak roughly to your little boy"—which Carroll's mother never did; she merely "kissed away" all his justifiable anger at being so soon deprived [by his younger sister] of her attentions. . . . The undisputed Queen (of Hearts!) of [*Wonderland*] is a Shiva, a tyrant whose fiat is "Off with his head!" In a matriarchal household ruled by velvet paws, the male mouse is in continual danger of emasculation—the *Wonderland* Mouse's attenuated tale ends in "death." Carroll's fight for identity in the nursery and later in the rectory garden was a Darwinian struggle for survival. The typical flower in the Looking-Glass-World garden is no wallflower, but a veritable virago—true Tiger-lily. Carroll's ego, a Humpty Dumpty (egg), was in perpetual peril of falling, never to be put together again. Indeed, Humpty Dumpty is the archetypal image of Platonic man—seen as the union of white and yolk, *yang* and *yin,* enclosed within a thin shell of brittle skin. His defensive hypersensitivity to a little girl's curiosity is a reflection of the touchiness of a boy too long exposed to feminine eyes. (p. 381)

Carroll's choice of a girl child, a heroine rather than a hero, is . . . significant in that it affirms the androgynous nature of the presexual self. (p. 383)

Alice as child-heroine undergoes the experiences ascribed by Jung to the mythical child—i.e. abandonment, invincibility, and hermaphroditism. The child is all that is abandoned and exposed and at the same time divinely powerful; the insignificant, dubious beginning, and the triumphal end. (p. 384)

The central riddle of *Wonderland* that must be solved is that which Alice asks the Duchess concerning the Cheshire Cat: "Please would you tell me . . . why your cat grins like that?" As the cat is traditionally feminine (as the dog is masculine), the Cheshire Cat's presence in the central, far-from-silent tableau of *Wonderland,* the emotionally (pepper) charged kitchen of the Duchess's house, is that of the Eternal Feminine. The mad grin of the appearing and disappearing gargoyle, which literally "hangs over" the heads of the participants in the game of life, is an insane version of the enigmatic smile of the "Mona Lisa," the mask of the Sphinx—supreme embodiment of the riddle of the universe.

The Duchess here plays the role of the Great Mother, the "loving and terrible mother" . . . the paradoxical Kali of Indian religion, a role she shares with the Queen of Hearts of the Trial scene. (pp. 385-86)

The heroic task that Alice as child-heroine must perform in *Wonderland* is to assert in the face of a primitive, threatening universe the reasonableness of her own (and the Knave of Hearts') right to exist, and actively to rebel against the social order that sentences to death ("Off with her head!") all those who demur from its mad decrees. (p. 386)

Alice wakes up from her dream-turned-nightmare—but the riddle of the Cheshire Cat remains unanswered.

In the Looking-Glass world that Alice next enters, she finds herself on a higher plane of existence than the Hell of Wonderland. As the heroine who dared challenge the tyranny of the Queen of that kingdom, she finds that she is to be made a queen herself if she can successfully complete her moves as White Pawn in the "great huge game of chess that's being played—all over the world—if this *is* the world at all, you know." She also admits to a secret desire—"I wouldn't mind being a Pawn, if only I might join—though of course I should *like* to be a Queen, best." The Red and White Queens of this kingdom are notably more agreeable than the Queen of Hearts and aid Alice in her journey. What has made this transformation possible?

The missing link between *Wonderland* and *Looking-Glass* and the real climax of their drama is the mythological event revealed in the "nonsense" of the famous **"Jabberwocky"** poem. The child-hero of this drama is, significantly, a boy—a miniature St. George: and like the traditional Christian hero, the deed he performs is that of rescuing a damsel in distress—i.e., the princess, or *anima,* about to be devoured by the dragon, which here symbolizes the evil attributes of the mother archetype. Here the threat of the terrible Queen of Wonderland is turned against herself in the apotheosized form of the Jabberwock:

> One, two! One, two! And through and through
> The vorpal blade went snicker-snack.
> He left it dead, and with its head
> He went galumphing back.

The awe-ful deed is done. The son-hero is received with joy by his father and the goal of atonement (at-one-ment) with the masculine principle is achieved.

At once Alice finds herself in the garden she has long sought to enter. The garden is here a positive mother symbol, no longer wild nature, but cultivated, tended, fostered—in short, the Garden of Live Flowers. (pp. 386-87)

The Red Queen, the governess-like mentor of Alice's *Looking-Glass* journey, is an extension of the positive character of the Duchess of *Wonderland.* . . . When Alice tenders her secret wish to be Queen, the Red Queen only smiles pleasantly and says, "That's easily managed. You can be the White Queen's Pawn. . . . When you get to the Eighth Square you'll be a Queen . . . we shall be Queens together, and it's all feasting and fun!" (p. 387)

In the last important move before her coronation, Alice is rescued from a Red Knight "brandishing a great club," by a White Knight—the apotheosis of the positive *animus,* the Jabberwock-slayer grown up, the "knight in shining armor" of chivalry and romance. Like Chaucer's "verray, parfit, gentil knight," he is the type of Christian hero whose function is to serve his Lady. Though it is his avowed function to conduct Alice safely to the end of the wood, it is in fact she who helps him by waving her handkerchief in encouragemen as he rides out of sight. It is not so much the actual help tendered her by her rescuer that Alice remembers, but the vividness of his presence, "the mild blue eyes and kindly smile of the Knight— the setting sun gleaming through his hair, and shining on his armour in a blaze of light that quite dazzled her—" This is the mystical moment for Alice. Not her own coronation, but that of the true King of the Looking-Glass World. Not a mighty world conquerer, but the gentle man, the pure and innocent hero, the risen Christ radiant with scars—Christ as Clown. . . . The White Knight is the advent of Christ the harlequin into the consciousness of an age that has forgotten how to laugh. Most of all, the very awkwardness of his comic falls constitute a clown—like choreography that is a mock parallel to the dance of David before the ark of the Lord. . . . (p. 388)

As absurd hero of his age, the White Knight sums up the history of Western civilization: he is at once Christ, St. George, the Knight of the Grail, Lancelot, Don Quixote, and finally modern man, none of whose ingenious "inventions" have really "worked"—in the sense that they have not brought him happiness. It is the paradox of her protector's power and powerlessness that evokes in Alice the "little scream of laughter" that marks the joyous epiphany of the book. She *sees* in her Knight's "gentle foolish face," in his "mild blue eyes and kindly smile," the face of the Lord of Life. (pp. 388-89)

[The] mock crowning and elevation of Alice to the position of Queen of the Looking-Glass World that also parallels the passion of Christ the clown. As He was deserted, denied, taunted in His royal robes, crowned with thorns and humiliated, made to drink the bitter vinegar of man's scorn and lifted up on the cross as "King of the Jews," so is she deserted by her sleeping companions, mocked by the powerful, crowned with a very heavy, tight golden crown, made to drink "sand [mixed] with cider," "wool [mixed] with the wine"; starved at her own triumphal banquet—the mock queen of a mad world. . . .

And what has really made Alice Queen of the Looking-Glass World? Throughout her journey she has exhibited (to enumerate the qualities Carroll attributes to her) curiosity, courage, kindness, intelligence, courtesy, dignity, a sense of humor, humility, sympathy, propriety, respect, imagination, wonder, initiative, gratitude, patience, affection, thoughtfulness, integrity, and a sense of justice in the face of an outrageous universe. It is notable that Alice assumes increasingly maternal characteristics in her journey. (p. 389)

Finally, then, it is her capacity for compassion that distinguishes Alice the Queen. . . .

Love is the golden crown that makes Alice the true Queen of Hearts. (p. 390)

> *Judith Bloomingdale, "Alice as Anima: The Image of Woman in Carroll's Classic," in* Aspects of Alice: Lewis Carroll's Dreamchild as Seen through the Critics' Looking-Glasses, 1865-1971, *edited by Robert Phillips (copyright © 1971 by The Vanguard Press, Inc.; reprinted by permission of the publisher, Vanguard Press, Inc.), Vanguard, 1971, pp. 378-90.*

KATHLEEN BLAKE   (essay date 1974)

Sylvie and Bruno and *Sylvie and Bruno Concluded* . . . add up to nine hundred odd pages of what Carroll calls in his preface to *Sylvie and Bruno,* "litterature," a peculiar narrative threading of "random flashes of thought" and "dream-suggestions." The "stringing together, upon the thread of a consecutive story" of these materials is most unusual. (p. 150)

To accept these novels, I believe the reader's state must be as incapable of rufflement as the Narrator's, who says at . . . [an] eerie seizure and the appearance of fairies in the drawing room, "'I felt no shock of surprise, but accepted the fact with the same unreasoning apathy with which one meets the events of a dream.'" (p. 152)

The Narrator is inclined in the *Sylvie and Bruno* books much more than in the *Alices* to direct philosophizing . . . (though the sentiment itself might suit either) because the later work is a "new departure" and intended to mix "some of the graver thoughts of human life" with "acceptable nonsense for children" . . . , an often incongruous and sometimes irritating mixture. Indeed, the nonsense itself sometimes fails to be entirely acceptable. Sometimes the wordplay has the spare, dry, not to say grim, humor of the *Alices*. . . . (p. 153)

We may not be entirely happy that Carroll chose to mix with his kaleidoscopically playful nonsense "thoughts . . . not wholly out of harmony with the graver cadences of Life" although we surely must concede that it *was* a new departure. Since I don't think that these graver thoughts, which are most interesting in themselves, really coalesce with the nonsense (except in the general sense that it is playful and some of the thoughts are on play) such that form and content must by rights be treated as one thing, I will consider now in semi-isolation the main theme in these books as it relates in particular to play, games, and sport. (p. 158)

[Let] us take play and games first. The *Sylvie and Bruno* books have something to say about the theoretical query, how does one pass the time, or what is pastime? Carroll presents two choices: (1) ecstatic bliss or nirvana, which makes time and consciousness cease to exist, or else (2) striving toward some self-proposed end, which gives time and consciousness a purpose and makes them pleasant. Carroll offers music and dance as emblems of the nirvana solution, but the solution he really backs appears to be diversions in time, an infinite stretch of them. Diversions of this sort, including all games, are characterized by highly defined time limits and goal orientation. Passages in *Sylvie and Bruno* and *Sylvie and Bruno Concluded* and their prefaces, which offer observations on a variety of subjects Carroll considered important, circle intriguingly around these characteristics and the problems that go with them.

As part of a moral disquisition on preparing for death inserted into the preface of *Sylvie and Bruno,* the unsettling specter is raised of a perpetual existence beyond the grave, more terrible than simple annihilation: "endless ages . . . , with nothing to do, nothing to hope for, nothing to love!" . . . (pp. 158-59)

The prospect of infinity is evoked again in a speech by the old Earl in *Sylvie and Bruno Concluded.* He is disturbed by the "nightmare" that in eternity men would run out of activities to occupy their minds. This would most obviously occur in practical fields like medicine, but could happen also in the theoretical field of mathematics. . . . (p. 159)

Carroll's Earl allows himself sometimes to evade the prospect of an eventual running out of things toward which to aspire, and worse, a running out of the energy of aspiration. He is sometimes tempted to pray for personal annihilation, or a type of Buddhist nirvana. . . .

On several occasions Carroll offers images of something not unlike a timeless, self-sufficient, nonstriving nirvana. One of these depends on a narrow confinement of time (one hour). This eliminates the necessity of consciousness of sequence, so that the experience may be imagined as an undivided moment of ecstasy. (p. 161)

In both novels Carroll is committed to an ideal of playfulness. (p.162)

The point is once explicitly made that heaven may begin on earth for the simple and childlike. Thus in one of Sylvie's and Bruno's adventures with the Narrator in which they perform good to the neighborhood, the harried, nagging drunkard's wife turns suddenly "playful" after her burden is relieved by her husband's vow to quit drinking. Playfulness and youthfulness are equated. . . . (p. 163)

However, Carroll's conception of play as basically games with rules of a highly competitive character inevitably gives a certain sharp edge even to the play of Sylvie and Bruno. . . . This abrasive edge becomes apparent in Bruno's attitude, for of the brother and sister pair he is the less excessively good. Bruno is highly conscious of the rules governing all activities, and he is at times gingerly rebellious (as Alice gets to be) in the face of those he doesn't care for. . . .

Bruno does dare to think and to challenge unpalatable codes. Nevertheless, he shows great deference to rules and authorities in those areas that he likes and accepts. (p. 164)

For loving sister and brother, the two are sharp, almost brutal with each other. Sylvie's tone in her fiat about rules, . . . is not gentle. The "sweet" Sylvie is capable of telling a story ostensibly for Bruno's amusement, though in fact it frightens him sadly, all about a fat, juicy little boy named Bruno who is pursued by a lion. . . . As a matter of fact, the stories told by both Sylvie and Bruno almost always concern one animal eating or trying to eat up another, with much emphasis on biting off or "nubbling" of heads.

Sylvie and Bruno are perpetually at each other in these novels. But it is very important to notice, as the Narrator reminds us, that theirs is a "new form of argument" that always ends in much hugging and kissing. . . . This is an abnormal ending for argument, which is after all a form of "collision." Its analogy to the physical collision of war is pointed out in Arthur's fanciful speculation on the possible communication between beings on a crescendo and diminuendo scale of relative size. To preserve fairness, argument would have to be substituted for war.

In their playful collision Sylvie and Bruno stop short of that normal issue of competitive games, the triumph of one over the other. (pp. 165-66)

The continuum linking playfulness, conceived in the form of games, and furious aggressiveness, constitutes a difficulty, I believe, for Carroll. He attempts to resolve it by providing for the intervention of love before the germ of aggressivity in play causes it to loose its innocence, an innocence he never denies. And yet he does certainly question the innocence of that form of play he calls sport. He is uneasy with the latter because it carries the implicit motive of self-aggrandizement into extreme destructiveness, of others and even of oneself. (p. 167)

Carroll's attitude [in the prefaces to the two novels] is mixed, but for the most part negative. He says hunting down a man-eating tiger may yield legitimate exultation, but not seeking one's pleasure in the easy slaughter of defenseless creatures. . . . When he treats the "Morality of Sport" in his second preface, Carroll confesses there is too much pro and con to cover, but he states his conclusion, that the infliction of pain, when there is no necessity, is cruel and wrong. . . .

Infliction of pain is a form of mastery, which when striven for without necessity makes an activity into play. That Carroll rejects the extreme manifestation of the destructive aspect of play can be gathered from the *Sylvie and Bruno* books. . . . (pp. 167-68)

> *Kathleen Blake, "Sport," in her Play, Games, and Sport: The Literary Works of Lewis Carroll (copyright © 1974 by Cornell University; used by permission of the publisher, Cornell University Press), Cornell University Press, 1974, pp. 149-79.*

ADDITIONAL BIBLIOGRAPHY

Atherton, J. S. "Lewis Carroll and *Finnegans Wake*." *English Studies* 33, No. 1 (1952): 1-15.*
    Considers the influence of Carroll on *Finnegans Wake*, and discusses Joyce's negative attitude toward Carroll's morals.

Auden, W. H. "Today's Wonder-World Needs Alice." *The New York Times* (1 July 1962): VI, 5.
    Discusses the validity of Alice as a contemporary heroine.

Collingwood, Stuart Dodgson. *The Life and Letters of Lewis Carroll*. New York: The Century Co., 1899, 448 p.
    A sympathetic and often intentionally obscure account of Carroll's life by his nephew, with some valuable primary source material.

Gaffney, Wilbur G. "Humpty Dumpty and Heresy; or, The Case of the Curate's Egg." *Western Humanities Review* XXII, No. 2 (Spring 1968): 131-41.*
    Identifies Humpty Dumpty as a parody of the British philosopher Thomas Hobbes.

Gernsheim, Helmut. *Lewis Carroll: Photographer*. New York: Chanticleer Press Inc., 1950, 126 p.
    A detailed look at Carroll's photographic technique. This book includes 64 plates, and a description of each.

Gregory, Horace. "On Lewis Carroll's Alice and Her White Knight and Wordsworth's *Ode on Immortality*." In his *The Shield of Achilles: Essays on Beliefs in Poetry*, pp. 90-105. New York: Harcourt, Brace and Company, 1944.*
    Discusses the White Knight's ballad of the "aged aged man" and its relation to Wordsworth's *Ode on Intimations of Immortality*.

Hinz, John. "Alice Meets the Don." *The South Atlantic Quarterly* LII, No. 2 (April 1953): 253-266.*
    Compares *Alice* and Cervantes's *Don Quixote* in character and incident, placing both in the mock-heroic tradition.

Kibel, Alvin C. "Logic and Satire in *Alice in Wonderland*." *The American Scholar* 43, No. 4 (Autumn 1974): 605-29.
    Analyzes Carroll's use of logical principles for the purpose of satire. This essay contends that Carroll saw a disjunction between the motives of one character and the purpose of the action as a whole.

Kurrik, Maire Jaanus. "Carroll's *Alice in Wonderland*." In her *Literature and Negation*, pp. 197-205. New York: Columbia University Press, 1979.
    Explores Alice's growth in the understanding of language as being. This essay concludes that *Alice* is more positive than books it prefigures, such as the works of Joyce and Beckett, in that it is in the end an affirmation rather than a denial of the self.

Lennon, Florence Becker. *Victoria through the Looking Glass: The Life of Lewis Carroll*. New York: Simon and Schuster, 1945, 387 p.
     The definitive biography of Carroll, containing analysis of his relationship with the Victorian age.

Levin, Harry. "Wonderland Revisited." *Kenyon Review* XXVII, No. 4 (Autumn 1965): 591-616.
     An essay commemorating *Alice*'s centennial, exploring the reasons it has lasted through the years as an important work of fantasy.

Parry, Judge. "The Early Writings of Lewis Carroll." *Cornhill Magazine* LVI, No. 334 (April 1924): 455-68.
     A discussion of Carroll's early poetry, most of it contributed to small magazines. Much of his early poetry was revised and incorporated in later versions in his later work.

Rackin, Donald. "Corrective Laughter: Carroll's *Alice* and Popular Children's Literature of the Nineteenth Century." *Journal of Popular Culture* I, No. 3 (Winter 1967): 243-55.*
     Claims that *Alice,* by satirizing popular children's books of its time, represented a return to an emphasis on imagination in children's literature.

Taylor, Alexander L. *The White Knight: A Study of C. L. Dodgson (Lewis Carroll)*. London: Oliver and Boyd, 1952, 209 p.
     Attempts to debunk both the "split personality" theory and the notion that the *Alice* books are "nonsense." Taylor's book contains logical explanations of what had previously been thought to be nonsense in Carroll's work.

Thody, Philip. "Lewis Carroll and the Surrealists." *The Twentieth Century* 163, No. 975 (May 1958): 427-34.*
     A humourous account detailing how the surrealists in France mistook Carroll for a social revolutionary.

Van Doren, Mark, Porter, Katherine Anne, and Russell, Bertrand. "Lewis Carroll: *Alice in Wonderland*." In *The New Invitation to Learning,* edited by Mark Van Doren, pp. 206-20. New York: Random House, 1942.
     Transcript of a radio interview in which the three speakers discuss their reactions to *Alice* as children, and their attitude toward it as adults.

George Darley

1795-1846

(Also wrote under the pseudonyms of Guy Penseval, Geoffrey Crayon, Jr., and John Lacy) Irish-born poet, short story writer, dramatist, essayist, and critic.

Darley is generally considered a writer of limited range but one who, in relative isolation and obscurity, created works that foreshadow trends in post-Romantic and Symbolist poetry.

Born in Dublin, Darley moved to London in 1822 after graduating with degrees in mathematics and classics from Trinity College. He was afflicted with an incurable stammer, and as this impediment grew stronger his confidence grew weaker, denying him both academic and social success.

As a contributor to the *London Magazine*, Darley was an often harsh drama and art critic. He also published verse and short stories in the journal. Although his first book, *The Errors of Ecstasie*, was largely ignored, Darley's drama *Sylvia; or, The May Queen*, was acclaimed by such well-known literary figures as Henry Cary, Charles Lamb, Elizabeth Barrett Browning, Alfred, Lord Tennyson, and Thomas Carlyle. However, the play met with little popular success. Darley turned to writing mathematics textbooks, which were much better received than his literary efforts.

Darley reached the highest point of his career with the poem *Nepenthe*. The dream imagery, meter, and symbolism used in *Nepenthe* demonstrate characteristics of late Romanticism, and foreshadow the Symbolist movement. Indeed, much of Darley's poetry seems particularly modern in its imagery, lyrical power, eloquent grace, and musical charm.

Darley's contribution to English poetry was not fully appreciated until the twentieth century. He is now regarded as a minor poet of originality and imagination.

©P. Seefert

PRINCIPAL WORKS

The Errors of Ecstasie (poetry) 1822
Labours of Idleness; or Seven Night's Entertainments [as Guy Penseval] (short stories) 1826
Sylvia; or, The May Queen (verse drama) 1827
It Is Not Beautie I Demande (poetry) 1828
The New Sketch Book [as Geoffrey Crayon, Jr.] (short stories) 1829
Nepenthe (poetry) 1835
Thomas à Becket (verse drama) 1840
Ethelstan; or, The Battle of Brunanburh (verse drama) 1841

THE LITERARY CHRONICLE AND WEEKLY REVIEW
(essay date 1822)

The Errors of Extasie, not withstanding the singularity of its title and its metaphysical speculations, is a very superior poem; there is an originality, an elegance, and a grandeur in its diction which is quite invigorating, and will rank it high among the productions of the day. (p. 213)

"'The Errors of Extasie: A Dramatic Poem','" in
The Literary Chronicle and Weekly Review, *No. 151,*
April 6, 1822, pp. 211-13.

CHARLES WENTWORTH DILKE (essay date 1824)

["**The Errors of Ecstasie**"] is in blank verse. Such a design cannot be good. . . . [A] work of which the scheme and construction is rhapsodical will never be read, and therefore it must be said to be bad, as all other things are when they will not answer the purpose they were made for. . . . [Those] who would be ready to apprehend at a glance a novel image, or a delicate peculiarity of expression, could not fail to perceive that the work is remarkable. There are passages in it, which, were they to be quoted as belonging to some poet of acknowledged pre-eminence, would not be considered as insufficient titles to his place. There is a good deal in it which is more characteristic of our earlier poetry than of the present, but there is an obvious ambition which belongs to our times. (p. 571)

There is sometimes a mixture of metaphysics in the poem which would be better expurgated. We never saw metaphysics and poetry combined with advantage, except in Mr. Coleridge's productions, and those too are in all other respects *sui generis,* and of a kind which the world seems to think more extraordinary than entertaining. (p. 572)

[If the poems included in **"The Errors of Ecstasie"** appear absurd, it is due] to the extravagance of the design. . . . (p. 573)

[Though the poems are a] work of youth, and . . . in parts deformed by extravagance, it will not be lightly treated by those who are capable of comprehending its merits. All its merits it is not to be expected that any large class of readers will perceive; . . . but here are passages which few will have read without admiring. The public have been satiated, and poetry is now little relished. With regard to that taste for it which is left, it is of a kind which we desire to see improved, and it belongs to such men as this author, in the approaching maturity of his powers, to correct and amend what is amiss in it. . . .

[Darley's] is a work as well of intellect as of temperament, although his fancy has been inadequately controlled. His poetry, though faulty enough, is to be blamed for the wildness of imagination, not the weakness of sensuality. There are no effeminacies, no allusions to the innocence of adultery and the omnipotence of love. His are not the tones of a discontented infidel or an emasculated melodist.

The language of the author is too abundant in uncommon words. We do not object to such words in moderation, especially when, as often in this book, they are peculiarly suitable to the verse. In this case also they belong to the language of a scholar and appear to have been derived from a familiarity with various branches of knowledge. But some belong too peculiarly to such branches to be fit for general use; and the frequency of their occurrence makes the whole appear somewhat whimsical and eccentric. (p. 575)

> *Charles Wentworth Dilke, "Review: 'The Errors of Ecstasie',"* in London Magazine, *Vol. X, December, 1824, pp. 571-76.*

MARY RUSSELL MITFORD   (essay date 1852)

Gifted certainly with high talents, and with the love of song, which to enthusiastic youth seems the only real vocation, [George Darley] offended his father, a wealthy alderman of Dublin, by devoting his whole existence to poetry, and found, when too late, that the fame for which he had sacrificed worldly fortune eluded his pursuit. It is impossible not to sympathize with such a trial; not to feel how severe must be the sufferings of a man conscious of no common power, who sees day by day the popularity for which he yearns won by far inferior spirits, and works which he despises passing through edition after edition, while his own writings are gathering dust upon the publisher's shelves or sold as waste paper to the pastry-cook or the chandler. What wonder that the disenchanted poet should be transmuted into a cold and caustic critic, or that the disappointed man should withdraw into the narrowest limits of a friendly society, a hermit in the center of London!

To add to these griefs, Mr. Darley was afflicted by a natural infirmity not uncommon with men of high talent and nervous and susceptible temperament. He stammered so much as to render conversation painful and difficult to himself, and distressing to his companions. The consciousness of this imped-

iment . . . increased its intensity, causing him to shrink from all unnecessary communications, except with the few to whom he was familiarly accustomed, and of whose appreciation he was sure. They seem to have esteemed him much. (pp. 503-04)

Never was so thorough an abnegation of all literary coxcombry as was exhibited in the outward form of . . . **"Nepenthe,"** unless there may be some suspicion of affectation in the remarkable homeliness, not to say squalidness, of the strange little pamphlet, as compared with the grace and refinement of the poetry. Printed with the most imperfect and broken types, upon a coarse, discolored paper, like that in which a country shopkeeper puts up his tea, with two dusky leaves of a still dingier hue, at least a size too small for cover, and garnished at top and bottom with a running margin in his own writing, such (resembling nothing but a street ballad or an old "broadside") is the singular disguise . . . of the striking poem. . . . There is no reading the whole, for there is an intoxication about it that turns one's brain. Such a poet could never have been popular. But he was a poet. (pp. 504-05)

> *Mary Russell Mitford, "Unrecognized Poets," in her* Recollections of a Literary Life; or, Books, Places, and People, *Harper & Brothers, Publishers, 1852, pp. 503-14.**

THE SATURDAY REVIEW   (essay date 1891)

[Darley was not] a great poet. He belonged to a class that was rather largely represented in his time, the men who were stimulated to write by an impassioned love of poetry, and by their admiration for the treasures of seventeenth-century work which had just been re-opened to the reading public. To appreciate Darley we must remember the early verses of Leigh Hunt and Keats, we must think of Reynolds, the friend of Keats, of Wade, the author of *Mundi et Cordis Carmina*, of Wells, the author of *Joseph and his Brethren*, of Barry Cornwall, of George Dyer. He is less than greatest of these, he is greater than the least; but we have to think of his work in this connexion not to do it an injustice. So far as counterfeiting the accent of the seventeenth-century went, Darley was not less skilful than the cleverest man of his generation. . . .

Darley tries to sing on his own account, and not in imitation of the seventeenth century, his magic leaves him. *Sylvia, the May Queen,* is the cleverest of his sustained pieces. It is a play of the class of Nabbes, and needs only to be raggeder in some places and bolder in others to seem a genuine antique of the Caroline decay. But it is difficult indeed to discover in the whole of it one scene, or even one lyric, quite good enough to quote, not as clever imitation, but for its own sake, as poetry. Better things, we believe, can be found in the rare and almost inaccessible **Ethelstan,** where some of the ballads are quite spirited, and the blank verse, if less sweet, more nervously sustained than in **Sylvia.**

[*Poems of the Late George Darley*] are, we suppose, the latest of Darley's poems. Many of them are graceful, a few of them are musical, but those which affect us most pleasantly are those in which imitation of others is most apparent. These newly-discovered lyrics do nothing to modify our conception of their author. Elegant, accomplished, tasteful, George Darley did not sing because he must, but because he would. His poetry lacks individuality, and could scarcely have attracted so much attention as it did in any generation less indulgent to poetic mediocrity than that which flourished between the death of Keats and the recognition of Tennyson. (p. 255)

"Reviews: George Darley," in The Saturday Review, London, Vol. LXXII, No. 1870, August 29, 1891, pp. 255-56.

THE SATURDAY REVIEW   (essay date 1892)

[With the re-issue of *Sylvia; or, the May Queen*] George Darley is at last given that opportunity of making his peace with the public which his troubled spirit so long desired, and desired in vain. We confess that we did not expect to see Darley re-issued. . . . Genuine lovers of Darley for his own sake, for Darley in blunt type and grey boards, will, we are sure, continue to be few, and those few, we are afraid, will continue to be lukewarm. The author of *Sylvia* is a curiosity, and nothing can galvanize him into a genius. All the king's horses—that is to say, the charms of tasteful *format*—and all the king's men—that is to say, indulgent and limp-minded critics—cannot put literary life into him again.

George Darley . . . was one of those ardent provincial youths who arrive in London equipped with more talent than force of character, and who are too deeply wounded in their first battle with indigence and disappointment ever to regain their resolution. He was not wanting in taste or talent, or intellectual resource, but he seems to have lacked fortitude, and to have allowed his misfortunes to tinge his nature with a feeble cynicism. As a poet, his gifts were checked and then crushed by his constant labours in journalism, and even in educational hackwork of a very dreary kind; but the character of his earliest lyrics gives no reason to suppose that his natural genius was very decided. (pp. 52-3)

Sylvia; or, the May Queen [is] Darley's pretty masterpiece, on which, if at all, his reputation as a poet must be based. . . . None of the elements of a play, in the ordinary sense, are to be met with in *Sylvia*. It is really the libretto of an opera, and the only chance it possesses of . . . popularity on the stage . . . would be found if some musical composer of the class of the late Mr. Goring Thomas should select it as a texture upon which to embroider his melodies.

It remains to see how this libretto is executed. We may reply at once, with very great skill and delicacy. It reads like a canto of pretty extracts from all the Jacobean poets of pastoral. . . . *Sylvia* is the *pastiche* of a *pastiche*, the copy of an imitation, and is of a rather tame and languishing order of gracefulness. The verse, whether lyrical or blank, is not merely correct, but skilful; the rhymes are rich, the conceits are numerous and appropriate, all the exterior parts of poetry are present. What is wanted is the spirit of life. Yet there are things in *Sylvia* which almost make us retract the harshness of our judgment. . . .

The texture of *Sylvia* is rendered the more closely Jacobean by buffooneries and horseplay, which seem as though they ought to become indelicate, or as if they once had been naughty, but had been very carefully revised. . . . We like Darley least when he is funny. This sort of thing has a hollow sound. . . . [Darley's] opera is a graceful and picturesque trifle which it does nobody any harm to reprint. Messrs. Dent have now restored [Darley] to a forgetful world. . . . We do not say that these men were poets, but they were curious writers, and the school was one which possesses, taken as a whole, a certain historical interest. (p. 53)

"Reviews: 'Sylvia'," in The Saturday Review, London, Vol. LXXIV, No. 1915, July 9, 1892, pp. 52-3.

THE ATHENAEUM   (essay date 1897)

Poet, mathematician, critic, George Darley was a remarkable man. . . .

We have read 'Nepenthe' with amazement. It is young as crocus and daffodil; it "smells April and May." Yet it is the work of a man of middle age. Something there is of Shelley, but, in the main, it follows the 'Endymion' of Keats, not wisely, but too well. Conceive a poet of forty-four imitating 'Endymion,' with all its youthful beauties. Evidently Darley at forty-four was very young. . . . He died five years afterwards, having never grown old. 'Nepenthe' has more wandering inconsequence than 'Endymion,' which is by comparison orderly, a poem with a backbone. Darley's poem has the merest pious desire of a plan, of an argument; and he adds confusion by occasional vague aspirations after an allegory, mere doubtful hints introduced to satisfy his conscience, when he would have done better frankly to own that he was following the unforeseen meanderings of his wild and untrained fancy. His style lavishes itself in every wilful extravagance the most youthful beginner can hit upon. Yet he is a poet, and 'Nepenthe' would be pronounced by all full of luxuriant promise, had it only been the work of twenty-four, instead of forty-four.

The first canto opens with great charm of expression and fancy; but before long it passes into a rhapsody, wherein the poet's powers are overstrained to a degree of almost insane abandonment. Yet always it is overstrained power, not overstrained weakness. . . .

[The] finest portion of the poem is the second canto. There is still the same inconsequence of so-called narrative; there is still abundant violence of diction and fancy pushed beyond its pitch. But here, more than in the first canto, there are 'Endymion' like compensations—descriptive fantasies ardently visioned and vividly expressed. If violence every now and again makes you overlook the richness of the diction, yet richness is constantly seducing you to overlook the violences of diction. Read with forbearance and patience, and you will not go unrewarded. Though we have dwelt so much on the degree to which Darley is inspired by 'Endymion,' [Darley] is no mere imitator, and there are distinct individualities in 'Nepenthe.' He has by no means Keats's power of imagery. His peculiar power lies in descriptive fantasy. He was born into the period when the Spasmodic School was prevalent, and shares its characteristics. . . . The power of the second canto of 'Nepenthe' consists in a luxuriant fancy, which shows itself not by way of imagery, but by way of description. The description is . . . what we may call phantasmal description, expressed in the most glowing diction. Again, the metre is mainly the metre of 'Endymion,' with much of its looseness; but there are passages which show a quite personal sense of metre, which might have come to something very perfect and distinctive. (p. 377)

[Darley] is often obscure through sheer loose grammar, a too impetuous and inartificial hurrying on of unconsidered clauses, hunched anyhow on each other's shoulders, or through curious perversities of construction. . . . His Latinisms and archaisms may appal the most daring. We delight in Latinisms and archaisms; but they must be archaisms and Latinisms. Darley has a greatly daring way of inventing would-be Latinisms in light-hearted defiance of scholarship, such as "reptilous" and "deluginous" And if he has no archaism to hand, he forges archaisms with blissful unconcern. "Bordure" seems to us suspicious, and "bittern"—not as the name of a bird, but as a synonym for "bitter"—has not a precedent to stand on. He exposes many such forged archaisms to the searching eye. But we are little disposed to insist on them.

George Darley, in conclusion, seems to us an extraordinary phenomenon in literature. How did it come to be—by what baffling from circumstance, by what inscrutable whim of nature—that a poet of luxuriant youthful power and promise was to the last a poet of luxuriant youthful power and promise; that the author of **'Nepenthe'** wrote **'Nepenthe'**—at forty-four? It is useless to speculate. We can read **'Nepenthe,'** and be thankful for what we have, yet sorrowful for what we have not. Could we ever have had it? If Darley had been born thirty years later—perhaps yes. (p. 378)

> *"Literature: 'Nepenthe: A Poem in Two Cantos',"*
> in The Athenaeum, *No. 3647, September 18, 1897,*
> *pp. 377-78.*

THE QUARTERLY REVIEW (essay date 1902)

Darley may very likely have been a minor poet, but, if he was so, he is no exception to the rule. He had very little in common with the age in which he lived. In the midst of the enthusiasm for Byron he declined to be Byronic, and so lived unread. In 1842 came the decisive appearance of Tennyson, which eventually killed Byronism. But even then Darley did not profit by the changed fashion; for the new poet carried all before him, and Darley was left stranded again. We can look back calmly enough now upon the literary rivalries of early Victorian days, and it may be that our cooler judgment will exalt Darley to the position which his contemporaries denied him. . . .

[Darley] was twenty-seven years old when [**'The Errors of Ecstasie'**] came out; but the poems which it contains show but little sign even of that degree of maturity which might be expected from a man of his age. Probably a good many of them were boyish efforts. . . . There are fine lines in it, but the blank-verse is monotonous and the Mystic's utterances are prolix and involved. The Moon, on the other hand, is a lady of strong common-sense, and expresses herself in language that is straightforward even to baldness. (p. 179)

'The Errors of Ecstasie' was, of course, a complete failure from the popular point of view, but it may have helped to introduce Darley to the literary world. (p. 180)

[**'Labours of Idleness'**] are written in a somewhat laboured style, but some of them have a touch of pathos, and others are not without power. The best of them are **'Lilian of the Vale,'** a pretty pastoral, which is the germ of his later work, **'Sylvia, or the May Queen,'** and a fantastic Poe-like piece of extravagance called **'The Dead Man's Dream,'** which, for all its exaggeration, contains some really imaginative writing. But to lovers of Darley the most interesting thing in the book is the first essay, **'The Enchanted Lyre,'** which may safely be taken as a piece of autobiography, and, so read, gives us a clearer picture of the poet's character and attitude towards life than all the comments and criticisms of his contemporaries. (pp. 181-82)

An attractive feature of **'The Labours of Idleness'** lies in the number of charming lyrics with which it is plentifully besprinkled. (p. 183)

Some of Darley's friends seem to have thought that **'Lilian of the Vale'** had the elements of a drama in it; and in response to their suggestions he wrote **'Sylvia, or the May Queen,'** in which the innocent little plot of his tale is made the basis of a kind of fairy opera. The appearance of **'Sylvia'** was, in a sense, the culminating point of Darley's career. With it he approached nearer to the confines of success than at any other time in his unhappy life. **'Sylvia'** is often referred to in the memoirs of the period, and never without eulogy. . . . But the public would none of it, and Darley had again to endure the bitterness of disappointed hopes. To tell the truth, **'Sylvia'** has few of the elements of success. So far as form goes, it more resembles one of the later Caroline masques or fairy pastorals than anything else, and it is a clever imitation, too; but the stuff of a dramatic poet was not in Darley. **'Sylvia'** begins brightly enough, but the poet soon tires of his puppets; and before the play is over their shadowy figures seem to have melted into thin air. Besides, Darley's blank-verse is often nerveless and monotonous, and he ventured to supplement the poetical parts of **'Sylvia'** with would-be humorous prose scenes, which are the most dismal fooling imaginable. The charm of **'Sylvia'** lies in the exquisite lyrics in which it abounds, and in the versified introductions to the various scenes, which recall the Elizabethan use of the Chorus. These 'scenical directions in verse,' as Lamb called them, are the distinguishing feature of **'Sylvia.'** In the earlier scenes they are brief and to the point; but, as the play goes on and the author gradually loses interest in his characters, he concentrates himself more and more upon these choral interludes, until towards the close of the play he presents us, *à propos des bottes,* with—of all things in the world—a piece of literary criticism in the shape of a comparison between Milton and Byron! Oddly as it occurs, there is some very fine writing in the passage. . . . (pp. 183-84)

The original **'Nepenthe'** is a curiosity in more ways than one. With a strange kind of affectation, Darley appears to have taken as much pains to repel a possible reader as the present-day poet takes to entice one to open his book. **'Nepenthe'** is printed in the most careless and unlovely manner upon coarse, dirty paper. It boasts no title-page, no author's name; the pagination is inaccurate and the original cover consisted solely of a couple of pieces of dingy brown paper.

The poem itself is in striking contrast to the squalor of its presentment. It glows with life and colour; it brims over with poetical invention. The great difficulty about it is to believe that it was written by a man of forty. It is instinct with the spirit of youth; it 'smells April and May.' Had it been the work of a boy of twenty, it would have been one of the most promising poems ever written. It has every conceivable fault that the extravagance of youthful fancy can suggest. It has no beginning and no end. The subject is dropped and picked up again a hundred times. . . . But with all its faults it establishes one fact in the plainest possible manner—that Darley was a genuine poet. (p. 187)

There is a woeful lack of order and symmetry in **'Nepenthe,'** but Darley often makes noble amends for the inconsequence of his story by the glowing beauty of isolated passages. The opening of the poem cannot fail to captivate the fancy of a sympathetic reader. (p. 188)

It is difficult to quote any passages from **'Nepenthe'** which shall give an adequate idea of its real value. In a short extract one inevitably misses the rush and swirl of the poetry. The Bacchic revels in the first canto are particularly spirited and vigorous. (p. 189)

But the finest thing in the poem is the beginning of the second canto, which opens with an apostrophe to Antiquity. Here Darley is in his richest and most sonorous vein. Here he has a sustained majesty of expression to which he rarely attains. His diction is almost Miltonic in its grandeur, and the metre which in the first canto has tripped with an airy lightness here takes to itself a measured dignity not unworthy of the author of 'Il Penseroso.' (p. 190)

A remark of Tennyson's about Alexander Smith has been applied to Darley—that he had fancy but not imagination. The application is singularly unjust, as any one who takes the trouble to read even [a] short extract from **'Nepenthe'** will perceive. Darley's fault was an excess rather than a lack of imagination, coupled with an indistinctness of mental vision which often rendered his images obscure and sometimes merely chaotic. Another fault, if it be a fault, is that he sometimes recalls other writers. . . . In structure ['Endymion' and **'Nepenthe'**] are by no means unlike, though, to tell the truth, 'Endymion' is a model of orderliness by the side of the labyrinthine extravagance of **'Nepenthe.'** Metrically, Darley owed little to Keats. The swift arrowy flight of **'Nepenthe'** is worlds away from the slow, voluptuous music of 'Endymion'; and Darley handles his metre with a surer touch than Keats—the Keats of 'Endymion' at any rate—possessed. One does not feel in **'Nepenthe,'** as one does all too often in 'Endymion,' that the rhyme has suggested and even compelled the thought. But, apart from the scheme of his poem, Darley's debts to Keats are sufficiently plain to the careful reader. His Bacchanals, 'light-trooping o'er the distant lea,' carry us back at once to the Indian damsel's song in 'Endymion.'. . . And often a word or phrase in **'Nepenthe'** rings with a memory of Keats. (p. 191)

Darley had imbibed to the full Keats's taste for quaint experiments in diction. Like Keats, he knew his Spenser well, and his fondness for using archaisms in season and out of season amounted to a mannerism. It is true, also, that the English language was sometimes not copious enough to satisfy his requirements; and then he never hesitated about coining a word to suit the emergency. (p. 192)

Next to Keats, we should say that Milton had the greatest share in the making of **'Nepenthe.'** The metre is Milton's, of course, and it is used with a good deal of Milton's technical mastery. Then, again, we detect Milton's influence in Darley's splendid and sonorous use of proper names . . . ; while towards the close . . . there is an exquisite echo of a famous passage in 'Lycidas'. . . . There is noble music in this [poem]; and, when all is said that can be said against **'Nepenthe,'** the poem remains an astonishing performance. Had Darley published it, it could scarcely have failed to make its mark, even though the time was unpropitious for a poem of this kind. (pp. 192-93)

With **'Nepenthe'** the chief interest in Darley's career ceases. Thenceforward, except for an occasional lyric in a magazine, he confined his energies entirely to the drama. For **'Thomas à Becket'** and **'Ethelstan,'** . . . we cannot profess much enthusiasm. . . . Undoubtedly there are beautiful passages in both plays; in fact Darley could hardly write a line without revealing the touch of a true poet; but he had very little dramatic power, and not much idea of characterisation. In both dramas he shows, it is true, a fuller mastery of blank-verse than in **'Sylvia,'** but even here, in spite of bursts of magnificent eloquence, the long speeches, of which here are many, are apt to become monotonous. Of the two plays, **'Thomas à Becket'** is the more vigorous, and perhaps, if subjected to the same process of curtailment and arrangement that turned Tennyson's 'Becket' into

a passable stage-play, it might face the footlights not without success. **'Ethelstan'** is impossible as a drama, but poetically it counts for more than **'Thomas à Becket,'** chiefly on account of the spirited songs of Runilda, the glee-maiden. Darley wrote a third play, **'Plighted Troth,'** which was produced . . . , but was never published. It failed completely, only surviving one performance. Its failure seems to be attributable chiefly to Darley's ignorance of stage technique, for as a poem it evidently had fine qualities. (pp. 194-95)

After his death [Darley] was soon forgotten. The rising sun of Tennyson extinguished the light of lesser stars. Since those days public taste in poetry has undergone many and strange changes. We have found that the idols of our fathers have feet of clay. (p. 196)

> *"A Forgotten Poet: George Darley," in* The Quarterly Review, *Vol. 196, No. 391, July, 1902, pp. 176-96.*

THE ACADEMY AND LITERATURE   (essay date 1902)

The question whether Darley was "forgotten" must, I think, be answered in the affirmative when we reflect that his resuscitation only dates from the "nineties." "Forgotten" poets have a way of being resuscitated, but the second life is never a genuine one. It is a soulless existence at the best. . . . As for Darley, he shares with better men a shady corner in oblivion, notwithstanding Charles Lamb's tribute to his "very poetical poems." He occupies no niche in Mr. T. H. Ward's *English Poets*; he was reduced to anonymity in the first edition of *The Golden Treasury*, and has apparently been omitted in more modern issues: and his fellow-countryman, William Allingham, while including his "modern antique" in *Nightingale Valley*, forgot to name the author. . . . Darley lived in a poetical age; he wrote poetry because his friends wrote it, and he chose a medium of expression which is in favour with exiguous talent; but the world is just, and declines to recognize his laborious pumping from the Pierian spring as a spontaneous welling forth. So Darley is "forgotten."

> *W.F.P., "Correspondence: George Darley," in* The Academy and Literature, *Vol. LXIII, August 9, 1902, p. 164.*

ROBERT BRIDGES   (essay date 1906)

I am not posing as advocate for all of Darley's poems; but I would say that a small and wisely made selection of his shorter pieces would have won him a very different reputation from what he now holds; and that he had great originality in learnedly perfecting rare or new forms of metre and rhythm. . . . **"The Palace of Ruin,"** and the two lyrics **"Down the Dardanelles,"** and **"Wind of the West arise"** in **"Nepenthe"** are sufficient proof of this claim. . . .

The rhythm [of **"Nepenthe"**] is treated with such mastery as to obviate monotony, and is also skilfully relieved by the introduction of a variety of other metres, and occasionally by great freedom, properly motived and harmoniously used. . . . [This] wholly imaginative poem, being like **"Endymion"** an allegory, gives also at first the same effect of a superabundant poetry with a minimum of obvious meaning. But while its general purport may elude or even defy comprehension, the verse and diction—if I may sternly except the first lyric . . .— are throughout masterly, rich and elevated, and one reads with almost unbroken pleasure. . . . As for the allegory, the closer one examines it the less doubt one has that every word was the approved expression of impassioned intention: but since language thus born will carry more than its contemplated interpretation, one cannot look to define the meaning in every detail. (p. 110)

In a good work of art, allegorical or not, the main effect appeals sufficiently to the senses at once, while every detail is good in itself; and from the first I always found plenty of this best kind of pleasure in reading "Nepenthe." (p. 111)

> Robert Bridges, "A Literary Causerie: 'Nepenthe'," in The Academy, No. 1787, August 4, 1906, pp. 110-11.

ALICE MEYNELL (essay date 1922)

It was Beddoes who gave this half-forgotten poet [George Darley], his contemporary, the name of violence. Being conscious of the brief and unimportant pause of poetic inspiration during which they lived, Beddoes wrote a letter of dismay wondering whether it were to the sentimental L.E.L. or to the violent George Darley that the trust of English poetry should be committed. (p. 82)

George Darley's violence, such as it was, had its way principally in a choice of words intended to retrieve the language from the Teutonism that began its fashion before he died in the middle of the century. He apparently did not hold the English language to be finally closed in, and in this he agreed with other and greater men who have used all their strength, at times with a single hand, to hold that door open. But perhaps Darley was not always careful enough of the difference between scholarly Latinisms and those whereof a poet in his haste might not stop to test the doubtful scholarship.

Apart, however, from the Latinisms, which are not many, [there] is with Darley a certain delight in quaintness which makes of Teutonic words a disagreeable kind of slang. 'Streamy vales', for example, is not a welcome phrase. Like to this is the prank of writing 'bittern ooze'. The ambiguity makes the words even grotesque; for the poet is writing of a marsh; is he then making the word 'bitter' more 'quaint', or is he taking the name of a bird for an adjective? Either way he is trifling. But as George Darley died a disappointed man, and as his poetry had light and space in it, and there was lacking the perception of these in his readers at the time, it is rather his beauties than his faults that shall be dealt with here. Life, light, and distance—in poetry—seem to leave on the mind's eye the impression of red, yellow, and blue, radiant less or more according as the life is less or more impassioned, the light celestial, and the space remote; though no red, not even red veiled by the blond and tender colours of humanity, shines in Darley's verse, there is assuredly no dimness in his gold nor dullness in his azure. At the first page of Nepenthe the reader takes a larger and more liberal view of the world of the poet before him, reading this line on the daytime sun

> High on his unpavilioned throne.

It is followed, unfortunately, by some commonplaces, but in itself it is fine. (pp. 82-4)

George Darley wrote of fairies—a dull subject, let us confess at last; and more than half of his drama of Sylvia, the May-Queen, is acted by fairies and fiends at war. But there are some happy fancies even in the prattle of fairy-queens to their courtiers. (p. 84)

Darley was as resolute an Elizabethan as Beddoes, but while Beddoes darkened his skies for the drama of passions graced with trivial flowers blooming in an angry light, Darley addressed himself rather to the imitation of the humour and the prettiness. He copied the Shakespeare of the Midsummer Night's Dream, and though the critics say that his rustics are tedious, it seems to me an unjust judgement. . . . [It] is not fair to say that Darley is really a bore. His Andrea in the May-Queen makes no bad sport of that kind. Darley has the situation and the quality of the laughter from Shakespeare, but the phrase is of his own exceeding ingenuity. . . . Darley had never got free from the habit of anapaestic vulgarities, out of date with all he wrote. . . . (pp. 84-5)

With how much perception, how pliant a turn of thought, how instant a reflection, how delicate a sense of mood and habit Darley could play the seventeenth-century poet is proved by his famous lyric, It is not beauty I demand. . . . In the first edition of the Golden Treasury [edited by F. T. Palgrave] this poem, of then unknown authorship, was placed, carefully timed, between [the seventeenth-century poets] Wotton and Carew. It seems to have been withdrawn altogether when its writer was found to be of the nineteenth century. (p. 86)

> Alice Meynell, "George Darley," in her The Second Person Singular and Other Essays, Oxford University Press, London, 1922, pp. 82-6.

CLAUDE COLLEER ABBOTT (essay date 1928)

The Errors of Ecstasie was probably written after Darley had realized that a fellowship at Trinity College was not for him. . . . It shows a mind in doubt, uncertain of its powers, too considerate of the many sides of the question; a mind that if it dares to fly will dare self-consciously. (p. 15)

It would be easy to pick out the many faults in this poem, such as the poverty of the dialogue, the melodramatic romance, the echoes of other poets, and the provoking neologisms and archaic words . . . which Darley scatters with a full hand. These things do not destroy the striking promise of the whole. At its best the blank verse is quiet, unrhetorical, musical. It has character, though that distinguishing quality is not strongly marked. The epithet often carries undue weight, yet the poet is one who knows the value of words. (p. 16)

There are . . . good things in Darley's prose. . . . The Labours of Idleness is an ambitious attempt by an amateur to write what may be termed imaginative prose. There are few marks of the practised hand in it. . . . The trouble is that there is not imagination enough. The author can embroider a slight fancy gracefully, but vigour of invention is wanting, there is a superfluity of sensibility, and the prose lacks coherence and restraint. He adventures too much of set purpose. My thoughts 'are irregular, venturous, vagabond', he writes, 'but I know them to be so.' The trouble lies in this self-consciousness. When he takes the air with his wings very soon we hear the loud beating and fluttering that betokens his attempt to keep flying. His successes are spasmodic. When these things have been said there is much to praise, particularly the nervous flexibility of the prose and the captivating delicacy of mind that sweetens the whole book. The Labours of Idleness is that notable thing, a failure worth many facile successes. In addition it contains sufficient verse to have established Darley's reputation as a lyric poet. But it attracted no attention. . . . Pedro Ladron, or The Shepherd of Toppledown Hill, is an exercise in the humorous grotesque. It is verbose and unsuccessful, a 'tall' story told by Pedro to astonish the vulgar. . . . The 'love' of the others is unearthly, a fanciful passion not warmed by human blood. Darley's characters are apt to wander unhappily on a plane between the spiritual and the real. The most ambitious tale of all, the elaborately introduced *Dead Man's Dream* . . . , is an excursion into the horrible demanding greater intensity than the author can achieve. The images of terror are painted as still life; they do not move our emotions. The plot of the tale owes much to [Thomas Beddoes's] *The Brides' Tragedy,* and the conduct of it is reminiscent of German romance. (pp. 51-2)

Darley's womenkind are gentle and modest wraiths who from unrequited love pine rapidly away. . . . [*Aileen Astore*] and *Lilian of the Vale,* the prose poem of a visionary loveliness that escapes the author's grasp, are the most distinctive [creations in *The Labours of Idleness*]. Both are set in the romantic wild Ireland of the poet's early memories. They are his escape from reality. (pp. 52-3)

[*Sylvia*] is the book by which [Darley] has been generally known . . . , though it did not establish his reputation with the world at large. (p. 62)

Sylvia will on the whole be regarded as a definite, though limited, success. There is nothing else quite like it in literature and it will keep its place. The wonder is that, being so good, it is not better. The machinery and verve are there, the metrical resource and cunning are almost prodigally apparent, and the author wrote with evident enjoyment. But though most of the poem is poetical only a small part of it is poetry. . . . Darley's first intention was sound: wedded to the right music *Sylvia* would have made an excellent light opera. (p. 63)

There are faults in plenty. *Sylvia* is altogether too long for a work that must dance with unlaboured lightness. Though it does not exactly 'tail off', towards the end of the third act interest weakens, and the catastrophes of the last two acts are needlessly involved. The action could be simplified with advantage. . . . Darley sometimes forgets that it is better for his characters to remain puppets. When he tries to breathe life into them the result is often weak and always astray. . . . Much of it is indeed sorry stuff; it is strange he did not see that a vigorous pruning was imperative. (pp. 63-4)

And yet there are many things to praise. The 'scenical directions' in tripping octosyllabic verse, the 'novel headings to each scene' recommended by Lamb, keep their grace. Much of the swiftly moving dialogue sings out for a musical setting. (p. 64)

The lavishly distributed lyrics are unequal. The best, Floretta's 'I do love the meadow beauties', Nephon's Autolyucs song 'Who wants a gown', and 'O May, thou art a merry time', have a Parnassian perfection of workmanship. (pp. 64-5)

Sylvia should have made Darley's reputation. The air of distinction and aloofness that it still carries should have been plain even to an age that rejoiced in the banalities of L. E. L. and Omnipresence Montgomery. Its significance lies in the fact that it is a craftsman's protest, possibly unconscious, against slipshod work and lazy sentimentality. To read the forgotten verse of the day . . . is to realize that *Sylvia* pointed in the right direction. (p. 65)

All Darley's lyric work is the pursuit of an ideal loveliness. For that reason, we think, he is particularly liable to error, and for that reason also he is likely at times to succeed greatly. . . . At his best he has an authentic voice and tune of his own,

depending in part on a carefully chosen and perfectly apt vocabulary, as remarkable for what it discards as for what it uses, avoiding excess of ornament, colour, and sentiment. Thence flows a gentle and delicately modulated music. . . . (pp. 86-7)

When all Darley's faults have been admitted there remain 'things unquestionable by any one who can get to the point of seeing them face to face as examples of verse'. English poetry in the nineteenth century did not, indeed, have to await the advent of Tennyson for the revelation of exquisitely ordered musical rhythm. . . . [The] lyrics in *The Labours of Idleness* and *Sylvia* show this unmistakably. (p. 94)

Darley's poetry could never have been popular. For that reason his reputation, upheld by the few, has not had to contend with the reaction that follows excessive lip-service. He is, in a sense, a poet's poet. His best work is beyond the reach of time and fashion. If poets must still be measured by the foot-rule let him be called a small classic. For a classic he is, undisputably. (p. 95)

[*Nepenthe*] was a strange intruder in an age of expensively produced Annuals, but most attractive in its strangeness, a poet's protest that poetry alone mattered. (p. 122)

Nepenthe is still, in essence, an obscure poem. (p. 125)

Nepenthe is best read neither as an allegorical poem with a purpose, nor as part of a projected work, but rather as a number of lyric episodes loosely strung together, forming a succession of spiritual adventures. (p. 127)

[Darley's] metrical mastery is apparent [in the first canto of *Nepenthe*]. The intensity of his vision makes him symbolical rather than allegorical. The poetry, at its best, has its own fervid and unmistakable distinction. But because of these qualities we forget, perhaps too readily, Darley's limitations. . . .

The second canto, more disjointed and obscure, shows a falling off. . . . The verse is sonorous rather than dignified, impressive without being convincing. In his use of resounding names Darley's touch is unsure and his epithets are often at fault. (p. 133)

There is much to be said for *Thomas à Becket.* It is an honest and sustained example of its kind. Its merits can be realized in part by reading it after encountering the mediocrities of Tennyson's *Becket,* which owes more than a little to the earlier play, without benefiting from it. Darley attempts to work out many of his dramatic theories, and with some success. The subject was momentous, national, and fit for tragedy. There is a fierce energy in the writing, and, generally, a quick cut and thrust in dialogue, which together prevent the play from becoming dull. He was careful to subordinate poetry to action, and to use, as far as he was able, the language of natural speech. Evidently he had been at great pains to study the period. Yet the brave attempt was foredoomed.

He would have had a better chance of success if he had taken a lesson from Scott and moved his leading historical figures to the background. (p. 220)

Ethelstan was his last attempt to gain the public ear or wring tribute from his friends. For twenty years he had devoted himself to literature, and with no apparent success. . . . Few poets or men of letters can have undergone so bitter and thankless an ordeal of devotion. It continued till his death, for he worked to the end. (p. 231)

Claude Colleer Abbott, in his The Life and Letters of George Darley: Poet and Critic *(reprinted by permission of Oxford University Press), Oxford University Press, Oxford, 1928 (and reprinted by Oxford University Press, Oxford, 1967), 285 p.*

[EDMUND BLUNDEN] (essay date 1929)

"Nepenthe" is the abstract and the many-jewelled crown of Darley's verse, a long and great poem distinct in rhythm, in idiom, and in fable from almost everything else in the nineteenth century. (p. 325)

"Nepenthe" scarcely succeeded in bringing home even the mild cordial which Darley's drooping spirit asked. Miss Mitford's applause was not quite enough. The poet allowed himself slowly to forget even "Nepenthe," and in deliberate fashion endeavoured to construct masterpieces such as his friends might admire and the public might demand—historical dramas. [*Thomas à Becket*] and *Ethelstan* may sometimes be found interred in those thick dreary volumes which ensepulchre the pseudodrama of the early Victorians. They are the most accessible, and the least, of Darley's publications. . . . The sense of "Nepenthe" in Darley's summary is that there is a harmful superflux of joy and of melancholy, and a serene human alliance between joy and melancholy. . . . But "Nepenthe," even imperfectly understood as a masque of Darley or of the passions, is so divine a singing, so seraphical an adventure, that beside its glowing transparency, its transferences of actual and spiritual, its heaven-impelled rapidity and zealous expectancy, most of our celebrated poetical illusions have a heaviness, and seem like painted ships on painted oceans. (pp. 326-27)

[Edmund Blunden,] "George Darley and His Latest Biographer" (originally published as "George Darley," in The Times Literary Supplement, *No. 1441, February 14, 1929), in his* Votive Tablets: Studies Chiefly Appreciative of English Authors and Books *(reprinted by permission of A D Peters & Co Ltd on behalf of the Estate of Edmund Blunden),* Harper & Brothers, Publishers, 1932, pp. 317-29.

A. J. LEVENTHAL (essay date 1950)

So long as Darley's characters, his young lovers, his peasants, his fairies, his demons—so long as they remain puppets who dance lightly on his poetic strings, so long do they hold our attention. We are in elfland—a land of Celtic imagination where imagery and metaphor reach great heights of fantasy. We are carried along by the very facility of the verse—its sheer exuberance—untramelled by considerations of ordinary everyday life. But when Darley, as he sometimes does, abandons the unreal for the real and attempts to graft flesh on his phantoms, he makes *their* blood run luke-warm at the best, and *ours* definitely run cold. (p. 10)

The libraries of the world are filled with the works of defunct authors. Many are irretrievably dead, but now and again we may stumble on some who have unjustly fallen into oblivion. George Darley was such a one and it does not require local patriotism as an impulse to bring him to public notice. His was a universal mind and a lofty purpose. He failed because he was before his time. But now, one hundred years after his death, his verse—particularly in *Nepenthe*—is in tune with some of the best poetry of modern times. (p. 17)

A. J. Leventhal, in his George Darley (1795-1846) *(originally a memorial discourse delivered at Trinity College, Dublin on June 5, 1950),* The Dublin University Press, Ltd., *1950, 17 p.*

PADRAIC COLUM (essay date 1950)

The publication of "Nepenthe" sixty years after the poet had it printed takes Darley out of the twilight zone of minor poetry. . . . "Nepenthe" is said to be unfinished; the poet had it in his mind to write three cantos and has written only two. But would a third canto have completed a poem in which there is no recognizable design? We should read "Nepenthe" not for any interest in the "Mythos" which Darley tried to mould his poem on, but for the pictures that come to us in a flight over mountains, through seas, and across deserts. . . . (p. 51)

The second canto opens with an apostrophe to Antiquity which the poet sets over against Time. I know no passage in poetry which gives so much of the sense of awe that comes to us from the sculptures of Babylon, Egypt, and Persia. . . . (pp. 51-2)

In the hills between Dublin and Wicklow where he spent his childhood he was always looking upon water—he had glimpses of the sea; wells, streams and tarns were in his familiar landscape. . . . When he writes about water he is most inspired. If, instead of the three poems of his that are given in the "Oxford Book," certain poems that came out of his feeling for this element had been given, George Darley would long ago have been praised for the verve I now claim for him. . . . ["**The Mermaidens Vesper Hymn**" and "**The Rebellion of the Waters**," in addition to "**Hymn to the Sun**,"] would certainly make us acknowledge the verve, not in all Darley's poems but in certain of them, and in many passages in "Nepenthe."

Poets are identified by a particular poem of theirs, and the poem that identifies Darley to most readers of collections of poetry is his "**It is not Beauty I demand**," a poem that was mistaken for an authentic Caroline relique. . . . The divergent images in the enumeration are properly fantastic, and yet they are related. As we read the first stanza we know what the conclusion will be, and yet we are carried on by its earnestness of statement. . . . [The] poem is remarkable, not only for the triumphant use of the convention in terms of brilliancy and inventiveness, but also for the gravity, the conviction that upholds it all. We will have to say that Darley contributed nothing to what we can name Irish poetry in English: the few attempts he made to link his imagination with anything that might seem Irish are half-hearted and only reproduce the 'Celticism' of Ossian. (pp. 52-4)

Padraic Colum, "Two Views on George Darley" (reprinted by permission of the Estate of Padraic Colum), in Irish Writing, *No. 12, September, 1950, pp. 50-4.*

L.A.G. STRONG (essay date 1950)

[Darley's] verse, despite flashes of brilliant technical success, remains for the most part uncontrolled in substance. He wrote lyrics of individual beauty, and had a welcome and unusual faculty of introducing into them an epigrammatic wit. But his longer works lack design. They have variety, and novelty, often very bold, of metre and rhythm: but there is an unfinished quality about them, an air of improvisation that reminds one of Shelley's off moments. Yet—and here I differ mildly from Padraic Colum [see excerpt above]—Darley's achievement at his height was a real addition to the technique and substance of poetry. . . .

I do not see how anyone can fail to recognize a new voice [in his poetry], an individual technique, and, what is evident in [many passages], though seldom consistent and never long sustained, a real control over the turbulent material of the dream. Dream was Darley's keynote. He opened the gates generously and for the most part fearlessly, but was too much at the mercy of what came through. Poets of his type resemble mediums who receive uncritically whatever enters their field; whereas the great medium, the great artist retains a measure of conscious control, not necessarily exercised at the time of writing, but manifest in revision and in the finished work which is put before the public. Darley had original gifts, but they were not quite strong enough. He himself was not strong enough. ". . . I have seldom the power to direct my mind, and must *only* follow it." (p. 58)

L.A.G. Strong, "Two Views on George Darley" (reprinted by permission of A D Peters & Co Ltd), in Irish Writing, *No. 12, September, 1950, pp. 54-9.*

JOHN HEATH-STUBBS   (essay date 1950)

[The] opening decades of the Victorian era saw the mature development of [a poet] whose natural place was in the succession of the Romantics, rather than with [his] Victorian contemporaries and successors. Darley's work received a little, though limited, recognition during his lifetime. (pp. 21-2)

[Darley], it seems to me, had at least as much potential poetic power as Browning or Tennyson, yet [he was] unable to weather the troubled seas of the nineteenth century. . . . The explanation, I believe, is this: Browning or Tennyson, like good Victorians, achieved a compromise—though at a great spiritual cost. . . . [There] was another factor—that of economics. . . . Now, though neither Browning nor Tennyson in their early years was in affluent circumstances, they were nevertheless in possession of sufficient private income to be able to devote themselves entirely to poetry even though that poetry was neglected by the public. This was not the case with . . . Darley, [who was] forced to dissipate [his] energies in journalistic work. Darley was also diverted from literature to the more profitable study of mathematics. . . . (pp. 22-3)

[The merits of Darley's poetry are] now generally recognized; yet I do not think [his] work will ever be widely popular. Compared with that of [his] Romantic predecessors there is a morbidity, a love of the strange and grotesque, above all a harshness in [his] imagery and conceptions, which is repellent to normal minds. . . . The mighty deserts and heaths of Darley's *Nepenthe,* the fantastic mythological and animal figures of the same poem, [and] the cold "syren" which appears so often in his minor lyrics, . . . are among the factors which give to [his] poetry an aura of harshness, strangeness, and sterility. (pp. 23-4)

[The harshness in Darley's poetry may be due to the fact that he was a Romantic] born too late into an uncongenial world. (p. 24)

The melody of [*It is Not Beauty I Demand*], and the genuine wit of some of the lines, might well have been struck out by Carew or other of the Caroline lyrists. But there is an excess of contemplative sensuality in some of the images, and a touch of sentimentality in the closing stanzas, which betray the poet of a later school, intellectually more undisciplined. Neverthe-

less, it is a favourable specimen of Darley's work. . . . The bulk of [Darley's work] is *pastiche*; but some modern critics have been too ready to use that word in a purely derogatory sense. At its best, *pastiche* may lead to the genuine recovery of a valuable mode of poetic feeling which has been lost. . . .

But there is one poem of Darley's—the two cantos of the unfinished *Nepenthe*—in which he reveals himself as a highly original writer, and in the direct line of succession from Keats and Shelley—and also from Blake. There is no other poem of like length in the English language which possesses such a continuous intensity of lyrical music and vivid imagery. Written in the four-stress couplet of *L'Allegro,* varied by the introducing of more complicated stanza forms, the whole poem, though narrative in subject, is really one intense, breathless lyric, hurrying the reader on with a truly Dionysiac inspiration. (p. 28)

Nepenthe remains a highly original and valuable contribution to the imaginative survey the early nineteenth-century Romantics made of the world of interior experience. It is also a poem of considerable technical interest; the freedom of its metrical plan, its sharp transitions and its vivid use of dream imagery, anticipate much that is characteristic of the poetry of our time. . . .

In the work of Darley, we can see Romanticism pushed to the limits of normal experience. (p. 37)

John Heath-Stubbs, "The Defeat of Romanticism," in his The Darkling Plain: A Study of the Later Fortunes of Romanticism in English Poetry from George Darley to W. B. Yeats *(reprinted by permission of David Higham Associates Limited, as agents for the author),* Eyre & Spottiswoode, 1950, pp. 21-61.*

JAMES REEVES   (essay date 1974)

Darley was a minor poet and, by his own standards, must be considered a failure. But this was in an age when to be minor and a failure was to some extent creditable. Writing after the full tide of Romanticism, from Wordsworth to Shelley, had subsided, and the influence of Byron, which Darley deplored, was paramount, he had strong and clearly formulated views on what poetry should be; but his personal qualities were not such as to enable him to impose these views on his time, or even, in any marked degree, imprint them on his own work. He lacked drive, assurance, perhaps even ambition. It was left to such poets as Tennyson and Mrs Browning to represent the ideals of early Victorian readers. Darley was only too painfully aware of his personal limitations. Indeed, he almost made a virtue of them. In an article entitled *The Enchanted Lyre* he wrote:

> I was, in fine, such an incomprehensible, unsystematised, impersonal compound of opposite qualities, with no overwhelming power of mind to carry off, as I have seen in others, these heterogeneous particles in a flood of intellectuality, that I quickly perceived obscurity was the sphere in which nature had destined me to shine, and that the very best compliment my friends could pay me, when I had left them, was to forget me and my thoughts for ever.

Darley believed that contemporary poetry had degenerated into the sentimentality and pretty-prettiness of popular poets such as Barry Cornwall on the one hand and the rhetorical hollowness of Byron and his imitators on the other. He expressed strong disapproval of Byron's influence on the poetic drama of the time; but in attempting this form, he himself followed a will o' the wisp that had misled others and was to mislead more. Poetic drama was dead long before the beginning of Victoria's reign, but the poets were very slow to acknowledge this. In any case, Darley's own views and inclinations were not in the direction of drama but of lyric. He believed that poetry should approximate to song, and that rhythm was the poet's central inspiration. He had a good ear which, however, sometimes failed him. Yet the sound of his poems is often fresh and refreshing when we are jaded by the almost mechanical impeccability of Tennyson. He sought a way out of the impasse at which poetry had arrived by going backwards— to the Middle Ages, to the Elizabethans and the seventeenth century. There are in his lyrics many echoes of Shakespeare. The diction which Darley accordingly adopted was artificial in the extreme. There is a time for artificiality, as distinct from naturalness, in the diction of poetry: although Darley's style never fully emerges from artificiality long enough to make a powerful impact, it is difficult to see what other course a man of his beliefs and his temperament could have taken. (pp. 136-37)

Darley's pastoral play *Sylvia* was a failure, and is chiefly remarkable for its lyrics. The best of his work, however, is to be found in *Nepenthe,* where his real command of striking and imaginative imagery, and richness and sonority of language find their best expression. His debt to Shelley and Keats, and especially to such symbolic dream-poems as *Alastor* and *Endymion,* is obvious. His best lyric, however, *O blest unfabled incense tree,* is immediately reminiscent of Coleridge. It deserves to be better known, and is one of the few nineteenth-century poems worthy to be judged alongside *Kubla Khan.* In other lyrics, such as *The Demon's Cave,* there is evidence of a macabre, Jacobean sensibility. *O May, thou art a merry time* is an effective exercise in Elizabethan lyric. In *Siren Chorus* the clear-cut imagery and imaginative range are notable, but lyrics such as *Final Chrous* will offend some readers by the artificiality of their over-poetic diction. *A Sea Dream* is an attractive evocation of a submarine landscape, and it is such poems as this which incline us to say that the further Darley is from mundane realities, the happier he is. It is, moreover, almost a truism to say that Darley's inspiration, as he himself knew, was almost wholly literary. In the end, this must count against him. But perhaps it is better to be a good, original and interesting literary poet than one of no technical accomplishment concerned with day-to-day realities. *It is not beauty I demand* is a successful and committed pastiche of seventeenth-century lyric. . . . (pp. 137-38)

James Reeves, "Commentary and Notes: George Darley" (© James Reeves 1974), in Five Late Romantic Poets, *edited by James Reeves, Heinemann, 1974, pp. 135-39.*

ANNE RIDLER (essay date 1978)

[Nothing] of Darley's is in print except a few often-repeated extracts in anthologies.

He deserves better than this. It is true that there is a great deal of dross among his poems. . . . Yet his ear for verse was as subtle and fine as Tennyson's, and at the moments when his imagination caught fire he created, as only the best poets can, a world which is unmistakably and delightfully his. For every

good poet makes his own verbal paradise, which his reader too can share: something derived from the work of others, and yet exclusively his own creation. (p. 11)

If Darley is to be assessed by his merits, it must be by the fineness of his ear for poetic rhythm, as well as by the flashes of imaginative power displayed in *Nepenthe.* . . . (p. 27)

Darley had indeed a highly-developed and subtle sense of rhythm, which enabled him not only to borrow stanza-forms for his own purposes, or to mimic the successes of other poets, but to develop forms of his own. . . . The metrical experiments begin early, and at first falter occasionally, as when, in some poems in *The Errors of Ecstasie,* a tricky rhythm is not sustained right through. But in one of the lyrics in that book, **'To a Stream',** which I have included in my selection, the simplicity of his best devices can be seen. The mere lengthening of a final line by a syllable, when the ear expects a triple-accented line, has the effect of an interrupted cadence in music, a faltering and a surprise. I quote one stanza, though it cannot give the full richness of the sound, for the final lines of each stanza rhyme with each other.

> Wild and silly Stream!
>   Ere the wish be vain,
> Turn to thy grassy spring,
>   Murmurer! again.
> Tears, tears of sorrow deep
> Rovers o'er their follies weep,
> For a dear and distant home.

Campion had used the same device in 'Never weather-beaten sail', and to express the same emotion of longing for a happier state. (p. 28)

It is only rarely that one can feel Darley's love poems to be addressed to a real human being, and his use of the bee's activities as a sexual metaphor (one which positively haunts the pages of his *Poetical Works*) is often embarrassingly coy. The poems addressed to Maria d'Arley, however, do convey a greater sense of reality, and the ones which adopt the seventeenth-century lyric form are none the less personal for that. Thanks to the fineness of his ear, and his sympathy with the genre, he was able to use a borrowed form to express a personal emotion, a genuine poetic experience. The 'distancing' which the form provided freed his tongue as a more direct way of expression could not have done.

One cannot call this pastiche, because a personal emotion is involved. (pp. 32-3)

'To mie Tirante', a pseudo-Elizabethan sonnet, is only a partial success, but **'The Promise',** which is one of his happiest and pleasantest love poems, surely has Marlowe's 'Come live with me and be my love' in the background. Both Marvell and Milton inspired the verse of *Nepenthe,* and Darley took from them just what he needed, even if occasionally the voice of the greater poet seems to drown the lesser. His least successful borrowing is the ballad form which he used for **'The Fight of the Forlorn',** a strained attempt to become excited over Irish history. . . . (p. 33)

Equally unsatisfactory is Darley's use of blank verse. The Shakespearian echoes overpower his own voice, and in *Sylvia,* his pastoral drama, the most successful parts are (apart from a few of the lyrics) the 'scenical directions in verse', as Lamb called them, which are in rhymed octosyllabics. . . . *Sylvia* cannot be called a success, yet as a kind of poetry that aspires to the condition of music (and Darley, who loved music, had at first intended it as an opera) it has a character of its own. (pp. 33-4)

In *Ethelstan* the songs of the Glee-Maiden, in Anglo-Saxon style, are quite successful . . . , and there are some vivid passages where the verse is descriptive and alliterative. . . . (p. 35)

Yet the self-knowledge that detects its own limitations and avoids exposing them, Darley did not possess, and unfortunately his ear for diction was not as reliable as his rhythmical sense. In his early poems he was constantly experimenting with unfamiliar or coined words, and that was natural enough. But he had very little instinctive sense of how to domesticate his recondite words, so that epithets like *indulcedinous, canorous, suspensive*, stand out uncomfortably from their surroundings. Even as late as *Nepenthe*, within a dozen lines one has *deluginous, bedreamed, undulous, purulent*, and *bittern* (for *bitter*). (p. 36)

Did Darley know what were his successes and what his failures? He did not prune his lyrics of their flaccid sentiments and stale imagery, so that few of them are without flaws. . . . Water and the sea almost always inspired him to his best effects, from some early lines in the *Errors of Ectasie* prologue, through *Nepenthe* to the haunting lyrics of **'The Sea-Bride'**. (p. 37)

[*Nepenthe*] was planned on an ambitious scale, and betrays Darley's weak sense of structure: it is well-nigh impossible to keep one's bearings or follow the narrative line. Yet the theme and the metre proved to be the right medium for a display of his powers at their best.

The *persona* of the hero is that of Darley himself in the character of imaginative poet, and if at one point he seems to be identified with Orpheus when torn in pieces by the Furies, that is appropriate enough, for one who spoke slightingly of women. (p. 38)

I have already remarked, à propos of *Sylvia*, that the octosyllabic couplet suited Darley's style. He sustains the metre through this longer stretch with a skilful variety of stress. (p. 41)

I do not think that Darley's reputation would be well served by an edition of all his extant poems and plays: much of his work is best left in obscurity. But it is extraordinary that his best poetry should be so neglected, and that no faithful text should ever have been printed. (p. 45)

> *Anne Ridler, "Introduction" (1978; copyright © Anne Ridler 1979; reprinted by permission of the author), in* Selected Poems of George Darley *by George Darley, edited by Anne Ridler, The Merrion Press, 1979, pp. 11-48.*

ADDITIONAL BIBLIOGRAPHY

Brisman, Leslie, "George Darley: The Poet as Pigmy." *Studies in Romanticism* 15, No. 1 (Winter 1976): 119-41.
> Reveals Darley's portrayal of himself in the characters of his works. This essay particularly focusses on Darley as Pedro in *Pedro Ladron, or the Shepard of Toppledown Hill.*

Brisman, Leslie. "George Darley: Bouyant as Young Time." In his *Romantic Origins*, pp. 183-223. Ithaca, London: Cornell University Press, 1978.
> Compares Darley's work to that of Keats, Shelley, Byron, Wordsworth, and Milton. This book gives a detailed analysis of the plots, intentions, and symbolisms in Darley's work.

Greene, Graham. "George Darley." In his *The Lost Childhood and Other Essays*, pp. 143-52. London: Eyre & Spottiswood, 1951.
> Excerpts criticism commenting on Darley's genius. This book also contains Darley's self-criticism, from letters and conversation.

Lange, Donald. "George Darley: New Manuscript Poems and Notes on 'It Is Not Beautie I Demand'." *The Review of English Studies* XXVII, No. 108 (November 1976): 437-45.
> Detailed study of the words and language used in Darley's poems.

"The Poet of Solitude." *The Times Literary Supplement*, No. 2338 (23 November 1946): 580.
> Discusses how Darley became inspired to write, and the reception his work received.

Benjamin Disraeli

1804-1881

English novelist, essayist, poet, and biographer.

One of the most distinguished British statesmen of the nineteenth century, Disraeli is considered the originator of the political novel and a significant historian and critic of the English system of government. As a member of Parliament, Chancellor of the Exchequer, and Prime Minister, Disraeli displayed a political acumen rivaled by few in his day. He exercised a particularly profound power on the Conservative party as the outstanding speaker for the Young England party. Though in his literary works his rationalist tendencies were often at odds with his romantic instincts, he nonetheless created a body of work which is considered a faithful, vivid recreation of Toryism in England.

Disraeli's father, Isaac, a celebrated biographer and critic, chose to educate Benjamin himself, hoping to prepare him for the law. However, Benjamin disliked legal pursuits, preferring to further his interest in literature and his political aspirations. While briefly working for a solicitor, Disraeli first observed the manners of the upper-middle class and developed a penchant for eccentricity in dress, which gave him the label of "dandy." Ironically, he shared the Anglican background of those he wished to emulate only because his Jewish father had quarrelled with members of his synagogue and chose to baptize his son a Christian. Disraeli's first novel, *Vivian Grey,* was the tale of a power-oriented young dandy. The book was published anonymously and became an immediate sensation in London. His thinly veiled satirical characterizations prompted someone to print a "key" which provided each character's true identity. The public assumed that a noted scholar or socialite had written *Vivian Grey;* the revelation that its author was a "twenty-one year old nobody—and a Jew!" was an affront to London literary circles. However, an anonymous novel by a "nobody" had become the rage of London society.

Disraeli was befriended by fellow-novelist and noted dandy Edward Bulwer-Lytton, who helped his friend gain entrance to society. Bulwer also provided Disraeli with advice on writing fashionable novels which depicted life in genteel society. In turn, Disraeli attempted to emulate Bulwer's dandy hero, Pelham. The people he met provided Disraeli with the attention he craved. His personal motto became "Affectation is better than wit." At a ball, when a woman asked Disraeli if he had read a recent novel, he flippantly replied, "Madame, when I wish to read a good novel, I write one!" While his eccentricity proved entertaining in London's social circles, it did not serve as a useful campaign tool for gaining a seat in Parliament, the object of Disraeli's new aspirations, and he soon began to modify his flamboyant behavior.

In 1837, Disraeli entered Parliament and became the leader of the Young England party. Formerly conservative Tories, the Young England party held that their country's hope lay in a revitalized feudalism and the glorification of its nobility. He expanded his views in *Coningsby; or, The New Generation,* considered the first English political novel. This, the first in Disraeli's trilogy of political novels, provides a romantic look at a fabricated golden past, which embodied Young England's

ideals. *Sybil; or, The Two Nations,* the second volume of his political trilogy, depicts the cause and nature of Chartism. In *Tancred; or, The New Crusade* Disraeli expressed his unorthodox views on the relationship between Christianity and Judaism. The trilogy unabashedly celebrates England's aristocracy while, paradoxically, it recounts the horrors of industrial England. These novels were Disraeli's political offerings to his readers, and they were popularly acclaimed.

Disraeli served as Prime Minister to Queen Victoria for a brief period in 1868. After his defeat for the office by Gladstone he wrote *Lothair,* a novel of political life and a commentary on the Roman Catholic Church. In 1874, Disraeli again became Prime Minister, and, in 1876, Victoria made him Earl of Beaconsfield. His relationship with the queen was very close: aggressive in his foreign policy, he made England an imperial power, and made Victoria Empress of India. Disraeli's final novel, *Endymion,* provides a concluding statement of his economic and political policies.

Disraeli knew well the importance of both his literary and political careers, stating that his life ambition was "to act out what I write." His novels provide an insightful commentary on political activity during the reign of Victoria, though his objective discussions of industrial England are rarely considered as interesting as his sensational romans à clef.

PRINCIPAL WORKS

Vivian Grey   (novel)   1826
The Young Duke   (novel)   1831
Contarini Fleming   (novel)   1832
The Wondrous Tale of Alroy. The Rise of Iskander   (novel and short story)   1833
Henrietta Temple   (novel)   1837
Venetia   (novel)   1837
Coningsby; or, The New Generation   (novel)   1844
Sybil; or, The Two Nations   (novel)   1845
Tancred; or, The New Crusade   (novel)   1847
Lothair   (novel)   1870
Endymion   (novel)   1880

THE LONDON LITERARY GAZETTE   (essay date 1826)

Vivian Grey is destined to occupy no trifling share of the attention of all those favoured persons, whose habits at once permit and impel them to fill up a regular and allotted portion of their time in turning over the leaves of those numerous piquant productions with which the press of the day so profusely teems.

We shall not pretend to give a detailed account of this singular and original work; partly, because it is so singular that we might not be successful in conveying to the reader any very satisfactory notion of it; but chiefly, because every body will read it who reads at all for amusement. We shall only say, therefore, that *Vivian Grey* professes to depict the history of an ambitious young man, of first-rate talent, various accomplishments, and high fashion, on his entry on the path of life; and that, besides developing the strong character of the hero himself, it presents the reader with sketches of all the persons with whom his views and adventures bring him into contact; and that all those persons have the air of being depicted from living individuals, known to every one who is acquainted with London, and mixes with its social Corinthian architecture, be it genuine or spurious. The characters, indeed, seem to us to have more than "the air" of being drawn from actual life: for that they are so drawn, and are even intended to be so considered, is pretty evident. But whether *Vivian Grey* and his friends and foes are real, or merely imaginary, certain it is that they are drawn with great spirit, vividness, and truth: we are afraid they belong to a class of which we never can approve in literature—personal portraits and satirical caricatures. . . .

[The] writer of *Vivian Grey* is a person who says whatever he has to say in the language and with the air of a man conscious of his own powers, and practised enough to venture saying what he likes in his own sharp and desultory manner. With respect to the plot, it consists simply in the formation and development of a political intrigue, which is set on foot by the hero for the purpose of lifting himself to place and power, and is baffled by the arts of a woman. But it is so slight and inartificial, that it has evidently only been devised as a vehicle for conveying the author's views on life, character, and society. (p. 241)

[It] includes some extremely spirited sketching, both of character and opinion, and . . . it cannot fail to create a general curiosity as to the future productions of its author. (p. 244)

> "Review of New Books: 'Vivian Grey'," *in* The London Literary Gazette, *No. 483, April 22, 1826, pp. 241-44.*

LONDON MAGAZINE   (essay date 1827)

Never did we observe the evidence of a more sincere, fervent, and devout admiration, than the author discovers of his own parts: he seems most potently persuaded that there is but one man in the world—the writer of *Vivian Grey:* and that the rest of mankind is divisible only into two classes—his pious worshippers and his unworthy detractors. These he treats with all magnanimity, blighting the one simply with his silent contempt, and blessing the other with the bounties of his great mind. . . . It is thus with *Vivian Grey:* he gives us the cobwebs and sweepings of that narrow cell, his cranium, with the air of one who confers inestimable treasures on a grateful world. (p. 472)

At Timbuctoo, they say that the author has painted his own character in *Vivian Grey;* and it has been malignly whispered in the Andes, that he wrote for the defunct Representative; at Kamtschatka too, he has been reproached for personality. "I am blamed," he pathetically observes, "for the affectation, the arrogance, *the wicked wit* of this ficticious character." Here we would entreat him, in some measure to be comforted. Believe us, Mr. Grey, no creature ever blamed you for your *wicked wit*, or any description of wit whatever—you are wholly free from the imputation. . . . But though Mr. Grey is not a wicked wit, he is a prodigious philosopher. His discoveries are, indeed, surprising. Doubtless much has been said of OBLIVION since the beginning of things; but it was reserved for this *wicked wit* to find out that "OBLIVION, *after all*, is a just judge." . . . What does he mean? Surely a delicate compliment to the venerable chancellor who forgets causes. OBLIVION stands for Eldon. The qualities of oblivion are certainly, when we come to consider it, highly judicial. But if it, *after all*, be a good judge, we think that Anticipation, before all, is a good Recorder. This is a pleasant manner of writing: we have half a mind to adopt it. (pp. 473-74)

Of the nature of HAPPINESS we had not the slightest conception, till we read the writings of Mr. Grey, who confidently informs us that it is A TALISMAN— . . . a poetic idea, which the reader will observe is as original, as that of the judicial capacity of OBLIVION is profound.

Of grammar, too, we had but very imperfect notions before we took up this book, wherein we find this mode of speech, "really these burghers have managed the business exceedingly *bad*." . . . [Again,] "*no one* now will own, by any chance, *they're* ever wrong." . . .

But in giving a passing notice of these rare beauties we are neglecting the story, about which, however, it is not our intention to say much, simply because it is an extremely fatiguing task to give a detailed account of a series of outrageous improbabilities, inconsistencies, and extravagances. (p. 475)

It must be confessed, that our author's production is a raiment of many colours, or rather it is a huge darn of motley hues. He works with one thread till it breaks or is exhausted; then, very coolly, takes another of a different tint, passes it through the eye of his needle, and stitches away with it again, most industriously and complacently, until he arrives at the knot, when he again repairs to his housewife, and botches on as before. The result is a piece of patch-work, which indicates more thrift than wealth. (p. 480)

He labours indefatigably to produce that kind of nonsense which vexes as in a dream. Let any one sup off half a pound of toasted cheese and we will engage that he shall see, at that moderate price, a vision which shall surpass the best scene of would-be grotesque in *Vivian Grey*. Let the author evert himself to the utmost—he is yet no match for the nightmare. Indigestion is superior to his invention, and the mightiest efforts of his brain will be excelled by the workings of a foul stomach. Imagination is a very fine faculty of the mind, when happily directed or judiciously controlled; but there is no kind of merit in the imagination of unalloyed nonsense; and when we give play to the imagination, we should have a care of playing the fool. This may seem a very unnecessary lecture to those who have not been fatigued with the unutterable folly of some imitations of the German in *Vivian Grey*. We refer particularly to the description of a debauch, which is indeed "an idiot's tale, full of sound and fury, signifying nothing." What may follow this performance we know not, for it ended our weary attempts to struggle through the book, as we flung it aside in disgust, and dropping into a doze, dreamt more reasonable things. (pp. 482-83)

> *"'Vivian Grey': Second Part,"* in London Magazine, *April 1, 1827, pp. 472-83.*

E. LYTTON BULWER　(essay date 1830)

I have read through your manuscript ['**The Young Duke**'] with great attention, and it has afforded me a very uncommon gratification.

I could fill my letter with praises of its wit, the terseness and philosophy of its style, and the remarkable felicity with which you make the coldest insipidities of real life entertaining and racy. One would think you had been learning at Laputa how to extract sunbeams from cucumbers.

In the *genius* of your work I see not a flaw—nothing to point out to your attention. In the *judgment* of it I think you are less invariably happy.

You do not seem to me to do justice to your own powers when you are so indulgent to flippancies. I do think you should look with a harsh, and even hypercritical, eye upon all those antithetical neatnesses of style which make the great feature of your composition.

Whenever they attain a witticism or a new truth (which is nine times out of ten) don't alter a syllable. But whenever you see that form of words which aims at a point and does not acquire it, be remorseless.

I would have you write a book, not only to succeed, but to have that form of success which will hereafter be agreeable to yourself. (pp. 317-18)

The flippancies I allude to are an ornate and showy effeminacy, which I think you should lop off on the same principle as Lord Ellenborough should cut off his hair. In a mere fashionable novel aiming at no higher merit, and to a mere dandy aiming at nothing more solid, the flippancies and the hair might be left: and left gracefully. But I do not think the one suits a man who is capable of great things, nor the other a man who occupies great places.

At all events, if you do not think twice, and act alike upon this point I fear you are likely to be attacked and vituperated to a degree which fame can scarcely recompense; and which, hereafter, may cause you serious inconvenience.

Recollect that you have written a book ('**Vivian Grey**') of wonderful promise, but which got you enemies. You have, therefore, to meet, in *this* book, a very severe ordeal, both of expectation and malice. You have attained in the book more than the excellences of '**Vivian Grey**:' but I do not think you have enough avoided the faults. (p. 318)

You have written a very fine, and a very original, thing. And all but a very sincere well-wisher would be perfectly satisfied with the display.

As a *trifle*—but not to be overlooked—I would give matured attention to the Duke's dress. I confess I think the blonde edgings too bold.

These are things (strange as it may seem) that make enemies, and scarcely make friends.

May Dacre is beautiful.

The egotisms I do not object to. They are always charming, and often exceedingly touching. Moreover, the interest of the story never flags; and you have agreeably belied my prediction of extravagance. (p. 319)

> *E. Lytton Bulwer, in his letter to Benjamin Disraeli on April 10, 1830, in* The Life, Letters and Literary Remains of Edward Bulwer, Lord Lytton *by Edward R. B. Lytton (reprinted by permission of Routledge & Kegan Paul Ltd),* Kegan Paul, Trench, Trubner & Co., Ltd., *1883, pp. 317-19.*

THE NEW MONTHLY MAGAZINE　(essay date 1832)

Mr. D'Israeli is a writer of very great genius, and "**Contarini Fleming**" is so vast an improvement on "**Vivian Grey**" and "**The Young Duke**," that it is difficult for me to believe it written by the same man. Nevertheless, the critics declare it could be written by no other. The tone of "**The Young Duke**" was painful; you felt that the Author should not have stooped to the performance; its vivacity was strained; its story unconnected; and the play of the writer's style too restless and unquiet. "**Contarini Fleming**" is the product of a far older mind—a travelled mind—a meditative mind—a mind gradually filtering itself of its early impurities of taste and discrepancies in judgment. The tone of it is more enlarged and benevolent than that of the former writings; and though, by the superficial, it is called extravagant, it is, in reality, remarkably succinct, whole, and uniform, in its plot, conduct, and purpose. The mass of readers will not perceive its object, and therefore it seems to them bizarre, merely because its meaning is not on the surface. In fact, "**Contarini Fleming**" is a delineation of abstract ideas, in which . . . the Author is often allegorical and actual at the same time. Each character is a personification of certain trains of mind; but in that personification the Author now and then forgets himself, and deals only with the external world, which he designed at first merely as the covering to metaphysical creatures. . . . The true nature of Mr. D'Israeli's talent is . . . vivid, sparkling, passionate. He writes much better when he paints the Outward which belongs to Passion, than the Inward, which belongs to Thought. One of the best parts of his book, and one of the best and most racy descriptions of life any work of fiction since Fielding . . . contains, is in volume the first, when the young Adventurer attempts the robber life, which was once so alluring to the youth of Germany. On the other hand, nothing but the dazzle of the diction can blind us to various contradictions, and to much hasty paradox, in all the reflective portions of the work. . . . But while Mr. D'Israeli is, we apprehend, yet a novice when he reflects, he often becomes a master when he creates. His personifications of idea are excellent, though his dilations on ideas may be crude. What a character he has made of Winter! I know nothing in the English language like it in conception, or more elaborately executed; it is only a pity that we have so little of this fine ideal. To sum up, in this work the Author has shown a power—a fertility—a promise—which we sanguinely trust will produce very considerable and triumphant results. He has shown, by much improvement, that he can improve more. A certain revolution is going on within his mind; right and deep ideas are gradually banishing wrong and erratic notions; and—striking, admirable in many most brilliant points, as every unprejudiced critic may allow **"Contarini Fleming"**—the Author will yet (he may believe me) far outshine it. (pp. 27-8)

"Asmodeus at Large: 'Contarini Fleming'," in The New Monthly Magazine, Vol. XXXV, No. CXXXIX, July 1, 1832, pp. 26-8.*

THE ATHENAEUM (essay date 1833)

Those who read to the fortieth page of [*The Wondrous Tale of Alroy*], then close the work for ever and call the author a wild enthusiast who deals in extravagant legends and supernatural fictions, will do him the greatest injustice. Wild his work is assuredly—extravagant sometimes to our utmost wish, and supernatural even to the very limits of poetic belief; but then genius is stamped on every page: feelings such as the muse delights in abound, nay overflow, while a true heroic loftiness of soul, such as influenced devout men of old when they warred for their country, glows and flashes through the whole narrative. Nor is this all—there is a deep infusion of the spirit of Judah in it—not the fallen and money-changing spirit of these our latter days, but of that martial and devout spirit which kindled in the Hebrew bosoms of old. . . .

[The author] has renounced the ordinary manner of legend writers, and imagined a style in harmony with his subject— more melodious, more elevated, more poetic, in short, than what is now the pleasure of story tellers to use. (p. 150)

The use of this new style has produced great defects, for the author is not seldom stilted and extravagant; it has produced also great beauties, for it has frequently—very frequently— given a buoyancy of thought and an elevation of sentiment, in harmony with the ruling spirit of the narrative. . . .

It will soon be heard and seen what the world and the critics say regarding the poetic style of the author of **'Alroy.'** For ourselves, we think he is right to a certain extent: the finest passages in all works which have moved us most, partake of the poetic character; if a page of history lingers on our memory, and many do, it is one in which the muse has had her influence in language as well as thought. (p. 151)

"'The Wondrous Tale of Alroy'," in The Athenaeum, No. 280, March 9, 1833, pp. 150-51.

THE EDINBURGH REVIEW (essay date 1837)

[**'Henrietta Temple, a Love Story'** and **'Venetia'**] are works of more than ordinary pretensions,—both dealing with difficult and elevated themes; the former professing to represent the passion of love in its most sudden and poetical form; the latter attempting, with scarcely even the shadow of disguise, to delineate the characters of Shelley and Lord Byron. Were we to say that in these bold attempts Mr D'Israeli (for we suppose it is now needless to treat the author as an anonymous novelist) has entirely failed, we should be doing injustice to the talent, liveliness, and eloquence which both works not unfrequently display: were we, on the other hand, to say that he has produced any very finished, striking, or original picture, either of passion or character,—or realized in any high degree the ideal conception at which he seems to have aimed, we should be doing still greater injustice to the cause of good sense, consistency of character, and moderation of expression. The marks of crudity in the conception, and of haste in the execution, which are everywhere visible, are not indeed difficult to be accounted for, when it is kept in mind that both these novels, each consisting of the established number of three volumes, have made their appearance within a year; and, even if a more patient attention had been bestowed on the plan of the story, or the details of character and dialogue, we have the greatest doubt whether the result would have been such as to satisfy our idea of a good novel or romance. But unquestionably much which at present mars and impairs the effect of some of the best scenes—many overwrought incidents and improbable changes of conduct in the characters—many redundancies, extravagances, and even vulgarities of expression, which seriously detract from the pleasure these volumes are calculated to afford,—might have been avoided by a more careful revision, and a little additional severity towards those *dulcia vitia* of style which seem to be the sin by which the author is most easily beset.

We have said that we doubt whether, even with all proper appliances, Mr D'Israeli could produce a really good work of fiction. He appears to us to want some of the most essential elements of a great novelist. The calm, the natural, the simply grand are not his field. *. . .* There is also a want of directness and reality about his passion; if he feels strongly, he has not the power of communicating a corresponding feeling to his readers; we perceive rather the reflection or shadow of feeling than the thing itself. . . . (pp. 59-60)

His passionate vein, too, such as it is, is not only too much prolonged, but is generally introduced too soon, and with too little preparation: ere we have time to get acquainted with the characters, we are expected to sympathize with the wildest burst of excited feeling; and the natural consequence is, first, that our sympathies must, in the course of the three volumes, be more than once worn out; and next, that the writer, like a musician who commences in too high a key, and is unable to play up to his opening strain, often appears cold, languid, and unimpassioned towards his conclusion. (p. 60)

The truth is, that Mr D'Israeli, in his **'Vivian Grey,'** chose at first, with very considerable tact and accuracy of perception, the precise department in which he was most fitted to excel— namely, the execution of rapid and dashing sketches of incident and character, unfettered by any close connexion or consistency; and that, though carrying into every thing he undertakes a portion of the same liveliness and cleverness of execution, he is obviously far less at home in the field of regular and systematic composition than in that fairy land of imagination, emancipated from all uneasy trammels of reality or probability, in which he chose in the outset to disport himself. (p. 61)

[**'Vivian Grey'**] made no more pretension to probability than a nursery tale; all connexion between causes and effects, as they are usually found to exist in the world, was coolly set at defiance; marvels, moral, political, and physical, were heaped upon each other; the hero moved through difficulties and dangers, unheard-of scrapes, and moving accidents of the most portentous character, with the ease and coolness with which some knight of old passed through the innocuous and unsubstantial flames that surrounded the enchanted castles of Fairy Land. (p. 62)

In the two productions which form the subject of this notice, Mr D'Israeli's aim has been of a more ambitious cast than in his '**Vivian Grey.**' He no longer contents himself with an avowed caricatura, in which the most inconsistent elements may find a place, but professes to throw aside the fantastic, and to place us in the world of reality. He ventures into the field of the regular novel, and courts the ordinary standard of comparison and criticism applicable to such compositions. The startling improbability and accumulation of incidents which characterised his first youthful production have in a great measure disappeared; the plots are in fact rather meagre than otherwise; the characters few, and less violently and melo-dramatically contrasted; and the author, though with questionable success, has at least aimed at the production of a whole instead of a mere series of scenes, blending tragedy, comedy, and broad farce in a compound so eccentric as to defy the application of any critical laws. Yet much of the old leaven of extravagance adheres to them still, though it has been transferred from the incidents and characters to the *tone* of the feelings represented. In both these novels there is a strained, *falsetto* vehemence of passion;—an obvious working up of situations for effect,—a wordiness and exaggeration in the language of feeling, which has in it something not a little theatrical and hollow, and altogether inconsistent with the excitement of any genuine emotion or sympathy. . . . We will not deny that some of his situations are powerfully painted, and that he is occasionally dramatic and forcible in the language of feeling; but we are confident that no one can peruse either '**Henrietta Temple**' or '**Venetia**' without a strong feeling that the effect of these scenes of strong passion would have been greatly heightened had they been less frequently introduced, more gradually prepared, and less perseveringly dwelt upon.

'**Henrietta Temple**' is denominated 'a Love Story'—*par excellence*, we suppose, because the whole plot of the novel hinges on that passion. The general conception which Mr D'Israeli seeks to embody is a fine and poetical one. His object is to paint the magic suddenness, the bewildering, the overpowering nature of a first passion in two beings of strong feelings, both educated under circumstances calculated to give to these feelings, when developed, a certain headlong and irresistible energy. The love which is here depicted is not that gradual feeling which only deepens into passion by time, and habit, and acquaintance; it is a fate, a destiny, the sudden awakening of a slumbering fire, which, kindled into life by an instantaneous and mysterious impulse, flames out at once into a wild and consuming glow. . . . [Mr D'Israeli's idea] is a good one; but he has done much to impair its proper development by the circumstances in which he has placed the hero of his story, at the supposed commencement of his passion. . . . [The] selfishness, dishonourable concealment, and disregard of former ties on the part of the hero, are utterly fatal to any real sympathy with the woes which his conduct accumulates upon his head. They are inconsistent with any ideal of *true* passion, which always merges self in the happiness of the beloved object, and could never have permitted him to involve that being in the misery which he *foresees* from the

first as the consequence of his rashness. This feeling, we say, intrudes itself in all the passionate scenes between the lovers, many of them certainly in themselves touching and beautiful. (pp. 63-5)

Mr D'Israeli may very naturally have thought many of the love dialogues of other writers stilted and artificial; but 'the simple-natural' also may be carried too far; and the 'silly 'sooth, that dallies with the innocence of love,' certainly does become somewhat luscious and lackadaisical when spread out before us in page after page of printed paper. (p. 65)

But, amidst these blemishes, we have already said we occasionally meet with ingenious and original observations on this master passion. . . . (p. 66)

Several of the subsidiary characters are happily drawn, particularly the mild, amiable Catholic tutor of the hero, Glastonbury, and the lively, light-hearted, but generous and kindly Count Mirabel,—a portrait *en beau*, we suppose, of the author's friend, Court D'Orsay, to whom, we observe, the novel is dedicated. (p. 68)

We do not think it would have been possible, by any talent, to have reconciled us to the subject [of '**Venetia**']. . . . [It] is still a little too soon to think of weaving three volumes out of the misfortunes of Byron, or the morbid peculiarities and too early fate of Shelley. Apart altogether from the taste and feeling of the choice, there is something exceedingly injurious to the effect of a work of fiction in attempting the treatment of such a subject; we feel in its perusal an uneasy consciousness of a strange mixture of reality and falsehood, identity and difference, which is fatal to any continuous and undivided interest. (pp. 68-9)

The best part of '**Venetia**' is undoubtedly the first volume. The early education of Lord Cadurcis and of Venetia—the development of the poet's wayward, generous, impetuous, and overbearing character—and the growth in the mind of Venetia of that passionate love and admiration of her unseen and unknown father, are powerfully and most interestingly described; though not without a touch of that exaggeration from which the writer is seldom free, even in his most successful pictures. (p. 69)

"'Henrietta Temple: A Love Story' and 'Venetia'," in The Edinburgh Review, Vol. 66, No. 133, October, 1837, pp. 59-72.

WILLIAM MAKEPEACE THACKERAY   (essay date 1844)

["**Coningsby; or, the New Generation**"] is quite as curious as it is clever. It is the fashionable novel, pushed, we do really believe, to its extremest verge, beyond which all is naught. It is a glorification of dandyism, far beyond all other glories which dandyism has attained. . . .

It is a dandy-social, dandy-political, dandy-religious novel. . . . The dandyism, moreover, is intense, but not real; not English, that is. It is vastly too ornamental, energetic, and tawdry for our quiet habits. . . . [However,] we believe this gentleman to be not only a dandy but a man of genius.

This superb coxcombry the author of "**Coningsby**" brings to bear upon a great number of very rare faculties and powers of mind. He has admirable humour, and scorn for *many* things which are base, not for all; and, in the midst of his satire, coxcombry intervenes, and one is irresistibly led to satirize the satirizer. He writes for a page or two in passages of the most admirable and pure English, thoughts finely poetical, fresh, startling, or ingenious; but one may be pretty sure of not being able to turn half-a-dozen leaves without coming upon something outrageous. Never was a moralist who laid himself more open to censure, a philosopher more personally weak, or a dandy and teacher of *ton* whose own manner was more curiously and frequently offensive. Politically, **"Coningsby"** is an exposure and attack of Whigs and Conservatives. Of Whigs much, but of Conservatives more. The author exposes the cant and folly of the name, and the lies of the practice. (pp. 40-1)

Numerous disquisitions find place in the volumes regarding various political fallacies. Many of them are well and ingeniously argued—the hits at both parties are severe and just, the evils are shown well enough; but it is only when the Young Englander comes to legislate for them that his reasoning becomes altogether unsatisfactory. (p. 42)

[Admiring] fully the vivid correctness of Mr. Disraeli's description of this great Conservative party, which conserves nothing, which proposes nothing, which resists nothing, which believes nothing: [we] admire still more his conclusion, that out of this nothing a something is to be created, round which England is contentedly to rally, and that we are one day to reorganize faith and reverence round this wretched, tottering, mouldy, clumsy, old idol. (p. 50)

> *William Makepeace Thackeray, "Disraeli's 'Coningsby'" (originally published in* Morning Chronicle, *May 13, 1844), in his* Contributions to the "Morning Chronicle," *edited by Gordon N. Ray, University of Illinois Press, 1955, pp. 39-50.*

[JAMES RUSSELL LOWELL]   (essay date 1847)

In *Coningsby* and *Tancred*, Mr. D'Israeli has interwoven a kind of defence of the Jewish race against the absurd prejudices of a so-called Christendom. (p. 213)

For once, Mr. D'Israeli seems to be in earnest, and we respect both his zeal and the occasion of it. The pen is never so sacred as when it takes the place of the sword in securing freedom, whether for races or ideas. But the earnestness of a charlatan is only a profounder kind of charlatanism. The moral of *Tancred*, if it have any, is, that effete Europe can be renewed only by a fresh infusion from the veins of Asia,—a nostrum for rejuvenescence to be matched only out of the pages of Hermippus Redivivus. According to Mr. D'Israeli, all primitive ideas have originated, and must for ever originate, in Asia, and among the descendants of Abraham. He would have us go to school to Noah in navigation, and learn the nicer distinctions of *meum* and *tuum* from Ishmael. He would make us believe that the Jewish mind still governs the world, through the medium of prime-ministers, bankers, and actresses. The chief excellence of this arrangement is, that we are profoundly ignorant of it. (pp. 213-14)

Mr. D'Israeli would be more endurable, if he himself thoroughly believed in the theory he promulgates. But it is evident that he only assumes his position for the sake of writing what one half of May Fair shall pronounce brilliant, and the other half profound. (p. 214)

Mr. D'Israeli is like the Irish gastronomer, who invited his friends to partake of a rich soup which he was to concoct out of a miraculous pebble. The entertainer liberally placed his whole mineralogical cabinet at the service of his guests, merely asking of each in return a *pro ratâ* contribution of a bit of beef, a trifle of pork, a few onions, a sprinkling of salt, and a kettle

wherein to try the thaumaturgic experiment. Mr. D'Israeli's characters are such wonderful pebbles. It is quite too heavy a tax upon the reader to expect him to fill up, with their appropriate lights and shades, the colossal outlines sketched by the author.

Tancred is one of these remarkable men, but there is nothing very remarkable in what he says or does. In the same way that old Gower enters as Chorus, and gives us to understand that we are now in Tyre, Mr. D'Israeli begs to inform us that we are now to enjoy the privilege of communion with a mind capable of vast "combinations." But Tyre turns out to be the same little canvas castle which was Tharsus a moment ago, and the vast combinations amount to the adding of two and two, and producing the surprising result of four. (p. 218)

If the book were intended as a satire, the end would be pertinent enough. But in the present case, it is as if a man, with infinite din of preparation, should set sail for a voyage round the world, and get no farther than a chowder on Spectacle island. At the beginning of the novel, we nerve ourselves for the solution of the great Asiatic problem, and, as long as X remains an unknown quantity, we feel a vague sort of respect for it. But when we arrive at the end of the demonstration, and Mr. D'Israeli, after covering the blackboard with figures enough to work out the position of the new planet, turns round to us, and, laying down his triumphant chalk, says gravely,—"Thus, Gentlemen, you will perceive that the square of the hypothenuse, &c., &c., Q.E.D.," we feel as if we might have found our way over the *pons asinorum* without paying him so heavy a fee as guide. (p. 219)

Tancred cannot be esteemed a work of art, even if that term may be justly applied in the limited sense of mere construction. There is in it no great living idea which pervades, moulds, and severely limits the whole. If we consider the *motive*, we find a young nobleman so disgusted with the artificial and hollow life around him, that he sacrifices every thing for a pilgrimage to what he believes the only legitimate source of faith and inspiration. We cannot, to be sure, expect much of a youth who is obliged to travel a thousand miles after inspiration; but we might reasonably demand something more than that he should merely fall in love, a consummation not less conveniently and cheaply attainable at home. If the whole story be intended for a satire, the disproportion of motive to result is not out of proper keeping. But Mr. D'Israeli's satire is wholly of the epigrammatic kind, not of the epic, and deals always with individuals, never with representative ideas. An epigram in three volumes post octavo is out of the question. The catastrophe has no moral or aesthetic fitness. Indeed, there is no principle of cohesion about the book, if we except the covers. Nor could there be; for there is no one central thought around and toward which the rest may gravitate. All that binds the incidents together is the author's will, a somewhat inadequate substitute for a law of nature. Every thing slips through our fingers like a handful of sand, when we grasp for a design. . . . [To] call upon Mr. D'Israeli for a work of art is to set a joiner to build an oak.

For want of due discrimination, such writers as Mr. D'Israeli are called *imaginative* authors. It is the same narrow view which has confined the name of poets to the makers of verse. Imagination is truly the highest exercise of that august faculty from which it is vulgarly esteemed so distant,—namely, reason. It is the instinctive (if we may so call it, in the absence of any readier term) perception of remote analogies; in other words, of the unity of truth. (pp. 220-21)

[We] cannot see any use that is to be answered by such books as *Tancred*. It is as dumb as the poor choked hunchback in the Arabian Nights, when we ask it what its business is. There are no characters in it. There is no dramatic interest, none of plot or incident. Dickens, with his many and egregious faults of style, his mannerisms, and his sometimes intolerable descriptive passages, is yet clearly enough a great genius, a something necessary to the world, and the figures upon his canvas are such as Emerson has aptly termed *representative,* the types of classes, and no truer in London than in Boston. Mr. D'Israeli, when he undertakes to draw a character, sketches some individual whom he happens to like or dislike, and who is no otherwise an individual than by the mere accident of being an actually living person, who has a name on the door in some street or other, who eats, drinks, and like the rest of us is subject to death and bores. (pp. 223-24)

In *Tancred* there are one or two excellent landscapes, and some detached thoughts worth remembering. There are a vast many girds at Sir Robert Peel, who, after all is said, has shown himself capable of one thing beyond Mr. D'Israeli's reach,—success, which always gives a man some hold or other, however questionable, upon posterity, and arms him in mail of proof against sarcasm. Mr. D'Israeli uses him as a militia company sometimes serve an unpopular politician. He sets up a rude likeness of him for a practising target; but, no matter how many balls may perforate the wooden caricature, its original still walks about unharmed, and with whatever capacity a politician has for enjoying life undiminished. . . . But we cannot undertake to give a sketch of the principal events in *Tancred*. . . . In this particular case, whenever we attempt to call up an individual impression of the book, our memory presents us with nothing but a painfully defiant blur. (p. 224)

> [*James Russell Lowell,*] *"'Tancred, or the New Crusade, a Novel',"* in *The North American Review, Vol. LXV, No. 136, July, 1847, pp. 201-24.*

HENRY JAMES   (essay date 1870)

"Lothair" is decidedly amusing. We should call it interesting at once, were it not that we feel this to be in a measure a consecrated, a serious word, and that we cannot bring ourselves to think of **"Lothair"** as a serious work. It is doubtless not as amusing as it might be, with the same elements and a little firmer handling; but it is pleasant reading for a summer's day. The author has great cleverness, or rather he has a great deal of small cleverness. In great cleverness, there must be an element of honest wisdom, we like to imagine, such as **"Lothair"** is fatally without. Still, he has cleverness enough to elicit repeatedly the reader's applause. A certain cleverness is required for getting into difficulties, for creating them and causing them to bristle around you; and of this peril-seeking faculty Mr. Disraeli possesses an abundant measure. Out of his difficulties he never emerges, so that in the end his talent lies gloriously entombed and enshrined in a vast edifice of accumulated mistakes. (pp. 303-04)

If it can be said to have a ruling idea, that idea is of course to reveal the secret encroachments of the Romish Church. With what accuracy and fidelity these are revealed we are not prepared to say; with what eloquence and force the reader may perhaps infer from what we have said. Mr. Disraeli's attempt seems to us wholly to lack conviction, let alone passion and fire. His anti-Romish enthusiasm is thoroughly cold and mechanical. Essentially light and superficial throughout, the au-

thor is never more so than when he is serious and profound. He indulges in a large number of religious reflections, but we feel inexorably that it is not on such terms as these that religion stands or falls. His ecclesiastics are lay-figures—his Scarlet Woman is dressed out terribly in the tablecloth, and holds in her hands the drawing-room candlesticks. As a "novel with a purpose," accordingly, we think **"Lothair"** a decided failure. It will make no Cardinal's ears tingle and rekindle no very lively sense of peril in any aristocratic brand snatched from the burning. . . . For ourselves, it has left us much more good-humored than it found us. . . . [In **"Lothair"** there is] thoroughly regenerate realism, and we find ourselves able to take all that Mr. Disraeli gives us. Nothing is so delightful, an objector may say, as sincere and genuine romance, and nothing so ignoble as the hollow, glittering compound which Mr. Disraeli gives us as a substitute. But we must take what we can get. We shall endure **"Lothair"** only so long as Lothair alone puts in a claim for the romantic, for the idea of elegance and opulence and splendor. . . . The author is like the gentleman who tells his architect that he will not have his house spoiled for a few thousand dollars. Jewels, castles, horses, riches of every kind, are poured into the story without measure, without mercy. But there is a certain method, after all, in the writer's madness. His purpose—his instinct, at least—has been to portray with all possible completeness a purely aristocratic world. He has wished to emphasize the idea, to make a strong statement. He has at least made a striking one. He may not have strictly reproduced a perfect society of "swells," but he has very fairly reflected one. His novel could have emanated only from a mind thoroughly under the dominion of an almost awful sense of the value and glory of dukes and ducal possessions. That his dukes seem to us very stupid, and his duchesses very silly, is of small importance beside the fact that he has expressed with such lavish generosity the ducal side of the question. It is a very curious fact that Mr. Disraeli's age and experience, his sovereign opportunities for disenchantment, as one may suppose, should have left him such an almost infantine joy in being one of the initiated among the dukes. (pp. 306-07)

> *Henry James, "'Lothair' by Lord Beaconsfield" (originally published in* Atlantic Monthly, *Vol. XXVI, No. CLIV, August, 1870), in his* Literary Reviews and Essays on American, English, and French Literature, *edited by Albert Mordell (copyright 1957, by Albert Mordell), Twayne Publishers, 1957, pp. 303-07.*

LESLIE STEPHEN   (essay date 1874)

Mr Disraeli's talents for entertaining fiction may not indeed have been altogether wasted in his official career; but he at least may pardon admirers of his writing, who regret that he should have squandered powers of imagination, capable of true creative work, upon that alternation of truckling and blustering which is called governing the country.

The qualities which are of rather equivocal value in a minister of state may be admirable in the domain of literature. It is hardly desirable that the followers of a political leader should be haunted by an ever-recurring doubt, as to whether his philosophical utterances express deep convictions, or the extemporised combinations of a fertile fancy, and be uncertain whether he is really putting their clumsy thoughts into clearer phrases, or foisting showy nonsense upon them for his own purposes, or simply laughing at them in his sleeve. But, in a purely literary sense, this ambiguous hovering between two meanings, this oscillation between the ironical and the serious, is always amusing, and sometimes delightful. Some simple-minded people are revolted, even in literature, by the ironical method; and tell the humorist, with an air of moral disapproval, that they never know whether he is in jest or in earnest. To such matter-of-fact persons Mr Disraeli's novels must be a standing offence; for it is his most characteristic peculiarity that the passage from one phase to the other is imperceptible. He has moments of obvious seriousness; at frequent intervals, comes a flash of downright sarcasm, as unmistakable in its meaning as the cut of a whip across your face; and elsewhere we have passages which aim unmistakably, and sometimes with unmistakable success, at rhetorical excellence. But, between the two, there is a wide field where we may interpret his meaning as we please. The philosophical theory may imply a genuine belief, or may be a mere bit of conventional filling in, or perhaps a parody of his friends or himself. The gorgeous passages may be intentionally over-coloured, or may really represent his most sincere taste. His homage may be genuine or a biting mockery. . . . The texture of Mr Disraeli's writings is so ingeniously shot with irony and serious sentiment that each tint may predominate by turns. It is impossible to suppose that the weaver of so cunning a web should never have intended the effects which he produces; but frequently, too, they must be the spontaneous and partly unconscious results of a peculiar intellectual temperament. Delight in blending the pathetic with the ludicrous is the characteristic of the true humorist. Mr Disraeli is not exactly a humorist, but something for which the rough nomenclature of critics has not yet provided a distinctive name. His pathos is not sufficiently tender, nor his laughter quite genial enough. The quality which results is homologous to, though not identical with, genuine humour: for the smile we must substitute a sneer, and the element which enters into combination with the satire is something more distantly allied to poetical unction than to glittering rhetoric. The Disraelian irony thus compounded is hitherto a unique product of intellectual chemistry.

Most of Mr Disraeli's novels are intended to set forth what, for want of a better name, must be called a religious or political creed. To grasp its precise meaning, or to determine the precise amount of earnestness with which it is set forth, is of course hopeless. Its essence is to be mysterious, and half the preacher's delight is in tantalising his disciples. (pp. 346-50)

Mr Disraeli, undoubtedly, has certain fixed beliefs which underlie and which, indeed, explain the superficial versatility of his teaching. Amongst the various doctrines with which he plays more or less seriously, two at least are deeply rooted in his mind. He holds with a fervour in every way honourable, a belief in the marvellous endowments of his race, and connected with this belief is an almost romantic admiration for every manifestation of intellectual power. . . . [The] most interesting of all objects to Mr Disraeli, if one may judge from his books, is a precocious youth, whose delight in the sudden consciousness of great abilities has not yet been dashed by experience. In some other writers we may learn the age of the author by the age of his hero. A novelist who adopts the common practice of painting from himself naturally finds out the merits of middle age in his later works. But in every one of Mr Disraeli's works, from **"Vivian Grey"** to **"Lothair,"** the central figure is a youth, who is frequently a statesman at school, and astonishes the world before he has reached his majority. The change in the author's position is, indeed, equally marked in a different way. The youthful heroes of Mr Disraeli's

early novels are creative; in his later they become chiefly receptive. Vivian Grey and Contarini Fleming show their genius by insubordinaiton; Coningsby and Tancred learn wisdom by sitting at the feet of Sidonia; and Lothair reduces himself so completely to a mere "passive bucket" to be pumped into by every variety of teacher, that he is unpleasantly like a fool. Mr Disraeli still loves ingenuous youth; but he has gained quite a new perception of the value of docility. . . . The audacity with which a lad of twenty solves all the problems of the universe, excites in Mr Disraeli genuine and really generous sympathy. . . . The exuberant buoyancy of his youthful heroes gives a certain contagious charm to Mr Disraeli's pages, which is attractive even when verging upon extravagance. (pp. 351-53)

Mr Disraeli's pictures may be, or rather they certainly are, too gaudy in their colouring, but his lavish splendour is evidently prompted by a frank artistic impulse, and certainly implies no grovelling before the ordinary British duke. It is this love of splendour, it may be said parenthetically, combined with his admiration for the non-scientific type of intellect, which makes the Roman Catholic Church so strangely fascinating for Mr Disraeli. His most virtuous heroes and heroines are members of old and enormously rich Catholic families. . . . The sensibility to such influences has a singular effect upon his modes of representing passion. He has frankly explained his theory. The peasant-noble of Wordsworth had learnt to know love "in huts where poor men lie," and a long catena of poetical authorities might be adduced in support of the principle. That is not Mr Disraeli's view. . . . All Mr Disraeli's passionate lovers—and they are very passionate—are provided with fitting scenery. The exquisite Sybil is allowed, by way of exception, to present herself for a moment in the graceful character of a sister of charity relieving a poor family in their garret; but we can detect at once the stamp of noble blood in every gesture, and a coronet is ready to descend upon her celestial brow. . . . "There is no love but at first sight," says Mr Disraeli; and, indeed, love at first sight is alone natural to such beings, on whom beauty and talent have been poured out as lavishly as wealth, and who need never condescend to thoughts of their natural needs. (pp. 380-84)

Mr Disraeli's lovers are apt to be . . . demonstrative and ungovernable in their behaviour. Their happy audacity makes us forget some little defects in their conduct. (pp. 384-85)

His "nobs" are so splendid in their surroundings, such a magical light of wealth, magnificence, and rhetoric is thrown upon all their doings, that we are cheated into sympathy. Who can be hard upon a young man whose behaviour to his creditors may be questionable, but who is swept away in such a torrent of gorgeous hues?. . . [For] the dazzling, brilliant forms of passion we must enter the world of magic, where diamonds are as plentiful as blackberries, and all surrounding objects are turned to gold by the alchemy of an excited imagination. The only difference is that, while other men assume that the commonest things will take a splendid colour as seen through a lovers eyes, Mr Disraeli takes care that whatever his lovers see shall have a splendid colouring. (pp. 387-88)

[His novels] have the faults of juvenile performances: they are too gaudy; the author has been tempted to turn aside too frequently in search of some brilliant epigram; he has mistaken bombast for eloquence, and mere flowery brilliance for warmth of emotion. But we might hope that longer experience and more earnest purpose might correct such defects. Alas! in the year of their publication, Mr Disraeli first entered Parliament. His next works comprised the trilogy, where the artistic aim has become subordinate to the political or biological; and some thirty years of parliamentary labours led to **"Lothair,"** of which it is easiest to assume that it is a practical joke on a large scale, or a prolonged burlesque upon Mr Disraeli's own youthful performances. May one not lament the degradation of a promising novelist into a Prime Minister? (pp. 392-93)

> *Leslie Stephen, "Mr. Disraeli's Novels" (orginally published in* Fortnightly Review, *Vol. 22, October 1874), in his* Hours in a Library, *second series, Smith, Elder & Co., 1876, pp. 344-93.*

GEORG BRANDES (essay date 1880)

Disraeli shows himself in his earliest works so amazingly precocious in worldly wisdom, in fashion, and in penetrating, sarcastic observation, that an inattentive reader might take him for a purely outward-bound character, who had, so to speak, overleapt that first stage of development, in which a youth is self-engrossed, searches deep into his own heart, weighs his capabilities in secret, and tries the elasticity and extent of his powers. But he could not really have escaped any of it; it only appears so because he passed through all these stages with great rapidity as a boy. . . . Neither vague dreams, fantastic visions of the future, doubt, nor lassitude were spared him. **"Contarini Fleming"** is witness that he was acquainted with it all; but the result of the ordeal was as favourable as it was rapidly attained. (p. 18)

No sooner did he begin to write than he began to portray prime ministers, and with equal imaginative faculty and political sagacity.

The two novels in which they occur, **"Vivian Grey"** and **"Contarini Fleming,"** both bear the stamp of psychological biographies, and each is the complement of the other. They contain forecasts of his own training, both as a politician and a novelist. Vivian Grey, the hero of the earlier work, is a young man inclined to politics, with talents for authorship; Contarini Fleming, on the contrary, is an imaginative youth, with talents for politics; both have a passion for power and fame. But that to Disraeli power appears to be the chief good, is betrayed most clearly in the career of the novelist, in which we should not, *a priori,* have expected to find love of power so strongly accented. (pp. 22-3)

"Vivian Grey" is a sparkling book; there is spirit in the dialogues, and wit in the reflections, which make it even now worth reading, and it produced an effect like the contact of flint and steel in English society. (p. 41)

In the mixture of truth and fiction which excited so much unaesthetic curiosity in Disraeli's first work there was something involuntary, which was to be attributed to the author's youth; but at the same time, one of his permanent characteristics was betrayed in it, and it has been repeated nearly every time he has set pen to paper as a novelist. In that character he never forgets the actual life around him; he does not care for a purely imaginative effect; he wants to strike in at the present moment, and in order to this nothing comes amiss to him. (pp. 41-2)

It has been stated almost as a certainty in England, that Disraeli, at twenty, found the original of Vivian Grey in the looking-glass, and the only youthful thing in the book has been said to be the *naïveté* with which the author displays the hard-headedness of age. There is, clearly enough, some personation of himself in Vivian Grey, for there is not the slightest irony

in the treatment of him: but the hard-headedness is affected rather than *naïve.* (p. 42)

The novel, as the reader will perceive, turns on politics; it is, so to speak, a rehearsal for real political chess moves, or the military manoeuvres in which our officers are prepared for the tactics of war. Nature has but little place in this book; here and there we have a moonlight night or a mountain landscape, but they only form a melodramatic background for the struggles and perils of the adventurer. Nature is to Mr. Disraeli never anything but—what he characteristically calls her in two of his works—an Egeria, that is, a source of political inspiration. He has taken refuge with her when weary of politics, like the tired soldier in the Vivandière's tent. But he never loved her for her own sake. (p. 44)

"Venetia" is a very peculiar book, a mixture of imagination and reality, to which even Disraeli's novels offer no parallel; it is an attempt to treat of characters and circumstances in the form of a romance, with whom and with which the whole first generation of readers were contemporary, and they are still so well known that the reader always feels put out and confused when historical truth ceases and fiction begins. (p. 94)

In spite of its violation of all aesthetic rules, it is a beautiful, impassioned, and spirited book; a good genius presides over it, and a waft of liberty flutters through its pages. (p. 96)

The romance of **"Venetia"** is a masterpiece of tact: it conducts the case of the two unjustly exiled men, without coming into too close quarters with any living person; it transfigures Lady Byron into a highly poetic being, though it fervently advocates Byron's cause; it does not condemn a single one of the enemies of the two poets, only the "despicable coterie," which had taken upon itself to represent England, and had driven Byron into exile in England's name, and had thus misled him into hurling his darts at his country, instead of at this miserable coterie alone; it is only on Lord Melbourne, husband of Lady Caroline, that a somewhat comical light is thrown, but he was purposely selected as a victim, being then the Whig Prime Minister. (pp. —)

Further, **"Venetia"** is a poetical work: it was a fine idea to allot to a woman, a young, pure, strong-hearted girl, the part of mediator, first between Byron and Shelley, and then between them both and the English people. With her brightness and golden hair, she comes before us as the dauntless genius of love, understanding all, forgiving all, and blotting out with her finger the stains in the lives of the two men of splendid genius, whom she adores and admires as daughter and *fiancée.* **"Venetia"** is the only one of Disraeli's romances in which he has introduced lyrics of no small value, for his verses generally leave much to be desired. (pp. 97-8)

Finally, **"Venetia"** is a fine piece of psychological criticism. The portraiture of the two poets is, on the whole, as spirited as it is correct; even their less conspicuous works, as, for example, Shelley's Essays, are introduced with great skill, and Shelley's influence on Byron is demonstrated with much penetration. There is a charming and truly Byronic humour in the passages where Byron acknowledges his plagiarism from Shelley, and laughingly confesses that he did not always quite understand what yet appeared to him so beautiful that he appropriated it. At the same time, it cannot be denied that we have only a sketch of Shelley, and not the finer physiognomical features. (p. 98)

"Henrietta Temple," the other novel written at this time, has for its second title, **"A Love Story,"** and it is an appropriate one. In this book the author has for once given the reins to this passion as he knew and felt it. He had, of course, treated of it in all his novels, for a romance without love is like a goblet without wine; but he had not, before writing "**Henrietta Temple,**" made it the main topic. In Disraeli's manner of writing about women and love, three stages may be noticed. In his early youth, in "**The Young Duke,**" he shows keen observation and freshness, much insight and surpassing irony; in his manhood, he depicts the ardent, admiring love of two young creatures, and, strongly affected by it himself, breaks forth into a song of praise in honour of Eros; in the third stage, woman is to him a higher, more representative being than man—she is the symbol of a great idea, and he describes her, and love for her, in the appropriate spirit, that of reverent tenderness. . . . But through all these stages, there runs, as the most essential feature, a growing, thoroughly English idealism. There is in this idealism obviously something inborn—the home of his soul was rather the inspired East of the Arab than the luxurious East of Hafiz—but there was still more that was acquired by adaptation to his surroundings. He was not originally wanting in sensuous fancy; he had a keen eye for colour, betrayed equally in delight in the contrast between the hue of the lobster and the whiteness of the flounder at a fishmonger's, or the play of the diamonds on a lady's neck at a ball; but he had not enough of nature in him, he lived too perpetually in abstract plans and schemes, to be able to distil a beautiful or poetic side from sensuous life. He does not once describe sensuous attraction as an element in love, not even as an idealist might describe it, with unimpassioned truthfulness, far less with poetical appreciation of this force of nature. For he desires, above all things, to be read by the general public; to be a drawing-room author, recommended by a mother to her daughter. He therefore allows the great naturalistic movement in English poetry to rush past him without learning anything essential from it. . . . The stages which I have indicated in Disraeli's treatment of love, . . . show rather his tendency to bring himself into accord with the spirit of the age and English taste, than the development of talent independent of the external world. (pp. 99-101)

Under George IV frivolity was the mode; consequently, in "**The Young Duke,**" Disraeli touches with a bolder and freer hand than he ever did afterwards the various mental and other conditions which result from frivolous or illegitimate love. The delineation of it is clever and in extremely good taste; the critical passages are passed over in jest or in a tragi-comic style. Still, erotic indiscretions have a place here, and are not, as afterwards, systematically excluded from the life of the hero. (p. 101)

In "**Henrietta Temple,**" love is treated in a totally different style. The praises of love are sung, its omnipotence is gravely described, and it is young, innocent love, sure of itself. All the difficulties with which it has to contend come from without, and do not finally separate the lovers. (p. 102)

"**Henrietta Temple**" is altogether a book that speaks from the heart. It may be that sighs and groans, superlatives and *fortissimos,* are rather superabundant. It becomes the author well, who is so fond of representing temporary political party questions as the great questions for the human race, to condescend to the common interests of mankind, and not to be above stenographing for us the talk of two lovers, or showing us their tenderly affectionate letters. It is in the courage exhibited in stenographing the language of love precisely as it is, without any dressing up by the author, that the originality of the novel consists. (p. 103)

[The purpose of "**Coningsby**"] was to assert the right of a select Tory party to be both a popular and a national party, as well as to serve as a programme to the clique, who here boldly appeared under the name of the "New Generation." Disraeli's experience with his "Vindication of the English Constitution" had convinced him of the impossibility of making abstract political essays a propaganda for his ideas among general readers; he resolved, therefore, to harness his talents as a novelist to these ideas, in order to open a wider sphere for them. The result was a novel without any artistic form, whose pages were permeated by political disscussions. . . .

The book at once arrested the reader by its impartiality; Tories and Whigs were assailed by the same merciless satire. (p. 125)

The strong point of ["**Sybil**"], as a work of fiction, is the series of well-drawn characters: the high aristocratic society, the young factory workers of both sexes, in whose rough *naïveté* there is a marked individuality, finally the "bishop" and his brother, a London attorney, who supports him without choosing to acknowledge the relationship; all these various groups are well conceived and truthfully drawn. In the pair last mentioned, especially, Disraeli is very successful in depicting lawless violence and worldly wisdom, and in throwing light on each by the contrast. (p. 145)

"**Tancred**" is unquestionably one of the most interesting and original of Lord Beaconsfield's works. It is a serio-comic, ironically mystic book; on the first reading, it seems too absurd to be subjected to serious criticism, but one takes it up again, and, although it falls asunder into two large fragments, its wit and brilliant Oriental scenes and conversations dwell in the memory. It comprises, moreover, Disraeli's whole field of vision, and ranges between the veriest frivolities of high life, an amusing gastronomic disquistion, and the highest religious pathos of which the author is capable, as well as the most far-reaching of his political schemes. . . . It is a book having, Janus-like, two faces—the one expressive of impenetrable irony, the other of almost pure mysticism; and the contrast is not done away with by *diversus respectus,* for the irony hovers over the mysticism, which is the pivot of the book, is to be found in reality in the mysticism itself, and thereby hits the Christian-religious enthusiasm for crusades, the cause of which he apparently advocates. It is usual to speak of Lord Beaconsfield's sphinx-like character, and "**Tancred**" affords more justification than usual for the term. . . . (pp. 170-71)

The strong point of the book is the masterly way in which Eastern life in the present day is sketched, especially where the introduction of European ideas and usages is illustrated. The dialogues of the natives are in harmony with the scenery of the desert, and the solitary castles beneath the Syrian hills. With the intuition of mental affinity, Disraeli has divined the Oriental way of looking at things, and imitates the mode of expression to a nicety. (p. 180)

["**Lothair**"] bears evident traces of the fact that the author was now advanced in years; it is the product of fuller and riper experience than his earlier works; it contains no mere political descriptions, no attacks on living personages; it has, in fact, the virtues of age; but taken as a whole, it is a repetition of his previous writings, especially of "**Tancred,**" and the style betrays the old man. During the years immediately preceding, a new element had crept into Disraeli's oratorical efforts, and his attitude as a Parliamentary speaker—a stamp of officialism. It is this which gives the final touches to his descriptions of character. (p. 217)

What makes "**Lothair**" psychologically interesting arises from the same position of affairs that has made the style official, namely, that the author stands at the summit of his wishes, and has realized his schemes, so that he no longer needs to take various circumstances into consideration. "**Lothair**" is a more straightforward book than the "Trilogy," so called, which preceded it. It is not only without false mysticism, but, in a religious point of view, it is the most openly free-thinking work that Disraeli has written, so opposed to miracles that it might be taken for the work of a Rationalist if the fantastic author had not signed it with his fantastic doctrine, never renounced, of the sole victorious Semitic principle. (pp. 217-18)

"**Lothair**" is an attempt to introduce representatives of the various prevailing views of life in the present day, and to make them carry on a decisive discussion. . . . The discussion of modern views of life on Oriental soil, is an ever-recurring reminiscence of Disraeli's own travels; it occurs in "**Contarini Fleming**" and in "**Tancred,**" where the race of Ansarey, with its beautiful queen, represents Hellenic worship of beauty, as Phoebus does in "**Lothair;**" but it can scarcely be said to have gained in depth in the author's latest production. It strikes one as rather comic when Phoebus, the zealous devotee of the Aryan principle, ends by setting up as Court painter in St. Petersburg, in order to paint Semitic subjects (incidents from the life of Jesus) for Mongolian connoisseurs. But one wearies of this perpetual and unscientific talk about race. Phoebus is not a real human being, only an affected counterpart of Disraeli himself as a Semitic theorist. While these everlasting discussions go on, whether Hellenism or Hebraism—which, after all, do not include everything—is the more profound or exalted way of looking at life, all-uniting, all-embracing nature is lost sight of. Everything resolves itself for our author into opposing systems, political and religious doctrines or fantasies, and is very characteristic that when at last Madre Natura does appear in his books, it is as the name of a secret and revolutionary society. One is inclined to say that she is not to be found in any other form with this enemy, on principle, of naturalism. (pp. 220-21)

> *Georg Brandes, in his* Lord Beaconsfield: A Study, *translated by Mrs. George Sturge, Charles Scribner's Sons, 1880 (and reprinted by Thomas Y. Crowell Company, 1966, 238 p.).*

THE QUARTERLY REVIEW (essay date 1881)

What [Disraeli] did at twenty-five, he is doing at seventy-five, only doing it better. Vivian Grey 'panted for a Senate.' The Prime Minister of England panted for a study. In the closing sentences of '**Coningsby,**' the author tells us that 'the youth of a nation are the trustees of Posterity.' In his youth he accepted that trust, and worked at it with ardent will. So much of his youth yet remains to him, that he is working at it still. 'Action,' says the General in '**Lothair,**' 'may not always bring happiness; but there is no happiness without action.' If we turn to '**Endymion,**' we read on almost every page the wise inculcation of the same truth, yet blent with tenderness for 'the heights of Meillerie.' There never was so harmonious and homogeneous a career. From the very first this man 'saw life steadily, and saw it whole.' He started with the conviction (might we not almost call it the instinct?) that life—real, full, complete life—should be divided, though without antagonism, between thought and action, between imagination and practice, between letters and politics, between the illimitable realms of fancy and the definite boundaries of a Senate, between the serious recreation

of the novelist and the fascinating responsibilities of the Statesman. What he saw he did. What he resolved he has accomplished. He sketched the outlines of a rounded and complete career; and then he proceeded to fill it in with himself—his own features, his own life, his own successes. It is given to few men to descry the Promised Land, and then to enter it. (p. 120)

How comes it that Lord Beaconsfield, who has for more than half a century diverted the world with the airiness of his invention, the shimmer of his wit, the originality of his ideas, and all the thousand and one resources of fresh and frolic genius, is transformed, when he approaches the business of life and the functions of government, into the most hard-headed statesman of his time; indeed, one so resolute in the cold clearness of his views, and so stubborn in the office of marking the just ends of action, and finding appropriate means for those ends, that he has been a thousand times reproached by his inconsequent critics with being too practical in his views, too deferential to facts, too devoid of what they are pleased to call sympathy, benevolence, and enthusiasm; in a word, with being all head, and no heart?

The answer to the question is eminently instructive. The author of '**Endymion**' has, all through life, rendered to Fancy the things that are Fancy's, and to Fact the things that are Fact's. He is a genuine man of letters, and yet a genuine statesman. A notable man of action, he is equally a notable man of imagination. (p . 121)

The first demand everybody makes upon a novelist is that he should not be dull. He must amuse, or he has failed. The novels of Lord Beaconsfield are amusing. They amused when they first appeared, and they amuse still. No doubt, '**Vivian Grey**' is longsome and occasionally tedious; '**Contarini Fleming**' must always be more or less caviare to the multitude; portions of '**Tancred**' could be dispensed with, even by an intelligent reader; and the description of the tournament in '**Endymion,**' though done with a light hand, rather too strongly recalls the padding of inferior writers. *Aliquando dormitat;* but, it must be added, the naps are few and short. '**Coningsby,**' '**Sybil,**' and '**Tancred**' are all obviously written with a moral purpose; and for a novelist to write with a moral, and more especially with an ethico-political purpose, is to venture upon a very risky experiment. In each instance alike, Lord Beaconsfield ran the risk, and triumphed over it.

How did he manage this? We wonder the secret should have escaped the commonest observer. That it should have eluded the vigilance of critics who talk about art, is indeed surprising. For it was by dint of art, and very consummate art, that the novelist succeeded where want of art would have indeed been fatal. But the art was essentially his own, because the difficulty to be overcome was one of his own creating, was entirely new, and had not been grappled with before. A lady is reported to have said of '**Lothair,**' 'I assure you it is not political; it is most amusing.' This naïve observation of a very ordinary person is worth volumes of criticism. If any one thinks it is easy to write a political novel that shall divert the whole world, the answer is, 'Let him try.' If he succeeds, his success will be considerable from more points of view than one. At the present moment there prevails among the general public the keenest interest in politics, and the passion for novel-reading is unabated. (pp. 124-25)

A good political novel means fame and emolument; but in acquiring them from this source, the author of '**Endymion**' stands alone. (p. 125)

[The] novels of Lord Beaconsfield are an integral portion of himself, the most vivid and vital expression alike of the man of letters and of the politician, of the man of thought and the man of action, of the novelist who is also a most dexterous artist and the orator and administrator who, thanks to his own intellect, force of character, and indomitable will, became Prime Minister of England. They are not 'a thing apart' from him; and if they are not his 'whole existence,' they have reflected and embodied his whole existence. They are the productions of the man of imagination, and of the man of action and experience, who also happens—and upon this, too, much might be said, if space were not running short—to be a man of infinite wit, and experienced in all the ways of the society of his time. (p. 126)

'Endymion' is the latest, we trust not the last, of Lord Beaconsfield's novels. It is different from the rest of them in many respects, but in many ways withal strikingly akin to them. It is very wise, and yet very young. Experience ripens, but imagination grows not old. (p. 128)

> *"'Endymion',"* in The Quarterly Review, *Vol. 151, No. 301, January, 1881, pp. 115-28.*

ANTHONY TROLLOPE   (essay date 1882?)

To me [Disraeli's novels] have all had the same flavour of paint and unreality. In whatever he has written he has affected something which has been intended to strike his readers as uncommon and therefore grand. Because he has been bright and a man of genius, he has carried his object as regards the young. He has struck them with astonishment and aroused in their imagination ideas of a world more glorious, more rich, more witty, more enterprising, than their own. But the glory has been the glory of pasteboard, and the wealth has been a wealth of tinsel. The wit has been the wit of hairdressers, and the enterprise has been the enterprise of mountebanks. An audacious conjurer has generally been his hero,—some youth who, by wonderful cleverness, can obtain success by every intrigue that comes to his hand. Through it all there is a feeling of stage properties, a smell of hair-oil, an aspect of buhl, a remembrance of tailors, and that pricking of the conscience which must be the general accompaniment of paste diamonds. I can understand that Mr. Disraeli should by his novels have instigated many a young man and many a young woman on their way in life, but I cannot understand that he should have instigated any one to good. (pp. 235-36)

Lothair, which is as yet Mr. Disraeli's last work, and, I think, undoubtedly his worst, has been defended on a plea somewhat similar to that by which he has defended *Vivian Grey.* As that was written when he was too young, so was the other when he was too old,—too old for work of that nature, though not too old to be Prime Minister. If his mind were so occupied with greater things as to allow him to write such a work, yet his judgment should have sufficed to induce him to destroy it when written. Here that flavour of hair-oil, that flavour of false jewels, that remembrance of tailors, comes out stronger than in all the others. Lothair is falser even than Vivian Grey, and Lady Corisande, the daughter of the Duchess, more inane and unwomanlike than Venetia or Henrietta Temple. It is the very bathos of story-telling. I have often lamented, and have as often excused to myself, that lack of public judgment which enables readers to put up with bad work because it comes from good or from lofty hands. I never felt the feeling so strongly,

or was so little able to excuse it, as when a portion of the reading public received *Lothair* with satisfaction. (pp. 236-37)

> *Anthony Trollope, "On English Novelists of the Present Day" (1882?), in his* An Autobiography, *Harper & Brothers, 1883 (and reprinted by Oxford University Press, 1923, pp. 221-37).**

EDMUND GOSSE   (essay date 1904)

Vivian Grey is little more than a spirited and daring boy's book; Disraeli himself called it "a hot and hurried sketch." It was a sketch of what he had never seen, yet of what he had begun to foresee with amazing lucidity. It is a sort of social fairy-tale, where everyone has exquisite beauty, limitless wealth and exalted rank, where the impossible and the hyperbolic are the only homely virtues. . . . In *The Young Duke* the manner is not so burlesque, but there is the same roughness of execution, combined with the same rush and fire. In either book, what we feel to-day to be the great objection to our enjoyment is the lack of verisimilitude. (p. xv)

Henrietta Temple is the boldest attempt he ever made to tell a great consecutive story of passion, and no doubt there have been those who have palpitated over the love-at-first-sight of Ferdinand Armine and Henrietta Temple. But Disraeli's serious vein is here over-luscious; the love-passages are too emphatic and too sweet. (p. xvi)

Of these imperfections fewer are to be found in *Venetia* and fewest in *Contarini Fleming.* This beautiful romance is by far the best of Disraeli's early books, and that in which his methods at this period can be most favourably studied. A curious shadow of Disraeli himself is thrown over it all; it cannot be styled in any direct sense an autobiography, and yet the mental and moral experiences of the author animate every chapter of it. (pp. xvi-xvii)

It is to be noted that the whole tone of *Contarini Fleming* is intensely literary. The appeal to the intellectual, to the fastidious, reader is incessant. This is an attitude always rare in English fiction, but at that epoch almost unknown, and its presence in the writings of Disraeli gave them a cachet. Under all the preposterous conversation, all the unruly turmoil of description, runs a strong thread of entirely sober political and philosophic ambition. Disraeli striving with all his might to be a great poet of the class of Byron and Goethe, a poet who is also a great mover and master of men—this is what is manifest to us throughout *Contarini Fleming.* It is almost pathetically manifest, because Disraeli,—whatever else he grew to be,—never became a poet. And here, too, his wonderful clairvoyance, and his command over the vagaries of his own imagination, come into play, for he never persuades himself, with all his dithyrambics, that Contarini is quite a poet. . . .

[In] his serious moments [Disraeli] had endeavored to accomplish in prose what the mysterious and melancholy poet of the preceding generation [Byron] had done in verse. The general effect of this Byronism, in spite of a certain buoyancy which carried the reader onwards, had been apt to be wearisome, in consequence of the monotony of effort. (p. xviii)

[In] *Contarini Fleming* we detect a new flavour, and it is a very fortunate one. The bitterness of Swift was never quite in harmony with the genius of Disraeli, but the *verve* of Voltaire was. The effect of reading *Zadig* and *Candide* was the completion of the style of Disraeli; the "strange mixture of brilliant fantasy and poignant truth" which he rightly perceived to be the essence of the philosophic *contes* of Voltaire, completed his own intellectual education. Henceforth he does not allow his seriousness to overweigh his liveliness; if he detects a tendency to bombast, he relieves it with a brilliant jest. (p. xix)

In spite of a certain insincerity, the volumes of *Contarini Fleming* cannot but be read with pleasure. The mixture of Byron and Voltaire is surprising, but it produces some agreeable effects. . . . But through it all he is conspicuously himself, and the dedication to beauty and the extraordinary intellectual exultation of such a book as *Contarini Fleming* are borrowed from no exotic source. (pp. xix-xx)

[In *Coningsby, Sybil, Tancred,* and the *Life of Lord George Bentinck*] we observe, in the first place, a great advance in vitality and credibility over the novels of the earlier period. Disraeli is now describing what he knows, no longer what he hopes in process of time to know. He writes from within, no longer from without, the world of political action. These three novels and a biography are curiously like one another in form, and all equally make a claim to be considered not mere works of entertainment, but serious contributions to political philosophy. (p. xxii)

In all these works, narrative pure and simple inclines to take a secondary place. It does so least in *Coningsby,* which as a story is the most attractive book of Disraeli's middle period, and one of the most brilliant stories of political character ever published. The tale is interspersed with historical essays, which impede its progress, but add to its weight and value. Where, however, the author throws himself into his narrative, the advance he has made in power, and particularly in truth of presentment, is very remarkable. In the early group of his novels he had felt a great difficulty in transcribing conversations so as to produce a natural and easy effect. He no longer, in *Coningsby,* is confronted by this artificiality. His dialogues are now generally remarkable for their ease and nature. . . . In *Coningsby* we have risen out of the rose-coloured mist of unreality which hung over books like *The Young Duke* and *Henrietta Temple.* (pp. xxii-xxiii)

Disraeli had a passion for early youth, and in almost all his books he dwells lovingly upon its characteristics. It is particularly in *Contarini Fleming* and in *Coningsby,* that is to say in the best novels of his first and of his second period, that he lingers over the picture of schoolboy life with tenderness and sympathy. (p. xxiii)

When we pass from *Coningsby* to *Sybil* we find the purely narrative interest considerably reduced in the pursuit of a scheme of political philosophy. This is of all Disraeli's novels the one which most resembles a pamphlet on a serious topic. For this reason, it has never been a favourite among his works, and his lighter readers have passed it over with a glance. *Sybil,* however, is best not read at all if it is not carefully studied. (p. xxv)

[Not withstanding] curious faults in execution, the book bears the impress of a deep and true emotion. Oddly enough, the style of Disraeli is never more stilted than it is in the conversations of the poor in this story. . . . A happier simplicity of style, founded on a closer familiarity, would have given fresh force to Disraeli's burning indignation, and have helped the cause of Devilsdust and Dandy Mick. But the accident of stilted speech must not blind us to the sincere and glowing emotion that inspired the pictures of human suffering in *Sybil.* (p. xxvi)

In *Tancred* [Disraeli] laid aside in great measure his mood of satirical extravagance. The whole of this book is steeped in the colours of poetry,—of poetry, that is to say, as the florid mind of Disraeli conceived it. . . . Real life is forgotten, and we move in a fabulous, but intensely picturesque, world of ecstasy and dream.

The prerogative of Judaism, as it had been laid down by Sidonia in *Coningsby,* is emphasized and developed, and is indeed made the central theme of the story, in *Tancred.* This novel is inspired by an outspoken and enthusiastic respect for the Hebrew race and a perfect belief in its future. (p. xxvii)

Tancred is written in Disraeli's best middle style, full, sonorous, daring, and rarely sinking into bombast. It would even be too uniformly grave, if the fantastic character of Fakredeen did not relieve the solemnity of the discourse with his amusing tirades. Like that of all Disraeli's novels, the close of this one is dim and unsatisfactory. If there is anything that the patient reader wants to know it is how the Duke and Duchess of Bellemont behaved to the Lady of Bethany when they arrived at Jerusalem and found their son in the kiosk under her palm-tree. But this is curiosity of a class which Disraeli is not unwilling to awaken but which he never cares to satisfy. He places the problems in a heap before us, and he leaves us to untie the knots. It is a highly characteristic trait of his mind as a writer that he is forever preoccupied with the beginnings of things, and as little as possible with their endings. (p. xxviii)

[*Lothair*] reads as if it were taken down from the flowing speech of a fine orator, not as if it were painfully composed in a study. It contains surprising ellipses, strange freaks of grammar. (p. xxx)

But if one thing is more evident than another to-day it is that this gorgeous story of a noble boy whose guardians, a Presbyterian earl and a Roman cardinal, quarrelled for his soul and for his acres, is an immense satire from first to last. In Disraeli's own words, used in another sense, the key-note of *Lothair* is "mockery blended with Ionian splendour." Never had he mocked so dauntlessly, never had his fancy been more splendid, and those who criticise the magnificence must realise that it was intentional. It was thus that Disraeli loved to see life, and most of all the life he laughed at. He had always been gorgeous, but he gave himself rein in *Lothair;* all is like the dream of a Lorenzo de' Medici or an Aurungzebe. Nothing is done by halves. (pp. xxx-xxxi)

There are perhaps too many temples in the landscape of *Lothair,* but they were put in on purpose. The splendour is part of the satire. (p. xxxi)

What marks the whole of Disraeli's writings more perhaps than any other quality is the buoyant and radiant temperament of their author. In *Lothair* he is like an inspired and enfranchised boy, set free from all the trammels of reality, and yet bringing to the service of his theme the results of an extraordinary inherited experience. If the picture is not real, we may take courage to say that it is far better than reality, more rich, more entertaining, more intoxicating. We have said that it is carelessly written, but that is part of the author's superb self-confidence, and when he is fortunately inspired, he obtains here an ease of style, a mastery which he had never found before. . . . He had developed, when he composed *Lothair,* a fuller sense of beauty than he had ever possessed before, but it revelled in forms that were partly artificial and partly fabulous. (pp. xxxii-xxxiii)

[His] books have not merely survived their innumerable fellows, but they have come to represent to us the form and character of a whole school; nay, more, they have come to take the place in our memories of a school which but for them would have utterly passed away and been forgotten. Disraeli, accordingly, is unique, not merely because his are the only fashionable novels of the pre-Victorian period which anyone ever reads nowadays, but because in his person that ineffable manner of the "thirties" reaches an isolated sublimity, and finds a permanent place in literature. But if we take a still wider view of the literary career of Disraeli, we are bound to perceive that the real source of the interest which his brilliant books continue to possess is the evidence their pages reveal of the astonishing personal genius of the man. (p. xxxiii)

> *Edmund Gosse, "The Writings of Benjamin Disraeli," in* Vivian Grey: A Romance of Youth *by Benjamin Disraeli (copyright, 1904, by M. Walter Dunne), Dunne, 1904, pp. xi-xxxiv.*

BLACKWOOD'S EDINBURGH MAGAZINE   (essay date 1905)

'Vivian Grey' is affected in style, in plot, and in character. Nevertheless, it possesses the quality of sincerity—a sincerity to youth and high spirits. The author was so splendidly convinced of his own omniscience, that there was no project, either active or literary, which he would not have essayed. Of course, he wrote in the fashion of the time, and if you had patience to compare 'Vivian Grey' with its forgotten contemporaries, you would see that it echoed the popular catchwords, and reflected the popular interests with some accuracy. It is Byronic, it is lackadaisical, it is fantastic. Its hero cares not for dinner so long as he is in time for the guava and liqueurs. But under the velvet glove of aestheticism there is the iron hand of action, and Vivian Grey, when he is not displaying his eloquence, is ready to manage mankind "by studying their tempers, and humouring their weaknesses." In other words, he has always "a smile for a friend, and a sneer for the world." But to whatever page you turn in this romance you find traces of the life and energy which were characteristic of its author. . . . [If] 'Vivian Grey' is puerile, as Disraeli called it, it still bears upon it the mark of genius. The mark of genius, indeed, is visible upon all that Disraeli ever wrote, save only the 'Revolutionary Epic'. . . . (pp. 287-88)

Disraeli wrote 'Vivian Grey' because he could not help it. He could not help being a man of letters any more than he could refrain from statesmanship, for he was born with the twin faculty of literature and politics. In brief, necessity is no more the cause of a book than a pot of ink and a quill pen. They are all three useful adjuncts, and that is all that can be said by the most hardened dogmatist. . . .

[The fragment of Disraeli's unfinished novel, 'Falconet,'] has been advertised like a popular encyclopaedia or a patent candle, and it might well have dispensed with this preliminary adulation. For it is a genuine fragment of the master. . . . In almost every line there are touches of the old irony and the familiar humour. . . . [Joseph] Toplady Falconet, the young statesman with more eloquence than humour, . . . would have been the most life-like portrait of Disraeli's most determined opponent, W. E. Gladstone. Nor did Disraeli's skill in making phrases desert him in this last fragment. . . . In brief, the very excellence of the fragment makes us regret the more deeply that we shall never know the fate of Joseph Toplady Falconet. Wellnigh seventy years separate the juvenility of 'Vivian Grey' from the assured irony of these unfinished chapters. But the hand that wrote them is the same, and of few novelists may it be said,

as of Disraeli, that he kept his talents undimmed unto the last. (p. 289)

> *"Musings without Method," in* Blackwood's Edinburgh Magazine, *Vol. CLXXVII, No. MLXXII, February, 1905, pp. 279-89.**

HOLBROOK JACKSON   (essay date 1908)

[*Vivian Grey*] is in reality a political satire and in effect the first political novel in the language. But nowadays its interest does not lie so much in its politics as in the light it throws on the early ambition of Disraeli. The motto of the book is characteristic of the young man:—

> Why, then, the world's mine oyster,
> Which with my sword I'll open.

Vivian is Disraeli, or rather the personification of Disraeli's ideas. He has the same ambitions and the same astounding self-confidence. Politics, fashions, and popular foibles are criticised and satirised with full-blooded impudence but excellent good humour. And although the calmly unscrupulous Vivian Grey is the author himself, poetic justice is done him in the frustration of all his calculated political schemes. Perhaps Disraeli for a moment doubted the worthiness of his cheerful egoism. The most interesting point about *Vivian Grey* is that in its pages appears the idea which not only appears in various forms throughout his works, but which was probably the underlying idea of his life: the idea that the really strong man, the unique individual, is not the man who is controlled by circumstances, but the man who controls not only his environment, but destiny. (pp. 197-99)

[In *Contarini Fleming*] his gift as a novelist becomes more apparent. Disraeli had been drawn towards poetry during his journey abroad, and Contarini is a portrait of himself in the rôle of poet. The most lasting thing about this novel, apart from the fine Byronic frenzy with which it is imbued, is its deep philosophical note. Disraeli is in a transition period, politics for a while seem vain and empty, and the whole outlook of his life is clouded and undetermined. Yet the philosophic egoism, enunciated so foppishly in *Vivian Grey,* becomes a profound idea in *Contarini Fleming*. A mystic note is struck which is new to the English novel. But the mysticism of Disraeli is not separated from life nor from robust inquiry. (p. 203)

Disraeli came upon Parliament at a time of flux. There were few commanding personalities and fewer vital ideas in the house. The new member for Maidstone had both personality and ideas; and although he looked to politics as a profession, he was none the less a man with a mission, and a sincere believer in the ideas behind his parliamentary tactics. These ideas exist in a permanent form in his novels, more particularly in the great trilogy which began with *Coningsby* in 1844, followed by *Sybil* in 1845, and concluded two years later with *Tancred*.

Disraeli saw England in the grip of a commercialism which, if not checked, would destroy her. . . . His desire was to revive the old sentiment of *noblesse oblige;* but he had as little faith in the ineffectual and pleasure-loving members of the aristocracy as he had in the money-loving Whigs and industrial overlords. (pp. 206-07)

In *Coningsby* he interprets the idea of a recreated nobility. He shows that if England is to be saved she must be saved by her aristocracy, but that can never come about until the aristocracy alters its ways and realises that its existence is not justified by self-indulgence, but by responsibility. In *Sybil* he deals with the condition of England, and shows how effete Parliament has become in the face of the immense difficulties before her. (p. 207)

All the wit and brilliance of the earlier novels are [in *Lothair*], but in a more masterly form. *Lothair* is the matured and experienced Disraeli,—the essential thought of the man of experience, who has seen the inside of the machinery of State, but whose romance, although not dead, has been taught to burn with a steady and dignified glow, rather than to flash its startling rays across the world. (p. 208)

The underlying idea of [Disraeli's] life was the translation of imagination into practical power. He is a part of that Romantic movement with which the eighteenth century closed and the nineteenth opened—the movement which has for its symbols Napoleon no less than Rousseau, Byron, Heine, and Shelley, as well as Ferdinand Lassalle and Benjamin Disraeli. All these romantic types find expression in the singular personality of Disraeli, and it is more than probable that his genius might have accomplished for England what his compatriot Lassalle began so brilliantly for Germany. His faith in imaginative power runs through all his novels, and his cleverest satires are criticisms of those great opponents of the imaginative faculty, rationalism and utilitarianism. . . . [In] *Coningsby*, he says, "Man is only truly great when he acts from the passions; never irresistible but when he appeals to the imagination." That is the keynote to his life, and for that idea his novels stand. They are not, like the novels of the earlier masters, portrayals of character or analyses of feeling; nor yet like the novels of Scott, impersonal romances; but more allied to the poems of Byron, they are the expression of an intensely personal view of life, revealed through types and customs rather than characters and feelings. They are novels of ideas, the brilliant interpretations of human ambition in terms of the imagination. (pp. 212-14)

> *Holbrook Jackson, "Benjamin Disraeli," in his* Great English Novelists, *Grant Richards, 1908, pp. 181-214.*

B. N. LANGDON-DAVIES   (essay date 1911)

[*Coningsby*] is essentially a study of young men, and in a great measure of certain particular young men—the Young England group. The *New Generation* is the second title of the work, and it is to the new generation that its teachings were addressed. Youth and the power of the individual are its constant theme. "It is a holy thing to see a state saved by its youth," said Coningsby. (p. xiv)

[What] made *Coningsby* so eagerly welcomed, so widely read, and so universally criticised at such a time? . . .

Coningsby cannot claim a plot which is in all respects ideal, for the incidents are liable to straggle in a somewhat disorderly manner after the fundamental ideas. Nor are all of the characters the delineations of a master-hand. Coningsby himself is a prig and is meant to be a hero; Sidonia is a perfect piece of intellectual and practical mechanism, and is meant to be an inspiring and powerful man; and indeed most of the characters leave upon us the impression of a set of opinions or a number of actions rather than of human beings. (p. xv)

A work of art to live must create. And the superficial excellences of *Coningsby* as a work of art would not have been enough to overcome its defects, had it not created something

which was of more than local and temporary power and interest. . . . [There] had not yet been a novel of political life. In an age of politics, the romance, the personnel, and the incidents of political life had, before the appearance of *Coningsby* with its initial experiments *Vivian Grey, Popanilla,* and *Contarini Fleming,* gone unrepresented. Disraeli had created a new type. The novel is essentially political, written to expound a political creed, and read in its own day to learn what that creed was. It is for this reason that, without a full appreciation and study of the purely political chapters, the book is only half appreciated. The lapse of sixty years has rendered the thinly disguised allusions and references obscure to the reader, and some analysis and explanation has become essential. A dozen such political stories might be written, which would never deserve to be exhumed. *Coningsby* is an exception. It is an exception because of the brilliance of its wit, the keenness of its satire, and the force of its ideals; it is also an exception because the political circumstances are less remote from our own than at first sight appears, and because it deals not only with isolated incidents and with party moves, but also with universal principles of government and statesmanship. (p. xvi)

> *B. N. Langdon-Davies, in his introduction to* Coningsby *by Benjamin Disraeli, E. P. Dutton & Co., 1911, pp. vii-xxvi.*

FRANK SWINNERTON   (essay date 1928)

["**Contarini Fleming**"] must be regarded as the most consciously autobiographical of the author's works, as it is the most ambitious of them all. It is very revealing, and it is very serious. That is one consequence of its false inspiration, because Disraeli seeks in the pages of "**Contarini Fleming**" to exhibit himself as a poet. He proved to be unequal to the task, for, while there is intellectual vigor in the book, there is a singular and admitted poetic sterility. (pp. 289-90)

In "**Venetia**," Disraeli continued to try to force inspiration. He was bent upon exploring mystery, and by setting the scene back in the eighteenth century he sought freely to reconstruct the lives and the final catastrophe of Byron and Shelley. The scheme is bold enough, but here again, as in "**Contarini Fleming**," the poetic is never captured, and the protagonists remain for the most part merely extravagant in action and speech. The defect of these ambitious books is clear. It is a want of creative imagination in the author, and a refusal at present to admit that his own deficiency was unconquerable by will. . . . It was his mistake all along to suppose that art and artifice, the grand, the grandiloquent, the sublime, the violent, the exaggerated, the noble, the beautiful, and the glorious, were all upon the same aesthetic level, and that he could force beauty as he could force argument. . . . The writer whose aim it is to be poetical is no poet. The heroes of Disraeli's psychological romances are called poets, but they are not poets. Disraeli, speaking of his own "poetic character," and aiming in his work at the effect of poetic character, was no poet. (pp. 290-91)

There have been other political novels, from those of Trollope to those of Mrs. Humphry Ward, but in the composition of this type of novel Disraeli has no equal. It gave him scope for all his gifts as a writer—for his wit, his love of political intrigue and political gossip, his apt portrayal of the life of the "saloons," his love of arch or satiric portraiture. It allowed him room in which to expound his sometime peculiar historical and political theories. It amused him to write, and it amused others—sometimes wildly—to read. These political novels are not great novels, and in places they are shockingly written; but they are supreme in their class. (p. 291)

Into his last five novels, therefore, are crowded the most notable achievements of Disraeli as a novelist. These books contain fewer falsenesses than the early novels, in the sense that they are most in accord—in theme and treatment—with the actual interests of Disraeli's and the true character of his genius. . . . [He] kept for the greater part of the time to the study of rich, witty, foolish, opinionated, intriguing, vain, ambitious, and preposterous people. He was amused by them because he was unceasingly amused by the superficies of life and unceasingly interested in the play of motive which it was so much a part of his work as a political leader to control. He knew what such human beings as he was describing would be likely to think and to plan and say. He knew the world, and he knew its ways. . . . From this knowledge, and from his own masked response to every move in the game of life and politics as he played it, came Disraeli's power as a writer. If not Olympian, he was detached. If he did not create, he decorated. And he was diverted by the spectacle of life in very much the degree in which we are diverted when we read his novels. (p. 292)

[In "**Coningsby**"] we are living in a world that is quite distinctly the real world of Disraeli. We live, not with the simulacra of ambitious poets, seen very earnestly by their author, but with politicians who are viewed with enchanting *sang-froid*. (p. 293)

["**Lothair**"] was and is the most popular and the most characteristic of all his books. It is astonishingly dexterous, and although its intrigue is poor the portraits and the gossip were never better, while the author's remarkable lightness and ease, unhampered by serious purpose, ran into delightful buoyancy. We have in "**Lothair**" Disraeli laughing and extravagant, absurd, full of rhodomontade, but relieved of the weight of ambition. . . . "**Lothair**" is by Disraeli the social success, the worldling, the observer of foibles, the wit, and the mask. . . . [This] is a bland book, happy, fluent, and entertaining. (pp. 295-96)

["**Endymion**"] is milder, quieter, and kinder. It is packed with forgiving portraits, as clear as ever, but it is less vivid. Great experience of the world is again Disraeli's principal quality, and he takes us into his own past friendships as he does nowhere else. "**Endymion**" is a very fitting close to a long literary career, for if we make a comparison of it with that other novel about a young man determined upon success in politics, Vivian Grey, we shall see that the writer has travelled far from his old cry of the oyster. Endymion has none of Vivian's impudence. He is more interested in others. He enjoys young society, which Vivian, precociously, never did. He is more successful than Vivian, because he submits to the ambitiousness of others upon his behalf. Looking back over his own career, Disraeli had been impressed anew by the part which had been played in it by his devoted women friends, and "**Endymion**," though it is tamer than "**Vivian Grey**," is also truer. It is a charming exhibition of Disraeli's loyalties, all the more charming because "**Endymion**" was his final gesture of acknowledgment to the world. (p. 296)

[The paradox of Disraeli is] that although he was probably ever dominated by ambition he was, amid all his calculation of chances and effects, an idealist. The idealism was as uncertain as his taste (he was as avid of beauty as he was of principles), and in both there was a readiness for the meretricious which appals some of his more fastidious admirers. . . . He was certainly not an artist, because it was his belief that the end (whether it was entertainment or propaganda) justified the most extravagant of means. His taste was faulty and flighty. His sense of character was never creative, but was always dominated by his wit. But he had his sincerities and consistencies, and if these often enough took the form of repetition of political, historical, and racial theory, they show that in so far as he was temperamentally able to grasp the world about him he was ready to depict it with candor and judgment. His pictures of society, accordingly, still have life and interest. . . . Coningsby, Egremont, Tancred, Lothair, Endymion—all are young men without natural importance. They are rich (with the exception of Endymion, who has greatness thrust upon him), bewildered, negative, and lacking in the power to impose themselves upon the dramatic action of the books in which they nominally play leading parts. They suffer; they do not create.

They are rich. This is one clue to their interest for Disraeli, who was in debt. Their movements are unhampered by the want of funds. They can indulge in the chosen delights of Disraeli. . . . From the beginning of his life, whether it was as poet or as politician, as leader of a recalcitrant party or as world diplomat, Disraeli saw himself idealized, as a being alone, dominating, immensely suave and powerful. He saw himself thus, but with deliberate romanticism. In his heart, he knew that he was still the little Jew boy. . . . [He] was gratifying his love of opulence and splendor in making his heroes rich men with magnificent gestures (for example, the young duke's spending efforts and Tancred's gift of jewels to Theodora) which most of us would think deplorable. (pp. 297-98)

The novels are his release from impassive calm. They show that he was free from passion, because passion as it is known to the majority of men either did not possess him or was never suffered to appear to do so. He was an Oriental, calm in all hours; but sensitive in a degree which those who allow passion to master them can never comprehend. For this reason the novels must be read, as they were written, as a kind of fairy tale. In them may be found nearly all Disraeli's opinions, many of his convictions, a number of his wishes. They are not first-class novels, but if they are read as revelations (conscious and unconscious) of Disraeli's personality, they will assist the reader very greatly in the imaginative reconstruction of a great figure, tenacious, ready to serve, full of wit and the bitterness of intellectual pride, affectionate, expert in ruse and counter-ruse, conscious in every failure and triumph of racial disadvantage, a lover of society, a despiser of baseness and futility, not much of a snob, but one whose taste strays towards the grandiose, the vast, the ornate, and—almost continually—the meretricious. He was a great figure. Not a great statesman or great novelist, but intensely interesting, both as statesman and novelist, as much for his limitations as for the picturesque qualities which give even his most striking statesmanship and even his most striking novels their characteristics of bland, romantic second-rateness. (p. 300)

Frank Swinnerton, "Disraeli as Novelist," in The Yale Review, *Vol. XVII, No. 2, January, 1928, pp. 283-300.*

WILHELMINA GORDON   (essay date 1945)

In linking [the] events of Disraeli's life with his three novels [*Coningsby, Sybil, Tancred*] . . . , it is important to realize how clearly he set forth, for all to read, his political ideals, his views of political reform, and to remember how eagerly and how far, many years later, he tried to put them into effect when he was in power as Prime Minister. But to turn the novels into biography, to try to identify each important character with an actual person whom Disraeli knew, is of no importance at all. Disraeli wrote biography, and he wrote novels; he did not produce that hybrid of modern literature, the novel which draws its interest from biography but escapes the responsibility of biography by using imaginary names and details. A creative artist, he drew from his experience material from which his imagination fashioned men and women and incidents in his novels; he was not concerned, like some story-tellers to-day, with protesting to his readers that any connection with actual persons and places should be regarded as accidental. One of the chief differences between these novels and others which deal with politics is that they are written from the inside. (p. 217)

In his novels, as in his temperament, Disraeli is both romantic and realistic. Romantic novels are often set in unfamiliar places or periods, with rugged or gloomy scenery, preferably seen by moonlight or in a storm; heroes and heroines are beautiful in face and feeling, villains are unmistakably black; the course of true love is beset only by external obstacles, not by inward misgivings; plot and atmosphere are complicated and coloured by the use of mystery and the supernatural; under stress of emotion speech becomes elaborate rather than abrupt. There is something of this in Disraeli's novels. . . . But in scenery the unusual is emphasized, especially in *Tancred*, where frowning mountains, treeless desert, and exotic gardens form the background for lovely women, lavish feasts and Arab steeds. (pp. 217-18)

Disraeli's men and women are often strikingly beautiful or at least attractive; it is characteristic of his tolerance that even unpleasant and selfish men are often shapely and dignified and his chivalry toward women seldom presents them as even plain. . . . [In] *Coningsby* Millbank's scathing comments on the peerage, with its alleged ancient lineage, suggests what a genuine aristocracy might be, if it were based on distinction.

The merely romantic novel makes no study of character; individuals are stock figures, little more than types or personified abstractions. Disraeli does not, like Dickens, amuse us with unforgettable figures, complete with name-tag and identifying gesture or phrase. His humour, like Scott's, is happiest when it plays on his less exalted persons, Tancred's home-bred servants in Syria, becoming more and more English as their master falls more and more under the spell of the East; the French *chefs* in London as they consult together in the early pages of *Tancred*, where their dwellings and manners are described in detail as crisp as Thackeray's but with kindly amusement. In the picture of Lord Marney, on the other hand, in *Sybil*, there is satire and insight, but little humour; Disraeli was ready to laugh at the flirt or the bore, man or woman, but the gentle, brow-beaten wife roused his tenderness and sympathy. (pp. 218-19)

Most of all in *Sybil* does Disraeli show his sympathy for the suffering and the down-trodden. (p. 219)

Sybil is, indeed, definitely a novel with a purpose. . . . (p. 221)

Disraeli presents the nation of the poor, their lives wasted when they might have been usefully and happily serving the country. In constant contrast he gives views, from his own experience, of the titled rich, in manor and castle and town house and club. There is little sympathy in this presentation, but keen satire. (p. 222)

Another theme which Disraeli treats with insistent eloquence is the great moral and intellectual contribution made to human civilization by the Hebrew race. In *Coningsby* and *Tancred* Sidonia appears, first as a mysterious stranger, then as the man of almost fantastic financial skill and power, "lord and master of the money-market of the world, and of course lord and master of everything else", proud of his descent from the Hebrew Arabs who were nobles in Arragon, a man of keen intellect, artistic tastes, wide and original benevolence and high imagination. No doubt the character was based on one or more of the Rothschilds—and almost with a sight of the future, for it was a Rothschild who made it possible for Disraeli, as Prime Minister, to give Britain control of the Suez Canal. But Sidonia is in a large measure an ideal figure; many of Disraeli's own hopes and ideas are expressed by him. (p. 223)

In many ways Disraeli stands alone. As man and novelist he left no descendants. Perhaps the last of the romantics, he looked to the East for his inspiration, and gave to his country the work of his life. Familiar with the Jewish ritual of cleanliness, he was appalled at the grimy and unhealthy surroundings of English workers in factories and on farms, and he laboured to improve them. Always a foreigner to many of the English, his more subtle intellect understood the devious working and the suave phrasing of the East, and in foreign affairs his consummate statesmanship could match all others. He did much to strengthen and establish the Empire which many to-day resent and would discard, and his constructive imagination gave a new meaning to that often misunderstood term. His novels were not to him a way of escape from the business of life and government; they were a means of making his ideas clear to himself, of rousing his countrymen to realize what needed to be done. Then he went into action. (p. 224)

Wilhelmina Gordon, "Disraeli the Novelist," in The Dalhousie Review, *Vol. 25, No. 2, July, 1945, pp. 212-24.*

V. S. PRITCHETT (essay date 1964)

[At the distance of] a hundred years, how exactly Disraeli has defined the English political situation. He is our only political novelist; I mean, the only one *saturated* in politics; the only one whose intellect feasts on polity. . . . Politics are a method, a humane technique of adjustment; and, in general, it must be said that this has been the English view throughout the nineteenth century and after. To Disraeli, the Jew and alien, such a theory was pragmatic and despicable. It also lacked theatre.

In his early years, at least, and especially in the trilogy of novels of which *Sybil* is the second volume, Disraeli brought to political thought the electric heat of the Jewish imagination and the order of its religious traditions. . . . [When] we pick up *Sybil* or *Coningsby*, with their captivating pictures of aristocratic life and their startling, documented pictures of the squalor of the industrial poor, we feel that here at last is a novelist who is impatient of immediate social issues and who has gone back dramatically to the historic core of the English situation. The tedium has gone. We may now be carried away by a faith, snared by a passion. How precise is the diagnosis of the failure of his own party; they are not Conservatives but concessionaries, a party without beliefs. As we read *Sybil* and *Coningsby* we are swept along by a swift exultant mind. It takes us, by a kind of cinematic magic, from the gold plate and languid peers of the Derby dinner to the delectable mansions and heavenly countenances of the exalted, and from them to the sunken faces of the starved and enslaved. . . . The secret of Disraeli's superiority as a political novelist is that he introduces imagination into politics; he introduces questions of law, faith and vision. He looked upon the English scene with the clear intellect of the alien who, as a Jew, identified himself with both the two English nations; with the race that was to be emancipated and with the aristocracy that ruled them. The romantic, Byronic pride of Disraeli—if we are to take the figure of Sidonia in *Coningsby* as a projection of himself, several times larger than life—is measureless. Under the ancient gaze of the hollow eye of Asia, the Norman family is as crude as a band of tourists standing before the ruin of Ozymandias, king of kings.

Disraeli's gift is for the superb and the operatic. And if there is more than a touch of the deluxe and meretricious in his understanding of the superb, that fits in with the political picture; politics is the world of façade and promises. Disraeli knew God and Mammon. So many political novels have known God, the party line, alone; and without Mammon the people fainteth. He was the romantic poet and yet the *rusé*, satiate, flattering and subtle man of the world. When we are exhausted by visions he can soothe us with scandal. No one, said Queen Victoria with delight when she read his letters—no one had ever told her *everything* before. The novels of Disraeli tell us everything. (pp. 75-7)

Coningsby is a novel of static scenes. . . . Where *Coningsby* is still, *Sybil* moves. We pass from the sight of society to the pictures of working-class starvation and slavery. Disraeli investigated the conditions of the poor for himself, and his remarkable eye and ear collected a number of unforgettable notes and dialogues. There is nothing as terrifying in Dickens, for example, as Disraeli's picture of the slum town of locksmiths run by the toughest working men alone, a kind of frontier town without institutions. (p. 79)

Sybil is melodramatic—it would make an excellent opera or film—it lacks the closely finished texture of *Coningsby* but is looser, bolder in argument, wildly romantic in scene. . . .

The rioting and the attack on Mowbray Castle at the end is tremendous theatrical stuff, though—it must be remembered—Disraeli claimed that all his material about the Chartists was carefully documented. The unreality of certain characters, especially Sybil herself, is, of course, comical; but such characters are not unreal in their context. They are ideals walking and so romantic in their carriage that, in the end, one accepts them and their theatrical lamentations over their stolen heritage. (p. 80)

> V. S. Pritchett, "Disraeli," in his The Living Novel and Later Appreciations (copyright 1947, © 1964, and renewed 1975 by V. S. Pritchett; reprinted by permission of Random House, Inc.; in Canada by Literistic, Ltd.), revised edition, Random House, 1964, pp. 74-80.

FRANÇOISE BASCH (essay date 1972)

In *Coningsby* and above all in *Sybil or the Two Nations* there is a striking diversity of female characters—some created by fantasy, others directly derived from the Blue Books and from personal observation.

In *Coningsby* the problem of the employment of young girls in factories is briefly described as it figures in the romantic imagination of Coningsby, a young aristocrat, who is travelling

around to find out for himself what the state of England is. . . . The young aristocrat discovering the miracle of mechanization and progress imagines a charming scene in which grace combines with ardour for work. The idyllic evocation is complete. (pp. 185-86)

The picture of industrial life is less poetic in *Sybil*. . . .

Disraeli was shocked by the clothing, the same for men and women and the crude language coming from what ought to be the pure lips of present or future mothers. But, he observes, how can we expect anything else from creatures reduced to the condition of slaves and beasts of burden? (p. 186)

When Disraeli described this 'second nation', the responsibility for which he wanted to persuade industrialists and aristocrats to assume, he was as resolutely hostile to degrading work for men as for women. . . .

Disraeli's portrait [of women in *Sybil*] traces their integration into a restored context and mode of life. The girls do not appear as passive and exploited victims or creatures lost through vice but as relatively stable creatures who had adapted to a new mode of production and a profound transformation of the family structure. In the new society that Disraeli points to it is the parents who are sacrificed for their incapacity to adapt to industrial society. (p. 187)

Disraeli and the Young England movement exalted the role of the artisan in a humane society where the aristocracy would watch over the wellbeing of the lowly. But the artisan in *Sybil* no longer has a place in the new capitalist society. He has lost his creative role. The worker's function is to watch over machines which enslave him. Disraeli certainly does not condemn the younger generation. The brief portrait of Harriet who abandoned her poor family dependent on her salary shows a degree of sympathy on the part of the author. These young workers have acquired an independence that Disraeli does not identify with the immorality which the majority of legislators feared and criticized. (p. 188)

Disraeli wanted implicitly to show that from a psychological as well as material point of view these young men and women show a new maturity that justifies their emancipation. He sketches the portrait of a young generation of working men and women, independent, stable and adapted to a new society. . . . In the general perspective of Disraeli's trilogy—of a Tory romanticism full of nostalgia for a return to the middle ages, of a hatred for contemporary utilitarian and liberal tendencies—these relatively modern views are remarkable. (p. 189)

> Françoise Basch, "A More Realistic Portrayal by Elizabeth Gaskell, Trollope and Disraeli," in her Relative Creatures: Victorian Women in Society and the Novel, translated by Anthony Rudolf (reprinted by permission of Schocken Books Inc.; translation copyright © 1974 by Françoise Basch; originally published as La femme victorienne: roman et société, 1837-1867, Université de Lille, 1972), Schocken Books, 1974, pp. 175-91.*

DANIEL R. SCHWARZ (essay date 1975)

The trilogy of the 1840s [*Coningsby, Sybil,* and *Tancred*] is Disraeli's Apologia. Behind the dramatization of the education of Tancred, Coningsby, and Egremont lies Disraeli's quest for the principles with which he could structure his public life. Disraeli continually asserted dogma to convince himself of its value, although as with Newman, the nature of the dogma was continually in flux. The political ideals discovered by his Young England heroes became, for a time, the tenets of his own political and moral credo. (p. 13)

The trilogy's three heroes—Coningsby, Egremont, and Tancred—are young scions of great families estranged from those charged with raising them. Each is expected by family circumstances and social convention to fulfill a predetermined pattern. But each gradually becomes disillusioned with his expected paradigm of development and those who counsel it, and is gradually reeducated to a new set of values. (p. 14)

According to Disraeli's intended argument, each of the protagonists overcomes dubiety and anxiety because he convinces himself that he possesses the unique intellectual and moral potential to shape not merely his own life, but the very fabric of historical process. Each protagonist's quest is conceived as a heroic quest to discover the values essential for a new breed of political leaders who will recognize the supremacy of the monarchy and the importance of serving the common people. Coningsby's ambition and self-confidence; Egremont's compassion and consciousness of the miseries of others; and Tancred's spiritual faith and willingness to act on behalf of his beliefs are the ideals to which others (and *others* for Disraeli meant his aristocratic audience and hence potential political leaders) must strive. (pp. 14-15)

In many significant ways, however, the three novels are separate and distinct and represent three different genres of fiction. *Coningsby* is a *Bildungsroman* concerned with the intellectual and moral development of the potential leader. *Sybil*, heavily borrowing from Blue Book material, is a polemical novel that primarily focuses on the socioeconomic conditions that need to be remedied. And *Tancred* is an imaginary voyage in the tradition of *Gulliver's Travels, Robinson Crusoe*, and Disraeli's own neglected *Popanilla*. . . .

The efficacy of *Coningsby* depends upon Disraeli's establishing a relationship between the private theme—the development of Coningsby's abilities as a potential leader; and the public theme—the need for revivifying England's political institutions. . . .

Coningsby's growth is measured by a kind of intellectual barometer: his acceptance of the views held by Sidonia (whose views generally echo the narrator's) is the index of his development. As is often the case in a *Bildungsroman* employing an omniscient third-person narrator, Disraeli's narrator expresses the values to which the protagonist evolves. (p. 15)

If *Coningsby* were written, as Disraeli claimed, simply "to vindicate the just claims of the Tory Party to be the popular political confederation of the country" it would seem a dreadful failure. Read alone, *Coningsby* is a rather dreary tract, but if read in conjunction with *Sybil*, it has substantial impact. In a sense, *Sybil* "completes" *Coningsby;* by illustrating the discontent and deprivation of the common people, the later novel implies the need for new leadership. . . . *Coningsby* is less effectual than *Sybil* because its intellectual and moral abstractions lack dramatized correlatives. . . . It remains for *Sybil* to illustrate how men lacking adequate political and spiritual leaders may totemize their own worst instincts in the form of a savage chieftain like the Wodgate Bishop; how Chartism appeals to men who feel a void in their lives; and how the church has become virtually a hollow anachronism. (pp. 15-16)

The inclusive structure of *Sybil* supplements the effects of Egremont's personal experience by presenting representative vignettes of life in England. Rapid alternation between scenes of luxury and scenes of poverty calls attention to the discrepancy between the idle, luxurious lives of the aristocracy and the struggle for economic and moral survival of the common people. . . .

Tancred does develop some of the social and political themes begun in *Coningsby* and *Sybil*. Tancred journeys to Jerusalem after convincing himself of the superficiality of contemporary English Civilization and the futility of its politics. The political world of the Mid-East parodies the intrigues of English politics; the major difference is that weapons rather than votes are the method of settling political disagreements. . . .

But despite superficial resemblances to its predecessors, *Tancred* does not function as the climactic volume of the political trilogy. Originally conceived as a novel about reviving the sacred position of the Anglican Church by means of rediscovering its spiritual principles, *Tancred* becomes, whether Disraeli intended it or not, a kind of clumsy metaphor for the discovery of the divine within oneself. . . .

Mimesis in *Tancred* is based on entirely different assumptions than in the rest of the trilogy. Verisimilitude of time and space is virtually absent. (p. 16)

Disraeli may well have believed that the art of *Tancred* demonstrated the "imagination" presently lacking in England. . . . As early as *Popanilla* and *Contarini Fleming* . . . , we can see his distrust of excessive logic and reason. In *Sybil*, Morley illustrated the emptiness of utilitarianism; once his own private designs are thwarted, the greatest good for the greatest number has little appeal, and repressed and unacknowledged atavistic impulses manifest themselves. The narrator in *Tancred* continually mocks scientific methodology and its inductive method, and implicitly proposes faith and intuition as superior alternatives. (pp. 16-17)

That the angel's revelation is not tested as a viable system is a failure of *Tancred* which severely affects the argument of the entire trilogy. The novel does not explore the meaning of the angel's message as a plausible alternative to political intrigue in Asia or to the decline of the monarchy and church in England. . . . Tancred becomes a ludicrous parody of, rather than—as Disraeli intended—an heir of, those biblical heroes to whom God and his angels spoke. (p. 17)

Tancred is as much a continuation of *Contarini Fleming* . . . as it is of the political novels of the 1840s. In *Tancred*, Disraeli transports himself as well as his title character from the demands of politics to a fantasy world populated by virtual demigods. . . . We can properly consider Disraeli a Romantic, shaping politics, religion, and philosophy to conform to his own private vision. Thus Tancred's search for spiritual faith may be a disguised version of Disraeli's unconscious desire to return to his racial and spiritual origins. (pp. 17-18)

Disraeli's motives for writing the trilogy were complex. He undoubtedly wanted to articulate political and moral principles, in part no doubt to erase the notoriety that he had acquired. . . . Disraeli created Sidonia as a mouthpiece to *argue* for the historical significance of the Jewish people in *Coningsby* and in the first two books of *Tancred*. But it is Tancred's pilgrimage to Jerusalem for "Asian spirituality" and his discovery of the Hebraic basis of Christianity that *dramatize* Disraeli's intense personal need to reconcile his Jewish origins with the Christian religion. Disraeli believed that Christianity was completed Judaism, although he may have unconsciously taken this position because of his need to justify his own conversion. . . . Disraeli's self-confidence in part depended upon his belief that the Jews deserved esteem as an especially gifted *race*. Often, and with considerable justification, Disraeli is accused of political expedience and intellectual legerdemain. But the defense of Jews was an article of faith. (p. 18)

Tancred, begun as an effort to reinvigorate spiritual values in England, really demonstrates Disraeli's disillusionment with Young England as a political movement. The hope voiced in *Coningsby* and *Sybil* has at best been partially fulfilled, for *Tancred* shows that the new generation of leaders is not yet governing and that political progress has been relatively slow. (pp. 18-19)

That Tancred becomes a fanatic, alternating between moments of meditation and spasms of frenetic activity when he is ready to sacrifice human life for his vague dreams, reflects Disraeli's disappointment with the demise of Young England and his frustration with his failure to obtain political power. I think, too, that Disraeli must have felt that he had not dramatized the enduring spiritual principles on which a revived church could be based and that *Tancred* did not provide an alternative to utilitarianism, rationality, and objectivity. As *Tancred* vacillates erratically from its political moorings to its concern with faith, subjectivity, and imagination, it destroys the expectation raised by *Coningsby* and *Sybil* for a major political trilogy based on a deft analysis of the past, a sustained indictment of the present, and a prophetic vision of the future. (p. 19)

> *Daniel R. Schwarz, "Progressive Dubiety: The Discontinuity of Disraeli's Political Trilogy," in* The Victorian Newsletter *(reprinted by permission of* The Victorian Newsletter*), No. 47, Spring, 1975, pp. 12-19.*

ADDITIONAL BIBLIOGRAPHY

Blake, Robert. *Disraeli*. London: Eyre and Spottiswoode, 1966, 819 p.
    Biography stressing Disraeli's personality and its emergence in his novels.

Bloomfield, Paul. *Disraeli*. Writers and Their Work, edited by Bonamy Dobrée, no. 138. London: Longmans, Green, & Co., 1961, 39 p.
    Survey of Disraeli's literary career.

Forbes-Boyd, Eric. "Disraeli the Novelist." In *Essays and Studies: 1950,* edited by G. Rostrevor Hamilton, pp. 100-17. London: John Murry, 1950.
    Finds Disraeli a novelist of great imaginative power, but one lacking in scope and variety.

Frietzsche, Arthur H. *Disraeli's Religion: The Treatment of Religion in Disraeli's Novels*. Logan, Utah: Utah State University Press, 1961, 46 p.
    A discussion of Disraeli's enthusiasm for Catholicism and Toryism.

Holloway, John. "Disraeli." In his *The Victorian Sage: Studies in Argument,* pp. 86-110. 1953. Reprint. Hamden, London: Archon Books, 1962.
    Examines the "serious and the rollicking" parts of Disraeli's novels and how he uses the latter to emphasize his message.

Kebbel, T. E. *Lord Beaconsfield and Other Tory Memories*. New York: Mitchell Kennerley, 1907, 360 p.
    Personal reminiscences of Disraeli as a statesman.

Maurois, André. "Disraeli and Victorian England." In *Lives of Today and Yesterday,* edited by Rowena K. Keyes, pp. 158-74. New York: Appleton, 1931.
    Brief sketch emphasizing Disraeli's literary development.

Monypenny, William Flavelle, and Buckle, George Earle. *The Life of Benjamin Disraeli, Earl of Beaconsfield*. 2 Vols. New York, Macmillan, 1910-20.
    The definitive biography of Disraeli.

More, Paul Elmer. "Disraeli and Conservatism." In his *Aristocracy and Justice: Shelburne Essays, ninth series,* pp. 151-89. Boston, New York: Houghton Mifflin Co., 1915.
    Expounds on Disraeli's conservative political philosophy.

O'Kell, Robert. "Disraeli's *Coningsby:* Political Manifesto or Psychological Romance?" *Victorian Studies* XXXIII, No. 1 (Autumn 1979): pp. 57-78.
    Discusses *Coningsby* as fiction reflecting upon the formation of Disraeli's political ideology.

Rosa, Matthew Whiting. "Disraeli." In his *The Silver Fork School: Novels of Fashion Preceding "Vanity Fair,"* pp. 99-115. New York: Columbia University Press, 1936.
    Discussion of *The Young Duke* and *Vivian Grey* as fashionable novels of the early nineteenth century.

Saintsbury, George. "Disraeli: A Portrait." In his *A Saintsbury Miscellany: Selections from his Essays and Scrap Books,* pp. 175-82. New York: Oxford University Press, 1947.
    Biographical view with short critical comments pertaining to Disraeli's novels.

Speare, Morris Edmund. "The Literary Significance of Benjamin Disraeli." In his *The Political Novel: Its Development in England and in America,* pp. 143-84. 1924. Reprint. New York: Russell & Russell, 1966.
    Praises Disraeli for his forcefulness and for his innovation of the political novel.

Fedor Mikhailovich Dostoevski

1821-1881

(Also transliterated as Feodor, Fyodor; also Mikhaylovich; also Dostoyevsky, Dostoievsky, Dostoevskii, Dostoevsky, Dostoïewsky, Dostoiefski, Dostoïevski, Dostoyévskiiy, Dostoieffski) Russian novelist, short story writer, and journalist.

Dostoevski is considered one of the most outstanding and influential writers of modern literature. His greatness lies in the depth and range of his vision, his acute psychological insight, his profound philosophical thought, and his brilliant prose style. In such works as *Prestuplenye i nakazanye (Crime and Punishment)* and *Brat'ya Karamazovy (The Brothers Karamazov)*, Dostoevski sought to reconcile the spiritual and the physical through his tormented heroes, characters capable both of the highest virtue and the lowest degradation.

Born into a strict family in Moscow, Dostoevski was sent away to school at an early age. Though his school years were lonely, they afforded him a release from the stern regime of his father's household. In his solitude he developed an interest in literature and spent most of his time reading. While Dostoevski was a young man, his father was brutally murdered by his serfs. Though he rarely mentioned his father's death, the theme of parricide provided the central focus of perhaps his greatest work, *The Brothers Karamazov*. Sigmund Freud suggested that the epilepsy that plagued Dostoevski throughout his life developed as a result of his father's murder.

At his father's insistence, Dostoevski attended engineering school, but upon graduation chose to pursue a literary career. His first published work, a translation of Honoré de Balzac's *Eugénie Grandet*, was published in a St. Petersburg journal in 1844. He completed his first novel, *Bednye lyudi (Poor Folk)*, in 1845. A naturalistic tale with a clear social message, the novel was acclaimed by the foremost literary critic of the day, Vissarion Belinski, who stated, "A new Gogol is born!" The work brought Dostoevski success and adulation that he was ill-equipped to handle. He became a member of Belinski's literary circle, but when Belinski reacted coldly to Dostoevski's subsequent work, a breach developed between them.

In 1848 Dostoevski joined a political group of young intellectuals led by Mikhail Petrashevski. The reactionary climate of Russia at that time was not receptive to a group which published illegal literature and discussed utopian socialism, and in 1849 the members were arrested and charged with subversion.

Dostoevski, whom the authorities considered "the most important member," was imprisoned and sentenced to death. In a scene that was to haunt him all of his life, Dostoevski and his friends faced a firing squad, but were reprieved when a messenger arrived with the announcement that their sentences had been commuted to hard labor in Siberia. Dostoevski described his life as a prisoner in *Zapiski iz myortvogo doma (The House of the Dead; or, Prison Life in Siberia)*, a novel reflecting both an insight into the criminal mind and an understanding of the Russian lower classes. His intense study of the New Testament, the only book prisoners were allowed to read, proved a major influence on his later work as he became convinced that redemption was only possible through suffering and faith.

Camera Press–PHOTO TRENDS

When Dostoevski returned to St. Petersburg in 1859, he began to write for several periodicals, some of which he helped to edit. He contributed articles expressing his belief that Russia should develop a social and political system based on values drawn from the spirit of the Russian people. These years were marked by personal and professional misfortune, including journalistic failures, the death of his wife and brother, and a passion for gambling which left him heavily in debt. It was in this atmosphere that Dostoevsky wrote *Crime and Punishment*. Initially published as a serial, the novel brought him widespread acclaim but provided little financial compensation. Considered one of the finest works in the history of literature, *Crime and Punishment* is his first novel concerned with the theme of redemption through suffering. The protagonist, Raskolnikov, is presented as the embodiment of spiritual nihilism and the novel depicts the harrowing confrontation between this "extraordinary man" and the power of immortal laws and judgment.

In 1867 Dostoevski fled to Europe to escape creditors. The years in exile proved creatively fulfilling and, following his second marriage, personally tranquil. His literary output continued to be prolific. *Idiot (The Idiot)*, influenced by Hans Holbein's *Christ Taken from the Cross* and Dostoevski's opposition to prevalent atheistic sentiment, depicts a hero's loss of innocence and experience of sin. Dostoevski's more conservative political attitudes, especially his reaction against nihilism and revolutionary socialism, provided the creative impetus for his great political novel, *Besy (The Possessed)*. This novel, published in the form of a political pamphlet and dealing with an actual incident, provoked a storm of controversy. In his striking portrayal of Stavrogin, the novel's central character, Dostoevski presented a figure possessed by the life-denying forces of nihilism.

Dostoevski returned to Russia in 1871 and began his final decade of prodigious literary activity. In sympathy with the conservative political party, he accepted the editorship of a reactionary weekly, *Grazhdanin (The Citizen)*. In *Dvevnik pisatelya (The Diary of a Writer)* which appeared in the journal, he published a variety of essays and short stories.

Dostoevski's final work, *The Brothers Karamazov*, was deeply influenced by the death of his son Alexey and the sense of guilt precipitated by his father's murder. It is considered by many to be his finest work, an awesome achievement published at the peak of his fame. *The Brothers Karamazov* includes "The Legend of the Grand Inquisitor," a work now famous in its own right, which explores the conflict between intellect and faith, and between the forces of evil and the redemptive power of Christianity.

To his contemporary readers, Dostoevski's books seemed, at first, to be painful to read because of their "horrible" content; however, it is evident that the author is as awed by the evil and horror of his creation as his audience. Dostoevsky sought to plumb the depths of the psyche, revealing the full range of human experience, from the basest of desires to the most elevated spiritual yearnings. Above all, he illustrated the universal struggle to understand God and self. Dostoevski was, as Katherine Mansfield said, a "being who loved, in spite of everything, adored life, even while he knew the dank, dark places."

PRINCIPAL WORKS

Bednye lyudi   (novel)   1846
   [*Poor Folk*, 1894]
Dvoynik   (novel)   1846
   [*The Double*, 1917]
Ynizhenye i oskorblenye   (novel)   1861
   [*The Insulted and Injured*, 1887; also published as *Injury and Insult*, 1887]
Zapiski iz myortvogo doma   (novel)   1862
   [*Buried Alive; or, Two Years Life of Penal Servitude in Siberia*, 1881; also published as *The House of the Dead; or, Prison Life in Siberia*, 1911]
Zapiski iz podpol'ya   (novel)   1864
   [*Notes from the Underground*, 1912; also published as *Letters from the Underworld*, 1913]
Igrok   (novel)   1866
   [*The Gambler*, 1915]
Prestuplenye i nakazanye   (novel)   1866
   [*Crime and Punishment*, 1886]
Idiot   (novel)   1869
   [*The Idiot*, 1887]
Besy   (novel)   1872
   [*The Possessed*, 1913; also published as *The Devils*, 1953]
Podrostok   (novel)   1876
   [*A Raw Youth*, 1916]

Dvevnik pisatelya   (essays and short stories)   1876-1880
   [*The Diary of a Writer*, 1949]
Brat'ya Karamazovy   (novel)   1880
   [*The Brothers Karamazov*, 1912]

VISSARION BELINSKI   (essay date 1846)

At first glance [in *Poor Folk*] it is apparent that Dostoyevski's talent is not satirical, not descriptive, but to the highest degree creative, and that the predominant characteristic of his talent is humor. He produces his effect not by that knowledge of life and of the human heart which comes from experience and observation; no, he knows them—and knows them deeply—a priori, therefore purely poetically, imaginatively. His knowledge is talent, inspiration. We do not wish to compare him with anyone, because such comparisons are in general childish and do not lead to anything, do not explain anything. We shall say only that this is an extraordinary and original talent, which immediately, in his very first work, set him quite apart from our whole crowd of writers who are more or less indebted to Gogol for their bent and character, and therefore for the success of their talent. (pp. 3-4)

In Makar Devushkin he showed us how much beauty, nobility, and holiness there is in the nature of a very limited human being. Of course, not all poor people . . . are like Makar Alekseyevich with his good qualities, and we admit that such people are rare. But at the same time one cannot but admit also that little attention is paid to such people, little concern for them is shown, little is known about them. . . .

Honor and glory to the young poet, whose muse loves people in garrets and basements and who says of them to the inhabitants of gilded palaces: These, too, are people; they are your brothers. (pp. 4-5)

In general, the tragic element permeates this whole novel. And this element is all the more striking in that it is conveyed to the reader not only in the words but also in the ideas of Makar Alekseyevich. To amuse and to move the reader deeply at one and the same time, to force him to smile through his tears— what skill, what talent! And no melodramatic springs, no theatrical effects. Everything so simple and ordinary, like that humdrum, everyday life which seethes around each one of us. . . . His talent belongs with those which are not immediately understood and recognized. In the course of his literary life there will appear many talented writers who will be compared with him, but it will end with their being forgotten at the very time when he reaches the height of his fame. (p. 5)

> *Vissarion Belinski, in his excerpt from "The Early 'Radical' Critics" (originally published in his "Petersburgskii," in* Otechestvennye zapiski, *Vol. XLV, No. 3, 1846), in* Dostoyevski in Russian Literary Criticism: 1846-1956, *by Vladimir Seduro (reprinted by permission of the publisher), Columbia University Press, 1957, pp. 3-10.*

V. G. BELINSKY   (essay date 1847)

[We must say a few] words about *The Landlady*, a remarkable story by Mr. Dostoevsky, but remarkable in a sense different from that we have hitherto used. Had it appeared over any other name we would not have said a word about it. The hero of the story is a certain Ordynov, a man deeply immersed in scientific pursuits, the exact nature of which the author does not specify, although the reader's curiosity on this score is a legitimate one. (p. 73)

Somewhere or other, Ordynov meets the beautiful wife of a merchant; we do not remember whether the author mentions the color of her teeth, but these are probably an exception, being pearl-white, for the sake of greater poetry in the narrative. . . . Curious scenes follow; the lady talks drivel, of which we cannot make out a single word, while Ordynov listens to her and constantly falls into fainting fits. The merchant with his fiery glances and sardonic smile frequently intervenes. What they said to each other to make them gesticulate so wildly, grimace, swoon and recover we positively do not know because we have not understood a single word in all these long and pathetic monologues. Not merely the idea but the very sense of this perhaps highly interesting story will remain a secret to our understanding until the author publishes the necessary commentaries and explanations to this strange riddle of his fantastic imagination.

What can this be, abuse or paucity of a talent that wishes to rise higher than it is able to, and is therefore afraid to follow the usual road and seeks a way that is unusual? We do not know. It merely strikes us that the author wished to try to reconcile Marlinsky and Hoffmann, adding to this mixture a little humor in the latest fashion, and thickly covering all this with the varnish of a Russian folk style. No wonder the result is a monstrosity reminiscent of the fantastic stories of Tit Kosmokratov, which amused the public in the twenties of the present century. Throughout the whole of this story there is not a single simple or living word or expression: everything is farfetched, exaggerated, stilted, spurious and false. What sentences we meet here: Ordynov is *scourged* by some strangely sweet and stubborn feeling; he passes by the *cunning* workshop of a coffinmaker; he calls his beloved his turtledove and asks from what skies she has flown into his heaven. But no more! If we were tempted to quote all the bizarre sentences from this story, we would never end. What in the name of wonder is this? It is mighty strange, a most incomprehensible thing! . . . (pp. 73-4)

> *V. G. Belinsky, "A Survey of Russian Literature in 1847: Part Two" (1847), in Belinsky, Chernyshevsky, and Dobrolyubov: Selected Criticism, edited by Ralph E. Matlaw (copyright, ©, 1962, by E. P. Dutton & Co., Inc.; reprinted by permission of the publisher E. P. Dutton), Dutton, 1962, pp. 33-82.*

NIKOLAI DOBROLYUBOV (essay date 1861)

I do not know whether I understand the basic idea of *The Double* correctly; in explaining it, no one, so far as I know, has been willing to get into it more than to say that "the hero of the novel is crazy." But it seems to me that if there must be a reason for every madness, then for madness about which a talented writer relates a story for 170 pages, all the more so. . . .

Something rose up from the bottom of his soul and was expressed in grim protest, of the only kind of which the unresourceful Mr. Golyadkin was capable—madness. . . . I do not say that Mr. Dostoyevski developed the idea of this madness in an especially artistic manner. But it must be acknowledged that his theme—the split personality of a weak, characterless, and uneducated man, fluctuating between timid uprightness of action and unrealized proclivities for intrigue, a duality under

the weight of which the reason of the poor man finally goes to pieces—this theme, in order to be executed well, requires very great talent. (pp. 14-15)

The spark of godliness nevertheless smolders in [his heroes], and as long as a man lives, there is no way whatever of extinguishing it. A man may be ground down, turned into a filthy rag, but still somewhere, in the filthiest folds of this rag, feeling and thought are preserved—voiceless and obscure as they may be, they are nonetheless feeling and thought. . . .

This is the merit of the artist: he discovers that the blind man is not completely blind; he finds in the stupid man flashes of very clear and sound reasoning; in the downtrodden, lost man who is deprived of individuality, he searches out and shows to us the living, never-stifled aspirations and needs of human nature, draws out of the very depths of the soul the hidden protest of the personality against external, violent suppression and offers it for our judgment and sympathy. (p. 15)

> *Nikolai Dobrolyubov, in his excerpt from "Early 'Radical' Critics" (originally published in his "Zabitze Lyodi," in Sovremenik, No. 9, 1861), in Dostoyevski in Russian Literary Criticism: 1846-1956 by Vladimir Seduro (reprinted by permission of the publisher), Columbia University Press, 1957, pp. 13-20.*

D. I. PISAREV (essay date 1867)

[In *Crime and Punishment*] Raskolnikov constructed his whole theory of the extraordinary man for one purpose only, to justify in his own eyes a quick and easy profit. He had to come quickly, at the first good opportunity, to dishonest means of wealth. The question arose in his mind: how is one to explain this desire to oneself? As a weakness or a strength? It would have been much more simple and believable to explain it as a weakness, but it was much more pleasant for Raskolnikov to consider himself a strong man and to justify his hand in someone else's pocket by this shameful thinking. By seeing this matter as a weakness and thus making himself an object of scornful and insulting sympathy, Raskolnikov would have had to rid himself of this kind of thinking to regain his self-respect. By seeing his theory as the very opposite, as a sign of a daring mind and strong character, Raskolnikov chose a very distinctive path. A man, according to him, becomes a criminal because he considers unsatisfactory the institutions under which he lives, the laws by which he is judged and the generally accepted conceptions which society uses against him. Raskolnikov, thus, confuses two kinds of crimes: those of need, expressed in the proverb that your own shirt is closest to your body, and those committed under the sway of enthusiastic love for an idea. Theorizing in this way Raskolnikov was able to prove to himself without much trouble that every improvement in the social sphere of life is itself a crime, because such improvement is possible only after destroying existing laws. And since humanity would have long ago disappeared from the face of the earth if it did not continue to move ahead and improve its institutions, then it follows that crime is in the highest degree useful for humanity. (p. 134)

In no way can one consider this theory to be the cause of the crime, any more than the hallucination of a sick person is the cause of his illness. This theory is merely the form in which Raskolnikov's weakened and perverted thinking has expressed itself. The theory is the direct result of those oppressive circumstances which Raskolnikov has been forced to struggle with and which have brought him to a point of exhaustion. The conditions of his surroundings come to be beyond the strength of our irritable and impatient hero; he finds it easier to throw himself at once into an abyss rather than to carry on, for a few months or even years, the lonely, dark, exhaustive struggle against privations. Raskolnikov does not commit the crime because, by way of varied philosophical considerations, he has convinced himself of its lawfulness, reasonableness, and necessity. On the contrary, the conditions he must live under drive him to commit the crime as they have moved him to philosophize about his intentions. In short, Raskolnikov makes the theory up for his own convenience. (p. 135)

[Why] exactly are [the consequences of this criminal act] so terrible to bear?

First of all, Raskolnikov is simply afraid of criminal punishment, for this will break up his whole life, cast him out of the society of honorable people, and close forever for him the road to a happy, respectable, comfortable life. . . . Knowing that what he has done is important enough to rouse the whole community and especially the police, Raskolnikov understands that he must watch with extreme care over all his acts and words, must weigh every step, think through every word, control the movement of every muscle of his body, and face and contrive everything so that this self-control and circumspection will not be obvious to anyone. There must be nothing artificial, secretive, or mysterious in his conduct; he must do nothing to attract attention. (p. 137)

Since he is in the habit of following with piercing eyes the action of others, Raskolnikov is naturally disposed to think that others are looking or can look at him in the same way. . . . Raskolnikov is too good a critic to be a good actor. Understanding to perfection the smallest faults in his game, he demands from himself an ideal of perfection that is in all probability unattainable not only by him but also by a man with cold steel for nerves. (pp. 138-39)

Raskolnikov's microscopic analysis hurts him not only because he looks too closely at his own words and acts, but also because he does the same with his imaginary antagonists. Because of his extraordinary ability to scrutinize every word and to go from spoken word to inner motive, Raskolnikov very often takes more from the words of others than was contained in them. He will often see a hint of something ominous in words uttered without any ulterior motive whatsoever, and he will prepare for an attack from a person who has not the slightest intention of becoming his enemy. Under such strenuous and completely superfluous watchfulness, Raskolnikov's anxiety has to grow not only daily but hourly, and in a short time must grow to such proportions that all self-possession becomes impossible.

Raskolnikov's struggle with the whole of society is particularly hard and hopeless because his faith in his own strength is broken. He knows that after the murder he had not had enough composure left to rob the old woman systematically and carefully, that he had been faint and his thoughts had been confused, and that his trembling hands could not make the key fit the locks. He knows that he has acted, for the most part, much more like a ten-year-old boy who is going to be whipped for stealing apples or nuts than like Napoleon executing his *coup d'état*. . . .

The thought of criminal punishment hangs like Damocles' sword over Raskolnikov's head, ready to fall at the first careless movement with its full weight. This thought in itself is tor-

menting enough to poison his whole life and to make it unbearable. The feeling of fright is probably the most torturous of all the physical sensations that afflict mankind. (p. 139)

A sick person who suffers from that kind of madness which is called "melancholia" will see threats on all sides of him, and experience a continuous feeling of mortal fright. These people search constantly for death, accepting any torture that will spare them the greatest of tortures, the feeling of mortal fright. Raskolnikov comes to experience the same tortures which melancholics experience. . . .

In addition to criminal punishment, Raskolnikov fears the horror of indignation and disgust with which all those who are dear to him will look upon his act. He believes that once his crime is known he will be rejected by all, that this terrible truth will kill his mother and force all his friends, and especially his sister, to recoil with repugnance before his lost soul. (p. 140)

We know already how intensely he loves his mother and sister. We can easily imagine how much he wants to rush to them, to open himself up to their embraces, and to make up for the three years of wearisome separation with a frank and heartfelt talk. We can well imagine what a deafening blow it is for him to find their caresses unbearable and repugnant. He realizes that they are repugnant and unbearable because they are not for him, but for the mask which hides his monstrous and disgraced face from everyone. (p. 141)

[The] essential elements of the inner suffering which Raskolnikov experiences are the fear of criminal punishment, the terror of contempt of people close and dear to him, the necessity of dissembling at every step with everyone without exception, and the clear premonition that all his feats of deception will sooner or later prove completely useless. Under the influence of these torments there takes place in Raskolnikov with surprising and frightening speed an inner process that one might call the disintegration of his mind and character. The first phase of this process had already taken place before the murder and was marked by his theory of comparing Newton and Kepler with ordinary thieves and murderers. The second phase is played out after the murder and ends when Raskolnikov, relinquishing the right to think his own thoughts and to act by his own judgment, gives himself up to the sage and saving care of the very good, very limited, and completely uneducated girl, Sonia Marmeladov. Once having killed the old woman and her sister, Raskolnikov loses completely the power to sustain any definite desire. He wants to give himself up voluntarily to the police, and he wants also to escape punishment and remain free. He himself is most definitely not capable of deciding which of these two desires is stronger and which in the next moment will direct his acts. (p. 142)

D. I. Pisarev, "A Contemporary View" (1867), translated by Edward Wasiolek; originally published in "Bor'ba za zhizn'," in F. M. Dostoevski v Russkoi Kritke, edited by A. A. Belkin, Profizdat, 1956), in "Crime and Punishment" and the Critics, edited by Edward Wasiolek (© 1961 by Wadsworth Publishing Company, Inc.; reprinted by permission of Wadsworth Publishing Company, Belmont, CA 94002), Wadsworth, 1969, pp. 134-42.

F. M. DOSTOIEVSKY (essay date 1873)

[In] my novel *The Possessed* I made the attempt to depict the manifold and heterogeneous motives which may prompt even the purest of heart and the most naïve people to take part in the perpetration of so monstrous a villainy. The horror lies precisely in the fact that in our midst the filthiest and most villainous act may be committed by one who is not a villain at all! This, however, happens not only in our midst but throughout the world; it has been so from time immemorial, during transitional epochs, at times of violent commotion in people's lives—doubts, negations, scepticism and vacillation regarding the fundamental social convictions. But in our midst this is more possible than anywhere else, and precisely in our day; this is the most pathological and saddest trait of our present time—the possibility of considering oneself not as a villain, and sometimes almost not being one, while perpetrating a patent and incontestable villainy—therein is our present-day calamity! (p. 149)

> *F. M. Dostoievsky, "One of the Contemporaneous Falsehoods," in his* The Diary of a Writer, *Vol. I, edited and translated by Boris Brasol (translation copyright 1949 by Charles Scribner's Sons; copyright renewed 1976, Maxwell Fassett Executor of the estate of Boris Brasol; reprinted with the permission of Charles Scribner's Sons; originally published as* Dnevnik pisatelia, *1873), Charles Scribner's Sons, 1949 (and reprinted by Octagon Books, 1973), pp. 142-56.*

LAFCADIO HEARN   (essay date 1885)

The power of [*Crime and Punishment*] lies in its marvelous dissection of intricate mental characteristics,—in its unaffected intensity of realism,—in a verisimilitude so extraordinary that the reader is compelled to believe himself the criminal, to feel the fascination of the crime, to endure the excitement of it, to enjoy the perpetration of it, to vibrate with the terror of it, to suffer all the nightmares, all the horrors, all the degradation, all the punishment of it. This is what causes so terrible a nervous strain upon the reader. He actually *becomes* Raskolnikoff the murderer, and feels, thinks, dreams, trembles as the criminal whose psychology is thus exposed for him! The perusal of the pages seems to produce a sort of avatar, a change of souls; if the reader is not wholly Raskolnikoff, he is at least wholly Dostoievsky the author, nearly crazed by his own thoughts. And all the personages of the narrative live with the same violence of realism. Gogol was Dostoievsky's teacher; but never did he write so puissant a book as this.

No book, moreover, has ever given so singular a revelation to French criticism. Here is an author, who, without attempt at style, without effort at form, without refinement of utterance, creates a book in open violation of all esthetic canons, and more powerful than any fiction written in strict obedience to them. A similar phenomenon,—though less pronounced perhaps,—may be discerned in most Russian writers, not excepting the most artistic of all, Tourgueneff. What is the secret of this immense superiority of the semi-barbaric Russian novel? Is it that the life of other civilizations, while more complex and refined, is also more factitious; and that Russian thought—Antaeus-like,—owes its power to a closer contact with mighty nature than our artificial existence allows of? (pp. 193-94)

> *Lafcadio Hearn, "A Terrible Novel" (originally published in the* Times-Democrat, *November 22, 1885), in his* Essays in European and Oriental Literature, *edited by Albert Mordell, Dodd Mead and Company, 1923, pp. 189-94.*

THE SPECTATOR   (essay date 1886)

In our opinion, [Dostoyevsky's] finest work is **The Crime and the Chastisement**. . . . We doubt, however, whether it will be very popular in this country; for it must be admitted that Dostoyevsky did not write with much regard for the prejudices of British Philistines. Though never Zolaesque, he is intensely realistic, calls a spade a spade with the most uncompromising frankness, and takes his characters from the "great army of miserables." The hero of his master-work is an assassin, the heroine a prostitute. But the assassin is a repentant sinner, the prostitute one of the noblest characters in fiction, the morality of the book that of the Sermon on the Mount. Dostoyevsky describes sin in its most hideous shapes; yet he is full of tenderness and loving-kindness for its victims, and shows us that even the most abandoned are not entirely bad, and that for all there is hope,—hope of redemption and regeneration. **The Crime and the Chastisement** may not be suitable for young people—we question if young people would care to read it—but we cannot believe that anybody who knows the difference between good and evil would be the worse for reading it; most people would probably be much the better. (p. 938)

[The keynote of the book is] suffering and sacrifice. But it is not a book that lends itself to citation, or which can easily be described. To be understood, it must be studied. Dostoyevsky sounded the lowest depths of human nature, and wrote with the power of a master. None but a Russian and a genius could draw such a character as Rodion Raskolnikoff, who has been aptly named the "Hamlet of the madhouse." (p. 939)

> *"A Russian Novelist," in* The Spectator, *Vol. 59, No. 3028, July 10, 1886, pp. 937-39.*

THE LITERARY WORLD   (essay date 1886)

The energetic exploitation of Russian literature which already has brought to us here in America so large a revelation of humanity, hitherto unappreciated because hidden in an unknown tongue, opens the gates of discovery still wider with the publication of the masterpiece of one of the Russian masters of fiction—the **Crime and Punishment** of Dostoyevsky. The author of this wonderful essay in psychology, notwithstanding certain traits of distinctive and unmistakable nationality, holds among the writers of modern Russia a place apart. His genius consisted in seizing upon personalities more or less morbid in their tendencies, in penetrating into their inmost thoughts, in tracing with consummate skill the genesis of the most complex motives, in following through their dread and certain course of development the ideas which inspire wrong-doing, and transform themselves into scorpion whips of remorse to drive the unhappy victim to madness or confession. Dostoyevsky's characters are all more or less diseased, but there can be no doubt that in choosing them he has been true to life as he saw it. All of his novels, and more particularly **Crime and Punishment,** are so many vivid illuminations of the gloomy underground passages of society where humanity, confined to an atmosphere of vice-engendering repression, appears in fantastic and horrible forms. (p. 364)

How, step by step, the victim of [the idea of murder] is led to the fatal deed; how, from the very first conception of the crime, its punishment begins to pass through all the phases of terror and uncertainty to the unbearable torture of remorse; how the criminal, existing in a lurid haze of madness, schemes and plans with a madman's cunning to evade the legal penalty of his act; and how, slowly but surely, he is brought to make a full confession—all this and more Dostoyevsky sets forth with a power of vivid realism that hurries the reader breathless from page to page, chained in a magic spell of the strange and terrible, and leaves him exhausted with the overpowering passions which, without any effort of his own, have been aroused within him. Each one of the characters, of whom there are many, is carefully elaborated, and each has a place in the gradual unfolding of the narrative which is made to seem inevitable, so firm and true is the author's every stroke, so keen his knowledge of the relations of cause and effect in the part that each plays in this heart-rending tragedy.

Can such a book, dealing with material so revolting, be of any possible service? We think it can—to those who can read it aright and understand fully the underlying principles of the art that brought it into being. In its microscopic fidelity it leaves no aspect of social degradation untouched, but it touches all with the unerring yet kindly skill of the trained physician who applies the knife and cautery to heal. In filth and crime and wretchedness, Dostoyevsky's characters retain the saving element of manhood, and their author never makes the error of depicting them as beasts. It is a book that gains in power by a second or a third reading, that takes hold upon the memory and leaves it peopled with new shapes, strange and often terrible in outline, yet pulsating with the universal longings that cry from the depths for the comprehension and sympathy of a common humanity. (p. 365)

> *"'Crime and Punishment'," in* The Literary World, *Vol. XVII, No. 22, October 30, 1886, pp. 364-65.*

JOHN LOMAS   (essay date 1886-87)

Of the four Russian writers—Tourgueneff, Dostoïewsky, Tolstoi, with their forerunner Gogol—who have within the last fifty years at once made and over-shadowed the literature of their country, shaping the course of thought, character, and event among their countrymen in a manner little less than phenomenal—of these four writers, Dostoïewsky is the one who seems to me to have most interest and importance for English readers; for, while his range of conception and expression is more limited than those of his great rivals, his materials are more solid and more solidly arranged, his purpose and plan more direct, and his analysis of human nature more searching, subtle and true. (pp. 187-88)

While his great comtemporaries, Gogol especially, betray a remarkable susceptibility to the charms and beauties of nature, and are often carried away from all soberness of language and simile by their enthusiastic love of her, Dostoïewsky's sympathies seem all absorbed by the scenes and dramas of the narrow streets and narrower homes of the city. (p. 188)

'**Poor Folk**' is simply grey. There is nothing in it that is not part of the dull average of every day misery, with only such picturesque, half-tragical, half-comical situations as commonplace misery yields, lighting them up, for those who look below the surface, with touches of tenderest humanity. There is a petty government servant, who spends his days in ignominious quill-driving, and in alternating struggles against want and the dictates of a proud self-respect. At first sight there is nothing at all interesting about the man; but to any one at all initiated into the peculiar virtues of the Russian people, there is in such a conception a grand opportunity for painting the spirit of unostentatious self-sacrifice and beautiful simplicity which are perhaps the most salient features in the character of the race. (p. 189)

I must join issue with those critics who regard Dostoïewsky's women as his finest creations. Save in one or two of his female characters there if always something a little repelling—either the absence of intuition and grateful perceptiveness, or the presence of a thread of selfishness—in their attitude towards the man who honours them with his devotion. It may pass as a piece of bitter satire—and as such I am bound to conclude the author intended it; but to make it a general rule is neither fair nor admirable, and sometimes turns an otherwise lovable woman into an irritating puppet. (pp. 189-90)

There is [in Dostoïewsky's work] no striving after effect, no mere fine writing for the sake of display, nor resort to any other of the recognised tricks of authorship. . . . We have just the plain, unvarnished tale of a man who has felt and suffered what he writes about; and very few will put down ['**Poor Folk**'] without the irrepressible thought that, if one half of what is here set forth is true—if poor burdened humanity is staggering thus secretly at our side under anything like these loads—one ought truly to spend one's life in some great and definite labour of helpfulness; or at least, if that be not possible, to tread with every careful and reverent tenderness over all the interlacing and interdependent ways which go to make up the strange community of life. (pp. 190-91)

['**A Region of the Dead**'] is doubly interesting, as being both a recital of his own daily existence [as a prisoner in Siberia] and a faithful representation of the scenes and experiences which he noted around him. (p. 192)

The realism of [the narrative in '**A Region of the Dead**'] is perhaps its most striking feature. No effort is required of us. We need no specially imported interest, no highly-coloured plot, in order to see and have fellowship with this great band of unfortunates at their hard, grinding tasks, or to follow them one by one into their dark retrospects. . . . [We] stand beside the deathbed of the man who has shrivelled away in his awful prison house; and the clank of his irons, as they trail after his body upon the floor, seems to startle us out of the rapt watching of his last agony. And then we understand that we really comprehend not the half of it: that, taken sentence by sentence, the writer has told us nothing; but has artfully led us to feel by the extreme simplicity and lucidity of his form, that, beyond our ken, there lies an experience and a woe to which we must for ever remain strangers, while such realisation as we have attained to is only the work of awakened sympathy.

It is something of a lesson to the reviewer to note how much of the effectiveness of the book is owing to what would, academically speaking, be reckoned its fault. In three directions this is apparent. There is, first, the barrenness in development of either character or story, to which allusion has already been made: a defect not only of all Dostoïewsky's conceptions, but working more or less havoc in those of all his great contemporaries. . . . When he attempts to outline [the future], hand and mind alike falter, and he turns quickly from the effort with evident relief. What a dangerous element this is in weak writing, or in a weak position, I need not stay to demonstrate. It is not always that power of description or diagnosis will prove sufficient—we may see in '**Oppressed**' how terribly this constructive defect could militate against even Dostoïewsky's success. And yet here, in '**A Region of the Dead**,' we only seem to be thereby left the more free to be dominated by the interests and impulses of the moment, as the drama moves disjointedly before us.

Then, springing perhaps out of this weakness in development, there is the unrelieved, and therefore exaggerated, spirit of hopelessness which broods over every character and every scene. . . . (pp. 193-94)

But, as 'Poor Folk,' so 'A Region of the Dead' is a work which cannot be harshly criticised: so deeply touching is it, so full of purpose to improve off the face of the earth the sorrows and evils under which the author himself had bowed. Repelled by its sickening details, and recognising here and there its short-comings and extravagances, we may long to put the book down, and free ourselves from its fascination, and yet it will finally conquer us. (p. 194)

['Oppressed'] was certainly composed at the best period of the author's life, and yet to me it is pre-eminently unsatisfactory. . . . Vania, the hero—Dostoïewsky himself—is, indeed, fairly life-like, but the rest of the characters are little else than puppets; while there is no real plot, but only disjointed threads of narrative leading up to no catastrophe, and action and dialogue are alike stilted. The author himself, in later years, wrote down his personages in this romance as "dolls," qualifying his expression by adding that they "have an artistic form," and are in reality "walking books." Herein, to my thinking, he showed a creator's partiality; for there can be no great art in forms which continually irritate the beholder, and the moral of the book can hardly fail to produce in a thoughtful mind an effect diametrically opposed to the design. (p. 195)

[In 'Crime and Punishment'], at least, there is a definite and coherent narrative: so coherent, in fact, and so subtle in its coherence, that not a word, hardly a gesture, certainly no minutest circumstance can be left unmarked without weakening the effect of the whole. But far transcending any dramatic interest—exciting as this is, and well-sustained until almost the last page —is the value of the narrative from a psychological point of view. . . . (p. 196)

[For us, with the appearance of 'Crime and Punishment,'] his figure ceases to have any special value. Dostoïewsky, the cosmopolitan in emotion and experience, is merged in Dostoïewsky the leader of a sect, and his writings become more and more the mere vehicle of a set of narrow opinions. All these—'The Possessed,' 'The Brothers Karamazof,' even the more valuable 'Note Book,' in which he returns now and again to his old artistic self and power—I lay aside willingly enough: content if, in some small way, I have been able to rouse the interest and sympathy of a few English readers in the works of a writer who at his best was surely one of the chiefs of his time. (p. 198)

John Lomas, "Dostoïewsky and His Work," in Macmillan's Magazine, *Vol. LV, No. 327, November-April, 1886-87, pp. 187-98.*

OSCAR WILDE (essay date 1887)

Doistoieffski differs widely from both his rivals [Tourgenieff and Tolstoi]. He is not so fine an artist as Tourgenieff, for he deals more with the facts than with the effects of life; nor has he Tolstoi's largeness of vision and epic dignity; but he has qualities that are distinctively and absolutely his own, such as a fierce intensity of passion and concentration of impulse, a power of dealing with the deepest mysteries of psychology and the most hidden springs of life, and a realism that is pitiless in its fidelity, and terrible because it is true. Some time ago we had occasion to draw attention to his marvellous novel "Crime and Punishment," where in the haunt of impurity and vice a harlot and an assassin meet together to read the story

of Lazarus and Dives, and the outcast girl leads the sinner to make atonement for his sin; nor is the book entitled "Injury and Insult" at all inferior to that great masterpiece. Mean and ordinary though the surroundings of the story may seem, the heroine Natasha is like one of the noble victims of Greek tragedy, she is Antigone with the passions of Phaedra, and it is impossible to approach her without a feeling of awe. . . . Aleosha, the beautiful young lad whom Natasha follows to her doom, is a second Tito Melema, and has all Tito's charm, and grace, and fascination. Yet he is different. He would never have denied Baldassare in the square at Florence, nor lied to Romola about Tessa. He has a magnificent, momentary sincerity; a boyish unconsciousness of all that life signifies; an ardent enthusiasm for all that life cannot give. There is nothing calculating about him. He never thinks evil, he only does it. From a psychological point of view he is one of the most interesting characters of modern fiction, as from an artistic standpoint he is one of the most attractive. As we grow to know him, he stirs strange questions for us, and makes us feel that it is not the wicked only who do wrong, nor the bad alone who work evil. And by what a subtle objective method does Doistoieffski show us his characters! He never tickets them with a list, nor labels them with a description. We grow to know them very gradually, as we know people whom we meet in society, at first by little tricks of manner, personal appearance, fancies in dress and the like; and afterwards by their deeds and words; and even then they constantly elude us, for though Doistoieffski may lay bare for us the secrets of their nature, yet he never explains his personages away, they are always surprising us by something that they say or do, and keep to the end the eternal mystery of life. Irrespective of its value as a work of art, this novel possesses a deep autobiographical interest also, as the character of Vania, the poor student who loves Natasha through all her sin and shame is Doistoieffski's study of himself. . . . [Almost] before he had arrived at manhood Doistoieffski knew life in its most real forms; poverty and suffering, pain and misery, prison, exile, and love were soon familiar to him, and by the lips of Vania he has told his own story. This note of personal feeling, this harsh reality of actual experience, undoubtedly gives the book something of its strange fervour and terrible passion, yet it has not made it egotistic; we see things from every point of view, and we feel, not that Fiction has been trammelled by fact, but that fact itself has become ideal and imaginative. Pitiless too though Doistoieffski is in his method, as an artist, yet as a man he is full of human pity for all, for those who do evil as well as for those who suffer it, for the selfish no less than for those whose lives are wrecked for others, and whose sacrifice is in vain. Since "Adam Bede," and *Le Pere Goriot*, no more powerful novel has been written than ["Injury and Insult"]. (pp. 77-9)

Oscar Wilde, "Dostoevsky's 'The Insulted and Injured'" (originally published as "A Batch of Novels," in Pall Mall Gazette, *Vol. XLV, No. 6902, May 2, 1887), in* The Artist as Critic: Critical Writings of Oscar Wilde, *edited by Richard Ellman, W. H. Allen, 1970, pp. 77-9.*

GEORGE BRANDES (essay date 1888)

Study the face of Dostoievsky: half a Russian peasant's face, half a criminal physiognomy, flat nose, little piercing eyes under lids quivering with nervousness, this lofty and well-formed forehead, this expressive mouth that speaks of torments innumerable, of abysmal melancholy, of unhealthy appetites, of infinite pity, passionate envy! An epileptic genius, whose exterior alone speaks of the stream of gentleness that filled his spirit, of the wave of acuteness almost amounting to madness that mounted to his head, and finally of the ambition, the immense effort, and of the ill-will that results from pettiness of soul.

His heroes are not only poor and pitiable creatures, but simple-minded sensitive ones, noble strumpets, often victims of hallucination, gifted epileptics, enthusiastic candidates for martyrdom—just those types which we should suspect in the apostles and disciples of the early days of Christianity. (pp. 96-7)

> *George Brandes, in his letter to Friedrich Nietzsche on November 23, 1888, in his* Friedrich Nietzsche, *Heinemann, 1914 (and reprinted by Haskell House Publishers Ltd., 1972), pp. 95-7.*

TEMPLE BAR   (essay date 1891)

['**The Memoirs of a Dead House**'], with its repetitions and irregular construction, is far from perfect; but the author tells his terrible story with such realistic power, and such a gift for simple narrative, that we are moved and interested in the highest degree. . . . (p. 246)

On reading ['**Crime and Punishment**'] for the first time, we may think that the terrible impression it produces is due only to the appalling nature of the subject and the vivid realism with which the events are described; but after repeated perusals, when the facts are no longer strange to us, we begin to feel the truth and delicacy of the psychological analysis; we are interested in the hero, because every trait of his character brings him nearer to us. The whole book, in spite of its diffuseness, vibrates with thoughts and feelings which enable us to understand the terrible act and the consequences it entails upon his mental and moral state. (p. 247)

The best of his later works is '**The Idiot,**' a strange, fantastic narrative, full of improbabilities and exaggerations, but containing two or three scenes of extraordinary power. The hero, the epileptic Prince Myschkin, is a very original conception, and his character is gradually unfolded to us with all Dostoiefski's peculiar skill. '**The Demons,**' the wildest, perhaps, of all his novels, deals with certain phases of Nihilism. '**The Diary of an Author**' . . . contains '**Krotkaja,**' a very original short story, full of genius, which probably no one but Dostoiefski could have written. In his last years he designed a great work which was to sum up all the thoughts and experiences of his life, and, as he fondly hoped, prove his masterpiece. But neither his mental nor physical health was equal to the task. The two volumes he lived to write of '**The Brothers Karamazov**' show a sad falling off, and add nothing to his reputation.

With all his faults and shortcomings, Dostoiefski will probably always possess an attraction for certain minds. He deals chiefly, not with normal, but abnormal individuals, and in the domain of mental disease reigns supreme. He hardly ever attempts to explain the motives of the strange characters he introduces to us, and often does not seem to understand them himself. He is a spectator, with a great gift as a *raconteur*, and the quickest, keenest powers of observation, who relates facts, conversations, and events to us with so intense an air of realism that his wildest fictions read like truth. And, in spite of much that is overstrained and repellent, the outcome of the wounds and bruises he could never forget, we can but sympathise with the warm heart that never ceases to bleed for every act of cruelty,

injustice, and oppression. No matter how steeped in sin a human being may be, if he is suffering justly or unjustly, Dostoiefski is ready to bind up his wounds and bid him sin no more. He passes no judgment on any man, but, with groans and tears, he entreats the injured and the injurers alike to pardon and forget. (pp. 248-49)

> *"Dostoiefski," in* Temple Bar, *Vol. 91, February, 1891, pp. 243-49.*

E. M. De VOGÜÉ   (essay date 1892)

In general we take up a novel to give us pleasure and not to make us ill; but to read *Crime and Punishment* is to harm oneself willingly, for the novel leaves behind a kind of moral bruise. The book is moreover quite dangerous for women and for impressionable natures. Every book is a duel between the writer, who wants to impose on us a truth, a fiction, or some terrifying impression, and the reader, who resists such imposition with the weapons of indifference and reason. In *Crime and Punishment* the author's power of frightening is far superior to the resistance of the average nervous system. The reader is quickly conquered and made to suffer indescribable agonies. . . . Hoffmann, Edgar Allan Poe, Baudelaire and all the classic representatives of the novel of terror are as nothing compared to Dostoevsky. One always sees in their work that the author is playing at terror. But in *Crime and Punishment* one feels that the author is as terrified as we by the character he has created.

The plot is very simple. A man conceives the idea of a crime. He thinks on it, he commits it, and resists for some time the efforts of the police. Finally, he is led to give himself up and he repents. For once, the Russian artist has observed the Western custom of unity of action. The drama is purely psychological and takes place completely in the struggle between man and his idea. (pp. 37-8)

All the dreary conditions of Raskolnikov's life are seen through the prism of his idea. And these conditions, now colored by the idea, come, by way of a mysterious chemistry, to further his plan to commit the crime. The force that drives this man is expressed with such plastic vividness that we see it as if it were itself a living actor, like the fate in Greek dramas. This force directs the hand of the criminal up to the moment when the hatchet comes crashing down on the two victims. (p. 38)

[After the crime, Raskolnikov's] whole soul is changed and he is in constant disharmony with life. This is not remorse in the classic sense of the word. Dostoevsky takes care to show the difference. Raskolnikov will not know remorse with its benevolent and redemptive virtue until he accepts expiation. No, the feeling that dominates him now is complex and perverse: it is a feeling of spite for having profited so little from an act he thought was well prepared; it is a feeling of revolt against the unexpected moral consequences which came to birth with the blow of the hatchet; and it is a feeling of shame for having found himself to be so weak and dependent. In the depths of Raskolnikov's character, there is only pride. (pp. 38-9)

Dostoevsky sees clearly that in the psychological state created by the crime, the feeling of love, like every other feeling, has become modified, has changed into a feeling of somber despair. Sonia, a humble creature, trapped into her profession by hunger, is practically unconscious of her disgrace, submitting to it as to an inevitable disease. Shall I reveal the intimate thought of the author at the risk of awakening incredulity before such mystic exaggerations? Sonia bears her disgrace like a cross, with holy resignation. She is attracted to the one man who has not treated her with contempt. She sees him tortured with his secret and she tries to share it with him. After many long struggles she wrenches the secret from him. But I express this wrongly, for she does not wrench the secret; no word is spoken between them when the secret is revealed. In a silent scene which is the height of tragedy, Sonia sees the monstrous secret in his eyes. The poor girl is struck dumb by the revelation, but she recovers quickly. She knows what to do, and this cry issues from her heart: "We must suffer together, pray, and expiate. Let us go off to prison together."

We are here on the familiar ground to which Dostoevsky always returns, which is also the fundamental conception of Christianity held by the Russian people: the goodness of suffering in itself, especially suffering undergone together, and the unique virtue of suffering to resolve all difficulties. (pp. 39-40)

Dostoevsky has not been able a single time to represent a love free of subtleties, a love which is the simple and natural attraction of two hearts for one another; he knows only extremes, either the mystic state of *compassion,* of devotion without desire; or the insane brutalities of the beast and even the perversions of nature. The lovers he gives us are not made of flesh and blood but of nerves and tears. (p. 40)

[As] Dostoevsky's art unfolds with increasing complexity, it is impossible to detach meaningfully any particular passage; what is infinitely curious is that the thread of the story and of the dialogues is woven as if with a mesh of electrical wires, through which one feels running an uninterrupted mysterious tremor. A word that one does not even notice, a small fact that takes up only a line, have their reverberations fifty pages later. One has to remember them to understand how the seed, dropped by chance, grew, and transformed a soul. (p. 41)

When the book appeared, a student in Moscow assassinated a pawnbroker in conditions similar in every point to those imagined by the novelist. One could probably compile a curious array of statistics showing that many such murders have been committed under the influence of the book since its publication. Surely, the intention of Dostoevsky was other than this; he hoped to turn the readers away from such actions by giving them a picture of the terrible torture that follows upon such a crime. But he himself did not foresee that the tremendous force of his art could operate in an opposite direction, that it could stimulate this demon of imitation which inhabits the irrational depths of the mind. (p. 42)

> *E. M. De Vogüé, "An Early French View," translated by Edward Wasiolek (originally published under a different title in his* Le roman russe, *third edition, 1892), in* "Crime and Punishment" and the Critics, *edited by Edward Wasiolek (© 1961 by Wadsworth Publishing Company, Inc.; reprinted by permission of Wadsworth Publishing Company, Belmont, CA 94002), Wadsworth, 1969, pp. 37-42.*

THE NATION   (essay date 1894)

As we read the simple, intensely pathetic story [of **"Poor Folk"**] told indirectly but with transparent lucidity in the letters of Mákar and Varvara, we cannot but share the feelings of the Russian readers and critics of half a century ago. The most elaborate attempt to depict squalid, hopeless poverty; the patient endurance of a wronged, ailing young girl; the kind heart, weak will, and magnificent unselfishness of a broken-down,

witless old Government clerk, would be hopeless beside the power of this narrative contained in a series of letters so full of true art that their inherent artificiality never once occurs to the enthralled reader. . . . As the ingenuous correspondence, which takes the place of the inadvisable visits, proceeds, we penetrate the innermost recesses of these two hearts and characters, and of the hearts and characters of all the persons who are mentioned as side issues. . . . Where all is so perfect, it is hard to single out any passage for special admiration; but the episode, in Varvara's sketch of her life, of the student Pokrosky's funeral, followed only by his loving but degraded old father, is one of the gems of literature. It must be read to be even imagined. (p. 181)

> *"Two Novels: 'Poor Folk'," in* The Nation, *Vol. LIX, No. 1523, September 6, 1894, pp. 181-2.**

PRINCE KROPOTKIN   (essay date 1901)

[Dostoyévskiy's] heroes speak in a slipshod way, continually repeating themselves, and whatever hero appears in the novel (especially is this so in *The Downtrodden*), you feel it is the author who speaks. Besides, to these serious defects one must add the extremely romantic and obsolete forms of the plots of his novels, the disorder of their construction, and the unnatural succession of their events—to say nothing of the atmosphere of the lunatic asylum with which the later ones are permeated. And yet, with all this, the works of Dostoyévskiy are penetrated with such a deep feeling of reality, and by the side of the most unreal characters one finds characters so well known to every one of us, and so real, that all these defects are redeemed. Even when you think that Dostoyévskiy's record of the conversations of his heroes is not correct, you feel that the men whom he describes—at least some of them—were exactly such as he wanted to describe them.

The *Memoirs from a Dead-House* is the only production of Dostoyévskiy which can be recognised as truly artistic: its leading idea is beautiful, and the form is worked out in conformity with the idea; but in his later productions the author is so much oppressed by his ideas, all very vague, and grows so nervously excited over them that he cannot find the proper form. The favourite themes of Dostoyévskiy are the men who have been brought so low by the circumstances of their lives, that they have not even a conception of there being a possibility of rising above these conditions. You feel moreover that Dostoyévskiy finds a real pleasure in describing the sufferings, moral and physical, of the down-trodden—that he revels in representing that misery of mind, that absolute hopelessness of redress, and that completely broken-down condition of human nature which is characteristic of neuro-pathological cases. By the side of such sufferers you find a few others who are so deeply human that all your sympathies go with them; but the favourite heroes of Dostoyévskiy are the man and the woman who consider themselves as not having either the force to compel respect, or even the right of being treated as human beings. They once have made some timid attempt at defending their personalities, but they have succumbed, and never will try it again. They will sink deeper and deeper in their wretchedness, and die, either from consumption or from exposure, or they will become the victims of some mental affection—a sort of half-lucid lunacy, during which man occasionally rises to the highest conceptions of human philosophy—while some will conceive an embitterment which will bring them to commit some crime, followed by repentance the very next instant after it has been done.

In *Downtrodden and Offended* we see a young man madly in love with a girl from a moderately poor family. This girl falls in love with a very aristocratic prince—a man without principles, but charming in his childish egotism—extremely attractive by his sincerity, and with a full capacity for quite unconsciously committing the worst crimes towards those with whom life brings him into contact. The psychology of both the girl and the young aristocrat is very good, but where Dostoyévskiy appears at his best is in representing how the other young man, rejected by the girl, devotes the whole of his existence to being the humble servant of that girl, and against his own will becomes instrumental in throwing her into the hands of the young aristocrat. All this is quite possible, all this exists in life, and it is all told by Dostoyévskiy so as to make one feel the deepest commiseration with the poor and the downtrodden; but even in this novel the pleasure which the author finds in representing the unfathomable submission and servitude of his heroes, and the pleasure they find in the very sufferings and the ill-treatment that has been inflicted upon them—is repulsive to a sound mind. (pp. 164-66)

The Brothers Karamázoff is the most artistically worked out of Dostoyévskiy's novels, but it is also the novel in which all the inner defects of the author's mind and imagination have found their fullest expression. The philosophy of this novel—incredulous Western Europe; wildly passionate, drunken, unreformed Russia; and Russia reformed by creed and monks—the three represented by the three brothers Karamázoff—only faintly appears in the background. But there is certainly not in any literature such a collection of the most repulsive types of mankind—lunatics, half-lunatics, criminals in germ and in reality, in all possible gradations—as one finds in this novel. A Russian specialist in brain and nervous diseases finds representatives of all sorts of such diseases in Dostoyévskiy's novels, and especially in *The Brothers Karamázoff*—the whole being set in a frame which represents the strangest mixture of realism and romanticism run wild. Whatsoever a certain portion of contemporary critics, fond of all sorts of morbid literature, may have written about this novel, the present writer can only say that he finds it, all through, so unnatural, so much fabricated for the purpose of introducing—here, a bit of morals, there, some abominable character taken from a psycho-pathological hospital; or again, in order to analyse the feelings of some purely imaginary criminal, that a few good pages scattered here and there do not compensate the reader for the hard task of reading these two volumes. (pp. 168-69)

[There] is certainly a great deal of power in whatever Dostoyévskiy wrote: his powers of creation suggest those of Hoffmann; and his sympathy with the most down-trodden and downcast products of the civilisation of our large towns is so deep that it carries away the most indifferent reader and exercises a most powerful impression in the right direction upon young readers. His analysis of the most varied specimens of incipient psychical disease is said to be thoroughly correct. But with all that, the artistic qualities of his novels are incomparably below those of any one of the great Russian masters: Tolstóy, Turguéneff, or Gontcharóff. Pages of consummate realism are interwoven with the most fantastical incidents worthy only of the most incorrigible romantics. Scenes of a thrilling interest are interrupted in order to introduce a score of pages of the most unnatural theoretical discussions. Besides, the author is in such a hurry that he seems never to have had the time himself to read over his novels before sending them to the printer. And, worst of all, every one of the heroes of Dostoyévskiy, especially in his novels of the later period, is a person suffering

from some psychical disease or from moral perversion. As a result, while one may read some of the novels of Dostoyévskiy with the greatest interest, one is never tempted to re-read them, as one re-reads the novels of Tolstóy and Turguéneff, and even those of many secondary novel writers; and the present writer must confess that he had the greatest pain lately in reading through, for instance, *The Brothers Karamázoff*, and never could pull himself through such a novel as *The Idiot*. However, one pardons Dostoyévskiy everything, because when he speaks of the ill-treated and forgotten children of our town civilisation he becomes truly great through his wide, infinite love of mankind—of man, even in his worst manifestations. Through his love of those drunkards, beggars, petty thieves and so on, whom we usually pass by without even bestowing upon them a pitying glance; through his power of discovering what is human and often great in the lowest sunken being; through the love which he inspires in us, even for the least interesting types of mankind, even for those who never will make an effort to get out of the low and miserable position into which life has thrown them—through this faculty Dostoyévskiy has certainly won a unique position among the writers of modern times, and he will be read—not for the artistic finish of his writings but for the good thoughts which are scattered through them, for their real reproduction of slum life in the great cities—and for the infinite sympathy which a being like Sónya can inspire in the reader. (pp. 169-70)

Prince Kropotkin, "Gontcharoff; Dostoyevskiy; Nekrasoff" (originally part of a series of lectures presented at the Lowell Institute, March, 1901), in his Russian Literature, *McClure, Phillips & Co., 1905 (and reprinted by Knopf, 1916), pp. 151-90.**

DMITRI MEREJKOWSKI   (essay date 1902)

With Dostoïevski there is throughout a human personality carried to the extremes of individuality, drawing and developing from the dark animal roots to the last radiant summits of spirituality. Throughout there is the conflict of heroic will with the element of moral duty and conscience, as in Raskolnikov; with that of passion, refined, deliberate, as in Svidrigailov and Versilov; in conflict with the will of the people, the State, the polity, as in Peter Verkhovenski, Stavrogine, and Shatov; and lastly in conflict with metaphysical and religious mystery, as in Ivan Karamazov, Prince Myshkine, and Kirillov. Passing through the furnace of these conflicts, the fire of enflaming passions and still more enflaming will, the kernel of human individuality, the inward *ego*, remains undissolved and is laid bare. (pp. 239-40)

In accordance with the predominance of heroic struggle the principal works of Dostoïevski are in reality not novels nor epics, but tragedies. (p. 240)

[With Dostoïevski,] the narrative portion is secondary and subservient to the construction of the whole work. And this is apparent at the first glance; the story, written always in one and the same hasty, sometimes clearly neglected language, is now wearisomely drawn out and involved, heaped with details; now too concise and compact. The story is not quite a text, but, as it were, small writing in brackets, notes on the drama, explaining the time and place of the action, the events that have gone before, the surroundings and exterior of the characters: it is the setting up of the scenery, the indispensable theatrical paraphernalia—when the characters come on and begin to speak then at length the piece beings. In Dostoïevski's dialogue is concentrated all the artistic power of his delineation: it is in the dialogue that all is revealed and unrevealed. (p. 241)

In Dostoïevski it is impossible not to recognize the personage speaking, at once, at the first words uttered. In the scarcely Russian, strange, involved talk of the Nihilist Kirillov we feel something superior, grating, unpleasant, prophetic, and yet painful, strained, and recalling attacks of epilepsy—and so too in the simple, truly national speech of "holy" Prince Myshkine. (p. 242)

Dostoïevski has no need to describe the appearance of his characters, for by their peculiar form of language and tones of voices they themselves depict, not only their thoughts and feelings, but their faces and bodies. (p. 243)

Not merely the mastery of dialogue, but other characteristics of his method bring Dostoïevski near to the current of great tragic art. At times it seems as if he only did not write tragedy because the outward form of epic narration, that of the novel, was by chance the prevailing one in the literature of his day, and also because there was no tragic stage worthy of him, and what is more, no spectators worthy of him. . . .

Involuntarily and naturally Dostoïevski becomes subject to that inevitable law of the stage which the new drama has so thoughtlessly abrogated, under the influence of Shakespeare, and by so doing undermined at the root the tragic action. It is the law of the three unities, time, place, and action, which gives, in my opinion, such incomparable power, as against anything in modern poesy, to the creations of the Greek drama. (p. 244)

Raskolnikov kills an old woman to prove to himself that he is already "on the wrong side of good and evil," that he is not "a shuddering being," but a "lord of creation." But Raskolnikov in Dostoïevski's conception is fated to learn that he is wrong, that he has killed, not "a principle," but an old woman, has not "gone beyond," but merely wished to do so. And when he realizes this he is bound to turn faint, to get frightened, to get out in the square and, falling on his knees, to confess before the crowd. And it is precisely to this extreme point, to this one last moment in the action of the story, that everything is directed, gathers itself up and gravitates; to this tragic catastrophe every thing tends, as towards a cataract the course of a river long confined by rocks.

Here there cannot, should not be, and really is not, anything collateral or extraneous, arresting or diverting the attention from the main action. The events follow one another ever more and more rapidly, chase one another ever more unrestrainedly, crowd together, are heaped on each other, but in reality subordinated to the main single object, and are crammed in the greatest possible number into the least possible space of time. (pp. 245-46)

To all the heroes of Dostoïevski there comes the moment when they cease "to feel their bodies." They are not beings without flesh and blood, not ghosts. We know well what sort of body they *had,* when they still felt its presence. But the highest ascent, the greatest tension of mental existence, the most burning passions—not of the heart and the emotions, but of the mind, the will, and the conscience—give them this divorce from the body, a sort of supernatural lightness, wingedness, and spiritualization of the flesh. (p. 247)

At times in Greek tragedy, just before the catastrophe, there suddenly sounds in our ears an unexpectedly joyous chant of the chorus in praise of Dionysus, god of wine and blood, of mirth and terror. (p. 248)

Dostoïevski is nearest of all to us, to the most inward and deeply-seated principles of Greek tragedy. We find him depicting catastrophes with something of this terrible gaiety of the chorus. (pp. 248-49)

At times, even in Dostoïevski's work, we lose our breath from the rapidity of the movement, the whirl of events, the flight into space. And what reviving freshness, what freedom there is in this breath of the storm! The most petty, paltry, and commonplace features of human life here become splendid under the lightning. . . .

As for Dostoïevski's Muse, we may doubt any other qualities of hers we please, only not her intelligence. He remarks in one place that an author ought to have *a sting;* "this sting," he proceeds to explain, "is the rapier point of deep feeling." I consider that no Russian writer, except Pushkin, was such a master of "the mental rapier of feeling" as Dostoïevski himself. (p. 249)

[The] principal heroes of Dostoïevski—Raskolnikov, Versilov, Stavrogine, Prince Myshkine, and Ivan Karamazov—are clever men first and foremost. Indeed it would seem that, taken on the whole, they are the cleverest, most rational, cultured, and cosmopolitan of Russians, and are European because they "in the highest degree belong to Russia."

We are accustomed to think that the more abstract thought is, the more cold and dispassionate it is. It is not so; or at least, it is not so with us. From the heroes of Dostoïevski we may see how abstract thought may be passionate, how metaphysical theories and deductions are rooted, not only in cold reason, but in the heart, emotions and will. . . .

Raskolniskov "sharpened his casuistry like a razor." But with this razor of abstractions he cuts himself almost fatally. His transgression is the fruit, as the public prosecutor Prophyry puts it, "of a heart outraged theoretically." The same may be said of all the heroes of Dostoïevski: their passions, their misdeeds, committed or merely "resolved on by conscience," are the natural outcome of their dialectic. (p. 250)

And the most abstract thought is, at the same time, the most passionate: the burning thought of God. "All my life God has tortured me!" owns the Nihilist Kirillov. And all Dostoïevski's heroes are "God-tortured." Not the life of the body, its end and beginning, death and birth, as with Tolstoi, but the life of the spirit, the denial or affirmation of God, are with Dostoïevski the ever-boiling source of all human passions and sufferings. (p. 251)

[Dostoïevski] has overcome the superstitious timidity, common to modern artists, of feeling in presence of the mind. He has recognized and showed us the connexion there is between the tragedy of our hearts and that of our reason, our philosophical and religious consciousness. This, in his eyes, is preeminently the Russian tragedy of to-day. (p. 252)

[After] reading Dostoïevski something is changed in our spiritual impressionability. It is impossible to forget, to either reject or accept him with impunity. His reasonings penetrate not only into the mind, but into the heart and the will. (pp. 252-53)

There are simple-minded readers, with the effeminate, sickly sentimentality of our day, to whom Dostoïevski will always seem "cruel," merely "a cruel genius." In what intolerable, what incredible situations he places his heroes! . . . Does it not sometimes seem as if he tortures his "dear victims" without object, in order to enjoy? Yes, of a truth he is one who delights in torture, a grand Inquisitor, "a cruel genius."

And is all this suffering natural, possible, real? Does it occur? Where has it been seen? And even if it occurs, what have we sane-thinking people to do with these rare among the rare, exceptional among the exceptional cases, these moral and mental monstrosities, deformities, and abortions, fancies of fever and delirium?

Here is the main objection to Dostoïevski, one that all can understand, unnaturalness, unusualness, apparent artificiality, the absence of what is called "healthy realism." "They call me a psychologist," he says himself; "it is not true, I am only a *realist in the highest sense of the word,* i.e. I depict all the soul's depths." (pp. 253-54)

But he is a searcher into human nature; also at times "a realist in the highest sense of the word"—the realist of a new kind of experimental realism. In making scientific researches he surrounds in his machines and contrivances the phenomena of Nature with artificial and exceptional conditions. He observes how, under the influence of those conditions, the phenomenon undergoes changes. (p. 254)

He submits his characters either to the rarefied icy air of abstract dialectics or the fire of elemental animal passion, fire at white heat. In these experiments he sometimes arrives at states of the human mind as novel and seemingly impossible as liquefied air. . . .

What is called Dostoïevski's psychology is therefore a huge laboratory of the most delicate and exact apparatus and contrivances for measuring, testing, and weighing humanity. It is easy to imagine that to the uninitiated such a laboratory must seem something of a "devil's smithy." (p. 255)

In Dostoïevski's novels there are peculiar passages as to which it is difficult to decide . . . whether they are Art or Science. At any rate they are not pure Art nor pure Science. Here accuracy of knowledge and the instinct of genius are mingled. It is a new "blend," of which the greatest artists and men of science had a prevision, and for which there is, as yet, no name.

And yet we have here "a cruel genius." This reproach, like some feeling of vague yet personal vexation, remains in the hearts of readers blessed with what is called "mental warmth," which we sometimes feel inclined to call "mental thaw." (p. 256)

There remains the question, more worthy of our attention—the question of the cruelty of Dostoïevski towards himself, his morbidity as an artist.

What a strange writer, in good sooth, with insatiable curiosity exploring only the maladies of the human soul, and for ever raving about plagues, as if he could not, or would not, speak of anything else! (pp. 256-57)

There is a notion current that Dostoïevski did not love Nature. But though he certainly but little and rarely describes it, that is, perhaps, just because his love for it is too deep not to be restrained. He does not wear his heart on his sleeve, but all the more in his rare descriptions there is more vigour than in anything of the kind in Tolstoi.

No, Dostoïevski loved the land not less than he loved the "body" of Russia, but less the "tangible" frame than the spiritualized face of that land. (p. 276)

Who knows St. Petersburg better, and hates it more, and feels more overcome by it, than Dostoïevski? Yet, as we see, there are moments when he suddenly forgives everything, and somehow loves the place. . . . "The foundling of nature," the most outcast of towns, of which even its inhabitants are secretly ashamed, Dostoïevski makes it, by the force of his affection, pathetic, piteous, almost lovable and homelike, almost beautiful; though curelessly diseased, yet with a rare "decadent" beauty not easily attained. (p. 277)

[Dirty] slummy inns, the "servants' halls" of St. Petersburg cosmopolitanism, are to be found in all Dostoïevski's stories. In them take place his most important, speculative, and impassioned conversations. And however strange it may be, yet you feel that it is just the platitude of this "cosmopolitan servants' hall" atmosphere, the sordid realism and the commonplaceness, that give to these talks their peculiarly modern, national flavour, and make their stormy and apocalyptic brilliance, like that of the sky before thunder, come into full relief. (p. 278)

All his heroes may be divided into two families, opposite, yet having many points of contact. Either, like Alesha, the Idiot, and Zosima, they are the men of "the city that is to come," of the holy Russia that is at once too old and too new, not yet in existence; or, like Ivan Karamazov, Rogojine, Raskolnikov, Versilov, Stavrogine, and Svidrigailov, they are the men of the existing city, of contemporary actual St. Petersburg, Petrine Russia. (p. 280)

Svidrigailov is the result of [Raskolnikov's] dream, and he himself is all a sort of dream, like a thick, dirty-yellow St. Petersburg fog. But if it is a ghost, then it is one with flesh and blood. In that lies the horror of it. There is nothing in it romantic, vague, indefinite, or abstract. In the action of the story Svidrigailov more and more takes form and substance, so that in the long run he proves more real than the sanguine, beefy heroes of Tolstoi. Gradually we learn that this "most vicious of men," this rascal, is capable of chivalrous magnanimity, of delicate and unselfish feelings. . . . Just before his death he concerns himself simply and self-sacrificingly, as if for his own daughter, on behalf of the orphan girl who is a stranger to him, and secures her fortune. Are we to believe that he has no existence? We hear the tones of his voice, we see his face so that we should "know him at once in a thousand." He is more living and real to us than most of the people we meet every day in so-called "real life."

But see, when we have grown finally to believe in him, then, just as he emerged from the fog, so, most prosaically, he vanishes into it. (pp. 282-83)

This phantasm Svidrigailov is convincing. And we, too, "are such stuff as dreams are made of."

The terror of "ordinary apparitions" lies partly in the fact that, as it were, they are conscious of their own paltriness and absurdity. (p. 284)

Not only do Dostoïevski's spectres pursue the living, but the living themselves pursue and terrify each other like spectres, like their own shadows, like their doubles. "You and I are fruit off the same tree," says Svidrigailov to Raskolnikov, and in spite of all his resistance, his callousness, the latter feels that it is true; that they have certain points in common; that, perhaps, even their personalities have a common centre. Svidrigailov has only gone immeasurably further along the road which Raskolnikov has barely begun; and shows him the inevitable super-scientific deductions from his own logic about good and evil—stands him in stead of a magic mirror. (p. 285)

[There] is no doubt that the Familiar of Ivan Karamazov is one of the greatest national creations of Dostoïevski, unlike anything else in the world's literature, a creation that has its roots seated in the inmost recess of his consciousness and of his unconsciousness. It is not for nothing that he expresses by the mouth of the Familiar his own most oracular thoughts. We might trace how Dostoïevski arrived at him all through his characters. As regards his essence, the Demon speaks in almost the same words as Dostoïevski himself of the essence of his own artistic creations, of the first source of that generative power from which all his works proceeded. (p. 287)

Dostoïevski first, and so far alone, among writers of modern times, has had the strength, while adhering to present-day actuality, to master and transform it into something more mysterious than all the legends of past ages. He was the first to see that what seems most trivial, rough, and fleshly marches with what is most spiritual, or, as he called it, "fantastic," i.e. religious. And he was the first that succeeded in finding the sources of the supernatural, not in the remote, but in penetrating the ordinary.

Not in abstract speculations, but in exact experiments, worthy of our present science, in human souls did Dostoïevski show that the work of universal history, which began with the Renaissance and the Reformation, the method of strictly scientific, critical, discriminating thought, if not already completed, is approaching completion. (p. 295)

> *Dmitri Merejkowski, "Tolstoi and Dostoïevski as Artists," in his* Tolstoi as Man and Artist, with an Essay on Dostoïevski, *G. P. Putnam's Sons, 1902 (and reprinted by Greenwood Press, 1970), pp. 163-310.**

ARNOLD BENNETT   (essay date 1910)

[I learned that **"The Brothers Karamazoff"**] is only a preliminary fragment of a truly enormous novel which death prevented Dostoievsky from finishing. Death, this is yet another proof of your astonishing clumsiness! The scene with the old monk at the beginning of **"The Brothers Karamazoff"** is in the very grandest heroical manner. There is nothing in either English or French prose literature to hold a candle to it. And really I do not exaggerate! There is probably nothing in Russian literature to match it, outside Dostoievsky. It ranks, in my mind, with the scene towards the beginning of **"Crime and Punishment,"** when in the inn the drunken father relates his daughter's "shame." These pages are unique. They reach the highest and most terrible pathos that the novelist's art has ever reached. And if an author's reputation among people of taste depended solely on his success with single scenes Dostoievsky would outrank all other novelists, if not all poets. But it does not. Dostoievsky's works—all of them—have grave faults. They have especially the grave fault of imperfection, that fault which Tourgenieff and Flaubert avoided. They are tremendously unlevel, badly constructed both in large outline and in detail. The fact is that the difficulties under which he worked were too much for the artist in him. . . . Nobody, perhaps, ever understood and sympathized with human nature as Dostoievsky did. Indubitably nobody ever with the help of God and good luck ever swooped so high into tragic grandeur. But the man had fearful falls. He could not trust his wings. He is an adorable, a magnificent, and a profoundly sad figure in letters. He is

anything you like. But he could not compass the calm and exquisite soft beauty of "On the Eve" or "A House of Gentlefolk." . . . (pp. 211-13)

> *Arnold Bennett, "Tourgenieff and Dostoievsky" (originally published in* New Age, *March 31, 1910), in his* Books and Persons: Being Comments on a Past Epoch, 1908-1911 *(copyright, 1917, by George H. Doran Company), Doran, 1917, pp. 208-13.**

THE SPECTATOR   (essay date 1912)

This extraordinary genius, known, if at all, in England simply as the author of one work, *Crime and Punishment,* is in Russia universally recognized as at least the equal, and possibly the superior, of Tolstoy. Above all, he is acclaimed as the most distinctively *Russian* of writers; and, no doubt, it is this very fact that has so far prevented his popularity in England. There is something so strange to English readers in Dostoievsky's genius—its essence seems so unfamiliar, so singular, so unexpected—that we are naturally repelled. But having swallowed Tolstoy, there is no reason why, in time, we should not also swallow Dostoievsky. (p. 451)

No doubt the most obviously disconcerting of Dostoievsky's characteristics is his form. Most of his works are not only exceedingly long, but—at any rate on a first inspection—extremely disordered. Even in *The Brothers Karamazov,* the last and the most carefully composed of his novels, the constructions seems often to collapse entirely; there are the strangest digressions and the most curious prolixities; we have an endless dissertation, introduced apparently *à propos de bottes,* on the duties of a Russian monk; we have a long, queer story, read aloud by one of the characters in a restaurant, about Christ and a Grand Inquisitor. In some of the most important of his other works—in *The Idiot, The Adolescent,* and *The Possessed*—this characteristic appears in a far more marked degree. The circumstances of Dostoievsky's life certainly account in part for the looseness and incoherence of his writing. Until his closing years he was always in difficulties, always desperately in want of money, and always pouring out a flood of fiction at the highest possible pressure. Thus it was only to be expected that his composition should not have been perfect; but it seems probable that a necessity for hasty work was not the sole cause. His mind, by its very nature, did not move on the lines of judicious design and careful symmetry; it brought forth under the stress of an unbounded inspiration, and according to the laws of an imaginative vision in which the well-balanced arrangements of the ordinary creative artist held no place. Thus, the more one examines his writings and the more familiar one grows with them, the more distinctly one perceives, under the singular incoherence of their outward form, an underlying spirit dominating the most heterogeneous of their parts and giving a vital unexpected unity to the whole. . . . The effect is like that of some gigantic Gothic cathedral, where, amid all the bewildering diversity of style and structure, a great mass of imaginative power and beauty makes itself mysteriously felt, and, with its uncertain proportions and indefinite intentions, yet seems to turn by comparison even the purest and most perfect of classical temples into something stiff and cold.

But, besides the looseness of his construction, there is another quality in Dostoievsky's work which is calculated to prove an even more serious stumbling-block to English readers. His books are strange not only in form, but in spirit. They seem to be written by a man who views life from a singular angle; everything in them is agitated, feverish, intense; they are screwed up above the normal pitch; they appear to be always trembling on the verge of insanity, and sometimes, indeed, to plunge over into the very middle of it. . . . Paradoxical as it may seem, it is yet certainly true that Dostoievsky, with all his fondness for the abnormal and the extraordinary, is a profoundly sane and human writer. In this respect, indeed, he is the exact opposite of Tolstoy, who conceals a neurotic temperament under the cloak of a strict and elaborate adherence to the commonplace. Dostoievsky, while refusing to turn away his eyes from what is horrible, grotesque, and disgraceful in life, does not, like the French writers of the Naturalistic School, take a pleasure in these things, and deal out pessimism with an acrimonious relish; on the contrary, he only faces the worst in order to assert, with a fuller courage and a deeper confidence, the nobility and splendour of the human spirit. . . . He can show us characters where all that is base, absurd, and contemptible is mingled together, and then, in the sudden strange vision that he gives us of their poignant underlying humanity, he can make us lay aside our scorn and our disgust, endowing us with what seems a new understanding of the mysterious soul of man. No other writer ever brought forth with a more marvellous power the "soul of goodness in things evil."

This power is but one manifestation of the wonderful intensity and subtlety of Dostoievsky's psychological insight. Here, no doubt, lies the central essence of his genius, the motive force which controls and animates the whole of his work. It is his revelations of the workings of the human mind that give him his place among the great creative artists of the world. But in other directions his ability is hardly less remarkable: in the unforgettable vividness of his descriptions, in his singularly original sense of humour, in his amazing capacity for crowding his stage with a multitude of persons, all interacting and all distinct, as in the famous account of the Convict's Bath in the *House of the Dead*. . . . [If] one seeks for comparisons, it is to the Elizabethan dramatists that one must turn to find kindred spirits with Dostoievsky. In his pages one finds again, as in an unexpected transmigration, the pathos, the terror, and the awful humour of Webster, the "inspissated gloom" of Tourneur, the tragic intensity of Middleton, the morbid agonies of Ford. The same vast and potent inspiration which filled so erratically and yet so gloriously those old poets of Renaissance England still seems to breathe and burn through the novels of the modern Russian. There is more than an echo in him of Shakespeare himself. The art which wove out of the ravings of three madmen in a thunderstorm the noblest and profoundest symphony that human hearts have ever listened to is, in its essence, the same art that went to the making of *The Idiot* and *The Possessed*. (pp. 451-52)

> "Dostoievsky," in The Spectator, Vol. 109, No. 4396, September 28, 1912, pp. 451-52.

LYTTON STRACHEY (essay date 1914)

[What] must first be apparent in [Dostoievsky's] works is the strange and poignant mixture which they contain of 'an almost maniacal acuteness' with 'the mild milk of human kindness'— of the terrible, febrile agitations reflected in those penetrating eyes and their quivering lids, with the serene nobility and 'infinite compassion' which left their traces in the expressive mouth and the lofty brow. These conflicting and mingling qualities are, in fact, so obvious wherever Dostoievsky's genius reveals itself in its truly characteristic form, that there is some danger of yet another, and a no less important, element in this complex character escaping the notice which it deserves—the

element of humour. . . . The group of novels . . . of which *Uncle's Dream, The Eternal Husband,* and *Another's* are typical examples show Dostoievsky in a mood of wild gaiety, sometimes plunging into sheer farce, but more often reminiscent of the Molière of *Le Médecin Malgré Lui* and *Georges Dandin,* in the elaborate concentration of his absurdities, the brilliance of his satire, and his odd combination of buffoonery and common sense. . . . [In *The Idiot* and *The Possessed*] Dostoievsky's humour appears in its final and most characteristic form, in which it dominates and inspires all his other qualities—his almost fiendish insight into the human heart, his delight in the extraordinary and the unexpected, his passionate love of what is noble in man, his immense creative force—and endows them with a new and wonderful significance.

The truth is that it is precisely in such cases as Dostoievsky's that the presence or the absence of humour is of the highest importance. . . . [The imaginary world of Dostoievsky] comes to us amid terror and exorbitance—not in the clear light of day, but in the ambiguous glare of tossing torches and meteors streaming through the heavens. Now writing of that kind may have many advantages: it may arouse the curiosity, the excitement, and the enthusiasm of the reader to a high degree; but there is one great risk that it runs—the risk of unreality. The beckoning lights may turn out to be will-o'-the-wisps, the mysterious landscape nothing but pasteboard scenery. And against that risk the only really satisfactory safeguard is a sense of humour. . . . [Dostoievsky] had humour; and so it happens that, by virtue of that magic power, his wildest fancies have something real and human in them, and his moments of greatest intensity are not melodramatic but tragic. In *The Idiot,* for instance, the unchecked passions of Rogozhin and Nastasya, the morbid agonies of such a figure as Ippolit, the unearthly and ecstatic purity of the Prince—all these things are controlled and balanced by the sheer fun of a hundred incidents, by the ludicrousness of Lebedyev and General Ivolgin, and, above all, by the masterly creation of Madame Epanchin. . . . (pp. 215-18)

But Dostoievsky's humour serves another purpose besides that of being a make-weight to those intense and extreme qualities in his composition which would otherwise have carried him into mere extravagance; it is also the key to his sympathetic treatment of character. There are many ways of laughing at one's fellow-creatures. . . . Dostoievsky, in his latest works, uses another sort of laughter—the laughter of lovingkindness. . . . Dostoievsky's mastery of this strange power of ridicule, which, instead of debasing, actually ennobles and endears the object upon which it falls, is probably the most remarkable of all his characteristics. *The Idiot* is full of it. . . . [The] most elaborate use of it occurs in *The Possessed,* where the figure of Stepan Trofimovitch, the old idealistic Liberal who comes to his ruin among the hideous realities of modern Nihilism, is presented to us through an iridescent veil of shimmering laughter and tears. The final passage describing his death inevitably recalls the famous pages of Cervantes; and, while it would be rash to say that the Russian writer surpasses his Spanish predecessor in native force, it cannot be doubted that he is the superior in subtlety. Stepan Trofimovitch is a nineteenth-century Quixote—a complex creature of modern civilisation, in whom the noblest aspirations are intertwined with the pettiest personal vanities, in whom cowardice and heroism, folly and wisdom, are inextricably mixed. So consummate is the portraiture that one seems to see the whole nature of the man spread out before one like a piece of shot silk, shifting every moment from silliness to saintliness, from meanness to dignity, from egoism to abnegation. This marvellous synthesis is the work of humour, but of humour which has almost transcended itself—a smile felt so profoundly that it is only shown in the eyes. (pp. 218-19)

Lytton Strachey, "A Russian Humorist" (originally published in The Spectator, *Vol. 112, No. 4476, April 11, 1914), in his* Literary Essays *(reprinted by permission of Harcourt Brace Jovanovich, Inc.; in Canada by The Society of Authors as agents for the Strachey Trust), Harcourt, 1949, pp. 215-19.*

J. MIDDLETON MURRY   (essay date 1916)

English criticism has generously praised Dostoevsky. It is pleasant to have discovered a writer of novels who can comfortably be called great, and to be precise as to the manner of his greatness. He is a novelist—for did he not write novels?—of deeper psychological penetration than his predecessors, who in the light of his intuition and sympathy has gone boldly into dark and undiscovered countries and brought back the results of his explorations. His form is the same as that his predecessors used, the novel; his purpose is the same as theirs, to represent life. (p. 24)

[But] the novels of this great novelist have in them explosive force enough to shatter the very definition of the novel.

It may be said that there is no such definition, and that each great novelist creates his own, and is to be judged after the fact. If this be so, and it is profoundly true, then Dostoevsky must be so judged. But to judge a novelist is to compare him with other novelists, and comparison to be valid and fruitful demands a common element in them all, even though this common element cannot be described with the exactness of a definition. The common ground of novelists is a commonplace of criticism. A novel, in the largest sense of the word, *represents* life. Life is a process, whose infinite variety cannot be staled; it is a movement in time. Therefore a representation of life must, like its exemplar, be permeated with this sense of process and movement. . . . (pp. 25-6)

When we first come into contact with [Dostoevsky's] novels, we are bewildered and grope about in darkness for [a] clue to reality. We read on as in a dream, and we are in a dream. We read one half *The Idiot,* one half even of *The Brothers Karamazov,* and in reading pass through a fire of spiritual experiences such as one hundred years could not have kindled—and we find that in the measurement of earthly time, but a day has been reckoned. . . . [The] correspondence of the physical day and its spiritual content is fantastic and unreal. It is no wonder that Dostoevsky made grotesque blunders in his registration of this earthly time. . . . Dostoevsky is immune from the discipline of time. There is in his works neither night nor day; the sun neither rises nor sets.

Therefore Dostoevsky's novels are not novels at all. They have not that element in their being upon which the novel itself depends. (pp. 26-8)

Dostoevsky is not a novelist. What he is is more difficult to define. . . . Our old methods and standards are useless to elucidate and to measure Dostoevsky, not because he is greater than the heroes of art who went before him, but because he is profoundly different. . . . Dostoevsky's rejection of time is an evidence of his newness. No drama that we know has room prepared for such portentous soliloquies as those of Dostoevsky's heroes. He may indeed have been nearer in spirit to the

drama than to the novel; but his drama is a new drama, and one for which the old can stand only as a vague symbol. (pp. 28-30)

Physical and actual events take place in Dostoevsky's novels. In reading them we are confounded not so much by the absence of time, as by a continual confusion between what may be called "the timeless world" and the world in time. We are carried from one to the other ruthlessly, and our minds are at the first involved in chaos. (p. 30)

Yet a memory as of some unsolved mystery hangs about us, compelling our return. We read again, and some of the dark places are made plain by a new light. Gradually upon the chaos of this pandemonium, with its ecstatic visions of unearthly beauty, simplicity descends. The new proportion, which was concealed from our eyes by the mere succession of the timeless world upon the world in time, is revealed. Some of the figures grow in stature until it seems that no integument of clay can contain the mightiness of their spirit. They pass beyond human comparison, and are no longer to be judged by human laws. (p. 31)

In their creation their author seems to have passed beyond some deep ordinance of human nature, saying, "Thus far shalt thou go and no further." In the mind they seek the company of their peers, which are few and far and hardly understood. That mocking cruel smile of the "Mona Lisa" seems to belong to their incarnation, and the spirits of Dostoevsky and Leonardo to seek each other across the ages, as those of men who have sought to pass beyond humanity.

I do not know whether my experience is common to all those who read and are fascinated by the works of Dostoevsky. There are times, when thinking about the spirits which he has conjured up—I use the word deliberately—I am seized by a suprasensual terror. For one awful moment I seem to see things with the eye of eternity, and have a vision of suns grown cold, and hear the echo of voices calling without sound across the waste and frozen universe. (p. 33)

[There] is an obscenity beyond the bodily world, a metaphysical obscenity, which consists in the sudden manifestation of that which is timeless through that which is in time.

This metaphysical obscenity was known to Dostoevsky, it creeps out again and again in his work. The thought of it haunts his great characters, as it haunted himself. It is in a peculiar sense the distinguishing mark of his imaginations. In different forms it recurs continually, either in the thoughts of his characters or in the fates which he devised for them. They are possessed by the horror of it, yet for all their agonised striving to escape it, they are caught by it at the last. For those who are sensible of these things there is more terror and cruelty to Dostoevsky's work than in all the literature of all the ages which went before him. . . . He represented that which he saw, and set down his torments in writing. He was obsessed by the *vision* of eternity.

Therefore he could not represent life. For a man who is obsessed by this awful and tremendous vision to represent life is impossible. It is an activity which demands a fundamental acceptance of life. But how should a man whose eyes saw life only too often as something which was cold and dead and infinitely small represent life? It was to him a mere mockery, and to represent it a barren labour. (pp. 36-7)

[Though] the characteristic creations of his imagination do for the most part date from the time at which his disease entered upon its most violent forms, they are nevertheless implicit in his work from its beginnings. There is no sign even in his earliest writing of that deep acceptance of life which would have saved him as it saves most men from the agonies of defying that which is immutable. His *Poor Folk* reveals him already as a youth fascinated by the awful fact of Pain. Never does what he was subsequently (in *A Raw Youth*) to call "the living life" appear in his work; to him that living life which is the material of the novelist's art remained either a miracle in his moments of self-distrust, or in his moments of belief in his own powers something profoundly ordinary and uninteresting. And deep down in his philosophy lay the conviction that that which is ordinary is in some sense unreal. (pp. 38-9)

There is no false step in the awful logic of Ivan Karamazov: If there is no God, then all things are lawful. Dostoevsky was the first writer to make that logic plain. His imagination conceived men who were driven by the force of their own humanity to confront the issue. However terrible they may appear—and they appear as portentous spirits—it is their humanity which compels them to know all things, and those things above all that some undying instinct tells us must not be known. For they seek a way of life, and that seeking is the very mark of humanity.

Beside these figures the myriad other characters of Dostoevsky's creation fade away. They are no more than the material out of which his own particular creations were fashioned. They are, as it were, the life upon which his great characters have brooded. They are suffering humanity, against whose suffering the giant minds have rebelled not merely in thought, but in act. Therefore they have but a small place in this book, not because they form one indistinguishable mass, for they do not, but because their creation was no more than the prelude to Dostoevsky's own achievement, which was to represent the mind of humanity rebellious against the life in which the suffering of the lesser creatures was inevitable, and with the ultimate courage of rebellion. This is but a part of what he did. His work is the record of a great mind's seeking for a way of life; it is more than a record of struggle, it is the struggle itself. . . . All that the human soul can suffer is somewhere expressed within his work; but there are lesser and greater sufferings, or rather there are sufferings and there is absolute suffering. Sufferings may be forgotten in happiness; but absolute suffering never. Dostoevsky's heroes are tormented by this absolute suffering: their minds are never free from the gnawing terror of the timeless world. Therefore they are not human. Man cannot suffer for ever. They are disembodied spirits. They have the likeness of men, we are told, but we know that we shall never look upon them. Nikolay Stavrogin's face was like a mask, says the story of *The Possessed*. They have all faces like masks, for no physical flesh could bear the lineaments of those spirits. Their bodies are but symbols, which may suggest that these are possibilities of the human spirit, possibilities which Dostoevsky alone had dared to contemplate. (pp. 45-8)

Dostoevsky was not a novelist, and he cannot be judged as a novelist. His superhuman and his human figures do not differ from each other in the degree of their humanity; they are absolutely different, and it is in them that the strangeness and the fascination and the power of Dostoevsky rests. They are the champions; the issue of the battle rests with them. (p. 48)

The slow emergence of his own essential conceptions, and their evolution to the final vision of *The Brothers Karamazov* can be traced through his books from the beginning, until at the

last each of his great novels seems to mark an epoch in the human consciousness. (pp. 48-9)

J. Middleton Murry, "Introductory," in his Fyodor Dostoevsky: A Critical Study *(reprinted by permission of The Society of Authors as the literary representative of the Estate of John Middleton Murry), Martin Secker, 1916 (and reprinted by Martin Secker, 1923), pp. 21-49.*

CHARLES GRAY SHAW (essay date 1918)

It is a terrible thing to fall into the hands of the living God, but that is what happened to Fydor Dostoievsky. It was not Russia, vast, fantastic, terrible, but real existence as such which wrung from his soul his tales of self-inquisition. "Reality has caught me upon a hook"; this chance expression in one of his romances of reality is the confessed secret of the anguished author. Dostoievsky is Russia, and "the Russian soul is a dark place." . . . Because of his pessimistic realism, Dostoievsky is not to be understood by any attempt to force his stubborn thought into the pens of conventional literature; "standard authors" afford us no analogies, so that it is only be relating the Russian to Job, Ezekiel, and the author of the Apocalypse that we are able to make headway in reading Dostoievsky. (p. 246)

[The] reader cannot comprehend Dostoievsky as artist unless the reader is prepared to look upon art as absolute. Style is swallowed up in significance, technique surrenders to subject; for the story *is* something, not about something. As architecture and music are arts which refuse to represent something other than themselves, but are real and representative together, so the art of Dostoievsky, instead of being pictorial and imitative, is so much reality spread out before one's gaze. The idea becomes fact, the mental solidifies, and that which is said is no more, no less, than that which took place. The story is a stream which carries river-bank and river-bed along with it, while huge cakes of reality float upon the surface. (pp. 246-47)

It is imperative to consider Dostoievsky's art from an intensive standpoint as so much psychology, but a psychology which would strain one of our modern laboratories, while its Russian aspects would disconcert what is popularly known as "sociology." The Russian writer chooses to style it "double-edged psychology," whose methods of analysis are so painful to the subject that he cries out, "Don't rummage in my soul; cursed be all those who pry into the human heart." Dostoievsky's fascinating fear of psychology was probably due to the fact that his most precious moments of introspection were enjoyed in connection with his experiences as an epileptic. In the midst of his mystical terror, the spirit rends his soul, while he screams as though another person were crying out within his own soul. Nevertheless, this epileptic experience has its heights of transfiguration, since the sufferer with his "special, sudden idea" is able to behold the "highest synthesis of life." (p. 247)

Two general principles seem to guide Dostoievsky's contemplation of life: one is anthropological in its attempt to define man and place him in a habitat; the other is racial, and seeks to analyze the Russian soul. As an anthropologist, Dostoievsky refuses to subsume man under the genus homo, just as he is unwilling to assign him to earth as his home. "Man," said Pascal, "is neither beast nor angel—*ni bête, ni ange*." According to Dostoievsky's calculation, *man is either beast or angel*, since he is never merely man; or, to use his own language, man is a "diamond set in the dirty background of life."

. . . In his mystic intuition of life, Dostoievsky could behold nothing between the black, barren earth and the endless shining of the sky; from which follows the fact that, as he says, "the man with the ideal of Sodom in his soul does not renounce the ideal of the Madonna." . . .

[The] interpretation of Dostoievsky must be carried on in the courts of a super-psychology and a major morality; if the reader clings to his traditional ideas of man as a creature of common consciousness and proper morality, he will soon be floundering in the flotsam of Dostoievsky's turbid soul-stuff. (p. 249)

Enthralled by the idea of a super-strong consciousness which turns human blood to lava or moulten iron, Dostoievsky makes Milton's Satan and Nietzsche's blond beast appear quite amateurish and unconvincing; the strong Slav is a reality in the artistic experience of the writer. . . . The most systematic treatment of undue strength is found in *The Brothers Karamazov,* which celebrates the "primitive force of the Karamazovs, a crude, unbridled earth-force, a thirst for life regardless of everything." Other nations, he tells us, may have their Hamlets, but the Russians have their Karamazovs. Dostoievsky's strong one turns to crime to cleanse his soul of the sense of power whose superabundance has become a burden to him. In this spirit, Rogozhin, in *The Idiot,* with a garden-knife slays a family of six for the sake of killing them, from which act of disinterested deviltry he turns to the murder of his beautiful bride. Prince Harry, in *The Possessed,* that Gadarean swine story, bites off the ear of the old count who in his deafness is trying to hear what the youth has to say. (p. 250)

Side by side with such frank frightfulness, for which even the German U-boat fleet can hardly prepare us, Dostoievsky loves to place accompanying tales of excessive want and extravagant self-abasement. From tropic to poles his art passes without literary inconsistency. In his hands, the story shifts from the Slavonic to the Sanskrit, while a word from him turns the Cossack into a Buddhist. Meanwhile, we are kept wondering just when man in the European and American sense will make his appearance. The underlying philosophy of Dostoievsky puzzles the eyes of reading-room and magazine-people, because this philosophy puts the negation of life upon a par with life-assertion. . . . Dostoievsky concludes that life is at its best when its tides are at their lowest ebb, its colors of an infra-red tint. The best man is the least of men, a kind of idiot who possesses just enough volition and ideation to continue diplomatic relations with life. Good and bad, life and death are one; at the same time, all souls are open to the one world; the endless publicity of Siberian existence had taught Dostoievsky that bitter lesson. (pp. 251-52)

Dostoievsky's theology is neither the latitudinarianism of Berlin nor the anthropomorphism of the Kaiser. Instead of accepting the idea of God, he finds no possible way of rejecting the notion. The Psalmist admitted that the fool might say, *non est deus,* even when he did not think it; but Dostoievsky cannot admit the possibility of the atheistic *dixit.* The atheist, he thinks, "will always be talking about something else." Like his favorite character, Alesha Karamazov, Dostoievsky seems to say, "I am not rebelling against God; I simply don't accept his world." Dostoievsky's rejection of the world is due to the pessimistic perception that the planet is the place of disorder, which fact makes possible the art of the Russian, even when his aesthetic capitalization of the cosmic chaos is not quite the same as that of the munition-maker's. . . . Of the Russian it may be said that this is perhaps the only place in his aesthetic system where the mystic becomes malicious; even here his

indignation assumes no more threatening an aspect than that of the "suffering smile."

If atheists are always talking about something else than the Deity whose existence they would deny, Dostoievsky showed his willingness to listen to their rash utterances. . . . (p. 253)

It was Dostoievsky's fate to be possessed of a primitive and patriarchal spirit and be called upon to display this in an age of industry. Place him in the world when creation was fresh and when the newest winds of Heaven fanned faces not yet furrowed by doubt and care, and your Dostoievsky had been fit and ready to join Enoch as he walked with God. But, finding himself in a world where economic systems have become superior to things and men, Dostoievsky could not help invoking the spirit of nihilism, even when he repudiated nihilistic politics as such. (p. 254)

Along with this spiritual nihilism which condemns the railway as a soteriological principle goes Dostoievsky's repudiation of science. He feels that science is selfish and tends to forbid pity, whence it will be folly to put one's trust in its princes. . . . Science, he believes, could not exist were it not for beauty, while the contrast between the aesthetical and the scientific makes it possible for one to conclude that "Shakespeare is better than boots, Raphael greater than petroleum, the Sistine Madonna finer than a pencil." (pp. 254-55)

Dostoievsky may not have found the integrating principle which shall not only bring men together, but persuade them that they belong together, but he has been of some service in showing us that our hope in horses and chariots, in steel cars and automobiles, is a vain and far-fetched consolation.

As to the terrified mystic himself, the reader of his unique works may close the several volumes with the conviction that, no matter what science may say about him, no matter what society may do to him, man exists. (p. 255)

Charles Gray Shaw, "Dostoyevsky's Mystical Terror," in The North American Review, *Vol. CCVII, No. 2, February, 1918, pp. 246-56.*

CONRAD AIKEN (essay date 1921)

Dostoevsky is perhaps the supreme instance of the compulsive nature of the artist's ideas. But if that means that we cannot take too seriously his "ideas," it does not mean that we cannot take him seriously as an artist. . . . [He] was also an injured soul, and his novels are the profuse, extraordinary record of that injury, the bewildered confession of an acutely sensitive but grievously wounded sensorium. Seen in this light, especially, but indeed seen in any light, his novels are "dreams": confused, wandering, crowded; lighted everywhere with the red light of fever.

Dostoevsky himself admitted more than once that he had little "control" of his story. . . . [But] he comes no nearer to lucidity or to the untroubled in *The Brothers Karamazov,* the only one of his novels composed at leisure. His novels are, in fact, dreams in a Freudian sense, since they are the projection, again and again, of his own difficulties in life. His characters all verge on the hysterical or epileptic—some of them project, as it were, one phase of the disease, and some another.

It is possible to carry too far this theory of genesis, but one hardly hesitates in ascribing to epileptic mysticism and euphoria the origins of Myshkin, of Sonia, of Alyosha, as one also is prone to see, on the other hand, in the "evil" or perverse phases of epilepsy, the origins of Rogozhin, Raskolnikov, Svidrigailov. One need not simplify excessively—there are other factors to be considered. There is, for example, Dostoevsky's metaphysical preoccupation with the problem of good and evil, a problem which essentially provides the core of all his greatest work: the theme, if we see it in abstract, of *The Idiot, The Possessed, Crime and Punishment, The Brothers Karamazov;* the theme, for once explicitly, of *Notes from Underground.* But do we not see the stigma of disease, once more, precisely in this excessive morbid preoccupation? It was a problem with which Dostoevsky was obsessed; the sense of "evil" rode him like a demon, a protean demon which at one moment was the monstrous symbol of pain, at another the symbol of the sense of horror and futility which arises from too acute a consciousness of the blank, empty, and indifferent determinism in which the human consciousness finds itself enmeshed.

In his analysis of the latter sensation, Dostoevsky went extraordinarily far—has anyone been more conscious, as it were, of consciousness, or so singularly and persistently endeavored to shed the light inward on himself? (pp. 166-67)

[We] are wise if we accept [Dostoevsky's novels] simply as amazing psychotic improvisations on a theme, psychological symphonies of unparalleled sensitiveness and richness; and if we are bound to wonder whether their characteristic extravagant vehemence is not a hint that the composition of them was often precisely an "epileptic equivalent," that need not lessen for us in the slightest our delight in abandoning ourselves to the torrent. What we come to is the fact that the later novels are not a transcription or representation of our actual world—they have their contact with it, obviously, their roots in it, but they flower, remotely and strangely, in another and translunar atmosphere. They approach, by this kind of singular abstraction and attenuated contact with the real, an "absoluteness" in fiction which we can perhaps only parallel, odd as the parallel seems, with the later novels of Henry James—*The Golden Bowl, The Wings of the Dove, The Awkward Age, What Maisie Knew, The Ambassadors.* I do not suggest any such absurdity as that these novels resemble, in any other remotest particular, *Crime and Punishment* or *The Brothers Karamazov.* Dostoevsky did not, as James did, calculate his effect; he was not even aware of it. He asked, in one of his letters, "Is not my fantastic *Idiot* the very dailiest truth?" Well, of course it is not; nor do we wish it to be. It is perhaps something better than the truth. (p. 167)

> *Conrad Aiken, "Dostoevsky, Feodor" (originally published as "Symphonies in the Psychotic," in* Freeman, *Vol. 4, No. 94, December 28, 1921), in his* Collected Criticism *(reprinted by permission of Brandt & Brandt Literary Agents, Inc.), Oxford University Press, New York, 1968, pp. 163-67.*

STEFAN ZWEIG (essay date 1922)

For Dostoeffsky, as for all his characters, "I am," "I exist," is the greatest triumph of life, the superlative sensation of belonging to the universe. Dmitri Karamazoff, in his prison cell, sings a hymn of praise on the subject of this "I exist," on the voluptuous pleasure of "existing"; and it is for the sake of this love of life that so much suffering is necessary. We see, therefore, that it is only on the surface of things that the sum total of suffering appears to be greater in Dostoeffsky's works than in those of any other author. For, if ever there was a world where nothing is inexorably fixed, where, from the

deepest chasm, a path leads up to safety, where every misfortune culminates in ecstasy, where every despair is crowned with hope, then that world is Dostoeffsky's world. (p. 156)

Each one of Dostoeffsky's heroes is asking himself the questions that are occupying the mind of all Russians: "Who am I? What am I worth?" He seeks himself, or, rather, the superlative essence of himself, in the unstable, in the spaceless, in the timeless. He wishes to see himself as God sees him; he wishes to acknowledge himself. Truth is more than a mere need to him; it is an excess, a voluptuousness, an avowal of the most intimate of his pleasures; it is his spasm, his orgasm. . . . It is here, in these combats for the revelation of the genuine ego, that Dostoeffsky reaches his greatest intensity. Here, in the arena of the inner man, the big tournaments take place. These are mighty epics of the heart, wherein what is purely Russian is purged away, and the tragedy broadens to include all mankind. The symbolical destiny of Dostoeffsky's figures then becomes explicit and staggering. Again and again, we live through the mystery of self-birth, of the myth created by Dostoeffsky himself: the birth of the new man from the universal humanity which resides in every pilgrim here below. (pp. 157-58)

[Dostoeffsky's characters], in the last analysis, experience the same fate, no matter how differently their lives are shaped at the outset. Each of them lives a variation upon one and the same theme: the process of becoming man. We must never forget that Dostoeffsky's art aims at the core of things; and, in so far as his works are psychological studies, he contemplates the man in humanity, the absolute or abstract man who lies far beyond the planes of civilization. (p. 158)

Dostoeffsky's heroes start from identical beginnings. True to their Russian temperament, they are rendered uneasy by their own vital energy. During puberty, the period of mental and bodily awakening, their cheerful and free sensibilities become clouded. They are dimly aware that a power is germinating within them, that a mysterious force is driving them on; something seems to be imprisoned, something that is growing, that is welling up and trying to escape from the garment of immaturity. (pp. 158-59)

Kirilloff, Shatoff, Raskolnikoff, Ivan Karamazoff, each of these solitaries has "his own" idea: nihilism, or altruism, or Napoleonic megalomania; each has incubated his fantasy in morbid isolation. Some of them wish to be armed against this new man who is to spring from their loins; their pride cannot suffer him, and they would crush him if they could. Others, again, hope that by over-stimulation they may get the better of this importunate life-pang, may weary it into quiescence. (p. 159)

What drives them into vicious paths is the urge of pain, not the prick of a thoughtless sensual appetite. They do not carouse in order to sink into a contented sleep . . . ; they drink for the sake of intoxication, that they may forget their delusions. . . . From the furnace of their lusts they rise upward to God's throne, or sink to the level of beasts; but their constant aim is to discover their own essential humanity. . . . If they are to fathom their own depths, if they are to be able to measure the greatness of their own humanity, they must plunge into every chasm: from sensuality they hurl themselves into depravity, from depravity into cruelty, and so on, downward into the nethermost abyss, a soulless region of ice and of deliberate wickedness. And they do all this out of a transmuted love and longing to know their own essential nature, out of a transmuted form of religious mania. (pp. 160-61)

The more they overtax their senses and their brains, the nearer do they approach to the essence of themselves; and the greater their desire for self-annihilation, the quicker is likely to be their salvation. Their sad bacchanalian orgy was, after all, no more than a convulsive seizure; and their crimes were nothing but the spasm of self-birth. In destroying themselves, they merely do away with the husk enclosing the inner man; such self-destruction is in reality self-preservation in the highest sense of the term. (p. 161)

Such, then, is Dostoeffsky's mythus: the individual ego, a compost of dim and amorphous ingredients, is impregnated with the seed of the true man, that archetypal being of mediaeval philosophy who is exempt from the taint of original sin. From each one of us the primal and absolutely divine essence can be born. It is our highest task, our supreme earthly duty, to bring forth this primal and everlasting man from the loins of the contemporary civilized human being. (p. 162)

Each of Dostoeffsky's novels ends with a catharsis, an emotional cleansing such as we find in Greek tragedy: this is the great atonement. Above the thunder-clouds, in the fresh and sweet atmosphere that follows the storm, flames a glorious rainbow, the Russian emblem of atonement.

Not until they have given birth to the true man, are Dostoeffsky's heroes allowed to enter the true community. Balzac's heroes triumph when they at last conquer society; Dickens's heroes attain their apogee when they settle down into their proper sphere of activity, into the life of a respectable citizen, when they found a family, and are successful in their careers. But the community towards which Dostoeffsky's heroes converge, is no longer social; it has, rather, the attributes of a religious community; these beings do not seek "society"; what they are in search of is world brotherhood. In that brotherhood, hierarchy as ordinarily understood has ceased to exist, for the only gradations are in the degree to which true inwardness, and therefore mystical community, has been achieved. It is of such beings that his novels have to tell. . . . These purified men no longer feel that there are any class distinctions; their souls, naked as in paradise, know not shame, or pride, or hatred, or contempt. Criminals and harlots, murderers and saints, princes and drunkards, they hold frank converse in the sphere of essential being, talking heart to heart and soul to soul. One thing alone differentiates them in Dostoeffsky's mind: how far they have attained their innermost and veritable selves, how far they have advanced along the road to a sterlingly genuine humanity. . . . In Dostoeffsky's cosmos, therefore, we find no hopelessly abandoned wretch, no hell with its lowest circle à la Dante, a hell whence Christ himself cannot deliver those who are condemned to suffer its torments. Purgatory he recognizes; and he knows that an erring mortal is filled with finer ardours and is nearer to the true man than the proud, cold, and perfectly mannered gentleman, in whose breast the true man has become congealed to a law-abiding citizen. . . . They possess that sublime faculty which Dostoeffsky tells us is peculiar to the Russian, namely, the incapacity to hate for any length of time; having this, they likewise possess an inexhaustible faculty for understanding all things terrestrial. . . . [This] mystery of universal reconciliation in brotherly identification, this orphic song of the spirit, accounts for the lyrical outbursts we hear ever and anon amid the gloomy music of Dostoeffsky's novels. (pp. 163-65)

Stefan Zweig, "Dostoeffsky," in his Master Builders, an Attempt at the Typology of the Spirit: Three Masters: Balzac, Dickens, Dostoeffsky, Vol. 1, *trans-lated by Eden Paul and Cedar Paul (translation copyright © 1930, copyright renewed © 1957, by the Viking Press, Inc.; reprinted by permission of the Estate of Stefan Zweig; originally published as* Drei Meister: Balzac, Dickens, Dostojewski, *Insel-Verlag, 1922), Viking Penguin Inc., 1930, pp. 99-238.*

ANDRÉ GIDE (essay date 1923)

Despite the extraordinarily rich diversity of his *Comédie Humaine*, Dostoevsky's characters group and arrange themselves always on one plane only, that of humility and pride. This system of grouping discomfits us; indeed, at first, it appears far from clear, for the very simple reason that we do not usually approach the problem of making a diversion at such an angle and that we distribute mankind in hierarchies.

[It] is not according to the positive or negative quality of their virtue that one can *hierarchize* (forgive me this horrible word!) his characters: not according to their goodness of heart, but by their degree of pride.

Dostoevsky presents on one side the humble (some of these are humble to an abject degree, and seem to enjoy their abasement); on the other, the proud (some to the point of crime). The latter are usually the more intelligent. We shall see them, tormented by the demon of pride, ever striving after something higher still.

His women, even more so than his characters of the other sex, are ever moved and determined by considerations of pride.

In all Dostoevsky we have not a single great man. "But what about that splendid Father Zossima in [*The Brothers Karamazov*]?" you may say. Yes, he is certainly the noblest figure the Russian novelist had drawn; he far and away dominates the whole tragedy. . . . At the same time we shall realize what in Dostoevsky's eyes constitutes his real greatness. Father Zossima is not of the great as the world reckons them. He is a saint—no hero! And he has reached saintliness by surrender of will and abdication of intellect.

His heroes' determination, every particle of cleverness and will-power they possess, seem but to hurry them onward to perdition, and if I seek to know what part mind plays in Dostoevsky's novels, I realize that its power is demonic.

His most dangerous characters are the strongest intellectually, and not only do I maintain that the mind and the will of Dostoevsky's characters are active solely for evil, but that, when urged and guided towards good, the virtue to which they attain is rotten with pride and leads to destruction. Dostoevsky's heroes inherit the Kingdom of God only by the denial of mind and will and the surrender of personality.

André Gide, in his Dostoevsky, *translated by Arnold Bennett (translation copyright © 1961 by New Directions Publishing Corporation; all rights reserved; reprinted by permission of New Directions Publishing Corporation; originally published as* Dostoïevsky, *Plon-Nourrit et Cie, 1923), New Directions, 1961, 181 p.*

JOSÉ ORTEGA Y GASSET (essay date 1925)

While other great names are setting, carried down into oblivion by the mysterious revolution of the times, that of Dostoevski has established itself firmly in the zenith. Perhaps the present fervent admiration of his work is a trifle exaggerated, and I would rather reserve my judgment for a serener hour. At any rate, he has escaped from the general shipwreck of nineteenth century novels. But the reasons usually given to explain his triumph and his ability to survive seem to me erroneous. The interest his novels arouse is attributed to their material: the mysteriously dramatic action, the utterly pathological character of the personages, the exotic quality of those Slavic souls so different in their turbulent intricacy from our clear and neat dispositions. All this may contribute to the pleasure we draw from Dostoevski; only it is not sufficient reason. Moreover, there is a certain questionable quality to these features that makes them as well suited to repelling as to attracting us. We remember that those novels used to leave us with a mingled feeling of pleasure and uneasy confusion. (pp. 74-5)

As it is, much has been said about what is going on in Dostoevski's novels and very little about their form. The extraordinary quality of the events and emotions this formidable writer describes has fascinated the critics and prevented them from penetrating into what, at first sight, seems accidental and extrinsic but in reality forms the essence of the work: the structure of the novel as such. Hence a curious optical delusion. The turbulent, wayward character of his personages is ascribed to Dostoevski himself, and the novelist is looked upon as one more figure in his own novels—which indeed seem begotten in an hour of demoniacal ecstasy by some nameless elemental power, akin to the thunder and brother of the winds.

But all this is mere fancy. An alert mind may indulge in such colorful pictures but will soon dismiss them for the sake of clear ideas. It may be that the man Dostoevski was a poor epileptic or, if one so desires, a prophet. But the novelist Dostoevski was an *homme de lettres,* a conscientious craftsman of a sublime craft, and nothing else. Many a time have I tried in vain to convince Pío Baroja that Dostoevski was, above all, a past master of novelistic technique and one of the greatest innovators of the form of the novel.

There is no better example of what I have called the sluggish character of the genre. Dostoevski's books are almost all extremely long. But the story that is told is usually quite short. Sometimes it takes two volumes to describe what happens in three days, indeed, in a few hours. And yet, is there anything more intense? (pp. 75-6)

The concentration of the plot in time and space, so characteristic of Dostoevski's technique, brings to mind, in an unexpected sense, the venerable unities of classical tragedy. This aesthetic rule, which calls for moderation and restraint, now appears as an efficient means of bringing about the inner density, the high pressure, as it were, within the body of the novel.

Dostoevski never tires of filling pages and pages with the unending conversations of his personages. Thanks to this abundant flow of words the imaginary persons acquire a palpable bodily existence such as no definition could contrive.

It is extremely interesting to watch Dostoevski in his cunning ways with the reader. To a perfunctory observation, he seems to define each of his personages. When he introduces a figure he nearly always begins by briefly giving a biography of that person and thus makes us believe that we know well enough with what kind of man we are dealing. But no sooner do his people begin to act—i.e., to talk and to do things—than we feel thrown off the track. They refuse to behave according to those alleged definitions. The first conceptual image we were given of them is followed by another in which we see their immediate life, independent of the author's definition; and the

two do not tally. At this point, the reader, afraid to lose sight of the personages at the crossroads of these contradictory data, sets forth in their pursuit by trying to reconcile the discrepant facts to make a unified picture. That is, he gets busy to find a definition himself. Now this is what we are doing in our living intercourse with people. Chance leads them into the ambit of our life, and nobody bothers officially to define them to us. What we have before us is their intricate reality not their plain concept. We are never quite let into their secret, they stubbornly refuse to adjust themselves to our ideas about them. And this is what makes them independent of us and brings it home that they are an effective reality transcending our imagination. But is not then Dostoevski's "realism"—let us call it that not to complicate things—not so much a matter of the persons and events he presents as of the way the reader sees himself compelled to deal with these persons and events? Dostoevski is a "realist" not because he uses the material of life but because he uses the form of life.

In this ruse of laying false scent Dostoevski indulges to the degree of cruelty. Not only does he refuse clearly to define his figures beforehand, but as their behavior varies from stage to stage they display one facet after another and thus seem to be shaped and assembled step by step before our eyes. Instead of stylizing the characters Dostoevski is pleased to have their ambiguity appear as unmitigatedly as in real life. And the reader, proceeding by trial and error, apprehensive all the time of making a mistake, must work out as best he can the actual character of those fickle creatures.

Owing to this device, among others, Dostoevski's books, whatever their other qualities, have the rare virtue of never appearing sham and conventional. The reader never stumbles upon theatrical props; he feels from the outset immersed in a sound and effective quasi-reality. For a novel, in contrast to other literary works, must, while it is read, not be conceived as a novel; the reader must not be conscious of curtain and stage-lights. (pp. 77-9)

> *José Ortega y Gasset, "Notes on the Novel" (originally published in his* La Dehumanizacion del arte e ideas sobre la novela, *Revista de Occidente, 1925), in his* The Dehumanization of Art: And Other Essays on Art, Culture, and Literature, *translated by Helene Weyl (translation copyright 1948; renewed © 1968 by Princeton University Press; reprinted by permission of Princeton University Press), Princeton University Press, 1968, pp. 57-103.**

JULIUS MEIER-GRAEFE   (essay date 1928)

Dostoevsky opens up new worlds: the regions he explores were previously unknown to literature. And he creates Upheaval. (p. 1)

It is no exaggeration to assume that in the near future Dostoevsky will exert as much influence as Goethe or Schiller, if indeed he has not already done so—perhaps even as much as Shakespeare. . . . Only a Russian could acquire this influence, this all-European influence, and only our age in which spiritual values are not allowed to exercise any kind of popular appeal has fashioned the conditions for his popularity. Whence the influence? Perhaps the most cogent factor is the more or less conscious superstition that Dostoevsky's creations are not literature and that he must not be counted amongst the poets. This fallacy is by no means based on the supposed plausibility of his plots, on the so-called naturalistic truth; on the contrary the plausibility is often a matter of doubt to the naïve reader. Moreover, Dostoevsky's outlook in no way justifies classifying him as a naturalist. Detailed description of externals is entirely eliminated. There is no painting of a *milieu* in its modern sense. The *milieu* grows with the action, or rather out of the action. Where Dostoevsky goes into details every external factor is merely auxiliary to an easily recognizable object, and this object, frank tension or tendency, is rejected by the naturalistic school. This partly consitutes the distinction between his writing and the current notion of modern literature. Such exciting stories are considered by the cultured reader as inartistic, particularly when coarse material is introduced. Dostoevsky seems to prefer this coarseness. It is nearly always a matter of crime or the possibility of crime. The plot of **Crime and Punishment** (which can be reduced to quite a simple theme) is the very thing for admirers of Sherlock Holmes. The same applies to the central *motif* of **The Brothers Karamazov**. In **A Raw Youth** the tension depends on a hardly tolerable film-trick, the famous letter which is never delivered and finally stolen. In **The Idiot, The Eternal Husband, The Possessed,** there is murder or attempted murder. The disguising of the gruesome *motif* does not render these stories different from the most vulgar concoctions of their kind. Blood flows, not behind the scenes, but in the full blaze of the footlights. In spite of that we read, we devour eagerly every line. . . . In Dostoevsky's novels blood is of the very essence of the mystery, always an indispensable factor. The action gains impetus from it, it produces a fascinating play of light and shade and, at times (consider the end of **The Idiot**), consecration. If we can tolerate this gory atmosphere, if murder not alone does not blunt but actually refines our spiritual senses—so refines them that they become sensitive to the most secret, the most delicate things of a complexity hitherto unpresentable—then it must be because the gruesome *motif* is introduced in some other way than is usual in stories of murder; it must be because the significance of what is revealed, not in spite of but by means of this *motif,* sweeps us beyond the point of blood-shyness.

These methods by which the murder-stories are brought to a higher level can be generally termed psychology; it is the psychological element which distinguishes these stories from commonplace productions, though they are not necessarily on that account brought within the realm of literature. . . . (pp. 2-4)

Dostoevsky is able to conceal his personality under the garb of a psychologist whose only concern is to reveal associations, the dark threads between thought and action, between heart and countenance, between two men who love one another whilst their hearts are overflowing with hatred, between enemies who smile while they rend one another, between two adjacent chambers of the same human heart. If this were regarded as literature, his arbitrary methods could not be overlooked; he could not be forgiven his reckless transitions, his apparent lack of economy, his irrelevancy and offences against the good manners of European prose. And still one thing more, the most important; it is because we look, not at the literary, but at the psychological side, that our interest is held. . . . He almost becomes an opponent at a committee-meeting whose intentions we have to divine before coming to any conclusion; or else the dreaded banker on whose whim depends the credit of the whole business. We do not say too much, do not show too much enthusiasm, but keep our wits about us. It might be worth while. Who knows?

That is just the point: we foresee certain advantages. Naturally we shall not imitate Stavrogin's vile deed and from pure bore-

dom torture a child of twelve to death. Who would think of attacking an old woman with a hatchet and then killing another one? And surely no one would be so mad as to stab in her bridal dress the woman he adored. (p. 5)

[Dostoevsky] cuts deep into us. Possibly other writers want, or are compelled, to remain on the surface because that is their only means of revealing their nature. On that surface which is affected by the nobility of an *Iphigenia* there must lie wonderful organs, organs more delicate, more carefully tended than the outstretched fingers with which we snatch the Karamazovs to us; organs which enable us to remain calm, to bring a smile to our furrowed countenance and to give dignity to our burdened gait. . . . It might be said that the *Iphigenia* appeals to other senses—for example to the musical sense—whilst Dostoevsky's appeal is to sight or touch. But that does not explain the different reaction of our spirit. Doubtless there are in the *Iphigenia* rhythmic notes which cannot be heard by Dostoevsky's reader. Is there adequate compensation in Dostoevsky? This question is discussed with fervour in the roof-garden. Those who miss the world of tone assume that Dostoevsky entirely lacks form. They assert that the spirit which finds refreshment in beautiful forms receives no nourishment from him. That is true to a certain point, up to the point, namely, when form becomes an end in itself. If we grant that form is a means to an end—and we shall have to find out how far this is possible—then form as commonly understood requires modifications which we shall have to accept even if the whole roof-garden stands on its head. Musical form is ignored by Dostoevsky, apparently if not actually. That is partly how he succeeds—in fact an indispensable factor of his success. He ignores the obvious as if he had more important things to attend to than to bother about the sound of his words. All the same, sound is not eliminated, for that is not possible—it is only subordinated to other conditions. If a relationship with the reader exists at all, it becomes so intimate that the traditional conception of narrator, event and listener acquires quite a new significance. In Dostoevsky's novels not alone is the hero's existence at stake, but also our own. (pp. 6-7)

There are, then, three consecutive effects; first the crude tension of a detective story, which is carried to its climax with the utmost subtlety; secondly, the enigmatic and intimate relationship of the stories to latent parts of our own existence which suddenly become roused and torment us; thirdly, the gladdening relaxation bringing spiritual harmony. It is understood, of course, that to the poet the most essential of these is the third. With the first two he wounds us, like a surgeon who is compelled to cut open the body in order to see what is inside it. The wound would soon heal again were it not that now follows the real interference, the laying bare of diseased and stunted organs. At last comes the promise of a healthier existence.

The painful operation is performed almost without anaesthetic. Our suffering is at times so agonizing that we feel like falling upon and murdering the man who is rummaging inside us. Hatred is our only redress. Sometimes he seems to torment us unnecessarily, prolonging the torture only because it gratifies his virtuosity. He is guided not by consideration for our well-being but by a hellish science, and we are the victims of his experiments. But every time we are on the point of condemning this as revolting literature, there is the dawn of a new salvation, and again we surrender. We become more and more convinced that his treatment is good for us and that we must endure it at any cost. In the end we bless the surgeon.

This benefaction renders his delving into souls something quite different from the usual psychology, and it thus brings his work a step nearer to the accepted standard of literature, though it is not in itself confined to art; a conscious moral aim might indeed depreciate literary value. (p. 8)

All Dostoevsky's ideas ascend from moral motives into the realm of art, and not, it would seem, from art into the realm of morals. All his principal works are tendentious. He wants to teach and to reform. But to him a doctrine is not an immutable law, it is a living organism in perpetual motion; it avoids a rigid formula because that would weaken its effect. A thoroughly Russian instinct. In The Beginning there is not the Word coined by invisible powers, but communion with others, with the whole people; and since this people is numerous and provided by nature with peculiarly associative organs, with the whole world. Anxiety for this communion makes him speak out without forcing him into the limelight. He does not rise to becoming the spokesman of the community but remains so essentially a part of it that he has only to talk to himself in order to speak to them. When Dostoevsky says "we," it is not the poetic licence of the Westerner who means only himself; Dostoevsky indicates a tangible living mass. The sinner does not stand isolated but is part of the mass. We all sin. Even the perpetrator of the most heinous crime is always surrounded by a crowd which is in some way his accomplice, which sins with him and encourages him. The greatest sinner is Dostoevsky himself; at all events he accepts that responsibility. He understands everything and, in the rôle of an older man who has once done the same himself, would not dream of reproaching the younger sinner. (pp. 9-10)

Dostoevsky neither considered literature in any way the reflex of an inner harmony, nor sought to bestow harmony by means of it. He struggled and endeavoured to make men fellow-strugglers. The aim of his creation was unrest from which others fled. And he knew what he was doing. To none of the great visionaries has the task been clearer. Though some detail often escaped his notice or even here and there some task, he was never unmindful of the significance of his calling. To no one has it come more naturally to turn the spirit of unrest to account in creative literature, unambiguously and without any element of vagueness. In spite of that, unrest drove him to the most ambitious aims. (p. 14)

There is a fundamental and easily recognizable idea in each of Dostoevsky's novels, as well as a few well-worked-out principal characters. Other ideas are ranged round the fundamental idea and secondary figures encircle the principal characters. The connexions between these secondary ideas and characters are often arbitrary or abstruse but never commonplace. We are never wearied by irritating, secondary figures usurping the functions of the principal actors. The object of padding is, as in Shakespeare, to complicate, retard or spread out the action and to contribute to the creation of the *spiritus loci*. If direct relationships to previous occurrences are at times scanty, indirect connexions with the author are so much the more convincing, for the latter depend on the dynamic force of Dostoevsky who never allows himself to be completely dominated by the idea underlying the work. At this juncture we will not stop to consider either the interpretation of his ideas or his dynamic force. Suffice it to observe that he was always reaching out beyond the things portrayed, and carried away by a momentary inspiration, yielded to the temptation. . . . Dostoevsky aimed at illuminating a darkness of gigantic volume without thereby detracting from its inherent value. It was not

his vocation as a poet which drove him to that, but his mission, as a Russian, Christian, servant and brother of mankind. In the darkness lay boundless possibilities of salvation and Dostoevsky's perceptive faculty rendered him a visionary in the twilight. It was not till he had dragged the particular incident into the light of day that he became the creative artist, and then he would mould it, toy with it, and forget the darkness for a time. That would never last very long. The passion of the artist would yield before his yearning for that mysterious treasure-chamber and once again he would plunge into the darkness. That was his fanaticism for toil. . . . Of course, if it is true to say that nothing can be added to or taken away from a work of art, Dostoevsky wrote nothing perfect, at least not till *The Brothers Karamazov,* and perhaps even in that book something could have been cut out here and there. But even an ideal Dostoevsky could not have attained our ideal standard; the very nature of so comprehensive a work precluded that possibility. . . . On the other hand Dostoevsky's form still invites criticism. In theory that cannot be silenced. (pp. 15-16)

Lack of proportion can only indicate an uneven relationship between content and extent, insufficient concentration. Instead of acting the author reflects, laments, regrets or rejoices, or recounts in ten sentences what ought to be given in one. Dostoevsky was at times long-winded. . . . There are many long-winded passages but they certainly do not belong to the species just mentioned. Dostoevsky's content, or at least parts of it, could not be set out more briefly. (p. 17)

But however much his lengthiness may irritate us, however obscure its object may seem at times, it was never merely the outcome of loquacity, least of all when it most appears so. Something very different behind it is soon enough noticeable. Dostoevsky's idea was guilt. His nervous tension could not resist the flow of his phantasy, and he seems at times to have been veritably obsessed by an aversion to all method, as though it were a cloak for lies and hypocrisy and everything which he found ridiculous and pernicious in the institutions of Europe. . . . His lengthiness did not lighten his task, nor was it an ornament, although one can, or at least thinks one can, imagine the novel without it; it was a medium, one of the thousand mediums of unrest. This leads to a curious result. The more one reads Balzac, the more tedious he becomes. If he relates the history of the paper industry in order to create a background for a pair of lovers, one feels tempted to apply the scissors. (pp. 17-18)

At first sight many of Dostoevsky's situations seem to invite similar treatment; the scissors are always applied on the first reading. Every one has done it. Every one begins by devouring and wants to reach the murder story as rapidly as possible. There are gluttons who never attain the poet because the path to the detective is too wearisome. This sensual craving has first to be satisfied; then in certain circumstances, circumstances which do not always exist, the other can come. There are two classes of people, those who read Dostoevsky once and those who read him again. . . . The more often we take up *The Brothers Karamazov* the more compact it appears. Dostoevsky needed length to ensure room for the action, to give himself, as well as us, a start, because there are never any of the normal links in the form of descriptions of nature or other transitional matter. (pp. 18-19)

One would be more easily reconciled to Dostoevsky's lengthiness—after all, whole works, which to the *bourgeoisie* have only one meaning, are borne with the patience of an angel—

if only it were not bound up with one annoying characteristic which has invited universal reproach; his obscurity. There are long and obscure passages which are heartily welcome to the European intent on education and sound sleep. . . .

But in Dostoevsky there is none of this pseudo-obscurity which is a mere illusion. With his obscurity he rouses somnolent emotions; the tired eyelid may will itself to recognize only obscurity; actually his is a sonorous colour scheme; it illuminates the darkness out of which it has arisen. But to perceive its brilliance the spirit must be willing. (p. 20)

From Dostoevsky's development is obvious the gradual perfecting of his form. What we are mainly concerned with is the æstheticism of the work freed, as far as possible, from extraneous matter. Already in *Poor Folk* the creative impulse was purely poetical. Those letters are the variations of a lyric poet which encircle the theme in ever-mounting spirals, like mountains surrounding the little church in the valley. The lyric quality is more important than the action. Things are just as they appear through the eyes of these two simple persons in the novel, thus and thus only, and their stolid mentality does not detract from the reality of events.

Dostoevsky adhered to variations. The subject-matter becomes richer and the mentality, the objective which focuses, becomes more and more complicated. The more the variations are differentiated the more the spirals extend, and again and again the *motif* resembles that of the church in the valley. The lyrical note in *Poor Folk* and other later stories would have been incompatible with the tension of the principal works, and had to be modified. The novel-drama developed from the monologues of the underworldling, his most audacious stroke, and was brought to perfection in his last work.

The history of the form is convincing because it portrays the history of Dostoevsky's thought. The novel-drama was not the invention of an artist seeking to display some new literary method, but of a visionary forced by the momentum of his figures to dramatic expression in order to achieve his variations. In most works until the last the subject-matter overshadowed the form and enforced a continuation. Not till *The Brothers Karamazov* was final balance attained.

The process of construction in each individual work is repeated in a masterly way in his work as a whole. The twofold *début*, *Poor Folk* and *The Double*, constitutes the fundamental theme which is worked out in immense variations and finally appears as the church in the valley. His profusion is overwhelming at first sight. There is breathless succession of events. . . . There are fifty characters in each of the principal works. That would make many hundreds if one had to add them up. But fifty characters would amply illustrate his entire works. The same thing is true of his themes. Dostoevsky constantly introduced new people and new themes, but, as in real life, they are mostly the same people and the same themes. Yet at every turn we experience something new. The inventive factor lies, not in the novelty, but in the variety of what is presented.

We have found four or five stages of development which are by no means chronological. His remarkable *début* was scarcely excelled till the underworld den, and in the long interval—particularly before and after the *katorga*—his work fell beneath that level. And if the underworld memoirs, as a novelty, as the bold flight of a man of genius, hold us much more forcibly than the *début*, yet they collapse formally, and at a superficial glance bear out the widely held opinion that they are not lit-

erature, but the work of a psychologist of peculiar intuition. (pp. 378-79)

We would not like to have missed even the least important of the interludes, for there was always something in them worth while, if only the process of development which reveals Dostoevsky's most phenomenal characteristic: growth of art without conscious effort; growth of idea which leads to consolidation; growth of tendency which emancipates. Were the interludes absent we should still have the whole of Dostoevsky in his last work. In *The Brothers Karamazov* he exhausts himself so completely that everything preceding could be regarded merely as preparatory sketches. (p. 380)

Dostoevsky is not more pure and noble in *The Brothers Karamazov* than in earlier works, but attains the peak of creative life. Purity and nobility are inadequate conceptions.

The attempt at analogy in the world of painting is not unfruitful. The fact that he attained the pinnacle of his creation at the end of his life is unique in world-literature, and similar examples are to be found but rarely in the world of painting. . . . In the nineteenth century only the development of Delacroix, whose *début* reminded us of Dostoevsky's first public appearance, can be considered in any way equivalent. . . . Who, when looking at his later work, thinks of that Dantesque attitude with which Delacroix embraced both art and people? What cultured eye would fail to notice his purification? What cultured eye would not secretly rejoice and forgo communion with the people for the sake of communion with the elect who are susceptible to such spiritual beauty? Would it not accept the exchange as a just and divine ordinance? Yet this is true only until a Dostoevsky illustrates that ultimate purification is not incompatible with communion, and that it is quite possible to begin as courageously as Delacroix and yet to discover the Dante's Bark at the end of one's path. In such conservation of power there is balance transcending artistic canons. With a final and overwhelming embrace of his people Dostoevsky perfects his creation. (pp. 381-82)

Dostoevsky fulfilled all expectations. Delacroix required of the painter to paint a person flinging himself out of the window within the space of time occupied by his fall. In that space of time Dostoevsky would have produced the entire history of a suicide and his family including a hundred variations. He invented facilely and to the point. The episode was at hand on the spot where he needed it. It was only necessary to write it down. Extremely pleasant both for him and for us, but at bottom only one of the minor features of his greatness. (pp. 390-91)

He still comforts and teaches us, helps us, laughs with us, a brother, and every youthful heart yearns for him. (p. 391)

> *Julius Meier-Graefe, in his* Dostoevsky: The Man and His Work, *translated by Herbert H. Marks, G. Routledge & Sons, 1928, 406 p.*

SIGMUND FREUD (essay date 1928)

Four facets may be distinguished in the rich personality of Dostoevsky: the creative artist, the neurotic, the moralist and the sinner. How is one to find one's way in this bewildering complexity?

The creative artist is the least doubtful: Dostoevsky's place is not far behind Shakespeare. *The Brothers Karamazov* is the most magnificent novel ever written; the episode of the Grand Inquisitor, one of the peaks in the literature of the world, can hardly be valued too highly. Before the problem of the creative artist analysis must, alas, lay down its arms.

The moralist in Dostoevsky is the most readily assailable. If we seek to rank him high as a moralist on the plea that only a man who has gone through the depths of sin can reach the highest summit of morality, we are neglecting a doubt that arises. A moral man is one who reacts to temptation as soon as he feels it in his heart, without yielding to it. . . . He has not achieved the essence of morality, renunciation, for the moral conduct of life is a practical human interest. . . . Dostoevsky threw away the chance of becoming a teacher and liberator of humanity and made himself one with their gaolers. The future of human civilization will have little to thank him for. (pp. 222-23)

To consider Dostoevsky as a sinner or a criminal rouses violent opposition, which need not be based upon a philistine assessment of crime. The real motive for this opposition soon becomes apparent. Two traits are essential in a criminal: boundless egoism and a strong destructive impulse. Common to both of these, and a necessary condition for their expression, is absence of love, lack of an emotional appreciation of (human) objects. . . . [It] must be asked why there is any temptation to reckon Dostoevsky among the criminals. The answer is that it comes from his choice of material, which singles out from all others violent, murderous and egoistic characters, thus pointing to the existence of similar tendencies in his own soul, and also from certain facts in his life, like his passion for gambling and his possible admission of a sexual assault upon a young girl. The contradiction is resolved by the realization that Dostoevsky's very strong destructive instinct, which might easily have made him a criminal, was in his actual life directed mainly against his own person (inward instead of outward) and thus found expression as masochism and a sense of guilt. Nevertheless, his personality retained sadistic traits in plenty, which show themselves in his irritability, his love of tormenting and his intolerance even towards people he loved, and which appear also in the way in which, as an author, he treats his readers. Thus in little things he was a sadist towards others, and in bigger things a sadist towards himself, in fact a masochist, that is to say the mildest, kindliest, most helpful person possible.

We have selected three factors from Dostoevsky's complex personality, one quantitative and two qualitative: the extraordinary intensity of his emotional life, his perverse instinctual predisposition, which inevitably marked him out to be a sadomasochist or a criminal, and his unanalysable artistic endowment. . . . But the position is obscured by the simultaneous presence of neurosis, which, as we have said, was not in the circumstances inevitable, but which comes into being the more readily, the richer the complication which has to be mastered by the ego. For neurosis is after all only a sign that the ego has not succeeded in making a synthesis, that in attempting to do so it has forfeited its unity. (pp. 223-25)

[The] formula for Dostoevsky is as follows: a person of specially strong bisexual predisposition, who can defend himself with special intensity against dependence on a specially severe father. This characteristic of bisexuality comes as an addition to the components of his nature that we have already recognized. His early symptom of death-like seizures can thus be understood as a father-identification on the part of his ego, permitted by his super-ego as a punishment. 'You wanted to kill your father in order to be your father yourself. Now you *are* your father, but a dead father'—the regular mechanism of hysterical symptoms. And further: 'Now your father is killing

you.' For the ego the death symptom is a satisfaction in phantasy of the masculine wish and at the same time a masochistic satisfaction; for the super-ego it is a punishment satisfaction, that is, a sadistic satisfaction. Both of them, the ego and the super-ego, carry on the role of father.

To sum up, the relation between the subject and his father-object, while retaining its content, has been transformed into a relation between the ego and the super-ego—a new setting on a fresh stage. (p. 232)

It can scarcely be owing to chance that three of the masterpieces of the literature of all time—the *Oedipus Rex* of Sophocles, Shakespeare's *Hamlet,* and Dostoevsky's *The Brothers Karamazov*—should all deal with the same subject, parricide. In all three, moreover, the motive for the deed, sexual rivalry for a woman, is laid bare. (p. 235)

It is a matter of indifference who actually committed the crime [in *The Brothers Karamazov*], psychology is only concerned to know who desired it emotionally and who welcomed it when it was done. And for that reason all of the brothers, except the contrasted figure of Alyosha, are equally guilty, the impulsive sensualist, the sceptical cynic and the epileptic criminal. . . . Dostoevsky's sympathy for the criminal is, in fact, boundless; it goes far beyond the pity which the unhappy wretch might claim, and reminds us of the 'holy awe' with which epileptics and lunatics were regarded in the past. A criminal is to him almost a Redeemer, who has taken on himself the guilt which must else have been borne by others. There is no longer any need for one to murder, since *he* has already murdered; and one must be grateful to him, for, except for him, one would have been obliged oneself to murder. . . . This may perhaps be quite generally the mechanism of kindly sympathy with other people, a mechanism which one can discern with especial ease in the extreme case of the guilt-ridden novelist. There is no doubt that this sympathy by identification was a decisive factor in determining Dostoevsky's choice of material. He dealt first with the common criminal (whose motives are egotistical) and the political and religious criminal; and not until the end of his life did he come back to the primal criminal, the parricide, and use him, in a work of art, for making his confession. (pp. 236-37)

Sigmund Freud, "Dostoevsky and Parricide," translated by D. F. Tait (originally published as "Dostojewski und die Vatertötung," in Die Urgestalt der Brüder Karamazoff, *Piper, 1928), in his* Collected Papers: Miscellaneous Papers, 1888-1938, *Vol. 5, edited by Ernest Jones, M.D. and James Strachey (reprinted by permission of Basic Books, Inc., Publishers; in Canada by The Hogarth Press Ltd.), Basic Books by arrangement with The Hogarth Press Ltd. and The Institute of Psychoanalysis, 1959, pp. 222-42.*

VIRGINIA WOOLF (essay date 1929)

[Dostoevsky] strikes out a character or a scene by the use of glaring oppositions which are left unbridged. Extreme terms like 'love' and 'hate' are used so lavishly that we must race our imaginations to cover the ground between them. One feels that the mesh of civilization here is made of a coarse netting and the holes are wide apart. . . . [Men and women] are free to throw themselves from side to side, to gesticulate, to hiss, to rant, to fall into paroxysms of rage and excitement. They are free, with the freedom that violent emotion gives, from hesitation, from scruple, from analysis. At first we are amazed by the emptiness and the crudity of this world compared with the other. But when we have arranged our perspective a little, it is clear that we are still in the same world—that it is the mind which entices us and the adventures of the mind that concern us. Other worlds, such as Scott's or Defoe's, are incredible. Of this we are assured when we begin to encounter those curious contradictions of which Dostoevsky is so prolific. There is a simplicity in violence . . . , but violence also lays bare regions deep down in the mind where contradiction prevails. . . . The simplification is only on the surface; when the bold and ruthless process, which seems to punch out characters, then to group them together and then to set them all in violent motion, so energetically, so impatiently, is complete, we are shown how, beneath this crude surface, all is chaos and complication. (pp. 126-27)

[*The Possessed*] appears to be written by a fanatic ready to sacrifice skill and artifice in order to reveal the soul's difficulties and confusions. The novels of Dostoevsky are pervaded with mysticism; he speaks not as a writer but as a sage, sitting by the roadside in a blanket, with infinite knowledge and infinite patience. (p. 127)

But in a novel the voice of the teacher, however exalted, is not enough. We have too many interests to consider, too many problems to face. Consider a scene like that extraordinary party to which Varvara Petrovna has brought Marya, the lame idiot, whom Stavrogin has married 'from a passion for martyrdom, from a craving for remorse, through moral sensuality'. We cannot read to the end without feeling as if a thumb were pressing on a button in us, when we have no emotion left to answer the call. It is a day of surprises, a day of startling revelations, a day of strange coincidences. For several of the people there (and they come flocking to the room from all quarters) the scene has the greater emotional importance. Everything is done to suggest the intensity of their emotions. They turn pale; they shake with terror; they go into hysterics. (pp. 127-28)

Yet though they stamp and scream, we hear the sound as if it went on next door. Perhaps the truth is that hate, surprise, anger, horror, are all too strong to be felt continuously. This emptiness and noise lead us to wonder whether the novel of psychology, which projects its drama in the mind, should not, as the truth-tellers showed us, vary and diversify its emotions, lest we shall become numb with exhaustion. . . . [So] convinced is Dostoevsky of some point of truth that he sees before him, he will skip and leap to his conclusion with a spontaneity that is in itself stimulating.

By this distortion the psychologist reveals himself. The intellect, which analyses and discriminates, is always and almost at once overpowered by the rush to feeling; whether it is sympathy or anger. Hence, there is something illogical and contradictory often in the characters, perhaps because they are exposed to so much more than the usual current of emotional force. Why does he act like this? we ask again and again, and answer rather doubtfully, that so perhaps madmen act. (pp. 128-29)

[In Dostoevsky] there is always an overflow of emotion from the author as if characters of such subtlety and complexity could be created only when the rest of the book is a deep reservoir of thought and emotion. Thus, though the author himself is not present, characters like Stephen Trofimovitch . . . can exist only in a world made of the same stuff as they are, though left unformulated. The effect of this brooding and

analysing mind is always to produce an atmosphere of doubt, of questioning, of pain, perhaps of despair. (pp. 129-30)

Virginia Woolf, "Phases of Fiction" (originally published in The Bookman, *New York, Vol. LXIX, Nos. 2, 3 & 4, April, May & June, 1929), in her* Granite and Rainbow, *Harcourt, Brace & World, Inc., 1958, pp. 93-148.*

DMITRI CHIZHEVSKY   (essay date 1929)

Dostoevsky's style is based on an interpenetration of "naturalistic" and "unrealistic" elements. The ordinariness of everyday life is strangely shot through with the fantastic, naturalistic portrayal alternates with the pathos of an abstract idea, the sober striving for reality with ecstatic visions of the world beyond the confines of reality. Dostoevsky's power as an artist lies precisely in his ability to avoid mixing or confusing these sharply contradictory elements, and to succeed in weaving them together, fusing them into an organic unity. . . . The important thing for us is to recognize that Dostoevsky's "realistically psychological" analysis is at the same time also "transcendentally psychological," "existential," and that all events and the whole pattern of his theme are always an ideological construct as well. . . .

From the very first pages of *The Double* Dostoevsky insists that the meaning of the younger Golyadkin's appearance lies exclusively in the peculiar psychic "situation" of the elder Golyadkin, even though the strange event might well be explained on the plane of reality. Just as in *The Landlady* the fantastic scenes appear always on the background of the almost delirious state of Ordynov, so also Golyadkin's double appears to him first while he is in an abnormal state of mind. . . . (p. 114)

Mr. Golyadkin's double—whatever may be the status of his physical reality—is conditioned psychologically: it rises from the depths of Golyadkin's soul. Even if one could show from the point of view of psychopathology that there is a causal necessity for this appearance, it matters only that Golyadkin's psychic situation, depicted at the beginning, must inevitably lead to a tragic end. At the beginning of the story the delusion has not yet entered Golyadkin's soul. But even then his whole behavior testifies to the pathological character of his split personality. Dostoevsky has us meet his hero at the moment when he has to make a decision, when he is getting ready for an action that is to change his whole life. He behaves "as if" he had such a plan. But only—"as if." His very first steps show that he is by nature incapable of making a decision. . . .

In the second part of *The Double,* after the appearance of the double, Dostoevsky gives at last—through Golyadkin—a formula containing the idea of his work. Against the background of the same constant vacillation between decisiveness and passive withdrawal, between "humility" and pathological retreat from imaginary or real dangers, a new and much deeper tone is sounded. Mr. Golyadkin's double crowds him out of all spheres of his life; he replaces, "impersonates," him in the office and with his fellow clerks, and in his "private life" in the family of Olsufy Ivanovich; or, as Golyadkin phrases it: "he forcibly enters the circle of my existence and of all my relations in practical life." (p. 115)

In order to make it perfectly clear that what matters is not the behavior of a real younger Golyadkin, but rather the feelings and introspection of the older Golyadkin, Dostoevsky expounds the same situation in a (consciously unreal) dream of the older

Golyadkin. In this dream the younger Golyadkin "takes his place in the service and in society" and succeeds in proving that "Golyadkin Senior was not the genuine one at all, but the sham, and that he—Golyadkin Junior—was the real one." Finally the Golyadkins multiply indefinitely. . . .

This weird dream is the center of the work. The answer to the question of "one's own place" is clear. Golyadkin (and here lies his typical—or, as Dostoevsky says, "social"—significance) has no place of his own, he has never achieved one in his life, he has no "sphere" of his own in life except possibly the corner behind the cupboard or the stove where he hides from the imaginary persecutions of his enemies. . . . There is something inhuman, thing-like in this lack of a place of one's own. (Golyadkin feels that he is being treated like a "rag.") The appearance of the double and his success in squeezing out Golyadkin from his place only shows that Golyadkin's place was completely illusory to begin with. For even the double can keep all his "places"—from the office to his Excellency's cabinet—only through the purely external traits of his character: by the flattery and servility which the older Golyadkin would have liked to master himself but which are no less superficial, unessential, and inhuman and incapable of ensuring him a "place" in life. Here Dostoevsky raises the ethical and ontological problems of the fixity, reality, and security of individual existence—surely one of the most genuine problems of ethics. The reality of human personality cannot be secured simply on the empirical plane of existence but needs also other (non-empirical) conditions and presuppositions. (p. 116)

> *Dmitri Chizhevsky, in his essay (reprinted by permission of the Estate of Dmitri Chizhevsky), in* O Dostoevskom: Sbornik Statei, *edited by A. L. Bem, Sklad uzd F. Svoboda, 1929 (translated by René Wellek and reprinted as "The Theme of the Double in Dostoevsky," in* Dostoevsky: A Collection of Critical Essays, *edited by René Wellek, Prentice-Hall, Inc., 1962, pp. 112-29).*

THE TIMES LITERARY SUPPLEMENT (essay date 1930)

It is common to say, in explanation of the white-hot intensity of Dostoevsky's ideological world, that he *felt* ideas; but it is perhaps more to the point to note that he invariably spiritualized ideas in his novels. He is, indeed, so thorough in this respect that his men and women are not so much men and women as human souls; they live in a region of experience from which all the accidents of human circumstance appear to have been eliminated and in which only the soul survives. From beginning to end the novel for Dostoevsky is a history of the soul. . . . More than any other novelist of the last century Dostoevsky helped to weaken the formal restraints of imaginative literature and to break down the conventional discipline of fiction. Under his influence the novel definitely ceased to be one of several distinct types, romantic novel, realistic novel, psychological novel, novel of adventure—**"Crime and Punishment"** was all these. It became something problematical, something specially interpretative of life: the question "What is a novel?" echoes the question "What is life?" What happened in effect, as the result of Dostoevsky's researches into the soul, was that artistic reality for the novelist tended to approximate more and more closely to spiritual reality—or to ideas of spiritual reality. . . .

[It] is by no means impossible to trace the legacy bequeathed by Dostoevsky to our novelists. It is not, perhaps, a strictly definable legacy; it is something in the air, a layer of the atmosphere in which the novelist breathes. Dostoevsky's preoc-cupation with the soul is, however, a definite starting-point for many of our novelists, who, having been brought there, move off in a direction of their own—doubtless more nearly parallel, if the Russian comparison is to be pursued, to Tolstoy or to Tchehov than to Dostoevsky. The naked soul, the metaphysical sensation of existence, the moral justification for this or that principle in human affairs—these are the dominant spiritual elements, one is inclined to say, in Dostoevsky's novels. . . .

Life at any given moment, the novelists say now, is not necessarily a link in a story with beginning, middle and end. What seems to be important is, not the few carefully chosen situations on which the story-teller must concentrate his vision of life, but the reality, the inward truthfulness and comprehensiveness of the vision he imparts. Truly the novel has changed in the last half-century in response to the stimulus of "War and Peace" and **"The Brothers Karamazov."**

Equally truly the novel is still changing. It is a living thing, forced to keep pace with other living things in a changing world. No influence lasts for ever; and perhaps no literary influence endures undiminished for more than one generation of writers. The example of the Russian novelists, and of Dostoevsky in particular, seems to have spent itself; it is a decaying influence at the present day. (p. 465)

Can we recapture the giddy excitement with which we first read Dostoevsky? Can we again respond so breathlessly to those bewildering novels? For that is what we remember best of all— our own nervous tension, the sensation of tumult, of chaos, of being caught up in a torrent, a storm of ideas, hurled into Heaven knows what struggle, battered by the winds of passion raging about us, emerging at last with senses dazed and mind confounded. Can we re-read those novels with the same sense of fatality, the same heightened awareness of the human soul in its moments of crisis? Let us consider the four great novels— **"Crime and Punishment," "The Idiot," "The Possessed,"** and **"The Brothers Karamazov."** How do they strike us today? Looking back at that vast and sombre stretch of country, we become aware of the peculiar bareness, the gloom and aridity of the scene. There are no pleasant places on which the eye can rest; there is no bright, natural colour in the entire landscape to relieve or distract our senses. Dostoevsky has few of the graces of literary art. His method is to pile up details in mountainous confusion. He is indifferent to the ordinary niceties of life: he has no feeling for form, no use for fancy; he is never light, never at ease, never at rest. He is without reticence and without discipline; ideas and passions tumble over one another in the wildest disorder, as though pressing towards some unknown destination. The intensity never abates, the speed never slackens. His characters are perpetually weeping tears of joy, tears of humiliation; they see visions and experience ecstacy; they aspire to be saints and are pursued by devils; they are for ever planning a universe in which there is no pain, or in which children do not weep, or in which love and sin and suffering are not inextricably mingled in someone's soul; they live perpetually on the edge of a volcano. Dostoevsky's nerves are always on edge; driven by obscure impulses, he cannot stop to compose himself. One of our strongest impressions is the frantic haste with which we have travelled through this strange territory. (pp. 465-66)

But the queer mounting excitement with which we first read him has not been destroyed, although, strangely enough, as we continue to read we now have the sensation that something unexpected is happening to us. The sensation grows more acute; this is excitement with a difference. Again we pause; again we look back on Dostoevsky's world. The unearthly light—to continue the metaphor—takes us for a moment completely unawares; we had not imagined it was quite so unearthly as that, or that the soul and the soul's salvation were so unrelated to earthly things. We were prepared in some measure for the distortion of the scene, for the exaggerated or grotesque appearance of every natural feature; but the abnormality of everything human suddenly strikes us as a travesty of human nature. . . .

It is easy, of course, to dismiss the world of Dostoevsky's imagining as a mere product of intellectual sensationalism by approaching it from a strictly naturalistic standpoint. It is not a part of Russia that the Karamazovs inhabit; it is a sort of waste land halfway between pathology and mysticism. There is some danger of denying it any significance at all; but there is a greater danger—to which many of us have succumbed at some time or other—of discovering in it a sort of promised land of literature. Dostoevsky's spiritual excesses are admittedly illuminating, but they are excesses. . . .

The test after all, is this: do we really believe in **"Crime and Punishment,"** for instance? Do we feel nowadays that these murders and sufferings and renunciations, these bouts of lacerating remorse and agonized argumentation, this prodigious assertion of the will and spectacular redemption of the moral sense—do we feel that these are true to experience? Is Raskolnikov's problem a real one? On a symbolical plane, yes, if you like; the novel is a novel of ideas, of metaphysical symbols, a history of the soul. . . . Now that we have recovered from the first shock of discovery, to what extent are we moved or convinced by the agonies and strivings of Dostoevsky's search for the absolute? . . .

Dostoevsky's profundities, we can realize now, are shallower than we had thought. It is not the flash of mysticism, not the sudden cry of agony or vision of beatitude—for these are in the last resort of doubtful integrity—which impresses us; it is the dramatic use to which the author puts them in a tale of crime or pathological obsession. No novelist has excelled Dostoevsky in the dramatic manipulation of extreme states of mind. . . .

[Dostoevsky] was a genius for immensities and incomprehensibles. Of the most intellectually adventurous of his heroes, Ivan Karamazov, it may be said that he repudiated all human values for life and "returned God his ticket" until such time as other and more perfect values might be established on earth. His was a large programme, and there is something awful and intimidating in the largeness of it. Dostoevsky's artistic programme is not dissimilar in this respect. He awes and intimidates by the boundlessness of his inquiries about the soul. His variations on the spiritual nature of man are illuminating, bewildering, exciting, stimulating, somewhat terrifying. They do not necessarily correspond to any reality in human experience.

His influence on the novel presents a strange paradox: it is founded on precisely that aspect of his achievement which is most open to suspicion. It is what Dostoevsky tried but failed to do, not what he genuinely accomplished, that has proved so powerful an inspiration. His desire to map out the whole uncharted territory of the human spirit erred on the side of rashness and pretentiousness, but it served as an example for writers of a less fevered turn of mind. Dostoevsky discovered no new ultimate values; he only affirmed the existence of the ultimate. Nor did he bring the soul into fiction; he merely sought to exclude everything else from it. It is in the looseness

and formlessness of the contemporary novel that we can find the clearest evidence of the effect he has had; it is in the growing emphasis on artistic form that we can detect the failure of his type of symbolism. It was, that is to say, his technical method as a novelist, not the sort of spiritual reality he postulated, which gave the novel new boundaries and a new vitality. He has bequeathed to later novelists the ambition to discover a less questionable reality in the region of experience he so ingeniously explored. (p. 466)

"Dostoevsky and the Novel," in The Times Literary Supplement (© *Times Newspapers Ltd. (London) 1930; reproduced from* The Times Literary Supplement *by permission), No. 1479, June 5, 1930, pp. 465-66.*

D. H. LAWRENCE (essay date 1930)

It is a strange experience, to examine one's reaction to a book over a period of years. I remember when I first read *The Brothers Karamazov,* in 1913, how fascinated yet unconvinced it left me. . . .

The story seemed to me just a piece of showing off: a display of cynical-satanical pose which was simply irritating. The cynical-satanical pose always irritated me, and I could see nothing else in that black-a-vised Grand Inquisitor talking at Jesus at such length. I just felt it was all pose; he didn't really mean what he said; he was just showing off in blasphemy.

Since then I have read *The Brothers Karamazov* twice, and each time found it more depressing because, alas, more drearily true to life. At first it had been lurid romance. Now I read *The Grand Inquisitor* once more, and my heart sinks right through my shoes. I still see a trifle of cynical-satanical showing-off. But under that I hear the final and unanswerable criticism of Christ. . . .

If there is any question: Who is the grand Inquisitor?—then surely we must say it is Ivan himself. And Ivan is the thinking mind of the human being in rebellion, thinking the whole thing out to the bitter end. . . .

And we cannot doubt that the Inquisitor speaks Dostoievsky's own final opinion about Jesus. The opinion is, baldly, this: Jesus, you are inadequate. (p. 283)

We may agree with Dostoievsky or not, but we have to admit that his criticism of Jesus is the final criticism, based on the experience of two thousand years (he says fifteen hundred) and on a profound insight into the nature of mankind. Man can but be true to his own nature. No inspiration whatsoever will ever get him permanently beyond his limits.

And what are the limits? It is Dostoievsky's first profound question. What are the limits to the nature, not of Man in the abstract, but of men, mere men, everyday men?

The limits are, says the Grand Inquisitor, three. Mankind in the bulk can never be "free," because man on the whole makes three grand demands on life, and cannot endure unless these demands are satisfied.

1. He demands bread, and not merely as foodstuff, but as a miracle, given from the hand of God.

2. He demands mystery, the sense of the miraculous in life.

3. He demands somebody to bow down to, and somebody before whom all men shall bow down.

These three demands, for miracle, mystery and authority, prevent men from being "free." They are man's "weakness." Only a few men, the elect, are capable of abstaining from the absolute demand for bread, for miracle, mystery, and authority. These are the strong, and they must be as gods, to be able to be Christians fulfilling all the Christ-demand. The rest, the millions and millions of men throughout time, they are as babes or children or geese, they are too weak, "impotent, vicious, worthless and rebellious" even to be able to share out the earthly bread, if it is left to them.

This, then, is the Grand Inquisitor's summing-up of the nature of mankind. The inadequacy of Jesus lies in the fact that Christianity is too difficult for men, the vast mass of men. . . .

Christianity, then, is the ideal, but it is impossible. It is impossible because it makes demands greater than the nature of man can bear. And therefore, to get a livable, working scheme, some of the elect, such as the Grand Inquisitor himself, have turned round to "him," that other great Spirit, Satan, and have established Church and State on "him." For the Grand Inquisitor finds that to be able to live at all, mankind must be loved more tolerantly and more contemptuously than Jesus loved it, loved, for all that, more truly, since it is loved for itself, for what it is, and not for what it ought to be. (pp. 284-85)

As always in Dostoievsky, the amazing perspicacity is mixed with ugly perversity. Nothing is pure. His wild love for Jesus is mixed with perverse and poisonous hate of Jesus: his moral hostility to the devil is mixed with secret worship of the devil. . . .

Dostoievsky's diagnosis of human nature is simple and unanswerable. We have to submit, and agree that men are like that. Even over the question of sharing the bread, we have to agree that man is too weak, or vicious, or something, to be able to do it. He has to hand the common bread over to some absolute authority, Tsar or Lenin, to be shared out. And yet the mass of men are *incapable* of looking on bread as a mere means of sustenance, by which man sustains himself for the purpose of true living, true life being the "heavenly bread." It seems a strange thing that men, the mass of men, cannot understand that *life* is the great reality, that true living fills us with vivid life, "the heavenly bread," and earthly bread merely supports this. (p. 285)

Dostoievsky was perhaps the first to realise this devastating truth, which Christ had not seen. A truth it is, none the less, and once recognised it will change the course of history. All that remains is for the elect to take charge of the bread—the property, the money—and then give it back to the masses as if it were really the gift of life. In this way, mankind might live happily, as the Inquisitor suggests. . . .

So far, well and good, Dostoievsky's diagnosis stands. But is it then to betray Christ and turn over to Satan if the elect should at last realise that instead of refusing Satan's three offers, the heroic Christian must now accept them. . . . But we now realize, no man, not even Jesus, is really "above" miracle, mystery, and authority. The one thing that Jesus is truly above, is the confusion between money and life. Money is not life, says Jesus, therefore you can ignore it and leave it to the devil.

Money is not life, it is true. But ignoring money and leaving it to the devil means handing over the great mass of men to the devil, for the mass of men *cannot* distinguish between money and life. It is hard to believe: certainly Jesus didn't believe it: and yet, as Dostoievsky and the Inquisitor point out, it is so.

Well, and what then? Must we therefore go over to the devil? After all, the whole of Christianity is not contained in the rejection of the three temptations. The essence of Christianity is a love of mankind. If a love of mankind entails accepting the bitter limitation of the mass of men, their inability to distinguish between money and life, then accept the limitation, and have done with it. Then take over from the devil the money (or bread), the miracle, and the sword of Cæsar, and, for the love of mankind, give back to men the bread, with its wonder, and give them the miracle, the marvellous, and give them, in a hierarchy, someone, some men, in higher and higher degrees, to bow down to. (p. 286)

And is that serving the devil? It is certainly not serving the spirit of annihilation and not-being. It is serving the great wholeness of mankind, and in that respect, it is Christianity. Anyhow, it is the service of Almighty God, who made men what they are, limited and unlimited.

Where Dostoievsky is perverse is in his making the old, old, wise governor of men a Grand Inquisitor. . . .

The man who feels a certain tenderness for mankind in its weakness or limitation is not therefore diabolic. The man who realises that Jesus asked too much of the mass of men, in asking them to choose between earthly and heavenly bread, and to judge between good and evil, is not therefore satanic. (p. 287)

[The] Inquisitor says that it is a weakness in men, that they must have miracle, mystery and authority. But is it? Are they not bound up in our emotions, always and for ever, these three demands of miracle, mystery, and authority? . . .

The thing Jesus was trying to do was to supplant physical emotion by moral emotion. So that earthly bread becomes, in a sense, immoral, as it is to many refined people to-day. The Inquisitor sees that this is the mistake. The earthly bread must in itself be the miracle, and be bound up with the miracle.

And here, surely, he is right. Since man began to think and to feel vividly, seed-time and harvest have been the two great sacred periods of miracle, rebirth, and rejoicing. Easter and harvest-home are festivals of the earthly bread, and they are festivals which go to the roots of the soul. For it is the earthly bread as a miracle, a yearly miracle. (p. 288)

The earthly bread is leavened with the heavenly bread. The heavenly bread is life, is contact, and is consciousness. In sowing the seed man has his contact with earth, with sun and rain: and he *must not* break the contact. . . .

Miracle and mystery run together, they merge. Then there is the third thing, authority. The word is bad: a policeman has authority, and no one bows down to him. The Inquisitor means: "that which men bow down to." Well, they bowed down to Caesar, and they bowed down to Jesus. They will bow down, first, as the Inquisitor saw, to the one who has the power to control the bread. . . .

How profound Dostoievsky is when he says that the people will forget that it is their own bread which is being given back to them. While they keep their own bread, it is not much better than stone to them—inert possessions. But given back to them from the great Giver, it is divine once more, it has the quality of miracle to make it taste well in the mouth and in the belly.

Men bow down to the lord of bread, first and foremost. For, by knowing the difference between earthly and heavenly bread, he is able calmly to distribute the earthly bread, and to give it, for the commonalty, the heavenly taste which they can never give it. (pp. 289-90)

It is not man's weakness that he needs someone to bow down to. It is his nature, and his strength, for it puts him into touch with far, far greater life than if he stood alone. All life bows to the sun. But the sun is very far away to the common man. It needs someone to bring it to him. It needs a lord: what the Christians call one of the elect, to bring the sun to the common man, and put the sun in his heart. The sight of a true lord, a noble, a nature-hero puts the sun into the heart of the ordinary man, who is no hero, and therefore cannot know the sun direct.

This is one of the real mysteries. As the Inquisitor says, the mystery of the elect is one of the inexplicable mysteries of Christianity, just as the lord, the natural lord among men, is one of the inexplicable mysteries of humanity throughout time. We must accept the mystery, that's all.

But to do so is not diabolic.

And Ivan need not have been so tragic and satanic. He had made a discovery about men, which was due to be made. It was the rediscovery of a fact which was known universally almost till the end of the eighteenth century, when the illusion of the perfectibility of men, of all men, took hold of the imagination of the civilised nations. It was an illusion. And Ivan has to make a restatement of the old truth, that most men *cannot* choose between good and evil, because it is so extremely difficult to know which is which, especially in crucial cases: and that most men *cannot* see the difference between life-values and money-values: they can only see money-values; even nice simple people who *live* by the life-values, kind and natural, yet can only estimate value in terms of money. So let the specially gifted few make the decision between good and evil, and establish the life-values against the money-values. And let the many accept the decision, with gratitude, and bow down to the few, in the hierarchy. What is there diabolical or satanic in that? (p. 290)

> *D. H. Lawrence, "Preface to 'The Grand Inquisitor'" (originally published as his preface to* The Grand Inquisitor *by Fedor Mikhailovich Dostoevskii, translated by S. S. Koteliansky, E. Mathews & Marrot, 1930), in* Phoenix: The Posthumous Papers of D. H. Lawrence, *edited by Edward D. McDonald (copyright 1936 by Frieda Lawrence; copyright renewed © 1964 by the Estate of the late Frieda Lawrence Ravagli; reprinted by permission of Viking Penguin Inc.), Viking Penguin 1936, William Heinemann, 1936, pp. 283-91.*

ERNEST J. SIMMONS (essay date 1940)

[One must] refuse to designate Dostoevski by any of the commonly accepted names which we apply to the literary artist and thinker. His divided soul rendered him incapable of unbroken allegiance to any credo of art or philosophy. Tolstoi said of him that his whole life was a struggle between good and evil, which is as true for the great characters of his novels as for their creator. Out of this struggle came his lifelong search for freedom—moral and spiritual freedom. . . . From the very beginning of his creative life, Dostoevski had profoundly distrusted the capacity of the intellect to establish those principles by which men may live in universal peace and happiness. He

felt that hate, not love, was the medium through which the socialists would attempt to achieve the unification of man. They did not understand that love, like God, was apprehended by the heart, not by the reason. This conviction led him to God and to His religion, for he perceived that without religion, morality was impossible. (pp. 386-87)

Often the famous works of an artist seem infinitely nobler than their creator; in the same sense, the novels of Dostoevski are more noble than the man himself and will outlive his religious and social thinking. Intellectuality can never be the sole measure of a great novelist; he achieves immortality, as it were, in spite of it. It is no mere accident or paradox that Dostoevski, a powerful if sometimes inconsistent thinker, should have been so deeply sceptical of reason as a key to the understanding of the individual and of life itself. His personal dualism continually led him into an impasse between the head and the heart. If God seemed to be the ultimate irrationality of man's mind, an unreasoning faith in Him appeared to be absolutely essential to assure the harmony of man's relation to the world in which he lived. Although Dostoevski's finest characters, the Doubles, reflect the mental struggle of his own split personality, his heart went out to his Meek creations, whose spirituality and goodness are expressed not through ratiocination, but through an outpouring of moral feeling.

Feeling, however, is not confined to the Meek characters, for the whole intellectual climate of Dostoevski's fiction is pervaded by it in the sense that he *felt* his thoughts. All the ordinary surface features of the consummate novelist he possessed to an extraordinary degree, but this quality of *feeling* suffuses them and gives to his best productions a high seriousness and a sense of vital experience. Unlike the rationalist, Ivan Karamazov, Dostoevski was more concerned with life than with the meaning of life. If he regarded life as a mystery, he did not seek to explain by reason what reason is powerless to explain. Life never became an abstraction, void of sense and value. Although he is commonly accepted as one of the most eminent precursors of the so-called psychological novelists, unlike many modern writers, he did not allow psychological analysis to become an end in itself. He emphatically believed that the novelist's business was not simply to explain life, but to see that life was lived in his books. . . . In his own life, he was never afraid of expressing his genuine feelings, sentiments, and emotions, nor did he ever deny these profoundly human attributes to the creatures of his imagination. If he is ever happy, he tells us, it is during the long nights when he sits with these men and women of his fancy as he would with real individuals. He loves them, rejoices and grows sad with them, and at times he even weeps sincere tears over their misfortunes. This is what is meant by *feeling*. He imaginatively and emotionally identifies himself with his characters, with all their experiences and actions. Even their political, religious, and social theories he apprehends passionately and sensitively so that they never seem like cold, artificial products of the mind. This quality of *feeling*, which we never fail to identify with life itself, contributes perhaps more than anything else to the deep and abiding experience we enjoy in reading his great novels. (pp. 387-89)

> *Ernest J. Simmons, in his* Dostoevski: The Making of a Novelist *(reprinted by permission of the Estate of Ernest J. Simmons), Oxford University Press, New York, 1940, 416 p.*

MONROE C. BEARDSLEY (essay date 1942)

The Russian title of the *Notes from Underground, Zapiski iz podpolya,* suggests (*pod,* "under"; *pol,* "floor") vermin spawning and wriggling like maggots in the dark under the boards, gnawing at the foundations of a house and peering out with bloodshot eyes through grimy cracks, brooding over destruction and chaos with a rat-like intensity, perverseness, and resentment against the forces that keep them imprisoned. . . . [It] is in the *Notes* that [Dostoyevsky] permits the undergroundling to draw his own portrait, which is filled in later with the browbeaten, mean, small, and narrow souls who swarm in all the novels and stories.

The undergroundling is, in his first embodiment, preëminently the man-worm, the common denominator of humanity, who is like everyone else and whose only motive is to be "original," that is, to do something—anything—which might for a moment relieve him of his terrible burden of nonentity. (p. 266)

The undergroundling is the cowed man; lacking any shred of individuality to distinguish him from his mob of brothers, he has only a raw pride that is continually trampled on by those who are cleverer, richer, bolder than himself. . . . [He] has no position and is the object of a universal contempt, which drives him into his lonely attic or compels him to wander feverishly about the Petersburg streets, and which builds in him that curious pride in loneliness which is the mark of the worm about to turn. For this absolute degradation of ugliness, awkwardness and poverty nourishes the seed of revolt in the peculiar resentment of the undergroundling. (p. 267)

Like the little outrages that break out all through *The Possessed,* his impulses are "quite unprovoked and objectless," quite irrational and pointless. That is, they have no motive or end other than the act itself. He will steal an apple, not for the fruit but for the theft, and if he is caught and punished, so much the better, for that proves he has bothered someone. . . . The undergroundling has chaos in his heart; he craves suffering and disorder as well as joy and peace. It is feeling itself which he needs, not any special quality of feeling, because if the feeling is sharp he escapes boredom and becomes a person. . . . The undergroundling's revolt against order is objectified in the demon within him who, at certain times, is projected as a second self. Stavrogin tells us that his devil is an undergroundling— "a little nasty, scrofulous imp, with a cold in his head, one of the unsuccessful ones." Ivan's devil appears as a poor relation who is the "incarnation" of his own "thoughts and feelings, but only the nastiest and stupidest of them." He is the "indispensable minus" which preserves the undergroundling from the universal reign of "good sense." (pp. 268-69)

[To] every manner in which the undergroundling is chained there corresponds a freedom to be won—freedom from economic exploitation, from political domination, from the necessity of choosing according to one's strongest motive, from the threat of science to predict the future, from, in short, all shapes and appearances of the drive of rationalism to render the world completely understood, ordered, and reasonable. In essence, the undergroundling's groping path is toward the truth, beyond "twice two is four," which holds in the four-dimensional world of God. (p. 269)

Monroe C. Beardsley, "Dostoyevsky's Metaphor of the 'Underground'," in Journal of the History of Ideas, *Vol. III, No. 3, June, 1942, pp. 265-90.*

KONSTANTIN MOCHULSKY (essay date 1942)

In Dostoevsky's novels there are no landscapes and pictures of nature. He portrays only man and man's world; his heroes are people from contemporary urban civilization, fallen out of the natural world-order and torn away from "living life." The writer prided himself on his *realism;* he was describing not the abstract "universal man," contrived by J. J. Rousseau, but the real European of the 19th century with all the endless contradictions of his "sick consciousness." The Russian novelist first discovered the real face of the hero of our "troubled time"—the "man from underground": this new Hamlet is struck by the infirmity of doubt, poisoned by reflection, doomed to a lack of will and inertia. He is tragically alone and divided in two; he has the consciousness of an "harassed mouse." (p. 649)

Special commentaries exist on Dostoevsky, the psychopathologist and criminalist. But his analysis was not limited to individual psychology; he penetrated the collective psychology of the family, of society, of the people. His greatest insights concern the soul of the people, the metapsychic "unity" of mankind.

Psychology is only the surface of Dostoevsky's art. It was for him not an end, but a means. The province of the inner life is only the vestibule of the kingdom of the spirit. Behind the psychologist stands the *pneumatologist*—the brilliant investigator of the human spirit. . . . Dostoevsky had his own doctrine of man—and in this is his great historical importance. He devoted all his creative forces to struggling for the spiritual nature of man, to defending his dignity, personality, and freedom.

In his own personal experience, the author of *Crime and Punishment* lived through the tragic epoch of the *shattering of humanism.* Before his eyes humanism tore itself away from its Christian roots and was transformed into a struggle with God. Having begun with the emancipation of man from "theology" and "metaphysics," it ended by enslaving him to the "laws of nature" and "necessity." Man was conceived as a natural being, subject to the principles of profit and rational egoism: his metaphysical depth was taken away from him, his third dimension—the image of God. Humanism wanted to exalt man and shamefully degraded him. Dostoevsky himself was a humanist, passed through its seductions and was infected by its poison. (pp. 649-50)

Dostoevsky lived through a period of crisis in Christian culture and experienced it as his personal tragedy. (pp. 650-51)

The Russian Dostoevsky, at the end of the 19th century, felt himself the only European who understood the significance of the world tragedy, which was being experienced by mankind. He alone "wept real tears." And now the "old idea" was gone and mankind was left on earth without God. The writer's "novel-tragedies" are devoted to depicting the fate of *mankind abandoned by God.* He prophetically indicated two paths: mangodhood and the herd.

Kirilov in *The Devils* declares: "If God doesn't exist, then I am God." In place of the God-man appears the man-god, the "strong personality," who stands beyond morality, "beyond the confines of good and evil," to whom "everything is permitted" and who can "transgress" all laws (Raskolnikov, Rogozhin, Kirilov, Stavrogin, Ivan Karamazov). Dostoevsky made one of his greatest discoveries: *the nature of man is correlative to the nature of God;* if there is no God, there is also no man.

In the man-god, the new demonic being, everything human must disappear. (p. 651)

The other path of atheistic mankind leads to the herd. The culmination of Dostoevsky's work is the *Legend of the Grand Inquisitor*. If men are only natural beings, if their souls are not immortal, then it is fitting that they be established on earth with the greatest possible well-being. And since by their nature they are "impotent rebels," then one must enslave and transform them into a submissive herd. The Grand Inquisitor will tend them with an iron rod. Then at last, an enormous anthill will be built up, the Babylonian tower will be erected, and now forever. Both ways—man-godhood and the herd—lead to one and the same result: the suppression of man.

Dostoevsky saw history in the light of the Apocalypse; he predicted unheard-of world catastrophes. "The end of the world is coming," he wrote. "The end of the century will be marked by a calamity, the likes of which has never yet occurred." The tragic world-outlook of the author of *The Devils* was inaccessible to the positivists of the 19th century: he was a man of our catastrophic epoch. But God's abandonment is not the last word of Dostoevsky's work; he depicted the "dark night," but had presentiments of the dawn. He believed that the tragedy of history would be culminated in the transfiguration of the world, that after the Golgotha of mankind would follow the Second Advent of Christ and "there would resound the hymn of the new and last resurrection."

To Dostoevsky belongs a place beside the great Christian writers of world literature: Dante, Cervantes, Milton, Pascal. Like Dante, he passed through all the circles of human hell, one more terrible than the mediaeval hell of the *Divine Comedy*, and was not consumed in hell's flame: his *duca e maestro* was not Virgil, but the "radiant image" of the Christ, love for whom was the greatest love of his whole life. (pp. 651-52)

> *Konstantin Mochulsky, "Conclusion" (1942), in his* Dostoevsky: His Life and Work, *translated by Michael A. Minihan (translation copyright © 1967 by Princeton University Press; reprinted by permission of Princeton University Press; originally published as* Dostoïevskii, *YMCA Press, 1947), Princeton University Press, 1967, pp. 649-50.*

ALBERT CAMUS (essay date 1942)

All of Dostoevsky's heroes question themselves as to the meaning of life. In this they are modern: they do not fear ridicule. What distinguishes modern sensibility from classical sensibility is that the latter thrives on moral problems and the former on metaphysical problems. In Dostoevsky's novels the question is propounded with such intensity that it can only invite extreme solutions. Existence is illusory *or* it is eternal. If Dostoevsky were satisfied with this inquiry, he would be a philosopher. But he illustrates the consequences that such intellectual pastimes may have in a man's life, and in this regard he is an artist. Among those consequences, his attention is arrested particularly by the last one, which he himself calls logical suicide in his *Diary of a Writer*. (p. 104)

[The] same theme is embodied . . . with the most wonderful generality, in Kirilov of *The Possessed*, likewise an advocate of logical suicide. Kirilov the engineer declares somewhere that he wants to take his own life because it "is his idea." Obviously the word must be taken in its proper sense. It is for an idea, a thought, that he is getting ready for death. This is the superior suicide. . . . He feels that God is necessary and that he must exist. But he knows that he does not and cannot exist. "Why do you not realize," he exclaims, "that this is sufficient reason for killing oneself?" That attitude involves likewise for him some of the absurd consequences. Through indifference he accepts letting his suicide be used to the advantage of a cause he despises. "I decided last night that I didn't care." And finally he prepares his deed with a mixed feeling of revolt and freedom. "I shall kill myself in order to assert my insubordination, my new and dreadful liberty." It is no longer a question of revenge, but of revolt. Kirilov is consequently an absurd character—yet with this essential reservation: he kills himself. But he himself explains this contradiction, and in such a way that at the same time he reveals the absurd secret in all its purity. In truth, he adds to his fatal logic an extraordinary ambition which gives the character its full perspective: he wants to kill himself to become god.

The reasoning is classic in its clarity. If God does not exist, Kirilov is god. If God does not exist, Kirilov must kill himself. Kirilov must therefore kill himself to become god. That logic is absurd, but it is what is needed. The interesting thing, however, is to give a meaning to that divinity brought to earth. That amounts to clarifying the premise: "If God does not exist, I am god," which still remains rather obscure. It is important to note at the outset that the man who flaunts that mad claim is indeed of this world. . . . Of the superman he has nothing but the logic and the obsession, whereas of man he has the whole catalogue. Yet it is he who speaks calmly of his divinity. He is not mad, or else Dostoevsky is. (pp. 105-07)

Kirilov himself helps us to understand. In reply to a question from Stavrogin, he makes clear that he is not talking of a god-man. It might be thought that this springs from concern to distinguish himself from Christ. But in reality it is a matter of annexing Christ. Kirilov in fact fancies for a moment that Jesus at his death *did not find himself in Paradise*. He found out then that his torture had been useless. "The laws of nature," says the engineer, "made Christ live in the midst of falsehood and die for a falsehood." Solely in this sense Jesus indeed personifies the whole human drama. He is the complete man, being the one who realized the most absurd condition. He is not the God-man but the man-god. And, like him, each of us can be crucified and victimized—and is to a certain degree.

The divinity in question is therefore altogether terrestrial. "For three years," says Kirilov, "I sought the attribute of my divinity and I have found it. The attribute of my divinity is independence." Now can be seen the meaning of Kirilov's premise: "If God does not exist, I am god." To become god is merely to be free on this earth, not to serve an immortal being. Above all, of course, it is drawing all the inferences from that painful independence. If God exists, all depends on him and we can do nothing against his will. If he does not exist, everything depends on us. For Kirilov, as for Nietzsche, to kill God is to become god oneself; it is to realize on this earth the eternal life of which the Gospel speaks.

But if this metaphysical crime is enough for man's fulfillment, why add suicide? Why kill oneself and leave this world after having won freedom? That is contradictory. Kirilov is well aware of this, for he adds: "If you feel *that*, you are a tsar and, far from killing yourself, you will live covered with glory." But men in general do not know it. They do not feel "that." As in the time of Prometheus, they entertain blind hopes. They need to be shown the way and cannot do without preaching. Consequently, Kirilov must kill himself out of love for humanity. (pp. 107-08)

This theme of suicide in Dostoevsky, then, is indeed an absurd theme. Let us merely note before going on that Kirilov reappears in other characters who themselves set in motion additional absurd themes. Stavrogin and Ivan Karamazov try out the absurd truths in practical life. They are the ones liberated by Kirilov's death. (p. 109)

Thus the novels, like the *Diary,* propound the absurd question. They establish logic unto death, exaltation, "dreadful" freedom, the glory of the tsars become human. All is well, everything is permitted, and nothing is hateful—these are absurd judgments. But what an amazing creation in which those creatures of fire and ice seem so familiar to us. The passionate world of indifference that rumbles in their hearts does not seem at all monstrous to us. We recognize in it our everyday anxieties. And probably no one so much as Dostoevsky has managed to give the absurd world such familiar and tormenting charms.

Yet what is his conclusion? Two quotations will show the complete metaphysical reversal that leads the writer to other revelations. The argument of the one who commits logical suicide having provoked protests from the critics, Dostoevsky in the following installments of the *Diary* amplifies his position and concludes thus: "If faith in immortality is so necessary to the human being (that without it he comes to the point of killing himself), it must therefore be the normal state of humanity. Since this is the case, the immortality of the human soul exists without any doubt." Then again in the last pages of his last novel, at the conclusion of that gigantic combat with God, some children ask Aliocha: "Karamazov, is it true what religion says, that we shall rise from the dead, that we shall see one another again?" And Aliocha answers: "Certainly, we shall see one another again, we shall joyfully tell one another everything that has happened."

Thus Kirilov, Stavrogin, and Ivan are defeated. *The Brothers Karamazov* replies to *The Possessed.* And it is indeed a conclusion. (pp. 110-11)

Consequently, it is not an absurd novelist addressing us, but an existential novelist. Here, too, the leap is touching and gives its nobility to the art that inspires it. It is a stirring acquiescence, riddled with doubts, uncertain and ardent. . . . [*The Brothers Karamazov*] is a work which, in a chiaroscuro more gripping than the light of day, permits us to seize man's struggle against his hopes. Having reached the end, the creator makes his choice against his characters. That contradiction thus allows us to make a distinction. It is not an absurd work that is involved here, but a work that propounds the absurd problem.

Dostoevsky's reply is humiliation, "shame" according to Stavrogin. An absurd work, on the contrary, does not provide a reply; that is the whole difference. Let us note this carefully in conclusion: what contradicts the absurd in that work is not its Christian character, but rather its announcing a future life. It is possible to be Christian and absurd. . . . The surprising reply of the creator to his characters, of Dostoevsky to Kirilov, can indeed be summed up thus: existence is illusory *and* it is eternal. (pp. 111-12)

> Albert Camus, "*Absurd Creation,*" *in his* The Myth of Sisyphe and Other Essays, *translated by Justin O'Brien (translation copyright © 1955 by Alfred A. Knopf, Inc.; reprinted by permission of Alfred A. Knopf, Inc.; originally published as* Le Mythe de Sisyphe, *Librarie Gallimard, 1942), Knopf, 1955 (and reprinted by Knopf, 1967), pp. 93-118.*

GEORG LUKÁCS   (essay date 1943)

Dostoevsky is a writer of world eminence. For he knew how during a crisis of his country and the whole human race, to put questions in an imaginatively decisive sense. He created men whose destiny and inner life, whose conflicts and interrelations with other characters, whose attraction and rejection of men and ideas illuminated all the deepest questions of that age, sooner, more deeply, and more widely than in average life itself. This imaginative anticipation of the spiritual and moral development of the civilized world assured the powerful and lasting effect of Dostoevsky's works. (p. 147)

In general, Dostoevsky does not like descriptions of external reality: he is not a *paysagiste,* as Turgenev and Tolstoy are, each in his own manner. But because he grasps with the visionary power of a poet the unity of the inner and the outer—the social and the psychic—organization here in the misery of the city, unsurpassed pictures of Petersburg emerge, particularly in *Crime and Punishment,* pictures of the new metropolis—from the coffinlike furnished room of the hero through the stifling narrowness of the police station to the center of the slum district, the Haymarket, and the nocturnal streets and bridges.

Yet Dostoevsky is never a specialist in milieu. His work embraces the whole of society, from the "highest" to the "lowest," from Petersburg to a remote provincial village. But the "primary phenomenon"—and this artistic trait throws a strong light on the social genesis of the books—remains always the same: the misery of Petersburg. (pp. 153-54)

But Dostoevsky is concerned with much more than a problem of artistic expression. The Petersburg misery, particularly that of intellectual youth, is for him the purest, classical symptom of his "primary phenomenon": the alienation of the individual from the broad stream of the life of the people, which to Dostoevsky is the last and decisive social reason for all the mental and moral deformations we have sketched above. One can observe the same deformations also in the upper strata. But here one sees rather the psychological results, while in the former the social and psychological process of their genesis comes out much more clearly. . . .

This divorce between the lonely individual and the life of the people is the prevailing theme of bourgeois literature in the second half of the nineteenth century. This type dominates the bourgeois literature of the West during this period—whether it is accepted or rejected, lyrically idealized, or satirically caricatured. But even in the greatest writers, in Flaubert and Ibsen, the psychological and moral consequences appear more prominently than their social basis. Only in Russia, in Tolstoy and Dostoevsky, is the problem raised in all its breadth and depth. (p. 154)

Dostoevsky investigates the . . . process of the dissolution of old Russia and the germs of its rebirth primarily in the misery of the cities among the "insulted and injured" of Petersburg. Their involuntary alienation from the old life of the people—which only later became an ideology, a will and activity, their—provisional—inability to "connect" with the popular movement which was still groping for an aim and direction, was Dostoevsky's "primary social phenomenon." (pp. 154-55)

[The] world of Dostoevsky lacks any trace of worldly skeptical coquetry, of vain self-consciousness, or of toying with his own loneliness and despair. (pp. 155-56)

Because this despair is genuine, it is a principle of excess, again in sharp contrast to the worldly polished forms of most of the Western skeptics. Dostoevsky shatters all forms—beautiful and ugly, genuine and false—because the desperate man can no longer consider them an adequate expression for what he is seeking for his soul. All the barriers that social convention has erected between men are pulled down in order that nothing but spontaneous sincerity, to the most extreme limits, to the utter lack of shame, may prevail among men. The horror at the loneliness of men erupts here with irresistible power precisely because all these pitiless destructions are still unable to remove the solitude.

The journalist Dostoevsky could speak consolingly in a conservative sense, but the human content, the poetic tempo and the poetic rhythm of his speech, have a rebellious tone and thus find themselves constantly in opposition to his highest political and social intentions. . . .

The poetic question, correctly put, triumphs over the political intentions, the social answer of the writer.

Only there does the depth and correctness of Dostoevsky's questioning assert itself fully. It is a revolt against that moral and psychic deformation of man which is caused by the evolution of capitalism. Dostoevsky's characters go to the end of the socially necessary self distortion unafraid, and their self-dissolution, their self-execution, is the most violent protest that could have been made against the organization of life in that time. The experimentation of Dostoevsky's characters is thus put into a new light: it is a desperate attempt to break through the barriers which deform the soul and maim, distort, and dismember life. (p. 156)

Every genuine man in Dostoevsky breaks through this barrier, even though he perishes in the attempt. The fatal attraction of Raskolnikov and Sonya is only superficially one of extreme opposites. Quite rightly Raskolnikov tells Sonya that by her boundless spirit of self-sacrifice, by the selfless goodness which made her a prostitute in order to save her family, she herself had broken the barrier, and transcended the limits—just as he had done by murdering the pawnbroker. For Dostoevsky this transcendence was in Sonya more genuine, more human, more immediate, more plebeian than in Raskolnikov.

Here the light shines in the darkness and not where the journalist Dostoevsky fancied he saw it. Modern solitude is that darkness. . . .

The ways that Dostoevsky points out for his characters are impassable. As a creator he himself feels these problems deeply. He preaches faith, but in reality—as a creator of men—he does not himself believe that the man of his age can have faith in his sense. It is his atheists who have genuine depth of thought, a genuine fervor for the quest.

He preaches the way of Christian sacrifice. But his first positive hero, Prince Myshkin in *The Idiot,* is fundamentally atypical and pathological because he is unable, largely due to his illness, to overcome inwardly his egoism—even in love. . . .

When, at the end of his career, Dostoevsky wanted to create a healthy positive figure in Alyosha Karamazov, he vacillated constantly between two extremes. In the extant novel Alyosha actually seems to be a healthy counterpart of Prince Myshkin, a Dostoevskean saint. But the novel as we know it—just from the point of view of the main hero—is only a beginning, only the story of his youth. (p. 157)

[The] world of Dostoevsky's characters dissolves his political ideals into chaos. But this chaos itself is great in Dostoevsky: his powerful protest against everything false and distorting in modern bourgeois society. . . .

The golden age: genuine and harmonious relations between genuine and harmonious men. Dostoevsky's characters know that this is a dream in the present age but they cannot and will not abandon the dream. They cannot abandon the dream even when most of their feelings sharply contradict it. This dream is the truly genuine core, the real gold of Dostoevsky's Utopias; a state of the world in which men may know and love each other, in which culture and civilization will not be an obstacle to the development of men.

The spontaneous, wild, and blind revolt of Dostoevsky's characters occurs in the name of the golden age, whatever the contents of the mental experiment may be. This revolt is poetically great and historically progressive in Dostoevsky: here really shines a light in the darkness of Petersburg misery, a light that illuminates the road to the future of mankind. (p. 158)

> *Georg Lukács, "Dostoevsky" (1943), in his Der russische Realismus in der Weltliteratur (© 1953 by Georg Lukács; reprinted by permission), Aufbau-Verlag, 1949 (translated by René Wellek and reprinted as "Dostoevsky," in Dostoevsky: A Collection of Critical Essays, edited by René Wellek, Prentice-Hall, Inc., 1962, pp. 146-58).*

JANKO LAVRIN (essay date 1947)

Ideas which had been lived, i.e. tested through one's entire consciousness and then embodied in living characters, were the mainspring of Dostoevsky's novels. (p. 29)

Dostoevsky's love of involved mysterious plots was [a] feature which connected him with romanticism. So was his love of extreme antitheses and particularly his interest in the irrational which he combined, however, with an uncanny psychological sense. Prying into the most hidden recesses of man's soul and spirit, he was the first European novelist to explore the unconscious and to annex it wholesale to modern literature. Yet he was too much of a brooding analyst to be a reliable observer of externals. Nor did he care for the traditional homogeneity of character, since he was only too familiar with the contrasts and contradictions of the human ego. What attracted him above all was that inner chaos which compels one to look for some outlet from among the greatest antinomies. (pp. 29-30)

Dostoevsky usually starts with some vital inner problem which determines the trend of his intuitions, observations and ideas. But instead of pasting the ideas upon his characters, he makes them an organic part of their inner make-up, no matter whether he himself agrees with what they say or not. Moreover, during the creative process his leading idea itself becomes split into its own conflicting antitheses which open up dramatic possibilities of a new kind. The very form of a Dostoevskian novel results from the dynamic tension between several contradictory planes and trends of one and the same consciousness— each of them with its own conclusions.

The principle of fugue, of 'symphonic' treatment, is possible in a novel only if the author gives the most opposite themes and motives an equal chance. And this is what Dostoevsky does. His favourite methods are those in which not only the inner life, but also the personal tone of the characters described comes out to the best advantage in the relationship to their own opposites. (pp. 30-1)

Dostoevsky confronts dramatically not only antinomic characters, but antinomic features in one and the same character. In doing this, he preserves complete spiritual and intellectual fairness, no matter how acute or how personal his own attitude may be. Entire chapters of his have a power of their own precisely because they are so ambiguous. (p. 31)

Only an author capable of projecting his own inner chaos and travail into living characters, in order to achieve a kind of *katharsis,* could have written as Dostoevsky did. For him art was a relentless urge, perhaps an alternative to madness. This explains why some of his creations are so intense as to haunt the reader's imagination like spooks. Sometimes they affect one as nightmares and symbols in one—even symbols of forces which seem to transcend our ordinary plane of existence. It is at this point that Dostoevsky's 'realism' asserts itself in a peculiar and original fashion.

We may perhaps find a clue to his realism by drawing a line between reality and actuality. The two are often regarded as identical. Yet reality is more than actuality. It includes all the hidden forces and agents of life, whereas actuality is confined to its external or else 'topical' aspects. The proportion between these two planes varies and is reflected in the two different although complementary directions in art, especially in the novel: the horizontal and the vertical.

The 'horizontal' novel is concerned with manners, with life as expressed in terms of external contacts and relationships of the persons described. But it must not stop here. Unless it has a fringe, suggestive of something more important and universal than what it shows, it will remain only a picture or document of a certain period—nearer to journalism than to art. The 'vertical' novel, however, concentrates above all upon human destinies as they work in and through the characters presented. Hence it is predominantly psychological. It is more intensive than extensive; for which purpose it reduces the number of characters, as well as the area of their background, to a minimum. If the 'horizontal' novel is analogous to the old epic on the one hand and to comedy on the other, the 'vertical' novel finds its counterpart in the drama. And as for social manners, it is interested in them in so far as they can be a matter of conflict with the individual who turns against tradition in the name of his own vision of life, or of his own inner freedom. The entire problem of evil, for example, with its ultimate metaphysical implications, is dealt with by Dostoevsky only on this plane. And so intensely, too, that some of his characters may even strike one as agents of cosmic forces of good and evil.

He thus enlarged and deepened the scope of the European novel. (pp. 31-3)

If a label were necessary at all, we could perhaps call his art *visionary* realism, as distinct from mere visual realism. He strains the actual and the average to its utmost limits mainly in order to reach that reality which lies beyond it. His wildest and cruellest situations are often but experiments upon the human soul with the object of extracting its 'inmost essence'. Hence there is something paradoxical about Dostoevsky's exaggerated characters: they are most real when they seem least realistic from the standpoint of the mere visual realism.

Dostoevsky's work (like that of any great author) can best be understood if regarded in the perspective of his general per-

ception and intuition of life. Yet in his case we must take into consideration the three planes which he usually intermingles. The first is the plane of *byt* or the social background. The second is the purely psychological plane. And the third—the most important among them—is the one in which 'psychology' passes into the sphere of spiritual experience and valuations.

The first of these three planes matters in so far as it expresses a complete absence of fixed or stable social forms. In Dostoevsky's writings everything is in a 'flux', including the social classes which are chaotically mixed up. His principal heroes are taken, as it were, out of all social causality—a fact which gives the author an even greater freedom in dwelling upon the fundamentals of human life, upon the tragic conflicts of mind and spirit. Yet while stripping his characters of external bonds and conventions, Dostoevsky adopted a number of external devices to keep the attention of his readers. A study of his technique may reveal tricks which resemble those of the sensational 'lower' fiction: the criminal or detective novel, the melodramatic newspaper serial, and even the penny shocker. . . . Only Dostoevsky could permit himself such cheap tricks and yet create great novels. He often adjusted his external plots to the level of the average reader; but at the same time he made them only scaffoldings for what lay beyond them. Thus the 'thrilling' detective element in *Crime and Punishment* is almost irrelevant as compared with the principal 'idea-force' of the novel: the idea of moral self-will.

Another reason why Dostoevsky loved to pile up so many unusual plots and events was his tendency to experiment with the human self: to put it into the most incredible situations, and watch its reactions. He was drawn towards such plots as would enable him to study the farthest limits of consciousness. Yet however complicated his plots may be, they develop with and through the characters. The motives of action thus remain internal. And once these motives have reached the intensity suggestive of supra-human agencies (whether of good or evil), Dostoevsky magnifies his characters accordingly; or at least his male characters, because his women are never treated on the same spiritual scale as his men. (pp. 33-5)

Dostoevsky had so much to say that the forms of the old novel proved inadequate. He had to work out a 'symphonic' form of his own whose style is often jerky, and composition uneven. . . . Most satisfactory, formally, are some of his smaller novels, such as *The Gambler* and *The Eternal Husband,* written at one sitting as it were. Among the big novels *Crime and Punishment* is best in construction, although the crime itself takes place before the motivation of the crime is given. The action begins right in the middle and then is gradually unravelled in concentric circles—from the periphery towards the focus. (pp. 35-6)

[A balance between art, psychology, and dynamic ideas is evident] in *The Brothers Karamazov,* Dostoevsky's last and longest novel. Each part of this monumental work is almost a novel in itself, yet they all converge towards the denouement in the finale. The contrast between the brothers is worked out with unsurpassed subtlety. Moreover, while reading this masterpiece, we actually follow its parallel development on the three mentioned planes. We watch the background of a Russian town, the involved psychological experiences of the main characters, and the spiritual import of it all. One of its great features is the delightful gallery of boys, each of them depicted with consummate understanding of a child's mind. In addition, Ivan Karamazov's **'Legend of the Grand Inquisitor'** gives us the most dramatic philosophy of history ever presented in literary form. (p. 36)

[Dostoevsky's] significance is enhanced by the manner in which he approached man's basic dilemmas, and at the same time refused all facile and superficial solutions. He never tired of fighting, and fiercely so, the facile optimism with regard to our progress, for example. Nor was he inclined to make any truce with those theories (whether socialistic or otherwise), the aim of which is to make human beings 'happy' by lowering their consciousness; by standardizing them into mere units of an efficient ant-hill.

His *Notes from the Underworld* was his first protest against such optimistic rationalism. At the same time it was an indirect defence of human personality as something autonomous; something which must insist on its own rights, without isolating itself, however, from the collective group or groups. An individual who remains exclusively in the group, within the sphere of social taboos and conventions, cannot develop into a personality. On the other hand, an isolated personality which has lost its organic contact with the collective or with the rest of mankind, is bound to become starved through its very isolation. The problem of personality thus becomes inseparable from the problem of mankind as a whole. The two are in fact one and the same problem, approached from its opposite ends. (pp. 55-6)

[Many] of Dostoevsky's characters are haunted by the question: 'Does God exist or not?' Dostoevsky himself tackled the problem not on the plane of theological formulae, but primarily as a psychologist interested in God as an active element in man's consciousness—an element which fills the latter not only with the highest longings, but also with the bitterest doubts and torments. . . . Unable to separate man's fundamental problems from the problem of God, Dostoevsky was anxious to explore the degree of reality of that 'mighty activity' in our soul. He wanted to know whether God exists also objectively, i.e. apart from and outside that activity. He demanded certainty in this matter mainly in order to see how the answer (one way or the other) would affect the fate of man. The search for God he thus identified primarily with the question as to whether there exists an incontestable, absolute Value towards which one's will and efforts could be directed for the sake of one's highest self-realization and 'way of life'. And since such a Value can only be given or sanctioned by an absolute Being, the answer as to whether God exists or not is bound to affect us. If the latter is in the negative, then our existence—taken not from the social, but from the spiritual angle—is turned into something accidental and devoid of any ultimate meaning. Once cognizant of that, an uncompromising conscience must either reject life and the world, or else proclaim man's will as the only law, and his ego as the only divinity on earth. (pp. 57-8)

Among the religious teachers it was Christ in particular who abolished the purely legalistic conceptions of God, by transferring Him from outside into the consciousness of man: 'The Kingdom of God is within you.' But this mystical attitude, even when practised whole-heartedly, failed to destroy the rebellious 'magical' element in man, since both attitudes represent the two polar unconscious tendencies of every human self. Hence the duality of man's inner life, and even of mankind's development as a whole. The antagonism between the spiritual and the secular aspects in our historical life may partly be traced back to this split. The latter can occur, however, also on the plane of spirit alone—a phenomenon which often leads

to unexpected conflicts, culminating in the antithesis of God-man and man-God, of Christ and Zarathustra.

The inner struggle of Dostoevsky's heroes, from Raskolnikov to Ivan Karamazov, is mainly due to this dilemma and to its two opposite sets of valuation, pushed to their final conclusions. During this process Dostoevsky realized that Christ has revealed to us the highest possible Value. In his opinion 'there is nothing lovelier, deeper, more sympathetic, more manly and perfect than the Saviour'. He even makes his 'superman' Kirillov exclaim that Christ is the One who gave the meaning to life, and that 'the whole planet, with everything in it, is mere madness without that Man'. Yet to see in Christ the Value and the meaning of life is not enough for an inquiring mind. One step farther, and we are confronted by the question: Does Christ Himself correspond to truth? Where is the certainty that the Value and the Way of Life, revealed by Him, are incontestable, with a reality behind, and not a mere illusion? In other words, is Christ Himself inside or outside the Truth? (p. 62)

Questions of this kind, prompted by incurable scepticism, crop up in all the chief novels of Dostoevsky, not as 'philosophy', but as living experience, as torments of the spirit. (p. 63)

He was so much afraid of the inner devastation, caused by modern scepticism, that he fought it with all the means at his disposal. . . . [He] asserted the priority of the irrational over the rational, and began to cling to Christ even in spite of reason. 'If any one could prove to me that Christ is outside the truth, and if the truth really did exclude Christ, I would prefer to stay with Christ and not with the truth,' he confessed candidly. On the other hand, he was too much of a dialectitian and a sharp thinker to be able to accept his religious intuitions without a rational sanction. As the two proved incompatible, he had to fight for his faith, step by step, during the whole of his creative life. (pp. 63-4)

The fight for belief is accompanied in [Dostoevsky's writings] by the most vigorous apology for unbelief. But for this very reason they are all the more poignant both as literature and as human documents. (p. 64)

Janko Lavrin, in his Dostoevsky: A Study *(reprinted by permission of the author),* Macmillan, 1947, 161 p.

RENATO POGGIOLI   (essay date 1952)

[For] a "realist" like Dostoevski, reality is primarily apprehended through the perspective of a personal, almost mystical intuition. Dostoevski's realism is therefore projection and introspection at the same time. . . .

In spite of the personal pathos of his inspiration, Dostoevski never indulged in self-contemplation and narcissism. The ego of the author never intruded in his work, and from this viewpoint he followed the standards of impersonality and objectivity, as understood by Western realism. It is worth remarking that, in spite of the fact that introspection was perhaps the source of his own psychological insight, and that his interest in the morbid side of psychic life was perhaps a projection of his inner conflicts, he was always unable or unwilling to report directly his extraordinary autobiographical experiences. He preferred to relate them in the third person, objectivizing them in the creatures of his imagination.

It is perhaps true that it was the fear of censorship that led him to adopt the literary device of pretending to be the editor, rather than the author, of *Notes From a Dead House,* perhaps his most "documentary" work. Yet that device creates an effect of esthetic distance, transforming the writer from a witness and a victim into a judge and a contemplator, and raising to the level of the dramatic an experience which otherwise would have been merely pathetic. (p. 24)

[Dostoevski thought] in terms of reconstructing the exceptional and the extraordinary from the raw materials of everyday reality. This is why he was able to foresee some of the psychological discoveries of the scientific school of Freud and his disciples, and to precede them in the field which later, almost in his own words, they would call "depth psychology." Before Freud, he knew how many "indecent thoughts" can be found in the minds of "decent people." (p. 25)

Dostoevski's liking for the unverisimilar in action, and the abnormal in psychology, must not lead us to believe that he favored the characterization, against a realistic background, of romantic heroes, of Titans and Supermen. He was equally interested in ordinary lives, and in the psychology of Everyman. He was well aware that the common or average man was becoming the protagonist of both Russian and Western fiction. Yet he felt that that human type must be made worthy not only of our sympathy, but also of our curiosity and interest. (pp. 25-6)

Dostoevski was never willing to see merely the "human beast" even in the most degraded human beings. Yet there are naturalistic elements in his work, as may be seen by the use in **The Brothers Karamazov** of the doctrine of "heredity," which, to be sure, is treated as a kind of ethical nemesis. (pp. 26-7)

Dostoevski's naturalism is below glamor, or beyond it. While his interest in the trivial and vulgar side of life led him to commit breaches of the code of manners and taste, which even a Zola would hesitate to commit, those very violations, on the other hand, opened for him the gates of the metaphysical and the transcendental.

No other writer would have dared to surprise his hero Dmitri, during the dramatic scene of his arrest, in the process of undressing himself and of showing to everybody, including the reader, his filthy socks. Yet these naturalistic details symbolize the tragic nakedness of human existence, the sense that man lives in the mud. Dostoevski used in the same way the animal and elemental reality of the human need for food. Generally, fictional heroes never eat: either they "dine," as in fashionable novels, or, as in proletarian fiction, they merely starve, yet without ever starving to death. Few writers would have thought of interrupting the hectic action of **The Possessed** to follow Petr Verkhovenski into those cheap restaurants where he suddenly orders, and coarsely devours, a rare, almost raw, beefsteak.

This is not the only case where a meaningless detail becomes a revealing symbol, or at least a significant fact. Sometimes the same effect is produced by the presence of odd, and yet common, things. Dostoevski treats them merely as such, yet, in the mind of the reader, they become also signs. (p. 27)

[The] naturalistic and the symbolic are interchangeable in the world of Dostoevski. This may be seen in the treatment of those "vile tales" which are so frequent in his fiction. They seem to transcend their coarseness and brutality by becoming "scandals" in the religious sense, while still remaining "scandalous scenes" in the everyday meaning of the term. In the same way, Dostoevski was able to transform an insignificant fact into a tremendous emotional experience, full not only of tragic meaning, but also of poetic awe. (p. 28)

Dostoevski has been praised not only as a poet, but also as a philosopher, or . . . as a "seer." There is no doubt that he worked with ideas, and with ideas of his own, yet we must never forget that those ideas were not superimposed, but embodied in the flesh of his heroes, and intimately connected with the living substance of his plots. For him, ideas are not only springs of action, but also modes of being: Dostoevski's is not an ideal, but an ideational universe. This is why his ideas become myths, while these myths spring from real life and from a prosaic world. Even his myth-making faculty accepts the conventions of realism, and operates within a naturalistic framework.

The complex myth of the "underground," according to which modern man is cornered between the disorder of a vitalistic consciousness and the order of a devitalized social design, is developed by Dostoevski in the homely metaphors of the mouse and the cellar, of the henhouse and the ant heap. (pp. 28-9)

Dostoevski always presents his own myths and ideas not as subjective revelations, but as objective visions: as spiritual realities taking place in the minds of his heroes. Very often, these visions take the shape of dreams. The idea of the end of our social order manifests itself in Raskolnikov's apocalyptic and prophetic dream of a future plague destroying the fabric of life and the house of man. Even more frequently, Dostoevski projects his myths and ideas into his fictions as conscious and active productions of his characters' minds, revealing them in the give-and-take of conversation, or in the very process of thought. (p. 29)

Dostoevski's method aims at suggesting the ambivalence of the real and the symbolic, of the naturalistic and the mythical. Sometimes he aims even at creating an atmosphere of ambiguity, veiling his own intentions and clouding his view of things. There is no doubt that Raskolnikov's crime is, in Dostoevski's interpretation, the monstrous child of intellectual pride and of radical thought. Yet he persistently insinuates through various characters that Raskolnikov's frame of mind and his criminal act have been determined by external factors and material circumstances. Raskolnikov's mother, his friend Razumikhin, the investigating attorney Porfiri, even the mysterious Svidrigaylov, point their accusing fingers not to Raskolnikov, but to his surroundings. The mother sees the dominating factor in that sickening garret where her son has been living, and which she likens to a tomb; others, apparently including both Raskolnikov and his creator, seem to share this opinion. (pp. 29-30)

This singular ambiguity seems to dominate Dostoevski's imagination whenever the supernatural makes its entrance into the material universe. How this effect of ambiguity is obtained may be seen in a conversation held by Raskolnikov and Svidrigaylov. Svidrigaylov confesses to seeing often the ghost of his deceased wife, to which Raskolnikov replies with the objection that ghosts appear only to diseased minds. Svidrigaylov, while admitting as much, denies however that from this fact we can logically deduce that ghosts do not exist.

The problematic mind of Dostoevski seems to accept both hypotheses at the same time. This can be seen in one of his highest creations, the conversation between Ivan Karamazov and the Devil. There is no doubt that Ivan is mentally sick, and that the Devil is a hallucination. Yet this imaginary devil plays in this realistic novel a role almost as important as Mephistopheles' in Goethe's *Faust*. Dostoevski's devil is, of course, not a romantic figure but a prosaic creature, a petty bourgeois in modern dress and shabby clothing. (p. 30)

It was on the foundation of this same ambiguity that Dostoevski built another magnificent episode of *The Brothers Karamazov*, an episode which is based on the problem of belief and disbelief in the matter of miracles. Every reader remembers the events attending the death of the saintly "elder," Father Zosima. His disciples are naïvely hoping that their master will give a sign of his saintliness by performing again a miracle reported in the pious legends of old. In brief, they expect that the body of the "elder" will be spared the degrading indignity of physical death, the breath of corruption and the decay of the flesh.

Against their expectations, and to the satisfaction both of the unbelievers and of those believers who were enemies of the "elder," what takes place instead of the miracle is a scandal, or, in material terms, a manifestation of the physical process of decay which seems almost unnaturally rapid and intense. Dostoevski does not stop here, but lists all the external factors to which the rapidity and the intensity of the process are due: the age and the frailty of the deceased, the heat, the pressing of the crowd, the closed windows and locked doors. (p. 31)

Dostoevski is never more realistic than in his moments of mystical insight. After all, he was a man of the nineteenth century, endowed, like Ivan Karamazov, with a "Euclidian mind." His "second sight" allowed him to contemplate also a non-Euclidian cosmic order, and in the desperate attempt to reconcile immanent and transcendental reality, his imagination achieved a paradoxical feat, by performing, so to speak, a "squaring of the circle." Dostoevski may have been a great seer, but he was primarily a great artist. In his work, the "spirit" lives because the "letter" is never dead: the "spirit" is not breathed into the "letter," but emanates from it. The metaphysical and the supernatural are the fourth dimension of his universe, yet they remain a projection of our three-dimensional world. Even the ideal and the symbolic spring in him from the Western sense of reality, and this is why all his work is a "prologue on earth." Dostoevski understood, like the Devil of Ivan, that only if it is given to him in "homeopathic doses" will modern man accept a reality beyond his reason and senses. (pp. 31-2)

> Renato Poggioli, *"Dostoevski, or Reality and Myth"* (originally published in an abridged version in The Kenyon Review, *Vol. XIV, No. 1, Winter, 1952*), in his The Phoenix and the Spider: A Book of Essays about Some Russian Writers and Their View of the Self *(copyright © 1957 by the President and Fellows of Harvard College; excerpted by permission), Cambridge, Mass.: Harvard University Press, 1957, pp. 16-32.*

PHILIP RAHV (essay date 1954)

[As an excursus on the theme of man's historical fate, its terror, despair, and absurdity, *The Legend of the Grand Inquisitor*] is nearly without equal in world literature. It enriches the ideological content of the novel in which it is embedded, enabling us to understand more fully the far-ranging implications of Ivan Karamazov's "rebellion," but it is even more meaningful in terms of Dostoevsky's development as a whole; and the figure of the Grand Inquisitor is dramatically compelling enough to stay permanently in our minds as a symbolic character-image of the dialectic of power. . . . Deceptively easy on the surface, it is at bottom one of the most difficult texts in the Dostoevskyean canon. By the same token, however, it is also one of the most rewarding. And the difficulty is not in its dramatic form but in the complexity of the ideas, their immense sugges-

tiveness and scope, and the dissonances of belief and emotional discords that sound in them.

But the dramatic form is indispensable to Dostoevsky. That he would have been capable of making substantially the same statement without recourse to the dramatized consciousness of a fictional character is extremely doubtful. . . . [The] felt disjunction between the qualities of his direct discourse and those emerging through the sustained imaginative projection of his fiction is due, I think, to the fact that when writing in the first person—out in the open so to speak—he at once loses the advantages of complicity. For it is complicity above all which is the secret of his creative triumph over the propagandist in himself. It arises in the process of his identification as novelist with his characters, but it is necessary to distinguish between its genesis and the larger uses to which he puts it. It saves him from the one-sidedness, the fanaticism of commitment, and the casuistry to which as an embattled reactionary ideologue he was all too prone. There is an ambiguity of feeling and attitude in him, a tension between sympathies and antipathies, finding its release in this complicity. He fully depends on it in the creation of his characters; and the few from whom he withholds it are reduced to stereotypes, as, for example, Grushenka's Polish suitor and the student-radical Rakitin in *The Brothers Karamazov*. Creatures of their author's political malice, they fall below the level of the world into which he injects them.

Ivan, on the other hand, it has frequently been observed, is the figure in the novel to whom as author he most readily gives himself in the process of identification. (pp. 130-31)

In his assault on God and the traditional faith Ivan proceeds in a way that transcends the rationalistic argumentation of the old-time atheists. For him it can no longer be a question of attempting to disprove God's existence logically. Ivan is not one to permit his intellectual faculties to linger in the modes of the past. He has made the essentially modern leap from the static framework of analytic thinking to thinking in terms of the historical process. But his leap is made in the typical Russian fashion of that epoch. That is to say, it lands him not in the somewhat placid "historicism" then prevailing in the consciousness of the West but in the eschatological frame of mind common to the Russian intelligentsia of the latter part of the past century. For whatever their outlook, whether revolutionary or not, inclined to nihilism or given to apocalyptic visions, in the main those people tended to see history as verging toward the ultimate and bringing forth a final solution compounded either of pure good or pure evil. (p. 131)

His version of atheism is all the more forceful in that it allows for God's existence, if need be, but not for the justifications of His world as revealed progressively *in* and *through* history. (p. 132)

Nor does Ivan dispute the ideality and supreme goodness of Christian teaching. On the contrary, it is this very ideality and goodness that he turns into the motive of his dissent from it when he depicts the Grand Inquisitor upbraiding Christ for thinking much too highly of man in endeavoring to augment his freedom of choice between good and evil instead of heeding the counsel of the wise and dread spirit of the wilderness to strip man of his freedom so that he might at long last live in peace and brutish happiness. God, confronted by the radical proofs of the meanness of His world, the senseless suffering prevailing in it and man's congenital inability to enter the promised spiritual kingdom, is disposed of through His works.

But if Ivan does not believe in God, neither does he believe in man. It is true that he loves man—there is no one else left to love and perhaps there has never actually been anyone else. Yet how can he believe in man's freedom in the face of the appalling testimony of history proving his incapacity to achieve it? And in what way does Ivan envisage the future? If we take the Grand Inquisitor as his *persona,* then he thinks that just as historical Christianity has failed man, so socialism—the Tower of Babel of the coming centuries—will fail him and afterwards the authoritarian theocrats will resume command. And the fault, from first to last, is in man himself because he is an "impotent rebel," a slave even if rebellious by nature. . . . Ivan torments himself with the question of what is to be done with man if you at once love and despise him. The ideology of the Grand Inquisitor, which repudiates freedom for the sake of happiness, is the means he devises for forcing a solution. Yet it also is a means of exposing it. The very manner in which Ivan develops this ideology expresses his loathing of it even as he despairingly accepts it.

This is but another way of saying that in the last analysis he is not really possessed by it, that his mind moves freely in and out of it. The *Legend* as a whole, in its interplay of drama and ideology, is to be taken, I think, as an experiment, one of those experiments in frightfulness with which modern literature has the deepest affinity. . . . Therefore to identify Ivan wholly with the Inquisitor, as so many commentators have done, is an error, though a lesser one than that of wholly identifying Dostoevsky with him. The fact is that the *Legend* has not one but two protagonists, Jesus and the Inquisitor, and that Ivan makes no real choice between them. Jesus is freedom and transcendent truth, whereas the Inquisitor typifies the implacable logic of historical reality; but so stark a confrontation in itself demonstrates that Ivan's dilemma is absolute. (pp. 132-33)

[If] Dostoevsky's Christ is so very Russian in his meekness, his Inquisitor is no less Russian in his cruelty. Though appearing in the role of a Catholic hierarch, he is in fact quite as Byzantine as he is Roman, if not more so. (p. 141)

The historian Kliuchevsky once summed up Russian history in a single sentence: "The state thrives while the people grow sickly." It is this brutalizing national experience which makes for the compelling force of the *Legend* and is by far the deeper explanation of it. Whatever Dostoevsky's manifest intention, actually it is one of the most revolutionary and devastating critiques of power and authority ever produced. What it comes to in the end is a total rejection of Caesar's realm, a rejection of power in all its forms, in its actuality as in its rationalizations; and it exposes above all the fatal effect of power on such ideals and aspirations of humanity as are embodied in the original Christian teaching. . . . [The] implications of the *Legend* belie the "official" national-religious thesis of the novel as a whole.

For implicit in the *Legend* is another thesis altogether, that of Russian Christian anarchism. (p. 142)

Dostoevsky's anarchism is fully as utopian as that of Tolstoy but with these important differences: it is latent rather than manifest in his work and it is mystical rather than rational in conception; its political aims are ill-defined and ambiguous; intrinsically it is more the expression of an apocalyptic mood than of a radical will to revolution as a practical enterprise. (pp. 143-44)

For Dostoevsky, as for the existentialists, it is above all through the experience of choice and decision, resolutely entered upon, that the individual comes to self-realization. But this grasp and possession of one's own being, which is the human creature's truest rapture, is at the same time inescapably associated with anxiety and suffering, and for this reason men are continually driven to shirk meaningful choices. However, the difference between some of the latter-day existentialists and Dostoevsky is that for him the act of choosing is wholly a moral if not always a religious act while for them it is an act unconditionally open to existence in all its sheerness and totality, not limited to any single sphere, ethical or otherwise.

Now in the *Legend* Dostoevsky so represents the truth of history—that is, the truth not of what ought to be but of what is and has been—that we see it as patently belonging to the Inquisitor, not to Christ. Dostoevsky nonetheless takes his stand with Christ. This should not surprise us; if we consider his biography in its temporal depth, so to speak, we find that he committed himself very early to this clinging to Christ in the face of all the malignant realities of history and man's nature. More than twenty-five years before composing the *Legend* he wrote in a letter from his place of exile in Siberia that if it were proven to him that Christ is "outside the truth, and if the truth really did exclude Christ, I should prefer to stay with Christ and not with the truth."

This paradoxical attitude is not to be taken as mere sentiment. It has its consequences. In the context of the *Legend* it means that if Dostoevsky rejects the wisdom of the Inquisitor, it is solely in the terms of the desperate paradox of his faith in Christ. Otherwise he apparently neither doubts nor denies that malign wisdom. What is to be observed, too, is that he thus indirectly fulfills his ideological aim of excluding any middle ground between Christ and the Grand Inquisitor. (pp. 147-48)

Philip Rahv, "'The Legend of the Grand Inquisitor'" (originally published in Partisan Review, *Vol. XXI, No. 3, May-June, 1954), in his* Essays on Literature and Politics: 1932-1972, *edited by Arabel J. Porter and Andrew J. Dvosin (copyright © 1978 by the Estate of Philip Rahv; copyright © 1978 by Arabel J. Porter and Andrew J. Dvosin; reprinted by permission of the Estate of Philip Rahv), Houghton Mifflin Company, 1978, pp. 129-48.*

ELISEO VIVAS (essay date 1955)

[Dostoevsky was] an artist in the immediate, concrete manner in which he seized the subject matter of experience. His lack of interest in nature has often been noticed. It is as if he had an eye capable exclusively of spiritual vision and for which, therefore, the inanimate ambient world could become visible only insofar as it is helped to disclose the fluid dynamism of the psychic. He saw human beings as concrete, actual agents of action, agonists of the drama of actual life. If we contrast him with Kafka, who in some respects is not unworthy of being put on the same plane as the Russian, we see the difference between an eye which is primarily dramatic and one which is metaphysical. (pp. 55-6)

It is true, of course, that Dostoevsky had strong convictions. He was, for instance, a committed Christian and a political conservative. But to take his Christianity without the careful qualifications forced on us by the dramatic manner in which he conceived human destiny would be to view it falsely; his faith is not a purely intellectual, logically simple, structure: it is an extremely complex and internally heterogeneous mass of living insights—affective, moral, and intellectual—in tension, and ordered not after the manner of the philosopher but of the dramatist. When therefore one asks oneself what were Dostoevsky's views on Christianity, one has to consider (simplifying for the sake of the illustration) not only what we can find out about one character or a class of characters, but what he tells us in the novels as a whole. (p. 56)

Dostoevsky fulfills the primary function of the artist, which so very few artists fulfill to the same extent. What he does is to organize or, better, to inform experience at the primary level and by means of animistic and dramatic categories. He does not undertake the philosopher's task, which is to abstract from experience already dramatically informed a formal structure in order to test its capacity to meet the exigencies of logical coherence and clarity of the rational intellect. What he does is to make life, insofar as man can do it, to be a poet and to give experience the form and intelligibility required by the whole mind, by the intellect and by the will. (p. 57)

[In] his books, which are pure stories, the story is the idea. However the word "idea" is not being used here in its ordinary sense, but as it is employed in musical aesthetics. His stories, however, pure drama though they are, exhibit two levels or aspects of human reality: the psychological and the metaphysical. . . . When we look at the relationship between these levels we find that the philosophical informs (in the technical Aristotelian sense) the psychological and the latter in turn informs the story. The matter of the story (the object of imitation, in terms of Aristotelian aesthetics) is human experience. (p. 58)

In the vast canvas of his major novels—and this is particularly true of the greatest of them, *The Brothers Karamasov*—one finds a series of "studies" of the various modalities through which certain types of human beings express themselves. The "type" however is gathered by us inductively from his unique specimens and it is not the former but the latter that interest Dostoevsky; nevertheless it is our intuition of the type in the individuals that makes them intelligible, while the individuals enable us to intuit the type, through the interrelationships of a complex system of similarities and contrasts which in this essay we cannot explore exhaustively but must be content to illustrate succinctly.

For illustration let us consider a type of individual with whom Dostoevsky was profoundly preoccupied and which, for lack of a better designation, we shall call "the liberal." In *The Brothers Karamasov* there are at least five or six fairly complete "studies" of this type: Ivan, Smerdyakov, Miüsov, Rakitin, and Kolya. But we could increase the number by adding some of the lesser characters. A liberal is, in religious matters, either an unbeliever or an agnostic; politically he is a reformist or a socialist; intellectually a "European" or Europeanized; and morally for Christian love he substitutes secular meliorism. (p. 59)

However it is not possible to understand an individual or a type through behavioral observation alone. We have to look into those secret crevices of the soul which ordinarily the individual does not suspect he has. In *The Brothers Karamasov* we become acquainted with Ivan in the ordinary manner—see him act, hear him express his attitudes and his ideas. In the famous Chapters 4 and 5 of Book V, entitled "Rebellion" and "The Grand Inquisitor," we see the depth of his concern for the religious problem and are given a first look into the nature of his difficulties. But Dostoevsky goes not only beyond Ivan's observed behavior, into his intellectual and moral structure, but into the unconscious double, which the Freudian would call the Id. . . . But Dostoevsky's grasp of hidden motives and

of instinctual processes which express themselves deviously differs in a very important respect from that exhibited by contemporary novelists who go to Freud for their knowledge of the human soul. Dostoevsky conceives the soul as fluid and he presents it, so to speak, directly for his reader's inspection. . . . And the result is that the conception of character of the novelist who has learned his human nature from Freud and not in the world, as Dostoevsky did, becomes the game of planting symbols according to a simple mechanical formula. (pp. 60-1)

Dostoevsky reveals Ivan's unconscious through the use of a Freudian device—the hallucination or delirium which Ivan undergoes when he is ill and in which he meets the Devil who, he tells us twice, is himself. Through this "visit" we find out that the man who is preoccupied with the relation between Church and State, and who clearly grasps the consequence of the denial of freedom to man in favor of happiness, is really, at bottom, a man whose soul is ripped by a contradiction of which he is perfectly aware, but which he is not able to resolve. (p. 61)

Through the delirium Dostoevsky has shown us the depths of Ivan's personality, but without the need to refer us to the Freudian code-book. Other devices which Dostoevsky employs in order to reveal the depths of the soul are not as easy to explain in general terms. One of the ways in which he does it is by having one character explain or reveal the meaning of another's actions; another is by having a character behave differently before each of the other characters with whom he has intercourse. Thus, Kolya, that delightfully lovable mischief-maker, is quite a different person with his fellows than he is with Alyosha or with the two children of the doctor's wife to whom his mother rented rooms. This device gives us the complexity of a person. But usually in order to reveal the duality of the soul Dostoevsky conducts the dramatic narrative on two planes, in such wise that while a character, let us say, is protesting love for another, he is revealing hatred. (p. 62)

Dostoevsky, of course, is not equipped to give a scientific explanation of those aspects of the personality which he discovered, nor is he interested in doing so. But he does more than give a mere phenomenological description of psychological processes. Indeed what gives his novels their depth and makes him one of the great thinkers of the modern world is that while positive science and naturalistic philosophy were straining to reduce man to purely naturalistic terms and to deny his metaphysical dimension in empirical terms, Dostoevsky was rediscovering that dimension in empirical terms which gave the lie to the modernists by reinvoking ancient truths whose old formulation had ceased to be convincing. With Kierkegaard, therefore, he was one of a small number of men who helped us forge the weapons with which to fend off the onrush of a naturalism bent on stripping us of our essentially human, our metaphysical, reality. (pp. 63-4)

[One] has not begun to understand him until one has grasped how, as Dostoevsky deepened his insight into human nature, he came more and more clearly to see that man's plight, his unhappiness, his divided soul, his need for self-laceration, his viciousness, his pride and his shame, his ills in short, flow from the same fountain-head, his unbelief. But unbelief is lack of love which in turn is hell. Dostoevsky progressively gains a firmer grasp of this insight through his creative work and in his last novel he is finally able successfully to bring into a comprehensive dramatic synthesis all his views of man and of his relations to his fellows and to the universe. At the heart of all questions, he comes to see, is the question of God, which is the question of love. (pp. 64-5)

This problem poses itself in Dostoevsky's mind in terms of a comprehensive metaphor possessing two conflicting terms, "Russia *versus* Europe." "Europe" promised happiness, but Dostoevsky saw that the price of an exclusively secular happiness was freedom. . . . On the other side one had "Russia," and the term, Dostoevsky believed passionately, had to be accepted, so to speak, "as was" and without bargaining. . . . Confronted with such an either/or Dostoevsky chose "Russia" in the belief that the Russian people would never accept atheistic socialism because they were too deeply and genuinely Christian. If we take the metaphor as intended we cannot fairly maintain that Dostoevsky was wrong. Indeed he came very close to the truth. But we must add in the same breath that one element of the metaphor's tenor, "Russia," was not in his day to be found and never will be either in history or in geography.

The other element of the tenor, "Europe," includes "the state" which is force, with its instruments, mysticism, miracle, and authority; justice without love, which involves blood; equality in things; and the multiplication of desires. Those at the controls of such a society are condemned to isolation and spiritual suicide and the ruled are sentenced to envy or murder. In contrast "Russia," which in justice to Dostoevsky we should remember he conceived as an ideal not yet adequately actualized, includes the church after it has absorbed the state, the denial of desires, the brotherhood of all living beings, spiritual dignity, justice in Christ and instead of pride and envy, humility and recognition of one's own sinfulness, and hence one's responsibility for the sins of all other men. The first term, "Europe," is of course exaggerated, and the second an improbable idealization. . . . Dostoevsky knew that the City of God is not of this world, but the route to it must be through "Russia" and not through "Europe," since the latter has been corrupted beyond redemption by the Grand Inquisitor, the Bernards and the socialists—who are three peas from the same pod. (pp. 65-6)

The question of God, however, is not a question that Dostoevsky settles easily by falling back on simple faith. Dostoevsky, who can easily be convicted of blindness to the evils of his own state and church, refuses flatly to compromise with the facts of individual experience, untoward as he knows them to be to his religious beliefs. (p. 66)

[In] the portraits of his great sinners and criminals Dostoevsky did not merely study the effects of vice but the effects of disbelief. He traces the effect of vice, pride, and hatred on the disintegration of the personality and he is most successful in drawing men in whom vice is connected with their repudiation of their condition as creatures and with their consequent effort to set themselves up wittingly or unwittingly as gods. And he shows how men who do not believe in God end up by believing in their own omnipotence.

Dostoevsky is not a propagandist and much less a dogmatist. He is, in the most important sense of that word of many meanings, a genuine philosopher, for he really inquired, questioned, sought the truth, instead of seeking bad reasons for what he already believed on faith. . . . (p. 67)

But then, how can one believe in God?—How, that is, if one is not a peasant woman of simple faith but has the brains, the education, and the range of experience of an Ivan? One cannot, is Ivan's answer, so long as the evil of the world remains to give the lie to God.

The furnace of doubt through which Dostoevsky said he had passed before he was able to arrive at his faith, consisted of at least two flames: the devastating knowledge he had of the criminal and depraved tendencies to be found at the bottom of the human soul and of which he gives us in *The Brothers Karamasov* three superb examples, Fyodor, Rakitin, and Smerdyakov; and the knowledge he has that injustice is inherent in the structure of human living and cannot be dislodged from it. These two flames, as I may continue to call them, cannot be smothered with social reforms or mechanical improvements. This is the hope of the rationalistic liberal, a hope that springs from his shallow grasp of human nature, and which, when it is not a mere pretense, as it is with Miüsov, is a diabolical lie, as it is with Rakitin. In "The Grand Inquisitor" he finally brought to full expression the implication of the conflict between God and freedom on the one hand and the atheistic effort to bring heaven to earth by dispensing with God on the other. (p. 68)

The alternative then to the ideal of The Grand Inquisitor is to accept God, freedom, and immortality. But this alternative has somehow to dispose of Ivan's dossier. To give man freedom is not only to open to him the door of eternal salvation, it is also to open the other door, whose threshold hope cannot cross. You cannot have Heaven without Hell; Heaven entails the General and his dogs. It is a terrible choice and no one knew more clearly than Dostoevsky how terrible it was: happiness without freedom, or freedom *and* hell. (p. 69)

The psychological and the metaphysical make up the concrete reality of Dostoevsky's human world. (p. 70)

Dostoevsky's great novels mirror comprehensively the bourgeois world of the nineteenth century, which is to say, a world in the first stages of an illness, which we today have the melancholy opportunity of seeing in a more advanced phase. Dostoevsky had a ground for optimism on which we cannot fall back: his faith that Zosima's "Russia" marked the direction toward which civilization would turn. But Rakitin and the other "Bernards" whom Dostoevsky dreaded have won, and the process by which man will destroy himself is already well under way. Thus the utopia of The Grand Inquisitor turns out to be a relatively pleasant morning dream as compared with the brave new world which our twentieth-century Bernards and Rakitins have begun to build. (pp. 70-1)

What Dostoevsky achieves is a definition of the destiny of Western man: he defines the alternatives and the corresponding values of each. Against the background of nineteenth-century humanity move the heroes of his books. In his inclusive world there is only one specimen lacking, the militant industrial proletariat, and the reason is that he did not have models of this type in his industrially backward native land. Saints, murderers, debauchees, intellectuals mad with pride, virginal whores and depraved ladies are the heroes. The mediocre, who lack the energy to become heroes, are pathetic rather than tragic, self-deceived rather than hypocritical, and unhappy, although ignorant of the malaise from which they suffer. Out of this mass emerge two groups of men who are in opposition: the saintly on the one side and those I have called "liberals" and the sensualists on the other.

Between sensualists and liberals there is a formal identity of ends, since the sensualist uses his body as instrument of pleasure and the intellectual his mind. As between these two types of men it may be hard to choose; but Dostoevsky seems to reveal in a man like Rakitin a greater depth of villainy than in

Fyodor, since he is the source of far-spreading corruption, while the power of evil of a man like Fyodor Karamazov is limited to himself and those he uses for his pleasure. The sensualist is consumed with self-hatred and shame, and his end is to destroy himself, but the intellectual, consumed with pride, seeks either to challenge God or to become God, and succeeds in wreaking havoc among men. Above the adult world is the world of the children, whom Dostoevsky could depict with inward fidelity, without sentimentality or condescension. (p. 71)

Dostoevsky views human destiny from the standpoint of an antirationalism which is more radical than that of Kierkegaard or Schopenhauer or Nietzsche. His rejection of "reason,"—"the stone wall constituted of the laws of nature, of the deductions of learning, and of the science of mathematics"—is clearly stated very early in his *Notes from the Underground.* But the full implications of "reason," and of his rejection of it, awaited the explorations which are to be found in his subsequent work, and particularly in the four major novels. It is his anti-rationalism which is the "source and head" of all his insights and attitudes, theological, psychological and political, and which therefore furnishes the ground on which he is often disposed of as a reactionary. . . . [The] meaning of human destiny which Dostoevsky reveals is not difficult to formulate: a life not built on love is not human, and a world without God is a world in which a triumphant cannibal frees the mass from the burden of their freedom in exchange for happiness. (p. 72)

> *Eliseo Vivas, "The Two Dimensions of Reality in 'The Brothers Karamazov'," in his* Creation and Discovery *(copyright © 1955 by Eliseo Vivas; reprinted by permission of the author), Noonday Press, 1955 (and reprinted in* "The Brothers Karamazov" and the Critics, *edited by Edward Wasiolek, Wadsworth Publishing Company, Inc., 1967, pp. 55-72).*

SAUL BELLOW (essay date 1955)

[As] I read *Winter Notes* I realized that to foreign eyes the French of 1862 were not substantially different from those of 1948. The great wars had not wrought too many changes. If wars could bring substantial changes, would we not all be deeply altered? If death and suffering had the power to teach us, would we of this century not all be wiser than our fathers? Hard, stubborn man, alas, does not easily correct himself but forgets what he has felt and seen.

Some of Dostoevsky's strictures repelled me by their harshness. He is as disagreeable as only a great radical can be. Recalling how evasive he had been when the Tsar's soldiers killed Polish patriots, I disliked his Slavophile notions. And then, too, a Jewish reader can seldom forget his anti-Semitism. It is, however, essential to remember that it was for his participation in the Petrashevsky "conspiracy" that Dostoevsky had been sent into exile. . . . Bourgeois France aroused his profoundest hatred. There is not a nation anywhere which does not contradict its highest principles in daily practice, but the French contradiction was in his eyes the worst because France presumed to offer the world intellectual and political leadership. (pp. 19-21)

It is the Western form of individualism that offends Dostoevsky. He invokes a higher individualism to which the desire for fraternal love is natural, an individualism which is self-effacing and sacrificial. . . . Elsewhere, and especially in the *Brothers Karamazov,* Dostoevsky asks the question that inevitably arises from this attitude: How Christian can a civilization be? And, as an artist must, he answers with ever more profound questions. But his severity towards the French never relaxes. In the French bourgeois character he sees a betrayal of the greatest hopes of the modern age.

It is in *Winter Notes* that his antagonism towards the French first appears. It culminates in his wild satire of *Bribri* and *Mabiche,* a funny and also rather ugly affair. The social criticisms of novelists and poets often contain concealed assumptions. Poets wish to see a poetic principle in human action, but they are not always gratified at the effects of literature on social behavior. Dostoevsky abhors "literary" bourgeois motives and the idolatry of culture. (pp. 21-2)

Winter Notes is often intemperate, worse than unfair and even frivolous. With his usual comic and cruel candor Dostoevsky concedes that his observations may be sour and jaundiced, and it is characteristic of him that he does not conceal his bias. For him this revelation of bias is a step toward the truth. "Good" principles tempt us to conceal ill-feeling and falsehood. Liberalism, whether it is Eastern or Western, is habitually deceitful. "Let us come forward as we are," Dostoevsky is forever saying, "in our native crudity. No disguises."

This is one of his important principles and he holds to it remarkably well. You may study his views of many topics in the huge, crazy, foaming, vengeful, fulminating book called *A Writer's Diary.* In this collection of his journalistic writings he records repeatedly his growing bitterness toward Europe. Europeans cannot understand Russia, he says. Even those who attempt "to grasp our Russian essence" do so in vain; they "will long fail to comprehend. . . ."

Yet Dostoevsky considered himself a most practical Christian. . . . Was Dostoevsky able to love Russians more because he detested Germans? Is it perhaps necessary to fix a limit to the number of people one can try to love? It does not surprise modern readers, acquainted with twentieth-century psychology, that the power to hate increases the power to love also. . . . Dostoevsky was not ignorant of it. But his personal opinions were not rational. As an artist he was both rational and wise. (pp. 24-6)

> *Saul Bellow, in his foreword to* Winter Notes on Summer Impressions *by Fyodor M. Dostoevsky, translated by Richard Lee Renfield (reprinted by permission of S.G. Phillips, Inc.; copyright © 1955 by S.G. Phillips, Inc.), Criterion Books, Inc., 1955 (and reprinted by McGraw-Hill Book Company, 1965), pp. 9-27.*

VLADIMIR ERMILOV (essay date 1956)

What does the meaning of the inner turmoil of *Crime and Punishment* consist of?

Raskolnikov carries out his monstrous "experiment" to settle for himself the question: What exactly is he? Can he "step over the bounds of morality with impunity"? Is he one of the extraordinary men who can do anything power and success demand without reproaching his conscience? Is he made of the stuff true leaders and masters of the world are made of? The murder of the moneylender was supposed to give him the answer.

Raskolnikov's "idea" is, for Dostoevsky, the product of the bourgeois society he must contend with. Raskolnikov comes to the conclusion after the crime that he is not made of the stuff which real leaders are made of, and of them Raskolnikov says: "No! those people are not made like that. A real leader, who has known only success, will plant a battery across a street and fire at innocent and guilty alike, not even deigning to explain? Bow down, trembling creatures and don't ask for reasons. That is not your concern.'' (pp. 142-43)

Raskolnikov asks himself, ''Am I fit to be among the leaders of the bourgeois world, the leaders who grind into exhaustion millions of people?'' The movement of the novel is the unfolding of this terrible experiment, which is at the same time a judgment of the bourgeois society.

Nietzsche's Zarathustra said, ''Man is what must be overcome!'' But the obvious conclusion to the inner struggle of *Crime and Punishment* can be briefly expressed as: ''No, man cannot be overcome!'' Raskolnikov did not prove to be too weak because, like Golyadkin, he could not become an actual despot. Dostoevsky had made Raskolnikov strong. (p. 143)

After the crime Raskolnikov separates himself from everything . . . , and the consciousness of his separation from everything human cuts into his soul like the fear of death. When Razumihin understood what Raskolnikov had undergone in bidding farewell to his mother and sister, he became frightened for him. ''Do you understand?'' Raskolnikov asked him with a face contorted with pain. He had loved his mother and sister more than anything else on earth and yet, disgusted with them and with himself, he felt himself beginning physically to hate them. He watches with terror over the loss of his right and even his capacity for feeling like a human being. But the desolation and the hate toward humanity that grow in his soul are loathsome to him. Spengler had sung the praises of the primitive man free of any social or human feeling; but in the portrait of Lara, inspired by folk creation, the young Gorky had dethroned the renegade who spurns society and whom reactionary thinkers of bourgeois individualism had tried to romanticize.

''I killed a principle,'' Raskolnikov says. What he wanted to kill was the principle of humanism. And this is so because the wolfish laws and morals of bourgeois society deny and kill humanism. This is the truth that Dostoevsky discovers. (p. 144)

Crime and Punishment is wholly, from first line to last, an excoriation of bourgeois selfishness and self-centeredness.

True, Raskolnikov to the very end of the novel cannot really understand *in logical terms* the wrongness of his ''idea.'' The ''idea'' continues to appear to him as *arithmetically correct.* But all the same he no longer believes in his ''idea'' with his whole nature, and he is punished, after the crime, in every situation he finds himself in and by every experience he undergoes. The whole movement of the novel, which from the outside looks only like a struggle between two strong logical minds—Raskolnikov and Porfiry, the struggle of the criminal with the consequences of his crime—serves to point up the unbearable sufferings of Raskolnikov, the sufferings of a renegade, the tortures of one who has cut himself off from humanity. The novel shows how unbearable it is for a man's consciousness to break with humanity; it shows the terror and emptiness of individualism, which can bring only agony and death to a man's soul. Dostoevsky shows logically, step by step, the gradual growth in the hero's soul of the utter terror of having broken his ties with mankind.

Yet Raskolnikov clutches desperately at any straw of hope that one may *live, still feel oneself a human being* after having committed such a crime. After the death of Marmeladov, for example, he suddenly feels as if a new life for him is possible. Taking upon himself the care of the Marmeladov family, he feels as if once again he has ties with humanity. (p. 145)

Raskolnikov has tried to become part of humanity once again by caring for the Marmeladovs, but he tries to do a contradictory thing also: he has tried to live like a human being while still asserting his right to commit such a crime, to be completely amoral and still be a human being. This explains Raskolnikov's dark attraction for Svidrigaylov. He does not understand that when he seeks out Svidrigaylov he is looking for a justification of his ''morality,'' or more properly, his ''immorality.'' (pp. 146-47)

Before the crime Raskolnikov could not live like a human being; after the crime he still cannot live like a human being and his sufferings are immeasurably greater. Yet he cannot kill the principle of humanity within him. This seems to be hinted at in his last dream when he tries again and again to kill the old woman with the butt end of an axe, and she remains unharmed and merely laughs at him. But perhaps one can say she laughs only at his weakness, at the fact that he is not made of the *right stuff*? So it might have seemed to Raskolnikov, but the whole artistic intent of the novel in all its particularity argues precisely for the opposite conclusion: that one cannot kill the principle of humanity within one. . . .

Though the novel is filled with terrible scenes of unbearable human experiences, there is something yet more horrible: this is the absence of any hint of tragic catharsis in the novel, the absence of any illumination or hope of resolution. Dostoevsky gives us a picture of humanity in an impasse. And such a picture is not true to reality. Humanity has never been and never will be in an impasse. You may lock it up, but it will always break out.

In condemning the revolt of Raskolnikov, Dostoevsky wanted to condemn along with it every social protest.

The chief and most terrible impasse to which Dostoevsky leads the reader is that there is no true alternative to boundless human suffering! . . . Dostoevsky's painful and cruel logic strove to show that every experience is overridingly hopeless and to show that life itself for man on earth is desperate and hopeless. (p. 147)

Vladimir Ermilov, ''A Soviet View: 1956,'' translated by Edward Wasiolek (an excerpt originally published in ''Prestuplenie i Nakazanie,'' in his F. M. Dostoevski, State Publisher of Arts and Letters, 1956), in Crime and Punishment and the Critics, *edited by Edward Wasiolek (© 1961 by Wadsworth Publishing Company, Inc.; reprinted by permission of Wadsworth Publishing Company, Belmont, CA 94002), Wadsworth, 1961, pp. 142-48.*

IRVING HOWE   (essay date 1957)

[Slavophilism may] be divided into at least three main tendencies: the pan-Slavists who provide a rationale for Tsarist imperialism; a middle group which fluctuates between its desire to retain Russian distinctiveness and its desire to reform Russian society within the framework of a constitutional monarchy; and the radicals who aspire toward a peasant democracy. Now the key—at least one key—to Dostoevsky is that he managed, with varying degrees of emphasis and clarity, to hold all three perspectives at once.

The dominant formal theme in his work is a conception of Russian destiny. (p. 55)

A disturbing though not unusual paradox: the writer whose most sacred image is that of Christ turning the other cheek demands the conquest of Constantinople, the almost craven apostle of humility exalts the use of brute power. Part of the truth about Dostoevsky is that this extraordinarily sensitive man who trembles for the slightest creature can also be a coarse and brutal reactionary.

For there *was* something coarse and brutal in Dostoevsky. He knew it perfectly well, hence his desperate straining for love and humility. The love-seeker or God-seeker is particularly vulnerable to self-torment if he inwardly believes that he seldom experiences true love and that instead of embracing God he merely celebrates his own ego. This is a central ambivalence of neurotic character—one is almost tempted to say of modern character; and it is nowhere more spectacularly illustrated than in Dostoevsky, whose spiritual imago is Alyosha Karamazov, but whose life is tainted by the lust of Dmitri, the skepticism of Ivan, the emotional torpor of Stavrogin.

At least in part, Dostoevsky's politics is a function of his psychology, that is, of his struggle to heal his moral fissure and of his horrified recoil from the sickness he finds in all men. Dostoevsky dreaded the autonomous intellect, the faithless drifting he had himself experienced and was later to portray in Ivan Karamazov; he feared that the intellectual, loosed from the controls of Christianity and alienated from the heart-warmth of the Russian people, would feel free to commit the most monstrous acts to quench his vanity. (pp. 55-6)

Though a tendentious moralist, Dostoevsky was an entirely honest novelist, and in his novels he could not but show that while the will to faith is strong in some modern intellectuals, it seldom leads them to the peace of faith. His God-seekers, like Shatov in *The Possessed,* are men peculiarly driven by anguish: the more serious their desire for God, the more must they acknowledge the distance separating them from Him— and the more they are tempted, in the manner of the radical Slavophiles, to assimilate God to the people. Since the quest of such characters is partly motivated by an intense dislike for commercial civilization, they often find themselves in unexpected conflict with society. Their ideas, it is true, have little in common with socialist doctrine, but their values lead them to an uneasy kinship with socialism as a critical activity.

Yet they cannot accept socialism. Dostoevsky despised it as "scientific," a bastard of the Enlightenment and the twin of rationalist atheism; he rejected it, also, because he feared that man might barter freedom for bread. (p. 56)

The Possessed is drenched in buffoonery. This itself is a major reason for the atmosphere of violent negation which hangs over the book. Dostoevsky's buffoonery means that while he takes seriously the problems raised in his novel he cannot do as much for the people who must face them, unwittingly, his book becomes a vote of no-confidence in society—both the seething Russian underworld and the stiffening overworld. (p. 58)

Buffoonery is appropriate to *The Possessed* because the characters are mainly pretenders. Stepan Trofimovich is a liberal pretending to heroism, a liberal who trembles before his shadow and is so lost in rhetoric that he cannot separate what he says from what he thinks. . . . Every character is a mockery of his own claims, a refutation of his own ideas; all are self-alienated in conduct and feverishly erratic in thought: even the saintly Father Tikhon suffers, suggestively, from a nervous tic.

A tone of buffoonery, a cast of pretenders—and a setting of provincial meanness. . . . The society of *The Possessed* is a society gone stale from lack of freedom, seedy from lack of cultivation. (pp. 58-9)

Stavrogin stands with Captain Lebyadkin, his brother-in-law and the most buffoonish of Dostoevsky's buffoons. It is raining. Stavrogin offers Lebyadkin an umbrella. In an oversweet voice Lebyadkin asks, "Am I worth it?" Stavrogin replies, "Anyone is worthy of an umbrella." And then Lebyadkin suddenly pours out: "At one stroke you define the minimum of human rights. . . ." Such a passage, deepening buffoonery into tragic statement, is the unique mark of Dostoevsky, possible only to the writer who had once said, "Man is a crook— and a crook is he who says so."

Stavrogin is the source of the chaos that streams through the characters; he possesses them but is not himself possessed. In the first part of the novel, where Dostoevsky plants several clues to his meaning, Stavrogin is likened to Pechorin, the Byronic protagonist of Lermontov's *A Hero of Our Time* who has lost the capacity for identifying or acting upon his emotions. Like Pechorin, Stavrogin seeks excitement because nothing excites him, experiments in sensuality because he wishes to *become* sensual. His tragedy is that he can replace the sense of cosmic fear only with the sense of cosmic void: the awareness of human limits which Dostoevsky regards as essential to life he entirely lacks. (pp. 61-2)

Stavrogin lives below, not beyond, good and evil; naturally so, for in the absence of desire, morality can hardly matter. The Nietzschean vision of "beyond good and evil" implies a harmonious resolution of desires to the point where moral regulation becomes superfluous; Stavrogin, by contrast, is on *this* side of morality. Yet it is no mere perversity on the part of his friends that they look upon him with awe, for in his wasted energies they see the potential of a Russia equally disordered and distraught. (p. 62)

In a sense he is We: all but one of the major characters are his doubles. Pyotr is his social double, Liza the Byroness his emotional double, and Marya, the cripple he has married, his double in derangement. Fedka the peasant murderer is a double through the link of the intellectual Kirilov, while Lebyadkin and Liputin are doubles in the dress of burlesque. The most important doubles are Kirilov and Shatov, who act out the two sides of Stavrogin's metaphysical problem. There is a significant political reason, though Dostoevsky would not accept it as a basic one, for the impasse in which these two find themselves. They have tried radicalism and recoiled, Shatov into hostility and Kirilov into indifference. . . .

Though at opposite poles ideologically, Shatov and Kirilov are in close emotional dependence, functioning as the split halves of an hypothetical self. Living in the same house yet tacitly avoiding each other, they represent in extreme form the issues thrown up by Stavrogin and debased by Verkhovensky. (p. 63)

Kirilov is one of Dostoevsky's most brilliant ideological projections but not, I think, an entirely satisfactory one. Is it really true, as Dostoevsky seems to assert, that the highest expression of the will is suicide? One would suppose that a higher heroism of the will might be a choice to live, a choice made with full awareness of the knowledge Kirilov has reached. In any case, Kirilov, having spontaneously helped Shatov, has lost his "right" to commit suicide, for by his act of help he has recognized a human obligation: he is no longer alone, he has acknowledged a "thou," he has granted the world a claim upon his life. And surely a man with his intellectual acuteness would recognize this. Still more troublesome is his readiness to take responsibility for the murder of Shatov. No doubt, Dostoevsky meant to suggest here that Kirilov's ideas make him indifferent to the fate of his friends and indeed of all men, but Dostoevsky himself has shown us otherwise: he could not help presenting Kirilov as a good man. For once—it does not happen very often—Dostoevsky the novelist has been tripped up by Dostoevsky the ideologue.

Shatov is conceived with greater consistency and depth. As he tells his wife, he is a Slavophile because he cannot be a Russian—which is another of Dostoevsky's marvelous intuitions, this one lighting up the whole problem of the intellectual's estrangement and the strategies of compensation by which he tries to overcome it. (p. 64)

In Shatov's mind, as in Dostoevsky's, God figures as a national protector rather than a universal mover, Christianity is seen as a radical morality committed equally to the extremes of ecstasy and suffering, and paradise, being realizable on earth, approaches the prescription Nietzsche offered for the good life. Before Nietzsche wrote, "What is done out of love always takes place beyond good and evil," Dostoevsky had written, "There is no good and bad." When Shatov declares the people to be the body of God, he offers a refracted version of nineteenth-century utopianism with its dream of a human fraternity that will dispense with the yardsticks of moral measurement. Together with this utopian faith, which cannot easily be reconciled with most versions of Christianity, Dostoevsky had a strong sense of the conservative and authoritarian uses of organized religion. . . .

Politics is left to Pyotr Verkhovensky, whose role in the book, as a Nechaev turned buffoon, is to bring the fantasies and fanaticisms of the Russian intelligentsia into visible motion. He reduces Kirilov's metaphysical speculations to petty problems of power, acts upon Stavrogin's nihilism by spreading confusion through all levels of society, and deflates the liberal rhetoric of his father, Stepan Trofimovich, to mere political maneuver. (p. 65)

Simply as a character in a novel, Verkhovensky is somewhat nebulous. What does he believe? Does he believe anything at all? Which of the many motives suggested for him are we to credit? How much sincerity, how much guile, can we allow him? Is he a revolutionist, a police spy or both? Twice he describes himself as "a scoundrel of course and not a socialist"—which is to imply that a socialist is something other than he, something other than a scoundrel. . . . Though Dostoevsky is often most remarkable for the life-like fluidity of his characterization, Verkhovensky is allowed to become too fluid, perhaps because Dostoevsky was never quite sure what to make of him. (pp. 65-6)

Toward the wretched little circle of plotters which revolves about Pyotr Verkhovensky, Dostoevsky shows no sympathy: *he does not need to,* he is their spiritual brother, his is the revilement of intimacy. Mocking and tormenting them with fraternal violence, Dostoevsky places each of the radicals exactly: Liputin, a cesspool of a man, frothing with gossip and slander, yet sincere in his reforming zeal; Virginsky, a pure enthusiast whom the latest apostle of the most advanced ideas will always be able to lead by the nose; Erkel, a fanatical youth searching for a master to worship and finding him in Verkhovensky; and Shigalov, a superb caricature of the doctrinaire. (p. 66)

Dostoevsky's politics are a web of confusion—few fears now seem more absurd than his fear that Rome and socialism would band together against the Orthodox Church; yet he is unequalled in modern literature for showing the muddle that may lie beneath the order and precision of ideology. Himself the most ideological of novelists, which may be half his secret, he also fears and resists ideology, which may be the other half. In our time ideology cannot be avoided: there is hardly a choice: even the most airy-minded liberal must live with it. Dostoevsky knew this, and would have mocked those cultivated souls who yearn for a life "above mere ideas." But ideology is also a great sickness of our time—and this is true despite one's suspicion of most of the people who say so. In all of his novels Dostoevsky shows how ideology can cripple human impulses, blind men to simple facts, make them monsters by tempting them into that fatal habit which anthropologists call "reifying" ideas. (pp. 67-8)

[All] but one of the major characters is a double of Stavrogin, and that exception is, of course, Stepan Trofimovich, the liberal with heroic memories. Toward him Dostoevsky is least merciful of all; he stalks him with a deadly aim; he humiliates him, badgers him, taunts him, and finally shatters him—and yet, he loves him. (p. 68)

In his portrait of Stepan Trofimovich, Dostoevsky incorporated every criticism Marx or Nietzsche or Carlyle would make of classical liberalism; and then he transcended them all, for Stepan Trofimovich in his ridiculous and hysterical way is a sentient human being whom one grows to love and long for, so that the actual man seems more important than anything that may be said about him. As the book progresses, Stepan Trofimovich moves through a number of mutations: the liberal as dependent, the liberal as infant, the liberal as fool (in both senses), the liberal as dandy, the liberal who tries to assert his independence, the liberal as spoiled darling of the radicals, as *agent provocateur,* as provincial, as bohemian, as bootlicker of authority, and the liberal as philosopher. . . . In each of these roles or phases, Stepan Trofimovich demonstrates the truth of Dostoevsky's remark that "The higher liberalism and the higher liberal, that is a liberal without any definite aim, is possible only in Russia."

Yet it is Stepan Trofimovich who is allowed the most honorable and heroic end. Driven to hysteria by the behavior of his son, his patroness and himself, he sets out in his old age on a mad pilgrimage, taking to the road, he knows not where, "to seek for Russia." Since for Dostoevsky salvation comes only from extreme suffering, Stepan Trofimovich begins to rise, to gather to himself the scattered energies of the book, after having been completely broken at the fete. (p. 69)

If we ask ourselves, what is the source of Dostoevsky's greatness, there can of course be no single answer. But surely part of the answer is that no character is allowed undisputed domination of the novel, all are checked and broken when they become too eager in the assertion of their truths. Once Stavrogin has asked Shatov the terrible question, "And in God?", Shatov can never control the book, and even after Stepan Trofimovich has soared to a kind of quixotic grandeur he is pulled down to reality by his old patroness who tells a priest: "You will have to confess him again in another hour! That's the sort of man he is."

Dostoevsky is the greatest of all ideological novelists because he always distributes his feelings of identification among all his characters—though putting it this way makes it seem too much an act of the will, while in reality it far transcends the will. . . . And Dostoevsky looks at the world through the eyes of all his people: Stavrogin and Father Tikhon, Stepan Trofimovich and Shatov, even Lebyadkin and Pyotr Verkhovensky. He *exhausts* his characters, scours all the possibilities of their being. None escapes humiliation and shame, none is left free from attack. In the world of Dostoevsky, no one is spared, but there is a supreme consolation: no one is excluded. (p. 70)

> Irving Howe, *"Dostoevsky: The Politics of Salvation," in his* Politics and the Novel *(copyright 1957; reprinted by permission of the publisher, Horizon Press, New York), Horizon, 1957 (and reprinted in* Dostoevsky: A Collection of Critical Essays, *edited by René Wellek, Prentice-Hall, Inc., 1962, pp. 53-70).*

MURRAY KRIEGER   (essay date 1960)

The Idiot is a novel of the desperate struggle for personal human dignity in a world that finds endless ways of depriving man of it. In the major action, in the minor actions like Ippolit's "Explanation" and mock suicide or like General Ivolgin's pitiable end at the hands of the pitiless Lebedyev, in the countless minor tales that are related to us along the way, always it is the beseeching human cry that asks that one may really matter and may be cherished for mattering. The youthful, deluded "liberals" demand dignity with such ferocity and spite that we are assured of the savage sickness that speaks through them and their program. Our openly demoniacal creatures have a purity and an integrity of demand so intense that, given the alloyed nature of what we can be given at best in life, they can be satisfied only when their life itself has been refined away to the nothingness they have sought. Myshkin seeks only to give dignity to each, even—or rather especially—at the cost of his own. But the bizarre enthusiasm of his relentless efforts appears as an inversion that, perhaps more surely than any alternative, would deny dignity to others through its very magnanimity. Thus he too must be rejected. And Yevgeny, the retiring critical intelligence that knows the futility of the problem too well to bother confronting it, helps us reject Myshkin's kind of offer as the others do. Myshkin retires to his wretched safety, and we are sorry to see him go—as is Yevgeny who really "has a heart." For we are left with no further alternative possibilities —where can one go beyond Myshkin?—since Yevgeny's way is also the way of retirement.

Or is there not another possibility, however imperfect, after all? The last words in the novel are spoken to Yevgeny and not by him. They are spoken by one of Dostoevsky's most magnificent creations, Lizaveta Epanchin, the general's wife and Aglaia's mother. Totally Russian and totally winning, if perhaps not totally sane, she is complaining about the unreality of Europe: ". . . all this life abroad, and this Europe of yours is all a fantasy, and all of us abroad are only a fantasy." . . . She is always a vigorous force for life, however messily she runs it. Even the ruin of Aglaia cannot long deter her. She must return to pick up her reality at home and must speak to the expatriate Yevgeny "almost wrathfully" and in warning against withdrawal. For Myshkin has not spoken the last word, although he has spoken the most extreme word. Whatever word is spoken beyond this is not spoken out of the tragic vision. (pp. 226-27)

> Murray Krieger, *"The Perils of 'Enthusiast' Virtue," in his* The Tragic Vision: Variations on a Theme in Literary Interpretation *(copyright © 1960 by Murray Krieger; reprinted by permission of Holt, Rine-*

hart and Winston, Publishers), Holt, Rinehart and Winston, 1960, pp. 195-227.*

EDWARD WASIOLEK   (essay date 1964)

There are no murderers, prostitutes, demonic wills, or child torturers in Dostoevsky's early works; no great dialogues on socialism, the rational organization of human happiness, free will, sin, suffering, or God. Everything we think of when we think of the great Dostoevsky seems to be missing. Yet much that was to become recurrent, insistent, and centrifugal in his later work is already in the early work. It may be hesitant, uncertain, and not always clear, but it is already there. (p. 3)

There is something else in the early works, too, and it is more basic and pervasive than either themes, character types, or situations. The psychology of Dostoevsky's mature works is already faintly present. God, crime, and the universal dialogues are missing, but the springs of human motivation that will bring to birth the great questions are unmistakably there in embryonic form.

The new psychology appears already in Dostoevsky's second published work, *The Double* . . . , and seems to his contemporaries to be willful obscurity. (p. 4)

From the perspective we now enjoy, *Poor Folk* promises less than many other of Dostoevsky's works in the forties. It is unconscionably long, repetitious, and dull. Its main point . . . is made over and over again: in a creature poorly endowed by nature and crushed by an unjust economic and social system, there glimmers nevertheless a golden heart, which is the pledge of the brotherhood of all men. (pp. 6-7)

We know why Makar suffers: he has to endure the smells of the kitchen, listen to the screams and racket of the lodgers, bear the jokes of his fellow lodgers, and he doesn't have enough money to buy Varenka grapes, candies, and frills. We know why he feels humiliated: the sole of his shoe comes off, he has to go slopping in the mud begging for a loan, with a cur at his heels, and the button of his uniform flies off in the presence of his excellency. We know what he wants: to be the protector of Varenka. And we know why he is unable to keep her: Bykov has more money, more power, and more guts. Makar's needs are real, and his desire to play the protector is understandable. He gets desperate when he cannot borrow money, and when there is a villain trying to take Varenka away from him; and he feels rebellious when he sees fools favored by fortune and better men trampled by fortune. There is no "causelessness" in the fortunes of Makar Devushkin. (p. 7)

The springs of his emotions and actions are largely economic. But where are the springs of Golyadkin's feeling and action? Makar can say that he is content when he is well dressed, shod, and fed; Golyadkin cannot. He is well dressed, well shod, and well fed, but there are no happy moments, only desperately busy ones meeting a thickening atmosphere of plots, intrigues, and impending destruction. He sees plots about him when there are no plots; people envy him when there is nothing to envy, dangers threaten him when there are no dangers. Yet these "causeless" fears are real enough to send him flying to do battle with them, and strong enough to drive him mad.

The real Golyadkin is a titular counselor living on Shestilavochnaya street; he serves in an office copying official documents; and he is the butt of his fellow workers' jokes. . . . Golyadkin hates gossips, toadies, and hypocrites because he knows he is one; he refuses to accept himself as he is. The distasteful Golyadkin, he thinks, is an invention of his enemies; the honorable, straight, courageous Golyadkin has been hidden, but will soon issue forth to chastise his enemies. (pp. 7-8)

Golyadkin's hatred of his wrong "self" has an important correlative: a desperate desire to be the right self. He has an overwhelming need to be a Golyadkin who is admired, respected, and envied. He will go to any lengths—even unto madness—to deny his bad self; he will go to any lengths to pursue his good self. It is his drive for *ambitsiya* (self-respect and dignity) that drives him to people his world with demons, enemies, and persecutors. He has to create the enemies so as to preserve for himself the image of a Golyadkin who is pure, well-intentioned, courageous, and straightforward.

What we get in Golyadkin—and admittedly it is not entirely successful—is the beginning of a new "logic" of human motivation. . . . Dostoevsky was already sensing dramatically what he was to say explicitly later in his career: that man's tragedy and his deepest problems do not spring from social and economic causes, but from his own insecurities and his own unquenchable drive for self-worth and dignity. Dostoevsky portrays not how social and economic facts act on Golyadkin, but how Golyadkin acts on social and economic facts. Golyadkin distorts reality, reshapes it, and remakes it to fit the needs that drive him. There are no enemies, no intrigues, and no plots against him—not at least as Golyadkin imagines them—but the insecurity that drives Golyadkin to imagine them and believe in them is real. *Golyadkin "creates" himself.* He tries to create a world that will answer to how he wants to see himself; he succeeds only in creating a world that mirrors his inner conflict.

Golyadkin remakes the world in the way he wants it to be, but he is not strong enough to sustain it. Reality presses on him with more force than he can project his image on reality, and, finally, in a kind of ultimate protection, he withdraws from reality entirely. His madness anticipates those frequent crises of "brain fever" in Dostoevsky's later novels. In the later novels, this "brain fever" is often a harbinger of rebirth; but Dostoevsky has as yet no conception of "rebirth," and must leave Golyadkin trapped between the reality of himself and the reality of the world. (pp. 9-10)

Golyadkin is motivated by some impulse to self-worth—as he understands it—and this impulse is powerful enough for him to deny what he is (as an economic and social unity), and powerful enough for him to try to create a new image. But still, this is what madmen do, and if Golyadkin and the kind of logic he represents are to be more than a case of growing insanity, the causes that drive him to insanity have to be a sign of something more than derangement. (pp. 10-11)

With Golyadkin, Dostoevsky had at the very outset of his career touched on the springs of action that were to motivate—in different settings and in a different philosophical and religious framework—his later heroes. But Dostoevsky himself was not strong enough to resist the misunderstanding of his contemporaries. Always sensitive to criticism, always ready to believe the worst of himself, he backs away from Golyadkin and experiments less successfully with different character types, themes, and forms. (p. 11)

The Underground Man is vain, nasty, petty, tyrannical, vicious, cowardly, morbidly sensitive, and self-contradictory. He hates his fellow workers, never forgets an insult, tyrannizes over those who offer affection, and offers affection to those who tyrannize over him. He turns love into lust, friendship into tyranny, and principle into spite. He respects neither love, nor affection, nor friendship, nor principle, nor logic. He is a sick and spiteful man. And yet Dostoevsky approves of him. Even more, he makes him his hero. For in this vain, petty, nasty, vicious, spiteful creature, indeed in the very marrow of that cold and malignant spite is a principle that is precious for him and for Dostoevsky: freedom. (p. 39)

The Underground Man is a man of "acute consciousness," and with his acute consciousness he sees what the laws of nature fully imply. The normal man of action believes at the same time in the laws of nature and in personal responsibility. The two are contradictory. (pp. 39-40)

The Underground Man refuses to accept the laws of nature. Against science, against the laws of reason, against the whole movement of man's systematic accumulation of knowledge, against the ideal of the Crystal Palace, which will envelop into one unified system not only inanimate nature but man himself—against all that man pursues and dreads—the Underground Man opposes his unique, capricious, subjective world of feeling: wish, dream, hope, and, yes, cruelty, suffering, pettiness, and viciousness. (p. 40)

Do the laws of nature exist? Is man a function of some infinite calculus, or is he free to follow the sweet curve of his foolish will? When the Underground Man talks about the "bulls," the normal men of action, he talks as if he believed the laws exist, and when he talks of the helpless delight he tastes when he sins according to his nature, he reasons as if the laws exist. (p. 41)

Still what man has always believed in and what he wants to believe in may not be what is. Man has always acted as if he had free choice, but he may have always deceived himself. We cannot prove one way or the other whether the laws of nature exist, but what we can know is what follows a belief in the laws of nature and what follows their rejection. The Underground Man does not believe in the laws, and what follows from this disbelief is brilliantly explained and dramatized by Dostoevsky.

As a man of acute consciousness, the Underground Man comes to understand—but not to believe in—the implacable laws of reason and nature. The more he is conscious of the "wall" (the laws of nature), the more his resentment and spite is kindled against it. It is in the defiance and spite that he finds the will to oppose the wall. His free, foolish, unfettered caprice is his only weapon against the laws of nature, and his only gauge of freedom. He can know his freedom only by acting his freedom. Consequently, he must dramatize to others, but most of all to himself, that he is free. (pp. 41-2)

The Underground Man does not want to be defined, and cannot be defined. At every moment he redefines himself by contradiction and denial. Why does he do this? Because such denial and contradiction and such constant and continual redefinition, are a pledge of his freedom. To the extent that he has a nature that is defined and knowable, to that extent his actions and his choices are a function of that nature. His nature must be the result of his choices, and not his choices the result of his nature. If he is to be free, he must make his nature, and he must make it with every choice. Like the French existentialists who were to follow three-quarters of a century later, he must be *"en marge"*; he must be in revolt not only against society, but against himself, not once, not only today or tomorrow, but in eternal revolt. . . . [The] Underground Man carries the principle of contradiction to every cranny of his consciousness, opposing every belief, action, thought, and attitude with their opposites in a ceaseless and unremitting struggle to assert his freedom by denying himself.

But this freedom implies an implacable and terrible truth about the actions of men and their treatment of others. If there are no laws to one's nature—and there cannot be if one is to be free—then man alone is his own law. And if he is his own end, he will make everything else serve that end, including other people. (p. 43)

[The] Underground Man wants to be insulted and humiliated, looks for insult, and provokes it when he cannot find it. Why? Because there is pleasure in being hurt, because it increases the self's consciousness of itself, and, most of all, because it provides the motive for hurting others. Seeking out hurt is the mechanism that keeps the vicious and barren circle of hurt and being hurt moving. This duel, which the self provokes and in which it is trapped, is even more apparent at the farewell party given by Zverkov, which the Underground Man insists on attending.

If the Underground Man is right and man is free—and Dostoevsky believes him to be right—then not only an implacable duel of wills follows upon this freedom, but every general truth becomes an illusion. If general truths are not illusions, then the general truths will exist prior to our choice of them; and if they exist prior to our choice, then the choice is not free but determined by them. Truth as something absolute, timeless, and pre-existing to our choices is impossible in Dostoevsky's dialectic of freedom. Truth like everything else in his world depends on our wills. If we continue to believe in general truths, then we are believing in illusions. The consequences of this dialectic of freedom are terrifying: every action of principle, every act of unselfishness, every good, beautiful, virtuous, reasonable act is only appearance. No matter how much the naïve and tender romantic soul may want to believe in them, the man of acute consciousness knows that they are deceptions, for beneath them is the reality of man's free will and his deadly duel with other "free" wills. For some, the battle is waged not only beneath the appearance of general truths, it is waged *with* them. For the will in its freedom will subvert all to its uses: weakness as well as strength; virtue as well as vice; good as well as evil; the beautiful as well as the ugly. All this is implied in the philosophical chapter of the first part [of *Notes from the Underground*] and in the incidents with Zverkov. The Underground Man comes to recognize, especially in his encounter with Liza, that the sublime and the beautiful are a lovely and unreal dream, a deception, and even more, a deadly weapon for the imposition of his will upon others. (pp. 47-8)

Because of his corrosive consciousness the Underground Man cannot believe in his dreams; he knows them to be improbable and unreal, and he knows that they are a kind of self-indulgence. All he can do is gnash his teeth and break into tears of frustration. But the incident with Liza intervenes, and in his duel with Liza comes a flash of insight: if he cannot believe in his dream, he can *use* it. After he has finished making love to the prostitute, the Underground Man sits silently in the darkness with the humiliation he has suffered at the hands of Zverkov and company burning in his heart. Liza sits silently and indifferently in her corner, and the Underground Man turns to move her from indifference. He tries to move her first by radiating sullen and silent hatred to her, and then by narrating a coarse and invented story about watery graves and the dropping of a coffin. She answers perfunctorily, neither frightened

nor interested. Irritated by her attitude and convinced that he has been too gentle with her, he begins to paint a picture of the sweetness of life even in sorrow as a contrast to her deplorable state, when suddenly "something flamed up in me, a sort of aim had *appeared.*" What follows is a moral lecture on the joys of familial and conjugal love. The point of the beautiful picture is to express concern and sympathy for Liza's plight and a desire that she, too, might enjoy these delights. The effect of his sympathetic and compassionate concern is to leave Liza in convulsive despair before the condition she finds herself in and with a desperate desire to leave her present way of life.

But it is his success in moving her to a desire for a better life that irritates the Underground Man afresh, for he understands that something other than concern for her life had prompted his compassionate moral lecture. What he had really intended, although only dimly apparent to him while he had waxed eloquent, becomes clear shortly after he leaves her. . . . The truth that had appeared dimly to him when he began to move her indifference and that had blazed out at him disgustingly after he had been successful is this: that though he had by his compassion and his eloquent picturing of a different kind of life reduced her to convulsive despair and to the desperate decision to give up her old life, he had been laughing at her the whole time. (pp. 50-1)

What the Underground Man discovers in his encounter with Liza is the effectiveness of "good" in exercising his will on another person. What he wants, as is clear from his fully developed psychology in the first and chronologically later part, is to feel the power of his will over other wills. (p. 52)

But Liza refuses at first to act as he has expected her to. She refuses to return insult with insult, hurt with hurt. At first she refuses because she takes his sympathy and concern to be sincere; and then, when he confesses that he has been laughing at her, she sees in a flash of insight his unhappiness, and through the warmth of true love she momentarily breaks through the vicious circle of hurt and being hurt. But it is not love but insult that the Underground Man wants, because by the return of insult, Liza will acknowledge and justify his "rules." Her love, however, is at once a "liberation" from the trap of hurting and being hurt and, because the Underground Man is a victim of his own psychology, a new motive for insult. . . . The Underground Man leaves Liza with an insult burning in her soul, convinced that "this highest form of consciousness" (consciousness of self) is better than the love he might offer her if he overtook her. And he leaves the pages of the novel with an insult to the reader, charging him with living only from books, afraid of life, and comfortable only as some stillborn, general man. (pp. 52-3)

[*Notes from the Underground*] is great because Dostoevsky's psychology, metaphysic, and craft first take mature form in it. The psychology which he uncertainly discerns in *The Double,* which he pursues erratically in the forties, which life confirms in prison, and which the threat of the radical critics raises to a philosophical level, finds its mature metaphysic in *Notes from the Underground.* (p. 53)

What is the psychology that takes mature form in the *Notes* and that will lie at the core of the motivations of the great characters to follow? It begins with characters who—like the Underground Man—are as sensitive as hunchbacks, quick to take offense, terrible in their hurt, boundless in their vanity, unforgiving in their grudges, and delighted in their pettiness.

And it begins and turns on the word *obida* (hurt). Hurt always generates another hurt; every hurt person wants immediately to make someone else bear his hurt. Thus, our abnormally sensitive hero is always paying back someone for something. (p. 54)

The Dostoevskian hero not only pays back for the hurt he suffers, but he looks for hurt to suffer. He likes being hurt. When he cannot find it, he imagines it, so that it will sting in his blood with the pungency of real hurt. He has a stake in being hurt: he seeks it, pursues it, and needs it. The vicious circle of "hurt-and-be-hurt" is something of his own making. He is at once provoker and sufferer, persecutor and victim.

But why does he do this? We can explain why the Dostoevskian hero hurts others by the law of self-preservation, but the desire to be hurt contradicts the same law. The answer lies in Dostoevsky's conception of the *will* as an unqualified first premise of existence. It finds satisfaction in hurting others and in hurting itself. In hurting others, it is conscious of its power over others; in hurting itself it is conscious of itself. What the will wants more than anything else is awareness of itself, and it will subvert every motive to gain this satisfaction. The will or the self for Dostoevsky is limited by nothing; it is boundless in appetite; and it is universal in presence. . . . The terror and freedom of the will are indissolubly linked. A freedom that is qualified is not freedom, and an unqualified freedom is a monstrous force unleashed on the world. Dostoevsky accepts the freedom, and he accepts the horror. (pp. 54-5)

Reason, despite conventional critical opinion, is not such a force. For Dostoevsky, reason can neither limit the horror nor preserve the freedom. In its pretensions—but they remain pretensions—it would destroy the freedom of the will. The Underground Man argues—and Dostoevsky agrees with him—that if rationally defined laws of nature exist, then the freedom of the will is impossible. The Underground Man's logic is impeccable: if the laws of human nature exist, then by their very comprehensiveness—like the laws of physical nature—they will be predictive of every human action.

But the laws of nature do not exist, because reason itself, as an objective entity, does not exist. There is no "reason" in Dostoevsky's world, only reasoners. . . . An idea for Dostoevsky is always someone's idea, and reason is always someone's reasoning. *Every act of reason for Dostoevsky is a covert act of will.*

Reason cannot control the terror of the will's freedom, but something else can, and this something else brings us to the core of Dostoevsky's moral dialectic and consequently to the core of what motivates his characters. The will is the primary fact of man's nature, but man can, for Dostoevsky, create a "new" nature in Christ. *Dostoevsky's moral world is dialectical: man is poised with every choice he makes between the self and God.* These two poles are absolute and unqualified, and man *makes* his nature by choosing his acts to serve one or the other. . . . Man in Dostoevsky's world does not choose what is already determined, but determines what he chooses. Self-sacrifice abstractly considered or as conventionally classified is "good," but it may be, in Dostoevsky's world, "bad." (pp. 55-6)

Man freely chooses the value his act shall have, and the value his act shall have comes from the choice—the most basic in Dostoevsky's moral world—of the act for *self* or for *God*. . . . Without God, the Dostoevskian hero is condemned to meet only himself, no matter how beautiful his intention, no matter how "good" his act.

Nor does Dostoevsky's moral dialectic introduce by the back door abstract moral distinctions in the form of acts that can be neatly and determinately classified as "for self" and "for God." . . . Nothing astonished Dostoevsky more, in his own world and in the world of his created characters, than the endless transformations the self could undergo, using for its own purposes any impulse, no matter how good, the infinite refinement of the mind in rationalizing any act, no matter how evil. (pp. 56-7)

Dostoevsky saw the world through the prism of a highly conscious metaphysic: man striving to express his will upon man and seeking confirmation of self in injuring and being injured; man meeting at every victory over himself a transmuted image and temptation of his self; man pursuing evil up the ladder of good, using the highest goods for the deepest injuries; and man, with God, occasionally wrenching himself out of these traps into selflessness. The Devil truly finds his most secure footing in Dostoevsky's world, as in traditional Christianity, in the most sublime virtues. For Dostoevsky's drama of the injured and the injuring, in its highest reaches, is translated into the drama of the forgiven and the forgiving. (p. 57)

The world view that takes mature form in *Notes from the Underground* and that will be refined in dramatic form in the great novels that follow is neither confused, nor contradictory, nor paradoxical. At its base lies the dialectic in which good may be chosen to be evil and evil chosen to be good. Not every character who does "good" in Dostoevsky's world is good, and not every character who does "evil" is evil. (pp. 57-8)

[The] oppositions that emerge in *Notes from the Underground* are not final. The individual freedom that contradicts the laws of universal rational harmony is in turn contradicted by what the freedom implies: a destructive will. The problem that Dostoevsky faces after writing the *Notes* is how to preserve the freedom and restrain its destructive implications. (p. 58)

The Dream of the Ridiculous Man is *blasphemy,* and yet it has been taken universally by Dostoevsky's interpreters as *sacrament.* If one can abstract the dream from the Ridiculous Man, then it is Dostoevsky's dream, for in every respect it is what Dostoevsky was convinced would follow a free choice grounded in the truth of Christ. But it cannot be abstracted, for no idea, no vision, no conviction in Dostoevsky's world can be abstracted. The dream of the Ridiculous Man is *his dream,* and it is as good as his motives, and his motives are self-interested. Dostoevsky has presented in this story what he has presented so often: he has placed some cherished truth in the mouth and being of a self-interested person. In the *Notes* he gave his argument against "compulsory rational happiness" to the Underground Man; in *The Possessed* he gave some of his most cherished ideas to the clown Lebedev; in *The Idiot,* some of his convictions to Ippolit. Dostoevsky criticism will always go wrong when it separates Dostoevsky's ideas from those characters who carry the ideas. In *The Dream of the Ridiculous Man* Dostoevsky shows, with great refinement, how even the most august truths can be corrupted to the service of the will. (pp. 145-46)

The Ridiculous Man . . . plays all the parts in his dream: he is the creator, corrupter, and redeemer of the "sinless" people. The shaft of pity he feels for the little girl is what gives birth to the dream of the golden age. But the pity that flickers in his heart is corrupted, and the dream tells us why he corrupts the Golden Age. He corrupts the Golden Age so that he can make it *his, and his alone*. The shaft of pity he feels for the small beggar is a threat to his conviction that nothing matters, and the dream is his way of coming to terms with the threat. And he comes to terms with the threat by killing the truth—hence the shot through his heart—and redeeming it in his own image. He corrupts the truth by making it his, and as is frequent in Dostoevsky's work, this corruption takes the form of a grotesque imitation of Christ. (pp. 146-47)

The Ridiculous Man wants to suffer for the people he has corrupted, and when he awakens, he continues to want to suffer for the people about him. He invites abuse and suffers gladly the taunts and charges of madness that his "preaching" brings. Why? So that the truth that has threatened his control of the world—through indifference—will be his weapon for controlling the world. The truth is something that he alone knows, and something that he alone will always know. He has even been careful enough to forget it somewhat, and indeed even boasts a little that perhaps he made it all up. Life and preaching are to be his goals; not—it can be noticed—"life and living." Can there be any doubt as to what the point of the "preaching" is to be? It is to emphasize again and again his special status. It is in his martyrdom to feel again and again—his superiority in truth and everyone else's inferiority in falsehood. The Ridiculous Man has carried the blasphemy of truth to its highest point, the blasphemy of Christ.

In Dostoevsky's moral dialectic the highest goods can be corrupted to the deepest evils, and it is often hard to see the difference. But the difference is there, and it is absolute. Arkady Dolgoruky, in perhaps an unintentional yet meaningful ambiguity, says of his father, Versilov: "I considered him a preacher [*propovednik*]: he carried the Golden Age in his heart and he knew the future about atheism." The Golden Age—without Christ—is atheism. The Golden Age the Ridiculous Man dreams of is a Golden Age without Christ; even more, it is a Golden Age by which he attempts to make of himself a Christ. (pp. 147-48)

> *Edward Wasiolik, in his* Dostoevsky: The Major Fiction *(reprinted by permission of The MIT Press, Cambridge, Massachusetts; copyright © 1964 by The Massachusetts Institute of Technology), The MIT Press, 1964, 255 p.*

V. S. PRITCHETT (essay date 1964)

The people of Dostoevsky's novels are notable not for their isolation but for their gregariousness. The infection is common. They run in crowds. If they plan to suicide or murder they tell everyone. They are missionaries in mass morbidity, mass guilt, and mass confession. Even when alone they are not absolutely alone; they have at least two selves. One hears not the private groan but the public lamentation. (p. 407)

The irrational is no longer the novelty it was, and we are consequently less struck by the madness of Dostoevsky than we used to be. A sensationalist he was; but now, whenever I open a novel of his, my first impression is one of realism and sanity. He knows the world from behind the scenes. The accent is decisive. The voice bristles with satire and expands with a capacious humor. Dostoevsky at his best writes like a hunted man who, for the moment, has fooled the bloodhounds and has time to confess and to laugh before the baying drives him on again. . . . Dostoevsky could see the terrors of our double natures, the fever in which our inner ghosts encounter each other, but he saw the raw comedy of this conjunction. . . . Look at *Uncle's Dream* for a moment. It is a farce; a masterful provincial lady in a scandal-mongering clique, attempts to marry off her beautiful daughter to a decrepit prince. One can picture the whole story as a very funny and quite unreal piece of theater. But even this mechanical piece of fooling lives on several planes. One moment the Prince, with his wig, his false beard and his derelict body, is a horror; the next moment he is ridiculous. Then, suddenly, he appears delightful. We long for him to appear again as we long for Stefan Trofimovitch in *The Possessed*. The Prince even attains a rickety dignity, and from dignity, he dwindles to a thing of pity. After all, we say, he did not really lie when he said his proposal of marriage was a dream. The conventional comic writer draws his characters to a single pattern of wit or makes the world a convenience for his joke. Dostoevsky does not do this. He is one of the great comic writers because, however satirically he may begin, he always grows into humor, and the humor is not imposed on life but arises out of it. He is aware of the collisions that take place in our natures. . . . Dostoevsky explored the whole, and the thing that is comic on one page may become tragic on the next. The profoundly humorous writers are humorous because they are responsive to the hopeless, uncouth concatenations of life. (pp. 407-09)

Each man and woman, I warn you (says Dostoevsky, the incurable novelist), is capable of becoming a novel in himself, a novel by Dostoevsky, moreover. I warn you it is impossible to do anything whatever with any human being, unless you are fully willing to take the tumultuous consequences of his being human. (p. 410)

[It] is odd that Dostoevsky should ever have been regarded as the novelist of the isolated soul. . . . In the great novels he is so blatantly the writer of spiritual headlines; in *The House of the Dead* he was content with the laconic news. No one who has read it can say that he ignored the problems of society. Like Balzac, on the contrary, he plunders society. . . . [In *The Eternal Husband*] it has been said that Dostoevsky parodied himself—it was written after *The Idiot* and *Crime and Punishment*—and certainly all his ideas are here: the double, the unconscious, the fantasies, dreams, persecutions, suspicions, shames and exchanges of personality. Even a child is tortured. But surely this comic masterpiece, a comedy which (as always in Dostoevsky) carries its own underworld along with it, stands completely on its own feet. In the first place the growth of Veltchaninov's sense of guilt from a vague irritation to mind and health into definite consciousness is described with wonderful objectivity and suspense. The value of psychological analysis to the novel lay, for Dostoevsky, in its latent dramatic quality. Psychology was dramatic; for us it becomes more and more a metaphor or explanation. (pp. 410-11)

The Eternal Husband is no doubt so refreshingly precise in its psychology, so well composed and economically written, so brilliant in its commentary because—for the time being—Dostoevsky had exhausted his anxiety for salvation. This is his one Western novel. It came from that part of him that liked to cut a social figure and was written during a rare period of equipoise and untroubled self-satisfaction. It has the genial air of a successful presumption, and it might easily have been written in our century, not his. And yet it could not have been. For the effect of psychological intuitions and discoveries upon our novel is to make it reminiscent, autobiographical, plotless; whereas in Dostoevsky's hands the novel became inventive, dramatic and far richer in plot than the rest of Russian fiction. (pp. 411-12)

V. S. Pritchett, "The Minor Dostoevsky," in his The Living Novel and Later Appreciations *(copyright 1947 © 1964; renewed 1975 by V. S. Pritchett; reprinted by permission of Random House, Inc.; in Canada by Literistic, Ltd.), revised edition, Random House, 1964, pp. 406-12.*

KENNETH REXROTH (essay date 1968)

[The] novels of Dostoievsky are not tragedies; they are enormously complicated farces. Dostoievsky is the first major novelist to make a literary virtue of the incorrigible immaturity of his people. . . .

[The] stylelessness of Dostoievsky; the pressure of serial deadlines, gambling debts, sickness, female trouble; his general buffleheadedness; and his utmost naïveté when confronted with general ideas, all conspired to release in Dostoievsky an irony of stylelessness, a literary subconscious that behind all the intellectual sentimentality and moral melodrama truly comprehended the simple absurdity of the human condition.

Superficially, the various conflicting "messages" of Dostoievsky, considered as he was for so long as a philosophical novelist, are the opposite of wisdom; they are general ideas reduced to foolishness and hysteria. So the relations of the Karamazov brothers and their father are not tragic, but embarrassing. (p. 255)

Yet something happens. Slowly, out of all the shambles, out of the profundity of a bottomless marsh, a formal vision emerges; life is reduced to the simplest terms, relationships to stark matter of fact, motives to behavior. When we go back and read one of the major novels over—*The Brothers Karamazov, The Idiot, The Possessed*—we discover that Dostoievsky has been mocking us, and himself, from the beginning. (pp. 255-56)

This self-mockery is consistent, and once we recognize it, we see it everywhere. It is most obvious in [*A Raw Youth,*] a novel seldom read nowadays. . . . It is almost a parody of *David Copperfield;* but it is also a comic variety show of all of Dostoievsky's own favorite characters and situations. Yet it is far from being a caricature—in fact, it has been called his greatest novel. The method of Dostoievsky, and he did have a method, becomes conscious and explicit; the messages dissolve, and the dilemmas along with them.

For a generation after it was written critics debated, "Who is the hero of *The Brothers Karamazov*?" That, of course, is the point. It is a tragedy without a hero—as it is a detective story without detectives, without a murderer, and without a murder. (p. 256)

And what is the solution of the detective story? Nobody knows. The trial is the greatest absurdity in all the book. . . . All that matters is that death is absurd, and against its absurdity the unadorned affirmation of the flesh is only just a little less so.

This is no message—it is tragic awareness; and it is the final statement of Dostoievsky, that man of many messages, a man in whom the flesh was always troubled and sick and whose head was full of dying ideologies—at last the sun in the sky, the hot smell of a woman, the grass on the earth, the human meat on the bone, the farce of death. (p. 257)

Kenneth Rexroth, "Dostoievsky: 'The Brothers Karamazov'," in his Classics Revisited *(copyright © 1965, 1966, 1967, 1968 by Kenneth Rexroth; reprinted by permission of the author), Quadrangle Books, 1968, pp. 253-57.*

PETER JONES (essay date 1975)

[Dostoevsky's] moral policies are not only baldly stated in *The Brothers Karamazov,* but their statement assumes importance in the plot and structure of the novel. (p. 112)

The structure of *The Brothers Karamazov,* on one level, is very simple. We are first presented with a characterization of different sorts of malaise, all fundamentally deriving from the same causes: the absence of faith in God, and the assertion of self. We are then given an explicit statement of moral and theological views which throw light on the types of malaise, and also point the way to effective regeneration. Finally, we are shown various stages in the regeneration of some of the central characters. The fundamental moral and religious views expressed in the novel cover nearly everything that happens in the novel, and this is appropriate, it might be thought, since there can be nothing to which God's laws do not apply.

The central characters may be taken as constituting a chain or scale of being, where 'being' is defined in terms of moral consciousness, and that, in turn, is defined in terms of faith in God, belief in immortality, and service to others. . . . Progress up the chain or scale depends upon recognition by an individual that he has a soul as well as a body and a mind, and that the soul must be made the centre of his being; the body is the source of experience, and also a prime driving force, while the mind is a mere tool, possessing no motive power of its own. The relative non-being represented by the lower members on the scale is associated not only with moral blindness, but also with falsehood, cruelty, self-interest, and failure to communicate with or to understand others. The moral policies and modes of living that are to be combated by the explicit moral doctrine of the novel, are themselves both stated and shown in action in the lives of the principal characters. . . . Dimitri and Ivan form the focus for the false doctrine, showing its embodiment and effects on persons. But there is also a more abstract attack upon types of reasoning; here, the law and science, represented by psychology, are pilloried. Both are essentially reductionist in form, and encumbered with their own rules of procedure—which they wield with morally dangerous aesthetic indulgence—they fail to recognize all the factors of which man is made; on the practical level, they fail, for example, to take account of such phenomena as self-punishment, and on the theoretical level, they fail to see that man has a soul over and above his mind and body. (pp. 113-14)

Although the novel is not an allegory, Dmitri, Ivan, and Alyosha may be seen as being under the primary influence of body, mind, and soul, respectively. And in connection with this three-part division we may also speak of three types of response and enquiry in the novel—personal, technical, and metaphysical. Personal enquiry is governed by an individual's psychology—his desires, habits, and mental constitution. All the Karamazov brothers sometimes fail to understand other people because of their own interests and preoccupations. . . . Personal traits may thus influence not only the collection and analysis of evidence, and the postulation of hypotheses, but even the selective application of the rules of inference needed for drawing conclusions from premises. Metaphysical enquiry belongs to the highest level of reflection shown in the novel, and it is concerned with spiritual truths, matters often regarded as abstract, but here claimed to have concrete realization in actual life—the theoretical pronouncements of Ivan and Zossima have their embodiment in the despair of Smerdyakov and the loving service of Alyosha, their beliefs and actions enforcing one another. (pp. 125-26)

In *The Brothers Karamazov* we are shown no character who achieved self-realization without the twin beliefs in God and immortality; but readers should recognize that it follows only that for *those* characters such beliefs were a sufficient condition for regeneration. It does not follow that such beliefs are the sole necessary condition for all men. . . . [The meaning] cannot be set out in a series of intelligible propositions for the benefit of those without faith; what can be done for such people is to characterize the life, thought, and deeds of men with and without faith, in the hope that such a presentation will awaken a favourable response. Although faith cannot be reached by argument there are practical steps that may be taken towards the leap of faith, steps designed to conform to, and mould, the psychological nature of man. Thus Zossima's advice to Alyosha to treat men as one treats children or the sick depends on the recognition that men find it easier to withhold their judgement and resentment of such persons. It is notable that whereas Ivan used the suffering of children for the purposes of accusing his hypothetical God, Dmitri used the dream of the 'babe' as a ground for 'accepting' what his brother could not; and Alyosha's stress on the memory of childhood . . . explicitly embraces the view that no man can ultimately deny to himself his own unselfconscious acts of loving. Such acts form the inner standards that constitute self-respect; but the outward-looking nature of these standards entail that the 'active love' of others is the fundamental practical policy; from it will follow the conditions and states that men mistakenly search for as preconditions of their concern for others. By loving his neighbour before all else a man comes not only to understand him, but also to achieve self-fulfilment and self-knowledge. (pp. 144-45)

> Peter Jones, "The Self and Others in 'The Brothers Karamazov'," in his Philosophy and the Novel: Philosophical Aspects of "Middlemarch," "Anna Karenina," "The Brothers Karamazov," "A la recherche du temps perdu" and of the Methods of Criticism (© Oxford University Press 1975; reprinted by permission of Oxford University Press), Oxford University Press, Oxford, 1975, pp. 112-46

ADDITIONAL BIBLIOGRAPHY

Baring, Maurice. "Dostoievsky." In his *Landmarks in Russian Literature,* pp. 80-162. New York: Barnes & Noble, 1960.
General view of Dostoevski's life and career.

Beach, Joseph Warren. "Philosophy: Dostoevski." In his *The Twentieth Century Novel: Studies in Technique,* pp. 94-102. New York: D. Appleton Century Co., 1932.
Philosophical analysis of *The Brothers Karamazov* and *Crime and Punishment.*

Beebe, Maurice. "The Three Motives of Raskolnikov: A Reinterpretation of Crime and Punishment." *College English* 17, No. 3 (December 1955): 151-58.
Finds Raskolnikov to be a character divided into three parts, with the intellectual, sensual, and spiritual sides of his personality in conflict. Beebe discerns the three motives for Raskolnikov's crime to be his desire to administer justice, or "to play God," his need to prove himself as an "extraordinary man," and his will to suffer.

Berdyaev, Nicholas. *Dostoevsky.* Translated by Donald Attwater. Cleveland, New York: The World Publishing Co., 1957, 227 p.
Discusses the depth of Dostoevski's religious and philosophical concerns. Berdyaev finds that Dostoevski's themes, "only latent in the 'seventies, came to life in the . . . great Russian revolutions."

Blackmur, R. P. "*Crime and Punishment:* A Study of Dostoevsky's Novel." *The Chimera* I, No. 3 (Winter 1943): 7-29.
General textual study.

Burchell, S. C. "Dostoiefsky and the Sense of Guilt." *The Psychoanalytic Review* XVII, No. 2 (April 1930): 195-207.
A discussion of Dostoevski's sense of personal guilt and how it was transmitted to his fiction.

Carr, Edward Hallett. *Dostoevsky (1821-1881): A New Biography.* London: George Allen & Unwin, 1931, 331 p.
A sensible, concise biography of Dostoevski.

Coulson, Jessie. *Dostoevsky: A Self-Portrait.* London: Oxford University Press, 1962, 279 p.
Biographical study based in large part on Dostoevski's correspondence.

Dostoyevsky, Aimee. *Fyodor Dostoyevsky: A Study.* New Haven: Yale University Press, 1922, 294 p.
A reminiscence by Dostoevski's daughter.

Fanger, Donald. *Dostoevsky and Romantic Realism: A Study of Dostoevsky in Relation to Balzac, Dickens, and Gogol.* Cambridge, Mass.: Harvard University Press, 1965, 307 p.
A discussion of the separate forms of romantic realism formulated by Balzac, Dickens, and Gogol, and their expression in the work of Dostoevski.

Frank, Joseph. *Dostoevsky: The Seeds of Revolt, 1821-1849.* Princeton: Princeton University Press, 1976, 401 p.
Detailed study of Dostoevski's early years, presenting his work as a "brilliant artistic synthesis of the major issues of his time." Frank states that Dostoevski "fused private dilemmas with those raging in the society of which he was a part."

Gissing, George. "Comparisons." In his *Charles Dickens: A Critical Study,* pp. 260-74. New York: Dodd Mead and Co., 1904.*
A critical comparison of the styles of Dickens and Dostoevski.

Goldstein, David I. *Dostoevsky and the Jews.* Austin: University of Texas Press, 1981, 231 p.
Study tracing the genesis and development of Dostoevski's anti-Semitism.

Grossman, Leonid, *Dostoevsky: A Biography.* Translated by Mary Mackler. Indianapolis: Bobbs-Merrill, 1975, 647 p.
A critical biography by an outstanding Soviet Dostoevski scholar.

Guerard, Albert J. "The Psychology of Dostoevsky: Conscious and Unconscious Understanding." In his *The Triumph of the Novel: Dickens, Dostoevsky, Faulkner,* pp. 160-203. New York: Oxford University Press, 1976.
A study of the Oedipal triangle and father-son conflict in *The Brothers Karamazov.*

Hingley, Ronald. *The Undiscovered Dostoevsky.* London: Hamish Hamilton, 1962, 241 p.
Survey of Dostoevski's life and writings, with particular attention paid to the early work.

Holquist, Michael. *Dostoevsky and the Novel.* Princeton: Princeton University Press, 1977, 202 p.
An analysis of Dostoevski's importance in literary history.

Huneker, James. "Dostoievsky and Tolstoy, and the Younger Choir of Russian Writers." In his *Ivory Apes and Peacocks,* pp. 52-88. New York: Charles Scribner's Sons, 1938.*
A stylistic comparison of Dostoevski and Tolstoy.

Ivanov, Vyacheslav. *Freedom and the Tragic Life: A Study in Dostoevsky,* edited by S. Konovalov, translated by Norman Cameron. New York: The Noonday Press, 1952, 166 p.
Scholarly study by an eminent Soviet critic. Ivanov calls Dostoevski's books "vehicles of Dionysus."

Magarshack, David. *Dostoevsky*. London: Secker & Warburg, 1962, 309 p.
  Detailed biographical study by a prominent translator of Dostoevski's work.

Maugham, W. Somerset. ''Dostoevsky and *The Brothers Karamazov*.'' In his *The Art of Fiction: An Introduction to Ten Novels and Their Authors*, pp. 245-71. Garden City, NY: Doubleday & Co., 1955.
  A study of the circumstances surrounding the creation of *The Brothers Karamazov*.

Milosz, Czeslaw, "Dostoevsky and Swedenborg." In his *Emperor of the Earth: Modes of Eccentric Vision*, pp. 120-43. Berkeley: University of California Press, 1977.
  An examination of the theme of self-love as manifested in the struggle between good and evil in Dostoevski's characters.

Mirsky, D. S. ''The Age of Realism: The Novelists (1).'' In his *A History of Russian Literature*, edited by Francis J. Whitfield, pp. 169-204. New York: Alfred A. Knopf, 1973.*
  Brief look at Dostoevski's early work and the influence of Gogol.

Oates, Joyce Carol. ''The Double Vision of *The Brothers Karamazov*.'' *Journal of Aesthetics and Art Criticism* XXVII, No. 2 (Winter 1968): 203-13.
  Discusses Dostoevski's style and fluctuations of his creative process.

O'Connor, Frank. ''Dostoevsky and the Unnatural Triangle.'' In his *The Mirror in the Roadway*, pp. 199-222. New York: Alfred A. Knopf, 1956.
  A short view of the image of the violated child in the fiction of Dostoevski.

Poggioli, Renato. ''Kafka and Dostoevsky.'' In *The Kafka Problem*, edited by Angel Flores, pp. 97-107. New York: Octagon Books, 1963.*
  A comparison of the literary styles of Kafka and Dostoevski.

Priestly, J. B. "The Broken Web: The Novelists." In his *Literature and Western Man*, pp. 222-73. London: Heinemann, 1960.*
  Describes Dostoevski's novels as a synthesis of ''psychological depth and symbolic dramatic intensity.''

Proust, Marcel. ''Dostoievski.'' In his *Marcel Proust on Art and Literature 1896-1919*, translated by Sylvia Townsend Warner, pp. 380-81. New York: Meridian Books, 1958.
  A short essay discussing Dostoevski's life as a convict and its effect on his literature.

Ramsey, Paul. ''No Morality Without Immorality: Dostoevski and the Meaning of Atheism.'' *The Journal of Religions* XXXVI, No. 2. (April 1956): 90-108.

  An analysis of atheism in *Crime and Punishment*.

Rowe, William Woodin. *Dostoevsky: Child and Man in His Works*. New York: New York University Press, 1968, 242 p.
  A study of Dostoevski's use of children in his works.

Seduro, Vladimir. *Dostoyevski in Russian Literary Criticism 1846-1956*. New York: Columbia University Press, 1957, 412 p.
  Study of a century of Russian critical response to Dostoevski.

Sewall, Richard B. ''*The Brothers Karamazov*.'' In his *The Vision of Tragedy*, pp. 106-26. New Haven: Yale University Press, 1959.
  A structural analysis of *The Brothers Karamazov*.

Slonim, Marc. *Three Loves of Dostoevsky*. New York: Rinehart & Co., 1955, 300 p.
  An account of Dostoevski's romantic interests and their influence upon him.

Snodgrass, W. D. ''Crime for Punishment: The Tenor of Part One.'' *The Hudson Review* XIII, No. 2 (Summer 1960): 202-53.
  A technical analysis of *Crime and Punishment*.

Steiner, George. *Tolstoy or Dostoevsky: An Essay in the Old Criticism*. New York: Alfred A. Knopf, 1971, 348 p.*
  A stylistic comparison of Tolstoy and Dostoevski.

Tate, Allen. ''The Hovering Fly.'' In his *On the Limits of Poetry: Selected Essays 1928-48*, pp. 146-62. New York: The Swallow Press and William Morrow & Co., 1948.
  A discussion of *The Idiot*.

Troyat, Henri. *Firebrand: The Life of Dostoevsky*. New York: Roy Publishers, 1946, 438 p.
  Detailed biographical study.

Tyler, Parker. ''Dostoievsky's Personal Devil.'' In his *Every Artist His Own Scandal: A Study of Real and Fictive Heroes*, pp. 53-69. New York: Horizon Press, 1964.
  An analysis of Stavrogin in *The Possessed*.

West, Rebecca. ''Redemption and Dostoevsky.'' *The New Republic* III, No. 31 (15 June 1915): 115-18.
  A reminiscence of the life of Dostoevski.

Wilson, Edmund. ''Dostoevsky Abroad.'' In his *The Shores of Light: A Literary Chronicle of the Twenties and Thirties*, pp. 408-14. New York: Farrar, Straus, and Young, 1952.
  Discusses Dostoevski's views of Europe.

Yarmolinsky, Avrahm. *Dostoevsky: His Life and Art*. New York: S. G. Phillips, 1957, 434 p.
  A critical biography by a noted Dostoevski scholar.

William Dunlap

1766-1839

American dramatist, historian, and artist.

Often regarded as "The Father of American drama," Dunlap was born in Perth Amboy, New Jersey, during the Revolutionary War. As a child, he was exposed to opposing political views: those of his Loyalist parents and those of the emerging new nation. A desire to express his own political feelings inspired many of his works, particularly his first drama, *The Modest Soldier; or, Love in New York*.

Dunlap's earliest aspiration was to become a painter, and he travelled to London to study with Benjamin West. However, while in London, his interest in the theater overcame his artistic ambitions, and his career as a painter suffered. Although he founded the National Academy of Design, for which he also served as vice-president and professor of historical painting, his greatest energy was always given to drama.

Critics feel Dunlap's best plays include *André* and *Leicester*, verse tragedies written in the Romantic style of the late eighteenth century, and a comedy of manners, *The Father; or, American Shandyism*. The success achieved by *The Father; or, American Shandyism* was so great that Dunlap decided to focus his attention on the stage. He experimented with employing Gothic elements in *Fontainville Abbey* and *Ribbemont; or, The Feudal Baron*, the first plays of their kind in America. Although often marked by a certain intelligence and exuberance, his work was often derivative, and because Dunlap's interests were so varied, he was unable to devote himself to one vocation for a long period of time.

In addition to his work with the National Academy of Design, he published and edited *The Monthly Recorder* and was assistant paymaster to the New York State Militia. His most important contributions as an artist and dramatist were his histories: *A History of the Rise and Progress of the Arts of Design in the United States* and *A History of the American Theatre*, which are still of considerable value.

Despite the dramatic talent evident in several of his plays, Dunlap was never considered a great dramatist, and few of his plays have survived. But the success which they achieved in their time inspired later American playwrights.

PRINCIPAL WORKS

The Modest Soldier; or, Love in New York (drama) 1787
Darby's Return (drama) 1789
The Father; or, American Shandyism (drama) 1789; also published as *The Father of an Only Child*, 1806
The Fatal Deception; or, The Progress of Guilt (drama) 1794
Fontainville Abbey (drama) 1795
Ribbemont; or, The Feudal Baron (drama) 1796
André (drama) 1798
The Glory of Columbia: Her Yeomanry! [adapted from *André*] (drama) 1803
The Voice of Nature (drama) 1803
The Italian Father (drama) 1810

Memoirs of the Life of George Frederick Cooke (biography) 1813
The Life of Charles Brockden Brown (biography) 1815
A Trip to Niagara; or, Travellers in America (drama) 1828
A History of the American Theatre (history) 1832
A History of the Rise and Progress of the Arts of Design in the United States (history) 1834
A History of New York, for Schools (history) 1837

*This was revised and retitled as *Leicester*.

THE GAZETTE OF THE UNITED STATES (essay date 1789)

The principal part of the entertainment at the *Theatre*, on Monday evening, was the new comedy, entitled **The Father, or American Shandyism,** the production of an American, a young gentleman of this city [William Dunlap].—This circumstance occasioned a crowded house; and from the reiterated plaudits which followed almost every exhibited incident, it is presumed that the public has very seldom been gratified in a higher degree.

The parts were very judiciously assigned, and supported with great animation and propriety.

The *Prologue* and *Epilogue* were finely adapted, and their delivery received uncommon applause.

A correspondent observes that sentiment, wit and *comique* humour are happily blended in that most ingenious performance *The Father, or American Shandyism,* nor is that due proportion of the pathetic which interests the finest feelings of the human heart, omitted. The happy allusions to characters and events, in which every friend to our country feels interested—and those traits of benevolence which are brought to view in the most favourable circumstances, conspired to engage, amuse, delight, and instruct the audience through five acts of alternate anticipations, and agreeable surprises.—This *Comedy* bids fair to be a favorite entertainment, and a valuable acquisition to the stage.

> *"William Dunlap's 'The Father',"* in The Gazette of the United States, *September 9, 1789 (and reprinted in* The American Theatre as Seen by Its Critics: 1752-1934, *edited by Montrose J. Moses and John Mason Brown, second edition, Norton, 1934, p. 26).*

THE GAZETTE OF THE UNITED STATES   (essay date 1789)

The Entertainment at the Theatre [John Street], on Tuesday evening last, appeared, by the repeated plaudits, to give the fullest satisfaction to a very crouded house: The selections for the Evening were made with judgment—and animated by the presence of the illustrious personages, who honored the exhibition, the Players excited their best abilities. The Pieces performed, were the *Toy—The Critic,* and a new Comic Sketch, entitled *Darby's Return.* The latter piece is the production of the same ingenious hand, who hath already contributed so much to the entertainment of the public by *The Father, or American Shandyism. Darby's Return* is replete with the happiest illusions to interesting events, and very delicately turned compliments. (pp. 26-7)

> *"Dunlap's 'Darby's Return',"* in The Gazette of the United States, *November 28, 1789 (and reprinted in* The American Theatre as Seen by Its Critics: 1752-1934, *edited by Montrose J. Moses and John Mason Brown, second edition, Norton, 1934, pp. 26-7).*

THE POLYANTHOS   (essay date 1807)

This catch-penny production [*The Glory of Columbia, Her Yeomanry!*] is attributed by some to William Dunlap, Esq. of New-York. . . . Where, in the name of wonder, could the author pick up such a gallimaufry of nonsense? Where did he get 'David Williams' and his 'Sister Sal,' with their 'mush and molasses,' and their long stories about 'milk-pails and cow yards, pigs and petticoats'? In what country did he find *Dennis O'Bog,* with his knapsack full of potatoes, and his mouth full of ridiculous tales of 'spectacles' and 'women without neses'?—*Glory of Columbia* truly!—

We can say nothing more of the performance than that it ended in smoke.

> *"'Glory of Columbia',"* in The Polyanthos, *Vol. 5, May, 1807, p. 139.*

THE AMERICAN QUARTERLY REVIEW   (essay date 1827)

[**"The Father of an Only Child"**] was, we believe, without doubt, the first American play represented on the stage; and if it possessed no other claim, would be entitled to particular notice on that account. It is, however, in our opinion, one of the best in all our collection. The plot is sufficiently dramatic, to carry an interest throughout; the characters are well drawn, and well employed; and the dialogue possesses, what is indispensable to genuine comedy, a brief terseness, and unstudied case, which few of the productions of the present era afford. (pp. 350-51)

There is a good portion of . . . colloquial ease and sprightliness, which unquestionably constitute the very essence of good comedy, in the dialogue, and a sufficiency of incident, as well as interest, we should think, to make this piece successful on the stage, in the hands of competent actors. It is only where these are wanting, that a dramatic writer is under the necessity of resorting to unnatural incidents, and inflated language, to amuse or interest the audience. (p. 352)

> *"American Drama: 'The Father of an Only Child',"* in The American Quarterly Review, *Vol. I, No. 2, June, 1827, pp. 350-52.*

THE NEW YORK MIRROR   (essay date 1830)

Dunlap has been distinguished as an author, as well as a painter. He has figured in biography as well as in the drama. He was admired among the scholars of an age gone by, and is honoured by the present, as a man of genius and of taste, and it is no easy matter to keep up with the march of improvement at this time. He has reared a monument to Brown the novelist, to Cooke the tragedian, and to others of less note. May he be rewarded according to his deeds.

> *"Literary Notices: Dunlap,"* in The New York Mirror, *Vol. VII, No. 52, July 3, 1830, p. 413.*

THE KNICKERBOCKER   (essay date 1833)

The whole life of Mr. Dunlap has been undeviatingly devoted to literature and the fine arts: to the cultivation of that which is the glory and safeguard of a nation—knowledge. From his last literary labor, the **"History of the American Theatre,"** with the very existence of which he is identified, we learn that the stage may *"hail him father,"* not only *"of an only child,"* but of more than FIFTY PRODUCTIONS, including every offspring of the dramatic family—Tragedy, Comedy, Melo-Drama, Opera, Farce, and Interlude, besides Prologues, Epilogues, and Addresses, to an extent of which the courtesy of a gentleman, and the pen of a ready writer, never fail to contribute. In addition to this long list of dramatic productions, Mr. Dunlap may probably point to other literary works of general interest and instruction, which for the possession of these qualities, are unsurpassed by any similar books in any country. The principal of these are the memoirs of *George Frederick Cooke,* the biography of *Charles Brockden Brown,* with whose personal friendship his early days were enriched, and the recently completed *History of the American Theatre.* (pp. 325-26)

Resolved, That as a testimony of our respect for the talents, character, and literary labors of WILLIAM DUNLAP, Esq. and of our esteem for the evidence which his dramatic works have furnished of the *moral influence* of the stage, a complimentary benefit be offered him in this city; and that we will individually use our best endeavors to produce a result that shall be serviceable to him, and in accordance with the literary and dramatic taste of this city. (p. 326)

> *"Correspondence of the Dunlap Benefit," in* The Knickerbocker, *Vol. 1, No. 5, May, 1833, pp. 323-29.*

WILLIAM DUNLAP (essay date 1834)

To your inquiry respecting my forthcoming work on art and arts, which I have dignified with the title of a **"History of the Rise and Progress of the Arts of Design in this country,"** it gives me pleasure to answer, it is nearly ready for the press, and I hope will appear in May or June next.

The interest which has been evinced in my undertaking by communication from every part of the Union is extremely encouraging, and has increased the very common and natural interest which every author feels in his own labours. I have said that "the progress made in America toward a high state of perfection in the arts, is one of the most prominent features in the moral physiognomy of the country," and those who know the pride I take in the democratic institutions of my native land, and in the name of American, can judge of the pleasure I experience in developing the causes of this progress, and exhibiting to my fellow-citizens the treasures they possess, and the prospects which are opened for a more glorious future.

My work, by giving a chronological series of biographical notices of our artists, will possess a variety, which, I think, adds to its interest; at the same time rendering it more amusing, and not less instructive, than it would have been in any other form. Biography admits of anecdote and gossip, and I believe the public love anecdote and gossip—*that I do,* I am quite certain.

> *William Dunlap, in his letter to the Editors in "Anecdote of American Artists," in* The New York Mirror, *Vol. XI, No. 31, February 1, 1834, p. 248.*

THE AMERICAN QUARTERLY REVIEW (essay date 1835)

That Mr. Dunlap has succeeded in compounding two very entertaining volumes, can scarcely be denied; but that he has been equally successful in accomplishing the object for which their appellation would indicate them to have been prepared, is not so sure. The **"History of the Rise and Progress of the Arts of Design in the United States,"** is a sounding title, and a sounding title is a dangerous affair. If the expectations which it arouses are not sufficiently realized, the reader is little disposed to be blind to the faults, and overkind to the merits of the work. . . . [The aspect of Mr. Dunlap's] title-page is more imposing than the character of his work, for one especial reason. He contrives to keep his readers in such good humour, for the most part, by the amusement which his pages afford, that it would be almost impossible for them to deal severely with his authorship. (pp. 143-44)

Mr. Dunlap's execution of his task is by no means deserving of unqualified praise. . . . There is little of the dignity of history in its gossiping chapters, and much more information is communicated about the men than the artists. Greater pains are taken to amuse us with traits and eccentricities of personal character, than to acquaint us with professional peculiarities. The original critical portions are for the most part meagre and

unsatisfactory, and almost together devoid of the *chiaro-oscuro* of criticism, if we may so speak. They are generally all light or all shade—all praise or all blame. The volumes, however, contain a great deal of valuable matter, calculated to render them admirable *Mémoires pour servir,* and Mr. Dunlap merits gratitude for the industry and perseverance with which he has sought information from the most authentic sources. (p. 144)

The autobiography with which he favours us, is without question the most original part of the work, there being no one to whom he could apply for information respecting the subject of the memoir, whom he might suppose more conversant with it than he is. It is also one of the most interesting and instructive portions—not, to be sure, in reference particularly to the light which it sheds upon the theme of the work, but from the variety of scenes through which the author has passed, and the salutary lesson which it teaches. With great ingenuousness and candour, he contrasts his own deportment with that of some of his brethren in the profession whom he holds up as examples of industry and the success which is the consequence; and exhibits its unsatisfactory results as an admonitory evidence of the evil of dissipation of time in early life, and subsequent want of perseverance and method. (p. 161)

Mr. Dunlap cannot be enrolled amongst our most distinguished artists. His two principal pictures, "Christ Rejected," and "Calvary," though not destitute of merit, are on the whole more remarkable for quantity than quality.

We do not like the manner in which the memoir of Colonel Trumbull [principally known for his paintings upon historical subjects] is written. The tone of asperity and disparagement by which it is pervaded, wears the appearance of a feeling of personal rancour altogether at variance with the spirit which should actuate the historian. We would not affirm that Mr. Dunlap has set down any thing in malice, but he assuredly does not appear to have been as anxious upon that point, as about that of extenuating nothing, to which he has adhered with the most scrupulous strictness. Even supposing that Colonel Trumbull is really obnoxious to the imputations here cast upon him, the mode in which they are thrown is calculated, we think, to weaken their force in a material degree. (p. 162)

Mr. Dunlap's volumes furnish abundant evidence that painting is the pursuit to which the genius of our land, as far as the fine arts are concerned, has the strongest affinity, and in which it is destined to obtain its most splendid triumphs. We might even go farther, and affirm, that it would be impossible to collect as great a number of names of persons who illustrate our annals in any other imaginative department, as is here displayed. (p. 176)

> *"'History of the Rise and Progress of the Arts of Design in the United States','" in* The American Quarterly Review, *Vol. XVII, No. 33, March, 1835, pp. 143-77.*

THE NORTH AMERICAN REVIEW (essay date 1835)

We have read [**History of the Rise and Progress of the Arts of Design in the United States**] throughout with great, though equally sustained interest. Mr. Dunlap has brought together in it a great variety of curious information about artists and the arts in the United States. . . . This task we think Mr. Dunlap has, on the whole, ably and laboriously fulfilled. Every source from which knowledge could be drawn, has been resorted to, and an extraordinary collection of materials, to illustrate the progress of the arts, in and out of the United States, has been gathered with untiring industry, and amazing minuteness of research. . . . The number of names which Mr. Dunlap has made the public acquainted with, would make the stoutest defenders of the superiority of American genius stare with wonder, and ought to make the cavillers hang their heads with shame. (p. 146)

Mr. Dunlap has relieved the body of his work by interspersing brief essays on the several arts. . . . In this way a great amount of information on the technical terms and manual processes of art, is brought within the reader's reach. This information, though not commonly possessed, is quite necessary to the right understanding of criticisms on the works brought into discussion. We think Mr. Dunlap has done wisely to give his readers this benefit, and hope it will prove a benefit to the sale of the book.

Some of the most interesting portions of the work are the autobiographical letters of living artists; published wholly or in part. . .

Mr. Dunlap's narrative style is easy and clear, though sometimes wanting in strength. There is, also, a want of arrangement, selection and compression; circumstances of little or no importance, are often related with as much gravity as those of the highest. The spirit of Mr. Dunlap's criticism, though not searching and profound, is, in general, full of good sense and candor. He praises heartily, and blames independently. He loves and respects the arts, and delights to honor those whose genius in the arts has made them illustrious. But we have some fault to find with him. He has been too free in showing up the private histories of artists, and blazoning abroad circumstances in their domestic or personal relations, which ought to have been held forever sacred from the public gaze. . . . He has taken up too many pages with the unimportant or merely local quarrels of artists, and sometimes shews a strength of personal feeling that must lessen his credit as an impartial historian. (p. 147)

> "Dunlap's History of the Arts," in The North American Review, Vol. XLI, No. 88, July, 1835, pp. 146-70.

THE NEW YORK MIRROR (essay date 1839)

We should not omit to take a more detailed notice, than has yet appeared in our columns, of one who has occupied, during the last century, a considerable space in the eyes of the world of art and of literature. The Commercial Advertiser contains the following biographical allusions, and we trust that a more minute account, from a competent hand, will soon be offered to the public:—"As an artist, Mr. Dunlap occupied a respectable rank, and as a man of letters a distinguished one. . . . He had a strong love for the drama, and did much towards its elevation in this country. . . . [His] reputation as a man of letters will be the most enduring. The productions of his pen have been numerous, and his works are to be found in the several departments of the drama, biography, history and fiction. His first biographical work, we believe, was the life of Charles Brockden Brown—which was soon followed by the life of George Frederick Cooke. More valuable still were his two able works of mingled history and biography, the *History of the American Stage*, and the *History of the Arts of Design in the United States*. His more recent works, with the exception of that clever and wholesome fiction, *The Cold Water Man*, have been historical. . . . We think [his *History of New York*] will be a valuable acquisition to our store of history—especially

as a repository of facts. It was as a collector of these rather than as a brilliant writer that Mr. Dunlap excelled. His diligence and his patience in research were remarkable and untiring. His mind was clear and vigorous down to the time of his attack by disease, and his memory was a grand store-house of facts and anecdotes, personal and historical. Hence he was one of the most interesting companions in conversation often to be met with."

> "The Late William Dunlap," in The New York Mirror, Vol. 17, No. 18, October 26, 1839, p. 143.

BRANDER MATTHEWS (essay date 1887)

When we begin to read Dunlap's play ['**André**'], we soon see that it is not in accord with the literary fashions of today; both in cloth and in cut it is of an old style. . . . '**André**' is a play adroitly contrived by one who had studied under Kotzebue, and who had seen frequent performances of . . . English heroic dramas, now equally faded and old-fashioned. In it we find sensibility and sentimentality more abundant than direct and simple pathos, conversation rather than action, set argument more often than emotion. There is vigor in the drawing of *Young Bland*, with whose fiery and boyish sincerity we may yet feel. There are character and dignity in the speeches of *Washington*. The blank verse in which the play is written is often involved and forced, but it has point, and it is the work of one who understood the exigencies of the acted drama. That Dunlap was not a poet, in any strict acceptation of the word, needs no discussion; he was a competent playwright, and he knew how to make a drama in accordance with the tenets of his time. '**André**' is a better piece of work than most of the plays even of high pretensions, which were produced in Great Britain and the United States toward the end of the last century. (pp. xii-xiii)

Of all the plays on the subject of Arnold's treason and André's sad fate, the '**André**' of William Dunlap is easily the best, both as literature and as a successful acting drama. (p. xxiv)

> Brander Matthews, in his introduction to André: A Tragedy in Five Acts by William Dunlap, The Dunlap Society, 1887 (and reprinted by Burt Franklin, 1970), pp. vii-xxiv.

ANNIE RUSSELL MARBLE (essay date 1907)

[William Dunlap's first performed play which met with success] was entitled *The Father; or, American Shandyism*. . . . The comedy abounds in melodrama, crude and complicated situations. . . . (p. 247)

The second play which was acted was a trifle, *Darby's Return*. . . . (p. 248)

[Anticlimaxes were] often found in Dunlap's plays. He chose this device to bring in humor and, in many cases, to speak a message of democracy. . . .

Dunlap [also] wrote the play that was printed later as *Lord Leicester*, but the title of which, as acted April 24, 1794, was *The Fatal Deception; or, The Progress of Guilt*. This play did not win much applause . . . ; but it had temporary fame. . . . (p. 249)

In spite of many technical defects and "wooden speeches" [in *André*], Dunlap achieved considerable success with the character of André. . . . The best portion of the play is in . . . the interview between André and Bland. . . . (p. 256)

The later lines . . . , in which André recites the incidents of his treason and capture, have a sustained interest, although many lines lack spontaneity and force. . . . (p. 257)

The interest awakened by this tragedy induced Dunlap to introduce some of the same characters—Washington, Arnold, Paulding, and André—in a melodrama, *The Glory of Columbia*. . . . Some of the songs, which formed a prominent feature of this play, were crude, but spirited. . . . (p. 258)

As one looks over the list of Dunlap's plays, with dates of writing, performance, and publication, he will note his years of plenty and of famine as a playwright. The climax of his popularity was at the close of the eighteenth century. . . . A brief revival of success came . . . when he produced *The Voice of Nature*. . . . Another period of desuetude, as regarded publication, followed for four or five years. Then came an awakening of interest in his . . . historical dramas *Rinaldo Rinaldini*, *The Battle of New Orleans*, and *The Soldier of Seventy-Six*, such translations as *Blue Beard, Lover's Vows*, and *The Africans*, and the opera *Yankee Chronology*. . . . (pp. 259-60)

[Dunlap was capable of summarizing] his chief faults—lack of a strong style and of much originality. Largely because of his rapid writing, but also from deficient training, his style was often loose and weak. There are a few passages of dramatic energy, and occasional characters with marked portraiture . . . but the mass of his plays lapse into mediocrity. His claim to remembrance cannot rest upon any individual play, with the possible exception of *André;* but he deserves some praise for skill in meeting the demands of his age, and for persistent efforts to cultivate a taste for pure, American drama. (pp. 261-62)

In general construction and adaptation to the fashions of his day, his plays were cleverly devised. They were always wholesome morally, whether of his own conception or translated. . . . He was sometimes extravagant in sensibility to suit the tastes of the time, but his tone was not prurient. . . . [He] never lost his patience nor his confidence in the public. (p. 262)

[As] a whole, his *History of the American Theatre* is not alone entertaining, but reliable, as a portrayal of characters and a graphic revelation of the dramatic impulse in America. . . . (p. 264)

In Dunlap's *History of the American Theatre* are delightful sidelights upon famous men and women of the past, especially among the actors and playwrights. (p. 265)

Turning from an estimate of his personal achievement to his influence on American drama and art, we must admit that Dunlap should be honored. His ideals were rudely treated in the struggle of life, but he never lost his faith in them nor in his countrymen. (p. 275)

> Annie Russell Marble, "William Dunlap: The Beginnings of Drama," in her Heralds of American Literature: A Group of Patriot Writers of the Revolutionary and National Periods, *University of Chicago Press, 1907, pp. 235-75.*

ORAL SUMNER COAD   (essay date 1917)

William Dunlap's first dramatic offspring has long slumbered in an unmarked grave. **"The Modest Soldier; or, Love in New York"** . . . is known to us only through the author's slight sketch of it in his **"History of the American Theatre"**: "A Yankee servant, a travelled American, an officer in the late revolutionary army, a fop, such as fops then were in New-York, an old gentleman and his two daughters, one of course lively and the other serious, formed the dramatis personæ." . . . **"The Modest Soldier"** was undoubtedly a comedy of sentiment. . . .

With his second attempt [**"The Father; or American Shandyism"**] Dunlap graduated into the meagre ranks of the successful American playwrights. (p. 137)

"The Father" is a thorough-going sentimental comedy. It could hardly have been anything else. Not only was the whole tendency of contemporary literature in that direction, but Dunlap was by nature susceptible to sentimentalism, being a moralist and a humanitarian. The main plot is of the lost-relative-found type, and involves the distressed-lover theme. The sub-plot is a reformed-rake episode. (p. 140)

As the second play of a youth of twenty-two, **"The Father"** is distinctly commendable. Without much claim to originality, it shows that ability to discover public taste which is one of the essentials of theatrical success. To be sure it is overcrowded with incident, and contains several scenes and figures which do not forward the action, yet it is brisk and entertaining, it is managed with discretion, and it should have gone well on the stage. (pp. 140-41)

The edition of 1806 made considerable alteration in the play, which was now called **"The Father of an Only Child."** The changes in the main were for the better. Some of the early crudity was removed, the style was more highly finished, and certain scenes and characters were more completely developed. . . . The increased moralizing tendency of this edition suggests that Dunlap's managerial experience had convinced him of the potency of the theatre as a social influence. (pp. 141-42)

"Darby's Return" is interesting as the first American ballad-opera to face the footlights. Though a brief affair of nine pages, it is a true ballad-opera because its two songs are set to popular airs.

The promise of worthy achievement held out in **"The Father"** was not belied in Dunlap's first tragedy, **"The Fatal Deception; or, The Progress of Guilt"** . . . , which was printed as **"Leicester."** The story is sufficiently exciting if somewhat extravagant. (p. 143)

"Leicester" obeys implicitly the three unities, yet in its medieval setting and in the freedom of its action it marks something of a break from the tradition which had dominated American drama since its inception. . . . **"Leicester"** may be classified as a semi-romantic tragedy, the product of many influences, namely: the Elizabethan revenge tragedy, the tragedy of fate, such semi-romantic tragedies as Home's "Douglas" . . . , and the recent Gothic plays.

It is written in a blank verse which is more poetic and more nearly adequate than anything before it in this country. The story is told with considerable skill throughout, and in the murder scene with more intensity and power than can be found previously in American drama. . . . To be sure, the play is loosely put together, and the action is often unmotivated, yet in force and stage effectiveness **"Leicester"** was the best native tragedy up to its time. (pp. 145-46)

Dunlap was the first American writer to take a visible part in the so-called Gothic revival. (p. 153)

"**Fontainville Abbey**" was more thoroughly Gothic than any of its dramatic precursors in England. . . . Dunlap took [great] pains to emphasize the setting; he carefully located each scene in unmistakably Gothic surroundings. Such startling devices as skeletons, blood-rusted daggers, subterranean passages, and howling storms were freely introduced. In the use of terroristic machinery he was not a little like that incomparable Gothic dramatist, Matthew Gregory Lewis, whose famous "Castle Spectre" did not make its appearance until four years after "**Fontainville Abbey**" was written.

Aside from its importance in the beginnings of American Gothicism, this piece has another claim to consideration. . . . "**Leicester**" departed to a large extent from the eighteenth century model, though still adhering to the unities. "**Fontainville Abbey**" broke entirely from this formal restraint, and became wholly and frankly a romantic tragi-comedy. As such it had but one predecessor, Mrs. Rowson's "Slaves in Algiers," acted a few months before. Dunlap's deliberate turning to the romantic type, exemplified in his first two serious plays, undoubtedly acted as one of the potent checks on conventional tragedy, for after 1795 that species almost disappeared from the United States.

William Dunlap's chief contribution to American opera was "**The Archers; or, Mountaineers of Switzerland.**". . . (pp. 154-55)

"**The Archers**" is devoid of anything like character drawing or intensity of effect. Nevertheless it furnishes opportunity for scenery, lovemaking, and martial pomp, the chief requirements of a musical play; so a theatrical success might have been expected. (pp. 156-57)

"**Ribbemont**" is another Gothic drama of the "**Fontainville Abbey**" type. It is as free from actual supernaturalism as the other, but its setting, its mysteries, and its wide departure from reality are hallmarks of the terroristic school. In the art of playmaking "**Ribbemont**" shows no advance over its author's previous productions. Unmotivated, unconvincing, and filled with lifeless figures, it has few redeeming features. Dunlap himself spoke disparagingly of it: "The play is not skilfully managed." "The characters and incidents were not in sufficient number, and the piece . . . is long since forgotten." The blank verse, which shows a careful study of Shakespeare, is superior to the average of that time, but the conventionally theatrical and useless speeches are too numerous to allow the style any claim to excellence. (pp. 158-59)

Several plays before "**André**" had dealt with American history, but Dunlap's tragedy surpassed them all. In general the early historical dramas were unusually poor affairs, and for this reason "**André's**" modest merit may be easily overestimated. . . . ["**André**"] must be classed among the most worthy efforts of our early dramatists. To be sure, it is artificial and sentimental, but on the whole it is rather satisfying. The characters are consistently if slightly drawn. The tone reaches a certain degree of intensity in places. . . . The blank verse is even and dignified, free both from puerility and from inspiration.

That Dunlap knew to some extent and admired Elizabethan drama is proved by "**The Italian Father.**". . . [He] considered this to be his best dramatic achievement. Unfortunately, a comparison of "**The Italian Father**" with [Dekker's] "The Honest

Whore," part two, reveals an amount of plagiarism which leaves him only a meagre remnant to call his own. (pp. 166-67)

With all respect to Dekker be it said that in certain respects Dunlap improved on his source. "**The Italian Father**" is simpler in construction and more closely knit, because several superfluous characters are removed, and the sub-plot is brought into closer relation with the main plot. Dunlap's prose diction is clearer than Dekker's mixture of prose, rhyme, and blank verse. In other words the American playwright used his well-developed technical skill to reconstruct the piece according to the canons of the contemporary stage. The result was a theatrically successful drama. But in its less superficial aspects the original far surpasses the imitation. (p. 169)

"**André**" was not a stage success. No wonder, since its hero was a British spy. Perhaps Dunlap saw the paradox and felt that the same episode presented from the American standpoint would have a greater claim to popularity. At any rate, in 1803 "**The Glory of Columbia—Her Yeomanry!**" again dramatized the Arnold-André conspiracy, but now the hero was the American common people, and the appeal was made frankly to national feeling. (p. 171)

"**The Glory of Columbia**" is one of Dunlap's poorest plays. The better parts were taken from "**André**" and arranged haphazard. The new material was constructed hastily and with the sole idea of capturing an ebullient Fourth of July audience. The Irish humor is painful and has no connection with anything else in the piece. The whole composition is a disjointed, operatic hodgepodge, sugar-coated with copious quantities of patriotism. That the American public of the time was uncritical is indicated by the fact that "**The Glory of Columbia**" was repeated over and over again, while the greatly superior "**André**" disappeared from the stage after three performances. When the subject was America, the playgoers demanded not art, but the screaming of the eagle. (pp. 172-73)

Dunlap's last play, "**A Trip to Niagara; or, Travellers in America**" . . . [was] no more than a farce intended as a running accompaniment to the scenery. The author confessed to using any material that might amuse the audience. (p. 176)

"**A Trip to Niagara**" is merely a series of disconnected and puerile scenes and irrelevant characters. No doubt a certain amount of low comedy could be extracted from it, for the humor is frequent and boisterous; but unless the scenery was strikingly excellent the audience with reason might have demanded its money back. Apparently, however, the uncritical playgoers were satisfied, inasmuch as this farce was given at least twenty-four performances, a run equaled only by "**The Glory of Columbia.**"

Not the least interesting feature of "**A Trip to Niagara**" is the dialect characters. Dunlap here made use of the four most common types to be found in early American plays: the negro, the Frenchman, the Yankee, and the Irishman. (p. 177)

[In] practically every instance Dunlap was indebted to some outside source for his central idea. Almost invariably he borrowed his essential elements from a novel, a historical event, or another play, as he always frankly admitted. To be sure, borrowing plots is a practice sanctioned by the most unimpeachable precedent, but the result is notable only when the borrowing is revitalized by the author's personality. Such an achievement requires creative power, and creative power was what Dunlap lacked. His mind could not evolve an original conception. Only when the idea came to him ready-made, could he produce a drama, and even then his accomplishment was frequently but little more than a change of form. His equipment consisted chiefly of a knowledge of stagecraft and a certain facility of composition, equipment which fitted him to be a dramatic remodeler rather than a creator. (pp. 182-83)

From first to last he showed a peculiar lack of improvement. Perhaps his best dramas are . . . "**The Father**" and "**Leicester.**" Certainly ["**A Trip to Niagara; or Travellers in America**"] is one of his poorest. (p. 183)

[Dunlap] was the first American to lay claim to the title of professional dramatist by writing a succession of moderately good plays that were actually staged. His mild superiority was the result of several qualities. He had a sense of humor. He could write smoother prose and more literary blank verse than his rivals. And, better still, he knew how to build a play to secure continuous interest and suspense. (pp. 186-87)

An important division of Dunlap's writing was the patriotic play. In this field he was not a pioneer, but he was the most generous contributor. Throughout his career this staunch patriot employed his pen in praise of his native land. At the outset he wrote "**Darby's Return**," the purpose of which was to glorify America. Then came "**André**," "**The Soldier of '76**," "**The Temple of Independence**," "**The Glory of Columbia**," "**Yankee Chronology**," "**The Battle of New Orleans**," and "**A Trip to Niagara.**" Perhaps he helped popularize this type, for national affairs became one of the commonest themes in our early drama.

In the history of ballad-opera Dunlap occupies a considerable place. Several operas had been written in this country before he attempted the form, but "**Darby's Return**" was the first to reach the stage. It was followed by "**The Archers**," "**Sterne's Maria**," "**The Wild Goose Chase**" (altered into an opera from Kotzebue), "**The Knight of Guadalquiver**," and "**The Glory of Columbia.**" No doubt it was partly as a result of these that plays interspersed with songs grew to be very numerous at the end of the eighteenth century and the beginning of the nineteenth. (pp. 188-89)

From this analysis of his original compositions, Dunlap's place in the history of American drama is apparent. He invented no new types and conceived no new ideas, but he was a pioneer in employing several types and ideas as yet almost, or wholly, untried in this country. (p. 191)

But, after all, the most memorable thing about our dramatist is not that he wrote good plays or bad plays, important plays or negligible plays, but that he wrote plays at all. He had a pleasant and remunerative business; and certainly the experience of his forerunners was not such as to tempt a young man from the selling of china to the writing of dramas. His motives were love of the art and a desire to be known as a playwright. He obeyed the urge of the author's instinct at a time when authorship was not encouraged. He rejoiced in the opportunity to give his countrymen the benefit of his talent. And in recounting William Dunlap's claims to an honorable remembrance, it should not be forgotten that commercialism had no part in the making of the Father of American Drama. (p. 192)

> *Oral Sumner Coad, in his* William Dunlap: A Study of His Life and Works and of His Place in Contemporary Culture, *The Dunlap Society, 1917 (and reprinted by Russell & Russell, Inc., 1962), 313 p.*

ALLAN GATES HALLINE (essay date 1935)

Dunlap's plays fall naturally into two groups: those which are chiefly of his own composition and those which are translations from foreign sources. The first group of plays is in some measure derivative, for Dunlap wrote scarcely a play which was not suggested by or based on some other play, novel, or historical incident. He altered, developed, or added to the original in a degree sufficient to justify his being called the author of the final product; but he did not synthesize his materials with that force of imagination which results in the creation of something new. (p. 43)

Among Dunlap's original productions it is possible to distinguish several different types. His first play, *The Modest Soldier; or, Love in New York,* has been lost; his second play, *The Father; or, American Shandyism,* belongs distinctly to the sentimental school. It concerns the separation and subsequent reunion of father and son, complicated by a drawing-room seducer who is trying to capture the son's betrothed for himself. The villain is exposed in his roguery and virtue is triumphant. *The Italian Father,* in its tearful feelings and perfect devotions, is also of the sentimental group. It is based largely on Dekker's *The Honest Whore* and shows the unsuccessful temptation of a daughter and her unwavering loyalty to husband and father. Other sentimental dramas of Dunlap's are *Sterne's Maria* and *The Natural Daughter.* . . .

[In] its exaggerated and lachrymal emotion, in its amorous intrigue, and in its explicit moralizing, [*Leicester*] is related to the sentimental drama; in its villainous plots and murders, it is suggestive of the Elizabethan tragedy of blood. . . . There appears also in *Leicester* the idea of fatalism. . . . This theme is to recur in *André*.

Another type of play which Dunlap experimented with and succeeded in is the Gothic. (p. 44)

The settings and atmosphere of [*Fontainville Abbey*] are completely Gothic: thunderstorms, ruined castles, dark, damp corridors, flickering lights, rumbling sounds—all these, together with fear, horror, murder, are the materials out of which Gothic romances are constructed. Thus we see how closely identified Dunlap was with various literary currents. *Fontainville Abbey* is based on Mrs. Radcliffe's *Romance of the Forest;* other plays of Dunlap belonging to this late eighteenth-century horror-romance are *Ribbemont; or, the Feudal Baron* and *The Man of Fortitude; or, the Knights Adventure,* the latter based on Godwin's *Caleb Williams* and Schiller's *Die Räuber.* There is good reason to believe that Dunlap introduced Gothic romance to America, his first works preceding Brown's by four years. That Dunlap considered himself something of an experimenter is suggested by the epilogue to *Fontainville Abbey* in which Cupid appears to complain that he is being neglected by the author for other interests. . . . (pp. 44-5)

[That] explicit moralizing is not to be regarded simply as a feature of sentimental literature, that it is, indeed, an expression of Dunlap's own views, integrated with his basic thinking on the drama, is clear when one bears in mind his *History of the American Theatre.* (p. 45)

Now, international though his borrowings and adaptations may be, and open-minded as many of his judgments are, yet Dunlap reflects, and in a conspicuous way, the nationalistic currents of the time. This is the case with his play having the enemy title *André;* dealing as it does, in many ways sympathetically, with the tragedy of this British officer and spy, yet the play is a piece of strong nationalism, crowded with patriotic actions and utterances. Perhaps most striking in this respect is the figure of Washington, dominating the action at nearly every point, and portrayed with the greatest respect and veneration, to be seen particularly in the forgiving calm with which he receives Bland's impetuous renunciation of the cockade. (p. 46)

[The nationalism of *André* is open-minded.] Strong as the patriotic utterances are, yet the title character of the play, enemy of America, is portrayed in a decidedly sympathetic light. . . .

[It appears] that nationalism with Dunlap is a strong interest, but one which does not exclude others nor prevent him from realizing the full value of foreign culture. . . . It appears further that the nationalism of *André* is Federalistic. . . . The philosophical concept of man's natural evil or weakness which lies behind the Federalistic view finds decided expression in the play. . . . (p. 47)

> Allan Gates Halline, "William Dunlap: 1766-1839,"
> in American Plays, *edited by Allan Gates Halline*
> *(reprinted by permission of D. C. Heath & Co.),*
> *American Book Company, 1935, pp. 43-9.*

ARTHUR HOBSON QUINN   (essay date 1943)

During the last decade of the eighteenth century and the first of the nineteenth, the dominating force in the American drama was the interesting figure of William Dunlap. From the pages of his *History of the American Theatre* and his *Arts of Design* emerges a real personality, an artist to his finger tips—enthusiastic, temperamental, and proud of his craft, whether it be that of the dramatist or the painter, yet capable of smiling even at his own performances, which never reached the shining level of his desires. (p. 74)

[*The Father, or, American Shandyism*] merits attention, both from the historical and the absolute points of view. (p. 76)

[The] combination of purpose, to amuse and instruct, was characteristic of the century, but, to Dunlap's credit, he did not overdo the moral lecture. Nor did he appeal to the morbid by dishing up contemporary scandal, sugar coated with moral reflections. . . . The plot of *The Father* is fairly conventional, but from the opening of the first scene . . . there is a sense of reality in the portraiture. . . . The play is lively: it reads well even to-day, for the conversation is bright at times and rarely stilted, and it leaves room for action. Of course, it was based on Dunlap's knowledge of other plays, and the most obvious dependence, that on *Tristram Shandy*, is acknowledged in the subtitle. (pp. 76-7)

The play [*The Mysterious Monk*] was published under the title of *Ribbemont, or the Feudal Baron*, in 1803. It is interesting in its criticism of false standards of honor, which probably was occasioned by the practice of dueling. Dunlap showed again in this play his ability, even in this period of romantic sentimentalism, to write direct blank verse, which afforded an actor an effective medium. (p. 84)

Dunlap's first translation of a foreign play [was] *Tell Truth and Shame the Devil*. . . . It was an adaptation of a French farce, *Jérôme Pointu*, by A.L.B. Robineau. . . . The adaptation has one original character, but Dunlap adds little to the piece, which owes its interest to the Gallic irony with which the original author represents his characters. . . . The language, which is not a slavish imitation of the original, is brisk and the comedy reads well. (pp. 84-5)

The play [*André*] is easily one of Dunlap's best. Its structure is admirable, especially from the point of view of unity. (p. 86)

The character of André himself is well drawn. As good a case as is possible is made out for him, and he acts with dignity and courage. The play was not a great stage success, since it was not frequently acted, but as a reading play it is well worth study. . . . Dunlap felt that it was too near the [actual] events to be successful, but it remains one of the best of our early plays.

Owing to the popular demand for patriotic spectacles, Dunlap rewrote *André* in 1803 as *The Glory of Columbia.* The unity of André was destroyed. . . . Some of the tragic scenes and the monologues of André are cut out. . . . Songs were inserted freely in *The Glory of Columbia,* and at the end the scene is transported to Yorktown and the captors of André are brought in, with a cheerful indifference to history. Dunlap had the sense of proportion which caused him to say in his *History* that *The Glory of Columbia* is "occasionally murdered for the amusement of holiday fools," but as a spectacle it is above the average. (p. 88)

[The play which Dunlap considered to be his best was *The Italian Father.* It] was received with great applause and was supposed to be by Kotzebue, since it was produced anonymously. When he published the play . . . Dunlap called attention to his debt to "old English dramatic literature," and in his history acknowledges his particular indebtedness to Thomas Dekker. *The Honest Whore* was his model, and he took from that play the main motive, a father's protecting care, shown in the disguise of a serving man, over the daughter whom he had formerly cast off and who even in her poverty and distress proves to be "mine own girl still." A comparison between the original play and its adaptation is interesting. Dekker has, of course, the supreme advantage of originality, but Dunlap was only following the custom of the Elizabethan playwrights themselves in making use of older material, and from the point of view of unity of construction, of swiftness of movement and stage effectiveness, there can be no question of the superiority of *The Italian Father.* He cut out entirely the tiresome subplot . . . , and he substituted an entertaining hoax played by a fool and a waiting woman upon a gentleman of the court. (pp. 93-4)

The result of these changes is a real gain in the sympathy of the audiences. Dekker built up an admirable character . . . in the First Part of *The Honest Whore;* in the Second Part he destroyed it. . . . There are, however, in *The Italian Father* four characters, Astrabel, Michael Brazzo, Beraldo, and Hippolito, in whose fortunes the audience is deeply interested, and the surest test of drama is, therefore, met.

Dunlap next adapted Schiller's *Don Carlos,* and produced it . . . "much shorn of its beams." (pp. 94-5)

Dunlap brought on the stage . . . his translation of Kotzebue's *False Shame, or the American Orphan in Germany,* which, according to him, "without scenery or decoration, by plain dialogue and natural character, supported the theatre through this season." . . . *False Shame* is a rather complicated play, with a strong appeal to good morals and sentimentality. . . . All these troubles are brought about by a false sense of delicacy.

After an unsuccessful adaptation from Boutet de Monvel's *Clémentine et Désormes* . . . under the title of *The Robbery,* Dunlap made a successful adaptation from Kotzebue's *Der Wildfang* in the form of an opera called *The Wild Goose Chase.* . . .

It is one of the most entertaining of Dunlap's plays, and he seems to have improved the original both in construction and dialogue. The sentences are crisp, the repartee sparkling, and while the whole thing verges on farce, it has a lightness of touch and a characterization rare in the farce of the period. (p. 96)

Dunlap broke away from Kotzebue to produce an opera, *The Knight of Guadalquiver*, . . . , but it was not approved by his audience. To make amends, he scored a success with *Abaellino, the Great Bandit*. . . .

Abaellino, the Great Bandit, is a romantic melodrama, laid in Venice. . . . The play is blood and thunder, but is skillfully put together, and has been the prototype of many other such plays. (p. 100)

The next of his adaptations that has survived is *Peter the Great*, an historical romance, from the German play, *Die Strelizen*, by Joseph Marius Babo. It . . . was not very successful, though it was revived. . . . However, the piece reads well, and the character drawing is above the average. (p. 101)

Seven years before his death, [Dunlap] published his invaluable *History of the American Theatre*, the first record of our stage. It is not only a mine of information about the beginnings of our theatre and our drama, it is a fascinating autobiography of a man who accomplished much through more than one failure. (p. 108)

Dunlap's achievement cannot properly be estimated by the methods of criticism that have hitherto been employed. . . . He was not provincial, and he was acquainted with the dramatic literature of England, both of an earlier time and of his own day. He kept himself informed of the current movements in French and German drama, and he selected with some discrimination from among all these foreign sources material for adaptation. That he had no contemporary masterpieces to select from was after all not his fault.

His versatility, too, must at least be noted. He began with the comedy of social life in *The Father*, he experimented with the romantic tragedy of history in *Leicester* and the Gothic melodrama in *Ribbemont*, then rose to his greatest height in the dignified if somber tragedy of American history in *André*, and he continued to reproduce American history on the stage with success. He made use of dramatic impulses of the past in *The Italian Father*, and he adapted with success French and German plays of his own period. The assumption of his necessary inferiority to European dramatists is dispelled at once by an actual comparison of his work, not with that of Shakespeare, but with those plays which were actually being written during the decades 1790-1810. (p. 109)

[It] is to be remembered that his original plays are his best. In *The Father*, his first acted play, he carried on the healthy impulse to describe real types of native character, and for a beginner succeeded well. In *André* he gave us the first adequate tragedy of American history, a play which can still be read without even implicit apology. *Darby's Return*, though a trifle, has no small merit in its sincerity, and it is a pity that Dunlap did not print all his patriotic plays, of which he composed seven. For one of his most likable qualities is his sturdy Americanism. (p. 111)

Of the remaining original plays, *Leicester* and *The Italian Father* are the best. . . .

[The character drawing] in both plays, especially in *The Italian Father* . . . , is of a quality that deserves much more than the faint praise accorded to it by those who, we must infer, have allowed the scarcity of his plays to discourage their attempts at first-hand criticism.

Dunlap's blank verse deserves, too, its share of praise. It is dignified, flexible, and straightforward. . . . But narrative verse is not dramatic verse, and Dunlap knew the difference. He never thought of being a great poet, but he could put verse into the mouths of characters on the stage and make it seem their natural utterance, which many have tried to do and failed. . . .

In short, William Dunlap had the soul of an artist and the intrepidity of the pioneer, and his place in our dramatic literature will remain secure. (p. 112)

Arthur Hobson Quinn, "William Dunlap, Playwright and Producer," in his A History of the American Drama: From the Beginning to the Civil War (reprinted by permission of Hawthorne Properties (Elsevier-Dutton Publishing Co., Inc.); copyright 1923, 1943, 1951, 1970 by Arthur Hobson Quinn), second edition, F.S. Crofts & Co., 1943 (and reprinted by Appleton-Century-Crofts, Inc., 1951), pp. 74-112.

ROBERT H. CANARY　(essay date 1963)

[William Dunlap] was, at one time or another, a dramatist, theatre manager-director, painter engraver, historian, biographer, essayist, novelist, poet and diarist. He was no mere dilettante, but a hard-working professional of some importance in several fields. It was Dunlap's misfortune to make his major contributions in drama, a field neglected by American literary historians, and painting, a field relatively neglected by everyone but art historians. Dunlap's endeavors kept him perennially insolvent in his lifetime; they have brought him only very limited recognition from posterity. (p. 45)

[His] *Life of Charles Brockden Brown* . . . , our first professional novelist, is a valuable if unreadable source of material on Dunlap's close friend. Readable, amusing and extremely valuable are Dunlap's *History of the American Theatre* and his *History of the Rise and Progress of the Arts of Design in the United States*. . . .

This wide experience in arts and letters and Dunlap's extensive acquaintanceships among artists and literary men make Dunlap a figure of significance in our cultural history, and lend interest to his comments on the problems of the arts in America. He was not a theorist by inclination, but he usually confined his comments to the art he was immediately concerned with at the time. (pp. 45-6)

[Dunlap] was not interested in writing closet drama; plays of his own which played badly on stage he filed away as "ineffective." While he would not accept the judgment of the far-from-ideal audience he faced on either his own plays or those of others, he was not too proud to write an occasional pot-boiler. He does not argue that society has a special duty to promote art, and he never argues that its service to morals is an important reason for supporting it. Instead, Dunlap held that art should make its own way in a commercial world.

William Dunlap believed that "The fine arts are all of one family." Very early in life he believed that the "sister Arts" of poetry, history and painting should "join and Mutually assist each other." His scattered remarks on the problems of various arts help us to understand some of the common problems of early American artists. His views are of especial interest, for Dunlap's generation set many of the basic patterns in the new nation, wrestled for the first time with problems which still occupy us today.

Dunlap stands as an early example of the American artist whose political faith in the people is unbounded, but who actively dislikes popular taste in the arts. Despite his fervent republicanism, Dunlap believed that only the educated upper classes had the developed sensibility needed to appreciate serious art.

Dunlap also stands as an early example of the perils of the marketplace. In order to carry on his serious work, he was constantly forced to serve the public what it wanted—accurate portraits, sentimental melodramas. (p. 49)

Dunlap's generation found an audience for the American arts, though not, perhaps, the ideal audience they sought. . . . On this question Dunlap's experience and historical importance entitle him to a hearing. (p. 50)

> Robert H. Canary, "William Dunlap and the Search for an American Audience," in Midcontinent American Studies Journal (copyright, Midcontinent American Studies Association, 1963), Vol. 4, No. 1, Spring, 1963, pp. 45-51.

NORMAN PHILBRICK   (essay date 1972)

If one analyzes the corpus of the dramatic writings of William Dunlap, the conclusion must be made that he was, if not by any means a distinguished playwright, certainly a more than competent one. His work, to be sure, is uneven, and it follows a sometimes derivative, sometimes imitative pattern. It is sentimental, moralistic, indulges frequently in excesses of the purple writing and Gothic atmosphere characteristic of its time, but its faults are often overcome by the sincerity and intensity of the writer as well as the technical control exercised by a playwright who was essentially an experienced man of the theatre. (p. 97)

André, unfortunately, was a failure, but there were extenuating conditions, causing its rapid demise, and these are related to the subject matter and the political environment of the time when it was produced in 1798. In examining the play, one is struck by its merits more than by its faults. Its worth as an example of early native drama and its superiority to many other plays of the eighteenth century, both English and American, should be emphasized. *André* is far from being a jerry-built, incompetent piece of work. One is impressed by its clarity, its several scenes of emotional validity, the slow but effective progression of its plot, and the honesty of its patriotic sentiments. The characters are not fully realized, but neither are they cut-out figures played against the explosions of chauvinistic effusions.

One of the chief weaknesses of *André* lies in the choice of a spy as hero, and Dunlap does not attempt to avoid the issue of the shocking nature of André's crime against a nation. He does mitigate it, however, and he obviously felt justified in doing so because of the character of the spy-hero and the romantic aura surrounding him. (pp. 97-8)

[Dunlap's excuse for *André*'s failure—that it was too close to the Battle of Bunker-Hill]—has some justification, but there were other more obvious reasons for the collapse of a well-intentioned endeavor.

Of major importance was the choice of subject. At first sight the story of André has within it many ingredients of a dramatic romance. . . . (p. 101)

Unfortunately for Dunlap, the realistic aspect of the business makes it impossible to treat the subject romantically or sentimentally, although he attempts to do so. . . . Dunlap did foresee, however, that he might have difficulties if he dramatized all aspects of the conspiracy. Consequently, he restricts his treatment of the event, beginning his play after the capture and trial of André, just the day before his execution. . . . Dunlap raises the hope that André may be allowed to die like a gentleman rather than a common criminal, but that hope is destroyed, and the spy is brought to the final catastrophe of an ignominious death. To these circumstances Dunlap adds the fiction of an ill-fated romance between André and Honora Sneyd. . . . In the play the pathetic separation of the lovers is made more poignant by the device of Honora's going mad when she cannot save André. There are then all the possibilities of an eighteenth-century tragedy in the grand manner—with a touch of Gothic thrown in.

Aware, however, that he is basing his drama on an actual occurrence and troubled by the fact that many of the participants in the affair are still alive, Dunlap cautiously threads his way through the historic facts of the case. He ignores some of them entirely, refers only slightly to others, and bases most of his evidence on the documents he has collected for publication with the first edition of the play. (pp. 101-02)

Dunlap makes full use of the excellent character of [André] and paints a hero just slightly more than life-size. His portrait is not idealized to such a degree that André appears to be a cardboard figure. To achieve the three-dimensional quality of the man, the playwright uses Bland, his close friend, as a dramatic counterfoil. Bland is tempestuous; André remains composed. Bland seeks excuses for André's conduct; André admits his errors. Bland betrays sentimental weaknesses in his character; André is an example of the typical reasonable man of the eighteenth century. . . .

[In] spite of the remembrance of the controversy dividing men eighteen years before the play was produced, Dunlap succeeded in convincing his audience that a spy could be a hero and at the same time added to the honor of Washington. . . . (p. 108)

There are then a number of reasons why *André* was not a success. The conditions for the failure of Dunlap's play . . . —the subject matter too close to the actual event, the attempt to make a hero of a former enemy and a spy as well, the weakness of the production on the opening night—separately might not have brought on disaster; together they created a great hazard. What effectively and finally ruined the chances of the play were its political aspects, something which Dunlap could not foresee. (p. 111)

André rings with patriotism and an unabashed love of country, a country, however, secured by union and not fragmented by separation of state against state, an idealized new world. . . . Yet Dunlap's cautionary theme throughout the play is that man is weak, "His tide of passion struggling still with Reason's/ Fair and favorable gale, and adverse/Driving his unstable bark upon the/Rocks of error." As in man, so in a nation. The solemn and sober moralizing represents the playwright's honesty and is part of his credo that the first duty of the stage is to raise the standards of society, to make the arts the living embodiment of public and private virtue and to teach by example. The fatal weakness of *André* is that Dunlap's high purpose was imbued with a political didacticism which ran counter to the rising and vociferous dissension of the common man. . . . *André* might have been successful if it had been produced in the triumph of Washington's first administration; in 1798, it had no chance of survival. (pp. 118-19)

> *Norman Philbrick, "The Spy as Hero: An Examination of 'André' by William Dunlap," in Studies in Theatre and Drama: Essays in Honor of Hubert C. Heffner, edited by Oscar G. Brockett (© copyright 1972 Mouton & Co. N.V.), Mouton Publishers, The Hague, 1972, pp. 97-119.*

JACK ZIPES (essay date 1974)

The plays of . . . Dunlap achieved their popularity because they . . . presented an illusion of the restoration of harmony after chaos. The plot and ideas work toward creating a sentimental idyll, whether the play is tragedy or comedy, in which evil . . . is overcome by good. . . . (p. 278)

[*The Italian Father*] is well constructed. The main plot is balanced by a comic sub-plot which makes the more serious scenes palatable. . . . Dunlap is a good craftsman. [However,] his critique of society becomes buried in sentiment and compromise. Obviously, Dunlap wants to criticize the puritanical standards in American society or society in general. . . . Dunlap clearly obfuscates all the criticism implicit in the play. . . . The crucial issues—sexual repression, arbitrary authority, and false moral standards—are left unexplored. A false harmony arises, and the curtain falls preventing the play from exposing social contradictions that had parallels in American society of that time. (pp. 280-81)

The theater of . . . Dunlap is illusionary theater. It appears to take the audience into its confidence; it appears to take their problems seriously, but it really means to distract, delight, placate, and indoctrinate the people into accepting compromises the [author himself was] making. . . .

It may seem a long jump from the . . . Dunlap drama to the American television series like *All in the Family*. But there is no doubt that the result of the compromise made by writers like . . . Dunlap at the end of the eighteenth century is the highly technical, flashy commercial dramatic production which works upon our consciousness so that we shall excuse our "ruling fathers" for their racism and bigotry because (deep down) they mean well, because all mistakes can be rectified in the end, all conflicts can be resolved. Such commercial productions of compromise contribute to the further destruction of historical consciousness and the cultivation of mass stupidity. This is not to say that . . . Dunlap [was an evil man]. There is nothing wrong with harmony and reconciliation, but there are more truthful and rational ways to portray the path to such harmony. The great European and American writers of bourgeois comedy and tragedy (the overly serious writers) also saw the need for harmony. Yet they did not make compromises in their works. They set out to expose social contradictions as honestly as possible and drew the consequences. Dunlap . . . worked to reduce the importance of these contradictions and failed to understand the ramifications that [his] work would have for future generations. The result in America can be seen in the pitiful productions on stage and television, and in your neighborhood movie theater. (p. 282)

> *Jack Zipes, "Dunlap, Kotzebue, and the Shaping of American Theater: A Re-evaluation from a Marxist Perspective," in Early American Literature (copy-*

righted, 1974, by the University of Massachusetts), Vol. VIII, No. 3, Winter, 1974, pp. 272-84.*

WALTER J. MESERVE (essay date 1977)

[William Dunlap] is frequently called the first professional dramatist in America. . . . [He] wrote biography and history, most notably his *History of the American Theatre.* Dunlap also brought a certain respectability to the American theatre. Considering its condition at the time, he deserves credit for a pioneering effort in an unproven field to which he brought a remarkable industry supported by talent and devotion. But it is his writing of at least sixty plays . . . that makes him a significant figure in the history of the American drama. He made people aware of the American dramatist. It was his *Tell Truth and Shame the Devil* . . . , for example, which, as the first American play given an English production, was performed at Covent Garden. . . . At a time when little was being accomplished in American drama, Dunlap's work was a torrent of light. . . . He appeared during a period when such a playwright as he was needed. Yet, in the larger view that time provides, his life appears as a succession of failures while his quantitative contribution to American drama is only occasionally distinguished by outstanding work. (pp. 102-03)

[By] following the sentiment of Laurence Sterne and by providing a complicated comic plot with disguises, devices, a good moral, an American soldier-hero, opportunity for much laughter, and a happy ending, Dunlap wrote [*The Father of an Only Child*, which] acted well and appealed to audiences. He also showed the necessary theatrical *savoir-faire* by providing a prologue which praised the moral tendency of the stage. (pp. 103-04)

Following an established pattern in American drama, *Darby's Return* was a satire but, different from other plays, a very gentle satire of the "gallant" soldier who returns to his village after the war. As Darby tells of his experiences, it is clear that the romantic concept of the soldier has no basis in actual military experience. Unfortunately, Dunlap's technique is narrative rather than dramatic and shows little of his later craftsmanship. In every sense the play is a trifle, but a delightful one with song and dance. (p. 104)

Written in average verse and boasting an exciting plot, [the] romantic tragedy [*Leicester*] suggests the type of heroic tragedy and melodrama toward which Dunlap would direct his talents either as playwright or as adaptor-translator. (p. 106)

In spite of the excessive romanticism, the sentiment, the obvious debts to English heroic tragedy and to Shakespeare, and the artificialities of the verse and the action, [*André*] manifests a certain provocative power in the sensitivity of its argument. The characters are secondary; particularly weak are the women, who are simply pawns of the dramatist. . . . Of the serious plays written in America before James Nelson Barker's *Superstition* (1824), *André* must be considered the best.

It is a comment on the times and on Dunlap that he felt obliged to rewrite *André* as a patriotic spectacle entitled *The Glory of Columbia—Her Yeomanry.* . . . The serious thesis of the original play was now replaced with scenic spectacle, song, and comic relief provided by America's soldiers and a spirited country girl as well as by a captured Irishman. The attempt to combine the story of André with the story of American soldiers fighting the British must seem a failure to all who read *André,* but it was a success on the stage for many years. Patriotic plays, generally, were extremely popular about this time, and Dunlap contributed his share. . . . *The Soldier of '76* . . . and *The Retrospect; or, the American Revolution* . . . were also patriotic pieces. Perhaps Dunlap's best-known effort in spectacle patriotism is *Yankee Chronology* . . . , which has been variously described as an anecdote, a sketch, and a monologue on stage. But mainly it is a song, "Yankee Chronology." . . . (pp. 109-10)

Dunlap deserves credit for his quantity and for his exuberance and idealism, which led him into situations where he could not cope although others under similar circumstances would later, and he made progress toward their success. If he was derivative in his playwriting, he at least imitated some of the appreciated dramatists of the time. By translating foreign dramas for American pleasure, he was in the foreground of a vast movement which for good or ill would come to fill a void and then stay to act as a deterrent to American creativity. With *André* he made a distinctive contribution to American drama; in his [*History of the American Theatre*] he gathered his impressions for others to consider. Perhaps it is simply wisest to say that at this early time, as the theatre and drama in America struggled to get started, a person of ideals, one of talent and imagination who could write what an audience could appreciate in a society not yet thoroughly comfortable with the institution of theatre and one of courage and a capacity for hard work, was desperately needed as a substantial if not brilliant basis on which to build. Dunlap was that person. (pp. 114-15)

> *Walter J. Meserve, "Early Dramatists of the New Republic," in his* An Emerging Entertainment: The Drama of the American People to 1828 *(copyright © 1977 by Indiana University Press), Indiana University Press, 1977, pp. 92-125.*

ADDITIONAL BIBLIOGRAPHY

Brooks, Van Wyck. "William Dunlap and His Circle." In his *The World of Washington Irving,* pp. 152-75. New York: E. P. Dutton & Co., 1944.*

> Historical material pertaining to Dunlap as an artist. This book discusses Dunlap's studies under Benjamin West, his acquaintance with fellow artists, and how he compiled *The History of the Rise and Progress of the Arts of Design in the United States.*

Campbell, William P. Introduction to *A History of the Rise and Progress of the Arts of Design in the United States,* by William Dunlap, pp. vii-xxxi. New York: Blom, 1965.

> Calls Dunlap's book "the definitive study of American Art."

McKee, Thomas J. Introduction to *The Father; or, American Shandyism,* by William Dunlap, pp. vii-xii. New York: The Dunlap Society, 1887.

> Biography of Dunlap focusing on his dramatic career. The book also contains a complete bibliography of Dunlap's published and unpublished plays.

Pickering, James H. "*Satanstoe:* Cooper's Debt to William Dunlap." *American Literature* XXXVIII, No. 4 (January 1967): 468-77.*

> Discusses the influence of Dunlap on James Fenimore Cooper's *Satanstoe.*

Quinn, Arthur Hobson. "Early Fiction and Drama." In *The Literature of the American People: An Historical and Critical Survey,* edited by Arthur Hobson Quinn, pp. 190-210. New York: Appleton-Century-Crofts, 1951.*

> Gives an inclusive history of all Dunlap's plays, discussing the basis for his ideas.

Gustave Flaubert

1821-1880

French novelist, short story writer, and dramatist.

The most influential French novelist of the nineteenth century, Flaubert is remembered primarily for the stylistic precision and dispassionate rendering of psychological detail found in his masterpiece, *Madame Bovary*. Although his strict objectivity is often associated with the realist and naturalist movements, he objected to this classification, and his artistry indeed defies such easy categorization. In pursuit of *le mot juste*, Flaubert struggled throughout his career to overcome a natural romantic tendency toward lyricism, fantastic imaginings, and love of the exotic past. A meticulous craftsman, his aim was to achieve a prose style "as rhythmical as verse and as precise as the language of science."

Flaubert was born in Rouen, where his father was chief surgeon at the city hospital and his mother was a well-known woman of provincial bourgeois background. After receiving his early education in Rouen, Flaubert reluctantly studied law in Paris for several years. During this period he wrote continuously, producing, among other works, the first version of *L'éducation sentimentale: Histoire d'un jeune homme (Sentimental Education; a Young Man's History)*. However, he chose never to publish these highly romantic early works and they only appeared posthumously. At age twenty-two, Flaubert suffered the first attack of a nervous disorder resembling epilepsy which plagued him throughout his life and which many critics feel partially explains his pessimistic view. This malady disrupted his law studies and thus Flaubert devoted himself wholly to literature. Following the deaths of his father and sister in 1846, he returned to the family estate of Croisset near Rouen, where he lived and wrote for the rest of his life.

Inspired by a painting by the elder Brueghel titled *The Temptation of Saint Anthony*, Flaubert dreamed of using this subject to create a French *Faust*. After several years of extensive research and meticulous composition, he gathered together his closest friends, Maxime Du Camp and Louis Bouilhet, and read them his manuscript. When he had finished and asked for their frank opinion, they declared the work a failure, saying, "We think you should throw it into the fire, and never speak of it again." Maintaining that the subject was an unfortunate choice because it encouraged his tendency towards excessive lyricism and lack of precision, they encouraged Flaubert to abandon historical subjects and begin a novel which would be contemporary in content and realistic in intent. Said Bouilhet: "Your Muse must be kept on bread and water or lyricism will kill her." Although devastated by this verdict, Flaubert respected his friends' advice and placed the manuscript in a drawer, where it remained unpublished for twenty-five years. When the final version was published after extensive revision, it was hardly the success that *Madame Bovary* had been. However, many critics feel that although *La tentation de Saint Antoine (The Temptation of Saint Antony)* is not so great a work as *Madame Bovary* or *Sentimental Education*, it represents more fully Flaubert's natural temperament.

After extensive travels with Du Camp to such countries as Egypt, Palestine, and Turkey, Flaubert returned to Croisset

to begin *Madame Bovary*. Although he found his bourgeois subject disgusting, he strove for stylistic perfection, working slowly and painfully for more than five years, often producing only one page in several days. This novel, his first to be published despite years of writing and several completed manuscripts, initially appeared in installments in *La Revue de Paris*. Although serious critics immediately recognized in *Madame Bovary* a work of immense significance, the French government was of a different opinion. Flaubert, his printer, and his publisher were tried together for blasphemy and offense against public morals. All were eventually acquitted, and both Flaubert and *Madame Bovary* acquired a certain noteriety. Flaubert came to resent the fame of *Madame Bovary*, which completely overshadowed his later works, saying he wished to buy all the copies, "throw them into the fire and never hear of the book again."

With *Madame Bovary* finally finished, Flaubert sought a new subject which would be far from the bourgeois provincial setting he had labored over for so long. Once again turning to the past, he traveled to Carthage to gather material for *Salammbô*, a historical novel whose exotic subject matter and opulent setting are reminiscent of the Romantic tradition and in which the descriptive technique is rigorously objective. Next he published *Sentimental Education*, depicting in panoramic porportions life under the July Monarchy. Although it has been criticized, like *Salammbô*, for its excessive documentation, *Sentimental Education* is noted by many for its excellent recreation of an erl, and is considered by some to be a finer work than *Madame Bovary*. A collection of short stories titled *Trois contes: Un coeur simple; La légende de Saint-Julien l'Hospitalier; Hérodias (Three Tales)*, published three years before Flaubert's death, is widely praised for its varied themes and exquisite style, and is noted by some as the fullest expression of his mature genius. Flaubert died before completing *Bouvard et Pécuchet (Bouvard and Pécuchet)*, a satirical novel of human folly which was intended to be his greatest attack on the bourgeois conventions he so detested.

Flaubert was burdened in his last years by financial difficulties and personal sorrow resulting from the deaths of his mother and several close friends. He was also disappointed by the failure of his theatrical works and saddened by the feeling that his works were generally misunderstood. However, he enjoyed close friendships with many prominent contemporaries including George Sand, Ivan Turgenev, Henry James and Guy de Maupassant; the latter served as his literary apprentice. A complex personality, obsessed with his art, Flaubert is perhaps best understood through his voluminous *Correspondance*. In these candid and spontaneous letters, Flaubert chronicles his developing literary philosophy and the meticulous research and writing of his works. Although many critics fault his pessimism, cold impersonality, and ruthless objectivity, it is universally acknowledged that Flaubert developed, through painstaking attention to detail and constant revision, an exquisite prose style which has served as a model for innumerable writers.

PRINCIPAL WORKS

Madame Bovary (novel) 1857
　　[*Madame Bovary*, 1881]
Salammbô (novel) 1863
　　[*Salammbô*, 1886]
L'éducation sentimentale: Histoire d'un jeune homme
　　(novel) 1870
　　[*Sentimental Education; a Young Man's History*, 1898]
La tentation de Saint Antoine (novel) 1874
　　[*The Temptation of Saint Antony*, 1895]
Trois contes: Un coeur simple; La légende de Saint-Julien
　　l'Hospitalier; Hérodias (short stories) 1877
　　[*Three Tales*, 1903]
Bouvard et Pécuchet (novel) 1881
　　[*Bouvard and Pécuchet*, 1896]
Correspondance. 4 vols. (letters) 1894-99
Premières oeuvres. 4 vols. (novels) 1914-20
The Selected Letters of Gustave Flaubert (letters) 1954

GUSTAVE FLAUBERT　(essay date 1852-53)

There are in me, literarily speaking, two distinct persons: one who is infatuated with bombast, lyricism, eagle flights, sonorities of phrase and lofty ideas; and another who digs and burrows into the truth as deeply as he can, who likes to treat a humble fact as respectfully as a big one, who would like to make you feel almost *physically* the things he reproduces. The former likes to laugh, and enjoys the animal side of man. . . .

[In *Saint Antoine*,] having taken a subject which left me completely free as to lyricism, emotions, excesses of all kinds, I felt in my element, and had only to let myself go. Never will I rediscover such recklessness of style as I indulged in during those eighteen long months. How passionately I carved the beads of my necklace! I forgot only one thing—the string. . . .

What seems beautiful to me, what I should like to write, is a book about nothing, a book dependent on nothing external, which would be held together by the internal strength of its style, just as the earth, suspended in the void, depends on nothing external for its support; a book which would have almost no subject, or at least in which the subject would be almost invisible, if such a thing is possible. The finest works are those that contain the least matter; the closer expression comes to thought, the closer language comes to coinciding and merging with it, the finer the result. I believe the future of Art lies in this direction. I see it, as it has developed from its beginnings, growing progressively more ethereal, from Egyptian pylons to Gothic lancets, from the 20,000-line Hindu poems to the effusions of Byron. Form, in becoming more skillful, becomes attenuated; it leaves behind all liturgy, rule, measure; the epic is discarded in favor of the novel, verse in favor of prose; there is no longer any orthodoxy, and form is as free as the will of its creator. . . .

It is for this reason that there are no noble subjects or ignoble subjects; from the standpoint of pure Art one might almost establish the axiom that there is no such thing as subject—style in itself being an absolute manner of seeing things. (p. 154)

　　·　·　·　·　·

Now [while writing *Madame Bovary*] I am in an entirely different world, that of close observation of the most trivial details. My attention is fixed on the mouldy mosses of the soul. It is a long way from the mythological and theological extravagances of *Saint Antoine*. And just as the subject is different, so I am writing in an entirely different way. I do not want my book to contain a *single* subjective reaction, nor a *single* reflection by the author. I think it will be less lofty than *Saint Antoine* as to *ideas* (which I don't think very important), but it will perhaps be stronger and more extraordinary, without seeming so. (p. 155)

　　·　·　·　·　·

Passion does not make verses; and the more personal you are, the weaker. I myself always sinned in that respect: I always put myself into everything I did. Instead of Saint Anthony, for example, *I* was in that book; my *Tentation* was written for myself, not for the reader. The less you feel a thing, *the more capable you are of expressing it as it is* (as it *always* is, in itself, in its universality, freed from all ephemeral contingencies). But one must be able to *make oneself feel it*. This faculty is, simply, genius: the ability to *see*, to have the model posing there before you.

That is why I abhor rhetorical poetry, pompous poetry. To express things that are beyond words, a look is enough. Exhalations of the soul, lyricism, descriptions—I want all that to be in the *style*. Elsewhere, it is a prostitution of art and of feeling itself. (p. 165)

　　·　·　·　·　·

Yes, it is a strange thing, the relation between one's writing and one's personality. Is there anyone who loves antiquity more than I, anyone more haunted by it, anyone who has made a greater effort to understand it? And yet in my books I am as far as possible from being a man of the antique world. From my appearance one would think I should be a writer of epic, of drama, of brutally factual narrative; whereas actually I feel at home only in analysis—in anatomy, if I may call it such. Fundamentally I am the man of the mists; and it is only by patience and study that I have rid myself of all the whitish fat that clogged my muscles. The books I am most eager to write are precisely those for which I am least endowed. *Bovary,* in this respect, will have been an unprecedented tour de force (a fact of which I alone shall ever be aware): its subject, characters, effects, etc.—all are alien to me. It should make it possible for me to take a great step forward later. Writing this book I am like a man playing the piano with lead balls attached to his knuckles. But once I have mastered my fingering, and find a piece that's to my taste and that I can play with my sleeves rolled up, the result will perhaps be good. In any case, I think I am doing the right thing. What one does is not for oneself, but for others. Art is not interested in the personality of the artist. So much the worse for him if he doesn't like red or green or yellow: all colors are beautiful, and his task is to use them. (pp. 166-67)

. . . . .

An author in his book must be like God in the universe, present everywhere and visible nowhere. Art being a second Nature, the creator of that Nature must behave similarly. In all its atoms, in all its aspects, let there be sensed a hidden, infinite impassivity. The effect for the spectator must be a kind of amazement. "How is all that done?" one must ask; and one must feel overwhelmed without knowing why. (p. 173)

. . . . .

It is perhaps absurd to want to give prose the rhythm of verse (keeping it distinctly prose, however), and to write of ordinary life as one writes history or epic (but without falsifying the subject). I often wonder about this. But on the other hand it is perhaps a great experiment, and very original. I know where I fail. (Ah, if only I were fifteen!) No matter: I shall always be given some credit for my stubbornness. (p. 182)

. . . . .

If the book I am writing with such difficulty turns out well, I'll have established, by the very fact of having written it, these two truths, which for me are axiomatic, namely: (1) that poetry is purely subjective, that in literature there are no such things as beautiful subjects, and that therefore Yvetot is the equal of Constantinople; and (2) that consequently one can write about any one thing equally well as about any other. The artist must raise everything to a higher level: he is like a pump; he has inside him a great pipe that reaches down into the entrails of things, the deepest layers. He sucks up what was lying there below, dim and unnoticed, and brings it out in great jets to the sunlight. (p. 189)

Gustave Flaubert, in extracts from five of his letters to Louise Colet from January 16, 1852 to March 31, 1853, in his The Letters of Gustave Flaubert: 1830-1857, *edited and translated by Francis Steegmuller (copyright © 1979, 1980 by Francis Steegmuller; excerpted by permission), Cambridge, Mass.: Belknap Press, 1980, pp. 154-55, 164-67, 173-74, 181-82, 188-89.*

CHARLES AUGUSTIN SAINTE-BEUVE (essay date 1857)

[With Gustave Flaubert's *Madame Bovary,* we come upon] a different mode of inspiration, and, to speak bluntly, another generation. The ideal is gone, lyricism has run dry. We are soberer. A severe, pitiless concern for truth, the most modern form of empiricism, has penetrated even into art. The author of *Madame Bovary* has lived in the provinces, in the country, in villages and small towns. . . . Now, what has he seen? Pettiness, squalor, pretentiousness, stupidity, routine, monotony, and boredom. The fields and villages, so natural and true, so full of the presence of the *genius loci,* will serve him only as a setting for portraying vulgar, banal, blindly ambitious creatures, totally ignorant or only semiliterate, whose love affairs are devoid of delicacy. The only person of refinement, the only one with an inner life whom fate has thrown there, and who aspires to something better, finds herself an alien, stifled. In the course of her sufferings, finding no one to understand her, she deteriorates, she becomes depraved, and in a vain pursuit of her dream amid ugly surroundings she comes step by step to her perdition and ruin. Is this moral? Is this comforting? The question does not seem to have occurred to the author. All he asked himself was one thing: Is it true? (pp. 260-61)

Another equally remarkable particularity of this work is that among all these very real, very living characters, not one can be supposed to be representing the author. . . . The author has remained completely uninvolved; he is there only as spectator, repeating and describing everything; nowhere in the novel do we catch so much as a glimpse of him. The work is entirely impersonal. This is a sign of remarkable power. (p. 261)

One precious quality distinguishes M. Gustave Flaubert from the other more or less exact observers who in our time pride themselves on conscientiously reproducing reality, and nothing but reality, and who occasionally succeed: he has *style.* He even has a trifle too much, and his pen delights in certain curiosities and minutiae of continuous description which at times injure the total effect. The things or the persons who should be kept most prominently in view are a little dimmed or flattened by the excessive projection of surrounding persons and things. Mme. Bovary herself, so charming when she first appears as Mlle. Emma, is so often described to us in minute detail that I cannot visualize her physically as whole, at least not clearly and distinctly. (p. 263)

We are led step by step into Mme. Bovary's heart. What is she really like? She is a woman; at first she is merely romantic, she has not been in the least corrupted. As he limns her for us, M. Gustave Flaubert does not spare her. Describing her dainty ways as a little girl and at school with the nuns, and showing her as given to extravagant daydreams, he exposes her pitilessly, and—shall I confess it?—we feel more indulgent toward her than he himself seems to be. Emma is unable to adjust herself to her new situation because she has one quality too many and one virtue too few: therein lies the root of all her transgressions, all her unhappiness. The quality is that she not only is a romantic nature but also has emotional and intellectual needs and ambitions, that she aspires to a higher, more refined, more elegant life than the one that has fallen to her lot. The virtue she lacks is that she never learned that the first condition of a good life is ability to endure boredom. (p. 264)

Emma's long solitary melancholy days, when she is left to herself during the first months following her marriage, her walks to the avenue of beeches at Banneville, accompanied by

Djali, her faithful greyhound bitch, the days during which she questions herself endlessly concerning fate and imagines what *might have been*—all this has been seen clearly and set down with the same analytical keenness, the same subtlety as can be found in older novels portraying people's intimate lives, the novels that set us dreaming. Impressions of rural nature, just as in the days of *René* [by Chateaubriand] or *Obermann* [by Étienne Pivert de Senancour], are mingled with sudden uprushes of capriciousness, spiritual boredom, and uncertain desires. . . . (p. 265)

The second half of the book is no less well handled and carefully composed than the first. I should like to point out a drawback, however, to the author's approach, which becomes apparent in the second half. To describe everything in exhausting detail and with the same emphasis has led him—surely inadvertently—to include scabrous details sufficiently vivid to risk arousing sensual emotions. In our opinion he should have stopped short of this. After all, a book is not and can never be reality itself. There is a point beyond which description defeats its own purpose. (pp. 270-71)

Mme. Bovary's atrocious end—her punishment, if you will—is presented and expounded in inexorable detail. The author has not played down the wretchedness of it all—he rasps our nerves. . . .

At certain moments and situations in this book, the author could easily have superimposed a coating of idealism over his implacable realism. By so doing he could have "patched up" a character and rounded it off—that of Charles Bovary, for example. A few more pats, and the clay the novelist was molding could have turned out a noble and touching figure instead of a vulgar one. The reader would not have complained—indeed, he all but begs him to do so. But the author refuses: he will not do it. (p. 271)

Although I appreciate the author's point of view—the keystone of his method, his poetics—I must reproach his book for the fact that there is no goodness in it. Not a single character represents goodness. . . . To be sure the book has a moral, one which the author has by no means dragged into it and which the reader must discover for himself. It is a rather terrible moral. But is it the duty of art to refuse all consolation to the reader, to reject every element of clemency and kindness under the pretext of being more truthful? . . . Modesty, resignation, devotion extending over long years—who among us has not seen examples of these virtues in the provinces? No matter how true to life your characters may be, they reflect the author's choice: it is he who has skillfully arranged the pattern of their shortcomings and absurdities. Why not arrange a pattern of good qualities—show us at least one character who captivates us or earns our respect? (p. 272)

Such are my objections to a book whose merits, however, I value very highly—observation, style (save a few blemishes), design, and composition.

In all its elements the work certainly bears the mark of its times. Begun, we are told, several years ago, it has come at the right moment. . . . For in many quarters and under various forms, I believe I discern signs of a new literature, exhibiting a scientific approach, a spirit of observation, maturity, power, and a certain tendency to callousness. These seem to me characteristics of the leaders among the younger writers. Son and brother of eminent doctors, M. Gustave Flaubert wields the pen as others wield the scalpel. (p. 273)

Charles Augustin Sainte-Beuve, "'Madame Bovary' by M. Gustave Flaubert" (1857; originally published as an essay in his Causeries du lundi, *1862?), in his* Sainte-Beuve: Selected Essays, *edited and translated by Francis Steegmuller and Norbert Guterman, (translation copyright © 1963 by Doubleday & Company, Inc.; reprinted by permission of the publisher), Doubleday, 1963, pp. 259-73.*

CHARLES BAUDELAIRE   (essay date 1857)

I cannot be grateful to Monsieur Gustave Flaubert for having at the first try [with the publication of *Madame Bovary*] obtained what others seek throughout their lifetimes. At the most I see in it a superrogatory symptom of power and shall seek to define the reasons which caused the author's mind to move in one direction rather than in another. (p. 91)

[When planning *Madame Bovary,* he] must have thought: "What is the surest means of stirring all these tired souls? They are really unaware of what they might love; they have a positive disgust only for what is great; naïve, ardent passion and poetic abandon make them blush and wound them. Let us therefore be vulgar in our choice of subjects, since the choice of too lofty a subject is an impertinence for the nineteenth-century reader. And also, let us beware of letting ourselves go and speaking our own minds. We shall be icy in relating passions and adventures that warm the blood of the common herd; as the school says, we shall be objective and impersonal.

"And also, since our ears have been buffeted in these recent times by childish school babblings, as we have heard of a certain literary process called *realism*—a disgusting insult hurled in the face of all analysts, a vague and elastic word signifying for the common man not a new method of creation but a minute description of accessories—we shall profit from the public confusion and universal ignorance. We shall apply a sinewy, picturesque, subtle, and exact style upon a banal canvas. We shall put the hottest and most passionate feelings into the most trivial adventure. The most solemn and decisive words will escape from the stupidest mouths.

"What is stupidity's stamping ground, the setting that is stupidest, most productive of absurdities, most abundant in intolerant imbeciles?

"The provinces.

"Who there are the most intolerable actors?

"The humble people, occupied with minor functions, the exercise of which falsifies their thinking.

"What is the most overdone and prostituted theme, the most hackneyed sob story?

"Adultery." (pp. 91-2)

"I need not worry about style, picturesque arrangement, the description of my settings; I possess all of these qualities more than amply. I shall proceed supported by analysis and logic, and I shall thus prove that all subjects are indiscriminately good or bad according to the manner in which they are treated, and that the most vulgar ones can become the best."

From that moment on, *Madame Bovary*—a wager, a true wager, a bet, like all works of art—was created.

It remained only for the author to accomplish this feat all the way, to strip himself (as much as possible) of his sex and to become a woman. A wondrous thing resulted from this: in spite of all his thespian zeal, he could not keep from infusing virile blood into the veins of his creature, and because of her energy and ambition and capacity for revery, Madame Bovary remained a man. Like the armored Pallas sprung from the forehead of Zeus, this bizarre androgyne has kept all of the seductive quality of a virile spirit in a charming feminine body.

Several critics have said: this work, truly lovely in the detail and lifelikeness of its descriptions, does not contain a single character representing morality or expressing the conscience of the author. Where is the proverbial and legendary character charged with explaining the fable and directing the intelligence of the reader? In other words, where is the indictment?

Absurdity! Eternal and incorrigible confusion of functions and genres! A true work of art needs no indictment. The logic of the work suffices for all postulations of morality, and it is up to the reader to draw conclusions from the conclusion.

As for the intimate, profound character in the fable, she is incontestably the adulterous woman. She alone, the dishonored victim, possesses all the graces of the hero. (pp. 92-3)

[Carried] away by the sophistries of her imagination, she gives herself magnificently, generously, in a completely masculine way, to wretches who are not her equals, exactly as poets give themselves to despicable women. (p. 93)

[This] woman is truly great. She is, above all, deserving of pity, and in spite of the systematic hard-heartedness of the author, who has tried his best to be absent from his work and to play the role of a manipulator of marionettes, all *intellectual* women will be grateful to him for having raised the female to so high a power, so far from the pure animal, and so close to the ideal man, and for having caused her to participate in that double character of calculation and reverie that constitutes the perfect being. (p. 94)

This essentially suggestive book could fill a whole volume of observations. For the moment I shall limit myself to observing that several of the most important episodes were at first either neglected or vituperatively attacked by the critics. Some examples: the episode of the unfortunate operation on the club-foot, and the one so remarkable, so full of desolation, so truly *modern,* in which the future adulteress—for she is still only at the beginning of her descent, poor woman!—goes to seek aid of the Church, of the divine Mother, of her who has no excuse for not being ever ready, of that Pharmacy where no one has the right to slumber! The good priest, Bournisien, concerned only with the little rascals in his catechism class playing games amid the pews and chairs in the church, replies ingenuously: "Since you are ill, Madame, and since Monsieur Bovary is a doctor, *why don't you consult your husband?*"

What woman, confronted with this curé's inadequacy, in the madness produced by such amnesty would not rush to plunge her head into the swirling waters of adultery? And who among us, in a more naïve age and in troubled circumstances, has not inevitably encountered the incompetent priest? (p. 95)

Charles Baudelaire, "'Madame Bovary'," translated by Raymond Giraud (originally published in L'Artiste, *October 18, 1857), in* Flaubert: A Collection of Critical Essays, *edited by Raymond Giraud (©1964 by Prentice-Hall, Inc.; reprinted by permission of Prentice-Hall, Inc., Englewood Cliffs, New Jersey 07632), Prentice-Hall, 1964, pp. 88-96.*

(essay date 1857)

[*The following is an excerpt from the obscenity trial of* Madame Bovary.]

[Opening speech for the prosecution by Ernest Pinard:]

[You may give **Madame Bovary**] another title and call it with justice *A History of the Adulteries of a Provincial Wife.* . . .

[Its] offense against public morals is in the lascivious pictures that . . . [Monsieur Flaubert has painted]; the offense against religious morals is in the mingling of voluptuous images with sacred things. (p. 329)

[Right from her first encounter with Rodolphe], from this first fall, [Madame Bovary] makes a glory of adultery, she sings a hymn to adultery, to its poetry, its pleasures. There, gentlemen, is what I find much more dangerous, much more immoral than the downfall itself! (p. 334)

Monsieur Flaubert knows how to beautify his paintings with all the resources of art, but without the circumspection of art. With him there is no reticence, no veil; he shows nature in all of its nudity, in all of its coarseness! (p. 340)

[After Madame Bovary poisons herself], without a regret, without a confession, without a tear of repentance for her present suicide and for her past adulteries, she is to receive the Last Sacrament. Why the Sacrament, when, in her thoughts just before, she is going into nothingness? Why, when there is not a tear, not a sigh of repentant Magdalen for her sin of disbelief, for her suicide, for her adulteries? . . .

[The words of the Last Sacrament] are holy and sacred words to us. It is with these words that we have closed the eyes of our forbears, of our fathers or our near ones, and it is with these same words that our children one day will close our own eyes. If one wants to reproduce them, it must be done exactly; at the very least they must not be accompanied by sensual images from the past. (p. 341)

It is for you to decide and to determine if [the death scene] is a mingling of the sacred and the profane, or if it would not be something worse, a mingling of the sacred and the sensual. . . .

[The] style Monsieur Flaubert cultivates, and which he achieves without the circumspection but with all the resources of art, is the descriptive style: it is the realistic school of painting. And you see to what lengths he goes. (p. 343)

I require only two scenes; for the offense against morality, will you not see it in the downfall with Rodolphe? Will you not see it in this glorification of adultery? Will you not see it, above all, in what takes place with Léon? And then, for the offense against religious morality, I find that in the passage about her confession . . . , in the religious period . . . , and finally in the last death scene. (p. 344)

As a general objection, the defense will say to us, "But, after all, is the novel not fundamentally moral, since the adulterous woman is punished?"

To this objection there are two replies: assuming a moral work, hypothetically speaking, a moral ending could not pardon the lascivious details that could be found in it. And therefore I say the book fundamentally is not moral.

I say, gentlemen, that lascivious details cannot be screened by a moral ending, otherwise one could recount all the orgies imaginable, one could describe all the depravities of a harlot, so long as she were made to die on a pallet in the poorhouse.

It would be permissible to study and to show all of her lascivious attitudes! It would be running counter to all the rules of common sense. It would be to place poison within the reach of all, and the remedy within the reach of a very few, if there is a remedy. . . . Lascivious paintings generally have more influence than dispassionate arguments. That is my reply to this theory; it is my first reply, but I have a second one.

I maintain that the story of Madame Bovary, considered from a philosophical viewpoint, is not at all moral. Doubtless Madame Bovary dies poisoned, and it is true that she has suffered much; but she dies at an hour of her choosing, and she dies not because she is an adulteress, but because she has wished to die; she dies in all of the glamour of her youth and beauty; she dies after having had lovers, leaving a husband who loves her, who adores her, who will find Rodolphe's portrait, who will find his letters and Léon's, who will read the letters of a wife who was twice an adulteress, and who after that will love her even more after she is dead. Who is there in the book who can condemn this woman? No one. That is the inference. There is not one character in the book who might condemn her. If you find in it one good character, if you find in it one single principle by virtue of which the adulteress is stigmatized, I am wrong. Consequently, if in all the book there is not an idea, not a line by virtue of which the adulteress is shamed, then it is I who am right: the book is immoral! (pp. 344-45)

Art without rules is no longer art; it is like a woman who throws off all her garments. To impose upon art the single rule of public decency is not to enslave but to honor it. (p. 347)

. . . . .

[Speech for the defense by Marie-Antoine-Jules Sénard:]

Gentlemen, Monsieur Flaubert is accused before you of having written an indecent book, of having committed flagrant offenses in this book against public morality and religion. Monsieur Flaubert is beside me; he swears before you that he has written an honorable book; he swears before you that the intention of his book, from first line to last, is a moral and religious intention and that if it is not misrepresented (and we have seen for a few moments what a great talent can do to misrepresent an intention), it would be for you (as it will shortly become again) what it has already been for its readers: an eminently moral and religious intention that can be described in these words: the incitement to virtue through horror of vice. (p. 348)

What Monsieur Flaubert has desired above all has been to take a theme from real life, has been to create and embody true middle-class prototypes and to arrive at a useful result. Indeed it is precisely this useful purpose that has most concerned my client in the study to which he has been dedicated, and he has pursued it by producing three or four characters from present-day society living in circumstances that are true to life, and by presenting to the reader's eye a true picture of what most often happens in the world.

In summarizing its opinion on **Madame Bovary,** the public ministry has said: "The second title of this work is *The Story of the Adulteries of a Provincial Wife.*" I emphatically protest this title. This alone would have proved what their constant preoccupation has been had I not already sensed it from beginning to end of the indictment. No! The second title of this work is not *The Story of the Adulteries of a Provincial Wife;* it is, if you must absolutely have a second title, the story of the education too often given in the provinces; the story of the dangers to which it can lead, the story of degradation, of vil-

lainy, of a suicide seen as the consequence of an early transgression, and of a transgression that was itself induced by the first misstep into which a young woman is often led; it is a story of an education, the story of a deplorable life to which this sort of education is too often the preface. (pp. 350-51)

He shows a woman turning to vice from an unsuitable marriage, and from vice to the last stages of degradation and misery. . . . [If] this book were placed in the hands of a young woman, could it have the effect of drawing her toward dissipation and toward adultery, or on the contrary, would it show her the danger from the start and cause her to shudder with horror? When the question is put in this way, your conscience will resolve it. (p. 351)

The public ministry is angered, and I think wrongly, on the grounds of conscience and human decency because . . . Madame Bovary takes a sort of pleasure, a joy in having broken out of her prison, and returns home [after her first sexual encounter with Rodolphe] telling herself: "I have a lover." You think that there we have no first cry of human distress! The burden of proof is between us. But you should have looked a little further on, and you would have seen that if the first moment, the first instant of that sin arouses a sort of transport of joy, of delirium in this woman, a few lines further on came disappointment; and in the author's phrase, she feels humiliated in her own eyes.

Yes, disappointment, sorrow, and remorse came to her at the same instant. The man to whom she had entrusted and given herself had taken her only to play with for an instant, like a toy; remorse consumes her; it rends her. What has shocked you has been to hear this called the "disillusionments" of adultery; you would have preferred the writer to have said "defilements" for this woman who, not having understood marriage, had felt herself defiled by her husband's touch, and who after having sought elsewhere for her ideal had found instead the disillusionments of adultery. . . . The man who speaks out strongly, gentlemen, and who uses the word "defilement" to express what we have called "disillusionment" uses a word that is true but vague, a word that does not help our understanding. I prefer a man who does not speak out strongly, who does not employ the word "defilement," but who warns the woman of disappointment and disillusionment, who says to her: "There where you think to find love you will find only libertinage; there where you think to find happiness you will find only bitterness. A husband who goes quietly about his affairs, who puts on his nightcap and eats his supper with you, is a prosaic husband who disgusts you. You dream of a man who loves you, who idolizes you, poor child! That man will be a libertine who will have taken you up for a moment to play with you. The illusion will occur the first time, perhaps the second; you will have returned home happy, singing the song of adultery: 'I have a lover!' The third time it will not have come to that; disillusionment will have set in. The man of whom you had dreamed will have lost all of his glamour; you will have rediscovered in love the platitudes of marriage, and you will have rediscovered them with contempt and scorn, with disgust and piercing remorse."

There, gentlemen, is what Monsieur Flaubert has said, it is what he has painted, it is what is in every line of his book; it is what distinguishes his work from other works of the same kind. With him the great failings of society figure on every page; with him adultery moves replete with disgust and shame. From the ordinary relationships of life he has drawn the most striking lesson that could be given to a young woman. (pp. 352-53)

And note one thing well: Monsieur Flaubert is not a man who paints you a charming adulteress only to have her rescued by a *deus ex machina*. No, you have leaped too quickly to that conclusion. With him, adultery is but a succession of torments, of regrets, of remorse; and finally it reaches a final expiation that is appalling. It is excessive. If Monsieur Flaubert sins, it is through an excess of zeal. . . . The expiation is not long in coming; it is here that the book is eminently moral and useful; it does not promise the young woman some of those wonderful years at the end of which she might say: "After that, let me die." No! From the second day, bitterness and disillusionments come. The conclusion in favor of morality is to be found in every line of the book. (pp. 353-54)

The book is written with a power of observation that is truly remarkable down to the smallest details. . . . What is striking in Monsieur Flaubert's book is that a number of descriptions have called forth an almost daguerrean fidelity in their reproduction of all types of intimate things, of thoughts and human feelings—and this reproduction becomes even more striking through the magic of his style. Note well that if he had applied this fidelity only to scenes of degradation, you would be able to say with justice: the author has been pleased to paint degradation with all the descriptive power at his command. From the first to the last page of his book he applies himself without any sort of reserve to all the events of Emma's life, to her childhood in her father's house, to her education in the convent, and he omits nothing. (p. 354)

Nevertheless, gentlemen, just as he likes to describe to us the pleasant bower where Emma played as a child, with its foliage, with the small pink or white flowers that came to bloom and its scented paths—just so, when she will have left there, when she will travel other roads, roads that will be muddy, and when she will soil her feet, when the stains will have splashed even higher—then he must not say so! But this would be completely to suppress the book; more than that, it would be to suppress the moral element on pretext of defending it, for if the transgression may not be shown, if it may not be pointed out, if in a painting from real life that aims by its attitude to show danger, downfall, and expiation—if you would forbid him to paint all that, this would obviously remove all meaning from the book. (p. 355)

You have accused us of mingling sensualism with the religious element in this picture of modern society! Rather accuse the society in which we live; do not accuse the man who, like Bossuet, cries out: "Awake and beware the danger!" Go rather and tell the fathers of families: "Take care, these are not good habits to give to your daughters; in all these mixtures of mysticism there is something that sensualizes religion." That would be to tell them the truth. It is on that account that you accuse Flaubert; it is on that account that I extol his conduct. Yes, he has done well to warn families in this way of the dangers of emotionalism to young girls attracted by petty practices instead of becoming attached to a strong and severe religion that would support them in their day of weakness. (pp. 365-66)

I am defending a man who, had he encountered some literary criticism on the form of his book, on some phrases, on the excess of details, or on some point or other, would have accepted this literary criticism with all his heart. But to see himself accused of outrage against morality and religion! Monsieur Flaubert cannot believe it; and here before you he protests such an accusation with all the astonishment and all the force at his command.

You are not the kind of men who condemn books on a few lines; you are the kind who judge the intention and the execution above all, and you will ask yourselves the question with which I opened my defense and with which I now close: Does the reading of such a book give a love of vice or does it inspire a horror of vice? Is not so terrible an expiation an inducement and an incitement to virtue? The reading of this book cannot produce in you any impression other than the one it has produced in us, namely: that the book is excellent as a whole, and irreproachable in its parts. (pp. 399-400)

. . . . . .

[The verdict:]

WHEREAS the work of which Flaubert is the author appears to have been labored over long and seriously from the viewpoint both of writing and character study; and whereas the passages challenged in the indictment are very few in comparison with the extent of the work; and whereas these passages, whether in the ideas they expound or in the situations they portray, all arise from the cast of characters the author wished to paint, while exaggerating and imbuing them with a coarse realism that is often shocking;

AND WHEREAS Gustave Flaubert protests his respect for decency and for all that pertains to religious morality; and whereas it does not appear that his book, unlike certain other works, has been written with the sole aim of gratifying the sensual passions or the spirit of licentiousness and debauchery or to ridicule the things that should be surrounded by the respect of all;

AND WHEREAS he has committed only the fault of sometimes losing sight of the rules that no self-respecting writer should ever break, and of forgetting that literature, like art, if it is to achieve the good work that is its mission to produce, must be chaste and pure in its form as in its expression;

In the circumstances, inasmuch as it has not been sufficiently established that Leon Laurent-Pichat, [director of *La Revue de Paris*] Flaubert, and Auguste-Alexis Pillet [printer of *La Revue de Paris*] have been found guilty of the offenses with which they have been charged;

The court acquits them of the accusation brought against them and dismisses the charges without costs against the defendants. (p. 403)

> *"The Trial of 'Madame Bovary'" (1857), translated by Evelyn Gendel (copyright © 1964 by Mildred Marmur; translation copyright © 1964 by The New American Library, Inc.; reprinted by arrangement with The New American Library, Inc., New York, New York), in* Madame Bovary *by Gustave Flaubert, translated by Mildred Marmur, New American Library, 1964, pp. 325-403.*

W. P. MORRAS (essay date 1870)

The author of *Madame Bovary* and *L'Éducation Sentimentale* appears to us especially interesting as a perfect type of the materialistic poet.

In keen observation of Nature, Flaubert can hardly be surpassed: not the most delicate difference in color, taste, warmth or electric tension escapes him. He is by no means merely a painter of Nature: he is a chemist, an anatomist, a physiologist, and subjects to his analysis, to his microscope, not only physical, but psychical creation. He sees everywhere atoms—no organisms, no interior spontaneousness. He treats the living soul exactly as he treats the dead body. In the storm of the Revolution he traces only the explosion of imprisoned steam: in the first love of a young girl only the sinister impulse of sensual desire. This leveling of the pressure and the impulse, the impulse and the sentiment, the sentiment and the conscious act, is in reality nothing else than a want of moral perspective. Stones, plants, furniture, works of art, human hearts,—all appear to the author the same, and he therefore describes each of them with precisely the same degree of care, fidelity and indifference. There is nothing omitted, nothing neglected, nothing left undescribed. But the mirror which is there held up to Nature has no focus: the picture it reflects has no conclusion. Where will the realist find a limit if the ideal does not fix one for his guidance? And while the whole remains unfinished, the several parts lack connection and proportion. It is the spirit that connects and unites things, that assigns a place to each. Flaubert, with all his accuracy of detail, is therefore incapable of inspiring us with the conviction that the whole is the truth. (p. 444)

Flaubert's style is in details always keen, incisive, clear, rich in coloring, plastic, overflowing with sensuality, rich in substantives and adjectives, which constitute the material of the language—but, as a whole, monotonous, cold and inarticulate. And as the poet finds no limit to his realism in what he says, so there is no end to the form in which he says it. (pp. 444-45)

But an objectivity which pretends that the entire spiritual and moral refinement of man is nothing save a fancy is a mere mask. Flaubert, it is true, neither praises vice nor condemns virtue, but, on the other hand, he condemns vice as little as he praises virtue. He does not represent evil as good, does not call the good good, or the bad bad, but acts as if he did not understand what these expressions meant. Such indifference is untrue, for it is inhuman. Flaubert wants to let things speak for themselves, which is impossible. (p. 445)

He wants to give us the full reality, while we feel it to be only half the truth—that his world is merely a world of a lower degree, and that only the weakness of his vision keeps him from seeing a higher world. Thus this realism, destitute of the ideal, is subjectively contracted, and therefore as untrue as the idealism which rejects reality. This one caricatures Nature, that one cripples her. The one invents misconceptions which are untenable—the other dissects corpses, thinking thus to learn the secret of life. (p. 446)

> W. P. Morras, "Gustave Flaubert, the Realist," in
> Lippincott's Magazine of Literature, Science and Education, *Vol. VI, October, 1870, pp. 439-46.*

GEORGE SAINTSBURY (essay date 1878)

The reproach usually brought against [M. Flaubert's *Madame Bovary*] is that it is too dreary, and that there is not a sufficient contrast of goodness and good humour to relieve the sombre hue of the picture. I believe myself that the author felt this, and that he intended to supply such a contrast in the person of M. Homais, the apothecary of Yonville. It has been suggested that Homais is not intended to be favourably drawn, but I think that this is a mistake. Homais has indeed the slight touch of charlatanism which half-educated and naturally shrewd men, whose lot is cast among people wholly uneducated and mostly

stupid, often acquire. But he is an unconscious humbug, and not a bad fellow as the world goes, besides being intensely amusing. Much of the amusement, indeed, results from the impassibly saturnine way in which M. Flaubert directs even the gambols of his puppets. This impassibility is the great feature . . . of all his books, and notably of this. The stupid commonplaceness of Charles Bovary's youth, the sordid dulness of his earlier married life, the more graceful dulness of the second, the humours of a county gathering and agricultural show at Yonville, the two liaisons with the vulgar roué squire and the dapper lawyer's clerk, the steps of Emma's financial entanglement, the clumsy operation by which Bovary attempts to cure a clubfoot, the horrors of the heroine's deathbed, and the quieter misery of her husband's end, are all told with the material accuracy of a photograph and the artistic accuracy of a great picture. (pp. 579-80)

There is no fault in the composition of the picture; every line tells, every line would be missed if it were away. Perhaps there is some unnecessary exaggeration in the loathsomeness, if not in the horror, of the deathbed. . . . But I am not sure—falling in to this extent with the tract theory—that M. Flaubert was not reprehensibly influenced in this particular by a desire to point a moral; and if this be the case it is certainly a painful instance of a lapse into the heresy of instruction on the part of a faithful servant of art.

Few greater contrasts can be found in fiction than the subject of M. Flaubert's first book and the subject of his second. Five years after *Madame Bovary* appeared *Salammbô*. From the dullest and flattest modernness the author had shifted to remote antiquity—to the nation of which less is known than of any other civilised nation, and which has to us the strangest and most unfamiliar characteristics and history. . . . All his scanty information he has woven into the narrative, supplementing it with the results of his vivid imagination and his endless patience. . . . [It] must be admitted that the indulgence in repulsive detail, which is one of the author's undoubted faults, is here rather painfully marked. The book is full of blood and torture, and, perhaps, this is justifiable enough by what we know of Carthage and Carthaginian institutions. But the way in which the leprosy of the suffete Hanno pursues us through it, is surely gratuitous. (pp. 581-82)

I do not know a more difficult book to judge than *Salammbô*. At the first reading . . . its absence of human interest, its profusion of hideous details, its barbaric and unreal world, where the figures seem half shadows, and the scenery and properties leave a confused impression of gold and blood, of gorgeousness and horror, on the mind, it is difficult to avoid experiencing [a] nervous impression. . . . But at every successive reading this disappears. The enormous genius which can thus reconstruct—or invent if you will—a world so different from the world we know, yet coherent, consistent, possible even, and tallying well with the few known facts of the matter, the absolutely unsurpassed excellence of the descriptions which have the matter-of-fact exactitude that Macaulay was pleased to laugh at in Dante, the power and art of the thing in short, grow on one strangely. . . . We grow accustomed to the grisly gorgeous world in which we find ourselves, the painting of God's judgments in purple and crimson becomes as natural as it was in a certain Hollow City, and the cruelty and the vigour, the hideous diseases and the hideous worship of the Semite, cease to affect us other than dramatically. (pp. 583-84)

[The greatest attraction of M. Flaubert's book, *L'Éducation Sentimentale*,] is the profusion of observation and knowledge of the intricacies of action and conduct which it displays, and which I do not hesitate to say is not excelled in the work of any contemporary writer. (p. 586)

The passionless review of folly and weakness which *L'Éducation Sentimentale* contains is too cold-blooded for most people to accept. They would rather have downright satire, even of the red-hot brand of Swift, than this cool depicting of failure and impotence. To a certain extent no doubt this is a question of taste and not arguable; to a certain extent, also, it is one proper to be argued, but not to be argued here. I should only say that to me it appears that M. Flaubert's process is a perfectly allowable one, and that the result certainly gives me pleasure. (p. 587)

[*La Tentation de Saint Antoine*] is my own favourite among its author's books. It is the best example of dream-literature that I know, and the capacities of dreams and hallucinations for literary treatment are undoubted. . . . One views all Antony's experiences exactly as Antony himself would have viewed them. The occasional misgiving of the supernatural is there: but the actually supernatural occurrences are related with strict simplicity and verisimilitude. (p. 589)

[*Trois Contes*] has the curious merit of giving in little examples, and very perfect examples, of all the styles which have made [M. Flaubert] famous. *Un Coeur Simple* displays exactly the same qualities of minute and exact observation, the same unlimited fidelity of draughtsmanship, which distinguish *Madame Bovary* and *L'Éducation Sentimentale*. *La Légende de Saint Julien l'Hospitalier* shows the same power over the mystical and the vague which is shown in *La Tentation de Saint Antoine*. *Hérodias* has the gorgeousness, the barbaric colours, and the horror of *Salammbô*. Of the three I have no hesitation in preferring *La Légende de Saint Julien*. The history of the Norman *bonne* Félicité, her fidelity, her narrow brain, her large heart, the way in which employers, relations, and all connected with her make use of her and owe her no thanks, is a wonderful *tour de force*, but it has the defects of its quality. One feels that the author is in effect saying, "I am going to make you, whether you will or no, take an interest in this commonplace picture of humble life"; and though he is successful, there is a certain sense of effort and of disproportion. *Hérodias,* again, has much the same defects as its prototype. The sketch of Aulus Vitellius is faithfully loathsome, and the scenery of the sketch is as a piece of scene-painting unsurpassable. The breath of the Dead Sea and the desert, the atmosphere of Jewish, Idumaean, and Arab savagery, is all over it; but the "nervous impression" still stands in the way. In *Saint Julien* this is no longer the case, and the effect is admirable. (p. 590)

No discussion of M. Flaubert's merits would be complete without some notice of the realism of which, it seems, he is the chief master. . . . This procedure is naturally more striking when the subject matter is of an unpleasant character, and hence the superficial critic runs away with the idea that realism means the choice of unpleasant subjects. . . . [M. Flaubert's] subjects are doubtless often unpleasant enough, but I cannot see that there is the faintest evidence of their having been chosen for their unpleasantness. It is, perhaps, a question whether unpleasantness would not predominate in the absolutely faithful record of any life. It has been said that no man would dare to write such a record of his own history; and all that can be said of M. Flaubert is that he has dared to do, for certain classes and types, what they dare not do for themselves. The ordinary novel is a compromise and a convention. Of compromises and conventions M. Flaubert knows nothing. He dares in especial

to show failure, and I think it will be found that this is what few novelists dare, unless the failure be of a tragic and striking sort. He draws the hopeful undertakings that come to nothing, the dreams that never in the least become deeds, the good intentions that find their usual end, the evil intentions which also are balked and defeated, the parties of pleasure that end in pain or weariness, the enterprises of pith and moment that somehow fall through. Perhaps this is realism, and, if it be, it seems to me that realism is a very good thing. (pp. 592-93)

[The] importance of this writer is very much greater as a maker of literature than as a maker of novels, though I am far from inferring that in the latter capacity he must not be allowed very high rank. His observation of the types of human nature which he selects for study is astonishingly close and complete; his attention to unity of character never sleeps, and he has to a very remarkable degree the art of chaining the attention even when the subject is a distasteful one to the reader. He has been denied imagination, but I cannot suppose that the denial was the result of a full perusal of his work. . . . [His imagination] is poetic rather than fictitious; it does not supply him with a rush of lively creations like the imaginations of the Scotts and the Sands, but with fantastic and monstrous figures, which his admirable writing power enables his readers to perceive likewise, and that not dimly, nor through a misty and hazy atmosphere. There are few things more curious than the combination of such an imagination with the photographic clearness of observation and reproduction which his less imaginative work displays.

His unpopularity as a novelist, such as it is, arises . . . in reality principally from the fact that he is a writer who not only deserves but demands to be read twice and thrice before he can be fully enjoyed. . . . One is struck at first by what can only be called the unpleasantness of the subject, and this colours the judgment. At the second reading the subject has ceased to engage the attention mainly, and the wonderful excellences of the treatment become visible, and at every subsequent reading this excellence becomes more and more apparent. (pp. 593-94)

[M. Flaubert] is in his own person a sufficient and victorious refutation of the theory which will have it that the artist's choice of subjects must express his personal tastes. M. Flaubert is altogether an outsider to his subjects; as Falstaff would say, they have lain in his way and he has found them. . . . We cannot imagine M. Flaubert suppressing an idea because it was troublesome to express or unpleasant to handle, or in any other way intractable. He is altogether of the opinion of Gautier in his contempt for the writer whose thoughts find him unequal to the task of giving them expression, and he may be assumed to be of Gautier's opinion also respecting the excellence of dictionaries as reading, for his vocabulary is simply unlimited. (pp. 594-95)

The immense labour which he has evidently spent upon his work has resulted in equally immense excellence. . . . M. Flaubert is a novelist and a great one. As a dramatist or a poet he might, had his genius so inclined him, have been greater still in the general estimation; but he could hardly have been greater in the estimation of those who are content to welcome greatness in the form in which it chooses to present itself, instead of suggesting that it should suit its costume to their preconceived ideas. (p. 595)

George Saintsbury, "Gustave Flaubert," in The Fortnightly Review, *Vol. 29, April 1, 1878, pp. 575-95.*

GEORG BRANDES (essay date 1881)

The work of [Flaubert's] life marks a step in the history of the novel.

He was a prose author of the first rank for several years; indeed, no one stood higher than he in France. His strength as a prosaist reposed upon an artistic and literary conscientiousness, which was exalted almost to the dignity of genius. He became a great artist because he was unsparing in his efforts, both when he was making preparations to write and when he was engaged in writing. . . . He became a master of modern fiction because he was sufficiently self-denying to be willing to represent those events alone that were true to the soul's life, and to shun all effects of poetic eloquence, all pathetic or dramatic situations which appeared beautiful or interesting at the expense of the truth. His name is synonymous with artistic earnestness and literary rigor. (p. 259)

No one could read ["**Madame Bovary**"] aloud without being astonished at the music of its prose. The style contains a thousand melodious secrets; it aims the keenest satire at human weakness, powerless yearnings and aspirations, self-deception and self-satisfaction, to an accompaniment of organ music. . . . If we should turn to a page in which a village apothecary utters his half scientific prattle, in which a diligence tour is depicted, or an old casket described, we would find it, viewed from a stylistic standpoint, as highly colored and enduring as a mosaic, owing to the freshness of its expression and the solid structure of its sentences. Each clause is so carefully put together that no two words could possibly be removed without destroying the entire page. The assured refinement of the imagery, the metallic ring of the musical flow of words, the rolling breadth of the rhythmic prose, invested the narrative with a marvellous power that was now picturesque, now comic. (pp. 264-65)

A singular book, written without the slightest degree of tenderness for its subject! Others had depicted the simple life of the country and of the province with melancholy, with humor, and at least with that attempt at idealizing which contemplation from afar is apt to bring with it. He regarded it without sympathy, and represented it as insipid and spiritless as it was. His landscapes were devoid of so-called poetry, and were painted briefly and with the utmost perfection. In his severe, masterly style he contented himself with reproducing the chief outlines and coloring, but gave thus an accurate presentation of the landscape. And he was wholly without tenderness for his principal character, a rare phenomenon in a poet whose principal character is a young, beautiful, and exceedingly attractive woman, who passes her life in yearning, languishing, and passionate desire, who errs and is deceived, is ruined, and finally perishes without so much as sinking beneath the level of her surroundings. But every dream, every hope, every delusion, every naïve and unhealthy desire that passes through her brain was investigated and brought to light without agitation, indeed with an overwhelming irony. There was scarcely a phase of her existence in which she failed to appear ridiculous or morally repulsive, and not until she dies a hideous death does the suppressed irony wholly recede, and she breathes her last, not as an object of sympathy, it is true, yet not as an object of contempt. (pp. 274-75)

His characters were all, without exception, commonplace, unlovely, vicious, or unfortunate. Nor did he attempt the slightest deviation from the standpoint taken. The young wife, for instance, dangerous though her instincts were, in her yearning for the beautiful, her aspirations after the ideal, and her per-

sistent faith in the romance of love, possesses attributes which, if portrayed differently, or with a more sparing hand, might have rendered the character noble, even in its errors. . . . The betrayed husband, likewise, notwithstanding his lack of skill as a physician and his awkwardness as a man, is kind-hearted, patient, upright, and truly devoted to Emma, and thus has elements which, under other circumstances, might have produced a most touching effect. . . . [However, Flaubert's] love of truth compels him to keep the form within the limits that to him appear the correct ones, and so he permits Bovary to remain, from beginning to end, a good-natured, undignified, inefficient, and unattractive person. (p. 276)

[With "**Salammbô**"] Flaubert had done his utmost to produce something that resembled ancient Carthage. He was artist enough, however, to know that he had not arrived at the outward truth, merely at the inner idea known as probability. (p. 280)

That Flaubert could not be classed among those who were copyists of actual truth, became clear [with the publication of this novel]. It was seen that his accuracy of description and information was rooted in a peculiar precision of imagination. He evidently possessed in an equally high degree the two elements that constitute the being of the artist: the gift of observation and the power of investing with form. . . . To speak now of photography in connection with him was impossible. For study implies activity, ardor, and an eye for the essential; while photography, on the other hand, is something passive, mechanical, and totally indifferent to the distinctions between essential and non-essential matters. . . . Style marks the difference between the artistically truthful delineation and a successful photograph, and style is omnipresent with Flaubert. (p. 281)

Flaubert believed in a passionate love which, although never gratified, was capable of enduring throughout life. Such a love he has depicted in the affection of Frédéric for Madame Arnoux [in "**L'éducation sentimentale**"]. It is utterly hopeless; it endures pangs of shame; it is suppressed; it only finds vent in certain unwise sacrifices for the husband of Madame Arnoux, and in certain half-uttered Platonic assurances of mutual sympathy. Nor does it lead to anything beyond a promise that is withdrawn by the lady, a few attempts which fail, and finally, after the lapse of twenty years, a fruitless confession and one single embrace, from which the lover recoils in terror, as the object of his affections has, meanwhile, grown old, and, with her white hair, inspires him with repugnance. (pp. 293-94)

The charm of the book . . . does not rest chiefly on the prevailing sentiment of its pages. Its main charm to me is the graceful, chaste manner in which the pen is wielded in passages descriptive of Frédéric's great love. This profound comprehension of the young man's dreamy devotion denotes personal experience. Nowhere has Flaubert written more directly from the depths of his own soul and gained less from the five or six imaginary souls which he, in common with every critically disposed and critically endowed nature, usually endeavored to give himself. (pp. 294-95)

It had been his desire to give an absolutely perfect picture of the times [in "**L'éducation sentimentale**"], and he had made it too elaborate. The historic apparatus is most wearisome in its effect. Flaubert's hatred of stupidity, as in so many other instances, had led him too far. . . . The picture of the times exceeds its proper limits: here, as well as in "**Salammbô**," the pedestal has become too large for the figure. . . . [He] was unable to keep in the background his descriptions of the surroundings of his theme and the general state of public sentiment and conditions in the country and period where the scenes were laid. (pp. 296-97)

[The **"Temptation of St. Antonius"**], failure though it is in some respects, displayed a quiet grandeur, in its melancholy monotony, and an absolutely modern stamp, attained by but few poetic works of French literature. (p. 300)

In this work of fiction we have Flaubert complete, with his sluggish blood, his gloomy imagination, his intrusive erudition, and his need of bringing to a level old and new illusions, ancient and modern faiths. . . . That he chose the legend of St. Antonius as a medium through which to free his mind, and utter some bitter truths to mankind, was because he was brought into contact by this material with antiquity and the Orient which he loved. Through it he could use the large cities and landscapes of Egypt as a background on which to lavish brilliant colors and gigantic forms. And with this theme he no longer painted the helplessness and stupidity of a society, but of a world. He depicted, quite impersonally, humanity as having waded up to its ankles until that hour of its existence, in faith and in blood, and pointed to science—which was as much shunned and dreaded as the devil—as the sole salvation.

The idea was as grand as it was new. The execution by no means attained the level of the plan. The book was crushed by the material used in its preparation. It is not a poetic work; it is partly a theogony, partly a piece of church history, and it is moulded in the form of a psychology of frenzy. There is in it an enumeration of details that is as wearisome as the ascent of an almost perpendicular mountain wall. Certain paths in it, indeed, are only thoroughly intelligible to savants, and seem almost unreadable to the general public. The great author had gradually passed into abstract erudition and abstract style. "It was a sorrowful sight," Émile Zola has pertinently remarked, "to see this powerful talent become petrified like the forms of antique mythology. Very slowly, from the feet to the girdle, from the girdle to the head, Flaubert became a marble statue." (pp. 305-06)

> *Georg Brandes, "Gustave Flaubert" (1881), in his* Eminent Authors of the Nineteenth Century: Literary Portraits, *translated by Rasmus B. Anderson (copyright © 1886 by Thomas Y. Crowell & Co.; reprinted by permission of Harper & Row, Publishers, Inc.),* Thomas Y. Crowell Co., Inc., 1886, pp. 259-309.

HENRY JAMES (essay date 1883)

Practically M. Flaubert is a potent moralist; whether, when he wrote [**"Madame Bovary"**], he was so theoretically is a matter best known to himself. . . . We may say on the whole, doubtless, that the highly didactic character of **"Madame Bovary"** is an accident, inasmuch as the works that have followed it, both from its author's and from other hands, have been things to read much less for meditation's than for sensation's sake. M. Flaubert's theory as a novelist, briefly expressed, is to begin on the outside. Human life, we may imagine his saying, is before all things a spectacle, an occupation and entertainment for the eyes. What our eyes show us is all that we are sure of. . . . Human life is interesting, because we are in it and of it; all kinds of curious things are taking place in it (we do not analyse the curious—for artists it is an ultimate fact); we select as many of them as possible. Some of the most curious are the most disagreeable, but the chance for "rendering" in the disagreeable is as great as anywhere else (some people think even

greater), and moreover the disagreeable is extremely characteristic. (pp. 201-02)

Some such words as those may stand as a rough sketch of the sort of intellectual conviction under which **"Madame Bovary"** was written. The theory in this case at least was applied with brilliant success; it produced a masterpiece. Realism seems to us with **"Madame Bovary"** to have said its last word. We doubt whether the same process will ever produce anything better. In M. Flaubert's own hands it has distinctly failed to do so. **"L'Éducation Sentimentale"** is in comparison mechanical and inanimate. The great good fortune of **"Madame Bovary"** is that here the theory seems to have been invented after the fact. . . . M. Flaubert knew what he was describing—knew it extraordinarily well. One can hardly congratulate him on his knowledge; anything drearier, more sordid, more vulgar and desolate than the greater part of the subject-matter of this romance it would be impossible to conceive. "Moeurs de Province," the sub-title runs, and the work is the most striking possible example of the singular passion, so common among Frenchmen of talent, for disparaging their provincial life. . . . The tale is a tragedy, unillumined and unredeemed, and it might seem, on this rapid and imperfect showing, to be rather a vulgar tragedy. Women who get into trouble with the extreme facility of Emma Bovary, and by the same method, are unfortunately not rare, and the better opinion seems to be that they deserve but a limited degree of sympathy. The history of M. Flaubert's heroine is nevertheless full of substance and meaning. In spite of the elaborate system of portraiture to which she is subjected, in spite of being minutely described, in all her attitudes and all her moods, from the hem of her garment to the texture of her finger-nails, she remains a living creature, and as a living creature she interests us. . . . We see the process of her history; we see how it marches from step to step to its horrible termination, and we see that it could not have been otherwise. It is a case of the passion for luxury, for elegance, for the world's most agreeable and comfortable things, of an intense and complex imagination, corrupt almost in the germ, and finding corruption, and feeding on it, in the most unlikely and unfavouring places—it is a case of all this being pressed back upon itself with a force which makes an explosion inevitable. . . . M. Flaubert keeps well out of the province of remedies; he simply relates his facts, in all their elaborate horror. The accumulation of detail is so immense, the vividness of portraiture of people, of places, of times and hours, is so poignant and convincing, that one is dragged into the very current and tissue of the story; the reader himself seems to have lived in it all, more than in any novel we can recall. At the end the intensity of illusion becomes horrible; overwhelmed with disgust and pity he closes the book.

Besides being the history of the most miserable of women, **"Madame Bovary"** is also an elaborate picture of small bourgeois rural life. Anything in this direction more remorseless and complete it would be hard to conceive. Into all that makes life ignoble and vulgar and sterile M. Flaubert has entered with an extraordinary penetration. The dullness and flatness of it all suffocate us; the pettiness and ugliness sicken us. Every one in the book is either stupid or mean, but against the shabby-coloured background two figures stand out in salient relief. One is Charles Bovary, the husband of the heroine; the other is M. Homais, the village apothecary. Bovary is introduced to us in his childhood, at school, and we see him afterwards at college and during his first marriage—a union with a widow of meagre charms, twenty years older than himself. He is the only good person of the book, but he is stupidly, helplessly good. . . . In Homais, the apothecary, M. Flaubert has really added to our knowledge of human nature—at least as human nature is modified by French social conditions. To American readers, fortunately, this figure represents nothing familiar; we do not as yet possess any such mellow perfection of charlatanism. The apothecary is that unwholesome compound, a Philistine radical—a *père de famille,* a free-thinker, a rapacious shopkeeper, a stern moralist, an ardent democrat and an abject snob. He is a complete creation; he is taken, as the French say, *sur le vif,* and his talk, his accent, his pompous vocabulary, his attitudes, his vanities, his windy vacuity, are superbly rendered. . . . The book is full of expressive episodes; the most successful, in its hideous relief and reality, is the long account of the operation performed by Charles Bovary upon the club-foot of the ostler at the inn. . . . The reader asks himself the meaning of this elaborate presentation of the most repulsive of incidents, and feels inclined at first to charge it to a sort of artistic bravado on the author's part—a desire to complete his theory of realism by applying his resources to that which is simply disgusting. But he presently sees that the whole episode has a kind of metaphysical value. It completes the general picture; it characterizes the daily life of a community in which such incidents assume the importance of leading events, and it gives the final touch to our sense of poor Charles Bovary's bungling mediocrity. Everything in the book is ugly; turning over its pages, our eyes fall upon only . . . one little passage in which an agreeable "effect" is rendered. It treats of Bovary's visits to Emma, at her father's farm, before their marriage, and it is a happy instance of the way in which this author's style arrests itself at every step in a picture. . . . To many people "Madame Bovary" will always be a hard book to read and an impossible one to enjoy. They will complain of the abuse of description, of the want of spontaneity, of the hideousness of the subject, of the dryness and coldness and cynicism of the tone. Others will continue to think it a great performance. They will admit that it is not a sentimental novel, but they will claim that it may be regarded as a philosophical one; they will insist that the descriptions are extraordinary, and that beneath them there is always an idea that holds them up and carries them along. We cannot but think, however, that he is a very resolute partisan who would venture to make this same plea on behalf of "L'Éducation Sentimentale." Here the form and method are the same as in "Madame Bovary"; the studied skill, the science, the accumulation of material, are even more striking; but the book is in a single word a *dead* one. "Madame Bovary" was spontaneous and sincere; but to read its successor is, to the finer sense, like masticating ashes and sawdust. "L'Éducation Sentimentale" is elaborately and massively dreary. That a novel should have a certain charm seems to us the most rudimentary of principles, and there is no more charm in this laborious monument to a treacherous ideal than there is interest in a heap of gravel. To nothing that such a writer as Gustave Flaubert accomplishes—a writer so armed at all points, so informed, so ingenious, so serious— can we be positively indifferent; but to think of the talent, the knowledge, the experience, the observation that lie buried, without hope of resurrection, in the pages of "L'Éducation Sentimentale," is to pass a comfortless half-hour. . . . The reader feels behind all M. Flaubert's writing a large intellectual machinery. He is a scholar, a man of erudition. Of all this "Salammbô" is a most accomplished example. "Salammbô" is not easy reading, nor is the book in the least agreeable; but it displays in the highest degree what is called the historical imagination. There are passages in it in which the literary expression of that refined, subtilized and erudite sense of the picturesque which recent years have brought to so high a development, seems to have reached its highest level. The "**Tentation de Saint Antoine**" is, to our sense, to "**Salammbô**" what "**L'Éducation Sentimentale**" is to "**Madame Bovary**"— what the shadow is to the substance. M. Flaubert seems to have had in him the material of but two spontaneous works. The successor, in each case, has been an echo, a reverberation. (pp. 202-10)

> Henry James, *"Charles de Bernard and Gustave Flaubert," in his* French Poets and Novelists, *B. Tauchnitz, 1883, pp. 186-210.**

JEFFERSON B. FLETCHER   (essay date 1890)

[*Madame Bovary*] deals with sickness rather than with vice; and although the symptoms of the disease are vicious, the viciousness is repulsive, not tempting. I can see no reason why this book should not be put into any hands with the most perfect safety. Innocence and the soft peach-bloom of illusion may go, perhaps, but a more robust virtue is left behind. Unless innocence is to be preferred to virtue, moral censure of *Madame Bovary*—and of sincere books like *Madame Bovary*—is not less unwise than unjust. (p. 18)

Artistically, however, just what makes the novel so severely moral is to me a defect. I mean the trail of the surgeon which is over it all. We are not surprised to learn that Flaubert—like Henrik Ibsen—was brought up to medicine. Both mistake pens for scalpels. *Madame Bovary* might well have been the report of a surgeon to his colleagues on an interesting case of *nymphomania*. It would have been an unusually literary report undoubtedly, but it has the proper judicial impassiveness. Even the term "judicial" implies too much, for Flaubert does not judge his creatures, but dissects their virtues or their follies just as he would their brains or bowels—with equal care, equal indifference. (pp. 18-19)

In a medical report, details into which this surgical instinct betrays Flaubert, would be unpleasant; in a work of art they are shocking. (p. 19)

Nor is this clinical method confined to mere external description—it eats into the very heart of the subject. Madame Bovary wanders from virtue unloving, unloved. She cares but little for the coarse Rodolphe and less for the trivial Léon; she is ready to desert either for the other or for almost anybody else—always excepting her husband. She is possessed to get somehow out of whatever rut she may happen to be in; she craves excitement, passion, without caring much how or whence it comes. Had drink or cards suggested itself instead of intrigue, she might have become a drunkard or a gambler. Flaubert is studying not woman, but *nymphomania*.

I said that this pathological treatment of life is an artistic defect—but why? Because it is untrue to a first principle of all art,—that life should be mirrored as the human eye sees it, not as it appears under the microscope of the specialist. What should we say of the painter who transferred to his canvas the hideousness and blotchiness of flesh magnified by a powerful lens? . . . [There] is a perspective as well in the representation of life by words as in its representation by forms and colors. In *Madame Bovary* I fail to find this literary perspective. (pp. 19-20)

A similar fault exists for me in Flaubert's descriptions. Painstaking, exact, full of keen observations and jealously chosen terms, his pen-pictures are marvellous bits of workmanship, but they picture to us—nothing at all. Feature after feature is pressed upon us with cruel impartiality, attention kept on the rack until its vigor breaks. (p. 20)

In spite of these defects of method, as I take to be Flaubert's cynical-clinical attitude towards life, and Chinese realism in painting life, there's no disputing the almost uncanny power of *Madame Bovary*. Flaubert has deep insights, and, when he puts aside his microscope, draws character admirably. The minor folk in *Madame Bovary* are more life-like than the heroine, just because they are not so unnaturally and unevenly magnified. . . .

Of all these life-like figures, however, not one is free from the cynical taint of its creator. Flaubert apparently intended M. Homais for a thoroughly likable man, as men go, and at any rate he is the cheerfullest in the gallery; but under a thin veneer of good-natured affability, Homais is vain, selfish, gossipy, unsympathetic, pharasaical. If this is the best that Flaubert, that realism can give us in the shape of human nature, do let's go back to idealism, and at last dream of the beautiful. (p. 21)

> *Jefferson B. Fletcher, "'Madame Bovary',"* in The Harvard Monthly, *Vol. X, No. 1, March, 1890, pp. 14-22.*

ERNEST NEWMAN   (essay date 1895)

It may seem somewhat paradoxical to affirm that it is to the very excellencies of his method and his conscientiousness of purpose that we have to trace Flaubert's defects as a novelist. When he confessed of his own *Salammbô* that the pedestal was too large for the statue, he indicated the danger that always beset his art. The difficulties of his method were just the difficulties that attend the operatic composer. Philosophical fiction stands, like vocal music, between two branching courses. The composer who tries to set to music a play of Shakespeare, for example, finds that he cannot hope to comprise within his scheme anything like the wealth of incident and situation possessed by the play. . . . And it is under this disadvantage, if we must call it such, that the philosophical fictionist also labours. He cannot hope to enliven his pages by romantic episode after episode; he will find it hard to make his work speak for itself, and tell its own message to any but the most careful of readers. If he chooses to go to the very springs of thought and passion and action, to exhibit life in motion, as it were, he can only do so by a laborious process of portraiture, in which every trait of character has to be led up to by subtle and unperceived ways. The more perfect the art he infuses into his work, the more difficult is it for the reader to discover at once the motives for this or that episode; and the hasty reader will regard that as asymmetrical and extraneous which is really the essential and supporting harmony of the composition. (pp. 822-23)

[An] instance of the difficulty attendant upon Flaubert's philosophic method is the episode of the club-foot in [*Madame Bovary*]. Its real purpose, of course, is to give further intensity to Emma's contempt for her husband's mediocrity of mind, by exhibiting the sorry figure he cuts in the failure of his surgical operation. Most novelists would have been satisfied to carry Emma's mind along this stage of added contempt by the easier method of abstract description. Flaubert chooses the longer and more arduous course of not telling the spectator of the evolution in Emma's mind of the twin passions of dislike for her husband and love for the more refined Rodolphe, but of making him see the evolution for himself. But to do so he has to expend fifteen pages in showing us what he could have told us, as a

matter of abstract fact, in fifteen lines. It is scarcely to be wondered at if the reader sometimes fails to get beneath the mere particular episode to the psychological underworld which it is designed to illustrate. More especially on a first reading of such a work as *Madame Bovary* is he apt to miss the connecting tissue of the book. But when, after a second or third reading—and nothing of Flaubert's can be understood in less than a second reading—he can let the episodes fall into their proper places, and see the world of the characters, as Flaubert saw it, in its artistic unity and purpose, he realises the colossal genius of the writer who could bend the intractable material to such obedient shapes.

And it goes without saying that if Flaubert at his best is apt to create an impression of occasional obscurity, his method when he is not at his best is likely to become pronouncedly wearisome. *L'Education Sentimentale* cost him as much as, or even more, trouble than *Madame Bovary,* yet the effect on the whole is decidedly less artistic. . . . Flaubert's careful objectivity of method here makes the book lacking in many places in fire and interest. That the colour is in low tone throughout, that it is a study of incompetence, of failure, of the commonplace, is of course no essential reason why it should not achieve high artistic perfection. Its comparative dulness is due not so much to its subject-matter as to the extreme length to which Flaubert has carried his theory of fiction. We can generally see the purpose of his episodes here, as we can see them in *Madame Bovary;* but while in that work they combine to make an artistic and symmetrical whole, in *L'Education Sentimentale* they have the misfortune to strike one simply as episodes rather than as essential links in the evolution of the story. (pp. 823-24)

It was the very sweep of Flaubert's genius, his Aristotelian love of logical working-out in art, that made it hard for him to weigh the merits of the individual portions of his work. . . . [The] defects of the *Tentation* as we have it are just those that followed from Flaubert's superiority in *ensemble* rather than in detail. Not all the magnificent scheme of the *Tentation* can blind us to the occasionally ludicrous effect of the book. There was in Flaubert's nature a rather unruly passion for occasionally tawdry ornament—probably it was the weaker side of his artistic appreciation of verbal and rhythmic beauty—and we sometimes become painfully conscious of it in *S. Antoine.* It is easy to decorate the page with gold and diamonds and peacock's feathers and all the gorgeous trappings of the East; but it is not so easy to give to all this the tone and texture and high restraint of art; and Flaubert's descriptions remind us sometimes all too glaringly of the front window of a pawnbroker's shop. The ultimate effect of the weakness of detail is to mar the artistic impression of the whole. One finds it rather hard to take this stupid old saint quite seriously, or to feel any illusion as to the reality of his temptations; while at times the scenes which Flaubert intended to be the most impressive of all rouse only a sense of the ludicrous. (p. 825)

That Flaubert's frequent inability to handle a large work with equal art in every department came from his undue insistence upon the general philosophical conception as compared with the interest of the details themselves, seems confirmed by the unique artistic success of his smaller stories. Here we get the impassible persistent calm that is so fundamental a characteristic of all his art, while the smaller scale on which he is working makes it impossible for him to elaborate his psychological scheme unduly, to keep on reaching out into circle after circle of detail. The result is that all the finer qualities of his genius have an opportunity to exhibit themselves, without the embarrassing companionship of his defects. In *Un Coeur Simple,* for instance, we see all the finer traits of *Madame Bovary*—the wonderful unity and tenacity of purpose, the consistency of the mental delineation, the pathos, the elevated sympathy for human suffering; while the shortness of the story and the small number of characters make it possible for him to avoid every episode that has not the strictest relevance to the central idea. And we get the finest example of his art which he has left us in the unsurpassable *S. Julien*—one of those works of such rare and faultless beauty as to leave the reader wondering how the total effect has been achieved. . . . It is on the side of his style that Flaubert's master-patience comes to its most artistic consummation. His theory that for each mood, each aspect, each situation, there was one true expression, and one alone, could not fail to give to his style the closest precision and the greatest psychological veracity. . . . He can utter volumes in a word, and give you far-reaching vistas of thought or emotion in a single phrase; he can play upon the inner life with the magic of a musician, and evoke the most wonderful dream-shapes at the bidding of a word. His prose at its best always gives us this sensation of new insight into things; a simple sentence will take its echoing course through the inner chambers of the mind, and the barest transcript of immediate experience swells into the solemnity of oceanic distances.

It was fitting that his grave and comprehensive philosophy of style should be accompanied by a philosophy of life of equal gravity and equal comprehensiveness. It was no mere craving after external finish that led him to desire such objectivity of method in his novels; it was his deep sense of the manifold complexities of life that made it essential for him to stand aloof from them in order to see them more clearly and completely. Hence his artistic power, his veracity, his verisimilitude, and at the same time his apparent pitilessness, and pessimism, and cynicism. (pp. 825-27)

To call [his philosophy] pessimism or cynicism is to make the grossest misuse of words; for Flaubert invariably keeps his characters and their motives in the ideal atmosphere of art, and never allows that personal note of contempt and bitterness to be heard that sounds so frequently in the work of Maupassant. *Bouvard et Pécuchet* may fail as a novel; but as a "human document" it ranks among the achievements of the century. Probably no other work can be named that so aptly characterizes the intellectual life of our time, in its shifting uncertainty, its break-up of received ideas, and the ever-pervading sense of futility and folly. (p. 828)

> Ernest Newman, "Gustave Flaubert," in The Fortnightly Review, *Vol. 64, December 1, 1895, pp. 813-28.*

BENJAMIN W. WELLS   (essay date 1898)

Madame Bovary is not only not romantic, it is the bitterest satire on romanticism. Its scene is the world of commonplace and the lesson of it is that in that world sentiment leads to shipwreck, and self-sufficient mediocrity to success. . . . [Flaubert] lays bare for us here first the weary banality of provincial life, and then the hopelessness of the romantic revolt against banality. (p. 246)

[No] summary can do justice to the many passages of vivid narration or of exquisite description, whose studied euphony appears first when they are read aloud, as Flaubert himself was wont to read repeatedly every paragraph that he wrote. . . . And then there are scattered up and down through the book a multitude of happily turned phrases, usually of irony, where we seem to see the author poising on his needle-point the acid drop and placing it with slow, delicate precision upon the quivering nerve.

The danger of romantic imagination—such had been the subject of *Madame Bovary,* and such continued to be the subject of *Salammbô* seven years later, but with a radical difference; for while in *Madame Bovary,* he had used the realistic method on his own Normandy, he undertook here to apply it to an age and land of which his ideas were inevitably the products of trained imagination, the Carthage of 240 to 237 B.C., during the revolt of the mercenaries that followed the first Punic War. He called this "epic realism." The result is an interesting literary feat. . . . [But] surely it is not so significant as *Madame Bovary*. It does not live as a whole. Its characters may be true or not for their country and time, but they are not true for us. We do not sympathise with them, because we do not understand them, and therefore their fate rouses a languid interest beside Emma's shipwreck and Homais' success. There seems to be, as an acute critic has said, a disproportion between the subject and the means used in treating it. [But] it contains passages, and they are not a few, which in picturesque brilliancy surpass anything attempted in the former novel. (pp. 251-52)

Taken as a whole . . . , *Salammbô* must be regarded as a failure, but it was a failure such as only a great, indefatigable, and high-souled artist could have made. Here more than in any other of his novels we feel the struggle between the old romanticism and the new scientific spirit. The book arouses wonder rather than sympathy. It will be admired, it will not be enjoyed. (pp. 253-54)

The story [of *Sentimental Education*] is of the slightest, slighter even than that of *Salammbô.* The book is the picture of a generation and of its political and moral bankruptcy culminating in the Second Empire. If it be urged that the novel lacks unity, Flaubert would reply that life lacks it, and that this is an advance in realistic art. . . . (pp. 254-55)

Such an attempt may show praiseworthy daring, and to it Flaubert gave the most minute and intense study, but it was inevitable that the result of this painful gestation should lack interest, because it lacked unity. We do not seek in a novel the reproduction of life, but the impression of life. And then the tendency . . . in *Madame Bovary* to present only characters of a contemptible mediocrity, whether of vice or virtue, is pushed here beyond reasonable limits. It might be as true as the multiplication table, but it would not be interesting. But is it true? Is not Flaubert the dupe of his own limitations? . . . One cannot but feel that *Sentimental Education* marks a growing sterility in Flaubert's genius. (p. 255)

Flaubert is not merely "implacable" to humanity, he is unjust. In *Madame Bovary* there was a corner left for true sentiment and honest pathos. Here there is nothing of this. Nobody is magnanimous, frank, or noble; all is petty, vulgar, contemptible. Flaubert's irony itself has no generous fire, and the strongest sentiment that we feel in finishing the novel is pity for the man who has such an outlook on the world. (pp. 255-56)

Throughout this long panorama of social disillusion and political incompetence the style is curbed, held rigidly down to the mediocrity of the subject. One cannot help feeling that it must have cost almost as much effort to the author as it does to the reader, though there are occasional flashes of irony that reveal the depths of human nature. Nor should the episodic scenes in the novel be forgotten. . . . Excellent, too, are the historical scenes, the joyous sacking of the Tuileries and the brutal desperation of the mobs of June, with their yet more brutal suppression. While, then, no one would claim that *Sentimental Education* is a good novel, it may be read with profit and even with pleasure as the imaginative projection of a close study of the national mind of France in a critical period of its evolution. (p. 256)

[With *The Temptation of Saint Antony,* Flaubert] has undertaken to exhibit to us, no longer the folly of provincial mediocrity as in *Madame Bovary,* or of the desires and ambitions of Parisian youth as in *Sentimental Education,* or of a sordid commercial state and an ancient faith as in *Salammbô,* but it is the folly and futility of thought itself and of the whole sentient world of which he has tried to put the quintessence in these three hundred pages of the most polished prose of our half-century. (p. 257)

The book is nihilistic to the core, but its pessimism is romantic. Flaubert's heart is the victim of his mind. He suffers, like Antony and Salammbô and Frédéric and Emma, from the pale cast of a thought that is ever bruising itself against reality. They all are projections of the world-pain of his generation, that undercurrent of materialistic sentiment that tells us in advance that all our ideals are dissolving views. So Flaubert says life seemed to him, even when a boy, "like the smell of a nauseating kitchen escaping through a ventilating hole. One had no need to taste to know that it was sickening," no need to study to learn that knowledge would but increase unsatisfied desire. Of this feeling the *Temptation* is the supreme expression in fiction. . . . The book cannot appeal, however, to any but literary artists, and it has hindered rather than aided the appreciation of his genius. . . . (pp. 257-58)

The Temptation of Saint Antony was followed . . . by three tales which represent in miniature the two sides of Flaubert's literary nature: the disgust at the sordidness of modern life, and the revels of imagination in the reconstitution of a grandiose past. . . . [The first of the tales contained in *Trois Contes, A Simple Heart* (Un coeur simple),] is told with a simplicity and restraint that is the height of art and pathos, so that it may be both read with pleasure and studied with advantage.

Equal praise in another kind may be given to *Julian the Hospitaller* (Julian l'hospitalier), the medieval patron saint of hosts and hospitality. Flaubert finds the legend of this saint "in a series of glass paintings in a church in my country" and undertakes to tell with medieval naïveté this story of the feudal noble, hunter, parricide, and penitent. The whole has something of the dim religious light of these ancient stained windows, something of their quaintness, of their sudden transitions, and of their atmosphere of miracle. (p. 258)

[In *Herodius*] there is more historic realism. The local colour is studied in detail, though not without an element of the grandiosely romantic, but the wild discord of jarring factions, the intensity of religious feeling in the seething brains of these Galileans, the haughty indifference of the materialised Romans, the morbid satiety of Antipas, the satanic passions of Herodias, the heartless, soulless grace of Salome, the fierce conviction of the prophet voicing itself in unbridled denunciation, all this is as wine to Flaubert's genius, and it seems at moments as though the sun of Palestine had touched his brain also, so that the effect of the whole may be described as dazzling. . . . It is here and in *Madame Bovary* that Flaubert shows the least effort and attains the greatest success. But by a strange and sad perversity of a great mind already verging on mania

he returned with saturnine humour to the harder and longer task, and in *Bouvard and Pécuchet* erected a monument to human stupidity, "the book of his revenge" he called it, with all the faults of the *Sentimental Education,* and with none of the redeeming elements that might overcome the unpleasant nervous impression and persuade us to listen to his doleful lesson.

Flaubert marks in fiction . . . the passage from idealism to realism, from the romantic to the naturalistic. He belongs to neither school and unites both. . . . It was because he was romantic that he was a pessimist, and that not from reason but from sentiment. . . . [His studious objectivity] makes him see his environments in wonderful detail, but takes something from the life of his characters. . . . And just as he tries to make the myriad little facts of environment support character, so he systematically substitutes sensations for feelings, the material image for the thought, and in thus making environment a link in the chain of association to evoke the past he contributed materially to the art of novelistic development. . . . (pp. 259-60)

The importance of Flaubert to the development of fiction for good or ill lies, not in his philosophy, but in his conception of the novel itself as the "synthesis of romanticism and science." To take a plain, straightforward tale of common life such as that of the servant in *A Simple Heart* or of Frédéric or of Emma Bovary or of Bovard and Pécuchet, to put it in an environment that should be minutely accurate, and to treat this "slice of crude life" in the most finished, polished style, a style that might win him the title of "the Beethoven of French prose," that is what Flaubert undertook to do, and it is what the whole naturalistic school have tried to do after him. . . . That he directed the development of the novel for a generation, and that he contributed essentially to maintain its place as a work of art, and keep it from the hands of the philistines of literature, are his titles to lasting remembrance. (pp. 260-61)

> *Benjamin W. Wells, "Gustave Flaubert," in his* A Century of French Fiction, *Dodd, Mead and Company, 1898, pp. 242-61.*

EMILE FAGUET (essay date 1899)

[*Salammbô* and *La Tentation de Saint-Antoine*] contain and characterise the whole of Flaubert's romanticism. (p. 50)

[Descriptive] romanticism; not sentimental, elegiac romanticism; not mediaeval, neo-Christian romanticism; but the romanticism of colour and of rhythm, pictural, sculptural, musical romanticism; that romanticism which, because of those tendencies, was ever attracted towards the East or towards classical antiquity as understood by Homer or by the Alexandrians, and thus preserved an Oriental tinge . . .—such is Flaubert's romanticism, and of it were born *Salammbô* and *La Tentation de Saint-Antoine.* (p. 54)

[An] historical novel only interests us in so far as the events which it unfolds engage or excite one of our passions, either eternal or contemporary. (p. 58)

In *Salammbô,* we witness the struggle between Carthage and the barbarian mercenaries in her pay, who, deceived by the city, have turned against it. Neither party interests us. It is of no consequence to us that either Matho or Hannon should triumph. Punic ferocity on the one side, barbaric ferocity on the other, it is equally indifferent to us that this or that should be victorious. . . .

There is another means of making an historical novel interesting; that is, to treat it as an ordinary novel, and to satisfy us by a curious description of the character's feelings. In that case the historical part of the novel is but the frame or the background of the picture. (p. 59)

Flaubert knew not how to employ that method. If we consider things in that way, the two heroes of his drama are Salammbô and Matho; now neither the one nor the other is at all penetratingly analysed. Matho is passionately in love and that is all. Salammbô is confused and enigmatical. (p. 60)

Yet another way of exciting interest is the attraction of mystey. . . . Flaubert sought that element of emotion; he invented the Zaimph or sacred veil which holds the fate of Carthage, as that of Troy was wrapt in the Palladium. Nothing could have been more happy as a poetical instrument, but he handled it badly. The Zaimph should have occupied our mind unceasingly, it should have held our attention and only let it go at rare intervals. Instead of which it disappears in that too prolific poem; we lose sight of it, then we find it again; we say to ourselves that that is what we must remember, but we do not remember it; the author has not succeeded in making us remember it, or at least in making of it our continual, subconscious, preoccupation.

Finally, it is absolutely necessary in a great poem that there should be a central character, distinctively, imperiously central, so to speak, and, since it is not the Zaimph, it should be a human being. . . . The principal character should have been Salammbô, and it is Matho. . . . Salammbô, like the Zaimph, sometimes appears, very brilliant, very curiously adorned, very mysteriously attractive, but she glides back again into shadows; her image disappears behind the struggling masses and the circling dust of the battle-field. Flaubert himself saw this, and admirably expressed it in this criticism of his own work . . . : 'The pedestal is too large for the statue.' That is it. Above the enormous bas-relief of that gigantic war, above that pile of battles, tumult and carnage, Salammbô appears like a statuette. If the subject of *Salammbô* is ill-chosen, the composition is absolutely defective. (pp. 61-3)

Salammbô and *La Tentation* represent the two sides of the medal. *Salammbô* is a material pessimistic novel, *La Tentation* an abstract pessimistic novel. The facts in *Salammbô* suggest a pessimistic thought as a conclusion, whilst a pessimistic idea gives birth to *La Tentation* and creates facts and pictures which are manifested and made palpable in the book. *Salammbô* is a nightmare of facts, *La Tentation* is a nightmare of ideas turned into pictures in order to become visible. . . . In Flaubert's final conception, the temptation of St. Anthony becomes the story of a man or rather of Man, mentally tempted by all the illusions of thought and of imagination. (pp. 67-8)

The idea was a great, even a dramatic one. (p. 68)

[However, the] execution is far below the design. As ever in Flaubert's work, the descriptions and pictures are the best part of the work. Only there is but one of them. It is the scenery of the beginning, the mountain in the Thebaid, the rocky enclosure in which the hermit turns backwards and forwards as in a voluntary prison, and the horizon of plains and valleys over which the saint's eyes wander from the height of his observatory. But the procession of deities, of animated things or beings, is very boring. It is monotonous, not from a lack of words, but from a lack of ideas. And there should have been an infinite variety of ideas, after the manner of Goethe, in order to fill and to diversify that immense programme. Then, very

soon, Flaubert's fundamental intellectual vice takes possession of him. He loves that which is grotesque, ridiculous, mean. And the mean, the ridiculous and the grotesque end by invading the whole of his work. (p. 71)

Philosophical thought itself, neither very strong nor very original, as is always the case with Flaubert, occasionally finds, however, some lucidity and some beauty in the *Tentation de Saint-Antoine*. (p. 75)

It is therefore possible to feel some admiration, and if not some emotion, some interest now and then whilst reading that philosophical poem. Still, besides being dull, it is weak in thought, it loses itself in things mean and grotesque without being amusing. And above all, it bears witness to a prodigious effort of which the traces have not been wiped away and which gives us a sensation of deadly fatigue. (pp. 77-8)

Madame Bovary gives an impression of life itself both in its complexity and in its precise detail. . . . [Flaubert's] descriptions of things mingle instantly and without confusion with his descriptions of people; his *dramatis personae* act as soon as they appear, and their surroundings become present to us as soon as they themselves do. (pp. 85-6)

As to the characters, no words are strong enough to say that they are truth itself, reality itself, and that, in my opinion, Flaubert far more than Balzac 'competes with civil registers.' Whether simple silhouettes or life-size portraits, all are perfect, every one of them living the minutest life without a moment's alteration of their outline. . . . [They] are marvellously distinct, each dwelling in our memory with his own admirably individual physiognomy. (pp. 89-90)

And, mark you, they are not *types*. They are not an epitome of humanity. . . . [They] are real persons, so powerfully alive that we recognise them, not because of our general knowledge of humanity, but apart from that knowledge, almost in spite of it, and only because we know a living being when we see it. (pp. 90-2)

M. Bovary, more so than Emma, marks the triumph of the author's talent. For the difficulty was to draw a characterless person and to give him some life and some individuality. And Flaubert has succeeded admirably. Bovary is nullity itself, and in that he is more of a 'type' than the other characters in the novel, representing as he does the immense majority of his social class; yet he has some individual features which give him precision and relief. (pp. 102-03)

Mme. Bovary, the immortal Mme. Bovary, as immortal as the immortal Homais, is the most complete woman's portrait I know in the whole of literature, including Shakespeare and including Balzac. (p. 107)

The essence of Mme. Bovary's soul is romance; and the various forms which this turn of mind assumes in her according to age and to circumstances constitute the whole of her life. (p. 108)

But Emma marries Bovary. . . . He bores her hopelessly, incurably. She immediately discovers in him the man of all men most opposite to her own nature. . . . He is the very thing she detests most in the world, he is reality. (p. 112)

At the moment when Rodolphe comes on the scene, Emma needs love in [the] sense that she yearns for a violent distraction from her boredom, for something unexpected in her life. (p. 116)

It is therefore Love itself that Emma loves, rather than Rodolphe. Later she will love Léon rather than Love itself. This evolution, in inverse ratio to the ordinary development, reveals a profound moralist. . . . The desire to become acquainted with love is the reason for her first sin; the second only will be caused by a wish to give herself to him whom she loves.

Moreover, her whole *liaison* with Rodolphe is chiefly an affair of imagination. . . . Rodolphe is not he whom Emma has loved most, but he who has satisfied her most, who has best responded to the artificial part of her nature, a nature such that the artificial part of it is the most essential. (pp. 117-18)

And so the disillusion, the rupture with Rodolphe, is the great, the tragical crisis of Emma's life. . . . When losing him in whom she had placed her romantic ideal, she loses her ideal itself, renounces it, believes in it no more. Her romantic turn of mind remains; it can never disappear because it forms the very basis of Emma's soul; but the hope of realising it and the conviction that it will be realised disappear or weaken. (p. 119)

For some time Mme. Bovary still feeds her romantic mind with fictitious food, deceiving it and deceiving herself. She makes elegies and romance of the languor of her convalescence; she acts the part of a sweet young invalid and finds some melancholy pleasure in the attitude. (pp. 119-20)

[This transition] does not last long. It indicates that, even after the crumbling away of her ideal, Mme. Bovary will always preserve some indelible traces of the romantic instinct. And now begins the process of degradation. (pp. 120-21)

[We] see her descend from a sentimental girl to a romantic woman, from a romantic woman to an amorous courtesan, and from a courtesan to a *cabotine*. This inevitable concatenation of character, in a life which began by a total absence of principle and a curiosity of the impossible, is a complete portrait of the romantic woman of the provinces, and constitutes the lesson taught by the book. (p. 122)

Emma, deprived of all element of romance, even merely apparent, can only die. For what would her life become henceforth? It would be a *real* life, as hopelessly real as the *bourgeois* life which she so hated. It is reality that Mme. Bovary never could admit. (p. 124)

The composition of the book is a wonder. The author has found means of making us live the life of a small town without allowing the thousand pictures of it which he shows us ever to impinge upon the principal character, or to draw our eyes away from her. . . . [All] the scenes are arranged in some analogous manner, and there is not one of them, however interesting by itself, which does not bring us back to the central character at the very moment when it seemed to take us away from it. . . . The general spirit of the book is that of a strict, haughty and conscientious writer. It shows first of all the desire to write what is true, rigorously and undeniably true. Then a too marked hatred and contempt for the provincial *bourgeois,* the man 'who has a low way of thinking and of feeling,' and no doubt we might consider, like Sainte-Beuve [see excerpt above], that too much care has been taken to admit no really generous soul, no lofty mind, into that small human agglomeration. It certainly is a misanthropical novel. But will it never be understood that a realistic novel is a picture of average humanity and that generous souls and lofty spirits are the exception? . . . [If] there is no virtuous character in **Madame Bovary,** neither is there a single scoundrel. Flaubert's characters are not even malicious. He makes no mention of hostility or of furious hatreds, so common in small towns. . . . They

are selfish and foolish, that is all. Is this, as seen by a misanthrope, so far from the average truth? (pp. 127-29)

[Frédéric Moreau of **L'Éducation Sentimentale**] is endowed with a marvellous incapacity for action. A soft, flabby being, he is not unlike Bovary. Only, as he has some intelligence and some imagination he is inactive and restless at the same time, and remains inactive in agitation as Bovary remains inactive in a sort of torpor. (p. 142)

Frédéric is something of a dilettante, and is eternally in love, simply because he seeks easy sensations, and also yearns to be ruled. It is in this that Frédéric resembles Mme. Bovary. He has the same fundamental indolence and the same constitutional dreaminess. . . . (p. 143)

On the whole, Frédéric might be the son of Bovary and of Mme. Bovary. . . . His end seems a little less sad than that of his spiritual parents, but it is not so in reality. It is *nothingness,* far more so than that of Bovary and Emma. . . . His portrait is well drawn, not in broad touches, but in short, too short, successive strokes; it is clear, solid and consistent, sometimes even not without vigour. Needless to say it is a true portrait, too true.

The secondary characters (save Arnoux . . . , who is excellent) are all colourless, almost indistinct and devoid of interest. After closing the book one does not know them very precisely from each other; one is inclined to confuse Sénécal with Régimbard, or to attribute some of Deslauriers' words to Hussonnet. They stand in our memory like a confused crowd. (pp. 147-49)

After Arnoux, the best secondary character is Deslauriers. He very nearly is a complete, living man, displacing a certain quantity of atmosphere and presenting three dimensions. In Flaubert's design, he is Frédéric's antithesis. He has an ardent will, with the corresponding faults, obstinacy and sudden ill-timed boldness, very little intelligence. . . . Deslauriers might have made a first-class character; it seems as if Flaubert had hesitated about him. He did not give him his full scope, and does not even give him the sequence he ought rigorously to have had. . . . In fact, in **L'Éducation Sentimentale,** Flaubert seems to have lost the secret of the astonishing relief with which the secondary or even third-class characters in **Madame Bovary** stood out before us. (pp. 149-50)

[One] of the author's intentions was to show us a picture of Paris and also of French society in 1840-55. He has not succeeded very well. . . . Flaubert has been betrayed by his peculiar turn of mind which led him to see in things the ridiculous, or rather the grotesque side only. His 1848 is exact but incomplete. It is exclusively a somewhat lively record of all the silly things which were said and thought at that time. It often is *piquant,* and the strong and lively satire of it carries us away; but it narrows the field prodigiously, apparently of set purpose, and that hinders our admiration and even our amusement. . . . Here again, as it happened to Flaubert so often, he has been mistaken as to 'realism.' He has mistaken satire for it because his own turn of mind was satirical. Lyrism is lyrism and satire is satire, but realism is not satire: it stands between the two. (pp. 151-52)

With all its merits mixed with faults of a slight nature, **L'Éducation Sentimentale** is not an interesting book. . . . I own that incidents do not command one another, do not *necessitate* one another; that many of them seem stuck in with no particular reason why they should be here instead of there; and that the book gives the impression of being made up of pieces put together with skill but with an obvious skill. It is so, no doubt, and the proof of it is that the interest *does not grow*. (pp. 152-53)

The true reason of the undeniable boredom with which this novel inspires us is that the principal person is himself a bore, the author having made a hero of the greatest bore he ever created. (p. 154)

Each of Flaubert's works was the result of one of the tendencies in his temperament. *Bouvard et Pécuchet* was the result of one of his manias, of his essential mania.

Flaubert's essential mania was a horror of stupidity and at the same time a sort of fascination which stupidity exerted over him. (p. 159)

Bouvard et Pécuchet is the history of a Faust who was an idiot. It was not at all necessary that there should be two. It is also the history of a Frédéric going through intellectual instead of sentimental experiences, and as the story of Frédéric is entitled *L'Éducation Sentimentale, Bouvard et Pécuchet* might be entitled *L'Éducation Intellectuelle.* (p. 164)

[Seen] from any point of view, this novel is a failure, and read in any manner it is wearisome. It occurs to one whilst finishing it that there was here hardly material enough for a short story. (p. 170)

There was nothing more in the subject, and Maupassant would have treated it thus. But it ever was Flaubert's failing to over-weight a subject with insistent repetitions, writing in six pages what only required four. This fault already appears in *Madame Bovary,* and is noticeable in *Salammbô* and in *La Tentation de Saint-Antoine.* It spoils the 'three tales'—*Un Coeur Simple,* so true and so touching; *La Légende de Julien l'Hospitalier* and *Herodias,* both marvels of picturesque style; and finally it crushes *Bouvard et Pécuchet,* which could and should have been a pretty tale in Voltaire's style, alert, merry and incisive. (p. 171)

Flaubert is one of the greatest writers in French literature. . . . No author seems ever to have brought more earnest, more obstinate attention to his style. . . . No writer ever deliberately put as great a distance between the style of conversation and that of a work of art. There is no likeness, save on very rare occasions, between the language of his correspondence and that of his novels. The language of his letters is copious, easy, almost purposely careless and trivial, disconnected, over-loaded, violent, emphatic and unbridled. That of his novels, without being concise, is careful, corrected, calculated to such a degree—and in this it becomes a fault—that nothing is ever left to the first flow, the spontaneous vivacity of his thought. (pp. 181-82)

Above all, he willed that his prose should be submitted to a hidden rhythm, a rhythm that the reader did not perceive, though real and unfailing. In the eighteenth century, it was said that verse should be as beautiful as beautiful prose; Flaubert desired that his prose should be as beautiful as beautiful verse. . . . (p. 183)

[His style] is always of a high order, and often really wonderful. It is only when Gustave Flaubert ventures to write in abstract style, a thing he hardly ever does, that he shows a slight awkwardness or embarrassment. Being as poor a philosopher as possible, abstract language was to him forbidden ground, and the handling of abstractions an impossibility. (p. 186)

Except for this case, which . . . is but rarely encountered, I see nothing that is not admirable, and Flaubert's style is a perpetual feast for the mind. Suitability, exactness, 'the word sticking to the idea,' we find nothing else in every page, in every line. (p. 187)

[As] a portrait-painter he was superior to Balzac. Balzac multiplies the features too much; one effaces the other and we become confused. . . . Flaubert paints after the manner of Saint-Simon, in broad and vigorous touches, with less power and less fury, but with more mastery and sobriety. (p. 192)

Flaubert's landscapes are precise hallucinations. They are of an absolute reality, and show that relief, that strong standing out of angles and contours that objects in our dreams sometimes assume suddenly against the black curtain of sleep. (p. 198)

Since Chateaubriand no one had known how to paint natural things with that prodigious clearness, that wonderful adaptation of the word to the object. Marvellous *invention* is necessary in order to see so correctly. (pp. 198-99)

[The] most admirable of all Flaubert's style effects is that the *key* is infallibly in tune. The key changes continually, especially in *Madame Bovary,* elsewhere there is an occasional feeling of monotony, and it is always true, always precisely appropriate to the object, circumstances and characters. (p. 200)

An admirable writer, born to be one, for he was capable of making efforts and of effacing the traces of his efforts; the books at which he worked most desperately are precisely those in which the labour, though not absolutely invisible, is least noticed at the first reading. (p. 204)

It is true that he seems to have spoken of men's errors with the single intention of mocking them cruelly. It is true that Flaubert's tone is almost continually satirical, and it remains to ask whether satire is a good use to make of talent. It certainly reveals a soul who is not kindly, who is soured, who is deeply wounded by the moral misery of humanity, and who writes not in order to cure them but to take revenge upon them. If one could choose one's own talent it would be a serious thing to choose the satirical style, and if one could choose one's temper it would be culpable to choose the inclination to evil speaking; but yet satire, like Molière's satirical comedy, which is but a variety of it, is of such immense social importance that it would be regrettable, though worthy of all respect, that a scruple should prevent those who have the gift for it to indulge in it. (pp. 230-31)

[Flaubert] had too much taste for human meanness; he is one of those of whom Gautier said, 'Some hearts are full of the sad love of ugliness'; but this sad complacence itself did not lead him to exaggerate or to darken the picture too much, because he was held back by the sense of truth and the taste for truth. That suffices to make us grateful to him not only as a great painter and a great writer, but also as one of those morose and bitter moralists, just nevertheless who are—and for that reason very salutary and even necessary—something like the harsh conscience of humanity. (p. 232)

> *Emile Faguet, in his* Flaubert, *translated by Mrs. R. L. Devonshire, originally published as* Flaubert *by Hachette et Cie, 1899), Houghton Mifflin Company, 1914, 238 p.*

ARTHUR SYMONS (essay date 1901)

Salammbô is an attempt, as Flaubert, himself his best critic, has told us, to 'perpetuate a mirage by applying to antiquity the methods of the modern novel.' By the modern novel he means the novel as he had reconstructed it; he means *Madame Bovary*. That perfect book is perfect because Flaubert had, for once, found exactly the subject suited to his method, had made his method and his subject one. On his scientific side Flaubert is a realist, but there is another, perhaps a more intimately personal side, on which he is lyrical, lyrical in a large, sweeping way. The lyric poet in him made *La Tentation de Saint-Antoine,* the analyst made *L'Education Sentimentale;* but in *Madame Bovary* we find the analyst and the lyric poet in equilibrium. . . . Flaubert finds the romantic material which he loved, the materials of beauty, in precisely that temperament which he studies so patiently and so cruelly. Madame Bovary is a little woman, half vulgar and half hysterical, incapable of a fine passion; but her trivial desires, her futile aspirations after second-rate pleasures and second-hand ideals, give to Flaubert all that he wants: the opportunity to create beauty out of reality. (pp. 130-31)

In writing *Salammbô* Flaubert set himself to renew the historical novel, as he had renewed the novel of manners. He would have admitted, doubtless, that perfect success in the historical novel is impossible, by the nature of the case. We are at best only half conscious of the reality of the things about us, only able to translate them approximately into any form of art. (p. 131)

Everything in the book is strange, some of it might easily be bewildering, some revolting; but all is in harmony. The harmony is like that of Eastern music, not immediately conveying its charm, or even the secret of its measure, to Western ears; but a monotony coiling perpetually upon itself, after a severe law of its own. (p. 134)

There should have been, as [Flaubert] says, a hundred pages more about Salammbô. . . . [She] is hardly more than an attitude, a fixed gesture, like the Eastern women whom one sees passing, with oblique eyes and mouths painted into smiles, their faces curiously traced into a work of art, in the languid movements of a pantomimic dance. The soul behind those eyes? the temperament under that at times almost terrifying mask? Salammbô is as inarticulate for us as the serpent, to whose drowsy beauty, capable of such sudden awakenings, hers seems half akin; they move before us in a kind of hieratic pantomime, a coloured, expressive thing, signifying nothing. Mâtho . . . has the same somnambulistic life; the prey of Venus, he has an almost literal insanity, which, as Flaubert reminds us, is true to the ancient view of that passion. He is the only quite vivid person in the book, and he lives with the intensity of a wild beast, a life 'blinded alike' from every inner and outer interruption to one or two fixed ideas. The others have their places in the picture, fall into their attitudes naturally, remain so many coloured outlines for us. The illusion is perfect; these people may not be the real people of history, but at least they have no self-consciousness, no Christian tinge in their minds. (pp. 134-36)

The style is never archaic, it is absolutely simple, the precise word being put always for the precise thing; but it obtains a dignity, a historical remoteness, by the large seriousness of its manner, the absence of modern ways of thought, which, in *Madame Bovary,* bring with them an instinctively modern cadence. (p. 137)

Compare the style of Flaubert in each of his books, and you will find that each book has its own rhythm, perfectly appropriate to its subject-matter. That style, which has almost every merit and hardly a fault, becomes what it is by a process very different from that of most writers careful of form. . . . Flaubert is so difficult to translate because he has no fixed rhythm; his prose keeps step with no regular march-music. He invents the rhythm of every sentence, he changes his cadence with every mood or for the convenience of every fact. He has no theory of beauty in form apart from what it expresses. For him form is a living thing, the physical body of thought, which it clothes and interprets. . . . Beauty comes into his words from the precision with which they express definite things, definite ideas, definite sensations. And in [*Salammbô*], where the material is so hard, apparently so unmalleable, it is a beauty of sheer exactitude which fills it from end to end, a beauty of measure and order, seen equally in the departure of the doves of Carthage, at the time of their flight into Sicily, and in the lions feasting on the corpses of the Barbarians, in the defile between the mountains. (pp. 138-40)

> Arthur Symons, "Gustave Flaubert" (1901), in his Figures of Several Centuries, *Constable and Company Ltd, 1916, pp. 130-40.*

JAMES HUNEKER   (essay date 1904)

The maker of a great style, a lyric poet, who selected as an instrument the "other harmony of prose," a master of characterization and the creator of imperishable volumes, Gustave Flaubert is indeed the Beethoven of French prose. . . . There never has been in French prose such a densely spun style,—the web fairly glistening with the idea. Yet of opacity there is none. Like one of those marvellous tapestries woven in the hidden East, the clear woof of Flaubert's motive is never obscured or tangled. . . . Flaubert was above all a musician, a musical poet. The ear was his final court of appeal, and to make sonorous cadences in a language that lacks essential richness—it is without the great diapasonic undertow of the Anglo-Saxon—was just short of the miraculous. . . . Omnipresent with him was the musician's idea of composing a masterpiece that would float by sheer style, a masterpiece unhampered by an idea. The lyric ecstasy of his written speech quite overmastered him. He was a poet as were De Quincey, Pater, and Poe. The modulation of his style to his themes caused him inconceivable agony. . . . Flaubert strove ceaselessly to overcome the antinomianism of his material. (pp. 228-30)

It was his fanatical worship of form that ranks him as the greatest artist in fiction the world has ever read. Without Balzac's invention, without Turgénieff's tenderness, without Tolstoy's broad humanity, he nevertheless outstrips them all as an artist. It is his music that will live when his themes are rusty with the years; it is his glorious vision of the possibilities of formal beauty that has made his work classic. . . . A student of detail, Flaubert gave the imaginative lift to all he wrote: his was a winged realism, and in *Madame Bovary* we are continually confronted with evidences of his idealistic power. Content to create a small gallery of portraits, he wreaked himself in giving them adequate expression, in investing them with vitality, characteristic coloring, with everything but charm. (pp. 231-32)

Relentlessly pursued by the demon of perfection, a victim to epilepsy, a despiser of the second-hand art of his day, is it not strange that Flaubert ever wrote a line? . . . He felt the immedicable pity of existence, yet never resorted to the cheap religious nostrums and political prophylactics of his contemporaries. He despised the bourgeois; this lifelong rancor was at once his deliverance and his downfall; it gave us *L'Education Senti-*

mentale, but it also produced *Bouvard et Pécuchet.* Judged by toilsome standards of criticism, Flaubert was a failure, but a failure monstrous, outrageous, and almost cosmical; there is something elemental in this failure. As satirical as Swift, he was devoured by a lyrism as passionate as Victor Hugo's. (pp. 236-37)

His was a realism of a vastly superior sort to that of his disciples. The profound philosophic bias of his mind enabled him to pierce behind appearances, and while his surfaces are extraordinary in finish, exactitude, and detail, the aura of things and persons is never wanting. His visualizing power has never been excelled, not even by Balzac,—a stroke or two and a man or woman peers out from behind the types. He ambushed himself in the impersonal, and thus his criticism of life seems hard, cold, and cruel to those readers who look for the occasional amiable fillip of Gautier, Fielding, Thackeray, and Dickens. This frigid withdrawal of self behind the screen of his art gave him all the more freedom to set moving his puppets. . . . Those who mortise the cracks in their imagination with current romanticism, Flaubert will never captivate. He seems too remote; he regards his characters too dispassionately. This objectivity is carried to dangerous lengths in *Sentimental Education,* for the book is minor in tone, without much exciting incident. . . . Five hundred pages seem too much by half to be devoted to a young man who does not know his own mind. Yet Frédéric Moreau is a man you are sure to meet on your way home. He is born in great numbers and in every land, and his middle name is Mediocrity. . . . He is not the hero, for the book is without one, just as it is plotless and apparently motiveless. Elimination is practised unceasingly, yet the broadest effects are secured; the apparent looseness of construction vanishes on a second reading. Almost fugal in treatment is the development of episodes, and while the rhythms are elliptical, large, irregular—rhythm there always is—the unrelated, unfinished, unrounded, decomposed semblance to life is all the while cunningly preserved. (pp. 237-40)

And the vanity, the futility, the barrenness of it all! It is the philosophy of disenchantment, and about the book hangs the inevitable atmosphere of defeat, of mortification, of unheroic resignation. It is life, commonplace, quotidian life, and truth is stamped on its portals. All is vanity and vexation of spirit. The tragedy of the petty has never before been so mockingly, so menacingly, so absolutely displayed. (p. 241)

> *James Huneker, "The Beethoven of French Prose," in his* Overtones, a Book of Temperaments: Richard Strauss, Parsifal, Verdi, Balzac, Flaubert, Nietzsche, and Turgenieff, *Charles Scribner's Sons, 1904 (and reprinted by Charles Scribner's Sons, 1928), pp. 228-55.*

WILLARD HUNTINGTON WRIGHT (essay date 1917)

[The] aesthetic standard I adhere to is at variance with the conventional one; for, while I am able to agree with those who acclaim Flaubert a master of rhythmic and tonal expression, I still hold that style, no matter how perfect, is not of chief artistic significance—that, in fact, it is only of secondary importance when compared with the internal architecture of art. This poised inner structure is a quality I fail to find in any of Flaubert's work; and, without it, I do not believe there can be the highest creation, however blinding the beauty of investiture. (p. 455)

The conception of his books—namely, the thematic structure which reveals the profundity of an artist's vision—was founded on a rigid externalism. Not only was it inspired by purely material observation, but its form was in large measure predetermined. It did not evolve naturally after certain forces had been set in motion. In brief, the content was not self-generating. Such organization as his books possessed was the result, first, of a single viewpoint toward which all the lines and volumes of the story were made to converge, and, secondly, of the verbal mould in which the document was cast. There was an order in his best works, but it was not organic. It was the order which follows a co-ordinating of data—that is, it was analytic, not synthetic. (p. 456)

We have recently learned that *Madame Bovary* was not an original story, but that both characters and incidents, with few variations, were adopted from life. Flaubert merely played the historian to actuality. Necessarily, therefore, he worked from the result back to the cause. It was the fact, and not the principle, with which he dealt. Also, in *Salammbô* and *La Tentation de Saint-Antoine* he attacked his problem by way of document. He built both stories on data he had unearthed in historical records. And, in *L'Éducation Sentimentale,* he sought only to reconstruct a certain political period. (pp. 456-57)

His primary concern was with external harmony; he strove almost exclusively for perfection in *matière.* Surface rhythm, and not profound rhythmic movement, was the goal toward which he struggled for thirty years. Whereas the incontestably commanding figures in art made their style a means of expressing an inner form of document, Flaubert used the aspects of document as a means for creating style. In this he was eminently successful, for not only was he willing to sacrifice everything to this end, but he possessed a faultless auricular sensitivity and an unerring instinct for pleasing color and tone. Furthermore, he was able to remove all trace of effort from his work and to give it an air of spontaneous serenity. (pp. 457-58)

Style should be merely the glass through which we can see the glories which reside underneath; but with Flaubert the style is like a beautiful stained window which shuts out our view of what is beyond. The stylistic standard by which he is commonly judged is, in the very nature of three-dimensional art, superficial. It is founded on idealistic and, to a great extent, theoretical considerations. There is an undeniable pleasure to be obtained from the precision of visual proportions, from the interplay of various and varied colors, from the flowing harmony and sequence of lines, from delicately balanced chiaroscura, and from the subtleties of tonal gradations. But all these sources of delight are possible in two dimensions, as is exemplified in Japanese paintings and in the melodies of Schumann. Poise and movement in the deeper sense—that is to say, the qualities which imply living realities—are possible only in objects which orientate in depth at the same time that they are moving on a given surface. And it is in proportion to an artist's ability to state life in all its dimensions, to reveal the undercurrents as well as the ripples, and to reproduce the subterranean order of forces as well as the external proportions, that he is great in the permanent aesthetic sense. (pp. 458-59)

The admitted fact that Flaubert loses more in translation than does almost any other prose writer, at once reveals the superficiality of his talents. *Madame Bovary,* stripped of its exquisite garb, is no more than a keenly analytic and wholly external account of a woman's disintegration under the corrosion of mediocrity. Flaubert places his characters under the microscope, observes every movement and change in their natures, and sets down each detail of their transmutation. We see them gradually taking shape as touch after touch is added; and in the end, when the picture is complete, we have a series of comprehensive and convincing portraits. But what we do not have is a complete vision of life brought to a small focus. We are not given a glimpse of the creative laws of nature. The mechanism of the human drama has not been revealed to us. We are affected because we have seen and felt a segment of life. We are not exalted because of having recognized and experienced the universal significance of life.

Herein Flaubert falls short of greatness. His creative method was not such as permitted the characters themselves to develop from within, as do the characters in Balzac. He did not set in action certain forces whose currents and cross-currents moulded and threw into relief the figures of his narrative. He traced back, from the person himself, the history of those currents, and showed the consecutive steps by which each character evolved. Flaubert revealed character: he did not create it. Emma Bovary, Homais, Salammbô, Frédéric, Antony—each one is particularized, consistent, and, in the personal sense, living. But none of them is universalized—that is, made genetically representative of all humanity. The difference, for instance, between Balzac's method of characterization and that of Flaubert is the difference between philosophy and reportorialism. In Balzac the whole is embodied in every part: in Flaubert the whole is visible only when every part has been laid in. In brief, Balzac was a subjective creator; Flaubert, an objective builder.

Flaubert, because he ushered in a new literary cycle—namely, that of naturalism,—has received the overvaluation which attaches to all pioneers; but we must not let his importance as an innovator blind us to his shortcomings as an artist. (pp. 460-61)

[Salammbô] exposes, perhaps better than any other book we possess, the limited possibilities of the naturalistic inspiration. The poverty of impersonal and dispassionate objectivity, as applied to aesthetic means, is here revealed in striking fashion. . . . A great artist can resuscitate the past for us and make it living because he is primarily concerned with causes. But the art of Flaubert, and of all the members of his school, being analytic and dealing wholly with effects, was capable of reproducing only the externals of antiquity. . . . In *Madame Bovary* we are temperamentally in touch with the conditions, and consequently can react to them. We are interested in Emma, but not in Salammbô. The one is relative to us, the other foreign. Aesthetically *Salammbô* was a failure; and so was *Madame Bovary*. But it was the failure of an entire creative system. In *Salammbô* the failure was more conspicuous merely because of the unfamiliar substance.

La Tentation de Saint-Antoine is even a less colorful reconstruction of history than *Salammbô*. It is deficient in Flaubert's usual lyricism, and its record of material is not seldom tiring. It is so highly intellectualized that its very naturalism is made difficult of access. (p. 462)

Flaubert once wrote: "Should you progress so far . . . that nothing, not even your own existence, seems to you to have any other purpose than to serve as an object for description . . . then come boldly forth and give books to the world." In these words we have an acute criticism of Flaubert's own writings. . . . In his implacable and unceasing pursuit of the simulacra, he ignored the meaning of life, which is its plastic content. And because no number of accurate trivialities can create an aesthetic unity unless they are related to the causes which produced them, he failed in the highest requirements of his art. (p. 463)

Willard Huntington Wright, "Flaubert: A Revaluation," in The North American Review, Vol. 206, No. 3, September, 1917, pp. 455-63.

MARCEL PROUST   (essay date 1920)

[Flaubert], by the entirely novel and personal use which he made of the past definite, the past indefinite, the present participle, and of certain pronouns and prepositions, has renewed our vision of things almost to the same extent as Kant, with his Categories, renewed our theories of knowledge and of the reality of the external world. It is not that I am particularly enamoured of Flaubert's style, as we find it in his various books. For reasons which I have not room to develop here, I believe that metaphor alone can give a species of eternity to style, and there is probably, in the whole of Flaubert, no single instance of a really beautiful metaphor. I would go even further and maintain that his images are, generally speaking, so weak that they scarcely rise above the level of those that his most insignificant characters might have used. . . . But, after all, there are other things in style besides metaphor. It would be impossibe for anyone to get on to the great Moving Staircase of Flaubert's pages, which go on and on, never stopping, never breaking their monotony, without colour and without clearness of outline—and not to realise that they are without their like in literature. . . . What tended to matter more and more to Flaubert, as his personality took form and became recognisably Flaubert, was the rendering of his vision without the slightest intervention of merely neat phrasing, or a hint of personal sensibility. In *Madame Bovary* the elements which are not wholly 'him' have not yet been completely eliminated. . . . Even in *Education Sentimentale* . . . there are occasional traces of something that is not Flaubert. . . . But, in spite of that, in *Education Sentimentale* the revolution has been accomplished, and what, up to the time of Flaubert, had been merely action, has become impression. Objects have just as much life as men, for it is the process of reasoning that, at a later stage, attributes external causes to visual phenomena. What reaches us in the form of a first impression contains no causal implication. . . . The subjective quality in Flaubert expresses itself by a novel employment of *tenses*, prepositions, adverbs—the two latter having, as a rule, merely a rhythmic value in his sentences. A continuous state is expressed by the use of the imperfect. . . . [This] imperfect, a newcomer to literature, entirely changes the look of people and of things, as, when the position of a lamp has been slightly shifted, the appearance of a new house may strike one as one enters it for the first time, or of an old one when one is in the process of moving. It is this kind of melancholy, made up of the breaking of old habits and of the flimsy unreality of the setting, that Flaubert's style produces, that style which, if only by reason of this single effect, strikes one as being so new. His use of the imperfect serves to narrate not only people's words, but their whole lives. *Education Sentimentale* is the prolonged narrative of a life, in which the human characters, so to speak, do not play any active part at all. Sometimes there is an incursion of the perfect into the clutter of imperfects, but when that happens, it, too, seems merely to mark something indefinite in process of prolongation. . . . There are, indeed, moments when the present indicative applies a corrective to the movement of the phrases down the inclined plane of these neutrally tinted imperfects, and casts a furtive beam of sunlight, which has the effect of picking out a more durable reality from the unceasing flow of objects. . . . (pp. 224-29)

The conjunction 'and' never, in Flaubert, plays the part assigned to it by grammar. It marks a pause in the beat of the rhythm, and acts as the means of dividing a picture into its parts. It is true to say that wherever one would normally put 'and', Flaubert suppresses it. This suppression provides the model, the form, of many admirable phrases. . . . In revenge, he makes use of it where no one else would have dreamed of doing so. It functions more or less as a sign that another part of the picture is beginning, that the moving wave is about to build itself up again. . . . The very slow process—and that it was slow I am ready to admit—of acquiring so many grammatical peculiarities . . . proves, in my opinion, not . . . that Flaubert was not a born writer, but, rather that he was. Since these grammatical singularities were, in fact, the means by which he registered a new vision, it must have needed an enormous amount of application to fix the contours of that vision, to make it pass from the unconscious into the conscious, to incorporate it in the various parts of his narrative. The only thing that really surprises me in so great a master is the mediocrity of his letters. . . . Since, however, we get to grips with Flaubert's genius only in the beauty of his conscious style and in the curiously rigid singularities of his distorting syntax, it may be well to point out a few more of them, such, for instance, as the way in which he constantly uses an adverb to conclude, not only a phrase, or a paragraph, but even a whole book. . . . With him, as with Leconte de Lisle, we feel the need of a certain solidity, even of a somewhat massive solidity to act as compensation for the—I don't say hollow, but certainly very light writing, in which too many interstices, too many gaps, have been allowed to show. But in Flaubert, adverbs and adverbial locutions, are always placed in the ugliest, the most unexpected, the heaviest, manner, as though they are intended to serve as cement for his compact phrases, so that each tiniest hole in the fabric shall be efficiently blocked. . . . For the same reason, he is never afraid of the *weight* of certain words, or of certain rather vulgar expressions. (pp. 229-32)

[One of Flaubert's literary merits] which touches me most nearly, because I find in it the successful solution of certain problems to which I have, in my own modest fashion, devoted a good deal of thought, is the masterly manner in which he managed to produce the effect of time *passing.* The finest thing, to my mind, in the whole of *Education Sentimentale,* is to be found, not in words at all, but in a passage where there comes a sudden moment of silence. Flaubert has just been describing, narrating, through many pages, the various trivial acts performed by Frédéric Moreau. His hero sees a policeman, with sword drawn, rush at a rioter who promptly falls dead: '*Et Frédéric, béant, reconnut Sénécal!*' Here there is an implied 'silence' of vast duration, and suddenly, without the hint of a transition, time ceases to be a matter of mere successive quarters of an hour, and appears to us in the guise of years and decades. . . . Flaubert was the first novelist to free this change from all parasitic growths of anecdote and historical scavenging. He treated it in terms of music. Nobody before him had ever done that. (pp. 234-35)

> *Marcel Proust, "About Flaubert's Style" (reprinted by permission of Georges Borchardt, Inc., as agents for the author; originally published in* Nouvelle Revue Française, *Vol. 8, January, 1920), in his* A Selection from His Miscellaneous Writings, *edited and translated by Gerard Hopkins, Allen Wingate, 1948, pp. 224-40.*

PERCY LUBBOCK (essay date 1921)

[Flaubert's *Madame Bovary*] remains perpetually the novel of all novels which the criticism of fiction cannot overlook; as soon as ever we speak of the principles of the art, we must be prepared to engage with Flaubert. (p. 60)

Flaubert handles his material quite differently from point to point. Sometimes he seems to be describing what he has seen himself, places and people he has known, conversations he may have overheard; I do not mean that he is literally retailing an experience of his own, but that he writes as though he were. His description, in that case, touches only such matters as you or I might have perceived for ourselves, if we had happened to be on the spot at the moment. His object is to place the scene before us, so that we may take it in like a picture gradually unrolled or a drama enacted. But then again the method presently changes. There comes a juncture at which, for some reason, it is necessary for us to know more than we could have made out by simply looking and listening. Flaubert, the author of the story, must intervene with his superior knowledge. . . . And so, for a new light on the drama, the author recalls certain circumstances that we should otherwise have missed. Or it may be that he—who naturally knows everything, even the inmost, unexpressed thought of the characters—wishes us to share the mind of Bovary or of Emma, not to wait only on their words or actions; and so he goes below the surface, enters their consciousness, and describes the train of sentiment that passes there. (pp. 64-5)

Flaubert is generally considered to be a very "impersonal" writer, one who keeps in the background and desires us to remain unaware of his presence; he places the story before us and suppresses any comment of his own. But this point has been over-laboured, I should say; it only means that Flaubert does not announce his opinion in so many words, and thence it has been argued that the opinions of a really artistic writer ought not to appear in his story at all. But of course with every touch that he lays on his subject he must show what he thinks of it; his subject, indeed, the book which he finds in his selected fragment of life, is purely the representation of his view, his judgement, his opinion of it. The famous "impersonality" of Flaubert and his kind lies only in the greater tact with which they express their feelings—dramatizing them, embodying them in living form, instead of stating them directly. (pp. 67-8)

It is a matter of method. Sometimes the author is talking with his own voice, sometimes he is talking *through* one of the people in the book—in this book for the most part Emma herself. Thus he describes a landscape, the trim country-side in which Emma's lot is cast, or the appearance and manners of her neighbours, or her own behaviour; and in so doing he is using his own language and his own standards of appreciation; he is facing the reader in person, however careful he may be to say nothing to deflect our attention from the thing described. He is making a reproduction of something that is in his own mind. And then later on he is using the eyes and the mind and the standards of another; the landscape has now the colour that it wears in Emma's view, the incident is caught in the aspect which it happens to turn towards her imagination. Flaubert himself has retreated, and it is Emma with whom we immediately deal. (p. 68)

Furthermore, whether the voice is that of the author or of his creature, there is a pictorial manner of treating the matter in hand and there is also a dramatic. It may be that the impression—as in the case of the marquis's ball—is chiefly given as a picture, the reflection of events in the mirror of somebody's receptive consciousness. The reader is not really looking *at* the occasion in the least, or only now and then; mainly he is watching the surge of Emma's emotion, on which the episode acts with sharp intensity. The thing is "scenic," in the sense in which I used the word just now; we are concerned, that is to say, with a single and particular hour, we are taking no extended, general view of Emma's experience. But though it is thus a *scene,* it is not dramatically rendered; if you took the dialogue, what there is of it, together with the actual things described, the people and the dresses and the dances and the banquets—took these and placed them on the stage, for a theatrical performance, the peculiar effect of the occasion in the book would totally vanish. Nothing could be more definite, more objective, than the scene is in the book; but there it is all bathed in the climate of Emma's mood, and it is to the nature of this climate that our interest is called for the moment. The lords and ladies are remote, Emma's envying and wondering excitement fills the whole of the foreground. (pp. 69-70)

In *Madame Bovary* the scenes are distributed and rendered with very rare skill; not one but seems to have more and more to give with every fresh reading of it. The ball, the *comices,* the evening at the theatre, Emma's fateful interview with Léon in the Cathedral of Rouen, the remarkable session of the priest and the apothecary at her deathbed—these form the articulation of the book, the scheme of its structure. To the next in order each stage of the story is steadily directed. By the time the scene is reached, nothing is wanting to its opportunity; the action is ripe, the place is resonant; and then the incident takes up the story, conclusively establishes one aspect of it and opens the view towards the next. And the more rapid summary that succeeds, with its pauses for a momentary sight of Emma's daily life and its setting, carries the book on once more to the climax that already begins to appear in the distance.

But the most obvious point of method is no doubt the difficult question of the centre of vision. With which of the characters, if with any of them, is the writer to identify himself, which is he to "go behind"? Which of these vessels of thought and feeling is he to reveal from within? . . . [Which] *is* the centre, which is the mind that really commands the subject? . . . In Flaubert's *Bovary* there could be no question but that we must mainly use the eyes of Emma herself; the middle of the subject is in her experience, not anywhere in the concrete facts around her. And yet Flaubert finds it necessary, as I said, to look *at* her occasionally, taking advantage of some other centre for the time being. . . . (pp.73-5)

If Flaubert allows himself the liberty of telling his story in various ways—with a method, that is to say, which is often modified as he proceeds—it is likely that he has good cause to do so. . . . [At] first sight it does seem that his manner of arriving at his subject—if his subject is Emma Bovary—is considerably casual. He begins with Charles, of all people. . . . (p. 77)

[His subject] is of course Emma Bovary in the first place; the book is the portrait of a foolish woman, romantically inclined, in small and prosaic conditions. She is in the centre of it all, certainly; there is no doubt of her position in the book. But *why* is she there? . . . Given Emma and what she is by nature, given her environment and the facts of her story, there are dozens of different subjects, I dare say, latent in the case. (p. 78)

Now if Emma was devised for her own sake, solely because a nature and a temper like hers seemed to Flaubert an amusing study—if his one aim was to make the portrait of a woman of that kind—then the rest of the matter falls into line, we shall know how to regard it. These conditions in which Emma finds herself will have been chosen by the author because they appeared to throw light on her, to call out her natural qualities, to give her the best opportunity of disclosing what she is. . . . If he had thought that a woman of her sort, rather meanly ambitious, rather fatuously romantic, would have revealed her quality more intensely in a different world—in success, freedom, wealth—he would have placed her otherwise. . . . Emma's world as it is at present, in the book that Flaubert wrote, would have to be regarded, accordingly, as all a *consequence* of Emma, invented to do her a service, described in order that they may make the description of *her*. . . . All this—*if* the subject of the book is nothing but the portrait of such a woman.

But of course it is not so; one glance at our remembrance of the book is enough to show it. Emma's world could not be other than it is, she could not be shifted into richer and larger conditions, without destroying the whole point and purpose of Flaubert's novel. She by herself is not the subject of his book. What he proposes to exhibit is the history of a woman like her in just such a world as hers, a foolish woman in narrow circumstances; so that the provincial scene, acting upon her, making her what she becomes, is as essential as she is herself. Not a portrait, therefore, not a study of character for its own sake, but something in the nature of a drama, where the two chief players are a woman on one side and her whole environment on the other—that is *Madame Bovary.* (pp. 79-80)

Obviously the emphasis is not upon the commonplace little events of Emma's career. They might, no doubt, be the steps in a dramatic tale, but they are nothing of the kind as Flaubert handles them. He makes it perfectly clear that his view is not centred upon the actual outcome of Emma's predicament, whether it will issue this way or that; *what* she does or fails to do is of very small moment. . . . The *events,* therefore, Emma's excursions to Rouen, her forest-rides, her one or two memorable adventures in the world, all these are only Flaubert's way of telling his subject, of making it count to the eye. They are not in themselves what he has to say, they simply illustrate it.

What it comes to, I take it, is that though *Madame Bovary,* the novel, is a kind of drama—since there is the interaction of this woman confronted by these facts—it is a drama chosen for the sake of the picture in it, for the impression it gives of the manner in which certain lives are lived. . . . Let Emma and her plight, therefore, appear as a picture; let her be shown in the act of living her life, entangled as it is with her past and her present; that is how the final fact at the heart of Flaubert's subject will be best displayed.

Here is the clue, it seems, to his treatment of the theme. It is pictorial, and its object is to make Emma's existence as intelligible and visible as may be. We who read the book are to share her sense of life, till no uncertainty is left in it; we are to see and understand her experience, and to see *her* while she enjoys or endures it; we are to be placed within her world, to get the immediate taste of it, and outside her world as well, to get the full effect, more of it than she herself could see. Flaubert's subject demands no less, if the picture is to be complete. She herself must be known thoroughly—that is his first care; the movement of her mind is to be watched at work in all the ardour and the poverty of her imagination. . . . And then there is the dull and limited world in which her appetite is somehow to be satisfied, the small town that shuts her in and cuts her off. . . . [Accordingly] Flaubert treats the scenery of his book, Yonville and its odd types, as intensely as he treats his heroine; he broods over it with concentration and gives it all the salience he can. (pp. 81-5)

Such is the picture that Flaubert's book is to present. And what, then, of the point of view towards which it is to be directed? . . . Where is Flaubert to find his centre of vision?—from what point, within the book or without, will the unfolding of the subject be commanded most effectively? . . . Part of his subject is Emma's sense of her world; we must see how it impresses her and what she makes of it, how it thwarts her and how her imagination contrives to get a kind of sustenance out of it. The book is not really written at all unless it shows her view of things, as the woman she was, in that place, in those conditions. For this reason it is essential to pass into her consciousness, to make her *subjective;* and Flaubert takes care to do so and to make her so, as soon as she enters the book. But it is also enjoined by the story, as we found, that her place and conditions should be seen for what they are and known as intimately as herself. For this matter Emma's capacity fails.

Her intelligence is much too feeble and fitful to give a sufficient account of her world. . . . Her pair of eyes is not enough; the picture beheld through them is a poor thing in itself, for she can see no more than her mind can grasp; and it does her no justice either, since she herself is so largely the creation of her surroundings. (pp. 85-6)

[The] poor creature cannot tell the story in full. A shift of the vision is necessary. And in *Madame Bovary,* it is to be noted, there is no one else within the book who is in a position to take up the tale when Emma fails. There is no other personage upon the scene who sees and understands any more than she; perception and discrimination are not to be found in Yonville at all—it is an essential point. The author's wit, therefore, and none other, must supply what is wanting. This necessity, to a writer of Flaubert's acute sense of effect, is one that demands a good deal of caution. The transition must be made without awkwardness, without calling attention to it. (p. 87)

[Flaubert deals with the difficulty] by keeping Emma always at a certain distance, even when he appears to be entering her mind most freely. He makes her subjective, places us so that we see through her eyes—yes; but he does so with an air of aloofness that forbids us ever to become entirely identified with her. . . . A hint of irony is always perceptible, and it is enough to prevent us from being lost in her consciousness, immersed in it beyond easy recall. The woman's life is very real, perfectly felt; but the reader is made to accept his participation in it as a pleasing experiment, the kind of thing that appeals to a fastidious curiosity—there is no question of its ever being more than this. The *fact* of Emma is taken with entire seriousness, of course; she is there to be studied and explored, and no means of understanding her point of view will be neglected. But her value is another matter; as to that Flaubert never has an instant's illusion, he always knows her to be worthless. (p. 89)

His irony, none the less, is close at hand and indispensable; he has a definite use for this resource and he could not forego it. His irony gives him perfect freedom to supersede Emma's limited vision whenever he pleases, to abandon her manner of looking at the world, and to pass immediately to his own more enlightened, more commanding height. (pp. 89-90)

[*Madame Bovary*] is a book that with its variety of method, and with its careful restriction of that variety to its bare needs, and with its scrupulous use of its resources—it is a book,

altogether, that gives a good point of departure for an examination of the methods of fiction. (p. 92)

Percy Lubbock, in his The Craft of Fiction *(reprinted by permission of Jonathan Cape Ltd, on behalf of the Estate of Percy Lubbock), J. Cape, 1921 (and reprinted by Charles Scribner's Sons, 1955, 277 p.).*

BENEDETTO CROCE   (essay date 1924)

[We] are rather sensible of a certain ferocity in laying bare every fold of Emma's soul [in *Madame Bovary*], in refusing to her a single flash of moral goodness and in degustating the torments that assail her, when she is hunted down and overcome by the deceptions in which she has become involved, like a rat caught in a trap. Yet it is impossible to deny to her a sort of greatness, as of one obsessed by a demoniac force, which at times becomes heroic. Emma is not base. With what ardour and resolution does she give all for all; how superior she feels herself to every law, which is not that of her dream, her longing, her passion; how, when she is hemmed in on every side, does she contrive to shake herself free of the chains, and then goes deliberately and without a word of complaint to meet her death! (p. 302)

Charles Bovary is treated in the same way, without the idealization of sympathy or pity, without the relief of a smile, and he too is finally presented as plunged in the desperation of his dreaming, after the death of Emma. . . . (p. 303)

Homais the chemist was the happiest of fathers and the most fortunate of men, impersonating all that Flaubert hates, together with his own self and his vain desires: life according to the laws, accommodating the laws to oneself and oneself to the laws, intent upon satisfying one's own mean needs of individual well-being and social respectability. Flaubert vibrates between these two hatreds of different colours, too refined to adopt the ethical ideals of Monsieur Homais, but not strong enough to cross the fiery furnace of his own morbid passions and attain to a new and loftier ethical ideal. For this reason, few books are so desolately pessimistic as *Madame Bovary.* (p. 304)

With *Madame Bovary* Flaubert had reached the greatest or rather the only dominion over himself of which he was capable. In the second of his novels, *l'Éducation sentimentale,* holding still the reins of this dominion, he merely repeats the same solution or lack of solution, at which he had stopped: the painful renunciation of dreams without anything more worthy taking their place. . . . The author seems to have been well aware that cupidity, egoism and stupidity are not the only things in the world, but that there are also goodness and self-sacrifice, and a going astray which is not wickedness, filling his narrative with these things: yet this does not change his pessimistic vision, but rather renders it more bitter and pungent. The *Éducation sentimentale* is almost a purgatory beside the inferno of *Madame Bovary,* not because it is crowned with hope, but on account of the more delicate tints which the same suffering there assumes. (pp. 305-06)

Salammbô is the blind spasm towards the barbaric-mysterious-luxurious-sanguinary, towards the voluptuously sacrilegious, and the true country of his heroine is certainly not Carthage, but that castle in Brittany where Chateaubriand conceived the first germ of his Atala and Velleda. Flaubert has seized with readiness the opportunity that offered itself of unchaining for a while, under the semblance of an archaeological reconstruction perfectly elaborated in style, the demon that he bore within himself, and had only allowed to come out of himself at first shut up and chastised in the body of the faithless wife of a country doctor. . . . The truth is that although Flaubert has given to *Salammbô* decent artistic form, he has not dominated his material, but covered it up, and although the style and the unified archaeological researches certainly cool its sensuality here and there, yet they do not conquer and dominate it. In this book he lacked the "internal form," in which art really consists, and which he had realized in the *Bovary* and the *Éducation.* In like manner, the *Tentations de Saint-Antoine,* notwithstanding the perfection of their prose versicles, are a chaos, oscillating between the coldness of the learned literary exercise on the one hand, and, on the other, a spasmodic nostalgia towards something inexpressible. (pp. 308-09)

That Flaubert tended always more and more as he grew older towards an art that has a dualism of imagination or, not to put too fine a point on it, of ill-humour to be poured out and of formalism in style, is confirmed by his last book at which he was working when he died, *Bouvard et Pécuchet.* Here, not satisfied with the extremely marked portrait that he had already given of Monsieur Homais, he set himself deliberately to utter his aversion for politics and for science in their every form, and in addition for anything else that rightly or wrongly had shocked his nerves, either because it really was something reprehensible or because he did not well understand and consequently did not like it. It is a work to which it is impossible to assign any critical value and of which the artistic value is slight. (p. 309)

Benedetto Croce, "Flaubert," in his European Literature in the Nineteenth Century, *translated by Douglas Ainslie (Canadian rights by permission of the Estate of Benedetto Croce), Alfred A. Knopf, 1924, pp. 297-311.*

WILL DURANT   (essay date 1931)

Gustave Flaubert is the apex of French literature in the nineteenth century because he bound [classicism, romanticism, and realism] together in his faultless art: because he established realism in *Mme. Bovary,* restored romanticism in *Salammbô,* and in all his writings achieved the simplicity and restraint of the consummate classic style. Never since has any man so profoundly influenced literature, or written so perfectly. (p. 227)

[In *Mme. Bovary* the] murderous dénouement is almost the only flaw in a book designed to banish sentimental unreality from literature and life. This book, and not a later one, should have been called *Sentimental Education;* it is the perfect diagnosis of the fantastic bourgeois soul. Never was realism calmer or more precise. Against this impartial accuracy the slumming expeditions of Zola read like partisan tracts. The observation is as subtle as in Stendhal, the description is as profound as in Balzac; but whereas Balzac describes first and narrates afterward, Flaubert describes only through narration, and only as his figures enter upon and perceive the scene. Each person in the drama is both a type and an individual, revealing all humanity through a single soul; taken together they form a text-book of psychology and a history of bourgeois civilization. Nothing could be more objective; the author recounts "good" and "bad" with the neutrality of an undertaker. . . . It was the first book of utter realism, and it is still the best. (p. 235)

If the book pretended to be all of life it would be unbearable; as the portrait of a phase, it is as true as a photographic plate.

With regard to morality, let every parson be of good cheer: sin is here exposed as the deadliest thing on earth—when it lasts as long as monogamy. (pp. 235-36)

The dominant element in Flaubert was the angry realism of outraged sentiment; the subject of all his books except one is romantic sentimentality exposed by ruthless description; his very pre-occupation with the subject tells how it possessed him; he denounced romanticism because it was in his blood, and he longed to be purified of it, to "be hard." (p. 237)

By a stroke of genius, or by the compulsion of passion, he resolved to pour all his suppressed romanticism into one tremendous book; to put behind him the bourgeois world of Croiset and France, the narrow peasants and merciless financiers, and lose himself, body and soul, in the Oriental past. (p. 238)

[*Salammbô*] is a marvelous story, in substance and in form; elemental in interest and passion, devotedly perfect in style, and marred only by its morbid lingering over scenes of suffering and slaughter. The sacrifice of Carthaginian children in the flames on the altar of Moloch is not only repulsive, but historically untrue; the final pages are a riot of flagellation, and every chapter reads like an obituary column. . . . And the construction is imperfect; we are prepared for more Salammbô than we get. . . . But what language! (pp. 242-43)

Nowhere is French more beautiful than Flaubert's in *Salammbô;* even in translation it shines and purrs and sings. . . . There is not a *cliché* here, not one trite phrase or metaphor; nothing nervous as in Taine, nothing crude and abrupt as in Balzac, nothing excitely rhetorical as in Hugo; here is the music of Bach and the splendor of Euripides; words reared and modeled like temples. This surely is Flaubert's masterpiece; no wonder he liked it best, and wrote it in a long delirium of joy. This, and not *Bovary,* made him a god of style for all Frenchmen, the patron saint of men of letters everywhere, the Keats of modern prose. (p. 244)

Will Durant, "In Praise of Flaubert," in his Adventures in Genius (copyright © 1931; renewed © 1958 by Will Durant; reprinted by permission of Simon & Schuster, a Division of Gulf & Western Corporation), Simon & Schuster, 1931, pp. 227-51.

MARY M. COLUM   (essay date 1937)

Madame Bovary not only crystallized the literary genre, but fixed the novel as the primary literary form, the one most favored by writers and readers for nearly a century; it also set the pattern for novel writing in subject, theme and construction down to our time, and still shows signs that it may continue into the future, side by side with new patterns that may be brought in. It is very important to note the theme of this first realistic novel—that is, the theme as apart from the plot and the content—for we find it repeated over and over again by realistic novelists. The theme of *Madame Bovary* is the attempt to make life, every-day life, conform to one's youthful dreams, and after the vain attempt to make it conform, the renunciation of all dreams. This is not only the theme of Flaubert's other realistic novel *L'Education Sentimentale,* but is the theme of all the great realistic novels. (pp. 162-63)

What had happened in [*Madame Bovary*] was that a writer for the first time in the history of literature had turned all his gifts, not to poetry or high romance or great drama, but to the revelation of people who might be encountered in any small town or any little suburb. . . . Nothing happens to [Emma] beyond the possibility of happenings in any little community. All the personages could be duplicated in any town, village or suburb, and none of them do or say anything that had not been done or said a million times before in the world. (pp. 163-64)

The personages who, whilst we are reading the novel, give the impression of being individuals become, in retrospect, types—that is, they are at once individual and typical. Emma Bovary herself, considered in turn by critics as the most complete feminine portrait in literature, as one of the most fascinating revelations of the soul of a woman, and—especially by Anglo-Saxon critics, like Percy Lubbock [see excerpt above]—as the portrait of a common, silly little person, foolishly romantic, meanly ambitious, in conflict with her environment, is in reality such an exceedingly subtle portrait that she is in some respects every woman. The portrait of Charles Bovary, good, stupid, with even a more limited expanse of consciousness than the average man, living a common, semi-animal, semi-plant life, with no desires or ambitions that his environment cannot more than satisfy, betrayed by his wife, represents the character of more men than any other type that up till then had appeared in literature. In the same way the character of Homais . . . is to be found by the score in every community. It is he, observing all the laws, habits and customs, keeping all the moralities, fulfilling all the ambitions of the ordinary man, who is the one happy person in the book, a contented husband and father, a success all round in his business and in his community. The vast irony of the portrait could not have been apparent to more than a fraction of the first readers of the novel; it is, perhaps, not apparent to the bulk of readers even now. . . . There is no portrait in *Madame Bovary* created with less irony than that of Emma herself: there is indeed less of Flaubert's well-known and often expressed contempt for humanity in his delineation of her than in that of any other character he has built up. (pp. 165-66)

[Flaubert] was the first author whose mentality represented strongly and clearly the two goals that the whole modern movement in literature, beginning with Lessing, was moving towards—the romantic and the every-day, the dream and the reality. A writer could depict the reality only if he thoroughly knew the dream, and he could realize the significance of the dream only by coming into conflict with reality. Flaubert was, like the bulk of humanity, a dreamer and a realist. In addition, he was a man with a lyrical temperament and an analytic mind, part idealist, part materialist, in his philosophic outlook a scholar with a profound knowledge of literature, an artist born with the sense of form, the very type of those who create new modes of expression.

At the same time, far from being the pure lyric and romantic he sometimes thought himself, he only understood the romantic and lyrical temperament when it was well anchored on one side to common sense and every-day realism. (p. 167)

In his realistic novels, Flaubert deliberately turned away from the accidental, the extraordinary and the dramatic which had so beguiled Balzac; he created neither remarkable persons nor heroes, though he did not blame anybody who did. . . . As for the meticulous power of observation shown in his books, he, like most men of genius, did not place too high a degree of importance on it; it was valuable, but subsidiary. "If I have arrived at some knowledge of life," he wrote, "it is by dint not of chewing a great deal of it but of having ruminated a lot on it." A little experience well pondered over—that gave him the matter for his novels. (p. 169)

Strange and even startling as was Flaubert's achievement, he was in form, even in technique, the heir of a long line not only of French writers but of the whole Latin tradition; in the psychological construction of his characters, as well as in his carefully wrought style, he showed himself of the same line as Racine: the shape of his plot, with its beginning, its crisis, its conclusion, was clearly in the classical manner. He used the old splendid tools on new material and as a new practitioner. (p. 171)

> *Mary M. Colum, "The Coming of the Realists," in her* From These Roots: The Ideas that Have Made Modern Literature *(copyright © 1937 by Charles Scribner's Sons, copyright renewed © 1965 by Columbia University Press, reprinted by permission of the publisher), Charles Scribner's Sons, 1937 (and reprinted by Columbia University Press, 1944), pp. 143-208.**

PAUL VALÉRY   (essay date 1946)

I confess to a weakness for *The Temptation of St. Anthony*. I may as well admit straight away that I have never cared for either *Salammbô* or *Bovary,* the one with its learned, gruesome, and extravagant imagery, or the other with its "truth" of a minutely reconstructed mediocrity.

Flaubert shared with his age a belief in the value of the "historical document" and in the raw observation of the present. But such things are vain idols. The only thing that is real in art is the art.

The best fellow in the world and a very tolerable artist, but without much grace or profundity of mind, Flaubert was defenseless against the very simple formulas propounded by Realism and against the naïve sense of authority which imagines that it can base itself on vast reading and "textual criticism." (p. 223)

One of [realism's] most disconcerting manifestations . . . lies in mistaking for "reality" the data that we find in "historical documents" belonging to some more or less remote period of history, and trying to reconstruct, with their help, a work which would give the impression of conveying "the truth" about that period. . . .

That is the trouble with *Salammbô,* which worries me when I read it. I get far more pleasure from tales of a quite frankly fabulous antiquity . . . , books that do not make us think of other books. (p. 225)

It is not impossible that some inkling of the difficulties created by the desire for realism in art, and the contradictions which emerge as soon as this desire becomes imperative, encouraged Flaubert in his idea of writing a *Temptation of St. Anthony.* The "Temptation"—a temptation that lasted all his life—was like a personal antidote against the boredom (which he admits) of writing his novels of contemporary manners, erecting stylistic monuments to the banality of provincial bourgeois life. . . .

[But] the real impulse that led him to conceive and to embark on the work seems to me to have come from reading Goethe's *Faust.* There is a similarity of origin and an obvious kinship between the subjects of *Faust* and the *Temptation:* the popular and primitive origin, the itinerant life of the two legends, which might be arranged in the form of "pendants" under the common rubric: Man and the Devil. In the *Temptation* the devil attacks the faith of the hermit and swamps his night with despairing visions, with contradictory doctrines and beliefs, with lewd and corrupting promises. (pp. 226-27)

Flaubert seems to me to have had no more than a glimpse of what the subject of the *Temptation* had to offer in the way of themes, possibilites, and opportunities for producing a really great work. His scrupulous concern for accuracy and verifying references alone shows how lacking he was in the decisive spirit and the constructive will which were essential for the invention and manufacture of a literary machine of great power.

A too obvious desire to impress by the number of episodes, apparitions, transformation scenes, arguments, and conflicting voices creates in the reader the growing sensation that he is trapped in a library where all the books, suddenly let loose in a wild uproar, bellow their billions of words at the same moment, and the rebellious portfolios fly open and, all together, disgorge their engravings and drawings. (pp. 227-28)

We have to admit that Anthony hardly exists.

His reactions are disconcenting in their feebleness. We are astonished that he is not more attracted or more dazzled by the spectacle, or more irritated or indignant at what he sees and hears; that he finds neither invective, mockery, nor violently ejaculated prayers to hurl at the obscene masquerade, at the elegant phrases pursuing him with a revolting stream of blasphemy. His passiveness is deadly; he neither yields nor resists; he waits for the end of the nightmare, during which he simply makes a few feeble exclamations from time to time. . . . Flaubert gives the impression of being carried away by the accessories at the expense of the main point. He was diverted by the décors, the contrasts, the "amusing" accents of detail, which he had picked up here and there in books he had seldom or only carelessly read. Thus, like Anthony hmself (but an Anthony who succumbs), he lost his soul—I mean the soul of his subject, which was its capacity to develop into a masterpiece. He spoiled one of the finest possible dramas, a work of the first order which was crying out to be written. By not making up his mind above all else to endow his hero with real vitality, he neglected the very substance of his theme; he failed to respond to the depth of its appeal. . . . I do not doubt that Flaubert was aware of the depth of his subject, but you might almost say that he was afraid to plunge into it, down to that depth at which everything that can be learned ceases to count. He therefore lost his way among too many books and too many myths; and that is where he lost sight of his strategy—I mean the unity of his composition which could only reside in an Anthony in whom Satan would have been one of the souls. . . . This work of his remains a diverse collection of moments and fragments; but among them there are some which were written to last forever. Such as it is, I regard it with reverence, and I never open it without finding reasons for admiring the author more than his book. (pp. 229, 231)

> *Paul Valéry, "The Temptation of (St.) Flaubert" (1946), in his* The Collected Works of Paul Valéry: Masters and Friends, Vol. 9, *edited by Jackson Matthews, translated by Martin Turnell, Bollingen Series XLV (copyright © 1968 by Princeton University Press; reprinted by permission of Princeton University Press), Princeton University Press, 1968, pp. 223-31.*

ERICH AUERBACH (essay date 1946)

[Flaubert's] opinion of his characters and events remains unspoken; and when the characters express themselves it is never in such a manner that the writer identifies himself with their

opinion, or seeks to make the reader identify himself with it. We hear the writer speak; but he expresses no opinion and makes no comment. His role is limited to selecting the events and translating them into language; and this is done in the conviction that every event, if one is able to express it purely and completely, interprets itself and the persons involved in it far better and more completely than any opinion or judgment appended to it could do. Upon this conviction—that is, upon a profound faith in the truth of language responsibly, candidly, and carefully employed—Flaubert's artistic practice rests. (p. 486)

[Both Emma and Charles Bovary are so immersed in their] own world—she in despair and vague wish-dreams, he in his stupid philistine self-complacency—that they are both entirely alone; they have nothing in common, and yet they have nothing of their own, for the sake of which it would be worthwhile to be lonely. For, privately, each of them has a silly, false world, which cannot be reconciled with the reality of his situation, and so they both miss the possibilities life offers them. What is true of these two, applies to almost all the other characters in the novel; each of the many mediocre people who act in it has his own world of mediocre and silly stupidity, a world of illusions, habits, instincts, and slogans; each is alone, none can understand another, or help another to insight; there is no common world of men, because it could only come into existence if many should find their way to their own proper reality, the reality which is given to the individual—which then would be also the true common reality. Though men come together for business and pleasure, their coming together has no note of united activity; it becomes one-sided, ridiculous, painful, and it is charged with misunderstanding, vanity, futility, falsehood, and stupid hatred. But what the world would really be, the world of the "intelligent," Flaubert never tells us; in his book the world consists of pure stupidity, which completely misses true reality, so that the latter should properly not be discoverable in it at all; yet it is there; it is in the writer's language, which unmasks the stupidity by pure statement; language, then, has criteria for stupidity and thus also has a part in that reality of the "intelligent" which otherwise never appears in the book.

Emma Bovary, too, the principal personage of the novel, is completely submerged in that false reality, in *la bêtise humaine*, as is the "hero" of Flaubert's other realistic novel, Frédéric Moreau in the *Éducation sentimentale*. How does Flaubert's manner of representing such personages fit into the traditional categories "tragic" and "comic"? Certainly Emma's existence is apprehended to its depths, certainly the earlier intermediate categories, such as the "sentimental" or the "satiric" or the "didactic," are inapplicable, and very often the reader is moved by her fate in a way that appears very like tragic pity. But a real tragic heroine she is not. The way in which language here lays bare the silliness, immaturity, and disorder of her life, the very wretchedness of that life, in which she remains immersed (*toute l'amertume de l'existence lui semblait servie sur son assiette*), excludes the idea of true tragedy, and the author and the reader can never feel as at one with her as must be the case with the tragic hero; she is always being tried, judged, and, together with the entire world in which she is caught, condemned. But neither is she comic; surely not; for that, she is understood far too deeply from within her fateful entanglement—though Flaubert never practices any "psychological understanding" but simply lets the state of the facts speak for itself. He has found an attitude toward the reality of contemporary life which is entirely different from earlier attitudes and stylistic levels, including—and especially—Balzac's and Stendhal's. It could be called, quite simply, "objective seriousness." . . . He wishes, by his attitude—*pas de cris, pas de convulsion, rien que la fixité d'un regard pensif* [no shrieks, no convulsion, nothing but a steady thoughtful gaze]—to force language to render the truth concerning the subjects of his observation. . . . Yet this leads in the end to a didactic purpose: criticism of the contemporary world; and we must not hesitate to say so, much as Flaubert may insist that he is an artist and nothing but an artist. The more one studies Flaubert, the clearer it becomes how much insight into the problematic nature and the hollowness of nineteenth-century bourgeois culture is contained in his realistic works; and many important passages from his letters confirm this. The demonification of everyday social intercourse which is to be found in Balzac is certainly entirely lacking in Flaubert; life no longer surges and foams, it flows viscously and sluggishly. The essence of the happenings of ordinary contemporary life seemed to Flaubert to consist not in tempestuous actions and passions, not in demonic men and forces, but in the prolonged chronic state whose surface movement is merely empty bustle, while underneath it there is another movement, almost imperceptible but universal and unceasing, so that the political, economic, and social subsoil appears comparatively stable and at the same time intolerably charged with tension. Events seem to him hardly to change; but in the concretion of duration, which Flaubert is able to suggest both in the individual occurrence (as in our example) and in his total picture of the times, there appears something like a concealed threat: the period is charged with its stupid issuelessness as with an explosive.

Through his level of style, a systematic and objective seriousness, from which things themselves speak and, according to their value, classify themselves before the reader as tragic or comic, or in most cases quite unobtrusively as both, Flaubert overcame the romantic vehemence and uncertainty in the treatment of contemporary subjects. . . . (pp. 489-91)

> Erich Auerbach, *"In the Hôtel de la Mole,"* in his Mimesis: The Representation of Reality in Western Literature, *translated by Willard R. Trask (copyright © 1953 by Princeton University Press; reprinted by permission of Princeton University Press; originally published as* Mimesis: Dargestellte Wirklichkeit in der abendländischen Literatur, *A. Francke, 1946), Princeton University Press, 1953, pp. 454-92.**

EDMUND WILSON (essay date 1948)

[Flaubert's] general historical point of view is, I believe, pretty well known. He held that 'the three great evolutions of humanity' had been 'paganisme, christianisme, muflisme [muckerism],' and that Europe was in the third of these phases. Paganism he depicted in *Salammbô* and in the short story *Hérodias.* The Carthaginians of *Salammbô* had been savage and benighted barbarians: they had worshiped serpents, crucified lions, sacrificed their children to Moloch, and trampled armies to death with herds of elephants; but they had slaughtered, lusted and agonized superbly. Christianity is represented by the two legends of saints, *La Tentation de Saint Antoine* and *La Légende de Saint Julien l'Hospitalier.* The Christian combats his lusts, he expiates human cruelty; but this attitude, too, is heroic: Saint Anthony, who inhabits the desert, Saint Julien, who lies down with the leper, have pushed to their furthest limits the virtues of abnegation and humility. But when we come to the *muflisme* of the nineteenth century—in *Madame*

Bovary and *L'Education sentimentale*—all is meanness, mediocrity and timidity.

The villain here is, of course, the bourgeois; and it is true that these two novels of Flaubert ridicule and damn the contemporary world, taking down its pretentions by comparing it with Carthage and the Thebaid. But in these pictures of modern life there is a complexity of human values and an analysis of social processes which does not appear in the books that deal with older civilizations; and this social analysis of Flaubert's has, it seems to me, been too much disregarded—with the result that *L'Education sentimentale*, one of his most remarkable books, has been rather underestimated.

In *Madame Bovary*, Flaubert is engaged in criticizing that very longing for the exotic and the faraway which played such a large part in his own life and which led him to write *Salammbô* and *Saint Antoine*. What cuts Flaubert off from the other romantics and makes him primarily a social critic is his grim realization of the futility of dreaming about the splendors of the Orient and the brave old days of the past as an antidote to bourgeois society. (pp. 76-7)

Flaubert had more in common with, and had perhaps been influenced more by, the socialist thought of his time than he would ever have allowed himself to confess. In his novels, it is never the nobility—indistinguishable for mediocrity from the bourgeoisie—but the peasants and working people whom he habitually uses as touchstones to show up the pretensions of the bourgeois. (p. 77)

[It is] in *L'Education sentimentale* that Flaubert's account of society comes closest to socialist theory. Indeed, his presentation here of the Revolution of 1848 parallels in [a striking] manner Marx's analysis of the same events in *The Eighteenth Brumaire of Louis Napoleon*. . . . (p. 78)

The only really sympathetic characters in *L'Education sentimentale* are, again, the representatives of the people. Rosanette, Frédéric's mistress, is the daughter of poor workers in the silk mills, who sold her at fifteen as mistress to an old bourgeois. Her liaison with Frédéric is a symbol of the disastrously unenduring union between the proletariat and the bourgeoisie, of which Karl Marx had written in *The Eighteenth Brumaire*. (pp. 79-80)

[*L'Education sentimentale*] is likely, if we read it in youth, to prove baffling and even repellent. The title may have given the impression that we are going to get a love story, but the love affairs turn out invariably to be tepid or incomplete, and one finds oneself depressed or annoyed. Is it a satire? The characters are too close to life, and a little too well rounded, for satire. Yet they are not quite vitalized enough, not quite responsive enough, to seem the people of a straight novel. But we find that it sticks in our crop. . . . Flaubert's novel plants deep in our mind an idea which we never quite get rid of: the suspicion that our middle-class society of manufacturers, businessmen and bankers, of people who live on or deal in investments, so far from being redeemed by its culture, has ended by cheapening and invalidating all the departments of culture, political, scientific, artistic and religious, as well as corrupting and weakening the ordinary human relations: love, friendship and loyalty to cause—till the whole civilization seems to dwindle.

But fully to appreciate the book, one must have had time to see something of life and to have acquired a certain interest in social and political dramas as distinct from personal ones. If one rereads it in middle age, one finds that the author's tone no longer seems quite so acrid, that one is listening to a muted symphony of which the varied instrumentation and the pattern, the marked rhythms and the melancholy sonorities, had been hardly perceptible before. There are no hero, no villain, to arouse us, no clowns to entertain us, no scenes to wring our hearts. Yet the effect is deeply moving. It is the tragedy of nobody in particular, but of the poor human race itself reduced to such ineptitude, such cowardice, such commonness, such weak irresolution—arriving, with so many fine notions in its head, so many noble words on its lips, at a failure which is all the more miserable because those who have failed in their roles have even forgotten what roles they were cast for. . . . Though *L'Education sentimentale* is less attractive on the surface and less exciting as a story than *Madame Bovary,* it is certainly the book of Flaubert's which is most ambitiously planned and into which he has tried to put most. And once we have got the clue to the immense and complex drama which unrolls itself behind the half-screen of the detached and monotonous style, we find it as absorbing and satisfying as a great play or a great piece of music. (pp. 81-2)

> *Edmund Wilson, "The Politics of Flaubert," in his* The Triple Thinkers: Twelve Essays on Literary Subjects *(reprinted by permission of Farrar, Straus & Giroux, Inc.; copyright Edmund Wilson 1938, 1948; copyright renewed 1956, 1971 by Edmund Wilson and 1976 by Elena Wilson, executrix of the Estate of Edmund Wilson), revised edition, Oxford University Press, New York, 1948 (and reprinted by Noonday, 1976), pp. 72-87.*

FRANÇOIS MAURIAC   (essay date 1949)

Art substituted for God leads [Flaubert] into dangerous paths as a flouted and despised art could not have done. It is not unintentionally that he makes use of mystical language to paint his life devoted to literary work. Knowingly, he usurps the place of the Infinite Being, not for himself probably, but for that continuation of himself, his work: *Bovary, Salammbô,* his charm and his torment. (pp. 89-90)

Metaphysics, morality, science, what does he not subordinate to esthetics? . . . Flaubert swallows up everything that touches on philosophy, religion, history, mechanics and applied arts, not to learn anything, nor to retain it, were it even a spark of the truth in some field, but to transform this immense acquisition into nightmares and false ideas with which he will stuff the brains of Saint Anthony, Bouvard and Pécuchet! (p. 90)

Doubtless, Bouvard and Pécuchet should not make us forget Charles and Emma Bovary, or Madame Arnoux, or the *Coeur Simple.* Thank Heavens, it was only at the end of his life that Flaubert attained the heights of absurdity. That was because art, his idol, had one important and fortunate exigency: life had to be observed first; this alone was demanded of the artist: to represent reality, what he observed of reality; and, in obedience to this commandment, Flaubert found the secret of his great works. But he only practiced it half-way; a defect in his mentality made him see only the outward appearance of his beings. (p. 91)

The Bourgeois, that *bête noire* which was poisoning his life, interposes itself between his eye and what he is looking at. It does not believe in that part of immortality which his ridiculous heroes contain within themselves. It is almost in spite of him that the soul of Madame Bovary or Madame Arnoux breaks

through sometimes. He thinks he is representing life, and he cuts off everything that does not stir up his nerves. He sees only what excites and nourishes his phobia until, in the excess of his distaste, he turns aside from that horrible world and takes refuge in the evolutions and restoration of abolished races: "Few people will guess how depressed I had to be to undertake to resuscitate Carthage," he writes. "That was a thebaid to which disgust for modern life drove me . . .". For he seems to think sometimes that no trace of all that he loathed in modern man was to be found among the ancients. The author of *Salammbô,* for his own greater happiness, sets up a universe without bourgeoisie, just as Renan, at the same epoch created, out of whole cloth, a Greece of professors and wise men, harmonious and reasonable. These scrupulous historians accumulate documents, and what they finally construct, are myths their own size; they relieve the passions of their souls.

But Flaubert was born clear-sighted and the Greek mirage hardly duped him long. . . . Flaubert, disappointed in the ancients, kept coming back to the bourgeoisie, because his artistic conscience would not give him any rest until he was again resigned to observing life.

Since he could no longer escape the study of the modern Prudhomme, well, he would look the beast in the face; he would take the bull by the horns; that huge bourgeois nonsense would become the subject of his book; he would incarnate it; that would be his masterpiece, he thought. Flaubert creates his nightmare with his own hands. The Bourgeois, under the guise of Bouvard and Pécuchet, sits down to his table, lies down in his bed, fills his days and nights, and ends by taking him by the throat. The Bourgeois has his skin at last; he has literally assassinated Flaubert. (pp. 91-3)

Was it his finical attachment to form that prevented him from "making live"? No, if life does not tremble in his work as in that of a Dostoyefsky or an Eliot, the writer's scruples must not be blamed for it. Doubtless, the anxiety he often betrayed in his letters by this expression "I am going to sit myself down to sentences" . . . helps us understand how dangerous such a work is for the direct expression of a still warm reality. On the other hand, this disadvantage is amply balanced by the composition of Flaubertian pictures, those symphonies in which, by means of art, complex reality is given back to us, and sometimes vibrates as strongly as in any other work spontaneously. But it is rare, very rare when Flaubert does not remain a little to one side of life. We remain outside of the drama he is relating to us. If we never feel pulled along or rolled over by the flow of the novel, if we watch it flow from the banks, we must not look for reasons of an esthetic nature; it is not because the author "sits down to sentences," takes a long time to choose epithets, exercises his mind with assonances. It is on the spiritual plane that the weakness of this art appears to us. (pp. 102-03)

> *François Mauriac, "Gustave Flaubert," in his* Men I Hold Great, *translated by Elsie Pell, originally published as* Mes grands hommes, *Éditions du Rocher, 1949), Philosophical Library, 1951, pp. 85-104.*

RENÉ DUMESNIL   (essay date 1955)

Considering that Flaubert made objectivity the indefeasible rule of his art, and that, throughout his career, he never stopped asserting that only an artist's work, and not his private life, belongs to the public, it may seem paradoxical to claim that his letters constitute his masterpiece. But in the end it is what he tells us about his inner self that we prefer even to those works which caused him the most trouble and suffering; it is the letters he wrote day by day that mean even more to us than the books he accomplished at the cost of so much labour. This is because, familiar and even trivial as they often are, they are so spontaneous, so vivid and idiosyncratic in style, that they are at once an encyclopaedia of literary method and an invaluable guide to living.

Such, it seems to me, are the reasons why we should turn our eyes once more towards the great man of Croisset. . . . [He] is one of those great masters who remain alive by virtue of the advice he can still dispense. And it is certain that that advice is worth following. (p. 570)

> René Dumesnil, "The Inevitability of Flaubert," translated by Edward Sackville-West, in The Golden Horizon, edited by Cyril Connolly (copyright, 1955, by University Books Inc.), University Books, 1955, pp. 562-70.

GEORGES POULET   (essay date 1956)

[Flaubert] is, primordially, a romantic: a romantic not so much for his love of the picturesque, as for the consciousness of an exceptional interior experience. But unlike that of the Romantics, the consciousness of this interior experience does not turn Flaubert in upon himself; it opens his mind to the sun; it turns him outward. Like Diderot, like Gautier, from the moment he makes use of his faculties for literary ends, those faculties which he exercises the most and which dominate all the others are precisely those which direct the mind not toward a knowledge of the self but toward a grasp of the non-self and a representation of the world. . . . (p. 21)

Self-awareness is fully experienced by him in the moment when he emerges from himself to become identified—by the simplest but most intense of the acts of the mental life, perception—with the object, whatever it may be, of this perception. Thus objectivity, far from being an acquired discipline with Flaubert, is a natural state, the only truly natural state of his thought. If it is realized fully only in exceptional instances, that is because ". . . man is so made that each day he can savor only a little nourishment, colors, sounds, feelings, ideas"; but this nourishment, made up in the first place of colors and sounds and secondarily of feelings and ideas, is the sole possible food. It is to it that one must turn for support and subsistence. Life exists, but only where there are colors, sounds, the outdoors, the sun. One must incline toward it, penetrate into it or be penetrated by it, and become what one feels by the very act of feeling. (p. 22)

A spiral, enveloping a thousand diverse images and traversing different zones of the past—such is the recreative synthesis which crowns the operation of memory in Flaubert. It does not consist in drawing upon a repository, in combining elements of different periods, but rather in allowing layers of images to rise in tiers in the mind, each of which keeps the particular form it occupied in time, but, on the other hand, takes color from the reflection of the others. Thus, the consciousness that evokes them appears to itself like a painting in perspective, in the depths of which there appear at unequal intervals with their particular hues—but in a unique ambience (which is the true self)—the phantoms of the past. . . . (pp. 26-7)

[In this manner, Emma in *Madame Bovary*], noticing on a letter from her father a little of the ashes with which he had the habit of drying wet ink, sees her father once more, "bending over

the hearth to pick up the tongs"; then, this first image leading to others, she recalls "summer afternoons full of sunlight"; and step by step, from memory to memory, she follows the course of her life down to the present moment. . . .

One feels that the whole force of this passage (leaving aside the feeling of the attrition of experience, of which more later) relates to the *depth of duration* which it suggests—a depth that is glimpsed through a descending perspective, in which the images are spaced out like milestones, along *the whole length of life*. The first memory is like the top of a slope; from that point there is nothing to do but descend again; and to redescend the slope is to retraverse the whole life, to render visible the very pathway of lived time. . . . (p. 27)

More rarely (for Flaubert's prospective imagination is poor), the same phenomenon is discovered with regard to time to come. . . . (p. 28)

There is in the *Première Éducation sentimentale* a passage that is particularly important because it seems to give us the profound reason for the difference, so visible in Flaubert, between the works of his youth and those of his maturity. This passage begins with a long, morose meditation that one of the characters pursues on the formlessness and dejection of his existence. Then gradually, the thought is transformed into images, and once again the past is put to unrolling a series of memory-pictures. But this time the dominating factor in this succession of images is neither the kind of spontaneous homogeneity which is given to the most disparate things by the current of emotions that carries them along nor, on the reverse side, the feeling of radical heterogeneity which reveals itself in them and between them when the current fails to link them together. This time, on the contrary, it is possible to find there a certain coherence. For the first time one can distinguish not only sensory and imaginative events but also events penetrable by the mind:

> Nevertheless from all that there resulted his present state, and this state was the sum of all those antecedents, one which permitted him to review them; each event had of itself produced a second, every feeling had been fused into an idea. . . . Thus there was a sequence and a continuity to this series of diverse perceptions.

It would be hard to imagine a reflection more ordinary or more commonplace. Nevertheless, it is around this reflection that Flaubert tried to reform a life and a work abandoned of themselves to the power of images. The solution he accepts is the middle solution, it is an option in favor of order—an order, moreover, which is perceived and which perhaps exists only when it is discovered as the order of accomplished facts. For it is discovered only in things that are completed and in the postulate that they are completed by reason of other things which have determined their completion. . . . Thus, the order does not depend on the assumption of any transcendence. It is an adequate relationship between what exists in this moment and what existed in all preceding moments. It is an *a posteriori* construction that the mind imposes upon the universe to make it hold together. Thanks to this formula, there are no more *gaps*, no more intervals between things, nor an abyss between the present and the past. We are in the kingdom of immanence, and of so integral an immanence that everything is representable and implied there. Beyond the chain of causes and effects as they are represented in the mind, there is the supposition that the same chain and the same interactivity of causes and effects persist indefinitely; there is nothing else; no mystery;

nothing veiled or inexpressible. What the imagination cannot revive the mind can represent to itself. (pp. 32-3)

[The] first movement of the Flaubertian reconstruction is the ascending movement by which thought climbs, in a series of inferences, the stairway of causes, and so progressively withdraws from the domain of sensation or of actual images, in order to pass into that of the order of things, into the domain of law. It is a method strictly opposed to that of Balzac, who, starting with an *a priori* creature, posits at the outset the existence of a law-force, of which there remains simply to express next, in terms more and more concrete, the descending curve into real life. Balzac, novelist of the *determining;* Flaubert, novelist of the *determined.*

But precisely by reason of the fact that in Flaubert that which is first given is this *determined* actual, indubitable, and resisting object upon which the representative faculty can rest all its weight, the Flaubertian construction, as high as it may rise, never risks becoming abstract. The law is not a non-temporal thing. It does not exist in itself but in the action by which it is exercised. In proportion as one ascends to it, one gathers up, at each step, the perceptible matter with which the human being has remodified itself in each of the antecedent moments of its duration. Thus the human being is somehow found to exist in two ways: by its sensations, whether immediate or remembered, which form its variable, contingent reality, though in intimate contact with the reality of things; and on the other hand, by the synthetic order that the concatenating series of causes imposes upon its existence. (pp. 34-5)

> Georges Poulet, "Flaubert," *in his* Studies in Human Time *(copyright © 1956 by The Johns Hopkins Press), Johns Hopkins University Press, 1956 (and reprinted in* Flaubert: A Collection of Critical Essays, *edited by Raymond Giraud, Prentice-Hall, Inc., 1964, pp. 21-35).*

RAYMOND GIRAUD (essay date 1957)

In all the nineteenth century there was probably no French writer who invested the word bourgeois with more savage contempt and bitter hatred than Gustave Flaubert. His hostility was not simply a hypertrophied romantic pose, a snobbish sense of identification with the nobility or an aggressive sympathy for the masses. Although Flaubert's romantic beginnings doubtless gave an important initial impetus to his feelings about the bourgeois, he later developed those feelings in an individual way that transformed the tradition that had transmitted them to him. (p. 132)

[In *L'Education sentimentale*] are discernible many of the ambiguities that make Gustave Flaubert's personality and work complex, particularly his representation of his own time and of the contemporary bourgeois. The central character of that novel, Frédéric Moreau, is neither a subjectively drawn Rousseauistic hero nor an impassively observed laboratory specimen. There is much in him that is reminiscent of the youthful Flaubert and his successive incarnations in *Mémoires d'un fou, Novembre* and the first *Education*. . . . But there is much more: The *Education* is not a personal story, but the "moral history" of Flaubert's entire generation; it is his judgment of his time, his condemnation of the entire bourgeois civilization of the late July Monarchy and early Empire, an important document for the study of the evolution of the artist's alienation from society. (p. 140)

Like most of the great novels of the nineteenth century, the *Education* is both a psychological novel and a novel of manners. These two aspects are joined in Frédéric Moreau's love for Marie Arnoux, which is not only a refashioning of Flaubert's own early passion for Elisa Schlesinger but also a symbol of Frédéric's weakness, which in turn is a symptom of the manners of his time. (p. 146)

All the great Flaubert novels—*Madame Bovary, Salammbô,* the *Education*—are love stories, in which the hero's or heroine's love represents a failure to realize the ideal. . . . One may legitimately ask to what extent these stories are "impassively" recounted bourgeois adventures and how much they are reflections or transpositions of Flaubert's own youthful romantic dreams and yearnings. In their composition Flaubert exploited two kinds of sources, the external and the internal, and his characters therefore have two kinds of ambiguities. (p. 147)

Frédéric Moreau is a bourgeois observed partly from within and partly from without. He cannot settle down to any steady productive work or get rid of many of his silly juvenile illusions. He is, however, potentially more noble than many of his friends and certainly on a much higher plane of contemporary bourgeois life than an Homais, a Roque or a Dambreuse. He is capable of an enthusiasm, of a fresh and naïve hunger for beauty and passion—qualities which Flaubert never really condemned. (p. 148)

Frédéric's central role in the *Education* is that of a lover. He falls in love with Mme Arnoux in the first pages of the novel, and this love is maintained as a unifying link throughout the book—which otherwise is very much a succession of vignetted tableaux. . . . There are, in particular, three aspects of Frédéric's manner of loving that seem to relate him intimately with the Flaubert of *Mémoires d'un fou, Novembre* and the first *Education:* These are the linkings-up of love with adultery, with reverie and with money. . . . Frédéric Moreau is neither a despised nor a "realistically" observed contemporary bourgeois; nor is he a totally sympathetic romantic hero; rather he is a hero who is weakened by being both romantic and bourgeois, and a bourgeois who is elevated by being both romantic and a sort of reflection of Flaubert himself. (pp. 151-52)

[One] aspect of Flaubert's dogged retention in later works of the themes, language and action of his juvenilia is Frédéric Moreau's association of dreams of passion with dreams of the Orient. This is already evident in the first chapter of the *Education* when, struck by a sort of romantic *coup de foudre*, Frédéric Moreau falls in love at first sight. Mme Arnoux is immediately put into a colorful and exotic setting, not only in the imagination of the character Frédéric, but by the will of the writer. . . . If Frédéric seems a silly, romantic dreamer, it is partly because Flaubert loaded the dice by creating circumstances especially favorable to his dreams. (p. 157)

In Frédéric's mind's eye the Jardin des Plantes and the Louvre undergo romanticized transformations. The sight of a palm tree suggests the Orient, and Frédéric imagines himself and Mme Arnoux, traveling together, "on the backs of dromedaries, under the canopy of an elephant's howdah, in the cabin of a yacht amidst blue archipelagos, or side by side mounted on two mules that ring bells as they stumble in the grass against the remains of ancient columns." At the Louvre, Frédéric substitutes Mme Arnoux's face for those in the portraits of past centuries, in scenes of the Middle Ages, in the splendid panoramas of ancient Rome, on the cushions of an Arab's harem. (p. 158)

This assemblage of romantic bric-a-brac, of ancient ruins, of the brilliantly colored and heavily perfumed Orient, with its strange and exciting fauna and flora, is not an unsympathetic caricature of the dreams of romantic adolescents. The studied rhythms of these jewel-studded sentences communicate a genuine lyricism and intoxication. The composite imagery, richly appealing to the senses, suggests comparison with the contemporary poetry of Baudelaire, Gautier, Leconte de Lisle and some of Hugo's *Orientales*. What is more, this imaginary voyage is no literary novelty for Flaubert; it is rather, on the contrary, a constant refrain in his work. It even makes its appearance in *Madame Bovary,* at a moment when Flaubert and the reader are warmly sympathetic with the unfortunate Emma, enclosed by ugliness and boredom, and longing for the passion and beauty she knows only from her childhood novels of love. (pp. 158-59)

The decline, sentimental atrophy or "bourgeoisification" of Frédéric Moreau can perhaps be illustrated best by relating his sentimental life to his conception of the kind of bourgeois life he wanted to lead and to the importance he attached to the role of money in that life. Like all the important characters in Flaubert's novels of modern life, Frédéric Moreau is inescapably a nineteenth century bourgeois, even though he is, like Emma Bovary, different from others because of his sensibility and his addiction to romantic dreams. (pp. 161-62)

Frédéric's financial history is an acknowledgement of the essential importance of money to himself and his mother. Money regulates their social relations with neighbors in Nogent; it is necessary for the preservation of an elevated status, to which Frédéric's mother clings, and for the realization of both his and her dreams for their future. To be sure, they are not avaricious or inclined toward the crude accumulation of wealth in the manner of various other bourgeois in Flaubert's novels— Roque, Dambreuse, Homais, Lheureux. These are the men who rise in Flaubert's fictional world and whose energy, aggressiveness and success constitute, shamefully, its major social dynamics. Frédéric Moreau is another kind of man. He has no great taste for making money, no real ambition for a trade, a profession or a career. . . . Soaked, like Emma Bovary, in his romantic dreams, Frédéric thinks of money only when threatened by its loss and faced with the prospect of being toppled from his high style of *rentier* living with all its pleasures, prestige and privileges. (pp. 162-63)

At [the] early stage of Frédéric's youth, wealth symbolizes a way of life, that of the elegant, idling dandy. . . . There is the added complication that this way of life is important to Frédéric mainly as a requirement for his continued courtship of Mme Arnoux. Frédéric does not seek actively to enrich himself; his material well-being is important to him primarily for sentimental reasons. (p. 165)

[In his marriage to Mme Dambreuse] alone, out of all Frédéric's sentimental adventures, is the pursuit of money and of social position unrestrained by the hero's feelings of disgust, guilt or contempt for his own behavior and untempered by the admixture of other motives and considerations that might evoke some sympathy from the reader. Once again, it is true, he delivers himself to his habit of dreaming. But this time, both the setting and the substance of his dreams are unsympathetic and revolting. (p. 168)

Although invested with none of the solitary greatness of the poet or even with the honorable and respectable dignity of a Larivière, Frédéric is, nevertheless, far from being a bourgeois

villain, and is less of a mediocrity than an Arnoux, a Charles Bovary or a Martinon. Like Emma Bovary, he is partially redeemed from total mediocrity by his sensibility and the idealism of his youthful desires. . . . Though by no means represented with total sympathy by Flaubert, Frédéric seems distinguished and, in a negative way, even moderately "heroic," in contrast with the more savagely hated bourgeois, Roque, Lheureux and Homais. (pp. 169-70)

Of all the characters in Flaubert's novels of modern life, Homais, Lheureux and Roque, and perhaps Bournisien, are the most outstanding symbols of what Flaubert hated and meant most by the word bourgeois. . . . They stand for the new world in which the moral sense is on the wane and in which meanness and mediocrity are triumphing; they are the bourgeois who are coming into possession of the present and are to inherit the future. (p. 174)

Flaubert's exaggerated and almost caricatural disgust for the humanity of the Second Empire is related to a general pessimism, a generally negative attitude toward life. . . . It seemed to him—and he was perhaps not wholly wrong—that mankind was coming to be governed by its lowest common denominator. Moreover, as the son of a scientist who had come into close contact with the medical realities of death, and as a representative of an era in which science was rapidly becoming immensely important, he was compelled to reject the concept of an anthropocentric universe and to view man in his true material proportions. (pp. 175-76)

> *Raymond Giraud, "Gustavus Flaubertus Bourgeoisophobus," in his* The Unheroic Hero in the Novels of Stendhal, Balzac and Flaubert *(copyright © 1957 by Rutgers, The State University; reprinted by permission of Rutgers University Press), Rutgers University Press, 1957, pp. 132-84.*

B. F. BART (essay date 1958)

Flaubert did not think of himself as an innovator or a revolutionary; rather he considered that he was a traditionalist. He is indeed one of the masters who moved the great line of western literature a step forward by a real return to the problem of Form. He was a classicist in the sense that he was in the Tradition, and he knew it. He was deeply irritated by those who set up little schools of the Beautiful—romantic, realistic, or classical for that matter: there was for him only one Beautiful, with varying aspects. . . . (p. 206)

To call Flaubert a realist (as opposed to noting realistic elements in his work) is to confuse the issue seriously. It was not, he felt, a good method to look at something and then go write about it; its essence had to be digested first. . . . Twenty-five years after writing the *Bovary,* Flaubert was still struggling to make himself understood, insisting that though he had always been incredibly scrupulous about reading all relevant documents and books, amassing all possible information and travelling wherever necessary, still he regarded all of this as secondary and inferior. So-called material reality should, he stated, never be more than a pattern used to mount higher. . . . Art completes reality; it does not reproduce it. And this doctrine is not and cannot be called realism.

Flaubert is not a realist, nor is he a romantic; nor, for that matter, is he a naturalist or a symbolist. He sought rather to include all of these partial views of life and of Art in a larger synthesis, the Beautiful. He was preoccupied with the basic problem of the great writers of all ages, life itself: what meaning it has, what its parts really are, and (lastly) how they may be portrayed so as to display life's meaning. (pp. 206-07)

The question of Flaubert's view of life, the meaning he attached to it and, hence, to his book, remains to be examined. . . . What was it that he had to say? What meanings did he discover and then display with such excellence? If a work is to reach the summits and take its place on the shelf, the very small shelf, of truly world literature, its form and its content, the what as well as the how, must both be superlative and must both fuse wholly into a totality which will speak cogently to later ages. *Madame Bovary* is good enough so that one may, without absurdity, ask whether it belongs on this select shelf. . . .

Flaubert's book had a point, and he knew it: "il découle de ce roman un enseignement clair. . ." [from this novel springs a clear message]. He went on, however, to say that it was a matter of perfect indifference to him and that style alone mattered. . . . But can it properly be a matter of indifference to the rest of us, his readers, who are not writers and for whom style is therefore less important? For my own part, I must answer "No," and must further urge that Flaubert himself in his better moments knew his assertion was an exaggeration.

If, then, we ask what the message of the book is, I think we must answer that it is one of distilled hatred and disgust, for romanticism, for the bourgeois, for provincial life, for orthodox religion: for nearly everything portrayed. Some parts of the book, some paragraphs or even short episodes show Flaubert as serene as he felt the masters had been, reaching beyond the exasperation and disillusionment which are the price of wisdom, to that calm which he knew was necessary to Art. It is these moments which produced the great pages, the scene by moonlight as Emma and Rodolphe plan their trip, the Catherine Leroux episode, Doctor Larivière's visit, the death of Charles, and a host of others.

Flaubert can, upon occasion, rise to the real heights of the great western tradition. Few books can ever do so, and it is great praise to say that some pages of his book do. But its essential message and its normal level are perhaps less than that. . . . (p. 208)

It is Flaubert's reiterated contention in his letters that life is hateful, farcical, grotesque; that it consists of ignominy and stupidity. . . . Like Baudelaire, Flaubert sees the evil in life; but unlike the poet, he does not see anything else. His is a limited view.

This is the burden of *Madame Bovary* as well. (pp. 208-09)

I am aware that life may be viewed as having no more significance than Flaubert attaches to it; I am aware of the pervasiveness now-a-days of the doctrine of irony, which Flaubert upheld truculently. But I do believe that, upon examination, the really great books of the western tradition counsel the understanding of life and urge terms in which it may be accepted. They go beyond the bitter taste of irony to some form of love. (p. 209)

> *B. F. Bart, "'Madame Bovary' after a Century," in The French Review (copyright 1958 by the American Association of Teachers of French), Vol. XXXI, No. 3, January, 1958, pp. 203-10.*

GEORG LUKÁCS (essay date 1962)

Flaubert's *Salammbô* is the great representative work of [a] phase of development in the historical novel. It combines all the high artistic qualities of Flaubert's style. Stylistically, it is the paradigm of Flaubert's artistic aims; which is why it shows so much more clearly than the writings of the mediocre and untalented writers of this period the unresolved contradictions, the irremovable inner "problematic" of the new historical novel.

Flaubert formulated his aims programmatically. He says that he wished to apply the procedure and method of the modern novel to antiquity. (p. 141)

Flaubert set himself a consistent programme: to reawaken a vanished world of no concern to us. It was precisely because of his deep hatred for modern society that he sought, passionately and paradoxically, a world which would in no way resemble it, which would have no connection with it, direct or indirect. (p. 143)

Flaubert wishes to portray this world realistically, using the artistic means which he himself had discovered a few years earlier for *Madame Bovary* and there brought to perfection. But now it is not the grey everyday reality of French provincial life to which this realism of minutely observed and exactly described detail is to be applied; instead it is the alien and distant, incomprehensible but picturesque, decorative, grandiose, gorgeous, cruel and exotic world of Carthage which is to arise before us. This explains Flaubert's desperate struggle to evoke a graphic picture of old Carthage by means of exact study and exact production of archaeological detail. (pp. 143-44)

[What] can a world thus re-awakened mean to us? Granted that Flaubert successfully solved all the problems which he raised artistically—has a world so represented any real living significance for us? Flaubert's paradoxes with regard to subjects which do not concern us, and which are artistic because they do not concern us, are very characteristic of the author's moods, but they also have their objective aesthetic consequences which are already known to us. (p. 144)

He chooses an historical subject whose inner social-historical nature is of no concern to him and to which he can only lend the appearance of reality in an external, decorative, picturesque manner by means of the conscientious application of archaeology. But at some point he is forced to establish a contact with both himself and the reader, and this he does by modernizing the psychology of his characters. The proud and bitter paradox which contends that the novel has nothing at all to do with the present, is simply a defensive paradox contending against the trivialities of his age. . . . *Salammbô* was more than just an artistic experiment. It is for this reason that the modernization of the characters acquires central importance; it is the only source of movement and life in this frozen, lunar landscape of archaeological precision.

Naturally it is a ghostly illusion of life. And an illusion which dissolves the hyper-objective reality of the objects. In describing the individual objects of an historical *milieu* Flaubert is much more exact and plastic than any other writer before him. But these objects have nothing to do with the inner life of the characters. . . . [In Flaubert there is no] connection between the outside world and the psychology of the principal characters. And the effect of this lack of connection is to degrade the archaeological exactness of the outer world: it becomes a world of historically exact *costumes and decorations*, no more than a pictorial frame within which a purely modern story is unfolded. (pp. 146-47)

[The] effect of Salammbô herself was to provide a heightened image, a decorative symbol, of the hysterical longings and torments of middle-class girls in large cities. History simply provided a decorative, monumental setting for this hysteria, which in the present spends itself in petty and ugly scenes, and which thus acquired a tragic aura quite out of keeping with its real character. The effect is powerful but it shows that Flaubert, because of his embitterment with the shallow prose of his time, had become objectively untruthful and distorted the real proportions of life. The artistic superiority of his bourgeois novels lies precisely in the fact that in them the proportions between emotion and event, between desire and its translation into deeds, correspond to the real, social-historical character of emotion and desire. In *Salammbô* the emotions, in themselves quite unmonumental, are falsely and distortedly monumentalized and hence inwardly unequal to such artistic heightening. (p. 147)

[The basis of the plot] is formed by two motifs which are only very externally connected: a "crown and state" conflict between Carthage and the rebellious mercenaries, and the love episode of Salammbô herself. Their involvement with one another is quite external and inevitably remains so. Salammbô is as much a stranger to the interests of her homeland, to the life-and-death struggle of her native city, as Madame Bovary is to the medical practice of her husband. But while in the bourgeois novel this indifference can be made the vehicle of a plot with Emma Bovary at the centre precisely because she is a stranger to provincial daily life, here instead we have a "crown and state" story, outwardly grandiose and requiring therefore extensive preparation, with which Salammbô's destiny has no organic connection. The links are all either pure accidents or external pretexts. But in the presentation of the story the external pretext must inevitably suppress and stifle the main theme. External occasions take up the major part of the novel; the main theme is reduced to a small episode.

This lack of relation between the human tragedy, which is what kindles the reader's interest, and the political action clearly shows the change already undergone by historical feeling in this age. The political plot is not only lifeless because it is cluttered up with descriptions of inessential objects, but because it has no discernible connection with any concrete form of popular life that we may experience. (p. 148)

[With *Salammbô* we] see the sharp opposition between the old and the new representation of history. The writers of the classical period of the historical novel were only interested in the cruel and terrible happenings of previous history insofar as they were necessary expressions of definite forms of class struggle . . . and also because they gave birth of a similar necessity to great human passions and conflicts. . . Flaubert begins a development where the inhumanity of subject-matter and presentation, where atrocity and brutality become ends in themselves. These features acquire their central position owing to the weak presentation of what is the chief issue—the social development of man; indeed for the same reason they assume even more importance than even this position warrants. Since real greatness is everywhere replaced by extensiveness—the decorative splendour of the contrasts replaces the social-human connections—inhumanity, cruelty, atrocity and brutality become substitutes for the lost greatness of real history. (p. 151)

[In both his historical novels and his pictures of modern society], hatred and disgust for the pettiness, triviality and meanness of modern bourgeois life are expressed with equal force, yet very differently in keeping with the difference of subject-matter. In his contemporary novels Flaubert concentrates his ironic attack on the portrayal of everyday bourgeois life and average bourgeois man. As an outstanding realist artist he thus achieves an infinitely nuanced picture of that dismal greyness which is a real aspect of this everyday life. Precisely his naturalist tendencies restrain Flaubert from any eccentricity in his treatment of the inhuman forms of capitalist life. But [in] his historical novel . . . he considered a liberation from the fetters of this monotonous flatness. All that his naturalist conscience had forced him to renounce in his picture of contemporary reality found a place here. In terms of form—the colourfulness, the decorative monumentality of an exotic *milieu;* in terms of content—eccentric passions in their fullest extent and uniqueness. And it is here that we clearly see the social, moral and ideological limitations of this great and sincere artist: while he sincerely hates the capitalist present, his hatred has no roots in the great popular and democratic traditions either of the past or present and therefore has no future perspective. His hatred does not historically transcend its object. Thus if, in the historical novels the suppressed passions break open their fetters, it is the eccentric-individualist side of capitalist man which comes to the fore, that inhumanity which everyday life hypocritically seeks to conceal and subdue. (pp. 152-53)

> *Georg Lukács, " 'Salammbô'," in his* The Historical Novel, *translated by Hannah Mitchell and Stanley Mitchell (copyright © 1962 by Merlin Press, Ltd.; reprinted by permission of Merlin Press, Ltd.), Merlin Press, 1962 (and reprinted in* Flaubert: A Collection of Critical Essays, *edited by Raymond Giraud, Prentice-Hall, Inc., 1964, pp. 141-53).*

ENID STARKIE   (essay date 1964)

A novel, with Flaubert, is as strictly composed as a five-act play, with all the pieces fitting into a pre-ordained scheme, which possesses the inevitability and balance of an architectural plan. (p. 123)

[He] wished to write for eternity, not to record the ephemeral. . . . *Madame Bovary* can be read today, more than a century after it was published, as readily as when it was written, with no historical effort, no trying to imagine the problems of that time, since the problems it studies are still ours today. Flaubert has chosen to depict the characteristics which do not alter from generation to generation, which are eternal and do not belong to one country or locality. . . . *Madame Bovary* is a classic which is read not only for its artistic excellence, not only because it represents its age, but also on account of the universal nature of its wisdom, because it is an eternal criticism of human life and destiny. (p. 124)

Flaubert has not given a picture of provincial life, but he has conveyed its essence, which is as true today as it was when the book was published, omitting the trivial outside details which would make it of one place and of one time, all things which date so soon. (p. 133)

[Flaubert] believed in fatality, but saw each man's character as his fatality, which he must learn to know. This did not preclude a belief in free will. As I see it, Flaubert considered fatality, or character, as the chain which binds the dog to his kennel. The dog is at liberty to move as he likes, or not to move at all, but he can only move to the length of his chain, and he must learn to take that into account. Bouvard and Pécuchet, in the posthumous novel of that title, embark on many intellectual pursuits for which they are totally unsuited by education, training, and practice. However, in the end, they know this, they learn wisdom and realize that all they are suited for is copying and they return to their former humble occupation. I believe that this is intentional with Flaubert.

In this method of characterization, Flaubert differs from his forerunner Balzac. Balzac was a physiognomist who believed that every inner quality is mirrored on the outward countenance, so that it was sufficient to give an exact picture of a person to convey his personality. . . . [It] is the behaviour of his characters that Balzac deals with rather than with their inner personalities. Flaubert, on the contrary, hardly considers outer characteristics at all. We see Emma as Charles saw her—little more than her hair, her cloud of dark hair, and her carefully tended hands, useless hands which amazed him after the work-worn hands he was used to in other women, and they became symbolical for him of her deepest quality. Her clothes also are described in the vaguest terms, and we apprehend their essence rather than their reality. (pp. 136-37)

Emma is an eternal type—not of any age—self-centred, thinking only of herself and of what is due to her femininity. . . . All through the ages women have used fiction as an escape from reality, but few have tried to live it really. Emma tried to turn her life into a novelette and that was her ruin. Although she is stupid she is a complicated character. She is vulgar, lazy, and vain—indeed one could make a whole catalogue of her deficiencies—nevertheless she has something which raises her above material considerations which arouses sympathy. Her dreams were great even if their quality was shoddy. Flaubert says that a soul is to be measured by the extent of its desires. Emma had all the dreams of a romantic heroine, but in vulgar taste and poor quality. (p. 137)

Although Emma is the main character, Charles is also drawn very fully, and indeed is essential for the complete unfolding of her character. It is not accidentally that the novel begins and ends with him. . . .

Charles may be the epitome of all the bourgeois characteristics which Flaubert abhorred—indeed his character is mercilessly described—nevertheless he is not wholly commonplace, and he possessed that quality, possessed by all Flaubert's characters, of having dreams beyond his powers of attainment. What raised him above the ordinary was his love for Emma. She is his exoticism, his romantic dream, the woman least suited to be his wife, but, without her, he would have sunk into total materialism. (p. 138)

The main characters are created in the round and are treated with compassion and little trace of irony. The secondary characters are drawn largely from the outside and with more than a touch of irony. There is Rodolphe at the agricultural show, beginning his campaign of seduction of Emma, as he utters all the emotional platitudes which the expert seducer has used since the beginning of time, and which the women have always believed. . . . There is Léon, with his literary pretensions, repeating the Lamartinian clichés of Romanticism. . . .

The minor characters—the chemist Homais and the parish priest Bournisien—are depicted through the external method of Balzac, and tend to be caricatures. . . . [Homais] is brilliantly drawn in an external way, but it seems to me that, in Father Bournisien, Flaubert has given a rare example of a psychological cliché, and that he is created from his author's anti-clerical prejudices. This is very unusual with Flaubert who believed that the author should not take sides, but should be in the midst of his creation, like God in his, all present but invisible. (p. 139)

Flaubert's novels are not read merely for pleasure, nor are they studied only as works of art. They are read for the wisdom they contain, and for what is learnt from them about human life and destiny. Flaubert had reflected a great deal about life and he wished to arrange his deductions and conclusions in a certain pattern to make them permanent. Instead of putting the result of his meditations in abstract form, he created living characters who revealed his conclusions.

He had a pessimistic view of life and he considered that those who were gross, insensitive, and self-interested generally prospered in life and were in control at the final curtain. In our moments of depression we are inclined to agree with this, nevertheless it is not a realistic view of life, and it is not universal experience that the Homais are always triumphant. Flaubert seemed incapable of believing that anyone of complexity and subtlety could possibly be worthy of admiration. . . . [Goodness] is found only in the simple and inarticulate—like Justin, or the peasant woman Catherine Leroux, or Félicité in the tale *Un Coeur simple*. (pp. 141-42)

Though he had a low view of life and human nature, Flaubert had great tenderness for the victims of Fate, great compassionate understanding. I think of little Justin, the chemist's assistant, who had loved Emma in his boy's way and who, when the whole town was asleep, went to weep on her grave. There is also the scene where Charles weeps beside the body of his wife, laid out in her wedding dress ready for burial. . . . It was no insensitive man who wrote these passages, nor one who was merciless or cynical. In all Flaubert's work there is pity for the wretched human creature, for his dreams, his weaknesses, and his failures. Life was a poor thing for Flaubert, but he himself had a powerful opiate to make bearable the painful operation of living, and that was his art. On that he lavished infinite devotion and care. Life existed only as material to be sacrificed to this insatiable God. (pp. 142-43)

> *Enid Starkie, "Flaubert and 'Madame Bovary'" (originally a lecture delivered at the Royal Society of Literature on March 19, 1964), in* Essays by Divers Hands, *Vol. XXXIII, edited by Richard Church (reprinted by permission of Oxford University Press), Oxford University Press, London, 1965, pp. 123-44.*

MARY McCARTHY (essay date 1964)

Madame Bovary is often called the first modern novel, and this is true, not because of any technical innovations Flaubert made (his counterpoint, his *style indirect libre*) but because it is the first novel to deal with what is now called mass culture. Emma did not have television, and Félicité did not read comic books in the kitchen, but the phenomenon of seepage from the "media" was already present in every Yonville l'Abbaye, and Flaubert was the first to note it.

Mass culture in *Madame Bovary* means the circulating library and the *Fanal de Rouen* and the cactus plants Léon and Emma tend at opposite windows, having read about them in a novel that has made cactuses all the rage. It means poor Charles' phrenological head—a thoughtful attention paid him by Léon—and the pious reading matter the curé gives Emma as a substitute for "bad" books. (pp. 86-7)

In Emma's day, mass-produced culture had not yet reached the masses; it was still a bourgeois affair and mixed up, characteristically, with a notion of taste and discrimination—a notion that persists in advertising. Rodolphe in his château would be a perfect photographic model for whiskey or tobacco. Emma's ''tragedy'' from her own point of view is her lack of purchasing power, and a critical observer might say that the notary's dining-room [which Emma envies in her last hours of life] simply spelled out the word ''money'' to her. Yet it is not as simple as that; if it were, Emma's head would be set straighter on her shoulders. What has happened to her and her spiritual sisters is that simulated-oak wallpaper has become itself a kind of money inexpressible in terms of its actual cost per roll. Worse, ideas and sentiments, like wallpaper, have become a kind of money too and they share with money the quality of abstractness, which allows them to be exchanged. It is their use as coins that has made them trite—worn and rubbed—and at the same time indistinguishable from each other except in terms of currency fluctuation. (pp. 87-8)

A meeting between strangers in *Madame Bovary* inevitably produces a golden shower of platitudes. This shower of platitudes is as mechanical as the droning action of the tax collector's lathe. It appears to be beyond human control; no one is responsible and no one can stop it. There is a terrible scene in the middle of the novel where Emma appeals to God, in the person of the curé, to put an end to the repetitive meaninglessness of her life. God is preoccupied and inattentive, and as she moves away from the church, she hears the village boys reciting their catechism. ''What is a Christian?'' ''He who being baptized . . . baptized . . . baptized. . . .'' The answer is lost in an echo that reverberates emptily through the village. Yet the question, although intoned by rote, is a genuine one—the fundamental question of the book—for a Christian means simply a soul here. It is Emma's demand—''What am I?''—coming back at her in ontological form, and there is no reply.

If this were all, *Madame Bovary* would be a nihilistic satire or howl of despair emanating from the novelist's study. But there *is* a sort of tongue-tied answer. That is Charles Bovary. Without Charles, Emma would be the moral void that her fatuous conversation and actions disclose. Charles, in a novelistic sense, is her redeemer. To her husband, she is sacred, and this profound and simple emotion is contagious.

He is stupid, a peasant, as she calls him, almost a devoted animal, clumsy, a dupe. . . . He has no imagination, Emma thinks, no ''soul.'' (pp. 88-9)

Yet this provincial, this philistine is the only real romantic in the novel—he and the boy Justin, Monsieur Homais' downtrodden apprentice, who dreams over Emma's fichus and underdrawers while Félicité irons in the kitchen. These two, the man and the boy, despised and rejected, are capable of ''eternal love.'' . . . [Charles] is a person of the utmost delicacy of feeling. If he is easy to deceive, it is because his mind is pure. It never enters his head that Emma can be anything but good. (pp. 89-90)

Charles is the hero of the book that, characteristically for him, bears someone else's name. *Madame Bovary* starts with his appearance among his jeering schoolfellows and ends with his death. Charles is docile. It does not occur to him to rebel. . . . He did not choose to be a doctor; he did not choose his name; he did not choose the widow. The only thing in life he chooses is Emma. She is his first and last piece of self-expression. Or not quite the last. When she is taken away from him, his reverence and gratitude to the universe turn to blasphemy. ''I hate your God!'' he bursts out to the curé, who is trying to console him with commonplaces. ''Still the spirit of rebellion,'' the priest answers, with an ecclesiastical sigh.

Now at first glance this appears to be an irony, since Charles has never rebelled until that moment against anything, let alone

God. But Flaubert's ironies are deceptive, and what sounds like an irony is often the simple truth, making a double irony. The priest is right. From the very beginning, Charles has been an obstinate example of passive resistance to the forces of the time and the milieu. A proof of this is that, in all his days, he pronounces only one platitude. His love for Emma is the deepest sign of that obstination. He loves her in the teeth of circumstance, opinion, prudent self-interest, in the teeth even of Emma herself.

This passive resistance of Charles', taking the form of a love of beauty, seems to come from nowhere. . . . No program for human improvement could be predicated on Charles' mute revolt against organized society. He is a sheer accident, nothing less than a placid miracle occurring among the notaries and tradesmen, the dyers and spinners of the textile city of Rouen, where he hankers, uncomplaining, for his country home, which was no arcadia either. He is a revelation, and at the same time his whole effort is to escape notice, to hide in his fleshly envelope like an animal in its burrow. Moreover, his goodness (for that is what it amounts to) has no practical utility and will leave no trace behind it. As a husband, he is a social handicap to Emma, and his mild deference probably contributes to her downfall. . . . Was he drawn from life? . . . All that can be said is that Charles Bovary, wherever he came from, dawning in a vision or patiently constructed out of treasured bits and pieces of reality, was cherished by his creator as a stubborn possibility that cannot be ruled out even from a pessimistic view of the march of events. (pp. 92-4)

Mary McCarthy, ''On 'Madame Bovary','' in her The Writing on the Wall and Other Literary Essays (© 1964 by Mary McCarthy; reprinted by permission of Harcourt Brace Jovanovich, Inc.), Harcourt, 1964, pp. 72-94.

VICTOR BROMBERT (essay date 1966)

Literary history has rendered Flaubert a poor service by indiscriminately linking his name with theories of realism and by presenting him to posterity as the founder, chief practitioner and high priest of a literary school. (p. 3)

[He] did not wish to be associated with any group, least of all with writers for whom literature was not the loftiest of exercises, and whom he suspected of cultivating sensationalism. . . . [It] was not merely the polemical noise made by the Realists and the Naturalists which he found unpalatable. It was a perspective on art with which Flaubert, out of the depths of his artistic convictions, could not possibly sympathize. If he held one consistent belief, it was indeed the priority of Art over life. (pp. 3-4)

There is another, more ambiguous reason behind Flaubert's violent reactions to the word and concept of realism: his hatred of reality. The very subject of *Madame Bovary*, and of so many of his works, is of course drawn from everyday life. But Flaubert never ceased proclaiming his abhorrence for these subjects, his nauseous contempt for the ''ignoble reality'' he forced himself to depict, partly out of self-imposed therapy to cure himself of his chronic idealism, partly also out of a strange and almost morbid fascination. . . . Flaubert always considered that the highest and purest pleasure of literature is its power to liberate those who practice it from the contingencies of life. Art was for him quite literally an escape. Its superiority over life was precisely its ability to transcend the conditions of living. For hatred of reality was in the case of Flaubert intimately bound up with an inherent pessimism; and pessimism in turn was one of the prime conditions of his ceaseless quest for ideal forms. (pp. 4-5)

His earliest works, such as *Smarh* or the autobiographical *Mémoires d'un fou* and *Novembre,* are clearly influenced by his exposure to the most extreme manifestations of Romanticism. (p. 7)

[Side] by side with the so-called realist whom he most often evinces, there appears another, perhaps more authentic Flaubert endowed with an irreducible faith in the evocative witchcraft of imagination or its substitute, memory. If Flaubert the realist exists, so does Flaubert the escapist, and even Flaubert the mystic. (p. 9)

An explosive exuberance, a permanent obsession with the formless and even the monstrous, underlie and determine the patterns of his imagination. . . . This taste for profusion, this fascination with elemental forces, repeatedly impelled him to stretch his fantasy to the very limits of the human. Horror, cruelty, dreams of destruction are permanent features of his most revealing texts, and are most often related to exotic yearnings. For exoticism, with Flaubert, marks the temptation of violence and disorder. (p. 11)

But above all, the exotic motifs which occur repeatedly in Flaubert's works—even when the setting is a village in Normandy—point to recurrent dreams of sexual frenzy and uninhibited orgies. . . . Often the exotic lyricism of the senses becomes more turbulent, and corresponds to imaginary orgies of violence and the most exacerbated sadism. In *Salammbô* and in the three versions of *La Tentation de saint Antoine,* Flaubert surrenders with immense relish to the goriest and most detailed visions of tortures, rapes, disembowelments, diseases and mutilations.

Flaubert's evocations of carnality and of orgiastic violence are, however, closely bound up with an unmedicable sense of sadness and futility. . . . [He] was obsessed by a very personal, almost unconscious association between lascivious and ascetic images. The silhouettes of streetwalkers in the rain are revealingly linked in his mind with fleeting evocations of monastic figures. . . . Marie, the prostitute-heroine of *Novembre,* embodies simultaneously an immense appetite for life and a desperate awareness of the tragedy of human desire precisely because desire, by its very nature, implies a yearning for that which is beyond reach, for that which cannot be possessed. It is in this sense that Marie—the prostitute—can paradoxically speak of her essential virginity. (pp. 12-13)

Flaubert is painfully aware, almost to a pathological degree, not only of death around him, but of the "necropolis" he carries within himself. Flaubert's pessimism, comparable in intensity to that of a Pascal, a Leopardi or a Schopenhauer, constitutes in itself a powerful poetic inspiration. In its extreme form, however, it can lead to dreams of self-annihilation. (p. 17)

Throughout his life he remained fascinated by medical lore, especially by descriptions of horrible maladies and infirmities. . . . It is "nature" itself which Flaubert the pessimist abhorred.

His is, however, not a negative, but a resilient pessimism. Flaubert finds inspiration in his very obsession with decay. He views the artist as an alchemist who creates beauty out of the very impurity of life. (p. 18)

In their intrinsic human and artistic interest, [Flaubert's] letters provide indeed invaluable insights into [his] literary temperament. Often preserving the rough vigor of the spoken sentence, they are at the same time familiar and yet elevated in spirit. They reflect a double Flaubertian requirement: friendships and intellectual contacts, but also the satisfactions of distance, independence and the dignity of isolation. Writing from his study in Croisset, Flaubert could at the same time feel very close and even intimate, and still protect his inner resources and the loftiness of his artistic dreams. There is much to commend these letters on the strictly human level: spontaneity, movement, a grouchy vivaciousness, pride and tenderness, and always a touching allegiance to his friends and to his ideals. But there is also far more.

The *Correspondance* is in fact one of the most moving documents concerning the anguish and problems of the literary artist. Flaubert is no doubt the first writer in France to display a systematic concern for the possibilities, technical difficulties, challenges and criteria of the novel as a dignified and important artistic genre. This was a new concern. (p. 19)

Flaubert was convinced that the novel had its laws which remained to be discovered, propounded and applied. He was convinced that steady meditation on the subject had endowed him with a clearer vision than anyone had ever had of the potentialities and of the limits of fiction. . . . One may smile at some of the more naïve claims in favor of a scientifically precise prose. The fact remains that Flaubert submits to an exacting apprenticeship, and that he imposes on himself a truly ascetic discipline. Did he not compare himself once to a pianist who practices with lead weights on every finger? As for his capacity to observe himself in the very act of composing, it reveals an almost clinical self-control. (pp. 19-20)

Flaubert knew that it was not the subject that mattered; that a novel, just as a poem, has its inner validity and logic, and that only the appropriate use of language and rhythm can provide the texture and the structure which alone make up literary beauty. Hence the corollary that "there do not exist in literature any beautiful artistic subjects" and the paradoxical belief that "beautiful" subjects could even be dangerous since they did not force upon the artist the realization that beauty in art can come only from his own *artistic* efforts. Style is thus more than a technical device or virtuosity; it represents the very vision of the novelist. (pp. 20-1)

[Flaubert] was convinced that private passions hampered, limited and falsified artistic creativity. Personal "emotions" were too close to nature, too unrefined, too despotic. . . . [Sensitivity] does not make the artist, just as passion does not make poetry. But there is also a serious dose of pessimism in this lesson of impersonality. The God-like perspective may well be a form of escapism. It implies a human condition for which there exists no adequate human compassion. (p. 22)

Flaubert's ideal of impersonality is really one of a majestic and quasi-universal mimesis: the artist's mind must, he feels, be as vast as the ocean, and the shores should be well out of sight. Flaubert's yearning for total experiences, his passionate dreams of the inaccessible are at the very heart of his theoretical pronouncements. (p. 23)

No survey of Flaubert's literary temperament as it reveals itself outside of his major novels can afford to neglect the rich mine of early texts, many of which have been collected under the title *Oeuvres de jeunesse inédites.* (p. 25)

If one looks closely at Flaubert's earliest works, those conceived between his fifteenth and his twenty-first years, one is struck indeed by a continuity of motifs and a recurrence of themes which help to understand the underlying unity of novels as dissimilar in appearance as *Madame Bovary, Salammbô* and *Bouvard et Pécuchet.* The patterns of his early fictional imagination, though influenced no doubt by current literary fashions, closely parallel the more permanent traits revealed in his correspondence: a taste for violent eroticism, an obsession with death, a metaphysical pessimism, an almost pathological attraction to decay and to the notion of nothingness, a blasphemous posture in the face of the very conditions of existence.

The erotic strains may at first seem like typical manifestations of adolescent ardor. Thus, in *Un Parfum à sentir,* the young Gustave composes dithyrambic lines in praise of women's breasts ("Oh! la gorge d'une femme . . ."). His voluptuous daydreams further find their habitual expression in exotic longings. M. Ohmlin, in *Rage et impuissance,* evokes the sensuous climate of the "Orient," and in particular the "brown, olive-colored skin of Asiatic women." Similarly, in the largely autobiographic *Mémoires d'un fou,* the seventeen-year-old author yearns for "quelque femme à la peau brune, au regard ardent. . . ." But sensuality and exoticism soon take on a more somber note. The very same passage leads to a vision of Roman debauches and to collective wallowings in orgies. Neronic images thus haunt Flaubert long before *La Tentation de saint Antoine, Salammbô* and *Hérodias.* (pp. 28-9)

The text most suggestive of the Romantic heredity, but also most personally revealing, is *Novembre.* . . . [It] is a true repertory of Romantic motifs: the antitheses of cynicism and tenderness, of enthusiasm and despondency; the cult of memories; the usual dose of algolagnia; hackneyed elegiac and lyric images (autumnal leaves, empty barrels, the echo of lost chords, evocative ruins, proud eagles); rhetorical questions on the meaning of life; a sense of ennui and tragic dissatisfaction; the suicidal urge coupled with a yearning for escape; the solipsistic veneration for one's own suffering. But it is also an intense, spiritual self-portrait of an adolescent, and as such it is a remarkably powerful text. (pp. 31-2)

Sexuality, in this early work, is already very profoundly linked to the dream of the impossible. Love thus assumes a dual value, symbolized by the dual reality of Marie (prostitute and idealized creature) as well as by the inner scission or *dédoublement* of the narrator. . . . (p. 32)

Sex and the modes of failure bear an intimate association in the Flaubertian vision. *Novembre* stresses a sense of premature fatigue which carries the incipient threat of paralysis. An inconsolable sadness accompanies the first manifestations of sensuality, finding its logical expression in the funereal embraces of Marie, and later in the "lugubrious" love-making of Emma Bovary. *Novembre* already provides the two key themes by means of which Flaubert transmutes eroticism into an ideal, impossible and absolute quest. The first is the theme of adultery. . . . The other theme is that of the double image of Marie, lascivious whore and pure virgin. . . . The paradox points to the lasting dream of lost innocence, which, in *L'Éducation sentimentale,* is so powerfully linked to defeat and degradation by means of a complex series of "prostitution" images. (p. 33)

Flaubert's patient weaving of images into elaborate patterns testifies to the supreme importance of larger motifs in his work. The stylistic prowess of the craftsman and artificer is rarely gratuitous. Whether it be the contrapuntal handling of tenses, the exploitation of the resources of free indirect discourse, or the artful marshalling of a massive yet supple prose, the results usually transcend the immediate effect. Style and form convey some of Flaubert's most haunting moods: immersion into an oppressive world of unassimilated phenomena; exposure to the mental landscapes of indefinite flow and destructive immobility; a stubborn yearning for precisely that which language cannot formulate. Gloom and weariness here nourish a latent idealism. Flaubert's pessimism feeds his poetic vision.

Neither heroes nor plots determine the meaning of Flaubert's fiction. Among the truly modern features of his work there is not only the steady perception of the eventlessness of events, and the ability to transmute triviality into a destiny, but the example of a novelistic construction in which the very characters and even the author's point of view are subservient to thematic developments. (p. 282)

Flaubert is a haunted writer. His so-called clinical and realistic approach, in works such as *Madame Bovary* and *L'Éducation sentimentale,* is intimately connected—not as a banal reaction, but as a tragic poetry of frustration and incipient idealism—to the agitated dreams which make up the substance of *La Tentation de saint Antoine* and, in a grotesque mode, of *Bouvard et Pécuchet.* Flaubert's achievement as a literary artist, and his relevance in historical terms, is largely due to a subtly intuited parallelism between his private obsessions and the social and intellectual tensions of his period. The apolitical Flaubert is thus simultaneously a diagnostician and a committed bard. So also, the critic of Romanticism is at the same time one of its most impressive victims and most glorious heirs. (p. 283)

Entrapment and failure are his basic terrors. Repeated images of confinement and obstruction alternate with images of horrendous proliferations with which neither the senses nor the intellect can cope. But more devastating still is the omnipresent sense of metaphysical ennui, the obverse of his spiritual longings, whose destructive yawn and paralyzing irony are as intense as Baudelaire's *monstre délicat* dreaming of sanguinous scaffolds. Pervading all of Flaubert's texts, there is a guilt of existing, a hatred of the flesh (and of the spirit too) which find their culmination in the acrid and strident pages of what perhaps stands out as his most revealing book, *La Tentation de saint Antoine.* (p. 284)

Desire and death are . . . firmly allied in Flaubert's imagination. Abundance, fecundity and multiplication of life are in fact constantly viewed as principles of ruin and decay. Disintegration and dissolution are central themes around which Flaubert develops manifold variations: the processes of time and of aging, the fatigue of living, the death of each instant, the circularity of events, deadly constriction and stasis. But the most characteristic manifestations of undoing are those which, in Flaubert's mind, are linked to the fascination with polymorphism. His obsession with unmanageable heterogeneity and with the gap between all phenomena is responsible for a latent sense of terror. His protagonists thus evolve in an atmosphere of nonassimilated reality, caught in the oppressive routine of a repetitive discontinuity. (p. 285)

Flaubert's pessimism is not the product of a petty, peevish disposition; it is an expression of indignation in the face of a reality so cluttered that it leaves no room for meaning. (pp. 285-86)

[His] concern is not so much with a given society as with a civilization sick with hate and false values. Or rather, it is with the very conditions of a culture, caught between the uncompromising claims of science and religion, suffering from surfeit, constipation, sterile relativism and a general collapse of values. . . . [His] denunciations of emptiness, false idols and sacrilegious denial of beauty are of a tragic and prophetic nature. (p. 287)

Flaubert proudly viewed himself as the last of the troubadours. He sensed that he was one of the late, but most imposing manifestations of the literary phenomenon known as Romanticism. . . . But if he is, in a sense, a splendid crepuscular figure, he also stands at the threshold of modern literature, as a direct link between Romanticism and our own visions of reality. The oppressive heterogeneity of phenomena, the fragmented immediacy of experience, the constant fading or alteration of forms, the disappearance of the conventional polarity of object and subject—all these were to become central assumptions as well as tragic motifs in twentieth-century writing. Similarly, Flaubert's awareness of Time as a qualitative, elastic and subjective principle of erosion, but also as a regenerative and liberating force, ushers in modern experiments in fiction. (pp. 288-89)

> *Victor Brombert, in his* The Novels of Flaubert: A Study of Themes and Techniques *(copyright © 1966 by Princeton University Press; reprinted by permission of Princeton University Press), Princeton University Press, 1966, 301 p.*

A. W. RAITT   (essay date 1973)

The broad vision, the grand design, the gift for synthesis required by the novel are not often combined in the one mind with that ability for terse concentration, for the selection of significant detail, for the distillation of meaning and emotion from a single action which are essential for excellence in the shorter form. Only a handful of the outstanding composers of narrative fiction have attained equal mastery of both genres: Balzac, Turgeniev, Joyce and, perhaps supreme among them, Gustave Flaubert. (p. 112)

Perhaps the first point to be made is that in many ways Flaubert's three tales [*Un Coeur simple, La Légende de Saint Julien l'Hospitalier,* and *Hérodias,* collected as *Trois Contes,*] are unique, and that their aims and methods are quite unlike those of the vast majority of short stories. . . . [Flaubert] was singularly impatient, in his maturity, with the whole idea of story-telling. His disdain for narration as such gives him a hankering after the unrealizable ideal of 'a book about nothing'. . . . [Plot for Flaubert is] subservient to the need to produce a particular impression, definable in terms of colour . . . , but perhaps also as a shape, as a texture, or as a rhythmic experience. . . . (pp. 113-14)

This is as true of his short stories as it is of his novels. There is in them no hint of that dramatic and suspenseful unfolding of a striking anecdote which characterizes so many nineteenth-century short stories; no unexpected twist in the action, no surprise ending, not even the single salient incident around which most writers like to construct their tales. . . . Of course, this is not to deny the meticulous attention which Flaubert pays to the mechanism of plot or the art with which he organizes and gradates dramatic effects. But he does stand alone among the writers of his time in regarding anecdote not as the essential object of a short story but as one element among many which combine to form a finished artefact the value and significance of which far transcend the sequence of events which it recounts.

One reason why anecdote in Flaubert's short stories loses the primacy it tends to have elsewhere lies no doubt in the remarkable process of maturation which the subjects of all three tales underwent. . . . The story of St. Julien had probably first come to his notice in 1835; in 1846 he had talked of one day writing his own version of it; he had done some desultory reading for it in 1856; but it was only in 1875 that he eventually committed it to paper. Adumbrations of *Un Coeur simple* likewise go back to his childhood: a character much like Félicité figures in a tale he wrote at the age of fifteen, and, strange as it seems, was almost taken as the heroine of *Madame Bovary*. . . . Only *Hérodias* seems to be a relatively new subject, but even there he had been taking notes for it five years previously, as well as reflecting on *Monsieur le Préfet* from which its underlying theme derives. The result is that the subjects had all acquired an extraordinary richness of texture and resonance through this long process of evolution: the alluvial deposits left by years of meditation, experience and feeling have given them a depth of fertility almost unequalled in the short story.

This quality of complex profundity is enhanced by the fact that Flaubert never makes explicit—perhaps not even to himself—precisely what significance he attaches to the subjects. . . . [In] the *Trois Contes* Flaubert points no morals, drops no hints, suggests no interpretations. Events are related with detachment; comment is eschewed. This is not only a function of that celebrated impersonality on which Flaubert laid such stress, and which is perhaps more perfectly realized in these tales than in any of his other works. It arises also from the singularly concrete quality of his imagination, which leads him from the outset to conceive a narrative in the uniquely individual terms of material reality, of particular people in a particular setting and in a particular light. . . . Flaubert sees plot, character and structure as an indivisible unity, endowed from the start with a presence and an individuality of its own, from which all abstract and generalizing elements are rigorously banished. . . . [The stories] acquire a three-dimensional quality extremely rare in works so short, and at the same time provide the reader with the sense of a reality which, like that of life itself, is meaningful, but with a meaning that cannot be circumscribed in abstract formulas or precise definitions.

A consequence of this mode of creation is that an entirely new role devolves upon description. In most short stories, as in most pre-Flaubert novels, descriptive passages serve essentially as background, as the stage setting in which the characters will appear to act out their parts. For Flaubert description serves a different purpose. It is an integral part of the whole experience of the figures whom he writes about and into whose lives we enter. Flaubert sees that no feeling and no event can exist in the abstract; it is always inseparably associated with the physical circumstances in which it occurred and can only be evoked by reference to them. Look for instance at the scene [in *Un Coeur simple*] where Félicité arrives at the convent after the death of her beloved Virginie. . . . Though this is one of the emotive climaxes of the tale, Flaubert says nothing at all about Félicité's feelings; instead, he puts us in her position so that we see the picture as she saw it and would recall it. The moment in time is fixed indelibly by visual means; the emotions are implied, not stated in what would inevitably have tended to be undifferentiated abstractions—grief, sorrow or whatever. The same technique, adapted to suit the aesthetic and technical postulates of each tale, is used throughout the book. . . . Each tale thus creates its own imaginative world which the reader can move into and inhabit as with perhaps no other short stories.

All this implies that, just as Flaubert assigns a special and unusual function to description in his stories, so he does with detail. . . . [The] relative fullness of detail gives the tales a texture more akin to that of novels than is usual in short stories, and obviates that feeling of somewhat contrived bareness that lesser authors may inadvertently convey in their desire for concision.

It is indeed noteworthy that each of the *Trois Contes* contains much more material, and material of a much more diverse kind, than authors usually think it wise to include in works of such brevity. . . . How has Flaubert carried off this exceptional feat? (pp. 114-18)

In *Un Coeur simple,* the main difficulty arises from the necessity of providing a sense of unity and a forward-moving impetus in the long and uneventful time-span of Félicité's existence, a difficulty increased by the obstacles in the way of involving the reader in the experiences of an illiterate and inarticulate serving-woman who communicates with nobody and who never reflects on her own situation. The key to Flaubert's resolution of the difficulty is to be found above all in his astonishingly subtle use of *style indirect libre,* the free use of the imperfect tense to convey the thoughts and feelings of a character without resorting either to direct quotation or to accurately reported speech. It is of course one of the outstanding features of Flaubert's style throughout his prose fiction, but nowhere is it put to better or more consistent use than in *Un Coeur simple,* where its peculiar advantage is that it enables the author, almost from one end of the story to the other, to be simultaneously within his character and outside her. The unity of point of view is thus more rigorously preserved than anywhere else in Flaubert's fiction, yet without limiting his expressive resources to the exiguous vocabulary and rudimentary mental equipment of his heroine. . . . A delicate balance is thus consistently maintained which enables Flaubert to create a unified work of art out of what at first blush might have seemed diffuse and unpromising material.

The problems of *La Légende de Saint Julien l'Hospitalier* are different. The legend with its contrasting scenes of hunting, parricide, expiation and apotheosis, has a dramatic energy of its own, which Flaubert exploits to the full. But he has added a further, unexpected dimension to it by viewing it not only as a story to be told in its own right, but also as a re-creation of medieval art. . . . The effect is created from the start by all manner of barely perceptible touches: an almost fairy-tale vagueness in the setting . . . , a naïve exaggeration in the descriptions . . . , a discreet use of archaic terms and old-fashioned constructions, a matter-of-fact acceptance of the supernatural, more ornate and colourful imagery, a deliberate stylization of the secondary characters. Avoiding the pitfalls of pastiche on the one hand and incongruity on the other, Flaubert has produced a highly original and successful medieval tonality in the language and presentation of *Saint Julien.* This achievement is all the more striking in that, despite appearances, the legend is more than an artificially ingenious aesthetic exercise. Running through it is not only a carefully and convincingly motivated study of a man in the grip of an uncontrollable blood lust, but also a disturbing complex of underlying themes interrelating cruelty, eroticism, guilt, and atonement through self-immolation. These undertones are all the more effective for remaining unspoken. The *Légende* is not only one of Flaubert's most elusively enigmatic works; it is also, in its very detachment and distance, one of his most personal. (pp. 119-20)

Hérodias is not a historical reconstruction, though it may look like one. As Flaubert once declared, 'I consider technical details, precise information, in short the historical and exact side of things, to be very secondary. Above all else, I am seeking for beauty, which my fellow-writers don't much care about.' That this principle is applied here is shown by the numerous historical anachronisms and mis-statements in *Hérodias,* which arise not from carelessness but from a conscious decision to sacrifice factual accuracy to a higher truth. This means that ultimately the reader has no need to remember the mass of detail about people, places, sects, parties, beliefs, politics and so forth which is so profusely supplied in the first part of the story. What Flaubert wants to do is to build up a vast network of pressures bearing down on the Tetrarch Herod and weighing on the administrative decision, fraught with consequences, that he has to take about the life or death of his prisoner Iaokanann (John the Baptist). It is of little moment if the reader cannot follow the daunting complexity of the factors involved, since Herod cannot either; and in the end, when Salome dances, everyone forgets them, united only in the lust for the girl. . . . The decision to execute Iaokanann is wrung from Herod by a frenzy of animal desire, not by a rational consideration of the rights and wrongs of the case. . . . And the totally unforeseen ironic consequence of Herod's decision, as we realize from the concluding tableau of the disciples bearing away the prophet's head, symbol of his message, is the spread of Christianity.

Once one reads the story in that light, it becomes clear that the detail in it, the multiplicity of characters, the constantly shifting point of view are essentially subservient to an impressionistic purpose, and the sensitive reader will understand that, implicitly, *Hérodias* constitutes a devastatingly misanthropic and pessimistic comment on the way humanity conducts its affairs. There is, in other words, a hidden design which justifies and binds together the apparently multifarious threads of which the story is composed. The unity of focus in *Hérodias* is less easy to grasp than in the other two tales; perhaps even it is less perfectly realized, at least on the surface. But its presence gives the tale its real strength and originality.

It appears then evident that, however belated and unorthodox Flaubert's cultivation of the short-story form may have been, he was intensely alive to the peculiar problems it posed and enormously skilful in solving them. . . . Whether Flaubert ever in so many words tried to distinguish the principles of short-story writing from those of the novelist's art is open to doubt, but it is certain that in practice he did not make the mistake of treating the tale as a truncated or embryo novel. Formally, the *Trois Contes* have an unmistakable identity of their own— or perhaps it would be fairer to say three separate identities, since there is no question of a threefold application of the same formula—and though they could certainly not have been written without the years of meditation and experience Flaubert had devoted to the novel, they show that the lessons of those years had been used flexibly and sensitively to fit in with the conditions of a different form. (pp. 121-23)

[*Un Coeur simple*] reverses the customary pattern of the world depicted in Flaubert's fiction, where idealism is trampled underfoot and mediocrity triumphs. Here, without commentary or sentimentality, we are shown a character who finds serenity and equilibrium amid adversity, and who dies happy, as the work moves to a soberly majestic conclusion. . . . Viewed objectively, Félicité's life is a long succession of disappointments, hardships, misunderstandings, and the world in which she moves is as grim and bleak as any Flaubert depicts. But because he constantly refuses to step outside her and judge her situation from above, and because she has none of the introspective intelligence which would enable her to see it for herself, as Emma Bovary eventually sees the reality of her position, she keeps her faith undimmed to the end. The vision of the celestial parrot may be an illusion, but it is an illusion which remains intact, and the reader is induced to acquiesce in it and to share in the sense of beatitude which descends on her. This tenderness towards Félicité and the extraordinary tact of feeling which permits Flaubert to preserve his customary pessimistic outlook while producing a work which is morally uplifting, make **Un Coeur simple** fundamentally different from everything else he wrote.

The **Trois Contes** do then in their different ways add something of their own to the greatness of Flaubert. . . . In both theme and technique he has treated the short story as of equal stature with the novel. This is indeed what gives these tales their peculiar and lonely eminence in the history of the nineteenth-century short story. . . . The **Trois Contes,** by their complexity, their density, the subtlety and power of their themes, the sense they convey of a depth and breadth of life extending far beyond their apparently restricted confines, stand alone among French and even among world short stories. (pp. 125-26)

> *A. W. Raitt, "Flaubert and the Art of the Short Story" (© A. W. Raitt; reprinted by permission of the author; originally a lecture delivered at the Royal Society of Literature on May 17, 1973), in Essays by Divers Hands, Vol. XXXVIII, edited by John Guest, Oxford University Press, New York, 1975, pp. 112-26.*

VLADIMIR NABOKOV   (essay date 1980)

[Can] we call **Madame Bovary** realistic or naturalistic? I wonder.

A novel in which a young and healthy husband night after night never wakes to find the better half of his bed empty; never hears the sand and pebbles thrown at the shutters by a lover; never receives an anonymous letter from some local busybody;

A novel in which the biggest busybody of them all, Homais—Monsieur Homais, whom we might have expected to have kept a statistical eye upon all the cuckolds of his beloved Yonville, actually never notices, never learns anything about Emma's affairs;

A novel in which little Justin—a nervous young boy of fourteen who faints at the sight of blood and smashes crockery out of sheer nervousness—should go to weep in the dead of night (where?) in a cemetery on the grave of a woman whose ghost might come to reproach him for not having refused to give her the key to death;

A novel in which a young woman who has not been riding for several years—if indeed she ever did ride when she lived on her father's farm—now gallops away to the woods with perfect poise, and never feels any stiffness in the joints afterwards;

A novel in which many other implausible details abound—such as the very implausible naiveté of a certain cabdriver—such a novel has been called a landmark of so-called realism, whatever that is.

In point of fact, all fiction is fiction. All art is deception. Flaubert's world, as all worlds of major writers, is a world of fancy with its own logic, its own conventions, its own coin-

cidences. . . . Flaubert may have seemed realistic or naturalistic a hundred years ago to readers brought up on the writings of those sentimental ladies and gentlemen that Emma admired. But realism, naturalism, are only comparative notions. What a given generation feels as naturalism in a writer seems to an older generation to be exaggeration of drab detail, and to a younger generation not enough drab detail. The *isms* go; the *ist* dies; art remains.

Ponder most carefully the following fact: a master of Flaubert's artistic power manages to transform what he has conceived as a sordid world inhabited by frauds and philistines and mediocrities and brutes and wayward ladies into one of the most perfect pieces of poetical fiction known, and this he achieves by bringing all the parts into harmony, by the inner force of style, by all such devices of form as the counterpoint of transition from one theme to another, of foreshadowing and echoes. Without Flaubert there would have been no Marcel Proust in France, no James Joyce in Ireland. Chekhov in Russia would not have been quite Chekhov. So much for Flaubert's literary influence. (pp. 146-47)

> *Vladimir Nabokov, "Gustave Flaubert: 'Madame Bovary'," in his Lectures on Literature, edited by Fredson Bowers (copyright © 1980 by the Estate of Vladimir Nabokov; reprinted by permission of Harcourt Brace Jovanovich, Inc.), Harcourt, 1980, pp. 125-78.*

ADDITIONAL BIBLIOGRAPHY

Bersani, Leo. "Flaubert and the Threats of the Imagination: *Madame Bovary*." In his *Balzac to Beckett: Center and Circumference in French Fiction*, pp. 140-91. New York: Oxford University Press, 1970.
> A stylistic analysis of *Madame Bovary*.

Blackmur, R. P. "Beauty Out of Place: Flaubert's *Madame Bovary*." In his *Eleven Essays in the European Novel*, pp. 48-74. New York: Harcourt Brace & World, 1964.
> An analysis of the "process of the objective imagination" in *Madame Bovary*.

Bowen, Elizabeth. "The Flaubert Omnibus." In her *Collected Impressions*, pp. 18-37. New York: Alfred Knopf, 1950.
> An excellent introductory overview of Flaubert's life and literary career.

Boyd, Ernest. "Flaubert and French Realism." In his *Studies from Ten Literatures*, pp. 3-20. 1925. Reprint. Port Washington, N.Y.: Kennikat Press, 1968.
> Asserts Flaubert's importance as the precursor of modern realism and naturalism, chronicling the progress of these movements following the publication of *Madame Bovary*.

Coleman, A. *Flaubert's Literary Development in the Light of His "Mémoires d'un Fou," "Novembre" and "Éducation sentimentale" (version of 1845)*. Baltimore: The Johns Hopkins Press; Paris: Librairie É. Champion, 1914, 154 p.
> Traces the genesis and development of Flaubert's artistic principles up to 1845 through the analysis of *Mémoires d'un fou, Novembre,* and *L'éducation sentimentale* (1845).

Cortland, Peter. *A Reader's Guide to Flaubert*. New York: Helios Books, 1968, 175 p.
> An introductory critical study of *Madame Bovary, Sentimental Education,* and *Three Tales,* including a brief guide to Flaubertian criticism and a critical biography.

France, Anatole. "The Ideas of Gustave Flaubert." In his *On Life and Letters, third series,* edited by J. Lewis May and Bernard Miall, translated by D. B. Stewart, pp. 285-94. London: John Lane the Bodley Head; New York: Dodd, Mead and Co., 1922.

Discusses Flaubert's ideas concerning life and literature.

Gordon, Caroline. "Notes on Faulkner and Flaubert." *The Hudson Review* I, No. 2 (Summer 1948): 222-31.*

Explores the influence of Flaubert's style upon William Faulkner.

Hearn, Lafcadio. "The Friends of Flaubert." In his *Essays in European and Oriental Literature,* edited by Albert Mordell, pp. 65-73. New York: Dodd, Mead and Co., 1923.

Discusses the reactions to Flaubert's works of such friends as Maxime du Camp and Louis Bouilhet.

James, Henry. "Gustave Flaubert." In his *Notes on Novelists with Some Other Notes,* pp. 65-108. New York: Charles Scribner's Sons, 1914.

An analysis of Flaubert's literary style with particular emphasis on *Madame Bovary.*

Kaplan, Harold. "*Madame Bovary:* The Seriousness of Comedy." In his *The Passive Voice: An Approach to Modern Fiction,* pp. 24-37. Athens, Ohio: Ohio University Press, 1966.

A close analysis of Flaubert's treatment of Emma Bovary.

Lapp, John C. "Art and Hallucination in Flaubert." *French Studies* X, No. 4 (October 1956): 322-34.

Explores the part played by Flaubert's epileptic hallucinations in forming the images and visions found throughout his work.

Levin, Harry. "Flaubert." In his *The Gates of Horn: A Study of Five French Realists,* pp. 214-304. New York: Oxford University Press, 1963.

An analysis of Flaubert as a crucial component of the realist movement with special attention to his insistence on stylistic perfection.

Lewisohn, Ludwig. "Gustave Flaubert." In his *Cities and Men,* pp. 163-66. New York: Harper, 1927.

Analysis of Flaubert as a "hero of letters."

Lucas, F. L. "The Martyr of Letters." In his *Studies French and English,* pp. 242-66. London: Cassell, 1934.

A study of Flaubert's hatred of the established world and the manifestation of that hatred in his literature.

Maugham, W. Somerset. "Gustave Flaubert and *Madame Bovary.*" In his *Great Novelists and Their Novels,* pp. 137-56. Philadelphia and Toronto: The John C. Winston Co., 1948.

A study of character treatment in *Madame Bovary.*

Mein, Margaret. "Flaubert, a Precursor of Proust." *French Studies* XVII, No. 3 (July 1963): 218-37.*

Finds that Flaubert anticipates Proust stylistically and in his treatment of the unity and disintegration within time.

Muir, Edwin. "Emma Bovary and Becky Sharp." In his *Essays on Literature and Society,* pp. 182-94. Cambridge: Harvard University Press, 1965.*

Compares and contrasts Emma Bovary with Becky Sharp from William Thackeray's novel *Vanity Fair.*

Pacey, Desmond. "Flaubert and His Victorian Critics." *University of Toronto Quarterly* XVI, No. 1 (October 1946): 74-84.

An excellent study of the Victorian critical response to Flaubert's works including many valuable references to early essays and reviews.

Sartre, Jean Paul. *The Family Idiot: Gustave Flaubert 1821-1857, Vol. I.* Translated by Carol Cosman. Chicago, London: The Chicago University Press, 1981, 627 p.

The first part of a comprehensive psychological and philosophical biography.

Smith, Garnet. "The Letters of Gustave Flaubert." *The Gentleman's Magazine* CCLXXIV, No. 1949 (May 1893): 550-67.

A discussion of Flaubert's literary development, personality, and opinions as revealed in his correspondence.

Starkie, Enid. *Flaubert: The Making of the Master.* New York: Atheneum, 1967, 403 p.

An extensive, well-documented portrait of Flaubert "the human being" as well as an informative analysis of Flaubert "the writer" up through the publication and trial of *Madame Bovary.*

Starkie, Enid. *Flaubert the Master: A Critical and Biographical Study (1856-1880).* New York: Atheneum, 1971, 390 p.

A continuation of Starkie's authoritative study *Flaubert: The Making of the Master* covering Flaubert's personal life and career from the year 1856 until his death. This volume "is intended to show Flaubert in full possession of his art and craft, and how he used them in different ways, without repeating himself; each novel being intended to solve a separate problem and to treat it in a different way, with a different style."

Steegmuller, Francis. *Flaubert and "Madame Bovary": A Double Portrait.* New York: Farrar, Straus and Co., 1950, 433 p.

An excellent biography concentrating on the periods when Flaubert was writing *La tentation de Saint Antoine* and *Madame Bovary.* Steegmuller also provides an extensive account, primarily using Flaubert's letters and travel notes, of his oriental journey with Maxime Du Camp, taken between the composition of these two novels.

Tarver, John Charles. *Gustave Flaubert As Seen in His Works and Correspondence.* New York: D. Appleton and Co., 1895, 368 p.

Seeks to define Flaubert's personality through his correspondence and works.

Thibaudet, Albert. "Flaubert." In his *French Literature from 1795 to Our Era,* translated by Charles Lam Markmann, pp. 298-305. New York: Funk & Wagnalls, 1968.

A brief synopsis of Flaubert's career.

Thorlby, Anthony. *Gustave Flaubert and the Art of Realism.* New Haven: Yale University Press, 1957, 63 p.

A critical survey of Flaubert's major works.

Trilling, Lionel. "Flaubert's Last Testament." In his *The Opposing Self,* pp. 173-205. New York: The Viking Press, 1955.

An examination of Flaubert's last novel, *Bouvard et Pécuchet.*

Turnell, Martin. "Flaubert." In his *The Novel in France,* pp. 247-316. New York: New Directions, 1951.

Analysis of Flaubert's narrative art, concluding that he was "a great technician, a great literary engineer rather than a great novelist."

Ullmann, Stephen. "Reported Speech and Internal Monologue in Flaubert." In his *Style in the French Novel,* pp. 94-120. Cambridge, England: Cambridge at the University Press, 1957.

Analyzes the development of free indirect speech in Flaubert's works.

Untermeyer, Louis. "Gustave Flaubert." In his *Makers of the Modern World,* pp. 91-101. New York: Simon and Schuster, 1955.

A biographical sketch.

Winegarten, Renee. "Literary Commitment versus Revolutionary Tradition: Flaubert." In her *Writers and Revolution: The Fatal Lure of Action,* pp. 170-82. New York: New Viewpoints, 1974.

Examines the degree to which Flaubert questioned the revolutionary mystique in *L'éducation sentimentale.*

Friedrich (Heinrich Karl) de La Motte Fouqué

1777-1843

(Also wrote under the pseudonym of Pellegrin) German novelist, poet, dramatist, and translator.

Fouqué's personal and literary philosophies were so extravagant that Joseph Eichendorff referred to him as the "Don Quixote of Romanticism." Though well received during the French occupation of Germany, Fouqué believed in a powerful nobility, and this opinion soon turned the public against him. His poems, dramas, and prose romances also advanced views of German superiority, and of the superiority of the upper classes; beliefs based in part on the linguistic theories of Johann Fichte. These opinions had helped to awaken patriotism before and during the Napoleonic wars, but increasingly, republican Germany found little use for them after the enemy had been driven out.

Fouqué was the descendant of a protestant French family, which was forced to move to Germany during a period of religious persecution. Like his grandfather, who was a well-known general under Friedrich II, Fouqué was a highly-patriotic German, and served for a long time in the military. In 1803, he retired to marry and write, rejoining the army in 1813 for two years to fight Napoleon. Fouqué's popularity declined after 1820, but he went on writing until his death, sometimes publishing anonymously, so that he might gain a hearing for his unpopular views. His royalist sympathies won him the favor of King Friedrich Wilhelm IV, however, and he was granted a pension, late in his life.

Fouqué was a master of Romantic literary excess: colorfully attired, gallant knights parade through his romances, fighting for the honor of their country or their women. *Der Zauberring* (*The Magic Ring*), his best known patriotic romance, and *Der Held des Nordens*, a trilogy in verse, are based on medieval German and Norse folklore, in which Fouqué was thoroughly knowledgeable. *Der Held des Nordens* is the first modern treatment of the *Nibelungenlied;* it was later adapted by Richard Wagner in his famous *Ring* cycle. Though highly regarded in their own day, Fouqué's works are regarded by most modern critics as melodramatic and unnatural, and are now of interest mainly to literary historians.

However, the public and the critics alike have always loved *Undine*, a fairy tale about a water spirit who acquires a human soul through marriage. Such diverse writers as Edgar Allan Poe, Walter Scott, and C. S. Lewis have joined Samuel Taylor Coleridge in his appraisal of *Undine* as "a most exquisite work." It has twice been made into an opera—once by E.T.A. Hoffmann (to which Fouqué contributed the libretto). Though now often published as a children's book, *Undine* is, in fact, a mature tale which discusses the universal themes of love, betrayal, revenge, and death.

Fouqué's other writings have barely survived him, but he remains important as a central figure in early German Romanticism.

PRINCIPAL WORKS

Der gehörnte Siegfried in der Schmiede [as Pellegrin] (dramatic sketches) 1803

*Aslauga (dramatic poetry) 1808
*Sigurd der Schlangentöter (dramatic poetry) 1808
*Sigurds Rache (dramatic poetry) 1808
Undine (fairy tale) 1811
  [Undine, 1818]
Der Zauberring (novel) 1813
  [The Magic Ring, 1825]
Sintram und seine Gefährten (novel) 1814
  [Sintram and His Companions, 1820]
Thiodolf der Isländer (novel) 1815
  [Thiodolf, the Islander, 1845]
Ausgewählte Werke (poetry, novels, dramas, dramatic poetry, short stories) 1841

*These three works make up the trilogy *Der Held des Nordens*.

LONDON MAGAZINE (essay date 1820)

[It would appear to us,] judging by **Sintram and his Companions**, that [Fouqué's] genius and disposition, are both impressed with a wild, dreary, shadowy character; that his power is gusty and unequal; that his feelings are fantastical as well as quick; that his creations, generally, are those of a phantasmagoria, rapid, striking, and poetical, but thin, uncertain, monstrous, and fleeting.—It is not because the interest of this tale depends, all the way through, on supernatural interference, that we are inclined to think the author has been unduly complimented with the peculiar faculty of giving the clearness and vivacity of life, and the vigour and genuine animation of nature to his personages and events. (p. 65)

[Ghosts,] seers, phantoms, and evil spirits, may, as it appears to us, be fashioned and introduced into a work, in a way to afford to the imagination of the reader an appropriate and lively feeling of their natural consistency and vigorous power of action. Ariel gives this assurance of itself, and Caliban:—but, to effect this, the genius of the author must be so identified with nature herself, as to be gifted with a share of her privileges, and have the power of varying the combination of her principles, without violating or contradicting their immutable and essential indications. When this is the case, we have on our minds an impression of reality, vigour, and healthiness in reading a composition: otherwise, it seems fantastical, sickly, and glimmering,—even though it may be interesting in its story, and distinguished by a rapid and poetical fancy.

The author of **Sintram,** we must confess, seems to us to belong to the latter division. A straining after effect, a theatrical taste, a style of language which we cannot otherwise characterize than by calling it *soft* and *greasy,* give us offence in it. It appears to us to be quite chargeable with the common German fault, of pushing the types of the feeling so much into display as to throw doubts on its reality. At the same time, there is a sort of night-mare sublimity about the characters, scenery, and events. Nothing is distinctly made out,—but the shadows roll about so as frequently to produce grand and awful pictures. It is often childish and often impotent; but the very signs of these qualities are marked with an earnestness and gravity, that give them the air of such monsters as infants with old men's countenances! (p. 66)

[The] German author has made of Folko the stiffest of gallants, long after he has become the most fortunate of spouses: the tip of his lady's little finger seems quite enough to put him in ecstasies,—and the consequence is, that all that is over seems to be thrown away on such a husband. The contrast which these two curious characters present to the rugged inmates of the Castle of Drontheim, has a powerful effect in the work; and we are pleased with them, in spite of the false, cold, artificial, and affected style in which they are delineated. They have no more of the heartiness of nature about them, than if they were wax-work figures; but in their own pompous, masquerading manner they are cleverly done,—being true to themselves, though false to all the principles of natural truth. (pp. 68-9)

The effect of the lady's charms on the wild northern mind of Sintram, is represented with a more masterly hand: the novelty of her beauty and of her manners fills his soul with an influence of a passionate, impetuous, yet not impure nature,—and here it struggles with those dark supernatural possessions to which the hero of the romance is subject. (p. 69)

The book is altogether a great curiosity, and in this respect it is well worthy of perusal. . . . [But,] it has also higher distinctions. It bears a northern, stormy, misty aspect—it is crowded with names and images of an icy, bleak, rugged, and frowning cast. It presents to our observation, nature in desolation, and

human beings, in savage gloom. Demons laugh throughout its pages; dead men's bones clatter; swords clash; and tempests howl. The inclemency of the fiction seems caught from the bleakness of the climate. (p. 71)

> *"Critical Notices of New Books: 'Sintram and His Companions',"* in London Magazine, *Vol. II, No. VII, July, 1820, pp. 65-71.*

THE MONTHLY REVIEW (essay date 1820)

[The] peculiar and metaphysical exemplification of human life is the subject of Baron Fouqué's works; and on this ground, aided by high poetic genius and descriptive powers, they deserve the attention of the critic and the reader. Thus, in pursuance of this singular principle, we find in the tale of **Undine** the evil influence of supernatural power, assisted by the weakness of human inclinations, as allegorized in the character of Sir Huldbrand of Ringstetten; while the unfortunate effects of ill-assorted unions are shewn in the fate of Undine. . . . Sintram [in **Sintram and his Companions**] on the other hand, exemplifies a moral victory, in the triumph of the mind over worldly sin and temptations. Though his patience and good resolutions are put to a severer proof than those of St. Antony of old, we are happy to acquaint our readers that he comes forth from the ordeal of Love only more purified in heart and spirit.

After having said thus much of the allegorical, we must dwell a little more closely on the real and tangible properties of the author. Without the finer qualities and more subdued tone of feeling which our English writers of a similar class evince, Fouqué contrives to exercise a more powerful influence over the imagination, and transports us in the enthusiasm of inventive genius into a fanciful world of his own. His writings are richly embued with a national spirit of romance, impressed with the same dark and shadowy character that belongs to the early legends and heroic traditions of the north. Strong, rapid, and contrasted feelings, and the passions of the moral world, are strangely mingled with the terrible and fleeting phaenomena of supernatural creation; haunting the human mind, and appearing and passing away in the nature of a dream. The chief characters are delineated by the hand of a master, stand prominently forward, and absorb the interest of the piece; the inferior figures are drawn also in strong and lively colours, representing the life and terror of a tragic picture: while the striking and rapid course of incident, passions, and events, like the contrasts of light and shade, seems busy in lending force and animation to the principal action of the whole. (pp. 187-88)

The Baron Fouqué appears, indeed, to unite the delicacy and rich pathos of [Torquato] Tasso with something of the wildness and terrible delineations of Shakespeare. He has also a portion of that intuitive power which is the surest proof of genius; and which, without actual observation, preserves truth and consistency in description, as well as in motives, action, and character. He has even too much imagination, not sufficiently corrected by taste and judgment; and he is thus frequently led to push the strength of his genius, and the beauty of his language and descriptions, to an extravagant and faulty degree, whether in violence or in simplicity of detail. The style and character of his works are singular, and somewhat paradoxical but we do not think that his genius depends alone on surprize and novelty, for the strong power which it certainly exercises over the mind. There is nothing weak and flimsy, though there is much "strange matter in his talk." He is altogether a very philosophic and metaphysical writer of romance; and those who are fond of exploring their own minds, and capable of deep and lasting impressions, with serious, disappointed, or sorrowful views of nature and the world, will feel highly interested, if not relieved and joyful, in dwelling on the strange and fearful imaginations of La Motte Fouqué. (p. 190)

[Fouqué] never thrusts the fashionable borrowed doctrine of *destiny* in our faces: but all things, in his romances, calmly reach their appointed end, drawn along as in nature gradually yet always progressively,—softly, yet irresistibly,—by an imperceptible chain. This is the right way to obtain for a book a permanent existence in the sympathies of man. . . . [Fouqué] in his seemingly wildest flights, preserves a beautiful consistency with himself. (p. 192)

In conclusion, we may illustrate by a simile our ideas of the powers of Fouqué as opposed to those of the author of the Scotch novels [Scott]. The inventions of the latter are fruits unequally ripened in our mutable climate, glowing and luscious on the one side, but green and tasteless on the other; while the fancies of the German are like those of the '*south countree*, the land with the beautiful blossoms,' gradually expanded, and plenteously fed with soft sun-beams till their full growth is accomplished. This comparison of the genius of Fouqué with that of our northern novelist may be derided by those who judge of quality by quantity; and it may strike the most unprejudiced reader of *modern* English literature as a startling and uncomfortable paradox. Nevertheless, we might even go farther, and state that the former is in a higher class, and is in its essence more permanent; inasmuch as he who developes the passions and sufferings of man in the abstract, from the depths and ponderings of his own mind, without becoming uninterestingly general, is a far more intellectual and commanding spirit than the mind which depends on diligent reading, and on a quick though not solid observation, aided by a lively fancy, rather than on an imagination lofty, clear, and pervading, and feelings intense in their natural state, though subdued and purified by solemn reflection and meditation. . . . [The] spirit of Fouqué is as essentially epic as that of Michel Angelo, and for that very reason will perhaps gain among us as few worthy admirers. The real and mysterious beauties of both must be "*caviare* to the general.'' (pp. 197-98)

> "*La Motte Fouqué's 'Undine', 'Sintram and His Companions',''* in The Monthly Review, *Vol. 93, October, 1820, pp. 184-98.*

THE MONTHLY REVIEW　(essay date 1822)

[The Baron de La Motte Fouqué,] whose powerful but excentric genius, deeply imbued with qualities of an uncommon kind, discovers at once both blemishes and beauties almost equally attractive and repulsive to English taste. He stands quite alone, forming an anomaly to the ordinary rules of composition even among his own most reflective and imaginative countrymen. In addition to its originality, his genius . . . is also abundantly productive in the slight fairy tales which he weaves with the playful art of a master, not less than in his more serious and pathetic romance. . . . Chiefly developed by an astonishing power of personification in the description of fairies and of demons, which typify the various modifications of good and evil,—the doubts, weaknesses, contentions, and triumphs of human reason over human passions, crimes, and follies,—the author's invariable purpose is to convey intellectual and philosophic truths under the veil of pleasing and fictitious stories;

at once gratifying the imagination and preserving a continued moral throughout. With such inventive powers, he gives new life and meaning to the old legends and superstitions of his country, which are thus invested with an importance altogether surprizing and new. (p. 203)

Of all the Baron's numberless productions, however,—epic, pastoral, poetic, and romantic,—perhaps none unite so many rich and pleasing qualities, proud chivalric feelings, and knightly and courtly graces, affording a bright and picturesque glimpse of "the olden times,'' as the tale of *Minstrel Love* now before us. *Sintram* may be more strange and terrible, or the fairy tale of *Undine* more wildly original and pathetic, or some of his epic pieces more daring and imposing:—but nothing is so full and complete in its way as the adventures of the Minstrel Knight of Maraviglia. He is a model of perfection, full of chivalric valor and platonic love, blooming in the charms of youth, beauty, and poetic fame; and we must not quarrel with the perfectibility of his nature, the success of his high adventures, and that unearthly spirit of love and fidelity with which it has pleased the author to invest him. . . . [The] German Baron, by boldly rushing directly into the world of spirits, claims exemption from all rules, builds aërial palaces that have no earthly foundations, and peoples them with beings of another order: but still shadowing forth the duties and the passions of mortals, and thus at once appealing to our reason through our imagination, like a subtle orator and a genuine master of his trade. Here we find no compromizing, no mincing with the object in view. His characters stand forth large and prominent, yet mysterious and obscure: his adventures and achievements are fairly above human calculation and attainment; his sentiments are high and honorable; his language, though vague and broken, is full of energy and eloquence: his reasonings are profound, and his moral is clear. This is as it should be in romance. . . . (pp. 204-05)

> "'*Minstrel Love*','' in The Monthly Review, *Vol. XCIX, October, 1822, pp. 202-08.*

THE MONTHLY REVIEW　(essay date 1825)

[La Motte Fouqué], we must confess, is inclined to stretch . . . a prerogative to the utmost; and he places his "*beau idéal*'' of fiction on such very high and fanciful ground, that he is often at a loss how to reconcile it even to the nature and semblance of his assumed adventures and characters. Such is, in particular, the defeat of [*Peter Schlemihl;*] which, however illustrative of his imaginary system . . . , with regard to a *shadowy* meaning and a moral, fails in justness and coherence of parts, and in assimilating what we are to suppose to be real and incidental with what he assumes as purely fictitious in the outset. Thus, while we grant him the power of conferring on a certain *black* gentleman the figure of 'a meagre, pale, tall, elderly, *grey* man', as he is here described to us, who boasts the singular art of purchasing and pocketing a person's own shadow, by loosening it from the body . . . , we cannot so easily go along with the author in his supposition of the subsequent disadvantages and disabilities, under which the hero so absurdly labors in consequence of such a deprivation. We can admit the supernatural part of the story, agreeably to certain arbitrary and established laws: but, this done, the subsequent incidents and results should be natural and probable. Now the inconveniences and miseries attributed by the author to his hero, on so singular a loss, are not such as would naturally occur: they are somewhat more serious, we think, and disastrous. Such a circumstance, in the first place, would fail to attract universal notice; and much less would the shadowless being subject himself to the derision and persecution of the world, and to a matrimonial disappointment, as long as he held the unlimited powers of purse which are here given to him. It is this defect in the framework and composition, casting a ludicrous and improbable air over the whole, which prevents the creation of the degree of illusion that is requisite in all works of fancy, before we can enter into the spirit and humor of the scene. In this respect, also, the present tale is inferior to most of the author's former productions; which exhibit a kind of *vraisemblance* and harmony of incident and action, founded on the supernatural ground-work, in a very superior degree.

The other features of this *shadowy* story, however, are better preserved: it is told with ease and simplicity of language; and the interest, such as it is, grows on us as we proceed, to a certain point. (pp. 202-03)

> *"'Peter Schlemihl',"* in The Monthly Review, *Vol. CVI, February, 1825, pp. 201-07.*

THOMAS CARLYLE   (essay date 1827)

Fouqué's genius is not of a kind to provoke or solicit much criticism; for its faults are negative rather than positive, and its beauties are not difficult to discern. The structure of his mind is simple; his intellect is in harmony with his feelings; and his taste seems to include few modes of excellence, which he has not in some considerable degree the power to realize. He is thus in unison with himself; his works are free from internal inconsistency, and appear to be produced with lightness and freedom. A pure sensitive heart, deeply reverent of Truth, and Beauty, and Heroic Virtue; a quick perception of certain forms embodying these high qualities; and a delicate and dainty hand in picturing them forth, are gifts which few readers of his works will contest him. At the same time, it must be granted, he has no pre-eminence in strength, either of head or heart; and his circle of activity, though full of animation, is far from comprehensive. He is, as it were, possessed by one idea. A few notes, some of them, in truth, of rich melody, yet still a very few, include the whole music of his being. The Chapel and the Tilt-yard stand in the background or the foreground, in all the scenes of his universe. He gives us knights, soft-hearted and strong-armed; full of Christian self-denial, patience, meekness, and gay easy daring; they stand before us in their mild frankness, with suitable equipment, and accompaniment of squire and dame; and frequently the whole has a true, though seldom a vigorous, poetic life. If this can content us, it is well: if not, there is no help; for change of scene and person brings little change of subject; even when no chivalry is mentioned, we feel too clearly the influence of its unseen presence. Nor can it be said, that in this solitary department his success is of the very highest sort. To body forth the spirit of Christian Knighthood in existing poetic forms; to wed that old *sentiment* to modern *thoughts,* was a task which he could not attempt. He has turned rather to the fictions and machinery of former days; and transplanted his heroes into distant ages, and scenes divided by their nature from our common world. Their manner of existence comes imaged back to us faint and ineffectual, like the crescent of the setting moon.

These things, however, are not faults, but the want of merits. Where something is effected, it were ungracious to reckon up too narrowly how much is left untried. . . . [Fouqué] is no primate or bishop in the Church Poetical; but a simple chaplain,

who merits the honours of a small but well-discharged function, and claims no other. (pp. 280-81)

Fouqué is a man of genius, with little more than an ordinary share of talent. His intellect is not richer, or more powerful than that of common minds, nor his insight into the world, and man's heart, more keen; but his feelings are finer, and the touch of an aerial fancy gives life and loveliness to the products of his other powers. Among English authors, we might liken him to Southey; though their provinces of writing are widely diverse; and, in regard to general culture and acquirement, the latter must be reckoned greatly his superior. Like Southey, he *finds* more readily than he *invents;* and his invention, when he does trust to it, is apt to be daring rather than successful. Yet his extravagant fictions are pervaded by a true sentiment: a soft vivifying soul looks through them; a religious submission, a cheerful and unwearied patience in affliction; mild, earnest hope and love; and peaceful, subdued enthusiasm.

To these internal endowments, he adds the merit of a style by no means ill adapted for displaying them. Lightness and simplicity are its chief characteristics: his periods move along in lively rhythm; studiously excluding all pomp of phraseology; expressing his strongest thoughts in the humblest words, and veiling dark sufferings or resolute purposes in a placid smile. A faint superficial gaiety seems to rest over all his images: it is not merriment or humour; but the self-possession of a man too earnestly serious to be heedful of solemn looks; and it plays like sunshine on the surface of a dark pool, deepening by contrast the impressiveness of the gloom which it does not penetrate. (pp. 282-83)

> *Thomas Carlyle, "Friedrich de La Motte Fouqué" (1827), in his* German Romance: Specimens of Its Chief Authors; with Biographical and Critical Notices, *Vol. I, William Tait and Charles Tait, 1827, pp. 273-83.*

THE FOREIGN QUARTERLY REVIEW   (essay date 1842)

[With] a delicate sense of beauty, with great felicity of graphic sensuous description, and with occasional bursts of mystic sublimity, Fouqué's imagination is still essentially one-sided and incomplete. Romance is his vocation, and the region in which he lives, and he is right in looking upon it as a grave reality. But it is a very different thing to look upon romance as the *only* reality of life; to make the mind of the artist a mere counterpart to his work; and to look in common things for the solemn meaning and heroic proportions, which were the proper objects of his creative faculty, only because they were peculiar and exceptional. We judge from the passages in which Fouqué speaks in his own person, or of himself, that he has fallen into this error. Finding himself at home in the region of earnest and high-strained fiction, he seems to have wrought up his mind to a permanent state of solemn and stiff enthusiasm, which enables him to shut his eyes to the contrast between every-day life and the scenes which his imagination has created. None but a man of real genius could be so much devoted to an ideal; but with more comprehensive genius, his worship of it would be less exclusive. Religious and knightly warriors have their proper place in the real world at fitting seasons, and always in the world of romance: but they do not constitute the whole of mankind: and when we have considered them sufficiently for the time, it is better to turn our thoughts to the rest of the universe, which contains many serious and many laughable objects; yet none so serious but that, contrasted with what is greater, it has its laughable side, and none so trifling but that it deserves in itself serious attention. It seems as if Fouqué could not satisfy himself of the reality of his creations, except by imitating them in his own person, and adopting their characteristics. A mind of the first order requires no external evidence of the truth of the ideal it has formed. (pp. 421-22)

As our present business is not with the author but with his works, we have only spoken of his peculiar turn of mind, because it illustrates and accounts for his characteristic excellences and defects as a writer. He has a warm feeling for greatness, but no sense of absurdity. His strength and his weakness may be described in three words: imagination without humour. He throws himself unreservedly into his subject, and indentifies himself with it so entirely, that if the interest is such that we can wholly sympathize with it, he has attained the perfection of art, where the workman is forgotten in his work. But if the story or character has a weak point, if it presupposes the existence of particular arbitrary associations, or special antiquarian knowledge, above all, if, however remote or obsolete the manners and scenery, it is not treated from the point of view in which it would naturally present itself to an educated man of the present day we cannot help feeling that the author is in a false position, and that, as he has not chosen to stand apart from or above his work, he shares in its incomplete and partial character. (p. 422)

As might be expected, Fouqué's comparative success depends more than ordinarily on his subject matter. The principal works in [*Ausgewählte Werke*] approach in various degrees to perfection. In the lowest place amongst them, though not in a low place, we are disposed to class the *Magic Ring,* which is, we think, inferior to *Sintram.* The *Hero of the North,* a trilogy composed of three dramas, *Sigurd the Serpent Killer, Sigurd's Revenge,* and *Aslauga,* possess great and various merit; and it may console any man under heavier failures than any which we attribute to our author, and under severer criticism than ours, to know that by a felicitous concurrence of genius and subject matter, he has created the faultless completeness of *Undine.* . . . We do not believe that the serious treatment of an old supernatural legend [as Fouqué attempts in *Hero of the North*] can be a thoroughly fit employment for modern art: but it was desirable that the experiment should be fairly made: and if ever the difficulty arising from a consciousness of unreality could have been overcome, we think the poet would have succeeded here. (p. 423)

The result of [Fouqué's] conscientious adherence to the true version of [the *Nibelungen-Lied*] as far as he could ascertain it, is, that although some apocryphal additions are admitted, the *Hero of the North* contains on the whole an authentic version of the legend as it was known in the north before the introduction of Christianity. Nor is this its only merit. The story is skilfully told; the lyrical poetry, constructed on the model of the northern songs, is wild and sometimes sublime; and above all the true tone of tragedy, the consciousness of a struggle with destiny, is so well kept up, as to remind us, in the midst of boundless dissimilarity, of the heroic drama of Greece. If we could forget that the poet is of the nineteenth century, and therefore shut our eyes to the pervading defect of unreality, there would be little drawback to our admiration. (p. 426)

The "**Magic Ring**" is written with a quaint and rich solemnity of style, which is useful in leading us away from the region of modern associations into a sphere where we can believe in the wonderful tale before us; and in the numberless adventures which take place in Norway, Gascony, or Carthagena, it is pleasant to feel the centripetal force by which the author grad-

ually draws them in to the common point of their completion in the Suabian castle on the Danube. But it is rather with the curiosity which watches a skilful conjurer, than with the interest excited by an artist, that we wait for the solution of the complicated problem. . . . Placed halfway between allegory and reality, the story offers one side to the fancy and feelings, and the other to the understanding: but the knights and ladies are neither living and lifelike enough to call out our sympathies strongly, nor so strictly typical as to amuse us by analogies or to instruct us by a moral. Attracted into the imaginary world presented to us, and yet unable to lose ourselves in it, and forget that it is unreal, we are at last carried on by the secondary impulse of love for wonderful events and picturesque scenes. (pp. 440-41)

The tale of *Sintram and His Companions* is written in a more elevated tone, and with greater unity of purpose. The attention is no longer distracted by multifarious adventures, and the conflict of good and evil, though still externally personified, is also carried on morally in the will and affections of the hero. (p. 441)

It would be easy to add many general considerations on Fouqué's genius, but we hope that the remarks which we have thrown out will be sufficient to explain our views, and in some degree to illustrate his works. We think he well deserves his wide reputation. (p. 450)

> "'*Ausgewählte Werke: Ausgabe letzter Hand*'," in *The Foreign Quarterly Review, Vol. XXIX, No. LVII,* 1842, pp. 421-50.

TAIT'S EDINBURGH MAGAZINE   (essay date 1845)

[In Fouqué's most elaborate production in verse,] the irregular dramatic poem called "**The Hero of the North**," we have always taken great delight. . . . Its conception, and many features in its execution, are directly traceable to the "Lay of the Nibelungen," the rude epic of Germany, which, when the first part of Fouqué's poem was composed, it was the fashion, in the literary circles of that country, to regard as standing in the same class with the Iliad. There is hardly a scene in the "**Hero of the North**" which does not exhibit instances, both of those faults which arose from the character of the poet's own mind, and of those impressed on his work by the laws of the [Romantic] school after which he had modelled his way of poetical thinking. But there is in it some deep pathos, infinite chivalrous vigour, and many touches of high poetic imagination.

In Fouqué's prose romances, the quality which determines the character is the pervading spirit of fine idealism. Those of them that are worth anything, owe their worth chiefly to the fact, that, if they have no other merit, their conception is poetical. Those of them that are quite worthless, are so because the main conception is one which did not admit of being treated poetically. Thus, nothing can be poorer than the attempts at humour; and the few tales built exclusively on this basis, are quite beneath criticism. And thus, also, where the leading idea is lofty and serious, the spirit is caught with a placid rapture, and represented, in its leading features, with a simple purity, which atone for all occasional lapses. Those who are acquainted with "**Undine**" will readily allow the truth of this remark; and they will also be disposed,—while those who have read the author's works more extensively cannot but be fully prepared,—to admit that he is a most wretched and bungling constructor of plots. He fails utterly in every attempt to do more than relate in natural order, the most simple series of incidents. . . . Not one of his larger tales is an exception of this censure. The **"Magic Ring"** is a perfect specimen of confusion worse confounded: and there is much of the same fault in a simpler, and more pleasing work, **"The Persecuted,"** (**"Der Verfolgte."**) It is only in some of his short tales and legends, that we are freed from the painful effort which his ravelled threads of narrative cost us. Nor is this the only fault in the outline of his works. The same deficiency in practical sense and judgement, which makes him incompetent to grapple with a complex group of facts,—co-operates with that systematic imitation of antique simplicity, which is a main characteristic of the literary sect he belongs to, in producing a forced and false naïveté, which often borders on childishness, and sometimes becomes absolutely silly.

Examples, pertinent enough, are furnished by the two romances last named. (p. 521)

[The nature of Fouqué's faults] is such, that, if our judgment on them be just, none of his most elaborate writings can be otherwise than seriously defective. And so, we think, the case stands. Even in **"Undine"** itself, a tale founded on a thought which is at once exquisitely fine and deeply touching, there is very much that causes the flow of feeling to stop painfully and abruptly. . . .

But every where, even in the least successful of the author's works, (excepting only **"The Tale of the Three Pictures,"** and one or two other melancholy attempts at the ludicrous,) there breaks out that fine spirit of poetry to which we alluded a little ago. . . . Some of the shorter pieces, throughout,—**"The Vow,"** for instance, . . . —**"The Champion,"** —**"The Repose on the Flight,"**—and many parts of the longer tales,—are inspired by a fine harmony of feeling, a quiet felicity of imagery, and an exquisite sense of the relations that bind together the spiritual and the material, which are worthy of a true poet, and fully entitle this author to claim the honourable name. And in that highest and most difficult branch of poetic art, which consists in the imagining of human character, we cannot, indeed, assert that he displays genius of the first order; but we can safely say, that the first touches of his outline are often vigorous as well as fine, and that the failure lies in the involvement of the conception rather than in its first formation. He is often exceedingly successful, likewise, in exciting, in favour of his characters, sympathetic emotion of a lofty as well as pure kind. . . .

[His] strength lies in the portraiture of the chivalrous character,—in its aspects of war, of love, and still more of religion; but of the chivalrous character, not in its full development, but in that rudimental state in which we may poetically imagine it to have existed in the earlier stages of its gradual formation. . . .

The story told in [**"Thiodolf, the Icelander,"**] is calculated to excite all its author's liveliest feelings. It is the history of a young Icelandic hero of the tenth century, whose adventurous wanderings through Europe bring him into relations with the knights of Provence and Italy, the Mahometans of northern Africa, the Emperor and nobles of Constantinople, and the barbaric hordes of the Bulgarian valleys. In the management of the materials thus collected, the author shows alike his besetting faults and his redeeming excellencies. He gives us much confusion of narrative, and a little silliness and insipidity. But these are only blots breaking out occasionally, in a picture painted with great spirit, and with fine poetic tenderness. (p. 522)

[We heartily recommend] it and Fouqué's other works to those who desire to become acquainted with one of the most curious sections in the recent history of literature. (p. 530)

"The Works of de La Motte Fouqué," in Tait's Edinburgh Magazine, *Vol. XII, No. CXL, August, 1845, pp. 520-30.*

EDGAR ALLAN POE   (essay date 1856)

[If] allegory ever establishes a fact, it is by dint of overturning a fiction. Where the suggested meaning runs through the obvious one in a *very* profound under-current, so as never to interfere with the upper one without our own volition, so as never to show itself unless *called* to the surface, there only, for the proper uses of fictitious narrative, is it available at all. Under the best circumstances, it must always interfere with that unity of effect which, to the artist, is worth all the allegory in the world. . . . Of allegory properly handled, judiciously subdued, seen only as a shadow or by suggestive glimpses, and making its nearest approach to truth in a not obtrusive and therefore not unpleasant *appositeness*, the **"Undine"** of De La Motte Fouqué is the best, and undoubtedly a very remarkable specimen. (p. 252)

Edgar Allan Poe, "Tale Writing—Nathaniel Hawthorne," in Godey's Lady's Book, *Vol. XXXV, No. 19, November, 1847, pp. 252-56.**

THE ENGLISHWOMAN'S DOMESTIC MAGAZINE (essay date 1871)

The list of Fouqué's works is a long one. We have observed that he tried his art on all branches of poetry. He has written ballads, which are not considered very successful, mahrchens (fairy tales) recommending themselves by their boldness and simplicity to childish admiration, epigrams of doubtful merit, idyls, lyric poetry of profound sentiment but not taking, patriotic rhymes which number scientifically among the better of their class, but have notwithstanding never been popular, dramas of various kinds and ages, written with marvelous facility at the rate of about one a year; but the writings on which he must depend for his enduring fame are his romances and novels. Fouqué's mind was best fitted for this class of composition. Here his exuberant imagination, his skill in blending the superhuman and the real, his refined and chivalrous sentiment, and his peculiar power of language had the best opportunity for telling. At best his writings have some little affectation and mannerism about them and in his dramas and rhymes that feature becomes unpleasantly prominent. (p. 273)

As Fouqué's first literary attempts were devoted to the dramatic plays, it may be convenient to consider his dramas first. Our author was an unusually prolific dramatist, writing no less than twenty-four plays in twenty years. . . . [There] are traces of talent and *esprit* visible in each; however, traces of such are not sufficient to constitute a work of lasting merit. The great disqualification in all is not the author but the school to which the author belonged; romanticism and dramaturgy do not seem to be compatible with one another; at all events their union has not produced any great results. . . .

Up to 1810 Fouqué lent his pen almost exclusively to dramatic writing. His best play of that period has also remained his best drama throughout—viz., a trilogy published in 1808, under the title of *The Hero of the North.* By this time Fouqué had fixed upon the class of subjects which best suited his personal temperament, and which remained his favourite to the end of his life—viz., the Scandinavian and old German tales. Beautiful as these tales are, their subjects hardly admit of dramatic treatment, being pre-eminently epic.

It must be allowed that Fouqué has made out of this in a dramatic way what he could, and there are scenes especially in the first part of the trilogy—viz., *Sigurd, the Dragon-killer*—which vie with the most effective from our best dramaturgic pens. But his object as a whole to revive the popularity of the ancient tales by putting them in a modern shape has not succeeded. (p. 274)

Our author's poetical writings claim higher merit in every respect than his dramatic compositions. Whenever he can bring himself to step beyond the regions of mysticism his verses are decidedly beautiful, but on relapsing into his ordinary strain he resumes an affected tone which detracts from their other excellence. . . . His *Yager's Songs and Poems of the War of 1813* number among the best popular verses in German literature. Some of his lyrics are very charming; his epigrams have a good deal of point, but his ballads have no great merit. The subjects are generally indifferently chosen and unsuitably handled. . . . The volume of *Religious Songs,* published three years after the author's death, comprise many excellent hymns. Without disparagement to the poet, the shortest poems are certainly the best on the whole; for in the longer ones he has given a loose to his mystic proclivities, and lost the poignancy of thought in breadth of mystic reverie.

It is as a novelist that Fouqué has been most successful. That speciality of literature he seems to have been specially made for, and in that field of labour he has hit upon the very task best suited to his talent. No work of his can compare with *Undine.* . . . It is not only the beauty of the romance which fascinates the reader, and the poetry of the ideas springing from Fouqué's fertile and creative imagination, but the elegance of the language and the refinement of the sentiment likewise stamp this novel one of the jewels of literature. (pp. 274-75)

The Magic Ring is a romance of chivalry in the truest conception of the romantic school, and one of the best of its class. The plot and *dénouement* is grand, and the whole is a beautiful creation whose merit is only impaired by the author's extravagance of sentiment, and the anachronism already referred to of imparting thoughts of the nineteenth century to knights of the Middle Ages. . . . *Alwin,* more than any of Fouqué's novels, betrays [his] discontented longing for a different state of things in Germany which, the author not having sufficient foreknowledge to see into the brilliant future in which the empire has become familiar to us, not unnaturally reverted to the glorious days of past history, decked out in all the beautifying colours with which distance and romance invests historical events. . . .

[Fouqué's later works, which expressed ultra-conservative political views,] discredited him with the public so seriously as almost to banish his name from the bookstalls. . . . Almost all his later compositions bear the stamp of political feudalism. The *Empires of the World* . . . , the *Pappenheim Cuirassier, Fata Morgana,* &c., have by the same trait been made unpalatable to the readers of his time, and are not likely to gain the favour of any succeeding generation.

It is not surprising that such flaws should detract from the popularity even of so successful a writer as De la Motte Fouqué among his own contemporaries; but after the period by which we are removed from that time they are simply forgotten, and to the present generation nothing remains but those brilliant

compositions which will secure our author a favourable hearing among refined minds in every age. (p. 275)

"The German Novelists: Friedrich Heinrich Karl de La Motte Fouqué," in The Englishwoman's Domestic Magazine, *Vol. XII, 1871, pp. 272-76.*

GEORG BRANDES (essay date 1873)

The Christian-Germanic reaction which was one of the results of the War of Liberation found very characteristic literary expression in a series of tales by a nobleman who had fought in the war as a cavalry officer, Baron de la Motte Fouqué. Fouqué is principally known to the reading world at large by his charming little story, *Undine.* As a specimen of Romantic "Naturpoesie" at its best, this tale is only inferior to Tieck's *Elfenmärchen* ("The Elves"). But Undine is the one really living figure which Fouqué has produced. The cause of his success in this case probably lay in the fact that he was depicting a being who was only half human, half an element of nature—a wave, spray, the cool freshness and wild movement of water—a being without a soul. . . . Fouqué, who was a poet without being a psychologist, found a subject exactly suited to his imaginative talent in this being, which corresponded to one of the elements, and hence itself consisted of but one life-element. . . . Although the theme is genuinely medieval (borrowed, in fact, from Paracelsus, whose theory of the elemental spirits is founded upon old popular beliefs), and although in the course of its elaboration the author often relapses into sentimental piety, yet, to its decided advantage, a fresh pagan note is predominant in the story. Undine's originality lies in her pagan nature, as it reveals itself before she is baptized; and there is something genuinely Greek in the idea of its not being the skeleton with the scythe which comes for the dying man, but an elemental spirit which brings him death in a loving kiss.

But at the same time that Fouqué was embodying such originality and genius as he possessed in this little tale, he was also, under the influence of the great national movement, projecting the long series of romances of chivalry which began with *Der Zauberring*. . . . To the romantic reactionaries *The Magic Ring* became a sort of gospel. Nobles and squires saw themselves reflected in all these old burnished shields and coats of mail, and rejoiced at the sight. But it was not a faithful historical picture which Fouqué exhibited. His age of chivalry is an imaginary age, in which stately, high-born men, clad in armour of burnished silver or of some dull metal inlaid with gold, and wearing silver helmets, plumed or unplumed, or iron helmets surmounted by golden eagles' wings . . . ride forth upon fiery chargers. . . . The knights are proud and brave, the faithful squires give their lives for their masters, the slender demoiselles award the prizes at the tourneys, and love their knights *"minniglich."* Everything is ordered according to the exact prescriptions of the book of the laws of chivalry.

Everything is conventional—first and foremost, the mawkish, languishing style, supposed to be peculiarly adapted to the glorification of this high-born society. Only examples can give any idea of it. Bertha, sitting by a rivulet, sees her reflection in the water. "Bertha blushed so brightly that it seemed as if a star had been kindled in the water." . . . A noble lady, pouring forth the tale of her misfortunes, takes time to interlard it with descriptions like the following: "I paced distractedly up and down my room, would hear nothing of the games in which the other noble maidens invited me to take part in the evening, and impatiently waved my maid away when she brought me a beautiful fishing-rod, *inlaid with mother-of-pearl,* with a *golden* line and *silver* hook.'' It is strange that the inhabitants of a world where all utensils seem to be made of mother-of-pearl, gold, and silver, should think it necessary specially to mention that the gift offered her was composed of these peerless materials.

The emotions are of the same material, all mother-of-pearl and cloth of gold—not one breath of unrestrained natural feeling, not one action dictated by pure, unreflecting passion. All the emotions and passions are as carefully trained as the knights' chargers. We know beforehand how everything will happen. (pp. 301-04)

[The] knights are not much more than stuffed suits of armour. They affect one much as do the figures one sees riding upon armoured wooden horses in the Tower of London or the great armoury in Dresden.

From the description of one of [the hero's] earliest single combats we gain an idea of the extraordinary influence attributed to attire. His opponent, Sir Heerdegen, wears a rusty suit of armour, and his *rusty* voice shouts from behind the bars of his *rusty* helmet: "Bertha! Bertha!" while from Otto's *silver* helmet comes in *silvery* tones the cry: "Gabriele! Gabriele!" (p. 305)

This literature is really literature for cavalry officers. The horses are the only creatures in the book whose psychology Fouqué has successfully mastered, and this for the same reason that he was successful with Undine, namely, that it is elementary psychology. (p. 306)

[The horses possess invincibility] until the destined master, he whose power over the heart is felt to be "of strange significance," appears, and from that moment onwards absolute devotion and the most tender caresses! What else, what more is there in Fouqué's young maidens of high degree? . . .

Thus does the psychology of the romance of chivalry culminate—psychology of the patrician, or psychology of the horse, call it which you will. In its portraiture of knights hailing from all the ends of the earth, *The Magic Ring* . . . confines itself to primary types of humanity and the colouring produced by the sun—we are able to distinguish a Moor from a Finn. (p. 307)

> *Georg Brandes, "Romantic Literature and Politics," in his* Main Currents in Nineteenth Century Literature: The Romantic School in Germany, Vol. II, *translated by Diana White and Mary Morison (originally published as* Hovedstromninger i det 19de aarhundredes litteratur, 1873), *Heinemann Ltd., 1902 (and reprinted by Boni & Liveright, Inc., 1924, pp. 293-309).**

GEORGE MACDONALD   (essay date 1895)

Were I asked, what is a fairytale? I should reply, *Read Undine: that is a fairytale; then read this and that as well, and you will see what is a fairytale.* Were I further begged to describe the *fairytale,* or define what it is, I would make answer, that I should as soon think of describing the abstract human face, or stating what must go to constitute a human being. A fairytale is just a fairytale, as a face is just a face; and of all fairytales I know, I think *Undine* the most beautiful. (p. 313)

> *George Macdonald in his* A Dish of Orts: Chiefly Papers on the Imagination, and on Shakspere, *Sampson, Low and Marston, 1895, 322 p.*

EDMUND GOSSE   (essay date 1896)

We, looking back to the beginning of the century, may now recognize in Fouqué the latest and the most uncompromising of the Romanticists, the man who accepted most unflinchingly the principles of that school, and who carried them out most thoroughly. 'Don Quixote', they called him, and wondered that he could venture to make his appearance two centuries after the death of his creator. To the mental vision, looking back some eighty years, Fouqué appears more as a rubicund officer of dragoons, sitting over a bivouac fire, and telling innocent fairy stories to the honour and glory of the King of Prussia. He belongs to an order of things now absolutely gone and done with, never, in all probability, to be seen again upon this world of ours. (pp. vii-viii)

The amount of literary work done by [Fouqué]—work in poetry, in drama, in prose fiction, in journalism—was positively prodigious, and most of it, so far as modern readers are concerned, might very well have been left undone. His *Theatre* is immense and perfectly unreadable. Time has found a great deal to 'pare away' from Fouqué's abundant fruitage. It has left four or five short romances which promise to be immortal, since the complete revolution of taste has not rendered them obsolete or uninteresting. Fouqué lives by *Sintram,* by *Der Zauberring,* and by *Thiodulf,* but most of all by *Undine*—that is to say, by the least considered of his productions from his thirty-third to his thirty-eighth year. In these stories he reveals a talent which is exquisite in its way, and quite unlike the talent of any one else. . . . (pp. viii-ix)

[Fouqué] produced the great patriotic trilogy on Sigurd, *The Hero of the North,* which, if not really a durable work, is certainly, from an historical point of view, the most interesting of his too abundant dramatic productions. (p. xiii)

[In] this Scandinavian trilogy he is vaguely and dimly, but unquestionably, leading the way for Wagner. At this time Fouqué was full of the *Nibelungenlied,* and in order to illustrate it more completely was reading Icelandic, Danish, and Swedish authorities with great assiduity. Nor did he stop here; he made this but the starting-point for the composition of other dramas, full of magnificent Teuton heroes who foreshadowed the greatness of Germany and her unbroken spirit. In these plays it seems almost certain that his zeal and fire were not equalled by his executive ability. He had little power of dramatic evolution, and no insight into character. The heroes ride through his dramas on very handsome steeds and in admirable armour, but we get little notion of their personal quality. (pp. xiii-xiv)

No element of humour, no smallest suspicion of the ridiculous, interfered with his perfect contentment in the composition of tales in which men and women of heroic mould, magnificently habited, were gently interfered with by supernatural beings and elemental influences. These stories were often instinct with beauty, and, of them all, *Undine* is certainly the most delightful. (p. xvii)

> *Edmund Gosse, in his introduction to* Undine *by Friedrich de La Motte Fouqué, translated by Edmund Gosse, Lawrence & Bullen, 1896 (and reprinted in* Undine and Other Stories, *Oxford University Press, London, 1932, pp. vii-xvii).*

W. J. LILLYMAN   (essay date 1971)

Undine is by no means a tale of simple contrasts, of good and of bad characters. Bertalda, for example, is not merely Undine's rival for Huldbrand's affection, but most importantly the girl who was wronged by the elemental spirits in being robbed of her true parents so that Undine might grow up in a human family. . . . [There] is considerable suggestion [in *Undine*] as my following analysis will attempt to show, that [Undine indeed got Huldbrand] at least partly through deception. These are some of the facets of the tale which make the distribution of guilt and innocence not quite as simple as has been maintained. (p. 95)

[In *Undine* the] human beings are completely at the mercy of the elemental spirits, utterly their victims, despite constant recourse to religious songs and to Christian ritual, and despite many appeals to God to protect them. (p. 96)

Huldbrand and Bertalda are . . . victimized by the elemental spirits. Having ventured into the forest to carry out a request of Bertalda's, Huldbrand is driven to the fisherman's dwelling by the spirits and marked by them as Undine's prospective husband. (pp. 96-97)

At this point we must consider one of the most important problems of the tale which is basic to any question of Huldbrand's guilt, namely, whether Huldbrand marries Undine of his own free will. Do the elemental spirits by their intervention merely create the opportunity for Huldbrand to marry Undine if he wishes to, or does their influence extend further than this? It is most revealing that Huldbrand is not just any knight who has wandered into the forest, but indeed the knight who has a certain attachment to and is carrying out an errand for Bertalda. Bertalda has already been robbed of her parents by the elemental spirits and they are now about to take her beloved too, although this latter point may not be immediately apparent. (p. 97)

It is indeed as though Undine has usurped Bertalda's total existence. The more "soulful" she becomes, the more "soulless" Bertalda appears.

Nevertheless, Fouqué's tale is not named after Huldbrand or Bertalda, and Undine's role in the story must therefore be considered further. In their view of Undine as an innocent girl of angelic goodness, critics ignore aspects of Undine's character *before* she obtains a soul, i.e., they ascribe little significance to the part she plays in the important events of the first seven of the nineteen chapters of the tale. Most especially, no critic has perceived that Undine intentionally lies to Huldbrand on their wedding night in order that nothing may hinder the consummation of their marriage and her obtaining of a soul. There is thus an objective basis for Huldbrand's feeling that Undine is a creature of deception beyond that of her being an elemental spirit. (p. 102)

It is Undine's tragedy that she can nevertheless not leave her past as an elemental spirit behind her, for Kühleborn and the other spirits continually interfere in her affairs, as they do in those of the humans in the tale, and contribute thereby to Huldbrand's rejection of Undine. Undine is finally, and ironically, therefore the most thorough victim of the elemental spirits.

Even from the beginning, however, Undine has been at the mercy of other spirits, for the task of obtaining a soul through marriage to a human being was not one she had set herself but one chosen for her by her parents. . . . Thus, also, Undine was not responsible for displacing Bertalda from her family nor for guiding Bertalda's knight to the fisherman's isolated abode, but she nevertheless suffers the consequences of these acts later when Huldbrand turns from her to Bertalda partly because of these machinations of the elemental spirits. (p. 103)

Even after receiving a soul, Undine is by no means free of the elemental spirits' dominance, for, as she warns Huldbrand, they would obtain "ein Recht über mich" [a right over me] . . . were he to curse her near a body of water. When this eventually does happen on the Danube, Undine has to return to the domain of the elemental spirits.

When Undine is forced by the elemental spirits to leave Huldbrand, she does not cease to exist or revert to being an elemental spirit as do her predecessors in this legend, but retains her soul. . . . This is an important innovation in the legend which adds to the characters' dilemma at the end, for, after the sorrow caused by Undine's disappearance has gradually diminished, Huldbrand's and Bertalda's feelings for each other reawaken and they wish to marry. The old fisherman also insists that his daughter, Bertalda, may not continue to live with Huldbrand out of wedlock. If Undine, however, still exists and still possesses a soul, are Huldbrand and Bertalda justified in marrying? (pp. 103-04)

When Undine kills Huldbrand in her embrace, the description is, on the surface, highly reminiscent of romantic love-deaths. . . . This is, however, not a scene of romantic transcendence. It rather illustrates Huldbrand's and Undine's total subservience to the will of the elemental spirits and represents the height of their suffering. It is indeed only at Huldbrand's funeral that there is the suggestion that Undine finally escapes the domination of the other elemental spirits and achieves a certain union with Huldbrand, although this is, intentionally, left somewhat ambiguous. . . .

To have a soul means, then, in Fouqué's tale being completely vulnerable, utterly a victim. . . . (p. 104)

> *W. J. Lillyman, "Fouqué's 'Undine'," in* Studies in Romanticism *(copyright 1971 by the Trustees of Boston University), Vol. 10, No. 2, Spring, 1971, pp. 94-104.*

ADDITIONAL BIBLIOGRAPHY

Bergmann, Frank. "The Roots of Tolkien's Tree: The Influence of George MacDonald and German Romanticism upon Tolkien's Essay 'On Fairy Stories'." *Mosaic* X, No. 2 (Winter 1977): 5-14.*
  Explains the pervasive influence of *Undine* on writers and theorists of fairy tales.

"Life and Writings of Fouqué." *Christian Remembrance Monthly* n.s. VII, No. XXXIX (March 1844): 304-17.
  A consideration of Fouqué's writings, with biographical anecdotes, citing Fouqué as an exception among German Romantics because of his superior morality.

Mornin, Edward. "Some Patriotic Novels and Tales by La Motte Fouqué." *Seminar* XI, No. 3 (September 1975): 141-56.
  Traces the roots of Fouqué's Romanticism and medievalism and comments on the political implications of his use of folk-legends.

Pollin, Burton R. "*Undine* in the Works of Poe." *Studies in Romanticism* 14, No. 1 (Winter 1975): 59-74.*
  A discussion of Poe's respect for *Undine* citing examples of its influence on his work.

Christian Dietrich Grabbe

1801-1836

German dramatist, poet, and satirist.

In the attitudes and techniques of his pessimistic, episodic dramas, Grabbe anticipated many features of the late nineteenth-century and the modern theater. Rejecting Romanticism and the classical idealism of Johann Wolfgang von Goethe and Friedrich Schiller, he depicted a senseless universe in which the individual's fate is controlled inexorably by history. Grabbe's work expresses concepts of realism and of existentialism that his contemporaries barely hinted at. With the montage arrangement of short, impressionistic scenes, Grabbe presaged the epic theater of Bertolt Brecht and moved toward the cinematic techniques of the twentieth century. Because Grabbe called for grandiose scenery and lighting in many of his plays, only one was produced in his lifetime. However, his plays have since been performed and studied for their unique style and innovative vision.

Grabbe's pessimistic artistic outlook grew from a life of constant failure, depression, and pain. The son of a prison warden, he received law degrees in Leipzig and Berlin and had a short, unsuccessful career as a military judiciary in his hometown, Detmold. He traveled to Düsseldorf where, with the encouragement of K. L. Immermann, Heinrich Heine, Ludwig Tieck and others, he began writing plays. Grabbe identified with the writers in the "Junge Deutschland" (Young Germany) movement, who aimed to expose the truth rather than to shroud it in Romanticism. One of Grabbe's first plays, *Scherz, Satire, Ironie und tiefere Bedeutung (Jest, Satire, Irony and Deeper Significance)*, achieved this aim in a satirical way, presenting a negativistic picture of society and of the literary community. His caustic criticism of the world of letters, coupled with his melancholic personality and anti-Semitism estranged him from many of his literary friends, alienating Grabbe more and more from society.

Grabbe's best-known plays are his historical dramas, which incorporate his most striking innovations. These plays, conceived as epic dramas, require elaborate, lifelike sets, huge crowd scenes, and unusual lighting. With their back lighting, enormous casts, and rapid scene development, they are precursors of twentieth-century films. *Hannibal* and *Napoleon oder die hundert Tage* represent heroic historical figures who are reduced to helpless puppets, unable to understand or determine their destinies. In *Napoleon oder die hundert Tage*, the hero's breakdown is traced through battle scenes, during which Napoleon becomes progressively more helpless against the tide of events. In a similar way, Hannibal's power and will are reduced visibly, scene by scene, as vast crowds vociferously assert their will, fulfilling history's inevitable course.

Grabbe's own fate was as tragic as his characters'. He lived in poverty and despair, and died at age 35 of tuberculosis, his literary work unrecognized. Critics and readers, however, soon acknowledged that, in his avant-garde themes and methods, Grabbe was a pioneer of modern dramatic theory and technique.

Courtesy of the German Information Center

PRINCIPAL WORKS

Marius und Sulla   (drama)   1823
Herzog Theodor von Gothland   (drama)   1827
Scherz, Satire, Ironie und tiefere Bedeutung   (drama) 1827
   [*Jest, Satire, Irony and Deeper Significance*, in *From the Modern Repertoire, Series Two*, edited by Eric Russell Bentley, 1952; published in England as *Comedy, Satire, Irony and Deeper Meaning*, 1955]
Don Juan und Faust   (drama)   1829
   [*Don Juan and Faust*, in *The Theatre of Don Juan*, edited by Oscar Mandel, 1963]
Hohenstaufen I: Kaiser Friedrich Barbarossa   (drama) 1829
Hohenstaufen II: Kaiser Heinrich der Sechste   (drama) 1830
Napoleon oder die hundert Tage   (drama)   1831
Aschenbrödel   (drama)   1835
   **[*Cinderella*, in *Poets and Poetry of Europe*, by Henry W. Longfellow, 1845]
Hannibal   (drama)   1835
   [*Hannibal*, 1964]

Die Hermannsschlacht (drama) 1838

*This is the date of first publication rather than first peformance.

**This is a partial translation of *Aschenbrödel*.

BLACKWOOD'S EDINBURGH MAGAZINE (essay date 1837)

Grabbe is a dramatic writer, of more genius than taste or judgment. His imagination is fertile enough; he often throws out striking and original thoughts; he sometimes sketches a character well, or brings out in single scenes, with considerable liveliness and truth, the expression of passion. But he wants the power of forming a whole; he wastes his strength in detail, and is unable to fuse together into any form of symmetry and beauty the scattered masses which lie in heaps about him. . . . [In *Cinderella*, Grabbe] has deserted the more elevated ground of tragedy for that of comedy, or rather of farce; and wisely, we think, for the sock seems to us to fit him more naturally than the buskin; and the purely fantastic character of the subject, by emancipating him from the restraints of probability, and allowing him free scope for the sallies and outbreakings of a lively imagination, and wild reckless humour, suits peculiarly well with his irregular and eccentric habits of thought. (p. 668)

[While Grabbe] contrives to make his comic scenes the vehicle of a good many sly hits at the humours, literary tastes, and political relations of the day, [he] has not pitched the tone of his dramatic tale entirely in the comic key; for he has mingled with the farcical part of the piece some serious scenes of no inconsiderable beauty and imagination. . . . Many of the allusions to existing individuals, or current topics of ridicule, we have no doubt have escaped us, but even as it is, we are indebted to Grabbe for not a few bursts of hearty laughter in the perusal of his whimsical performance. (p. 669)

> "'Cinderella': A Dramatic Tale," in Blackwood's Edinburgh Magazine, Vol. XLI, No. CCLIX, May, 1837, pp. 668-81.

F. W. KAUFMANN (essay date 1940)

Grabbe betrays even more than Grillparzer the inner disharmony and disillusionment of the Restoration period. His birth placed him between the bourgeois and the proletarian classes: he shares with the bourgeois of the late-romantic and Biedermeier period the political disinterestment and contemplative characteristics while the proletarian in him tends towards an anti-idealistic, concrete positivism. . . . In Grabbe himself are combined qualities which, at least in part, seem incompatible: industry, intelligence, contentment as against an unrestrained imagination, and boundless intemperance. Grabbe is a man who longed for inner harmony and the sympathy of his environment, but again and again he was agitated by his uncontrolled vitality and demoniacally driven to the wildest extremes, only to be thrown back into a stage of exhaustion and apathy. Correspondingly, his work is characterized by the antagonism between romantic subjectivism and an intense desire for exaggeration, on the one hand, and a realistic objectivity, a critical valuation, and a recognition of the limitations of concrete existence, on the other. In particular, the emotional side,—the organ of romantic self-transcendence—is counteracted by an-

alytical reason, the organ of self-limitation and self-control. The opposing tendencies within his character reflect the general situation of a time which begins to turn from patriarchal self-sufficiency and the modest pleasures of the smallest sphere to a materialistic and utilitarian mode and aspect of life. This disharmony and consequent reorientation, which stirs Grabbe and his period, is also characteristic of his dramatic work, in which these opposite tendencies seek a tolerable balance. For this reason alone earlier interpretations must be rejected which find in Grabbe's work chiefly the problem of the leader-personality who fails through the stupidity of the masses. Such an interpretation presupposes a belief in the absolute value of the great individual which Grabbe, despite the fact that he possessed qualities of genius, was just as incapable of endorsing as his contemporaries Grillparzer and Schopenhauer.

There is no direct evidence for Grabbe's earlier belief in the values of the idealistic world view. Its significance, however, for his formative years can be inferred from the desperate disillusionment of his first dramatic works. His tragedy *Herzog Theodor von Gothland* can be compared, with respect to the part which it played in his development, with Grillparzer's *Blanka von Kastilien* and even more with *Die Ahnfrau*. Grabbe's struggle with traditional views and values in the first drama is even more desperate and pathetic than Grillparzer's, and its dynamic exuberance is almost pathological. . . . [Grabbe] makes blind emotionalism responsible for the catastrophe of human relations: Gothland's tragedy is that of disregarded reality. . . . Subjective Romantic idealism . . . ends in a complete nihilism of values. This negative result, however, is the first stage of Grabbe's search for a world view, in which the individual is not considered as a detached self, but as existentially integrated in a human environment. (pp. 80-3)

Herzog Theodor von Gothland is a document characteristic of the decline of Romanticism and Idealism with its passionate violation and exaggeration of all realistic probabilities. Exaggeration even appears in the structure as a whole. In its single scenes and in the dialogue, it is almost entirely built upon such contrasts as Christianity and Satanism, immortality and nihilism, love and basest harlotry, humanity and bestial sadism. (pp. 83-4)

The comedy *Scherz, Satire, Ironie und tiefere Bedeutung* emphasizes less Grabbe's despairing doubt of the fundamental values of idealism. Rather it criticizes a world which has accepted the ideas of previous periods in their most distorted form. In this play, Grabbe derides almost everything which the conventional mind has taken over as a secure possession or with the claim of infallibility. The pretenses of the nobility are caricatured in the superficiality and avarice of von Wernthal and in the brutality of the Freiherr von Mordax. The rage for titles in an empty-headed society is ridiculed by the friendly reception of the devil, who introduces himself with papal titles. The world of the lower bourgeoisie is presented as so hopelessly stupid that it entrusts the education of its children to a drunkard and considers the possession of intestinal worms as a sign of aptitude for the study of theology. . . . The intellectual products of this society are, of course, on a corresponding level. The ladies enjoy the sentimentalities of late-Romanticism, but reject everything which is of a more concrete vitality as coarse imagination. This society worships the theologians whose beliefs are criticized by Grabbe as primitive and fetishistic. It has the highest esteem for the conceited, but actually stupid, scientists, who repudiate any factual evidence which might shake the validity of their preconceived theories. It has the same deep respect for those idealistic philosophers who content themselves with reducing the concrete world to an empty formula such as "the essence of all existence.". . . This satire reaches its climax when, at the end of the drama, a strong punch is served and the "vermaledeite Grabbe" appears in person to join the drinking party; for this indulgence is the only thing which the author believes himself to have in common with such company. Society is treated in this comedy as a group deprived of any intelligence, and held together by a few traditional valuations, unreasonable formalities and primitive needs. The author here shows he has lost his belief in any inner community of man which would derive its force from living values. Only one choice seems to remain, the choice between the nihilistic despair of Herzog Theodor or else some kind of an adjustment to reality, which, however, he finds extremely disappointing, since he has approached it with the expectations of an idealist. This explains why the prevailing mood of this so-called comedy is not a self-sufficient humor which can consider the weakness of man as an imperfect manifestation of a perfect idea, but is, to use Grabbe's own words, "das Lachen der Verzweiflung"; he is deeply stirred by the imperfection of reality and tries to face the intolerable by refusing to take it too seriously. The grotesque and apparently chaotic structure of the play is, therefore, not mere license or lack of artistic capability, but an adequate expression of the inner rift in Grabbe's relation to the outside world. Disharmony pervades even the details of the scenes; time and again the author creates a mood of sublimity and suddenly interrupts it by a remark or a situation of coarse and caustic realism. . . . As a grotesque comedy it differs, in spite of many similarities, from the Romantic comedy. . . . Grabbe is still under the influence of [Romantic] ideas, but he has lost his faith in them, and so the comparison between idea and experience poisons his attitude towards reality, which, after all, he cannot fail to recognize.

The fragment of the tragedy *Marius und Sulla,* marks a certain progress towards solving Grabbe's dilemma. Earlier Grabbe had doubted the validity of idealism and disdained reality; in *Marius und Sulla* we see him gradually attaining a more positive attitude toward reality. (pp. 84-6)

[In this play] the sentimental and retrospective Marius is defeated by the positivistic and rational Sulla. The romantic victim of incontinence is contrasted with a character of realistic self-determination and self-limitation. This corresponds to Grabbe's own inner development from the disharmony of "Gefühlszerrüttung" to a more objective attitude towards life—in part as a result of his work on this dramatic fragment. [The] same polarity, the same antagonism between two views of the relation of man to reality, the same tendency of development from idealistic detachment to realistic acceptance of the world is dramatically symbolized in the tragedy *Don Juan und Faust.* Grabbe's testimony supports this interpretation when he says that the author's own spirit seems to be engaged in a death struggle with itself. In *Don Juan und Faust* he attempts to show the "destruction of the too sensual and the too spiritual nature in man." With these words he ascribes to his drama the function of establishing a balance between these two opposite tendencies which oppressed the poet and his contemporaries; thus he wishes to counteract the menace of a materialistic reaction to the idealism of past generations. (p. 88)

Like Grillparzer, [Grabbe] arrives at a conception of life which places the individual in a definite environment and forces him into tragedy through detachment from his environment. Such tragedy could already be traced in Grabbe's first drama *Herzog Theodor von Gothland.* In *Don Juan und Faust,* it is the final truth which Faust at last realizes. In *Kaiser Friedrich Barbarossa,* the dependence of man upon his time and environment is treated in a way which reminds one of Grillparzer's *Sappho* and *König Ottokars Glück und Ende.* (p. 90)

In Grabbe's development from idealism to realism, *Herzog Theodor von Gothland* is the dramatic expression of the first revolt against a traditional world view; emotional perturbation obscures the recognition of the real issue, and scepticism regarding the reliability of the emotions causes doubt of all social and moral values, of all human relations and beliefs. A cynical contempt for man and a fatalistic resignation to the meaninglessness of existence itself characterize Grabbe's first examination of his philosophical heritage, a heritage which his feeling and imagination is disposed to accept. In *Scherz, Satire, Ironie und tiefere Bedeutung,* Grabbe turns with equal despair against a society which thrives on traditional judgments and habits, and has lost all spontaneity and inner responsibility, together with all understanding for the immediate moral demands of reality. In *Marius und Sulla,* Grabbe proceeds to a more positive attitude toward life. . . . [In *Don Juan und Faust*] Grabbe tries to find the human mean between animalistic sensualism and cynical materialism on the one hand, and the "idealistic" detachment from all living contact on the other.

A similar balance is sought in the later historical dramas for the relation between leader and people. The outstanding leader personality is here conceived in the same problematic relation to his people as the mind in its relation to the body in *Don Juan und Faust.* The leader's ability to envisage the more remote potentialities of the future makes him neglect the realistic conditions necessary for executing his projects and, thus, he exposes himself to that tragic isolation which is equivalent to catastrophe. In this way, Barbarossa and Heinrich VI are by their phantastic projects of conquest drawn away from the concrete basis of their power, the German soil, and both meet their fate as soon as they approach the realization of their goal; this very approach parallels their growing isolation. Similarly, Napoleon's efforts to attain his phantastic ends are vain, for he fails to consider the concrete political conditions and the spiritual tendencies of his time. In *Hannibal* the emphasis is shifted to the side of the people; the success of the leader depends absolutely upon the cooperation of his followers, and the harmony of the "intellectual" and the "material" principles is made the basic prerequisite of survival. Harmonious cooperation is emphasized even more in *Die Hermannsschlacht,* since Hermann partly achieves his aims, although the unachieved part of his projects can only be realized in the future when his people will have overcome their primitive stage of materialistic narrowness. Here we find at least a first pregnant, functional explanation of the tragic surplus of energy in the leader personality: the distant, unrealized aim seems to provide the necessary impulse which alone can awaken the inert masses to action; the prospect of eventual realization of this remote aim stimulates them.

The development in Grabbe's dramas indicates a progressive adaptation to the demands of reality. The extraordinary individual is gradually deprived of his superhuman halo, and the mass of the people is increasingly recognized as the spatial and temporal condition for the realization of heroic action. Simultaneously, leader and people are brought into closer organic relation; the leader becomes a life-function of the people, its thinking and directive organ. (pp. 100-01)

Grabbe's view of life develops in and through his dramas from a desperate, nihilistic conception to a moderately tragic one;

the denial of all tragedy would, of course, be an unworthy superficiality, since tragedy is an inescapable consequence of the natural limitation of all human will. In a quite rational development he arrives at a relative harmonization of the two antagonistic poles which we found in extreme tension at the beginning of his dramatic career. . . . [Grabbe never] succeeds in relieving the extraordinary individual entirely of tragedy; but [finds] a meaning for his surplus of will and intelligence in the fact that these provide an aim for further development and the impulse for its realization. . . . [However,] Grabbe remains entirely within the sphere of reality and in this respect stands in closer contact with the realistic tendencies of the nineteenth century than [do several of his contemporaries]. (p. 102)

> *F. W. Kaufmann, "Christian Dietrich Grabbe" (originally published in a somewhat different version as "Die realistische Tendenz in Grabbes Dramen,"* in Smith College Studies in Modern Languages, *Vol. XII, No. 4, July, 1931), in his* German Dramatists of the 19th Century *(reprinted by permission of the Estate of Friedrich Wilhelm Kaufmann), Lymanhouse, 1940, pp. 81-102.*

AUGUST CLOSS   (essay date 1957)

[In the works of C. D. Grabbe] life becomes utterly futile and senseless. According to his *Herzog Theodor von Gothland,* man reads goodness into history, since he is too cowardly to confess its horrible truths to himself. . . . The only way out of the senselessness of life would be to purify the earth with fire and sword, war and plague, like Attila or Caesar. The poet, according to Grabbe, is the surgeon or the satyr who plays with chaos.

Instead of belief in the divine order of things, only sorrow rules in a world in which the deeds of heroic virtue become deeds of crime. Even death does not free—it is no illusion, no triumph as with Goethe's Egmont. Death, like life, is a means of torture and pain. This earth is hell—not guilt—but we must take this hell upon ourselves, otherwise we are cowardly philistines. We are humans (in Grabbe's sense), humans with eagles' heads, but our feet are rooted in the mud.

In his tragedy *Hannibal* the noble hero goes under in a chaos of commonness. Yet the one solace remains: 'We don't fall out of this world.' Napoleon, too, is conscious of his historical mission even at the hour of his defeat when he says: 'It is my fortune which falls, not I.'

A short comparison of Goethe's *Faust* with Grabbe's *Don Juan und Faust* also clearly indicates how very much Grabbe's Nihilism differs from the Classic belief in the divine world order. Grabbe's Faust is a wretched person, self-destructive and grotesque. He is, as the devil mocks, much less than a devil—only a human being. But the imposing thing about this drama is that volcanic 'will to power' which, in spite of knowing suffering, is fulfilled in activity alone, even if nothingness waits furtively behind sorrow and desire. If he cannot create, he can still destroy. (pp. 156-57)

> *August Closs, "Nihilism and Modern German Drama: Grabbe and Büchner," in his* Medusa's Mirror: Studies in German Literature *(reprinted by permission of Barrie & Jenkins Ltd, a division of the Hutchinson Publishing Group Limited), The Cresset Press, 1957, pp. 147-63.**

JAMES TRAINER   (essay date 1966)

In grandeur of conception at least, Grabbe's first play, *Herzog Theodor von Gothland* . . . can measure up adequately to the first plays of Goethe, Schiller or Hebbel, none of them distinguished for its subtlety of approach. . . .

The inspiration of the drama, with its central theme of noble-minded brothers torn apart by misunderstanding and wilful deceit, is not hard to find—in Shakespeare, whose works Grabbe had described to his parents as "the first book in the world, more regarded by some people than the Bible", and in the *Sturm und Drang* writers whose characters came always and only in the giant size. But it is not at bottom a purely literary experience, for the awareness of social divisions, the call for the overthrow of the established order, in a word the stark and bitter theme of *revenge* against a hostile world, was . . . a formative element from [Grabbe's] earliest days. . . . The tone throughout is that of desperation. (p. 276)

When he turned briefly from tragedy to comedy, [Grabbe] took the nihilistic tone with him. . . . *Scherz, Satire, Ironie und tiefere Bedeutung* hardly smacks of desperation to the ordinary reader, indeed he may find himself regretting that Grabbe abandoned the comic genre as quickly as he did, but the iconoclastic tendency is immediately obvious, the sacred cows of society are ridiculed out of town and a wide range of themes, heaven and hell, the frailty of human effort compared with the infinity of the universe, are so elaborated as to invoke a cumulative sense of desperation about man and his condition. The view expressed in *Gothland* that the world was created and ruled over by some satanic monster is here expanded, except that, since the play is also literary satire in the manner of Tieck's *Der gestiefelte Kater,* the image is changed to accord with the new situation. (pp. 276-77)

[In *Don Juan und Faust,* Grabbe] wished to form a bridge between what he considered the two greatest German artistic triumphs, Goethe's *Faust* and Mozart's *Don Giovanni,* and as pontifex he hoped to succeed in placing himself in the same rank as these.

In fact neither character in Grabbe's play *Don Juan und Faust* shows much resemblance to his form in these earlier works, for everything that Grabbe touched turned to Grabbe. Here too he has succeeded chiefly in attracting them into his own ideological orbit and making them bearers of that opposition to the *status quo* which is the function of nearly all his major characters in the early plays. And whereas in *Scherz Satire* Grabbe, in imitation no doubt of Tieck's satirical comedies, came on to the stage himself to be ridiculed . . . , he now transfers his self-pity to an identification of himself with the anti-bourgeois attitudes of Don Juan who dislikes Octavio for the many social accomplishments which he possesses and which Grabbe never possessed. . . . Here [as in *Scherz, Satire, Ironie und tiefere Bedeutung*] the stress is on the awareness of physical unattractiveness and the lack of social graces, a further projection of the author himself upon his hero. (pp. 277-78)

What was merely satirical in *Scherz Satire* had become by the time of *Don Juan und Faust* a necessity to deflate each idea as soon as it was formed, to extract a sense of hollowness from every lofty ideal expressed, as if the parodist were looking over his shoulder to make fun of the poetic vision which he possessed. And so Grabbe became his own parodist accompanying each heroic impulse with a lashing of sarcasm lest the gaoler's son should sound to be laying claim to the mantle of Schiller. The ruin was completed by turning his "sehr tiefes Stück" [very serious piece] into a kind of intellectual pantomime by the provision of a ballet of gnomes and a musical setting within which serious tragedy could never hope to survive. At all events the illusion must be shattered, and just as *Scherz Satire* ends with Grabbe himself appearing on stage to scold his characters, so *Don Juan und Faust* slowly moves away from the sphere of metaphysical speculation concerning man's senses and his intellect to the point where the two heroes reach identical conclusions on every point and the whole purpose of the contrast is vitiated.

The shattering of such illusions has nothing to do with alienation or dramatic theory of any kind. What we have here is talent of a high order ruled by a temperament which was chronically unstable. For that reason it is hard to refuse to forgive him the resultant *Grabbage*. (pp. 279-80)

> James Trainer, *"Grabbe and Grabbage"* *(copyright © by* Forum for Modern Language Studies *and James Trainer), in* Forum for Modern Language Studies, *Vol. II, No. 1, January, 1966, pp. 274-80.*

A. W. HORNSEY (essay date 1966)

Gothland expresses the distress of a young man who has found that the world is not the ideal place he had hoped it might be. Benno von Wiese has described it as the nightmare of a disillusioned eighteen-year-old who sets out to destroy the world so that he can bewail its loss and the end of God's creation. All that is left is the terrible hopelessness which will dominate the later tragedies. We need not admire this first wild outburst, but we may note that it contains and expresses an emotional experience that is essential for the understanding of the later works.

It is inevitable that Grabbe's first work should give evidence of his previous reading and his interest in the theatre. It is a succession of impressions, imitations, borrowings and reminiscences of the world of letters as he knew it. The play has been a happy hunting ground for those who are primarily interested in looking for sources, and critics . . . tend when discussing the play to draw parallels rather than to examine the intentions and attitude of the author. (p. 41)

Most important in *Gothland* is the hero's realisation that all is not well in the world, that good and evil are close neighbours, that bestial impulse may override civilised instinct, that God is dead, that life is empty and boring, that truth and falsehood are tantalisingly ambiguous and that death is materially destructive but neither heroic nor inspiring. Bereft of ideals, a man is the impoverished victim of reality. In *Gothland* is to be found the theme of all Grabbe's early dramas, namely that man's thoughts may soar to the vault of heaven but his feet are sunk deep in the mire of earth. . . . (pp. 43-4)

Gothland was intended to shock and to disillusion. The characteristics of the ephemeral literature of Grabbe's day were pure, vapid love, prudery and that kind of silvan romanticism which has lost touch with reality. Grabbe dealt these a vicious blow. Gustav is an idealistic, heroic lover; but Berdoa soon teaches him what love is 'in natura', and all ideals are soon forgotten in the arms of a comely whore. She is all that the chaste, pure maidens of the popular novel were not. She is a regimental harlot, she is dispensable, she is not credited with any human feelings.

Grabbe shocks his audience or reader not only by his portraiture of vice and immorality but also by cold-blooded actions—

Manfred's death is described in detail: head cut open, blood and mangled brains, which in his agony he tears out with his own hands. Rolf's description of the night he spends in a tomb is horrifically macabre. Worms gnaw at the flesh on the corpses. When they catch the scent of Rolf's living flesh, they crawl lustfully towards him, eager for the feast. He is saved in the eleventh hour but his frightful experience destroys his will to live. (p. 44) .

Gothland is intolerably long, episodic and fitful. The language starts at screaming-pitch and it does not relax until we are nearly deafened by over five thousand lines of it. The climax is reached in Act V in the episode of the 'Schwarzwildbretjagd'. Gothland and Berdoa play a murderous game of hide-and-seek on the battlefield. The scene is not intended to be comic, but a sophisticated, critical audience must find its unintentional buffoonery absurd. After this episode Grabbe then tries to end the play with the victory of good over evil. The exiled Swedish king returns with friendly auxiliary forces. It is May, the birds are singing, the trees are green—a scene hopelessly misplaced after the violence of the foregoing events. A conciliatory happy-ending would, on any terms, be ludicrous. Gothland and Berdoa are the violent masters of a grotesque drama. (pp. 57-8)

For the Grabbe who had already written *Marius und Sulla* and who wished to write dramas with a solid, 'real' background, *Gothland* was a curiosity expressing a bygone state of mind. It was a violent attempt to free himself from romantic ideals in which he had once believed but which contact with the cruel real world had destroyed. Already in *Gothland* romantic hopes and ideals are tested and are found to be fraudulent. The emotional impact of a word like 'hero' is 'unmasked' when put to the test of reason. . . . (p. 59)

It was for a different reason that the 'Naturalists' liked Grabbe's works. In an attempt to convey an impression of the 'formlessness' of reality, Grabbe wrote formless plays. Sentences are left unfinished, incoherent exclamations are poured forth, scenes change rapidly to give an impression of the many sides of reality. The 'Naturalists' understood this desire to 'compose' according to 'nature' rather than according to strict, formal rules. Particularly the later historical dramas excited their admiration, because Grabbe does not select his material to support an idea but tries to reproduce faithfully a 'slice' of history.

Grabbe's heroes are intellectuals and rationalists—Marius and Heinrich der Löwe are notable exceptions—and they seem to belong to a world based on rational principles. In the early works, however, their 'rationalism' does not stand the test of close inspection. They are, in fact, the inadequate creations of Grabbe's thwarted hopes and ideals. Throughout Grabbe's works it becomes progressively more clear that he is attempting to set fantastic heroes—men who reflect himself in his dreams—into a real world which has no place for the dreamer. Gothland, Faust, Heinrich VI, Napoleon, Hannibal and Hermann are all thwarted dreamers. They are the 'unreal exceptions' in a world which is all too real. . . . Grabbe makes his heroes absurdly unreal by mixing up the fantastic dreamers with concrete reality and by letting them rationalize their feelings and intentions. Gothland's monologues are incredibly ludicrous.

The excesses in the scale and design of the plot of *Gothland,* the juvenile bombast of the idiom, the almost cretinous banality of the 'thought', disqualify the drama from consideration as a portrayal of real life under whatever aspect. If it is not to be dismissed as ludicrous, it must be justified on some other terms, and they could only be terms acceptable to the 'Romantics'—

or perhaps the later expressionists—or even modern Existentialism. As a projection of Grabbe's personality, as an expression in dramatic form of his fervid mind: on these terms it is worthy of attention. Looking back from *Don Juan und Faust,* we can see that *Gothland* served to 'clear the air'. It is Grabbe's personal 'Sturm und Drang', a profession of disbelief in the possibility of having and keeping ideals in an evil world.

The 'Schwarzwildbretjagd' was comedy in tragedy, Grabbe's second drama *Scherz, Satire Ironie und tiefere Bedeutung* is tragedy in comedy. It was called a 'Lustspiel' by Grabbe, but shows the same chaotic world as *Gothland* from which it differs only in size and title. *Scherz, etc.* is only a comedy because we are capable of laughter in spite of everything. . . . It is indeed no more than a mocking description and criticism of a contemporary society as hopeless as the world of *Gothland* on a smaller scale. (pp. 59-61)

Sanity has disappeared from Grabbe's world, the whole fabric of society has gone awry. . . . There is no guiding principle; all is burlesque. The world has gone mad and sense and reason are lost. Only ignorant and insensitive people are happy. A surfeit of wine is the only cure for sorrow, for reality is ugly, hopeless and evil.

Nannette und Maria plays no part in the development of Grabbe's tragedy and is merely a curiosity. It was written to make amends for the wildness of *Gothland*. . . . (p. 61)

[*Nannette und Maria* has been described] as the weakest of Grabbe's works. It is slight, unlikely and excessively sentimental. It was a child of contemporary taste and of the sentiments of the effeminate novel. This was probably Grabbe's intention, for he wanted to lure the reading public into reading his works and demanding that they be produced. . . . [It has been argued] that this is only a retrospect excuse for bad writing, but it is improbable that Grabbe could have taken such a play seriously. The sentiments it expresses are certainly not in accord with his life or his character. . . . It is more logical and less preposterous to believe Grabbe, and to take *Nannette und Maria* at its face value, namely as a bait to lure those romantics who had been repelled by *Gothland*. (pp. 63-4)

Faust and Don Juan [in *Don Juan und Faust*] are not strictly antagonists, nor does Grabbe succeed in making a unified plot involving both of them equally. The drama is the loosely constructed picture of the notable representatives of two different ways of life who travel towards the same goal. Different as they are, they represent together the 'active' principle in a world which is being lulled to sleep in the cradle of bourgeois ordinariness. Neither is prepared to compromise with convention and risk losing—zest for knowledge on the one hand, and zest for life on the other. While the stress in the drama is on their differences, their similarity is striking. Both are borne away to the nether regions; but we know that even there there will be no question of placid acceptance of a merely passive existence. Both, as the Ritter, Grabbe's devil, so succinctly puts it, had the same end in view but were making for it on two different waggons. . . . For Grabbe, both are 'great' because they fulfil his demand that men should be active. It is far better to be creative in criminal ways than to stagnate in smug ordinariness. (pp. 65-6)

In *Don Juan und Faust* the social criticism of *Scherz, Satire, Ironie und tiefere Bedeutung* is heard again. It is characterized by Don Juan's frequent criticism of honour and patriotism. (p. 67)

Don Juan und Faust fulfils for Grabbe an inner need. Not by chance did he leave *Marius und Sulla* unfinished and return to metaphysics from the reality of history. In *Marius und Sulla* Grabbe had 'sketched' two types of man—the man of reason (Sulla) and the man of feeling (Marius). In the historical drama, the 'clash' of these two types had not been fully developed; in *Don Juan und Faust* Grabbe was able to give it his full attention. Faust is Grabbe's last dreamer and Don Juan is his first down-to-earth realist. Faust wants to conquer heaven; Don Juan is satisfied to remain on earth and enjoy life. . . . Don Juan will live on in the 'great men' whose boundless vitality creates history, but who, like Don Juan, are also mortal. But something of Faust lives on too—just as it lived on in Grabbe who was never able to reconcile his dreams with reality. Even Heinrich VI will want to conquer the heavens and even Hermann dreams in vain of a united and strong Germany. In *Don Juan und Faust* Grabbe had shown beyond all doubt the failure of the hopes of a dreamer. The aspirations of his historical heroes are just as hopeless, but they never give them up. (p. 68)

For Grabbe, history is action. Kleist's *Hermannsschlacht* is about political intrigue, Grabbe's is about a battle in its complete course and elemental force. Heroes are for Grabbe active and mighty, but they are mortal; they cannot allow themselves the luxury of ideals. Sulla retires from history lest he should become an anachronism; Marius is an anachronism, for he curiously fights for ideals and a way of life which history has left behind. Grabbe's heroes set history in motion but do not control it. Sometimes it leaves them behind. (p. 79)

It is inevitable that Grabbe will from time to time be compared with Hebbel, but the difference is clear: Hebbel was convinced that history had a 'shape', that it followed a pattern, Grabbe was not. Grabbe talks about the 'iron necessity of fate' in reference to history, but even this was seen as a *random* force. History is a flood-tide without form. (p. 79)

Grabbe's historical dramas are then an attempt to reproduce historical reality, and great actions, the 'movement of history', are embodied in heroes. They are those men of action which the 'Restaurationszeit'—Grabbe's own age—lacked. They are also men who die tragic deaths, the victims of that reality for which they had stood as representatives and champions. They could have achieved so much, but their strength was limited by the world as it is or was in their time—by 'reality'. Another hero might appear, to defeat them (Marius), a new age might disillusion them (Hannibal, Tancred), death might carry them away in the midst of their glory (Barbarossa, Heinrich VI). The fate of Carthage depends on the outcome of a battle; but Hannibal, being no superman, is unable to win the battle whilst depending on the people, for they are more interested in the profit and loss of petty commercial transactions than in the war. (pp. 79-80)

Both Hohenstaufen plays [*Kaiser Friedrich Barbarossa* and *Kaiser Heinrich der Sechste*] are, as a whole, too diffuse and unwieldy. Grabbe is not sufficiently selective, and the work is a concatenation of episodes rather than an organic series of events. Some of the themes and episodes are well depicted. The tension between the personalities of the North and South Germans is impressively worked out and portrayed, so that the two ways of life are drawn into an inevitable conflict. But such qualities do not disguise the formlessness of the dramas. It is clearly essential for Grabbe to describe battles, yet he is equally clearly unable to present battle-scenes in which the behaviour of the participants is reasonably natural and convincing. . . .

In the course of Grabbe's stage battles his characters have far too much to say. (p. 89)

Grabbe called *Napoleon* 'ein dramatisches Epos' [a dramatic epos] and thereby characterised its hybrid form. The rise and fall of its hero's fortune is essentially a dramatic subject, but it is the epic qualities of the work which carry the day. Napoleon plays a relatively small part in the stage action and the impression left by the play in that it is an epic description of one hundred turbulent days. The great armies, the remnants of an antiquated monarchy, the Paris mob and finally the Battle of Waterloo itself are represented. Much too vast for the theatre, *Napoleon* would be thought today more suitable as the material for a film of 'epic' dimensions.

In *Napoleon* Grabbe was not interested in individuals; he could not even concentrate his attention on a single hero and Napoleon is in consequence the least convincing of his 'great men'. We are not exclusively preoccupied with Napoleon's fate; he is merely a piece of history. It is true that Napoleon is the person the play 'is about', but he is in fact painted with a few broad, quick sweeps and is then abandoned, in so far as the action is concerned, in favour of a Jouve, a Blücher, a Wellington or a simple Prussian soldier. Napoleon is the figure 'behind' an exciting phase of European history, but Grabbe fails to convince us that his defeat means the end of all 'vitality'. That had been Grabbe's intention, but the work is too diffuse for us to attach such paramount importance to the final defeat of one single man.

The first act of *Napoleon* is a masterpiece of historical scene-painting and shows what Grabbe might have achieved, had he been able to control his wild, chaotic impulses. The France of 1815 is reflected in four mirrors: the people of Paris, the aristocracy, the court and finally the exiled Emperor himself, whose memory had lingered behind him. These are the four elements of supreme importance in the events of the hundred momentous days. (pp. 100-01)

The first drafts of *Hannibal* were in verse but, on Immermann's suggestion, Grabbe changed to an austere, subdued prose. Immermann edited the work, advising Grabbe against including certain episodes which were not strictly relevant and also to divide the play into five acts. As a result *Hannibal* is formally Grabbe's best play.

The Hannibal of history was a tough, unfeeling general and Grabbe was faced with the task of making him into an understandable tragic hero. He was able to succeed because Hannibal . . . had gained his own undivided sympathy. . . . *Hannibal* is the most intensely personal of Grabbe's historical studies. Grabbe had hitherto been as arrogant, and sought to be as unfeeling as, his Napoleon, but now, as he saw his last hopes of success slipping away, he identified himself completely with the fall of Hannibal. The scene of Hannibal's departure from Italy is the most moving that Grabbe wrote, for in it his hero renounces all hope of winning the prize for which he had been struggling so long. (p. 105)

Hannibal is his most tragic work, for whereas previous heroes had, at least, some weakness in their make-up which had contributed to their downfall, Hannibal has none. We see that even the strongest hero (even the greatest poet, as Grabbe interpreted it) is helpless when the masses around him are ignoble and indifferent. (p. 109)

Hermannsschlacht bears witness to Grabbe's failing strength. More loosely constructed than any of his works, it is a series of scenes broken off where the lulls in the battle occur. The battle scenes—they compose the greater part of the play—are improbable and full of unnecessary discourse: two Cheruskans argue in the heat of the fray—spears are flying around them—about who should stand in the first and who in the second row in the battle!

Hermannsschlacht is the last expression of a sick man's bitterness and of his view of the inadequacy of human greatness. . . The drama is very slight, but it does say the final word on the subject that had troubled all of Grabbe's works, namely that the great individual is limited because he is surrounded by masses of petty, unworthy people. (pp. 111-12)

[Three] factors combine to produce such relentlessly pessimistic dramas; Grabbe's unhappy life, his uncongenial literary and social environment, and his own pathological condition. His life, like that of his heroes, was one of frustrated ambition. He failed to achieve the personal glory he desired. Behind his work is not only a desire to express himself but also a wish to achieve fame for doing so. We can trace this feeling throughout his dramas. In adolescence Grabbe found that he was not the centre of the universe and that the kind of security he had felt at home with his mother was not easily found elsewhere. His resentment seeks expression. The characters in *Gothland* are incited to action by a desire for revenge—vengeance on what he believed to be an evil world—which inspired the drama. He also wanted to shock this world into recognition of his existence—going so far as to write an insincere play (*Nannette und Maria*) in order to attract popular attention. (p. 114)

Grabbe longed for power. He tried for a short while to translate this yearning into patriotic terms in his *Hohenstaufen*—but even Heinrich VI proved to be mortal. The last heroes were an expression and portrayal of Grabbe's own inadequacy; he enacted in his tragedies his own various frustrated attempts to come to terms with life. So closely did he identify himself with his own creations that he was able to feel himself the victim of all of Hannibal's disappointments. . . . Grabbe had unlimited aspirations, yet he remained almost unknown. Himself insecure, he saw all secure writers and friends as his potential enemies. He grew to hate them all and clearly came to see himself as the only hero in a barren age. For this reason he depicted the contemporary literary scene as so outrageously bad (*Scherz, Satire, etc.*) and for this reason he had to turn to history to find men of his own kin and kind—other great men who had been deserted by their times. (pp. 114-15)

Grabbe's first drama is excessive and too wild to be taken seriously. Whatever virtues the subsequent dramas may have, it is impossible to escape the feeling that Grabbe repeatedly bewails his own spiritual and physical inadequacy. (p. 115)

It is possible to select good passages in Grabbe's works—Benno von Wiese admires the powerful delineation of the characteristics of the North and South Germans in *Barbarossa;* others praise the first act of *Napoleon;* and *Hannibal* is even well composed and is certainly a moving drama. These few examples do not, however, allow us to acclaim Grabbe as a great dramatist. We can laugh at *Scherz, etc.*, and be stirred by the intensity of feeling in *Hannibal,* but our experience is not enriched by a reading of Grabbe's works. Grabbe creates an empty world without a valid hope or message. (pp. 116-17)

Grabbe, having first tried to shatter the whole fabric of the world, shows admiration only for the selected few. He has nothing positive to offer us. He leaves us with a view of man who is incapable of over-coming the narrow restrictions of reality—a reality which is in any case not worth the candle. Even if we condone Grabbe's inability to give his tragedies coherent form, we are still unable to find satisfaction in their content. The hero whose fame lives on after him is Grabbe's only hope in a worthless world. He creates chaos in chaotic terms and all that is left is the brief glory of the 'great exception'. Grabbe's works are his consolation for his *own personal* deficiencies. They are too excessively concerned with the 'exception', too excessively individual for us to feel deeply concerned with them. (p. 117)

> A. W. Hornsey, in his Idea and Reality in the Dramas of Christian Dietrich Grabbe *(copyright © 1966 Pergamon Press Ltd.)*, Pergamon Press, 1966, 120 p.

ROY C. COWEN (essay date 1967)

For several generations of literary criticism it has been customary to link Georg Büchner's *Dantons Tod* and Christian Dietrich Grabbe's *Napoleon*. Quite correctly, most critics point to a similar technique in the mass-scenes, with which these two poets created a new dramatic realism. . . . [Yet] despite the obvious importance of the masses in the lives of Danton and Napoleon, no attempt has yet been made to examine and compare the two protagonists' relationships to them. It is hoped that the following observations will cast light on these relationships and consequently on Büchner's and Grabbe's approaches to their subjects. (p. 316)

Both Büchner and Grabbe see the masses of the Revolution as the controling factor in the fate of these supposedly great individuals, who in reality merely ride on the masses like "foam on the waves," like the "banner on a ship." And their common emphasis on mass-scenes must be considered more significant than a coincidental similarity in dramatic technique. . . .

Jouve [of *Napoleon*] symbolizes the Revolutionary element whose resurgence must be suppressed by Napoleon when he returns from Elba. The forces unleashed by Jouve on Paris represent a more important historical factor than mere anarchy during the interim between the flight of the Bourbons and the return of Napoleon; they represent a revival of the Revolutionary spirit of 1789. . . . Jouve is probably more bloody than any of Büchner's Revolutionaries, for in him we see a rebirth not only of the horrors of the storming of the Bastille, but also of the September Massacre, the very act of violence that haunts Büchner's Danton.

Jouve incorporates not only the lewdness and energy but also the cynicism that Büchner associates with the Revolutionaries. (p. 317)

[In one speech Jouve] denies the importance of humanity in general, for he asks why the forces of Hell or Heaven should even be angered by beings that are in a state of constant decay. Because he emphasizes the folly of human endeavor in the face of man's subjection to decay, Jouve even seems to anticipate one of the most important themes in Danton's speeches. But while Danton is unable to transcend his consciousness of his own materiality, Jouve not only denies any further interest in mankind's fate but also asserts his own feeling of affinity with the *Höllenlegionen* [legions of hell]. . . .

Jouve incites his followers by appealing to their emotions, not to their sense of social injustice, and he himself has Satanic overtones suggested by the fact that his desire for destruction has no tangible motives. On the other hand, Büchner's "Erster Bürger" in a violent speech appeals to the mob's sense of social injustice, not to its bestial instinct. (p. 318)

The most obvious personal difference between [Büchner's] Simon and Jouve is the fact that the latter is essentially a serious character while the former is comic. Whenever Jouve does laugh, it is the laughter of a beast of prey. His laughter is always intentional, for it represents a ridicule of the values and systems that he considers worthless and empty. It is Satanic laughter. . . . Simon laughs seldom, and his position as a comic character is determined by his unintended comedy rather than by his humor. Often he is ridiculed by the other characters. . . . [Simon] of the Revolution, drifts between the upper and lower extremes of both society and human sensibility. (p. 319)

Simon also lacks the cynical perception of Jouve. He mouths the phrases of the Revolution and carries out its handiwork with neither the imagined power nor the bestial pleasure of Jouve. Like Satan, Jouve can look with contempt on the activities of mankind to better its lot, but Simon is the eternal dupe of mankind in its futile efforts to change the course of events. Yet Jouve and Simon, each in his own way, ultimately reveal a common premise underlying both pictures of the Revolution: that there is no progress toward a higher ideal to human history.

Napoleon is a drama of events, and its author makes no strong effort to develop conflicting personalities. Napoleon stands alone at the top, so much so that his role is virtually that of a monologue. But . . . he is but a flag being carried on the ship of the Revolution. . . . Like a flag, he is, for all the world to see, the symbol of Revolutionary values. Napoleon's personality, as well as his personal aims, are no longer important, for as a "symbol" his role is already determined. He can no longer separate himself from the forces that created him, just as he cannot escape the enemies that he, as the "son" and symbol of the Revolution, has brought into being.

The Revolution, says Grabbe, lives on after Napoleon. Napoleon's fate is at an end because he is but the temporal symbol of the Revolution and as such has no further influence on events. . . . Like Napoleon, Danton is a dead saint because he no longer exercises an influence on the course of events, yet he, like Napoleon, continues to exist as an individual. Herein lies the difference between the structures of the two plays. Grabbe's *Napoleon* reveals the forces in the creation and downfall of an idol, i.e., the *Geschicht* [story], not the man. Büchner shows the isolated soul that is left behind after the events have toppled the idol. (pp. 320-21)

In a very specific sense Napoleon's existence depends on historical factors, and Grabbe's play about him is in the most literal sense a historical drama because it reveals the irresistible forces creating and destroying a historical myth. . . . Büchner's play is one of persons, not of events. . . . (p. 321)

Despite many common techniques in their dramatizations of the masses, Büchner and Grabbe have completely opposite concepts of the relationship of the protagonist to the masses: the former sees the masses as being led by Robespierre and Danton, while the latter conceives of the masses as a force exerting pressure from beneath, a pressure that excludes the possibility of fatigue as well as of a meaningful assertion of the protagonist's own will. Although we hear from both dramatists that the hero has been created by the Revolution rather than the other way around, it should now be obvious that the actual "drama" of *Dantons Tod* is far more indebted to an essentially ahistorical concept of man than that of *Napoleon*.

Grabbe's interest in Napoleon was based mainly on the inherent "drama" of the historical facts, for it was his conviction: "Der Stoff ist groß, von selbst dramatisch" [The vast subject is automatically dramatic]. Indeed, Grabbe's concept of the historically *dramatic* seems even more dependent on Büchner's well-known dictum of a "Fatalismus der Geschichte" [fatalism of history] than Büchner's own. (p. 322)

> Roy C. Cowen, "*Grabbe's Napoleon, Büchner's Danton, and The Masses,*" *in* Symposium *(copyright © 1967 by Syracuse University Press), Vol. XXI, No. 7, Winter, 1967, pp. 316-23.*

ROGER A. NICHOLLS   (essay date 1967)

The fairy tale comedy as a dramatic mode has never enjoyed a high critical estimate and the somewhat cursory studies on this genre fail to distinguish Grabbe's [*Aschenbrödel*] from numerous experiments of the later Romantics. . . . [Yet the] play has, above all in its comic scenes, a curious attraction and vitality. It is the only other work besides *Scherz, Satire, Ironie und tiefere Bedeutung* in which Grabbe gave free vent to his irrational and often grotesque sense of farce. Moreover, despite the limitations of this somewhat constraining literary form, we see here as clearly as anywhere in Grabbe the clash between idealist and skeptic, between the dreamer and the man of bitter and desperate disillusion. (p. 68)

Essentially characteristic of Grabbe's *Aschenbrödel,* and an element that takes it beyond its predecessors, is the intense contrast between the idealism in the story of the King and Cinderella and the realism, even bitter cynicism, of the comic episodes. . . . This spirit of an interplay between the fairy tale world of wonder and more realistic social comment is essentially characteristic of certain comedies by Tieck, as well as by Raimund, Platen, and others, but Grabbe has given new emphasis both to the nature of the longing of the hero and heroine for love and to the comic counterpoint of disenchantment and pessimism.

The character of the two lovers has been subtly developed by Grabbe and each reveals under stress a surprising intensity of feeling. No longer merely puppets serving the action, they have been infused with the poet's own passions so that they become themselves a genuine source of dramatic interest. This is perhaps more clearly evident in the King than in Aschenbrödel herself. In Grabbe the King seeks a wife . . . in order to escape the isolation of the throne. At first sight this seems to be very much in accordance with the normal requirements of the Romantic hero. It is only to be expected that the girl he seeks should possess "innocence and grace," as the King's counsellor Alastor suggests, and not be deceived by false appearance of empty show. But here, as in the comparable figure of Leonce in Büchner's *Leonce und Lena,* there is an undertone that points beyond the accepted Romantic language of the hero and suggests a disturbing depth of passion. This is not so apparent at the beginning when only an occasional phrase suggests a serious and personal tone, but comes clearly to the surface when the violence of the King's anger shows the extent of his passions. In Act 3, where he is disguised, and he looks on with contempt at the hypocritical flattery paid to the Court Jester in the King's clothes, the revulsion he expresses can only come from ideals betrayed. We realize the power of his desire and the inherent dangers of disillusion. . . . Such passion works against the atmosphere of fairy tale harmony. For a moment we forget the happy resolution that is assured through the presence of the fairy queen. Yet a similar anger appears more than once. In the fourth act, when he is looking for Aschenbrödel, who has run away, the King's scorn for the people, "despicable, lying and greedy" breaks out again as he sees them thronging to try their luck with the glass slipper. The dangers intrinsic to his nature come to the surface. . . . Only the strength of his passion justifies the strangely grotesque image with which he exults when he finds Olympia again, proclaiming the "giant snake of desire" trodden under heel. Desire, which had been so ready to turn on itself and drive him to destruction, is seen as an enemy which he can finally master. (pp. 71-3)

Reflected against such destructive elements in his nature, the ardor of the King's idealism becomes more impressive. We feel the seriousness of his character and his genuine nobility of feeling. Even amidst the lively jokes of his court followers he cannot restrain himself. The cynical comments of the court fool and the court poet about morality and truth he calls the freedom of the irresponsible. In comedy, he asserts, where fancy has free play, one may joke with the moral order, for everyone knows you are only joking. But in life one must act nobly. . . . He is also true to himself, one feels, when he proclaims that the goal of art is not the reproduction of everyday emotion and incidents, as in Iffland, but the glorification of life, the recreating of the world in ultimate harmony. . . . Strange as it is to find in Grabbe an ideal of art so frankly confessed which brings such echoes from Schiller and comes close to the Romantic dictum of "das Unendliche endlich dargestellt" it nonetheless carries conviction.

It is to this idealism that the King's adviser Alastor appeals. In an interesting exchange at the end of Act 3, at a time when Aschenbrödel seems lost to the King, Alastor insists that even without her he should not give up hope, but learn to act according to his highest principles even when inflicted by the sorrows and torments of life. (pp. 73-4)

The possibility that [happiness] should be achieved without Aschenbrödel is not tested. The workings of the fairy powers make sure that happiness is in store for him. But we are aware of the danger that the King, like other of Grabbe's heroes, might remain torn between an unfulfilled desire for the ideal and his recognition in reality of a contemptible and false-fronted world. . . .

[In Aschenbrödel] the basic charm of the fairy tale heroine is retained—she is still the poor, neglected, sweetnatured and loving girl who gains her true reward. . . . But it is more than her fairy tale purity that wins the attention of the King. He is attracted by the depth of her character as well as the genuineness and truthfulness of her feelings. Where others pretend and are deceived by their own selfish desires, she responds to her own heart. The royal clothes the court fool wears mean nothing to her; she sees only the wretched man underneath. (p. 74)

For all her modesty, however, Aschenbrödel is not without longings. Her dreams are all the greater because of her loneliness. She pleads repeatedly with her stepmother to be allowed to go to the ball and feels most oppressively the power of Spring that touches all things but leaves her bereft. (pp. 74-5)

[By introducing the King and Aschenbrödel into] a fear of ideals and dreams rejected, the sense of all-embracing harmony controlling their lives is threatened. It is as though a particular miracle saved them; though we are from the beginning aware that fortune will make all things right, there are still moments in which we are very conscious of the possibility of a world without such benevolent divinities.

Many features of the comic action add to this impression of danger. Some of the comic scenes are, it is true, straightforward and uncomplicated enough. The activities of the gnome who is the companion of the fairies, for example, when he sneaks unnoticed behind the guests at the court ball and drinks their wine or when he projects his voice into those of Aschenbrödel's sisters . . . are amusing variations on standard farcical proceedings. . . . But other elements are disturbing. The misanthropic outbursts of Aschenbrödel's father, the Baron, suggest in their violence a world ludicrously out of keeping with the harmony of the poetic fairy scenes. The hypocrisy of the Baroness and Aschenbrödel's half-sisters or of the courtiers around the King seems a genuine, if outrageous, reflection of normal human behavior while the Court Jester, watching their calculation and cunning, offers a sardonic and despondent commentary. A similarly disturbing picture emerges from other details: the parody of love, for instance, in the scenes between Cinderella's unwilling servants, the rat turned coachman and the cat transformed into a lady's maid, or the almost maniacal greed and selfishness of the Jewish money lender Isaak. The happy ending scarcely offers any resolution to the realities of the human situation that these figures represent. (pp. 75-6)

[The relationship of the rat coachman and feline lady's maid] provides a curiously flavored humor when the rat is ridiculed because he is frightened of the girl and the maid in her pursuit of the man inadvertently reveals a cat on the prowl. The result is something more than the normal comic device whereby a secondary pair of lovers affords a humorous echo of the main love affair on a lower level. We have here an incipient attack on the human dream of love. To the rat who thinks they are biting each other when they are kissing, the human lovers seem victims of absurd and incomprehensible desires. The longing that is the source of nobility to the King and Aschenbrödel is to the cat merely an uncontrollable instinct. . . . [These] are animals dominated by their instincts and unable to understand anything except the satisfaction of their own needs. Yet in the context their directness and realism seems to cast doubt on the possibilities of any values beyond their own. On what grounds, we are forced to wonder, can men claim to be anything more? (pp. 76-7)

In portraying [Aschenbrödel's stepmother and two half-sisters] Grabbe uses clearly traditional elements of the story, but certain characteristics are interestingly emphasized. Above all, it is clear for the girls that marriage is their only possibility for advancement. Endless intrigue and cunning is involved in achievement of the best possible match. (p. 77)

In the end inordinate ambition gets the better of them. One reasonably good prospect after another is discarded because they finally hope to win the King himself. While they may be out of their depth in the court circle, their naive assurance that they are doing the only thing possible, is not at all different from the cynicism of those around them. . . . This narrow self-seeking is reflected on a more ingenuous level in the mobs who try to fit their daughters' clumsy feet into the delicate slipper Aschenbrödel has inadvertently left behind. All are agreed in a search for wealth and fortune irrespective of any qualities or merit they may possess.

The Baron's main creditor Isaak provides an even more striking example of man completely the victim of the instinctive demands of his own self-interest. Isaak is one of the most lively and interesting personages in the play, and despite some unpleasant anti-Jewish elements in the portrayal it is worth while examining his role in some detail. Isaak is in part a farcical

figure, the comic Jew who is the absurd victim of his own monomania, but the scenes in which he appears have a vitality that derives from the individuality of his character. In an opening scene with the Baron Isaak's greed is purely ludicrous. He forces in his face, first at the door then at the window, to persuade the Baron to pay his debts, and finally comes down the chimney to carry off all the goods he can—some even in his mouth. But later at the court, when he appears as a kind of comic Shylock insistent on his bond, his relentless pursuit of the money owed him verges on the insane. Nothing can dissuade him from his pound of flesh. This limitless irrational greed is no longer simply comic, but disturbingly grotesque and frightening. . . . [To Isaak, money] and possessions are so necessary that nothing else in the world matters. It may be this separation from all other values that Grabbe sees as characteristically expressed in the Jew. Being isolated from the traditional standards of the community, he is completely dependent on the material. Hence when a Jewish father brings his daughters to try their luck with the glass slipper, the father's advice to the girls to squeeze their feet and bear any suffering for the moment by thinking of the future profits is a kind of parody of the rewards of Christian faith. (pp. 77-8)

Isaak interprets history in terms of business transactions. He explains that Joseph bought corn cheaply in order to sell at a fine profit in the lean years, and even when Joseph's brothers sold him into captivity they made a good profit on their goods. As a result, the Court Fool with mock enthusiasm proposes to employ Isaak as financial advisor to the court. Here Grabbe seems to be broadly satirizing the economic conditions of his time. . . . Isaak's prospective role in court policies, however, seems to go beyond any specific satirical objective. It is a grossly exaggerated reflection of the progressively triumphant materialism of the nineteenth century in which all values were subordinate to considerations of wealth and profit and the individual man became the victim of large scale economic speculation. His plans for raising more money, by having the state declaring itself bankrupt and paying only a fraction of its debts or establishing a monopoly in basic areas of production and raising prices accordingly, are startlingly modern in tone and free of all moral inhibitions.

If Isaak points to the triumphant future, it may be the Baron represents the decayed past. Where Isaak is all aggressive self-assertion, the Baron is void of all will to action and his indolence has left the field open to his enemies. Like his fellow Baron in *Scherz, Satire, Ironie und tiefere Bedeutung,* he sits and watches the world's illusion, finding relief for his pent-up resentment against life in outbursts of anger at the nature of women, or on occasion and less pertinently, at the absurdly high reputation enjoyed by second-rate writers. . . . He is a living example that man never learns from experience. Having escaped one unpleasant woman by her fortuitous death he has married another equally unpleasant. (pp. 78-9)

Whereas Isaak, the Baroness and her daughters, as well as the cat and the rat, are all victims of their desires, the Baron stands outside the world and observes its misery. This situation might be validly expressed in Schopenhauerian terms. . . . [Unlike the other characters, who are creatures of will, the Baron], and perhaps the Court Jester as well, find themselves for moments at least free from the demands of the will. In humorous outbursts or under the influence of wine the Baron is able to stand aside and observe the world as an idea or concept; the Court Jester, quite in the manner of Shakespeare's fools, offers a sad but authoritative commentary on events from his privileged position of comic irresponsibility. To that extent the wheel of Ixion stands still. Naturally this independence is gained at the cost of all will to action. They are impotent, detached observers. The parallel may be taken one step further. For the Baron reminds us of Schopenhauer himself. Beneath his pessimism he is healthy and robust enough. There is a certain gaiety in his revengeful and vindictive attacks on the world and on women, reminiscent of the colorful and vivid way in which Schopenhauer exposes the miseries and inadequacy of life.

The primacy of the will over morality must also be a challenge to Aschenbrödel and the King. It seems that the violence of the King's reaction to the iniquities of man, his desperate hatred of the sycophantic courtiers and the greedy mob, can be explained by the fear that his own ideals of true love and a life of service to his people are illusory. The question arises whether anything exists beyond the desire for one's own advantage and whether he and Aschenbrödel are not equally creatures of blind forces.

The disturbing implications of the comic scenes and of the characters of the King and Aschenbrödel threaten to destroy the simple Cinderella theme at the center of the work. In the end, however, the idyll of the lovers and the harmony of the fairy tale prevails. . . . It may well be that the very emphasis on the disruptive gives new meaning to the contrasting harmony. Because we see characteristic Grabbian features in the individuality of the lovers or the problems of the comedy, we are more likely to understand the meaning of the fairy tale scenes. While he is certainly following a fashion that indulges our most obvious desires of wish-fulfillment, it would be a mistake to consider these episodes as purely derivative. While, to our taste, these lyrical scenes are the weakest feature of the play, the fairy tale world . . . offers an escape from the destructive drives in Grabbe's own thinking. The lyrical mood often fails to convince and Grabbe's verses are inadequate to compensate for the lack of dramatic tension inherent in the fairy tale drama. But in this world of the fairy tale all things have meaning. True love and a life of service are possible because man's life is guided by loving hands. Whereas in *Scherz, Satire, Ironie und tiefere Bedeutung* the love story is constantly tinged with irony and we can scarcely believe in a match between Liddy and the misshapen hero Mollfels . . . here the love idyll has its own rights and arouses a genuine response. Purity of heart sees through all worldly illusions. (pp. 80-1)

Roger A. Nicholls, "Idealism and Disillusion in Grabbe's 'Aschenbrödel'," in The German Quarterly (copyright © 1967 by the American Association of Teachers of German), Vol. XL, No. 1, January, 1967, pp. 68-82.

MAX SPALTER   (essay date 1967)

[In his *Concerning the Shakespeare Madness* Christian Dietrich Grabbe] tries to show that Shakespeare's reputation is meretricious, not only because of the way it has developed, but also because of Shakespeare's aesthetic failings, which Grabbe finds egregious enough to make him say: "Shakespeare does not deserve to be identified with the most exemplary form of tragedy." (p. 39)

Concerning the Shakespeare Madness remains, in the final analysis, a document less valuable for its cultural substance than for the light it sheds on the psychology of a very strange man, a man who admits that there has never been anyone quite like Shakespeare but who belittles Shakespeare every chance he gets; who ascribes great value to the literary taste of the average German but finds that same taste offensively spurious; who gives the distinct impression of writing as much out of chauvinistic emotionalism as out of aesthetic discernment—all in all, a weird mixture of contradictions.

Grabbe's plays intensify this impression. Like Lenz, he speaks with two voices which would seem to be mutually exclusive but which interact oddly. A corrosive cynicism which spares nothing is joined to a powerful sense of pathos. Again like Lenz, Grabbe has a very strong need to be concretely realistic about the very things which inspire his strongest enthusiasm. But what links Grabbe most importantly to Lenz is his use of the episodic structure. He, too, employs this structure as an element of illustrative realism. Episodic development allows him to pinpoint whatever social and historical forces control the action of the play and, by implication, human action in general. (pp. 40-1)

In Grabbe's first play, *Theodore, Duke of Gothland* . . . , the structure is not episodic; it is, in fact, very much that of the typical classical-idealistic play written in verse a generation earlier. But it deserves attention, if only because it proves again that the youthful emotions of a dramatist clarify all later attitudes. *Gothland* has been called a pile of filth, and it is easy enough to see why; it is not quite so easy to discern that the emotions Grabbe puts into his first play will be less apparent in his more mature work but nonetheless decisively present. (p. 41)

Gothland need occasion little speculation as to Grabbe's tendency therein to shift back and forth between lyrical pathos and brutal sensualism. Both postures have the same obvious cause—seething frustration at a world which leaves Grabbe agonized when it is not merely making him bitter. The note of repelled alienation sounded here would re-echo in all of his succeeding works.

Gothland gives us the emotional mechanisms of Grabbe's art; *Marius and Sulla* reveals intellectual processes which anticipate his most mature work. . . . For the first time he employs the episodic structure in order to convey panoramically what happened in a crucial period of history. . . . [With] regard to *Marius and Sulla,* Grabbe informs us that his play is to make obvious history's need for the strong leader.

In this latter aim Grabbe does not succeed, and the reason may well be laid to his epic technique. Individual episodes tend to lack focus; they are provocative enough for the observation of life in general that Grabbe works into them but not for their relevance to his central theme. . . . Grabbe wastes no time striking cynical chords. Like Brecht, he is aware that the major events of history are not in the least glamorous from the bottom up. (pp. 43-4)

But if *Marius and Sulla* ends on a cynical footnote, this hardly makes up for a great deal of extremely naïve matter in the body of the play. The later Grabbe would realize that no hero functions in a historical vacuum, that no action is divorced from a multiplicity of other actions. The early Grabbe, in contrast, seems to suggest that while the hero rides high, he is a supreme, autonomous force constituting the one and only key to historical developments; the spirit of the age speaks with his imperious voice. *Marius and Sulla* is permeated with a respect for heroism which Grabbe was soon to qualify by the knowledge that heroes are all too mortal and in no sense divorced from the complexities of the time in which they live. Only in Marius—and in the Sulla of the final scene—does Grabbe approximate that latter attitude.

Grabbe's notes leave little doubt that the many separate episodes of *Marius and Sulla* were intended to depict persuasively the chaotic mess which once-great Rome had become. But the illustration pattern leaves much to be desired; individual episodes sacrifice historical insight for immediate dramatic effect; far too often Grabbe tries to devise interludes of horror so as to demolish with a vengeance any idyllic notions one might have about the distant past; one's reaction to the play is clouded by misgivings about a writer prone to relish evocations of carnage. . . . Quite plainly, a good deal of this is history melodramatized by a writer fascinated with personalities devoid of conscience. Not to be dismissed, however, in Grabbe's first episodic play are adumbrations of maturer work. . . . Some of his scenes, though sensationalistic, are quite effective in getting across an utterly cynical vision of history as a barbarous process; and one must say that if there is sickness here, there is also imaginative brilliance. Most important, in *Marius and Sulla* Grabbe breaks radically with the classical-idealistic tradition; this time his hero is not an overemotional idealist, but a realist so cold and hard as to repel civilized taste. (p. 48)

[The two Hohenstaufen dramas, *Kaiser Friedrich Barbarossa* and *Kaiser Heinrich der Sechste*,] as well as *Don Juan and Faust* . . . and *Jest, Satire, Irony, and Deeper Meaning* . . . , are by no means of secondary importance; but they do not give us that fusion of historical awareness and episodic form which links the Grabbe of *Marius and Sulla* to his best work. (p. 49)

The Hohenstaufen dramas are flooded with rhetoric and are not devoid of comic-strip heroics, but it would again be unfair to overlook those moments which afford glimpses of Grabbe's final vision. All sorts of romantic fantasies are deflated by hard facts. . . . The world goes on in spite of its leaders, who are far less important than the fear inspired by them would suggest; one should be awed only by time's ceaseless continuity.

Grabbe's last phase begins with *Napoleon*. . . . Once and for all he leaves behind the classical rhetoric which makes parts of his Hohenstaufen so unreadable today; and he settles upon the episodic structure. From now on, language as well as form will serve to give his dramas a strikingly modern tone and make him, along with Büchner, an anticipator of Brechtian theater in particular and twentieth-century realistic drama in general. (pp. 49-50)

Napoleon begins in a kind of whirl. . . . Grabbe is trying to depict simultaneously two worlds—the world of yesterday, which centered around the brief efflorescence of the French Revolution and is now flickering out, and the new world in the process of developing, whose distinguishing marks seem to be displacement and disillusion. More than anything else, Grabbe impresses upon us in [the] first scene the reality of a historical period coming to an end, and the mark it has left on those unfortunate enough to survive it. (pp. 50-1)

In spite of its title, *Napoleon* is not a heroic play; and in spite of the way Grabbe avoids making Napoleon a conventional hero, it is easy to fall into the error of expecting conventional characterization. . . . Actually, Grabbe is trying to demolish the idea of a single Napoleon; such a Napoleon would indeed be the wax-works dummy Grabbe has been accused of fashioning. . . . Just as Grabbe pictures the spirit of a nation as a spectrum of intellectual and emotional reactions, so he pictures the personality of a great leader as a spectrum of adaptations

and postures. Grabbe was well aware that in the modern world adaptation would be barely distinguishable from pose.

The importance of *Napoleon* was not recognized until recently. (pp. 56-7)

Surely the emergence of Brecht has something to do with the revaluation of Grabbe. . . . Looking backward, it is hard not to single out *Napoleon* as one of the most significant episodic plays of the nineteenth century. Like Brecht, Grabbe uses the episodic structure to say something about the nature of the modern world, and like Brecht, he makes the episodic structure a perfect mold for his own peculiar way of seeing things. There is so much in *Napoleon* that is worth noting that one can hardly sympathize with the view that the work fails because it lacks an over-all integrating idea. (p. 57)

Napoleon recalls Shakespeare, the *Sturm and Drang,* and Grabbe's first historical play, but it fully deserves the recognition given it as a truly original work. Like Lenz, Grabbe enriches his drama with implication by such techniques as episodic reinforcement, scenic juxtapositions, and generalized commentary. Unlike Lenz, he knows exactly what he is doing and does not try to make *Napoleon* say something at odds with the dominant effect. . . .

The way Grabbe links up his scenes in *Napoleon* produces an overwhelming panoramic effect. From moment to moment we jump to the various power centers of France, and the swift transitions of atmosphere create an almost kaleidoscopic effect, Grabbe stopping only long enough for us to get the feel of another place, another pocket of ambition or discontent, another seat of forces. Aristotle is left behind, first of all, because Grabbe feels history is made not in one single place but whenever men are ready to go into action, or wherever they are content to do nothing.

Much more radically than Lenz, Grabbe splits the action of his play into units which are independent of a dominating plot line. Anticipating Büchner, he makes the scene in front of us hang together by its own intrinsic dynamism and by its presentation of action that is immediately significant. The *Guckkastentechnik* is refined in the direction of maximum exposure, and the exposure is achieved in scenes which are not designed to milk suspense from what would seem to be potentially a very suspenseful situation. (p. 58)

Scenes commence with jarring abruptness and conclude quite desultorily as Grabbe makes the very linear outlines of his actions communicate dissonance. Like Büchner, he combines scenes whose implications complement one another in order to avoid distortion by omission. . . .

In the street scenes we do not get one action so much as a multiplicity of actions—Grabbe proceeding to create a mosaic of dialogues. To the front of the stage comes whichever little group Grabbe wishes us to see in action, and in a matter of moments the group dissolves back into the crowd. . . .

Lenz's use of language to suggest gesture was integral to his approach to theater. Grabbe, too, employs language in this fashion. In the street scenes, especially, it is difficult not to visualize the expressions and postures which spoken words suggest. (p. 59)

Grabbe, like Lenz, wants theater to make an immediate impression, not to come alive principally through developments of plot punctuated by climactic speeches. Though Grabbe is often taken to be antitheatrical, he is not really. His handling of some of the most minor action of *Napoleon* shows him to be very much aware of the interactions possible between audience and actors on a level independent of literary contexts.

The Hohenstaufen suffered from the forced quality of dialogue which was often versified quite mechanically. This artificiality is gone in *Napoleon*. Here Grabbe writes some of the most striking dramatic prose in the history of German theater. Like Brecht, he sheds the linguistic habits which, perhaps more than any other factor, explain the resistance of the modern reader to much of classical drama. Like Brecht, he seems to have been nourished by the strong phrasings of the Lutheran Bible, which stimulated him to make his own compromise between the language of everyday life and stage language. As it is, Grabbe's dialogue may often catch something of the careless and telegraphic quality of ordinary speech under pressure, but it is not naturalistic. Like Lenz's dialogue, it is designed to convey inner agitation when there is such agitation and in general to come through with a vividness and directness which bespeaks a minimum of literary stylization. But it is stylized nonetheless to reinforce Grabbe's general view that history is a maelstrom of quickly passing events occurring in anything but a related, logical fashion. Choppy dialogue indicates each person is spinning around on his own treadmill, that human speech is far more an outlet for aggression than communication. Following the lead of the *Sturm und Drang*, Grabbe frequently reduces a portion of dialogue to one or two exclamations which it takes the speaker no more than a moment to get out. (p. 60)

Grabbe's dialogue is not always swift or adrenalized, but it is always crisp and concise, and when a character gives utterance to the kind of pithy observations or memorable aphorisms which are sprinkled throughout the play, it seems entirely natural. In fact, after a while we begin to expect striking words or phrases, so casually does Grabbe have recourse to vivid expressions. (p. 61)

By the time the final episode of *Napoleon* has unfolded, it is quite clear that for Grabbe concreteness does not imply simplicity, at any rate not the kind of simplicity which would allow us to reduce Napoleon's downfall to a specific material cause; for Grabbe takes pains to invest *Napoleon* with an overriding sense of fatalism. . . . There is little doubt that what fascinates Grabbe is the vast mechanism of history, which makes use of a great man for a while and then consigns him to the scrapheap. Grabbe's achievement is that he does not make Napoleon's fate ultimately a function of tangible factors; he sees all tangible factors themselves under the sway of inexorable dark forces which play with human and territorial destinies. If history favors anything, it is the conglomerate mass, never the highly individuated hero.

In *Napoleon* Grabbe anticipates Brecht by virtue of the relationship he sets up between drama and audience. Emotional identification between spectator and character there is almost nil, if for no other reason than Grabbe's abrupt changes of scene; but even if the scenes were sustained longer, there would be little identification with characters who generally come through as marionettes tied to a single emotional string. . . . [When] Grabbe is not deliberately grotesque and caricatural, he is usually cool enough for us to sense objectively what is going on. The result is that we experience *Napoleon* very much the way we experience a Brecht play, conscious as we are that everything happening in front of us illustrates a certain attitude toward life in general, that the dramatist takes greater pains to share his cynical perception than to communicate a moving experience, that he wants us to see through what he sees through.

In *Hannibal* . . . Grabbe remains fatalistic, but with a difference. Here the episodic structure is once more adopted, and the play is divided into sections rather than acts, each one with a legend which identifies broadly the subject to be dramatized. . . . (pp. 65-6)

The most noteworthy change revealed by *Hannibal* is in Grabbe's language. . . . Hannibal's speech is pregnant with incisive cynicism and mental toughness, with a hardness of heart Grabbe attributed to no other leader. . . . [Hannibal] is never sentimentalized by Grabbe, who shows him to be in his way every bit as vicious as his enemies. (p. 67)

Hannibal has an exotic atmosphere such as Grabbe aimed at in no other work. But its theme is hardly exotic. It may well be that Grabbe wrote here a play that is only too modern. For what destroys Hannibal? In a word, the profit motive. Grabbe hated the increasing commercialization of his day, and in *Hannibal* he states the issue quite bluntly: either the commercial spirit or the heroic spirit—you can't have both. When we realize that for Grabbe the heroic spirit is synonymous with the totalitarian spirit, we can break his dichotomy down to capitalism versus autocracy. The final choice is between scum and Führer. Is it any wonder Grabbe has so long been a prophet without honor in Germany?

As interesting as *Hannibal* is for the tragic overtones with which Grabbe invests the futile quest of the great leader in a banal world, the play is less relevant to modern epic technique than *Napoleon*. Going back to the world of *Marius and Sulla*, Grabbe once more occupies himself with those customs and habits of ancient life which lend themselves to sensationalistic presentation. If anything, the illustration pattern is too obvious, as Grabbe fills scenes with unsavory details to make his point. . . . [A] note of self-pity is unmistakable. There is more sadness than cynicism here. (pp. 68-9)

There is always a deliberate homeliness in Grabbe's depiction of the lower elements, but this technique is most pronounced in [his *The Hermann Battle*]. . . . Much more than in any other historical drama, Grabbe depicts here the concrete aspects of historical developments, and this includes the rainy climate, the perilous terrain, all the geographical and climatic factors which affected the day-to-day life of the Teutons. He even catalogs the foods carried in knapsacks. Aside from this, there is emphasis on local custom, idiosyncrasies of language, and folk habit to a degree which makes the life of these forest-dwellers come alive with a remarkable vividness, which makes us feel with our senses what it must have been like to live in a jungle of rocks and trees, with oppressive moisture, unseasonal colds, dense thickets, and threatening hillocks. In a way, Grabbe gives us the archetypal jungle.

Grabbe does not romanticize the ancient Germans. In scene after scene he shows them to be the deficient human material which their leader Hermann realizes they are too late. They are barbaric to the core, stupidly shortsighted, and every word they speak reveals their savage nature. Their language has a rough guttural quality, a gruff abruptness, a harsh, clipped rhythm which seems the ultimate in linguistic dehumanization. (p. 69)

The Hermann Battle may not strike us as relevant to modern epic theater. But surely what comes out here is *emotionally* relevant to what came out in all of Grabbe's earlier work. . . . In *The Hermann Battle* the psychic pressures which one finds present in everything Grabbe wrote come out most uninhibitedly. Significantly, Grabbe chooses as the locale of his last play a dark hermetic place where the civilized superego is yet to be born. Here aggression is the very spirit of life and dictates almost every word or action. Here Grabbe can present more bluntly than ever his view of man as mere beast.

In his last play Grabbe is once more out to paint a picture of a particular time in such a way that he cannot be accused of sentimentalizing anything or of making anything abstract. Once again he is deliberately harsh and choppy and caustic at every opportunity. The general run of man is, as usual, presented as scum. . . . *The Hermann Battle* says little that is new, but what it does say, it says with a ferocity that may well be available only to those driven by pathological aggressions. More than any other, this play makes pertinent the reputation of Grabbe's psychopathology, his violent anti-Semitism, his belief in nothing but the rightness of his contempt for common mankind. (pp. 69-70)

When we experience the action of a scene in a Brecht play, our reaction is hardly a simple one, and the same applies to Grabbe. At the same time that we respond to uproarious grotesquery, we are conscious of tragic overtones; while we laugh, we *know* that the implications of what is making us laugh should make us quite sad or angry. We realize that the dramatist is exaggerating to the point of caricature: still his characters are disturbingly real. Episode after episode shows what little basis exists for a high opinion of the human species, but rare is the scene that leaves us feeling the driving forces of life are not at bottom relished. (p. 72)

Perhaps what links Grabbe and Brecht most significantly is the nature of an inner conflict neither could resolve. Both viewed the world as grotesquely impossible. Brecht's solution was communism, but this never altered the nature of reality implied by his drama. . . . Turning to Grabbe, we get an idea of his conflict from his powerful need to identify himself with Schiller rather than Shakespeare and his conviction that Schiller created with his spirit. The implication seems to be that Grabbe was very much for the spirit as against coarse materialisms. But he hardly lives up to this image; the truth of the matter is that with all his contempt for material reality, he realized bitterly that such contempt really had no basis. Like Brecht, he could not escape the conviction that material reality is all there is, that it makes irrelevant any outraged attitude one adopts toward it. Here, perhaps, is the ultimate source of that strange mixture of social concreteness and cynical detachment which entered German drama with the emergence of epic theater. (p. 73)

> *Max Spalter, "Christian Dietrich Grabbe," in his*
> Brecht's Tradition *(copyright © 1967 by The Johns*
> *Hopkins Press), The Johns Hopkins University Press,*
> *1967, pp. 39-73.*

ROGER A. NICHOLLS (essay date 1969)

[In] Grabbe we are aware of the richness of his genius and the potentialities that were never totally fulfilled. In his gift for the creation of character and scene, in the range of emotions, in his ability to impose on to history the vitality of the human struggle, Grabbe seems rightly to stand comparison with Shakespeare himself. It is also true that his work all too often ends in disappointment. . . . We cannot, however, so easily ascribe Grabbe's failures to weaknesses of character or temperament, the excesses of fever or madness or what Heine calls the "spiritual intoxication of genius". For all the eccentricities of Grabbe's character we see in fact in his life much evidence of determination and endurance. . . . He was totally serious in his

devotion to his work and altogether conscious of the problem he faced. The causes of failure lay in his time. Grabbe's vision of the world shocked and baffled his contemporaries as it did the 19th century as a whole. He in turn responded with contempt for those who seemed to find their way all too easily to success.

If Grabbe's work tends to wander without direction, the cause lies in his inability to accept the carefully structured dramatic form that the German theatre of Goethe and Schiller had constructed on the basis of French classicism. The lapses of taste, the excesses of the action and the uncertainty of the language are the reflection of a world of disorder experienced without any clear central focus and point of control. . . . Grabbe is not able to formulate his experience into any kind of tragic sequence. Only in his earliest drama *Herzog Theodor von Gothland* do we find anything of a traditional tragic development, but already here we are aware of a desperately poignant crisis of faith so overwhelming that it threatens to shatter all dramatic form and control. (pp. 254-55)

Possibly, for all the interesting qualities of his later work, [Grabbe] was most successful earlier when he openly adopted remote and eccentric dramatic forms as in *Scherz, Satire, Ironie und tiefere Bedeutung* and *Don Juan und Faust*. Even here . . . he was partly dependent on accepted modes and conventions. *Scherz* has its roots in Romantic comedy and reflects the influence of Ludwig Tieck. *Don Juan und Faust* is in part a recreation of much developed themes. But in the extravagances and vitality of the comedy Grabbe achieved a strikingly original manner whereby he was able to express without pathos his own vision of a disordered world. . . . In *Don Juan und Faust* Grabbe found a means to express openly the extent and intensity of human desires and ambitions. The idea of putting two such superhuman heroes into one play seems like a characteristic Grabbe extravagance yet he was able legitimately to limit and control the material. (pp. 255-56)

When he turned to the history drama Grabbe was not able openly and directly to present his sense of spiritual crisis. The plays reflect and partly reproduce the neutral colors of history itself. But the mood and spirit of these plays is only comprehensible if we understand the current of disillusion that runs through them. (p. 256)

Grabbe organizes events into a dramatic pattern but only in order to impose some kind of structure on the inevitable confusion of historical events. . . . [He] was not able to accept a dominating idea behind the multiplicity of human events. When he speaks as he does on occasion of expressing "the spirit of history" he means only that he is not tied to precise accuracy in reproducing historical events. He aims to penetrate history with his own vision but only in order to reveal the disorder and confusion, as well as the strengths and weaknesses, of human aims.

In the two Hohenstaufen dramas Grabbe attempted to encompass this incoherent and many sided world within a largely traditional form. He wanted to attract his audience by the pageantry and color of the medieval scene. He makes use of the traditional iambic pentameter and injects into his language and imagery a heroic tone and patriotic flourish that might appeal to his time. Even in the structure of the plays which are carefully divided into 5 acts and can be more or less satisfactorily analyzed in terms of a normal exposition, climax and dénouement, he seems to impose an orthodox order on to events. . . . On the one hand individual scenes suggest the real incoherence of the many sided world. The whole significance of the action [in *Friedrich Barbarossa*] is not encompassed within the imperial conflict. The multiple ambitions and valuations of men cannot so easily be incorporated within a single theme. As a result the very stress on this central conflict seems like an artificial imposition of the author's. At the same time the picture of the medieval ruler takes on a curiously Romantic coloring. Grabbe indulges the possibilities of an earlier age where men carried in themselves the self-assurance that imposes meaning on life. (pp. 257-58)

In the Hohenstaufen plays and especially *Heinrich VI* the contrast between Grabbe's novelty of purpose and orthodoxy of structure leaves us uncertain in our reactions. For all their interesting qualities these plays remain dramatically ambiguous. But in the later histories Grabbe boldly broke new ground. *Napoleon oder Die Hundert Tage* reveals an essentially new dramatic plan. Here the action of the play is dictated by historical events. . . . Grabbe's aim now is to show the reality of the forces that determine history. (pp. 258-59)

A drama of this kind has no necessary beginning, middle and end. . . . Recurrent motifs of the play emphasize the cyclical nature of human events. . . . Individual scenes take on greater dramatic importance. They carry their own center of gravity and cannot be interpreted only as stages moving towards the tragic outcome. Grabbe's techniques themselves are intensely dramatic. It is characteristic of his work what he always externalizes, sacrificing verisimilitude often in order to reveal events directly in front of our eyes. Yet the action as a whole takes on epic proportions. Inevitably the play has to be related to the new objectives of Brecht's "epic theatre". For in Grabbe as in Brecht we are not totally involved in the dramatic sequence. There is no central figures or figure with whom we may unconsciously identify. In the end we are left outside, awed observers reflecting on what we have seen.

In *Hannibal* a central theme returns. The betrayal of the leader by his own people at home provides an emotional center to the variegations of the action. But once again the world reveals a chaotic clash of contending forces. Here the action moves in leaps, through rapidly shifting scenes that reflect in transient episodes the vast sweep of events. A grotesque light is thrown on the human scene and the brutal desperation of man's endeavors. The disillusion that lay under the surface in the earlier history dramas, coming to appear only indirectly through the absence of valid human purposes, now comes into the open. The objective reflection of history is penetrated with the sense of tragic betrayal. If *Napoleon* seemed like a forerunner of the epic theatre, *Hannibal* points to other features of contemporary drama, above all to expressionism and the theatre of the absurd. In his use of leaping techniques, rapidity of movement and sharply illuminated episodes, Grabbe challenges as does expressionism our normal sense of a clearly structured and ordered world. At the same time his use of deliberate distortions and grotesque associations, overlying a melancholy sense of futility, emphasizes the absurdity of the human condition and the total limitations of our rational control.

The absence in Grabbe's work of a clear symbolic structure may well be a source of appeal to us. A classical tragedy with its implicit pattern of human fate may seem too arbitrary and to leave too much out. We too share Grabbe's skepticism and are glad to see the world in its ambiguity, fragmented, many-sided, lacking any center. Grabbe's work must be judged in relation to a rebellious tradition that may be traced back to the "Sturm und Drang", and especially to Lenz, and which continues through Büchner and Wedekind to Dürrenmatt and innumerable other modern figures. (pp. 259-61)

Grabbe's emphasis [is] on the brutal strains in human nature. The frightening excesses of *Gothland* reoccur just as horribly in *Marius und Sulla*. . . . He seems deliberately to shock us by the contrast between our own humane predilections and the bitter cruelty exemplified by the man of power. (p. 262)

[Everything within Grabbe] drove him to resist the pressure towards futility which he saw in the world around him. His heroes deny all protective illusions and assert themselves irresistibly against the world. There are times when Grabbe seems to linger in dreams of a simpler and more harmonious age. Don Juan and Faust feel that something in the present time has gone wrong, that being themselves the fragmented victims of a world that has lost its center, they can only dream of a previous harmony. In *Friedrich Barbarossa* Grabbe created a medieval world of faith in which the Emperor lives in the security of his God-given role. In the fairy tale comedy *Aschenbrödel* and more ironically in *Scherz, Satire, Ironie und tiefere Bedeutung* he indulged the possibility of a world of happy endings where lovers find in each other the comfort to face the disorders of life. Even in *Die Hermannsschlacht* we see once more the hero buoyed up by his inner relation to his people. Yet each of these dreams fails to satisfy, and at other times Grabbe seems tempted by the attractions of pure defiance. More than once he broaches the possibility of superman. In *Don Juan und Faust* through the speculations of his heroes, in *Heinrich VI* and *Marius und Sulla* through direct action and decision, he suggests the hope of a life beyond normal human restrictions and all common values of good and evil. But there are times also, especially in *Napoleon* and *Hannibal,* as well as to a large extent in his comedies, when Grabbe faces the reality of an unheroic world and accepts the nature of the mass age that is upon us. These plays offer no obvious consolation. They bring no message and no program to us. Yet there is an element of confidence and hope. The heroes, touched by common human weakness, share a vital spirit which spurs them on. We recognize and rejoice in the energy with which they pursue the varied purposes of life. (pp. 262-63)

> *Roger A. Nicholls, in his* The Dramas of Christian Dietrich Grabbe *(© copyright 1969, Mouton & Co. N.V., Publishers; reprinted by permission of the author), Mouton Publishers, The Hague, 1969, 268 p.*

K. F. JAY   (essay date 1969)

While the dramatic sequence is often unskilled and motivation not always convincing, [*Herzog Theodor von Gothland*] is nevertheless a work of extraordinary and dynamic strength, reminiscent of the best Sturm und Drang creations, but profounder, and touching continuously upon the fundamental issues of human existence, dealing not only with the relationships of man to man, but also of man to fate and exploring the nature of Good and Evil. It is, at the same time, a witness to deep-seated inner conflicts in the adolescent author. (p. 111)

Grabbe's next dramatic attempt, probably designed to curry favour with the powerful Tieck, an attempt to create a romantic comedy under the title of *Scherz, Satire, Ironie und tiefere Bedeutung* must be deemed a failure. Grabbe lacked a genuine sense of humour and the lightness of touch required. He succeeds better with his satirical allusions, but his development as a satirist had to wait until much later. . . .

Grabbe's comedy is comic only in the sense of a vulgar Punch and Judy show, in which despicable puppets hit one another and a devil performs tricks. The true comedian is in sympathy with his characters while Grabbe despises them. (p. 112)

The first play [in Grabbe's historical series, the Hohenstaufen cycle], which he calls a tragedy, is his **Kaiser Friedrich Barbarossa,** largely a colourful pageant, romantic in tone, interspersed with anachronist compliments for contemporary dynasties. . . . In the second play of the series, **Kaiser Heinrich der Sechste,** more powerful and less diffuse than the previous one, the author seems to have abandoned the original idea of presenting a popular spectacle to the German nation. (pp. 113-14)

Grabbe's **Napoleon oder die hundert Tage** represents a new departure in the poet's development: his hero is almost what we could call in modern parlance a "non-hero", part of a more important historical setting, a mere link in the flow of events. . . . **Napoleon** is a strangely diffuse work, no longer a stage play in the accepted sense of the word, an epic dramatisation in prose. . . . (p. 114)

[Some critics considered **Hannibal**] Grabbe's maturest and greatest tragedy, completed after **Napoleon.** . . . This awesome and deeply moving work gives us an idea of what Grabbe might have become had not physical illness and dark forces within prematurely destroyed him. The new hero is intensely human, he does not speak in hyperboles, he is a man and not a "superman". His aims are not excessive, nor is he ambitious for himself. His stature both as a feeling human being, a patriot and a leading military and political figure is expressed with great economy of words and reflected in the hatred of his enemies and the loyalty of his followers. . . . The action [of the play] has the compelling and metallic quality of Greek drama. . . . (p. 115)

Don Juan und Faust [was] Grabbe's only excursion into metaphysical tragedy. . . . [Next] to Marlowe's **Doctor Faustus** and possibly Goethe's **Faust**—Part I, Grabbe's creation is probably the dramatically and intellectually most satisfactory rendering of the combined themes, granting also the tremendous difficulty facing the author when confronting two dramatic prototypes of almost universal significance, figures which had appeared in innumerable shapes on the contemporary stage. . . . [The] poet's concern is with two opposing life principles. Grabbe avoided Byron's mistake, whose **Manfred** offers almost nothing but meditative recitation, and created a central plot: the conflict between the sanguine southern hedonist Don Juan and the nordic polymath Faust, who clash over the possession of a beautiful woman. Most of the traditional trimmings of the two themes are employed. . . . Grabbe paints a marvellous picture of a possessed megalomaniac, describes the pathology of a self-destroyer, of a hero who utterly defeated descends to hell, but promises us a continued fight in the hereunder. To have been able to create a Faust, almost totally different from existing models, alone is an appreciable achievement. . . . By contrast, the figure of Don Juan is one of Grabbe's most attractive creations. It is as if Grabbe, the ugly little man and the domed brow of the thinker and the weak chin, the one whom life was in the process of defeating, the shy one and the failure with women, had projected his wish dreams upon the greatest of all lovers and sensualists, Don Juan, the man of action for action's sake, the enemy of metaphysical reflection, the gambler at high stakes, the hero who has "neither in front of him nor behind him a luminous realm of values". (pp. 116-17)

[Grabbe's] work, however faulty in parts, *forms the vital link between the German classics and Kleist on the one hand and Friedrich Hebbel on the other.* . . . Because a fervent conviction propelled him, his dramas are still discussed, praised, or condemned, while the plays of his contemporaries, so well received in their day, now hardly figure in the histories of German literature. (p. 117)

Grabbe prophetically anticipated the age when the masses would play their part in political history, and certainly in **Napoleon** and **Die Hermannsschlacht** action depends not so much on the will of the great hero than upon the interplay of hero and multitudes—a situation characteristic of the modern era. Of less importance, but nevertheless significant, is Grabbe's mastery of battle scenes. With bold strokes this little civilian grasped the essentials of campaigns and engagements, and went successfully far beyond the token battles of past plays.

Grabbe's overall importance as a dramatic force is therefore undeniable, but his evaluation in purely poetical terms poses a much more difficult question. Taking his verse first: his lines do not appear to come easily to him. Much is sheer Shakespearean and Schillerian imitation or strongly reminiscent of the winged trochaic rhythm of the fate dramatists. Certainly in his early plays bombast and ranting declamation are frequently found. Moreover, Grabbe's lack of refined culture and variance of eroticism prevented him from presenting satisfactory love scenes. Here his verse is reminiscent of a bad libretto. And yet, when his own psychological problems invade action or characters, some truly good and deeply expressed lines make their appearance. He fails in an epic description of Nature; his paean to the Alps in **Don Juan und Faust** is but a faint reflection of Byron's majestic lines in **Manfred,** but he does succeed if, as in an El Greco, nature becomes intimately linked with the soul of his hero, when the external scene becomes expressive and reflexive of interior states. (pp. 118-19)

[It] is prose and not verse that is Grabbe's true medium, and one wonders how much bombast and forced rhetoric could have been avoided, had Grabbe adopted prose earlier than he did. (p. 119)

[Not] only do we find in Grabbe a continuous development of dramatic expression, culminating in the excellent prose of **Hannibal,** but we also find a refinement of the very experience of disaster. Grabbe has become superior to the bombastic self-pitying hero. Grabbe's growing maturity of the conception of historical key figures no longer permits him to cast them in the mould of supermen. One of the criticisms levelled against Grabbe is that he uses a heavy-handed sledge hammer approach. This may be valid for his earlier work, but the very fact that in his last plays he shows definite satirical gifts disproves the accusation. Both in **Napoleon** and in **Hannibal** satire is skilfully used to deepen the characterisation of persons and periods. (p. 120)

Because of Grabbe's ignorance of the nobler side of eroticism and of "ladies", practically all his heroines remain puppetlike, reciting stock phrases. Nor does he succeed with "normal" and balanced characters, such as the Emperor Barbarossa. His vision was too introspective to enable him to encompass character traits other than his own. (p. 122)

Grabbe left no school and no literary heirs. He seems to have been a "dead man" before he disappeared from the scene. . . . There is no trace of an influence on either Schopenhauer or Nietzsche. Grabbe's merits as a pioneer were overshadowed by Georg Buchnër's work. Grabbe's tragedy of isolation and frustration thus continued even after his death. (p. 125)

K. F. Jay, "Christian Dietrich Grabbe," in German Men of Letters: Twelve Literary Essays, Vol. V, edited by Alex Natan (© 1969 Oswald Wolff (Publishers) Limited), Oswald Wolff, 1969, pp. 110-30.

ROY C. COWEN (essay date 1972)

Finding faults in [Herzog Theodor von Gothland] does not demand great critical acumen on the part of the "reader." . . . The drama is much too long, possibly because Grabbe was reluctant to discard entirely his two earlier, rejected plays. It also seems too long because there is too much repetition that does not move the plot, which, in terms of Gothland's development, reaches its climax in the third act.

Too many problems are created or implied for any one drama to satisfy within the limits imposed by an audience's patience. Moreover, Grabbe does not do much beyond suggesting these problems. For instance, the socio-cultural aspect is evoked, then dropped. The North-South conflict, which will, in later dramas, play a significant role, is not yet fully developed. Gothland's relationship to his family . . . is treated in a cursory manner.

The language, as full of obscenities as it is by the standards of the nineteenth century, is often bombastic, and its pathos frequently becomes self-parodying in its exaggeration. In terms of the number of scenes and characters the play exceeds both the audience's comprehension and the demands of the stage. Motivations of the characters are too often missing entirely or merely suggested. One might almost say that each character is playing the part of a literary predecessor whose motivation is readily accepted. . . .

We feel that Grabbe, while indirectly attacking the traditional theater of his time, remains heavily indebted to it. Over and over again Gothland rejects fate and ascribes everything to "chance." Yet much of this play obviously stems from the "fate tragedies" of Grabbe's time. (p. 43)

The deficiencies of Grabbe's first published play are so patent that naming them seems like beating a dead horse to death. But wherever we touch upon Grabbe's life and works, we find excesses on both the positive and negative sides, and here as well. Gothland is unquestionably a work of genius. . . . [Several] aspects of Grabbe's play certainly merit praise. Above all, we are favorably struck by many of the monologues, by occasional flashes of ingenuity, and by the sheer scope of the action.

Moreover, although his coordination and execution is far from mature, Grabbe introduces into this play almost all of the themes and motifs that characterize his later dramas. This fact alone makes Gothland an important work. Perhaps we are disturbed by the pathetic frenzy with which certain ideas are stated, but this very overstatement offers an advantage. It allows us to perceive Grabbe's attitudes more clearly than in the later plays, for which these attitudes frequently form only a background. It has been correctly stated that no single play can represent Grabbe, but certainly Gothland and its comic complement, Scherz, Satire, Ironie und tiefere Bedeutung, come as close as any to fulfilling this role. . . .

Unlike his Austrian contemporary, Franz Grillparzer, Grabbe never showed any pronounced desire to provide an extensive psychological foundation for the actions of his characters. But to say that he neglected the problem of motivation even in this play, his first and most disorganized, would be misleading. (p. 44)

Although Grabbe deals extensively with the pseudohistorical aspects of the action, the play does not impress us as being historical. Most critics maintain that the play degenerates into a family tragedy not unlike the mediocre fate tragedies of the times. This contention bears a fair amount of credence. But the main reason for the play's lack of conviction as a historical drama lies in the fact that the sociopolitical action is subordinated to Gothland's personal disillusionment and to the effect of this disillusionment on him as a metaphysical being, not as a nobleman, brother, or soldier.

Gothland derives its tension from violent confrontations: Finns against Swedes, heathens against Christians, African against European, brother against brother, son against father, subject against king, individual against homeland, and so forth. Yet almost all these conflicts are either left unrealized in their potential or lack a clear profile of issues and decisions. They are only symptomatic of the primary conflict lying within the protagonist himself, a conflict that is, in turn, projected on all of the other events. (pp. 45-6)

There is no "idea" inherent in history, and each event is lived only for its own excitement. The real world is all we have. Although Gothland is not a truly historical drama and its characters are far from credible as historical persons, Grabbe's emphasis on time as the only meaningful criterion forms the basis for his increasing realism. Man as a blind captive of the present time, of his present emotions and of the thrill of the moment for its own sake—this is man as he will later appear as the subject of Grabbe's truly historical dramas. (p. 50)

[Scherz, Satire, Ironie und tiefere Bedeutung] is a very entertaining comedy. Its effectiveness on the stage is demonstrated by the fact that it has been performed every year for the last decade in at least one important German theater. In retrospect we may regret that Grabbe did not write more comedies. . . .

In Scherz, Satire, Grabbe uses a characteristically Romantic form, but he does so, not to pay homage to Tieck or Romanticism, but to reject Romantic values. This fact stamps him as a Weltschmerzler. (p. 55)

[In Scherz, Satire] Grabbe blends the fantastic and earthy, caprice and realism, imagination and realism. All the characters reflect Grabbe's feeling for, and observation of, lower-class, unsophisticated life, as well as his knowledge of literary and intellectual fads. On a realistic level, we cannot quite believe in the true existence of these characters, yet we are not prepared to assert that there is no such drunken Schoolmaster or no such emancipated young lady as Liddy. (p. 57)

Grabbe also ridicules any system, be it artistic, scientific, or philosophical. Like Tieck, he makes it clear that he does not believe in creating or thinking according to given rules. . . . [In Scherz, Satire] we have lost the security provided by a substitution for the notions and values under attack. For that reason, Grabbe's satire seems to be far more subjective and personally revealing, but also more nihilistic. (p. 58)

Taken together, Gothland and Scherz, Satire present a tragicomic world of absurdity, a world of moral and physical chaos, in which ideal meaning cannot be found. . . . Grabbe brings the tragic and comic elements increasingly closer to each other, until he arrives at one of his most important modes of expression: the tragicomedy. In *Hannibal,* which shows true mastery of this genre, Scipio the Elder says, ''What is tragic is also amusing, and vice versa. For I have, after all, often laughed in tragedies and have almost been moved in comedies.'' . . . Throughout his career, Grabbe's propensity for the tragicomic will be inseparably tied, as in *Gothland* and its comic counterpart, with the problem of fate. Over and over again we shall see how Grabbe attempts to resolve the conflict between his belief in a personal fate and a meaningless, chaotic world that seems to reveal no timeless principles as a guiding force.

Touching on the fate problem represents about the only redeeming feature of *Nannette und Maria.* It is certainly the only feature in this rather banal work that links it with the rest of Grabbe's dramas. (pp. 64-5)

Scherz, Satire is an intentional, seriously comic parody of *Gothland* with a truly deeper significance. *Nannette und Maria* is simply, like Mollfels' nose, ''flat as a story by Karoline Pichler'' (a feminine novelist satirized in *Scherz, Satire*). In trying to give his contemporaries what they wanted, Grabbe betrayed himself and his talent. (p. 67)

[The first version of *Marius und Sulla*] is, in its mass scenes, largely indebted to Shakespeare. But the second version, stemming, as it does, from the time of Grabbe's critical essay on Shakespeare and Shakespearianism, introduces a new, truly original technique. The new technique will present the ''spirit'' and the idea of history, something that Grabbe felt was often missing in Shakespeare's chronicles. . . .

Grabbe restricts himself to the specific historical idea in a specific period. . . . The later historical dramas, like *Marius,* carry out this program because Grabbe renounces, except by tone and implication, the revelation of universal truths and ideas in history. (p. 73)

Like Gothland, all of Grabbe's historical characters live for the ''moment,'' and the ''spirit'' that pervades his histories is created by the ''facts'' devoid of all abstract, metaphysical principles implying knowledge beyond the present moment. Not only does such a ''spirit'' imply the negation of progress and development; in Grabbe's works it becomes more and more commensurate with history seen as a senseless cycle into which man ''reads the good.'' (pp. 73-4)

[Grabbe praises his mass scenes in *Marius und Sulla,*] and rightfully so. Several of them effectively evoke the atmosphere and spirit of the times. But they are not merely naturalistic re-creations of details. There is an undercurrent of cynicism in them that anticipates the scenes in Grabbe's great historical dramas on Napoleon and Hannibal. To achieve his own, individual ''tone'' Grabbe uses two techniques: a sort of caricatured realism and a so-called commentary technique. (p. 74)

[A] principle of selectivity becomes obvious in the scenes which seem almost chaotic in their abundance of characters. But— and this is one of Grabbe's most significant achievements— these characters are not merely the standard bearers of abstract ideas. By and large they all have dimension. At the same time, we note that Grabbe's types tend toward caricature. . . . No better example of this quality in Grabbe's first truly historical play can be found than in Saturninus, who also represents the second technique, the ''commentary technique.''

Some critics, Max Spalter, for example, view Saturninus as being superfluous to the plot. This point could be conceded as far as the main plot is concerned, but Saturninus is nevertheless absolutely essential for the drama as a whole. . . . Through

him we see and hear how fickle the masses are, how susceptible they are to a demagogue, and how they will abandon their leader as soon as he no longer has the physical power to force obedience. These times are made for an opportunist, and Saturninus is one. These are times in which the voices of rationality and moderation are drowned out, the times of fear, irrationality, and injustice, all of which Saturninus uses to his own advantage. A forerunner of Jouve, the old revolutionary in *Napoleon,* Saturninus shows us as well, however, that the man who leads the masses against their exploiters does not do so out of idealism or a love of humanity. (pp. 74-5)

As much as is new in *Marius und Sulla,* many of the problems from the other plays recur here. The technical innovations, in many cases, only serve basic attitudes that have changed but little since *Gothland.* Nevertheless, Grabbe has also developed new variations on some of his fundamental ideas. (p. 75)

In a sense, *Don Juan und Faust* fulfills its promise to summarize the ideas in the previous dramas, particularly *Gothland* and *Scherz, Satire,* the most strongly anti-Romantic works. But we also have many indications that this work does not simply stem from a look backward. Before it was completed, Grabbe stated his intention to devote himself to historical subjects. Following *Marius und Sulla, Don Juan und Faust* might seem like a mere excursion or simply another experiment. Experiment it is, but one that reveals a continued interest in history. Too often neglected by critics, the relationship between *Don Juan und Faust* and Grabbe's historical dramas should not be underrated, mainly because it makes his sole drama of ideas seem less isolated and, therefore, helps us to see the continuity from *Marius und Sulla* to the Hohenstaufen dramas. (p. 94)

In its original form, *Aschenbrödel* contains more and stronger literary satire. (p. 111)

In *Scherz, Satire,* we perceived a pronounced ''laughter of desperation,'' a tendency toward cynical contempt for mankind. The same qualities recur in the first version of *Aschenbrödel* but are deleted in the second. (p. 112)

The moderation of the later version can be interpreted as a sincere effort on Grabbe's part to find a positive solution and to show that the ideal can occasionally be realized.

Nevertheless, satire on the court and its decadence is still present, though meliorated, in the second version, completed after *Napoleon* and before *Hannibal.* In the two major historical plays, the presentation of the court, symbolic of the ''system'' and artificiality, has, however, tragicomic implications more in keeping with the first *Aschenbrödel,* which can, therefore, be viewed as a transition piece to the major works. The revised, more idealistic *Aschenbrödel* appears, on the other hand, to have provided a respite between the bitter portraits of the established, fruitless, corrupt, and ignorant systems depicted in *Napoleon* and *Hannibal.* Indeed, it seems to be a last, desperate attempt to reconcile ideality and reality, for Grabbe's last drama, *Die Hermannsschlacht,* offers little more consolation than *Hannibal.*

Yet, even in its final form, *Aschenbrödel* still incorporates many themes and motifs from the earlier works, particularly *Scherz, Satire.* In turn, it continues the line of development from the previous plays to *Hannibal,* as well as having many features of *Napoleon.* No harmless interlude like *Nannette und Maria,* it is, despite its latent attempt to find a way out of the Graggian conflict between ideality and reality, typical for the author of *Gothland.* (pp. 113-14)

Although virtually all of Grabbe's dramas treat the question of fate or destiny in some manner, the theme occurs only once [in *Aschenbrödel*], and at that it seems almost a blind motif. . . . *Aschenbrödel* represents a regression back to the purely Romantic form of comedy.

Nowhere is Grabbe's increased realism more apparent than in the opening scenes of this play. . . . As in *Scherz, Satire,* there are really two parallel plots: the Cinderella story with Olympia and the King, and the story of the Baron's attempt to extricate himself from financial difficulties. In terms of the play's structure, the uniting element is the coachman-rat, who gains human form through the fairy queen's intercession for Olympia. He brings the Baron's story to a happy end by eating the mortgage held by Isaak, who, in the end, however, receives his money from the King. In both Olympia's and the Baron's situations, the solution to their problems is both magical and realistic. . . . In both cases, the magical episodes are almost unnecessary adornments.

On the other hand, Grabbe suggests a plea for the supernatural as a part of the realistic world. . . . Many German writers of the day who were producing such a banal realism had learned from Iffland and Walter Scott, both of whom Grabbe attacks in *Aschenbrödel*. In *Gothland* and his historical plays, Grabbe uses his superdimensional heroes as a counter to the *Biedermeier* glorification of everyday life. Here, however, Grabbe is trying to prove, by example, that there can be a bit of beauty and humor in the real world. (pp. 115-17)

[Grabbe's] last three plays provide the best measure of his originality. In their themes, motifs, and attitudes they ensue directly from the previous works, but their technique represents at least partial fulfillment of the tendencies latent in the earlier plays, representing Grabbe's increasing divergence from the main line of dramatic tradition in the nineteenth century. (p. 119)

Napoleon is Grabbe's first serious play couched completely in prose. It is also his most immediate drama, for in it he shows his ability to make history relive its course on the stage. . . .

The characters in *Napoleon* express themselves without a stiffness of conventional stage characters, yet they manifest a terseness, succinctness, and wit that gives the scenes dramatic impact and concentration. This original stage language represents one of Grabbe's great accomplishments, and it will also characterize the speech patterns in *Hannibal* and the *Hermannsschlacht*. Indeed, many of the linguistic innovations attributed to Büchner and to Hauptmann can already be found in Grabbe's major historical dramas. . . .

[In *Napoleon* Grabbe] earns the designation as one of the masters of the stage. Almost every scene is, in itself, a small masterpiece. Such is the underlying assumption of all attempts to evaluate Grabbe's skill as a dramatist. (p. 125)

Here, in Grabbe's most "realistic" drama up to that time, we nevertheless sense the typically Grabbean tone, a "laughter of desperation." Napoleon is a special case in history—he received a "second chance." By limiting himself to the period of this second chance—the "Hundred Days"—Grabbe shows not only what made Napoleon great the first time, namely the revolution, but also what gave him his second opportunity. There exists a need for him, for a time of excitement, for a stimulus to greatness. (pp. 132-33)

The language of [*Hannibal*] is a masterful exercise in understatement. It is language without flow and beauty. . . . [The] language of *Hannibal* approaches pure expression, not as description of one's feelings, but as a series of ejections, as a forced reply to a world that does not allow any beautification or explanation. Pared to its essence, Grabbe's dialogue here is a direct precursor of Expressionism and Absurdism. (pp. 143-44)

There is little discrepancy in the critical opinions about *Die Hermannsschlacht:* it is generally considered to be the weakest of Grabbe's later works. Most critics emphasize its essentially "undramatic" character. The flaws are usually ascribed to Grabbe's declining health, for one of the most obvious weaknesses lies in the author's inability to infuse into this play the same dramatic force, unity of purpose, and sharpness of characterization found in *Napoleon* and *Hannibal*. (p. 149)

[The minor characters in *Napoleon oder die Hundert Tage* and *Hannibal*]—indeed, in all of Grabbe's historical plays—are in the main drawn with the deftness, sharpness, and economy of an artist. The sure hand which, with a few strokes, portrayed Saturninus in *Marius und Sulla*, Jouve, Vitry, Chasseceour, the Berlin Jew in *Napoleon,* Brasidas, Turnu, and Alitta in *Hannibal*—that hand seems to have lost its precision and to betray the physical deterioriation of the man. . . . The mass scenes, elsewhere Grabbe's forte, are, in *Die Hermannsschlacht,* almost banal enough to give them . . . the effect of satire. The realism of these scenes cannot be underestimated, yet they lack the inner vitality, the dynamic force of the earlier ones. . . . [They] are, moreover, not as successfully integrated into the play as a whole. (pp. 149-50)

Rejecting the *Hermannsschlacht* merely as a product of a degenerating mind and body is grossly unfair, for, although Grabbe no longer had the physical qualities necessary for the execution of his ideas, he did have ideas, new ideas, that stem directly from his previous works. . . . [He] pursued a line that obviated either unbridled patriotism or its antithesis, satire of a national myth. Either view presupposes a one-sidedness which Grabbe—despite his many other failings—never evidenced.

Quite simply stated, Grabbe tries to reveal the problematic nature of culture in a historical sense. In most of his later dramas, the main problem concerns some historical form of the conflict between the "system" and the "chaotic," between tradition and revolution, decadence and vitality, security and danger, reason and imagination. In *Die Hermannsschlacht,* Grabbe once again dramatizes these issues. . . . But the playwright goes beyond the simplified conflict implied by this dualism. (pp. 150-51)

Die Hermannsschlacht is not a good play. Yet its failure cannot be ascribed simply to Grabbe's inability to reveal, once again, an important problem and a meaningful paradox of human existence. In his conception of the issues, as in his formal innovations, Grabbe may well have achieved the dubious honor of having written the best play about Arminius. (p. 153)

Roy C. Cowen, in his Christian Dietrich Grabbe *(copyright © 1972 by Twayne Publishers, Inc.; reprinted with the permission of Twayne Publishers, a Division of G. K. Hall & Co., Boston), Twayne, 1972, 176 p.*

ADDITIONAL BIBLIOGRAPHY

Cowen, Roy C. "Satan and the Satanic in Grabbe's Dramas." *The Germanic Review* XXXIX, No. 2 (March 1964): 120-36.

A study of the imagery of evil in Grabbe's dramas.

Cowen, Roy C. "Grabbe's Faust—Another German Hamlet?" *Studies in Romanticism* 12, No. 1 (Winter 1973): 443-60.*

  Discusses the resemblances in plot and character in Shakespeare's *Hamlet* and Grabbe's *Faust*.

Edwards, Maurice. "Grabbe's *Jest, Satire, Irony, and Deeper Significance:* An Introduction." In *Jest, Satire, Irony, and Deeper Significance: A Comedy in Three Acts,* by Christian Dietrich Grabbe, pp. vii-xxi. New York: Frederick Ungar Publishing Co., Inc., 1966.

  A brief analysis of Grabbe's comedy.

Heald, David. "A Dissenting German View of Shakespeare—Christian Dietrich Grabbe." *German Life and Letters* XXV (1971-1972): 67-78.*

  A comparison of Shakespeare and Grabbe, discussing the ways in which Grabbe incorporated Shakespeare into his works.

Hoch, Horace Lind. "Shakespeare's Influence upon Grabbe." Ph.D. dissertation, University of Pennsylvania, 1910?*

  Analyzes the striking similarities in the works of Shakespeare and Grabbe.

Kuehnemund, Richard. "The Struggle for National Freedom and Union: Heinrich von Kleist and His Successors." In his *Arminius or the Rise of a National Symbol in Literature,* pp. 86-104. Chapel Hill: University of North Carolina, 1953.*

  Studies the nationalistic war themes and epic characteristics of Grabbe's *Hermannsschlacht*.

Nathaniel Hawthorne

1804-1864

American novelist, short story writer, and essayist.

Nathaniel Hawthorne is considered one of the greatest of American fiction writers. *The Scarlet Letter: A Romance,* with its balanced structure, simple, expressive language, and superb use of symbols is a recognized classic of American literature. The novel examines the questions of pride, sin, guilt, and retribution within the milieu of Puritan America, a period which fascinated Hawthorne.

Hawthorne's preoccupation with Puritan history grew from his own heritage. His first American ancestor was William Hathorne (Hawthorne himself added the "w" to his name), who participated in the persecution of the Quakers in seventeenth-century New England, and whose son presided over the Salem witch trials. The sins of his forefathers haunted Hawthorne, who suspected that his family's failing fortunes and his father's early death were the product of divine retribution. Hawthorne's childhood was somber and sheltered, spent with his mother and two older sisters in Salem and, briefly, Lake Sebago, Maine. An avid reader with a taste for John Bunyan and Edmund Spenser, Hawthorne began to write at Bowdoin College, where he met Franklin Pierce and Henry Wadsworth Longfellow. After graduation, Hawthorne returned to his mother's home in Salem where he passed a twelve-year literary apprenticeship, occasionally publishing unsigned tales in journals but more often than not destroying his work. He published a novel, *Fanshawe: A Tale,* but later withdrew it from circulation and burned every available copy.

Twice-Told Tales, Hawthorne's first signed work, contained historical sketches and tales displaying the dark themes and skillful technique that characterize his later work. Although the book was overlooked by the reading public, it drew favorable criticism from writers, including an enthusiastic review by Longfellow. Soon after the book's publication, Hawthorne fell in love with Sophia Peabody, a frail neighbor who had admired his work. Hoping to find a permanent home for himself and Sophia, Hawthorne joined the Brook Farm community but left after six months, uncomfortable with communal life and unconverted to transcendentalism. He and Sophia married in 1842 and moved to the Old Manse, a house in Concord, where they spent the happy years recorded in the first sketch of *Mosses from an Old Manse.*

Hawthorne was forced by poor finances to accept a post as surveyor in the Salem Custom House, a position he lost in 1849. Troubled about money and saddened by the recent death of his mother, Hawthorne began a novel that he had brooded over for years. *The Scarlet Letter,* a culmination of the best characteristics of his earlier tales, brought Hawthorne recognition and some financial security, despite the resentment of his Salem neighbors, who took the sardonic "Custom House" introduction to the book as a criticism of their community. The Hawthornes, with their son and two daughters, moved to Lenox where Hawthorne befriended Herman Melville, who dedicated *Moby Dick* to Hawthorne. In the next several years, Hawthorne wrote *The House of the Seven Gables,* set in contemporary New England and dealing with the theme of an-

Culver Pictures

cestral sin. *The Blithedale Romance,* also written at this time, was based on Hawthorne's experience at Brook Farm and dealt explicitly with the vanity of human pride.

In 1852, Hawthorne wrote a campaign biography for Franklin Pierce who later appointed Hawthorne consul to Liverpool. The Hawthornes spent three years in England and two in Italy, where Hawthorne wrote *The Marble Faun; or, The Romance of Monte Beni.* This is a novel with an Italian setting which probes more deeply the question of good and evil. The book received good reviews, however its structure, language and symbolism, which in Hawthorne's other work had been subtle and natural, appeared to many critics to be stilted and poorly integrated.

The last years of Hawthorne's life were marked by declining health and creativity. He continued to write and to struggle with the themes of ancestral sin and mortality, but was unable to translate his thoughts into fiction. The works which occupied his last years, published posthumously, are mere fragments which show little of Hawthorne's former power. He is nonetheless considered among the greatest American authors. By projecting profound moral concerns on a distinctly American background, Hawthorne sought to interpret the spiritual history of a nation. But his art is not parochial. In his acute portrayals of the struggle of the human soul, Hawthorne transcended locale and history. Today, as strongly as in his own time, the comment made about him by Emily Dickinson applies: he "appalls, entices." (See also *Dictionary of Literary Biography, Vol. 1: The American Renaissance in New England.)*

PRINCIPAL WORKS

Fanshawe: A Tale (novel) 1828
Twice-Told Tales (sketches and short stories) 1837
Twice-Told Tales (second series) (sketches and short stories) 1842
Mosses from an Old Manse (sketches and short stories) 1846
The Scarlet Letter: A Romance (novel) 1850
The House of the Seven Gables (novel) 1851
The Snow Image, and Other Tales (short stories) 1851
The Blithedale Romance (novel) 1852
Life of Franklin Pierce (biography) 1852
A Wonder-Book for Girls and Boys (short stories) 1852
Tanglewood Tales for Girls and Boys; Being a Second Wonder-Book (short stories) 1853
The Marble Faun; or, The Romance of Monte Beni (novel) 1860; published in England as *Transformation; or, The Romance of Monte Beni,* 1860
Our Old Home (essays) 1863
Passages from the American Notebooks of Nathaniel Hawthorne (journal) 1868
Passages from the English Notebooks of Nathaniel Hawthorne (journal) 1870
Passages from the French and Italian Notebooks of Nathaniel Hawthorne (journal) 1872
Septimius Felton; or, The Elixir of Life (unfinished novel) 1872
The Dolliver Romance and Other Pieces (unfinished novel) 1876
Doctor Grimshawe's Secret: A Romance (unfinished novel) 1883

[HENRY W. LONGFELLOW] (essay date 1837)

In the stream of thought, which flows so peacefully deep and clear, through the pages of [*Twice-Told Tales*], we see the bright reflection of a spiritual star, after which men will be fain to gaze "with the naked eye, and with the spyglasses of criticism." This star is but newly risen; and ere long the observations of numerous star-gazers, perched up on arm-chairs and editors' tables, will inform the world of its magnitude and its place in the heaven of poetry. . . . (p. 59)

To this little work we would say, "Live ever, sweet, sweet book." It comes from the hand of a man of genius. Every thing about it has the freshness of morning and of May. These flowers and green leaves of poetry have not the dust of the highway upon them. They have been gathered fresh from the secret places of a peaceful and gentle heart. There flow deep waters, silent, calm, and cool; and the green trees look into them, and "God's blue heaven." The book, though in prose, is written nevertheless by a poet. [Hawthorne] looks upon all things in the spirit of love, and with lively sympathies; for to

him external form is but the representation of internal being, all things having a life, an end and aim. (pp. 59-60)

[Extracts] are sufficient to show the beautiful and simple style of [*Twice-Told Tales*], its vein of pleasant philosophy, and the quiet humor, which is to the face of a book what a smile is to the face of man. . . . Like children we say, "Tell us more." (p. 73)

[Henry W. Longfellow,] "Hawthorne's 'Twice-Told Tales'," in The North American Review, Vol. XLV, No. XCVI, July, 1837, pp. 59-73.

[CHARLES FENNO HOFFMAN] (essay date 1838)

The "Twice-told Tales" are well worth twice telling. They are the offspring of a calm, meditative fancy, enlivened at times with a flickering ray of humor. (p. 281)

When a noble spirit, like Hawthorne, condescends to throw open to us the leaves of his private life, and to make us familiar with him in his little household of joys and sorrows, we should deal kindly with his errors, if any there be; and admire his gentle beauties with generous and heart-deep enthusiasm. The erusal of the "Twice-told Tales" has excited in us many feelings "too deep for tears." (p. 282)

Some rending and ever-remembered sorrow seems to hover about his thoughts, and color them with the shadow of their presence. Almost every story in the volume is filled with a pervading sadness. In these pages sunshine is a transient visiter; cloud and darkness and a softer gloom, perpetual guests.

We think that the main peculiarity of Hawthorne, as a writer, and that which distinguishes him from any other with whom we are acquainted, is this same fine tone of sadness that pervades his best tales and sketches. One class of writings in this volume reminds us of Lamb, although without the antique, humorous, and high-sounding phrases which render the style of Elia so singular and profound of its kind. **"The Rill from the Town-Pump"** is very much in this vein.

A second class of Hawthorne's sketches rivals Irving himself in occasional graphic thoughts and phrases, and partakes not a little of his picturesque mode of viewing a topic. We would instance **"Dr. Heidegger's Experiment,"** where four venerable personages, in the withered extreme of age, are transformed into as many gay, frisking creatures in "the happy prime of youth," by a draught from the famous Fountain of Youth. It struck us as a very apt companion-piece to Irving's "Mutability of Literature." **"Fancy's Show-Box"** has a sentence, here and there, flavored strongly with the Sketch Book humor. In the third species of writing in this volume, Hawthorne follows no model, imitates no predecessor, that we can recollect. He is himself. And these, to our mode of thinking, appear to be the gems and jewels of the work. The style is flowing, smooth, serious. The tone of the pieces, mellowed, calm, meditative. The manner of diffusing his subject, peculiar to himself, and original. The sketches and stories in which these characteristics predominate, outnumber, as might be expected, those of a different kind. **"Sunday at Home," "The Wedding Knell," "The Minister's Black Veil," "The Prophetic Pictures," "Sights from a Steeple,"** are as fine essays of their kind as may be found in the English language. In fact, we scarcely know where to look for productions with which to compare them.

Many have written pathetic and mournful stories, many have indulged in a tender, moralizing sorrow, as they looked upon the world and humanity: this many have accomplished admirably—Addison, Mackenzie, Lamb, and others. But nowhere do you find the new strain in which Hawthorne so eloquently pours forth his individual feelings.

His pathos, we would call New England pathos, if we were not afraid it would excite a smile; it is the pathos of an American, a New Englander. It is redolent of the images, objects, thoughts, and feelings that spring up in that soil, and nowhere else. The author of **"Twice-told Tales"** is an honor to New England and to the country. (pp. 282-83)

> [*Charles Fenno Hoffman*,] *"Reviews: 'Twice-Told Tales',"* in The American Monthly Magazine, Vol. XI, March, 1838, pp. 281-83.

[EDGAR ALLAN POE]   (essay date 1842)

[*Twice-Told Tales*] professes to be a collection of *tales,* yet is, in two respects, misnamed. These pieces are now in their third republication, and, of course, are thrice-told. Moreover, they are by no means *all* tales, either in the ordinary or in the legitimate understanding of the term. Many of them are pure essays, for example, **"Sights from a Steeple," "Sunday at Home," "Little Annie's Ramble."** . . . We mention these matters chiefly on account of their discrepancy with that marked precision and finish by which the body of the work is distinguished. . . .

[The Essays] are each and all beautiful, without being characterised by the polish and adaptation so visible in the tales proper. A painter would at once note their leading or predominant feature, and style it *repose.* There is no attempt at effect. All is quiet, thoughtful, subdued. Yet this repose may exist simultaneously with high originality of thought; and Mr. Hawthorne has demonstrated the fact. At every turn we meet with novel combinations; yet these combinations never surpass the limits of the quiet. We are soothed as we read; and withal is a calm astonishment that ideas so apparently obvious have never occurred or been presented to us before. Herein our author differs materially from Lamb or Hunt or Hazlitt—who, with vivid originality of manner and expression, have less of the true novelty of thought than is generally supposed. . . . The Essays of Hawthorne have much of the character of Irving with more of originality, and less of finish. . . . [In the case of Mr. Irving,] repose is attained rather by the absence of novel combination, or of originality, than otherwise, and consists chiefly in the calm, quiet, unostentatious expression of commonplace thoughts, in an unambitious unadulterated Saxon. In them, by strong effort, we are made to conceive the absence of all. In the essays before us the absence of effort is too obvious to be mistaken, and a strong under-current of *suggestion* runs continuously beneath the upper stream of the tranquil thesis. In short, these effusions of Mr. Hawthorne are the product of a truly imaginative intellect, restrained, and in some measure repressed, by fastidiousness of taste, by constitutional melancholy and by indolence. . . .

But it is of his tales that we desire principally to speak. The tale proper, in our opinion, affords unquestionably the fairest field for the exercise of the loftiest talent, which can be afforded by the wide domains of mere prose. (p. 298)

We have very few American tales of real merit—we may say, indeed, none, with the exception of "The Tales of a Traveller" of Washington Irving, and these **"Twice-Told Tales"** of Mr. Hawthorne. . . .

Of Mr. Hawthorne's Tales we would say, emphatically, that they belong to the highest region of Art—an Art subservient to genius of a very lofty order. . . .

Mr. Hawthorne's distinctive trait is invention, creation, imagination, originality—a trait which, in the literature of fiction, is positively worth all the rest. But the nature of originality, so far as regards its manifestation in letters, is but imperfectly understood. The inventive or original mind as frequently displays itself in novelty of *tone* as in novelty of matter. Mr. Hawthorne is original at *all* points.

It would be a matter of some difficulty to designate the best of these tales; we repeat that, without exception, they are beautiful. **"Wakefield"** is remarkable for the skill with which an old idea—a well-known incident—is worked up or discussed. A man of whims conceives the purpose of quitting his wife and residing *incognito,* for twenty years, in her immediate neighborhood. Something of this kind actually happened in London. The force of Mr. Hawthorne's tale lies in the analysis of the motives which must or might have impelled the husband to such folly, in the first instance, with the possible causes of his perseverance. Upon this thesis a sketch of singular power has been constructed. . . .

"The Minister's Black Veil" is a masterly composition of which the sole defect is that to the rabble its exquisite skill will be *caviare.* The *obvious* meaning of this article will be found to smother its insinuated one. The *moral* put into the mouth of the dying minister will be supposed to convey the *true* import of the narrative; and that a crime of dark dye, (having reference to the "young lady") has been committed, is a point which only minds congenial with that of the author will perceive.

"Mr. Higginbotham's Catastrophe" is vividly original and managed most dexterously.

"Dr. Heidegger's Experiment" is exceedingly well imagined, and executed with surpassing ability. The artist breathes in every line of it. . . .

"The White Old Maid" is objectionable, even more than the **"Minister's Black Veil,"** on the score of its mysticism. Even with the thoughtful and analytic, there will be much trouble in penetrating its entire import. . . .

In **"Howe's Masquerade"** we observe something which resembles a plagiarism—but which *may be* a very flattering coincidence of thought. (p. 299)

[The idea] is, that the figure in the cloak is the phantom or reduplication of Sir William Howe; but in an article called "William Wilson," one of the "Tales of the Grotesque and Arabesque," we have not only the same idea, but the same idea similarly presented in several respects. . . .

[Not] only are the two general conceptions identical, but there are various *points* of similarity. In each case the figure seen is the wraith or duplication of the beholder. In each case the scene is a masquerade. In each case the figure is cloaked. In each, there is a quarrel—that is to say, angry words pass between the parties. In each the beholder is enraged. In each the cloak and sword fall upon the floor. The "villain, unmuffle yourself," of Mr. H. is precisely paralleled by a passage . . . of "William Wilson."

In the way of objection we have scarcely a word to say of these tales. There is, perhaps, a somewhat too general or prevalent *tone*—a tone of melancholy and mysticism. The subjects are insufficiently varied. There is not so much of *versatility* evinced as we might well be warranted in expecting from the high powers of Mr. Hawthorne. But beyond these trivial exceptions we have really none to make. The style is purity itself. Force abounds. High imagination gleams from every page. Mr. Hawthorne is a man of the truest genius. (p. 300)

[*Edgar Allan Poe,*] *"Review of New Books: 'Twice-Told Tales',"* in Graham's Magazine, *Vol. XX, No. 5, May, 1842, pp. 298-300.*

THE AMERICAN REVIEW (essay date 1846)

We don't mean to say that Nathaniel Hawthorne is necessarily a *"nonpareil,"* and therefore above or beyond any body or thing else in all the land! . . . [But we do say] that taking the plain level of results aimed at and ends accomplished, our author covers the broadest and the highest field yet occupied by the Imaginative Literature of the country, and deserves to be set forth, in very many particulars, as "the glass of fashion and the mould of form" to those who are to come after, at least! . . . [In his fine satires, Hawthorne] has lashed the vices of his countrymen and times with unequaled keenness and effect, and yet has handled his cat-o'-nine-tails of scorpions with such exquisite dexterity and benevolent humor, that even those who winced and suffered most have been compelled to smile and look in his eyes, that they might drink out healing from the Love there. . . . [The placid universality of Hawthorne's mind]—which recognizes all things that may be presented to its life, and gives them out with a profusion royal as the benedictions of our mother Nature—[teaches] that Truth wears not one form alone, but many. (pp. 302-03)

[We] are very happy to perceive in [Hawthorne] something of that breadth, depth, repose, and dignified reliance, which we have, perhaps unreasonably, asked as worthy characteristics of a truly National Literature—as they certainly are of a polished and elegant cultivation. It is very sure, if we ever aspire to any higher rank than that of mere imitators, we must fall back with an entire and unhesitating confidence upon our own resources. . . . Hawthorne is national—national in subject, in treatment and in manner. We could hardly say anything higher of him, than that he is Hawthorne, and *"nothing else!"* He has never damned himself to the obese body of a Party. He belongs to *all of them!* but spurns the slippery cant, and the innocent malignity of expletive, with which each one assails the other. His writings say plainly to the world, "I am that I am!" . . . [It] is greatly refreshing to meet with a straight-up-and-down flat-footed man, who stands on his own bottom, and asserts himself as Hawthorne does. (pp. 304-05)

One of [Hawthorne's] finest traits is a sort of magical subtlety of vision, which, though it sees the true form of things through all the misty obscurations of humbug and cant, yet possesses the rare power of compelling others to see their naked shapes through a medium of its own. . . . It is a favorite expression with regard to Hawthorne, that he *"Idealizes"* everything. Now what does this Idealization mean? Is it that he *improves* upon Nature? Pshaw! . . . Hawthorne does not endeavor to improve upon the Actual, but with a wise emulation attempts—first to reach it, and then to modify it suitably with the purpose he has to accomplish. (p. 309)

[Hawthorne] sees a "halo over common things," and so brings up his readers, whether they will or not, to his point of view. Though it may be "the difficult air o' the iced-mountain tops" to them at first, yet he has a wonderous soft persuasion in his manner, which wins them to go with him, until, all at once, they find themselves unconsciously seeing with his eyes, and informed with "the spirit of his knowledge." We know no modern writer more eminent than Hawthorne in this particular faculty. He is to the Present and the Future what Charles Lamb was to the Past. (p. 310)

There are many minor points of coincidence in which Charles Lamb and Hawthorne may be fairly contrasted. They both have a quietly permeating humor, which searches "the joints and marrow" of the ludicrous; and with this keen-edged shrewdness they both have a mild and patient benevolence which interpenetrates and sweetens what might otherwise be called the acrimony of wit! They are the most loving and lovable of Satirists; but then they differ widely in their purposes! One merely burlesques Progress by a cruel and unfair reference to the Past:—the other encourages Progress by a swift "showing up" of old errors, and an acute illustration of the "wherein" a fundamental Reformation consists! One would reform the manners and the fashions of his time—the other would reform the body and soul! Here we are content to dismiss the contrast; for certainly if Lamb has made us in love with the Past, Hawthorne has presented us with the undying Hope for the Future, and fired us with a zeal which can never decay, for bringing forth its Promise! . . . It is certain that neither Lamb, nor any other modern Prose Writer has ever walked more critically that difficult and narrow line between the Natural and Supernatural. This is a most perilous place to tread; and Hawthorne's clear eye and calm nerve does it with a steadiness and skill scarcely equaled. Take the first story in the **"Legends of the Province House,"** for example, in his earlier book, **"Twice-told Tales."** We defy anybody, after reading **"Howe's Masquerade"** to decide at once whether the "mysterious pageant" with which the entertainment of the last Royal Governor of Massachusetts is interrupted, comes really from the Shadow-Land, or is merely a skillfully devised Masque of the rebellious Citizens! . . . [The] Real and Unreal have been mingled throughout with so many consummate touches. . . . This is the highest accomplishment of a peculiar skill which all imaginative writers have emulated. Its perfect type is found in the Old Ballads. Walter Scott and Fouque have been masters; while in Poetry Coleridge has triumphed supremely in "Christabel." Hawthorne equals either of them in skill—but his subjects do not possess the breadth or Histrionic Grandeur of Scott's. His style and treatment have not equaled, though they have approached the airy grace and tenderness of [Fouque's] "Undine," or attained to the mysterious dread which creeps through music in [Coleridge's] unequaled "Christabel." Yet we think his story of **"Young Goodman Brown"** will bear to be contrasted with anything of this kind that has been done. The subject of course wants many imposing elements—for it is merely an Allegory of simple New England Village Life—but as a Tale of the Supernatural it certainly is more exquisitely managed than anything we have seen in American Literature, at least! He wins our confidence at once, by his directness and perfect simplicity. (pp. 310-11)

The singular skill with which our sympathy is kept "halting between two opinions"—by which we are compelled throughout to recognize the flesh and blood reality of Goodman Brown; and necessarily, to enter into all the actual relations of the man, is only surpassed by the terrible elaboration with which this human embodiment of Doubt is compelled, through awe and madness, to struggle with the beings—almost equally human—of a self-created Hell. . . . But such effects are not, by any means, all that Hawthorne is capable of producing. We see through everything that he has done, the same faculty, not of

Idealizing the Real—as it is called—but of Humanizing the Unreal—giving it thews, sinews and a life-blood! . . . [With] all Hawthorne's stories—we never stop to ask whether they are "sure 'nough" or not—it is sufficient that *he has made them Real*, and beguiled us for a time into the belief, that we are as wise as our Childhood was! Ineffable wisdom of Simplicity! Why are there so many Infants among us, with foreheads in which "the big imagination" is swelled out as we may conceit it to have been in the matured Shakespeare . . .? Will "Infantine" Wisdom answer us—or will Hawthorne? Hawthorne *might* do it!—for we see "glimpses" in him that make him worthy. (p. 315)

The true Poet is the highest Philosopher; and it is as the true Poet that we most profoundly respect Hawthorne. . . . Hawthorne constantly writes Poems while he only pretends to be writing Tales! Who of our Poets can point to a deeper Poetry than is expressed in **"Rappaccini's Daughter."** . . . Not only in this, but in a dozen other Allegories—or Stories, as you choose to call them—can we point out "Our Hawthorne" as "Noticeable!". . . . [In] the **"Moses of an Old Manse,"** it seems to us that his Life has deepened since that which gave us **"The Twice-told Tales,"** and . . . we hope and pray he may not spare us a future volume, though they may be even the Thrice-told Tales of Hawthorne! (pp. 315-16)

> *"Hawthorne," in* The American Review, *Vol. IV, No. III, September, 1846, pp. 296-316.*

EDGAR A. POE   (essay date 1847)

In the preface to my sketches of New York Literati . . . I thus alluded to Nathaniel Hawthorne:—

> For example, Mr. Hawthorne, the author of **'Twice-Told Tales,'** is scarcely recognized by the press or by the public, and when noticed at all, is noticed merely to be damned by faint praise. Now, my own opinion of him is, that although his walk is limited and he is fairly to be charged with mannerism, treating all subjects in a similar tone of dreamy *innuendo,* yet in this walk he evinces extraordinary genius, having no rival either in America or elsewhere. . . .

The reputation of the author of **"Twice-Told Tales"** has been confined, indeed, until very lately, to literary society; and I have not been wrong, perhaps, in citing him as *the* example, *par excellence,* in this country, of the privately admired and publicly-unappreciated man of genius. (p. 252)

The fact is, that if Mr. Hawthorne were really original, he could not fail of making himself felt by the public. But the fact is, he is *not* original in any sense. Those who speak of him as original, mean nothing more than that he differs in his manner or tone, and in his choice of subjects, from any author of their acquaintance—their acquaintance not extending to the German Tieck, whose manner, in *some* of his works, is absolutely identical with that *habitual* to Hawthorne. (pp. 252-53)

[The] critic (unacquainted with Tieck) who reads a single tale or essay by Hawthorne, may be justified in thinking him original; but the tone, or manner, or choice of subject, which induces in this critic the sense of the new, will—if not in a second tale, at least in a third and all subsequent ones—not only fail of inducing it, but bring about an exactly antagonistic

impression. In concluding a volume, and more especially in concluding all the volumes of the author, the critic will abandon his first design of calling him "original," and content himself with styling him "peculiar." . . .

There is a species of writing which, with some difficulty, may be admitted as a lower degree of . . . the true original. . . . This kind of composition (which still appertains to a high order) is usually designated as "the natural." It has little external resemblance, but strong internal affinity to the true original, if, indeed, as I have suggested, it is not of his latter an inferior degree. It is best exemplified, among English writers, in Addison, Irving and *Hawthorne*. The "ease" which is so often spoken of as its distinguishing feature, it has been the fashion to regard as ease in appearance alone, as a point of really difficult attainment. This idea, however, must be received with some reservation. The natural style is difficult only to those who should never intermeddle with it—to the unnatural. It is but the result of writing with the understanding, or with the instinct, that the *tone,* in composition, should be that which, at any given point or upon any given topic, would be the tone of the great mass of humanity. (p. 253)

The "peculiarity" or sameness, or *monotone* of Hawthorne, would, in its mere character of "peculiarity," and without reference to what *is* the peculiarity, suffice to deprive him of all chance of popular appreciation. But at his failure to be appreciated, we can, *of course,* no longer wonder, when we find him monotonous at decidedly the worst of all possible points—at that point which, having the least concern with Nature, is the farthest removed from the popular intellect, from the popular sentiment and from the popular taste. I allude to the strain of allegory which completely overwhelms the greater number of his subjects, and which in some measure interferes with the direct conduct of absolutely all.

In defence of allegory, (however, or for whatever object, employed,) there is scarcely one respectable word to be said. . . . (pp. 253-54)

The obvious causes, however, which have prevented Mr. Hawthorne's *popularity,* do not suffice to condemn him in the eyes of the few who belong properly to books, and to whom books, perhaps, do not quite so properly belong. These few estimate an author, not as do the public, altogether by what he does, but in great measure—indeed, even in the greatest measure—by what he evinces a capability of doing. In this view, Hawthorne stands among literary people in America much in the same light as did Coleridge in England. . . . [There is a simple truth] that the writer who aims at impressing the people, is *always* wrong when he fails in forcing that people to receive the impression. How far Mr. Hawthorne has addressed the people at all, is, of course, not a question for me to decide. His books afford strong internal evidence of having been written to himself and his particular friends alone. (p. 254)

[Hawthorne] is peculiar and *not* original—unless in those detailed fancies and detached thoughts which his want of general originality will deprive of the appreciation due to them, in preventing them forever reaching the *public* eye. He is infinitely too fond of allegory, and can never hope for popularity so long as he persists in it. This he will not do, for allegory is at war with the whole tone of his nature, which disports itself never so well as when escaping from the mysticism of his Goodman Browns and White Old Maids into the hearty, genial, but still Indian-summer sunshine of his Wakefields and Little Annie's Rambles. Indeed, *his* spirit of "metaphor run-mad'' is clearly imbibed from the phalanx and phalanstery atmosphere in which he has been so long struggling for breath. He has not half the material for the exclusiveness of authorship that he possesses for its universality. He has the purest style, the finest taste, the most available scholarship, the most delicate humor, the most touching pathos, the most radiant imagination, the most consummate ingenuity; and with these varied good qualities he has done *well* as a mystic. But is there any one of these qualities which should prevent his doing doubly as well in a career of honest, upright, sensible, prehensible and comprehensible things? Let him mend his pen, get a bottle of visible ink, come out from the Old Manse, cut Mr. Alcott, hang (if possible) the editor of ''The Dial,'' and throw out of the window to the pigs all his odd numbers of ''The North American Review.'' (p. 256)

> *Edgar A. Poe, "Tale Writing—Nathaniel Hawthorne," in* Godey's Lady Book, *Vol. XXXV, No. 19, November, 1847, pp. 252-56.*

[JAMES RUSSELL LOWELL]   (essay date 1848)

[*The following is taken from James Russell Lowell's poem,* A Fable for Critics.]

> There is Hawthorne, with genius so shrinking
>   and rare
> That you hardly at first see the strength that is
>   there;
> A frame so robust, with a nature so sweet,
> So earnest, so graceful, so lithe and so fleet,
> Is worth a descent from Olympus to meet;
> 'T is as if a rough oak that for ages had stood,
> With his gnarled bony branches like ribs of
>   the wood,
> Should bloom, after cycles of struggle and
>   scathe,
> With a single anemone trembly and rathe;
> His strength is so tender, his wildness so
>   meek,
> That a suitable parallel sets one to seek,—
> He's a John Bunyan Fouqué, a Puritan Tieck;
> When Nature was shaping him, clay was not
>   granted
> For making so full-sized a man as she wanted,
> So, to fill out her model, a little she spared
> From some finer-grained stuff for a woman
>   prepared,
> And she could not have hit a more excellent
>   plan
> For making him fully and perfectly man.
>
>   (pp. 47-8)

> *[James Russell Lowell,] in his* A Fable for Critics: A Glance at a Few of Our Literary Progenies, *second edition, G. P. Putnam, 1848, 80 p.**

[GEORGE RIPLEY]   (essay date 1850)

[Hawthorne] derives the same terrible excitement from those legendary horrors, as was drawn by Edgar Poe from the depths of his own dark and perilous imagination, and brings before us pictures of death like, but strangely fascinating agony, which are described with the same minuteness of finish—the same slow and fatal accumulation of details—the same exquisite coolness of coloring, while everything creeps forward with irresistible certainty to a soul harrowing climax—which made the last-named writer such a consummate master of the horrible and infernal in fictitious composition. Hawthorne's tragedies, however, are always *motived* with a wonderful insight and skill, to which the intellect of Poe was a stranger. In the most terrific scenes with which he delights to scare the imagination, Hawthorne does not wander into the region of the improbable; you scarcely know that you are in the presence of the supernatural, until your breathing becomes too thick for this world. It is the supernatural relieved, softened, made tolerable, and almost attractive, by a strong admixture of the human; you are tempted onward by the mild, unearthly light, which seems to shine upon you like a healthful star; you are blinded by no lurid glare; you acquiesce in the necessity of the wizard journey; instead of being provoked to anger by a superfluous introduction to the company of the devil and his angels.

The elements of terror, which Mr. Hawthorne employs with such masterly effect, both in the original conception of his characters and the scenes of mystery and dread in which they are made to act are blended with such sweet gushes of natural feeling, such solemn and tender relations of the deepest secrets of the heart, that the painful impression greatly mitigated, and the final influence of his most startling creation is a serene sense of refreshment, without the stupor and bewilderment occasioned by a drugged cap of intoxication.

The **"Scarlet Letter,"** in our opinion, is the greatest production of the author, beautifully displaying the traits we have briefly hinted at, and sustained with a more vigorous reach of imagination, a more subtle instinct of humanity, and a more imposing splendor of portraiture, than any of his most successful previous works. . . .

[Roger Chillingworth], who holds a principal place in the development of the plot, is depicted with such fearful directness and vigor that his infernal presence must long haunt the chambers of memory.

[Pearl, a] creation of a different order, but of no less originality and power, gleams in fairy brightness through the sombre scenes of the narrative, surpassing in artistic harmony, and in mystic, thrilling grace, the similar productions of Goethe and Scott. . . .

[The **"Scarlet Letter"** is] a genuine native romance which none will be content without reading for themselves. The moral of the story—for it has a moral for all wise enough to detect it— is shadowed forth rather than expressed in a few brief sentences near the end of the volume. . . .

The introduction, presenting a record of savory reminiscences of the Salem Custom House, a frank display of autobiographical confessions and a piquant daguerrotype of his ancient colleagues in office, while Surveyor of that port, is written with Mr. Hawthorne's unrivalled force of graphic delineation, and will furnish an agreeable amusement to those who are so far from the scene of action, as to feel no wound in their personal relations by the occasional too sharp touches of [caustic acid]. . . .

> *[George Ripley,] "Reviews of New Books: 'The Scarlet Letter'," in* New York Daily Tribune, *April 1, 1850, p. 2.*

THE ATHENAEUM   (essay date 1850)

['Scarlet Letter'] is a most powerful but painful story. . . . We rate [Mr. Hawthorne] as among the most original and peculiar writers of American fiction. There is in his works a mixture of Puritan reserve and wild imagination, of passion and description, of the allegorical and the real, which some will fail to understand, and which others will positively reject,—but which, to ourselves, is fascinating. . . . [We] recollect no tale dealing with crime so sad and revenge so subtly diabolical, that is at the same time so clear of fever and of prurient excitement. The misery of the woman is as present in every page as the heading which in the title of the romance symbolizes her punishment. Her terrors concerning her strange elvish child present retribution in a form which is new and natural:—her slow and painful purification through repentance is crowned by no perfect happiness, such as awaits the decline of those who have no dark and bitter past to remember. . . . [If] Sin and Sorrow in their most fearful forms are to be presented in any work of art, they have rarely been treated with a loftier severity, purity, and sympathy than in Mr. Hawthorne's **'Scarlet Letter.'** The touch of the fantastic befitting a period of society in which ignorant and excitable human creatures conceived each other and themselves to be under the direct "rule and governance" of the Wicked One, is most skilfully administered. The supernatural here never becomes grossly palpable:—the thrill is all the deeper for its action being indefinite, and its source vague and distant.

"'The Scarlet Letter: A Romance'," in The Athen-aeum, No. 1181, June 15, 1850, p. 634.

HERMAN MELVILLE (essay date 1850)

It is curious how a man may travel along a country road, and yet miss the grandest or sweetest of prospects by reason of an intervening hedge, so like all other hedges, as in no way to hint of the wide landscape beyond. So has it been with me concerning the enchanting landscape in the soul of this Hawthorne, this most excellent Man of Mosses. His [*Mosses from an Old Manse*] has been written now four years, but I never read it till a day or two since. I had seen it in the book-stores—heard of it often—even had it recommended to me by a tasteful friend, as a rare, quiet book, perhaps too deserving of popularity to be popular. But there are so many books called "excellent," and so much unpopular merit, that amid the thick stir of other things, the hint of my tasteful friend was disregarded and for four years the *Mosses on the Old Manse* never refreshed me with their perennial green. It may be, however, that all this while the book, likewise, was only improving in flavor and body. (pp. 54-5)

What a wild moonlight of contemplative humor bathes [Hawthorne's] Old Manse!—the rich and rare distilment of a spicy and slowly-oozing heart. No rollicking rudeness, no gross fun fed on fat dinners, and bred in the lees of wine,—but a humor so spiritually gentle, so high, so deep, and yet so richly relishable, that it were hardly inappropriate in an angel. It is the very religion of mirth; for nothing so human but it may be advanced to that. The orchard of the Old Manse seems the visible type of the fine mind that has described it—those twisted and contorted old trees, "they stretch out their crooked branches, and take such hold of the imagination that we remember them as humorists and odd-fellows." And then, as surrounded by these grotesque forms, and hushed in the noonday repose of this Hawthorne's spell, how aptly might the still fall of his ruddy thoughts into your soul be symbolized by: "In the stillest afternoon, if I listened, the thump of a great apple was audible, falling without a breath of wind, from the mere necessity of

perfect ripeness." For no less ripe than ruddy are the apples of the thoughts and fancies in this sweet Man of Mosses.

Buds and Bird Voices. What a delicious thing is that! "Will the world ever be so decayed, that spring may not renew its greenness?" And the *Fire Worship.* Was ever the hearth so glorified into an altar before? The mere title of that piece is better than any common work in fifty folio volumes. (pp. 57-8)

The sketch of *The Old Apple Dealer* is conceived in the subtlest spirit of sadness; he whose "subdued and nerveless boyhood prefigured his abortive prime, which likewise contained within itself the prophecy and image of his lean and torpid age." Such touches as are in this piece cannot proceed from any common heart. They argue such a depth of tenderness, such a boundless sympathy with all forms of being, such an omnipresent love, that we must needs say that this Hawthorne is here almost alone in his generation,—at least, in the artistic manifestation of these things. . . . All over him, Hawthorne's melancholy rests like an Indian-summer, which, though bathing a whole country in one softness, still reveals the distinctive hue of every towering hill and each far-winding vale.

But it is the least part of genius that attracts admiration. Where Hawthorne is known, he seems to be deemed a pleasant writer, with a pleasant style,—a sequestered, harmless man, from whom any deep and weighty thing would hardly be anticipated—a man who means no meanings. But there is no man, in whom humor and love, like mountain peaks, soar to such a rapt height as to receive the irradiations of the upper skies;—there is no man in whom humor and love are developed in that high form called genius; no such man can exist without also possessing, as the indispensable complement of these, a great, deep intellect, which drops down into the universe like a plummet. (pp. 59-61)

How profound, nay, appalling, is the moral evolved by the *Earth's Holocaust;* where—beginning with the hollow follies and affectations of the world,—all vanities and empty theories and forms are, one after another, and by an admirably graduated, growing comprehensiveness, thrown into the allegorical fire, till, at length, nothing is left but the all-engendering heart of man; which remaining still unconsumed, the great conflagration is naught. (pp. 61-2)

The Christmas Banquet, and *The Bosom Serpent,* would be fine subjects for a curious and elaborate analysis, touching the conjectural parts of the mind that produced them. For spite of all the Indian-summer sunlight on the hither side of Hawthorne's soul, the other side—like the dark half of the physical sphere—is shrouded in a blackness, ten times black. But this darkness but gives more effect to the ever-moving dawn, that forever advances through it, and circumnavigates his world. Whether Hawthorne has simply availed himself of this mystical blackness as a means to the wondrous effects he makes it to produce in his lights and shades; or whether there really lurks in him, perhaps unknown to himself, a touch of Puritanic gloom,—this, I cannot altogether tell. Certain it is, however, that this great power of blackness in him derives its force from its appeals to that Calvinistic sense of Innate Depravity and Original Sin, from whose visitations, in some shape or other, no deeply thinking mind is always and wholly free. . . . [Perhaps] no writer has ever wielded this terrific thought with greater terror than this same harmless Hawthorne. Still more: this black conceit pervades him through and through. You may be witched by his sunlight,—transported by the bright gildings in the skies he builds over you; but there is the blackness of darkness beyond; and even his bright gildings but fringe and play upon the edges of thunder-clouds. (pp. 62-3)

[It] is that blackness in Hawthorne, of which I have spoken that so fixes and fascinates me. It may be, nevertheless, that it is too largely developed in him. Perhaps he does not give us a ray of light for every shade of his dark. But however this may be, this blackness it is that furnishes the infinite obscure of his background,—that background, against which Shakespeare plays his grandest conceits, the things that have made for Shakespeare his loftiest but most circumscribed renown, as the profoundest of thinkers. (p. 64)

Nor need you fix upon that blackness in [Hawthorne], if it suit you not. Nor, indeed, will all readers discern it; for it is, mostly, insinuated to those who may best understand it, and account for it; it is not obtruded upon every one alike.

Some may start to read of Shakespeare and Hawthorne on the same page. They may say, that if an illustration were needed, a lesser light might have sufficed to elucidate this Hawthorne, this small man of yesterday. But I am not willingly one of those who, as touching Shakespeare at least, exemplify the maxim of Rochefoucauld, that "we exalt the reputation of some, in order to depress that of others";—who, to teach all noble-souled aspirants that there is no hope for them, pronounce Shakespeare absolutely unapproachable. But Shakespeare has been approached. (p. 67)

Now I do not say that Nathaniel of Salem is a greater man than William of Avon, or as great. But the difference between the two men is by no means immeasurable. Not a very great deal more, and Nathaniel were verily William. (p. 70)

[My] countrymen, as an excellent author of your own flesh and blood,—an unimitating, and, perhaps, in his way, an inimitable man—whom better can I commend to you, in the first place, than Nathaniel Hawthorne. He is one of the new, and far better generation of your writers. The smell of young beeches and hemlocks is upon him; your own broad prairies are in his soul; and if you travel away inland into his deep and noble nature, you will hear the far roar of his Niagara. Give not over to future generations the glad duty of acknowledging him for what he is. Take that joy to yourself, in your own generation; and so shall he feel those grateful impulses on him, that may possibly prompt him to the full flower of some still greater achievement in your eyes. And by confessing him you thereby confess others; you brace the whole brotherhood. For genius, all over the world, stands hand in hand, and one shock of recognition runs the whole circle round. (pp. 75-6)

But I cannot leave my subject yet. (p. 77)

I feel that this Hawthorne has dropped germinous seeds into my soul. He expands and deepens down, the more I contemplate him; and further and further, shoots his strong New England roots into the hot soil in my Southern soul. . . .

Here, be it said to all those whom this poor fugitive scrawl of mine may tempt to the perusal of the Mosses, that they must on no account suffer themselves to be trifled with, disappointed, or deceived by the triviality of many of the titles to these sketches. For in more than one instance, the title utterly belies the piece. (p. 79)

[With] whatever motive, playful or profound, Nathaniel Hawthorne has chosen to entitle his pieces in the manner he has, it is certain that some of them are directly calculated to de-

ceive—egregiously deceive, the superficial skimmer of pages. To be downright and candid once more, let me cheerfully say, that two of these titles did dolefully dupe no less an eager-eyed reader than myself; and that, too, after I had been impressed with a sense of the great depth and breadth of this American man. "Who in the name of thunder" (as the country people say in this neighborhood), "who in the name of thunder, would anticipate any marvel in a piece entitled *Young Goodman Brown*?" You would of course suppose that it was a simple little tale, intended as a supplement to *Goody Two Shoes*. Whereas, it is deep as Dante; nor can you finish it, without addressing the author in his own words—"It shall be yours to penetrate, in every bosom, the deep mystery of sin". . . . (pp. 80-1)

I allude to [*Young Goodman Brown*] now, because it is, in itself, such a strong positive illustration of the blackness in Hawthorne, which I had assumed from the mere occasional shadows of it; as revealed in several of the other sketches. . . . [This is a] direct and unqualified manifestation of it.

The other piece of the two referred to, is entitled *A Select Party*, which, in my first simplicity upon originally taking hold of the book, I fancied must treat of some pumpkin-pie party in old Salem; or some chowder party on Cape Cod. Whereas, by all the gods of Peedee, it is the sweetest and sublimest thing that has been written since Spenser wrote. Nay, there is nothing in Spenser that surpasses it, perhaps nothing that equals it. And the test is this. Read any canto in *The Faerie Queene* and then read *A Select Party*, and decide which pleases you most,—that is, if you are qualified to judge. Do not be frightened at this; for when Spenser was alive, he was thought of very much as Hawthorne is now,—was generally accounted just such a "gentle" harmless man. (pp. 82-3)

Gainsay it who will, as I now write, I am Posterity speaking by proxy—and after times will make it more than good, when I declare, that the American, who up to the present day has evinced, in literature, the largest brain with the largest heart, that man is Nathaniel Hawthorne. Moreover, that whatever Nathaniel Hawthorne may hereafter write, *Mosses from an Old Manse* will be ultimately accounted his masterpiece. For there is a sure, though secret sign in some works which proves the culmination of the powers (only the developable ones, however) that produced them. But I am by no means desirous of the glory of a prophet. I pray Heaven that Hawthorne may yet prove me an impostor in this prediction. (pp. 85-6)

Once more—for it is hard to be finite upon an infinite subject, and all subjects are infinite. By some people this entire scrawl of mine may be esteemed altogether unnecessary, inasmuch "as years ago" (they may say) "we found out the rich and rare stuff in this Hawthorne, who you now parade forth, as if only you *yourself* were the discoverer of this Portuguese diamond in your literature." But even granting all this—and adding to it, the assumption that the books of Hawthorne have sold by the five thousand,—what does that signify? They should be sold by the hundred thousand; and read by the million; and admired by every one who is capable of admiration. (p. 86)

> Herman Melville, "Hawthorne and His Mosses" (*originally published in* Literary World, *Vol. 7, No. 7, August 17-24, 1850), in his* The Apple-Tree Table and Other Sketches, *Princeton University Press, 1922, pp. 53-86.*

NATHANIEL HAWTHORNE (essay date 1850)

Much to the author's surprise, and (if he may say so without additional offence) considerably to his amusement, he finds that his sketch of official life, introductory to [*The Scarlet Letter*], has created an unprecedented excitement in the respectable community immediately around him. . . . As the public disapprobation would weigh very heavily on him, were he conscious of deserving it, the author begs leave to say that he has carefully read over the introductory pages, with a purpose to alter or expunge whatever might be found amiss, and to make the best reparation in his power for the atrocities of which he has been adjudged guilty. But it appears to him, that the only remarkable features of the sketch are its frank and genuine good-humor, and the general accuracy with which he has conveyed his sincere impressions of the characters therein described. As to enmity, or ill-feeling of any kind, personal or political, he utterly disclaims such motives. The sketch might, perhaps, have been wholly omitted, without loss to the public, or detriment to the book; but, having undertaken to write it, he conceives that it could not have been done in a better or a kindlier spirit, nor, so far as his abilities availed, with a livelier effect of truth.

The author is constrained, therefore, to republish his introductory sketch without the change of a word.

> *Nathaniel Hawthorne, in his preface to his* The Scarlet Letter, *second edition, Ticknor, Reed & Fields, 1850 (and reprinted in* The Complete Novels and Selected Tales of Nathaniel Hawthorne, *edited by Norman Holmes Pearson, The Modern Library, 1937, p. 82).*

HENRY T. TUCKERMAN (essay date 1851)

[Hawthorne] shadows forth,—hints,—makes signs,—whispers,—muses aloud,—gives the keynote of melody—puts us on a track;—in a word, addresses us as nature does—that is unostentatiously, and with a significance not to be realized without reverent silence and gentle feeling—a sequestration from bustle and material care, and somewhat of the meditative insight and latent sensibility in which his themes are conceived and wrought out. Sometimes they are purely descriptive, bits of Flemish painting—so exact and arrayed in such mellow colors, that we unconsciously take them in as objects of sensitive rather than imaginative observation; the "**Old Manse**" and the "**Custom House**"—those quaint portals to his fairyland, as peculiar and rich in contrast in their way, as Boccacio's sombre introduction to his gay stories—are memorable instances of this fidelity in the details of local and personal portraiture; and that chaste yet deep tone of colouring which secure an harmonious whole. Even in allegory, Hawthorne imparts this sympathetic unity to his conception; "**Fire Worship**," "**The Celestial Railroad**," "**Monsieur de Miroir**," "**Earth's Holocaust**," and others in the same vein, while they emphatically indicate great moral truth, have none of the abstract and cold grace of allegorical writing; besides the ingenuity they exhibit, and the charm they have for the fancy, a human interest warms and gives them meaning to the heart. On the other hand, the imaginative grace which they chiefly display, lends itself quite as aptly to redeem and glorify homely fact in the plastic hands of the author. "**Drowne's Wooden Image**," "**The Intelligence Office**," and other tales derived from common-place material, are thus moulded into artistic beauty and suggestiveness. Hawthorne, therefore, is a prose-poet. He brings together scattered beauties, evokes truth from apparent confusion, and embodies the tragic or humorous element of a tradition or an event in lyric music—not, indeed, to be sung by the lips, but to live, like melodious echoes, in the

memory. We are constantly struck with the felicity of his invention. . . . There is a certain uniformity in Hawthorne's style and manner, but a remarkable versatility in his subjects; and each as distinctly carries with it the monotone of a special feeling or fancy. . . . (pp. 343-44)

Although he seldom transcends the limited sphere in which he so efficiently concentrates his genius, the variety of tone, like different airs on the same instrument, gives him an imaginative scope rarely obtained in elaborate narrative. Thus he deals with the tragic element, wisely and with vivid originality, in such pieces as "**Roger Malvern's Burial**" and "**Young Goodman Browne;**" with the comic in "**Mr. Higginbotham's Catastrophe**," "**A Select Party**," and "**Dr. Heidegger's Experiment**," and with the purely fanciful in "**David Swan**," "**The Vision of the Fountain**," and "**Fancy's Show Box**." Nor is he less remarkable for sympathetic observation of nature than for profound interest in humanity; witness such limning as the sketches entitled "**Buds and Bird Voices**," and "**Snowflakes**"—genuine descriptive poems, though not cast in the mould of verse, as graphic, true and feeling as the happiest scenes of Bryant or Crabbe. . . . [Hawthorne] has performed for New England life and manners the same high and sweet service which Wilson has for Scotland—caught and permanently embodied their "lights and shadows." (pp. 346-47)

To clothe a familiar scene with ideal interest, and exalt things to which our senses are daily accustomed, into the region of imaginative beauty and genuine sentiment, requires an extraordinary power of abstraction and concentrated thought. (p. 347)

In our view the most remarkable trait in [Hawthorne's] writings is this harmonious blending of the common and familiar in the outward world, with the mellow and vivid tints of his own imagination. . . . [The] most elaborate effort of this kind . . . is "**The Scarlet Letter**." With all the care in point of style and authenticity which mark his lighter sketches, this genuine and unique romance, may be considered as an artistic exposition of Puritanism as modified by New England colonial life. In truth to costume, local manners and scenic features, "**The Scarlet Letter**" is as reliable as the best of Scott's novels; in the anatomy of human passion and consciousness it resembles the most effective of Balzac's illustrations of Parisian or provincial life, while in developing bravely and justly the sentiment of the life it depicts, it is as true to humanity as Dickens. . . . "**The House of the Seven Gables**" is a more elaborate and harmonious realization of these characteristics. The scenery, tone and personages of the story are imbued with a local authenticity which is not, for an instant, impaired by the imaginative charm of romance. . . . In these details we have the truth, simplicity and exact imitation of the Flemish painters. So life-like in the minutiae and so picturesque in general effect are these sketches of still-life, that they are daguerreotyped in the reader's mind, and form a distinct and changeless background, the light and shade of which give admirable effect to the action of the story: occasional touches of humor, introduced with exquisite tact, relieve the grave undertone of the narrative and form vivacious and quaint images which might readily be transferred to canvass—so effectively are they drawn in words. . . . [In "**The House of the Seven Gables**," Hawthorne's skill in evoking atmosphere] is also as apparent: around and within the principal scene of this romance, there hovers an alternating melancholy and brightness which is born of genuine moral life; no contrasts can be imagined of this kind, more eloquent to a sympathetic mind, than that between the inward consciousness and external appearance of Hepzibah or Phoebe and Clifford, or the Judge. They respectively symbolize the poles of human existence; and are fine studies for the psychologist. . . . [Magnetism] and socialism are admirably introduced; family tyranny in its most revolting form, is powerfully exemplified; the distinction between a mental and a heartfelt interest in another, clearly unfolded; and the tenacious and heriditary nature of moral evil impressively shadowed forth. (pp. 347-48)

[We deem that one of Hawthorne's most felcitious merits is] that of so patiently educing artistic beauty and moral interest from life and nature, without the least sacrifice of intellectual dignity. . . .

As earth and sky appear to blend at the horizon though we cannot define the point of contact, things seen and unseen, the actual and spiritual, mind and matter, what is within and what is without our consciousness, have a line of union, and, like the colour of the iris, are lost in each other. About this equator of life the genius of Hawthorne delights to hover as its appropriate sphere. . . . (p. 349)

> *Henry T. Tuckerman, "Nathaniel Hawthorne," in*
> The Southern Literary Messenger, *Vol. XVII, No. 6,*
> *June, 1851, pp. 343-49.*

THE LITERARY WORLD   (essay date 1851)

Mr. Hawthorne, one of the best of all possible writers for children, has conferred a new favor on the youthful people of America, by unfolding to them the pleasant resources of his [*Wonder-Book for Boys and Girls*]. The imagination he has so well under control and in his power that he may direct its forces either to the terror of age or the amusement of childhood. Whether he write SCARLET LETTERS to the world, or disclose the remarkable inventions of wonderland to children, his resources are alike adapted to the occasion. He knows the passion for the marvellous in the young and how it may be gratified, submitting exaggeration to the gentler uses of pity and good conduct. Natural, because he is sincere, his stories for children are at once entertained by the youthful mind—a home where all crude thoughts, half conceptions, bungling style, and made up stuff, knock in vain for admittance. . . .

This new *Wonder-Book for Boys and Girls* is a series of half a dozen tales from the old Classical stories, the strange invention and incidents of which drop as naturally as ripe cherries into the open-mouthed attention of childhood. . . . [The stories are handled] at once in the spirit of the original, and with a modern fringe and embroidery of new ideas and conceptions. Life, from whatever view he paints it, always comes forth an harmonious picture from Hawthorne's pen. (p. 424)

[We] had better send our young friends at once to the book. (p. 425)

> *"Hawthorne's 'Wonder-Book for Boys and Girls',"*
> *in* The Literary World, *Vol. IX, No. 252, November*
> *29, 1851, pp. 424-25.*

NATHANIEL HAWTHORNE   (essay date 1851)

The point of view in which [*The House of the Seven Gables*] comes under the Romantic definition lies in the attempt to connect a bygone time with the very present that is flitting away from us. It is a legend prolonging itself, from an epoch now gray in the distance, down into our own broad daylight, and bringing along with it some of its legendary mist, which

the reader, according to his pleasure, may either disregard, or allow it to float almost imperceptibly about the characters and events for the sake of a picturesque effect. The narrative, it may be, is woven of so humble a texture as to require this advantage, and, at the same time, to render it the more difficult of attainment.

Many writers lay very great stress upon some definite moral purpose, at which they profess to aim their works. Not to be deficient in this particular, the author has provided himself with a moral,—the truth, namely, that the wrong-doing of one generation lives into the successive ones, and, divesting itself of every temporary advantage, becomes a pure and uncontrollable mischief. . . . When romances do really teach anything, or produce any effective operation, it is usually through a far more subtle process than the ostensible one. The author has considered it hardly worth his while, therefore, relentlessly to impale the story with its moral as with an iron rod,—or, rather, as by sticking a pin through a butterfly,—thus at once depriving it of life, and causing it to stiffen in an ungainly and unnatural attitude. (pp. vi-vii)

> *Nathaniel Hawthorne, "Preface" (1851), in his* The
> House of the Seven Gables, *Washington Square Press,*
> *Inc., 1961, pp. v-viii.*

NATHANIEL HAWTHORNE   (essay date 1851)

[*The Twice-Told Tales*] have the pale tint of flowers that blossomed in too retired a shade—the coolness of a meditative habit which diffuses itself through the feeling and observation of every sketch. Instead of passion, there is sentiment; and even in what purport to be pictures of actual life we have allegory, not always so warmly dressed in its habiliments of flesh and blood as to be taken into the reader's mind without a shiver. Whether from lack of power, or an unconquerable reserve, the Author's touches have often an effect of tameness; the merriest man can hardly contrive to laugh at his broadest humor; the tenderest woman, one would suppose, will hardly shed warm tears at his deepest pathos. The book, if you would see anything in it, requires to be read in the clear, brown, twilight atmosphere in which it was written; if opened in the sunshine, it is apt to look exceedingly like a volume of blank pages.

With the foregoing characteristics, proper to the productions of a person in retirement (which happened to be the Author's category at the time), the book is devoid of others that we should quite as naturally look for. The sketches are not, it is hardly necessary to say, profound; but it is rather more remarkable that they so seldom, if ever, show any design on the writer's part to make them so. They have none of the abstruseness of idea, or obscurity of expression, which marks the written communications of a solitary mind with itself. They never need translation. It is, in fact, the style of a man of society. Every sentence, so far as it embodies thought or sensibility, may be understood and felt by anybody who will give himself the trouble to read it, and will take up the book in a proper mood.

This statement of apparently opposite peculiarities leads us to a perception of what the sketches truly are. They are not the talk of a secluded man with his own mind and heart (had it been so, they could hardly have failed to be more deeply and permanently valuable), but his attempts, and very imperfectly successful ones, to open an intercourse with the world. (pp. xiv-xv)

Nathaniel Hawthorne, "Preface" (1851), in his Twice-Told Tales and Other Short Stories (copyright, ©, 1960, by Washington Square Press, Inc.), Washington Square Press, 1960, pp. xiii-xvi.

THE NEW QUARTERLY REVIEW AND DIGEST OF CURRENT LITERATURE, BRITISH, AMERICAN, FRENCH, AND GERMAN (essay date 1852)

The final moral of *The Blithedale Romance* appears on the face of it morbid and exaggerated. But this is characteristic of Hawthorne. He is a morbid and moody man, who seems to have got out of his proper orbit, so as "never to see the world in its true aspect" himself. He is in his element when dissecting a corpse, and smelling putrefaction. Always he gives you the dark side of humanity, and always paints it in such beautiful colours that you are charmed even by what is inexpressibly painful. Anguish utters no shriek but what is musical, and the voice of villany itself is melodious. Hawthorne could charm you into admiration of a dunghill. He has an eye for the beautiful, but only dim perceptions of the right, the good, and the true. Your moral faculties are unhealthily excited, when excited at all. This is a serious defect in a work of so much purity and power, and is the source of several artistic faults, which would have been remedied by greater moral earnestness in the writer. It makes him timid, hesitating, and slow in his movements. With all his originality, there is no bold stroke of art, but only a succession of beautiful sketches, all on the same level, and often sprawling and monotonous, for want of that concentration of purpose and fulness of design which can only emanate from an earnest and even tumultuous nature. With the general effect, therefore, of this work, we are dissatisfied; with most of its scenes and sentiments we are delighted. Hawthorne is a painter, not a sculptor. He excels in pictorial colouring, not in correct harmony of design. Notwithstanding the ease with which he now handles his pencil, he has reached his present position by slow and laborious effort. His latest production is his best, and gives promise of something still better. In point of mere style, he stands at the head of American writers, and is one of the few among them who write for immortality. (pp. 414-15)

"'The Blithedale Romance'," in The New Quarterly Review and Digest of Current Literature, British, American, French, and German, *Vol. I, 1852, pp. 413-15.*

[GEORGE ELIOT] (essay date 1852)

"The Blithedale Romance" will never attain the popularity which is vouchsafed (to borrow a pulpit vocable), to some of its contemporaries, but it is unmistakably the finest production of genius in either hemisphere, for this quarter at least—to keep our enthusiasm within limits so far. Of its literary merits we wish to speak, at the outset, in the highest terms, inasmuch as we intend to take objection to it in other respects. (p. 318)

[We] cannot pretend to give even a faint outline of a tale which depends for its interest altogether upon the way of telling it. Hawthorne's *forte* is the analysis of character, and not the dramatic arrangement of events. . . . Not more than six or seven characters are introduced, and only four of them are prominent figures. They have, therefore, ample room for displaying their individuality, and establishing each an independent interest in the reader's regards. But this is not without disadvantages, which become more apparent towards the close. The analysis of the characters is so minute, that they are too

thoroughly individualized for dramatic co-operation, or for that graduated subordination to each other which tends to give a harmonious swell to the narrative, unity to the plot, and concentrated force to the issue. They are simply contemporaries, obliged, somehow, to be on familiar terms with each other, and, even when coming into the closest relationship, seeming rather driven thereto by destiny, than drawn by sympathy. It is well that the *dramatis personae* are so few. They are always a manageable number, and are always upon the stage; but had there been more of them, they would only have presented themselves there in turns, which, with Hawthorne's slow movement, would have been fatal to their united action and combined effect. Even with a consecutive narrative, and a concentration of interest, the current flows with an eddying motion, which tends to keep them apart, unless as happens once or twice, it dash over a precipice, and then it both makes up for lost time, and brings matters to a point rather abruptly. But the main tendency is toward isolation—for the ruling faculty is analytic. It is ever hunting out the anomalous; it discovers more points of repulsion than of attraction; and the creatures of its fancy are all morbid beings—all "wandering stars," plunging, orbitless, into the abyss of despair—confluent but not commingling streams, winding along to the ocean of disaster and death: for all have a wretched end. . . .

Poor Miles Coverdale! so genial, so penetrative, so candid—he begins by mocking others, and he ends with mocking himself! Hollingsworth's life teaches a solemn lesson to traffickers in humanity, and with due solemnity is it enforced. Priscilla's life is too shadowy and colourless to convey any lesson. She is a mere straw upon the current. And what of Zenobia? It is difficult to say what we may gather from her life—so many lives were in her! She discusses it herself with Coverdale (quite characteristic) on the eve of her fall. It is a wise point to settle, but she makes it out thus:—

> A moral? Why this: that in the battle-fields of life, the downright stroke that would fall only on a man's steel head-piece, is sure to light upon a woman's heart, over which she wears no breastplate, and whose wisdom it is, therefore, to keep out of the conflict.
>
> (p. 319)

There is something very unartistic in such formal applications of moral or social truths. . . . It indicates imperfection in the construction and colouring of the picture. So many morals—one a-piece for Coverdale and Hollingsworth, and two and a half for Zenobia—are symptomatic of weak moral power, arising from feebleness of moral purpose. Hawthorne has a rich perception of the beautiful, but he is sadly deficient in moral depth and earnestness. His moral faculty is morbid as well as weak; all his characters partake of the same infirmity. Hollingsworth's project of a penitentiary at Blithedale is here carried out in imagination. Hawthorne walks abroad always at night, and at best it is a moonlight glimmering which you catch of reality. He lives in the region and shadow of death, and never sees the deep glow of moral health anywhere. He looks mechanically (it is a habit) at Nature and at man through a coloured glass, which imparts to the whole view a pallid, monotonous aspect, painful to behold. And it is only because Hawthorne can see beauty in everything, and will look at nothing but beauty in anything, that he can either endure the picture himself, or win for it the admiration of others. The object of art is the development of beauty—not merely sensuous beauty, but moral and spiritual beauty. Its ministry should be one of pleasure, not of pain; but our anatomist, who removes his subjects to Blithedale, that he may cut and hack at them without interference, clears out for himself a new path in art, by developing the beauty of deformity! He would give you the poetry of the hospital, or the poetry of the dissecting-room; but we would rather not have it. . . . Zenobia is the only one in the group worthy to be the Trustee of Human Right, and the Representative of Human Destiny; and she, at least, should have come out of all her struggles in regal triumph. But, after the first real trial of her strength with adversity, and when there was resolution yet left for a thousand conflicts, to throw her into that dirty pool, and not even to leave her there, but to send her base-hearted deceiver, and that lout of a fellow, Silas Foster, to haul her out, and to let the one poke up the corpse with a boat hook, and the other tumble it about in the simplicity of his desire to make it look more decent—these, and many other things in the closing scene, are an outrage upon the decorum of art, as well as a violation of its purpose. That such things do happen, is no reason why they should be idealized; for the Ideal seeks not to imitate Reality, but to perfect it. (pp. 319-20)

We are cautioned, in the preface, against the notion (otherwise very liable to be entertained) that this is a history of Brook Farm under a fictitious disguise. . . . There are problems both in biography and in history which imagination only can solve; and in this respect, **"Blithedale,"** as a whole, may tell a truer tale with its fictions than Brook Farm with its facts. Hence it is that our author, while expressing an earnest wish that the word may have the benefit of the latter, felt that it belonged to him to furnish it with the former. A poetic soul sees more in history that it can reproduce in a historical form, and must, therefore, create a symbolism for itself, less inexorable in its conditions, and more expressive of his latest thought. The historical result of the experiment at Brook Farm, and its direct didactic value, may have been inconsiderable enough, but its reproductive capacity in a fruitful mind might have issued in a work which would have rendered that bubble a permanent land-mark in the progress of humanity.

But here, again, Hawthorne disappoints us, and again through his lack of moral earnestness. Everybody will naturally regard this, whether fact or fiction, as a socialistic drama, and will expect its chief interest as such to be of a moral kind. In **"Blithedale,"** whatever may be its relation to Brook Farm, is itself a socialistic settlement, with its corresponding phases of life, and, therefore, involves points both of moral and material interest, the practical operation of which should have been exhibited so as to bring out the good and evil of the system. But this task he declines, and does not "put forward the slightest pretensions to illustrate a theory, or elicit a conclusion favourable or otherwise to Socialism." He confines himself to the delineation of its picturesque phases, as a "thing of beauty," and either has no particular convictions respecting its deeper relations, or hesitates to express them. It was necessary for him to pass judgment upon the theories of Fourier or Robert Owen. He had nothing to do with it as a theory; but as a phase of life it demanded appropriate colouring. Would he paint an ideal slave-plantation merely for the beauty of the thing, without pretending to "elicit a conclusion favourable or otherwise" to slavery? . . . ["**Blithedale,**"] as a socialistic community, is merely used here as a scaffolding—a very huge one—in the construction of an edifice considerably smaller than itself! And then, the artist leaves the scaffolding standing! Socialism, in this romance, is prominent enough to fill the book, but it has so little business in it, that it does not even grow into an organic

part of the story, and contributes nothing whatever toward the final catastrophe. . . . [Socialism] forms a circumference of circumstances, which neither mould the characters, nor influence the destinies, of the individuals so equivocally situated,— forms, in short, not an essential part of the picture, but an enormous fancy border, not very suitable for the purpose for which it was designed. Zenobia's life would have been exhibited with more propriety, and its moral brought home with more effect, in the "theatre" of the world, out of which it really grew, and of which it would have formed a vital and harmonious part. Zenobia and Socialism should have been acted in the ready-made theatre of ordinary humanity, to see how it would fare with them there. Having occupied the ground, Hawthorne owed it to truth, and to a fit opportunity, so to dramatize his experience and observation of Communistic life, as to make them of practical value for the world at large. (pp. 320-21)

[George Eliot,] "Contemporary Literature of America: 'The Blithedale Romance'," in The Westminster Review, Vol. LVIII, No. CXIV, October, 1852, pp. 318-21.

[A. P. PEABODY] (essay date 1853)

It is difficult to refer Hawthorne to any recognized class of writers. So far as our cognizance extends, he is the only individual of his class. In the popular sense of the word, he writes no poetry. . . . [His language] is often crisp and harsh, betraying little sensitiveness to musical accords and cadences; and we should despair of finding a paragraph of his, in which the sound could, by the most skilful reading, be made to enhance the impression of the sense. Yet more, we cannot remember a single poetical quotation in all his writings. . . . (p. 227)

[Yet] Hawthorne is preëminently a poet. It belongs to his genius not merely to narrate or describe, not merely to invent characters and incidents of the same constituent elements with those in history or in real life; but to create out of nothing —to place before the imagination objects and personages which derive their verisimilitude not from their resemblance to the actual, but from their self-coherency. . . . A year or two ago, he conceived the plan of reëditing some of the fables of the classic mythology; but the result [The Wonder-Book] was a Pantheon all his own, rigidly true, indeed, to the letter of antiquity, and thus vindicating his title to genuine scholarship, while yet gods and heroes, Gorgons and Chimerae, Atlas and Pegasus, all bore as close kindred to him as Minerva to Jupiter. In fine, his golden touch is as unfailing as was that of Midas, and transmutes whatever he lays hand upon. . . . [His golden touch] imposes no superficial glitter, but brings out upon the surface, and concentrates in luminous points, the interior gilding, which is attached to the meanest objects and the lowliest scenes by their contact with the realm of sentiment, emotion, and spiritual life. He literally transforms, draws the hidden soul of whatever he describes to the light of day, and often veils exterior phenomena from clear view by the very tissue of motives, loves, antipathies, mental and moral idiosyncrasies, which they are wont to conceal. He thus, often, when least successful in the development of a plot, gives us portraitures of character as vivid as if they were wrought in flame-colors, and transcripts of inward experience so graphic that to read them is to live them over. (pp. 228-29)

As a writer of stories, whether in the form of tales, novels, or romances, Hawthorne will not bear comparison with his contemporaries in the same department, or measurement by any conventional rule. The most paltry tale-maker for magazines or newspapers can easily excel him in what we might term the mechanical portion of his art. His plots are seldom well devised or skilfully developed. They are either too simple to excite curiosity and attract interest, or too much involved for him to clear them up to the reader's satisfaction. His conversations, too, are not such as seem natural, in the sense of being probable or possible, but natural only because they are more rigidly true to fact and feeling than speech ever is. There is also, not infrequently, an incompleteness in his choicest productions, not as if he had been careless or hurried in their execution, but as if they had been too intimately a portion of his own being for separate existence,—as if they had been too deeply rooted in their native soil to bear transplanting. But, if he lacks skill in the management of his plot, he is independent of it. Were he to eliminate every thing of a narrative character from the best of his stories, we doubt whether their currency or his reputation would suffer detriment. Indeed, he is often most successful, where he does not even attempt narration, but selects some single scene, object, or incident, as the nucleus for a cluster of fancies and musings. . . . (p. 230)

Hawthorne has written nothing more likely to survive his times than several simply, yet gorgeously, wrought and highly suggestive allegories, among which **"The Celestial Railroad"** holds the first place, and deserves an immortality coeval with that of the great prose-epic which furnished its theme. (pp. 230-31)

[Hawthorne's] stories are generally written to illustrate some idea or sentiment, to which, and not to the personages or incidents, the author manifestly solicits his reader's heed. He is a philosopher, with a strong dash of the humorist in his composition; human life and society constitute his field of speculation; and his queries and conclusions tend, through his poetic instincts, to concrete rather than abstract forms. With him, a tale takes the place of an apophthegm; an allegory, of a homily; a romance, of an ethical treatise. . . . [There is] in his writings a philosophical completeness and unity, even when, in an artistical point of view, (as is often the case,) they are fragmentary or desultory. (pp. 231-32)

[The story of the bold and startling fiction, *The House of the Seven Gables*, is] portrayed with a vividness and power unsurpassed, and rarely equalled. The terrible Nemesis that waits on the extortion of the ancestor, and pursues the wages of his iniquity till the injured family receives its own again, reminds one of the inexorable fate of the Greek tragedy; and, in describing the successive footfalls of the angel of retribution in that ill-starred mansion, the author rises into a fearful sublimity worthy of the theme. In other portions, the narrative is sprightly, quaint, and droll, the dialogues seldom otherwise than natural and well managed, (though the daguerreotypist talks more than anybody but Phoebe could care to hear,) and the *denouement* free, for the most part, from abruptness and improbability. (pp. 236-37)

As a story, we are inclined to esteem [*The Blithedale Romance*] inferior to either of its predecessors in similar form. . . . [The] dialogues of the Blithedale optimists are often prolix, wearisome, and we should say unnatural, were it not for our ignorance of the way in which people thrown into the closest society, with no preëxisting bond of kindred or of sympathy, would be likely to talk. But whether from the life or not, a great deal of Arcadian material is wrought into the sayings and doings of this community, and it makes but an incongruous woof on the homespun warp of New England farm life. . . .

But with all these drawbacks, [*The Blithedale Romance*] is a work of no ordinary power, and indicative of all its author's mental affluence. (p. 241)

> [A. P. Peabody,] *"Nathaniel Hawthorne's 'The House of the Seven Gables: A Romance',"* in The North American Review, *Vol. LXXVI, No. CLVIII, January, 1853, pp. 227-48.*

THE LITERARY WORLD   (essay date 1853)

The good work which Charles Lamb begun for young readers in disentangling the stories upon which Shakespeare's plays are founded from the intricacies of plot and poetry, . . . has been continued in a congenial spirit by Nathaniel Hawthorne, in these [*Tanglewood Tales*]. (p. 99)

[These stories of the ancient classics,] which have always furnished healthy food for the profound moralist, come forth from the mind of Hawthorne pure and graceful, their essential force preserved, while they are decently draped in modern language and incident. In his own happy way, an art and nature possessed by so few, Hawthorne has in effect created a new world for childish sympathy and admiration. He has taken the wisdom and entertainment of the childhood of the world, and found their sympathetic, congenial reception in the fable-loving, imaginative period of the childhood of life. Wiser or grander fables are not to be found. Be sure they lose nothing of their real vitality or kindling power to virtue and the imagination in such hands as Nathaniel Hawthorne's. (pp. 99-100)

The merit of [Hawthorne's] style must be apparent to the most careless reader. It is neither too big for children or too little for father and mother. The whole family may find equal delight in it. *The Tanglewood Tales* is a book which will be a treasure to the household for many generations to come. (p. 101)

> *"Hawthorne's 'Tanglewood Tales',"* in The Literary World, *Vol. XIII, No. 345, September 10, 1853, pp. 99-101.*

DUBLIN UNIVERSITY MAGAZINE   (essay date 1855)

With not a few points of resemblance to recent English and American authors, Hawthorne has yet many peculiarities of his own, so nicely characterised that we cannot think of anything like a complete prototype to him in literature. Now, the quaint, still humour of his thoroughly English style, reminds us of Washington Irving; now the delicate, imperceptible touches of Longfellow become apparent; now the calm, genial, effortless flow of Helps. We have often fancied, also, that we could detect a resemblance to John Foster, but we suspect, were we to attempt a comparison of parallel passages, it would turn out to be rather imaginary. There is a tendency, no doubt, in both, to pry into all the odd nooks, and corners, and dark places of the mind; but the firm, strong, practical nature of Foster never suffers him to carry this beyond a certain point, and always shapes his researches to some masterly conclusion, while Hawthorne often runs riot in the pursuit from mere apparent wantonness. Yet, undoubtedly, it is this ruling feature of Hawthorne's mind that invests his writings with much of their peculiar charm;—producing extravagant and overdrawn description in some; in others it is the zest and spirit of the whole. In reading the works of Macaulay or Bulwer Lytton, there is often a disagreeable consciousness that all is splendidly got up; but with Hawthorne all seems to flow from the heart. . . . (pp. 463-64)

Like almost every original author, Hawthorne occasionally verifies our great dramatist's remark about vaulting ambition o'erleaping itself and falling on the other side, giving utterance to the veriest drivel, such as scribblers of the lowest order could hardly be guilty of perpetrating. It would be hard to say how many readers he has lost who have had the misfortune to take up, say the **"Twice-Told Tales,"** and opened with **"Tales of the Province House,"** or **"The Threefold Destiny."** Even in the **"Mosses from an Old Manse,"** which abounds in unmistakable evidences of his genius, abundance of pieces might be cited which would require the utmost stretch of charity to pass by. . . .

Were we particularly anxious to impress a reader favourably with Hawthorne at starting, we do not think we could succeed better than by directing him to take up the **"Mosses from an Old Manse,"** and begin at the beginning, when, if he did not go the end of the first article, we should certainly pronounce him an incorrigible dullard. . . . [Yet as one continues to read how] breezy and wholesome the picture of the old manse, the river, the woods, and the garden [appear]! . . . (p. 464)

To the merits of the **"House of the Seven Gables,"** the most pleasing and complete of Hawthorne's tales, an adverse critic, in our opinion, unconsciously pays a high compliment, when he complains that the author seizes on the reader by the button, as it were, and, like the Ancient Mariner, compels him to hear the story to an end, which, after all, turns out to be no story at all—that is to say, there is no grand *denouement,* no long a-missing marriage-certificate is discovered, nor is any hitherto supposed plebeian elevated to patrician rank. An original idea, truly, to censure an author for contriving so to rivet your attention that you must read his book through, even though, as the saying is, there is nothing in it! . . . **"The House of the Seven Gables"** may be very faulty as a story, and we certainly would not recommend it as a model to apprentice fiction-mongers; but . . . we think such an author as Hawthorne may be allowed to let his genius find its own vent, and diverge as often as it pleases from any path it may ostensibly follow. **"The House of the Seven Gables,"** we venture to say, would have wanted the best part of its attractions, had the author rigidly repressed the promptings of his luxuriant fancy, and closely pursued the even tenor of his narrative, even though the plot and winding-up had been exciting enough to please our fastidious censor.

As might be expected from Hawthorne's peculiar idiosyncrasy, he possesses, in a remarkable degree, the faculty of indicating by imperceptible shades the approaching event long ere it is announced, like the hush becoming stiller and stiller as the noiseless battalia of clouds creep denser and denser together before the storm. . . . [Only Dickens] could rival the incidental touches immediately antecedent to the death of Judge Pyncheon. (pp. 464-65)

"The Blithedale Romance," one of Hawthorne's most recent publications, lies more open than any other to unsparing and well-deserved ridicule—in the characters especially: one being inflated to bursting with about as much success as the frog of old; another insipid; another wofully wishy-washy; and the hero of the tale himself, who tells the story in the first person, an impertinent sort of eavesdropper. . . . Yet, with all drawbacks, there is hardly one of his works we could read over with more

pleasure than this eccentric production. . . . The mode of life at [the model farm] is the great charm of the book, for Hawthorne can hardly fail to delight when he catches a glimpse of nature. To use his own words, he speaks of her "like the very spirit of earth imbued with a scent of freshly-turned soil." In his sketches and essays, American scenery comes before us in all its rich luxuriance and unfettered gladness. . . . (p. 465)

The rest of Hawthorne's works consist principally of tales and sketches; and in these . . . allegory is frequently employed, with masterly effect, to give life to his conceptions. His most brilliant and finished effort of this kind is **"The Celestial Railroad,"** in which the mantle of Bunyan appears to have descended on him with a double portion of his spirit—the quaint, nervous simplicity of the prince of dreamers blending with his own rich vividness of descriptive power, and quiet under-current humour. (p. 466)

Most of Hawthorne's other allegorical compositions sound as incomplete half utterances, hinting but vaguely at the meaning intended to be conveyed, though we are not sure if we should call this indefiniteness a defect—the power of negative suggestion thus displayed being often perfectly magical. Yet we cannot say that allegory is made much more attractive to us by Hawthorne than by his predecessors. . . . It is pleasant enough now and then to step out of the material world; but we do not like to be incessantly reminded that all is unreal, mist and shadow. The mind craves a firmer foothold, and prefers swallowing downright impossibilities, if presented with an unblushing air of veracity, and imbued with a sufficient tinge of the *vraisemblable.* This has not escaped Hawthorne; and he has very happily embodied ideas in this form in one or two papers, telling his tale as if perfectly prepared to vouch for the authenticity of the whole. **"The Artist of the Beautiful"** is a fine instance of this; and the moral conveyed loses none of its effect, that the reader is left to find it out for himself. . . .

Perhaps, on the whole, the walk in which Hawthorne most excels is in that blending of the essay, sketch, and tale, for which we have no definite term as yet. . . . A volume of Hawthorne's compositions of this nature, selected from his works, and cleared from all surrounding rubbish, would be a perfect *chef-d'oeuvre* of its kind. . . . There is one paper [**"PVs Correspondence"**] in his **"Mosses from an Old Manse"** which would have made the fortune of any ordinary literary aspirant— original, so far as our memory serves us, in conception, and rivalling the happiest efforts of Goldsmith and Irving in execution. (p. 467)

There is one other work of Hawthorne's in a totally different vein, which we must not pass by in concluding, though we should not have regretted its non-publication very much—his **"Life of General Pierce, the American President."** We could not help thinking it a pity . . . that in his zeal for [the Democrats, Hawthorne] should have been led to step so far out of his own sphere, and descant on patriotism, the union, anti-and-pro-slavery, in a style bordering somewhat on that of the stump orator. Occasionally, no doubt, faint reflections of his former self may be detected, but these partake in some measure of the character of features distorted in the bowl of a spoon. . . . [We] hope, for his own sake, Mr. Hawthorne will in future give no more political lucubrations to the world. It is evident that dealing with the dry, practical doings of life is not his forte, and the field over which his genius can range is so wide and varied that we can well dispense with any excursions beyond it.

In the desultory remarks we have been making, we must not be understood as putting forward any claims for Hawthorne to rank as a model anything. Exceptions of every kind may be taken to his works, which, though perhaps *sans peur*, are certainly not always *sans reproche*. But withal he is a man of genius, and as such without any farther "peroration" we leave him to our readers. (pp. 468-69)

> "Nathaniel Hawthorne," in Dublin University Magazine, *Vol. XLVI, No. CCLXXIV, October, 1855, pp. 463-69.*

NATHANIEL HAWTHORNE   (essay date 1859)

[*The Marble Faun*] was sketched out during a residence of considerable length in Italy. . . . The author proposed to himself merely to write a fanciful story, evolving a thoughtful moral, and did not propose attempting a portraiture of Italian manners and character. He has lived too long abroad not to be aware that a foreigner seldom acquires that knowledge of a country at once flexible and profound, which may justify him in endeavoring to idealize its traits.

Italy, as the site of his Romance, was chiefly valuable to him as affording a sort of poetic or fairy precinct, where actualities would not be so terribly insisted upon as they are, and must needs be, in America. No author, without a trial, can conceive of the difficulty of writing a romance about a country where there is no shadow, no antiquity, no mystery, no picturesque and gloomy wrong, nor anything but a commonplace prosperity, in broad and simple daylight, as is happily the case with my dear native land. It will be very long, I trust, before romance-writers may find congenial and easily handled themes, either in the annals of our stalwart republic, or in any characteristic and probable events of our individual lives. Romance and poetry, ivy, lichens, and wall-flowers, need ruin to make them grow.

In rewriting these volumes, the author was somewhat surprised to see the extent to which he had introduced descriptions of various Italian objects, antique, pictorial, and statuesque. Yet these things fill the mind everywhere in Italy, and especially in Rome, and cannot easily be kept from flowing out upon the page when one writes freely, and with self-enjoyment. And, again, while reproducing the book, on the broad and dreary sands of Redcar, with the gray German Ocean tumbling in upon me, and the northern blast always howling in my ears, the complete change of scene made these Italian reminiscences shine out so vividly that I could not find it in my heart to cancel them. (p. 590)

> Nathaniel Hawthorne, in his preface to his The Marble Faun, *Ticknor & Fields, 1859 (and reprinted in* The Complete Novels and Selected Tales of Nathaniel Hawthorne, *edited by Norman Holmes Pearson,* The Modern Library, *1937, pp. 589-91).*

[JAMES RUSSELL LOWELL]   (essay date 1860)

The nineteenth century has produced no more purely original writer than Mr. Hawthorne. A shallow criticism has sometimes fancied a resemblance between him and Poe. But it seems to us that the difference between them is the immeasurable one between talent carried to its ultimate, and genius,—between a masterly adaptation of the world of sense and appearance to the purposes of Art, and a so thorough conception of the world of moral realities that Art becomes the interpreter of something

profounder than herself. In this respect it is not extravagant to say that Hawthorne has something of kindred with Shakspeare. But that breadth of nature which made Shakspeare incapable of alienation from common human nature and actual life is wanting to Hawthorne. He is rather a denizen than a citizen of what men call the world. We are conscious of a certain remoteness in his writings, as in those of Donne, but with such a difference that we should call the one super- and the other subter-sensual. Hawthorne is psychological and metaphysical. Had he been born without the poetic imagination, he would have written treatises on the Origin of Evil. He does not draw characters, but rather conceives them and then shows them acted upon by crime, passion, or circumstance, as if the element of Fate were as present to his imagination as to that of a Greek dramatist. . . . [It] is marvellous how subtilely and with what truth to as much of human nature as is included in a diseased consciousness he traces all the finest nerves of impulse and motive, how he compels every trivial circumstance into an accomplice of his art, and makes the sky flame with foreboding or the landscape chill and darken with remorse. . . .

It is commonly true of Hawthorne's romances that the interest centres in one strongly defined protagonist, to whom the other characters are accessory and subordinate,—perhaps we should rather say a ruling Idea, of which all the characters are fragmentary embodiments. (p. 509)

Nothing could be more original or imaginative than the conception of the character of Donatello in Mr. Hawthorne's new romance [*The Marble Faun*]. His likeness to the lovely statue of Praxiteles, his happy animal temperament, and the dim legend of his pedigree are combined with wonderful art to reconcile us to the notion of a Greek myth embodied in an Italian of the nineteenth century; . . . we feel, that, while we looked to be entertained with the airiest of fictions, we were dealing with the most august truths of psychology, with the most pregnant facts of modern history, and studying a profound parable of the development of the Christian Idea.

Everything suffers a sea-change in the depths of Mr. Hawthorne's mind, gets rimmed with an impalpable fringe of melancholy moss, and there is a tone of sadness in this book as in the rest, but it does not leave us sad. In a series of remarkable and characteristic works, [*The Marble Faun*] is perhaps the most remarkable and characteristic. (p. 510)

> [James Russell Lowell,] "Reviews and Literary Notices: 'The Marble Faun'," in The Atlantic Monthly, *Vol. V, No. XXX, April, 1860, pp. 509-10.*

[E. P. WHIPPLE]   (essay date 1860)

The style [of Hawthorne's early books], while it had a purity, sweetness, and grace which satisfied the most fastidious and exacting taste, had, at the same time, more than the simplicity and clearness of an ordinary school-book. But though the subjects and the style were thus popular, there was something in the shaping and informing spirit which failed to awaken interest, or awakened interest without exciting delight. Misanthropy, when it has its source in passion,—when it is fierce, bitter, fiery, and scornful,—... this is always popular; but a misanthropy which springs from insight,—a misanthropy which is lounging, languid, sad, and depressing,—... this is a misanthropy which can expect no wide recognition; and it would be vain to deny that traces of this kind of misanthropy are to be found in Hawthorne's earlier, and are not altogether absent from his later works. He had spiritual insight, but it did not penetrate to the sources of spiritual joy; and his deepest glimpses of truth were calculated rather to sadden than to inspire. A blandly cynical distrust of human nature was the result of his most piercing glances into the human soul. He had humor, and sometimes humor of a delicious kind; but this sunshine of the soul was but sunshine breaking through or lighting up a sombre and ominous cloud. There was also observable in his earlier stories a lack of vigor, as if the power of his nature had been impaired by the very process which gave depth and excursiveness to his mental vision. . . . As psychological portraits of morbid natures, his delineations of character might have given a purely intellectual satisfaction; but there was audible, to the delicate ear, a faint and muffled growl of personal discontent, which showed they were not mere exercises of penetrating imaginative analysis, but had in them the morbid vitality of a despondent mood.

Yet, after admitting these peculiarities, nobody who is now drawn to the "Twice-Told Tales," from his interest in the later romances of Hawthorne, can fail to wonder a little at the limited number of readers they attracted on their original publication. For many of these stories are at once a representation of early New-England life and a criticism on it. They have much of the deepest truth of history in them. . . . In the "Prophetic Pictures," "Fancy's Show-Box," "The Great Carbuncle," "The Haunted Mind," and "Edward Fane's Rose-Bud," there are flashes of moral insight, which light up, for the moment, the darkest recesses of the individual mind; and few sermons reach to the depth of thought and sentiment from which these seemingly airy sketches draw their sombre life. . . . Interspersed with serious histories and moralities like these, are others which embody the sweet and playful, though still thoughtful and slightly saturnine action of Hawthorne's mind,— like "The Seven Vagabonds," "Snow-Flakes," "The Lily's Quest," "Mr. Higgenbotham's Catastrophe." . . . (pp. 615-16)

The "Mosses from an Old Manse" are intellectually and artistically an advance from the "Twice-Told Tales." . . . In description, narration, allegory, humor, reason, fancy, subtilty, inventiveness, they exceed the best productions of Addison; but they want Addison's sensuous contentment and sweet and kindly spirit. . . . The defect of the serious stories is, that character is introduced, not as thinking, but as the illustration of thought. The persons are ghostly, with a sad lack of flesh and blood. They are phantasmal symbols of a reflective and imaginative analysis of human passions and aspirations. The dialogue, especially, is bookish, as though the personages knew their speech was to be printed, and were careful of the collocation and rhythm of their words. The author throughout is evidently more interested in his large, wide, deep, indolently serene, and lazily sure and critical view of the conflict of ideas and passions, than he is with the individuals who embody them. He shows moral insight without moral earnestness. He cannot contract his mind to the patient delineation of a moral individual, but attempts to use individuals in order to express the last results of patient moral perception. Young Goodman Brown and Roger Malvin are not persons; they are the mere, loose, personal expression of subtile thinking. "The Celestial Railroad," "The Procession of Life," "Earth's Holocaust," "The Bosom Serpent," indicate thought of a character equally deep, delicate, and comprehensive, but the characters are ghosts of men rather than substantial individualities. . . . [In "The Scarlet Letter," Hawthorne] first made his genius efficient by penetrating it with passion. This book forced itself into attention by its inherent power. . . . (p. 617)

Two characteristics of Hawthorne's genius stand plainly out, in the conduct and characterization of the romance of "The Scarlet Letter," which were less obviously prominent in his previous works. The first relates to his subordination of external incidents to inward events. . . . Hawthorne relies almost entirely for the interest of his story on what is felt and done within the minds of his characters. Even his most picturesque descriptions and narratives are only one-tenth matter to nine-tenths spirit. The results that follow from one external act of folly or crime are to him enough for an Iliad of woes. (p. 618)

The second characteristic of his genius is connected with the first. With his insight of individual souls he combines a far deeper insight of the spiritual laws which govern the strangest aberrations of individual souls. But it seems to us that his mental eye, keen-sighted and far-sighted as it is, overlooks the merciful modifications of the austere code whose pitiless action it so clearly discerns. In his long and patient brooding over the spiritual phenomena of Puritan life, it is apparent, to the least critical observer, that he has imbibed a deep personal antipathy to the Puritanic ideal of character; but it is no less apparent that his intellect and imagination have been strangely fascinated by the Puritanic idea of justice. . . . Throughout "The Scarlet Letter" we seem to be following the guidance of an author who is personally good-natured, but intellectually and morally relentless.

"The House of the Seven Gables," . . . while it has less concentration of passion and tension of mind than "The Scarlet Letter," includes a wider range of observation, reflection, and character; and the morality, dreadful as fate, which hung like a black cloud over the personages of the previous story, is exhibited in more relief. Although the book has no imaginative creation equal to little Pearl, it still contains numerous examples of characterization at once delicate and deep. . . . The whole representation, masterly as it is, considered as an effort of intellectual and imaginative power, would still be morally bleak, were it not for the sunshine and warmth radiated from the character of Phoebe. In this delightful creation Hawthorne for once gives himself up to homely human nature, and has succeeded in delineating a New-England girl, cheerful, blooming, practical, affectionate, efficient, full of innocence and happiness. . . . (pp. 618-19)

[In "The House of the Seven Gables"] there is also more humor than in any of his other works. It peeps out, even in the most serious passages, in a kind of demure rebellion against the fanaticism of his remorseless intelligence. In the description of the Pyncheon poultry, which we think unexcelled by anything in Dickens for quaintly fanciful humor, the author seems to indulge in a sort of parody on his own doctrine of the hereditary transmission of family qualities. (p. 619)

[It] is necessary to say a few words on the seeming separation of Hawthorne's genius from his will. He has none of that ability which enabled Scott and enables Dickens to force their powers into action, and to make what was begun in drudgery soon assume the character of inspiration. Hawthorne cannot thus use his genius; his genius always uses him. This is so true, that he often succeeds better in what calls forth his personal antipathies than in what calls forth his personal sympathies. His life of General Pierce, for instance, is altogether destitute of life; yet in writing it he must have exerted himself to the utmost, as his object was to urge the claims of an old and dear friend to the Presidency of the Republic. The style, of course, is excellent, as it is impossible for Hawthorne to write bad English, but the genius of the man has deserted him. General

Pierce, whom he loves, he draws so feebly, that one doubts, while reading the biography, if such a man exists. . . . (pp. 619-20)

[In **"The Wonder-Book"** and **"Tanglewood Tales"**] Hawthorne's genius distinctly appears, and appears in its most lovable, though not in its deepest form. These delicious stories, founded on the mythology of Greece, were written for children, but they delight men and women as well. . . .

[**"The Blithedale Romance"**] is far from being so pleasing a performance as **"Tanglewood Tales,"** yet it very much better illustrates the operation, indicates the quality, and expresses the power, of the author's genius. His great books appear not so much created by him as through him. They have the character of revelations,—he, the instrument, being often troubled with the burden they impose on his mind. His profoundest glances into individual souls are like the marvels of clairvoyance. It would seem, that, in the production of such a work as **"The Blithedale Romance,"** his mind had hit accidentally, as it were, on an idea or fact mysteriously related to some morbid sentiment in the inmost core of his nature, and connecting itself with numerous scattered observations of human life, lying unrelated in his imagination. . . . On the depth and intensity of the mental mood, the force of the fascination it exerts over him, and the length of time it holds him captive, depend the solidity and substance of the individual characterizations. In this way Miles Coverdale, Hollingsworth, Westervelt, Zenobia, and Priscilla become real persons to the mind which has called them into being. He knows every secret and watches every motion of their souls, yet is, in a measure, independent of them, and pretends to no authority by which he can alter the destiny which consigns them to misery or happiness. They drift to their doom by the same law by which they drifted across the path of his vision. (p. 620)

"The Marble Faun" [his current book], which must, on the whole, be considered the greatest of his works, proves that his genius has widened and deepened in [the interval since **"The Blithedale Romance"** was published]. . . . The most obvious excellence of the work is the vivid truthfulness of its descriptions of Italian life, manners, and scenery; and, considered merely as a record of a tour in Italy, it is of great interest and attractiveness. The opinions on Art, and the special criticisms on the masterpieces of architecture, sculpture, and painting, also possess a value of their own. The story might have been told, and the characters fully represented, in one-third of the space devoted to them, yet description and narration are so artfully combined that each assists to give interest to the other. . . .

[Hawthorne writes] the sweetest, simplest, and clearest English that ever has been made the vehicle of equal depth, variety, and subtilty of thought and emotion. His mind is reflected in his style as a face is reflected in a mirror; and the latter does not give back its image with less appearance of effort than the former. His excellence consists not so much in using common words as in making common words express uncommon things. (p. 621)

In regard to the characterization and plot of **"The Marble Faun,"** there is room for widely varying opinions. Hilda, Miriam, and Donatello will be generally received as superior in power and depth to any of Hawthorne's previous creations of character; Donatello, especially, must be considered one of the most original and exquisite conceptions in the whole range of romance; but the story in which they appear will seem to many

an unsolved puzzle, and even the tolerant and interpretative "gentle reader" will be troubled with the unsatisfactory conclusion. It is justifiable for a romancer to sting the curiosity of his readers with a mystery, only on the implied obligation to explain it at last; but this story begins in mystery only to end in mist. . . . The central idea of the story, the necessity of sin to convert such a creature as Donatello into a moral being, is also not happily illustrated in the leading event. When Donatello kills the wretch who malignantly dogs the steps of Miriam, all readers think that Donatello committed no sin at all; and the reason is, that Hawthorne has deprived the persecutor of Miriam of all human attributes, made him an allegorical representation of one of the most fiendish forms of unmixed evil, so that we welcome his destruction with something of the same feeling with which, in following the allegory of Spenser or Bunyan, we rejoice in the hero's victory over the Blatant Beast or Giant Despair. Conceding, however, that Donatello's act was murder, and not "justifiable homicide," we are still not sure that the author's conception of his nature and of the change caused in his nature by that act, are carried out with a felicity corresponding to the original conception.

In the first [section], and in the early part of the second, the author's hold on his design is comparatively firm, but it somewhat relaxes as he proceeds, and in the end it seems almost to escape from his grasp. Few can be satisfied with the concluding chapters, for the reason that nothing is really concluded. (pp. 621-22)

In intellect and imagination, in the faculty of discerning spirits and detecting laws, we doubt if any living novelist is [Hawthorne's] equal; but his genius, in its creative action, has been heretofore attracted to the dark rather than the bright side of the interior life of humanity, and the geniality which evidently is in him has rarely found adequate expression. In the many works which he may still be expected to write, it is to be hoped that his mind will lose some of its sadness of tone without losing any of its subtilty and depth. . . . (p. 622)

> [*E. P. Whipple,*] *"Nathaniel Hawthorne," in* The Atlantic Monthly, *Vol. V, No. XXXI, May, 1860, pp. 614-22.*

WILLIAM JAMES   (essay date 1870)

I little expected so great a work. [*The House of the Seven Gables* is] like a great symphony, with no touch alterable without injury to the harmony. It made a deep impression on me and I thank heaven that Hawthorne was an American. It also tickled my national feeling not a little to notice the resemblance of Hawthorne's style to yours and Howells's. . . . That you and Howells with all the models in English literature to follow, should needs involuntarily have imitated (as it were) this American, seems to point to the existence of some real American mental quality. (p. 332)

> *William James, in an extract from his letter to Henry James on January 19, 1870 in* The Thought and Character of William James, *edited by Ralph Barton Perry, Little, Brown, and Co., 1935 (and reprinted in "'The Wizard Hand': Hawthorne, 1864-1900" by Edwin H. Cady, in* Hawthorne Centenary Essays, *edited by Roy Harvey Pearce, Ohio State University Press, 1964, pp. 317-34).*

G. S. HILLARD   (essay date 1870)

The difference between [*Our Old Home* and *Passages from the English Note-Books of Nathaniel Hawthorne*], inspired by English life, manners, and scenery is simply the difference between full dress and undress. (p. 264)

Our Old Home was carefully prepared for the press, but the *English Note-Books* were kept for [Hawthorne's] own use. . . . Thus the former work has a minute and matchless finish not found in the latter. In point of form, grace of expression, and beauty of style, *Our Old Home* is entitled to stand at the head of all his works; as the same place is due to *The Scarlet Letter* in creative power and tragic grandeur. The two together represent the whole circle of his genius, his vision, and his faculty, his originality in invention, his imaginative conception of character, his depth of light and shade in moral portraiture, his piercing insight, his power of passionless contemplation, his shrewd apprehension of every-day life, his feminine sympathy, and his unequalled skill in the use of the instrument of language.

The *English* and the *American Note-Books* have alike a peculiar value as illustrating the mind and character of the author. (pp. 264-65)

In these *Note-Books* we have an expression of Hawthorne's feeling both towards nature and art. He was a lover of nature, but not an impassioned or a fastidious lover. The sort of rapture and passion which Wordsworth reveals in his poetry and Ruskin in his prose was not felt by him. (p. 268)

[Hawthorne] describes the beautiful, but does not describe beautifully. . . . He sets down his impressions of what he sees with inimitable grace, but much in the same quiet way as a sailor puts down in his log-book the course of a storm at sea. (p. 269)

[We] have in the *English Note-Books* a book of permanent interest and value, both from its essential literary merit and from its autobiographical character, as illustrating the mental and personal traits of the most original genius in the sphere of imaginative literature that our country has yet produced. (p. 272)

> *G. S. Hillard, "The English Note-Books of Nathaniel Hawthorne," in* The Atlantic Monthly, *Vol. XXVI, No. CLV, September, 1870, pp. 257-72.*

[HENRY JAMES, JR.] (essay date 1872)

[*Passages from the French and Italian Note-Books of Nathaniel Hawthorne*] throw but little light on [Mr. Hawthorne's] personal feelings, and even less on his genius *per se*. Their general effect is difficult to express. They deepen our sense of that genius, while they singularly diminish our impression of his general intellectual power. There can be no better proof of his genius than that these common daily scribblings should unite so irresistibly a charm with so little distinctive force. They represent him, judged with any real critical rigor, as superficial, uninformed, incurious, inappreciative; but from beginning to end they cast no faintest shadow upon the purity of his peculiar gift. Our own sole complaint has been not that they should have been published, but that there are not a dozen volumes more. The truth is that Mr. Hawthorne belonged to the race of magicians, and that his genius took its nutriment as insensibly—to our vision—as the flowers take the dew. He was the last man to have attempted to explain himself, and these pages offer no adequate explanation of him. They show us one of the gentlest, lightest, and most leisurely of observers, strolling at his ease among foreign sights in blessed intellectual irresponsibility, and weaving his chance impressions into a tissue as smooth as fireside gossip. . . .

These volumes of Italian notes, charming as they are, are on the whole less rich and substantial than those on England. . . . The book is full, nevertheless, of the same spirit of serene, detached contemplation; equally full of refined and gently suggestive description. . . . [Mr. Hawthorne] walks about bending a puzzled, ineffective gaze at things, full of a mild, genial desire to apprehend and penetrate, but with the light wings of his fancy just touching the surface of the massive consistency of fact about him, and with an air of good-humored confession that he is too simply an idle Yankee *flâneur* to conclude on such matters. The main impression produced by his observations is that of his simplicity. They spring not only from an unsophisticated, but from an excessively natural mind. Never, surely, was a man of literary genius less a man of letters. He looks at things as little as possible in that composite historic light which forms the atmosphere of many imaginations. There is something extremely pleasing in this simplicity, within which the character of the man rounds itself so completely and so firmly. His judgments abound in common sense; touched as they often are by fancy, they are never distorted by it. His errors and illusions never impugn his fundamental wisdom; even when (as is almost the case in his appreciation of works of art) they provoke a respectful smile, they contain some saving particle of sagacity. Fantastic romancer as he was, he here refutes conclusively the common charge that he was either a melancholy or a morbid genius. He had a native relish for the picturesque greys and browns of life; but these pages betray a childlike evenness and clearness of intellectual temper. (p. 172)

Mr. Hawthorne's minute and vivid record of [his journey from Rome to Florence] is the most delightful portion of these volumes, and, indeed, makes well-nigh as charming a story as that of the enchanted progress of the two friends in the *Marble Faun* from Monte Beni to Perugia. . . .

His pictures of the strange, dark little mountain-cities of Radicofani and Bolsena, on his [return] journey, are masterpieces of literary etching. It is impossible to render better that impression as of a mild nightmare which such places make upon the American traveller. . . . [Mr. Hawthorne's] was a rich simplicity. These pages give a strong impression of moral integrity and elevation. And, more than in other ways, they are interesting from their strong national flavor. Exposed late in life to European influences, Mr. Hawthorne was but superficially affected by them—far less so than would be the case with a mind of the same temper growing up among us to-day. We seem to see him strolling through churches and galleries as the last pure American—attesting by his shy responses to dark canvas and cold marble his loyalty to a simpler and less encumbered civilization. This image deepens that tender personal regard which it is the constant effect of these volumes to produce. (p. 173)

> *[Henry James, Jr.,] "Hawthorne's French and Italian Journals," in* The Nation, *Vol. XIV, No. 350, March 14, 1872, pp. 172-73.*

G. P. LATHROP (essay date 1872)

[In "Septimius Felton" the central figure's] character is nothing more nor less than a mood which occurs to many, but is transient with most, developed into a real person. This mood is his permanent constitution; and it is thus that a natural and sufficiently ordinary and probable set of incidents becomes imbued with an aspect suiting his disposition. So that throughout the book we enter into the brain of this half-crazy youth, and dwell there, taking these incidents just as he has colored them, until, despite the impossibility of the thing, and un-heeding those turnings of the fabric by which the author occasionally hints a reverse side, showing the rude stitches which back his tapestry, we come to think and feel with the hero, and look forward with trembling eagerness to the anticipated consummation of his desire. In the execution of this story Hawthorne would appear to have realized the conditions he himself prescribes for the romancer, namely, that he should be always "careering upon the utmost verge of a precipitous absurdity," the skill lying in "coming as close as possible without tumbling over." At the last, however, he lets in the daylight with a ruthless hand; and the acute sense of disap-pointment we feel in the event is perhaps the best proof of the success with which he has thrown us into Septimius's point of view. (p. 459)

In the development of the persons there is perceptible an ad-herence to the rough exteriors of real life, a reproduction of idiomatic and defective ways of speaking, . . . which gives them a verisimilitude, a color and rotundity, lacking in the characters introduced to our acquaintance by the earlier efforts of the author, noticeably his short tales. . . . After granting something to the untrimmed condition in which the work finds its way to us, I think there is still reason for believing that Hawthorne meant to leave about these figures more tangible vestiges of every-day wear than it had been usual with him to do; and there is enough in what is here given us to show how perfect might have been the union between his smooth refine-ments of style and a treatment of character heartily real in tone. Through the individuals thus brought before us, he has let fall the central radiance of his thought, until each has become a living and illuminated symbol of some one of its various phases. (pp. 459-60)

G. P. Lathrop, "History of Hawthorne's Last Ro-mance," in The Atlantic Monthly, *Vol. XXX, No. CLXXX, October, 1872, pp. 452-60.*

T. W. HIGGINSON   (essay date 1872)

[In *Septimius Felton,* the title character] must go through all the alternations of hope, fear, toil, obstruction, success, im-plied [in his search for immortality]; and as he approaches final triumph, there must come new and profounder alternations of joy and despair. Every fine gradation of infinitely varied feel-ing, by which his strange lot foreshadows itself, must be painted into the canvas; a hundred separate tragedies would be easier to depict than this which combines so many in one. The element of the supernatural must here be projected on a mortal life; the hero is mortal in his ties, immortal in the realization of his dreams. It costs an effort even thus feebly to draw the outline of what such a creation must be. Yet Hawthorne created it. . . .

The manner in which Hawthorne by sheer power of fancy antedates for us the actual experience of [Septimius Felton], and makes his ultimate failure yield to our imagination the same fruit as if the poor fellow had succeeded, seems to me one of the very greatest triumphs in all literature. The romancer has in a manner discounted for us the debt of nature, and whether it is ever actually paid in full, in this particular case, is of no importance. Instead of being "in at the death" we have to all intents and purposes been in at the deathlessness. (p. 102)

Few things in the English language, I fancy, are more subtle and delicate than the analysis of [Septimius Felton]. And with

what unsurpassed fineness of touch is the general regimen laid down, as quoted from the imaginary scroll, for his who would concentrate all his powers on the mere prolongation of life! I know not where to find, since the famous "Indenture" in Goethe's *Wilhelm Meister,* so much profound insight in so few words; and Hawthorne's statement indeed differs from that only as the blade of Saladin from that of Richard. (p. 103)

With easy and unerring delineation, Hawthorne . . . touches the points where selfishness and unselfishness apparently blend into one, so that each may wear the mask of the other. The precise middle ground where angel might meet fiend, and fiend meet angel, and each be bewildered on finding in the other's action some semblance of his own, was never so marked out before. (p. 104)

Painful as may be the theme of this book, I do not see how any one can help dwelling with delight on the fine details of its execution. The annotations and memoranda, made here and there by Hawthorne himself, only add to the interest; it is delightful to have constantly these glimpses at his process, and to see the master's hand not in the architecture alone, but in the fragments of scaffolding that still stand. (pp. 104-05)

For one, I confess to having found in this painful book an irresistible and entangling charm; partly, perhaps, because its strangest scenes are still laid amid the familiar rural scenery of Concorord, but more, no doubt, because it is the last in-tellectual bequest we can hope to receive from its author. No other important fragment of his unpublished literary work is likely to reach our hands; nor is there any quarter whence we can look for any work of kindred quality, within the limits of the English tongue. (p. 105)

T. W. Higginson, "Hawthorne's Last Bequest," in Scribner's Monthly, *Vol. V, No. 1, November, 1872, pp. 100-05.*

ANTHONY TROLLOPE   (essay date 1879)

There never surely was a powerful, active, continually effective mind less round, more lop-sided, than that of Nathaniel Haw-thorne. . . . [From] Hawthorne we could not have obtained that weird, mysterious, thrilling charm with which he has awed and delighted us had he not allowed his mind to revel in one direction, so as to lose its fair proportions.

I have been specially driven to think of this by the strong divergence between Hawthorne and myself. It has always been my object to draw my little pictures as like to life as possible, so that my readers should feel that they were dealing with people whom they might probably have known, but so to do it that the every-day good to be found among them should allure, and the every-day evil repel. . . . Hawthorne, on the other hand, has dealt with persons and incidents which were often but barely within the bounds of possibility,—which were sometimes altogether without those bounds,—and has deter-mined that his readers should be carried out of their own little mundane ways, and brought into a world of imagination in which their intelligence might be raised, if only for a time, to something higher than the common needs of common life. (pp. 204-05)

How was it that [Hawthorne's] mind wandered away always into those fancies, not jocund as are usually those of the tellers of fairy tales, not high-flown as are the pictures generally drawn by the poets, with no fearful adventures though so sad, often by no means beautiful, without an attempt even at the picturesque, melancholy beyond compare, as though the writer had drawn all his experiences from untoward accidents? That some remnant of Puritan asceticism should be found in the writings of a novelist from Concord, in Massachusetts, would seem natural to an English reader,—though I doubt whether there be much of the flavor of the Mayflower left at present to pervade the literary parterres of Boston. (pp. 205-06)

[Hawthorne's] is a mixture of romance and austerity, quite as far removed from the realities of Puritanism as it is from the sentimentalism of poetry. He creates a melancholy which amounts almost to remorse in the minds of his readers. There falls upon them a conviction of some unutterable woe which is not altogether dispelled till other books and other incidents have had their effects. The woe is of course fictitious, and therefore endurable,—and therefore alluring. . . . [In] the world of melancholy romance, of agony more realistic than melancholy, to which Hawthorne brings his readers, there is compensation to the reader in the feeling that, in having submitted himself to such sublime affliction, he has proved himself capable of sublimity. . . . [Hawthorne,] when you have studied him, will be very precious to you. He will have plunged you into melancholy, he will have overshadowed you with black forebodings, he will almost have crushed you with imaginary sorrows; but he will have enabled you to feel yourself an inch taller during the process. (pp. 206-07)

["**The Scarlet Letter**"] is so terrible in its pictures of diseased human nature as to produce most questionable delight. The reader's interest never flags for a moment. There is nothing of episode or digression. The author is always telling his one story with a concentration of energy which, as we can understand, must have made it impossible for him to deviate. The reader will certainly go on with it to the end very quickly, entranced, excited, shuddering, and at times almost wretched. His consolation will be that he too has been able to see into these black deeps of the human heart. (p. 208)

[Hawthorne] has intended that the reader's heart should run over with ruth for the undeserved fate of [the wretched Hester Prynne]. . . . [The] reader's heart glows with a longing to take her soft hand and lead her into some pleasant place where the world shall be pleasant and honest and kind to her. I can fancy a reader so loving the image of Hester Prynne as to find himself on the verge of treachery to the real Hester of flesh and blood who may have a claim upon him. Sympathy can not go beyond that; and yet the author deals with her in a spirit of assumed hardness, almost as though he assented to the judgment and the manner in which it was carried out. In this, however, there is a streak of that satire with which Hawthorne always speaks of the peculiar institutions of his own country. The worthy magistrates of Massachusetts are under his lash throughout the story, and so is the virtue of her citizens and the chastity of her matrons, which can take delight in the open shame of a woman whose sin has been discovered. Indeed, there is never a page written by Hawthorne not tinged by satire. (pp. 210-11)

Hatred, fear, and shame are the passions which revel through the book. To show how a man may so hate as to be content to sacrifice everything to his hatred; how another may fear so that, even though it be for the rescue of his soul, he can not bring himself to face the reproaches of the world; how a woman may bear her load of infamy openly before the eyes of all men,—this has been Hawthorne's object. And surely no author was ever more successful. (p. 211)

But through all this intensity of suffering, through this blackness of narrative, there is ever running a vein of drollery. As Hawthorne himself says, "a lively sense of the humorous again stole in among the solemn phantoms of her thought." He is always laughing at something with his weird, mocking spirit. The very children when they see Hester in the streets are supposed to speak of her in this wise: "Behold, verily, there is the woman of the scarlet letter. Come, therefore, and let us fling mud at her." Of some religious book he says, "It must have been a work of vast ability in the somniferous school of literature." . . . Through it all there is a touch of burlesque,—not as to the suffering of the sufferers, but as to the great question whether it signifies much in what way we suffer, whether by crushing sorrows or little stings. (pp. 212-13)

As a novel "**The House of the Seven Gables**" is very inferior to "**The Scarlet Letter**." . . . [Ideally, a novelist] has characters to draw, lessons to teach, philosophy perhaps which he wishes to expose, satire to express, humor to scatter abroad. These he can employ gracefully and easily if he have a story to tell. If he have none, he must concoct something of a story laboriously. . . . All the good things I have named are there in "**The House of the Seven Gables**"; but they are brought in with less artistic skill, because the author has labored over his plot, and never had it clear to his own mind. (p. 213)

The unraveling of [the mysteries of the house of the seven gables] is vague, and, as I think, inartistic. The reader is not carried on by any intense interest in the story itself, and comes at last not much to care whether he does or does not understand the unraveling. He finds that his interest in the book lies elsewhere,—that he must seek it in the characters, lessons, philosophy, satire, and humor, and not in the plot. (p. 214)

But no one should read "**The House of the Seven Gables**" for the sake of the story. . . . It is for the humor, the satire, and what I may perhaps call the philosophy which permeates it, that its pages should be turned. Its pages may be turned on any day, and under any circumstances. To "**The Scarlet Letter**" you have got to adhere till you have done with it; but you may take this volume by bits, here and there, now and again, just as you like it. There is a description of a few poultry, melancholy, unproductive birds, running over four or five pages, and written as no one but Hawthorne could have written it. There are a dozen pages or more in which the author pretends to ask why the busy Judge does not move from his chair,—the Judge the while having dree'd his doom and died as he sat. There is a ghastly spirit of drollery about this which would put the reader into full communion with Hawthorne if he had not read a page before, and did not intend to read a page after. To those who can make literary food of such passages as these, "**The House of the Seven Gables**" may be recommended. To others it will be caviare. (p. 216)

[The stories in "**Mosses from an Old Manse**"] are, rather than tales, the jottings down of the author's own fancies, on matters which have subjected themselves to his brain, one after the other, in that promiscuous disorder in which his manner of thinking permitted him to indulge. (p. 217)

"**The Procession of Life**" is perhaps the strongest piece in the book,—the one most suggestive and most satisfactory. Hawthorne imagines that, by the blowing of some trumpet such as has never yet been heard, the inhabitants of the world shall be brought together under other circumstances than those which at present combine them. . . . The scope for irony and satire which Hawthorne could get from such a marshaling as this was unbounded. (pp. 218-19)

The great fault of ["**The Marble Faun**"] lies in the absence of arranged plot. The author, in giving the form of a novel to the beautiful pictures and images which his fancy has enabled him to draw, and in describing Rome and Italian scenes as few others have described them, has in fact been too idle to carry out his own purpose of constructing a tale. We will grant that a novelist may be natural or supernatural. Let us grant, for the occasion, that the latter manner, if well handled, is the better and the more efficacious. And we must grant also that he who soars into the supernatural need not bind himself by any of the ordinary trammels of life. . . . But there must be some plot, some arrangement of circumstances, with an intelligible conclusion, or the reader will not be satisfied. . . . [Hawthorne's] readers will hardly be so gentle as not to require from him some explanation of the causes which have produced the romantic details to which they have given their attention, and will be inclined to say that it should have been the author's business to give an explanation neither tedious nor unsatisfactory. The critic is disposed to think that Hawthorne, as he continued his narrative, postponed his plot till it was too late, and then escaped from his difficulty. . . . (pp. 220-21)

In "**The Marble Faun**," as in all Hawthorne's tales written after "**The Scarlet Letter**," the reader must look rather for a series of pictures than for a novel. It would, perhaps, almost be well that a fastidious reader should cease to read when he comes within that border, toward the end, in which it might be natural to expect that the strings of a story should be gathered together and tied into an intelligible knot. This would be peculiarly desirable in regard to "**The Marble Faun**," in which the delight of that fastidious reader, as derived from pictures of character and scenery, will be so extreme that it should not be marred by a sense of failure in other respects.

In speaking of this work in conjunction with Hawthorne's former tales, I should be wrong not to mention the wonderful change which he effected in his own manner of writing when he had traveled out from Massachusetts into Italy. As every word in his earlier volumes savors of New England, so in "**The Marble Faun**" is the flavor entirely that of Rome and of Italian scenery. His receptive imagination took an impress from what was around him, and then gave it forth again with that wonderful power of expression which belonged to him. . . . In Hawthorne's Roman chronicle the tone of the telling is just as natural,—seems to belong as peculiarly to the author,—as it does with "**The Scarlet Letter**" or "**The House of the Seven Gables**." (p. 222)

> Anthony Trollope, "The Genius of Nathaniel Hawthorne," in The North American Review, Vol. CXXIX, No. CCLXXIV, September, 1879, pp. 203-22.

HENRY JAMES, JR. (essay date 1879)

[The] valuable element in [his early tales] was not what Hawthorne put into them consciously, but what passed into them without his being able to measure it—the element of simple genius, the quality of imagination. This is the real charm of Hawthorne's writing—this purity and spontaneity and naturalness of fancy. For the rest, it is interesting to see how it borrowed a particular colour from the other faculties that lay near it—how the imagination, in this capital son of the old Puritans, reflected the hue of the more purely moral part, of the dusky, overshadowed conscience. The conscience, by no fault of its own, in every genuine offshoot of that sombre lineage, lay under the shadow of the sense of *sin*. . . . [Haw-

thorne] had ample cognizance of the Puritan conscience; it was his natural heritage; it was reproduced in him; looking into his soul, he found it there. But his relation to it was only, as one may say, intellectual; it was not moral and theological. He played with it, and used it as a pigment; he treated it, as the metaphysicians say, objectively. He was not discomposed, disturbed, haunted by it, in the manner of its usual and regular victims, who had not the little postern door of fancy to slip through, to the other side of the wall. It was, indeed, to his imaginative vision, the great fact of man's nature; the light element that had been mingled with his own composition always clung to this rugged prominence of moral responsibility, like the mist that hovers about the mountain. . . . [Hawthorne] speaks of the dark disapproval with which his old ancestors, in the case of their coming to life, would see him trifling himself away as a story-teller. But how far more darkly would they have frowned could they have understood that he had converted the very principle of their own being into one of his toys! (pp. 56-8)

[Hawthorne] is no more a pessimist than an optimist, though he is certainly not much of either. He does not pretend to conclude, or to have a philosophy of human nature; indeed, I should even say that at bottom he does not take human nature as hard as he may seem to do. . . . What pleased him in [gloomy] subjects was their picturesqueness, their rich duskiness of colour, their chiaroscuro; but they were not the expression of a hopeless, or even of a predominantly melancholy, feeling about the human soul. Such at least is my own impression. He is to a considerable degree ironical—this is part of his charm—part even, one may say, of his brightness; but he is neither bitter nor cynical—he is rarely even what I should call tragical. There have certainly been story-tellers of a gayer and lighter spirit; there have been observers more humorous, more hilarious—though on the whole Hawthorne's observation has a smile in it oftener than may at first appear; but there has rarely been an observer more serene, less agitated by what he sees and less disposed to call things deeply into question. . . . [Hawthorne's *Note-Books*] are full of this simple and almost childlike serenity. That dusky pre-occupation with the misery of human life and the wickedness of the human heart which [critics speak of] is totally absent from them. . . . (pp. 58-9)

Hawthorne was a man of fancy, and I suppose that, in speaking of him, it is inevitable that we should feel ourselves confronted with the familiar problem of the difference between the fancy and the imagination. Of the larger and more potent faculty he certainly possessed a liberal share; no one can read *The House of the Seven Gables* without feeling it to be a deeply imaginative work. But I am often struck, especially in the shorter tales, of which I am now chiefly speaking, with a kind of small ingenuity, a taste for conceits and analogies, which bears more particularly what is called the fanciful stamp. The finer of the shorter tales are redolent of a rich imagination. (p. 60)

There is imagination in [*Young Goodman Brown*]; but as a general thing I should characterise the more metaphysical of our author's short stories as graceful and felicitous conceits. They seem to me to be qualified in this manner by the very fact that they belong to the province of allegory. Hawthorne, in his metaphysical moods, is nothing if not allegorical, and allegory, to my sense, is quite one of the lighter exercises of the imagination. . . . Certainly, as a general thing, we are struck with the ingenuity and felicity of Hawthorne's analogies and correspondences; the idea appears to have made itself at home in them easily. Nothing could be better in this respect than *The Snow Image* (a little masterpiece), or *The Great Carbuncle*, or *Doctor Heidegger's Experiment*, or *Rappaccini's Daughter*. But in such things as *The Birth-Mark* and *The Bosom-Serpent* we are struck with something stiff and mechanical, slightly incongruous, as if the kernel had not assimilated its envelope. But these are matters of light impression, and there would be a want of tact in pretending to discriminate too closely among things which all, in one way or another, have a charm. The charm—the great charm—is that they are glimpses of a great field, of the whole deep mystery of man's soul and conscience. They are moral, and their interest is moral; they deal with something more than the mere accidents and conventionalities, the surface occurrences of life. The fine thing in Hawthorne is that he cared for the deeper psychology, and that, in his way, he tried to become familiar with it. This natural, yet fanciful, familiarity with it; this air, on the author's part, of being a confirmed *habitué* of a region of mysteries and subtleties, constitutes the originality of his tales. And then they have the further merit of seeming, for what they are, to spring up so freely and lightly. The author has all the ease, indeed, of a regular dweller in the moral, psychological realm; he goes to and fro in it, as a man who knows his way. His tread is a light and modest one, but he keeps the key in his pocket.

His little historical stories all seem to me admirable. . . . [They] are full of a vivid and delightful sense of the New England past; they have, moreover, the distinction, little tales of a dozen and fifteen pages as they are, of being the only successful attempts at historical fiction that have been made in the United States. . . . [Hawthorne's] fancy, which was always alive, played a little with the somewhat meagre and angular facts of the colonial period, and forthwith converted a great many of them into impressive legends and pictures. There is a little infusion of colour, a little vagueness about certain details, but it is very gracefully and discreetly done, and realities are kept in view sufficiently to make us feel that if we are reading romance, it is romance that rather supplements than contradicts history. The early annals of New England were not fertile in legend, but Hawthorne laid his hands upon everything that would serve his purpose, and in two or three cases his version of the story has a great deal of beauty. *The Grey Champion* is a sketch of less than eight pages, but the little figures stand up in the tale as stoutly, at the least, as if they were propped up on half-a-dozen chapters by a dryer annalist. . . . Hawthorne had, as regards the two earlier centuries of New England life, that faculty which is called now-a-days the historic consciousness. He never sought to exhibit it on a large scale; he exhibited it, indeed, on a scale so minute that we must not linger too much upon it. His vision of the past was filled with definite images. . . . (pp. 61-6)

[The sketch *The Custom House* which precedes *The Scarlet Letter*] is, as simple writing, one of the most perfect of Hawthorne's compositions, and one of the most gracefully and humorously autobiographic. (p. 103)

The Scarlet Letter contains little enough of gaiety or of hopefulness. It is densely dark, with a single spot of vivid colour in it; and it will probably long remain the most consistently gloomy of English novels of the first order. [But it is] the author's masterpiece, and I imagine it will continue to be, for other generations than ours, his most substantial title to fame. . . . It is simpler and more complete than his other novels; it achieves more perfectly what it attempts, and it has about it that charm, very hard to express, which we find in an artist's work the first time he has touched his highest mark—a sort of straight-

ness and naturalness of execution, an unconsciousness of his public, and freshness of interest in his theme. (pp. 106-07)

[*The Scarlet Letter*] is beautiful, admirable, extraordinary; it has in the highest degree that merit which [is] the mark of Hawthorne's best things—an indefinable purity and lightness of conception, a quality which in a work of art affects one in the same way as the absence of grossness does in a human being. . . . In spite of the relation between Hester Prynne and Arthur Dimmesdale, no story of love was surely ever less of a "love-story." To Hawthorne's imagination the fact that these two persons had loved each other too well was of an interest comparatively vulgar; what appealed to him was the idea of their moral situation in the long years that were to follow. The story, indeed, is in a secondary degree that of Hester Prynne; she becomes, really, after the first scene, an accessory figure; it is not upon her the *dénoûment* depends. It is upon her guilty lover that the author projects most frequently the cold, thin rays of his fitfully-moving lantern, which makes here and there a little luminous circle, on the edge of which hovers the livid and sinister figure of the injured and retributive husband. The story goes on, for the most part, between the lover and the husband . . .—between this more wretched and pitiable culprit, to whom dishonour would come as a comfort and the pillory as a relief, and the older, keener, wiser man, who, to obtain satisfaction for the wrong he has suffered, devises the infernally ingenious plan of conjoining himself with his wronger. . . . The attitude of Roger Chillingworth, and the means he takes to compensate himself—these are the highly original elements in the situation that Hawthorne so ingeniously treats. None of his works are so impregnated with that after-sense of the old Puritan consciousness of life to which allusion has so often been made. . . . I say this not because the story happens to be of so-called historical cast, to be told of the early days of Massachusetts, and of people in steeple-crowned hats and sad-coloured garments. The historical colouring is rather weak than otherwise; there is little elaboration of detail, of the modern realism of research; and the author has made no great point of causing his figures to speak the English of their period. Nevertheless, the book is full of the moral presence of the race that invented Hester's penance—diluted and complicated with other things, but still perfectly recognisable. Puritanism, in a word, is there, not only objectively, as Hawthorne tried to place it there, but subjectively as well. Not, I mean, in his judgment of his characters in any harshness of prejudice, or in the obtrusion of a moral lesson; but in the very quality of his own vision, in the tone of the picture, in a certain coldness and exclusiveness of treatment.

The faults of the book are, to my sense, a want of reality and an abuse of the fanciful element—of a certain superficial symbolism. The people strike me not as characters, but as representatives, very picturesquely arranged, of a single state of mind; and the interest of the story lies, not in them, but in the situation, which is insistently kept before us, with little progression, though with a great deal, as I have said, of a certain stable variation; and to which they, out of their reality, contribute little that helps it to live and move. (pp. 108-111)

[There is a passionless quality in] Hawthorne's novel, [an] element of cold and ingenious fantasy, its elaborate imaginative delicacy. These things do not precisely constitute a weakness in *The Scarlet Letter;* indeed, in a certain way they constitute a great strength; but the absence of a certain something warm and straightforward, a trifle more grossly human and vulgarly natural . . . will always make Hawthorne's tale less touching to a large number of even very intelligent readers, than a love-story told with the robust, synthetic pathos. . . . [Hawthorne's imagination leads his theme on] such a dance through the moon-lighted air of his intellect that the thing cools off, as it were, hardens and stiffens, and, producing effects much more exquisite, leaves the reader with a sense of having handled a splendid piece of silversmith's work. (pp. 112-13)

In *The Scarlet Letter* there is a great deal of symbolism; there is, I think, too much. It is overdone at times, and becomes mechanical; it ceases to be impressive, and grazes triviality. The idea of the mystic *A* which the young minister finds imprinted upon his breast and eating into his flesh, in sympathy with the embroidered badge that Hester is condemned to wear, appears to me to be a case in point. This suggestion should, I think, have been just made and dropped; to insist upon it and return to it, is to exaggerate the weak side of the subject. Hawthorne returns to it constantly, plays with it, and seems charmed by it; until at last the reader feels tempted to declare that his enjoyment of it is puerile. In the admirable scene, so superbly conceived and beautifully executed, in which Mr. Dimmesdale, in the stillness of the night, [calls Hester and Pearl to come and stand on the scaffold beside him,] . . . the effect is almost spoiled by the introduction of one of these superficial conceits. (pp. 113-14)

[What leads up to it] is imaginative, impressive, poetic; but when, almost immediately afterwards, the author goes on to say that "the minister looking upward to the zenith, beheld there the appearance of an immense letter—the letter *A*—marked out in lines of dull red light," we feel that he goes too far, and is in danger of crossing the line that separates the sublime from its intimate neighbour. We are tempted to say that this is not moral tragedy, but physical comedy. In the same way, too much is made of the intimation that Hester's badge had a scorching property, and that if one touched it one would immediately withdraw one's hand. Hawthorne is perpetually looking for images which shall place themselves in picturesque correspondence with the spiritual facts with which he is concerned, and of course the search is of the very essence of poetry. But in such a process discretion is everything, and when the image become importunate it is in danger of seeming to stand for nothing more serious than itself. . . . Hawthorne devotes a chapter to [the] idea of [Pearl's] having, by putting the brook between Hester and herself, established a kind of spiritual gulf, on the verge of which her little fantastic person innocently mocks at her mother's sense of bereavement. This conception belongs, one would say, quite to the lighter order of a story-teller's devices, and the reader hardly goes with Hawthorne in the large development he gives to it. He hardly goes with him either, I think, in his extreme predilection for a small number of vague ideas which are represented by such terms as "sphere" and "sympathies." Hawthorne makes too liberal a use of these two substantives; it is the solitary defect of his style; and it counts as a defect partly because the words in question are a sort of specialty with certain writers immeasurably inferior to himself.

I had not meant, however, to expatiate upon his defects, which are of the slenderest and most venial kind. *The Scarlet Letter* has the beauty and harmony of all original and complete conceptions, and its weaker spots, whatever they are, are not of its essence; they are mere light flaws and inequalities of surface. One can often return to it; it supports familiarity, and has the inexhaustible charm and mystery of great works of art. It is admirably written. Hawthorne afterwards polished his style to

a still higher degree; but in his later productions—it is almost always the case in a writer's later productions—there is a touch of mannerism. In *The Scarlet Letter* there is a high degree of polish, and at the same time a charming freshness; his phrase is less conscious of itself. (pp. 115-17)

[*The House of the Seven Gables*] is a rich, delightful, imaginative work, larger and more various than its companions, and full of all sorts of deep intentions, of interwoven threads of suggestion. But it is not so rounded and complete as *The Scarlet Letter;* it has always seemed to me more like a prologue to a great novel than a great novel itself. I think this is partly owing to the fact that the subject, the *donnée,* as the French say, of the story, does not quite fill it out, and that we get at the same time an impression of certain complicated purposes on the author's part, which seem to reach beyond it. I call it larger and more various than its companions, and it has, indeed, a greater richness of tone and density of detail. The colour, so to speak, of *The House of the Seven Gables* is admirable. But the story has a sort of expansive quality which never wholly fructifies, and as I lately laid it down, after reading it for the third time, I had a sense of having interested myself in a magnificent fragment. Yet the book has a great fascination. . . . If it be true of the others that the pure, natural quality of the imaginative strain is their great merit, this is at least as true of *The House of the Seven Gables,* the charm of which is in a peculiar degree of the kind that we fail to reduce to its grounds—like that of the sweetness of a piece of music, or the softness of fine September weather. It is vague, indefinable, ineffable; but it is the sort of thing we must always point to in justification of the high claim that we make for Hawthorne. In this case, of course, its vagueness is a drawback, for it is difficult to point to ethereal beauties; and if the reader whom we have wished to inoculate with our admiration inform us, after looking awhile, that he perceives nothing in particular, we can only reply that, in effect, the object is a delicate one.

The House of the Seven Gables comes nearer being a picture of contemporary American life than either of its companions; but on this ground it would be a mistake to make a large claim for it. It cannot be too often repeated that Hawthorne was not a realist. . . . *The House of the Seven Gables* has, however, more literal actuality than the others, and if it were not too fanciful an account of it, I should say that it renders, to an initiated reader, the impression of a summer afternoon in an elm-shadowed New England town. It leaves upon the mind a vague correspondence to some such reminiscence, and in stirring up the association it renders it delightful. . . . But the mild provincial quality is there, the mixture of shabbiness and freshness, the paucity of ingredients. The end of an old race—this is the situation that Hawthorne has depicted, and he has been admirably inspired in the choice of the figures in whom he seeks to interest us. They are all figures rather than characters—they are all pictures rather than persons. But if their reality is light and vague, it is sufficient, and it is in harmony with the low relief and dimness of outline of the objects that surrounded them. They are all types, to the author's mind, of something general, of something that is bound up with the history, at large, of families and individuals, and each of them is the centre of a cluster of those ingenious and meditative musings, rather melancholy, as a general thing, than joyous, which melt into the current and texture of the story and give it a kind of moral richness. . . . The drama is a small one, but as Hawthorne does not put it before us for its own superficial sake, for the dry facts of the case, but for something in it which he holds to be symbolic and of large application, something that points a moral and that it behoves us to remember, the scenes in the rusty wooden house whose gables give its name to the story, have something of the dignity both of history and of tragedy. Miss Hephzibah Pyncheon, dragging out a disappointed life in her paternal dwelling, finds herself obliged in her old age to open a little shop for the sale of penny toys and gingerbread. This is the central incident of the tale, and, as Hawthorne relates it, it is an incident of the most impressive magnitude and most touching interest. . . . [Hephzibah] is exquisite—admirably conceived and executed, with a kind of humorous tenderness, an equal sense of everything in it that is picturesque, touching, ridiculous, worthy of the highest praise. . . . Hephzibah Pyncheon is a masterly picture. I repeat that she is a picture, as her companions are pictures; she is a charming piece of descriptive writing, rather than a dramatic exhibition. But she is described, like her companions, too, so subtly and lovingly that we enter into her virginal old heart and stand with her behind her abominable little counter. Clifford Pyncheon is a still more remarkable conception, though he is, perhaps, not so vividly depicted. It was a figure needing a much more subtle touch, however, and it was of the essence of his character to be vague and unemphasised. Nothing can be more charming than the manner in which the soft, bright, active presence of Phoebe Pyncheon is indicated, or than the account of her relations with the poor, dimly sentient kinsman for whom her light-handed sisterly offices, in the evening of a melancholy life, are a revelation of lost possibilities of happiness. (pp. 119-23)

[Judge Pyncheon] is, in spite of the space he occupies, an accessory figure, and, . . . even more than the others, he is what I have called a picture rather than a character. . . . Judge Pyncheon is an elaborate piece of description, made up of a hundred admirable touches, in which satire is always winged with fancy, and fancy is linked with a deep sense of reality. . . . Holgrave is intended as a contrast; his lack of traditions, his democratic stamp, his condensed experience, are opposed to the desiccated prejudices and exhausted vitality of the race of which poor feebly-scowling, rusty-jointed Hephzibah is the most heroic representative. . . . [Evidently] what Hawthorne designed to represent was not the struggle between an old society and a new, for in this case he would have given the old one a better chance; but simply, as I have said, the shrinkage and extinction of a family. (pp. 124-25)

I will add that Holgrave is one of the few figures, among those which Hawthorne created, with regard to which the absence of the realistic mode of treatment is felt as a loss. Holgrave is not sharply enough characterised; he lacks features; he is not an individual, but a type. But my last word about this admirable novel must not be a restrictive one. It is a large and generous production, pervaded with that vague hum, that indefinable echo, of the whole multitudinous life of man, which is the real sign of a great work of fiction. (p. 126)

[*The Wonder-Book* and *Tanglewood Tales*] are among the most charming literary services that have been rendered to children. . . . Hawthorne's stories are the old Greek myths, made more vivid to the childish imagination by an infusion of details which both deepen and explain their marvels. (pp. 126-27)

I hardly know what to say about [*The Blithedale Romance*], save that it is very charming; this vague, unanalytic epithet is the first that comes to one's pen in treating of Hawthorne's novels, for their extreme amenity of form invariably suggests it; but if, on the one hand, it claims to be uttered, on the other it frankly confesses its inconclusiveness. Perhaps, however, in

this case it fills out the measure of appreciation more completely than in others, for *The Blithedale Romance* is the lightest, the brightest, the liveliest, of this company of unhumorous fictions.

The story is told from a more joyous point of view—from a point of view comparatively humorous—and a number of objects and incidents touched with the light of the profane world—the vulgar, many-coloured world of actuality, as distinguished from the crepuscular realm of the writer's own reveries—are mingled with its course. The book, indeed, is a mixture of elements, and it leaves in the memory an impression analogous to that of an April day—an alternation of brightness and shadow, of broken sun-patches and sprinkling clouds. Its *dénoûment* is tragical—there is, indeed, nothing so tragical in all Hawthorne, unless it be the murder of Miriam's persecutor by Donatello, in *Transformation,* as the suicide of Zenobia; and yet, on the whole, the effect of the novel is to make one think more agreeably of life. The standpoint of the narrator has the advantage of being a concrete one; he is no longer, as in the preceding tales, a disembodied spirit, imprisoned in the haunted chamber of his own contemplations, but a particular man, with a certain human grossness. (pp. 128-29)

[Miles Coverdale is] a portrait of a man, in a word, whose passions are slender, whose imagination is active, and whose happiness lies, not in doing, but in perceiving—half a poet, half a critic, and all a spectator. He is contrasted excellently with the figure of Hollingsworth, the heavily treading Reformer, whose attitude with regard to the world is that of the hammer to the anvil, and who has no patience with his friend's indifferences and neutralities. (p. 129)

The finest thing in *The Blithedale Romance* is the character of Zenobia, which . . . strikes me as the nearest approach that Hawthorne has made to the complete creation of a *person*. She is more concrete than Hester or Miriam, or Hilda or Phoebe; she is a more definite image, produced by a greater multiplicity of touches. . . . [The] picturesqueness of Zenobia is very happily indicated and maintained; she is a woman in all the force of the term, and there is something very vivid and powerful in her large expression of womanly gifts and weaknesses. Hollingsworth is, I think, less successful, though there is much reality in the conception of the type to which he belongs—the strong-willed, narrow-hearted apostle of a special form of redemption for society. (pp. 130-31)

The portion of [*The Blithedale Romance*] that strikes me as least felicitous is that which deals with Priscilla, and with her mysterious relation to Zenobia . . . [and with] her Sibylline attributes, as the author calls them. Hawthorne is rather too fond of Sibylline attributes—a taste of the same order as his disposition, to which I have already alluded, to talk about spheres and sympathies. As the action advances, in *The Blithedale Romance,* we get too much out of reality, and cease to feel beneath our feet the firm ground of an appeal to our own vision of the world—our observation. I should have liked to see the story concern itself more with the little community in which its earlier scenes are laid, and avail itself of so excellent an opportunity for describing unhackneyed specimens of human nature. I have already spoken of the absence of satire in the novel, of its not aiming in the least at satire, and of its offering no grounds for complaint as an invidious picture. Indeed, the brethren of Brook Farm should have held themselves slighted rather than misrepresented, and have regretted that the admirable genius who for a while was numbered among them should have treated their institution mainly as a perch for starting upon an imaginative flight. But when all is said about a certain want of substance and cohesion in the latter portions of *The Blithedale Romance,* the book is still a delightful and beautiful one. Zenobia and Hollingsworth live in the memory; and even Priscilla and Coverdale, who linger there less importunately, have a great deal that touches us and that we believe in. (pp. 132-33)

Life of Franklin Pierce belongs to that class of literature which is known as the "campaign biography," and which consists of an attempt, more or less successful, to persuade the many-headed monster of universal suffrage that the gentleman on whose behalf it is addressed is a paragon of wisdom and virtue. Of Hawthorne's little book there is nothing particular to say, save that it is in very good taste, that he is a very fairly ingenious advocate, and that if he claimed for the future President qualities which rather faded in the bright light of a high office, this defect of proportion was essential to his undertaking. (p. 136)

[Hawthorne's] *Note-Books* are provincial, and so, in a greatly modified degree, are the sketches of England, in *Our Old Home;* but the beauty and delicacy of this latter work are so interwoven with the author's air of being remotely outside of everything he describes, that they count for more, seem more themselves, and finally give the whole thing the appearance of a triumph, not of initiation, but of the provincial point of view itself. (p. 143)

Our Old Home is charming—it is most delectable reading. The execution is singularly perfect and ripe; of all his productions it seems to be the best written. The touch, as musicians say, is admirable; the lightness, the fineness, the felicity of characterisation and description, belong to a man who has the advantage of feeling delicately. His judgment is by no means always sound; it often rests on too narrow an observation. But his perception is of the keenest, and though it is frequently partial, incomplete, it is excellent as far as it goes. The book gave but limited satisfaction, I believe, in England, and I am not sure that the failure to enjoy certain manifestations of its sportive irony has not chilled the appreciation of its singular grace. (pp. 144-45)

[The book] is full of a rich appreciation of the finest characteristics of the country. But it has a serious defect—a defect which impairs its value, though it helps to give consistency to such an image of Hawthorne's personal nature as we may by this time have been able to form. It is the work of an outsider, of a stranger, of a man who remains to the end a mere spectator (something less even than an observer), and always lacks the final initiation into the manners and nature of a people of whom it may most be said, among all the people of the earth, that to know them is to make discoveries. (pp. 146-47)

[*Transformation*] has a great deal of beauty, of interest and grace; but it has, to my sense, a slighter value than its companions, and I am far from regarding it as the masterpiece of the author, a position to which we sometimes hear it assigned. The subject is admirable, and so are many of the details; but the whole thing is less simple and complete than either of the three tales of American life, and Hawthorne forfeited a precious advantage in ceasing to tread his native soil. Half the virtue of *The Scarlet Letter* and *The House of the Seven Gables* is in their local quality; they are impregnated with the New England air. . . . [It may] very well be urged in Hawthorne's favour here, that in *Transformation* he has attempted to deal with actualities more than he did in either of his earlier novels. He has described the streets and monuments of Rome with a close-

ness which forms no part of his reference to those of Boston and Salem. But for all this he incurs that penalty of seeming factitious and unauthoritative, which is always the result of an artist's attempt to project himself into an atmosphere in which he has not a transmitted and inherited property. . . . There is in *Transformation* enough beautiful perception of the interesting character of Rome, enough rich and eloquent expression of it, to save the book, if the book could be saved; but the style, what the French call the *genre,* is an inferior one, and the thing remains a charming romance with intrinsic weaknesses.

Allowing for this, however, some of the finest pages in all Hawthorne are to be found in it. The subject, as I have said, is a particularly happy one, and there is a great deal of interest in the simple combination and opposition of the four actors. It is noticeable that, in spite of the considerable length of the story, there are no accessory figures; Donatello and Miriam, Kenyon and Hilda exclusively occupy the scene. This is the more noticeable as the scene is very large, and the great Roman background is constantly presented to us. The relations of these four people are full of that moral picturesqueness which Hawthorne was always looking for; he found it in perfection in the history of Donatello. . . . Donatello is rather vague and impalpable; he says too little in the book, shows himself too little, and falls short, I think, of being a creation. But he is enough of a creation to make us enter into the situation. . . . Hawthorne has done few things more beautiful than the picture of the unequal complicity of guilt between his immature and dimly-puzzled hero, with his clinging, unquestioning, unexacting devotion, and the dark, powerful, more widely-seeing feminine nature of Miriam. Deeply touching is the representation of the manner in which these two essentially different persons—the woman intelligent, passionate, acquainted with life, and with a tragic element in her own career; the youth ignorant, gentle, unworldly, brightly and harmlessly natural—are equalised and bound together by their common secret, which insulates them, morally, from the rest of mankind. The character of Hilda has always struck me as an admirable invention—one of those things that mark the man of genius. (pp. 160-62)

Like all of Hawthorne's things, [*Transformation*] contains a great many light threads of symbolism, which shimmer in the texture of the tale, but which are apt to break and remain in our fingers if we attempt to handle them. These things are part of Hawthorne's very manner—almost, as one might say, of his vocabulary; they belong much more to the surface of his work than to its stronger interest. The fault of *Transformation* is that the element of the unreal is pushed too far, and that the book is neither positively of one category nor of another. . . . This is the trouble with Donatello himself. His companions are intended to be real—if they fail to be so, it is not for want of intention; whereas he is intended to be real or not, as you please. He is of a different substance from them; it is as if a painter, in composing a picture, should try to give you an impression of one of his figures by a strain of music. The idea of the modern faun was a charming one; but I think it a pity that the author should not have made him more definitely modern, without reverting so much to his mythological properties and antecedents, which are very gracefully touched upon, but which belong to the region of picturesque conceits, much more than to that of real psychology. . . . And since I am speaking critically, I may go on to say that the art of narration, in *Transformation,* seems to me more at fault than in the author's other novels. The story straggles and wanders, is dropped and taken up again, and towards the close lapses into an almost fatal vagueness. (pp. 163-64)

I am at a loss to know how to speak of *Septimius Felton, or the Elixir of Life;* I have purposely reserved but a small space for doing so, for the part of discretion seems to be to pass it by lightly. I differ, therefore, widely from [G. P. Lathrop,] the author's biographer and son-in-law in thinking it a work of the greatest weight and value, offering striking analogies with Goethe's *Faust* [see excerpt above]. . . . It seems to me almost cruel to pitch in this exalted key one's estimate of the rough first draught of a tale in regard to which the author's premature death operates, virtually, as a complete renunciation of pretensions. It is plain to any reader that *Septimius Felton,* as it stands, with its roughness, its gaps, its mere allusiveness and slightness of treatment, gives us but a very partial measure of Hawthorne's full intention; and it is equally easy to believe that this intention was much finer than anything we find in the book. Even if we possessed the novel in its complete form, however, I incline to think that we should regard it as very much the weakest of Hawthorne's productions. The idea itself seems a failure, and the best that might have come of it would have been very much below *The Scarlet Letter* or *The House of the Seven Gables.* . . . The weakness of *Septimius Felton* is that the reader cannot take the hero seriously—a fact of which there can be no better proof than the element of the ridiculous which inevitably mingles itself in the scene in which he entertains his lady-love with a prophetic sketch of his occupations during the successive centuries of his earthly immortality. I suppose the answer to my criticism is, that this is allegorical, symbolic, ideal; but we feel that it symbolises nothing substantial, and that the truth—whatever it may be—that it illustrates is as moonshiny, to use Hawthorne's own expression, as the allegory itself. Another fault of the story is, that a great historical event—the war of the Revolution—is introduced in the first few pages . . . and then drops out of the narrative altogether, not even forming a background to the sequel. It seems to me that Hawthorne should either have invented some other occasion for the death of his young officer, or else, having struck the note of the great public agitation which overhung his little group of characters, have been careful to sound it through the rest of his tale. I do wrong, however, to insist upon these things, for I fall thereby into the error of treating the work as if it had been cast into its ultimate form and acknowledged by the author. To avoid this error, I shall make no other criticism of details, but content myself with saying that the idea and intention of the book appear, relatively speaking, feeble, and that, even had it been finished, it would have occupied a very different place in the public esteem from the writer's masterpieces. (pp. 172-74)

[Hawthorne's] work will remain; it is too original and exquisite to pass away; among the men of imagination he will always have his niche. No one has had just that vision of life, and no one has had a literary form that more successfully expressed his vision. He was not a moralist, and he was not simply a poet. The moralists are weightier, denser, richer, in a sense; the poets are more purely inconclusive and irresponsible. He combined in a singular degree the spontaneity of the imagination with a haunting care for moral problems. Man's conscience was his theme, but he saw it in the light of a creative fancy which added, out of its own substance, an interest, and, I may almost say, an importance. (pp. 176-77)

Henry James, Jr., in his Hawthorne, *Harper & Brothers, Publishers, 1879, 177 p.*

THE ATHENAEUM (essay date 1883)

[It] is impossible to ignore the fact that ['**Dr. Grimshawe's Secret'**] has come into the world in a somewhat questionable shape. . . .

There is no cohesion whatever between the parts, and the second part sometimes becomes absolutely unmeaning. The first part is written in Hawthorne's most careful style, though even there we find much that needs correction and revision. The second part is full of inconsistencies and extravagances. We fail to see the middle of the story, and there is no end at all. (p. 9)

[Much of the first half of '**Dr. Grimshawe's Secret'**] has already appeared in a slightly different form in ['**Septimius Felton'**]. Dr. Grimshawe himself is Dr. Portsoaken again, and "crusty Hannah" is first cousin to Aunt Keziah. The same strange room, hung round with cobwebs, is common to both, and the great spider "Orontes" reappears in a still more terrific form. . . .

The description of the doctor's house with its cobwebs, and the two beautiful children who live with the "grim doctor" and fear nothing, is told in Hawthorne's best way. He plays with his subject, holds it up, turns it round, lets rays of light fall upon it from every side, and, half moralizing, half dreaming, he invests it with that strange interest so peculiarly his own. Though, as we have said, there is a good deal which recalls '**Septimius,**' and though the action of the story moves slowly, the "artistic merit" (as we may learn to call it) is very great. (p. 10)

The smaller inconsistencies—the whole book is full of them—are hardly worth noticing after the inconsistency of the plot itself. What is the meaning of the picture of the man with a noose round his neck? Why did Colcord tell the doctor that he had some papers "still recoverable by search," and a few hours afterwards say, "I have them about my person"? . . . [We] might fill a column with such questions.

However, this incoherency is in one aspect satisfactory, as it seems another warrant for the genuineness of this fragment, or rather these fragments. Hawthorne might hereafter have worked up these rough notes for an English story. Surely no one could deliberately set himself to write for publication such crude nonsense as some of it undoubtedly is. Besides in nearly all we can recognize Hawthorne's touch, and even where that seems occasionally to fail, as in the dull political conversation with the warden, we can still see traces of Hawthorne's thought. Delightful descriptions of scenery, quaint pathetic suggestions, wild imaginings of every kind, lie strewn about; but, without form and void as it now is, no one who respected Hawthorne's memory should have permitted the publication of this book. (pp. 10-11)

"Literature: 'Doctor Grimshawe's Secret: A Romance'," in The Athenaeum, *No. 2880, January 6, 1883, pp. 9-11.*

BLISS PERRY (essay date 1904)

Some ideas committed to [Hawthorne's mind] become refined, over-refined, refined away. Symbolism, always a mode of art congenial to Hawthorne, is sometimes allowed to take the place of expression. The individual loses color and precision of outline, and becomes a mere type. Hawthorne's imagination seldom misled him; it had the inevitableness of genius. But his fancy, playing upon superficial resemblances, sporting with trivial objects, was his besetting weakness as a writer. . . .

To the task of describing the landscape and people most familiar to him, Hawthorne brought an extraordinary veracity, and a hand made deft by years of unwearied exercise. Yet he is equally effective in dealing with the Pilgrims, or the stately days of the Massachusetts Province. He loves, in stories like the *Seven Gables,* to bring the past, gray with legendary mist, into the daylight of the present. Here the foreground and background are perfectly harmonized; the present is significant in proportion as its tones are mellowed and reinforced by the sombre past. Thus Hilda and Kenyon, New Englanders of Hawthorne's day, walk over the bloodstained pavements of old Rome, and the ghostly shadows of the Eternal City are about them as they move. Hawthorne himself considered the *House of the Seven Gables* and the *Marble Faun* his best achievements. They belong to the same type. Time and place and circumstance conformed to his feeling for the Romantic. (p. 203)

[His plots,] various as they are, have the simplicity of true Romance. His most widely read production, [*The Scarlet Letter*], has practically no plot whatever; it is a study of a situation. . . . The action of [Hawthorne's] romances is seldom dramatic, in the strict sense of the word. To dramatize the *Scarlet Letter* is to coarsen it. The deliberate action, the internal moral conflict, the subtle revelation of character, are all suited to the descriptive, not the dramaturgic method. They are in perfect keeping with the tone which Hawthorne instinctively maintained. He placed the persons who were to exemplify his themes now in the present, now in the past, if possible in the half-light of mingled past and present, and out of the simplest, most familiar materials he learned to compose a picture so perfect in detail, so harmonious in key, that even were the theme of slight significance, he would still vindicate his right to a high place among literary artists.

Yet perhaps the most convincing test of Hawthorne's merit is one of the most obvious. Open one of his books anywhere, and read a page aloud. Whatever else there may be, here is style. Hawthorne was once asked the secret of his style. He replied dryly that it was the result of a great deal of practice; that it came from the desire to tell the simple truth as honestly and vividly as he could. . . .

But the facts, as such, were not enough to hold Hawthorne long; he pressed on beyond the fact to the truth behind it. As he developed, he collected certain facts to the neglect of others. He observed, but he also philosophized. If, therefore, the technique of his descriptive work often reminds us of the great realists, the use he makes of his talent as an observer and reporter forbids us to group him with them. He was born with too curious an interest in the unseen world. (p. 204)

[What] a writer this provincial New Englander is! . . . The sentences move in perfect poise. Their ease is perhaps a little self-conscious;—pains have been taken with their dressing,— it is not the careless inevitable grace of Thackeray,—but it is a finished grace of their own. It is a style exquisitely simple, except in those passages where Hawthorne's fancy gets the better of him, and leads him into forced humor, all the worse for its air of cultivated exuberance. Yet even when he sins against simplicity, he is always transparently clear. The certainty of word and phrase, the firmness of outline are marvelous. . . . (pp. 204-05)

[Yet the most marked quality of Hawthorne's style is] its unbroken melody, its verbal richness. Its echoes linger in the ear;

they wake old echoes in the brain. The touch of a few other men may be as perfect, the notes they evoke more brilliant, certainly more gay; but Hawthorne's deep-toned instrument yields harmonies inimitable and unforgettable. The critics who talk of the colorless life of New England and its colorless reflection in literature had better open their Hawthorne once more. His pages are steeped in color. (p. 205)

No one would claim that [Hawthorne's] genius was faultless in all its divinations. Feeble drawing, ineffective symbolism, morbid dallying with mortuary fancies, may indeed be detected in his books. . . . In repeating his Pater Noster, the stress falls upon *Forgive us our trespasses* rather than upon *Thy Kingdom come.*

Yet he believed that the sin and sorrow of humanity, inexplicable as they are, are not to be thought of as if we were apart from God. . . . Hawthorne was no natural lover of darkness, but rather one who yearned for light. The gloom which haunts many of his pages is the long shadow cast by our mortal destiny upon a sensitive soul, conscious of kinship with the erring race of men. The mystery is our mystery, perceived, and not created, by that finely endowed mind and heart. The shadow is our shadow; the gleams of insight, the soft radiance of truth and beauty, are his own. (p. 206)

Bliss Perry, "The Centenary of Hawthorne," in The Atlantic Monthly, *Vol. 94, No. 2, August, 1904, pp. 195-206.*

ARTHUR SYMONS   (essay date 1904)

With Tolstoi, [Hawthorne] is the only novelist of the soul, and he is haunted by what is obscure, dangerous, and on the confines of good and evil; by what is abnormal, indeed, if we are to accept human nature as a thing set within responsible limits, and conscious of social relations. . . . [Finding] the soul, in its essence, so intangible, so mistlike, so unfamiliar with the earth, he lays hold of what to him is the one great reality, sin, in order that he may find out something definite about the soul, in its most active, its most interesting, manifestations. (p. 52)

All Hawthorne's stories are those of persons whom some crime, or misunderstood virtue, or misfortune, has set by themselves, or in a worse companionship of solitude. Hester Prynne "stood apart from moral interests, yet close beside them, like a ghost that revisits the familiar fireside, and can no longer make itself seen or felt." The link between Hester and Arthur Dimmesdale, between Miriam and Donatello, was "the iron link of mutual crime, which neither he nor she could break. Like all other sins, it brought along with it its obligations." Note how curious the obsession by which Hawthorne can express the force of the moral law, the soul's bond with itself, only through the consequences of the breaking of that law! And note, also, with how perfect a sympathy he can render the sensation itself, what is exultant, liberating, in a strong sin, not yet become one's companion and accuser. "For, guilt has its rapture, too. The foremost result of a broken law is ever an ecstatic sense of freedom." (pp. 53-4)

[Hawthorne] is interested only in those beings, of exceptional temperament or destiny, who are alone in the world; and yet what he represents is the necessity and the awfulness, not the pride or the choice, of isolation. . . . His men and women are no egoists, to whom isolation is a delight; they suffer from it, they try in vain to come out of the shadow and sit down with the rest of the world in the sunshine. Something ghostly in their blood sets them wandering among shadows, but they long to be merely human, they would come back if they could, and their tragedy is to find some invisible and impenetrable door shut against them. (p. 55)

[Hawthorne's attitude was] that of a sensitive but morbidly clear-sighted friend, or of a physician, affectionately observant of the disease which he cannot cure. It was his sympathy with the soul that made him so watchful of its uneasy moods, its strange adventures, especially those which remove it furthest from the daylight and perhaps nearest to its true nature and proper abode. (pp. 55-6)

To Hawthorne it was the wonder and the mystery which gave its meaning to life, and to paint life without them was like painting nature without atmosphere. Only, in his endeavour to evoke this atmosphere, he did not always remember that, if it had any meaning at all, it was itself a deeper reality. And so his weakness is seen in a persistent desire to give an air of miracle to ordinary things, which gain nothing by becoming improbable; as in the sentence which describes Hester's return to her cottage, at the end of **"The Scarlet Letter"**: "In all these years it had never once been unlocked; but either she unlocked it, or the decaying wood and iron yielded to her hand, or she glided shadowlike through these impediments—and, at all events, went in." His books are full of this futile buzzing of fancy; and it is not only in the matter of style that he too often substitutes fancy for imagination.

Hawthorne never quite fully realised the distinction between symbol and allegory, or was never long able to resist the allegorising temptation. Many of his shorter stories are frankly allegories, and are among the best of their kind, such as **"Young Goodman Brown,"** or **"The Minister's Black Veil."** But, in all his work, there is an attempt to write two meanings at once, to turn what should be a great spiritual reality into a literal and barren figure of speech. He must always broider a visible badge on every personage: Hester's "A," Miss Hepzibah's scowl, the birthmark, the furry ears of the Faun. In all this there is charm, surprise, ingenuity; but is it quite imagination, which is truth, and not a decoration rather than a symbol? He passes, indeed, continually from one to the other, and is now crude and childish, as in the prattle about the Faun's furry ears, and now subtly creative, as in the figure of the child Pearl, who is in the true sense a living symbol. . . . He has used the belief in witchcraft with admirable effect, the dim mystery which clings about haunted houses, the fantastic gambols of the soul itself, under what seem like the devil's own promptings. But he must direct his imps as if they were marionettes, and, as he lets us see the wires jerking, is often at the pains to destroy his own illusion. (pp. 56-7)

[Hawthorne] is at home in all those cloudy tracts of the soul's regions in which most other novelists go astray; he finds his way there, not by sight, but by feeling, like the blind. He responds to every sensation of the soul; morbidly, as people say: that is, with a consciousness of how little anything else matters.

Yet is there not some astringent quality lacking in Hawthorne, the masculine counterpart of what was sensitively feminine in him? . . . No one has ever rendered subtler sensations with a more delicate precision. . . . Yet there is much in his sentiment and in his reflection which is the more feminine part of sensitiveness, and which is no more than a diluted and prettily coloured commonplace. That geniality of reflection, of which we find so much in **"The House of the Seven Gables,"** is really

a lack of intellectual backbone, a way of disguising any too austere truth from his sensibilities. The two chapters, in that often beautiful and delightful book, written around Judge Pyncheon, as he sits dead in his chair, show how lamentable a gap existed in the intellectual taste of Hawthorne. (pp. 57-8)

His style, at its best so delicately woven, so subdued and harmonious in colour, has gone threadbare in patches; something in its gentlemanly ease has become old-fashioned, has become genteel. There are moments when he reminds us of Charles Lamb, but in Lamb nothing has faded, or at most a few too insistent pleasantries: the salt in the style has preserved it. There is no salt in the style of Hawthorne. Read that charming preface to the **"Mosses from an Old Manse,"** so full of country quiet, with a music in it like the gentle, monotonous murmur of a country stream. Well, at every few pages the amateur peeps out, anxiously trying to knit together his straying substance with a kind of arch simplicity. In the stories, there is rarely a narrative which has not drifted somewhere a little out of his control; and of the novels, only **"The Scarlet Letter"** has any sort of firmness of texture; and we have only to set it beside a really well-constructed novel, beside "Madame Bovary," for instance, to see how loosely, after all, it is woven. . . . [Hawthorne seems incapable of looking at things] without thinking of something else, some fancy or moral, which he must fit into the frame or the cube, or else drape around it, in the form of a veil meant for ornament. Yet, in all this, and sometimes by a felicity in some actual weakness, turned, like a woman's, into a fragile and pathetic grace, there is a continual weaving of intricate mental cobwebs, and an actual creation of that dim and luminous atmosphere in which they are best seen. And, in the end, all that is finest in Hawthorne seems to unite in the creation of atmosphere. (pp. 59-60)

Something unsubstantial, evasive, but also something intellectually dissatisfied, always inquiring, in his mind, set Hawthorne spinning [his] arabesques of the soul, in which the fantastic element may be taken as a note of interrogation. Seeing always "a grim identity between gay things and sorrowful ones," he sets a masquerade before us, telling us many of the secrets hidden behind the black velvet, but letting us see no more than the glimmer of eyes, and the silent or ambiguous lips.

Hawthorne's romances are not exactly (he never wished them to be) novels, but they are very nearly poems. And they are made, for the most part, out of material which seems to lend itself singularly ill to poetic treatment. In the preface to **"Transformation"** he says: "No author, without a trial, can be conscious of the difficulty of writing a romance about a country where there is no shadow, no antiquity, no mystery, no picturesque and gloomy wrong." Yet this shadow, this antiquity, this mystery, this picturesque and gloomy wrong, is what he has found or created in America. . . . [Each of his novels] is not so much a narrative which advances, as a canvas which is covered; or, in his own figure, a tapestry "into which are woven some airy and unsubstantial threads, intermixed with others twisted out of the commonest stuff of human existence." A Puritan in fancy dress, he himself passes silently through the masquerade, as it startles some quiet street in New England. Where what is fantastic in Poe remains geometrical, in Hawthorne it is always, for good and evil, moral. It decorates, sometimes plays pranks with, a fixed belief, a fundamental religious seriousness; and has thus at least an immovable centre to whirl from. And, where fancy passes into imagination, and a world, not quite what seems to us the real world, grows up about us with a new, mental kind of reality, it is as if that arrangement or transposition of actual things with which poetry begins had taken place already. I do not know any novelist who has brought into prose fiction so much of the atmosphere of poetry, with so much of the actual art of composition of the poet. It is a kind of poetry singularly pure, delicate, and subtle, and, at its best, it has an almost incalculable fascination, and some not quite realised, but insensibly compelling, white magic. (pp. 60-2)

Arthur Symons, "Nathaniel Hawthorne," in his Studies in Prose and Verse, E. P. Dutton & Co., 1904 (and reprinted by E. P. Dutton & Co., 1922), pp. 52-62.

PAUL ELMER MORE   (essay date 1905)

When, with the coming of the nineteenth century, the fierce democracy of those Northern States asserted itself against priestly control and at the same time shook off the bondage of orthodoxy, it only moved the burden from one shoulder to the other, and the inner tyranny of conscience became as exacting as the authority of the Church had been. But this shifting of the centre of authority from without to within was at least fruitful in one important respect: it brought about that further transition from the conscience to the imagination which made possible the only serious literature this country has yet produced. In that shift from the conscience to the imagination lies the very source of Hawthorne's art. The awful voice of the old faith still reverberates in his stories of New England life and gives them their depth of consciousness; the dissolution of the commands of a sectarian conscience into the forms of a subtle symbolism lifts them from provincial importance merely to the sphere of universal art. (p. 129)

[Ethan Brand stands at the center of the circle of Hawthorne's works.] So manifestly do the doctrines of Cotton Mather stalk through that tale under the transparent mask of fiction that it might almost seem as if Hawthorne had taken . . . [passages from Mather's] Magnolia as a text for his fancy. . . . [We] have Ethan Brand, the lime-burner, dwelling in the fragrant solitude of the mountains, watching his kiln through the long revolutions of the sun and the stars, perplexing his mind with no problem of predestination and free-will, but with the meaning of life itself, with its tangle of motives and restraining intelligence. . . . [In] place of remorse over one act of surrender to impulse against the arbitrary dictates of religion, we have a strange reversal of Puritan faith through the lens of the imagination. Ethan Brand returns to his long-abandoned lime-kiln after wandering over the world, bringing with him the sense that he has sought and found at last in his own heart the Unpardonable Sin, the sin of banishing from the breast all those natural, spontaneous emotions in the pursuit of an idea. He bears the mark, not of an artificial atheism, like that which abased the soul of the young divine, but of that ananthropism (if I may use the word) which was the real sin of New England, symbolised by the strange nature of his successful search. "He had lost his hold of the magnetic chain of humanity. He was no longer a brotherman, opening the chambers or the dungeons of our common nature by the key of holy sympathy, which gave him a right to share in all its secrets; he was now a cold observer, looking on mankind as the subject of his experiment." There lies the tragedy not of Ethan Brand alone, but of the later New England. The dogmas of faith had passed away and left this loneliness of an unmeaning idealism; the enthusiasm which had trampled on the kindly emotions of the day has succumbed, and the comtempt of the human heart has given place to this intolerable loneliness.

And last of all there is the "splenetic malady," the melancholy that pursues this thwarting of nature and drives the wanderer to lay violent hands on himself. The burning of Ethan Brand in the lime-kiln, within the circle of whose crimson light he had pondered the Unpardonable Sin, is not, in the sense of Cotton Mather, one of the unsearchable judgments of God, but a cunningly devised symbol of literary art.

This is the second act of the New England drama: [from the religious intolerance of Cotton Mather to the imaginative isolation of Hawthorne.] . . . The great preacher sought to suppress all worldly emotions; the artist made of the solitude which follows this suppression one of the tragic symbols of human destiny. . . . (pp. 129-31)

The tragedy of New England came when Hawthorne wrought the self-denial of the ancient religion into a symbol of man's universal isolation, when out of the deliberate contemning of common affections he created the search for the Unpardonable Sin. (p. 133)

Paul Elmer More, "Hawthorne: Looking Before and After," in his Shelburne Essays, Second Series, Houghton Mifflin Company, 1905 (and reprinted in his Shelburne Essays on American Literature, edited by Daniel Aaron, Harcourt Brace Jovanovich Inc., 1963, pp. 126-35).

W. C. BROWNELL   (essay date 1909)

[Hawthorne's works] are thoroughly original, quite without literary derivation upon which much of our literature leans with such deferential complacence. Even the theme of many of them—the romance of Puritan New England—was Hawthorne's discovery. They are works of pure literature and therefore in a field where competition is not numerous. They altogether eschew the ordinary, the literal, and they have the element of spiritual distinction, which still further narrows their eminence and gives them still greater relief. Withal they are extremely characteristic, extremely personal. They represent, only and all, their author and no one but their author. . . . (pp. 63-4)

A recluse in life, [Hawthorne] overflows to the reader. He does not tell very much, but apparently he tells everything. His confidences are not ample. Nothing is ample in his writings but the plethora of detail and the fulness of fancies. But he has no reticences. If he communicates little, he has nothing to conceal. (p. 66)

[Hawthorne thought his status of recluse] the most material fact about both him and his work, as is plain from his calling his reserve "unconquerable." So that it is impossible to share his uncertainty as to whether the tameness of his touches proceeds from this reserve or from lack of power. The answer clearly is: both. And to go a step further, and as I say to the root of the matter, his unconquerable reserve proceeds in all probability from his lack of power—at least of anything like sustained, unintermittent power that can be relied upon and evoked at will by its possessor.

Power at all events is precisely the element most conspicuously lacking in the normal working of this imagination. . . . Repeatedly he seems to be on the point of exhibiting power, of moving us, that is to say; but, except, I think, in "The Scarlet Letter," he never quite does so. His unconquerable reserve steps in and turns him aside. He never crosses the line, never makes the attempt. He is too fastidious to attempt vigor and fail. . . . [Hawthorne] follows his temperamental bent with tranquil docility instead of compelling it to serve him in the construction of some fabric of importance. The latter business demands energy and effort. And if he made so little effort it is undoubtedly because he had so little energy. His genius was a reflective one. . . . Reality repelled him. What attracted him was mirage. Mirage is his specific aim, the explicit goal of his art—which thus becomes inevitably rather artistry than art. His practice is sustained by his theory. Speaking of a scene mirrored in a river he exclaims, "Which, after all, was the most real—the picture or the original?—the objects palpable to our grosser senses, or their apotheosis in the stream beneath? Surely the disembodied images stand in closer relation to the soul." . . . [Hawthorne preferred] the vague and the undefined in nature itself as nearer to the soul of the poet. Nearer to the soul of the poet it may be, not to that of the artist. The most idealizing artist can count on enough vagueness of his own—whether it handicap his effort or illumine his result in dealing with his material. And it is not near to the soul of the poet endowed with the architectonic faculty—the poet in the Greek sense, the maker. It is the congenial content of contemplation indeterminate and undirected. (pp. 69-71)

In general, one imagines [Hawthorne] did not have to set fancy resolutely to work, but merely to give it free play. The result was amazingly productive. How many **"Mosses"** and **"Twice-Told Tales"** are there? Certainly a prodigious number when one considers the narrowness of their range and their extraordinary variety within it. Their quality is singularly even, I think. Some of them—a few—are better than others, but mainly in more successfully illustrating their common quality. What this is Hawthorne himself sufficiently indicates in saying, "Instead of passion there is sentiment; and even in what purport to be pictures of actual life we have allegory." (p. 72)

Sentiment replaces passion, it is true. But the sentiment is pale for sentiment. It is sentiment insufficiently *senti*. Allegory, it is true, replaces reality, but the allegory itself is insufficiently real. The tales are not merely in a less effective, less robust, less substantial category than that which includes passion and actual life, but within their own category they are—most of them—unaccented and inconclusive. They are too faint in color and too frail in construction quite to merit the inference of Hawthorne's pretty deprecation. . . . There is not a shiver in them. Their tone is lukewarm and their temper Laodicean. Witchery is precisely the quality they suggest but do not possess. Their atmosphere is not that of the clear brown twilight in which familiar objects are poetized, but that of the gray day in which they acquire monotone. The twilight and moonlight, so often figuratively ascribed to Hawthorne's genius, are in fact a superstition. There is nothing eerie or elfin about his genius. He is too much the master of it and directs it with a too voluntary control. . . . There is no greater sanity to be met with in literature than Hawthorne's. The wholesome constitution of his mind is inveterate and presides with unintermittent constancy in his prose. Now caprice, conducted by reason, infallibly incurs the peril of insipidity, and it is not to be denied that many of the tales settle comfortably into the category of the prosaic. (pp. 73-4)

[Hawthorne's tales] won and have kept their classic position, it is not to be doubted, because of their originality, their refinement, and their elevation. There is certainly nothing else like them; their taste is perfect; and, in general, they deal with some phase of the soul, some aspect or quality or transaction of the spiritual life. . . . [Their] informing purpose lies quite outside the material world and its sublunary phenomena. No small portion of their originality consists, indeed, in the association of their refinement and elevation with what we can now see is their mediocrity. Elsewhere in the world of fiction mediocrity is associated with anything but fineness of fibre and spirituality. The novelty of the combination in Hawthorne's case was disconcerting, and it is small wonder that for a time at least . . . the importance of the **"Twice-Told Tales"** and the **"Mosses"** was argued from their distinction. Finally, some of them—too few assuredly—are good stories.

The rest are sterilized by the evil eye of Allegory. . . . [Allegory] is art only when its representation is as imaginatively real as its meaning. The mass of allegory—allegory strictly devoted to exposition and dependent upon exegesis, allegory explicitly so called—is only incidentally art at all.

Hawthorne's is of this order. His subject is always something other than its substance. Everything means something else. Dealing with the outer world solely for the sake of the inner, he is careless of its character and often loses its significance in mere suggestiveness. His meaning is the burden of his story, not the automatic moral complement of its vivid and actual reality. (pp. 74-7)

[Hawthorne's] faculty of discovering morals on which tales could be framed is prodigious. . . . It is, as one may say, a by-product of the Puritan preoccupation. He did not find sermons in stones. He had the sermons already; his task was to find the stones to fit them. And these his fancy furnished him with a fertility paralleling his use for them. But his interest in shaping these was concentrated on their illustrative and not on their real qualities. Instead of realizing vividly and presenting concretely the elements of his allegory, he contented himself with their plausibility as symbols. (pp. 78-9)

[Hawthorne] was, in fact, allegory-mad. Allegory was his obsession. Consequently, he not only fails to handle the form in the minimizing manner of the masters, but often fails in effectiveness on the lower plane where the moral occupies the foreground. **"The Birthmark"** is an instance. Nothing could be finer than the moral of this tale. . . . But it is a moral even more obscurely brought out than it is fantastically symbolized. In the same way, the moral of **"Rappaccini's Daughter,"** distinctly the richest and warmest of Hawthorne's productions, is still less effectively enforced. It is quite lost sight of in the development of the narrative, which is given an importance altogether disproportionate to the moral, and which yet is altogether dependent upon the moral for significance—sustained as it is, and attractive, as it might have been, had it been taken as a fairy tale frankly from the first. . . .

[The] tales in which he leaves [allegory] alone altogether or at all events does not lean upon it, are the best, I think. His excellent faculty is released for freer play in such tales as **"The Gentle Boy,"** in which if he is less original, he is more human, and takes his place and holds his own in the lists of literature—instead of standing apart in the brown twilight and indulging his fancy in framing insubstantial fictions for the illustration of moral truths. . . . (p. 81)

[The] real misfortune of Hawthorne—and ours—was the misconception of his talent, resulting in this cultivation of his fancy to the neglect of his imagination. (p. 82)

I do not suppose anything could have been made of **"Septimius Felton, or the Elixir of Life"** in any case, except under the happiest circumstances and with the nicest art. But it is a capital instance of what Hawthorne's fancy can do with a theme of some suggestiveness in the way of emptying it of all significance. . . . [Its] profound and sombre power resides in its appalling reality. *This* is what a draught of the Elixir of Life would produce if the puerile decoction over which Septimius Felton labors through so many wearisome pages had crowned his hopes—this, and not the insipid experiences foreshadowed in the vaporings of his infatuated fancy.

But "Septimius Felton" is a posthumous production and one of Hawthorne's failures. Consider a work of far more serious ambition if not in all respects of more representative character—"The Marble Faun." There is the same *kind* of ineffectiveness and for the same reason, the frivolity of fancy. The theme of "The Marble Faun," the irretrievableness of evil conjoined with its curious transforming power—the theme in short of that profoundly imaginative masterpiece, the myth of the Fall of Man—is rather stated than exemplified in the story, overlaid as this is with its reticulation of fantastic unreality. Its elaboration, its art, tends to enfeeble its conception; its substance extenuates its subject. . . . Probably its admirers considered that the treatment poetized the moral. That is clearly the author's intention. But a truth is not poetized by being devitalized. . . . The lack of construction, of orderly evolution, in the book is an obvious misfortune and shows very clearly Hawthorne's artistic weakness, whatever his poetic force. But its essential defect is its lack of the sense of reality, to secure which is the function of the imagination, and through which alone the truth of the fundamental conception can flower into effective exposition. (pp. 85-7)

[However Hawthorne's] divorce from reality and consecration to the fanciful may have succeeded in giving him a unique position and demonstrating his originality . . . there is one vital respect, at all events, in which he almost drops out of the novelist's category. . . . [A Hawthorne character] has not enough features for an individual and he has not enough representative traits for a type. His creator evokes him in pseudo-Frankenstein fashion for some purpose, symbolical, allegorical, or otherwise illustrative, and has no concern for his character, apart from this function of it, either for its typical value or its individual interest. . . . Consequently his dramas have the air of being conducted by marionettes. This is less important in the short stories, of course. It may be said that of such a character as the minister in "The Black Veil" the reader needs to be told nothing, that his character is easily inferred and, anyhow, is not the point, that the point is his wearing the veil and thereby presenting a rueful picture illustrative of our uncleansed condition from secret faults. In that case the idea is enough, and a hortatory paragraph would have sufficed for it. And in any case it is easy to see how immensely the idea would have gained in effectiveness, in cogency, if the minister had been characterized into reality. . . . (pp. 89-91)

[Hawthorne's] characters, indeed, are not creations, but expedients. Roger Chillingworth is an expedient—and as such the only flaw in "The Scarlet Letter," whose impressive theme absorbed its author out of abstractions, . . . except in the case of Chillingworth, to create the only real people of his imaginary world. In creating Dimmesdale and Hester—and I am quite sure Pearl, also—Nature herself, as Arnold says of Wordsworth, "seems to take the pen out of his hand and write for him." (pp. 91-2)

[Hawthorne's novels elude reality] not only in their personages but in their picture of life in general. "The Scarlet Letter" itself is the postlude of a passion. Just so much of the general Salem scene as is necessary for the setting of the extremely concentrated drama is presented and no more. Nowhere else is the scene treated otherwise than atmospherically, so to speak. It does not constitute a medium or even background, but penumbra. The social picture does not exist. The quiet Salem streets of "The House of the Seven Gables," the community life of Blithedale, the village houses and hillocks and gossip and happenings of "Septimius Felton," though the War of Independence is in progress and Concord fight is actually an incident, contribute color, not substance, to the story. (p. 93)

The incompleteness of Hawthorne's characters, the inadequacy of his social picture, the lack of romantic richness in his work, have, to be sure, been attributed largely to the romantic poverty of his material—his environment. (p. 95)

[One] may well doubt if Ibsen . . . would ever have suggested Shakespeare, even to the order of appreciation to which he does suggest Shakespeare, if he had had to deal with a world remotely approaching Shakespeare's in richness of material. But as to Hawthorne there is no possible question. His environment furnished him material exactly, exquisitely, suited to his genius. His subject was the soul, and for the enactment of the dramas of the soul Salem was as apt a stage as Thebes. . . . "The Scarlet Letter" is so exclusively a drama of the soul as to be measurably independent of an elaborate setting in a social picture. But if Hawthorne's other works were as well placed, as firmly established, as deeply rooted in their environment, they would be works of very different value. That they are not is not the fault of their *milieu,* but of their author. (p. 97)

Hawthorne's style, doubtless less original than his substance, is nevertheless indubitably his own. . . . It is, to begin with, difficult to define, and its lack of positive qualities quite exactly parallels the insubstantiality of its subject-matter. Only by a miracle, one reflects, could subject-matter of much vital importance be thus habited—so plainly, placidly, unpretendingly presented, though in such an exceptional instance as "The Scarlet Letter" the latent intensity of the theme is doubtless set off by the sobriety of its garb, to which also it gives a deepened tone. But the harmonious, rather than contrasting, services of such a style as Hawthorne's in general, could be useful only for the direct expression of something bordering on informing insipidity. It is above all a neat style. It wears no gewgaws of rhetoric and owes little or nothing to the figures of speech. . . . Nothing shows more clearly the dilettante character of Hawthorne's exercise of his fancy than this neatness, which is never discomposed by fervor or thrown into disarray by heat.

It is in fact the antithesis of heat, and the absence of heat in Hawthorne's genius appears nowhere so markedly as in his style. His writings from beginning to end do not contain an ardent, or even a fervent passage. They are as empty of exaltation as of exhilaration. (pp. 123-25)

[Hawthorne] writes as the scribes, and lacks the conviction, the assurance of his vocation, the authentic literary and artistic commission for exclamation or utterance with any fire or particular fervor. It is simply extraordinary that so voluminous a writer should care so little for writing as an art of effective expression, should practise it so exclusively as an exercise—as mere record and statement. (p. 126)

[But Hawthorne's style] has the great merit of ease, conjoined with exactness. One without the other is not uncommon, but the combination is rare. The kind of care that goes with deliberateness he undoubtedly took, though he certainly took none that demanded strenuous and scrupulous effort, or his result would have been more distinguished instead of being purely satisfactory. . . . [Hawthorne's] style has in some degree the classic note. . . . And though often as familiar in tone as it is simple in diction its smoothness never lacks dignity and often attains grace. Why has it not in greater degree the truly classic note? Why is it that after all—perfectly adapted as it is to the expression of its substance, to the purpose of its author —it lacks quality and physiognomy? Or at all events why is its quality not more marked, more salient? Because it *is* such an adequate medium for its content, for the expression of a nature without enthusiasm, a mind unenriched by acquisition and an imagination that is in general the prey of fancy rather than the servant of the will. Hawthorne should have taken himself more seriously at the outset—in his formative period—and less so in the maturity of powers whose development would have produced far more important results than those achieved by their leisurely exercise in tranquil neglect of their evolution. (pp. 129-30)

> W. C. Brownell, "Hawthorne," in his American Prose Masters *(copyright 1909 Charles Scribner's Sons; copyright renewed 1937 by Gertrude Hall Brownell; reprinted with the permission of Charles Scribner's Sons), Charles Scribner's Sons, 1909, pp. 63-130.*

LESLIE STEPHEN   (essay date 1909)

No modern writer has [Hawthorne's skill in so] using the marvellous as to interest without unduly exciting our incredulity. He makes, indeed, no positive demands on our credulity. The strange influences which are suggested rather than obtruded upon us are kept in the background, so as not to invite, nor indeed to render possible, the application of scientific tests. We may compare him [to Charlotte] Brontë, who introduces, in "Villette," a haunted garden. She shows us a ghost who is for a moment a very terrible spectre indeed, and then, very much to our annoyance, rationalises him into a flesh-and-blood lover. Hawthorne would neither have allowed the ghost to intrude so forcibly, nor have expelled him so decisively. The garden in his hands would have been haunted by a shadowy terror of which we could render no precise account to ourselves. . . . His ghosts are confined to their proper sphere, the twilight of the mind, and never venture into the broad glare of daylight. We can see them so long as we do not gaze directly at them; when we turn to examine them they are gone, and we are left in doubt whether they were realities or an ocular delusion generated in our fancy by some accidental collocation of half-seen objects. So in the **"House of the Seven Gables"** we may hold what opinion we please as to the reality of the curse which hangs over the Pyncheons and the strange connection between them and their hereditary antagonists; in the **"Scarlet Letter"** we may, if we like, hold that there was really more truth in the witch legends which colour the imaginations of the actors than we are apt to dream of in our philosophy; and in **"Transformation"** we are left finally in doubt as to the great question of Donatello's ears, and the mysterious influence which he retains over the animal world so long as he is unstained by bloodshed. In **"Septimius"** alone, it seems to me that the supernatural is left in rather too obtrusive a shape in spite of the final explanations; though it might possibly have been toned down had the story received the last touches of the author. The artifice, if so it may be called, by which this is effected . . . sounds, like other things, tolerably easy when it

is explained; and yet the difficulty is enormous, as may appear on reflection as well as from the extreme rarity of any satisfactory work in the same style by other artists. With the exception of a touch or two in Scott's stories, such as the impressive Bodach Glas, in "Waverley," and the apparition in the exquisite "Bride of Lammermoor," it would be difficult to discover any parallel.

In fact Hawthorne was able to tread in that magic circle only by an exquisite refinement of taste, and by a delicate sense of humour, which is the best preservative against all extravagance. Both qualities combine in that tender delineation of character which is, after all, one of his greatest charms. His Puritan blood shows itself in sympathy, not with the stern side of the ancestral creed, but with the feebler characters upon whom it weighed as an oppressive terror. He resembles, in some degree, poor Clifford Pyncheon, whose love of the beautiful makes him suffer under the stronger will of his relatives and the prim stiffness of their home. He exhibits the suffering of such a character all the more effectively because, with his kindly compassion there is mixed a delicate flavour of irony. The more tragic scenes affect us, perhaps, with less sense of power; the playful, though melancholy, fancy seems to be less at home when the more powerful emotions are to be excited; and yet once, at least, he draws one of those pictures which engrave themselves instantaneously on the memory. The grimmest or most passionate of writers could hardly have improved the scene where the body of the magnificent Zenobia is discovered in the river. Every touch goes straight to the mark. (pp. 182-84)

> Leslie Stephen, "Nathaniel Hawthorne" *(originally published in a different form in* The Cornhill Magazine, *Vol. XXVI, No. 156, December, 1872), in his* Hours in a Library, *Smith, Elder & Co., 1909, pp. 158-85.*

FRED LEWIS PATTEE   (essay date 1923)

Hawthorne wrote in the period when American authors tended toward the grandiose in style and diction. The writer of romance, as none better than he understood, galloped constantly on the brink of absurdity, and most of the American writers fell hopelessly over, but *Twice-Told Tales* and the others which followed it are never extravagant, never ornamented for the sake of ornament, never, even when viewed in the cold light of to-day, ridiculous. They were uninfluenced by the popular material by which they were surrounded. Many of them were written while the Dickens wave was sweeping over English fiction, but there is no slightest trace of Dickens in Hawthorne. So far as style is concerned his tales might have been written in the eighteenth century. His was a style that had been molded by an early knowledge of Greek and Latin classics, of the English Bible, which seems to have been read aloud daily in the Hawthorne home, and of the early English masterpieces brooded over for years in solitude. It is a classical style: finished yet seemingly spontaneous; artistic, yet simple even to childlikeness.

Poe in 1847 professed to have found the secret of Hawthorne in Tieck [see excerpt above]. . . .

One may indeed "liken" Hawthorne's work to Tieck's and even to Töpffer's, but it is doubtful if one may go much farther. Certainly one finds in him Tieck's brooding, poetic fancy, his tendency at times to symbolism and allegory, and his conception of romantic art as the ability to "lull the reader into a dreamy mood.'' Both, moreover, handled the *Mährchen*, or legendary tale, in the poetic manner and both in some instances made use of the same materials. (p. 105)

The likeness between [Hawthorne and Tieck] came from similarity of soul and from the fact that both were working in an atmosphere charged with the German romantic spirit. Like his own artist in **"Prophetic Pictures,"** Hawthorne worked not in life, but in an idealization of life. ''A subdued tinge of the wild and wonderful is thrown over a sketch of New England personages and scenery, yet . . . without entirely obliterating the sober hues of nature.'' It is the very essence of the later romanticism and both romancers made full use of it, Tieck often with wild abandon, Hawthorne always sanely and with due reverence for the essential Puritan foundations from which his feet never wandered. (pp. 106-07)

[Hawthorne] wrote to please himself, using for models, if he used any at all, the older classics, the dramas of Shakespeare, and the English novel which, according to his sister's testimony, he had studied for its technique. As a result his tales, from the standpoint of form, show surprising merits and, on the other hand, equally surprising defects. . . . It is not hard now, in the light of modern rules, to point out Hawthorne's failures: his leisurely, expository openings; his frequent discursiveness; his characters which for the most part are as abstract and bloodless as Spenser's creations; his distance from the warm currents of actual life; his moralizing endings. But these defects, serious as some of them may be, are overbalanced by equally important excellencies, even in technique, for if we are to judge him by his work, by a dozen or more tales universally admitted now to be masterpieces, tales like **"Rappaccini's Daughter," "The Birthmark," "The Great Stone Face," "The Wives of the Dead," "The Great Carbuncle," "The White Old Maid," "The Minister's Black Veil," "Ethan Brand,"** the four **"Legends of the Province House," "The Snow Image,"** and a few others, we shall find that even in the matter of form Hawthorne was a pioneer, in advance of all his contemporaries save Poe.

He conceived of his tales in terms of culminating action; there is always a dramatic moment for which everything before has been a preparation. (pp. 107-08)

Perhaps his emphasis of a single climactic moment rather than of a growing series of happenings in chronicle form came from the sermonic habit, which, like every other indigenous New Englander, he had inherited from his Puritan ancestors. His tales came to him as texts to be illustrated and driven home. (p. 108)

In the second place, Hawthorne had a keen eye for situation. Here again was he a pioneer, the first prominent writer whose tales may be defined in terms of situation. So far as I have been able to find, the first to perceive and record this fact was the English *National Review* in 1861:

> All his tales embody single ideal situations, scarcely ever for a moment varied in their course. . . . His longer works are ideal situations expanded by minute study and trains of closely related thought into the dimensions of novels. . . . He prefers to assume the crisis past and to determine as fully as he can the ideal situation to which it has given rise when it is beginning to assume more of a chronic character. ´

No one has expressed more clearly than this what Hawthorne really added to the short story. If it be true—and no one has disputed it—then the author of the *Twice-Told Tales* rather than Poe stands as the father of the American short story. At least he was the first to direct it into its modern form.

Hawthorne was the first in America to touch the new romanticism with morals, at least the first to touch it in the department of its fiction. His situations are almost invariably moral culminations, and for presenting them he had several devices. Often he sought for a symbol that would grip and shake the reader's imagination. . . . Sometimes the situation is presented in order to study the psychological reactions of the victim and to probe into the depths of personality, as in **"Wakefield."** Most often of all, the situation is presented in order to point out a fundamental characteristic or a subtle besetting sin of humanity. . . . If each of his tales were cut to bare single-sentence texts, as their severe unity renders it possible to do, as, for example:

> In every heart there is secret sin, and sad mysteries which we hide from our nearest and dearest, and would feign conceal from our own consciousness.—**"The Minister's Black Veil"**;

> Does it not argue a superintending Providence that, while viewless and unexpected events thrust themselves continually athwart our path, there should still be regularity enough in mortal life to render foresight even partially available?—**"David Swan"**; . . .

if all his tales were so reduced and the resulting texts were gathered into a chapter, it would be a fairly complete summary of the best elements of his philosophy. His stories, the best of them, are, therefore, sermons, each with a text to which its author rigidly adheres, made vivid by a single illustration dwelt upon lingeringly, presented from new angles again and again until it becomes a haunting presence that lays its hands upon one's very soul. (pp. 108-10)

Hawthorne, therefore, did four things for the short story: he turned it from its German romantic extravagances and frivolity and horrors into sane and moral channels; he made of it the study of a single intense situation; he deepened it and gave it beauty; and he made it respectable even in New England, a dignified literary form, admitted as such even by the most serious of the Transcendentalists. After *Twice-Told Tales* and *Mosses From an Old Manse* the short story had no longer to apologize for its existence and live a vagabond life in the corners of weekly papers and the pages of lady's books and annuals: it had won so secure a place that even before Hawthorne had died *The Atlantic Monthly*, . . . mouthpiece of the Brahmins of New England, could print seventeen specimens of it in its first volume. (p. 110)

Fred Lewis Pattee, "Nathaniel Hawthorne," in his The Development of the American Short Story: An Historical Survey (copyright 1923 by Harper & Row, Publishers, Inc.; renewed 1950 by Fred Lewis Pattee; reprinted by permission of Harper & Row, Publishers, Inc.), Harper, 1923, pp. 91-114.

D. H. LAWRENCE   (essay date 1923)

The Scarlet Letter isn't a pleasant, pretty romance. It is a sort of parable, an earthly story with a hellish meaning. (p. 83)

That blue-eyed darling Nathaniel knew disagreeable things in his inner soul. He was careful to send them out in disguise.

Always the same. The deliberate consciousness of Americans so fair and smooth-spoken, and the under-consciousness so devilish. *Destroy! destroy! destroy!* hums the under-consciousness. *Love and produce! Love and produce!* cackles the upper consciousness. And the world hears only the Love-and-produce cackle. Refuses to hear the hum of destruction underneath. Until such time as it will *have* to hear.

The American has got to destroy. It is his destiny. It is his destiny to destroy the whole corpus of the white psyche, the white consciousness. And he's got to do it secretly. As the growing of a dragon-fly inside a chrysalis or cocoon destroys the larva grub, secretly. (pp. 83-4)

So the secret chrysalis of *The Scarlet Letter,* diabolically destroying the old psyche inside.

Be good! Be good! warbles Nathaniel. *Be good, and never sin! Be sure your sins will find you out. . . .*

Then listen to the diabolic undertone of *The Scarlet Letter.*

Man ate of the tree of knowledge, and became ashamed of himself.

Do you imagine Adam had never lived with Eve before that apple episode? Yes, he had. As a wild animal with his mate.

It didn't become "sin" till the knowledge-poison entered. That apple of Sodom. (p. 84)

The sin was the self-watching, self-consciousness. The sin, and the doom. Dirty understanding. (p. 85)

The Scarlet Letter gives the show away.

You have your pure-pure young parson Dimmesdale.

You have the beautiful Puritan Hester at his feet.

And the first thing she does is to seduce him.

And the first thing he does is to be seduced.

And the second thing they do is to hug their sin in secret, and gloat over it, and try to understand.

Which is the myth of New England.

Deerslayer refused to be seduced by Judith Hutter. At least the Sodom apple of sin didn't fetch him.

But Dimmesdale was seduced gloatingly. Oh, luscious Sin!

He was such a pure young man.

That he had to make a fool of purity.

The American psyche.

Of course, the best part of the game lay in keeping up pure appearances. (pp. 87-8)

A. The Scarlet Letter. Adulteress! The great Alpha. Alpha! Adulteress! The new Adam and Adama! American!

A. Adulteress! Stitched with gold thread, glittering upon the bosom. The proudest insignia.

Put her upon the scaffold and worship her there. Worship her there. The Woman, the Magna Mater. A. Adulteress! Abel!

Abel! Abel! Abel! Admirable!

It becomes a farce.

The fiery heart. A. Mary of the Bleeding Heart. Mater Adolerata! A. Capital A. Adulteress. Glittering with gold thread. Abel! Adultery. Admirable!

It is, perhaps, the most colossal satire ever penned. *The Scarlet Letter.* And by a blue-eyed darling of a Nathaniel.

Not Bumppo, however.

The human spirit, fixed in a lie, adhering to a lie, giving itself perpetually the lie.

All begins with A.

Adulteress. Alpha. Abel, Adam. A. America.

The Scarlet Letter.

(p. 88)

Hester Prynne is the great nemesis of woman. She is the KNOWING Ligeia risen diabolic from the grave. Having her own back. UNDERSTANDING. (p. 89)

Mr. Dimmesdale also wasn't at the end of his resources. Previously, he had lived by governing his body, ruling it, in the interests of his spirit. Now he has a good time all by himself torturing his body, whipping it, piercing it with thorns, macerating himself. It's a form of masturbation.

It is the old self-mutilation process, gone rotten. The mind wanting to get its teeth in the blood and flesh. The ego exulting in the tortures of the mutinous flesh. I, the ego, I *will* triumph over my own flesh. Lash! Lash! I am a grand free spirit. *Lash! I* am the master of my soul! *Lash! Lash!* I am the captain of my soul. *Lash!* Hurray! "In the fell clutch of circumstance," etc., etc. (p. 90)

Hester was scared only of one result of her sin: Pearl. Pearl, the scarlet letter incarnate. The little girl. When women bear children, they produce either devils or sons with gods in them. And it is an evolutionary process. The devil in Hester produced a purer devil in Pearl. And the devil in Pearl will produce— she married an Italian Count—a piece of purer devilishness still.

And so from hour to hour we ripe and ripe.

And then from hour to hour we rot and rot.

There was that in the child "which often impelled Hester to ask in bitterness of heart, whether it were for good or ill that the poor little creature had been born at all".

For ill, Hester. But don't worry. Ill is as necessary as good. Malevolence is as necessary as benevolence. (p. 96)

Pearl is perhaps the most modern child in all literature.

Old-fashioned Nathaniel, with his little-boy charm, he'll tell you what's what. But he'll cover it with smarm.

Hester simply *hates* her child, from one part of herself. And from another, she cherishes her child as her one precious treasure. For Pearl is the continuing of her female revenge on life. But female revenge hits both ways. Hits back at its own mother. The female revenge in Pearl hits back at Hester, the mother, and Hester is simply livid with fury and "sadness", which is rather amusing. (pp. 96-7)

A little demon! But her mother, and the saintly Dimmesdale, had borne her. And Pearl, by the very openness of her perversity, was more straightforward than her parents. She flatly refuses any Heavenly Father, seeing the earthly one such a fraud. And she has the pietistic Dimmesdale on toast, spits right in his eye: in both his eyes. (p. 97)

Poor little phenomenon of a modern child, she'll grow up into the devil of a modern woman. The nemesis of weak-kneed modern men, craving to be love-drawn.

The third person in the diabolic trinity, or triangle, of the Scarlet Letter, is Hester's first husband, Roger Chillingworth. (pp. 97-8)

He is no Christian, no selfless aspirer. He is not an aspirer. He is the old authoritarian in man. The old male authority. But without passional belief. Only intellectual belief in himself and his male authority. . . .

[Chillingworth] keeps on the *intellectual* tradition. He hates the new spiritual aspirers, like Dimmesdale, with a black, crippled hate. He is the old male authority, in intellectual tradition.

You can't keep a wife by force of an intellectual tradition. So Hester took to seducing Dimmesdale.

Yet her only marriage, and her last oath, is with the old Roger. He and she are accomplices in pulling down the spiritual saint. (p. 98)

A black and complementary hatred, akin to love, is what Chillingworth feels for the young, saintly parson. And Dimmesdale responds, in a hideous kind of love. Slowly the saint's life is poisoned. But the black old physician smiles, and tries to keep him alive. Dimmesdale goes in for self-torture, self-lashing, lashing his own white, thin, spiritual saviour's body. The dark old Chillingworth listens outside the door and laughs, and prepares another medicine, so that the game can go on longer. And the saint's very soul goes rotten. Which is the supreme triumph. Yet he keeps up appearances still.

The black, vengeful soul of the crippled, masterful male, still dark in his authority: and the white ghastliness of the fallen saint! The two halves of manhood mutually destroying one another.

Dimmesdale has a "coup" in the very end. He gives the whole show away by confessing publicly on the scaffold, and dodging into death, leaving Hester dished, and Roger as it were, doubly cuckolded. It is a neat last revenge.

Down comes the curtain, as in Ligeia's poem.

But the child Pearl will be on in the next act, with her Italian Count and a new brood of vipers. And Hester greyly Abelling, in the shadows, after her rebelling.

It is a marvellous allegory. It is to me one of the greatest allegories in all literature, *The Scarlet Letter.* Its marvellous under-meaning! And its perfect duplicity.

The absolute duplicity of that blue-eyed *Wunderkind* of a Nathaniel. The American wonder-child, with his magical allegorical insight.

But even wonder-children have to grow up in a generation or two.

And even SIN becomes stale. (pp. 98-9)

D. H. Lawrence, "Nathaniel Hawthorne and 'The Scarlet Letter'," in his Studies in Classic American Literature *(copyright 1923 by Thomas Seltzer, Inc.; copyright renewed 1950 by Frieda Lawrence; copyright © 1961 by The Estate of the late Mrs. Frieda Lawrence; reprinted by permission of Viking Penguin Inc.; in Canada by Laurence Pollinger Ltd and the Estate of Frieda Lawrence Ravagli), Thomas Seltzer Inc., 1923, William Heinemann Ltd., 1924 (and reprinted by Viking Press, 1964, pp. 83-100).*

YVOR WINTERS   (essay date 1937)

Of Hawthorne's three most important long works—*The Scarlet Letter, The House of the Seven Gables,* and *The Marble Faun*—the first is pure allegory, and the other two are impure novels, or novels with unassimilated moral elements. The first is faultless, in scheme and in detail; it is one of the chief masterpieces of English prose. The second and third are interesting, the third in particular, but both are failures, and neither would suffice to give the author a very high place in the history of prose fiction. Hawthorne's sketches and short stories, at best, are slight performances; either they lack meaning, as in the case of *Mr. Higginbotham's Catastrophe,* or they lack reality of embodiment, as in the case of *The Birthmark,* or, having a measure of both, as does *The Minister's Black Veil,* they yet seem incapable of justifying the intensity of the method, their very brevity and attendant simplification, perhaps, working against them. The best of them, probably, is *Young Goodman Brown.* In his later romances, *Septimius Felton, Dr. Grimshaw's Secret, The Ancestral Footstep,* and *The Dolliver Romance,* and in much of *The Blithedale Romance* as well, Hawthorne struggles unsuccessfully with the problem of allegory, but he is still obsessed with it. (p. 157)

That New England predisposed Hawthorne to allegory cannot be shown; yet the disposition . . . is obvious. And it can easily be shown that New England provided the perfect material for one great allegory, and that, in all likelihood, she was largely to blame for the later failures.

The Puritan theology rested primarily upon the doctrine of predestination and of the inefficaciousness of good works; it separated men sharply and certainly into two groups, the saved and the damned, and, technically, at least, was not concerned with any subtler shadings. This in itself represents a long step toward the allegorization of experience, for a very broad abstraction is substituted for the patient study of the minutiae of moral behavior long encouraged by Catholic tradition. Another step was necessary, however, and this step was taken in Massachusetts almost at the beginning of the settlement, and in the expulsion of Anne Hutchinson became the basis of governmental action: whereas the wholly Calvinistic Puritan denied the value of the evidence of character and behavior as signs of salvation, and so precluded the possibility of their becoming allegorical symbols, for the orthodox Calvinist, such as Mrs. Hutchinson would appear to have been, who trusted to no witness save that of the Inner Light, it became customary to regard as evidence of salvation the decision of the individual to enter the Church and lead a moral life. . . . Objective evidence thus took the place of inner assurance, and the behavior of the individual took on symbolic value. That is, any sin was evidence of damnation; or, in other words, any sin represented all sin. (pp. 158-59)

[In] examining Hawthorne, we are concerned with two historical centers: that of the first generation of Puritans in New England, in which occurs the action of *The Scarlet Letter;* and that of the post-Unitarian and Romantic intellectuals, in which was passed the life of Hawthorne.

Hawthorne, by nature an allegorist, and a man with a strong moral instinct, regardless of the condition of his ideas, found in the early history of his own people and region the perfect material for a masterpiece. By selecting sexual sin as the type of all sin, he was true alike to the exigencies of drama and of history. In the setting which he chose, allegory was realism, the idea was life itself; and his prose, always remarkable for its polish and flexibility, and stripped, for once, of all superfluity, was reduced to the living idea; it intensified pure exposition to a quality comparable in its way to that of great poetry.

The compactness and complexity of the allegory will escape all save the most watchful readers. Let us consider the following passage as a representative example. Hester has learned that the magistrates and clergy are considering whether or not she ought to be separated from her child, and she waits upon Governor Bellingham in order to plead with him:

> On the wall hung a row of portraits, representing the forefathers of the Bellingham lineage, some with armor on their breasts, and others with stately ruffs and robes of peace.
>
> (pp. 164-65)

> At about the center of the oaken panels, that lined the hall, was suspended a suit of mail, not, like the pictures, an ancestral relic, but of the most modern date; for it had been manufactured by a skillful armorer in London, the same year in which Governor Bellingham came over to New England.
>
> (p. 165)

> Little Pearl—who was as greatly pleased with the gleaming armor as she had been with the glittering frontispiece of the house—spent some time looking into the polished mirror of the breast-plate.
>
> "Mother," cried she, "I see you here. Look! Look!"
>
> Hester looked, by way of humoring the child; and she saw that, owing to the peculiar effect of the convex mirror, the scarlet letter was represented in gigantic and exaggerated proportions, so as to be greatly the most prominent feature of her appearance. In truth, she seemed absolutely hidden behind it. Pearl pointed upward, also, at a similar picture in the headpiece; smiling at her mother with the elfish intelligence that was so familiar an expression on her small physiognomy. . . .

The portraits are obviously intended as an apology for the static portraits in the book, as an illustration of the principle of simplification by distance and by generalization; the new armor, on the other hand, is the new faith which brought the Puritans to New England, and which not only shone with piety—"especially the helmet and breastplate", the covering of the head and heart—but supported them in their practical struggles with physical adversaries, and which in addition altered their view of the life about them to dogmatic essentials, so that Hester was obliterated behind the fact of her sin, and Pearl transformed in view of her origin. Governor Bellingham, in his combination of legal training with military prowess, is representative of his fellow colonists, who displayed in a remarkable degree a capacity to act with great strength and with absolutely simple directness upon principles so generalized as scarcely to be

applicable to any specific moral problem, which mastered moral difficulties not by understanding them, but by crushing them out. (p. 166)

It is noteworthy that in this passage from *The Scarlet Letter* Hawthorne turns his instrument of allegory, the gift of the Puritans, against the Puritans themselves, in order to indicate the limits of their intelligence; it is noteworthy also that this act of criticism, though both clear and sound, is negative, that he nowhere except in the very general notion of regeneration through repentance establishes the nature of the intelligence which might exceed the intelligence of the Puritans, but rather hints at the ideal existence of a richer and more detailed understanding than the Puritan scheme of life is able to contain. The strength of *The Scarlet Letter* is in part safeguarded by the refusal to explore this understanding; the man who was able in the same lifetime to write *The New Adam and Eve,* to conceive the art colony described in *The Marble Faun,* and to be shocked at the nude statues of antiquity, was scarcely the man to cast a clear and steady light upon the finer details of the soul.

The conception of the book in general is as cleanly allegorical as is the conception of the passage quoted. Hester represents the repentant sinner, Dimmesdale the half-repentant sinner, and Chillingworth the unrepentant sinner. The fact that Chillingworth's sin is the passion for revenge is significant only to the extent that this is perhaps the one passion which most completely isolates man from normal human sympathies and which therefore is most properly used to represent an unregenerate condition. (pp. 168-69)

Once Hawthorne had reduced the problem of sin to terms as general as these, and had brought his allegory to perfect literary form, he had, properly speaking, dealt with sin once and for all; there was nothing further to be said about it. It would not serve to write another allegory with a new set of characters and a different sin as the motive; for the particular sin is not particular in function, but is merely representative of sin in general, as the characters, whatever their names and conditions may be, are merely representative of the major stages of sin— there is no escape from the generality so long as one adheres to the method. There was nothing further to be done in this direction, save a few footnotes to the subject in the form of sketches.

The only alternative remaining was to move away from the allegorical extreme of narrative toward the specific, that is, toward the art of the novelist. The attempt was made, but fell short of success. In *The House of the Seven Gables* and in *The Marble Faun* alike the moral understanding of the action—and there is a serious attempt at such understanding, at least in *The Marble Faun*—is corrupted by a provincial sentimentalism ethically far inferior to the Manicheism of the Puritans, which was plain and comprehensive, however brutal. And Hawthorne had small gift for the creation of human beings, a defect closely allied to his other defects and virtues: even the figures in *The Scarlet Letter* are profoundly unsatisfactory if one comes to the book expecting to find a novel, for they draw their life not from specific and familiar human characteristics . . . , but from the precision and intensity with which they render their respective ideas; the very development of the story is neither narrative nor dramatic, but expository. When, as in *The Marble Faun* or *The House of the Seven Gables,* there is no idea governing the human figure, or when the idea is an incomplete equivalent of the figure, the figure is likely to be a disappointing spectacle, for he is seldom if ever a convincing human being and is likely to verge on the ludicrous. (pp. 169-70)

[Hawthorne's] effort to master the novelist's procedure, however, was not sustained, for his heart was not in it. In *The Blithedale Romance,* he began as a novelist, but lost himself toward the close in an unsuccessful effort to achieve allegory; the four unfinished romances represent similar efforts throughout.

His procedure in the last works was startlingly simple; so much so, that no one whom I can recollect has run the risk of defining it.

In *The Scarlet Letter* there occurs a formula which one might name the formula of alternative possibilities. In the ninth chapter, for example, there occurs the following passage: . . .

> At first, [Roger Chillingworth's] expression had been calm, meditative, scholar-like. Now, there was something ugly and evil in his face, which they had not previously noticed, and which grew still more obvious to sight the oftener they looked upon him. According to the vulgar idea, the fire in his laboratory had been brought from the lower regions, and was fed with infernal fuel; and so, as might be expected, his visage was getting sooty with smoke.

In such a passage as this, the idea conveyed is clear enough, but the embodiment of the idea appears farfetched, and Hawthorne offers it whimsically and apologetically, professing to let you take it or leave it. . . . Similarly, in *The Marble Faun,* one never learns whether Donatello had or had not the pointed ears which serve throughout the book as the physical symbol of his moral nature; the book ends with the question being put to Kenyon, who has had opportunities to observe, and with his refusing to reply.

This device, though it becomes a minor cause of irritation through constant recurrence, is relatively harmless, and at times is even used with good effect. If we reverse the formula, however, so as to make the physical representation perfectly clear but the meaning uncertain, we have a very serious situation; and this is precisely what occurs, in some measure toward the close of *The Blithedale Romance,* and without mitigation throughout the four unfinished romances. We have in the last all of the machinery and all of the mannerisms of the allegorist, but we cannot discover the substance of his communication, nor is he himself aware of it so far as we can judge. We have the symbolic footprint, the symbolic spider, the symbolic elixirs and poisons, but we have not that of which they are symbolic; we have the hushed, the tense and confidential manner, on the part of the narrator, of one who imparts a grave secret, but the words are inaudible. Yet we have not, on the other hand, anything approaching realistic fiction, for the events are improbable or even impossible, and the characters lack all reality. (pp. 170-72)

In *The Scarlet Letter,* then, Hawthorne composed a great allegory; or, if we look first at the allegorical view of life upon which early Puritan society was based, we might almost say that he composed a great historical novel. History, which by placing him in an anti-intellectual age had cut him off from the ideas which might have enabled him to deal with his own period, in part made up for the injustice by facilitating his entrance, for a brief time, into an age more congenial to his nature. Had he possessed the capacity for criticizing and or-

ganizing conceptions as well as for dramatizing them, he might have risen superior to his disadvantages, but like many other men of major genius he lacked this capacity. In turning his back upon the excessively simplified conceptions of his Puritan ancestors, he abandoned the only orderly concepts, whatever their limitations, to which he had access, and in his last work he is restless and dissatisfied. The four last romances are unfinished, and in each successive one he sought to incorporate and perfect elements from those preceding; the last, *The Dolliver Romance,* which he had sought to make the best, had he lived, is a mere fragment, but on the face of it is the most preposterous of all. His dilemma, the choice between abstractions inadequate or irrelevant to experience on the one hand, and experience on the other as far as practicable unilluminated by understanding, is tragically characteristic of the history of this country and of its literature. . . . Hawthorne, when he reversed his formula of alternative possibilities, and sought to grope his way blindly to significance, made the choice of the later Romantics; and his groping was met wherever he moved by the smooth and impassive surface of the intense inane. (pp. 174-75)

> *Yvor Winters, "Maule's Curse, or Hawthorne and the Problem of Allegory," in his* Maule's Curse: Seven Studies in the History of American Obscurantism *(© 1938 by New Directions; copyright renewed © 1965 by Yvor Winters; reprinted by permission of Ohio University Press, Athens,) New Directions, 1938 (and reprinted in his* In Defense of Reason, The Swallow Press Inc., *1947, pp. 157-75).*

F. O. MATTHIESSEN   (essay date 1941)

[*Fanshawe,* Hawthorne's first novel,] shows a remarkable finish. . . . [To] be sure, the style is still all a matter of surface skill, for the plot of a romantic love story, with an abduction and pursuit, belongs to the school of Godwin, and had . . . little to do with Hawthorne's maturing interests. . . . So far as the construction of the book shows anything of his later method, he seems to have learned it from Scott, the beginning of whose *Waverley* series had been one of the great events of Hawthorne's boyhood. . . . He was likewise indebted to Scott both here and later for many devices that were in turn a faroff echo of Shakespearean drama: the habit of dividing his characters into groups and of carrying along the actions of each group separately; the way of developing his plot by means of a few spot-lighted scenes, with speeches of an exalted pitch, as those between Hester and the minister; the occasional interweaving of oddities of low comedy, as in Uncle Venner and the frequenters of the cent-shop in *The Seven Gables,* or in Silas Foster, the farmer whose 'great, broad, bottomless yawn' interrupted the evening conversations of the cultivated community at Blithedale.

In *Fanshawe,* this comic strain called out his best efforts both in style and characterization. He had not belonged at college to the literary society with Longfellow, but the experience that had led to his being fined for playing cards may readily have included such a type as he tried to draw in Hugh Crombie, the landlord of the Hand and Bottle, the composer of rowdy ballads. . . . The humor of this [portrait] is not entirely derived from Hawthorne's reading, and the language is already unmistakably his in its peculiar mixture of so high a proportion of latinate words with a relaxed, if hardly colloquial manner.

The serious characters in the book have scarcely the thickness of cardboard, though the solitary scholar Fanshawe, 'independent of the beings that surrounded him,' is a faint sketch of the type that, as Hawthorne grew more aware of the falseness of such a position, was to take on tragic proportions in Arthur Dimmesdale. (pp. 203-04)

[In **'The Hollow of the Three Hills,'** one of Hawthorne's earliest tales, the very opening clause introduces the particular approach that he was destined to make throughout his work to the relation between appearance and reality: 'In those strange old times, when fantastic dreams and madmen's reveries were realized among the actual circumstances of life . . .' . . . . [Hawthorne] was already aware of the implications that were to lead him to say there that 'modern psychology' might well endeavor to reduce the alleged powers of sinister influence into 'a system, instead of rejecting them as altogether fabulous.' Through his own meditation he found a psychological equivalent for the witch's evil eye in the contemporary abuse of mesmerism. . . . His desire to probe spiritual reality beneath all manner of guises made [Hawthorne] willing to suspend disbelief concerning whatever human hearts had long held to be true; but his hard critical sense equipped him to see through not only the distortions and delusions of Puritanism, but likewise through the sleight-of-hand of contemporary 'sciences' like phrenology and mesmerism, and thus to occupy a more serious domain than Poe. (p. 205)

Compared with Thoreau, the diction seems archaic, and Hawthorne's way of describing nature, despite his sustained pattern of subdued colors, is highly artificial. It makes you think of Yeats' remark that whenever language has been 'the instrument of controversy,' it has inevitably grown abstract. For behind Hawthorne's formality you can sense several New England generations in which rhetoric had served for public uses, for sermons and political deliberation, but scarcely at all for literature. And though renouncing the role of preacher as Emerson never did, Hawthorne kept a taste for other aspects of the age just previous to his own, for the Augustan authors who had gradually stimulated New England's enlightenment, and whom Emerson and Thoreau had joined Carlyle in dismissing as superficial to man's soul. (p. 206)

[Hawthorne] showed his clear perception of the value of simplicity when he said that learned ministers possessed every gift save that of being able to speak 'the heart's native language' and so to convey 'the highest truths through the humblest medium of familiar words and images.' . . . [Yet he] seems frequently to have wanted to move away from the colloquial, as when 'small' is dressed up as 'diminutive,' 'good' as 'beneficent,' 'loud' as 'obstreperous.' When some impressions that he had gathered in the mountains emerged, ten years later, as the setting for **'Ethan Brand'** and a 'great, old dog' became a 'grave and venerable quadruped,' you sense his relish for the rounded period, and for the heightened dignity that the eighteenth century had believed must characterize serious art. Sometimes his conscious artificiality was part of a witty intention, as where he said of the adventist Father Miller . . . that he appeared to have 'given himself up to despair at the tedious delay of the final conflagration.' . . . [But] Hawthorne's device is not just a matter of vocabulary. He believed that he could bring out the full effect of an ironic perception by deliberate rhetorical expansion, as when he remarked of a young barkeeper that 'he had a good forehead, with a particularly large development just above the eyebrows; fine intellectual gifts, no doubt, which he had educated to this profitable end; being famous for nothing but gin-cocktails.' . . .

Too often, however, this expansion led to mere diffuseness of detail, as when 'all such trash' as he found in Dr. Ripley's

library became 'other productions of a like fugitive nature.' Its effect is the tameness which Hawthorne himself recognized in his preface to the *Tales* [see excerpt above]. . . . (p. 213)

[It] may be adequate to suggest that a comparison between ['**The Gentle Boy,'** the] first of his real successes and **'Ethan Brand,'** one of the last short pieces he was to write, will show no progress in essentials. . . . [The] fact that most of his early manifestations of artistic skill deal with the seventeenth century might indicate that his imagination could gain release only when it gave up the problem of confronting the bare present. But **'The Shaker Bridal'** was suggested by his visit to the community at Canterbury, New Hampshire; and **'Ethan Brand,'** the deftly presented sensuous details of which are as evocative even as those in **'Young Goodman Brown,'** was based on his observation of scenes and people near North Adams. The test for Hawthorne's success, therefore, would seem to be not whether his material was contemporary or from the past, but whether it could be impregnated with his kind of inner theme. The human problems that he scrutinized were the same in both settings. (pp. 218-19)

[Hawthorne formed] imaginative release primarily in reflections, in fountains and the fluid mirrors of streams. Why these became such favorite symbols for Hawthorne is elaborated in the description, in **'The Old Manse,'** of his excursions on the Concord with Ellery Channing. The original draft in his notebook was even more detailed:

> I have never elsewhere had such an opportunity
> to observe how much more beautiful reflection
> is than what we call reality. The sky, and the
> clustering foliage on either hand, and the effect
> of sunlight as it found its way through the shade
> . . . all these seemed unsurpassably beauti-
> ful. . . . I am half convinced that the reflection
> is indeed the reality—the real thing which Na-
> ture imperfectly images to our grosser sense.
> At all events, the disembodied shadow is near-
> est to the soul.
>
> (p. 259)

As [Hawthorne] repeated that memory too is a mirror, his habit of symbolizing extended that metaphor diversely. Most frequently it became the glass of introspection, as at several critical moments in *The Scarlet Letter.* When Hester stood on the scaffold in the opening scene, her spirit relieved itself from the pressure of the crowd's eyes by summoning into this 'dusky mirror' a succession of 'phantasmagoric forms' from her happier past. In the chapter called **'The Interior of a Heart,'** Dimmesdale sometimes punctuated his long vigils by staring at his own face in a looking-glass under the strongest light that he could throw upon it, and 'thus typified the constant introspection wherewith he tortured, but could not purify himself.' (pp. 259-60)

Elsewhere, this 'mind's eye,' as Hawthorne calls it, extends its range and becomes equivalent to the universal memory. That extension is the function of the fountains that he used as a device for breaking through the restrictions of the given moment, by projecting into their bubbling life imaginative hints of both the past and the future. The signal instance is [in *The House of the Seven Gables*], Maule's Well, the spring in the Pyncheon's garden, the name of which is a reminder that the land whereon the mansion stands was originally wrested from a poorer family. It may seem strange that Hawthorne thought at one time of calling the book by this name, for only passing attention is paid to the well. But one sentence of its first description shows the kind of significance it held for him: 'The play and slight agitation of the water, in its upward gush, wrought magically with these variegated pebbles, and made a continually shifting apparition of quaint figures, vanishing too suddenly to be definable.'

What is created from those images depends on the beholder. To Clifford's broken mind, as, with childish delight in the open air after his long imprisonment, he hangs over the fountain, 'the constantly shifting phantasmagoria of figures' seemed like faces looking up at him, beautiful faces, except when suddenly he would cry out in anguish, 'The dark face gazes at me.' Matter-of-fact Phoebe could see nothing of this, 'neither the beauty, nor the ugliness,' but only colored pebbles disarranged by the force of the water. Nor did she comprehend the meaning of the daguerreotypist, a descendant of the Maules, who, thinking of the traditional curse on the house, pronounced this dark spring, in the midst of a garden long since run to seed, to be 'water bewitched.' On the last page of the book, after they have all gone away from the house to more hopeful surroundings, Maule's Well, 'though left in solitude, was throwing up a succession of kaleidoscopic pictures, in which a gifted eye might have seen foreshadowed the coming fortunes.'

Thus the imagination, by merging itself with 'the universal memory' of events, can perform its function of projecting the past into the future. I deliberately repeat Yeats' term, for though there are many differences between his account of the imagination and Hawthorne's, they share the belief, which is common also to Emerson and other 'Platonists,' that the individual imagination, like the disembodied reflections in the stream, is part of the Divine Mind.

By detaching Hawthorne's descriptions of the well from their context, the delicate spell he designed by them may have been broken. He was himself always aware of the destructibility of his imaginative life. In the preface to *The Scarlet Letter,* where he showed his full understanding of his creative process, he remarked that the atmosphere of a custom-house was so little adapted 'to the delicate harvest of fancy and sensibility' that his imagination had become 'a tarnished mirror.' 'It would not reflect, or only with miserable dimness, the figures with which I did my best to people it.' (pp. 260-61)

Every syllable of this account, which extends to several pages, is germane to the interpretation of what Hawthorne wrote, and of why he wrote it as he did. . . . [The] final ingredient in the circumstances . . . stimulated him most: 'Glancing at the looking-glass, we behold—deep within its haunted verge—the smouldering glow of the half-extinguished anthracite, the white moonbeams on the floor, and a repetition of all the gleam and shadow of the picture, with one remove further from the actual, and nearer to the imaginative. Then, at such an hour, and with this scene before him, if a man, sitting all alone, cannot dream strange things, and make them look like truth, he need never try to write romances.'

For, under these conditions, all the ordinary objects—the center table with its work basket, the sofa, a child's shoe—suffered a remarkable change. Seen afresh by the unusual light, they seemed 'to lose their actual substance' and to be 'invested with a quality of strangeness and remoteness,' to be so 'spiritualized' that they became figments of the mind, and thereby susceptible of fresh and unexpected combinations. 'Thus . . . the floor of our familiar room has become a neutral territory, somewhere between the real world and fairy-land, where the Actual and the Imaginary may meet, and each imbue itself with the nature of the other.'

This climax, with its juxtaposition of the terms 'actual' and 'imaginary,' compels consideration of what I may have seemed to pass by too easily in Hawthorne's description of the river, the question of what he meant by the more inclusive term 'reality.' (p. 262)

Essential truths of the human situation are exactly what Hawthorne's imagination could not shrink from–not even, as we have seen, when he wanted it to. Nor does his matured conception of art neglect the 'real' for the 'ideal'; it posits the relation that he believed should exist between them. In the opening paragraph of *The Marble Faun,* before he had had a chance to adulterate his pages with any of his odd 'literary' notions about the fine arts, he voiced a fundamental conviction. In leading up to his description of the Faun of Praxiteles, he spoke of how the great figures of antique sculpture are 'still shining in the undiminished majesty and beauty of their ideal life.' That phrases the function of idealization in art in a way that marks it off sharply from romantic escapism; it reaffirms the truth that art, both in its intention and its lasting result, raises its material to the level of contemplation, freed from accidents and irrelevancies. But Hawthorne did not forget where the artist's material must be found. . . . He expressed the contrast between what he believed to be the true attitude and the false one when he described how a sunset in Edinburgh had irradiated a cluster of old houses into a spelled realm of the picturesque, quite obliterating the fact that 'layer upon layer of unfortunate humanity' were massed there in squalor. 'The change symbolized the difference between a poet's imagination of life in the past—or in a state which he looks at through a colored and illuminated medium—and the sad reality.' Save for his personal fondness for Longfellow, Hawthorne had no respect for that kind of poet. 'The ideal' that Hawthorne wanted to project in art was 'the real': not actuality transformed into an impossible perfection, but actuality disengaged from appearance. (pp. 263-64)

[Hawthorne's] fascinated use of fountains and mirrors often enabled him to bring his material to artistic concentration, as well as to endow his scenes with depth and liquidity. He set his stage for Endicott's grim act of cutting the red cross from an English flag to show that neither Pope nor Tyrant had further part in the colony, by describing the Salem green as it was mirrored in this soldier's polished breastplate. In another of his most affecting tales, **'Dr. Heidegger's Experiment'** . . . , a grotesque search for the fountain of youth is dramatized by four old people drinking an ambiguous fluid, which sparkles like champagne and, in the half light of the doctor's room, seems to gleam with a moonlike splendor. But at the moment of their exhilarated transformation, when the three now young gentlemen dance in a circle around the girl-widow, enamored by the freshness of her charms, 'by a strange deception, owing to the duskiness of the chamber, and the antique dresses which they still wore, the tall mirror is said to have reflected the figures of the three old, gray, withered grandsires, ridiculously contending for the skinny ugliness of a shrivelled grandam.' No wonder that Melville, consumed with interest in any manifestation of the contrast between appearance and reality, marked [in his copy of the book] this subtle instance where the reflection in a mirror, as well as in the glass of memory and imagination, kept the truth that had been lost by the characters' frantic delusion. (pp. 273-74)

[It] never occurred to Hawthorne that art is more fundamental than nature. . . . [We can find] the kind of discrimination he made—though he did not use these terms—between mechanical copying and imaginative imitation. He had that difference in mind when putting his finger on the secret of Thoreau's power. Hawthorne judged that 'Natural History of Massachusetts' was an accurate 'reflection of his character,' and that it conveyed too 'a very fair image of his mind . . . so true, minute, and literal in observation, yet giving the spirit as well as letter of what he sees, even as a lake reflects its wooded banks, showing every leaf, yet giving the wild beauty of the whole scene.' There could hardly be a more sensitive analogy for the enchanted wholeness of imaginative composition. (p. 274)

[Hawthorne reiterated in *The Snow-Image*] his belief that the moon creates, 'like the imaginative power, a beautiful strangeness in familiar objects.' . . . [It is] true that an extraordinary number of his major scenes are played out under these rays. Or rather, the light does not remain a dramatic property, but becomes itself a central actor. Such is the case with the meteoric exhalations that harrow Dimmesdale with the thought that knowledge of his hidden guilt is spread over the whole broad heavens; and an even more dynamic role is played by the rising moon during Judge Pyncheon's night watch, since, as it fingers its way through the windows, it is the only living thing in the room. And simply to mention, out of many more, the two most effectively presented crises in the other romances, we remember the midnight stream from which the dead-white body of Zenobia is recovered; and the maddened instant when Donatello, seeing Miriam's sinister model emerging from the shadows into the moonlight, cannot resist the impulse to hurl him off the Tarpeian rock.

In all these scenes Hawthorne draws on every possible contrast between lights and darks; and the way he invariably focuses attention on the thought-burdened faces of his characters justifies the frequent comparison between his kind of scrutiny and Rembrandt's. Moreover, despite his relative ignorance of painting, he deliberately created, throughout his work, sustained landscapes of low-pitched tones to heighten the effects of his foreground. He generally visualized his outdoor scenes in neutral 'gray and russet,' against which he projected such symbols as the brilliant crimson and purple blossoms that hang over the fountain in Rappaccini's garden, and hide deadly poison in their beauty. Or, again at night, the dark woods on the mountain side, where the final agony of Ethan Brand is enacted, are shot through not only by occasional moonbeams, but by streaks of firelight from the limeburner's roaring furnace. More complex than this effect, or that whereby the tragedy of Ilbrahim is begun in lingering twilight and ended on a night of violent storm, is the continual manipulation of the lighting in both *The Scarlet Letter* and *The Seven Gables*. From the opening description of the elm-clustered old house, the sense that 'the shadow creeps and creeps, and is always looking over the shoulder of the sunshine' on the great vertical dial on one of the gables is raised to the level of a central theme, for it symbolizes how the actions of the fragile present are oppressed with the darkness of the past. (pp. 281-82)

> *F. O. Matthiessen, "Problem of the Artist as New Englander" and "Allegory and Symbolism," in his* American Renaissance: Art and Expression in the Age of Emerson and Whitman *(copyright 1941 by Oxford University Press, Inc.; reprinted by permission), Oxford University Press, New York, 1941, pp. 192-241, 242-315.**

Q. D. LEAVIS   (essay date 1951)

The essential Hawthorne—and he seems to me a great genius, the creator of a literary tradition as well as a wonderfully

original and accomplished artist—is the author of *Young Goodman Brown, The Maypole of Merry Mount, My Kinsman Major Molineux, The Snow-Image, The Blithedale Romance, The Scarlet Letter,* and of a number of sketches and less pregnant stories associated with these works such as *The Gray Champion, Main Street, Old News, Endicott of the Red Cross, The Artist of the Beautiful.* This work is not comparable with the productions of the eighteenth-century "allegorical" essayists nor is it in the manner of Spenser, Milton, or Bunyan—whom of course it can be seen he has not merely studied but assimilated. The first batch of works I specified is essentially dramatic, its use of language is poetic, and it is symbolic, and richly so, as is the dramatic poet's. . . . [In Hawthorne's work,] the "symbol" is the thing itself, with no separable paraphrasable meaning as in an allegory: the language is directly evocative. Rereading this work . . . , one is constantly struck by fresh subtleties of organization, of intention, expression and feeling, of original psychological insight and a new minting of terms to convey it, as well as of a predominantly dramatic construction. (pp. 181-82)

The aspect of Hawthorne that I want to stress as the important one, decisive for American literature, and to be found most convincingly in the works I specified, is this: that he was the critic and interpreter of American cultural history and thereby the finder and creator of a literary tradition from which sprang Henry James on the one hand and Melville on the other. . . . [The problems of] the relation of the individual to society, the way in which a distinctively American society developed and how it came to have a tradition of its own, the relation of the creative writer to the earlier nineteenth-century American community, and his function and how he could contrive to exercise it—the exploration of these questions and the communication in literary art of his findings—[are Hawthorne's] claim to importance. It is true that he is most successful in treating pre-Revolutionary America, but that, after all, is, as he saw it, the decisive period. . . . Hawthorne's sense of being part of the contemporary America could be expressed only in concern for its evolution—he needed to see how it had come about, and by discovering what America had, culturally speaking, started from and with, to find what choices had faced his countrymen and what they had had to sacrifice in order to create that distinctive "organic whole." . . . Though he was the very opposite of a Dreiser . . . yet I should choose to describe Hawthorne as a sociological novelist in effect, employing a poetic technique which communicates instead of stating his findings. The just comparison with *The Scarlet Letter* is not *The Pilgrim's Progress* but *Anna Karenina*, which in theme and technique it seems to me astonishingly to resemble. . . . Hawthorne in his best work is offering in dramatic form an analysis of a complex situation in which he sides with no one party but is imaginatively present in each, having created each to represent a facet of the total experience he is concerned to communicate. The analysis and the synthesis help us to find our own "way of salvation" (not a form of words I should have chosen). . . . To analyze the way in which Hawthorne actually works as a writer is the only safe way to come at the nature of his creation, to make sure we are taking what he has written and neither overlooking it nor fathering on the author some misreading of our own or of inert traditional acceptance. (pp. 182-85)

The Maypole of Merry Mount is an early work bearing obvious signs of immaturity but it also shows great originality. . . . We are, or should be, struck in this early piece by the mastery Hawthorne achieves in a new form of prose art, by the skill with which he manages to convey ironic inflexions and to control transitions from one layer of meaning to another, and by which he turns, as it was to become his great distinction to do, history into myth and anecdote into parable. The essential if not the greatest Hawthorne had so soon found himself. (p. 185)

[The distinctive quality of *The Maypole of Merry Mount*] is its use of symbols to convey meaning, and a boldness of imagination and stylization which while drawing on life does not hesitate to rearrange facts and even violate history in that interest. The outline of the historically insignificant Merry Mount affair . . . was a godsend to Hawthorne, who saw in it a means of precipitating his own reactions to his forefathers' choice. While Hawthorne's imagination was historical in a large sense, he was never an imaginative recreator of the romantic past, a historical novelist: he had always from the first very clearly in view the *criticism* of the past. The past was his peculiar concern since it was the source of his present. He always works through the external forms of a society to its essence and its origin. He felt that the significance of early America lay in the conflict between the Puritans who became New England and thus America, and the non-Puritans who were, to him, merely the English in America and whom he partly with triumph but partly also with anguish sees as being cast out (here is a source of conflict). He saw this process as a symbolic recurring struggle, an endless drama that he recorded in a series of works—*The Maypole, My Kinsman Major Molineux, Endicott of the Red Cross, The Gray Champion, The Scarlet Letter, The Blithedale Romance,* among others—that together form something that it would not be fanciful to describe as a ritual drama reminding us of, for instance, the Norse Edda. If his artistic medium is primitive, his intention is not. It is a kind of spiritual and cultural casting-up of accounts: what was lost and what gained, what sacrificed to create what? he is perpetually asking, and showing. (pp. 186-87)

Hawthorne adapted [the theological myth of *The Maypole at Merry Mount*] to convey subtle and often ironic meanings, just as he freely adapts the historical facts. . . . He starts with the Maypole as the symbol of the pagan religion for "what chiefly characterized the colonists of Merry Mount was their veneration for the Maypole. It has made their true history a poet's tale." A living tree, "venerated" for it is the center of life and changes with the seasons, it is now on the festival of Midsummer's Eve hung with roses. . . . Here we have the earliest use of one of Hawthorne's chief symbols, the rose, and we notice that the native wild rose and the cultivated rose carried as seed from England (with generations of grafting and cultivation behind it) are in process of being mingled at Merry Mount. (pp. 187-88)

Hawthorne had realized that religion is a matter of symbols, and his choice of appropriate symbols is not at all simple-minded. The Maypole worshipers are not, it turns out, to be accepted without qualification. They have another symbolic quality attached to them, they are "silken." . . . Everyone was "gay" at Merry Mount, but what really was "the quality of their mirth"? "Once, it is said, they were seen following a flower-decked corpse, with merriment and festive music, to his grave. But did the dead man laugh?" . . . Hawthorne is preparing a more complex whole for us, and preparing us to receive it. The term for the Puritans corresponding to "silken" for the settlers is "iron." . . . A party comes "toiling through the difficult woods, each with a horse-load of iron armour to burden his footsteps." A little later they are "men of iron," and when they surround and overpower the Maypole-worshipers their leader is revealed as iron all through. . . . [The references to iron suggest] the rigid system which burdens life, the metal that makes man militant and ultimately inhuman, and it is spiritually the sign of heaviness and gloom, opposed in every way to the associations of lightness—silken, sunny, gay and mirthful, used for the followers of the old way of life. (pp. 191-92)

The Puritans' religion is expressed in their rites—acts of persecution, oppression and cruelty. . . . While the Merry Mount way of life embodies something essential that is lacking in the Puritans', making theirs appear ugly and inhuman, yet Hawthorne's point is that in the New World the old way could be only an imported artifice; New England, he deeply felt, could never be a mere reproduction of the Old. The fairies, as John Wilson says in *The Scarlet Letter,* were left behind in old England with Catholicism. And Hawthorne implies that the outlook of Merry Mount is not consonant with the realities of life in the New World, or the new phase of the world anywhere perhaps. The Puritans may be odious but they have a secret which is a better thing than the religion of the nature and humanity. The May Lord and Lady, at Endicott's command, leave their Paradise—the reference to Adam and Eve driven from the Garden is unmistakable, as others to Milton in this tale—and there is a general suggestion that the "choice" imposed on New England is like that made by Adam and Eve, they sacrifice bliss for something more arduous and better worth having. . . . The close parallel between the Merry Mount drama and the corresponding conflict in Milton's poem between the Brothers and the followers of Comus must be intentional— there are explicit references—and intended by Hawthorne as a criticism of Milton's presentment of the case. Virtue and Vice are a simple-minded division in Milton's *Comus,* however his symbolism may be interpreted. In Hawthorne's view that contest was quite other than a matter of Right and Wrong; his Puritans are an ironic comment on Milton's cause and case. Hawthorne's rendering shows two partial truths or qualified goods set in regrettable opposition. What Hawthorne implies is that it was a disaster for New England that they could not be reconciled. Hawthorne is both subtler and wiser than Milton, and his poem, unlike Milton's, is really dramatic and embodies a genuine cultural and spiritual conflict. Milton is a Puritan and Hawthorne is not; to Hawthorne, Milton is a man of iron. (pp. 192-94)

Just as the rose, the flower that symbolizes human grace and whose beauty is essentially something cultivated, the product of long training—just as the rose is used from *The Maypole* onwards, so the concept of the iron man becomes basic thereafter. The meaning is expounded in a remarkable section of *Main Street* which concludes:

> All was well, so long as their lamps were freshly
> kindled at the heavenly flame. After a while,
> however, whether in their time or their chil-
> dren's, these lamps began to burn more dimly,
> or with a less genuine lustre; and then it might
> be seen how hard, cold and confined, was their
> system,—how like an iron cage was that which
> they called Liberty.

I believe the image was taken by Hawthorne, consciously or unconsciously, from Bunyan; it may be remembered that in the Interpreter's House Christian is shown a Man in an Iron Cage as an awful warning of what a true Christian should never be. . . . [These] writings of Hawthorne's, to yield all they offer, must be studied as a whole, as a poet's works are, each illuminating and strengthening the rest. This is not the case with the fictions of any English nineteenth-century novelist. . . . [His] recurrent drama is a poet's vision of the meaning of his world, and it is communicated by poetic means.

Young Goodman Brown, visibly a much later and more practiced work than the last, is also more powerful and more closely knit than anything else of Hawthorne's with the possible exception of the very complex and ambitious [*My Kinsman, Major Molineux*]. . . . It demands the same approach, as has been already outlined, and is even more unmistakably a prose poem. . . . Young Goodman Brown is Everyman in seventeenth-century New England—the title as usual giving the clue. He is the son of the Old Goodman Brown, that is, the Old Adam (or Adam the First as he is called in Bunyan), and recently wedded to Faith. We must note that every word is significant in the opening sentence: "Young Goodman Brown came forth at sunset into the street of Salem Village; but put his head back, after crossing the threshold, to exchange a parting kiss with his young wife." She begs him to "put off his journey until sunrise," but he declares he cannot. . . . [It] should not escape us that she tries to stop him because she is under a similar compulsion to go on a "journey" herself— "*She* talks of dreams, too," Young Goodman Brown reflects as he leaves her. The journey each must take alone, in dread, at night, is the journey away from home and the community, from conscious, everyday social life, to the wilderness where the hidden self satisfies, or is forced to realize, its subconscious fears and promptings in sleep. We take that journey with him into the awful forest. We note the division, which is to be the basis of *The Scarlet Letter,* between the town (where the minister rules) and the forest (where the Black Man reigns). . . . [In his depiction of the forest, we] see Hawthorne making timely use of the traditional Puritan association of trees, animals, and Indians as the hostile powers, allies of the fiend. . . . The nightmare poetry gathers volume and power as [Goodman Brown] approaches the flaming center of the forest, but Hawthorne's poetic imagination is as different as possible from Poe's—there is no touch of the Gothic horrors one might anticipate. (pp. 194-97)

When Young Goodman Brown returns to Salem Village . . . his eyes have been opened to the true nature of his fellowmen, that is, human nature; he inescapably knows that what he suspected of himself is true of all men. . . . Hawthorne has made a dramatic poem of the Calvinist experience in New England. The unfailing tact with which the experience is evoked subjectively, in the most impressive concrete terms, is a subordinate proof of genius. I should prefer to stress the wonderful control of local and total rhythm, which never falters or slackens, and rises from the quiet but impressive opening to its poetic climax in the superb and moving finale. . . . (p. 197)

Hawthorne has imaginatively recreated for the reader that Calvinist sense of sin, that theory which did in actuality shape the early social and spiritual history of New England. But in Hawthorne, by a wonderful feat of transmutation, it has no religious significance, it is as a psychological state that it is explored. Young Goodman Brown's Faith is not faith in Christ but faith in human beings, and losing it he is doomed to isolation forever. (pp. 197-98)

Hawthorne never anywhere surpassed [*My Kinsman, Major Molineux*] (written when he was not more than twenty-seven) in dramatic power, in control of tone, pace, and tension, and in something more wonderful, the creation of a suspension between the fullest consciousness of meaning and the emotional incoherence of dreaming. (p. 200)

[The climax of the story is the nightmarish tar and feather scene, which is] seen to represent a tragedy and is felt by us as such; it arouses in Robin [the protagonist] the appropriate blend of emotions—the classical "pity and terror." But Hawthorne has by some inspiration—for how could he have known except intuitively of the origins of tragedy in ritual drama?— gone back to the type of action that fathered Tragedy. . . . We seem to be spectators at that most primitive of all dramatic representations, the conquest of the old king by the new.

If the story had ended here, on this note, it would have been remarkable enough, but Hawthorne has an almost incredible consummation to follow. I mean incredible in being so subtly achieved with such mastery of tone. From being a spectator at a tragedy, Robin has to fulfill his premonitions of having "to bear a part in the pageantry" himself. He is drawn into the emotional vortex and comes to share the reactions of the participants. He has felt intimately the dreadful degradation of his English kinsman, but now he is seized with the excitement of the victors, his fellow-countrymen, and sees their triumph as his own. . . . Then in a sudden calm that follows this orgy "the procession resumed its march. On they went, like fiends that throng in mockery around some dead potentate, mighty no more, but majestic still in his agony." We are left in the silent street, brought back into the world of problems in which the tale opened. Robin still has to settle with reality and decide his future, the future of his generation. (pp. 204-05)

Hawthorne has been blamed for failing to provide a "solution" and for not being optimistic as a good American should be, but it seems to me that here, as in *The Maypole,* he ends in reasonable, sober hopefulness for the future of life. Provided we recognize the facts and fully comprehend the positions, we can cope with it, if not master it, he implies. Declining to be, perhaps incapable of being, a naturalistic novelist, he was true to his best perceptions of his genius when he did the work of a dramatic poet, the interpreter and radical critic of [society]. . . . (p. 205)

. . . . .

[In *The Scarlet Letter,* Hawthorne's stress falls] on the sociological and not the "moral" in the popular sense at all, since he is clearly demanding sympathy for the anti-social members of the community, victims of a theocratic society where "religion and law were almost identical." (p. 429)

Just as [*Anna Karenina*] is framed to evoke the response: This is the society that condemned Anna! so Hawthorne makes Hester the critic of the society that similarly rejects and victimizes her. And just as in *Anna* Tolstoi managed to find room for all his interests, experiences, and problems, so *The Scarlet Letter* has a richer life than any other of Hawthorne's works because it is the most inclusive. What he had worked on and crystallized out in *The Minister's Black Veil, Endicott and the Red Cross, Young Goodman Brown, Main Street, Rapaccini's Daughter,* and *The Maypole of Merry Mount* he swept into a finely organized whole, so that every portion is concentrated with meanings and associations and cross-references. (p. 430)

[The introductory chapter, **"The Prison Door,"**] wonderfully concentrates the theme of the book. Hawthorne describes in one pregnant sentence a Puritan throng waiting outside a prison door, and we realize that that is an index of the nature of their life. He continues, with that disturbing likeness to Swift that shows another formative influence in his literary heredity:

> The founders of a new colony, whatever Utopia
> of human virtue and happiness they might of-

ficially project, have invariably recognized it among their earliest practical necessities to allot a portion of virgin soil as a cemetery, and another portion as the site of a prison.

The graveyard and the prison: the existence of Death and Sin as primary factors in that way of life, equally inescapable, have thus been indicated. (p. 431)

Hawthorne's preoccupation with something that is at once the cultural and the psychological classes him with George Eliot and Tolstoi and Conrad. . . . His profound concern with the history of his local civilization and its importance for himself distinguishes him even among his kind there. (pp. 432-33)

[In *The Scarlet Letter*,] Hawthorne's undisguised "message" is that the evil lay in [Arthur's concealment of his sin]—"Thou wast not bold, thou wast not true," Pearl accuses her father. The tragedy consists in the separation of the genuinely united couple by an inhuman society and originated in the false relation imposed on a girl by an unlovable husband (as in *Anna*). . . . Hawthorne points his unorthodox position by ending, it may seem incongruously, with a regenerated Hester promising to other unhappy women a brighter future "when the world should have grown ripe for it" and "a new truth would be revealed" which will "establish the whole relation between man and woman on a surer ground of mutual happiness." . . . [*The Scarlet Letter* is] a perfect sociological tragedy—given this kind of society and this situation occurring in it, with principals of such a nature and so conditioned, only this can result, there is no escape but in death. And the theological disputation between Hester and her husband is genuinely distilled from the action and its religious environment, not [an imposed "philosophy"]. . . . (pp. 437-38)

If *The House of the Seven Gables* has been consistently overrated (it seems to me quite uninteresting, illogical in conception and frequently trivial in execution, proof of the mischief of the pressure that forced Hawthorne to try and write something like the popular idea of a novel), *The Blithedale Romance* has never as far as I can make out had justice done it. Its style is more consistently distinguished than that of *The Scarlet Letter,* its tone ranges with remarkable command from the drily critical to the poetic. . . . Blithedale is the contemporary Merry Mount, the symbol of a life superior in the theory on which it is based and in the possibilities it offers to the form of life forced on one by the society in which one finds oneself by birth. Its existence represents the possibility of a choice—there is none in *The Scarlet Letter,* hence the Labyrinth is the comprehensive image used in that. (pp. 440-41)

There are no irrelevancies in Hawthorne's best works and when we seem to find one it should be read with particular care as it will undoubtedly turn out to be structural. A first reading [of *The Blithedale Romance*] leaves most people bewildered, asking questions about the unresolved mysteries of the drama. . . . The stress seems to fall in the oddest places. A truly inward reading however sees how everything is part of a whole and in its appropriate place; the book is uncanny because unconventional, not incompetent, original as *Women in Love* or *Nostromo* had to be. (p. 441)

We have in *Blithedale* even more than in the other works I've discussed the [proof of Hawthorne's genius]. . . . The true artist, he has the indispensable genius for knowing, and communicating, where life flows and wherein lies its value and health. He has consistently shown Zenobia as a creature radiant with life, the splendid human animal, but the stress falls on

"human"; she is not only contrasted with the run of New England women who lacked sensual experience, she is also characterized by her "noble and beautiful motion" and we are told of her then: "Natural movement is the result and expression of the whole being, and cannot be well and nobly performed, unless responsive to something in the character." Her death by drowning is the most poignant of all Hawthorne's writing. (pp. 452-53)

Hawthorne's sense of the truly human included intellectual freedom, passion and tenderness and he can thus bring home to us in the concrete the tragedy for New England life of the Puritan's rejection of the human possibilities represented by Zenobia who is drowned, Hester who is starved and outlawed, and the Maypole which is cut down, all by the death-dealing Puritan judge. . . . Hawthorne, we see, required man to be humane, and his ideal opposite he represents by the image of the iron man, whether it takes the form of Endicott, or Governor Bellingham with his head separated from his body, or "that steel engine of the devil's contrivance, a philanthropist." (p. 453)

Hawthorne's moral sense is not something in conflict with these instinctive preferences, it is a corresponding form of sensitiveness. He believed—the proof is in his art—that human beings have no right to take up attitudes of rejection and condemnation toward life. The Prison is Hawthorne's symbol of the society that condemns and punishes, and his heroes and heroines are its victims. The eternal pattern that he saw behind all social life in his America from the beginning has in *Blithedale* been traced in the Nineteenth Century too: the ideal community is disintegrated for the Puritan and hence the Devil cannot be kept out; the separation of rich and poor is insuperable in this age; the Puritan always masters the scene, and as always he rejects Zenobia for Priscilla and what Zenobia stands for is destroyed and lost to society. (p. 454)

Not unrelated to Hawthorne's recurrent theme, but more directly personal, is the class of stories to which *The Snow-Image* belongs, which includes *The Devil in Manuscript* and *The Artist of the Beautiful,* the equivalents of Henry James's stories about writers. . . . The finest of these, *The Snow Image*—significantly sub-titled **"A Childish Miracle"**—at first sight might seem merely a translation into the New England idiom of a Hans Andersen story. But it is not playful nor a fairy-tale, it is an exposition of Hawthorne's predicament as an artist in an entirely bourgeois society such as he found himself doomed to write for. . . . "Snow-images" occurs in the introduction to *The Scarlet Letter* as symbolic of what the artist makes—"the forms which fancy summons up." . . . Literature needs collaboration; the Snow-Image is the creation of the artist's imagination but it is only by sympathetic participation, by an imaginative sharing of the whole community (the father and mother in the story, as well as the children) that it can continue to be kept alive or valid. It is destroyed by the uncomprehending spirit that has no belief in anything but the materially profitable. *The Artist of the Beautiful* puts the same case rather differently. . . . [We find Hawthorne] concluding that "It is requisite for the ideal artist to possess a force of character that seems hardly compatible with its delicacy; he must keep his faith in himself while the incredulous world assails him with its utter disbelief." . . . There are few things more impressive in the history of the novel than the determination of the first great American novelists to find a non-naturalistic form for their work and to reject the English novelists' tradition of social comedy and melodrama, derived from the theater. Hawthorne was truly "empirical." He can be seen consciously trying, or somehow discovering for himself, the various possible techniques for his purpose: the märchen (*Young Goodman Brown*), the allegory of Bunyan (*The Celestial Railroad*), of Spenser and Milton, the romance, the morality play, the legend (*The Gray Champion* follows the widespread Holgar the Dane pattern), the myth, the masque, drama of various kinds in the light of Shakespeare, the panorama (*Main Street*), the pageant, the fable, the parable. As became a pioneer, Hawthorne instinctively kept close to the sources of literature. His stage is the platform stage of early drama, his settings of the traditional sort such as are provided for by a tree, an archway, a street, a public square, a forest clearing, the outside of a church, a fountain or well or pool. (pp. 454-56)

Hawthorne's concern for his culture is positively religious and never gets out of touch with the sources of a religious drama. His folklore element is always notably more serious than Scott's, though he has nothing so picturesque as *Wandering Willie's Tale* and many of his attempts to write American folk-story are failures (like **Mr. Higginbotham's Catastrophe**) from poverty of the raw material. The apparent oddities of his writings are not due to incompetence but are inherent in their nature; he is fragmentary as are Shakespeare's *Winter's Tale* and the old Ballads. . . .

Hawthorne's claim does rest on a small body of work, but even ignoring his importance as a trail-blazer, an infector and literary ancestor, that work is sufficient. It is slight only in being tense, sensitive, elegant as a mathematical proof, sinewy, concentrated as a poem and incorruptibly relevant. (p. 457)

> *Q. D. Leavis, "Hawthorne as Poet," in* The Sewanee Review *(reprinted by permission of the editor; © 1951, copyright renewed © 1979, by The University of the South), Vol. LIX, Nos. 2 & 3, Spring and Summer, 1951, pp. 179-205, 426-57.*

EDWARD H. DAVIDSON (essay date 1964)

In [Hawthorne's] last writings, the major burden is that of posing the real and the conceptual dimensions of life, between, that is, what a character is actually doing and what Hawthorne, the writer, meant to show in the behavior of that character. The meditative asides, the reminders, and the long conjectures which fill so many manuscript pages of these last writings— all deal with the central problem of Romance: it is the attempt to deal generally and conceptually with human experience and to reach conclusions about experience without first being able to particularize the living details which give rise to that experience. (p. 145)

In quite extraordinary ways, Hawthorne was capable of bringing great theoretical and imaginative force to bear upon his art; but the force had to be mustered and resolved before the workmanship, the actual composition of sentences, had begun. The speed with which he wrote his four major novels testifies to the planning, the power of thought, and the sheer imaginative dexterity which were his when he was at his best. . . . The true imaginative force Hawthorne brought to his art was in bridging the speculative distance between the real and the abstract, between the commonplace and the conceptualized, and between the trivial and the grand, even the divine; it was a power both of devising an abstract moral idea of experience and of particularizing just those elements and just those human beings which would make that idea vivid and meaningful. In these last romances Hawthorne seems to be, in each of the four fragments, only at the beginning of that inquiry which, in the

major writings, had been accomplished before the action got under way. (pp. 146-47)

When [Hawthorne] was not able to specify what this central idea ought to be—whether the American traveler in England should be lured into subservience to England's charm or remain stalwartly American; whether the experimenter in elixirs of life should be high- or low-minded—then Hawthorne had to stop, retrace his steps, and try to set down a satisfactory, if provisional, statement of his "moral." In these last romances, the warnings that he must resolve this initial premise become sharper as the pages of manuscript increase. "I have not yet struck the true key-note of this Romance," he remarks in *The Ancestral Footstep*, "and until I do, and unless I do, I shall write nothing but tediousness and nonsense. I do not wish it to be a picture of life, but a Romance, grim, grotesque, quaint. . . . If I could but write one central scene in this vein, all the rest of the Romance would readily arrange itself around that nucleus." (p. 147)

A writer like Hawthorne may suffer from too great a moral and imaginative sophistication and thereby come to have contempt for the very workmanship which had brought him his earlier success. The breakdown came, therefore, first, because of a method of composition which had served Hawthorne very well throughout his whole career; secondly, because of a method of characterization; and thirdly, because of this rift between real and conceptualized experience—a rift which widened perilously and then disastrously as these last years moved on. (p. 148)

On first reading the meditative asides in *Doctor Grimshawe's Secret*, one is struck by the apparently hit-or-miss method of planning and workmanship; yet it is not the improvisation of a man who does not know quite where he is going. It is the craft and practice of an artist who knows that life is touched, not forced, that the meaning of an action may lie in the power of the questing imagination, and that, quite without anyone's knowing how it comes to pass, the "central idea" may release itself by virtue of its own inner necessity. Nowhere is Hawthorne closer to Melville than in his awareness that both the statement and the form of an idea may inhere in the most jumbled and incongruous exposition of life. It is what he called, in a striking phrase in *The Ancestral Footstep*, "imaginative probability": a moral abstraction, a human action, even a fantastic legend such as the bloody footstep may, Hawthorne noted, "bring its own imaginative probability."

Yet what was that "probability"? One cannot say with respect to these unfinished romances simply because the end of a question in probability rests not on its hypothetical or abstract statement but rather on its fulfilment. Dealing as we must with only portions and fragments, we must be wary of supposing that Hawthorne had in mind a formal and coherent artistic presupposition; the very waywardness of his imagination as he worked through these unfinished drafts testifies both to the improvisation and even to the chance of the moment.

We can suppose, nevertheless, that the central subject of these last romances was, as it had been for *The Marble Faun*, the dependence of modern life, of progress, even of human restoration and redemption, on antecedent decay, corruption, and fall. . . . The subject of the romances would be, accordingly, on the theme of the Fall—the fall of a single traveler and then his restoration or, conversely, the fall of a whole society in the upheaval of war.

Yet the Fall is not, in Hawthorne's fiction, an incident in a man's life or a single event in history; it is a continuing, pervasive condition of nature and of the whole of mankind whereby human beings are permitted, if they are privileged to be enlightened, to understand themselves in their degradation and in their truth. (pp. 148-50)

The conceptualized idea of the Fall was, for Hawthorne, both a principle and a method of workmanship. When he got into trouble, as he did so frequently in these fragmentary romances, he tended to improvise on the question of the Fall; he sought to work backward in the lives of his characters; he tried to deepen the "imaginative probability" by construing any number of ancillary events as rightly pertaining to the "central effect" and to the main action. The Fall took him ever toward that antecedent corruption and decay by which he sought to invest his characters with the vivid lineaments of Romance. Indeed, the Fall and the idea of Romance joined: one equaled the other in the logic of imaginative probability. (p. 150)

[Hawthorne] longed for some emblem of buried evil which, festering through centuries, might darken the sunlight of the contemporary world: he conjured up a coffin supposedly full of gold which, on being opened, contained only masses of golden hair into which a woman's body had been transformed. Hidden documents, secret nostrums promising eternal life, relics long buried in the earth or a tomb—these might be the embodiments of man's perpetual sharing in the world's core of evil. Hawthorne had a similar way of studying or "deepening," as he called the method, his characters: generally speaking, he devised his protagonists by going backward. He began with a man or woman at the last and dramatic occasion of the romance; then he worked his way through the earlier life of that person until, as in *Doctor Grimshawe's Secret,* he was at the very beginning of his hero's story. (pp. 150-51)

Yet to accuse Hawthorne of merely playing with one of his central themes and of crudely piling up incidents is to falsify a great writer's craft. The difficulty was not that Hawthorne's method of composition was failing him; indeed, it was the very force of his improvisation which gave him so many directions to follow and so many variations to play on his central theme. The difficulty in these last expositions of the Fall was that Hawthorne's imaginative and critical faculty was being brought to bear, with really too great emphasis, on men and women who were somehow outside or freed from the implications of the very Fall in which they were supposedly involved. (p. 151)

Hawthorne's method of characterization was based in large part on his embodying in human form certain abstract moral truths such as Innocence, Hardness of Heart, Sympathy, Ambition, and so on. Hawthorne was, however, intelligent enough to consider these somewhat shadowy human figures ambiguous for the very reason that an abstraction can never be fully informed with human life. . . . In the last romances, however, Hawthorne essayed both to invest his characters with the dark lineaments of the past and yet somehow to bring them into the light of a new day which had none of the implications of that age-old system, or of the Fall. Indeed, the movement of human life might come from individual impulse, as if men were finally freed from the tragic imputation of original sin; experience could now be presented as though it were lived now and as though the new privilege of life were that it could be self-sufficient, self-contained, and self-understanding. (pp. 151-52)

In these fragmentary romances, Hawthorne's characters are not yet privileged to have experience; they have not begun to experience anything but are forced by the unwitting and heedless world of conjecture and possibility to assume a simple, temporary guise and thereby to exclude the many-sided values which might lend them interest and importance. Thus these romances pose the good-heartedness, sometimes the whimsical and stubborn recalcitrance, of self-asserting human beings against a proven, a durable ethical system—against, that is, the Fall. . . . In the end, Hawthorne's characters in these unfinished novels cast serious doubt on the validity of an ethical system which had remained unchallenged throughout Hawthorne's literary career; these seekers of ancestral wealth and magical nostrums pursue most high-minded aims and yet, at every turn of the action, countermand the moral principles which allow them their only right to exist. (pp. 152-53)

Sometimes Hawthorne tried to cast experience in the form of a dream, as though the hazy intangibility of dream would mediate between the disparate claims of life. . . . When, as it so often happened, the hero could not be budged farther than the most sedate, or intransigent, flatness of the commonplace, then Hawthorne again had recourse to the strange and the spectacular—to the bloody footstep, the coffin filled with golden hair, the unraveling of a long-buried mystery; and when they refused to yield their secret and thereby limn the dark underside of human consciousness, Hawthorne felt only contempt for his creatures and broke out into such self-condemnatory remarks as "What unimaginable nonsense!" He had events, more than he could ever employ; he had human beings, some copied from men he had known in England and Italy, others, like the old pensioner of the charity in England, modeled directly on his neighbor Alcott. Experience was there to be lived; yet he had no one fit to live it. On the one side was "the reality," the commonplace existence which is the lot of most of mankind—"the point of view where things are seen in their true lights." On the other side was "the true world . . . like dark-colored experience," "the absolute truth . . . all outside of which [is] delusion." The narrative and the characters must join these two visionary possibilities; when they failed, then the romance failed utterly. The pathos and the tragedy of these last romances is that, as his problems deepened and the confusion worsened, Hawthorne's characters were no longer capable of those discriminations, of tenuous or profound moral judgment, or of those dark, ambiguous probings of their own sensitive minds; they were moral incompetents in a morally incompetent world; and their creator's vengeance on them was dire and terrible. (pp. 154-55)

[In these last romances,] Hawthorne's power of invention, his "Gothicism," which conjured strange and suggestive events, was forced to yield to the form of the action in which the characters should move and have their being: that "form" was a lifetime's habit of conceptualizing, of thinking abstractly about the otherwise common exigencies of life, and then of adding, as though in an afterthought, the elements and particulars out of which concepts are made. The interest of these posthumous fragments is that, while he had tentatively resolved the marvelous and the moral requirements, Hawthorne was trying to make clear to himself just those minute particularities out of which concepts are made. He kept reminding himself that he must "Specify, specify"; it was not the marvelous and the supernatural which were lacking; it was the simplest investment of the common day, those most ordinary details that writers like Dickens and Trollope made the very stuff of their writings.

In attempting to mediate between the marvelous and the commonplace, Hawthorne effected a curious and almost imperceptible transformation in the heroes of these fragmentary novels. They began as creatures in a world of Romance, whether in Salem, in a midland county in England, or in Hawthorne's own Wayside in Concord during the opening months of the Revolutionary War; and they became more and more recognizable as men in the busy world of the present, of Liverpool, of American military and political life. As he went on tirelessly and painfully, Hawthorne abandoned his theory of romance and tried to write a moral fable for his own time. (pp. 155-56)

[The protagonist was] a very modern hero, whose unbending desire for self-satisfaction and for worldly success, both in England and in America, is set grotesquely amid the peaceful relics of a long-past time. Middleton, Etherege, Redclyffe, Septimius Felton, or whatever the provisional name this young man bears is the new middle-class hero of Dickens or Trollope—a young man with no parentage, with meager beginnings, with a rude, canny intelligence, and with an overweening passion to get ahead in the world; yet he is for a time inhabiting a special place in which commercial greed, modern industry, and the moral advantages of poverty do not exist.

The Ancestral Footstep and *Doctor Grimshawe's Secret* required that this commercial hero should come upon a long-established ethical system, be quite unaware of his own moral incompetence, and never understand the havoc he may be causing by reason of his researches into his family history. Yet, instead of setting a self-reliant hero against an intractable ethical system and allowing that system to come under harsh surveillance such as would be the hallmark of the bourgeois romance from Defoe through Dickens to Orwell, Hawthorne made the ethical establishment the final moral authority and thereby tried to effect, in his own words, "a bitter commentary" on the presumption of a man to be a claimant for anything in this shifting and fallible world. (pp. 156-57)

In the **"Romance of Immortality,"** the premise is reversed. . . . [Here] Hawthorne placed a most moral young man in a time of moral disarray, even collapse. Thus human virtue abides only in this young man, Septimius Felton; he seeks not for wealth or a lost patrimony but for some relief from that most dread burden of existence, namely death. . . . (p. 157)

Hawthorne tried to draw a metaphysical rebel, one who sought to overthrow everything that sustained society, and in doing so fashioned once again the man with the diabolized heart—the cold-blooded villain whose very excellence of mind and motive is his own and others' doom. Hawthorne might have been devising a bitter commentary on nineteenth-century meliorism, Utilitarianism, and the illusion of earthly progress. Perhaps he was: the Blithedale community of an earlier time revealed the corruption which lies just beneath the ruminative surface of man's most exalted intentions. *Septimius Felton* reveals, more suggestively, that when he had not clearly informed himself of the moral theme for his romance—the fragments reveal a distressing improvisation with almost palpably felt ideas—Hawthorne sought refuge in the most errant inventiveness or "romancing," as if the very piling up of incident and detail would magically solve the difficulty. In the last fragment, *The Dolliver Romance,* Hawthorne tried to invest his hero with all goodness and sweetness of temper; the projected narrative would not risk a protagonist who should become a fool. Here, for the last time in his career, Hawthorne would again have that distinctly moral man whose life is all in the past and who has the power to invest experience with those glowing colors which moral insight can give it. (p. 158)

In these unfinished romances, Hawthorne was less interested in the way the story moved and more concerned with what at every turn the narrative might reveal. This is not to say that in his major writings Hawthorne had not been the allegorist; it is to say that, in the earlier writings, he brought greater imaginative and moral force to the action, to the symbolic design, and to the human beings who should exemplify the subject of the romance than to the subject itself. In the posthumous romances, Hawthorne directed his very considerable imaginative power, not toward disclosures of his ideas in the lives of men and women, but toward the themes themselves; he took them with profound seriousness; he felt oppressed by them; and, when he could not effect that "imaginative probability" in the lives of his characters, he turned on them with ruthlessness and contempt. Thus, when they failed him, as they did every time, Hawthorne made them the victims of a critical intelligence which was scrupulous, exacting, and severe. (pp. 158-59)

The failure of these last romances would be only a minor incident in American literary history and of interest only as a coda to Hawthorne's great career if that failure were merely of biographical and personal moment. The failure is, however, an occasion in the continuous history of the American imagination and bears striking relevance to events in the lives of other writers—Melville, Mark Twain, and Emily Dickinson, to name only a few. The issue was fundamentally that of the artist and his subject. In order to function properly, the artist in American letters had three gaps to fill: through knowledge and experience he must discover the past, the evil in the world, and those people who would illustrate for him the ideas he considers imaginatively probable. He must show his men and women as losing their innocence and then becoming purified by their recognition of, and their triumph over, sin and corruption. And the artist, together with his creations, must emerge with the capacity to deal, if not profoundly, at least cogently with the basic issues of his art. (pp. 159-60)

In his last years Hawthorne found himself cut off from his central subject, namely, the peril and the wonder of moral man finding his way to, and his place in, a God-ordained and, therefore, ethical universe. When he set this presumably moral man in a time very close to the present—the English romance would be as contemporary as Hawthorne's own life in Liverpool—Hawthorne became painfully aware of his impotence and unworthiness to understand his hero's destiny.

The difficulty was not really with the subject, or with the times, but with art itself—that continuing and pervasive difficulty with which American writers of the nineteenth century struggled. Hawthorne may not be adequately representative of them all; yet, behind his questions concerning his shadowy characters and their futile dreams of wealth and elixirs of life, he does reveal that the imaginative power he had formerly expended on the display of moral ideas in the lives of men and women was now turning inward and being brought directly to bear on the issue of art and the imagination. The question was not so much, What is the writer doing when he writes?, as it was, What must be the writer's ethical warrant and place in the diffuse and indeterminate life of his world and time? Perhaps the only nineteenth-century American writer who found a satisfactory answer to this question was Henry James, one of whose distinctions was that he admitted his debt to Hawthorne. (pp. 160-61)

[Through] the nineteenth century, there was a pervasive discontinuity in the art of fiction of such proportions that Dickens'

Pip could inhabit the Gothic world of Mrs. Radcliffe and that Twain's *Huckleberry Finn* could be the moral picaresque of a heedless Everyman. In either case, this lack of any logical congruence in modern life lies at the moral center of much American, and for that matter English, fiction of the nineteenth century: it was that the artist sought to work through his creations in order to deal cogently, perhaps profoundly, with certain quite well-defined moral issues but that, especially with American writers, the larger problem of art itself eventually triumphed over and submerged those men and women who should have been the living representatives of ethical ideas. (pp. 161-62)

Hawthorne's expositions of moral ideas came as a result of very considerable and concentrated thought, not on the particular lives his characters might lead, but rather on abstract forms of living which would somehow lift these transitory lives of men and women above the commonplace requirements of daily existence. Human life did not give dignity and vividness to moral ideas, quite the contrary: moral abstractions bestowed distinction on life. "Imaginative probability" was the infinite calculus of possible relevance between the world's timeless law of good and evil and the energetic, haphazard, and oftentimes futile actions of human beings. Thus the effective moral thought of the writer grants to life more than it deserves to have; even in the fragmentary romances of the final years, we can see these people beginning with the most trivial self-deceits and then be almost mysteriously lifted up by the impelling power a moral idea can bestow on them; and when Hawthorne could not decide what this "central effect" or "moral center" ought to be, the characters disintegrate or become the objects of his scorn. (pp. 162-63)

[Even] in these final years of despair, Hawthorne well knew the state of his mind; he did not have the effrontery to blame the troubled times in which he lived. If he did turn on his half-formed characters the venom of his frustration, he knew that he alone was the cause of his trouble. That trouble was too great for contempt, for pathos, even for understanding. It was fortunate that Hawthorne died before he had said his own last word on it; that word might have been the bitterest of all. (p. 163)

> *Edward H. Davidson, "The Unfinished Romances," in* Hawthorne Centenary Essays, *edited by Roy Harvey Pearce (copyright © 1964 by the Ohio State University Press; all rights reserved), Ohio State University Press, 1964, pp. 141-63.*

ADDITIONAL BIBLIOGRAPHY

Alcott, A. Bronson. "Hawthorne." In his *Concord Days*, pp. 193-97. Boston: Roberts Bros., 1872.
Character sketch by Hawthorne's Concord neighbor.

Astrov, Vladimir. "Hawthorne and Dostoevski as Explorers of the Human Conscience." *The New England Quarterly* XV, No. 2 (June 1942): 296-319.*
Examines the many points of contact in the moral and psychological ideas of Hawthorne and his Russian contemporary.

Brooks, Van Wyck. "Hawthorne in Salem." In his *The Flowering of New England: 1815-1865*, pp. 210-27. New York: E. P. Dutton & Co., 1940.
Describes Hawthorne's solitary years in Salem and traces their effect upon his writings.

Carpenter, Frederic I. "Puritans Preferred Blondes: The Heroines of Melville and Hawthorne." *The New England Quarterly* IX (June 1936): 253-72.*
Discusses Melville and Hawthorne's use of blonde and brunette hair to symbolize good and evil heroines.

Carpenter, Frederic I. "Scarlet A Minus." *College English* 5, No. 4 (January 1944): 173-80.
Asserts that Hawthorne flawed *The Scarlet Letter* by confusing Hester's transcendental morality and Puritan morality.

Cowley, Malcolm. "Hawthorne in the Looking Glass." *Sewanee Review* LVI (1948): 545-63.
Discusses the importance of Hawthorne's mirror imagery in his literature and life.

Cowley, Malcolm. "Five Acts of *The Scarlet Letter*." *College English* 19, No. 1 (October 1957): 11-16.
Proposes that by dividing *The Scarlet Letter* into essentially five scenes, Hawthorne innovated an architectural form for the novel and captured for New England the essence of Greek tragedy.

Crews, Frederick. *The Sins of the Fathers: Hawthorne's Psychological Themes*. New York: Oxford University Press, 1966, 279 p.
Important psychological interpretations of several works.

Curl, Vega. *Pasteboard Masks: Fact as Spiritual Symbol in the Novels of Hawthorne and Melville*. Cambridge: Harvard University Press, 1931, 45 p.*
An analysis of Hawthorne's view of the Transcendentalist philosophy.

Feidelson, Charles, Jr. "Four American Symbolists: Hawthorne." In his *Symbolism and American Literature*, pp. 6-16. Chicago and London: The University of Chicago Press, 1953.
Discusses symbolism and allegory in Hawthorne's novels.

Fiedler, Leslie A. "The Scarlet Letter: Woman as Faust." In his *Love and Death in the American Novel*, pp. 485-519. New York: Criterion Books, 1960.
Presents Hester as the "first Faust of classic American literature." This is an important discussion of *The Scarlet Letter*.

Fields, James T. *Yesterdays with Authors*. Boston: Houghton, Mifflin and Company, 1893, 419p.*
Affectionate personal reminiscence by Hawthorne's publisher and lifelong friend.

Fogle, Richard Harter. *Hawthorne's Fiction: The Light & the Dark*. Norman, Okla.: University of Oklahoma Press, 1952, 219 p.
Examines the stories and novels as instances of Hawthorne's use of "light and dark:" his clarity of design and lucid language versus tragic complexity and black tonality.

Fogle, Richard Harter. *Hawthorne's Imagery: The "Proper Light and Shadow" in the Major Romances*. Norman, Okla.: University of Oklahoma Press, 1969, 175 p.
Explores Hawthorne's use of light and shadow as a means of unifying narratives and illuminating characters. This is intended as a companion volume to the work listed above.

Gerber, John C., ed. *Twentieth-Century Interpretations of "The Scarlet Letter"*. Englewood Cliffs, NJ: Prentice-Hall, Inc., 1968, 120 p.
Essays by various critics examining the background, form, technique, and critical reception of Hawthorne's masterpiece.

Hawthorne, Julian. *Nathaniel Hawthorne and His Wife: A Biography*. 2 vols. Boston and New York: Houghton, Mifflin and Company, 1893, 970 p.
Detailed biography of Nathaniel and Sophia Peabody Hawthorne by their only son.

Hoeltje, Hubert H. *Inward Sky: The Mind and Heart of Nathaniel Hawthorne*. Durham, N.C.: Duke University Press, 1962, 579 p.
Examines Hawthorne's character through his writings.

Kaul, A. N., ed. *Hawthorne: A Collection of Critical Essays*. Englewood Cliffs, N.J.: Prentice-Hall, Inc., 1966, 182 p.

Essays and excerpts from longer works, focusing on the major novels and tales.

Lathrop, George Parsons. *A Study of Hawthorne.* 1876. Reprint. New York: AMS Press, 1969, 350 p.
> An early, influential study by Hawthorne's son-in-law.

Lawrence, D. H. "Hawthorne's *Blithedale Romance.*" In his *Studies in Classic American Literature,* pp. 101-10. New York: The Viking Press, 1961.
> A sardonic assessment of the characters and action of *The Blithedale Romance.*

Lawton, William Cranston. "Hawthorne: A Lonely Life." In his *The New England Poets: A Study of Emerson, Hawthorne, Longfellow, Whittier, Lowell, Holmes,* pp. 48-104. New York: The MacMillan Company, 1898.
> Biographical and critical survey.

Levin, Harry. "Camera Obscura." In his *The Power of Blackness,* pp. 36-67. New York: Knopf, 1958.
> Examines the somber and supernatural element in Hawthorne's work.

Lewis, R.W.B. "The Return into Time: Hawthorne." In his *The American Adam: Innocence, Tragedy and Tradition in the Nineteenth Century,* pp. 110-26. Chicago: University of Chicago Press, 1955.
> A textual analysis of *The Marble Faun.*

More, Paul Elmer. "The Origins of Hawthorne and Poe." In his *Shelburne Essays on American Literature,* pp. 86-98. Edited by Daniel Aaron. New York, Burlingame, Calif.: Harcourt, Brace & World, Inc., 1963.*
> Examines literary and historical precedents which lent Poe and Hawthorne's writings the "force and realism of profound moral experience."

Pearce, Roy Harvey. "Hawthorne and the Sense of the Past: Or, the Immortality of Major Molineux." *ELH: A Journal of English Literary History* XXI, No. 4 (December 1954): 327-49.
> Traces the theme of the pervasiveness of history through Hawthorne's oeuvre.

Pearce, Roy Harvey, ed. *Hawthorne Centenary Essays.* Columbus: Ohio State University Press, 1964, 480 p.

Essays on Hawthorne's art, philosophy, and critical heritage by Harry Levin, R.W.B. Lewis, Lionel Trilling, and other distinguished critics.

Spiller, Robert E. "The Artist in America: Poe, Hawthorne." In his *The Cycle of American Literature,* pp. 61-75. New York: The American Library, 1957.*
> Examines aesthetic detachment in Hawthorne's novels.

Stein, William Bysshe. *Hawthorne's Faust: A Study of the Devil Archetype.* Gainesville: University of Florida Press, 1953, 172 p.
> A depiction of the Faustian myth in the work of Hawthorne.

Stewart, Randall. Introduction to *The American Notebooks by Nathaniel Hawthorne,* pp. xiii-xcvi. New Haven: Yale University Press, 1932.
> Describes Sophia Hawthorne's revisions of her husband's notebooks and discusses his use of them as a source for plots and themes.

Stubbs, John Caldwell. *The Pursuit of Form: A Study of Hawthorne and the Romance.* Urbana: University of Illinois Press, 1970, 170 p.
> Explores Hawthorne's exploitation of nineteenth-century romance, emphasizing his skill as an "artificer."

Turner, Arlin. *Nathaniel Hawthorne: An Introduction and Interpretation.* New York: Barnes and Noble, Inc., 1961, 149 p.
> A "brief history" of Hawthorne's mind, as revealed in his stories and novels.

Van Doren, Carl. "The Flower of Puritanism." *The Nation* CXI, No. 2892 (8 December 1920): 649-50.
> Contrasts the Puritan philosophy of *The Scarlet Letter,* set in New England, with that of *The Marble Faun,* set in Italy.

Van Doren, Mark. *Nathaniel Hawthorne.* New York: The Viking Press, 1949, 279 p.
> Graceful critical biography.

Waggoner, Hyatt H. *Hawthorne: A Critical Study.* Cambridge, Mass.: The Belknap Press of Harvard University Press, 1963, 278 p.
> Critical survey of Hawthorne's oeuvre.

Warren, Austin. "*The Scarlet Letter:* A Literary Exercise in Moral Theology." *Southern Review* n.s. I, No. 1 (January 1965): 22-45.
> Detailed examination of the theological and philosophical background of *The Scarlet Letter.*

Ernst Theodor Amadeus Hoffmann

1776-1822

German short story writer, novelist, and music critic.

Composer, musician, and artist, Hoffmann is best known as a writer of bizarre and fantastic fiction. Drawing from English Gothic romance, eighteenth-century Italian comedy, the psychology of the abnormal, and the occult, he created a world where everyday life is infused with the supernatural.

Hoffmann's tales were influential in the nineteenth century throughout Europe and America. Edgar Allan Poe, Charles Baudelaire, Fedor Dostoevski, Heinrich Heine, and George Meredith are among the authors who derived plots, characters, and motifs from Hoffmann. Yet twentieth-century critics and readers have tended to overlook him. Hoffmann was, as René Wellek commented, "like a forgotten well from which many have drunk, but which has dried out today." Since the 1950s, however, critics have revaluated Hoffmann and have come to appreciate his inventiveness and vision.

The child of estranged parents, Hoffmann lived with his uncle, a pragmatic civil servant who did not encourage his nephew's prodigious talents. Hoffmann studied law and accepted a government appointment, but cared for music above all and devoted himself to composing theatrical scores, opera, and ecclesiastical pieces. A public official by day and a composer of romantic music by night, Hoffmann experienced the conflict that became a recurring theme in his fiction: the opposition between artistic endeavors and mundane concerns and the struggle of the artist to create in an unsympathetic, philistine society.

In 1806, Hoffmann lost his bureaucratic post and joined the Bamberg theater as musical conductor and stage director. His theatrical experience provided Hoffmann with an understanding of character, dialogue, and dramatic structure that enriched his fiction. Significant, too, was Hoffmann's passionate attachment to Julia Marc, a gifted voice student whom he idealized in his writings as a representation of music incarnate. In Hoffmann's life, however, as in his fiction, the ideal is inviolable, and his love for Julia remained platonic.

Hoffmann's first published works were reviews of Beethoven, Bach, Gluck, and Mozart, the last of whom Hoffmann honored by changing his own third name from Wilhelm to Amadeus. Believing that music was the supreme mode of expression, Hoffmann tried to replicate in his fiction music's superior traits, such as its immediacy, emotional power, and supernatural qualities. Hoffmann hoped to transport readers beyond the physical realm by thrusting them into an environment palpably real, yet strangely unfamiliar.

Hoffmann's stories range from fairy tales to traditional narratives, but his most characteristic works feature doppelgänger, automata, and mad artists and each has a dark, hallucinatory tone. The author's potent language and images sometimes offended his contemporaries. Johann Wolfgang von Goethe remarked on Hoffmann's "sickness," and Sir Walter Scott wrote that Hoffmann required "the assistance of medicine rather than of criticism." Many critics, however, still appreciate the grotesque humor, social satire, and extravagant

artistry beneath the horrific surface. The extent of Hoffmann's influence is obvious in the work of his literary descendants, from Poe and the symbolists to the surrealists and modernists.

PRINCIPAL WORKS

Fantasiestücke in Callots Manier. 4 vols.   (short stories)
  1814-15
Die Elixiere des Teufels (novel) 1815-16
  [*The Devil's Elixir*, 1824; also published as *The Devil's Elixirs*, 1963]
Nachstücke. 2 vols. (short stories) 1816-17
Klein Zaches gennant Zinnober (novella) 1819
  [*Little Zack* published in *Fairy Tales*, 1857; also published as *Little Zaches, Surnamed Zinnober* in *Three Märchen of E.T.A. Hoffmann*, 1971]
Seltsame Leiden eines Theater-Direktors (novella) 1819
Die Serapions-Brüder. 4 vols. (short stories) 1819-21
  [*The Serapion Brethren*, 2 vols., 1886-92]
Lebens-Ansichten des Katers Murr nebst fragmentarischer Biographie des Kapellmeisters Johannes Kreisler in züfalligen Makulaturblättern (unfinished novel) 1820-21

[*The Educated Cat* in *Nut-Cracker and Mouse-King, and, The Educated Cat*, 1892; also published as *The Life and Opinions of Kater Murr: With the Fragmentary Biography of Kapellmeister Johannes Kreisler on Random Sheets of Scrap Paper* in *Selected Writings of E.T.A. Hoffmann: The Novel; Vol. 2*, 1969]
Prinzessin Brambilla: Ein Capriccio nach Jakob Callot (novella)   1821
[*Princess Brambilla* published in *Three Märchen of E.T.A. Hoffmann*, 1971]
Meister Floh: Ein Märchen in seiben Abenteuern zweier Freunde (novella)   1822
[*Master Flea*, 1826]
Die Letzten Erzählungen (short stories)   1825
The Golden Pot (short story)   1827
Hoffmann's Strange Stories (short stories)   1855
Hoffmann's Fairy Tales (fairy tales)   1857
Weird Tales. 2 vols. (short stories)   1885
The Elementary Spirit (short story)   1888
The Mines of Falun (short story)   1926
German Short Stories (short stories)   1934
Tales of Hoffmann (short stories)   1959
Selected Writings of E.T.A. Hoffmann. 2 vols. (short stories and novel)   1969

BLACKWOOD'S EDINBURGH MAGAZINE (essay date 1824)

The Devil's Elixir is, we think, upon the whole, our chief favourite among the numerous works of [E.T.A. Hoffman,] a man of rare and singular genius. It contains in itself the germ of many of his other performances; and one particular idea, in which, more than any other, he, as a romancer, delighted, has been repeated by him in many various shapes, but never with half the power and effect in which it has been elaborated here. (p. 55)

[This idea is] what he calls, in his own language, a *doppelgänger*. . . . [In some works using the *doppelgänger*,] the idea is turned to a half-ludicrous use—and very successfully too—but by far the best are those romances in which it has been handled quite seriously—and of all these, the best is [*The Devil's Elixir*]. (pp. 56-7)

The superior excellence of the **Devil's Elixir** lies in the skill with which its author has contrived to mix up the horrible notion of the double-goer, with ordinary human feelings of all kinds. He has linked it with scenes of great and simple pathos—with delineations of the human mind under the influences of not one, but many of its passions—ambition—love—revenge—remorse. He has even dared to mix scenes and characters exquisitely ludicrous with those in which his haunted hero appears and acts; and all this he has been able to do without in the smallest degree weakening the horrors which are throughout his *corps de reserve*. On the contrary, we attribute the unrivalled effect which this work, as a whole, produces on the imagination, to nothing so much as the admirable art with which the author has married dreams to realities, the air of truth which his wildest fantasies draw from the neighbourhood of things which we all feel to be simply and intensely human and true. Banquo's ghost is tenfold horrible, because it appears at a regal banquet—and the horrors of the Monk Medardus affect our sympathies in a similar ratio, because this victim of

everything that is fearful in the caprices of an insane imagination, is depicted to us as living and moving among men, women, and scenes, in all of which we cannot help recognizing a certain aspect of life and nature, and occasionally even of homeliness. (p. 57)

> "'The Devil's Elixir'," in Blackwood's Edinburgh Magazine, Vol. XVI, No. XC, July, 1824, pp. 55-67.

[WALTER SCOTT] (essay date 1827)

The author who led the way in [the Fantastic style] of literature was Ernest Theodore William Hoffmann; the peculiarity of whose genius, temper, and habits, fitted him to distinguish himself where imagination was to be strained to the pitch of oddity and bizarrerie. He appears to have been a man of rare talent,—a poet, an artist, and a musician, but unhappily of a hypochondriac and whimsical disposition, which carried him to extremes in all his undertakings; so his music became capricious,— his drawings caricatures,—and his tales, as he himself termed them, fantastic extravagances. (p. 74)

We do not mean to say that the imagination of Hoffmann was either wicked or corrupt, but only that it was ill-regulated and had an undue tendency to the horrible and the distressing. Thus he was followed, especially in his hours of solitude and study, by the apprehension of mysterious danger to which he conceived himself exposed; and the whole tribe of demi-gorgons, apparitions, and fanciful spectres and goblins of all kinds with which he has filled his pages, although in fact the children of his own imagination, were no less discomposing to him than if they had had a real existence and actual influence upon him. (p. 81)

It is no wonder that to a mind so vividly accessible to the influence of the imagination, so little under the dominion of sober reason, such a numerous train of ideas should occur in which fancy had a large share and reason none at all. In fact, the grotesque in his compositions partly resembles the arabesque in painting, in which is introduced the most strange and complicated monsters, resembling centaurs, griffins, sphinxes, chimeras, rocs, and all other creatures of romantic imagination, dazzling the beholder as it were by the unbounded fertility of the author's imagination, and sating it by the rich contrast of all the varieties of shape and colouring, while there is in reality nothing to satisfy the understanding or inform the judgment. Hoffmann spent his life, which could not be a happy one, in weaving webs of this wild and imaginative character, for which after all he obtained much less credit with the public, than his talents must have gained if exercised under the restraint of a better taste or a more solid judgment. . . . [Notwithstanding] the dreams of an overheated imagination, by which his taste appears to have been so strangely misled, Hoffmann seems to have been a man of excellent disposition, a close observer of nature, and one who, if this sickly and disturbed train of thought had not led him to confound the supernatural with the absurd, would have distinguished himself as a painter of human nature, of which in its realities he was an observer and an admirer.

Hoffmann was particularly skilful in depicting characters arising in his own country of Germany. Nor is there any of her numerous authors who have better and more faithfully designed the upright honesty and firm integrity which is to be met with in all classes which come from the ancient Teutonic stock.

There is one character in particular in the tale called "**Der Majorat**" ["**the Entail**"]. . . . (pp. 81-2)

[The central character] is indeed an original: having the peculiarities of age and some of its satirical peevishness; but in his moral qualities he is well described by La Motte Fouqué, as a hero of ancient days in the night-gown and slippers of an old lawyer of the present age. The innate worth, independence, and resolute courage of the justiciary seem to be rather enhanced than diminished by his education and profession. . . .

Having known two generations of the baronial house to which he is attached, he has become possessed of their family secrets, some of which are of a mysterious and terrible nature. This confidential situation, but much more the nobleness and energy of his own character, gives the old man a species of authority even over his patron himself, although the baron is a person of stately manners, and occasionally manifests a fierce and haughty temper. (p. 83)

[The concluding passage of "**the Entail**"], while it shows the wildness of Hoffmann's fancy, evinces also that he possessed power which ought to have mitigated and allayed it. Unfortunately, his taste and temperament directed him too strongly to the grotesque and fantastic,—carried him too far "extra moenia flammantia mundi," too much beyond the circle not only of probability but even of possibility, to admit of his composing much in the better style which he might easily have attained. The popular romance, no doubt, has many walks, nor are we at all inclined to halloo the dogs of criticism against those whose object is merely to amuse a passing hour. . . . But we do not desire to see genius expand or rather exhaust itself upon themes which cannot be reconciled to taste; and the utmost length in which we can indulge a turn to the fantastic is, where it tends to excite agreeable and pleasing ideas. (pp. 92-3)

Hoffman has in some measure identified himself with the ingenious artist [Callot] by his title of "**Night Pieces** *after the manner of Callot*" ["**Phantasiestüeke in Callots Manier**"], and in order to write such a tale, for example, as that called "**the Sandman**," he must have been deep in the mysteries of that fanciful artist, with whom he might certainly boast a kindred spirit. We have given an instance of a tale in which the wonderful is, in our opinion, happily introduced, because it is connected with and applied to human interest and human feeling, and illustrates with no ordinary force the elevation to which circumstances may raise the power and dignity of the human mind. [The narrative "**the Sandman**"] is of a different class:

> half horror and half whim,
> Like fiends in glee, ridiculously grim.
>
> (p. 94)

This wild and absurd story is in some measure redeemed by some traits in the character of Clara, whose firmness, plain good sense and frank affection are placed in agreeable contrast with the wild imagination, fanciful apprehensions, and extravagant affection of her crazy-pated admirer.

It is impossible to subject tales of this nature to criticism. They are not the visions of a poetical mind, they have scarcely even the seeming authenticity which the hallucinations of lunacy convey to the patient; they are the feverish dreams of a light-headed patient, to which, though they may sometimes excite by their peculiarity, or surprise by their oddity, we never feel disposed to yield more than momentary attention. In fact, the inspirations of Hoffmann so often resemble the ideas produced by the immoderate use of opium, that we cannot help considering his case as one requiring the assistance of medicine rather than of criticism; and while we acknowledge that with a steadier command of his imagination he might have been an author of the first distinction, yet situated as he was, and indulging the diseased state of his own system, he appears to have been subject to that undue vividness of thought and perception of which the celebrated Nicolai became at once the victim and the conqueror. Phlebotomy and cathartics, joined to sound philosophy and deliberate observation, might, as in the case of that celebrated philosopher, have brought to a healthy state a mind which we cannot help regarding as diseased, and his imagination soaring with an equal and steady flight might have reached the highest pitch of the poetical profession. (p. 97)

[Hoffmann's] works as they now exist ought to be considered less as models for imitation than as affording a warning how the most fertile fancy may be exhausted by the lavish prodigality of its possessor. (p. 98)

> [*Walter Scott*,] "*On the Supernatural in Fictitious Composition," in* The Foreign Quarterly Review, *Vol. I, No. 1, July, 1827, pp. 61-98.*

FYODOR M. DOSTOEVSKI   (essay date 1861)

[Edgar Allan] Poe merely supposes the outward possibility of an unnatural event, though he always demonstrates logically that possibility and does it sometimes even with astounding skill; and this premise once granted, he in all the rest proceeds quite realistically. In this he differs essentially from the fantastic as used for example by Hoffmann. The latter personifies the forces of Nature in images, introduces in his tales sorceresses and specters, and seeks his ideals in a far-off utterly unearthly world, and not only assumes this mysterious magical world as superior but seems to believe in its real existence. . . . (p. 61)

Poe has often been compared with Hoffmanan. . . . [We] believe such a comparison to be false. Hoffmann is a much greater poet. For he possesses an ideal, however wrong sometimes, yet an ideal full of purity and of inherent human beauty. You find this ideal embodied even oftener in Hoffmann's nonfantastic creations, such as "**Meister Martin**" or the charming and delightful "**Salvator Rosa**," to say nothing of his masterpiece, "**Kater Murr**." In Hoffmann, true and ripe humor, powerful realism as well as malice, are welded with a strong craving for beauty and with the shining light of the ideal. (p. 62)

> *Fyodor M. Dostoevski, "Three Tales of Edgar Poe," translated by Vladimir Astrov (originally published in* Wremia, *Vol. I, 1861), in* The Recognition of Edgar Allan Poe: Selected Criticism Since 1829, *edited by Eric W. Carlson, University of Michigan Press, 1970, pp. 60-2.**

GEORGE BRANDES   (essay date 1873)

[For the Romanticists, it is not enough] to transpose the personality into the past, or to deck it with the bright peacock's tail of future existences. They split the Ego into strips, they resolve it into its elements. They scatter it abroad through space, as they stretch it out through time. For the laws of space and time affect them not. (p. 161)

To Hoffmann the Ego is simply a disguise worn on the top of another disguise, and he amuses himself by peeling off these disguises one by one. (p. 162)

He relies for effect, in a manner which soon becomes mannerism, upon the sharp contrasts with which he ushers in his terrific or comical scenes. From the commonest, most prosaic every-day life we are suddenly transported into a perfectly distorted world, where miracles and juggling tricks of every kind so bewilder us that in the end no relation, no species of life, no personality, seems definite and certain. We are always in doubt as to whether we are dealing with a real person, with his spectre, with his essence in another form or other power, or with his fantastic "Doppelgänger." (pp. 165-66)

In creating these doubled and trebled existences, the character, for instance, of the Archive Keeper [in *The Golden Jar*], who is a Registrar by day and a salamander at night, Hoffmann obviously had in his mind the strange contrast between his own official life, as the conscientious criminal judge, severely rejecting all considerations of sentiment or aestheticism, and his free night life as king of the boundless realm of imagination— a life in which reality, as such, had no part. (p. 167)

Dreams, dipsomania, hallucinations, madness, all the powers which disintegrate the Ego, which disconnect its links, are [familiar friends of Hoffmann and other Romanticists]. Read, for instance, Hoffmann's tale, *The Golden Jar,* and you will hear voices issue from the apple-baskets, and the leaves and flowers of the elder-tree sing; you will see the door-knocker make faces, &c., &c. The strange, striking effect is here specially due to the way in which the apparitions suddenly emerge from a background of the most humdrum, ordinary description, from piles of legal documents, or from tureens and goblets. All Hoffmann's characters . . . are considered by their neighbours to be either drunk or mad, because they always treat their dreams and visions as realities.

Hoffmann created most of his principal characters in his own image. His whole life resolved itself into moods. We see from his diary how anxiously and minutely he observed these. We come on such entries as: "Romantically religious mood; excitedly humorous mood, leading finally to those thoughts of madness which so often force themselves upon me; humorously discontented, highly-wrought musical, romantic moods; extremely irritable mood, romantic and capricious in the highest degree." . . . (pp. 172-73)

We seem to see the man's spiritual life spread and split itself up fan-wise into musical high and low spirits. (p. 173)

Romanticism having thus dissolved the Ego, proceeds to form fantastic Egos, adding here, taking away there.

Take, for an example, Hoffmann's *Klein Zaches,* the little monster who has been endowed by a fairy with the peculiarity "that everything good that others think, say, or do in his presence is attributed to him; the result being that in the society of handsome, refined, intelligent persons he also is taken to be handsome, refined, and cultured—is taken, in short, for a model of every species of perfection with which he comes in contact." . . . [The hero Zaches] grows in greatness, becomes an important man, is made Prime Minister, but ends his days by drowning in a toilet-basin. Without overlooking the satiric symbolism of the story, I draw attention to the fact that the author has here amused himself by endowing one personality with qualities properly belonging to others, in other words, by dissolving individuality and disregarding its limits. (pp. 173-74)

Here we have Romanticism amusing itself by adding qualities to human nature; but it found subtracting them an equally attractive amusement. It deprives the individual of attributes which would seem to form an organic part of it; and by taking these away it divides the human being as lower organisms, worms, for example, are divided into greater and smaller parts, both of which live. (p. 174)

[In Hoffmann's] clever little *Story of the Lost Reflection,* the hero leaves his reflection in Italy with the entrancing Giulietta, who has bewitched him, and returns home to his wife without it. . . . [The hero Spikher tries to prove to his wife] that it is foolish to believe that a man can lose his reflection, but that even if the thing be possible, it is a matter of no importance, seeing that a reflection is simply an illusion. Self-contemplation only leads to vanity, and, moreover, such an image splits up one's personality into truth and imagination.

[In *Story of the Last Reflection*] we have the mirror chamber developed to such a point that the reflections move about independently, instead of following their originals. It is very amusing, very original and fantastic, and, as one is at liberty to understand by the reflection whatever one chooses, it may even be said to be very profound. (pp. 178-79)

> George Brandes, "Romantic Duplication and Psychology," in his Main Currents in Nineteenth Century Literature: The Romantic School in Germany, Vol. II, translated by Diana White and Mary Morison (originally published as Hovedstromninger i det 19de aarhundredes litteratur, 1873), Heinemann Ltd., 1902 (and reprinted by Boni & Liveright, Inc., 1924, pp. 152-80).*

THE SATURDAY REVIEW London   (essay date 1884)

[Although] the French can boast of a respectable translation of [Hoffmann's] more famous stories, we have had to content ourselves with a version of some half-dozen of them which, with the exception of one that engaged the attention of Mr. Carlyle's indefatigable genius [*The Golden Pot*], are all more or less feeble efforts at translation. Thus this singular fact presents itself, that while Hoffmann had achieved a considerable popularity upon the Continent, in England his works were well-nigh unread, and certainly unappreciated. The cause of this, we are inclined to think, was the early publication of his perhaps most ambitious, but certainly weakest and most disagreeable work, *Elixiere des Teufels.* . . . It was in his short, vigorous, fantastic pieces, . . . which he collected together under the titles of *Fantasiestücke in Callots Manier, Serapionsbrüder,* and *Nachtstücke,* that Hoffmann was at his best; and we have evidence that he himself set no value on those works which called for more sustained effort, for he never liked the *Elixiere des Teufels,* and never completed *Lebensansichten des Katers Murr* ("Tom Cat Murr's Philosophy of Life"), which, though a masterpiece as far as it goes, we cannot doubt the author felt himself unable to finish. These short pieces, originally written for no other purpose than to replenish a chronically empty purse, are full of most exquisite humour, brilliant wit, and trenchant satire. At times, it is true, he deals in horrors which are rather apt to disgust than attract the reader; but in the tales [included in *Les Contes d'Hoffmann*] this fault is scarcely to be detected. There are many persons, doubtless, who will fail to see the beauties and eagerly point out the blemishes of these extraordinary tales; but that is only natural where so many are incapable of appreciating genuine humour and prone to resent anything but commonplace situations in fiction as the greatest of crimes. Our advice to all such is to abstain from an attempt to understand Hoffmann, for certainly he did not write these tales for such readers. (p. 145)

"E.T.W. Hoffmann," in The Saturday Review, *London, Vol. 57, No. 1475, February 2, 1884, pp. 145-46.*

THE LITERARY WORLD   (essay date 1885)

Hoffmann is one of the idols of literature whose powers are spoken of with traditional reverence, but whose works few take the trouble to read. How much we heard in our younger days of the fearful joys to be snatched from the pages of this uncanny romancer, and how little did the result appear in the full measure of breathless expectation! And now, after an interlude of Trollope, and Daudet, and Howells, we find it more difficult than ever to awaken a sympathetic thrill over the antiquated psychological horrors of the *Serapionsbrüder.* Clever the tales undoubtedly are, but their fantastic episodes and characters are the fruit of a diseased imagination, rather than of poetical genius. Hoffmann's mental traits were akin to those of Poe (the comparison is general) but the German lacked Poe's marvelous faculty of concentration. His representations of character, as such, have no value, for they are devoid of coherency, they are marionettes, and are wholly at the mercy of the grotesque whims of their creator.

Where, then, lies the secret of Hoffmann's fascination? It is in the consummate art with which he conveys passing impressions, and the unflagging fertility of invention which is constantly bringing forth new and startling episodes.

> Master Martin, as was his wont, threw his head back into his neck, played with his fingers upon his capacious belly, and, opening his eyes wide and thrusting forward his under-lip with an air of superior astuteness, let his eyes sweep round the assembly.

Later on, you may get a wholly different portrait, but here, for the time being, is Master Martin, as if reflected from the author's mind into a mirror. This wonderful gift of expression lends a seemingly vivid realism to the most improbable of Hoffman's productions. . . . And yet, a careful perusal of Hoffmann's tales brings no feeling of gratification. The mind is perturbed with all this fantastic imagery; the satire is acrid and leaves unpleasant traces; the passion is too much like brute instinct; the magic wand of the enchanter is thrust too often on our notice; the grim, unyielding doctrine of fatalism, which the author takes occasion to profess so often, stimulates an instinct of revolt. Hoffmann's tales are to be read, if read at all, as one would take hasheesh or opium—to note the effects upon the mind and cull therefrom an interesting experience. Of no other series of romances can it be said so absolutely that the effects vary with the temperament of the reader. Only an abnormal intellect could find in them genuine and habitual enjoyment. (pp. 111-12)

"Hoffmann's Weird Tales," in The Literary World, *Vol. 16, No. 7, April 4, 1885, pp. 111-12.*

THE SATURDAY REVIEW London   (essay date 1892)

[The tales in *The Serapion Brethren*] are all more or less characterized by the weird and humorous imagination, half real, half fictitious, and altogether fascinating in bewilderment, which

is so remarkable a feature in Hoffmann's work, and which, as one of the Brethren remarks, after having related the story of **"Albertine's Wooers,"** has "something of a kaleidoscope character that, in spite of its crackiness . . . does ultimately form interesting combinations." . . . The somewhat ghastly story of **"The Uncanny Guest"** is followed by . . . **"Mademoiselle Scudéri,"** a most enthralling "shocker" of the time of Louis XIV. . . . [This is a] perfect little romance of crime. . . . **"Gambler's Fortune"** strikes a different note, and is, perhaps, one of the most dramatic stories in the volume. . . .

[The longest story] is a *novella* in the style of Boccaccio. . . . The boisterous fun which runs through this tale smacks somewhat of the pantomime, with its cudgelling and horseplay; but it has a true Italian ring about it, and we pity the man who can read the story without thoroughly enjoying it. **"The Life of a Well-known Character," "Phenomena,"** and **"The Mutual Interdependence of Things,"** are all stories which would make the fortune of any sixpenny magazine; but **"The King's Betrothed,"** with which the volume ends, is a tale in the true vein of Hoffmann humour. (pp. 400-01)

"'The Serapion Brethren'," in The Saturday Review, *London, Vol. 74, No. 1927, October 1, 1892, pp. 400-01.*

SIGMUND FREUD   (essay date 1919)

It is only rarely that a psycho-analyst feels impelled to investigate the subject of aesthetics even when aesthetics is understood to mean not merely the theory of beauty, but the theory of feeling. . . . But it does occasionally happen that he has to interest himself in some particular province of that subject; and then it usually proves to be a rather remote region of it and one that has been neglected in standard works.

The subject of the 'uncanny' is a province of this kind. (p. 368)

[The] 'uncanny' is that class of the terrifying which leads back to something long known to us, once very familiar. (pp. 369-70)

In proceeding to review those things, persons, impressions, events and situations which are able to arouse in us a feeling of the uncanny in a very forcible and definite form, the first requirement is obviously to select a suitable example to start upon. (p. 378)

[In his paper 'Zur Psychologie des Unheimlichen,' E. Jentsch says]: 'In telling a story, one of the most successful devices for easily creating uncanny effects is to leave the reader in uncertainty whether a particular figure in the story is a human being or an automaton; and to do it in such a way that his attention is not directly focussed upon his uncertainty, so that he may not be urged to go into the matter and clear it up immediately, since that, as we have said, would quickly dissipate the peculiar emotional effect of the thing. Hoffmann has repeatedly employed this psychological artifice with success in his fantastic narratives.'

This observation, undoubtedly a correct one, refers primarily to the story of **'The Sand-Man'** in Hoffmann's *Nachtstücken.* . . . But I cannot think—and I hope that most readers of the story will agree with me—that the theme of the doll, Olympia, who is to all appearances a living being, is by any means the only element to be held responsible for the quite unparalleled atmosphere of uncanniness which the story evokes; or, indeed, that it is the most important among them. Nor is this effect of the story heightened by the fact that the author himself treats the episode of Olympia with a faint touch of satire and uses it to make fun of the young man's idealization of his mistress. The main theme of the story is, on the contrary, something different, something which gives its name to the story, and which is always re-introduced at the critical moment: it is the theme of the 'Sand-Man' who tears out children's eyes. (pp. 378-79)

[There is] no doubt that the feeling of something uncanny is directly attached to the figure of the Sand-Man, that is, to the idea of being robbed of one's eyes; and that Jentsch's point of an intellectual uncertainty has nothing to do with this effect. Uncertainty whether an object is living or inanimate, which we must admit in regard to the doll Olympia, is quite irrelevant in connection with this other, more striking instance of uncanniness. It is true that the writer creates a kind of uncertainty in us in the beginning by not letting us know, no doubt purposely, whether he is taking us into the real world or into a purely fantastic one of his own creation. . . . But this uncertainty disappears in the course of Hoffmann's story, and we perceive that he means to make us, too, look through the fell Coppola's glasses—perhaps, indeed, that he himself once gazed through such an instrument. For the conclusion of the story makes it quite clear that Coppola the optician really is the lawyer Coppelius and thus also the Sand-Man.

There is no question, therefore, of any 'intellectual uncertainty'; we know now that we are not supposed to be looking on at the products of a madman's imagination . . . ; and yet this knowledge does not lessen the impression of uncanniness in the least degree. The theory of 'intellectual uncertainty' is thus incapable of explaining that impression.

We know from psycho-analytic experience, however, that this fear of damaging or losing one's eyes is a terrible fear of childhood. . . . A study of dreams, phantasies and myths has taught us that a morbid anxiety connected with the eyes and with going blind is often enough a substitute for the dread of castration. In blinding himself, Oedipus, that mythical lawbreaker, was simply carrying out a mitigated form of the punishment of castration—the only punishment that according to the *lex talionis* was fitted for him. We may try to reject the derivation of fears about the eye from the fear of castration on rationalistic grounds, and say that it is very natural that so precious an organ as the eye should be guarded by a proportionate dread. . . . (pp. 382-83)

[But] I would not recommend any opponent of the psycho-analytic view to select precisely the story of the Sand-Man upon which to build his case that morbid anxiety about the eyes has nothing to do with the castration-complex. For why does Hoffmann bring the anxiety about eyes into such intimate connection with the father's death? And why does the Sand-Man appear each time in order to interfere with love? He divides the unfortunate Nathaniel from his betrothed and from her brother, his best friend; he destroys his second object of love, Olympia, the lovely doll; and he drives him into suicide at the moment when he has won back his Clara and is about to be happily united to her. Things like these and many more seem arbitrary and meaningless in the story so long as we deny all connection between fears about the eye and castration; but they become intelligible as soon as we replace the Sand-Man by the dreaded father at whose hands castration is awaited. [Freud elaborates in a footnote: In the story from Nathaniel's childhood, the figures of his father and Coppelius represent the two opposites into which the father-imago is split by the ambiva-

lence of the child's feeling; whereas the one threatens to blind him, that is, to castrate him, the other, the loving father, intercedes for his sight. That part of the complex which is most strongly repressed, the death-wish against the father, finds expression in the death of the good father, and Coppelius is made answerable for it. Later, in his student days, Professor Spalanzani and Coppola the optician reproduce this double representation of the father-imago, the Professor is a member of the father-series, Coppola openly identified with the lawyer Coppelius. Just as before they used to work together over the fire, so now they have jointly created the doll Olympia; the Professor is even called the father of Olympia. This second occurrence of work in common shows that the optician and the mechanician are also components of the father-imago, that is, both are Nathaniel's father as well as Olympia's. I ought to have added that in the terrifying scene in childhood, Coppelius, after sparing Nathaniel's eyes, had screwed off his arms and legs as an experiment; that is, he had experimented on him as a mechanician would on a doll. This singular feature, which seems quite out of perspective in the picture of the Sand-Man, introduces a new castration-equivalent; but it also emphasizes the identity of Coppelius and his later counterpart, Spalanzani the mechanician, and helps us to understand who Olympia is. She, the automatic doll, can be nothing else than a personification of Nathaniel's feminine attitude towards his father in his infancy. The father of both, Spalanzani and Coppola, are, as we know, new editions, reincarnations of Nathaniel's 'two' fathers. Now Spalanzani's otherwise incomprehensible statement that the optician has stolen Nathaniel's eyes so as to set them in the doll becomes significant and supplies fresh evidence for the identity of Olympia and Nathaniel. Olympia is, as it were, a dissociated complex of Nathaniel's which confronts him as a person, and Nathaniel's enslavement to this complex is expressed in his senseless obsessive love for Olympia. We may with justice call such love narcissistic, and can understand why he who has fallen victim to it should relinquish his real, external object of love. The psychological truth of the situation in which the young man, fixated upon his father by his castration-complex, is incapable of loving a woman, is amply proved by numerous analyses of patients whose story, though less fantastic, is hardly less tragic than that of the student Nathaniel.]

[We] venture, therefore, to refer the uncanny effect of the Sand-Man to the child's dread in relation to its castration-complex. (pp. 384-85)

Hoffmann is in literature the unrivalled master of conjuring up the uncanny. His *Elixiere des Teufels* [**The Devil's Elixir**] contains a mass of themes to which one is tempted to ascribe the uncanny effect of the narrative; but it is too obscure and intricate a story to venture to summarize. Towards the end of the book the reader is told the facts, hitherto concealed from him, from which the action springs; with the result, not that he is at last enlightened, but that he falls into a state of complete bewilderment. The author has piled up too much of a kind; one's comprehension of the whole suffers as a result, though not the impression it makes. We must content ourselves with selecting those themes of uncanniness which are most prominent, and seeing whether we can fairly trace them also back to infantile sources. These themes are all concerned with the idea of a 'double' in every shape and degree, with persons, therefore, who are to be considered identical by reason of looking alike; Hoffmann accentuates this relation by transferring mental processes from the one person to the other—what we should call telepathy—so that the one possesses knowledge, feeling and experience in common with the other, identifies himself with another person, so that his self becomes confounded, or the foreign self is substituted for his own—in other words, by doubling, dividing and interchanging the self. And finally there is the constant recurrence of similar situations, a same face, or character-trait, or twist of fortune, or a same crime, or even a same name recurring throughout several consecutive generations. (pp. 386-87)

[The] 'double' was originally an insurance against destruction to the ego, . . . and probably the 'immortal' soul was the first 'double' of the body. . . . [Such ideas] have sprung from the soil of unbounded self-love, from the primary narcissism which holds sway in the mind of the child as in that of primitive man; and when this stage has been left behind the double takes on a different aspect. From having been an assurance of immortality, he becomes the ghastly harbinger of death. (p. 387)

[Even after close consideration of] the manifest motivation of the figure of a 'double', we have to admit that none of it helps us to understand the extraordinarily strong feeling of something uncanny that pervades the conception. . . . The quality of uncanniness can only come from the circumstance of the 'double' being a creation dating back to a very early mental stage, long since left behind, and one, no doubt, in which it wore a more friendly aspect. The 'double' has become a vision of terror, just as after the fall of their religion the gods took on daemonic shapes.

It is not difficult to judge, on the same lines as his theme of the 'double', the other forms of disturbance in the ego made use of by Hoffmann. They are a harking-back to particular phases in the evolution of the self-regarding feeling, a regression to a time when the ego was not yet sharply differentiated from the external world and from other persons. I believe that these factors are partly responsible for the impression of the uncanny, although it is not easy to isolate and determine exactly their share of it. (pp. 388-89)

Sigmund Freud, "The 'Uncanny'," translated by Alix Strachey (originally published in Imago, *Vol. 5, 1919), in his* Collected Papers: Papers on Metapsychology, Papers on Applied Psycho-Analysis, Vol. 4, *authorized translation under the supervision of Joan Riviere (reprinted by permission of Basic Books, Inc., Publishers; in Canada by The Hogarth Press Ltd.), Basic Books by arrangement with The Hogarth Press Ltd. and The Institute of Psychoanalysis, 1959, pp. 368-407.**

PAUL ROSENFELD   (essay date 1946)

[It] was with the communication of the shudders of fantastic fiction—a category of fiction which was his forte—that [E.T.A. Hoffmann] fascinated the world. (p. 51)

[Hoffmann's *The Devil's Elixir*], conveys the horror of the experience of an insane mind, a disintegrating personality, by setting us, as it were, squarely in [the hero's] shoes and making us "live" his world. Simultaneously, it conveys horror by showing our reflective intelligence a deadly case of the mysterious mechanism of what the psychoanalysts call "projection," the unconscious externalization of what is entirely subjective. We see Hoffmann half amusing himself and us with his horror story; half standing with us curious and aghast before an unillumined realm which may be that of the devil, and certainly is some "nightside" of the psyche alien to consciousness and to the conditions of consciousness. It is probably

the source of personality and also the seat of a tricky, destructive power which if not the devil is practically as strong as he and as capable of man's ruin. (p. 52)

[Hoffmann's stories often put us solidly on the ground of the contemporary psychological study, as in one of his last and best works, *Mademoiselle de Scudery*.] This story is a grandiose piece of symbolization of a deadly irrational trait, common to many artists and to as many nonartists, in the form of a detective or criminal romance. . . . Cardillac, a goldsmith of seventeenth-century Paris, a second Benvenuto Cellini, is the maker of beautiful jewelry with universal appeal. But each purchaser or recipient of his jewelry, some time after its acquisition, is found murdered, and the jewelry gone. The murderer is, of course, Cardillac himself. What is symbolized is the mysterious desire of so many artists and nonartists to take back what at one time they have given freely, to kill the person whom they have enriched but cannot possess. . . .

These psychological analyses were, of course, facilitated for Hoffmann [and other German fantastic writers] by their capacity to dissect themselves. (p. 53)

[That out of Hoffmann's contemporaries it was neither Ludvig Tieck, Achim von Arnim, nor Clemens Brentano] but Hoffmann himself who actually passed the taste for fantastic fiction to the entire world was because he was a more versatile and varied storyteller than was Tieck; and while possessing less sheerly poetic magic than von Arnim or Brentano, he was a better craftsman of the story than they were. A brilliant thematic inventor, he constituted one of those imaginative greenhouses under whose glass new ideas—an author's own and those of his contemporaries—come to ripeness. Besides, he possessed a grotesque but appealing sense of humor. Whatever the ultimate reason, the effect of his work was practically universal. (p. 54)

[Hoffmann's] appearance in our day from out of the past flows partly from his qualities as a writer, qualities which provide a reason for placing him in his category alongside Poe. While Hoffmann's narrative, for example, lacks the characteristic American swiftness of Poe's, his fiction is enveloped in an atmosphere of quaint but authentic culture and reflects a personal acquaintance with, and enjoyment of, intelligent society and good art. But the main reason for his return, as we have seen, is the similarity of the spiritual conditions of our period and his own. We, too, are in a restless interregnum. For years Freudianism has been exploring one of the realities posited by Hoffmann and his contemporaries, casting fierce light onto the "night-side" of the psyche whose immensity and power he and they divined, illuminating the mechanism of projection which fascinated and terrified them, clarifying the huge extent to which imagination and fantasy form part of the waking psyche's machinery. (pp. 55-6)

[This] has brought Hoffmann close to us. Brilliant entertainer that he is, he entertains us doubly, for he also entertains our reflective minds, which understand his attitude and perceive in it a more terrified forerunner of our own. (p. 56)

Paul Rosenfeld, "E.T.A. Hoffmann and Fantastic Fiction," in Tomorrow, *Vol. V, No. 12, August, 1946, pp. 51-6.*

ALFRED R. NEUMANN   (essay date 1953)

In the search for his artistic self Hoffmann underwent a major development from lawyer to musician to author. His interest in visual arts was always in the background. His path is outlined by many biographers and critics. However, none of them . . . venture a satisfactory answer to the question: Why does Hoffmann the musician become Hoffmann the author, in the popular mind as well as in fact? The creative development of a personality that could express itself in three artistic dimensions must be explored. The preoccupation with one form or the other at various times also must have left its mark upon the other genres. (pp. 174-75)

The gradual process [in Hoffmann] toward the use of language in lieu of music took place between 1809 with *Ritter Gluck,* and 1814, when, on the one hand, the opera *Undine* was practically finished while, on the other, Hoffmann's literary success was assured. Still, he could not always bring himself to employ the word in an objective manner. The result to be achieved was still the dream-reality of the romantic musical experience, the vague chaos of surging emotions with only a hint of the real. Hoffmann finally found the medium best suited for his purposes in the "**Märchen.**" The early stages of his authorship, however, are of the greatest interest here, as they show the transition from music to literature.

The dream-reality just mentioned is probably the most impressive in the early tales *Ritter Gluck* and *Don Juan.* Both are imbued with the atmosphere of an impressionistic tone-painting. We are left with a sense of elevation, exhilaration, and dreaminess that is normally caused only by music. In *Ritter Gluck* the uncertainty is caused by the fact that we never really know if the stranger is an insane old man or a phantom of Kreisler's imagination. He seems to come out of a vague fog. In *Don Juan* the situation is almost identical: the reader is never sure whether Donna Anna is only the product of a sixth sense of the Traveler or a real person. Both music and somnambulism forge a relationship between the characters. The listener co-experiences the opera in both tales to such a degree that he identifies himself with it. Thus Hoffmann created an appeal on two planes: he described the effect of music upon an individual and simultaneously created an independent effect upon the reader which strangely resembles the effect of music upon the listener.

This musical impression is heightened by the reference to somnambulism, a matter of current interest in Hoffmann's day, somewhat as psychoanalysis is today. . . . If one remembers the sleepwalking atmosphere in Kleist's *Käthchen von Heilbronn* (1808-10) and *Prinz von Homburg* (1810-11), Hoffmann's reference to the same heightened reality in his *Don Juan* is in keeping with the spirit of the era. What does not seem possible in strict reality is here made conceivable, as in a dream, in a state of sleepwalking. In the perception of music the same superreal state may be achieved.

In turn in *Ritter Gluck* the Old Man says about Gluck's compositions :"Alles dieses, mein Herr, habe ich geschrieben, als ich aus dem Reich der Träume kam" [All of these, Sir, I have written, but I came from the realm of Dreams.] Hoffmann therefore wishes to reiterate the contention that music originates in the same sphere as dreams, in the subconscious. . . . Without a doubt music can have just such an effect. Again and again Hoffmann reminds his readers that the state of mind which he is attempting to portray is that of a dream-reality, not dissimilar to the way in which some romanticists tended to listen to music. . . . [It seems] that music as well as what Hoffmann calls somnambulism bring man in contact with a higher reality. One is as if drugged, as if understanding intuitively all the things that reason keeps hidden. Music is capable

of causing a Dionysian intoxication, which elevates the listener beyond earthly reality, and exhausts him in the awakening. In his soaring he appears to lose all impedimenta, to rise in space. In dream the same thing happens. Under musical and dream intoxication Hoffmann created in his tales a gravity-defying atmosphere that can only be explained by his conscious attempt to express in words what he failed to transmit through his music.

Hoffmann presented this relation of dream and actuality in numerous works. The climax of the trend appears in *Der goldene Topf,* where the two worlds are masterfully interlocked. . . . In *Der Magnetiseur* again there is the view of a dream as a glance into the subconscious. Everywhere Hoffmann's attempt to break through the barriers of reality to the origin and essence of things becomes clear. To transgress the bounds of musical laws and traditions was a much more severe task than to liberate himself from verbal realism. Hoffmann's emancipation from the rigidity of musical composition was the result of his attempt to express the same longing, the same atmosphere in words.

While Hoffmann's literary career was thus born of his musical life, he had achieved, and overcome, a compromise art form that such a torn personality was predisposed to seek. On August 5, 1814, he had finished the composition of his outstanding musical work, his opera *Undine.* It is Hoffmann's attempt to integrate the poet, musician, and painter within him. . . . This opera occupies the central position in Hoffmann's life and thinking as the practical compromise and synthesis of one of his lifelong problems: the choice between music and literature as his most personal and effective mode of expression. Here he was able to apply all three of his talents to the creation of a work of art in which the major arts were fused. (pp. 178-81)

The concept of such a fusion of the arts in Hoffmann's life and work is therefore the direct product of his indecision as to a final choice of art medium. After exploring numerous musical and literary forms Hoffmann finally decided to devote himself mainly to literature, through the realization that only here could he break classical tradition as well as the technical barrier between his potential audience and himself. . . . [Hoffmann] was able to forge a link between literature and music. His medium of expression, the tale, was a popular, critical, and financial success. No further did he need to experiment with a new genre on the borderline of literature and music. (p. 181)

Alfred R. Neumann, "Musician or Author? E.T.A. Hoffmann's Decision," in Journal of English and Germanic Philology *(© 1953 by the Board of Trustees of the University of Illinois), Vol. LII, No. 2, 1953, pp. 174-81.*

V. S. PRITCHETT (essay date 1953)

What is the lineage of the detective story? It begins, presumably, with the first detective: Vidocq. After that important invention, Hoffmann's *Mlle de Scudéri* seems to be next in the succession and here the moral and technical basis are properly laid down. (p. 179)

Mr. J. M. Cohen's acute analysis of Hoffmann . . . has explained to me why (when it comes to the test) I prefer Hoffmann's kind of tale . . . to nearly all works of detective fiction. "There are for Hoffmann three realms", says Mr. Cohen, "a comfortable Philistia—comically drawn in *The Golden Pot*— a borderland of dangers and hidden significances, and a third region of spiritual power and serenity.'' [In detective novelists] there is Philistia alone. . . . (pp. 179-80)

Hoffmann's world [unlike the world of detective fiction] is the underworld or overworld of Romance, the world of Good and Evil, not of Right and Wrong. We shall meet the flesh and the devil, wickedness and virtue, imagination and the world. A tale like *The Golden Pot* is a charmed allegory of the life of the artist. Those who find German fantasy repugnant, who groan before its archaic paraphernalia and see in its magic, its alchemy, its visions, its hypnotic dreams and trances, its ghosts and its diabolism, all the disordered tedium of the literary antique shop, will find Hoffmann more engaging, more concrete, and cleverer than he seems at first sight. He is a wonderful story-teller, his humour is gracious, he is circumstantial and his invention is always witty. In *The Golden Pot,* for example, where the artist takes to drink, he is represented not as a drunkard but as a little creature imprisoned in a bottle. *The Entail* is a vivid and satisfying *nouvelle* and the management of the two sleep-walking scenes is the work of a master of ingenuity. And if his world is Romance, then it defines what Romance ought to be: not extravagance, but life reflected perfectly in a mirror or a lake, true in detail, but mysteriously ideal. (pp. 180-81)

Hoffmann is a sweet dessert wine, but he has that extra clear-headedness in a restricted field which is often noticeable in the fuddled; he was a startlingly complete artist, though in miniature. He had grasped the lesson of folklore; that the extraordinary, the unheard of, must be made minutely, physically real, and the pleasure he gives is that of exactitude and recognition. (p. 182)

> V. S. Pritchett, "The Roots of Detection," in his Books in General (*copyright © 1953 by V. S. Pritchett; reprinted by permission of Literistic, Ltd.; in Canada by A D Peters & Co Ltd*), Chatto & Windus Ltd., 1953, pp. 179-84.*

GEORGE C. SCHOOLFIELD   (essay date 1956)

[Hoffmann] possessed a more thorough musical training than any other important literary man of his day. . . . [His] personal adventures invite incorporation into the life of Kreisler [Hoffmann's most complete musical character].

What we know of Johannes Kreisler we have in a fragmentary form. The first of the *Kreisleriana, Kreislers musikalische Leiden,* appeared in September 1810; *Kater Murr,* the last of the works concerning the musician, saw the publication of its second volume in 1821. Into the period between the publication of the *Leiden* and *Kreislers Lehrbrief* (1814) fall the *Kreisleriana* proper together with some other musical stories; in 1816 and 1817 Hoffmann composed other tales (such as *Das Sanctus*) which cast light upon the character of the musician. *Murr* was begun in 1819. Hoffmann was therefore occupied with the figure of Kreisler throughout most of his literary career, but the picture of the musician is by no means complete. The *Krisleriana* are a series of illuminating sketches on music which say perhaps too little about the man himself. . . . Whoever wishes to know Kreisler must piece together his information from a number of sources. A tendency on the part of German scholars has been to fill the gaps with information from Hoffmann's own life. It should be remembered that Kreisler is not a thinly disguised attempt at autobiography but the literary portrayal of the Romantic musician par excellence, and the outstanding musical hero in German literature.

Hoffmann created the inner Kreisler first and then gave him outward form, surrounding him with friends and enemies. Yet even in the *Kreisleriana* the themes of the composer's battle with society and of his passion for Julia are briefly presented. The prelude to the *Kreisleriana, Musikalische Leiden,* shows the wretched Kreisler at a party in Councilor Röderlein's home. While the elderly people play cards, the young ladies of the house are ordered to sing by their mother, and Kreisler must accompany them. Their errors and the absurd remarks of the guests drive Kreisler to despair. The only consolation for Kreisler is Amalia, the niece of Röderlein. . . . She can essay such roles as Gluck's Armida or Mozart's Donna Anna. The niece is Julia Marc, and the society that of Bamberg; the piece was originally intended as a satire on musical life in the Franconian city. Beneath the satire we detect Hoffmann's eternal quarrel with society, which is to take various forms; he struggles both to be accepted as a musician by the general public and as a human being (and an equal) by his social "betters." And Hoffmann's search for the ideal is revealed in the figure of the niece, who embodies all that Hoffmann reveres in music. These two tendencies may be considered as the most important features of Kreisler's relationships with others. . . . (pp. 17-19)

[Hoffmann's attacks against the upper levels of society,] written both from the standpoint of the musician and of the protester against social injustice, make up a great part of *Kater Murr.* The Kreisler portion of the novel takes place at the court of Prince Irenäus. . . . (p. 19)

[In this milieu, Kreisler] is insulted by the functionaries and by such visitors as Prince Hector, who demands that the "lackey" show him proper respect; he sees the final degradation of music in the aftermath to a performance given by Julia and himself before the Prince. Crying that he is overcome by the music, the Prince rushes forward and attempts to kiss Julia. (Only once, in a moment of the highest musical inspiration, has Kreisler allowed himself to call Julia "du".) Kreisler drives him away, but as far as we know, Julia later is married off to Prince Ignatius and so falls prey to the brutal aristocracy after all. Music and the musician are debased in every way, and Kreisler is powerless to act. His only defense is his scurrilous humor. (pp. 20-1)

Much has been made of the fact that the origin of these unpleasant scenes was the union between Julia Marc and [the man she actually married,] the merchant Gröpel, yet most critics have overlooked the fact that Hoffmann was too fine an artist to repeat the theme again and again simply to vent his personal feelings. Hoffmann has given an extremely pessimistic meaning to the defilement of the Julia-figure; it is characteristic of his attitude toward music that he mentions the sufferings of Julia far more often than he does his own. He remains the servant of music, Julia is music itself.

Hoffmann's eulogies of the feminine voice are among his least ironic creations, an indication of his deep feeling. Written over a period of years, they still bear a close resemblance to one another; Hoffmann cannot vary his description of absolute musical beauty. Whatever the name of the heroine may be, Amalie, Ombra adorata, Caecilie, or Julia Benzon, the essentials of her song and her character remain the same. Other feminine singers not connected with Kreisler bear similar features: Antonie in *Rat Krespel* and "Donna Anna" in *Don Juan.* In each case the most important (and at times the only) feature of the ideal is her heavenly voice, which frees the musician from the trammels of life. The portion of the *Kreisleriana* entitled *Ombra adorata* is perhaps the purest example of Hoffmann's cult of the female voice. The *Ombra adorata* is tacitly dedicated to Julia Marc; her name is never mentioned. The voice remains unidentified and unattached to any human form; we know it as the guide which leads the composer into the dream world of art. Later the voice takes the form of Caecilie and Julia Benzon; but even after Julia appears fully developed in *Kater Murr,* she remains an ethereal figure. Hoffmann provides a detailed account of her musical abilities; otherwise she is still the "adored shadow" who neither knows sensual feeling for Kreisler nor arouses this feeling in him. The sensual function is assumed by the Princess Hedwiga, in her humors a feminine counterpart of Kreisler. That Julia arouses the lust of Hector detracts nothing from her essentially spiritual nature; here Hoffmann indicates . . . the debasement of art by the non-artist. In the conversation with Rätin Benzon, Kreisler carefully points out the difference between the love of the "bad musicians" and the "good musicians." The "bad musicians" are enamored of a pair of beautiful eyes and generally wed their possessor, leading her home into the prison of marriage; the "good musicians" see transported to earth the image of the angel which had secretly rested in their breast. . . . Kreisler modestly says "die guten Musikanten" [the good musicians]; he means the creative musicians like himself who are able to appreciate the nature of the ideal and therefore do not wish to disturb it.

We have as yet said nothing of Hoffmann's technical thoughts on music; in the passages on the Julia-figure Hoffmann does not concern himself with the details of music as an art, although he does cite the texts which his heroines sing. . . . At no time does one of his heroines sing a work by a composer whom music history classifies as a Romantic; a possible exception would be "Donna Anna" in *Don Juan,* where Mozart receives Hoffmann's "Romantic" interpretation. (Hoffmann's own compositions are remarkably "classical.") Nevertheless, the *Kreisleriana* provide conclusive proof that Kreisler is a Romantic musician in his technical thought as well as in his attitude towards life and art.

In the *Kreisleriana* and their paralipomena Hoffmann attempts to erase the division between musician and poet. Hoffmann, himself both literary man and composer, saw no reason why one art could not assume certain of the functions of the other—why language could not become more musical and music closer to the word. This idea is first given complete expression in the dialogue, *Der Dichter und der Komponist* . . . , and is already hinted at in *Don Juan* . . . , where the opera is thought of as a music drama. . . . [In the dialogue, the musician Ludwig expresses the idea that poet] and musician must be in complete harmony, an anticipation of Wagner's ideal of the Gesamtkunstwerk; music must win new means of expression closer to those of literature. Hoffmann develops his theory in that section of the *Kreisleriana* called *Kreislers musikalisch-poetischer Klub.* At the club's present meeting Kreisler decides to improvise at the piano. . . . What follows is a series of chords, played one after another, each specifically designated as to key and dynamics. To every chord is assigned a particular picture, in every case an emotion, in most cases a figure or a color. A soft A flat major chord calls forth a picture of spirits with golden wings, the A flat minor carries the musician into the realm of eternal yearning. The A minor causes a beautiful girl to appear; her lover embraces her in heroic F major. . . . The passage indicates unmistakably what path Hoffmann's musical thought has taken. Music is no longer an interweaving of melodies, of polyphony; it is essentially a matter of tonal combinations and their modulations. The musician is not to confine himself to the intellectual task of polyphonic construction; he can make use of the emotional effects inherent in harmony. Each chord is assigned a definite emotional connotation; the exactitude of the connotation is increased through the use of instruments, and to a degree through the mingling of color and sound. Ludwig Tieck applies the same synaesthetic device in his early poetry, but there it is not based upon musical knowledge; Hoffmann has laid the groundwork for a manual of Romantic compositional technique.

Hoffmann's Kreisler, like Thomas Mann's Leverkühn in *Doktor Faustus,* reveals much of his character in his thoughts on music; in both cases it is difficult to say which is the product of the other, character or musical thought. In the *Klub* Kreisler shows his extreme changeability; within a few moments he runs the gamut from reverence to eroticism, from charming landscapes to macabre graveyard scenes, from heroic confidence to fear of madness. . . . Music is usually the most noble of the arts; yet Hoffmann suspects that a dangerous power exists in music—that music may be the destroyer as well as the savior. While this thought does not entirely disappear in the last works, it is most clearly expressed in the *Kreisleriana,* in particular in *Der Freund,* where Kreisler's insanity is depicted. The friend attempts to heal the madman through musical therapy, as it were; Kreisler listens attentively at first, but soon falls into such a rage that the friend ceases to play. The friend then places a small piano and a guitar in Kreisler's room, and the musician involuntarily touches the strings of the latter instrument. At the sound of the C major chord (that chord associated with the devil in the *Klub*) Kreisler smashes the instrument. Hoffmann recognizes that evil lies hidden in music's beneficence. The theme of music's danger is later given a one-sided development by such writers as Lenau, for whom music becomes almost entirely harmful in its influence. Hoffmann transforms the factor of evil, making his musician a demonic figure whose life is possessed by music. The strength of this possession may drive him to destruction or prove to be his salvation. (pp. 21-5)

The conclusion of *Kater Murr* is unknown, and the sketches for the initial Kreisler novel point unmistakably to the madness of the musician. Kreisler is not the first demonic musician; that title must belong to [Joseph] Berglinger, whose demon takes the form of religious inspiration. In Kreisler the demonic begins to assume a more evil aspect, although music is still regarded by and large as beneficent. After Kreisler, musical characters appear who themselves have become evil, a perversion of Hoffmann's thought. Thomas Mann borrows from Hoffmann in this respect too: his hero, himself a good man, is forced to enter a pact with evil as a necessary concomitant of his genius.

Hoffmann's Kreisler figure produced certain offspring in Romantic literature; these other examples of the creative musician appear in the works either of less inspired literary men or of artists not primarily writers but rather composers. The fact that Hoffmann alone among the writers of Romanticism has produced a full length portrait of the composer is not astonishing when we remember that he is simply describing that phase of life and artistic effort which he knows best. Neither Tieck nor Wilhelm Hauff, two Romanticists who have also treated the composer, possessed the necessary technical knowledge—or indeed the interest in the art—to stay the course; the *Davidsbündler*-series of Robert Schumann, a third follower of Hoffmann's tradition, remains the work of a talented amateur. (p. 29)

George C. Schoolfield, "Romanticism," in his The Figure of the Musician in German Literature *(copyright 1956 by The University of North Carolina Press),*

University of North Carolina Press, 1956, pp. 10-55.*

WOLFGANG KAYSER (essay date 1957)

[The title of *Phantasiestücke in Callots Manier*], as well as the author's preface, in paying homage to Callot suggests its appropriateness in the [context of the grotesque]. Actually, even those of Hoffmann's stories which were composed before the *Nachtgeschichten* are full of grotesque elements. In many of them a connection with subjects previously dealt with is directly or indirectly established. Callot's and Bruegel's names are repeatedly mentioned, and occasionally they appear side by side. "Don't drink—look at her closely!" people are warned of beautiful Julia in *Abenteuer in der Sylvesternacht* (Adventures on New Year's Eve), "Haven't you seen her before on the warning signs put up by Bruegel and Callot?" This admonition is given in a dream which contains a perfect grotesque; in it trees and plants become disproportioned, the "little one" turns into a squirrel, and the other figures are transformed into candy creatures that come to life and creep about in an ominous manner—until the dreamer awakes with a cry. Whereas in this instance Hoffmann employs motifs from Callot and the ornamental grotesque, a dream from *Die Elixiere des Teufels* (Elixirs of the Devil) reads like the literary equivalent of certain of Bosch's or Bruegel's infernal visions. . . .

> Heads moved along on crickets' legs attached to their ears and sneered at me. Strange fowl—ravens with human faces—whirled in the air. I recognized the concertmaster from B. with his sister, who danced madly to the tune of a waltz which her brother played on his chest, which served as a violin. Belcampo, with an ugly lizard's face and mounted on a ghastly winged worm, violently approached me and wanted to comb my beard with a red-hot iron comb. . . . Satan stridently laughs, "Now you are wholly mine."

While Aurelia is here transformed into Satan, the grotesquely drawn figure of Dr. Dapertutto in *Die Abenteuer* turns out to be the devil, and Giulia his creature. As soon as the reader is certain of this fact, the grotesque scenes in which the world was alienated lose part of their strangeness, and some of the grotesque has disappeared since it ceases to puzzle us. If the devil himself appears, we are prepared for all sorts of infernal tricks. What at first reading struck us with the full force of the grotesque seems milder or different in retrospect. When the stranger in the novella *Aus dem Leben eines bekannten Mannes* (From the Life of a Well-known Man) favorably impresses the inhabitants of Berlin by his politeness, but jumps six feet high and twelve feet wide across the street when offered help by a compassionate pedestrian; when at night, dressed in a white shroud, he knocks at doors; when he acts most strangely but explains his actions (though never satisfactorily)—the world begins to be alienated. But when we are informed that it was the devil (for Hoffmann is retelling a Berlin chronicle of 1551), we are sobered and loath to reread the story. Expressions like "Callot's and Bruegel's warning signs" and Hoffmann's preface to his *Phantasiestücke* indicate that the German author wanted to see the works of these painters interpreted in a special manner, namely—in spite of his fascination with the grotesque—as a Christian mode of indoctrination. This confirms an observation derived from certain traits of the *Phantasiestücke* as well as some of Hoffmann's earlier stories: that a full inter-pretation and organization of the "secret realm of spirits" weakens the force of the grotesque, no matter how much Hoffmann likes and manages to portray the ominous alienation of the world in other places. There are sufficient genuinely grotesque elements still remaining in these stories; Hoffmann is much too preoccupied with this phenomenon not to use it even in passages totally unrelated to the infernal sphere and which are in no way illuminated by it when seen in retrospect.

In the opening section of *Sylvesternacht*, Victor Hugo could have found an excellent illustration for the clash between the grotesque and the sublime, a clash which becomes abysmal through grotesque exaggeration. The excited narrator has rediscovered his lost sweetheart, whom he finds to be more angelic than ever. Music from Mozart's "sublime E Flat Major Symphony" is heard. "I shall never let you go, your love . . . inspiring higher life in art and poetry . . . but didn't you return in order to be mine forever?—Precisely at that moment, a clumsy, spider-legged figure with protruding frog's eyes came stumbling in, laughed foolishly, and shrieked: 'Where the devil has my wife gone?'" With a few precise strokes Hoffmann has drawn a grotesque figure composed of human and animal traits whose models could easily be found in Callot's engravings. (pp. 68-70)

Ornamental grotesques, Bosch, Bruegel, and Callot—all these manifestations of the grotesque reappear in Hoffmann's writings, as do the two other closely related strains which we have isolated. Almost all of Hoffmann's stories yield examples of the eccentric gestic style of eccentric figures which [are] derived from the *commedia dell'arte*. Take the following passage: "The innkeeper covered the mirror, and immediately afterwards a little thin fellow dressed in a coat of a strange, brownish hue came rushing into the room. He moved with an awkward speed, clumsily, quickly, I am tempted to say. As he hopped about in the room, his coat with the oddest folds and wrinkles moved around his body in such a peculiar way that in the candlelight it almost looked as if many figures were moving toward, and away from, each other." This example is taken from *Sylvesternacht*, which also contains a caricature that is on the point of becoming grotesque. The reader had just witnessed a hellish grotesque, in which the infernal tempters appeared to the narrator and almost persuaded him to sell his wife and child to the devil—an act that would damn his soul forever. But his wife's good graces have saved him at the very last moment. He now steps up to her bed in order to listen to her farewell speech, which begins as a caricature of the pedantic housewife but ends grotesquely: "'When you reach Nuremberg, however, add a brightly colored hussar, and a piece of gingerbread, as a loving father. Fare thee well, my dear Erasmus.' The woman turned over and went to sleep." This passage is obviously not only intended to satirize the mixture of common sense and insensitivity but also is designed to render the world strange and ridiculously ominous in the face of such inhuman, puppet-like behavior.

In E.T.A. Hoffmann's works we thus encounter the various types of the grotesque which emerged in the [previous] three centuries. . . . Hoffmann is a master in the composition of grotesque scenes; still we get the impression that the grotesque effect is usually weakened by the conclusions of his works. The novellas so far discussed ultimately turned out to have a meaning, since the intruding hostile and alienating forces were mostly seen as infernal temptations. The figures rose out of hell, and not out of the void. Some of the ominous qualities of the grotesque are lost, no matter how vaguely defined the hellish mythology. This is also true of *Der goldene Topf* (The Golden Pot), in which certain scenes are models of the grotesque (the name of the Hell Bruegel [Pieter the younger] is significantly mentioned). Seen as a whole, however, the novella turns out to be a fairy tale illuminated by allegory. The good and evil powers which struggle for the artist's soul are carefully delineated, and once again the question concerning the relation of part to whole becomes appropriate. It is apparently quite easy to enter the realm of the grotesque, but outside help is needed if one wants to leave it. The grotesque pushes one into an abyss, and if the story is to be continued, another level is needed for its enactment. . . . Hoffmann was fond of countering the horizontal movement of a story of temptation—or, in *Der goldene Topf,* of a story of temptation and salvation—with the vertical movement of the grotesque scenes. But the meaning inherent in the story of temptation detrimentally affected the grotesque in retrospect. (pp. 71-2)

Der Sandmann concludes with Nathanael's fall into the abyss. The hostile power which enters his life is not a devil but the dealer in barometers Coppola, who appears to be identical with the lawyer Coppelius, who had acted so hostilely toward the boy. (It is typical of Hoffmann's art that the doubts concerning their identity are never fully resolved.) In Nathanael's description, Coppelius himself, however, again appears as a Callot grotesque composed of human and animal traits and merges with the sandman. His nurse had told him that this creature visits children "who don't want to go to bed and throws handfuls of sand into their eyes, causing them to fall bleeding out of their sockets." . . . The eyes are a leitmotif of the novella, often in conjunction with the motif of the doll. The eyes of Clara, Nathanael's fiancée, are like a lake "in which the pure azure of the cloudless sky is mirrored." In a dream Nathanael sees himself standing with Clara before the altar, when Coppelius touches the latter's eyes and causes them to fall like bloody sparks into the dreamer's breast. The mechanical doll Olympia has everything—limbs, gait, and voice; only her glance lacks the "ray of life." The barometer dealer offers Nathanael a pair of sharply ground spectacles, that is, an artificial means of improving his vision; Nathanael finally buys a telescope, which he will always carry about him, and which symbolizes his dimmed and alienating glance. Or is it that he sees more sharply than other people? . . . This remarkable emphasis on realistic details is typical of the style of the grotesque and reminds one of the cold and wiry strokes in the etchings of Callot or Goya. Taken by itself, the isolation of the eyes has an ominous and alienating effect. It forces us, moreover, to acknowledge the full meaning which they have here assumed: the eyes as an expression of the soul, as a link with the world; the eyes as the actual seat of life.

One of the most grotesque scenes in the novella is Nathanael's encounter with the doll Olympia. While everybody else regards this mechanized image of life as both ridiculous and sinister (the solution of the puzzle is not furnished by the narrator but by the events themselves), Nathanael, who has fallen in love with her after seeing her through the telescope, is blind. He disregards the mechanical aspects and is ecstatic in the doll's presence. When he finally learns the deception, madness takes hold of him, since the excitement was too great and his contact with reality too tenuous. (pp. 72-4)

Madness is the climactic phase of estrangement from the world. The whole novella is an account of the triumph of the inner life of a highly gifted, imaginative, artistic individual (Nathanael is a poet)—a process set in motion by the author and accelerated through repeated encounters with an ominous power. And this in spite of the fact that this power (Coppola, Coppelius) does not directly interfere with the action but merely functions as a catalyst. . . . [In *Der Sandmann*] a certain amount of guilt is involved. An ounce of justice too much and in the wrong place . . . , and an ominous force immediately answers the provocation. Little Nathanael . . . offends when he desires to see the sandman and hides behind the curtain in order to achieve his goal. [In this instance] the punishment is out of proportion to the guilt, and, basically, [the ethical category] cannot encompass the events depicted in the story, for the "guilt" was . . . preformed in the nature of the [protagonist]. . . . Nathanael's character, moreover, merely enhances certain traits of his father, whose alchemistic experiments—which drove him into Coppelius' arms and, finally, into death—resulted from the urge to gain access to the secret forces behind reality. The abysmal nature of Hoffmann's story consists in the very fact that the artist, whose existence rests on his rich imagination, is in danger of being exposed to other forces which estrange the world for him. Time and again in Hoffmann's stories it is the artist who provides the point of contact between the real world and the ominous forces, and who loses hold of the world because he is able to penetrate the surface of reality.

In the story of such an estrangement of the world Hoffmann has found the horizontal action which enabled him, or rather forced him, to compose grotesque scenes. There was no need for him to produce devils or infernal monsters. It is a sign of Hoffmann's gradually acquired mastery that even those aspects of Coppelius' and Coppola's appearance and behavior which seem unnatural and improbable, permit a doubt or encourage the reader to seek an explanation within the limits of verisimilitude. At the very beginning of the novella, he makes Clara write a letter in which she describes Nathanael's youthful experiences and his harrowing encounter with the weathermaker in so reasonable a fashion that the reader is led to trust her. He feels she is justified in stating that the dark powers are victorious only if man's soul receives them willingly and grants them authority over the Self. . . . By putting these words into Clara's mouth Hoffmann causes his readers to believe, like her, in the existence of the "dark powers" and thereby increases the horror stemming from Nathanael's experiences. Let Nathanael exaggerate the ominousness of Coppola's character; his doing so is in itself a symptom of the estrangement which leads him toward what goal? It is possible to give comic expression to the fact that he mistakes a doll for a human being, thinks that she loves him, and confesses his love to her, but Hoffmann's presentation of the matter is so genuinely grotesque that its effect upon us is humorous and horrible at the same time. Hoffmann gains still another advantage by leaving the reader in doubt as to how things are in reality: who Coppelius is, whether he returns in Coppola, what is wrong with the telescope, etc.; a satisfactory explanation of these matters is not provided. The narrator, whose task begins after the presentation of the opening letters, initially seems to adopt a familiar attitude. He claims to be poor Nathanael's friend and appears to know his entire story. But gradually he abandons this bird's-eye view, moves very close to the events themselves, occasionally fuses with the other characters (and adopts their perspective) or turns into a deeply affected eyewitness of the events—an example of the new narrative point of view, the perfection of which is one of Hoffmann's great and lasting achievements. But since this narrator, when he began to speak, introduced himself as one of those people whose excitable soul leads to conflicts and causes them to be at odds with the outside world (he is an "author"), and since, at the same time, he appeals to the highly imaginative reader, we tend to identify ourselves with Nathanael and regard his fate as a latent possibility of our own existence. (pp. 74-6)

Wolfgang Kayser, "The Grotesque in the Age of Romanticism," in his The Grotesque in Art and Literature, translated by Ulrich Weisstein (translation copyright © 1963 by Indiana University Press; originally published as Das Groteske: Seine Gestaltung in Malerei und Dichtung, Gerhard Stalling Verlag, 1957), Indiana University Press, 1963 (and reprinted by McGraw-Hill Book Company, 1966), pp. 48-99.*

MARIANNE THALMANN (essay date 1964)

[Hoffmann's] avid interest in the occult and in the esoteric sciences, not found anywhere else to this degree except in French literature, reflects his need for artificial magic. By combining the urban reality of gaslights with the oriental pomposity of cheap literature, he produces a world of grotesque obscurities in which the foreground of life ceases to be real. (p. 88)

[Hoffmann's "Serapion principle, for which *Serapion-Brüder* is named, demands that the material for fiction] be taken from our actual environment, in which, one must admit, there is something inherently theatrical, but that this material then be separated from the objective world so that we are filled with consternation. This means that these stories must condition themselves to a definite pace and, what is more, to a definite content. Until now such subject matter had not necessarily been fairy-tale material, and when it was used that way, it was received with a sceptical shake of the head. The usual and commonplace in Hoffmann does not merely contain the wonderful and strange; it has become unfathomable. Here Hoffmann departs from early romanticism. (p. 90)

E.T.A. Hoffmann was greatly influenced by the *opera buffa*. *Poet and Composer (Dichter und Komponist)* in the *Serapion Brothers* sheds light on this subject. In addition to the everyday events which Tieck required for the fairy tale, Hoffmann demands something decidedly contemporary, the fairy tale "in tails," so to speak. In doing so, he affirms his [dual existence as burgher and poet]. . . . What he loves about the *opera buffa* is the wild leaps and bounds of his neighbor "in his familiar cinammon-colored Sunday suit with the gold-covered buttons" in which there is no trace of tragedy. Here the strange combines with the banal, the comical with the grotesque. The realism of a Breughel and a Callot has taken hold of him. This leads him to a strikingly modern confession: he recognizes in the tragicomical a legitimate form of expression for his time, one hundred years before it avowedly became that for us. . . . What Hoffmann introduces into romanticism is the buffoonish fairy tale where, out of the adventurous flight of individual figures, out of the bizarre game of chance, the fantastic is born which "propels" our daily lives "at the top and at the bottom". . . . In limiting himself to "the serious people, senior court judges, archivists, and students," who are given a ghostlike quality, he makes resounding laughter a new indispensable note in the fairy tale. The fairy tale has changed over from the monotony of daily life in Tieck to the major events of the official calendar in Hoffmann, who singles out from contemporary society a particular titled group of the middle class to play the leading roles. (pp. 91-2)

[Hoffmann's] ironic tone paves the way for the grotesque, which Hoffmann adopts in his later works. Hoffmann has also deviated from the early romantic fairy tale in rejecting "little verses in the story" . . . , and he condemns the mixing of forms, a must for the Schlegel circle, because this is, in his view, an attempt to conceal "some weakness of the material." There is nothing lyrical about Hoffmann. Even in his comical little verses that occasionally crop up he is leftish. He is only interested in narrating. . . .

From the very start [Hoffmann] is not only an author, but also a storyteller. More than anyone else, he holds all the strings in his hand. He candidly shoves aside the pretense that someone is reading the story aloud and establishes direct contact with the reader himself. He is always the author who tries to fascinate his audience. From the standpoint of art, this becomes sensationalism, but at the same time, a capricious form of irony. He sets up his figures in front of us and with us like a complicated chess problem. (p. 92)

Hoffmann introduces his main characters before the first move is made. He describes their clothing, their appearance. . . . He lets us look in every direction. We see how he controls the game, how he moves the figures back and forth, dismissing them and conjuring them back again. . . . [Hoffmann] addresses his reader intimately: "Perhaps you, oh my reader, like me are of the opinion that the human mind itself is the most wonderful fairy tale of all.—What a magnificent world lies buried in our breast". . . . Such excursuses often assume an unusual length, particularly at the beginning of the fairy tales, continuing for several paragraphs. This form of ironic textual interpolation increases precariously in the later fairy tales. As a result the material is to a large extent taken out of the carefree atmosphere of the fairy-tale past and moved up into the loquacious yesterday of realism.

The same narrative devices also serve Hoffmann in staging the conclusion of his fairy tales. With the skill of the professional director, which he has, he sets up a final tableau. There must be weddings at the end. It must be a gay ending in which the tricks of fate and the bizarre complications of life dissolve in laughter. (pp. 93-4)

[In *The Golden Pot*, subtitled **"Fairy Tale of our Times"**, Hoffmann] touches upon the fundamental substance of all his fairy tales—the sidewalk and coffeehouse character of their plot. What does this "of our times" imply? It is not a "once upon a time" in the old-fashioned sense of smug memories. It is the news item from yesterday's paper, an accident, a club announcement, fireworks in the Linkisch Bad in Dresden. . . .

[Every] plot follows the church calendar of feast days and week days—in this particular case, from Assumption Day to Veronica's birthday. The days themselves are carefully divided into office hours, hours for coffee, strong beer, and punch, and finally hours for sleep. The events also have their geographic reality in the Koselschen Garten in Dresden, at the Rossmarkt in Frankfurt, at the Porta del Pòpolo in Rome. (p. 97)

The hero of [*The Golden Pot*], the student Anselmus, comes from the same middle-class stratum of society. He lacks logic, is a Philistine, a genius, and a hypochondriac all in one. . . . [In] presenting this figure, Hoffmann goes far beyond the instability of Tieck's heroes. He stands much closer to the outer edges of experience; he is not afraid of approaching the margins of sanity. His hero is not merely a dreamer; he is already inwardly impaired; he exhibits schizophrenic traits, he lives in hallucinations, and experiences reality on different levels of consciousness, making a grotesque impression on the people around him. (pp. 97-8)

[Anselmus] is imperceptibly guided from outside. Strange things take him by surprise; they assail him. He does not expect them, nor does he actually conjure up this enchanted world, as Tieck's heroes do. He is afraid of it even before it appears. His fear can already be clinically defined. He becomes clay in the hands of older men who have overcome their taste for folly and are acquainted with the wounds of life, although they themselves have remained unscarred. In these figures Hoffmann has translated the heroes of the Masonic novel into wise and attractive personalities. The emissaries of the order as they are found in the cheap literature of the eighteenth century have developed into bourgeois characters who have acquired a certain mastery over the pain of daily life and, at the same time, radiate the light of their humorous relationship to it. They know the inadequacies of the Philistine, the tears it costs to be young and to want to be gifted. They laugh with the bureaucrats, and they make fun of the tormented, something that Hoffmann himself could never do. We realize that both sides are ridiculous. (pp. 98-9)

[In *Nutcracker* and *The Strange Child,* which were written for children,] it is again a master who takes [the characters] in hand: the godfather Drosselmeier (*Nutcracker*) and the fairy child (*The Strange Child*). Both love what is childlike: they love the time of life when one may still dream, when one quite naturally imagines and even sees a wonderful world behind the objects of reality. Both the godfather and the fairy child tell a story which associates children's lives with strange happenings in distant places and casts the first shadows over their childhood. What they tell is another Phosphorus fairy tale, translated into a youthful language so that children feel involved in it. These fairy tales within fairy tales, a play within a play, so to speak, represent a continuation of a romantic structural concept, and are part of every one of Hoffmann's fairy tales. In them the battle between powers and opposing powers is so intensified that they become fantastic. By portraying the conditions that undermine the Philistine world, Hoffmann briefly exposes his own time. He alienates the world of the petty bourgeoisie by implicating it in a past which presupposes a very different kind of reality. (pp. 101-02)

After these two children's fairy tales, Hoffmann approaches the middle class with growing sarcasm in his questionable fairy tales about success and politics. Balthasar, the hero of *Klein Zaches,* is an Anselmus whom life treats somewhat more kindly, even though he was "not worth much" as a poet. . . . We find in the Hoffmann fairy tale the beginnings of a future army of misfits: the tormented person, Burgher Schippel, Professor Unrat, the Tesmanns, and Ejlerts. His need for amassing such figures grows. The hero is reflected in his friend, powers and adversaries are doubled, even the figure of the master doubles: Alpanus supports Balthasar who is endowed with "an inner music," and Rosabelverde supports Klein-Zaches, whose loathsomeness she finds touching. Men look to see how the mechanism works, while women become the prey of their own sentiment. The game of influence and success, truth and deception, goes back and forth between these two figures. Balthasar also must endure the trials of inner conflict and doubt and must risk the battle with Klein-Zaches before he wins his Candida in a now prosaic world and may call Dr. Alpanus' estate his own. With tongue in cheek, Hoffmann lets morality win: young married couples are generously remembered by good uncles, everyone receives his title at the right time, and every virtuous girl of the suburbs finds her well-to-do Peregrinus Tyss. There is nothing so lasting as these vulgarities. Hoffmann does not deny that such a world still exists. It is

becoming more and more difficult, however, for the unusual person to live in it. (pp. 102-03)

[*The King's Bride*] is the fairy tale of fairy tales. The Schikaneder pattern is grotesquely exaggerated from the beginning to the end. It treats the theme of the alienation of man and object throughout, and hence it becomes "le comique absolu," as Baudelaire said, who greatly admired this fairy tale. The leading lady is a Veronica without a bit of imagination. For her only things with names exist, commodities, her household, yet from the lettuce, beans, and carrots in her garden, from the independence of these plants as they go through the world conforming to human beings, she experiences enchantment, for not even the dullest wit can escape it completely. A ring on a carrot which she pulls out of the ground suddenly slides onto her finger. And who could resist such a pretty little harmless thing?

The master who sees through the hostility between objects and wants to control it is Herr Dapsul, Ännchen's father. . . . But the master is no longer the lord of creation as before. The adversaries trip him; he slips, he falls on his bottom, he is thrown into the frying pan along with the chopped eggs, he is transformed into a mushroom. The machinery of magic of the Masonic novel has become independent, and human existence now merely evokes laughter. (p. 105)

It is above all in the grotesque form of [the plot of *The King's Bride*] where E.T.A. Hoffmann gains full control over the traditional trappings of magic without sacrificing the artistic, something that cannot always be said of him. *The King's Bride* is the fairy tale of an expert who delights his audience at the end by even giving it a glimpse into his studio. It is a grotesque of boorish existence, and what could be more ridiculous than that at a time of crisis for man and society. . . . The happy ending is not only in harmony with fairy-tale practice, but also with the ironic tone of a story whose aim is to amuse. It needs this game with the pretty tableau at the end. . . . (p. 106)

Hoffmann came to literature by way of the opera and the theater and hence, he loved scenery. Indeed, even the staging of the action imbibed Schikaneder's talent to make the ending of every act a hit and to sanction jokes. That means rich scenery, many stage settings, and a good deal of equipment. (p. 107)

Houses watch us right and left. Street corners trip us. Something giggles in the vegetable bed, and there is whispering in the lilac bush. . . . The tangible rooms with their sofas, dining-room tables, and sewing baskets, which feign a certain closeness because everything in them is correctly labeled and deciphered, become both comical and malicious because Hoffmann feels that his own surroundings are absurd. He is sceptical about this reality with its gaping background behind which one senses the sinister lurking. But the fact that the technique of presentation seems realistic probably explains why he has almost been numbered among the realists who castigate the bourgeoisie for their sins. The truth is, however, that it was more Hoffmann's horror of bourgeois virtues which pursued him through life.

We return from romantic flights into space to the narrow confines of the living room, cluttered with objects and figures. Hoffmann has a preference for small intimate rooms, as was so often true of the painters of the grotesque. His people live uncomfortably close to each other but set in motion, the walls burst and the room is extended to fantastic dimensions. The parade of the toy figures in *Nutcracker*—the brave gardeners, Tirolese, Tungus, barbers, harlequins, tigers, long-tailed monkeys, and apes, the crowds in the capital of Fairyland, all the figures of sugar and tragacanth, the shepherds and lambs, mailmen and dancers, enlarge the play room to a playground of terrifying proportions. . . . Hoffmann creates the most oppressive kind of fear in these grotesques of overcrowded rooms. (pp. 107-09)

But inasmuch as a fairy tale also needs some room to breathe, Hoffmann likes to turn to the capital of a small principality, to a narrow little provincial city where the dignitaries, petty princes, and their bureaucrats, live together in security. This locale also has an uncomfortable closeness. It is filled to the bursting point with rushing, laughing, stumbling, pushing. And even where Hoffmann goes beyond the street corner to the village, the woods, the pond, or the cliff, it does not become real, but remains scenery in which the decorative element, the frosting on the cake, so to speak, is the most important thing. Without going far astray, one may say that Hoffmann does not invent nature symbols, but simply uses the ready-made landscape terminology gained through his wide reading. It is a collapsible scenery which can be set up in a flash. He is not a lover of nature. . . . He needs company and people; he comes to life in overcrowded restaurants; he is at home in the streets. He has no affinity to nature and compensates for this lack by overcrowding his sets. He sees with the eyes of the Sunday stroller: pretty slender birch trees, tall dark fir trees, lovely flowers, flowery fields, charming villages, golden clouds, golden beetles, golden harps, golden purple. There is no skimping when it comes to gilding. Hoffmann is not a master of spiritual coloring, but an expert on brilliant gloss. (pp. 109-10)

The landscape adapts itself to his purposes in a profusion of verbs. . . . Objects and color, fragrance and thing, part company and realign themselves to produce new effects. Shrubs sparkle like "green-glowing carbuncles," the water of the rivers is "dark-yellow," fish are "rose-red" and mingle "with gold-scaled dolphins" and "silver soldiers." Language and content scarcely coincide anymore; however, this is less apt to lead to something spiritual than to something ostentatious and cheap. (pp. 110-11)

[Of] all his elaborate landscapes, none can surpass the confectioner's landscape in *Nutcracker*. Marie is led by Nutcracker along the orange brook, over the candy meadows, through the almond gates, past the cake trees to the marzipan castle. It is a landscape in which everything smells sweet, glistens, and gushes. . . . One cannot help but think that this is Hoffmann's way of giving his reader a gentle rap on the knuckles for having gullibly swallowed such enormous quantities of poetic sweets without noticing how grotesquely they were dished out. (pp. 111-12)

[Hoffmann] transforms what is dull in the writings of the past so that they reflect the condition of his own day, a condition between laughter and fear, in which the spiritual person is destroyed and the bourgeois form of life becomes a caricature. An alienation of reality appears, because what is behind this reality, the sur-reality of dreams, fears, and abysses, becomes significantly more important. The caricature is not a criticism of society. Hoffmann has a natural talent for it, and in it he expresses his fear of the deformation which is taking place all around him and which is also corroding him.

With equal artistic skill Hoffmann also gives his language a grotesque turn. Nouns are strung together so that his scenes become oppressively overcrowded and each individual object takes on a threatening life of its own. . . . And yet it is not the language which makes Hoffmann's fairy tales. It is not a question of artistic language here. Even words are merely a means of transforming the world into grotesque proportions and relationships. (pp. 112-13)

What evolves as a natural result of Hoffmann's analysis of [the] hazy world of mediocrity where the usual and the unusual clash with such force, is the grotesque of a tragicomical world in which an exalted mood is a delusion and a declaration of love merely ridiculous. With that the new image of man has entered a precarious border zone. Hoffmann himself, to be sure, is not at home there, but he can already look into it from a distance. The breach in society between the well-balanced person who can always snap back into what has been certified as balance, and those who are less balanced, as Hoffmann no doubt felt deeply with respect to himself, appears in his fairy tales as the fundamental enmity between the Philistine and the genius. What results is the distortion of the burgher as the Philistine who has freed himself from the sublime and tragic. In his devotion to the Nutcrackers, moreover, Hoffmann begins to justify the man of genius and the dark side of life outside the bourgeois sphere by means of exhaustive effects. In any tragicomical situation, which has its greatness but no nobility, the bohemian takes the place of the poet. He has left the romantic behind and has become the product of a deformed society, so that no God can bring solace any more. (p. 117)

[*The King's Bride*, in which Hoffmann perfects his type of] grotesque fairy tale and arrives at the irony of irony, is his masterpiece. A surplus of wit, laughter that does not offend, this is Hoffmann's highest trump. The unhappiness one feels over the people of means and the inflationary values of society dissolve in this laughter and become something which in the last analysis no longer hurts. An artistic solution presents itself here which spiritualizes, even though it is not a story of redemption. It is not a plot that is governed by reason, it is not about a Satan, a Cain, or a Wandering Jew, but simply about the horror of the most common everyday things in which the tragicomical and the grotesque unite in a natural bond. They stand there before us, all those respectable people, and each one has a screw loose in his head. . . . The irony with which Hoffmann portrays these simple people who have accidently slipped over into the realm of the fantastic has a charm no longer mixed with bitterness. The fairy tale has become a work of artistic subtlety. E.T.A. Hoffmann did not write another *Golden Pot*, it is true, but in the *The King's Bride* he finally wrote the grotesque without tears. (pp. 119-20)

Marianne Thalmann, "The Hoffmann Fairy Tale," in her The Romantic Fairy Tale: Seeds of Surrealism, *translated by Mary B. Corcoran (copyright © by The University of Michigan 1964), University of Michigan Press, 1964, pp. 88-120.*

S. S. PRAWER   (essay date 1965)

In the opening paragraph of *Der Sandmann* two worlds confront each other; and this confrontation determines the structure of the whole story that is to follow. We need only list the adjectives of this paragraph: 'Hold', 'süss', 'hold' again, 'freundlich', 'hell', [gracious, sweet, gracious again, amiable, bright]— all attributes of Clara who represents (as her very name tells us) a realm of light, clarity and simplicity that stands in dialectical relationship to another realm of which the following adjectives speak: 'zerrissen', 'dunkel', 'grässlich', 'drohend', 'schwarz' [confused, dark, terrible, menacing, black]. . . . These two realms belong together, and it is only because we are given so plain a vision of the first that the second has such power to terrify. . . . [The tension between these two worlds] constitutes the ultimate theme of this as of so many other of Hoffmann's tales.

That is one important pattern of which the opening of the story makes us aware; but there are others that are no less important. The first paragraph rises to a climax of apprehension . . . and seems suddenly to swoop down, bathetically, into the banal everyday. . . . But this is not really an anticlimax at all, for Hoffmann's subject is precisely the terror that lurks in the most apparently ordinary and everyday. . . . [We] have an exact reversal of the structural pattern of, say, Mrs Radcliffe's novels, in which 'supernatural' events are given a 'natural' explanation at the end. Hoffmann's explanations explain nothing at all: they point, instead, to the real mystery, to the connexion between the familiar and the uncanny; they suggest the working of unknown powers in a world in which we feel at home.

Yet a third important pattern may be observed in the opening paragraphs of *Der Sandmann.* We are taken into a comfortable family circle—all the members of the family are disposed about a round table at which the father smokes his pipe, drinks his glass of beer and tells the children fantastic stories. Into this circle breaks the terrifying figure of the Sandman, at first in the nurse's tale, then in the shape of the lawyer Coppelius; there is a climax of terror, until, it seems, the Sandman is cast out and the family circle closes again protectively about the child. . . . But this is nothing but a *reculer pour mieux sauter* [drawing back in order to spring forward], for soon afterwards all 'Gemütlichkeit' [good feeling] is dispelled and the family group shattered by the father's death.—The pattern of Nathanael's childhood reminiscence is repeated exactly in the second part of the story, where we find the idyllic love of Nathanael and Clara disturbed by the appearance of Coppola and Olimpia; instead of the swoon of the earlier episode we now have a fit of madness, until the protective circle closes, or seems to close, again. . . . But this too proves to be nothing but the calm before the real storm, before the last appearance of Coppelius and Nathanael's incurable madness and death.

What appears in *Der Sandmann* as a structural principle is made explicit when Cyprian, in *Die Serapionsbrüder,* comments on a story significantly entitled *Der unheimliche Gast.* . . . A stranger, an 'uncanny guest', who appears at first banal and undistinguished, destroys the family idyll. The very form of the sentence which introduces him, however, shows that he really belongs to this family idyll—that he is witness to a realm with which the family was seeking contact at the very moment of his irruption. . . . The stranger is 'unheimlich' [uncanny] not only in the sense that after his appearance men no longer feel 'at home' in their world, but also in that deeper sense of which [Freud spoke]. . . .

[In his essay on the 'Uncanny' (see excerpt above)] Freud discusses *Der Sandmann* as a notable example of the Uncanny in literature. He lays particular stress, not so much on the motif of the mechanical doll . . . as that of 'fear for the loss of one's eyes'. The Sandman threatens the boy's eyes in the nurse's tale and in the scene in which Coppelius and Nathanael's father are observed at their alchemistic experiments; and he later comes between Nathanael and the consummation of his love. Freud sees in Coppelius—Coppola, Spalanzani and Nathanael's father parts of a single image, a 'split type figure' like the two fathers of Hamlet; fear for the loss of one's eyes is a disguise assumed by fear of castration; and Olimpia, the mechanical doll, is an objectified complex of Nathanael's, a sign

that his father-fixation has made him incapable of normal love. (pp. 298-300)

The possibility that everything in the story which transcends ordinary experience may be taken as Nathanael's delusion is an important part of the effect of *Der Sandmann.* This does not mean, however, that the story has only private significance. In *Die Serapionsbrüder,* Lothar defends the fascination that insanity has for him . . . and Kreisler is shown, in *Kater Murr* and elsewhere, to see more deeply into the heart of things than his more obviously 'sane' contemporaries. . . . The 'dark powers', 'uncanny powers', 'inimical principles' of which Hoffmann likes to speak work through men's minds, but are not necessarily identical with men's minds, are not necessarily merely signs of our personal unconscious. There is something devilish, something motivelessly malign in Coppelius—Coppola, something which connects him with that more than natural realm of evil which is hinted at in the nurse's story. (p. 301)

For Hoffmann the personal unconscious is a means of gaining contact with something larger and deeper . . . which we may equate, without serious distortion, with Jung's 'Collective Unconscious'. . . . [*Der Sandmann*]—which may be regarded as the reversal or 'Zurücknahme' of *Der goldne Topf*—has many elements that would seem to demand a Jungian analysis. Coppelius—Coppola may be seen as the hero's 'Shadow'; Lothar and Siegmund give us (rather colourlessly, it must be admitted) the archetype of the 'Seelenfreund'; Clara and Olimpia clearly represent two opposing aspects of the Anima; and the 'circle of fire', which plays so prominent a part in Nathanael's visions and poems, may be seen as a perverted Mandala.

The important point, here and elsewhere, is that *Der Sandmann* must not be regarded . . . as a mere capriccio or arabesque; that it reproduces through its figures, incidents and structure, the logic of the unconscious. And this leads us back to a motif which we have already seen to be of central importance: the irruption of an 'uncanny guest' into a cosy family-circle to which he seems, somehow, to belong. We may now interpret this as the irruption of dark images from below the threshold of consciousness, images that push past the 'censor' or 'Acciseofficiant' of the conscious mind. (p. 302)

[Another manifestation of the image of the 'uncanny guest' is presented through the characters Coppelius and Spalanzani. They] objectify feelings of alienation that we meet again and again in the literature of the last century and a half: the alienation of man from the world he has created; the alienation of man from parts of his own personality that have been repressed only to return as spectral 'doubles' to hound and torment him. Here Hoffmann must be seen together with Poe, with Dickens, with Dostoevsky; with all those writers who have depicted the city as the home of uncanny presences that haunted, in earlier times, the castles of the Gothic novel and of [Marquis] de Sade, or the mountains and woods of [Ludwig] Tieck's first 'Märchen'. Once again we are confronted by the image of the 'uncanny guest'. Coppola *seems* an outsider, an itinerant Italian in the world of the small German town: but is he not identical with the lawyer Coppelius, who belonged to that world and whom Nathanael's father venerated above all his fellow-citizens? The neurotic constitution that makes Nathanael appear predestined to madness, gives him at the same time a clear insight into social realities; and his 'Zerrissenheit' [inner strife] makes him into a drastic paradigm for the fate of a sensitive, artistically gifted man in the world of cities. (p. 304)

In reading *Der Sandmann* and other, similar, stories one has the impression that the wondrous, the transcendent, the demonic are playing a game of hide-and-seek—or, more accurately, of cat-and-mouse—with the characters; and this game seems to have materially determined the structure of such stories too. Everywhere in **Der Sandmann** we meet on the one hand motifs of dressing up and disguising, of keeping secret and mystifying; and on the other motifs of peeping from a hiding-place, peering out from cupboards and curtains, peering across into strange houses with the aid of telescopes. (This 'Peeping Tom' motif is of course connected with the 'eye' images whose prominence has already been noted.) The cat-and-mouse game, however, determines not only *what* Hoffmann tells but also his manner of telling it. The author retreats behind a fictitious narrator, an imagined friend of Nathanael's engaged in piecing his story together. This narrator, in his turn, sometimes identifies himself with his readers' tastes, sometimes ironically distances himself from them, ascribing Philistine imperceptiveness to his 'dear reader'; sometimes he seeks to draw the reader into his spell by every possible rhetorical device, then again he retreats in a cloud of witticisms à la Jean Paul. The somewhat bizarre construction of the tale—hovering between epistolary and third person narrative, between flashback and straightforward time-sequence interrupted, again and again, by an ironic excursus—this too is part of the pervading cat-and-mouse game. Zigzagging narrative hides an action that is logical and symmetrical: twice Nathanael's life moves from idyll to a crescendo of terror; this is followed, on each occasion, by a fit of swooning or of madness, after which the idyll is re-established; and only after this false reassurance does fate show its hand completely, bringing death at first to Nathanael's father and then to Nathanael himself.

The shifts in tone imposed by the 'game' that has just been noticed affect the structure of Hoffmann's sentences, too; paratactic, breathless sentences alternate startlingly with hypotactic, long-winded, encapsulated ones. . . . These are Hoffmann's two voices, which stand in the same relationship to one another as the worlds of Clara and Coppelius, or the fantastic and realistic elements of the tale: the voice of the visionary who wants to draw the reader into his spell by fair means or foul, and the voice of the ironic artist who knows how to distance himself from his creation. It is the co-presence in him of visionary and coolly weighing craftsman which makes Hoffmann find such exact expression for the physiology as well as the psychology of fear; makes him experiment so successfully with grotesquely distorted language and gradations of sound; enables him to blend so perfectly exactly observed vignettes of German small-town life with terrifying fantasy. Only occasionally he writes too quickly and takes the easy way out—then he produces passages (like his description of the abortive duel between Nathanael and Lothar) that read like parodies of [Christian Heinrich] Spiess, Benedicte Neubert or even [Heinrich] Clauren.

For all their occasional lapses of taste, Hoffmann's tales of terror have not lost their fascination for us today. It is not their plot that draws us (for that is often melodramatic) nor is it the characters Hoffmann presents (for these are often either colourless or grotesquely incredible). We read them for the complicated and tortured personality that shows itself behind and within plot and characters, revealing itself in rhetoric of terror, in play of irony, in complex narrative structures. We read them for the strange and haunting visions that are evoked as precisely as the familiar setting into which they break. We read them because they exemplify perfectly what Hoffmann called the 'Serapiontic principle': the ability to mould the materials of the outer world (men, landscapes, events, literary reminis-

cences) into images for an exactly apprehended inner world. In one sense such visions are private—they are clearly connected with Hoffmann's experiences. . . . But they also have representative force: they constitute powerful symbols of the experience of artists in a world of cities, of Germans in the early nineteenth century, of men in a world which they have themselves made but which now confronts them in strange, hostile, terrifying shapes. . . . [Twentieth-century readers] are able to sense the experienced truth behind Hoffmann's luminous fantasies; they feel a shudder of intimate recognition when they are shown, again and again and in ever new ways, the irruption of an 'uncanny guest' into a homely, familiar and interpreted world. (pp. 305-07)

> S. S. Prawer, "Hoffmann's Uncanny Guest: A Reading of 'Der Sandmann'," in German Life & Letters, Vol. XVIII, No. 4, July, 1965, pp. 297-308.

E. F. BLEILER (essay date 1966)

[Hoffmann's best work] is sui generis. There are few writers who can match him where the principle of Serapionism is concerned—the technique of presenting the supernatural convincingly. He can arouse momentary conviction and acceptance for even the most outrageous fantasy, leading the reader, as in **"The Golden Flower Pot,"** from the prosaic Biedermeier streets of Dresden into the wildest wonderland achieved in literature up to his time. The greatness of his achievement here can be seen by comparing his work with the Romantic short stories that preceded it. Hoffmann is also a very subtle writer, with a remarkable ability to merge levels of explanation, blending literalistic fantasy with allegory, symbolism, philosophy, and the psychology of the day. The result is a very personal amalgam which is worlds removed from the crudities of *The Horrid Mysteries* and similar Gothic material that stimulated him when he was young. And yet he is often elusive and tricky, and the reader may often discover that he has not always fathomed Hoffmann's true meaning at first reading.

Technically, Hoffmann at his best was very strong. Characterization was one of his fortes, and strange personality after personality emerged from his pen. No matter what their origin—whether very deliberate embodiments of contemporary psychological theories, or fragments of himself, or caricatures of his friends, or whatever else—they carry conviction. Experimental forms in which stories are told from the point of view of the "wrong" character, where letters alternate with editorial reflections, where essays on musicology interrupt the narrative, where characters split and combine, where his characters reflect back on Hoffmann's works—all of these are handled masterfully. Hoffmann usually remains in control and does not lose his individuality or become swallowed in confusion as so often happened to his Gothic prototypes. (pp. xv-xvi)

Yet Hoffmann does have faults, despite his many excellences. He is sometimes too sentimental, particularly when he is writing under the influence of Jean Paul Richter. This sentimentality, however, is an isolated phenomenon, and seldom affects the hard brilliance of his work. His experiments with form, in addition, occasionally do not come off. At times he seems to have arrived at the end of a story with no clear idea of how to close it convincingly. In such cases he gives the impression of having cleared the stage as rapidly as he could, with some impatience. His personality sometimes obtrudes into his work, and he is not always a well-balanced writer. Much of his thought, if stripped below the narrative level, and, sometimes, placed in his life situation, is not pleasant. Goethe, who could admire aspects of **"The Golden Flower Pot,"** applied to Hoffmann's work as a whole the 19th-century equivalent of "sick, sick, sick."

Still, if Hoffmann lacks the serenity and balance of a Goethe, and is an excited and exciting man, his very lack of balance often creates a drive and motion in his work that Goethe's sometimes lacks. Hoffmann is seldom dull. One of his strongest assets is his tremendous nervous energy and narrative drive; he must surely be one of the most rapid authors in all literature. His motion is breath-taking.

In the opinion of many modern scholars Hoffmann's work represents not only the last chronological work of the German Romantic period, but also its culmination. . . . For Novalis the supernatural was numinous, poetic, and ethical; for the Schlegels it was philosophical and critical; for Tieck it was self-laughter; for the minor writers, it was emotion—thrills and longing; and for Hoffmann it was science. Once the misty ideas of the anti-Enlightenment were themselves organized into the clarity and logic of a legal brief, and the supernatural became merely a division of abnormal or depth psychology, the creative impulse could go no farther.

Most critics agree that **"The Golden Flower Pot"** (**"Der goldne Topf"**) is Hoffmann's best story. (pp. xvi-xvii)

On the most superficial level, it can be read simply as a fantastic thriller, in which the supernatural emerges and invades the world of everyday life, just as supernaturalism within a pseudohistorical setting did in the Gothic novels that Hoffmann delighted in reading. Some of Hoffmann's minor fiction, indeed, is written on this level, but it is very unlikely that **"The Golden Flower Pot"** is to be taken this way.

Beyond the external events of magic in Dresden and the emergence of the elemental world of the Renaissance Rosicrucians, for example, there lie several themes that appear in much of Hoffmann's other work: that loss of faith or denial of revelation can be destructive; that there is a connection between madness and the suffering world; and that art and life do not mingle, but must be separated.

Individuation, in the modern psychological sense, offers one of the most plausible symbolic interpretations of **"The Golden Flower Pot."** This amounts to a statement (in fantastic terms) of character growth. It is thus the story of the awakening of poetic sensibility in Anselmus, and of the upheaval which the new developments cause in Anselmus's personality. . . . According to this interpretation the entire story of **"The Golden Flower Pot"** is the projection of Anselmus's mind. His emergent sense of ecstasy colors and transforms everything he beholds, and the daily life of a staid, bourgeois early 19th-century city is seen as a mad scramble of occult powers, half-insane super-humans, strange perils and remarkable benisons as Anselmus becomes a poet.

Yet beyond this there are other possible levels of interpretation. It has been noticed that the characters and ideas of **"The Golden Flower Pot"** are arranged in two series, each with one pole in the world of reality and another in the world of fantasy. Indeed, there is even a sort of identity between the two forms: Serpentina with Veronica, Anselmus with the Registrator Heerbrand, Archivarius Lindhorst with Conrector Paulmann, and so on. According to this interpretation, Anselmus is simply a projection of the Registrator which disappears in the world of fantasy, while the Registrator, giving up his dreams, marries Veronica. She, in turn, recognizes that she cannot possess the Anselmus complex but must be content with the Conrector-turned-Geheimrat.

Both of these interpretations may seem to be far-fetched interpretation for its own sake, but the fact remains that some justification exists for them or comparable unriddlings. Hoffmann's work is permeated with the concept of personality fragments coming to separate identity and acting as characters. (pp. xviii-xix)

The heart of **"The Golden Flower Pot"** is the märchen, or literary myth, that the Archivarius begins in the tavern; it is concluded by a strange glossologia from an Oriental manuscript that Anselmus is copying. The archphilistine of the story calls this märchen "Oriental bombast," but as the Archivarius replies, it is not only true but important. It recapitulates the central thought of **"The Golden Flower Pot"** sub specie aeternitatis, stripped of the accidentals of time, space, and personality.

The central idea of this märchen is the birth of poetry, expressed in terms of cosmic symbols drawn from the Naturphilosophie. It tells of the divine spark (phosphorus was the chemical symbol for the nervous fluid or intelligence in some of the systems of the day) which awakens and fertilizes a vegetative life. This in terms of mounting triads (a concept borrowed from the philosophical systems of the day) must die to give birth to a higher principle.

Lindhorst's märchen is thus a combination of several elements: a pseudobiblical creation statement; an allegory in which details have special meaning, although it is not always clear now what each point means; a fanciful statement of the human situation; and perhaps an ironic spoofing of some of the philosophical systems of the day. Hoffmann, although he was greatly interested in the outgrowths of Schelling's philosophy and accepted much of it, could be expected to retain a pawky incredulity at certain aspects of it. But perhaps analysis should not be pushed too far; it may be enough to say that this is a numinous statement of life, in which both profound and trivial concepts are fused. (pp. xix-xx)

E. F. Bleiler, "Introduction" (1966), in The Best Tales of Hoffmann *by E.T.A. Hoffmann, edited by E. F. Bleiler (copyright © 1967 by Dover Publications, Inc.), Dover, 1967, pp. v-xxxiii.*

RENÉ WELLEK (essay date 1967)

Much of Hoffmann's writing is couched in an almost formulaic sentimental diction which may be hard to take, though Hoffmann is obviously laughing at himself. Much of the satire is directed against an extinct society: the petty courts of tiny German principalities, the pompously stolid burghers, and the weepy, ethereal girls of the German middles classes of the time. Much of the technique of narration will strike us as old-fashioned: the addresses to "dear reader," the insertion of letters, the opportune coincidences, the substitutions of children at birth, and other paraphernalia of romance.

We must not, however, be deterred by this. (p. 50)

Hoffmann has a complex vision of the world. It is, at first, easiest to think of it simply as a scale which extends from brute matter to supernal beauty—"supernal" in the vague, mystical sense in which Poe spoke of it. Many of Hoffmann's stories revolve around a conflict between mind and matter, soul and body, art and life. His writings are pervaded by a nostalgia for a happier world in which the artist and all spiritual men must find consolation for the failure of life. . . . The artist is a visitor from [another] world—misunderstood and even persecuted by the cloddish world of the Philistines. He can never make his peace with them. Even in his love for a woman he must remain resigned and pure. His love of art must be disinterested, all-absorbing. Music is the highest art; it takes us into the upper world most quickly. (pp. 50-1)

Music is only one of [the means of emotional release and exultation]; the other (or is it the same?) is imagination, the creative imagination of the poet and the unconscious workings of our dream-life. The dream, as with so many poets of the time—from Novalis to Nerval—is the ivory gate through which we enter the realm of truth and beauty.

This almost Neo-platonic vision in Hoffmann remains, however, only a private hope; there is nothing Messianic or Utopian about it. Rather, one suspects it to be a consolatory scheme which he imbibed from the German romantic surroundings while, existentially, most personally, this radiant vision is denied or distorted by his profoundest experience: the horror behind the surface of the world, a sense of the malignity of fate, of the powers which dispose of us arbitrarily and make life rather a nightmare than a hope or, at best, a silly and inconsequential dream.

There is much in Hoffmann which is merely sinister and weird, and this earned him the reputation of "spooky" Hoffmann— though he rarely introduces ghosts into his stories and deals rather with phenomena explainable by telepathy, hypnosis, or hallucination. But there is much more in Hoffmann which shows a profound sense of the precariousness of our existence, for which he found unforgettable symbols and myths ever since he professed to have heard the Devil's voice as a boy on the seashore in East Prussia: a weird sound which filled him with profound terror and piercing compassion. This other world is not the Atlantis of **"The Golden Pot."** It is a world of demons who govern us and even enter into us. We hang helplessly between this and the other world or are ourselves divided between them. Thus, many of Hoffmann's most interesting characters are split personalities, even physical "doubles." . . . The double is for him the question mark put to the concept of the human self, a symbol of the doubt we have of human identity and the stability of our world. The automatons, puppets, and even the stock figures of the Italian *commedia dell' arte* so prevalent in his tales represent the sense of man's dependence on superior powers, the determinism in which Hoffmann believes. (pp. 51-2)

This whole contradictory world, almost Manichean in its division into good and evil, light and darkness, even within an individual, rarely is allowed to degenerate into melodrama or farce because it is seen with a sense of detachment and irony, viewed with a feeling of superiority. The rapid changes of mood, the piquant mixture of tears and laughter, the whole tragicomedy of life is pointed up by a technique of telling in which the teller of the tale is always present and prominent. A sense of make-believe and play is never absent.

The extreme of such technical virtuosity is reached in his novel *The Life and Opinions of Tomcat Murr*. . . . [The] story of the tomcat is interrupted by the story of the musician [Kreisler] but his story is and remains fragmentary. . . . The effect of the sandwiching of the two stories is rather one of simple contrast: the satire of the tomcat story clashes oddly, even

brutally, with the highly poetical intricate artist's novel set in a tiny German court. The Murr story, which is only about a third of the book's length, is a parody of the educational novel, of Goethe's *Wilhelm Meister* and its romantic imitators. The titles of the sections—**"Months of Youth," "The Experience of the Adolescent," "Et ego in Arcadia," "The Months of Apprenticeship," "The More Mature Months"**—comically parallel, in the shorter time span of a cat's life, the stages of the growth of a young German. . . . The cat's flowing eloquence makes trivial the vocabulary and thought of the time, its ideals of education and culture, fatherland and humanity, enlightenment and optimism, sentimental love and the romantic cult of nature. All these ideas and feelings are ridiculed by having them expressed through a cat's mouth. By direct or indirect quotation, the cat turns the German classics into absurdities. (pp. 52-3)

Against these prosaic ruminations, the world of Kreisler's exalted art shines with lyrical beauty. But it is also a sinister world dominated by a dark fate. . . . [The mysterious musician Kreisler is,] as always in Hoffmann, is the artist-outsider dedicated to his music, but also cursed by it. (p. 53)

[Among Hoffmann's tales,] we can distinguish three main groups of stories: retellings of traditional stories elaborated to suit Hoffmann's moods and taste, fantastic fairy tales, and grotesques of his own invention. The first group contains some of Hoffmann's most successful writing, if we judge in terms of traditional construction, formal story line, and adherence to the conventions of realism. The sources in a memoir or history provide some restraint and an anchorage in the world of concrete things. **"Mlle de Scudéry,"** among our examples, is the more effective because Hoffmann controls the method of telling the story superbly. The cutback describing the events of some twenty-three years is dramatized by the situation of telling: the murder charge against Olivier, the despair of Madelon, and the change which Mlle de Scudéry experiences in listening to the story, her growing conviction of Olivier's innocence preparing for the happy ending.

The fantastic fairy tale, best represented by **"The Golden Pot,"** breaks completely with the world of cause and effect. In a riot of capricious fancy, everything comes to mean everything else: a rhetoric of metamorphoses changes man into plant, plant into animal, an applewoman into a doorknocker, a turnip into a king. One can see in these stories anticipations of the irresponsible dream world of the surrealists, a stream of free association, a melting of all the senses, colors, sounds, and perfumes (long before Rimbaud). One may even look for deeper meanings in the symbolism drawn from Masonic rites—sometimes suggested by Mozart's *Magic Flute*—from alchemy, from the world of sylphs and gnomes best known to us from Pope's *Rape of the Lock,* or from the stock figures of the Italian Pantalone, Scaramuccia, Brighella, etc. But it may be wiser to enjoy these fairy tales simply as gorgeous capriccios, as the kind of spectacle the Russian ballet provided. (pp. 54-5)

The third group is probably closest to Hoffmann's heart and mind: The horrifying and grotesque world of his eccentrics, automatons, mad scientists, and wild musicians clashing with dreamy students and unsophisticated girls. **"Councillor Krespel"** is possibly the most impressive story of its kind. It is only seemingly disjointed. . . . The three parts of the story, though unrelated in tone, move easily from the oddities of the house being built to the weird dissecting of ancient violins, from the comic dispatch through the window of Krespel's Italian *prima donna* wife to the funeral procession, and are nevertheless balanced with consummate art. They yield the propitious mixture of grotesquerie, lyrical rapture, and sinister menace.

Ultimately, Hoffmann should be judged as an artist who created a unique world of the imagination. His art should appeal to us because of its ingredients which are, in many ways, kindred to the art of our time. Hoffmann, one must say, is hardly a committed writer, though he detests the stifling atmosphere of post-Napoleonic Germany. Unconcerned as he may be with a social utopia, he nevertheless has something in common with our time: a sense of the absurd, of the tragicomedy of life. A single mood, a single tone, is unknown to him. He mixes his colors deliberately, insistently. He comes up to T. S. Eliot's conception of the artist. He composes poetry, falls in love, reads Spinoza, smells cooking—all at the same time. He attains a tense though precarious equilibrium of opposites, dark and light, mad and sane, grotesque and nostalgic, tragic and comic. A time which appreciates Gogol and Kafka, Dostoevsky and Beckett, might well go back to Hoffmann, not primarily because of historical curiosity but for the enjoyment of the spectacle of an artist struggling to define a world of the imagination which is akin to the world of our most admired and representative writers. (pp. 55-6)

> René Wellek, "Why Read E.T.A. Hoffmann?" in
> Midway *(reprinted by permission of the author;* ©
> *1967 by The University of Chicago), Vol. 8, No. 1,*
> *June, 1967, pp. 49-56.*

JOHN REDDICK   (essay date 1969)

[Due to the profound multivalence of Hoffmann's work,] the reader can hope to find no one universal pattern . . . that will account for everything: the labyrinth ultimately always proves too large.

All the same, though, it does seem possible to isolate certain recurrent patterns and modes in the stories, and to identify certain persistent, formative pre-occupations. . . . Hoffmann may well have been reflecting his own conception of his art when, in [*Kater Murr*], he figured Meister Abraham and his paper-cutting

> Master Abraham had a way of cutting sheets
> of cardboard in such a way that although you
> could at first make nothing of the confusion of
> cut-about patches, you only had to hold a light
> behind the sheet for all kinds of groups of the
> strangest figures to form in the shadows cast
> on the wall:

Before we can look for these significant patterns, however, we must recognise some of the cardboard components in Hoffmann's world for what they are. It is no coincidence that "Celionati", one of Hoffmann's fictive characters who most fascinatingly reflects him *qua* creator, is repeatedly described as a "Charlatan" . . . or that Meister Abraham, a similar figure is referred to as a "Taschenspieler" (conjurer): Hoffmann is undoubtedly a charlatan himself in certain respects, a purveyor of false contrivances. One level at which this applies is that of *plot*, for Hoffmann is sometimes quite happy to contrive ramshackle, disjointed intrigues, blatantly unmotivated entrances and exits, transparently stagey setpieces of moonlight witchery, dark intrigue, cloaks and daggers etc. . . . Another level at which Hoffmann can ring false is notoriously that of language. This is particularly true when he writes within particular "genres" such as the Idyllic (e.g. "nature", "beautiful girls", "domestic bliss") or the Tragick; but it is also often true when he is trying to convey ordinary human emotion—as August Langen remarked: even in Kreisler's most passionate utterances in *Kater Murr* the words are "nur Klischee" (nothing but clichés). Summarily speaking, the reader finds that Hoffmann's style almost always tips over into derivative mediocrity when the author attempts to don cothurns and "play it straight". Significantly, it is precisely this pattern that is dwelt on in *Prinzessin Brambilla,* the work in which Hoffmann plays most fascinatingly on the question of the artist and his true mode of "delivery": so long as the actor Giglio Fava remains committed to tragedy, his existence is one of blindness and false postures; it is only when he experiences the validity of the *ironic* mode of the commedia dell'arte that he becomes genuine at last. This is most profoundly true of Hoffmann himself: he is only fully genuine, and therewith fully effective and luminous, when he manipulates his created world as a detached *ironist*.

If this contention is a valid one, then it renders dubious one of the most inveterate and cherished of Hoffmann interpretations, whereby he is held to be essentially a "metaphysicist" and "myth-creator" in the best Romantic tradition. . . . This kind of view does seem to me to be a radical misconception. However much Hoffmann was influenced by such as Novalis, G. H. Schubert, Schelling, Fichte, and however many of their notions may have found their way into the "décor" of his writings, there is little evidence that . . . [the generative "Hauptidee" (governing notion) of his work is] in any meaningful way Romantic or metaphysical. (pp. 78-80)

But if Hoffmann's "Hauptidee" is not to create transcendental myths, but to contrive situations in which everyday reality is turned topsy-turvy, what then is the purpose and method of this process? There is one particular metaphor that Hoffmann repeatedly uses which symbolises it most effectively: that of the *mirror*. (p. 80)

An ironical reflecting of the given social reality . . . is one function of Hoffmann's creative mirror. But it has another function, more persistent and much more profound: it reflects an *outward visible image* of the *otherwise secret inner being* of individual characters, that is to say of the fictive people whom Hoffman invents as representatives, perhaps, of that given reality. . . . *Prinzessin Brambilla* explicitly illuminates the process, for the mirror-like waters in the "Urdargarten" allegory are . . .

> nothing other than what we Germans call 'hu-
> mour', that wondrous power of a man's mind,
> born of the deepest insight into nature, to create
> its own ironical double, in whose strange buf-
> foonery he recognises and enjoys the spectacle
> of his own and also—I allow myself the im-
> pertinent phrase—the spectacle of the buffoon-
> ery of all existence here on earth. . . .

In this particular case, the confrontation with the "ironischen Doppelgänger" [ironical double] that manifests inward being is blithe and beneficial. . . . But there is also an opposite pole to this, whereby the ironic mirror reveals an inward being of desperate brokenness and distortion. In *Kater Murr,* Hoffmann creates a sharp paradigm of this kind of process: after having already established a mirror relationship between Kreisler and the mad, savage artist, Leonard Ettlinger . . . , Hoffmann suddenly confronts the hero with his seemingly corporeal "Eben-bild, sein eignes Ich, das neben ihm daherschritt" (images, his own ego, striding along beside him)—Kreisler's normal ironic defences prove useless: he is "vom tiefsten Entsetzen erfaßt, [. . .] zum Tode erbleicht" (gripped by the deepest horror, pale as death), and even his most essential power of music is frozen. . . . It is only then that Kreisler and the reader discover the "Mechanik" . . . behind the apparition, the actual mechanical device, i.e. the "Hohlspiegel" that Meister Abraham has set up outside his door. Hoffmann has Kreisler complain that it was just a "Fopperei" (bit of dupery), a meaningless trick ("Kunststückchen")—but the retort that is put in Abraham's mouth . . . is crucial, for it indicates that fundamental principal behind Hoffman's mirror process: that it is *not* gratuitous trickery, but a device for bringing out into the open that otherwise secret inner being. . . . (pp. 81-2)

Hoffmann never illuminates society through its institutions as such, but exclusively through its inhabitants and their attitudes. . . . What specifically interests him is the relationship of people (*a*) to themselves, and (*b*) to other people—and therewith to "society" and to "existence". This produces a wide span of dramatic personae whose fictive existences range from the "largely private" to the "totally public", but who mostly oscillate, with characteristic ambivalence, between the two. (p. 82)

When we take a closer look at those figures whom Hoffmann created as representative of *society,* we soon find that their identifying characteristic, in one or another form, is *ungenuineness;* that is to say: they have no personal, organic Self, but possess an identity only in terms of their society; they are in fact prisoners of what Sartre was later to define as "mauvaise foi". This phenomenon is projected in numberless forms. A remark in **Kater Murr** is typical: "der Hof verwirft überhaupt, jedes tiefere Gefühl als unstatthaft [. . .] und gemein" (the court rejects every deeper feeling of whatever kind as vulgar and inadmissable). (pp. 82-3)

One of Hoffmann's most persistent metaphors for "ungenuineness" is significantly the "mechanical". Thus for instance an ironical passage in the **Kreisleriana** claims that music's true function is to relax a man so that he may return refreshed "zu dem eigentlichen Zweck seines Daseins [. . .], d.h. ein tüchtiges Kammrad in der Walkmühle des Staats sein" (to the proper purpose of his existence, i.e. to be an industrious cog in the pounding mill of state). . . . This metaphor, together with its associate one of "puppets" . . . is, of course, one that countless other writers of the period found it apt to use as well, from, say, Lenz through "Bonaventura", Kleist and Tieck to Büchner (to name only a few!). But it also ties up with a timeless fascination of ironic, comic writers for *robot-like rigidity* in human behaviour, as exploited most classically by Molière. Repeatedly in Hoffmann we find an ironic illumination of cerebral "plans" and "schemes" that are fatuous and false in direct proportion to their blind inflexibility. . . . Hoffmann reflects this basic pattern time without number, and it is worth noting that, however pessimistic he undoubtedly was about the viability within society of "true being", he almost without exception has his exponents of "false being" come a cropper in the end, just as Molière has his Tartuffe fail at the last for all his pernicious interim success. (pp. 83-4)

It comes as no surprise to find that Hoffmann reflects this pattern of falseness and of antagonism to individuality as having been in turn falsely legitimised by being rationalised into a formal moral code. (p. 84)

We move here into one of the most crucial areas that Hoffmann probes and mirrors: the obscure background from which the falseness and dissonances of society derive. And instead of metaphysical notions, we repeatedly find him positing an empirical causation, namely *some form of severe dislocation* within or amongst those social creatures that are humans. A programmatic passage in **Kater Murr** on the upbringing of children is revelationary, a passage put in the mouth of that pedagogic pillar of society, Professor Lothario: . . .

> The Professor was in favour of open force, as the ordering of things to the public good demanded that every individual should, regardless of any attempts at resistance, be squeezed as early as possible into that mould which is determined by the relationship of constituent parts to the whole, since a corruptive monstrousness would otherwise arise which would wreak all manner of ruinous damage.

This undoubtedly reflects the theory and practice in society as Hoffmann saw it. . . . But in fact it is precisely such practices which, far from preventing "Monstruosität" [monstrousness], actually encourage it, as Hoffmann suggests via Meister Abraham's retort that the same principle applies with the young as with "Partiell-Wahnsinnigen" (the partially mad). . . . This helps to mark out what is perhaps the most fundamental polarity of all in Hoffmann's world: at one end, monstrous, sterile, false patterns of existence, with constraint, dislocation, conflict as their cause; on the other, a fruitful wholeness and sanity, with genuine, personal awareness as its base. And it is important to note that a distribution chart of Hoffmann's characters would show them more heavily clustered towards the former pole. (pp. 85-6)

[We] can say that Hoffmann's concern with "true inward being", his concern with people's relationships with (*a*) themselves, and (*b*) other people, is figured exclusively in terms of the notion of "identity". Is there a fruitful identity between a man's image of himself, and his actual inward reality? Is there a fruitful identity between a man's genuine reality and the reality of his environment? It is these questions that are the source of artistic tension in almost every story that Hoffmann ever wrote.

The figure of Medardus in the **Elixiere** is . . . exemplary of the one pole: . . .

> I am what I seem, and seem not what I am; an unaccountable riddle even to myself, I am divided utterly against my ego. . . .

Medardus dons a multitude of different clothes and assumes a multitude of different "identities"—but feels himself in real possession of none of them for very long. His every sense of stability is illusive, whether it be in the "Handelsstadt", in the Court or on return to the monastery. The one bitter constant of his existence is the irremediable syndrome of lust-violence-guilt. And it is this that gives rise to a motif which, together with that of "rôles", is the paramount structure of the book: the motif of "Doppelgänger". The reader is faced with a haunting, most remarkable situation: in this book the fiction of "real people" has gone almost completely by the board. The Prior, the Fürst, the Doctor and other auxiliaries may be fictively "real". But Viktorin? the mad, savage "monk"? Hermogen? Aurelie? the Maler? Each of these seems to have a "reality" only as a "projection" of Medardus' distorted "Bewußtsein" [awareness]. (pp. 91-2)

The structure of [**Die Elixere des Teufels**] as a whole is so arranged that even the reader experiences its multivalence at every turn. With its leitmotifs, its multiple-mirror-image characters, its narrations of single events from multiple standpoints, it achieves the sometimes astonishing effect of imposing on the reader the spectacle of an indeterminate number of figures scurrying vainly through an indeterminate mirror-lined labyrinth. And one passage, the assessment of the situation by the Prior towards the novel's end . . . , is so created that it conveys a dislocated sense of "reality" that one might normally think was the invention of Kafka. True: the novel ends limply and has a hundred gross faults; but it has at least as many virtues.

At the opposite pole from Medardus, of course, we find Giglio Fava [in *Prinzessin Brambilla*]. He, too, has a severe crisis of identity, coming into physical conflict with himself . . . , and being characterised in terms of the same topoi of "illness" and "madness" as Medardus and many others. . . . But: unlike Medardus . . . , Giglio's "jewelled potential" is not distorted or deformed but simply dormant and hidden; thanks to the mirror of irony and humour, he perceives his true being, "kills" his false self in a comic duel, and thus attains to a genuine "identity" and integrity. (pp. 92-3)

Medardus and Giglio Fava, then, mark the opposite limits in Hoffman's figurations of the "identity" motif in respect of "people's relationships with themselves", and almost every central character in his stories can be located somewhere on the scale. (p. 93)

On this particular scale of the motif of "personal" identity, the distribution of characters is clearly fairly even. How then is the earlier assertion justified that Hoffmann's figures cluster more towards the pole of dislocation than the pole of integrity? This soon becomes evident when we illuminate that other motif of "identity between people and their surroundings". And it likewise becomes rapidly evident that we are concerned here with probably the most central and certainly the most plangent themes of all Hoffmann's writing. It is characteristically Johannes Kreisler—Hoffmann's greatest creation—in whom the fundamental dislocated pattern is most grievously manifest. . . . [But while the topos of "madness" is with Medarus a reflection of *his*] inward falsity and distortion, it is with Kreisler . . . a reflection of the non-identity between [his] inward *genuineness* and that falsity in society which we have previously evinced. With Kreisler, Hoffmann characteristically extends the pattern right into his childhood: we have seen how his family, in its false aspirations and norms, blinded him to his true potential . . . , and misled him into taking up a legal career. . . . (pp. 93-4)

Few indeed are the people who, once exposed to society, . . . can keep any kind of mine-shaft open to that pristine jewelled potential which Hoffmann optimistically posits (in this respect he is of course an heir of the Enlightenment and of Classical humanism . . .). It is as a result of this that we find a notion in Hoffmann that clearly prefigures Stendhal's "Happy Few": a kind of scattered fraternity of kindred spirits—"verwandte Geister" in Hoffmann's recurrent phrase—who know to some greater or lesser extent what "genuineness" means. The cardinal question remains, though: how far, and in what way, can a member of this vulnerable fraternity enter into a viable relationship with his environment? (pp. 94-5)

[While] a "genuine" individual may conceivably integrate with his empirical environment at a private domestic level, like Peregrinus Tyss [in *Meister Floh*], there is no chance at all, in Hoffmann's view, of his identifying with the larger, public reality. He will always be an alien, a "Fremdling in der Welt"

[stranger in the world], because of the irretrievable discrepancy between his "genuineness" and society's gross falsity. . . . (p. 96)

Did Hoffmann see any solution? Did he see any means whereby the "genuine" could ease their grievous position in an alien society? One pat answer lay ready to hand: to escape; to evaporate into incorporeal dream and fantasy and so waft through the bars of the cage and out into the insubstantial air. . . . It is this kind of response to reality that Hoffmann figured in personae such as Anselmus [in *Der goldne Topf*] and *Serapion*—and in Kreisler, too, in the form of his theme of "artistic love", thereby there is no external physical object, but instead an inward idol, born of his own creative being. . . . But this easy escapist response clearly did not satisfy Hoffmann as genuine. The real question was not "how to opt out", but: how to stay firmly *within* the given social reality, however alien, and establish some kind of viable relationship to it. And when we survey those "genuine" figures in the stories who are imperilled by society in its falseness, we repeatedly find that Hoffmann's solution to the problem is a defensive stance of *ironic insight and detachment*. (pp. 96-7)

It is, of course, Kreisler in whom this motif of ironic detachment is most emphatically figured. In the characteristic phrase prefacing the second set of *Kreisleriana:* "So wurde oft sein höchster Schmerz auf eine schauerliche Weise skurril" (Thus in a horrible way his deepest suffering often turned into comedy). He is supremely one of those whose stance of "Humour" is born "aus der tieferen Anschauung des Lebens in all seinen Bedingnissen, aus dem Kampf der feindlichsten Prinzipe" (of a profounder insight into life with all its restrictions, of struggle with the most antagonistic forces), and it is thanks to this stance, thanks to the protective comic mask pressed close to his face, that, far from evaporating into the nether air, he can walk in amongst the "ungenuine" masses. . . . The alternatives are clear: the richly genuine can either try to involve themselves emotionally in society, try to attain their true goals through the corrupt social reality—and become inevitably an eternal "Fremdling in der Welt"; or they can maintain a safe emotional detachment behind a Harlequin's mask, and so acquire at least a kind of citizenship, however much of a pale and fragile surrogate that may be. (p. 97)

[This] ironical stance is one that characterises not only Kreisler . . . and a host of others amongst his fictive personae: it is also Hoffmann's own most luminous and characteristic stance, his own vibrant "Hauptidee", as the beginning of the essay tried to show. And is it not a meaningful tautology to assess Hoffmann in terms of his own polarity of "genuine"—"false", and to say that it is only as a mirror-wielding Ironist that he is properly genuine and effective? to say that he is in principle always a false posturer when he quits this ironic mode?—If this is valid, it is easy to see that E.T.A. Hoffmann's main and true position in the European literary tradition is *not* that of "Romanticist" or "myth-creator", *not* that of "Realist", *not* that of "purveyor of the dark side of existence", but that of being an heir to the aristocratic line of such as Rabelais, Grimmelshausen, Reuter, Lesage, Sterne, Smollett; and more significantly: a most remarkable forebear of such as Heine, Stendhal, Fontane, Gide, Thomas Mann, Kafka, Grass. And whatever else he may contingently be, E.T.A. Hoffmann is a great Ironist. (p. 98)

John Reddick, "E.T.A. Hoffmann," in German Men of Letters: Twelve Literary Essays, Vol. V, *edited by Alex Natan (© 1969 Oswald Wolff (Publishers) Limited), Oswald Wolff, 1969, pp. 77-109.*

LEONARD J. KENT   (essay date 1969)

[Hoffmann] has a divided allegiance: on the one hand, a true romantic, he exults in the pursuit of the unknown, prefers the enigma to the solution, the unintelligible to the rational, but, on the other, there is textual evidence that the *Aufklärung* [Enlightenment] had not left him unaffected, for the miraculous is sometimes explained—much to the chagrin of a character who, expressing Hoffmann's own proclivity, prefers to be left in the dark. The occult attracted Hoffmann the romantic; it sated him emotionally. Pushing his imagination to extremes, the detestable world of philistines (and their attachment to the sane, safe, controlled, complacent) was exorcised. For Hoffmann, the occult meant nothing less than emancipation from mediocrity, from what he called "zu viel Wirklichkeit" [far too much reality]. There is reality in Hoffmann, but it is a reality born of the implications of nonreality, a reality of singular meaning because it transcends the prosaic existence which, in the context of the mundane, has no meaning at all.

Hoffmann's fictional world is also divided, sometimes maddeningly. . . . [The] prosaic and the fantastic coexist, but . . . the very closely detailed fantastic becomes more real than the real itself. So too is it with the extrinsic and intrinsic; they reach beyond their normal confines, flow, silently and unobserved, one into the other; hence, doubles become a normal symptom of abnormal conditions. In such stories as Hoffmann's chilling *Die Doppeltgänger* we see what the intimate coexistence of the disparate accomplishes—and we gain insight into the Hoffmann technique: layers of the unintelligible build into a nightmare; the setting, seemingly prosaic, is imbued with the fantastic; there is a heavy concentration on words which recur with great frequency in Hoffmann, words which create and complement his tone. . . . And there is the ironic, the laugh at the expense of self . . . and the grotesque. . . . (pp. 48-9)

Even more to my point, a hero (or, more properly, half a hero) such as Deodatus, sent away under mysterious circumstances to somehow see a creature he had created in his dreams, no sooner walks into an inn than he is confused for someone else. . . . (p. 49)

In Hoffmann we read of chronic illness, of letters not written by one, yet in his handwriting. Strangers suddenly appear; there are rustling sounds and incantations, croaking ravens—it is a world of madness which helps explain why the hero feels his sanity slip away. It is a terrifying solipsistic world created out of dreams. How is it possible, for example, for two men identical in appearance to be in love with the same girl, though one of them has never seen her? It is not; that is, it is not unless one accepts the occult or the psychological as explanations. Perhaps we are witnessing nothing less than the total disintegration of personality, schizophrenic multiplicity. The subversion of a single self, in turn subverts the whole concept of reality. (p. 50)

[Cardillac, in *Mademoiselle de Scudery*,] was schizophrenic. So too is the Danish Major in *Der Magnetiseur,* a torn demon of wildly alternating moods, withdrawn one moment, charming and gregarious the next.

Schizophrenia in Hoffmann may be attributed to the occult extrinsic forces, to the disparate elements of personality, to subconscious guilt, or to a traumatic experience. The erosion of sanity makes the projection of self on to another figure comprehensible. Hoffmann's insight into the causes and manifestations of clinical madness are, even within the context of the frenetic scientific and pseudo-scientific activity of his age, remarkable.

The dream and the dream world are crucial features in Hoffmann. The reader is often invited to define the distinction between the world of dreams and that of reality. In *Die Bergwerke zu Falun*, there is a strange anticipatory dream—and in Hoffmann even traditional devices become unique—which not only foreshadows but directs; that is, extrinsically formed by some occult power, it appears to Elis Fröbom and dictates his actions which ultimately lead to his doom. Another puppet, Fröbom is destroyed by fate in the surreptitious guise of a dream.

Dreams may be telepathic: in *Das Gelübde* the exact moment of death is described in a dream; in *Das Majorat,* the old justiciar dreams of the simultaneous experiences of his nephew. Medardus, in *Die Elixiere des Teufels,* dreams psychologically comprehensible dreams, is haunted by his guilt, by a past inconsistent with his present psychological and moral condition.

In *Kater Murr,* Hoffmann's mad world reaches its brilliant peak in inventiveness, satire, romantic irony, the disintegration of reality. . . . Confusing even when relatively coherent, [*Kater Murr*] juxtaposes sense and nonsense, for the pretentious cat [Murr] has written his memoirs on the proofs of Kreisler's biography, and the sheets are bound together. Unfinished, there yet emerges from this novel a marvelous hero, *Kapellmeister* Kreisler, on whom Hoffmann lavishes his sympathy because he is Hoffmann. If Kreisler is mad because he cannot come to terms with the philistine world, his madness is only ironic. His is the world of sanity, the exalted world of sensitivity and acute imagination. Hoffmann again has turned reality inside out, has forced the reader to reorient his concepts. It is typical that we do not even really know, for example, who Kreisler is, for his memories are often Hoffmann's, cannot be correlated to the text. The novel is "a mystery wrapped in an enigma", but there is about it the quiet panic of desperation, the aura of the absurdity of reality, the delineation of the glory of madness. It is a world that never existed, and one whose exuberant glory casts a pallor over the one that does.

Hoffmann, fascinated by the abnormal and the occult, was possessed of a fecund imagination that made its recreation possible. He is not an early clinical psychologist; abnormality and the subconscious and supernatural appeal to him esthetically, not scientifically. The real world, too confining, is squeezed dry and, as pulp, left behind, but the fantasies are significant because their implications reflect on reality: there is an absurdity about realness, a complexity about the seemingly simple, a meaningfulness about the apparently trivial; above all, there is man, controlled like a robot from without, a many-layered creature from within.

Hoffmann's world is the world of hyperbole, a world where anything is possible, a world between dream and reality, where reality and the subconscious create the dream and the dream creates the reality of divided man. It is a world of engulfing and identity—destroying reality, the descent into the endless darkness of life and the flight from it. Most significant of all, man's identity, crushed in the relentless machine of conformity and reality, is threatened; he becomes less than one self even as he becomes more than one self. He cannot be merely a physically functioning animal, nor can he be merely rational. The occult functions from without and the irrational, "sidereal" self, from within. (pp. 50-2)

Leonard J. Kent, "Towards the Literary 'Discovery' of the Subconscious," in his The Subconscious in Gogol' and Dostoevskij and Its Antecedents *(© copyright 1969 Mouton & Co. N.V., Publishers; reprinted by permission of the author), Mouton Publishers, The Hague, 1969, pp. 15-52.*

GLYN TEGAI HUGHES (essay date 1979)

Hoffmann's two main definitions of his narrative theory are linked to the titles of two of his collections of Novellen and Märchen. . . . Hoffman had considered calling [his first volume of Märchen] 'Bilder nach Hogarth' (Pictures after Hogarth) but decided eventually on [*Fantasiestücke in Callots Manier,* after Jacques Callot]. . . . Hoffmann admired in Callot the great technical ingenuity, the thousands of figures and details in a confined space and yet each individualized the audacity, power, life and naturalness of the depiction. . . . Yet Hoffmann was equally attracted by the strangeness of the prints, by the way the most ordinary feature takes on a romantic, fantastic quality, by the grotesque deformations that allow mysterious allusions. For the writer the analogy with Callot lies in his receiving into [what Hoffmann called] his 'inner romantic imagination' . . . all the myriad detail of the phenomenal world, and reproducing it in strange attire.

The procedure seems, at first sight, to be reversed in the 'Serapion principle' [of *Die Serapions-Brüder*]. . . . The opening tale is that of the supposed hermit Serapion whose fancies are so vivid and objective that they entirely replace reality for him. This becomes the 'Serapion principle' (das serapiontische Prinzip), according to which the more powerful the imagination, the more realistic the product. One can only bring effectively to life what one has seen within oneself; and one is reminded of Caspar David Friedrich's prescription that 'the painter should not just paint what he sees before him, but also what he sees within himself'. (pp. 113-14)

The Callot and Serapion principles are both aspects of the same aesthetic conviction: sensory observation is fired by imagination, and imagination must express itself concretely in the world of the senses. This productive tension between Hoffmann's capacity for myth-making and his evidential observation of the everyday ensures that an aesthetic echoing Novalis and Schelling does not lead to bloodlessness and insubstantiality. Creative energy in its unconscious working throws up images and forms (perhaps it is more than a soothing ploy when he keeps assuring his publisher that the next work is well on the way—in his imagination it no doubt is). Hoffmann's head one might irreverently describe as a nourishing compost-heap hot with speculatory novelties from magnetism to cabbalism, with frenzied personal griefs and disappointments, with raucous comedy—where else in Romanticism would one find an Irish joke? All this is then exteriorized in a much more deliberate way than has often been thought. The juridical mind creates its own patterns of witnesses' statements, of written and oral evidence, of logic and counter-logic, all within the courtroom, all safely in a frame. Thus, though Hoffmann's subject may be the irreparable dualism or heterogeneity of existence, his art-forms offer a reconciling prospect, somewhere on the edge of the real world.

We see this in [the story *Ritter Gluck,* from *Fantasiestücke in Callots Manier*]. . . . Much ingenuity has gone into speculating whether the musician [in the story] is mad, a reincarnation, a dream, an incorporation of the spirit of music, an expression of the duality of existence, of the coexistence of two realities.

Two points may be more worth our attention: the ambivalent position of the narrator and the primacy of the realm of art. Doubt is the narrator's chief characteristic; we are never sure of his position and it seems more than just idiomatic that at the end he should be 'beside himself' (außer mir . . .). He is standing at some strange point which is and is not the Berlin of 1809, and is caught up in the creative power of an artist, who in a sense is also his creature. This creative power torments Gluck, his dreams unfit him for bourgeois life even as they break down the barriers between reality and illusion. Any harmony comes in the final artistic product, symbolized by Gluck's soft clasp of the narrator's hand and his strange smile.

Hoffmann's Märchen pursue the theme of the disjointed world and the possibility of aesthetic reconstruction, of redemption within the sphere of art. They are, in his new formulation, ideal vehicles in which to link the everyday and the supernatural, as implied indeed in the title of *Der goldene Topf.* . . . (pp. 116-17)

In *Der goldene Topf* crystal is one motif of many through which the everyday world is penetrated by the energy of the poetic world. But the motifs are, until late on in the story, presented in an ambiguous light, so that the reader is kept puzzled as to the nature of reality. What Anselmus had taken for a fire-lily bush turns out to be Archivarius Lindhorst's dressing gown; when he seems to see the Archivarius fly away into the darkness a large bird of prey rises screeching before him—that is what it must have been, and yet how *did* the Archivarius disappear? Changes of perspective, half-concealed shifts of the narrative point of view, rationalizations by the characters themselves, matter-of-fact accounts of the inconceivable, all deliberately serve to confuse the reader. Archivarius Lindhorst's brother has not gone to the dogs but to the dragons, as he relates, taking a pinch of snuff; he adds that he is in mourning for his father who died quite recently, three hundred and eighty-five years ago. . . . This naturally contributes to the comic effect which, in Hoffmann, has many facets other than the often cited grotesque and ironic. . . . *Der goldene Topf* satirizes elements in contemporary philosophy, uses bureaucratic style for incongruous communications, sets the most philistine objects and professions alongside mythic projections, makes play with clumsiness and with other peculiarities of physique, teases the reader with hints or obfuscations, follows an impassioned argument about whether Lindhorst really is a salamander with a knockabout description of a morning-after hangover. Hoffmann's comedy often reminds one of a grimace, a desperate manic grin. The surprise is that he generally brings it so well under control; well enough, for instance, to eliminate the original intention that the golden vessel should be a chamber-pot (though *Klein Zaches* reverts to the motif).

In *Prinzessin Brambilla* . . . Hoffmann makes an explicit allegorical defence of humour as a reconciling force, summing up the dramatic context of the 'capriccio', as the work is called. Looking into the crystal prism (symbolic of the purity of nature) that is the Urdar lake—as one might look at a stage comedy—the characters in an interpolated Märchen see the antics of their own mirror-image, recognize the nonsense of all existence here below, and are amused. Reversing the order of things is a releasing experience; when the self is exteriorized at the same time as the rest of the world a degree of harmony is achieved. . . . (pp. 117-18)

The mythic elements in the Märchen are reminiscent of Novalis, whom Hoffmann greatly admired; but the unusual feature is that the mythic is now itself viewed ironically. Both in *Der goldene Topf* and *Prinzessin Brambilla* the interpolated or interwoven Märchen derive from G. H. von Schubert, and present the disruption of a golden age (a paradisal garden) by the intrusion of reflective consciousness. Themes from astrology, Indian and Nordic mythology, folk magic, demonology, mesmerism and contemporary psychiatry fill out the mythic structure. Anselmus, in *Der goldene Topf,* escapes from the world of philistinism to the aesthetic realm of Atlantis where love reveals the harmony of all things; he has become a poet. (pp. 118-19)

Klein Zaches, gennant Zinnober . . . can be said to continue the contrast between the bourgeois world and that of the imagination, but in less exalted terms and with much bizarre complication. The philistine, rationalistic world, in which much contemporary thought and many aspects of society are satirized, shows itself to be a world of appearance; reality is found only in the aesthetic experience. In the context of the fiction this resides in the humour, the dominating experience in this Märchen. (p. 119)

[Hoffmann's last work] *Meister Floh* is, if anything, even more marked by grotesque inventiveness than its predecessors, though there is at times an air of contrivance or of downright muddle. . . . [A just appreciation of at least the content of this Märchen may] be provided by the satire on the exact sciences, especially in the persons of Leuwenhöck (Leeuwenhoeck) and Swammerdamm, the seventeenth-century Dutch scientists still apparently alive in Frankfurt in the 1820s; Leuwenhöck indeed calls attention to this mythic abolition of time and space when he says to Pepusch, 'you are the only one in Frankfurt who knows that I have been lying in my grave in the old church at Delft since the year 1725'. . . . The two are 'crazy retail dealers of nature' . . . and are condemned because they seek to examine nature's secrets microscopically and competitively instead of lovingly, reverently. Inner, organic, unifying growth, allegorized here in plant life, passes them by. And it is unity with the organic whole that Peregrinus finds at the end of the Märchen through fidelity and love. (p. 120)

[The] themes of Doppelgänger and automata are to be seen in *Die Automate* and *Der Sandmann*. . . . Their fictional impact . . . goes far beyond trickery; they raise questions about the nature of personality and of knowledge, about the relationship between the inner creative core in man and the dead mechanical construct without; gravest of all they question the necessity of the self. It is not, as some critics claim, that these automata are meant to induce feelings of mystery and horror in us; for the modern reader their implausibility would prevent this. What Olimpia in *Der Sandmann* does to us she does through Nathanael, for in him we see a descent into madness that a shifting narrative perspective enables us to accept as purely pathological or as accompanied by incursions from some fatal magic realm, some dark creative unconscious. The motif of the eye and the fear of losing one's eyes, which Freud equated in this story with the fear of castration [see excerpt above], suggests more strongly the loss of identity, the destruction of the mediator between self and world. The feeling of alienation, of metaphysical abandonment is strong. (p. 121)

Recent criticism has . . . tended to emphasize, and perhaps to overemphasize, Hoffmann's conscious manipulation of narrative structure in his two published novels. . . . There is no need to underplay the influence on [*Die Elixiere des Teufels*] of the Gothic horror novel tradition, notably that of Matthew Gregory Lewis's *The Monk* (1795) and Karl Grosse's *Der Genius* (1790-4); but Hoffmann is both psychologically more sub-

tle and fictively more complex. 'Monk' Lewis proceeds in a series of improvisations, piling horror upon horror as invention allows. Hoffmann, too, provides a rich and improbable variety of action, with apparently inextricable confusion (resolved by an operetta-type denouement) and the most complex family relationships—including the motifs of incest and family guilt that also underlie Brentano's *Romanzen,* and that no doubt have some basis in contemporary biological speculations on heredity. (p. 122)

We travel with [the monk Medardus] the road to self-knowledge, though his later narrative self sometimes breaks through to forewarn, and the fragmentary and enigmatic nature of personal identity reveals itself in the hallucinatory exteriorization of the self that reaches its climax in the figure of the Doppelgänger (or Doppeltgänger in Romantic usage). The double is indeed a physical one, Medardus's half-brother Viktorin; but the effect is almost wholly psychological, a projection of the evil impulses in a part of his nature. The reader, certainly, cannot tell whether the double is really there or not. The breakup of personality also takes the form of madness, which like dreams and visions, somnambulism, mesmerism and other borderline states stands guard at the portals of mystery. Madness transforms the world, rearranges the combinations within it: so that in Medardus's grotesque vision there are Bosch-like ravens with human faces, a skeleton horse whose rider has a luminous owl's head, ants with dancing human feet. . . . It may also be an idyllic release from the pressure of life; that is what gives Belcampo's eccentricity its comic edge, as he 'often doubts the existence of the present'. . . . (pp. 122-23)

[In *Die Elixiere des Teufels*] Hoffmann is, above all, creating an atmosphere, exploiting the trappings of the horror novel to create fear and tension. For the rest, how much does Hoffmann believe? What significance is there for him in fate, in family curses, unexplained supernatural intervention, the resolute power of evil, the redemptive power of the Catholic Church? Perhaps not all that much; and yet what makes it different from the ordinary Gothic novel is that Hoffmann's feet, too, have dangled over the pit of self-loss; Narcissus with a stone to crack the mirror. Mystery and terror lie not just in the events but in the whole nature of things.

Hoffmann's greatest achievement is, without much doubt, the novel *Lebensansichten des Katers Murr nebst fragmentarischer Biographie des Kapellmeisters Johannes Kreisler in zufalligen Makulaturblättern.* . . . (p. 123)

[Its] narrative structure, the parallels and contrasts between the Murr and Kreisler episodes are, in fact, the meaning of the novel. Murr's story, as many critics have pointed out, is a parody of the Bildungsroman or, more pointedly, of contemporary society's inadequate concept of education and culture (Bildung), and this is emphasized by the chapter headings: 'The Youth's Experiences of Life. I too was in Arcady' or 'The Months of Apprenticeship: The Capricious Play of Fortune'.

Murr is a pretentious, self-satisfied philistine, who has absorbed enough contemporary philosophical and literary jargon to dress up his selfish instincts as high-flown principles, and to give superficial justification to his claim as a writer. Through him, and he is after all a cat and earns our good-humoured if patronizing smile, Hoffmann satirizes contemporary bourgeois society and literary fasions. . . . Kreisler is, as he himself points out, a 'circler'. . . . He *turns* helplessly in a dual attempt to relate to society, a vain task for an artist in a world full of limitations (not least the intrigues and pretensions of petty aristocracy), and to achieve a vaguely apprehended paradisal state theoretically, though not actually, attainable through love (tainted by sensuality) or art (which has still to be translated into the signatures of the everyday). A commonplace of older criticism was that this dichotomy, this inability to attain harmony, was biographical; a third section [which Hoffmann promised but never wrote] could not have produced a resolution, other than the collapse inherent in Kreisler going mad. The novel is, however, an organized fiction, all appearances notwithstanding. There are cross-illuminations between the Murr and Kreisler episodes, with a detached, ironic narrator holding in balance the alleged autobiography of Murr, who is not without traits from Hoffmann himself, and the narrated life of Kreisler, with the imperfectly informed biographer supplemented by information from Murr and Meister Abraham. These narrative devices are themselves statements about the contingency of an artist's life, and of human life; and the whole is a paradigm of the fragmentary nature of reality and our imperfect hold on it. The fierce comedy of **Kater Murr** lies on a road from Sterne to Joyce. The disenchanted eye makes use of all the resources of fictional technique.

There is a good deal to criticize in Hoffmann: an often cliché-ridden and overblown style, an over-ready commitment to the modish tricks of his day's best sellers, an uncritical dabbling in fashionable ideas, a willingness to let theatrical props invade his fiction. Yet the exploitation of the subconscious, the examination of the alienated self, the attempt to show creatures of the imagination placed in the real world and, above all, the holding of these in balance by irony, by narrative point of view, by the resources of art, are a major contribution to modern literature. (pp. 124-25)

> *Glyn Tegai Hughes, "The Risks of the Imagination: Hoffmann, with Chamisso, Fouqué and Werner," in his* Romantic German Literature *(© Glyn Tegai Hughes 1979; reprinted by permission of Holmes & Meier Publishers, Inc.; in Canada by Edward Arnold (Publishers) Ltd), Holmes & Meier, 1979, Edward Arnold, 1979, pp. 112-26.**

ADDITIONAL BIBLIOGRAPHY

Chambers, Ross. "The Artist as Performing Dog." *Comparative Literature* XXIII, No. 1 (Winter 1971): 312-24.*
　　Examines the portrayal of the "artist as performing dog," a concept originated by Hoffmann, in the works of Hoffmann, Baudelaire, and Beckett.

Daemmrich, Horst S. *"The Devil's Elixirs:* Precursor of the Modern Psychological Novel." *Papers on Language and Literature* VI, No. 1 (Winter 1970): 374-86.
　　Views Medardus, protagonist of *Die Flixiere des Teufels,* as a precursor of the modern antihero.

Dunn, Hough-Lewis. "The Circle of Love in Hoffmann and Shakespeare." *Studies in Romanticism* II, No. 2 (Spring 1972): 113-37.*
　　Detailed comparison of *Prinzessin Brambilla* and three Shakespeare comedies: *A Midsummer Night's Dream, As You Like It,* and *Twelfth Night.*

Findlay, Charles. "The Opera and Operatic Elements in the Fragmentary Biography of Johannes Kreisler." *German Life and Letters* XXVII, No. 1 (October 1973): 22-34.
　　Discusses the "interpenetration of music and action" in the Kreisler sections of *Kater Murr.*

Hertz, Neil. "Freud and the Sandman." In *Textual Strategies: Perspectives in Post-Structuralist Criticism,* edited by Josué V. Harari, pp. 296-321. Ithaca, NY: Cornell University Press, 1977.*
　　Examines Freud's analysis of "Der Sandmann."

Hewett-Thayer, Harvey W. *Hoffmann: Author of the Tales.* 1948. Reprint. New York: Octagon Books, 1971, 416 p.
　　Survey of the life and works of Hoffmann.

Nock, Francis J. "E.T.A. Hoffmann and Nonsense." *The German Quarterly* XXXV, No. 1 (January 1962): 60-70.
　　Asserts that, because it contains an element of fun seldom found in German literature, Hoffmann's humor is misunderstood by his compatriots.

Passage, Charles E. *The Russian Hoffmannists.* The Hague: Mouton & Co., 1963, 261 p.*
　　Detailed study examining the connections "between some seventy Tales of Hoffmann and some fifty Russian prose narratives," including works by Pushkin, Gogol and Dostoevski.

Peters, Diana Stone. "E.T.A. Hoffmann: The Conciliatory Satirist." *Monatshefte* LXVI, No. 1 (Spring 1974): 55-73.
　　Presents Hoffmann's work as his "attempt to grasp and resolve the fundamentally dualistic nature of the universe through . . . irony and humor."

Raraty, M. M. "E.T.A. Hoffmann and His Theatre." *Hermathena,* No. XCVIII (Spring 1964): 53-67.
　　Examines how aspects of Hoffmann's fiction—dialogue, setting, characterization, point-of-view—were influenced by the theater.

Taylor, Ronald. *Hoffmann.* London: Bowes & Bowes, 1963, 112 p.
　　Critical overview stressing the importance of Romanticism and music to Hoffmann's work.

Taylor, Ronald. "Music and Mystery: Thoughts on the Unity of the Work of E.T.A. Hoffmann." *Journal of English and Germanic Philology* LXXV, No. 4 (October 1976): 477-91.
　　Discusses the influence of music on Hoffmann's literary works.

Washington Irving

1783-1859

(Also wrote under the pseudonyms of Geoffrey Crayon, Diedrich Knickerbocker, Jonathan Oldstyle, and Launcelot Langstaff) American short story writer, essayist, historian, biographer, journalist, and editor.

Irving is considered both the first American man of letters and the creator of the American short story. Though best known for his tales of rural Americana, Irving later became a prolific and accomplished biographer as well as a distinguished statesman.

Born in New York, Irving was the youngest son of indulgent parents who did not insist that he attend college, as his older siblings had. Though he read the law and eventually entered a law office, his legal studies were half-hearted. He much preferred writing for his brother Peter's journal, *The Morning Chronicle*. In 1802, Irving wrote a series of letters to the *Chronicle* under the pseudonym of Jonathan Oldstyle. These letters gently mocked New York society and brought Irving his first recognition as a writer. Failing health forced him to seek a change of climate, and he traveled to Europe. In 1806, he returned home and was admitted to the bar; however, his legal interest waned, and he chose to pursue a literary career.

Irving, his brother William, brother-in-law James Kirke Paulding, and others of their friends were known as the "Nine Worthies of Cockloft Hall," named after their favorite place for "conscientious drinking and good fun." They collaborated on the satirical journal, *Salmagundi; or, The Whim-Whams and Opinions of Launcelot Langstaff, Esq., and Others*, which included many essays by Irving and which reflected his Federalist political attitudes and social stance. The venture proved unprofitable, however, and the young men were forced to abandon the publication.

A History of New York, Irving's first book, commences as a humorous parody of historical scholarship but evolves into a tale of Dutch colonization. Though Dutch people claimed to resent Irving's parody, it is considered his most consistently optimistic work. Through the voice of Diedrich Knickerbocker, Irving could expound on native themes with affection and candor; indeed, the name "Knickerbocker" has become synonymous with a period of early American culture.

Irving's untroubled life changed drastically when his fiancée, Matilda Hoffman, died in 1809. Grief dominated Irving's life for a long time thereafter, and his works were never again to be light-spirited. In an effort to forget his sorrow, Irving entered a period of fervid activity. He acted as his brother's law partner, helped in the family hardware business, and edited the *Analectic* magazine. Finally, "weary of everything, and myself," Irving left again for Europe to assess his own talents. After reappraising what he had written, he reworked Knickerbocker's *History*, but feared he had lost much of his creative ability.

However, the appearance of *The Sketch Book of Geoffrey Crayon, Gent.* insured Irving's reputation as a man of letters. Its timing proved opportune because no one had yet produced a universally appealing piece of American literature. *The Sketch*

Book is considered the finest example of Irving's artistry, containing the well-known "Rip Van Winkle" and "The Legend of Sleepy Hollow," and presenting, in a humorous vein, the mythology and traditions of America. In a sequel, *Bracebridge Hall*, Geoffrey Crayon again provided a decorous and polished voice. In 1826, Irving traveled as a member of the American diplomatic corps to Spain, where he wrote *A History of the Life and Voyages of Christopher Columbus*. A subsequent tour of Spain produced *A Chronicle of the Conquest of Granada* and *The Alhambra*. In 1842, Irving became minister to Spain. Though he enjoyed his role as a diplomat, he returned to the United States to further his career as a biographical writer. His biography of Oliver Goldsmith is considered a particularly fine example of Irving's concise, balanced style. His last years were spent at work on a biography of George Washington. Though overly elaborate and lacking his former naturalness of tone, the work expresses Irving's belief in a glorious American past.

Irving's funeral was attended by thousands of admirers who mourned the death of an author they loved. Contemporary critics do not all share such devotion, but those who appreciate Irving consider him an outstanding romantic historian and an accomplished, witty re-creator of America's mythic past. (See

PRINCIPAL WORKS

Salmagundi; or, The Whim-Whams and Opinions of Launcelot Langstaff, Esq., and Others [with William Irving and James Kirke Paulding]   (satirical essays) 1807-1808
A History of New York [as Diedrich Knickerbocker] (historical parody)   1809
The Sketch Book of Geoffrey Crayon, Gent. [as Geoffrey Crayon]   (short stories)   1819-20
Bracebridge Hall [as Geoffrey Crayon]   (sketches)   1822
Tales of a Traveller [as Geoffrey Crayon]   (travel sketches) 1824
A History of the Life and Voyages of Christopher Columbus (biography)   1828
A Chronicle of the Conquest of Granada   (history)   1829
The Alhambra [as Geoffrey Crayon]   (travel sketches) 1832
The Crayon Miscellany [as Geoffrey Crayon]   (travel sketches)   1835
A Tour on the Prairies   (travel sketches)   1835
Oliver Goldsmith   (biography)   1849
The Life of George Washington   (biography)   1855-59

[RICHARD HENRY DANA]   (essay date 1819)

[We] have to thank Mr. Irving for being the first to begin and persevere in works which may be called purely literary. His success has done more to remove our anxiety for the fate of such works, than all we have read or heard about the disposition to encourage American genius.

Mr. Irving's success does not rest, perhaps, wholly upon his merit, however great. *Salmagundi* came out in numbers, and a little at a time. With a few exceptions it treated of the city— what was seen and felt, and easy to be understood by those in society. It had to do with the present and real, not the distant and ideal. It was exceedingly pleasant morning or after-dinner reading, never taking up too much of a gentleman's time from his business and pleasures, nor so exalted and spiritualized as to seem mystical to his far reaching vision. (p. 334)

Mr. Irving has taken the lead [in *The Sketch Book of Geoffrey Crayon, Gent.*], in the witty, humourous and playful cast of works—those suited to our happier feelings. . . . He has not modelled himself upon any body, but has taken things just as he found them, and treated them according to his own humour. So that you never feel as when looking at [*The Sketch Book*], that you have gotten a piece of second-hand furniture, scraped and varnished till made to look fine and modern, that it may be put to a new use. His wit and humor do not appear to come of reading witty and humorous books; but it is the world acting upon a mind of that cast, and putting those powers in motion. There are parts, it is true, which remind you of other authors, not, however, as imitations, but resemblances of mind. (pp. 335-36)

Amidst the abundance of his wit and drollery, you never meet with any bilious sarcasm. He turns aside from the vices of men to be amused with their affectation and foibles; and the enter-

tainment he finds in these seems to be from a pure goodness of soul—a sense that they are seldom found in thoroughly depraved and hardened hearts. (p. 336)

Amiableness is so strongly marked in all Mr. Irving's writings as never to let you forget the man; and the pleasure is doubled in the same manner as it is in lively conversation with one for whom you have a deep attachment and esteem. There is in it also, the gayety and airiness of a light, pure spirit—a fanciful playing with common things, and here and there beautiful touches, till the ludicrous becomes half picturesque.

Though many of the characters and circumstances in *Salmagundi* are necessarily without such associations, yet the Cock-lofts are not only the most witty and eccentric, but the most thoroughly sentimental folks in the world. . . . With a very few exceptions, [Irving's] sentiment is in a purer taste, and better sustained, where it is mixed with witty and ludicrous characters and circumstances, than where it stands by itself. He not only shows a contemplative, sentimental mind, but what is more rare, a power of mingling with his wit, the wild, mysterious and visionary. (pp. 336-37)

It looks a little like impertinent interference to advise a man to undertake subjects of a particular sort, who is so well suited for variety in kind. Nor do we wish that Mr. Irving should give up entirely the purely witty, of humorous, for those of a mixed nature. We would only express our opinion of the deep interest which such writings excite, and of his peculiar fitness for them; and at the same time suggest to him the great advantages he gains by changing from one to the other. For ourselves, we have no fear of being tired of his wit or humour, so long as they come from him freely. He is much more powerful in them, than in the solely sentimental or pathetic.

We give him joy of making his way so miraculously, as not to offend the dignity of many stately folks, and pray him go on and prosper. It was a bold undertaking in a country where we are in the habit of calling humour, buffoonery—and wit, folly. (p. 337)

Mr. Irving's style in his lighter productions, is suited to his subject. He has not thought it necessary to write the history of the family of the Giblets as he would that of the Gracchi, nor to descant upon Mustapha's Breeches in all the formality of a lecture. He is full, idiomatic and easy to an uncommon degree; and though we have observed a few grammatical errors, they are of a kind which appear to arise from the hurry in which such works are commonly written. There are, likewise, one or two Americanisms. Upon the whole, it is superior to any instance of the easy style in this country, that we can call to mind. That of the Foresters is more free from faults than Mr. Irving's, but not so rich. The principal defect in his humorous style is a multiplying of epithets, which, making no new impression, weaken from diffusion. It is too much like forcing a good thing upon us till we think it good for nothing. We make no objection to a style rich with epithets, which have fitness and character, unless they are strung along so as to look like a procession. But Mr. Irving's are sometimes put upon a service for which they were never intended, and only occasion confusion and delay.

Another fault, and one easily to be avoided, is the employing of certain worn out veterans in the cause of wit. Indeed, we owe it to him to say, that we believe he has now dismissed them, as we do not meet with them in the *Sketch Book*. (p. 338)

Another fault, which is found principally in *Knickerbocker,* is that of forcing wit as if from duty—running it down, and then whipping and spurring it into motion again—as in that part upon the different theories of philosophers. Wit must appear to come accidentally, or the effect is lost. (p. 339)

Salmagundi is full of variety, and almost every thing good of its kind. Though upon an old plan, nothing can be better done than some of Mustapha's letters, particularly those upon a Military Review, and the City Assembly. (p. 342)

At parting company with *Salmagundi,* we cannot but say again, that though its wit is sometimes forced, and its serious style sometimes false, upon looking it over, we have found it full of entertainment, with an infinite variety of characters and circumstances, and with that amiable, good natured wit and pathos, which show that the heart has not grown hard while making merry of the world.

There is but little room left for **Knickerbocker,** of which we are glad to say, a third and very neat edition has lately been put out. As our remarks upon *Salmagundi* will apply equally well to this work, and an analysis of a story, which every one has read, is dull matter, we the less regret it. It has the same faults and same good qualities in its style, its wit and humour; and its characters are evidently by the same hand as the leading ones in *Salmagundi,* though not copies from them. They are perfectly fresh and original, and suited to their situations. Too much of the first part of the first volume is laborious and up hill; and there are places, here and there, in the last part to which there is the same objection. (pp. 344-45)

It was delightful meeting once more with an old acquaintance who had been so long absent from us; and we felt our hearts lightened and cheered when we, for the first time, took the *Sketch Book* into our hands. Foreigners can know nothing of the sensation; for authors are as numerous and common with them, as street acquaintances. We, who have only two or three, are as closely attached to them, as if they were our brothers. And this one is the same mild, cheerful, fanciful, thoughtful, humorous being that we parted with a few years ago, though something changed in manner by travel. We will be open with him, and tell him that we do not think the change is for the better. He appears to have lost a little of that natural run of style, for which his lighter writings were so remarkable. He has given up something of his direct, simple manner, and plain phraseology, for a more studied, periphrastical mode of expression. He seems to have exchanged works and phrases, which were strong, distinct and definite, for a genteel sort of language, cool, less definite, and general. It is as if his mother English had been sent abroad to be improved, and in attempting to become accomplished, had lost too many of her home qualities. . . . He too often aims at effect by a stately inversion of sentences. Another and a greater error, which is found principally in his serious and sentimental writings, is an incorrect use of figurative language, which is, frequently, from connecting a word, strictly an image, with one which is not, so as to present a picture to the mind's eye, and the next moment rub it out. This appears to be owing to a mere oversight, a want of considering that any figure was used. Another is, connecting two words which are figures, but quite hostile to one another, so that they seem brought together for no other purpose than to put an end to each other. (pp. 348-49)

We have made these short remarks, and given these few instances, because it is faults of this kind which make our style feeble and impure, rather than the use of Americanisms, as they are called. . . . This defect of vision in picturesque language is the more singular in Mr. Irving, as he has an eye for

nature, and all his pictures from it are drawn with great truth and spirit. *The Sketch Book* is extremely popular, and it is worthy of being so. Yet it is with surprise that we have heard its style indiscriminately praised.

We have already stated, why we consider Mr. Irving's former works, though more obviously bad in places, still, as a whole, superior in point of style to the *Sketch Book* The same difference holds with respect to the strength, quickness and life of the thoughts and feelings. The air about this last work is soft, but there is a still languor in it. It is not breezy and fresh like that which was stirring over the others. He appears to us to have taken up some wrong notion of a subdued elegance, as different from the true, as in manners, the elegance of fashion is from that of character. There is an appearance of too great elaboration. (p. 350)

"**The Broken Heart**" has passages as beautiful and touching as any that Mr. Irving has written, but they are frequently injured by some studied, unappropriate epithet or phraseology which jars upon the feelings. The general reflections have a deep and tender thoughtfulness in them, and are much too good for the story. It is enough to meet in life with those who can make themselves over to one man, for lucre, or something worse or better, while their hearts are with another; but in a work of sentiment it is revolting. (p. 352)

Another fault—which is from the same false theory—is laying open to the common gaze and common talk, feelings the very life of which is secrecy. (p. 353)

"**Rip Van Winkle**" is our favorite amongst the new stories. We feel more at home in it with the author, than in any of this collection. Rip's idle good nature, which made him the favorite of the boys—his 'aversion to all kinds of profitable labour,' 'thinking it no use to work upon his own farm because every thing about it went wrong, and would go wrong, in spite of him,' yet always ready to help his neighbours—'the foremost at husking frolics, and building stone fences,' and ready at running errands for all the old wives in the village—and toiling all day at fishing and shooting—these show a thorough understanding of the apparent contradictions in character, and are set forth in excellent humour. . . . The mountain scenery is given with great beauty, and the ghostly party at ninepins is at the same time laughable and picturesque. The author's mind is highly fanciful and exactly suited to such scenes. (pp. 353-54)

Mr. Irving's scenery is so perfectly true—so full of little beautiful particulars, so varied, yet so connected in character, that the distant is brought nigh to us, and the whole is seen and felt like a delightful reality. It is all gentleness and sunshine; the bright and holy influences of nature fall on us, and our disturbed and lowering spirit is make clear and tranquil—turned all to beauty, like clouds shone on by the moon. Though we see in it nothing of the troubles and vices of life, we believe Mr. Irving found all he has described. If there be any thing which can give purity and true dignity to the character of man, it is country employments and scenery acting upon a cultivated mind. (p. 355)

> [*Richard Henry Dana,*] "*'The Sketch Book of Geoffrey Crayon, Gent.',*" *in* The North American Review, *Vol. IX, No. 2, September, 1819, pp. 322-56.*

BLACKWOOD'S EDINBURGH MAGAZINE (essay date 1820)

Mr Washington Irving is one of our first favourites among the English writers of this age—and he is not a bit the less for having been born in America. He is not one of those Americans who practise, what may be called, a treason of the heart, in perpetual scoffs and sneers against the land of their forefathers. He well knows that his "thews and sinews"are not all, for which he is indebted to his English ancestry. . . .

The great superiority, over too many of his countrymen, evinced by Mr Irving on every occasion, when he speaks of the manners, the spirit, the faith of England, has, without doubt, done much to gain for him our affection. But had he never expressed one sentiment favourable to us or to our country, we should still have been compelled to confess that we regard him as by far the greatest genius that has arisen on the literary horizon of the new world. The *Sketch Book* has already proved, to our readers, that he possesses exquisite powers of pathos and description. . . .

[*History of New York*] is a *jeu-d'esprit,* and, perhaps, its only fault is, that no *jeu-d'esprit* ought to be quite so long as to fill two closely printed volumes. Under the mask of an historian of his native city, he has embodied, very successfully, the results of his own early observation in regard to the formation and constitution of several regular divisions of American society; and in this point of view his work will preserve its character of value, long after the lapse of time shall have blunted the edge of these personal allusions which, no doubt, contributed most powerfully to its popularity over the water. (p. 361)

Mr Irving has, as every good man must have, a strong affection for his country; and he is, therefore, fitted to draw her character *con amore* as well as *con gentilezza.* The largeness of his views, in regard to politics, will secure him from staining his pages with any repulsive air of bigotry—and the humane and liberal nature of his opinions in regard to subjects of a still higher order, will equally secure him from still more offensive errors. . . .

[It] strikes us that [Irving] writes, of late, in a less merry mood than in the days of *Knickerbocker* and the *Salmagundi.* If the possession of intellectual power and resources ought to make any man happy, that man is Washington Irving; and people may talk as they please about the "inspiration of melancholy," but it is our firm belief that no man ever wrote any thing greatly worth the writing, unless under the influence of buoyant spirits. . . . The amiable and accomplished Mr Irving has no evil thoughts or stinging recollections to fly from—but it is very possible that he may have been indulging in a cast of melancholy, capable of damping the wing even of *his* genius. *That,* like every other demon, must be wrestled with, in order to its being overcome. And if he will set boldly about *An American Tale, in three volumes duodecimo,* we think there is no rashness in promising him an easy, a speedy, and a glorious victory. Perhaps all this may look very like impertinence, but Mr Irving will excuse us, for it is, at least, well meant. (p. 369)

> "Diedrich Knickerbocker's 'History of New York',"
> in Blackwood's Edinburgh Magazine, Vol. VII, No.
> XL, July, 1820, pp. 360-69.

THE EDINBURGH REVIEW   (essay date 1820)

Though [Geoffrey Crayon's **'Sketch Book'**] is a very pleasing book in itself, and displays no ordinary reach of thought and elegance of fancy, it is not exactly on that account that we are now tempted to notice it as a very remarkable publication,— and to predict that it will form an era in the literature of the nation to which it belongs. It is the work of an American, entirely bred and trained in that country—originally published within its territory—and, as we understand, very extensively circulated, and very much admired among its natives. Now, the most remarkable thing in a work so circumstanced certainly is, that it should be written throughout with the greatest care and accuracy, and worked up to great purity and beauty of diction, on the model of the most elegant and polished of our native writers. (p. 160)

But though it is primarily for its style and composition that we are induced to notice this book, it would be quite unjust to the author not to add, that he deserves very high commendation for its more substantial qualities; and that we have seldom seen a work that gave us a more pleasing impression of the writer's character, or a more favourable one of his judgement and taste. There is a tone of fairness and indulgence—and of gentleness and philanthropy so unaffectedly diffused through the whole work, and tempering and harmonizing so gracefully, both with its pensive and its gayer humours, as to disarm all ordinarily good-natured critics of their asperity, and to secure to the author, from all worthy readers, the same candour and kindness of which he sets so laudable an example. . . . The manner perhaps throughout is more attended to than the matter; and the care necessary to maintain the rythm and polish of the sentences, has sometimes interfered with the force of the reasoning, or limited and impoverished the illustrations they might otherwise have supplied. (pp. 161-62)

The English writers whom the author has chiefly copied, are Addison and Goldsmith, in the humorous and discursive parts— and our own excellent Mackenzie, in the more soft and pathetic. In their highest and most characteristic merits, we do not mean to say that he has equalled any of his originals, or even to deny that he has occasionally caricatured their defects. But the resemblance is near enough to be highly creditable to any living author; and there is sometimes a compass of reasoning which his originals have but rarely attained. (p. 162)

It is consolatory to the genuine friends of mankind—to the friends of peace and liberty and reason—to find [patriotic] sentiments gaining ground in the world; and, above all, to find them inculcated with so much warmth and ability by a writer of that country which has had the strongest provocation to disown them, and whose support of them is, at the present moment, by far the most important. . . . It is impossible, however, in the mean time, to disguise that much more depends upon the efforts of the American writers, than upon ours; both because they have naturally the most weight with the party who is chiefly to be conciliated, and because their reasonings are not repelled by that outrageous spirit of party which leads no small numbers among us, at the present moment, to reject and vilify whatever is recommended by those who are generally opposed to their plans of domestic policy. (pp. 172-73)

In justice to the work before us, however, we should say, that a very small proportion of its contents relates either to politics, or to subjects at all connected with America. There is a **'Legend of Sleepy Hollow,'** which is an excellent *peudant to* **'Rip Van Winkle;'** and there are two or three other papers, the localities of which are Transatlantic. But out of the thirty-five pieces which the book contains, there are not more than six or seven that have this character. The rest relate entirely to England; and consist of sketches of its manners, its scenery, and its characters, drawn with a fine and friendly hand—and remarks on its literature and peculiarities, at which it would be difficult for any rational creature to be offended. (p. 173)

There is a great deal too much contention and acrimony in most modern publications; and because it has unfortunately been found impossible to discuss practical questions of great interest without some degree of heat and personality, it has become too much the prevailing opinion, that these are necessary accompaniments to all powerful or energetic discussion, and that no work is likely to be well received by the public, or to make a strong impression, which does not abound in them. The success of such a work as this before us, may tend to correct this prejudice, and teach our authors that gentleness and amenity are qualities quite as attractive as violence and impertinence: and that truth is not less weighty, nor reason less persuasive, although not ushered in by exaggerations, and backed by defiance. (p. 176)

"'The Sketch Book'," in The Edinburgh Review, *Vol. XXXIV, No. 67, August, 1820, pp. 160-76.*

BLACKWOOD'S EDINBURGH MAGAZINE   (essay date 1822)

Bracebridge Hall, certainly does not possess the spirit of the *Sketch Book.* And the worthy family to whom we are introduced, and whose habits and peculiarities form the chief subject of the work, are on the whole rather dull. . . . The great blemish of the work indeed is, that is is drawn not from life, but from musty volumes, and presents a picture of habits no where to be met with, except among those whom our author has formerly ridiculed as diurnal visitants of the British Museum. He has here fallen under his own ban, and so palpably, that the essay on **"Book-Making,"** in the *Sketch Book,* looks like a prospective quiz upon *Bracebridge Hall.* . . .

But for all this, there are redeeming beauties even in the portion of the work we censure. The pictures of English life, though fraught with the defects above mentioned, are at times exceedingly humorous and just. (p. 689)

On the work are ingrafted three tales; the first of which, **"the Student of Salamanca,"** is but middling. The last, **"Dolph Heyliger,"** by Diedrich Knickerbocker, is very good, in the style of **"Rip Van Winkle,"** full of those pictures of North American life and scenery, to us so interesting and so new. The other tale, called **"Annette Delarbre,"** is indeed exquisitely beautiful, and displays stronger powers over the pathetic than are evinced even by the *Sketch Book.* (p. 691)

"'Bracebridge Hall'," in Blackwood's Edinburgh Magazine, *Vol. XI, No. LXV, June, 1822, pp. 688-92.*

THE NORTH AMERICAN REVIEW   (essay date 1822)

We have no hesitation in pronouncing [*Bracebridge Hall*] quite equal to any thing, which the present age of English literature has produced in this department. In saying this, we class it in the branch of essay writing. It may, perhaps, be called a novel in disguise; since a series of personages are made the subject or authors of the sketches of life and manners, which it contains, and it is conducted to a wedding, the regular *denouement* of a novel. . . . [We] may venture to put it in comparison with any thing else of the kind in English literature, for accuracy and fidelity of observation, for spirit of description, for a certain peculiar sly pleasantry, like the very happiest touches of the Addisonian school, and for uncommon simplicity and purity of style. In this last respect, however, we do not know that it is any way superior to the former writings of its author. (p. 209)

Mr Irving gained his reputation as an American writer, as a painter of American life, an observer of our humors, as the happy delineator of a very peculiar and deeply marked variety in character and manners, which he had witnessed from early life, and on which his mind had exercised itself habitually. He was so identified with the Salmagundi and Knickerbocker, that he could not, without labor, form himself to a different circle of topics, and if he did, it would remain for his readers here to become acquainted with him in his new dress, to feel familiar with an old friend under a new character, and then make the comparison between the two; a comparison never to be tempted by a writer so popular as the author of *Salmagundi* and *Knickerbocker.* Mr Irving, however, has now chosen to appear in a new character: the observer of English life and manners, and the describer of them in a style of writing more correct perhaps, in the freedom from a few specific faults, but in our judgment less original and nervous. . . . Mr Irving traverses Bracebridge Hall, explores the grounds, goes in and out of the housekeeper's room, and the hunter' lodge, visits the village school and the rustic fair, not like the stranger from another world, struck at the sort of life, which he had never before witnessed, but as one of the inmates. In so doing, we maintain that he has mistaken his powers. . . . Mr Irving has aimed to engraft himself, manner and matter, on the English stock. In so doing, he has merely proved his happy facility, and no more. He has shown with what ease and freedom he can write on English scenery and manners, after two or three years passed in England; and this is agreeable. We are not saying that the *Sketch Book* and *Bracebridge Hall* are not pleasing, finely written works; but we do say that they wave almost wholly that peculiar interest, which the author's position enabled him to give them; and in the main can be read through and through, without causing a thrill in the heart of a countryman. (pp. 212-14)

[However] in *Bracebridge* there is one story, the longest, and in our opinion the best in the work, called **"Dolph Heyliger"**, which is of the true *Knickerbocker* and **"Rip Van Winkle"** school, though not equal to the best efforts of the author, in the same department. (p. 215)

There are other passages also of great merit in the piece; but we do not regard it on the whole as a happy effort.—The lore of alchemy is somewhat trite, and Mr Irving in search of originality has gone somewhat too deeply into it, and quoted freely the names of authors too long forgotten to awaken any association.—The incidents are commonplace, and the interest of the story but moderate.—Few writers might be able to produce so agreeable a piece, but we suppose Mr Irving could write a score such, with no additional effort, but that of the mechanical labor. (pp. 216-17)

[We] should not have spoken so freely of the work before us, had we not thought it in the author's power to write a better one. . . . But though we cannot allow that Mr Irving has done all that ought to have been expected from the pen of an American in England, we have much to admire and praise, in his works. Beside the episodical tales, he has given us admirable sketches of life and manners, highly curious in themselves, and rendered almost important by the goodnatured mock gravity, the ironical reverence, and lively wit with which they are described. (pp. 223-24)

"'Bracebridge Hall, or the Humorists, a Medley, by Geoffrey Crayon, Gent','" in The North American Review, *Vol. VI, No. 1, July, 1822, pp. 204-24.*

TIMOTHY TICKLER (essay date 1824)

I have been miserably disappointed in the "Tales of a Traveller." Three years have elapsed since the publication of "Bracebridge Hall," and it had been generally given out that the author was travelling about the Continent at a great rate, collecting the materials for a work of greater and more serious importance. Above all, it was known that Mr Irving had gone, *for the first time*, to Italy and to Germany; and high expectations were avowed as to the treasures he would bring back from these chosen seats of the classical and the romantic, the beautiful and the picturesque. With the exception of a very few detached pieces, such as the description of the Stage-coachman, and the story of the Stout Gentleman, Mr Irving's sketches of English life and manners had certainly made no lasting impression on the public mind. . . . [However, it] was said that the author had been too hasty, in his anxiety to keep up the effect he had produced in his "Sketch-book"; and that, having dressed up all his best English materials in that work, he had, *ex necessitate,* served up a hash in the successor. . . .

The more benign the disposition, the worse for Mr Irving now. He has been not only all over Germany, but all over Italy too; and he has produced a book, which, for aught I see, might have been written not in three years, but in three months, without stirring out of a garret in London, and this not by Mr. Irving alone, but by any one of several dozens of ready penmen about town. . . . The ghost stories, with which the greater part of the first volume is occupied, are, with one exception, old, and familiar to everybody conversant in that sort of line. The story of the Beheaded Lady, in particular, has not only been told in print ere now, but much better told than it is in Mr Irving's edition. To say the truth, a gentleman like this, who goes about gaping for stories to make up books withal, should be excessively scrupulous indeed, ere he sets to work upon anything he hears. (p. 294)

The matter of these ghost stories of his, however, is not the only, nor even the chief thing, I have to find fault with. They are old stories, and I am sorry to add, they are not improved by their new dress. The tone in which Mr Irving does them up, is quite wrong. A ghost story *ought* to be a ghost story. Something like seriousness is absolutely necessary, in order to its producing any effect at all upon the mind—and the sort of half-witty vein, the little dancing quarks, &c. &c. with which these are set forth, entirely destroy the whole matter. . . . There were some ghost stories in the Album, well worth half a ton of these. ''"The Fox-hunters" are *crambe recocta*, and bad *crambe* too; for Mr Irving no more understands an English fox-hunter, than I do an American judge. The same thing may be said of the whole most hackneyed story of Buckthorne, which is a miserable attempt at an English Wilhelm Meister; and yet one can with difficulty imagine a man of Mr Irving's sense producing this lame thing at all, if he had read *recently* either that work or the *Roman Comique.* "Buckthorne" is really a bad thing—*nulla virtute redemptum.* A boarding-school miss might have written it.

But the German part of the adventure has turned out exactly nothing, and this will perhaps be the greatest mortification to those who open Mr Irving's new book. Anybody, at least, who had read "Knickerbocker," and who knew Deutchland, either the upper or the nether, *must* have expected a rich repast indeed, of Meinherren and Mynheers. All this expectation is met with a mere cipher. There is nothing German here at all. . . . (p. 295)

The Italy, too, is a sad failure—very sad, indeed. Here is an American, a man of letters, a man of observation, a man of feeling, a man of taste. He goes, with a very considerable literary repution, as his passport at once and his stimulus, to the most interesting region, perhaps, in the old world, and he brings from it absolutely nothing except a few very hackneyed tales of the Abrussi Bandits, not a bit better than Mrs Maria Graham's trash. . . . [The] use Mr Irving has made of his Italian travels, must sink his character very woefully. It proves him to be devoid not only of all classical recollections, but of all genuine enthusiasm of any kind; and I believe you will go along with me when I say, that without enthusiasm of some sort, not even a humourist can be really successful. If Mr Irving had no eyes for tower, temple, and tree, he should at least have shewn one for peasants and pageants. But there is nothing whatever in his Italian Sketches that might not have been produced very easily by a person (and not a very clever person neither) who had merely read a few books of travels, or *talked* with a few travellers. Rome, Venice, Florence, Naples—this gentleman has been over them all, crayon in hand, and his Sketch-book is, wherever it is not a blank, a blunder.

Mr Irving, after writing, perhaps after printing one volume, and three-fourths of another, seems to have been suddenly struck with a conviction of the worthlessness of the materials that had thus been passing through his hands, and in a happy day, and a happy hour, he determined to fill up the remaining fifty or sixty pages, not with milk-and-water stuff about ghosts and banditti, but with some of his own old genuine stuff—the quaintnesses of the ancient Dutch hoers and frows of the delicious land of the Manhattoes. The result is, that this small section of his book is not only worth the bulk of it five hundred times over, but really, and in every respect, worthy of himself and his fame. This will live, the rest will die in three months.

He has most certainly made no progress in any one literary qualification since [the "History of New York"]. There is far keener and readier wit in that book,—far, far richer humour, far more ingenious satire, than in all that have come after it put together; and, however reluctant he may be to hear it said, the style of that book is by miles and miles superior to that in which he now, almost always, writes.

Long ere now, Mr Irving must, I should think, have made considerable discoveries as to the nature and extent of his own powers. In the first place, he must be quite aware that he has no inventive faculties at all, taking that phrase in its proper and more elevated sense. He has never invented an incident—unless, which I much doubt, the idea of the Stout Gentleman's story was his own;—and as for inventing characters, why, he has not even made an attempt at that.

Secondly, the poverty and bareness of his European Sketches alone, when compared with the warmth and richness of his old American ones, furnishes the clearest evidence that he is not a man of much liveliness of imagination; nothing has, it seems, excited him profoundly since he was a stripling roaming about the wild woods of his province, and enjoying the queer *fat* goings-on of the Dutch-descended burghers of New York. . . .

Thirdly, Mr Irving must be aware that he cannot write anything serious to much effect. This argues a considerable lack of pith in the whole foundations of his mind, for the world has never seen a great humourist who was nothing but a humourist. . . . If he wishes to make for himself a really enduring reputation, he must surpass considerably his previous works—I mean he must produce works of more uniform and entire merit than any of them, for he never can do anything better than some fragments he has done already. He must, for this purpose, take time, for it is obvious that he is by no means a rapid collector of materials, whatever the facility of his penmanship may be. Farther, he must at once cut all ideas of writing about European matters. He can never be anything but an imitator of our Goldsmith here,—on his own soil he *may* rear a name and a monument, *ere perennius*, for himself. No, he must allow his mind to dwell upon the only images which it ever can give back with embellished and strengthened hues. He must riot in pumpkin pies, grinning negroes, smoking skippers, plump jolly little Dutch maidens, and their grizzly-periwigged papas. (p. 296)

Perhaps there would be no harm if Mr Irving gave rather more scope to his own real feelings in his writings. A man of his power and mind must have opinions of one kind or another, in regard to the great questions which have in every age and country had the greatest interest for the greatest minds. Does he suppose that any popularity really worthy a *man's* ambition, is to be gained by a determined course of smooth speaking? Does he really imagine that *he* can be "all things to all men," in the Albemarle Street sense of the phrase, without emasculating his genius, and destroying its chances of perpetuating fame? . . . Does he suppose that we should be either sorry or angry, if he spoke out now and then like a Republican, about matters of political interest? He may relieve himself from this humane anxiety as to our peace of mind. There is no occasion for lugging in politics direct in works of fiction, but I must say, that I cannot think it natural for any man to write in these days so many volumes as Mr Irving has written, without in some way or other expressing his opinions and feelings. (p. 297)

> *Timothy Tickler, in his letter to Christopher North, in* Blackwood's Edinburgh Magazine, *Vol. XVI, No. XCII, September, 1824, pp. 291-304.**

BLACKWOOD'S EDINBURGH MAGAZINE   (essay date 1825)

The *Sketch-Book*—is a timid, beautiful work; with some childish pathos in it; some rich, pure, bold poetry: a little squeamish, puling, lady-like sentimentality: some courageous writing—some wit—and a world of humour, so happy, so natural—so altogether unlike that of any other man—dead or alive, that we would rather have been the writer of it, fifty times over, than of everything else, that he has ever written.—

The touches of poetry are everywhere; but never where one would look for them. Irving has no passion: he fails utterly, in true pathos—cannot speak, as if he were carried away, by anything. He is always thoughtful; and, save when he tries to be fine, or sentimental, always at home, always natural. . . . We hate his affectation; despise—pity his daintiness, trick and foppery, but cannot refuse to say, that in his delicate, fine, exquisite adaptation of descriptive words, to the things described, in his poetry he has no equal. (pp. 64-5)

We hardly know how to speak of [the sad affair of *Tales of a Traveller*]—when we think of what Irving might have done—without losing our temper. It is bad enough—base enough to steal that, which would make us wealthy for ever: but—like the plundering Arab—to steal rubbish—anything—from anybody—everybody—would indicate a hopeless moral temperament: a standard of self-estimation beneath everything.—No wonder that people have begun to question his originality—when they find him recoining the paltry material of newspapers—letters—romances.—In the early part of these two volumes we should never see any merit, knowing as we do, the sources of what he is there serving up, however admirable were

his new arrangement of the dishes; however great his improvement.

A part of the book—a few scenes—a few pages—are quite equal to anything, that he ever wrote. But we cannot agree with anybody, concerning those parts. Irving is greatly to blame—quite unpardonable, for two or three droll indecencies, which everybody, of course, remembers, in these *Tales*:—not so much because they are so unpardonable, in themselves—not so much on that account—as because the critics had set him up, in spite of Knickerbocker; in spite of *Salamagundi*; in spite of the Stout Gentleman—as an immaculate creature for this profligate age. . . . [We] cannot applaud anybody's courage or morals—who under a look of great modesty—with an over-righteous reputation—ventures to smuggle impurity into our dwellings—to cheat our very household gods.

The latter part of these *Tales,* we firmly believe, were old papers lying by. (pp. 66-7)

One word of advice to him, before we part—in all probability, *for ever*.—No man gets credit by repeating the story of another. . . . You cannot write a novel; a poem; a love tale; or a tragedy. But you *can* write another *Sketch-Book*—worth all that you have ever written: if you will draw only from yourself. You have some qualities, that no other living writer has—a bold, quiet humour—a rich beautiful mode of painting, without caricature—a delightful, free, happy spirit—make use of them.—We look to see you all the better for this trouncing. God bless you! Farewell. (p. 67)

> *"American Writers: No. IV," in* Blackwood's Edinburgh Magazine, *Vol. XVIII, No. XCVI, January, 1825, pp. 48-69.**

ECLECTIC REVIEW   (essay date 1825)

[The] *Tales of a Traveller* may be considered as a continuation of the *Sketch Book*. The same facility of touch, the same elegance, sustained without labour, and polished without art, may be traced in each. No author writes better English; and he is the solitary instance in which an American may read a salutary, though mortifying lesson to many of our native writers, in whose eyes Transatlantic literature is not likely to find much favour. (p. 65)

Yet, if we have been amused by the *Tales of a Traveller,* it is not because they are highly finished or skilfully contrived. With one or two exceptions, they seem all wanting in those satisfactory conclusions for which we pant so ardently, when our curiosity has been put to the rack, and our sympathies worked to a considerable fermentation. . . . Such, however, is the power of our friend Crayon, that we are pleased even while we are disappointed, and follow him with delight through the different avenues of his story, though they 'lead to nothing.' It is, moreover, an undeniable proof of the talent and taste of the writer, that he has conferred upon sketches comparatively so light and unfinished, the full interest of more complete and systematic pictures. (pp. 65-6)

"The Mysterious Stranger" and the **"Young Italian"** are powerfully written; but we were better pleased with Buckthorn and his friends, in the second part of the first volume. The Author exhibits some singular pictures of literary life; and here we must be allowed to remark, that although some of the caricatures may have had prototypes in real nature, yet, the finish of the pictures, and the grouping of the figures, must be the product of pure imagination. (p. 71)

On the whole, these volumes have yielded us considerable entertainment; and those who take no pleasure in invidious comparisons between the last and the former productions of the writer, and who will consent to be carried along without cheating themselves of a great portion of rational amusement, by mingling with the sensations excited by the *Tales of a Traveller,* the recollections of what they felt on the perusal of the earlier productions of Geoffrey Crayon,—by those, in fact, who have not sate down to the perusal with unreasonable expectations, which it is no sin in him not to have gratified; they will be welcomed as an agreeable accession to the stock of light reading. Mr. Crayon's great excellence lies in serving up a variety of dishes to please a variety of tastes. There is tenderness for the sentimental, and (for humour and sensibility are seldom far distant from each other in the human bosom) force and caricature for those who are inclined to be innocently merry. . . . We regret that we cannot dismiss these volumes, however, with an unqualified sentence of commendation. (p. 74)

> *"'Tales of a Traveller',"* in Eclectic Review, *n.s.,*
> *Vol. XXIV, July, 1825, pp. 65-74.*

WILLIAM HAZLITT   (essay date 1825)

[Mr. Washington Irving] is not bottomed in our elder writers, nor do we think he has tasked his own faculties much, at least on English ground. Of the merit of his *Knickerbocker* and New York stories we cannot pretend to judge. But in his *Sketch-book* and *Bracebridge-Hall* he gives us very good American copies of our British Essayists and Novelists, which may be very well on the other side of the water, or as proofs of the capabilities of the national genius, but which might be dispensed with here, where we have to boast of the originals. Not only Mr. Irving's language is with great taste and felicity modelled on that of Addison, Goldsmith, Sterne, or Mackenzie: but the thoughts and sentiments are taken at the rebound, and, as they are brought forward at the present period, want both freshness and probability.

Mr. Irving's writings are literary *anachronisms.* He comes to England for the first time, and being on the spot, fancies himself in the midst of those characters and manners which he had read of in the *Spectator* and other approved authors, and which were the only idea he had hitherto formed of the parent country. Instead of looking round to see what *we are,* he sets to work to describe us as *we were*—at second hand. . . . Whatever the ingenious author has been most delighted with in the representations of books he transfers to his portfolio, and swears that he has found it actually existing in the course of his observation and travels through Great Britain. Instead of tracing the changes that have taken place in society since Addison or Fielding wrote, he transcribes their account in a different handwriting, and thus keeps us stationary, at least in our most attractive and praise-worthy qualities of simplicity, honesty, hospitality, modesty, and good-nature. (pp. 343-44)

The first Essay in the *Sketch-book,* that on National Antipathies, is the best; but, after that, the sterling ore of wit or feeling is gradually spun thinner and thinner, till it fades to the shadow of a shade. Mr. Irving is himself, we believe, a most agreeable and deserving man, and has been led into the natural and pardonable error we speak of by the tempting bait of European popularity, in which he thought there was no more likely method of succeeding than by imitating the style of our standard authors, and giving us credit for the virtues of our forefathers. (p. 344)

> *William Hazlitt, "Elia, and Geoffrey Crayon" (1825),*
> *in his* The Spirit of the Age; or, Contemporary Por-*
> *traits, edited by W. Carew Hazlitt, fourth edition,*
> *George Bell and Sons, 1886, pp. 333-46.**

AMERICAN QUARTERLY REVIEW   (essay date 1828)

Hitherto we have been accustomed to regard Irving wholly as a voyager in the world of fiction. In [*A History of The Life and Voyages of Christopher Columbus*], he presents himself in the new light of the grave historian of perhaps the most memorable event in the annals of the world; that by which an entire hemisphere was opened to the view of the nations of the ancient continent. . . . If, in assuming the character of the historian, Irving may have given up many advantages, such as his brilliant and inventive imagination, his powers of description and intense sense of natural beauty, and still more, his vein of delicate, yet keen-edged humour; attributes which have rendered his former works so fascinating; still he may find a compensation in the overpowering interest of his subject, while the graces of his chaste and simple, yet polished diction, remain to attract and delight his readers. (p. 175)

Furnished with . . . ample sources of information, our author has employed them to the best advantage, in developing the early habits and education of his hero, by which he was trained for his enterprise, and that mixture of the highest knowledge of his age, both practical and theoretic, with the enthusiasm of a crusader, the patience and humility of a martyr. It is, in this respect, that the work before us is novel, and most interesting. Other writers have recorded the bare facts of the voyages of Columbus, the glory that seemed to repay his success, and the severe reverses he experienced from the ascendency of envy and malignity. In that of Irving, we have seen for the first time fully illustrated, his extensive learning, his patient devotion under delay and suffering, sustained by the hope of extending the dominions of the cross, to regions of paganism and darkness; the holy, even if mistaken zeal, with which he proposed to dedicate the hard-earned profits of his success, not to his own personal ease or the establishment of his family, but to the recovery of the sepulchre of Christ from the infidels. (p. 176)

> *"'A History of the Life and Voyages of Christopher*
> *Columbus',"* in The American Quarterly Review,
> *Vol. III, No. 5, March, 1828, pp. 173-90.*

THE NORTH AMERICAN REVIEW   (essay date 1832)

Mr. Irving, who possesses the true poetical temperament, must . . . have found, in every part of the Spanish Peninsula, abundant materials for his sketches [in his *Alhambra*]; and we may confidently anticipate that other collections will follow that with which he has now favored us. . . .

The work before us contains . . . a description of the author's journey from Seville to Granada, and an account of his residence in the Alhambra, interspersed with some of the legends of love and war, of hidden treasures, magic spells, and spectral apparitions, in which which the Arabians took so much delight, and which are still current, wherever they were established. (p. 269)

The introductory chapter, which narrates the events of the journey from Seville to Granada, is one of the most agreeable in the book. In general, we think that Mr. Irving's style is more nervous and spirited, when he is employed in embellishing facts that have come within his own observation, than when he attempts a wholly fictitious narrative. (pp. 270-71)

It would be superfluous to follow the ingenious and elegant author in detail through the several portions of a work, which has already preceded our notice in the hands of most of our readers. It is marked substantially with the qualities that distinguished his former productions of the same class, excepting that there is no mixture of the pathetic. The tone is throughout light and pleasant, and the tales are all, if we rightly recollect, of a comic cast. We are not sure that this tone is quite in keeping with the character of the subject; and if there be any defect in the general conception of the work, it consists in selecting the ruins of a celebrated ancient palace, which seem to lead more naturally to grave meditations on the fall of empires, and melancholy musings on the frailty of human greatness, as the scene of a series of sportive caricatures and comic stories. (pp. 275-76)

The high and deep things, whether of philosophy or feeling, are in a great measure foreign to [Mr. Irving]; and, as he more than intimates in the present work by several sly innuendoes about metaphysics, are, in his opinion, secrets not worth knowing. In the midst of the scenes and objects that most naturally suggest them, he reverts instinctively to the lights and shadows that play upon the surface of social life. (p. 276)

The best articles are those, in which the author gives a description of scenes and persons that have come directly within his own observation: such as the **"Journey,"** the **"Balcony,"** the **"Haunted Tower,"** the **"Author's Chambers,"** and the **"Visitors."** Although some of these subjects might appear, as we have intimated, light and trifling, if viewed under the impression of the feelings most natural to the scene, they are all wrought up with great felicity, and are among the most finished and elegant specimens of style to be found in the language. (p. 277)

The tales, though not to us, as we have said, the most agreeable portion of the work, and though, in fact, not distinguished by any particular power or point, are written in the correct and graceful style peculiar to the author, and will be read with pleasure, were it only for the beauty of the language, which is in fact their principal merit. **"The Moor's Legacy"** and **"Governor Manco"** are perhaps the best. **"Prince Ahmed, or the Pilgrim of Love,"** though evidently among the more elaborate, appears to us somewhat less successful than the others, which is rather remarkable, considering the attractive character of the subject, and the profusion of machinery which the author has brought into action. . . . On the whole, we consider the work before us as equal in literary value to any of the others of the same class, with the exception of the *Sketch Book*, and we should not be surprised, if it were read as extensively as even that very popular production. We hope to have it in our power, at no remote period, to announce a continuation of the series, which we are satisfied will bear, in the bookseller's phrase, several more volumes. (p. 281)

> *"Irving's 'Alhambra',"* in The North American Review, *Vol. XXXV, No. 77, October, 1832, pp. 265-82.*

THE NORTH AMERICAN REVIEW   (essay date 1835)

We regard Washington Irving as the best living writer of English prose. Let those who doubt the correctness of this opinion name his superior. Let our brethren in England name the writer, whom they place before Washington Irving. He unites the various qualities of a perfect manner of writing; and so happily adjusted and balanced are they, that their separate marked existence disappears in their harmonious blending. His style is sprightly, pointed, easy, correct, and expressive, without being too studiously guarded against the opposite faults. It is without affectation, parade, or labor. If we were to haracterize a manner, which owes much of its merit to the absence of any glaring characteristic, we should perhaps say, that it is, above the style of all other writers of the day, marked with an expressive elegance. Washington Irving never buries up the clearness and force of the meaning, under a heap of fine words; nor on the other hand does he think it necessary to be coarse, slovenly, or uncouth, in order to be emphatic. (p. 1)

In bestowing upon Mr. Irving the praise of a perfect style of writing, it must not be understood, that we commend him, in a point of mere manner. To write as Mr. Irving writes, is not an affair, which rests in a dexterous use of words alone; at least not if we admit the popular, but unphilosophical distinction, between words and ideas. Mr. Irving writes well, because he thinks well; because his ideas are just, clear, and definite. He knows what he wants to say, and expresses it distinctly and intelligibly, because he so apprehends it. There is also no affectation in the writer, because there is none in the man. There is no pomp in his sentences, because there is no arrogance in his temper. There is no overloading with ornament, because with the eye of an artist, he sees when he has got enough; and he is sprightly and animated, because he catches his tints from nature, and dips his pencil in truth, which is always fresh and racy. (p. 3)

From Mr. Irving we have the humors of contemporary politics and every-day life in America. . . . When he writes the history of Columbus, you see him weighing doubtful facts, in the scales of a golden criticism. You behold him, laden with the manuscript treasures of well-searched archives, and disposing the heterogeneous materials, into a well-digested and instructive narration. Take down another of his volumes, and you find him in the parlor of an English country-inn, of a rainy day, and you look out of the window with him upon the dripping, dreary desolation of the back-yard. (pp. 4-5)

To what class of compositions [*A Tour on the Prairies*] belongs, we are hardly able to say. It can scarcely be called a book of travels, for there is too much painting of manners, and scenery, and too little statistics;—it is not a novel, for there is no story; and it is not a romance, for it is all true. It is a sort of sentimental journey, a romantic excursion, in which nearly all the elements of several different kinds of writing are beautifully and gaily blended into a production almost *sui generis*. (pp. 5-6)

Washington Irving possesses, in the highest degree, the gift of the poet, *the maker*. And delightful it is to reflect, as in a case like this, how little it imports to the man, to whom this divine gift is imparted, what materials he shall take in hand to employ it upon, or where he shall lay the scene of his creations. . . . We are proud of Mr. Irving's sketches of English life, proud of the gorgeous canvass upon which he has gathered in so much of the glowing imagery of Moorish times. We behold with delight his easy and triumphant march over these beaten fields; but we glow with rapture as we see him coming back from the Prairies, laden with the poetical treasures of the primitive wilderness,—rich with spoil from the uninhabited desert. (pp. 12-14)

It cannot be necessary to attempt anything like what, in the technical language of criticism, would be deemed a review of

Mr. Irving's work. It has already delighted all our readers;— We wish only, in this desultory notice, to utter the feelings of deep and grateful emotion, with which we have perused it. (p. 14)

> "'A Tour on the Prairies'," in The North American Review, Vol. XLI, No. 88, July, 1835, pp. 1-28.

SOUTHERN LITERARY MESSENGER (essay date 1835)

We hailed with pleasure the appearance of the first number of the **Crayon Miscellany,** but we knew not what a feast was preparing for us in the second. In **Abbotsford** and **Newstead Abbey** the author of the **Sketch Book** is at home. By no one could this offering to the memories of Scott and Byron have been more appropriately made. It is the tribute of genius to its kindred spirits, and it breathes a sanctifying influence over the graves of the departed. The kindly feelings of Irving are beautifully developed in his description of the innocent pursuits and cheerful conversation of Sir Walter Scott, while they give a melancholy interest to the early misfortunes of Byron. He luxuriates among the scenes and associations which hallow the walls of Newstead, and warms us into admiration of the wizard of the north, by a matchless description of the man, his habits, and his thoughts. The simplicity and innocence of his heart, his domestic affections, and his warm hospitality, are presented in their most attractive forms. The scenes and the beings with which Sir Walter was surrounded, are drawn with a graphic pencil. All conduce to strengthen impressions formerly made of the goodness and beneficence of Scott's character, and to gratify the thousands who have drawn delight from his works, with the conviction that their author was one of the most amiable of his species. No man knows better than Washington Irving, the value which is placed by the world (and with justice) upon incidents connected with really great men, which seem trifling in themselves, and which borrow importance only from the individuals to whom they have relation. . . . The whole of the details respecting Miss Chaworth, and Byron's unfortunate attachment to that lady, are in his best manner. The story of the White Lady is one of deep interest, and suits well with the melancholy thoughts connected with Newstead. An instance of monomania like that of the White Lady, has seldom been recorded; and the author has, without over-coloring the picture, presented to his readers the history of a real being, whose whole character and actions and melancholy fate belong to the regions of romance. In nothing that he has ever written, has his peculiar faculty of imparting to all he touches the coloring of his genius, been more fully displayed than in this work. (p. 646)

> "Literary Notices: 'The Crayon Miscellany, No. II'," in The Southern Literary Messenger, Vol. 1, No. 11, July, 1835, pp. 646-48.

[JAMES RUSSELL LOWELL] (essay date 1848)

[The following excerpt is taken from James Russell Lowell's poem, A Fable for Critics.]

> What! Irving? thrice welcome, warm heart and
>   fine brain,
> You bring back the happiest spirit from Spain,
> And the gravest sweet humor, that ever were
>   there
> Since Cervantes met death in his gentle despair;
> Nay, don't be embarrassed, nor look so
>   beseeching,—
> I shan't run directly against my own preaching,

> And, having just laughed at their Raphaels and
>   Dantes,
> Go to setting you up beside matchless Cervantes;
> But allow me to speak what I honestly feel,—
> To a true poet-heart add the fun of Dick Steele,
> Throw in all of Addison, *minus* the chill,
> With the whole of that partnership's stock and
>   good will,
> Mix well, and while stirring, hum o'er, as a
>   spell,
> The fine *old* English Gentleman, simmer it well,
> Sweeten just to your own private liking, then
>   strain,
> That only the finest and clearest remain,
> Let it stand out of doors till a soul it receives
> From the warm lazy sun loitering down through
>   green leaves,
> And you'll find a choice nature, not wholly
>   deserving
> A name either English or Yankee,—just Irving.
>
> (p. 65)

> [James Russell Lowell,] in his A Fable for Critics; A Glance at a Few of our Literary Progenies, second edition, G. P. Putnam, 1848, 80 p.*

WILLIAM CULLEN BRYANT (essay date 1860)

I have just read this **History of New York** over again, and I found myself no less delighted than when I first turned its pages in my early youth. When I compare it with other works of wit and humor of a similar length, I find that, unlike most of them, it carries forward the reader to the conclusion without weariness or satiety, so unsought, spontaneous, self-suggested are the wit and the humor. The author makes us laugh, because he can no more help it than we can help laughing. . . . The mirth of the **History of New York** is of the most transparent sort, and the author, in even the later editions, judiciously abstained from any attempt to make it more intelligible by notes.

I find in this work more manifest traces than in his other writings of what Irving owed to the earlier authors in our language. The quaint poetic coloring, and often the phraseology, betray the disciple of Chaucer and Spenser. We are conscious of a flavor of the olden time, as of a racy wine of some rich vintage. . . .

Of all mock-heroic works, **Knickerbocker's History of New York** is the gayest, the airiest, the least tiresome. (p. 302)

It was during [the interval between the **History of New York** and the **Sketch Book**] that an event took place which had a marked influence on Irving's future life, affected the character of his writings, and, now that the death of both parties allows it to be spoken of without reserve, gives a peculiar interest to his personal history. He became attached to a young lady whom he was to have married. She died, unwedded, in the flower of her age; there was a sorrowful leave-taking between her and her lover, as the grave was about to separate them on the eve of what should have been her bridal: and Irving, ever after, to the close of his life, tenderly and faithfully cherished her memory. . . .

Whoever compares the **Sketch Book** with the **History of New York** might, perhaps, at first fail to recognize it as the work of the same hand, so much graver and more thoughtful is the strain in which it is written. A more attentive examination, however, shows that the humor in the lighter parts is of the same peculiar and original cast, wholly unlike that of any author who ever wrote. . . . Yet one cannot help perceiving that the author's spirit had been sobered since he last appeared before the public, as if the shadow of a great sorrow had fallen upon it. The greater number of the papers are addressed to our deeper sympathies. . . . (p. 303)

The *Sketch Book* and the two succeeding works of Irving—*Bracebridge Hall* and the *Tales of a Traveller*—abound with agreeable pictures of English life, seen under favorable lights and sketched with a friendly pencil. Let me say here, that it was not to pay court to the English that he thus described them and their country; it was because he could not describe them otherwise. It was the instinct of his mind to attach itself to the contemplation of the good and beautiful wherever he found them, and to turn away from the sight of what was evil, misshapen, and hateful. . . . If there are touches of satire in his writings, he is the best-natured and most amiable of satirists, amiable beyond Horace; and in his irony—for there is a vein of playful irony running through many of his works—there is no tinge of bitterness. (p. 304)

[Simplicity is the first quality of Irving's *Life of Washington*] which impresses the reader. Here is a man of genius, a poet by temperament, writing the life of a man of transcendent wisdom and virtue—a life passed amidst great events and marked by inestimable public services. There is a constant temptation to eulogy, but the temptation is resisted; the actions of his hero are left to speak their own praise. (p. 309)

A closer examination reveals another great merit of the work, the admirable proportion in which the author keeps the characters and events of his story. I suppose he could hardly have been conscious of this merit, and that it was attained without a direct effort. Long meditation had probably so shaped and matured the plan in his mind, and so arranged its parts in their just symmetry, that, executing it as he did conscientiously, he could not have made it a different thing from what we have it. There is nothing distorted, nothing placed in too broad a light or thrown too far in the shade. (pp. 309-10)

I confess that my admiration of this work becomes the greater the more I examine it. In the other writings of Irving are beauties which strike the reader at once. In this I recognize qualities which lie deeper and which I was not sure of finding—a rare equity of judgment, a large grasp of the subject, a profound philosophy, independent of philosophical forms and even instinctively rejecting them, the power of reducing an immense crowd of loose materials to clear and orderly arrangement, and forming them into one grand whole, as a skilful commander, from a rabble of raw recruits, forms a disciplined army, animated and moved by a single will. (p. 310)

His facility in writing and the charm of his style were owing to very early practice, the reading of good authors and the native elegance of his mind, and not, in my opinion, to any special study of the graces of manner or any anxious care in the use of terms and phrases. Words and combinations of words are sometimes found in his writings to which a fastidious taste might object; but these do not prevent his style from being one of the most agreeable in the whole range of our literature. It is transparent as the light, sweetly modulated, unaffected, the native expression of a fertile fancy, a benignant temper, and a mind which, delighting in the noble and the beautiful, turned involuntarily away from their opposites. His peculiar humor

was, in a great measure, the offspring of this constitution of his mind. (p. 311)

In his pages we see that the language of the heart never becomes obsolete; that truth and good and beauty, the offspring of God, are not subject to the changes which beset the inventions of men. We become satisfied that he whose works were the delight of our fathers, and are still ours, will be read with the same pleasure by those who come after us. (p. 312)

> *William Cullen Bryant, "Bryant on Washington Irving" (originally a discourse before the New York Historical Society on April 3, 1860), in* The Living Age, *Vol. LXV, No. 831, May, 1860, pp. 298-312.*

EVERT A. DUYCKINCK (essay date 1860)

In estimating the genius of Irving, we can hardly attach too high a value to the refined qualities and genial humor which have made his writings favorites wherever the English language is read. The charm is in the proportion, the keeping, the happy vein which inspires happiness in return. It is the felicity of but few authors, out of the vast stock of English literature, to delight equally young and old. The tales of Irving are the favorite authors of childhood, and their good humor and amenity can please where most literature is weariness, in the sickroom of the convalescent. Every influence which breathes from these writings is good and generous. Their sentiment is always just and manly, without cant or affection; their humor is always within the bounds of propriety. They have a fresh inspiration of American nature, which is not the less nature for the art with which it is adorned. The color of personality attaches us throughout to the author, whose humor of character is always to be felt. This happy art of presenting rude and confused objects in an orderly pleasureable aspect, everywhere to be met with in the pages of Irving, is one of the most beneficent in literature. The philosopher Hume said a turn for humor was worth to him ten thousand a year, and it is this gift which the writings of Irving impart. (pp. 25-6)

> *Evert A. Duyckinck, in an excerpt from his "Memoranda of the Literary Career of Washington Irving," in his* Irvingiana: A Memorial of Washington Irving, *Charles B. Richardson, 1860 (and reprinted in* A Century of Commentary on the Works of Washington Irving: 1860-1974, *edited by Andrew B. Myers, Sleepy Hollow Restorations, 1976, pp. 18-28).*

HENRY WADSWORTH LONGFELLOW (essay date 1876)

> Here lies the gentle humorist, who died
> In the bright Indian Summer of his fame!
> A simple stone, with but a date and name,
> Marks his secluded resting-place beside
> The river that he loved and glorified.
> Here in the autumn of his days he came,
> But the dry leaves of life were all aflame
> With tints that brightened and were multiplied.
> How sweet a life was his; how sweet a death!
> Living, to wing with mirth the weary hours,
> Or with romantic tales the heart to cheer;
> Dying, to leave a memory like the breath
> Of summers full of sunshine and of showers,
> A grief and gladness in the atmosphere.

> *Henry Wadsworth Longfellow, "In the Churchyard at Tarrytown" (1876), in his* Kéramos and Other Poems, *Houghton, Osgood & Company, 1878 (and reprinted in* A Century of Commentary on the Works of Washington Irving: 1860-1974, *edited by Andrew B. Myers, Sleepy Hollow Restorations, 1976, p. 39).*

CHARLES DUDLEY WARNER   (essay date 1880)

Irving was always the literary man; he had the habits, the idiosyncrasies, of the literary man. I mean that he regarded life not from the philanthropic, the economic, the political, the philosophic, the metaphysic, the scientific, or the theologic, but purely from the literary point of view. He belongs to that small class of which Johnson and Goldsmith are perhaps as good types as any, and to which America has added very few. (pp. 404-05)

Like Scott, he belonged to the idealists, and not to the realists whom our generation affects. Both writers stimulate the longing for something better. Their creed was short: "Love God and honor the king." . . . The bent of Irving's spirit was fixed in his youth, and he escaped the desperate realism of this generation, which has no outcome, and is likely to produce little that is noble. (p. 405)

He seems to have been born with a rare sense of literary proportion and form; into this, as into a mold, were run his apparently lazy and really acute observations of life. . . . As an illustration, his *Life of Washington* may be put in evidence. It is impossible for any biography to be less pretentious in style, or less ambitious in proclamation. . . . [While] he has given us a dignified portrait of Washington, it is as far as possible removed from that of the smileless prig which has begun to weary even the popular fancy. The man he paints is flesh and blood, presented, I believe, with substantial faithfulness to his character. . . . Irving's grasp of this character; his lucid marshaling of the scattered, often wearisome and uninteresting details of our dragging, unpicturesque Revolutionary War; his just judgement of men; his even, almost judicial moderation of tone; and his admirable proportion of space to events, render the discussion of style in reference to this work superfluous. (pp. 405-06)

[Irving's] mood is calm and unexaggerated. Even in some of his pathos, which is open to the suspicion of being "literary," there is no literary exaggeration. He seems always writing from an internal calm, which is the necessary condition of his production. If he wins at all by his style, by his humor, by his portraiture of success or of character, it is by a gentle force, like that of the sun in spring. . . . I think the calm work of Irving will stand when much of the more startling and perhaps more brilliant intellectual achievement of this age has passed away. (pp. 407-08)

His books are wholesome, full of sweetness and charm, of humor without any sting, of amusement without any stain; and their more solid qualities are marred by neither pedantry nor pretension. (p. 408)

> *Charles Dudley Warner, "Washington Irving," in* The Atlantic Monthly, *Vol. XLV, No. CCLXIX, March, 1880, pp. 396-408.*

GEORGE W. CURTIS   (essay date 1883)

Knickerbocker's History was the work of a young man of twenty-six, who lived fifty years afterward with a constantly increasing fame, making many and admirable contributions to literature. But nothing that followed surpassed the joyous brilliancy and gay felicity of the earliest work. Appearing in the midst of the sober effusions of our Puritan literature, and of a grave and energetic life still engrossed with the subjugation of a continent and the establishment of a new nation, *Knickerbocker's History* was a remarkable work. To pass the vague and venerable traditions of the austere and heroic founders of the city through the alembic of a youth's hilarious creative humor, and turn them out in forms resistlessly grotesque, but with their identity unimpaired, was a stroke as daring as it was successful. The audacious Goth of the legend who plucked the Roman senator by the beard was not a more ruthless iconoclast than this son of New Amsterdam, who drew his civil ancestors from venerable obscurity by flooding them with the cheerful light of a blameless fun.

The skill and power with which this is done can be best appreciated by those who are most familiar with the history which the gleeful genius burlesques. Irving follows the actual story closely, and the characters that he develops faithfully, although with smiling caricature, are historical. Indeed, the fidelity is so absolute that the fiction is welded with the fact. The days of Dutch ascendency in New York are inextricably associated with this ludicrous narrative. (pp. 68-9)

> *George W. Curtis, in an excerpt from "Editor's Easy Chair," in* Harper's New Monthly Magazine, *Vol. LXVI, No. CCCXCV, April, 1883 (and reprinted in* A Century of Commentary on the Works of Washington Irving: 1860-1974, *edited by Andrew B. Myers, Sleepy Hollow Restorations, 1976, pp. 66-70).*

EDWIN W. BOWEN   (essay date 1906)

"Knickerbocker's History of New York" was a happy conception and was largely indebted for its success to the author's characteristic abundant sense of humor. It was this quality that redeemed the burlesque from mere caricature in execution and stamped it an artistic production. The book was written in the vein of Swift, but the satire lacked the sting and bite which the famous Dean of St. Patrick's generally infused into his work. Irving's satire is of a mild type, and his prevading humor robs it of its sting, causing the victim to be amused, not exasperated, at his own foibles. The portraits of the old Dutch governors are sketched with evident pleasure and ease by a hand altogether untrammeled by literary traditions. The freshness and buoyancy of the narrative and the whimsical, charming style combine with the rollicking humor to make the book quite without a parallel in English literature. It is, however, but just to observe that the first few chapters which, by the way, are the product of the collaboration of his brother with Irving, appear somewhat stilted, pompous and pedantic and make the unhappy impression that the authors were feeling their way and were not yet sure of their footing. But the illusion cast over the reader later, as he progresses, makes him forget the weakness of grip which the authors show in the opening chapters. Each of the old Dutch governors of New York is depicted with such minuteness of detail and with such a vividness of incident and with such a mock seriousness of style withal, as they were in turn confronted with the various problems of state, that the narrative is invested with an air of reality and might readily be taken, on first blush, as veritable history. All in all, the fanciful idea of this piece of historical burlesque and its clever execution seem a stroke of genius, and the result is a masterpiece of humor, unsurpassed in American or English literature. (pp. 173-74)

The **"Sketch-Book"** is distinctively American, racy and smacks of the soil. The old legends of the Hudson are here clothed with life and beauty and are now recognized almost as a part of our national history. (pp. 174-75)

The treatment of the "**Sketch-Book**" is somewhat unequal. Some of the sketches are naturally better than others. A popular vote would probably put "**The Wife**," "**Rip Van Winkle**" and the "**Legend of Sleepy Hollow**" easily first, and this verdict would be confirmed by critical judgment. While all are good, these three sketches are felt to be the finest. Their tender pathos, imaginative humor, simplicity and grace have already endeared these three to the hearts of thousands of readers who have lingered, almost spellbound, over their pages; and their charm and beauty will, no doubt, commend them to generations of readers yet unborn. (p. 175)

["**Life of Goldsmith**"] is by far the best of Irving's later productions and has much of the charm and freshness of his earlier work. The subject was doubtless congenial to the biographer. The vagabondish life of the generous-hearted, improvident Goldsmith appealed to Irving's sympathies and kindled once more his waning imagination till it glowed again as if with its earlier accustomed warmth. The result is a biography showing deep insight into the character and worth, and tender sympathy with the foibles and frailties, of one of the most beloved authors of English literature in the eighteenth century. (p. 181)

Irving richly deserves the distinction usually accorded him of being the first American author to win for himself a conspicuous and unfading name in the department of letters. His star now for wellnigh half a century has shone with undimmed lustre and shows no sign of being immediately eclipsed. This honor has been achieved not by our author's intellectual force and acumen, nor by his creative imagination and incisive literary touch, but by the free play of his romantic fancy, his pervading sentiment, his unfailing, delightful humor and his charming style. Herein lies the secret of his success. The charm of Irving's style is remarkable, and proves clearly, as Shakespeare's brilliant example does, that the literary art and vital spark are not confined exclusively to academic halls.

Irving appeals to the sensibilities rather than to the intellect, to the heart rather than to the head. His register, to use a musical term, is not great; his range is not wide. There are notes he never sounded, depths and heights he never reached. The tragedy of life, the profoundest problems of human existence, the realm of philosophical speculation—these were to Irving an unexplored country which his creative mind never entered. The subtle analysis of Poe and the perplexing social problems and deep mysteries of Hawthorne had for Irving no special interest or attraction. He did not make his works a medium for communicating to the world mere metaphysical exercises of marvelous originality, or great moral truths. Such studies awaken in us the spirit of inquiry and speculation, disturb our peace of mind and tend to unsettle our convictions. Irving's works, on the other hand, induce to repose and quiet musing; they do not agitate or ruffle our spirits. They reflect their author's own quiet and reposeful nature, as that nature is enlivened by a delightful vein of humor and sentiment. (pp. 181-82)

Irving did not share the restless energy of the typical American. Unlike most of his countrymen he seems to have found more to interest him in the past than in the present or future. Janus-like, his face was set both toward the east and toward the west. However, Irving's inclination to the east with its Old World traditions, some think, made his love for the west kick the beam. It is true he found in the historic personages and romantic traditions of the past the chief sources of his inspiration. The Old World exercised over him a preponderating influence. Yet Irving was American to his finger-tips. Where can we find a bit of literature more distinctively American than "**Knicker-**

bocker's History of New York," or the "**Sketch-Book**," or "**Captain Bonneville**," or "**Astoria**," or "**A Tour of the Prairies**"? Surely, these smack of the soil and have the genuine, unmistakable American flavor. We treasure them as a part of Irving's valuable legacy to American literature. (pp. 182-83)

> *Edwin W. Bowen, "Washington Irving's Place in American Literature," in* The Sewanee Review, *Vol. XIV, No. 1, January, 1906, pp. 171-83.*

FRED LEWIS PATTEE (essay date 1923)

For the short story as we know it to-day Irving performed perhaps nine distinctive services:

1. He made short fiction popular. He was peculiarly endowed for writing the shortened form and he used it exclusively. . . .

2. He was the first prominent writer to strip the prose tale of its moral and didactic elements and to make of it a literary form solely for entertainment. (p. 140)

3. He added to the short tale richness of atmosphere and unity of tone.

4. He added definite locality, actual American scenery and people. Though only seven of his forty-eight tales are native in setting, these seven have been from the first his best loved and most influential work. They were the result of no accident. Deliberately he set out to create for his native land that rich atmosphere which poetry and romance had thrown over the older lands of Europe. . . . (pp. 140-41)

5. He was the first writer of fiction to recognize that the shorter form of narrative could be made something new and different, but that to do it required a peculiar nicety of execution and patient workmanship. . . .

6. He added humor to the short story and lightness of touch, and made it human and appealing. A pervasive humor it was, of the eighteenth-century type rather than of the pungent American type that was to be added by Aldrich and his generation, but nevertheless something new and something attractive.

7. He was original: he pitched the short story in a key that was as new to his generation as O. Henry's was to his. (p. 141)

8. Though his backgrounds may often be hazy . . . , his characters are always definite individuals and not types or symbols. . . .

9. And finally, he endowed the short story with a style that was finished and beautiful, one that threw its influence over large areas of the later product. . . .

But in many respects Irving was a detriment to the development of the short story. So far as modern technique is concerned he retarded its growth for a generation. He became from the first a model followed by all: unquestionably he was in America the most influential literary figure of the nineteenth century. To him as much as even to Scott may be traced the origin of that wave of sentimentalism and unrestrained romance that surged through the annuals and the popular magazines for three decades. (p. 142)

Of form as we know it to-day the tales of Irving, even the best of them, have little. He had begun as an eighteenth-century essayist, and according to Dr. Johnson an essay is "a loose sally of the mind; an irregular, undigested piece; not a regular or orderly composition"; he had ended as a romanticist, and romanticism may be defined as lawlessness. His genius was not dramatic. He delighted to saunter through his piece, sketching as he went, and chatting genially about his characters. . . .

To Irving plot seemed unessential. He had evolved with deliberation a form of his own that fitted him perfectly. (p. 143)

But there is a more serious indictment. . . . Irving lacked robustness, masculinity, "red-bloodedness." He was gentle to the verge of squeamishness. . . . Beyond a doubt this lack of robustness in Irving must be reckoned with as one cause of the general effeminacy and timid softness that characterized so much of American fiction during the greater part of the century.

But criticism of Irving's defects is thankless labor. It is best to overlook his faults and be profoundly thankful for him, for with him began American literature. (p. 144)

> *Fred Lewis Pattee, in an excerpt from his "Washington Irving," in his* The Development of the American Short Story: An Historical Survey *(copyright 1923 by Harper & Row, Publishers, Inc.; renewed 1950 by Fred Lewis Pattee; reprinted by permission of Harper & Row, Publishers, Inc.), Harper, 1923 (and reprinted in* A Century of Commentary on the Works of Washington Irving: 1860-1974, *edited by Andrew B. Myers, Sleepy Hollow Restorations, 1976, pp. 137-46).*

VERNON LOUIS PARRINGTON (essay date 1930)

Irving proposed to make the field of western romance his own, with the result that he published in quick succession [*A Tour on the Prairies*], *Astoria,* and *The Adventures of Captain Bonneville.*

On the whole the new venture did not prosper. The spirit of the West was not to be captured by one whose heart was in Spain. In [*A Tour on the Prairies*] there is a certain homely simplicity and straightforwardness that spring from a plain recital of undramatic experience; and in *Astoria* there is an unembellished narrative of appalling hardship and heroic endurance, with none of the tawdry romantics that mar the work of Flint and Hall. Yet neither is creatively imaginative, neither stirs one with a sense of high drama. The atmosphere of Snake River could not be created in the quiet study at the "Roost"; it needed the pen of a realist to capture the romance of those bitter wanderings in mountain and sagebrush. It is journeyman work, and on every page one is conscious of the professional man of letters faithfully doing this day's allotment. It is much the same with his *Life of Washington.* In this last great undertaking Irving no longer writes with gusto. The golden days of Diedrich Knickerbocker and Rip Van Winkle are long since gone; the magic is departed from his pen; and a somewhat tired old gentleman is struggling to fulfill his contract with his publisher. (pp. 168-69)

The most distinguished of our early romantics, Irving in the end was immolated on the altar of romanticism. The pursuit of the picturesque lured him away into sterile wastes, and when the will-o'-the-wisp was gone he was left empty. A born humorist, the gayety of whose spirits overflowed the brim, he was lacking in a brooding intellectuality, and instead of coming upon irony at the bottom of the cup—as the greater humorists have come upon it after life has had its way with them—he found there only sentiment and the dreamy poetic. As the purple haze on the horizon of his mind was dissipated by a sobering experience, he tried to substitute an adventitious glamour; as romance faded, sentiment supplied its place. So long as youth and high spirits endured, his inkwell was a never-failing source

of gayety, but as the sparkle subsided he over-sweetened his wine. This suffices to account for the fact that all his better work was done early; and this explains why the Knickerbocker *History* remains the most genial and vital of his volumes. The gayety of youth bubbles and effervesces in those magic pages, defying time to do its worst. The critic may charge the later Irving with many and heavy shortcomings, but the romantic smoke-clouds that ascend from Wouter Van Twiller's pipe cannot be dissipated by the winds of criticism. (p. 169)

> *Vernon Louis Parrington, in an excerpt from his "Two Knickerbocker Romantics," in his* Main Currents in American Thought, an Interpretation of American Literature from the Beginnings to 1920: The Romantic Revolution in America, 1800-1860, *Vol. 2 (copyright 1927 by Harcourt Brace Jovanovich, Inc.; copyright 1955 by Vernon L. Parrington, Jr., Louise P. Tucker, Elizabeth P. Thomas; reprinted by permission of the publisher), Harcourt, 1930 (and reprinted in* A Century of Commentary on the Works of Washington Irving: 1860-1974, *edited by Andrew B. Myers, Sleepy Hollow Restorations, 1976, pp. 159-60).**

HENRY SEIDEL CANBY (essay date 1931)

Irving's reputation is the remarkable achievement of a style that sometimes rests upon little else than its own suavity. (p. 70)

[Irving] was not a man of letters who wrote history, he was a chronicler-historian who wrote like a man of letters. He was not creative, a fact that has been obscured by his successful use of legend and anecdote. He was more dependent upon his style than his famous predecessors, to whom he gladly admitted his debt, because the congenial task he chose for himself was to illumine history, myth, and character that appealed to him, by romance and wit gracefully expressed. In his authentic history—of Columbus and his companions, of Granada, of George Washington—he merely adds color to an assemblage of facts, which he brings together in a skilful narrative order without the slightest evidence of a trained historian's power of criticism and interpretation. Myth, anecdote, and picturesque historical incident he suffuses with his own romantic sentiment or with ironic humor, according to the subject and his mood, and with real imagination builds into charming edifices of style. The Knickerbocker **"History,"** **"The Alhambra,"** and **"Rip Van Winkle"** are masterpieces of this kind. Real life he sometimes quite literally transcribed, as in the **"Tour on the Prairies,"** sometimes suffused with sentiment and handled freely as in the feudal scenes of **"Bracebridge Hall."** When he tells stories of contemporary life, as in **"The Wife"** and that one-time favorite, **"The Broken Heart"** in **"The Sketch Book,"** he is an arrant sentimentalist and conventional also, with no compensation for his lachrymosity except the unfailing suavity of his style.

To sum up, with no real power of character analysis, with no originality of thought, with no sense either of horror or pathos (his battles are usually humorous), quite immune to the great ideas sweeping through his world, Washington Irving relied upon a humorous, romantic temperament that mirrored with a difference the scenes that attracted such a mind—and upon a style. He was right, and he knew that he was right. (pp. 71-2)

It was only when his style became as easy as penmanship that Irving attempted long books—and they were formal, second-hand histories.

These histories, which Irving attempted in the hope that large, solid books would bring him in a steady income, did little for his reputation, which rests as he foresaw upon his miniatures and vignettes. . . . The enormous achievements of his elder contemporaries, Jefferson and Hamilton, are at the very base of American life, political, social, economic, but who reads their works? And who ever read **"Rip"** without pleasure, or missed a word! It is as fresh as the day it was written, and as indisputably a work of genius as it is certainly in thought and subject the "bagatelle" that Irving called it. **"The Alhambra"** deserves the word "charming" as richly as the essays of Lamb. I can think of few books of prose that in this attribute excel it. If Irving is often *vox et præterea nihil,* and never more sonorous in the literary orchestra than his own favorite flute, yet in the earthy paradise of Sleepy Hollow, or the martial romance of the Moors, or the humors of Bracebridge Hall, he is a master of lovely rhythm. If his style gilds fustian, it can ornament the occasional nuggets of gold, and if it is monotonous, it is the monotony of fair weather. (p. 73)

Style always has its secret, and the secret of Irving's suavity is well hidden in that native environment which through all his years abroad he professed to love, and did love, best. The student of sources has had his say, and it has not been enough. Irving is more than Goldsmith served cold, and far more than German romanticism brought overseas. He owes much to Goldsmith, but he is not cold. He is a romantic, but very definitely not German. (p. 74)

[It was] no blighted heart but something much more common that made Irving a ready victim of the fashionable melancholy of the period and touched with the grace of sincerity the gentle sadness of his prose. It is clear that he was homesick, in the literal sense of the word. In all his books there is a longing for stability, for ease in surroundings to his taste, and for a home, which he never possessed until well into middle age. He makes the Alhambra domestic, and has drawn the classic picture of home life in the English country. Yet both ambitious poverty and the exigencies of his career compelled him to wander, and to wander single. . . . [The] pathos, the loneliness, the love, the tragedy in Irving's books reflect the emotions of a wandering bachelor deprived of an ideal domesticity, which he first dared not attempt lest something he valued more should be lost, then could not find. (p. 76)

If any outside influence is to account for Washington Irving's really remarkable success with only a humorous temperament and a sensitive soul to go on, then that influence will be found in American Federalism. For Irving, so far as his instrument permitted, represented the Federalist spirit in American literature, and this relationship is the key to much that is otherwise puzzling in a man at the same time so gentle and so famous. Not that Irving was ever interested in politics. He loathed them consistently through a long life in which he owed more to politics than most men. . . .

And yet, if Federalism as an ideal of living was to find literary expression, it was bound in that age of the romantic movement to have its Irving. For Federalism was essentially an aristocratic ideal struggling to adapt itself to the conditions of a republic and the equalities of a new country. (p. 77)

Irving was not interested in the political aims of either [the Republican or Federalist parties]. In his letters and occasional writings he calls a plague on both their houses every time an election stirs the muddy minds of the populace. . . . [A] young wit and beau, pretending to read law in a worldly little seaport where polite affiliations were almost as much European as American, could not be expected to sympathize either with ward politics, or with the moral intensities of a Dwight who believed that God had given America into the government of respectable church members, or with that Virginia idealism which proposed to erect a newfangled state utterly different from anything in the romances of Sir Walter Scott. In the England of Coleridge, Shelley, Byron, Wordsworth—to cite literary names merely—he was to see nothing but the picturesque, and the relics of Moorish Spain were to mean far more to him than Germany in its golden age. The ideas, great and small, of the formative period of the United States naturally passed over his head.

Indeed, when he does defend the American system he is a little absurd. . . . It was not merely old age that led him to end the **"Life of Washington"** at the moment when a heroic life of glory became involved in questions of domestic politics and a great career was used by partisans for their not very creditable purposes. Politics, for Irving, were New York politics, which meant a squabble between the ins and the outs.

And yet Irving, in spite of his indifference to party, was more Federalist than the Federalists, more Federalist essentially than the Hartford wits, who adumbrated in their vast poems a government by moral didacticism that was New Englandism rather than aristocracy. He was keenly aware of the deeper struggle of which the brawls of politicians and the ideology of statesmen were only symptoms. . . . **"Salmagundi,"** like the "Spectator," and still more curiously like the "columns" of modern New York papers, is an onslaught upon manners, an attempt to give detachment, gaiety, civility, to a sodden town. Diedrich Knickerbocker's **"History of New York"** in its purely Dutch aspects is a satire upon a thoroughly bourgeois civilization, in its attacks upon the Yankees a satire on the ideals of traders and business men. . . . Half of Irving's heart is in **"Rip Van Winkle,"** where the picturesque Rip and his cronies, so full of humor and honest if stupid happiness, are set in contrast to the shabby pretentiousness of the village twenty years later. And the other half is in **"Bracebridge Hall"** and **"The Alhambra,"** for in each is a life tinged with the melancholy of departing, yet rich in loyalty, solidity, and human worth instead of human rights. (pp. 78-81)

America of the early eighteen hundreds was alive in all its parts, perhaps more so than the standardized and accomplished America of the twentieth century. Pathetic, from this point of view, is the young Irving's illusion that he and the few like him could create and keep a milieu of taste in hustling young New York, but strong the pressure, far stronger than if he had lived in contemporary Europe, to do something, be something, that expressed his loves and his hates. . . . But what could he do that he wanted? The answer was to write, to write like an aristocrat, like a gentleman, like a Federalist.

For Federalism . . . was much more than a political and economic system. It was a government by the best, the ideal to which all philosophic statesmen have aspired. It was, more specifically, an aristocracy, not of birth or of privilege, but of achievement, with the entrance door always open but a censor of manners, of morals, of capability, at the threshold. (p. 82)

It was to this intangible spirit of Federalism that Irving owed allegiance, a spirit deeper than economic theory, deeper than the struggle for power, a spirit which outlived the party that professed to represent it, so that it is still possible to call a man or a book Federalist in the United States. Irving shared the Federalist respect for the tried, its distrust of the new, its hatred of the vulgar. . . . Irving's feeling for England was magnified by his love for English literature, which was the basis of his education. . . . [If] George Washington was an English country gentleman, with a difference, Irving was an English man of letters, with a difference, who turned in disgust from the sprawlings for food and water of the gigantic infant, his country, and in protest against the crude and new sought to write as elegantly as he could. Yearning for civilized urbanity in a continent designed to be great in quite another fashion, he perfected a style, and only then ceased to feel beaten, discouraged, and futile.

Irving as the arch-Federalist of American literature is much more interesting than Irving as a custodian of the romantic movement in America. . . . It is true that the romantic haze that still hangs over the noble estuary of the Hudson rose from his pen, and the romantic past of that least romantic of American cities, New York, is his contriving. True, too, that he made Europe picturesque for Americans. England was not picturesque to Richard Mather, or to Benjamin Franklin, but Irving imbued it with all that the rest of us have ever since felt of romantic veneration. Yet, although as a maker of glamour he was a pupil of Walter Scott, his inspiration was not all literary. He spoke for the nostalgia of the Federalists, for the decorum, the stability, of colonial days, for the richness of living of the mother country. . . . The best of all this, and very little of the worst, is in Irving. As a romantic among the greater romantics of Europe he is humble and usually derivative, but as an American and as a Federalist he speaks in his own right, and had a motive to speak well.

To read Irving's works again with these facts in mind is to form a new estimate of the man as a writer. When he was young and heady . . . there was more edge than sentiment in his romance. . . . It is only when the Dutch come to New Amsterdam that [the Knickerbocker "History"] takes life, and why? Because these stupid Dutch with their sluggish bourgeoisity, their absurd parodies of courage, the "happy equality" of their intellects, their lack of fire, energy, grace, are perfect symbols of that sodden materialism which Irving found ridiculous in others and hated for himself. In spite of its comforts, which he did not disdain, it was the very opposite of all qualities of romance. . . . Indeed, if the "History" is, as I believe, the meatiest of Irving's books, and excelled in style only by a few of the best of his later sketches, the reason is that never again did he have so much of his own observation, his own prejudice and rooted dislike, to add to the documents he drew upon. (pp. 83-6)

The Knickerbocker "History," erudite, polished, suave, antibourgeois, a satire upon the unromantic, an attack upon democracy, a challenge to all ideologues, pedants, moralists, fanatics, a lampoon on besotted commercialism, stands at the head of Federalist literature. (pp. 86-7)

His histories are admirable for style, but they are not literature, though often more literature than history. Indeed, Irving if he had lived in the twentieth century would have been a magazine writer, if not a columnist. . . . "The Sketch Book" is a miscellany, a travel book, sweetened to the taste of the times by romantic sugarplums, and rising to literature only when Irving was more Federalist than romanticist, or more story-teller and essayist than an adorner of sentiment by style.

There was of course some truth, and a good deal of insight, in the romanticizing of jolly old England that makes up so much of "The Sketch Book." And it is Irving, not Dickens, who is chiefly responsible for the glamour that ever since his day has hung about Christmas in the old hall, the stagecoach, the waits, the loyal tenantry, and all the paraphernalia of merry England. It is only romantic truth, as can readily be ascertained by reading in order from "The Sketch Book" and from the contemporary pages of Jane Austen. Nevertheless, the literary symbolism that he found for the picturesque as he saw it at Abbotsford and Newstead Abbey took such hold on his readers on both sides of the water that it became to them history, and is as vivid in the imagination of the American tourist as manor houses and crumbling castles to his eye. (pp. 87-8)

Without the two Dutch stories, however, "The Sketch Book" would not have worn so well. They are perfect examples of what Irving best loved to do, and naturally he did them well. "Rip Van Winkle" and "The Legend of Sleepy Hollow" are history of that legendary character which he fed upon—history that preserves, with little care for too minute reality, the memories of a period. . . . He himself, in "The Sketch Book," was Rip, gentle, pleasure-loving, inadaptable to the crudities of business and family support. He loved the rascal because he was as Irving might have been without brothers and friends. Dame Rip was the urge of hustling, unsubtle America that threatened to drive him away from the pleasant loafing that he loved into a mode of life he most philosophically disapproved of. The Catskills were those hills of romantic dreaming in which he wandered seeking the future—and the harsh disillusion of the bustling ugly village of twenty years afterward, where no one knew Rip, or wanted him, was no bad similitude of the future in those depressing years from 1816 to 1819 when the failure of his brother's business roused in his imagination the spectre of a return, *auctor ignotus*, to job-hunting in New York. No such symbolism, I suppose, was in Irving's consciousness, but he wrote these humorous idylls of picturesque living from his heart, and told them superbly in a prose so pure and harmonious as to speak of a master at his best. (pp. 88-9)

The sense for style in 1819-20 had not yet been sicklied by the welter of romanticism. Houses were still being built with that easy mastery of form and proportion which was the gift of the eighteenth century, and if the crisp outlines of English prose were blurring under the pen of a Walter Scott, and if the quaintness of Charles Lamb and the profuseness of De Quincey were beginning to be preferred to the cool clarity of Goldsmith, the conception of measure, harmony, restraint, was to last as long as good architecture. Indeed, it is perhaps not altogether a coincidence that Irving and good architecture died in the same decade in America. A delightful temperament, a pleasing play of sentiment and humor upon fortunate themes, and a triumph of style—this was the current estimate of "The Sketch Book." And it remains our estimate, except that the "sob stories," as they would be called in the modern vernacular, can no longer be regarded as fortunate.

The rest of Irving that really matters is implicit in the books I have already discussed. "The Alhambra," that romance of history mellowed in a style that is too pure and clear to permit of turgid extravagance, is of course another "Sketch Book," with the single theme of a lost and beautiful civilization. The earlier "Tales of a Traveller" are less admirable because, paradoxically, they are more original. Here Irving trusted too much to invention, and when he left legend and history and scenes that he knew by deep experience he fell almost invariably into mawkishness or into rhetorical display. Irving could write well on any theme, but rhetoric alone never turned a bad theme into literature. . . . "**A Tour of the Prairies,**" a work that deserves more reputation, was conceived as another "**Sketch Book,**" with included stories, and, like "**The Alhambra,**" with a single romantic theme—the march of the Rangers through the Indian country. But here Irving was too close to his subject. The Indian stories were not in his vein, the companions of his voyage did not project their shadows against historic backgrounds. . . . The material that Cooper found so rich was, for him, too thin. . . . He was, after all, a bookish writer, and the life he best interpreted was seen through books or under their influence. For the frontier he had no books with the flavor of history and hence no perspective. (pp. 89-91)

He did little to illumine American life and character although so much to enrich the American romantic imagination. He endowed the Hudson Valley with a past of legend and fable borrowed from the old world, but his Dutch are quite false, except as satire, his Yankees no more true than Yankee Doodle, his New Amsterdam a land of Cocaigne, which has bequeathed to posterity an idea that New Netherlands was the comic relief of colonial history.

He was not a great romantic, if Scott and Byron and Shelley be taken as models of romanticism. His gentle melancholy is more akin to Collins, and his humor to Goldsmith. In truth, where Irving was most eighteenth century in manner he has best survived, for his humor, his sense for the quaint, and his admirable feeling for proportion are more valuable than his attempts at pathos, terror, and grandeur in the style of the Teutonized romance of his own period. (p. 91)

The romanticist in Irving powerfully influenced a century of American writers ("**The Sketch Book**" was Longfellow's first school of literature) and usually to their hurt. They sucked sentiment from him and left the humor behind. But equally strong, and much more fortunate, has been the ideal of excellence set up by his style. Every American writer who has cherished the Federalist hope of urbanity and a counsel of perfection in the midst of democratic leveling may claim Irving as his spiritual father.

The textbooks call him the first ambassador of the new world to the old. That is to look at him through English eyes and is in fact a repetition of his first authentic praising, which came from abroad. . . . Call him rather an American Marco Polo, bringing home the romance of other countries, bearing their gifts of suavity, detachment, ease, and beauty to a raw country dependent upon its vulgar strength, stronger in brains than in manners, yet not devoid of a craving for civility. (p. 92)

Irving might well have written, for his own epitaph, that his writings belonged to the best school of English prose. . . . Great American themes, native to our development, were later to find both prose and verse; they are not in Irving. He was the type of that American, always commoner than Europe believes, whose nostalgia in the midst of prosperity, strenuosity, and progress is genuine and enduring. (p. 94)

He wrote like a European, but with the desires, the mentality, the outlook (already defined), of an American. His style is English, but made in America, for an American need.

And because in order to speak for Federalist America he learned to write with a vanishing grace and a suavity not again to be attained on this side of the Atlantic, his future is more secure than that of his successors in the historical vein. . . . Irving's lighter craft is well trimmed for the shifting gales of fame. He

had a style, he had a temperament, he had an eye for the humors, he was born a New Yorker, he could say, as New Englanders would not say, as Philadelphians and Virginians and Carolinians could not say effectively: While we create a new society in a new republic, let us not forget the mellowness of the age we have left behind us overseas, let us not forget the graces of life, let us not forget to be gentlemen. And if this was all he said, it was put admirably, in a time of need, and with apposite and succinct example. He made Spain glamorous, England picturesque, and his own land conscious of values not to be found in industry, morals, or politics. A slight achievement beside Wordsworth's, a modest ambition by comparison with Byron's, but enough. Not a great man, not even a great author, though a good chronicler, an excellent storyteller, a skilful essayist, an adept in romantic coloring; not in accord with progress in America but the most winning spokesman for the Federalist hope; a musician with few themes, and the minor ones the best, and many played perfectly—that is Washington Irving. (pp. 95-6)

> *Henry Seidel Canby, "Washington Irving," in his* Classic Americans: A Study of Eminent American Writers from Irving to Whitman, with an Introductory Survey of the Colonial Background of Our National Literature *(copyright 1931, 1958 by Henry Seidel Canby; reprinted by permission of the Literary Estate of Henry Seidel Canby), Harcourt, Brace & Company, 1931 (and reprinted by Russell & Russell Inc., 1959, pp. 67-96).*

STANLEY T. WILLIAMS (essay date 1935)

A shambling, windy book—such is the first impression [of *A History of New York*]. Yet a probing of its sources, contents, and fame kindles respect. One returns, for example, more and more thoughtfully to the reading of this young provincial. Unquestionably the most allusive of all American literary compositions written before 1825, *A History of New York* defines the current reading of cultivated Americans living in the little seaport in 1809. . . . Here, in many a gleeful passage, at least once in hidden verse, Irving played with that pseudo-epical manner which was to aid him in writing *The Conquest of Granada*. (p. 114)

It was love of history, after all, which carried Irving on to the end of this long book; history stuffed these notebooks with laborious excerpts. He was developing his passion for dusty tomes, the subject of an essay in *The Sketch Book,* and for dim manuscripts, which form the backgrounds for three of his works. He was also displaying that impatience of final, decisive investigation which was to restrict him as an antiquarian and hamper him as a scholar. He used secondary material and translations with numerous thefts and few ascriptions; his plagiarisms in *A History of New York* were unscrupulous, lighthearted. . . .

This huddling together of odds and ends shows Irving confused among his materials; these had mastered him. A comparison of his rough notes with his book discovers these to be often identical. He experimented little and polished less . . . , but dumped pell-mell his first drafts into the printer's copy. Assimilation and excision, in which he was later an adept, troubled him not at all; he felt, apparently, that he must use up all his stores. Repetition of ideas, and even of phrases, lies like a blight upon the pioneer version of *A History of New York*. (p. 115)

Whatever the edition, *A History of New York* is still amusing. Our sides do not ache with laughter, like Sir Walter Scott's; we do not wear out a copy, carrying it about, as did Dickens, or break down over it, as did Fanny Kemble and Bryant— incredible legend!—or enjoy it as did Byron and Coleridge. Yet the pipe plot, the ponderosities of William Kieft, the amours of Antony the Trumpeter among the corn-fed lasses of Connecticut, the duel between Jan Risingh, doughty Swede, and Peter Stuyvesant, more doughty Hollander, with his tragic fall upon a natural bovine cushion—these are less musty than some time-worn jests. Irving's laughter is at everything in the history of the proud city—explorers, aldermen, New England saints, close-fisted Yankees, avaricious Swedes, cock-fighting Virginians, soap-mad Dutch housewives, heavy colonial chroniclers, hidalgos, smoking, bundling, and the author himself. It is dangerous to speak of the book as a burlesque on a single theme; its satire is social, literary, and political, and it assails the foibles of humanity. It is not a rapier, like that used by one of Irving's teachers, Swift, but a true Dutch blunderbuss, shooting in all directions at those idiosyncrasies in men and women which so amused the Salmagundians.

This whole-hearted laughter is the life in the book, the gold in the alloy. Yet, if we read on, we may enjoy also Irving's use, in this early period of American literature, of our own legend and history. (p. 116)

Again and again, if we are familiar with Irving's life story, *The Sketch Book* rings true. Neither his nature nor his writings bear severe analysis, but his sorrows made his humble book more honest and more beautiful. His reading, his imaginative observation of old England, his ordinary, human struggles with life—these all confirmed him in his particular bent in writing. Out of these he built *The Sketch Book*. (p. 181)

Irving's workmanship in *The Sketch Book* is best in this skillful union of his reading and his own experience. The most graceful example of such technique is **"Stratford-on-Avon,"** in which he adorns every step of his actual walk through village, church, and meadow with Shakespearean allusion. (p. 182)

Test *The Sketch Book,* as it stands among the sets of English classics. Test it not, as did the first American critics, by single essays or groups of essays, nor, like the first English readers, by the two separate collections, but as one book, the first serious writing of Washington Irving. It will then appear to be a miscellaneous and, especially, an uneven work. As literature, at least a half-dozen essays are worthless; twice that number bear the stigma of mediocrity. With its prolix prefaces and appendices, the book overflows, lacking form, into a delta, with sands of sentiment and pools of quiet thought. In these last Irving is persuasive, but sand predominates. . . .

To-day the reader turns, in *The Sketch Book,* to a few essays. These are different; they live on in the speech of men, in quotation and allusion, in painting and the drama, and in innumerable reprintings. However tepid, however archaic *The Sketch Book* as a whole, these few essays seem to have life. (p. 185)

In all are Irving's long, indolent sentences, with their select vocabulary and their perfect concatenation. In all is the tranquil manner which engaged the admiration of Poe; the felicity of phrase, whose attainment may be traced in the notebooks; and the clever turn of incident, as in the conclusion of **"Rip Van Winkle."**

In these, that bookishness so tiresome in **"Rural Funerals"** illumines, and the observations on English character so tedious

in **"John Bull,"** so puerile compared with, say, the penetration of Emerson in *English Traits,* are engaging and even wise. Though **"Westminster Abbey"** is but a postscript to a thousand homilies, but one more repetition of *omnibus mors,* one more overtone of *Urn-Burial,* the measured sentences depict reposefully the sanctuary's dark splendor and retell in not unworthy accents the story of man's glory and doom. (p. 186)

Mutability, indeed, the poet's strain—this is the motif of the six essays. In his five years in England this feeling overshadowed all others in Irving's mind; and in moments it found a not ignoble expression. Certainly the emotion of Rip Van Winkle, after his descent from the mountains, reflects the dejection, so unescapable in the notebooks, of the pathos of changes effected in absence. To state airily that Irving, depressed by his own isolation, was like the prodigal of the village, is to go too far. Yet symbolism is in the rôle; it was Irving's way of intimating his dismay in the face of this law of life. Even amid his good humor in the **"Boar's Head,"** fingering the japanned tobacco box and the "parcel-gilt" goblet, he brooded over the silence where once rang out Falstaff's laughter. . . .

The "dilapidations of time"! The phrase is everywhere in the journal, and now it reappears in *The Sketch Book.* Platitude, yet more than platitude! Where was it more devastating than in his own craft? (p. 187)

[Setting] and incident differ, but each essay sets free the same emotion. Sometimes this mood is casual, as in the ending of **"The Legend of Sleepy Hollow."** Near the decaying schoolhouse, the plowboy hears the melancholy hum of psalms from the spirit of Ichabod Crane. At other times, mutability is the essence of an essay, as in **"Westminster Abbey,"** with its peroration upon transitory fame. Yet, whether incidental or basic, this mood has won for a few essays in *The Sketch Book* a place in English literature. (p. 188)

The Sketch Book was robust compared with [*Bracebridge Hall,* a] bloodless assembly of lovers, mistresses, huntsmen, servants, and antiquarians idling in castles and forests. The penalty attached to Irving's plan as suggested by Moore was the thinnest of plots and the most trivial of subjects. (pp. 207-08)

For this reason *Bracebridge Hall* is to-day defunct. The sincere sentiment and the gamy humor of the best essays of *The Sketch Book* were swallowed up in what Irving himself was fond of calling black-letter dilettantism. His veneration for England had become effusive, watery. The repetitions were innumerable, including even Diedrich Knickerbocker himself. The shorter sketches were sometimes mere digests of Elizabethan passages; the quotations were long and trite; the moralizing on marriage was tedious. . . . (p. 208)

Bracebridge Hall, in brief, though not equal to *The Sketch Book,* defined still more sharply the nature of Irving's contribution in both writing and personality to literature and society. (p. 210)

[Next] to his miscellaneous writings, *Tales of a Traveller* is perhaps the most slovenly of all Irving's books. Each of the four parts has faults unpardonable to-day. Both the ghost stories and the robber tales, designed for a public in love with German romantics and Gothic prestidigitators, are obsolete, as dead as the fashions which begot them. In Parts I and III we yawn over the machinery of haunted *châteaux,* sinister storms, mysterious footsteps, and hidden panels. Spirits sigh in the darkness; portraits wink; furniture dances; and brooding, sensitive heroes woo melancholy maidens—in vain.

Indeed, the strength and weakness in Irving's treatment of the supernatural is that he is partly satiric; he loves to end a wild tale with a good-humored chuckle. But *Tales of a Traveller* lacks the deft touch of "**Rip Van Winkle.**" Thus we can never read these stories as we pore over the serious narratives of Charles Brockden Brown, with possibly a smile at their absurdity but with respect for Brown's sincere rendering of the Gothic tradition; nor are they effective as satire. Irving's success has depended rather, as in "**The Spectre Bridegroom**" or "**The Legend of Sleepy Hollow,**" upon the naturalness of his laughter at the end. In these two tales, when his good sense normalizes his supernatural fancies, his mirth is convincing. But in *Tales of a Traveller* it is hollow. Moreover, his hasty composition affected the quality of these historiettes. The Van Tassels and even the Katzenellenbogens are persons; but the Marquis and Gottfried Wolfgang, the German student, are less than moonshine. The pranks of Sir Herman Von Starkenfaust and Brom Bones still amuse; but the sleepless night of the Bold Dragoon is merely dull. The tales are too brief, too wanting in substance to provoke either an honest shudder or an honest smile. "**The Story of the Young Italian,**" the longest, most solemn, most frequently translated of all the stories, is a tedious study in exaggerated sensibility. Most of all, in both these groups of tales, is lacking that indefinable something, that mood of repose, which remains with us after reading "**Rip Van Winkle.**" These are bagatelles. (pp. 274-75)

> Stanley T. Williams, in his The Life of Washington Irving, Vol. I (copyright, 1935, by Oxford University Press, Inc.; copyright renewed 1963 by Charles R. Williams; reprinted by permission of the Estate of Stanley T. Williams), Oxford University Press, New York, 1935 (and reprinted by Octagon Books, 1971, 501 p.)

EUDORA WELTY   (essay date 1944)

[*The Western Journals of Washington Irving*] is charmingly put together. . . . There are maps and reproductions of Irving's casual and fluent pencil sketches, and a sample chapter from the "**Tour on the Prairies**" resulting from the notes, for comparison's sake, rounding out the book in a satisfying and scholarly manner.

That Irving spent his days in delight is evident everywhere. He seemed to meet new things, new people, the excitements and pleasures of a strange life with an emotion somewhere justly between intoxication and amusement, between curiosity and pleasant objectivity. The notes are set down with an unselfconsciousness that is still elegant. Their directness and spontaneity have the charm which Irving himself would probably shrink to consider achieved until his writing was "finished". . . .

Chances are, such delicacy seldom went West. The writing that was to spring out of the West would never be like this, and Irving's work is unique in Western annals because it is not robust nor rambunctious nor raw; there is not any smartness or swaggering in any word of Irving's writing any more than there was in any bone of his body.

Perhaps the most appealing thing about Irving here is his marvelous eye for detail—that dateless quality. . . . The notes are generally pictorial, often beautiful—he remarks ahead the "blue lines of untrodden country." He is swift to compose a whole little landscape; then fill it with action. . . .

These word-pictures, set down in their immediacy, make valuable records of their time. They prove that Irving was a good reporter. Especially, he was fascinated by Indians, as he always was by the romantic and legendary in American life which related it to the Old World. . . .

He was equally meticulous to enter little bits of Indian legends when he ran across them: "An old squaw left alone when her party had gone hunting prayed the Great Spirit to make something to amuse her—he made the mosquito." But there is marked absence of any of our own Western tall tales in this book, samples of our wild humor or ways of talking. . . .

He remained ever the detached gentleman and observer, seeing the pageant through urban eyes. When the Western scene threatened vulgarity, he suddenly saw it romantically, instead. . . .

Irving does not consciously condescend—and is a great defender, of course, of the Indians—but he does refer to the guides and such in the party as "servants" and the Frenchman Antoine as "the half-breed," and there is a quiet impression that everybody else waited on Mr. Irving. There is appraisal without rapport.

The West was a curiosity; Irving was the visiting New Yorker. He rather expected to find things romantic, and he did: "Fires lit in dell—looks like a robbers' retreat." He enjoyed himself. He never did learn to spell "prairie," though.

> Eudora Welty, "Skies without a Cloud," in The New York Times Book Review (© 1944 by The New York Times Company; reprinted by permission), December 24, 1944, p. 3.

GEORGE SNELL   (essay date 1947)

Irving exerted a marked influence on other American writers of his time, some of whom, greater than himself, in turn handed on the peculiar qualities first prefigured in his writing. For this reason it is quite possible to say that Irving unconsciously shaped a principal current in American fiction, whatever may be the relative unimportance of his own work.

Irving's own derivations are fairly explicit. That he was a passionate Anglophile has been repeatedly pointed out, and indeed he admitted it. (p. 105)

For Irving the appeal of the "old home" was entirely romantic. He sought that established traditionalism which, he thought, alone provided the requisite backdrop for true literature. . . . But however romantic Irving may have been in his original aspirations toward Europe, he managed to set down a not unrealistic picture of it. Some of the best pages of the *Sketch Book* and *Bracebridge Hall* are precisely those in which romantic predisposition dissipates and he tells of things as he actually saw them. If he had done so oftener, the books would have been better; but it is impossible to doubt that his intention was realistic, if his disposition was incorrigibly romantic. (p. 106)

It is generally thought that the *Sketch Book* is the ultimate expression of Irving's romanticism; but actually this book shows how far Irving had gone along the road to a quasi-realism, an attenuated realism that found more artistic expression in the work of Hawthorne. What he was attempting, he says, was a sketch of scenes and manners similar to the work in a different medium by his friend Leslie, whose closely worked Dutch miniatures were so popular. Geoffrey Crayon was to paint his times in words, mixing his colors as assiduously and working in details with the indefatigable patience of a water colorist painting a baroque interior.

Geoffrey Crayon's *feeling* toward his subject was unmitigatedly romantic. He was often deluded by surface appearances; he stood in awe of many commonplaces in English life; he venerated customs that, to an American and presumably a democrat, ought to have occasioned his censure. But Geoffrey Crayon *approached* his material with only a half-hearted romanticism. His eyes were on the central object, and he described what he saw, though his vision was impaired by the aura of supposed romance which surrounded all he saw. This pilgrim was more reverent than passionate. The interpretative faculty was usually absent, but when present, missed the logical interpretation. . . . On the other hand, when he was able to find a theme consonant with the nostalgic reverence informing all the English portions of the book (and drenching *Bracebridge Hall* to the drowning point), he rose to adequate expression. (pp. 107-08)

It is, however, with the American stories that we are principally concerned, since they represent Irving at his best. He actually spent much time among the country people of New York state; and when he drew upon his observation, and not upon romantic preconceptions or upon his reading, he was most successful both in delineating character and approaching that romantic realism which became a broad stream in American fiction after him. (pp. 108-09)

It must be admitted though that his studies yielded little in the way of psychological insight. They did produce a gallery of striking types seen exteriorly: Rip Van Winkle, his wife, Ichabod Crane, Brom Bones, Farmer Van Tassel and old Baron Katzenellenbogen. Ichabod Crane is the trusty forerunner of a myriad scapegraces in our literature; and not so much because we know anything about what went on in the poor pedagogue's psyche as because we know for a fact what he looked like and what happened to him. Irving saw clearly the external lineaments; but the mind's labyrinth and the heart's paradoxes were a closed book to him. Geoffrey Crayon painted what he saw; like the Dutch miniature colorists, he wished to portray nothing more. And it would be difficult to find, even in the work of those who succeeded Irving and widely extended his tendencies, more striking caricatures than those of Rip and Ichabod. (p. 109)

In Irving's happiest work he made the most of the juxtaposition of solid realism and tenuous myth. The telling effect of **"Sleepy Hollow," "Rip Van Winkle"** and **"The Spectre Bridegroom"** arises from the fact that the legendary is so firmly interwoven with earthy realism. Here again we see the foreshadowing of what might be better done by the hand of a Hawthorne. Acting on this principle, Irving soundly conceived his system of inducing a suspension of disbelief. **"Sleepy Hollow"** is firmly grounded in the everyday, and when the supernatural appears, it gains our whole acceptance. Whether this was Irving's conscious intention is questionable; but it was a wholly successful rule. Doubtless his ill-defined inclination toward realism tended to bring about the happy result; and, in fact, there is a nice correspondence between the technique of the Irving short story and the general philosophy of his composition which tempts one to emphasize it unduly.

Balzac enumerating the furnishings of a room, or Zola describing the death of a harlot, was not more circumspectly naturalistic than Irving when he set about to paint a scene. (p. 110)

On the whole, the *Sketch Book* proved to be enspiriting for diverse American writers. The effect was not immediately apparent, and it was probably a diffuse stimulation, arising more from Irving's manner than from his content. The gentlemanly essay, the Christmas book, the modest homily, were still to be popular for many years; but the *Sketch Book*'s chief influence upon the imagination of other writers was its style. . . . Poe, Hawthorne, Prescott, Longfellow and Holmes deferentially remarked the debt American literature owed to Irving, though Hawthorne alone according to internal evidence inherited to any striking degree his method and matter. As a young man shut up in his dark Salem chamber, Hawthorne studiously emulated the Irving style, and it is incredible that the peculiar charm of the mythlike and legendary in **"Rip Van Winkle"** and **"The Spectre Bridegroom"** did not enormously stimulate the author of "The Great Stone Face" and "Young Goodman Brown." (pp. 113-14)

The *Alhambra* has a sort of unity that even the *Sketch Book* lacked, achieved by the simple device of encompassing all the fantasy and observation within the walls of the great palace. On the other hand, there is a monotony, an unrelieved evenness of tone which, apart from the frequent sentimentalism, vitiates our interest in the work, as it lies outside the taste of our time. This latter criticism, the matter of temper, can of course be levied against the whole of Irving's work; but once we concede the conventions of his time and accept the limitations of early nineteenth-century American taste, it is quite possible to appreciate the excellences that first elevated Irving in critical esteem. . . .

Almost the only productions that have currency today . . . are the essays and stories in the *Sketch Book,* but if they did nothing more than bring to a higher degree of development the tale of the miraculous and adumbrate that successful turning toward England, the spiritual home of such an orphan of tradition as Henry James, they performed a vital service to our literature. (p. 116)

George Snell, "Washington Irving: A Revaluation," in his The Shapers of American Fiction: 1798-1947 *(reprinted by permission of the publisher, E. P. Dutton), E. P. Dutton & Co., Inc., 1947, pp. 105-16.*

DANIEL G. HOFFMAN (essay date 1953)

[In the York State valley of **"Legend of Sleepy Hollow"** Irving's Dutch braggart, Brom Bones,] concocts the perfect backwoodsman's revenge on the Yankee. This first statement of the theme is among the most memorable it has ever received in our literature; it is with us yet and ever has been. . . . (p. 432)

The rustic hero may be naive and honest, with only his common sense to help him make his way in the world. . . . [He] represents the American élan, the pioneer, the Natural Man rebelling against the burden of guilt of the ages. . . .

Who is his adversary? Perhaps an insufferable fop from the city to the East—traditions, culture, lineage, class distinctions always come from the East in American mythology: from New England, from Europe. Perhaps he is a shrewd, narrow-nosed Yankee peddler. No matter; in either form he stands for that ancient heritage of useless learning and inherited guilt against which the American, in each succeeding generation, must rebel.

Such are the roles in this ever-recurring fable of the American destiny. (p. 433)

But what of Ichabod Crane? Did the pumpkin kill him? Of course not! Our folk heroes never die. Wearing the magic cloak of metamorphosis, they stave off death forever by simply changing their occupations. The ungainly pedagogue is no more—long live the New York City lawyer! For that is what Ichabod becomes after he makes his way from Sleepy Hollow. And onward and upward he goes: from the bar into politics, from his office to the press, thence to the bench. Far be it from Washington Irving to analyze or criticize the great American myth; where he finds a mythology of humor, he improves it on its own grounds. Responding instinctively to his fabulous materials, he makes Ichabod unforgettable in a stunning caricature. Brom, who is much more like life, is not so memorable, even though Americans always love a winner.

Yet Ichabod is not ultimately the loser in this legend. All he has lost is a farm girl's love and a measure of self-respect; the former was no real passion, the latter can be repaired. Ichabod Crane is a sorry symbol of learning, of culture, of sophistication, of a decayed religious faith, of an outworn order in the world. His very name suggests decrepitude: "And she named him Ichabod, saying, The glory is departed from Israel" (I Sam.iv.21). But Ichabod Crane is no Israelite; although an anachronism in all other respects, he is yet an American. And therefore he is immortal. (pp. 433-34)

Ichabod also knew two emotions, and two only. His were fear, and ambition. He is not the loser, because he leads a full and prosperous life, experiencing to the brim the two emotions which give meaning to his existence: fear, in Sleepy Hollow, and ambition, in New York City. For it is the same ambition which led him to court Katrina Van Tassel that takes him later to the bar and the polls, to the editor's chair and the juror's bench. Ambition of this magnitude requires for its satisfaction a culture sufficiently complex to be capable of corruption. It cannot be gratified in the folk society of Sleepy Hollow Village, where the good people are as pure as the air.

Fear and ambition are Ichabod's, but not love. That is because Ichabod Crane is not wholly human. A sterile intellectual, his head aswim with worthless anachronisms, his heart set on material gain, Ichabod is gracelessly devoid of the natural human affections. He is the bumpkin's caricature of what life in the seat of a corrupt civilization can make of a man.

When one compares "The Legend of Sleepy Hollow" to the bulk of Irving's work it seems anomalous that he could have mustered the imaginative power to enrich us so greatly, for most of Irving's writing betrays a lack of creative energy, a paucity of invention. . . . *Bracebridge Hall, Tales of a Traveller,* most of *Wolfert's Roost* and *The Sketch Book* itself make tedious reading today. They show all too plainly Irving's faults: his dependence upon secondary sources, and the restricted range of emotional experience from which he was able to create fiction. But in the characters of Ichabod and Brom Bones, Irving found archetypal figures already half-created by the popular imagination. Among all of Irving's characters only Rip Van Winkle has as great a power to move us; and Rip, too, is what the highly developed but narrow gift of a storyteller whose milieu was the fabulous has made of a character from folklore. . . . Rip is indeed close to an aspect of the American national character—that yearning for escape from work and responsibility which is exemplified by a host of gadgets and the daydream dramas of contemporary popular culture. Irving's Knickerbocker Dutchmen were . . . remote caricatures resurrected from a distant past. But when Irving dramatized the homely comic figures he found in native American folk tra-

ditions, his Ichabod and Brom pass so readily into the reader's own imagination that they seem to be persons we have always known. "**The Legend of Sleepy Hollow**" sketches the conflict of cultures which the rest of our literature has adumbrated ever since. One could predict *that* from Irving's story; both Ichabod Crane and Brom Bones lived lustily ever after. They are rivals yet. (pp. 434-35)

> Daniel G. Hoffman, "Irving's Use of American Folklore in 'The Legend of Sleepy Hollow'," in PMLA, 68 (copyright © 1953 by the Modern Language Association of America; reprinted by permission of the Modern Language Association of America), Vol. LXVIII, No. 1, March, 1953, pp. 425-35.

STANLEY T. WILLIAMS   (essay date 1955)

If we forget, in reading *The Conquest of Granada,* the would-be historian and listen only to the romancer, we find at times his natural powers at their best, as in his account of Boabdil's return to captivity or of his farewell to Granada ("El último suspiro del moro") or of the final assault on the city ("El día de toma"). When Irving's prose flowed directly from his pleasure in an incident or character he wrote well. In particular, Boabdil, who on the monument in Tarrytown stands shoulder to shoulder with Diedrich Knickerbocker and Rip Van Winkle, comes to life in this book, at least to a kind of dream life. . . . Boabdil, like another Spanish hero in our fiction whom Irving would have understood, [Melville's] Benito Cereno, was unfit for rule, as Irving himself in some ways was unfit for the ways of men, even for the writing of history. Boabdil was a man after his own heart. He could delineate this type of human being. The Moorish king lives again as a hero of romance in this strange, composite book, *The Conquest of Granada.* (p. 42)

In some respects Boabdil is also the hero of *The Alhambra,* in which he reappears, amplified by Irving's supplementary studies in Luis del Mármol Carvajal. . . . [We] can hail *The Alhambra* as the most distinguished literary work on Spain written by an American before 1850. Behind it lay two of the most indelible experiences of Irving's life: his residence in the palace and his friendship with Fernán Caballero. . . . This autobiographical element brings Irving back again, in this sheaf of graceful essays and stories on Spain, to his old role, renounced since *Bracebridge Hall,* of the observer of picturesque ways of life. For this point of view his stay in the Alhambra with Mateo and Dolores was indispensable.

This intimate knowledge of the Spanish peasant was, unless we prefer the pretty fairy tales of princesses and buried gold, the charm of this new *Sketch Book.* (p. 43)

The Alhambra, in echoing the *artículo de costumbres,* not only linked the American with the European essay of manners but introduced into the beginnings of our literature across the Atlantic a note of exoticism. (p. 44)

Irving's seven years in Spain, as well as his several thousand pages of history and fiction inspired by this country, make his interpretation peculiar to himself. No other major American writer of the nineteenth century became through residence and use of materials so deeply identified with any one Continental nation. . . . In spite of Irving's ventures into scholarship his interpretation was essentially poetic. Without powers, like Bryant's or Longfellow's, to translate Spanish poetry, his adaptations of Moorish legends and ancient Spanish lore were, nevertheless, those of the poet. What Longfellow attempted in *Outre-Mer,* Irving achieved in *The Alhambra.* Master and disciple—for in regard to romantic Europe this was their relationship—complemented each other. (pp. 44-5)

Stanley T. Williams, "Washington Irving," in his The Spanish Background of American Literature, Vol. II (copyright, 1955, by Yale University Press), Yale University Press, 1955, pp. 3-45.

WILLIAM L. HEDGES (essay date 1965)

At nineteen Irving was calling himself "Jonathan Oldstyle"—not exactly the signature to a declaration of independence. In the folklore of the period "Jonathan" signified the unsophisticated, if not uncouth, American, jealous of the freedom he had recently won from John Bull. The irony of yoking him to an "Oldstyle" points to the precariousness in Irving's situation as a writer. Unwilling or unable in the nine epistolary essays that he published in his brother Peter's New York *Morning Chronicle* to present his comment on local manners, especially in the theater, in his own voice, he is nonetheless not entirely comfortable speaking as Oldstyle. The dilemma is that of a provincial writer pretending to urbanity. The reader—and perhaps the writer—cannot be sure whether the mimicry expresses respect or mockery, is an effort to see through adult eyes or to prolong and accentuate youth. (p. 17)

There ought to be a voice between that of Oldstyle and the countryman, one more suited to Irving, a plain, direct voice, affecting neither ornateness nor vulgarity. Indeed, a somewhat different environment might have induced him to give greater prominence to those qualities of vigor and directness which are often a part of his style, even though they may be toned down. In the backwoods, for instance, writing in his notebook, he could manage by a simplicity of imagery and diction to render experience starkly. But the social climate of New York was not conducive to the growth of a closemouthed and workmanlike prose. (pp. 28-9)

Used ironically, however, as when Oldstyle pretends to admire an inept or overly ornate decoration, or when used in tandem with blunt informality, [his flamboyant] style becomes a useful instrument for exposing the smallness and pretentiousness of a youthful culture. At the beginning of the nineteenth century the attempts of the fledgling literature of the United States to develop a soaring style tend to become tiresome, and it is with some relief that one turns to the relentless ridicule that distinguishes what was to be known as the "Knickerbocker" manner in the literature of New York. (p. 30)

It is fortunate that Irving, having started on the road to nonsense, does not turn back. In the end he reduces Oldstyle to utter absurdity. Thus the hilarious ninth letter serves as a rousing finale to a divertimento whose central theme has become, perhaps inadvertently, growing confusion. Here the comedy of manners almost breaks up into slapstick. (p. 32)

[Irving's] *Notes and Journal of Travel in Europe, 1804-05* often reveal little more than the delight of a young man on an extended vacation, but the trip as a whole is best viewed as part of an early American quest for style. It is here that one sees most clearly Irving's encounter with ideas and attitudes that were standard equipment for the cultivated man of his day. (p. 34)

Yet, lacking the assurance and sophistication of the young English gentleman in the eighteenth century on the Grand Tour, he did not play the dilettante particularly well. His immediate reactions to what he saw were larded over with recollections of, or references to, books he had read or paintings he had seen. Often, his comments echo one or another of the eighteenth-century guidebooks he used. (p. 35)

Inevitably, his own descriptions of Italian scenes struggled for picturesque effects, sometimes verging on the sublime.

The picturesque was an acquired taste. For all his fondness for picturesque views, Irving sensed distortions in them, fearing that they were not quite real. (p. 40)

Irving's picturesque feeling for ruins came close to being a concept, the one intellectual frame he had to put around his picture of the world. His sense of inevitable decay was to be his substitute for a theory of history or a philosophy. As he stood between the conflicting claims of past and present, it suited his needs, though it gave no permanent satisfaction. It explained everything and nothing—explained everything by reducing it to nothing. Its annoying aspect, for an American, was that it made one picture ruins in the path of progress. But this was, as we shall see in a later chapter, an American writer's cramp that did not wear off easily. When Irving a few years later packed eleven pages of a commonplace book with extracts from the *Consolations* of Boethius, he was doing more than preparing to mock the cult of sensibility in *Knickerbocker*. The old story of the transience of human existence, the vanity of earthly endeavor, the corruptibility of virtue, the "mutability" of fortune, and the consequent "anxiety" attendant upon prosperity was one that never ceased to move him. (pp. 42-3)

First and last, *Salmagundi* manifests a great deal of interest in travelers and traveling. Much of the concern, complementing the anticockneyism, consists of resentment at the pompous ignorance and flagrant misrepresentations of American life in the works of foreign travelers. (p. 52)

But often *Salmagundi*'s satire is directed as much at "travelmongers" in general. Moreover, in the very act of satirizing foreign travelers for trying to read European meanings into America, the magazine is not above exposing the barrenness of certain native scenes and institutions. (p. 53)

To accept *Salmagundi* with all its contradictions is to respond to the cultural frustration which it represents and which is its abiding significance. (p. 56)

The key to Irving's achievement in the *History of New York* is the ingenious device of Diedrich Knickerbocker, who manages to sound at once like Sterne's first person narrators, and Fielding's cultivated omniscience going berserk in mazes of irony. Knickerbocker is totally eccentric and solitary, even more "extravagant" (in the root sense) than Tristram Shandy, Yorick, or the bachelors in *Salmagundi*. He is, from the Addisonian point of view, a candidate for Bedlam, though quite harmless and capable of serious insight and reflection in the midst of his grossest misunderstandings. At one moment he is guilty of utterances so absurd that we must conclude that they express exactly the opposite of Irving's view; at the next, he is ready with opinions that simply cannot be taken ironically. (p. 65)

Knickerbocker longs for greatness but seems afraid of the responsibilities that greatness entails. He would have a civilized society but shrinks from the conflicts through which decent institutions are established and maintained. As he reveals the compulsion of some of his characters to monumentalize themselves for eternity, on occasion the impotence behind his conscious longing for greatness almost turns to rage. Whether he applauds or secretly abhors what he describes we cannot always be sure: his almost frantic tone at times might imply either. (pp. 67-8)

Knickerbocker thus sometimes shows a deep antipathy to history, and the interinvolvement of his attraction to, and fear of, memorable historical achievement is a central irony of the book. (p. 68)

Knickerbocker retains his good humor only at the expense of ignoring, for all his desire to be logical, his ultimate inconsistencies. (p. 69)

The *History of New York* consistently ridicules the possibility of acquiring certain or reliable knowledge. (p. 72)

Trying desperately to inflate his narrative and turn history into epic, Knickerbocker only betrays himself by consciously or unconsciously revealing to the reader his actual sense of the meagerness of the present he inhabits and the past he has inherited. The praises he intends to sing keep turning in his mouth to ridicule or loathing. (p. 76)

[The] total effect of the *Knickerbocker History* is to emphasize the relativity of judgment to point of view and to suggest that a position can always be found from which even the greatest achievements will appear small. (p. 78)

The nonsense of *Salmagundi* and *Knickerbocker* tended to reduce the world to words, but one went on using words, trying to compose fiction and find order in the records of the past. What Irving needed was a theory of imagination or Transcendental Reason. What he had was a flair for style and a sense of the picturesque. A thoroughgoing organicism might have stabilized the flux of impressions to which his experience seemed reduced. But for those unable to reach a clear intuition of an infinite coherence of parts and parcels within a single Whole, there was apt to be more mutability than stability, and a groping or rioting about in what often seemed merely private associations. (p. 107)

After reducing history almost to blank enigma in *Knickerbocker,* [Irving] began to take the past more seriously, yet his change of attitude hardly amounted to a new conception. The Irving of *The Sketch Book* was simply less averse to enjoying in public his subjective responses to relics of the past—even when he suspected the irrelevancy of his emotions or the inaccuracy, or perhaps unverifiability, of his ideas. If the world seemed to leave him nothing but the freedom of his own associations, he had at least to try to take satisfaction in them. (p. 108)

The character of Irving's best work was always "superficial"—a word used here not in a necessarily derogatory, but in a simpler denotative, sense. Generally, he assumed that he could not have knowledge (which Knickerbockerism had seen only as opinion anyway) of the "inside" of experience unless he started with observations on the surface. (p. 117)

More than many writers', his mind worked on associative or assimilative principles. He looked for resemblances even when he could not be sure what to do with them. (p. 118)

His sense of the fitness of folklore, tradition, and terrain for one another is another outgrowth of the same habit of mind. (p. 119)

[The] fact that Irving used a pseudonym [for *The Sketch Book*] suggests a desire for a kind of unity in the miscellany. A sense of coherence emerges in patterns of imagery functioning in relation to the central figure of Crayon, the shy spectator who

wishes he had close friends or relatives, the aging bachelor who would half like to be married, the American in England searching for a past, the traveler trying to get to something like home. Crayon is a prompter of good feeling among others who finds it impossible to get himself finally settled. He serves as go-between for temporarily estranged husbands and wives, for American readers and British writers; he mediates between present and past; he sympathizes with broken hearts and mourns at funerals in country churchyards. Yet the morbid implications in his own sentimentality frighten him. His interest in the past often seems to him a fascination with gradual decay. His sympathy with the losses of others sometimes masks but thinly an awareness of something he has lost, or perhaps never had. He is haunted by the image of the dark, isolated, and forgotten person he may turn into.

One has to admit Crayon's shortcomings. His avowed susceptibility to sentiment only in part excuses his sentimentality. And he ought to know that there are some inconsistencies not permitted even in a man who pretends to have no head for philosophy. Nevertheless, a cumulative impression develops in *The Sketch Book* which justifies its being read as a whole. There is a network of relationships among the various items in the miscellany that catches up again and again and lifts up out of the murk of the past, tentative, half-formed, anxious attitudes toward questions of national character, heritage, and culture. (pp. 129-30)

[The sense of mutability] is everything in *The Sketch Book.* If it is not old books or buildings, it is old men who, even though he responds to them whimsically, haunt Crayon. (p. 134)

Again and again Irving affirms the values of hearth and home, yet he seems to have doubts and questions about the family that, as a bachelor, he can't dispel or answer completely. This may be in part why the specter of economic failure (and thus of success) plagues *The Sketch Book.* . . .

It is in "**Rip Van Winkle,**" however, for all its humor, that the questioning becomes most intense. "If left to himself," Rip Van Winkle "would have whistled life away in perfect contentment; but his wife kept continually dinning in his ears about his idleness, his carelessness, and the ruin he was bringing on his family." Rip's wife is the spirit of industry, a *Poor Richard's Almanac* made flesh, a combination of puritan conscience and Protestant ethic. (p. 137)

If in the end the story remains comic rather than tragic, it is because Rip is able to parlay his loss into a positive asset, to make a success of inadequacy or failure. He acquires a new identity as a result of having a tale to tell. (p. 140)

There is not much of Knickerbocker in the tone of these stories. "**Rip**" may contain a few phrases that recall the eccentricities of the old historian, but the essential quality of Knickerbocker, the rather desperate need to inflate limp subjects with a flourish of rhetoric, is quite lacking. It is, in effect, Geoffrey Crayon who is telling the stories, that is, an American who is in England and who has aspirations to an English style of gentility but who nevertheless has fond recollections of settings which he frequented as a boy and a young man. (p. 141)

Irving's general tendency is to avoid the detailed and relatively objective descriptions of people and places in which someone like Mary Russell Mitford specialized, and instead to create a kind of fiction in which something that happens or does not happen to Crayon is of primary concern, in which his responses to people and places are as important or more important than the people and places are in themselves. (p. 146)

The essential characteristic of Irving's stories is that they are told by a man who is not altogether sure of himself. Hence they take the form of legends, of hearsay; they are stories picked up at second or third hand, not eyewitness accounts. The disavowal of responsibility carries over into the more or less whimsical tone that persists in most of Irving's fiction. (p. 161)

Irving's is a fiction of dreams, fantasies, symbolic projections; it is heavily loaded with imagery functioning as metaphor. Its heroes or protagonists tend to be variations of, or foils to, the personality of the Crayonesque observer or the author behind the story. It alternately sympathizes with, laughs at, and turns in fear from the stranger, the homeless or orphaned young man, the provincial abroad, the recluse, the eccentric scholar, the dreamer, the enthusiast, and the teller of tales. Whether these heroes come to good or bad ends, are lucky or unlucky, succeed or fail, come home or get lost seems to depend largely on the precise shade of Crayon that they have in them. (pp. 161-62)

The beginning of *Bracebridge Hall* . . . shows an Irving highly conscious of the mask he had created for himself in *The Sketch Book*. (p. 164)

[It] was thought to be a falling-off from its predecessor. One disappointment is the diminution of the personal, wistful quality, a consequence of Irving's not utilizing fully the Crayonesque viewpoint. The emphasis is again on place, landscape, environment, atmosphere, manners, customs. But, whereas the Christmas sketches, which started with Geoffrey Crayon on the road and stopping over at random inns, had rescued him from solitude and found him a temporary home, *Bracebridge* largely dispenses with this narrative prop. (p. 165)

The sentimentality, the heavy emphasis on home and harmony that one might have expected after *The Sketch Book,* on the whole fails to materialize in *Bracebridge.* Irving does provide a few outright sops for sentimental readers, including two of the four interpolated tales in the book, the pathetic "**Annette Delarbre**" and "**The Student of Salamanca**," a dreadful gothic melodrama. But for the most part contemporary readers had to satisfy their appetite for sentiment by ignoring, or discounting the full import of, the quasi-satirical humor that surrounds all the flocking about the nest. . . . (p. 171)

Without quite realizing it, Irving in *Bracebridge Hall* joins in that prolonged American search for a middle-class hero that reaches fruition in Howells and James. It is a complicated quest, and when the hero finally evolves, he comes trailing clouded origins behind him, compounding qualities that in the beginning belonged to stations both lower and higher than his own. He is asked to do the nearly impossible—which is perhaps what makes him heroic—to be middle class without being morally middlebrow, to be neither pure farmer nor pure bourgeois, but somehow a combination of rural innocence and urban know-how, to synthesize the apparently opposed but nonetheless essential components often fictionalized in "nature's nobleman" and the "good squire." *Bracebridge Hall* does not advance American literature very far in this quest. But it does refuse, finally, to take the landed gentry seriously as the guardians and custodians of the social welfare. (pp. 179-80)

Tales of a Traveller is the work of a short-story writer who had not quite discovered his form. . . . Consciously Irving was attempting to write, not short stories, but a series of relatively short narratives that could somehow be combined into a book. He thought of himself as a bookman, not as a magazine hack. (p. 194)

Irving seldom managed to achieve a structural unity or compactness comparable to Poe's, but he understood the importance of tonal unity or consistency. By experimenting with pseudonyms and narratives-within-narratives he largely avoided those disconcerting shifts back and forth between high seriousness and comic relief that mar so much nineteenth-century fiction presented under the aspect of omniscience. The shifts are disconcerting because they presuppose as narrator a being who may laugh when he should be moved to tears, or vice versa. But Irving is apt to modulate by changing narrators: the new voice justifies the change in tone. . . . Furthermore Irving's efforts to establish a relationship between story and narrator edge toward a conception of fiction as the revelation of character. By emphasizing the telling as much as the novelty or surprise which the popular audience demanded, he, like Poe, was able to bring out connections between action and character, gesture and motive, spectacle and response. (pp. 204-05)

Columbus is—as much as any American novel—a romance. It makes the career of the discoverer of America a fabulous quasi-allegorical quest. It sees the New World as a land of wonder and enchantment, where nature contrives effects with bewildering lavishness. In one sense the newness turns out to be an illusion, part of the enchantment. Irving, however, remains unsure of the values of the ordeal of innocence to which he subjects his early American hero. (p. 250)

The *Conquest of Granada* begins as a joke. Irving pretends to be presenting parts of an old chronicle compiled by Fray Agapida. . . .

But to go from the book to the sources is to be surprised by its substantial reliability—that is, if one has assumed that when an author bothers to invent a chronicler he may as well invent the chronicle to go with him. (p. 251)

Through Agapida, Irving simply excuses himself from having to take infinite pains. The pen name of an historian frees him from the pretense of being an impartial scientific scrutinizer and enables him to tell the story in whichever way it sounds best, without having to worry about refined criteria for testing the reliability of evidence. . . . The book, however, is not a mock-history like *Knickerbocker*. Agapida is mildly amusing, but although Irving is still poking fun at historians, he is trying to take fiction fairly seriously.

In the long run one regrets the lack of historical detail. The recurrence of disaster tends to wear the book down. (pp. 252-53)

Shortly after completing the *Conquest,* he was on the road through the mountains to Granada, a sort of Quixote, as he pictures himself in *The Alhambra,* looking for adventures. . . . In Irving's mind the trip became a kind of flight from time, his personal quest for a terrestrial paradise, doomed, however (as he knew in advance), to failure. For the Alhambra proved to be only one more inn. . . . (p. 263)

His imagination seems to transform landscapes and interiors into settings for romances and Arabian tales. Transports of joy lift him out of the present and carry him back into a timeless fictitious past, although he likes to think that he is only playing with illusions, temporarily keeping the everyday world at a safe distance. He still has one eye on a present which lives in the shadow of the past he now inhabits. . . . (pp. 263-64)

For Irving there was no rebirth of creative power in the withdrawal to the Alhambra, no imaginative rejuvenation. He left the Moorish paradise, at best a man with much of his youth and vigor behind him, a man to whom time now seemed to make less difference, who was becoming more content or resigned to seeing it pass, a man satisfied, like Van Winkle, to tell charming but inconsequential stories. The final version of *The Alhambra* suggests that there had been a kind of death; the procession that escorts Irving from the palace, past his own last sigh and into an exile like Boabdil's, is almost a funeral. . . . (pp. 265-66)

The Alhambra of 1850 is a better book than the original because it is unified around the author's often poignant identification with Boabdil. . . . A melancholy sense of loss, it is true, does dominate the first third of the 1832 text, but thereafter an unevenness of tone becomes a distraction. A breezy comic element figures more prominently in the style than it is allowed to in the final version, where changes of phrasing have been made and additional material has tipped the balance in another direction. It is in the 1850 version, especially as a result of two new stories, the **"Grand Master of Alcantara"** and the **"Legend of the Enchanted Soldier,"** that one gets the stronger sense of Irving repeating his one basic story of loss and disillusionment. . . . In the end, in the final version, he seems too preoccupied with enshrining a memory, coating it over with a glossy prose, to attend to commonplace details. Imaginative escape from the mundane was the religion he had been flirting with all his life, the religion now fully tolerated in an increasingly sentimental age by an emotionally indulgent public, which, for all its surface convictions, had its own deep uneasinesses.

The sense of time had helped make his fiction. He had prized time enough to pay careful attention to recording its passage. His ability in the better stories and sketches to get the illusion of time right was part of an important development in the history of fiction. But in *The Alhambra,* even in the original version, the sense of inevitability tends to inundate time. The stories, one knows, are all going to be pretty much the same. Irving was no longer interested in lingering over them. (pp. 266-67)

> *William L. Hedges, in his* Washington Irving: An American Study, 1802-1832 *(copyright © 1965 by The Johns Hopkins Press), The Johns Hopkins University Press, 1965, 274 p.*

LEWIS LEARY   (essay date 1972)

[Washington Irving] was an author whom his countrymen could pridefully and safely accept as an exemplar of their conviction that Americans, in literature as well as in trade or in politics, were as good as anyone else.

Few recognized that that was precisely where Geoffrey Crayon failed them: he was as good as almost anyone else, but not to any degree better. He was courteous, kind, urbane, and cheerful. No intrusive thoughts penetrated the veneer of his polished prose. He was an observer whose carefully wrought sketches were lightened with humor and delicately colored with sentiment. . . . As he wrote of English villages and bygone English customs, of rural churches and deserted graveyards, or as he recalled traditional Christmas festivities—the roaring fire, the roasted pig, the good brown ale—he summoned nostalgic memories, even among American readers. His languishing backward glances caught fleetingly again what once had been, but

which in the onrushing nineteenth century could not be expected to return again.

But, though his gaze was retrospective, his touch was sure. He wrote admirably, and cautiously, well, surpassed by few men before his time or since. His sentences were smoothly polished, with exquisite care. Yet Geoffrey Crayon was as a writer without a subject—except as he found it in other men's books or in scenes which, catching his fancy, were deftly transcribed. His intention was placative, to soothe and smooth and gracefully narrate, to recall old times and moods of quiet reminiscence. . . . However deft his strokes, Geoffrey Crayon was more copyist than creator. (pp. 14-15)

Geoffrey Crayon's tranquil phrases provide an effectively traditional patina, which disguises—and not unattractively—the thin fragility of the vessel which holds them. More important than the scene is the mood which it calls forth, of serenity, of "classic sanctity." . . . Geoffrey Crayon's still waters have little depth. His still-life sketches contain significantly more stillness than life. His writing is clear, even to transparency, reflecting quivering trees, limpid waters, and rustic quietness, but undisturbed by the ruffling or ruggedness of thought. Picturesque, nostalgic, correct, and utterly acceptable, it has proved to be a fare quite too bland for many appetites.

But when the first installment of *The Sketch Book* appeared in New York in the spring of 1819, its popularity was guaranteed, not by the transatlantic voice of Geoffrey Crayon, but by the intrusion, as the last item in that small pamphlet, of a more resonant second voice, almost as if a last-minute afterthought. Speaking is the bluff and less verbally timorous old gentleman named Diedrich Knickerbocker. . . . (pp. 15-16)

For many [Diedrich Knickerbocker's *History of New York*] remains Irving's most successful book, the "only authentic history of the times that hath been or ever will be published." Fact is frolicsomely jumbled with fiction; dates are distorted, footnotes are often spurious, but it is a gay and mirth-filled book, written with abandon and assumed authority by a younger man who had not yet learned the efficacy of caution. (p. 16)

What is living and lively in the book are not the local references, the sly jibes at individuals, which made some of Irving's contemporaries so angry, any more than what is living and lively in *Gulliver's Travels* are the detailed contemporary references which students discover there. . . .

His laughter is directed at historians, explorers, and antiquarians; at plump and dumpling-like Dutch matrons and robust, red-cheeked Connecticut girls; at Yankee skinflints and parsons, cock-fighting Virginians, the cozy advantages of bundling, and—in luscious detail—the joys of overeating. (p. 17)

More often than not, the humor is broad, sometimes mirthfully vulgar, as when Knickerbocker speaks slyly of the tumbling skirts of dancing Dutch maidens. . . . Small wonder that his countrymen were disturbed when he compared a Dutch ship to a typical maiden of New York: "both full in the bows, with a pair of enormous cat-heads, a copper bottom, and a most prodigious poop." (p. 18)

Old Diedrich speaks a lusty and frolicsome language such as rarely had been heard in English before. He is native, colloquial, and direct. Better than any man before him, and better also than many who came later, he catches the swing and rhythm of everyday, rough-and-ready language. . . .

Diedrich knows about politicians and their talent for making jokes which do not quite come off. (p. 20)

And Diedrich Knickerbocker himself is a forward-looking man. Forty years before Charles Darwin, he speaks of men being descended from monkeys. . . . He irreverently suggests that liberty of speech is only another way of saying "gift of the gab."

Legend and language are created as Diedrich shapes from whatever comes to his nimble fingers a mirage of tradition, through which characters move in quixotic grandeur. Their noble intentions are made to seem absurd, though no less noble, because of the provincial background against which they suffer inevitable, and comic, defeat. (p. 21)

There was theme and scheme behind the "coarse caricature" of Diedrich Knickerbocker's burlesque *History*. . . .

But Irving cared not to recognize what he had done. When he revised the *History* a few years later, he cleansed it of much colloquial coarseness, and of caricature which might wound his countrymen or his own literary reputation. So intent did he seem on being liked as Geoffrey Crayon that he failed to realize that as Diedrich Knickerbocker he had written the first American book capable of outliving the man who made it. (p. 22)

When Diedrich Knickerbocker was resurrected later in *The Sketch Book* and other miscellanies, he was seldom allowed to speak so irrepressibly well again. Something more than style has kept Rip Van Winkle alive, to become, as Hart Crane once explained, our "guardian angel" as we journey through our past. He remains a kind of native conscience, amusing and accusing at the same time. As Irving gave local habitation to a myth, as old as any which has beguiled the mind of man . . . he added familiar elements of popular lore. . . . (pp. 22-3)

In Rip was created the symbol of the mythic American. . . . He is a carefree, overgrown child, incapable of understanding the world of adults, even that of his wife. He is "one of the boys," off for an evening of pleasure or a long day of hunting, released from responsibility. But he is a Lazarus also, come back to warn his countrymen, and a comic figure besides, whimsically an innocent, undisturbed at having slept his life away. His son is like him, and his grandson is another Rip, who will become an old Rip in his turn. (p. 23)

Almost all of Diedrich Knickerbocker's best-remembered tales . . . celebrate victory for the practical man, defeat for the dreamer—as if they were modest, but masochistic parables of Irving's own career. Men like Brom, who understand or defy superstition, knowing so well that visions are illusionary that they can use them to their own ends—these come out well. The exuberance of fancy, old Diedrich seems to say, must be replaced by common sense as one grows older; tales of goblins, or even burlesque of high adventure and romance like his *History,* are for children or childish men. What an ironic twinkle there may be in his eye when he tells readers in a postscript that even ungainly, visionary Ichabod Crane could succeed, when he left daydreaming, as Irving had not, and turned to law, which Irving as a younger man had spurned.

Diedrich is adept at broadly sketched native caricature, and he relishes sensuous delights. (pp. 24-5)

Even [the] later Diedrich Knickerbocker, taught by Geoffrey Crayon to be polite and cautious so that he could become popular, keeps his eyes open and speaks with simple verve which Irving managed nowhere else so well. It is little to be wondered at that he is not forgotten, and that his descendants multiply. . . . His name has come to signify more than baggy Dutch breeches; it describes a period in the history of native culture, and an attitude toward literature and life. And his literary sons and grandsons are legion, finding, as he found, in native idiosyncracy and native scene and native idiom sources for a native literature.

The ventriloquist Washington Irving did speak in two voices—perhaps in three, for another may be discovered in his Spanish tales. As Geoffrey Crayon he became most successful in his own time, for his pose seemed correct; he looked backward and spoke in accents which, because they echoed accents of the past, fell pleasantly, because familiarly, on the ears of his listeners. As Diedrich Knickerbocker he spoke a plainer language and explored subjects of the future, his head held irreverently high, his words echoing colloquial words of ordinary men. His humor was native, in the same comic spirit which motivated tall tales of the western frontiers, and which became serious, though none the less comic, when spoken by men like Mark Twain and William Faulkner. It is to the credit of Irving's contemporaries that, while they honored him as Geoffrey Crayon, who broke the literary embargo with England, they reacted to him most quickly, though not always with instant approval, when he spoke in the less politely modulated voice of Diedrich Knickerbocker. (p. 26)

Lewis Leary, "The Two Voices of Washington Irving," in From Irving to Steinbeck: Studies of American Literature in Honor of Harry R. Warfel, *edited by Motley Deakin and Peter Lisca (copyright © 1972 by the State of Florida), University of Florida Press, 1972, pp. 13-28.*

E. CURRENT-GARCIA (essay date 1973)

Crayon's *Bracebridge* reflections on the various levels of English society—and on the attitudes of their representative members toward one another—attain a degree of sophistication which anticipates de Tocqueville's by more than a decade, rather than simply reflecting a nostalgic, sentimental glorification of outmoded forms.

Apart from its account of persons and activities within Bracebridge itself, the book contains only four pieces of short fiction, none of which quite equals, artistically, either "**Rip Van Winkle**" or "**The Legend of Sleepy Hollow.**" Yet each reveals an extension of Irving's narrative technique for achieving varied effects as well as a scarcely perceptible species of literary and social criticism, subtly dropped into his framework references. . . . Irving here suits each story to the particular occasion and to the individual member of the Bracebridge menage who is allegedly responsible for getting it told. Thus, "**The Stout Gentleman**" (which opens the tale-telling sessions and is on the whole the most successful), is an amusing example of the hoax tale, related to the assemblage by "a thin, pale, weazen-faced man, extremely nervous," who turns up later as an important narrator in *Tales of a Traveller.* (p. 330)

In sharp contrast to this jocular take-off of romantic fiction, the next two stories told at Bracebridge—"**The Student of Salamanca**" and "**Annette Delarbe**"—are so saturated with sentimentality as to be virtually unreadable today. Yet they too clearly fit the circumstances of the moment which inspired them: namely, Lady Lillycraft's request for a tender love story "to make the day pass pleasantly" on the first occasion, and her desire to reciprocate with another one like it a few days later on May Morning. They not only show Irving's versatility in working with romantic and gothic materials in novella form, but also suggest his own carefully half-concealed ironic attitude toward this type of fiction.

In cranking up "**The Student of Salamanca**," for example, Irving employed *two* persona devices to secure aesthetic distance. (p. 331)

Irving contrived an even more elaborate framework for placing his fourth story, "**Dolph Heyliger**," in a climactic position within the context of *Bracebridge Hall*. Essentially an American tall tale, "**Dolph Heyliger**" is based on the same fund of Dutch legend he had worked up in the *Knickerbocker* and later in the *Sketch Book* tales. . . . (pp. 331-32)

This, at last, is the story of Dolph Heyliger, deservedly called "the real hero of *Bracebridge Hall*." For despite its structural weaknesses and cumbersome length, it is the typical rags-to-riches tale of a roguish but good-natured middle-class American boy, whose pluck and luck, good looks, and charm bring him riches and a winsome bride in the end. . . .

Dolph is indeed a worthy successor to Rip, Ichabod Crane, and Brom Bones, since he possesses energy, courage, and imagination, along with a superb talent "for making ghosts work for him." Had Irving felt confident enough to continue developing fully in his next collection the vein of fiction Dolph represented, his work might have received the acclaim he felt it deserved. For in "**Dolph Heyliger**," as in "**Rip Van Winkle**" and "**Sleepy Hollow**," his modified mock-heroic approach was transforming American life into legend. . . . (p. 332)

With his emphasis upon "nicety of execution," Irving's effort to achieve a new departure in fiction brought him to the threshold of the modern concept of the short story, though he fell short of it perhaps because the genre itself, conceived as a self-contained fictional form based on its own artistic principles, had not yet been defined. (p. 333)

[In] reading each group of stories consecutively, one becomes increasingly aware, first, that Irving's effort to establish a relationship between the narrator and his tales is moving toward a conception of fiction as the revelation of character; and secondly, that the development of mood engendered in each sequence of tales subtly progresses from one of whimsy and fun-poking to one of terror, violence, or serious introspection. (p. 335)

[The theme of "**The Story of the Young Italian**"] is concerned with the question of what terrifying inner forces would drive a gifted, sensitive individual to commit a crime that implants an indelibly bloody image on his conscience; and in developing the life story of the young painter as a murderer capable of arousing the reader's sympathy, Irving displays a foretaste of Hawthorne's skillful probing of a soul in torment, as well as his ability to suggest through symbolic imagery in setting, characterization, and events the corrosive effects of violent impulse, guilt, and remorse. Presented from his own first-person point of view, Ottavio is, we see, a highly emotional young man seeking his identity in a hostile world. . . . With a touch worthy of Hawthorne, the horror of Ottavio's remorse compels him to attempt, futilely, to exorcize the tormenting phantom of his crime by committing it to a canvas and then to bequeath both the picture and his confession to the sympathetic Englishman before giving himself up to justice at the latter's behest. By contrasting the violence of the young Ital-

ian's passionate fervor and the staid Englishman's reaction to it, Irving anticipated both Hawthorne's and James's fascination for the beauty and terror of Italy. Yet his own whimsicality prevails in the end. . . . (p. 337)

In Part II of the *Tales*—"**Buckthorne and His Friends**"—Irving shifted both the focus and the style of his narrative, as the ten connected pieces making up this portion of the volume play variations on the theme of authorship rather in the manner of the Addisonian periodical essay than in that of the gothic tradition involving sensational actions and events. Here, Irving's basic purpose was to draw a series of ironic contrasts between the aims and aspirations of the artist and the harsh realities of the practical world confronting him. (pp. 337-38)

Neither this nor the other shorter tales in Part II enhance Irving's stature as a fiction writer, though they offer interesting symbolic reflections of his own doubts and fears regarding the role of the artist in "the seductive but treacherous paths of literature." . . .

[But in] "**The Italian Banditti**," he displayed perhaps his greatest versatility and boldness as both parodist and craftsman. . . . Here as before Irving's basic purpose is satiric; for while the stories again begin by contrasting English reserve and Italian passion, they repeatedly undercut the allure of illicit sex as a dominant appeal in much of the popular sentimental and gothic fiction of the era. (p. 338)

Irving slyly introduces a variety of sexual innuendo through successive contrasts between innocence and experience. The naiveté of a drooping young heroine miraculously rescued in the tale of "**The Belated Travellers**," for example, is set off against the bawdy sophistication of an old Spanish princess who, along with her handsome nephew, is also being held captive by bandits at an isolated tavern. Gradually the accounts of these and other narrow escapes intensify the "fair Venetian's" suppressed sexual curiosity, as well as her apparently unconscious desire to arouse an amorous response from the bland Englishman. Thus, as the stories build up to a violent climax of overt sexuality in "**The Story of the Young Robber**," a brutal tale of mass ravishment and ritual murder which was severely condemned by American reviewers, it seems clear that Irving was boldly carrying the vein of sensational gothic fiction as far as he dared, without, however, abandoning his parodic aim. (p. 339)

Finally, in Part IV of the *Tales* Irving returned again to his favorite American scenes and subject matter, presenting in the four concluding stories lumped under the rubric of "**The Money Diggers**" the familiar type of legendary lore that had characterized his best work in the *Knickerbocker History* and *The Sketch Book*. Here he abandoned parody and burlesque, resorting instead to the more leisurely form of the folk tale. And though the theme of the tales in Part IV remains essentially the same as that of the preceding ones—namely, the vanity and mutability of what are called "**Great Expectations**" in "**Buckthorne**" and "**Golden Dreams**" in "**Wolfert Webber**"—Irving again demonstrated his versatility by showing that in fiction the subject matter is less important than the way the story is told.

The basic story throughout the *Tales* has to do with unfulfilled promises or the disillusionment born of experience, but whereas it is told with passion and inflated gothic rhetoric in Parts I and III, and with philosophic dispassionateness in Part II, in these concluding pieces it is frankly set forth in the venerable guise of folk superstitions concerning the age-old quest for buried treasure—which oftener than not proves illusory in the end. Yet Irving's stylistic skills are nowhere more prominently displayed than in his handling of this ancient chestnut. . . . ["The Devil and Tom Walker,"] despite its wildly improbable plot, foreshadows the best of Hawthorne's fictional exposure of Yankee shrewdness and Puritan hypocrisy.

In developing the Faustian character of Tom Walker, his termagant wife, and their separate confrontations with the devil, Irving once more achieved not only the subtle blend of sericomic pathos seen in "Rip Van Winkle," but also a species of much starker imagery that transforms such commonplace American activities as money lending, timber cutting, slave trading, treasure hunting, and Bible reading into grotesque emblems of spiritual deprivation, emotional sterility, hypocrisy, and lovelessness. . . . Irving's consummate mastery of word play, alliteration, hyperbole, metaphor, and allusion bears out his claim that what he valued most in his treatment of fiction was "the play of thought, sentiment, and language [that shadowed forth] a half-concealed vein of humor."

Although these values are likewise evident in the remaining stories told about Wolfert Webber, a comic Dutch colonial whose frantic disembowelment of his cabbage farm in search of non-existent gold nearly impoverishes his family before the paternal acres are transformed eventually into a profitable real estate subdivision, these rambling narratives seem tedious beside the concentrated effect of "The Devil and Tom Walker." But Irving had already proved in that tale, as well as in various others in the volume, that he well deserved the encomiums which Poe, twenty years later, pointedly bestowed upon his artistry. If he did not actually invent the short story, he had indeed set the pattern for the artistic re-creation of common experience in short fictional form—a pattern to which the superior genius of Poe and Hawthorne alike paid an even higher compliment by imitating, extending, and refining it in the short stories they produced in the 1830s and '40s. (pp. 340-41)

> E. Current-Garcia, "Irving Sets the Pattern: Notes on Professionalism and the Art of the Short Story," in Studies in Short Fiction (copyright 1973 by Newberry College), Vol. X, No. 4, Fall, 1973, pp. 327-41.

ROBERT A. FERGUSON (essay date 1981)

In the first decade of the nineteenth century, Irving was a historian rejecting a progressive view of country, a citizen questioning republican virtue, and, above all, an unhappy lawyer spurning a nation of laws. Unmistakably, vocational resentments lie at the center of a larger hostility that controls Irving's most important fiction. (p. 23)

[A] fear of failure lies behind Irving's sharpest contribution to *Salmagundi*, "On Greatness," and its satire of the alternative he could never realize. Timothy Dabble has all the assurance of a young man on the make, the "little great man" who pushes immediately into "the highways and marketplaces" in search of political advancement, throwing himself into "the scrubrace for honor and renown." Here Irving trivializes the conventional ambitions and virtues that every young lawyer was supposed to possess on the road to honor and preferment. "On Greatness" lumps great men together with pimps, bailiffs, and lottery brokers and turns to the dung beetle and jackass for its only images of energy, resolution, and application. (p. 24)

A History of New York contains a similar but much darker spirit of negation. (p. 25)

Part anodyne, part an expression of sorrow, bitterness, and relief, *A History of New York* is at once a light burlesque comedy set in the colonial past and an acerbic satire of republican society. Irving's double escape from the law and from the marriage associated with it figures prominently on each level so that the lawyer's private alternative to professional ambition becomes the writer's formal act of rebellion. In fact, Irving's emotional rejection of law—fictionally portrayed through the collapse of New Amsterdam—supplies a dramatic unity and thematic coherence that set *A History of New York* apart from his other imaginative works. As many have noted, Irving borrowed slavishly from Sterne, Goldsmith, Swift, Addison, Butler, Fielding, Cervantes, and Rabelais. . . . Even so, *A History of New York* is a distinctly American creation and a unified work of the imagination in a sense that the subsequent, more polished books of fiction are not. Crazy old Diedrich Knickerbocker—himself a composite from *Tristram Shandy, A Tale of a Tub,* and *The Spectator*—brings all external sources under the capacious umbrella of his own anger and frustration. If the Dutch historian constantly wanders, his larger objective, "hunting down a nation," never varies, and his sights remain fixed upon "the self-satisfied citizens of this most enlightened republick." His driving force is anger, an anger that has little to do with the more genial Irving who dilutes all spirit of rancor in later editions. (p. 26)

Throughout the declension of New Amsterdam, Irving's narrator rants compulsively against the "galling scourge of the law." . . .

Irving's comic narrative of a golden age in New Amsterdam celebrates a masculine idleness that is divorced both from the need for law and from the intrusive industry of a world of women. His placid Dutch burghers do little but eat, sleep, and pull on their pipes in ever obscuring clouds of smoke. "Making but few laws, without ever enforcing any," they enjoy life precisely because they are satisfied with obscurity and lack all interest in vocational activity, public honor, and civic service. . . . (p. 27)

The symbol of Irving's America, and focal point of his displeasure in *A History of New York,* is Thomas Jefferson's administration of 1801 to 1809. . . . Early republicans had little trouble in recognizing their third president in the figure of William the Testy. Here, as in the earlier *Salmagundi,* Irving satirizes Jefferson's character (his clothes, intellectuality, scientific enthusiasms, and passion for fine horses), his ideas (the stresses upon education, patriotism, democracy, and republican virtue), as well as Jefferson's specific programs as president (naval, economic, and foreign policies in general, and the inaugural addresses, the Non-Importation Act of 1806, the Embargo Act of 1807, and the Non-Intercourse Act of 1809 in particular). But more than politics informs Irving's hostility. Jefferson and Irving occupied extremes on the American spectrum. Virginia's imposing aristocrat, patriarch, and agrarian theorist intimidated the unprepossessing youngest child in an urban, middle-class family of northeastern merchants. It was intellectual versus dilettante and cynic, the man of affairs and practical energy against an adolescent daydreamer, the leading legal mind in America through the eyes of an uncertain law student. As imaginative projection, *A History of New York* seeks to reverse this context of defeat. (p. 28)

Diedrich Knickerbocker's raillery contains a very serious theoretical point. Through the satire of Jefferson, Irving calls into question the whole legal vision of America upon which Jeffersonianism is based. . . . [The] law as deliberate sham covers an even starker reality: the law as dangerous illusion. Diedrich Knickerbocker will have none of the design for order that law pretends to supply. (p. 29)

A History of New York is the first American book to question the civic vision of the Founding Fathers, and Diedrich Knickerbocker is the natural enemy of Publius, Novanglus, the Pennsylvania Farmer, and other rational, legal spokesmen in early American literature. Irving's comic historian easily ridicules the high seriousness of these republican mythmakers, but the real success of his challenge depends upon his manipulation of basic intellectual affinities. . . .

Though short, *A History of New York* faithfully reproduces the elaborate organizational format of a standard legal compendium. Irving divides his little book into volumes, books, chapters, and headings and supplies a plethora of footnotes in mock replication of the formal machinery in eighteenth-century legal analysis. (p. 30)

At the outset Irving rejects the Enlightenment's assumption of a discernible relation between natural order and social harmony—an assumption that encourages an epistemology based upon the connection of natural law and positive or manmade law and that supports the theory of social contract from Locke to Rousseau. Diedrich Knickerbocker finds too much mystery in Nature to justify such exercises in scholasticism. (p. 31)

All of Knickerbocker's nonsense has a serious goal in mind. Books I and II of *A History of New York* demolish the intellectual foundations for a progressive interpretation of American culture. Conventional beliefs in natural law, the virgin land, manifest destiny, and republican order and virtue all become impossible aboard the Dutch historian's "crazy vessel." . . . Steeped in Homer, Herodotus, Thucydides, Plato, Cicero, Plutarch, and Boethius, Knickerbocker finds history to be cyclical rather than progressive. . . . He and his contemporaries actually live within degenerate times. (pp. 32-3)

Irving begins by unmasking republican pretensions to order and control of the kind one finds in *Common Sense, The Federalist,* and *Notes on the State of Virginia.* In *A History of New York* every plan and method of insuring a virtuous society founders upon the organic spontaneity of new world growth. (p. 33)

Irving's reliance upon humor is immediate and obvious in *A History of New York,* but his methods and the underlying safeguards they contain deserve closer attention. Knickerbocker is the first in a long line of literary personae who trade upon a subversive vein of humor in American literature—a humor that plays upon chaos and affirms common individual traits (cunning, endurance, physical prowess) over and against civic identities and the ideological building blocks of republican culture. (pp. 36-7)

What distinguishes Irving from other comic writers of the day is the courage of one who has stepped completely outside of the welter of incongruities that he is seeking to describe. He holds nothing back in *A History of New York.* At the same time, his stance as a thoroughly alienated, outside observer allows the artistic detachment upon which all good satire depends. . . . To accept that voice on its own terms—and the reader has no choice in this matter—is to be doubly disarmed from protesting the views it secures. (p. 37)

Since irony must work through indirection, there is no one moment for seizing upon and denying the image of America that accompanies Knickerbocker's gradual embrace of his au-

dience. When, for example, the Dutch historian reveals his fat, sleepy burghers placing a "scrupulously honest" hand or foot upon the scales in fur trade with the Indians, we laugh at reality through the appearance. . . . [The] indirection of irony allows Irving to make his point while evading the responsibility of a stance for or against. . . . [One cannot] divorce an accepting laughter at Knickerbocker's New York from Irving's critical presentation of America. (p. 38)

As a blend of satire and comedy, *A History of New York* undermines more than it attacks. More precisely, it uses a "comedy of confusion" to ridicule order and system within the world. (p. 39)

At his angriest, Irving is unsuited for the more bitter art of a Swift or a Pope, but craft as well as temperament is responsible for the lighter humor and more cautious piquancy of *A History of New York.* Diedrich Knickerbocker instinctively knows that direct attack will not meet with a receptive audience—an assumption in keeping with the intellectual movement of the eighteenth century away from satire and toward a more joyful and kindly theory of laughter. Irving's criticizing voice has to be comic because the more negative art of satire cannot reach the needs of an American culture still straining for affirmations. (p. 40)

A History of New York flows from the bewilderment of one who has just realized the unfair pain that life inflicts upon the living. *The Sketch Book,* in contrast, represents a calculated move by Irving the bankrupt to regain lost caste or, as he also puts it, "to reinstate myself in the worlds thoughts." The first book strikes against; the second seeks to reconcile and rejoin. Diedrich Knickerbocker gleefully juxtaposes starving poets to "a fat round bellied alderman" of a world, while the gentlemanly Crayon avoids every incongruity in search of a dignified, harmonious stance for the writer as observer. (p. 42)

The great irony of Washington Irving's career is that the dead ends of *A History of New York* produce far more energy and originality than the fresh start of *The Sketch Book* and everything that follows. Geoffrey Crayon's muted tones are harder won and based upon a deeper understanding, but Knickerbocker's insistent voice is more clearly original, creative, and authentic. Trapped in grief and aimlessness, the younger writer swings wildly but with telling effect. Geoffrey Crayon, on the other hand, is trying to make his way in the world. . . .

Harsh realities do appear in *The Sketch Book,* but, as Irving suggests, they have been softened and tinted. Typically, his ordeal of bankruptcy surfaces in **"Roscoe," "The Wife,"** and **"Rip Van Winkle,"** but the bitterness and humiliation Irving personally felt have been filtered from these fictional accounts. (p. 44)

Everywhere in *The Sketch Book* death, sickness, and squalor are limned by delicate colors and framing discourse. The dead are cared for by the living, the sick by the hale, the poor by the rich, allowing Irving to draw the sting from life's terrors. . . . **"Rip Van Winkle"** and **"The Legend of Sleepy Hollow"** captivate because they consciously reach back toward the more jaundiced eye and sharper tongue of the earlier persona.

"Rip Van Winkle" opens with a comic defense of Knickerbocker's stance *against* his culture. The idle Rip, as many have shown, is a natural renegade. His "insuperable aversion to all kinds of profitable labor" and final success make him a subversive force within republican culture. **"The Legend of Sleepy**

Hollow" comes even closer to the residual source of Knickerbocker's sardonic strength. . . . Sleepy Hollow represents a retreat from the world and its distractions, the one peaceful exception within a restless country of incessant change. Ichabod is its mortal enemy because he is from the outside and holds such worldly ambitions. (pp. 45-6)

Ichabod's eventual and inevitable climb in the world represents both an unpleasant memory and a final barb from the author. For Ichabod ultimately succeeds as a New York lawyer who takes the traditional path to public office and succeeds as a justice of the city courts. Like Timothy Dabble before him, he is another "little great man" in republican culture. Irving's concluding postscript reaches back to former tirades against the legal profession and is an echo of problems not forgotten. Here Knickerbocker uses "pepper and salt" and "a triumphant leer" to point out that those who "have reason and the law on their side" will never understand Ichabod's story. Here too is the satirist's parting shot. (p. 46)

> *Robert A. Ferguson, "Hunting Down a Nation: Irving's 'A History of New York'," in* Nineteenth-Century Fiction *(©1981 by the Regents of the University of California), Vol. 36, No. 1, June, 1981, pp. 22-46.*

ADDITIONAL BIBLIOGRAPHY

Aderman, Ralph M., ed. *Washington Irving Reconsidered: A Symposium.* Hartford: Transcendental Books, 1969, 66 p.
    A collection of essays discussing varied aspects of Irving's work.

Brooks, Van Wyck. "Irving and Cooper Abroad." In his *The World of Washington Irving,* pp. 315-36. New York: E. P. Dutton and Co., Inc., 1944.*
    Examines Irving's connections with American authors and artists while in Europe.

Callow, James T. *Kindred Spirits: Knickerbocker Writers and American Artists, 1807-1855.* Chapel Hill: The University of North Carolina Press, 1967, 287 p.*
    A study of Irving's literary circle in New York City during the first part of the nineteenth century.

Clark, William Bedford. "How the West Won: Irving's Comic Inversion of the Westering Myth in 'A Tour on the Prairies'." *American Literature,* L, No. 3 (November 1978): 335-47.
    Traces Irving's use of comic techniques in "A Tour on the Prai-
ries" and discusses his inversion of the classic "winning the west" theme.

Leary, Lewis. *Washington Irving.* University of Minnesota Pamphlets on American Writers, edited by William Van O'Connor, Allen Tate, Leonard Unger, and Robert Penn Warren, no. 25. Minneapolis: University of Minnesota Press, 1963, 48 p.
    Overview of Irving's career. Leary concludes that Irving had "little of final importance to write about."

Lynch, James J. "The Devil in the Writings of Irving, Hawthorne, and Poe." *New York Folklore Quarterly* VIII, No. 2 (Summer 1952): 111-31.*
    An analysis of Irving's view of Satan as reflected in his writings.

Martin, Terence. "Rip, Ichabod, and the American Imagination." *American Literature* XXXI, No. 2 (May 1959): 137-49.
    Presents "Rip Van Winkle" and "The Legend of Sleepy Hollow" as reflections of the tension between artistic endeavors and American culture.

Melville, Herman. "Rip Van Winkle's Lilac." In *A Century of Commentary on the Works of Washington Irving: 1860-1974,* edited by Andrew Myers, pp. 75-93. Tarrytown, NY: Sleepy Hollow Restorations, 1976.
    A poem about the character of Rip Van Winkle.

Myers, Andrew B., ed. *Washington Irving: A Tribute.* Tarrytown, NY: Sleepy Hollow Restorations, 1972, 86 p.
    A collection of commemorative essays.

Prescott, William H. "Irving's 'Conquest of Granada'." In his *Biographical and Critical Miscellanies,* pp. 73-101. London: George Routledge and Sons, 1845.
    Discusses Irving's ability as a historian in his account of the conquest of Granada.

Reichart, Walter A. *Washington Irving and Germany.* Ann Arbor: University of Michigan Press, 1957, 212 p.
    Biographical discussion of Irving's experiences in Germany. The author points out the similarity between Irving's short stories and German folktales.

Roth, Martin. *Comedy and America: The Lost World of Washington Irving.* Port Washingtion, NY: Kennikat Press, 1976, 205 p.
    Overview of Irving's comic sense.

Thackeray, William Makepeace. "Nil Nisi Bonum." In *Prose Masterpieces from Modern Essayists,* edited by George Haven Putnam, pp. 177-92. New York: G. P. Putnam's Sons, 1893.
    An analysis of Irving's reputation abroad.

Wagenknecht, Edward. *Washington Irving: Moderation Displayed.* New York: Oxford University Press, 1962, 223 p.
    Biographical study focussing on the complexity of Irving's temperament and its effect on his work.

Douglas William Jerrold

1803-1857

English playwright, humorist, and journalist.

As the son of the manager of the Sheerness Theatre in London, Jerrold became familiar with the stage at an early age. However, the promise of a career with the Royal Navy enticed him more than did his interest in the theater, and he enlisted to serve as a midshipman in the Napoleonic Wars (1813-1815). Although he never actually fought in a battle, Jerrold was deeply moved by the destruction of war, and his experiences in the navy proved to be an inspiration for his plays, particularly the nautical melodrama, *Black-Eyed Susan; or, All in the Downs*.

British audiences were unwilling to accept the sophisticated comedy of Jerrold's early plays. *The Mutiny at the Nore* and *The Rent Day* are typical examples of the high forms of humor Jerrold strove to achieve, for they satirically portray the pomposity of the royalty and are perhaps the best examples of Jerrold's humor. His most successful plays, *Black-Eyed Susan*, *The Bride of Ludgate*, and *Time Works Wonders*, are noted particularly for their wit and skillful construction of dialogue. These native melodramas were more popular with audiences than the Gothic dramas which had been previously performed on the English stage. Critics generally agree that his other theatrical works are of little value.

In 1836, Jerrold began a partnership with his brother-in-law as manager of the Strand Theatre. The failure of this association, combined with the lack of interest in his plays, caused Jerrold to turn his attention from the theatre to magazine writing. He contributed essays to *Freemason's Quarterly Review*, *The London Athenaeum*, and *Blackwood's Magazine*, served as editor of *The Heads of the People*, the *Illuminated Magazine*, *The Shilling Magazine*, and *Lloyd's Magazine*, and also began his own newspaper and magazine, but they were short-lived.

Jerrold is best-known for work which appeared in the magazine, *Punch*, particularly for his weekly series, *Mrs. Caudle's Curtain Lectures*, written under the pseudonym "Q." He furthered the aims of the magazine: "To seek to instruct and cease to punish." As a regular contributor, Jerrold exposed the oppression of the poor and wrote with the intention of improving the human condition. He earned the title "Mr. Punch" for the warm humor and liberal tendencies of his contributions. These made several of his less outspoken contemporaries envious, among them William Makepeace Thackeray. Jerrold was truly an innovative writer, introducing comic journalism to England, and surpassing all others in the art form he helped to create.

Hawthorne, after the death of Jerrold, said, "He wrote with an honest and manly purpose; he was thoroughly sincere; he earnestly desired to make the world better, to lighten its suffering, and give noble dignity to life." Jerrold's literary achievement, distinguished by his strong sense of purpose and humor, mark him as an important contributor to English journalism and drama.

PRINCIPAL WORKS

*More Frightened Than Hurt (drama) 1821
Fifteen Years of a Drunkard's Life (drama) 1828

Culver Pictures

Black-Eyed Susan; or, All in the Downs (drama) 1829
The Mutiny at the Nore (drama) 1830
The Bride of Ludgate (drama) 1831
The Rent Day (drama) 1832
Men of Character (short stories) 1838
Bubbles of the Day (drama) 1842
Cakes and Ale (short stories) 1842
Prisoner of War (short story) 1842
Punch's Letters to His Son (satirical essay) 1843
Story of a Feather (short story) 1844
Mrs. Caudle's Curtain Lectures (satirical essays) 1845
Punch's Complete Letter Writer (essay) 1845
Time Works Wonders (drama) 1845
Chronicles of Clovernook (short stories) 1846
The English in Little (satirical essay) 1846
A Man Made of Money (short story) 1849
The Catspaw (satirical essay) 1850
St. Giles and St. James (satirical essay) 1851

**This drama was originally entitled *The Duellists*.

CHARLES DICKENS　(essay date 1844)

I am truly proud of your remembrance, and have put the **'Story of a Feather'** on a shelf (not an obscure one) where some other feathers are, which it shall help to show mankind which way the wind blows, long after *we* know where the wind comes from. I am quite delighted to find that you have touched the latter part again, and touched it with such a delicate and tender hand. It is a wise and beautiful book. I am sure I may venture to say so to you, for nobody consulted it more regularly and earnestly than I did, as it came out in *Punch*.

> *Charles Dickens, in his letter to Douglas Jerrold in May, 1844, in* The Life and Remains of Douglas Jerrold *by W. Blanchard Jerrold, Ticknor and Fields, 1859 (and reprinted in* The Letters of Charles Dickens: 1844-1846, *Vol. 4, edited by Kathleen Tillotson, Oxford University Press, Oxford, 1977, p. 120).*

WILLIAM MAKEPEACE THACKERAY　(essay date 1845)

[The Caudle Papers] are still more pleasant and profitable to read, than when they appeared dispersed through the pages of *Punch*. They form a body of conjugal morality. Swift's Directions to Servants were not more awful lessons for the kitchen and pantry in the last century, than the Caudle Lectures for the parlours of the present age; and, indeed, if one may be permitted to speculate upon the chances of future reputation for works of humour, we should say that [*Mrs. Caudle's Curtain Lectures*] is as likely to last as any other that has been produced in modern days. It is quite as keen as the satirical book of the Dean before alluded to, contains wit and sarcasm quite as brilliant, and gives (in caricature) the most queer, minute, and amusing picture of English middle-class life. (pp. 93-4)

[To create the realities of this book] is the greatest triumph of a fictitious writer—a serious or humorous *poet*. (pp. 94-5)

[The] credibility of Mr. and Mrs. Caudle is a greater charm than the wit and humour with which their lives are recorded. These come next, and in them the author was never wanting. You come perpetually upon turns of expression the most ingenious, thoughts and sarcasms the most novel, curious, and laughter-provoking. These sparkling, odd, sudden quips and fancies surprise you everywhere amidst the Caudle dialogues. (p. 95)

> *William Makepeace Thackeray, "Christmas Books, No. II: Jerrold's 'Mrs Caudle's Curtain Lectures', Taylor's 'Fairy Ring'" (originally published in* Morning Chronicle, *December 26, 1845), in his* Contributions to the "Morning Chronicle," *edited by Gordon N. Ray, University of Illinois Press, 1955, pp. 93-100.**

JOHN TAYLOR SINNETT　(essay date 1847)

Who has not heard of Douglas Jerrold? Who has not seen the touching drama of the **"Rent Day,"** that noble interpretation of Wilkie's picture? And who has not laughed a hundred times over those most admirable letters, which he wrote under the pleasant name of *Punch*, dealing out to all England, in the person of his son, the soundest admonitions, with all the jocund hilarity of Falstaff? What depth of observation there is lurking beneath those facetious remarks! What keen sagacity and wisdom in that quiet irony! What point in that humor! Alack! how does he contrive it? In this age of excitement, turmoil, and confusion, when other people hedge, jostle, knock against each other, and every man tears his way along this bustling world as best he can, without snatching a moment of leisure to husband his remarks, if he make any, his mind at least has been able to settle his thoughts down upon the manners and spirit of the age, and to seize them with the perceptions of a true master. Moreover, he is a living proof that the old genius of the land, though torpid, is not extinct, for he writes with the Saxon pith of yore, and with Saxon simplicity; in an age when many a writer of note does not even read the old authors, he emulates them; *he steps into the footprints of their muses*. He has got the true trick of the old craft; he is every inch a classic.

"Rent Day," plainly stamped as it was with the lineaments of a forcible mind, nobly and justly directed, did not afford its author that extensive reputation which he deserved. Certainly it gave Jerrold the esteem of the thinking and inquiring, and won golden opinions from those of his profession; but his name did not yet become a household word at the family hearths of his countrymen. His character was growing; but large reputations are slow in coming to maturity, nor was it his fortune to acquire his present universal fame, till he and other fine spirits had founded the immortal *Punch,* that admirable galaxy of *mirth without malice.* . . . (p. 443)

Douglas Jerrold has generally been considered one of the principal founders of this popular paper, and his excellent **"Story of a Feather," "Punch's Letters to his Son,"** and the famous **"Curtain Lectures of Mrs. Caudle,"** have been the most successful contributions to the work.

Although these successive stories and epistles were written in detached pieces, at isolated periods, they abound everywhere with that robust argument, that liberal and manly spirit, which so few can express happily and lastingly; and the child-like drollery and humor to which the author stoops his mind, only renders the instruction more shapely by the amusement in which it is dressed. Many people have thought that the **"Curtain Lectures of Mrs. Caudle"** were extended too far, and passed the limits of truth, and that the witty author was too severe upon the sex. Perhaps he was so. Douglas Jerrold has shown in all his works that he had read Fielding, that he had not studied him in vain; he has great skill in irony, and a very marked propensity to satire. Besides, Mrs. Caudle was written *for a country, not for a class,* and if her frivolity, ardent temper, and persecution, seem excessive when applied to some sweet tyrants, there are others whose propensity to subjugate their lords by vocal thunder leave even her example behind. . . .

The **"Men of Character"** is an amusing series of essays, written in a jaunty, magazine style, but not so closely and concisely as Jerrold's other productions; they all point an admirable moral to the reader. **"Adam Buff, the Man Without a Shirt,"** is one of the best of these light pieces. (p. 444)

Among the dramatic works of Douglas Jerrold, [**"Black-Eyed Susan"** and **"The Rent Day"**] are probably the most interesting, and will continue to be standard plays. . . . He has, however, written several others of considerable merit: **"The Schoolfellow," "The Prisoner of War," "The Bubbles of the Day,"** and **"Time Works Wonders"**; four comedies sparking with wit, and directed against the follies, foibles, and frippery of the times we live in. No man has been more successful on the stage in touching the national heart. He may, perhaps, want the fine philosophic theory, the poetic diction of Sheridan Knowles; he may not possess the delicate suavity of Bulwer, but he can clutch the passions and the feelings of the people as well as either of them: for he possesses as deep a pathos as the author of "The Hunchback," and far more virility than the author of "Money." He has his defects, certainly, as well as his beauties. We often think he writes too hurriedly, that he does not linger enough upon a fine thought, which is of all secrets the greatest in the great arts of writing and painting, for when a moralist has got an idea which is striking, he should show it again and again under various phases before he passes from it, leaving the reader ample time to feel its purport and to relish its pleasantry. . . . Again, Douglas Jerrold is accused of being too caustic, of forgetting the advice of that courtly gentleman, Sir Lucius O'Trigger: "Let your courage be as keen, but at the same time as polished, as your sword." "He not only," say his detractors, "cuts, but hacks and mangles his victims." Such, indeed, is the spirit of the age; but we do not allow Jerrold to be guilty of this fault: the seeming defect often lies rather in the honest bluntness of his language than in the virulence of his charges. Translate his fiercest attacks upon men and manners into the decorous and courtly language of Lesage or Marivaux, of Fielding or Scott, and they would lose two-thirds of the lacerating cruelty they seem to portray. (pp. 444-45)

In all [Jerrold's] enterprises, literary and political, this able moralist had embraced with uncommon ardor the cause and interests of the great body of the people, to all which he gave "a local habitation and a name." . . . Few men have shown the generous audacity that he has displayed in advocating the rights of the INDUSTRIOUS CLASSES; none have more vividly described the inborn and gallant virtues of the English heart. We think, however, that his proper province is rather in letters than in politics; because his mind is too vigorous to be plastic and compliant, and there is too much sincerity in his nature . . . to stoop to party views and objects. Nor is it easy for such solid mineral as his, to liquify and pour itself out with that rapid abundance that political writing demands. . . . [Jerrold] wrote only when his sympathy was touched, when his spirit was in flame, when his mind, like the teeming breast of a mother, panted for effusion. Rousseau only dealt in masterpieces. He has the sublime eloquence of Bossuet, the searching tenderness of Massillon; his argument is closer than Bourdaloue's or La Bruyère's, his humor not so frequent, but perfectly as quaint as Montaigne's, and his diction has all the music, if not all the graces of Voltaire.

We do not blame Douglas Jerrold for the volubility of his pen; but we regret that he cannot practise a husbandry less prodigal; because we think so highly of his powers that we believe if he gave his thoughts all the maturity they might derive from composure, there is hardly any height he might not attain to in his wit and argument. But, at all events, to speak of him in all justice and candor, he is allowed to be one of the master spirits of the day, and his name shall live after him, and become one of the surviving symbols of the age, when this our busy generation, like the broad wave of a cataract, shall have swept on for ever adown the gulf of time. (p. 445)

John Taylor Sinnett, "Mr. Douglas Jerrold," in The Eclectic Magazine, Vol. XI, No. IV, August, 1847, pp. 443-45.

THE ATHENAEUM (essay date 1848)

The fact on which the moral of [A Man Made of Money] is founded is as old as the introduction into society of a circulating medium—and almost as common as the circulation itself. A man tempted by the constant demand him for money beyond his means to supply, and goaded by the vexations to which the disproportion subjects him, is driven to the impatient expression of a wish which thousands have uttered before him:—"I wish to Heaven," said Mr. Jericho, "I was made of money!" This wish it is the object of the work here in progress to rebuke. Mr. Jerrold brings down upon his hero, for his ulterior purposes, the curse of its fulfilment. . . .

The reader will scarcely fail to see what fine truths may be worked by the machinery which Mr. Jerrold has invented,— and how well the working of them is suited to his peculiar talent. (p. 1000)

If we might venture a hint without making that encroachment upon the future intentions of the author which we have disclaimed, we should say that Mr. Jerrold has prepared for himself a difficulty in the characters which he has adopted as the agents of his morals. . . . How the finer and deeper meanings which reside in his scheme are to be brought out through the medium of one so wanting in sentiment as the hero, we do not foresee. But, as we have said, it is the author's secret:—and the earnestness that conceived the idea will, it is reasonable to suppose, be brought to its adequate working out. (p. 1002)

"'A Man Made of Money'," in The Athenaeum, No. 1093, October 7, 1848, pp. 1000-02.

THE BRITISH QUARTERLY REVIEW (essay date 1849)

[In] that one quality called wit, in the power of sharp and instant repartee, and, above all, in the knack of demolishing an opponent by some restless pun upon his meaning, Douglas Jerrold is, among London literary men, unrivalled. On paper there are some who may come near him; but in witty talk among his friends he is *facile princeps*. (p. 192)

[On] the other hand, Mr. Jerrold is more vaguely known as the author of numerous favourite theatrical pieces, including two standard comedies; as one of the principal contributors to *Punch,* in whose pages he has brought out successively **'The Story of a Feather,' 'Punch's Letters to his Son,'** the **'Caudle Lectures,'** and other miscellanies of the same nature; as the writer of various tales and essays that have appeared elsewhere; as recently the proprietor and editor of a weekly newspaper, devoted to the advocacy of liberal opinions, and especially earnest in its denunciations of the practice of Capital punishments; and, finally, as the author of a serial work of fiction, in six parts, entitled, **'A Man made of Money,'** less successful, it is said, than the similar publications of Dickens and Thackeray, but still by no means a failure. (pp. 192-93)

Mr. Jerrold is no mere man of wit: he is something higher and better; he is a man of clear thought; of no mean amount of knowledge; and of most keen and strong feelings. . . . [If] friendly readers were first to correct their misconception of Mr. Jerrold as a man whose sole or even chief endowment is wit, they would find both [the **'Man made of Money'**] and all his other writings to possess a merit higher and more essential than that of being pleasant to read—the merit, we mean, of being amply and closely representative of their author. (pp. 193-94)

Fully to bring out all that it seems necessary to say respecting Mr. Jerrold's peculiarities as a writer, it may be well to regard him separately for a little in each of those two phases that we have marked as characteristic of him. We shall, therefore, in what follows, consider him first as the man of wit, the comic author; and secondly, as the essayist, the man of higher opinions, the political and philanthropic partisan. We shall select our examples in both cases, chiefly, though not exclusively, from '**The Man made of Money,**' the latest and perhaps most complete of his publications. (p. 195)

Mr. Jerrold's comic writing . . . is, in some respects, more like a *liqueur* than a wine; one discerns the alcoholic ingredient of strong personal feeling in it, drugging and firing the true juice of the grape. Hence, probably, it is that one can read less of him at a time than of either Dickens or Thackeray. They, having more of the specially artistic spirit, which finds delight in merely depicting, lure the reader on, page after page, without fatiguing him; he, the moralist too strong in him, soon heats and chafes you with his pungent and bitter sentences.

One thing it may be worth while to remark regarding Mr. Jerrold's manner as a comic writer—the small use he makes of the pun. That this is not because of any inability to use it, every one acquainted with him knows, no man alive can wield that weapon in talk better than he. Neither is it, we believe, because of any resolution against it, as too mean for literary use. It is only when the pun usurps undue prominence, and is applied to subjects that should be deemed beyond its range, that it becomes odious. It must, therefore, be from some unconscious change of his mental attitude when he takes his pen in hand, that Mr. Jerrold so seldom puns when he writes. (p. 198)

Another thing to be remarked respecting Mr. Jerrold's writings is, that they contain fewer perfectly successful comic portraits than those of either Thackeray or Dickens. . . . [Mr. Jerrold] always excepting his inimitable Mrs. Caudle, and one or two delineations in the same favourite vein, as, for example, Mrs. Jericho, in the '**Man of Money,**' and Miss Tucker, in '**Time Works Wonders,**' has not contributed any such happy sketches to our picture-gallery of comic characters. His writings, indeed, abound with all sorts of comic men and women—Browns, Snubs, Pigeons, Canditufts, &c., often cleverly hit off, and sufficiently distinct as one reads the scenes in which they figure; but, placed there to serve a purpose, they do not remain with one after that purpose is over. Even when his characters are labelled, by recurring descriptive phrases put into their mouths, . . . they rapidly evanesce from the memory. . . . Mr. Jerrold is almost uniformly less happy than Mr. Dickens or Mr. Thackeray in the names he selects for his characters. The power of inventing a good name for a character seems, in fact, to be but a variety of the power that conceives the character itself. And where Mr. Jerrold succeeds in the conception, as in Mrs. Caudle, there also the name is good. The truth is, as we have already hinted, that in Mr. Jerrold, the moralist, the satirist, prevails over the artist. His creations are, in most cases, but vehicles for some feeling or opinion; and it is more rarely that, laying aside intention and preference, he rollicks in his own fancies. . . . [Some] of the little tales that Mr. Jerrold has given to the public, first in periodicals, and afterwards in a collected form, in the two series entitled '**Men of Character,**' and '**Cakes and Ale,**' are really fine pieces of writing. The latter series is the superior; many of the tales in it, like some of those in the former, are questionable tissues of grotesque fun to amuse idle people; others have shrewd, keen sense in them; while a few are altogether of a higher species, and show a bright and poetic fancy.

From what has been said, it will be seen that the wit and humour in Mr. Jerrold's writings must naturally lie more in passages of express and direct dialogue between himself and his reader,

and in casual outbreaks of his own individual sense of the comic, than in sustained comic delineation. (pp. 198-200)

Mr. Jerrold, as we have already said, is no mere wit, no mere satiric observer, no mere maker of amusing jests and conceits. He is something more; he is a man of highly emotional nature, armed to the teeth with keen sensibilities and convictions, and as ready as any man we know to leave jest for earnest when the moment requires it. There is no sneering with him at high art, exalted virtue, or recondite science—cheap resource of mean natures; no uneasy striving to keep down the discourse so low that it may still be possible to pun and joke. On the contrary, he has a native sympathy with what is elevated. . . . It is this very inner seriousness of nature that gives his wit its force. . . . Mr. Jerrold is to be placed out of the category of merely comic writers; for at least half of what he has written consists of perfectly serious matter—pathetic story, fanciful description, or bitter and vehement satire. (p. 202)

[The] moral of the '**Man made of Money**' . . . is one that Mr. Jerrold has often repeated. Contempt for money . . . , generous and bountiful dealing with one's fellow creatures, is a principal part of the morality that Mr. Jerrold inculcates. In the structure of the . . . story the imagination of the author has possibly been allowed to take too great a liberty with the understanding of the reader. The natural in the moral loses considerably in its effect from its relation to the unnatural in the fiction. His teaching, too, on the points in question, is often too vague and lax; mere sentimental generosity, it is to be feared, sometimes prevailing in his philanthropic theory, over the moral element of justice. . . . Here, we think, his own earnestness, and powers of scorn, would step in to save him. And, as regards his theory itself, one cannot but respect it when it takes the form, as it often does, of enthusiastic argument in behalf of political equality, popular education, and other specific measures of social improvement. . . . Upon occasions, all the virtues seem to pass over somewhat too readily, at his bidding, from the side of the washed to that of the unwashed. (pp. 204-05)

On no topic is Mr. Jerrold more fierce than on that of war. . . . No partizan of the peace movement could go farther than he in his denunciations of the folly of the sword, and the delusion of military glory. There is scarcely one of his writings that does not contain some passage of satire against the occupation of a soldier. Here, however, his superior intellect, and his generosity of sentiment, preserve him from a certain gross and narrow mode of thinking, to which men of less cultivation are liable—a mode of thinking which reveals itself in the constant and indiscriminate use of sweeping phrases of condemnation against all characters of the past that have acted on the condition of the world by any other than a peaceful instrumentality. (p. 206)

Mr. Jerold, we should imagine to be, on the whole, a careful writer. His language is pregnant, clear, and terse; exhibiting, sometimes, as is natural in an author who feels strongly, a certain hurry and confusion of metaphor; but rarely weak or redundant. He has evidently read much. . . . Occasionally, however, we remark a tendency towards coarseness, towards a too liberal use of what we should call the Stokes element in human life. . . . There is a special department of this general Stokes element, in which, perhaps more than in any other, Mr. Jerrold is apt to offend—that which, to use a favourite word of his own, we would designate 'the toothsome,' and which consists in too detailed allusions to viands, especially if in course of preparation, and to unaesthetic beverages. Leaving such criticisms, however, one is glad to be able to notice, in conclusion, one fact relating to Mr. Jerrold as a literary man—to wit, the manifest progress that he has made since he began to write, and the increased strength and freedom of his later as compared with his earlier works. His last production, the **'Man made of Money,'** seems to us decidedly the best. (pp. 207-08)

"'A Man Made of Money'," in The British Quarterly Review, *Vol. X, No. XIX, August 1, 1849, pp. 192-208.*

DOUGLAS JERROLD   (essay date 1851)

It has been my endeavour [in **"St. Giles and St. James"**] to show in the person of St. Giles the victim of an ignorant disregard of the social claims of the poor upon the rich; of the governed million upon the governing few; to present—I am well aware how imperfectly; but with no wilful exaggeration of the portraiture—the picture of the infant pauper reared in brutish ignorance; a human waif of dirt and darkness. Since the original appearance of this story, the reality of this picture, in all its vital and appalling horror, has forced itself upon the legislature; has engaged its anxious thoughts; and will ultimately triumph in its humanising sympathies. I will only add that upon an after revision of this story, I cannot think myself open to the charge of bedizening St. Giles at the cost of St. James; or of making Hog Lane the treasury of all the virtues to the moral sacking of May Fair.

The completion of the first volume of a collected edition of his writings—scattered over the space of years—is an opportunity tempting to the vanity of a writer to indulge in a retrospect of the circumstances that first made authorship his hope, as well as of the general tenor of his after vocation. I will not, at least, in these pages, yield to the inducement; further than to say that, self-helped and self-guided, I began the world at an age when, as a general rule, boys have not laid down their primers; that the cockpit of a man-of-war was at thirteen exchanged for the struggle of London; that appearing in print ere perhaps the meaning of words was duly mastered—no one can be more alive than myself to the worthlessness of such early mutterings.

In conclusion, I submit this volume to the generous interpretation of the reader. Some of it has been called "bitter": indeed, "bitter" has, I think, a little too often been the ready word when certain critics have condescended to bend their eyes upon my page: so ready, that were my ink redolent of myrrh and frankincense, I well know the sort of ready-made criticism that would cry, with a denouncing shiver, "aloes; aloes." (pp. iii-iv)

Douglas Jerrold, in his preface to his The Writings of Douglas Jerrold: "St. Giles and St. James," *Vol. I, Bradbury and Evans, 1851, pp. iii-iv.*

THE ECLECTIC MAGAZINE   (essay date 1854)

[The] wits and satirists, at the head of whom we place a Dickens, a Thackeray, and a Douglas Jerrold, are entitled to take as high a rank in the scale of intellect as the most lauded of their predecessors, while they unquestionably claim a far higher one on the score of morality. . . . [We] believe there is no author of equal ability whose writings are so little known in the general community, and none whose merely comic writings are more heartily appreciated in London society. . . . Jerrold's power as a writer has never been fully known. By some men

he is regarded as flippant, by others as sardonic. One class objects to him on the score of his political prejudices, while another considers him to be a cynic, with more than the cynicism of Diogenes.

Mr. Jerrold occupies a position somewhat different from that of most contemporary writers of equal or even greater eminence. His works, in point of subject and style, as well as in respect of their peculiarities of thought and their moral bearing, represent some of the leading characteristics of the literary mind more thoroughly than those of any other author who has written things of a similar character. It is not only the combination of wit and humor with deep feeling and earnest thinking, that gives them the uniqueness which we allude to, for some of his contemporaries greatly excel him in the finer and purer qualities of humor. . . . With Jerrold the satire is always marked by a certain everyday character, and invariably suggests something within the range of every-day experience. The feeling expressed in his works is quite as free from any approach to sentimentality as that of Thackeray; and although it is by no means so genial, or likely to be so generally effective as that of Dickens, yet we are disposed to think that it is deeper than that of either. There is a more sternly practical character about all Jerrold's writings than we have been able to find in those of any modern author in the same departments of literature. He seems to us a man much more intimately acquainted with the varied aspects of city life than most of his contemporaries; and as a distinguishing feature—more marked, perhaps, than any other—all that he writes is highly colored by strong and decided political opinions. Hence we find that he has never been more successful than when employing fictitious incidents and ludicrous circumstances to express his scorn of hollow conventionalities either in social usages or political dogmas. His wit is never brought into play for the mere sake of seeming witty; his arrows are always pointed, and pointed, too, with a cutting sharpness. Shot with that directness of aim which he gives them, they never fail to pierce wherever they hit. (pp. 167-68)

Although Mr. Jerrold has been regarded rather too exclusively as a comic writer and a wit, that phase of him is undoubtedly the most prominent one. The serious, earnest nature of the man is seen in his broadly comic writings almost as plainly as in those of a graver and more reflective character. In such things as the **"Caudle Lectures,"** it is true, the pungency of the wit, the success with which certain social or domestic features are hit off, and the artistic conception and consistency of the whole, are most notable, and suffice to render them unique. The moral tendency, where it is seen at all, is much less apparent than it is even in some of his other and less successful comic writings. It is inserted here and there more by suggestion than direct expression, and the nature of the productions is not such as to give it any weight. But for its unique character and the flashes of wit which it contains, we should have been disposed to regard this part of Mr. Jerrold's writings as belonging rather to the fugitive or ephemeral order. . . . In thoroughly comic character, Mr. Jerrold has produced nothing so complete as **"Mrs. Caudle."** . . . [But] we have an impression that the author's predilection for making his characters appear as representatives of his own ironical views of life tends in some degree to mar the comic effect of such characters. With Jerrold, wit and humor, whether expressed in impersonation or in his own descriptions, are never made use of without a very apparent aim. . . . Several of the tales in the **"Men of Character,"** and in **"Cakes and Ale,"** contain passages of what we may be permitted to call pure and gratuitous fun; but it is not in these that we find the best specimens of Mr. Jerrold's comic manner. The satirist invariably prevails over the artist, and even in his most playful moods it is impossible for him to write a page without dashing into it some stinging sarcasm. **"Punch's Letters to his Son,"** those singularly felicitous imitations of Lord Chesterfield's "Letters," in spite of all their comicality, are satirical from beginning to end. The text of each is taken from social shams and follies; and it is so with almost every thing Mr. Jerrold has written, if we except his plays, which seem to have been composed for the most part on the principle of enjoying and communicating the enjoyment of drollery.

It is as a satirist, then, rather than as a comic writer . . . that we must consider Mr. Jerrold—as one, in short, who makes his comic vein subservient to the purposes of satire. . . . [Mr. Jerrold's wit] plays momentarily around its object, showing in a lurid light its moral deformity, or its formal hollowness, and then strikes it with a withering stroke. . . . All worldly distinctions—all the forms and shows of things—are to Mr. Jerrold so many masks which he must tear off and show the abstract thing, the living, practical reality behind. . . . It is not to be denied, however, that while Mr. Jerrold's satire is sometimes rather grim, it has on the whole a healthful character; and it is never directed against things which will bear a close moral scrutiny, or which are in any way allied to the nobler feelings and motives of humanity. His warmest sympathies are with the poor and his sarcasm is never more pitiless than when it is directed against those prejudices which arise from differences of social position. His most contemptible characters are invariably those whose sole claim to the position they occupy rests upon titles or wealth. He detects and exposes with merciless severity the meanness, the cupidity and the vices which obtain in high places. . . . Such being the general scope of his works, it is scarcely necessary to say that he is a firm believer in the doctrine of progress. He is perhaps the ablest and most energetic exponent in his own literary walk, of the more advanced views of that doctrine. Full as his writings are of fine chivalric sentiment, and the admiration of nobleness in all ranks of life, he has no sympathy with those who conceive that progress has not been made in all that is conducive to social well-being. (pp. 168-70)

One of his most recent and perhaps least known works, **"The Man made of Money,"** proceeds wholly on the ground of the retribution which follows an indulgence of avaricious propensities; and by incidents sometimes of the most telling and effective character, but often wildly extravagant, it expresses its author's ideas of the miseries arising from that inordinate love of gain which he seems in the strictest sense to consider the root of all evil. . . .

Mr. Jerrold has drawn too strongly on the intelligence of his readers in this tale. In his wish to give the moral of it an extraordinary force, he has overstepped altogether not only the bounds of probability . . . but the very wide bound allowed to the writer of fiction. His purpose in the story is weakened by the very efforts made to give it an additional strength, and the consequence is, that where we ought to have had the impressive, we have simply the horrible. Nor is this the only offence against good taste which this tale manifests; there are passages of it which cannot be justified by any reference to the moral aim which the writer has had in view: passages in which, as it seems to us, there is an unnecessary exhibition of the evils which he designs to expose, and, what is much worse, a resort to melo-dramatic effects and language as offensive as it is

uncalled for. As a whole, then, we consider **"The Man made of Money"** the least successful of Mr. Jerrold's works. The purpose of it comes out far more distinctly, because more naturally, and with greater effect, in some of his other works. The tendency to make too much of the moral designed to be conveyed in the story is apparent, it is true, in each of these—so apparent sometimes as almost to make us think that Mr. Jerrold considers money in its very abstract an evil, and poverty a virtue rather than a necessity: but delicacies of feeling and beauties of expression, not less than a clear and piercing irony, give a healthier and higher tone to the means by which the moral is brought out. (p. 170)

If, however, the reader would form a correct opinion respecting the true character of our author's genius—for genius of a high order he undoubtedly possesses—he should read **"St. Giles and St. James,"** and **"The Story of a Feather."** These are his most important, and we may perhaps add, his most finished works. In both, the serious as well as the comic phase of his mind is seen to advantage, and his peculiar vein of sarcasm runs through both. Of these two books, the first is, in some respects, the most successful. It has an artistic completeness which the subject of the other scarcely requires; it contains some of its author's finest thoughts, and most of those peculiarities or prejudices which have occasionally subjected him to adverse criticism. . . .

[Now, it has been asserted] that Mr. Jerrold has magnified the evils arising from social distinctions, overstated the claims of the poor, and overdrawn the picture of their misery. There is undoubtedly a tendency, in all his more serious writings, to make the most of the responsibilities of the rich; but that he can be charged with giving a false color to the virtues of the poor, or of exaggerating the evils arising from ignorance, no one who reads the story to which we now refer with any thing like the attention which it deserves, will, we think, be disposed to admit. . . . Mr. Jerrold has done no more in this novel than exhibit, in the light in which a writer of fiction is permitted to do so, the effect of a neglect of . . . duties. He has shown at once the demoralizing nature of an indulgence of the selfish principle, and the evil thereby entailed on those who are the victims of the neglect of duty consequent on that indulgence. In so doing, he has only more forcibly exhibited truths obvious enough to all, than is quite palatable to those whom they more immediately concern, and has in effect done no more than has been done by other writers. Nor do we think he can be charged with exaggerating the evils of our social system. . . . (p. 171)

Mr. Jerrold seldom if ever descends to the use of such language as is often employed in the condemnation of war. His intelligence, not less than his good taste and generous feeling, restrain him from the fulmination of coarse invectives or sweeping charges against those who have been the agents of what he conceives to be a false idea. Yet, on this as on other subjects which provoke his sarcasm, Mr. Jerrold may very fairly be regarded as taking up a position from which he might be easily driven by weapons of his own forging. . . .

We have thus endeavored briefly to point out some of the more prominent characteristics of Mr. Jerrold's literary character, giving illustrations of what we conceive to be the chief element of it—viz., a serious and earnest nature working with the materials, so to speak, of a comic and satirical writer. (p. 172)

Although we are disposed to regard Mr. Jerrold as in some respects the most practical of our modern novelists—as giving us, upon the whole, the most ordinary pictures of human life in those aspects in which he looks at it—it would be a great mistake to suppose that his writings are destitute of those expressions of feeling which are, in the strictest sense of the word, poetical. While it must be admitted that there is occasionally a tendency towards the use of language and metaphors which are the very reverse of tasteful or elegant, for the most part his style is clear and terse—singularly so for a writer of such strong feelings, and yet necessarily so, we should be disposed to think, for the effect of his satire. So pregnant and complete are some of his sentences, that it would seem as if in a few words he had struck out a meaning which could not have been better conveyed in a page. (pp. 172-73)

The love of nature, and of all things beautiful, as evinced in such passages, marks, in a greater or less degree, almost every one of Mr. Jerrold's works, except such as are broadly and exclusively comic. He turns aside, as if for relief and refreshment, from the city scenes of misery and the haunts of profligacy, to the quiet of the sunny lanes and the breezy downs of England. His landscapes are all unmistakably English. (p. 173)

There is a geniality about the **"Chronicles of Clovernook,"** and on the whole an absence of the author's more extreme opinions, which has always led us to regard it as among his most successful comic writings. . . .

The ironical enters so largely into every thing of a comic character which Mr. Jerrold has written, that it would be impossible, even did our limits permit, to quote a passage of any length in which it does not occupy a marked prominence. Nor is his irony at all of the delicate or obscure kind. (p. 174)

[It is manifest, we think] that Mr. Jerrold has made great progress since the earliest of his works was published; it is certainly not too much to expect that he will yet attain to a much higher position than the one he now occupies. As it is, his writings are worthy of more attention than they receive from the large class to whom his qualities, both of mind and heart, are little known. We trust it has been shown that he is no mere wit; not simply a satirist of social follies, but a man of strong convictions and keen sensibilities, equally alive to what is grave and serious, to the ludicrous and the mirthful. His errors—and they arise as often from the strength of his feelings as from his repugnance to all that is formal and hollow—are not those of a man who lacks charity, but are frequently the result of a too ready acquiescence of the judgment in the dictates of a heart easily and strongly moved. He has contributed much that is healthful and invigorating to the literature of the day, and we think his faults may be lightly passed over in consideration of his sympathy with so much that is true and elevating. (p. 175)

"Genius and Writings of Douglas Jerrold," in The Eclectic Magazine, *Vol. XXXII, No. II, June, 1854, pp. 166-75.*

THE ATHENAEUM (essay date 1854)

[A rereading of Mr. Jerrold's works] serves to confirm our original opinion, that their object is to advance the good of mankind; that to this object there has been a devotion of rare skill, undoubted originality, imperturbable good temper,—concealed, perhaps, occasionally under an apparent fierceness of phrase and a force and flash of wit at once dazzling and delightful. A body of works more original, either in the artistic construction or in the informing spirit has not been added to the national literature in our time.

An especial charm in these works is, the visible earnestness of purpose of their author. . . . [He] teaches invaluable truths. . . . Our feeling that Mr. Jerrold speaks under conviction renders the arguments and illustrations in his stories doubly powerful and attractive. . . .

We do not, however, indorse all Mr. Jerrold's sentiments. . . . [In '**St. Giles and St. James**'] there are conclusions which do not naturally follow the premises, and effects traced to causes which have not produced them. . . . Still the story is a fearful story. . . .

We may add, with respect to '**St. Giles and St. James,**' that . . . [it] especially excels in touches of character. . . .

La Bruyère wrote "Characters" which have charmed many generations and will charm many more; so graceful are they, so eloquent, so lightly, yet so strikingly, outlined. When he draws at full length he puts a fictitious name to his handiwork, as Gilray used to do at the foot of his portrait-caricatures. Mr. Jerrold's "characters" are of another complexion and quality. His gallery is all alive and in action, there is less of sentiment appended to his personages or put in their mouths than is to be found in any of his other works; but then the sentiment is acted, if not spoken, and seldom has wisdom played under so merry, so shifting, and so attractive a mask, or masks, as on this occasion. It is not all merry, however,—there is rue among the flowers, and an occasional savour of bitterness for which the author himself apologizes—in his own ironical humour. Of the eight "characters" we have heard each in turn pronounced to be the best. . . .

The originality of conception and expression in these "characters" authorizes us to distrust the old classical legend, that Aesop gained the last intellectual gift which Mercury had to bestow. . . . Mr. Jerrold has succeeded to the inheritance of Aesop,—has improved the property,—and is liberal with it to boot. Witness the rich prodigality of his '**Cakes and Ale**,'— cakes of every variety, ale for all palates, and abundance of both;—with "bitter ale" for those who need a tonic.

We hope Mr. Jerrold will take advice as well as give it. . . . Mr. Jerrold, then, we would strongly advise to look to the application of some of his "morals." More than one concluding paragraph to the stories in '**Cakes and Ale**' cannot be accepted as the "morals" for which they are intended. (p. 1293)

'**The Chronicles of Clovernook**' may not be the most attractive or popular, but it is perhaps the most philosophical,—and, with all its fun, the most serious of Mr. Jerrold's works. . . .

We say nothing of the construction of this story. It has its faults, doubtless . . . ; but these are minor matters, and we forget them in the philosophy which pervades the work throughout. How pleasantly in this way does Mr. Jerrold extend, perhaps without deliberately intending it, the elementary principles, or the system, which Descartes himself only succeeded in establishing after sublime and persevering efforts, "Cogito, ergo sum." Most people have been content to stop at the definition as conclusive; but the Clovernook philosophy goes a step further, and when a man says *I think, therefore I am,* he is made to add the really fearful question, "and *Who are you?*" . . .

[Many wrongs,] social or otherwise, [are] discussed, with suggestions for remedy, in this volume. Some have a serious, some a comic aspect; a few seem to defy a treatment that shall interest, but Mr. Jerrold, however we may dissent from some of his details, is one of those happy writers who, if he cannot always convince you, can win interest by putting warmth into the coldest subjects. (p. 1294)

We have little space left us to speak of those two able works, the **'Story of a Feather,'** and **'A Man made of Money.'** The former is in the hands of more young people than any of Mr. Jerrold's works; and in the hearts of youthful England his popularity rests on this light, graceful, and instructive story. A general reader will, however, observe that light as is the book, it carries a heavy freight of wisdom, and that it is written in a vein for all perusers. We would not pause to censure light faults where beauty hangs upon the blade of every feather. . . .

The **'Man made of Money'** reminds us at once of Hoffman, Chamisso, and Balzac. Of the first, in the mingling of the grotesque and the terrible; of Chamisso in the simplicity and air of truthfulness in the characters who are outside the circle of terror, and of Balzac, because Jericho's skin is a more genuine *"Peau de Chagrin"* than that which forms the basis of the story so named, by the French writer. . . .

If there be any who have not read [**'A Man made of Money'**], they will thank us for not further describing it; and they who have would take description as impertinence. (p. 1295)

> *"Reviews: The Writings of Douglas Jerrold',"* in The Athenaeum, *No. 1409, October 28, 1854, pp. 1293-95.*

LITTELL'S LIVING AGE   (essay date 1857)

With the exception always of Mrs. Caudle, and perhaps of Mrs. Jericho and Sir Arthur Hodmadod in *The Man made of Money,* [Jerrold] has not, by his tales, added to our British gallery of comic portraits characters that remain so distinctly and permanently in the popular memory. . . . "The truth is," says one of his critics, "the moralist, the satirist, prevails in Mr. Jerrold over the artist. His creations are in most cases but vehicles for some feeling or opinion . . . and it is more rarely that, laying aside intention and preference, he revels in his own fancies. . . . Consider Mr. Jerrold as a man of thought and feeling working in the element of fiction; and then, giving him all the more credit when he does from time to time contribute an original physiognomy to our portfolio of comic portraits, you will yet cease to regard this as his proper business, and will be content if his tales are so constructed that each of them, the names and figures vanishing, shall leave its impression as a whole." To this we may add, that the moral fiction, if not so popular a form of art as the fiction pure and poetical, still is a form of art. And in this style of art, not only are some of Mr. Jerrold's shorter tales, as in his two series entitled *Men of Character* and *Cakes and Ale,* fine specimens, but even his longer and continuous fictions, such as *The Man made of Money,* have striking points of merit. The canons of invention are here different from those which hold in the pure novel; but there are canons of invention here too. When Mr. Jerrold, in his *Man made of Money,* makes the hero literally what the name implies,—a living personage, whose flesh consists miraculously of bank-notes,—it is clear that he had in his mind a type of comic fiction different from that of the natural comic novel. The type may not be popular; but it is legitimate, and has precedents in Swift and other authorities in our fictitious literature.

But whatever may have been Mr. Jerrold's success compared with some of his contemporaries in the direct fiction or tale, there is a kindred department of imaginative literature in which

his supremacy is admitted. He is almost alone as a writer of genuine English comedies. . . . The thirteen dramas which he has reprinted among his collective works, beginning in order of time with his *Black-eyed Susan* and his *Rent Day,* and ending with his *Time works Wonders,* and others lately represented, have upheld on the stage, and uphold still, wherever they are acted, the reputation of simple and classic English comedy; and when read at home, they charm equally by their plot and construction, and their brilliant and witty dialogue. Indeed, those very peculiarities of his genius which operate against him in the novel, fit him for mastery in the comic drama. Here also his English style is seen to perfection. . . . (pp. 315-16)

Many of his writings are rather essays, or descriptive sketches or fantasies in prose, than satires or compositions of mere wit; and in all his writings, even the most purely witty, there are touches and passages of pathos, simple description, criticism, and argument. Some of his shorter tales are pathetic and poetical throughout. His earnest nature . . . is perpetually breaking forth in direct invective; and occasionally he couches his meaning imaginatively in an apologue, or in a species of ghastly allegory. . . . [It] is in his writings as a journalist that his direct opinions are most explicitly manifested. . . . [As] a journalist on what is called the "liberal side," he is consistent with himself from first to last. (p. 316)

> *"Douglas Jerrold,"* in Littell's Living Age, *Vol. LIII, No. 675, May 2, 1857, pp. 313-16.*

THE ATHENAEUM   (essay date 1857)

Death has taken from among us a man of vast and peculiar force. . . . Douglas Jerrold was the greatest marvel to those who knew him best. His reading was wide, and his memory for what he read prodigious. . . . [The] powers which made his fame were native. He was most widely known perhaps by his wit. . . . And his wit was very nimble, crackling, and original. No man could resist its spontaneity and sparkle, and it wrote its daily story in London life as a thing apart and institutional. But his wit, however brilliant, was not his finest gift. . . . His wit made only one side of his genius—sprung indeed from a central characteristic—the extraordinary rapidity of his apprehension. He saw into the hearts of things. He perceived analogies invisible to other men. These analogies sometimes made him merry, sometimes indignant. And as he never hung fire, dull people often saw his wrath before they understood his reason; and they blamed him, not in truth because he was wrong, but because they were slow. (p. 758)

Indeed, no dramatic work of ancient or modern days ever reached the success of [**'Black-Eyed Susan'**]. It was performed, without break, for hundreds of nights. . . .

Many dramas, comic and serious, followed this first success— all shining with points and colours. Among these were **'Nell Gwynne,' 'The Schoolfellows,'** and **'The Housekeeper.'** Drury Lane opened its exclusive doors to an author who had made fortune and fame for [theatre managers] Elliston and Cooke. . . . He returned to the theatre after a while with his **'Bride of Ludgate,'** the first of many ventures and many successes [of stories at sea]. **'The Mutiny at the Nore'** had followed the first nautical success, and his minor pieces . . . continued to run long and gloriously. . . .

A selection from the early writings for the stage, made by himself, has been published in the 'Collected Edition' of his works. But many were unjustly condemned, and among those rejected plays the curious seeker will find some of the most sterling literary gold. His wit was so prodigal, and he prized it so little, save as a delight to others, that he threw it away like dust, never caring for the bright children of his brain, and smiling with complacent kindness at people who repeated to him his jests—as their own! At the least demur, too, he would surrender his most happy allusions and his most trenchant hits. . . .

The best part of many years of his life was given up freely to . . . theatrical tasks,—for his genius was dramatic—his family belonged to the stage—and his own pulpit, as he thought, stood behind the footlights.

In **'The Prisoner of War,'** in parts cast for them, the two Keeleys harvested their highest comic honours. **'Bubbles of a Day'** followed,—the most electric and witty play in the English language; a play without story, scenery, or character, but which, by mere power of dialogue, by flash, swirl, and coruscation of fancy, charmed one of the most intellectual audiences ever gathered in the Haymarket. Then came **'Time works Wonders,'** remarkable as being one of the few works in which the dramatist paid much attention to story. **'The Catspaw,'** produced at the Haymarket,—**'St. Cupid,'** an exquisite cabinet piece, first produced at Windsor Castle, and afterwards at the Princess's Theatre, . . . one of the most dainty and tender assumptions of this charming artist,—and **'The Heart of Gold'** . . . complete the series of his later works. We are glad to announce, however, that the dramatist has left behind a finished five-act comedy, with the title of **'The Spendthrift.'** . . .

Contemporaneously, he had worked his way into notice as a prose writer of a very brilliant and original type—chiefly through the periodicals. His passion was periodicity—the power of being able to throw his emotions daily, or weekly, into the common reservoirs of thought. Silence was to him a pain like hunger. . . . All the chief writings of our author—except **'A Man made of Money'**—saw the light in magazines, and were written with the devil at the door. **'Men of Character'** appeared in *Blackwood's Magazine,*—**'The Chronicles of Clovernook'** in the *Illuminated Magazine,* of which he was founder and editor,—**'St. Giles and St. James'** in the *Shilling Magazine,* of which he was also founder and editor,—and **'The Story of a Feather,' 'Punch's Letters to his Son,'** and **'The Caudle Lectures'** in *Punch.* The exquisite gallery of Fireside Saints which appear in *Punch's Almanack* for the present year is from his hand. Most of these works bear the magazine mark upon them—the broad arrow of their origin; but the magazine brand in this case, like the brands of famous vintages, if testifying to certain accidents of carriage, attests also the vigour and richness of the soil from which they come. **'Clovernook'** is less perfect as a work of art than many a book born and forgotten since the Hermit fed on dainty viands and discoursed of sweet philosophy. Some of his essays contributed at an early time to the *Athenaeum* and to *Blackwood's Magazine* rank among the most subtle and delicate productions of his muse. (p. 759)

[The] depth of [Jerrold's] insight, the subtlety of his analysis, the vividness of his presentation must strike every one who reads. His place among the wits of our own time is clear enough. He had less frolic than Theodore Hook, less elaborate humour than Sydney Smith, less quibble and quaintness than Thomas Hood. But he surpassed all these in intellectual flash and strength. His wit was all steel points,—and his talk was like squadrons of lancers in evolution. . . . His wit stood nearer to poetic fancy than to broad humour. . . . In his earlier time,

before age and success had mellowed him to his best, he was sometimes accused of ill-nature, a charge which he vehemently resented and which seemed only ludicrous to those privileged with his friendship. To folly, pretence, and assumption he gave no quarter, though in fair fight; and some of those who tried lances with him long remembered his home thrust. . . . No man ever used such powers with greater gentleness. Indeed, to speak the plain truth, his fault as a man—if it be a fault— was a too great tenderness of heart. . . . If every one who received a kindness at his hands should lay a flower on his tomb, a mountain of roses would rise on the last resting-place of Douglas Jerrold. (pp. 759-60)

"Douglas Jerrold," in The Athenaeum, *No. 1546, June 13, 1857, pp. 758-60.*

SIR NATHANIEL (essay date 1857)

Of [Jerrold's] novels and tales, the two most ambitious, in length and breadth of treatment, are **"A Man made of Money"** and **"St. Giles and St. James."** The construction of a story, with its evolution or development as a work of art, was by no means Mr. Jerrold's forte. He was not good at a plot, nor showed any wealth of resources in carrying it out. He had little of that surprising tact in the adjustment of the main plan, and the harmonious arrangement of its parts. . . . The longest of them, **"St. Giles and St. James,"** has been called, by one of the author's most thorough-going admirers, a fearful story. . . . It is allowed, however, that the close of the story is faulty. . . . [It] is in bits of character and practical philosophy that the book is mainly attractive. Some of the characters are naught. . . . But the reader finds amends in [other] sketches. . . . (pp. 410-11)

It is said that the **"Story of a Feather"** is in the hands of more young people than any of Mr. Jerrold's works, and that his popularity in the hearts of youthful England rests on this light, graceful, and instructive story. The same authority pronounces the **"Chronicles of Clovernook"** the most philosophical, and, with all its fun, the most serious, of his *opera omnia.* . . . To the same category may be referred some portions of **"Cakes and Ale"**—cakes of the spiciest, and ale of the strongest, sometimes more than a little *hard,* but never lacking a liberal proportion of the hop-bitter.

There is an extravagance and farcical exertion, a sort of mechanical want of repose, about **"Men of Character,"** which makes the reading of their exploits and experiences a rather fatiguing business. It must be owned that when the author is at what we may call his middlemost, he is very middling indeed. And, writing on the scale and for the purposes he did, he very frequently kept for a long time together in this mediocre track, this not at all golden mean. He is then strained and stagey in his seriousness—abounding with melodramatic phrases . . . ; while his humour drags heavily, is fuller of grotesque antics than genial inspirations, rather labours than makes holiday, and, thus far losing the very essence of humour, is forced out by undue pressure, rather than oozes out, from a ripe exuberance of its own. We feel this in several of the stories included in **"Cakes and Ale"** . . .—papers that recall, in various particulars, the heart and soul, as well as the manner and penmanship, of two real humorists to whom the writer was not very remotely akin, though by no means so nearly as we could wish, or as some, perhaps, will affirm—Charles Lamb, to wit, and Thomas Hood. But in **"Men of Character"** the grotesque is predominant, the fun is almost ever far-fetched and fussy, and proves more of a damper than a fillup to the spirits. . . . [We fail to realise the characters] as the phrase goes; they are caricatured allegories, or distorted abstractions, anything but probable, practicable, flesh-and-blood personages. They are quaint embodiments of an idea, and the idea is one-sided in the conception and burlesqued in the embodiment. We feel as we read that the author as he wrote had before his eye a theatrical stage, actors, and audience; that he aimed at effect such as would tell there. . . . The writers of successful farces, it has been laid down as a general rule, do not make good tellers of stories, because they are not congradual unfolding of natural events, but they must "distil" human beings "above proof"— go out of their way in search of broad effects, and call into use exaggerated dialogues, full of ultra puns, rugged points, and broken English. (pp. 412-13)

Incomparably superior is **"Punch's Complete Letter Writer."** Here we have Mr. Jerrold producing a far greater effect without a twentieth part of the effort. . . . But of all his works the most successful we take to be **"Mrs. Caudle's Curtain Lectures."** . . . [Mrs. Marsh in an early chapter of "Emilia Wyndham" wrote—". . .] It is no very difficult matter to draw a Mrs. Caudle, and publish how in a popular journal; and with such success, that she shall become a byword in families, and serve as an additional reason for that rudeness and incivility, that negligent contempt, with which too many Englishmen still think it their prerogative, as men and true-born Britons, to treat their wives." (p. 414)

Few writers suffer so little as Douglas Jerrold by being seen in quotations. In fact, he not unfrequently appears to more advantage in this mutilated form than when studied as a whole: one is apt to become fatigued by such a sustained crackle of fireworks, such a recurring series of witty sayings, such a prolonged succession of retort and repartee. The comedies he wrote in his prime are richer and racier in this quality than the dramas he dashed off in his youth; but even in these dramas the most note-worthy point is the same scintillating, epigrammatic character in dialogue and diction. (p. 416)

Of [Jerrold's] larger and later works we may say . . . that they are defective in the art and practice of construction, the plot being often a failure as regards ingenuity of design and a gradually accumulating interest; but that in his characters and dialogue the author is indeed an "approved good master"—smartness of repartee being peculiarly his forte. . . . Hardly a scene throughout **"Bubbles of a Day,"** or the grave and gay fluctuations of **"Time Works Wonders,"** or the mixed modes of **"Retired from Business,"** or the active and passive voices of the **"Catspaw,"** or the crosses and contrarieties of **"Saint Cupid,"** but supplies proof positive, and superlative, of the dramatist's facility and felicity in this line of things. But as acting plays their fortune has been, on the whole, untoward, and no doubt disappointed him in a high degree. In effect, and for the playgoer, they are now shelved; but on shelves whence the *reader* will often take them down, to enjoy in the closet what the stage has perhaps too willingly let die. Meanwhile the shorter pieces, some of them, flourish still, and bid fair to flourish long; for there is safety in predicting an extended lease of popularity to **"Black-ey'd Susan,"** the **"Rent Day,"** and the **"Prisoner of War."** (p. 417)

Sir Nathaniel, "Notes on Note-Worthies, of Divers Orders, Either Sex, and Every Age: Douglas Jerrold," in New Monthly Magazine, Vol. CX, No. CCCCXL, August, 1857, pp. 407-17.

[J. HANNAY] (essay date 1857)

[Douglas Jerrold] was in a singular degree a representative man of his age; his age having set him to wrestle with it,—having tried his force in every way,—having left its mark on his entire surface. Jerrold and the century help to explain each other, and had found each other remarkably in earnest in all their dealings. This fact stamps on the man a kind of genuineness, visible in all his writings,—and giving them a peculiar force and raciness, such as those of persons with a less remarkable experience never possess. We are told, that, in selling yourself to the Devil, it is the proper traditionary practice to write the contract in your blood. Douglas, in binding himself against him, did the same thing. You see his blood in his ink,—and it gives a depth of tinge to it. (p. 2)

Tradition and family connection must have led him chiefly [to the theatre]; for though he had some of the most important qualities of a dramatist, very few of his dramas seem likely to live,—and even these are not equal to his works in other departments. The **"Man made of Money"** will outlast his best play. His most popular drama,—**"Black-eyed Susan,"** though clever, pretty, and tender, is not, as a work of art, worthy of his genius; nor did he consider it so himself. In his dramas we find, I think, rather touches of character, than characters,— scenes, rather than plots,—. . . dramatic genius, rather than harmonious creations of it. He could not separate himself from his work sufficiently for the purposes of the higher stage. As Johnson says of "Cato," "We pronounce the name of Cato, but we think on Addison,"—so one may say of any character of Jerrold's that it suggests and refers us to its author. . . . There is always the wit of the man, whether the play be **"Gertrude's Cherries,"** or **"The Smoked Mixer,"** or **"Fifteen Years of a Drunkard's Life,"**—or what not. *That* quality never failed him. He dresses up all his characters in that brilliant livery. But dialogue is not enough for the stage and compared with the attraction of an intense action is nothing. . . .

His first fame and success, however, were owing to the Drama; and though his non-dramatic labors were greater and still more successful, he never altogether left the stage. I repeat, that I value his plays, most because they helped to discipline him for his after-work; and I thank the theatre chiefly for ripening in its heat the philosophic humorist. That was the real character of the man. He tried many things, and he produced much; but the root of him was that he was a humorous thinker. He did not write first-rate plays, or first-rate novels, rich as he was in *the elements* of playwright and novelist. He was not an artist. But he had a rare and original eye and soul—and in a peculiar way he could pour out himself. In short, to be an Essayist was the bent of his nature and genius. (pp. 3-4)

He is often *quaint,*—a word which describes what no other word does,—always conveying a sense of originality, and of what, when we wish to be condemnatory, we call egotism, but which, when it belongs to genius, is delightful. . . .

[**"Men of Character"** is] a curious collection of philosophical stories;—for artist he was not; he was always a thinker. He had a way of dressing up a bit of philosophical observation into a story very happily. He had much feeling for symbol, and like the old architects, would fill all things, pretty or ugly, with meaning. When one reads these stories, one does not feel as if it were the writer's vocation to be a story-teller, but as if he were using the story as a philosophical toy. (p. 5)

Jerrold's first papers of mark in "Punch" were those signed "Q." His style was now formed, as his mind was, and these papers bear the stamp of his peculiar way of thinking and writing. Assuredly, his is a *peculiar* style in the strict sense; and as marked as that of Carlyle or Dickens. You see the self-made man in it,—a something *sui generis,*—not formed on the "classical models," but which has grown up with a kind of twist in it, like a tree that has had to force its way up surrounded by awkward environments. Fundamentally, the man is a thinking humorist; but his mode of expression is strange. The perpetual inversions, the habitual irony, the mingled tenderness and mockery, give a kind of gnarled surface to the style, which is pleasant when you get familiar with it, but which repels the stranger, and to some people even remains permanently disagreeable. It think it was his continual irony which at last brought him to writing as if under a mask; whereas it would have been better to write out flowingly, musically, and lucidly. . . . His wit is not to the head only, but of the heart,—often sentimental, and constantly *fanciful,* that is dependent on a quality which imperatively requires a sympathetic nature to give it to full play. Take those "Punch" papers which soon helped to make "Punch" famous, and Jerrold himself better known. Take the **"Story of a Feather,"** as a good expression of his more earnest and tender mood. . . . How moral, how stoical, the feeling that pervades it! (pp. 5-6)

A basis of philosophical observation, tinged with tenderness, and a dry, ironical humor,—all, like the Scottish lion in heraldry, "within a double tressuretleury and counterfleury" of wit and fancy,—such is a Jerroldian paper of the best class in "Punch." It stands out by itself from all the others,—the sharp, critical knowingness, sparkling with puns, of a Beckett—the inimitable, wise, easy, playful, worldly, social sketch of Thackeray. In imagery he had no rivals there; for his mind had a very marked tendency to the ornamental and illustrative,—even to the grotesque. In satire again, he had fewer competitors than in humor;—sarcasms lurk under his similes, like wasps in fruit or flowers. (p. 7)

["**Man of Money**"] bids fair, I think, to be read longer than any of his works. It is one of those fictions in which . . . the supernatural appears as an element, and yet is made to conform itself in action to real and everyday life, in such a way that the understanding is not shocked. . . . The conception is fine and imaginative, and ought to rank with the best of those philosophical stories so fashionable in the last century. Its working-out in the every-day part is brilliant and pungent; and much ingenuity is shown. . . . In short, I esteem this Jerrold's best book,—the one which contains most of his mind. . . . ["**The Man made of Money**"] is the completest of his books as a creation, and the most characteristic in point of style,—is based on a principle which predominated in his mind,—is the most original in imaginativeness, and the best sustained in point and neatness, of the works he has left. (pp. 8-9)

> [*J. Hannay,*] *"Douglas Jerrold," in* The Atlantic Monthly, *Vol. I, No. 1, November, 1857, pp. 1-12.*

THE NORTH AMERICAN REVIEW   (essay date 1859)

Douglas Jerrold has passed away forever from the earth; but he has left behind him such memorials of his wit, genius, and intellectual ability, as the world will not willingly let die. Nor are these his only triumphs. Time and death have their separate, inalienable sovereignties, and exercise with remorseless despotism, their conscriptive rights over individuals, and all personal and historic achievements,—often diminishing what seemed great in human character, and enlarging what at first

sight, and in the common estimation, was regarded as mean and insignificant; but neither time, death, nor eternity can change that which is essentially true in the soul of man, nor rob it of its moral grandeur and sublimity. (p. 431)

In truth, in stern loyalty to his principles and convictions lies the crowning glory of Jerrold. . . . Sydney Smith alone among moderns is worthy to compare with Jerrold, not only in the sudden promptness and keen edge of his retort, but in the fine morality of his humor and sarcasm. Jerrold exceeds him, however, in fancy, in the symbolism of truth, and in those grand attributes of intellect and imagination which render this wit equally a man of genius and of profound practical wisdom. It is true that the jovial and learned divine is also a man of genius, and that he possesses faculties and acquirements which cannot be claimed for Jerrold,—elaborate humor, for example, and scholarship; but, large and liberal as he was in mind and character, and ever ready . . . to lend his lance for the succor of the oppressed and the punishment of the oppressor, he was necessarily, from his position and profession, walled round by many obstructions to the free play of his intellect, and lacked, as we think, that keen, instinctive recognition and appreciation of truth in its absolute nature, which are so characteristic of Jerrold, in his graver and professedly artistic writings. (pp. 431-32)

Although a hard-working, laborious writer, Jerrold was a fragmentary man, and expressed himself best in fragments. Those short, piquant pieces in Punch, how admirable they are! How he adapts himself to the space he has to occupy, and how well he fills it! . . .

A catalogue of his printed performances, including his plays, magazine articles, pamphlets, Punch contributions, and books, would be a startlingly voluminous affair, and we dare not attempt it in these pages. Nor indeed would it be worth the trouble, so far as the literary merit of many of them is concerned; but it would illustrate better than many sounding sentences could the indomitable energy and industry of the author. Jerrold himself set small value upon his plays, although he naturally enough loved the salt-water smack of **"Black-Eyed Susan,"** the flavor of which so well suited the popular taste, and established him, while yet a very young man, as a solid power in the realm. **"Time Works Wonders"** is one of his most mature plays; but we doubt if it will survive the present century.

His prose writings are far better than his plays. There are whole poems of great beauty in his **"Chronicles of Clovernook,"**—a book in which is revealed, we think, more of his real nature than in any other of his works. It sparkles with poetic genius,—contains much profound thinking, imaginative suggestion, and wise practical teaching. The style, too, is more artistic than his usual method, which, while it possesses sufficient originality, is sometimes crooked, distorted, and unmusical. (p. 438)

> "'The Life and Remains of Douglas Jerrold'," in The North American Review, *Vol. LXXXIX, No. 185, October, 1859, pp. 431-50.*

JAMES HUTCHISON STIRLING   (essay date 1860)

Some of [Jerrold's plays], like **"Black-eyed Susan,"** are eminently successful, replenishing the coffers of vulgar, dissipated, greedy managers, but bringing to their author a renewal only of neglect, disappointment, and injustice. . . . Few authors have ever undergone a more protracted ordeal or passed through a longer novitiate than Jerrold. And when, at last, his bark did—after veerings, and tackings, warpings-in, and warpings-out, in the dirtiest weather and the most intricate of channels—reach the open sea, and the fog rose up and showed the shoals behind and the whole ocean of success in front, it was wonderful to find it still so hale and hearty, still so true and cheery, still so sound and pure at the core, if at the same time, also, it must be confessed, somewhat dull and indifferent, somewhat sceptical and incredulous as to the advantages of the voyage at all, and inclined rather to drop anchor and enjoy the sunshine. (pp. 22-3)

In later life, [the products of Jerrold's literary activity] were, for the most part, condemned as worthless by their own author, who spoke even of the remarkably successful **"Black-eyed Susan,"** and the equally successful **"Mrs. Caudle's Curtain Lectures,"** as trash and lollipop, and desired to assume the honours of paternity for such works only as **"St. Giles and St. James," "Time works Wonders," "A Man made of Money,"** and **"The Chronicles of Clovernook."** . . . Indeed, it is doubtful if even these latter works possess themselves any very certain germ of an enduring vitality. For the conditions of literature are involved, now-a-days, in processes of transformation that are as yet neither explained nor explored; and there is now the ever-increasing possibility of the existence of both talent and genius—clothed, too, in forms that, two or three generations ago, would have appeared marvels magnificent as palaces of Aladdin—but without the least chance of either eminence or permanence of place in the progression of the ages. . . . [We] may say with assurance that, on the whole—despite one or two exceptions, which are themselves but temporary, perhaps—Jerrold's literary works have never struck deep root into public estimation, or enjoyed any very extended genuine popularity. (pp. 23-5)

We have done our best to love the writings of the brave Jerrold; but images and ideas . . . will ever intrude, and we wander from the book to theorize endlessly on the evils of premature and professional authorship. And yet we admit at once that Jerrold is a writer who has widely influenced the literary, political, and social opinions of his period; that he is an able writer, a vigorous writer; a man as dexterous with his pen as any master of fence with his rapier; a coiner and utterer of richest, raciest, subtlest sayings. We admit, too, that with the names of Dickens and Thackeray that of Jerrold also must be always associated; but even while conceding him this parity of place beside both, we assert that this place has mainly a mere external foundation, and that his writings have never exercised a tithe of the influence or acquired a tithe of the renown of those of either.

Like that of some of the wits of the bygone century, his fame, indeed, may, at the last, prove an affair of tradition rather than document. He is essentially, even in his best writings, the sayer of good things, of strong things—the wit of clubs. His works are not so much carefully-meditated, carefully-elaborated, carefully-finished literary wholes, in which the fervid soul of an original author has accomplished the embodiment of the deep feelings and deep thoughts which he knows to be his own, which seem to him to have been born with him, which seem to him to live and move in him, tormenting him to speech—not so much these collections rather of hard, sharp, effective hits in words. He writes, *saccadé*, as if in blows. We feel as if we had to do with a master of attack whose rapid upper-cuts and unexpected back-handers were perpetually surprising and confounding us. His style and manner faithfully reflect his

experiences, and declare him to have been a fighter, a bitter fighter, against adverse fortune and opposing circumstances. As we said already, contrast reigns; contrast is his secret. (pp. 26-8)

How keen he is, how bright, how swift, how polished! the points in his writing are like the points of needles. One feels sometimes, indeed, as if Jerrold thought in needles—wrote in needles. His very handwriting, "smaller than printed types," seems to have been the work of just such an implement. (p. 28)

Jerrold's manner of writing will be found, throughout his works, generally similar. If there be any exception it is in the inaugural chapters, which, for the most part, are written freshly, flowingly, triumphantly, as if from a full heart and a full soul. Jerrold, indeed, is always buoyant, elastic, alert at the start: he is not long-breathed, however; he soon flags—inspiration fails, and work grows drudgery. [Then the writing] looks artificial and mechanical; the deft hand turns it and turns it till it shines again, but the *hand* seems only there; the *heart* seems otherwise: the heart, in fact, seems to be constantly saying to itself: "This *is* weariness of the flesh; this *is* but the trick of the trade: if I had my own will it is not here I should be sitting, playing upon words and ringing the changes upon sentences!" (p. 35)

We do not contemplate here any regular and complete criticism of Jerrold's writings; but we must remark, in passing, that the characters and conduct of [**"St. Giles and St. James"**] display faults quite similar to those we signalize. The characters are never creations, and seldom portraits: these Jerichos, and Cuttlefishes, and Canditofts, and Capsticks, and Bright Jems, and Tom Blasts, have no life of their own; they have the life only of their author; they are but his puppets, and discourse at his motion and in his dialect. . . . The incidents are few; each is made the most of, nor passes till its ultimate drop is wrung. The finale is merely arbitrary, and, as is to be expected, comes at last by a simple pulling down of the curtain.

In fact, we are carried always back to the evils of premature authorship. When Jerrold reached middle-life, and had acquired his audience, he was already *blasé;* he had now no longer enthusiasm, and hardly hope. Sitting there at his desk, and having with ready alacrity and prompt vigour stamped with his own brand the living interests and current topics of the day for the columns of *Punch,* it was only with unwillingness, we fancy, that he turned him to his other writings. These things in *Punch* were alive; they had the red blood of the day in them: but those others, the creatures of his fancy, in his other and apparently more proper tasks, were but pale abstractions. The world was no longer what the golden boy had dreamed it was. His illusions were all gone. The evils of life were too gigantic; he heard them roaring all too unappeasably around him: he could no longer believe in a transforming "Presto" of the pen. His fancy was no longer an inspiration; it lay in his hands a tool—a tool that he could most dexterously use, but still a tool. Ever to cut and carve out weapons wherewith to pierce the wrongs he could no longer hope to redress, was irksome to him. His past lay behind him like a fearful dream. . . . So the club became his arena, and the solitary chamber, deserted of the enthusiasm that once had made it bright, was chill to him as the cell of monk.

The estimate we have thus put upon his writings may appear to many much too narrow, much too niggardly. We may seem to have flung but coldly, summarily, into the scales the products of a life for which we professed so much sympathy. Formal criticism has not been our object, however; and we hope that, while endeavouring to trace in the tissue the thread derived from the prematurity and necessity of the authorship, we have not unduly depreciated the signal and essential merits of the tissue itself. To that tissue, genius, as well as talent, has set its stamp; and it is heavy with gems with which, hereafter, many a pilgrim will seek to decorate his own plainness. (pp. 37-40)

> *James Hutchison Stirling, "Douglas Jerrold" (originally published in* Meliora, *April, 1860), in his* Jerrold, Tennyson and Macaulay: With Other Critical Essays, *Edmonston & Douglas, 1868, pp. 1-50.*

EDWARD COPPING (essay date 1892)

Douglas Jerrold had long gained a very wide reputation in literature, and took rank with the foremost authors of the day. . . . Douglas Jerrold was a wit, a brilliant and a ready wit. . . . Even now fresh illustrations of his wit are given to us from time to time by our writers of memoirs. A recent critic, Mr. J. Logie Robertson, is indeed of opinion, that it is his sayings, rather than his writings, which keep his name before the public. (p. 362)

Douglas Jerrold was accused of setting class against class by his writings, and it cannot be denied that the most moving passages in his works are those in which he depicts the sufferings of the poor and the harshness of the world towards them. It is these passages which explain the charge of bitterness so frequently brought against him. How keenly he resented that charge is known to all who have read his works. It evidently wounded him deeply and filled his sensitive nature with acute pain, whether directed against himself or his writings. . . . In his indignation he spares no sarcasm to give effect to his invectives; he strives to the utmost to make each sentence as pointed as possible, nay, as one of his critics remarked, every word seems to have been specially sharpened before being used. He wrote, as Hawthorne says, with an honest and a manly purpose; he was thoroughly sincere; he earnestly desired to make the world better, to lighten its suffering, and give a nobler dignity to life. But like Carlyle he lacked the higher qualities of the teacher: gentleness, forbearance, patience. He was too impulsive, too eager, too desirous of enforcing his views with peremptory sternness. An author who sees scarcely anything but the imperfections of human nature and the injustice of the world, who is so severe upon our faults, and who shows so little indulgence for our weakness, seems to take up a position outside the range of our sympathies, and thus alienates himself from his fellow men. There can be no doubt that Douglas Jerrold's writings fail of their full effect from this cause. We feel that we are not so black as we are painted; that the world is not so selfish, so mean, and so cruel as the satirist represents. (pp. 363-64)

It is impossible to resist the inference that [Jerrold's works] are no longer generally read. They have secured a place in our literature; but it is not the place their author strove to reach. (p. 364)

> *Edward Copping, "Douglas Jerrold," in* The New Review, *Vol. VII, No. 40, September, 1892, pp. 358-64.*

LEWIS MELVILLE (essay date 1903)

It is always with a feeling akin to sadness that one writes of an author who, once ranked too highly, has by succeeding

generations been dispossessed of his stripes and degraded to the ranks. On the rare occasions when the name of Douglas Jerrold is mentioned, the memory conjures up the picture of a brilliant, caustic wit and raconteur: yet in his day he was regarded by many as equal in humour to Thackeray and Dickens. (p. 149)

One of the few dramatic successes that Jerrold achieved was a comedy, **"Time Works Wonders,"** produced at the Theatre Royal, Haymarket, when it ran for seventy nights. The dialogue of this play is really brilliant, and often epigrammatic; but the plot is not well constructed. . . .

Jerrold was at his best when writing short humorous papers, like the **"Caudle Lectures."** He was ill-equipped for the writing of novels. His characters were not creations. Jericho, Capstick, Canditoft, Bright Jem, to mention a few, are the merest puppets. His philosophy was narrow; and he frequently interrupted the narrative to state his opinions, which, as a rule, were very superficial. He was always sincere, no doubt, but he trusted to his feelings rather than to his intellect; and, after all, the sentimentalist is not always in the right. **"A Man Made of Money"** is, perhaps, his best story. It deals with the supernatural. . . . The idea is well conceived, but indifferently carried out. The book gives the impression of having been written in a hurry.

He had a gift of describing characters. Of Jericho, a matter-of-fact man, he wrote: "Talk to him of Jacob's ladder, and he would ask the number of the steps"; of a pessimist, "He would not allow that there was a bright side to the moon"; and of a third, Capstick, "He wore his hatred of mankind as he would have worn a diamong ring: a thing at once to be put in the best light and to be very proud of." Occasionally he was epigrammatic "Beauty! it's like a guinea; when it's once changed at all, it's gone in a twinkling." "Patience is the strongest of strong drinks, for it kills the giant despair." "Wit, like money, bears an extra value when rung down immediately it is wanted. Men pay severely who require credit." "Despair of freedom, even at the worst, is atheism to the goddess Liberty." These are clever, but they are not polished. Nor was his humour polished. It was crude, and often laboured. It was middle-class humour. . . . He was not an artist. His style was not very literary. But his satire was trenchant, and his brilliancy undeniable. He was, however, a wit rather than a humourist. The best that may be said of him as an author is that he wrote several amusing sketches. (p. 150)

> *Lewis Melville, "The Centenary of Douglas Jerrold," in* The Bookman, London, *Vol. XXIII, No. 136, January, 1903, pp. 149-52.*

RICHARD KELLY (essay date 1967)

It is unfortunate that Jerrold's [series of satirical papers entitled **"The English in Little"**] I has never been reprinted, because it offers an interesting example of the high quality of comic journalism in the Victorian period. Furthermore, Jerrold has the ability to make his characters come to life and to entertain us even when the events of his day, which first called them forth, have passed.

Drawing on current topics, Jerrold satirizes the societies of both England and America. The dual satire is effective, achieved by having the papers written in dialect under the persona of Tom Thumb. Jerrold superficially pokes fun at the gullibility of the English and their preference for foreigners. . . . As one of England's most popular playwrights, Jerrold crusaded vehemently against the pernicious effects of mere spectacle upon the legitimate stage.

By dangling Thumb like a rash puppet in the midst of Buckingham Palace and making him raise the regal roof, Jerrold mocks royalty for lavishly favoring the foreign performer over many of England's gifted writers and artists. The aristocracy, upon whom Jerrold heaped the blame for most of England's ills, are also attacked for neglecting their country's poor and applauding the American visitor. . . . The characteristic frankness of Thumb also allowed Jerrold to expose the deplorable state of the drama, the inhuman conditions found in the workhouses, and the general hypocrisy of English society.

Interwoven and contrasting with the local satire is a critical and satiric portrayal of American society—its vulgarity and egotistical patriotism, its pragmatic ethical standards, and its hypocrisy in proclaiming itself a Free Republic while practicing slavery. On the other hand, one may discern beneath the satire Jerrold's respect for the forthrightness and stamina inherent in the American's brash independence. (p. 28)

It is a curious fact that **"The English in Little"** was not as popular with readers of *Punch* as was [Thackeray's] "The Snobs of England." . . . Viewed apart from the reputations of their creators, it seems that **"The English in Little"** has been unjustly ignored in favor of a work whose merit derives chiefly from the later fame of its author. (pp. 30-1)

> Richard Kelly, *"The American in England: An Examination of a Hitherto Neglected Satire by Douglas Jerrold,"* in The Victorian Newsletter *(reprinted by permission of* The Victorian Newsletter*), No. 31, Spring, 1967, pp. 28-31.*

RICHARD KELLY (essay date 1969)

In **"Mrs. Caudle's Curtain Lectures"** [Jerrold] raises comic journalism to an art, for he has created a world that continues to live independent of the social milieu which it mirrors.

The popularity of the **"Curtain Lectures"** sent [*Punch's*] circulation up by leaps and bounds. . . . The Caudles soon began to appear on commercial advertisements for items as various as soap and liver pills. . . . Even Jerrold's co-workers on *Punch* capitalized upon the popularity of his serial. . . . Unscrupulous publishers began using pirated versions of the **"Lectures"** and hack playwrights were busily adapting them into comic sketches and musicals that were played to laughing thousands both in London and in the provinces. (pp. 295-96)

Although consisting basically of loosely connected psychological episodes, the serial has unity. . . . The action is confined almost exclusively within the minds of the characters, and the effect of movement obtained by the several changes of scene is restricted by the exclusive focus upon the bedroom as the center of the Caudles' world. (p. 298)

The **"Curtain Lectures"** satisfy a desire for realistic portrayal of characters in humour. . . . Not only is Mrs. Caudle a convincing character, but the entire family life of the Caudles emerges, in Thackeray's words, "the most queer, minute, and amusing picture of English middle-class life" [see excerpt above].

The "low" subject matter of the **"Curtain Lectures"** contrasts with the high society of the "silver-fork novels," and the confined bedroom setting contrasts with the adventure stories of Marryat. The very choice of a bedroom for the setting and

the intimacy of marriage for the theme provided a release from prudery and was open to the charge of indelicacy. (p. 300)

Jerrold draws all of his characters, Job, his wife, and his friends, from the middle or working classes of the 1840s. They are all without exceptional endowments and have lived through the ordinary experiences of love, marriage, and parenthood. Life is rather unhappy and dull for them, and their world is largely limited to domestic affairs. (pp. 300-01)

Mrs. Caudle's rhetoric attests both to her unique personality and to her credibility. Her speech consists of plain statements in simple sentences, expressive of a wide range of moods, strategically deployed against her defenceless husband. . . . She threatens, flatters, cajoles, and condemns, but to no avail. The dramatic potential of such a character, who gradually convinces us that people talked, acted, and thought like her, is obvious.

Jerrold's ambiguous attitude towards the Caudles also contributes to their credibility. During the late thirties and early forties in his writings on social and political themes he consistently sided with the economically oppressed lower class. Now, in 1845, he sympathizes with the psychologically oppressed Job who is presented as an object of both pity and contempt. Jerrold does not identify completely with the husband and at times he obviously gets some relish from exercising his own powers of invective through Mrs. Caudle. The ambiguity adds another dimension of reality to their characters to the degree that it parallels the mixed feelings we experience towards actual people.

Although Job expresses sympathy towards his wife only after she dies, calling her his "sainted creature," Jerrold carefully enlarges her character with pathos. . . . This pathos comes as a shock to the reader, who has long been accustomed to think of Mrs. Caudle as an unfeeling shrew. Suddenly to be made aware that she possesses a sensibility revitalizes her as a character, and the subsequent lectures are all colored by this new understanding. Mrs. Caudle's final lecture, delivered from her deathbed, eschews sentimentality in favor of genuine pathos. . . . (pp. 301-02)

Jerrold's **"Curtain Lectures"** helped bring fiction to terms with real life. They not only satirized the ideal Victorian home but too clearly portrayed families that fell short of the ideal. (p. 303)

Mrs. Caudle's death greatly affected readers of *Punch*. In Thackeray's words, "though Mrs. Caudle had her faults, perhaps there was no woman who died more universally lamented than she. The want of her weekly discourse was felt over the kingdom." At the end of the last installment of the **"Curtain Lectures"** there was a note to the effect that other **"Caudle Papers"** are extant that reveal "what an aggravating man Caudle really was" and that may appear in the next volume. Jerrold had obviously conceived of **"Mr. Caudle's Breakfast Talk"** before the **"Curtain Lectures"** ran out in order to lessen the disappointment his readers received at their conclusion. (p. 307)

Compared to Margaret Caudle, Job's character is flat, his complaints unfunny, and his transformation into a tyrant too sudden to be convincing. **"Mr. Caudle's Breakfast Talk"** serves by contrast to reveal the basic ingredient of the **"Curtain Lectures"** which guarantees its survival as literature: the presence of characters who convince us of their reality and of the reality of the world they inhabit. Recalling Thackeray's comment that "to create these realities is the greatest triumph of a fictitious writer," one may recognize in the **"Curtain Lectures"** the presence of a genuine artist who, unlike Thackeray, remained a dedicated contributor to *Punch* and assured a place of respectability for the profession of comic journalism. (p. 308)

> *Richard Kelly, "Mrs. Caudle, a Victorian Curtain Lecturer," in* University of Toronto Quarterly *(reprinted by permission of University of Toronto Press), Vol. XXXVIII, No. 3, April, 1969, pp. 295-309.*

RICHARD M. KELLY (essay date 1972)

It is hardly necessary to point out that Jerrold's plays have no place in the modern theater; they are not serious works of art. On the other hand, they are first-rate melodramas and, when transformed from the printed page to the theater, his plays could doubtless still elicit laughter from the sober audience. Even more than most forms of the drama, farce and melodrama seem to require the magic of lights, setting, costume, and skilled actors for their success. They are also interesting for their revelation of popular taste and convention and for their role in the evolution of the melodrama into the new theater of Pinero and Shaw. Similarly, Jerrold's novels are of more concern to the literary historian than to the modern reader seeking entertainment and illumination. (p. 145)

Jerrold, as Mr. Punch—attacking the status quo, setting Thackeray's teeth on edge, stirring French antipathy, and lampooning the professional practitioners of cant and humbug—shines at his best. Not only may the literary historian discover a powerful satiric force at work in the world of *Punch,* but anyone today can find lively reading in *Mrs. Caudle's Curtain Lectures, The English in Little,* or *Punch's Letters to His Son.* The whole concept of comic journalism as a distinct genre, worthy of careful study, has been ignored in recent scholarship. Too often the trade of journalism has been viewed merely as an apprenticeship grimly undertaken by promising novelists who, after they develop a distinctive style, graduate to the respectable world of novels. Perhaps because Jerrold himself felt this way, he made his awkward attempt to follow in the path of Thackeray and Dickens. But Jerrold was a pioneer in the new genre of comic journalism; and, as its foremost expositor, Jerrold surpasses his contemporaries and successfully communicates his humor to the present age. No discussion of Victorian humor can be complete that does not take into account the satire, wit, parody, and burlesque of Douglas Jerrold. (p. 146)

> *Richard M. Kelly, in his* Douglas Jerrold *(copyright © 1972 by Twayne Publishers, Inc.; reprinted with the permission of Twayne Publishers, a Division of G. K. Hall & Co., Boston), Twayne, 1972, 168 p.*

ANGUS EASSON (essay date 1973)

The "Q" Papers are the best of the unfamiliar Jerrold; he hits out at magistrates, welcomes the birth of the Prince of Wales . . . , deprecates public executions, and ridicules the Robert Peel who still supports the Corn Laws. Jerrold's outspokenness is often refreshing; his liberal attitudes tie in well with those of Hood and Dickens . . . ; and the serious purpose underlying the articles justifies their facetious tone (with the shining exception of *Gentlemen Jews*). . . . (p. 104)

Still, Jerrold remains a journalist. . . . The journalist emerges as we read *Mr. Punch's Letters:* like most journalistic series its formula guarantees that the writer can keep going from week to week. The success (and this is true of the *Complete Letter Writer* and *Mrs. Caudle* as well) lies in the initial happy idea,

and reading through such series shows a diminishing return. In bodying forth the character of Mrs. Caudle, Jerrold does provide hints of something more than a formula: themes are extended over several lectures. . . . (pp. 104-05)

Jerrold is not a major figure, but he is a useful minor one. . . . (p. 105)

> *Angus Easson, "Reviews: 'The Best of Mr. Punch: The Humorous Writings of Douglas Jerrold'," in* Notes and Queries *(© Oxford University Press 1973), Vol. 20, No. 3, March, 1973, pp. 104-05.*

ANTHONY BURGESS (essay date 1974)

[What] has appealed to me for the last forty years about *Mrs. Caudle's Curtain Lectures* is the skill with which Douglas William Jerrold has recorded the Eternal Sound of Woman, especially In Bed. (p. 11)

[Mrs. Caudle] is as little hampered by the values of a middle-class education as any of the heroines in my catalogue [of literary figures]. Of Mr. Caudle's own lack of social pretensions we can be equally sure, though we make mostly indirect contacts with him. He is a "toyman and doll-merchant" and he likes a drink. There is nothing original in the reproofs his wife deals out at him when he wants to sleep, nor in the other domestic grouses: the fun lies in the recognizability of the rhythms of reproach, the capturing of a tone that does not advance all that far into parody. . . . One's attitude to Mrs. Caudle is complex, certainly ambivalent. One wants her to stop but wants her to go on. It is love-hate with a vengeance (the latter supplied by Mr. Jerrold). It is the recognition of Eternal Woman, to whom terms like love and hate are probably irrelevant, from which we obtain our small but complex *frisson.* She is a ghastly and intolerable bednag who deserves to die, but she is life, not the Circumlocution Office. (p. 13)

[Douglas William Jerrold] is not now much read for anything except this small classic. To read that alone is to have the illusion of being in the presence of a remarkably modern writer, whereas, of course, he has merely tapped the eternal, as Joyce did in the last chapter of *Ulysses.* . . . [Jerrold] wrote plays— like *Black-ey'd Susan* and *The Bride of Ludgate*—which were highly thought of in their time but would now probably seem singularly lacking in the very qualities that keep the *Lectures* alive. He also wrote for *Punch* social and political satires of a progressive tone. . . . (p. 14)

[It] may be noted that without *Punch* some of the funniest books of the Victorian era would never have got themselves, like hash, accumulated. . . . *Mrs. Caudle's Curtain Lectures,* which I am happy to introduce to a new generation, remains for me one of the funniest books in the language. (p. 15)

> *Anthony Burgess, "Foreword" (© Anthony Burgess 1974), in* Mrs. Caudle's Curtain Lectures *by Douglas Jerrold, Harvill Press, 1974, pp. 11-15.*

ADDITIONAL BIBLIOGRAPHY

Dickens, Charles. *The Letters of Charles Dickens: 1844-46, Vol. 4.* Edited by Kathleen Tillotson. Oxford: Oxford University Press, 1977, 725 p.

Contains a letter from Dickens to Jerrold concerning *Time Works Wonders*. Dickens calls the play ''incomparably the best of your dramatic writings.''

Jerrold, Walter. In his *Douglas Jerrold and ''Punch.''* London: Macmillan and Co., 1910, 447 p.
   A discussion of Jerrold's contributions to *Punch* and a history of the magazine and its contributors. This book contains a complete bibliography of Jerrold's contributions to the magazine.

Kelly, Richard M. Introduction to *The Best of Mr. Punch,* by Douglas Jerrold, pp. 2-23. Knoxville: The University of Tennessee Press, 1970.
   Excellent biographical sketch focusing on the writing career of Jerrold, citing the impression his works made in the past and continue to make in the present. This essay introduces a collection of Jerrold's contributions to *Punch*.

Gottfried Keller

1819-1890

Swiss novella and short story writer, novelist, poet, and essayist.

Keller, a chief exponent of poetic realism, is considered one of the masters of the novella. Born in Zurich, he first tried to make a career of landscape painting but failed. A scholarship following the publication of his first book, *Gedichte,* allowed him two years of study at Heidelberg. From there he went to Munich, where he wrote the greater part of *Der grüne Heinrich* (*Green Henry*), the autobiographical novel which announced his arrival on the literary scene.

Green Henry is a *Bildungsroman* in the tradition of Johann Wolfgang von Goethe's *Wilhelm Meister* cycle; it both glorifies and satirizes the concept of the artist as a young man. Later Keller wrote a different version of *Green Henry.* In the second version, the protagonist is able to lead a decent life after repenting for his sins, while in the original the main character discovers the error of his ways too late to make amends. Keller's next and most acclaimed work was *Die Leute von Seldwyla* (*The People of Seldwyla*), a collection of novellas about the residents of a fictional Swiss town. Both setting and characters are portrayed with poetic realism, a technique which adds lyrical description of detail to naturalistic theme and content. Critics have claimed that Keller's Seldwylans represent all that is best and worst in the Swiss character. The most famous of the *Seldwyla* tales is "Romeo und Julia auf dem Dorfe" ("A Village Romeo and Juliet"), in which Keller blends naturalism and mysticism in his attempt to evoke powerful pathos.

Keller returned to Zurich and became a government official in 1861, leading a quiet life for fifteen years. During this time he published *Sieben Legenden* (*Seven Legends*), novellas about the early Christian era, and a second volume of Seldwyla tales. After his retirement, Keller produced two more novella cycles, *Die Züricher Novellen* and *Das Sinngedicht,* as well as the revised version of *Green Henry,* and *Martin Salander,* a novel with distinctly political overtones.

Although *Martin Salander* is generally regarded as a failure, it is important in that it demonstrates Keller's growing disillusionment with democracy. In *Martin Salander,* we see the unscrupulous backroom dealings of Swiss politics in the late nineteenth century. Generally, however, Keller was an optimist who believed in the natural goodness of people. His satire tends to be more gentle than vitriolic, his tone in general is more sympathetic than harsh and all his works are tempered with a gentle humanism. He remains one of the most beloved of Swiss authors.

PRINCIPAL WORKS

Gedichte (poetry) 1846
Neuere Gedichte (poetry) 1851
Der grüne Heinrich (novel) 1855
Die Leute von Seldwyla (novellas) 1856
   [included in *The People of Seldwyla,* 1929]
Sieben Legenden (novellas) 1872
   [*Seven Legends,* 1911]

Die Leute von Seldwyla (novellas) 1874
   [included in *The People of Seldwyla,* 1929]
Die Züricher Novellen (novellas) 1878
**Der grüne Heinrich* (novel) 1880
   [*Green Henry,* 1960]
Das Sinngedicht (novellas) 1881
Gesammelte Gedichte (poetry) 1883
Martin Salander (novel) 1886
A Village Romeo and Juliet (novella) 1914
Gesammelte Werke. 24 vols. (novels, novellas, poetry, short stories, essays, and letters) 1926-49

*These two volumes were published separately, but with the same title. Both are collected in the English translation.

**This is a revision of the 1855 version, and is significantly different. The first version has not been translated into English.

HELEN ZIMMERN (essay date 1880)

[Of Switzerland Keller] is a faithful son, owning its idiosyncrasies in fullest measure. He is simple, strong, concrete, unsentimental, yet not devoid of feeling. The granite of his Alps brings forth men of granite, powerful and rugged, yet sound to the core. Such a man is he, and such live in his books. In confining his imagination to Switzerland, Keller has an advantage over his German colleagues. . . . [The] air not being so full of doctrines and systems as in Germany, a Swiss novelist stands on firmer ground. He deals with a homely nation of a certain slow persistency of character, who form a sober commonwealth of practical persons, devoid of romanticism, whose aspirations do not arise beyond the preservation and increase of their goods and chattels. But if all ideal flights, all imaginative subtleties, are lacking, whimsical, eccentric, angular characters flourish in this confined soil. Of this community Keller has constituted himself the chronicler, and, sharing most markedly many of its characteristics, he has both consciously and unconsciously reproduced these in a series of inimitable romances.

Yet to Keller's first production, **'Der grüne Heinrich,'** these remarks do not altogether apply. Nothing that Keller ever penned is imitative, even his firstborn is *sui generis,* and springs from a fancy that has been unbiassed and unrestrained. It is a strange work, full of glaring faults of construction; capricious, unequal, an incongruous medley, which nevertheless contains so many beauties that we cannot lay it down unsatisfied, for it is full of that ineffable youthful fire of a first effort which carries the reader over many a rugged path. . . . Keller's romance is a medley of truth and fiction, the autobiographical part telling of his own struggles as an artist. The hero is called 'green' because of the colour of his coats, but we also trace a symbolical meaning in this appellation, namely, that we are dealing with an unripe nature. It is the history of an irresponsibly contemplative character working itself out to maturity. . . . The end is clumsy, and open to sharp censure. It offends against all artistic canons, and leaves an unpleasant, harsh impression. Was it for this, we ask ourselves, that Heinrich suffered and made others suffer and sacrifice themselves for him, in order that he should die just when his strangely commingled nature had come to an harmonious issue, and has forced its way through the hampering enclosure?

The best portion of this work is the hero's autobiography, which occupies two out of the four volumes, and deals with his childhood. We follow the development of an observant, silent, introspective child, endowed with a poet's nature, lacking stability of purpose, full of fantasy and intensity of emotion, with good and evil impulses struggling for mastery. And as background to the whole, Zurich with its lovely lake, and the country around, with its snowy mountains, its green swards, its purling streams, and its châlets. In none of his later writings has Keller so keenly reproduced the atmosphere of Switzerland, or told us as much of its national life and customs. The descriptions of landscape are full of intense sympathy with nature, of a semi-mystical and pantheistic kind, reminding of Wordsworth's treatment, but more simple and unaffected, because more unconscious, than the poet's method. But these descriptions are not the only exquisite thing in the work. The episode of Heinrich's childish innocent love for a young girl, Anna, recalls Longus's 'Daphnis and Chloe' in its delicacy of narrative and treatment. The continuation of Heinrich's life-story is not so good; the author has lost sight of perspective, he grows too didactic, the narrative is too often interrupted by disquisitions. These are frequently excellent in themselves, and sometimes necessitated by the current of the story, but proportion has not been observed. Our author allows his pen to meander, the maxims and reflections do not always apply to the particular case. At last our conception of Heinrich grows confused amid this extraneous matter, and he disappears from our grasp into a nebulous dreamland. There is a casual air about the whole which destroys its epic character. It is a grave novel, strong in just those points to which the ordinary novel-reader is, as a rule, indifferent. It is best characterised as a serious character-study, a psychological investigation of the most secret folds of the human heart, the analysis of an artistic nature that withdraws from customs and rules of ordinary life, and finds the laws for its conduct in its inner self. In every point the **'Grüne Heinrich'** is a first attempt, and at once stamped its creator as a bizarre writer. . . . (pp. 460-62)

But **'Die Leute von Seldwyla'** is the work that founded Keller's fame. It is a series of novelettes that may be classified as peasant stories. . . . While all the scenes and incidents are somewhat remote from real life, with its hot, busy strife, they are yet true to nature. Only the everyday vulgarities and commonplace elements do not thrust themselves into notice. Keller mingles ideality with the inflexible necessity of material things, the plummet of reality may be sunk into his depths, but a moonlit atmosphere suffuses the surface. (pp. 462-63)

Each volume [of **'Die Leute von Seldwyla'**] contains five stories. **'Romeo and Juliet of the Village'** [**'Romeo und Julia auf dem Dorfe'**] is the gem of the series; indeed it deserves the palm above all else that Keller has ever penned. (p. 465)

[This story] is told with simple earnestness and pathos. Its construction is masterly. This, however, is far from being the case as a rule. In point of construction there is usually much to condemn in Keller: it is often lax and shapeless, his stories are apt to plunge like fairy tales into the midst of their subject. He seems to fancy that we too are Seldwylers and have known our neighbours and their concerns since childhood, that it is only needful to mention so-and-so for the whole bearings to rise up before us. This literalness, however, throws so powerful an air of reality over Keller's creations that even when these points are exaggerated we do not feel the exaggeration as we read, but are carried along by the stream of his persuasive plausibility. Into the **'Romeo and Juliet'** there enters no element of the burlesque, rarely absent from Keller's stories. Its Nemesis is Hellenic in its remorselessness. Nor is there anything forced or unnatural in the feelings and acts of these youthful peasants. (p. 467)

Between the publication of the first and second volumes of **'The People of Seldwyla'** falls a work of a somewhat different kind, namely, a cycle of **'Seven Legends'** [**'Sieben Legenden'**]. These stories (*Märchen*) are perhaps the most individual of Keller's productions, in which his comic instincts, his mirth, now purely genial, now underlaid with earnestness, his fantastic humours, have full play. The legends are all constructed upon the basis of Church traditions. In some cases Keller has merely expanded these, in others he has caught the spirit and form of the narrative but changed the conditions. The fundamental idea, however, is in all cases subverted. It is the human and natural elements in man that are made to triumph over the unnatural asceticisms of religious fanatics. . . . Their whole purport is to show that while we are in the world we must do the world's work, and have no right thus to withdraw ourselves from its duties and temptations for the selfish gratification of our own inclinations. Keller is a free-thinker in the best and noblest sense of the word, a profoundly religious soul unfettered by forms, and it is against the worship of mere forms that he combats in these legends. But his purpose is hidden under airy conceits, and it is possible to read and enjoy these dainty stories without a guess at their deeper aim. Written in the spirit of the middle ages, which saw no irreverence in familiarity with divine things, they are carried out in the pure and delicate spirit of noble humanism. (p. 471)

We now come to the last book published by Keller. He is not, therefore, as we see, a prolific writer, and hence has the right to be heard, as he only speaks when he has something to say. **'Zurich Novelettes'** (**'Zürcher Novellen'**) is the collective title of the series. The fair city of Zurich was till lately full of old-fashioned ways and things, and boasts a long and agitated history, which furnishes rich matter to a chronicler. Keller traces this from mediæval times down to the present day, connecting the whole by a loose framework, which probably serves an allegorical purpose. (p. 472)

As a type of excellence the first stories introduce us to the old Zurich family of Manesse, and we follow their fortunes from the end of the thirteenth to the middle of the fifteenth century. . . . [The story] consists of a series of episodes, and is somewhat rambling and discursive. As is the case with all Keller's stories, its charm lies in the telling. There are no stirring incidents, but there is much *naïveté* and many pretty scenes. Mediæval Zurich is conjured before us; we live among its worldly bishops and nuns, its knights and ladies. . . . There was still one Manesse, a degenerate scion, who was known as the Fool, and inhabited the ruined family castle until it was burnt down over his head. This man's one aim in life was to pass off as something different from what he was, and over this endeavour his character warped and his brain gave way. . . . Distinction at all hazards was his craving, but when the moment came to prove the reality of his boasts his courage evaporated like Falstaff's. He is a grotesque and ludicrous figure, conceived and delineated with power and psychological insight.

So far the symbolical has been uppermost in these stories, and there is less of the humorous element than usual. This comes forward again in the next, **'The Landvogt of Greifensee,'** a story that misses excellence from its prolixity, but which would be delicious if tersely told. . . . We are transported back into a windstill period, where life did not tear along so fast, where love endured, where feuds were hotly waged and not soon forgotten, where hurry and speed were words unknown. It is perhaps because he realised this too vividly that Keller has spun out this story unduly.

This censure does not apply to **'Ursula.'** Here in a condensed narrative is brought before us with bold and powerful strokes the Zurich of Zwingli's day, introducing the religious and political changes wrought by this Reformer. Keller's story deals chiefly with the Anabaptist movement, which he regards as one of the inevitable ugly excrescences produced by every great revolution, and he reproduces with horrible fidelity the delirious speeches and deeds of this misguided faction. In this story the plot is nothing, the accessories are everything. **'The Flag of the Seven Upright Ones'** is perfect all round, and a worthy pendant to the **'Romeo and Juliet of the Village.'** Plot, treatment, *mise en scène,* all are original and equally excellent, and give full scope to Keller's peculiar talents. His best quips and quirks, his best vein of drollery, his gentle satire, his tenderness, are all represented here. . . . [**'The Flag of the Seven Upright Ones'**] contains strongly emphasised a distinctive feature of Keller's genius. This is the genial nature of his humour. He makes us smile at his characters without injury to their dignity. While we are amused at the weaknesses of poor humanity, we never lose our respect for the persons in whom these weaknesses are embodied. We smile gently over the heads of the seven upright veterans, while at the same time their creator forces us to bow down with respect for their integrity and high-minded purposes.

We must still say a word about Keller's manner, which is no less his own than his matter. He handles the German language with rare skill; no conventional phrases, no rhetorical flourishes, no affectations or mannerisms disfigure his pages. His style is simple and unadorned, and hence perfectly in keeping with the homely republican nature of his characters; yet withal so pithy, piquant, quaint, that the most ordinary expressions acquire a new force under his pen, and the whole effect is far removed from commonplace. Not the least of Keller's charms lies in his style, his happy mode of narration. Such, briefly, is the Swiss writer whose remarkable originality we have tried faintly to indicate. (pp. 472-76)

> *Helen Zimmern, ''A Swiss Novelist,'' in* Fraser's Magazine, *April, 1880, pp. 459-76.*

CHARLES H. HANDSCHIN   (essay date 1917)

In discussing Keller's attitude towards tragedy, now, we need to call to mind that his early works tend to end tragically, *e.g., Der grüne Heinrich, Romeo und Julia auf dem Dorfe,* and especially *Theresa,* a dramatic fragment, conceived probably under the influence of [Friedrich] Hebbel's *Maria Magdalena.* All of these were conceived not later than 1847 to 1849, and Keller never again wrote a tragic work, or a work with a tragic end, with the exception of *Regina* in the *Sinngedicht,* planned in 1851. And, while we cannot, here, go into the various changes later introduced into these works, I wish merely to state the fact that the tragic in the above mentioned works was either changed to a happy ending, as in the revised edition of *Der grüne Heinrich* and in *Dorotheas Blumenkörbchen* in the *Sieben Legenden,* or remained uncompleted, as *Theresa,* except in the case of *Romeo und Julia,* and *Regina,* where to give up the tragedy would have been to give up the story. *Die drei gerechten Kammacher,* which dates from the early period, and which some would count as tragic, is not tragic because the bearers of the action do not possess the qualities of tragic persons. Moreover, there are various statements of Keller's which substantiate the fact that he grew more and more averse to tragedy with the years. (pp. 274-75)

In Keller's mature view of life there was no place for the future world, either of the Christians, or of the panlogists; nor for pessimism, so prominent in the philosophy and in the theory of tragedy of the period; nor was there any place for fatalistic polytheism nor, incidentally, for the hot-house optimism of such a man as Nietzsche. . . .

Keller considered drama the highest form of poetic art. We know also that Keller was no dramatist, but that is not because he had not well-defined views of tragedy but because of the nature of his poetic faculty. (p. 275)

As an esthetic means Keller saw no objection to the *fatum* if it did not interfere with clearness and simplicity, Keller's first prerequisites. . . . [When] Keller condemns the predominant use of the *fatum,* as he does, he is thinking of contemporaries who had abused the fatalistic motive, and especially of certain heavy-footed pessimists who were, in Keller's generation, construing a new *fatum* which was far more depressing than the Grecian fatum ever thought of being. (pp. 275-76)

Keller dislikes a predominant use of chance as a tragic motive, first, because of his desire for clearness and simplicity, and furthermore because its predominant use overemphasizes its place in the government of the world. The question might be formulated thus: Is depending mainly upon chance, in any undertaking, a good progressive policy? As to the question of tragic guilt, Keller stands half-way between the two schools, one of which never construes tragic guilt for the hero, while the other always does. In this he follows the popular feeling, which, no doubt, has good ground: namely, that the guiltless tragic hero is not the only kind to be found in the world. . . .

Keller also has examples of tragedy in which no tragic guilt is construed for the tragic persons, namely, in *Romeo und Julia,* and *Regina.* But here there is nothing of the pessimistic, fatalistic. Here we have a psychological tragedy which follows in the steps of Charles Darwin. . . . (p. 279)

We come to our conclusion regarding Keller's view of tragedy. In the first place we may say that he, like Goethe, was averse to tragedy. . . . [Morever,] panlogism is not to his way of thinking, and merely asserting his freedom of will against fate and by a free act of the will giving up existence does not avail Keller anything. Nor could he go very far with the Schopenhauer-Nietzsche idea of *tragische Weltanschauung* for the very obvious reason that Keller is a meliorist, and again, the pessimistic ferment of this school availed him nothing, since his art is not for art's sake but for humanity's sake, and he felt that their pessimism was not a progressive human force. (pp. 279-80)

> *Charles H. Handschin, "Gottfried Keller and the Problem of Tragedy," in* Modern Language Notes, *Vol. XXXII, No. 5, May, 1917, pp. 273-80.*

CAMILLO von KLENZE   (essay date 1926)

It may be doubted whether the entire nineteenth century, with its insistence upon life itself as the problem of problems, produced anywhere a figure more typical of his time than the Swiss narrator Gottfried Keller. Keller stands as a robust reaction against both the religious dogmatism which would relegate this vale of tears to a position of minor importance, and to the Hegelian and other German Romantic philosophies (still regnant in his day) which in their search for the extra-mundane sources of existence turned away from the daily round of life. To Keller the life of man, even when he trudges the road of the commonplace, is the ever-bubbling source of inspiration, the never-failing guide to deepest truths. From the loving and concentrated perusal of life's daily script man must learn all the lessons which the universe has to teach. Hence, not crass materialism indeed, but rather a deification of experience animates Keller. To use his own words: God radiates Reality.

Keller's personality and his work reflect his native soil: that doughty little Switzerland which by dint of bravery and commonsense had early won its independence from powerful neighbors and which later, during Keller's own time, succeeded in welding its loose conglomerate of mutually jealous cantons into a firmly articulated confederacy. The share which Keller himself bore in this great national achievement quickened his being to higher issues and informed his work with its most characteristic tone. (pp. 105-06)

This extraordinary individual has left a deep trace upon German letters. He expressed himself in lyrics, tales (*Novellen*), and in novels. The lyrics which charm rather by their spontaneity than by their finish of form, reveal his inner struggles as well as a healthy, buoyant view of the world. They throb with a passionate love for even the minutest phenomena of nature, which they render with an accuracy startling for his day and generation. . . . [His] verses affiliate him with that group of modern poets who like Tennyson and Browning observed with a keener retina than their predecessors "things as they are." Nor does he shrink from touching upon such matters as politics and even machinery (so shocking to Ruskin's sensibilities). Thus he rebukes the Romantic poet Justinus Kerner who in 1845 had bewailed the possible advent of the airship as a destroyer of poetry, whereas Keller would acclaim it a manifestation of energy and thus an added stimulus to poetic expression (*An Justinus Kerner*). Keller belongs to the generation of Courbet who exclaimed: *"Il faut encanailler l'art."* [We must degrade art]. (pp. 120-21)

Keller never wrote anything more magnificent than *A Village Romeo and Juliet,* published in 1856 as one of the collection [*Die Leute von Seldwyla*], which deserves special mention as one of the five or six really great short-stories of the nineteenth century. An age-old tragedy is here retold in the setting of a simple village community with such power and subtlety that a shaft seems to be sunk down to the very heart of things and we are vouchsafed a glimpse of the mysterious underprops of life.

This great narrator was also a great stylist. He had the typically German gift of extracting its poetic essence from the homespun word or phrase. His style is characterized not so much by Gallic charm and elegance as by unrivalled spontaneity, virile adequacy, and lyric savor. (p. 130)

> *Camillo von Klenze, "Realism and Romanticism in Two Great Narrators: Keller and Meyer," in his* From Goethe to Hauptmann: Studies in a Changing Culture *(copyright 1926 by The Viking Press; reprinted by permission of Viking Penguin Inc.), The Viking Press, 1926 (and reprinted by Biblo and Tennen, 1966), pp. 105-58.* *

E. K. BENNETT   (essay date 1934)

For Keller the characteristic form is that of the cyclical framework Novelle, the grouping together of a series of stories, which are connected by a similarity of theme or motive or intention, and held together by a framework, which is variously elaborated. This habit or perhaps constitutional tendency to see things in groups, amplifying and complementing one another, is in itself a proof of the wider, more organic and systematic view of life which is symptomatic of the epic standpoint. Keller's lyrical poems do not play the same important part in his literary output as the poems of Storm in his creative work. Though the Swiss writer began as a lyric poet, his whole tendency was away from the personal subjective lyric to the more objective art of the narrator. . . . His early novel, *Der grüne Heinrich*—afterwards entirely rewritten—has in its form a certain likeness to the framework narrative. Though it is in intention an autobiographical work, and in its inner form an Erziehungsroman [novel of initiation] in the manner of *Wilhelm Meister,* it will be seen on examination to be rather a collection of episodic events held together by the framework of a biography. This impression is further heightened by the inclusion of various narratives which do not really form part of the immediate experience of the characters of the novel but are, as it were, let into the main narrative. . . . (pp. 176-77)

Apart from his two novels, *Der grüne Heinrich* at the beginning of his career, and *Martin Salander*—his least successful production—at the close, all Keller's prose work is in the form of Novellen, and consists of four groups of stories. . . . *Die Leute von Seldwyla* and the *Sieben Legenden* are framework Novellen only implicitly; that is to say, there is no narrative framework to connect them outwardly; their interconnection consists in a unity which is imposed upon them by the similarity of subject matter in the various stories. In *Die Leute von Seldwyla* they are grouped round a certain entirely imaginary town and its inhabitants; in the *Sieben Legenden* the connection lies not only in the subject matter but in the consistent attitude of mind to all these miraculous stories of mediaeval saints which Keller presents. . . . In *Die Züricher Novellen,* however, the framework is more explicit. The first three stories are framed in a narrative which has independent value. (pp. 178-79)

The three stories are entitled *Hadlaub, Der Narr auf Manegg,* and *Der Landvogt vom Greifensee*—the action of the first two taking place in the Middle Ages, that of the third in the eighteenth century. With regard to this latter—one of Keller's most delightful works—it may be pointed out that it is itself a framework Novelle within a framework Novelle, for all of the principal characters who appear in it—seven in all—have their life histories related. *Die Züricher Novellen* are in so far an imperfect cyclical Rahmengeschichte [series of frame stories], because the enclosing narrative comes to an end after the third story, and the two remaining stories are added without any reference to it. . . . In *Das Sinngedicht* the framework is itself a Novelle and indeed the *raison d'être* of the work, whilst the individual stories are there to support and elucidate the theme of the framework. And all the stories have a common motive: the problem of marriage. . . . The organic nature of the whole work is further heightened by the dialectical method employed in the story-telling: one story illustrates one point of view, whereupon the next story serves as a criticism thereof by representing another point of view. There are individual stories in the other collections which are as good as or better than any included in *Das Sinngedicht,* but no complete work of Keller has the same perfection of artistry as a whole—unless it be the *Sieben Legenden,* where the organic nature of the work is less obvious. (pp. 180-81)

Keller is amongst all these writers of Novellen the one who is most centrally epic, holding the balance almost perfectly between the two functions of narrating and describing but with that slight tendency to lay the greater stress upon description, which is entirely consistent with the principles of the literary movement of Poetic Realism, and consists in a feeling for the actual value and interest of natural things as such. . . . [The] richness and inventiveness of his imagination reveals itself in his delight in curious detail. Actual material things are a source of pleasure to him, and he will describe a whole catalogue of oddities—such as the collection of Züs Bünzlin in *Die drei gerechten Kammacher*—or elaborate a fantastical character, or paint in great detail a piece of pageantry, not merely for its value in the development of the story, but because it is in itself a source of pleasure to him. All this detracts from the purity of the form as the theorists of the Novelle usually conceive it. . . . In all the stories of Keller it is not a question of the mere 'event' being sacrificed to any other element; but rather of its being enriched and loaded, perhaps even overloaded with a wealth of attendant circumstance which to anyone but a sheer purist for style must be added delight. (pp. 182-84)

In Gottfried Keller's works the German Novelle reaches a maximum, beyond which no development is possible, except in the development of some individual and one-sided tendency

at the expense of totality and comprehensiveness. What distinguishes the Novellen of Keller from the classical prototypes of the Novelle is not so much that they are different in form, but that the severe outlines of the original form have been considerably filled out—the slim figure of the maiden has acquired the opulent contours of the matron. 'To load every rift with ore' was the aim of Keats in writing poetry, and that is the achievement of Keller as a writer of Novellen. The austere line of the original form has given place to a richly coloured and detailed painting. The subject matter of some of the stories might be equally well treated by Boccaccio: *Romeo und Julia auf dem Dorfe* for instance, or *Der Schmied seines Glückes*—one can easily imagine what mischievous delight Boccaccio would have taken in the telling of the latter—but what Boccaccio would have told in five or ten pages Keller tells in fifty or a hundred, and the additional pages are filled with that detailed and localized account of reality, which is one of the most precious elements in Keller's art—but one which the theorists of the Novelle regard as lying outside its scope. . . . In most German Novellen the centre of gravity is shifted from the incident to some more internal interest: in the best of Keller's Novellen, though this internal interest is present, the stress is fairly distributed between event, material surroundings and the inner interest, which can generally be described as education of personality. (pp. 191-92)

E. K. Bennett, "The Novelle of Poetic Realism," in his A History of the German Novelle from Goethe to Thomas Mann, *Cambridge at the University Press, 1934 (and reprinted by Cambridge at the University Press, 1949), pp. 124-92.**

J. G. ROBERTSON   (essay date 1935)

Spiritual attunement between the poet and his audience is essential to that subjective art in which the literatures of the northern races are so rich; it is the secret of the eternal appeal of that art, from the mediaeval German *Parzival* to the eighteenth-century *Faust.* Such works are, as one of the later Middle High German poets said of his poem, "seas into which many rivers pour", but also seas beneath whose surface lies the sunken Vineta of the reader's own soul; he hears from the depths the pealing of the bells of a submerged city.

Der grüne Heinrich by Gottfried Keller is a book of this kind. This huge, formless, badly proportioned novel, with its irrelevant episodes and often distracting aimlessness, is the "Dichtung und Wahrheit" [fiction and reality] of its author's life. Keller is himself the young Heinrich Lee, whose green clothes, cut down out of his father's uniforms, are the occasion of his sobriquet. It is his own childhood in the great beehive of a house in the Zürich Rindermarkt which he describes with such irresistible charm in the first volume of the work. The changes he has made are not great, and are to be regarded rather as a veil drawn over reality than as an attempt to falsify it in the interests of a more engaging fiction. (pp. 62-3)

Opinion is divided between the two forms of [*Der grüne Heinrich*]. The later edition has the advantage of being shorter: of having the many excrescences lopped off, the proportions improved; but I am not sure that it is not still more satisfying to read *Der grüne Heinrich*—if one does not shrink from its enormous and unnecessary length—in its old unwieldy form. The first edition ends tragically; Heinrich has failed in life; his mother is dead; he has nothing to live for, and he finds rest beneath the green sod. . . . The change [for the second edition] involved the elimination of much in the early version that pointed to a tragic ending, and Keller did his best to soften its acerbities; but he has not altogether succeeded. Such satisfaction as we can draw from the new close is frankly due to the fact that we still feel it to be essentially tragic: after all, there are more tragedies in life than those that end in death. . . . In the new version Keller avoids the clumsy technique, in accordance with which he began with Heinrich Lee's journey to Munich and then inserted the account of his early life as a "manuscript" written by the hero himself. By converting the whole novel into a narrative in the first person, a greater unity is attained, and also perhaps some exoneration for its subjective formlessness; but much that is related about fictitious personages cannot be told by themselves in the first person, and Keller's efforts to give the narrative a semblance of probability are often clumsy. (pp. 69-70)

[Like] Heine, like so many German men of letters who wrote at the middle or shortly before the middle of the century, Keller illustrates the great transition of his time, that from the spiritual "otherworldliness" of Romanticism to the hard realities of science and industrialism; and it is on the threshold of the new time that *Der grüne Heinrich* stands. It is a "Bildungsroman", a type which elsewhere I have claimed as the national type of German fiction, that is to say, the history of a soul in its search for its mission in life. . . . The heroes of these typical German novels are subjected to a sentimental education—"sentimental" not in the Flaubertian sense, but in that of Sterne or Schiller. *Wilhelm Meisters Lehrjahre* is the type, and one can see it evolving in the eighteenth century from Wieland's *Agathon* onwards; and to this type the Romantic movement of the nineteenth century remained faithful through a long line of mainly fragmentary soul-histories—*Franz Sternbalds Wanderungen, Heinrich von Ofterdingen, Ahnung und Gegenwart, Maler Nolten.* It is to this royal line that *Der grüne Heinrich* belongs. It presents us with the picture of a romantic soul in its progress through art and poetry to life; and, just as *Wilhelm Meister* evolved from a specific "artist novel"—a novel of the theatre—into a work dealing with man's attitude to the problems of the individual life, . . . *Der grüne Heinrich* outgrows its original plan of describing the education of a painter, and becomes the history of a young soul struggling in the spiritual fermentation of eighty years ago. And *Der grüne Heinrich* is what *Wilhelm Meister* was not: a tragedy. Green Heinrich is shipwrecked on the ideal he fails to attain; or, might we not rather say, he comes to grief, because the Romantic world in which he had striven to make himself a denizen, had itself passed away before his apprenticeship was at an end? Keller's novel is not merely in the royal line, not merely the last of the Romantic novels, and the fullest and richest of them all: but a novel that stands on the threshold of the modern world.

There is another aspect of Keller's *Grüne Heinrich* which may be regarded as a finger-post for his subsequent development: embedded in the autobiography of the novel are several detachable stories; and there is a tendency, in the parts which were written last, to segregate into episodes. As a matter of fact, Keller's real strength, as he ultimately discovered, lay not in the long novel at all, but in the "Novelle". . . . Keller's next work . . . was a collection of short stories, *Die Leute von Seldwyla.* . . . (pp. 73-4)

In [his] framework of not unkindly satire Keller encases a series of short stories. *Pankraz, der Schmoller,* which opens the first volume, begins admirably in the spirit of the Preface; there is much of the author himself in the sulking hero . . . ; but the method by which the hero is cured of his sulking, by a lion,

savours of Romantic extravagance. Keller, like most writers that matter, was not a good inventor of plots; and his genius, when not held in check by a realism imposed from without, was inclined to run to exaggeration. *Frau Regel Amrain und ihr Jüngster* is a much better example of Keller's powers; it is a real slice of personal experience, with a considerable infusion of the national enthusiasm for education: not perhaps quite interesting enough to stand by itself, or sufficiently welded together into an artistic whole, but essentially true and free from extravagance. Between these two items lies a very different type of story, in which Seldwyla and its amiable foibles hardly matter. *Romeo und Julia auf dem Dorfe* is a "Novelle" of peasant-life, and has been justly praised as the finest of its type in German literature. The basis of the story was a brief and commonplace newspaper report from Saxony, which described how two young lovers had been found dead in a field near Leipzig; and on this report Keller built up an engrossing village tragedy. . . . The introduction of the touch of Romantic fantastry in the "black fiddler"—a legacy possibly from E.T.A. Hoffmann—is a little out of keeping with the realism of the picture; for it is just in its bed-rock veracity that Keller's art makes its overwhelming appeal. Here he stands out as the legitimate successor of the first European master of the "peasant-novel," Jeremias Gotthelf, of whom our own Ruskin was so warm an admirer. The realism of *Romeo und Julia auf dem Dorfe* is the realism, freed from the dross of details that do not matter, of *Uli der Knecht* and *Elsi, die seltsame Magd:* it is the essentially national element in Keller's work; the romanticism is only the German literary varnish. One cannot help regretting that in after years, Keller, distrustful, it may have been, of his nation's ability to stand alone, and insistent on German Switzerland's solidarity in literature with the North, gave his *Romeo und Julia* no successor. He fell back—unfortunately, if one may say so without seeming ungrateful for not a few masterpieces—into that complacent mid-century German "idealism", which for a generation successfully resisted the clamorous knocking at the door of a more virile literary art.

Die drei gerechten Kammacher with its admirably characterized types of Saxon, Bavarian and Swabian, and still better, the delightful Züs Bünzlin, to whose hand they aspire, shows Keller's powers as a humorist at their best. The Keller devotee is, indeed, inclined to regard the ability to appreciate this story as a kind of passport to the circle of the faithful. Most readers, however, would probably have liked to see a little less farcicality in the baroque close . . . , and a little less acerbity in the decision of their ultimate fates. But that is perhaps, after all, the real Keller flavour in the story.

The second volume of Seldwyla novels . . . is of inferior interest to the first. *Der Schmied seines Glückes,* and *Die missbrauchten Liebesbriefe* are both early productions, written in Keller's Berlin days. The former seems to me, with its grotesque humour, to deserve a higher place than Keller's admirers are inclined to give it; but *Die missbrauchten Liebesbriefe* falls badly asunder into literary satire and a story which has no organic connection with the satire; while the last item in the volume, *Das verlorene Lachen* is, as a story, dull and uninteresting; at best, it may be regarded as a forerunner of the political novel of *Martin Salander* with which Keller's career closes. One has most pleasure from *Kleider machen Leute.* . . . Keller's management of the "peripeteia" is fresh and skilful; his humour is kept within stricter bounds than in the *Kammacher,* and is free from the touch of cynicism which created something of a dissonace in the earlier work. On the other hand, the fifteenth-century tale, *Dietegen,* in spite of many fine touches, suffers from the artificiality of its plot, and the lack of reality in its pseudo-historical background. The theme is a kind of echo of *Romeo und Julia auf dem Dorfe,* but it is set in the framework of an unreal fairy-tale, and ends without tragedy. (pp. 76-9)

[In the *Züricher Novellen* Keller] has chosen to group together his stories in a framework; but the framework this time is not strong enough to support its burden. (p. 79)

In the hearts of many of Keller's admirers the *Sieben Legenden* holds the first place. Three of the legends, *Eugenia, Dorotheas Blumenkörbchen* and *Der schlimm-heilige Vitalis* are old church stories, which permit, with not too tragic consequences, the mingling of the naïve piety of the early Christian world with a strain of amiable worldliness. Three are legends of the Virgin, *Die Jungfrau und der Teufel, Die Jungfrau als Ritter,* and *Die Jungfrau und die Nonne,* in which the Virgin appears as the peacemaker and the conciliator in very worldly conflicts and troubles; and the collection is rounded off by the most ethereal blend of poetry and music in modern literature, *Das Tanzlegendchen,* a veritable poem in prose. One is almost reluctant to endorse the high claim that is made for this collection, lest it should seem to suggest a depreciation of the great stories of the earlier books; but of the beauty and delicacy of the *Sieben Legenden* there can be no question. That genial harmony, which is the most precious quality of Keller's mind in its maturity, lies over them; his rich imagination touches no false notes; he blends a naïve and primitive religious romanticism with a kindly, healthy, commonsense outlook, which expresses itself neither in crude scepticism, nor ridicule: but adds rather a richer, deeper gold to the aureole round the heads of the sanctified. In these legends . . . Keller has broken, more definitely than in the *Züricher Novellen,* with the realism of his *Village Romeo and Juliet,* and has gone back to the old Romantic wonderland that knows neither time nor place. Might we not say that they, too, belong to the literature of mid-century transition, that in them Keller has, by virtue of his harmony-loving art, found a basis for reconciling the spiritualism of Romanticism with the scepticism that had been instilled into him by Feuerbach?

Less important is the cycle of "Novellen" which bears the title *Das Sinngedicht.* . . . The book bears the stamp of that artificiality and estrangement from life's realities which were in favour in Germany in the middle of the nineteenth century, as an antidote to the prosaic literature of commonplace experience, and of political and social reform, for which "Young Germany" and its successors were responsible. . . . These stories are for the most part exotic, and exotic in more than the obvious sense that Keller went abroad for his subjects; they seem to me to give him little opportunity for that personal sympathy which is the compelling charm in the masterpieces of the Seldwyla series and the *Züricher Novellen*—some of them, indeed, are even just a little tedious—but the close, again in its artificial Romantic way, is quite delightful. (pp. 83-5)

There remains but one other greater work of Keller's, the novel of *Martin Salander* . . . , again a specifically Swiss work, dealing with essentially Swiss problems and Swiss political aspirations. The old spirit of satire creeps in again; and if Keller had first thought of calling his novel *Excelsior,* after Longfellow's poem, it was rather in ironic depreciation of the optimistic aspirations of young Switzerland than to encourage them. The apparent bankruptcy of the Swiss liberalism of 1869 did not allow him to take a very roseate view of his country's future. *Martin Salander* is a novel with which a foreign reader, at least, has a difficulty in getting into real sympathy. Somehow the magic of Keller's style seems to have missed fire; he himself confessed that there was "too little poetry" in it; one feels that the hermit of the Zürich Bürgli was beginning to grow old. (pp. 85-6)

[The supreme mastery of the short story] lies not with Germany, but with Switzerland. . . . Keller, indeed, is the greatest colourist among the writers of the short story; he had not begun life as a painter and lived through the dreary disillusionment of his **"Green Heinrich"** for nothing; what he failed to put on canvas he has reproduced in all its pristine freshness in his writings. The brilliancy and yet delicacy of colouring in the finest of Keller's Swiss novels recalls the art of his famous countryman and friend, Arnold Böcklin, in many respects a kindred spirit: both men possessed the power of captivating the modern mind, in spite of its leanings toward a drabber naturalism; both form a bulwark of the romantic spirit in Europe in an unromantic age. For this I regard as Keller's peculiar "poetic mission": he succeeded better than any of his German contemporaries in keeping the old romantic ideals alive in the later nineteenth century. And this he achieved not by artificial imitation, nor by turning his back upon the aspiration of his own time. Rather did he, this disciple of Herwegh and Feuerbach, take his stand frankly in the unromantic, materially-minded present, and, wrestling with the spirit of the past, conquer it anew for his contemporaries. (pp. 87-8)

J. G. Robertson, "Gottfried Keller," in his Essays and Addresses on Literature, G. Routledge & Sons, Ltd., 1935 (and reprinted by Books for Libraries Press, 1968), pp. 62-88.

WALTER SILZ (essay date 1954)

[In *Romeo und Julia auf dem Dorfe*] Keller, like all the great masters of the Novelle beginning with Kleist, while maintaining the general type, has enlarged and deepened it in a new way. He has shown that the Novelle can be made the medium for one of the great themes of the world's literature and, treating this theme in terms of his familiar homeland and its plain folk, he has given a superlative example both of "Heimatkunst" [native art] and of middle-class tragedy. He pictures virtually the whole lifetime of his two chief personages from infancy to death—evincing as fine an understanding of the psychology of adolescence as of childhood—and in addition conveys an impression of their entire surrounding world. He condenses the essential substance of a novel into a Novelle of one hundred pages, and he does this in the main by throwing light on certain critical turns in the protracted action. (pp. 80-1)

Romeo und Julia is an excellent example of Poetic Realism, showing how its Romantic heritage is blended with a sharpened sense for the hard realities of everyday life. Keller has a certain amount of Romantic imagination, even a Romantic love for the extraordinary and bizarre; but his imagination never runs away with him; it is restrained by an unerring sense of fact. His landscape pictures in this story, as in so many of his actual watercolors, are full of definitely outlined reality, overlaid with the dreamy blue haze of the "romantische Landschaft" [romantic landscape]. His theme is the "romantic" one of Romeo and Juliet, but it is set in the harsh workaday reality of a Swiss peasant village. Yet the language throughout, though lifelike, is held to a certain level, and this is characteristic of Poetic Realism. (pp. 81-2)

It is the way of the Poetic Realist to observe accurately the things of actuality, but to select certain of their traits for an artistic purpose and raise these into a higher, significant reality. There is a wonderfully sharp quality, a *plein-air* lighting, in the opening scene of the two peasants plowing over a rise of ground in the bright sun of a September morning. . . . As we draw near, the figures show the distinct and characteristic detail of a portrait. We see the lines in the men's well-shaven faces, the creases in their breeches, the jarring of their shirtsleeves as they hold the plow. . . . [Keller] likens them to two constellations rising and setting behind earth's round, thus accenting their exemplary character and suggesting a deeper significance behind their doings.

The manifest symmetrical patterning of the whole story is an element of the "poetic" superimposed on the "real." . . . [This] is reality, not falsified, but seen and selected with a poet's and philosopher's eye that invests mere fact with higher meaning.

In the account of the Manzes' removal to town and in the picture of the wretched "inn" which they take over . . . , the realistic details are carefully chosen to contribute to the oppressive atmosphere of deterioration. The same is true of the corresponding picture of Marti's run-down farm . . . , where the neglected well is singled out as a special "symbol of shiftlessness." But Keller shows a painter's appreciation for the picturesque aspects of this dilapidation, and he even humanizes them. (pp. 82-3)

Romeo und Julia is not merely the tragedy of young and ill-starred love; it is also a "middle-class tragedy" . . . of impressive proportions and compelling motivation. It deals with social deterioration and loss of caste and the unhappy consequences thereof in two generations. (p. 86)

Romeo und Julia is pure bourgeois tragedy, in the sense of Hebbel's *Maria Magdalene:* the tragic conflict is no longer, as it was in Schiller's *Kabale und Liebe,* a conflict between the middle and higher social class, but a conflict within the middle class itself; it is based on the tragic limitedness of the bourgeois mind, immolating itself to its own ideals of respectability. Keller, however, has made these ideals more admirable, and treated the theme more poetically, than has Hebbel.

To these young people, with the ingrained convictions of their class, the mere dissension and degradation of their elders present a formidable barrier. (p. 89)

Near the end of his story . . . , Keller summarizes the irresistible forces that are closing in on the young lovers, and the one he makes the most of is their frustrated craving for an irreproachable bourgeois station in life. . . .

Thus the tragic circle is completed. . . . The very vestige of "bürgerliches Ehrgefühl" [bourgeois sense of honor] which persists in the children after the decay of their families, is what brings about their destruction. Had they been less honorable, less bound by the code of honor proper to their class, there would have been for them no tragedy nor death. But they have cherished in their minds the original "Urmass" of what constitutes the desirable life. Indeed, one reason for their passionate and utter love is that each sees in the other the incorporation of fortune and happiness lost but never forgotten. . . .

They thirst for happiness, but only on reputable bourgeois conditions. . . . But neither will their fiery passion be denied, and so they take the way out which to them, and to the reader who has followed Keller's presentation of the situation, must seem the only way out. The marvel is that to this very end, in the midst of their glowing passion and their wicked environ-

ment, the poet has kept his pair innocent and pure. He has thus made their fate deeply pathetic, yet genuinely tragic; they exemplify that maturest species of tragedy in which a character is ruined not by outward circumstances merely, but by his own mind and will, and not by his worse, but by his better nature. (p. 91)

Walter Silz, "Keller, 'Romeo und Julia'," in his Realism and Reality: Studies in the German Novelle of Poetic Realism *(copyright 1954 The University of North Carolina Press), The University of North Carolina Press, 1954, pp. 79-93.*

HERBERT W. REICHERT   (essay date 1956)

[The main misconception in Keller research is that *Der Grüne Heinrich*] is to be esteemed primarily for its psychological realism. No one would, of course, venture to deny the autobiographical nature of the content, but to ignore the sense of conscious artistry and the didactic realism from which the work sprang is to ignore the source of much of its peculiar, almost indefinable charm. . . .

[It] would appear that a study of caricature in *Der Grüne Heinrich* at this time might help to bring about a more correct and fuller appreciation of the novel. . . . (p. 372)

It may be well to explain at the outset what is meant here by caricature. The word is used according to Webster to denote "a distortion by exaggeration, producing a grotesque or ridiculous effect, as in a picture." Caricature has been preferred to the term satire, since the latter usually carries with it the implication of trenchant wit or sarcasm and does not refer as frequently to persons. With Keller the distortion is largely of a humorous nature and concerns primarily his characters.

A key question that will serve to introduce the actual consideration of Keller's use of caricature is why he utilized such a device, when his ostensible desire was to present a realistic account of how a young man grew to intellectual maturity. In this regard it must first be made clear that although Keller was a great friend of the truth, he was not an out-and-out realist. Both his ethics and aesthetics demanded simplification for the sake of clarity. The moral pedagogue in him was anxious that his point get across to the reader. The artist felt that simplicity was the main key to the *Übersicht* essential to good writing. But the desire for simplicity does not supply the whole answer. . . . Keller's desire to simplify was not restricted solely to his caricatures, but also included those characters who symbolized good. Dorothea and the count lack the realism of Heinrich and his relatives largely because Keller sought to idealize them. Anna and Judith, convincing as they are, reveal elements of stylizing to emphasize the contrast implicit in them between the ideal and the real. Simplicity, then, cannot account exclusively for the use of caricature. Beyond the factor of simplicity, it must be remembered that Keller, although he wanted to expound his views forcibly and sincerely, did not feel that polemic writing belonged to great literature. . . . To answer our question then, one fundamental reason why Keller employed caricature was that he was often not so anxious to give a realistic account as he was to achieve the simplicity and necessary objectivity with which to portray evil and to warn against it.

Keller's conception of evil is important to an understanding of his use of caricature. . . . [He] felt enlightenment concerning one's own true nature was the key to morality and happiness. As a result he extolled humility as the greatest virtue and condemned as the greatest vice the vanity that kept a man from having an open mind and learning to know himself. . . . Vanity in the broadest sense, as a more or less conscious aberration from one's intrinsic nature, is without exception the basic attribute of all of Keller's humorous villains. (pp. 372-73)

Keller made abundant use of caricature in both versions of the novel, and . . . , as indicated earlier, he employed this device whenever he wished to symbolize and chastise vice and folly, particularly vanity and its related evils. Caricature was used in varying degree in proportion to the wickedness of the person involved, except for those evil characters who were apparently still too close to the author, autobiographically speaking, to permit them to be portrayed in an ironic fashion. Since caricature was restricted to the minor characters, care must be taken when speaking of their realism; the fact is, they appear realistic only when they personify neither good nor bad. Most important of all is the conclusion that Keller did not conceive his novel solely as an autobiographical confession or as an elegiac revival of his past, but to a large degree as a pedagogic-aesthetic medium designed to point out and eradicate evil wherever he saw it. To be sure, the psychological realism in the novel enhances its value. But much of its unique charm comes from its unrealistic aspects, from the assortment of queer little men and women whom Keller created out of the depths of his poetic fancy to illustrate the vices he wished to scourge. (p. 379)

> Herbert W. Reichert, "Caricature in Keller's 'Der grüne Heinrich'," in Monatshefte (copyright © 1956 by The Board of Regents of the University of Wisconsin System), Vol. XLVIII, No. 7, December, 1956, pp. 371-79.

ROY PASCAL (essay date 1956)

[*Der grüne Heinrich,* the] one great novel of the Swiss author, Gottfried Keller is curiously like [Goethe's] *Wilhelm Meister's Apprenticeship.* It is the story of the growth of a child to manhood, of a would-be artist who discovers that his true calling is service to society, the Canton of Zürich. His error is not unprofitable. Heinrich's devotion to art, to his imagination, detaches him from the conventional round of life, from the vulgar concepts of success and failure, from the thoughtless egoism of the Philistine. He learns both to renounce, and to pursue the ideal purposes of social living; in his final capacity as a modest administrator he becomes a man of trust, a mediator, a representative of communal life. But, much as Keller avowedly learned from Goethe, and in particular from *Wilhelm Meister,* his novel is no glib imitation. It is, as Keller repeatedly said, 'the fruit of personal experience'; its problems were those of Keller himself, and its material is often autobiographical. He toiled at it for many years, and the labour of composition bears witness to Keller's own severe struggle with his experience. (pp. 32-3)

It was only as a result of a long experience that Keller came to see that in this personal story he was describing a fate 'for which no-one is guilty, or everyone'; that there is a 'psychological-social' solution to a guilt like Heinrich's, through nature and work, even though his feeling of guilt, his consciousness of error, remains with him as the principle of his personal renunciation. The culmination of the first version forces everything into the perspective of the fate of an individual; that of the final version asserts the vitality of social life and makes the individual, even in his eccentric course, a representative man. (pp. 34-5)

On one level we have a story rich in reality . . . ; on another level, a series of experiences, including anecdotal digressions, which as they accumulate build up a human life in terms of its basic factors. Though the novel was 'the fruit of personal experience', Keller had much more than an autobiographical purpose. . . . His 'experience' included his thought, and his novel was the fruit of his whole wisdom. The principle of its composition is in fact Keller's search for the fundamental structure of a human life. (p. 35)

As rich an account of childhood as *David Copperfield, Great Expectations,* or *Jane Eyre,* [*Green Heinrich*] surpasses them in two ways: the child is more contaminated, and his moral growth, more endangered, is more substantial, while at the same time his experience acquires a social representativeness. (p. 39)

[There] is a consistent interweaving in *Green Heinrich* of incident and general theme, a consistent symbolism of structure. In the early parts of the book fusion of symbol and reality is perfect. But after Heinrich's arrival at Munich this fusion is less satisfactory. Something of the emptiness of Heinrich's life as an artist enters into the work itself. . . . The incidents of his years in Munich have nothing of the spatial and atmospheric precision of his earlier life. . . . The long dream at the end, which introduces Heinrich's decision to go back home, is an inappropriate form to indicate his change of mind; the stay at the Count's mansion, the introduction to Feuerbach's philosophy, is poorly motivated and somewhat forced. And the return home, the acceptance of social duty, is told in summary, general terms. . . . The novel has, from a formal point of view, much the same weakness as *Wilhelm Meister.* As we come closer to Heinrich's decision to leave the world of imagination for the world of reality, the writing itself loses in plasticity, the theme emerges in an abstract didactic form and loses its poetic quality. Keller perhaps deliberately avoids describing this Swiss society as it actually was, with its factories, banks and social conflicts; he shows the process of Heinrich's development, but not the life into which he enters. (pp. 43-4)

[The] first version of *Wilhelm Meister* was composed as the straightforward consecutive story of the hero, and . . . in the final version, Goethe made the story of Meister's childhood retrospective and told by the hero himself. Keller reversed the process. The childhood was originally inserted, as Heinrich's autobiography, after an opening section describing his arrival at Munich, and the whole of Heinrich's later artistic career was recounted in the third person. In the final version, the novel begins with the story of Heinrich's childhood, and the whole novel is written in the first person as Heinrich's own account. (p. 44)

It is imaginable that the whole novel might have been written in the third person; it is certain that it would have lost thereby. By retaining and extending the use of the first person, Keller was able to find a simple and unifying principle for the selection of episodes, and was freed from any concern for insignificant biographical detail. The imagined author remembers only what is significant for him, those incidents where something important was at issue; he is seeking to clarify his purpose and his problem, and the moments of crisis (using the word in its widest significance) naturally remain prominent in his consciousness. But Keller was concerned not only to portray, but also to comment, to make the meaning of events explicit. This current commentary, which extends to general questions such as religion and politics, was not only less mature in the first version; in the parts written in the first person it was often inappropriate to the youth of the pseudo-author and, in the parts written in the third person the intrusions of the author were oppressively frequent. In the final version, purified by a wiser head and a riper taste, the commentary is that of the hero himself, and as such is an organic part of the tale. We know who it is that is making the comments—in this sense the conclusion of the book, the mature wisdom of Heinrich, is present from the beginning, and the actual story only confirms what is subtly and sometimes vigorously evident in each incident. The dualism of author and incident that sometimes vexes in the earlier version has disappeared, and in the final form, the political, philosophical, aesthetic or moral comments form an organic part of the hero's reality.

Keller therefore never seeks to reproduce the world simply as a child, a 'greenhorn', might see it. His style reflects, without disguise, the mature man who recaptures, through memory and imagination, the world of the child, illuminated by the understanding. It is a peculiarly dense style, inclining even to clumsiness at times. It is thronging with things, with material, psychological and social actuality; yet impregnated with reflexion, which gives a shape to the experiences recounted and builds up, with them, the process of the book, the 'Bildung' [education] of Heinrich. (pp. 46-7)

In relating the hero's imaginative world with the actuality for which it is his compensation, Keller provides a running criticism of this actuality. The theme of the book, the discovery of 'the poetry of what is living and reasonable', is not only Heinrich's spiritual development, but also the development of the social reality to which he learns to devote himself. Keller does not idealise the Canton of Zürich as an idyllic corner of the world. . . . His affirmation of the Zürich democracy was not the result of a practical commonsense acceptance of an inescapable reality; it arose from his conviction that, imperfect as it was, it still provided a satisfactory framework for human relationships and humane aspirations. . . . Keller's humour, which fuses his sympathy and his criticism, is never passive and sentimental; its basis is his belief that the aberrations he describes can be corrected, and that the society in which his characters are placed offers the possibility of improvement. . . . This positive critical realism is not only the social message of the book; it is the secret of its poetic quality. The book belongs to Switzerland, to Keller's generation; no German or Austrian author of the time could be so fully at home in his world, and could come to so harmonious a reconciliation of beauty and reality. (pp. 50-1)

> Roy Pascal, "Gottfried Keller: 'Green Heinrich'," in his The German Novel: Studies (copyright ©, U.K., 1956 by Manchester University Press; reprinted by permission of Manchester University Press), Manchester University Press, 1956, pp. 30-51.

J. M. RITCHIE (essay date 1957)

In most of the major histories of German literature Keller's last work, Martin Salander, hardly merits two or three lines' mention. Keller is neatly described as the classic example of poetic realism, and the disturbing last work is conveniently ignored, and indeed, it must be admitted, with some justice, for the book cannot be read with pleasure for its own sake. . . . Suddenly, with Martin Salander there is definite change of style, and while the opinions of the experts vary widely, one thing is certain; Keller has left poetic realism far behind him. This paper will stress the significance of this stylistic development, though of course the subject-matter of Martin Salander

will not be entirely ignored. It hopes to show that, while Keller in his last work adopted the techniques of the contemporary objective social novel, content and purpose of his work remained essentially unchanged.

The dominant feature of Keller's poetic realism is that it is stylized. He employs a unified language which strives after absolute grammatical correctness. Colloquial expressions, exclamations, abbreviations, etc., are used sparingly in preference to the language and forms of recognized literary standards. . . . [For Keller, the] written and the spoken languages are irreconcilable; literary work should be carried out exclusively in the literary language. . . . [But] opposed to these stiff literary forms Keller's language and style are constantly enriched by their deep roots in popular expression, proverbs, metaphors and similes drawn from everyday life, and his constant use of diminutive forms. The fusion of these literary and popular elements into one unified whole produces the often-praised artistry of the language of poetic realism.

Keller stresses the importance of this unified style. . . . A story must have a basic tone, the harmony and unity of which nothing should disturb. Hence there is about Keller's works a certain monotony—as he called it, 'jener ruhige, trockene Ton' [that quiet, dull tone]—for all their richness and variety of content. Dialogue, which is comparatively rare in his short stories and rarely involves more than two people, is seldom dramatic. (p. 214)

Martin Salander, we shall see, displays a gradual abandoning of the old Märchensprache, but it also reveals a complete abandonment of the old Märchenland, for example, Seldwyla which had been the setting for all his previous prose writings. . . . In Martin Salander the terrain is no longer that of the earlier works; the action takes place in a growing city of the Gründerzeit which overruns the paths and gardens Keller loves so much. . . . [In Martin Salander the setting] is strictly realistic; Seldwyla . . . has been devoured by the growth of modern civilization. But though, as in the novels of the naturalists, the scene of action is the big city, after the first chapters there are no descriptions of milieu and the action unfolds itself in vacuo. Not even the Salander home is described. But not only the background of nature is missing; in Martin Salander the people are missing too. In Der grüne Heinrich the hero is brought into contact with all classes and professions. Similarly the Novellen are played against an unanimistic body of Seldwyler and Züricher. This choir of active onlookers is entirely missing from Martin Salander; the action takes place in the narrowest family circle and there is never the suggestion of the pulsating throb of the big city. Keller had no interest in it, and therefore does not bring it to life as Zola and Dickens did.

On its appearance Martin Salander roused heated discussion in the democratic, socialist camp. But literary critics as well as party politicians objected to the overpolitical nature of the book. Yet an examination of the text shows that Keller was completely consistent in his political position. The novel was based on the excesses consequent upon the acceptance of the democratic Swiss constitution of 1869, and the evils which Keller scourges are the same as those on which he sits in judgement in Der grüne Heinrich and the Novellen, only now the presentation is more realistic and the humour gone. (pp. 215-16)

Apart from this main theme of democracy and the revision of the constitution, the contemporary scene is treated in very general terms, the political parties and religious sects are hardly mentioned by name, and the major conflict between the So-cialists and the Democrats is only lightly touched upon. Such problems do not really interest Keller. . . . Keller, unlike the naturalists, had more feeling for moral and ethical factors than for purely practical and political ones. (p. 216)

Similarities between *Der grüne Heinrich* and *Martin Salander* were early recognized by the critics. The theme of the political education of the hero into a true Swiss *Bürger,* his development into a man who could take his place in public life, a theme which had only lightly been touched upon in the early work, is now the intention of the author in *Martin Salander.* Hence *Martin Salander* is in a sense the sequel to *Der grüne Heinrich.* There is no fundamental difference between the nebulous en-thusiasm of the artist and the blind idealism of the secondary schoolteacher, Martin. Closer examination of the two texts shows even more striking similarities. The disappointments which Heinrich experiences in public life point directly to the presentation of the abuses of democracy in *Martin Salander.* The basic situations at the end of *Der grüne Heinrich* and the beginning of *Martin Salander* are the same. . . .

But how different is the technique in the two novels! Instead of Keller's normal general characterizations, dramatic action introduces the characters. The exposition is presented by means of dialogue. Dialogue prevails everywhere, Keller's usual avoidance of long stretches of direct speech is no longer no-ticeable. Keller here strives after dramatic presentation. . . . [The] general tendency of the novel [is] to move away from the slower techniques of poetic realism towards dramatic pre-sentation through action and dialogue. . . . (p. 217)

Martin Salander shows distinct traces of the naturalist concep-tion of the novel. Keller's preliminary sketches show that he had intended to develop the theme of socialism and anarchy, although nowhere in the novel does the revolutionary socialist tendency appear. The masses, the proletariat, play no part, though the scene of the action is a big city during a period of capitalist expansion. Keller was a liberal republican, not a revolutionary socialist. However, the basic situation of the novel, the attempt to tell the history of a period through the fates of the members of a single family, to present the totality of all social conditions in one main event, does reflect the naturalistic conception of the novel as a sociological study. (p. 218)

Hence in spite of his proclaimed aversion to the new literary movement, the naturalistic novel was not without influence on Keller. If one also considers the style of *Martin Salander,* techniques are found which were widely used by the French naturalists, though the influence of Spielhagen may have been more direct. . . . One characteristic of this style is the constant repetition of the same words to portray characteristics, to reveal a state of mind, to recall a *Stimmung* [atmosphere], or to fulfil an architectonic purpose in linking otherwise disconnected parts of the novel. Whole sentences (and in Zola whole pages) are repeated in this way. Repetition of significant words or phrases is particularly effective in the last words of a chapter. Zola and Daudet, like Dickens, also like to characterize their figures by particular external features or stereotyped expressions, which are repeated like *leitmotivs.* All these techniques, which Keller had condemned in the Dickens imitator Otto Ludwig. . . , are employed for the first time in *Martin Salander*! Keller tries to temper the schematic nature of his repetitions as far as possible, though not always with success. . . . (p. 219)

Der grüne Heinrich is not a planned novel in which everything fits into a prearranged concentric scheme. *Martin Salander* is

entirely different. Here is no longer the organic development of one life story, but a rigidly planned novel in which a de-liberate parallelism is pursued. (pp. 219-20)

Whereas in *Der grüne Heinrich* the unity is preserved by centr-ing the action on Heinrich's development, in *Martin Salander* the action centres on the Salander family. But there is no real unity of action. The characters are not all brought into contact with each other. . . . [The] interrelationship between otherwise disconnected parts of the story is established by means of rep-etition of significant phrases and episodes. (p. 220)

[In *Martin Salander* no] personal opinion on the events related is ever expressed, nor does the author introduce his characters and comment on the part they play in the novel as a whole. The characters present themselves. The facts speak for them-selves. The novel, as we have seen, becomes dramatic, epi-sodic, presented by means of action and dialogue instead of narrative and reflexion. All theoretical discussions, reflexions, explanations etc., are placed in the mouths of the actors. Char-acterization and psychological motivation are presented by in-ner monologues. . . , with which the novel now abounds. (p. 221)

But the effect of this objective technique is disastrous. The 'innere Heiterkeit', the glow, the gentle warmth which per-vaded all Keller's works is gone. . . . In Keller the poet is always present in his works, but his presence warms romantic irony into true humour. In *Martin Salander,* however, the dual-ity between the humorous judge and the objective story-teller is destroyed. The poet disappears entirely behind his charac-ters. . . . Humour is gone and nothing remains but a sharp satire of bitter reality. (pp. 221-22)

Yet *Martin Salander* does not in any way upset the essential unity of Keller's works. While the technique is new, content and pedagogical purpose are as before. The old Keller is still recognizable under the new garb. (p. 222)

> *J. M. Ritchie, "The Place of 'Martin Salander' in*
> *Gottfried Keller's Evolution as a Prose Writer," in*
> The Modern Language Review *(© Modern Human-*
> *ities Research Association 1957), Vol. LII, No. 2,*
> *April, 1957, pp. 214-22.*

STANLEY EDGAR HYMAN (essay date 1961)

The psychological acuity of [*Der grüne Heinrich*], published the year before Freud was born, is staggering. A 15-page ac-count of Henry's dreams, imaging sex as food and money, is a triumph of careful observation and what amounts to pre-science. Henry himself is a curiously modern case history of mother-fixation and repression. (p. 218)

The sociological penetration of the novel is equally impressive. Henry, like Keller himself, is a child of the new class, the son of a journeyman mason who by self-education and industry had become an architect and contractor. The conservatism and greed of the Swiss landowners, the old owning class, are re-lentlessly satirized in the book, while the peasants are typified by the lout Henry beats up. The promising social elements for Keller, as for his contemporary Karl Marx, are the self-edu-cated journeymen like his father; the intellectual aristocrats like the Count, enlightened by reading Feuerbach; and the prole-tariat.

Keller is more visibly ambivalent about the latter two than Marx was. . . . The life of the urban working class is at once seen as a pastoral idyll and patronized. (p. 219)

Green Henry often seems surprisingly modern. Some of its intellectual conversations will remind readers of Thomas Mann, and some of its ironic touches of the short stories of Isaac Babel. In its constant tension between passionate young women and a repressed and mother-fixated young man, Keller's novel is curiously reminiscent of modern Irish fiction. Most of all, in its blending of absurdity and the deepest insight, it very much resembles Melville's *Pierre*.

What makes *Green Henry* great, ultimately, is its powerful affirmation of life. (p. 220)

It is as a life symbol that Henry is "Green" Henry. His one clear memory of his father is in a green coat, showing the child a green plant; later Henry wears only green clothes, cut down from his father's (thus the nickname); he informs us: "I had grown up like a blade of grass"; Judith tells him that his cruel innocence is a "green soul"; he writes a book (the first part of this book) and has it bound in green cloth; he recognizes that he has been "a young greenhorn"; Judith eventually returns to her "green lad" and he finishes his book "in order once again to walk the old green path of remembrance." (pp. 220-21)

> *Stanley Edgar Hyman, "Salad Days, Green and Cold" (originally published in* The New Leader, *Vol. XLIV, No. 22, May 29, 1961), in his* The Critic's Credentials: Essays & Reviews, *edited by Phoebe Pettingell (copyright © 1978 by Phoebe Pettingell; reprinted with the permission of Atheneum Publishers), Atheneum, 1978, pp. 217-21.*

F. M. LINDSAY　(essay date 1961)

For the most part [Keller's] tendentious political poems impress us as rather naive, even ridiculous nowadays. The *Jesuitenzug,* for instance, which is intended to be menacing, even frightening, now seems merely funny. . . . The nature poetry from [*Gedichte*] has worn better, and often in only slightly modified form his early nature poems were preserved by the aged poet in his *Gesammelte Gedichte*. . . . Keller's genuine feeling for nature, his keen painter's eye, his evident liking for his fellow-men and the plants and animals of the field, and an occasional moment of high poetic inspiration combine to make his verse memorable and important as a personal document of the poet's life.

In the *Gesammelte Gedichte* the *Spielmannslied,* which is the first poem in the collection, characterizes Keller's poetry most effectively; he makes no excessive claims for himself, but he does through the parable of the sower make it clear that he regards himself as a true poet; he would not claim that he has always made the most of himself, that he has never been slack or heedless or missed an opportunity; yet now and again "a hungry little bird" has gathered nourishment from him, he has provided the sustenance that sent the bird soaring heavenwards again, and he has therefore not entirely betrayed his mission. (pp. 174-75)

[*Unter Sternen,*] with its joy in the beauties of creation, places Keller among the true nature poets of Europe, side by side with Goethe or Wordsworth. His famous *Abendlied an die Natur* is a hymn of homage to the benign and refreshing influence of Nature to which he turns for comfort in every difficult situation in life. . . . (p. 175)

Abend auf Golgatha is the most direct evidence we possess that Keller may have turned away from Feuerbach towards the end of his life. This is a beautiful and subtle short poem about Christ on the cross. . . . Keller handles the hexameter here with great skill, and this is undoubtedly one of his best lyrics.

We do not remember Keller primarily as a lyric poet, but in the poems mentioned and a handful of others he has produced work which ranks with the best written in the German tongue. His best known and best loved poem, *Abendlied (Augen, meine lieben Fensterlein)* is the work above all others in which the quintessential Keller, the man of the seeing eye, who treasures the precious gift of life, reveals himself. Here Keller achieves that rare synthesis of thought, emotion and form which constitutes a true work of art. *Winternacht,* a delightful poem in which the imprisonment of natural forces in the winter is symbolized by the nixie's struggle to emerge from below the ice of a frozen pond, is another poem that haunts the memory. (p. 176)

A little artificial [*Das Sinngedicht*] certainly is, with its elaborately stylized setting and the constantly recurring symbolism of the epigram, but it has a charm and polish all of its own. In this work Keller shows himself to be not merely a profound writer, but also extremely accomplished. *Das Sinngedicht* is the greatest work of Keller's old age, as *Der grüne Heinrich* is the greatest work of his youth. (p. 189)

> *F. M. Lindsay, "Gottfried Keller," in* German Men of Letters: Twelve Literary Essays, *Vol. V, edited by Alex Natan (© 1961 Oswald Wolff (Publishers) Ltd), Oswald Wolff, 1961, pp. 169-92.*

NORBERT FUERST　(essay date 1966)

In classical fiction the turns of the narrative are the real revelations, the fully symbolic events. Keller's pages are so spiked with fictions that it hurts our thin skins. In the following half-century several first-rate writers (James, Proust, Joyce, Mann) made models of the modern novel of their importance to create stories. In Keller, analysis is undisguised and terse, but a means of fiction, not its master.

In this predominance of 'pure' fiction over the other ingredients, Keller is representative of the German Novelle, which genre dominated German literature in the whole 'Victorian' period, 1830-1890. . . . The German Novelle cannot be understood as an undersized novel or an overblown story; it can be understood as the prose-epic, the prose-poem, and especially the prose-drama of the period. Almost every outstanding writer contributed some masterpiece to it, but four other authors made it their chief vehicle, each excellent in a different thing: Gotthelf in natural substance, Stifter in intense still-life, Storm in lyrical mood, Meyer in well-staged drama. So many writers, so many forms. But with Keller it is: so many stories, so many forms. He is the easiest inventor, he has stories within Novellen, and anecdotes within stories. All his fiction reminds one of the original meaning of anecdote, 'unedited.' (p. 117)

'The Smiles Gone' ['Das Verlorene Lachen'] is one of the best examples of what Keller dared to do to the Novelle. He packed into it all the virtues and vices of the novel. Precipitations and retardations; poetic, metaphoric shortcuts and prosy dissertations; dependable cultural history and reckless yarnspinning; leaps from realism into fairytale; sudden transitions from the tender to the grotesque, peripateias from comedy into tragedy, but also sudden turnings from tragedy into idyll. He is often hard to follow, as he leads us from room to room, each decorated in a different style. But those who follow him will soon see that it is the variety of a huge talent, which in the end forces all contrasts into a powerful synthesis. We have only to look at the way his individual stories have of complementing each other in a cyclical fashion, in the *Züricher Novellen,* in the exquisite *Epigram,* and above all in his most difficult and heterogeneous *Green Henry.* The mysteries of cyclical composition apply also to his individual stories: they too are loosely constructed, somehow more spacious than their outward dimensions. (pp. 124-25)

It is surprising both how many pages in [Keller's] works are given to sermonizing, and how these meditations are lost in the other riches. They are converted; they reach into the fictional substance and dignify it; the fiction reaches into them and makes them poetic. Keller is never theoretically sure of his means, but practically he uses them with a sort of compulsion—which afterwards he finds hard to justify: he abounds in deprecating, even harsh judgments of his works. He alternates his means because he does not aim at a single vision, but rather at a whole, fictional world. And the relation of that fictional to the real world is not at all that the former imitates the latter, but rather the opposite, that reality please learn a lesson, now and then, from fiction. Therefore his only steady rule is to make the fictional world as rich and spacious as he can. (p. 126)

To many Keller represented first and foremost the essence of the middle-class. The solution of his great novel was intransigently bourgeois: renounce art, better renounce all 'higher' aspirations, do what others need to have done, and you will be safe. Much in Keller looks like this solution, on the surface. But it is only the modest brown into which all bright colors flow together if we mix them. Seen as they are, his canvasses are made of the brightest and boldest colors. The main impression is perhaps that of *Buntheit,* variegation. In none of his stories do we find an affinity for the monochrome, everywhere colorfulness made by contrasts. His whole work is a set of paradoxical compensations. His preaching was only just as good as his deflating. He was sometimes the most fanciful and whimsical, but more often the most earthy and humorous. This apostle of normality was also the chief crank of the time. He was both the most bourgeois and the most bohemian, the most civic and the most artist. (p. 127)

Norbert Fuerst, "Gottfried Keller," in his The Victorian Age of German Literature: Eight Essays, *The Pennsylvania State University Press, University Park, 1966, pp. 103-27.*

J. M. LINDSAY   (essay date 1968)

In *Das Sinngedicht* Keller took up a theme dear to his heart and dwelt upon it with greater depth and concentration than ever before. The relationship between the sexes had often engaged his attention in the past, but here he explores the subject systematically and from the different points of view of man and woman. Written before it became generally fashionable to talk of a war between man and woman, the book is largely concerned with the fundamental antagonism between the sexes. Keller was well aware of this, and the reader constantly perceives "nature red in tooth and claw" behind the civilized conversations and sophisticated but always tendentious storytelling. This tale—with illustrations—of the courtship of two gifted people is told with great delicacy and finesse by an author who, having lost all illusions about the nature of love and

marriage retains goodwill towards his fellow men and women. (p. 211)

The stories are based on Friedrich von Logau's epigram:

Wie willst du weiße Lilien zu roten Rosen machen?
Küss' ein weiße Galatee; sie wird errötend lachen.

(How will you make white lilies into red roses?
Kiss a white Galatea; she will blushingly laugh.)

The seventeenth-century moralist and epigrammatist formulates neatly the moral conflict between law and freedom, sensuality and morality. The phrase "blushingly laugh" illustrates this contrast perfectly. While laughter conveys wholesome, natural pleasure in the kiss, the blush shows that the person concerned recognises certain moral restraints. Keller took Logau to mean that an ideal relationship between man and woman would be one in which instinct and restraint would co-exist and complement one another.

The young scientist Reinhart has lived for years a hermit-like life among his books and experiments. His life has been impoverished and his eyesight impaired by his excessive preoccupation with his scientific experiments. (p. 212)

From this restrictive and graceless existence he instinctively turns in the end to seek the qualities in which he knows himself to be deficient. Keller points out rather censoriously how much Reinhart is missing by this self-imposed scientific discipline. Fortunately, Reinhart has enough commonsense to draw the appropriate conclusion when his eyes begin to hurt during his spectroscopic enquiries. Reinhart's situation as a man with scientific and intellectual interests which threaten to take over and destroy or at least impair his life is meant, I think, to indicate the danger to which men in particular are subject of allowing professional cares and ambitions to dominate their whole lives. (p. 213)

Reinhart's first glimpse of Lucie reads like the climax of a fairy-tale, and indeed the setting of the marble fountain in front of the great house with the white-clad maiden sorting red roses in the evening sunshine contributes in no small measure to this atmosphere. (p. 214)

The early part of the *Sinngedicht* introduces with much charm and lightness of touch the issues which will dominate the whole work. It must be admitted that the extreme care and art shown in these early pages are not consistently maintained throughout the work; one or two of the stories are comparatively trivial in content and disappointing in execution. However, the cycle as a whole is remarkable for its organic unity, to which the artfully constructed framework largely contributes. (pp. 214-15)

Among the distinguishing features of this cycle of *Novellen* are its leisurely pace and careful construction. Basic assumptions of *Das Sinngedicht* are aristocratic standards of conduct, a sophisticated yet generous ideal of the cultivated individual and a reserved but free manner of life. The milieu is no longer the petty bourgeois world of small tradesmen, shopkeepers and publicans; we are here moving among leisured members of the upper classes. Keller never discusses directly the social position of his characters, but this becomes clear from the surroundings in which we find them and from their evident freedom to spend their time as they prefer.

Corresponding to the change in milieu as compared with Keller's earlier works is the development which has taken place in his style. . . . [He] liked to load his pages with descriptive detail, sometimes almost to the point where there was a risk of allowing descriptive passages to assume a life of their own. This tendency could even on occasion disrupt the narrative economy of a *Novelle*. Also he liked to use occasional outré metaphors and similes, which had the effect of startling the reader into paying closer attention. Compared with the style of *Die Leute von Seldwyla* that of the present work seems spare, economical, restrained; it is lucid, formal, rather severe. (pp. 222-23)

Das Sinngedicht does not demand in any crude or superficial way woman's "emancipation", in which Keller did not believe. Nevertheless, Lucie often adopts feminist and emancipated attitudes. In this respect perhaps she reflects Keller's acquaintance with intellectual women in the Berlin salons during the 1850s. The *Sinngedicht* does embody a conception of life in which each of the sexes has a separate but equally important place. It is perhaps worth while recording that Lucie is more nearly self-sufficient without Reinhart than he is without her; her way of life is more reasonable and satisfying than his. The work reflects both Christian and Goethean thinking about the place of man and woman as partners in marriage. (p. 223)

The whole conception of the cycle is somewhat artificial; the idea of the epigram sending the hero out on his search, and of Reinhart and Lucie sorting out their opinions on love and marriage by means of telling tendentious stories to one another sounds more like an intellectual or artistic exercise than like life. Matching the unreality of the conception we have the ideal remoteness of the beautiful house on the hill, the gentlemanliness of Reinhart, the aristocratic self-assurance, poise and highly idiosyncratic personal culture of Lucie. The occasional romantic traits found in *Das Sinngedicht* are introduced with self-conscious skill, and are never allowed to assume excessive importance.

Nowhere in Keller's works has he taken such trouble over the cyclic construction of a group of *Novellen*. The framework story of Reinhart's and Lucie's courtship is furthered stage by stage by the various *Novellen*, each of which illustrates a different aspect of the relationship between man and woman in love and marriage. The *Novellen* help to enlighten and purify the lovers' understanding of one another and of the respective functions of man and woman in marriage. Oddly enough physical passion is nowhere mentioned; indeed it scarcely ever appears in Keller's works after the original version of *Der grüne Heinrich*. The stories explore the effects of riches and poverty, differing religious beliefs, race and a person's general view of the world on marriage. (pp. 224-25)

Das Sinngedicht may be said to offer Keller's conscious and generous tribute to a somewhat more elevated, formal, even aristocratic pattern of existence than that in which he had grown up. The framework story possesses considerable importance from this point of view. It is evident from the care which Keller lavishes upon the description of Lucie's house and garden that he wishes us to applaud her style of life. . . . Into this ideal setting Keller projects his vision of the good and civilised life, in which man, and woman learn to curb and control the tensions which naturally arise between them and to find fruitful and productive outlets for potentially destructive forces. Keller wrote in the finale of *Das Sinngedicht* not of life as he had known it but as he would have wished it, and we cannot fail to see in this work his most carefully planned and most fully pondered, as well as his most delicately and delightfully presented commentary on life. Because *Das Sinngedicht* shows such careful

and calculated construction, because Keller handles so many traditional motifs of literary art with such superb control and discrimination, because of the variety of narrative matter which he offers for our consideration, because of his lucid yet profound symbolism, because of the tolerance and charity which underlie the whole work, it represents Keller's finest artistic achievement. *Der grüne Heinrich* obviously deals at greater length with many aspects of life, but the selection, handling and presentation of the material used in *Das Sinngedicht* has been performed with the skill, breadth of perception and psychological finesse of the mature artist. For all these reasons we must undoubtedly acclaim it as Keller's masterpiece. (pp. 227-28)

> J[ames] M[artin] Lindsay, in his Gottfried Keller: Life and Works (© 1968 Oswald Wolff (Publishers) Limited, London), Wolff, 1968 (and reprinted by Dufour Editions, Inc., 1969), 258 p.

BARRY G. THOMAS   (essay date 1971)

A basic theme in most, if not all, of the tales from *Die Leute von Seldwyla* is the need for the individual to gain a fuller understanding of himself so that he might develop a better relationship to his fellow man and function more effectively as a member of society. To gain this understanding it is usually necessary that the individual retreat for a time from the cares and pressures of society, for only from a distance can he obtain the proper perspective on community participation. (p. 63)

With the possible exception of the figure of Judith in the revised version of *Der grüne Heinrich*, Keller never realized this ideal in his two novels: Heinrich Lee dies soon after his return home (first version), or leads a mediocre existence as a public official (second version), and in *Martin Salander* the son Arnold Salander . . . remains a shadowy and unconvincing figure.

In *Die Leute von Seldwyla* Keller makes several attempts to represent the ideal member of society whose "Zeitüberlegenheit" [superiority to his times] does not preclude his ability to be "tätig umgestaltend, wirkend" [active, transforming, effective]. Here the first step toward gaining the necessary perspective is found usually in the peace and solitude of nature. After the ball-scene in *Kleider machen Leute,* for example, when Strapinski's true identity is revealed, the rebuilding of the relationship between Nettchen and Strapinski begins as Nettchen finds the tailor lying in the snow by the woods . . . and in this stillness begins the mutual recognition of each other's qualities behind the appearances. . . . A similar quiet prevails in *Die missbrauchten Liebesbriefe* when Wilhelm and Gritli find themselves in a cathedral-like clearing in the woods. . . . A similarly peaceful and idyllic scene in *Dietegen* conveys the idea of rebirth and a new beginning in the relationship between the two main characters. . . . Perhaps the most obvious example of the association of silence and nature with the rebirth of the individual can be found in *Das verlorene Lachen*. Here Jukundus and Justine have met again after their alienation and long separation, and they stroll through the woods on a peaceful Sunday morning. . . . Keller makes it quite clear that the renewal of love between Jukundus and Justine, and the effort of the people behind the tree-nursery project, spring from the same ideals of community and humanity. . . .

In these examples the retreat from the community is viewed as a positive experience; the periods of peace and quiet serve as a time of introspection for the individual, after which he can re-establish on a firmer basis his connection to society and its individual members. (pp. 63-5)

In other instances, however, Keller indicates that the attempt to remove oneself from the demands of society may also have a negative side. It can happen that man will come to regard the idyllic situation as an end in itself, as the final answer to his problems, and not as a means for meeting those problems. . . . The thesis that the individual order and the general social order must find common expression is given negative expression in three tales from *Die Leute von Seldwyla: Romeo und Julia auf dem Dorfe, Die drei gerechten Kammacher,* and *Der Schmied seines Glückes.* Common to each of these stories is the attempt by the characters to find fulfillment in a kind of paradise-on-earth. . . . (p. 65)

Self-imposed death [as in *Romeo und Julia*] is the most drastic expression of the individual's inability to reconcile the personal order with the general, and is found chiefly in Keller's early works, some of whose conclusions were later moderated. Keller's tendency to avoid tragic situations has been noted previously, but this should not suggest that he became any less aware of the possibilities for tragedy in man's struggle to find his identity as part of the whole. . . . Keller did not choose to dwell on the fact of man's "lost paradise," as exemplified in the negative examples of *Romeo und Julia* and *Die drei gerechten Kammacher,* but rather attempted in the majority of his works to present those ideals of humanity which might serve as a positive example and goal for mankind. (p. 76)

> Barry G. Thomas, "Paradise Lost: The Search for Order in Three Tales by Gottfried Keller," in The Germanic Review (copyright 1971 by Helen Dwight Reed Foundation; reprinted by permission of Heldref Publications), Vol. XLVI, No. 1, January, 1971, pp. 63-76.

J. P. STERN (essay date 1971)

Keller places [the hero of *Der grüne Heinrich*] in a fairly well-defined social context that is governed by a simple and unprobing 'bürgerlich' morality. His task is to adjust the predetermining aspects of the genre to the claims of realism. . . . The episode of Heinrich's dealings with one of his art teachers, a man called Römer, is one of several instances which point up the novelist's task.

Römer is presented as that which Heinrich Lee is not, a genuine artist. He has come to Heinrich's native town (Zürich) after many failures, accompanied by sinister rumours concerning his past life. Heinrich lends him some of his mother's money. At a crucial point in Römer's haunted life, Heinrich, in a pique of vanity and self-righteousness, asks for the return of the money in a letter that is little short of blackmail. Römer instantly pays up and leaves, and is never seen again. In a subsequent venomous letter from Paris, addressed to 'my dear young friend', Römer makes it abundantly clear that Heinrich's action was the *coup-de-grâce* which has pushed him into abject poverty and moral disintegration. Some time later . . . Heinrich confesses his perfidy to Judith, the more mature of the two girls to whom he is attached. He does so contritely, adding that 'the story will be a warning to me'; by his self-reproaches, he feels, he has as good as atoned for the misdeed. Judith indignantly repudiates the suggestion. . . . In such forthright statements of the irretrievable nature of past experience, of the finality of wrong-doing, Keller's novel presents an advance on Goethe's *Wilhelm Meister*. For there the genre itself, with its

underlying view of experience as a series of experiments, had run counter to the making of such clear-cut moral judgements. However, in the next few lines the solipsistic philosophy of the genre reasserts itself. Heinrich doesn't reply to Judith's accusation. But in his own mind he finds it only too easy to assimilate the experience, 'because, after all, it belongs to my person, to my story, to my nature, otherwise it wouldn't have happened!' The objective aspect of the deed recedes behind its subjective meaning. In the moral indictment, the Goethean view of character-development is briefly widened, but in Heinrich's self-conscious rationalisation of the deed the genre catches up with the judgement and neutralises it.

Keller's engaging honesty consists quite simply in his refusal to do what almost every other author of a '*Künstlerroman*' has done—to make Heinrich into a great artist who is misunderstood. . . . Keller exposes [Heinrich's] dilettantism in detailed stages, unsparingly revealing the process at work in all inauthentic displays of talent, which he is old-fashioned enough to regard as a piece of self-indulgence. . . . All this is anti-romantic and honest, involving Heinrich in the kind of disillusionment that is germane to realistic fiction; but alas it is also somewhat undramatic. Bad art is equated with irresponsibility, which may come as something of a relief to readers saturated with literature about the 'a-moralism' or 'demonism' of art. But Keller seems unaware of slipping into the opposite (and equally egregious) attitude—I mean into the philistinism, writ large by the 'socialist realists' of our own time, which equates good art with social responsibility. . . . The message Heinrich discovers is simply 'This way is no way.' If the paean in praise of adult social responsibility on which the novel closes is unexciting, not to say insipid, then here again the genre asserts itself; the journey, in this kind of novel, is always so much more absorbing than its goal. Finally, as for the journey's relevance to the goal, the reader remains less than fully convinced. The prospect before him at the end is a lifetime's loyal service as a municipal pen-pusher. (pp. 125-27)

More than any other kind of novel, the [*Bildungsroman*] answers to the feeling we have for the fleetingness of experience, for the promise of fulfilment just around the next corner and always in the moment to come. It takes the sting of finality out of experience, and replaces it not only (as we have seen) by the notion of development but also by a *plan*. . . . [The] heroes all discover that their progress has been benevolently watched over—not by a divine Providence but by a philosopher, a club of freemasons, a wise old man or (in Heinrich Lee's case) a rich count. It is a half-hearted solution, which pays lip service to realism by employing a human agency, and at the same time disrupts it by showing how innocuous and harmless were the hero's acrobatics in the world when all the while there was a safety-net spread out under him. (p. 127)

No character in fiction is more bent on 'experiences', more determined to enrich his self, than Stendhal's Julien Sorel. Yet it is in a comparison with *Le Rouge et le Noir,* another variation on the theme of 'development', that the weakness of Keller's novel becomes clear. . . .

The most obvious thing to insist on in such a comparison is the unabating vitality of almost every one of Stendhal's characters. By this I mean that the forces in conflict with each other in his novel are incomparably greater, incomparably more violent. The social inertia, the *resistance* which the world offers to Julien Sorel's ambitions, is magnificently powerful. The measure of these forces is not so much that they will lead to his violent end but that each, hero *and* world, gives as good as it gets. . . . To compare the political cabbala in which Julien gets involved in Paris with the lengthy discussions on road planning and civic duties which teach Heinrich Lee how to become a responsible member of the Helvetic Confederation is like moving from a city jungle of predatory animals to the bovine economy of alpine pastures. (p. 128)

The irony with which Stendhal reports on Julien's progress has none of Keller's gentleness and bemused detachment. Stendhal's almost Flaubertian wryness implies a supreme narrative confidence, a perfect rapport between author and public that is free from didacticism and high-mindedness alike—and again this confidence has no equivalent in the German literature of the age outside the pages of Heine. The *Bildungsroman* makes of the hero's entry into the world something of a problem— shall he, shan't he?—as though he could somehow avoid it. For Stendhal the idea that world and society are anything but the firm *données* of the hero's situation doesn't arise. The idea that society will in some mysterious way yield before the hero's *weaknesses*—which is what it does in Keller's novel—is quite alien to Stendhal's scheme of things; and, it may not be irrelevant to add, to life as we know it. . . . Whatever Sorel wants he must fight for. The passion displayed in the course of that fight gives Stendhal's novel a dimension that is lacking in Keller's. Hence the scheme of moral values challenged through Julien's actions is consistently more important and interesting. Heinrich is engaged in a protracted tussle with his art and his conscience; in a conflict with selfishness, heartlessness, irresponsibility. Yet all these are *his* qualities: once he has sorted them out, the world offers no challenge. . . . [The] circle of the self is merely widened, never breached. All *comes* at him, a means to his end; the world is hardly more than his world: not exactly unreal but malleable. (pp. 129-30)

Keller's presentation of 'the world', then, lacks a last degree of seriousness. And this defect is paralleled—necessarily so— in his portrayal of the two women in Heinrich's life. Representatives of spirit and flesh respectively, they are mere literary clichés, they have been done over and over again throughout the nineteenth and early twentieth centuries, all the way down to Hermann Hesse. . . . The comparison with Stendhal is once more revealing. Unlike Mme de Rênal and Mathilde de La Mole, Anna and Judith don't exist outside the hero's emotional need of them (two souls, alas, live in his breast), and even on that doubtful premiss they don't come to life. (pp. 130-31)

Some of Keller's difficulties in the writing and rewriting of *Der grüne Heinrich* were no doubt due to his misgivings about telling his story through a first-person narrator. But that was not the only problem he encountered. Seeing that several chapters of the novel in its final version are apt to stand away from the main story as self-contained *Novellen*, we may wonder whether he had the narrative gift to 'go through to the end' with an extended novel—whether he had that energy which is the hallmark of the great novelist. (pp. 132-33)

> J. P. Stern, "Gottfried Keller: Realism and Fairytale," *in his* Idylls & Realities: Studies in Nineteenth-Century German Literature *(© 1971 J. P. Stern), Methuen, 1971, pp. 123-38.*

MARTIN SWALES (essay date 1977)

What Keller suggests . . . in his introduction to the Seldwyla tales is both the questionableness and the charm of the Seldwyla ethos. Keller also suggests, by implication, that the experience of the outsider who enters this community, or, conversely, the

experience of the insider who is forced to break with his home community, is the decisive area where this little Swiss world yields its full moral and social implications. As the stories themselves show, it is this marginal area—both literally and metaphorically—that will provide Keller with the material he recounts. . . . He points out that, given the character of the Seldwyla community, there can be no shortage of strange life histories. However, he continues: "Yet in this little volume I do not want to tell such stories as are inherent in the character of Seldwyla as I have described it—but rather a number of strange oddities, which happened from time to time, exceptions as it were, but they could only occur in Seldwyla." . . . Perhaps we should push Keller's argument a stage further and suggest that these experiences are typical precisely because they are exceptional, precisely because they involve the radical and explicit enactment of what is always latent in the workings of the community. . . . Marginal experience—whether in the form of the alienated outsider or of the alienated insider— constitutes a challenge to the Seldwyla ethos. The radicalism of this challenge—interpretatively—is the measure of Keller's own honesty in confronting the problem he has set himself.

Die drei gerechten Kammacher opens with a general introduction that recalls to the reader's mind several of the arguments advanced in the preface to the stories. We are told that the Seldwyler have shown that frivolous people can just about get along together—whereas the three *Kammacher* (combmakers) prove that three upright, "righteous" men cannot live under the same roof without getting on each other's nerves. Here, Keller immediately defines the prevailing ingredient of the Seldwyla ethos—*"Ungerechtigkeit"* ("unrighteousness") or *"Leichtsinn"* ("frivolity"). He goes on to indicate that the three combmakers are "righteous" *("gerecht")*: they embody an ethos that is diametrically opposed to the lighthearted, frivolous climate of the town. Keller is careful to introduce an immediate qualification of the notion of *Gerechtigkeit*—"righteousness." It is, we are told, neither divine righteousness, nor the "natural righteousness of the human conscience," but it is "that bloodless righteousness which has removed from the Lord's Prayer the sentence 'and forgive us our debts as we forgive our debtors'—because it never makes any debts." (pp. 161-62)

Keller goes on to give further examples of the creed of *Gerechtigkeit* that is to play such an important part in the story. It involves joyless commitment to hard work and the obsessive hoarding of money. *Gerechtigkeit* is an inherently individualist, competitive ethic, and its practitioners derive sustenance from the degree to which they can be seen to surpass all others in their ascetic aloofness from the shallow worldliness of a frivolous society. . . . In this story, Keller with a precise artistic and social sense confronts [the Protestant] ethic with the easygoing ethic of Seldwyla. That he should find the code by which the combmakers live monstrous and horrific is scarcely surprising. However, the greatness of Keller's story resides in the careful dialectic that it sustains, whereby the *Gemütlichkeit* of the Seldwyler, for all its appealing qualities—particularly when compared to the existence of the Kammacher—is ultimately no more a genuinely humane value than is the righteousness that it so strenuously—and rightly—repudiates. (p. 163)

On the whole, the Seldwyler [figure] in a positive light in the story. Certainly, beside the obsessiveness of the Kammacher, their lightheartedness and gaiety seem immensely human and appealing. However, their *Leichtsinn* is not, in itself, a humane value; the ethos of *Gemütlichkeit* is no guarantee of moral rightness. The three combmakers challenge this ethos in the most radical way imaginable. Yet the challenge serves to bring into sharp illumination the human basis on which this ethos rests—and it is a basis that is squalid. In this story, Keller is anything but the apologist of Seldwyler virtues. The presence of the combmakers in the town, as it were, forces Seldwyla to show its hand—with deeply disquieting results.

It is this radicalism in the story that accounts for its humor, for its imaginative and stylistic intensity, for its critical energy. The story is, in the spirit of Keller's remarks in the preface to the Seldwyla tales, both exceptional and typical, both unique and utterly characteristic. In this sense the story manifestly belongs within the loosely defined framework that is the social *donnée* of the tales. The combmakers are the figures from outside, who bring a foreign ethos into the community. The friction between the two ways of life, between *Gerechtigkeit* and *Leichtsinn* shows us exactly what the Seldwyla community is made of. . . . The Kammacher, in their utter alienation from Seldwyla, in their manifest and uncompromising marginality, force an exceptional enactment of what the Seldwyla ethos stands for. By means of this constellation—one that is characteristic of the novelle—Keller is able to give a suggestive examination not only of a small Swiss community in the nineteenth century, but also of some important issues in nineteenth-century bourgeois society. In effect, he polarizes the social situation into two extreme possibilities: on the one hand, *Leichtsinn*, the irresponsibility of speculative existence, of monetary lightheartedness involving the incurring of debts and the scorn for practical work, for a properly acquired trade; and, on the other hand, *Gerechtigkeit*, the obsessive concern for hard work, for accumulation of savings, for the relentless production of goods, for self-defeating competitiveness. Moreover, he suggests that both extremes harbor an inherent moral falseness, a reduction and degradation of man. The radicalism of the challenge to the familiar world of Seldwyla is the measure of Keller's artistic success. With that artistic success goes a thematic energy that transcends the provincialism of his setting. (pp. 178-79)

> *Martin Swales, "Keller: 'Die drei gerechten Kammacher'," in his* The German Novelle *(copyright © 1977 by Princeton University Press; reprinted by permission of Princeton University Press), Princeton University Press, 1977, pp. 158-79.*

ADDITIONAL BIBLIOGRAPHY

Fife, Hildegarde Wichert. "Keller's Dark Fiddler in Nineteenth-Century Symbolism of Evil." *German Life & Letters* XVI, No. 2 (January 1963): 117-27.
> Explains how Keller uses a naturalistic character as a mystic proclaimer of evil in *Romeo und Julia auf dem Dorfe*.

Frank, Barbara R. "Irony in Keller's *Sieben Legenden*." *The Germanic Review* XLIX, No. 2 (March 1974): 129-45.
> Contends that characters in *Sieben Legenden* are led to confusion by organized religion.

Furst, Norbert. "The Structure of *L'education sentimentale* and *Der grüne Heinrich*." *PMLA* LVI, No. I (March 1941): 249-60.*
> An analysis of the internal structure of the two novels which cites philosophical and psychological parallels and contrasts.

Hauch, Edward Franklin. *Gottfried Keller as a Democratic Idealist*. New York: Columbia University Press, 1916, 96 p.
> Contends that Keller's optimistic idealism and belief in democracy allowed him to integrate romantic and realistic tendencies in his works.

Jennings, Lee B. "Gottfried Keller and the Grotesque." *Monatshefte* L, No. 1 (January 1958): 9-20.
> Shows how the grotesque has a vital function in Keller's system of imagery.

Lemke, Victor J. "The Deification of Gottfried Keller." *Monatshefte* XLVII, No. 3 (March 1956): 119-26.
> Argues that Keller was a strict realist, and that attempts to show him as "good-natured" are misconceived.

Radandt, Friedhelm. "Transitional Time in Keller's *Züricher Novellen*." *PMLA* LXXXIX, No. 1 (January 1974): 77-84.
> Describes how *Die Züricher Novellen* deal with the concept of living in a time of social and cultural transformation.

Richert, Herbert W. *Basic Concepts in the Philosophy of Gottfried Keller*. Chapel Hill: The University of North Carolina, 1949, 164 p.
> Disputes the claim that Keller's social philosophy derives mainly from Ludwig Feuerbach, and instead points to Friedrich von Schiller as Keller's main influence.

Schreiber, William I. "Gottfried Keller's Use of Proverbs and Proverbial Expressions." *The Journal of English and German Philology* LIII, No. 4 (October 1954): 358-84.
> Shows how Keller used proverbs to give his final judgement on characters or situations.

Shaw, Michael. "The Mirror and Its Uses: A Study of a Pattern in Gottfried Keller's Prose." *Symposium* XXII, No. 4 (Winter 1968): 358-84.
> Explains Keller's use of reflection as a shock of recognition for his characters, leading to their transformation.

John Pendleton Kennedy

1795-1870

(Also wrote under the pseudonyms of Mark Littleton, Esq. and Solomon Second-thoughts) American novelist, essayist, and biographer.

In an era when European critics insisted that American authors had nothing American worth writing about, Kennedy demonstrated that the new country's history was a colorful adventure which could be brought to life. His experiences in the War of 1812 inspired his romantic idealism but they also enabled him to write accurate, first-hand accounts of military life, which he vividly portrayed in several of his novels.

Kennedy's works were devoted to those causes which he felt would improve the fledgling nation—especially the stories which opposed debt imprisonment and slavery. As a novelist, he examined the political and cultural life of early America, and supplied accurate interpretations and insights into the American way of life. He contributed to several magazines, publishing the *Red Book* (a periodical similar to the *Spectator* and the *Salmagundi*) with Peter Hoffmann Cruse, and collecting his editorials from the Washington *National Intelligencer* for *Mr. Ambrose's Letters on the Rebellion.* Mark Littleton, Esq. is the name of the narrator of Kennedy's first novel, *Swallow Barn; or, A Sojourn in the Old Dominion,* an account of travels in Virginia. This novel describes the pastoral atmosphere and serene country life which Kennedy enjoyed during summer visits to relatives. His second novel about Virginia, *Horse-Shoe Robinson: A Tale of the Tory Ascendancy,* contains humorous character delineation. This is a historical novel of the American Revolution, reflecting Kennedy's experiences of the War of 1812 and written in the Romantic tradition. The first historical account of the Revolution with a southern setting, *Horse-Shoe Robinson* mixes a nationalist tone and pastoral setting, a combination that the nineteenth-century reading public found appealing. In *Rob of the Bowl: A Legend of St. Inigoe's,* Kennedy wrote a romance of his home state, colonial Maryland. Awkwardly written and of little interest to readers, the book marked the end of his career as a novelist.

The abrupt end of Kennedy's literary career was not entirely due to the failure of *Rob of the Bowl.* Throughout his life, his first preoccupation was with American politics and most of his energy was spent campaigning, pamphleteering, and lecturing. An important member of the Whig party, Kennedy also served in Congress, was Speaker of the Maryland House of Delegates, and was Secretary of the Navy under Millard Fillmore.

*Many critics feel that the turning point of Kennedy's literary career came after his marriage to Elizabeth Gray, daughter of a wealthy cotton-spinner. She encouraged him to combine his literary and political talents, embrace the precepts of capitalism, and advocate them in his nonfiction. Memorable among these later works are *Annals of Quodlibet,* a satire on Jacksonian democracy, and *Memoirs of the Life of William Wirt, Attorney General of the United States,* a full-length biography of a much-admired friend.

Kennedy was a devout Romantic who celebrated the national character and was innovative in depicting scenes from Amer-

ican life. We see mirrored in his fiction something of the development of the United States. (See also *Dictionary of Literary Biography, Vol. 3: Antebellum Writers in New York and the South*).

PRINCIPAL WORKS

Swallow Barn; or, A Sojourn in the Old Dominion [as Mark Littleton, Esq.] (novel) 1832
Horse-Shoe Robinson: A Tale of the Tory Ascendancy (novel) 1835
Rob of the Bowl: A Legend of St. Inigoe's (novel) 1838
Annals of Quodlibet [as Solomon Second-thoughts] (novel) 1840
Memoirs of the Life of William Wirt, Attorney General of the United States (biography) 1849
Mr. Ambrose's Letters on the Rebellion (essays) 1865

[EDWARD EVERETT]　　(essay date 1833)

[*Swallow Barn, or a Sojourn in the Old Dominion*] is a work of great merit and promise. It is attributed to [John Pendleton Kennedy], already advantageously known to the public by several productions of less compass, and in various styles, but all excellent in their respective ways. The present attempt proves that he combines, with the talent and spirit which he had previously exhibited, the resource, perseverance and industry, that are necessary to the accomplishment of extensive works. We do not know that we can better evince our friendly feeling for him than by expressing the wish, that the success which this production has met with may induce him to withdraw his attention from other objects, and devote himself entirely to the elegant pursuits of polite literature, for which his taste and talent are so well adapted, and in which the *demand for labor* . . . is still more pressing than in law, political economy, or politics. . . .

The texture of [*Swallow Barn*] is natural, and sufficiently ingenious, though from the nature of the plan, it does not excite a very deep and strong interest. (p. 519)

The talent of [Mr. Kennedy] is probably not inferior to that of Mr. Irving. Some of the smaller compositions to which we have already alluded, and in which the author depends merely on his own resources, exhibit a point and vigor of thought, and a felicity and freshness of style, that place them quite upon a level with the best passages in the *Sketch Book*. In the present work, his genius, if our impression be not incorrect, is throughout partially rebuked by the consciousness that he is not proceeding entirely upon his own spontaneous impulses, but following, to a certain extent, at least, in the footsteps of another writer. . . . [We] think we can assure him, that when he shall tempt again the uncertain sea of public favor, he has only to launch forth boldly, and steer his course independently of all other guidance than the great lights of nature, and the compass of his own taste and judgment, in order to make a still more fortunate and productive voyage than the present. (pp. 543-44)

> [*Edward Everett*,] "'*Swallow Barn*'," *in* The North American Review, *Vol. 36, No. LXXIX, April, 1833, pp. 519-44.*

[EDGAR ALLAN POE]　　(essay date 1835)

We have not yet forgotten, nor is it likely we shall very soon forget, the rich simplicity of diction—the manliness of tone—the admirable traits of Virginian manners, and the striking pictures of still life, to be found in *Swallow Barn*. The spirit of imitation was, however, visible in that book, and, in a great measure, overclouded its rare excellence. This is by no means the case with Mr. Kennedy's new novel [*Horse-Shoe Robinson*]. If ever volumes were entitled to be called original—these are so entitled. We have read them from beginning to end with the greatest attention, and feel very little afraid of hazarding our critical reputation, when we assert that they will place Mr. Kennedy at once in the very first rank of American novelists.

Horse-Shoe Robinson . . . is a tale, or more properly a succession of stirring incidents relating to the time of the Tory Ascendency in South Carolina, during the Revolution. (p. 522)

It will here be seen at a glance that the novelist has been peculiarly fortunate in the choice of an epoch, a scene and a subject. We sincerely think that he has done them all the fullest justice, and has worked out, with these and with other materials, a book of no ordinary character. . . . [Mr. Kennedy] has

ventured, at his own peril, to set at defiance the common ideas of propriety . . . , and, not having the fear of the critic before his eyes, has thought it better to call his work by the name of a very singular personage, whom all readers will agree in pronouncing worthy of the honor thus conferred upon him. The writer has also made another innovation. He has begun at the beginning. We all know this to be an unusual method of procedure. It has been too, for some time past, the custom, to delay as long as possible the main interest of a novel—no doubt with the very laudable intention of making it the more intense when it does at length arrive. Now for our own parts we can see little difference in being amused with the beginning or with the end of a book, but have a decided preference for those rare volumes which are so lucky as to amuse us throughout. And such a book is the one before us. We enter *at once* into the spirit and meaning of the author—we are introduced *at once* to the prominent characters—and we go with them *at once*, heart and hand, in the various and spirit-stirring adventures which befall them. . . .

We think [Mr. Kennedy] has been particularly successful in the delineation of his female characters; and this is saying a great deal at a time when, from some unaccountable cause, almost every attempt of the kind has turned out a failure. (p. 523)

With the exception of now and then a careless, or inadvertent expression, such for instance, as the word *venturesome* instead of *adventurous,* no fault whatever can be found with Mr. Kennedy's style. It varies gracefully and readily with the nature of his subject, never sinking, even in the low comedy of some parts of the book, into the insipid or the vulgar; and often, very often rising into the energetic and sublime. Its general character, as indeed the general character of all that we have seen from the same pen, is a certain unpretending simplicity, nervous, forcible, and altogether devoid of affectation. This is a style of writing above all others to be desired, and above all others difficult of attainment. Nor is it to be supposed that by simplicity we imply a rejection of ornament, or of a proper use of those advantages afforded by metaphorical illustration. . . . We have called the style of [Mr. Kennedy] a style simple and forcible, and we have no hesitation in calling it, at the same time, richly figurative and poetical. . . .

While we are upon the subject of style, we might as well say a word or two in regard to *punctuation*. It seems to us that the volumes before us are singularly deficient in this respect—and yet we noticed no fault of this nature in *Swallow Barn*. How can we reconcile these matters? Whom are we to blame in this particular, the author, or the printer? It cannot be said that the point is one of no importance—it is of very great importance. A slovenly punctuation will mar, in a greater or less degree, the brightest paragraph ever penned; and we are certain that those who have paid the most attention to this matter, will not think us hypercritical in what we say. A too frequent use of the *dash* is the besetting sin of the volumes now before us. It is lugged in upon all occasions, and invariably introduced where it has no business whatever. Even the end of a sentence is not sacred from its intrusion. Now there is no portion of a printer's fount, which can, if properly disposed, give more of strength and energy to a sentence than this same *dash;* and, for this very reason, there is none which can more effectually, if improperly arranged, disturb and distort the meaning of every thing with which it comes in contact. But not to speak of such disturbance or distortion, a fine taste will intuitively avoid, even in trifles, all that is unnecessary or superfluous, and bring nothing into use without an object or an end. . . .

The second of [Mr. Kennedy's] volumes is, from a naturally increasing interest taken in the fortunes of the leading characters, by far the most exciting. But we can confidently recommend them both to the lovers of the forcible, the adventurous, the stirring, and the picturesque. They will not be disappointed. A high tone of morality, healthy and masculine, breathes throughout the book, and a rigid—perhaps a too scrupulously rigid poetical justice is dealt out to the great and little villains of the story. . . . In conclusion, we prophecy that *Horse-Shoe Robinson* will be eagerly read by all classes of people, and cannot fail to place Mr. Kennedy in a high rank among the writers of this or of any other country. (p. 524)

> *[Edgar Allan Poe,]* "'Horse-Shoe Robinson'," in The Southern Literary Messenger, *Vol. I, No. 9, May, 1835, pp. 522-24.*

THE ATHENAEUM (essay date 1850)

[It may] seem to many unnecessary to have endowed [William Wirt] with the public honours of biography,—at least on the colossal scale adopted by Mr. Kennedy; who has thought it right to expend more ink on the memoirs of this obscure American lawyer than Thucydides considered necessary for the whole record of the Peloponnesian War!

Nevertheless, . . . we are not sorry to have received [*Memoirs of the Life of William Wirt, Attorney-General of the United States*]—nor do we rise from their perusal with the feeling that our time has been thrown away on a profitless task. . . .

In itself the Memoir is not what the reading world calls intersting. There is no action and little incident. The letters are the best portion. (p. 867)

We have no idea of going over the *Memoir* methodically. . . . [It] yields little in the shape of result. [The] moral is, however, forcibly exhibited in the Letters—though it never once catches the attention of the biographer. . . . Mr. Kennedy has done what he had to do with zeal and ability. But the book is not likely to take much hold of English readers, from the absence of all stirring interest in the narrative. (p. 868)

> "'Memoirs of the Life of William Wirt, Attorney-General of the United States'," The Athenaeum, *No. 1190, August 17, 1850, pp. 867-68.*

SOUTHERN QUARTERLY REVIEW (essay date 1852)

It is all times pleasant to be reminded of this delightful author [J. P. Kennedy]. Few of our gifted countrymen, with so many and such varied excellencies, are chargeable with so few defects. He is at the same time a bold and exquisite painter—his touches, to suit the subject and occasion, equally free and delicate. [Mr. Kennedy's] style, as pure and chaste as Washington Irving's, and finished as in his most elaborate efforts, is always full of life. It possesses the charm of a never-failing freshness, buoyancy and raciness. It is singularly graceful and easy—the wing of a swallow is not more nimble and alert. And though his style is made the medium of a humour, most free, hearty and exuberant, yet it never itself becomes extravagant or oversteps the modesty of nature, or runs into . . . inanity and verbiage. His humour lies in the conception, and the style is simply the apt expression of it. He does not seek to make too much of a thought—to over-dress it, to dwell upon it with a lover-like tediousness and tenacity, and fatigue by iteration upon iteration. (pp. 71-2)

All who appreciate the past of Virginia, and the peculiar elements which rendered her so attractive in social life, and so great in arms and politics, will feel obliged to Mr. Kennedy for the portrait he has given of the mother of states and of men [in *Swallow Barn*]. His pleasant work, so full of delightful mirth, will provoke many a sigh from those who cling fondly to the past, and, passing away themselves, mourn over a style of character, customs and manners, which are fading rapidly to extinction among us. (pp. 75-6)

There is much sage reflection upon grave matters of public concern to provoke and stir the politician; a modest, sweet little love story trickles in and out through its pages, with its mysteries, its varied fortunes, its uncertainty, so attractive and refreshing to all youthful hearts; and for the boys of this or the last generation, there is a possum hunt. . . . (pp. 77-8)

[Mr. Kennedy] speaks of his portrait of the social life of Virginia as a strong likeness, if a daub. . . . The author and the subject might well felicitate each other. The theme became the artist and the artist the theme. The work has been executed *con amore,* with all the affection of the lover, but none of his blindness. For a Virginian himself to have seen and described Virginia as Mr. Kennedy has seen and described her, he must first have travelled. He has brought out all that is noble, genial and generous in her character—not a feature that would do her honour, that is not rendered with loving fidelity and glowing warmth, and the picture is set in the very best lights too, yet the little weaknesses, the odd points, the obvious vanity, and the unconscious assumption of the good and stately old mother, are slyly insinuated and sufficiently indicated, as to make it a very decided portion of the picture. (p. 78)

[The] negro never appears in this work but in his natural, always amiable, and always happy character. The author shows singular happiness in painting him, physically and morally, and we could wish that all who approached the question of negro slavery itself, had treated it with the wise distrust, the modesty and admirable good sense which distinguish the grave reflections of the author of this volume. (p. 82)

> *G.S.B., "Kennedy's 'Swallow Barn',"* in Southern Quarterly Review, *Vol. V, No. IX, January, 1852, pp. 71-86.*

[WILLIAM GILMORE SIMMS] (essay date 1852)

Mr. Kennedy has acquitted himself with a great credit, and acquired permanent reputation, in sundry departments of literature—the biography, the satire, the descriptive narrative and the novel. His **"Life of Wirt"** takes rank among the best of the American biographies. His **"Quodlibet,"** unacknowledged, but generally understood to be from his pen, was a trenchant whig satire. . . . His **"Swallow Barn"** . . . affords a lively and piquant portraiture of domestic life in Virginia. . . . **"Rob of the Bowl"** did not seize upon the popular fancy, and, upon the whole, was rather a languid performance, though with some scenes of great interest and spirit. As a novelist, the reputation of the author rests wholly upon **"Horse-Shoe Robinson."** This romance . . . at once took firm hold upon the public fancy. It soon passed to a second edition, and became a popular favourite. Its material was comparatively fresh. . . . As a story, . . . it was of little value. Mr. Kennedy is not distinguished as a raconteur. His merits lie in portraiture of character, and, especially, in a happy perception of the piquant and the humorous. The love legend of the **"Horse-Shoe"** is its smallest attraction. The lover is little more than the walking gentleman of the conventional drama. The heroine is only a pleasing child, with the tenderness of the woman. Their course of love lacks originality. The true attraction of the work lies wholly in the character of ''Horse-Shoe Robinson.'' (pp. 203-04)

This book is . . . one that, as conspicuously as any other, illustrates the importance of truthful and salient characterization, in a work, without regard to its simple incidents. Not that the incidents in the novel are not full of life and interest; but, as they serve only for the development of the characters they are, necessarily to be held subordinate. Without Horse-Shoe, the story would be flat; with him in the foreground, full of genuine hearty humour, great courage, excellent sense, and a calm, deliberate judgment, there are few purely American stories which can be assigned the superiority over it.

Such, in general terms, is the sufficient estimate which may be made of this production. . . . The publication of the new and beautiful edition before us, after an interval of twenty years, sufficiently shows that the story is regarded as an American classic, and must take its place, without question, in the national library. This being the case, it is matter of regret that the author has not been a little more severe in his revision of its pages. We note sundry little particulars which needed the file and burnisher, and a scrupulous care would have pruned away many luxuriances, which impair the effect of the better portions of the picture. In some of his dialogues, our author has not possessed himself of the right idiom of the country; and, in others, he sometimes forgets to make his speaker consistent in the patois which he uses. (p. 206)

Mr. Kennedy is one of those gentlemen whom we highly esteem, as well for his great private worth, his purity and integrity of character, and for his endowments as a literary man. But Mr. Kennedy, like many others, has been misled by the false statements of superficial or corrupt historians, who are quite too numerous in our country, and who abuse the confidence of the reader, sometimes through their own ignorance and haste, sometimes through sectional prejudices, and, not unfrequently, because they aim to subserve the purposes of party. (p. 212)

The reader will understand us, as joining issue with our author in a friendly spirit, and with no purpose to impute to him a single injustice, or wilful or unkind assumption. He is one of our favourites, whom we hold in great respect as an author, and in great regard as a man. His book we cordially commend, as truthful in its spirit, and lively and attractive in its interest. Our dissent from some of its details must not be construed into any disposition to decry its genuine claims, or to detract, in any wise, from its real merits. (p. 220)

[*William Gilmore Simms,*] *''Kennedy's 'Horse-Shoe Robinson','' in* Southern Quarterly Review, *Vol. VI, No. XI, July, 1852, pp. 203-20.*

RUFUS WILMOT GRISWOLD   (essay date 1852)

[*Swallow Barn, or a Sojourn in the Old Dominion*] appears to have been commenced as a series of detached sketches of old or lower Virginia, exhibiting the habits, customs and opinions of the people of that region, and to have grown into something with the coherence of a story before it was finished. The plan of it very much resembles that of Bracebridge Hall, but it is purely American, and has more fidelity as an exhibition of rural life, while it is scarcely inferior in spirit and graceful humour. (p. 341)

No works could be more unlike each other than [*Horse-Shoe Robinson, A Tale of the Tory Ascendancy*] and *Swallow Barn*. They have no resemblance in style, in construction, or in spirit; but *Horse-Shoe Robinson* was even more successful than its predecessor. . . . [The characters of *Swallow Barn*] are sketched with singular skill and felicity, but they are less essentially creations than [they are] free-hearted, sagacious, and heroic. . . . [But in *Horse-Shoe Robinson* there are] original and admirably executed characters, whose individuality is distinct and perfectly sustained amid all varieties of circumstance; and skilful underplots, in which are imbodied beautifully-wrought scenes of love and touching incidents of sorrow. . . .

[*Rob of the Bowl, a Legend of St. Inigoe's*] was evidently written with much more care than the others, but it was less successful. Though dealing largely in invention, it is, like *Horse-Shoe Robinson,* of an historical character. . . . The characters are numerous, various, and strongly marked; but several of them are so prominent and so elaborately finished that the interest is much divided, and it has been remarked with some reason, that the story wants a hero. The historical impression which it conveys is as accurate as the most careful study of the incidents and temper of the times enabled the author to render it; the costume throughout is exact and in keeping; and the descriptions of scenery are spirited and picturesque in an eminent degree. . . .

[The *Annals of Quodlibet*] is full of wit, humour, and pungent irony, but is too exclusive in its reference to events of the day to possess much interest now when those events are nearly forgotten.

Each of the four works that have been mentioned is marked by distinct and happy peculiarities, and from internal evidence it probably would never have been surmised that they were by one another. (p. 342)

[*A Defence of the Whigs*] is purely political, and is remarkable for clearness, vigour, and amplitude of statement and illustration. (pp. 342-43)

Mr. Kennedy is altogether one of our most genial, lively, and agreeable writers. His style is airy, easy, and graceful, but various, and always in keeping with his subject. He excels both as a describer and as a raconteur. His delineations of nature are picturesque and truthful, and his sketches of character are marked by unusual freedom and delicacy. He studies the periods which he attempts to illustrate with the greatest care, becomes thoroughly imbued with their spirit, and writes of them with the enthusiasm and the apparent sincerity and earnestness of a contemporary and an actor. He pays an exemplary regard to the details of costume, manners, and opinion, and is scarce ever detected in any kind of anachronism. There are some inequalities in his works, arising perhaps from the interruptions to which a man in active public life is liable; there is occasional diffuseness and redundance of incident as well as of expression; but his faults are upon the surface, and could be easily removed. (p. 343)

Rufus Wilmot Griswold, ''John Pendleton Kennedy,'' in his The Prose Writers of America, *revised edition, A. Hart, 1852 (and reprinted by Garrett Press, Inc., 1969, pp. 341-53).*

[WILLIAM GILMORE SIMMS]   (essay date 1854)

[Kennedy's *Rob of the Bowl*] is not so successful a story as *Horseshoe Robinson,* but it is not unworthy of the accomplished author, and exhibits some of the most agreeable characteristics of taste and manner. There are several scenes of great force and vivacity, and much picturesque portraiture.

> [*William Gilmore Simms,*] *"Critical Notices: 'Rob of the Bowl',"* in Southern Quarterly Review, *Vol. X, No. XIX, July, 1854, p. 269.*

J. R. LOWELL (essay date 1860)

I have found [your **"Legend of Maryland"**] particularly interesting, and shall be truly gratified to see it in the "Atlantic." Forgive me for making you the victim of a confidence, but (apart from all other considerations of intrinsic merit) it is so seldom that the editor of an American Magazine has the luck to meet with a contributor who writes altogether like a gentleman, that such an event gives him a particular pleasure. There is so much cleverness and so little *style!* (p. 206)

> *J. R. Lowell, in his letter to John Pendleton Kennedy on April 26, 1860, in "The Kennedy Papers (Second Article): Letters from Dickens, Macaulay, Cooper, Holmes, Lowell, and Others," edited by Killis Campbell, in* The Sewanee Review *(reprinted by permission of the editor and the publisher, the University of the South), Vol. XXV, No. 2, April, 1917, pp. 193-208.*

EDWARD M. GWATHMEY (essay date 1929)

We greet Kennedy's *Swallow Barn* upon its republication with the same pleasure that we feel in greeting a friend of our youth who has been absent from our midst for a long time and who suddenly reappears. *Swallow Barn* deserved a better fate than that of being consigned to oblivion for the many years which have elapsed since the last edition of it was published. The modern craze for antique collecting is recalling to our minds with redoubled force the beauty of old time furniture, which beauty shows more beautiful with the mellowness of age upon it. Such is the case with a book like *Swallow Barn*. . . . It is a book to be read for relaxation. In it Kennedy does not burden his readers with an intricate plot; so that it may be read with equal pleasure either in parts or in its entirety. I can think of no book which I should prefer to have for a traveling companion on a wearisome journey. (p. 225)

> *Edward M. Gwathmey, "Book Reviews: 'Swallow Barn, or a Sojourn in the Old Dominion',"* in *American Literature, Vol. 1, No. 2, May, 1929, pp. 225-26.*

VERNON LOUIS PARRINGTON (essay date 1930)

[Kennedy's] three best-known books, written between the ages of thirty-six and forty-five, are unlike enough to have been written by different men. *Swallow Barn* like the youthful sketches of *The Red Book*, is Irvingesque, and the Irving influence crops out again in a late book *Quodlibet;* but *Horseshoe Robinson* is substantial Revolutionary romance, done in sober narrative with touches of realism; and *Rob of the Bowl* is light and whimsical cavalier romance, all atmosphere and small talk, utterly unlike Irving. It is in this latter book . . . that Kennedy really found himself; he seems to move through the scenes more easily and with greater delight than in any other of his pages. (pp. 50-1)

Quite too much . . . has been made of [the way in which *Swallow Barn* imitates Irving's work]—it is an imitativeness

rather of method than of theme or style. If it was not quite a pioneer work in the field of local description, it was amongst the earliest. . . . Intrinsically as well as historically the work is curiously suggestive. Nowhere else does the plantation life of the Old Dominion in the days before its decline appear so vividly as in these discursive pages. . . . (p. 51)

Surely the romance of Old Virginia, preserved in these light-hearted discursive pages, is worth remembering by later generations who have forgotten how to live so genially. (p. 52)

Slavery in *Swallow Barn* is kept in the background. . . . The result is what one could have foreseen. The plantation master was the victim of a benevolent romanticism that vaguely looks for a solution to colonization schemes that will return the negro to Africa; but like other southern gentlemen he is somewhat testy at the suggestion of outside interference. Slavery he regards as an exclusive southern problem, to be solved by those who understand its complex domestic implications. It would be better for everybody if Abolition busybodies would mind their own affairs and cease stirring up feelings where no good can come of it. To prove that Virginia gentlemen are aware of their responsibility, Meriwether offers a half humorous suggestion that negro emancipation might well follow the example of English villeinage, with a slow break-up of the system, the emancipated negro to remain in a protective feudal relation to his master. It was an amiable notion to play with, and it fitted the feudal psychology of the plantation.

In these early sketches Kennedy revealed an easy knack at writing that gave promise of excellent work later. He has lightness, grace, refinement, an eye sensitive to picturesque effects, delight in line and texture and color, an agreeable wit and playful sentiment, a relish for English idiom and the literary colloquial. In *Horseshoe Robinson* . . . he abandoned the essay-sketch and turned to the school of historical romance then in full swing. . . . There is quite obvious concern for authentic reality. The title-hero, a shrewd homespun scout, is carefully drawn from life; the background of bushwhackings and forays and onsets, and the numerous company of blackguards and honest folk, are painted in skillfully; and the whole conducts to a dramatic finale in the battle of King's Mountain. It is an excellent tale, quiteworth reading today, . . . [but realism] was not Kennedy's forte and after *Horseshoe Robinson* he abandoned the field of the Revolution. . . . (pp. 52-3)

In *Rob of the Bowl* Kennedy opened a promising vein that he never adequately explored—the vein of the cavalier romantic. Temperamentally he was ill fitted to deal with rollicking action or picaresque adventure; he preferred the leisurely, discursive romantic, subdued to gentle raillery or humorous tenderness. . . . Here is the raw stuff of a true bloody-bones thriller. . . . (p. 53)

But in the handling the story is far removed from a bloody-bones tale. The action is deliberately subdued to the humoresque; atmosphere is studiously created; adventure is held in strict subjection to the whimsical; and a mellow old-time flavor is imprisoned in the leisurely pages. Kennedy had an appreciative eye for picturesque characters, and in *Rob of the Bowl* he has gathered a choice group, limned—as he would choose to say—with a partial hand. . . . [The stock character's] abundant talk is well seasoned, and if the action sometimes drags, the company is good and the drinking is a sufficient end in itself. . . . [Kennedy's] vocabulary is saturated with the homely old speech, and his characters talk as if they had culled all the simples of English cottage gardens to garnish the staple of their wit. He has a keener delight than Simms in the picturesque archaic. He far surpasses Irving in easy mastery of the old-fashioned colloquial, as indeed he surpasses all our early novelists. He delights in the courtly wit of the Cavalier equally with the humors of Dogberry and Falstaff and Captain Bobadil, and he quite evidently is seeking to cross the sparkle of Congreve with the robustness of the Elizabethans. The result may sometimes appear a bit self-conscious; his phrases too often seem to be on dress parade; but he can plead his precedents in justification. In its fondness for the literary colloquial his prose style almost suggests Thackeray. . . . (p. 54)

Rob of the Bowl is certainly Kennedy's best work, as it is one of the most finished and delightful of our earlier romances. . . . [It] has scarcely received the recognition its lightness of touch deserves. . . . *Quodlibet* . . . is a surprising successor to *Rob*— a satire on Jacksonian democracy, done with a light touch and great good humor. . . . The book is keen, vivacious, sparkling. The supposed follies of Jacksonianism—its deification of the majority vote, its cant of the sovereign people, its hatred of all aristocrats, its demagoguery and bluster and sheer buncombe—are hit off with exuberant raillery. (pp. 54-5)

The satire sparkles amusingly, but it is drawn from the old Federalist vintage and it preserves the flavor of a time when gentlemen frankly resented the rule of the unwashed majority. For that very reason *Quodlibet* is an unusually interesting document. It is the most vivacious criticism of Jacksonianism in our political library, one of our few distinguished political satires, and it deserves a better fate than to gather dust on old shelves. . . .

[*Memoirs of the Life of William Wirt, Attorney General of the United States*] seems to have met with approval, for it ran to six editions. Our grandfathers liked stately narrative that portrayed their subjects in full dress; and Kennedy gave them an impeccably respectable work in which all the rugosities of character were ironed out neatly and a fine starchy effect achieved. It is hard to understand how a writer so keen to detect the whimsical should have drawn so lifeless a picture of the genial Attorney-General. Perhaps the memory of Wirt's reputed greatness rested too heavily upon him; or it may have been that a lawyer in old Virginia lived as colorless a life as the narrative suggests; at any rate the novelist who never had failed to breathe life into the characters of his fiction, somehow failed in depicting this excellent gentleman of the old school. . . . [In] his *Letters of Mr. Paul Ambrose on the Great Rebellion in the United States,* [Kennedy] showed that he could keep his temper and argue calmly. It was a difficult theme for which he was inadequately equipped. His constitutional argument is not impressive and it makes an ill showing. . . . He was a man of letters rather than a lawyer, and if he had eschewed politics and law and stuck to his pen our literature would have been greatly in his debt. Few Americans of his day were so generously gifted; none possessed a lighter touch. He has been somewhat carelessly forgotten even by our literary historians who can plead no excuse for so grave a blunder. (p. 56)

> Vernon Louis Parrington, ''Adventures in Romance,'' in his Main Currents in American Thought, an Interpretation of American Literature from the Beginnings to 1920: The Romantic Revolution in America, 1800-1860, Vol. 2 (copyright 1927 by Harcourt Brace Jovanovich, Inc.; copyright 1955 by Vernon L. Parrington, Jr., Louise P. Tucker, Elizabeth P. Thomas; reprinted by permission of the publisher), Harcourt, 1930 (and reprinted by Harcourt, 1958), pp. 41-60.*

JOHN EARLE UHLER   (essay date 1932)

It is [John Pendleton Kennedy's] miscellaneous works, some of which appeared in newspapers and magazines or as pamphlets and most of which were included in three posthumous volumes . . . that give the reader the most helpful material for an understanding of Kennedy and his novels. They impress us with the fact that he should be judged, not as a Southerner, not as an imitator of Irving and Cooper, but as an independent and alert student, a historian, an antiquarian, with a taste for a story, an eye for the picturesque, and a whim for the satirical.

To appraise Kennedy's work as that of a Southern writer is misleading. He was not Southern in birth or in political or economic sympathy. . . . [In] his essay *The Border States* and in his *Letters of Mr. Ambrose,* even acrimonious in his criticism of the Southern attitude towards secession, he looked upon the South (Virginia), not as a native, but as a visitor, an acute observer, tolerant of what he called the feudalism of the South and appreciative of what he considered the quaintness of a passing order. And as for his imitation of Irving and Cooper, only his youthful essays in *The Red Book* resemble Irving, and only *Horseshoe Robinson* resembles Cooper. His *Swallow Barn,* so often compared with *The Sketch Book* and *Bracebridge Hall,* differs radically from both in possessing two narrative threads that closely knit all the character sketches and episodes, including the stories of Mike Brown and the slave boy Abe, into an organic whole. Even if the similarity were closer, what of *Rob of the Bowl,* ''A Legend of Maryland,'' and *Quodlibet,* for which we find no exact parallel in either American or English literature? (pp. 471-73)

Beginning with *Swallow Barn,* we note that only in this work does [Kennedy] picture plantation life and customs of the South. . . . [He] takes, with the exception of some literary privileges, the point of view of the unbiased historian.

The miscellaneous works indicate that the distinctive Southern views he expresses in this first novel are mainly those of his characters rather than his own. (p. 473)

Kennedy's second novel, *Horseshoe Robinson,* has only a general connection with the posthumous work in that it further reveals the author's interest in the history of his country and his insistence on the authenticity of character and incident. It is strange that to the specific interest in the background and events of this story, on which his fame has largely rested, he never again recurs. (pp. 474-75)

In *Rob of the Bowl,* Kennedy taps a supply of literary material which he continues to exploit with industry and apparent pleasure. . . . (p. 475)

Concerning Kennedy's attitude toward the current political questions on which he based his satirical novel *Quodlibet,* the posthumous works afford much detailed information. On the controversy relating to the banks, and on Jackson's maladministration of public affairs—in which connection Kennedy makes, in *Quodlibet,* his most vigourous attacks on the Democratic party. . . . [The] satire in *Quodlibet* on such general subjects as demagoguery, inflated progress, and the treachery of office-holders is echoed, although less dramatically, in the essay on ''**Demagogues**,'' his address on ''**The Spirit of the Age**,'' and ''**The Confessions of an Office-Holder**.'' Of these posthumous works, the political writings—the speeches, the report on the currency, and ''**The Defence of the Whigs**,''— are of singular interest in that they display very little of the author's ability at satire as we find it in the narrative works and most of the essays. When he deals with ideas alone, he is apparently sobered by their seriousness. It is only when he places characters in the background of ideas that he rises to the type of satire that impels him to take the opposite side of a question and, with apparent ingenuousness, deliver his enemies to his friends.

A study of the posthumous works, together with the novels, gives us a new conception of Kennedy as a literary man. He is too cosmopolitan to warrant the provincial appellative of "Southern" or "Northern." He is too broad in his interests and abilities to deserve the criticism that he apes Irving and Cooper, who are no more his masters than Dickens and Emerson and Carlyle and Jane Austen and Disraeli and Poe and Daniel Webster. Too discerning and forceful in character for servile imitation, he rather possessed the sophistication, audacity, and power which we notice today in such writers as Sinclair Lewis and H. L. Mencken. . . . (pp. 477-78)

Kennedy is, in general, to be understood as a man of affairs and a student of his time, with a strong antiquarian interest—as a member of Congress and Secretary of the Navy and yet a Professor of History in the University of Maryland. Although active in the controversies of his day he takes time for the study of old documents and musty books and old songs and antiquated pleasures like falconry, which plays an important part in *Swallow Barn, Rob of the Bowl,* and **"A Legend of Maryland."** He possesses the social acumen of a politician, the scholarship and culture of a student of history, and the imagination of the literary man. (p. 479)

> *John Earle Uhler, "Kennedy's Novels and His Posthumous Works," in* American Literature, *Vol. III, No. 4, January, 1932, pp. 471-79.*

ALEXANDER COWIE (essay date 1948)

[*Swallow Barn*] is rather less a novel than a series of descriptive essays, character sketches, digressory episodes, and miscellaneous wisdom set forth in language which is at once leisurely in tone and brilliantly epigrammatic in style. (pp. 259-60)

Setting and characterization are superbly handled in *Swallow Barn,* and they have been a source of inspiration to countless later novelists. . . . Few American novels are richer in characterization that is searching without being profound. . . . [Kennedy] added much from his own observation. Whether a plot is forthcoming or not, the reader is content to know the people. (p. 260)

[*Horse-Shoe Robinson* is an historical romance.] The locale was new . . . and the plot utilized new episodes in the history of the nation; but the situations and for the most part the characters were already somewhat stereotyped when Kennedy began to write. . . . [In] reporting history accurately Kennedy did not seriously impair the "romantic" plot, which is a perfectly adequate one if the test of originality is not too rigorously applied. . . . Invention was not Kennedy's forte. This much is proved by the number of elements which he seems to have borrowed. . . . (pp. 262-63)

[Horse-shoe Robinson] is one of the best-drawn characters in the American historical romance, and he has kept *Horse-Shoe Robinson* from the utter neglect into which it otherwise might have fallen. . . . [Genuine] characters survive changing fashions. Despite its prolixity . . . *Horse-Shoe Robinson* is read even today. It has other virtues—an almost flawless . . . style and moments of good description as well as unity of time and

of tone . . . , but these would not have kept the book alive without [Horse-Shoe] Robinson. (p. 264)

In *Rob of the Bowl* Kennedy tells a good story, but he tells it to please himself as much as the reader. He writes in a ruminative, meditative, almost muted manner that is full of charm. To be sure, no gourmet of the historical romance could be disappointed at the spicy ingredients of the story. . . . Yet one suspects that the author was not mainly interested in the action as such. Certainly the plot was not highly original. Nor were the characters wholly unknown before *Rob of the Bowl* was published. Rather they are brilliant transitional figures borrowed, relimned, and passed over to later writers. . . . The gallery of characters in *Rob of the Bowl,* indeed, is so brilliant that complaint has been made of Kennedy's failure to create one central figure. The point is unimportant in view of the rich texture of the whole book. . . . *Rob of the Bowl* is one of the minor classics in a semi-popular genre. (pp. 265-67)

Though a man of convictions, Kennedy was not a writer of great power. . . . Yet in his domain he was one of the most finished writers in the history of American fiction. (p. 269)

> *Alexander Cowie, "Contemporaries and Immediate Followers of Cooper, II," in his* The Rise of the American Novel *(reprinted by permission of D. C. Heath & Co.)* American Book Company, 1948 (and reprinted by American Book Company, 1951), pp. 228-75.*

ERNEST E. LEISY (essay date 1950)

[The] importance of [*Rob of the Bowl*] does not lie in originality of plot or characters. The introduction of the smugglers, and the author's manner of alternating history with fiction and then blending the two, mark Kennedy as a devoted follower of Scott, although his style is more brisk. There are overtones, also, of Elizabethan drama. Garret Weasel and his wife, keepers of the Crow and Archer, are well realized, and the scenes at the fisherman's hut are excellent. Albert appears too saintly, but the proprietary, Lord Calvert, is well portrayed. He is tolerant toward Protestants, even though their active antagonism is shown to underlie much of the trouble in the colony. The things, then, that make *Rob of the Bowl* a satisfying work for the reader of historical romance are a beautiful heroine, a hero with clouded ancestry, smugglers plying their trade, picturesque tavern scenes, an abduction and a rescue, excitement, and a happy ending. All this is presented in a style that knows no lassitude, and the story is readily enjoyable today. (p. 35)

> *Ernest E. Leisy, "Colonial America," in his* The American Historical Novel *(copyright 1950 by the University of Oklahoma Press; copyright renewed © 1977 by Mrs. Ernest Erwin Leisy), University of Oklahoma Press, 1950, pp. 21-67.*

CHARLES H. BOHNER (essay date 1961)

Although an unexpected successor to the historical romance *Rob of the Bowl, Quodlibet* was a natural book for Kennedy to write. Politics to Kennedy, as to most men of his generation, was what really mattered. . . . In taking up his pen in support of his political principles, Kennedy at the age of forty-five fused his vocations of politician and author to produce what V. L. Parrington called "the most vivacious criticism of Jacksonianism in our political library [and] one of our few distinguished political satires" [see excerpt above].

Kennedy could write of the American political scene with authority. He had been deeply involved in politics. . . . (pp. 84-5)

Although politically inspired, *Quodlibet* is not narrowly political in its orientation but is in the broadest sense a penetrating criticism of Jacksonian America. Kennedy intended the Borough of Quodlibet as a microcosm, "an abstract or miniature portrait of this nation." More concerned with doctrinaires than with doctrines, his chief target was a new breed of men, impudent, grossly ignorant and wanting in political morality. His was the contempt of an intelligent, respectable conservative for "mushroom banks" and their "swarms of scrub aristocrats in the shape of presidents, cashiers, directors, and clerks." He saw in their subterfuge a scheme to entrench a political faction by arraying class against class. (pp. 88)

Quodlibet is full of scenes minutely observed and sharply rendered, vivid with the devotion to detail of a limner's portrait. Yet the book, for all its wit, exudes the musty flavor of ancient jests. The cutting edge of some of its humor has been blunted by buried allusions and battles fought and forgotten, but many of its best thrusts are universal in their application. Kennedy was writing in the classic tradition of English satire, and his debt, particularly to Swift and Sterne, is on every page.

Yet *Quodlibet* is also in the native grain. . . . Kennedy's ear was tuned to the racy, idiomatic diction, the incongruous but peculiarly apt adjectives, and the homely metaphors drawn from common speech. His best scenes amusingly rendered this American vernacular. (p. 89)

Charles H. Bohner, "J. P. Kennedy's 'Quodlibet': Whig Counterattack," in American Quarterly *(copyright, Spring, 1961 Trustees of the University of Pennsylvania), Vol. XIII, No. 1, Spring, 1961, pp. 84-92.*

CHARLES H. BOHNER   (essay date 1961)

If *Swallow Barn* deserves attention as an authentic document in the social history of the South, it also holds a significant place in literary history as the prototype of a persistent and influential theme in American literature—the southern plantation tradition. *Swallow Barn* stands at the head of a long stream of novels of the Old South. . . . (p. 73)

[It] is superb characterization rather than plot which gives *Swallow Barn* its continuing interest and charm. (p. 80)

Kennedy skillfully evoked the atmosphere of the plantation. He captured "the mellow, bland, and sunny luxuriance of her [Virginia's] old time society—its good fellowship, its hearty and constitutional *companionableness,* the thriftless gayety of the people, their dogged but amiable invincibility of opinion, and that overflowing hospitality which knew no ebb." What was so attractive in this civilization was its rural simplicity, a blend of rustic open-heartedness and naive parochialism which permeates this comic pastoral. . . . The satiric tone is skillfully maintained, the author laughing at personal idiosyncracies without sarcasm and criticizing institutions without malice. The style is well adapted to the material—leisurely in pace, unobtrusively didactic, and on occasion brilliantly epigrammatic. (p. 83)

Swallow Barn abounds with memorable vignettes of plantation life. . . . Kennedy lingered over these descriptions of country amusements with the loving attention of a connoisseur. They could be savored as an exotic, but not regarded with unmixed praise. On the contrary, *Swallow Barn,* far from a nostalgic

lament for a vanishing golden age, is permeated by a genial but nonetheless penetrating irony. (p. 85)

Swallow Barn is the first important novel in the plantation tradition, it stands apart from the novels that come after it by virtue of its authenticity. . . . Kennedy had sought authenticity, and that is what he achieved; he is one of the pioneers in our literature in the use of local color. (p. 88)

Charles H. Bohner, "Virginia Revisited," in his John Pendleton Kennedy: Gentleman from Baltimore *(©1961 by The Johns Hopkins Press), The Johns Hopkins University Press, 1961, pp. 72-88.*

J. V. RIDGELY   (essay date 1966)

Kennedy's over-all design [in *Swallow Barn* was to give] an extended satirical portrait of the way of life of . . . an archetypal Virginia planter proud of his family and state, arrogant of manner, and short of cash. (p. 37)

[The] sketches of the inhabitants of Swallow Barn . . . suggest minor plot lines . . . , and the book for a time assumes the pace of a conventional novel. . . . [The] construction of the main love plot and the dialogue [Kennedy uses] is clearly an echo of the eighteenth-century comedy of manners. . . . (p. 39)

From the date of its original publication to the present, critics of *Swallow Barn* have commended its "fidelity" or the "realism" of its representation of the Old Virginia scene. Its earliest readers . . . were struck by the verisimilitude of the book; and they reasonably assumed that the characters and events must have been drawn directly from personal observation. (p. 46)

[To] speak unqualifiedly of the value of *Swallow Barn* as authentic social record is to mislead the present-day reader. . . . *Swallow Barn* stuck to the plausible and did not rely on mysterious doings, incredible plot twists, or a diabolical villain for reader interest. . . . [*Swallow Barn*'s] method is *not* closely reportorial; it is *not* an objective rendering of an observed scene. [Its] techniques are derived from a wide range of stock devices, and its flavor everywhere is "literary." This is not to say that Kennedy did not draw details from his own memories of Virginia; it is to emphasize that he could not decide whether the "true" Virginia was to be sought in the ideal or in the actual. The book is *both* myth and countermyth, and what is most significantly "real" is its revelation of Kennedy's own dilemma in trying to apprehend reality. (pp. 46-7)

[*Swallow Barn* indeed seems] to be what Kennedy called [it in his 1851 preface—a volume that is "utterly unartistic in plot and structure." Certainly to the modern taste it is too bulky, too digressive, too anchored to literary prototypes. It is, furthermore, neither a pure work of the fancy nor an entirely trustworthy factual account of its announced subject of life on a Virginia plantation. Nevertheless, in spite of all its easily tabulated defects, it remains in other important ways one of the most engrossing books produced by an American in the 1830's. (pp. 52-3)

[The] modern reader may find the most basic meanings of *Swallow Barn* in the very "flaw" from which Kennedy wished to divert attention: the fact that neither he nor his fictional mouthpiece, Mark Littleton, could maintain a consistent stance. His proposal to sketch life in western Virginia as an amused spectator from the outside world could not be entirely excised. . . .

What finally emerges from *Swallow Barn* . . . is a double attitude about society which tells much about the dilemma of the American writer who—at the critic's urging—did choose the native scene for his subject matter. (p. 53)

[Part] of *Swallow Barn* is legend-making and uncritical. It is backward-looking and "historical"; it counts upon our memory of literary models to supply an atmosphere of age, status, and solidarity. It praises individual liberty, rejoices in "characters," assesses slavery as chiefly a local problem, and opposes central government whenever its power is bent upon wiping out all regional peculiarities. From the other angle of vision, the book accepts the reality of man's progress and argues the necessity of further change; it satirizes the provinciality and folly of this closed society, lets its members damn themselves through their tirades against outside interference and internal improvements, and scorns cherished States' rights. Kennedy's difficulty in synthesizing his views was not . . . merely literary. . . . The dichotomy of *Swallow Barn* . . . contributes instead to an understanding of the tension in the mind of a man who could be drawn both to the Southern past and the national future. (pp. 53-4)

Few other writers besides Kennedy in the America of this period could so neatly have hit off [as in *Swallow Barn*] so many foibles: intellectual pretension, meaningless legal wrangles, romantic yearnings, rhetorical flourish—in short, the self-revelations of a society which preferred façade to backbone, lofty words and manners to workaday deeds, literary posturing to solid character. (p. 63)

Swallow Barn remains a true document in [the sense that] it is a valid reflection of the divided mind of John Pendleton Kennedy, a man who looked forward but understood the pragmatic value of legend—one who, like many of his countrymen, yearned for roots in the past and for the America that was to be, and was not at all sure how the two could be reconciled. (p. 64)

[*Horse-Shoe Robinson*] strikes the modern reader as slow-moving and needlessly prolix.

Purely in terms of plot, the chief structural flaw of the book is that its nominal hero, Major Arthur Butler, languishes in captivity during the action of thirty-eight out of the fifty-eight chapters. . . . Furthermore, Kennedy's two carefully preserved "secrets" evoke no sustained interest and provide no startling surprises. The first—that Butler and Mildred have been man and wife for some time before the action of the book opens—is a mild fillip at best. The second involves the mysterious character called Tyrrel. . . . Kennedy rather inexplicably lets his villain meet his death by hanging. . . . The "mystery" [turns] out to be mystification for its own sake.

But it must at once be reiterated that, while the plot of *Horse-Shoe Robinson* as mere plot may only bore the modern reader, the thematic conflicts embedded in its story do much to redeem Kennedy's ineptness. (pp. 72-3)

As in *Swallow Barn*, Kennedy develops [the themes in *Horse-Shoe Robinson*] slowly, relying in the opening section more on extended character analyses than on action to draw the reader into the story. (p. 75)

[In] spite of its wit and occasional sharp strokes, *Quodlibet* is today a dead book. . . . [The] fact remains that the satire is chiefly directed at a specific contemporary situation, and only the special student of this period can grasp all the secondary meanings. . . . [His] subject is too parochial to allow any . . . universal application. (p. 118)

Nothing but laborious footnoting could really restore full meaning to the text, and few readers would find the result worth such a venture. (p. 119)

Despite all the care which Kennedy lavished upon it, *The Life of William Wirt* is for the modern reader a dreary production. Since it was intended to be commemorative, the reader would expect to find Wirt's virtues magnified and his faults minimized—yet he would nonetheless anticipate some life in a *Life*. Unfortunately it has little; it is padded out with Wirt's documents . . . ; it is slanted according to Kennedy's own political views; it is "official" in all the bad senses of that word. (p. 123)

J. V. Ridgely, in his John Pendleton Kennedy *(copyright © 1966 by Twayne Publishers, Inc.; reprinted with the permission of Twayne Publishers, a Division of G. K. Hall & Co., Boston), Twayne, 1966, 156 p.*

ADDITIONAL BIBLIOGRAPHY

Osborne, William S. Introduction to *Rob of the Bowl: A Legend of St. Inigoe's* by John Pendleton Kennedy, pp. 5-27. New Haven, Conn.: College & University Press, 1965.
    Biographical essay with brief critical comment.

Heinrich von Kleist

1777-1811

German dramatist, novella and short story writer, essayist, and journalist.

Though Kleist is now considered one of the greatest of German dramatists, he was unappreciated in his own time. Despite his ardent patriotism, Kleist's political writings were not printed until half a century after his death. His fellow writers held Kleist in low esteem, deepening the introspective depression which informed his works. The stylized, fiery content of Kleist's dramatic verse reveals the struggles plaguing him throughout his life, which eventually ended in suicide.

Born into an old Prussian military family, Kleist served in the Prussian army for several years. He grew disillusioned by its sterile atmosphere, however, and chose to enroll in the University of Frankfurt. Kleist believed that self-improvement and the development of one's intellect were steps to a better life; however, his optimism waned as he became preoccupied with the uncertainty of human destiny. Education suddenly proved futile. In 1800, Kleist traveled throughout Europe. When he returned, his view of the world had altered. After his voyage, Kleist tried to establish a new world view by reading Immanuel Kant's *Critique of Pure Reason*. But Kant's reliance on pure forms of intuition, space, and time indicated to Kleist that even knowledge can be illusory. Kleist retreated to Switzerland to reevaluate his philosophy and his goals.

His first play, *Die Familie Schroffenstein (The Feud of the Schroffensteins)*, reflects both his revolt against what were then the prevalent aesthetic influences and his own inner turmoil. A subsequent drama, *Robert Guiskard,* became what Kleist considered his creative redemption. As with his later works, he became obsessed with the play's creation. The character of Robert Guiskard, a dying army commander, is a character of Promethean ambition whose ultimate despair at his own ineffectiveness matched Kleist's own. Like his other plays, *Robert Guiskard* concerns a world on the brink of destruction. Kleist's struggle with the work proved overpowering; alternating between his creative drive and growing self-doubt, he destroyed the manuscript. Later, he attempted to reconstruct the play; however, only a fragment remains.

Kleist repeatedly attempted to reconcile his artistic potential with his philosophical turmoil. He traveled widely, and met Johann Wolfgang von Goethe and Friedrich Schiller. Goethe recognized Kleist's ability immediately, but found his work to be disturbing, noting a certain "sick element," and offering little encouragement or support. Goethe, perhaps, resented Kleist's talent and determination to surpass the works of other playwrights. He supervised the production of Kleist's only comedy, *Der zerbrochene Krug (The Broken Jug)*, and altered its structure; thus he effected the play's critical failure.

Kleist retreated to Königsberg, where he held a civil service position and, for the first time, experimented with prose. With renewed confidence, he resigned his post, hoping to support himself through his writing. His short stories of this period reflect his keen perception of human emotion and ironically depict the merits of leading a moderate life, a way of life Kleist himself was unable to adopt.

Courtesy of the German Information Center

The political climate in Germany was intensely anti-Napoleonic, and Kleist, like his fellow countrymen, dreamed of a successful uprising against the French leader. Ironically, his country's political failure was synonymous with his own. En route to Dresden, Kleist was arrested by the French as a spy, and imprisoned. Upon his release, he and critic Adam Müller founded a short-lived literary journal, *Phöbus*. At this time, Kleist wrote fiercely patriotic poetry and a political play, *Die Hermannsschlacht*, indicating his fervent support for Germany's liberation. He also wrote *Prinz Friedrich von Homburg (The Prince of Homburg)*. Considered by many critics to be his finest work, this play depicts the Prussian nation as a union of justice and mercy. Kleist also enjoyed limited success with his short stories, and edited the daily paper *Berlin Abendblätter*. However, pressures of censorship forced him to cease publication. Once again he had to admit defeat.

In 1811, Kleist's despondency manifested itself again in a recurring death wish. He befriended Henriette Vogel, a woman afflicted with cancer. Bound together only by a common desire to die, they entered into a suicide pact. Once Kleist had found a companion for his "final adventure," as he called it, his depression disappeared. The purpose he had searched for all his life suddenly emerged. **On November 11, 1811, Kleist shot Vogel, and then himself.**

Kleist's critical acclaim came long after his death. Later poets and dramatists were influenced by his perception and honesty, though in his time, many critics dismissed him as a nationalist poet. However, scholars of the twentieth century value Kleist's psychological insight and probing of human vulnerability, and his posthumous reputation places him with Goethe and Schiller as one of the most important German dramatists of the nineteenth century.

PRINCIPAL WORKS

Die Familie Schroffenstein (drama) 1803
   [*The Feud of the Schroffensteins,* 1916]
Amphitryon [adapted from a play by Molière] 1807
   [*Amphitryon,* 1962]
Penthesilea (drama) 1808
   [*Penthesilea,* in *The Classic Theatre,* Vol. II, ed. by Eric
   Bentley, 1958]
Robert Guiskard (drama) [fragment] 1808
Der zerbrochene Krug (drama) 1808
   [*The Broken Jug,* in *German Plays of the Nineteenth
   Century,* ed. by T. M. Campbell, 1930]
Das Kätchen von Heilbronn oder Die Feuerprobe (drama)
   1810
   [*Kate of Heilbronn,* 1841]
Erzählungen. 2 vols. (short stories) 1810-11
   [*The Marquise of O and Other Stories,* 1960]
Die Hermannsschlacht (drama) 1821
Prinz Friedrich von Homburg (drama) 1821
   [*The Prince of Homburg,* 1875]

*This is the date of first publication rather than first performance.

JOHANN WOLFGANG von GOETHE (essay date 1808)

I am most grateful to you for the copy of **'Phoebus'.** I have enjoyed reading the essays in prose very much. I knew some of them already. I have not yet been able to come to terms with your **'Penthesilea'.** She belongs to such an unusual race and moves in so strange a region that I must take time to get used to both. And allow me to say—for unless one is honest, it would be better to say nothing at all—that it always disturbs and saddens me to see really talented and gifted young men waiting for a theatre that is still to be. A Jew waiting for the Messiah, a Christian for the New Jerusalem, a Portuguese for Don Sebastian, is not to my mind a more distressing sight. Before any trestle-stage I would say to the true theatrical genius; *'Hic Rhodus, hic salta!'* On any fair-ground, even on planks put across barrels, I could—*mutatis mutandis*—bring the highest enjoyment to the masses, cultured and uncultured, with Calderon's plays. Forgive my plain speaking, it shows my sincere affection. I realise one might say this kind of thing with friendlier phrases and more attractively. I am content now to have got something off my chest.

> *Johann Wolfgang von Goethe, in his letter to Heinrich von Kleist on February 1, 1808, in his* Letters from Goethe, *translated by Dr. M. von Herzfeld and C. Melvil Sym, Edinburgh at the University Press, 1957, p. 347.*

THE FOREIGN QUARTERLY REVIEW (essay date 1828)

[Compositions such as the **"Prince of Homburg"**] never will pass muster along with those of Müllner, Howald, [and Raupach]. . . . That Kleist's conceptions were clear and accurate, we are fully disposed to admit; but his natural impatience and irritability prevented him from acquiring that power of eloquence, without which a dramatic composition will be found to differ [from the best models]. . . . (pp. 695-96)

In the **"Katharine von Heilbronn,"** the leading source of interest consists in the persevering—the intense and pure affections of the heroine, towards the chivalrous hero of the piece, in despite of the most cruel sufferings, insults, misfortunes, and persecution, amid all which her inexhaustible love exists changeless and triumphant. The idea is beautiful, exalted and affecting; but here, also, though Kleist evinced all the best feelings of a poet, the "accomplishment of art" was wanting, and the work, though it keeps its place on the stage, is extremely unequal and defective. (p. 696)

> *"Works of Henry Kleist," in* The Foreign Quarterly Review, *Vol. II, No. IV, May, 1828, pp. 671-96.*

GEORG BRANDES (essay date 1873)

[When] we read the one fragment that remains to us of the never-completed drama, *Guiscard,* we are filled with astonishment. It was as little within the power of this work as of any other to remove the crown of honour from the brow of the genius whose spirit dominates two centuries; but the fact remains that the fragment of it which we possess stands on a level with much of the best produced by Goethe.

Kleist has drawn on his imagination for the picture of a great man, a great leader; and he at once successfully impresses us with his hero's greatness by showing how much depends upon him, upon his life, how thousands upon thousands look up to him as their ruler and only saviour. (p. 262)

And there is profound meaning as well as grandeur in this conception of Kleist's. This Guiscard, who stands there erect and unflinching while mortal disease is gnawing at his vitals, who is he but Kleist himself, his whole unhappy life long? He himself is the great genius whose plans are foiled by the pestilence without and within him. (p. 263)

What distinguishes Kleist's characters from those of the other Romanticists is that there is nothing blurred and vague about them; the essential quality which his and theirs have in common is morbidity. In every passion Kleist seizes upon that feature which betrays kinship with the fixed idea or with helpless insanity; he probes every mind, however sound, till he finds the diseased point where it loses control over itself—somnambulistic tendency, overpowering animal appetites, absent-mindedness, cowardice in the face of death. Take such a passion as love; it is certainly not of a rational nature, but it has a side from which it may be seen to be connected with reason and intellect. Kleist almost invariably, and with admirable skill, depicts it as of the nature of disease, as mania. (pp. 263-64)

Side by side with much that is ridiculous and repulsive, *Käthchen von Heilbronn* contains much that is really grand. It is plain enough that [an overpowering and unrequited] passion, which comes on as suddenly as a fit of apoplexy—which, moreover, as a fixed idea, destroys every other idea, and, itself a miracle, performs miracles with the aid of an angel—oversteps the bounds of the natural and the healthy. Yet there is something fine in it. It gave intense satisfaction to Kleist, who had such a rooted aversion for mere phrases, to represent a loving woman, in whom everything was truth and reality which in other women is mere words. (p. 265)

[*Der Prinz von Homburg* is] probably the finest drama produced by the Romantic School. In it all the important characters stand out as if hewn in stone. The dialogue is vigorous and clear; every word tells. (p. 266)

[It] is curious to see how the mystic element, the strange trinity of sensuality, religion, and cruelty, insinuates itself into all Kleist's dramas. . . . [In *Penthesilea,* the heroine] has conceived quite as fatal a passion for Achilles as Käthchen's for Count Strahl. But in Penthesilea love shows itself in a different way; it takes the form of cruelty. . . .

It is plain that it is his own temperament with which Kleist has endowed the Amazon queen. She cares for nothing, will take nothing, but Achilles, just as he refused to aim at anything, to be content with anything, but the highest place of honour. Her wild haste to conquer her beloved corresponds with his desire to attain his aim at one blow, with his drama, *Robert Guiscard*. Like Kleist, she can only live when she is striving after what her soul desires. (p. 268)

Nowhere in all Kleist's writings has mysticism taken such strange possession of a perfectly pagan, not to say wanton, theme as in his *Amphitryon*. . . . (pp. 273-74)

The interest of the play centres in the character of Alcmene, the interest of her character in the vigour with which she refuses to allow her peace of mind to be disturbed and her feelings confused, and the interest of her tragic story in the anguish she suffers when, in spite of herself, her inmost feelings are agitated and perplexed by the appearance of her husband in different forms.

Goethe, whose genius enabled him, though he did not understand Kleist's character, to understand much of the working of his mind, made the profound remark that what he chiefly aimed at was "confusion of feeling." . . . Confusion of feeling was to [Kleist] the truest tragedy.

His own strong, undivided feeling was unsettled and perplexed again and again. (pp. 277-78)

We have the idea very plainly in . . . *Die Marquise von O.* The Marquise knows as little as Alcmene who it is that has embraced her in the dark; her feelings, too, are perplexed and confused; her nearest and dearest suspect her; and when the Russian officer, whom she looks upon as her saviour, but who proves to be the delinquent, returns to her, loving and repentant, her innocent soul is rent by alternate paroxysms of hatred and love. In much the same manner, the sense of justice, originally so strong in the soul of *Michael Kohlhaas,* is confused by the wrongs he suffers. (p. 278)

It is this same confusion of feeling which gives their morbidness to all his productions. Even *Michael Kohlhaas,* that masterpiece of the art of story-telling, at the beginning of which each character is drawn with the precision of genius, ends in a kind of dream-like confusion. (p. 279)

No one could prize decision, unity of character, more than [Kleist] did, and never was there a more uncertain, divided, morbid man. He was always despairing, always wavering between the highest endeavour and the inclination to commit suicide. This explains how it is that we see him, the greatest of the Romanticists, liable to almost all the errors which dis-

tinguish his contemporaries. His own really fine, noble nature was spoiled very much as are most of the characters in his works, by sinister, disastrous peculiarities, which slacken the will and destroy the elasticity of the mind. Yet Heinrich von Kleist has assured himself a place in literature, like all others who have won places there, by the vigour and the passion with which he lived and wrote. (pp. 282-83)

> *Georg Brandes, "Mysticism in the Romantic Drama,"
> in his* Main Currents in Nineteenth Century Literature: The Romantic School in Germany, Vol. II,
> *translated by Diana White and Mary Morison (originally published as* Hovedstromninger i det 19de aarhundredes litteratur, *1873), William Heinemann, 1902
> (and reprinted by Boni & Liveright, Inc., 1924, pp.
> 253-92).**

BARKER FAIRLEY (essay date 1916)

So intensely does Kleist concentrate his vision that the foreground of his spectacle of energies becomes dominant; the individual blocks the prospect, obscuring the middle distance with its collective human chorus, and almost crowding out the background of the material world. He violently deranges the balance in favor of the immediate and personal; it is almost entirely from the actual characters—often from a single character—that the vigor derives. He is careless of the larger canvas; he is at no pains to weave the special action into union with the vaster life without; humanity at large is a neglected force. In his hands the material world is mainly visual, rarely dynamic, rarely emerging into the interference of circumstance; it is a mere playground, with no power of stealthy influence or prerogative of intervention. (pp. 330-31)

Penthesilea is the most complete title in all drama, since nowhere else does the title-rôle so tyrannize the play. It is only after an immersion in the play's atmosphere that what is here said of it can be tested. And clearly any measure of dramatic excess is relative; elements essential in all life can be minimized, never eliminated. The propelling forces can never be wholly gathered from one element alone; an external analysis will always point to a mixed origin. Thus it is from her dead mother that the initial fillip is given to Penthesilea's conduct, and the changing fortune of war is essential in the development of the crisis. But in the real world of the play the personal energy of Penthesilea alone is felt. (p. 331)

It is interesting to observe some of the characteristics of this amazing play and to consider how far they contribute to the peculiar dominant effect. It will at once be noticed that the sententious is almost entirely lacking. Reflection is as remote from Penthesilea, her friends, and her opponents, as if the lives of them all had begun with the play's opening and the very basis of reflection were absent. . . . The events lie in a remote past, a different world almost. Their life is not the life of the play. . . . In *Penthesilea* the very clearness of the pictorial vision robs the things seen of their true energy. . . . There is no atmosphere in it, no impressionism, only color and outline and brightness. It has the flat, inert falseness of a color photograph. It astonishes the eye, but leaves the spirit hungry. (pp. 332-33)

The play cannot command our affection; it must always evoke a large measure of disapproval; but the sheer energy of its central figure will remain a thing not easy to put aside. . . .

The same tendency influences every play of this disconcerting author. His earliest play, *Die Familie Schroffenstein,* is the only one with a deliberate attempt to employ the energy of blind forces in vitalizing the action, and this feature of the work seems, from an inspection of the variants, to have been an afterthought. . . . The variety of the characters, the strongly differentiated scenes—there is a witch's kitchen with cauldron and incantations as well as some woodland love-making—the presence of a fair amount of general reflection, all these do indeed create a feeling of balance, which makes the play, immature as it is, the most normal in general impression of all Kleist's dramas and gives promise of a development far more on traditional lines than proved to be the case. But even here the mood which makes puppets of mankind is felt to be on the wane and the unfathomable personality asserts itself. (p. 334)

[Kleist's ability to conceive and organize dramatically is] exactly in line with his personal conviction about life. Just as he remained more completely than most adults the center of a disorderly universe, so his natural tendency in play-writing was to throw full energy into a single character and to surround it with passive material, human and inanimate, which it illumines, quickens, or annihilates at will. And just as this sole constant, the personality, was to Kleist a riddle, incalculable and fraught with unsuspected potentialities, so in his plays these central figures, violent as they are, are not usually fully revealed as consistent entities but only flashed into the eye from the particular angle of immediate observation. (pp. 337-38)

It can be seen . . . that throughout Kleist's plays, his extraordinary bias toward the personal, as the controlling energy, determines or, at least, in large measure affects the impression they convey to the student. . . . [The *Prinz von Homburg* and *Der zerbrochene Krug*] retain in restrained form the virtues of Kleist's genius and powerfully correct his great excess. Both contain a rich gallery of portraits; both touch the healthier national traditions. . . . [While] the relation of these two plays to the main characteristics of Kleist's other works can easily be traced, it is unobtrusive, and the whole manner of them is on altogether broader lines. (pp. 338-39)

[In] serious drama the *Prinz von Homburg,* with its superlative deftness, holds a unique and distinguished place.

For theorists in literature Kleist has done still more. The critic who is not content with masterpieces alone, where poets so ungenerously cover their traces, will find in a fuller study of Kleist a most welcome insistence on the real *point de départ* in literary judgments. In order to point the physician's finger at Kleist's poetic constitution, its basis of energy, not its basis of dexterity, must be regarded. He insists, all unconsciously, on the underlying arrangement of vitalities which sustains the whole of literature. The application of accepted Classical and Romantic standards to his work shows how external, not to say superficial, are such criteria. Drama is at bottom a system of energies, and it is to Kleist's enormous credit that he defies examination on any shallower basis. (pp. 339-40)

> *Barker Fairley, "Heinrich von Kleist," in* Modern Philology, *Vol. XIV, No. 6, October, 1916, pp. 321-40.*

BENEDETTO CROCE   (essay date 1922)

In practical life, having sought and failed to find his proper path, [Kleist's poetic] blindness ended by slaying him.

What should we call the blindness of a poet? The incapacity of seeing particular passions in the light of human passion, aspirations in the fundamental and total aspiration, partial and discordant ideals in the ideal which shall compose them in harmony: what at one time was called incapacity of "idealizing." For poetic idealization is not a frivolous embellishment, but a profound penetration, in virtue of which we pass from troublous emotion to the serenity of contemplation. He who fails to accomplish this passage, but remains immersed in passionate agitation, never succeeds in bestowing pure poetic joy either upon others or upon himself, whatever may be his efforts. (p. 52)

[Kleist's literary works] are intrinsically documents rather than works of genius.

Completely dominated by the emotions of the moment, Kleist was led to express them sensually in his writing, because an emotion, however noble may have been its origin and tendency (and Kleist certainly had noble ardours and impulses), if it be regarded only on its external side, if it be not entirely dominated and its place assigned on the vast background of reality, appears as nothing but an instinctive movement, animal or mechanical, and with the one-sided revelation of its sensible aspects alone, these aspects are exaggerated and deformed. Hence the horror which his Penthesilea has always aroused. Full to overflowing with the one longing to conquer and bind to herself Achilles whom she loves, seeing that she fails to conquer him, she slays him in a delirium of fury, inflicting blows and bites upon the corpse of the hated loved one. This was not due to any pleasure taken by Kleist in the libidinous, sanguinary, and horrible, as might have been the case with other writers; on the contrary, the original motive lies in the vain longing after a most lofty ideal and in despair at having failed to attain it. But the motive remains symbolical and almost allegorical, beyond the representation which clothes it with a garment of gross sensuality, taking the form of hysterical fury. . . . Kleist's stories, so swift, precise, and compact in detail, appear to sink and be drowned in the course of the narrative, giving an impression of the strange, the curious, or the terrifying, but not of the moving or tragical. (pp. 53-5)

When Kleist sets to work translating and adapting that light and graceful play of Molière, *Amphitryon,* upon what aspect of the story does he dwell? Upon the irremediably shocked modesty and the desolate and invincible sadness of Alcmena, when she learns that she has been possessed by another than her husband, although that other is neither more nor less than Jove and from their union is to spring a divine son. . . . [This] idea is in bad taste, and the figure of Alcmena thus renewed by means of the unconsolable sadness that envelops it is foolish and out of place in this smiling fable. It is also impure, owing to the anguish experienced at the loss of purity, whereas it would have been pure in art if it had remained in the sphere of jest. (p. 56)

Kleist, since he remained permanently materialistic, was induced, in order to confer life upon his work, intentionally to exaggerate it, either in the sphere of morality or of politics. Hence the intellectualistic element of which we are sensible in his plays that often closely resemble an *opus oratorium*, attaining sometimes to the level of the edifying tale, such as the *Prinz von Homburg,* where material details are met with less often, but are not, on the other hand, altogether absent—the dozing and waking of the prince, his wandering while the orders for the battle are being given, his physical terror at the idea of death. Here Kleist is more successful in suggesting a sort of calm, the result rather of a moral than of an artistic conception. So intellectualistic is Kleist's method that he is often unable to avoid banality, superficiality and puerility of treatment. The

Prinz von Homburg, for instance, inclines to melodrama, with its scenes and dialogue, suitable to a play of the "happy ending" sort. (pp. 56-7)

Kleist shows himself to possess little poetic talent, notwithstanding, and indeed just because, he is endowed with limitless ambition towards the great and important in art. This ambition, this search, is proper to those who are naturally feeble in gifts, without that pure impulse which achieves what is great without proposing it as an object, without knowing that it does so, as a simple expansion and manifestation of itself. His gifts were secondary, gifts proper to the orator, such as clarity in dramatic exposition, lively description, energy of tone. There is, perhaps, not a single truly poetical passage in all his work. (p. 58)

Kleist still pleases many, because many delight (and in Germany more than elsewhere) in the colossal, the noisy, the roll of the drum, the sound of the trumpet, that hubbub in which pure poetry is suffocated like Cordelia, whose voice was low and whose words were few. (p. 59)

> Benedetto Croce, "Kleist" (1922), in his European Literature in the Nineteenth Century, *translated by Douglas Ainslie (Canadian rights by permission of the Estate of Benedetto Croce), Alfred A. Knopf, 1924, pp. 52-9.*

STEFAN ZWEIG   (essay date 1925)

Robert Guiscard was to be something more than the mere literary mirror of [Kleist's] inner self. The titanic figure of the great Norman adventurer was to represent the tragedy of Kleist's existence, the boundless cravings of the spirit of one whose body was weakened by unsuspected infirmities. The completion of his work would symbolize the taking of Byzantium, the attainment of world-empire, the realization of the dream of universal power, which the resolute conquistador was to win despite the flaws in his body and the reluctance of his people. Kleist longed to tear out the flames that consumed him; he wanted to escape from the daimon by hunting the hunter out of himself into an emblem, an image. For him, completion of his *Guiscard* would signify cure; victorious achievement would bring deliverance; ambition was the outcome of the impulse to self-preservation. That was why his nerves were twitching with eagerness, his every muscle tensed for the fray. It was a life-and-death struggle. (pp. 400-01)

[Kleist's] art became an obsession. That accounts for the strangely coercive character of his plays, which remind the reader of the explosion of a shell. With the exception of *The Broken Pitcher* (which, written for a wager, is light in touch, though strong), they are outbreaks of feeling, expressions of the escape from the inferno of his soul. They have an intensely irritable tone, like the cry of a man able to draw breath freely after he has been on the verge of suffocation; they twang like an arrow from the bowstring as they are discharged from overstrained nerves; they are ejaculated (the reader must pardon the image, for it so aptly embodies the truth) like semen in the sexual orgasm. Only to a minor degree fertilized by the intelligence, no more than faintly tinctured by reason, naked and unashamed, they are spurted into the infinite by an unquenchable passion. Each of them condenses feeling to a superlative degree; each of them represents an explosion of the overwrought mind and of one which has blindly followed the promptings of instinct.

In *Guiscard* he spewed forth his Promethean ambition; in *Penthesilea* he gave violent expression to his sexual ardours; in *Hermannsschlacht* his animal ferocity found vent. All of them show the fever of the author's blood rather than the usual temperature of the environment. Even in the works that are less intimately representative of Kleist's ego, in his gentler writings such as *Käthchen von Heilbronn* and the short stories, we feel the vibration of his nerves and are aware of the swiftness of transition from epic intoxication to sobriety.

Wherever we follow Kleist, we find ourselves in the sphere of magic, in a region where the affective life is intense though overshadowed by gloom—to be irradiated from time to time by lightning-flashes that pierce the sultry atmosphere. It is this coercive element, together with the sulphurous and fiery discharges, which make his dramas so strange and so splendid. Goethe's plays embody vital transformations, but no more than episodically; they are disburdenings, self-justifications, flight and release. They never have the explosive character of Kleist's, in which lava and scoriae are vomited from the unconscious. This ejection upon the borderline betwixt life and death is what distinguishes Kleist's works on the one hand from those of Hebbel, which are thoughts in fancy dress, where the problems derive from the superficial strata of the intelligence; and on the other hand from those of Schiller, which are works of art, but untroubled by the primal needs and perils of existence. No other German writer has incorporated his own inmost being into his works to the same extent as Kleist, tearing out his vitals (as it were) to fashion them. (pp. 406-07)

Kleist was not, as was Schiller, an author who mastered the problems he mooted or solved, but one who was obsessed by them; and it was this constraint that they imposed on him which made his outbursts so violent and so convulsive. His creative work was not the outcome of a deliberate exteriorization; it resulted from a frenzied endeavour to escape from internal and almost fatal stresses. Every character in his plays feels, as the author himself felt, that the cross laid upon him is the one important thing in the world; each of them is the slave of his passions; each of them stakes the limit, hazards his very life. Whatever happens to Kleist, and therefore whatever happens to his dramatis personae, cuts to the bone. His country's distresses, which for other authors are topics for fine writing; philosophy, which Goethe dallied with in a sceptical mood and so far as was requisite to his own spiritual growth; Eros and the sorrows of Psyche—to Kleist, all these became a fever, a mania, and placed him on the rack. Kleist's problems were not, like Schiller's, poetical fictions; they were personal tragedies, cruel realities, which gave his writings their unique atmosphere. The polar contrasts of his nature found vent in them. (p. 408)

Nothing but tragic drama, could give adequate expression to the agonizing oppositions of Kleist's temperament. The epic vein lends itself to more conciliatory, more easy-going formulations; but tragedy demands meticulous finish, and was more accordant with the extravagance of his character. This became his chosen method of expression. Yet "chosen" is not the apt word. He did not choose this method, but was driven to it. . . . Goethe spoke sarcastically of the "invisible theatre" for which these plays must have been composed. Now, for Kleist there did exist an invisible theatre, and it was the daimonic world which by forcible cleavage, by establishing diametrical oppositions, created such stresses as could not fail to shatter a concrete and visible stage. Their themes are too vast for the "boards." Kleist was never "practical," and to write with an eye to the necessities of dramatic production would have conflicted with the passionate unrest of his nature.

His themes and his conceptions are always casual and careless; the ties that bind the different parts of his work together are loose; his technique is hastily devised. Consequently, whenever his genius ceases to sustain him, he becomes stagy and melodramatic; lapsing, at times, into the mannerisms of third-rate comedy, . . . of the pantomime. Then, of a sudden (like Shakespeare), he soars from clownish gambols to the sublimest altitudes. His topic is a pretext, is the clay he moulds; the essence of his work is that it is suffused with passion. (pp. 408-09)

The machinery is crude; the arrangements are faulty and trivial; slowly and by devious paths he finds his way to the heart of the conflicts he is describing: but thereupon, with a vigour that is unrivalled, comes the discharge of pent-up feelings in a dramatic explosion. . . . In the opening of his plays (*The Broken Pitcher, Robert Guiscard, Penthesilea*), details and situations seem hopelessly thronged—as if he were massing the clouds from which alone the thunderstorm could burst. He loves this dark and oppressive atmosphere because it is that of his inmost being. . . . Kleist's dramas irritate before they bring relief to our strained feelings. (pp. 409-10)

Except in the case of *Homburg,* one always feels with Kleist that the characters have run away from their creator into some fourth-dimensional sphere beyond the range of his waking imagination. . . . Each character becomes one of the irresponsible fiends called up by a magician's apprentice. Kleist is no more accountable for their doings than any of us is for words uttered in sleep, words which (uninhibited) reveal longings hidden from our conscious mind.

The form as well as the substance, the language no less than the thought-content, of Kleist's dramatic writing, are subject to like coercions, to the same dominance of unconscious passion over conscious intelligence and will. (pp. 410-11)

Kleist, regarding the world as fundamentally tragical, could never (as did Goethe) "uplift his voice to its worth"; and for this very reason he could never "rejoice in his own worth." All the creatures of his fancy are destroyed because of his dissatisfaction with the cosmos; offspring of a tragedian, they never cease kicking against the pricks and running their heads against the impenetrable wall of fate. . . . [Kleist] was heroically unwise; he had the courage to plumb the depths; voluptuously he followed his dreams into the uttermost gulfs, knowing that they would drag him down to doom. Contemplating the world as a tragedy, he fashioned tragic dramas out of his world, and of these dramas his own life was the greatest tragedy of all. (pp. 412-13)

Kleist knew very little of reality, but was intimately acquainted with the essence of things. . . . His psychology was weaponless, perhaps blind, in face of common types, in face of ordinary phenomena; his clairvoyance began only when he had to deal with abnormal feelings, with persons dwelling in ultra-dimensional space. Only through his volcanic passions was he linked with the outer world. . . . He never described people. All that happened was that the daimon in him recognized its brother in them behind the veil of the earthly and was in tune with nature.

That is why his heroes lack balance, why they transcend the limitations of daily life, why they suffer from excess of passion. These unruly children of an unrestrained imagination seem to derive (as Goethe said of Penthesilea [see excerpt above]) from a generation peculiar to themselves; each of them exhibits Kleist's own traits, his unconciliatory disposition, bluntness, obstinacy, mulishness, immalleability. (pp. 414-15)

Invariably the trivialism in Kleist's leading personalities, which might have sufficed to make them popular ideals, is tinctured by a drop or two of some perilous ingredient which estranges them from the folk. . . . Kleist saw clearly, and detested pettiness of feeling. He was more likely to lack taste than to be trivial, to be stubborn and hyperbolical than saccharine. To him—the blunt, the acerb, the man of many trials, the man who had known suffering—gush was utterly uncongenial; with the result that he was deliberately unsentimental, and put the controls on at the point where, in commonplace authors, the romantic stop is pulled out. Especially was he reticent in his love-scenes, allowing his characters no words, nothing more than a blush, a stammer, a sigh, or an impassioned silence. The hero, to Kleist's way of thinking, must not make himself common. . . . [His heroes] are inharmonious, incongruous; they share their creator's self-will and unconciliatoriness and therefore each of them is a lonely figure. (pp. 415-17)

His world was as remote and as timeless as himself, a Saturnian sphere, turning away from daylight and clarity. Kleist was interested in nature, in the world, as in man, only at that uttermost bourne where it grows daimonic; where the natural passes into the magical; where the mundane shades into the supramundane, transcending the limits of the customary and the probable; where (I might even say) it becomes monstrous, vicious, abnormal. In events, as in human beings, his interest is riveted only by deviations from the rule (the Marquise von O., the Beggar-Woman of Locarno, the earthquake in Chile); always, therefore, at moments when they seem to be breaking away from God's appointed orbits. . . . Kleist was most at home in the peculiar, the eerie; in desolate regions where, amid shadows and chasms, he could sense the presence of the daimon by whom he was so strangely allured, where he was not embarrassed and intimidated by the proximity of the commonplace—to him always uncongenial. Thus did he, ever lacking restraint, plunge deeper and deeper into the enigmas of nature. In the cosmos, as in the realm of feeling, he was incessantly searching for the superlative.

At the first glance there would seem to be a kinship, because of this revolt from the obvious and the trite, between Kleist and his contemporaries the Romanticists. Yet in truth a gulf yawns between them and him, between their partly deliberate and partly spontaneous superstition and devotion to fable, on the one hand, and his obsession with the fantastic and the abstruse, on the other. For the Romanticists, the cult of the "wonderful" was tantamount to a religion; whereas for Kleist, the strange, the inexplicable, was a malady of nature. . . . [He] took an uncanny pride in a sober relation of the incomprehensible, boring through stratum after stratum until he tapped the depths where the magical in nature and the daimonic in man are inexplicably wedded. In this respect he resembles Dostoeffsky more closely than does any other German writer. Kleist's figures, too, are burdened with all the morbid and exacerbated energies of the nerves; and these nerves are somewhere and somehow painfully interconnected with the daimonic elements of the cosmos. Like Dostoeffsky, Kleist is not only sincere, but sincere to a fault, and that is why the "atmosphere" of his writings is often obscured by a blight—the chill clarity of the intelligence being suddenly replaced by the sultry obscurity of fantasy and troubled by windy outbursts of passion. Kleist's spiritual atmosphere is often exhilarating. He has a profound insight into essentials, profounder maybe than that of any other German imaginative writer. Yet the air he makes us breathe is irrespirable for long (he himself could endure it for only a decade), since it tenses the nerves unduly, tormenting our senses with its crude contrasts of heat and cold, and making repose impossible. Even as an artist this man, cloven in sunder, was homeless. There was no solid ground beneath the rolling wheels of his perpetual flight. He lived in the realm of the wonderful without believing in it, and he created realities while having no love for them. (p. 419)

Kleist's mind dwelt in two worlds: in the torrid zones of fancy, and in the sober, cold, and concrete region of analysis. That was why his art was bifid, pushing in either direction to an extreme. Kleist the playwright and Kleist the teller of tales have often been treated as one, or the teller of tales has been regarded as a variant of the dramatist. In reality, however, the two forms of literary art were for him contrasted expressions of the ambivalence of his temperament. As playwright, he seized his material without restraint, and heated it red-hot in his fires; as writer of nouvelles, he put the curb on his participation, held scrupulously aloof, so that none of the breath of his own life should inspire the narration. In his dramas it was himself that he was fanning into flame, but in his novels it was others, his readers, whom he wished to render ardent; in his plays he spurred himself forward, in his stories he reined himself back. (p. 420)

In his novels, Kleist excluded his ego, suppressed his passions, or (rather) switched them onto a different track. (p. 421)

Through repression, Kleist betrayed all that was not good, all that was hidden away out of sight; betrayed them because calm and self-mastery were alien to his temperament. Absolute freedom (the artist's supreme magic) was lacking to him when he wished to impose upon himself a tranquillity foreign to his nature. (p. 422)

[With] Kleist there ensued a passion for dispassionateness, with the result that his own tensions were transferred to his readers. Always we feel the excess which was natural to him, and for this reason the ablest and strongest of his stories is the one which was an appropriate embodiment of the motive force of his own personality—"**Michael Kohlhaas**," the most splendid, most symbolical type Kleist ever created; the man whose forces are destroyed by lack of control, the man in whom level-headedness degenerates into obstinacy, and a craving for justice into litigiousness. Kohlhaas (though Kleist probably was not aware of it) was the emblem of his creator, one whose best qualities became his greatest peril, and who was pushed over the edge by the fanaticism of his will. (p. 423)

In every one of his plays Kleist was a self-betrayer; in each of them the molten lava of his soul erupted into the outer world, giving objective shape to his passion. Through them, therefore, we can gain a partial acquaintance with the contradictions of his nature; but he would not have become one of the immortals, his personality fully disclosed, had he not been able in the last of his works [*The Prince of Homburg*] to give a picture of himself and his limitations. In . . . *The Prince of Homburg*, he depicted (with that outstanding genius which fate rarely grants to an artist more than once in his life) himself, the conflict that had always raged in him, the tragic antinomy of passion and discipline. In *Penthesilea*, in *Guiscard*, in *Die Hermannsschlacht,* one impulse dominated, an urge towards the infinite. In *Homburg* the interplay of impulses finds expression—pressure and resistance in which neither is victorious, but in which counterpoise and suspense ensue. Now, what is suspense of the energies other than the most perfect harmony? (p. 425)

In *Homburg* Kleist gained control over the daimon for an instant, ridding himself of the haunter by incorporating him into the written work. He did not—as in *Penthesilea*, in *Guiscard*,

in *Die Hermannsschlacht*—merely cut off one head of the hydra whose tentacles entwined him. Seizing the monster in an irresistible grip, he embodied it wholly in his creation. Here, then, we feel his power, because force is not dissipated in the void, because passion does not hiss aimlessly like the steam escaping through the safety-valve of a superheated boiler, but energy wrestles with energy. Nothing runs to waste in *Homburg*. Kleist found deliverance through a restraint which brought redoublement. The opposing forces are no longer destructive, inasmuch as they no longer leave outlets for this or that unregulated impulse. (p. 426)

For the first time there emanates from Kleist's work a muted tone of kindliness, an aroma of sympathy; as he fingers his harp, we hear what we have never heard before in his melodies, the notes of the silver strings. There is a gathering together of every variant of human motives. Just as it is sometimes said of the dying (especially of those who die by drowning) that their last thoughts are a condensed recapitulation of a lifetime's memories, so does Kleist's whole past, a seemingly misspent existence, sketch itself here in outline, sketch itself so dexterously that his errors, his omissions, his follies, and his futilities, are seen to have significance. (pp. 427-28)

The Prince of Homburg is the sincerest of Kleist's dramas because it embodies the totality of his life. The criss-crossings and complications of his temperament are there: his love of life and his craving for death, his discipline and his indiscipline, his heritage and his acquirements. (p. 428)

Stefan Zweig, "The Struggle with the Daimon: Kleist" (originally published under a different title in his Der Kampf mit dem Damon, Insel-Verlag, 1925), *in his* Master Builders: A Typology of the Spirit, *translated by Eden Paul and Cedar Paul (translation copyright © 1939, copyright renewed © 1966, by the Viking Press, Inc.; reprinted by permission of the Estate of Stefan Zweig), Viking Penguin Inc., 1939, pp. 369-440.*

THOMAS MANN   (essay date 1926)

What is loyalty? It is loving without seeing; it is triumph over a hated forgetfulness. We meet a face we love, and after some looking at it during which our feeling is confirmed, we are parted from it. . . .

It is after this fashion I have loved Kleist's *Amphitryon;* forgotten it, yet treasured it, even during a forgetting due to lack of time and opportunity to see it again. . . . I read it again and the response of my nature to this work is true to its old form. I am delighted, I glow with pleasure. It is the wittiest, charmingest, the most intellectual, the profoundest and most beautiful theatre piece in the world. I knew that I loved it—now, praise God, again I know why.

I mean to talk about it as though it were new, as though I were the only person who had ever read it or talked about it. I will take care neither to read what other people have written about it, nor to admit to myself that I could possibly have read what they said. (p. 202)

So far as Kleist's *Amphitryon* goes, Plautus and the French comedies are simply material. . . . (p. 203)

Kleist shows the childlike facility that makes an artist take over elements either from reality or from a naïve model. . . . (p. 204)

[There] are survivals from the earlier version: amusing social comments that smile their way into a poetry full of mystical intellectuality and extraordinary sensitiveness—for that is what Kleist's translation has made of the material. For a translation it is, in the very strongest sense of the word: the actual and incredible transference, kidnapping, and captivation of a work of art out of its own sphere into another one originally quite foreign to it; from one century into another, one nationality into another. It is a radical Germanization and romanticization of a masterpiece of French art. (p. 205)

[The] piece as a whole is not distressing, it preserves a high degree of gaiety and tolerableness; it is, by its intellectual appeal, saved from the charge of lightness; and the aesthetic demand for justice, for a sense of sympathy and fellow-feeling, is nowhere seriously infringed on. The poet has a care for this requirement from the first, taking thought for it both in the pathetic and in the vulgar. (p. 231)

My love for [*Amphitryon*], my loyalty through the years, reaped the joyful reward of once more knowing why, as I reread its subtle lines. The blitheness of its mysticism, the warmth of its humour, are incomparable. Played as it deserves to be played, it would be a diversion in which atmosphere and intellect would both be celebrated in their equal due. (p. 239)

> Thomas Mann, "Kleist's 'Amphitryon'" (originally published in Neue Rundschau, 1926), in his Essays of Three Decades, translated by H. T. Lowe-Porter (copyright 1947 by Alfred A. Knopf, Inc.; reprinted by permission of Alfred A. Knopf, Inc.), Knopf, 1947, pp. 202-40.

FRIEDRICH WILHELM KAUFMANN   (essay date 1940)

[Kleist's work is] the reflection of an existence tragically torn between authority and flight to freedom, between self-discipline and passion, between ambition and despair. This extreme dynamic tension is reflected in the characters of Kleist's dramas, whose fate depends on the excesses of passion and devotion, of cruelty and fear. In this respect, he is accordingly a poet of the conflict between rational control and an irrational and creative emotion. In and through his dramatic works he finds the solution of those problems which he fails to resolve in his life. (p. 28)

[Kleist's] revolt against a rationalized and standardized attitude towards life is responsible for the beginning of his dramatic art. Rationalism becomes the negative pole, and the search for a new principle becomes the positive meaning of his whole work.

The first drama to express this problem is the tragedy *Die Familie Schroffenstein*. The two branches of the noble house of Schroffenstein are held together by an old agreement of succession. Once in the past, this agreement may have been the expression of a friendly relation, but as a rationalization of an emotional bond it only leads to catastrophe. (pp. 29-30)

Reason, detached from immediate contact with reality, isolates man in distrust; its triumph is identical with ruin. The tragedy of man . . . lies in the fact that whatever is perceived only through the senses is ambiguous, and that all purely abstract reasoning about human relations prevents one from understanding one's fellow-men and thus contributes to the destruction of human values. The dramatic presentation of such a destruction is, however, not only the expression of disillusionment;

it also implies the postulate that human relations should be such that human values may survive and be furthered. . . .

In the dramatic fragment *Robert Guiskard, Herzog der Normänner,* the power of the outside world is even more oppressive, and the power of the will to shape and to reorganize this world around a spiritual center is here represented as being less effective than in *Familie Schroffenstein.* Guiskard experiences the intolerable tragedy of a man who feels in himself the urge to live a free, creative life and who encounters one insurmountable obstacle after another in his effort to reach the goal for which he is striving. It is—to use the Fichtean terminology—the tragedy which results when man fulfills his duty to transform the non-ego into the ego. (p. 31)

Robert Guiskard seems to express only the despair of a man who realizes the futility of all human endeavor. . . . [Yet] this most dreadful hopelessness of fate, as portrayed in the certainty of death just before the goal is reached, is but a transitory stage in Kleist's development. It is this utter pessimism with regard to man's power which he tries to overcome; and his struggle constitutes the deeper meaning of the heroism with which he endows his protagonist.

It is fundamentally the same problem in Kleist's comedy *Der zerbrochene Krug.* Although the comic form suggests a more optimistic approach, the content of the play reveals a close relation to Kleist's first tragedy *Die Familie Schroffenstein.* Again it is a world dominated by prejudice and material interests which menaces the happiness of the lovers, and again it is extreme and unperturbed devotion which points the way out of the chaos. The environment is as unproblematic and as near to life as one can possibly imagine, for the play concerns peasants with robust senses and an unspoiled joy in life. That is why we feel the more keenly the potential tragedy inherent in man's nature: man's reason enables and forces him to transcend the immediate experience of reality; but this human ability at the same time serves to undermine man's natural relation to others by causing misunderstanding, dissension, and antagonism. . . . The comic element in the play is, however, only a means of emphasizing the underlying problem: is reason as such capable of regulating the relations of man? . . . [The] play shows that reason without a deeper foundation in human sympathy may become the source of any calamity. (pp. 32-3)

[*Amphitryon*] has been interpreted by bourgeois moralists as a glorification of matrimonial fidelity. Others, who have applied the classical pattern of Schiller, have thought that Kleist intended to present the rise of a character from worldly affection to absolute devotion to the ideal. Still others have considered the drama as a symbolic presentation of the Christian mystery of the Immaculate Conception. Others, again, have not been able to discover in it anything but a psychological study of the confused ways of human passion. These misinterpretations clearly show that one can read almost anything into a work of art so long as one takes it in its isolation and not as an integral part of the author's whole work and expression of his fundamental problem. Kleist's desire, however, was to establish an emotional contact with this world and thereby to come to an understanding of its deepest and most vital reality. . . . Romantic estheticism may consider as a value the enjoyment of the "beautiful moment" in which all consciousness recedes, so far as enjoyment symbolizes the freedom of transcending individual boundaries. For Kleist, however, there is neither a transcendent idea, nor an esthetic, passive submersion in the infinite. The essence and the foundation of his universe is the individual concrete self, which transcends its own limited sphere in active emotional experience.

Alkmene's refusal to renounce her mortal husband for her divine seducer expresses Kleist's firmly established conviction that the self is the center of all life, and that the non-self is recognized only in so far as it becomes a concrete emotional experience of the self. . . . The identity of love and marriage, which is accepted in this drama as a matter of course, is closely related, however, to the main issue, the conflict between the rationalized norm and the individual will, and is therefore submitted to further poetic analysis.

This is the theme of the tragedy *Penthesilea.* Here again the subject matter, as such, is but an interesting psychological analysis of the erotic affinity between love and hatred, between fulfillment and disillusion, as carried to the extremes of voluptuousness and perversion in the annihilation of the beloved and in self-destruction. (pp. 33-5)

Kleist's conception of morality differs essentially from the classical idea of the universal validity of moral principles. [Penthesilea's] death is rather the supreme liberation from all heterogeneous determination and the absolute assertion of the spontaneous individual. The attitude of the Amazons towards men is intended to show the extent of demoralization to which the rationalization of human relations may lead. The abstract and objective order is thus represented in this tragedy as the arch-destroyer of the highest personality values. The tragic end of the play demands rather that the inner sympathetic relation should be acknowledged as the fundamental principle of human conduct. The ideal of humanity can be attained only on the basis of sympathy and love.

The aim, in other words, is to replace the heteronomy of a rational and inflexible order by a dynamic order which expresses the sympathetic relation of human personalities. . . . *Penthesilea* leaves no doubt that the order must be such that its laws can be obeyed by the individual without detriment to his inner freedom. Such synthesis of authority and inner freedom, however, is possible only if law and order are manifestations of the moral will of the individual and derive their validity from his will only, that is if law and order become identical with the moral will of the individual. (pp. 37-8)

In *Penthesilea* the emphasis is still on the negative side of the problem; with *Käthchen von Heilbronn* it shifts to the positive presentation of the emotional foundation underlying human relations. Käthchen is the impersonation of nature in its primal purity, naïvely free from the considerations and inhibitions of reflective reason, unerringly devoted to her love and ever willing to sacrifice her life in the service of others. (p. 38)

On first examination of the theme it might seem that the play is but a dramatization of the Cinderella fairy-tale or of the disenchanted princess who is saved by a prince and then marries him. As in the fairy-tale, good and bad are sharply contrasted, and the solution of the conflict is a fabulous triumph of goodness, while wickedness is completely put to shame. . . . This particular nature of the fairy-tale thus made it especially suitable as a substratum for the presentation of Kleist's problem, for his ideal of a revitalization of the world from the inner center of the emotional self could best be presented in its imaginative setting. . . .

The optimism which distinguishes *Käthchen von Heilbronn* from Kleist's earlier dramas reflects Kleist's own growing confidence in himself and his ability as a playwright. His more

positive attitude toward life may be seen in this play's unmistakable insistence that sympathy be the guide in human relations. In this drama, in contrast to *Der zerbrochene Krug* and in comparison with *Penthesilea,* the ideal order prevails without the intervention of a kind of *deus ex machina.* (p. 39)

The real hero of the drama is the people, with its absolute claim to existence, with its inner activity. It is the people as an organism which constantly creates from within its individual integrity and which therefore has the absolute right to its country as the condition of its existence and it has the moral duty to defend its own integrity. The people also is the hero of the play in a deeper sense. It is the people who surpasses in its fight the limitations set by its own greed as well as by a foreign rule and thus achieves its realization in national self-assertion.

Since the play had its origin in a tense and passionate political situation, the emphasis is more upon the national issue, and the inner relation of the individual to the national community is left somewhat obscure. In Kleist's next drama, *Prinz Friedrich von Homburg,* this relation is elucidated as thoroughly as is possible in dramatic presentation. This leaves no doubt that the individual should *not* be subservient to the state and its objective laws. Any other interpretation of Kleist's meaning would be incompatible with the whole development of his thought; it would be in absolute contrast to the rejection of the rational and heterogeneous order in *Penthesilea.* We have no right to suppose of *Prinz Friedrich von Homburg* that Kleist had opportunistically yielded to the pressure of the moment and thus rob the striving and the suffering of his life of its meaning. . . . Kleist's idea of the fatherland is more than the real condition of ideal freedom; it is the concrete manifestation of the will of a natural group of people aiming at the highest realization of their individual potentialities. This fatherland is never merely existent; rather it continues to realize its existence through the active will of the individual; it is an ever-creative regeneration. As the final goal was anticipated in Käthchen's and von Strahl's dreams, so the conclusion is foreshadowed in the dream of Prinz Friedrich von Homburg in the first scene of the drama: the wreath and the chain are the symbols of his striving for love and glory. (pp. 43-4)

The incipient rationalism in Kleist's development remains the negative pole even in this last drama; its most distinctive representative is Prince Hohenzollern, especially in the argumentation with which he tries to save his friend from execution. He attributes the real guilt for Homburg's insubordination to the prince-elector himself, who gave the wreath and the chain to Homburg in his somnambulistic dream and thereby weakened his will-power so that he disobeyed the military instructions; therefore, the prince-elector rather than Homburg should be held responsible. The prince-elector reveals the absurdity of this rationalistic argument by pointing out that a causal explanation would, in the last analysis, reduce to absurdity any concept of guilt and would undermine the entire organization of the state. . . . This drama . . . establishes a synthesis between the objectivity of reason and the pure subjectivity of sentiment; it makes the individual subject the creator of the law of the state and makes the law dependent upon the active will of the individual to establish a superindividual order.

Kleist's poetic creation began as a revolt against the rationalism which dominated his own life and thinking as well as that of his environment. Rationalism became the negative pole and the search for an emotional principle of life the positive pole of his work. (pp. 46-7)

Every one of Kleist's dramas is . . . evidence of a fight against the traditions of a rationalistic order of life, and of a search for a new order in which every form and every relation of life is constantly being created out of immediate contact with persons and situations. His work as a whole may be considered as a progressive solution of this problem. It is the expression of a relentless fight for an immediate experience of existence, for the dynamic penetration of the object-world with the creative will of the subject, for the transformation of the non-ego into the ego. (p. 49)

> *Friedrich Wilhelm Kaufmann, "Heinrich von Kleist," in his* German Dramatists of the 19th Century *(reprinted by permission of the Estate of Friedrich Wilhelm Kaufmann), Lymanhouse, 1940 (and reprinted by Books for Libraries Press, 1970; distributed by Arno Press, Inc.), pp. 27-49.*

STEN FLYGT   (essay date 1943)

Kleist's existential problem is neatly revealed as the tension between feeling and understanding. Throughout his plays and stories the two poles of this tension find expression in various symbolic disguises. Feeling is represented in the spontaneous and unreasoned action of the characters; understanding, in their logical interpretation of what their senses tell them and their trust in material evidence. . . .

[Kleist] consciously recognized that he had already abandoned belief in the rational as a guiding principle, and . . . he embraced an ardent belief in the sanctity of the irrational and its infallibility. With this change came another: heightened aesthetic sensitivity and the need to find poetic expression.

He found it first in *Die Familie Schroffenstein,* a dark and passionate tragedy of souls misguided by reason. (p. 515)

This play shows that for Kleist at this time the immediate and personal cause of tragedy is the corruption or blinding of the spontaneous urge by logical deduction. But the larger tragic problem is the question why this cause can exist. Kleist is tentatively dealing with the problem of fate, while the other cause of tragedy, although perhaps the tool of fate, is in the forefront of attention. The bitter hopelessness of the play comes from Kleist's inability to believe absolutely in anything as an infallible guide, and in the last act his mocking skepticism turns the whole thing into a horrible joke.

In *Robert Guiskard* there seems to be no struggle between understanding and feeling. Perhaps this circumstance is due to the fact that we have so little of the play. At any rate, Guiskard himself seems to be . . . a man in whom reason and artifice are in the service of an overpowering will. But the background situation of *Die Familie Schroffenstein,* namely the problem of fate, is very prominent in this play. Guiskard, whose feeling is strong and unimpaired, is crushed by an outside force. . . . [As] in *Die Familie Schroffenstein,* feeling is an imperfect shield against the blows of fate.

None the less, Kleist does not give up his ardent belief in the spontaneous, as the two plays which follow testify. He continues to ask the same questions, but the answers are not so terrifyingly negative. In fact, they are a vigorous affirmation of feeling, and doubts are resolutely suppressed.

The tension of feeling and understanding is clear and central in *Amphitryon.* It exists within the personality of both Amphitryon and of Alkmene and from it comes the extremely problematical nature of the play.

In Amphitryon's character the conflict is relatively uncomplicated: he fails to trust his feeling of love where the evidence of his senses leads him to make a mistaken inference. This is a typical situation of the Kleistian man. . . . The main psychological and dramatic interest of the third act lies in the expiation Amphitryon must make for having allowed his mind to discredit the sure intuition of his heart. Tragedy threatens Amphitryon from this uncomplicated cause but it is averted.

The tragedy which threatens Alkmene does not have so simple a cause. . . . Alkmene's suffering poses the problem of whether the principle of feeling, the guide which Kleist wished to follow as infallible, might not itself prove false. The doubt here raised of course, is plainly related to what I have termed the residual factor of *Die Familie Schroffenstein,* but there is a difference. In the earlier play the doubt remains, but here it is swept away before Alkmene's perfection of feeling. . . . The whole problem for Alkmene has been: has her feeling deceived her so that she has without knowing it, given her love to someone who is not Amphitryon? If this has happened, then life is, indeed, over for her, since the holy and absolute guide of her life, her feeling, has proved to be fallible. But her feeling has been right all the time: she has never given her love to someone who is not Amphitryon, for the god *is* Amphitryon, just as he is all things. The outcome is a triumph for Alkmene, a cosmic vindication of intuitional knowledge.

It is also a twofold exposure of the evil of the rational principle, for the tension of feeling and understanding within Amphitryon as well as within Alkmene ends in the complete discrediting of understanding. None the less, the threat of the evil rational principle to cause men to abandon the infallible guide of feeling does not constitute the whole of the tragic problem. The residual factor is prominent in this play, being identical with Jupiter, who caused the internal tension of Amphitryon and Alkmene, and Jupiter, in his baffling character, is a symbol for the universal godhead.

Jupiter as a dramatic character is not consistent, cannot be. First of all he is a human god with human desire and individual existence. . . . [In] another and more concrete sense Jupiter is the real Amphitryon because he is the ideal Amphitryon. But Jupiter is more than just the human god, he is all things, the world, fate, present, past, and future.

The mysterious inconsistency of Jupiter, who is both individual and all pervasive, is a symbol, whether actual in Kleist's consciousness or not, of the mysterious inconsistency of the world. Therefore, the change that takes place in him from disregard of Alkmene's feelings to purest love is also a symbol of Kleist's belief that feeling so perfect as Alkmene's must invoke divine aid. . . . In *Die Familie Schroffenstein* the question was asked, How can God allow such cruel fate to overtake men? In *Amphitryon* God not only allows but even causes the shadow of tragedy to fall upon men. None the less, the play proclaims Kleist's desperate faith that the man whose feeling is perfect will be saved.

Der zerbrochene Krug, a true comedy, is another optimistic play. In it we find again the tension of feeling and understanding, the latter symbolized by the court, the judge, and the judge's specious arguments. (pp. 517-20)

Das Erdbeben in Chili deals with a tragedy which comes from the triumph of the evil rational principle over the irrational principle. But in this story the tension of the two principles is not within the main characters, Jeronimo and Josephe. There is never any doubt or question about the unerring feeling of the two lovers. In the community, however, understanding is embodied in the state and particularly the church. This is a natural symbolism, with parallels in *Die Familie Schroffenstein, Penthesilea,* and *Die Hermannsschlacht.* . . . [Upon] first examination, the central problem of the story seems to be a simple instance of the corruption of good natural feeling by the evil rational principle.

But the case is not as simple as it seems, for the residual factor is very prominent, in fact, almost as prominent as the persistent central problem. The disaster itself causes terrible anguish, which Kleist here treats as problematical; not only does the earthquake cause suffering and death directly, but it also releases cruelty and inhumanity among the people. Plundering breaks out and violent repressive measures are taken without regard to the question of guilt or innocence. . . . The feeling of the lovers and their friends is fine and sound, the natural feelings of humanity in a crisis may be heroic and good, and the most poignant tragedy comes from "der unglückselige Verstand" [the unfortunate understanding], the evil rational principle as embodied in the state and the church, but Kleist must raise the question, why does God permit terrible disasters? Clearly the good principle of spontaneity is no bulwark against tragedy. In writing the story Kleist must have wrestled in agony with this inescapable fact. (pp. 521-22)

The tensions in *Die Marquise von O* are complicated. First and simplest is the relationship of the Marquise to her parents, in whom the rational principle temporarily stifles their feeling of trust and belief in their daughter, causing great unhappiness for them all. Then there are two different struggles within the Marquise's mind, one succeeding the other. The first is caused by the necessity of growing adjusted to the fact that she is pregnant, and is the familiar tension of feeling and understanding. Her mind cannot grasp what her inner feeling tells her is true, that she is to have a child. The tension between feeling and reason nearly causes madness but then logic is forced to yield to feeling and she accepts the fact. When her reason has thus yielded she becomes an independent person, resolved and able to face whatever may come. This means an adjustment to the residual factor of tragedy, an acceptance of what the mind cannot grasp: the inevitable existence of suffering and its mysterious causes. The Marquise is thus a kind of symbol of humanity, which endures tragedy without knowing why or how. . . . [She] must face a new and more terrible crisis when she learns that the count is the unknown father of her child. He now seems like a devil to her because he had at first seemed to be an angel and she is in real terror of him, so real that he can win back her trust and love only by sternest self-abnegation and only after a rather long time, about a year. The new dilemma when she learns that the count has violated her most sacred feelings is a reversal of the first. . . . If it is true that the count is unworthy, then her own feeling is fallible, her purity is corruptible, and, moreover, she has no staunch and perfect shield against misfortune. (pp. 522-23)

The count's love is really true and steadfast, but it had the terrible defect. In him the spontaneous principle itself is corrupt. This is a problem which Kleist sees clearly and grapples with, but he can get nowhere in his struggles. . . .

Penthesilea marks the culmination of this crucial phase in Kleist's struggle with the problem of feeling. The old familiar conflict is there, to be sure, and until examined more closely, it seems to be only that and nothing more. Penthesilea is torn by an inner tension caused by her being loyal to the rational state of which she is the queen and therefore the defender, and, at the same time, being loyal to feeling as her highest personal law. (p. 523)

Penthesilea is even more grim than *Die Familie Schroffenstein,* but the residual factor is not prominent. In fact, in this regard the contrast is strong between the two plays: in the earlier play as well as in the latter, feeling is stifled by understanding and the result is tragic, but in the earlier play Kleist was greatly concerned with the ultimate cause of tragedy, the mysterious riddle of God. Not so in *Penthesilea.* Here the ultimate cause is not a cosmic riddle; it is, rather, the rational history and foundation of the Amazon state. . . . In *Penthesilea* reason is the total evil.

But even though reason is the total evil, feeling is not absolutely infallible. It is, indeed, fallible in the striking new way that marks a turning point in the history of Kleist's mind. We have seen that the rational principle is condemned in the breaking of the law of Tanais. And the irrational principle is thereby vindicated, by a natural inference from the condemnation of the rational and by the fact that the Amazons are given back to a natural life. Still, the play does not show a triumph of the irrational principle, for the tragedy is not optimistic but profoundly, even hysterically, pessimistic, and the solution it reaches is extinction and oblivion. What makes the tragedy particularly savage and nihilistic is that reason corrupts Penthesilea's feeling of love and perverts it to its opposite, loathesome and inhuman madness. . . . In his ceaseless agonized struggle with the problem of feeling Kleist drives himself to the point where he wonders whether the very principle he so desperately trusts and believes in cannot itself betray him. But he is not yet ready to draw the final inexorable conclusion. In fact, he may not, in *Penthesilea,* be completely aware of what the conclusion must be, but the doubt which finds only incomplete expression here is completely worked out in *Michael Kohlhaas,* which had its inception at the time when *Penthesilea* was begun. The present mental revolution is, so to speak, the reverse of that early overthrow of belief in reason: Kleist had once thought he trusted completely and desperately in understanding, doubts grew until they could no longer be kept down, and then with his relentless, exclusive extremism, he proclaimed feeling as the only road to salvation. Now in the same uncompromising struggle to learn the truth he is on the point of recognizing that this road to salvation leads only to new eternal fires. . . . [Underneath] the manifested activity of his mind he pursues the thread which comes to view in *Penthesilea* and *Die Marquise von O* and which began to be the leading motif of *Michael Kohlhaas,* until in the completed version of *Michael Kohlhaas* he is able to affirm the dread discovery that once more his highest values have been lost. Thus, the essay on the marionettes ["**Über das Marionettentheater**"] sums up his deepest experience: banished from Paradise he must go all the way around to enter from the other side.

Das Käthchen von Heilbronn exhibits the conflict of feeling and understanding in several uncomplicated ways. Käthchen herself is the embodiment of the spontaneous principle: reflection has no share whatever in determining her conduct. The rational principle is embodied in the Vehmgericht, and primarily in Kunigunde, a creature of artifice and synthetic beauty. . . . [Rarely] has Kleist so simplified the conflict as here in the struggle between Käthchen and Kunigunde: one is pure feeling and goodness and the other is pure artifice and evil. (pp. 524-25)

Of Kleist's plays *Die Hermannsschlacht* is the least problematic and the poorest. In it there is very little struggle and Kleist's fundamental problem is solved by reason being completely in the service of feeling—a solution which Kleist did not feel but which he merely constructed for the sake of his external purpose in writing the play. . . . Its real importance is that it shows a transition in Kleist's struggle with the problem of feeling to the conception of the state as embodying a higher principle than feeling—a complete reversal of his old attitude to the state. . . . In *Die Hermannsschlacht* is a new national spirit, an acknowledgment of the subordination of the individual to his country. (pp. 525-26)

[At] the outset of his career as a writer Kleist staked everything on the principle of spontaneity and condemned the principle of logical deduction, and . . . his doubts about the validity of the spontaneous principle grew until he was forced to admit that there is a higher principle. But acknowledging the fallibility of feeling did not solve the problem, for there now arose the question: what of the rational principle? A complete reversal was the most obvious possibility, but that would have meant completely denying everything he had lived by. In following the principle of feeling and condemning the principle of understanding Kleist had followed a law of his inner self, not to be overthrown at one stroke. And still he had now arrived at a clear realization that the principle of reason may make demands upon the individual superior to the demands of feeling. To meet the new dilemma Kleist did as he always did when, as he puts it, he found himself outside of the locked gates of Paradise: he went all the way around to see whether there might not be a means of entering again from the other side. This means in this particular case the postulation of a new kind of reason which can make justified claim to be the absolutely trustworthy guide. In the essay *Über das Marionettentheater* he gives an account of the new transcendent principle. (pp. 529-30)

It seems almost as if the essay on the marionettes had been written as commentary upon *Prinz Friedrich von Homburg*, and it is certain that the essay, the play, and the story *Michael Kohlhaas* all are products of the latest phase of Kleist's struggle with the problem of feeling. The play is evolutionary in essence, the famous scene of collapse constituting the crisis which separates the first phase from the last. (p. 530)

The first phase, before the crisis, has three phases of its own: before the battle, the battle, and after the battle. The scene which opens the play and shows the Prince walking in his sleep dreaming of victory and love, is symbolic. That is, it is an explanation, not a cause, of the subsequent events, and its function is to show the Prince under the domination of feeling. . . . [The] Prince's dream really continues even into his normal waking life and he makes no adjustment to the real situation in which he finds himself. He hears the orders given him, he even partially repeats them, but they have no reality save as they complete his dream and fit into his own feelings. The fact that he is preoccupied when the plan of battle is explained does not furnish a cause for his subsequent failure to obey orders—in fact, elaborate precautions are taken by the officers that the commands be impressed upon the Prince and when he orders the charge he knows that he is acting contrary to plan—but his preoccupation is a symptom of his character. He has no interest whatever in a rational plan of battle, but he takes his orders only from his heart. (pp. 530-31)

The state of *Homburg* is not the state of *Kohlhaas*, which was conceived as a social contract, but it is the conscious realization of that community of feeling which received its first expression in *Die Hermannsschlacht*. . . . The new principle of reason

which has been made active in the Prince through his tragic experience is, therefore, very much like unspoiled intuition. When reason has passed through the infinite, original grace is restored. This is the teaching of the essay on the marionettes. (p. 535)

The solution of the existential problem which Kleist finally attained may be regarded as a synthesis of the antithetical principles of feeling and understanding. Bitter experience and suffering taught him that he could not trust exclusively either one or the other of the two opposing principles and his uncompromising quest of truth made him give up his most cherished belief. Unhappily, it did not give him what he had so earnestly sought all his life: an infallible guide to be followed in every practical situation. The rational principle of *Homburg* and the *Marionettes* does not represent a real advance in Kleist's struggle with the problem of feeling but rather another turn of the wheel. The new reason is not so different from the old feeling and the synthesis probably could not have been a permanent solution. Kleist's work shows an almost futile struggle to resolve an impossible tension. But he does achieve a solution which may be summarized as follows: Man, by virtue of his being man, cannot walk the road of life by sure-footed unthinking instinct. Reason must light his way. But only infinite reason casts no deceiving shadows. (pp. 535-36)

> *Sten Flygt, "Kleist's Struggle with the Problem of Feeling," in* PMLA, LVII, *Vol. LVII, No. 2, June, 1943, pp. 514-36.*

THOMAS MANN (essay date 1960)

[There] is only one Kleist in all the world, and that is the one who wrote *Penthesilea, Michael Kohlhaas,* and the one tremendous act of *Robert Guiscard,* which is so superb that it is impossible to imagine its continuation. . . .

What confusion and childishness must have reigned in this mind! . . . Kleist's ambition was in its very essence damaged by *hubris*, jealousy and envy, always overreaching itself, the passion of one pretending to a crown that is not rightfully his and which must be torn from the head of its true owner, in this case the most great, most richly blest Goethe. (p. 10)

Nevertheless, it is Kleist's plays alone, lacking as they are in harmonious proportion and decorum, that give us the archaic shudder of myth the way Sophocles and Aeschylus do. This is especially true of . . . the *Guiscard* fragment. (pp. 11-12)

Kleist's narrative is something altogether unique. To account for it by the cliché of "historical perspective" won't do: even in his own time Kleist's singularity stood out; no other contemporary writer resembled him in the least. His method of storytelling is as eccentric as his plots, and with very few exceptions—among whom Ludwig Tieck was the most notable—Kleist's contemporaries found his fiction intolerably mannered, unpalatable in fact. And yet how is it possible to accuse a writer of affectation who proves on every page that he has looked at life closely and rendered it responsibly? We are faced with a style hard as steel yet impetuous, totally matter-of-fact yet contorted, twisted, surcharged with matter; a style full of involutions, periodic and complex, running to constructions like "in such a manner . . . that," which make for a syntax that is at once closely reasoned and breathless in its intensity. (p. 14)

All Kleist's stories are told in this unusual style, and none of them fails of extraordinary effect. (p. 15)

Kohlhaas seems to me to have a peculiar relevance to the present time, when apathy toward the law, callousness toward injustice, a limp acceptance of "the way things are" exercise a paralyzing influence all over the world. Kleist shows us, incidentally, with a superb, mordant humor, the predicament into which a society accustomed to constant abuse of the law is thrown by a man who refuses to put up with such abuse; how his associates gradually withdraw from the doltish robber baron who created the whole mess—with whom they would have continued to get along easily had it not been for the unpleasant consequences of his insolent act. (p. 17)

The idea of suspense is closely bound up with the idea of fiction. This is as it should be; to tell a story is to create suspense, and the art of the storyteller resides in this ability to make dull subjects sound entertaining and plots whose solution everyone knows in advance, exciting. Kleist, however, creates a very different kind of suspense. His tales conform closely to the Italian archetype—the *novella*— and *novella* means news. What he tells us so coldly and dispassionately is news of the most extraordinary kind, and the suspense his stories create has a specificity, a concreteness, that is positively alarming. We are filled with anxiety and terror, shudder in the face of mystery, doubt in the powers of reason and, indeed, in the power of God himself—all our "affects are confounded." Kleist knows how to put us on the rack and—such is his triumph as an artist—succeeds in making us thank him for that torture. (p. 23)

> *Thomas Mann, "Preface," translated by Francis Golffing (copyright © 1960 by Harper & Row, Publishers, Inc.; reprinted by permission of Harper & Row, Publishers, Inc.), in* The Marquise of O—and Other Stories *by Heinrich von Kleist, translated by Francis Golffing, Criterion Books, 1960, pp. 5-23.*

MARTIN GREENBERG (essay date 1960)

Kleist remained unknown to the world for so many years, and even his own countrymen ignored him for almost a century, because of those very qualities which today create an atmosphere of breathless excitement in his work. What makes him exciting is his modernity. Like Stendhal, like Georg Büchner, Kleist was an avant-garde writer in the true sense of the term; he was not only ahead of the literary fashions of his time, he was not only ahead of his generation, he was ahead of his age. (p. 28)

[The quality of Kleist that makes this work so startlingly modern is] the *questionableness* at the heart of his world, the almost diabolical ambiguity of its atmosphere, the way things tremble and shift and make one wonder if they are what they seem. This is a characteristic of the modern age in the most literal sense: the world seemed flat but it turns out to be round, seemed fixed but it moves—nevertheless it moves, and when we have learned to appreciate, with Galileo and Freud, that things are not what they seem, we are into modern times. What Kleist does, in a way that is as radical as it is subtle, is to question the traditional, apparently self-evident moral, psychological, sexual and political conceptions. He subverts the solid, rational, customary foundations of the world order; suddenly everything begins to sway and we are in fear of falling. Kleist *frightens* one. . . . But the fear inspired by his horror stories is not the delicious, half-nonsensical shudder of Romantic sensationalism; it is a metaphysical fear, as it were, a fear of what is revealed by the glimpse he gives one into the deepest interior and heart of things. (pp. 29-30)

[The narrative of "**Beggar Woman of Locamo**,"] which rushes along with the speed of an express train, makes one morally dizzy: one irritable action and the Marquis is utterly destroyed! A ghost story, it is not the ghost that scares you but the implied statement that the moral order is not rational and just, but cruel, impatient and insensate. It does not argue the point, it embodies it; the story fires itself off like a gun, leaving you not to reflect on it but to recover from it.

Michael Kohlhaas calls the political order into question, or rather the superb body of the story does; the concluding section, which ostensibly resolves the issues of Kohlhaas' "case," only does so formally; it does not really answer the radical doubts raised in the course of the narrative, and seems to me, with its fairytale super naturalism, a good deal less forceful and serious. What Kleist does is evoke a powerful sense of dread and dismay which is never adequately accounted for just by the story of what happens to Kohlhaas, with the result that the accumulated feelings of terror remain undispelled when the story itself comes to an end. Or to put it another way, the horse dealer's agony becomes a metaphor for what Kleist calls the imperfect state of the world, the fundamental irreconcilability of the social order with justice and decency; the formal justice done Kohlhaas at the end of the *novella* does nothing to allay the feelings of anxious dread inspired all along by his fate. (p. 30)

Until the final section, when the gypsywoman of Jüterbock appears on the scene and the *novella* suddenly veers into a shadowy Gothic fantasticness serving to obscure its unsatisfactory conclusion, *Michael Kohlhaas* is a masterpiece of realism. It is written in a German that is extraordinarily compact, complicated, yet impetuous; peremptory to the point of ruthlessness, abrupt in its manner and its transitions, dry and impersonal, it is deliberately anti-literary. . . . Kleist's style expresses a revulsion against the artifice and "lies" of literature, and the search for new truth.

The imperfect state of the world is considered from an altogether different side, and with an altogether different attitude, in the marvellous story *The Marquise of O—*. If *Michael Kohlhaas* hints at a rejection of the social and political order because of all its radical faults and imperfections, *The Marquise of O—* hints at contradictions of the soul and hidden antagonistic movements of the affections which it embraces in a sweeping affirmation of life. (pp. 32-3)

Kleist does not hesitate to tamper with equally sacred conceptions. In the intense, supercharged scene in which the Marquise is reconciled with her father the Commandant, Kleist describes them as two lovers; there is an explicit suggestion of incestuous feeling. But again, Kleist's motive is not the commonplace one of wishing simply to shock. This astonishing writer who dwelt almost exclusively on themes of violence and horror in his plays and stories, of fanaticism, murder, lynching, rape, and cannibalism, had a deep and unafraid understanding of love and sex. The sexual, incestuous element in the feeling between father and daughter does not throw a lurid light on the scene and make their emotion questionable; it is rather an expression and intensification of their tenderness for one another. Kleist understood how false our distinctions often are; he understood the unity in life of what our fearful consciousness tries to separate. (pp. 34-5)

> *Martin Greenberg, "Introduction" (copyright © 1960 by Martin Greenberg; reprinted by permission of Harper & Row, Publishers, Inc.), in* The Marquise of O—and Other Stories *by Heinrich von Kleist,*

translated by Martin Greenberg, Criterion Books, 1960, pp. 27-38.

E. L. STAHL   (essay date 1961)

[The] importance of at least three major intellectual influences on Kleist's life and work has been generally recognized. They are: first, his assimilation of pre-Kantian philosophy; secondly, the impact of Kant or the followers of Kant on his thought; and thirdly, his interest in the ideas of G. H. von Schubert and of Adam Müller. Although it is not possible to establish complete agreement about the precise effect of these intellectual experiences on Kleist's work, and although we may never know to what extent these experiences determined his psychological and artistic development or were determined by it, the influence of Kant, Schubert and Müller appear to be the most clearly recognizable milestones indicating his spiritual progress from pessimism to a guarded optimism.

Of another order, but equally significant, is the effect of the Napoleonic Wars on Kleist's mind and art. Their importance lies in the fact that they took the place of the earlier intellectual influences and that, to a large extent, they effaced these earlier experiences. They closed an important chapter in Kleist's life and opened a new one. The Napoleonic Wars turned his mind from his previous preoccupation with the metaphysical conditions of existence and directed it towards the acceptance of practical values, and they impelled him to portray characters who represented social and national causes and conflicts. (pp. 2-3)

The underlying unity of his work is revealed in his persistent treatment of the themes of error and deceit. (p. 3)

In Kleist's tragedies the suspicions of the parties opposing each other are the result of an inherent weakness of human nature, the inability to distinguish the true from the false, but ultimately the responsibility for the ensuing misfortunes lies with Fate rather than with the human beings. The prejudices engendered in men are provoked by an incalculable higher being. The genesis of this thought . . . is of great importance in his tragedies. (p. 16)

In his persistent use of certain images we may discover a symbolical significance and find a key to understanding the fusion of Kleist's intellectual powers with the pathological forces that also governed him. His images are vivid and lucid and their symbolical application is characterized by a careful, almost logical employment of detail. . . . [Images] which are symbolically significant bear traces of their origins in Kleist's irrational attitude to life, in his distrust of the powers which, he believed, thwarted the happiness of man, or in his own sexual frustrations. The image of the oak in the storm [in *Die Familie Schroffenstein*] is an instance of the first kind. (p. 18)

Kleist's view of tragedy combined two opposite notions, and in his dramas two different conceptions of the tragic may be found. On the one hand tragic happenings are for him the result of human weakness, of the fallibility of human reason and human feelings; on the other hand they are the product of the exalted strength of human passion which provokes the intervention of a higher power in the life of those who experience this passion, and causes their tragic destruction. (p. 19)

Tragic sublimity for Kleist resides in the capacity of experiencing great passions, but with dignity. His most tragic characters, Alkmene and Penthesilea, are sublime because they are endowed with great emotions and they are tragic because, by virtue of these emotions, they become the victims of higher powers. The storm of Fate destroys them because they possess exalted qualities, in excess of those which enable lesser men and women to live in obscurity and hence in safety. (p. 20)

[For] Kleist tragedy lay in man's inability to distinguish between the true and the untrue, an incapacity inherent in his very nature. . . . In Kleist's pessimism there is scarcely a trace of self-criticism. Human fallibility, the weakness of man's cognitive faculties, is a fault for which man cannot be held responsible. Like Thomas Hardy he blamed an inscrutable higher force for the ravages of human life. Man is the victim of Fate and in the battle of life his powers are crippled from the start. He is blinded before the battle begins and in his mistaken efforts to achieve self-realization he destroys his fellowmen and is destroyed by them. (pp. 22-3)

Kleist's characters err because they cannot understand the desires of others. They are not suspicious of their own motives, but suspect those of their fellow-men, and such is the ill-fated constellation of events in their lives, that they cannot know the correct facts of the situation or judge the behaviour of other characters. . . .

Kleist only rarely makes his characters analyse their own motives or justify their own behaviour, as an examination of his use of monologues and dialogues in his dramas will show. He used the monologue not as other dramatists do, in order to reveal the deeper springs of self-doubt and hesitation in the principal characters, but as a means of exposing their growing suspicion and distrust of others. . . . (p. 23)

Another reason for Kleist's infrequent use of monologues may be sought in a different aspect of his poetic genius. His work is singularly lacking in lyric qualities. Not only are the drama and the 'Novelle' the only literary forms which he practised with success—his poetry was purely occasional and epigrammatic and possesses little merit—but in his dramas and in his prose writings themselves there is scant evidence of an interest in lyric values. . . . (p. 24)

Kleist's figures are engrossed in their own thoughts and feelings, they do not listen to the arguments of those with whom they are speaking. Hence their speeches often are not dialogues in the accepted sense of the term. His dramas at their climax frequently give an impression of presenting a series of self-contained, rather than inter-related exchanges of thought and feeling. (p. 25)

Another feature of Kleist's technique is revealed in his lack of attention to the material aspect of the dramatic plot. The physical events remain in the background of the action and our interest is primarily aroused by the spiritual condition of the characters and the emotional relations between them. (p. 28)

Kleist's principal consideration in fashioning his style was expressiveness. To this end he sacrificed the values which were of supreme importance for other poets—the enchanting epithet, the mellifluous phrase, the happy cadence—and he eschewed all forms of embellishment for its own sake. . . .

Kleist's passionate desire to be truthful accounts for the naturalistic elements in his work. Just as he did not conform to the view that it is the purpose of the tragedian's art to temper the emotions, but set out to give them the greatest intensity, so also he was impelled by the aim to express with utmost veracity and cogency and without suppression or modification, the thoughts and feelings within him. (p. 30)

Viewing together *Die Familie Schroffenstein, Amphitryon* and *Penthesilea* we arrive at the conclusion that the ultimate, if unacknowledged source of his pessimism, and thus the core of the motivation in his tragedies, is his conception of the attitude of God to man. . . . [In these plays God] is either indifferent to human suffering, or intervenes in human affairs to produce suffering. . . .

However, in *Penthesilea,* Kleist does not use this theme for the motivation of the whole tragedy as he did in earlier dramas, and indeed after completing this work he abandoned the writing of tragedies. His last three plays exhibit a more hopeful attitude to life. He never achieved a stable relationship with his fellow-men, but his distrust of human nature and of the powers that rule man's existence became less pronounced and gave way to a more optimistic outlook. (p. 32)

In his last plays, however, Kleist does not so much solve the tragic problems of his earlier dramas, as override them. . . . The outlook of the later dramas is simply the reversal of that displayed in the tragedies. . . .

Nor do the elements of his later belief form a consistent whole. The positive attitude to life revealed in *Käthchen von Heilbronn* is different from that displayed in *Die Hermannsschlacht* and both differ from *Prinz Friedrich von Homburg.* In the first play we observe a new attitude to the problem of the relation of God to man, hence a new estimate of human relationships, in the second drama Kleist's patriotic beliefs are expressed, in the last work we have a portrayal of human relationships without reference to the overruling problem of the nature of God and man. (p. 33)

The fundamental unity of Kleist's work, however, is revealed by the fact that [a] valuation of instinct does not appear for the first time in his later work. It is an essential feature of his tragic representations no less than the cardinal principle of his romantic drama. (p. 38)

Kleist's fundamentally critical temperament, however, did not allow him to base his philosophy of life permanently on the acceptance of a belief in the miraculous order of things. A more stable affirmation of the values of life is found only in *Prinz Friedrich von Homburg,* where the problem is no longer the relation between God and man, but that between the individual and the state. . . . Here Kleist reveals an astonishing sense of balance, in his psychological emphases as well as in his use of formal values. The metaphysical disorders of his youth reverberate only as faint echoes and the fanciful constructions of *Käthchen von Heilbronn* have been put aside. Those 'romantic' fancies had their educative value for Kleist, for, once achieved they made all further speculation on the subject of the ultimate nature of life unnecessary. (p. 39)

> *E. L. Stahl, in his* Heinrich von Kleist's Dramas *(©Basil Blackwell, 1961), revised edition, Basil Blackwell, 1961, 145 p.*

E. K. BENNETT (essay date 1961)

[The Novellen of Kleist] are not only in their objectivity, in the uncommented way in which they are presented, but also in their emotional intensity the work of a poet who is primarily a dramatist and not an epic writer; one whose business it is to stir the feelings of an audience by heightening his effects to the utmost. . . . [The home and origin of these Novellen] are in no sort of society whatever, but in solitude and anguish.

Nor can one imagine the sort of society in which they could be narrated as a form of entertainment.

This absence of the social element in Kleist's treatment of the Novelle is certainly partly due to the character and temperament of the author who was by nature as well as by force of circumstance a solitary man among his fellow beings. But actual political and social conditions must also be taken into account. All of the Novellen were written during the years in which the Napoleonic wars were destroying the fabric of an ordered society in Germany. (p. 38)

Kleist's Novellen—like Kleist himself—stand on the dividing line between classical and romantic. They still possess in their outward form something of the self-contained quality which is the characteristic of classical literature. In two of them at least, *Michael Kohlhaas* and *Die Marquise von O.,* the principal characters achieve a self-mastery, the attainment of which is the ethical problem in the classical works of Goethe and Schiller. But the world in which the action of all Kleist's stories is laid is no longer the world with secure foundations which Goethe and Schiller had constructed, but one whose foundations are floating in incomprehensibility. [The irrational] . . . is an element in the Novelle—the event as such, which strikes into the lives of the characters from without, is irrational. (p. 39)

[With Kleist the irrational element is] an expression of a fundamental quality of the universe: the faulty nature of the world—of the world as he experienced it, as a conflict of irreconcilable antitheses. What Kleist achieved for the development of the Novelle in respect of its content was not, as has been often said, that he made the tragic Novelle possible—already in Boccaccio there are tragic Novellen—but that he created the metaphysical Novelle. . . . The Novellen have the same quality of having burst inevitably out of Kleist's being as the dramas have and they present the same characteristics. One of these characteristics of all Kleist's work is the harshness of conflicting antitheses, which finds expression sometimes in the character of his persons, sometimes in the situation. It is a presentation by means of concrete examples of that inherent dualism of the universe of which the tragic dramatist is so acutely aware. (p. 40)

[The] Novelle in its original form might be said to provide something in the nature of a picture of actual life. Nothing of the sort, however, can be said of Kleist's Novellen. He makes the utmost use of the liberty accorded to the writer of Novellen to deal with the strange, the unusual, the extraordinary. Earthquakes, war, revolution, murder, rape—these are the aspects of life which he presents. But though such events may be regarded as exceptional and abnormal from the point of view of the ordered bourgeois existence with which the Novelle had hitherto concerned itself—uncharacteristic events—in the world of Kleist's imagination they are symbols and typical expressions of the cleavage and internecine strife in the universe as it appeared to him. In this respect again the tragic dramatist reveals himself, for the tragic dramatist, as Hebbel points out, has specifically to deal with the abnormal conditions of life. (pp. 41-2)

The word monstrous which has been used to describe the events which occur in Kleist's Novellen seems to be the most suitable one to designate with him that element of the 'unusual' which is an essential in all Novellen. Under the pressure of events surpassing their comprehension or power of credibility the characters of Kleist, who in themselves are in no way striking or out of the ordinary, develop a greatness or force which gives them a monumental quality, transforms them into exceptional beings. (p. 44)

The idea of the Novelle as a form of social entertainment is entirely discarded, and with it the sense of a narrator who is present and narrates to a society of his equals. The Novellen of Kleist come like a voice out of the void and re-echo into emptiness.

The subject matter is shifted from the contemporary and familiar (sublimated gossip) into an exotic distance of place or time. It has certainly in itself interest and power to hold the attention of the reader, but its specific quality is due to the fact that the incident in every case serves as an illustration of the metaphysical problem of Kleist's relation to the universe, which is basically that of an agonized questioning and seeking for certainty. Thus all the characters are faced with problems which shake their credibility and faith in their world order to the utmost. . . . The irrational element, which is an essential of the Novelle, is no longer the equivalent of chance, as revealed in the event, but is conceived as the incomprehensible, irresponsible forces of the universe, which break into the ordered life of man and shake his faith in existence. (pp. 44-5)

> *E. K. Bennett, "The Metaphysical Novelle: Kleist," in his* A History of the German Novelle, *edited by H. M. Waidson, second edition, Cambridge University Press, 1961 (and reprinted by Cambridge University Press, 1965), pp. 37-46.*

WALTER SILZ   (essay date 1962)

Über das Marionettentheater is not the epitome of Kleist's wisdom on life and literature, but a *geistreiches Feuilleton;* an occasional essay for a newspaper, not a flawless and perdurable edifice of aesthetic theory. . . .

The popular character and intent of the piece are evident in its very form. Contrary to Kleist's usual style, in his major narratives, it is broken up into many brief paragraphs of short, uncomplicated sentences. (p. 71)

[Discrepancies soon become evident in the essay.] To begin with a practical consideration: one finds it difficult to visualize the mechanism of Kleist's puppets, and one wonders whether he wrote on the basis of observation or of sheer imagination. (p. 73)

On closer view, the professional reality of Kleist's puppets appears indeed suspect. Near the beginning of the conversation, the author-interlocutor asks Mr. C. how it is possible to govern the dolls without having a myriad strings in one's hands, and Mr. C. assures him that it is by no means necessary to control the individual limbs, but only the *Schwerpunkt der Bewegung* [center of motion] in the interior of the figure; when this is moved, the limbs, being mere pendulums, follow mechanically, by gravity. . . . In any case, meaningful dance movement, to say nothing of expressive dramatic action, could hardly be achieved by dolls attached to single wires, with limbs dangling and incapable of individual motion. (pp. 73-4)

The impressive-sounding dictum on which the essay ends, when we look at it more closely, is not wholly convincing. If eating of the tree of knowledge got us into trouble, eating of it *again* will hardly get us out. A second eating, as any boy who has indulged in unripe apples knows, does not undo the first eating, but adds to its unhappy effects. The only logical and physiological reversal of eating is regurgitation. Furthermore, no amount of retrogression will ever restore us to being puppets, because

we never *were* puppets. The marionette is not the most primitive stage of humanity, at the opposite extreme from the god: it is a human artifact, indeed a product of a comparatively advanced stage of human development.

But even *geschichtsphilosophisch betrachtet,* return to a state of innocence is impossible: we cannot go back home. Hence, this essay, which has been taken to voice an optimistic philosophy of civilization, ends in fact on a hopeless note. (p. 79)

[In "**Über das Marionettentheater**"] Kleist is coping with a fundamental antinomy of human nature: the contradiction between our inborn desire for the primitive and unknowing and our equally inborn desire to know more and more. (p. 80)

Kleist felt a recurrent longing for a life free from mental demands and complications. For this longing he found various symbols: the simple man of unquestioning faith whom he observed and envied in the Catholic church in Dresden; the peasant secure at the motherly bosom of Nature, such as he hoped to become in Switzerland; the carpenter in Koblenz whom he wanted to work for. (p. 81)

The marionette may be taken as one more symbol—and, as it proved, the last one—for this craving for peace, for relief from mental pressure, for uncomplicated self-fulfillment. But the marionette is not, it seems to me, the happiest symbol Kleist might have chosen, and that is one more difficulty about his essay. This symbol involves an inevitable antinomy in Kleist's mind. In his early letters, he declared himself aghast at the idea of being *eine Puppe am Drahte des Schicksals*—better by far to be dead. In his first play, too, the puppet concept has a pejorative value. Yet in the essay the marionette is held up as something man should envy and emulate. That Kleist was aware of the fallacy in this is perhaps betrayed by the interlocutor's humorous thought that the puppets should not be given credit for not erring when they do not have the capacity to err. . . . The marionette, being a thing without consciousness, volition, or thought, cannot seriously serve as a model for man, whose problem is precisely that he *has* those capacities. (pp. 81-2)

Kleist's own Käthchen, almost invariably cited as the best personification of his ideal, is a much less satisfactory embodiment [of the puppet], for in her case the question is begged by the superhuman agencies of the fairy tale. And Prinz Friedrich, sometimes nominated as the ideal "puppet," cannot be characterized by such a simple tag. (pp. 82-3)

It is perhaps a symptom of the lack of compelling logic in the essay that one can imagine it, written in a different mood and with a slight change of emphasis, reaching a quite different conclusion. Kleist could equally well have chosen to emphasize the puppeteer instead of the puppets. Instead of showing that grace is unattainable to man, he might then have shown what grace man, committed as he is to consciousness and intellect, can still attain through his puppets, his instruments, the work of his hand and brain. . . . It is idle to argue about the consciousness or unconsciousness of the puppets. The only consciousness they can possibly express is that of the person who works their strings. The very simplicity of the instrument poses a challenge to the expressive powers of the modern mind. (pp. 83-4)

The very capacity to delight in the primitive or mindless is a prerogative of thinking man. The ocean wave has no consciousness; it is the product of physical forces; its beauty and grace are not *its* achievement but a mental experience of the human observer. (p. 84)

The very fact that one is stimulated to enlarge on Kleist's essay in this manner is perhaps a further indication of its character: it is . . . full of ideas, if not of flawless reasoning; lively, *fesselnd* [enthralling], provocative of thought and also of contradiction—in short, if left and judged in its minor genre, a highly successful performance. But it is not a reasoned treatise yielding a formula applicable to the whole of Kleist. (p. 85)

Walter Silz, in his Heinrich von Kleist: Studies in His Works and Literary Character *(© 1961 by the Trustees of the University of Pennsylvania), University of Pennsylvania Press, 1962, 313 p.*

SIGURD BURCKHARDT   (essay date 1964)

Prussia's sense of order was Hobbesian, a desperately functional shoring against chaos. The prose of its political habitus was no self-denying ordinance; it claimed to be the last word, the definitive proposition. Like its army, it was so fully and tautly articulated that it seemed to leave no room for spontaneous communion and free creativity. Into this Prussia Kleist was born. . . . He could not rebel in the name of a higher patriotism—to restore his fatherland to its true self. Prussia *was* itself, the state *an sich* as it were, the very thing he was rebelling against. Thus the question of a higher legitimacy—in the name of what do I rebel?—assumed for him from the start an extraordinary bareness and urgency. (p. 103)

[The] ideas and ideals of his time stood ready to furnish Kleist with an answer to his question; the great legitimator of rebellion was Nature. For a brief space he thought the answer would do. He had only to believe that Nature was innocent and existing society unjust, that simple men were noble and benevolent—in short, that the Fall was reversible. In one of his earliest stories—"**The Earthquake in Chile**"—he shows how the destruction of a merciless, petrified order releases men, now stripped of law and rank and prejudice, to join in natural fellowship and harmony. But even in this story the end is tragic; it turns out that the shattering of the order releases not only benevolence but likewise fear and brutal unreason. . . .

[What] is unusual even here is that Kleist measures the order, not so much by a higher order, whether natural or divine, but by its capacity, or incapacity, or *inclusion*. Morally, the element before which the order breaks is a pitiful and disreputable datum: an illegitimate child. With this story, illegitimacy becomes one of Kleist's major motifs. But unlike many of his contemporaries, he does not celebrate it as an assertion of nature over artificiality and convention; he uses it, in what I will call a characteristically Prussian manner, to test the orders men live by.

What is order? There are those—Goethe was perhaps their last great spokesman—for whom it is the outer expression of an inner harmony, something that is generated rather than imposed. But there are others—more numerous and, I fear, more modern—for whom order is a construct, moral, legal, or conceptual, which divides the world of phenomena into an inside and an outside, which purchases intelligibility at the cost of inclusiveness, coherence at the cost of relevance. This kind of order is wholly explicit and tends to justify itself by the tautological perfection of its interior workings. (p. 104)

To seek refuge in such an order, to condemn in oneself and others what the order defines as irrational and illegitimate, is a great temptation. No man can live for long in chaos, a rebel without a cause; and where he has no higher order to appeal to, he must, it seems, succumb to the positive and explicit one, which rewards his submission by assigning him a place and a role. There are many who make this submission with a mental reservation, who cling to the sentimental belief that there is a public sphere and a private one, who learn to split their individuality and their moral responsibility, until finally as men they can grow roses while as functionaries they run concentration camps. But there are others, though few, who will not recant, with or without mental reservation, but will keep faith with the inchoate and incomprehensible stirrings within them. Of these Kleist was one.

It was, he found, his art that was illegitimate; the words, images, and tales he felt himself unaccountably pregnant with were offensive and disorderly in an order that was, within its own terms, definitive and complete. And so he shaped a style and a series of great fables which are unmistakably his own and have, nevertheless, an authoritative impersonality. . . . [In the "**Marquise von O.**", the descent from the sphere of classical and religious myth] to the level of prose and ordinary reality is Kleist's decisive step, for it forces his characters to find *within themselves* the strength to defend their inner truth against the legitimate claims of the establishment. The Marquise's pregnancy seems to defy reason as well as morality; it is an inexplicable novum, which everyone tries his utmost to deny and ignore, until at last it can be ignored no longer. At that point the pressure to recant and repent becomes almost irresistible; the order puts all its vast authority into the effort to sustain itself, to compel submission. But at the decisive moment the Marquise does not break; she stands by the reality within her and submits only, to quote Kleist, "to the great, holy and inexplicable scheme of things." Because she does so and at the same time honors the claims of legitimacy enough to wish to find her child's father and to marry him, she succeeds in solving the mystery and in establishing a truer, *i.e.* more encompassing order. (pp. 105-06)

What Kleist does is to call into question the easy rationality of the classical sentence, which gains its victories by keeping out unfitting detail—the streaks of the tulip that Samuel Johnson forbade the artist to paint. What the rational order—which claims to be "natural" but in fact is as positive as Prussia—proscribes as illegitimate, accidental, and irrelevant, Kleist forges into a larger, tenser structuring. He does so, not with the naturalist's comfortable faith that out of accumulation order will somehow arise, but from the positivist's knowledge that there can be no truth without order, yet that every order stands under the judgment of what it can*not* admit.

But self-vindication, however impersonal and unsentimental, was not enough for Kleist. As a poet he was bound to aspire to being a founder of unions in his own right, to perform what Shakespeare calls "the marriage of true minds," independent of, even in opposition to the social order. . . . [He] took the classical test case—the Romeo-and-Juliet situation—and divested it of its consoling elements. Shakespeare had shown the way when he made his lovers re-enact their story in the guise of Troilus and Cressida and watched with bitter cynicism how a love that is buttressed by nothing but private faith and feeling turns into betrayal. (p. 106)

It is easy to interpret [*Penthesilea*], and much else in Kleist, as evidence of a deep psychic disturbance, an obsessive sado-masochism. But such an interpretation misses the essential point: that the play is a test, arranged with a scientist's cunning guard against specious solutions. Unsupported by any common order—of thought or custom or law—what promised to be the sweetest fulfilment turns into the most savage tragedy. . . . As Achilles lies mutilated and Penthesilea is killed by the comprehension of what she has done, the *tertius ridens* appears to be the authority Kleist had desperately tried to prove superfluous—Prussia.

But before I pass beyond this tragic failure, let me stress once more that its being a failure is its greatness. Kleist did not pride himself on his "tragic sense of life," did not try to provide us the inhuman satisfaction of being able to look unflinching into the face of horror. (p. 107)

Kleist painfully discovered that as a poet he could not escape from the state, any more than man could; that man is a political animal, and if the political is subtracted only the animal is left. . . .

To poetize Prussia—to dissolve its explicit, denotative outlines in the soft focus of patriotic feeling, to give the harsh rectangularity of its matrix the gentler curvature of a womb—this must have seemed to Kleist a very seductive way out of his dilemma. (p. 108)

Kleist now set himself to writing what he called a patriotic drama, which he intended as his last word and testament as a poet and a Prussian. The play, *The Prince of Homburg,* celebrates the victory won by the Great Elector over the invading Swedes in the battle of Fehrbellin. . . .

The subsequent fate of this play is in the highest degree ironic; it is hardly too much to say that by its gradual acceptance on the German stage we can measure the progress of a creeping political malaise. . . . It was interpreted to show that the individual, acting in arrogant reliance on his private judgment, is bound to fall, but that the state, personified in the Elector can reclaim him by wise pedagogic management. By judicious dosages of power and manipulation, the erring individual can be made to acknowledge the state's overriding claims; by a genuine inner acceptance of his fault and the state's justice, he can regain grace and reinstatement. There was, in fact, greater rejoicing over one reclaimed sinner than over a hundred of the just.

The religious analogy underlying this interpretation is obvious; and it means that the divine and the political orders have become one. (p. 109)

There can be no question that Kleist himself saw the Prince's fate under the aspect of the archetypal drama of man's fall and redemption—nor that he saw the state as an ultimate order, with no possibility of appeal to a higher jurisdiction. But what this meant to him was not that the state had to be deified so as to provide man with an *ersatz* heaven, but that the divine order had become secularized. . . .

The remarkable thing about Kleist's play is that it does not in any way soften the rigor of this polar opposition but on the contrary increases it. More and more, ruler and subject withdraw from each other until at the climax the subject is *mere* man, stripped of all the dignity and dignities society has to give, while the ruler has retreated into the order, a wholly impersonal embodiment of the law. The spheres no longer touch each other.

The moment has come, it would seem, for either tragedy or compromise. But Kleist gives us neither. When the Elector is made aware of the total irrelevance of the absolute order to the absolute individual, he abdicates. (p. 110)

[The Prince] has no divine warranty; his inner voice was not infallible but has led him into an act which, by the only possible criterion—the law—must be defined as a crime. (p. 111)

But when he gets the Elector's note, his situation becomes still more confusing: he is put into the strange position of being whatever he *says* he is. . . . Since whatever he says becomes true by his saying it, to say that he is innocent is nothing more than if he said: "I am that I am"—an empty tautology.

Thus, at this moment two tautologies face each other, self-referential, without meaning each for the other: the absolute law and the sovereign individual. . . . He would encapsule himself in an unchallengeable emptiness, without reference or relation. He would, to put it differently, be a Poet, with a capital P, the kind whose utterances do not mean but are. This, then, would be one way out of Kleist's dilemma: to become a "pure" Poet.

If, on the other hand, Homburg pronounces himself guilty, his judgment merely endorses that of the law; his voice and the state's will be one, and he signs his death warrant, not merely in the sense that he is killed, but that he confirms the law in *its* self-defining perfection. (pp. 111-12)

But in this seemingly hopeless dilemma the Prince does keep hold of one saving fact: that, like Socrates, he has been addressed and asked to reply. . . . He has no God to speak for; he can speak only in his own name. But he speaks *to* some one, and though he does not surrender to the state, he does deliver himself over, as every true speaker does, to the man he answers. . . .

It is his sovereign utterance because he has chosen to speak, freely and truly, rather than let himself be enslaved by the deadly alternative of absolutes.

[He] has also spoken to some purpose. True speech is between men, and by his answer he has freed the Elector, who, in fear of destroying the state, had retreated behind the gates of the law. (p. 112)

The first risk and action the Elector takes is the tearing up of the death sentence. He can take the risk now, not because the Prince has contritely acknowledged the necessity of absolute obedience—learned his Prussian lesson, in other words—but because he has demonstrated that where there is no divine law to fall back on, the burden of order need not be carried entirely by the state's positive law. Autonomous man can bear his share and yet not diminish the order's authority but rather increase it. While God can be merciful because He is omnipotent, the secular power can grant mercy because the risk rests not on it alone. Nor need law assume the certainty of self-definition, because where there is meaning, ambiguity can be chanced. (p. 113)

Sigurd Burckhardt, "Heinrich von Kleist: The Poet As Prussian," in The Centennial Review *(© 1964 by* The Centennial Review*), Vol. VIII, 1964 (and reprinted in his* The Drama of Language: Essays on Goethe and Kleist, *Johns Hopkins Press, 1970, pp. 101-15).*

HANS JOACHIM SCHRIMPF   (essay date 1966)

Kleist's inner tragedy is his shattering awareness of the basic contradiction of life: the irreconcilable paradox of a world relentlessly deceiving mankind and the human need for certainty and incontrovertible truth. Knowledge, science, social institutions, even the most personal relationships prove unreliable. They entice and deceive the individual who seeks refuge in them, loses himself in them, and ultimately sees himself deprived of his individuality. Kleist calls this the "infirm world" (die gebrechliche Einrichtung der Welt), in which he finds the unique "feeling" of the individual soul to be the only fixed and absolute value. He struggles to restore and preserve a last certainty. As a dramatist he envisions the ultimate tragedy when this last value: *self-assurance*, is jeopardized by inescapable reality. . . .

All of Kleist's literary production in the tragic vein, his dramas and his Novellen alike, represents a desperate attempt to liberate the true being of man, that special inner self, from a reality which is hostile and antagonistic. For this reason a strange discordance and inconsistency is found throughout his work, which is sometimes strident and violent, sometimes delicate and dreamily graceful. (p. 195)

What Kleist's dramatic productions—as well as his Novellen—from the *Schroffensteiner* to the *Prinz von Homburg* depict and what determines their dramatic structure is the presentation, at once realistic and visionary, of the extreme test of man as a human being and as an individual in exceptional situations. These are existentially revealing tests, in which finally a connection is established between reality and the human soul, involving unconditional decisions and unfailing deference to inviolable sensitivity. In Kleist's dramas the way to such a revelation, in which man gains a new and deeper knowledge of his real, self-determined existence, usually leads through a tormenting condition of dissociation from the self and extreme schism and inner torment. . . .

In *Die Familie Schroffenstein* the destructive madness of two families, brought on by insidious and misleading circumstances, produces the rupture of consciousness and the horror. Although innocent, both families are driven ever more deeply into a state of deadly hatred, ruining one another in their blind fury. (p. 197)

In *Penthesilea* too Kleist depicts the tragic disintegration of man, the splitting of consciousness as a result of conflict between the individual soul and reality. Again it is love, unconditional love, which is sacrificed to relativity, being subjected to an investigation into its right to exist. (p. 198)

The examination to which Kleist's characters are subjected in many situations in order to elicit a hidden truth from them as if putting them on the rack to extract it from them—this is the basic pattern of his dramatic technique. (p. 199)

The fearful and oppressive elements in the characters and in the comical contrasts always become more apparent when the total analytical development is more prominent and the plot thickens. At such moments, anxiety combines with laughter, choking us. . . . In Kleist's tragedy it is always the beauty of the human soul, the mystery of pure unconsciousness, that stands forth in tragic circumstances. In *Der zerbrochene Krug* such a factor is lacking. In place of destruction—we are dealing, of course, with a comedy—we have scandal and unavoidable humiliation. It is only possible to comprehend that tormenting, oppressive gloom when reality breaks down, when it begins to be deceptive, merciless, and sinister, when we lose the ground from under our feet—as Kleist once said of himself in a letter—and for this only *one* stylistic category seems suitable—namely the Grotesque. (pp. 202-03)

In Kleist's play the grotesque element is present, for example, in the cold mechanics of the court proceedings, which take on

a life of their own, and in the fine net that closes in more and more tightly around Adam. . . .

The grotesque features in this comedy are found not only in the plot and in the characters, but also in individual gestures and in stylistic elements; for instance, deformed humanity as such is grotesque. (p. 203)

[In *Amphitryon*] Kleist makes out of Molière's social comedy about a deceived husband—at least in essence—a tragic drama about a problem of human identity. What Goethe calls confusion of the emotions is precisely the crucial point, the point of departure from which this playwright makes the characteristic turn to the tragic. (p. 205)

[In contrast to Molière's treatment of the play, Kleist's *Amphitryon* deals] not with society and its rules but with the loneliness of the individual soul and with the identity of the self. For Kleist, Alkmene's "fall" is faithfulness *in* unfaithfulness, vindication *in* failure, and self-possession *in* self-alienation. As Adam, the village judge, stumbles into the fall of man, Alkmene stumbles into the precincts of the divine. (p. 206)

[The] realms of the comic and the tragic do not fuse into a tragicomic effect, but rather alternate, and hence contrast sharply with one another.

Two spheres—that of primitive, sensual, earthy comedy and that of more profound and mysterious solemnity illuminated by heaven—are woven together here: the lowest and the highest, creature-like existence (typical), and the most sublime (individual) feeling, but both are essentially human. . . .

It must not be overlooked that the tormenting examination of Alkmene appears tragic from a human perspective only, and that the same happening, viewed from Olympus, appears like a gay experiment, a game of the gods, although a dangerous one. Kleist has included this perspective also in his work. As we have understood *Der zerbrochene Krug* to be pure comedy, but in the spirit of the grotesque, so we may in closing say of *Amphitryon* that the playwright here depicts a tragic comedy, in which human tragedy and divine comedy synchronize in an astounding manner. (p. 208)

Hans Joachim Schrimpf, "Tragedy and Comedy in the Works of Heinrich von Kleist," in Monatshefte *(copyright © 1966 by The Board of Regents of the University of Wisconsin System), Vol. LXIII, No. 3, 1966, pp. 193-208.*

JAMES M. McGLATHERY (essay date 1967)

[Kleist's dialogue in *Über das Marionettentheater*] is less a commentary on human destiny than an expression of a death wish and . . . the puppet dance described by Herr C— is a dance of the dead, not of the living. (p. 325)

In his letters Kleist speaks disparagingly of the great mass of people who are content to live like puppets suspended from the thread of fate . . . yet Herr C— praises his puppets as worthy of emulation. Obviously, Herr C— values gracefulness above free will, or rather he is able to imagine a situation in which destiny and free will are no longer in conflict. In an absolute sense, this requirement can be fulfilled only in death. Kleist's choice of the puppet image further reinforces this conclusion, if we view the allegory from the perspective of tradition. Virtues conventionally are personified by artistic representations of living beings. Only Death is personified by a copy of the lifeless human form. Herr C—'s puppets, then, may personify Death as well as Grace, and the dancing of the puppets may be explained as a mystical rejoicing over the marriage of the soul to God in death. (pp. 326-27)

There is an element of cunning in Herr C—'s gospel of salvation through puppetry. Herr C—is willing to sacrifice intellect in order to gain paradise, but as a descendant of Adam he is unable to give up the dream of becoming God's equal. For this reason, he envisions the ideal relation between puppet and puppeteer as a mystical union. If man sacrifices his intellect, God will no longer need to sit in judgment on him. (pp. 327-28)

If Herr C—really believed that his dream of an ideal puppet theatre held the key to human happiness, we would expect him to seek out a forum for the promulgation of his ideas. Quite the contrary. It is left to the narrator, who is characterized as something of a busybody, to remark on Herr C—'s visit to the puppet theatre. This would seem a golden opportunity for Herr C— to discuss a favourite subject, yet he is perfectly willing to let the narrator pursue the topic or to drop it, as he sees fit. It is significant that the narrator provides most of the impetus in the discussion by raising the important questions about the mechanics involved in the manipulation of puppets, the role of the puppeteer, the degree of intellect required on his part, and the advantage which puppets have over human dancers. (p. 329)

[Although] Herr C— is obviously the exponent of profound Kleistian ideas in the dialogue, Kleist identifies himself with the narrator by signing [the essay] 'H. v. K.'. . . This is, of course, only a mask. The narrator is the sort of philosophical idealist and pedant we find often in Kleist's letters. . . . Kleist no doubt both resented the necessity of the mask and delighted in his skill at such masquerading. He takes final revenge on this enforced *alter ego* in *Über das Marionettentheater*. The dialogue is conceived as an ironic self-mystification. We are treated to a tragi-comic confrontation of the real Kleist, the cynical psychologist, with the naive idealist. (p. 330)

> *James M. McGlathery, ''Kleist's 'Über das Marionettentheater','' in* German Life & Letters, *Vol. XX, No. 4, July, 1967, pp. 325-31.*

JOHN GEAREY (essay date 1968)

[There] has been a tendency to regard Kleist as typical of the poet whose personal problems distort his view of things and whose works, therefore, though important to an understanding of his life and thought, can hardly lay claim to truly great significance as art. But the matter is not nearly so simple. It was not that Kleist really lacked the wisdom necessary to a clear understanding of man and the human situation, nor that he always encountered the tragic things in life, but that he actually acquired much of the general knowledge given to his time and place, and yet could not quite use it, that he often experienced what might be called the right things, and yet, ironically, at the wrong time. (p. 189)

He was not, of course, the only writer of the period who had read Kant, nor was he alone in his deep concern with the implications of Kant's critical theories. The question of knowledge, of seeming and being, had already been faced, and in part answered, in the preceding generation, and was being analysed in a new light in his own, both in philosophy and in literature. . . . There were in the air, one might say, as many plausible answers to the problem of knowledge as there were

puzzling questions; and apparently Kleist knew of these answers.

Not that he was necessarily directly acquainted with all the ideas of his contemporaries, nor was he trained in philosophical thinking. But he had experienced the same intellectual event, the dethroning of Reason, and was responding in a similar fashion, more frantically than they, it is true, but then with all the more dispatch. He seems to have thought out, within a surprisingly short span of time, virtually all the alternatives to the Kantian critical position which the older and the younger generation had adopted, and to a reexamination of which he himself was later to return. Into his first drama, *Die Familie Schroffenstein,* went not only the tragic insights born of the recognition of the limitations of human understanding, but also the rudiments of his positive and prolonged reaction to this recognition. Even in this early work, conceived immediately after the crisis in his thought, he was already attempting, like Schiller before him, to trace the causes and ingredients of tragic delusion to the character or temperament of the individual, for example, Rupert, rather than to a basic flaw in the nature of man; and though the counter-argument to this moral approach is also presented in the play, and with equal force, it cannot be said that Kleist was unaware of the former possibility, particularly when we recall that in *Michael Kohlhaas* and *Penthesilea* he was to resume the question of the relationship of character to fate. . . . [Though] he had definite reservations concerning the validity of this spontaneous spiritual urge as a guide to truth, he could never bring himself to reject it completely. . . . [If] Kleist was indeed attempting to justify faith in feeling despite the facts of immediate existence, then he was already ranging in thought beyond Schiller toward that more extreme idealistic philosophy of Fichte's in which the individual was regarded as a world or reality or law unto himself. . . . [There] was hardly a philosophical, moral, or existential approach to the problem of knowledge of which he was not aware, and at a relatively early stage in his development.

But these various concepts, attitudes, and beliefs which were serving his contemporaries in different ways as tolerable, if not always ideal, solutions to the questions that Kant had raised, were of little actual or lasting value to Kleist. His problem, first of all, was not the same as theirs. . . . [The] conscious elements in his thinking represented only one level or aspect of the views he held. Often what he said and believed, or had the characters in his works say and believe, was not a direct and reliable index of his deeper sense of life. Rather, it was only another symptom or indirect reflection of his struggle to resolve the conflicts inherent in his underlying thought or, to speak in terms of his art, in the fictional situations he created. And just as this underlying pattern tended in the early period to undermine his professed belief in the essential order and justice in the universe, and in the period of revolution colored his interpretation of Kant, so, too, in the extended period of reaction, it led him again and again hastily to accept principles or adopt attitudes which, like his former enlightened views, would seem to offer solutions to his problems but would prove either incompatible with his basic presuppositions or, if logically compatible with them, emotionally untenable under their strain. It was a constant accepting, rejecting, and reexamining. (pp. 189-92)

The contradictions and injustice in the world which, since the essay on happiness, he had regarded as typical of life, as the *facts* of existence, would leave little hope, once the trust in the infallibility of reason had been destroyed, for any kind of constant, secure, and meaningful good fortune, regardless of one's attitude. . . . [In the end] he arrived not at a brighter solution, not at the ultimately consoling, since metaphysically justifiable, concept that there was after all a personal moral deficiency in his tragic figure which had caused his fall, but at a profound insight into the paradoxical nature of a world in which the very strength and purity of an individual's ideals stood in almost inverse proportion to true happiness; where an unfailing sense of justice could logically lead to disorder and crime. Kleist may have been intellectually indebted to Schiller for some of his positive moral precepts, and even have proposed them, as in *Der Zweikampf* and *Die Verlobung in St. Domingo,* as directing principles in life, but ultimately he could not integrate them into his own world view without altering, which could hardly be expected, his whole way of thought. (pp. 192-93)

Because he differed in thought from his contemporaries, he differed in his art even more. He was the realist of his literary generation, but a realist of a separate order. One does not easily guess at the beginning of his dramas and stories how they will end. Bent as he was on emphasizing the fortuitous and puzzling nature of reality, he tended to choose as a base for his works the very type of situation which would almost defy conjecture as to the probable course of its development. If other realists were concerned in their art with those factors in human experience which reflect the laws of natural and inevitable cause and effect, he, not only unlike them but directly opposed to them, preferred to deal with the exceptional, the unheard-of, the event which by virtue of its occurrence subverts rather than confirms our sense of order in the objective world. In fact, the problem in many of his works, we said, is simply that his characters do not know this. They are continually attributing a reasonable or meaningful cause to what is actually a chance effect and, reacting accordingly, are ultimately confronted with realities which contradict their assumptions and anticipations, or, in more drastic cases, their firmest hopes and beliefs. We have bewildered heroes who have been blessed by fate, and disillusioned heroes who have been wronged, but we do not have, with the exception of Kohlhaas and Penthesilea, "tragic" figures who through their own failings or even ideals set in motion a series of events the relentless workings of which they are powerless to stop. Such figures belong to a literature of inevitability, a literature in which one is aware of the basic force of necessity behind any apparent disorder. Kleist's characters live in an essentially hazardous fictional world, and the events that occur in it are, as often as not, the sort which, despite the seemingly logical or plausible nature of their occurring, leave one with the feeling that they should *not* have occurred. (pp. 193-94)

But there is a logic behind the sequence of events that forms the reality in his dramas and stories. Kleist was not simply giving vent to his unconscious anxieties by emphasizing in his art the frustrating aspects of human experience. If he was doing that in part, he was also endeavoring, like any other artist, to understand, objectify, and transcend his subjective sense of things. (p. 194)

[However, whether] or not he could find in contemporary thought, and in the realm of his own experience, logical reasons and tangible examples to support his assumption of the prevalence of disorder in the world, he had still as an artist to meet the demand of giving a poetic order to the content of his works. It was a difficult task: witness the failure of the majority of his contemporaries to create realistically convincing expres-

sions of their new feeling for life. Kant's critical thought, on which Kleist and the younger generation as a whole based their view of the world, had not only challenged in philosophy the formerly unchallenged presupposition of an underlying purpose in creation, it had also made questionable in literature the long-established Aristotelian principles of probability, verisimilitude, and cause and effect, all of which, if not founded directly on rationalism, were at least parallels in aesthetics to it. . . . But how was the poet who, like Kleist, saw in the empirical world not the reflection of eternal design but the clear suggestion of the fortuitousness of things, to adhere to artistic precepts which were unrelated and even opposed to his views? And if he did not, to what was he to turn? (pp. 195-96)

The fate dramatists of the early nineteenth century . . . whom Kleist overall most resembles, though they deliberately avoided introducing purely fantastic elements into their works, still emphasized the weird and portentous to such an extent that their "realism" was soon lost in a haze of symbols and dark moods. Kleist, however, attempted to make a more natural poetic order out of disorder, to work out the dream or, in its tragic form, the nightmare of life in the broad light of day.

He accomplished this in a way both unique and yet wholly in keeping with his view of reality. [The] unheard-of event, the trick of fate, the chance happening are not the only, or even the most important factors he employs to create the sensation in his art of the baffling nature of experience. Such factors represent rather the coming to a head of a series of contradictions and oppositions subtly but consistently woven into the texture of his narratives or the scene-to-scene action of his plays. When at the end of *Die Familie Schroffenstein, Die Verlobung in St. Domingo, Amphitryon,* or *Das Erdbeben in Chili*—to mention only the most striking examples—a reality abruptly arises to strike down the aspirations or anticipations of the characters involved, it marks only the dramatic eruption of a force already exerting itself in a less acute way in the constant jarring of minor factors and feelings. For it is more than mere confusion that reigns in this world, it is an almost methodical contrariness of things. It is true that even when we recognize the method in this seemingly disordered world of contradiction and adversity, and are aware of the consistent creative impulse guiding the course of events, we will still be left with the impression of a perverse occurring of things which we feel emotionally and intellectually should not have occurred. But that is precisely the author's intent, and it is precisely what the characters themselves, of course, are continually experiencing at all levels of thought and feeling. So persistent, in fact, is this pattern of opposites and oppositions that once we become aware of it, we begin to read this new type of tragic realism in that peculiar state of mind which one otherwise only experiences in comedy, where one no longer awaits the inevitable but begins actually to expect the unexpected. And so seldom does Kleist fail us in this respect that we might say that it is here, perhaps, if anywhere, that we come closest to understanding both the deeper laws of his artistic creation and the deeper origins of his view of life. (pp. 196-97)

> *John Gearey, in his* Heinrich von Kleist: A Study in Tragedy and Anxiety, *University of Pennsylvania Press, 1968, 202 p.*

DONALD H. CROSBY (essay date 1969)

In reading *Penthesilea* . . . we are compelled to think on two levels; one purely descriptive, often lying wholly within an unrealistic framework, the other purely psychological, the human or realistic plane of the drama. . . .

The equation of overwrought sexual passion with madness—or more accurately the equation of lack of sexual inhibition with temporary madness—an equation which is clearly justifiable within accepted norms of human behavior—is one of the basic themes of the drama, indeed one having almost the character of a *leitmotif*. (p. 6)

Within the context of the drama, Penthesilea's near-cannibalistic attack on Achilles is not an act of hatred at all, but rather the climax of a passion no longer expressible within accepted norms of behavior. Kneeling next to her dogs, vying with them in ferocity, Penthesilea is less a mortal woman than a manifestation of the archetypal feminine, the earth mother who tries to incorporate her mate. Having carefully shaped Penthesilea's love for Achilles into an emotion of cosmic dimensions and of elemental intensity, Kleist doubtless intended his conclusion as its psychological and structural counterweight. Literally attacking the beloved with tooth and nail is, of course, perverse by all accepted norms of behavior, but at the same time the act must be judged in the light of the author's intentions. Given the intensity of Penthesilea's love for Achilles, given Kleist's elevation of her beyond mere womanhood into a feminine principle, Penthesilea's orgiastic attack on Achilles is the logical-psychological consequence of her total commitment, her total surrender of self to the Greek hero. Even removed from the context of the play, Penthesilea's attack on the body of Achilles retains a certain proximity to accepted sexual norms—to what one might call the healthy temporary derangement of sexual excitement present in so-called "normal" sexual behavior patterns. (p. 8)

Unlike the drama *Penthesilea,* in which . . . the realism of the play lies wholly apart from the plot, Kleist's novella *Die Marquise von O* . . . remains within the sphere of a fairly consistent realism; and yet it may be argued that what is most realistic in this work, too, is precisely that which is *not* explained but which operates on the psychology of both characters and readers alike. (p. 9)

[It] is clear that Kleist's realism is limited by a strong mixture of coincidence and contrivance, and that any number of events in the tale—especially the "central event," the Count's furtive rape of the Marquise—could not stand up to a strict definition of realism. More relevant to this investigation, however, are certain scenes in the novella which, on a purely literal level, *seem* unrealistic but upon closer study reveal a higher—or more accurately—a psychological realism. The first of these is not, strictly speaking, a scene at all, but only a mark of punctuation, a mere dash, set in the story just after Count F . . . had rescued the Marquise from the would-be rapists. . . . [To] exclude what is obviously the most important event of the story, the Count's rape of the unconscious Marquise; to censor this action and to substitute for it an utterly mute, barely visible punctuation mark is, of course, in one sense the very negation of realism. Yet at the same time this device is the key to a psychological realism far more vivid than any description may have been able to supply. For gradually, as the story progresses and the clues to the identity of the unknown father mount up, the reader is forced mentally to return to that dash in the text, as it were, and to think out for himself the scene of the Count's rape of the Marquise. . . . (p. 10)

[The] foolhardy bravery of the Count helps unravel the complicated psychological motivation of the crime itself, for the Count's actions make it clear that his very masculinity has been his undoing. His excessive virility—the word for which in several languages is identical with that for courage—was in large part responsible for the outrage that took place under the cover of the dash earlier in the text. (p. 11)

In order to maintain the "inner" tension of the novella—that is, to maintain the Marquise's ignorance of what the reader already knows—Kleist had to contrive to keep his heroine from guessing the truth about Count F . . . until the end of the story. On the conscious level, at least, the Marquise in fact does not connect the Count's importunate proposals of marriage with his "rescue" of her some months earlier until he makes his dramatic entrance in the closing pages of the novella—this despite numerous "hints," especially that of the swan-anecdote. In striking contrast to this unrealistic blindness to what should have been an obvious connection of facts is the Marquise's psychological perceptiveness, which at two points in the story almost overcomes what is obviously her mental block to a conscious, rational solution of the mystery: her veneration of her rescuer as an "angel of heaven." (p. 12)

The final scene of *Die Marquise von O* . . . , the oft-criticized conciliatory ending which unites the Marquise and her errant Count in a second wedding and then populates their domicile with bouncing Russian babies, seems to me precisely the logical and realistic ending of the novella. Kleist's fictional world is a flawed one, one in which to be human is to err. Repeatedly he places his characters into situations in which the characters are bent almost to the breaking point, and indeed, sometimes beyond it. And yet, flawed as they are, Kleist's most representative characters have an inner reserve of resilience and tenacity upon which they call when they are threatened by the existential crises inevitable in life. The Prince of Homburg, hero of Kleist's final and finest drama, shows this tenacity when, after having groveled on his knees in cowardly—should one not say human?—fear of death, he can pull himself together, stare into his open grave, and set a hero's example by his willingness to die for a principle of state. Mankind had to go through generations of wars, through generations of prison camps and death camps, through generations of degradation and starvation before it realized how precious life can be, even to a hero, and therefore how real, how human the Prince's plea for life really is. (p. 14)

Donald H. Crosby, "Psychological Realism in the Works of Kleist: 'Penthesilea' and 'Die Marquise von O'," in Literature and Psychology *(© Morton Kaplan 1969), Vol. 19, No. 1, 1969, pp. 3-16.*

MICHAEL HAMBURGER (essay date 1970)

Error, and more often than not the very impossibility of discovering the truth, assumes a metaphysical significance in Kleist's works; it is the Purgatory through which all his characters must pass, and from which the tragic ones do not emerge. Already his first play, *Die Familie Schroffenstein,* was a tragedy of errors. (p. 132)

In comic situations, the sinister enigma of most of Kleist's works may give place to a paradox that can be unraveled by ingenuity; this is the case in *Der Zerbrochene Krug*. Sometimes, as in *Die Marquise von O.,* the events themselves finally offer a solution; in the weaker works that do not end tragically, such as *Käthchen,* a *deus ex machina* is required. There are many variations: *Das Erdbeben in Chili* begins with a *deus ex machina,* the earthquake itself, but this only serves to sharpen the tragic irony of the denouement. In *Amphytrion,* Kleist's admirable adaptation of Molière's comedy, we see the given enigma deepen into a mystery; the error, which was a mere pretext for social comedy in Molière, strikes such deep roots in Alcmene, her perplexity is so greatly intensified by her deeper response to Jupiter's divinity, that the play hangs on the verge of tragedy.

What is constant in all these works is the error itself; and the disorientation of those involved in the error. When error has wholly obscured the truth, they fall into the excessive passions that destroy them. In some cases, as in *Michael Kohlhaas,* the error takes the form of injustice; but injustice is a suppression of the truth on the ethical plane. The resulting disorientation is the same. (pp. 133-34)

The crowning irony of Kleist's career is that his last play and his last story point to a resolution of the metaphysical, moral, and emotional dilemma to which all his personal failures were due. His literary works were always well ahead of his personal development; for even if he did not know it, they were action as much as thought. Kleist did not live to catch up with *Friedrich Prinz von Homburg* and *Der Zweikampf.* It was not till these last works that he was able to present a love relationship free from confusion and excess. The love between Homburg and Natalie is as far removed from the mixture of sensuality, heroism, and cannibalism that passes for love in *Penthesilea* as from the self-obliterating, abject devotion of Käthchen von Heilbronn (whom Kleist, in one of his rare comments on his own works, described as the minus corresponding to Penthesilea's plus, "the reverse side of Penthesilea, a creature as mighty by virtue of submission as the other by virtue of action"). (p. 134)

Kleist was one of the first German writers to face—or at least to suffer—the full implications of those peculiarly modern processes, the isolation of the individual consciousness and the fragmentation of reality into islands of pure subjectivity on the one hand, mere mechanistic phenomena on the other. . . . That is why Kleist was inclined to judge his own art in terms of a conflict between reality and imagination—or, in other words, between the individual and his environment. The antinomy between "thought" and "action" is only another variant of the same conflict, the conflict between what Blake called Reason and Energy. The peculiar and admirable tautness of Kleist's blank verse and narrative prose owes much to the tension between them, to Kleist's strenuous endeavors to impose the curb of plausibility on the anarchic products of his imagination. (p. 136)

[The] vitalism and antirationalism that [*On the Gradual Formation of Thought during Speech* and *On the Puppet Theater*] propound were counterbalanced by Kleist's inflexible control over his artistic media. Kleist knew very well that spontaneity is not enough. . . . It is the intensity of this struggle in Kleist's case that justifies the analogy of music, of a mathematical structure raised on a foundation of unreason. Kleist's works are like products of the successful collaboration between a maniac and a mathematician. That is why Kafka could learn from Kleist to illuminate nightmare with a daytime lucidity; not to explain his paradoxes, but to render them; and, however outrageous his visions, to maintain the outward assurance of a somnambulist. . . .

I have already alluded to his ingenious use of metaphor and simile. The entire significance of *Die Marquise von O.* can be shown to hinge on a few words almost casually scattered over the narrative: "god" and "angel" on the one hand, "devil" and "dog" on the other. If, as one might well argue, the introduction of these words was involuntary, the dualism that they convey still remains essential to the story; and it matters very little whether we praise the maniac or the mathematician for finding so subtle a way of conveying it. (p. 137)

Kleist could theorize as lucidly as any critic who knows from his own experience what he is talking about; but he left his theories behind as soon as he started work on a story or a play. Here all his thinking was dramatic, preceded and precipitated by action. However carefully, even painfully, executed, his works created the illusion that he leapt before he looked. In his stories, he plunged straight into the action, skillfully regulating its speed, but rarely stopping to moralize, analyze, or reflect. . . . The long sentence, with its wealth of subsidiary clauses, is typical of Kleist's narrative style, designed to convey as much detailed information as possible without interrupting the flow of action. For the same reason he preferred reported speech, which can be packed into similar sentences, so that the reader is swept on from shock to shock, with no time to formulate his objections.

The dramas demand a little more exposition; but Kleist reduces it to a minimum by avoiding introductory scenes, explanatory soliloquies—still the rule of his time—and all other devices that hold up the action. But his greatest advantage as a dramatist was his extraordinary capacity for reproducing the very processes of thought in his dialogue. . . . We do not need to be told about the state of mind of Kleist's characters. As soon as Homburg speaks, his manner conveys the precise state of almost trancelike distraction that Kleist wished to convey. Both his plays and his stories are singularly lacking in passages of "poetic" abandonment; in the plays there is a single dominant tension, never relaxed by irrelevant emotions, in the stories a single current of action, never broken by intrusions on the author's part. The lyrical moment does not matter; and Kleist's short poems are by far the least distinguished part of his work.

As a dramatist and storyteller, Kleist belonged to no school. His personal contacts with his contemporaries, the Romantics, had little or no effect on his works, though he shared some of their extravagances and some of their ideals, notably nationalism. . . . It is true that Kleist was at his worst when he consciously compromised with the taste of his public, as in the case of *Käthchen;* but his own variety of heroism owes much more to his age and country than he was aware. Though his lack of moral inhibitions and didactic ambitions made it easier for him than for his humanistic predecessors, Lessing, Goethe, and Schiller, to arouse the tragic emotions, he was as far as they were from renewing the religious and cultural function of Greek tragedy. His distinction is that he treated barbarous subjects with a hard precision, which is that of the scientific intellect, disciplined to record phenomena with a steady hand, a cold eye; yet the experiments he recorded were those of passion itself, of passion endured in a social and metaphysical void. His excellence as an artist is unmistakably modern in character: perfect control of the means to an uncontrollable end. (pp. 138-39)

Michael Hamburger, "Heinrich von Kleist" (originally published in a different form as "Heinrich von Kleist: An Introduction," in Partisan Review, *Vol. XXII, No. 1, Winter, 1955), in his* Contraries: Studies in German Literature *(copyright © 1957, 1965, 1970 by Michael Hamburger; reprinted by permission of the author), E. P. Dutton & Co., Inc., 1970, pp. 101-39.*

J. M. ELLIS (essay date 1970)

The structure of [*Prinz Friedrich von Homburg*] . . . concerns an antithesis between two different sides of human behavior, and an exploration of the relation between them in which their differences begin to disappear. . . .

The most obvious of [the features of the play's construction that show its antithetical structure] are the settings of the play. The middle part of the drama is in strong contrast to the first and final scenes. The former, which includes the main events of the play, takes place in the daytime; the latter at night. The contrast is between light and dark in a symbolic sense as well. In the daylight scenes the actions of the characters seem to be in plain view, with no concealment; but in the garden at night the darker side of human nature is not easily open to scrutiny, although it is briefly illuminated by "Fackeln." The contrast is not merely of light and dark, night and day, but of the realm of nature and the sphere of civilization. (p. 14)

A further striking set of antitheses and dualities consists in the double roles played by most of the characters, which give rise to double relationships; this too is part of the play's concern with the coexistence of two levels of behavior. The list of characters can be analyzed in two quite different ways: in their public role, as officials of the state, army officers, and so forth; and as friends and relatives. They have public duties and private loyalties, responsibilities involved in their positions but also responsibilities to friends and relatives. Again the former are comparatively clear and easily formulated, pertaining to the sphere of objective behavior and conscious reason, while the latter are complex in ways that are not easily perceptible. (p. 15)

A further aspect of the two-level structure of the play emerges when we consider the sequence of events. Two distinct patterns emerge. On the one hand, there is a clear plot outline, a story of a subordinate who disobeys an order and is condemned to death for it. It is possible to give a scene-by-scene résumé of the way the plot moves forward and tells this story, very much as one might summarize the historical source. But, on the other hand, this clear outline, corresponding to the objective and rational side of the play, is interspersed with numerous enigmatic episodes which do not (apparently) contribute to the development of the plot, and are not even clearly motivated. (p. 17)

That the play is concerned with the relation of two levels of behavior and, as a result of this, with two kinds of interpretation of behavior is seen also in the fact that in the text two different types of explanation are frequently in conflict. When events occur which for the other characters are not easily and rationally explicable, for example the sleepwalking of the Prince, two distinct attitudes are taken. The major female characters both assert that the Prince is sick. They consider that what they see is to be taken seriously and not laughed at, and that it indicates the Prince's general condition. But the male characters dismiss the Prince's behavior as unimportant. (pp. 20-1)

[The] play contains two kinds of interpretation of behavior: on the one hand, a narrowly rationalistic one, which concentrates on the obvious motivation of people when they perform the duties and actions expected of them in their everyday lives, and dismisses all else as insignificant or foolish; and, on the other hand, an attitude that all behavior is important and must be reckoned with.

There is, however, a third class of interpretations which attempts to avoid significant facts . . . : important actions are considered as mere jests. . . . That there are jokes and comedy in the play is true; but they have a serious basis, and are often better indicators of attitudes than what is said in a more guarded way. (pp. 22-3)

The language of the play presents more evidence of its dual structure. . . . For every feature of the play's language that can be noted, its opposite is just as much in evidence. (p. 24)

[When] we attempt the positive task of relating the language of the play to its meaning, it becomes apparent that the antitheses of language are part of the basic thematic antithesis of the play—the antithesis between the public sphere of reason, clarity, and objectivity, on the one hand, and the private, unclear, and irrational world on the other hand. The well-formed prose carries the assertions of one sphere; the luxuriant images and linguistic confusion, the deeper attitudes of the other sphere. . . . [The] play explores the relation between . . . prelinguistic dispositions and the rational formulations superimposed on them. Ambiguous utterances occur in unclear situations, and are then taken unambiguously, though in different senses, according to what the listener wishes to hear in the given situation. (p. 28)

The nature of the conflict between the Prince and the Elector is the central issue in the interpretation of the play. But this conflict must be analyzed in the light of the two levels of behavior with which the play is concerned. . . .

If the play is read entirely on the level of the rational and objective world and the external plot events, it is easy to decide in the Elector's favor. When the Prince is ordered to play a certain part in the battle, his duty is made clear to him, but he disobeys orders, thereby endangering the outcome of the battle. . . .

The fact of the Prince's disobedience and condemnation is certainly a reality of the play—a fact with which the characters themselves have to contend. An interpretation, however, must take this view—that the Prince is culpable—and its opposite as elements to be assimilated, with others, into a more complete view of the conflict of Prince and Elector; insubordination and its punishment are only one part of their complex relationship. (p. 30)

[The] relationship of the Prince and the Elector, on the surface one of mutual love and respect, conceals elements of rivalry and competitiveness. The rivalry is most dangerous on the Elector's side simply because it is disguised by a more rational mode of behavior; the Elector justifies himself in objective terms much more easily than can the Prince. This hypothesis, I believe, accounts for the strangeness of the Elector's behavior—his hesitations, odd jokes, silences, and miscalculations. . . .

The Elector's rivalry with the Prince, his sensing that the Prince as a young and dashing general wins far more acclaim in battle than he himself does, affects his judgment as to what is in the best interest of the state. It is obvious that the Prince is unable to function responsibly as a strategic general; his dreams of grandeur get in the way. But both Prince and Elector are in the grip of forces they cannot control. The import of the play lies both in this similarity and in the difference between the two: that the Prince is out of control is obvious, whereas the Elector's lack of control is masked by rational behavior and rationalization. And this raises the real theme of the play: the relation of reasonable behavior to underlying attitudes. . . .

[The] matter is not simply that the best use of the Prince is conspicuously avoided: he is actually placed in a role in which he can be expected to do very badly. The Elector's planning shows more than mere inefficiency; he is downright negligent. (p. 33)

Kleist's Elector is a man who sees things very plainly on the surface, but is subject to pressures that he does not understand. His conscious sense of doing right and his well-meaning handling of situations obscure his instinctive responses to challenges to his prerogatives. And this is why by the end of Act II he has produced the situation in which he can respond to these challenges by prosecuting the Prince, and have an objective reason for doing so.

The Prince is in some ways a more simple and easily understood character. He is a young man behaving expansively and trying, so to speak, to increase his personal territory. . . . It is [a] pressure to expand and extend his sphere of influence and acclaim that produces the crisis; the dispute over the Prince's disobedience is a late symptom, not a cause, of the underlying conflict between the two men. It has overtones of the classic situation in which the status quo of the older generation is disturbed by a vigorous young man who instinctively exerts pressure to make it yield a more important place for him. As a result the older man is torn between his regard for the younger as a loved son and his fear of him as an aggressive competitor. Part of the Elector's instinctive reaction is a destructive one, and yet he cannot react unambiguously and consciously. (pp. 40-1)

In Kleist's play the rational order asserts itself in everyday events which are apparently motivated by ordinary considerations and arguments. The imagery of the play, however, conveys deeper motives and attitudes that are ultimately far more important. . . .

Although individual images are often very striking, it is more useful to deal with groups of them when investigating their function. One notable group is that of plants and all that is related to them—trees, flowers, cultivation, and areas of cultivation. (p. 58)

The horticultural imagery has an obvious general place in the thematic structure of the play: it is the sphere where reason and nature meet, where human planning and control are in contact with unpredictable nature. Gardening may be a science, but not an exact one; plants can be guided but not controlled. The image thus pertains to the play's theme of the relation of conscious control to natural tendencies.

One would expect "der Gärtner" [the gardener] to be identifiable as the Elector, the planner and reasoner who attempts to control and direct everything. This identification is in fact corroborated by his persistent appearance in the role of the gardener in the plant imagery throughout the play. He plans the battle, in which the soldiers are a "Saat" [standing crop], in which his victory will eventually "erblühen" [bloom], and he "mows" the flags of the enemy. Alas, his battle plans go wrong in the meantime; the fortuitous "Eisenregen" [sleet] mows down his men: the enemy is thus seen as cruel and uncontrollable weather. A more important aspect of his activity as the gardener is his control of people. (p. 61)

The gardener must have a garden: and here the horticultural images broaden to include the question of sphere of influence. When the Prince turns to thoughts of escaping from his sentence, he must, at some level of his mind, realize that his attempt to expand his influence within the Elector's sphere of authority has been the cause of his downfall, for he now pro-

poses to avoid the problem by going off to a country estate to sow and reap there; in the language of the symbol, he is getting out of the master-gardener's territory to leave the latter's authority undisputed: he will sow and reap elsewhere, where he does not compete with the Elector. (pp. 61-2)

The extensive imagery, patterned in a highly systematic way, is vital for the interpretation of the play. Parallelism and contrast are the most important of the patterns it displays. Behind the bold and often forced metaphor for which Kleist has long been noted there is a clever and interesting, however bizarre, linking of things which seem separate but are for the play's purposes closely related. Throughout, the analysis of the central characters is the focus of interest, and the discrepancy between their surfaces and depths is the main point of the parallels and contrasts articulated in the imagery. (p. 82)

The play has subtly probed beneath the surface of clichés and attractive superficial notions which serve to mask what is happening below that surface. . . . (pp. 98-9)

The end of the play, instead of solving problems, leaves them open. But this is not simply inconclusiveness; it is an important part of the play that in one sense there should be no solution, and even no real change in the situation. The basic problem of the conflict of the Prince and Elector cannot be removed, for the relation between reasoned behavior and underlying motives must continue to be obscure and problematic. The play has probed but not solved the problem, nor could it. The Prince and Elector must, as human beings, remain exposed to the forces which brought them into dangerous conflict. (p. 99)

> *J. M. Ellis, in his* Kleist's "Prinz Friedrich von Homburg": A Critical Study *(copyright © 1970 by The Regents of The University of California; reprinted by permission of the University of California Press), University of California Press, 1970, 132 p.*

ROBERT E. HELBLING (essay date 1975)

It would be a serious mistake to reduce Kleist's tragic vision of life merely to his own personality traits, the seemingly pathological withdrawal of his genius into a world of its own reflected in the inward stance of the protagonists in his dramas. He gave the many intellectual crosscurrents of his age a hearing and found them wanting. His tragic sense of reality could not be blunted by theory. (p. 46)

Reduced to its simplest expression, the single most important theme in Kleist's tragic view is the conflict between the "realities" of the world and the individual's inner vision of them. This theme is rendered more complex through the intense search of the Kleistian character for his own being based on his "feeling" of self, often done in defiance of the world. . . . But in the midst of seeming debacle, the "heroic" individual safeguards the integrity of his soul. While he must go through a tormenting experience of inner schism, he finally seems to arrive at greater self-possession in life or in death. . . . And it is questionable whether Kleist's hero or heroine—if they survive—will find life more livable after their sobering experiences. They might find it more difficult, since they have experienced the fragility of their own self-assurance. Most likely, they will be more wary of their soul's intimations about the realities of the world. (pp. 46-7)

What one can say with certainty, however, is that through disturbing events the Kleistian character profoundly experiences his unique subjectivity, which heretofore had been dormant. The very nature of one's subjectivity can hardly be grasped abstractly and encapsulated in words. It is a matter of inner experience. . . . But precisely because a strong upsurge of subjectivity cannot be fully distilled in intellectual categories of thought, he remains as much a mystery to himself as to those around him. This may be the "modern" and somewhat existential element in Kleist's tragic vision.

However, the religious or metaphysical dimension is not banned from Kleist's world. For all their inner solitude and anxiety, his protagonists are not existential heroes moving about in a world bereft of transcendence. . . . They do not arrive at an explicit profession of faith or lie prostrate before their Judge. Rather, in relying on an inner summons they hope to be properly related not only to themselves but also to God, to be the tools of God as is the marionette in Kleist's essay [on the *Marionettentheater*]. Yet, they hardly ever venture to utter even just trembling assertions about God, for they are as much baffled by His ways as by their own. . . .

It is rather Kleist himself who invents situations and episodes or describes personal reactions which suggest the divine presence in his characters' lives. (p. 48)

It is precisely because Kleist looks at the human quest for inner certainty *sub specie aeternitatis* that he also has a strikingly acute sense of its many ironies. He knows of the metaphysical aspirations of human "feeling," but is equally aware of its historic and finite limitations. . . . [Kleist's characters] commit tragic blunders, not through willful self-assertion, as in Shakespearean tragedy, but by relying naïvely on the promptings of their feeling. (p. 49)

The tragic irony in Kleist's works is heightened by indirect author interference. . . . Kleist succeeds in introducing a subtle element of doubt suggesting new inner and outer developments just as his characters utter protestations to the contrary. . . .

But unlike Shakespeare's typical hero, the character of the Kleistian hero is not exclusively his own undoing. It is equally due to the unfathomable motives of other human beings, the frail social institutions of man, or even the cryptic manifestations of supernatural powers. From this basic dramatic clash between "inner" and "outer" world derive all of the corollary themes found in Kleist's works, such as remnants of a supposedly Rousseauist belief in the natural goodness of the individual as opposed to the monstrous artificiality of certain social institutions, the tragic shortcomings of mere reason in disentangling the web of confusion enveloping the world, the impossibility of communicating directly the essence of one's subjective awareness to another human being equally enclosed in his own inner experience. (p. 50)

Expressed in traditional dramaturgic parlance, Kleist's dramas and *Novellen* show the conflict between "character" and an inexorable "fate." "Character" denotes in his case the individual's inner "feeling" while "fate" appears in various guises as the deceptive world. Kleist always achieves a subtle balance between these two entities, but in the ensuing dramatic tension, it is clear that his sympathies lie with those individuals who must defend their inner integrity against deceptive appearances. . . .

The basic existential insight that man must seek his being through torment and error and largely without immediate divine aid is responsible for the feeling of unrelieved anxiety that pervades Kleist's world. It also colors his notion of "chance" as a manifestation of "fate." (p. 51)

Although Kleist's feeling of the "absurd" is tempered later on by his concern with man's inward search for his destiny, strange coincidences continue to play an important role even in his more adult vision of the world. If Kleist suggests that human life must be viewed *sub specie aeternitatis,* then he does it with daring irony, as in **"The Duel,"** where in the plot itself he shows how misguided are the pretenses under which man-made laws presumably embody the divine will. (pp. 51-2)

On the other hand, the phenomenal world is but the outward, visible manifestation of a mysterious *thing-in-itself.* Similarly, irrational chance is but the visible, immediate revelation of an invisible, remote fate. In the drama, this may be more difficult to suggest than in the *Novelle,* for there human life is portrayed through the earthly dialog of the characters—unless the modern dramatist resorts to devices reminiscent of the ancient chorus, as in the Epic Theater or the "play within the play"—while in the *Novelle* the author may allow himself the luxury of a more omniscient viewpoint. However, the very nature of the *Novelle* lends itself to a conversion of mere chance into ominous fate. Without dwelling on character development or psychological motivation, it shows how an event strikes a human life from the outside with sudden force. (p. 52)

In a world of unrelieved tension and seemingly hostile, irrational forces the Kleistian hero is often overcome by an intense feeling of powerlessness. In Kleist's world, man is hardly the master of his fate, he is at best the captain of his soul, and then only at the cost of great inner stress. He is the chattel of his inner destiny, "condemned" to be himself. Man is in this sense *ohnmächtig,* "powerless." It is not surprising that in Kleist's works *Ohnmacht,* denoting primarily "fainting spell," but also "lack of power," is a recurring motif. . . . *Ohnmacht* epitomizes the effect of a dramatic clash between inner "truths" and outer "realities"; it is not mere melodrama.

Ohnmacht, then, serves as a symbolic "gesture" intimating the unfathomable depth of the human soul. As such it is also an extralingual means of expressing the individual's inner solitude. (pp. 52-3)

Kleist's vantage point varies, although the fundamental irony he portrays remains the same. At times, his lens zooms in on the comic of isolated occurrences; other times, its field of vision broadens to encompass the universal forces that shape man's destiny. **The Broken Pitcher** is set in the homespun atmosphere of a little Dutch village; its characters are drawn with all their personal idiosyncrasies, their fate entangled in the network of their modest daily pursuits. **Penthesilea,** on the other hand, is steeped in a mythological atmosphere; its protagonists are symbols of cultures in conflict while their fate is determined by the existential and metaphysical aspirations concealed in the human soul. . . .

As regards the *Novelle,* its "objective" form lends itself to a portrayal of apparently isolated, though unusual events in the perspective of a portentous fate and with seeming dispassion on the part of the author. In most of Kleist's *Novellen,* the unusual events which constitute their fictional matter suggest tragedy. But in a *Novelle* such as **"The Marquise of O—,"** the theme of the apparent immaculate conception by a blameless woman seeking the unknown father of her unborn child through a newspaper ad has lascivious overtones bordering on cynical humor. In others, such as **"Saint Cecilia,"** an element of the grotesque intrudes itself. (p. 55)

And in one sense, the grotesque portrays unfulfilled tragedy, a lack of catharsis provoking agonized laughter mixed with a recognition of horror which may freeze our guffaws into deadly silence. . . . The notion of *Versehen*—misapprehension—which plays such a large part in Kleist's view of human life, is itself grotesque, in the sense of "incongruous," when measured against the unspeakable grief that comes to some of Kleist's characters as a result of their misapprehension of reality. But it also highlights the tragic and comic elements that inhere simultaneously in Kleist's artistic vision of man. . . . In the Kleistian world, deception is not placed in the full consciousness of the tragic hero. It is rather built into the very nature of things—the "fragile constitution of the world"—and forever threatens the human quest for certitude. Even when a tragic character embarks upon conscious deception, as is the case with Achilles who intends to submit to Penthesilea under false pretenses, the "intrigue" illustrates the naïveté of the hero's frame of mind, his way of thinking or, more precisely, nonthinking. Intrigue is not an important aspect of the plot in Kleist's works, in contrast to Schiller's drama where the hero's destiny is enmeshed in the political and historic realities of his time. Kleist, though not entirely oblivious of such realities, rather shows the solitary quest of the individual for the wholeness of his being. In this sense, he portrays an "alienated hero" seeking the meaning of his life in loneliness and terror. (p. 56)

> *Robert E. Helbling, in his* The Major Works of Heinrich von Kleist *(copyright © 1975 by Robert E. Helbling; reprinted by permission of New Directions Publishing Corporation), New Directions, 1975, 275 p.*

JAMES M. McGLATHERY (essay date 1975)

[In *Amphitryon*] Kleist's pushing of husband and wife to the brink of despair is subordinate to his romantic portrayal of erotic love as inseparable from a subconscious transcendent longing.

In adapting Molière's *Amphitryon* to the bent of his own poetic genius, Kleist shifted the psychological interest from Amphitryon's reaction at being cuckolded to Alkmene's realization that she has been seduced. Even more radical is Kleist's exploring whether Alkmene's heart belongs to her seducer or to her husband. Molière largely avoids this offense against decorum and sensibility by excluding Alcmène from the play's last act. Kleist's emphasis on Alkmene's reaction to the seventeen-hour night of lovemaking with Jupiter is important, however, for his investigation of how the chaste, pious young wife is affected by the realization that she has unknowingly had sexual intercourse with a god.

Piety would demand that Alkmene rejoice at this revelation. Her failure to do so may imply only resentment at Jupiter's imposture as her husband, leaving open the possibility that under other circumstances she might have been willing to accept the Olympian as lover in fulfillment of a religious obligation. Yet Alkmene consistently maintains that the thought of making love to anyone other than her husband is abhorrent to her. Because Alkmene extends society's prohibition against adultery to include intercourse with the gods, her chastity seems more than conventional virtue. . . . Alkmene's tragedy consists in the shattering of her illusion about the nature of her conjugal love. (pp. 327-28)

Kleist's Jupiter, unlike Molière's, desires not only a night of lovemaking with Alkmene but also the satisfaction of having her guess his identity. This is reason enough for his appearing to Alkmene incognito; that he must impersonate Amphitryon

is dictated, of course, by Alkmene's chasteness. In Kleist's play, though, Jupiter seems also to relish the imposture as a chance to prove his superiority over the husband. (p. 329)

Jupiter's achievement of his related aim—Alkmene's sexual preference of himself over Amphitryon—is far more significant for Alkmene's tragic role in Kleist's play than is the triumph of her virtue in failing to guess his identity. As protagonist, she clings desperately to the belief that she has remained faithful to her husband and that the enhancement of their love is attributable to Amphitryon's elation over returning from battle as a conquering hero and to her increased appeal as a result of his prolonged absence. (pp. 329-30)

To what extent then has Jupiter succeeded in winning Alkmene's heart? In the end she is forced to admit to herself that she bestowed her preference on the god. When Jupiter reveals his identity, she faints in her husband's arms. On the conscious level the revelation comes as a complete surprise; but her faint also results from the dreaded confirmation of intimations which she struggled throughout to suppress. In idolizing her husband she has succumbed to the seductions of a god incarnate. For a woman whose piety and humility involve feelings of awe engendered by sexual and spiritual tabus, this self-admission must sever the ties which bound her to life. It is Alkmene's personal mysticism which now leaves her equally unable to find happiness in life or to escape into dreams of immortality. (p. 332)

Alkmene's sigh at the play's end may express a feeling of relief, but certainly not without a note of despair. Her tragic self-revelation poses the question often asked by German Romantics from Tieck to Eichendorff, whether erotic love is not expressive of a subconscious, transcendent yearning for immortality. As Kleist's Herr C . . . insists in the dialogue, **"Uber das Marionettentheater,"** the story of the Fall is basic to an understanding of man and history. (p. 333)

> *James M. McGlathery, "Kleist's Version of Molière's 'Amphitryon': Olympian Cuckolding and 'Unio Mystica',"* in Molière and the Commonwealth of Letters: Patrimony and Posterity, *edited by Roger Johnson, Jr., Editha S. Neumann, and Guy T. Trail (copyright © 1975 by the University Press of Mississippi), University Press of Mississippi, 1975, pp. 327-33.*

ILSE GRAHAM (essay date 1978)

In **"Die Verlobung in St. Domingo"** Kleist has chosen to symbolize the perceptual flaw which vitiates our experiencing at an unreachably deep bodily level in the color of the natives, and the fear aroused by it. Toni's uncertain hue—she is a mestizo—constitutes the same physical barrier to true perception which in the case of Penthesilea has found expression in the amputated breast. (p. 12)

Such radical distortion of experience through the faultiness of our bodily medium—and the impossibility to relate in the face of such distortion—have found their articulation in a number of interrelated symbolisms, all deployed with a maximum of ambiguity: the most important of these being color at the sheer physical level, the linking of hands as a token of trust, and tying. (pp. 12-13)

In Kleist's story . . . hands are deployed in . . . a twilight realm between communication and aggression. Hands reach out, hands beseech, hands caress, hands grasp and snatch, hands hurt and hands kill. Thus the act of linking hands becomes profoundly ambiguous. Gustav is asleep when Toni covers his hand with kisses. When he wakes, her own will be busied tying Gustav's hands and feet with a rope. How can her gesture—she ties her lover to ensure his safety—communicate its message? (p. 13)

In the end, it is the dead lovers' hands that will be linked as their rings are exchanged before they are committed to the earth.

The act of tying itself is similarly embedded in a web of occurrences in which it signifies overt hostility or defensive cunning. Thus the true meaning of Toni's deed is lost on a man whose trust is undermined by meanings as slippery as the shifting patterns of a kaleidoscope. (pp. 13-14)

Kleist's poetic idiom, be it his verse or his prose, by its violent dislocations fairly thrusts itself upon the attention, enveloping thought, winding itself about it like a cerecloth and choking it, or else tearing it apart by the multitudinous interpolations that are packed into it. It is a tacky and glutinous medium, as close to the sculptor's clay as language has ever been allowed to become in a poet's hand. And this is all to the good: for Heinrich von Kleist's gnarled, tormented, kinaesthetic and utterly idiosyncratic idiom is not the least part of his glory. Furiously he attacked it so as to make visible through its distorting mirror the threatened vision—that of the speaker for instance who, carving his path through a veritable thicket of semantic twists and torsions, sustains his waylaid impetus and triumphantly completes his utterance in life and about it—as furiously and expressively as van Gogh used the roughnesses of his canvas and the thickness of his paint or as Michelangelo fought the resistance of the stone he worked, as furiously indeed as a wrestler will hold his adversary in the vice of his embrace. (pp. 15-16)

Does Kleist leave off having his characters strain after the unadulterated vision because he knows their subjectivity to be a hopelessly distorted, and distorting medium, like his own? Far from it. . . . [He] has yet implanted in them all the same avid thirst for the Absolute: absolute knowledge, absolute love, absolute trust and absolute faith. And in the deep naturalness of that need—it drives them onward like a homing instinct—lies their innocence. Most of them seek it *in* the bewildering complexity of their predicament, in and through the impenetrable corona of misconceptions that shrouds their own sensibility and that of their protagonists from each others' view. Kohlhaas and Penthesilea and Alkmene and the Marquise von O., they all want to understand and be understood, to love and be loved, to trust and be trusted "*in* meiner Tat" [within the context of my deed], as Eve has it in *Der zerbrochene Krug* . . . , that is to say, *within* the highly idiosyncratic, deceptive and seemingly corrupt context in which they are entrapped. Others, fewer, long once and for all to shed an embodiment that prevents them from seeing the Absolute face to face. . . . (p. 16)

But all alike are made to endure the rigors of their incarnate condition, most of them thickheaded and literalminded, blinkered and obtuse, all of them condemned to gravity and the matter they indwell as perhaps only Dostoevsky and Kafka have dared condemn the creatures of their imagination, yet with their eyes turned obstinately upward, straining for illumination to come to them in their very imprisonment or to be altogether released from it. . . .

[Heinrich von Kleist] through his reticences and indirections, through the obliqueness of pantomime and gesture, through scenic enactment of inner events and featherlight metaphors of transcendence as much as through what he spelt out, gave utterance to the all but ineffable—the innocent vision flowering clean above the treachery of words and a sense-environment riddled with self-doubt and distrust; and therein lies the miracle of his art. But then, this strange genius was at home in the unspeakable. (p. 17)

Ilse Graham, "Heinrich von Kleist: The Captive Vision," in The German Quarterly *(copyright © 1978 by the American Association of Teachers of German), Vol. LI, No. 1, January, 1978, pp. 1-18.*

MARVIN MUDRICK   (essay date 1979)

["**The Foundling**"] isn't tragic, nothing here has the effect of irresolution or waste or loss: indeed Piachi fulfills himself, overcomes all his enemies, dies triumphant—"unrepentant" would give a false impression—and glowing with anticipation; rather, this extravagance of energy is comic or farcical or even transcendent, comparable to the effect of *Oedipus at Colonus,* whose hero is also a furious old man who embraces his death in a sublimity of self-approbation.

Kleist is less concerned with the momentousness of issues or events than with the momentum of feeling. (p. 57)

The title character of "**Michael Kohlhaas**" begins as an innocent bystander . . . , but the world—in the persons of brutal lackeys, mean-spirited knights, and graceless princes—makes the mistake of passing him off as a nobody to whom the inadvertent and impersonal injustices of the world will be as sourly acceptable as they are to the rest of us. (p. 58)

It's a very long story, a comedy of self-interest and circumstance that couldn't have been expected to open out more or less accidentally toward such possibilities; but Kohlhaas is a man in touch with the quick of his uncharted nature, and, as the Elector discovers, there are dragons out there.

Kleist (by the evidence of a friend's letter) saw himself as a dramatist and regretted the time he had to spend on his stories, which he considered pot-boilers and occasional pieces; and it's a fact that the critics and outline-histories classify him as a dramatist who also wrote some impressive and idiosyncratic fiction. But in this respect Kleist resembles Chekhov: each is less an instrument through which powerful stories tell themselves than an authoritative voice which tells them; each, in his plays, having lost his voice delegates authority to the protagonist. . . . (p. 60)

Prince Frederick of Homburg is said to be Kleist's masterpiece, but prodigies of interpretive gymnastics don't dissipate the aura of neurotic self-dramatization. . . . Kleist's "tragedy," *Penthesilea,* seems to be about the awful violence of passionate love (it does come up with one interesting character, Achilles, presented as a shrewd and amiable ladies' man), has Greek pretensions, and concludes with a peripeteia in which—offstage of course—the heroine not only kills her lover Achilles, she bites chunks out of him too; but when Kleist's voice isn't there reporting matter-of-factly on the palpable brains that Piachi or Kohlhaas splatters over nearby floors and walls, the characters speaking for themselves have such an attack of stage fright they can't do better than make like the woe-is-me or oy-vay school of drama. . . . Kleist's only play in which the medium doesn't hopelessly cramp his style is *Amphitryon,* a rather grim adaptation of Molière's witty and uncommitted comedy of appearances. . . . [It isn't] Molière with a Prussian accent; it's an interesting if coarse-grained personal adjustment of one of the theater's great plots to a characteristic theme of Kleist's. Maybe adaptation was more congenial to Kleist than invention when he was writing drama: anyhow, in this instance he had the luck to be working with characters none of whom—divine or human—had the kind of sensibility he couldn't as a playwright resist identifying with and losing himself in. But none of them sounds at all like Kleist either, and we miss him.

Writing fiction Kleist has no problems, he can be himself without being at the mercy of himself: it may have helped that writing fiction seemed to him a waste of his time which he ought to have spent writing those heroic dramas suffused with Shakespearean pathos which represented his notion of masterpieces. . . . In Kleist's fiction, which is heroic as his plays never are, the personal is always besieged by social proscriptions or social or natural or even supernatural catastrophes and always a match for them. (pp. 61-3)

> Marvin Mudrick, "I Don't Care What Mama Don't Allow," in his Books Are Not Life But Then What Is? (copyright © 1979 by Marvin Mudrick; reprinted by permission of Oxford University Press, Inc.), Oxford University Press, New York, 1979, pp. 52-64.

BENJAMIN BENNETT   (essay date 1979)

[In *Prinz Friedrich von Homburg*] Kleist actually attempts to make a "poem" out of dramatic criticism and theory.

This theoretical tendency is already present in the first scene, where the Elector, in taking the wreath and winding his chain around it, *stages a poetic vision for the Prince.* By symbols the Elector expresses the idea that heroic energy or individual freedom (the wreath) must somehow undergo a synthesis with law (the chain) and that this synthesis cannot be achieved once and for all but must remain in the distance as an object of endless desire and striving. . . .

As the play progresses, . . . we become more and more aware that the opening scene had presented us with a picture of our own situation as recipients of a symbolic vision in the theater, and Kleist thus obliges us to think about the relation of play to audience; he sets the stage for the unfolding of a theory of drama. (p. 23)

Prinz Friedrich is psychologically subtle but not psychologically obscure; the intentions and motives of the characters are not quite so mysterious as they have been made out to be. For example, the Elector never really entertains the notion of marrying Natalie to the Swede. . . .

In the second place, when Natalie describes the Prince's abject plea for his life, the Elector is genuinely shocked. . . .

Another and more important question of intent, however, must be disposed of first, the question whether the Elector ever intends to allow the Prince to be executed. Again, I think the answer is no. . . .

[Two] pieces of evidence show that the Elector never intends to carry out the sentence. First, when he carefully frames the wording of his letter, he is hoping that the Prince will reject his offer; and again, therefore, since he knows that Natalie is in love with the Prince, it would be exceptionally cruel of him to send her with the letter (thus forcing her to witness the Prince's hoped-for decision) if he did not intend to give the affair a happy ending. (p. 25)

[What] are the Elector's principal motives and values? We have understood something about what he does not intend, but what are his positive goals? (p. 26)

Of course the Elector has an interest in upholding the law, but is this his principal conscious aim in what he does? At least within the action of the play one object is clearly more important to him than either law or today's victory, and that is the education of the Prince. . . . At first glance there appears to be a conflict of motives, between the Elector's educational goal and his duty to the "sacred" fatherland . . . ; but in fact there is no real conflict, and the idea of such a conflict is based on a misunderstanding of the Elector's political thought. Given his official position, the Elector must profess publicly a strict insistence upon law; in truth, however, his idea of the state is a good deal more flexible than he admits, and . . . it not only allows but requires him to be concerned primarily with the Prince's education.

The Prince, at any rate, apparently needs to be educated. His courage and tactical flair are unquestioned, but he must learn discipline and a respect for larger strategic and political considerations. The need for combining heroic energy with respect for law and for the state is what gives the Elector his idea for the chain-and-wreath symbol, and is also the reason for the "ineptness" of his battle plan. (p. 27)

[*Prinz Friedrich*] is psychologically subtle and interesting, but not psychologically obscure; it employs psychology but is not about psychology. It is, rather, *a drama about drama,* and its true principal intention, its center of gravity, is thus indicated by its critical allusiveness as well as by the ironic structure of play-within-play.

The Elector's political thinking is best approached by way of the question of what is wrong with the Brandenburgian polity and army, what internal problems the Elector is faced with. . . . Both Golz and Dörfling, at crucial and conspicuous points in the play, are afraid to say anything that might displease their superiors—and this is a symptom of what is really rotten in the state of Brandenburg: not too little discipline and subordination, but rather too much. The play stresses not the need for law as a corrective to energy but rather the need for energy and initiative as correctives to excessively literal reliance on law. (pp. 31-2)

This idea—of the insufficiency of law and the need for energy and free initiative in a state or army—is not merely the play's main political burden, but it also represents the Elector's own thinking. The Elector cannot express himself verbally in this vein for two simple reasons. In the first place, his position prohibits it. If the ruler or general, the man who embodies the law, states out loud that he does not consider the law absolutely holy, the result among his subordinates will be carelessness and eventually chaos. In the second place, one cannot foster energy and initiative by advocating them in words; these qualities, by definition, must originate in the person who possesses them. (p. 32)

The Elector therefore cannot express himself verbally, but he does express himself unambiguously in his otherwise unaccountable actions. The reason for his overriding interest in the Prince's education, for example, now becomes clear. The Prince is a young man in whom the qualities of energy and initiative are abundant; this man must therefore be trained as a true leader for the army, in order that the rest may profit from his fiery example. (pp. 32-3)

There is some question about whether the Elector's education of the Prince can be said to have succeeded; but the success of his education of his army, or at least of his officer corps, his successful use of the Prince as a vital spark, seems quite clear. At the beginning of the play the officers are all timidly pedantic in carrying out their orders; even old Kottwitz is careful to disclaim responsibility . . . before following the Prince into battle. But at the end of the play, without committing any actual insubordination, the officers are willing to stick their necks out quite a bit in disputing with their commander-in-chief. (p. 33)

Hohenzollern's case is especially instructive. At the beginning, when he brings the Elector to witness the Prince's dreaming, . . . he is quite obviously telling tales out of school. His emotional situation is deeply (but not Freudianly) ambivalent. He has genuine affection for the Prince, but at the same time he is disturbed and a bit envious that the Elector has granted so much favor and responsibility to a man whose record as a general is hardly even promising. . . . (pp. 33-4)

By the end of the play, however, he has undergone considerable development (perhaps more than the Prince) and is now prepared to assert that the Elector had been at fault in disrupting the battle plan. . . . [This] kind of growth, the awakening of initiative and of confidence in their convictions, is precisely what the Elector had desired from his officers.

A number of other questions about the play now resolve themselves with no difficulty. The Elector's reason for not dismissing immediately the Swedish Count Horn, for example, is that he does not know until the last act exactly what course he must pursue in negotiations. (p. 34)

We can now also understand that the essence of the contrast between the Elector and Wallenstein is that the latter, who does sacrifice his daughter, is interested only in political advantage for himself, whereas the former is interested in forming a healthy body politic (where rigidity of law is counteracted by vital energy) for the sake of future generations. (pp. 34-5)

[There] is no special reason to look for personal development in the Elector either. Like the Prince, in fact, the Elector is the same at the end of the play as at the beginning, shaken but ultimately confirmed in his basic nature and purposes. I do not mean by this that he is a symbol of changeless divinity—any more than the Prince is—or that he possesses infallible wisdom. He does have very sound and sensible political attitudes, conducive to the future health of his country. (p. 38)

And yet, for all his good sense, he is still only a man. He has, at the beginning of the play, quite a reasonable plan for testing and educating the Prince, by ordering him to watch the battle rather than participate, thus forcing him to exercise self-control. But in his overintentness upon his goal (comparable to the Prince's over-eagerness) he makes two serious mistakes. First, when he is shown the Prince in the garden, he thinks he sees an opportunity for reinforcing his educational scheme by working on the pupil's unconscious mind; but the result is to inflame the Prince beyond all possibility of control, so that the original plan cannot work any longer. . . . The Prince's insubordination is thus not only the Elector's fault, but it is a fault the Elector has himself long been wary of. Hence also the Prince's outrageous optimism when he is first imprisoned, and then his collapse into utter despair. (pp. 38-9)

And after inadvertently sentencing the Prince to die, when the Elector thinks he sees an opportunity to make up the educational ground that has apparently been lost on the battlefield, he lets the sentence stand as long as possible; but again he is mistaken. The Prince is not chastened by his imprisonment but bewildered, because of what he knows from the evidence of his own eyes and Natalie's glove. (p. 39)

[However, the Elector still] appears in the end to have achieved his ultimate aim, the revitalization of his army and state. Again, therefore, our reading is supported by a simple unifying structure in the work. Just as the Prince sets out to win his fortune (including Natalie) in the most direct way, then makes a mistake that apparently dashes his hopes, but in the end finds himself very close to his goal, so also the Elector makes a mistake that eventually seems to profit him more than the successful completion of his original plan would have. This—not only in the fictional action but also in the meaning for an audience—is the play's *master pattern* (and bears a fairly clear relation to the pattern of characters' speaking against their own true wishes). (pp. 39-40)

The problems of the state of Brandenburg are a symbol for the problem of the revitalization or reactivation of the human race, and it is essentially this problem which the Elector deals with by declining to express his true intentions—by attempting, that is, to avoid contributing to the insidiously self-perpetuating and self-potentiating fabric of human self-consciousness—and by placing his subordinates, *without their knowledge,* in a situation where energy and initiative, coupled with self-discipline, are likely to arise spontaneously, inspired in others by the example of the Prince.

Herein, however, lies the difficulty in our reading. If the problems of Brandenburg are equivalent to the problem of the human race, then Kleist is attempting to educate his audience in the same way that the Elector educates his army. And yet the Elector's true purposes, hence by analogy the author's true purposes, are known to the audience. Has the author failed in his purpose, then, since he has only managed to involve those who understand his meaning more deeply in the complexities of self-consciousness? . . .

This philosophical and political problem, from the late eighteenth century on in Germany, had come to be associated especially with drama. (p. 41)

[These ideas are] the basic considerations which had generated the national-theater movement in Germany—and which also underlie the maneuvering of Kleist's Elector, who hopes for a rebirth of free initiative in such a way as to strengthen rather than endanger the communal order.

Once we understand the relation between these ideas and drama or theater, it becomes easier to see the connection between the Elector's *mistake* and the ironic structure, the play-within-play, of *Prinz Friedrich.* In particular, the Elector's communication to the Prince (in the latter's "dream") of more than he intends to communicate, corresponds to an inherent difficulty in drama. (p. 42)

Drama, like the Elector, who communicates to the Prince more than serves his purpose, tends to say too much for its own good. We recall, moreover, that in the first scene a clear parallel is drawn between the Prince and the audience—in that both are presented with deliberately contrived symbolic visions—and we can now understand that the Prince's confusion in interpreting his vision is meant to illuminate a general problem about audiences. The audience of a drama always, as it were, snatches a real glove from the imaginary vision presented it; it always interprets what it sees and attempts to apply its interpretation to real life. But in the case of *Prinz Friedrich*—or in the case of any work that attempts to fulfil Kleist's idea of the function of drama, to revitalize human community—this process of application must always lead to confusion. (pp. 42-3)

The Elector's plan to educate the Prince quite clearly fails; nothing is *learned* in the fictional world but something still *happens,* and perhaps, by analogy, something is meant to happen in the real world of the theater, to the audience. At any rate nothing is learned in the theater, because of the nature of the play's message; there is no such thing as a teachable "philosophy of action."

The Prince, if our reasoning so far is correct, is a kind of projection of the audience—not an *image,* not an typical German theater-goer of the period, but a larger-than-life *projection.* The contrived symbolic vision he is presented with is parallel to the symbolic vision which is the play as a whole; the mistake made by the Elector, the presenter of this intendedly educational vision, reveals a difficulty in the form of drama itself, a "mistake" that every dramatist makes by being a dramatist; and this mistake in turn necessarily leads the audience into a confusion (our consciousness of the play's meaning endangers that meaning) which is then projected in the Prince's confused application of the meaning of the garden scene. But once we have come this far, what do we do? Evidently we must abandon any attempt to apply the play's meaning. . . . (p. 44)

And yet, even this hopelessness (as it arises in the audience) is projected in the Prince's despair. Just as we are forced to abandon all hope of deriving from the play "a sure way to find and enjoy happiness," so the Prince must abandon his hopes of possessing Natalie and glory, the two prizes promised him in his vision. . . . [When] we leave the Garden of Eden, as the Prince then does, we take two curses with us, our self-consciousness and our mortality, and the two are clearly equivalent. . . .

But self-consciousness, the legacy of Eden, is what makes the audience's situation hopeless. We understand what the play means; we know that ultimately we are free and that our freedom belongs harmoniously in the general order of things, that the chain and the wreath are somehow intertwined. But we also recognize that our consciousness of this truth divides us from ourselves and excludes us from our own unified being, so that we can never realize the perfect union of freedom and order in actual experience. (p. 45)

[This] is a projection, not an image. We do not merely see our self-consciousness on the stage—. . .—but rather we see what our self-consciousness implies; we are faced with the full potential horror of our condition. (pp. 45-6)

The play does not and cannot teach us how to be free; what it does, rather, is make us free by leading us to the true seat of our freedom. Once again, the process of understanding the play, if we understand it correctly, is identical with the process of penetrating into our own self-consciousness to the point where its tragic potential is revealed, to the point where the mere act of thinking about ourselves becomes a constant recognition and (in that we still carry out this act) a constant affirmation of the incomprehensible but inexorable sentence of death under which we stand. . . . Now, however, in the theater, we experience self-consciousness as itself the shadow of death, and we therefore experience our freedom as a heroic freedom, which we express merely by existing in man's in-

tolerable condition. . . . [This] sort of freedom tends naturally to strengthen the communal order, for its nature is to affirm and so overcome death, the most outrageously arbitrary of all externally imposed necessities, the absolute necessity in relation to which all particular requirements of law become mere symbols. . . . Thus the play's master pattern appears once again on the level of meaning. The unavoidable failure of the play to circumvent our self-consciousness, its failure to teach effectively the unity of freedom and duty, in the end brings us closer to this unity—by complicating and intensifying our self-consciousness. (pp. 46-7)

[We] do not learn about freedom, but rather, by affirming and enjoying our own self-consciousness as we sit in the theater, we *are* free, with a freedom we also see projected before us, a freedom that requires no particular action of us but rather resides in our very being. This is the aim of tragedy—to effect a liberation of the audience here and now, in the theater.

But *Prinz Friedrich* is not a tragedy. It cannot be a tragedy, for we have known from the start what the Elector's true intentions are. . . . The Prince's death is made necessary, as the capstone of the tragic structure of the work's relation to its audience; but it is also made impossible. Why does Kleist do this? (p. 48)

Suppose the Prince were executed. The result, for the audience, would be a climactic image of the heroism of human existence. Our ability to watch and enjoy the Prince's death would be testimony to our own triumph. (p. 49)

Kleist understands that there is no such thing as knowledge of our "highest freedom," since such knowledge would have to be more than a feeling of "the mind's superiority"; it would have to be a "philosophy of action," an understanding of the absolute unity of freedom and duty or freedom and fate, which is impossible. The Prince's death . . . would confirm our feeling of freedom, and this confirmation, this reduction of freedom to a lesson or feeling, must be avoided if we are to retain the experience of *freedom itself,* which is the constant re-overcoming of an abject terror ceaselessly inherent in our self-conscious existence. . . . Therefore the play at the end, like the Elector at the beginning, thrusts us "back into Nothingness" . . . , back into that realm of utter uncertainty where the experience of freedom is born. In this sense the play does truly come full circle and lead us back to the original garden.

And yet, this withdrawal of tragic confirmation is not carried out arbitrarily; the Prince is not saved by a *deus ex machina.* His pardon, rather, forces us to look back over the work as a whole and recognize that we have known all along what would eventually happen, that the play's tragic tension, out of which our sense of freedom has grown, is nothing but illusion, nothing but our own mental contrivance. . . . The tragic aspect of the play corresponds to our sense of the heroism inherent in our own self-conscious condition, thus to our knowledge of true human freedom, which knowledge cannot really exist. By being denied this knowledge, therefore, or by recognizing that the play's tragic aspect is illusory, we are cast back into that "Nothingness" where our freedom is in truth generated. (pp. 49-51)

Benjamin Bennett, "'Prinz Friedrich von Homburg': Theory in Practice," in his Modern Drama and German Classicism: Renaissance from Lessing to Brecht *(copyright © 1979 by Cornell University; used by permission of the publisher, Cornell University Press), Cornell University Press, 1979, pp. 22-56.*

ADDITIONAL BIBLIOGRAPHY

Blankenagel, John Carl. *The Attitude of Heinrich von Kleist toward the Problems of Life*. Hesperia: Schriften zur germanischen Philologie, edited by Hermann Collitz and Henry Wood, no. 9. Baltimore: The Johns Hopkins Press, 1917, 84 p.
> A discussion of Kleist's personal philosophy as reflected in his letters.

Crosby, Donald. "The Creative Kinship of Schiller and Kleist." *Monatshefte* LIII, No. 5 (October 1961): 255-64.*
> A comparison of the work of Schiller and Kleist, noting thematic and technical similarities.

Ellis, John M. "Kleist: 'Das Erdbeben in Chili'." In his *Narration in the German Novelle: Theory and Interpretation*, pp. 46-76. Cambridge: Cambridge University Press, 1974.
> An analysis of "Das Erdbeben in Chili" as a "detective story on a cosmic scale."

Hamburger, Michael. "Kleist." In his *Reason and Energy: Studies in German Literature*, pp. 107-44. New York: Grove Press, 1957.
> Biographical study focusing on Kleist's emotional difficulties.

March, Richard. *Heinrich von Kleist*. New Haven: Yale University Press, 1954, 60 p.
> General biographical study.

Ossar, Michael. "Kleist's 'Das Erdbeben in Chili' and 'Die Marquise von O'." *Revue des Langues Vivantes* XXXIV, No. 2 (1968): 157-69.
> A stylistic comparison of "Das Erdbeben in Chili" and "Die Marquise von O."

Perry, Henry Ten Eyck. "Sentimental and Fantastic Comedy: Lessing and Raimund." In his *Masters of Dramatic Comedy and Their Social Themes*, pp. 275-313. Cambridge, Mass.: Harvard University Press, 1939.*
> Brief analysis of *Der zerbrochene Krug*.

Stamm, Israel S. "A Note on Kleist and Kant." In *Studies in Honor of John Albrecht Walz*, pp. 31-40. Lancaster, Pa.: The Lancaster Press, 1941.*
> Philosophical study of Kleist's experience with the writings of Kant.

Wellek, René. "The Younger German Romantics: Arnim and Kleist." In his *A History of Modern Criticism 1750-1950: The Romantic Age, Vol. II*, pp. 288-91. New Haven: Yale University Press, 1955.*
> Brief view of themes in *Amphitryon* and "Über das Marionettentheater".

Wittels, Fritz. "Heinrich von Kleist—Prussian Junker and Creative Genius." In *The Literary Imagination: Psychoanalysis and the Genius of the Writer*, edited by Hendrik M. Ruitenbeek, pp. 23-42. Chicago: Quadrangle Books, 1965.
> Psychological analysis stating that the violence and force of Kleist's writing stems from suspected latent homosexuality.

Henry Wadsworth Longfellow

(1807-1882)

American poet, novelist, essayist, and translator.

Although Longfellow was the most popular American writer of the nineteenth century, his reputation suffered a serious decline after his death. The very characteristics which made his poetry popular in his own day—gentle simplicity and a melancholy reminiscent of the German Romantics—are those that fueled the posthumous reaction against his work. However, despite the continuing debate over Longfellow's stature, he is credited with having been instrumental in introducing European culture to the American readers of his day. Moreover, he simultaneously popularized American folk themes abroad, where his works enjoyed an immense readership.

Contrary to his father's wish that he study law, Longfellow preferred a literary career and began publishing poems in numerous newspapers and periodicals while attending Bowdoin College. Before graduation, the college trustees offered him a professorship of modern languages, provided he first prepare himself for the post by traveling in Europe. Grateful for the opportunity to make literature his profession, he accepted and sailed for Europe. This journey particularly contributed to his future life and work, evidenced in a unique blend of both American and foreign influences in his later work.

Following three years in Europe, Longfellow returned as a professor to Bowdoin and soon published a book of travel sketches titled *Outre-mer; a Pilgrimage Beyond the Sea*. Recognizing the obvious influence of Washington Irving's *Sketch Book,* many contemporary critics considered *Outre-mer* overly derivative and inferior to its model. Restless at Bowdoin, Longfellow accepted a position at Harvard as the Smith Professor of Modern Languages, a post he held for eighteen years. He again traveled to Europe and, in Heidelberg, discovered the German Romantic poets. Greatly impressed, he incorporated much of their artistic philosophies into his later writing. After returning and settling in Cambridge, Longfellow developed lasting friendships with American literary figures, such as Charles Sumner, Washington Allston, and Nathaniel Hawthorne.

Longfellow devoted himself to scholarly pursuits as well as to poetry. He published textbooks, literary essays, and numerous translations of European poets. His most ambitious translation was of *The Divine Comedy of Dante Alighieri,* completed late in his life and still ranked among the finest translations of that work. Another monument to Longfellow's achievement as a scholar is his anthology, *The Poets and Poetry of Europe.* Consisting of translations from the works of nearly four hundred poets and representing ten modern languages, it includes poetry from the early Middle Ages to the nineteenth century.

Longfellow made his debut as a professional poet at age thirty-two with *Voices of the Night,* a collection which achieved immediate popularity. This work contained his poems "A Psalm of Life" and "The Light of the Stars." During the same year he published *Hyperion,* a romantic novel drawing heavily upon his European experience; this is, however generally considered a flawed success in prose fiction. *Hyperion,* in addition to

Outre-mer and his translations of European poets, was important in introducing European thought and art to the American public.

Following *Voices of the Night* and another collection titled *Ballads and Other Poems,* Longfellow began writing the longer narrative poems for which he is primarily remembered. *Evangeline, A Tale of Acadie,* written in classical dactylic hexameters, was immediately acclaimed for its lyrical grace and poignant storyline. *The Song of Hiawatha* was another popular success. Inspired by the Finnish folk epic *Kalevala,* the work is drawn directly from the tribal folklore and mythology of the North American Indians. Although it is still enjoyed by children, the poem's mature audience is now considerably diminished. *Tales of a Wayside Inn,* a series of narrative poems reminiscent of Chaucer's *Canterbury Tales,* is perhaps the best example of Longfellow's versatility and mastery of the narrative form. It also contains one of his and America's most famous poems, "Paul Revere's Ride."

In 1872, Longfellow published what he considered his masterpiece: a trilogy of dramatic poems composed of *The Golden Legend, The New England Tragedies,* and *The Divine Tragedy,* entitled *Christus: A Mystery.* This work treats the subject of

Christianity from its beginnings through the Middle Ages to the time of the American Puritans. Although these works contain some beautiful and effective writing, critics generally agree that Longfellow's creative gift was poetic rather than dramatic, and that the scope of this particular work was well beyond his range.

The debate over Longfellow's literary merit, begun shortly after his death, still continues. While some critics call his work derivative, sentimental, didactic, and excessively symbolic, others insist that, although he was not a great poet, Longfellow holds a unique and important place in American literature. Said Odell Shepard: "To every educated American it should be a pride and pleasure to know Longfellow well, to defend him wisely, and to hold him dear." (See also *Dictionary of Literary Biography, Vol. 1: The American Renaissance in New England.*)

PRINCIPAL WORKS

Outre-mer; a Pilgrimage Beyond the Sea. 2 vols. (travel
    sketches) 1833-34
Hyperion (novel) 1839
Voices of the Night (poetry) 1839
Ballads and Other Poems (poetry) 1842
*The Spanish Student (verse drama) 1843
Poems (poetry) 1845
The Poets and Poetry of Europe [editor and translator]
    (poetry) 1845
Evangeline, A Tale of Acadie (narrative poetry) 1847
Kavanagh (novel) 1849
The Seaside and the Fireside (poetry) 1850
*The Golden Legend** (verse drama) 1851
The Song of Hiawatha (narrative poetry) 1855
The Courtship of Miles Standish, and Other Poems
    (poetry) 1858
Tales of a Wayside Inn (narrative poetry) 1863
The Divine Comedy of Dante Alighieri. 3 vols. [translator]
    (poetry) 1865-67
*The New England Tragedies** (verse dramas) 1868
*The Divine Tragedy** (verse drama) 1871
In the Harbor (poetry) 1882
The Complete Writings of Henry Wadsworth Longfellow. 11
    vols. (poetry, dramas, novels, travel sketches, and
    translations) 1904

*This is the date of first publication rather than first performance.

**These were published together as *Christus: A Mystery* in 1872.

THE AMERICAN MONTHLY REVIEW   (essay date 1833)

With much to remind the reader of [Washington] Irving, there is no lack of originality in the style, as well as the subjects of [*Outre-mer; A Pilgrimage beyond the Sea*]. It is the first number of a series of over-sea sketches, from the pen of a gentleman, whose reputation as an elegant scholar, an easy and graceful writer, a poet of no little celebrity, and a distinguished professor in one of our colleges, is already widely spread through our country. It is modestly put forth; claiming but little, and is anonymous. (pp. 157-58)

[The various sketches] embrace many beautiful descriptions of scenery, touching incidents in our pilgrim's experience, and interesting legends founded upon associations with the places and people which he met with in his wanderings. (p. 158)

If we are not very wide of the truth in our suspicions of the authorship of *Outre-mer*, we think we risk nothing in assuring the lovers of elegant literature, that the part of the "pilgrimage" which yet remains in manuscript, will present attractions far stronger than those contained in the number before us. (p. 159)

Our author, in closing his "Epistle Dedicatory," expresses the modest hope that the reader of his pages will say, upon finishing them, "in the words of Nick Bottom, the weaver, 'I shall desire you of more acquaintance, good Master Cobweb,'"— to which, in parting, we would heartily respond, in the language of that worthy's address to a more pungent personage among his fairy attendants,—"I promise you, your kindred hath made my eyes water ere now. I desire your more acquaintance, good Master Mustard Seed!'" (p. 160)

> "'Outre-mer. A Pilgrimage beyond the Sea'," *in* The American Monthly Review, *Vol. IV, No. II, August, 1833, pp. 157-60.*

THE SOUTHERN LITERARY MESSENGER   (essay date 1839)

[Professor Longfellow's *Hyperion, a Romance,*] it is probable, will fail to please many. Those who are merely and strictly of the novel-reading class—who look with eagerness for incident and plot and dramatic effect, and are dissatisfied if they do not find them—will lay it down after they have read a few pages. But those who appreciate the creations of intellect, who love the stamp of genius and know it when they see it, will pore over its beautifully-printed pages with delight. Its plot is simple enough. A mere thread upon which the pearls are strong. But these *are* pearls. *Hyperion* gives full evidence that its author is a man of refined intellect. . . . It will therefore be read, and it will survive the ephemeral productions of the day. (p. 840)

> "New Works: 'Hyperion, a Romance'," *in* The Southern Literary Messenger, *Vol. V, No. XII, December, 1839, pp. 839-41.*

[C. C. FELTON]   (essay date 1840)

[Longfellow's] Romance of **"Hyperion"** must not be judged by the principles of classical composition. It belongs, preëminently, to the Romantic School. The scene is laid in the very centre of all that is romantic in the land of recollections and ruins of the Middle Ages. It is steeped in the romantic spirit. The language is moulded into the gorgeous forms of Gothic art. The illustrations and comparisons are drawn wholly from the sphere of romantic literature. In tender and profound feeling, and in brilliancy of imagery, the work will bear a comparison with the best productions of romantic fiction, which English literature can boast. Some tastes will be offended by the luxuriance of the language, and the brocaded aspect which it occasionally presents. A mind educated in exclusive admiration of the ancient classics, or in the modern schools formed upon their principles, may naturally be displeased with many things which occur in **"Hyperion."** We are ourselves by no means insensible to the force of strictures, which may be made upon it. But we remember, on the other hand, that nature is limited to no age or country; and art may select from the whole range of nature those objects which suit her purposes, whether they have been handled by the ancient masters or not, provided she do not transcend the limits of morality on the one side, nor sink to the region of common place, on the other. **"Hyperion"** must be judged wholly with reference to this view. The term *romance* has probably misled a great many readers. We have been accustomed to expect, in a work bearing this title, a prodigious amount of diabolical mysteries, trap-doors without number, subterranean dungeons, and the clanking of chains; fortunate, if we escaped with half a dozen ghosts, to say nothing of wizards and enchanters. . . . **"Hyperion"** is no romance of this description. Its quiet, delicate, and beautiful pictures contrast with the terrific scenes of old romance, like a soft, autumnal scene, compared with the landscape swept by the tropical hurricane.

In simplicity of plan, **"Hyperion"** is also distinguished from what a romance is commonly understood to be. The action, if action it may be called, is carried on by as few personages as that of an ancient Greek drama. Nor are there any heroic achievements, which transcend the vigor of moral arm; no battles astound as with their din, or shock us with their bloodshed. Why, then, is the book called a romance? The answer to this question is intimated in the remark we have already made; because its materials, thoughts, feelings, scenery, and illustration, are drawn from the regions of romantic sentiment and poetry. Two paths lay open to the author. He might have constructed a romance, which should have represented the romantic ages in their living reality. He might have gone back a few centuries, summoned the old knights from their tombs, repeopled the ruined castles of the Rhine, and told a tale of love, such as the passion was felt in the olden time. But this would have been a work of a more artificial character than the present. It would have had less connexion with the feelings and aspirations of the present age; it would have been less a part of life, and an outpouring of the heart. The other course was the one which the author has followed. He has represented his hero under all the influences of the romantic age, which a man of modern times may be supposed to feel. . . . This hero, with all his delicate sensibilities, his poetical reveries, his quick feeling of the beauties of natural scenery, and his familiar acquaintance with the storied past, he places in the very heart of the region of old romance. He is a traveller and a student. His memory is peopled with the tales and legends of the Rhine; he sees, in the mighty ruins of the Middle Ages, noble monuments of a glorious and poetical period, and his heart beats with rapture in the contemplation of them. There is something striking in the mode by which the author has reconciled the demands of the past, and those of the present; in his delicate adaptation of the character of his hero to the impression, which it was desirable that the romantic scenes and monuments around him should produce, and the picture which he proposed to give. We are carried back to the illusions of the past, and yet we never desert the familiar present. We see the poetry and architecture of the romantic ages visibly mirrored in a modern mind; and yet that modern mind is such as may naturally be formed by the peculiar circumstances, and the heavy sufferings, which the author represents it to have passed through.

The passions which are unfolded in the course of the story are conducted upon the same principle. There is no modern complication of plot; there are no petty difficulties and entanglements, such as impede the progress of most modern heroes. There is a tale of love; but it is so taken out of the ordinary accompaniments of that passion, that it seems to belong more to a past and distant age than to the present. The passion remains; but it is so surrounded with the halo of poetry, and the recollections of other times, that its connexion with the real

life of to-day, is like that of a cloud picture in the distant horizon, with the landscape of the solid earth beneath it. To keep up the consistency of the representation, the love-tale is one of unrequited passion. Thus the dreamy character, which ought to mark a literary work blending present realities and past illusions, is preserved throughout. (pp. 145-47)

There are a few points . . . which deserve a more particular consideration. The first is the suitableness of the style to the scenes described. The scenery, we have said, is wholly of the romantic character; and the language, descriptive of such scenery, should be such as to awaken romantic associations, and no other, if possible. (p. 147)

[The] most expressive and picturesque and national parts of our complicated language are the remains of the Anglo-Saxon. They speak the wants of the national heart; they recall the imagery that surrounded the national childhood; they carry us back to the associations, which blend with all our recollections of departed days; they touch the deepest chords of English feeling, and draw from the readiest response, and the most powerful harmonies. They take us back to the rude old Saxon times, and the romantic manners, of the Middle Ages. Now, it is precisely this element which is most suitable to a romance, and especially one whose scenes are laid in Germany; and a careful examination of the style of **"Hyperion,"** will show that this old Saxon element predominates in it to a very remarkable degree. And it is this element that makes the style so picturesque. . . . It would be difficult, we fancy, to find a book more remarkable for this picturesque character than **"Hyperion."**

Another point deserving of more particular remark, is the literary criticism contained in the book. The author's mind and heart are full of the poetical literature of Germany; and he writes about it with the eloquence and enthusiasm of a lover. The criticisms, which he puts into the mouth of his hero, are plainly his own; and, without adopting them for ours, we hold it but justice to say, that they are marked by a clearness and warmth, which indicate a sagacious head as well as a sympathizing heart. . . . We do not perceive, that the mistiness and obscurity, which are the besetting sin of German authors, have spread over the radiant pictures of **"Hyperion";** on the contrary, the author more than once takes occasion to reprove the supersublimated nonsense of the Transcendentalists. But it cannot be denied, that the sentimental feelings, which belong more to German than to English poetry, are perceptible in the general tone of the work; and that this sentimentality occasionally transcends the bounds of English reserve. Nor are we prepared to vindicate the tone of expression in every case. We would by no means hold up **"Hyperion"** as a model of style for our countrymen. With all its excellences, it has defects,— *splendida vita,*—which, in any attempt at imitation, would degenerate into intolerable faults. With this *caveat,* we must say, that we have been borne away upon its golden tide of brilliant language, in spite of critical objections, and sometimes against our better judgment; and its rich discussions of letters and art have always given materials for reflection, and often feelings of delight. (pp. 148-49)

[*C. C. Felton,*] "'*Hyperion*'," in The North American Review, *Vol. L, No. 106, January, 1840, pp. 145-61.*

THE NORTH AMERICAN REVIEW   (essay date 1840)

[The poems of Longfellow's **"Voices of the Night"**] are among the most remarkable poetical compositions, which have ever appeared in the United States. They are filled with solemn pathos, uttered in the most melodious and picturesque language. . . . [How] rare is it to find poetry to compare with . . . the **"Psalm of Life."** (p. 266)

The poetry of Mr. Longfellow is marked by a very vivid imagination, great susceptibility to the impressions of natural scenery, and a ready perception of the analogies between natural objects and the feelings of the human heart. But, besides this, he possesses an extraordinary command over the powers of language, and turns it to any form at will. . . .

If we analyze any one of the poems . . . , we shall find that each thought, and each illustration, is clothed in the words that precisely fit it; that the author's tact in this respect is most felicitous. (p. 268)

The earlier pieces, which make the second division of the volume, are already well known to the readers of poetry. They are beautiful compositions, characterized by good taste, a flowing and easy versification, and quiet and gentle feelings; but they are occasionally rather timid and subdued, and show here and there traces of the influence of the recent schools of English poetry; an influence perfectly natural, and almost irresistible to a youthful poet's mind. They show the same nicely attuned ear, the same lively susceptibility, the same descriptive powers, though not fully unfolded, that have appeared in his later productions. (p. 269)

> *"Longfellow's 'Voices of the Night',"* in The North American Review, *Vol. L, No. CVI, January, 1840, pp. 266-69.*

THE CHRISTIAN EXAMINER   (essay date 1840)

There is a period in the life of most men, when they are addicted, with more or less earnestness, to what is called wooing the muse. In our condition of society, this task is commonly begun and ended in about the same space of time, that is alloted to wooing of a less ethereal kind; or, in general, between the age of sixteen and the important period of twenty-one. Then, it is admitted to be necessary for the temporary bard to lay aside such vanities, and stretch to his oar on the perilous voyage before him. . . . Poetry has as little chance to be heard amidst [the] stern realities of life, as a whisper in the din of a cotton factory. But there is, nevertheless, here and there an individual, very happily born or circumstanced, in whom the fire continues to burn, after its first wild blaze has gone down; and of this fortunate class, and high in its scale, is Mr. Longfellow. He has been for some years very favorably known to the public, not by any poetical work of great extent or labor; but by productions of taste and talent, indicating little ambition for display, but rich with all the promise which a delicate observation of nature, polished versification, and pure and elevated thought can give.

Apart from the merits which most commonly attract attention, one of the characteristics of the poetry of Mr. Longfellow, is its tone of sincerity and manliness. Some may regard this as faint praise; but if the end of the art be to improve and elevate as well as please, it should surely be regarded as the greatest praise of all. (p. 243)

It would not be easy to find a "strain in a higher mood" than [**"A Psalm of Life"** from Mr. Longfellow's *Voices of the Night*]; it is equally admirable for its simplicity, manly fervor, dignity, and truth. . . .

The same spirit reigns throughout [*Voices of the Night*]; not only is there nothing in it at variance with true sentiments, but, in the later pieces particularly, those sentiments are expressed with a force and beauty, which go directly to the heart. (p. 245)

The larger portion of this volume is occupied by the author's earlier writings, now for the first time collected, and by translations, principally from the Spanish. His version of the "Coplas di Manrique" has been often noticed with high and merited praise; but there are others, which we regard as equally happy. . . . This power of transfusing the spirit of another language into ours, though, even when most successfully displayed, inferior to that of original creation, requires some higher qualities than the mere art of reproducing the same thoughts in graceful rhyme; yet the highest glory of the translator falls very short of that which is due to him, in whom the fire of inspiration is not borrowed from another's altar. . . . [The sequence entitled **"Voices of the Night"** abounds] in elevated thoughts, and true poetical feeling; the expression is in general glowing and felicitous, though occasionally liable to the charge of quaintness; nor are we quite certain, that the allusions to the death-scene of Lear, in the **"Midnight Mass for the Dying Year,"** however striking and ingenious, are consistent with perfect taste. It is, nevertheless, a proud testimony of Shakespeare's genius, that the comparison of one of the mighty changes in the aspect of nature, with that of the infirm, wronged old king, when his accumulated sorrows are closing in the welcome relief of death, betrays no want of nature or of dignity. (p. 246)

> *"Longfellow's 'Voices of the Night',"* in The Christian Examiner, *Vol. XXVIII, No. 2, May, 1840, pp. 242-48.*

[EDGAR ALLAN POE]   (essay date 1842)

Much as we admire the genius of Mr. Longfellow, we are fully sensible of his many errors of affectation and imitation. His artistic skill is great, and his ideality high. But his conception of the *aims* of poesy *is all wrong.* . . . His didactics are all *out of place.* He has written brilliant poems—by accident; that is to say, when permitting his genius to get the better of his conventional habit of thinking—a habit deduced from German study. We do not mean to say that a didactic moral may not be well made the *under-current* of a poetical thesis, but that it can never be well put so obtrusively forth as in the majority of his compositions.

We have said that Mr. Longfellow's conception of the *aims* of poesy is erroneous; and that thus, laboring at a disadvantage, he does violent wrong to his own high powers; and now the question is, what *are* his ideas of the aims of the Muse, as we gather these ideas from the *general* tendency of his poems? It will be at once evident that, imbued with the peculiar spirit of German song (in pure conventionality) he regards the inculcation of a *moral* as essential. Here we find it necessary to repeat that we have reference only to the *general* tendency of his compositions; for there are some magnificent exceptions, where, as if by accident, he has permitted his genius to get the better of his conventional prejudice. But didacticism is the prevalent *tone* of his song. His invention, his imagery, his all, is made subservient to the elucidation of some one or more points (but rarely of more than one) which he looks upon as *truth.* And that this mode of procedure will find stern defenders should never excite surprise, so long as the world is full to overflowing with cant and conventicles. (pp. 376-78)

In common with all who claim the sacred title of poet, [Professor Longfellow] should limit his endeavors to the creation of novel moods of beauty, in form, in color, in sound, in sentiment; for over all this wide range has the poetry of words dominion. To what the world terms *prose* may be safely and properly left all else. The artist who doubts of his thesis, may always resolve his doubt by the single question—"might not this matter be as well or better handled in *prose*?" If it *may,* then is it no subject for the Muse. (pp. 381-82)

Of the pieces which constitute ["**Ballads and Other Poems**"], there are not more than one or two thoroughly fulfilling the ideas we have proposed; although the volume, as a whole, is by no means so chargeable with didacticism as Mr. Longfellow's previous book ["**Voices of the Night**"]. We would mention as poems *nearly true*, "**The Village Blacksmith**"; "**The Wreck of the Hesperus**," and especially "**The Skeleton in Armor**." In the first-mentioned we have the *beauty* of simple-mindedness as a genuine thesis; and this thesis is inimitably handled until the concluding stanza, where the spirit of legitimate poesy is aggrieved in the pointed antithetical deduction of a *moral* from what has gone before. In "**The Wreck of the Hesperus**" we have the *beauty* of child-like confidence and innocence, with that of the father's stern courage and affection. But, with slight exception, those particulars of the storm here detailed are not poetic subjects. Their thrilling *horror* belongs to prose, in which it could be far more effectively discussed, as Professor Longfellow may assure himself at any moment by experiment. . . . In "**The Skeleton in Armor**" we find a pure and perfect thesis artistically treated. We find the beauty of bold courage and self-confidence, of love and maiden devotion, of reckless adventure, and finally of life-contemning grief. Combined with all this, we have numerous *points* of beauty apparently insulated, but all aiding the main effect or impression. The heart is stirred, and the mind does not lament its mal-instruction. The metre is simple, sonorous, well-balanced, and fully adapted to the subject. Upon the whole, there are fewer truer poems than this. It has but one defect—an important one. The prose remarks prefacing the narrative are really *necessary*. But every work of art should contain within itself all that is requisite for its own comprehension. And this remark is especially true of the ballad. . . . [Its] effect will depend, in great measure, upon the perfection of its finish, upon the nice adaptation of its constituent parts, and, especially, upon what is rightly termed by Schlegel *the unity or totality of interest*. But the practice of prefixing explanatory passages is utterly at variance with such unity. . . . [The] totality of effect is destroyed.

Of the other original poems in the volume before us, there is none in which the aim of instruction, or *truth*, has not been too obviously substituted for the legitimate aim, *beauty*. We have heretofore taken occasion to say that a didactic moral might be happily made the *under-current* of a poetical theme . . . ; but the moral thus conveyed is invariably an ill effect when obtruding beyond the upper-current of the thesis itself. Perhaps the worst specimen of this obtrusion is given us by our poet in "**Blind Bartimeus**" and "**The Goblet of Life**," where it will be observed that the *sole* interest of the upper-current of meaning depends upon its relation or reference to the under. (pp. 382-85)

Of the translations we scarcely think it necessary to speak at all. We regret that our poet will persist in busying himself about such matters. *His* time might be better employed in original conception. (p. 385)

[Edgar Allan Poe,] "Longfellow's Ballads" (originally published as "'Ballads and Other Poems'," in Graham's Magazine, *Vol. XX, Nos. 3 & 4, March-April, 1842), in* The Complete Works of Edgar Allan Poe, *Vol. VI,* Colonial Press Company, *1856, pp. 374-91.*

[C. C. FELTON]   (essay date 1842)

Mr. Longfellow's profound knowledge of German literature has given a very perceptible tincture to his poetical style [in *Ballads and Other Poems*]. It bears the Romantic impress, as distinguished from the Classical, though at the same time it is marked by a classical severity of taste. Nothing can exceed the exquisite finish of some of his smaller pieces, while they also abound in that richness of expression and imagery, which the Romantic muse is supposed to claim as her more especial attribute. The melody of his versification is very remarkable; some of his stanzas sound with the richest and sweetest music of which language is capable. (p. 115)

[C. C. Felton,] "Longfellow's 'Ballads and Other Poems'," in The North American Review, *Vol. LV, No. 116, July, 1842, pp. 114-44.*

MARGARET FULLER   (essay date 1846)

We must confess to a coolness towards Mr. Longfellow, in consequence of the exaggerated praises that have been bestowed upon him. When we see a person of moderate powers receive honors which should be reserved for the highest, we feel somewhat like assailing him and taking from him the crown which should be reserved for grander brows. And yet this is perhaps ungenerous. It may be that the management of publishers, the hyperbole of paid or undiscerning reviewers, or some accidental cause which gives a temporary interest to productions beyond what they would permanently command, have raised such a one to a place as much above his wishes as his claims, and which he would rejoice with honorable modesty to vacate at the approach of one worthier. We the more readily believe this of Mr. Longfellow, as one so sensible to the beauties of other writers and so largely indebted to them *must* know his own comparative rank better than his readers have known it for him. (pp. 382-83)

Mr. Longfellow has been accused of plagiarism. We have been surprised that anyone should have been anxious to fasten special charges of this kind upon him, when we had supposed it so obvious that the greater part of his mental stores were derived from the works of others. He has no style of his own growing out of his own experiences and observations of nature. Nature with him, whether human or external, is always seen through the windows of literature. There are in his poems sweet and tender passages descriptive of his personal feelings, but very few showing him as an observer at first hand of the passions within or the landscape without.

This want of the free breath of nature, this perpetual borrowing of imagery, this excessive because superficial culture which he has derived from an acquaintance with the elegant literature of many nations and men out of proportion to the experience of life within himself, prevent Mr. Longfellow's verses from ever being a true refreshment to ourselves. (pp. 383-84)

Let us take, for example of what we do not like, one of his worst pieces [in *Poems*], the "**Prelude to the Voices of the Night**"—

> Beneath some patriarchal tree
> I lay upon the ground;
> His hoary arms uplifted be,
> And all the broad leaves over me
> Clapped their little hands in glee
> With one continuous sound.

What an unpleasant mixture of images! Such never rose in a man's mind as he lay on the ground and looked up to the tree above him. The true poetry for this stanza would be to give us an image of what was in the writer's mind as he lay there and looked up. But this idea of the leaves clapping their little hands with glee is taken out of some book; or at any rate is a book thought and not one that came in the place, and jars entirely with what is said of the tree uplifting its hoary arms. (p. 384)

Such instances could be adduced everywhere throughout the poems, depriving us of any clear pleasure from any one piece, and placing his poems beside such as those of Bryant in the same light as that of the prettiest *made* shell, beside those whose every line and hue tells a history of the action of winds and waves and the secrets of one class of organizations.

But do we therefore esteem Mr. Longfellow a willful or conscious plagiarist? By no means. It is his misfortune that other men's thoughts are so continually in his head as to overshadow his own. The order of fine development is for the mind the same as the body, to take in just so much food as will sustain it in its exercise and assimilate with its growth. If it is so assimilated—if it becomes a part of the skin, hair, and eyes of the man, it is his own, no matter whether he pick it up in the woods or borrow from the dish of a fellow-man or receive it in the form of manna direct from Heaven. (p. 385)

But Mr. Longfellow presents us not with a new product in which all the old varieties are melted into a fresh form, but rather with a tastefully arranged museum, between whose glass cases are interspersed neatly potted rose trees, geraniums, and hyacinths, grown by himself with aid of indoor heat. Still we must acquit him of being a willing or conscious plagiarist. Some objects in the collection are his own; as to the rest, he has the merit of appreciation and a rearrangement not always judicious, but the result of feeling on his part.

Such works as Mr. Longfellow's we consider injurious only if allowed to usurp the place of better things. The reason of his being overrated here is because through his works breathes the air of other lands, with whose products the public at large is but little acquainted. He will do his office, and a desirable one, of promoting a taste for the literature of these lands before his readers are aware of it. As a translator he shows the same qualities as in his own writings; what is forcible and compact he does not render adequately; grace and sentiment he appreciates and reproduces. Twenty years hence when he stands upon his own merits, he will rank as a writer of elegant if not always accurate taste, of great imitative power, and occasional felicity in an original way where his feelings are really stirred. He has touched no subject where he has not done somewhat that is pleasing, though also his poems are much marred by ambitious failings. As instances of his best manner we would mention **"The Reaper and the Flowers," "Lines to the Planet Mars," "A Gleam of Sunshine,"** and **"The Village Blacksmith."** His two ballads are excellent imitations, yet in them is no spark of fire. In **"Nuremberg"** are charming passages. Indeed, the whole poem is one of the happiest specimens of

Mr. L.'s poetic feeling, taste and tact in making up a rosary of topics and images. (pp. 385-86)

And now farewell to [*Poems*], with its Preciosos and Preciosas, its Vikings and knights, and cavaliers, its flowers of all climes, and wild flowers of none. We have not wished to depreciate these writings below their current value more than truth absolutely demands. We have not forgotten that if a man cannot himself sit at the feet of the Muse, it is much if he prizes those who may; it makes him a teacher to the people. Neither have we forgotten that Mr. Longfellow has a genuine respect for his pen, never writes carelessly, nor when he does not wish to, nor for money alone. Nor are we intolerant to those who prize hothouse bouquets beyond all the free beauty of nature; that helps the gardener and has its uses. But still let us not forget—*Excelsior!* (p. 388)

> *Margaret Fuller, "American Literature," in her* Papers on Literature and Art, *Wiley and Putnam, 1846 (and reprinted in her* The Writings of Margaret Fuller, *edited by Mason Wade, The Viking Press, 1941, pp. 358-88).**

NATHANIEL HAWTHORNE   (essay date 1847)

[The theme of Longfellow's *Evangeline* is], indeed, not to be trusted in the hands of an ordinary writer, who would bring out only its gloom and wretchedness; it required the true poet's deeper insight to present it to us, as we find it here, its pathos all illuminated with beauty,—so that the impression of the poem is nowhere dismal nor despondent, and glows with the purest sunshine where we might the least expect it, on the pauper's death-bed. We remember no such triumph as the author has here achieved, transfiguring Evangeline, now old and gray, before our eyes, and making us willingly acquiesce in all the sorrow that has befallen her, for the sake of the joy which is prophesied and realized within her.

The story is told with the utmost simplicity—with the simplicity of high and exquisite art, which causes it to flow onward as naturally as the current of a stream. Evangeline's wanderings give occasion to many pictures both of northern and southern scenery and life; but these do not appear as if brought in designedly, to adorn the tale; they seem to throw their beauty inevitably into the calm mirror of its bosom, as it flows past them. So it is with all the adornments of the poem; they seem to have come unsought. Beautiful thoughts spring up like roses, and gush forth like violets along a wood-path, but never in any entanglement or confusion; and it is chiefly because beauty is kept from jostling with beauty, that we recognize the severe intellectual toil, which must have been bestowed upon this sweet and noble poem. It was written with no hasty hand, and in no light mood. The author has done himself justice, and has regard to his well-earned fame; and, by this work of his maturity—a poem founded on American history, and embodying itself in American life and manners—he has placed himself on an eminence higher than he had yet attained, and beyond the reach of envy. Let him stand, then, at the head of our list of native poets, until some one else shall break up the rude soil of our American life, as he has done, and produce from it a lovelier and nobler flower than this poem of Evangeline!

Mr. Longfellow has made what may be considered an experiment, by casting his poem into hexameters. The first impressions of many of his readers will be adverse; but, when it is perceived how beautifully plastic this cumbrous measure becomes in his hands—how thought and emotion incorporate and identify themselves with it—how it can compass great ideas, or pick up familiar ones—how it swells and subsides with the nature and necessities of the theme—and, finally, how musical it is, whether it imitate a forest-wind or the violin of an Acadian fiddler—we fully believe that the final judgment will be in its favor. Indeed, we cannot conceive of the poem as existing in any other measure. (pp. 334-35)

> Nathaniel Hawthorne, "Hawthorne's Contributions to 'The Salem Advertiser': Longfellow's 'Evangeline'," edited by Randall Stewart (originally published as "Longfellow's 'Evangeline'," in The Salem Advertiser, November 13, 1847), in American Literature, Vol. 5, No. 4, January, 1934, pp. 333-35.

JOHN GREENLEAF WHITTIER   (essay date 1848)

Eureka! Here, then, we have it at last,—an American poem [*Evangeline*], with the lack of which British reviewers have so long reproached us. Selecting the subject of all others best calculated for his purpose,—the expulsion of the French settlers of Acadie from their quiet and pleasant homes around the Basin of Minas, one of the most sadly romantic passages in the history of the Colonies of the North,—[Professor Longfellow] has succeeded in presenting a series of exquisite pictures of the striking and peculiar features of life and nature in the New World. The range of these delineations extends from Nova Scotia on the northeast to the spurs of the Rocky Mountains on the west and the Gulf of Mexico on the south. Nothing can be added to his pictures of quiet farm-life in Acadie, the Indian summer of our northern latitudes, the scenery of the Ohio and Mississippi Rivers, the bayous and cypress forests of the South, the mocking-bird, the prairie, the Ozark hills, the Catholic missions, and the wild Arabs of the West, roaming with the buffalo along the banks of the Nebraska. The hexameter measure he has chosen has the advantage of a prosaic freedom of expression, exceedingly well adapted to a descriptive and narrative poem; yet we are constrained to think that the story of *Evangeline* would have been quite as acceptable to the public taste had it been told in the poetic prose of the author's *Hyperion*.

In reading it and admiring its strange melody we were not without fears that the success of Professor Longfellow in this novel experiment might prove the occasion of calling out a host of awkward imitators, leading us over weary wastes of hexameters, enlivened neither by dew, rain, nor fields of offering.

Apart from its Americanism, the poem has merits of a higher and universal character. It is not merely a work of art; the pulse of humanity throbs warmly through it. The portraits of Basil the blacksmith, the old notary, Benedict Bellefontaine, and good Father Felician, fairly glow with life. The beautiful Evangeline, loving and faithful unto death, is a heroine worthy of any poet of the present century. (p. 280)

The natural and honest indignation with which, many years ago, we read for the first time that dark page of our Colonial history—the expulsion of the French neutrals—was reawakened by the simple pathos of the poem; and we longed to find an adequate expression of it in the burning language of the poet. We marvelled that he who could so touch the heart by his description of the sad suffering of the Acadian peasants should have permitted the authors of that suffering to escape without censure. The outburst of the stout Basil, in the church of Grand Pré, was, we are fain to acknowledge, a great relief

to us. But, before reaching the close of the volume, we were quite reconciled to the author's forbearance. The design of the poem is manifestly incompatible with stern "rhadamanthine justice" and indignant denunciation of wrong. It is a simple story of quiet pastoral happiness, of great sorrow and painful bereavement, and of the endurance of a love which, hoping and seeking always, wanders evermore up and down the wilderness of the world, baffled at every turn, yet still retaining faith in God and in the object of its lifelong quest. It was no part of the writer's object to investigate the merits of the question at issue between the poor Acadians and their Puritan neighbors. Looking at the materials before him with the eye of an artist simply, he has arranged them to suit his idea of the beautiful and pathetic, leaving to some future historian the duty of sitting in judgment upon the actors in the atrocious outrage which furnished them. With this we are content. The poem now has unity and sweetness which might have been destroyed by attempting to avenge the wrongs it so vividly depicts. It is a psalm of love and forgiveness: the gentleness and peace of Christian meekness and forbearance breathe through it. (p. 281)

> John Greenleaf Whittier, "'Evangeline'" (originally published in The National Era, Vol. II, January 27, 1848), in The Achievement of American Criticism: Representative Selections from Three Hundred Years of American Criticism, edited by Clarence Arthur Brown, Ronald Press, 1954, pp. 280-84.

EDGAR ALLAN POE   (essay date 1849?)

For the *Evening Mirror* of January 14 (1846), before my editorial connection with the *Broadway Journal*, I furnished a brief criticism on Professor Longfellow's **"Waif."** . . . The criticism ended thus:

We conclude our notes on the **"Waif"** with the observation that, although full of beauties, it is infected with a *moral taint*—or is this a mere freak of our own fancy? We shall be pleased if it be so;—but there *does* appear, in this little volume, a very careful avoidance of all American poets who may be supposed especially to interfere with the claims of Mr. Longfellow. These men Mr. Longfellow can continuously *imitate* (*is* that the word?) and yet never even incidentally commend.

Much discussion ensued. (p. 258)

[To] show, in general, what I mean by accusing Mr. Longfellow of imitation, I [ask the reader to compare] his **"Midnight Mass for the Dying Year,"** with "The Death of the Old Year" of Tennyson. (p. 309)

I have no idea of commenting, at any length, upon this imitation, which is too palpable to be mistaken, and which belongs to the most barbarous class of literary piracy: that class in which, while the words of the wronged author are avoided, his most intangible, and therefore his least defensible and least reclaimable, property is appropriated. Here, with the exception of lapses which, however, speak volumes (such for instance as the use of the capitalized "Old Year," the general peculiarity of the rhythm, and the absence of rhyme at the end of each stanza), there is nothing of a visible or palpable nature by which the source of the American poem can be established. But then nearly all that is valuable in the piece of Tennyson, is the first conception of personifying the Old Year as a dying old man, with the singularly wild and fantastic *manner* in which that conception is carried out. Of this conception and of this manner he is robbed. What is here not taken from Tennyson is made up, mosaically, from the death scene of Cordelia, in "Lear"—to which I refer the curious reader.

In *Graham's Magazine* for February, 1843, there appeared a poem, furnished by Professor Longfellow, entitled "The Good George Campbell," and purporting to be a translation from the German of O.L.B. Wolff. In "Minstrelsy Ancient and Modern," by William Motherwell, published by John Wylie, Glasgow, 1827, is to be found a poem partly compiled and partly written by Motherwell himself. It is entitled "The Bonnie George Campbell." (pp. 313-14)

Professor Longfellow defends himself (I learn) from the charge of *imitation* in this case, by the assertion that he *did* translate from Wolff, but that Wolff copied from Motherwell. I am willing to believe almost any thing than so gross a plagiarism as this seems to be—but there are difficulties which should be cleared up. In the first place how happens it that, in the transmission from the Scotch into German, and again from the German into English, not only the versification should have been rigidly preserved, but the *rhymes* and *alliterations*? (pp. 314-15)

Were I disposed, indeed, to push this subject any further, I should have little difficulty in culling, from the works of the author of **"Outre Mer,"** a score or two of imitations quite as palpable as any upon which I have insisted. The fact of the matter is, that the friends of Mr. Longfellow, so far from undertaking to talk about my "carping littleness" in charging Mr. Longfellow with imitation, should have given me credit, under the circumstances, for great moderation in charging him with imitation alone. Had I accused him, in loud terms, of manifest and continuous plagiarism, I should but have echoed the sentiment of every man of letters in the land beyond the immediate influence of the Longfellow coterie. (pp. 323-24)

Having brought the subject, in this view, to a close, I now feel at liberty to add a few words, by way of freeing myself of any suspicion of malevolence or discourtesy. The thesis of my argument, in general, has been the definition of the grounds on which a charge of plagiarism may be based, and of the species of ratiocination by which it is to be established: that is all. It will be seen by anyone who shall take the trouble to read what I have written, that I make *no* charge of moral delinquency against [Mr. Longfellow] . . .—indeed, lest in the heat of argument, I may have uttered any words which may admit of being tortured into such interpretation, I here fully disclaim them upon the spot. (p. 325)

> *Edgar Allan Poe, "Longfellow and Other Plagiarists" (1849?), in* The Complete Works of Edgar Allan Poe, Vol. VI, *Colonial Press Company, 1856, pp. 258-327.*

JOHN GREENLEAF WHITTIER   (essay date 1850)

We welcome with real pleasure another volume of poems from the pen of one of the sweetest poets of our time. The pieces in [**"The Seaside and the Fireside"**] have the careful moulding and patient polish by which art attains the graceful ease and chaste simplicity of nature. There are no rugged lines nor uncouth rhymes, to break the harmony of these felicitous numbers. All whose ears have been tortured by Browning's burlesque of rhythm, should resort at once to the healing influences of **"The Seaside and Fireside"** melodies of Longfellow.

There are two poems in this little volume which will live, for the common heart of humanity to which they address them-

selves will not willingly let them die. **"The Fire of Drift-wood"** shines over some of the dark problems of life, and **"Resignation"** is full of that tender sympathy and Christian consolation, which, in the language of Scripture, gives "the oil of joy for mourning, and the garment of praise for the spirit of heaviness." A considerable portion of the volume is occupied by a spirited translation of a poem by Jasmin, the Barber-poet of Gascony, which will excite the curiosity of the reader to know more of the author.

> *John Greenleaf Whittier, "Longfellow: 'The Seaside and the Fireside'" (originally published under a different title in* The National Era, *Vol. IV, No. 1, January 3, 1850), in his* Whittier on Writers and Writing: The Uncollected Critical Writings of John Greenleaf Whittier, *edited by Edwin Harrison Cady and Harry Hayden Clark, Syracuse University Press, 1950, p. 162.*

BLACKWOOD'S EDINBURGH MAGAZINE   (essay date 1852)

We have no hesitation in expressing our opinion that there is nearly as much fine poetry in Mr. Longfellow's *Golden Legend* as in the celebrated drama of Goethe [*Faust*]. (p. 213)

Mr. Longfellow will, in all probability, not receive that credit which is really his due, for the many exquisite passages contained in his *Golden Legend,* simply on account of its manifest resemblance to the *Faust.* Men in general look upon the inventive faculty as the highest gift of genius, and are apt to undervalue, without proper consideration, everything which appears to be not original, but imitative. This is hardly fair. The inventive faculty is not always, indeed it is very rarely, combined with adequate powers of description. The best inventors have not always taken the trouble to invent for themselves. . . . But it must be confessed that Mr. Longfellow does not possess the art of disguising his stolen goods. It is one thing to take a story, and to dress it up anew, and another to adopt a story or a plot, which, throughout, shall perpetually put you in mind of some notorious antecedent. (p. 215)

In respect of melody, feeling, pathos, and that exquisite simplicity of expression which is the criterion of a genuine poet, Mr. Longfellow need not shun comparison with any living writer. He is not only by nature a poet, but he has cultivated his poetical powers to the utmost. No man, we really believe, has bestowed more pains upon poetry than he has. He has studied rhythm most thoroughly; he has subjected the most beautiful strains of the masters of verbal melody, in many languages, to a minute and careful analysis; he has arrived at his poetical theories by dint of long and thoughtful investigation; and yet, exquisite as the product is which he has now given us, there is a large portion of it which we cannot style as truly original. In the honey which he presents to us—and a delicious compound it is—we can always detect the flavour of the parent flowers. He possesses, more than any other writer, the faculty of assuming, for the time, or for the occasion, the manner of the poet most qualified by nature to illustrate his immediate theme. He not only assumes his manner, but he actually adopts his harmonies. . . . He is a great master of harmonies, but he borrows them too indiscreetly. He gives us a very splendid concert; but then the music is not always, nor indeed in the majority of instances, his own.

Do we complain of this? By no manner of means. We are thankful that the present age is graced by such a poet as Mr. Longfellow, whose extraordinary accomplishment, and research, and devotion to his high calling, can hardly be over-rated. His productions must always command our deep attention, for in them we are certain to meet with great beauty of thought, and very elegant diction. . . . To the wideness of [his] harmonic range we should be inclined to ascribe many of his shortcomings. It is not an unqualified advantage to a poet to be able to assume at will the manner of another, and even, as Mr. Longfellow frequently does, to transcend him. Every poet should have his own style, by which he is peculiarly distinguished. He should have his own harmonies, which cannot be mistaken for another's. When such is not the case, the poet is apt to go on experimenting too far. He is tempted, in versification, to adopt new theories, which, upon examination, will not bear to be tried by any aesthetical test. . . . Mr. Longfellow, within the compass of the same poem, presents us with various theories. This surely is a blemish, because it necessarily detracts from unity of tone and effect. We are no advocates for close poetical precision, or the maintenance of those notes which, a century ago, were deemed almost imperative; but we think that poetic license may sometimes be carried too far. In various passages of *The Golden Legend*, Mr. Longfellow, acting no doubt upon some principle, but one which is wholly unintelligible to us, discards not only metre, but also rhyme and rhythm. . . . [The] dialogue may be sweetly and naturally expressed, but the reader will no doubt be at a loss to determine whether it belongs to the domain of poetry, or to that of prose. . . . (pp. 215-16)

[Mr. Longfellow] is one of the most accomplished and skilful versifiers of his time, and therefore we regret the more that he will not confine him to the safe, familiar, and yet ample range of recognised Saxon metres. . . . Surely he must see, on reflection, that there are natural limits to the power and capacity of each language, and that it is utterly absurd to strain our own in order to compass metres and melodies which peculiarly belong to another. There can be no doubt that the German language, from its construction and sound, can be adapted to many of the most intricate of the Grecian metres. But the English language is not so easily welded, and beyond a certain point it is utterly hopeless to proceed. Mr. Longfellow thoroughly understands the value of pure and simple diction—why will he not apply the same rules to the form and structure of his verse? As sincere admirers of his genius, we would entreat his attention to this; for he may rely upon it that, if he continues to give way to this besetting sin of experiment, he is imperilling that high position which his poetical powers may well entitle him to attain. (p. 217)

[*The Golden Legend*] does undeniably exhibit many proofs of genius, accomplishments, power of expression, and learning; . . . nevertheless, we cannot accept [it] as a great work. It is like an ornament in which some gems of the purest lustre are set, side by side with fragments of coloured glass, and even inferior substances. The evident presence of the latter sometimes shakes our faith in the absolute value of the jewels, which are deserving of better association; and we cannot help wishing that the whole work could be taken to pieces, the counterfeit materials thrown aside, and the remainder entirely reconstructed on a new principle and design. There is ever an intimate connection between the design and the material. Thoughts, however rich in themselves, lose their effect when ill displayed; and the want of the knowledge of this has ere now proved fatal to the fame of many a promising artist. The language and sentiments of Elsie, however beautiful in themselves—and that they are beautiful we most unhesitatingly maintain—excite in our minds no sympathy. They are simply portions of an ill-

constructed drama, almost aimless in purpose, and without even an intelligible moral; they do not tend to any point upon which our interest or expectations are concentrated, and therefore, in order to do justice to them, we are forced to regard them as fragmentary. Mr. Longfellow has not succeeded in giving a human interest to his drama. His story is poor, or rather incomprehensible, and his plan essentially vicious; and these are faults which no brilliancy of execution can ever serve to redeem. We are deeply disappointed to find that such is the case, for we can assure the author that we have watched his poetical career with no common interest—that we have long been aware of the great extent of his powers—and that we have waited, with much anxiety, in the expectation of seeing those powers exhibited in their full measure. We fear that we must wait a little longer before he shall do justice to himself. . . . His radical error, we think, may be traced to two things—the want of a life-like plot, and the introduction of supernatural machinery.

No reader of *The Golden Legend* will venture to aver that he has derived the highest interest from the story, apart from the poetry with which it is surrounded. (p. 224)

We hope hereafter to find Mr. Longfellow engaged on some subject more worthy of his genius. Of his powers there can be no doubt, nor of his success, provided he will apply those powers properly. We are fully sensible of the many beauties contained within the compass of this volume; and our only regret, while laying down the pen, is that we cannot yet congratulate the author on having achieved a work, fully developing his excellencies, natural and acquired, and entitling him to assume a higher rank among the masters of English song. (p. 225)

> *"Longfellow's 'Golden Legend',"* in Blackwood's Edinburgh Magazine, *Vol. LXXI, No. CCCCXXXVI, February, 1852, pp. 212-25.*

THE DUBLIN UNIVERSITY MAGAZINE (essay date 1856)

[It] seems to have been left for Longfellow to push the explorations of his countrymen into nature and into legendary lore—into the wilderness of space and of tradition—to a limit before unreached. By one or two of his earlier works he had given indications of what his more matured genius might arrive at. In **"Evangeline,"** and those lesser hymns of the hunting-grounds, he had fired the bush, as it were, before him, and he can now advance by the light kindled by himself. This is not too much praise, perhaps, to bestow on a poet whom we were quite as ready to censure when, mistaking his course, he followed the dim, mediaeval swampfire, and for a time lost himself in the **"Golden Legend."**

That he should have recovered the path—we might call it the *trail*—speaks loudly to his credit. Few poets have found their way back to their own vein when they have struck away from it. Longfellow is once more conspicuous, because he is once more American. He may indeed still be natural and pleasing, as he always has been, when he stands alone with his own thoughts, be they caught from what country or clime they may. But he will never continue to be—what he is now—*original*, unless he abandons, once for all, the moulds of conventionalism, and abjures as thoroughly as he has just done, everything that is not native to him. Such is our general estimate as regards the career of a national poet. Some one or two may be lifted, by transcendent genius, above the necessity of preserving the *couleur locale;* but, as a general rule, it must be adhered to. (p. 91)

The "Song of Hiawatha" is founded, as the author tells us, "on a tradition prevalent among the North American Indians, of a personage of miraculous birth, who was sent among them to clear their rivers, forests, and fishing-grounds, and to teach them the arts of peace." Into the Indian song—or Edda—thus derived, have been woven other Indian legends. . . . But, in constructing what bears the outward semblance of a mere fable, it appears to have formed part of the author's design to convey, in the guise of allegory, a further meaning. Hiawatha, the hero, is a type of the progress which was alone possible to the savage. The virtues, the powers, the faults, and the absurdities of the red man are depicted in colours as bold as those with which his person is bedaubed. The gentle, artless thing, presiding over the female department of the native wigwam has her representative in Hiawatha's wife—Minnehaha—"Laughing Water." And the allegory is kept up to the end; for the story concludes with the retreat of the aboriginal hero into the recesses of the westward forests, as soon as the stranger has set foot on the soil he is destined to appropriate to himself with such cool and cruel effrontery.

With sound good sense, Longfellow, instead of aiming at such novelties of versification as Tennyson has been lately experimenting upon, has chosen as his medium of expression a monotonous, rhymeless chant—said to be Finnish—uncouth to the ear at first, but after a time, from its very monotony, lending a weird character to the wild tales it accompanies; so that when we get to the end the rhythm continues to drone on, like the *bourdon* of a bagpipe, calling for any additional amount of legendary articulation. The vehicle is, no doubt, *as a vehicle,* a good one. That detached passages could be familiarly quoted for their poetic beauty, in such a dress, is scarcely possible. The "song" must be sung out. (pp. 91-2)

The command of language and imagery displayed by Longfellow in this attempt of his, we are bound to say, is far greater than a superficial reader might imagine. To relieve a long poem, hampered by a monotony of cadence, from a monotony of diction and metaphor, needs all the force and compass of a practised hand. In proportion as the framework is uniform, must the details be varied. To vary these details, without destroying the *simplicity* the scene and characters demand, is a task requiring no ordinary skill. We gladly admit that here the poet has displayed very high powers. (p. 92)

That a bold plunge has been made into untrodden tracts, may be safely affirmed. That these regions teem with the productions of a virgin soil, there is as little reason to deny;—that they present rather the promise of a return to further and future enterprise, than the substantial fruits of a full cultivation, the intelligent reader will, perhaps, have already discovered for himself. (p. 98)

["The Song of Hiawatha" proves] how completely unimpaired are the powers of a genuine living poet; and likewise [conspires] to show how greatly more remains to be done in the same field. Beauties now detached would then be continuous. Legend would underlie narrative, instead of overflowing it. Metrical effects would enhance the interest and pathos, which would call for more finished and less Finnish harmonies.

What scope there is for the genius of America upon her own soil! Let Longfellow, who has now established himself on the outskirts of all previous imaginative exploration in this direction, not content himself with reproducing the legends of the past, but *repeople* it. . . .

For our own part, we take upon ourselves to assign Longfellow his future function amid these scenes. We forbid him, with friendly severity, all access to the Old World. We close up the Atlantic against him. Having high regard for his real fame, implicit faith in his powers, and a warm, brotherly interest in the progress and destiny of his country's literature, we would say to him—Abide where you are—build a wigwam where you have pitched a tent—settle yourself down where you have hunted—and make acquaintance with the *men*, as well as the myths, of primeval America. (p. 99)

> *"Longfellow's 'Song of Hiawatha',"* in The Dublin University Magazine, *Vol. XLVII, No. CCLXXVII, January, 1856, pp. 90-9.*

[EDWARD EVERETT HALE]   (essay date 1856)

The old favorite has sung us his new song. [With *The Song of Hiawatha* Mr. Longfellow] has broken the silence of four years. He has compelled us to listen. He has lighted up the old legends, he has given zest and voice to them quite new. (p. 272)

For ourselves, we confess that in this "North American" blood of ours there is enough of the native element to induce a thorough "Ugh" of satisfaction. We could not have written a better Indian poem, and we do not think Mr. Longfellow could, and we do not think anybody else could. We do not believe that a series of Indian legends should be written in the state or dignity of *Paradise Lost;* nor do we believe that they should have been wrought into an epic, because other countries and times have loved epics, nor into a string of rhymed ballads, because other countries and times have loved such. (p. 273)

The essential characteristic of Indian life, and so of Indian literature, is that it is childlike. . . . There is nothing "Runic" about him. There is nothing of "Romance" about him. There is nothing "Classical" about him. He cannot graduate at a classical college. He cannot fight in an English regiment. He cannot make his bow at a French court. And for all these reasons, he cannot be sung about in an epic poem.

Yet he has his legends,—he has his mythology,—has his unwritten literature. (pp. 273-74)

These are the materials which Mr. Longfellow, with the happiest taste, has selected from. Of these legends, thanks to him, there are now a dozen or more, which will be known at every fireside of those who have driven the hunting-lodges that loved them farther to the westward. He tells the stories as those who told them first would be glad to have them told to pale faces. . . .

In short, Hiawatha is the first permanent contribution to the world's *belles-lettres* made from Indian authorities. We have had a great many mock Indians, like the Indians of the stage. Here is the first poem which savors of the prairie or the mountain hunting-trail. (p. 274)

> [*Edward Everett Hale,*] *"Critical Notices: 'The Song of Hiawatha',"* in The North American Review, *Vol. LXXXII, No. 170, January, 1856, pp. 272-75.*

JAMES RUSSELL LOWELL   (essay date 1859)

Longfellow's translation of "The Children of the Lord's Supper" may have softened prejudice [against the hexameter] somewhat, but "Evangeline" . . . , though encumbered with too many descriptive irrelevancies, was so full of beauty, pathos, and melody, that it made converts by thousands to the hitherto ridiculed measure. (pp. 118-19)

While we acknowledge that the victory thus won by **"Evangeline"** is a striking proof of the genius of the author, we confess that we have never been able to overcome the feeling that the new metre is a dangerous and deceitful one. It is too easy to write, and too uniform for true pleasure in reading. Its ease sometimes leads Mr. Longfellow into prose . . . and into a prosaic phraseology which has now and then infected his style in other metres. . . . We think one great danger of the hexameter is, that it gradually accustoms the poet to be content with a certain regular recurrence of accented sounds, to the neglect of the poetic value of language and intensity of phrase.

But while we frankly avow our infidelity as regards the metre, we as frankly confess our admiration of the high qualities of **"Miles Standish."** In construction we think it superior to **"Evangeline";** the narrative is more straightforward, and the characters are defined with a firmer touch. It is a poem of wonderful picturesqueness, tenderness, and simplicity, and the situations are all conceived with the truest artistic feeling. Nothing can be better, to our thinking, than the picture of Standish and Alden in the opening scene, tinged as it is with a delicate humor, which the contrast between the thoughts and characters of the two heightens almost to pathos. (pp. 119-20)

Mr. Longfellow has been greatly popular because he so greatly deserved it. He has the secret of all the great poets—the power of expressing universal sentiments simply and naturally. A false standard of criticism has obtained of late, which brings a brick as a sample of the house, a line or two of condensed expression as a gauge of the poem. But it is only the whole poem that is a proof of the poem, and there are twenty fragmentary poets, for one who is capable of simple and sustained beauty. Of this quality Mr. Longfellow has given repeated and striking examples, and those critics are strangely mistaken who think that what he does is easy to be done, because he has the power to make it seem so. We think his chief fault is a too great tendency to moralize, or rather, a distrust of his readers, which leads him to point out the moral which he wishes to be drawn from any special poem. (p. 121)

[We] have seen some very unfair attempts to depreciate Mr. Longfellow . . . for qualities which stamp him as a true and original poet. The writer who appeals to more peculiar moods of mind, to more complex or more esoteric motives of emotion, may be a greater favorite with the few; but he whose verse is in sympathy with moods that are human and not personal, with emotions that do not belong to periods in the development of individual minds, but to all men in all years, wins the gratitude and love of whoever can read the language which he makes musical with solace and aspiration. [**"The Courtship of Miles Standish"**], while it will confirm Mr. Longfellow's claim to the high rank he has won among lyric poets, deserves attention also as proving him to possess that faculty of epic narration which is rarer than all others in the nineteenth century. In our love of stimulants, and our numbness of taste, which craves the red pepper of a biting vocabulary, we of the present generation are apt to overlook this almost obsolete and unobtrusive quality; but we doubt if, since Chaucer, we have had an example of more purely objective narrative than in **"The Courtship of Miles Standish."** Apart from its intrinsic beauty, this gives the poem a claim to higher and more thoughtful consideration; and we feel sure that posterity will confirm the verdict of the present in regard to a poet whose reputation is due to

no fleeting fancy, but to an instinctive recognition by the public of that which charms now and charms always,—true power and originality, without grimace and distortion; for Apollo, and not Milo, is the artistic type of strength. (pp. 122-23)

> James Russell Lowell, "Longfellow: 'The Courtship of Miles Standish'" (originally published in The Atlantic Monthly, Vol. III, No. XV, January, 1859), in his The Function of the Poet, and Other Essays, Houghton Mifflin Company, 1920, pp. 115-23.

THE SOUTHERN LITERARY MESSENGER   (essay date 1859)

[Mr. Longfellow] is a real poet,—in our judgment, take him all for all, the noblest of our American poets. Ideal and spiritual in conception, yet keenly observant of the actual, and true to nature, rich in lore, high-minded, pure in thought, picturesque, scholarly, careful in diction, and melodious in versification (the hexameter mania excepted) he appreciates the poet's mission, and labours as the gods love to see mortals labour, to accomplish it. He is an honour to our country, and to refuse him the highest meed of his calling, would show want of patriotism. (p. 118)

The formula for the honest criticism of a work of imagination, is reduced to two very simple questions. Does it please? and why? . . .

Thus, every one who reads **"The Courtship of Miles Standish,"** would say without hesitation—"Yes,—it is a pleasant book—decidedly so." . . .

That point is therefore settled—the book pleases the common, candid reader. *Bene*, then let it please the critic too. If you ask our representative friend, why it pleases,—most likely he will say without much thought or method—"Because the story is told in an agreeable way: I like the old Puritan pictures: the staple sentiments of Love, Friendship, Courage and Religion always please where well exhibited. Longfellow has undoubtedly a genius for figurative language, and without saying that I admire those milliped verses, there is a quaintness about them that titillates the ear."

Now, we think, the general reader has answered very fairly the two questions, and given sufficient reasons for his judgment as far as it goes. . . . [But] many would push the questions somewhat further and ask—How much does it please? Has Mr. Longfellow, in his last poem, maintained his relative eminence, as compared with other poets, or as compared with himself in his other poems? (p. 119)

[We] have prepared the way to say with the least possible offence, that in our poor judgment, **"The Courtship of Miles Standish"** is just a good, readable poem,—that it gives, in a general way, *satisfaction*. As every body agrees to this proposition, we are not called to maintain it affirmatively. But as against those who claim that it is a great poem, we will justify ourselves by a little specialising upon the elements introduced in the verdict of the general reader, already given, but in a reverse order.

First, as to the versification. We will not plunge into the question of longs and shorts. The state of the controversy is briefly this. Many writers deny that the English language is capable of being moulded into tolerable verse. . . . Nevertheless, Mr. Longfellow insists that it can be done, and to prove it, he does it, and continues to do it. (pp. 119-20)

[He] who reads aloud these hexameters, will find that it is a matter of no little difficulty to keep either the canter or the pacing of a butcher's pony. Hardly by whip or spur is it possible to overcome the tendency to subside into the sober walk of downright prose. . . . In plain words, we read it as plain prose, and our auditors said that it was read to edification. Some of the prominent passages in Miles Standish *must* be read thus, or they will lose half their effect. (p. 120)

Now, if Mr. Longfellow could do nothing better than write dreary, weary, draggle-tailed hexameters upon a model of Greek that never existed, he ought to be pitied and let alone. But few poets can charm the ear more deftly than he, when he chooses, as every body knows, who has read **"The Golden Legend"**; and therefore, he ought to be told plainly, for his good and ours, that these draggle-tailed hexameters *are* dreary and weary. He writes them, no doubt, conscientiously and upon theory; but people cannot hear conscientiously, and upon theory: so, having done enough for his conscience, he ought, henceforth to have regard to our ears.

The Poem is cast in the mould of story. If a story does not awaken interest by its development, it is, as a story, a failure. We would not say that in this poem, there is no interest belonging to the narrative; but we think the stimulus it gives to curiosity, is very slight. . . . [In **"The Courtship of Miles Standish"**] Mr. Longfellow has selected an epigrammatic anecdote, and undertaken to expand it into a story. Now, if you expand an epigram, you necessarily flatten its point, and to build a fine poem upon a damaged anecdote, is a task so difficult, that we cannot be surprised that even Mr. Longfellow should have failed in it. That a fair maiden should say to a young man who was wooing her for an old widower too stiff to undertake the performance for himself—*"Why do'n't you speak for yourself, John?"* is a specimen of *naiveté* that has a flavour which we have relished repeatedly, with various adaptations, since first we heard it as a boy. Mr. Longfellow manipulates all the elasticity out of it. He approaches it so tediously, and presents it so tamely, that we scarce know whether to receive it as jest or sentiment. As this incident is the basis of the poem, it necessarily finds a place near the beginning: and as the story is virtually told out as soon as it occurs, the poem, if continued, must, of necessity, be without a story. When the denouement occurs at the beginning, a difficulty arises; as to what shall fill the place of the denouement which is usually presented at the close. Mr. Longfellow meets the difficulty by furnishing two episodes and a commonplace. The two episodes are, the campaign of Miles Standish against the Indians, and the sailing of the Mayflower—both dull; and the commonplace is the wedding of the lovers, good enough, but nothing more. (pp. 120-21)

The Poem has another aspect, in which it may be viewed: that of a historical picture. . . . We must confess to a disappointment here. The spirit of the time is not embodied in any very palpable way. Except the profuse use of Scripture, which versifies into Mr. Longfellow's hexameters better than anything he has introduced, we do not find much that is characteristic. Indeed, as this is a Love Poem, it would not be easy to introduce a great deal of characteristic Puritanism. Doubtless the Puritans loved and married, and the unaffected inquiry addressed by "Priscilla the Puritan maiden" to young John Alden, proves that they, or at least, the young maidens, had the right notion about it. Still, love was not their forte, and a love-story is not the best form of history for them. True, they fought Indians well; but Mr. Longfellow is not the best hand to describe battles. (p. 121)

As a Love Poem, **"The Courtship of Miles Standish"** might have been expected to delineate, in a striking way, the sentiments of the parties concerned, especially of the young people. But in the places where we look for this, the poet is either cold, or a little bombastic. In truth, we cannot admire John Alden as a lover. (pp. 121-22)

In the imagery of the poem, Mr. Longfellow is himself. If he has in any poem failed to embellish his subject by comparisons, varied, rich, apposite, classic, natural and rare, we have never read that poem. . . .

And so we part with **"The Courtship of Miles Standish."** We have not said that it is not a good poem—but only that Mr. Longfellow has written many things better: and we conclude by giving expression to the confident expectation that his busy pen will give us many better things in due time to come. (p. 122)

S.L.C., "Miles Standish," in The Southern Literary Messenger, *Vol. XXVIII, February, 1859, pp. 118-22.*

ECLECTIC MAGAZINE   (essay date 1859)

The causes of [his] rapid and remarkable popularity are easily traceable in Mr. Longfellow's poems, especially his earlier ones. His merits certainly do not consist in any imaginative originality. The moral and intellectual quality of the *Voices of the Night,* is such as appeals to the sympathies, and falls within the comprehension, of every reader. They are written from what may be called every body's point of view; they express, always neatly, sometimes gracefully, and now and then beautifully, what nine tenths of their readers think and feel on the subject, or rather what they know they ought to think and feel. . . . *The Footsteps of Angels, The Reaper and the Flowers, The Light of Stars, Midnight Mass for the dying Year,* merely develop, prettily and fancifully, common ideas, and ideas, too, suggested in their entirety by the very titles of these poems. So intelligible and unobjectionable is Mr. Longfellow's thought, so obvious and universally admitted his moral tendency, that we can quite believe what we have heard, that people who neither understand nor care for other poetry buy his as a sort of thing that "deserves encouragement."

The same common-placeness of intellectual character is shown in those of Mr. Longfellow's poems in which the interest is historical. His impressions here also are those which ought to be made on "any well-constituted mind." (p. 460)

Mr. Longfellow has the abstract and generalized impressions of the past which every one derives from reading history; and where he endeavors to reproduce it, he gives us the conventional idea and traditional costume of the period. *The Belfry of Bruges, Nuremburg,* and similar poems, are merely a fluent and musical expression of thoughts and fancies which would at once occur to any intelligent visitor of those famous towns with Murray's Hand-book under his arm. His imagination never properly throws itself into the past; but sees it through the haze of distance, and so catches only its familiar and general outline and most prominent features. The emperors are "rough and bold;" the burghers "brave and thrifty;" the monks "merry" or "holy;" in every case the regular stock epithet embodying the popular idea. Any one of his poems of this kind will illustrate this. (pp. 460-61)

As a describer of nature, Mr. Longfellow holds a higher place than as an interpreter of the life of man, either in the present or the past. He sees further into the forest than into the crowd; and his limited range of experience and of sympathy are, of course, not so directly and palpably felt. The American poets are all, as far as we have observed, comparatively strong in depicting natural scenery, while deficient in thought and culture. Man, with his passions and struggles and perplexities, plays but a secondary part in their writings; he is dwarfed and subdued in the presence of the vast and impressive scenery by which he is surrounded. (p. 461)

It is scenery of [a] vast and impressive kind that Mr. Longfellow describes best. He has a true eye for its salient features, though his sight does not reach much beyond these. He is a steady and truthful though not profound or minute observer. Except in the case of some of the grander natural objects, such as forests and the sea, Mr. Longfellow describes in a fresh and unaffected way not only what would strike every spectator, but what every spectator would find little difficulty in putting into words. He never gives us any of those surprising touches which, like the scent of May blossom, place us at once in the midst of long-forgotten sights and sounds, with all their indescribable associations. He takes in just so much of a landscape as harmonizes with the thought or feeling in his mind, and apart from these his descriptions have comparatively little value. In Tennyson, and generally in poets of a high class, the thought and meaning of the poems are more profound and less obvious; the corresponding natural scenery is less consciously selected, and therefore less superficially appropriate. . . . We do not say that the natural scenery in Mr. Longfellow's poems is merely *illustrative,* or that his thought is merely the reflection of the natural scenery; we believe that there is in many of his poems the real fusion of the two which must take place in the minds of all genuine poets, only that this fusion is less thorough than in the case of Tennyson and some other poets. . . .

Mr. Longfellow is less successful in his descriptions of natural scenery in those poems in which it is introduced in combination with human thought and feeling, than in those in which it is an object of direct contemplation. His poetry of this kind has been called "looking-glass poetry;" and as regards the clearness and literalness, if not the minuteness, with which it gives back some aspects of nature, the expression is a good one. (p. 463)

None of Mr. Longfellow's poems show much creative or dramatic power except *Hiawatha;* in which a small germ of Indian tradition has been expanded into an altogether unique story— a strange mixture of mythology, romance, and fable, as unlike all other poems with which we are acquainted as a savage in his war-paint is unlike all civilized people, but not without some vigorous pictures of forest life and scenery, and a certain soft and noiseless grace like that of the people it describes. This is undoubtedly the most original of all the author's poems; and it has a certain humor of its own—a quality not possessed by any of Mr. Longfellow's other poems. (pp. 463-64)

Mr. Longfellow is quite unrivaled when he has Indian demigods, beavers, sturgeons, and woodpeckers for his characters; and we think he succeeds next best where, as in *Evangeline,* the characters are about half-way between the "Hiawatha" people and educated English or Americans of the present day. His poetical faculty is well adapted for the narration of some simple story which keeps the even tenor of its way among the pastoral occupations and fireside incidents of a primitive people: and such have been the subjects he has chosen for two of his longest poems, *Evangeline* and *The Courtship of Miles Standish;* of which the earlier poem is in our opinion far better than

the later one. Both the story and the characters are more interesting, the scenery is more varied and more richly colored, and the later poem contains no incident nearly as good as the passing of Evangeline and her lover close by each other in their boats without either being aware of it. Both of them are stories from the annals of Mr. Longfellow's own land; and with these, from the simpler and more elementary character of the events recorded in them, he is less incompetent to deal than with the earlier stages of European civilization. (p. 464)

In intimating that a certain commonplace and superficial character belongs to all Mr. Longfellow's poetry, we by no means imply that he is not a true poet. His mind more readily and naturally and sufficiently expresses itself in poetical forms than that of many poets whose productions contain elements of far higher quality; his poems are more harmonious, more complete as specimens of the art, than theirs. Indeed, his very success in what he aims at is greatly owing, not of course to his powers being limited, but to their being equally limited in every direction. With more thought, he might have been acceptable to a higher class of readers; but he would, *coeteris paribus,* have produced poems inferior, as poems, to his present ones. What his writings would have gained in originality and power, they would have lost in symmetry and completeness. A tithe of Browning's psychological subtlety, or Tennyson's ripened wisdom, would have checked Mr. Longfellow's facile and melodious utterance of fallacious commonplaces and popular half-truths; but it would also have deprived us of many graceful fancies, salutary thoughts, and pretty and finished pictures. The easy symbolism in which Mr. Longfellow delights, would not have served to convey thoughts derived from a profounder insight and a wider experience, or emotions of a more refined and complex character; and his employment of it is of itself sufficient to show that he is not one of those who have become wise by "deeply drinking in the soul of things." Yet this forms the ground-work of many of his most attractive and most popular poems, and in one or two cases is employed with really beautiful and poetical effect, as in his recent poem of *The Two Angels,* in which he has transcended his usual limits in depth of feeling and force of expression. Mr. Longfellow has much genuine religious earnestness; and this has given some of his poems on slavery, the hymn for his brother's ordination, and one or two others, an unusual firmness and a fervency of tone. (pp. 464-65)

Mr. Longfellow's plays have, in our opinion, less merit even than his longer poems. He has no dramatic power; and it is impossible to take the slightest interest in the colorless and unreal personages of *The Spanish Student* and *The Golden Legend.* There are occasional descriptions in them marked by a certain weak grace and delicacy of language; and the venerable traditions of the playwright as to the duty of breaking up the serious business at due intervals by snatches of song and that peculiar species of comic repartee among the minor characters which makes the deepest tragedy an intense relief, are all faithfully observed. On the whole, they are neither better nor worse than the general run of those plays, one or more of which so many clever and cultivated men think fit in their lifetime to publish, we suppose as a sacrifice to oblivion.

Of Mr. Longfellow's prose works, the best known, *Hyperion,* has little continuous interest; its slender thread of a love-story being altogether lost amid the profuse and gaudy descriptions and sentimental and high-flown musings. *Kavanagh* is decidedly better; there is more story, and the characters . . . are drawn with a quiet humor one would scarcely have expected from Mr. Longfellow. *Kavanagh* is altogether a very pleasant and freshly-colored tale of American village-life, with its primitive conditions, its transparent and amusing affectations, its homely joys and sorrows. But prose fiction, or indeed prose or fiction of any kind, is not Mr. Longfellow's *forte*. He is a born poet, though not a poet of the highest rank; and his strength lies in the melodious and graceful expressions of some

> Familiar matter of to-day,
> Some natural sorrow, loss, or pain,
> That has been, and may be again.

(pp. 465-66)

"Poems of Longfellow," in Eclectic Magazine, *Vol. XLVI, No. IV, April, 1859, pp. 459-66.*

THE LIVING AGE (essay date 1864)

Longfellow is certainly chiefly characterized by the crystal grace of his poems. Nor is it mere refinement of *style* by which he is principally distinguished; for that would tell us little of him as a poet. Even in *subjects* there is a greater and a less capacity for what we may call the crystal treatment; and Longfellow always selects those in which a clear, still, pale beauty may be seen by a swift, delicate vision, playing almost on the surface. Sometimes he is tempted by the imaginative purity of a subject . . . to forget that he has not adequate vigor for its grasp, as in the series in [**"Tales of a Wayside Inn"**] on the Saga of King Olaf, which is, in his hands, only classical, while by its essence it ought to be forceful. But, on the whole, every volume he has published has been filtered into purer and brighter beauty than the last, and—if we except **"Hiawatha,"** where his subject was peculiarly suited to the graceful surface humor of his genius,—this is, to our minds, the pleasantest of all his volumes. His reputation was acquired by a kind of rhetorical sentimental class of poem, which has, we are happy to say, disappeared from his more recent volumes,—the "life is real, life is earnest" sort of thing, and all the platitudes of feverish youth. Experience always sooner or later filters a genuine poet clear of that class of sentiments, teaching him that true as they are, they should be kept back, like steam, for working the will, and not let off by the safety-valve of imaginative expression. In this volume such beauty as there is, is pure beauty, though it is not of a very powerful kind. Mr. Longfellow has adopted the idea of Chaucer . . . , of making each of a group of friends relate a tale at a "wayside inn," and, as generally happens in such cases, perhaps, the best part of the poem is the prelude which introduces and describes the various guests and storytellers in the Massachusetts wayside inn. (p. 43)

This is not a very powerful species of poetry, and yet it is very pleasant, and to our ears much more truly poetical than the sentimental verse which first obtained for Longfellow his wide popularity. Longfellow does not catch the deepest beauty or the deepest passions which human life presents to us. His tale of **"Torquemada"** and the consuming fire of persecuting orthodoxy, is comparatively feeble and ineffectual. But he catches the surface bubbles,—the imprisoned air which rises from the stratum next beneath the commonplace,—the beauty that a mild and serene intellect can see issuing everywhere, both from nature and from life,—with exceedingly delicate discrimination; and his poetry affects us with the same sense of beauty as the blue wood-smoke curling up from a cottage chimney into an evening sky. . . . Longfellow does not attempt to deal with rich or various materials. He seizes on the ligher phases of gentle loveliness, and distils them at once into his verse.

And he does this with a true poetic felicity of language that shows how keenly he *feels* the expressive associations of the words he uses, which are never far fetched, though often fetched from afar. . . . In describing the falcon's dream in his story of Sir Frederigo he says:—

> Beside him, motionless, the drowsy bird
> Dreamed of the chase, and in his slumber heard
> *The sudden scythelike sweep of wings that dare*
> The headlong plunge through eddying gulfs of air.

The beauty of the adjective "scythelike," as applied to the sweep of the falcon's wings, is by no means exhausted when you have thought of the motion and of the sound it suggests. It calls up, besides, a hundred associations with dewy summer mornings and "wet, bird-haunted English lawns" that help the beauty, the freshness, and the music of the thought. Of such delicate touches as these this last volume of Mr. Longfellow, though by no means of the highest order of poetry, is very full. And few influences on the imagination are more resting and sunny, though there may be many more bracing and stimulating. The poem on **"The Birds of Killingworth"** is full of such beauties. (p. 44)

"Mr. Longfellow's New Poems," in The Living Age, *Vol. 80, No. 1022, January 2, 1864, pp. 43-4.*

[C. E. NORTON] (essay date 1867)

Mr. Longfellow's translation [of Dante's *The Divine Comedy*] is the mature work of a poetic genius, long accustomed to exercise itself not only in original composition, but also in the reproduction of foreign poetry. The felicity of his minor translations has been universally acknowledged, and the same art and taste shown in them are shown in still fuller measure in this version to which he has devoted, with a sense of what was due to the character of his original, the most patient labor, and the service of his ripest faculties. (p. 124)

A version of a great poem which shall be true to the original in rendering all its qualities, is an achievement beyond human faculties. To the production of the effect of a work of art all its original elements are essential, while the differences inherent in different languages, and in which the differences of race and civilization are embodied, cannot be neutralized or overcome, so that an English Odyssey or Divine Comedy shall be to us what the originals were in their time to the Greeks or the Italians. (p. 126)

The spirit of *realism*, which is so marked a characteristic of the so-called formative or representative arts in these times, prevails also in literary art. Truth not only to the outer and actual fact, but also to the essence, and to the facts of imagination, is the one thing needful alike in original composition and in the reproduction of the works of other men. (p. 133)

Mr. Longfellow has performed his work in full sympathy with this prevailing spirit, and with entire recognition of the force of these distinctions. His translation is the most faithful version of Dante that has ever been made. He is himself too much a poet not to feel that, in one sense, it is impossible to translate a poem; but he is also too much a poet not to feel that sympathy with his author which enables him to transfuse as much as possible of the subtile spirit of poesy into a version of which the first object was to be faithful to the author's meaning. His work is the work of a scholar who is also a poet. Desirous to give to a reader unacquainted with the Italian the means of knowing precisely *what* Dante wrote, he has followed the track of his master step by step, foot by foot, and has tried, so far as the genius of translation allowed, to show also *how* Dante wrote. The poem is still a poem in his version, and, though destitute, by necessity, of some of the most beautiful qualities of the original, it does not fail to charm with its rhythm, as well as to delight and instruct with its thought. (pp. 133-34)

[The] translator's success is not to be achieved by formal fidelity and lip-service: it must finally and absolutely depend on his genuine respect for, and sympathy with, his author, and on his poetic sense, faculty, and culture. It is when judged by this test that the merit of Mr. Longfellow's work is most conspicuous. The method of translation which Mr. Longfellow has chosen is free alike from the reproach of pedantic literalism and of unfaithful license. In freeing himself from the clog of rhyme, he secures the required ease of expression; and in selecting a verse of the same metre as that of the original, and in keeping himself to the same number of verses, he binds himself to the pregnant conciseness of the poem, and to a close following of its varied tone. His special sympathy and genius guide him with almost unerring truth, and display themselves constantly in the rare felicity of his rendering. (p. 137)

In fine, Mr. Longfellow, in rendering the substance of Dante's poem, has succeeded in giving also—so far as art and genius could give it—the spirit of Dante's poetry. Fitted for the work as few men ever were, by gifts of nature, by sympathy, by an unrivalled faculty of poetic appreciation, and by long and thorough culture, he has brought his matured powers, in their full vigor, to its performance, and has produced an incomparable translation,—a poem that will take rank among the great English poems. (pp. 145-46)

> [C. E. Norton,] "Longfellow's Translation of 'The Divine Comedy'," in The North American Review, Vol. CV, No. 216, July, 1867, pp. 124-48.

GEORGE SMITH   (essay date 1868)

[The] poetry of Longfellow is . . . his own; a result following mostly from the circumstances by which he is surrounded. True, he is only one of the stars before the dawn. There is nothing in him to indicate that he is able to cope with the stupendous and magnificent wonders of nature visible in his native clime. He is deficient in proportion, anything but colossal in conception, and at times feeble in execution. Some of his finest poems are hung upon a thread; and for a lyric poet he is too frequently deficient in fire. Hence, his very best effusions in the manner of some of our own poets—[Thomas] Campbell, for instance—fall far below theirs. But one of his greatest claims to our admiration is the fact that he has not swerved from declaring at all times what he deems to be his vocation. There is a purity breathing through every one of his poems which is an honour to the time; in truth, his principal trait is the Christianity, not of creed but of faith, apparent in his works. Though there may be some extravagance in assuring youths at mechanics' institutes—as the young man is alleged to have assured the psalmist—that because others have made their lives sublime they may make theirs also, the general effect of Longfellow's poems is to raise the dignity of nature, to show that the grossness of our mortal energy is capable to a great extent of subversion by patient and constant effort, and to point the way by which a wandering race may return to the bosom of the great Father. An elegant and accomplished scholar, a considerable linguist, and withal a most amiable man, we yet cannot concede to him the possession of any great creative faculty. Of many men it may be said that they are greater than their works; of him, not. His mind was not cast in a colossal mould. The good, the beautiful, and the true he can appreciate; and his sympathy for the struggling spirit will always give him a place in the human heart. His utterances, however, are like the sweet tones of the harp—they do not partake of the grand roll and sweep of the organ. As a translator, Longfellow has few equals among his own craft. We are almost astonished on reading some of his graphic "transferred" pictures, that one so gifted should not have been able to produce a work of his own that should stand the test of devouring time. . . . Longfellow's blank verse is a failure. He has not the power of sustaining that majestic rhythm as it demands; and where the lines are not stilted, they are halting, grotesque, and frequently imperfect. The want of dramatic power, too, is apparent in all his poems. "The Spanish Student" is a work far beneath, on the whole, similar productions of poets acknowledged to be inferior to its author. Character is not intricately and minutely delineated, and those persons drawn, are drawn in a slovenly manner, whilst the plot is of the most meagre and palpable description. But if Longfellow fails here, he fails in company with many otherwise distinguished men, who have attempted that which is the exclusive right of those only who possess the cosmopolitan intellect. It is as a writer of stanzas that he will be remembered, if at all, by posterity. And we are prepared to affirm that several poems which he has penned will live for generations, not on account altogether of their intrinsic merit, but because they have seized upon certain stages of feeling belonging to the universal man—the man both of the Old World and the New—and have caused, as it were, "a light to shine in the darkness," and hope to spring in the bosom of despair. Of scepticism there is nothing in his composition—at least judging from his poetry. The divine economy is taken for granted, and he has simply fulfilled what he deems to be his duty in insisting upon it. He is almost childlike in his simplicity, and shrinks from committing to paper anything that would offend the most fastidious eye. . . . Though we cannot give him a high place amongst the recognised examples of creative genius, we nevertheless pass upon him a high eulogium when we say that the world will have been the better for his living in it. (pp. 62-4)

> George Smith, "On Three Contemporary Poets," in Bentley's Miscellany, Vol. LXIV, 1868, pp. 61-9.*

WALT WHITMAN   (essay date 1882)

Longfellow in his voluminous works seems to me not only to be eminent in the style and forms of poetical expression that mark the present age (an idiocrasy, almost a sickness, of verbal melody), but to bring what is always dearest as poetry to the general human heart and taste, and probably must be so in the nature of things. He is certainly the sort of bard and counteractant most needed for our materialistic, self-assertive, money-worshipping, Anglo-Saxon races, and especially for the present age in America—an age tyrannically regulated with reference to the manufacturer, the merchant, the financier, the politician and the day workman—for whom and among whom he comes as the poet of melody, courtesy, deference—poet of the mellow twilight of the past in Italy, Germany, Spain, and in Northern Europe—poet of all sympathetic gentleness—and universal poet of women and young people. I should have to think long if I were asked to name the man who has done more, and in more valuable directions, for America.

I doubt if there ever was before such a fine intuitive judge and selecter of poems. His translations of many German and Scandinavian pieces are said to be better than the vernaculars. He does not urge or lash. His influence is like good drink or air. He is not tepid either, but always vital, with flavor, motion, grace. He strikes a splendid average, and does not sing exceptional passions, or humanity's jagged escapades. He is not revolutionary, brings nothing offensive or new, does not deal hard blows. On the contrary his songs soothe and heal, or if they excite, it is a healthy and agreeable excitement. His very anger is gentle, is at second hand, (as in **'the Quadroon Girl'** and **'the Witnesses'**).

There is no undue element of pensiveness in Longfellow's strains. Even in the early translation, 'the Manrique,' the movement is as of strong and steady wind or tide holding up and buoying. Death is not avoided through his many themes, but there is something almost winning in his original verses and renderings on that dread subject. . . .

To the ungracious complaint-charge (as by Margaret Fuller many years ago, and several times since [see excerpt above]), of his want of racy nativity and special originality, I shall only say that America and the world may well be reverently thankful—can never be thankful enough—for any such singing-bird vouchsafed out of the centuries, without asking that the notes be different from those of other songsters;—adding what I have heard Longfellow himself say, that ere the New World can be worthily original and announce herself and her own heroes, she must be well saturated with the originality of others, and respectfully consider the heroes that lived before Agamemnon.

Without jealousies, without mean passions, never did the personality, character, daily and yearly life of a poet, more steadily and truly assimilate his own loving, cultured, guileless, courteous ideal, and exemplify it. In the world's arena, he had some special sorrows—but he had prizes, triumphs, recognitions, the grandest.

Extensive and heartfelt as is to-day, and has been for a long while, the fame of Longfellow, it is probable, nay certain, that years hence it will be wider and deeper. . . .

> Walt Whitman, *"Death of Longfellow,"* in The Critic, *Vol. II, No. 33, April 8, 1882, p. 101.*

GEORGE EDWARD WOODBERRY (essay date 1903)

As a scholar Longfellow was cosmopolitan; but in that portion of his life which was the fruit of his poetic gift he was distinctively American. If the mildness of his nature be considered, the fervor of Longfellow's patriotism was a very marked quality; his habitual artistic control conceals its real force, but does not hide its clear depth; from the early days when he was all for Americanism in literature, through his manhood friendship with [Charles] Sumner and his antislavery poems, to the darker days of the sinking of the *Cumberland* and the prayer for the ship of state, he was one with his country's aspiration, struggle, and trial, one in heart with her life; but he showed this patriotic prepossession of his whole nature, if less touchingly, still more significantly, by his choice of American themes for what were in no sense occasional poems, but the greater works in which he built most consciously and patiently for his fame in poetry,—in **"Hiawatha," "Evangeline,' "Miles Standish,"** and the like.

It is the fashion to decry these poems now; yet the fact cannot be gainsaid that each of these remains the only successful poem of its kind, one of the Indian life, one of colonial pastoral, one of the Puritan idyl, while the trials made by others have been numerous; and in each of these, but especially in the first two, there is in quality a marvellous purity of tone which for those who are sensitive to it is one of the rarest of poetic pleasures. It is the fashion to decry also the shorter poems by which Longfellow entered into the homes of the people; but if heaven ever grants the prayer that a poet may write the songs of a people, it is surely in such poems as these that the divine gift reveals its presence. . . . Say what one will, the **"Psalm of Life"** is a trumpet-call, and a music breathes from **"Resignation"** in which the clod on the coffin ceases to be heard, and dies out of the ear at last with peace. In the grosser spirit of life that now everywhere prevails even among the best, and is not confined to any one sphere of politics, art or letters, nor to any one country or capital, it is not surprising that the fame of Longfellow should be obscured; but his silent presence must still be deeply and widely felt in those simpler and million homes that make up the popular life which, as the whole history of poetry shows, can never be corrupted. Longfellow had this remarkable and double blessing: he was the product of the old Puritan stock at its culminating moment of refinement, its most cultivated gentleman, and he enters most easily at lowly doors. (pp. 427-28)

> George Edward Woodberry, *"The Literary Age of Boston,"* in Harper's Monthly Magazine, *Vol. CVI, No. DCXXXIII, February, 1903, pp. 424-30.*

W. D. HOWELLS (essay date 1907)

[The] courage in frankly trusting the personal as the universal, is what made Longfellow not only sovereign of more hearts than any other poet of his generation, and more than any other poet who has lived, but now, on the hundredth anniversary after his birth, when a generation has passed since his death, has established him a master of such high degree that one who loves his fame may well be content without caring to ascertain precisely his place among the other masters. (p. 472)

He is the most literary of our poets; but to him literature was of one substance with nature, and he transmuted his sense of it into beauty by the same art, by which he transmuted to beauty the look of the familiar landscape, the feel of the native air, the scent of the mother earth. (p. 473)

Longfellow's talent was graced by a scholarship so hospitably responsive to the appeal of what was beautiful, in any aspect of literature or of nature, that we are continually tempted to forget how deeply Puritan he was by race and tradition. . . . We hardly realize how very introspective he was, and how much given, in the old Puritanic fashion, to self-question, to the interrogation of his motives, and to the judgment of his actions. (p. 475)

It has been with surprise, in my latest reading of his verse, that I have seen how intensely Longfellow has said himself in the intimate things in which a man may say himself without shame. These are pure utterances of personal feeling, but their effect is in that high ether where the personal is sensible of mergence in the universal, purified of what is transient, impermanent, extrinsic. It has been noted that, among all his poems, there is only one that may be called a love poem; but a great many of them are poems of feeling such as comes before passion, and endures with it and remains after it, and is the clear note of supreme song, in which childhood and manhood and age find themselves joined. It is among these poems of pure feeling, personal, universal, eternal, that Longfellow's art wholly frees itself from the sense not only of technic, of material, but of ethical purpose. (p. 476)

A poet is not only imaginative for what he does, but for what he makes us do, for the imagination which he creates in us, and Longfellow has this magic power upon us in a score of pieces, in a hundred passages, through a sort of spiritual intimacy, which owns us close akin, whether we are young or old, great or mean, so only we are mortal. . . .

It is on the face of it mere statement, mere recognition, but it is the finest art; the power of imparting emotion, unhindered by apparent effort, can have no effect beyond it. (p. 477)

Longfellow was, above everything and before everything, unaffected. His sincerity was without [the] alloys of motive, those grudges and vanities which debase and limit our universality and dwarf us from men to individuals. He had always imagined in his loyalty to his native air, a sort of duty he had to give his country, a poem which should be not only worthily, but distinctively American, and such a poem he did give her in the "**Evangeline.**" He gave it on his own terms, of course, and this most American, and hitherto first American, poem of anything like epic measure, remains without a rival, without a companion.

The poet's art is mere story-telling is admirably structural in it; he builds strongly and symmetrically, as he always does, though sometimes the decoration with which he heaps the classic frame distracts us from the delight of its finely felt proportion. Here again he is entirely unaffected, while being as far from simplicity as convention itself can go. The characters are not persons, but types. . . . But the poet brings to them his tender sense of their most moving story, and he so adds his own genuine nature to theirs that they live as truly and strongly as if they had each been studied from people of the real world, to an effect of such heartache in the witness as is without its like in poetry. (p. 479)

["**The Courtship of Miles Standish**"] in its lower level of comedy is of a perfection which the "**Evangeline**" does not always keep on its heights of tragedy. It is as humorously as that is pathetically imagined, and in the handling of the same verse it shows more of what is like native ease and colloquial habit. (p. 480)

It is in an advance beyond the "**Evangeline**" that the people of the "**Miles Standish**" tend to be more of characters and less of types, though so typical, so universal, so eternal in their personal relation that no lovers of any time could fail to read themselves into the hero and heroine.

Like the "**Evangeline**" and the "**Hiawatha**" it has the unity of design which is wanting to "**The Tales of a Wayside Inn,**" where the pictures are set successively in such a frame as many artists have used before, each having to make its effect with the spectator, unaided by strong common relation. But what charming pictures they are, how good every one in its way! . . . The poet tells again some strange or familiar story, something far-brought in date or place from the reaches of his measureless reading, or found in the memories of his first years, and each story takes his quality, and renews or matures itself at his touch. (pp. 480-81)

Longfellow wished above everything to be true; and the constant pressure of his genius was towards clarifying his emotion and simplifying his word. (p. 482)

In his earlier work, as in his earlier taste, he was very Romantic, or to use an apter word, Gothic; but he became more and more Hellenic. It will be interesting for those who are interested in this point, to contrast his earliest dramatic piece, "**The Spanish Student,**" with the later, and almost latest, attempts in that form, "**The New England Tragedies.**" In the first, Chispa and Baltasar speak their drolleries in unmodulated prose, as Shakespeare's clowns do; in the last Kempthorn and Butter express themselves in the blank verse which the poet subdues to the occasions of their level.

But the whole is of a simplicity in the words which the passion of the drama lifts out of vulgar associations. Say what we will of the inadequacy of these dramas as we imagine them across the footlights, there can hardly be just question of their high solemnity, their sombre and serious beauty. Longfellow would not have been Longfellow if he had not wished to touch our hearts in them, not only as men, but also as fellow men, and have us feel the ache which wrings the soul in the presence of mistaken or unjust suffering a thousand years ago with a grief as fresh and keen as that in which we read ourselves into the martyr who died yesterday. The fact that the pieces are not theatricable does not of itself impeach their dramatic quality, and I do not know that the poet could have given them any narrative shape without loss to the beauty, in which they were imagined. As they show in his final disposition, the "**New England Tragedies**" form the climax of the larger dramatic whole which he called "**Christus: A Mystery,**" and in which he, perhaps too arbitrarily, assembles with them "**The Divine Tragedy**" and "**The Golden Legend.**" The poet's design is clear enough, and each part is firmly wrought, but the parts are *welded*, not *fused*, together. In "**The Golden Legend,**" his love of the humor and pathos of old Germanic and Latin lands, where the generous American of his day so fondly dwelt, plays so long that the fancy wearies a little; and the meaning of the fable more nebulously than his wont.

He is more truly, with all his love of the mediaeval past, at home in his native air, and the "**New England Tragedies**" are more convincing than either of the other parts. (pp. 482-83)

I find the pieces in which he charms and teaches far outnumbering those in which he teaches and charms; that first he is an artist and then a moralist. It was so from the beginning; but there was recurrently with these two kinds a middle species, in which he lapsed from the lyric to the didactic; and, though the lyrical prevailed with him more and more, the very last of the poems which he is known to have written, "**The Bells of San Blas,**" returns to the explicit intentionality of some of his earlier pieces, while it is characteristically graced with that tender feeling for the past, for the alien, in which error and truth are reconciled and the consolation flows from their reconcilement. (p. 484)

W. D. Howells, "The Art of Longfellow," in The North American Review, Vol. CLXXXIV, No. DCX, March 1, 1907, pp. 472-85.

LAFCADIO HEARN (essay date 1915)

Within the last fifteen or twenty years it has become too much of a practice with the young scholars and many critics to speak disparagingly of the American poet Longfellow, who exercised over Tennyson's generation an influence and a charm second only to that of Tennyson himself. For this sudden reaction against Longfellow, the critics are only partly responsible; the character of the present generation may partly account for it.

The critics say what is very true, that Longfellow is only a second class poet, because his versification was never brought to that high point which the greatest poetry demands. But this does not mean that he should not be studied. Second class poetry may often be quite as important in its way as first class poetry; it may possess emotional beauty that the first class poetry can not show. Perfect verse means only perfect form, and form is not the most important quality of poetry by any means. Nevertheless, as soon as it had been shown that Longfellow's hexameters were faulty, young scholars set the fashion of sneering at Longfellow. This fashion has now become rather general; and I want to protest against it. Some of its utterances have been quite unreasonable, not to say unjust. . . . If you have followed the course of the English literary movement, during the Victorian age, you will recognise that the reaction against Longfellow was almost coincident with the movement in favour of realism. (pp. 167-68)

Now during the realistic enthusiasm, it was natural that Longfellow should have been for a moment despised. Of all the poets of the age, none was so completely romantic as Longfellow, so ideal, so fond of the spiritual and the impossible. He is the most dreaming of dreamers, the least real among romantics. But with the present reaction I believe that he will, for this very reason, rise into worldwide favour again. I can not think that genius of this sort can possibly be pushed aside for any length of time, merely because some of his verse happens to be defective in construction.

Now let us speak about the good qualities in his work, and try to discover what its distinguishing characteristic is. He has been for nearly two generations the favourite poet of youth; and there must be a good reason for that. He has written a great many things which stay in memory forever after you have once read them; and there must be a good reason for that. His appeal, nevertheless, is not an appeal to sense or passion, such as Byron was once able to make. Neither can he be called an innovator such as Sir Walter Scott was; I mean that he had not the advantage of coming before the world with an entirely new story to tell. On the contrary, he is particularly a poet of old thoughts and old customs and old legends. Yet there are very few persons with any taste for poetry who have not been charmed by him in their youth; and if I meet a grown-up scholar to-day, no matter how great, who has read Longfellow during boyhood and now denies the charm of his poetry, I am quite sure that there is something defective in that man's organisation. (pp. 168-69)

[If] you should ask me what particular quality makes the charm of Longfellow, in his work itself, I should answer "ghostliness." There is something of ghostliness in the work of nearly all our great poets, but it is not so frequently met with in such thrilling form as we find it in Longfellow. In his most trifling pieces there is always some suggestion of the spirit behind the matter, the ghost beyond the reality. Now young people always like this, and Longfellow has given it to them better than anybody else. (p. 171)

The value of Longfellow is that of a composer of hundreds of short poems, short poems of a kind different from anything else written during the age. It is in these short poems that you will especially find the ghostly quality about which I have spoken, and it is by these short poems that Longfellow became a great educator, not only of the American, but also of the English public. By "educator" here I mean a teacher of new beauties and new values and new ideas. Before his time very little was known about the charm of many foreign poets whose work he first either translated or paraphrased. Norwegian, Danish, Swedish, Spanish, German, Portuguese, Finnish, Russian, and even Persian poetry of the popular school, together with some specimens of Tartar verse—all these were presented to English readers for the first time in a way that could please the mind and touch the heart of the simplest person. How much variety of matter does this range of selection suggest! But this represents only a part of what has been given to us in the short poems. Almost every episode of European history, ancient, mediaeval and modern, is represented in these brief compositions. Thousands of young persons were first persuaded to study with interest the old heroic stories of Spanish and German and Norwegian history by reading something about them in the pages of Longfellow. If only for this reason, Longfellow should be more valued than he would now seem to be. Yet again, his own original work in these directions is not a fourth part of his work in the same direction as an editor. You will find in your library a collection of thirty-one volumes, entitled "Poems of Places"—examples of poetry written about all the famous places in all parts of the world, from England to Japan, from northern Asia to southern Australia. There is no other work of this kind in the English language, and its value can scarcely be too highly spoken of. Almost all the poets of the world are represented there. Besides, you must recollect that Longfellow made perhaps the best metrical translation of Dante that has ever been made in modern times. Surely these productions ought to compel recognition of his importance as an educator in the best sense of the word. (pp. 173-74)

Longfellow is neither English nor American; at his best he is without nationality and without personal idiosyncrasy. Even when he takes up a foreign subject, with which we can not be naturally expected to feel sympathy, he can make us feel it, by insisting upon some human element that belongs to it. Take, for example, his poem about Peter the Great of Russia. . . . [Longfellow] made the reader feel for a moment as the Russian peasant feels toward his sovereign–inasmuch as the feeling of loyalty is not peculiar to any one country or time or people. (p. 177)

[Softness] and dreaminess and ghostliness make most of the charm of Longfellow. Yet with these tender and almost ethereal ways of utterance he can often wake the strongest kind of enthusiasm. Mere force of words does not always produce forcible effects; the sense of beauty may be more powerful than any recognition of strength, on the same principle that an electric shock may effect even more than the blow of a sledge-hammer. (p. 188)

[Longfellow] is not a painter in oil colours. He is only an artist in water colours; but so far as poetry can be really spoken of as water colour painting, I do not know of any modern English poet of his own rank who can even compare with him. Think of him, therefore, if you can as one who paints very charming pictures in very charming aquarelle. Secondly, remember that he is a ghost-like story teller. There are many story tellers among the poets of this age, besides the great story tellers of the first rank, such as Tennyson or Rossetti. There was Morris, for example, writing stories in verse quite as skilful as Sir Walter Scott's. Longfellow I should nevertheless put very much above Morris. Sometimes his verse is not so correct as that of Morris; but Morris is often tiresome, and Longfellow never is. I think the great merit of Longfellow as a story teller is that he always knows when to stop. . . .

Longfellow perceived the beauty of the world in quite a special way, feeling the ghostliness of nature in all her manifestations, and reflecting it in his simple verse, without calling to his help any religious sentiment. Now this is not a common virtue. Most of the poets who are great nature lovers and take nature seriously have been very apt to mingle religious idealism with their pictures. Longfellow does not do this. There is no narrow religious feeling to be found in any of his work. Indeed, he was the most generous-minded of poets—looking everywhere for beauty and finding it everywhere, and always indifferent as to whether it was Christian or pagan, domestic or foreign, old or new. All he required was that it should be beautiful in itself, morally or otherwise. (p. 198)

> *Lafcadio Hearn, "On a Proper Estimate of Long-fellow," in his* Interpretations of Literature, Vol. II, *edited by John Erskine (copyright 1915 by Mitchell McDonald; copyright renewed 1942 by Kazuo Ko-izumi), Dodd, Mead and Company, 1915 (and re-printed by Kennikat Press, 1965, pp. 167-99).*

G. R. ELLIOTT (essay date 1929)

The mildness of [Longfellow's] style, now so much misconceived, was inevitable. It was due ultimately to the limits of American poetry, which, as still today, was not strong-grown enough to apprehend very much of America's life without losing too much of its own. Only an artist of the unintensity and detachment of Longfellow could so dedicate himself, under American conditions, to the world of poetry. Moreover, his work represents a golden moment. The old narrow puritanical intensity, incapable of poetry, had faded; the new industrial-democratic intensity, disruptive for poetry, had not arrived. It is significant that the fair moment could not be seized by Emerson, our profoundest worshipper of poetry. His verse shows how naïve, impatient, and fitful, how much lacking in clear grasp of poetic mode, our American devotion to poetry can be, even when most exalted and pure—how long a way toward the heights of poetic form we have to go. Our basic need is the patient and thorough zest in poetry—a zest not to be warped from its aim by our thronging cults and gusty "vitalities"—that Longfellow achieved for us. "Achieved" is the word! His poetic gentility, so far from being in its essential nature a deficiency of the Victorian New-England school, now outgrown or outworn, is a positive achievement of American poetry, needing to be continually resumed and built upon.

To be sure, the achievement had to be paid for. The price was the genteel and angelic aspects of Longfellow's style—ghostly offspring of the pioneer and the Puritan. . . . In Longfellow's verse the lineaments of the pioneering Puritan gentleman hover in the form of a genteel angel, cultivating flowers instead of clearing stumps, bringing us airs from heaven, screening off and perfuming the blasts from hell. Yet at bottom the scented style had in Longfellow the same source as in Keats,—an exceptional desire, in a century full of harsh and cross purposes, for sheer poetic beauty of expression. He succumbed to the lure of obvious aesthetic effects. But it is to *our* advantage to think rather of his successful avoidance of *un*poetic effects. Didacticism spread its claws on every side of him; but excepting a few awkward scratches—worst of all the dreadful translation of *The Children of the Lord's Supper*—he escaped and passed on fancy-free. (pp. 73-5)

Longfellow grew up in a community which liked its verse sentimental when not moralistic, and could not much encourage the real nobility of art. In avoiding moralism Longfellow's muse was thrown much upon sentiment and fancy. Yet he continually tried for a mode of style that would be elevated

without ceasing to be poetic. Emerson under the same circumstances produced the grand style jerky. Longfellow, vowed at least to other than broken music, produced the grand style flat . . . yet not flatulent, like Tennyson's, nor moving, as the Miltonic vein of Wordsworth often does, with a sort of bumptious bounce. In *Morituri Salutamus, John Endicott, The Golden Legend, Michael Angelo,* Longfellow is bearer of a high poetic tradition which at least he will not debauch. But in particular passages he could not often attain the impressiveness which belongs to his poetry as a whole, to his entire poetic mood, which holds in solution a fine personal character. This way of looking at a poet's work is not countenanced by those who, under the sway of imagism and the élan vital, desire briskness in detail and some impersonal throb of nature in the whole. Nevertheless the firm, sweet, and laborious living of the man Longfellow, devoted to the aims of poetry and free from the cult-spirit, goes on like a stream through the whole territory of his work, and gives it a recurrent freshness of poetic appeal lacking in many artists of a more originative genius.

And surely his work has a certain shadowy loveliness quite its own. . . . His melancholy, I think, is mainly that of Poetry herself in a locale where the flow of verse cannot yet be beautifully strong. At the same time his realization of his limits, and his will to do what he could for poetry within them, won him a clear distinction in the total history of poetry. Worshiping the epic gods afar off, he created near at hand the limpid shadowy eagerness of *Hiawatha.* . . . No other poet has a style at once so homely and so cultivated. No other style has the peculiar quiet gleaming of his whenever it touches a shadow. . . . [Regarded] in its whole mood, his style is not a foreign importation. Its gentle sombreness is the natural outcome of a true poetic spirit growing in this neighbourhood, and having in the background a constant sense of the pioneer labour of America, so long, and so often fruitless, and fruitful mainly in material things.

He could not "hear America singing" like Walt Whitman: he could not listen so widely and so confidently to her various workers "singing with open mouths their strong melodious songs." For he experienced poetry, and life, not mainly as an outpouring but as an arduous shaping; and he felt our American need of long constructive labour in the spirit. He was spiritually realistic at the point where Whitman was a simple visionary. Whitman underestimated the length of our American road to eternity. He sprinkled our very "leaves of grass" with our pseudo-religious optimism. He was a freedman of democratic Christianity, more or less consciously wooing the primitive. Longfellow, through education and the tradition of poetry, became a citizen of a *civilized* world older than Christianity, and, more or less unconsciously, was much of a pagan. Excepting in a few angelic passages, he did not slur over the great and plain human meaning of death; and his consciousness of the continued presence of the dead is not essentially Christian. He reverenced, to be sure, the high Christian reaches of eternity, especially when in Dante's presence. But he felt the difficulty of them, and the difficulty of turning them into human poetry, in America. The spirit-region characteristic of Longfellow lies somewhere between the peace of the old cathedral and the rush of the modern street, and somewhere between the ancient pagan shrines of the dead and the fireside of the New-England home. . . . In the work of no other poet of the century does the world of the dead become so constant and so real a presence without distorting the issues of life. It is a presence that excludes the incoherent egotism of romantic mystics even while it detaches us from the egotism of our everyday selves.

It blends indivisibly with personal and historic memories. It surrounds us with a cloud of witnesses who neither disturb nor illuminate our workaday life, but sustain us with the intimate sense that "such as these have lived and died." Longfellow wrote the poetry of plain laborious effort in the human spirit, refreshed by the most simple loveliness of its Shades.

A greater American poet would fuse and lift the labour and faith of America in a grander design—in a narrative poem, let us say, which would go far beyond *Miles Standish* and *Hiawatha.* But America is not yet capable of such poetry. We feel that Whitman was prophetic of it. But we cannot proceed toward it through a mode of verse which rejects, instead of developing, the avenues of character and memory opened by Longfellow; which stops its memory at Whitman and only superficially remembers him. Whitman's vision of a great national spirit and verse in America has dwindled to an Aeolian attachment of a vitalistic cult. To resume and carry forward his vision, and eventually to realize it, demands the patient zest of memory and design achieved for us by Longfellow. (pp. 75-7)

A national poetry that has become intensely eager in aim but fearfully thin in accomplishment, cannot safely neglect its most accomplished master. In America we should not neglect Longfellow at least until we can overtop *The Golden Legend* and the *Tales of a Wayside Inn,* not only in picayune jewels of expression but in human scope and in narrative power. (p. 80)

> G. R. Elliott, "Gentle Shades of Longfellow," in his The Cycle of Modern Poetry: A Series of Essays toward Clearing Our Present Poetic Dilemma (copyright 1929 by Princeton University Press; reprinted by permission of Princeton University Press), Princeton University Press, 1929, pp. 64-82.

ODELL SHEPARD (essay date 1934)

[Longfellow] has long been an American institution. His poems, whether good or bad, are woven in among our heartstrings, so that the effort to see them as they really are involves the strain of self-analysis and adverse criticism of them seems to tear at our very roots. (p. xi)

Longfellow's work is of utmost value to America in her effort to see what she has been and what, therefore, she is and is to be. In studying him we study ourselves. It is true that he has little to say about the America of his time, and that his remarks about the America of any time are seldom acute; yet in the total temper of his mind he represents us, without fully intending it, more truly than other poets do who intend little else. Considering this, and also the range and depth of his influence upon us, it is clear that no view of American culture which leaves him out or treats him with contempt can be either sound or complete. Those who think him a great poet may be naïve, but those who think him unworthy of careful consideration are something worse than that. (p. xii)

From whatever angle we consider Longfellow's relation to his environment, . . . we find that his grasp of contemporary fact was weak and incomprehensive. Between him and the actual American scene there intervened an Indian-summer haze, dreamily dim, which blurred and softened every hue and line and angle, hiding the coarse and the familiar, substituting the colors of the heart's desire. This haze it is that we see in his writings, and not the crude reality behind it. Machinery, science, labor disputes, social unrest, the roar of industry and the din of war, all the strife and toil and anxious mental questing

up and down which must be forever associated with his century, make little stir in his still pages. (pp. xxvii-xxviii)

Whether a fault or not, this is a major trait of Longfellow's, that he does not bring the force of his mind to bear upon things near at hand. His thoughts and loves are otherwhere. Self-indulgently romantic, he uses imagination rather for escape from reality than for penetration of it. And even when concerned with things remote, his thought needs to dally with superficial hues and contours and seldom pierces to essences. This we feel in reading his several attempts at dramatic writing such as the inanimate *New England Tragedies,* and even more in his prose fiction. The stage is set for action, but no actors that draw the breath of life appear upon it. In an early story called "The Baptism of Fire," published in *Outre-Mer,* he writes a cool description of an execution by fire and hanging which gives, at first, the effect of a callous brutality. One soon realizes, of course, that the writer is half asleep, that he has failed to bring the terrible experience home to himself as a thing that once actually happened—as a thing the like of which was happening in his own country in his time as in ours. Had he keenly realized this, either he would not have written the story at all or else he would have written it with an anguish of mind that would have made it live. But it remained for him, as it does for us, merely something in a book, distant in time and place, a faintly lurid spot in the light and shade of history.

The haze that dimmed and all but hid Longfellow's America from his eyes was composed, so to speak, of time. That is, he looked at the present through the past—through an illusory and highly romantic past, to be sure, of his own dreaming. What he saw in America was chiefly the enduring of the old rather than the emergence of the new. In fancy and imagination he was at least as antiquarian as Washington Irving, whose writings he admired as a boy, imitated as a young man, and never quite outgrew. Like Hawthorne, whose fancy clothed with mosses a house not seventy years old when he went to live in it, Longfellow had a deep delight in all things established and timeworn—a delight all the stronger because the America about him had so few of such things. (pp. xxviii)

Longfellow failed to establish living contact either with his own time or with the earlier ages into which he retreated. Even the world of nature was for the most part a blur to him, or a storehouse of metaphors and similes. His poems of the sea are indeed uniformly excellent, possibly because the images in them were stamped upon his mind before he began the rhetorician's quest of analogies, but elsewhere his observation was slight, superficial, and inaccurate. (p. xxx)

The harsh facts of life seldom touched him. He knew to the full the grief of personal bereavement, but the world's woe and misery never lay heavy upon his heart. He knew even less of sin, apparently, than Emerson did, and far less of moral and intellectual struggle. (pp. xxxiv)

There is an important sense . . . in which we may say that this man, who spent his long life in reading and discussing and writing books, simply did not know enough, in the more vivid and poetic ways of knowing. One looks vainly through his pages for any sign of the amateur's acquaintance with science that gives bone and sinew to the writing of Emerson, providing it with a thousand flashing metaphors and profound analogies. He had none of Thoreau's knowledge of nature and skill in handicraft. He had nothing to correspond with Whittier's passionate concern about politics, with Melville's knowledge of the outer world of toil and danger, or with Hawthorne's grasp of the inner realities of the conscience. He lacked, moreover, a precious trait clearly seen in all these men—the sense of place and of utter devotion to it. Although he loved Portland and Cambridge, he could not have said, with Hawthorne, that New England was the largest lump of earth his heart could hold, nor did he draw strength of mind and spirit, as Whittier and Thoreau and Emerson learned to do, from the old familiar scene. In his *wanderjahre* he escaped provincialism in its good as well as in its bad aspects, to that—absurd though it is to regard him as a man without a country—even in his Americanism there is something diffuse, diluted, and faintly German. (pp. xxxv-xxxvi)

Though the stream of his thought may be shallow, it is clear, and it flows. Always chiefly concerned to convey his thought and feeling, he used verse not as an end in itself but as a vehicle of communication. He had the good craftsman's liking for the finished task, and he felt that the task of the creative artist is not finished so long as there remains in his work anything difficult or obscure which a greater care of his might clear away. Thus, for example, he used the normal prose order of words rather more consistently than other poets of his time, consulting not his own ease but that of his reader. . . . His art is of that good kind which conceals itself. What may seem at first to be mere triteness in his style often turns out to be exact rightness. That stultifying fear of the hackneyed expression by which the poets of our day are tormented was unknown to him, partly because he wished to say not new and clever and startling things but the things that had been tried by the ages and found true. Moreover, he wished to hold attention upon his thought or story and not upon himself. (pp. xli)

Longfellow's ability to sink himself and his own moods out of sight enabled him to excel as a translator and as a narrative poet. There are, to be sure, many dull passages in *Evangeline* and many shallows in the *Tales of a Wayside Inn,* which betray the hand of a professional writer doing his hundred lines a day. Longfellow's deficiency in first-hand experience and his shrinking from violence enfeebles not a few of his stories. Even the most decided success in his narrative writing, the account of the fight between Miles Standish and the Indians, falls far short of the terrible tale told in his source. On the other hand, most of his narrative work is straight-grained, objective, moving steadily onward with a strong sense of the goal.

In every poem he wrote Longfellow had a definite thing to say. This might be, and often it was, a platitude. For that he had little care, because he knew that we live in an old and iterative world and that the mere novelty of an idea is a supposition against it. Together with his thought, he had at the same moment a clear notion of the form in which it could be expressed most effectively. Form and substance seem to have occurred to him at the same instant, as two aspects of one thing, and it is for this reason that in all his better work the thought seems to fill the form without crowding or inflation.

Even the more acute readers of Longfellow have seldom recognized that his sense of form was at all uncommon, partly because the simple stanzas and meters of his familiar work—most of them derived from the popular ballad, Protestant hymnology, and the Romantic poets of Germany—are seldom associated with this Latin trait. Close reading of even his feebler early lyrics will show, however, that they usually contain little that could be dispensed with. For all their apparent laxity or ease, they are likely to be succinct, though seldom terse or laconic. Nearly everything irrelevant has been pruned away.

Only when this is realized are we prepared to understand Longfellow's remarkable success in the sonnet. It is here, more clearly than elsewhere, that we see him working as a conscious artist, making beauty for its own sake, shaping form unhastily with a slow-pulsed hand that never trembles. And it is perhaps from his sonnets that the sophisticated reader is most likely to gain that respect which may induce an intelligent re-reading of the poet's entire work. In the single sonnet **"Nature"** the best of his qualities are all implicit. Without a word too many or too few it phrases an ancient unchanging verity with quiet precision. The thought is obvious and the feeling familiar; the "as-so" design is hackneyed; the metaphor is by no means fresh; yet the poem is so beautifully constructed, its music is so delicate an echo of the mood, it is so perfectly one and indivisible, that it lives in memory as a piece of still perfection.

The beauty of this sonnet is not in the single lines and not in any of its aspects taken separately, but in the architectonic, the just proportion, the harmony and unity of the whole composition. And it is precisely in what may be called his sense of the whole that Longfellow is most remarkable as technician and creative artist. Herein, and not in the verbal virtuosity of a Swinburne or the finished texture of a Tennyson, lies his chief aesthetic excellence. In this important respect, moreover, his art improved and ripened with the years. (pp. xlii-xliv)

Both the verse and the prose of Longfellow reveal a habit of mind, common in his time but not in ours, which impedes his direct communication with the reader. For our taste he is too heavily metaphorical. Moreover, his metaphors are often used rather for decorative purposes than for clarification. . . . This is due to that vice of professional and self-conscious phrase-making which the ancient rhetoricians foisted upon western literature, making it appear that the work of the literary artist is that of external adornment rather than that of imaginative penetration. Of this vice Longfellow was a late though not a flagrant example. He acquired it in his schooling, from public oratory, from sermons, and from the prevailing philosophy of his time. (pp. xliv-xlv)

Longfellow's function in our literature was to release energy and not to restrict or guide it, certainly not to suggest that it might come to a tragic end. He was the poet of sentiment. The steeps of ecstasy and the pits of despair he never scaled or descended. He did what his times demanded and made possible, or, in a sense, necessary. . . . Different men, to be sure, were even then doing a different work. While Longfellow sat by the fire in his luxurious study, dreaming out the acquiescent lyrics that would soon lull a million readers to his mood, there was a young man sitting by a sheet-iron stove not fifteen miles away, in a shanty he had built with his own hands beside a lake in the woods, and this young man was writing a prose book intensely, even bitterly, critical of nearly all that was then going on in the land. But the poems of Longfellow were sold by the hundred thousand in some twenty languages, and the full fame of Thoreau has not even yet arrived. (p. xlviii)

[Longfellow] considered the past our chief guide through the present and our best clue to the future; and also he thought it a main task of the poet to appraise the work of those who have gone before and so make it live anew in each generation. Such work he thought particularly urgent in America, where there had been so sharp a break with tradition. He thought America needed to be enriched in mind and spirit before she was corrected, and he set himself to the task of bringing her the wealth of other times and lands. Dominated by this motive, he did not wish to be unique, bizarre, eccentric. He wished to be faithful, sane, normal, and representative. (p. xlix)

What [this literary retrospection has] cost is obvious. It withdrew Longfellow's attention from events and ideas of the first magnitude, thus giving apparent sanction to the belief that the business of poetry and of the arts in general is to provide a temporary escape from actuality, rather than to pierce and illumine that actuality and so to transform it. . . . Thus he relegated art to a Sabbatical position, leaving the Philistine free for at least six days of unrestricted Philistinism. True though it may be that if he had claimed more he might have secured less, we cannot suppose that his actual claim was the result of any such calculation. He asked for poetry what he thought it deserved, and in asking so little he represented the attitude of his country. (pp. xlix-l)

If Longfellow had been able to see precisely what sort of poetry America needed and had been endowed with the will and the power to make precisely that, it is not clear that his work would have been in many ways different. She needed a deeper sense of beauty, respect for the arts, wider mental horizons, veneration for the past, and tradition. He provided at least the means of getting these. There were other things equally necessary, such as restraint, humility, depth of thought, free play of ideas, but most of these are the gift of the critic. It was Longfellow's task to initiate the difficult transition from a moralistic to an aesthetic regime in literature. He did this the more effectively because he himself stood halfway between the extremes, and it is interesting to observe how, as the decades went by, the didactic element in his work was steadily subordinated. The pressure of necessity was lessening for many thousands in America. They were untrained in leisure or delight, which they regarded as dangerous if not reprehensible. Any such pure beauty as that in the Odes of Keats they would have ignored. They had enjoyed so little "schooling in the polite pleasures" that these had to come at first in the familiar guise of edification. In the poems of Longfellow they did so come. Moreover, he drew us gently back, after a long period of intellectual isolation, toward the main currents of the world's thought. As scholar and teacher, translator and editor, travel-writer and poet, he did much valuable work in what Barrett Wendell called the "transplanting of culture." He deepened our sense of the American past. His example taught us that a life devoted to thought and artistic creation may be dignified and useful. He probably did more than all our other poets together to enlarge in America the audience for poetry, and certainly he did more than all of them combined to apprise the rest of the world that we are not entirely songless. In his unquestioning idealism, in his moral simplicity and directness, in his natural honesty of mind and heart which could afford to go unadorned because it was beautiful in its essence, Americans have always recognized qualities to which they aspire. (pp. lii-liii)

In reading him we read ourselves. His poetry provides a bridge by means of which we may return at will into an America simpler and quieter than that of the present, yet indefeasibly our own. It lends depth and distance to our time, linking what we are with what we have been. Here is an assurance and a serenity not easy to find elsewhere. Here is beauty and charm and glamour that are part of our birthright. If this treasure is lost through our ignorance or impatient scorn of the past, we shall all be the poorer. To every educated American it should be a pride and a pleasure to know Longfellow well, to defend him wisely, and to hold him dear. (pp. liv-lv)

Odell Shepard, in his introduction to Henry Wadsworth Longfellow: Representative Selections *by Henry*

Wadsworth Longfellow, edited by Odell Shepard (reprinted by permission of D. C. Heath & Co.), American Book Company, 1934, pp. xi-lv.

ALEXANDER COWIE (essay date 1948)

Longfellow began to write at an early age, but he matured his art slowly. . . . He blossomed lazily when conditions were propitious. Steady growth, not spurts, revealed the law of his nature. The ambition to succeed was no stronger in him than the instinct to perfect his work. His productions were quiet-toned; his colors were pastels. He uttered few piercing notes of sudden grief or shouts of exultant joy. All was measured, settled, and slow. The poet of the fireside was at his best when the fire had reached the stage of embers. The prose writer too was unhurried, pensive, dreamy. He waited for his thoughts to mature; he was content if growth continued. He may be said to have ripened his stories rather than constructed them. Accordingly they are stories to be enjoyed for their flavor and texture, rather than for the stimulation they afford. Longfellow was a good prose writer but not a very good narrative writer.

Most of his prose exhibits the same properties. *Outre-Mer* was a skilful blending of the same sort of sentiment and picturesqueness as Irving had purveyed in the *Sketch Book*. His two long stories [*Hyperion* and *Kavanagh*] . . . were almost wholly lacking in the dynamic qualities that are popularly associated with novel and romance. They are both drowsy books—bred out of dream and mist, heavy with reminiscence, reluctant to deliver their burden of plot. Generations since their time have largely passed these books by with a vague phrase of recognition. Yet they deserve better than the fate that has befallen them. Their defects of plot are obvious to him who runs; their pallid characterizations are as easy to overlook as many of Hawthorne's. Nevertheless in most respects they are quite the equal of most of the poetical pieces of Longfellow that appear perennially in the "litercher books" of our school children. They are not so well proportioned as many of the poems, but they contain much extremely skilful writing, and they contain more that is of interest to the adult mind than do most of the poems. Their practical defect is that they are books of miscellany. Likewise, although they are "earnest" books, they lack profundity. Their general aspect is one of tameness and simplicity. Yet it is a mistake to reserve the laurel for those writers who undertake an enterprise of obvious magnitude, weight, and scope. A writer should not be condemned because it is not his gift to plumb the depths of the ocean in its farthest reaches; he may be reflecting life with as much truth and brilliance in cove or estuary. Not timidity but a true discernment of his real powers kept Longfellow from the truly sublime and terrible. He could translate, but not emulate, the author of *The Divine Comedy*. (pp. 309-10)

[In *Hyperion*,] the novel is unrecognizable. Even the "romance" gets lost if by romance one means a knot of adventure cunningly tied and untied by a conscious craftsman. But the romantic quest of Paul Flemming exists in the warm emotion created by contemplation of an ancient atmosphere and old pageantry. This dreamy re-creation of old Germany and some of its modern exemplars serves as a matrix wherein is born a pattern of faith, a mode of life for a hero in the strife of life. The book is as unordered as a field of flowers; its atmosphere uncertainly alternates between mist and sunshine. The hero stumbles from time to time on his uneasy pilgrimage but finally reaches a resolution of his doubts. *Hyperion* is a sort of spiritual journal of Paul Flemming.

Kavanagh [is] Longfellow's only other extended piece of prose fiction. . . . By this time Longfellow had had the narrative experience of writing *Evangeline,* but he had not tasked himself in the stricter demands of the story-writer's art. He succeeded in narrative in spite of rather than because of his narrative habits. Only about half as long as *Hyperion, Kavanagh* is somewhat more unified than its predecessor, but it is just about as guileless in narrative technique. Compared with a narrative of Poe, it would seem to be the work of an amateur story-teller. Once this defect has been granted, the book can be enjoyed for its idyllic tone—its utterly simple and natural quality. Passing through summer into the first frosts of autumn, it is not without sadness for some of its characters, but it preserves an air of tranquillity. *Kavanagh,* for all its technical defects is a charming book, and a valuable contribution to the literary history of New England—a kind of extended elegy of a village people. (pp. 313-14)

> Alexander Cowie, "The Mixed Thirties," in his The Rise of the American Novel *(reprinted by permission of D. C. Heath & Co.), American Book Company, 1948 (and reprinted by American Book, 1951), pp. 276-326.**

NORMAN HOLMES PEARSON   (essay date 1950)

Taken by and large Longfellow is what he is said to have been: derivative, sentimental, and minor. But there is no reason why we should continue to take him "by and large," if he can appear to better advantage. The remembered quality of a poet's work frequently is no more than a residuum. Reputations have been maintained on the evidence of a handful of poetic craft. It is questionable whether any of even the most moderately critical sensibilities of Longfellow's own age regarded him as a major poet in terms of the achievements of poetry. Yet they recognized, what we are not always presently willing to admit, that to be a good minor poet is an excellence. (p. 245)

There were in fact two Longfellows, whose careers were in conflict. There was the "better maker" who, like an Ezra Pound *de ses jours,* wished to bring to the craft of American poetry and to the resources of the court of Cambridge and of the Harvard Yard all that was dextrous and ennobling from the resources of the past; and there was the familiar bard, he who for the middle classes and the populace could now through periodicals and collected-editions sing to the people by their firesides, in strains as uplifted from crudity as their new government was from old cruelty, of the valor and the virtue of the race.

To both circles he tried to maintain a benign loyalty. (pp. 245-46)

That the public was grateful for his kindness finds its evidence in the love which they maintained for so many of his popular ballads and lyrics, and for the tales which he spun from the thinnest threads. They gave him their highest tribute, that of memory. His poems they recited until Longfellow became *a per se* the poet laureate of the common man. . . . (p. 246)

Poems so commonly popular as certain of Longfellow's take on the characteristics of old saws. It should be within the critic's powers to achieve something of the resharpening which the situation demands. Given this facility one can recognize, for example, Longfellow's great mythopoeic powers. This was an element of the literary imagination which he possessed perhaps beyond the capacities of any other American poet of his time or later. Though Walt Whitman, the American master, can be

said to have created a *mystique* of the body, such a *mystique* was operative chiefly in terms of emotional thrust. Far greater in absolute value and significance as Whitman's poetical powers were, there is nothing in his poems quite like the firm outlines with which Longfellow endowed such figures as Paul Revere, John Alden and Priscilla, or even the village blacksmith. Their appearance was not an accident. One of Longfellow's expressed objectives as a poet was to supply his country with the mythical figures lacking to its psyche. His success was immense. Its achievement lay beyond any mnemonic gifts which verse or rhyme alone could have brought. These enriching characters were his own creations; they exist in and because of his poems.

"Paul Revere's Ride" can only be regarded as a distinguished artistic success within its genre. It is by intent not a reflective piece, nor is its purpose to present the imponderables of ambiguity. No definition of poetry as the precise presentation of the imprecise will obtain in its case. Its purpose is to create a figure from the past whose virtues of immediate decision and action will coincide with and catch up the virtues of what had been America's chief moral action as a nation. (pp. 246-47)

The enforcing merit of Longfellow's metrics [in "Paul Revere's Ride"] should be as obvious as the swift pace of the ride. Longfellow is blanketed with the accusation of sentimentality, but only critical predisposition can detect sentimentality in the actual tone of the poem. Nor is it derivative in any ascertainable degree. . . . Paul Revere is, as he was intended to be, a national hero. The poem is, as it was intended to be, a popular ballad. It effects, as Longfellow hoped it to do, a successful restoration of a past function of poetry.

"The Children's Hour" is another popular poem that deserves to be rescued from predisposition and parody. The occasion of the poem differs from that of "Paul Revere's Ride." Here the circumstance and the mood are meditative. There is leisure for speculative fancy and for affection. The time is set in a twilight of reality in which the demands of pure reason have been softened by conventional attitude. What is desired is not the magnified hero but the common denominator. The nature of sentimentality has been described as "emotional response in excess of the occasion." But that a father should love his daughters is not so much a matter of excess emotion as of natural affection, and Longfellow has given us its presentation in terms of organic suitability. (pp. 247-48)

Longfellow was discerning but seldom valiant in his poetry, and one is struck, in reading his poems, with how little he used the resources of the metaphor as a device. . . . Such a reliance on simple similitude as Longfellow pursued tended to give a kind of flatness to his poetry, a deft but not multidimensionally suggestive relation between things or situations which was based on externals. Longfellow chiefly concerned himself with craftsmanship.

It was his concept of the poet as craftsman rather than as divinely endowed seer that makes Longfellow closer in spirit to the poets of the late eighteenth century than to such American contemporaries as Emerson and Whitman who in their importations took over Romantic philosophy rather than manners. Longfellow's desire was to develop not so much a personal style as one correct in conformity. Though his method allowed for a wealth of formal variety, this was cosmopolitanism rather than individual idiom. . . . Longfellow's was on the whole a secular mind. His mode of communication therefore was not so much through the resources of the imagination as through those of reason. For such purposes it is the simile which serves the poet better than the metaphor does. The results, however, are as relatively limited as is the secular mind itself. (pp. 249-50)

[What] so frequently trips Longfellow in the achievement of maintained distinction through poems as a whole is perhaps to be found in a combination of his habit of the simile with the conflict between the two Longfellows. The poetic presentation of a situation in and for itself was not enough. Having presented it he must determine an analogy, point out and all too frequently spell out its implication. The principle of such relationship is that of the simile extended into gross structure. What was true for him in terms of unexpected likenesses between otherwise disparate objects was also true in terms of the relevance of a physical situation to a moral one. This was a possible way of gaining extra dimension for his poems, but one limited to the resources of Fancy. For one of Longfellow's particular personality it held a special danger. What might have been in its presentation suited to the court often was in its moral analogy cut down and fitted to the middle-class and the people. (pp. 251-52)

What is chiefly disturbing in Longfellow's poems is his confusion of audiences, the frequency with which a poem for the court is turned by simile into a poem for the people. To serve both at once is a democratic concept, but it makes for awkward poetical relationships. (p. 252)

It seems reasonably obvious that the greatest service to be rendered to Longfellow's confused reputation would be to pare down the body of his poems to a core, or two cores, which can be regarded without undue condescension. Such, I am afraid, is not the present situation as represented either in anthologies or in criticism. If the necessary paring seems too ruthless in its excisions, when subsequent additions are made the acts will bring a sense of increased and perhaps unexpected profit. (pp. 252-53)

> *Norman Holmes Pearson, "Both Longfellows," in* The University of Kansas City Review, *Vol. XVI, No. 4, Summer, 1950, pp. 245-53.*

ARTHUR H. QUINN   (essay date 1951)

It is significant that the poet who represented American life most truly should also strike most successfully the international note. "A national literature," Longfellow records in his *Journal* in 1847, "is the expression of national character. We have, or shall have, a composite one, embracing French, Spanish, Irish, English, Scotch and German peculiarities. Whoever has within himself most of these is our truly national writer."

It was because Longfellow's interests were so wide, and his love of his native land so deep that his study of other literatures enriched his poetry with a background against which he depicted scenes and characters of American life so true and so universal in their appeal that they have become part of the intellectual and emotional being of his own and of other nations. So free of artifice, so honest in their artistry are his poems that they seem to spring directly from his heart to that of the reader.

Through this quality he has revealed to millions grace and beauty in the things of which their lives are made. There are other functions than this in poetry; there are none greater. He belongs to the patrician democrats of literature, who view men not as units of a social or political caste but as human beings.

His democracy did not manifest itself in standing on the housetops and crying out that he had arrived and must be reckoned with, and it did not confuse democracy, whose essence is conservatism, with revolt. He realized that to reveal humanity to itself it is by no means necessary to be new.

His immediate appeal has blinded the critic who distrusts anything he can understand, and after the great popularity Longfellow enjoyed in his lifetime there grew up a critical reaction which threatened for a time his proper position. Fortunately the rarer quality of his sonnets and many others of his lyrics, the splendid sweep of his narratives and his remarkable mastery of the technique of versification are now fully recognized by the discriminating, and the platitudes concerning his unoriginality and his foreign inspiration are uttered only by the conventional critic, unable to come out of the shadow of the obvious. (pp. 322-23)

> *Arthur H. Quinn, "Widening Horizons in Poetry," in* The Literature of the American People: An Historical and Critical Survey, *edited by Arthur Hobson Quinn, Appleton-Century-Crofts, 1951, pp. 322-46.*

GEORGE ARMS   (essay date 1953)

At the outset of any study of Longfellow and all the way along, we must recognize that as a poet he had fully pledged his work in the interest of morality. To this in itself we cannot object, unless we are willing to dispense with most classics and the best modern literature. But negatively we question the profoundness of his moral view, and positively we object to the manner of fulfilling the pledge: an open didacticism which frequently seems to relegate the other parts of the poem to no more than a shifty preparation for a lesson. Though along with [W. D.] Howells we may point to many nondidactic poems or suggest the avoidance of the didactic parts, in so doing we avoid the issue. The didactic poems are so many and didacticism permeates the tone of the writings so thoroughly that we cannot overlook it. (p. 207)

In his poem *The Singers* he accepts several purposes for poetry, whether its gift is to charm, strengthen, or teach, but the kind of poetry which he wrote is not well described by any of the three (which Longfellow glossed as lyric, epic, and devotional or didactic) or by a combination. Possibly his incomplete syntax in one stanza of *The Poet and His Songs* is significant of his own inability at self-appraisal and forbearance from it:

> His, and not his, are the lays
>   He sings; and their fame
> Is his, and not his; and the praise
>   And the pride of a name.

Even if he had conscious purpose, he probably did not have enough of it. As with Lowell, though less disastrously, he did not fully know where his best parts lay. There are certainly plenty of examples of lack of humor in his verses. (pp. 216-17)

Just as Longfellow many times misses that perfection of mood which can have poetic pleasure for us, so his placid faith in mankind and his lack of profundity will leave us with a sense of inadequacy. In part our response is sound, but in part we seem to be making demands upon the poet that we have no right to urge. Though Longfellow does not go deeply into human experience, he sees with a good deal of clarity and poise that life which comes to his view. Without prophetic insight, he has perceptive everyday understanding, and he is willing to use diverse materials which show considerably larger spread than we might expect from our judgment of the genteel predilections of his background.

Most of all, I suppose that we think of his use of European and American scene and legend, and we are apt to say that he avoided his own culture by using the first and that when he went to the second his method was to Europeanize native materials. Both charges have truth. Yet concerning his use of Europe we should not forget that pressure was greater in Longfellow's time than ours for native material. In going to Europe (though he was following in the footsteps of Irving) he was moving against the literary currents of his day. A number of passages in the *Tales of a Wayside Inn* show his awareness of the problem and the reasons for his solution.

We next think of Longfellow as a domestic poet, singing the joys and sorrows of the family circle. This too is a sound judgment, but like the others it leaves out much. Longfellow went well beyond. *The Seaside and the Fireside* . . . suggests that he had a larger view than of the home. Through his friendships, he wrote on many public figures in a variety of activities (the sequence *Three Friends of Mine*). Though inadequately, he concerned himself with slavery and the Civil War, he attempted the industrial scene (*The Ropewalk*), he wrote on literature from Chaucer to Bayard Taylor and on its past (*The Singers*) and future (*Possibilities*). We miss his dealing with natural fact, sensuous detail, and the life of the time as we see it through our greater perspective. All the same, we should remember him as almost like the periodical essayist in his constant search for subjects and his welcoming use of a large variety of material.

In not going deep and in keeping on a social level, he exemplifies the manner of the periodical essayist. Yet because of this he should not be branded as genteel. *The Falcon of Ser Federigo* . . . , derived from Boccaccio's *Decameron*, shows the extent of Longfellow's willingness to follow material which, though not sordid, is far from prettified. (pp. 217-18)

[There is] a pathetic sense of transiency exhibited in such poems as *Aftermath* and *The Tide Rises*, but there is not a terrible sense and not a full recognition of the urgency of human experience.

Lack of recognition, however, does not prove that there is no awareness. The "comfort" which Hawthorne found in Longfellow's poetry and which the poet himself consciously proposed is based upon an assumption of turbulence. We see it in many of his poems that have to do with poetry, and in . . . *Seaweed,* in which the "wild emotion" reaches the repose of "hoarded household words," and in *Jugurtha,* which provides no resolution. But generally resolution is offered, whether implicitly in the early *Prelude* or explicitly and rather naïvely in the later *Epimetheus, or the Poet's Afterthought*. Our poet saw himself as moving from the early period of *Sturm und Drang* to the wisdom and balance of the elder Goethe. Unlike Goethe he neglected the affirmation of turbulence that is the basis of dynamic resolution, and in contrast with contemporary thought he does not urge turbulence as the major part of experience. Yet we should grant his awareness of it and admit that since his prevailing mood lies between pathos and comedy the aesthetic need of conflict is less great than it would be otherwise. (p. 219)

We can never perhaps fully understand why Longfellow and his contemporaries regarded their means of climax, use of analogy, and leisurely presentation as artistic values. But . . .

we can achieve a greater comprehension than we have, and for the satisfaction of our intelligence and feeling we owe it to ourselves to try. With all his faults Lowell still said that Donne "wrote more profound verses than any other English poet save one only," and with his faults Longfellow still strove to make his steps "keep pace" with Dante. Since Donne and Dante were the masters of Lowell and Longfellow, as fellow servants we should recognize our common bond. (p. 222)

> *George Arms, "Longfellow," in his* The Fields Were Green: A New View of Bryant, Whittier, Holmes, Lowell, and Longfellow, with a Selection of Their Poems *(with the permission of the publishers, Stanford University Press; copyright 1953 by the Board of Trustees of the Leland Stanford Junior University),* Stanford University Press, *1953, pp. 204-37.*

NEWTON ARVIN (essay date 1963)

A reader who was familiar with Longfellow's boyish poems, and who opened *Voices of the Night* when it first appeared, would surely have been struck very soon by the tones of a new manner. . . . [One is] aware at once of a firmness of tone, a boldness in attack, a freshness of image, that one would have found nowhere in Longfellow's juvenilia. (p. 63)

[*Voices of the Night*] is pervaded, as its title promises, by . . . nocturnal symbolism. . . . The author of these poems was always to be, in one of his roles, a poet of the Night, or the Twilight; Night was to have for him an emotional significance that the day never quite had. . . . Almost always it brings thoughts, as it does in "**Hymn to the Night**," of repose, assuagement, release from care. At moments one discerns a longing for unconsciousness, even oblivion, in this poet, that runs strangely counter to other reaches of his feeling. (pp. 64-5)

There is no wildness of terror or fierceness of anger in this melancholy of Longfellow's, as there is in Poe's or Melville's, and no such dull and continuous pain as he himself saw in Hawthorne's; at its most acute, it never goes beyond a bearable despondency. It could be described as romantic nostalgia of the less passionate and rebellious sort, but it is as far as possible from being a mere literary convention; it was as inherent in Longfellow's temperament as a similar vein of feeling was in Heine's—without, as a rule, the recoil of irony. (p. 67)

There was never a time, however, when Longfellow was willing, as some greater and even some lesser writers have been, to yield himself wholly to the evidence of his sensibilities and make a coherent world-view out of his sufferings. His aversion to the tragic was as temperamental as his sensitiveness to pain, and as all mankind knows, or once knew, he insisted from the outset on correcting—one might say, on contradicting—the evidence of his sensibilities by opposing to it a doctrine of earnest struggle, of courageous resolution, of cheerful and productive action. . . . His resolute hopefulness is quite as genuine as his melancholy, only it is the product not of spontaneous emotion but of conscious effort and self-discipline. Perhaps it is expressed most acceptably in "**The Light of Stars**," one of the two or three better poems in *Voices of the Night*. In this poem he confesses that in his breast, as in the night, there is no light but a cold and starry one, and especially the light of "the red planet Mars," to which he declares he is giving the first watch of the night. Mars, cold as he may be, is the planet of heroic action, and the poet is determined to accept that stern influence. . . . "**The Light of Stars**" was never one of Longfellow's extravagantly popular pieces, perhaps because there is too nice a balance in it between the confession of suffering and the voice of the resisting will. There was no such balance, and no such expressive metaphor, in **"A Psalm of Life"** or **"The Village Blacksmith"** or **"Excelsior"**; and the slack commonplace of these inferior poems insured their universal currency for many decades. (pp. 67-8)

Longfellow's moralizing poems fail, either wholly or relatively, because he was not a moralist. His gifts were quite different from that. Nothing, to repeat, could be more sincere than his moral convictions, but they are at second hand; they were not the fruit, as Emerson's (for example) were, of solitary and independent cogitation. . . . [Honorable] as they were, they have no intrinsic intellectual interest, and they usually do nothing for his poetry but enfeeble it. All this is only too evident.

Longfellow was obeying a truer instinct when he turned to the equally popular, but for him less treacherous, form of the ballad or short balladlike poem. He had a strain of the genuine folk poet in his make-up—in his unaffected naïveté, his simplicity of mind and heart, his love of rapid and usually pathetic storytelling, and his power of improvisation—for some of these poems were written with as little effort as a folksinger puts into a new ballad on an old and familiar kind of subject. Hackneyed as it is, **"The Wreck of the Hesperus"** could hardly be surpassed as a literary imitation of the border ballad. . . . It is a poem for the young, of course, without any more under-feeling than the subject itself carries with it, but on its youthful level, it has in it the authentic terror of the sea. So, too, has the equally familiar **"The Skeleton in Armor,"** which is a little triumph of seaworthy narrative verse. (pp. 69-70)

[Few poets] have had a stronger sense of the sea than Longfellow; and the best poems in *The Seaside and the Fireside,* for the most part, are the poems in the section, **"By the Seaside,"** to which both **"Sir Humphrey Gilbert"** and **"The Secret of the Sea"** belong. The longest of these is **"The Building of the Ship."** One regrets that this poem, like some others of Longfellow's, was staled and shopworn almost from the beginning by constant use in school readers and in youthful recitation, for, flawed as it is by some of Longfellow's habitual faults—the too facile family sentiment of one or two passages, for example—it has, to a robust taste that can overlook these flaws, a vivacity, a swiftness of movement, and a painterly concreteness of detail, as in an old-fashioned genre-painting or print, that save it from simple banality. (pp. 70-1)

It goes without saying, now, that there is much that is facile and flaccid in [his collections of poetry]; like most minor poets who have been prolific as well as minor, Longfellow had no clear sense of the distinction between his weaknesses and his real strength. He seems to have taken as much pleasure in some of his inferior poems as in the better ones. . . . His nature was so genuinely sensitive and *gefühlvoll* that, with the best conscience in the world, he could fall a victim to the bad sentimental taste of his age—there is of course a good sentimental taste—and there were subjects that normally betrayed him into the sort of false and misplaced feeling that one finds in Lydia Hunt Sigourney. One of these subjects was childhood (**"To a Child"**); he is almost always at his feeblest on this theme. Another treacherous subject for him was that of innocence or simple unstained purity (**"Maidenhood"**); one need not make light of this virtue in order to find Longfellow's celebration of it painfully wanting in moral complexity or edge. Death, too, sometimes inspired in him a soft and second-rate moral response, not a tragic one (**"Footsteps of Angels"**); and the fact

that he shared this weakness with greater writers of the age—Dickens, Tennyson, and others—does not conduce to greater patience with him.

Both morally and artistically speaking, when such subjects are in question, there is something suspect in emotions that well up so easily as these do, and that express themselves with so little stress or struggle. In general, it was a double-natured gift that the gods bestowed on Longfellow when, as it were in his cradle, they endowed him with the talents of an improvisator. . . . [When] thoughts or feelings sprang up in him that needed to be resisted, he gave them as free a rein as the thoughts or feelings that could safely be trusted. (pp. 78-9)

His art, with some ups and downs, was to go on refining and enhancing itself perceptibly to the very end, but already the poems down to *The Seaside and the Fireside* furnish pretty much the measure of his capacities as a lyrical and narrative poet. There are states of feeling that remain this side of either ecstasy or despair—sadness, weariness, a half-pleasurable fear, elation, the simple apprehension of beauty—that Longfellow could express with a veracity that has nothing in it of falseness or the meretricious. Moods of the weather, seasons of the year, divisions of the day or night—to these external states he was delicately sensitive, and they often become the expressive equivalents of his emotions. . . . He had something like a genius for narrative poetry—not, to be sure, of the psychologically or philosophically interesting sort, but in the popular and romantic sense—and he could almost always draw, to happy effect, on legend or literary tradition. His sense of form was fallible, but at his best he is an accomplished, sometimes an exquisite, craftsman, like a master in some minor art, a potter or a silversmith; and his command of his materials, at such times—language, meter, rhyme, imagery—though it is not that of a great artist, is wholly adequate to his purposes. (pp. 80-1)

Evangeline suggests a minor poetic form, not the epic, and it suggests a more archaic literary form than the novel. It is enough if the tenderness and the tenacity of the lovers' devotion to each other—for, after all, Gabriel does prove constant—are made credible, as they are; enough if the two of them move through the poem not as realistic lovers of the mid-eighteenth century in the colonies, but as figures of the frankest romanticism, dimly outlined, quietly moving, grave and gentle, and speaking hardly at all. Gabriel's father, the blacksmith Basil Lajeunesse, has enough choler and enough heartiness to give him a certain definition, but it is no more than that; and Evangeline's father, the prosperous farmer Benedict Bellefontaine, who dies of heartbreak on the sea beach during the night before the deportation, is a figure of pure pathos. The minor characters . . . fill in the human scene pleasantly and rescue it from the bareness that might so easily have impoverished it. (pp. 107-08)

[Plenty] of readers and critics at the time protested vigorously, as plenty have done since, against the metrical form in which Longfellow chose to cast his poem. This was of course the very controversial form of the allegedly classical hexameter. No really successful English poem had yet been written in this form, though experiments with it had been made ever since Elizabethan times. . . . (p. 109)

[*Evangeline* stands or falls] not on the correctness of its hexameters, classically speaking, but on their intrinsic charm and their appropriateness to its inner character. When we read *Evangeline* in this spirit, we are likely to feel that, at its most successful, the verse has a kind of grave, slow-paced, mellif-luous quality, like a slightly monotonous but not unmusical chant, which is genuinely expressive of its mournful and minor theme. (p. 111)

The real interest of *Hyperion,* only too obviously, lies not in the moral action, but in the divagations of one sort or another—they bulk too large to be called digressions—that make up the staple of the book. It was a great age of travel literature, not in the heroic Elizabethan sense, but in a more personal and impressionable one; and what doubtless most attracted Long-fellow's readers at the time was *Hyperion*'s character as a pleasantly fictionalized guidebook. (p. 118)

Not that Longfellow proves himself, here any more than in *Outre-Mer,* a descriptive writer of great power; side by side with the great writers of this kind—with Ruskin, let us say—he is meager and hasty. He relies, for his effects of romantic wandering, not so much on sustained pieces of landscape paint-ing or architectural evocation, as on his general genial move-ment from place to place by stagecoach or on foot; on his stops at inns with picturesque names, the White Horse or the Rhein-ischen Hof or the Golden Ship; and indeed, to a considerable extent, on the mere suggestive charm of the storied place-names themselves. . . . The whole narrative is bathed in so sunny and ingenuous an atmosphere of vagrant nostalgia that the mere name of a village or a lake, a river or a mountain, is enough to set the fancy vibrating pleasantly, if not with much sonority. And so of the glimpses one is furnished of "real" life in Germany and Austria; they never draw one's eye to the re-actionary realities of the thirties—the censorship, the repres-sion, the political imprisonments—any more than similar glimpses in *Outre-Mer* draw one's eye to the Italy of the early Risorgimento. (p. 119)

Much more than to [the] rather set pieces of social description, however, *Hyperion* owes its undeniable, and even now appre-ciable, flavor and color to its pervasive and almost obsessive literariness. Longfellow, when he wrote it, was still living in the first glow of his enthusiasm, his *Begeisterung,* for German literature, and *Hyperion* is the engaging memento, like a gift-book or album, of his love affair with the German mind. No one before him, in this country, had plunged so eagerly into those romantic waters, or come up with so rich a haul of literary impressions; and he poured them out, in *Hyperion,* with a youthful prodigality. No doubt he was rifling his own lectures at Harvard when he did this, but if so, his stylistic sense saved him from an obvious error; he does not merely thrust passages from his lectures, like inorganic lumps of commentary, into the structure of his narrative. The literary talk in which the book abounds is always, and with real naturalness, worked into the fabric of the whole. (pp. 119-20)

[On the strength of such talk,] Longfellow is entitled to a small but secure niche in the history of our literary criticism. His critical writing, it is true, like his lecturing, is frankly subjec-tive, appreciative, affirmative; his general literary *principles* are the commonplaces of romantic aesthetics, and his taste, fine as it often was, often too went sadly astray. At his best, however, he wrote sensitively, warmly, and imaginatively, like the poet he was, about the writers who delighted him. (p. 121)

It is characteristic of his criticism to express itself not only in metaphor but in metaphor that depends for its appreciative effect on allusions and references that are charming in them-selves. . . . But it is not only in his criticism that Longfellow's mind habitually reveals its natural grain through metaphor and

allusion: his prose in general sparkles with imagery and ref-erence, fanciful, pretty, sometimes witty, sometimes inapt, but almost always delightful in itself. The prose of *Hyperion* owes its pleasantness, to a considerable extent, to this rococo or-nament. (p. 122)

[*Kavanagh,*] is even slighter and more imponderous than *Hy-perion;* one feels that the merest puff from the lips of criticism would shatter it, and indeed it seems to have proved to Long-fellow himself that prose fiction was not, for him, a mode worth pursuing any further. Yet it was written, as he said, *con amore,* and an indulgent criticism will find, even now, ele-ments of tenuous, but not merely imaginary, interest in it. . . . It *has* a certain veracity, just as it has a certain faint and flowerlike fragrance.

It is the fragrance of American pastoral. Like the stories of the local colorists which began to appear some time afterward, *Kavanagh* is an elegy on the old-fashioned village life of New England that was already, when he wrote, beginning to recede into oblivion, though Longfellow felt this before it had become a commonplace. (pp. 124-25)

The main action of *Kavanagh* [however] is wholly without fictional solidity or serious truth. Longfellow had some but not most of the specific gifts of the novelist, and *Kavanagh,* despite the pleasure he took in writing it, seems to have taught him this. Very fortunately, on the whole, he was done with prose fiction for the rest of his literary life. (p. 129)

[Whatever his success in the writing of the *Song of Hiawatha*], Longfellow was attempting an interesting experiment, and one that had not been made before. The Indian, of course, had already figured for decades in our literature; the subject, in a general way, may be said to have become hackneyed. Yet it had been viewed in only a few of its aspects. For the poets, the Indians of their time were appealing almost solely for the pathos of their fate, as members of a doomed and tragic race. . . .

What none of these writers, not even Cooper, had done, except in the most incidental way, was to interest themselves in the Indians' own mythology; in what had already begun to be called the "folklore" of this primitive race, the tales and legends inherited from a remote, ante-historic past, and preserved for generations in the form of oral tradition. This, and not the prowess of splendid savages or even the tragedy of their pass-ing, was what now fascinated Longfellow. (p. 155)

Longfellow's self-chosen task was to select among [the Amer-ican Indian legends], translate them into his own imaginative terms, and make a coherent poem of them. This is what he did in *Hiawatha.* (p. 156)

If "primitive" means only savage, bloodthirsty, and fierce, then Longfellow's Hiawatha is a romantic caricature of the real culture-hero of primitive peoples. . . . [He] is essentially hu-man in his proportions, despite his magic resources; eternally young, slender, graceful, and kindly. . . . Hiawatha is not the Savage as Devil—the savage of the Puritans—or the Noble Savage of Cooper or the Heroic Savage of Melville; he has to be called something like the Gentle Savage. (pp. 157-58)

If we can regard Hiawatha indulgently in this milder light, he has a minor but genuine imaginative truth not merely to Indian but to human reality. He is a composite product—the image of an Indian prophet conjured up by a sensitive nineteenth-century imagination, with its own freshness and naïveté, which had steeped itself in the somewhat expurgated legends that the early ethnologists had brought together. . . . [He] has a quasi-primitive veracity of his own—a childlike seriousness, an archaic ingenuousness, that ring perfectly true to one aspect of primordial human experience. (p. 159)

There is no recondite symbolism in [the Indian] myths or legends as Longfellow retells them; if there is any symbolism, it is perfectly transparent, and Longfellow saw in them no such suggestiveness for romantic allegory as Melville, in *Mardi*, saw in his Polynesian myths and legends. They lack a certain resonance as a result, a certain penumbra of emotion or intellectual meaning. But Longfellow's mind was both more and less "primitive" than Melville's; he delighted in these traditions simple-mindedly for their own sake, and as a result they have, in his handling of them, a clarity of shape, an unambiguous freshness, which they would have lost in the handling of a greater poet. This points to a defect in the poem, but the defect is not without its compensations, and between them they signalize the weakness and strength of *Hiawatha* as a whole. There is another aspect, too, in which its qualities and its defects may be viewed. There was next to no *negative* strain in Longfellow's cult of the primitive; it was not—as it was with most writers in his time—the reverse of any deep loathing he may have felt for civilization or progress. . . . There is thus no painful complexity, no rich contradictoriness, in what Longfellow does with primitive life, and this keeps *Hiawatha* from having the intensity one finds in the work of more passionate men like Thoreau or Melville or even Cooper. The compensation is that it has a greater simplicity of truth to some aspects of primitive life. Was it a fatal mistake for Longfellow to pitch upon the meter that he thought the only right one for what he called his "Indian Edda"? . . . It is not only the meter, of course, but the trick of reiteration, especially at the beginning of lines . . . that has affected so many readers as laughable; but it is the meter that has been the real sticking-point. Is it not as hopelessly monotonous and even maddening as a primitive drumbeat, without the excuse that no better instruments are available to civilized composers? It is a painful question to any reader who cannot forswear the modest pleasure-giving quality of the poem as a whole. Does this quality simply survive in spite of the meter?—for a poem need not be utterly shipwrecked even by an infelicitous pattern. (pp. 166-67)

Both the meter and the language come to life, and the poem frees itself from mere monotony, when the action is playful, innocent, or *märchenhaft*, or even when it is violent if the violence is half sportive. . . . [In] the description of Pau-Puk-Keewis's dancing there is a fine kinetic sense of choreographic movement, slow at first, then accelerated, and finally whirling. So with the hunting of Pau-Puk-Keewis; the verse keeps pace with the swift, unflagging movement of the flight and pursuit, and the mannerisms of style fall away almost completely.

This is even truer of the passages in which the moods of external nature—of languor or drowsiness, stillness or hush, even grimness—are in harmony with the emotions of the human figures. The most genuine feeling in the poem is the feeling that is reflected back from the landscape or the season or the time of day, and the verse is capable of expressing this without deflation. (p. 170)

Even now Longfellow had not done with the Indians; they reappear in *The Courtship of Miles Standish,* only now they are not legendary prophets and singers, boasters and tricksters, but historical Wampanoag Indians, such as the settlers of Plymouth had encountered in all their solid actuality on the shores and in the woods of Massachusetts. As a result, they are seen not through an Indian Summer haze of poetic primitiveness but

with a certain harshness of "realism." They are seen, as a matter of fact, as if through the eyes of the Pilgrims themselves, and if that is a distorting medium, it is clearly the right one for this poem. (pp. 173-74)

The hexameters of *The Courtship* are looser, more relaxed, more frequently trochaic, and less sonorous than those of *Evangeline;* sometimes, in their colloquial ease, . . . they are merely jejune, and sometimes they are painfully prosaic. . . . [Yet] *The Courtship* has a sharp tonality of its own—to which the verse and the language of course contribute—somewhat reminiscent of the "primeval" opening and close of *Evangeline,* but quite unlike its luxuriant and subtropical middle passages. (pp. 177-78)

The Puritan color of the poem is kept up not only by the austere landscape and seascape, but by the constant and always natural recurrence, as in a sacred cantata, of Scriptural language and imagery, usually in an Old Testament spirit. Alden and Priscilla, on their way home from the wedding, recall . . . Rebecca and Isaac; and earlier, when John has been plunged in remorse for his "excessive" love of Priscilla, he accuses himself of "worshipping Astaroth blindly, and impious idols of Baal." . . . [The] poem comes to an end in a burst of feeling that is both Israelitish and pastoral. It has that kind of truth to the life of the Plymouth Colony; and *The Courtship of Miles Standish,* modest as it is in the claims it makes, is a minor but honorable achievement in poetic narrative. (pp. 179-80)

[Longfellow] had reached a kind of upland of his powers as a lyric poet with *The Seaside and the Fireside,* and after that he held his ground with no really startling ascents or descents until perhaps his late sixties, when there is an appreciable, but by no means a miserable, failure of energy. Almost everything he was later to say had been said, or implied, by the time of *The Seaside and the Fireside,* and what remained was, fortunately, not mere self-repetition, but a steady, slight, unsensational, but beautiful refinement and enhancement of what he had already done. (p. 181)

It remained for Longfellow in his middle fifties, and after the crushing blow of his wife's death, to hit upon the most fortunate plan—of an ambitious sort, that is—in his whole career as a poet, the plan of a series of tales in verse contained within a narrative frame [and titled *Tales of a Wayside Inn*]. No literary undertaking could have made a happier or more fruitful use of his powers and his equipment than this—of his storytelling genius, his sense of narrative form, his versatility, and the opulence of his literary erudition. He had considered projects of this sort long before, but nothing had come of them—in part, surely, because the right *kind* of frame had not suggested itself to him, as it did now. (p. 205)

As we read the *Tales of a Wayside Inn,* we feel ourselves in the presence of a poet who is at work in his most natural and spontaneous vein, a poet whose matter and form are at one with each other, and who has found his happiest means of expression. As we read Longfellow's dramatic poems, we feel ourselves, a good deal of the time, baffled and, sometimes, bored by writing that clearly expresses an aspiration, an ambition, but that is somehow not quite naturally directed; writing that is willed, even determined, but only intermittently borne up and carried along by a true afflatus. (p. 258)

Never did he undertake a task more mistakenly than when he set himself to compose a first panel for his sacred trilogy, *Christus: A Mystery,* and attempted, as he did in *The Divine Tragedy,* to dramatize poetically the life of Christ. It is a subject beyond the powers of any poet, certainly of any poet since the Middle Ages, as even *Paradise Regained,* even Klopstock's *Messias,* should have demonstrated, and it was wholly beyond the powers of a poet whose Christian faith, sincere as it certainly was, was New England Unitarianism in its coolest, most reasonable, and most optimistic form. . . . Longfellow's awareness of human evil, of sin, was almost nonexistent, or so intermittent as to be largely ineffectual in his work, and the redemption of mankind from its burden of guilt by a transcendent Saviour was a theme of which he was utterly unable to make dramatic poetry of any but the most unconvincing sort. (pp. 259-60)

The two *New England Tragedies,* **"John Endicott"** and **"Giles Corey of the Salem Farms,"** have a kind of vitality that is missing from *The Divine Tragedy:* in writing them, Longfellow was not oppressed by the constraint and self-consciousness that evidently weighed on him in writing the first part of the trilogy. The subjects themselves were fresher, closer at hand, and more purely human than the Gospel subject, and Longfellow could, and did, handle his historical authorities with much greater freedom. Neither play succeeds in arousing the emotions of tragedy in any profound way, but of the two **"John Endicott"** comes closer to doing so, no doubt because the heroism of the Quakers in resisting persecution had a reality for Longfellow that the suffering of the "witches" at Salem did not quite evoke. (p. 268)

"John Endicott" communicates something of the emotional tension of a community in the grip of heresy-hunters; **"Giles Corey"** fails, in the end, to communicate with any real power the emotional tension of a community pathologically attacked by a peculiarly virulent hysteria. There was a morbid horror in the subject of Salem witchcraft, unlike that of theological persecution, which Longfellow's kindly spirit shrank, perhaps half-consciously, from rendering with any real sternness or rigor; the poisons of panic terror, of malignant hostility, of superstitious cruelty were so alien to his own nature that, in this connection at least, he could not master them imaginatively, and though they are present in **"Giles Corey,"** they are never represented with full dramatic conviction. Correspondingly, Longfellow fails to evoke any deep tragic sense of the heroism, the moral grandeur, of those who held out against the hysteria and, in some cases, went to their deaths in unavailing innocence. (pp. 273-74)

The subject of *Judas Maccabaeus* was almost as unsuitable a subject for Longfellow's gifts as *The Divine Tragedy* had been, and the poem has even fewer elements of interest than the other has. It is on an almost perversely small scale—five tiny acts divided into even tinier scenes and amounting to hardly a thousand lines in all. As a result, the poem produces somewhat the effect of an epic drama in a puppet theater or an oratorio reduced to a few brief and rather thin recitatives. Naturally, the theme that had struck Longfellow as so fruitful for a play—the collision of Judaism and Hellenism—could not be, and is not, developed in this space with any real richness or complexity: it is broached, but it is not worked out; grazed lightly, but not seriously *treated.* (pp. 277-78)

The character and career of a great artist made less unnatural demands on Longfellow's power than the character and career of a great patriot-warrior, and the "Fragment" of *Michael Angelo,* which he never regarded as finished, has too much vitality, autumnal as that vitality mostly is, to be disposed of as a mere failure. (p. 279)

As a whole, *Michael Angelo,* whatever its shortcomings, is by no means unimpressive as a poetic and even as a "dramatic" treatment of its difficult and complex subject; fragmentary as it is, along with *The Golden Legend* it is the most interesting of all Longfellow's dramatic experiments. (p. 287)

Certainly Longfellow will never again "enjoy" the excessive popularity he enjoyed in his own time and for some years afterward, and this is as it should be. (p. 324)

Longfellow may continue to seem minor, but one rebels against describing him as small. There is a certain largeness not only in his conception of his role but in his actual performance, which is inconsistent with the label of littleness, even of perfection in littleness; his mind was simply, with all its limitations, too venturesome to allow him to remain content with the mastery of one or two forms or modes, and if this meant that he sometimes essayed to do a larger kind of thing than his gifts warranted, the result often has the value of interesting failure, and sometimes a greater value than that. The author of *Hiawatha,* of *Tales of a Wayside Inn,* of *Michael Angelo* was a lesser but not a little writer, a minor poet but not a poetaster. (p. 326)

In the great bulk of his work, . . . he is a demotic poet pure and simple, like Bryant, Whittier, and Holmes—only richer in resources, more various, more *genialisch* than any of them. And there are poems, early and late, which do not belong to the sphere of popular poetry at all; poems that are simply expressions of an authentic poetic gift, of course of a secondary order. These are the poems most worth holding on to, but much of the rest of his work deserves to be retained in the literary memory in much the same spirit in which Byron's narrative poems, or Tennyson's ballads, or the best of Whittier's demotic pieces deserve to be retained. It is still pleasure-giving to a catholic taste; it still speaks appealingly, for an American mind, to the sense of the American past; and now and then it disengages itself from historic circumstances and takes on the aspect, modestly and even obscurely, of timelessness. Our literature is not so rich in writing of this kind that we can afford to discard any of it. (pp. 328-29)

> *Newton Arvin, in his* Longfellow: His Life and Work *(© 1962, 1963 by Newton Arvin; reprinted by permission of Little, Brown and Company in association with the Atlantic Monthly Press), Atlantic-Little, Brown, 1963, 338 p.*

EDWARD L. HIRSH   (essay date 1964)

The major ideas underlying Longfellow's poetry are characteristically expressed in a conventional nineteenth-century terminology that invites partial misreading, partly because of subsequent changes in meaning, especially in connotation, and partly because important terms are often so inclusive as to seem indeterminate. Longfellow's constant appeal to the heart is frequently understood as the consequence of a vague, sentimental notion that the gentler emotions could resolve problems and order life, to the near-exclusion of thought. His usage, however, like that of his contemporaries, reflects an older and wider meaning of *heart.* The word refers not only to the emotions, but also to will and intuitive reason. The heart is the source of insight as well as of joy or grief; it embraces the moral sensibility that accepts or rejects truth and that acts as conscience in its unstudied response to generally self-evident laws. . . . [In] his simple division of man into body and soul, Longfellow assigned all thoughts, all feelings, all desires to the soul, not the body, which is only the instrument. "It is the soul," he insisted, "that feels, enjoys, suffers . . ." Thus the affections themselves are spiritual, and, directed to good ends, can properly be called "holy."

Longfellow's frame of ultimate reference is formed by his religious convictions. . . . Like his father, Longfellow in general accepted the teaching of William Ellery Channing: that man is fundamentally good, endowed by God with reason, conscience, and an intuitive awareness of the divine; and that Christianity, the purest faith known to man, is progressing toward a full realization of its ideals in a universal church of the future. (pp. 136-37)

For so optimistic a belief, the chief problem is that of sin and evil, and the greatest imaginative failure of Longfellow's poetry is its inability to probe life's dark or sordid aspects. . . . Especially in his long poems, Longfellow represents or alludes to the malicious, fanatic, and selfish behavior men are capable of, but he suggests no deeper cause than a defect incidental to man's present condition, reformable although not yet reformed. (p. 137)

The simply held ideas by which Longfellow attempted to order experience are frequently unable to contain the strong current of feeling that is a distinctive quality of his romantic sensibility. Although he was sharply critical of what he considered the excesses and absurdities of romanticism, his own poetry is saturated with a romantic sense of life's fragility. . . . However tempered in expression by his almost classical restraint and social poise, the dominant mood of Longfellow's poetry is a melancholy not unlike that of Washington Irving, compounded of nostalgia, the sadness of personal loss, and the painful awareness of transience and mortality. (p. 138)

Like much nineteenth-century poetry, Longfellow's seems in retrospect leisurely, even too relaxed. The slow development of ideas, the elaboration of details, the multiplication of parallels, the explication of the already-evident are practices that destroy some of his poems and in varying combinations and degrees characterize most of them. The language, too, bears the stamp of its time in its tendency to expansive statement, its often predictable vocabulary and phraseology, and its fondness for literary diction. . . . Historically considered, the kind of poetry Longfellow wrote lay within a poetic tradition that with various adaptations served the larger part of a century, and was imaginatively satisfying to the romantic-Victorian sensibility. Within the age's literary conventions, Longfellow used language skillfully and sensitively. At its best, his language is simple and economical, natural in movement, emotionally exact in its use of words and phrases, and restrained in statement. Furthermore, Longfellow's handling of language is largely responsible for his achievement of an impressive tonal range from the formality of semi-epic narrative to the humor-seasoned easiness of the discourse of polite society. He makes the traditional poetic language, with often minimal alteration, express distinctively his own insights and feelings.

As a poet more evocative than creative of experience, Longfellow employs language with a notable awareness of the way in which it becomes charged with meaning from the inescapable situations of human life. Frequently he depends not upon connotations or overtones developed within the context of a poem, but upon a resonance provided immediately by general experience itself and renewed in the poem by allusions to the appropriate common events or situations, or by brief descriptions of them. (pp. 144-45)

Like other aspects of his poetry, Longfellow's prosody is remarkable for resourcefulness and variety within traditional limits. His uncommon talent in versification and his absorption in its technical problems led to no prosodic revolution; indeed, a dangerous facility, combined with a taste for euphony, brings his verse at moments close to that of the typical Victorian "sweet singer." Within accepted bounds, however, Longfellow's versatility in rhythmical, metrical, and rhyming patterns and his constant experimentation, directed toward the creation of a unique effect for each poem, reveal a technical mastery rarely approached in American poetry. Although his prosodic variety is most obvious in the surprisingly various patterns of his stanzaic verse, it is perhaps more subtly displayed in meeting the resistance of a set form like the sonnet, where, employing the Italian pattern and almost invariably observing a strict octet-sestet division, Longfellow achieves striking rhythmic differences by ingenious handling of metrical substitution, run-on and end-stopped lines, and caesuras. In freer forms, his skill is no less evident: the extremely uneven blank verse of *The Divine Tragedy* has reflective passages in which comparative rhythmic freedom works with approximately normal word order to produce lines that sometimes collapse into prose but that occasionally attain a thoroughly natural movement barely but unmistakably tightened into poetry. . . . (p. 146)

The technical virtuosity of Longfellow's art is manifested in several accomplishments: the successful maintenance of falling rhythm in spite of English poetry's strong tendency to rising rhythm; the dexterous control of varied rhythm and free rhyming by an organization based on parallelism, balance, and alliteration; and the giving of widely varied movement to such uncomplicated verse forms as the quatrain. (p. 147)

The major irony of Longfellow's literary career was the commitment of his hopes for distinctive major achievement to the form in which he was most consistently unsuccessful, the poetic drama. From 1849 to 1872 he intermittently labored over what he regarded as "his loftier song" in "sublimer strain," as his greatest work, "the equivalent expression for the trouble and wrath of life, for its sorrow and mystery." The completed *Christus: A Mystery* consists of three parts comprising four poetic dramas, all so manifestly closet dramas that they could be properly described as dramatically organized poems. The first part is *The Divine Tragedy,* the last to be published; the second part is *The Golden Legend,* the first published; the third part, *The New England Tragedies,* consists of two dramas, *John Endicott* and *Giles Corey of the Salem Farms.* The three parts are linked by interludes and the whole *Christus* is provided with an "Introitus" and "Finale." No other works of Longfellow's had such intended scope or received such dedicated attention; and none were so disappointing in result. (pp. 154-55)

Longfellow's general failure in dramatic form is understandable. His talent was narrative and lyrically meditative, and he could not refrain from reliance on narration and exposition, even to the destruction of dramatic effect. . . . It is his least pretentious dramatic work, the early *Spanish Student,* that is in many respects the most successfully realized; in spite of its lack of intellectual significance, it is a colorful, pleasant comedy of intrigue, technically more proficient than the later poetic dramas. Two minor dramatic works, *Judas Maccabeus* and *The Masque of Pandora,* have interesting themes but are extremely weak in execution. Only the partly completed *Michael Angelo,* closely related to Longfellow's own life and work, and containing in a few passages some of his strongest poetry, shows an apparently emerging mastery of dramatic form in the 1870's.

The fundamental obstacle to the *Christus'* success, however, is not simply a flawed dramatic technique, but an internal conflict in the work between its ostensible intention and its meaning. Originally planned as a dramatizing of the progress of Christianity, the *Christus* loosely employs the theological virtues of faith, hope, and charity as the basis of organization, *The Divine Tragedy* expressing hope through its representation of Christ's life and mission, the *Golden Legend* depicting faith in its full medieval flowering, and the *New England Tragedies* pointing to the religious freedom of the age of charity or love. The optimism of the design is realized in some scenes and is recurrently asserted as a proposition, but it is not borne out in the *Christus'* development and accumulated feeling, which are finally somber and even pessimistic in their tendency. Longfellow's emotional recoil from several aspects of the contemporary religious scene apparently caused him to lose much of his professed hope for the future and left its mark especially on the first and third parts, the latest composed, of the *Christus*. (pp. 155-56)

Perhaps the most successful part of *Christus* is the *Golden Legend,* which, in spite of an elementary plot, an unmedievally melancholy hero, and a sentimentalized heroine, effectively profits from Longfellow's knowledge of the Middle Ages. Although the deepest intellectual and spiritual life of the medieval world is not mirrored here, the varied contrasts and conflicts of the medieval surface, as well as the immediately underlying crosscurrents, are colorfully represented through skillfully shifted scenes presented in a freely handled answerable verse. (p. 157)

> *Edward L. Hirsh, in his* Henry Wadsworth Longfellow *(American Writers Pamphlet No. 35; © 1964, University of Minnesota), University of Minnesota Press, Minneapolis, 1964 (and reprinted as a chapter in* Six Classic American Writers: An Introduction, *edited by Sherman Paul, University of Minnesota Press, 1970, pp. 122-59).*

LOUIS UNTERMEYER   (essay date 1967)

Few poets have run the gamut from the world's devotion to critical dismissal as completely as Henry Wadsworth Longfellow. Idolized in his time—the only American poet to be honored with a bust in Westminster Abbey—and condescendingly suffered in our own, he is due for a thorough reappraisal. Too many know him only through textbooks that have enshrined his worst, featuring the banal maxims of **"A Psalm of Life,"** the sugared sententiousness of **"The Arrow and the Song,"** and the bland absurdities of **"Excelsior"** with its unintentionally comic quatrains. . . .

Andrew Hilen's meticulously edited *The Letters of Henry Wadsworth Longfellow* represents . . . [a significant] effort to establish the man instead of the myth, the instinctive poet rather than the too frequently facile poetaster.

Professor Hilen's project is a multi-volume edition that will bring together for the first time letters written by the poet, most of which have never appeared in print. These first two volumes cover the period 1814-1843, from Longfellow's seventh to his thirty-sixth year, and contain 805 letters. . . .

What about the letters themselves? Alas, unlike most poets, Longfellow was not an impassioned, provocative, or even interesting letter-writer. His letters fail to move us because, although a courteous correspondent, he hated to write them. As a youth he informed his father that he actually and utterly abominated the business of composing a letter. "I write so exceedingly slow that it is really a waste of time to no purpose—neither I nor my correspondent can be wiser for what is written." The result, as might be expected, is that most of the letters are dull, packed with perfunctory descriptions, dutiful replies, and a vast flotsam of trivia. . . .

The reader keeps on hoping that the letters will (perhaps unconsciously) disclose something of the inner life of the young and maturing poet. Professor Hilen tries to assure us; he believes the reader will tend to find that the letters "reveal Longfellow as having a keen and expansive mind." This not-too-captious reader cannot agree. Keen? At times. Expansive? Never. Chiefly what they reveal is a pleasant but certainly not penetrating mind.

As an appreciator of poetry, the young Longfellow liked verse that was both prim and platitudinous. . . . As a thinker, he was conservative to the point of complacent conformity. As an observer of his country's political activities, he was, except for some rather prettified antislavery poems, passive rather than critical. There is scarcely anything [in these early letters] to indicate that some day Longfellow would plunge his hands in native clay and mold it into such indigenous stuff as *The Song of Hiawatha, Paul Revere's Ride, The Courtship of Miles Standish,* and *The New England Tragedies.* Nor is there more than a hint that surprisingly, in a voice resembling Whitman's, Longfellow could say: "We want a national literature commensurate with our mountains and rivers, a national epic, a national drama in which scope shall be given to our gigantic ideas and to the unparalleled activity of our people."

> *Louis Untermeyer, "Poet or Poetaster?" in* Saturday Review *(copyright © 1967 by* Saturday Review; *all rights reserved; reprinted by permission), Vol. L, No. 26, July 1, 1967, p. 27.*

LESLIE A. FIEDLER   (essay date 1971)

[It] has become clear to us, as it always does at revolutionary moments, cultural as well as political, that in order to possess the future we must first repossess the past; in order to invent the future, first reinvent the past—if need be, a *new* past, a history we never lived. In terms of creating a new poetry, this means finding in that past, counterfeiting out of it if necessity compels, a model, a set of ideal ancestors. It is intriguing to speculate, while prophecy is still possible in this regard, who these half-imaginary ancestors will be: who will play for the poetic revolution in the last three decades of the twentieth century the role played by John Donne (Eliot's John Donne) during the first three decades and by Walt Whitman (Allen Ginsberg's Walt Whitman) during the two that followed. And my answer . . . is Henry Wadsworth Longfellow, plus, perhaps, Stephen Collins Foster; Longfellow and Foster will be our Donne and Whitman. (pp. 168-69)

[We need] figures who closed the gap before most readers in America quite knew it had opened; figures who stood at the center of an age when popular song and printed verse still drew on a single implicit notion of what poetry was, when the serious contemporary anthologist (E. C. Stedman, for example) could put the most popular of the songwriters and the most widely read of the printed poets side by side in the same collection—with no sense of doing something radical or superchic, or even a little daring. It is, then, to the mid-nineteenth century that we must return, back through the intervening years during which the divorce between popular song and serious verse grew ever more extreme. . . . (p. 169)

[It is not] to the mid-nineteenth century of Walt Whitman that we must return, or even to that of Herman Melville . . . ; not to F. O. Matthiessen's "American Renaissance" at all, but to the *other* mid-nineteenth century defined by Longfellow and James Russell Lowell and Oliver Wendell Holmes, by Harriet Beecher Stowe and Julia Ward Howe and Stephen Foster—not to the alienated symbolist works prized exclusively (I hope we shall continue to prize them forever, though not to the exclusion of the counter-Renaissance, the bourgeois "white" Romantics) in the recent past by critics, including me, who assumed a hierarchy of literary works in prose and in verse, which provided at its broad, not-quite-respectable base a vast demi-literature available to everyone, but at its narrow summit offered only a few winnowed works to be appreciated by select handful of readers, who turned out to be, in fact, not merely adults as opposed to children, sophisticated as opposed to naive, ironical as opposed to sentimental, but also male as opposed to female, white as opposed to black.

It was Longfellow and Foster . . . who, not absolutely to be sure, but approximately at least, joined together an audience of men and women, children and adults, privileged and underprivileged. Of Harriet Beecher Stowe, Emerson was moved to say from the other side of the barricades, as it were, that she was read in the parlor, the kitchen and the nursery; and Longfellow pleased an audience analogously heterogeneous— as attested by the story that when he went to England for an audience with Queen Victoria, he was asked first to go down into the servants' quarters to receive the plaudits of the larger and more demonstrative group of readers awaiting him there. (pp. 169-70)

[A] creative, dissenting minority among the young, from whose midst the storytellers and minstrels who give a special savor to our time almost entirely come, have been rejecting or radically undercutting traditional concepts of "growing up"— questioning not merely Freudian doctrine, which preaches that maturity entails moving on from the polymorphous-perverse sexuality of infancy to full genitality, but also the Arnoldian theory that adulthood entails a surrender of fairy tales and comic books, science fiction and pornography and Westerns, in favor of the kind of literature that makes one feel old and established merely by virtue of appreciating it: the novels of Henry James, for instance, or the poetry of T. S. Eliot.

We are living, in short, in the Children's Hour come round once more, and who can more appropriately be resurrected to serve as its laureate than the author who presided over a similar era more than a century ago? The very name which comes to my mind when I try to describe the moment at which we stand is the title of what was once Longfellow's best-loved short poem [**"The Children's Hour"**], the lines of which have never ceased to ring in my head. . . . (pp. 170-71)

It is, however, a poem which has not survived (critics and editors seem convinced) the Modernist revolution in taste, which for a while banned Longfellow completely from the loftier levels of art and, even when its spokesmen relented enough to let him back in with the status of minor poet, insisted he be loved for quite other poems than the ones which had compelled tears and sighs of admiration at the time of his greatest popularity. . . . For them, at least, that poem was relegated to the nursery once and for all. Yet if we would really revive Longfellow in a time when living politics has become a Children's Crusade and fewer and fewer of the young are content to surrender the privileges of childhood at any point short of the grave, it is Longfellow the children's poet (rather than Long-

fellow the fully adult translator of Dante or the maker of sonnets about him) we must be willing to evoke.

Not where he is most like the *Symbolistes,* but where he is furthest from them, Longfellow is capable of redeeming us, teaching us why we have continued to love Blake's *Songs of Innocence* and the songs of Burns in a time not really congenial to such work, and permitting us, without reservation or shame, to love also Will Carleton and James Greenleaf Whittier, Eugene Field and Robert Service, along with the poems of A. E. Housman, Oscar Wilde's "The Ballad of Reading Gaol" and "Woodman, Spare That Tree!" by G. P. Morris, laureate-before-the-fact of all modern ecologists. For too long we have honored only the difficult and far-fetched metaphor, catachresis or the conceit, that yoking of dissimilars which stirs us to admire the virtuosity of the author and the subtlety of our own minds. Under the aegis of Longfellow, we will remember to pay homage, too, perhaps first of all, to the easy metaphor, the obvious connection, those marriages not of Beauty and the Beast, but of neighbors and friends, which create immediately (it takes no repetition to make a real cliché) figures we feel we have always known, might well have invented ourselves and therefore have no scruples about borrowing. (pp. 171-72)

> *Leslie A. Fiedler, "The Children's Hour; or, the Return of the Vanishing Longfellow: Some Reflections of the Future of Poetry," in* Liberations: New Essays on the Humanities in Revolution, *edited by Ihab Hassan (copyright © 1971 by Wesleyan University Press; reprinted by permission of Wesleyan University Press), Wesleyan University Press, 1971, pp. 149-75.*

ADDITIONAL BIBLIOGRAPHY

Allen, Gay Wilson. "Henry Wadsworth Longfellow." In his *American Prosody,* pp. 154-92. New York: American Book Co., 1935.
  A detailed examination of Longfellow's stanzaic devices and metrical forms.

Brooks, Van Wyck. "Longfellow in Cambridge." In his *The Flowering of New England, 1815-1865,* pp. 147-71. New York: The Modern Library, 1936.
  Portrays the professional and social atmosphere of Cambridge to which Longfellow was exposed when he began his teaching career at Harvard.

Fiske, John. "Longfellow's *Dante.*" In his *The Unseen World, and Others Essays,* pp. 237-65. Boston: Houghton, Mifflin and Co., 1876.
  A textual analysis of Longfellow's translation of Dante's *The Divine Comedy,* with background on Longfellow's philosophy of translation and technique.

Franklin, Phyllis. "The Importance of Time in Longfellow's Works." *Emerson Society Quarterly,* No. 58, Part 1 (First Quarter 1970): 14-22.
  Examines Longfellow's interpretation of the past and its effect on progress, concluding that "like many others in the nineteenth century, Longfellow did not conceive of the present as an absolute and isolated point in time. He could not look at the present without, at the same time, seeing the past and considering the future."

Frothingham, O. B. "Henry Wadsworth Longfellow." *Atlantic Monthly* XLIX, No. CCXCVI (June 1882): 819-29.
  A general overview of Longfellow's career, defending his reputation as an important American poet.

Griffin, Gerald R. "Longfellow's 'Tegnér's Drapa': A Reappraisal." *The American Transcendental Quarterly,* No. 40 (Fall 1978): 379-87.

A close textual analysis of the poem "Tegnér's Drapa," Longfellow's eulogy for the Swedish poet Esaias Tegnér, which has proven to be an ambiguous work to many Longfellow scholars.

Higginson, Thomas Wentworth. *Henry Wadsworth Longfellow*. Boston, New York: Houghton Mifflin Co., 1902, 336 p.
A detailed account of Longfellow's personal and professional life, featuring numerous excerpts from correspondence and valuable information concerning early critical evaluation of his works.

Howells, W. D. "The White Mr. Longfellow." In his *Literary Friends and Acquaintance: A Personal Retrospect of American Authorship*, pp. 178-211. New York, London: Harper & Brothers Publishers, 1900.
Howell's personal reminiscence of his friendship with Longfellow which provides considerable insight into Longfellow's personality.

Littlefield, Daniel F., Jr. "Longfellow's 'A Psalm of Life': A Relation of Method to Popularity." *The Markham Review* 7 (Spring 1978): 49-51.
Explores the reasons for the considerable popularity of "A Psalm of Life" despite critics' general dismissal of the poem as a literary failure.

Millward, Celia, and Tichi, Cecelia. "Whatever Happened to *Hiawatha*?" *Genre* VI, No. 3 (September 1973): 313-32.
Examines the metric and poetic devices used in *The Song of Hiawatha* and also discusses its relationship to other epic-heroic poetry.

More, Paul Elmer. "The Centenary of Longfellow." In his *Shelburne Essays on American Literature*, edited by Daniel Aaron, pp. 136-54. New York: Harcourt Brace Jovanovich, Inc., 1963.
Discusses the contrast between Longfellow's popular appeal and his critical reception, noting both the accessibility and the lack of originality of his work.

Moyne, Ernest J. *"Hiawatha" and "Kalevala."* Helsinki: Suomalainen Tiedeakatemia, Academia Scientiarum Fennica, 1962, 146 p.
A study of the relationship between *The Song of Hiawatha* and *Kalevala*, the Finnish epic which influenced both the form and content of Longfellow's poem.

Nemerov, Howard. "On Longfellow." In his *Poetry and Fiction: Essays*, pp. 143-58. New Brunswick, N.J.: Rutgers University Press, 1963.
Discusses Longfellow's desire to create a national literature and debates the worthiness of the international reputation achieved during his lifetime. Nemerov also discusses the effects of Longfellow's career as professor and translator upon his art, emphasizing his heavy reliance upon secondary sources.

Pattee, Fred Lewis. "Longfellow and German Romance." *Poet Lore* XVII, No. 1 (Spring 1906): 59-77.
Examines the artistic influence of Longfellow's European travels and the influence of German Romantics on his work.

Pauly, Thomas H. "*Outre-Mer* and Longfellow's Quest for a Career." *The New England Quarterly* L, No. 1 (March 1977): 30-52.
Chronicles the events in Longfellow's life which inspired *Outre-Mer* and emphasizes the importance of its publication in establishing his literary career. Pauly states that "in writing *Outre-Mer* Longfellow was laying a valuable conceptual and aesthetic basis for his future career."

Poe, Edgar Allan. "Mr. Longfellow, Mr. Willis, and the Drama." In his *The Complete Works of Edgar Allan Poe*, pp. 328-73. Boston, New York: Colonial Press Co., 1856.*
Debates the originality and merit of *The Spanish Student*, concluding that "its plot is no plot; its characters have no character; in short, it is little better than a play upon words, to style it 'A Play' at all."

Saintsbury, George. "Longfellow's Poems." In his *Prefaces and Essays*, pp. 324-44. London: Macmillan and Co., Limited, 1933.
A general consideration of Longfellow's work which, in acknowledging the poet's flaws, finds the greater part of the oeuvre simple but not simplistic.

Wagenknecht, Edward. *Longfellow: A Full-Length Portrait*, London: Longmans, Green & Co., 1955, 370 p.
A well-researched biography concentrating on Longfellow's inner life, social relationships, and the details of his career as a scholar, professor, and man of letters.

James Russell Lowell

1819-1891

American poet, critic, essayist, and editor.

Lowell is considered among the most erudite and versatile American authors. In his earnest, formal verse, he sought to advance liberal causes and establish an American aesthetic. While such poems as "Ode Recited at the Commemoration of the Living and Dead Soldiers of Harvard University, July 21, 1865," (commonly referred to as the Commemoration Ode), and "The Vision of Sir Launfal" were widely admired in his day, Lowell's poetry is now considered diffuse and dated, and is rarely read. Modern critics generally agree that his outstanding literary contributions were in the areas of satire and criticism.

His Brahmin ancestry and Harvard education provided Lowell with access to the New England literati, and as a young man he became acquainted with Ralph Waldo Emerson, Henry David Thoreau, and Henry Wadsworth Longfellow. A natural conservative, Lowell turned increasingly toward liberal humanitarianism after his marriage to Maria White, a poet and abolitionist who encouraged her husband to contribute poetry to the *National Anti-Slavery Standard* and the *Pennsylvania Freeman*.

In 1848, Lowell achieved national acclaim with the publication of three of his best-known works: *Poems: Second Series, A Fable for Critics: A Glance at a Few of Our Literary Progenies*, and *The Biglow Papers*. Two of these are often cited by critics as his finest writing. *A Fable for Critics*, a witty diatribe written in lively though sometimes careless verse, is remarkable for its numerous critical appraisals which have endured through time and changing styles. The first volume of *The Biglow Papers* records the sardonic observations of Hosea Biglow, a New England farmer, and his neighbors, as the United States enters the Mexican War. Modern critics generally cite *The Biglow Papers* as Lowell's masterpiece, an ingenious combination of humor, poetry, and trenchant satire written in brisk Yankee dialect.

After his wife's death in 1853, Lowell concerned himself more with editing, scholarship, and criticism than with poetry. In 1855, he succeeded Longfellow as Smith Professor of Modern Languages at Harvard, a post which allowed him to travel abroad and study European languages and literatures. Two years later, Lowell assumed additional responsibilities as first editor of the *Atlantic Monthly* and later joined Charles Eliot Norton as coeditor of the *North American Review*. In 1877, President Rutherford B. Hayes appointed Lowell, by then a thorough conservative, as minister to Spain. James Garfield, in 1880, transferred Lowell to England where he charmed London literary society and became godfather to Sir Leslie Stephen's daughter, Virginia Woolf.

The astuteness and scope of Lowell's criticism, despite charges that it is merely impressionistic, have moved literary historians to place him beside Poe as a major nineteenth-century American critic. He is praised as well for his general prose pieces, which are personable essays with a wryness and buoyancy absent from the verse. Ironically, Lowell's serious-mindedness, well-intended though it was, may have kept his poetry

Courtesy of Princeton Photograph Division, Library of Congress

from greatness. It is in the satire and criticism where his wit is in evidence, that Lowell's power is revealed. (See also *Dictionary of Literary Biography, Vol. 1: The American Renaissance in New England*.)

PRINCIPAL WORKS

A Year's Life (poetry) 1841
Poems (poetry) 1844
Conversations on Some of the Old Poets (criticism) 1845
The Biglow Papers (poetry) 1848
A Fable for Critics: A Glance at a Few of Our Literary Progenies (verse criticism) 1848
Poems: Second Series (poetry) 1848
The Vision of Sir Launfal (poetry) 1848
Fireside Travels (essays) 1864
Ode Recited at the Commemoration of the Living and Dead Soldiers of Harvard University, July 21, 1865 (poetry) 1865
The Biglow Papers: Second Series (poetry) 1867
Under the Willows and Other Poems (poetry) 1868
Among My Books (criticism) 1870
The Cathedral (poetry) 1870

[GEORGE S. HILLARD] (essay date 1841)

[*A Year's Life*] abounds with proofs of unquestionable poetical talent, sufficiently so to make us hope well of the author's literary progress, in spite of the defects with which nearly every page is more or less alloyed.

Mr. Lowell, poetically speaking, is the child of his age, belonging to that class of poets in whom the imaginative and reflective element predominates over the passionate, and who are now occupying the highest place in the general favor. . . . [This] class of poets has been obviously growing in general esteem during the last ten or fifteen years; and among them Mr. Lowell is to be ranked, though he is by no means a servile imitator, and has a spontaneous and native vein of poetry.

It is unfortunate for the success of his book, that its most substantial and prominent fault is of that kind which will prejudice most readers against it, even more than it deserves. We allude to its very strong infusion of personality. A considerable portion of its contents is occupied by versified confessions. Upon the subject of that passion which has ever twined its myrtles with the poet's laurels, his disclosures are more ample and confidential than good taste warrants. Love-letters have little attraction, except to the eye of the person to whom they are addressed, nor is the matter much mended by throwing them into a poetical garb. . . . [We regret that Mr. Lowell] should have printed so many of these poems. The nature of the subject exacts from love-poems a higher degree of literary merit than from any others, and one which our young friend is seldom successful in attaining. Had he taken counsel of a judicious adviser, we think he would have excluded from his volume much which adds nothing to its merit, and which provokes the sneer of the cynic and the harsh judgment of the intolerant. (pp. 452-54)

[In *A Year's Life*] there is much of the ore of poetry, but little of it in its purified and polished state. We have found in it much, certainly, that is striking and beautiful. The author has seen things for himself, and not transcribed the impressions made on other minds. His love of nature is genuine, and the beauty of her majestic countenance has evidently sunk deep into his soul with refreshing and elevating influences. His imagination is vivid, and his fancy fruitful in fine images. We are frequently struck with a nice and delicate power of observation, and sometimes detect a searching glance, which shows the power of looking deeper into man's nature than he has usually done. We are pleased, too, with his purity and elevation of feeling. Morally speaking, there is not a line which, dying, he could wish to blot. Especially do we like the reverence which he shows for woman, and that love of ideal beauty which takes from the passion and adds to the sentiment of love. (pp. 454-55)

["**Irené**," for instance,] shows a power of discerning and describing the retiring graces and reserved charms of woman-

hood, not often found in a masculine intellect, and an appreciation of, and reverence for, the higher excellencies of the female character, which does honor to his moral sense and purity of taste. . . . With many of Mr. Lowell's characteristic excellences, [**"Irené"**] also is by no means free from his characteristic defects,—his neglect of the laws of rhythm, his want of precision, and his love of superfine phraseology. (p. 458)

[**"The Syrens"**], as a whole, is a fine [poem], in spite of some characteristic prettinesses, such as "restful voices," "gurgle longingly," &c. The poet has caught the spirit of the sea, and his verse flows like the undulating movement of its waves. . . . "The leaden eye of the sidelong shark" is a fine line, and shows the eye of a true poet, and the image of the seaweed, waving and beckoning with its lank and brown arms, is vivid and picturesque. "The singing waves *slide* up the strand," is a happy expression, of which the eye and the ear recognise the fidelity. We would, however, enter our respectful protest against the transformation of "mariner" into "marinere." A poet has no right to deal with his words as a sailor with his ropes, splicing them where they are not long enough. (pp. 462-63)

Among the contents of the volume are thirty-five sonnets, many of which are entitled to high praise for their essential excellence, their truth and dignity of sentiment, their purity and elevation of feeling, their love of the true and the beautiful, their hopeful spirit, and the high moral purpose which breathes through them. But there is not one, which has that mechanical finish and faultless execution, which is rigorously exacted from poems of this class. An occasional carelessness of expression, a halting line, an imperfect rhyme, may be tolerated in a longer poem, which is not endurable in a sonnet, just as we pardon a blemish in a statue, which is fatal in a cameo. (p. 463)

[Mr. Lowell] has much to learn as well as to unlearn, before he can take high rank among his tuneful brethren. In all that belongs to the form and garb of verse, there is room for great improvement. In rhyme and the structure of his verse, he is a "chartered libertine." We are constantly meeting with lines, that have too many and too few feet, that want the rhythm and cadence of verse, and have nothing but the capital letter to distinguish them from prose. There is a good deal, too, of that cloudy and misty phraseology, which is so fashionable now in prose and verse, which tantalizes us with glimmerings of meaning, but does not satisfy us with a full revelation of it. A familiar thought gains nothing by ambitious language, as an awkward man is not made graceful by fine clothes. The following lines may be cited as a specimen of the fantastic jargon to which we have recently grown familiar, and which, in attempting to combine poetry and philosophy, succeeds only in producing what is not far removed from old-fashioned nonsense.

> Of Knowledge Love is master-key,
> Knowledge of Beauty; passing dear
> Is each to each, and mutually
> Each one doth make the other clear;
> Beauty is Love, and what we love
> Straightway is beautiful,
> So is the circle round and full,
> And so dear Love doth live and move
>   And have his being,
> Finding his proper food,
>   By sure inseeing,
> In all things pure and good. . . .
>
> (pp. 464-65)

Another conspicuous fault of Mr. Lowell's poetry is the perpetual presence of daintinesses and prettinesses of expression. His thoughts are overdressed. He abounds with those affected turns, with which the poetry of Tennyson (which we suspect our friend has studied more than is good for him) is so besprinkled. He is too liberal in the use of the poetical vocabulary. . . . He uses too liberal a license in compounding words, as "spring-gladsome," "vine-bowered," "leaf-checkered," "rapture-quivered," "organ-shaken," &c. He is also too fond of the solemn termination *eth*, as "dwelleth" for "dwells," which gives an air of stiffness to some of his pieces. To all these and many more which might be cited, we may justly apply Sir Hugh Evans's pithy observation upon Pistol's grandiloquence, "The tevil and his tam! what phrase is this, *He hears with ear?* Why, it is affectations." (p. 465)

> [*George S. Hillard*,] *"Lowell's Poems," in* The North American Review, *Vol. LII, No. 111, April, 1841, pp. 452-66.*

THE NORTH AMERICAN REVIEW   (essay date 1844)

In Mr. Lowell's first volume, we thought we saw a tendency to . . . second-hand poetizing; a disposition to mimic the jingle of [Alfred Tennyson], who, with much genius and an exquisite ear for musical rhythm, has also a Titanian fondness for quaint and dainty expressions, affected turns, and mawkishly effeminate sentiment; and who would be the worst model, therefore, not only for a young poet to imitate, but even to read; so contagious are the vices of his manner.

[But in his new volume, *Poems*,] the symptoms have, to a great degree, passed off, or Mr. Lowell has nearly outgrown the disease with which his literary childhood was threatened, if not actually assailed. We recognize in his later productions a firmer intellect, a wider range of thought, a bolder tone of expression, and a versification greatly improved. We feel that he is now becoming master of his fine powers, and an artist in the execution of his conceptions. The character of his more elaborate productions is, in general, noble and elevated, though tinged somewhat with the vague speculations which pass current in some circles for philosophy. There is a similar vagueness in the expression of religious feeling; positive religious views, though not rejected, are kept far in the background. Many of the poems are devoted to the utterance of sentiments of humanity; and here, though the feelings expressed are always amiable and tender, the youth and inexperience of the poet are clearly manifested. He is a dreamer, apparently, brooding over the wrongs which are endured in the present state of society, and rashly inferring that the existing institutions are bad, and should be overthrown. Such radical opinions are not perhaps directly uttered, but the general tone tends that way. (p. 286)

Mr. Lowell's poems want compression. In the words of Taylor, the *whey* needs pressing out. Redundancy, both of thought and expression, is the principal fault which we think the critical reader will be disposed to find with them. The subjects of many of his poems are drawn out to a wearisome length, by interweaving, not only the leading thoughts which belong to their proper treatment, but all the subordinate ideas and commonplace moralities, which should be taken for granted, as understood of themselves. To borrow an expression from the writers on metre, they abound in *logacedic endings;*—they are poetry terminating in prose. Sometimes, at the end of a fine poetical piece, a long moral application is appended, like the "improvements" in the old Puritanical sermons. Now, either the moral conclusion would naturally be drawn by the attentive reader, or else the telling of the story, or the wording of the parable, is deficient in point and clearness. But there is no such deficiency in any of Mr. Lowell's poetical effusions of this class. The **"Prometheus"** is an instance of injuring the effect of an otherwise noble poem by too great prolixity. The conception of this piece is not only beautiful, but sublime; it is a Christian reproduction of the old myth, and, in general, is treated not only with high poetical beauty, but with a dignified elevation of moral feeling; but Prometheus is not characteristically represented. His soliloquy runs too far into minute details and ornamented expression, as if he were a gentleman a great deal more at his ease than he really was under the circumstances. . . . Lowell's **"Prometheus"** is masterly, and sustained at a high point of elegance and calm beauty; but it is precisely this elegance and calm beauty which are out of keeping with the subject, considered with reference to the character and condition of the gigantic sufferer.

A good instance of the second fault,—that of the unnecessary enforcement of a moral application,—is in the delightfully written poem of **"Rhœcus."** All after the conclusion of the story . . . were much better omitted; that is, something more than two pages of very well expressed, but quite uncalled for, moralizing. Striking out all that, and some lines at the beginning, the poem is nearly faultless, as our readers will have an opportunity, by and by, of seeing.

Of Mr. Lowell's poetical style in general, the present volume has given us a high opinion. Not that it is by any means free from defects; but it has the elements of a clear, vigorous, and pure form of expression. It shows the marks of a profound study of the English language, in the best authors; and though the influence of particular writers is at times perceptible, his style is generally formed from the substantial materials taken from the heart of the language. For the most part, the constructions are clear, and the order of the words is free from those inversions which disfigure so much of the overstrained poetical composition of this age. Sometimes, though rarely, we find a studied quaintness of turn, a finical expression, or an extravagant simile or metaphor. Again, we are offended by words absurdly compounded, or used in a distorted sense. The termination of the imperfect tense, or passive participle, in *ed* is too frequently made an independent syllable. But all of these faults might easily be avoided. (pp. 288-89)

We have no great fondness for sentimentality in type. Much of this in the present volume would have been better omitted. *Subjective* feelings, to use the jargon of philosophical criticism, should be but rarely and reservedly expressed in books. The sonnets are the least successful pieces; especially those addressed to Wordsworth, which, so far as they have any meaning at all, have an assuming one. (p. 297)

[That Lowell will] create a noble sphere for the exercise of his fine powers, and give additional lustre to a name already crowned with the honors of professional, literary, and mercantile eminence is what we not only hope, but, in the faith of achievements already performed, confidently predict and believe. (p. 299)

> *"Lowell's Poems," in* The North American Review, *Vol. LVIII, No. 123, April, 1844, pp. 283-99.*

ELIZABETH BARRETT BARRETT   (essay date 1845)

[Mr. Lowell] has a refined fancy & is graceful for an American critic, but the truth is, otherwise, that he knows nothing of

English poetry or the next thing to nothing, & has merely had a dream of the early dramatists. The amount of his reading in that direction is an article in the Retrospective Review which contains extracts,—& he re-extracts the extracts, re-quotes the quotations, &, 'a pede Herculem,' from the foot infers the man, or rather from the sandal-string of the foot, infers & judges the soul of the man—it is comparative anatomy under the most speculative conditions. How a /man›writer/ of his talents & pretentions could make up his mind to make up a book [*Conversations on Some of the Old Poets*] on such slight substratum, is a curious proof of the state of literature in America. Do you not think so?—Why a lecturer on the English Dramatists for a ''Young Ladies' academy'' here in England, might take it to be necessary to have better information than he could gather from an odd volume of an old review! And then, Mr. Lowell's naïveté in showing his authority . . . as if the Elizabethan poets lay mouldering in inaccessible manuscript somewhere below the lowest deep of Shakespeare's grave . . . is curious beyond the rest!—Altogether, the fact is an epigram on the surface-literature of America. As you say, their books do not suit us. . . . If they *knew* more they could not give parsley crowns to their own native poets when there is / more›greater/merit among the rabbits. . . . Mr. Lowell himself is, in his verse-books, poetical, if not a poet—& certainly this little book we are talking of [*Conversations on Some of the Old Poets*] is grateful enough in some ways—you would call it a *pretty book*—would you not? (pp. 332-33)

> *Elizabeth Barrett Barrett, in her letter to Robert Browning on December 19, 1845, in* The Letters of Robert Browning and Elizabeth Barrett Barrett 1845-1846, *edited by Elvan Kintner (copyright © 1969 by the President and Fellows of Harvard College; excerpted by permission), Cambridge, Mass.: Harvard University Press, 1969, pp. 332-33.*

[JAMES RUSSELL LOWELL] (essay date 1848)

[*The following excerpt is taken from James Russell Lowell's poem,* A Fable for Critics.]

> There is Lowell, who's striving Parnassus to
> climb
> With a whole bale of *isms* tied together with
> rhyme,
> He might get on alone, spite of brambles and
> boulders,
> But he can't with that bundle he has on his
> shoulders,
> The top of the hill he will ne'er come nigh
> reaching
> Till he learns the distinction 'twixt singing and
> preaching;
> His lyre has some chords that would ring
> pretty well,
> But he'd rather by half make a drum of the
> shell,
> And rattle away till he's old as Methusalem,
> At the head of a march to the last new
> Jerusalem.
> (pp. 70-1)

> [*James Russell Lowell,*] *in his* A Fable for Critics; or, A Glance at a Few of Our Literary Progenies, *second edition, G. P. Putnam, 1848, 80 p.**

[FRANCIS BOWEN] (essay date 1849)

We are not quite sure that ''The Biglow Papers'' will be added to the list of successful humorous publications. All the persons concerned in them have a political object in view, and are so earnest in the pursuit of it, that they sometimes quite forget that their only vocation is to laugh at the follies of others. (p. 186)

[But ''The Biglow Papers'' are] very fair fun. The rhymes are as startling and felicitous as any in Hudibras, and the quaint drollery of the illustrations is in admirable keeping with the whole character of [Hosea Biglow,] the forlorn recruit from Massachusetts. Of the almost numberless imitations of the Yankee dialect, this is decidedly the best that we have seen. (p. 188)

To show our friend Biglow's almost marvellous facility in versification, we . . . [cite] what he calls a debate in the Senate, set to a nursery rhyme. The laughable manner in which the names of honorable Senators are hitched into jingle will remind the reader of some of Sheridan's lampoons in the same key, against the chiefs of the party who were opposed to him. . . . (p. 189)

We cannot say much for the copious prose commentary, the prefatory and illustrative matter, in which the Biglow rhymes, in this edition, are imbedded. Most of Parson Wilbur's *lengthy* annotations are as heavy as his own sermons, from which, indeed, a large part of them profess to have been borrowed. Hosea Biglow, with his father 'Zekiel, and Birdofredom Sawin, are true and lifelike creations, admirably sustained throughout, and made up of materials with which the writer is evidently familiar. But the Parson is a quaint jumble of half a dozen characters whom we know only in books, and is a tedious old fellow to boot. There is not a bit of the Yankee in him, and his elaborate pedantry is far-fetched and wearisome to the last degree. He is a compound of Jedediah Cleishbotham, Thomas Carlyle, and an American antislavery haranguer,—the attempt to fuse together these discordant elements being quite a failure. (p. 190)

We pass to the next book on our list, ''**A Fable for Critics.**'' Common rumor attributes it to the same pen which wrote ''**The Biglow Papers**''; and if there was no other reason for this conjecture but the author's extraordinary command of Hudibrastic rhymes, and the easy flow of his versification, we should think it must be well founded. The ''**Fable,**'' which, by the way, is no fable at all, is really a very pleasant and sparkling poem, abounding in flashes of brilliant satire, edged with wit enough to delight even its victims. It is far more spirited and entertaining than one would expect from the labored conceits of its title-page and preface, which, with their forced and concealed jingle, are but melancholy introductions for the lively and half-grotesque rhymes that follow. The framework of the poem is too slight to merit notice; the writer evidently began with some idea of a plot or an apologue, but soon tired of it, and throwing the reins upon the neck of his Pegasus, allowed the verse to ''wander at its own sweet will.'' Goldsmith's ''Retaliation'' was certainly his model, and though he comes far short of that exquisite mixture of playful satire and discriminating portraiture of character, under which the good-nature of the kind-hearted poet appears so constantly that not one of his glittering shafts leaves a painful wound, he quite equals it in the easy flow of his rhymes, and surpasses it in wit and sauciness. We are doubtful about his puns, though most of them are very good, and they sometimes fall as rapidly as drops in a shower; but at best, they are only wit's bastard offspring, and become tedious enough in print, though they enliven small-talk. Condensation is the quality in which the writer is most deficient; if his poem were pruned down to the length of the "Retaliation," we venture to predict that it would become almost as universal a favorite. (pp. 191-92)

We cannot say much for the consistency of the poet now before us, who has no sooner done with roasting the critics than he forthwith turns critic himself, thinking, apparently, that the world could not get along without the services of at least one of the fraternity. His **"Fable"** is simply a very witty review article, done into rhyme. . . . The sketches are drawn in a very free and bold manner, though they have the usual defect of caricatures, that the most prominent and peculiar feature is brought out in high relief, and maliciously magnified, so that the likeness is instantly recognized, though the remainder of the face is left out altogether, or so drawn as to bear no resemblance to the original. (p. 192)

Another and frequent fault of our bard as a critic is, that he often gives us the features of the man in place of a character of the author, and, as a natural consequence, mixes up so much of personal liking or aversion with his drawings, that they lose all claim to fidelity. This fault is seen even in his choice of subjects. One or two of the most flattering portraitures in the book are of persons whom nobody ever heard of beyond the corner of the next street from that in which they live; and to make the matter worse, these are mixed up with sarcastic and depreciating sketches of bards whom, with all their faults, the whole civilized world has long since learned to admire. (p. 194)

But enough of fault-finding, which has been forced upon us only by our author's claim to be considered as a faithful critic; his pretensions as a poet and a wit we admit without question. As a general rule, we believe that poets make very poor critics; they are too apt to look at their brother bards through the medium of their own verses. To give our author his revenge, we will very gladly allow that reviewers would write shocking bad poetry; only we never heard of one who was insane enough to make the trial. (p. 197)

[*Francis Bowen,*] *"Humorous and Satirical Poetry," in* The North American Review, *Vol. LXVIII, No. 142, January, 1849, pp. 183-203.**

EDGAR ALLAN POE (essay date 1849)

The **"Fable for the Critics,"** just issued, has not the name of its author on the title-page; and, but for some slight foreknowledge of the literary opinions, likes, dislikes, whims, prejudices, and crotchets of Mr. James Russell Lowell, we should have had much difficulty in attributing so very *loose* a brochure to *him*. The **"Fable"** is essentially "loose"—ill-conceived and feebly executed, as well in detail as in general. Some good hints and some sparkling witticisms do not serve to compensate us for its rambling plot (if plot it can be called) and for the want of artistic finish so particularly noticeable throughout the work—especially in its versification. In Mr. Lowell's prose efforts we have before observed a certain *disjointedness*, but never, until now, in his verse—and we confess some surprise at his putting forth so unpolished a performance. The author of **"The Legend of Brittany"** (which is decidedly the noblest poem, of the same length, written by an American) could not do a better thing than to take the advice of those who mean him well, in spite of his fanaticism, and leave prose, with satiric verse, to those who are better able to manage them; while he contents himself with that class of poetry for which, and for which alone, he seems to have an especial vocation—

the poetry of *sentiment*. This, to be sure, is *not* the very loftiest order of verse; for it is far inferior to either that of the imagination or that of the passions—but it is the loftiest region in which Mr. Lowell can get his breath without difficulty.

Our primary objection to this **"Fable for the Critics"** has reference to a point which we have already touched in a general way. "The malevolence appears." We laugh not so much at the author's victims as at himself, for letting them put him in such a passion. The very title of the book shows the want of a due sense in respect to the satirical essence, *sarcasm*. This "fable"—this severe lesson—is meant *'for the Critics.''* "Ah!" we say to ourselves at once—"we see how it is. Mr. L. is a poor devil poet, and some critic has been reviewing him, and making him feel very uncomfortable; whereupon, bearing in mind that Lord Byron, when similarly assailed, avenged his wrongs in a satire which he called 'English Bards and Scotch Reviewers,' he (Mr. Lowell) imitative as usual, has been endeavoring to get redress in a parallel manner—by a satire with a parallel title—**'A Fable for the Critics.'**"

All this the reader says to himself; and all this tells *against* Mr. L. in two ways—first, by suggesting unlucky comparisons between Byron and Lowell, and, secondly, by reminding us of the various criticisms, in which we have been amused (rather ill-naturedly) at seeing Mr. Lowell "used-up."

The title starts us on this train of thought, and the satire sustains us in it. Every reader versed in our literary gossip, is at once put *dessous des cartes* as to the particular provocation which engendered the **"Fable."** Miss Margaret Fuller, some time ago, in a silly and conceited piece of transcendentalism, which she called an "Essay on American Literature," or something of that kind, had the consummate pleasantry, after *selecting* from the list of American poets, *Cornelius Mathews and William Ellery Channing,* for especial commendation, to speak of *Longfellow* as a booby, and of *Lowell* as so wretched a poetaster "as to be disgusting even to his best friends." (pp. 236-38)

Mr. Lowell has obviously aimed his **"Fable"** at Miss Fuller's head, in the first instance, with an eye to its ricochétting so as to knock down Mr. Mathews in the second. Miss F. is first introduced as Miss F.—, rhyming to "cooler," and afterward as "Miranda"; while poor Mr. M. is brought in upon all occasions, head and shoulders; and now and then a sharp thing, although never very original, is said *of* them or *at* them; but all the true satiric *effect* wrought, is that produced by the satirist against himself. The reader is all the time smiling to think that so unsurpassable a—(*what* shall we call her?—we wish to be civil)—a transcendentalist as Miss Fuller, should, by *such* a criticism, have had the power to put a respectable poet in *such* a passion.

As for the plot or conduct of this **"Fable,"** the less we say of it the better. It is so weak—so flimsy—so ill put together—as to be not worth the trouble of understanding:—something, as usual, about Apollo and Daphne. Is there *no* originality on the face of the earth? Mr. Lowell's total want of it is shown at all points—very especially in his preface of rhyming verse written without distinction by lines or initial capitals, (a hackneyed matter, originating, we believe, with *Frazer's Magazine*)—very especially also, in his long continuations of some particular rhyme—a fashion introduced, if we remember aright, by Leigh Hunt, more than twenty-five years ago, in his "Feast of the Poets"—which, by the way, has been Mr. L.'s model in many respects.

Although ill-temper has evidently engendered this **"Fable,"** it is by no means a satire throughout. Much of it is devoted to panegyric—but our readers would be quite puzzled to know the grounds of the author's laudations, in many cases, unless made acquainted with a fact which we think it as well they should be informed of at once. Mr. Lowell is one of the most rabid of the Abolition fanatics; and no Southerner who does not wish to be insulted, and at the same time revolted by a bigotry the most obstinately blind and deaf, should ever touch a volume by this author. (pp. 239-40)

His prejudices on the topic of slavery break out everywhere in his present book. Mr. L. has not the common honesty to speak well, even in a literary sense, of any man who is not a ranting Abolitionist. With the exception of Mr. Poe, (who has written some commendatory criticisms on his poems,) no Southerner is mentioned *at all* in this "**Fable.**" It is a fashion among Mr. Lowell's set to affect a belief that there is *no such thing* as Southern literature. Northerners—people who have really nothing to speak of as men of letters,—are cited by the dozen, and lauded by this candid critic without stint, while Legaré, Simms, Longstreet, and others of equal note are passed by in contemptuous silence. Mr. L. cannot carry his frail honesty of opinion even so far South as New York. All whom he praises are Bostonians. Other writers are barbarians, and satirized accordingly—if mentioned at all.

To show the general *manner* of the fable, we quote a portion of what he says about Mr. Poe:

> Here comes Poe with his Raven, like Barnaby Rudge—
> Three fifths of him genius, and two fifths sheer fudge;
> Who talks like a book of iambs and pentameters,
> In a way to make all men of common sense d—n metres
> Who has written some things far the best of their kind;
> But somehow the heart seems squeezed out by the mind.

We may observe here that *profound* ignorance on any particular topic is always sure to manifest itself by some illusion to "common sense" as an all-sufficient instructor. So far from Mr. P.'s talking "like a book" on the topic at issue, his chief purpose has been to demonstrate that there exists *no* book on the subject worth talking *about;* and "common sense," after all, has been the basis on which *he* relied, in contradistinction from the *un*common nonsense of Mr. L. and the small pedants.

And now let us see how far the unusual "common sense" of our satirist has availed him in the structure of his verse. First, by way of showing what his *intention* was, we quote three accidentally accurate lines:

> But a boy / he could ne / ver be right / ly defined.
> As I said / he was ne / ver precise / ly unkind.
> But as Ci / cero says / he won't say / this or that.

Here it is clearly seen that Mr. L. intends a line of four anapæsts. (An anapæst is a foot composed of two short syllables followed by a long.) With this observation we will now simply copy a few of the lines which constitute the body of the poem; asking any of our readers to *read them if they can*—that is to say, we place the question, without argument, on the broad basis of the very commonest "common sense":

> They're all from one source, monthly, weekly,
>   diurnal . . .
> Disperse all one's good and condense all one's
>   poor traits . . .
> The one's two thirds Norseman, the other half
>   Greek . . .

He has imitators in scores who omit . . .
Should suck milk, strong will-giving brave,
    such as runs . . .

(pp. 240-42)

But enough:—we have given a fair specimen of the *general* versification. It might have been better—but we are quite sure that it *could not have been worse.* So much for "common sense," in Mr. Lowell's understanding of the term. Mr. L. should not have meddled with the anapæstic rhythm: it is exceedingly awkward in the hands of one who knows nothing about it and who *will* persist in fancying that he can write it by ear. Very especially he should have avoided this rhythm in satire, which, more than any other branch of letters, is depending upon seeming trifles for its effect. Two thirds of the force of [Pope's] "Dunciad" may be referred to its exquisite finish; and had the "**Fable for the Critics**" been (what it is *not*) the quintessence of the satiric spirit itself, it would, nevertheless, in so slovenly a form, have failed. As it is, no failure was ever more complete or more pitiable. By the publication of a book at once so ambitious and so feeble—so malevolent in design and so harmless in execution—a work so roughly and clumsily yet so weakly constructed—so very different, in body and spirit, from any thing that he has written before— Mr. Lowell has committed an irrevocable *faux pas* and lowered himself at least fifty per cent in the literary public opinion. (pp. 242-43)

> *Edgar Allan Poe, "James Russell Lowell" (originally published in* Southern Literary Messenger, *March, 1849), in his* The Complete Works of Edgar Allan Poe, *Colonial Press Company, 1856, pp. 233-43.*

JOHN GREENLEAF WHITTIER (essay date 1850)

We regret that our Congress-crowded columns will not allow us to notice in a fitting manner this handsome collection [*Poems* by J. R. Lowell] of one of the strongest and manliest of our writers—a republican poet who dares to speak brave words for unpopular truth, and refuses to submit to the inquisitorial expurgation of book-selling caterers to prejudice and oppression. Since his first appearance in public, he has happily overcome a slight tendency to mysticism and metaphysics, and in his later poems he stands out clear and strong in the light of truth and simple nature. He is no longer afraid of the sharp outlines of reality; and so that his thought is fully and forcibly expressed, and his illustration apposite, he seems at times quite careless of the niceties of diction and metaphor. The stamp of the man is on all he does—he is always himself, and none other. He is yet a young man, and, in view of what he has already attained, we have a right to expect a good deal of his future. May he have strength and long life to do for freedom and humanity, and for the true and permanent glory of American literature, all that others less gifted, and subject to less favorable circumstances, have striven in vain to accomplish.

"**The Present Crisis**" is in our view the noblest poem in the collection. We have read it often, and never without being deeply moved by the magnificent flow of its thought-charged verses. (p. 163)

> *John Greenleaf Whittier, "Lowell's Poems" (originally published in* National Era, *January 17, 1850), in his* Whittier on Writers and Writing: The Uncollected Critical Writings of John Greenleaf Whittier, *edited by Edwin Harrison Cady and Harry Hayden Clark, Syracuse University Press, 1950, pp. 163-64.*

IRISH QUARTERLY REVIEW (essay date 1855)

The leading peculiarity of James Russell Lowell, is energy of the most active kind: he grasps his thoughts as Jupiter his thunderbolts, and hurls them to their destined aim, with as much accurate velocity as the Autocrat of Olympus. His knowledge of human nature is vast and subtle, his ethics sound and uncompromising, diction copious and flexible, and he knows no political creed distinct from the welfare of his country. He is not always so happy in his ontological and psychological speculations, and we shall expect to see it evidenced in his future productions, that his ears have been rigidly closed against the alluring whispers of the syren voice, which has, in some instances, beguiled his footsteps. Analytic power, indeed the love of analysis, is another of Lowell's distinguishing traits. He delights to dissect his subjects with the nicety of a metaphysician, and to peer with microscopic exactness, into the dim recesses of its contemplative materials. One other of his characteristics . . . is the wizard potency of his descriptive talent. This, however, has never induced the subject of our remarks to indulge in rhapsodical prolixity; for as he himself tells us, man should constitute the theme of the Poets of the new world. This comprehensive doctrine . . . acknowledges Lowell as its most earnest advocate: to him it principally owes its promulgation, and already acquired celebrity; and in his hands it may yet achieve its sublimest triumphs. His superhuman vigor, perceptive intellect, and undisguised reverence for this principle, mark him out as the apostle who will most eminently develope the tenet it commands. **"The Vision of Sir Launfal"** is a specimen of the perfect ballad, written in a spirited and interesting manner; the language is appropriate, and might well have been chaunted by the minstrels of Provence. (pp. 578-79)

"The Sirens," is a poem containing abundant instances of sparkling, and playful fancy: it is not unlike the "Merman and Mermaid" of Tennyson in spirit. If we delight (as who does not) in a beautiful idealized picture, **"Irene"** affords us one such as we shall seldom happen to feast our eyes upon: it demonstrates in the most lucid manner, the author's individualizing power, exhibits great loftiness of thought, much veneration for virtue, and is clothed in a becoming solemnity of language. . . . (p. 579)

Like all true poets, Lowell "Touched each key of the lyre, and was master of all." His flexible and comprehensive genius can create, not only the massive master-piece of intellectual origin, but in like manner can revel in the dazzling and sportive regions of fancy: **"The Fountain"** serves as an excellent specimen of his lyric power. (p. 580)

An excellent satire on the great short-comings in some branches of our modern poetry, is contained in **"An Ode"**; . . . it takes a most comprehensive, and apparently prophetic view of the poetry which after ages will bring forth: the passionate aspirations for the extension of philanthropy which it manifests, the rugged energy of the language, with its masterly analysis of things, speaks volumes for the future achievements of its author. . . .

It would be almost impossible for any poet to evince more gigantic power of description than Lowell has compressed into his **"Summer Storm,"** a masterly production of its kind, and replete with wonderful energy and truthfulness. As it is particularly characterized by much minute sketchings of natural objects, hitherto untouched by either the pen of the poet or the brush of the painter, it would be high treason against good taste to pass over unnoticed **"The Indian Summer Reverie."** (p. 581)

"Studies for two Heads" is graphic, and the portraits are taken in that spirit of analysis, and with that great knowledge of human nature, which Lowell constantly evinces. Metaphysical beauty, religious confidence, and philanthropy, lend their important influence in adorning the **"Elegy on the Death of Dr. Channing,"** and the **"Fable for Critics"** establishes the author's right to membership in that awful association. (p. 583)

"The Poets of America," in Irish Quarterly Review, *Vol. 5, No. 19, September, 1855, pp. 561-90.**

CHRISTIAN EXAMINER (essay date 1864)

If [*Fireside Travels*] were the work of a young man, and with his foot on the first round of the tedious ladder of literary renown, we should call it promising, and expect better things from the maturity of its author. Graceful it is certainly, and something more; it shows tender feeling and delicate humor, a quiet perception and hearty enjoyment of out-of-the-way people and of the peculiar traits of everyday people, to an extent which few books of travel can equal. Its sentiment is healthy, its retrospection cheerful, its memory discriminating. Still it is like the book of a young man. The paper on **"Cambridge Thirty Years Ago"** is the only portion of it which would indicate to any reader unacquainted with the author's name that he might possibly have passed middle age; and even here there is this peculiarity, that the style seems at wide variance with the subject. The style is brisk, not flowing; with the flash of wit oftener than the glow of humor, and the wit itself seeming not always to kindle without some poking. There are, however, some charming pictures in this little essay. . . . (p. 376)

With the exception of [**"Cambridge Thirty Years Ago"**] the book is made up of reminiscences of travel, partly on the waters and shores of Moosehead Lake, but for the most part of Italian travel. . . . [Mr. Lowell's] is a model diary, and as we jog contentedly along with him in the company of his not very mysterious friend Storg, and their guide Leopoldo, over the mountains and through the ravines about Tivoli and Subiaco, the whole freshness and flavor of that delightful travel come back to us, and we lose all taste for criticism amid the crowding memories of the days. . . . In such temper we drop our pen and exclaim, Stupid indeed must he be who cannot be entertaining when he writes of Italy! Mr. Lowell is certainly not stupid, and is pretty sure to be entertaining, whatever he writes. But he would be quite as much so with less effort at smartness. (pp. 376-77)

Mr. Lowell seems likely to end where most writers begin. At one-and-twenty, his literary promise was brighter than that of any rival, and was not merely the promise of a brilliant and cultivated intellect, but also and equally of a vigorous and earnest reformer. . . . The principles which he advocated with such warmth of enthusiasm at the beginning of his career he still advocates, but the enthusiasm has disappeared, and the generous and hot indignation is sometimes replaced by a sarcastic bitterness, which, even when attacking the old enemies, leaves room for an occasional sneer at the old friends. So true it is, as Bacon says, that "the counsels of youth stream more divinely." (p. 377)

"Review of Current Literature: 'Fireside Travels'," in Christian Examiner, *Vol. LXXVII, No. III, November, 1864, pp. 376-77.*

THE NATION (essay date 1866)

It is in his character of a satirical and humorous poet that we now have to do with [Lowell], for a second series of the famous **"Biglow Papers"** is just put forth. Certainly no one will gainsay us when we say that in this particular walk no one can be for a moment compared to Lowell. First and last, hundreds of people have attempted the portraiture of the Yankee; but, notwithstanding these pictures, numerous *ad nauseam, . . .* the Yankee would still be awaiting the true artist if it were not for Professor Lowell—if Hosea Biglow had not been drawn for us, and Parson Wilbur, and Mr. Birdofredum Sawin. . . . (p. 387)

[It is only with himself that] Mr. Lowell can be compared. Tried by the former series, this series will probably be put in the second place, because there is more poetry in this one than in that. Great as was the success achieved by the author in the creation of such characters as the parson, the Yankee farmer, and the New Englander turned loafer—characters so life-like and, in the main, so true to nature—so good as individuals and as types that we do not know where in our literature to look for three others that excel them—great as was the success in this particular achieved in the first series there seems to us to have been a blemish there which we also find in this series. Mr. Lowell must be mistaken; the Rev. Homer Wilbur never wrote those imitative newspaper notices prefixed to the work. And we doubt if he is the author of that essay upon the newspaper which the first series contains, and which seems to us rather an effort of some clever disciple of Professor Teufelsdröckh than of the pastor of the First Church in Jaalam. But, in the second series this fault is found, as it seems to us, in the poems themselves. Mr. Lowell's authority is great; probably no man is so well informed upon all that relates to the real character of the New Englanders, but a passage in his preface makes us bold to express an opinion formed before the preface was printed. Mr. Biglow says now things as good, as characteristic as he said in 1845; his natural force seems to have not abated; but he is now sometimes Mr. Lowell. (pp. 387-88)

> *"The New Biglow Papers," in* The Nation, *Vol. III, No. 72, November 15, 1866, pp. 386-88.*

THE NATION (essay date 1870)

[In **"The Cathedral,"** Lowell recalls four happy days of youth.] He speaks of them not in a certain mood with which his poetry has made readers of it familiar, though it may be doubted if it is so much his favorite one as he seems to say—that mood in which all the shows of nature affect the beholder who remembers old times with a joy, or else with

> A pathos, from the years and graves between.

Nor yet does he speak of them in the mood, of frequent recurrence with him, in which he looks, baffled, on the imperturbable face of enduring, constant Nature, self-sufficing, unintelligible, immovable, the open secret. Both of these moods are discoverable in the poem. But of late the latter seems to be tempered by a religious trust which forbids overmuch questioning; or even dismisses the problem. And the former was always held in check by the poet's mere delight in the sights and sounds of nature, and by the high enjoyment, almost animal in its character, which these stirred in him. Then, again, this sentimental way of making nature tributary and subservient to our own joys and woes of spirit has almost always been well

held in check by still another power in Mr. Lowell—by his gift of objective perception and presentation of what passes around him. It is, for instance, winter pure and simple—that is, winter plus no more of the poet's self than there is of realistic artist in the poet—that we see in the admirable scene in Quompegan Street. (p. 60)

The descriptions of the other three days are less realistic than [the winter-day piece]; they painted themselves less instant and less vivid on the brain of the beholder. But [Lowell's] delicate susceptibility to the influences surrounding him they show quite as plainly; and more plainly they show his capacity of being moved by things vaguer and more impalpable to the mind than mental influences. In short, we see made evident in these four happy days the two things which are made manifest in what we have been accustomed to consider our author's very best and most enduring work, whether in verse or prose—namely, his wonderful power of sympathy, and his power as an objective painter of things conceived or observed objectively. And it would not be fanciful to say that we may see in the boy, affected as he here sets forth, the maker of the **"Biglow Papers,"** so far as that work is sharp delineations of typical characters which are everywhere about us; and so far, also, as it is truthful pictures of individual men. The sympathetic diviner of other personalities whom we respect in the maturer critic and painter of character, and the observer who sees the thing as it is, seem to us clearly visible in the first half-dozen of these pages before us, which relate the boy's impressions.

We may say here that a jarring expression in the . . . [winter-day piece] is an indication of a fault in our author which, while it has never detracted from what is called the interest of his works, rather, indeed, has added to it, has yet almost always more or less injured their beauty and final satisfactoriness. That "young savage in his age of flint" is a young savage, sure enough; if only for his barbarous intrusion. The mind goes off at a tangent from the matter in hand, the poet once letting go his hold upon it in that abrupt manner, and there is no reason why it should come back till after the age of "lake dwellings" and then all the metallic ages have had a little attention. Mr. Lowell says himself, as he is going away from the cathedral at which he had planned to spend happy hours of abandonment:

> I, who to Chartres came to feed my eye,
> And give to Fancy one clear holiday,
> *Scarce saw the minster for the thoughts it stirred.*

And so it often happens with him. The self-pleasing activity of a mind remarkably quick and remarkably open to suggestion, wide-reaching and subtle, and which has at command numberless treasures with which to play, often prevents him from keeping himself steadily to the artistic elaboration of the piece of workmanship in hand. Thus we get many jewels, but not often the perfect jewel. (pp. 60-1)

> *"Lowell's 'Cathedral'," in* The Nation, *Vol. X, No. 239, January 27, 1870, pp. 60-1.*

[J. R. DENNETT] (essay date 1870)

Containing the deliberate words of perhaps the best of living English critics—his final judgments on many of the great names of literature; judgments which are the result of long and wide study and reading, of marvellous acuteness of sight and delicacy of sympathy; containing a poet's opinion of other poets, a wit's opinion of other wits; in short, the careful opinions of a man of cultivated genius concerning other men of genius who are near and dear to all of us, but to all of us partly unintelligible without an interpreter—["**Among my Books**"] is one of the best gifts that for many years has come to the world of English literature; and to say this, still is to say one of the best gifts that has for many years come to the world of literature. . . .

There will not be two opinions among readers of the volume before us whether the finest piece of criticism in it is not the essay entitled "**Shakespeare Once More;**" and we doubt if the sincerest hater of the superlative would not be willing to admit that, on the whole, in virtue of its combined penetration and comprehensiveness, this is the best single essay that has yet been written on the poet and his works. For our own part, we felt an inclination to go further, and to acknowledge to ourself a preference of this to any equal quantity of Shakespearean criticism that is to be found anywhere else. . . . (p. 258)

A little further on, in the same essay, Mr. Lowell says: "Whether I have fancied anything not Hamlet which the author never dreamed of putting there, I do not greatly concern myself to enquire;" and he goes on to give an ingenious reason for his want of concern. But it seems a reason ingenious rather than conclusive in favor of a practice to which it is not unfair to say that Mr. Lowell certainly is addicted. . . . More than one or two or ten instances we might cite where Mr. Lowell seems to put into his authors more than they meant should be found in them, or puts into their mouths something somewhat different from what they said.

Of kin to this fault of overingeniousness is another, which still more interferes with the reader's enjoyment, and that is the disturbing sparkles of wit in which our author indulges himself, and with which, too, he gives his readers pleasure—a momentary pleasure, for which by-and-by they make him pay. Perhaps it is that such incessant wit, read by us ladies and gentlemen who all our lives have been talking prose, not without knowing it, we are apt to resent. Or perhaps it may be that we care more for what our author thinks and feels than for his play with his thoughts and feelings. However this may be, no doubt Mr. Lowell's point does, as a matter of fact, count to his disadvantage with many of his readers, whether these are of the envious and malicious type, or among the willing admirers of genius. (pp. 258-59)

The opening paper of "**Among my Books**" is upon Dryden, and seems to us exhaustive. It is a model essay of the sort of which the men of Dryden's time have now for some time been the subjects —essays which do more to keep alive certain of our English poets than they themselves are still able to do. But this essay comes a great deal nearer to making it possible to dispense with the reading of its subject's own works than any similar essay with which we are acquainted. . . .

"**New England Two Centuries Ago,**" "**Rousseau and the Sentimentalists,**" "**Lessing,**" we have left ourselves no space to speak of. Each is, in its own way, so good that it would be easy to speak of it at great length; but this, we hope, is in no way necessary to call the attention of all our readers to the best body of criticism, best expressed, that American literature has to show. (p. 259)

> [*J. R. Dennett,*] *"Lowell's Essays," in* The Nation, *Vol. X, No. 251, April 21, 1870, pp. 258-59.*

H. D. TRAILL   (essay date 1882)

[One] cannot help wondering, though it may perhaps be impertinent to wonder, whether [Mr. Lowell] is satisfied to be known and popular as a humourist alone, or whether he would have preferred fame and remembrance as a serious poet. If he cares at all for reputation of the latter sort, he has certainly a right to complain of the niggardly spirit in which contemporary opinion has behaved to him. It may be that the *Biglow Papers* have exacted from him a converse penalty. . . . It may be that Mr. Lowell's sins as Hosea Biglow or Birdofredum Sawin have blinded the eyes of incurious readers to those exquisite vignettes of rural life which he has given them in *Under the Willows* and many of its companion pieces, and hardened their hearts against his truly splendid **Commemoration Ode,** ringing from end to end with the note of passionate patriotism if ever that has been sounded by the human voice. (pp. 82-3)

It is to the lack of [the commonplace] in Mr. Lowell's own verse that it owes, one may suspect, its comparatively narrow circle of admirers. . . . The knack of infusing [the commonplace] into his poetry in the proportion approved of by the popular palate did not come naturally to Mr. Lowell, and he has never acquired it. His poetic faculty, as we trace it through some thirty years of productive effort, shares the healthy growth of a healthy mind, but has never developed that useful form of adipose tissue which serves, at the expense no doubt of the higher quality of beauty, to keep warm the poetry—and the poet. On the other hand, it is but just to Mr. Lowell to add that he has not allowed his verse to run, in revenge, into that angularity of manner which too many poets not accepted by the multitude are wont to cultivate of malice prepense—the overstrained protest of classic severity of outline against the too buxom contours of the "popular" muse. Mr. Lowell's poetry has simply gone on perfecting itself in form and finish, until now he is as complete a specimen of "a literary man's poet," of the consummate artist in expression—whom the lover of the art of expression is hard put to it to judge impartially, from sheer delight in his workmanship—as it would be easy to find in a summer day's hunt through a well-filled library.

It is not difficult to trace the literary influences which have moulded this highly-wrought, this artless-artful poetic manner. In the introduction to the *Biglow Papers* Mr. Lowell observes with pride that the nineteenth-century New Englander "feels more at home with Fulke Greville, Herbert of Cherbury, Quarles, George Herbert, and Browne than with his modern English cousins." And the studies to which the ancestry of this New England poet has attracted him have done [much for his verse]. . . . (pp. 83-4)

[In his poem *Seaweed,* the imagery] construction, choice words, the "conceit" which has suggested the poem, and the *kind* of fancy which gives us the "pale shepherdess" for the moon; the kind of diction which gives us the "dear recurrence of thy law;" the continuous maintenance of that contrast which Coleridge has so acutely noticed in George Herbert and his contemporaries, between a somewhat far-fetched thought and its nobly simple expression—all recall the period in which Mr. Lowell evidently loves to dwell. We seem to catch the very breath of the seventeenth century. (p. 85)

The popular instinct which has seized upon the *Biglow Papers* and will insist on regarding Mr. Lowell as the author of that comic masterpiece and of nothing else, is in one sense a sound one. For while it is just open to argument whether Mr. Lowell is an actual or an adopted son of the Muses, he is unquestionably a born humorist. He possesses a humour of thought which is at once broad and subtle; his humour of expression is his American birthright. The mere characterisation of the *Biglow Papers* have perhaps been overpraised, though Birdofredum

Sawin certainly appears original and typical to an outsider, whatever may be said of Parson Homer Wilbur; but the graphic power of statement, the gnomic faculty of sententious utterances, the extraordinary fluency and facility of the versification, make the book a perpetual delight. . . . It is the fashion to talk of the second series of the papers, published from thirteen to sixteen years afterwards during the progress of the American Civil War, as inferior to its predecessor; but it would be hard to find any better ground for this opinion than the particular fact that it *was* a second series, and the general truth that seconds are not firsts. In no respect save that of novelty does it seem to me inferior in workmanship to the earlier volume. . . . (pp. 86-7)

As a critic of *belles lettres* [Mr. Lowell] has scarcely any living equal; and if we are allowed—as surely we should be—to give more marks for sanity than for any other quality of criticism, he ranks higher, perhaps, than any rival. Great delicacy of perception and a discriminative faculty, "piercing, even to the dividing asunder of soul and spirit," in a piece of literary work, are accompanied, in Mr. Lowell's case, by a most commendable freedom from crotchet and affectation, and a consistent sobriety of judgment. His paper on Chaucer in *My Study Windows* is at once as stimulating and satisfying, as suggestive of new ideas, and as adequate in its development of familiar ones, as any paper of forty odd octavo pages on an almost inexhaustible subject well could be. Nor is there anywhere out of Charles Lamb (who, moreover, as a cockney, could not have written it) a more charming piece of English prose writing of the half poetic, half humorous wholly nature loving order, than a *Good Word for Winter* in the same columns. (pp. 87-8)

H. D. Traill, "Mr. J. R. Lowell," in The Fortnightly Review, *Vol. XXIV, 1882, pp. 79-89.*

THE NATION   (essay date 1886)

An essay is the freest, an address one of the most enslaving, forms of literary expression. . . . [This consideration prepares] one for what seems a lack of customary freedom in [Lowell's *Democracy, and Other Addresses*], and for a novel attitude of the author, which may be expressed by saying that he does not talk with you, as he was wont to do, but at you. Tact is an admirable quality, and when one must observe so many and various amenities as a foreign minister who enters into the intellectual and social life of a great nation, it is of incalculable utility; but the necessity to employ it is an inconvenience to the thinker.

In the address which Mr. Lowell made before the Wordsworth Society, for example, his position as the retiring president was evidently an embarrassment to him as a critic, and the windings he makes, not, like Burke, into his subject, but out of it, are a lesson how to tell the truth without making a martyr of one's self, which the most skilled master of literary fence might lay to heart. In the Harvard address, on the contrary, the constraint of the hour was evidenced by the complete liberty of speech which he sensibly accorded to himself: as one in the house of his friends, he magnanimously determined to say his say, irrespective of who might be critical, sure of amiable tolerance if not of cordial agreement. But in an essay he would not have apologized for plain-speaking. The moral is this: that however successful these addresses were, and however delightful in themselves, let us not be flattered into believing that the man of letters can be so admirable as a speaker as he is as a writer. . . .

The address, nevertheless, has proved a fruitful form of expression for [Lowell's] later thought. One would not say that he was in earlier writings characteristically discursive, but the extraordinary fulness of his mind and the restless spontaneity of its action make him seem so. This copiousness was always his, and age has brought a mellower ripeness and more of charm. For a man whose mental wealth is so constituted, and who yet has never shown a disposition to reduce and systematize thought, any literary form which takes the surplusage of the mind and holds it, is sure to be serviceable. This is the essential character of the contents of this volume, which is less a reasoned criticism of books or life or institutions than the overflow of an opulent mind. It would be as impossible to submit such work to criticism as it would be unfruitful; and it is unnecessary to notice anew the traits of style, the felicities of phrase, the charm, eloquence, and humor which are familiar to two generations of our people. (p. 525)

[The address **"Democracy"** is not,] as it has been called, a profound and full exposition of the democratic principle. It has rather the consecutiveness of life than the sequence of logic, as indeed Mr. Lowell himself conceived it. . . . The sanity of [Lowell's] remarks is the most striking of their qualities; they are altogether free from panic, a liability to which is the political weakness of culture, and they thus keep proportion marvellously. (p. 526)

[The] two most noticeable traits of the ripened convictions of Mr. Lowell as made known in this volume [are] the democratic and the idealistic temper in forms of extraordinary purity. . . . [Lowell's addresses] are a better defence of the rights of humane study than any advocate could frame. The best moral is implicit in things, not explicit in words; and in this volume there is the authentic impress of the classical spirit—age seasons every page and yet every page is young. (pp. 526-27)

"Mr. Lowell's New Volume," in The Nation, *Vol. XLIII, No. 1121, December 23, 1886, pp. 525-27.*

BRET HARTE   (essay date 1891)

[Although] Mr. Lowell had humour, it was subordinate to his controversial purpose, and, undoubted as was his lyric power, in his most stirring passages the moral effort was apt to be painfully and Puritanically obvious. . . . Whatever ideal Mr. Lowell may have had in his own inner consciousness—in spite of the playful portrait he has given of himself in the **"Fable for Critics"**—outwardly at least the work of his manhood seemed to have fulfilled the ambition, as it had the *promise,* of his youth. A strong satirical singer, who at once won the applause of a people inclined to prefer sentiment and pathos in verse; an essayist who held his own beside such men as Emerson, Thoreau, and Holmes; an ironical biographer in the land of the historian of the Knickerbockers; and an unselfish, uncalculating patriot selected to represent a country where partisan politics and party service were too often the only test of fitness—this was his triumphant record. His death seems to have left no trust or belief of his admirers betrayed or disappointed. The critic has not yet risen to lament a wasted opportunity, to point out a misdirected talent, or to tell us that he expected more or less than Mr. Lowell gave. (pp. 193-94)

Yet it has always seemed to me that his early success as well as his strength lay in his keen instinctive insight into the personal character of the New Englander. He had by no means created the "Yankee" in literature, neither had he been the first to use the Yankee dialect. . . . It remained for Mr. Lowell alone to discover and portray the real Yankee—that wonderful evolution of the English Puritan, who had shaken off the forms and superstitions, the bigotry and intolerance of religion, but never the deep consciousness of God. It was true that it was not only an allwise God but a God singularly perspicacious of wily humanity; a God that you had "to get up early" to "take in"; a God who encouraged familiarity, who did not reveal Himself in vague thunders, nor answer out of a whirlwind of abstraction; who did not hold a whole race responsible—but "sent the bill" directly to the individual debtor. It was part of Mr. Lowell's art to contrast this rude working-Christian Biglow with the older-fashioned Puritan parson Wilbur, still wedded to his creed and his books. The delightful pedant is no less strong and characteristic than his *protégé,* though perhaps not as amusing and original. . . . [Clever] as was the "swaller-tailed talk" of the parson, one is conscious that it is mere workmanship, and that at best it is but humorous translation artistically done. It is the rude dialect of Hosea that is alone real and vital. For this is not the "Yankee talk" of tradition, of the story books and the stage—tricks of pronunciation, illiterate spelling, and epithet—but the revelation of the character, faith, work, and even scenery of a people, in words more or less familiar, but always in startling and novel combination and figurative phrasing. New England rises before us, with its hard social life, its scant amusements, always sternly and pathetically conjoined with religious, patriotic, or political duty. . . . [One] may take that perfect crystallisation of New England—the white winter idyl of **"The Courtin'."** In the first word the keynote of the Puritan life is struck:—

> "*God* makes sech nights, all white and still."

The familiar personal Deity is there—no Pantheistic abstraction, conventional muse, nor wanton classic Goddess, but the New Englander's Very God. Again and again through the verses of that matchless pastoral the religious chord is struck; weak human passion and grim piety walk hand-in-hand to its grave measure. . . . (pp. 194-96)

Equally strong and true . . . are the few touches that discover the whole history of the Revolution and its "embattled farmers" in the "Old Queen's arm" over the chimney; that reveal the economic domestic life in the picture of the hardworking mother utilising her discreet propinquity by "sprinklin' clo'es agin to-morrow's i'nin'" in the next room, and the fair Huldy herself dividing her blushes with "the apples she was peelin'." The hard realistic picture is lifted into the highest poetry by two or three exquisite similes—conceits that carry conviction because they are within the inventive capacity of the quaint narrator, and the outcome of his observation. Take such perfect examples as:—

> But long o' her his veins 'ould run
> All crinkly like curled maple,
> The side she brushed felt *full o' sun*
> *Ez a south slope in Ap'il.*
>
> . . . . .
>
> All ways to once her feelins flew
> Like sparks in burnt up paper.
>   (p. 196)

[As to the origin and genius of this wonderful dialect, one] is not concerned to know that much of the so-called dialect is Old English, and that among the other things the Puritan carried over with him was the integrity of the language. Enough for us that it was the picturesque interpretation of the New England

life and character. Critic of the New Englander as [Lowell] was, he was first and last always one of them. Like Bramah he may have been the "Doubter and the Doubt," but he was also "the hymn the Brahmin sings."

But Mr. Lowell was more of an Englishman than an American—in the broadest significance of the latter term. His English blood had been unmixed for two generations, with the further English insulation of tradition, family, and locality. . . . He knew little of the life and character of the West and South—it is to be feared that he never greatly understood or sympathised with either. His splendid anti-slavery services were the outcome of moral conviction, and not the result of a deliberate survey of the needs and policy of a nation. In his most powerful diatribes, there was always this reiteration of an abstract Right and Wrong that was quite as much the utterance of Exeter Hall as of Elmwood. Only once does a consideration of the other side occur, and that is a note of human compassion:—

> My eyes cloud up for rain; my mouth
> Will take to twitching roun' the corners;
> I pity mothers too down South,
> For all they sot among the scorners.
>   (pp. 197-98)

But if Mr. Lowell failed in a sympathetic understanding of the whole nation . . . , he never erred in his complete and keen perception of the section whose virtues and vices he portrayed. With his instincts as a true artist he knew that his best material lay at the roots of the people, close to the common soil, and with his instincts as a gentleman he heeded not the cry of "vulgarity" at his choice. We cannot be sufficiently grateful to him that he did not give us perfunctory, over-cultivated, self-conscious, epigrammatic heroes and heroines, as he might have done, and that his perfect critical faculty detected their unartistic quality, as his honest heart despised their sham. His other creative work had little local colour, might have been written anywhere, and belonged to the varying moods of the accomplished singer and thinker, whether told in the delicate tenderness of the **"First Snowfall,"** of **"Auf Wiedersehen,"** and **"After the Burial,"** or in the gentle cynicism of **"Two Scenes from the Life of Blondel."** His critical essays are so perfect in their literary quality that one forgets that they are or are not criticism. (p. 200)

Bret Harte, "A Few Words about Mr. Lowell," in The New Review, Vol. V, No. 28, September, 1891, pp. 193-201.

HORACE L. TRAUBEL (essay date 1892)

A good eye will detect here and there a suspicion that in Lowell the critical and the scholarly overpasses the creative and the intuitional—that, after all, he interprets books better than nature, and is more easily fitted to the ways of the student than the ill quarters of wanderers on social wastes. . . .

We will not dispute Lowell's gifts. Talent of a very high order veined and ennobled verse and prose and public life. If he gave literature no new forms, he gave it honest combinations of the old. Next to discovery is rehabilitation. Little that method and art can do for man was left undone for Lowell and his fame. (p. 23)

The **"Biglow Papers,"** the Essays, the **Lincoln Ode,** the **"Poems"** and Papers, always combed and curled and dressed after the best inheritances of taste; the pure life; the disposition to give literary history its area of practical benevolence; his faith that things were feeling, however they may as yet have failed to realize, nobler entrances and a wider stage; his reverence for art, and the high ideals to which he austerely paid tribute; his domestic relations, and service to college and government—all these splendid qualities and distillations, none of them to be scorned or dispensed with, go far to justify the historic necessity and grandeur of [Lowell's] achievement. Lowell espoused, he did not bring, a message. He was conservator; he was not creator.

Here, then, is the popular mistake. Lowell's office is magnified by being misunderstood. Aspiration is mistaken for inspiration. (p. 25)

Lowell brings us the life of books. His poetic line is chiselled to antique measurements. Exquisite proportion, abundant demonstration of effective and perfect anatomy; but stone, withal, and color lost in form. (p. 26)

Lowell comes into our history dragging along an old heritage too cumbersome to allow the spirit its free play. Organization, tradition, the accumulated and magnified principles and rules of art, the harassing littlenesses of pettifogging orthodoxies, impale and limit him. He could soar beyond them, and did; he could take long flights and short; but, always returning, he in fact acknowledged their claims. His grace, beauty, music—his loving armory, serviced for man—his supreme determination to be and remain clean and clear—his creation of noble songs and honest, if not indulgent and inclusive, criticism—his courageous assertion of personality, so far as the conviction of it existed—his command of knowledge and ease of speech—his eye, undimmed to the last in discrimination and perception of color—his real contribution to the hour and to the future—are not laurels to be mocked at or denied. Yet this finally remains to be said: serving life as he saw it, and from ancestral and collegiate backgrounds, as he had them, and never freed from the subtle bonds of that relationship and heredity, it would be our wrong and shame to profess him greatest where there are greater. . . . (pp. 29-30)

> *Horace L. Traubel, "Lowell—Whitman: A Contrast," in Poet Lore, Vol. IV, No. 1, January 15, 1892, pp. 22-31.**

THE ATHENAEUM   (essay date 1896)

Lowell was never, in any proper sense of the term, a first-rate, or even a second-rate poet; but some injustice cannot but be done to an occasionally resonant rhetorician, a frequently humorous versifier, by the publication of such tame, tasteless, and incompetent verse as most of that included in [*Last Poems*]. One piece ['**The Nobler Lover**'], indeed, there is which is redeemed from the commonplace by a Browning-like touch of sentiment, and a note of rhetoric somewhat gentler and more human than usual; yet even this is impassioned speech rather than poetry. . . .

This [poem] reminds one of some of those graceful early pieces in which Lowell was at all events simple in form and downright in sentiment. Elsewhere, however, in the book it is scarcely the qualities of simplicity and directness which are the most obvious or the most typical. The writing is more generally heavy and surcharged, striving after a fulness which does but end in repletion, as in these lines, for instance, from a poem addressing '**Turner's Old Téméraire, under a Figure symbolizing the Church**' (such is the title of the piece):—

> How didst thou trample on tumultuous seas,
> Or, like some basking sea-beast stretched at ease,
> Let the bull-fronted surges glide
> Caressingly along thy side,
> Like glad hounds leaping by the huntsman's knees!

What a confusion of metaphors, and how ineffectually they are flung about! Metaphor was always a pitfall to Lowell. Alike in verse and prose he was convinced that good writing meant metaphorical writing, and that the best style was the style most packed with metaphors. The figure of speech was to him speech at its finest elevation; and he laid violent and indiscriminate hands on everything that could be compared to anything else. Sometimes his comparisons are curiously out of place, as when he speaks of two floating goldfishes,

> Grave as a pair of funeral urns;

and, still addressing the goldfishes, alludes to "your prose-bounded day." At other times he is somewhat too mechanically accurate in his elaboration, as in the opening lines of the same poem . . . :

> What know we of the world immense
> Beyond the narrow ring of sense?
> What should we know, who lounge about
> The house we dwell in, nor find out,
> Masked by a wall, the secret cell
> Where the soul's priests in hiding dwell?
> The winding stair that steals aloof
> To chapel mysteries 'neath the roof?

Here we have a certain ingenuity, an ingenuity cleverly and deliberately applied to the manufacture of an article of fancy. It is not poetical ingenuity at all; it has not even the pretence of having been found by the way, or in dreams; we can but praise the skill of its making. With Lowell a very genuine, though extraordinarily unpoetical, humour adds, not infrequently, to the strained and prosaic effect of these experiments in fancifulness. . . . [In a poem] serious in sentiment, he tells us

> Thought is lumpish, Thought is slow,

and presently figures Thought in Love's "deserted nest," as he

> Sits to hold the crowner's quest;

Thought finally following Happiness to

> ——a brink
> Whence too easy 'tis to fall
> Whither's no return at all;
> Have a care, half-hearted lover,
> Thought would only push her over!

"Thought would only push her over"! Conceive of a poet with any fine sense of the eternal soul or the musical speech of true poetry thinking, writing, and printing such a line! But after all it is not the prevalence of bad lines, of false metaphors, of any other external blemish, that forbids us to assign Lowell any place among the conspicuous poets of his time; it is his radically prosaic attitude of mind and his radically prosaic construction of verse. His work is full of fancy, but he seems to take his fancy out of pigeon-holes. He gets the right number of syllables in his lines, but he seems to get them by counting on his fingers. No incommunicable charm ever for a moment descends upon his altar to the Muses in light, or ascends from it in fire. That he should ever have seemed to the American critic or the

American public a poet of national importance is, perhaps, the severest criticism on itself that the American nation has ever made. (pp. 12-13)

"Literature: 'Last Poems'," in The Athenaeum, *No. 3558, January 4, 1896, pp. 12-13.*

EDINBURGH REVIEW (essay date 1900)

Lowell would have been the last to wish to be judged by a provincial standard: he would have preferred that his work should be tested by the classics of that language which is common to the whole English-speaking world. And if we judge him by this standard, charming writer though he is, the verdict of posterity will be that he does not live among the great poets of the nineteenth century. . . . Much that he wrote was thin, because he was, as he himself said, 'a good versifier.' He had the poetic faculty—a charming fancy, there are lines which live, sometimes as from an inspiration; no line has ever hit more suggestively the whole feeling of the great seas than that in which he addresses the

Ocean men's path and their divider too.

But in truth Lowell had almost a fatal facility of verse; he could turn every subject, grave or gay, every emotion, every glint of humour into rhyme, and, as he said of Wordsworth, 'he wrote too much to write always well.' Such a faculty, unusual and delightful, needed to be carefully watched; the course of Lowell's life, so far from confining it, gave it play, and prevented that perfect form, that strength of mental supply, without which poetry is not, and a man becomes chiefly a versifier. (p. 174)

[In] reading Lowell's verse it is impossible not to be often aware of an absence of concentration—on the contrary, of the weakening of the original thought. There is a great quantity of agreeable verse—feeling for natural beauty, a perception of the undertones of life. It is as walking through delightful but not remarkable scenery—we are never displeased, but we are never deeply moved. We are inclined rather to be struck with the personality of the writer than with his poetry. (p. 175)

When we peruse the immense quantity of agreeable verse in his collected works, and compare it with the comparative smallness of the **'Biglow Papers,'** we cannot but be struck with the superiority of these poems. Their setting, in the shape of the letters of the Rev. Mr. Wilbur, is sometimes tedious to English readers, but the poems themselves will remain Lowell's most permanent addition to American literature. They are animate with the life of a great mass of the people; they are often a passionate and yet humorous expression of contemporary thought, the writer is voicing his age, and he is in earnest. A memorable moment has come, and a strong movement of feeling impels him to expression. The subjects are serious, large. The very fact that these poems are written in a dialect, that they realise types of the people, gives them a truth which adds to their completeness and their permanence. . . . The intense provincialism of [the **'Biglow Papers'**] was in a great measure its strength. In **'The Courtin','** . . . we perceive how well he could represent the feelings of the countrypeople of New England. It has a simplicity, a charm, and a truth which makes it of greater worth than any of his more general work. It is a picture of New England life. We can see the snow long lying on the hills of Maine, the sparse farms, the warm parlour, the home of more than one generation of those sturdy farmers who still live prosperous and contented in this hard country. . . .

[In **'The Courtin'**] is the true metal, nothing forced and nothing weak, far removed from those poetical efforts which, though they show cultivation and quick feeling, are without character. Whittier well said that Lowell was one

Who in the language of their farm-fields spoke
The wit and wisdom of New England folk.

What the world regrets is that Lowell did not write more which could be regarded as distinctively American work.

As a critic, Lowell is what might be expected from his character and temperament. A critic is born, not made; no one can be a critic of the first rank without natural imagination, sympathy, and quickness of perception. Lowell had these qualities in a marked degree, and they were in constant course of expansion and activity. . . . But the impression which his criticisms leave is that Lowell never delved very deeply into the subject of them. In his letters are constantly to be found flashes of insight which illuminate quickly and for the moment the book or the writer on which his intellect is turned. His more elaborate work has the same characteristics—it is scarcely sufficiently well pondered. (pp. 177-79)

The essence of Lowell's critical writings is a sympathetic and cultured common sense. Ambiguity of phrase, uncompleted thought producing embryonic ideas, a hostile frame of mind towards his subject, a narrowly bounded view, are never to be found in his writings. Thoughts are sometimes too quickly transferred from his brain to his paper, but they are always clear—not a very powerful stream, but pleasant, pure, and healthy. . . .

But if there are some shortcomings in Lowell's purely literary criticisms, on the other hand, as a critic of men, of the movements of society, of the literature of life, he is admirable. Perhaps nowhere is this better exemplified than in the brilliant address on Thoreau; it is full of insight, it is marked by memorable and suggestive phrases. Thoreau 'was not a strong thinker, but a sensitive feeler.' Of the transcendental movement in which he was so noticeable, Lowell said, 'Communities were established where everything was to be common but common sense.' It would be difficult within the same space to find a keener yet a more sympathetic review of a remarkable man, and of a noticeable intellectual and moral movement, than is contained in this address. (p. 180)

Among the writers known to the English-speaking race in the last fifty years no man arrests attention more than James Russell Lowell. If greatness be measured by signal achievements in a single branch of human endeavour, it cannot be declared that Lowell has attained the highest rank. But if with more catholicity of opinion we estimate greatness by remarkable efforts and results in various fields, Lowell reached a high position among men of letters of the nineteenth century. As a journalist in the best and widest sense, as an essayist and critic, and in some degree as a poet, he will long be memorable. (p. 181)

"James Russell Lowell," in Edinburgh Review, *Vol. CXCI, No. CCCXCI, January, 1900, pp. 157-81.*

JOHN MACY (essay date 1913)

In [his] lampoon of himself in the clattering **"Fable for Critics"** [see excerpt above], Lowell confesses one of his defects, and he exhibits another—his verbal carelessness and lack of metrical finesse. He also displays very attractive virtues, genial willingness to apply his critical candour to his own talents, and freedom from the more solemn sort of literary pose. He began his career with some slight verses, sincere in thought and not unskilful, though technically stiff and hasty with the haste that betrays itself. He was moved, at least in his youth, by noble enthusiasms; he studied the poets ancient and modern with unfeigned ardour; he became a competent, even acute, analyst of the technique of poetry; his impulse to utter his feelings in song did not abate with youth but continued all his life. Yet he wrote no perfect poem in classic English (if classic is the word to discriminate what is not in dialect); no poem of his sings itself, flies on its own wings or, to use its own words, "maintains itself by virtue of a happy coalescence of matter and style." The old way of expressing his failure is to say that he was not a born poet, which explains nothing but suggests what is wanting in the verse of a man who had most of the namable abilities and motives that make a poet. Life-long devotion to poetry, an unusually wide acquaintance with the resources of language, elevated thoughts and an intense desire to say them, all are his; the music simply does not happen. (pp. 189-90)

The best of all [Lowell's] verse, except that in dialect, is the passage about Lincoln in the **"Commemoration Ode";** it is so good that it ought to be great, but the light fades from it when it is put beside Whitman's elegies. The Ode was written in a rush of inspiration which left Lowell exhausted, a true case of the poet's pouring his heart's blood (that is, his nervous energy) into his work. But it leaves at least one reader, who is eager to like it, almost cold. The metaphors shine, but do not glow. Lowell's strong, capricious intellect seems not to have guided firmly the flow of his emotion but to have intercepted it and diluted it with rhetoric and conceits. Some of his other high-pitched and sober verse, intended to be in the grand style and strong with the very effort to be poetry, is confused and perplexing. The metaphors are manufactured and inserted; they are not of one substance with the thought. (pp. 191-92)

The themes of Lowell's poems in pure English are all sung better by some other poet. In **"Appledore,"** one cannot hear the sea as one hears it in Swinburne and Whitman. **"The Washers of the Shroud"** does not thrill with the ominous voice of War. It is intellectually interesting, and has, like much of Lowell's verse, every virtue but *the* virtue. (pp. 192-93)

"Talent," says Lowell, "is that which is in a man's power; genius is that in whose power he is." . . . That epigram is too sharp to be true, but it has truth in it, and it is applicable to Lowell's verse. He had poetic talent; the genius of poetry did not possess him. (pp. 193-94)

[There is one portion of Lowell's poetry] for which nothing but praise can be spoken—**"The Biglow Papers."** They have no rivals. Custom has not staled them. Occasional poems, they have wings that lift them above occasion to immortality. In them Lowell is possessed by his genius, by a genius that never visited any one else in the same shape. The dialect, artificial from the point of view of a philological naturalist, becomes Lowell's native speech. In it he can say anything. . . . (p. 194)

A New Englander can read **"The Biglow Papers"** aloud with hardly more consciousness that he is reading a dialect than an educated Scotsman (probably) feels in reading Burns. To say that it is a dialect that no people ever spoke is merely to say that New Englanders do not talk in verse. Neither would a Scotch farmer before Burns have said, "A woe-worn ghaist I hameward glide"; for that is the idiom not of speech, but of literature reshaping a dialect. Biglow's turn of phrase falls

familiar on the ear of one who knows New England farmers— farmers that did leave "the ax an' saw," "the anvil an' the plow," who believe that the best way to settle "is to settle an' not jaw"—and then argue an hour to prove it. Lowell's enthusiasm for the dialect and his delight in the Yankee mixture of common sense and mystic nearness to God find expression in the essay which prefaces the collected works of Mr. Biglow and Parson Wilbur. Can the literature of philology show such a truly literary and genuinely philological essay as Lowell's? He knows the subject as a scholar, and he feels it as a poet. The dialect is his most effective literary idiom; in it he can "let himself go," and he is freed from the weight of his bookishness. (p. 195)

Did not Lowell read too much? Did not his vigorous mind become smothered in more traditional ideas than it could assimilate and master? (p. 200)

His biography portrays him hurrying home from lectures, half ironically congratulating himself for having overcome his indolence and "done a day's work," then incontinently sinking into his armchair and reading till midnight. . . . [Lowell's] mind was crammed with literature, that is, with the expressions of outworn states of society, and even his large nature had no room for any thing fresh from life. Literature is a food and a stimulant up to a certain point. Beyond that it becomes a drug. . . . One is jealous in behalf of real literature at the surrender of such a splendid mind as Lowell's to the inferior work, the secondary work, of studying books. That work, which is necessary and requires talent, can be well enough done by men who could not write **"The Biglow Papers"** or the essay on Lincoln. Moreover, less reading, the study of fewer men, would not have hurt [Lowell's] bookish essays, but might have improved them. He quotes too much directly and indirectly; transfers to his pages in too great abundance, and to the disturbance of order, the marked passages in his beloved library.

Lowell's submersion in books was, to be sure, not motived entirely by the sin of indolence and willingness to let other men determine the course of his thought; he was devoted to great thinkers, and his devotion is more than justified by the work he did as a teacher and critic. In company with Longfellow, Emerson, and others of the New England Illuminati, he introduced modern literature into a cultivated society that had hitherto depended wholly on the ancient classics. . . . (pp. 200-02)

He was a discoverer, and his critical essays tingle with the fervour of discovery. . . . Lowell made his reading fruitful for other men. Therefore he is a true critic. He did his work at a time when it was greatly needed. Yet one cannot help thinking that he was reading other men's work when he ought to have been rewriting his own, that another poem as good as **"The Courtin',"** and better versions of many of his other poems got lost in the library where there was so much French Romance and Dante and Chaucer. (pp. 202-03)

As an amateur enjoying himself in a wide range of literature, Lowell sometimes misjudges. Many commonplace instructors in English could point out where he was wrong, but they are wrong, too, and are not interesting. . . . What difference does it make if Lowell is wrong in his contention about Chaucer's nine-syllable line? The significant thing is that no other American professor, not even Child with all his knowledge, has written an essay on Chaucer which like Lowell's is itself literature.

Lowell illuminates even where he misjudges and therein he differs from critics who write with such modified judgments and well-tempered compensations that they elaborately kill their discourses. Lowell's essay on Thoreau is unjust. But even one who regards Thoreau as very great will find himself unable to improve upon Lowell's praises on the last atoning page. (pp. 204-05)

The opening pages of the same essay are an acid caricature of a whole era of thought and are good reading if not taken too seriously. They are written by a man who is more than a literary critic, who is a satirist of human nature, the same satirist who wrote the double-edged commentaries of Hosea's friend, the Rev. Homer Wilbur. Lowell's essay on Carlyle measures exactly the place in nineteenth-century thought that now, looking back, we can see Carlyle had come to at that time. (pp. 205-06)

Lowell has the true essayist's inability to stick to his subject. Apropos of a book or a writer he talks of anything that happens to be suggested to him. . . . Some formalistic critics, who seem to think that the whole universe of literature depends on their saying just the right thing, object too strongly to Lowell's habit of kicking up his heels in the midst of a fine passage. Lamb, the greatest of critics, does the same thing. It comes from irrepressible high spirits, delight in life, which is a good thing in literature, and is correspondingly good in the criticism of literature. No other writer about books after Lamb and Hazlitt is more continuously readable than Lowell. His very prejudices are entertaining; they lead him to some bold hard hitting which, we are told, passed out of good society with the days of Macaulay and Poe; perhaps that is the reason some of us read Macaulay and Poe in preference to critics of finer amenity. Lowell always talks like an honest man, never like a literary poseur. His affectations are not really affectations, for he expects you to know what he is doing, to play-act with him in a momentary interruption before he goes on again with the lesson in hand. He tells what books mean to him, not what they ought to mean to him because some other critic has said so. He is capable of fine eloquence, and he has a habit of bringing his eloquence quickly down by whimsical change of mood. He has variety of style because he has variety of feelings. The irregularities of his prose are due not wholly to carelessness, but partly to exuberance and to the impulsive pursuit of his idea.

All Lowell's prose is good to read. One volume of it is indispensable to an American, the **"Political Essays."** We can read somebody else's essays on Gray and Keats, but no one of the time has left us a better volume of its kind than Lowell's papers on political affairs. (pp. 206-07)

> *John Macy, "Lowell," in his* The Spirit of American Literature *(copyright 1913 by Doubleday, Page & Co.; copyright renewed 1940 by William M. Rockwell, as literary executor to the Estate of John Macy; reprinted by permission of Doubleday & Company, Inc.), Doubleday, 1913, pp. 189-209.*

WILLIAM HENRY HUDSON   (essay date 1914)

[The contents of **"A Year's Life"**] testify in the imitative quality of their form and manner to [Lowell's] dependence upon certain chosen masters, and notably upon Keats, to whom he was ardently devoted, and Tennyson, who was just then beginning to lay his spell upon the New England public. At the same time it is the purely personal note that dominates this early verse. Lowell hardly looks beyond the narrow horizon of his own life for his motives; it is with his love and the meaning of that love for him that he is almost wholly occupied; and the value of what he writes is to be sought chiefly in the combination of intensity and purity with which his passion is revealed. (p. 31)

Some three years only separated Lowell's first venture from [**"Poems,"** his] second volume of verse; but in these three years he had gained greatly by wider contact with the world, and his mind had grown rapidly both in depth and in breadth. A purely "literary" and imitative quality is still conspicuous here and there in the **"Poems"** as, notably, in the longest in the collection, **"A Legend of Brittany,"** which in the character of its theme, its mediæval atmosphere, its stanza-form, and the richness of its language and imagery, is unmistakably reminiscent of Keats's "Isabella." But elsewhere a new note—a distinctive and individual note—is struck with no uncertain hand, and what is more significant, Lowell begins to assert his high sense of the functions and responsibilities of the true poet as the inspirer and teacher of men. (p. 35)

It may be that [**"Poems"**] was circumscribed and one-sided; that it threw altogether too much stress upon the didactic function; that it tended to some extent to repudiate the claims of art as art, and to confound the aims and methods of the artist with those of the teacher. Such questions must be left for each individual reader to settle for himself. (p. 43)

[The] work which, perhaps, beyond all others of the period embodies the full spirit of Lowell's early manhood [is] **"The Vision of Sir Launfal."** (p. 57)

[A reference that Lowell made] to Tennyson's "Sir Galahad" suggests that the literary inspiration of **"Sir Launfal"** is probably to be found in that fine poem. . . . Since [Tennyson, like Lowell,] was emphatically a moralist, and fashioned his old tales to a modern didactic purpose, it is natural that some comparison should be made between the ethical significance of his Arthurian poems and that of Lowell's excursion into the same field. This comparison must not, indeed, be pushed too far. Yet the essential difference between the moral implications of the two versions is as interesting as it is obvious. Tennyson makes his Arthurian stories the vehicle of a characteristic warning against sensuous license and morbid anti-social perversions of religion. Lowell's narrative is a parable of democracy, a sermon on his great text of human brotherhood and the common divinity of all men. Yet the author of "The Holy Grail" and the author of **"Sir Launfal,"** it should be noted, are at one in this—that love of God for both of them is most conclusively shown in love of man. (pp. 58-9)

[The real beauty of **"Sir Launfal"**] lies, not in the narrative parts of it, but in the descriptive framework. The two landscapes are painted with wonderful fidelity and pictorial power, and their contrast is most effective. Nature was lovely to Lowell in all her moods and changes, and the December piece which introduces the second part gives us a sense, not only of the severity but also of the delicate beauty of the season in a way which is entirely worthy of the man who was presently to devote a whole essay to the praise of winter. But, after all, it is in the superb prelude to Part I, with its wealth of colour, its lavish profusion of details, and the full-throated music of its verse that Lowell reaches his highest mark as an interpreter of nature. It is not unusual for a poet to have his special season as well as his special landscape. Chaucer, for instance, was preeminently the poet of the spring; Bryant of the autumn. Lowell's chosen season is the early summer, when the fresh glory bursts "on field and hill, in heart and brain," and tardy May's hesitating promise is fulfilled in a sudden outbreak of adolescent life. (p. 71)

[It] is a striking example of his versatility that the very year in which "The Vision of Sir Launfal" appeared saw also the production of another poem so different from this in matter, spirit, and style, that it is not easy to realise that it came from the same pen. This is "A Fable for Critics," a literary satire of amazing force and audacity. The piece has conspicuous defects. It is much too long; it drops at times into mere doggerel; in places it irritates by its digressions, its over-emphasis, its too obvious straining after the clever phrase and the surprising sally. But its high spirits are contagious, and there is still amusement to be found in its rollicking fun, its nimble punning, and its gymnastic achievements in double and triple rhymes. It has, moreover, substantial value as an essay in criticism, for it presents an admirable survey of American literature at the time of its production, and its judgments upon contemporary writers are for the most part astonishingly penetrative and just. (pp. 75-6)

The critical essays in which Lowell garnered up and condensed the best results of his academic study and thought are justly regarded as the finest contribution yet made by America to the literature of criticism. As a prose-writer he has many defects; he often lacks simplicity and sometimes dignity; he is occasionally intricate and laboured in style. But at his best he is wonderfully racy and stimulating; and he is never anything or anybody but himself. His scholarship was thoroughly sound; his range and versatility were remarkable; he wandered over the widest fields with all the assurance of a master; and he never failed to say something fresh and illuminating upon every subject he selected for discussion. . . . (p. 121)

The reader who compares Lowell's literary essays with his poetry must inevitably be struck by the fact that, while his critical standards were extremely high and his judgments apt to be severe, his own verse is rarely characterised by sustained excellence, and is often, indeed, marred by unevenness and extravagances which he would have been the first to detect and condemn in the work of others. What is the explanation of this contradiction? It must be sought chiefly, I think, in the difference between Lowell in his critical and Lowell in his creative mood. As an arbiter and censor he was strict even to fastidiousness. But his genius upon the poetical side was essentially volatile and impetuous. (pp. 133-34)

In his essay on Rousseau [Lowell] says, "We value character more than any amount of talent." . . . [This sentence is extremely significant, because it not only shows where he himself always laid the emphasis, but also indicates] the basis of his own enduring greatness. It is character and all that we mean by it which give a distinctive stamp to everything that Lowell wrote. We prize and love his poetry because it is the work of one who was at once a true poet and a true man. (p. 136)

> *William Henry Hudson, in his* Lowell & His Poetry *(reprinted by permission of Harrap Limited), Harrap, 1914, 136 p.*

BLISS PERRY (essay date 1919)

[Although in pure literary fame many outrank him,] Lowell stands with both Emerson and Whitman in the very center of that group of poets and prose-men who have been inspired by the American idea. (p. 133)

Of both series of "Biglow Papers" we may surely exclaim, as did Quintilian concerning early Roman satire, "This is wholly ours." It is true that Lowell, like every young poet of his generation, had steeped himself in Spenser and the Elizabethans. They were his literary ancestors by as indisputable an inheritance as a Masefield or a Kipling could claim. He had been brought up to revere Pope. Then he surrendered to Wordsworth and Keats and Shelley, and his earlier verses, like the early work of Tennyson, are full of echoes of other men's music. It is also true that in spite of his cleverness in versifying, or perhaps because of it, he usually showed little inventiveness in shaping new poetic patterns. His tastes were conservative. He lacked that restless technical curiosity which spurred Poe and Whitman to experiment with new forms. But Lowell revealed early extraordinary gifts of improvisation, retaining the old tunes of English verse as the basis of his own strains of unpremeditated art. He wrote "A Fable for Critics" faster than he could have written it in prose. "Sir Launfal" was composed in two days, the "Commemoration Ode" in one.

It was this facile, copious, enthusiastic poet, not yet thirty, who grew hot over the Mexican War and poured forth his indignation in an unforgettable political satire ["Biglow Papers," First Series] such as no English provincial poet could possibly have written. What a weapon he had, and how it flashed in his hand, gleaming with wit and humor and irony, edged with scorn, and weighted with two hundred years of Puritan tradition concerning right and wrong! For that, after all, was the secret of its success. Great satire must have a standard; and Lowell revealed his in the very first number and in one line:

> 'Taint your eppylets an' feathers
> *Make the thing a grain more right.*
>
> (pp. 137-38)

The Second Series of "Biglow Papers" is more uneven than the First. There is less humor and more of whimsicality. But the dialogue between "the Moniment and the Bridge," "Jonathan to John," and above all, the tenth number, "Mr. Hosea Biglow to the Editor of the Atlantic Monthly," show the full sweep of Lowell's power. Here are pride of country, passion of personal sorrow, tenderness, idyllic beauty, magic of word and phrase.

Never again, save in passages of the memorial odes written after the war, was Lowell more completely the poet. (p. 139)

[In the "Commemoration Ode,"] and in the various Centennial Odes composed ten years later, Lowell found an instrument exactly suited to his temperament and his technique. Loose in structure, copious in diction, swarming with imagery, these Odes gave ample scope for Lowell's swift gush of patriotic fervor, for the afflatus of the improviser, steadied by reverence for America's historic past. To a generation beginning to lose its taste for commemorative oratory, the Odes gave—and still give—the thrill of patriotic eloquence which Everett and Webster had communicated in the memorial epoch of 1826. The forms change, the function never dies. (pp. 141-42)

Contemporary critics have . . . betrayed a certain concern for some aspects of Lowell's criticism. . . . Candor compels the admission that he often had no thesis to maintain: he invented them as he went along. Sometimes he was a mere guesser, not a clairvoyant. . . . It is true, finally, that a deeper interest in philosophy and science might have made Lowell's criticism more fruitful; that he blazed no new paths in critical method; that he overlooked many of the significant literary movements of his own time in his own country. (pp. 144-45)

[But the whole tradition of the English familiar essay] has always welcomed copious, well-informed, enthusiastic, disorderly, and affectionate talk about books. It demands gusto rather than strict method, discursiveness rather than concision, abundance of matter rather than mere neatness of design. "Here is God's plenty!" cried Dryden in his old age, as he opened once more his beloved Chaucer; and in Lowell's essays there is surely "God's plenty" for a book-lover. Every one praises **"My Garden Acquaintance," "A Good Word for Winter," "On a Certain Condescension in Foreigners,"** as perfect types of the English familiar essay. But all of Lowell's essays are discursive and familiar. They are to be measured, not by the standards of modern French criticism—which is admittedly more deft, more delicate, more logical than ours—but by the unchartered freedom which the English-speaking races have desired in their conversations about old authors for three hundred years. . . . Lowell, like the rest of us, is to be tested by what he had, not by what he lacked. (pp. 145-46)

> *Bliss Perry, "James Russell Lowell," in his* The Praise of Folly and Other Papers *(originally an address delivered at the Cambridge Historical Society on February 22, 1919; copyright 1923 by Bliss Perry; copyright renewed 1950 by Bliss Perry; reprinted by permission of Houghton Mifflin Company), Houghton, 1923 (and reprinted by Kennikat Press, Inc., 1964), pp. 130-50.*

JENNETTE TANDY (essay date 1925)

[James Russell Lowell produced in Hosea Biglow of the *Biglow Papers*] a satiric figure which, however well it satisfied his own generation, is sixty years later almost forgotten. For a pitfall awaits every political satirist. The more minutely he caricatures the affairs of his own day, the more obscure and uninteresting he will appear to those that follow. If he assumes whole-heartedly the party animosity of his time, he will by later critics be accused of bigotry. Lowell ran the risk, and suffers from these imputations. Though his political message seems at times ungenerous and hard, his Yankee portraits are always masterly, and his pictures of office-seekers and petty politicians will live as long as democracy. (pp. 43-4)

Of all the hundred Yankee wanderers [in American Literature] from Brother Jonathan down, [Lowell's Birdofredum Sawin] is the most adventurous and the most amusing. Though cut on a time-frayed pattern, the incidents of his argonautic voyage are without precedent. As a psychological study he is unique. There is consistency in the rascal's adaptation of principle to expediency, and the truth of mockery in his mixed fate of good and bad fortune. . . . If Lowell intended B. S. in the beginning for a clown, the buffoon soon developed a strong individuality. After a blow of the slapstick he always tumbles to his feet, with a bow. He is as resourceful as he is ingenious in self-excuse. Above all he stands as the first, best, and only study of the development of the Yankee rascal. (pp. 57-8)

Lowell might be said to have divided himself into compartments. In the *Biglow Papers* we see nothing of the man of letters, the diplomat, the graceful verse-writer. The poems and the literary essays, the political articles give no hint of the creator of Hosea and Birdofredum. (p. 63)

In comparison with Whittier and Longfellow and Hawthorne and Emerson as interpreters of New England life and tradition, [Lowell] the comic satirist looms large. Though he skims over the depths and subtleties of the Puritan heritage, he avoids also the shallows of Mid-Victorian sentimentalism. And he cuts deeper than any other into the gnarled fibers of the cross-grained Yankee. Hosea, Birdofredum, John P. Robinson, the Pious Editor, the Candidate, are a Hogarthian company. Lowell's range and penetration in satirical portraiture are unsurpassed in America.

As a piece of sustained irony the *Biglow Papers* has escaped the careful study of present-day critics. We have no other satirist at once so witty and so racy. Still, one would hardly venture to accord him the unqualified praises of Thomas Hughes:

> Greece had her Aristophanes; Rome her Juvenal; Spain has had her Cervantes; France her Rabelais, her Molière, her Voltaire; Germany her Jean Paul, her Heine; England her Swift, her Thackeray; and America has her Lowell.

No, on the whole, Mr. Lowell is a little lower than these angels. (pp. 63-4)

> *Jennette Tandy, "The Biglow Papers," in her* Crackerbox Philosophers in American Humor and Satire *(reprinted by permission of the publisher), Columbia University Press, 1925 (and reprinted by Kennikat Press, Inc., 1964), pp. 43-64.*

NORMAN FOERSTER (essay date 1928)

In no other American of the nineteenth century has the critical spirit manifested itself so comprehensively as in James Russell Lowell. Despite the fact that he leaves an impression of comparative superficiality and futility—shortcomings to which we are keenly sensitive today, perhaps because they are our own—he must still be regarded as our most distinguished literary critic. While there is far more of original vigor in both Poe and Emerson, he was free of the special purposes that limited their achievement as critics. The bulk of Poe's work was journalism, book-reviewing, ephemeral commentary on the books of the day; Emerson, at the other extreme, characteristically chose for his literary essays themes that are timeless; Lowell, however, attempted rounded portraits and estimates of so many authors of the past that he virtually wrote a critical history of literature from Dante to his own age. . . . Poe and Emerson were at their best in critical theory; Lowell, wanting their turn for speculation, excelled in practice. Poe and Emerson have certain aesthetic doctrines associated with their names; but the name of Lowell suggests nothing of the kind, suggests, rather, gusto and flashes of insight, the free play of feeling and intelligence.

From what has just been said—that aesthetic doctrines are so inconspicuous in Lowell, and that he excelled in practice rather than theory—it might reasonably be inferred that he was an impressionist. . . . In substantiation of this inference, it might be urged that we read his literary essays much as we read his charming letters—for their personal qualities—and that if we subtracted these personal qualities the essays would dissolve into nothingness, while in the case of Poe and Emerson the skeleton of ideas would remain. At a glance, one has reason to say of Lowell: his criteria are negligible, the man is all, he was an impressionist. (pp. ci-cii)

In the present instance, the important facts are twofold. In the first place is the obvious fact that the impressionist is not a critic without criteria, but a critic who refuses to delimit his criteria by deliberate formulation and application. To call Lowell an impressionist is not to dispose of his criteria. In the second place, a thorough scrutiny of Lowell's criticism would show that his criteria, far from being negligible, are really distinct and impressive. It could probably be demonstrated, indeed, that his weakness was the very reverse of that which is commonly alleged; that, instead of having insignificant criteria and effective personal qualities, he possessed a set of controlling ideas that wanted only the impetus of great personal qualities to make them in the highest degree significant and useful. (p. cii)

Intellectually indolent, Lowell was attracted to impressionism. Although in his best years he appealed to standards, he was always, late and early, something of an impressionist. (p. civ)

[Lowell] remained in large measure the discoverer, the adventurer in the realms of gold, full of zest and waywardness, recording impressions on senses not a little remarkable for ductility. As an impressionist of the romantic and not of our realistic age, he was concerned with the culling of beauties. "I string together a few at random," he says, a few being seventeen, but "I shall excuse myself from giving any instances" of the author's faults. Instead of regarding quotations as a documentation and illumination of purposeful discourse, he tended to look upon himself as a kind of showman, displaying this, that, and the other, with comments expressing his own pleasure in the objects. (p. cv)

[Lowell's comprehensive vision of the task of the critic] involves sensitiveness to impressions, historical understanding, and an aesthetic-ethical judgment. Upon these he bases his placement of the great authors—a habit of his more naïve than dogmatic—ranking Homer, Æschylus, Dante, and Shakespeare as the four supreme poets, and Wordsworth as "fifth in the succession of the great English Poets." Of Donne he said that he "wrote more profound verses than any other English poet save one only"—not telling us whom he meant by the one. It must be admitted that Lowell was a little childish in his love of superlatives. But it must also be admitted (to apply a superlative to Lowell himself) that beneath all his surface caprices lies a literary creed, aesthetic and moral, that is the most representative of man's artistic experience through the ages yet attained in America. (pp. cxiii-cxiv)

The unifying principle in the artistic and literary creed of Lowell lies in his attempt to use the best ideas offered by the two great critical traditions, the classic and the romantic. (p. cxiv)

To the Greeks Lowell was indebted for the principles or qualities that constantly guided his aesthetic criticism: *unity, design, proportion, clearness, economy, power, control, repose, sanity, impersonality,* all of which are involved in the conception of self-subsistent form. Among nineteenth-century English critics we think of Matthew Arnold as almost solitary in urging impressively the claims of form as understood by the Greeks; but Lowell was a more frequent champion, who lacked impressiveness largely because his doctrine on this subject as on all subjects was set forth somewhat in the manner of *obiter dicta,* which is to say that he himself was deplorably wanting in that sense of design that he includes among his immutable principles. (p. cxvi)

[But form] is Lowell's primary criterion of a work of art, sometimes conceived in its structural effect, sometimes in its organic cause. So far he may be termed an Aristotelian, an exponent of the "Poetics" and of romantic critical theory that amplified Aristotle's conception of a work of art as an organism. We may next observe that he again follows Aristotle in requiring not merely organic form but *ideal* form, "that sense of ideal form which made the Greeks masters in art to all succeeding generations." (p. cxix)

From romantic theorists, Coleridge most of all, Lowell derived a theory of the imagination that runs everywhere through his writings. (p. cxxii)

[Imagination] is for Lowell the main instrument in the attainment of understanding of life, and of the happiness that springs from understanding. It was consequently natural for him to tend to measure a work of art by the vitality of its ethical or spiritual insight. This would determine its quality of beauty, and quality, he everywhere implies, is the *final* and highest consideration. (p. cxxvi)

If it is necessary to relate to some tradition Lowell's view of the end of literature, let us refrain from the facile and false assumption that he was a "Puritan" (as was Milton for that matter) and instead label him an "Aristotelian." In a dozen passages he protests, as outspokenly as Poe, against the heresy of the didactic involved in the deliberate teaching of morals through literature—it is gravel in strawberries and cream. The primary object in tragedy, for example, "is not to inculcate a formal moral"; and yet the moral is there, for, "representing life, it teaches, like life, by indirection." (p. cxxxi)

A poet, [Lowell] says, must not be judged historically, relatively to his age; but absolutely, according to the artistic qualities of his work and according to the man's genius and his vision. "We may reckon up pretty exactly," says Lowell, "a man's advantages and defects as an artist; these he has in common with others, and they are to be measured by a recognized standard." The quantity of beauty, we might say, can be measured with fair accuracy. But the quality eludes our makeshift instruments. . . . (p. cxxxii)

If it were possible for us to lay aside our memory of the personality of Lowell and of the weaknesses of his essays, and to concentrate our minds solely upon [his] system of ideas . . . , we should certainly be drawn to the conclusion that we have here the sanest and most comprehensive conception of literature formed in America prior to the twentieth century. Laying aside also our twentieth-century predilections (if we have them) for various limited kinds of art denominated realistic, we are bound to admit the impressiveness of a creed that offers justification, at one and the same time, for Æschylus, for Aristophanes, for the "Arabian Nights," for Dante, for Chaucer, for Cervantes, for Shakespeare, for Milton, and for Wordsworth. As Aristotle based his "Poetics" upon the attainment of the writers before his day, so did Lowell seek his principles in the achievement of an immensely rich past. (p. cxxxvii)

As the leading humanist of the renaissance of New England, [Lowell] made it his twofold task to belittle the specious attractions of the recent moderns, and to establish the high claims of those halfway moderns or halfway ancients, from Dante to Milton, whom the American public had not rightly valued. From the romanticism that resounded about him in his early manhood, he derived chiefly a part of his terminology, notably the term "imagination," which he used with romantic frequency and unromantic caution. The result of his entire procedure (doubtless in the main an unconscious one) was a conception of literature that one would find it perilous to assail unless with the weapons of a skepticism that logically destroys itself along with everything else. Lowell's creed is almost the unwritten constitution of the republic of letters.

Why is it, then, as we acknowledged at the beginning, that the critical essays of Lowell leave an impression of comparative superficiality and futility? The answer is inescapable: it is not his creed that is weak, but the man himself. Lowell is a capital instance of the fact that it is possible to think both rightly and feebly, just as it is possible to think both wrongly and energetically. (p. cxxxviii)

Poet, scholar, teacher, critic, essayist, editor, abolitionist, patriot, ambassador to the Old World; possessing an extraordinary assortment of qualities—sensuousness, emotionality, imagination and fancy, facility of expression, moral earnestness, common sense and logic, wit and humor—Lowell stood forth among his contemporaries because of his accomplished versatility rather than because of high attainment. Once or twice, as in the **"Biglow Papers"** and the Harvard **"Commemoration Ode,"** he was able to fuse most of his powers in adequate expression, but the rest of the time he was a man of parts, a man of shreds. Capable of growth—more capable than Poe or even Emerson—he was unhappily incapable of self-mastery, no part of his nature being strong enough to force the rest into submission. Nor did he find help in the age in which he lived, which suffered his own difficulties writ large. (p. cxxxix)

> *Norman Foerster, "Lowell As Critic," in his* American Criticism: A Study in Literary Theory from Poe to the Present *(copyright 1928 by Norman Foerster; copyright © renewed 1956 by Norman Foerster; reprinted by permission of Houghton Mifflin Company), Houghton Mifflin, 1928 (and reprinted in* James Russell Lowell: Representative Selections *by James Russell Lowell, edited by Harry Hayden Clark, American Book Co., 1947, pp. c-cxxxix).*

GRANVILLE HICKS (essay date 1935)

As a poet [Lowell] never conquered the diffuse romanticism that had marred his juvenilia; rather, he became increasingly derivative, and his major efforts, the various commemorative odes, are, despite the nobility of mood and the dignity of expression, palpably without either depth of thought or freshness of language. As a critic he was erudite, perhaps beyond all other American critics, and thoroughly familiar with the greatest writers of western culture. Nor was the range of his criticism narrow: he could speak as historian or philologist; he could write with the gusto of an epicure or assume the manner of a judge. But the incoherence of his critical studies, his preference for a casual attack in the manner of the informal essay, points straight to the deep-seated indolence of mind that prevented him from molding out of his insight and information a solid and consistent theory of literature. Principles he had in abundance, but, like all borrowed principles, they were a poor substitute for that organic body of fundamental ideas that the great critic cultivates, with the aid of his imagination, out of the soil of study and experience.

To the development of American literature he contributed almost nothing, except insofar as he may have furthered a thoughtful reading of the European masters. In addition to two brief and not particularly valuable papers on the national literature, one written at the beginning and the other at the end of his life, he left, if we exclude casual reviews and the tren-

chant but largely personal comments in *A Fable for Critics,* few discussions of American writers. He did write on Emerson and Thoreau, praising the former for his spirit without analyzing his work, and attacking the latter in such a way as to betray a complete lack of understanding. The younger writers he welcomed were the perpetuators of the genteel tradition he came more and more to embody—Howells the essayist, Stedman, Aldrich, and Gilder—whereas to Whitman he was utterly indifferent, taking the trouble only to say, on the strength of what Norton had told him about *Leaves of Grass,* that such things wouldn't do. In short he made not the slightest effort to understand the peculiar conditions under which American writers were working, and did nothing, either by example or counsel, to help the men who were trying to understand them. Even to Howells, whose work he praised, he made it clear that he liked the novels because he liked the man, and that ordinarily he preferred romance to realism. (pp. 16-17)

It is clear that we must dismiss Lowell and all that he stands for from any just account of the forces that were making for the development of American literature. . . . (pp. 20-1)

> *Granville Hicks, "Heritage," in his* The Great Tradition: An Interpretation of American Literature since the Civil War *(copyright © 1933, 1935 by Macmillan Publishing Co., Inc.; originally published in 1933 by The Macmillan Company, New York; new material in the revised edition copyright © 1969 by Granville Hicks; reprinted by permission of Russell & Volkening, Inc., as agent for the author), revised edition, Macmillan, 1935, Quadrangle Books, 1969, pp. 1-31.**

H. L. MENCKEN (essay date 1945)

The first masterpiece of [a genuinely colloquial and national style of writing] was Lowell's **"The Biglow Papers."** . . . Lowell not only attempted to depict with some care the peculiar temperament and point of view of the rustic New Englander; he also made an extremely successful effort to report Yankee speech. His brief prefatory treatise on its peculiarities of pronunciation, though it included a few observations that had been made long before him by Witherspoon, was the first to deal with the subject with any approach to comprehensiveness, and in his introduction to Series II he expanded this preliminary note to a long and interesting essay, with a glossary of nearly 200 terms. (pp. 129-30)

Unhappily, Lowell labored under the delusion that he had sufficiently excused the existence of any given Americanism when he had proved that it was old English, and so a large part of his essay was given over to that popular but vain exercise. But despite his folly in this respect and his timorousness in other directions [In a footnote Mencken states: "He permitted himself, for example, to denounce slang on the ground that it 'is always vulgar,' and he thought it worthwhile to defend Hosea Biglow at some length against the idiotic change of 'speaking of sacred things familiarly.'"] he did a great service to the common tongue of the country, and must be numbered among its true friends. His writing in his own person, however, showed but little sign of it: he gradually developed a very effective prose style, but it did not differ materially from that of his New England contemporaries. The business of introducing the American language to good literary society was reserved for Clemens. . . . (pp. 130-31)

> *H. L. Mencken, "The Views of Writing Men," in his* The American Language: Supplement I *(copy-*

right 1945 by Alfred A. Knopf, Inc.; copyright renewed © 1972 by the Estate of the author; reprinted
by permission of Alfred A. Knopf, Inc.), Knopf, 1945,
pp. 114-35.*

WILLIAM SMITH CLARK II   (essay date 1948)

Lowell's serious poetry in general contains too many echoes
of patterns and styles from classic English poesy to permit the
authentic note of originality. More often than not his lyrics
lack, as Emerson once [remarked in his *Journals*], "the uncontrollable interior impulse . . . which is felt in the pervading
tone, rather than in brilliant parts or lines; as if the sound of
a bell, or a certain cadence expressed in a low whistle or
booming, or humming, to which the poet first timed his step,
as he looked at the sunset, or thought, was the incipient form
of the piece, and was regnant through the whole." Yet he
chose to labor most in the field of the formal lyric, because it
was surrounded with a lofty tradition. (p. xxxiii)

[Lowell] made the mistake of persisting in over-lofty Parnassian dreams which distracted him from the essential originality
of his own muse. His forte in verse had been clearly revealed
before his thirtieth year in *A Fable for Critics* and *The Biglow
Papers, First Series*. These works display nothing of the stilted
teaching and bookish language so prevalent in his serious poems
of that period. The lighter, more informal tone which their
character permitted freed Lowell's tongue from all imitative
inhibitions. Here he spoke with a wit and a satiric deftness of
greater potency than that achieved by any other American poet
of the nineteenth century. (p. xxxv)

[Lowell] in a second series of *Biglow Papers* did exploit the
vein of homely Yankee humor somewhat further. To the political material he added descriptive lyrical touches, the choicest of which appear in *Sunthin' in the Pastoral Line*. . . . [This
poem] is Lowell's masterpiece in his unique genre of poetry.
It is an achievement of considerable artistry, for, despite the
provincialism of its style, it portrays with superb vitality those
elements in a local speech, environment, and morality which
provoke universal appreciation. (p. xxxvi)

[Lowell] followed out the dramatic bent visible in *Sunthin' in
the Pastoral Line* and others of *The Biglow Papers* by composing
in formal English verse a full-fledged narrative of Yankee life
and character, *Fitz Adam's Story*. Though much of the Biglow
quality lurks in its lines, the piece is a decidedly more ambitious
effort in poetic art. The tale of Deacon Bitters, while it is
copiously decorated with pungent observations of the New
England locale, moves forward with tension sustained, and
reaches a perfect dramatic climax. Sly whimsy colors the depiction of both characters and setting. . . . Fitz Adam's description of October weather and of its effect on himself finds
Lowell startlingly close to that quiet tone of elfish irony so
characteristic of a later member of the New England poetic
fraternity, Robert Frost:

> Well, there I lingered all October through,
> In that sweet atmosphere of hazy blue,
> So leisurely, so soothing, so forgiving,
> That sometimes makes New England fit for living.
> I watched the landscape, erst so granite glum,
> Bloom like the south side of a ripening plum. . . .

The piquancy of this New England flavor and the excellence
of the structural design combine to place *Fitz Adam's Story*
among the best of Lowell's poetic creations.

Its superior merit offers decisive evidence that Lowell's muse
was most happily inspired when under the spell of Yankee
background. The homespun beauty and humor of rural New
England provided the proper outlet for that raciness of imagination and language which constituted his choicest gift. Then,
as at no other time, his singing took on a notable individuality
and revealed the honorable position which is his in the great
choir of the poets. The rightful place of Lowell the poet will
always be as a seer of perhaps the purest Yankee spirit produced
by New England. (pp. xxxvii-xxxviii)

Throughout the prose writings of Lowell a conservatism, at
once vigorous and humane, expresses itself. Lowell cultivated,
more than any other of the critic's faculties, the capacity to
saturate one's self with age-ripened feeling and thought.
(p. xxxviii)

Lowell grew up with an enthusiasm for the cultural heritage
of the Old World, but he early perceived that his countrymen
in general lacked a feeling of allegiance to any such common
body of cultural ideals as the nations of the Old World possessed. This need in American society for the stabilizing force
of traditions caused him, both as a man of letters and as a
public speaker, to urge upon his fellow citizens the value of
closer acquaintance with their English and European inheritance. . . . (p. xxxix)

Lowell's conviction was so intense that he took pains to warn
against an American overestimate of the creative values to be
derived from "the flavor of the climate," and the "gift of the
sun peculiar to the region." Because he foresaw the artistic
dangers, he gave rather guarded approval to the idea that, in
the development of American writing, "the novel aspects of
life under our novel conditions may give some freshness of
color to our literature." Such deliberately untraditional endeavor as Walt Whitman's *Leaves of Grass* at once aroused
his hostility. (pp. xl-xli)

Lowell did not hesitate to condemn [Whitman's] poetry as
"downright animality." He also castigated the young English
poet Algernon Swinburne for immorality. (p. xlii)

Lowell's voice in his critical pieces is not always, of course,
enchanting. The music sometimes dies away, and the spell is
broken by the prosaic tones of pedantic argument or historical
digression. At intervals there intrudes also a superabundance
of quotation. The form then betrays the commentator rather
than the disciplined formal essayist. His procedure, he admitted, was often rather discursive. He liked to browse along the
path and allow both his mind and imagination to lead him
where they so desired. It is therefore surprising that he did not
more copiously express himself in the personal essay. Therein
he could range with only the continuing thread of experience
to preserve as it twists around the self. Such few informal
compositions as Lowell did undertake—for example, *At Sea*
or *Cambridge Thirty Years Ago*—allow him to chat engagingly
within the wide orbit of a reminiscent topic, and to interlard
his reminiscences with acute observations of human destiny.
But perhaps he appears to even better advantage in the loosest
of his essay forms, the journal, for here he is able to build in
mosaic pattern. Day by day, bits of changing color and varying
substance are added in accordance with the imaginative fortunes of the moment. In *A Moosehead Journal* Lowell's whimsical mind seizes delightfully upon a tessellated literary structure in which it can depict a rich medley of scenes from the
Maine backcountry. There is dramatic interplay of Yankee
humor and sensuous fancy, of deft characterizations in dialogue

and sharp pictures of setting. And constantly these variegated tones and materials are blended into a pleasing mosaic harmony of ''a little nature, a little human nature, and a great deal of I.'' Nowhere does Lowell show more versatility as a prose writer and as a critic of humanity than in this lively travelogue.

It is, however, in his letters that the genius of Lowell finds perhaps its ideal medium. In personal correspondence the utmost liberty may be granted to the habit of scintillating discursiveness—a habit preëminently characteristic of Lowell, who doted on all the allurements and provocations concealed in the coverts of language. Style, . . . rather than Form, becomes the essential artistic element in letter-writing. Lowell's was a genius which best precipitated itself in perfect, if detached and unrelated, crystals, flashing back the light of our common day tinged with the diviner hue of his own recording powers. His epistolary comment reveals an energetic and richly stored mind seething with multitudinous associations. . . . The gracious wisdom and the tonic style should secure for Lowell's letters a prominent place in American literature. (pp. xliv-xlvi)

> *William Smith Clark II, in his introduction to* Lowell: Essays, Poems, and Letters, *edited by William Smith Clark II (reprinted by permission of The Bobbs-Merrill Co., Inc.), The Odyssey Press, 1948, pp. xv-xlix.*

RICHARD H. FOGLE   (essay date 1952)

Many men, including himself, have denied to James Russell Lowell any firm central identity. Professor Foerster [see excerpt above] and Professor Clark [see additional bibliography], on the other hand, have vigorously defended his claims to centrality. Where lies the truth? It shifts, perhaps, according to one's views on the location of the center. In Lowell it is less within himself, and more outside himself in the main stream of European and American culture. He has the chameleon quality which is proper to an academic and a professional critic, the shape-changing sensitivity and the caution which faithfully register the work as it is, within a broad context of its cultural surroundings. The conservatism for which Lowell has been taxed, his inhospitality to new writers, has perhaps two causes, which are at bottom one. He comes at the end of a great tradition, which at the last failed in energy to revitalize itself; and there really was much in the new generations which Lowell did well to reject.

Lowell is in the organic tradition of Herder, Goethe, and Coleridge in seeking the life principle of a man or work intrinsically, within themselves. His early criticism of Emerson's poetry in *A Fable for Critics* has almost all of the organicist ideas. . . . [According to this early criticism, a poem] should be an organic expression of the soul (''Some poems have welled / From those rare depths of soul. . . .''). It is to be judged from within, through the critic's intuition of its vital impulse. Consequently the problem of genre is only superficial at most (''A grassblade's no easier to make than an oak''), and the old neoclassical ranking by kinds no longer has validity. Instead the criterion is the genuineness of the creative urge (the organic life of the work). If form and content are truly one, this organic unity will be manifested in unity of tone, which is the outward evidence of the inner life (''The something pervading, uniting the whole''). A genuinely organic work must be judged as a whole (''Now it is not one thing nor another alone / Makes a poem''), since its parts are organically inseparable; insofar as any part of it can be without harm abstracted, so far the work is imperfect. Finally, the work should be not the sum of its

parts (mechanical unity by arrangement or aggregation), but more than the sum of its parts (organic unity by fusion).

> Roots, wood, bark, and leaves singly perfect may be,
> But, clapt hodge-podge together, they don't make a tree.

Lowell's criticism is eclectic, but organicist in its very eclecticism, since its method is determined by the requirements of his subject. He shows the organicist willingness to sympathize, to assimilate, to absorb before he passes judgment. And his judgments generally stand up well. His essay on Keats, for example, written in 1854, contains in the germ all that modern scholarship has fathomed of Keats's identity, his unique fusion of experience and thought, his sensuous power and his idealism. Although less well-known, his essay is better than Arnold's on Keats. The organicist Lowell, unlike the judicial Arnold, is not led astray by his own social and moral prejudices.

His criticism is most completely organic when it deals with established, unshakeable masters. In treating of Dante and Shakespeare he is expounding on the foundation of the organic principle of life and unity, the presence of which he is able to assume. (pp. 108-09)

> *Richard H. Fogle, ''Organic Form in American Criticism: 1840-1870'' (originally a paper read at the annual meeting of the American Literature Group of the Modern Language Association in December, 1952), in* The Development of American Literary Criticism, *edited by Floyd Stovall (copyright, 1955, by The University of North Carolina Press), University of North Carolina Press, 1955, pp. 75-112.**

ROY HARVEY PEARCE   (essay date 1961)

[In his lecture,] **''The Function of the Poet,''** James Russell Lowell granted that his age was ''materialistic,'' an age of ''common sense.'' But, he argued, in the modern world materialism and common sense were themselves poetic, having given us in railroads ''the shoes of swiftness,'' in ''patent pills'' our own ''Aladdin's lamp,'' etc. He concluded that ''the office of the poet seems to be reversed, and he must give back these miracles of the understanding to poetry again, and find out what there is imaginative in steam and iron and telegraph-wires.'' And later: . . . ''We are in our heroic age, still face to face with the shaggy forces of unsubdued Nature, and we have our Theseuses and Perseuses, though they may be named Israel Putnam and Daniel Boone. It is nothing against us that we are a commercial people. . . . The lives of the great poets teach us that they were the men of their generation who felt most deeply the meaning of the present.'' Like the Whitman of the 1855 Preface, Lowell had learned the lesson of Emerson's ''The Poet'' —almost.

True enough, in his later life Lowell, chameleon-like figure that he was, somewhat muted his call for an American poetry—as earlier, for a time bedazzled by transcendentalism, he had insisted that a genuine poetry would not be sullied by commercialism. The important point is that he knew well what the issues were and that his way of resolving them was precisely the reverse of that of great poets of his age: instead of hoping to conceive railroads, patent pills, etc. in the image of the men, the central man, who used them, to conceive of men as they might be themselves, fully ''spiritual,'' in spite of their material achievements. He is therefore in the end obliged to shrink back from the Emersonian implications of the passage just quoted.

He was not at all disturbed by the problem of the anti-poetic. For he wanted to save man *from,* not *in,* his world. "The poet," he said in this lecture, "is he who can best see and best say what is ideal—what belongs to the world of soul and of beauty." Later: "Every man is conscious that he leads two lives, the one trivial and ordinary, the other sacred and recluse; the one which he carries to the dinner-table and to his daily work, which grows old with his body and dies with it, the other that which is made up of the few inspiring moments of his higher aspiration and attainment. . . ." Lowell wanted then, instead of a poetry which charges day-to-day life with the values it may discover, a poetry which makes day-to-day life bearable, because it promises retreat and surcease.

The problem for the poet who would reach the great audience was to attain a poetic level just a little high for those whose lives were too much defined by the day-to-day, and yet not too high, not beyond their reach. For Lowell, solution of this problem meant finally a decision that all great poetry actually did exist at this level. Or so he argues in his numerous essays in criticism and his almost as numerous essays on poetry and culture in general.

In his poems (from full-dress performances like *A Fable for Critics* to small pieces like the sonnet **"To the Spirit of Keats"**) Lowell tends to understand all poets in the light of his concern to make of poetry a means of withdrawing, if only temporarily, from the busyness of day-to-day life. (His political poems are perhaps a partial exception here; but even they are not exactly *engagé*—since it is not James Russell Lowell but a crackerbarrel New Englander who is found the right sort to exhort Americans into political action.) . . . [Lowell is dissatisfied] with his crackerbarrel *persona.* Still it is in his preaching poems, exercises in rhetoric wherein he confronts his readers with a problem which must be argued through, that he does his best work. With his commitment to a poetry somehow beyond (but not too far beyond) preachment and "rational" analysis, he steadily produced poems which are vague, sentimental, acutely tender—generating something even less than metaphysical pathos. (pp. 214-16)

[Lowell,] with his frigid sonnets on love and great spiritual issues, with—to recall two celebrated examples—his **"Rhoecus"** and his *Vision of Sir Launfal,* could never quite touch upon the realities of the day-to-day. He had not even Bryant's "sublime" power or Longfellow's essential homeliness, or the metrical dexterity of either of them. (pp. 216-17)

It is as the poet of *The Biglow Papers* and the later odes that Lowell assumes his proper stature. . . . Yet [these] poems are essentially documents—splendid documents, but still documents—and their proper history could be told only in a history of American oratory and political debate. Lowell is at his best when he puts aside problems of "poesy."

So too with the later odes. Anticipated by his earlier political poems, they serve to assuage their readers' well-founded doubts as to the meaningfulness of the terrible destruction and sacrifice which have necessarily been part of the American idea of progress. Here Lowell is altogether the poet as patriarch; spokesman for his community as a whole, rather than those who, as individuals, make it up. And this is only proper; for the occasions of the odes are communal, in which men want to know that what they suffer they suffer in common and for a common cause. Ironically, Lowell's tendency to preachment, when fully realized, makes him most able to fulfill his ideal as a poet. Thus the end of the 1865 Harvard **"Commemoration Ode"** is

in its own way a triumph: for the speaker, who has raised the members of his audience phoenix-like out of the ashes of their despair to a sense of their mutual dedication; for the audience, which has again discovered a common cause and so can, as audience, continue to live with itself. . . . The slow movement here, the loose use of figurative language . . . , the reinforcing power of the rhymes, the argument conducted at the level of the hortatory, not the dialectical—all such effects make for a wholly "public" poetry and pull the reader, or auditor, into that public. (pp. 217-18)

[In the poem **"An Incident in a Railroad Car"**] Lowell tells of hearing Burns being read to enthralled "men rough and rude." He meditates at some length the problem of writing poems for such an audience and concludes: . . .

> To write some earnest verse or line,
>   Which, seeking not the praise of art,
> Shall make a clearer faith and manhood shine
>   In the untutored heart.
>
> He who doth this, in verse or prose,
>   May be forgotten in his day,
> But surely shall be crowned at last with those
>   Who live and speak for aye.

The closest that Lowell could get to this sort of poem was the sixth of the second series of *Biglow Papers*, **"Sunthin' in the Pastoral Line"**. . . . Even the epic simile could be domesticated when Lowell spoke through the *persona* of just the sort of man to whom Burns was read on that railroad car. Moreover, only here, in a passage of natural description, could he get down to cases; beside this, the June day of *The Vision of Sir Launfal* fades into deserved nothingness. This poem can be read as much in spite of its politics as because of them. . . . In *this* Hosea the created speaker takes over; or rather, the scene in which he has his being takes over. Nonetheless, his is a provincial dream-vision. So too in the *Atlantic Monthly* letter . . . and **"The Courtin'"**—where Lowell does almost as well as he does in **"Sunthin' in the Pastoral Line."** Only in the natural world might the would-be people's poet find the material which he could freely treat in a wholly evocative way.

Yet shortly before he wrote **"Sunthin' in the Pastoral Line,"** Lowell declared in his famous exasperated essay on Thoreau: "I look upon a great deal of the modern sentimentalism about Nature as a mark of disease. It is one more symptom of the general liver-complaint. To a man of wholesome constitution the wilderness is well enough for a mood or a vacation, but not for a habit of life." Ironically enough, only in a common man's "sentimentalism about Nature" might Lowell find a world in which a semblance of objectivity could be assumed. This was not enough. The pressures of day-to-day practicality, the reality and earnestness of life, demanded even of the common man that he do no more than vacation in such a world. Otherwise he would cut himself off from the real world. Lowell wanted to make poems which would help his great audience know that real world for what it was. He came to conceive of poetry as the product of neither the "natural" nor the "real" world, but of an "ideal" world. The ideal was there to give direction and coherence to men living in the real world and save them from their temptation to take seriously the natural world. The poet came to be not seer but schoolteacher; read not on railroad cars, but in schoolrooms; not by coarse men, but by well-scrubbed children and their anxious parents. (pp. 218-20)

Roy Harvey Pearce, "American Renaissance: The Poet and the People," in his The Continuity of American Poetry *(copyright © 1961 by Princeton University Press; reprinted by permission of Princeton University Press), Princeton University Press, 1961, pp. 192-252.**

THOMAS WORTHAM (essay date 1977)

[Hosea Biglow] belongs to, just as he helped create, the tradition of New England rustic or Down East humor; but in Lowell this Yankee type is primarily a voice, a point of view, a center of consciousness: a fine commentator but a poor actor.

[Birdofredum Sawin], on the other hand, provided rich possibilities both for humor and irony. He is a true picaro; his responses to and reflections on his adventures in Mexico and the South and his unfortunate career in politics portray his character more fully than Lowell managed to achieve with either Wilbur or Hosea. He is a supporting actor who nearly steals the show. For all this, he is nonetheless a type, what Howells would later call the Puritan rebel. But he is a human type; Birdofredum never becomes a monster, either of drollery or of wickedness. The men he admires—Cushing, Taylor, the petty politicians surrounding them—seem monstrous, however, largely because we have seen sympathetically, and with no slight regret, the flaws in a pathetic fellow who believes he can emulate their glory. A man who believes the lies by which he and his society live is too common to be despised. Increase D. O'Phace is a hypocrite, Birdofredum merely a fool. (pp. xxiv-xxv)

[It] is not in characterization, though it has been generally praised, that the greatest strength of *The Biglow Papers* lies. Fine characterization is rarely remarkable in humorous satire; the chance for a hit, for humor, understandably diverts the author from anything so literary as consistency of character. What holds *The Biglow Papers* together, what makes it a book, are irony and its form, unique both in conception and execution. From its beginning in deft parodies of contemporary literary notices to its outrageous "Index," *The Biglow Papers* is a masterpiece of sustained irony, the irony of an earnest young man who sees the good sense of truth and justice, but realizes the blindness of those about him. It is irony that permits much humor, because the ironist believes that conflicts between the fact and the ideal may be resolved. It is irony not yet directed against the self, though there are times—for instance, Wilbur's last paragraph in the last paper—when this final irony is strongly suggested: where the fun is turned on one's self, where the limits of society are glimpsed as limits—perhaps unchangeable—of that self. (pp. xxvi-xxvii)

> *Thomas Wortham, in his introduction to his* James Russell Lowell's "The Biglow Papers": A Critical Edition *(copyright © 1977 by Northern Illinois University Press), Northern Illinois University Press, 1977, p. ix-xxxiv.*

ADDITIONAL BIBLIOGRAPHY

Clark, Harry Hayden. "Lowell's Criticism of Romantic Literature." *PMLA XL* (March 1926): 209-28.
> Refutes numerous negative appraisals of Lowell's critical ability. Clark argues that although Lowell's philosophy may lack consistency, his critical judgement was sound and his vision keen.

Duberman, Martin. *James Russell Lowell.* Boston: Houghton Mifflin, 1966, 516 p.
> A thorough critical biography.

Greenslet, Ferris. *James Russell Lowell: His Life and Work.* Boston and New York: Houghton Mifflin Co., 1905, 309 p.
> Biography including copious excerpts from Lowell's correspondence and minimal critical commentary.

Howard, Leon. *Victorian Knight-Errant: A Study of the Early Literary Career of James Russell Lowell.* Berkeley and Los Angeles: University of California Press, 1952, 388 p.
> Examines why Lowell failed to live up to the promise of his early poetry.

Howells, W. D. "Studies of Lowell." In his *Literary Friends and Acquaintance : A Personal Retrospect of American Authorship,* pp. 212-50. New York and London: Harper & Brothers Publishers, 1900.
> Reminiscences of Lowell in Europe and in Cambridge.

[James, Henry]. "Men and Letters: Conversations with Mr Lowell." *Atlantic Monthly* 79, No. 471 (January 1897): 123-30.
> Memoir of Lowell in London, painting him as something of a Judaeophobe.

Mott, Wesley. "Thoreau and Lowell on 'Vacation': *The Maine Woods* and 'A Moosehead Journal'." *Thoreau Journal Quarterly* X, No. 3 (1978): 14-24.*
> Comparison of separate accounts by Lowell and Thoreau of trips through Maine. Mott highlights similarities in tone, theme, and style, and discusses these analogies in light of Lowell's later critical attacks on Thoreau.

Reilly, Joseph J. *James Russell Lowell as a Critic.* New York & London: G. P. Putnam's Sons, 1915, 228 p.
> Detailed examination of Lowell's criticism. Reilly concludes that Lowell is merely an impressionist, yet, compared with his contemporaries, an outstanding nineteenth-century American critic.

Voss, Arthur. "Background of Satire in *The Biglow Papers.*" *The New England Quarterly* XXIII, No. 1 (March 1950): 47-64.
> Description of political figures and events—connected mainly with slavery and the Mexican War—which inspired Lowell's *The Biglow Papers.*

Wurfl, George. *Lowell's Debt to Goethe: A Study of Literary Influence.* The Pennsylvania State College Studies, Vol. 1, No. 2. State College, Pa.: The Pennsylvania State College, 1936, 89 p.*
> Closely detailed document of Goethe's influence on Lowell's critical method.

James Kirke Paulding

1778-1860

(Also wrote under the pseudonym of Launcelot Langstaff and Hector Bull-Us) American novelist, dramatist, poet, historian, and editor.

Paulding was born during the Revolutionary War in Putnam County, New York. The hostilities between England and America made a deep impression on him, and throughout his life he produced works which rejected the influence of the British and proclaimed his fervent nationalism.

At the age of eighteen while working at a public office, Paulding met Washington Irving and his brother William. This association stimulated Paulding's literary interests, and they, along with several others, formed "The Nine Worthies of Cockloft Hall," an informal writing club. In 1807, they began publishing *Salmagundi; or, The Whim-Whams and Opinions of Launcelot Langstaff, Esq., and Others*, a humorous periodical in the style of the London *Spectator*. The publication lasted only a year. Its sequel, *Salmagundi; Second Series*, published later, met with less success than the original.

Paulding's firm patriotic stance forms the central focus of his works. He contributed lively, acerbic criticism of the English people to American periodicals, matching British writers' disparaging comments point for point, and praising democracy. In such works as *The United States and England, Letters from the South, Written during an Excursion in the Summer of 1816, A Sketch of Old England by a New England Man*, and *John Bull in America; or, The New Munchausen*, Paulding incorporated the ideals of Jeffersonian democracy.

Sensitive to Britain's disapproval of American writing, Paulding also wrote in defense of his country's emerging literature. He encouraged readers to discover native themes and settings, rather than to imitate foreign ideals. His efforts on behalf of America's literary independence won him recognition, and President James Madison appointed him to the Board of Navy Commissioners. In 1824, President James Monroe assigned him the position of Navy agent at New York, and in 1838, President Martin Van Buren named him to his cabinet as Secretary of the Navy.

Paulding's novels are realistic and satirical accounts of historical subjects. *The Lay of the Scottish Fiddle*, which ridicules the romanticism of Sir Walter Scott, is an example of his wit. Paulding attacked the literary styles of Lord Byron and Scott in *Tales of the Good Woman* and *The Book of St. Nicholas*. *Koningsmarke, the Long Finne: A Story of the New World*, his first important work of fiction, is a historical romance depicting the settlement of the Swedes on the Delaware River. This book anticipated and may have influenced James Fenimore Cooper's *Satanstoe*; it has been cited by many critics as Paulding's best book. *The Dutchman's Fireside*, an account of life in upper New York during the French and Indian War, is considered an excellent depiction of the Dutch of New Amsterdam.

"Rational fiction," as he called it, was the aim of Paulding's later novels, moreover, he detested the "bombast and inflated

rhetoric" which he felt plagued many nineteenth-century authors. Praised by Edgar Allan Poe, Paulding was also an admitted influence on Nathaniel Hawthorne. Paulding is an important, if minor, figure in American literature. (See also *Dictionary of Literary Biography, Vol. 3: Antebellum Writers in New York and the South.*)

PRINCIPAL WORKS

Salmagundi; or, The Whim-Whams and Opinions of Launcelot Langstaff, Esq., and Others [with William Irving and Washington Irving]   (satirical essays) 1807-1808
The Diverting History of John Bull and Brother Jonathan [as Hector Bull-Us]   (satire)   1812
The Lay of the Scottish Fiddle   (poetry)   1813
The United States and England   (history)   1815
Letters from the South, Written during an Excursion in the Summer of 1816   (satire)   1817
The Backwoodsman   (poetry)   1818
Salmagundi; Second Series [as Launcelot Langstaff] (essays) 1820

THE NORTH AMERICAN REVIEW   (essay date 1818)

[Paulding] hits off characters very happily and gives some fine descriptions and narrations. These indeed constitute all the excellence of [*Letters from the South*]; but they are frequently half spoiled by the intermixture of insipid puns, flat witticisms, and degrading and impertinent allusions to the classicks and to distinguished characters. . . . We know not whether this and a great deal more of the same sort is of the author's own invention, but whether it is or not, it seems to us, if it raise a laugh at all, it is likely to be at his expense.

The writer of these letters is . . . a vehement enemy of imitation; he sometimes waxes more earnest and serious than is befitting for such a droll, and becomes downright angry with our ladies for copying the French and English fashions of dress, and our authors for adopting their modes of thinking. . . . Leaving our modes of dress then, we will say a word concerning our modes of thinking, in regard to which it seems to us that of all nations composing what we call the civilized world or christendom, we Americans are the least inclined to a stupid imitation of our predecessors, or a blind adoption of the habits and practices of other nations. (pp. 379-80)

On the whole, our general impression, concerning these letters from the south, is, that as far as they are made up of descriptions, sketches of character, and narrations, they are very amusing, pleasant reading, always excepting however the mawkish drollery with which these, as well as the rest of the work, are more or less dashed; and that in other respects the performance has very little merit;—it is meagre of information, the wit is in general poor, and the opinions and speculations are the result of superficial thinking. (p. 382)

> *"'Letters from the South',"* in The North American
> Review, *Vol. VI, No. 3, March, 1818, pp. 368-82.*

ECLECTIC REVIEW   (essay date 1819)

[*The Backwoodsman*] is certainly the most favourable specimen of transatlantic literature that has yet fallen under our notice. It is a poem which would be its author's passport to celebrity in any country; and unless we are greatly deceived in our estimate of its merits, it will satisfy the most sceptical as to the possible existence of such an anomaly as native poetical genius in an American. . . . America has hitherto produced no genuine poet, scarcely any one, indeed, who has been able to make his name heard across the ocean. Mr. Paulding, how-ever, deserves to be heard and honoured as a brilliant exception. . . . (p. 394)

The Backwoodsman is professedly a descriptive poem. The Author, that he 'may not be charged with having failed in what he did not attempt,' is anxious to have it understood that the extent of his design was

> to indicate to the youthful writers of his native country, the rich poetic resources with which it abounds, as well as to call their attention *home,* for the means of attaining to novelty of subject, if not to originality in style and sentiment. The story was merely assumed as affording an easy and natural way of introducing a greater variety of scenery, as well as more diversity of character; and whether the writer shall ever attempt to complete his original intention in the construction of a regular plan, will principally depend on the reception given to this *experiment*.
>
> (p. 395)

[We] shall hope to see the volume reprinted in this country. (p. 400)

> *"'The Backwoodsman',"* in Eclectic Review *n.s.*
> *Vol. XII, October, 1819, pp. 394-400.*

JOHN NEAL   (essay date 1825)

[Paulding is a good prose writer who had the] audacity enough, some years ago, to publish a volume of poetry [*The Lay of the Scottish Fiddle*], which others have had impudence enough to praise. . . . [It is] a small book, . . . giving some account, in the style of the Scripture, as we see it, in the Chronicles, of our squabbles with America.—We have not seen it, for many years; have no safe recollection of it; and shall, therefore, pass it over. . . . Papers in *Salmagundi,* . . . most of which are capital, [are] ill-tempered. . . . [*Letters From the South* is] a well-written book—not very malicious—nor very able; [it gives] some account, but a very imperfect one, of the *southern* habits; and *western* habits of his countrymen. . . . *The Backwoodsman—Nature and Art* . . .—purporting to be poetry—[is] absolute prose, nevertheless. . . . A new *Series of Salmagundi,* [Paulding has written] altogether by himself: quite equal to the first; but—such is the miserable caprice of popular opinion—altogether neglected. . . . Mr. P. is charged with having written *Letters on Old England by a New England Man.* [It is] a mischievous, wicked, foolish book: with little or no plain truth in it: a few downright lies—a multitude of misrepresentations. . . . [Paulding] is a man of good, strong talent; a hearty republican; a sincere lover of his country—a cordial hater of ours—with little or no true knowledge concerning us, or it: of a most unhappy disposition; sarcastic humour; and—we are afraid—not a very good heart.—His caricatures are too serious for pleasantry. There is nothing like fun or frolic in his misrepresentations. . . . (p. 172)

> *John Neal, "American Writers: Paulding" (originally published in* Blackwood's Edinburgh Magazine, *Vol. XVII, No. XCVII, February, 1825), in his* American Writers: A Series of Papers Contributed to "Blackwood's Magazine" (1824-1825), *edited by Fred Lewis Pattee, Duke University Press, 1937, pp. 172-73.*

FRASER'S MAGAZINE FOR TOWN AND COUNTRY
(essay date 1832)

[We] have before us a book [Paulding's *The Dutchman's Fireside*] written by as genuine an American as ever abused mother country . . . , a work in which we were exposed to considerable satire of a singular kind. . . . [The] little touches of nice observation are quite refreshing; and the character bestowed upon the English nation is deduced from particulars . . . correctly noticed. . . . (p. 343)

[Paulding's novel] has been in no small degree extolled in divers quarters in this country, and has received a unanimous tribute of approbation in his own. . . . To speak plainly, there is some good writing in the book. . . . The story is trifling— it is only just to Paulding to say that he does not make any pretension to the formation of a regular novel—and the work derives its interest from the sketches of individual and national character which it contains. (pp. 343-44)

Paulding can describe character which he has seen, and his prejudices are, to the last degree of absurdity, anti-English. (p. 346)

[The] staple wit of Paulding's book shews the low estimation in which the ladies are held among his countrymen. They are the general common-place butts of his very common-place jests. An English officer is abused whenever it is possible; but a woman is at all times the regular subject for petty jeering and low sarcasm. (p. 348)

This, we think, strongly indicates that, in Mr. Paulding's opinion, it is the fashion of *this* time in America to belie, cheat, and overreach everybody. (p. 349)

Society uncivilised, neglected women, impertinent and selfish men, corrupt or ignorant legislators, want of decency, civilisation, and refinement, figure in [Paulding's book] as the characteristics of the American Whites. . . . He, determined that no class of his countrymen should be shewn in colours too favourable, depicts the Blacks of the present day as the wretched victims of a rash, miscalculating philanthropy, whose last refuge is the prison or the penitentiary; the uncivilised Red race as "kritters" fit only for indiscriminate slaughter; and those of their tribes whom attempts have been made to bring towards European habits, as the most mischievous of mongrels, a compound of the ferocity of the savage, and the cunning, deceit, and sensuality of the civilised scoundrel.

Mr. Paulding, as we have already remarked, knows his countrymen, and can accurately describe what he sees. His *Dutchman's Fireside,* valueless as a novel, may be safely referred to as a record of American character. (p. 350)

"Trollope and Paulding on America," in Fraser's Magazine for Town and Country, *Vol. V, No. XXVII, April, 1832, pp. 336-50.**

THE SOUTHERN LITERARY MESSENGER   (essay date 1832)

[Mr. Paulding] may be classed as the secondary [novelist] of this country, though in general literature, Paulding is equal if not superior to Cooper. His tales are usually short and want interest; but his characters are well sketched, his incidents natural, and his opinions and observations characterized by good sense. There is, however, an affectation of humor in what he writes, that does not please me. It seems to consist more in the employment of quaint terms and odd phrases, than in the incident or character itself, and would appear to be the

result of an early and frequent perusal of the works of Swift and Rabelais. His productions are neat and sensible, but not very imaginative or striking. The interest or curiosity of the reader is never powerfully excited, but he never fails to please by the manner in which he conducts his plots; the easy and perspicuous style he employs, the clear and happy illustration of the vice or folly he holds up to indignation or scorn, and the successful though sometimes exaggerated developement of the character he wishes to portray. . . . Mr. Paulding has not displayed any great depth or expansion of mind in anything he has yet written, though he has tried his wing in both prose and verse. His forte is satire, which . . . is more playful than mordant and bitter. (p. 602)

"Letters on the United States of America" (1832), in The Southern Literary Messenger, *Vol. I, No. 11, July, 1835, pp. 602-04.**

[EDGAR ALLAN POE]   (essay date 1836)

We have read Mr. Paulding's *Life of Washington* with a degree of interest seldom excited in us by the perusal of any book whatever. We are convinced . . . that, as it grows in age, it will grow in the estimation of our countrymen, and, finally, will not fail to take a deeper hold upon the public mind, and upon the public affections, than any work upon the same subject, or of a similar nature, which has been yet written—or, possibly, which may be written hereafter. . . . Mr. Paulding has completely and most beautifully filled the *vacuum* which the works of Marshall and Sparks have left open. . . . He has done all this . . . in a simple and quiet manner, in a manner peculiarly his own, and which mainly because it is his own, cannot fail to be exceedingly effective. . . . Such books as these before us, go down to posterity like rich wines, with a certainty of being more valued as they go. . . .

The rich abundance of those delightful anecdotes and memorials of the private man which render a book of this nature invaluable . . . is the prevailing feature of Mr. Paulding's *Washington*. (p. 396)

In regard to the style of Mr. Paulding's *Washington*, it would scarcely be doing it justice to speak of it merely as well adapted to its subject, and to its immediate design. Perhaps a rigorous examination would detect an occasional want of euphony, and some inaccuracies of syntatical arrangement. But nothing could be more out of place than any such examination in respect to a book whose forcible, rich, vivid, and comprehensive English, might advantageously be held up, as a model for the young writers of the land. There is no better literary *manner* than the manner of Mr. Paulding. . . . We repeat, as our confident opinion, that it would be difficult, even with great care and labor, to improve upon the general manner of the volumes now before us, and that they contain many long individual passages of a force and beauty not to be surpassed by the finest passages of the finest writers in any time or country. (pp. 398-99)

[Edgar Allan Poe,] *"Paulding's Washington,"* in The Southern Literary Messenger, *Vol. II, No. VI, May, 1836, pp. 396-99.*

THE ATHENAEUM   (essay date 1849)

Without any disparagement of such reputation as Mr. Paulding may have gained in his own country, the English have never ranked him among their favourite American novelists. According to our estimation, Cooper, Miss Sedgwick, Ware, and even Bird, come before him; to say nothing of writers who have succeeded in the short story. . . . We know few authors to whom the epithet ''tiresome'' can be more deliberately and justly applied than to Mr. Paulding. He conceives himself to be jocose when he is only dreary. . . . But we must still remind the reader that such are precisely the qualities on which national tastes and sympathies are apt to disagree. . . . [Ours] is but an *English* estimate of the author of **'The Dutchman's Fireside'**; and it is possible that what appears to us forced, wearisome, and affected, . . . may be cordially relished on the other side of the Atlantic.—For the English reader's guidance it is enough further to state that one-half of **'The Puritan and His Daughter'** is carried on in England and the other in America; and that it does not contain a single combination, character, digression, or speculation which has not been presented to us a dozen times at least by former romancers.

> *''Our Library Table: 'The Puritan and His Daughter','' in* The Athenaeum, *No. 1153, December 1, 1849, p. 1206.*

RUFUS WILMOT GRISWOLD   (essay date 1852)

[The success of *The Dutchman's Fireside*] was decided and immediate, and it continues to be regarded as the best of Mr. Paulding's novels. . . . The characters are natural, and possess much individuality. From the outset the reader feels as if he had a personal acquaintance with each of them. . . . The work is marked throughout with Mr. Paulding's quaint and peculiar humour, and it is a delightful picture of primitive colonial life, varied with glimpses of the mimic court of the governor, where ladies figure in hoops and brocades, and of the camp in the wilderness, and the strategy of Indian warfare. (pp. 143-44)

Mr. Paulding's writings are distinguished for a decided nationality. He has had no respect for authority unsupported by reason, but on all subjects has thought and judged for himself. He has defended our government and institutions, and has imbodied what is peculiar in our manners and opinions. There is hardly a character in his works who would not in any country be instantly recognised as an American.

He is unequalled in a sort of quaint and whimsical humour, but occasionally falls into the common error of thinking there is humour in epithets, and these are sometimes coarse or vulgar. Humor is a quality of feeling and action, and like any sentiment or habit should be treated in a style which indicates a sympathy with it. He who pauses to invent its dress will usually find his invention exhausted before he attempts its body.

He seems generally to have no regular schemes and premeditated catastrophies. He follows the lead of a free fancy and writes down whatever comes into his mind. He creates his characters, and permits circumstances to guide their conduct. Perhaps the effects of this random and discursive spirit are more natural than those of a strict regard to unities. It is a higher achievement to maintain an interest in a character than to fasten the attention to a plot. (p. 144)

> *Rufus Wilmot Griswold, ''James Kirke Paulding,'' in his* The Prose Writers of America, *revised edition, A. Hart, 1852 (and reprinted by Garrett Press, Inc., 1969, pp. 143-51).*

THE ATLANTIC MONTHLY   (essay date 1867)

[Paulding's writings bear] a very marked resemblance to Washington Irving's manner in the prose, which is inevitably, of course, less polished than that of the more purely literary man, and which is apt to be insipid and strained in greater degree in the same direction. It would not be just to say that Paulding's style was formed upon that of Irving; but both had given their days and nights to the virtuous poverty of the essayists of the last century; and while one grew into something fresher and more original by dint of long and constant literary effort, the other, writing only occasionally, remained an old-fashioned mannerist to the last. . . . The last delicacy of touch is wanting in all his work, whether verse or prose; yet the reader, though unsatisfied, does not turn from it without respect. If it is second-rate, it is not tricksy; its dulness is not antic, but decorous and quiet; its dignity, while it bores, enforces a sort of reverence which we do not pay to the ineffectual fire-works of our own more pyrotechnic literary time. (p. 124)

> *''Reviews and Literary Notices: 'The Literary Life of James K. Paulding','' in* The Atlantic Monthly, *Vol. XX, No. CXVII, July, 1867, pp. 124-25.*

AMOS L. HEROLD   (essay date 1926)

Paulding's novels exemplify his theory of rational fiction. (p. 93)

[*Koningsmarke, the Long Finne: A Story of the New World*] has the marks of an initial, imitative effort. It is deficient in unity and cumulative force, and for two volumes there is too little action. The mood or tone sometimes shifts unnaturally from serious to comic and vice-versa. The principal white characters, however, have vital individuality, and the Indians, though somewhat Dutchy and unskilled as fighters, are convincingly real. The satire on Scott's romances, sordid ministers, and gossipy old ladies would not increase the popularity of the novel. The thunder scene is finely conceived and convincingly written; it presents a dramatic clash of characters and contending interests involving love, hate, revenge, superstition, charity, and reverence for the Great Spirit. (pp. 96-7)

The Lion of the West demonstrated Paulding's skill in dialogue and in comedy. His fiction of this period had much good talk, and some of his stories were related in the first person. His earlier play, **''The Bucktails; or, Americans in England,''** . . . is a five-act prose comedy with echoes from Shakespeare. . . . Parts of the comedy satirize the English king and the nobility. Besides two pretty love scenes, the chief complication arises from Noland's abduction of Jane Warfield, an American heiress. At one point the feeling rises to the dignity of blank verse. The play is both readable and actable.

Paulding's second and best novel, *The Dutchman's Fireside* . . . [contains] many lines of interest, [and] made a deep impression on contemporary readers. (pp. 99-100)

Though the plot gets off in leisurely Dutch fashion and sags somewhat at the satiric middle, it pulls itself together for a dramatic finish. Containing little action, the early chapters present Dutch character sketches, poetical descriptions, and wise reflections. (p. 101)

[Though *Westward Ho!*] begins as a story of adventure, it develops into an unpleasant psychological study, shifting its emphasis from the outer to the inner world. Consequently, it suffers from too much introspection and too little action, and reveals the author's literary kinship with Hawthorne. (p. 104)

[After leaving his cabinet position as naval secretary], Paulding wrote two more novels. The first was *The Old Continental: or the Price of Liberty*. . . . Substantially written several years before and revised before publication, the work is more finished than *Westward Ho!* It is probably his second best novel. (p. 106)

Had Paulding maintained the pace that he set in the earlier portions of the story, *The Old Continental* would be his best novel. As it stands, it is a memorable narrative, depicting the neutral ground more truly than did Cooper's *The Spy*. The author had become seasoned; he had digested and mastered his materials; he wrote with ease and persuasiveness. Action, scene, characters, dialogue, humor, love of nature, and knowledge of life are successfully fused together. . . .

Towards the end, however, some of the incidents are trite and unnecessary, and some of the dialogue is cheap and superfluous. (p. 107)

The last and least successful of Paulding's novels, *The Puritan and His Daughter* . . . , gives many indications of a decline of his mental powers. Strangely enough, this child of his old age was his favorite. Its defects are clearly indicated by the manner of composition. (pp. 108-09)

[The] novel is loose, rambling, and as a whole ineffective. . . . The story has a mild interest, a vein of humor and satire, and frequent descriptions. (p. 109)

In a romantic and sentimental age, Paulding was a realist. Since his tendency to satirize and philosophize detracted from his ability as a narrator, his novels are somewhat deficient in action. His plots are simply and plainly constructed. In exposition and argument he had native ability, but he learned to tell a story only after long and arduous practice. Hence, he was more successful in the delineation of character, as shown by the portraits in the *The Dutchman's Fireside*. His dialogue is usually natural and character-revealing. As a novelist, he is at his best in presenting the New York Dutch. Beautiful threads in his fiction are the bits of philosophy and the poetical descriptions of nature. He is witty rather than sentimental; realistic rather than romantic; and to adventure he adds a psychological interest. (pp. 109-10)

In several volumes the dominant element is social criticism. *The Merry Tales of the Three Wise Men of Gotham* . . . is a misnamed volume, for the narrative is so slight that the pieces in the collection should not be called tales. They are really narrative essays. . . . These papers present Paulding as a conservative student of life without romantic delusions or impossible dreams. (p. 114)

[*The Backwoodsman*] was Paulding's major poetic experiment, and the first book unluckily that carried the author's name. . . . The poem aims to present a typical pioneer, but is the gloomiest of Paulding's works. Written in a period of ill health, it shows that the author's mind was then occupied with the problem of suffering, evil, and death. (pp. 121-22)

[Paulding] was so absorbed in the writing of neat couplets that he almost forgot to tell the story. Besides, though condensed and thoughtful, the verses lack vivacity, and inevitably become monotonous. There is much description of a rather gloomy sort. (p. 122)

Paulding's love of and joy in nature were highly poetical. From youth to old age he found delight in observing the wonders of creation. In a sane appreciation of nature he may be compared with Wordsworth himself. (p. 123)

Though neither wholly original nor especially rhythmical, [his poems] are concrete, picturesque, and sincere. . . . [They are] poetical and worthy of preservation. They illustrate Paulding's

theory that definite thought should be the basis of poetry, and they indicate his kinship as a nature poet to Bryant and Wordsworth. . . .

But Paulding's poetry and criticism were usually incidental and fragmentary. He did not develop or show his full strength either as poet or as critic. Indeed, he rated creative work so much higher than criticism that he scorned the professional critic. His stricture on the American prose and poetry of a century ago is no less creditable than the commendation that his own prose won from Edgar Allan Poe [see excerpt above]. His estimate of the great authors is usually sound. That he shared Carlyle's adverse opinion of Byron is noteworthy; that he conceded a pre-eminent position to Shakespeare, Fielding, Milton, and Dryden, and admired Chaucer and Burns will not lower his rating as a critic. As to his theoretical preference of realism to romanticism, Paulding's practice in the composition of his ghost and fairy stories proved that he did not reject the valid claims of romanticism. Perhaps the soundest theory is that realism and romanticism are complementary and that the supreme literary achievement is their successful fusion. Is it not true that Homer, Dante, and Shakespeare blend the two? Surely, dreams and vivid imaginings may influence human conduct as powerfully as the facts of history or the conclusions of science. (pp. 126-27)

As an author [Paulding] developed slowly but steadily. He did his best work between the ages of fifty and seventy. He was an independent thinker. He theorized over politics, fiction, prose and poetical style, slavery, states' rights, and other subjects. His active mind and facile pen missed little of contemporary interest, and he was urged on by a strong and persistent impulse to write. . . . He was wit and realist, journalist and politician, essayist and poet, philosopher and public official, critic and biographer, and author of tales and novels. (p. 146)

> *Amos L. Herold, in his* James Kirke Paulding: Versatile American *(reprinted by permission of the publisher), Columbia University Press, 1926, 167 p.*

VERNON LOUIS PARRINGTON   (essay date 1927)

A writer so consciously and completely American would find abundant occasion to put his pen to the service of his country at a time when every English traveler turned critic and on his return home published a volume of truculent disparagement of ways and things American. For the most part those volumes were a defense of Toryism by the easy method of attacking democracy, and they annoyed Paulding beyond measure. He would not let them go unanswered, and from *The Diverting History of John Bull and Brother Jonathan* . . . to *John Bull in America* . . . , he published five different replies, varying his attack from argument to burlesque. Something more than loyalty to his country seems to have spurred him on. His dislike of England was inveterate, partly because of the old Revolutionary feud, partly because of later antagonisms. (p. 214)

Paulding was persuaded that America constituted the hope of the future. Here in this land he believed that men should eventually achieve a measure of well-being undreamed of in the old world; already the old tyrannies had been destroyed, the ancient poverty abated. From this stubborn idealism nothing could turn him aside. It finds expression in an early poem, and it provides the theme for his last novel. *The Backwoodsman* . . . is a rambling and somewhat plethoric idyll of the West, the hero of which is an archetype of the oppressed and exploited, who finds a generous asylum in the free land beyond the Alleghenies, and . . . expands the horizons of his mind under the beneficent touch of freedom. *The Puritan and His Daughter* . . . deals with a different phase of the same general theme. It is a vivid picture of the strife engendered in America by immigrant families who bring hither their old-world feuds and animosities, and the curative influence of the free environment that, in discovering the good rather than the bad in neighbors, draws together the younger generation despite the jealous parental authority that would keep them apart. (p. 215)

[Paulding] was partisan to no cause or party, literary or political, of the old world. He was content to be American and suffer his native land to bound his loyalties. In his own literary practice he refused to imitate the current English fashions and he spoke his mind freely to the American reading public for its greedy swallowing of cheap imported food. He did not take kindly to the English romantic writers, and went often out of his way to have a dig at his two pet aversions, Scott and Byron. His amusing tale of *Koningsmarke, the Long Finne,* is a good-natured burlesque of certain romantic mannerisms of the Waverley novels, and a defense of Cooper's *Pioneers* for its homely realism. Paulding's dislike of the "blood-pudding" fiction that had come over from England, and that proved so disastrous to the genius of Gilmore Simms, was inveterate, and in his whimsical dedication of *The Puritan and His Daughter* to the sovereign people he comments on the public taste. . . . (p. 216)

Koningsmarke is Paulding's most interesting work, and the utter neglect that has overtaken it is far from deserved. It is native and original, full of shrewd comment and sly satire, and it embodies most of Paulding's pet theories and aversions. Few books of the time are more amusing than this tale. . . . [His] wit still preserves its freshness after a hundred years. It is a whimsical satire on the ways of the hour, literary and other, set against the background of an old Swedish settlement on the banks of the Delaware; but the chief purpose of its quizzical pages is the pouring of a broadside into the picturesque hull of contemporary fiction. . . . Paulding cleverly hits off the high-flown and ghostly, the love of blood pudding, the snobbish contempt for the homely and native. (pp. 219-20)

In some of his later work the line between burlesque and serious is not so clearly marked, and one hesitates to pronounce whether *Westward Ho!* is a sober attempt at popular romance or a *reductio ad absurdum* of the current romantic flummery. Certainly it is a preposterous story. . . . *Westward Ho!* is not an amusing book; it is quite lacking in local color, and its casual bits of realism and occasional satire are too inconsequential to signify. *The Dutchman's Fireside,* written at about the same time, is far more successful. . . . [It] contains some lovely pictures of old times that one reads with pleasure; but it indulges somewhat freely in adventure . . . , and its love story is needlessly romantic. Although Paulding still protests against a blood-pudding diet, he indulges occasionally in the high-flown, to the detriment of the idyllic note. . . . Too casual in his work, too undisciplined in the craft of writing, he remained to the end an amusing amateur, a homespun man of letters who never took the trouble to master his technic. There was excellent stuff in him . . . , but his failure suggests the difference between the journeyman and the artist. (pp. 220-21)

> *Vernon Louis Parrington, "Two Knickerbocker Romantics," in his* Main Currents in American Thought, *an Interpretation of American Literature from the Beginnings to 1920: The Romantic Revolution in America, 1800-1860, Vol. 2 (copyright 1927 by Harcourt Brace Jovanovich, Inc.; copyright 1955 by Vernon L. Parrington, Jr., Louise P. Tucker, Elizabeth*

> *P. Thomas; reprinted by permission of the publisher), Harcourt, 1930 (and reprinted by Harcourt, 1958), pp. 203-21.**

CARL VAN DOREN (essay date 1940)

[James Kirke Paulding] had considerable merit as a novelist, particularly in the matter of comedy. . . . He was too facile in lending his pen, as parodist or follower, to whatever fashion prevailed at any given moment to do any very individual work, but *The Dutchman's Fireside* . . . , his masterpiece, deserves to be mentioned with Cooper's *Satanstoe,* considerably its superior, as a worthy record of the Settlement along the Hudson; and his *Westward Ho!* . . . significantly reveals the charm which the West—especially Kentucky, in which the scene of this novel is chiefly laid—had for the natives of the older states. (pp. 48-9)

> *Carl Van Doren, "Romances of Adventure," in his* The American Novel: 1789-1939 *(reprinted with permission of Macmillan Publishing Co., Inc.; © 1940 by Macmillan Publishing Co., Inc.; renewed 1949 by Carl Van Doren; renewed © 1968 by Anne Van Doren Ross, Barbara Van Doren Klaw and Margaret Van Doren Bevans), revised edition, Macmillan, 1940, pp. 43-57.**

ALEXANDER COWIE (essay date 1948)

The ruthless winnowing process of time removes from general view not only scores of worthless writers but also a considerable number of writers whose productions are but a little short of first-rate. Among the latter group is James Kirke Paulding. In his day he was so popular that some of his works were translated into as many as five languages. Critically he was so well received that there seemed little reason to question Poe's assertion (about 1835) that there was "no better literary *manner* than the manner of Mr. Paulding" [see excerpt above]. He appealed to many tastes and offended few. For a number of years he was accorded honors virtually on a par with those received by Cooper. This was the more remarkable in that Paulding was a competitor in Cooper's own field of operations, the historical romance. In retrospect it is clear that Paulding was a writer of less weight and power than Cooper. It is clear, too, that some of his many literary gifts tended to cancel each other. Nevertheless a tidy balance of credit remains, and Paulding is still respected and admired for his colorful stories of Colonial life in the Middle states, especially New York. (p. 185)

Paulding's earliest writing, it seems odd to recall, was the result of a collaboration with Irving, gentle Washington Irving. In 1807-08 he participated in those ebullient, bantering studies of social life in adolescent New York which were published as *Salmagundi.* Although the wit he there displayed never deserted him, Paulding later lost the amateur charm of youth and acquired in its place the purposeful and occasionally acerb manner of a vigilant observer of the political scene and of human motive and behavior in general. Political issues, foreign and domestic, interested him passionately. He became one of the most conspicuous champions of America during that literary warfare with England which became an inglorious substitute for powder and ball as a means of expressing hostility between the nations. Irving deplored such warfare and sought to allay it. But if Irving was oil, Paulding was acid, and he etched many a satiric portrait of John Bull in the years between 1812 and 1822. Other literary interests had not entirely lapsed during this period, witness *The Backwoodsman* . . . , a long poem cele-brating the life and exploits of a New Yorker who emigrated to the Ohio Valley. But Paulding's poem was dull, and it was not until 1823 that he made a fair popular success with non-controversial material. In that year he published *Koningsmarke, the Long Finne: A Story of the New World.* (pp. 185-86)

Koningsmarke is more—and also less—than an historical ro-mance. It is more in that it has greater variety than generally characterized the form. The personnel is more real and more diversified than was usual. . . . At times Paulding's treatment of the doughty Swedish governor recalls Irving's treatment of the Dutch governors of New Amsterdam, but Paulding is on the whole less burlesque in his treatment and also less kindly. . . . [The] hero and the heroine, though mainly types, share in Paulding's effort to make his characters psychologically plau-sible. . . . However arbitrarily arranged, the impasse [of the hero and heroine] is handled with skilful detail. . . . Paulding was good in describing adventure, but he was finally more interested in character and motive than in mere excitement. He was also interested in natural scenery, and his skill in describing outdoor scenes was distinctly superior to that of most of his confrères in the historical romance. To some modern readers, *Koningsmarke* may seem more valuable as a regional story than as an historical romance. For others the chief value of the story may lie in the author's mastery of a terse, epigrammatic style. Paulding's humor . . . imbues *Koningsmarke* with vitality throughout. Few writers of the historical romance offered so much variety to their readers. (pp. 187-88)

Koningsmarke is also less than a good historical romance. . . . That same vitality which raises *Koningsmarke* to distinction is associated with the partial defeat of his romance as such. Too often he adopted a tone of mockery which either irritates or puzzles the reader of romance. . . . Paulding's [comments make sense, but they impair the pleasure of the] thoroughgoing reader of romance, who can endure endless absurdities if delivered with sufficient solemnity but grows restive under jocose treat-ment. . . . [His] inveterate habit of dissecting motives was often embarrassing. . . . [Paulding] provided *Koningsmarke* with introductory chapters containing brilliantly written com-ments, but these comments . . . do the author no good in an ostensibly imaginative tale. A friend and erstwhile collaborator of Irving, Paulding lacked Irving's genial nature. Irving wanted to make the reader laugh; Paulding wanted to make him laugh and think. A writer of historical romance par excellence is not troubled by afterthoughts, and it is as well if his humor is used sparingly—and never at the expense of his principal characters. (pp. 188-89)

Paulding varied the genre of the historical romance—for better or worse as the reader may decide. When he wrote straight adventure he was thoroughly competent. When his witty or satiric vein is quiescent the story goes through phases that are as thrilling or chilling as one may care to read. . . . Paulding, when he chose, could write in the popular vein. (pp. 190-91)

The Dutchman's Fireside is probably the best of Paulding's novels. Most of the characteristics observable in *Koningsmarke* reappear in *The Dutchman's Fireside,* but the author's mocking and satiric tone is heard less frequently. (p. 191)

The story manifestly is based in good American sentiment: an inarticulate rural lad finally carries off the prize of a fashionable but virtuous girl in the face of heavy competition by moneyed, titled suitors with glamorous European backgrounds. The hero is not a hero at the beginning but must prove himself one by

pluck and resourcefulness. This is one advantage *The Dutch-man's Fireside* has over Cooper's yet-to-be-written *Satanstoe,* which it resembles in much of its narrative agenda and portions of its setting. It is also a livelier and more varied book than *Satanstoe,* and its re-creation of old Dutch life seems more authentic than that of Cooper's story. (p. 192)

[*Westward Ho!*] and the two novels which succeeded it added more to Paulding's royalties than to his permanent reputation, for in none of them did he marshal his abilities with sustained success. Yet each has substantial elements which refuse to be dismissed lightly.

Westward Ho! proved to be a none-too-happy blending of ad-venture and psychology. The westward trek of Cuthbert Dan-gerfield from Virginia (which Paulding knew) to Kentucky (which he had read about—especially in Timothy Flint's *Rec-ollections of the Last Ten Years*) entailed dangerous adventures which had been common matters of record in the period just after the Revolution. This aspect of the story is well handled. Dudley Rainsford, however, a religious fanatic in love with Dangerfield's daughter Virginia, is the subject of more psy-chological analysis than the action can well sustain. (pp. 192-93)

[*The Old Continental: or, The Price of Liberty*] as a whole is vigorous and racy, but it falls off in power toward the end. . . . Paulding again proved in *The Old Continental* that he found climaxes uncongenial or too taxing. He excelled in detail rather than in mass. . . . [The climax of the story], which should have called forth all the author's powers as a writer of adven-ture, proved to be very inadequate as a climax. Paulding's novels as a whole, in fact, suggest that he might have been more at home in a sort of satirico-picaresque narrative with frequent philosophical stop-overs somewhat after the fashion of Brackenridge's *Modern Chivalry.* But satirical fiction . . . was not the wanted type in America of the forties and fifties. Paulding was doing his best to splice his talents to a form, the historical romance, to which they were not perfectly suited.

The last of Paulding's novels, *The Puritan and His Daughter* . . . , was at once the author's favorite and his poorest long story. . . . [The] novel exhibits a geographical dispersion that is not compensated for by focus of character or action. Nor is the story completely redeemed by Paulding's use of the inter-esting thesis that the noxious gases of New England sectari-anism can best be dissipated in the beneficent air of the freer West. (pp. 193-94)

In retrospect it appears that at the very centre of his talents Paulding was a commentator first and a story-teller second. He was always brimful of opinion, which he often managed to suppress for moderate intervals but which he took his keenest pleasure in expounding. The stories should in effect be illus-trations or examples of the author's views. He himself admitted almost as much when he described the introductory chapters of the eight books of *Koningsmarke* as the "very cream" of the book. (p. 194)

Paulding's literary theories and criticisms are scattered through a score of volumes dating from his young manhood to his old age. The itch to comment on writing, whether his own or others', was one of his most persistent traits. Consistency he did not always maintain, but most of his detailed criticism stems from his creed of "rational fictions." Inasmuch as he himself often traveled the popular route of the historical ro-mance, it is easy to understand that on occasion he was not a little pinched by his own insistence on common sense as the basic literary virtue. Indeed he never did achieve a comfortable coalition of opposing forces in his own theory and practice. While ostensibly writing romance he was in the position of sabotaging his own efforts by ridiculing the form or at least needlessly exposing its machinery.

It is certain that Paulding was no dyed-in-the-wool romanticist. So much might be guessed of a writer who referred to Dryden as "the best critic of modern times." His roving imagination was firmly tethered to a stake of realism in his most exciting tales. He believed that the facts of history can be as exciting as extravagant concoctions of "Gothic or Grecian" wonders, and real characters as interesting as synthetic ideals or mechanized villains. His robust Americanism explains his preference for national themes and his independent spirit forbade slavish imitation—especially imitation of supercilious British writers. (p. 196)

The essay called **"National Literature"** is a remarkable document for the period. It is also unlike much, perhaps most, of Paulding's other reflections on the art of authorship in that it is coolly and objectively written. Its direct style is in strong contrast to the ironical vein in which he wrote in many of his prefatory chapters in *Koningsmarke* and in other works such as *Letters from the South* which incidentally touch the same subject. Time and again he lashes out against the feeble British writers who overinfluence their American colleagues for the worse. (p. 197)

Paulding's criticism, caustic in content, ironical in form, [helps] to explain the malaise which always affected him more or less. The historical romance was vogue when he came into his maturity, but he could not hope to marry his art to a form he was only half in love with. His perpetual harping on what a novel or romanc should and should not be must have wearied his readers as much as the fashionable writers irritated him. (p. 199)

[Connoisseurs] of fine prose recognize in Paulding a master of a keen, incisive idiom ready to serve alike the purposes of humor and critical reflection. But the broad public insists on story and sentiment, and from the point of view of maintaining popularity it would appear that a certain idyllic charm in his descriptions of rural and village life might well have been more fully capitalized by Paulding. His greatest defect . . . was his lack of illusion in scenes devoted to high adventure. In his studies of character and light episode on a less grandiose scale, he needed no "illusion," for he was drawing from the life. (p. 200)

> *Alexander Cowie, "Contemporaries and Immediate Followers of Cooper, I," in his* The Rise of the American Novel *(reprinted by permission of D. C. Heath & Co.), American Book Company, 1948 (and reprinted by American Book Company, 1951), pp. 165-227.**

RALPH M. ADERMAN (essay date 1962)

In attitude and style of writing Paulding was a transitional figure who combined elements of the neoclassical tradition and the romantic movement. In this combination lie the reasons for Paulding's contemporaneous popularity and his relative neglect today. . . . Paulding in his public writing developed a style which was dignified and decorous and soon out of fashion by most literary standards. Notwithstanding, Paulding retained it because it met the demands he put upon it. His slashing invective, pungent satire, and homely didacticism all benefited from the examples of [such] eighteenth-century models [as Jonathan Swift, Henry Fielding and Oliver Goldsmith]. With the emergence of the romantic temperament and its emotionalism and enthusiasm, its fondness for combining native American materials with Gothic details, and its propensity toward didacticism, Paulding found another mode suited to his purposes and consequently often combined the romantic and the neoclassical to produce a literary hybrid found in many other American writers of the early nineteenth century. Even so, Paulding showed his partiality for the neoclassical approach by condemning the deleterious effects of Scott and Southey upon the literature of the day. (pp. xiii-xiv)

With Paulding the compulsion to write was so great that he yielded to it unresistingly, with the result that writing became for him a form of relaxation and enjoyment. His letters, as well as his other outpourings, reveal the ease and fluency of one who enjoyed what he was doing, who set down his ideas as they flowed from his pen without benefit of revision of any sort. Consequently, some of his ideas are roughly but vigorously expressed, and in this expression we come close to the man himself. (p. xv)

> *Ralph M. Aderman, in his introduction to* The Letters of James Kirke Paulding, *edited by Ralph M. Aderman (copyright © 1962 by the Regents of the University of Wisconsin), University of Wisconsin Press, 1962, pp. xiii-xxiv.*

ADDITIONAL BIBLIOGRAPHY

Blankenship, Russell. "New York, the Cosmopolitan City." In his *American Literature as an Expression of the National Mind*, pp. 244-71. New York: Holt, Rinehart and Winston, 1949.*
    Finds Paulding a neglected but significant writer.

Gerber, Gerald E. "James Kirke Paulding and the Image of the Machine." *American Quarterly* XXII, No. 3 (Fall 1970): 736-41.
    Discusses the machine imagery throughout Paulding's works.

Owens, Louis D. "James K. Paulding and the Foundations of American Realism." *Bulletin of the New York Public Library* 79, No. 1 (Autumn 1975): 40-50.
    Discusses how Paulding strove to express the ideals of realism in American literature.

Watkins, Floyd C. "James Kirke Paulding and the South." *American Quarterly* V, No. 3 (Fall 1953): 219-30.
    Discusses Paulding's sympathy for the South and its expression in his writings.

Charles Reade

1814-1884

English novelist, playwright, and journalist.

One of the most eccentric of the English authors of his time, Reade exhibited power, passion, and pathos in his work. He studied law at Magdalene College, Oxford, and was later called to the bar at Lincoln's Inn, but chose not to practice. Though he never defended anyone in a court room, Reade was aware of the injustice and inhumanity around him, and aimed his novels at alleviating these wrongs. Reade's works also reflect a strong moralistic and spiritual upbringing, for his parents raised him hoping he would enter a religious order.

Reade took pride in the fact that his novels inspired reform. Of his most didactic efforts, five are particularly outstanding: *A Woman-Hater*, an attempt to bring about the admission of women into the traditionally male field of medicine in England, *Foul Play*, an exposé of the insurance fraud of the shipping industry, *Hard Cash; a Matter-of-Fact Romance*, which revealed the pathetic conditions of English private insane asylums, *It Is Never Too Late to Mend*, an attack on the English penal system, and *Put Yourself in His Place*, which brought to public view the terrorism of the English trade unions. His most successful novel, *The Cloister and the Hearth: A Tale of the Middle Ages*, is a historical romance which A. C. Swinburne placed "among the very greatest masterpieces of narrative."

Despite the popular reception Reade's novels achieved, he wished to be remembered as a dramatist rather than a novelist. His best works for the stage were written with Tom Taylor and other dramatists. He also successfully adapted foreign plays, such as *Drink* from Émile Zola's *L'Assommoir*. It has often been noted that his dramas appear compiled, rather than written, for he gathered as much information as possible from reliable printed sources and personal testimony. Critics praise Reade's powerful narration and vivid description, but feel his works suffer from didacticism.

While today the social concerns in his novels are outdated, Reade is nonetheless recognized as an author of what he termed "matter-of-fact romances": a writer of didactic novels, with a mind devoted to humanitarian purposes.

PRINCIPAL WORKS

The Ladies' Battle (drama) 1851
Masks and Faces [with Tom Taylor] (drama) 1852
Christie Johnstone (novel) 1853
It Is Never Too Late to Mend (novel) 1853
Peg Woffington [adapted from the novel *Masks and Faces*] (novel) 1853
Cream: Jack of all Trades; a Matter-of-Fact Romance (novel) 1858
Love Me Little, Love Me Long (novel) 1859
The Cloister and the Hearth: A Tale of the Middle Ages (novel) 1863
Hard Cash; a Matter-of-Fact Romance [also published as *Very Hard Cash*] (novel) 1863
Griffith Gaunt; or, Jealousy (novel) 1866

Foul Play [with Dion Boucucault] (novel) 1869
Put Yourself in His Place [adapted from the drama *Free Labour*] (novel) 1870
A Woman-Hater (novel) 1878
Drink [adapted from the novel *L'Assommoir* by Émile Zola] (drama) 1879
A Perilous Secret (novel) 1884

BLACKWOOD'S EDINBURGH MAGAZINE (essay date 1855)

We suppose a Scotsman's national pride ought to be gratified by *Christie Johnstone;* But Scotsmen, like other people, are apt to be perverse, and we are afraid we do not quite appreciate the compliment paid by a "Southron" who can only handle it imperfectly, to our native Doric. There is a certain sweet and subtle charm in a language which only those to the manner born can express or understand. The Scotch of Mr. Reade . . . is *too* Scotch to be genuine. . . . [In *Christie Johnstone* the] *words* are broadly, coarsely, elaborately Scotch, but the idiom and construction are purely English, and the bloom is gone from this uncouth dialect, which loses the fragrance of its own spirit without gaining the inspiration of the other. . . .

Christie Johnstone, nevertheless, is a clever book. . . . [There] is a great deal that is very good in the conception of Christie. . . . We prefer *Peg Woffington,* however, to her Scottish sister. The artist has no difficulty here with his tools, and is at liberty to put all his strength upon his subject; and he has produced a very animated, bright, good picture. . . . (p. 567)

> *"Modern Novelists—Great and Small," in* Blackwood's Edinburgh Magazine, *Vol. LXXVII, No. CCCCLXXV, May, 1855, pp. 554-68.**

GEORGE ELIOT　(essay date 1856)

[Mr. Charles Reade's novel **'It is Never Too Late To Mend'** is] a remarkable fiction, and one that sets vibrating very deep chords in our nature. . . . Mr. Reade's novel opens with some of the true pathos to be found in English country life. . . . It then carries us . . . to the gaol, and makes us shudder at the horrors of the separate and silent system. . . . Then it takes us to Australia, . . . first through the vicissitudes of the Australian 'sheep-run', and then through the fierce drama of gold-digging. . . . (p. 328)

In all the three 'acts' of this novel, so to speak, there are fine situations, fine touches of feeling, and much forcible writing. . . . In short, **'It is Never Too Late to Mend'** is one of the exceptional novels to be read not merely by the idle and the half-educated, but by the busy and the thoroughly informed.

Nevertheless, Mr. Reade's novel does not rise above the level of cleverness: we feel throughout the presence of remarkable talent, which makes effective use of materials, but nowhere of the genius which absorbs material, and reproduces it as a living whole, in which you do not admire the ingenuity of the workman, but the vital energy of the producer. . . . [Mr. Reade] seems always self-conscious, always elaborating a character after a certain type, and carrying his elaboration a little too far—always working up to situations, and over-doing them. The habit of writing for the stage misleads him into seeking after those exaggerated contrasts and effects which are accepted as a sort of rapid symbolism by a theatrical audience, but are utterly out of place in a fiction, where the time and means for attaining a result are less limited, and an impression of character or purpose may be given more nearly as it is in real life—by a sum of less concentrated particulars. (pp. 328-30)

In everything, Mr. Reade seems to distrust the effect of moderation and simplicity. . . . [He] wearies our emotion by taxing it too repeatedly. . . . But the most amazing foible in a writer of so much power as Mr. Reade, is his reliance on the magic of typography. We had imagined that the notion of establishing a relation between magnitude of ideas and magnitude of type was confined to the literature of placards, but we find Mr. Reade endeavouring to impress us with the Titanic character of modern events by suddenly bursting into capitals at the mention of 'THIS GIGANTIC AGE!' It seems ungrateful in us to notice these minor blemishes in a work which has given us so much pleasure, and roused in us so much healthy feeling as **'It is Never Too Late to Mend;'** but it is our very admiration of Mr. Reade's talent which makes these blemishes vexatious to us, and which induces us to appeal against their introduction in the many other books we hope to have from his pen. (pp. 330-31)

George Eliot, *"Three Novels" (originally published as part of an essay in* The Westminster and Foreign Quarterly Review, *Vol. LXVI, No. CXXX, October 1, 1856), in her* Essays of George Eliot, *edited by Thomas Pinney, Columbia University Press, 1963, pp. 325-34.**

THE NORTH AMERICAN REVIEW　(essay date 1857)

[In **"It is Never too Late to Mend"**] we have a story embracing a wonderful variety of scenes, events, and characters, all so developed as to leave no obscurity, so harmonized as never to clash or become entangled, and so grouped as to bring out, without obtrusive moralizing, a manifold illustration of the maxim that forms the title, and of not a few fundamental moralities beside. . . . The entire work is pervaded by a strong and high moral purpose; and by means of it the author has assumed and fortified his position, as that of one whose office it is not to amuse, but to instruct, reform, and elevate.

> *"Critical Notices: 'It Is Never Too Late To Mend'," in* The North American Review, *Vol. LXXXIV, No. 174, January, 1857, p. 280.*

THE ATHENAEUM　(essay date 1861)

Whatever Mr. Reade writes is sure to have some good substance in it. . . . In this present work he gives his readers plenty for their money. . . . **'The Cloister and the Hearth'** is full to overflowing of adventures of the most marvellous and heart-thrilling description, dangers so imminent and escapes so hairbreadth, that the reader will feel almost as nervous as if they had ended fatally. . . . Mr. Reade has caught the spirit and colour of the age he has selected. In all the conversations, actions, manners and customs the reader is taken back to the everyday life of [the mid-fifteenth century]. . . . [In] Mr. Reade's pages it wears the kindly aspect of an old-remembered time, instead of being a stiff imitation of a bygone state of things. The characters are all warm; the descriptions are vivid; the tone of thought and the turn of speech are consistent and probable. The first volume is the best; there is more action—the story moves briskly: and the foundation of it is well laid, giving no indication of its future course. (pp. 576-77)

As the story proceeds it begins to drag heavily. Mr. Reade is more anxious to show forth his own reading and research in the records of the life and times of the age than to attend to the business of the story. Indeed, his characters for awhile become mere pegs on which to hang the incidents he has gathered from books; and the pedantry spoils the interest. The knowledge he has obtained is not sufficiently assimilated; it is given too much as he found it, as though he had copied whole pages of an itinerary. Throughout the whole of the second volume the story stagnates. The style itself, being quaint and deliberate, aids this effect. . . . In summing up our judgment on this work, we must say that it has many merits; but that there is a coarseness of workmanship which takes away both from the value of the story and the pleasure of the reader. The work contains materials enough for half-a-dozen ordinary novels; but they need a thorough supervision and compression to make the book as good as, with the labour and research bestowed to gather those materials together, it ought to be. . . . Readers will accept the novel, and read it, with omissions, according to the measure of their patience. (p. 577)

"New Novels: 'The Cloister and the Hearth: A Tale of the Middle Ages'," in The Athenaeum, *No. 1775, November 2, 1861, pp. 576-77.*

NATIONAL REVIEW (essay date 1862)

[Mr. Reade] may rise to the level above him, or he may sink to that below him. He has great gifts and great industry, but he has also great defects and enormous wilfulness, which seems to be rather on the increase than on the decline.

We do not intend to comment upon the novels of Mr. Reade one by one. *Christie Johnstone, Peg Woffington, It's never too late to mend, White Lies, Love Me little love Me long,* and *The Cloister and the Hearth,* if they do not complete the list, comprise all that are necessary to be taken into account. They show Mr. Reade at his best and his worst; indeed, each story does that, with the exception of *Love Me little love Me long,* which shows him persistently at his worst. (p. 135)

Mr. Reade's novels strive to be what *Never too late to mend* is called on the title-page, "matter-of-fact romances." This circumstance, and many confessions, direct and indirect, show the goal which the author aims at, if not that which he has reached. . . . Mr. Reade falls short, however, of [his] questionable success. There are four obvious reasons for his failure. In the first place, he has little insight into the real springs of human action, and the deep hidden bases on which the fabric of human character reposes. He shrinks from working down to them. If he has ever attempted to look into the abysses, he has turned, dizzy and blinded, away. Mr. Reade, indeed, unwittingly makes confession of this fact, though he mistakes an individual incapacity for a universal human limitation. (pp. 135-36)

Mr. Reade philosophising is a spectacle to gods and men. He is not frequently weak enough to assume an attitude as natural to him as dancing to a dog, and it is cruel to exhibit him in one of these unguarded moments. Still the mental defect . . . pervades all Mr. Reade's writings, and, if unconquered or unconquerable, will keep him on a lower level of art than he otherwise might attain to. . . . It is because Mr. Reade will not look into his own heart that he sees such a little way into the hearts of others. Only the most superficial emotions, and the most strongly marked distinctions of character, are discerned by him. He sketches life from the outside. We feel that we know, and that the author knows, as little of his heroes and heroines as of the casual acquaintances whom we meet and pass by, and talk superficially with, every day. If Mr. Reade would really rise to the eminence which perhaps fancies he has already gained, he must follow, instead of sneering at, the advice of "Herr Cant." He must look into his own heart, and write. . . . Mr. Reade, relying solely on external observation, necessarily passes over or misinterprets many external indications even which a subtler discrimination and a deeper insight would turn to account for purposes of true artistic delineation. (pp. 136-37)

Mr. Reade's realism is too much that of the stage. . . . [His] characters have life and movement, they have body and substance, they are not lay figures, puppets pulled by a string, nor mere abstractions. But they always recall to our minds the side-scenes and the foot-lights. Mr. Reade's novels in plot, in character, and in dialogue, are not dramatic merely, but theatrical. *Peg Woffington,* for example, without a single change in incident, or in the order of the events, or in the dialogue, makes, as *Masks and Faces,* one of the most effective acting dramas

of our time. Mr. Reade never portrays much more of a character than a clever actor could delineate on the stage. . . . The dialogue of his most homely personages is always such as an intelligent pit would approve, and suggests a clapping of hands and a stamping of feet. The incidents, again, are essentially theatrical. . . . What we cite as a defect, Mr. Reade may plausibly contend to be in it consummate art, and to have been directed by a purpose. He may allege that he has made *Peg Woffington* theatrical on the same principle on which he has made *White Lies* French in tone and colouring. But his other stories, which deal with English country life, and open-air adventure in Australia, or with French camps and châteaux, or with Scottish ports and fish-wives, are, if less perfect in construction, just as theatrical in dialogue, in incident, in character, as *Peg Woffington.* (pp. 137-38)

In *White Lies* the plot turns entirely upon the sudden reappearances of characters supposed to be dead or otherwise disposed of, that is, on unexpected meetings and partings of a melodramatic character. In *Never too late to mend* the villanous contrivances of Meadows, and the extraordinary means by which they are defeated . . . are essentially theatrical. . . . [The] conversation, in like manner, is stage dialogue. It is very good dialogue. Its wit is that of the comedy of Sheridan or Jerrold; its earnestness the earnestness of the best domestic drama or melodrama. But nothing can be more remote from the sort of thing that goes on in real life. His characters meditate also in protracted soliloquies, containing many effective "points." His personages, too, are of the boards. In his several heroes, we see the same *jeune premier* acting various parts. The difference is of costume, of situation, of incident, of dialogue only. Mr. Reade, misled by his stage models, and by his views as to the study of character, never goes beyond those qualities which all well-disposed and spirited young men have in common. George Fielding in *Never too late to mend,* Captain Dujardin in *White Lies,* Gerard in *The Cloister and the Hearth,*—the modern English yeoman, the French officer of the Revolutionary era, the Dutch artist and novice of the fifteenth century,—are at bottom one and the same. . . . All of Mr. Reade's characters run in couplets or in triplets.

The substance, then, of Mr. Reade's stories,—their plot, incidents, personages, and dialogue,—show the student of human nature on the stage rather than in the out-of-doors world. Whatever is drawn from life off the boards appears to be put into a theatrical mould, and unconsciously adapted for representation. The admiration and the imitation of the modern French novelists, which is evident in Mr. Reade's style, in the very structure and connexion of his sentences, has probably acted in the same direction. *White Lies* is intended to be French: it is probably the most French novel ever written in English or by an Englishman. It is designed to be so, says the author, and the desire is in conformity with the laws of artistic congruity. But his other works, of which the themes are drawn from England, Scotland, Ireland, Europe in the middle ages, have a French tone about them, in the manner of thinking and writing, though not in the things thought and written about. Mr. Reade is perfectly correct when he says: "True art is a severe battle, not only against egotism, but against monotony. Books should not emulate peas. Each work should add to the features of literature, not merely to its lamentable bulk." Judging the author by his own test of excellence, in the battle of art against egotism, Mr. Reade has been signally worsted. In the battle of art against monotony,—which we must not confound with tiresome dullness,—he has had but an imperfect success. An egotist must be more or less monotonous, and Mr. Reade is a consummate egotist. The delineator of life who would depict the characters of other men without first looking into his own heart, will never discriminate with the nicety needful to give variety to his portraitures, especially if the stage and the French novelists have in any considerable degree supplied his materials and suggested the manner of treating them.

Allowing for these qualifications, we have nothing but praise for Mr. Reade. He is perfectly master of his own resources, such as they are. His style is incisive and pungent; his outlines bold and distinct; his colouring vivid; his descriptions of nature are fresh and keen, though a little too hard and glittering, in a word, too metallic. The interest which depends on a situation, on highly-wrought interest and protracted suspense, is created, developed, intensified by him, until the catastrophe comes, with really marvellous power. The simpler emotions and passions, whether tender or violent, and incomplex characters, are also well drawn by him. His old soldiers are perhaps the best. . . . Mr. Reade has a rough manly tenderness, as different as possible from the ''Ah me!'' sort of moralising into which Mr. Thackeray falls, when he thinks it necessary to be sentimental. There is a blunt honest cynicism about him quite remote from the covert sneer which pervades the works of the author of *Vanity Fair*. These qualities give him insight into and sympathy with the rude warmth and plainspoken honesty of the *vieux militaire* class, and contribute to the success of his delineations of them.

These preliminary remarks will serve to clear our way to the more detailed consideration of Mr. Reade's latest and, in some respects, his best work, *The Cloister and the Hearth*. (pp. 140-41)

[In *The Cloister and the Hearth*, Mr. Reade is consciously misstating facts and] seems to us to go beyond the proper limits of historic romance. Artistic necessity is no excuse for real falsification. . . . The novelist's variations may perhaps be excused on the ground of charity. They put those whose conduct is attacked by them in a fairer light than the original document does. (p. 143)

Mr. Reade set out, it is evident, with the intention of telling the story of Gerard and Margaret [the parents of Erasmus], so as to send it home to the sympathy and imaginations of his readers. That intention he has carried out with a success which we do not think any of his contemporaries could have surpassed, or even approached. . . . The author has not merely acquired the erudition needful for [the purpose of depicting the proper setting and characters], but has thoroughly assimilated it, and formed thence a vivid picture of men and things. . . . As a work of art, Mr. Reade has injured his novel by not knowing when to hold his hand. He should have given just so much of the century . . . to his hero, and no more. As it is, the first two volumes of this story drag. The work might have been reduced to half its bulk with advantage to its interest as a romance.

Still we should have been sorry to lose sketches so vigorous and so instinct with vitality as even those parts of the work which are in a way excrescences upon the tale at present. Mr. Reade's disposition towards outward observation enable him to give, with admirable effect, such a picture of society as would fall under the eye of a traveller rapidly moving from Rotterdam to Rome. He unrolls a vivid panorama of country and town, road and river, with their varied groups and scenery. The period is one particularly interesting. The age immediately preceding a great revolution is more momentous than that in which the revolution itself takes place. (pp. 148-49)

We cannot speak too highly of the power and pathos of those portions of *The Cloister and the Hearth,* which relate to the later fortunes of [the major characters]. Mr. Reade, if he is deficient in the power of minute analysis, excels in painting the action of strong emotions upon simple characters. . . .

We do not know any thing in prose fiction more tender and ennobling than Mr. Reade's delineation of the short-lived happines, the much tribulation, and the final peace other than of this world, which mark the lonely history of the parents of Erasmus. (p. 149)

> ''*Mr. Charles Reade's Novels: 'The Cloister and the Hearth'*,'' *in* National Review, *Vol. 14, No. XXVII, January, 1862, pp. 134-49.*

THE QUARTERLY REVIEW   (essay date 1864)

Very Hard Cash is in many respects one of the very best novels in the English language, and is far superior to any thing the author had previously given us reason to suppose him capable of producing. . . . [We] regard it as one of the best models of what a novel should be that we have ever seen; in some purely artistic points of view superior to any single production of the great Wizard of the North [Sir Walter Scott]. . . . [In] *Very Hard Cash,* the interest of the story centres where it should, around the principal persons, begins with the opening of the book, and is sustained throughout, and never for a moment flags till you reach the end. The management of the story is for the most part natural, easy; things fall out as they should, without violence; every thing follows in its order, and the conclusion intended is forseen and reached without any *tour de force*. The author keeps to reality, and preserves the *vraisemblable*. He has no exaggeration, no straining after effect, nothing affected, nothing out of the range of common life. (pp. 229-30)

[We] do not pretend that Reade has the original or creative genius, or the ability of [Scott or Thackeray], nor that *Very Hard Cash* is a work of as high an order as *Old Mortality, Ivanhoe,* or *The Heart of Midlothian,* as *Vanity Fair, Pendennis,* or *The Virginians*. . . . [It] is more complete and perfect in its kind, and its kind is by no means despicable, even beside them. Its great merit is in its truthfulness, its realism, and its just and unexaggerated, though not *unideal,* view of life. We meet in it no false sentimentality, no weak or weakening romance, which makes one weary of the world in which he lives, and yet deprives him of strength to gain or even to strive after a better. It never sets us on a wild goose chase after the unattainable. There is love, true and undying love in it, but no wild and ungovernable passion. . . . There is in *Very Hard Cash* true love . . . such as a modest Christian maiden may confess, such as an honorable gentleman may cherish without debasing himself or humiliating its object, but no other love is chanted, whether veiled or unveiled. The imagination of the author is as chaste as his words or the conduct of his hero and heroine. . . . The author has no faith in the *fatality* of love. (pp. 230-31)

The characters are sufficiently marked and well sustained throughout; but we may add that they are not characters that grow on you. They are presented at once full grown and perfect as they ever become. The author presents, he does not develop them; none of them ever surprise you, or do any thing or turn out any thing you do not forsee and expect. This may be an artistic defect. . . . You know every one as soon as introduced, the way in which he or she will act, and what he or she will do; you understand at once the part or lot of each. . . . Yet though you forsee it all, the story loses nothing in its interest.

The author never overburdens you with descriptive passages, though his descriptive powers are of the highest order, and his command of language marvellous. He has the faculty of making you present at the scene he is describing, and of enabling you to see it as an eye-witness. . . . This faculty of making the reader present, and enabling him to see what is going on, Mr. Reade possesses in a degree seldom surpassed. It is a true dramatic power, and adds immensely to the interest of his writings. . . .

The characters are well sustained, we have said, but we ought to add that they are not characters far removed from every day life. They have no extraordinary merits or demerits. The good are not extravagantly good, nor the bad extravagantly bad. (p. 232)

We do not pretend that Mr. Reade has given us in this novel any striking original creations. He has kept himself within the region of common life and placed us among every day people, and his great merit lies in his having been able to invest these every day people with all the charms of genuine poetry and romance, without exaggerating or transforming their characters. In this is the power as well as the originality of his genius. His work is intensely interesting, exciting even, but the excitement is a healthy, not a morbid excitment; you rise from its perusal fresh and strong, not jaded and exhausted. . . . The moral and religious tone of *Very Hard Cash* is unexceptionable, far superior to that of most professedly religious novels. It is free from cant, from all affectation, strict but not rigorous. . . . Mr. Reade has a very just appreciation of real religious worth, and one who really loves his religion and seeks to live as a man loving God and doing his will, can always read him with pleasure. His religion is in the life, and expresses itself in deeds, not words. We can, therefore, commend his work as a novel free from nearly every thing that creates a prejudice against novel reading. (pp. 236-37)

> *"Reade's 'Very Hard Cash',"* in The Quarterly Review, *Vol. 1, April, 1864, pp. 223-37.*

THE ATLANTIC MONTHLY   (essay date 1864)

Charles Reade is not a clever writer merely, but a great one,—how great, only a careful *résumé* of his productions can tell us. We know too well that no one can take the place of him who has just left us, and who touched so truly the chords of every passion; but out of the ranks some one must step now to the leadership so deserted, for Dickens reigns in another region,—and whether or not it shall be Charles Reade depends solely upon his own election: no one else is so competent, and nothing but wilfulness or vanity need prevent him,—the wilfulness of persisting in certain errors, or the vanity of assuming that he has no farther to go. He needs to learn the calmness of a less variable temperature and a truer equilibrium, less positive sharpness and more philosophy; he will be a thorough master, when the subject glows in his forge and he himself remains unheated.

He is about the only writer we have who gives us anything of himself. Quite unconsciously, every sentence he writes is saturated with his own identity; he is, then, a man of courage, and . . . courage in such case springs only from two sources, carelessness of opinion and possession of power. Now no one, of course, can be entirely indifferent to the audience he strives

to please; and it would seem, then, that that daring which is the first element of success arises here from innate capacity. Unconsciously, as we have said, is it that our author is self-betrayed, for he is by nature so peculiarly a *raconteur* that he forgets himself entirely in seizing the prominent points of his story; and it is to this that his chief fault is attributable,—the want of elaboration,—a fault, however, which he has greatly overcome in his later books, where, leaving sketchy outlines, he has given us one or two complete and perfect pictures. His style, too, owes some slight debt to this fact; it has been saved thereby from offensive mannerism, and yet given traits of its own insusceptible of imitation,—for by mannerism we mean affectations of language, not absurdities of type.

There is a racy *verve* and vigor in Charles Reade's style, which, after the current inanities, is as inspiriting as a fine breeze on the upland; it tingles with vitality; he seems to bring to his work a superb physical strength, which he employs impartially in the statement of a trifle or the storming of a city. . . . There is no trace of the stale, flat, and unprofitable here; the books are fairly alive. (pp. 137-38)

The Breton novel of Mr. Reade, **"White Lies,"** although somewhat crude, otherwise ranks with his best. The action is uninterrupted and swift, the characters sharply defined, if legendary, the dialogue always sparkling, the plot cleanly executed, the whole full of humor and seasoned with wit. So well has it caught the spirit of the seene that it reads like a translation, and, lest we should mistake the *locale,* everybody in the book lies abominably from beginning to end. . . .

There is a good deal of picturesque beauty in this volume. (p. 139)

Our author is evidently a great admirer of Victor Hugo, though he is no such careful artist in language: he seldom closes with such tremendous subjects as that adventurous writer attempts; but he has all the sharp antithesis, the pungent epigram of the other, and in his freest flight, though he peppers us as prodigally with colons, he never becomes absurd, which the other is constantly on the edge of being. (p. 140)

[In **"White Lies"**] are combined the true elements of modern sensational writing: there are the broad canvas, the vivid colors, the abrupt contrast, all the dramatic and startling effects that weekly fiction affords, the supernatural heroine, the more than mortal hero. What, then, rescues it? It would be hard to reply. Perhaps the reckless, rollicking wit: we cannot censure one who makes us laugh with him. Perhaps nothing but the writer's exuberant and superabundant vitality, which through such warp shoots a golden woof till it is filled and interwoven with the true glance and gleam of genius. . . . Indeed, Charles Reade has a great deal of . . . pictorial power. A single sentence will sometimes give not only the sketch, but all its tints. (pp. 142-43)

When **"Peg Woffington"** first fell upon us, a dozen years ago or so, . . . it was like setting one's teeth in a juicy pear fresh from the warm sunshine. Then came **"Christie Johnstone,"** a perfect pearl of its kind, in which we recognize an important contribution to one class of romance. If ever the literature of the fishing-coast shall be compiled, it will be found to be scanty, but superlative. . . .

Charles Reade makes an exclamation-and an interrogation-point together say as much as many novelists can dibble over a whole page. Nevertheless, in his latest work these eccentricities are greatly modified. (p. 143)

A much less venial fault than any typographical trifle is a tendency belonging to this author to repeat both incident and colloquy. This of course is merely the result of negligence,—and negligence no one likes to forgive. . . . [We] doubt if Mr. Reade so much as looks his [manuscripts] over a second time. (p. 144)

Mr. Reade's latest novel, "**Very Hard Cash**," is a continuation of a previous one, "**Love me Little, Love me Long.**" A great charm of Thackeray's books was, that in every fresh one we heard a little news of the dear old friends of former ones; and "**Very Hard Cash**" has all the advantage of prepossession in its favor. Its forerunner was a startling thing to the circulating-library, for the hero was an entirely new character, dashing among the elegancies of the habitual hero like a shaggy dog in a drawing-room; and though the author admires him to the core of his heart, he never once hesitates to put him in ridiculous plight, and sets at last this diamond-in-the-rough in his purest and most polished gold. It is a delightful book, with one scene in it, the memorable night as sea, worth scores of customary novels, and, apart from the noble and beautiful delineation of David Dodd, would be invaluable for nothing else but its faultless portraiture of that millinery devotee, Mrs. Bazalgette. (p. 147)

Youth never was painted so well as here; both Julia and Alfred are aureoled in its beauty; they are not reasonable mortals with the accumulated perfections of three-score and ten, but young creatures just brimmed, as young creatures are, with the blissfulness of being. Nobody ever appreciated youth as this writer does, nobody has so entered into it; he never fails, to be sure, to make you laugh at it a little, but all the time he confesses a kind of loving worship of that buoyant time when the effervescence of the animal spirits fills the brain with its happy fumes, of that fearless, confident period. . . . (pp. 147-48)

We have often wondered that no one ever before grappled with the material of this last volume. . . . Perhaps one of the ablest portions of the treatment which this book affords the theme is in the singular collocation of characters,—the hero being wrongfully imprisoned as insane, the heroine's father really made so by medical malpractice, the hero's sister dying of injuries received from another maniac, his uncle being imbecile, and his father and one of his physicians becoming monomaniac. Nicer shades than these allow could not be drawn, and the subject stands in bold relief as a monument of dauntless courage and enthusiasm.

No one can hesitate to declare this novel, as it is the latest, to be also the finest of all that Charles Reade has given us. In saying this we do not forget the "**Cloister and Hearth**," which, however tender and touching and true to its century, is rather a rambling narrative than an elucidated plot. "**Very Hard Cash**" is wrought out with the finest finish, yet nowhere overdone; it so abounds in scenes of dramatic climax that we fancy the stage has lost immensely by the romance-reader's gain; yet there is never a single situation thrown away, every word tends in the main direction, and after that the prolific mind of the writer overflows in *marginalia*. There are one or two striking improbabilities, which Mr. Reade himself excuses by asserting that the commonplace is neither dramatic nor evangelical. . . . But the characterization in this book is wonderful; every name becomes an acquaintance. (p. 148)

The real charm of the book, however, lies in the beautiful relation which it pictures between mother and children, and in the nature of the daughter herself, so exuberant, so dancing,

yet the foam subsiding into such a luminous body of clearness, which so lights up the page with its loveliness, that, seeing how an artless woman is foreign to Mr. Reade's ideas, we are forced to believe that Nature was too strong for him and he wrote against the grain. Nevertheless, there is enough of his own prejudice retained for piquancy. . . . [The whole novel was] done at a touch, with a light, loose pen, but showing beyond compare the soul of the poet through the flesh of the novelist. (pp. 148-49)

In conclusion, we must pronounce Mr. Reade's merit, in our judgment, to belong not so much to what he has already done as to what, if life be allowed him, he is yet to do. All his previous works read like 'studies,' in the light of his last. For "**Very Hard Cash**" is the beginning of a new era; it shows the careful hand of the artist doing justice to the conceptions of genius, in the prime of his vigor, with all his powers well in hand. The forms of literature change with the necessities of the age,—to some future generation what illustration the dramatists were to the Elizabethan day the knot of superior novelists will be to this, and among them all Charles Reade is destined to no subordinate rank. (p. 149)

"*Charles Reade,*" *in* The Atlantic Monthly, *Vol. XIV, No. LXXXII, August, 1864, pp. 137-49.*

THE ATLANTIC MONTHLY   (essay date 1866)

There has been much doubt among many worthy people concerning Mr. Reade's management of the moralities and the proprieties, but no question at all, we think, as to the wonderful power he has shown, and the interest he has awakened. . . . (pp. 767-68)

It is not as a moralist that we have primarily to find fault with Mr. Reade, but as an artist, for his moral would have been good if his art had been true. [In "**Griffith Gaunt: or, Jealousy**"], up to the conclusion of Catharine Gaunt's trial, is in all respects too fine and high to provoke any reproach from us; after that, we can only admire it as a piece of literary gallantry and desperate resolution. . . . It is courageous, but it is not art. It is because of the splendid *élan* in all Mr. Reade writes, that in his failure he does not fall flat upon the compassion of his reader. . . . But it is a failure, nevertheless; and it must become a serious question in aesthetics how far the spellbound reader may be tortured with an interest which the power awakening it is not adequate to gratify. Is it generous, is it just in a novelist, to lift us up to a pitch of tragic frenzy, and then drop us down into the last scene of a comic opera? We refuse to be comforted by the fact that the novelist does not, perhaps, consciously mock our expectation.

Let us take the moral of "**Griffith Gaunt**,"—so poignant and effective for the most part,—and see how lamentably it suffers from the defective art of the *dénouement*. . . .

If the fable teaches anything . . . , it is this: Betray two noble women, and after some difficulty you shall get rid of one, be forgiven by the other, come into a handsome property, and have a large and interesting family. If the reader will take the fate of Griffith Gaunt [the hero] and contrast it with that of Tito Melema, in [George Eliot's] "Romola," he shall see all the difference that passes between an artificial and an artistic solution of a moral problem. (p. 768)

[If] the conclusion of the fiction is weak, how great it is in every other part! The management of the plot was so masterly, that the story proceeded without a pause or an improbability until the long fast of a month falling between the feasts of its publication became almost insupportable. It was a plot that grew naturally out of the characters, for humanity is prolific of events, and these characters are all human beings. They are not in the least anachronistic. They act and speak a great deal in the coarse fashion of the good old times. . . . They are of an age that was very gallant and brutal, that wore goldlace upon its coat, and ever so much profanity upon its speech; and Mr. Reade has treated them with undeniable frankness and sincerity. . . . Griffith Gaunt himself is the most perfect figure in the book, because the plot does not at any period interfere with his growth. We start with a knowledge of the frankness and generosity native to a somewhat coarse texture of mind, and we readily perceive why a nature so prone to love and wrath should fall a helpless prey to jealousy. . . .

The character of Kate Gaunt is treated in the *dénouement* with a violence which almost destroys its identity, but throughout the whole previous progress of the story it is a most artistic and consistent creation. (p. 769)

> *"Reviews and Literary Notices: 'Griffith Gaunt: or, Jealousy'," in* The Atlantic Monthly, *Vol. XVIII, No. CX, December, 1866, pp. 767-69.*

CHARLES READE (essay date 1869)

You side with fools and liars against me. You have published, without a word of disclaimer, a diatribe in which George Eliot is described as the first of English novelists, and her style, which is in reality a mediocre, monotonous style, with no music and no beauty in it, is described as perfect, and my style, which on proper occasions, is polished beyond the conception of George Eliot, or any such writer, is condemned wholesale as sadly rugged, &c. And this in a monthly [*Galaxy*] which contains a story by me. It does appear strange to me that you, who have got the cock salmon, should allow this ass * * * to tell your readers that the trout is a bigger fish than the cock salmon.

Now hear the real truth. George Eliot is a writer of the second class, who has the advantage of being better read than most novelists. She has also keen powers of observation and reasoning.

She has no imagination of the higher kind, and no power of construction, nor dramatic power. She has a little humour, whereas most women have none; and a little pathos. But she has neither pathos nor humour enough to make anybody laugh nor anybody cry.

Her style is grave, sober, and thoughtful; but it lacks fire, tune, and variety.

She has been adroit enough to disavow the sensational, yet to use it as far as her feeble powers would let her. Her greatest quality of all is living with an anonymous writer, who has bought the English press for a time and puffed her into a condition she cannot maintain, and is gradually losing.

Why lend yourself to a venal English lie? This George Eliot is all very well as long as she confines herself to the life and character she saw with her own eyes down in Warwickshire when she was young. But the moment imagination is required she is done. Let any man read true books about the Middle Ages and then read *Romola*—he will at once be struck with two things: That the records of the Middle Ages are a grand romance full of noble material and character and situation, and that this unhappy scribbler of novels has so dealt with that

gigantic theme as to dwarf it to her own size. When you have waded through the watery waste of *Romola*, what remains upon the mind?

A little Florence, a faint description of petty politics not worth mentioning. A little Savonarola depicted, not sculptured. A young lady called Romola, who is not mediaeval at all, but a delicate-minded young woman of the nineteenth century and no other. And a hero who is—Mr. George Lewes.

Now read a mediaeval novel by Scott, or even *The Cloister and the Hearth* by Charles Reade. Do these works miss all the grand features of the Middle Ages as this poor unimaginative scribbler has done; or do they transport you out of this ignorant present into a ruder and more romantic age? Verbum sapienti.

I will only add that in all her best novels the best idea is stolen from me and her thefts are not confined to ideas and situations; they go as far as similes, descriptions, and lines of text. Believe me, the pupil is never above her master.

This last fact coupled with the persistent detraction I meet from my fair pupil's satellites in the English press will, I hope, excuse this burst of bile.

Seriously, however, and setting my personal feelings out of the question, do not you underrate the judgment of the American public in this case; nor overrate the judgment of the English press.

The public is an incorruptible judge; the press is a corruptible judge, and peculiar facilities were offered in G. Eliot's case for buying the English press, and they have been purchased and repurchased accordingly. (p. 253)

> *Charles Reade, in his letter to the editors of* Galaxy, *June 8, 1869 (and reprinted in "Charles Reade's Opinion of Himself and His Opinion of George Eliot," in* The Bookman, *New York, Vol. XVIII, November, 1903, p. 254).*

BLACKWOOD'S EDINBURGH MAGAZINE (essay date 1869)

[It] would take half a hundred ordinary novelists to make up a shadow of the power, the wonderful swing of life and energy, the human insight and splendid graphic force of the author of the '**Cloister and the Hearth.**' (p. 488)

[Mr. Reade's volumes] stand before us, a little library of fiction, sound, wholesome, and vigorous, with many faults and many beauties, the real utterance of a real human being; full of the heartiest human sentiments, noble indignation, noble pity, daring sufficient to carry the lamp of imagination into very dark corners indeed, and to flash its revelation upon actual deeds of darkness, with all the imperious will of genius, and that true insight which only sympathy can give. . . . [He] is now and then coarse, as in '**Griffith Gaunt**'—not that he intends it, but that, having chosen to build his story upon a certain course of incidents, it was necessary for him to note certain events not generally chronicled; and he does so in plain, brief language, without thought of delicacy or the reverse. This may be coarse, but it is not nasty; nor is there any suggestion of nastiness in the sudden and curt record. . . . Mr. Reade's faults are so lost in the brilliancy of his power, . . . in the mingled force and softness of his sympathy, in the noble ideal he so often sets before us, and the fine, keen sense of excellence which shines through everything he does, that we have not the heart to reproach him with [his failures].

There is, perhaps, no writer of equal eminence who has so clearly shown the character and principles of his genius from the very beginning of his career. **'Peg Woffington,'** his earliest work, is at once an epitome and adumbration of all he has done. Mr. Reade's *repertoire* is limited. . . . Such a limitation is no doubt a weakness in point of art; but we doubt much whether it is not an additional charm to the ordinary reader. . . . [Making opposites equal] is the thing of all others which Mr. Reade has done best; and we know not one of his contemporaries, and few of his predecessors, who have given such an idea to the world. (pp. 489-91)

['**Peg Woffington'** does have] faults, no doubt, and there is a touch of extravagance in it, an extravagance the result of his power and mastery over his materials, which is one of Mr. Reade's standing defects. (p. 492)

['**Griffith Gaunt'** is the] author's noblest romance—a book which will no doubt take its place among the immortals, and live beyond the limits of the nineteenth century. . . . (pp. 495-96)

[The conclusion of **'Griffith Gaunt'**] is the ruin of the book. The horror has been piled so high, the tragic strength and devotion of the two female characters, the tragic weakness, vacillation, and misery of the wretched man, have been set before us so forcibly, that we are quite unprepared for sugar and rose-water at the end. Mr. Reade's paternal affection has deceived him, and made him forget those fine instincts of the poet which are strong in him by nature. . . . It is a mistake on Mr. Reade's part to make [Griffith] so despicable and to make his shame so public just as it is a mistake to make Vane [in **'Peg Woffington'**] such a weak villain, and Gatty [in **'Christie Johnstone'**] so poor a creature. . . . This is to make Love, the most clear-sighted, the most long-suffering, the most exquisite and sad of all spirits, into a simple fool. . . . This is false to nature, and altogether a mistake in art. . . . [Let] us adjure Mr. Reade another time, by our admiration for his genius. . . . (pp. 498-99)

[**'Love Me Little, Love Me Long'**] is not a book which it is usual to distinguish as Mr. Reade's masterpiece; but of all the little library before us, it is the one to which we personally turn with the warmest partiality. There is so little in it that we can wish out of it—so little redundancy, so much originality—such truth and naturalness, such charming ease and undemonstrative power. . . . It is a little idyl, a homely poem. . . . [There] are few sensational events, . . . yet the story attracts us like music. (pp. 500-01)

David [in **'Love Me Little, Love Me Long'**] is Mr. Reade's *preux chevalier.* As there is little excellence on the stage without a little extravagance, so Mr. Reade's picturesque and dramatic genius is never quite free from a *soupçon* of exaggeration. (pp. 501-02)

The book which reintroduces us to the . . . bridal happiness [of **'Love Me Little, Love Me Long'**] is entitled **'Hard Cash,'** and it is a book which has been mightily canvassed, and of which it remains an open question whether the ground it goes over is ground permitted or not to fiction. (p. 506)

'Never too Late to Mend' is a book which is full of all [Reade's] characteristic faults, and has few of his equally characteristic excellences. (p. 510)

Very different is the character of the **'Cloister and the Hearth.'** It is, as everybody knows, a historical novel; and historical novels, as everybody knows, are generally heavy work to both reader and writer. . . . But Mr. Reade's historical study is alive. . . . [Our] author's fault, if fault it can be called, is always a little too much movement and activity. His imagination is so rich and full, and his invention so unbounded, that, like a medieval painter, he enriches every inch of his canvas with its own special story. Indeed the book altogether reminds us of a picture. . . . Mr. Reade, as we have said, cannot but be somewhat theatrical. His genius is so dramatic that its weakness falls on the side of castastrophes and situations. . . . The author, it is evident, has not thought much about probability. He goes on [in **'The Cloister and the Hearth'**], as life does, at a pace which leaves little time for the selection of incidents. Let us add, that were the pace less violent, and the incidents less crowded, it is quite possible that the story might be more effective. But this is simple speculation. (pp. 510-11)

In this [story], however, as in Mr. Reade's other novels, we have to reproach him with the bad management of his villany. It is poorly done—it is unsuccessful—the villains are contemptible. . . . Their motive is not sufficient for so much rascality, and themselves are poor creatures, not worth a second glance. Another weakness which is visible in almost all his works recurs here also. Doctors are great bunglers, let us allow, and medicine a science which goes very much in the dark, making a series of fortunate or unfortunate guesses; but why the profession should be made to stand up on a stool of repentance in the middle of the sixteenth century, and receive a hearty blow . . . , in no way enforced by the story or the necessities of its course, we are quite unable to guess. . . . [There is] a certain air of fanaticism and monomania to the author's principles. It is a mistake in art as well as in chronology, and shows with what bonds of iron Mr. Reade's opinions and prejudices bind him.

There is one other special criticism besides, which refers exclusively to the **'Cloister and the Hearth.'** The wonderful variety and animation of the scenes in the background become almost a defect when considered in their relation to the unity of the tale. They are all so full of life and character that the reader is tempted to forget their entirely subsidiary rank. . . . (pp. 511-12)

Mr. Reade—who attempts no moralities, who has been reproached with coarseness, who is often theatrical, and almost always extravagant—who calls one of his books a matter-of-fact romance, and is constantly thrusting himself into the discussion of actual and existing evils in a manner considered by the critics as quite incompatible with fiction—is nevertheless a workman who keeps the ideal constantly in sight. Whatever his books may be lacking in, they never fail in the persistent testimony that there is something in the world beyond the mere commonplace virtues; that high generosities and charities are, after all, more interesting to humanity than records, however exact, of bores and dunces; and that it is possible to be real flesh and blood, and yet show God's image. . . . Mr. Reade, while taking from the theory of realism all that is best in it, has never been carried away by this common stream [of undistinguishable characters]. With all his rapidity and sweep of movement, and all his vivid power of observation and detail, he has always preserved the ideal in his mind. He sets before us men and women whom it is no shame to admire, who are not occupied solely by the aimless loves and labours of mediocrity, but who are able to mould their own fortunes, to stand fast before the assaults and bear the hardships of life, and who are actuated by motives and meanings beyond the mean level of the ordinary. His eyes are always aglow with that perennial worship of excellence which comes natural to genius. (p. 513)

It will be seen that we have left entirely aside Mr. Reade's last completed work. We are not sure that **'Foul Play'** is [capable of much criticism.] . . . Yet even in this strange production, which surpasses all the rest in extravagance, and falls infinitely short of them in reality, there is yet the high natural grace of a conception perfectly noble, an attempt at the portrayal of a man above all selfishness, full of delicacy, generosity, purity, and honour. . . . The book is to a great extent a mistake, and is not worthy either of its author's reputation or his power. But yet there is a soul even in this unsuccessful effort, which goes a world beyond many a work more secure of fame. (pp. 513-14)

Mr. Reade is no philosophical maker, calmly projecting his creatures into existence, to take their own way and follow their own impulses; he does not watch them with good-humoured cynicism as some writers do, calmly explaining their ways and their motives, and deriving a certain amusement from their blunders. On the contrary, he is the warm and tender and impassioned partisan of his children. He weeps with them, and rejoices with them, and suffers in their sufferings. He admires them with an ingenuous frankness which is beyond artifice. Real or not to us, they are real to him. Their magnanimity and generosity which are his favourite virtues, their breadth of understanding which is his favourite talent, move him, not as if he had made them with his own hands, but as they would do did he meet them in the world. . . . Fiction, as Mr. Reade pursues it, all deficiencies and errors apart, is poetry in the true sense of the word. It is more voluminous, more familiar, enters more minutely into the details of life, but nothing mean, or paltry, or frivolous is in the art, which never contents itself with vulgar reproduction, but always aims at a lofty soul under the garments of individual existence. A man with so rich an imagination, and resources so abundant, should leave us something better still to illustrate our age. And for this purpose, if he will listen to a friendly word of counsel, it is not stimulation that he requires, but restraint—not excitement, but self-denial. . . . There are few writers to whom such advice is necessary. It is almost the only counsel which a sympathetic critic feels bound to offer, with respect and admiration, to the author of **'Christie Johnstone,'** of [**'Hard Cash'**] and of the **'Cloister and the Hearth.'** (p. 514)

> *"Charles Reade's Novels," in* Blackwood's Edinburgh Magazine, *Vol. 106, No. 648, October, 1869, pp. 488-514.*

THE NATION   (essay date 1870)

Mr. Reade has done once more what he has never yet failed to do. He has written a thrilling and passionate novel, from the perusal of which one could pause about as easily as he could linger in the act of going over a precipice. As the story appeared in monthly parts, the reader's progress through it may be described as dropping from one sharp and piercing point of interest to another, which, like so many projections of rock from the sides of the precipice, are each one more poignant than the last, and renders his course more and more terrific, until he is hurled at last into the abyss of bliss below. (p. 423)

"And Fiction," says Mr. Reade, as if he thought something of the kind ought to be said, "whatever you may have been told to the contrary, is the highest, widest, noblest, and greatest of all the arts;" which may be true, though, honestly, things

in this book have made us doubt it; and, to tell the truth further, fiction does not appear to have been used as an art toward the end, where characters and catastrophes have been heaped down pell-mell together. At the same time, we are bound to believe, from thorough conviction by Mr. Reade's former books, that, when he ceases to be an artist, it is of his own motion. We only wonder that he cares so little for the public that honors him so much, for it seems to us that he finally sacrifices to theatrical effects what was first and best in the conception of his story, and the early development of that conception. . . . We hedge again, by allusion to the constantly recurring strokes of wit, and the human nature which Mr. Reade shows by flashes in his people; and then let us doubt if this will atone for their general lapse and collapse. The most egregious catastrophes are painted with force and probability, but you wish they had not needed so much painting.

Let us say once more that **"Put Yourself in his Place"** is intensely interesting, and then let us say, it is a pity that it is not less interesting and better. We do not forget "George Eliot" when we say, as we do say, that the author of **"Put Yourself in his Place"** is now the greatest living writer of English fiction; and that makes it all the more melancholy that he will do what he has here done. But it is consoling to think that a literary excess or blunder is not retroactive, and that though **"Put Yourself in his Place"** exists, none of Mr. Reade's former novels has therefore ceased to be. (pp. 423-24)

> *"Mr. Reade's Last Novel," in* The Nation, *Vol. X, No. 261, June 30, 1870, pp. 423-24.*

[CHARLES READE]   (essay date 1872)

[Charles Reade] is the greatest living English writer of fiction; his two splendid stories, *A Good Fight* and *Foul Play*, did so much for the success of *Once a Week*.

A Good Fight, with three volumes of new matter added to it, was subsequently called *The Cloister and the Hearth*.

Charles Reade's earliest stories were followed . . . by that powerful work of his genius, *It Is Never too Late to Mend*. The book created a great sensation: was read by everybody: effected its author's purpose—viz., compelled the public to insist that the Model Prisons' system should be looked searchingly into.

From the publication of *Peg Woffington*, Charles Reade has continued to apply his great talents to the work of writing novels and dramas; with what success, every reader of fiction knows. (p. 254)

Now it certainly argues some want of real knowledge or study in the critics of this day, that they cannot assign his place, whatever that may be, to this writer. They can place inferior authors; but they really and honestly have no notion where this man stands either as a novelist, or dramatist, or both. Perhaps it may tend to clear this absolute fog, enveloping the judgment of our contemporaries, if we descend from the indefinite to the definite, and compare him with a writer of acknowledged excellence. We are so fortunate as to possess in this country a novelist who, if contemporary criticism were to be trusted, is the greatest writer of fiction the world ever saw. With regard to Shakespeare, contemporary criticism has left but two remarks in print, both of them unfavourable. Corneille was so often lashed, and so little praised. . . .

Molière was denounced as a plagiarist. Voltaire was well lashed. Scott did not quite escape. Bulwer has been severely criticised.

Even Dickens was always roughly handled in certain respectable prints.

But George Eliot is faultless. This is the sober and often-repeated verdict of every quarterly, monthly, and daily critic in the empire. . . .

Now perhaps some people will open their eyes if we tell them that this prodigious writer often borrows ideas from Charles Reade, and sometimes improves them, sometimes bungles them. But as in matters of art it is sometimes kind to open people's eyes, we shall assure you that this is so; and moreover that in a single instance the two writers have come into competition on fair terms, and the comparison is so unfavourable to the favourite, that the said comparison, though obvious, has always been dexterously avoided. . . .

Reade uses few words, after his kind; and Eliot uses many words, after her kind. But amplification is not invention: the inventor and the only inventor of [the famous scenes in Eliot's plays] is Charles Reade. (p. 256)

[The] fertile situation in [Eliot's] *Felix Holt* was supplied by Charles Reade. The true literary patent is in him. (p. 257)

The Cloister and the Hearth is a gallery of . . . portraits, painted in full colours to the life. *Romola* is a portfolio of delicate studies. *Romola* leaves on the memory—1, a young lady of the nineteenth century, the exact opposite of a mediaeval woman; 2, the soft egotist, an excellent type; 3, an innocent little girl; 4, Savonarola emasculated. The other characters talk nineteen to the dozen, but they are little more than voluble shadows.

The Cloister and the Hearth fixes on the mind—1, the true lover, hermit and priest, Gerard; 2, the true lover, mediaeval and northern, Margaret of Sevenbergen; 3, Dame Catherine, economist, gossip, and mother; 4, the dwarf with his big voice; 5, the angelic cripple, little Kate; 6, the Burgomaster; 7, the Burgundian soldier, a character hewn out of mediaeval rock; 8, the gaunt Dominican, hard, but holy; 9, the patrician monk, in love with heathenism, but safe from fiery faggots because he believed in the Pope; 10, the patrician Pope, in love with Plutarch, and sated with controversy; 11, the Princess Claelia, a true mediaeval; 12, the bravo's wife, a link between ancient and mediaeval Rome. (p. 258)

You can find a thousand Romolas [as in Eliot's *Romola*] in London, because she is drawn from observation, and is quite out of place in a mediaeval tale. But you cannot find the characters of *The Cloister and the Hearth,* because they are creations. (pp. 258-59)

[*Foul Play*] is a novel of immense power, of the greatest originality, and is one of [Charles Reade's] works that shows best the boundless resource of the writer. This feature must strike every reader of [his] novels; his resource is unlimited; his incidents, novel and striking, yet always possible and natural, follow one another with startling rapidity. *Foul Play* showed off to perfection his ingenuity. The plot is intricate: the characters—several of them quite new in fiction—are real men and women, living and acting in his pages as men and women live and act and speak in real life, and in few novels but his own. It is a story of what is called the sensational type: yet so great is the power of art: so mighty the skill of the artist: that all the incidents seem natural and consequent. . . . It is a work of genius. The effect of the book is perfectly marvelous. . . . (p. 259)

Of *The Cloister and the Hearth* it is impossible to speak too well. The author's perfect knowledge of mediaeval life, just before the time of Erasmus, is wonderful. The plot is full of incident of the newest and most striking, yet most probable and natural sort: the characters live, and seem to us real persons we know well: the France, Italy, Holland, and Germany of the time of Erasmus are faithfully reproduced. The interest never flags: there is always something to command attention and excite curiosity. *The Cloister and the Hearth* is one of the most scholarlike and learned, as well as one of the most artistic and beautiful, works of fiction in any language. . . . Although we place these two books first in their respective classes—*Foul Play* in the class of novels called sensational, and *The Cloister and the Hearth* in that of the purely imaginative—yet Charles Reade's books, taken throughout, are of more even merit than those of almost any other novelist. They are written in English as pure, as simple, and as truly Saxon as any this century has produced: in a literary style—nervous, vigorous, and masculine—with which the most captious and partisan critic cannot find any fault.

Read him: resign yourself to the magic spell of his genius : and be lifted above the cares of everyday life into the regions of imagination, peopled by his real creations. You may be trusted then to draw your own conclusions as to the merit of his books.

By the million readers of the time to come, Reade, Dickens, and Thackeray will be handed down to fame together in every English-speaking country.

To the scholar and the man of culture, *The Cloister and the Hearth* may possibly be dearer than the humorous and wonderful creations of Dickens's fertile genius, or the life-like characters and satirical digressions of Thackeray. (pp. 259-60)

[*Charles Reade,*] *"Charles Reade's Opinion of Himself and His Opinion of George Eliot"* (originally published as *"Charles Reade,"* in Once a Week, January 20, 1872), in The Bookman, New York, Vol. XVIII, November, 1903, pp. 253-60.*

THE SPECTATOR   (essay date 1882)

Mr. Reade is of novelists, perhaps, the most unequal. . . . [To] this reviewer, who confesses to a cordial admiration for some of his novels, *The Wandering Heir* seems terribly tiresome . . . ; *The Double Marriage,* tedious as well as unnatural; *The Simpleton,* good only when . . . Mr. Reade's power of realising distant and exciting scenes comes into play; and *The Terrible Temptation,* very nearly disgusting. . . . [*The Terrible Temptation*] is like a protracted *double entendre.* . . . [The] story is dull, devoid of the naturalness and half-conscious pathos which . . . redeem *Griffith Gaunt;* and full of evidence of Mr. Reade's great intellectual defect,—his inability to distinguish between originality and cynicism. . . .

Mr. Reade's real power, which we acknowledge to be considerable, appears to us to consist in three things. He can depict the outsides of his characters admirably. He cannot or does not make them thoroughly intelligible, but he can and does make them real, so real that even when they do unexpected things, you think those persons would have done them. . . . Mr. Reade can both invent and describe incident, stirring incident, with a force which has been given to a few novelists. The movement, bustle, and "go" of some chapters in *Hard Cash, The Cloister and the Hearth, Christie Johnstone,* and *Never Too Late to Mend* . . . are simply admirable. . . . [Finally], Mr. Reade has a command of pathos which he very rarely indeed exerts, but which is of a very genuine and rare kind. . . .

The power of building up, though not of dissecting, character, unusual command of dramatic incident, and great though little used knowledge of the springs of pathos, these are great qualities in a novelist; yet Mr. Reade himself will probably regard the reviewer who acknowledges them as a slightly malignant idiot, because he sees in the writing more of metallic iridescence, than of true, self-derived flash. Well, each one has the defect of his qualities, and a modest man could not have written Charles Reade's novels at all.

"The Works of Charles Reade," in The Spectator, *Vol. 55, No. 2,820, July 15, 1882, p. 928.*

WALTER BESANT (essay date 1882)

[It] has always been to me matter of great astonishment that the appearance of a novelist among us like Charles Reade should not have been received—I do not say with wider popularity—but with a more ready and more generous appreciation on the part of the critical press. . . . I, for one, consider that Reade takes rank with Fielding, Smollett, Scott, Dickens, and Thackeray: that is to say, in the great and delightful art of fiction, wherein the English—who are always, in every age, doing something better than their neighbours—have surpassed the world, Charles Reade stands among the foremost and best.

First, then, he is a scholar. This means, among other things, that he brought to the study of living man and woman a knowledge of ancient men and women; he knew what to expect. (pp. 198-200)

Secondly, Charles Reade is a dramatist. Observe that the drama permits almost everything except verbosity and tameness. A drama may have nearly every fault, and yet succeed if it be lively and not verbose. But the great majority of novels are verbose to the last degree, without action and without incident. If such a story as **"Griffith Gaunt,"** for instance, be compared with almost any ordinary novel of the day, the first note of difference will be found in the overwhelming amount of incident in the former as compared with the latter; the second, that the descriptions of persons, scenery, place, voice, gesture, &c., necessary in every novel, are much shorter in **"Griffith Gaunt"** than the other. The third, that the conversations do not drag and seem too long or discursive, but that they carry on the action and develop the characters. . . . Charles Reade in his novel work resembles the old dramatists. If he takes his reader to a North Country fishing village, he does not make up an elaborate picture of the houses, the boats, the nets spread out upon the seashore, the smell of the fish, the narrow streets, the reek and the dirt of it. I do not say that in some hands such a description is not pleasing, but it is not part of Reade's method. He is not a painter of scenery nor of houses; he does not care for picturesque "bits" and effects of light unless they help his story; he is a painter of men and women. Therefore, in the space of half a page or thereabouts, he introduces us briefly to the kind of folks we are to meet, and then sets them to talk for themselves. Not a bit of furniture; not an inch of tapestry; no blue china; no cabinets; yet, when all is told and the curtain drops we know the place where the people live better than if we had read pages of description. This is the art of the dramatist. (p. 201)

Looking, therefore, upon his story always as a dramatist considers his plot, Reade, at the outset, seems to have considered strength as the first essential in his work. He aims continually at strength; he achieves strength in three ways: first, by a style which is always reined in, nervous and vigorous, in the purest English; next by clearness of vision in his own mind. You *cannot* draw a portrait when you do not see the face. . . . Thirdly, Reade's strength is achieved by his conscientious fidelity to truth. Not only is he true to his characters, but he is *true to his plots.* I mean this: there are so many complications possible in life, that there is no difficulty whatever in finding the materials for a story; but the artist must have story and characters to match. He must have players who can play the parts and look the characters; he must have a plot which springs naturally from the given conditions, and does not appear manufactured. The age, the position, the very names of his characters must belong to his story. Now all Reade's stories are strong, and strong in their studied art, which seems so unstudied; many of them depend upon situations which in less skilful hands would be merely melodramatic. In his, they belong to the natural development of the plot. Thus, **"It is Never too Late to Mend"** is one long series of striking incidents; it is like a French play in Five Acts and Cinquante Tableaux. There is material enough in it to make a dozen three-volume novels, with the word-spinning and "character-drawing" which fill them out. In **"Love me Little, Love me Long,"** the contrast between David Dodd and Reginald Talboys, struck almost at the opening, is a situation in itself maintained throughout with wonderful skill and success. Then, is there anything more delicious than Peg Woffington pretending to be a portrait in Triplet's studio? In **"Put Yourself in His Place"** he covers the canvas with incidents, he is prodigal of incident, as becomes one who is fertile in devising situations continually new; while in the short **"Wandering Heir"** he has at least half-a-dozen situations all new and all strong. One need not continue the list. Enough has been said to show my meaning, that strength is the main quality desired by this author. (pp. 202-03)

Reade never introduces a needless character.

Nothing more hinders a play, nothing more endangers its success, than a character not wanted. Reade, as I have said before, writes his novels as if he were writing a play. Scene after scene, act by act, the story advances. What does not help the story along must be cut out. And as in a play a man does not come on the stage with a paper tacked on his back describing his character, but proceeds to show himself by words, so in these novels every character shows who and what he is by words and deeds. Many weak writers can imagine vividly and can describe, more or less, what they imagine their characters to have done and why they did it. Reade, on the other hand, I repeat, does not describe; he makes his puppets act their own story, and tell it themselves, putting in only here and there the necessary explanation, the *callida junctura,* which must never be beside the subject, and must, like the conversation, advance the story. He is not himself a narrator so much as a dramatist. His works are almost ready for the stage, his characters portray themselves.

Strength, truth, animation—these are three excellent qualities for a novelist to possess; they will not be denied to Charles Reade even by his enemies. There is, however, a great deal more. (p. 203)

All his books, again, represent life in action. Thackeray loved to sit at a club window and watch the procession along the pavement of old fogies, old bucks, old warriors, old dowagers, young dandies, girls in carriages, actresses, gamblers, brave young country lads, admiring colonials, and the rest who make up the world of clubs and of society. Reade, who cannot be compared with Thackeray, because there is no single point at which they touch, loves the life of action. It is the brave workman fighting single-handed against a Union; it is the young sailor, handsome, gallant, and simple-hearted, against the man of the world; it is the girl disguised as a man; it is the wretched criminal struggling upwards to the level of self-respect, or the husband tortured by jealousy; always real life, with flesh and blood temptations and a hatred of hot-house and artificiality; all his characters—yes, all—are men and women, because, if he flings a figure even for a moment on the canvas, he finishes it with a few bold strokes, and it remains a portrait, not an uncertain phantom: the true artist will not scamp any part of his work. Everybody is real; everything seems to happen as it might happen to all of us, even when the scenes are the most romantic, and the situations are the most unexpected; and this because he weaves his fact with his inventions, so that one hardly knows where reality ends and romance begins. And the novels, taken altogether, cover so wide an area, that we may certainly accord to Reade the glory of being the chief painter of English modern life in its many forms, from the belle of the season to the fish-fag, and from the peer to the convict. I believe, however, that the great uninteresting stratum of life known as the "lower middle class" has been left quite untouched by him, probably because he knows nothing of it.

He gathers his material where he can, like Molière and Shakespeare. If he wants to write about modern times, there are the daily papers, the essays of the monthly press, the blue-books, the pamphlets—all kinds of things. If he wants to write about the past, there is the literature of the age to teach him. (p. 205)

[I think] that the collected volumes of Reade's novels present a more complete picture of English modern life than can be found in the works of any other novelist. There are separate novels by Trollope, Hardy, Mrs. Oliphant, sketches by Laurence Oliphant, stories by Miss Mulock, and plenty of others, invaluable as pictures of contemporary manners and touching on portions of life outside the field of Charles Reade; but not one has covered so wide an area, or studied so carefully or represented so successfully the living, moving, struggling, acting life. I do not wish to set up comparisons between Reade and Trollope, or any other good writer. To each his gifts. It is, however, a very remarkable and suggestive thing about Reade that he cannot be compared. You cannot lay hold of Reade here and of Trollope there, and compare their treatment. He is absolutely unlike Thackeray; he bears no resemblance to Dickens; with Blackmore, Hardy, or George Meredith, the three who seem to me to come next to Thackeray, Dickens, and Reade, he has not one single point in common. The impossibility of either comparing or classifying Reade, or of judging him from a critical point of view which admits any other writer, is, to my mind, one of the strongest proofs of his excellence. (p. 208)

I find ["**Christie Johnstone**"], almost the earliest outcome of Charles Reade's genius, the most significant and the most characteristic. There are in it the contrasts which he loves between the conventional and the real, the conscious artificial and the unconscious natural; there is the life of action, the truth and fidelity of fact, the dramatic situations, the freedom from verbosity, the clearness of vision, the epigrammatic talk, and the indignation of the moralist; above all, it strikes the note of the True Woman.

Reade, in fact, invented the True Woman. That is to say, he was the first who found her. There have been plenty of sweet and charming women in stories—the patient, loving Amelia; the bouncing country girl, Sophy Western; the graceful and *gracieuses* ladies of Scott; the pretty dummies of Dickens; the insipid sweetnesses of Thackeray; the proper middle-class (or upper-class) girl of Trollope; the conventional girl of the better lady novelists. There have also been disagreeable girls, especially the bad-style, detestable girl of the "worser" lady novelists; but Reade—the *trouvère*—has found the real woman. You will meet her on every page of all his novels. . . . [She] is not, at all events, insipid; no real women are; if she is artificial, he shows the real woman beneath. What he loves most is the woman whom fashion has not spoiled; the true, genuine woman, with her natural passion, her jealousy, her devotion, her love of admiration, her fidelity, her righteous wrath, her maternal ferocity, her narrow faith, her shrewdness, even her audacity of falsehood when that can serve her purpose, and her perfect abnegation of self.

An objection has been made to Reade on the ground that he is wanting in fun. He is not, certainly, a comic writer, nor is he even one who writes mirthfully; but he is always a cheerful writer. His studies have led him to think, on the whole, well of humanity; he is hopeful. More than this it would be absurd to expect of a man who makes of each "case" before him a study of human life. But he is eminently hopeful.

There remains one book of his on which I have as yet said nothing. It is his greatest work—and, I believe, the greatest historical novel in the language. I mean "**The Cloister and the Hearth.**" . . . [In it] there is portrayed so vigorous, lifelike, and truthful a picture of a time long gone by, and differing in almost every particular from our own, that the world has never seen its like. To me it is a picture of the past more faithful than anything in the works of Scott. As one reads it, one feels in the very atmosphere of the century; one breathes the air just before the Great Dawn of Learning and Religion; it is still twilight, but the birds are twittering already on the boughs; it is a time when men are weary of the past; there is no freshness or vigour in the poetry; all the tunes are old tunes. There is plenty of fanaticism, but no faith; under the tiara the Pope yawns; under the scarlet cloak the cardinals scoff; in his chamber the scholar asks whether the newly found Greek is not better than all the ecclesiastical jargon; in the very cloister are monks secretly at work on the new learning, and cursing the stupid iteration of the bell; even the children of the soil are asking themselves how long—Alas! they must wait till the Greater Jacquerie of 1792 relieves them; there is uncertainty everywhere; there is the restless movement which goes before a change. There is, however, plenty of activity in certain directions. Soldiers fight, and great lords lead armies; there are court ceremonies at which knights feast and common people gape; prentice lads go a-wandering along the roads; with them tramp the vagrant scholars; the forests are full of robbers; the beggars are a nation to themselves, and a very horrible, noisome, miserable nation; the towns are crowded within narrow walls; fever and the plague are constantly breaking out; there is no ladder by which men can climb except that lowered for them by the Church; where a man is born, there he sticks. A fine picturesque time; with plenty of robberies and murders; vast quantities of injustice; with lords among the peasants, like locusts among corn, devouring the substance; with fierce punishments for the wicked, but not so fierce as those which certainly await most people in the next world; with gibbets, racks, red-hot pincers, wheels, processions of penitents, heavy wax candles, cutting off of hands, and every possible stimulus to virtue; yet a world in which virtue was singularly rare. All this life—and more—is in **"The Cloister and the Hearth"**; not described, *but acted*. . . . The reader who does not know, or does not enquire, presently finds himself drawn completely out of himself and his own times; before he reaches the end, he thinks like the characters in the book; he feels like them; he talks like them. This is the general effect of the book; but, besides, there runs through it the sweetest, saddest, and most tender love story ever devised by wit of man. There is no heroine in fiction more dear to me than Margaret; she is always real; always the true woman; brave in the darkest hour; and for ever yearning in womanly fashion for the love that has been cruelly torn from her. (pp. 210-13)

I do not suppose that by these remarks one can add anything to the real reputation of Charles Reade or to the admiration with which the English-speaking races regard his works. They may, however, lead others to consider the position occupied by this writer, which is, and has been, since the death of Thackeray and Dickens, alone in the front rank. He resembles no other writer living or dead. His merits are his own, and they are those of the first order of writers. He cannot be classified: in order to be classified, a man must be either a leader or one of a following. Reade cannot, certainly, be accused of following. In fine, he paints women as they are, men as they are, things as they are. What we call genius is first the power of seeing men, women, and things as they are—most of us, being without genius, are purblind—and then the power of showing them by means of "invention"—by the grafting of "invention" upon fact. No living man has shown greater power of grasping fact and of weaving invention upon it than Charles Reade. (p. 214)

Walter Besant, *"Charles Reade's Novels," in* The Gentleman's Magazine, *Vol. CCLIII, No. 1820, August, 1882, pp. 198-214.*

WILLIAM ARCHER (essay date 1882)

[Mr. Charles Reade is a dramatist] who has at least that first requisite of greatness, faith in himself. In speaking of him I should perhaps confess that my estimate may be warped by the personal repulsion which Mr. Reade's style tends to create in me. He is always in a bad temper. Anger is not with him a "short madness." His controversial style is violent to a degree, and he carries the same mannerism out of the sphere of controversy into that of art. It is a question of temperament, and to me such a temperament is antipathetic. Hence I may possibly be unjust in my estimate of his absolute merits.

That he is a great dramatist, if not *the* great dramatist of the age, he himself has perseveringly informed us, in the manifestoes and controversial effusions which every now and then ornament either the advertising or the correspondence columns of the newspapers. His theory is that he is a born dramatist driven into prose fiction by unjust and unwise copyright laws. In this theory there is a certain amount of truth. Let any one compare **"Peg Woffington"** with **"Masks and Faces"** and he will find in the spasmodic style of the novel a defect which disappears in the play. On the other hand let any one sit out **"The Scuttled Ship"** or **"It's Never Too Late to Mend"** and he will find it difficult to believe that such crude, ill-digested, and often conventional matter is the work of one of "nature's dramatists." . . . A dramatist must be "made," as well as born. Mr. Reade may have been born a dramatist, but he has certainly not been shaped into one.

"Masks and Faces" is probably his best work. It is a genuine comedy of interesting intrigue and well-marked character. The dialogue, too, is above the usual level. It is true that in many cases, the wit belongs to the "comedy of no-manners" school, which seems strangely inappropriate in a piece whose dresses and surroundings are eminently those of a comedy of manners. Half the fun of the piece, moreover, is got from two or three themes mechanically worked out to the very last echo. . . . But with all [its faults] the dialogue remains more than usually interesting from its occasional touches of true wit and genuine feeling.

Its construction is in several respects interesting. The first point to be observed, as a peculiarity rather than a fault, is that, like **"Vanity Fair,"** it is a play without a hero. More correctly, it has in Triplet a hero who is almost entirely unconnected with the plot. He is concerned in the *dénouement*, it is true, but quite passively. . . . (pp. 27-9)

A much more serious defect is the conduct of the *dénouement*. . . . [The] authors seem to have lost all grasp of their subject. They needlessly protract the action through several tedious and illogical scenes, which have to be led up to by means of very strained devices. . . . The play is like the human body as represented by the Darwinian theory—it has caudal vertebrae which seem to indicate that, at some earlier stage of its development, it rejoiced in a tail. (p. 30)

[I believe **"Masks and Faces"**] is the only one of Mr. Reade's works, so far as they are known to me, which is likely to hold the stage. He, on the other hand, believes in the immortality of **"It's Never Too Late to Mend,"** which, he says, has outlived a hundred French dramas, and will outlive a hundred more. This is in a sense unquestionable—my only wonder is that it does not outlive its audiences. It has outlived me twice, so that after mature deliberation I have come to the conclusion that there is an M too much in its name, and that **"It's Never Too Late to End"** was the title to which it was "specially written up." (pp. 31-2)

[Mr. Reade] has informed us that **"Drink,"** his adaptation of **"L'Assommoir,"** is the greatest drama of the century, and it is certainly a very remarkable play. It is hard to over-estimate the difficulties with which he had to contend. He had to transplant a piece depending for its success on its realistic reproduction of the lights and shadow of low life in Paris, to a theatre whose audiences, for the most part, have no special knowledge of or interest in Parisian life. Another dramatist might probably have destroyed the reality and diminished the picturesqueness by removing the scene to England. Not so Mr. Reade. . . . I am no great believer in the direct and immediate moral effect of stage representations, but if there ever was a drama which could cause instant conversions from evil ways, **"Drink"** was that drama. . . . My contention is that, art or no art, **"Drink"** was an instructive play of distinctly moral tendency. . . . It rose in several respects above the level of conventional melodrama, and was a more or less truthful illustration of life. (pp. 35-8)

William Archer, *"Playwrights of Yesterday," in his* English Dramatists of To-day, *Sampson Low, Marston, Searle, & Rivington, 1882, pp. 19-48.**

A. C. SWINBURNE (essay date 1884)

To a country and a century in which the higher form of drama has been supplanted and superseded by the higher form of novel, the loss of an energetic and able craftsman in the trade of narrative fiction must naturally seem more or less considerable. The brilliant industry of Mr. Charles Reade, his vivid and vehement force of style, his passionate belief and ardent delight in the greatness of his calling, would have conferred a certain kind of interest on a literary figure of less serious pretentions to regard. It is not at all wonderful that on the morrow of his death there should have arisen in the little world of letters a little noise of debate as to the proper station and definition of so remarkable a writer. Whether he was or was not a man of genius—whether his genius, if he had such a thing, was wide or narrow, deep or shallow, complete or incomplete—became at once, for the moment, a matter in some quarters of something like personal controversy. If he had often written as well as he could sometimes write—or, again, if he had often written as ill as he could sometimes write—there would be no possibility of dispute on the subject. He has left not a few pages which if they do not live as long as the English language will fail to do so through no fault of their own, but solely through the malice of accident, by which so many reputations well worthy of a longer life have been casually submerged or eclipsed.

On the other hand, he has taken good care that few of his larger and more laboured works shall have so much as a fair chance for their lives. No man was ever at more pains to impair his own prospects of literary survival. His first two stories were the very quintessence of theatrical ability—and were now and then something more. But if some of his best effects were due to his experience as a dramatic aspirant, not a few of his more glaring faults as a novelist are traceable to the same source. The burlesque duel in *Christie Johnstone*, the preposterous incident of the living portrait in *Peg Woffington*, might have made the fortune of a couple of farces; but in serious fiction they are such blemishes as cannot be effaced and can hardly be redeemed by the charming scenes which precede or follow them—the rescue of the drowning dauber by his discarded bride, and the charity of the triumphant actress to the household of the stage-struck poetaster. These are small matters; but there are errors of the same stamp in the more important works of the maturer novelist. (pp. 550-51)

One of the most important and indispensable figures in [*It is never too late to mend*] might have done well enough on the boards of a theatre, but does very much less than well between the boards of a novel. [The character] 'Levi the Jew' has been unjustly, I think, dismissed as an elaborate and absolute failure: . . . the remnants of the chosen people seem seldom to bring their admiring students a stroke of good luck in the line of sentimental or enthusiastic fiction: but it is when set aside or between such living and complete figures as George Fielding and Tom Robinson that the grateful and vindictive Hebrew appears out of his place by day, so far from the footlights behind which he could be seen in due relief and measured by the proper standard.

A far more absolute failure is the athletico-seraphic chaplain—[similar to Eugène Sue's] Prince Rodolphe (of the *Mystères de Paris*) in Anglican orders, and much astonished to find himself translated into a latitude less congenial than the slums of the Seine riverside. . . . That in this case the hideous and nauseous narrative is unmistakably inspired by no baser instinct than a pure and genuine loathing of cruelty is more than enough to exculpate the man, but by no means enough to exculpate the artist. (p. 551)

There is not, however, in all the range of his work, another as flagrant instance of passionate philanthropy riding rough-

shod over the ruins of artistic propriety. In *Hard Cash* the crusade against the villainous lunacy of the law regarding lunatics was conducted with more literary tact and skill—with nobler energy and ardour it could not be conducted—than this precious onslaught on the system which made homicide by torture a practical part of such prison discipline as well deserved the disgrace of approbation from the magnanimous worshipper of portable gallows and beneficent whip: the harsher and the humaner agents of an insane law who figure on the stage of the narrative which attacks it are more lifelike as well as less horrible than the infernal little disciples of Carlyle who infest and impede the progress of the earlier tale.

In the brilliant story of *A Simpleton* there are passages of almost as superfluous dulness as the dullest superfluities of the self-styled naturalist whose horrors Mr. Reade undertook to adapt for presentation on the English stage: and the dullness is . . . deliberate and systematic, based on [M. Zola's] great principle, that a study from life should be founded on what he calls 'documents'—nay, that it should be made up of these, were they never so noisome or so wearisome: but the second half of the book redeems and rectifies the tedious excesses and excursions of the first. (p. 552)

Mr. Reade, by far the greatest master of narrative whom our country has produced since the death of Scott, was as much his superior in dramatic dexterity as he was inferior to Dumas in the art of concealing rather than obtruding his natural command and his practical comprehension of this peculiar talent. It is the lack of that last and greatest art—not the art to blot, but the art to veil—it is the inability to keep his hand close, to abstain from proclamation and ostentation, to be content with a quiet and triumphant display of his skill and knowledge and experience in all the rules and all the refinements of the game—it is this that sets him, as a narrative artist, so decidedly below Dumas; it is the lack of seeming unconsciousness and inevitable spontaneity which leaves his truest and finest pathos less effective and less durable in its impression than the truest and finest pathos of Scott. (pp. 553-54)

The variety of life, the vigour of action, the straightforward and easy mastery displayed at every step in every stage of the fiction, would of themselves be enough to place *The Cloister and the Hearth* among the very greatest masterpieces of narrative; while its tender truthfulness of sympathy, its ardour and depth of feeling, the constant sweetness of its humour, the frequent passion of its pathos, are qualities in which no other tale of adventure so stirring and incident so inexhaustible can pretend to a moment's comparison with it—unless we are foolish enough to risk a reference to the name by which no contemporary name can hope to stand higher or shine brighter, for prose or for verse, than does that of Shakespeare's greatest contemporary by the name of Shakespeare.

The wealth and splendour, of invention, the superb command of historic resource, and the animating instinct which gives life to every limb and feature of the story, interest to every detail of various learning, and the charm of perfect credibility to the wildest phases of passion or of faith, the strangest adventure or coincidence, the boldest strokes of worse or better fortune which influence or modify the progress of character and event, would need more time and space to indicate and to praise with any show of adequacy than I can hope to afford them here. But this book is foundation enough, if any ground for prophecy may be supplied by the fortunes of other books, for a fame as durable as any romancer's ambition could desire. It is so copious and various that the strength and skill with which the unity of interest is maintained through all diversities of circumstance and byplay of episodes may almost be called incomparable: Dumas has never shown such power and tenderness of touch in the conduct and support of a story so pure and profound in its simplicity of effect through such a web of many-coloured adventure. And for vivid play of incident, for versatile animation of detail, Dumas himself seems no longer incomparable in his kind to the reader of this book. (pp. 556-57)

It seems singular that any important work of the hand which has given us so noble and high-toned a book as this great romance should ever have been taxed with immorality; and more singular still that it should in any sense be fairly liable to such a charge. Of the two among Mr. Reade's novels which were assailed on this score at the date of their first appearance, the later, *A Terrible Temptation,* seems to me the more easily and the more thoroughly defensible. Such attacks on it as I remember to have seen were not generally based on the simple fact that it contained a remarkably lifelike and brilliant study of a courtesan—ultimately transfigured by conversion into a field-preacher: they were based on the imputation that the married heroine of the story was represented as hovering more or less near the edge of adultery. How such a notion can ever have slipped into the head, I do not say of any rational and candid reader, but of the most viciously virtuous reviewer that ever gave tongue on the slot of an imaginary scandal, I have never been able to imagine. It requires not merely a vigorous effort of charity, but a determined innocence in the ways of the world of professional moralists, to believe that any reader of the book, at any stage of the story, can have really mistaken the character of the 'terrible' and most natural temptation which besets the tender and noble nature of the heroine: a temptation, not to illicit love, but to legal fraud instigated by conjugal devotion. To me this has always seemed one of the very best and truest in study of character, most rich in humour and interest, most faithful and natural in evolution and result, of all Mr. Reade's longer or shorter stories.

But for tragic power, for unfaltering command over all the springs and secrets of terror and pity, it is not comparable with the book which would beyond all question be generally acknowledged by all competent judges as his masterpiece, if its magnificent mechanism were not vitiated by a moral flaw in the very mainspring of the action. This mainspring, if we may believe the sub-title of *Griffith Gaunt,* is supplied by the passion of jealousy. But the vile crime on which the whole action of the latter part of the story depends, and but for which the book would want its very finest effects of pathos and interest, is not prompted by jealousy at all: it is prompted by envy. (pp. 557-58)

We do not forbid an artist in fiction to set before us strange instances of inconsistency and eccentricity in conduct: but we require of the artist that he should make us feel such aberrations to be as clearly inevitable as they are confessedly exceptional. If he can do this, but not otherwise, he has a right to maintain that fiction, like wisdom, is justified of all her children. . . . Now it seems to me undeniable that Charles Reade has not succeeded in making us feel it inevitable—and therefore has not succeeded in making us feel it possible—that an honourable man should be so mastered by the temptation or provocation which assails Griffith Gaunt as to throw all sense of honour to the winds rather than endure the momentary sting of insult from an inferior. . . . (pp. 558-59)

No language can overpraise what hardly any praise can sufficiently acknowledge—the masterly construction, the sus-

tained intensity of interest, the keen and profound pathos, the perfect and triumphant disguise of triumphant and perfect art, the living breath of passion, the spontaneous and vivid interaction of character and event, the noble touches of terror and the sublimer strokes of pity, which raise [*Griffith Gaunt*] almost as high as prose can climb towards poetry, and set it perhaps as near as narrative can come to drama. The forty-third chapter is to my mind simply one of the most beautiful things in English literature: and no fitter praise can be given to the book than this—that so exquisite an interlude is not out of keeping with the rest.

Great as was usually the care displayed in the composition of Mr. Reade's other works, and great as was sometimes the skill which ensured success to this ungrudging and conscientious labour of love, there is not another of his books which as an all but absolute and consummate work of art can be set beside or near this masterpiece. . . . The best of Mr. Reade's romances are certainly not more finished works of higher or more faultless art than the best plays of Ford or Webster: their faults are generally not less gross and glaring than such as disfigure the masterpiece of Decker or of Middleton. (pp. 561-62)

All we can say is that, if not, the loss will be theirs who shall have let such good merchandise go to wreck. It will be a loss—whatever good work of its own age which utterly neglects them may produce—to know nothing of a book so full of keenly refined humour and nobly moving incident, such good studies and such good scenes, as that which carries the rather silly label, 'Love me little, love me long.' (p. 562)

A man's most perfect work is not likely to be his greatest, unless the man himself be one of the very greatest writers of all time; and the full energy of Mr. Reade's genius is conspicuous rather in works less free from his besetting sins of pretension and prolixity. For, concise as was his usual method of narrative or comment, and indeed sometimes rather defiantly demonstrative of this excellent faculty of concision, he could be tediously prolix in the reiteration and reinforcement of theories and arguments by illustration and exposition at far greater length than was necessary or suitable to the very effect at which he aimed. (p. 563)

[*The Autobiography of a Thief*] is nothing less than a masterpiece of tragicomedy: the fellow's style is perhaps the very finest evidence of his creator's dramatic faculty which could be adduced from the whole collection of Charles Reade's romances. That faculty however, brilliant and versatile as it is, is never so thoroughly or so strikingly displayed in the full completion or consummation of the work undertaken as in the vivid energy of single scenes, the vivid relief of single characters. (pp. 564-65)

That I am no lukewarm admirer of Mr. Reade's genius will hardly, I presume, be questioned by any reader of these lines; and his warmest admirers have the best right to place on record their regret that he should have made it necessary for them to remark on the singular lack of taste and judgment displayed in the collection and preservation of his most unwise and violent extravagances in the field of personal or critical controversy. Honest indignation is a great thing when it makes great verses, and a good thing when it makes good prose: but the fact is no less obvious than lamentable that Reade's, however unaffected it may have been, had only too often no foothold in reason, no ground of common sense to stand on.

From a writer capable of such vehement follies and such high-toned ambitions, a rational reader would naturally have expected nothing better, if nothing worse, than Reade has left behind him. What Mr. Trollope says of Charlotte Brontë is more exactly true, it seems to me, of Charles Reade. 'If it could be right to judge the work of a novelist from one small portion of one novel,'—or rather, in this case, from sundry small portions of various novels—'and to say of an author that he is to be accounted as strong as he shows himself to be in his strongest morsel of work,'—then, to finish the sentence for myself, I should say that the station of Charles Reade would be high among the very highest workers in creative fiction. As a painter of manners, and of character as affected by social conditions, he is never much above Trollope at his best; indeed I doubt if he has ever done anything at all better than the study of that hapless, high-souled, unmanageable and irrational saint and hero, whose protracted martyrdom and ultimate deliverance give such original and unique interest to *The Last Chronicle of Barset*. More delightfully actual and life-like groups or figures than the Grantlys, the Luftons, and the Proudies, it would be impossible to find on any canvas of Mr. Reade's: and these leading figures or groups of Barsetshire society are sketched with such lightness of hand, such an attractive ease and simplicity of manner, that the obtrusive and persistent vehemence of presentation which distinguishes the style and the method of Charles Reade appears by comparison inartistic and ineffectual. Perhaps he did not think better of his own characters than they deserved: but he would seem to have thought worse than it probably deserves of his average reader's intelligence, in supposing it incompetent or slow to appreciate, with quiet recognition and peaceable approval, the charm of the force of character, the strength or the subtlety of motive displayed in the conduct of action or dialogue, without some vigorous note of more or less direct and personal appeal to the attention and admiration required by the writer as his due.

But this and all other defects or infirmities of his genius disappear or become transfigured when it suddenly takes fire and spreads wing for heights far beyond the reach of the finest painter of social manners, the most faithful and trustworthy spokesman or showman of commonplace event and character. Were there not a twang of cant or rant about the epithet, I should venture to say that there is something of a more Homeric quality about his narrative power at its highest than could without absurdity be attributed to the work of any among his contemporary countrymen: a vivid force which informs even prose with something of the effect of epic rather than dramatic poetry. There is more romantic beauty, more passionate depth of moral impression, in the penultimate chapter of *Westward Ho!* than in any chapter of Reade's; but it hardly attains the actual and direct force of convincing as well as exciting effect which we recognise in the narrative of the Agra's last voyage homeward. That magnificent if not matchless narrative is the crowning evidence of its author's genius: if it should not live as long as the language, so much the worse for all the students of the language who shall overlook so noble an example of its powers. As much, in my poor opinion, may be said for the narrative of Gerard's adventures in the company of Denys the Burgundian; this latter, with all deference to the sounder judgment and the finer taste of Mr. Anthony Trollope, 'a character that will remain' as long as most figures in English fiction. There are characteristic and serious faults in the story called *Put yourself in his place;* the sublimely silly old squire is a venerable stage property not worth so much refurbishing as the author's care has bestowed on it; the narrative is perhaps a little overcharged with details of documentary evidence; but the hero, the villain, and the two or three heroines are all excellently well drawn; the construction or composition of the story is a

model of ingenuity, delicacy, and vigour; and the account of the inundation is another of those triumphant instances of masterful and superb description which give actually the same delight, evoke the same admiration, stimulate and satisfy the same intense and fervid interest, on a tenth as on a first reading. There is nothing nearly so good as this in *A Woman Hater;* but here again the villain is a very creditable villain, the story is well arranged and sustained, the characters generally are well handled and developed. *The Double Marriage* is best in its martial episodes, towards the close; there is in these an apparently lifelike vivacity which makes them seem good enough to be matched against anything I know of the kind in fiction or in history except Stendhal's incomparable picture of a young soldier's experience and emotion—or lack of emotion—on such a field as that of Waterloo. The opening of *La Chartreuse de Parme* remains of course unapproached for concise realism of impression and terse effect of apparent accuracy; but Reade, as a painter of battle, is at once credible, comprehensible and interesting beyond the run of historians and other dealers in more or less conscientious fiction. In *Foul Play* there is very good writing, with some genuine pathos and much industrious ingenuity; but it is not, I think, by any means to be counted among its author's more distinct and triumphant successes.

Of his shorter stories, *The Wandering Heir* seems to me very decidedly the worst, *Clouds and Sunshine* as decidedly the best; for the *Autobiography of a Chief* is not so much of a story as an episodic study of character, cast with superb ingenuity and most sensitive tact into the form of a prose monodrama. Midway between these I should place *Jack of all Trades,* with the posthumous story of *Singleheart and Doubleface.* But Charles Reade's place in literature must always depend on the ultimate rank assignable to a writer whose reputation has mainly to rely on the value of splendid episodes and the excellence of single figures rather than on the production of any work, in any line of his art, at once so thoroughly single in its aim and so thoroughly perfect in its success. . . . What this rank may be I certainly do not pretend or aspire to foretell. But that he was at his very best, and that not very rarely, a truly great writer of a truly noble genius, I do not understand how any competent judge of letters could possibly hesitate to affirm. (pp. 565-67)

> *A. C. Swinburne, "Charles Reade," in* The Nineteenth Century, *Vol. XVI, No. 92, October, 1884, pp. 550-67.*

W. D. HOWELLS   (essay date 1895)

[Charles Reade had a great effect] with our generation. He was a man who stood at the parting of the ways between realism and romanticism, and if he had been somewhat more of a man he might have been the master of a great school of English realism; but, as it was, he remained content to use the materials of realism and produce the effect of romanticism. He saw that life itself infinitely outvalued anything that could be feigned about it, but its richness seemed to corrupt him, and he had not the clear, ethical conscience which forced George Eliot to be realistic when probably her artistic prepossessions were romantic.

As yet, however, there was no reasoning of the matter, and Charles Reade was writing books of tremendous adventure and exaggerated character, which he prided himself on deriving from the facts of the world around him. He was intoxicated with the discovery he had made that the truth was beyond invention, but he did not know what to do with the truth in art after he had found it in life, and to this day the English mostly do not. We young people were easily taken with his glittering error, and we read him with much the same fury that he wrote. *Never Too Late to Mend; Love Me Little, Love Me Long; Christie Johnstone; Peg Woffington;* and then, later, *Hard Cash, The Cloister and the Hearth, Foul Play, Put Yourself in His Place*—how much they all meant once, or seemed to mean! (pp. 193-94)

[A few months ago I read *Christie Johnstone*] again, after not looking at it for more than thirty years; and I read it with amazement at its prevailing artistic vulgarity, its prevailing aesthetic error shot here and there with gleams of light, and of the truth that Reade himself was always dimly groping for. The book is written throughout on the verge of realism, with divinations and conjectures across its border, and with lapses into the fool's paradise of romanticism, and an apparent content with its inanity and impossibility. But then it was brilliantly new and surprising; it seemed to be the last word that could be said for the truth in fiction; and it had a spell that held us like an anaesthetic above the ache of parting. . . . (p. 196)

> *W. D. Howells, "Charles Reade," in his* My Literary Passions, *Harper & Brothers Publishers, 1895, pp. 191-97.*

EDWARD WAGENKNECHT   (essay date 1943)

Charles Reade may well go down to posterity with a single book in his hand—*The Cloister and the Hearth* . . .—that magnificent historical novel which modern criticism values above all the rest of his work together. (p. 243)

Sometimes language fails Reade altogether. Then he uses pictures set into the text. . . .

Reade's eccentricities are not always stylistic. When a character is in danger, the author may cry out a warning as if he were a small boy in the gallery at a melodrama theater; he also apostrophizes himself. He does not address the reader so often as do Thackeray and Trollope, but he surely breaks the illusion when he does. . . . (p. 244)

Peg Woffington, though always popular, is an extremely artificial book. . . . Its companion piece, *Christie Johnstone* . . . is better. . . . But it was not until *It Is Never Too Late to Mend* came out . . . that Reade really began to show what was in him. . . .

It was to this work that Reade first applied the elaborate system of documentation. . . . (p. 245)

Put Yourself in His Place has its realistic element, for it includes a description of the "rattening" (sabotage) practiced by "the dirty oligarchy" which Reade saw in the labor unions. Outside of that, however, it is better, because more consistent, undiluted melodrama than *Never Too Late*. . . . There is nothing so painful in *Put Yourself in His Place* as the prison scenes of *Never Too Late;* and it has more picturesque material, some of it of great charm. . . .

Reade uses suspense, more elaborately, perhaps, than any other standard English novelist has ever used it. He is following Scott's method here, but he goes much further than Scott. He cuts in anywhere, moving from one group of characters to another; no matter if the arrangement is purely arbitrary. (p. 247)

Yet Reade often fails to thrill us, for he moves so rapidly that we are never left in doubt long. His insane speed gave him a

natural affinity with short books, and while it is true that his principal works are very long, he achieves this length by combining great masses of often disparate material. Even so, he always seems rushing to catch a train. (p. 248)

There are more learned novels than *The Cloister and the Hearth,* but few of them have assimilated their learning so well.

Griffith Gaunt has had many distinguished admirers. . . . Reade tried to be psychological in this book, but many melodramatic elements carried over. . . .

Other books of Reade's introduce no fresh elements of much importance. (p. 250)

> *Edward Wagenknecht, "The Disciples of Dickens: Charles Reade," in his* Cavalcade of the English Novel: From Elizabeth to George VI *(copyright © 1943 by Henry Holt and Company, Inc.; copyright renewed, 1971, by Edward Wagenknecht; reprinted by permission of the author), Holt, Rinehart and Winston, 1948 (and reprinted by Holt, Rinehart and Winston, 1954, pp. 243-50).*

EMERSON GRANT SUTCLIFFE   (essay date 1944)

The most significant feature of the novelistic technique of Charles Reade is his thorough dependence on fact, usually documentary fact. . . . One cause which brought him to this technique was his distrust of his imagination. . . . He could invent, and he continued to invent, but he spurred invention on with materials drawn from life or from others' imaginations.

Such materials he did not gather and classify systematically in notebooks till after the publication of his first "matter-of-fact romance," *It is Never Too Late to Mend*. . . .

When he wrote *Hard Cash* . . . his documentary method was fully developed. (p. 582)

Novels upreared on such substantial foundations may yet differ widely in their styles, depending on their period and the personality of their architects. Reade's have a buoyancy which belongs both to him and his era; and an *outré*, melodramatic cast which reflects his own desire for publicity as well as theatrical fashion. (p. 583)

No artist can long herd together such droves of facts without conceiving creative attitudes toward them. Reade drew his inspiration from facts, but he remained Reade. He chose facts which were as violently colored as his own temperament. They were essentially the same kind of facts, after all, whether they enabled him to denounce social injustice or to narrate swift and vivid incident—whether they related to instruments of torture in prisons or fights in Australian gold-fields, to sabotage in Sheffield or to a bursting reservoir. He felt that his sensational novels were better than those of some of his contemporaries because they had "a leading idea,"—an attack on some social malpractise, whereas their novels were "unideaed melodramas for unideaed girls." But really the incidents in his novels which exemplify these leading ideas are indistinguishable in character from those that are just intrinsically exciting—"unideaed." Furthermore, facts to the contrary notwithstanding, Reade remained for the most part a Victorian with a Victorian's code of morals—fictionally, at least. Yet his accumulations of data undoubtedly tended toward an increase in the realism, even, at moments, the naturalism of his fiction. And though he lustily defended himself against those whom he labeled "prurient prudes," and who accused him of indecency, his novels occasionally showed the influence of much clipping from the newspapers. (pp. 583-84)

Reade's object is to dramatize facts, past or present, so that they will take on personal, vital semblance to his readers, whom he conceives as spectators in the theatre of his novels. For his readers he himself plays all the parts intensely. . . .

Reade had no doubt that facts must be caught up and energized in the glow of the artist's personality. At the same time he was sure that the artist proved his greatness by founding his fictions on fact. (p. 584)

Reade, however, was uncertain whether fact or fiction had the greater meaning, and in particular he could not decide how much freedom the historical novelist might allow himself in dealing with matters of fact. He is evidently cynical in *Put Yourself in His Place* when he sums up the conditions affecting Sheffield workmen and then says: "Having thus curtailed the Report, I print the remainder in an Appendix, for the use of those few readers who can endure useful knowledge in works of this class." He makes in a single novel, *A Wandering Heir,* three incongruous statements. He can speak as roundly as this: "Let us have no more of the miserable cant about truth being superior to fiction"; yet three chapters before he lamented that "Hard fact holds me with remorseless grasp; and I am constrained to show how all this bright picture was shivered in a day, and by the man's own hand"; and then again in the last chapter he proclaims the law of liberty. . . . (p. 586)

In gathering facts Reade apparently found it easier to rely on printed sources of information than on facts derived from conversation with authorities. When he first determined to use the factual method, in writing *It is Never Too Late to Mend,* he felt the need of corroborating books by personal testimony. . . . That materials obtained at second-hand through print were somehow out of focus he undoubtedly realized. (pp. 586-87)

Basing his fiction on facts, Reade was interested in the way in which life sometimes apparently imitated fiction—in those close parallels between real circumstances and similar events previously described in novels. He is thinking not only of those deliberate imitations which critics have cited to prove the novelist's social importance and responsibility, but of accidental resemblances. (p. 587)

Reade's dependence on document was one cause of the frequent accusations of plagiarism which were leveled at him. He was reproached for stealing Erasmus's *Colloquies* and using some of them almost verbatim in *The Cloister and the Hearth,* though he acknowledged in the novel itself that "Some of the best scenes in this new book are from his mediaeval pen." A similar charge was brought against him for basing an eighteenth century Dublin scene in *A Wandering Heir* on Swift's verse. (p. 588)

In proposing never to guess where he could know, Reade was not necessarily committing himself to the writing of realistic novels. Indeed, his intentions are described definitely in the phrase which appeared on the title-page of *It Is Never Too Late to Mend,* and which he applied to *The Cloister and the Hearth* and *Hard Cash:* "a matter-of-fact romance." The phrase shows his allegiance to the story of rapid, startling, strange incident. Strange incidents but true ones—it is a divided allegiance. Though in tone predominantly romantic, even melodramatic, his fiction is realistic in parts, and realistic because of his dependence on document. His feminine characters, though undeniably predetermined by his own attitude towards women,

and not genuinely objective, are yet colored realistically by the information about "foemina vera" which he found in the newspapers and collected in his notebooks. His studies of the woman still in love with the man whom she knows untrue, and of the woman strongly masculine in one way or another, are especially authentic.

A neglected short story, *Reality,* undoubtedly derived from a newspaper account, suggests the kind of fiction Reade might have written if he had lived in the twentieth century rather than in the day of the sensational novel. (pp. 590-91)

There is plenty of love-making in Reade's novels, but some of it, apparently, Reade put in with his tongue in his cheek. In *A Woman Hater* he says ironically: "The true business of the mind was resumed; and that is love-making, or novelists give us false pictures of life, and that is impossible." He especially prides himself on avoiding the overtly sentimental. "If love was not directly spoken," he assures the readers of *Put Yourself in His Place,* "it was constantly implied, and, in fact, that is how true love generally speaks. The eternal *Je vous aime* of the French novelist is false to nature, let me tell you." In *Love Me Little, Love Me Long* he asks pardon for such indirect love-making, "for relating things as they happen, and not as your grand writers pretend they happen." Julia in *Hard Cash* objects to a novel which the *Criticaster* said was a good novel to be read by the sea-side: "It was an ignoble thing; all flirtations and curates,"—which, perhaps, is Reade's opinion of Trollope. He comments on an affectionate speech in *A Terrible Temptation:* "This is mawkish; but it will serve to show on what terms the woman and boy were. On second thoughts, I recall that apology, and defy creation. 'The Mawkish' is a branch of literature, a great and popular one, and I have neglected it savagely." (pp. 591-92)

On the subject of married life, Reade assembled data and bibliography in his notebooks under the head of *Conjugalia.* In several of his novels, accordingly, the hero and the heroine marry early in the story: in *The Cloister and the Hearth, White Lies, Griffith Gaunt, Singleheart, and Doubleface, A Simpleton.* In the last-named, he endeavors to hold the sentimental readers whom this event might drive away, on the ground that there is more novelty and excitement in marriage than in single blessedness. . . . In other words, Reade finds in increased realism an opportunity for increased romance. (pp. 592-93)

In the portrayal of those actual details which might revolt the person of delicate sensibilities, Reade was comparatively unabashed, though such details never become so nauseous and numerous as in Zola or much of our contemporary fiction. His method, however, led him into one kind of untruth which characterizes many propaganda novels based on fact. Though, as Reade pointed out to those who doubted the factual bases of his stories, he had authority for all the incidents questioned, and though he was careful to describe both good and bad prison wardens, and humane and unscrupulous owners of private asylums, his stories yet gave false impressions, in one important respect. No one British jail ever held so many horrors as that in *It is Never too Late to Mend,* and no one British asylum was probably ever so completely and evilly mismanaged as that in *Hard Cash.* And even if exceptions have existed, Reade's pictures, true in detail, are yet not true as wholes, because they are composite and not typically true. Such exaggeration may make effective propaganda, but it does not make either history or art. (pp. 593-94)

Fiction, Reade says in the last chapter of *Put Yourself in His Place,* "studies, penetrates, digests, the hard facts of chronicles and blue books, and makes their dry bones live.'' Thus it performs a valuable social service, in making ''readers realize those appalling facts of the day which most men know, but not one in a thousand comprehends.'' This the novelist can do not only for contemporary facts which it will be valuable for people to know, but for those facts of the past associated with the lives of ''obscure heroes, philosophers, and martyrs,'' of whom Gerard, the hero of *The Cloister and the Hearth*, is a particular instance. Bare facts lack sympathetic emotion, interpretation, the coloring of art, and are thus socially useless. . . . (p. 598)

> Emerson Grant Sutcliffe, ''Fact, Realism, and Morality in Reade's Fiction,'' in Studies in Philology, Vol. XLI, No. 4, October, 1944, pp. 582-98.

WAYNE BURNS (essay date 1947)

[*Hard Cash* is certainly Reade's] best social novel, even though it is marred by his usual shortcomings—his inadequate understanding and philosophy, his abnormal interest in physical violence, his almost hysterical indignation against supposed injustices, and the greatest of all his handicaps, his naïve documentary realism. Why these weaknesses are not so disastrous as usual in *Hard Cash* cannot be explained here. But it is true, as any reader can discover for himself. And it is also true that in this novel Reade does justice to his greatest gift, his ability to write sustained and absorbing narrative. . . . At best, *Hard Cash* is not what Reade intended—a serious and realistic novel of social purpose. It is acceptable only as masterful melodrama.

To characterize *Hard Cash* in this way is not, however, to place it on a lower artistic level than *The Cloister and the Hearth*. It too is masterful melodrama, but melodrama with certain differences which in no small measure have caused it to be regarded as a great historical fiction. It is one of Reade's best novels certainly, perhaps the best, but it is not best for the reasons usually given, and it is by no means great. Reade wrote it according to his usual ''sensation'' formulas and with no more skill or insight than he showed in some of his other works. Its exceptional virtues, such as they are, do not spring from ''inspiration,'' or even from conscious artistic planning; they are, in almost every single particular, the result of a fortunate concatenation of circumstances. (pp. 72-3)

[By] grace of the Goddess Fortuna, Reade was able to overcome, at least in part, some of his most glaring weaknesses— his overplotting, his emotional aberrations, his almost hysterical indignation, his lack of psychological and intellectual insight, and some of the worst features of his melodramatic realism. By partly eliminating these weaknesses Reade succeeded in freeing *The Cloister and the Hearth* from many of the faults that characterize his other novels. Moreover, though he himself was probably not aware of it, the absence of these self-imposed handicaps gave him an unusually good opportunity to capitalize on his one great artistic gift, his ability to transform even the most unlikely materials into a rousing good story. At any rate, he was at his best in dealing with his great mass of fifteenth-century sources. (pp. 76-7)

Reade was ''a great master of narrative'' in every single one of his better novels—as accomplished a master as in *The Cloister and the Hearth*. To repeat, the extraordinary virtues of this novel, such as they are, do not derive from Reade's conscious artistry, but from his being able, quite by chance, to overcome some of the deficiencies which mar his other works, and to do

full justice to his limited artistic abilities. . . . Reade himself did not understand what he had achieved or how he had achieved it. He did not consider *The Cloister and the Hearth* his masterpiece, did not understand its strength and weakness. That is why he could never repeat his triumph.

Although the many fine qualities of *The Cloister and the Hearth*, whether largely fortuitous or not, may justify its being placed slightly above Reade's other fiction, these qualities are by no means sufficient to justify its being considered a great novel, fundamentally superior to his other works. Intrinsically it is not a better novel than *Hard Cash* or *Griffith Gaunt*. Despite his many advantages, Reade simply was not able to rise above his fundamental limitations. Unquestionably he had the knowledge, the understanding, the documentary techniques, and the narrative ability necessary to the writing of a first-rate novel. What he lacked were those prime insights and abilities that mark the difference between a merely gifted storyteller and a great novelist—that enable the novelist to give new and significant re-creations of human beings and social relationships.

In characterization—which is of primary importance—Reade was woefully weak, and this despite all the favorable circumstances that have been mentioned. He could not comprehend the mind and emotions of either Gerard or Margaret, the microcosms of his major theme. Or if he could—and this is all that really matters—he was unable to objectify his understanding in fictional form. (pp. 77-8)

[His minor characters] too are little more than cleverly devised puppets, transparently of the usual Readeian construction. Even Denys, thoroughly charming in his first appearances, eventually becomes insufferably sweet and tiresome—a kind of medieval version of Dickens's George Rouncewell. As for the best of the other minor characters, they do have human qualities, and it must be admitted that Reade's vigorous manipulation almost brings them to life at times; but, for the most part, one can see Reade using them to complicate the plot, offer comic relief, supply exciting episodes, or spout sentimentalized emotion—all in the best tradition of Adelphi melodrama. (p. 78)

Reade's narrative art could not—or at any rate did not—transform the other and weaker elements of the novel. They remained what they were. Consequently, Reade's final achievement is at best little more than a long sequence of excellent melodramatic scenes (complete with historical settings), very neatly worked into the form of a ''good story''—one that makes ''the audience want to know what happens next.''

More than this can hardly be claimed for the novel as an artistic whole. . . . [Reade] was in an ideal position to understand Gerard and his problems, but his melodramatic preconceptions distorted his vision. As a result, he could not see and reproduce Gerard's struggles as they were, in relation to his fifteenth-century background; he could recreate them only as they should have been according to a conventional ''sensation'' pattern. (p. 79)

The Cloister and the Hearth is of the same bone and sinew as the other ''matter-of-fact romances.'' Like the best of them, it is informative, intelligent, and humane, and a masterpiece of narrative art; but also, like all the other novels that Reade wrote, it is lacking in those qualities that mark the difference between a great novel and a good story—the difference between Thackeray's *Henry Esmond* and Kingsley's *Westward Ho! The Cloister and the Hearth* is not an individual and perceptive re-creation of life; it is a coruscating but arbitrary forcing of historical materials into melodramatic formulas. In relation to the best of Reade's other fiction, its points of superiority are superficial, mere surface brilliances, and by no means sufficient to justify the repute in which it is held; that is, unless *Hard Cash, Griffith Gaunt,* and perhaps a few of Reade's other "romances" are to be elevated to the rank of great novels.

Historical narratives as learned and exciting as *The Cloister and the Hearth* are rarely to be met with, and for this reason it deserves a place in our literary heritage. But we should recognize it for what it is, and not confuse ourselves by trying to endow it with the qualities of a great novel. It is superb fictional melodrama, neither more nor less, and that is praise enough. (p. 81)

> Wayne Burns, "'The Cloister and the Hearth': A Classic Reconsidered," in The Trollopian (copyright, 1947, copyright renewed © 1975, by The Regents of the University of California; reprinted by permission of the University of California Press), Vol. 2, No. 2, September, 1947, pp. 71-81.

SHEILA M. SMITH   (essay date 1958)

Although Charles Reade is now remembered chiefly as the author of *The Cloister and the Hearth* . . . , he himself thought the novel inferior to the drama as an art-form, and mistrusted written words . . . as the medium for his ideas. . . .

The play in which he first exploited spectacle to any extent was *Gold.* . . . It told the story of the success of the failed farmer, George Sandford, and his ex-convict friend Robinson, in the Australian gold-fields. . . .

[Much] of the effect was achieved by means of real objects— pumps, spades, wheel-barrows—on the stage. . . . [These realistic stage effects attracted] people to the theatre, especially the scene in the Australian gold-field with the working mechanisms of the cradles and the testing of the metal. . . . (p. 94)

In [*It is Never Too Late to Mend*] one of his aims was to denounce the 'separate system' as practised in the 'model' prisons, and the tyranny of a prison governor. . . .

It is Never Too Late to Mend [his own adaptation of the novel] was the first of Reade's plays to embody a problem of contemporary society. One of its main faults lies in its construction. . . . [A] certain sense of continuity achieved in the novel is lost in the drama. . . .

Because [Reade] wanted his audience to share his indignation he tried to translate the prisoners' sufferings into an impressive visual experience for theatregoers. And so he attempted to use the startling realistic effects of the popular 'sensation' drama . . . not solely for pleasure, but to make people aware of contemporary evils, think about them, and do something to alleviate them. (p. 95)

[Such] a serious use of realistic effects was not usual. The drama . . . was for entertainment, not to incite people to agitate for social reform.

Reade used realistic spectacle again in a didactic drama, *Free Labour* . . . , in which he depicted the struggle of a clever craftsman . . . against the outrages of the Trade Unions. . . .

The 'realism' of Reade's plays can be considered from three angles: the reality of the stage effects; artistic reality; and truth to the actual conditions of human life.

Although in *It is Never Too Late to Mend* and *Free Labour* Reade used realistic scenic effects to emphasize a contemporary evil, he more often used them for the pleasure of the effects themselves. They were popular in *Gold,* which had no propaganda purpose, and in *It is Never Too Late to Mend* they were not confined to the prison scenes. (p. 96)

In the plays Reade wrote after *It is Never Too Late to Mend* the realistic effects were even more startling and sensational, such as the explosion in *Free Labour* . . . and the colliery explosion in *Love and Money.* . . .

Reade used his realistic effects largely for the sake of sensation, to provide his audience with the spectacle and exciting incidents they loved. His efforts to produce a serious social drama decreased after *It is Never Too Late to Mend.* The forging of the real tools in *Free Labour* cannot be justified by the plea that it makes more impressive the dramatist's protest against Trade Union terrorism—it is spectacle for spectacle's sake. And *Love and Money* has no serious social purpose whatever. So, apart from . . . *It is Never Too Late to Mend,* Reade's realistic effects were meant to thrill rather than make more evident a contemporary wrong. The social purpose became a subsidiary issue.

It is also true that when he was concerned with social problems in his dramas he emphasized their crudely external aspect rather than their subtler human implications. (p. 97)

[In] *It is Never Too Late to Mend* psychological truth is often sacrificed so that the audience shall be certain to receive the full thrill of physical action. . . .

[Even] in the scenes which were meant particularly to expose a contemporary evil Reade lost sight of the problem in the sensational effect. (p. 98)

[Only] four of Reade's plays can be described as having a social purpose—*It is Never Too Late to Mend* and *Free Labour* advocate reforms in the organization of society, *Foul Play* . . . is vaguely concerned with the villainy of big businessmen who try to cheat insurance companies, and *Drink.* . . . attacks intemperance. Nevertheless, it is true that Reade had a passionate belief in the utilitarian function of art, and that when he wanted to publicize a problem or an evil he used every sensational device to get his 'message' across. And his sensational tricks worked towards 'realism' because by transplanting the actions and events of 'real life' to the stage he believed that his drama would thereby acquire artistic reality, because both these and the realistic scenery would then be 'hard facts' to which Reade, the artist, pinned so much faith. This attempt to equate factual and artistic reality was fatal to any serious achievement as a dramatist.

Reade's social dramas, for all their concern with contemporary human problems, were no nearer to human life than were his other plays. The Bluebook data had its basis in fact, but the human emotions were often spurious. . . . In the same way that Reade's desire for incident and spectacle led him to concentrate on the sensational aspects of social wrongs, so his genuinely indignant awareness of an abuse or an injustice was disastrously entangled with contemporary stage conventions. . . . (pp. 98-9)

The simple realism of stage effects became in [Reade's] hands crude spectacle, and the presentation of social problems was falsified by subservience to contemporary stage conventions. Reade's social dramas are interesting to the modern reader for two main reasons. He found the material for them in the lives of ordinary or down-trodden people—small farmers, workmen, ex-convicts, sailors, ticket-of-leave men: the people who formed part of the living human activity in which nineteenth-century drama was at last to find renewal of life after its incredible excursions into melodrama and its coy flirtations with the poetic muse in the plays of, for example, Sheridan Knowles. Also, he is to be commended for attempting, however briefly, to make the drama a vehicle for serious thought, not simply a drug to the senses and a purveyor of well-worn moral tags. But he was not a great enough artist to shape his awareness of contemporary wrongs into powerful drama. He could not create a form to express his new subject-matter; he could only attempt to force his subject-matter into the old form. (pp. 99-100)

> *Sheila M. Smith, "Realism in the Drama of Charles Reade," in* English, *Vol. XII, No. 69, Autumn, 1958, pp. 94-100.*

ARTHUR POLLARD   (essay date 1975)

Reade's place in the popular mind, so far as he still retains one, rests no doubt on his historical novel *The Cloister and the Hearth* . . . , if only because it is (or was) a favourite in G.C.E. syllabuses. Yet *Griffith Gaunt* . . . has claims different from, and in some ways superior to, those of any of the other novels. Reade's biographer, Malcolm Elwin, considered it 'one of the most important novels of its generation', whilst a contemporary critic, no less a person than Henry James, gave it a special mention when he referred to 'those great sympathetic guesses with which a real master attacks the truth, and which, by their occasional occurrence in the stories of Mr. Charles Reade (the much abused **"Griffith Gaunt"** included), make him, to our mind, the most readable of living English novelists, and prove him a distant kinsman of Shakespeare'. . . . And this was in a comparison favouring Reade at the expense of George Eliot! (p. 221)

[*Griffith Gaunt*] was too outspoken on various aspects of sexual relationships to be acceptable to many Victorians. Ever ready to detect antagonism, Reade wrote to the American J. T. Fields of the 'dead silence anything but encouraging' . . . which had greeted the early numbers of the serial and later he complained that 'in this country I must fight against a powerful cabal'. . . . It was, however, the American *Round Table* which came out fiercely in condemnation of the handling of sexual relationships in the novel. Reade was roused. He wrote a letter to the American press, 'The Prurient Prude', in which he defends himself with characteristic pugnacity. . . . (p. 222)

Griffith Gaunt is concerned with 'a great and terrible passion, Jealousy, and . . . its manifold consequences'. The opening of the novel is characteristically dramatic—a snatch from a quarrel, which will only be fully described much later, and then a brief description of the speakers 'who faced each other pale and furious . . . man and wife, and had loved each other well'. Gaunt's jealousy is double—first, his pre-marital hatred of his rival Neville . . . , and later, urged on by the villainess Caroline Ryder, his passion against his wife. . . . From the first comes his duel with Neville and from the second his flight and bigamous marriage, his suspected drowning and the trial of his wife. (p. 224)

[Reade's experience in the theatre] shows in the very construction of the novel. One can see how easily it would adapt into three acts—courtship . . . ; marriage and jealousy . . . ; bigamy and its consequences. . . . The choice of incident indicates similar forces at work. Events are striking, even sensational, sometimes gruesome. The recovery of the flesh-stripped corpse

from the lake is of the essence of spine-chilling melodrama. Reade knows too the value of confusion and its resolution, of mistaken identity and the fear that the truth may not be discovered until too late. He recognises also the need for recurring climaxes; this is indeed the function of some of the striking events of the novel such as the duel. But there are other such climaxes which are less dependent on mere external action, events which really bring the reader face to face with the deep passionate issues of the novel. . . . Most impressive of all, however, the book's full climax, is the scene in which Griffith comes upon his wife and Leonard together in the wood. . . . This is the book's crisis, and there are those who wish it might also have been its conclusion. All the rest . . . is in a sense anti-climax. Reade says:—'A great fault once committed is often the first link in a chain of acts that look like crimes, but are, strictly speaking, consequences' . . . , and he must indeed rely upon this doctrine of inevitability. Nevertheless, one cannot help but feel at times a certain strain. (pp. 224-25)

Yet Reade's melodrama is balanced by a sort of realism. In some ways this . . . is less evident in *Griffith Gaunt* than in the social-problem novels. He claimed that he was writing a historical novel, but apart from a few casual references such as those to the recent Jacobite uprising there is little to suggest the atmosphere of the mid-eighteenth century. How much he could have learned from Thackeray, had he wished to do so! His own *Peg Woffington* could have taught him something. Yet Reade is realistic where it matters most—at the beginning, where he creates a sense of the society of minor gentry which forms the basis of the book's setting. . . .

But more important than external detail is interior experience, such as Reade portrays in his main characters. *Griffith Gaunt* has obvious parallels with George Eliot's *Romola*, but, despite James, we should not look to Reade for that psychological perception which characterised the work of his fellow novelist. 'Great sympathetic guesses' there may be, but not the delicate appreciation of nuances of behaviour nor the sensitive suggestion of the overwhelming significance of the ordinary that marks the achievement of George Eliot. Reade is content to 'note the tiny seeds of events to come'; the dull years of Griffith's marriage with the imperceptibly but nonetheless definitely widening gap between himself and his wife are passed over in a few brief pages. . . . One feels that George Eliot—and James—would have made a book of this alone. Yet here we see two of Reade's virtues. One is his economy and directness (this shows itself, incidentally, in the far greater proportion of dialogue in his work than in that of most of his contemporaries); the other is his awareness both of his strength and his limitations, what he knew he could do and, equally, what he apparently knew he could not do. (p. 225)

Griffith Gaunt leaves us realising the underlying paradox of Victorian melodrama. It both over-states and under-states. The broad emphatic strokes of its brush are somehow able to suggest the subtleties it omits. Reade, by concentrating on the striking scene, somehow compels us to imagine those subtleties of characterisation that he disregards. . . . Reade belongs in the succession of the novelists of feeling. He deals in strong emotions, unusual incidents and high dramatisation. . . . [He] is his own man—direct, simple, sometimes even crude, but also sharp, powerful and at his best impressively memorable. (p. 227)

> *Arthur Pollard, "'Griffith Gaunt': Paradox of Victorian Melodrama," in* Critical Quarterly *(reprinted by permission of Manchester University Press), Vol. 17, No. 3, Autumn, 1975, pp. 221-27.**

A. BROOKER THRO   (essay date 1978)

Charles Reade, the novelist who criticizes George Eliot's style for lacking "fire" and praises Harriet Beecher Stowe's for being "all . . . red ink and . . . biceps muscle," endorses energy directly. In *Griffith Gaunt* Reade embraces without reservation *both* the extremes of melodrama. What he does not do, surprisingly, is consider how these extremes relate to one another. (p. 369)

[Reade] makes no attempt to improve upon or even to criticize goodness and energy because he is somehow able to promote them both without discovering that they contradict and implicitly devaluate one another. His open advocacy of energy leads him, then, not to comprehend melodramatic incongruity . . . , but only to expose it more glaringly by making themes of his novel's clashing opposites. . . . (p. 370)

Reade gratifies his craving for excitement by giving his novel an incongruous subordinate plot. But self-indulgence carries him even beyond this. . . . (p. 371)

> A. Brooker Thro, "An Approach to Melodramatic Fiction: Goodness and Energy in the Novels of Dickens, Collins and Reade," in Genre (© copyright 1978 by the University of Oklahoma; reprinted by permission of the University of Oklahoma), Vol. XI, No. 3, Fall, 1978, pp. 359-74.*

ADDITIONAL BIBLIOGRAPHY

Buchanan, R. "Charles Reade: A Personal Reminiscence." *Harper's New Monthly Magazine* 69, No. 412 (September 1884): 600-06.
   An elegaic biography.

Burns, Wayne. In his *Charles Reade: A Study in Victorian Authorship*. New York: Bookman Associates, 1961, 360 p.
   Contains Reade's personal comments about his work and artistic motivation.

Campbell, O. J., Jr. "Charles Reade and the Experimental Novel." *The Nation* 100, No. 2596 (1 April 1915): 352-54.
   Cites the goals Reade strived to achieve, and the new strategies he developed for writing novels and dramas.

Coleman, John. In his *Charles Reade As I Knew Him*. London: Anthony Treherne & Co., 1903, 428 p.
   Discusses Reade's collaborative and individual dramatic efforts. This book, although often criticized as being an unreliable source, is nonetheless an often quoted source.

Elwin, Malcolm. In his *Charles Reade*. London: Jonathan Cape, 1931, 388 p.
   Acclaimed as one of the most important biographies.

Haines, Lewis F. "Reade, Mill, and Zola: A Study of the Character and Intention of Charles Reade's Realistic Methods." *Studies in Philology* 40, No. 3 (July 1943): 463-80.*
   A discussion of Reade's realistic method and how he anticipated the writings of Emile Zola.

Orwell, George. "Charles Reade." In his *The Collected Essays, Journalism and Letters of George Orwell: My Country Right or Left 1940-1943, Vol. II*, edited by Sonia Orwell and Ian Angus, pp. 34-7. London: Secker & Warburg, 1968.
   Discusses the vast amount of "useless information" Reade accumulated, and how he imaginatively incorporated this knowledge in his works.

Reade, Charles L. and Compton Reade. In their *Charles Reade, D.C.L., Dramatist, Novelist, Journalist: A Memoir Compiled Chiefly from His Literary Remains*. New York: Harper and Brothers, 1887, 448 p.
   A biography of Reade, covering almost every aspect of his personal, social, and literary life. Based largely on his memoirs, this work devotes several chapters to Reade's principal works and unpublished essays.

Sutcliff, Emerson Grant. "Plotting in Reade's novels." *PMLA* XLVII, No. 3 (September 1932): 834-63.
   Traces Reade's method of plot development and the didactic purpose of his fiction.

Turner, Albert Morton. "Charles Reade and Montaigne." *Modern Philology* XXX, No. 3 (February 1933): 297-308.
   Discusses Reade's borrowing of character, plot, and detail from Montaigne.

Turner, Albert Morton. In his *The Making of "The Cloister and the Hearth."* Chicago: The University of Chicago Press, 1938, 230 p.
   A detailed investigation of the sources Reade used in preparing this novel, and his inspiration in writing it.

Christina Georgina Rossetti

1830-1894

English poet, short story, and prose writer.

Rossetti is ranked among the finest English poets of the nineteenth century. Although she also published a great deal of prose, critics generally consider her poetry to be superior. Closely associated with the Pre-Raphaelites, Rossetti was equally influenced by the asceticism of the Oxford Movement. Her poetry thus treats such opposing forces as sensuality and asceticism, human passion and divine love, and love of life and anticipation of death. Her poetry is marked by a diversity of stanzaic patterns and displays an impressive facility in rhyme.

Rossetti's father was an Italian exile who settled in London four years before her birth. Although she grew up in England, her Italian heritage remained an important influence throughout her life and provides an interesting contrast to the predominantly English sensibility found in her work. She demonstrated her poetic gifts early, writing sonnets in competition with her brothers William Michael and Dante Gabriel, a practice which undoubtedly developed her command of metrical forms. Always an avid reader, at age eighteen Rossetti began studying Dante whose works became a major and lasting influence. Among English poets, she favored Samuel Taylor Coleridge, John Keats, Percy Bysshe Shelley, and William Blake.

Rossetti's first published poem appeared in *The Athenaeum* when she was eighteen. When Dante Gabriel Rossetti founded the Pre-Raphaelite journal, *The Germ*, in 1852, she became a frequent contributor. Her first collection of poetry, *Goblin Market and Other Poems,* gained her immediate recognition as a skilled and original poet. *Goblin Market and Other Poems* was also the first great success for the Pre-Raphaelites and shows their influence in its symbolism, allegory, and rich, sensual imagery. This volume and her next collection, *The Prince's Progress and Other Poems,* contains much of her finest work and established Rossetti's reputation as an important poet.

Rossetti's poetic production diminished as she grew older and became increasingly committed to writing religious works. A succession of serious illnesses strongly influenced her temperament and outlook on life. Because she often believed herself close to death, religious devotion and mortality became persistent themes in both her poetry and prose. In 1871 she developed Graves' disease and though she published *A Pageant and Other Poems* in 1881, following this illness she concentrated primarily on works such as *The Face of the Deep: A Devotional Commentary on the Apocalypse.* Critics often remark on the inferior quality of the later prose works, but Rossetti's extreme religious devotion was not entirely detrimental to her poetic output for much of her finest verse was obviously inspired by her all-consuming faith.

Rossetti's religious convictions dominated her personal as well as her literary life. As a young woman, she declined two marriage proposals because her suitors' beliefs failed to conform exactly to the tenets of the Anglican Church. Rather than marry, she chose to remain with her mother, an equally devout Anglican. The beautiful sonnet sequence "Monna Innomi-

nata," included in *A Pageant and Other Poems,* celebrates Rossetti's denial of human love for the sake of religious purity.

The contradictions and complexities of her own intellect and experience served as Rossetti's richest subject matter. Rather than grappling with the social problems which preoccupied such contemporary literary figures as Thomas Carlyle, John Ruskin, and William Morris, she chose to explore the enduring themes of love and death. Faulted by some critics for an alleged indifference to social issues, she is praised by many more for her simple diction, timeless vision, and consummate stylistic technique. Although she is remembered by many merely as the ethereal symbol of Pre-Raphaelitism evoked in Dante Gabriel Rossetti's paintings, Rossetti also produced a unique body of work that transcends the limits of any single movement and which secures her place in nineteenth-century literature. Upon her death, Arthur Symons wrote that "by the death of Christina Rossetti, literature, and not English literature alone, has lost the one great modern poetess. . . . [She] possessed, in union with a profoundly emotional nature, a power of artistic self-restraint which no other woman who has written in verse, except the supreme Sappho, has ever shown; and it is through this mastery over her own nature, this economy of her own resources, that she takes rank among poets rather than among poetesses.''

PRINCIPAL WORKS

Goblin Market and Other Poems (poetry) 1862
The Prince's Progress and Other Poems (poetry) 1866
Commonplace and Other Short Stories (short stories) 1870
Sing-Song (children's verse) 1872
A Pageant and Other Poems (poetry) 1881
Poems (poetry) 1882
The Face of the Deep: A Devotional Commentary on the Apocalypse (religious prose) 1892
Verses (poetry) 1893
New Poems (poetry) 1896
The Poetical Works of Christina Georgina Rossetti (poetry) 1904

THE ATHENAEUM (essay date 1862)

[The poems of *Goblin Market and other Poems*] by Miss Rossetti have the charm of a welcome surprise. They are no mere reflections and echoes of previous beauty and music, but, whatever their faults, express both in essence and form the individuality of the writer. To read these poems after the laboured and skilful, but not original, verse which has been issued of late, is like passing from a picture gallery, with its well-feigned semblance of nature, to the real nature out-of-doors which greets us with the waving grass and the pleasant shock of the breeze.

'Goblin Market,' the most important of Miss Rossetti's poems, has true dramatic character, life and picture for those who read it simply as a legend, while it has an inner meaning for all who can discern it. Like many of its companions, it is suggestive and symbolical without the stiffness of set allegory. (p. 557)

The poems that follow are of various merit, both in kind and degree; but even in the case of those which we least like— 'Sister Maude,' for example,—there is not one without an idea for its root, or without the complete unfolding of that idea for its purpose. Sometimes, as in 'Love from the North' and 'Maude Clare,' the idea is rendered with a vividness and roundness that leave nothing to be added or desired. In other cases, both thought and expression are so delicate that the full meaning can only be discerned by a poetic eye. The reader, for instance, must himself bring imagination to the poem called 'An Apple Gathering,' or he will lose much of its significance. Its simple beauty of description and plaintive melody cannot well be missed; but it needs deeper insight to find in the young girl who plucks apple-blossoms for her adorning, a type of those prodigal affections that forestall their future, and are thus barren when less ardent natures are fruitful. . . .

The sweetness of [the poem] lingers on the ear, and makes us regret that Miss Rossetti, who is, when she chooses, a mistress of verbal harmony, should at times employ discords with a frequency which aims at variety but results in harshness. From this flaw, however, her strains are generally free when their burden is sad; but we could well wish that the minor key which she uses so effectively were used less often. Sorrow for its own sake—sorrow unimproved into faith or resignation—has

but a dangerous charm,—and, indeed, a poor one when compared with that nobler influence of which this writer is capable. Her poem, 'From House to Home,' and her devotional pieces generally, rebuke the vain laments which she elsewhere utters. Still, we must not be ungrateful, nor repine too much that, while gathering the ripe vintage, we meet also with the hectic leaf. Miss Rossetti's poems are not all of equal merit, and there is more than one from the teaching of which we dissent; but the entire series displays imagination and beauty which are both undeniable and unborrowed. (p. 558)

> "Goblin Market and Other Poems ," in The Athenaeum, No. 1800, April 26, 1862, pp. 557-58.

THE SATURDAY REVIEW (essay date 1862)

Miss Rossetti's poetical power is most undeniable. She is gifted with a very good musical ear, great strength and clearness of language, and a vivid imagination, which only now and then wants to be restrained. Some of the shorter pieces in [*Goblin Market and Other Poems*] are as faultless in expression, as picturesque in effect, and as high in purity of tone as any modern poem that can be named. It is a pleasure to meet an authoress who has obviously given such conscientious labour to the tasks she has set herself to accomplish, and who has succeeded so frequently in saying the right thing to be said in the best and shortest way.

Yet there is one ground upon which we are inclined to quarrel with Miss Rossetti; and that ground is the poem which is placed in the front of her volume and of its title. *Goblin Market* is a story of too flimsy and unsubstantial a character to justify or to bear the elaborate detail with which it is worked out. As it deduces a moral at the close in favour of sisterly affection, it may be presumed to be in some sense or other an allegory. But what the allegory is, or how far it runs upon all-fours with that of which it is the shadow, we cannot undertake to say. . . . Where the moral inculcated is so excellent and proper, it may seem ungracious to complain of the unreal texture of the fable through which it is conveyed. The language of the story is very graceful and musical, and the picture of the sisters in their daily labour and rest is drawn with a pretty simplicity which gives a momentary substantiality to the dreamland in which they live. . . .

An artist of Miss Rossetti's power ought to know by instinct a theme which will bear filling out with shape and colour, from one of which the inconsecutiveness and unreality show only the more strongly in proportion to the labour used in its embodiment and ornament. A picture of which half is a photographically accurate representation of nature, and the other half a purely symbolical imagination worked out with equal distinctness and detail, can never be really harmonious or satisfactory; and the same may be said of a story. The eye and the ear equally like to know to what extent they are bound to believe what they see and hear, and what is the result of it all. The reader of *Goblin Market* may be carried on by the pleasant flow of sound and stream of imagery; but the real thought of the poem is a mere rope of sand, carrying no deeper consistency or meaning than the revelations from the unseen world interpreted now-a-days by a professional spirit-medium.

Miss Rossetti's genius appears to tend very naturally towards symbolical expression. One of the most perfect little pieces in the volume is the statement of a very serious enigma called *Up-hill*. It is remarkable for saying not more than is needed on a text which tempts many sermonizers to be prolix. . . .

There is a subdued and grave simplicity about . . . [the poem] which very clearly marks Miss Rossetti's power of accommodating her style to the subject. Equal simplicity, combined with a more detailed picturesqueness and a more plaintive tone, is to be found in *An Apple-Gathering*. . . . (p. 595)

[In this poem, the] idea of the composition is rather pictorial than poetical; and it is so graceful when regarded in this light that we can afford to overlook the slight artifices of the verbal interpretation which Miss Rossetti has given to her own painter's imaginings. The foundation of the whole picture is a genuine and human sentiment, quite different from the sheer unreality which underlies the conception of the *Goblin Market;* and for the strength and success with which this sentiment has been caught and impressed upon the sense of the reader, it is prudent to forgive some of the questionable truth of detail.

The devotional poems which fill a large portion of this volume are excellent in tone, and generally very clear and good in expression. Every reader of one of these called **"From House to Home,"** will be forcibly reminded of the manner of Mr. Tennyson's "Palace of Art and Dream of Fair Women;" but the poem is not wanting in originality of thought. The highest specimens of Miss Rossetti's power, however, will be found in the secular division of her works. . . .

It would be easy to point out various instances of a slight affectation in language and in rhythm, and an unnecessary preference for the use of unfamiliar in lieu of familiar terms. Such faults are, perhaps, theoretically, less excusable in an authoress who shows her thorough command of metre, and of a very sufficient vocabulary of good sterling English. Yet in such a case these errors are practically the more venial, as they may be expected to correct themselves in the course of study. Miss Rossetti displays the talent of conscientious hard work in her verses, as Mr. [Dante Gabriel] Rossetti does in his very remarkable and original paintings. Sooner or later they will both, as we trust, work out for themselves in their respective arts the desirable conviction that quaintness is not strength, and that it generally interferes with beauty. (p. 596)

> "Reviews: 'Goblin Market and Other Poems'," in The Saturday Review, *London, Vol. 13, No. 343, May 24, 1862, pp. 595-96.*

THE ATHENAEUM   (essay date 1866)

The pathos which springs from a sense of what is deep and abiding in human love and desire, and of what is casual and brief in human fortune, would seem to give the tone to Miss Rossetti's musings. With her the perception of beauty, however, is as keen as that of pathos, and these together form an imagination sadly sweet—one, moreover, which has been long and sedulously disciplined. In [*The Prince's Progress; and other Poems*] this imagination is seen in its prime: the sentiment is warm, the observation fresh, the art subtle and mature. We have the summer of the writer's genius, which sits less, indeed, in the sunshine than where

> The cedar sheds its dark green layers of shade,

or the yew overshadows the mound. The foliage above is thick and dark, but the foliage of summer still. . . .

In a great measure Miss Rossetti redeems her work from stiffness and artificial ingenuity—generally the besetting weakness of allegory—by painting scenes which, though touched by the light of imagination, are yet as vividly true as if they were photographs of familiar objects. (p. 824)

She seldom offers to us pictures of *present* emotion. She does not unveil to us the face of humanity until the flush of human impulse has died away. We do not see the conflict of the heart, but the sequel of that conflict. Hence there is in some of her best pictures the air of the cathedral rather than that of the world without. Her saints and heroes have not the stir and dust of life about them; but they smile to us in a repose almost mournful, like effigies from a stained window or the sculptured forms of knight and dame in the coloured light of the aisle. We notice, indeed, not without regret, that most of these poems are set in a minor key—that a strain of suffering insinuates itself even into the author's devotional pieces. . . . [We] cannot but lament that the tone of Miss Rossetti's poetry—always, be it remembered, religiously submissive—should be that of the dirge rather than of the anthem. Setting aside this objection, and warning the reader that the volume is not poetry made easy, but a book which requires a co-operating imagination on his own part, we warmly commend it to perusal. There is scarcely a poem (if we make any exception it is to **'Under the Rose'**) which does not evolve a distinct idea or feeling with finished charm of manner. (p. 825)

> "'The Prince's Progress; and Other Poems'," in The Athenaeum, *No. 2017, June 23, 1866, pp. 824-25.*

THE SPECTATOR   (essay date 1866)

Miss Rossetti has never again come up to the level she reached in *Goblin Market*. There was a freshness, simplicity, and originality in that little goblin story which reminded us of Hans Christian Andersen, and yet a sweet, refined current of poetical feeling which kept it far above the level of a mere child's tale. We cannot say the same for the poem which gives the name to this little volume [*The Prince's Progress and Other Poems*]. The *Prince's Progress* is rather a common-place allegory of the delays and temptations which men allow to intervene between themselves and the beauty or truth to which they profess to dedicate their lives. And the execution does not redeem the poem itself from the charge of a certain want of drift, vigour, and *raison d'être*. There are much better things in the book than the *Prince's Progress*. . . . [However, with] few exceptions the fugitive insights and glimpses of beauty with which these poems abound have little to bind them together, and leave little mark on the mind. They are full of snatches of fancy, of floating musical notes, gleaming wings, rustling leaves, and glowing skies, such as we might bring together in a summer-day dream, but the single pieces are not penetrated by single conceptions; they are rather fancies idly strung on a single mood of mind, without force and without effect. And Miss Rossetti yields the rein to her fancy so completely and helplessly that sometimes it betrays her, leading her into mere caprices that have neither the form and glow of beauty about them, nor any individuality of their own to give them a claim to poetic existence independently of beauty, by mere right of the fascination they exert over the imagination. Take, for instance, the very silly poem, so we must call it, called **"A Bird's Eye View,"** which describes, from a croaking raven's point of view, the hapless voyage of a royal bride whose ship founders at sea, and so fulfils the bad omen which the bird of ill omen predicted. The idea of the poem is poor, and the execution is worse than the idea, capricious to the verge of imbecility. . . . (p. 974)

But though the fault of the book consists in the excessive vagrancy and loose texture of the fancies which Miss Rossetti strings together, often almost with the arbitrariness of the little bits of coloured glass in a kaleidoscope, we should be very sorry not to recognize fairly the beauty,—often indeed evanescent beauty, which it is difficult to remember, and the impression of which vanishes almost with the reading of the piece,—of many of the stanzas it contains. There is no doubt that Miss Rossetti has a genuinely poetic temperament, and that what she wants is rather original conceptions and strongly marked subjects, than variety of illustration and warmth of sentiment with which to clothe such thoughts as she has. The finest poem, we think much the finest poem, in the volume, is the one called **"Light Love."** . . . [There] is the true ring of tragedy in the verses, and a finesse in the scornful cruelty of the traitor's language which impresses us far more powerfully than any other of these webs of brightly coloured fancy, and warm, often hectic, sentiment. . . . The imagination which conceived *Goblin Market* and [this] very different kind of poem . . . ought to be capable of other original efforts, and we think would be, if Miss Rossetti would only concentrate her powers more, and instead of throwing off so many slight snatches of mere prettiness, would cherish one or two subjects long in her imagination, and not attempt to write upon them till they had really taken root,—taken possession of her mind. (p. 975)

> *"Miss Rossetti's New Poems," in* The Spectator, *Vol. 39, No. 1992, September 1, 1866, pp. 974-75.*

THE SPECTATOR   (essay date 1870)

[With *Commonplace, and Other Short Tales* Miss Rossetti] has diverged into an entirely different region, and the exuberance and delicacy of fancy, which are such charming characteristics of her poems, have not much play in short stories like these—principally of ordinary life. We sigh to find the spell broken, and that the authoress of such exquisite verses can indeed write commonplace; not that evidence of the same fancy is entirely wanting, but it is chiefly exhibited in the grotesque variety of the wares offered for our acceptance, and which are adapted to such opposite classes of customers, and belong to such different periods of life, that we are involuntarily reminded of her own goblin merchantmen crying to the passers, "Come buy, come buy!" and offering fruits of every clime and season, "all ripe together." . . . The fairy tales, only, remind us of their beautiful half-sisters, the poems, and have to sustain alone, as far as they can, the reputation of their common mother, and to introduce and to plead for their less attractive relatives, who are received out of respect for their parentage, and retained because all or none must be taken—as we put up with the uninteresting brothers of a family for the sake of the sweet and graceful girls. But even the fairy tales do not quite suit our ideas; they are fanciful and delicate, and the morals inculcated unexceptionable; but Miss Rossetti is a little out of her depth, and creates marvels which, judged even by the broad and liberal minds that arranged the natural laws of the fairy world, would seem to be impossibilities. . . .

We do not mean that the other stories in the volume have no merit; they are all characterized by purity of language and refinement of thought and a spirit of gentle affectionateness, and the sketches are drawn with a delicate and, at the same time, faithful touch. . . .

Nevertheless the stories are, with [certain exceptions], wanting in originality and power, and the interest is of the very slenderest kind. . . . (p. 1292)

On the whole, we cannot help regretting that Miss Rossetti has collected into a volume such very slight and incongruous materials. (p. 1293)

> *"Miss Rossetti's Short Tales," in* The Spectator, *No. 2209, October 29, 1870, pp. 1292-93.*

SIDNEY COLVIN   (essay date 1872)

It is pleasant to see children's literature get better as it does year by year in England. This season in particular has produced a crop of books that are delightful for them—for the children—but more delightful still, perhaps, for some among their elders. . . . (p. 23)

[*Sing-Song*] by Miss Rossetti, and illustrated by Mr. [Arthur] Hughes (not, by the way, a matter of story-telling but of song-singing), is one of the most exquisite of its class ever seen, in which the poet and artist have continually had parallel felicities of inspiration—each little rhyme having its separate and carefully engraved head-piece. In the form of the poetry the book answers literally to its title, and consists of nothing but short rhymes as simple in sound as those immemorially sung in nurseries—one only, of exceptional length, containing as many as nine verses—and having always a music suited to baby ears, though sometimes a depth of pathos or suggestion far enough transcending baby apprehension. But both in pictures and poetry, provided they have the simple turn, and the appeal to everyday experience and curiosity, which makes them attractive to children at first sight and hearing, the ulterior, intenser quality of many of these must in an unrealised way constitute added value, we should say, even for children. . . . In tuning the simplest fancies or hints of fragmentary idea, Miss Rossetti cannot lose the habit or instinct of an artist; and the style and cadence of these tiny verses are as finished and individual, sometimes as beautiful in regard of their theme, as they can be, and not much recalling any precedent, except in a few cases that of Blake. (pp. 23-4)

> *Sidney Colvin, "'Sing-Song'," in* The Academy, *No. 40, January 15, 1872, pp. 23-4.*

CATHOLIC WORLD   (essay date 1876)

Christina Rossetti is, we believe, the queen of the Preraphaelite school, the literary department of that school at least, in England. To those interested in Preraphaelites and Preraphaelitism the present volume [*Poems*], which seems to be the first American edition of this lady's poems, will prove a great attraction. (p. 122)

Miss Rossetti we take to be a very good example of the faults and virtues of her school. Here is a volume of three hundred pages, and it is filled with almost every kind of verse, much of which is of the most fragmentary nature. Some of it is marvellously beautiful; some trash; some coarse; some the very breathing and inspiration of the deep religion of the heart. In her devotional pieces she is undoubtedly at her best. . . . [Her] other pieces are not so satisfactory. The ultra-melancholy tone, the tiresome repetitions of words and phrases that mark the school, pervade them. (p. 123)

[Whatever] merits the Preraphaelite school of poetry may possess, cheerfulness is not one of them. As a proof of this we only cull a few titles from the contents of the book before us. **"A Dirge"** is the eighth on the list; then come in due order, **"After Death," "The Hour and the Ghost," "Dead before**

Death," "Bitter for Sweet," "The Poor Ghost," "The Ghost's Petition," and so on. But Miss Rossetti is happily not all melancholy. The opening piece, the famous **"Goblin Market,"** is thoroughly fresh and charming, and, to our thinking, deserves a place beside "The Pied Piper of Hamlin." (p. 124)

Something much more characteristic of the school to which Miss Rossetti belongs is **"The Poor Ghost."** . . . But this is too lugubrious. There are many others of a similar tone, but we prefer laying before the reader what we most admire. We have no doubt whatever that there are many persons who would consider such poems as [**"The Poor Ghost"**] from the gems of the volume. To us they read as though written by persons in the last stage of consumption, who have no hope in life, and apparently very little beyond. The lines, too, are as heavy and clumsy as they can be. Perhaps the author has made them so on purpose to impart an additional ghastliness to the poem; for, as seen already, she can sing sweetly enough when she pleases. Another long and very doleful poem is that entitled **"Under the Rose,"** which repeats the sad old lesson that the sins of the parents are visited on the heads of the children. A third, though not quite so sad, save in the ending, is **"The Prince's Progress,"** which is one of the best and most characteristic in the volume. (pp. 125-26)

So far for the general run of Miss Rossetti's poems. It will be seen that they are nothing very wonderful, in whatever light we view them. They are not nearly so great as her brother's; indeed, they will not stand comparison with them at all. The style is too varied, the pieces are too short and fugitive to be stamped with any marked originality or individuality, with the exception, perhaps, of the **"Goblin Market."** But there is a certain class of her poems examination of which we have reserved for the last. Miss Rossetti has set up a little devotional shrine here and there throughout the volume, where we find her on her knees, with a strong faith, a deep sense of spiritual needs, a feeling of the real littleness of the life passing around us, of the true greatness of what is to come after, a sense of the presence of the living God before whom she bows down her soul into the dust; and here she is another woman. As she sinks her poetry rises, and gushes up out of her heart to heaven in strains sad, sweet, tender, and musical that a saint might envy. (pp. 126-27)

> *"Christina Rossetti's Poems," in* Catholic World, *Vol. XXIV, No. 139, October, 1876, pp. 122-30.*

T. HALL CAINE (essay date 1881)

Anything sweeter or more beautiful and, at the same time, more subtly conceived than the title poem of Miss Rossetti's new volume [*A Pageant and other Poems*] it would be difficult to desire and unfair to expect. Those who long for something simply thought and felt, and yet informed throughout by strength and fervour, will find the **"Pageant"** grateful and charming. The personifications presented are the months of the year, represented half as boys and half as girls, and the dramatic element in the poem is concerned with the race of the seasons to overtake each other. Simple as the scheme is in outline, it affords opportunity for many a collateral touch of passion to which a more elaborate design might not so naturally lend itself. Even the stage directions are made the channel for the display of the closest insight into the workings of Nature, and are in themselves as poetic as anything communicated in the text. Indeed, though admirably adapted for representation by children, the pageant would even lose something in the acting by

the difficulty of conveying by action the subtle sense of natural phenomena which finds perfect expression in the unspoken prose. . . . As to Miss Rossetti's especial vocation for depicting Nature's changeful aspects, it must be said, her prefatory "key-note" notwithstanding, that she is never so happy as when realising the gentler side of Nature's temper—her stillness, which the rippling of rivers or twittering of birds makes yet more still, her cloudlessness, her hopefulness and peace. With Nature's less tractable moods of mist and wind, and with her sterner heights of hill and fell, the poet displays less sympathy, and it may be doubted if, together with her love of loveliness, she could possess the gift that compasses them. This point is the worthier of remark from the clear tendency Miss Rossetti has shown, more than ever in recent years, to drop into a despondent personal tone, which, though wholly natural and unforced, is clearly somewhat pampered, even in the face of robuster promptings. Such a tone as I speak of finds vent in the admirable **"Ballad of Boding"** (a poem full of symbol, and surpassed for truth and fervour by nothing in this volume), and in certain sonnets distinguished by strength of exceptional ascetic passion. . . .

"Brandons Both," though touched with the poet's characteristic sadness, is a sweet little idyl written in a rarely musical tripping metre of which I do not remember to have met with any other example. . . . The interweaving of various movements in this metre is very ingenious—lending itself to a most happy variety of feeling. . . . The lyrics in this volume have that mingled music, sweetness, emphasis, and condensation which should belong to all examples of pure song, whose first function is to live in the air.

> *T. Hall Caine, "'A Pageant and Other Poems'," in* The Academy, *No. 486, August 27, 1881, p. 152.*

RICHARD Le GALLIENNE (essay date 1891)

[In Christina Rossetti's *Poems*] we have the exquisite product of a life which cannot yet have left off singing, poems of as fair an art, lyrics of as fresh a note, dreams of as strange a phantasy, as ever made blessed the English tongue.

To say that Miss Rossetti is the greatest English poet among women is to pay regard to a distinction which, in questions of art, is purely arbitrary—a distinction which has given us the foolish word "poetess," a standing witness in our language to the national obtuseness. How little must the artistic constitution—the third sex—be understood among a people with such a word in their dictionary. How inorganic such distinctions are, of course, needs no illustration, though, if such were necessary, Miss Christina Rossetti's genius would form an admirable text; for, to my mind, she is, in right of its rarest quality, our one imaginative descendant of the magician of "Kubla Khan" [Coleridge]. No English poet till the appearance of **"Goblin Market"** ever again found the hidden door to Xanadu save she. . . .

In that power of dream, that gift of the child's imagination, is the most absolute distinction of these poems. All things are seen in that light, the whole world is still a child's vision of wonder, every hill is a presence, every flower a gnome, and that "mysterious face of common things" which every poet intermittently realises is for her their constant aspect. That is the individual charm of her many exquisite natural pictures; the light of the miracle is about them all; their fresh morning scent and bloom come breathing a sense of the mystery of their existence, not "the burden," but the glamour. . . .

But this, though so much, is only one aspect of a genius which is singularly many-sided. A gift of simple singing, an artless perfection of art, a pulse of unpremeditated passion, an ideal spiritual exaltation—all these powers go to the making of these poems, with a spontaneity in their exercise rare indeed in our self-conscious age. In no other modern poet is "the fine care-less rapture" so surely heard. (p. 130)

[A note of loss] is another distinctive characteristic of Miss Rossetti's singing. It wells through all, like the sadness of the spring. Her songs of love are nearly always of love's loss; of its joy she sings with passionate throat, but it is joy seen through the mirror of a wild regret. Yet she is not as those who sorrow without hope—she can still say from the heart: "Or in this world, or in the world to come."

And though, of course, many of her poems are directly "de-votional" as her brother Dante Gabriel's are not, it is interesting to trace the same strain of mystic materialism running through them as gave us [his] "The Blessed Damozel." . . . And, to turn once more to purely artistic considerations, here and there also in her poems the verse has occasionally that "decorative" quality, as of cloth of gold stiff with sumptuous needle-work design, which is a constant effect in the painter's poetry—that rich material symbolism such as finds its most perfect illus-tration in a poem like the Song of Solomon. . . .

Sometimes in her best poems we come across a word insensitive or out of colour. This, obviously, cannot be from lack of the power of art, it can only be because her exercise of the power is mainly unconscious. We find the same flaws in the early work of Keats; but he, on the other hand, soon learnt to train his song by a mature study of style. I should say, however, that Miss Rossetti has never done this; and so great is her instinctive power of art that she has really been able to afford the neglect, her poetry retaining thereby a charming *naiveté* which by a self-conscious culture might have been lost to us. (p. 131)

> Richard Le Gallienne, "Christina Rossetti's Poems," in The Academy, *No. 979, February 7, 1891, pp. 130-31.*

THE INDEPENDENT   (essay date 1892)

[*The Face of the Deep, A Devotional Commentary on the Apoc-alypse* is veritably] a poet's book; the work of a poet, and for poetic minds, but inspired by a faith that rises into the rhapsody of open vision. The book is not a commentary in any sense recognized hitherto among the makers of that kind of sad col-ored literature. Possibly in the sense of some transformation of the letter into spirit, or of a poetic mind sanctified and inspired to reveal the deep things of God, this may be a com-mentary, tho made of stuff that poets only know how to weave. . . . [The book] flashes with almost supernal light, the splendid corruscations of genius inspired by faith. There is a line of mystic symbolism running through the whole rhapsody, but it is too objective to be absorbed in mystical contemplations except in the rapturous objectivity of Dante and Beatrice. It is not a book of deep spiritual penetration. But for lofty flights and soaring far and away into the depths of adoring contem-plation we have seen nothing like this last book of Christina Rossetti.

> "Literature: 'The Face of the Deep: A Devotional Commentary on the Apocalypse'," in The Indepen-dent, *Vol. XLIV, No. 2291, October 27, 1892, p. 1524.*

KATHERINE (TYNAN) HINKSON   (essay date 1893)

[Miss Rossetti] would not be the exquisite poet she is if she were not full of human sympathies, if she had not the human capacities for joy and pain. (p. 78)

[In her] early days Miss Rossetti wrote of things such as make the dreams of any imaginative girl; and the finer the imagination the more pensive the dreams. Love, dreams, and death made the warp and woof of her poetry, and the spiritual note, learnt early from a deeply religious and worshipped mother, was not yet dominant. Miss Rossetti's poetry has always been mel-ancholy, melancholy then with the half sweet trouble of a young imagination, later with the melancholy of one to whom the world is but as a day, and the desires of it dust and ashes; melancholy, now that it has become the poetry of a saint, with the yearnings of an exile. Of itself it was not essentially sad; such a poem as **"A Birthday,"** for example, is full of joy; and several of the early poems have a very placid and unclouded atmosphere. Hers is never a sadness that disturbs, as it would in the poetry of a lesser poet. . . . In any but your most ex-quisite poet, sadness in time becomes dreariness. (pp. 78-9)

[The] art in her poems is so fine and consummate that very simple souls may find in them exquisite satisfaction, without discovering that the limpid clearness is anything so far beyond them as the finest art. Her "half-in-love with easeful Death" has nothing lowering in it; it is not the roof of the grave she desires, but the Country and the Presence that lie beyond that threshold. The note of spiritual rapture is very dominant in her last book, **'The Face of the Deep.'** . . .

Many hearts will faint before the spiritual heights of **'The Face of the Deep,'** yet turn again and again to those early songs, to the sonnets of the volume called **'A Pageant,'** and the many other poems in which Miss Rossetti sings of earthly love and sorrow with as poignant sweetness as later she was to sing of Paradise. One can see in the later poems how the grave and the gradual plucking away of human joys have translated them-selves for her into the promise and the joy of eternity.

As a mere personal judgment, I should rank the poetry of no living English poet beside Miss Rossetti's. She has the impulse, the intensity, and the unexpectedness of genius, with an art that was born in her, not made. Those poems of hers which, in her later volumes of meditations, she pours out in great numbers, are each one absolutely perfect of its kind, a fine jewel not facetted, but crystal clear and with a white light at its heart. (p. 79)

> Katherine (Tynan) Hinkson, "The Poetry of Chris-tina Rossetti," in The Bookman, *London, Vol. 5, No. 27, December, 1893, pp. 78-9.*

THE ATHENAEUM   (essay date 1893)

[*Verses*] is a book which will no doubt be largely, and suitably, read for its devotional tendency by people who will not see the difference between such verse and the verse of the late Frances Ridley Havergal. But it will be appreciated for its actual poetical value by all who care for Miss Rossetti's work, that is to say, by all who care for poetry.

There is nothing in this volume quite equal to such earlier masterpiece as **'Despised and Rejected,' 'Passing away, saith the World, passing away,'** or **'Advent.'** But, on the other hand, there is scarcely a single piece, scarcely a snatch or fragment, which is not a satisfying piece of work, an adequate work of art. These little pieces, so short, simple, fragmentary in character, so intangible very often, and so elusive in their charm, are a sort of noting of the sensations of the soul—sensations almost "too simple and too sweet for words," too fleeting to be seized and recorded. . . . [In her religious poems, Miss Rossetti] has certain definite things to say; her subject absorbs her, and seems, itself, to find for her the appropriate words, the simplest, the sincerest, the most direct and vivid. For her art is concerned absolutely with the essentials, needing neither elaboration nor ornament, so sufficing, in their proper beauty, are the words which interpret the beauty of her emotions and sensations. . . . Very often her simplicity is attained by an elaborate and difficult process, as in the continuous rhyming of the same word, a favourite device, loved, doubtless, for the cumulative effect of its fervent monotony. And sometimes there is a touch of the fantastic (after her earlier secular manner) in the symbolism (p. 842)

But always there is the same subtle use of simple words, and there are generally simple rhythms, or rhythms which are constrained to have an air of the instinctive and the unpremeditated, with a certain attractive homeliness in the handling of the abstract, which has always been one of her characteristics, from the days of **'Goblin Market'** till now. . . .

[Her religious poetry] is the only purely religious poetry now being written in this country, or, indeed, easily to be found in recent literature. It is not the soaring rapture of [Richard] Crashaw, which shrieks aloud, almost, in the fever of its devotional ecstasy; much less is it akin to the dusty, daily pieties of George Herbert. Hers is, indeed, a rapture, but contained, constrained, saddened with a conscious unworthiness, grave with the sorrow of the world. It has its own peculiar note of personal sorrow, an undertone always, if only an undertone. Though written, doubtless, with a definitely religious intention, it is never didactic, never attempts (what is of all things most impossible to poetry, and most abhorrent) the heresy, as it has been called, of teaching,—is edifying after all, one might almost say, by accident. Here is a poet, one of the greatest of living poets; she is deeply religious by nature, and consequently her verse is suffused with religious emotion. The sequence is inevitable; it is but the blossoming of the tree after its kind. (p. 843)

"Literature: 'Verses'," in The Athenaeum, *No. 3451, December 16, 1893, pp. 842-43.*

EDMUND GOSSE (essay date 1893)

Severely true to herself, an artist of conscientiousness as high as her skill is exquisite, [Miss Rossetti] has never swept her fame to sea in a flood of her own outpourings. . . . I desire to pay no more than a just tribute of respect to one of the most perfect poets of the age—not one of the most powerful, of course, nor one of the most epoch-making, but to one of the most perfect—to a writer toward whom we may not unreasonably expect that students of English literature in the twenty-fourth century may look back as the critics of Alexandria did toward Sappho and toward Erinna. (p. 138)

What is very interesting in her poetry is the union of [a] fixed religious faith with a hold upon physical beauty and the richer parts of Nature which allies her with her brother and with their younger friends. She does not shrink from strong delineation of the pleasures of life even when she is denouncing them. (p. 148)

There is no literary hypocrisy here, no pretence that the apple of life is full of ashes; and this gives a startling beauty, the beauty of artistic contrast, to the poet's studies in morality. Miss Rossetti, indeed, is so didactic in the undercurrent of her mind, so anxious to adorn her tale with a religious moral, that she needs all her art, all her vigorous estimate of physical loveliness, to make her poetry delightful as poetry. That she does make it eminently delightful merely proves her extraordinary native gift. (pp. 148-49)

[*Goblin Market*] is one of the very few purely fantastic poems of recent times which have really kept up the old tradition of humoresque literature. Its witty and fantastic conception is embroidered with fancies, descriptions, peals of laughing music, which clothe it as a queer Japanese figure may be clothed with brocade, so that the entire effect at last is beautiful and harmonious without ever having ceased to be grotesque. I confess that while I dimly perceive the underlying theme to be a didactic one, and nothing less than the sacrifice of self by a sister to recuperate a sister's virtue, I cannot follow the parable through all its delicious episodes. Like a Japanese work of art, again, one perceives the general intention, and one is satisfied with the beauty of all the detail, without comprehending or wishing to comprehend every part of the execution. . . . [It is] astonishing to me that the general public, that strange and unaccountable entity, has chosen to prefer *Goblin Market,* which we might conceive to be written for poets alone, to *The Prince's Progress,* where the parable and the teaching are as clear as noonday. The prince is a handsome, lazy fellow, who sets out late upon his pilgrimage, loiters in bad company by the way, is decoyed by light loves, and the hope of life, and the desire of wealth, and reaches his destined bride at last, only to find her dead. This has an obvious moral, but it is adorned with verse of the very highest romantic beauty. Every claim which criticism has to make for the singular merit of Miss Rossetti might be substantiated from this little-known romance. . . . (pp. 149-50)

[Her lyrics] are eminent for their glow of colouring, their vivid and novel diction, and for a certain penetrating accent, whether in joy or pain, which rivets the attention. Her habitual tone is one of melancholy reverie, the pathos of which is strangely intensified by her appreciation of beauty and pleasure. . . . Her lyrics have that *desiderium,* that obstinate longing for something lost out of life, which Shelley's have, although her Christian faith gives her regret a more resigned and sedate character than his possesses. In the extremely rare gift of song-writing Miss Rossetti has been singularly successful. Of the poets of our time she stands next to Lord Tennyson in this branch of the art, in the spontaneous and complete quality of her *lieder,* and in their propriety for the purpose of being sung. (pp. 151-52)

Her music is very delicate, and it is no small praise to her that she it is who, of living verse-writers, has left the strongest mark on the metrical nature of that miraculous artificer of verse, Mr. Swinburne. . . . Miss Rossetti, however, makes no pretence to elaborate metrical effects; she is even sometimes a little naïve, a little careless, in her rough, rhymeless endings, and metrically her work was better in her youth than it has been since.

The sonnets present points of noticeable interest. They are few, but they are of singular excellence. (pp. 153-54)

It is in certain of her objective sonnets that her touch is most firm and picturesque, her intelligence most weighty, and her style most completely characteristic. The reader need but turn to **"After Death, "On the Wing," "Venus's Looking Glass"** . . . , and the marvellous **"A Triad"** to concede the truth of this; while in the more obvious subjective manner of sonnet-writing she is one of the most successful poets of our time. In **"The World,"** where she may be held to come closest to her brother as a sonneteer, she seems to me to surpass him.

From the first a large section of Miss Rossetti's work has been occupied with sacred and devotional themes. Through this most rare and difficult department of the art, which so few essay without breaking on the Scylla of doctrine on the one hand, or being whirled in the Charybdis of commonplace dulness on the other, she has steered with extraordinary success. Her sacred poems are truly sacred, and yet not unpoetical. As a religious poet of our time she has no rival but Cardinal Newman. . . . (pp. 155-56)

> *Edmund Gosse, "Christina Rossetti" (1893), in his* Critical Kit-Kats, *Dodd Mead and Company, 1896 (and reprinted by Scholarly Press, Inc., 1971, pp. 133-62).*

EDMUND K. CHAMBERS (essay date 1894)

Miss Rossetti's gifts, unfairly, as I think, obscured for some time by the marvellous genius of her brother, have none the less won recognition in the hearts of many men. Her poetry has always been reticent and unassuming, but always stamped with a rare distinction, a perfection of form, and an elevation of spirit which are as welcome as flowers in May. It is with a pride of possession that one puts her new volume [*Verses*] upon the shelf, to return to again and again for refreshment of the appropriate mood. . . . In various ways [these poems] are not without traces of their origin. A cycle of verses written, as some of Miss Rossetti's are, to fit the feasts and fasts of the Prayer Book, must needs, one would think, want something at times of spontaneity. The spiritual moods of the most devout do not follow precisely the order of the ecclesiastical year, nor can those who are nearest in sympathy to John write with equal felicity of Paul and Didymus. A little discreet pruning might have made this book even more representative of the author's powers than it is, by the removal of repetitions and weaknesses accidental to the method of its composition. But this may not be everyone's view, and even so much of criticism appears ungracious, where the only desire is to praise rightly.

It is natural, after this long interval, to look back to Miss Rossetti's earlier work, and attempt to measure the growth which divides it from that of to-day. Certain elements in that earlier work have disappeared; certain others have become fixed and dominant. The note of paganism, so inconsistent with the writer's general standpoint, has ceased the sound; there are no more dirges for dead love, no more tears over life or yearnings for the rest of oblivion. The sense that the world is a vanity of vanities has survived, but it has been transformed: no longer an ultimate criticism of existence, it has become the foil to a religious philosophy. And so, too, the veil of unearthliness, of detachment, which was always present in her most characteristic and serious moods, has extended itself over the whole field of vision. The direct human view of things, the fresh impulse of the senses, the keenness of simple emotion, have become dim in the shadow of all time and all eternity. There is abundance of love for humanity still; but it is a reflected love, for man as the image of the Most High, for man as the beloved of Christ, not for man simply as man. When Miss

Rossetti speaks of love now she means not clinging but charity. . . . In this sense Love is the keynote of Miss Rossetti's book. It is the final outcome of all her disciplines and raptures, her message, as it was St. John's, to her generation. She rings changes on the beloved word of Love, filling her heart with its music. But the individual, personal love of the **Monna Innominata,** that is no longer a subject of her song. An exactly similar change has come over her outlook upon nature. It has been etherealised, spiritualised. The primal sensuous delight in flowers and the song of birds, the heart that beat in sympathy with June, have vanished. She is still sensitive to the beauty of earth, but chiefly to those aspects of that beauty which suggest the unearthly, the symbolic aspects, in which the spiritual shines most clearly through the material veil: not the full hearted, aggressive, jubilant moods, but the quiet tints, the serener landscapes, the gentle breezes. . . . In a word, Miss Rossetti has become definitely and exclusively a religious singer. (pp. 162-63)

I do not know whether Miss Rossetti is a Catholic or a Protestant. . . , but it is quite certain that with her Italian blood she has inherited tones of speech and manners of thought which do not belong to our country; and in this fact you have a physiological expression of the unique character of her work. She stands in definite and easily intelligible relations to her brother on the one hand, and to the artistic tendencies of Dante and the Pre-Raphaelite painters on the other. There is the same intimate sense of spiritual beauty, and the same desire to embody this beauty in a concrete symbol. Some of her verses are almost archaic in this respect; they are one in spirit with those groups of heavenly figures drawn rather stiffly with trumpets and uplifted faces on a gold background. . . . Miss Rossetti is almost equally felicitous in her handling of imagery, whether she elects the traditional inheritance of religious poets, the well-worn store of scriptural metaphor, rich with its association; or whether she goes further afield, to seek a spiritual suggestion in the harvest of her own quiet eye. . . . She displays also a remarkable command of metrical form. As of old, the sonnet seems to be the mode of expression most natural to her: a sonnet constructed with infinite art, with the very spirit of music in its rhythms, and with a subtle and audacious disposition of irregular accents to dispel all danger of monotony. But outside this special sphere she is at her case alike with the simplest lyric and the most complicated stanza. (p. 163)

Miss Rossetti's philosophy is as low-toned, as full of half-tints, as her art. It is no robust, jubilant, self-satisfied, Christianity that she has to offer. She has seen the world and the bitterness thereof. The shadows of its disappointments and perplexities still cloud her mental horizon. And yet through all she retains a moderate optimism: she is content to walk dimly, to hold a humble faith, that in some unknown way things will work out all right, that man will have a chance of fulfilling his high destinies, and that Love will still be lord of all. It is a philosophy of resignation, a creed for the evening of life, of acceptance rather than endeavour, waiting rather than working. (p. 164)

> *Edmund K. Chambers, "Literature: 'Verses',"* in The Academy, *No. 1138, February 24, 1894, pp. 162-64.*

ALICE MEYNELL (essay date 1895)

There is assuredly but one opinion as to the poet who has lately passed from earth, though that opinion varies in degree. All who have human hearts confess her to be a sad and a sweet poet, all who have a sense of poetry know how rare was the quality of poetry in her—how spiritual and how sensuous—somewhat thin, somewhat dispread in her laxer writing, but perfectly strong, perfectly impassioned in her best. (p. 201)

Christina Rossetti allows us to see how purely poetic was all her least success and her unsuccess. We willingly linger in an easy world which is, with her, not only easy but perpetually beautiful. No less easy was her supreme success: for it is impossible to think that she did herself any violence by close work upon her art. All she touches is fine poetic material, albeit material that is often somewhat scattered. She has no unhandsome secrets of composition, or difficulties of attainment. She keeps the intimate court of a queen. The country of poetry is her home, and she is a "manifest housekeeper," and does nothing out of it. As for the stanzas and passages—but they are oftener whole brief lyrics—in which she reaches the point of poetic passion, they have the stress of purpose which, when it knows how to declare itself, is art indeed. (p. 202)

We are not to reverence the versification of Christina Rossetti as we have learnt to reverence that of a great and classic master. She proves herself an artist, a possessor of the weighty matters of the law of art, despite the characteristic carelessness with which she played by ear. That thought so moving, feeling so urgent, as the thought and feeling of her *Convent Threshold* are communicated, are uttered alive, proves her an artist. . . . In this poem—it is impossible not to dwell on such a masterpiece—without imagery; without beauty except that which is inevitable (and what beauty is more costly?); without grace, except the invincible grace of impassioned poetry; without music, except the ultimate music of the communicating word, she utters that immortal song of love and that cry of more than earthly fear: a song of penitence for love that yet praises love more fervently than would a chorus hymeneal. . . . (p. 203)

In *Amor Mundi*, also, there is terror, though it be terror that is not instant, but that flies and sings, as ominous as a bird of warning—terror suggested, not suffered, as it is profoundly suffered in *The Convent Threshold*. In *The Three Enemies*, again, fear is uttered, not sharply but, with a constant sense of

> The sadness of all sin
> When looked at in the light of love.

And, by-the-bye, while the lax ways of Christina Rossetti's versification are matters of frequent criticism, the artistic perfection of these twelve stanzas of *The Three Enemies* should be insisted on. Equally perfect are *Uphill, Advent,* and some ten more: all pieces written with the full number of syllables. She has here a strong and gentle brevity without haste, a beauty of phrasing, a finality, a sense of structure and stability, with the freedom of life, scarce possible to surpass. Wherever she writes by rule, she uses that rule admirably well. It is only in the lax metres which keep—more or less—musical time rather than account of numbers, that one might wish she had more theory. Her versification then is apt to be ambiguous and even incorrect. Take the beautiful lyric at the end of *The Prince's Progress,* though many other passages might be cited. It seems, in one stanza, that the poet has chosen to let the beats of her time fall—punctually and with full measure of time—now upon a syllable and now upon a rest *within the line;* so that the metre goes finely to time, like a nursery song for the rocking of a cradle. But then the succeeding stanza is, as often as not, written with no rule except that of numbers and accents. One stanza throws doubt upon the others. Read the poem which

way you will, there is no assurance as to the number of beats which she intended. (pp. 203-04)

Now, even if Christina Rossetti has more than the inevitable ambiguity, and really mingles her measures, she has done a very serious service to English versification by using afresh this voice of poetry—the voice that sings in musical time. (p. 205)

Her lovelier example is in the motive of all her song. Its sadness was the one all-human sadness, its fear the one true fear. She, acquainted with grief, found in grief no cause of offence. She left revolt to the emotion of mere spectators and strangers. . . . The poet and saint who has now passed from a world she never loved, lived a life of sacrifice, suffered many partings, unreluctantly endured the pains of her spirituality; but she kept, in their quickness, her simple and natural love of love and hope of joy, for another time. Such sufferings as hers do indeed refuse, but they have not denied, delight. Delight is all their faith. (pp. 205-06)

Alice Meynell, "Christina Rossetti," in The New Review, *Vol. 12, No. 69, February, 1895, pp. 201-06.*

ALICE LAW (essay date 1895)

[It is her] power of reducing to poetic expression elements that are by nature fleeting and volatile, which, broadly speaking, lends such a characteristic air of charm and immateriality to Miss Rossetti's verse. Like some magic web, it seems woven of a substance so elusive, intangible, and of such an almost gossamer tenuity as defies handling, and constitutes at once the critic's ecstasy, wonder, and despair. . . .

Miss Rossetti's poetry is characterised by its extreme felicity of manner, its ease of style. At times, and especially in her Nature lyrics, it can only be likened to the loosening of the imprisoned notes in a bird's throat, so richly do the sounds swell and fall, and burst upon one another in their hurry to be out. (p. 445)

[The] keynote of much of Miss Rossetti's word-music is its aesthetic mysticism and rich melancholy. It is associated . . . , as in the works of her brother and the other Pre-Raphaelites, with the deep mediaeval colouring, and quaint bejewelled setting of an old thirteenth- or fourteenth-century manuscript. The women of Miss Rossetti's pages have much in common with the long-tried Griseldas of ante-Renaissance type, with the slow fading Isabella of Boccaccio, or the olive-wreathed, flame-robed virgins of the *Divine Comedy.* Miss Rossetti's verse, like her brother's canvas, bears the deep impress of that Dantean intensity, which, despairing of all material comparisons, could only liken the dazzling beauty of Beatrice to the glorious purity of fire. . . . (p. 447)

[It] is specially in the *Prince's Progress* that Miss Rossetti's subtle and mysterious art finds its most perfect expression. Here we seem to breathe the very atmosphere of old-world charm and mysticism: the stanzas as it were exhale that almost indescribable aesthetic aroma of mingled flowers and herbs—rosemary, thyme, rue, and languorous lilies. . . . (pp. 447-48)

Not only is the atmosphere of her poems old-world, but in all Miss Rossetti's pages we seem to see the mediaeval heroine herself looking out at us, from an almost cloistered seclusion, with sad patient eyes. We hear the song of her overflowing heart, longing to spend and to be spent for love. There is nothing modern about the singing, unless it be its hopelessness, its troubled emotion and despair. The attitude is throughout that of the old-world heroine—pensive, clinging, *passive*. It is the tearful, uplifted accent of her who, in the silence of barred cell or rush-strewn chamber, weeps and prays for victory to crown the arms of others; of her whose only warfare is with the fears and fightings of her own bursting heart. (p. 449)

How eagerly, how jubilantly, Miss Rossetti anticipated the thought of death, how she dwelt on it as on the prospect of endless, soothing peace, may be discovered from her sonnet, *Rest,* or from the glad metre of **When I am dead, my dearest, sing no sad songs for me**. Death had no terrors for her; it was to her but as cool, refreshing sleep. She envies the dead. Nothing of its kind can exceed the beauty of the poem *Dream Land,* which perhaps more than any other embodies Miss Rossetti's feeling about death. . . . (p. 451)

[It] is this prevailing mediaeval Pre-Raphaelite attitude which so markedly separates Miss Rossetti's—as also her brother's—poetry from that of all her predecessors and contemporaries, in particular from that of her great English contemporary, Elizabeth Barrett Browning. It is curious that, while both were eminently religious-minded women, their individual expression of faith should have been so diametrically opposite; there may be more philosophy, but there is certainly less art, in Mrs. Browning's plain, all-round outlook. What she lost in diffuseness and breadth of view, Miss Rossetti gained in intensity and concentration.

It is commonly remarked that Mrs. Browning is the greater poet of the two by reason of her wider sympathy and more extended vision. But a strict and impartial literary criticism must guard against the tendency to confuse quality with quantity, and to mistake a noble-minded desire to remedy crying abuses of the day for the supreme expression of poetic art. . . .

[Miss Rossetti], though rarely posing as teacher, philosopher, or moralist, is yet always a consummate artist; open her pages where we will, we must needs light upon beauty. (p. 452)

As the author of *Goblin Market, The Prince's Progress, Maiden Song,* of numerous exquisite sonnets—among which the *Monna Innominata* threaten to rival Mrs. Browning on her own ground—as the author of these, I repeat, Miss Rossetti's name is attached to a monument of finished work that almost dwarfs the volume of Mrs. Browning's similarly finished productions. (p. 453)

Alice Law, "The Poetry of Christina G. Rossetti," in The Westminster Review, *Vol.143, No. 4, April, 1895, pp. 444-53.*

WILLIAM MORTON PAYNE   (essay date 1895)

[It is upon the contents of the collections 'Goblin Market and Other Poems,' 'The Prince's Progress and Other Poems,' and 'A Pageant and Other Poems'] that Miss Rossetti's reputation must rest, although she did a considerable amount of other literary work. . . . [Her] devotional books, which have both found and deserved a large and appreciative audience, are distinctly out of the common, but the spirit which finds expression in them finds utterance still more intense and rapturous in the three volumes of song to which we now turn. (pp. 237-38)

The longer pieces which introduce Miss Rossetti's three volumes are not the most successful of their contents. It is rather to the lyrics, ballads, and sonnets that the lover of poetry will turn to find her at her best. Who, for example, could once read and ever forget such a sonnet as **'Rest'?** (pp. 239-40)

Miss Rossetti's verses sometimes suggest those of other poets, but we always feel that her art is distinctly her own. . . . As for the influence of the great Italian [Dante], which shaped so powerfully the thought of every member of the Rossetti family, it is less tangible here than in the work of her greater brother, yet to it must be attributed much of the tenderness and the pervasive mysticism of her poems. It is perhaps most apparent in the two sonnet-sequences, **'Monna Innominata'** and **'Later Life,'** both included in [**'A Pageant and Other Poems'**]. . . . But we must repeat that Miss Rossetti's genius was too original to be chargeable with anything more than that assimilation of spiritual influence from which no poet can hope wholly to escape, and which links together in one golden chain the poetic tradition of the ages.

If in most of the provinces of the lyric realm Miss Rossetti's verse challenges comparison with that of our greater singers, it is in the religious province that the challenge is most imperative and her mastery most manifest. Not in Keble or Newman, not in Herbert or Vaughan, do we find a clearer or more beautiful expression of the religious sentiment than is dominant in Miss Rossetti's three books. In this respect, at least, she is unsurpassed, and perhaps unequalled, by any of her contemporaries. In her devotional pieces there is no touch of affectation, artificiality, or insincerity. Such poems as **'the Three Enemies'** and **'Advent'** in the first volume, **'Paradise'** and **'The Lowest Place'** in the second, and many of the glorious lyrics and sonnets of the third, will long be treasured among the religious classics of the English language. (pp. 242-44)

William Morton Payne, "Christina Georgina Rossetti," in his Little Leaders, *Way & Williams, 1895, pp. 237-45.*

LIONEL JOHNSON   (essay date 1896)

Miss Rossetti, artist through and through, mistress of her craft, faultless in tone and taste, completely conscious of her powers and of their extent, may suffer awhile, in coming generations which knew her not, from the intensely personal limitations, the wonderfully individual intentions of her Uranian Muse. Doubtless [**"New Poems"** includes] many a piece of airy fantasy, many a laughing lyric, many a poem born of external circumstance; but her characteristic greatness lies in her most intimate, most severe, most passionate and sacred poems. . . . And by this it is not meant that her obviously and ostensibly sacred poems are alone her greatest: many others, poems of meditation or of passion, with no distinct Christian cry in them, stand side by side with the poems divine and devout. Her fair and stern philosophy of life, which never fails to draw to itself her choicest powers of art, is that which marks out her poetry for distinction and for admiration. Her more external work, with its gaieties and beautiful imaginings, is full of delights, but a thing less high and moving. . . . Miss Rossetti, in her sacred poems, brings together all the elements of art's excellence and of a Christian's faith. Their chief note, their unique interest and delight, is a tenderness in them, a tremulous and wistful beauty of adoration, rising and passing, at times, into something like a very joyous adoration of friend by friend. *Sed quid invenientibus!* we think: this is more than imagination, it is nothing else than vision. . . . The Paradisal imageries, crowns, palms, flames, all the "furniture of heaven," become to us in her poetry as real, visible, tangible, as altars upon earth; the golden trumpets and harps, the multitudinous music of the Saints and Angels, ring through the triumphing chaunts of her later verse. But it is a lyrical, a momentary power, which touches the heart of mystery, sings it, and falls silent; not the prolonged utterance of a pilgrim travelling the far-off land. And the fervour lacks no humility; it is always tremulous, always wistful. . . . These poems have the homesickness for Heaven, amid an infinitely strong desire to endure the exile and the dereliction. And from this longing, that makes the verse quiver and thrill, springs another affection: that merry appropriation of the Holy Child, with all the holy hospitalities of Christmas; the spirit, more delicately refined, of medieval carollers and minstrels, who expressed in good, simple, whole-some ways the full theological purport of the Incarnation—the true Humanity, the true Divinity, the two Natures in the one Person. These poems, a whole succession of them, follow the year of the Church, changing from tone to tone: not, in the more mild and obvious fashion of [John] Keble, discoursing pretty or persuasive thoughts, sermons in verse, daintily touched, but with the more profound interior sympathy, the more learned mysticism, of the greatest Latin hymns. The succession of poems becomes a tragedy, lyric upon lyric developing the sweet and bitter theme: the lilies and the thorns, the incense and the ointment, the tears and the jubilation, the prostrate penitent and the redeemed in glory, all do their part, helping forward the ritual of Christian life, adorning the times and seasons of meditation. And this, without any artifice, any forced treatment of ideal feeling: it is as natural in its beauty and in its rare effect as the loveliness of the *Fioretti*. In all the simplicity, there is the mystically enamoured spirit of true theology, that flaming faith and love of Saints. . . . In her three hundred sacred poems we find all possible tones of feeling and thought. There are poems with a homely, carolling air about them, in their grace and sweetness, as though they were (*salva reverentia*), the nursery songs of Heaven. There are poems, metrically and imaginatively marvellous, surging and sweeping forward with a splendour of movement to their victorious, their exultant close, as though they were the national hymns of Heaven. (p. 59)

I have dwelled upon this side of Miss Rossetti's incomparable work, because in these **"New Poems"** the divine are by far the finest and the most welcome. We may have doubts here and there about the editor's decision to publish some of the other poems, full of interest as they are; but these poems have all their writer's perfection of religious and poetical power. The others, some seven or eight of which have, by a natural oversight, been republished here, though already published in previous volumes, date from Miss Rossetti's girlhood to within a few years of her death. They show her style in process of formation, but not her imaginative bent and tendency: that, from first to last, set firmly in the same one direction, toward lyrical intensity, whether in brief dramatic story, in song of bright or solemn music, in pieces of pondering contemplation, above all, in sonnets massive, poignant, most memorable. Her sonnets have, far beyond most, that singleness of a dominant emotion, piercingly felt and craving expression, joined to a rich magnificence of strict rhythm, which is the sonnet's perfect praise. (pp. 59-60)

> Lionel Johnson, "*Miss Rossetti and Mrs. Alexander*," in The Academy, *No. 1264, July 25, 1896, pp. 59-60.**

ARTHUR SYMONS   (essay date 1897)

By the death of Christina Rossetti, literature, and not English literature alone, has lost the one great modern poetess. There is another English poetess, indeed, who has gained a wider fame; but the fame of Mrs. Browning, like that of her contemporary, and, one might almost say, companion, George Sand, was of too immediate and temporary a kind to last. . . . In Miss Rossetti we have a poet among poets, and in Miss Rossetti alone. Content to be merely a woman, wise in limiting herself within somewhat narrow bounds, she possessed, in union with a profoundly emotional nature, a power of artistic self-restraint which no other woman who has written in verse, except the supreme Sappho, has ever shown; and it is through this mastery over her own nature, this economy of her own resources, that she takes rank among poets rather than among poetesses.

And, indeed, the first quality that appeals to one in Miss Rossetti's work is its artistic finish; and this finish is apparent in a simplicity so intense, so expressive, and so casual in seeming, as only the finest elaboration could extract from the complexities and confusions of nature. Her preference was for the homeliest words, and for the rhythms in which the art consists in a seeming disregard of art. No one who ever wrote in verse used so many words of one syllable, or so few words not used in ordinary conversation. No one ever used fewer inversions, or was less dependent on the unusual in sound or colour, or found less need or less room for metaphor. . . . And yet, with these plain, unadorned words, the words that come first to our lips when we speak to one another, she obtained effects, not merely of vivid sincerity, of downright passion, of religious conviction, but also of fantastic subtlety, of airy grace, of remote and curious charm. (pp. 135-36)

This felicitously simple art, in which style is never a separate grace, but part of the very texture, so to speak, of the design, is the expression of a nature in which intensity of feeling is united with an almost painful reserve. . . . The words seem as if wrung out of her, and it is in their intense quietness that one realizes the controlling force of the will that has bound them down. Alike in the love poems and in the religious poems, there is a certain asceticism, passion itself speaking a chastened language, the language, generally, of sorrowful but absolute renunciation. This motive, passion remembered and repressed, condemned to eternal memory and eternal sorrow, is the motive of much of her finest work; of **"The Convent Threshold,"** for instance. . . . Its recurrence gives a certain sadness to her verse, in spite of so much that is quaint, playful, and childlike in it. . . . [In] her religious poems, which are perhaps the finest part of her work in verse, it is with a mainly tragic ecstasy that she sends up her soul to God, out of the depths. . . . Hers is, indeed, a rapture, but contained, constrained, saddened with a conscious unworthiness, grave with the sorrow of the world. . . . Here, as in the love-poems, depth of feeling is made no excuse for laxity of form; but the form is ennobled, and chastened into a finer severity, in proportion to the richness of the sentiment which it enshrines. It is by this rare, last quality of excellence, that Christina Rossetti takes her place among the great poets of our century, not on sufferance, as a woman, but by right, as an artist.

A power of seeing finely beyond the scope of ordinary vision; that, in a few words, is the note of Miss Rossetti's genius, and it brings with it a subtle and as if instinctive power of expressing subtle and yet as if instinctive conceptions; always clearly, always simply, with a singular and often startling homeliness, which is the sincerity of a style that seems to be innocently unaware of its own beauty. (pp. 137-40)

Miss Rossetti's power of seeing what others do not see, and of telling us about it in such a way that we too are able to see it, is displayed nowhere more prominently than in those poems which deal, in one way or another, with the supernatural. . . . In one poem of Miss Rossetti's we find the most perfect expression ever given to [the] milder aspect of the supernatural. **"Goblin Market"** is surely the most naïve and childlike poem in our language. Miss Rossetti's witchcraft is so subtle that she seems to bewitch, not only us, but herself, and without trying to do either. The narrative has so matter-of-fact, and at the same time so fantastic and bewildering an air, that we are fairly puzzled into acceptance of everything. The very rhythm, the leaping and hopping rhythm, which renders the goblin merchantmen visible to us, has something elfin, and proper to "the little people," in its almost infantile jingle and cadence. In **"The Prince's Progress"** we are in quite another corner of the world of faëry. The poem is more mature, it is handled in a more even and masterly way. . . . The narrative is in the purely romantic manner, and the touch of magic comes into it suddenly and unawares, like the green glitter that comes into the eyes of the milkmaid as she casts her glamour over the Prince on the way. The verse is throughout flexible and expressive, but towards the end, just before and during the exquisite lament, bride-song and death-song at once, it falls into a cadence of such solemn and tender sweetness as even Miss Rossetti has rarely equalled.

Yet another phase of the supernatural meets us in a little group of poems (**"The Ghost's Petition," "The Hour and the Ghost," "At Home," "The Poor Ghost"**) in which the problems of the unseen world are dealt with in a singular way. (pp. 140-42)

These strange little poems, with their sombre and fantastic colouring, the picturesque outcome of a deep and curious pondering over unseen things, lead easily, by an obvious transition, to the poems of spiritual life, in the customary or religious sense of the term. Miss Rossetti's devotional poetry is quite unlike most other poetry of the devotional sort. It is intensely devout, sometimes almost liturgical in character; surcharged with personal emotion, a cry of the heart, an ecstasy of the soul's grief or joy: never didactic, or concerned with purposes of edification. She does not preach; she prays. . . . In all these poems we are led through phase after phase of a devout soul; we find a sequence of keen and brooding moods of religious feeling and meditation; with, in the less sombre pieces, a sort of noting of the sensations of the soul; with, also, something of the ingenious quaintness, the solemn curiosity of Donne, allied to something of the instinctive and unaccountable felicity of Shelley. (pp. 142-43)

There is one subject to which Miss Rossetti returns again and again, a subject into which she is able to infuse a more intense feeling than we find in any but her devotional pieces: that of a heart given sorrowfully over to the memory of a passion spent somehow in vain, disregarded or self-repressed. In such poems as that named **"Twice,"** she has found singularly moving words for the suppressed bitterness of a disappointed heart, the anguish of unuttered passion reaching to a point of ascetic abnegation, a devout frenzy of patience, which is the springing of the bitter seed of hope dead in a fiery martyrdom. It is in **"The Convent Threshold"** that this conception obtains its finest realization. Passion, imagination, the romantic feeling, the religious fervour, the personal emotion, all her noblest gifts and qualities, with her noblest possibilities of style and versification, meet here as one. In this poem the passion is almost fierce. In **"Monna Innominata: a Sonnet of Sonnets,"** the masterpiece of a later volume, a much quieter, perhaps only

a sadder, voice is given to the same cry of an unsatisfied and unweariable love, the love of an "unnamed lady" for one between herself and whom there is a barrier, "held sacred by both, yet not such as to render mutual love incompatible with mutual honour:" self-repression and self-abnegation keep down its heart, a dignified prisoner behind very real bars. This sonnet-sequence should and will take its place among the great works of that kind. . . . (pp. 144-45)

To her, nature is always a relief, an escape; certain aspects she responds to with a peculiarly exhilarating joyousness. It is always the calm aspects of natural things, and chiefly growing nature, that waken sympathy and delight in her. What we call scenery she never refers to; nor to mountains, nor often to the sea. But nowhere in poetry can we get such lovingly minute little pictures of flowers, and corn, and birds, and animals; of the seasons, particularly of spring. She delights in just such things as are the delight of a child; her observation is, as of set purpose, very usually that of a thoughtful and observant child. Children, we must remember, especially very small children, play a great part in the world of Miss Rossetti's poetry. They have, indeed, a book all to themselves [*Sing-Song: A Nursery Rhyme-book*], one of the quaintest and prettiest books in the language. (pp. 146-47)

What renders these little songs so precious is their pure singing quality, what Matthew Arnold calls the "lyrical cry;" and the same quality appears in a really large number of exquisite lyrics scattered throughout Miss Rossetti's volumes; some of them being, perhaps, in the most ethereal and quintessential elements of song, the most perfect we have had since Shelley, whom she resembles also in her free but flawless treatment of rhythm. The peculiar charm of these songs is as distinct and at the same time as immaterial as a perfume. (p. 147)

[Finished workmanship] we find in almost every poem [of Miss Rossetti's] and workmanship of such calm and even excellence that it is not at first sight we are made aware of the extremely original, thoughtful, and intense nature which throbs so harmoniously beneath it. (p. 148)

> Arthur Symons, "Christina Rossetti," in his Studies in Two Literatures, *Leonard Smithers, 1897, pp. 135-49.*

FORD MADOX HUEFFER [FORD MADOX FORD]
(essay date 1904)

It is convenient to call [Christina Rossetti's] verse lyric, but the term is not strictly correct. . . . It is assuredly not Epic; it is never exactly Elegiac, nor is it ever really Narrative verse. Most particularly it is not philosophic, hortatory, or improving. Even her devotional poetry is seldom other than the expression of a mood. It is a prayer, an adoration of the Saviour, a fear of the Almighty, a craving for pardon and for rest. . . . But her verse is never a sermon; it never preaches, and that, no doubt, is why it lives. In that matter she had the Latin temperament, the instinct that makes you see that if you want to convince you must interest, and if you want to interest you must draw concrete pictures, leaving your hearer to draw the morals. That too, as far as the presentation of her matter goes, is the "technique" of her secular poetry; she had the gift of just, simple, and touching words, and with them she drew pictures that expressed her moods.

The expression of moods—that after all is the only business of the lyric poet. And when he has conveyed those moods to others he has succeeded. It is very decidedly not his business to look at things on the large scale, to "write poetic," to be more impracticable, frenzied, or romantic than Nature has made him. He has to appeal rather than to overwhelm, to hang in the ear rather than to sweep you away with organ peals. It is for these reasons that Christina Rossetti deserves to live.

This new edition [*The Poetical Works of Christina Georgina Rossetti*] challenges a readjustment of our views of her. It emphasises her other sides; it brings forward her larger flights. It groups together in a prominent place works in which, if the modelling is not broader, the outlines at least contain more canvas. This does not much affect one's view of her technique; she remains still the poet of lines, of stanzas, of phrases, and of cadences that are intimately right. But, with the grouping together of her longer verse, there stands out a buoyancy of temperament, a profuseness, a life, and, as far as the metre of the verse is concerned, an infectious gaiety. There appears too, more strongly defined, her little humour, her delicate playfulness, her major key.

"Goblin Market," with which the volume opens, moves breathlessly. Its metre is short, its rhymes are concealed enough not to hinder you with a jingle of assonances, and accurate enough to keep the stanzas together. (pp. 396-97)

The whole poem goes in one breath. Yet it is treated with so much detail as to give the impression of profusion and of value. It is succeeded in the volume by . . . earlier poems of some length. "Repining," and the "Three Nuns," are juvenile efforts, rather dry in tone, and a little formal, but austerely worded. They show interestingly how, in the girl, the organ, the vehicle of expression, was already formed and waiting for the afflatus. (pp. 397-98)

"The Lowest Room" and "From House to Home" were both written before "Goblin Market," and both after she had attained to maturity, the one in 1856, the other two years later. They indicate change of temperament, a hardening of point of view as well as of technical attainment. (p. 398)

But "Goblin Market" was written next year, and from that time onward all her longer verse kept its level of inspiration. It has a profusion of imagination, a power of painting pictures; here and there it has dramatic places, and always a level austerity and restraint in the wording. . . .

The last of the longer poems here given is "**Later Life, a double Sonnet of Sonnets,**" and this suggests, after all, the clue to all her longer pieces. The throwing these thus together challenges, as I have said, a readjustment in our minds, a revision of our mental image of Christina Rossetti's structural technique. It holds out, as it were, this rearrangement, the idea that here was a writer of "sustained" verse, who had, at least potentially, epic as well as lyric gifts. But "**Later Life**" is a sequence of sonnets and careful examination will reveal that the "**Processional of Creation**" is a sequence of pictures, and so, too, the "**Prince's Progress**" and "**Goblin Market**" are sequences— as you might say, strings of beads. They prove, if proof be needed, that, by very careful handling, the lyrical method may be applied to make long poems that are readable and entrancing. (p. 399)

Christina Rossetti arrayed herself very little in the panoply of poetic phrases; she wrote as she spoke. And, indeed, when she was in the mood, she wrote nearly as easily as she spoke. . . . [It] is the distinguishing characteristic of her best poems that they open always with a line that is just a remark, not the

"strong first line" of a song. She seems to utter a little sentence like, "I wonder if the sap is stirring yet," and the spring is presented. For the most part she kept to that conversational key. . . . Indeed, her choice of words was rather limited, and, along with it, her choice of images. She used words like "rest" and "rain" over and over again, without troubling to find synonyms. . . . This implies of course, limitations, both of vocabulary and of temperament. It means, too, that every word that she used was her own; it means, perhaps, an overscrupulousness.

Scrupulous she was to a degree beyond that of common humanity. She suppressed her work for fear of repeating herself, she suppressed still more of it for fear it was too pagan or too sensual. And how much of herself she suppressed in that fear we cannot do more than guess. . . . Suppressions, of course, are legitimate enough aesthetically, when they are made for aesthetic reasons. But it is a loss to both humanity and to art when they are made for reasons so personal—out of a fear for one's soul, that if it is not purely pagan, is at least in essence a survival of devil worship and of the dark ages of the soul.

But if Christina Rossetti suppressed, as far as she was able, whatever was sensual and joyous in the matter and in the temperament of her poems, her faculty for pure delight and for aesthetic enjoyment was expressed all the more strongly in her metre. For her verse is neither musical nor lyrical, it has not the unconscious quality of "lilt," or of the song that merely bubbles. It is rhythmical and even intricate; it is a faculty that, coming from very deep in the sources of enjoyment, moves us for deep and unexplained reasons just as the rhythms of music do. If it has not the quality of lilt it has not the defect; it is never mechanical with numbered syllables. (pp. 401-02)

In Christina Rossetti's verse it is [the] quality of the unexpected, the avoidance of the *cliché* in metre, the fact that here and there you must beat time in a rest of the melody, that gives it its fascination and its music. (p. 403)

She wrote a great deal of verse that to one taste or another is comparatively poor. . . . But nearly all her poems are "authentic" in tone; they yield generally a touch of her flavour here and there, even if the general quality be thin. The very quantity will probably help her fame to stand in the long run. (p. 404)

[She] had one characteristic which should make her gain upon all her distinguished contemporaries—she held aloof from all the problems of her day. She was not greatly esteemed as a teacher in the nineteenth century, because she had not any lessons for that strenuous age. (pp. 404-05)

She was comparatively self-centred, but, inasmuch as the succeeding centuries will cease to be interested in the problems of yesterday, she escapes a danger if she missed some love. . . .

Christina Rossetti, with her introspection, studied her soul; with her talent she rendered it until she became the poet of the suffering—and suffering is a thing of all the ages. (p. 405)

> *Ford Madox Hueffer [Ford Madox Ford], "The Collected Poems of Christina Rossetti," in* The Fortnightly Review, *Vol. 75, March 1, 1904, pp. 393-405.*

PAUL ELMER MORE (essay date 1905)

Probably the first impression one gets from reading the [*Poetical Works*] of Christina Rossetti . . . , is that she wrote altogether too much, and that it was a doubtful service to her memory to preserve so many poems purely private in their nature. . . . For page after page we are in the society of a spirit always refined and exquisite in sentiment, but without any guiding and restraining artistic impulse; she never drew to the shutters of her soul, but lay open to every wandering breath of heaven. In comparison with the works of the more creative poets her song is like the continuous lisping of an æolian harp beside the music elicited by cunning fingers. And then, suddenly, out of this sweet monotony, moved by some stronger, clearer breeze of inspiration, there sounds a strain of wonderful beauty and flawless perfection, unmatched in its own kind in English letters. (p. 124)

Purer inspiration, less troubled by worldly motives, than [**"Passing Away, Saith the World, Passing Away"**] cannot be found. Nor would it be difficult to discover in their brief compass most of the qualities that lend distinction to Christina Rossetti's work. Even her monotone, which after long continuation becomes monotony, affects one here as a subtle device heightening the note of subdued fervour and religious resignation; the repetition of the rhyming vowel creates the feeling of a secret expectancy cherished through the weariness of a frustrate life. If there is any excuse for publishing the many poems that express the mere unlifted, unvaried prayer of her heart, it is because their monotony may prepare the mind for the strange artifice of this solemn chant. But such a preparation demands more patience than a poet may justly claim from the ordinary reader. Better would be a volume of selections from her works, including a number of poems of this character. It would stand, in its own way, supreme in English literature,— as pure and fine an expression of the feminine genius as the world has yet heard.

It is, indeed, as the flower of strictly feminine genius that Christina Rossetti should be read and judged. She is one of a group of women who brought this new note into Victorian poetry,—Louisa Shore, Jean Ingelow, rarely Mrs. Browning, and, I may add, Mrs. Meynell. She is like them, but of a higher, finer strain than they. . . . (pp. 126-27)

There is in her a passive surrender to the powers of life, a religious acquiescence, which wavers between a plaintive pathos and a sublime exultation of faith. (p. 127)

It is this perfectly passive attitude toward the powers that command her heart and her soul—a passivity which by its completeness assumes the misguiding semblance of a deliberate determination of life—that makes her to me the purest expression in English of the feminine genius. (p. 133)

> *Paul Elmer More, "Christina Rossetti," in his* Shelburne Essays, Third Series, *Houghton Mifflin Company, 1905, pp. 124-42.*

PERCY LUBBOCK (essay date 1918)

The peculiar gift of Christina Rossetti is one of the rarest in poetry, if not of the greatest: it is the gift of song. She had a fountain of music within her which never ceased altogether in her life, strangely as her life seemed to narrow itself and her shy difficult spirit to shrink from experience. . . . Her fine powers of mind and imagination were kept in a narrow groove by a puritan rule which she adopted from the very first and held to the end. She would not move outside it, surrounded though she was with some of the fullest and most striking opportunities, æsthetic and intellectual, of her generation. It is

a curiously grey and insular story for a poetess of her origin and endowment, and the strangest part of it all is that her vivid lyrical impulse never entirely left her or lost its freedom. (p. 286)

There is to be found in her earlier poems, and not only in these, a franker and simpler delight in the budding and flowering and fruiting of nature, in the turn of the quick tractable English seasons, in the happy grace of birds and furry creatures, than has often been seen in a literature in which, for the most part, the natural world is made the very groundwork of philosophy. . . . The dawn and flush of spring, the rapture of young love, the lark-song of a summer cornfield—she knew and uttered such moments with a music that has their very own sense of wonder and newness and liberation. She does not study or describe, but her verse is continually full of country weather, airs blowing and sunlight falling—images caught and reflected in a memory as lucid, as keen and thoughtless, as a child's.

The beautiful originality of her poems in this mood is of a kind that makes her the truest "Pre-Raphaelite" of all the famous group. If the word was meant to imply a way of looking at things with new eyes and an ingenuous mind, it suited her long after her brother and the rest had diverged upon their different lines. . . . She could let her fancy riot, as in *Goblin Market,* with wayward profusion; but its opulence is that of a dream, with no attachment to life and ready to vanish in a moment. It was an imagination acutely sensitive to the colour and shape and touch and taste of things—of queer and grotesque things as much as any other. But the mere world could not lay hold on it, and for this very reason it stands out with a singular shining freshness. If ever in her work she ventured, as she seldom did, into actual life, it was evidently because she was tempted by the example of Mrs. Browning; and she was then betrayed into a kind of sentimentality very unlike Mrs. Browning's passionate intellectual honesty. In the world of dreams her brilliance, audacity, even humour, are always alive and true. (pp. 287-88)

The flame of her spirit was bright, by its own human virtue, through all her long and grievous self-vexation; and there are poems of hers, those that are now perhaps most often returned to, in which it glows with a profoundly attaching and appealing beauty. It might be a slender handful of experience that fed the fire; but there could be nothing loftier than the sincerity with which the single-minded votaress of an ideal passion refused to misunderstand or to misprize the memory she guarded. The poetry she dedicated to it has the charm of a perfect loyalty to the sweetness of earthly love. If, for trust in its power, she lacked a certain generosity of soul, she would not for that deny it, or attempt to give it any name but its own. No songs or elegies of love show a simpler and straighter sense of its magic than do hers, and in few is it expressed with a melody more fervent and eager. Their pathos is very great, for even in disappointment and disillusion they retain the sensitive candour of youth, with all its power of suffering and all its instinct for happiness.

But the burden of her creed lay heavily on her—so heavily, so little to her encouragement or even her peace of mind, that it seems alien to her, as though it must have been imposed, as perhaps it was to some extent, by a stronger will from without. . . . A monotony of mood asserted itself more and more in her work. She held fast to the idea that the only road to harmony is through renunciation; but the passion she poured into the act of self-sacrifice, strong as it was, had not the substance, had rather, perhaps, a too pure and artless simplicity, to create a positive life for her in the ideal. She missed the freedom of adventure and exultation that is discovered there by the true mystic. The poetry of Christina Rossetti touches this height at moments, but generally it is caught by the way on the thorny sense of her own ingratitude and faithlessness, and preoccupied to excess with the stern contrast between the enchantments of the world and the promises of eternity.

None the less her "devotional" poetry, though wanting vigour of thought, is always distinguished, and of rare splendour at its best. The movement of her genius had a peculiar dignity; and though she wrote much that has no great value, much that is merely tentative and but half-expressed, she wrote almost nothing which does not show the controlled nerve of an admirable style. Her command of rhythm and metre, by no means faultless, had a very remarkable scope. She adopted or invented a great variety of measures, and used them with an ease which falls short of real mastery only through lacking the last edge of care; her spontaneity is equally unforced, whether it flings out its own irregular but living shape or whether it fills a traditional one, and some of her effects of repeated rhymes and refrains have the happiest originality. And mastery, with no qualification whatever, is displayed in the robustness and purity of her diction. . . . If she could marshall a pomp of words with prophetic fervour, she could give to homely turns and phrases a stateliness and gravity which at times is not far from the art of Dante. Such sympathy for words, such perception of their value and ring, is for whatever reason rarely a feminine gift; and in all this Christina Rossetti had a wider reach and a surer taste than any woman who has written our language—she, the one to whom it was not native.

But her place among all great poets is not less certain. In spite of her limitations and her thwarted development, she had the true heart of song; and by virtue of it she has her own supremacy. Song which seems to draw its life from the dew and breeze of summer, warm ripeness that is yet freshness, transparent sunshine that has still the suggestion of clean showers—such is the song of Christina Rossetti, and her slender achievement is in its way unique. Life should have fostered a genius and nature like hers. Her instinct was entirely lyrical, and even when she wished to write allegories and moralities, *The Prince's Progress* or the *Convent Threshold,* pure irresponsible music would break out uncontrollably in her argument. It must seem one of the calamities of poetry that she should have missed a fuller growth and that so much of her work should have been overhung with sterile shadows. Away from them she uttered some of the most singing melodies, blithe and sad, to be found in English verse. (pp. 288-90)

> *Percy Lubbock, "Christina Rossetti," in* The English Poets, Selections with Critical Introductions by Various Writers and a General Introduction by Matthew Arnold: Browning to Rupert Brooke, Vol. V, *edited by Thomas Humphrey Ward (copyright, 1918 by the Macmillan Company; copyright renewed © 1946 by Dorothy Ward; reprinted by permission of Macmillan, London and Basingstoke), Macmillan, 1918, pp. 286-90.*

WALTER de la MARE (essay date 1926)

Christina Rossetti's finer poems are, for the most part, and as she herself confessed, subjective. If they are instructive, the knowledge they convey is not matter of fact, but imaginative truth, and it is invariably charged with feeling. . . . If she preaches, it is in the first place to her own heart and spirit. She asks, Am *I* saved? rather than Are you? And in her finest

work, thought and feeling, idea and emotion, the theme and her treatment of it are so much at one that to attempt to divide them, or to discriminate between them, would be like that of drawing and quartering a man in the hope of discovering his sense of humour. (p. 84)

[It] cannot be questioned that the prevalent themes of Christina Rossetti's poems echo the writer of Ecclesiastes. They express a curious absorption in the ravages of time, in the seductiveness and disaster of sin, in death and the grave. Some of them, it is true, are tinged with her own quiet humour; a few jet up like fountains in a garden out of the happiness of her heart. But optimistic is certainly the last doubtful compliment we should bestow on her intelligence. These poems assure us that all is *not* right with her world, and many even of the happiest of her poems are wistful in tone, and tinged with regret or foreboding.

Why, then—since the world . . . has troubles enough of its own—why does Christina Rossetti remain among the English poets? Why do those who love her work find a unique beauty, solace, reconciliation, enjoyment in it? Because while she wrote even her most desperate and tragic poems, her mind was exalted, at a hazardous rest, and not only happy in the presence of the truth and reality she was striving to express, but in the achievement of expressing them fully and truly. (pp. 84-5)

A large proportion of Christina Rossetti's poems, and nearly all her best poems, are, as we say, in "a minor key," and what major key is lovelier in effect? They enshrine the emotions of a homesick, tortured spirit, and of a temperament and imagination not cold of the North, but passionate of the South, for she was three parts Italian. To charge her with emotionalism, however, to assert that she had little restraint, and less than her fair share of practical, calm, English common sense, would be as ludicrously false from anyone who had read her family letters as it would be to charge Keats with being a mere sensuous dreamer after reading his.

The most conspicuous quality of her letters . . . is their freedom from the very things which many of us expect of a poet—the "poetical." However generous and considerate the feeling and sentiments they express, those feelings are always in complete control. The style is natural and easy, though occasionally touched with the ceremonious. They are at times a little stilted, even frigid, and sometimes demure. Here, again, we find her quiet humour and sensitive spirit, but cries from the heart are as rare as gymnastics of the intellect. It would be difficult to find in them a single passage that vividly and passionately surrenders the writer of the poems. (pp. 86-7)

As with her letters, so with the volumes of prose that she wrote late in life—'**Anno Domini,' 'Seek and Find,' 'Called to be Saints,'** and the rest. They reveal her profoundest interest, are vigorous and sensitive, and have beauties of their own, and those proper to prose. They are the work of a poet, yet no critic, I think, could fully divine *this* poet in them. (pp. 88-9)

[In] her letters we become conscious of a human being of a vigorous and even formidable character, of an inflexible will and determination, less tender than just and compassionate. She was resolute in suffering, faithful to one ideal, absolutely assured that life, apart from all its delights and dreams, is an arduous discipline and preparation for a death that shall be the drawing aside of a veil from the face of the true reality. (p. 93)

Again and again her poems reiterate certain convictions—the fleetingness of beauty; the vanity of human wishes; the fickleness of hope and joy; that all things obey one law, one will; that as man makes his world, his universe, so shall it thin and fade away into meaninglessness or become charged with an eternal significance. (p. 104)

It is possible—and it is a happy thing—to delight in Christina Rossetti's poems for their pure sensuousness and naturalness; but to ignore or to attempt to refute their implications is to ignore what is essential to them. But whatever final artistry went to their making, one and all were the outcome of purest impulse. Habitually silent and reserved though she might appear to be, that quiet mind was a reservoir of impassioned memories; and as naturally as a wild flower out of the half-frozen ground, her lyrics sprang into beauty out of her austerity. They are her own speech. The very onset of them is as natural as a smile, a sigh or an exclamation of delight. . . . Bare statements, little imagery, no striving for effect; no decoration, nothing literary. It is their poise, rhythm, cadences, that convey her inmost implications and emotion; it is their secret congruity of sound that is the very essence of their poetic meaning. (p. 105)

[Just] as the most commonplace remark may be made infinitely significant and personal and characteristic by the tone in which it is said, by the expression or gesture which accompanies it, so by means of a rhythm and verbal music peculiar to herself she floods her simplest speech with her own delight and imagination. For this reason Christina Rossetti is at once one of the simplest of modern poets, and yet within her chosen range one of the most profound; one of the least elaborate and self-conscious of modern artists, yet one of the most delicate and sure. (p. 106)

Her poetry at its best is simple as Herbert's, yet it rarely falls into mere conceit. Like Vaughan's, it reveals a spiritual vision which is one of the rarest of all poetic qualities. Its range of thought, of interest, like theirs too, is limited. It reflects a life and personality unusually isolated and secluded from the ambitions, aspirations, achievements, rewards of the great world of society and affairs. Its interests were never in the nature of that ephemeral merchandise called "good copy." Crystal clear it springs and fountains from the depths of her being; and Italian by birth and tradition though she was, though indeed one of the most intimate of her poems was actually written in Italian, her English speech as perfectly expresses her own nature as the blossoms of a hawthorn, or the singing of a nightingale express theirs. It is never obscure, except by reason of the fact that the flowers of the imagination flourish in the secret and remote recesses of the mind. And it is never cynical, fantastic or grotesque.

Christina Rossetti's attempts on the other hand, to depict or create character or story, unlike those of Keats, do not suggest that she had any great dramatic or narrative power—none comparable, at any rate, with Emily Brontë's at one extreme, or with Jane Austen's at the other. But, with Emily Brontë, she is supreme among English lyric writers of her own sex up to her own day and as yet in ours. And she takes her place among the English poets by virtue of course of the very qualities which were peculiarly her own, and which were, therefore, in some degree essentially feminine.

It is said that every man of genius shares the hospitality of his heart with a woman and a child. Christina Rossetti was that still rarer thing, a woman of genius. She had the insight of genius; its power of divination. None the less she was sharply conscious of the differing gifts and faculties in mind and temperament innate in men and women, and was keenly apprehensive of the least vital sacrifice of those differences. She accepted the conditions which are at the very root of mortal and earthly life: and in that acceptance, triumphed. (pp. 114-16)

Walter de la Mare, "Christina Rossetti," in Essays by Divers Hands, Vol. VI, *edited by G. K. Chesterton (reprinted by permission of Oxford University Press), Oxford University Press, London, 1926, pp. 79-116.*

EDITH BIRKHEAD　(essay date 1930)

The fame of Christina Rossetti has been overshadowed unduly by that of her brother, Dante Gabriel. . . . Dante Gabriel Rossetti is, in fact, a figure whom it is impossible to overlook in the history of nineteenth-century art. Christina Rossetti, on the other hand, is more obscure and withdrawn. . . . Her work, with the exception of **"Goblin Market"** and a few isolated lyrics, is generally subdued in tone and colouring. Her diction is natural and unstudied. Her verse rarely "surprises by a fine excess." She did not, like Dante Gabriel, ransack old romances in the British Museum in the search for "stunning words for poetry." . . . Yet in its different way her artistry is as fine as his. Her effects are subtler and more elusive. The beauty of her lyrics lies rather in unity of composition than in separate felicities that detach themselves from the context. Although at the first glance Christina Rossetti, in her poetry and in her life, seems to have cultivated a "fugitive and cloistered virtue, unexercised and unbreathed," her strenuous pursuit of an ideal becomes evident on closer scrutiny. Beneath her quiet exterior the flame of life burnt ardently. Believing that "virtue is like precious odours, most fragrant when they are incensed and crushed," she refused resolutely to follow impulse. The artist's fierce desire for self-expression was tempered in her nature by a religious humility that demanded renunciation. Although in this way she narrowed deliberately the range of her verse, she did not destroy its intensity. The struggle between desire and denial inspired some of her finest poetry. . . . Christina, though she spared no pains to make her devotional poems technically perfect, sometimes published undistinguished work, because she believed it might minister to the service of her faith. She came to be regarded as a writer of religious verse, which it would be a profanation to judge from an artistic point of view. William Michael Rossetti, who was responsible for the collected edition of her work, made it still more difficult to arrive at a final impression of her poetry by rescuing from the oblivion of her notebooks many of the verses which she herself withheld from publication. Some of them were obviously written in a tumult of emotion, when she was struggling unsuccessfully for expression. They were fragments of a painfully intimate journal, but they were not poetry. Only when she was calm enough to stand aloof from her experience while she re-created it did it assume the final and enduring form of art. (pp. 13-15)

Nearly all the poems that Christina Rossetti had written up to 1858 had been concerned with her own emotions, and yet many of them reveal how ardently she longed for a refuge from herself. . . . [Only] once, in **"Goblin Market"** . . . , does she allow herself to enter for more than a brief moment the enchanted country of which she was free. Here she lets her fancy roam, untrammelled by allegory or symbolism. **"Goblin Market"** is a revel of the senses; the swart-headed mulberries, bright-fire-like barberries, bloom-down-cheeked peaches, plump unpecked cherries, melons icy-cold, appeal to sight and touch and taste. Although the story itself, as it winds along, unfolds an ever-changing pageantry of strangeness and beauty, she adorns it with lovely imagery. (pp. 62-3)

As she grew older Christina Rossetti began to distrust the senses. Musing in her prose work **"The Face of the Deep"** . . . , she decided that hearing was the least sensual of the five senses. That Christina Rossetti appreciated the external beauty of the senses **"Goblin Market"** alone would serve to show, but her later poetry seems to appeal chiefly to the ear. Even her visual imagery becomes vague and indefinite compared with the heightened sense-perceptions of this early fantasy.

In **"The Prince's Progress"** . . . Christina Rossetti had another opportunity of revisiting the land of romance. The poem hovers on the fringe of that country, without ever stepping over the border. It is marred by the light touch of sentimentality derived from Tennyson and ill-suited to Christina Rossetti's entirely serious temperament. That narrative is a mere *tour de force,* attempted at the suggestion of her brother. The song of the bride, to be seen no more save of Bridegroom Death, reveals the melancholy mood and cadence characteristic of her verse. . . . The lines drift us back inevitably to Christina Rossetti herself. She seems to have lost the impulse to write objectively. She turns within into the world of her own feelings.

Her view of life remained to the end profoundly melancholy. In spite of the consolation of her faith, she realized as bitterly as Hardy the pain of human existence. . . . The gloom cast by her sense of life's "thwarted purposings" is seen at its darkest in one of the sonnets in **"Later Life."** . . . Accepting this bleak conception of life, she set herself to endure hardness. The decision was made, but the conflict was not so easily resolved. A rebellious anger against life smoulders beneath the resignation she struggles to express. Again and again her baffled and thwarted instincts forced themselves to the surface. (pp. 81-5)

She tended as she grew older to dedicate her art more and more to the service of her faith. She no longer revelled in colour and beauty for their own sake. The golden flash of angelic wings or the saints in their aureoles relieve the sober tones of some of her religious poems, but the bright hues in which she had once revelled gradually vanish out of her poetry. The flowers of the field once loved for their own sake become symbols of Christian virtues. (pp. 91-2)

The rapture of escape Christina Rossetti never realized. Her spirit did not take the final bound. It remained on tiptoe for a flight. The soul's wings were almost free—"measuring the gulph it stoops"—but it never soared clear away from the earth it despised. She remained hovering like a lonely wraith on the confines of the two worlds and conscious of belonging to neither, knowing that she was herself her own prison. . . . Her lyrics rose often out of this unresting conflict. The flower of her poetry was not rooted and grounded in faith. It blossomed rather out of the common soil of human feeling. Besides the life of prayer and piety to which she vowed herself she continued to live a life of memories and sighs. It is from these filaments that some of her finest poetry is woven. (pp. 105-06)

When the burden of herself became intolerable Christian Rossetti found in the practice of her art a solace comparable to that which she experienced, in her religious life, in confession. The composition of such a poem as **"Twice"** must not only have given her the alleviation of expression, but have filled her with the conscious pleasure that comes through triumphant

mastery of an artistic medium. The sorrow that the poem embodies is tempered by the harmony of language and the sense of difficulty overcome. The quiet concentration of a bitter and prolonged experience within the narrow compass of this simple lyric suggests that it was written in a mood both of intense feeling and of great calm. It seems to illustrate the truth of Wordsworth's statement that poetry takes its origin in "emotion recollected in tranquillity." (p. 106)

[**"Passing Away"**], rising to a note of subdued exaltation, is a masterpiece of craftsmanship. The twenty-six lines are based on a single rhyming sound that lingers on the ear with a haunting and insistent melancholy; but monotony is avoided by the deliberate irregularity of the rhythm and by the introduction of the shortened lines at the end of the stanzas. The composition is a highly organized work of art. In **"Marvel of Marvels"** she again carries through triumphantly another experiment in monorhyme. The long resonant lines suggest the solemn tolling of the passing bell, but the artifice is so unobtrusive that the impression it leaves is one of harmonious unity of sound and feeling. . . . (pp. 109-10)

She was by no means a conventional metrist. Trusting her own sense of harmony, she is not afraid to vary her rhythms subtly according to the theme. Though her verses often defy the ordinary rules of scansion, they rarely fail to satisfy the ear. Possessed of an unusually beautiful voice and a fine sense of sound, she took a conscious pleasure in the melody of verse and of prose. (p. 119)

She turned to poetry as an outlet for feelings that poisoned her peace of mind. As she wrote, grief and pain became mysteriously transfigured. Denying herself many of the joys of existence, she knew at least the supreme joy of creation. (p. 120)

> *Edith Birkhead, in her* Christina Rossetti & Her Poetry *(reprinted by permission of Harrap Limited), Harrap, 1930 (and reprinted by Folcroft Press, 1970), 126 p.*

VIRGINIA WOOLF   (essay date 1930)

[If we follow the various schools of criticism regarding Christina Rossetti's poetry] we shall only come to grief. Better perhaps read for oneself, expose the mind bare to the poem, and transcribe in all its haste and imperfection whatever may be the result of the impact. In this case it might run something as follows: O Christina Rossetti, I have humbly to confess that though I know many of your poems by heart, I have not read your works from cover to cover. I have not followed your course and traced your development. I doubt indeed that you developed very much. You were an instinctive poet. You saw the world from the same angle always. Years and the traffic of the mind with men and books did not affect you in the least. You carefully ignored any book that could shake your faith or any human being who could trouble your instincts. You were wise perhaps. Your instinct was so sure, so direct, so intense that it produced poems that sing like music in one's ears—like a melody by Mozart or an air by Gluck. Yet for all its symmetry, yours was a complex song. When you struck your harp many strings sounded together. Like all instinctives you had a keen sense of the visual beauty of the world. Your poems are full of gold dust and "sweet geraniums' varied brightness"; your eye noted incessantly how rushes are "velvet-headed", and lizards have a "strange metallic mail"—your eye, indeed, observed with a sensual pre-Raphaelite intensity that must have surprised Christina the Anglo-Catholic. But to her you owed perhaps the fixity and sadness of your muse. The pressure of a tremendous faith circles and clamps together these little songs. Perhaps they owe to it their solidity. Certainly they owe to it their sadness—your God was a harsh God, your heavenly crown was set with thorns. No sooner have you feasted on beauty with your eyes than your mind tells you that beauty is vain and beauty passes. Death, oblivion, and rest lap round your songs with their dark wave. And then, incongruously, a sound of scurrying and laughter is heard. There is the patter of animals' feet and the odd guttural notes of rooks and the snufflings of obtuse furry animals grunting and nosing. For you were not a pure saint by any means. You pulled legs; you tweaked noses. You were at war with all humbug and pretence. Modest as you were, still you were drastic, sure of your gift, convinced of your vision. A firm hand pruned your lines; a sharp ear tested their music. Nothing soft, otiose, irrelevant cumbered your pages. In a word, you were an artist. And thus was kept open, even when you wrote idly, tinkling bells for your own diversion, a pathway for the descent of that fiery visitant who came now and then and fused your lines into that indissoluble connection which no hand can put asunder. . . . Indeed so strange is the constitution of things, and so great the miracle of poetry, that some of the poems you wrote in your little back room will be found adhering in perfect symmetry when the Albert Memorial is dust and tinsel. (pp. 263-64)

Virginia Woolf, "I Am Christina Rossetti" (1930), in her The Second Common Reader *(copyright 1932 by Harcourt Brace Jovanovich, Inc.; copyright 1960 by Leonard Woolf; reprinted by permission of the publisher; in Canada by the Literary Estate of Virginia Woolf and The Hogarth Press Ltd; published in Britain as* The Common Reader, *second series, Hogarth, 1932), Harcourt, 1932, pp. 257-65.*

FREDEGOND SHOVE (essay date 1931)

['**Goblin Market**'] shows most clearly Christina Rossetti's unusual powers of visualisation. The description of the maidens, of the fruit and of the goblins are things of astonishing vigour. They seem to spring straight from Christina Rossetti's soul, carried on an uprush of creative energy, with brilliant and fantastic inspiration and without the smallest strain. Strain, affectation or staleness would most quickly have been apparent in a poem of this kind, but the colours in this artist's box were never stale. She was mistress of every pure, keen tint, from spring's rash green to autumn's damson hue, and with her beautiful eye for colour went an exquisite ear for melody. But these gifts could not have accounted for '**Goblin Market**' without the presence of a third—her actual imagination, which delighted in the delineation of the grotesque beings, seized their pace, apprehended their gait, their speech, their demeanour and their awful spiritual significance. (pp. 36-7)

Akin to '**Goblin Market**' in that it is a narrative poem of length and vivid beauty is '**The Prince's Progress**'. It has the metrical distinction of all the author's best work and the rhymes in it are most skilfully arranged. . . . [She] sometimes brings in for the sake of a rhyme a word which does strike one as clumsy and unwelcome; but this does not often happen, since she had an amazingly good vocabulary as well as an inborn sense of the fitness of words which is quite one of her most enviable gifts. The story of '**The Prince's Progress**' is not so fresh nor so original as that of '**Goblin Market**', but it gave scope for some very lovely writing. . . . (pp. 40-1)

['**Maiden Song**' is] one of the most successful of her narrative poems. It is a kind of simple fairy tale, the story of three sisters, two of whom went wandering into the spring meadows to find their happy fates awaiting them, whilst the third and fairest waited at home and is sought in marriage by a king. In the treatment of their beauty, the beauty of the daylight, the flowers, the sunlight deepening, the moon-rise, and the joy of the maidens in their innocent loves, there is a magical freshness, unequalled by any other of the authoress's poems. No hint of sorrow, pain or weariness is present. The whole is a picture of joy, most difficult of all atmospheres to present because so easily confused with commonplace cheerfulness and mechanical liveliness. (p. 45)

[The sonnets of '**Monna Innominata**'], called after some imaginary and forgotten Italian lady, bear really, of course, the impress of Christina Rossetti's own heart. Here and there she seems actually to lift the veil of her sensitive reticence and to show us a glimpse of that inner and heartrending struggle between inclination and what seemed to her to be duty which was then going on in her life. Read without biographical reference, however, the sonnets, though dignified and always indicative of a nobly sensitive, fastidiously high-minded nature, do not bear the stamp of her highest talent and cannot be rated with her best purely lyrical work. (p. 48)

Some will be reminded of Blake in reading [*Sing Song*]. They have not the weight of symbolical sorrow that drops from the wings of the *Songs of Innocence*, causing the cries of the birds and lambs and babies to be more awful than words of judgment or doom, so piercing is the poet's pity for the wrongs of tiny children and all God's innocent creatures. Christina Rossetti was like Blake in her love and veneration for innocence—children, lambs, birds, dogs, cats, rabbits, bees, caterpillars, flowers and sea beasts—but in *Sing Song* she is telling children about these creatures, showing their innocence, their gaiety, their meekness, their drollery, fun and jollity, without relation to the cruel facts of life that surround them. Yet, even if we take *Sing Song* as being what it is, merely a collection of short poems for children, full of intimate vision, fancy and fun, there is in each of them that drop of distilling genius which makes of their very drollery and innocence something, not indeed as in Blake's 'Chimney Sweep's Song' marrow-dissolving and haunting, but something so charged with the unconscious pathos which is the soul of childhood itself that it leaves one with the sense of sadness mingling in the sunbeams and the taste of tears in all the honey. A great deal has been said about the sadness of Christina Rossetti's devotional poems, about the morbidity of her mind as expressed in these and others which reveal conflict and the actual struggles that went on in her personal life. To my mind, the whole sadness together with the final sweet and satisfying firmness of faith and cheerfulness of the woman seem most noble, because most unconscious, in these childlike but never childish verses. (pp. 59-61)

Then there must be mentioned a special quality of hers, noticeable in a latent sense in the '**Pageant**', more obvious in *Sing Song*—namely, her humour. It is a thread of gold in all the homely warp of her letters. It is seldom, one feels, at all absent from her mood even when she writes with melancholy, although it is difficult to explain how one feels this humorousness, which must not be confused with the occasional flash of irony she sometimes showed. (p. 62)

The root, the main stem of [her] genius, is God-loving, beauty-loving, spiritualised, earth-loving *observation*: the same translated on the one side into vivid, glowing colours and on the other into instant, spontaneous music—I had almost written bird-song, for the notes are so natural; they are like Shakespeare's 'wood notes wild' and bring no echo of the academy. (pp. 62-3)

[We] could understand little Christina Rossetti's mind unless we were prepared to recognise that the mainspring of its beauty, the core in all this living growth, colour and radiance of song was her love of God. Whether she writes directly or indirectly of that love, we feel it. . . . (pp. 73-4)

[Just] as Christina Rossetti had variety of moods and modes of expression in her secular, so in her devotional work she was various. All the devotional poems bear her mark. They are, as it were, a flock, easily recognisable by something at once simple (she never searched for the uncommon word although it sometimes came, she searched for and generally found the right word), direct, intense in feeling, unaffected; feminine in being so direct, so untrammelled by tiresome ponderous learning, always reverent, self-forgetting. There are, indeed, occasionally monotonies in her religious verse, and these could sometimes becloud her other work. They came, perhaps, from the weakness of her body; anaemia sometimes tinges her work with a tragic suggestion of what might have been, and there is a rare, but very rare, tendency to fall into the commonplace of poetic idea. But it is still astonishing to notice in how many ways Christina Rossetti could and did approach her central religious theme of the love of God. (pp. 77-8)

[This] love is seen always or almost always under one aspect; for her God was oftener though of in the glorious second Person of the Trinity than in either the first or the third. . . . Our blessed Lord's Passion, His agony on the Cross, were her constant pre-occupations and it is not too much to say that her religious life was indeed rooted on Calvary. She was, as I have said before, extremely scrupulous and inclining towards self-accusation, thus her poems have a constantly recurring straining note of repentance. (p. 84)

[Viewed] as a prose writer, she is interesting, distinguished, but far less significant than she is when viewed as a poet. (p. 92)

[In her prose works] she is so much more conscious, heavier and more constrained than when writing poetry. They suggest somehow to me a careful pruning, almost a self-distrust—the artist is now waiting in humble attendance upon the student of self-discipline and the disciple in the house of pain.

The Face of the Deep is rich in noble litanies and exquisite verses, in wise and gentle precept. But somehow . . . I feel it to be a little over-elaborate. The Book of Revelation is surely too astounding in its other-worldly simplicity, its sheer realism of the spirit, to be studied in this literal manner. Nevertheless, for those who have a mind to read slowly with digestion in quiet and reflective moments, this long commentary, with its tender upshooting of verse and its grave and penitential tone, will yield many glories for inspection. (pp. 93-4)

In *Time Flies* and *Called to be Saints* we have examples of quite a different kind of writing, one that in minute observation and picturesque vision does bear a ceratin resemblance to Dorothy Wordsworth's descriptive passages and the authoress' own poetry. . . . (pp. 95-6)

Seek and Find, The Face of the Deep and the other fine prose books live mainly on account of the wonderful uprushing of lyrical poetry that is in them. They are like marsh beds silently filled with waters—the waters spring up here and there with a

welcome bubbling of music and gladden both the ear and the eye by their glittering joyful beauty and their godly rhythm. A poet she was first and last, and one is grateful for the knowledge that as such she discerned herself, and as such she was recognised during her lifetime. (p. 104)

Fredegond Shove, in her Christina Rossetti: A Study, *Cambridge at the University Press, 1931 (and reprinted by the Folcroft Press, Inc., 1969), 120 p.*

VIRGINIA MOORE   (essay date 1934)

No good poet has been read more superficially than Christina Rossetti. Readers are intimidated by the size and bulk of her *Poetical Works,* half of which is mediocre, and only half distinguished in quality. The impatient judge her by requoted anthology pieces, such as **"Passing Away," "Goblin Market,"** and **"Remember,"** being ignorant of poems as fine or finer, like **"The Bourne," "Three Stages," "Who Shall Deliver Me?" "Up Hill," "Autumn Violets,"** and **"From House to Home"** It is unfortunate that her work was not pruned at publication. But this was not the fault of the poet, who was meticulous in self-criticism, but of her brother Michael, who, without authority for the presumption, printed every scrap he could find after her death.

For forty years . . . her ability waxed and waned very little: it simply was. Her technical innovations were fortuitous. Alive or dull, the poems all but wrote themselves. At best they are clear as spring water which, in unexpected places, bubbles to the surface. They are simple statements of all but fathomless emotion, in the tone of voice of one so close to the judgment day when all will be told that candour gains nothing, loses nothing, but is a kind of peace. This directness is in contrast to the circuitousness usually, and rightly, attributed to women. Reticent and stern of spirit, something in her willingly pays a difficult price. . . . One recognizes the hallmarks of integrity, and spirit approves of spirit.

Recognizes how? By signs incompatible with spiritual hypocrisy—by simplicity, exactness of word choice, the personal colour which suffuses an idea once that idea has been taken into a mind, later to be given out individualized and fresh. The spirit requires concrete images as bright points of departure. It is a bird rising from its ground-nest.

Christina Rossetti's claim to high poetic distinction is because of her ability to saturate a poem with values beyond temporary considerations, so that one forgets, as one reads, all other values. Genius obeys a hidden law; it has a sweet and self-conditioned reasonableness. Whoever finds her poetry forbidding is like the poet herself when, on a visit to the Continent, she beheld for the first time the high snowy Alps.

"Their sublimity impressed me like want of sympathy," she said, "because my eyes were unaccustomed." (pp. 56-8)

Virginia Moore, "Christina Rossetti," in her Distinguished Women Writers *(copyright, 1934, by E. P. Dutton & Co., Inc.; copyright renewed © 1962 by Virginia Moore; reprinted by permission of the publisher, E. P. Dutton), Dutton, 1934, pp. 45-58.*

C. M. BOWRA   (essay date 1949)

The Pre-Raphaelite poets left Christianity alone and pursued their own schemes of salvation. Yet among these powerful and turbulent personalities there moved with shy assurance and self-effacing modesty a woman who was at least their equal in the art of words and those outlook was very different from theirs. Christina Rossetti has a place not far from the highest among English religious poets. She learned her art from the Pre-Raphaelites and has many affinities with them, but she turned her genius to a different end and won her own special triumphs. (pp. 245-46)

Christina's poetry reveals an almost dual personality. One side of her was Pre-Raphaelite, fond of pictorial effects and unusual images, capable of telling a story with a proper sense of its dramatic possibilities, and, what was rarer in her circle, with a certain whimsical humour and playful fancy. She was often enough content to withdraw into fancies and dreams and to find a full satisfaction in the world of her imagination. . . . [*Goblin Market, and Other Poems*] shows how naturally and how well she practised a Pre-Raphaelite art without surrendering any of her originality. The charming poem which gives its title to the book is an authentic feat of the creative imagination, an extension of experience into an unknown world which she has invented and made real. It shows perhaps some traces of influence from Coleridge and Hood and Allingham, but they are few and unimportant. Christina speaks in her own voice and in her own way. Her command of a rippling metre and the fersh conversational simplicity of her language, so unlike her brother's elaborate majesty, reveal a talent which has fully found itself and translated into its own idiom the vague ideals of her friends. She advances at one step into her own special sphere and finds her way with confident ease. "Goblin Market" lives of its own right in its own world as an ingenious and brilliant creation. (pp. 246-47)

"Goblin Market" represents one side of Christina's character, the side which fitted easily into the Pre-Raphaelite circle and was honoured by it. But she had another side, grave and serious and intimately bound with her inner life. Even in "Goblin Market" there is an undercurrent of this seriousness, and though she herself said that she did not "mean anything profound by this fairy-tale," it has its little moral: that it is dangerous to play with the unknown and that human beings who so do pay for it. (pp. 248-49)

The two sides of Christina's nature account for the twofold character of her poetry. On the one side is her poetry of imagination and fancy, whether in long pieces like "Goblin Market" and "The Prince's Progress," or in short pieces in which, with an uncommon charm and delicacy, she sketches some situation which has touched her heart or appealed to her love of the living scene. On the other side are her many devotional pieces, not indeed always of equal merit, and sometimes rather perfunctory, but at their best unsurpassed for their sureness of touch and their passionate sincerity. Nor were the two sides always kept separate. Indeed, some of her most characteristic poems are those in which she allows her conscientious attachment to the sacred texts to be enlivened by her love of decorative details. (pp. 249-50)

The conflict in Christina between the woman and the saint was hers almost until the end, though with the passing of years her religion became more absorbing and more insistent and allowed her only at intervals to indulge her more human feelings. How strong these were can be seen from more than one poem in which she forgets for the moment her divine calling and laments the emptiness and failure of her life. In her religious hours she believed that the world was as nothing, and then suddenly it would assert its claims, and she would regret her lost chances and her vanishing dreams. She would indeed accept her fate,

but not altogether willingly and not without regret. Though she knew that the world passes away and that mortal things wither and die, she loved them too well to be insensitive to their destruction. In tones of agonizing sweetness she sings of her anxieties and fears, and in the same moment knows that regret is useless. . . . (p. 262)

Against these regrets and these misgivings, Christina's other self set its faith and its intermittent hopes. If love could not be realized in this world, there was still the hope that it might be in another, and this was her consolation. If she could not give herself to a man, she must give herself to God, and in doing this she trusted that in the end her earthly love would be fulfilled in heaven. (p. 263)

[Her] poetry of the soul's search for God and its struggles towards perfection is written in a language of remarkable simplicity. The more serious Christina is, the less she adorns her verse. Her images become rarer and more traditional, and the words are the unpretentious words of every day. But each word expresses exactly what she feels, and her sense of rhythm is so subtle that even in her darkest moments she can break into pure song. She varies her effects with consummate skill, and though she often writes in a very quiet key, her touch is so sure that every movement tells, and her constant changes of tone produce endless delightful surprises. Few poets have her gift of beginning a poem with the most homely and humble words or of using phrases which are consciously trite or commonplace, only to rise to some sudden burst and thereby to show that even in the drabbest conditions there are possibilities of dazzling spendour. Her sonnet **"In Progress"** illustrates this subtle art, and though it claims to be written about another person, it is a true account of Christina herself as those who knew her saw her. . . . Each phrase seems to have been reduced to the lowest possible emphasis and to keep rigorously to an unpretentious account of humdrum facts, but in every sentence there is a special charm and strength, until the end comes with an astonishing glory of light and flame.

The same fusion of matter and form can be seen in Christina's use of metre. She was not a great inventor of metres, but she made many variations inside existing forms, and shaped each to some special need of her imaginative moods. She is equally at home with the sonnet and the song, with staid iambics and the more lively anapaests and dactyls. She has a remarkable gift for varying the speed of a line partly by punctuation, partly by stressing the important words. Her results are so natural that we hardly notice what control of her craft she has: everything seems to fall so easily into its right place and to reflect so exactly what she feels. (pp. 264-65)

[Her] poetry has a remarkable concentration. Everything seems to be directed towards a central point and related to it. Once a subject has been started, there is not much development in its treatment, and the element of surprise is kept for small effects inside a narrow compass. It is characteristic of Christina that she loves a kind of rondel in which a phrase is repeated several times, and this device gives a great compactness and concentration. (p. 266)

Christina Rossetti presents in a remarkable manner the case of a poet whose naturally Romantic tendencies were turned into a different channel by the intensity of her religious faith. But for it she might have continued to write in the spirit of "Goblin Market" and have illustrated many delightful corners of consciousness by her ingenious and sprightly art. But this spirit was in conflict with her devotion to God and her search for salvation. From this conflict and the sacrifices which it entailed, she wrote a different kind of poetry, deeply personal and intimate and often painful, in which she dramatized her secret feelings in passionate song. This too was a kind of Romantic art, an escape from her actual troubles and at the same time a comment on them, by which she was able to penetrate many hidden corners of her consciousness and to present them in compelling, concrete forms. Indeed, it was this conflict between her human self and her divine calling which created her most characteristic poetry. But her purely religious work owed little to it. In this she might sometimes allow herself a small flight of decorative fancy, but as a whole the subject was too serious for her to stray far from what orthodoxy told her to be true. Her achievement suggests that though the Romantic spirit is concerned with another world, this other world is not that of common faith. It is what the poet finds and fashions for himself, not what has been sought and sanctified by millions of men and women. So when she spoke of it, Christina did not try to create it for herself but conformed to traditional ideas of it. In the end she passed beyond the Romantic spirit by the intensity of her faith, and in so doing showed a weakness in that spirit which seems to have no peace for this kind of vision.

Painful though her conflict often was, Christina solved it to her own satisfaction. When she passed beyond her early fancies and beyond even her poems of unsatisfied love, she found something else more absorbing and more inspiring. Nor did her poetry lose by this. The eternity for which she hungered brought all her emotions into play and enabled her to give a final, irresistible power to her words. Because she disciplined herself so sternly to the tasks of religion, she kept a singularly direct approach to many kinds of experience and assessed their worth with uncompromising candour. She had her own peculiar insight into the mystery of things, and it was all the keener because it was supported by the full resources of her rich nature. Her faith, with its passionate honesty and its extremely personal emotions, was the fulfilment of her devoted and tender soul. In the end she is a great religious poet, because religion called out in her all that was essentially and most truly herself. Only in God could she find a finally satisfying object for the abounding love which was the mainspring of her life and character. (pp. 269-70)

> *C. M. Bowra, "Christina Rossetti," in his* The Romantic Imagination *(copyright ©1949 by the President and Fellows of Harvard College; copyright renewed © 1977 by The Estates Bursar, as executor of C. M. Bowra; excerpted by permission), Cambridge, Mass.: Harvard University Press, 1949 (and reprinted by Oxford University Press, 1961), pp. 245-70.*

W. W. ROBSON (essay date 1957)

It is significant that one finds oneself appraising [Christina Rossetti's] work in . . . negative terms. For negation, denial, deprivation are the characteristic notes of Christina's religious poetry: and it must be admitted that an extensive reading of it is depressing. The sadness, often morbidity, which is felt even in her delightful poetry for children, even in **Goblin Market,** certainly in **The Prince's Progress;** the felt absence of any outlet for aggressive impulses, deepening into depression or resignation; the compensating yearning for death imagined as an anodyne, an eternal anesthetic—these are familiar to every reader of her poetry. And it is difficult to find many poems in

which she either transcends them or turns them into the conditions for major creation.

One of the rare occasions on which her religion appears in her poetry as a source of revival and refreshment is the (significantly titled) sonnet *A Pause.* . . . The exquisite good taste and spiritual good manners (if the expression be permitted) of the way in which the two worlds are related—the religious and the everyday—are characteristic distinctions of Christina's poetry. And a comparison of her better-known *Sping Quiet* ("Gone were but the Winter") with Hopkins's early *Heaven-Haven* ("I have desired to go") brings out a certain community of temperament. . . . But it reminds us also that *Heaven-Haven,* unlike *Spring Quiet,* by no means represents a high point of its author's achievement.

The distinctiveness and the limitation of Christina Rossetti's talents are alike illuminated by the parallel her sonnet **"Remember"** offers to Shakespeare's 71st sonnet ("No longer mourn . . ."). . . . The superficial similarity of theme does not disguise the deep difference between the two poems. Shakespeare's sonnet, though not one of his greatest, is characteristic of his best work in the Sonnets, in the effect it produces of a mind intent upon its argument, charged with the determination to deliver its meaning, and taking the emotional effect of that meaning so much for granted, that the poet can afford to deploy his statement in a highly formal, "logical" progression. For all the element of poignancy, the total effect is therefore akin to wit; the satisfactory following-through of an exaggeration, a hyperbole, to its completion. The result is that a poem which, on the face of it, expresses as much loving self-abnegation and tender humility as Christina's, conveys at the same time a graceful compliment and a hint of rebuke. And thus the *precise* value we are to give to Shakespeare's overt humiliation of himself and his poetry has been beautifully defined, and the beauty of this defining is the beauty of the poem. Christina's poem calls for no such subtle adjustment; the shy reserve, tenderness, and wistfulness of the speaker are presented simply and truthfully, and our acceptance of her truthfulness is bound up with our recognition of her authentic speaking voice. . . . But by the time we reach the closing lines, with their (hardly successful) epigrammatic turn of phrasing which sends us back to the Shakespeare sonnet, we feel a slight discomfort with the poem; its modest acceptance of very limited pretension which makes it seem, if not mawkish, a little *mièvre.* . . . (pp. 185-87)

The deprived, depressed, monotonous quality of her poetry is to be accounted for, as we know, very largely by the circumstances of her life and her renunciation. But in one form or another this is a common feature of Victorian Romantic poetry. And if we ignore the personal accent of Christina Rossetti, and the devotional vocabulary and setting of her poems, their moods and tones are immediately recognizable as moods and tones of the period. This is certainly not because of any affectation of fashionable melancholy on Christina's part: no poet could be more touchingly sincere and disinterested. Yet we may wonder if, had she been in contact with a tradition allowing the exercise, in serious verse, of her sharp wits and her astringency, the substance of her work might not have been more considerable and its styles more various. (p. 188)

> *W. W. Robson, "Pre-Raphaelite Poetry," in* The Pelican Guide to English Literature, *Vol. 6 (copyright © by Penguin Books, 1957; reprinted by permission of Penguin Books Ltd.), Penguin Books, 1957 (and reprinted in* British Victorian Literature: Recent

Revaluations, *edited by Shiv K. Kumar, New York University Press, 1969, pp. 172-94).**

IFOR EVANS (essay date 1966)

Certain persistent motives govern [Christina Rossetti's] creative work, varying in their outward form, in the shape and fashion of the symbol, but recognizably the same in origin. However she may have appeared in daily life, that portion of herself which she converted into poetry is possessed of a singular consistency, a definable continuity of desire. Even in her juvenile pieces there arises the same poetic argument that one finds in her mature work. A warm desire kindles within her for joy and love, the pleasurable and sensuous acceptance of life. Before she can gain this breath of warm experience, fear chills her: life is insecure, refusing to yield what it has promised, its joys but brief preludes to enduring sin. Her early poetry dwells in a latent conflict between these two motives. They resolve themselves, a little sadly, in a faith in Christianity which is at once passionate and sombre. This devout otherworldliness leaves Christina Rossetti with a deep, somewhat baffled antagonism to life. (pp. 89-90)

This central conflict gains frequent expression and colours moods and incidents which seem at first sight unrelated. The ubiquity of a single theme has often been suggested as the most limiting factor in Christian Rossetti's poetical work. . . . Yet these circumscribed motives give her work a consistency and integrity, as if its many parts, *Goblin Market,* her nature poetry, and *The Convent Threshold,* were but contributory to one symbolic intention. (pp. 90-1)

In *Goblin Market* itself she evolved a completely Pre-Raphaelite poem, and yet one whose elements could be easily assimilated and accepted without hostility. . . . Yet the poem cannot be adequately described in the terms of Pre-Raphaelitism, and its contact with the movement seems more accidental than deliberate. *Goblin Market* is one of the mysterious poems of the period, raising the same problems as *The Ancient Mariner,* though a solution cannot be gained as completely as with Coleridge's poem. In both a moral is suggested, as an incongruous anticlimax to a poetic narrative full of glamour and magic. In both the metre has novel elements and an unusual importance in producing the poetic effect. In both the coherent witchery of the poem seems to have developed from wide associations of reading and memory. . . . Prosodically [*Goblin Market*] is cunningly contrived, and yet the form seems a mass of irregularities which by design or instinct she has succeeded in manipulating to serve her poetic purposes. . . . Yet throughout there is the sense of control, even, at times, of restraint. It is gained by repeating lines of the same rhythm as if a motive were repeated, by adjusting the rhythm, particularly in its speed, to the meaning, and by asserting regular decasyllabics or octosyllabics after passages in which all regular movement seems in danger of being lost. . . . In much of her work Christina Rossetti was careless prosodically, flat, and occasionally incompetent. Here she achieved that rare prosodic success of giving a poem the only form in which, one feels, it could ever have been held. (pp. 92-3)

The other poems in *Goblin Market* are lyrics, many possessing an originality of atmosphere unequalled by any woman poet of the century. In a number of pieces, *Cousin Kate, Noble Sisters,* and particularly in *Maude Clare* and *Sister Maude,* she uses the ballad form with poignant and tragic themes and a consciousness that the ballad demands quick and allusive presentation. A love motive dominates a number of the most memorable poems. (p. 94)

[The] sense of a love grown dead leads to world-weariness and a desire for death, and so are produced two of the best-known pieces in the volume, *Up-hill* and *Song.* . . . (p. 95)

Closely allied to this theme are the nature poems *The First Spring Day, Bitter for Sweet, Spring,* and *Winter Rain.* Throughout the motive is that out of winter comes spring, and out of spring, winter, with the symbol suggested that in the human heart the spring that turns to winter remains winter, always. . . . [Usually] nature is for her not a theme for description but a symbol, an image of warmth and cold, of sun and frost, of hope followed by despair. In thus avoiding the complex emotions which the romantics had found in nature she gives to her poems the poignant simplicity of a medieval 'seasons' poem. (pp. 95-6)

[Her] devotional poems conquer the difficult problem of conveying mystical experience in poetical form, which can only be achieved by arresting the mind of the reader with an adequate imagery, and by resolving devoutness and mysticism into the terms of normal activity. This she achieves in such poems as *A Better Resurrection,* which possesses a greater simplicity than the work of the seventeenth-century religious poets, but does not lack their urgency. (p. 96)

Disappointment must attend a reading of her second volume, *The Prince's Progress.* . . . The same motives predominate as in *Goblin Market*—the sister theme, the lost-love theme, temptation poems, love-ballad poems, nature 'seasons' poems, devotional poems, and the narrowness of interest, already a marked feature of her poetry, gains emphasis. (p. 97)

Despite similarities with *Goblin Market,* this volume has an increased emphasis on personal weariness and distress which now appears more persistently and penetrates deeper. In *Life and Death* she demands an annihilation of all that is life in a desire for rest. . . . Elsewhere, in *What would I Give?* and *Autumn,* a more distinctly personal element is added to this pessimism. *Memory* is the only poem in the volume where this sickness of the spirit emerges into original poetic expression. The theme attaches itself to that motive of lost love and broken betrothal which pursues all her love poetry, but it is maintained with such strong and consistent imagery that the poem has the lucid clarity of a single symbol. The imagery is one which she has used before, and so is the motive, but it is represented with freshness and urgency. . . . (pp. 97-8)

[In *A Pageant and Other Poems*] outstanding expression can be found in the poetic allegory, *A Ballad of Boding,* where in a dream the poet sees three ships—one of Love, filled with revel and feasting; one, the ship of the Worm, of wealth and strife; and a third, a ship of Suffering without brightness or display. . . . The allegory is a simple one: the Love ship and the Worm ship go down, but the third survives the storms. The poetic manipulation of this theme lifts it out of the commonplace. (p. 99)

Later Life is less a sequence than a miscellaneous collection of sonnets, though a certain unity is gained by the prevalence of religious themes. It is the aftermath of *Monna Innominata,* the renunciation of earthly love for spiritual salvation. The Elizabethan intrusions in the earlier sequence have disappeared; one seems to sense an increased severity and distress. . . . Occasionally a more genial imagination lingers to give a keen and successful interpretation to the religious theme. Usually this occurs in poems where the personal element and the emphasis on weariness have been obviated, as in *Sonnet 10* ('Tread softly! all the earth is holy ground''). (pp. 101-02)

[*A Pageant*] shows a fuller preoccupation with religious themes, and the last volume, *Verses* . . . , is entirely religious and devotional in character. Nowhere in this later religious verse does she show the imaginative power which sustained *Sleep at Sea, The Three Enemies,* and *A Ballad of Boding.* Her distinctive achievement had been to reveal in poetical terms the conflict of the world and the spirit in the religious soul. In this later verse the spirit has conquered: the Church, its feasts and fasts, are celebrated, and the relation of the worshipper to God. Yet neither imagery nor emotion converts these poems into great religious verse such as that of Donne or Herbert. Even when she records experience she lacks the reality of the earlier pieces and approaches at times the luxury of spiritual self-flagellation. (p. 102)

Few writers united so fully the two main and usually distinct movements of the period—the poetry with Pre-Raphaelite décor and the poetry of religious sensibility. In however narrow a range, there exist in her work both the enthusiasms which began with Rossetti and those which find their ultimate source in the Oxford Movement. (p. 103)

> *Ifor Evans, ''Christina Georgina Rossetti,'' in his* English Poetry in the Later Nineteenth Century *(© Ifor Evans, 1966), revised edition, Methuen & Co Ltd, 1966, pp. 87-103.*

STUART CURRAN (essay date 1971)

[Christina Rossetti] was a prodigy of enormous potential, whose best poetry was written before she was twenty. Her first major volume, *Goblin Market and other Poems* . . . , consisting mostly of these early writings, was the first wide-spread literary success of the Pre-Raphaelite Movement. Later she exploited a sound knowledge of technique with only rare moments of mental electricity, never again achieving such a sustained level of creative energy. (p. 288)

A large number of the poems in the initial volume are religious. Indeed, the largest single section of Christina Rossetti's *Poetical Works* is devotional, a reflection of the intense religious focus of her life. . . . There is little in any of Christina Rossetti's religious poetry that does not ring a very pronounced bell. Her sources are the King James Bible and the Book of Common Prayer, both of which she melodically rewrites. Even in the early religious verses the reader can sense her later development as a writer of uninspired poetic tracts. The tone is almost unpleasantly pedantic, her mentor almost exclusively Ecclesiastes. She writes one reverent sermon after another which, though in verse, are far from being poetry. Sometimes, even technique fails her (or overwhelms her, as the case may be). A lesser poet would not have attempted the recurrent feminine rhymes that make an unintentionally comic poem of ''I Will Lift Up Mine Eyes.'' . . . (p. 289)

And yet, this attitude is overly harsh, for Christina Rossetti was a poet, an introspective and serious craftsman, not merely a versifier for the popular press. As a whole, the devotional poems do not achieve the success of her secular efforts, but occasionally they strike fire. . . . Occasionally, too, the religious picturing takes its impetus from a profoundly personal feeling. In this respect, and, indeed, in most respects, **''The Convent Threshold''** is Christina Rossetti's finest poem. . . .

The brooding melancholy that is the predominant emotional substance of **''The Convent Threshold,''** as of most of the poems, was clearly the result of her scrupulous preoccupation with the New Jerusalem and with the manifestations of her rigorous ideals in life. (pp. 289-90)

One tends to speak of this poet as though all her writing were seriously flawed. This is by no means true. But that is not to say that she is without serious limitations. The sentimentality that is not disagreeable in ''Oh roses for the flush of youth'' inundates lesser poems that lack its classical poise. She has only one real subject, mortality, and the variety of her treatment is never extensive. This is in great degree the result of an almost total lack of what the modern critic calls ''texture.'' Her stock of images is small, and they are seldom developed in striking or suggestive ways. This is poetry of sometimes precise pictures but vague statements; and because of that— because, too, of a temperamental austerity—its range is small.

But, granted these limitations, Christina Rossetti is a poet of great gifts. Basic to the unsatisfying mixture of good and bad that composes her poetry may well be her attitude toward writing. . . . That Christina Rossetti is essentially a spontaneous poet means that she never labors the magic out of her lyrics, but also that she never invests the poetry with a depth of image or of complicated thought.

The consistently lovely **''Twilight Calm''** exemplifies her ''spontaneous'' capabilities. This picture of a rural sunset adds nothing beyond the scope of its subject, draws no implications, but is content to employ a rich technical facility on the slightest of materials. Landscape painting of a pleasing hue, it is without passion or intentsity. The eye wanders tunefully, allowing the description to unfold as it will, never forcing a compression of material for the sake of enriching the poetic fabric, never striking the reader's attention with original diction or rhetoric. (pp. 291-92)

A somewhat more aggressive poem on the same order is **''Venus's Looking-Glass,''** a poetic exercise in subject far beyond the usual range of Christina Rossetti's poetry. . . . This, again, is a pretty, decorative piece that is arresting only in the alliteration of its third line and in the pleasant, unruffled ease of the last two lines. The poem is meant to be read quickly, assimilated in the brief perusal, and not worried over. More than a cursory glance reveals how tenuous a piece of verse it is, pretty though it may also be. The diction is generally simple: the nouns are obvious, the verbs common. . . . Because of the poet's disregard for all but the superficial aspects of her craft, the whole is as ''weightless'' as Venus and her court.

To Christina Rossetti's credit, however, is a willingness to grapple with form, an endeavor in which she achieves generally distinguished results. Like all of the Pre-Raphaelites she was adept at difficult stanzaic patterns. Her most consistently remarkable poetic attribute is her facility in rhyming and fitting thought into form without a trace of awkwardness. The awesome pyrotechnics of *Goblin Market* recur only occasionally (poetic exuberance is after all a sign of the weaknesses of the flesh), but always with a charming evanescence. Most Victorian poets in writing of the wind would see it as correlative of life's vicissitudes, of man's uncertainties, or of his separation from nature. In **''Hollow-Sounding and Mysterious''** one senses the presence of all of these issues, but they are at best secondary to the onomatopoetic skill which Christina lavishes on her trifle. . . . (pp. 293-94)

''Venus's Looking-Glass'' exemplifies Christina Rossetti's customary approach to the sonnet. She uses the form felicitously but seldom conquers it and perhaps only once achieves that burning unity for which the sonnet writer aims. In this particular poem the form is academic and the treatment lacking the tautness requisite for imparting life to the structure. (p. 294)

[A] close look reveals the poet's constant experimentation with the sonnet form. The sestet of sonnet 14 of *"Monna Innominata"* almost languishes in its exquisite self-pity, but the tendency is countered by daring echoes which culminate in a trailing appositive of rhetorical force. . . . Hiding a flaccidity of diction and thought behind striking effects is not a singular mark of poetic integrity. It is perhaps, then, fair to portray Christina Rossetti's technique at its soundest and most sustained level, in the first of a trinity of sonnets on a verse from Proverbs, **"If Thou Sayest, Behold, We Knew It Not."**. . . It is not an anthology piece, and yet the poem displays an emotional sincerity as well as a freedom from clichéd pieties, which places it far above the normal course of the poet's religious verse. (pp. 294-95)

The entire sonnet is bold from the twisted word order of the first line to the stretched rhetoric of the last. About the success of the opening line—"I have done I know not what,—what have I done?"—critics could disagree. One could easily say that such padding so early in a sonnet strains the sides; but on the other hand, padding is not responsible for the meek pathos that results from restating the opening words in a question. The weight of monosyllables contributes greatly to this, disarming us with the masculine force of the initial statement so that we are unprepared for the collapse into a child-like plea for enlightenment. From this point the poem, doubling in on itself, moves painfully forward, avoiding the obvious break in the middle of the octave, once again accumulating extraordinary weight through a rhetorical series in which each clause echoes its predecessor before establishing a new thought, appositive in turn to the next clause. The result is an astonishing fabric of interwoven threads paralleling the labyrinth of religious questioning from which the poet seeks to extricate herself. (p. 295)

If this sonnet never quite achieves the high passion of the best of Hopkins' religious sonnets, it must stand—with its indisputable power and carefully molded structure—as one of the monumental expositions of the form in Victorian poetry. Yet it must be accepted that one cannot expect this kind of formal energy very often in a poet who had little capacity for creating drama in such close quarters and whose muse was an essentially tuneful one. She is much more at home in her loose but harmonic short stanzas, or in the pyrotechnics for which *Goblin Market* is famous. (p. 296)

Ease, of course, she never lacked: it is her single most prominent poetic attribute. But a sense of direction, both within individual poems and within her corpus of works, is not one of her gifts. She has so little to say that she can seldom venture beyond a very small effort. Christina Rossetti possessed considerable technical skill, but she lacked the mental prowess to develop it. She was a simple and a pious woman who loved the orthodox God of her Anglican parish-house. A very few poems reveal doubts and questioning, but her main purpose was to affirm God's personal benevolence and to wish for deliverance from life's pains. She does not concern herself with the state of man or with the state of the church: her subject is herself. Hers is a natural theology without concrete dogmas or concrete problems; God is the all-embracing fact; she is humble and submissive before Him.

Humble and submissive: entirely unpretentious. But a great poet cannot be unpretentious: he dares and questions; he attempts to answer, not only in matters of the human being and his universe but in the less glamorous matters of diction and meter, of dramatic imagery and formal necessities, of all the mundane materials out of which great poetry is forged. Christina Rossetti's universe was settled before she came of age, and it neither changed nor developed. She is never deeply unsure, and thus she states, almost never suggests. Her poetry is largely devoid of sharp observation, whether intellectual or imaginative. She is neither an intellectual nor an imaginative woman for the most part, but she has the not inconsiderable gift of felicitous music. She falls back on pretty language, the bane of so many women poets. Whereas Emily Dickinson can sustain a totally feminine tone without sacrificing a crystalline perception and a subtle imagination, this woman's tone is too often merely effeminate, weak and nebulous. She is a good poet, an able poet, but not a great one. With few exceptions her gifts were for lyrics of great felicity, but somehow removed from a world in which real tragedies happen and in which man is confronted with real conflicts, real doubts, real decisions, and indeed real truths—all of which are painful and even agonizing. A major poet can retreat from them, as Herrick did in his "Hesperides," and remain major. But the laurel is conferred for total perfection and poetic integrity within a limited sphere. Even this Christina Rossetti did not possess.

Her aims were small and her gifts were small. (pp. 298-99)

> *Stuart Curran, "The Lyric Voice of Christina Rossetti," in* Victorian Poetry, *Vol. 9, No. 3, Autumn, 1971, pp. 287-99.*

MARTINE WATSON BROWNLEY   (essay date 1979)

The wide appeal of Christina Rossetti's **"Goblin Market,"** her most famous poem and her greatest work, rests on the richness of the various levels of meaning available to the reader of the poem. The different kinds of language Rossetti employs in the Pre-Raphaelite verse romance reflect these levels. On the surface, a simple and direct storytelling style marked by childlike expressions makes **"Goblin Market"** appear to be a mysterious fantasy, an entertaining romance spun from the elements of folklore and fairy tale. At the same time, the use of language with theological overtones combines with the motif of temptation to support the reading of the poem as a Christian allegory. Readily explicable as either Christian allegory or fairy tale, **"Goblin Market"** poses problems of interpretation on another level of meaning, represented by language which carefully delineates states of mind in detail. On this level Rossetti explores certain psychological and emotional states using Lizzie's and Laura's experiences at the goblin market as the symbolic terms for her portrayal of a feminine initiation into adult sexuality. . . .

The kind of sexual experience that goblin men symbolize is suggested both by Laura's feast and its aftermath. The sensuality of the experience is reflected by the descriptions of the fruit, expressed in terms of the rich color and sensuousness characteristic of the Pre-Raphaelites, with images reminiscent of the rich fruit described in the *Song of Solomon*. But more than the fruit is important in the experience; the goblins at least partially endow the fruit with significance. That their presence is important becomes clear later in the poem when they refuse to let Lizzie buy fruit and leave, insisting instead that she eat it with them. (p. 179)

A strange amalgam of the human and the animal, the goblins are more than whimsical denizens of fairyland. Words such as "prowled," "crawled," and "sly" . . . give their strangeness a sinister and predatory quality. "Leering" . . . adds prurient overtones. The descriptions of the goblins' appearances, attributes, and actions suggest the inhuman, animalistic nature of any experience in which they are participants. Sexual experience with goblin men requires payment with a part of the self. . . . Penniless, Laura can only pay by clipping a golden curl, reflecting the traditional association of hair with sexuality.

The description of Laura's eating the fruit adds the final touches to an experience which has as background sensuality, animality, and sacrifice of personal essence. Though the goblins have to be present when the feast occurs, the eating is a solitary action; Laura autoerotically indulges herself. The intense pleasure results in slight physical discomfort which suggests harmful overindulgence: "She sucked until her lips were sore." . . . The oral pleasure of the experience is emphasized: "She sucked and sucked and sucked the more" . . . , the oral stage, the earliest in the Freudian progression to sexual maturity, is hypnotic to Laura. Rossetti's description of the experience thus suggests that the sexual knowledge that Laura buys from the goblins at such a price is an immature, self-centered sexuality, which involves a deep violation of the self within a context of non-human elements.

The aftermath of the experience further defines what has happened to Laura. First of all, as she turns to go home, she "knew not was it night or day." . . . Intoxication is suggested, but inherent in the idea of intoxication, of being stimulated and excited, is the root meaning of the word, "to be poisoned." Laura's inability to distinguish day and night suggests that after the goblin feast she is beginning to lose touch with the natural processes in her world, and further details elaborate this idea. Her alienation from ordinary life increases as the poem progresses. (p. 180)

Along with alienation, part of the aftermath of eating goblin fruit is continuing self-deceit. . . . The rich intensity of experience which blunts Laura's responses to ordinary reality also deceives her about the origins of her stimulants. At the beginning of the poem Rossetti points out that the fruit is "sweet to tongue and sound to eye," . . . and the seductive appearance effectively hides the dangerous emotional and intellectual dimensions inherent in the experience with the fruit. As long as Laura remains deceived about the nature and meaning of her sexual experience, she can only pine for more of the same. . . .

Yet she cannot get any more satisfaction. Alienated from her surroundings, confusing appearance for reality, Laura after the experience becomes totally trapped within herself. She becomes obsessed with the idea of autoerotic, narcissistic pleasure, and she thinks only of herself and her own gratification. Characteristically enough for a person in this totally self-centered state, she cannot even respond to the external stimuli which might gratify and release her. She is too self-absorbed even to hear the goblins any more. . . . Sexual pleasure based purely on sensuality and centered in the self can lead only to sterility and destruction. Locked into the oral stage of sexuality, Laura can progress no farther. (p. 181)

Laura's eating of the fruit has created a destructive psychological state which can be altered only by death or by another kind of love more powerful than the sexual one she has discovered with the goblins. Her hold over herself is finally broken at great cost by Lizzie's act of unselfish love. Lizzie goes out to meet the goblins because of Laura, but it is clear that in some sense it is necessary for Lizzie personally to face the goblin feast and what it means. . . . Laura's plight forces Lizzie to confront the problems of sexuality which she wants to avoid. (p. 182)

Lizzie can stand against the temptations of the goblins' self-absorbing and destroying love because she represents another kind of love. Like Laura, she is intoxicated when she leaves the goblins; she, too, "knew not was it night or day." . . . But her intoxication stems not from poisonous sexual pleasure called from goblin fruit but from her exaltation that her love for Laura has triumphed over evil. . . . (pp. 182-83)

Lizzie can experience narcissistic sensuality and not allow it to destroy her because she is motivated by a pure and selfless love. Not only does she refuse to pay with any part of herself for goblin love, but she does not even lose her money. Lizzie loses nothing in the confrontation and gains everything. . . . Through her ordeal, her stand for unselfish love which looks beyond the physical, she is the agent by whom Laura is brought back to life. The goblins find that they cannot break her resistance, and they vanish in defeat.

The central symbolic action of the poem is Laura's licking the juice of the goblin fruit from Lizzie. . . . With Lizzie as a symbol of the Christ who willingly undergoes suffering to redeem a sinner, this imagery of communion is brilliantly effective and appropriate. What is readily apprehensible as a theological symbol of communion, however, becomes more problematical and delicate to deal with in sexual terms. . . . Laura's horror at Lizzie's courageous defiance of the goblins in the first step in releasing her from her self-entrapment. For the first time in the poem since she has eaten the goblin fruit, Laura responds to something outside of herself. In her fear for Lizzie, tears come to her eyes, water at last after her lengthy arid burning. Just as for Coleridge's Ancient Mariner, redemption for Laura begins in instinctive caring for something beyond the self, and in both poems water is an early sign of salvation. But this caring is not enough to release Laura; she has to again taste goblin fruit and re-enact her traumatizing experience. Her sexual fall requires a sexual redemption. This time, however, her experience of oral sexuality is with another person rather than solely with herself. Laura's stimulus is Lizzie, who stands for a love that gives, rather than the goblins, who represent a love that takes, that requires the sacrifice of personal essence. Lizzie replaces the goblins and removes the animalistic, inhuman element from the experience. (p. 183)

[Laura] confronts before her in Lizzie what she herself can be; in seeing Lizzie she comes to share finally in Lizzie's vision of what love is. Lizzie embodies an alternative to narcissistic, sensuous sexuality, a selfless love which knows the proper relationship of the physical and the spiritual. Once Laura recognizes this alternative to the goblin fruit which has enslaved her, she hates its taste. . . . Nevertheless, the process of purging her former desires is a violent one; in releasing the self from an obsession so complete and encompassing, the risk is that the personality cannot emerge whole and unscathed from the difficult process of freeing itself from the emotional tyranny.

Rossetti heralds Laura's survival through a characteristic antithesis in the line "Life out of death," . . . a succinct statement of the central paradox of the Christian religion. The line also functions significantly in the context of the sexual level of meaning in the poem. Adult sexuality, rooted in selfless and mature love, can emerge from the death-in-life of immature, self-centered sensuality. Loveless sensuality can only be barren and destructive, but sexual experience rooted in mutual love can be revitalizing and redemptive. After a long night Laura awakens in the morning and laughs in "the innocent old way," . . . but she has arrived at a new kind of innocence. Light dances in her eyes, replacing the fire in her breast, just as adult sexuality has succeeded adolescent sensuality. Through Lizzie, Laura has come to a mature understanding of the proper relationship between sensuality and love, between the body and the soul. Both sisters are ready for marriage and for the children to whom Laura tells her story in the last stanza. (p. 184)

Christina Rossetti never duplicated her achievement in **"Goblin Market."** . . . Small wonder that Rossetti insisted to the end that **"Goblin Market"** was a simple fairy tale with no hidden meanings. Undoubtedly that was the only way that the quiet, devoted recluse could tolerate what she had produced in her poem. The woman who pasted pieces of paper over the more explicit lines in Swinburne's poetry could never have faced the actual implications of the stunningly effective parable of human sexuality which somehow welled up from her unconscious self into unforgettable form in **"Goblin Market."** Her reticence in facing these implications accounts for her tacking on to the end of **"Goblin Market"** the most inadequate "moral" placed on a poem since Coleridge had tagged his "Ancient Mariner." "There is no friend like a sister" is a nice maxim and a comforting thought, but it is hardly the central conclusion to be drawn from **"Goblin Market."** D. M. Stuart notes that Rossetti "was always better able to suggest realities of which she had no personal knowledge." This ability of hers is nowhere more apparent than in **"Goblin Market."** (p. 185)

> *Martine Watson Brownley, "Love and Sensuality in Christina Rossetti's 'Goblin Market'," in* Essays in Literature *(copyright 1979 by Western Illinois University), Vol. VI, No. 2, Fall, 1979, pp. 179-86.*

ADDITIONAL BIBLIOGRAPHY

Bald, Marjory A. "Christina Rossetti." In her *Women Writers of the Nineteenth Century*, pp. 233-66. Cambridge: Cambridge University Press, 1923.
    Discusses the literary sources of Rossetti's poetry and examines her poetic use of symbol, allegory, and dream.

Bell, Mackenzie. *Christina Rossetti: A Biographical and Critical Study*. 1898. Reprint. New York: Haskell House Publishers, 1971, 405 p.
    The earliest critical biography of Rossetti. Bell's account is enhanced by his acquaintance with Rossetti and other Pre-Raphaelites and serves as a good introduction to her life and works.

Fass, Barbara. "Christina Rossetti and St. Agnes' Eve." *Victorian Poetry* 14, No. 1 (Spring 1976): 33-46.
    Examines the influence of Keats's poetry on Rossetti's work.

Fredeman, William E. "Christina Georgina Rossetti." In his *Pre-Raphaelitism: A Bibliocritical Study*, pp. 176-82. Cambridge: Harvard University Press, 1965.

A selected bibliography of critical works concerning Rossetti's works and her importance to the Pre-Raphaelite movement.

Garlitz, Barbara. "Christina Rossetti's *Sing-song* and Nineteenth-Century Children's Poetry." *PMLA* LXX, No. 3 (June 1955): 539-43.
    Discusses *Sing-Song* in relation to other nineteenth-century children's poetry.

Greene, Kathleen Conyngham. "Christina Georgina Rossetti." *Cornhill Magazine* n.s. LXIX, No. 414 (December 1930): 662-70.
    A study of Rossetti's works marking the centenary of her birth.

Hueffer, Ford Madox. "Christina Rossetti and Pre-Raphaelite Love." In his *Memories and Impressions: A Study in Atmospheres*, pp. 60-77. New York, London: Harper & Brothers Publishers, 1911.
    Asserts that Rossetti's importance as a Modernist transcends her acquaintance with the Pre-Raphaelite circle.

Packer, Lona Mosk. "Symbol and Reality in Christina Rossetti's 'Goblin Market'." *PMLA* LXXIII, No. 5, Part I (December 1958): 375-85.
    Discusses the symbolic, allegorical, and psychological levels of meaning in the poem "Goblin Market."

Packer, Lona Mosk. *Christina Rossetti*. Berkeley, Los Angeles: University of California Press, 1963, 459 p.
    A biography which concentrates on Rossetti's emotional life, "for it is in these subterranean depths that the source and mainspring of Christina's poetic energy may be found." Packer hypothesizes that the clue to Rossetti's poetry can be found in a secret love relationship with the Pre-Raphaelite poet and painter William Bell Scott.

Rosenblum, Dolores. "Christina Rossetti: The Inward Pose." In *Shakespeare's Sisters: Feminist Essays on Women Poets*, edited by Sandra M. Gilbert and Susan Gubar, pp. 82-98. Bloomington: Indiana University Press, 1979.
    Explores a "doubleness" of opposing themes in Rossetti's poetry which the critic feels resulted from the restrictions of being a woman in Victorian England.

Sharp, William. "Some Reminiscences of Christina Rossetti." In his *Papers Critical & Reminiscent*, edited by Mrs. William Sharp, pp. 66-103. London: William Heinemann, 1912.
    Impressions of Rossetti drawn from various meetings.

Thomas, Eleanor Walter. *Christina Georgina Rossetti*. New York: Columbia University Press, 1931, 229 p.
    A critical biography in which the critic endeavours to "call attention to the relation of Christina Rossetti's work to the literature of her time, to study her prose books for the light which they throw upon her poetry, and to indicate the association of some of her poems with the experiences of her life."

Waugh, Arthur. "Christina Rossetti." *The Nineteenth Century* CVIII, No. DCXLVI (December 1930): 787-98.
    A laudatory critical appreciation of Rossetti's poetry, calling her "the most perfect of all the English woman poets, if not indeed of all the women poets of the world."

Winwar, Frances. *Poor Splendid Wings: The Rossettis and Their Circle*. Boston: Little, Brown, and Co., 1933, 413 p.*
    A detailed account of the private lives and personal relationships of the Pre-Raphaelite artists and writers.

Zaturenska, Marya. *Christina Rossetti: A Portrait with Background*. New York: The Macmillan Co., 1949, 311 p.
    A general overview of Rossetti's life and literary career.

George Sand

1804-1876

(Pseudonym of Amandine Aurore Lucile Dupin Dudevant)
French novelist, dramatist, and essayist.

Sand was one of France's most celebrated and controversial writers. Extremely prolific, she wrote effortlessly, as she said, "much as another person might garden." Yet despite her spontaneous method of composition, she maintained an amazing richness of style and unity of construction. Henry James said of her, "no writer has produced such great effects with an equal absence of premeditation." She produced nearly sixty novels, a lengthy autobiography, numerous essays, twenty-five plays, and approximately 20,000 letters. Relatively few of her works are studied today, however, and she is primarily remembered for her bold behavior as a young woman, wearing trousers, smoking cigars, and openly engaging in love affairs with prominent artistic figures. The fascination with Sand, first, as a personality is evidenced in the numerous biographies detailing every facet of her life, but serious critical studies of her work are lacking.

Sand's parents, who married one month before her birth, were of dissimilar backgrounds: her mother was a bird trainer's daughter while her father was an officer, only a few generations removed from royalty. Following her father's death when she was four, Sand was entrusted to her paternal grandmother's care and was raised at the family estate of Nohant in Berry. At eighteen, Sand married a local army officer, Casimir Dudevant, and soon became the mother of two children. Although the first years of marriage and motherhood were happy, Sand became increasingly restless and, in 1831, left her husband and moved to Paris, determined to pursue a literary career. Following the publication of two novels written in collaboration with her lover Jules Sandeau and signed J. Sand, she began her career in earnest, writing independently under the name of George Sand.

After arriving in Paris, Sand began a series of colorful and notorious affairs. Following a brief encounter with Prosper Mérimée and a longer involvement with Alfred de Musset, Sand fell in love with and actively pursued Frédéric Chopin. Initially put-off by her unusual way of life, Chopin soon became enchanted by Sand's unique charm and intelligence. Their liaison lasted nine years and culminated in a period of great artistic productivity for both. In addition to her romantic involvements, Sand developed lasting friendships with such great contemporaries as Honoré de Balzac, Charles Sainte-Beuve, and Eugène Delacroix. One of her most significant literary friendships was with Gustave Flaubert, begun later in life and well-documented in their published correspondence. Opposites in virtually every respect, they vigorously debated their conflicting literary philosophies. Following her death, Flaubert said, "One had to know her as I knew her to realize . . . the immensity of tenderness in that genius. She will remain one of the splendors of France and unmatched in her glory."

Critics usually divide Sand's literary career into four periods. The works of her first period reflect her rebellion against the bonds of marriage and deal largely with the relationships between men and women. Clearly influenced by Byron and Rous-

seau, they are romantic works full of passionate personal revolt against societal conventions and an ardent feminism, an attitude which outraged her early British and American critics. These early novels, including *Indiana, Lélia,* and *Jacques,* were extremely successful and established Sand as an important literary voice for her generation. Her second period, characterized by such novels as *Consuelo* and *Le meunier d'Angibault (The Miller of Angibault),* reflects Sand's increasing concern with contemporary social and philosophical problems. These novels were strongly influenced by Pierre Leroux, and deal specifically with humanitarianism, Christian socialism, and Republicanism. Considered by many to be her least plausible works, their tone is often didactic and their plots obviously contrived. Sand next wrote pastoral novels, depicting rural scenes and peasant characters. Set in her native Berry *La mare au diable (The Haunted Marsh)* and *François le champi (Francis the Waif)* were inspired by her love of the French countryside and her sympathy with the peasants. Realistic in background detail and distinguished by their gentle idealism, they are considered by many critics to be Sand's finest novels. Although she continued writing until her death, few of the works written after her pastoral period are remembered today. The most interesting and lasting products of her later years are her autobiography, *Histoire de ma vie (My Life)*, and her voluminous correspondence.

Considering the moral climate of her time and her open hostility to societal conventions, it was perhaps inevitable that Sand should become better known for her personal life than for her considerable literary accomplishments. From the beginning of her career, Sand's flamboyant lifestyle interfered with serious critical assessment of her works. However, although moral prejudice dominated British and American criticism of her works through the 1860s, she eventually won acceptance as an artist during her own lifetime and is now noted for her bold exploration of such issues as sexual freedom and independence for women. While Sand is not ranked among the finest French writers, the importance of her contribution to nineteenth-century French literature is acknowledged.

PRINCIPAL WORKS

Indiana (novel) 1832
   [*Indiana*, 1881]
Valentine (novel) 1832
   [*Valentine*, published in *The Masterpieces of George Sand*, 1902]
Lélia (novel) 1833
   [*Lélia*, 1978]
Jacques (novel) 1834
   [*Jacques*, 1847]
André (novel) 1835
   [*André*, 1847]
Lettres d'un voyageur (travel sketches) 1834-36
   [*Letters of a Traveller*, 1847]
Mauprat (novel) 1837
   [*Mauprat*, 1847]
Spiridion (novel) 1839
   [*Spiridion*, 1842]
Le compagnon du tour de France (novel) 1841
   [*The Companion of the Tour of France*, 1847]
Consuelo (novel) 1842-43
   [*Consuelo*, 1846]
Jeanne (novel) 1844
Le meunier d'Angibault (novel) 1845
   [*The Miller of Angibault*, 1847]
La mare au diable (novel) 1846
   [*The Haunted Marsh*, 1848]
François le champi (novel) 1848
   [*Francis the Waif*, 1889]
La petite Fadette (novel) 1849
   [*Little Fadette*, 1849]
Histoire de ma vie. 20 vols. (autobiography) 1854-55
   [*My Life*, 1979]
Elle et Lui 1859
   [*She and He*, 1978]
Le marquis de Villemer (novel) 1861
   [*The Marquis of Villemer*, 1871]
Flamarande (novel) 1875
Correspondance, 1812-1876. 6 vols. (letters) 1883-95

THE ATHENAEUM   (essay date 1833)

[The] favourite French novelist of the year 1832, was unquestionably the author of '**Indiana**' and '**Valentine**,'—avowedly Mr. George Sands; but . . . now known to be Madame Dudevant.

Her first work, '**Indiana**,' was very popular, and as much talked of in the salons as an opera by Rossini. It is a work that would not have been tolerated, despite its talent, in England. . . . The characters, with the exception of the Scotchman, who is passing absurd, are of the present day, and of great truth. The selfish rudeness of the imperial soldier is well depicted, as well as the heartlessness of the man of fashion;—the latter being a sentiment identically the same indeed with what hundreds of romancers have depicted; but the personage is very different from theirs.

['**Valentine**'] is not such a favourite with the French reader as '**Indiana**.' . . . The first volume is charming for its warmth, its simplicity, and its nature: being love from beginning to end, we will not attempt a specimen: it would be like taking a coal out of a furnace, for the same purpose; what is glowing in the volume, would prove but a cinder in extract. The second volume is as detestable as the first is excellent; being said love conjugated a little too far—consisting of seduction, suicide, intrusion into bridal chambers, and an utter contempt for all the obstacles of decorum, possibility, time, or place.

What is most remarkable respecting these volumes, is not so much their merit as their vogue. In England, they would not be tolerated, not only on account of their immoral tendency and licentious descriptions, but that really two volumes of all love, and nothing but love, would be palling to English taste.

> "'*Indiana*' and '*Valentine*'," in The Athenaeum, *No. 281, March 16, 1833, p. 163.*

THE ATHENAEUM   (essay date 1833)

[George Sand's *Lélia*] is the book of the season—of the month—of the day; but, as we have not, in truth, cast its nativity, we had better not offer any prophetic anticipations as to the duration of its fame: enough, then, that it is the book of the hour—the fashionable novelty—the romance the most sought after in the reading rooms, and the most talked of in the literary saloons, of Paris. Whether it should be considered as a novel, a philosophical essay, a poetical invective, or a picture of manners, it somewhat puzzles our philosophy to determine.

It is, no doubt, a brilliant work. The lady . . . seems to have taken for her model the symbolic and mystical school of Germany. '**Lélia**' is one of that class of works in which fiction and reality, truth and untruth, assimilate and mingle in "most admired confusion"; in which living men and unreal shadows cross our path and perplex our understanding, coming and departing at the mysterious waving of the magician's wand.

This style is new to the writer: there is nothing like it in her '**Valentine**' and '**Indiana**.' But, though she has certainly succeeded in producing something "rare and strange," . . . we cannot look upon it but as an "unreal mockery"—a bold, brazen paradox, born, fostered, and nourished, in the very hot-bed of scepticism, in the whirl and turbulence of Parisian politics, manners, and questionable morality.

Lelia is herself a repulsive being: a woman who fain would love, and pray, and have a faith, but who finds in her heart an utter incapacity either to love, pray, or believe. Her soul is withered. The drama in which she acts exhibits her under a double and contradictory light: she is at once young and enthusiastic, yet old in heart and dead in feeling. You meet everywhere with exalted sentiments, high-sounding rhetoric, soul-touching poetry, hand in hand with unbelief, scorn for what is gentle and good, contempt of the world, and inability to appreciate all that is mental and spiritual in it; the result is a monster, a Byronic woman—endowed with rich and energetic faculties, delicate perceptions, rare eloquence, fine talents, but no heart—a woman without hope and without soul. Religion, morals, human sympathies, but "sear her eyes"; she holds them all to be false, deceitful, ridiculous. Unable to feel any pure, true, and devoted affection, she finds her chastisement and torture in that very inability. Virtue is with her a hoax, and she is too wise to be deceived; so, keeping her eyes steadfastly fixed upon the objects of her unattainable desires, she writhes and dies in the agonies of an irremediable despair. (p. 646)

Such is '**Lélia.**' You may find in it an apology for every crime, a panegyric on every vice: debauchery is here a sublime expansion of human power; gaming, a magnificent heroism; a murderer is a bold contemner of the laws of social life; and a *forçat,* a galley slave, is a strong-minded man, at war with society, but greater and nobler than his fellow-creatures. If you condescend to be lectured by Lelia, she will teach you that the bold face of vice is a proof of strength, and the humbleness of virtue a proof of weakness. She will bid you admire the giant-like crime, which towers above the prejudices, opinions, feelings, and morality of the everyday world, as the frozen summit of the Jungfrau towers above the plains. (pp. 646-47)

The whole romance is illustrative of this axiom: "Virtue is inferior to vice, in strength, in greatness, and in beauty." If written in England, the work would have been pursued by the hue-and-cry of every critic in the kingdom.

We feel some difficulty in giving an analysis of a novel without incident, the actors in which are pure creations—mere allegorical beings—and the tendency of which is to prove the stupidity of being anything but a thorough-paced scoundrel. . . .

We shall not again dip our pen in this mire of blood and dirt, over which, by a strange perversity of feeling, the talent of the writer, and that writer a woman! has contrived to throw a lurid, fearful, and unhallowed light. (p. 647)

> "'Lélia: A Novel'," in The Athenaeum, *No. 309, September 28, 1833, pp. 646-47.*

THE ATHENAEUM   (essay date 1834)

[George Sand] is undoubtedly the most gifted and most original female writer of her country and times, a sort of female Jean Jacques Rousseau. She has the same eloquence, the same pathos, the same voluptuousness of style, the same perverted philosophy, the same hatred to social restraints. As he assailed the institutions of his country and the social system of his era, she, with no feebler hand, wages a perpetual war against the nuptial vow. Her writings are especially directed against matrimony: she has no faith in it; she impugns, insults, and tramples under her indignant feet, what we have been accustomed to think the holiest ties, the most hallowed feelings of the heart. An adept in the school of sensation, a despiser of customs, however old and however sanctified, she never holds up *virtue* and *duty* as the aim and hope of human life. The indulgence of passions, of sympathies, of super-refinements, of a sensibility so nervous and trembling as to resemble a morbid egotism, such are her idols. She displays everywhere an admirable

finesse of the understanding; a ready and ever-flowing eloquence; a deep knowledge of the female heart, such, at least, as the highly heated atmosphere of Parisian life has made it. She is, in fact, a woman of genius, whose cradle was rocked in the stormy billows of Jean Jacques's prose and Byron's poetry; whose youth felt the scorching influences of an ill-assorted marriage; and whose deep-rooted despair looks with a cold eye on her past tortures and her still-bleeding wounds. Her anathema is sadder and more harrowing than the curse which Byron threw upon the world. . . .

Criticism on such a plot [as that of *Jacques,* Mrs. Sand's latest novel,] is quite needless in England. Of the characters, we may observe, that Sylvia is unnatural, and the magnanimity of Jacques is false; his philosophy is but the coldness of egotism, and his behaviour to his wife is unfeeling and unreasonable. We shall not attempt to refute the false philosophy on which the work is founded, nor drag into notice the immorality which infects it, even for exposure. We must, however, express our regret at these perversions of genius, for it is impossible not to admire the wonderful truth of feeling and observation—the rapid and burning eloquence—the marvellous insight into the human heart, which is discoverable in the work. Whenever the writer condescends to draw natural incidents, and to copy human life as it is, she is admirable. (p. 883)

> "'Jacques'," in The Athenaeum, *No. 371, December 6, 1834, pp. 883-84.*

[JOSEPH MAZZINI]   (essay date 1839)

[George Sand] has suffered—she revolted,—she has struggled—she has sought, hoped, found; and she has told us *all.* The long series of her compositions form a grand confession. Spirits young, pure, and innocent, not worn by unhappiness, whom contact with the world has not yet endowed with the knowledge of evil, may well—perhaps, should—abstain from reading it; but let the rest, numerous as they are, boldly go through the whole; they cannot, we say it with profound conviction, but rise the better. (p. 27)

[Her works] contain the history of her soul's life—the most complete autobiography, the most striking in its truth, and useful truth, that we know. Taken as a whole, they offer us an ascending line of progress towards good that is going on even whilst we are writing. *Indiana, Lélia, Jacques,* the *Lettres d'un Voyageur, Spiridion,* appear to us to mark the culminating points; her other productions come in, as valleys between the mountains, among the five books we have just named, and establish in some sort their continuity.

We know not in what manner "**Indiana**" has been read, so that an accusation of immorality against the author could be drawn from it; but we do know, that we read it before knowing this accusation, that we have re-read it before writing these lines, and that, on both occasions, we have found in it weighty precepts and a powerful lesson of morality. . . . The morality of a literary performance appears to us to consist far less in the choice of the things represented, of topics, than in the manner in which they are treated, in the final effect which the book, by whatever means, produces on the soul. Whether virtue be unsuccessful or triumphant, whether evil finds its penalty or remains unpunished, in the work, matters little, if we are taught to revere and love virtue notwithstanding its misfortunes, to abhor evil notwithstanding the seductiveness of the temporal and temporary good fortune that may attend it. Not to the eyes, but to the heart, should the author speak; to our own hearts in particular should he remit the hatred of evil and the punishment of the guilty. . . . Towards this kind of emotion it appears to us the soul must be impelled in reading **"Indiana;"** and the end, the inevitable consequence, is aversion for the seducer. Wherefore has it been said that **"Indiana"** is a *plea* against marriage? It is not even one against the husband. Certainly the inconveniences of a union between two persons whose incompatibility is beforehand written on every feature of their existence, are there strongly pointed out. But is that doing a work of immorality? Delmare, old, infirm, in character violent and domineering, is he, in the opinion of most persons, a suitable companion for a very young, beautiful, and impassioned woman, whose heart rebounds at all oppression? Unions like that, destructive of all happiness, are they not themselves a covert for great immorality, by rendering seduction a hundred times more to be feared? George Sand has made this thoroughly felt. . . . Never was there a portrait sketched with so absolute an intention of calling forth disgust, as that of Raymon; never any with so much art not to render the individuality too hateful at the risk of destroying the effect of the lesson. Raymon, with his talents and success in society—a seducer by liking, and indefatigable from the love of triumph . . . is the very type of the dangerous seducer so often to be met in the world: his love is thoroughly that *love-passion,* a hideous compound of sensuality and vanity, that exercises so powerful a charm—fascination we might say—over the weakness of inexperience. And in **"Indiana,"** he is laid bare to the eye—a hundredfold beneath the husband-oppressor, cowardly, cruel, criminal as selfishness, of which he is the very highest expression. And the consequences of the seduction stand before the face of each of them, all frightful and irremediable; before the seducer, the corpse of poor Noun; before the seduced, the wreck of her illusion. For Indiana is *illusion:* she believes in goodness beyond the line of duty; she trusts blindly to the realisation of the ideal love that she bears in her own bosom, to the sincerity of the passion expressed, to the man's constancy, to a few glowing words whose source she has never studied. It is sufficient to read the letter of Indiana . . . to understand the mystery of her unhappiness; the secret of the book is contained in the ejaculation that the author puts into the mouth of Indiana herself, when Raymon reproaches her with having learnt love from romances, in the usual fashion of waiting-maids: *"What alarms and terrifies me is, that you are right,"* says Indiana. These words appear to us to contain—and we appeal to the sex as judges—a warning for all women of hearts ready to sacrifice duty to hope, more efficacious than twenty commonplaces of morality. How is it that puritanical criticism has forgotten these? How has it been forgotten that the author was writing, not an apology, but the history of Indiana—that the epithet *crime* is not spared to the flight of Indiana—that a passage of the tenth chapter reproaches her "with being too soon disheartened with her lot, and with not having given herself the pains of trying to make her husband better?" And why is there forgotten the love of Ralph—a love of the heart, respectful, and devoted, uniting in itself something of the threefold affection of the lover, the husband, and the father, a happy contrast with Raymon's harassing, unrestrained, and daring love of the imagination—which, till then mute, dares not manifest itself but at a moment of solemnity, and when the tomb of the *husband* has long been closed? Strange that the criticism which stigmatised the book as *immoral* should have quietly got rid of Ralph by calling him "a stupid cousin." (pp. 28-30)

In a class more elevated, more open to exceptions—near [Goëthe's] Faust and [Byron's] Manfred—must be placed **"Lélia."** This is not a immoral work—far from it; but for young spirits, who have not passed the double initiation of meditation and suffering, **'Lélia''** is a dangerous book. . . . **"Lélia"** is food for the strong; let the weak abstain, for there is in it that which may be the salvation of strong and tried organisations, but which may kill the tender and frail. It is a lesson whose aim is sanctified; but the details are horrible—such, perhaps, as may be necessary to act on society in a state of gangrene. Doubtless, courage was required to trace this picture of desolation, in which hope after hope is unlinked, torn by some diabolical hand from the tree of life, and falling, like dead leaves, into the sepulchre of decay and nothingness. . . . Courage also is required to read it to the end; for we fear, at each step we take, that we are bordering on the desert of spiritual suicide: as before every general formula we feel a sensation of dizziness; and it is a formula of destruction, of negation without change, that **"Lélia"** undertakes to teach us. And yet hers is truly a high and sacred formula. The work of destruction that she fulfils, is that of a world worn out and corrupted, that rules over us yet, though in its agony. It is the world of *individuality,* the world that proposed to itself no other end, no other reason for its existence, than the search after prosperity. This, taken as the end of life, necessarily results in selfishness.

Lelia, whether the author intended it or not, is a symbol. The *dramatis personae* exist not as human beings; they are speaking and moving formulas; and hence it is that they strike on the brain rather than on the heart; they cause us not to weep, as **"Indiana"**—they make us think. Trenmor is human *reason*— reason pure, solitary, dry, deprived of impulse and sensibility. Stenio is *passion,*—not that of the heart, but empthatically that of the imagination. Pulcherie is *sensualism,*—calm, logical, and clevated even to theory. Magnus is still sensualism, but that of the instinct, fiery, unreflecting, and at enmity with superstition. Lelia is the wandering spirit on the search amid all these varieties; she is the other half of Faust, the woman-Faust. . . . What secks she? Temporal happiness. And what seek all these personifications, all these *ideas* we would say, that are revolving round her like spectres, whom she follows each in turn? Temporal happiness: the one by the enjoyments of the flesh, or by repentance and humiliation before God; another by the exaltation of the poetic faculties; a third by the philosophic calm of stoicism; but all, whatever they may say, are only occupied with their existence. This, indeed, is the mother-principle in Faust; only as man lives more by the brain, and woman by the heart, whilst Faust seeks happiness in knowledge, Lélia seeks it through love; we feel that there rules in Faust a deep craving for power—in Lélia, a deep craving for life, for the expansion of sympathy. In Goëthe, Mephistophiles is destined to destroy power by doubt, much as he appears desirous of satisfying it by degrees. In George Sand, Trenmor destroys love, much as he appears to protect Stenio by his sympathies. Trenmor—Reason—the being who thinks, but whose heart beats not—who, instead of thinking how to *direct* the passions—instruments that God has placed at our disposal for good—fancies "that where they finish, man begins," and in whom the extinct passions have left only a mass of recollections and reflections, whose life is only the intellectual life, the *me* that contemplates and communes not—in a word, the being that muses . . .—Trenmor sways Lélia. She has a heart less ardent and less powerful than his mind; her faculties are inferior to his musings. Tormented by a lively thirst for love, but bent on there meeting with absolute and infallible happiness, when she finds it not there,—when in submitting her experience to the cool analysis of individual reason, she finds only the *finite* to satisfy a spirit full of aspirations for the infinite, she curses life and love;—she leaves herself to be tossed between scepticism and faith, and resumes her internal struggle, her desires and her impotence, with this sorrowful cry. "Happy those who can love." (pp. 32-3)

Bound as she is in the folds of a philosophy that steps not beyond the *individual,* she never rises to the conception of the *social* life of her mission in the world; between her and the crowd there is no exchange; "she has no sympathy for the human race, though she suffers the same evils, and sums up in herself all the sorrows scattered on the face of the earth." She comprehends not God in humanity; she prays not with it; she looks aside at her own weak and solitary individuality; thence it is she fears it, and feels ready to revolt from it. . . . In causing us to be born from one man, and in making us beings eminently social, God willed that our power for good should be enlarged just so much as we shall be careful to steep it in the common spring, and he has condemned to barenness all philosophy that aims at confining itself within the circle of individuality.

Lélia is the development of this principle as to woman, as Faust—more perhaps by the instinct of genius, and by a logical necessity, than from the intention of the author—is as to man. Goëthe found man marching in the path of science without any other aim than *his* pride and *his* happiness; George Sand found woman marching in the path of love without any other aim than the full budding of *her* faculties, *her* happiness; and both have inscribed at the goal of these two courses—"Impotence and nothingness." By what fatality, by what injustice—so much the greater that Goëthe stopped there, and George Sand has advanced—has the first had absolution, while the latter remains under the burden of an accusation of immorality. Why has it been made a crime for one to have proved by a *tableau*—frightful we confess—that it is an illusion to desire happiness in life and love, of what kind soever it may be, while the other has been praised for having taught that to seek happiness in knowledge and power is an illusion often criminal? Is it from weakness of perception, or from malignity, that criticism has persisted in reading and judging as a vulgar tale what evidently is not so? (p. 34)

["**Lélia**" and "**Indiana**"] are, of the longer works of Madame Aurore Dupin, those which have called forth the most exclamations against the immorality of the author; and if we have succeeded in pointing out a more just and more favourable route for the appreciation of these works, our task is nearly completed. We only desire to provoke a fresh and more considerate examination. We ask this, upright in conscience, proud of being the first to demand it in this country, and convinced . . . that there is benefit in reconciling society with genius. . . .

Those who shall undertake the examination we ask, will certainly find some hasty passages, some crude descriptions, that we should like better to be able to suppress; they will find some phrases hazarded, in which the abuses, the absurdities, the prejudices, and the vices of society are expressed by the collective word "*society,*" some where there is used "*marriage*" in place of "*persons married.*" But, looking over a few details to get at the *ensemble,* judging the spirit rather than the letter, we are sure they will find true and high morality where superficial critics have pronounced themselves scared. . . . [Never] in the pages of George Sand is vice presented in a way to seduce the young imagination, never does virtue appear but surrounded with that glory of art that impels us to prostrate ourselves before it; there is always a protest in the face of crime, aspiration after good in the face of evil. They will find that it is not the *institution* of marriage, but the corruption of

that holy institution; that not husbands, but *bad* husbands are dealt with; that if she has been led to think that "the scandal and disorder of women are *very often* provoked by the brutality or infamy of men, and that a husband who wantonly neglects his duties in idle talk, merriment, and drinking, is sometimes less excusable than the wife who betrays hers in tears, in affliction, and in repentance," she is at the same time ready to revere "that grand, noble, excellent, *voluntary,* and *eternal* love," which is marriage such as Christianity made it, such as St. Paul explained it. . . . (p. 35)

And above all this, if they shall desire to reflect more conscientiously than has yet been done, they will discover that cry of deep and solemn sadness that springs from almost all the writings of Madame Aurora Dupin. . . . They will then demand, astonished, how this woman, a writer that fulfils with extraordinary powers a mission in the world of Art so substantially austere, could have been so mistaken, so little understood, so calumniated? And, thinking on the storm of misfortune that swept over her years of youth . . . , they will pardon the errors and the reaction that has signalised the first part of her course who has never betrayed the cause of truth, who has always pleaded the cause of suffering, and who has never, under trial, lost sight of the goal that alone could save her. (p. 36)

> [*Joseph Mazzini,*] "*George Sand,*" *in* Monthly Chronicle, *Vol. IV, July-December, 1839, pp. 23-40.*

[WILLIAM MAKEPEACE THACKERAY]   (essay date 1840)

[George Sand] teaches her wisdom in parables, that are, mostly, a couple of volumes long; and began, first, by an eloquent attack on marriage, in the charming novel of "**Indiana.**" "Pity," cried she, "for the poor woman who, united to a being whose brute force makes him her superior, should venture to break the bondage which is imposed on her, and allow her heart to be free."

In support of this claim of pity, she writes two volumes of the most exquisite prose. What a tender, suffering creature is Indiana; how little her husband appreciates that gentleness which he is crushing by his tyranny and brutal scorn; how natural it is that, in the absence of his sympathy, she, poor clinging confiding creature, should seek elsewhere for shelter; how cautious should we be, to call criminal—to visit with too heavy a censure—an act which is one of the natural impulses of a tender heart, that seeks but for a worthy object of love. But why attempt to tell the tale of beautiful Indiana? Madame Sand has written it so well, that not the hardest-hearted husband in Christendom can fail to be touched by her sorrows, though he may refuse to listen to her argument. Let us grant, for argument's sake, that the laws of marriage, especially the French laws of marriage, press very cruelly upon unfortunate women.

But if one wants to have a question of this, or any nature, honestly argued, it is better, surely, to apply to an indifferent person as an umpire. . . . Madame Sand having, according to the French newspapers, had a stern husband, and also having, according to the newspapers, sought "sympathy" elsewhere, her arguments may be considered to be somewhat partial, and received with some little caution. (pp. 236-37)

[If] we examine what the personal character of the preacher is, we begin pretty clearly to understand the value of the doctrine. Any one can see why Rousseau should be such a whimpering reformer, and Byron such a free and easy misanthropist, and why our accomplished Madame Sand, who has a genius and eloquence inferior to neither, should take the present condition of mankind (French-kind) so much to heart, and labour so hotly to set it right. (p. 237)

[After "**Indiana**"] came "**Valentine**," which may be said to exhibit her doctrine, in regard of young men and maidens, to whom the author would accord, as we fancy, the same tender licence. "**Valentine**" was followed by "**Lélia**," a wonderful book indeed, gorgeous in eloquence, and rich in magnificent poetry: a regular topsy-turvyfication of morality, a thieves' and prostitutes' apotheosis. This book has received some late enlargements and emendations by the writer; it contains her notions on morals, which, as we have said, are so peculiar, that, alas! they can only be mentioned here, not particularized. . . . (pp. 237-38)

[In "**Spiridion**"] the lady asserts her pantheistical doctrine, and openly attacks the received Christian creed. She declares it to be useless now, and unfitted to the exigencies and the degree of culture of the actual world; and, though it would be hardly worth while to combat her opinions in due form, it is, at least, worth while to notice them, not merely from the extraordinary eloquence and genius of the woman herself, but because they express the opinions of a great number of people besides: for she not only produces her own thoughts, but imitates those of others very eagerly. . . . (p. 238)

With regard to the spelling and grammar, our Parisian Pythoness stands, in the goodly fellowship, remarkable. Her style is a noble, and, as far as a foreigner can judge, a strange tongue, beautifully rich and pure. She has a very exuberant imagination, and, with it, a very chaste style of expression. She never scarcely indulges in declamation, as other modern prophets do, and yet her sentences are exquisitely melodious and full. She seldom runs a thought to death (after the manner of some prophets, who, when they catch a little one, toy with it until they kill it), but she leaves you at the end of one of her brief, rich, melancholy sentences, with plenty of food for future cogitation. I can't express to you the charm of them; they seem to me like the sound of country bells—provoking I don't know what vein of musing and meditation, and falling sweetly and sadly on the ear.

This wonderful power of language must have been felt by most people who read Madame Sand's first books, "**Valentine**" and "**Indiana**:" in "**Spiridion**" it is greater, I think, than ever; and for those who are not afraid of the matter of the novel, the manner will be found most delightful. The author's intention, I presume, is to describe, in a parable, her notions of the downfall of the Catholic church; and, indeed, of the whole Christian scheme. . . . (p. 240)

I think that Madame Sand's novel of "**Spiridion**" may do a vast deal of good, and bears a good moral with it; though not such an one, perhaps, as our fair philosopher intended. For anything he learned, [the protagonist] Samuel-Peter-Spiridion-Hebronius might have remained a Jew from the beginning to the end. Wherefore be in such a hurry to set up new faiths? Wherefore, Madame Sand, try and be so preternaturally wise? Wherefore be so eager to jump out of one religion, for the purpose of jumping into another? See what good this philosophical friskiness has done you, and on what sort of ground you are come at last. You are so wonderfully sagacious, that you flounder in mud at every step; so amazingly clear-sighted, that your eyes cannot see an inch before you, having put out,

with that extinguishing genius of yours, every one of the lights that are sufficient for the conduct of common men. (pp. 249-50)

In what a state . . . does Mrs. Sand and her brother and sister philosophers, Templars, Saint Simonians, Fourierites, Lerouxites, or whatever the sect may be, leave the unfortunate people who have listened to their doctrines, and who have not the opportunity, or the fiery versatility of belief, which carries their teachers from one creed to another, leaving only exploded lies and useless recantations behind them! (p. 251)

I don't wish to carry this any farther, or to say a word in defence of the doctrine which Mrs. Dudevant has found "incomplete;"—here, at least, is not the place for discussing its merits, any more than Mrs. Sand's book was the place for exposing, forsooth, its errors: our business is only with the day and the new novels, and the clever or silly people who write them. Oh! if they but knew their places, and would keep to them, and drop their absurd philosophical jargon! Not all the big words in the world can make Mrs. Sand talk like a philosopher: when will she go back to her old trade, of which she was the very ablest practitioner in France? (p. 258)

> [*William Makepeace Thackeray,*] *"Madame Sand and the New Apocalypse" (1840), in his* The Paris Sketchbook, *Crowell, 1905, pp. 233-60.*

THE NORTH AMERICAN REVIEW (essay date 1841)

[Whatever garb George Sand's] works assume externally, they are all pervaded with one purpose, and tend constantly in one direction. The same morbid imagination, the same gloomy and passionate spirit, at war with the world and the allotments of Providence, and discontented with itself, appear everywhere in her writings, and give a sad image of the temperament and feelings of the author. None but a mind and heart thoroughly diseased could pour forth such effusions, while the impetuosity of manner, the vivid descriptions, the eloquent portraiture of passion, and the richness of style prove, but too evidently, that a noble nature has gone astray. In point of vigor and originality of genius, she may well be classed with Rousseau, or, if the comparison be confined to her own sex, she may be placed even higher than Madame de Staël. She is less affected than the latter, and her style, equally rich, is more condensed and energetic. For eloquent and imaginative writing, the most brilliant passages of "**Corinne**," when placed beside many chapters of "**Indiana**," or "**Valentine**," will gain nothing by the contrast. Her pages bear no marks of the various, but rather superficial, learning, which appears in the "**Allemagne**," but her observation of life, though tinged by a morbid temperament, is even more keen, while her picturesque and glowing descriptions display a more perfect appreciation of external nature.

But the parallel, which these volumes naturally suggest, lies between their author and "the self-torturing sophist, wild Rousseau." We see in each the same wayward direction of a richly gifted spirit, the same ardent delineations and intense sensibility, pictures of life shadowed with similar gloom, and an equal command over the sympathy of the reader. Both quarrel with the present institutions of society, and, setting its laws and censure at defiance, lose themselves in dreams about another condition of mankind, as fantastic and impracticable as a sick brain and a corrupted moral sense could well devise. A similar vein of egotism pervades their writings,—a disposition to make a confidant of the whole world, and to call for its sympathy by a free disclosure of individual passions and sufferings, of wearied affections and buried hopes, of both external and inward causes of unhappiness peculiar to themselves. (pp. 107-08)

There is a difference between the two writers, however, in the manner and purport of these auricular confessions to the public. Rousseau tells every thing, down to the most trivial details. George Sand exposes, not the history of her life, but her character and feelings. She is silent about the external facts, but eloquent in expounding the sentiments and passions, to which the incidents have given rise. She is continually drawing her own portrait, though not writing her autobiography. The heroine in nearly all her tales, the central figure about whom all the interest and scenery are grouped, is a sister image to Byron's half fanciful, half real personation of self,—a proper consort for his gloomy and perpetually recurring hero. Of the two conceptions, perhaps hers is the more life-like and striking; it seems to embody more of actual experience, to be copied more faithfully from the life. Such a character is that of Indiana, in the novel of the same name, a work conceived and written with a greater flow of feeling, . . . than any other of her productions. (p. 108)

As a theorist, our author is not entitled to the praise of originality. She would destroy the whole constitution of society as it exists at present, but has nothing to offer as a substitute except some indefinite notions, borrowed from Rousseau, respecting the freedom, simplicity, and happiness of mankind in a state of nature. The restraints imposed by human legislation are to be done away, the yoke of superstition is to be broken, the comforts and luxuries of civilized life to be resigned, and man is to become again an inhabitant of the woods, following no rule but that of appetite and impulse. A fierce attachment to the doctrines of liberty and equality, manifested as much by hatred towards all rulers and governments, as by sympathy with the governed, or pity for the oppressed, is the basis of her political creed. Join to these opinions the wildest form of Mary Wolstonecraft's doctrine respecting the rights of woman, and you have the whole system of opinions, the inculcation of which appears to George Sand a more important object, than to interest her readers by pictures of real life, or astonish them by the products of an ardent and fertile imagination. Such doctrines are more the growth of temperament and passion, than of unsound reasoning, or of a curious and speculative understanding. They exist as feelings rather than reflections, and are supported not by sophisticated arguments, but by appeals to sentiment and by varied illustration. They are avowed and defended with perfect earnestness and sincerity; and one might even be pleased with the eloquent and fanciful garb in which they are arrayed, perfectly secure against any danger from such extravagances, if the enjoyment were not checked by the gloom and misanthropy, which are continually breaking forth throughout these remarkable writings. (pp. 109-10)

There are many passages in [George Sand's *Oeuvres*] which repel sympathy by the spirit of gloom and violence which they exhibit, and not a few which will shock merely English readers from their indelicacy. The writer is resolute in her determination to unsex herself in the general tone and execution of her works, in the boldness of her theories, and the warmth and freedom of her descriptions. But, in spite of her efforts, the woman's pen appears throughout,—in the keen-sighted observation of life, the susceptibility to strong passion excited by comparatively trivial causes, and in the feminine acquaintance with all the intricacies and windings of the human heart. Not-

withstanding many objectionable passages, she does not appear an intentionally licentious writer. . . . There is matter enough for regret and indignation in the view of George Sand's works, but we do not believe her style to be intentionally gross and corrupting. (pp. 111-12)

Some of her later tales are evidently made to sell; they repeat the objectionable peculiarities of the former ones, but do not bear the impress of equal vigor and originality of mind. Though always well written, there is a repetition in the sentiment and characters, a poverty of invention in the plot, and a general languor of execution, which mark the indolent or exhausted author. Sometimes her admiration of German models leads to an affected mysticism and inflation of style, which are not wholly redeemed by great exuberance of language and forcible delineations of passion. (p. 112)

The least exceptionable of her writings, which affords also some glimpse of her theories and shows much of her peculiar genius, is the novel of **"Mauprat."** The plot is exceedingly simple, and the incidents rare, which is the case indeed with most of her tales. (p. 113)

Far different from this generally pleasing tale is the novel of **"Valentine,"** which is even more rich in flashes of genius, but shows more vividly also in its invectives against society, and in its pictures of ardent and gloomy passions, the unhappy and diseased condition of the writer's mind. There is nothing of the cynical spirit, the devilish sneer, with which some of George Sand's contemporaries and countrymen have imitated Voltaire in treating of the institutions of man and the higher interests of his better nature. Our author is too good a hater to assume this careless and mocking air, or to fight with such indifferent weapons. She wars against the moral creed, the existing opinions of the whole civilized world, with a hate that is too concentrated to vent itself in sarcasm. What the law of God and man has branded as crime, she boldly, fiercely, declares to be virtue, and the doer of the act, who suffers from its consequences, either through the natural course of events or from the punishment directly inflicted by an outraged community, is eulogized by her as a hero and a martyr. . . . [The] lesson which the writer seeks to inculcate in **"Valentine,"** if we understand it aright, is, that passion and impulse, when sincere, should be allowed their own way, for they have a sanctifying power, and purify from every taint of guilt all actions, however gross, that are committed under their influence. And the work is executed with so much power, such command of pathos in the description of suffering, and so much eloquence of invective, that the reader's feelings are enlisted before he is aware, and he goes on under a species of fascination, though tempted at every moment to throw the atrocious book into the flames. (p. 122)

There is much, which is offensive to sound principle and a pure moral taste, in the very design of such a book; and its execution and details often outrage, still more directly, all the fixed opinions and delicate feelings of a well-balanced mind. (p. 129)

[A] single passion,—the favorite one, it is true, of imaginative writers,—forms the groundwork in most of her plots, and supplies the chief interest of the story. Her harp has but one string; the burden of her song is "love,—still love." It is a dangerous topic to speculate about, and her philosophizing turn gives rise to theories, which are fanciful and erratic enough. The most singular of her whims is . . . the idea of representing woman as the victim of this passion, as the first to acknowledge its power, and, therefore, as compelled to beg a return of affection from those by whom it is grudgingly yielded, or totally withheld. Nearly all her heroines fall in love before they are asked to do so, and then go whining about, complaining of the coldness of other people's hearts, when they ought only to strive against the overwarmth of their own. This notion of our author is the more remarkable and inconsistent, because, in every other respect, she shows herself such a resolute champion of the rights and superior endowments of her sex. The tyranny of man is the constant object of her invective, and the contrasts which she draws between the various characters in her novels, are often any thing but flattery to the male part of creation. (p. 130)

One of the most pleasing, yet melancholy, of our author's shorter stories, **"André,"** comes directly in point in this connexion. (p. 131)

Nothing can be more simple and touching, than the outline and filling up of this interesting story. It is written with spirit and tenderness, the characters are sketched with graphic force, and the scenes of pathos are skilfully touched, without being overwrought. The heroine is a charming ideal, a floweret, which seems so fragile, that a breath would scatter its leaves, yet clinging to its stem with a tenacity that marks a really vigorous growth. By her side, the poor-spirited and wavering André, yielding to the storm which he has not the resolution to face, sinks almost below pity. It forms an affecting picture, this being of superior station, education, and sex, looking for consolation and guidance to one for whom nature and circumstances seemed to point him out as a guardian and protector. . . . The relation between the two parties in her story is striking, because it is new, and the chances are not much in favor of its frequent occurrence in real life. It is the good fortune of woman, occupying her present position in society, that exigencies do not often call forth such traits of character, even if they exist, and she ought rather to rejoice at the absence of any such occasion, than to long for a struggle with circumstances, that might exhibit her latent energies. But our author is not satisfied with this state of things, and returns to the defence of her speculations on this head in her dramatic sketch of **"Gabriel."** In this little work, more power is displayed, than in the one just noticed, though the morality of it is more questionable, and the chief incidents of the plot are fantastic, not to say extravagant and absurd. But there is great liveliness in the piece, . . . much spirit in the characters, and variety in the action. . . . (p. 132)

[An] able and earnest champion the modern doctrine respecting the rights of woman has found in George Sand. . . . Those who wish to know more of her views respecting the evils of the social state and the remedies which are applicable to them, may be satisfied by reading **"Lélia";** if curious further to ascertain something about her daring speculations on the subject of religion, we refer them to **"Spiridion."** For our own part, notwithstanding the vigor and eloquence with which both these works are written, far superior in point of style to either of her other publications, we have no heart to dissect and exhibit them, whether for exposure or refutation. A long wail of discontent and anger with the actual condition and opinions of the civilized portion of our race strikes harshly and gloomily upon the ear; and as we believe it proceeds from a mind incurably diseased, we are willing to let it die away without remark or censure. (pp. 134-35)

> *"Works of George Sand," in* The North American Review, *Vol. LIII, No. CXII, July, 1841, pp. 103-39.*

[G. H. LEWES]   (essay date 1844)

George Sand is a moral writer; but some of her works are, it is true, immoral in their tendency. This is a distinction generally lost sight of. She is a moral writer because an earnest one. She puts forth *convictions.* Her works are immoral in their tendency when these convictions are erroneous; and sometimes, when her descriptions of scenes of passion border too closely on reality, their warmth being too unsubdued. . . . George Sand holds some few opinions on religious, moral, and political subjects, which are at variance with those generally received, and these she has either put distinctly forth, or else implied, in several of her works. While admitting that she has thereby injured those works, we cannot conscientiously condemn her for the deed. She was bound to utter what she thought the truth, and to utter it in her own way. It is absurd to contend that novels are not the places for such ideas. The artist must use his art as a medium—as the journalist would use the journal, as the politician would use the pamphlet.

And after all, the immorality of George Sand's works has been very grossly exaggerated. Her private history has been so much the theme of scandal, and that so exaggerated with the usual prodigality of report, that people have unconscientiously attributed to her books the character of her actions. (pp. 266-67)

[George Sand], considered with reference to marriage, is decidedly not an immoral writer; and if compared with her contemporaries, is purity itself. With reference to 'lawless love' and St. Simonian licence, we may say that whatever her private opinions, whatever her personal actions may imply, her works give no countenance of such a notion. Her heroines are singularly chaste. Valentine, Fiamma, Yseult, Edmée, Laurence, Quintilia, Consuelo, &c., are so many tributes to the beauty of chastity. With the exception of Valentine, they are women of great character, and although placed within reach of temptation, are preserved by their own resolute dignity and feminine virtue. (p. 270)

Besides the sincerity of her longing after truth, which most readers have admitted, George Sand always exhibits a vivid sympathy with greatness of thought and feeling. She loves to contemplate the victory of mind over matter. Generous herself to a high degree, she everywhere manifests a love of generosity and integrity. Self-dependent, self-sustained, she is fond of exhibiting her heroines relying solely on their own will and dignity; without however making them Amazons: Fiamma, Consuelo, Yseult, &c., have nothing masculine but their energy and courage. The only fault in this is her fondness for making women independent of society: pursuing a line of conduct they have laid down for themselves, rather than that laid down for them by society. This, in as far as it may be supposed to influence the actual conduct of women, we admit to be immoral in its tendency. On the whole, however, the effect of her works, upon the reader's mind, cannot but be beneficial. . . . (p. 271)

This requires some qualification, if the reader be young, inexperienced, or a female. To such we would say do not open **'Lélia,' 'Spiridion,' 'Leone Leoni,'** nor, perhaps, **'Jacques.'** **'Lélia'** is a profound poem, but a very dangerous novel. It should be read only by the strong. . . . It is the most terrible outcry of scepticism ever heard. The whole anarchy of the epoch is mirrored in its pages. . . . We say the same of **'Spiridion,'** from a different cause. **'Leone Leoni'** and **'Jacques'** are not suited to an English taste, nor to English ideas. But with these exceptions, we think her works perfectly harmless, nay, decidedly beneficial. (pp. 271-72)

The style of George Sand, in her earlier works, is perhaps the most beautiful ever written by a French author. It has recently become occasionally wordy and emasculated; but in **'Indiana,' 'Valentine,' 'Jacques,' 'Lélia,' 'Mauprat,' 'Lettres d'un Voyageur,'** and **'Les Sept Cordes de la Lyre,'** it is unequalled for freshness, vigour, grace, and harmony. There is a magic in many passages which is beyond all example in the French language. Its music is as fresh as that of a spring that bubbles underneath the grass; and its harmonies have sometimes the grandeur of a cathedral organ. **'Lélia,'** which is alternately a hymn to the majesty of nature, and an elegy on the nothingness of life, is perhaps the most extraordinary piece of writing extant. (pp. 279-80)

[It is not] in description alone that George Sand excels. Her style has every excellence by turns. Now grave, now epigrammatic; now exhibiting the lightness and delicacy of Voltaire, with the exquisite felicity of Racine; now the solemn energy of Bossuet, and the rhetorical vehemence of Rousseau or Lamennais. Always clear as crystal; always unaffected; always musical. Style, which in almost every writer is the result of infinite labour, is, with her, impassioned inspiration. . . . Poetry flows from her pen as water from the rock; she writes as the birds sing: without effort, but with perfect art. (p. 281)

In delineation of character it would be difficult to choose between Balzac or George Sand; both are great in this department, and both very opposite in method. . . . Sand is a poet, and creates characters; Balzac is a philosopher, and criticises them. Sand places her men and women dramatically before you: they reveal their characters in their thoughts and deeds. . . . Sand seldom analyses, and only the more subtle and obscure passions and motives. The difference in their delineation of character is precisely similar to that of their delineation of scenery: Balzac describes by accumulation of details, Sand by a few rapid strokes, bringing before you the scene with all its attendant emotions. Sand, like a poet, has known and felt life; Balzac has observed it. The one gives you her experience; the other his observation. The experience of Sand is shown in types. The observation of Balzac is conveyed through details of great accuracy and value, but they are details, and no more. It is also worthy of remark, that while George Sand's knowledge of passion is extensive and profound, that of Balzac is comparatively slight; at the same time his knowledge of motive is much greater. Sand, in her rich experience of life, knows passions because she has felt them, because she has been able to deeply scrutinize them in herself, as in others. (pp. 283-84)

> [G. H. Lewes,] *"Balzac and George Sand," in* The Foreign Quarterly Review, *Vol. XXXIII, No. LXVI, July, 1844, pp. 265-98.* *

GRAHAM'S MAGAZINE (essay date 1846)

George Sand has expended much composition on the rights and wrongs of woman, but in the delineation of Consuelo she has done more to exalt the sex than she could have achieved by a thousand thunders of declamation. Those who have imbibed strong prejudices against her, from the offensive scenes and opinions in some of her other novels, should not omit reading [*Consuelo*], her purest and greatest work. To us it appears to be one of the best and noblest fictions produced within the last twenty years, and to evince a power and originality of genius unmatched by any woman of the time. The character of Consuelo is wrought out with the most assiduous care, is exhibited under the severest trials, and comes forth from the fiery furnace of temptation and difficulty pure, high-hearted, more noble and beautiful than before. It is an exquisite ideal creation, distinguished by so many natural traits, and appealing so continually to the heart's deepest and finest sympathies, that the impression it leaves on the mind is of the most beautiful and lasting kind. The other characters evince a wide knowledge of life, and a keen insight into the springs of action and passion. Occasionally, however, the authoress allows the didactic spirit to overcome the representative, especially in the delineation of her base and vicious characters. As regards the morality of the book, it seems to us, judging from the impression it leaves on the mind as a whole, and not taking particular scenes as a ground for judgment, to be eminently moral. The author's mind, as displayed in this book at least, seems to have the utmost horror and disgust for profligacy, both in man and woman. To a person acclimated to Shakespeare, or even to Richardson, the freedom of representation in some chapters is not calculated to surprise. Indeed, we should think it ridiculous in an Englishman, tolerant of Byron, Moore and Bulwer, to be offended with this work of George Sand—which, less open to the censure even of prudery than their popular writings, is infinitely higher in principle.

> *"Review of New Books: 'Consuelo'," in* Graham's Magazine, *Vol. XXIX, No. 1, July, 1846, p. 107.*

[GEORGE HENRY LEWES] (essay date 1846)

'Jeanne' betrays not only a want of that profound truth which generally characterises George Sand's creations, but also a want of that animation and passion which irradiates them. There is somewhat of languor in the style, very unusual with her; which may probably arise from the false conception she is struggling to make real; a suspicion which seems confirmed by the vigour of some of the scenes, in which secondary persons and real passions come into play. On the whole, **'Jeanne'** may be recommended as a work which even girls may read: it contains nothing to ruffle the most delicate fastidiousness, nothing to scandalise the most inquisitive 'propriety.'

'Isidora' is rightly called a fragment. It is a careless affair; written probably for some feuilleton, and written in such haste, or with such carelessness, that no regard whatever has been paid to the most ordinary rules of construction. It begins by pretending to be extracts from two journals kept by a poor, ambitious youth, who lives in a garret communing with his thoughts. This stale device is quickly forgotten, and the narrative pursues its course, as if nothing of the kind had preceded. By the time we get to the second part, the narrative changes again, and is no longer told by the hero, but by the author. All this without a word of explanation. (p. 22)

This negligence, trivial in itself, is important as in indication of the state of literature. Of all the abuses of the press none need more vigilant repression, than the growing irreverence of Art manifested by the 'Free Pencils,' all over Europe. To write much is daily becoming a greater ambition than to write well. The demand is for quantity. Instead of exquisite stories in one or two volumes, carefully meditated, slowly written, we are now confronted on all sides with stories sprawling over ten volumes, written recklessly—or rather not written at all, but *dictated;* in which plan, probability, characterisation have to shift for themselves: if the can be improvised, so much the better; if not, we must put up with the loss. (p. 23)

Above all existing novelists, [George Sand] is the last who should succumb. There is not one, in any country, who can compete with her as an artist, or as a painter of passion and character. Few have had her deep and varied experience of life; none have had her power of pourtraying it. . . . Did she ever reflect that in those novels of hers, in which she pours forth that impassioned philosophy which she is so anxious should get a hearing, are wasted on a feuilleton, where readers have only time to scramble through and glance at the story? Evidently the feuilleton is the last place she should choose; and hers is the last sort of talent to succeed there.

We have been led into these remarks by the small fragment, entitled **'Isidora,'** which is quite unworthy of its author, being nothing more than a reproduction of old materials. Isidora herself is a fusion of **'Lélia'** and **'Pulcherie'**—but somewhat feeble; and the hero is one of those pale aspiring young men, without character, without force, whom the author has recently taken an affection to, but for whom we have no respect, in spite of their love of poetry, their reveries, and their purity. Madame Sand has seldom been happy in her heroes. Hitherto almost all her well-drawn young men were rascals; her pencil seemed to delight in drawing women and old men; her lovers were heartless or weak; now they are drivellers. (p. 24)

Let us add, however, that Madame Sand does not seem much to sympathise with them. Her better instincts constantly turn her elsewhere and force her, as it were, to ridicule her own creation. Thus in **'Le Meunier d'Angibault,'** Grand Louis is the real hero; the man after her heart; and in **'Le Péché de M. Antoine,'** the effervescence of Emile is contrasted with the practical head of Cardonnet, and the patient calmness of Bois-guilbault. We should be happy to see these better instincts gaining complete predominance; for we are heartily tired of the dreamy ineffectual young gentlemen. . . .

We had begun to despair of George Sand. The feebleness of the **'Comtesse de Rudoldstadt,'** and **'Jeanne,'**—the careless-ness and nothingness of **'Isidora'**—though all contained oc-casional passages such as no one else could pen—led us to suspect that the cry of 'George Sand has written herself out,' might not be one of envy, but of regret. Many were the mor-alising reflections this suspicion aroused in us; and we were beginning to accustom ourselves to the idea; for, said we, why should she not write herself out? has she not already presented an immense variety of characters—has she not given us the rich experience of a life, the profound thoughts of an extraor-dinary mind? The source must be dry some day; why not suppose it dry at present? Having consoled ourselves as we best could, there came **'Le Meunier d'Angibault'** to overthrow all our conclusions and once more to awaken our enthusiasm. How much of the rapture which this work roused may be owing to the force of contrast with the three preceding novels, we cannot determine; certain it is that in the **'Meunier,'** we recog-nised with delight the hand that wrote **'Valentine,' 'Simon,' 'Le Compagnon du Tour de France,'** which is not saying little. (p. 25)

The only fault with which we would reproach **'Le Meunier d'Angibault'** is [the] false conception of Marcelle and Henri. . . . All the rest is excellent in conception and execution; the style generally worthy of her pen, though sometimes more diffuse and vague than befits the author of **'Lélia'** and **'Jacques.'** It may not be uninteresting to add, that the present novel is quite unexceptionable on the score of morality; and may be read by any female of any age, provided she have no objection to an occasional Utopian tirade. . . .

'Teverino' came next. It is entitled 'une fantaisie,' and ap-peared in the feuilleton of *La Presse*. Here again the lovers are thrown into the shade, and the whole affair of their love is somewhat feeble and uninteresting. Teverino himself is a remarkable sketch, and though exaggerated, yet consistent. The Bird-catcher is a genuine bit of poetry; and the old *Curé* is well hit off. We see the traces of the author's genius; but we see also the fatal effects of the *feuilleton*. When one is gifted with a mind like that of George Sand, it is *lese-littérature* to abuse such gifts by squandering them upon trivialities. One who can create, should not descend to trifle. A 'fantaisie' is very well; but if the poet's imagination take such vagabond flights, it should at least be artistic in its plan. (p. 31)

'Le Péché de M. Antoine' is the last on our list, and has the merit at least of being a serious work. (p. 35)

The story is full of interest and the mystery well kept up. But we remark here, as elsewhere, how very pale are the colours in which George Sand now paints the passions she once de-picted with such unrivalled energy and truth. The impassioned author of **'Indiana,' 'Jacques,' 'Valentine'** and **'Mauprat,'** is scarcely to be recognised in **'La Comtesse de Rudoldstadt,' 'Jeanne,' 'Teverino,' 'Le Meunier'** and **'M. Antoine.'** The fire that glowed with such energy is exhausted. Timid readers are no longer startled by the vehement impetuosity and daring truth with which the human heart was laid bare; it beats feebly now; and if the timid be not startled, neither are they led away by irresistible fascination. Many worthy people will applaud the change; it makes the works more *moral,* as they say. We cannot but deplore it, for it makes the works commonplace. We cannot forget that the author was once a great poet, uttering in har-monious language the deep experience of life. (pp. 35-6)

Whence arises this feebleness? Is her genius exhausted? We can hardly think it. The early parts of **'Consuelo'** and the intense passion of **'Horace'** are too recent for us to suppose their author exhausted. But she had not descended into the *feuilleton* in those days. . . .

We may be wrong; but we venture on this friendly warning to Madame Sand: to quit the noisy feuilleton and to write once more slowly and exquisitely. . . .

Her recent novels are far inferior to their predecessors, and this inferiority coincides with her entrance into the feuilleton. The conclusion is obvious: either she has written herself out, or the feuilleton is fatal to her genius. (p. 36)

[*George Henry Lewes,*] *"George Sand's Recent Nov-els,"* in The Foreign Quarterly Review, *Vol. XXXVI, No. LXXIII, 1846, pp. 21-36.*

THE LITERARY WORLD   (essay date 1847)

[George Sand's *Jacques*] is bought and will be read; but a slight knowledge of its contents would operate as a timely warning, and certainly prevent many from introducing it into their fam-ilies. It is a false bad book, calculated to do great evil.

In saying this, we do not wish to be understood as underrating the talents of the author, or joining in the hasty condemnation of all her writings. She is a woman of great powers of mind, of a philosophical insight in the discrimination of character, of imagination expressed in her acute sympathies, and she conveys all this in a style of pure harmony. We must however stop short at *what violates the laws of decency,* not forbidding pictures of evil in a work of art, knowing that if they are historically true to human life, according to the just intentions of art, they will vindicate their morality by their warning. . . .

Jacques is a corrupt book; yet it has many noble and refined thoughts. Its heroism is spurious, its morality is contemptible; yet the ideas of morality and heroism are valiantly kept up, and need only the introduction of a few sound principles, with the consequent omission of some discreditable incidents, to make them not only endurable, but honorable. This need is everything. Jacques is a hero and a model of unconquerable self denial. Yet what a pitiable representative of nobleness he is! If this be any tribute to the author, and it certainly is, she gives us a much higher idea of the man than is realized in her descriptions and incidents. . . . Any unsophisticated reader, long before he gets through with these volumes, will sigh many times for one good kick of an Anglo-Saxon foot applied to the sneaking, seducing Octave. Yet this book, if justified at all, is to be justified by the heroism of Jacques. What is to be said of it then, when, making every allowance for the sentiments and fine expressions of this heroism, it occupies but a subordinate part of the volumes. For one hour of Jacques we have twenty-four of the seducer Octave, who is on a footing, in the house, of the most sickening domesticity. This portion of the work is disgusting. It could not have entered the mind of any English writer above the level of the stews. Compared with the indecencies of a writer like Swift, it is the stain of oil alongside that of mud. (p. 8)

The grand error of the work is its theory of passional harmony, and that too not of the development of all the passions, but of the morbid excesses of a single one; love is the business and sole thought of every personage in this book; life is to be devoted to the one object, the attainment of these affinities in a happy union. . . . If the book has any meaning at all, and it is didactic in every page, it inculcates this lesson, that the positive laws of God and man are to be set aside for the convenience of our self-love, inclination and will. . . .

As a picture of real life the book is naught, no such realities have existed in the world: as a work of Art it is in contradiction to one of the first principles of Art, unless we rake into the filth of Pompeii for a precedent, that the selection of the subject must not be injurious to good morals. . . .

The admirers of George Sand will probably say, that it is one of her earliest works, written in what is called the tumultuous period of her life, one of her few writings devoted to seduction, and that there are far better specimens of her morality and genius. If so, we can only say, that the choice of this work for translation and publication has been peculiarly unfortunate. (p. 9)

> *"'Jacques'," in* The Literary World, *Vol. I, No. 1, February 6, 1847, pp. 8-9.*

THE CHRISTIAN EXAMINER AND RELIGIOUS MISCELLANY (essay date 1847)

[George Sand's] pet notion of the wrongs of women drives her into peevish and aimless complainings, and without so much as endeavouring to point out a remedy, she vents, through pages of discontented declamation, her uneasiness and her disgust with the age, and with its husbands in particular. The darkest feature in her conjugal creed is, that she shows us no ray of hope, no method of relief. . . . In her ardent rebellion at marital abuses, she concedes no advantages and no peace to our present matrimonial alliances. By ridicule, by argument,

by sarcasm, by paradoxes, by picturing, by attacks direct and allusions indirect, she holds them up as preposterous and debasing. Her genius is essentially destructive. She is a thoroughpaced radical, and, forsaking the course of wise reformers, she gives us no hint of the form or proportions of the structure that is to rise from the proposed ruins. (p. 209)

We are quite sure that the sort of cure demanded for the matrimonial evils of this age is not [to be found in her characters]. . . . [We] can discover hardly a female in all the group of her creations who is not thrusting upon us, *ad nauseam,* some wearisome evidence of the omnipresent influence of the sexual appetite. Such ceaseless harping on that single passion is to the last degree disgusting. We had supposed pure-minded women made the topic a stranger to their thoughts.

But, according to our author's standard, it would seem that female experience, of a high, thrilling order, must be shockingly incomplete without a lapse or two from virtue. A life of uniform, chaste contentment, domestic self-denial and forbearance, is altogether too tame, commonplace, stupid, for romantic moralists of your women-in-pantaloons school. This is precisely the pernicious, seductive, mischief-working stuff which ought to be ejected from all righteous and home-loving society. It is as contemptible as it is unblushing. (pp. 210-11)

[A] writer whose experience has been of that mournful character, whose path has been in places forbidden of God and every high and holy sentiment in the soul, should certainly show us, in her Magdalen confessions, no taint of remaining passion, no delight in the polluted scenes she has forsaken. She should either observe the modesty of silence, or speak language lifted far above suspicion,—language betokening regrets unspeakably solemn, breathing an unsullied purity, and never rousing one ambiguous emotion. This indicates the charge we have to bring against George Sand. It is not that she pays no formal and verbal homage to virtue; for she has many beautiful tributes to that heavenly power which every human soul, in its inmost depths, must sometimes revere with a feeling akin to worship. . . . It is not that she jests at crime, and ridicules purity,—the abominable sin of so much of English literature; her disposition is not of the jocose or even humorous order. It is not that she does not sometimes make vice reap a harvest of wretchedness. It is not that she has a base intention, and *means* to preach impurity at all. But it is that, by the infelicitous and terrible sway of a diseased and abused nature, there creeps into her writings a subtle and almost indefinable spirit which the instinct of a pure heart revolts from. It is that vague but ugly something, which the quick moral sense detects instantly as corrupt, and shuns as poisonous, insinuating itself into her descriptions by force of an inward coarseness long indulged and not yet quite subdued,—herself not willing it, probably unconscious of it. . . . (p. 214)

[We] have repeatedly laid down her books with the feeling of having been in an unwholesome presence,—with much the same sensation as that with which one escapes from an ill-ventilated apartment into the open air.

We cannot omit to say, in passing, that this lady has a way of recommending petty falsehoods. She attributes, not to her worse or doubtful characters alone, but to those that are in other respects quite exemplary, this vicious trick of lying. And so far from representing the habit as objectionable, she leaves us to infer that it is a very pretty accomplishment. (p. 220)

By far the most weighty fault in George Sand's writings pertains, however, not to her views of any one specific subject or statute of morality, but to the principle that lies at the very foundation of her religious philosophy. There is a fatal absence of any believing recognition of Christ and Christianity. (p. 221)

[Aesthetics] is the substitute for theology; art, for Christian faith; associations of artists and artisans, for the Christian Church; the admiration of the beautiful, for piety towards God; and homage to genius, for the worship of the Father. (p. 222)

Of the literary execution of George Sand's writings, in general, it is not easy to speak in terms of too high commendation. Apart from an occasional extravagance . . . which finds its way sometimes from her strain of feeling into her style, that style is one of rare excellence. She writes always with beauty, often with singular power. (p. 223)

Among the intellectual manifestations of the age she is one of the more remarkable phenomena. With a mind capable of diversified and intense action,—with large resources, derived rather from an eager and penetrating observation, from an intuitive perception of the significance and relations of things, not unassisted by reflection, than from learned investigations, informed rather by insight than by research,—with an imagination vivid and not easily fatigued in its flights,—with a strong command of pathos, and a stronger of satire,—with an extraordinary mastery of the flexible qualities of the French language,—with these brilliant endowments, she is equal, intellectually, to high endeavours and unusual achievements. . . . Unfortunately, the strength of her moral principles has not balanced the vigor of her mind. Accordingly, we see in her one of those sad spectacles of which literary history exhibits too many;—genius wandering from rectitude; conscience unsettled from its throne; no firm faith to harmonize and tranquillize the motions of a soul, deploring in bitter lamentations, now in whinings of discontent, now in shrieks of anguish, its desolation and its misery. She has deep, fervent sympathies with her kind, and she would rejoice to deliver them from the inequalities, wrongs, sufferings, that burden them. But for the office of a genuine reformer it is to be feared she has unfitted herself. Her spirit has not the healthful, genial tone which to the true reformer is indispensable. . . . Her energy has not the magnificence of a surface in repose, hiding invincible powers beneath. She chafes peevishly, and raves frantically, and sometimes rails almost spitefully. Some of her most eloquent and splendid passages, like that at the conclusion of **"Lelia"** for example, lose a great part of their force and beauty by their exaggerations; they are not true, they grossly misrepresent the age, and abuse humanity. For the prophet's vocation, the loftiest human calling, she has not the needed consecration. . . . She drank too deeply of the world's most poisonous cup; and though she has repented with a sorrow that we would not doubt is accepted of Heaven, yet the dregs have left disease and imbecility in her constitution. . . . [The books that] chronicle the vagaries of her struggling philosophy, can do little service to the substantial welfare of men. (pp. 224-26)

> F.D.H., *"Writings of George Sand,"* in The Christian Examiner and Religious Miscellany, *Vol. VII, No. II, March, 1847, pp. 201-27.*

BENTLEY'S MISCELLANY   (essay date 1850)

The intellectual power of George Sand is attested by the suffrages of Europe. The use to which she has put it is another question. Unfortunately, she has applied it, for the most part, to so bad a use, that half the people who acknowledge the ascendancy of her genius, see too much occasion to deplore its perversion.

The principles she has launched upon the world have an inevitable tendency towards the disorganization of all existing institutions, political and social. This is the broad, palpable fact, let sophistry disguise or evade it as it may. Whether she pours out an intense novel that shall plough up the roots of the domestic system, or composes a proclamation for the Red Republicans that shall throw the streets into a flame, her influence is equally undeniable and equally pernicious.

It has been frequently urged, in the defence of her novels, that they do not assail the institution of marriage, but the wrongs that are perpetrated in its name. Give her the full benefit of her intention, and the result is still the same. Her eloquent expositions of ill-assorted unions—her daring appeals from the obligations they impose, to the affections they outrage—her assertion of the rights of nature over the conventions of society, have the final effect of justifying the violation of duty on the precarious ground of passion and inclination. . . . A writer who really meant to vindicate an institution against its abuses, would adopt a widely different course; and it is only begging George Sand out of the hands of the jury to assert that the *intention* of her writings is opposed to their *effect,* which is to sap the foundations upon which the fabric of domestic life reposes. (pp. 506-07)

But time that mellows all things has not been idle with George Sand. (p. 508)

And now comes an entirely new phase in the development of George Sand's mind. . . . [She] has recently produced a work . . . which is in the highest degree chaste in conception, and full of simplicity and truthfulness in the execution. This work is in the form of a three-act comedy, and is called **"François le Champi."** (pp. 508-09)

The domestic morality, the quiet nature, the *home feeling* of this comedy may be described as something wonderful for George Sand; not that her genius was not felt to be plastic enough for such a display, but that nobody suspected she could have accomplished it with so slight an appearance of artifice or false sentiment, or with so much geniality and faith in its truth. (p. 509)

The actual story of **"François le Champi"** . . . is so slight as to throw the whole interest into the dialogue. Action, there is little or none; the vital charm of the piece consisting in the truthfulness of treatment. . . . (p. 510)

The character of Madeleine is exquisitely drawn; frank, gentle, transparent to the depths of her truthful nature, and swaying all around her by the mere force of love and goodness. The open, honest, strong, and tender-hearted François is every way worthy of her. All the members of this domestic group, even down to Catherine, whose fidelity lifts her into importance, put forward irresistible claims to our sympathy and admiration. They belong to the real world of country life—even the malice of Sévére is full of the meannesses and pettinesses, the low spite and gossiping slander of the village mischief-maker. The art of the author is deficient only in one point—the history of François himself. Being a foundling, and having a large sum of money sent to him mysteriously by his mother, we look forward to a sequel or explanation which never comes. As he is the hero of the piece, we have a right to know all about him, or at least not to be tantalized, and then left in the dark. (pp. 510-11)

"The Genius of George Sand," in Bentley's Miscellany, *Vol. XXVII, 1850, pp. 506-13.*

THE LIVING AGE   (essay date 1857)

The novels of George Sand are seldom entertaining; and the last she has written, *La Daniella,* is perhaps less entertaining than any of its predecessors. Whatever may be the merits of the writer, it is hard work reading through two thick volumes of a fiction where there is scarcely any plot—where the characters are sketched faintly, and hinted at rather than fully delineated—and where there is little to startle, amuse, or touch us. *La Daniella* has the great fault which marks all the recent productions of George Sand—it is very much too long. It is spun out with an audacious prolixity, as if the writer were amusing herself with seeing how much she could make the public read. Perhaps this prolixity may arise from a wish to meet the demands of the publisher for a two-volumed story; or possibly, it springs from what is a very prominent characteristic of the writer's mind. George Sand is essentially reflective and self-contemplative—she writes because she feels, and as she feels. It is the world within, and not the world without, with which she occupies herself. Being, however, of an impulsive and passionate nature, certain subjects, such as the problems of social life and the range of artistic excitement, have taken a deep hold on her imagination. While these subjects were new to her, she worked them with a spontaneous life and freshness which enabled her in a great measure to dispense with action and incident in her fictions. Now that she has grown calmer, sadder—in one word, older—she gives us reflections as original and as suggestive as ever, but which, from the very fact that they are truer to life and nature, more soberly expressed, and more patiently elaborated, have less to stimulate and fascinate the reader. It is not that her powers have decayed, but their maturity itself makes her productions less effective. Secure of an attentive audience, she goes on page after page writing whatever comes uppermost, without regard either for those whom she addresses, or for the puppets of her romance. But, although *La Daniella,* in which she has indulged her genius to the uttermost, is tedious, spiritless, and flat, it bears abundant traces of a master-hand. It contains many passages which no one but George Sand could have written—passages full of subtlety, of a nobleness of aspiration, and of nice observation, and expressed with that wonderful grace, ease and *abandon,* the command of which is the greatest of her gifts. (p. 574)

The scene of the story is laid in the vicinity of Rome. There are many authors who can describe scenery more distinctly and effectively than George Sand; but there is no one who can surpass her in the power of giving an impression of the deep feeling with which the scenery described has possessed itself of the mind of the writer, or who more thoroughly carries the charm of personality, and of a subjective richness of meaning, into representations of the external world. She has a singular facility in marking out some features of what she wishes to paint, which stamp the scenery portrayed forever in our recollection. (p. 575)

But although there are many fruits of this artistic sensibility scattered through the work, it is not these fruits that constitute the chief excellence of *La Daniella.* It is in the analysis of the less obvious relations of the sexes—of the treacherous delights of female friendship, and the rough differences of married lovers—that George Sand shows the full scope of her genius. *La Daniella* has much of this analysis wherewith to reward the patient reader. As a novel, it can never be popular; but it is

not without importance as a sample of French literature, and it cannot fail to interest all who wish to watch the course through which so remarkable a mind as that of its author is carried in the progress of its development. (p. 576)

"'La Daniella'," in The Living Age, *Vol. 55, No. 705, November 28, 1857, pp. 574-76.*

[JULIA WARD HOWE]   (essay date 1861)

Was [George Sand] not to all of us, in our early years, a name of doubt, dread, and enchantment? Did not all of us feel, in our young admiration for her, something of the world's great struggle between conservative discipline and revolutionary inspiration? We knew our parents would not have us read her, *if they knew.* We knew they were right. Yet we read her at stolen hours, with waning and still entreated light; and as we read, in a dreary wintry room, with the flickering candle warning us of late hours and confiding expectations, the atmosphere grew warm and glorious about us,—a true human company, a living sympathy crept near us,—the very world seemed not the same world after as before. She had given us a real gift; no criticism could take it away. The hands might be sinful, but the box they broke contained an exceeding precious ointment.

At a later day we saw these things rather differently. The electric intoxication over, which book or being gives but once to the same person, its elements were viewed with some distrust. Passing from ideal to real life, as all pass, who live on, we shook our heads over the books, sighed, ceased to read them. Grown mothers ourselves, we quietly removed them as far as possible from the young hands about us, and would rather have deprived them of the noble French language altogether than have allowed it to bring them such lessons as *Jacques* and *Valentine.* Yet we retain the old love for her; the world of literature still seems brighter for her footsteps; and should we live to learn her death, tears must follow it, and the sense of void left by the loss of a true friend, noble and loyalhearted, if mistaken. (p. 514)

[Julia Ward Howe,] "George Sand," in The Atlantic Monthly, *Vol. VIII, No. XLIX, November, 1861, pp. 513-34.*

EUGENE BENSON   (essay date 1867)

George Sand could not be silent; she is the voice of her age; through her, not France alone, but Europe, has spoken. . . . [She] has sought to express the spiritual and moral needs of her age, to unmask established forms of injustice, to expose the pretensions of customs derived from an old and different order of society, to weaken social bonds that retard and often paralyze the best impulses, and destroy the free activity of men. It was for this that George Sand, artist in her genius and in her instincts, has been the conscience, the moral sense, and the intellectual protest of her time; it was for this that she has been forced to produce such an amazing quantity of work, as from an inexhaustible source; it was for this that she has been animated by a genius at once artistic and moral, at once unrestrained and self-possessed. Madame George Sand, who has shocked moral people in England, American and France, is among French writers an example of purity and nobleness. But she is altogether too grand and impassioned a type of woman, too comprehensive in her mind, covers too much of the moral and intellectual world, to be measured by the literary retailers, and the literary yard-sticks of our ordinary or average life. We need to extend the scale when we wish to estimate her proportions. The New Testament, Rousseau, Byron, the revolutions of '89 and '48 (the first before her birth), Europe, the whole of art, ancient and modern, and nature—most loving and intimate and intelligent intercourse with nature from childhood—went to form Madame George Sand, to enter and possess, and become a part of her genius. No woman ever lived who has been subjected to such varied and powerful influences. (pp. 243-44)

[Though] love is the vivifying and dominant sentiment of her life, nay more, the passion of her life, an ideal at once half pagan and half Christian—pagan in its voluptuous and natural beauty, Christian in its vague and infinite spirituality—yet her literary and socialistic work covers more ground than that intense and comprehensive passion. . . . The riotous *abandon* of antique passion modified or spiritualized by the Christian sentiment, is what Madame George Sand means when she writes the word *love*. But she has another great word and another great inspiration—*nature*. Taught by nature, moved by love, she formed generous ideas of the liberation of man and the restoration of society. She has carried the idea of nature, the idea of love, the idea of worship, throughout her life, and her various works either illustrate one or all of these ideas, and in every case show a strong and intelligent sentiment of art. Whatever relates to or affects the social being of man has possessed her and agitated her; through her agitation, through her unrest, she has revealed the social disorders of the time, she has struggled and lifted up her voice of despair or of warning. She has written books mournful as music, yet so full of the beautiful that, like pictures, they hold us by indescribable charms. She has passed through every possible sensation; but revolt against society and its monstrous iniquities, and the consequent indignation of her outraged moral sense, religious questionings and seekings, and passion for the beautiful have led every other feeling and conquered every other idea. The bitterness, and sadness, and magnetic beauty of her books cannot be equalled. (p. 246)

. . . . .

George Sand is not the Parisian writer—the writer who best represents the common idea of "French style and spirit;" she is rather a continental mind that uses the French language. Her work has an infusion of the German spirit, but shows the dominance of the love of form which belongs to the Latin race. George Sand is French in her ideas, in her courage, in her ardor; she is continental in her comprehensiveness and in her sympathies. . . . Among novel-writers George Sand has often been called the literary expression of the artistic spirit. It is unquestionable that she has understood best, and sympathized most deeply with that spirit; but to most persons such a definition of her work limits it to the idea of the beautiful and the impulse of lawlessness. But as a writer she cannot be so limited. She has made her works expressive of the whole scale of modern life—its religion, morality, and sentiment of the beautiful. Yet not once has she consented to the mercenary or prosaic spirit of modern life. Her whole effort has been to react against the mercenary and prosaic, and it was this reaction which outraged and made uncomfortable more prudent persons. The great charm of her works is their spontaneity, their unforced fulness of expression; and their chief trait is flexibility. George Sand's mind may be characterized as noble, flexible and lucid. . . .

[Say] she has a vast and vital appreciation of form; that she is firm, large, lucid, and, though ample, not diffuse, and you have spoken the best words to describe her genius. (p. 619)

As an example of genius, harmonious and unrestrained, and a woman, I do not know her peer among contemporary names. And one of the most beautiful facts about her works is the dominance of the benevolent spirit. You recognize the *maternal* element as strongest. She yearns to do good, to influence, to ennoble, to stimulate; and by common consent, she is the noblest mind that, among European writers, has used the novel as a means of acting on the great reading public. (p. 620)

> Eugene Benson, "George Sand and Her Works," in The Galaxy, *Vol. III, February 1 and March 15, 1867, pp. 240-48, 618-24.*

HENRY JAMES (essay date 1876)

[George Sand's novels] are a very extraordinary and splendid series, and certainly one of the great literary achievements of our time. . . . She was an *improvisatrice,* raised to a very high power; she told stories as a nightingale sings. No novelist answers so well to the childish formula of "making up as you go along." Other novels seem meditated, pondered, calculated, thought out and elaborated with a certain amount of trouble; but the narrative with Madame Sand always appears to be an invention of the moment, flowing from a mind which a constant process of quiet contemplation, absorption and reverie keeps abundantly supplied with material. It is a sort of general emanation, an intellectual evaporation. There had been plenty of improvisation before the author of **"Consuelo,"** but it had never been—and it has never been in other hands—of so fine a quality. She had a natural gift of style which is certainly one of the most remarkable of our day; her diction from the first ripe and flexible, and seemed to have nothing to learn from practice. The literary form of her writing has always been exquisite, and this alone would have sufficed to distinguish it from the work of the great body of clever scribblers who spin their two or three plots a year. Some of her novels are very inferior to others; some of them show traces of weariness, of wandering attention, of a careless choice of subject; but the manner, at the worst, never sinks below a certain high level—the tradition of good writing is never lost. In this bright, voluminous envelope, it must be confessed that Madame Sand has sometimes wrapped up a rather flimsy kernel; some of her stories will not bear much thinking over. But her great quality from the first was the multiplicity of her interests and the activity of her sympathies. She passed through a succession of phases, faiths and doctrines—political, religious, moral, social, personal—and to each she gave a voice which the conviction of the moment made eloquent. She gave herself up to each as if it were to be final, and in every case she turned her steps behind her. . . . She accepted as much of every influence as suited her, and when she had written a novel or two about it she ceased to care about it. This proves her, doubtless, to have been a decidedly superficial moralist; but it proves her to have been a born romancer. It is by the purely romantic side of her productions that she will live. It is a misfortune that she pretended to moralize to the extent that she did, for about moral matters her head was not at all clear. It had now and then capital glimpses and inspirations, but her didacticism has always seemed to me what an architectural drawing would be, executed by a person who should turn up his nose at geometry. Madame Sand's straight lines are straight by a happy chance—and for people of genius there are so many happy chances. She was without a sense of certain differences—the difference between the pure and the impure—the things that are possible for people of a certain delicacy, and the things that are not.

When she struck the right notes, and so long as she continued to strike them, the result was charming, but a sudden discord was always possible. Sometimes the right note was admirably prolonged—as for instance in her masterpiece, **"Consuelo."** . . . [As] she advanced in life she wrote her stories more and more for the story's sake, and attempted to prove nothing more alarming than that human nature is on the whole tolerably noble and generous. After this pattern she produced a long list of masterpieces. Her imagination seemed gifted with perpetual youth; the freshness of her invention was marvelous. Her novels have a great many faults; they lack three or four qualities which the realistic novel of the last thirty or forty years, with its great successes, has taught us to consider indispensable. They are not exact nor probable; they contain few living figures; they produce a limited amount of illusion. Madame Sand created no figures that have passed into common life and speech; her people are usually only very picturesque, very voluble, and very "high-toned" shadows. But the shadows move to such a persuasive music that we watch them with interest. The art of narration is extraordinary. This was Madame Sand's great art. The recital moves along with an evenness, a lucidity, a tone of seeing, feeling, knowing everything, a reference to universal things, a sentimental authority, which makes the reader care for the characters in spite of his incredulity and feel anxious about the story in spite of his impatience. He feels that the author holds in her hands a stringed instrument composed of the chords of the human soul. (pp. 133-35)

> *Henry James, "George Sand" (originally published in the* New York Tribune, *July 22, 1876), in his* Literary Reviews and Essays: On American, English, and French Literature, *edited by Albert Mordell, Twayne Publishers, 1957, pp. 130-35.*

F. M. DOSTOIEVSKY (essay date 1876)

[George Sand] was unreservedly one of our (*i.e.*, *our*) contemporaries—an idealist of the Thirties and Forties. Hers is one of those names of our mighty, self-confident, and at the same time sick, century, replete with most obscure ideals and unattainable desires—those names which, having arisen over there, in "the land of sacred miracles," have enticed from us, out of our Russia, which is eternally in a state of creation, all too many thoughts, all too much love, holy and noble enthusiasm, *élan vital*, all too many dear convictions. . . . Let these words of mine cause no surprise—especially as applied to George Sand, about whom even in our days there may be arguments, and whom half of the people in Russia, if not nine-tenths of them, have forgotten. But, nevertheless, in the past she did accomplish in Russia her task, and who if not we—her contemporaries of the whole world—should gather at her grave to say a word in her memory? . . . Oh, of course, many will smile maybe when reading what significance I attribute to George Sand; but those who might be amused would not be right. . . . [Everything] in the being of this poetess that constituted a "new word," all that was "universally human" in her—all this, at the time, was promptly reflected in our Russia as a strong and profound impression; it did not escape us, thereby proving the fact that every poet-innovator in Europe, everyone who appeared there with a novel thought and with fresh vigor, cannot help but become forthwith a Russian poet, cannot avoid Russian thought, and almost becomes a Russian force. (pp. 342-44)

[At] the very beginning of the Thirties, we took cognizance of that immense European literary movement. The names of many newly appearing orators, historians, tribunes and professors were already known. Though partly and only superficially, it became known whither this movement tended. And most passionately it has revealed itself in art, in fiction, and principally—in George Sand. (p. 345)

At that time people in Europe were saying that she preached a new status for woman and she prophesied "the rights of free wifehood." . . . But this was not quite so, since her sermons were by no means confined to woman alone; nor did she ever invent the term "free wifehood." George Sand belonged to the whole movement, and not to the mere sermons on women's rights. True, being a woman herself, she naturally preferred to portray *heroines* rather than heroes, and, of course, women of the whole world should now don mourning garb in her memory, because one of their loftiest and most beautiful representatives has passed away, and, in addition, an almost unprecedented woman by reason of the power of her mind and talent—a name which has become historical and which is destined not to be forgotten by, or to disappear from, European humanity.

As for her heroines . . . , I was astonished from the very start—ever since the age of sixteen—by the strangeness of the contradiction between what people had been writing and saying about her, and what in reality I personally perceived. In fact, many—at least, several—of her heroines represented a type of such elevated moral purity that it could not have been conceived without an immense ethical quest in the soul of the poetess herself; without the confession of most complete duty; without the comprehension and admission of most sublime beauty and mercy, patience and justice. True, side by side with mercy, patience and the acknowledgment of the obligations of duty, there was the extraordinary pride of the quest and of the protest; yet it was precisely that pride which was so precious because it sprang from the most sublime truth, without which mankind could never have retained its place on so lofty a moral height. This pride is not rancour *quand même*, based upon the idea that I am better than you, and you are worse than me; nay, this is merely a feeling of the most chaste impossibility of compromise with untruth and vice, although—I repeat—this feeling precludes neither all-forgiveness nor mercy. Moreover, commensurately with this pride, an enormous duty was to be assumed. These heroines of hers thirsted for sacrifices and heroic deeds. I was then particularly fond of several girl characters in her early works, which were portrayed, for example, in the then so-called Venetian novels . . .—types which culminated in the romance *Jeanne*, an altogether ingenious work setting forth a serene and, perhaps, an incontestable solution of the historical question of Joan of Arc. In a contemporary peasant girl she suddenly resurrects before the reader the image of the historical Joan of Arc, and graphically justifies the actual possibility of that majestic and miraculous event. This is a typically Georgesandesque task, since no one but she among contemporary poets bore in the soul so pure an ideal of an innocent girl—pure and so potent by reason of its innocence. These girl characters, to which I am referring, reiterate in several successive works one and the same problem, one and the same theme (not only girls, however: this theme was later reiterated in the magnificent novel *La Marquise*, also one of her early works). (pp. 347-48)

George Sand was not a thinker but she was one of the most clairvoyant foreseers (if this flourishing term be permitted) of a happy future awaiting mankind, in the realization of whose ideals she had confidently and magnanimously believed all her life—this because she herself was able to conceive this ideal in her soul. The preservation of this faith to the end is usually the lot of all lofty souls, of all genuine friends of humanity. . . . [George Sand] was perhaps, without knowing it herself, one of the staunchest confessors of Christ. She based her socialism, her convictions, her hopes and her ideals upon the moral feeling of man, upon the spiritual thirst of mankind and its longing for perfection and purity, and not upon "ant-necessity." All her life she believed absolutely in human personality (to the point of its immortality), elevating and broadening this concept in each one of her works; and thereby she concurred in thought and feeling with one of the basic ideas of Christianity, *i.e.,* the recognition of human personality and its freedom (consequently, also of its responsibility). Hence, the recognition of duty and the austere moral quests, and the complete acknowledgment of man's responsibility. And, perhaps, in the France of her time there was no thinker and no writer who understood as clearly as she that "man shall not live by bread alone." As to the pride of her quests and of her protest—I repeat—this pride never precluded mercy, forgiveness of offense, or even boundless patience based upon compassion for the offender himself. On the contrary, time and again, in her works George Sand has been captivated by the beauty of these truths and on more than one occasion she has portrayed characters of the most sincere forgiveness and love. (pp. 349-50)

> *F. M. Dostoievsky, "The Death of George Sand. . . . A Few Words about George Sand" (1876), in his* The Diary of a Writer, *edited and translated by Boris Brasol (translation copyright 1949 by Charles Scribner's Sons; copyright renewed 1976 by James Maxwell Fassett, Executor of the Estate of Boris Brasol; reprinted with the permission of Charles Scribner's Sons), Charles Scribner's Sons, 1949 (and reprinted by George Braziller, 1954), pp. 341-49.*

FREDERIC W. H. MYERS (essay date 1877)

A great spirit has passed from among us; and many, no doubt, have of late been endeavouring to realise distinctly what kind of pleasure they have drawn, what lessons they have learnt, from the multitudinous writings of the most noteworthy woman, with perhaps one exception, who has appeared in literature since Sappho.

To estimate the general result and outcome of a series of romances like George Sand's is no easy task. For while on the one hand they contain implicitly what amounts to a kind of system of philosophy and theology, yet on the other hand the exposition of this system is so fluctuating and fitful, so modified by the dramatic necessities of varied plots, that it is hard to disentangle the operative and permanent from the inert and accidental matter. (p. 221)

In the earlier romances, the Romances of Search, we hear her appealing with passionate earnestness for light and revelation to an irresponsive heaven. And in the Romances of Exposition, which constitute the great bulk of her works, we have the scheme of the universe, at which she ultimately arrived, enforced upon us in a hundred different ways. . . . Briefly stated, it is much as follows:—There is a God, inconceivable and unknown, but approachable by prayer under the aspect of a Father in Heaven; there is a Holy Spirit, or ceaseless influx of grace and light, receivable by sincere and ardent souls: and among the beings who have been filled fullest with this divine inspiration the first place belongs to Jesus Christ, whose life is the highest model which humanity has known. Progress is

the law of the universe; the soul's progress, begun on earth, is continued through an infinite series of existences; nor is there any soul which may not ultimately rise to purity and happiness. Unselfish love is the best and most lasting of earthly experiences, for a love begun on earth may endure for ever. Marriage affords the best and the normal setting for such love; but under exceptional circumstances it may exist outside the married state. Religious aspiration and unselfish love should form, as it were, the spirit of life; its substance is best filled out by practical devotion to some impersonal ideal,—the scientific or meditative observation of Nature, the improvement of the condition of the people, or the realisation of our visionary conceptions in a sincere and noble art. (p. 223)

[The] characteristic moral of George Sand's books—the doctrine that every elevation, whether of a class or of an individual, must be effected primarily from *within*—is as strongly insisted on in the case of the working classes as in the somewhat similar case of the female sex. . . . And, in fact, few of her books are without some example of a working man (or woman) whose self-reverence and self-control end by placing him on an acknowledged equality with those whose original station was far above his own. And, like the author of *Felix Holt*, George Sand is always anxious to show that a true rise in life does not necessarily consist in a man's quitting the class in which he was born, but rather in his rendering the appropriate work of that class worthy of any class by thoroughness, honesty, artistic or scientific skill. (p. 226)

[Concerning] George Sand's treatment of the duties and position of *women*, we find that the distinction between the two periods of her writings, between what we have called the Romances of Search and the Romances of Exposition, is very marked. Her first few books were written when the world seemed crumbling around her, when distressing doubt had succeeded to Christian ecstasy, and a most unsuitable and painful marriage to the tranquil affections of her convent and her country home. These books, of which **Lélia** is the type, are the cry of a bewildered child for the light: they are the dizzy and Byronic phase of a nature essentially just and serene. . . . But it is not from these immature and dreamy productions that she ought to be judged.

In the Romances of Exposition, of which **Consuelo** is one of the earliest, and one of the best, examples, we find the question of Women's Rights treated in an eminently sound spirit; that is, we find a series of impressive but temperate protests against such injustices towards women as are sanctioned in France by society and law, but coupled herewith a continual encouragement to women to begin by developing and respecting themselves—to *deserve* at any rate the respect of men, and to be confident that the state of any class of human beings will ultimately conform itself to their intrinsic deserts. This is the chief lesson of Consuelo's history. . . . (p. 227)

In a series of works, one of whose main themes is the power which women possess of elevating their character, and rectifying the injustices of their position by the exercise of 'self-reverence, self-knowledge, self-control,' it is painful to observe the frequent recurrence of the pervading fault of French literature—even of much of that literature which is meant to have, and has, a direct moral tendency—namely, a want of reticence and delicacy in matters connected with the relation between the sexes. Probably this disagreeable characteristic of so many of the best French books should in great measure be considered simply as a branch of that general want of dignity and reserve, to which the French character is so unfortunately prone. (pp. 227-28)

George Sand is capable of maintaining a level of lofty and militant purity; many of her books are wholly free from any kind of taint; but in others we feel the need of that instinctive incapacity to dwell on anything gross or morbid which is the glory of the best English literature, and of that literature almost alone. It should be observed, however, that one accusation, which has been brought against George Sand's novels, that they tend to bring the institution of marriage into contempt, can certainly not be maintained. Few authors have more convincingly insisted on the paramount excellence of a single, a permanent, a wedded affection. Few have more unshrinkingly exposed the misery which follows on the caprices of selfish and transitory passion. (p. 228)

George Sand is before all things *catholic* in her conception of human passion; . . . her romances are not mere illustrations of some favourite theory or special pleadings in defence of some personal cause.

There is no doubt one form of love which occurs oftenest in her books, especially where a woman is telling her own story— namely, the protective and admiring compassion which a woman of strong nature may feel for a gifted, but weak or faulty man. This form of affection was abundantly illustrated by George Sand's own history; and seems to be allied to that eager maternal instinct which was the dominant emotion of her life. . . . (p. 230)

The results of [her] excessive haste are most marked in her earlier writings. She has not had time to make them short. The grace of her language never fails, but she is often tedious and full of repetitions, and before she has gained experience of life she tends to be fantastic and unreal. Much of *Lélia,* though the book created so great a sensation, seems now unreadably dull. As time goes on her style improves its dignity and melody remain; its *longueurs* gradually disappear. From *Consuelo* onwards she seems able to say whatever she wishes in admirable form. . . . With maturity she gained simplicity; her pastoral romances are models of pastoral speech, and her latest works, *Flamarande, La Tour de Percemont,* &c., are almost as concise and clear as Voltaire himself.

But certain characteristics remain unchanged through the five-and-forty years of her literary life. In almost all the books there is the same air of unlaboured spontaneity and irresistible inspiration; in almost all there is the same subordination of the verisimilitude of minor events to the development of one central character, one dominant idea, one absorbing passion. And the defects of a class of romances which aim so high are almost inseparable from their merits. (pp. 232-33)

> *Frederic W. H. Myers, "George Sand," in* The Nineteenth Century, *Vol. 1, No. 2, April, 1877, pp. 221-41.*

MATTHEW ARNOLD   (essay date 1877)

[In the evolution of] three elements,—the passion of agony and revolt, the consolation from nature and from beauty, the ideas of social renewal,—in the evolution of these is George Sand and George Sand's life and power. Through their evolution her constant motive declares and unfolds itself . . . : 'the sentiment of the ideal life, which is none other than man's normal life as we shall one day know it.' This is the motive, and through these elements is its evolution; an evolution pursued, moreover, with the most unfailing resolve, the most absolute sincerity.

The hour of agony and revolt passed away for George Sand, as it passed away for Goethe, as it passes away for their readers likewise. It passes away and does not return; yet those who, amid the agitations, more or less stormy, of their youth, betook themselves to the early works of George Sand, may in later life cease to read them, indeed, but they can no more forget them than they can forget *Werther.* . . . How the sentences from George Sand's works of that period still linger in our memory and haunt the ear with their cadences! Grandiose and moving, they come, those cadences, like the sighing of the wind through the forest, like the breaking of the waves on the sea-shore. (pp. 322-23)

George Sand is one of the few French writers who keep us closely and truly intimate with rural nature. . . . Nowhere has she touched her native Berry and its little-known landscape, its *campagnes ignorées,* with a lovelier charm than in *Valentine.* (p. 328)

How faithful and close it is, this contact of George Sand with country things, with the life of nature in its vast plenitude and pathos! And always in the end the human interest, as is right, emerges and predominates. What is the central figure in the fresh and calm rural world of George Sand? It is the peasant. And what is the peasant? He is France, life, the future. And this is the strength of George Sand, and of her second movement, after the first movement of energy and revolt was over, towards nature and beauty, towards the country, towards primitive life, the peasant. She regarded nature and beauty, not with the selfish and solitary joy of the artist who but seeks to appropriate them for his own purposes, she regarded them as a treasure of immense and hitherto unknown application, as a vast power of healing and delight or all, and for the peasant first and foremost. Yes, she cries, the simple life is the true one! but the peasant, the great organ of that life, 'the minister in that vast temple which only the sky is vast enough to embrace,' the peasant is not doomed to toil and moil in it for ever, overdone and unawakened, like Holbein's labourer, and to have for his best comfort the thought that death will set him free. (pp. 331-32)

Joy is the great lifter of men, the great unfolder. (p. 332)

In all this we are passing from the second element in George Sand to the third,—her aspiration for a social new-birth, a *renaissance sociale.* It is eminently the ideal of France; it was hers. (p. 334)

[For] almost every Englishman Madame Sand's strong language about equality, and about France as the chosen vessel for exhibiting it, will sound exaggerated. 'The human ideal,' she says, 'as well as the social ideal, is to achieve equality.' France, which has made equality its rallying cry, is therefore 'the nation which loves and is loved.' . . . The republic of equality is in her eyes 'an ideal, a philosophy, a religion.' She invokes the 'holy doctrine of social liberty and fraternal equality, ever reappearing as a ray of love and truth amidst the storm.' She calls it 'the goal of man and the law of the future.' She thinks it the secret of the civilisation of France, the most civilised of nations. (p. 338)

How comes the idea to be so current; and to be passionately believed in, as we have seen, by such a woman as George Sand? It was so passionately believed in by her, that when one seeks, as I am now seeking, to recall her image, the image is incomplete if the passionate belief is kept from appearing. (p. 339)

The people is what interested George Sand. And in France *the people* is, above all, the peasant. . . . The peasant was the object of Madame Sand's fondest predilections in the present, and happiest hopes in the future. The Revolution and its doctrine of equality had made the French peasant. What wonder, then, if she saluted the doctrine as a holy and paramount one? (pp. 339-40)

Whether or not the number of George Sand's works,—always fresh, always attractive, but poured out too lavishly and rapidly,—is likely to prove a hindrance to her fame, I do not care to consider. Posterity, alarmed at the way in which its literary baggage grows upon it, always seeks to leave behind it as much as it can, as much as it dares,—everything but masterpieces. But the immense vibration of George Sand's voice upon the ear of Europe will not soon die away. Her passions and her errors have been abundantly talked of. She left them behind her, and men's memory of her will leave them behind also. There will remain of her to mankind the sense of benefit and stimulus from the passage upon earth of that large and frank nature, of that large and pure utterance,—the *large utterance of the early gods.* There will remain an admiring and ever widening report of that great and ingenuous soul, simple, affectionate, without vanity, without pedantry, human, equitable, patient, kind. She believed herself, she said, 'to be in sympathy, across time and space, with a multitude of honest wills which interrogate their conscience and try to put themselves in accord with it.' This chain of sympathy will extend more and more. (pp. 346-47)

> Matthew Arnold, "George Sand" (originally published in The Fortnightly Review, Vol. XXVIII, No. CXXVI, June 1, 1877), in his Mixed Essays, The Macmillan Company, 1903, pp. 315-47.

ANATOLE FRANCE   (essay date 1889)

Realist art is not a whit truer than idealist art. M. Zola does not see man and nature with more truth than Madame Sand saw them. He has only his eyes to see them with, just as she had hers. . . . Naturalists and idealists are alike the playthings of appearances; they are both the prey of the idols of the Den. . . . Since, then, the witness that any one of us gives of nature is no better than that of any other, since every image of things that we form corresponds, not to the things themselves, but to states of our own souls, why should we not preferably seek and enjoy appearances that inspire charm, beauty, and love? Dream for dream, why not choose the pleasanter? (pp. 302-03)

The truth is, the realists want to render life odious, while the idealists seek to beautify it. And how right they are! What an excellent task they perform! There is in mankind an incessant desire, a perpetual need for ornamenting life. Madame Sand has very well said: "By a natural law, the human mind cannot hinder itself from beautifying and elevating the object of its contemplation." In order to beautify life, what have we not invented? . . . The whole immense effort of civilisation has for its end the beautifying of life. (pp. 303-04)

Madame Sand was a great artisan of the ideal; it is the reason why I love and venerate her. . . .

George Sand's novels, too forgotten to-day, will yet find readers. I desire it. I would like people to read not only the wisest

and the most tranquil of them, but also the most ardent, those of her first period, "**Lélia**" and "**Jacques**." They doubtless contain a very audacious vindication of the rights of passion. There is in them, as Chateaubriand said when he had grown old, an offence against uprightness of life. But had not the author of "René" also sown burning words throughout the world? Besides, what is the good of denying the rights of passion? (p. 304)

Madame Sand was always quite convinced that the great business of men is love. She was half right. Hunger and love are the two axes of the world. All humanity turns on love and hunger. What Balzac saw above all in man was hunger. . . . He showed with extreme precision all the functions of the claw, the jaw, and the stomach, all the habits of the man of prey.

George Sand is not the less great for having shown us only lovers. (pp. 305-06)

> Anatole France, "George Sand and Idealism in Art," in his On Life & Letters, first series, translated by A. W. Evans (originally published in La vie littéraire, Vol. I, Calmann-Lévy, 1889), John Lane Company, 1911 (and reprinted by Dodd, Mead and Company, 1924, pp. 299-306).

THE QUARTERLY REVIEW   (essay date 1890)

George Sand divides with Madame de Staël the honours of French female literature; and if, in point of moral reputation, one is a little embarrassed to choose between them, as regards genius it may be affirmed that the Sibyl of Nobant was a far more consummate artist than her Swiss predecessor and rival. (pp. 301-02)

[A] likeness has been suggested, not absurdly, between [Goethe] and George Sand. In both we find a high artistic perfection, a versatility and abundance, and a marvellously soft yet clear colouring, which combines something of Raffaelle with the Caracci gracefulness. Again, they were both distinguished for a singular *bonhomie*, free from pretence or affectation; while, when we compare their first works with their later, we cannot but see in them a certain purifying of the flame from smoke. But, above all, they resembled one another in their complete detachment from persons once passionately loved. Always their chief aim appears to have been the development of their own character at whatever cost. Goethe tells his sentimental experiences with unruffled composure. 'Werther' may be a lyrical outburst, and the story of Frederika of Sesenheim a very charming pastoral, but never once does the narrator let slip his self-control. He stands outside his own creations, though they have sprung from his heart. With no less suppression of the personal element does George Sand describe her relations with Alfred de Musset in '**Elle et Lui.**' It is an admirable canvas, full of fire and passion, artistically considered; but she has ground her poet into paint, and lays on the colour without giving a second thought to the life-blood which has supplied its crimson. Again, she takes up her parable, and writes of herself and Chopin in '**Lucrezia Floriani.**' . . . To what lengths Madame Sand's audacity of self-portraiture could reach, those will know whom duty or inclination has led to the study of that remarkable, if not very exhilarating, story. Like '**Valentine,**' it belongs to a world—we cannot say an unfallen one—in which shame is not. (pp. 303-04)

The fixed starting-point in this very strange and comical realm is the violability of the marriage-contract. It becomes what Sophie Arnould called it, 'The sacrament of adultery.' From

'Indiana,' with its lovely rhythmical prose and its reminiscences of 'Paul et Virginie,' to 'La Marquise' and 'Constance Verrier,' we listen to the same unvarying tale. Everywhere the 'sensibilities of the heart' rule as a first principle; duty does not count; or it becomes, as in 'Jacques,' the French duty of the husband committing suicide that his wife and her lover may be happy. Nor are we to suppose these things burlesque. They have been written in sober sadness, for our instruction. Their drift is not irony; they are simply due to the false ideal which the keenest-witted nation in Europe has set up and diligently worshipped, as Titania doted on the ass's head of bully Bottom. . . .

Love is always to be in excess, always a blind motion, always criminal, always disastrous. There is but one virtue, self-sacrifice. . . . The atmosphere of 'Lélia' is impregnated with suicide like a miasma. But George Sand, like Goethe, outlived that doctrine. Jacques might fling himself over the glacier; his creator never did. (pp. 304-05)

Much of George Sand's earlier writing, especially 'Lélia,' 'Spiridion,' and the series of religious rhapsodies to which they belong, almost overpowers one with voluble discourse concerning Love, Doubt, Freedom, and Fraternity. It is the very false gallop of the sublime, and will remind the irreverent, to whom Pierre Leroux is no more an apostle than any other Pierre, not so much of Pegasus in harness, as of a well-trained circus pony, going round the ring or vaulting through hoops at the crack of his master's whip. The ultra-masonic initiation which takes up so many weary chapters of 'La Comtesse de Rudolstadt' probably exhibits these rushlight illuminations, and this sham theatrical thunder,—the rolling of sheet-iron distinctly perceptible throughout,—at its perfection. All is calculated for an audience in pit and boxes, to be startled or seduced into applause.

But in George Sand's volatile yet passionate nature there was always one sound element, with which Romanticism might and did achieve great things. . . . [Unquestionably] her noblest work was done in painting the quiet landscape, so full of delicious touches, of her native Berri. When we think of George Sand, it is La Vallée Noire, rather than palaces on the Grand Canal, with which we associate her. The warm tropical scenery of 'Indiana,' and still more the lovely descriptions wrought into the otherwise shameful tragedies of 'Valentine' and 'Jacques,' announced that, when the fires of her passion should be a little spent, the author would turn for consolation, perhaps even for cleansing from the stains of youth, to nature, and to the simple, true-hearted peasantry among whom she had been brought up. (pp. 309-10)

[Few] have known the ways of the French peasant as George Sand knew them. To have gone down, so to speak, into the heart of his existence, to have eaten of his bread and drunk of his cup of sour *piquette*, when it was not unmixed water, was a condition of her astonishing exactitude in drawing him as he lives and moves. But she needed, likewise, to stand away from it, to view it as a whole, before she could render its meaning transparent. Experience was plainly not enough, for who among the millions of rustic France could have given a true account, as she has done, of their curious customs; their neighbourly kindnesses and jealousies, loves and quarrels; their dumb feeling with the beasts of the field and the stones of the brook; their superstitions, fears, traditional religion; their cloudy horizon of knowledge on which things foreign and distant gleam as faintly as stars in a fog? The genius which could render

these things faithfully was unique; it has had no successor. (p. 311)

"The Modern French Novel," in The Quarterly Review, *Vol. 170, No. 340, April, 1890, pp. 287-317.**

GEORGE BRANDES   (essay date 1890?)

Most undoubtedly [George Sand] was the idealist, all her life long; but it was not really the desire to delineate human beings as "they ought to be" which inspired her to write, but the desire to show what they could be if society did not hamper their spiritual growth, corrupt them, and destroy their happiness; hence, in her delineations of the representatives of "society" no leniency was shown. What George Sand originally meant to give was a picture of life as it is, of reality as she had experienced and observed it; what she gave was the feminine enthusiast's view of reality. The section she saw was a patch of earth with the brightness of heaven over it. Her clearsightedness was the clear-sightedness of the poet. (p. 133)

[*Indiana, Valentine, Lélia,* and *Jacques* are books] which possess little literary interest for the reader to-day: the characters are vague idealisations; the plots are improbable, as in *Indiana,* or unreal, as in *Lélia* and *Jacques;* the harmonious sonority of her style does not save the author from the reproach of frequent lapses into magniloquence; in the letters and monologues she is often the poetical sermoniser. And yet there is a fire in these works of George Sand's youth which gives light and warmth to this day; they struck a note which will go on sounding for ages. They emit both a wail and a war-cry, and where they penetrate they carry with them germs of feelings and thoughts, the growth of which this age has succeeded in checking, but which in the future will unfold and spread with a luxuriant vigour of which we can only form a faint conception. (p. 137)

It was in the rôle of the psychologist and story-teller, not in that of the reformer, that she at first appeared before the public. In *Indiana,* as in *Valentine,* the fervour, the poetical impulses, the enthusiastic passions and stormy protests of youth, are the proper contents of the book; there is much psychological and little personal history. Nevertheless there was in the nature of the feeling described (feelings free from any trace of viciousness, yet at variance with the decrees of society), and still more in the reflections interspersed throughout the tale, something which actually struck at the foundations of society. (p. 141)

[In *Lélia* and *Jacques*] their authoress's Byronic "Weltschmerz" and declamatory tendency reach high-water mark. In *Lélia* she represented her ideal great, unsensual, profoundly feeling woman, and provided her with an opposite in her sister, Pulchérie, a luxurious courtesan. Taking her own character and separating the two sides of it, she formed Lélia after the Minerva-image, Pulchérie after the Venus-image in her own soul; the result being, not unnaturally, rather two symbolic personages than two human beings of flesh and blood. In *Jacques* she approached the problem of marriage from a new side. In *Indiana* she had portrayed a brutal, in *Valentine* a refined, cold husband; but now she equipped the husband with the qualities which in her eyes were the highest, and wrecked his happiness upon the rock of his own elevated character, which his insignificant young wife is not capable of understanding and continuing to love. The authoress has endeavoured to impart additional force to her own opinions by putting them into the mouth of the wronged husband. He himself excuses his wife. . . . The extravagance of Romanticism is most noticeable in the final catastrophe. Jacques can think of no better means of liberating Fernande than a suicide committed in a manner which to her will give it the appearance of an accident. This transports us at once into the region of unreality. But the unreality in this novel is, generally speaking, more apparent than actual. It is easy for modern criticism to point out the absence of any indications of locality, of real occupations, &c., &c.; the personages in George Sand's early novels have no occupation and no aim but to love. The reality of these books is a spiritual reality, the reality of feeling. . . . [We] must remember that George Sand's characters are not supposed to be average men and women. She describes unusually gifted beings. Indeed, in these early works she has done little else than delineate and explain her own emotional life. She places her own character in every variety of outward circumstance, and then, with a marvellous power of self-observation and unerring skill, draws the natural psychological conclusions. It is interesting to observe how the constant craving to find a masculine mind which is the equal of her own, leads her to a kind of self-duplication in two sexes. Ardently as she exalts love, strongly as she allows it to influence the life of the great woman and of the great man, nevertheless both of these, Jacques as well as Lélia, are inspired by a still stronger, still more ideal feeling, that of friendship for a noble member of the opposite sex, by whom they are understood. In comparison with this profound mutual understanding, Lélia's love for Sténio, Jacques' for Fernande, seem merely the weaknesses of these two great souls. Lélia has an understanding friend and equal in Trenmor, Jacques in Sylvia. Jacques would love Sylvia if she were not his half-sister, or rather if he were not compelled to suspect that she is; but there is a beauty in their mutual relationship, such as it is, to which merely erotic relations could hardly attain. (pp. 143-45)

Characters such as these illustrate the strong instinct of friendship which George Sand possessed, and which was quite in the spirit of the youthful Romanticism of the period. Her *Lettres d'un Voyageur,* which follow the first group of novels, and begin immediately after the separation from Alfred de Musset in Venice, give us an insight into her friendships. (p. 146)

In no other of her works is she so eloquent, in none of the later ones do her periods flow in such long, lyrically rhetorical waves. Nowhere better than here can we study her personal style, as distinguished from the dialogue of her novels. Sonority is its most marked feature. It rolls onward in long, full rhythms, regular in its fall and rise, melodious in joy, harmonious even in despair. The perfect balance of George Sand's nature is mirrored in the perfect balance of her sentences—never a shriek, a start, or a jar; a sweeping, broad-winged flight—never a leap, nor a blow, nor a fall. The style is deficient in melody, but abounds in rich harmonies; it lacks colour, but has all the beauty that play of line can impart. She never produces her effect by an unusual and audacious combination of words, seldom or never by a fantastic simile. And there is just as little strong or glaring colour in her pictures as there is jarring sound in her language. She is romantic in her enthusiasms, in the way in which she yields unresistingly to feelings which defy rules and regulations; but she is severely classical in the regularity of her periods, in the inherent beauty of her form, and the sobriety of her colouring. (pp. 146-47)

[Of the purely poetic tales of the second period of her literary career,] *La Marquise* is, in my estimation, undoubtedly the best; indeed, taking nothing but art into consideration, it is possibly her most perfect work. I fancy it must have been inspired by the memory of her kind-hearted, dignified grand-mother. It fascinates by its combination of the spirit and customs of the eighteenth century with the timid, more spiritually enthusiastic amatory passion of the nineteenth. (p. 151)

George Sand has written nothing more graceful. The sly sarcasm in [the] conclusion, a quality which also distinguishes the equally charming and equally suggestive little tale, *Teverino,* but which is not frequently met with in her writings, is quite in the spirit of the eighteenth century; and the style has that conciseness which is, as a rule, an indispensable quality in a work destined to descend to future generations. *La Marquise* has a rightful claim to a place in every anthology of French masterpieces.

Amongst the works which George Sand now proceeds to write is a whole series in which she represents her conception of woman's nature when it is uncorrupted. The women she draws are chaste and proud and energetic, susceptible to the passion of love, but remaining on the plane above it, or retaining their purity even when they yield to it. She inclines to attribute to woman a moral superiority over man. But the natures of her heroes, too, are essentially fine, though in the ruling classes tainted by the inherited tendency to tyrannise over woman and the lower classes. . . . Women like Fiamma in *Simon,* Edmée in *Mauprat,* Consuelo in the novel of the same name . . . , are fine specimens of George Sand's typical young girl. Her rôle is to inspire, to heal, or to discipline the man. She knows not vacillation; resolution is the essence of her character; she is the priestess of patriotism, of liberty, of art, or of civilisation. (p. 153)

Side by side with the books which have the high-minded young girl as heroine, we find one or two in which the mature woman is the central figure—in which George Sand has given a more direct representation of her own character. Such are *Le Secrétaire intime,* a comparatively weak story, and *Lucrezia Floriani,* one of the most remarkable productions of her pen. Of this latter book, it may with truth be said that it is not food for every one. . . . To most readers it will seem a forbidding or revolting literary paradox; for it aims at proving the modesty, nay, the chastity of an unmarried woman (an Italian actress and play-writer) who has four children by three fathers. But it is a book in which the authoress has successfully performed the difficult task she set herself, that of giving us an understanding of a woman's nature which is so rich and so healthy that it must always love, so noble that it cannot be degraded, so much that of the artist that it cannot rest content with a single feeling, and has the power to recover from repeated disappointments. (pp. 153-54)

The contrast between *Lucrezia Floriani* and the short series of simple, beautiful peasant stories which follow it after a short interval . . . seems at first sight a very marked one. In reality, however, the gulf separating *Lucrezia* from *La Mare au Diable, François le Champi,* and *La petite Fadette* is not so wide as it appears. What attracted George Sand to the peasants of Berry, to the rustic idylls of her native province, was the very same Rousseau-like enthusiasm for nature that had lent impetus and weight to her protests against the laws of society. . . . Her French peasants are very certainly not "real" in the same sense as Balzac's in *Les Paysans;* they are not merely represented with a sympathy which is as strong as his antipathy, but are made out to be amiable, tender-hearted, and sensitively delicate in their feelings; they are to real French peasants what the shepherds of Theocritus were to the real shepherds of Greece. Nevertheless, these tales have one merit which they owe entirely to their subject-matter and which George Sand's other novels lack—they possess the charm, always rare, but doubly rare in French literature, of naïveté. All that there was of the peasant girl, of the country child, in George Sand; everything in her which was akin to the plants that grow, to the breeze that blows, knowing not whence it cometh nor whither it goeth; all that which, unconscious and dumb, was so legible in her countenance and behaviour, but was so often nullified in her works by sentimentality and phrase-mongering, revealed itself here in its childlike simplicity. (pp. 156-57)

[*La Mare au Diable*] is the gem of these village tales. In it idealism in French fiction reaches its highest level. In it George Sand gave to the world what she declared to Balzac it was her desire to write—the pastoral of the eighteenth century. (p. 157)

> *George Brandes, "George Sand," in his* Main Currents in Nineteenth Century Literature: The Romantic School in France, *Vol. V, translated by Diana White and Mary Morison (originally published as* Hovedstromninger i det 19de aarhundredes litteratur, *1872-1890), Heinemann Ltd., 1904 (and reprinted by Boni & Liveright, Inc., 1924, pp. 132-57).*

CHARLES WHIBLEY   (essay date 1904)

For forty years [George Sand] composed novels, stories, and articles without number, the most of which are long since forgotten. Though her critics disagree in many points, they are unanimous in this—that she was a mistress of the famous *style coulant*. . . . [While] Flaubert tortured himself to find a word, George Sand sat down and saw a novel invent itself. . . .

In the end, of course, the difficult method triumphs. Books that are so easily made seldom stand the test of time; and George Sand's romances have another fatal defect besides facility. Not merely did they grow as by a happy accident,— they are packed with declamation, which long since lost its excuse. Nothing wears so faint and faded an air as an old sermon, whose lot is too often that of a worn-out shoe. New ills require new remedies; the moral surrenders of to-day cannot be stayed by the old exhortations; and George Sand's rhetoric long since lost its meaning. She stood with invincible courage for the impossible ambitions, the fantastic beliefs, the absurd, magnificent sympathies of her period; but her period is not ours, and we can profess little more than an archaeological interest in her speculations. And the strange thing is that, when once she deserted her serious imaginings for the plain countryside, which she knew so well, she composed masterpieces whose immortality is assured. None will ever again be interested in the false sentiment of **'Mauprat,'** in the shallow argument of **'Spiridion';** but so long as the French language is read, so long will **'La Mare au Diable'** win admirers, so long will the character of Germain hold the interest of the world. The truth is, that when George Sand wrote of what she understood, she instantly affected a gracious parsimony of word and thought. The quiet life of labourers, the simple trials of simple folk, are a poor excuse for philosophic harangues; and in recording sincerely what was sincere to herself, George Sand attained that general truth, which too often escaped her. In other words, this fervent romantic did her best work when she strayed for a moment within the fold of the classics, and forgot a while the preacher in the artist. (p. 256)

> *Charles Whibley, "Two Centenaries," in* Blackwood's Edinburgh Magazine, *Vol. CLXXVI, No. MLXVI, August, 1904, pp. 255-62.**

FRANCIS GRIBBLE   (essay date 1904)

It is difficult, if not impossible, for a writer to be both voluminous and vital. George Sand wrote many books that made a noise, but no book that can really be said to live, or to deserve to live. In two of the qualities which give permanent value to the written word, her work was lamentably lacking. She was not a penetrating observer of externals, and her grip of life was not intellectual but purely emotional. She worked with her heart, and not with her head, and wrote down not what she had thought out, but what she felt; and that is always a dangerous practice for those who desire to include posterity in their public. For intellectual values are constant, whereas emotional values vary from one generation to the next. . . . George Sand is out of date for the same reason for which Chateaubriand is out of date—because the receptivity of the reading public is not what it was when she wrote. She commands our interest not as a creator but as a phenomenon—as the exaggerated type of an emotional epoch that has passed away. (pp. 274-75)

In so far as the novels conduct an argument, the method is purely deductive. Almost all of them could be cast in the form of a syllogism; and the major premiss of all the syllogisms is the same. Love comes from God, and obedience to its dictates is a duty. Indiana, or Lelia, or whoever it may be, loved her lover. Therefore, she was right to be unfaithful to her husband, and he had no cause to complain of her conduct. That is the formula, continually re-stated with ingenious and pathetic variations. . . .

[George Sand] was putting herself forward as the prophetess of a new moral code. She did deliberately proceed from premises to conclusions. Consequently, one feels warranted in pointing out, not indeed that her premises do not contain her conclusions, but that, precisely because they prove so much, and prove it so easily, the premises are themselves the objects of a reasonable suspicion. The real point at issue is not whether the particular case is covered by the general proposition but what is the evidence for the general proposition itself. If sexual anarchism is the ideal, then clearly Lelia or any other sexual anarchist merits our sympathy and even our applause. But what is the philosophic case for sexual anarchism? How are we to defend it without, by implication, simultaneously defending the anarchism of the man who, being hungry, steals, or being angry, kills? That is the ultimate problem, and George Sand does not face it. She does not even face the practical consequences of the anarchism which she advocates. As often as there is an awkward tangle, the god descends from the machine to cut the knot. Inconvenient children die; inconvenient husbands commit suicide. By these mechanical devices a happy ending is secured. (p. 276)

The essential doctrine is that the obligations of love are paramount, overriding all legal contracts, and all extra-legal promises. The only alternative to the view that George Sand preached sexual anarchism would be the view that she wrote simply as a literary artist, and must not be regarded as having preached any doctrine at all. But even so the doctrine of sexual anarchism is certainly in the novels, whether she intentionally put it there or not. If it is not the conclusion, it is the postulate. (p. 278)

> *Francis Gribble, "Two Centenaries," in* The Fortnightly Review, *Vol. LXXVI, August 1, 1904, pp. 260-78.**

PROSSER HALL FRYE   (essay date 1908)

English literature is distinguished from French by its preference, at least in effect, for improvisation and inspiration. And it is for this reason, because these are so exactly the characteristics of her writing, that George Sand deserves the attention of the English reader. . . . Her spontaneity, ease, and fluency, her individuality, sensibility, and inventiveness are the positive virtues which most please the English sense; while the vices of their reverse—her diffuseness, confusion, and haziness, her irregularity, extravagance, and wilfulness, in fine her lack of discipline—are all defects which the English least notice or most readily excuse. She had no art in the strict sense; but she had inspiration, its virtues and vices, its qualities and defects. (p. 41)

[In] spite of the charm of her writing, almost irresistible in the wooing of the soft slow sentences, the inevitable weaknesses of the facility which stood her in place of literary method have been observed over and over, particularly where they are most noticeable, in her construction. Her lack of fundamental plan, of architectural design, has impaired a work that otherwise would have in perfection, as it now has in bulk, few peers. Sentences she could write, and chapters, exquisite in touch and feeling,—few better; but alas! for all their delicacy, fragments. When it comes to building up piece by piece a single whole, an entire fabric with the subdual of many parts to the perfect harmony of one great purpose,—there her weakness, the weakness of facility, is manifest. (p. 42)

With her quick, sensitive, and rather shallow nature she was by no means so likely to distinguish herself through the manifestation of intellect and will in literature as through the manifestation of sentiment and emotion—not so much in composition as in style. . . . [George Sand's writing] is full of colour and feeling, it is splendidly romantic; but when one comes to consider it as a whole, to look toward its end and reflect upon its tendency, one is struck by its ineptitude to its purpose. (p. 45)

For the careful and consistent reader one of the most painful experiences is prepared by the frequency with which she falls away in the latter part of her novels from the high standard of her beginnings,—and that not merely in her early work, when she was learning her trade, but in the work of after periods as well, when she had served along apprenticeship to her art. . . . And it is sadder still to find for oneself a book of such fair promise, which might have been completed faultlessly within the limit of three hundred pages, running on into a wreck of diminishing climaxes and crises and feeble after-thoughts, until it expires tardily of sheer exhaustion, without the needed apology for being so long a-dying, at more than twice its natural age,—spoiled for no other apparent reason than that the writer wrote too easily to stop when she had finished. . . . It is hardly exaggeration to advise one wishing to read George Sand's best work to read only the first halves of her novels.

And yet the difficulty were not to be so escaped. This fault of saying too much, this plethora of words occurs again and again over smaller areas than an entire book. With the inveteracy of disease it infects the whole system. The author is not willing to make the reader a suggestion, to drop him a hint, to risk herself to his perspicacity. She must needs explain—often more for her own sake than for his, it would appear—until there is left over event and motive hardly a single shadow for him to penetrate, but everything lies exposed in an even glare of revelation, like the monotonous landscape of our great western prairie, without concealment or mystery. There are no skeletons in George Sand's closet; she has got them all out into the middle of the floor. And her dialogue is as prolix as her analysis. Her characters seem possessed with her own fondness for expli-

cation, and invariably talk matters out to a finish, however trivial, so that the reader is constantly outrunning the writer with a sense at the end of disillusion and disappointment. (pp. 46-8)

Perhaps this faultiness, behind which lies always her too ready fluency, may be explained, or at least illustrated, by her manner of work. It is well known nowadays, when the personal habits of authors are more studied than their books, that she wrote at night for certain fixed hours with the regularity of a day-labourer. . . . The story goes of her that if she happened to finish the novel on which she was employed an hour or even less before her time was up for the night, she would calmly set the manuscript away, the ink still damp on the page, and placidly begin another, composing rapidly as she went until the clock released her. Whether rightly or wrongly one misses something here—the fond lingering over the old work, the patient review and minute revision, the reluctance to part with the child of the brain which makes every *finis* to the author a lover's parting and which is so characteristic of the French writers of the century. (pp. 48-9)

[However] there is something very like grandeur—the grandeur of renunciation, perhaps—in this ability of hers to put away the past when she was done with it, to leave her work to its deserts without just one more backward look, just one more correction, and to pass on confidently to the next duty without worrying over what was gone. . . . At all events it shows a self-detachment, a sobriety and moderation which is often sadly to seek in French literary workmanship of the modern school, with its long brooding, its slow coagulation, its overlaid and half-addled conception. . . . (pp. 50-1)

But for all this excess of care we might well wish that George Sand had, without going too far, shown a little more concern for what she had done, a little more for what she was about to do, were it reasonable to suppose that all her errors were due to her habits of work and could have been retrieved by revision. Much, however, of her defective construction must be charged to another cause. A certain indefiniteness of conception, a failure to decide the end from the beginning and write up to it—in short, a powerlessness to fix and realise the idea of a book, is equally a condition of her structural frailty. (p. 52)

[As a result of] the vivacity of her feelings, she was at her best when she centred her novels neither in a doctrinal *motif* nor a merely personal emotion, but in some simple episode of common life which she had noticed and been touched by. Her masterpieces are few in number—as any one's must be—but they are perfect in their kind:—*la Mare au diable, la Petite Fadette, François le champi. Les Maîtres sonneurs,* of the same attempt as the others, errs by excessive development; it overreaches and outruns itself and in spite of much good grows wearisome by its length; while *Jeanne* and the *Meunier d'Angibault,* which are sometimes classed with these, show traces of confusion due partly to the introduction of extra-literary ideas and partly to the mixture of idyllic and social elements; so that none of these latter three can be ranked as masterpieces beside the former. Her own district of Berri, which she always loved and to which she returned more and more in later life, furnished her with the setting for these flawless gems. . . . The simple, unpretentious life of the peasant amid his fields with his robust loves and hates, hopes and fears, was a discovery in comparative humanity to French letters. The healthfulness and freshness of these idyls, full of the air of wood and lawn, the breath of morning and evening, is a revelation after the stale intrigue skulking away in the close and tainted atmosphere of city rooms. They justify to the English reader the existence of French fiction. It may be, as [the French critic M. Vincent de Paul] Brunetière declares, that George Sand made the French novel capable of sustaining thought; it is of infinitely greater credit to her to have shown that it was possible for the French novel to carry good, clean, wholesome sentiment. No reader of modern French fiction can return to these stories without feeling that there life, as well as literature, has been triumphantly vindicated against *naturalism*, and without feeling, too, that his heart has been purified and gladdened by contact with a simple and sincere art. (pp. 60-2)

> *Prosser Hall Frye, "George Sand," in his* Literary Reviews and Criticisms, *G. P. Putnam's Sons, 1908, pp. 29-62.*

RENÉ DOUMIC (essay date 1909)

On comparing George Sand with the novelists of her time, what strikes us most is how different she was from them. She is neither like Balzac, Stendhal, nor Mérimée, nor any storyteller of our thoughtful, clever, and refined epoch. She reminds us more of the "old novelists," of those who told stories of chivalrous deeds and of old legends, or, to go still further back, she reminds us of the *Aedes* of old Greece. (p. 307)

George Sand did not employ a versified form for her stories, but she belonged to the family of these poets. She was a poet herself who had lost her way and come into our century of prose, and she continued her singing.

Like these early poets, she was primitive. Like them, she obeyed a god within her. All her talent was instinctive, and she had all the ease of instinctive talent. When Flaubert complained to George Sand of the "tortures" that style cost him, she endeavoured to admire him. (p. 308)

This was merely her charity, for she never understood that there could be any effort in writing. Consequently she could not understand that it should cause suffering. For her writing was a pleasure, as it was the satisfaction of a need. As her works were no effort to her, they left no trace in her memory. She had not intended to write them, and, when once written, she forgot them. (pp. 308-09)

Her novels were like fruit, which, when ripe, fell away from her. George Sand always returned to the celebration of certain great themes which are the eternal subjects of all poetry, subjects such as love, nature, and sentiments like enthusiasm and pity. The very language completes the illusion. The choice of words was often far from perfect, as George Sand's vocabulary was often uncertain, and her expression lacked precision and relief. But she had the gift of imagery, and her images were always delightfully fresh. She never lost that rare faculty which she possessed of being surprised at things, so that she looked at everything with youthful eyes. There is a certain movement which carries the reader on, and a rhythm that is soothing. She develops the French phrase slowly perhaps, but without any confusion. Her language is like those rivers which flow along full and limpid, between flowery banks and oases of verdure, rivers by the side of which the traveller loves to linger and to lose himself in dreams.

The share which belongs to George Sand in the history of the French novel is that of having impregnated the novel with the poetry in her own soul. She gave to the novel a breadth and a range which it had never hitherto had. She celebrated the hymn

of Nature, of love, and of goodness in it. She revealed to us the country and the peasants of France. She gave satisfaction to the romantic tendency which is in every one of us, to a more or less degree.

All this is more even than is needed to ensure her fame. She denied ever having written for posterity, and she predicted that in fifty years she would be forgotten. It may be that there has been for her, as there is for every illustrious author who dies, a time of test and a period of neglect. . . . [However, we] are gradually coming back to a better comprehension of what there is of "truth" in George Sand's conception of the novel. This may be summed up in a few words—to charm, to touch, and to console. Those of us who know something of life may perhaps wonder whether to console may not be the final aim of literature. George Sand's literary ideal may be read in the following words, which she wrote to Flaubert:

"You make the people who read your books still sadder than they were before. I want to make them less unhappy." She tried to do this, and she often succeeded in her attempt. What greater praise can we give to her than that? And how can we help adding a little gratitude and affection to our admiration for the woman who was the good fairy of the contemporary novel? (pp. 309-11)

> *René Doumic, "The Genius of the Writer," in his* George Sand: Some Aspects of Her Life and Work, *translated by Alys Hallard (originally published as* George Sand: dix conférences sur sa vie et son oeuvre, avec quatre portraits et un fac-similé d'autographe, *Perrin, 1909), G. P. Putnam's Sons, 1910, pp. 290-311.*

BENEDETTO CROCE (essay date 1923)

We read to-day with effort the hundred and more volumes of Georges Sand, which made our grandmothers shiver and grow pale, and the re-reading of them fails of giving pleasure, like a game that has ceased to amuse, because the trick of it has been discovered. (p. 206)

Georges Sand was undoubtedly one of the most noteworthy representative of European moral life in the twenty years prior to the revolution of 1848. She represented this practical side of life chiefly and energetically by means of a strange Utopia, which may be termed "the religion of love." . . . From the point of view of this religion, the value and meaning of life are to be found in love, just in love, understood sexually; and Eros is the god, although the rhetorical phraseology of the day preferred to formulate its thought with a certain degree of unction and spoke of "love" as "coming from God."

Love, being the highest and indeed the only act of the religious cult, does not recognize any law as superior to itself: as soon as it appears, it has the right of obtaining satisfaction, "the right of passion." And it is sovran: it does not tolerate a division of its kingdom with other affections: every other passion must serve it, receive orders from it and submit to it. It is also unique and eternal; and when it seems to vary in its objects, the fault lies with society, which embarrasses it with its foolish and tyrannical laws, or with material accidents, which trouble it, for in its essence it is constancy and fidelity. He who loves without return should respect the passion for another object in the beloved, and love ordains self-sacrifice, in order that passion may celebrate the sacred rite in full joy and freedom: in making this sacrifice, duty is performed, the heroism of the perfect lover is attained. (pp. 208-09)

When we recognize . . . the altogether sensual and pathological origin of Sand's theories, of her religion of love, and admit the accusation of immorality brought against them, we have already implicitly granted that they are without doctrinal or philosophical importance, and without any value as truth. Truth, however bitter it may be and pessimistic it may seem to be, is always moral and a source of morality. Sand was unable to extract truth from her nervous spasm, which she expressed in formulas possessing only the semblance of being theoretical. But her ideology did not even become poetry and art, when translated into the form of fiction, because art too is truth and demands sincerity towards one's self, a superior sincerity which vanquishes one-sided practical interest and penetrates to the recesses of the soul, dissipating or clearing the clouds that obscure it. Sand's was not a profound mind . . . , she was absorbed in dreaming; in weaving the web of her imaginings, as the woman she was. And being a woman, she never conceived that art should be respected, but always held it to be the natural outlet for her own sensibility and for her own intellectuality. As woman again, she brought practical sense into the things of art, domestic economy and commercial knowledge, aiming always at making above all what is called the romance, the pleasing book, and at making many of them, because many produced much fruit. She observed reality, but who does not? She even observed it with attention; but her work consisted, as she said, in "idealizing it." . . . [It] is generally admitted and recognized . . . that Georges Sand's novels are defectively composed or lack composition, but it is not observed that this was due in her case to the lack of vigorous thought, or rather of an inspiring poetic motive, owing to which she abandoned herself to chance as regards personages and events, which might be this or the opposite, and since they had little cohesion, it was not difficult for her to change or turn into its opposite this or that one of her novels, to change the fate of *Indiana* or of *Lélia,* making Indiana and Ralph marry or making Lélia die in a convent. She frequently also began her narratives, such as *Mauprat,* with force and vigour; but when we anticipate that a theme from such a beginning should attain to its full significance in the course and ending of the story, we find her losing herself in the conventional, in intrigues and in trivial adventures.

Lyricism as "setting" and the "agreeable" side of romantic love are to be found in all her works in different proportions, sometimes the one, sometimes the other preponderating. In *Lélia,* which is her greatest poetical effort, the former predominates: here everything sparkles and echoes, so that the eye becomes, as it were, dimmed, the ear seduced and deafened. The personages of *Lélia* are neither allegories nor poetical individuals: they are not allegories, because they lack definite concepts, nor poetical individuals, because they lack definiteness of character. This poem in prose, this feminine *Faust,* also fails to resolve itself into a succession of lyrics, because instead of lyrics, it abounds in emphasis and declamation. (pp. 214-17)

The characters of *Jacques* are also dreams of erotic sensuality: the hero himself, mysterious, most perfect, an idler, whose supreme need and occupation is pure love (not love that is pure), and all the more agreeable to women, since he is capable of sometimes disappearing, so that they may occupy themselves with their pleasures undisturbed. . . . (pp. 218-19)

The art is there all the more easy, because the story is developed by letters, all of them in the same florid style, letters that are not letters save by means of a gross artifice, discussing and recounting previous events and informing the reader of what is necessary for his information. This is art of a second-rate quality, like that of the first romance, *Indiana,* which gave fame to the authoress, and is the type of so many others of her novels, in which the craftsmanship predominates. There is not one poetical motive or idea in the whole of that celebrated romance: the theme . . . is treated externally and materially, complicated but not developed by means of strange events, surprises and suicides, crossings of the ocean, and the like. (p. 219)

Certainly qualities of a secondary order are very much in evidence in Sand. She is an authoress of extraordinary fluidity and abundance, although giving but slight relief to her characters, and she knows how to tell a story with vivacity. But perhaps the only places where her writing is illuminated with a touch of poetry are her descriptions of "natural scenery," universally praised, which corresponded to a true emotion in her, to a small melody that sang itself in her soul, in the midst of the din caused there by the passions artificially intensified and by ill-thought-out ideas, and in the midst of conventionalisms and expedients of the craft. Something of the florid, rhetorical and verbose is to be found in them also; but sometimes these are able to render rather successfully the feeling of waiting, of melancholy, of abandonment, of purification, of gladness, which Sand infused into the spectacles of nature. (pp. 220-21)

As is well known, Georges Sand gave herself to the cultivation of humanitarian and especially of socialistic ideals in the second period of the four into which critics are wont to divide her too copious production. (p. 222)

Consuelo belongs to [this] period, standing between the historical novel—as it was then understood, introducing great historical personages and placing them in relation to other imaginary personages and showed them as immersed in politics, intrigues and love affairs with one another—and the novel of socialistic tendencies. Consuelo is another incarnation of Lélia, an extraordinary woman, daughter of a street singer, herself a singer, but in some unknown manner endowed with the greatest possible knowledge of things in general and of the human heart, of the greatest will-power, of the greatest rectitude, of the greatest tact and practical sense, and in addition acutely intellectual and critical with a mind that meditates upon God and human destiny. In the novel, the miracles that she accomplishes follow one another: the idealization or idolization usual with Sand, unites with adventures piled upon one another, to compose a perfect novel in supplements. . . . How little capable was Sand of going deeply into anything is to be seen in the figure of Count Albert. . . . This figure is well conceived, but quickly becomes superficialized and lost in narratives of strange events, terrifying apparitions and intrigues.

It is true that Sand, in the third period of her production as classified by the critics . . . , is supposed then to have composed at last her masterpieces, the idyllic novels, and to have thus bestowed upon France a kind of literature that she still lacked. I do not deny that *La mare au diable, La petite Fadette, François le champi, Les maîtres sonneurs,* and one or two like them, are very graceful books, full of gentleness and goodness, far better arranged and proportioned than the foregoing, written with greater care and with an able adaptation of peasant speech. But, to tell the truth, there does not seem to be anything poetical that comes to light in these novels, but rather the virtuosity of the expert authoress of pleasing books. A certain preparatory tone makes itself indeed felt in the best of them, *La mare au diable:* we feel there the intention of moving and delighting us with a story of innocence and tenderness. (pp. 224-26)

The accuracy of Georges Sand in portraying the life of peasants in this and others of her novels has been contested, and, as is always the case, under the guise of an unjust criticism is to be found concealed another criticism which is just, namely, annoyance at the mannered style of these edifying and consoling narratives. (p. 227)

And what shall we say finally as to the last manner, that of the fourth period of Georges Sand, when she returned to love stories no longer of the fields but of the city, returned appeased and without the fictions of rebellion and apostolate which had shaken her in the past? The recognized masterpiece of this period is *Le marquis de Villemer.* . . . . It is one of those novels read with delight by young ladies, married women and gentlemen, and enjoys the favour of good society, being praised there as an *exquise.* If, however, you are simply a lover of poetry, I would counsel you to avoid it and others like it, because they would seem to you to be insipid and would perhaps arouse your indignation at their pretence of art. (pp. 228-29)

> Benedetto Croce, "Georges Sand," in his European Literature in the Nineteenth Century, *translated by Douglas Ainslie (Canadian rights by permission of the Estate of Benedetto Croce; originally published as* Poesia e non poesia, *G. Laterza & Figli, 1923), Alfred A. Knopf, 1924, pp. 206-29.*

GAMALIEL BRADFORD (essay date 1930)

Through all [her] mad adventures and strange experiences the distinguishing feature and the fundamental characteristic of George Sand's temperament was her essential idealism. . . . [Always] she retained an extraordinary, persistent power of self-delusion about persons and things. The remarkable point is that, especially in earlier years, the delusion was accompanied by the most piercing bursts and flashes of clear vision, of cynical disillusion, when for the moment all the bare ugliness of fact and truth stood out in its prevailing horror. No one could appreciate this horror or state it more clearly or violently, for the time, than she did. (pp. 206-07)

The most striking illustration of George Sand's idealism is her Autobiography, the **'Histoire de Ma Vie.'** Here everything is in a sense veracious. There is truth of detail, undeniable record of indisputable fact. Yet somehow, over everything, there is a sweet, sunlit glow, a pervading atmosphere of gentle tenderness, which transforms and transfigures, gives a touch of unreality, or more properly of ideality, to the most unpromising incidents and the most unattractive people. (p. 208)

The climax, the fine flower, the full embodiment of George Sand's ideal instinct and genius for friendship, appear in the correspondence between her and Flaubert, which, like those between Goethe and Schiller, or between Emerson and Carlyle, is one of the great spiritual exchanges of the world, and is perhaps the most remarkable. What is striking is the complete difference of the two correspondents. Flaubert, in theory at any rate, was the least idealistic of men, cold-blooded, keen-sighted, cynical, realistic in his mental attitude. George Sand was visionary, imaginative, a weaver of dreams. Yet by sheer breadth of character and loftiness of spiritual purpose and level, they were able to understand, to respect, to enjoy, and to love each other. And what is further notable is the way in which George Sand secures and maintains her spiritual superiority. (pp. 211-12)

If George Sand was an idealist in artistic method and attitude, she was quite as much so in artistic achievement. Not for her was the slow, laborious rendering of the sordid detail of the surface of life, but there was always the impetuous effort to transfigure reality with ideal beauty. Sometimes this was accomplished by artistic climaxes, and when these grew naturally and logically out of the movement and development of the story, they were often in a high degree impressive and effective, as with the admirable theatrical triumphs of Consuelo, which it is impossible for any sympathetic reader to resist. And again there was deference to the cheap romantic devices of the day, the hidden trapdoors, the mysterious caverns, the tricks and passwords, which make the later portion of this same 'Consuelo' rather wearisome to the modern reader. Even in the best of her novels George Sand was too much inclined to claptrap of this sort. . . . (pp. 266-27)

The same idealism of handling appears in the region of character. This was never George Sand's strong point, and her range and variety of human types is comparatively limited. For women it may well be said that the only figure she drew with real power and success was herself. There is always a contrasted type, for purposes of conflict and comparison, the Anais of **'Valentine,'** the Pulchérie of **'Lélia,'** the Amélie of **'Consuelo.'** But in all the novels the same heroine appears, strong, modest, self-contained, unpretentious but dominant and dominating, Valentine, Indiana, Consuelo, the Thérèse of **'Elle et Lui,'** Lucrezia Floriani, above all, Lélia, and always this heroine is George Sand. It is curious to see how the same personage is manifest in the autobiography, **'Histoire de Ma Vie,'** and always with the leading position, the *beau rôle.* The extraordinary thing is that this figure should be so dominant and so charming, and every one of these heroines commends herself with a winning magic that is difficult to understand.

It is far otherwise with the heroes. . . . The men of George Sand fall into two distinct types. There is the spoiled, high-strung, over-sensitive child, who is chiefly embodied in Alfred de Musset, the Bénédicts, the Sténios, man as George Sand really saw him, a creature to be petted and nursed and fostered and despised. And there is the hero whom she would have liked to see, the Trenmor of **'Lélia,'** Albert in **'Consuelo,'** who combines the passions of the man with the intellect of the god. And under it all you cannot help feeling a vast instinctive contempt, a sense that the sole function of the male is to fecundate the female and then die. (pp. 227-28)

It is curious to reflect that this conception of the great feminine idealist finds its counterpart, to a large extent, in the treatment of the world's great realistic artist, Shakespeare. The men of Shakespeare certainly appear—to other men—more real than those of George Sand, but their reality is to the full as earthy as that of her men. And Shakespeare's women have the same ideal superiority, the Portias, the Violas, the Imogens, have all the celestial, sustained perfection that belongs to Lélia and Consuelo.

But undoubtedly what most idealizes these various elements in George Sand is the charm and the magic of her style. It is not in all ways a perfect style. It is too facile, too flowing, at times almost approaching the slipshod. But its very quality of improvisation gives it a divine ease and grace which all the long labor of Flaubert could never equal. There is a depth and a delicacy of rhythm, which no translation can suggest, but which is hardly surpassed in any French prose anywhere. (p. 229)

ALBERT THIBAUDET (essay date 1936)

George Sand herself said that she was "a fool." What she said must not always be taken literally. But it is a fact that, gifted in an extraordinary way for thinking, for producing, for putting life into eloquence, into characters and into stories, she had no personal spirit, she does not attract the reader, especially today, to her sources, her inner world; she rings hollow. If the quality of a great artist is measured by the imagined world that he adds to the real world as a supplement or that he sets up in competition with it, it does not take long to circumnavigate the world of George Sand. She left no "message," and she does not make us dream. (pp. 212-13)

But, of all the great novelists of this period, it was she who most resembled the great romantic poets. The poetic power of *Indiana* explodes like the poetic power of *Notre-Dame de Paris.* Not only is the novel tropical in its evocation of the country in which it is set, tropical in the excess of distracted passion that runs through it, it is tropical in the temperature of its poetry. (p. 213)

Not only did George Sand make poetry flow through the novel; she erected her poetic inspiration, her unsatisfied feminine ardor, her protests against the marriage bond, her challenges to society, into real and solid novels. All that Ovid thought became verse; all that George Sand thought took without effort the shape of novels that, undertaken always with the "thank God!" of inspiration or a happy chance, always without a preconceived plan, are ingenious and interesting novels, constantly varied in composition, sustaining interest according to the best recipes (she was born a quick-lunch operator and immediately became a *cordon bleu*), with parts that dragged and parts that lagged, drawing on the reader's reserve of patience, but no more than in Balzac and much less than in Dumas. Has Dumas written a more spirited novel with a more skillfully evolved plot than *Les Beaux Messieurs de Bois-Doré?* *Mauprat* and *Le Marquis de Villemer* were read with so much enthusiasm not for their preachments on marriage, for their thesis, but for their technique, which can still be admired today, like the chestnut timbers, the forest of the rafters in a deserted mansion. (pp. 213-14)

The most-talked-about works of George Sand, those to which immortality has long been promised, are the rustic trilogy of *La Mare au diable, La Petite Fadette,* and *François le champi.* . . . Though they are somewhat old-fashioned, there is no occasion to challenge that opinion too strongly. *La Mare au diable* is a masterpiece of delicacy and narration, but diffuse: Maupassant and Paul Arène would have made it a short story, more perfect, in perhaps thirty pages. We will not reproach George Sand, any more than Mistral, for having idealized her peasants, but rather for having made them speak an artificial language, like the stage language in plays that are too well written. (pp. 214-15)

George Sand's style has long been called the best style of the novel. Like the greater part of romantic prose, it is oratorical in nature, with a riverlike movement, slow and strong, that carries the load of narrative admirably and dialogue much less so. . . . This dialogue has no grip, no features; it does not bite

the paper. George Sand was the soul of facility, of regularity. . . . If Balzac was a force of nature, George Sand represents its facile, generous gift. It must not be forgotten that, if George Eliot and Colette came after her, she was the first woman to make the career and the manifold, abundant work of a novelist consubstantial with the nature of a woman. With the same limitations and the same weaknesses, she practiced on people that transplantation of motherhood that Mme. de Staël dedicated to ideas. As an initiator of great feminine literature in the West she is on a par with the prophetic Germaine. Have their literary sisters so much widened the circle whose two halves were drawn by these two women of genius? (p. 215)

STEPHEN ULLMANN (essay date 1957)

With the progress of Romanticism, the problem of speech-reporting became more acute. The widening of literary horizons and the social sympathies of the Romantics brought the lower classes, urban as well as rural, within the orbit of fiction. Balzac was faced at quite an early stage with the problem of dialect in literature. After some experiments in *Les Chouans* (1829), he made a more sustained effort fifteen years later, in *Les Paysans,* to reproduce the speech of the peasantry. But he was not sufficiently familiar with their language; his technique was uncertain, and he failed to distinguish between dialect and argot. . . . It fell to George Sand to evolve a linguistic medium which would serve as a vehicle for a new *genre,* the 'roman champêtre'.

George Sand started with one great asset: she had a thorough first-hand knowledge of the Berry region, which is the scene of her rustic stories, and of the local dialect. . . . Yet she did not find it easy to develop a rustic style to her own satisfaction. Her first experiments (*Valentine* . . .) were still rather timid. It was not till twelve years later, in the novel *Jeanne,* that she set herself in all seriousness to reproduce the dialect spoken by her characters. In the intervening period, she had acquired progressive social views and had become associated with the so-called 'proletarian' movement in literature, centred on Pierre Leroux's *Revue Indépendante.* Under the influence of Rousseau and Leroux, she had formed an ideal picture of the peasant who had remained free from the debasing and corrupting effects of urban civilization. Her enthusiasm extended to the speech of the countryside. . . . (pp. 74-5)

The mood of naive enthusiasm in which *Jeanne* was written accounts for the extravagant use of linguistic colour in the novel. (p. 75)

Such an extraordinary style could hardly commend itself to the common reader. The author herself was not happy about it; she felt in particular that the way her heroine spoke was out of harmony with her idealized portrait and also with the style of the narrative itself. . . . She therefore promptly abandoned this manner; in *La Mare au Diable* . . . and other stories from the same period, linguistic colour is considerably toned down, and no attempt is made to give an exact transcription of local speech. The characters talk in a kind of Basic French, with some dialect terms and grammatical peculiarities thrown in here and there to remind the reader of their background. . . . (p. 76)

Even this solution failed to satisfy the exacting taste of the author, and only a year later, she tried yet another manner in *François le Champi.* . . . Some of the rustic novels of this period (*François le Champi, Les Maîtres Sonneurs*) are actually told by peasant speakers, and there is an obvious tendency to strengthen linguistic colour, lexical as well as grammatical.

La Mare au Diable, then, represents a transitional stage, a trough between two crests, in George Sand's method of speech-reporting. But this does not mean in any way that the novel is lacking in local colour. There is a sprinkling of dialect terms and features throughout the story—some fifty in all, which is not inconsiderable in a book of this size. (pp. 76-7)

La Mare au Diable is a simple, unpretentious story, hardly a novel at all. The vivid colours and strong contrast effects of a *Carmen* or a *Notre-Dame* would have been quite out of place in such a stylistic milieu. Discouraged by her previous failures, George Sand was aiming at a style which would be in harmony with the general tone of the narrative and with the mentality of the people portrayed. Hence the sparing use of linguistic colour; hence also the protest in the preface: 'Je n'ai voulu ni faire une nouvelle langue, ni me chercher une nouvelle manière.' The result was a somewhat diluted form of regionalism which would be acceptable both to the local and to the general reader. At the same time, there is sufficient local colour in the novel to evoke the idyllic and old-world atmosphere of the countryside as George Sand saw it, to give the story an air of authenticity, and to show that the author was thoroughly familiar with the dialect and genuinely fond and proud of it. (pp. 80-1)

Stephen Ullmann, "Some Romantic Experiments in Local Colour," in his Style in the French Novel, Cambridge at the University Press, 1957, pp. 40-93.*

NANCY ROGERS   (essay date 1979)

[The] question of Sand's sexual contradictions is an interesting one in light of her depiction of sexual roles, especially the crossing of the boundaries of individual sexual identity, in her early novels. (p. 19)

The comparatively bold depiction of sex in George Sand's early novels is somewhat surprising in light of [the general predilection during her day] for veiled eroticism; this is doubly true since the author was a woman. . . . [Love] between man and woman as George Sand describes it is hardly the spiritually uplifting, ethereal bond which is exalted by Chateaubriand. Rather than presenting love as a soft, feminine, passive union of two souls, Sand's novels display a daring, active, violently physical sensation defined as love. (pp. 20-1)

The imagery of fire, fever, and vertigo is almost constantly associated with "love" in Sand's first novel [*Indiana*], so much so that "love" must be equated to "sex"—a violent physical reaction which renders the lover almost physically ill. The second novel, *Valentine,* presents an even stronger picture of love as physical sensation. . . . The touch of a hand, an emotionally and erotically charged game of hide and seek, or an unexpected look is enough to cause breasts to heave and blood to rise, leading to a state resembling death. . . . The intensity of this kind of physical disorganization is a central feature of the sexual encounter as Sand envisions it; the body is disturbed

and disoriented to the extent that the lover loses total control of his corporeal self. . . . [The] disintegration of both the body and mind by the intensity of sexual passion is a major theme in [*Lélia*], in which the ossianic priest, Magnus, is driven mad by his desire for the statue-woman. . . . In this novel Sand examines the conflict between spiritual and physical love, the psychology of sexual frustration and frigidity, and the notion of idolatry in love, a concept which she condemns. Here, sexual satisfaction is "le but inconnu," a tormenting need which is never satisfied. Erotic images fill the pages of *Lélia,* but sexual encounters, although voluptuous, violent, and tumultuous, are never complete, at least for the heroine: the lovers are left unfulfilled, their passion a destructive force. Sand describes this void with an almost cruel authenticity, making *Lélia* one of the boldest of romantic novels. And yet physical passion and pleasure are praised in this ethereal, spiritual novel; the courtesan Pulchérie . . . , Lélia's sister, exists for pleasure and is the only satisifed and complete character in the work, for she understands the limits of happiness and accepts life as it is. . . . [She] is a vibrant, positive personage in the work, serving as the incarnation of physical pleasure as a genuine means of human fulfillment.

The breadth of Sand's erotic imagination is demonstrated by her investigation of the darker elements of sex, those erotic possibilities such as violence, pain, masochism, and death explored by the Marquis de Sade and the Gothic novelists. (pp. 21-2)

However, she does not imply that sex is limited to the "darker" elements: indeed, these novels exhibit a wealth of light, "innocent" features which arouse passion. The sounds, odors, and forms of nature, for example, are presented as temptations to sexual union. . . . Sand also sees other seemingly innocent elements as stimuli to sexual passion: music, for example, is described as "le langage de toute passion forte," and lovers are aroused by its message; articles of clothing, such as Indiana's scarf and Valentine's handkerchief, are capable of becoming objects of fetishism; and prayer, seemingly a spiritual activity, is a catalyst to passion as well. . . . Thus we see that the young Sand examines myriad elements of sexuality with an originality which reveals a fertile imagination and a curiosity about sex which distinguishes her from many of her fellow romantics. The author refuses to shy away from subjects considered taboo at the moment; instead she goes so far as to imply that sex is a major component of many human behavior patterns which are usually considered "pure." (pp. 23-4)

The existential questions "Who am I?" and "Who is he?" were a key element in the dilemma of romantic man as he wrestled with his inner self, alienated from his milieu. This dilemma figures prominently in Sand's method of portraiture, for characters seem to have more than one identity depending upon who is looking at them. Sand profoundly explores changing identities, the masks and disguises that people wear, and the various social roles which individuals assume. But it is one particular manifestation of the Sandian question of identity which interests us here: the merging or metamorphosis of identity, especially in the sexual act.

Sand's first three novels display a phenomenon which was initially manifested in the work *Rose et Blanche,* written . . . with Jules Sandeau. The two women of the title are an actress and a nun, respectively, whose temperaments and tastes are diametrically opposed but who serve, at least implicitly, as alter egos. Each of Sand's next three works contains a pair of young women counterparts whose fusion is of central importance to the structure of the work.

In *Indiana* the two women, Indiana and her "femme de chambre créole" Noun, are both desired by the callous Raymon de Ramière. This sexual triangle will be repeated in the next two novels, but there the ultimate merging of the two women is perhaps presented in the most dramatic manner. . . . The robust Noun and the sickly Indiana seem to represent, on the surface at least, the active and passive elements of human sexuality: Noun forcefully pursues love, . . . becomes pregnant, and in a half-wild state, commits suicide; Indiana, on the other hand, passively accepts Raymon's love, hopes that their relationship will remain spiritual, faints when kissed, and uses her will and reason to resist him until she finally gives in to her passion. . . . [It is] through Raymon that the two become physically metamorphosed; in a powerful erotic scene . . . he finally possesses Indiana through the body of Noun.

Valentine, as well, examines the relationship between two young women counterparts and a man who is attracted to both of them. In this instance the two, Valentine and Louise, are sisters and they act out both sibling and feminine rivalry in a way which would have been impossible for the Creole "soeurs de lait." Here, the brunette Louise is the active one: she has pursued love, become pregnant (like Noun), and sacrificed her material well-being for sexual passion. . . . She is also capable of intense jealousy, even of her own sister, and is so cruel to Valentine that her rebukes hasten the latter's death soon after that of Bénédict. The gentle, blond Valentine is more cautious, prudent, and modest, pulling away from love and attempting to extinguish her passion for Bénédict; she is incapable of understanding the violent jealousy and cruelty of her sister, yet accepts it as her just punishment for having committed adultery. . . . The intimate ties between Louise and Valentine are further strengthened by the convention of naming, a device which solidifies the fusion of their beings by means of a complex, convoluted interrelationship. Valentine was reared as a small child by her older sister, and the two refer to each other as if they had enjoyed a mother/daughter relationship. So, naturally, when Louise has a son, she names him Valentin after her sister/daughter. The young man is blond like his aunt and so closely resembles her in both appearance and character that his mother soon becomes jealous of their attachment. In addition, Valentine and Bénédict take charge of the education of Valentin, treating him as if he were their own son and thus usurping the mother's role. And when Valentin marries Athénais, the *fermière* to whom Bénédict had been engaged, his daughter is named Valentine; this pale blond child is not reared by her mother but by her grandmother, Louise, who has now reintegrated the roles of sister and mother to take charge of another Valentine. Thus, the female roles of mother/sister/daughter/aunt/lover are in a constant state of flux in this novel, shifting and changing so that no one role remains distinct. One other facet of the naming convention completes the fusion of Louise and Valentine: this is the fact that Valentine's full name is Louise-Valentine, proof that each is merely one portion of a complete woman. (pp. 24-6)

The third set of sisters in Sand's first novels consists of Lélia and Pulchérie, two women who overtly represent contrasting possibilities of existence. Their psychosexual profiles are the basis of their ideologies; thus, the question of identity is a more serious problem here. The heroine Lélia, as a single entity, is viewed by others as a mass of impossible contradictions: angel/devil, fire/ice, monster/mistress, man/woman, sister/mother/

lover. She never becomes a fully integrated being for either Magnus or Sténio, both of whom fail to possess her. The Rose/Blanche, actress/nun syndrome is dramatically manifested here by the sensual courtesan Pulchérie and the spiritual poetess Lélia. The two meet at an orgiastic feast after years of separation, and the central portion of *Lélia* relates their reunion, culminating in a merging of their identities as Sténio possesses Pulchérie's body, convinced that she is Lélia. (pp. 26-7)

It is evident that George Sand is attempting to analyze and define female sexuality through these pairs of sister heroines. Each pair represents a shifting, unstable psychosexual nature, a kind of sexual schizophrenia which must be resolved. The author accomplishes the reunion of the many facets of female eroticism through a kind of metamorphosis of two identities, roughly representing the binary oppositions of body and soul, senses and emotions, active and passive, male and female. Such union is achieved in erotic scenes which, although varied in each novel, involve violent sexual fusion. The central triangle in each case is the same: a male figure is attracted to and caught between two different, almost opposite, females. The androgynous fission which has occurred to produce these two types can only be resolved through this figure of a third, the "other," the desiring male; metamorphosis occurs with him as the mediator, either in his mind, as in *Valentine,* or through his body, as in *Indiana* and *Lélia.* The repetition of this pattern in the three novels indicates an underlying subconscious network through which Sand explores the ambiguities and contradictions of sexual identity. She thus applies the existential question "Who am I?" to two (or more) facets of the same personality.

Whether the young author uses her novels as a means of defining her own psychosexual orientation is difficult, if not impossible, to state definitively. . . . The erotic nature of her first novels seems to indicate that Sand was never able to integrate her diverging sexual tendencies, thus justifying, to a certain extent, the critics' perplexity.

What is more important for her art, however, is the undeniable richness of her erotic imagination; of the romantic novelists, only Balzac rivals her in this aspect of creativity. Her perhaps intuitive perception of sexual schizophrenia and the consequent hunger for fusion is all the more striking when one considers the comparative temerity of the romantic novel in general. Sand has been called the first modern, liberated woman; her gloriously pre-Freudian explorations of female psychosexuality support that claim. (pp. 34-5)

Nancy Rogers, "Psychosexual Identity and the Erotic Imagination in the Early Novels of George Sand," in Studies in the Literary Imagination *(copyright 1979 Department of English, Georgia State University), Vol. XII, No. 2, Fall, 1979, pp. 19-35.*

V. S. PRITCHETT   (essay date 1979)

[George Sand] is shamelessly autobiographical. The love affair of the week, month or year, along with mysticism, socialism and The People was transposed into the novel that promptly followed; she spoke of herself as 'the consumer' of men and women too, and the men often turned out to be projections of herself. The passions of her characters, their powerful jealousies, their alternations of exaltation and gloom, were her own. She was half Literature.

Her finer powers emerged when her fame as a novelist declined, above all in her *Histoire de ma vie,* in her lively travel writing and her letters. In her letters there is no need of Gothic castles or dreadful ravines: her mundane experience was extraordinary enough in itself. As a traveller she had eyes, ears and verve. The short pastoral novels *La mare au diable (The Haunted Pool)* or *François le Champi (The Country Waif)* are serene masterpieces drawn from her childhood and her love of nature, which awakened her senses as they awakened Colette's. She was close to the peasants of Nohant. The self is in these tales, but it is recollected or transposed in tranquility—in her own early life she had known what it was to be a waif, albeit a very fortunate one. These works have never lost their quiet, simple, truth-telling power. . . . (p. 117)

[George Sand's] inner class conflict enriched both [her] exuberant imagination and those sympathies with the poor which took her into radical politics; strangely like Tolstoy—but without his guilt or torment—she turned to presenting the peasantry not as quaint folk or a gospel, but as sentient, expressive beings. . . . She had the humility and concern to discard dramatic earnestness without losing her psychological acumen or her art as a story teller who keeps her people in focus as the tradition of Pastoral does: very often her best work is a gloss on traditional forms.

In the feminist foreground of the present revival [of interest in George Sand] is *Lélia,* the confessional novel which she wrote at the age of twenty-nine. . . . Lélia is intended to be a Romantic heroine, a doomed but indomitable soul, one pursuing a mystical quest for spiritual love. She is beautiful, intellectual, independent, yet tormented by a sensuality that is nevertheless incapable of sexual happiness. She cannot be a nun like Santa Teresa nor can she be a courtesan or married woman. (pp. 117-18)

It is important to remember . . . that George Sand's prose feeds on a sensibility to music which dated from her childhood; she was alert to all sounds in nature and to all delicacies and sonorities of voice and instrument. (Her novels might be described as irresistible overtures to improbable operas which are—as they proceed—disordered by her didactic compulsion.) *Lélia,* I think, rises above this, because it is so personal and arbitrary in its succession of sounds and voices, and we are bounced into accepting the hyperbole as we would be if it were sung, though we may be secretly bored by the prolonging of the moans.

In *Lélia* we listen to five voices: there is the voice of Sténio, the young poet lover whom Lélia freezes with Platonic love; she is an exalted *allumeuse;* there is Trenmor, the elderly penitent gambler and stoic—her analysis of the gambler's temperament is the best thing in the book: George Sand was at heart a gambler—there is Magnus, the fanatic priest who is made mad by the suppression of his sexual desires and who sees Lélia as a she-devil; there is Pulchérie, Lélia's sister, a genial courtesan living for sexual pleasure; and Lélia herself, defeated by her sexual coldness, horrified by the marriage bed, the mocker of a stagnant society, religion and the flesh. She is sick with self-love and her desires approach the incestuous: she seeks weak men who cannot master her, to whom she can be either a dominating mother, sister or nurse.

In chorus these voices sing out the arguments for and against spiritual love. As in opera, the plot is preposterous and scenes are extravagant and end without warning. (pp. 120-21)

Lélia is one of those self-dramatizations that break off as mood follows mood. She asks what God intended for men and women: whether he intended them to meet briefly and leave each other

at once, for otherwise the sexes would destroy each other; whether the hypocrisy of a bourgeois society is the enemy; whether intellectual vision must be abnormal; whether poetry and religion corrupt. All the voices are George Sand herself—and very aware, as she frankly said, that she belonged to a generation which, for the moment, was consciously out to shock. . . .

One can see how much of the book comes out of Hoffmann and even more precisely from Balzac's equally chaotic and melodramatic *La Peau de chagrin.* . . . Both writers feel the expanding energies of the new century; both have the confident impulse toward the Absolute and to Omniscience; but hers is the kind of imagination and intellect that breaks off before suggesting a whole. Balzac and Sand were both absorbed by an imaginative greed; they worked themselves to the bone, partly because they were like that, partly because they created debts and openly sought a vast public. Their rhetoric was a nostalgia for the lost Napoleonic glory.

How thoroughly she toiled in her social-problem novels! The tedious *Compagnon du Tour de France* is a garrulous study of the early trade unions, a politically pious book, enlivened by her strong visual sense. In the far more sympathetic *Mauprat* she goes to the heart of her life-long debt to Rousseau. . . . (p. 123)

George Sand herself did not think we should be punished for our sins or our grave faults of character, but that we were called upon to learn from them: they were—*grace à* Rousseau—opportunities for interesting self-education and reform. She is not a doctrinaire like Gorki in his communist phase. Her advantage as a woman is that she is a psychologist who gives hostilities their emotional due: they are indications of the individual's right to his temperament. She may have been a domineering, ruthless woman and very cunning and double-minded with it, but there is scarcely a book that is not redeemed by her perceptions, small though they may be.

She understands the rich very well—'There are hours of impunity in château life'—and she thinks of the poor as individuals but flinches from them as a case. Two words recur continually in her works: 'delirium,' which may be ecstatic, bad, or, more interestingly, a psychological outlet; and 'boredom'—energy and desire had been exhausted. One can see that she is woman but not Woman. The little fable of *François de Champi* shows that she used every minute of her life; for not only was she in a fortunate sense a waif, as I have said, but an enlightened waif; and we note that when François grows up he marries the widow who has been a mother to him. Most of George Sand's men were waifs in one way or another; the Higher Incest was to be their salvation. Women were the real power figures, whereas men were consumable. She liked to pilfer their brains. (p. 124)

V. S. Pritchett, "George Sand," in his The Myth Makers *(copyright © 1979 by V. S. Pritchett; reprinted by permission of Random House, Inc.), Random House, 1979, pp. 115-27.*

ADDITIONAL BIBLIOGRAPHY

Babbitt, Irving. "George Sand and Flaubert." In his *Spanish Character and Other Essays*, pp. 121-40. Boston, New York: Houghton Mifflin Co., Cambridge: The Riverside Press, 1940.*

A discussion of Sand's correspondence with Flaubert including excerpts from letters detailing their debate on literature.

Blount, Paul G. *George Sand and the Victorian World*. Athens: The University of Georgia Press, 1979, 190 p.
    Traces the evolution of Victorian attitudes towards Sand's work from early disapproval to later admiration. Blount provides valuable references to important early reviews and essays.

Cate, Curtis. *George Sand: A Biography*. Boston: Houghton Mifflin Co., 1975, 812 p.
    The first major biography of Sand since André Maurois's *Lélia: The Life of George Sand*. Drawing on previously unpublished correspondence, Cate offers a thorough and complex portrait.

Duclaux, Madame Mary. "George Sand, the Romantic" and "La Bonne Dame de Nohant." In her *The French Procession: A Pageant of Great Writers*, pp. 162-75, 231-46. New York: Duffield & Co., 1909.
    Chronicles Sand's relationships, using published correspondence, with Alfred de Musset, her daughter Solange, and Flaubert.

Howe, Marie Jenney. *George Sand: The Search for Love*. New York: The John Day Co., 1927, 351 p.
    By exploring her many love affairs, this biographer attempts "to throw light on George Sand's inner life, to explain the secret of her suffering, the reasons for her loneliness, and the unprecedented situation which made her the most misunderstood woman in the history of literature."

Jones, Howard Mumford. "American Comment on George Sand, 1837-1848." *American Literature* 3, No. 4 (January 1932): 389-407.
    Discusses American critical reaction to Sand's novels during the years 1837-1848.

Kennard, N. H. "Gustave Flaubert and George Sand." *Nineteenth Century* 20, No. 117 (November 1886): 693-708.*
    Discusses the opposing literary styles of Sand and Flaubert as reflected in their published correspondence.

Maurois, André. *Lélia: The Life of George Sand*. Translated by Gerard Hopkins. New York: Harper & Brothers, 1953, 482 p.
    An authoritative biography.

Moore, Virginia. "George Sand." In her *Distinguished Women Writers*, pp. 83-95. New York: E. P. Dutton & Co., 1934.
    Provides a brief overview of Sand's personal life.

Ponsonby, Mary E. "George Eliot and George Sand." *The Nineteenth Century and After* L, No. 296 (October 1901): 607-16.*
    A comparison of Sand's and Eliot's novels, focussing on their contrasting attitudes towards life.

Rea, Annabelle. "Maternity and Marriage: Sand's Use of Fairy Tale and Myth." *Studies in the Literary Imagination* XII, No. 2 (Fall 1979): 37-47.
    Analyzes elements from fairy tales, myths, legends, and archetypal patterns found in Sand's novels.

Thomson, Patricia. *George Sand and the Victorians: Her Influence and Reputation in Nineteenth-Century England*. New York: Columbia University Press, 1977, 283 p.
    A study of the effect of Sand's novels on Victorian England.

Vest, James M. "Dreams and the Romance Tradition in George Sand's *Indiana*." *French Forum* 3, No. 1 (January 1978): 35-47.
    Examines references to nocturnal dreams and daydreaming in *Indiana*. Vest asserts that many of these passages are crucial to the character development and thematic unity of the work.

West, Anthony. "George Sand." In his *Mortal Wounds*, pp. 225-306. New York: McGraw-Hill Book Co., 1973.
    A "behavioral study" of Sand depicting her as a vindictive woman. West states that she "gave almost as much to falsifying the record of her own behavior as she did to the more immediately rewarding work of destroying her wretched husband's reputation and happiness."

Esaias Tegnér

1782-1846

Swedish poet and scholar.

Tegnér is remembered for his philosophical lyrics which combine precise language, fine characterization, patriotic expression, and metrical variety. These qualities won Tegnér the post of national poet of Sweden and helped to earn Sweden a place in world literature.

Tegnér was the youngest of eight children of a poor clergyman who died when Tegnér was a boy. His mother arranged for him to be tutored by the crown bailiff Branning, who recognized Tegnér's brilliance and helped him to attend the University of Lund, where he received a philosophy degree in 1802. In 1811, after winning the grand prize of the Swedish Academy for the poem *Svea* (Sweden), Tegnér was appointed professor of Greek at the university, where he taught for twenty-two years.

His early poetry is written in a style of academic classicism and based on Icelandic sagas and Norse folktales. Condemning the obscurantism of the Swedish Romantics, Tegnér adhered to the Gustavian tradition of elegant rhetoric. Greatly influenced by the philosophies of the German Romantics Emmanuel Kant and Friedrich Schiller, and the Danish poet Adam Oehlenschläger, Tegnér's verse is marked by vivid imagery and keen insight. Such pieces as *Den Vise* (The Wise One), *Kulturen* (Culture), and *Ungdomen* (Youth), also reflect Tegnér's personal melancholy and basic pessimism, qualities which pervade all of his work.

In 1824 Tegnér was named Bishop of Växjö. As bishop, his youthful liberalism shifted gradually toward conservatism, a tendency demonstrated in the epic cycle *Frithiofs saga (Frithjof's Saga)*, the first Swedish poem to gain worldwide recognition. Unfortunately, the pressures of Tegnér's religious duties, his literary work, and his marital problems caused him to suffer periods of mental illness. *Mjältsjukan (Hypochondria)* is an expression of Tegnér's despair and anticipation of death.

Henry Wadsworth Longfellow, who translated *Nattvardsbarnen (The First Communion)* said: "Esaias Tegnér stands first among the living poets of Sweden; a man of grand and gorgeous imagination, and poetic genius of high order." For his unique synthesis of diverse philosophies and careful, expressive language, Tegnér has earned his place as Sweden's national poet.

PRINCIPAL WORKS

Krigssång för skånska lantvärnet (poetry) 1808
Svea (poetry) 1811
Hjälten (poetry) 1813
Sång till solen (poetry) 1813
Nattvardsbarnen (poetry) 1820
 [*The First Communion*, 1842]
Axel (poetry) 1821
 [*Axel*, 1837]
Mjältsjukan (poetry) 1824
 [*Hypochondria*, 1825]

Frithiofs saga (poetry) 1825
 [*Frithiof's Saga*, 1833]
Afsked (poetry) 1842

BLACKWOOD'S EDINBURGH MAGAZINE (essay date 1828)

The Saga, or adventures of Frithioff . . . has always been held as one of the finest relics of northern antiquity. . . .

[The modern Swedish poet, Esaias Tegnér,] has adhered faithfully to the ancient Saga [in his *Frithiofs saga*]; and whatever slight departures he may have occasionally indulged in, are such as in no degree to impair the antique cast of the characters and sentiments. . . .

[Tegnér] had, in his poem of "Axel," given, perhaps, to a simple tale of love and jealousy, all the tender pathos of which it is susceptible. That short work teemed with beautiful and original images, the peculiarity and felicity of which betrayed an imagination revelling amid a field whose treasures had been skimmed, not exhausted. . . .

But Frithioff is a composition of a bolder and loftier character. . . . The polished languor of modern poesy derives marvellous and superhuman energy from the contact. . . . (p. 138)

> "'*Frithioff*—a Swedish Poem," in Blackwood's Edinburgh Magazine, *Vol. XXIII, No. CXXXV, February, 1828, pp. 137-59.*

[HENRY WADSWORTH LONGFELLOW]   (essay date 1837)

[Esaias Tegnér] stands first among the living poets of Sweden; a man of a grand and gorgeous imagination, and poetic genius of a high order. His countrymen are proud of him, and rejoice in his fame. If you speak of their literature, Tegnér will be the first name upon their lips. They will speak to you with enthusiasm of *Frithiofs Saga;* and of *Axel,* and *Svea,* and *Nattvardsbarnen,* (the Children of the Sacrament). Here, at least, the prophet is not without honor in his own country. . . . The modern Scald has written his name in immortal runes; not on the bark of trees alone, in the "unspeakable rural solitudes" of pastoral song, but on the mountains of his fatherland, and the cliffs that overhang the sea, and on the tombs of ancient heroes, whose histories are epic poems. Indeed we consider the **"Legend of Frithiof"** as one of the most remarkable productions of the age. . . . [It contains] a novel idea; and perhaps thereby the poem loses something in sober, epic dignity. But the loss is more than made up, by the greater spirit of the narrative; and it seems to us a very laudable innovation, thus to describe various scenes in various metre. (pp. 150-51)

It may be urged against Tegnér . . . that he is too profuse and elaborate in his use of figurative language, and that the same figures are sometimes repeated with very little variation. But the reader must bear in mind, that the work before him is written in the spirit of the past; in the spirit of that old poetry of the North, in which the same images and expressions are oft repeated. . . . (p. 151)

We must visit, in imagination at least, that distant land, and converse with the Genius of the place. It points us to the Past. . . . (p. 152)

[We] are but too well aware that by a brief analysis and a few scattered extracts, we can give only a faint idea of the original [inspiratory scenes which took place during the time Tegnér was writing *Frithiofs Saga,*] and that consequently the admiration of our readers will probably lag somewhat behind our own. If the poem itself should ever fall into their hands, we hope that [some] foregoing remarks on Sweden . . . [will] enable them to enter more easily into the spirit of the poem, and to feel more truly the influences under which it was written. The German translation of Frau von Helvig is very spirited and faithful, and moreover preserves the measure of the original in each canto. We regret, that we cannot award the same praise to the English version now lying before us. "There are," says Göthe, "two maxims of translation; the one requires that the author of a foreign nation be brought to us in such a manner that we may regard him as our own; the other, on the contrary, demands of us that we transport ourselves over to him, and adopt his situation, his mode of speaking, his peculiarities." We recognise only one of these maxims of translation,—the last. The English translators of Frithiof . . . seem to recognise neither. In hardly a single instance has the measure of the original been preserved. Entire passages are introduced which

do not belong to the poem; and others omitted which not only belong to it, but are essential to its beauty; and sometimes a single line, or even part of a line, is spread out into three or four. (pp. 158-59)

> [Henry Wadsworth Longfellow,] "Tegnér's 'Frithiofs Saga'," in The North American Review, *Vol. XLV, No. 96, July, 1837, pp. 149-85.*

CHRISTIAN EXAMINER (essay date 1840)

[*Frithiof's Saga, or the Legend of Frithiof*] is the first production of the Swedish muse, which has fallen in our way, and had for us the charm of a literary curiosity. Well acquainted with the useful but unromantic exports of the Baltic shores, . . . we have not been in the habit of finding among these precious commodities the intellectual recreation of a leisure hour. The history of Sweden has formed but a small part of the usual course of historical studies in this country. . . . Few interesting volumes of travels in these sequestered regions have reached us; and we doubt not that many of our readers will be as much surprised at encountering a highly poetical effusion from a Swedish mind. . . . (p. 343)

We confess that our own interest in this poem has been derived rather from the glimpses it affords us into the actual operation of that religious system, which was once so wide spread in all the north of Europe, than from its intrinsic poetical merit, or its nationality. Strongly marked, however, in these latter respects, it has seemed to us worthy the attention of our readers. It resembles rather the productions of the English mind, than those of the Germans, Italians, French, or Spanish. . . . Still the merits and demerits of *Frithiof's Saga* are of a different stamp from those of the other literatures of Europe, and it ought not, perhaps, to be judged by the standard of English taste. . . .

The author has thrown himself back into those rude ages [of the eighth and ninth centuries] with power, and, as it seems to us, with singular success. The supernatural agency introduced is, of course, that of the gods and goddesses worshipped in ancient Norway and Sweden; and the allusions to these fearful beings, their attributes and influence, are not so numerous as to confuse and disgust a foreign reader; but rather, in our opinion, serve to give a peculiar value to his imagery and interest to his simple plot. (p. 346)

[We] have faithful sketches of the superstitions and manners of those remote times. They are full of imagination; but it is not altogether the imagination of Tegner. He has taken what he found, but he has used his materials well. . . . The modern Swede has shown much discretion in the adoption of his machinery, availing himself of the picturesque legends of the Norzemen, and generally rejecting absurdities unendurable by the taste of the present day. (p. 348)

That Tegner is a man of genius none can doubt, who read *Frithiof's Saga,* even through the medium of a translation. . . . [If] we admire the glowing imagination of the poet, pouring forth a redundancy of images and illustrations like a fountain of fire, corruscating like the Aurora Borealis of his native skies, still deeper homage do we pay to his fine moral sense, which has portrayed a character so exalted as that of Ingeborg. The narrative is beautifully pure; the contrasts of character well managed; that between the brothers Helge and Halfdan, though the latter be only an outline, is distinct; and that between Frithiof and Ingeborg, both true to nature and well sustained. Her gentleness, her integrity, her tenderness of conscience,—that loveliest trait of innocence,—and her firmness of purpose, are so mingled with a womanly strength of affection, as to raise her far above the ordinary standard of heroines. Indeed, a common-place poet or novelist would have disposed of her very differently; and instead of wedding her to King Ring, would have striven to interest us by her sufferings in a mad flight with her lover; or would have bidden us weep over the fair and youthful self-murderess. Tegner has painted one who can rule herself, despising the romantic and dangerous sentiment, on which so many bewitching fictions have been based, so much real usefulness and happiness wrecked. Frithiof, on the other hand, stands forth, the wild and fiery child of impulse; headstrong and headlong, he listens only to the first hasty promptings from within; and well has Tegner painted the ever recurring regrets, the outward violence, the inward restlessness and misery of such a being. We think, therefore, that this poem has a moral, and a fine one. If there be an anachronism in the production, it is the pervading one of carrying on the action in a pagan land, with pagan agents, yet allowing the whole poem to breathe a Christian spirit, a Christian moral. But we cannot quarrel with our author for this; our hearts tell us he has done right. (p. 357)

> "'Frithiof's Saga, or The Legend of Frithiof'," in Christian Examiner, Vol. XXVIII, No. III, July, 1840, pp. 339-58.

THE CORNHILL MAGAZINE   (essay date 1875)

The poem which first made Tegnér famous throughout Sweden was *Svea*, a song to his native land, which gained the prize of the Swedish Academy in 1811. It was received with a thrill of enthusiasm throughout the country, although it contained the heaviest invectives against the morals and manners of the time, and despite the singularly senatorical *laudatio temporis acti* with which the song teems. Now followed poetical works, one after the other, in rapid succession, the most remarkable among which are the *Candidates for Confirmation, Axel,* and *Frithjofs Saga,* the one of Tegnér's works which has made his fame world-wide. (p. 350)

As a poet Tegnér has been a bone of contention amongst the critics almost up to the present time. In Sweden no poet before nor after, except Runeberg, who is not a Swede, has enjoyed anything like Tegnér's popularity. No Swedish poet has become so famous out of Sweden, and no Swedish poet has been so persistently translated into foreign languages as Tegnér. . . . Tegnér was gifted with great poetical talent; he exhibited it in perhaps unexampled clearness of language and aptness of illustration, qualities which in themselves constitute the popular favourite. But his vivid imagination sometimes carried him into illustrative researches which led him into such homely quaintnesses as to jar upon the tender nerves of the art critic with too shrill a note in the midst of a wealth of harmonious sweetness; and this is his chief sin in the critic's eyes. . . . Tegnér's poetry centres round no single philosophical ideal, but is sporadic and the unsystematic result of impulse; the one prevailing thought in his writings is intense love of fatherland, and of all that is noble and good in the national character.

In Tegnér's lyric of the *Passage Birds* we see no embodiment of a philosophic idea, no illustration of transcendental laws, but simply a beautiful example of that love of home and fatherland towards which his ideas for the most part gravitated. (pp. 350-51)

> "'Birds of Passage'," in The Cornhill Magazine, Vol. XXXII, No. 189, September, 1875, pp. 346-53.*

DUBLIN UNIVERSITY MAGAZINE   (essay date 1877)

[*Fridthjof's Saga: A Norse Romance*] possesses the recommendation of having passed through twenty editions in Sweden, and nearly as many in Norway, a circumstance which speaks strongly in favour of its accordance with the national taste and character. Mr. Longfellow the poet, describes it as "the noblest poetic contribution which Sweden has yet made to the literary history of the world:" and Mr. Bayard Taylor says, "no poetical work of modern times stands forth so prominently and peculiarly a representative of the literature of a race and language." (p. 401)

We have failed to discover the great merit either in the substance of the story or the translation, which others ascribe to them. The cantos, of varied length and metre, are not well connected together, and there is often great obscurity for want of necessary explanation, as to who is speaking, and under what circumstances. Out of such romantic materials, a more effective work might have been anticipated. (p. 403)

> "Literary Notices: 'Fridthjof's Saga': A Norse Romance," in Dublin University Magazine, Vol. 89, No. 531, March, 1877, pp. 400-03.

THE SATURDAY REVIEW   (essay date 1885)

With the single exception of Runeberg, who, though he wrote in the Swedish tongue, was a Russian subject, Tegnér alone among the many poets of Sweden has attained a European reputation. Triumphing over a disadvantage which has robbed the poets of Russia, Poland, and Hungary of half their glory— the necessity of writing in a language but little understood abroad—he ascended to fame early in the present century, with a rapidity which was surpassed by Byron alone, to enjoy a popularity well-nigh as cosmopolitan as his. (p. 280)

The genius of Tegnér was not precocious. He was twenty-seven when his **"Song for the Skaane Militia"** [*Krigssång för skånska lantvärnet*] procured him universal recognition; he was forty before his first narrative poem, *Axel,* was given to the world. . . . [In 1811] the poet's reputation was established by the publication of the patriotic ode, *Svea,* the ancient name for Sweden. . . .

[*Svea*] was crowned by the Swedish Academy, and in the following year its author received the appointment at Lund which has been alluded to. Innumerable minor pieces flowed from Tegnér's pen during this portion of his career, when versification was evidently treated merely as a pastime. Among the most interesting are his odes in celebration of historical personages, written on the anniversary of their death or the performance of some notable public action. . . .

Partiality to France is a trait characteristic of the Swedes, the result of long political connection, and from this Tegnér was by no means exempt. We may look in vain, therefore, in his writings for any trace of sympathy with our own heroes of the revolutionary period. . . .

It is now time to glance at the poet's longer and better known productions. In 1820 appeared the *Children of the Lord's Supper* [*Nattvardsbarnen*], which, as translated by Longfellow, is presumably familiar to the public. In 1822 came *Axel;* written in the style of Byron's tales, but with no trace of the idiosyncrasies of that poet; in fact, it wears the faithful impress of its author's native genius. The narrative itself is of a popular character. . . . The poem, which is very beautiful, though its diction may perhaps seem too luxuriant, has been translated into English. The year 1825 saw the production in its complete form of the poet's masterpiece, the *Tale of Frithiof* [*Frithiofs saga*], which has been so frequently rendered into English. . . . It has been objected that this poem is less an epic than a collection of ballads composed as it is of four-and-twenty short pieces—a defect, if such it be, which originated in its publication piece-meal in the detached numbers of a periodical. A more serious blemish may perhaps be detected in its anachronistic treatment; the poet has overlaid his theme, which is founded on the Icelandic saga of *Fridthiof hinn Frækinn,* or "the Bold," with a veneer of modern civilization which is quite out of place from a realistic point of view—the rugged viking of history has been pared down to a hero of modern romance. The climax of this ideal is reached in the final song, where a glimmer of Christian faith is represented as penetrating the still Pagan North. . . .

The *Crown Bride,* written in 1841, may be regarded as the child of Tegnér's old age. He had then long been in tranquil occupation of the see of Vexiö, and this charming idyl reveals the picture of his patriarchal existence in the midst of his flock. (p. 281)

> *"Tegnér," in* The Saturday Review, *London, Vol. 60, No.1557, August 29, 1885, pp. 280-82.*

HJALMAR HJORTH BOYESEN (essay date 1895)

The genius of the Scandinavian north has never found a more complete and brilliant incarnation than the Swedish poet Esaias Tegnér. Strong, cheerful, thoroughly wholesome, with a boyish delight in prowess, adventure, and daring deeds, he presents a most agreeable contrast to the moonshine singers and graveyard bards of the phosphoristic school, who were his contemporaries. (p. 219)

[In regards to Tegnér's style,] it is primarily the man who is impressive; and the author is interesting as the revelation of the man. He has no literary airs and graces, but speaks with a splendid authority, *e pleno pectore,* from the fulness of his manly conviction. . . . His vision of the world is bright and vivid, and he swims with a joyous ease in the high-tide of the moment, like a beautiful fish in the luminous summer sea. (pp. 220-21)

That wholesome robustness in his acceptance of life which finds utterance in his early songs must have established a quick bond of sympathy between him and his youthful hearers. The instincts of the predatory man were yet strong in him. The tribal feeling which we call patriotism, the juvenile defiance which carries a chip on its shoulder as a challenge to the world, the boastful self-assertion which is always ridiculous in every nation but our own—impart a splendid martial resonance to his first notable poem, **"War-Song for the Scanian Reserves".** . . . There was a charming, frank ferocity in this patriotic bugle-blast which found an echo in every Swedish heart. The rapid dactylic metres, with the captivating rhymes, alternating with the more contemplative trochees, were admirably adapted for conveying the ebullient indignation and wrath which hurls its gauntlet into the face of fate itself, checked, as it were, and cooled by soberer reflections and retrospective regret. It is the sorrow for the yet recent loss of Finland which inspires the elegiac tones in Tegnér's war-song; and it is his own ardent, youthful spirit, his own deep and sincere love of country, which awakes the martial melody with the throbbing of the drum and the rousing alarum of trumpets. (p. 232)

As long as we have wars we must have martial bards, and with the exception of the German, Theodor Körner, I know none who can bear comparison with Tegnér. English literature can certainly boast no war-poem which would not be drowned in the mighty music of Tegnér's **"Svea," "The Scanian Reserves,** and that magnificent, dithyrambic declamation, **"King Charles, the Young Hero."** Tennyson's "Charge of the Light Brigade" is technically a finer poem than anything Tegnér has written, but it lacks the deep virile bass, the tremendous volume of breath and voice, and the captivating martial lilt which makes the heart beat willy nilly to the rhythm of the verse. (p. 233)

It was in 1811 that Tegnér's poem **"Svea"** received the prize of the Swedish Academy. . . . It is not in any sense an imitation; but there is an audible reminiscence which is unmistakable in the metre and cadence of the short-lined verses, descriptive of the vison. Never, I fancy, had the Swedish language been made to soar with so strong a wing-beat, never before had it been made to sing so bold a melody. To me, I admit, **"Svea"** is too rhetorical to make any deep impression. It has a certain stately academic form, which, as it were, impedes its respiration and freedom of movement. . . . But Tegnér seems himself to have been conscious of the strait-jacket in which the old academic rules confined him, for in the middle of the poem he suddenly discards the stilted Alexandrines with which he had commenced and breaks into a rapturous old-Norse chant [with its] abrupt metres. . . . (pp. 236-37)

Soon after **"Svea"** followed, in 1812, **"The Priestly Consecration."** . . . Here the oratorical note and a certain clerical rotundity of utterance come very near spoiling the melody. **"At the Jubilee in Lund"** . . . is very much in the same strain. (p. 237)

Tegnér enriched Swedish literature with a series of lyrics which in point of lucidity of thought and brilliancy of diction have rarely been surpassed. . . . [He] stimulated [Sweden's] national self-respect without which independence is impossible. (pp. 241-42)

[In his **"Children of the Lord's Supper"** run] beautiful, stately hexameters, which . . . are delightfully adapted for epic narrative in any fairly polysyllabic language. And Swedish, which is the most sonorous of all Germanic tongues, and full of Gothic strength, produces the most delectable effects in the long, rolling line of slow-marching dactyls and spondees. The tempered realism of Tegnér, which shuns all that is harsh and trite, accords well with the noble classical verse. (pp. 245-46)

The romantic tale of **"Axel"** . . . rejoiced in a greater popularity, in spite of the carping criticism with which it was received by the *Svensk Litteratur—Tidning,* the organ of the Phosphorists. Though, to be sure, the merits of the poem are largely ignored . . . , it is undeniable that the faults which are emphasized do exist. First, the frequent violations of probability . . . draw tremendous draughts upon the reader's credulity; and secondly, the lavish magnificence of imagery rarely adds to the vividness of the situations, but rather obscures and confuses them. . . . The metaphors exist for their own sake, and are in nowise subordinate to the themes which they profess to illustrate. (pp. 246-47)

[The] images tread so close upon each other's heels, that they come near treading each other down, and tumbling together in a confused jumble. (p. 247)

["**Frithjof's Saga,**" from beginning to end,] has a lyrical intensity which sets the mind vibrating with a responsive emotion. It is not a coldly impersonal epic, recounting remote heroic events; but there is a deeply personal note in it, which has that nameless moving quality . . . which brings the tear to your eye, and sends a delicious breeze through your nerves. (p. 262)

[Tegnér's] passionate intensity of soul was, indeed, part of his poetic equipment; and he would not have been the poet he was if he had been cool, callous, and self-restrained. . . . A glimpse of this experience which transformed the powerful, joyous, bright-visaged singer into a bitter, darkly brooding pessimist, fleeing from the sinister shadow which threatened to overtake him, is afforded us in the poem "**Hypochondria.**" . . . (p. 280)

The Swedes have been called the Frenchmen of the North, and there is no doubt that delight in this toga-clad rhetoric is inherent in both. It was because Tegnér, in appealing to this delight, was so deeply representative that he extinguished the old school and became the national poet of Sweden. (p. 288)

> *Hjalmar Hjorth Boyesen, "Esaias Tegnér," in his* Essays on Scandinavian Literature, *Charles Scribner's Sons, 1895, pp. 219-88.*

MARGARET WATSON   (essay date 1897)

The whole poem of "**Frithjof's Saga**" is most interesting, and parts of it are very fine. I believe it is considered Tegnér's best work. . . .

Its story is that of a fine nature [in the character Frithjof], driven, half-unwittingly, into wrong-doing; of his repentance, atonement, and final forgiveness.

The other characters, even that of Ingeborg [the heroine], are but accessories. Ingeborg is too submissive, and claims our pity rather than our admiration, except in one scene, where she holds to her own idea of right in spite of Frithjof's appeals. . . . [Ingeborg's brothers,] the fanatical Helge and weak Halfdan, though powerfully, are lightly sketched. (p. 30)

> *Margaret Watson, "'Frithjof's Saga'," in* The Dublin Review, *Vol. CXXI, July, 1897, pp. 30-40.*

PAUL ROBERT LIEDER   (essay date 1914)

To present-day readers [Tegnér's poetry] seems overburdened with figures of speech, many of which are fine-spun. . . . With the exception of a few poems written in the dark years of his life, his work . . . is optimistic and fresh, not mournful and brooding. . . . [Though the material in *Frithiofs saga*] is ancient, its treatment is modern. . . . A characteristic feature of the poem is the use of a different metre in each of the twenty-four cantos, often with variations within the canto itself, to fit the scene in hand. In other words, though a narrative, the poem is lyric. Its form and its contents, in so far as it takes a saga story for its plot, was inspired, Tegnér frankly admitted, by Oehlenschlaeger's *Helge.* . . . *Frithiof,* however, with its exuberant glee, soon eclipsed its gloomier model in popularity and influence.

It is distinctly a poem for the young, and Frithiof is a typical boy's hero. (pp. xii-xiii)

Frithiof is not a character to be analyzed like Faust or Hamlet. Tegnér does not seem to have fashioned his poem . . . to mean more than meets the ear. Its greatness lies in its intense emo-

tion, its vividness of imagination, and its artistic beauty, rather than in the profundity of its thoughts. . . .

Axel, an excellent piece, though somewhat fantastic in plot, reveals, like *Svea,* Tegnér's patriotic side. The *Nattvardsbarnen* shows the sincerity and depth of his appreciation of Swedish peasant life. The characteristics of both works are essentially those of *Frithiof.* As an example of Tegnér's later style may be mentioned his *Mjeltsjukan (Ode to Melancholy),* "one of the most despairing poems," says Brandes, "of all literature."

Tegnér's writings have the individual note that we expect in a man of power. His short pieces have unquestionably "the lyric cry," his narratives are full of action, his war-songs beat with patriotism, and the love scenes in his longer poems, despite the sentimentality of the age and country in which they were written, still make a strong appeal. Whether or not critics agree with him in valuing imagery above thought in poetry, they can but acknowledge that in revealing sensuous beauty in verses of great melody Tegnér shows nothing less than genius. (p. xiv)

> *Paul Robert Lieder, in his introduction to* Poems by Tegnér: "The Children of the Lord's Supper" and "Frithiof's Saga," *translated by Henry Wadsworth Longfellow and Rev. W. Lewery Blackley, The American-Scandinavian Foundation, 1914 (and reprinted by The American-Scandinavian Foundation, 1930), pp. ix-xxvii.*

ADOLPH B. BENSON   (essay date 1938)

Tegnér has laid the rich colours of his palette [in *Frithiof's saga*]. Epical recitations, dramatic scenes, lyric songs, all are found here. In the development of his subject he has given attention so far as choice of form is concerned only to the movement of the action and to the various passions of the characters. (p. 106)

Frithiof's saga is the favourite poem of the Swedes, the work of their great national poet that up to the present time is without peer. After this composition, the one they prefer is the little poem of the *First communion* . . . , which Tegnér has invested with all the fascination of his sacred character as Bishop. . . . (p. 107)

Axel [is] one of the finest poetic monuments of the Swedish language.

Preserved also are Tegnér's lectures and the sermons which he gave in his capacity of bishop; the former serve to demonstrate with what zeal and profundity he was dedicated to the bettering of teaching in Sweden; they are masterpieces of oratorical art, notable contributions to the science of pedagogy. The sermons are unsurpassed examples of Protestant religious oratory. (p. 109)

> *Adolph B. Benson, "Romanticism," in* The History of the Scandinavian Literatures: A Survey of the Literatures of Norway, Sweden, Denmark, Iceland and Finland, from Their Origins to the Present Day, Including Scandinavian-American Authors, and Selected Bibliographies, *edited and translated by Frederika Blankner (copyright © 1938 by The Dial Press; reprinted by permission of The Dial Press), Dial, 1938, pp. 101-09.*

ADDITIONAL BIBLIOGRAPHY

Brandes, Georg. "Esaias Tegnér". In his *Creative Spirits of the Nineteenth Century,* translated by Rasmus B. Anderson, pp. 106-83. New York: Thomas Y. Crowell Co., 1923.
> An account of the most important features of Tegnér's life and works. Brandes portrays the individuality of Tegnér by including the historical, psychological, and aesthetic atmosphere of his time.

Franzen, Gösta. "Tegnér's *Skeppet Ellida:* The Icelandic Background and the Etymology." *Scandinavian Studies* 34, No. 4 (November 1962): 237-44.
> Discusses Tegnér's knowledge of language and history, and how he applied it to *Frithiof's saga.*

Sturtevant, Albert Morey. "The Character of Ingeborg in Tegnér's *Frithiofssaga.*" *Scandinavian Studies* 7 (February 1927): 31-51.
> Detailed character analysis of Ingeborg in *Frithiof's saga.*

Tegnér, Esaias. Introduction to his *Frithiof's Saga, a Legend of the North,* translated by G. S., pp. 43-9. Stockholm: A. Bonnier, 1839.
> A translated version of Tegnér's letter to the translator of *Frithiof's saga.* Here, Tegnér reveals his purpose for writing the novel, and responds to some of the critical reviews he has received.

Paul (Marie) Verlaine

1844-1896

(Also wrote under the pseudonym of Pablo de Herlagñez) French poet, essayist, autobiographer, and short story writer.

Many critics have contended that Verlaine captured the musicality of the French language more than did any other poet. By using rhyme structures and meters that had previously been rare in French poetry, he is said to have liberated French poetics from the strictures of classicism and the rhetoric of Romanticism. And although he led a life of poverty and dissipation, Verlaine wrote verse that is generally recognized as among the most beautiful in all poetry, giving expression to thoughts and feelings that few poets have been able to describe. Verlaine took as his motto "no color, only nuance," and thus helped to define the Symbolist theory of poetics, which demands that the poet never name an emotion, but merely suggest it. Thus, in its evocative power, poetry was to resemble music rather than prose.

Born in Metz to middle-class parents, Verlaine began his bohemian ways as a student at the Lycée Bonaparte, where one of his teachers called him the filthiest, most slovenly student in the school. Barely obtaining his degree, he took a minor clerical position in the city government of Paris. This job required little work and enabled him to spend much of his time in cafés, and to begin writing poetry. In 1866, he published a book of poems which were influenced by Baudelaire and titled *Poèmes saturniens.* Though this volume and his next, *Fêtes galantes,* were well received by other poets, the public ignored them, and Verlaine continued his decadent lifestyle.

In 1869, he became engaged to Mathilde Mauté. He celebrated their marriage in *La bonne chanson,* a volume that contains the verse of Verlaine at his happiest, a Verlaine who truly thought that love and marriage would save him from his dangerous way of life. But he could not anticipate the effect of one man—Arthur Rimbaud—upon his life and work. Rimbaud, whom he met in 1871, was an almost satanic figure in the life of Verlaine and soon drove him away from his wife and back to a life of insecurity and depravity. The two poets traveled through Europe. This separation from Mauté destroyed Verlaine's marriage and whatever stability his life had. The relationship between the two poets is chronicled in Rimbaud's *Un saison en enfer (A Season in Hell).* In 1873, Verlaine shot and wounded Rimbaud in a quarrel, and was imprisoned for a year and a half, ending the tumultuous affair. Though he converted to Catholicism while in prison, Verlaine never was able to change his ways, and spent the rest of his life repenting his excesses. He was a creature of the moment, as intuitive in his poetry as in his actions, and critics often attribute the greatly varying quality of his poetry to Verlaine's ephemeral nature. In his later years, his poverty was also a contributing factor to his often inferior verse.

Though many French critics prefer *Sagesse, Romances sans paroles* is generally considered to be Verlaine's greatest work, and expresses the best qualities of his writing: musicality, personal feeling, and the evocation of sorrow and regret. Though Verlaine has been attached to various movements in poetry, he was one of the few French poets who did not hold an artistic

theory for more than a year or two at a time. His poetry is highly original, but never explicit or forceful. In all of his poems, it is his distinct, yet whispered voice that is heard.

PRINCIPAL WORKS

Poèmes saturniens   (poetry)   1866
Les Amies [as Pablo de Herlagñez]   (poetry)   1868
Fêtes galantes   (poetry)   1869
La bonne chanson   (poetry)   1870
Romances sans paroles   (poetry)   1874
Sagesse   (poetry)   1881
Jadis et naguère   (poetry)   1884
Les poètes maudits   (essays)   1884
Amour   (poetry)   1888
Parallelement   (poetry)   1889
Bonheur   (poetry)   1891
Chansons pour elle   (poetry)   1891
Hombres   (poetry)   1891
Mes hôpitaux   (essays)   1891
Liturgies intimes   (poetry)   1892
Elégies   (poetry)   1893
Mes prisons   (essays)   1893

J. K. HUYSMANS (essay date 1884)

[The following excerpt is taken from J. K. Huysmans's novel *Against the Grain.*]

[After the masters, Des Esseintes] betook himself to a few writers who attracted him all the more because of the disdain in which they were held by a public incapable of understanding them.

One of them was Paul Verlaine who had begun with a volume of verse, the *Poèmes Saturniens*, a rather ineffectual book where imitations of Leconte de Lisle jostled with exercises in romantic rhetoric, but through which already filtered the real personality of the poet in such poems as the sonnet *Rêve Familier.* (p. 277)

[In] some of his books, *Bonne Chanson, Fêtes Galantes, Romances sans paroles,* and his last volume, *Sagesse,* were poems where he himself was revealed as an original and outstanding figure.

With rhymes obtained from verb tenses, sometimes even from long adverbs preceded by a monosyllable from which they fell as from a rock into a heavy cascade of water, his verses, divided by improbable caesuras, often became strangely obscure with their audacious ellipses and strange inaccuracies which none the less did not lack grace.

With his unrivalled ability to handle metre, he had sought to rejuvenate the fixed poetic forms. He turned the tail of the sonnet into the air, like those Japanese fish of polychrome clay which rest on stands, their heads straight down, their tails on top. Sometimes he corrupted it by using only masculine rhymes to which he seemed partial. . . . He had employed other rhymes whose dim echoes are repeated in remote stanzas, like faint reverberations of a bell.

But his personality expressed itself most of all in vague and delicious confidences breathed in hushed accents, in the twilight. He alone had been able to reveal the troubled Ultima Thules of the soul; low whisperings of thoughts, avowals so haltingly and murmuringly confessed that the ear which hears them remains hesitant, passing on to the soul languors quickened by the mystery of this suggestion which is divined rather than felt. (pp. 277-79)

It was no longer the immense horizon opened by the unforgettable portals of Baudelaire; it was a crevice in the moonlight, opening on a field which was more intimate and more restrained, peculiar to Verlaine who had formulated his poetic system in those lines of which Des Esseintes was so fond:

Car nous voulons la nuance encore,
Pas la couleur, rien que la nuance.
Et tout le reste est littérature.

(p. 279)

After his ***Romances sans paroles*** . . . , Verlaine had preserved a long silence, reappearing later in those charming verses, hauntingly suggestive of the gentle and cold accents of Villon, singing of the Virgin, "removed from our days of carnal thought and weary flesh." Des Esseintes often re-read *Sagesse* whose poems provoked him to secret reveries, a fanciful love for a Byzantine Madonna who, at a certain moment, changed into a distracted modern Cydalise so mysterious and troubling that one could not know whether she aspired toward depravities so monstrous that they became irresistible, or whether she moved in an immaculate dream where the adoration of the soul floated around her ever unavowed and ever pure. (p. 280)

> *J. K. Huysmans, in a chapter in his* Against the Grain: A Rebours, *translated by John Howard (originally published as* A Rebours, *G. Charpentier, 1884),* Albert and Charles Boni, 1930, pp. 265-301.

EDWARD DELILLE (essay date 1891)

Were I called on to declare in a word what I think the keynote of Verlaine, I should reply—it is to be found in his peculiar thrill of *grief.* . . . What Verlaine has invented, is a new shade of woe.

In the attempt to define in its full distinctness and uniqueness the particular, mournful, world-weary, world-wounded thrill which is the Verlaine *leit-motiv,* recourse must be had to negatives. It is not wistfully cold and pure like the melancholy of [Alfred] De Vigny; not raging and wailing by turns like the angry sorrow of [Alfred de] Musset; not deliberately and calmly desperate like the pessimism of Leconte de Lisle; not quivering continually at the precise point between tears and smiles like the pathos of [Heinrich] Heine, and not consistently, logically agonising like the world-horror of [Giacomo] Leopardi. Something less material it is than even the least material of these. . . . Something imperceptibly faint and slight, like the liliputian wreath of vapour that might rise from hot tears shed silently one by one in secret; something throbbing in a sort of reproachful dumbness of amaze, a dulness and deadness of pain, like some very frail and small creature crushed bleeding to the ground by a big and brutal force or being that it cannot rightly understand. . . .

In the Jardin des Plantes at Paris, in a fine grassy enclosure, is a group of tiny animals, the smallest antelopes known. . . . [Such] is the effect of their littleness, their timorousness, their almost absurd delicacy—so small, so delicate, those little, little hoofs, those little tender limbs, those fragile fawn-coloured sides, that little humid twitching muzzle; so small, and yet so keenly, tremulously perceptive and sensitive so intensely; so little, yet all alive and quivering with nerves; so small, so weak, so helpless, and apparently so unfitted for aught except to apprehend; such minute atoms and specks of sentient being, so lost amid a universe's vast incomprehensibility—that my heart has been smitten to look upon those miniature living things, with the quite inordinate frailty of their body and the disproportionate bigness of their eyes. (p. 394)

I think those antelopes are symbols of a state of soul rare enough among men, and yet too frequent. A somewhat similar combination of hopeless powerlessness to resist with the most unbounded capacity to suffer . . . is reflected in Verlaine's verse. (pp. 394-95)

Verlaine makes somewhat frequent, and always most felicitous use of casually recurrent rhymes within the verse. Another characteristic of Verlaine's manner is his employment of irregular nine-foot, eleven-foot, and thirteen-foot metres, giving results of lightness, fluidity, and softness not to be obtained with the artificial, Versailles-park trimness of such forms as the classic Alexandrine for example. (p. 395)

If in the art, literature, politics and society of France since 1870 Verlaine has found but little to appease his nature's inner cravings for fitness ethic and aesthetic, neither have the exterior aspects of Paris itself brought unquestioning delight to his mind or eye:

> La 'grande ville.' Un tas criard de pierres blanches
> Où rage le soleil comme en pays conquis.
> Tous les vices ont leur tanière, les exquis
> Et les hideux, dans ce désert de pierres blanches.

Such are the thoughts, distasteful, with which the "décor" of outward Paris inspires him. The theme, however, is not always treated by Verlaine in this moralising vein. White streets, gay parks, bustling suburban fêtes, busy faubourgs, banal *banlieue*, the varied Parisian scenery familiar in [François] Coppée's verse, [Giuseppe] De Nittis's and [Jean] Béraud's paintings, [Jean Louis] Forain's sketches and aquarelles: there is much of this in Verlaine, done with a smartness, brightness, vividness of touch quite delightful. Instantaneous photographs, only artistic. . . .

In passing let me note how readily, for all his intense Parisianism, modernism, impressionism, Verlaine turns to allegory, that simplest, yet profoundest, of poetic moral effects. He is naturally allegorical, like Baudelaire, Hawthorne, Poe. (p. 400)

Of Verlaine's sense for love in the abstract, meaning, in the concrete, woman—and as everyone knows who *quâ* critic knows anything, 'tis the nature and degree of his sense for love that give the truest measure of the poet—I shall only say that it is most delicate, most exquisite at once and most unhappily questioning and revolted. The core of animalism in even the feminine nature is apparent odiously to Verlaine's sense. . . .

The cruel faculty of the analyst is Verlaine's: the painfully piercing glance, painful alike to him and to his victim, that gazes half-involuntarily upon the nudeness of the poor flawed stigmatised clay:

> Tu m'as, ces pâles jours d'automne blanc, fait mal,
> A cause de tes yeux, où fleurit l'animal. . . .

Never, to Verlaine, is woman so divine as when her animal nature sinks into latency, quiescence, and may, for one moment, be lost to his perception. . . .

[Carnality], *per se,* Verlaine abhors. To him it seems a loathsome thing, the slimy slug upon the plant. . . .

But if carnality pure and simple repels him, depravity in its more refined forms exercises a quite morbid attraction for his spirit. Take as proof his *Fêtes Galantes.* Redolent it is, of all possible loveliness of sin; all imaginable grace, charm, force, terror, diabolism, delight, of the thoroughly corrupt. A tiny wreath, woven with delicate, delicious art, of the rarest, subtlest, sweetest flowers of passional aberrance and unhealth, insinuating—so strongly!—on the sense the languor, torpor,

from which there may be no awaking. The fullest essence is herein, of that dangerous eighteenth-century compound of sensuality the most determined, refinement the most delightful, intelligence the most vivid, elegance the most extreme. Twenty little pieces, as cunningly coquettish, suggestive as scientifically, of all by which depravity may be, has been, rendered stronger than love and than death. . . . Yet, by a touch here and there, as of an organ note note now and again among the "pleasing" of flutes and lutes, is made to be felt the poet's own occasional interior thrill at the thought of the essential horror underlying this "gallantry" and these "fêtes." (p. 402)

He has lived for his art alone, and by reason of his art he must die; because, full of art, he is void of many things else. Void of broad general humanity, void of the deeper world-wisdom, void of the eloquence most penetrating and profound that coming from the heart goes to the heart not of the time merely but of all time, and speaks, a lofty Voice, along the ages.

No great poet, no world-poet, is Paul Verlaine. But the exquisite, delightful, diseased, lacerated poet of a morbid *élite*. In the main, however, a touching figure, with the intensity of his emotion, elevation of his impulse, and fatal weakness of his will. . . . Yes, poor wandering, worsted Knight, wandering and worsted and woeful and utterly downcast, but not, when all is said and done, not ignoble, and so painstricken, and so pitiable! (p. 405)

Edward Delille, "The Poet Verlaine," in The Fortnightly Review, *Vol. XLIX, March 1, 1891, pp. 394-405.*

STÉPHANE MALLARMÉ   (essay date 1891)

[Verlaine] was the first to react against the impeccable and impassible Parnassian attitudes. His fluid verse and certain of his intentional dissonances were already evident in *Sagesse.* . . . [The] father, the real father of all the young poets is Verlaine, the magnificent Verlaine. The attitude of the man is just as noble as the attitude of the writer. For it is the only possible attitude at a time when all poets are outlaws. Think of absorbing all the grief that he has—and with his pride and his tremendous pluck! (pp. 22-3)

Stéphane Mallarmé, "The Evolution of Literature" (originally published in Echo de Paris, *March 14, 1891), in* Mallarmé: Selected Prose Poems, Essays, & Letters, *translated by Bradford Cook (© 1956, The Johns Hopkins Press), The Johns Hopkins University Press, 1956, pp. 18-24.**

ARTHUR SYMONS   (essay date 1891)

Bonheur is written very much in the style of *Sagesse,* and a great part of it might be assigned, on internal evidence, to a period anterior to *Amour* and *Parallèlement.* It has none of the perversity, moral and artistic, of the latter book, despite a few experiments upon metre and rhyme. Nor is space devoted, as occasionally in *Amour,* to the mere courtesies of literary friendship. The verse has an exquisite simplicity, a limpid clearness, a strenuous rejection of every sort of artistic "dandyism." . . .

The verse in *Bonheur* is indeed, "*bien* simple." There is a poem addressed to a friend—"Mon ami, ma plus belle amitié, ma meilleure"—which even Verlaine has hardly excelled in a kind of plaintive sincerity, full of the beauty of simple human feeling, seeking and finding the most direct expression. . . . Verlaine speaks to his friend as if he would say more for friendship than has ever been said before. He would fain find words close and gracious enough to express all the intimacy and charm of their friendship. . . . "Remembrances to be, and hopes returned again"—how lovely a verse, French or English! And the emotion, temperate and restrained through most of the poem, rises at the end into exaltation:

> Afin qu'enfin ce Jésus-Christ qui nous créa
> Nous fasse grâce et fasse grâce au monde immonde
> D'autour de nous alors unis—paix sans séconde!—
> Définitivement, et dicte: Alleluia.

I quote this stanza not only because of its place in the poem—its expression of the culminating emotion—but because it is an excellent example of Verlaine's most characteristic technique. Note the rhyme at the beginning of the first line and at the end of the second, the alliteration, the curious effect produced by the repetition of "fasse grâce" (itself an assonance), the tormented rhythm throughout, the arbitrary and extraordinary position and transposition of accents. It cannot be said that all these experiments are always and equally successful; but it is useless to deny that Verlaine has widened the capacities of French verse. He has done what Goncourt has done in his prose: he has contributed to the destruction of a classical language, which, within its narrow limits, had its own perfection. But how great a gain there has been, along with this inevitable loss! (p. 362)

Almost all the poems in *Bonheur* are closely personal—confessions of weakness, confessions of penitence, confessions of "l'ennui de vivre avec les gens et dans les choses," confessions of good attempts foiled, of unachieved resolutions. . . . [Here] as in *Sagesse,* the really distinguishing work is an outpouring of desires that speak the language of desire, of prayers that go up to God as prayers, not as literature; of confessions that have no reticences.

One of the finest pieces tells the story of that endeavour to rebuild the ruined house of life which Verlaine made at the time of his conversion, after those calm and salutary eighteen months' of seclusion. This intensely personal poem, which is really a piece of the most exact autobiography, becomes a symbol of all lives that have fallen, that have struggled to rise, that have failed in the endeavour. Towards the end the emotion rises in a crescendo, half of despair, half of hope, as he cries out in the very fury of helplessness against the worst of foes. . . . (pp. 362-63)

> *Arthur Symons, "Literature: 'Bonheur'," in* The Academy, *No. 989, April 18, 1891, pp. 362-63.*

GEORGE MOORE (essay date 1891)

[Verlaine's] instincts are neither patriotic nor popular, but entirely aesthetical—the religious emotion of a monk painting the joys of heaven above the dim altar, and the sensuousness of the same monk delineating the tall adolescent angel. He loves language and every cadence the French language may inflect haunts in his ear. So natural and instinctive is the music of his verse that it often seems no more than the melancholy inarticulate voice which nature speaks, penetrating and profound by reason of its vagueness and utterness. (p. 86)

Verlaine is exclusively a poet, and may leave for no moment the immortality of his verse for the daily bread of prose. His rhythms become disintegrated in prose, his thoughts—gentle reveries—die in the looseness of prose. (p. 87)

In one of his essays Edgar Poe says that no one is original by temperament; that we become original by a deliberate effort of reason, by desiring originality, and declining to write in this way and that way, because these methods have been appropriated by other writers, and not because they are unnatural to us. . . . Nature is more subtle than our logic, even more subtle than Poe's. Verlaine believes in the Roman Catholic Church as earnestly as the Pope himself, but in Verlaine there is only belief—practice is wholly wanting in him. Nor do I think he ever quite realises how he lives or how he writes. (p. 89)

I feel sure that [Verlaine's] strange cadences are an integral part of the man's ear, and are as spontaneous and unconscious as the thought. In Verlaine, mental and corporeal life are distinct and separable things working almost unconsciously of each other. (p. 90)

In considering Verlaine's claims to high poetic fame we are more concerned with his last two volumes, *Sagesse* and *Amour,* than with the earlier ones, beautiful though they all most certainly are. For it is in *Sagesse* and *Amour* that we are most fully treated to the astonishing spectacle of a man writing purely devotional poetry while leading notoriously a more than profligate life. . . . [To] find the seed whence sprang the devotional verses of Verlaine, I look in vain through French poetry until I happen across Villon's Ballade to his Mother. Unconsciously and without suspicion of plagiarism, Verlaine has elaborated that beautiful poem into many volumes, and were Villon unknown to me and I were shown the refrain of the ballade in question: *"Dans cette foi je veux vivre et mourir,"* I would stake my very existence that it was a line of Verlaine's, and probably to be found in *Sagesse*. . . . Some poets write to tell how well women have loved them, others seek to record their exploits in the battle or the huntingfield, others desire to convince the reader of their excessive erudition; all show pride more or less hidden on some point, and they write with the object of acquainting the world with their excellence or their peculiarity in this or that respect; but I am not aware of any other poet except Verlaine who has written solely to tell how weak, helpless, and undistinguished he is in all ways and things. Nowhere do we find a trace of personal pride; even his afflictions he relates gently and without bitterness. (pp. 91-2)

The whole man—his poetry, his life, his literary success, and his failure—is contained in an all-embracing sense of his own unworthiness; he keeps it continually before you; he tells you of it in a hundred different ways, for he is the most personal of poets. He writes of nothing but himself; his own life is his only theme. Sometimes he confides it by a personal narrative, sometimes it assumes some slight and obvious disguisement. His unworthiness is all he has to tell you, and it is most affecting, for it is the whole man. (pp. 92-3)

> *George Moore, "A Great Poet," in his* Impressions and Opinions, *Charles Scribner's Sons, 1891 (and reprinted by T. Werner Laurie, Ltd., 1913, pp. 85-94).*

ANATOLE FRANCE (essay date 1891)

[The *Poèmes saturniens,*] certainly never foreshadowed the most singular, monstrous, mystical, complicated, simple, nervous, eccentric, and undoubtedly most inspired and truest of contemporary poets. Still, through these manufactured poems, and in spite of the manner of the [Parnassian] school, one divined a kind of strange, unhappy and tormented genius. (p. 297)

[It] was only a slim volume. But Paul Verlaine had already shown himself therein in his perturbing candour, and something of his slight, awkward and inexpressible charm. . . .

Verlaine, who is one of those musicians who play false by refinement, has put many discords in these minuet airs, and his violin sometimes scrapes horribly; but all at once some note tugs at your heart-strings. The wicked fiddler has stolen your soul. (p. 298)

The accent is new, peculiar, and profound. . . .

Suddenly Paul Verlaine disappeared. . . . Nothing further was heard of him. For fifteen years he kept silence; after which it was learnt that the penitent Verlaine was publishing a volume of religious poetry [*Sagesse*] with a Catholic publishing-house. What had happened in these fifteen years? I know not, and what does anybody know? The true history of François Villon is ill known. And Verlaine much resembles Villon: they are two "bad hats," to whom it was granted to say the sweetest things in the world. As for those fifteen years, we must adhere to the legend which states that our poet was a great sinner. . . . (p. 299)

Doubtless it is but a legend, but it will prevail. It must. This detestable and charming poet's verses would lose their value and meaning if they came not from the dense atmosphere "lacking all light" where the Florentine [Dante] saw carnal sinners who subordinated reason to lust. . . .

Moreover, the fault must be real for the repentance to be genuine. In his repentance Paul Verlaine returned to the God of his baptism and of his first communion with the completest candour. He was entirely sentimental. He never reflected nor argued.

No human thought, no intelligence ever troubled his idea of God. We have seen that he was a faun. Those who have read the Lives of the Saints know how easily the fauns, who are very simple, allowed themselves to be converted to Christianity by the Apostles to the Gentiles. Paul Verlaine wrote the most Christian verses we have in France. (p. 301)

This conversion was truly sincere, but not enduring. Like the dog of Holy Scripture, he returned to his vomit. Once more his relapse inspired him with exquisite candour. What, then, did he do? As sincere in sin as in repentance, he accepted the alternatives with cynical innocence. He resigned himself to taste in turn the pleasures of crime and the horrors of despair. Even more, he so to speak tasted them together: he kept the affairs of his soul in two separate compartments. Hence the curious collection of verse entitled *Parallèlement*. It is doubtless perverse, but of such artless perversity that it almost seems pardonable.

And then, this poet must not be judged like an ordinary man. He has rights which we have not, for he is at once greater and smaller than we are. He has no conscience, and is a poet such as is not met with once in a hundred years. (pp. 303-04)

You say he is mad? I agree. And if I did not think so, I should not have written what I have. He is certainly mad. But remember that this lunatic has created a new art, and there is a chance that some day it will be said of him, as it is now said of François Villon, with whom he may be well compared: "He was the greatest poet of his time." . . .

Count Tolstoi tells us the history of a poor, drunken, wandering musician, who, with his violin, expresses all that can be imagined of heaven. After having wandered throughout a whole winter's night, the wretched man falls dying in the snow. Then a voice says to him: "You are the best and the happiest of men." Were I a Russian, at least if I were a Russian saint and prophet, I feel that after reading *Sagesse* I should say to-day to the poor poet lying in a hospital bed: "You fell, but you confessed your fault. You were unhappy, but you never lied. Poor Samaritan, between your childish babble and your invalid's hiccoughs, it has been granted you to utter a few heavenly words. We are Pharisees. You are the best and the happiest of men." (p. 304)

Anatole France, "Paul Verlaine," in his On Life & Letters, *third series, edited by J. Lewis May & Bernard Miall, translated by D. B. Stewart (originally published as* La vie littéraire, *Vol. 3,* Calmann Lévy, *1891), John Lane Company, 1922, pp. 295-304.*

ARTHUR SYMONS   (essay date 1893)

[Verlaine's] verse, from the moment when, in *Romances sans Paroles,* it attains complete individuality, has been true to [his] theory of subtlety in simplicity, alike in the evocations of twilight landscapes and twilight moods which we find in his earlier work, in the poignant intensity of the spiritual conflict expressed in the work written later, and in the sometimes brutal sensuality which finds expression in some of his very latest work.

It is all very wrong, no doubt, and perhaps incredible, from one standpoint, that a man should sin and repent, sin and repent, with such absolute good faith, such tumultuous helplessness, and that he should write it all down as the mood takes him, addressing now "vous, cocodette un peu mûre," and now—

Vous, maitresse de la mort
Et reine de la vie, o Vierge immaculée.

But Verlaine is always faithful to himself, to the two sides of himself, and he has thus succeeded in rendering, as no one ever has before, the whole *homo duplex,* the eternal conflict of humanity. And the verse which he has fashioned to his use with such *finesse,* the verse which can sing as French verse has never yet sung, which can express the last fine shade of emotion and of sensation, has, in opening up a new future for French verse, become in his hands the vehicle of a new kind of truth. Verlaine has often protested against the fallacy which attributes to him a school. He has shown others, it is true, that verse can have a new texture, as Whistler, for instance, has shown that paint can be handled in a new way. But he has done so incidentally, and where he is most himself he is least of all to be followed, for with Verlaine, as with every great writer, the style is the man. (pp. 611-12)

The poet, the man of genius, is fundamentally abnormal, for genius itself, we were once told figuratively, we are now assured scientifically, is a form of madness. It is the poet against society, society against the poet, an irreconcilable antagonism, the shock of which, however, is often possible to avoid by some admitted compromise. So much license is allowed on the one side, so much liberty foregone on the other. The consequences are not always of the best, art being generally the loser. But there are certain natures to which compromise is impossible, and never was there a nature more absolutely impelled to act itself out, more absolutely alien to every conceivable convention, than that of Verlaine. (p. 615)

Arthur Symons, "Paul Verlaine," in The New Review, Vol. IX, No. 55, December, 1893, pp. 609-17.

ARTHUR SYMONS (essay date 1896)

More than any man of letters of his time, Verlaine has been a sort of public figure, typifying, for all the world, the traditional vagabond character of the poet. As the whole of his work was personal, one long confession of the joys and sorrows, the sins and repentances, of his strange, troubled, intensely living life, it is perhaps natural that an undue attention should have been given, not always quite sympathetically, to these private accidents of existence. . . . What really concerns us is that Verlaine was a great poet, certainly the greatest French poet since Baudelaire, and with a subtlety and sincerity of genius which not even Baudelaire possessed. As a verse-writer he extended the bounds of the French language, he brought into it or out of it a "lyrical cry" with which it had never thrilled. As a poet he expressed a wonderful personality, a personality as interesting as any of our time, with a directness, a poignant simplicity, equal to that of Villon. As an influence, he has controlled almost the whole poetic writing of the younger generation in his own country, and much of the poetic writing of the younger generation in other countries. And I cannot end these lines, written hurriedly on hearing the news of his death, without saying that to those who knew him intimately he has left the memory of one of the most intrinsically fine, one of the most sensitively sympathetic, of temperaments, essentially the temperament of genius, the poetic temperament.

Arthur Symons, "M. Paul Verlaine," in The Athenaeum, No. 3559, January 11, 1896, p. 54.

THE SPECTATOR (essay date 1896)

["*Invectives*"] must be judged not as poetry, but as a confidence. Written in a loose, familiar style, it is essentially prosaic, and reveals merely the bitter, if justified, hatreds of the man. To appreciate its acridity one must recall the poet's sinister career. Born with an exquisite talent for verse—a talent which neither poverty nor misfortune has impaired—Verlaine was also born into a modern, logical world with the careless habit of the gipsy. (p. 237)

To the ignorant his name is a synonym for impropriety, but, if you put aside a single volume—**"Parallèlement"**—there is not one of his works which could offer the slightest affront to a proper modesty. And where in modern literature shall you find a daintier set of impressions than **"Romances sans Paroles,"** a more delicate expression of love than **"La Bonne Chanson,"** or a nobler piece of devotion than **"Sagesse"**? That he resented the misappreciation, in which his own recklessness had helped to involve him, there was no proof until to-day. But in his **"Invectives"** he makes clear his own sensitiveness, and attacks all those who have patronised his poetry and defamed his life. The book is packed with material of offence, and perhaps it would have been better to publish it before death had made reparation impossible. None the less, it completes the character of the poet, and shows that for all his simplicity he fiercely resented the infamy of his enemies and the lamentable indiscretion of his pretended friends. Among the victims of his invective are journalists, critics, doctors, magistrates, and anarchists. . . .

"Invectives," in brief, will not affect the reputation of Verlaine the poet. It is rather a pamphlet than a work of art. Moreover, it is marred by grave faults of taste and temper. But now it is plain that Verlaine from the first felt and resented the constant aspersions that were cast upon his character. He did not, as the foolish man believed, pocket the insult with a silent shrug. (p. 238)

"The Posthumous Verlaine," in The Spectator, Vol. 77, No. 3556, August 22, 1896, pp. 237-38.

REMY de GOURMONT (essay date 1896)

Verlaine is a nature and as such undefinable. Like his life, the rhythms he loves are of broken or rolling lines; he ended by disjoining romantic verse, and having destroyed its form, having bored and ripped it so as to permit too many things to be introduced, all the effervescences that issued from his crazy skull, he unwittingly became one of the instigators of vers libre. Verlainian verse with its shoots, its incidences, its parentheses, naturally evolved into vers libre; in becoming "libre," it did no more than reflect a condition.

When the gift of expression forsakes him, and when at the same time the gift of tears is removed, he either becomes the blustering rough iambic writer of *Invectives,* or the humble awkward elegist of *Chansons pour Elle*. Poet by these very gifts, consecrated to talk felicitously only of love, all loves; and he whose lips press as in a dream upon the stars of the purifactory robe, he who wrote the *Amies* composed those Canticles of the month of Mary. And from the same heart, the same hand, the same genius,—but who shall chant them, O hypocrites! if not those very white-veiled Friends.

To confess one's sins of action or dreams is not sinful; no public confession can bring disrepute to a man, for all men are equal and equally tempted; no one commits a crime his brother is not capable of. That is why the pious journals or the Academy vainly took upon themselves the shame of having abused Verlaine, still under the flowers; the kick of the sacristan and scoundrel broke on a pedestal already of granite, while in his marble beard, Verlaine was everlastingly smiling, with the look of a faun hearkening while the bells peal. (pp. 251-53)

Remy de Gourmont, "Verlaine," in his The Book of Masks, translated by Jack Lewis (originally published as Le livre des masques: Portraits symbolistes, Vol. I, Mercure de France, 1896), J. W. Luce & Co., 1921 (and reprinted in Books for Libraries Press, 1967; distributed by Arno Press, Inc.), pp. 251-53.

ARTHUR SYMONS (essay date 1899)

French poetry, before Verlaine, was an admirable vehicle for a really fine, a really poetical, kind of rhetoric. . . . "Take eloquence, and wring its neck!" said Verlaine in his *Art Poétique;* and he showed, by writing it, that French verse could be written without rhetoric. It was partly from his study of English models that he learnt the secret of liberty in verse, but it was much more a secret found by the way, in the mere endeavour to be absolutely sincere, to express exactly what he saw, to give voice to his own temperament, in which intensity of feeling seemed to find its own expression, as if by accident. . . . [With] such a personality as Verlaine's to express, what more has art to do, if it would truly, and in any interesting manner, hold the mirror up to nature?

For, consider the natural qualities which this man had for the task of creating a new poetry. "Sincerity, and the impression of the moment followed to the letter": that is how he defined his theory of style, in an article written about himself. . . . Take, then, his susceptibility of the senses, an emotional susceptibility not less delicate; a life sufficiently troubled to draw out every emotion of which he was capable, and, with it, that absorption in the moment, that inability to look before or after; the need to love and the need to confess, each a passion; an art of painting the fine shades of landscape, of evoking atmosphere, which can be compared only with the art of Whistler; a simplicity of language which is the direct outcome of a simplicity of temperament, with just enough consciousness of itself for a final elegance; and, at the very depth of his being, an almost fierce humility, by which the passion of love, after searching furiously through all his creatures, finds God by the way, and kneels in the dust before him. (pp. 87-9)

There are poems of Verlaine which go as far as verse can go to become pure music, the voice of a bird with a human soul. It is part of his simplicity, his divine childishness, that he abandons himself, at times, to the song which words begin to sing in the air, with the same wise confidence with which he abandons himself to the other miracles about him. . . . He knows that words are suspicious, not without their malice, and that they resist mere force with the impalpable resistance of fire or water. They are to be caught only with guile or with trust. Verlaine has both, and words become Ariel to him. . . . They transform themselves for him into music, colour, and shadow; a disembodied music, diaphanous colours, luminous shadow. They serve him with so absolute a self-negation that he can write *romances sans paroles,* songs almost without words, in which scarcely a sense of the interference of human speech remains. The ideal of lyric poetry, certainly, is to be this passive, flawless medium for the deeper consciousness of things, the mysterious voice of that mystery which lies about us, out of which we have come, and into which we shall return. (pp. 89-90)

With Verlaine the sense of hearing and the sense of sight are almost interchangeable: he paints with sound, and his line and atmosphere become music. (p. 90)

[With] the same attentive simplicity with which he found words for the sensations of hearing and the sensations of sight, he found words for the sensations of the soul, for the fine shades of feeling. From the moment when his inner life may be said to have begun, he was occupied with the task of an unceasing confession, in which one seems to overhear him talking to himself, in that vague, preoccupied way which he often had. Here again are words which startle one by their delicate resemblance to thoughts, by their winged flight from so far, by their alighting so close. (pp. 91-2)

[In] Verlaine I find that single, childlike necessity of loving and being loved, all through his life and on every page of his works; I find it, unchanged in essence, but constantly changing form, in his chaste and unchaste devotions to women, in his passionate friendships with men, in his supreme mystical adoration of God.

To turn from *La Bonne Chanson,* written for a wedding present to a young wife, to *Chansons pour Elle,* written more than twenty years later, in dubious honour of a middle-aged mistress, is to travel a long road, the hard, long road which Verlaine had travelled during those years. (p. 94)

The poems to Rimbaud, to Lucien Létinois, to others, the whole volume of *Dédicaces,* cover perhaps as wide a range of sen-

timent as *La Bonne Chanson* and *Chansons pour Elle.* The poetry of friendship has never been sung with such plaintive sincerity, such simple human feeling, as in some of these poems, which can only be compared, in modern poetry, with a poem for which Verlaine had a great admiration, Tennyson's *In Memoriam.* Only, with Verlaine, the thing itself, the affection or the regret, is everything; there is no room for meditation over destiny, or search for a problematical consolation. (pp. 95-6)

In spite of the general impression to the contrary, an impression which by no means displeased him himself, I must contend that the sensuality of Verlaine, brutal as it could sometimes be, was after all simple rather than complicated, instinctive rather than perverse. In the poetry of Baudelaire, with which the poetry of Verlaine is so often compared, there is a deliberate science of sensual perversity which has something almost monachal in its accentuation of vice with horror, in its passionate devotion to passions. . . . With Verlaine, however often love may pass into sensuality, to whatever length sensuality may be hurried, sensuality is never more than the malady of love. It is love desiring the absolute, seeking in vain, seeking always, and, finally, out of the depths, finding God. (pp. 96-7)

Arthur Symons, "Paul Verlaine," in his The Symbolist Movement in Literature, *William Heinemann, 1899, pp. 77-102.*

EDMOND LEPELLETIER   (essay date 1907)

The *Poèmes Saturniens* have a twofold inspiration, and are of a composite character: two or three of the pieces, and those not the least beautiful, among them the poems specially quoted and praised by Sainte-Beuve, *César Borgia* and *La Mort de Philippe II.,* are entirely in the descriptive and pompous manner of [Victor Hugo's] *La Légende des Siècles* and [Leconte de Lisle's] *Poémes Barbares.* Others show signs of the influence of Baudelaire, *Mon Rêve familier, e.g.,* evokes a recollection of some piece out of *Les Fleurs du Mal,* in spite of the lucidity and precision which Verlaine introduced into the expression, however studied and subtle, of exquisite sensations, mysterious correspondences, and mental affinities. The lines, charged with ideas and suggestions, with which the poem ends, are of a consistent and original beauty very characteristic of the author, and have no trace of the influence of Baudelaire. There was, moreover, in the *Poèmes Saturniens* . . . an intent to dogmatise and create a poetic creed. Verlaine was in fact the first to formulate the theory of the *Impassibles* (the immovable ones), as the poets of the new school were called to begin with; afterwards the term "Parnassiens" carried the day, although less appropriate and more pedantic.

In the introductory poem, as in that which forms the epilogue, he rebels against the school of [Alphonse de] Lamartine (and delights in Madame Desbordes-Valmore), the unlyrical brilliance of Alfred de Musset (*"Allons! dieu mort descends de ton autel d'argile!"* he cries furiously to the shade of Rolla), and the political satire of Auguste Barbier, [Jean Jacques] Barthélemy, Hégésippe Moreau, and even Victor Hugo. He proclaims the abstention of the poet, in the midst of struggles for public office, his indifference to the quarrels which agitate statesmen and citizens. He preaches isolation, and admires the ivory tower. (pp. 121-22)

[It] was Verlaine who first presented, in the strong, lucid verse of the prologue to the *Poèmes Saturniens* the theory of poetical abstraction, the isolation of the poet in modern society, making the writer—the apostle extolled by Victor Hugo—a fanatical egoist, a sort of *bonze* of art, shutting himself up in a temple into which penetrates only a softened and poetised rumour of the doings, cries, complaints, and acclamations of the multitude.

In the epilogue to the poems he completes his idea. Not only must the poet live, think, and feel apart from his contemporaries, but he must keep his conscience and his thoughts from certain promiscuities. He must in the beginning distrust his inspiration. (p. 123)

Such was the poetic method which characterised the Verlaine of the *Poèmes Saturniens,* deaf to all the calls, complaints, and exaltations of the world within him, projecting his sensations outside, materialising his dreams, exteriorising his impressions and treating poetry as plastic material. He was to change in its entirety this manner of seeing, feeling, and expressing his ideas, sensations, reveries, and visions.

The same impersonality, and an even more refined and artistic objectivity, dominates that precious and surprising volume the *Fêtes galantes.* No borrowed inspiration is to be found here; it is a synthesis of the Art of the eighteenth century, a presentment of the manners, conversations, and diversions of that dainty and superficial period. (p. 129)

La Bonne Chanson is a transition from objective, descriptive, plastic verse to personal expression, the soul's confession. It is the substitution of one method of art for another. To sentiments received, suggested, and developed rather than felt, to imaginary passions, invented sorrows, sensations obtained from reading, conversation, hypothesis, and human companionship, has succeeded intimate, subjective, personal poetry, the result of feeling, living, and suffering.

It was no longer the Victor Hugo of *La Légende des Siècles,* but the [Hugo] of the *Feuilles d'Automne,* and the *Contemplations,* whose influence was henceforward in the ascendant. (p. 204)

In the hour when the poet sang *La Bonne Chanson,* that unforgettable hour which most of us have experienced, and the delights of which only an artist can transcribe, he cast away the cloak of abstraction, and poured forth his love like the wild bird of the woods, forgetful of all but the one for whom his melodies arose like a fountain at night among the marbles.

How magnificent in its abandonment to genuine feeling is that enthusiastic appeal to the Beatrice henceforward his guide, his rescuer from the hungry maw of that Hell into which he had been rapidly disappearing; it begins:

Puisque l'aube grandit, puisque voici l'aurore,
Puisqu 'après m'avoir fui longtemps, l'espoir veut bien.

This is an echo of De Musset, the poet Verlaine violently decried, the dead god he desired to throw down from his altar of clay; it is one of those Titanesque sobs of despair and disgust with which Verlaine was afterwards to be shaken by his intense desire to follow in peace and happiness the smooth and tranquil path along which the "heart's companion found at last" beckoned him. (p. 205)

Verlaine's *Bonne Chanson,* with its beautiful artistic title, is an autobiography only in its details. It is rather a stanza taken from the eternal poem of youthful love, and therefore it will live. (p. 207)

The *Romances sans Paroles* bears witness to a mental revolution. He is no longer the poet of the *Fêtes galantes* describing the familiar features of the Belgian landscapes. . . . His ideas, sentiments, desires, and opinions underwent a radical alteration, and with this change in his mind was a corresponding change in his method of writing. He entered upon a new existence. He dreamed of a new style of verse. (p. 326)

It was in prison, recalling the discourses of Arthur Rimbaud and his peculiar ideas with regard to metre, that he thought out lyrical combinations, in which a new music of verse played an important part, not only accompanying the idea, but evoking feeling, recollection, association, just as a perfume to the refined senses of certain beings calls up actual visions, distinct images, beings, and things almost tangible. The admiration he had long felt for Baudelaire had part in the new conception. The title, *Romances sans Paroles,* determined upon long after the varied poems which make up this interesting collection were composed, although apparently suggested by [Felix] Mendelssohn, was a summing-up, a synthesis, of this new theory of verse. With the misfortunes that darkened his life came, as is the case with every poet, the desire to unburden his woe, to perpetuate it in his work. Art was a powerful anesthetic. He treated himself to a course of personal impassioned verse. He renounced the poetry of his early years. The *Poèmes Saturniens* and the *Fêtes galantes* were like flowers cultivated scientifically in the classic *parterres,* French or exotic, of the *Parnasse,* while the *Romances sans Paroles* and *Sagesse* [and other poems] . . . were fruits of bitterness, watered by tears, ripened in gloom, the untended wild flowers of solitude, like those plants of phosphorescent gleam and extraordinarily contorted shapes, their interiors filled with ashes, which grow in dense forests wherein no sun nor joyous life ever penetrates. (pp. 336-37)

It may be said that in *Jadis et Naguère,* the seven cords of the lyre sound, vibrate, mutter, sigh, murmur, menace, and sing. It is not Verlaine's most perfect volume, and many of the pieces of which it is composed were severely omitted by him from the MSS. of previous volumes; they did not satisfy the poet, and appeared to him to require further consideration and polishing. He discovered imitations among them, and these he grouped together under the ingenuous sub-title: *A la Manière de Plusieurs.* In short the poems, diverse in tone, character, subject, and inspiration, which make up this volume, give it the appearance of a collection of selected pieces. . . . (p. 407)

Edmond Lepelletier, in his Paul Verlaine: His Life—His Work, *translated by E. M. Lang (originally published as* Paul Verlaine: Sa vie, son oeuvre, *Société du Mercure de France, 1907), Duffield & Co., 1909 (and reprinted by AMS Press, Inc., 1970), 463 p.*

REMY de GOURMONT (essay date 1912)

[Verlaine] was the little child who piously recites his prayer and the faun who prowls about like an ogre. He was Saint Teresa, drunk with divine love, and also Sappho, who loved only her own kind. He was the dreamer touched by the autumn nightfall, who quivers at a whirling leaf as he would at a fluttering scarf; and he was also the bad *gallant* who slept in taverns. Verlaine was intimate with all feelings and all sensations.

I do not know how those people read who see in *Poèmes saturniens* nothing but poetic exercises or impersonal notations. It is possible that he might have intended to obey Leconte de Lisle's rule of impassivity, but his nature refused. His sensibility was already overflowing. (p. 192)

All of Verlaine's poems are in bud and the leaves already visible in the *Poèmes saturniens*. Certain prosodic liberties, concealed here and there, make me doubt that he had ever been a true Parnassian in the bottom of his heart, in the bottom of his nerves. Whoever swoons on hearing

> Les sanglots longs
> Des violons,

was not Parnassian, nor was anyone who wove new metaphors of love:

> Baiser! rose trémière au jardin des caresses!

or who wrote as a prelude to his future poetic art:

> De la douceur, de la douceur, de la douceur.
>
> (pp. 192-93)

Verlaine was a great poet and he has had a great influence on French poetry. One can say that whatever the material form our poetry has affected—free verse, liberated verse, romantic verse—it has been entirely and still is under the domination of Verlaine. . . . [Generations of poets have found their justification in Verlaine's **"Art poétique"**]: "Music above all.—Do not be too precise: fear excessive clarity.—Not the color but the shading.—Avoid epigram, wit, laughter.—No eloquence: strangle it.—Rhyme? It is a cheap bauble that rings hollow and false under the file. (p. 197)

Despite certain licenses, as Théodore de Banville used to say, it is rather in the language itself than in the prosody that Verlaine is an innovator. His phrases rise and fall in tone, suddenly split up, are forgotten as in a suspension of distracted thought, set out again, arrive at the goal of which caprice never loses sight. Verlaine's verses never suggest effort, erasures, or repeated starts. The short poem, often a sonnet, unrolls with a perfect certainty, in conformity to a free unity of rhythm, a music that sings from within. Verlaine's poetry, form and thought, is entirely spontaneous. . . . Nothing suggests a retouching. The style does not change: whether the inspiration be religious or libertine, it is the same pure fluidity; whether the stream flows over grass or gravel, the voice sings always the same amorous song; whether his love laughs at women or angels, it is nearly the same sensuality. He himself has blended, in his *Parallèlement,* these two nuances of his dream: eroticism and mysticism. (pp. 197-98)

> *Remy de Gourmont, "Paul Verlaine" (originally published as "Paul Verlaine," in* Promenades littéraires: 4. série, Mercure de France, 1912), in his Selected Writings, *edited and translated by Glenn S. Burne (copyright © by The University of Michigan 1966), The University of Michigan Press, 1966, pp. 191-98.*

HAROLD NICOLSON (essay date 1921)

[*Poèmes saturniens*] covers the first eight years of Verlaine's literary life, and for this reason contains many experiments in different manners. There is a long and uninteresting poem entitled **"Nocturne parisien,"** which is in date the earliest of any of Verlaine's publications; there are experiments in the objective manner, such as **"César Borgia"** and **"La Mort de Philippe II"**; there are recollections of Baudelaire and Hugo; and over it all is hoisted, not wholly with conviction, the fresh standard of the Parnassus. In spite of their mixed character, Verlaine has in all these poems tried very hard to be Parnassien. . . . But in the latter poems—and the whole volume contains some of the best that Verlaine ever wrote—he is carried away by the lilt of his own music, and the Parnasse is forgotten in the plaintive cadence of his curious lyricism. . . . (pp. 28-9)

Verlaine was at this time untouched by any real emotion, and yet these poems equal in poignancy any that were to be wrung out of him by the real tragedies and tribulations of the future. Nor is this surprising. The strange mechanism of his sensitory faculties were syntonised only to the currents of secondary emotions. To the deeper currents of feeling his nerves, as so often with the artistic temperament, failed to respond. And hence the minor key of most of his melodies, and the avoidance of the octaves and diapasons of more important poetry. (pp. 29-30)

The *Poèmes saturniens* are memorable also for the light they throw upon Verlaine's character at this period, in which we can clearly trace the lines of future disastrous development. He forecasts for himself, as one of those unfortunates whose birth has fallen beneath the planet Saturn,

> Bonne part de malheur et bonne part de bile;
> L'Imagination, inquiète et débile,
> Vient rendre nul en eux l'effort de la Raison.

Even the more subtle sides of his nature are apparent; his extreme dependence; his continual desire to rely on some calm, strong nature; on some one who would love and understand and forgive; on some one who would act as the flywheel to his intermittent will-power; on some one who would treat him as a wise mother treats a sickly child. . . . (p. 30)

All this intimacy was taking Verlaine very far from the cold austerity of the Parnassus, and he had made matters worse by those tricks of versification and syntax which were to be so characteristic of his later style. His "curious felicity" for placing words in a verse, such as the soft thud of the "feuille morte" at the end of the **"Chanson d'Automne,"** his love of inverted diction, such as "la spontanéité craintive des caresses," were not likely to attract the scholarly susceptibilities of the earnest young Parnassiens. (p. 31)

If regarded purely as an evocation of the eighteenth century the *Fêtes galantes* are not successful. Verlaine was too modern, too animal, too *canaille,* to catch the necessary atmosphere. (p. 33)

As purely decorative writing, however, the *Fêtes galantes* are in their way unique. . . . The whole volume contains pieces of rare skill, such as **"Les Coquillages"** and **"Les Indolents,"** and some of gentle beauty, such as **"En Sourdine"** and **"Les Ingénus."** Even the passages in which Verlaine fails to catch the tender dignity of the eighteenth century are not without a certain personal charm. . . . It is in the *Fêtes galantes,* moreover, that Verlaine's mastery of cadence is at its most perfect. . . . (p. 34)

Sagesse is considered by most French critics to be the supreme achievement of Verlaine's poetical talent, or, if you prefer it, of his genius. The English reader will perhaps be disinclined to endorse this judgement. In the first place, the majority of the poems are religious in character, and to the Anglo-Saxon ear the hackneyed phrases of religious expression adapt themselves awkwardly, and with a faint sense of farce, to the gay precision of the French language. This impression is illogical, of course, and fortuitous, but it arises from the first, and from the first it casts a shadow of unreality over *Sagesse.* The sense of unreality is increased by the actual circumstances of Verlaine's conversion; by the sobbing impulsiveness of his self-humiliation; by the cheery acceptance of the ensuing absolution. . . . The whole business, to our slow-moving minds, was too hectic, too scrambled, to be very real; and in addition there is the undeniable fact that while writing *Sagesse* he was also toying with *Parallèlement*. For some of us this unreality will cause the poems of *Sagesse* to seem insincere; to others it will merely make them dull. Personally I do not feel that [the] charge of insincerity has much meaning. Verlaine was too self-centred to be self-conscious. He was too intimate to be insincere. His very conception of including in *Sagesse* the pornographic poems of the same period indicates his intention of presenting a complete picture of his emotions during that intricate sojourn. Taken as such a picture the poems are real enough. (pp. 119-20)

[*Mes Hôpitaux*] is perhaps the best of his prose works. It is humorous, elusive and very brave. It is written in the loquacious and slangy style at which no one, until the days of [Colette], was to be his equal. (p. 171)

Even a cursory reading, even the most exclusive anthology of Verlaine's poems, must give a very vivid sense of intimacy, a feeling of a definite and immensely human personality. The methods by which this impression is conveyed are perfectly obvious; they require no very detailed analysis. The intimacy of Verlaine's better poems is no idle exhibitionism. . . . Its effect resides firstly in the sparing and skilful use of attributes, in an apparently incidental but vivid reference to minor objects which for him radiate with emotional significance. It is not that such objects are of themselves of any interest to us, it is not that we are really affected by their relation to Verlaine's emotions; it is simply that our sentiment of association is set vibrating by these references, that a pleasurable chord is struck by the thought of other objects, intimate to us, which have precisely such a connexion in our own experience. The device is one which can be effective only if used with the most skilful precision, if introduced with consummate musical tact. And it is in this that Verlaine is, at least in his earlier poems, so complete a master. (pp. 239-40)

The device of association is not, however, the only method by which Verlaine attains to the peculiar intimacy of his manner. He secures a similar effect by the garrulous confidences of his poems, by the way in which he renders the casual moods and habits of his life interesting and emotional. . . . With the frankness of a child babbling to some stranger of its toys and its relations, Verlaine is convinced that the most trivial events of his experience are tremendously interesting, are of almost cosmic significance. . . . For him the value of an emotion is not its depth, not even its intensity, but its truth. He knew full well that his peculiar poetic quality was not attuned to the grandiose, he knew that the deeper emotions would always elude him, and he preferred, therefore, to deal with the more incidental sensations, and to reflect in them the passions and tragedies in which his life was involved. In this he was abundantly right: the minor key can convey its message only by the indirect method; in order to be wistful one must above all be elusive. Where Verlaine was to go wrong was in the exaggeration of this manner, and in his later poems he loses all selective faculty; he becomes too garrulous: he becomes a bore. (pp. 241-42)

There is a further medium, and one which he employed abundantly, through which Verlaine was able to suggest the something beyond. It was a constant practice of his to open a poem with a suggestion of exterior conditions through which, by some vague transition, he would explain and illustrate his moods.

This method had many advantages. It enabled him to catch the fleeting sensation inspired by some sudden aspect of nature and to modulate his verse accordingly. The human heart was thus fused with the sadness of tree and sky, and infinite scope was thereby given to his rendering. (p. 248)

Such, therefore, was the manner in which Verlaine was able to voice the twin elements of intimacy and suggestion which were to play so large a part in the machinery of Symbolism. His contribution in this respect was vital to the new school, the coherence which he gave to these two doctrines was definitely constructive in quality. His influence, however, was to go further. He was to succeed more than any other man in enfranchising the French speech, and in rendering French prosody the servant of the poet rather than his master. (p. 250)

For generations the French have placed lucidity in the forefront of literary virtues; for them precision has become at once an art and a science. In extreme cases, and in France quite mild cases are terribly apt to become extreme, this fetish of precision has played havoc with their intelligence. . . . [For] many bright and charming people over there in France it does not matter so much what one says so long as one says it lucidly. In serious or simple matters this ideal is not disadvantageous; but in poetry it hampers and it disconcerts, it leads either to a cold reserve or to a turgid rhetoric; it leads either to sterilisation or unreality. Neither of the so Parisian movements of the Romanticists or the Parnassiens had availed to any permanent extent in overturning this oligarchy of words. It was left to the alien immigration of the Symbolists to achieve the final revolution. It was left largely to Verlaine really to vulgarise the poetic diction of the French. And they, for their part, were never wholly to forgive him.

It must be admitted, indeed, that the vocabulary, the syntax and the versification of Verlaine were the "enfants terribles" of the Parnassien movement. He would insist on using expressions which were often affected, sometimes vulgar and sometimes merely odd: he would insist on twisting his grammar into the most derogatory convolutions: he would insist in playing disrespectfully with the Alexandrine, in wallowing shamelessly in shattered caesura and gaping hiatus: he would insist in treating the French language as a cheery contemporary and not as an aged and unassailable tradition. . . . Verlaine, who was far from being precious, preferred on the whole to use ordinary and current words and to give them personality by strange attributes or still stranger tricks of syntax and phraseology. (pp. 250-52)

[One] can exaggerate the extent and importance of Verlaine's own innovations in the mere diction of French poetry. In this direction he was to be equalled and outdistanced by most of the new generation of writers. He figures, indeed, rather as the executant of the new diction than as its inventor, and even in this capacity his function was rather to reconcile the public to the audacities of others than to be particularly audacious himself. . . . He treated the French language as an equal, but he did not, as the others, treat it as an inferior. His originality was to manifest itself less in his diction than in his prosody. And here at least he was to be apocalyptic; here at least he was to become, and to remain, enormously unpopular. (pp. 253-54)

He was not as great a man as Mallarmé, his influence to-day is less than that of Rimbaud. He was not as intensely literary as [Jules] Laforgue, he had not the energy of [Maurice] Barrès, nor the intellect of André Gide. He was above all personal, and for this reason he stands to some extent in an isolated position. His influence is all-pervading rather than concentrated. He left behind him an atmosphere rather than a doctrine. He is universal rather than particular.

There is one field, however, in which he was quite consciously to innovate. There is one direction in which his place in literary history will, whatever his intrinsic value, be permanently assured. He was the first to restore to French poetry that wide gamut of melody which it had so unfortunately relinquished. (pp. 254-55)

[In French poetry] the stress of the spoken word is almost entirely absent, and their verse is for this reason obliged to fall back upon balance and rhyme. In other words, the rhythm of verse is attained not by the ebb and sway of the spoken language, but by the artificial orchestration of prosody. It is merely the intrinsic beauty of the French language which has prevented this system from becoming gravely defective: it had not, however, until Verlaine's arrival, prevented it from becoming monotonous. (p. 256)

[By] the time Verlaine arrived on the scene French metrics were labouring under two separate tyrannies, the first representing what remained of the old pre-Hugo doctrines, the second centering in the essential importance of rhyme. (p. 259)

Verlaine, with his sensitive ear for music, felt these limitations instinctively. He determined to free French verse from the distressing monotony which menaced it, and he was able, while not denaturalising the essential quality of the language, to introduce a new and sensitive method by which the slightest tremor of feeling could be registered and expressed. (pp. 259-60)

The prosody of Verlaine is indeed an interesting subject, but it is one which a foreigner can only approach with diffidence. To a foreign ear the poetry of Verlaine is without a doubt the most musical in the French language. It is not so for all his compatriots. . . . Does it mean that the foreign ear catches a deliberate intonation in Verlaine's poems to which the French ear is not attuned? Or does it mean, simply, that we, with our habit of a tonic accent, actually mispronounce the verses, and that we read into them a melody which Verlaine himself had not intended? The truth lies probably between the two. (pp. 261-63)

The essence of Verlaine's style is its gentleness, or, as his detractors would say, its effeminacy. He secures this effect by the profuse employment of labial consonants, and broad vowels, and by the avoidance of all dentals, sibilants or closed vowel-sounds. Verlaine, to a greater degree than other lyric poets, had a predilection for the alliteration or alternation of "l," "m," "n" and "r," and the tune of his most characteristic poems is based on the interchange of these weak and fluid consonants. . . . There was another and even more obvious method by which Verlaine secured the characteristic gentleness of his verse, namely, by his use of feminine rhymes. The rules of French prosody divide, as is well known, all rhymes into either "masculine" or "feminine." Masculine rhymes are those which end with the syllable which contains the tonic vowel: feminine rhymes are those in which the rhyme-syllable is followed by another containing an "e muet." The rule is that the masculine and feminine rhymes should alternate throughout the verse, and this rule, until Verlaine's day, was rarely violated. In some of his more plaintive poems, however, Verlaine has deliberately omitted the masculine couplets and based the whole structure on a feminine sequence. . . . Nor is

this all. Even in those poems where he abides by the rule and alternates his masculine with his feminine couplets he is able, by the unsparing use of labials, to render his masculine rhymes as epicene as possible, to render them indeed almost hermaphroditic. The effect obtained is one of fluid simplicity and of plaintive impotence, and that, after all, was the effect which he himself desired. (pp. 266-68)

Verlaine's verses, in their shrouded music, can be appreciated instinctively and without elaboration. Some technical dissection is necessary, of course, if only to disprove the school of criticism which accuses him of ignorance and clumsiness; but the vital essence of his lyrical powers will inevitably elude analysis. It will always remain intuitive in that it was so sincere. (p. 269)

Harold Nicolson, in his Paul Verlaine *(reprinted by permission of the Estate of Harold Nicolson), Constable & Company Limited, 1921, 271 p.*

PAUL VALÉRY (essay date 1937)

Nothing is simpler, and until recently nothing would have appeared more natural, than to compare François Villon and Paul Verlaine. It is child's play to the connoisseur of historical parallels, that is to say, imaginary parallels, to show that these two literary figures resemble one another. Both are admirable poets; both were rascals; the work of both is a mixture of the most pious feelings with descriptions or observations which are exceedingly frank; and both pass from one to the other tone with extraordinary ease. Both are truly masters of their art and of the language of their time, which they use like men in whom culture is combined with an instinctive sense of the living language, of the very speech of the people among whom they lived, which creates, modifies, and blends words and forms to its own fancy. Both have an adequate knowledge of Latin and an excellent command of slang; both haunt church or tavern according to their mood; and both, for very different reasons, found themselves condemned to harsh confinement, where they managed not so much to make amends for their faults as to extract from them their poetic essence of remorse, regret, and fear. Both fall, repent, fall again, and rise up great poets! The parallel suggests itself and works out quite well.

But what can be brought together and superposed so easily and so speciously can be separated and dissociated without great difficulty. It would be a mistake to attach any great importance to it. (pp. 232-33)

[The] Villon-Verlaine parallel, this obvious and attractive conjunction of . . . two exceptional beings . . . , though it holds together reasonably well and can be reinforced by certain biographical details, weakens or collapses as soon as we compare their works in the same way that we have compared the men. . . . (p. 233)

If we insist on comparing [Verlaine] with Villon, not as a criminal character with a police record but as a poet, we shall find—or at any rate I find, for it is only a personal impression—I find to my surprise that Villon (vocabulary apart) is in certain ways more "modern" than Verlaine. He is more precise and more pictorial. His language is markedly firmer. *Le Débat du coeur et du corps* is constructed out of dialogue as clear and crisp as a passage from Corneille. And his work is full of unforgettable phrases, each of which is a *trouvaille* of the *classical* type. . . . But first and foremost, to Villon belongs the glory of a truly great work—the famous *Testament,* a work unique in conception, complete, a *Last Judgment* pronounced on men and things by a man who, at the age of thirty, had already lived too much. (p. 249)

As for Verlaine, if I tell you (at my own risk) that he seems to me to be less literary than Villon, I do not mean *more naïve:* neither of them is more naïve than the other, nor more naïve than La Fontaine; poets are only naïve when they do not exist. I mean that the poetry which is special to Verlaine, like *La Bonne Chanson, Sagesse,* and so on, suggests at a first glance a shorter literary tradition behind it than the poetry of Villon; but this is only apparent: the impression can be explained by the remark that the latter wrote at the beginning of a new era in our poetry, and at the end of the poetic tradition of the Middle Ages—that of allegories, moralities, romances, and pious stories. Villon is, in a way, oriented toward the period soon to follow, when poetry will be written in full consciousness of itself and for itself. The Renaissance was the birth of art for art's sake. Verlaine is completely the reverse: he came out of, departed from, and escaped the Parnassian Movement; he was, or thought he was, at the end of an aesthetic paganism. He reacted against Hugo, against Leconte de Lisle, against [Théodore de] Banville. . . . (pp. 250-51)

Verlaine's reaction led him to create a form the complete opposite of the one whose perfections had become irksome to him. . . . We sometimes have the impression that he is fumbling among syllables and rhymes, that he is seeking the most musical form of expression of the moment. . . .

For this apparently *ingenuous* individual was a highly organized primitive, a primitive of a kind never seen before, evolved out of a highly skilled and very conscious artist. None of the authentic primitives is like Verlaine. He may perhaps have been more accurately classified when, about 1885, he was called a "decadent." Never was there a more subtle art than this, which assumed that it was leaving another behind, and not that it had a precedent. (p. 251)

> *Paul Valéry, "Villon and Verlaine" (originally published as* Villon et Verlaine, A.A.M. Stolls, 1937), *in his* The Collected Works of Paul Valéry: Masters and Friends, Vol. 9, *edited by Jackson Mathews, translated by Martin Turnell, Bollingen Series XLV (copyright © 1968 by Princeton University Press; reprinted by permission of Princeton University Press), Princeton University Press, 1968, pp. 232-52.**

CHARLES MORGAN   (essay date 1944)

In [Verlaine] naïveté took a peculiar form, completely divorced from the idea of simplicity. A less simple man can seldom have lived or a more naïf, for in him naïveté was a projection of weakness—a carrying of weakness to such an extreme that what, in other men, halts at mere flabbiness and indecision became, in him, a unique power to receive impressions. He had no armour, no resistances, no crust of consistency. . . . This appears in his life disastrously; and in his work, because the gift of an unsurpassed music had been added to it, as aeolian genius without parallel in literature. Others have searched the spirit and the flesh of man more profoundly than he, have sung of greater worlds with nobler and more compassionate music, but none has given a more vibrant and, for the moment, a more passionate response to every touch and whisper of experience. He was terribly alive. (p. 161)

Never did any man's style respond to his subject with so wonderful a combination of suppleness and precision. But nothing,

be it remarked, made Verlaine stammer. The deeper his emotion, the clearer his rhythm, the purer his note.

> Mon Dieu, mon Dieu, la vie est là,
> Simple et tranquille.
> Cette paisible rumeur-là
> Vient de la ville!
>
> Qu'as-tu fait, ô toi que voilà
> Pleurant sans cesse,
> Dis, qu'as-tu fait, toi que voilà
> De ta jeunesse.

The poem is in every anthology. To requote it is self-indulgence and yet unavoidable, for the essence of Verlaine is in it: his longing for tranquillity, his astonishment by it, his instant acceptance of it; his power of surrender, in his life an abject weakness, in his art an ecstasy; above all, his naïveté which, expressed in his music of an interior innocence as though there were angels in his head, enabled him to say that the sky is blue and calm—

> Le ciel est, par-dessus le toit,
> Si bleu, si calme!

—in two opening lines that can never be analysed but are flowing with the milk of paradise. (pp. 165-66)

> *Charles Morgan, "Paul Verlaine" (originally published as "Menander's Mirror," in* The Times Literary Supplement, April 1, 1944), *in his* Reflections in a Mirror *(reprinted by permission of Macmillan, London and Basingstoke),* Macmillan, 1946, pp. 159-67.

ANTOINE ADAM   (essay date 1953)

[In *Sagesse*] appears, in all its splendor, that genuine symbolism which was the great discovery of 1873, that advance over impressionism and its too facile charms. Let us look closely at "Les faux beaux jours ont lui. . . ." There is no question here of impressions gathered on a stormy evening. The subject of these lines is a sinner's soul, returned to virtue, which feels old temptations rumbling. This agitation, this anguish, this flight toward the Lord of Mercy are not directly expressed by the poet as formerly the joys and purities of *La Bonne Chanson* were. His whole poem is one single metaphor. A stormy landscape, a lurid light, the slopes of the valley lashed by the downpour. But in the distance another prospect—one of clear skies, of silence, and of prayer. A woman passes, eyes lowered, hands clasped: the soul of the poet as it must become and must remain.

Side by side with these pieces that continue and crown previous effort, that are allied with and extend that effort, are others that put us in the presence of an unexpected poetic world. In these, allegories come to life. Here the brave knight Misfortune plunges his iron fingers into the poet's breast and causes a new heart to be born therein. And here a lady in snow-white raiment descends from the sky and puts the monster, the fierce giant, Flesh, to flight. This lady is Prayer. And there the allegory of a besieged city, maintained despite betrayals from within, betrayals that would hand over the keys of the city to the usurping enemy. These works show a new impulse in Verlaine's work. (pp. 109-10)

Sagesse is the sincerest kind of statement, an impassioned declaration of faith, the confession of a man who put himself wholly into his work. Sincerity is not a literary virtue, and it is not because of its genuineness that *Sagesse* is an admirable book. But since there are some historians who would claim that these outpourings are mendacious, it is necessary to set the facts straight and to assert that Verlaine wrote this book with his whole soul.

On the other hand, it is absurd to praise *Sagesse* as a "highly coherent" work, for the sole fault one may truly attribute to this volume is that of being a composite work, of mixing together poems of quite obviously different date, impulse, and quality. (p. 115)

But this same ensemble has as well a richness, variety, and more often than not a beauty that make *Sagesse* Verlaine's masterwork. We are perhaps ill prepared for understanding what was original and valuable about this book. We are not sufficiently aware of the degree to which French poetry during the previous fifteen years had tended to restrict itself to the description of appearances. Whether it gave itself over to the empty mannerisms of exoticism or, contrarily, concentrated on recording the familiar picturesque quality of everyday life, poetry, in the work of many, had hardly any aim but that of seeing and describing. Sometimes an effort was made to convey modern anxieties and despairs; but again, this effort did not go beyond the level of appearances. The mysterious reality of the soul, the backgrounds, the perspectives, were lost to this poetry. It remained still and solely a matter of impressionism. *Sagesse,* for the few men who read this slim volume, was a message of freedom and resurrection, for it informed them that beyond the sensible world lay another, and that attaining that beyond is the poet's sole real task, his only duty. (pp. 115-16)

Amour, to [Verlaine's] mind, was to be a kind of continuation and extension of *Sagesse.* It was to show the place that love had occupied in his life. Cause of his misfortunes, source of his redemption, it was the secret law responsible for the true grandeur of life. This idea gives the book unity despite the variety of recollections that are called up. For here, as in *Sagesse,* Verlaine brings together pieces that extend over a period of more than ten years. . . .

Those who remain unmoved by this poetry of purity, tenderness, and resignation are to be pitied. Beneath the hand of God great and terrible, Verlaine bows his head. . . .

Poetry of humble submission. But poetry, too, of purity. Everything in these beautiful poems becomes suspect and distressing if one supposes for a moment that they are founded on deceit. But they themselves contain evidence that does not lie. If it is wise to be wary of defenders of Verlaine, it is impossible to mistake the involuntary affirmation, the implicit declaration that emerges from his poems, the atmosphere of joyous and childlike purity, the Eden-like atmosphere in which they are steeped.

Verlaine was an adventurer in love; that is the idea implicit in the whole collection:

  J'ai la fureur d'aimer. Mon coeur si faible est fou.

  I am infected with love's frenzy. My poor weak heart is
  mad.

His past misfortunes were born of that frenzy, that madness. When the call of love sounds within him, he throws himself into the breach without thinking, without looking ahead. (pp. 130-31)

Amour is a tough and forceful book. It has its faults. It is sometimes overelaborate, excessively clever, pedantic. But, on the other hand, how many beauties! What an attempt at innovation, what determination to find a tone, to create a style, to achieve hitherto unknown effects! One figure from the past inspires Verlaine: Villon. He wants to be the Villon of the end of his century. That is why he writes ballads and employs a discreetly archaic language. Christian poet, man of the Middle Ages strayed into the sad times in which we live, he continues to have recourse to allegory. Moral life presents itself to his mind in the guise of entities that have their source, one might say, in the *Roman de la Rose* (Romance of the Rose). He is in pursuit of Happiness, but he has found nothing but Error in his path; Pride has clipped his wings. A questionable enterprise, doubtless, as is any return to the past. But not one to be scorned, for in the case of this poet it is less a matter of carrying on a dead tradition than of reviving an ancient form of beauty.

Rather than over these attempts, however interesting, one should pause, in *Amour,* over what it offers that is unquestionably totally new. And that is, to begin with, an art of description very far removed from the methods of impressionism. The beautiful poem, **"Bournemouth,"** for instance, contains none of the juxtaposed notations dear to the Goncourt brothers. It is dominated rather by the humble worship of beauty. Landscape is no longer a plethora of colors, but a harmony presented to the poet; and it is this harmony he concentrates on. Whence the predominance, in his depiction, of essential values, and the care taken to establish their relationships. (pp. 131-32)

Antoine Adam, in his The Art of Paul Verlaine, *translated by Carl Morse (reprinted by permission of New York University Press; translation copyright © 1963 by New York University; originally published as* Verlaine, l'homme et l'oeuvre, *Hatier-Boivin, 1953), New York University Press, 1963, 180 p.*

LOUIS UNTERMEYER   (essay date 1955)

[*Poèmes Saturniens*] are scarcely as saturnine as the title promised. On the contrary, instead of being morose or ominous, they are extraordinarily light in texture and delicate in tone. A visual impressionism is enhanced by a fluctuating music, sensuous but serene. The violin-like sounds of long, low-sobbing winds which hurt the remembering heart are not only suggested but heard in the strange assonances of:

> Les sanglots longs
> Des violons
>   De l'automne
>
> Blessent mon coeur
> D'une langueur
> Monotone.

(pp. 198-99)

A mixture of resentment and experiment shows through Verlaine's second volume *Fêtes Galantes* (Gallant Festivities), but only faintly. The poems, which have been compared to the nimble melodies of Mozart and the naughty delicacies of Watteau, are lightly cynical, spiced with the badinage of **"Colloque Sentimental," "Sur l'Herbe," "L'Allée,"** the Pierrotic raillery of **"A la Promenade," "Mandoline,"** and the pseudo-archaic loveliness of **"Clair de Lune."** . . .

The radiance of [Verlaine's] betrothal and the simple delight of marriage—the sweetness of evening, the rosy hearth, the "dear fatigue," the benignly approving stars—glow through

La Bonne Chanson (The Good Song) which, in contradistinction to the preceding "Parnassian" verse, is warm, intimate, and romantically unsophisticated. (p. 199)

While he was a prisoner Verlaine [wrote] some of the tenderest lyrics in the language. Assembled in *Romances Sans Paroles (Romances Without Words)* they are unsurpassably moving, naïve yet full of subtle nuances, superficially as simple as a nursery rhyme yet, beneath their placid surfaces, darkly troubled—a poetry of the nerves but also a poetry which sounded like the songs of the people. Such plangent lines as "Il pleure dans mon coeur" ("It weeps in my heart"), with its subtitle from Rimbaud, had the same appeal for readers (and composers) as the bittersweet stanzas of Heine. (p. 201)

[Rejected in his forties by the French Academy], Verlaine was more disbalanced than ever; he swung ambivalently from excessive sensuality to the extremes of mysticism. Although his books had received little praise and small recompense, he continued to write and publish poems rich with the utmost refinements of poetic form, studded with lines that were sometimes tenuous, sometimes turbulent, but always characterized by the piquant oddities and delicate dissonances which began to be echoed in the altered tone of modern poetry. (pp. 202-03)

> *Louis Untermeyer, "Paul Verlaine," in his* Makers of the Modern World: The Lives of Ninety-two Writers, Artists, Scientists, Statesmen, Inventors, Philosophers, Composers, and Other Creators Who Formed the Pattern of Our Century *(copyright © 1955 by, Louis Untermeyer; reprinted by permission of Simon & Schuster, a Division of Gulf & Western Corporation), Simon & Schuster, 1955, pp. 198-203.*

PHILIP STEPHAN   (essay date 1961)

While the numerous commentaries on Verlaine's **"Art poétique"** have placed understandable emphasis on the questions of music and rime, they have ignored the fact that Verlaine devotes almost as much space to wit, or humor, as he does to rime and music. Why does Verlaine attack wit so vehemently, when we are not aware that he wrote humorous verse? That is a question which this article proposes to take under consideration. . . .

[The] esthetic basis of humor is the spectator's dissociation from the comic character. Thus, we laugh at the players in a comedy because we feel they are different from us and we suffer with the protagonist of a tragedy because we identify ourselves with him. While not all Verlaine's impassive poetry is humorous, all his humorous poetry springs from the same sense of personal detachment that we find both in the Parnassian poems of *Poèmes saturniens* and in the eighteenth-century poems of *Fêtes galantes.* (p. 196)

Even in Verlaine's early Parnassian poems, one can see that two types of impassivity are present. In one type appears the young poet's debt to his poetic predecessors, such as Gautier and Baudelaire. In the poem, **"Une Grande Dame"** . . . , the emphasis on the tactile, enduring qualities of the lady's beauty, the use of artistic terms like *sertir* and *bleu de Prusse*, the clever *pointe* and Baudelairian sadism of the conclusion, all suggest imitation of older, established poets. (p. 197)

In a second type of impassivity, Verlaine's treatment of prostitutes and beautiful women reveals, we feel, something more than his desire to imitate the Parnassians. While Spain, the sea, and medieval scenes are typically Parnassian subjects, the

courtesan is a less frequent theme of the *Parnasse*. On the contrary, we believe that Verlaine has chosen a subject emotionally near to him—biographically, we know that he was already frequenting *filles de joie* at the time *Poèmes saturniens* were composed—and that the impassivity of these poems is a mask for his personal anxieties. . . . Although he often describes women and love, he keeps them distant by impassive description or by consigning them to the unreal world of dream and memory.

Such distant emotions occur on a wider and more complex scale in *Fêtes galantes,* where the poet is separated from emotion, not by his own impassivity, but by his use of "dramatic space" to isolate both the characters of his poems and the emotions they undergo. (pp. 197-98)

A noteworthy trait of [**"Sur L'Herbe"**] is that it consists almost entirely of dialogue, which establishes mood and expresses ideas as in a play. The theatrical analogy is heightened by the title and the opening sentence, "L'Abbé divague," which can be construed as stage direction. . . . A poem composed as a play suggests a spectator-actor relationship between the reader and the characters of the poem. While the reader is open to the characters' emotions and even shares them to a certain degree, still those emotions tend to remain distant; they belong to the actors, not to the reader, not even to the poet. . . . The reader is an onlooker and not a party to the situation and, as an onlooker, he is separated not only by psychological distance, but also by physical distance. The spectator relationship suggests, at least by implication, that the reader is as far from the scene as the audience is from the players on a stage. (pp. 198-99)

Furthermore, the pictorial quality of the term "dramatic space" is exemplified by the poems **"Pantomime"** and **"Fantoches,"** where the visual description of the characters and of their actions suggests, indeed, a painting. . . .

This is not to say that Verlaine expresses himself with diminished effectiveness in the dramatic poems of *Fêtes galantes,* but we do mean to assert that there is not the same intimacy, the same immediacy of feeling for the reader that we find in poems where the poet speaks directly, expressing himself without the intermediary of dramatic characters.

As with the reader, so with the poet. Verlaine places his emotions in other persons, away from himself, entrusting them with the expression of his own feelings. . . . Instead of talking to the reader, he has his characters speak to the reader for him. . . . In his use of dramatic space, Verlaine writes emotion-filled verses, if not coldly, at least with the dispassionate craft of a dramatist.

Verlaine's humor and irony serve to alienate him from the emotional situations of his poetry; this statement is especially true, in *Fêtes galantes,* of love. By treating amorous relationships humorously, Verlaine dissociates himself from them, implying that he, too, is remote and unmoved. . . . (p. 199)

That Verlaine uses humor consciously in order to establish a distance between himself and the emotion of love is apparent, we feel, in poems where wit disintegrates and a more authentic expression of emotion emerges. Such as poem is **"La Chanson des ingénues,"** where, in the initial stanzas, Verlaine presents, again in somewhat theatrical fashion, the reaction of a group of innocent girls, the *ingénues*, who ridicule love because they fail to understand it. (p. 200)

In his comic portrayal of lovers, Verlaine emphasizes their exaggerated poses and sighs, their complete failure with the frivolous girls, who, in their innocence, cannot understand why the men act as they do. Here is a fitting example of humor as detachment, for it is only in their ignorance of an emotion they have not yet experienced that the girls are able to take such a humorous view. In contrast to this is the last stanza, suddenly serious, where the girls' prescience destroys the comic aspect and causes their hearts to beat harder. . . . Thus, in a poignant ending, Verlaine abandons the distance which he has established between himself and emotion, to bring it closer to himself and to the reader in a moment of intimacy and empathy. (p. 201)

Verlaine develops the idea of psychologically distant emotion further by emphasizing the superficiality of characters in *Fêtes galantes*. Just as the girls of **"Les Ingénues"** ridicule the love which they do not yet understand . . . , so the persons in **"Sur L'Herbe"** and **"En Bateau"** . . . give themselves over to a mood of reckless and irresponsible gaiety. Love is the subject of their witty remarks, yet we know that love for them is not a sincere affection, but a gay farce; indeed, in spite of the sensuous tenor of *Fêtes galantes*, in some of these poems one is inclined to wonder if the characters carry their feelings as far as physical gratification. On the contrary, the hilarity of such poems seems suspended at an indefinite point in time, with no tomorrow to reckon with, without even the possibility of further development of the emotions which Verlaine sketches deftly and almost, it seems, hastily. (p. 202)

By their façade of inane gaiety, by their failure to understand personal sentiment, Verlaine's *personnages* show the distance that separates them from genuine pathos or joy. (p. 203)

While Verlaine's emotions are distant from him in many poems of his first two collections of verse, in subsequent volumes the poet is closely identified with his emotions, locating them within himself. In *La Bonne Chanson* he expresses his feelings directly and without reservation. If the enthusiastic lyricism of that collection appears poetically less sophisticated than *Poèmes saturniens* or *Fêtes galantes*, a new refinement of method appears in *Romances sans paroles*, which represent another effort to express emotions in an intimate, subtle fashion.

A distinction should be made between distant emotions and those which, while close to the poet, are expressed in restrained and indirect language. Particularly in *Romances sans paroles* Verlaine expresses close emotions indirectly, often by fusing physical sensation and personal sentiment in a description of landscape, as in a poem of the **"Ariettes oubliées"** series:

> O bruit doux le la pluie
> Par terre et sur les toits!
> Pour un coeur qui s'ennuie,
> O le chant de la pluie! . . .

Here the poet's sadness is stated impersonally, by the figure of "a heart" and by the suggestion that the "gentle sound of the rain" comforts his heart. . . . Verlaine does not commit the pathetic fallacy of projecting his emotions into the landscape; rather, physical sensation serves as a meeting point between man and nature, and by comparing his emotions to the sensations he feels, the poet is able to ascribe his emotions to the scene before him in "an intimate interpenetration of man and nature." Thus the landscapes of *Romances sans paroles* do not remove the poet's sentiments from him, as do the dramatic poems of *Fêtes galantes;* neither do these careful, Impres-

sionist descriptions represent the objectivity of Parnassian descriptions like **"Une Grande Dame"** or **"Un Dahlia."**

Furthermore, it should be pointed out that both in *Poèmes saturniens* and in *Fêtes galantes* poems where emotions are close to the poet exist along with poems of distant emotion. . . . The poems representing distant emotions are, then, one current among several. It is important to note, however, that this attitude of emotional distance, or detachment, forms an audibly distinct note on Verlaine's many-toned lyre, and that, beginning with a few poems of Parnassian impassivity, it is highly developed in *Fêtes galantes*, only to die out with that volume.

It is only five years later, in [*Romances sans parole*], that Verlaine returns to the idea of distant emotions, and this time it is to condemn humor in his **"Art poétique"**. . . . The target at which this attack is aimed would be unclear, were it not for the extensive use of humor in Verlaine's own poetry. It is not likely that Verlaine would attack so explicitly a few humorous poems such as **"L'Enterrement"** . . . or **"Femme et chatte"** . . . , or that he would comment on the work of other poets when most of **"Art poétique"** deals with trends in his own work. Rather, the stanza refers, we feel, to his humorous, ironic treatment of love in *Fêtes galantes*. By extension, we may infer that Verlaine here is also turning his back on all his poetry where emotions are dealt with distantly. (pp. 204-05)

[The] assertion "Car nous voulons la Nuance encor, / Pas la coleur, rien que la nuance!" indicates a particular method of expressing emotions, that of suggesting nice distinctions of feeling. Verlaine's use of nuance reaches a high level of achievement in the landscape poems of *Romances sans paroles*, in which physical description suggests, rather than states, his mood with remarkable precision. . . . [In] 1874, date of composition of **"Art poétique"** and of many poems of *Romances sans paroles*, Verlaine . . . decided to concentrate on this method of treating emotion, to the exclusion of others.

It is appropriate, therefore, to consider why, having developed such an efficacious expression of distant emotions, Verlaine returns to a position of emotional immediacy. (p. 206)

At the period of *Poèmes saturniens* . . . and *Fêtes galantes* . . . , Verlaine was single, unhappy, and desperately searching for the great love that would, he hoped, bring him happiness. . . . Although he engaged in the more sordid aspects of love, as is seen in the clandestine, pornographic volume, *Les Amies*, . . . these activities did not satisfy his desire for a sincere, noble affection leading to marriage. On the contrary, love seemed to him, in real life as well as poetically, a distant and inaccessible ideal. . . .

After the publication of *Fêtes galantes*, the situation was radically changed by Verlaine's marriage in 1870 to Mathilde Mauté; and while the marriage did not last very long, it was followed immediately by his affair with Arthur Rimbaud in 1872-74. These two events are reproduced poetically by *La Bonne Chanson* . . . and *Romances sans paroles*. . . . If he was disillusioned by marriage, at least love was no longer a distant ideal, it was a close, immediate experience, something he had lived through and seen from the inside. To have attained his ideal, even though it proved to be a disillusionment, altered his poetic treatment of the ideal by bringing it closer to him, so that he no longer treats the emotions connected with it distantly. (p. 207)

If biographically we find a maturation of personal experience in Verlaine's amorous adventures, then poetically there is a parallel growth in the development of his style. As a beginning poet he is subject to several outside influences—hence the eclecticism apparent in *Poèmes saturniens*—as well as to divergent but original tendencies from within himself. Not only is Verlaine open to outside influences—more so, perhaps, than other poets—but he has a particular flair for adopting divergent styles; hence, his numerous *pastiches,* in which he mimics not only other poets but even, in his later years, his own poems. . . .

Poetically, Verlaine's situation in 1874, when he wrote **"Art poétique,"** was as different from that of 1866 as was his private life. The company of Rimbaud was a very real stimulus to his poetic creativity, and discussions with Rimbaud led him to reflect on poetic problems. Not only did Rimbaud's influence lead him to freer and bolder techniques, but the very act of reflecting on poetic theory led him to analyze his own methods more incisively than he had ever, perhaps, done before. Certainly **"Art poétique"** is a much deeper and more methodical outline of artistic principles than the random, *Parnasse*-inspired suggestions of the **"Prologue"** and **"Epilogue"** of *Poèmes saturniens.* Verlaine was, of course, a much maturer and more experienced poet, too. (p. 208)

Intent on perfecting his new system of poetry, more experienced in life itself, Verlaine abandons some of his earlier styles of writing. A more efficacious way of presenting emotion supplants the idea of placing emotion in the distance; similarly, a more complete experience of life renders unnecessary the view of love as a distant ideal. Verlaine has progressed beyond questions of impassivity and of distantly expressed emotions, to reach a new fusion of emotion and symbol, with the poet discreetly involved in both. (p. 209)

> *Philip Stephan, "Verlaine's Distant Emotions," in* The Romanic Review *(copyright © by the Trustees of Columbia University of the City of New York; reprinted by permission), Vol. LII, No. 3 (October, 1961), pp. 196-209.*

ANNA BALAKIAN   (essay date 1967)

For reasons that were tragic, the names of Verlaine and Rimbaud have been coupled in the annals of literary history, particularly in connection with the development of poetic theory revolving around the notion of symbolism. (p. 54)

The fact that Rimbaud was a greater innovator than any of the Symbolists has nothing to do with the fact that he is not really in their orbit. His inclusion among the ranks of the precursors of symbolism has simply complicated the history of the Symbolist movement, bringing many a critic to the conclusion that Symbolism is heterogeneous, or at least a wavering between two contradictory commitments. (p. 56)

Although *Romances sans paroles* and **"Art poétique"** . . . spring out of the same years and are written practically side by side with [Rimbaud's] *Les Illuminations,* in the most intimate personal relationship that could exist between two artists, they are not merely two sides of the same coin, they are as different as the coins of two separate countries. So much opportunity for cross-influence, yet so much difference of vision, of character, and of poetic communication! (p. 61)

Both *Les Illuminations* and *Romances sans paroles* consist of a series of kaleidoscopes in which the outer landscape provides the target for the inner mood. In both cases there is the will not to communicate the subjective state directly to the reader, but to veil the purely biographical by means of metaphoric devices. There the similarity ends. . . .

Verlaine had already practiced the art of suggestive writing in *Fêtes galantes;* he had already linked the landscape of the soul with the man-made tapestries of a Watteau scene and shown how much more subtle is the bittersweet of emotions than either the sweet or the bitter. (p. 62)

In suggesting the characteristic quality of the beloved [in **"Clair de lune"**], Verlaine says that her soul is a landscape where they sing of gay things in minor keys. He had also discovered in the same volume that the half-light is richer in suggestive power and for stimulating the imagination than the bright sunlight, and that words which *imply* emotion are more powerful in communicating that emotion than words which designate it. These discoveries come into greater fulfillment in *Romances sans paroles,* where the slices of scenery act as a prism between the poet's delicate sensitivity and the reader's receptivity. With the simplest words in the French language . . . he sets moods, as a musician sets a key: skies, clouds, the moon, the wind, the snow, the crows, rain, the plain—these nouns, so often used by Verlaine, were to become in symbolist vocabulary recognizable, unfortunately too recognizable, as symbols, losing eventually what concrete attributes they may have retained in Verlaine's poetry. They were to be coupled with the most non-specific adjectives possible—grey, pale, uncertain, white, placid, deep, fleeting, soft—and with verbs suggestive of melancholy rather than of passion—such as to cry, to whimper, to be bored, to blow, to sigh, to tremble, to flee—sounds as muted as the grey of skies, as the sound of water on moss.

The stage is indeed set for symbolist imagery. (pp. 63-4)

[Rimbaud's] notion of suggestive rather than direct discourse is quite different from Verlaine's. Whereas Verlaine seeks the infinite possibilities of the vague and the uncertainties of nuance, Rimbaud provides in his landscapes stark, concrete details—disconnected yet juxtaposed, so as to remain even more tantalizingly ambiguous than vague language. . . . But the Symbolists of the 1880's were to adhere to the manner of Verlaine, to which they had been exposed for some ten years, rather than to that of Rimbaud, which had fallen like a meteor into sudden view in the mid-1880's. The sotto voce suggestiveness of Verlaine's images conveyed a sense of *intimacy;* the naked fragments communicated by Rimbaud were to give him an almost total *privacy* of meaning, which to this day his commentator are trying indefatigably to break through. Verlaine won out, for intimacy was to be the dominant tone of the Symbolists. (pp. 67-8)

> *Anna Balakian, "Verlaine, Not Rimbaud," in her* The Symbolist Movement: A Critical Appraisal *(copyright © 1967 by Random House, Inc; reprinted by permission of Random House, Inc.), Random House, 1967, pp. 54-71.*

C. CHADWICK   (essay date 1973)

Jadis et Naguère is a decidedly second-rate piece of work. The poems that come nearest to the kind of quality that has been encountered in 'Soleils couchants', 'Colloque sentimental', 'La lune blanche . . .', 'Il pleure dans mon coeur . . .' and 'Je ne sais pourquoi . . .', to choose just one example from each of the five previous volumes, are, not surprisingly, those that were composed in 1873 and 1874. One such is 'Sonnet boiteux', given this title presumably because it is in 'vers impairs' with the unusual number of thirteen syllables to each line, but also perhaps because the two tercets do not observe the pattern of rhymes that is customary in a sonnet. . . . Although [the] condemnation by Verlaine [in this poem] of the life he had led in London with Rimbaud lacks the customary sad and melancholy note, creating instead an impression of extreme violence and impotent rage, it nevertheless deserves a high place in Verlaine's poetry for the way in which this mood, though unusual, is conveyed in characteristic fashion with a certain casualness of language and syntax. (pp. 70-1)

Jadis et Naguère did at least contain four or five poems of considerable interest as regards Verlaine's religious and literary ideas and of considerable merit as regards their poetic quality. The same cannot, unfortunately, be said of *Amour,* which is a uniformly dull volume of verse, all too full of the long discursive kind of poem that Verlaine seemed increasingly able to turn out at will. (p. 82)

[A] single quatrain from a sonnet addressed to the composer Emmanuel Chabrier will serve to indicate the level of the occasional verse which forms a substantial part of this ostensibly religious volume of verse:

> Chez ma mère charmante et divinement bonne,
> Votre génie improvisait au piano,
> Et c'était tout autour comme un brûlant anneau
> De sympathie et d'aise aimable qui rayonne . . .

One could forgive such lines, just as one forgives **'Birds in the Night'** and **'Child Wife'** in *Romances sans Paroles* and **'Prince mort en soldat . . .'** in *Sagesse* if, as in those two volumes, there were other poems in *Amour* of true Verlainian quality, but, as the vast majority of critics would agree, there is not a single memorable poem in the entire volume. (p. 84)

[*Parallèlement*] is largely the same kind of ragbag as *Jadis et Naguère.* It opens with half a dozen Lesbian poems under the general sub-title *Les Amies,* that Verlaine had already published clandestinely over twenty years before in 1868 under the pseudonym of Pablo de Herlagnez, and these set the tone for the volume as a whole which, ostensibly, is a collection of sensual poetry parallel to the ostensibly religious poetry of *Amour.* But just as *Amour* soon drifts, after the first few pages, into decidedly secular verse, so *Parallèlement,* after a further half dozen poems of recent composition under the general sub-title *Filles,* drifts into the poems from *Cellulairement* . . . , which have nothing whatever to do with the sins of the flesh, and ends with a couple of dozen poems on a variety of subjects that were clearly added simply to bring the volume up to an acceptable size rather than to pursue the theme of profane love parallel to the sacred love of the previous volume. (p. 90)

> *C. Chadwick, "The Minor Poetry," in his* Verlaine, *(© C. Chadwick 1973), The Athlone Press, 1973, pp. 70-90.*

ADDITIONAL BIBLIOGRAPHY

Carrière, Jean. "Paul Verlaine." In his *Degeneration in the Great French Masters,* pp. 169-96. London: T. Fisher Unwin, Limited, 1922.
> Graceful biographical-critical essay portraying Verlaine as a "'bad master,'" a "propagator of moral cowardice."

Carter, A. E. *The Idea of Decadence in French Literature: 1830-1900.* Toronto: University of Toronto Press, 1958, 154 p.*
> Discusses Verlaine in the context of the decadent movement, insightfully commenting on Verlaine's ideas of homosexuality.

Carter, A. E. *Verlaine: A Study in Parallels.* Toronto: University of Toronto Press, 1969, 255 p.
> An informative biography, interweaving the study of Verlaine's life and works. Carter's conclusion is that Verlaine's personality was such that his genius would always remain prodigal.

Coulon, Marcel. *Poet Under Saturn: The Tragedy of Verlaine.* Translated by Edgell Rickwood. 1932. Reprint. Port Washington, NY: Kennikat Press, 1970, 206 p.
> A bio-critical study which stresses the emotional realism of Verlaine's works.

Ellis, Havelock. "The Approach to Verlaine." In his *From Rousseau to Proust,* pp. 269-83. Boston and New York: Houghton Mifflin Company, 1935.
> A psychological analysis which defines Verlaine's genius as quintessentially primitive.

Hanson, Lawrence, and Hanson, Elizabeth. *Verlaine: Fool of God.* New York: Random House, 1957, 394 p.
> A sensitive and sympathetic biography that treats Verlaine's works as a natural outgrowth of his personality and refrains from condemning him as a man.

Harris, Frank. "Talks with Paul Verlaine." In his *Contemporary Portraits,* pp. 269-82. New York: Mitchell Kennerly, 1915.
> Personal recollections of Verlaine and his wife, providing insights into both their characters.

Nalbantian, Suzanne. "The Symbolists: The Failing Soul." In her *The Symbol of the Soul from Holderlin to Yeats: A Study in Metonomy,* pp. 66-85. New York: Columbia University Press, 1977.*
> Describes how Verlaine and other Symbolists treat the soul as a static and material entity, incapable of transcendence.

Richardson, Joanna. *Verlaine.* New York: The Viking Press, 1971, 432 p.
> The definitive critical biography, scholarly and readable.

Sonnenfeld, Albert. "The Forgotten Verlaine." *Bucknell Review* XI, No. 1 (December 1962): 73-80.
> Contends that Verlaine's "musical" poetry is balanced by hostile, rebellious, and nonlyrical poetry that is usually ignored.

Stephan, Philip. *Paul Verlaine and the Decadence: 1882-1890.* Manchester, England: Manchester University Press, 1974, 216 p.
> Paints Verlaine as a central figure in the rise of decadence and chronicles his ascent to the status of a major poet.

Appendix

THE EXCERPTS IN NCLC, VOLUME 2, WERE REPRINTED FROM THE FOLLOWING PERIODICALS:

The Academy
The Academy and Literature
American Literature
The American Monthly Magazine
The American Monthly Review
American Quarterly
The American Quarterly Review
American Transcendental Quarterly
The Analectic Magazine
Antijacobin Review
The Antioch Review
The Athenaeum
The Atlantic Monthly
Augustan Review
Baldwin's London Magazine
Bentley's Miscellany
Blackwood's Edinburgh Magazine
Blackwood's Magazine
The Bookman (London)
The Bookman (New York)
British Critic and Quarterly Theological
　Review
The British Quarterly Review
British Review
Bucknell Review
Catholic World
The Centennial Review
The Christian Examiner
The Christian Examiner and Religious
　Miscellany
Concerning Poetry
The Cornhill Magazine
The Critic
Critical Quarterly
The Dalhousie Review
The Dublin Review
Dublin University Magazine
Early American Literature

The Eclectic Review
The Edinburgh Review
Educational Theatre Journal
English
The English Journal
The Englishwoman's Domestic Magazine
Essays in Literature
ETC
The Foreign Quarterly Review
The Fortnightly Review
Forum for Modern Language Studies
Fraser's Magazine
Fraser's Magazine for Town and Country
Freeman
The French Review
The Galaxy
The Gazette of the United States
Genre
The Gentleman's Magazine
German Life & Letters
The German Quarterly
The Germanic Review
Godey's Lady Book
Graham's Magazine
Harper's Monthly Magazine
Harper's New Monthly Magazine
The Harvard Monthly
The Independent
Irish Quarterly Review
Irish Writing
Journal of American Studies
Journal of English and German Philology
Journal of the History of Ideas
Journal of Negro History
The Knickerbocker
The Liberator
Lippincott's Magazine of Literature,
　Science, and Education

The Literary Chronicle and Weekly Review
The Literary World
Literature and Psychology
Littel's Living Age
The Living Age
The London Literary Gazette
London Magazine
Macmillan's Magazine
Meliora
Midcontinent American Studies Journal
Midway
Modern Language Notes
Modern Language Review
Modern Philology
Monatshefte
Monthly Chronicle
Monthly Review
Morning Chronicle
The Nation
The National Era
National Review
New Age
The New Englander
The New Leader
The New Monthly Magazine
The New Quarterly Review and Digest of
　Current Literature, British, American,
　French, and German
The New Review
New Statesman
New York Daily Tribune
The New York Mirror
The New York Times
The New York Times Book Review
The New Yorker
The Nineteenth Century
Nineteenth-Century Fiction
The North American Review

Notes and Queries
Once a Week
Pall Mall Gazette
Partisan Review
PHYLON: The Atlanta University Review
  of Race and Culture
Poet Lore
The Polyanthos
The Quarterly Review
Quarterly Review of Literature
Queen's Quarterly
The Romanic Review
The Salem Advertiser
Saturday Review
The Saturday Review (London)

Scot's Magazine
Scribner's Monthly
The Sewanee Review
Southern Literary Messenger
Southern Quarterly Review
Studies in English Literature
Studies in the Literary Imagination
Studies in Philology
Studies in Romanticism
Studies in Short Fiction
Symposium
Tait's Edinburgh Magazine
Temple Bar
Times-Democrat
The Times Literary Supplement

Tomorrow
The Trollopian
The University of Kansas City Review
University of Toronto Quarterly
The Victorian Newsletter
Victorian Poetry
The Westminster and Foreign Quarterly
  Review
The Westminster Review
The Yale Review

THE EXCERPTS IN NCLC, VOLUME 2, WERE REPRINTED FROM THE FOLLOWING BOOKS:

Abbott, Claude Colleer. The Life and Letters of George Darley: Poet and Critic. *Oxford University Press, 1967.*

Adam, Antoine. The Art of Paul Verlaine. *Translated by Carl Morse. New York University Press, 1963.*

Aderman, Ralph M., ed. The Letters of James Kirke Paulding. *University of Wisconsin Press, 1962.*

Aiken, Conrad. Collected Criticism. *Oxford University Press, 1968.*

Archer, William. English Dramatists of To-day. *Sampson Low, Marston, Searle, & Rivington, 1882.*

Arms, George. The Fields Were Green: A New View of Bryant, Whittier, Holmes, Lowell, and Longfellow, with a Selection of Their Poems. *Stanford University Press, 1953.*

Arnold, Matthew. Mixed Essays. *The Macmillan Company, 1903.*

Arnold, Matthew. Essays in Criticism, first and second series. *Dutton, 1964.*

Arvin, Newton. Longfellow: His Life and Work. *Atlantic-Little, Brown, 1963.*

Auden, W. H. The Dyer's Hand and Other Essays. *Random House, 1962.*

Auerbach, Erich. Mimesis: The Representation of Reality in Western Literature. *Translated by Willard R. Trask. Princeton University Press, 1953.*

Balakian, Anna. The Symbolist Movement: A Critical Appraisal. *Random House, 1967.*

Baring, Maurice. An Outline of Russian Literature. *Williams & Norgate, 1915.*

Basch, Françoise. Relative Creatures: Victorian Women in Society and the Novel. *Translated by Anthony Rudolph. Schocken Books, 1974.*

Beerbohm, Max. Around Theatres, Vol. 1. *Alfred A. Knopf, 1939.*

Bellow, Saul. Foreword *to* Winter Notes on Summer Impressions *by Fyodor M. Dostoevsky. Translated by Richard Lee Renfield. Criterion Books, Inc., 1955, McGraw-Hill Book Company, 1965.*

Bennett, Arnold. Books and Persons: Being Comments on a Past Epoch, 1908-1911. *Doran, 1917.*

Bennett, Benjamin. Modern Drama and German Classicism: Renaissance from Lessing to Brecht. *Cornell University Press, 1979.*

Bennett, E. K. A History of the German Novelle from Goethe to Thomas Mann. *Cambridge at the University Press, 1949.*

Bennett, E. K. A History of the German Novelle. *Rev. ed. Edited by H. M. Waidson. Cambridge at the University Press, 1965.*

Birkhead, Edith. Christina Rossetti & Her Poetry. *Harrap, 1930, Folcroft Press, 1970.*

Blake, Kathleen. Play, Games, and Sport: The Literary Works of Lewis Carroll. *Cornell University Press, 1974.*

Blankner, Frederika, ed. The History of the Scandinavian Literatures: A Survey of the Literatures of Norway, Sweden, Denmark, Iceland and Finland, from Their Origins to the Present Day, Including Scandinavian-American Authors, and Selected Bibliographies. *Translated by Frederika Blankner. Dial, 1938.*

Bleiler, E. F., ed. Introduction *to* The Best Tales of Hoffmann *by E.T.A. Hoffmann. Dover, 1967.*

Blunden, Edmund. Votive Tablets: Studies Chiefly Appreciative of English Authors and Books. *Harper & Brothers, Publishers, 1932.*

Bohner, Charles H. John Pendleton Kennedy: Gentleman from Baltimore. *The Johns Hopkins University Press, 1961.*

Bowra, C. M. The Romantic Imagination. *Harvard University Press, 1949, Oxford University Press, 1961.*

Boyesen, Hjalmar Hjorth. Essays on Scandinavian Literature. *Charles Scribner's Sons, 1895.*

Bradford, Gamaliel. Daughters of Eve. *Houghton Mifflin, 1930.*

Brandes, Georg. Lord Beaconsfield: A Study. *Translated by Mrs. George Sturge. Charles Scribner's Sons, 1880, Thomas Y. Crowell Company, 1966.*

Brandes, Georg. Eminent Authors of the Nineteenth Century: Literary Portraits. *Translated by Rasmus B. Anderson. Thomas Y. Crowell Co., Inc., 1886.*

Brandes, Georg. Main Currents in Nineteenth Century Literature: The Romantic School in Germany, Vol. II. *Translated by Diana White and Mary Morison. Heinemann Ltd., 1902, Boni & Liveright, Inc., 1924.*

Brandes, George. Friedrich Nietzsche. *Heinemann, 1914, Haskell House Publishers Ltd., 1972.*

Brockett, Oscar G., ed. Studies in Theatre and Drama: Essays in Honor of Hubert C. Heffner. *Mouton Publishers, 1972.*

Brombert, Victor. The Novels of Flaubert: A Study of Themes and Techniques. *Princeton University Press, 1966.*

Brown, Clarence Arthur, ed. The Achievement of American Criticism: Representative Selections from Three Hundred Years of American Criticism. *Ronald Press, 1954.*

Brownell, W. C. American Prose Masters. *Charles Scribner's Sons, 1909.*

Burckhardt, Sigurd. The Drama of Language: Essays on Goethe and Kleist. *Johns Hopkins Press, 1970.*

Burgess, Anthony. Foreword to Mrs. Caudle's Curtain Lectures *by Douglas Jerrold. Harvill Press, 1974.*

Byron, Lord. The Poetical Works of Lord Byron. *John Murray, 1837, Henry Frowde, 1904.*

Calvert, William J. Byron: Romantic Paradox. *University of North Carolina Press, 1935, Russell & Russell, Inc., 1962.*

Camus, Albert. The Myth of Sisyphus and Other Essays. *Translated by Justin O'Brien. Knopf, 1967.*

Carlson, Eric W., ed. The Recognition of Edgar Allan Poe: Selected Criticism Since 1829. *University of Michigan Press, 1970.*

Carlyle, Thomas. German Romance: Specimens of Its Chief Authors; with Biographical and Critical Notices, Vol. I. *William Tait and Charles Tait, 1827.*

Chadwick, C. Verlaine. *The Athlone Press, 1973.*

Chesterton, G. K. Twelve Types. *Arthur L. Humphreys, 1902.*

Chesterton, G. K., ed. Essays by Divers Hands, Vol. VI. *Oxford University Press, 1926.*

Chesterton, G. K. A Handful of Authors: Essays on Books & Writers. *Edited by Dorothy Collins. Sheed and Ward, 1953.*

Chew, Samuel C., Jr. The Dramas of Lord Byron: A Critical Study. *The Johns Hopkins University Press, 1915, Russell & Russell, Inc., 1964.*

Church, Richard, ed. Essays by Divers Hands, Vol. XXXIII. *Oxford University Press, 1965.*

Closs, August. Medusa's Mirror: Studies in German Literature. *The Cresset Press, 1957.*

Coad, Oral Sumner. William Dunlap: A Study of His Life and Works and of His Place in Contemporary Culture. *The Dunlap Society, 1917, Russell & Russell, Inc., 1962.*

Colum, Mary M. From These Roots: The Ideas that Have Made Modern Literature. *Charles Scribner's Sons, 1937, Columbia University Press, 1944.*

Connolly, Cyril, ed. The Golden Horizon. *University Books, 1955.*

Cowen, Roy C. Christian Dietrich Grabbe. *Twayne, 1972.*

Cowie, Alexander. The Rise of the American Novel. *American Book Company, 1951.*

Croce, Benedetto. European Literature in the Nineteenth Century. *Translated by Douglas Ainslie. Alfred A. Knopf, 1924.*

Crossman, Richard; Highet, Gilbert; and Kahn, Derek, eds. The New Oxford Outlook. *Basil Blackwell, 1933.*

Davis, John P. The American Negro Reference Book. *Prentice-Hall, 1966.*

Deakin, Motley and Lisca, Peter, eds. From Irving to Steinbeck: Studies of American Literature in Honor of Harry R. Warfel. *University of Florida Press, 1972.*

de la Mare, Walter. Lewis Carroll. *Faber and Faber Ltd., 1932.*

Doren, Carl Van. The American Novel: 1789-1939. *Rev. ed. Macmillan, 1940.*

Dostoievsky, F. M. The Diary of a Writer. *Edited and translated by Boris Brasol. Charles Scribner's Sons, 1949, George Braziller, 1954.*

Doumic, René. George Sand: Some Aspects of Her Life and Work. *Translated by Alys Hallard. G. P. Putnam's Sons, 1910.*

Duff, J. D. Translator's Preface to Years of Childhood *by Serge Aksakoff. Translated by J. D. Duff. Edward Arnold Inc., 1916, Hyperion Press, Inc., 1977.*

Duff, J. D. Introduction to A Russian Gentleman *by Serghei Aksakoff. Translated by J. D. Duff. Oxford University Press, 1923.*

Durant, Will. Adventures in Genius. *Simon & Schuster, 1931.*

Duyckinck, Evert A. Irvingiana: A Memorial of Washington Irving. *Charles B. Richardson, 1860.*

Eliot, George. Essays of George Eliot. *Edited by Thomas Pinney. Columbia University Press, 1963.*

Eliot, T. S. On Poetry and Poets. *Farrar, Straus and Cudahy, 1957.*

Elledge, W. Paul. Byron and the Dynamics of Metaphor. *Vanderbilt University Press, 1968.*

Elliott, G. R. The Cycle of Modern Poetry: A Series of Essays toward Clearing Our Present Poetic Dilemma. *Princeton University Press, 1929.*

Ellis, J. M. Kleist's "Prinz Friedrich von Homburg": A Critical Study. *University of California Press, 1970.*

Ellmann, Richard, ed. The Artist As Critic: Critical Writings of Oscar Wilde. *W. H. Allen, 1970.*

Empson, William. Some Versions of Pastoral. *Chatto & Windus, 1935.*

Ermilov, Vladimir. F. M. Dostoevski. *Translated by Edward Wasiolek. State Publisher of Arts and Letters, 1956.*

Evans, Ifor. English Poetry in the Later Nineteenth Century. *Rev. ed. Methuen & Co Ltd, 1966.*

Faguet, Emile. Flaubert. *Translated by Mrs. R. L. Devonshire. Houghton Mifflin Company, 1914.*

Farrison, William Edward. William Wells Brown: Author & Reformer. *University of Chicago Press, 1969.*

Flaubert, Gustave. The Letters of Gustave Flaubert: 1830-1857. *Edited and translated by Francis Steegmuller. Belknap Press, 1980.*

Foerster, Norman. American Criticism: A Study in Literary Theory from Poe to the Present. *Houghton, 1928.*

France, Anatole. On Life & Letters, first series. *Translated by A. W. Evans. John Lane Company, 1911, Dodd, Mead and Company, 1924.*

France, Anatole. On Life & Letters, third series. *Edited by J. Lewis May and Bernard Miall. Translated by D. B. Stewart. John Lane Company, 1922.*

Frye, Northrop. Fables of Identity: Studies in Poetic Mythology. *Harcourt, 1963.*

Frye, Prosser Hall. Literary Reviews and Criticisms. *G. P. Putnam's Sons, 1908.*

Fuerst, Norbert. The Victorian Age of German Literature: Eight Essays. *The Pennsylvania State University Press, 1966.*

Fuller, Margaret. Papers on Literature and Art. *Wiley and Putnam, 1846.*

Fuller, Margaret. The Writings of Margaret Fuller. *Edited by Mason Wade. The Viking Press, 1941.*

Gayle, Addison, Jr. The Way of the New World: The Black Novel in America. *Anchor Press, 1975.*

Gearey, John. Heinrich von Kleist: A Study in Tragedy and Anxiety. *University of Pennsylvania Press, 1968.*

Gide, André. Dostoevsky. *Translated by Arnold Bennett. New Directions, 1961.*

Giraud, Raymond. The Unheroic Hero in the Novels of Stendahl, Balzac and Flaubert. *Rutgers University Press, 1957.*

Giraud, Raymond, ed. Flaubert: A Collection of Critical Essays. *Prentice-Hall, 1964.*

Goethe, Johann Wolfgang von. Letters from Goethe. *Translated by Dr. M. von Herzfeld and C. Melvil Sym. Edinburgh at the University Press, 1957.*

Goode, Clement Tyson. Byron as Critic. *R. Wagner, 1923, Haskell House, 1964.*

Gosse, Edmund. Critical Kit-Kats. *Dodd Mead and Company, 1896, Scholarly Press, Inc., 1971.*

Gosse, Edmund. Introduction to Undine *by Friedrich de La Motte Fouqué. Translated by Edmund Gosse. Lawrence & Bullen, 1896, Oxford University Press, 1932.*

Gosse, Edmund. Introduction to Vivian Grey: A Romance of Youth. *by Benjamin Disraeli. Dunne, 1904.*

Gourmont, Remy de. The Book of Masks. *Translated by Jack Lewis. J. W. Luce & Co., 1921, Books for Libraries Press, 1967.*

Gourmont, Remy de. Selected Writings. *Edited and translated by Glenn S. Burne. The University of Michigan Press, 1966.*

Greenberg, Martin. Introduction to The Marquise of O—and Other Stories *by Heinrich von Kleist. Translated by Martin Greenberg. Criterion Books, 1960.*

Griswold, Rufus Wilmot. The Prose Writers of America. *Rev. ed. A. Hart, 1852, Garrett Press, Inc., 1969.*

Griswold, Rufus Wilmot. The Prose Writers of America: With a Survey of the Intellectual History, Condition, and Prospects of the Country. *Rev. ed. Porter & Coates, 1870.*

Guest, John, ed. Essays by Divers Hands, Vol. XXXVIII. *Oxford University Press, 1975.*

Halline, Allan Gates, ed. American Plays. *American Book Company, 1935.*

Hamburger, Michael. Contraries: Studies in German Literature. *E. P. Dutton & Co., Inc., 1970.*

Hamilton, Catherine J. Women Writers: Their Words and Ways, first series. *Ward, Lock, Bowden and Co., 1892.*

Hassan, Ihab, ed. Liberations: New Essays on the Humanities in Revolution. *Wesleyan University Press, 1971.*

Hawthorne, Nathaniel. Preface to The Scarlet Letter. *2d ed. Ticknor, Reed & Fields, 1850.*

Hawthorne, Nathaniel. Preface to The Marble Faun. *Ticknor & Fields, 1859.*

Hawthorne, Nathaniel. The Complete Novels and Selected Tales of Nathaniel Hawthorne. *Edited by Norman Holmes Pearson. The Modern Library, 1937.*

Hawthorne, Nathaniel. Preface to Twice-Told Tales and Other Short Stories. *Washington Square Press, 1960.*

Hawthorne, Nathaniel. Preface to The House of the Seven Gables. *Washington Square Press, 1961.*

Hazlitt, William. The Spirit of the Age; or, Contemporary Portraits. *4th ed. Edited by W. Carew Hazlitt. George Bell and Sons, 1886.*

Hearn, Lafcadio. Interpretations of Literature, Vol. II. *Edited by John Erskine. Dodd, Mead and Company, 1915, Kennikat Press, 1965.*

Hearn, Lafcadio. Essays in European and Oriental Literature. *Edited by Albert Mordell. Dodd, Mead and Company, 1923.*

Hearn, Lafcadio. A History of English Literature in a Series of Lectures, Vol. II. *The Hokuseido Press, 1927.*

Heath-Stubbs, John. The Darkling Plain: A Study of the Later Fortunes of Romanticism in English Poetry from George Darley to W. B. Yeats. *Eyre & Spottiswoode, 1950.*

Hedges, William L. Washington Irving: An American Study, 1802-1832. *The Johns Hopkins University Press, 1965.*

Heermance, J. Noel. William Wells Brown and "Clotelle": A Portrait of the Artist in the First Negro Novel. *Archon Books (Shoe String Press, Inc.), 1969.*

Helbling, Robert E. The Major Works of Heinrich von Kleist. *New Directions, 1975.*

Herold, Amos L. James Kirke Paulding: Versatile American. *Columbia University Press, 1926.*

Hicks, Granville. The Great Tradition: An Interpretation of American Literature since the Civil War. *Rev. ed. Macmillan, 1935, Quadrangle Books, 1969.*

Hirsh, Edward L. Henry Wadsworth Longfellow. *University of Minnesota Press, 1964.*

Hornsey, A. W. Idea and Reality in the Dramas of Christian Dietrich Grabbe. *Pergamon Press, 1966.*

Howe, Irving. Politics and the Novel. *Horizon, 1957.*

Howells, W. D. My Literary Passions. *Harper & Brothers Publishers, 1895.*

Hudson, William Henry. Lowell & His Poetry. *Harrap, 1914.*

Hughes, Glyn Tegai. Romantic German Literature. *Holmes & Meier, 1979, Edward Arnold, 1979.*

Hugo, Victor. Things Seen (Choses vues): Essays. *Estes and Lauriat, 1824(?).*

Huneker, James. Overtones, a Book of Temperaments: Richard Strauss, Parsifal, Verdi, Balzac, Flaubert, Nietzsche, and Turgenieff. *Charles Scribner's Sons, 1928.*

Huysmans, J. K. Against the Grain: A Rebours. *Translated by John Howard. Albert and Charles Boni, 1930.*

Hyman, Stanley Edgar. The Critic's Credentials: Essays & Reviews. *Edited by Phoebe Pettingell. Athenaeum, 1978.*

Jackson, Holbrook. Great English Novelists. *Grant Richards, 1908.*

James, Henry. French Poets and Novelists. *B. Tauchnitz, 1883.*

James, Henry. Literary Reviews and Essays: On American, English, and French Literature. *Edited by Albert Mordell. Twayne Publishers, 1957.*

James, Henry, Jr. Hawthorne. *Harper & Brothers, Publishers, 1879.*

Jerrold, Douglas. Preface to *The Writings of Douglas Jerrold: "St. Giles and St. James," Vol. I. Bradbury and Evans, 1851.*

Jerrold, W. Blanchard. The Life and Remains of Douglas Jerrold. *Ticknor and Fields, 1859.*

Johnson, Roger, Jr.; Neumann, Editha S.; and Trial, Guy T. Molière and the Commonwealth of Letters: Patrimony and Posterity. *University Press of Mississippi, 1975.*

Jones, Peter. Philosophy and the Novel: Philosophical Aspects of "Middlemarch," "Anna Karenina," "The Brothers Karamazov," "A la recherche du temps perdu," and of the Methods of Criticism. *Oxford University Press, 1975.*

Jump, John D., ed. Byron: A Symposium. *Barnes & Noble, 1975.*

Katz, William Loren, ed. Five Slave Narratives: A Compendium. *Arno Press, 1968.*

Kaufmann, Friedrich Wilhelm. German Dramatists of the 19th Century. *Lymanhouse, 1940, Books for Libraries Press, 1970.*

Kayser, Wolfgang. The Grotesque in Art and Literature. *Translated by Ulrich Weisstein. Indiana University Press, 1963, McGraw-Hill Book Company, 1966.*

Kelly, Richard M. Douglas Jerrold. *Twayne, 1972.*

Kent, Leonard J. The Subconscious in Gogol' and Dostoevski, and Its Antecedents. *Mouton Publishers, 1969.*

Kintner, Elvan, ed. The Letters of Robert Browning and Elizabeth Barrett Barrett 1845-1846. *Harvard University Press, 1969.*

Klenze, Camillo von. From Goethe to Hauptmann: Studies in a Changing Culture. *The Viking Press, 1926, Biblo and Tannen, 1966.*

Knight, G. Wilson. The Golden Labyrinth: A Study of British Drama. *Phoenix House, 1962.*

Krieger, Murray. The Tragic Vision: Variations on a Theme in Literary Interpretation. *Holt, Rinehart and Winston, 1960.*

Kropotkin, Prince. Russian Literature. *McClure, Phillips & Co., 1905, Knopf, 1916.*

Kumar, Shiv K., ed. British Victorian Literature: Recent Revaluations. *New York University Press, 1969.*

Langdon-Davies, B. N. Introduction to Coningsby *by Benjamin Disraeli. E. P. Dutton & Co., 1911.*

Lavrin, Janko. An Introduction to the Russian Novel. *Methuen & Co. Ltd., 1942.*

Lavrin, Janko. Dostoevsky: A Study. *Macmillan, 1947.*

Lawrence, D. H. Studies in Classic American Literature. *Thomas Seltzer Inc., 1923, William Heinemann Ltd., 1924, Viking Press, 1964.*

Leisy, Ernest E. The American Historical Novel. *University of Oklahoma Press, 1950.*

Lepelletier, Edmond. Paul Verlaine: His Life—His Work. *Translated by E. M. Lang. Duffield & Co., 1909, AMS Press, Inc., 1970.*

Leventhal, A. J. George Darley (1795-1846). *The Dublin University Press, Ltd., 1950.*

Lieder, Paul Robert. Introduction to Poems by Tegnér: "The Children of the Lord's Supper" and "Frithiof's Saga" *by Esaias Tegner Translated by Henry Wadsworth Longfellow and Rev. W. Lewery Blackley. The American-Scandinavian Foundation, 1930.*

Lindsay, J[ames] M[artin]. Gottfried Keller: Life and Works. *Wolff, 1968, Dufour Editions, Inc., 1969.*

Loggins, Vernon. The Negro Author: His Development in America to 1900. *Columbia University Press, 1931, Kennikat Press, Inc., 1964.*

Longfellow, Henry Wadsworth. Kéramos and Other Poems. *Houghton, Osgood & Company, 1878.*

Lowell, James Russell. A Fable for Critics; or, A Glance at a Few of Our Literary Progenies. *2d ed. G. P. Putnam, 1848.*

Lowell, James Russell. The Function of the Poet, and Other Essays. *Houghton Mifflin Company, 1920.*

Lowell, James Russell. James Russell Lowell: Representative Selections. *Edited by Harry Hayden Clark. American Book Co., 1947.*

Lubbock, Percy. The Craft of Fiction. *J. Cape, 1921, Charles Scribner's Sons, 1955.*

Lukács, Georg. The Historical Novel. *Translated by Hannah Mitchell and Stanley Mitchell. Merlin Press, 1962.*

Lytton, Edward R. B. The Life, Letters and Literary Remains of Edward Bulwer, Lord Lytton. *Kegan Paul, Trench, Trubner & Co., Ltd., 1883.*

Macdonald, George. A Dish of Orts: Chiefly Papers on the Imagination, and on Shakspere. *Sampson, Low and Marston, 1895.*

Macy, John. The Spirit of American Literature. *Doubleday, 1913.*

Mallarmé, Stéphane. Mallarmé: Selected Prose Poems, Essays, & Letters. *Translated by Bradford Cook. The Johns Hopkins University Press, 1956.*

Mann, Thomas. Essays of Three Decades. *Translated by H. T. Lowe-Porter. Knopf, 1947.*

Mann, Thomas. Preface to The Marquise of O—and Other Stories *by Heinrich von Kleist. Translated by Francis Golffing. Criterion Books, 1960.*

Marble, Annie Russell. Heralds of American Literature: A Group of Patriot Writers of the Revolutionary and National Periods. *University of Chicago Press, 1907.*

Marchand, Leslie A. Byron's Poetry: A Critical Introduction. *Houghton Mifflin, 1965.*

Marshall, William H. The Structure of Byron's Major Poems. *University of Pennsylvania Press, 1962.*

Martin, L. C. Byron's Lyrics. *The University of Nottingham, 1948.*

Matlaw, Ralph E. Introduction to The Family Chronicle *by Sergey Aksakov. Translated by M. C. Beverly. Dutton, 1961.*

Matlaw, Ralph E., ed. Belinsky, Chernyshevsky, and Dobrolyubov: Selected Criticism. *Dutton, 1962.*

Matthews, Brander. Introduction to André: A Tragedy in Five Acts *by William Dunlap. The Dunlap Society, 1887, Burt Franklin, 1970.*

Matthiessen, F. O. American Renaissance: Art and Expression in the Age of Emerson and Whitman. *Oxford University Press, 1941.*

Mauriac, François. Men I Hold Great. *Translated by Elsie Pell. Philosophical Library, 1951.*

McCarthy, Mary. The Writing on the Wall and Other Literary Essays. *Harcourt, 1964.*

McDonald, Edward D. Phoenix: The Posthumous Papers of D. H. Lawrence. *Viking Penguin, 1936, William Heinemann, 1936.*

Meier-Graefe, Julius. Dostoevsky: The Man and His Work. *Translated by Herbert H. Marks. G. Routledge & Sons, 1928.*

Melville, Herman. The Apple-Tree Table and Other Sketches. *Princeton University Press, 1922.*

Mencken, H. L. The American Language: Supplement I. *Knopf, 1945.*

Merejkowski, Dmitri. Tolstoi As Man and Artist, with an Essay on Dostoïevski. *G. P. Putnam's Sons, 1902, Greenwood Press, 1970.*

Meserve, Walter J. An Emerging Entertainment: The Drama of the American People to 1828. *Indiana University Press, 1977.*

Meynell, Alice. The Second Person Singular and Other Essays. *Oxford University Press, 1921.*

Minto, William. The Literature of the Georgian Era. *Edited by William Knight. William Blackwood and Sons, 1894.*

Mirsky, D. S. A History of Russian Literature from Its Beginnings to 1900. *Edited by Francis J. Whitfield. Vintage Books, 1958.*

Mitford, Mary Russell. Recollections of a Literary Life; or, Books, Places, and People. *Harper & Brothers, Publishers, 1852.*

Mochulsky, Konstantin. Dostoevsky: His Life and Work. *Translated by Michael A. Minihan. Princeton University Press, 1967.*

Moore, George. Impressions and Opinions. *Charles Scribner's Sons, 1891, T. Werner Laurie, Ltd., 1913.*

Moore, Virginia. Distinguished Women Writers. *Dutton, 1934.*

More, Paul Elmer. Shelburne Essays, second series. *Houghton Mifflin Company, 1905.*

More, Paul Elmer. Shelburne Essays, third series. *Houghton Mifflin Company, 1905.*

More, Paul Elmer. Shelburne Essays on American Literature. *Edited by Daniel Aaron. Harcourt Brace Jovanovich Inc., 1963.*

Morgan, Charles. Reflections in a Mirror. *Macmillan, 1946.*

Moses, Montrose J. and Brown, John Mason, eds. The American Theatre as Seen by Its Critics: 1752-1934. *2d ed. Norton, 1934.*

Mudrick, Marvin. Books Are Not Life But Then What Is? *Oxford University Press, 1979.*

Murry, J. Middleton. Fyodor Dostoevsky: A Critical Study. *Martin Secker, 1923.*

Myers, Andrew B., ed. A Century of Commentary on the Works of Washington Irving: 1860-1974. *Sleepy Hollow Restorations, 1976.*

Nabokov, Vladimir. Lectures on Literature. *Edited by Fredson Bowers. Harcourt, 1980.*

Natan, Alex, ed. German Men of Letters: Twelve Literary Essays, Vol. V. *Oswald Wolff, 1969.*

Neal, John. American Writers: A Series of Papers Contributed to "Blackwood's Magazine" (1824-1825). *Edited by Fred Lewis Pattee. Duke University Press, 1937.*

Nicholls, Roger A. The Dramas of Christian Dietrich Grabbe. *Mouton Publishers, 1969.*

Nicolson, Harold. Paul Verlaine. *Constable & Company Limited, 1921.*

Ortega y Gasset, José. The Dehumanization of Art: And Other Essays on Art, Culture, and Literature. *Translated by Helene Weyl. Princeton University Press, 1968.*

Parrington, Vernon Louis. Main Currents in American Thought, an Interpretation of American Literature from the Beginnings to 1920: The Romantic Revolution in America, 1800-1860, Vol. 2. *Harcourt, 1958.*

Pascal, Roy. The German Novel: Studies. *Manchester University Press, 1956.*

Pattee, Fred Lewis. The Development of the American Short Story: An Historical Survey, *Harper, 1923.*

Paul, Sherman, ed. Six Classic American Writers: An Introduction. *University of Minnesota Press, 1970.*

Payne, William Morton. Little Leaders. *Way & Williams, 1895.*

Pearce, Roy Harvey. The Continuity of American Poetry. *Princeton University Press, 1961.*

Pearce, Roy Harvey, ed. Hawthorne Centenary Essays. *Ohio State University Press, 1964.*

Perry, Bliss. The Praise of Folly and Other Papers. *Houghton, 1923, Kennikat Press, Inc., 1964.*

Phillips, Robert. Aspects of Alice: Lewis Carroll's Dreamchild as Seen Through the Critics' Looking-Glasses, 1865-1971. *The Vanguard Press Inc., 1971.*

Poe, Edgar Allan. The Complete Works of Edgar Allan Poe, Vol VI. *Colonial Press Company, 1856, A. C. Armstrong & Son, 1884.*

Poggioli, Renato. The Phoenix and the Spider: A Book of Essays about Some Russian Writers and Their View of the Self. *Harvard University Press, 1957.*

Poulet, Georges. Studies in Human Time. *Johns Hopkins University Press, 1956.*

Praz, Mario. The Romantic Agony. *Translated by Angus Davidson. Oxford University Press, 1951, Meridian Books, 1956.*

Priestley, J. B. I for One. *John Lane, 1923, Books for Libraries Press, 1967.*

Pritchett, V. S. Books in General. *Chatto & Windus Ltd., 1953.*

Pritchett, V. S. The Living Novel and Later Appreciations. *Random House, 1964.*

Pritchett, V. S. The Myth Makers. *Random House, 1979.*

Proust, Marcel. A Selection from His Miscellaneous Writings. *Edited and translated by Gerard Hopkins. Allen Wingate, 1948.*

Quinn, Arthur Hobson. A History of the American Drama: From the Beginning to the Civil War. *2d ed. F. S. Crofts & Co., 1943, Appleton-Century-Crofts, Inc., 1951.*

Quinn, Arthur Hobson, ed. The Literature of the American People: An Historical and Critical Survey. *Appleton-Century-Crofts, 1951.*

Rahv, Philip. Essays on Literature and Politics: 1932-1972. *Edited by Arabel J. Porter and Andrew J. Drosin. Houghton Mifflin Company, 1978.*

Redding, J. Saunders. To Make a Poet Black. *University of North Carolina Press, 1939, McGrath Publishing Company, 1968.*

Reeves, James, ed. Five Late Romantic Poets. *Heinemann, 1974.*

Reiman, Donald H. Introduction to The Family Legend and Metrical Legends of Exalted Characters *by Joanna Baillie. Garland Publishers, 1976.*

Reiman, Donald H. Introduction to Miscellaneous Plays *by Joanna Baillie, Garland, 1977.*

Reiman, Donald H., ed. The Romantics Reviewed, Contemporary British Romantic Writers: Byron and Regency Society Poets, Vol. III. *Garland Publishing, Inc., 1972.*

Rexroth, Kenneth. Classics Revisited. *Quadrangle Books, 1968.*

Richardson, E. P. Washington Allston: A Study of the Romantic Artist in America. *University of Chicago Press, 1948, Thomas Y. Crowell Company, 1967.*

Ridgely, J. V. John Pendleton Kennedy. *Twayne, 1966.*

Ridler, Anne. Introduction to Selected Poems of George Darley *by George Darley. Edited by Anne Ridler. The Merrion Press, 1974.*

Robertson, J. G. Essays and Addresses on Literature. *G. Routledge & Sons, Ltd., 1935, Books for Libraries Press, 1968.*

Ruskin, John. The Works of John Ruskin: Early Prose Writings, 1834 to 1843, Vol. I. *Edited by E. T. Cook and Alexander Wedderburn. Longmans, Green, and Co., 1903.*

Rutherford, Andrew. Byron: A Critical Study. *Stanford University Press, 1961.*

Sainte-Beuve, Charles Augustin. Sainte-Beuve: Selected Essays. *Edited and translated by Francis Steegmuller and Norbert Guterman. Doubleday, 1963.*

Schoolfield, George C. The Figure of the Musician in German Literature. *University of North Carolina Press, 1956.*

Scott, Walter. The Miscellaneous Prose Works of Sir Walter Scott: Biographical Memoirs of Eminent Novelists, and Other Distinguished Persons, Vol. IV. *Robert Cadell, 1834.*

Scott, Walter. Familiar Letters of Sir Walter Scott, Vol. I. *Houghton Mifflin & Company, 1894.*

Seduro, Vladimir. Dostoyevski in Russian Literary Criticism: 1846-1956. *Columbia University Press, 1957.*

Shepard, Odell. Introduction to Henry Wadsworth Longfellow: Representative Selections *by Henry Wadsworth Longfellow. Edited by Odell Shepard. American Book Company, 1934.*

Shore, Fredegond. Christina Rossetti: A Study. *Cambridge at the University Press, 1931, Folcroft Press, Inc., 1969.*

Silz, Walter. Realism and Reality: Studies in the German Novelle of Poetic Realism. *The University of North Carolina Press, 1954.*

Silz, Walter. Heinrich von Kleist: Studies in His Works and Literary Character. *University of Pennsylvania Press, 1962.*

Simmons, Ernest J. Dostoevski: The Making of a Novelist. *Oxford University Press, 1940.*

Slonim, Marc. The Epic of Russian Literature: From Its Origins Through Tolstoy. *Oxford University Press, 1964.*

Smith, William, ed. Lowell: Essays, Poems, and Letters. *Odyssey Press, 1948.*

Snell, George. The Shapers of American Fiction: 1798-1947. *E. P. Dutton & Co., Inc., 1947.*

Spalter, Max. Brecht's Tradition. *The Johns Hopkins University Press, 1967.*

Stahl, E. L. Heinrich von Kleist's Dramas. *Rev. ed. Basil Blackwell, 1961.*

Stephen, Leslie. Hours in a Library. *Smith, Elder & Co., 1909.*

Stepto, Robert B. From Behind the Veil: A Study of Afro-American Narrative. *University of Illinois Press, 1979.*

Stern, J. P. Idylls & Realities: Studies in Nineteenth-Century German Literature. *Methuen, 1971.*

Stirling, James Hutchinson. Jerrold, Tennyson and Macaulay: With Other Critical Essays. *Edmonston & Douglas, 1868.*

Stovall, Floyd, ed. The Development of American Literary Criticism. *University of North Carolina Press, 1955.*

Strachey, Lytton. Literary Essays. *Harcourt, 1949.*

Swales, Martin. The German Novelle. *Princeton University Press, 1977.*

Swinburne, Algernon Charles. Essays and Studies. *2d ed. Chatto and Windus, 1876.*

Symons, Arthur. Studies in Two Literatures. *Leonard Smithers, 1897.*

Symons, Arthur. The Symbolist Movement in Literature. *William Heinemann, 1899.*

Symons, Arthur. The Romantic Movement in English Poetry. *Archibald Constable & Co. Ltd., 1909.*

Symons, Arthur. Figures of Several Centuries. *Constable and Company Ltd, 1916.*

Symons, Arthur. Studies in Prose and Verse. *E. P. Dutton & Co., 1922.*

Tandy, Jennette. Crackerbox Philosophers in American Humor and Satire. *Columbia University Press, 1925, Kennikat Press, Inc., 1964.*

Thackeray, William Makepeace. The Paris Sketchbook. *Crowell, 1905.*

Thackeray, William Makepeace. Contributions to the ''Morning Chronicle.'' *Edited by Gordon N. Ray. University of Illinois Press, 1955.*

Thalmann, Marianne. The Romantic Fairy Tale: Seeds of Surrealism. *Translated by Mary B. Corcoran. University of Michigan Press, 1964.*

Thibaudet, Albert. French Literature from 1795 to Our Era. *Translated by Charles Lam Markmann. Funk & Wagnalls, 1967.*

Tillotson, Kathleen, ed. The Letters of Charles Dickens: 1844-1846, Vol. 4. *Oxford University Press, 1977.*

Trollope, Anthony. An Autobiography. *Harper & Brothers, 1883, Oxford University Press, 1923.*

Ullmann, Stephen. Style in the French Novel. *Cambridge at the University Press, 1957.*

Untermeyer, Louis. Makers of the Modern World: The Lives of Ninety-two Writers, Artists, Scientists, Statesmen, Inventors, Philosophers, Composers, and Other Creators Who Formed the Pattern of Our Century. *Simon & Schuster, 1955.*

Valéry, Paul. The Collected Works of Paul Valéry: Masters and Friends, Vol. 9. *Edited by Jackson Mathews. Translated by Martin Turnell, Bollinger Series XLV. Princeton University Press, 1968.*

Vivas, Eliseo. Creation and Discovery. *Noonday Press, 1955.*

Wagenknecht, Edward. Cavalcade of the English Novel: From Elizabeth to George VI. *Holt, Rinehart and Winston, 1954.*

Ward, Thomas Humphrey, ed. The English Poets, Selections with Critical Introductions by Various Writers and a General Introduction by Matthew Arnold: Browning to Rupert Brooke, Vol. V. *Macmillan, 1918.*

Wasiolek, Edward. Dostoevsky: The Major Fiction. *The MIT Press, 1964.*

Wasiolek, Edward, ed. ''Crime and Punishment'' and the Critics. *Wadsworth, 1961.*

Wasiolek, Edward, ed. ''The Brothers Karamazov'' and the Critics. *Wadsworth Publishing Company, Inc., 1967.*

Wellek, René, ed. Dostoevsky: A Collection of Critical Essays. *Prentice-Hall, Inc., 1962.*

Wells, Benjamin N. A Century of French Fiction. *Dodd, Mead and Company, 1898.*

West, Paul. Byron and the Spoiler's Art. *Chatto & Windus, 1960.*

Whiteman, Maxwell. Bibliographical note to The Escape; or A Leap for Freedom: A Drama in Five Acts *by William Wells Brown, Rhistoric Publications, 1969.*

Whittier, John Greenleaf. Whittier on Writers and Writing: The Uncollected Critical Writings of John Greenleaf Whittier. *Edited by Edwin Harrison Cady and Harry Hayden Clark. Syracuse University Press, 1950.*

Williams, Stanley T. The Spanish Background of American Literature, Vol. II. *Yale University Press, 1955.*

Williams, Stanley T. The Life of Washington Irving, Vol. I. *Oxford University Press, 1935, Octagon Books, 1971.*

Wilson, Edmund. The Triple Thinkers: Twelve Essays on Literary Subjects. *Rev. ed. Oxford University Press, 1948, Noonday, 1976.*

Wilson, Edmund. The Shores of Light: A Literary Chronicle of the Twenties and Thirties. *Farrar, Straus & Giroux, 1952.*

Winters, Yvor. Maule's Curse: Seven Studies in the History of American Obscurantism. *New Directions, 1938.*

Winters, Yvor. In Defense of Reason. *The Swallow Press Inc., 1947.*

Woolf, Virginia. The Second Common Reader. *Harcourt, 1932.*

Woolf, Virginia. The Moment and Other Essays. *Harcourt, 1948.*

Woolf, Virginia. Granite and Rainbow. *Harcourt, Brace & World, Inc., 1958.*

Wortham, Thomas. James Russell Lowell's ''The Bigelow Papers'': A Critical Edition. *Northern Illinois University Press, 1977.*

Wright, Nathalia. Introduction to Lectures on Art and Poems (1850) and Monaldi (1841) *by Washington Allston. Scholars' Facsimiles & Reprints, 1967.*

Yellin, Jean Fagin. The Intricate Knot: Black Figures in American Literature, 1776-1863. *New York University Press, 1972.*

Zweig, Stefan. Master Builders, an Attempt at the Typology of the Spirit: Three Masters, Balzac, Dickens, Dostoeffsky, Vol. 1. *Translated by Eden Paul and Cedar Paul. Viking Penguin Inc., 1930.*

Cumulative Index to Authors

Cumulative Index to Critics

CRITIC INDEX

CRITIC INDEX

Saintsbury, George
Elizabeth Barrett Browning
1:126
Maria Edgeworth 1:261
Gustave Flaubert 2:226
Théophile Gautier 1:345
Franz Grillparzer 1:386
Edgar Allan Poe 1:508

Salisbury, Lord
Theodor Storm 1:535

Sanborn, F. B.
Amos Bronson Alcott 1:22

Sandbach, F. E.
Friedrich Maximilian von
Klinger 1:426

Sayers, Dorothy L.
Wilkie Collins 1:183

Schmidt, Hugo
Franz Grillparzer 1:395

Schoolfield, George C.
Ernst Theodor Amadeus
Hoffmann 2:346

Schrimpf, Hans Joachim
Heinrich von Kleist 2:453

Schwartz, Daniel R.
Benjamin Disraeli 2:152

Schwarz, Egon
Manuel Tamayo y Baus 1:567

Scott, Walter
Jane Austen 1:30, 32
Joanna Baillie 2:35
George Gordon Byron, Lord
Byron 2:68
John Galt 1:330
Ernst Theodor Amadeus
Hoffmann 2:339

Sharp, William
Guy de Maupassant 1:447

Shaw, Bernard
Edgar Allan Poe 1:502

Shaw, Charles Gray
Fedor Mikhailovich Dostoevski
2:170

Shepard, Odell
Amos Bronson Alcott 1:24
Henry Wadsworth Longfellow
2:487

Shilstone, Frederick W.
George Gordon Byron, Lord
Byron 2:103

Shove, Fredegond
Christina Georgina Rossetti
2:571

Silz, Walter
Franz Grillparzer 1:390
Gottfried Keller 2:416
Heinrich von Kleist 2:451
Theodor Storm 1:541

Simmons, Ernest J.
Fedor Mikhailovich Dostoevski
2:183

Simms, William Gilmore
Washington Allston 2:21

Simpson, Richard
Jane Austen 1:34

Sinnett, John Taylor
Douglas Jerrold 2:395

Sivert, Eileen
Jules Amédée Barbey
d'Aurevilly 1:77

Slonim, Marc
Sergei Timofeyvich Aksakov
2:14
Nikolay Chernyshevsky 1:161
Ivan Andreevich Krylov 1:436

Smith, Albert B.
Théophile Gautier 1:352

Smith, Alexander
Wilkie Collins 1:174

Smith, Fred Manning
Elizabeth Barrett Browning
1:129

Smith, George
Henry Wadsworth Longfellow
2:482

Smith, L. Pearsall
Sergei Timofeyvich Aksakov
2:12

Smith, Sheila M.
Charles Reade 2:551

Snapper, Johan Pieter
Friedrich Maximilian von
Klinger 1:431

Snell, George
Washington Irving 2:382

Soto, Rafael A.
Pedro Antonio de Alarcón 1:14

Sowerby, Benn
Gérard de Nerval 1:484

Spacks, Patricia Myer
Lewis Carroll 2:118

Spalter, Max
Christian Dietrich Grabbe 2:280

Speare, Morris Edmund
Benjamin Disraeli 2:149

Spector, Ivar
Ivan Alexandrovich Goncharov
1:365

Spiller, Robert E.
James Fenimore Cooper 1:218

Stahl, E. L.
Heinrich von Kleist 2:449

Starkie, Enid
Jules Amédée Barbey
d'Aurevilly 1:74
Gustave Flaubert 2:252

Stedman, Edmund Clarence
Elizabeth Barrett Browning
1:121

Steegmuller, Francis
Guy de Maupassant 1:462

Steeves, Harrison R.
Maria Edgeworth 1:271

Stempel, Daniel
Friedrich Maximilian von
Klinger 1:432

Stepanov, Nikolay
Ivan Andreevich Krylov 1:438

Stephan, Philip
Paul Verlaine 2:629

Stephen, Leslie
Benjamin Disraeli 2:141
Nathaniel Hawthorne 2:321

Stepto, Robert B.
William Wells Brown 2:55

Stern, J. P.
Franz Grillparzer 1:391, 393
Gottfried Keller 2:424

Stern, Madeleine B.
Amos Bronson Alcott 1:27

Stevenson, Robert Louis
Edgar Allan Poe 1:499

Stilman, Leon
Ivan Alexandrovich Goncharov
1:367

Stirling, James Hutchinson
Douglas Jerrold 2:404

Strachey, Lytton
Fedor Mikhailovich Dostoevski
2:168

Strange, William C.
Gérard de Nerval 1:484

Strauss, Walter A.
Gérard de Nerval 1:481

Strong, L.A.G.
George Darley 2:131

Sullivan, Dennis G.
Gérard de Nerval 1:482

Sullivan, Edward D.
Guy de Maupassant 1:466, 468

Sumichrast, Frédéric César de
Théophile Gautier 1:347

Sutcliffe, Emerson Grant
Charles Reade 2:548

Swales, Martin
Gottfried Keller 2:425

Swinburne, Algernon Charles
George Gordon Byron, Lord
Byron 2:71
Wilkie Collins 1:179
Charles Reade 2:544

Swinnerton, Frank
Benjamin Disraeli 2:149

Symons, Arthur
George Gordon Byron, Lord
Byron 2:77
Alphonse Daudet 1:240
Gustave Flaubert 2:236
Théophile Gautier 1:346
Nathaniel Hawthorne 2:316
Leigh Hunt 1:414
Guy de Maupassant 1:454
Gérard de Nerval 1:475
Christina Georgina Rossetti
2:564
Paul Verlaine 2:618, 620, 621

Tandy, Jennette
James Russell Lowell 2:517

Tasistro, Louis Fitzgerald
Edgar Allan Poe 1:492

Tate, Allen
Edgar Allan Poe 1:519

Tayler, Neale H.
Manuel Tamayo y Baus 1:565

Thackeray, William Makepeace
Edward Bulwer-Lytton 1:138,
141
Benjamin Disraeli 2:139
Douglas Jerrold 2:395
George Sand 2:584

Thalmann, Marianne
Ernst Theodor Amadeus
Hoffmann 2:350

Thibaudet, Albert
George Sand 2:605

Thomas, Barry G.
Gottfried Keller 2:423

Thompson, James R.
Leigh Hunt 1:422

Thoreau, Henry David
Ralph Waldo Emerson 1:277

Thorpe, Clarence DeWitt
Leigh Hunt 1:418, 421

Thro, A. Brooker
Charles Reade 2:553

Tickler, Timothy
Washington Irving 2:369

Tolstoy, Leo N.
Ivan Alexandrovich Goncharov
1:361
Guy de Maupassant 1:452

Traill, H. D.
James Russell Lowell 2:509

Trainer, James
Christian Dietrich Grabbe 2:273

Traubel, Horace L.
James Russell Lowell 2:511

Trodd, Anthea
Edward Bulwer-Lytton 1:154

Trollope, Anthony
Edward Bulwer-Lytton 1:148
Wilkie Collins 1:176
Benjamin Disraeli 2:146
Nathaniel Hawthorne 2:308

Tuckerman, Henry T.
Nathaniel Hawthorne 2:298

Turgenev, Ivan
Nikolay Chernyshevsky 1:158

Turner, H. F.
Pedro Antonio de Alarcón 1:15

Twain, Mark
James Fenimore Cooper 1:208

Twitchell, James
George Gordon Byron, Lord
Byron 2:100

Tymms, Ralph
Clemens Brentano 1:98

Uhler, John Earle
John Pendleton Kennedy 2:432

Ulam, Adam B.
Nikolay Chernyshevsky 1:165

Ullmann, Stephen
George Sand 2:605

Untermeyer, Louis
Henry Wadsworth Longfellow
2:498
Paul Verlaine 2:628

CRITIC INDEX

CRITIC INDEX